To Linda,
My star pupil!
Viel Spaß!
Viel Glück!
Viel Wein!
Bis bald!

Love

The Pocket
Oxford-Duden
German
Dictionary

English—German
German—English

Edited by the Dudenredaktion
and the German Section of the
Oxford University Press
Dictionary Department

Chief Editors
M. CLARK
O. THYEN

OXFORD UNIVERSITY PRESS
1997

Oxford University Press, Great Clarendon Street, Oxford OX2 6DP

Oxford New York
Athens Auckland Bangkok Bogota Bombay
Buenos Aires Calcutta Cape Town Dar es Salaam
Delhi Florence Hong Kong Istanbul Karachi
Kuala Lumpur Madras Madrid Melbourne
Mexico City Nairobi Paris Singapore
Taipei Tokyo Toronto

and associated companies in
Berlin Ibadan

Oxford is a trade mark of Oxford University Press

Published in the United States by
Oxford University Press Inc., New York

British Library Cataloguing in Publication Data
Data available

Library of Congress Cataloging in Publication Data
Data available
ISBN 0–19–860136–0
ISBN 0–19–860131–X (pbk)

Printed in Great Britain by
Mackays of Chatham
Chatham, Kent

The Pocket Oxford-Duden
German Dictionary

Foreword

The *Pocket Oxford–Duden German Dictionary* has been designed to meet the needs of students, tourists, and all those who require quick and reliable answers to their translation questions. It provides clear guidance on selecting the most appropriate translation, numerous illustrative examples to help with problems of construction and usage, and precise information on grammar, style, and pronunciation.

Based on the much acclaimed *Oxford–Duden German Dictionary*, this easy-to-use pocket dictionary carries the authority of two of the world's foremost dictionary publishers, Oxford University Press and the Dudenverlag, making use of the unparalleled databases maintained and continually expanded by the two publishers for their celebrated native-speaker dictionaries. Its reliability and clarity make it an invaluable aid to understanding, speaking, and writing everyday idiomatic German in the nineteen nineties.

MICHAEL CLARK
Oxford University Press

Editors and Contributors

in Oxford

Michael Clark
Bernadette Mohan
Maurice Waite
Ursula Lang
Trish Stableford
Tim Connell
Neil Morris
Ting Morris

in Mannheim

Olaf Thyen
Werner Scholze-Stubenrecht
Brigitte Alsleben
Ulrike Röhrenbeck
Magdalena Seubel
Eva Vennebusch

Key to entries

- pronunciation given in IPA
  *Aussprache in internationaler
  Lautschrift*
- indication of approximate
  equivalence
  Angabe ungefährer Entsprechungen

bailiff ['beɪlɪf] *n.* ≈ Gerichtsvollzieher, *der*

- cross-reference to a synonymous headword
  Verweis auf synonymes Stichwort

barrow ['bærəʊ] *n.* **a)** Karre, *die;* Karren, *der;* **b)** *see* **wheelbarrow**

- stress mark
  Betonungszeichen
- irregular plural
  unregelmäßige Pluralform

basis ['beɪsɪs] *n.., pl.* **bases** ['beɪsiːz] Basis, *die;* Grundlage, *die*

- regional/national label
  räumliche Zuordnung
- gloss where no translation is possible
  Umschreibung, wenn eine Übersetzung nicht möglich ist

Belisha beacon [bəliːʃə 'biːkn] *n.* *(Brit.)* gelbes Blinklicht an Zebrastreifen

- compound block with a swung dash representing the first element of each compound
  Kompositablock mit Tilde für den ersten Teil jeder Zusammensetzung

black: **~berry** ['blækbərɪ] *n.* Brombeere, *die;* **~bird** *n.* Amsel, *die;* **~board** *n.* [Wand]tafel, *die;* **~currant** *n.* schwarze Johannisbeere

- idiomatic phrase
  feste Wendung
- swung dash representing the headword
  die Tilde vertritt das Stichwort
- style labels
  (also given for translations)
  *Stilschichtangaben
  (auch für Übersetzungen)*

boot [buːt] **1.** *n.* **a)** Stiefel, *der;* **give sb. the ~** *(fig. coll.)* jmdn. rausschmeißen *(ugs.);* **b)** *(Brit.: of car)* Kofferraum, *der.* **2.** *v. t. (coll.: kick)* kicken *(ugs.)*

- irregular past tenses
  unregelmäßige Verbformen

break [breɪk] **I.** *v. t.*, **broke** [brəʊk], **broken** ['brəʊkn] **a)** brechen

- grammatical categories
  Gliederung nach grammatischen Gesichtspunkten

- phrasal verbs listed under main verb
  Verben in festen Verbindungen mit Präpositionen oder Adverbien (Phrasal verbs) im Anschluß an das jeweilige einfache Verb

break 'down 1. *v. i.* zusammenbrechen; ⟨*Verhandlungen:*⟩ scheitern; ⟨*Auto:*⟩ eine Panne haben. **2.** *v. t.* **a)** aufbrechen ⟨*Tür*⟩; brechen ⟨*Widerstand*⟩; niederreißen ⟨*Barriere, Schranke*⟩; **b)** *(analyse)* aufgliedern. **break 'in 1.** *v. i. (into building etc.)* einbrechen. **2.** *v. t.* **a)** zureiten ⟨*Pferd*⟩; **b)** einlaufen ⟨*Schuhe*⟩; **c)** ~ **the door in** die Tür aufbrechen. **break 'into** *see* ~ **2 b. break 'off 1.** *v. t.* abbrechen; abreißen ⟨*Faden*⟩; auflösen ⟨*Verlobung*⟩. **2.** *v. i.* **a)** abbrechen; **b)** *(cease)* aufhören. **break 'out** *v. i.* ausbrechen; ~ **out in spots/a rash** Pickel/einen Ausschlag bekommen

- semantic categories
  Gliederung nach Bedeutungsunterschieden

- collocators
  Kollokatoren

- sense indicator
  Indikator

- information on syntax
  syntaktische Angabe

feature ['fiːtʃə(r)] **1.** *n.* **a)** *usu. in pl. (part of face)* Gesichtszug, *der;* **b)** *(characteristic)* [charakteristisches] Merkmal; **be a ~ of sth.** charakteristisch für etw. sein; **c)** *(Journ. etc.)* Feature, *das;* **d)** *(Cinemat.)* ~ [film] Hauptfilm, *der*

- usage example
  Anwendungsbeispiel

- subject labels
  Bereichsangaben

- cross-references for additional information
  Verweise auf zusätzliche Informationen

fifty ['fɪftɪ] **1.** *adj.* fünfzig. **2.** *n.* Fünfzig, *die. See also* **eight; eighty 2**

Erläuterungen zum Text

- grammatische Angaben
  grammatical information

- Bereichsangaben
  subject labels

- Verweise auf das Grundwort
  (bei einer Ableitung)
  *references to root word
  (from a derivative)*

- Betonung und Quantität
  stress and vowel length

beschneiden *unr. tr. V.* **a)** cut ⟨*hedge*⟩; prune ⟨*bush*⟩; cut back ⟨*tree*⟩; **einem Vogel die Flügel ~:** clip a bird's wings; **b)** *(Med., Rel.)* circumcise. **Beschneidung die; ~, ~en a)** s. **beschneiden a:** cutting; pruning; cutting back; **b)** *(Med., Rel.)* circumcision

beschummeln *tr. V. (ugs.)* cheat; diddle *(Brit. coll.)*

- Aussprache in internationaler
  Lautschrift
  pronunciation given in IPA

Balkon [bal'kɔn, bal'koːn] *der;* **~s, ~s** [bal'kɔns] *od.* **~e** [bal'koːnə] **a)** balcony; **b)** *(im Theater, Kino)* circle

- Kollokatoren
  collocators

- Indikatoren
  sense indicators

beschreiben *unr. tr. V.* **a)** write on; *(vollschreiben)* write ⟨*page, side, etc.*⟩; *(darstellen)* describe

- die Tilde vertritt das Stichwort
  *swung dash representing the
  headword*

bestanden *Adj.* **von** *od.* **mit etw. ~ sein** have sth. growing on it; **mit Tannen ~e Hügel** fir-covered hills

- Verweis auf ein Synonym
  *cross-reference to a synonymous
  headword*

berappen *tr., itr. V. (ugs.)* s. **blechen**

- Anwendungsbeispiel
  usage example

Beruf *der;* **~[e]s, ~e** occupation; *(akademischer)* profession; *(handwerklicher)* trade; **was sind Sie von ~?** what do you do for a living?

- Redensart
  idiomatic phrase

- Sprichwort
  proverb

Besen *der;* **~s, ~** broom; **ich fress' einen ~, wenn das stimmt** *(salopp)* I'll eat my hat if that's right *(coll.)*. **neue ~ kehren gut** *(Spr.)* a new broom sweeps clean *(prov.)*

- Kompositablock
  compound block

- Angaben zur Syntax
  information on syntax

- Gliederung nach grammatischen Gesichtspunkten
  grammatical categories

- Gliederung nach Bedeutungsunterschieden
  semantic categories

- Kompositionsfuge
  dot between elements of a compound

- räumliche Zuordnung des Stichworts/der Übersetzung
  regional labels for the headwords/translations

- zusätzliche Glosse zur Bedeutung des Stichworts
  additional gloss specifying the sense of the headword

- Angaben zur Stilschicht
  style labels

blut-, Blut-: ~**unterlaufen** *Adj.* suffused with blood-*postpos.*; bloodshot *(eyes)*; ~**vergießen** das; ~s bloodshed; ~**vergiftung** die bloodpoisoning *no indef. art., no pl.*; ~**wurst** die black pudding

beschweren 1. *refl. V.* complain *(über + Akk., wegen about)*; 2. *tr. V.* weight down

beschränkt 1. *Adj.* **a)** *(dumm)* dullwitted; **b)** *(engstirnig)* narrowminded; 2. *adv.* narrow-mindedly

Bei·name der epithet

Beis[e]l das; ~s, *od.* ~n *(österr.)* pub *(Brit. coll.)*; bar *(Amer.)*

Benzin das; ~s petrol *(Brit.)*: gasoline *(Amer.)*; gas *(Amer. coll.)*; *(Wasch~)* benzine

Bütten·papier das handmade paper *(with deckle-edge)*

bestatten *tr. V. (geh.)* inter *(formal)*; bury; **Bestattung** die; ~, ~en *(geh.)*

Contents

Proprietary Names

This dictionary includes some words which are, or are asserted to be, proprietary names or trade marks. The presence or absence of such assertions should not be regarded as affecting the legal status of any proprietary name or trade mark.

Die für das Englische verwendeten Zeichen der Lautschrift

ɑː	barb	bɑːb	m	mat	mæt
ã	séance	'seɪãs	n	not	nɒt
æ	fat	fæt	ŋ	sing	sɪŋ
æ̃	lingerie	'læ̃ʒərɪ	ɒ	got	gɒt
aɪ	fine	faɪn	ɔː	paw	pɔː
aʊ	now	naʊ	ɔɪ	boil	bɔɪl
b	bat	bæt	p	pet	pet
d	dog	dɒg	r	rat	ræt
dʒ	jam	dʒæm	s	sip	sɪp
e	met	met	ʃ	ship	ʃɪp
eɪ	fate	feɪt	t	tip	tɪp
eə	fairy	'feərɪ	tʃ	chin	tʃɪn
əʊ	goat	gəʊt	θ	thin	θɪn
ə	ago	ə'gəʊ	ð	the	ðə
ɜː	fur	fɜː(r)	uː	boot	buːt
f	fat	fæt	ʊ	book	bʊk
g	good	gʊd	ʊə	tourist	'tʊərɪst
h	hat	hæt	ʌ	dug	dʌg
ɪ	bit, lately	bɪt, 'leɪtlɪ	v	van	væn
ɪə	nearly	'nɪəlɪ	w	win	wɪn
iː	meet	miːt	x	loch	lɒx
j	yet	jet	z	zip	zɪp
k	kit	kɪt	ʒ	vision	'vɪʒn
l	lot	lɒt			

: Längezeichen, bezeichnet Länge des unmittelbar davor stehenden Vokals, z. B. boot [buːt].

' Betonung, steht unmittelbar vor einer betonten Silbe, z. B. ago [ə'gəʊ].

(r) Ein „r" in runden Klammern wird nur gesprochen, wenn im Textzusammenhang ein Vokal unmittelbar folgt, z. B. pare [peə(r)]; pare away [peər ə'weɪ].

Phonetic information given in the German-English section

The pronunciation of German is largely regular, and phonetic transcriptions have only been given where additional help is needed. In all other cases only the position of the stressed syllable and the length of the vowel in that syllable are shown: a long vowel is indicated by an underline, e.g. Maß, a short vowel by a dot placed underneath, e.g. Masse.

Phonetic symbols used in transcriptions of German words

a	hạt	hat	ŋ	lạng	laŋ
a:	Bahn	ba:n	o	Morạl	mo'ra:l
ɐ	Ọber	'o:bɐ	o:	Boot	bo:t
ɐ̣	Ụhr	u:ɐ̣	ǫ	loyạl	lǫa'ja:l
ã	Ensemble	ã'sã:bl̩	õ	Fondue	fõ'dy:
ã:	Abonnement	abɔnə'mã:	õ:	Fond	fõ:
ai	weịt	vait	ɔ	Pọst	pɔst
au	Haut	haut	ø	Ökonọm	øko'no:m
b	Bạll	bal	ø:	Ọ̈l	ø:l
ç	ịch	ıç	œ	göttlich	'gœtlıç
d	dạnn	dan	œ̃:	Parfum	par'fœ̃:
dʒ	Gịn	dʒın	ɔy	Heu	hɔy
e	egạl	e'ga:l	p	Pạkt	pakt
e:	Beet	be:t	pf	Pfahl	pfa:l
ɛ	mästen	'mɛstn̩	r	Rạst	rast
ɛ:	wählen	'vɛ:lən	s	Hạst	hast
ɛ̃	Mannequin	'manəkɛ̃	ʃ	schạl	ʃa:l
ɛ̃:	Cousin	ku'zɛ̃:	t	Tạl	ta:l
ə	Nase	'na:zə	ts	Zạhl	tsa:l
f	Fạß	fas	tʃ	Mạtsch	matʃ
g	Gạst	gast	u	kulạnt	ku'lant
h	hạt	hat	u:	Hụt	hu:t
i	vitạl	vi'ta:l	ụ	aktuẹll	ak'tuɛl
i:	viẹl	fi:l	ʊ	Pụlt	pʊlt
ị	Studịe	'ʃtu:dịə	v	wạs	vas
ı	Bịrke	'bırkə	x	Bạch	bax
j	jạ	ja:	y	Physịk	fy'zi:k
k	kạlt	kalt	y:	Rübe	'ry:bə
l	Lạst	last	ỹ	Nuance	'nỹã:sə
l̩	Nạbel	'na:bl̩	ʏ	Fülle	'fʏlə
m	Mạst	mast	z	Hạse	'ha:zə
n	Nạht	na:t	ʒ	Geniẹ	ʒe'ni:
n̩	baden	'ba:dn̩			

'	Glottal stop, e. g. beạchten [bə'|axtn̩].
:	Length sign, indicating that the preceding vowel is long, e.g. Chrom [kro:m].
~	Indicates a nasal vowel, e. g. Fond [fõ:].
'	Stress mark, immediately preceding a stressed syllable, e. g. Ballon [ba'lɔŋ].

English abbreviations used in the Dictionary/ Im Wörterverzeichnis verwendete englische Abkürzungen

abbr(s).	abbreviation(s)	Footb.	Football
abs.	absolute	Gastr.	Gastronomy
adj(s).	adjective(s)	Geog.	Geography
Admin.	Administration, Administrative	Geol.	Geology
		Geom.	Geometry
adv.	adverb	Her.	Heraldry
Aeronaut.	Aeronautics	Hist.	History, Historical
Agric.	Agriculture	Hort.	Horticulture
Amer.	American, America	imper.	imperative
Anat.	Anatomy	impers.	impersonal
arch.	archaic	incl.	including
Archaeol.	Archaeology	indef.	indefinite
Archit.	Architecture	Information Sci.	Information Science
art.	article		
Astrol.	Astrology	int.	interjection
Astron.	Astronomy	interrog.	interrogative
Astronaut.	Astronautics	Ir.	Irish, Ireland
attrib.	attributive	iron.	ironical
Austral.	Australian, Australia	joc.	jocular
Biol.	Biology	Journ.	Journalism
Bookk.	Bookkeeping	lang.	language
Bot.	Botany	Ling.	Linguistics
Brit.	British, Britain	Lit.	Literature
Chem.	Chemistry	lit.	literal
Cinemat.	Cinematography	masc.	masculine
coll.	colloquial	Math.	Mathematics
collect.	collective	Mech.	Mechanics
comb.	combination	Mech. Engin.	Mechanical Engineering
Commerc.	Commerce, Commercial		
		Med.	Medicine
compar.	comparative	Metalw.	Metalwork
condit.	conditional	Meteorol.	Meteorology
conj.	conjunction	Mil.	Military
def.	definite	Min.	Mineralogy
Dent.	Dentistry	Motor Veh.	Motor Vehicles
derog.	derogatory	Mus.	Music
dial.	dialect	Mythol.	Mythology
Diplom.	Diplomacy	n.	noun
Dressm.	Dressmaking	Naut.	Nautical
Eccl.	Ecclesiastical	neg.	negative
Ecol.	Ecology	N. Engl.	Northern English
Econ.	Economics	ns.	nouns
Educ.	Education	Nucl. Phys.	Nuclear Physics
Electr.	Electricity	obj.	object
ellipt.	elliptical	Ornith.	Ornithology
emphat.	emphatic	P	Proprietary name
esp.	especially	Parl.	Parliament
euphem.	euphemistic	pass.	passive
excl.	exclamation, exclamatory	Pharm.	Pharmacy
		Philos.	Philosophy
expr.	expressing	Photog.	Photography
fem.	feminine	phr(s).	phrase(s)
fig.	figurative	Phys.	Physics

Physiol.	Physiology	Scot.	Scottish, Scotland
pl.	plural	sing.	singular
poet.	poetical	sl.	slang
Polit.	Politics	Sociol.	Sociology
poss.	possessive	St. Exch.	Stock Exchange
postpos.	postpositive	sth.	something
p.p.	past participle	subord.	subordinate
pred.	predicative	suf.	suffix
pref.	prefix	superl.	superlative
prep.	preposition	Surv.	Surveying
pres.	present	symb.	symbol
pres. p.	present participle	tech.	technical
pr. n.	proper noun	Teleph.	Telephony
pron.	pronoun	Telev.	Television
prov.	proverbial	Theol.	Theology
Psych.	Psychology	Univ.	University
p.t.	past tense	usu.	usually
Railw.	Railways	v. aux.	auxiliary verb
RC Ch.	Roman Catholic	Vet. Med.	Veterinary Medicine
	Church	v. i.	intransitive verb
refl.	reflexive	v. refl.	reflexive verb
rel.	relative	v. t.	transitive verb
Relig.	Religion	v. t. & i.	transitive and
rhet.	rhetorical		intransitive verb
sb.	somebody	Woodw.	Woodwork
Sch.	School	Zool.	Zoology
Sci.	Science		

German abbreviations used in the Dictionary/ Im Wörterverzeichnis verwendete deutsche Abkürzungen

a.	anderes; andere	berlin.	berlinisch
ä.	ähnliches; ähnliche	bes.	besonders
Abk.	Abkürzung	Bez.	Bezeichnung
adj.	adjektivisch	bibl.	biblisch
Adj.	Adjektiv	bild. Kunst	bildende Kunst
adv.	adverbial	Biol.	Biologie
Adv.	Adverb	Börsenw.	Börsenwesen
Akk.	Akkusativ	Bot.	Botanik
amerik.	amerikanisch	BRD	Bundesrepublik
Amtsspr.	Amtssprache		Deutschland
Anat.	Anatomie	brit.	britisch
Anthrop.	Anthropologie	Bruchz.	Bruchzahl
Archäol.	Archäologie	Buchf.	Buchführung
Archit.	Architektur	Buchw.	Buchwesen
Art.	Artikel	Bürow.	Bürowesen
Astrol.	Astrologie	chem.	chemisch
Astron.	Astronomie	christl.	christlich
A. T.	Altes Testament	Dat.	Dativ
attr.	attributiv	DDR	Deutsche
Bauw.	Bauwesen		Demokratische
Bergmannsspr.	Bergmannssprache		Republik

Dekl.	Deklination	jur.	juristisch
Demonstrativ-	Demonstrativ-	Kardinalz.	Kardinalzahl
pron.	pronomen	kath.	katholisch
d. h.	das heißt	Kaufmannsspr.	Kaufmannssprache
dichter.	dichterisch	Kfz-W.	Kraftfahrzeugwesen
Druckerspr.	Druckersprache	Kinderspr.	Kindersprache
Druckw.	Druckwesen	Kochk.	Kochkunst
dt.	deutsch	Konj.	Konjunktion
DV	Datenverarbeitung	Kunstwiss.	Kunstwissenschaft
ehem.	ehemals, ehemalig	landsch.	landschaftlich
Eisenb.	Eisenbahn	Landw.	Landwirtschaft
elektr.	elektrisch	Literaturw.	Literaturwissenschaft
Elektrot.	Elektrotechnik	Luftf.	Luftfahrt
engl.	englisch	ma.	mittelalterlich
etw.	etwas	MA.	Mittelalter
ev.	evangelisch	marx.	marxistisch
fachspr.	fachsprachlich	Math.	Mathematik
fam.	familiär	Med.	Medizin
Ferns.	Fernsehen	Meeresk.	Meereskunde
Fernspr.	Fernsprechwesen	Met.	Meteorologie
fig.	figurativ	Metall.	Metallurgie
Finanzw.	Finanzwesen	Metallbearb.	Metallbearbeitung
Flugw.	Flugwesen	Milit.	Militär
Forstw.	Forstwesen	Mineral.	Mineralogie
Fot.	Fotografie	mod.	modifizierend
Frachtw.	Frachtwesen	Modalv.	Modalverb
Funkw.	Funkwesen	Münzk.	Münzkunde
Gastr.	Gastronomie	Mus.	Musik
Gattungsz.	Gattungszahl	Mythol.	Mythologie
Gaunerspr.	Gaunersprache	Naturw.	Naturwissenschaft
geh.	gehoben	Neutr.	Neutrum
Gen.	Genitiv	niederdt.	niederdeutsch
Geneal.	Genealogie	Nom.	Nominativ
Geogr.	Geographie	nordamerik.	nordamerikanisch
Geol.	Geologie	nordd.	norddeutsch
Geom.	Geometrie	nordostd.	nordostdeutsch
Handarb.	Handarbeit	nordwestd.	nordwestdeutsch
Handw.	Handwerk	ns.	nationalsozialistisch
Her.	Heraldik	N. T.	Neues Testament
hess.	hessisch	o.	ohne; oben
Hilfsv.	Hilfsverb	o. ä.	oder ähnliches;
hist.	historisch		oder ähnliche
Hochschulw.	Hochschulwesen	od.	oder
Holzverarb.	Holzverarbeitung	Ordinalz.	Ordinalzahl
Indefinitpron.	Indefinitpronomen	ostd.	ostdeutsch
indekl.	indeklinabel	österr.	österreichisch
Indik.	Indikativ	Päd.	Pädagogik
Inf.	Infinitiv	Papierdt.	Papierdeutsch
Informationst.	Informationstechnik	Parapsych.	Parapsychologie
Interj.	Interjektion	Parl.	Parlament
iron.	ironisch	Part.	Partizip
intr.	intransitiv	Perf.	Perfekt
Jagdw.	Jagdwesen	Pers.	Person
Jägerspr.	Jägersprache	pfälz.	pfälzisch
jmd.	jemand	Pharm.	Pharmazie
jmdm.	jemandem	Philos.	Philosophie
jmdn.	jemanden	Physiol.	Physiologie
jmds.	jemandes	Pl.	Plural
Jugendspr.	Jugendsprache	Plusq.	Plusquamperfekt

Postw.	Postwesen	Sup.	Superlativ
präd.	prädikativ	Textilw.	Textilwesen
Präp.	Präposition	Theol.	Theologie
Präs.	Präsens	thüring.	thüringisch
Prät.	Präteritum	Tiermed.	Tiermedizin
Pron.	Pronomen	tr.	transitiv
Psych.	Psychologie	Trenn.	Trennung
Raumf.	Raumfahrt	u.	und
Rechtsspr.	Rechtssprache	u. a.	und andere[s]
Rechtsw.	Rechtswesen	u. ä.	und ähnliches
refl.	reflexiv	ugs.	umgangssprachlich
regelm.	regelmäßig	unbest.	unbestimmt
Rel.	Religion	unpers.	unpersönlich
Relativpron.	Relativpronomen	unr.	unregelmäßig
rhein.	rheinisch	usw.	und so weiter
Rhet.	Rhetorik	v.	von
röm.	römisch	V.	Verb
röm.-kath.	römisch-katholisch	verächtl.	verächtlich
Rundf.	Rundfunk	veralt.	veraltet; veraltend
s.	siehe	Verhaltensf.	Verhaltensforschung
S.	Seite	verhüll.	verhüllend
scherzh.	scherzhaft	Verkehrsw.	Verkehrswesen
schles.	schlesisch	Versiche-	Versicherungswesen
schott.	schottisch	rungsw.	
Schülerspr.	Schülersprache	vgl.	vergleiche
Schulw.	Schulwesen	Vkl.	Verkleinerungsform
schwäb.	schwäbisch	Völkerk.	Völkerkunde
schweiz.	schweizerisch	Völkerr.	Völkerrecht
Seemannsspr.	Seemannssprache	Volksk.	Volkskunde
Seew.	Seewesen	volkst.	volkstümlich
Sexualk.	Sexualkunde	vulg.	vulgär
Sg.	Singular	Werbespr.	Werbesprache
s. o.	siehe oben	westd.	westdeutsch
Soldatenspr.	Soldatensprache	westfäl.	westfälisch
Sozialvers.	Sozialversicherung	Wieder-	Wiederholungs-
Soziol.	Soziologie	holungsz.	zahlwort
spött.	spöttisch	wiener.	wienerisch
Spr.	Sprichwort	Winzerspr.	Winzersprache
Sprachw.	Sprachwissenschaft	Wirtsch.	Wirtschaft
Steuerw.	Steuerwesen	Wissensch.	Wissenschaft
Stilk.	Stilkunde	Wz.	Warenzeichen
Studentenspr.	Studentensprache	Zahnmed.	Zahnmedizin
s. u.	siehe unten	z. B.	zum Beispiel
Subj.	Subjekt	Zeitungsw.	Zeitungswesen
subst.	substantivisch;	Zollw.	Zollwesen
	substantiviert	Zool.	Zoologie
Subst.	Substantiv	Zus.	Zusammensetzung
südd.	süddeutsch	Zusschr.	Zusammenschreibung
südwestd.	südwestdeutsch		

A

A, ¹a [eɪ] *n.* A, a, *das*

²a [ə, *stressed* eɪ] *indef. art.* ein/eine/ ein; **he is a gardener/a Frenchman** er ist Gärtner/Franzose; **she did not say a word** sie sagte kein Wort

AA *abbr. (Brit.)* **Automobile Association** *britischer Automobilklub*

aback [ə'bæk] *adv.* **be taken ~:** erstaunt sein

abandon [ə'bændən] *v.t.* verlassen ⟨*Ort, Person*⟩; aufgeben ⟨*Prinzip*⟩

abase [ə'beɪs] *v.t.* erniedrigen

abashed [ə'bæʃt] *adj.* beschämt

abate [ə'beɪt] *v.i.* nachlassen

abattoir ['æbətwɑː(r)] *n.* Schlachthof, *der*

abbey ['æbɪ] *n.* Abtei, *die*

abbot ['æbət] *n.* Abt, *der*

abbreviate [ə'briːvɪeɪt] *v.t.* abkürzen.

abbreviation [əbriːvɪ'eɪʃn] *n.* Abkürzung, *die*

abdicate ['æbdɪkeɪt] *v.t.* abdanken.

abdication [æbdɪ'keɪʃn] *n.* Abdankung, *die*

abdomen ['æbdəmɪn] *n.* Bauch, *der*.

abdominal [æb'dɒmɪnl] *adj.* Bauch-

abduct [əb'dʌkt] *v.t.* entführen. **abduction** [əb'dʌkʃn] *n.* Entführung, *die*

aberration [æbə'reɪʃn] *n.* Abweichung, *die*

abet [ə'bet] *v.t.*, **-tt-** helfen (+ *Dat.*); **aid and ~:** Beihilfe leisten (+ *Dat.*)

abhor [əb'hɔː(r)] *v.t.*, **-rr-** verabscheuen. **abhorrent** [əb'hɒrənt] *adj.* abscheulich

abide [ə'baɪd] **1.** *v.i.* **~ by** befolgen ⟨*Gesetz, Vorschrift*⟩; [ein]halten ⟨*Versprechen*⟩. **2.** *v.t.* ertragen; **I can't ~ dogs** ich kann Hunde nicht ausstehen

ability [ə'bɪlɪtɪ] *n.* **a)** *(capacity)* Fähigkeit, *die;* **have the ~ to do sth.** etw. können; **b)** *(cleverness)* Intelligenz, *die;* **c)** *(talent)* Begabung, *die*

abject ['æbdʒekt] *adj.* elend; bitter ⟨*Armut*⟩; demütig ⟨*Entschuldigung*⟩

ablaze [ə'bleɪz] *adj.* **be ~:** in Flammen stehen

able ['eɪbl] *adj.* **a)** **be ~ to do sth.** etw. können; **b)** *(competent)* fähig. **ablebodied** ['eɪblbɒdɪd] *adj.* kräftig; tauglich ⟨*Soldat, Matrose*⟩. **ably** ['eɪblɪ] *adv.* geschickt; gekonnt

abnormal [æb'nɔːml] *adj.* abnorm; a[b]normal ⟨*Interesse, Verhalten*⟩. **abnormality** [æbnɔː'mælɪtɪ] *n.* Abnormität, *die*

aboard [ə'bɔːd] **1.** *adv.* an Bord. **2.** *prep.* an Bord (+ *Gen.*); **~ the bus** im Bus; **~ ship** an Bord

abode [ə'bəʊd] *n.* **of no fixed ~:** ohne festen Wohnsitz

abolish [ə'bɒlɪʃ] *v.t.* abschaffen. **abolition** [æbə'lɪʃn] *n.* Abschaffung, *die*

abominable [ə'bɒmɪnəbl] *adj.* abscheulich; scheußlich

aborigine [æbə'rɪdʒɪnɪ] *n.* Ureinwohner, *der*

abort [ə'bɔːt] *v.t.* abtreiben ⟨*Baby*⟩. **abortion** [ə'bɔːʃn] *n.* Abtreibung, *die.* **abortive** [ə'bɔːtɪv] *adj.* mißlungen ⟨*Plan*⟩; fehlgeschlagen ⟨*Versuch*⟩

abound [ə'baʊnd] *v.i.* **~ in sth.** an etw. *(Dat.)* reich sein

about [ə'baʊt] **1.** *adv.* **a)** *(all around)* rings[her]um; *(here and there)* überall; **all ~:** ringsumher; **b)** *(near)* **be ~:** dasein; hiersein; **c) be ~ to do sth.** gerade etw. tun wollen; **d) be out and ~:** aktiv sein; **e)** *(approximately)* ungefähr. **2.** *prep.* **a)** *(all round)* um [... herum]; **b)** *(concerning)* über (+ *Akk.*); **know ~ sth.** von etw. wissen; **a question ~ sth.** eine Frage zu etw.; **what was it ~?** worum ging es?

above [ə'bʌv] **1.** *adv.* **a)** *(position)* oben; *(higher up)* darüber; **b)** *(direction)* nach oben. **2.** *prep.* *(position)* über (+ *Dat.*); *(direction, more than)* über (+ *Akk.*); **~ all** vor allem. **abovementioned** *adj.* oben genannt

abrasion [ə'breɪʒn] *n. (graze)* Hautabschürfung, *die*
abrasive [ə'breɪsɪv] **1.** *adj.* **a)** scheuernd; Scheuer-; **b)** *(fig.: harsh)* aggressiv. **2.** *n.* Scheuermittel, *das*
abreast [ə'brest] *adv.* **a)** nebeneinander; **b)** *(fig.)* **keep ~ of** sth. sich über etw. *(Akk.)* auf dem laufenden halten
abroad [ə'brɔːd] *adv.* im Ausland; *(direction)* ins Ausland
abrupt [ə'brʌpt] *adj.*, **a'bruptly** *adv.* **a)** *(sudden[ly])* abrupt; plötzlich; **b)** *(brusque[ly])* schroff
abscess ['æbsɪs] *n.* Abszeß, *der*
abscond [əb'skɒnd] *v. t.* sich entfernen
absence ['æbsəns] *n.* Abwesenheit, *die;* **the ~ of** sth. der Mangel an etw. *(Dat.)*
absent ['æbsənt] *adj.* abwesend; **be ~ from school/work** in der Schule/am Arbeitsplatz fehlen. **absentee** [æbsən'tiː] *n.* Fehlende, *der/die;* Abwesende, *der/die.* **absent-minded** [æbsənt'maɪndɪd] *adj.* geistesabwesend; *(habitually)* zerstreut
absolute ['æbsəluːt] *adj.* absolut; ausgemacht *(Lüge, Skandal).* **abso'lutely** *adv.* absolut; völlig *(verrückt);* **you're ~ right!** du hast völlig recht; **~ not!** auf keinen Fall!
absolve [əb'zɒlv] *v. t.* **~ from** entbinden von *(Pflichten);* lossprechen von *(Schuld)*
absorb [əb'sɔːb] *v. t.* **a)** aufsaugen *(Flüssigkeit);* **b)** abfangen *(Schlag, Stoß);* **c)** *(fig.: engross)* ausfüllen. **absorbent** [əb'sɔːbənt] *adj.* saugfähig. **ab'sorbing** *adj.* faszinierend
abstain [əb'steɪn] *v. i.* **~ from** sth. sich einer Sache *(Gen.)* enthalten; **~ [from voting]** sich der Stimme enthalten
abstemious [əb'stiːmɪəs] *adj.* enthaltsam
abstention [əb'stenʃn] *n. (from voting)* Stimmenthaltung, *die*
abstinence ['æbstɪnəns] *n.* Abstinenz, *die*
abstract ['æbstrækt] **1.** *adj.* abstrakt. **2.** *n.* Zusammenfassung, *die*
absurd [əb'sɜːd] *adj.* absurd; *(ridiculous)* lächerlich. **absurdity** [əb'sɜːdɪtɪ] *n.* Absurdität, *die.* **ab'surdly** *adv.* lächerlich
abundance [ə'bʌndəns] *n.* **[an] ~ of** sth. eine Fülle von etw.
abundant [ə'bʌndənt] *adj.* reich **(in** an + *Dat.)*
abuse 1. [ə'bjuːz] *v. t.* beschimpfen. **2.**

[ə'bjuːs] *n.* Beschimpfungen *Pl.* **abusive** [ə'bjuːsɪv] *adj.* beleidigend; **become ~:** ausfallend werden
abysmal [ə'bɪzml] *adj. (coll.: bad)* katastrophal *(ugs.)*
abyss [ə'bɪs] *n.* Abgrund, *der*
AC *abbr.* **alternating current** Ws
academic [ækə'demɪk] *adj.* akademisch
academy [ə'kædəmɪ] *n.* Akademie, *die*
accede [æk'siːd] *v. i.* **a)** zustimmen **(to** *Dat.);* **b) ~ [to the throne]** den Thron besteigen
accelerate [ək'seləreɪt] **1.** *v. t.* beschleunigen. **2.** *v. i.* sich beschleunigen; *(Auto, Fahrer:)* beschleunigen. **acceleration** [əkselə'reɪʃn] *n.* Beschleunigung, *die.* **accelerator** [ək'seləreɪtə(r)] *n.* **~ [pedal]** Gas[pedal], *das*
accent ['æksənt] *n.* Akzent, *der.* **accentuate** [ək'sentjʊeɪt] *v. t.* betonen
accept [ək'sept] *v. t.* **a)** annehmen; entgegennehmen *(Dank, Spende);* übernehmen *(Verantwortung);* **b)** *(acknowledge)* akzeptieren. **acceptable** [ək'septəbl] *adj.* akzeptabel; annehmbar *(Preis, Gehalt).* **acceptance** [ək'septns] *n.* **a)** Annahme, *die;* **b)** *(acknowledgement)* Anerkennung, *die*
access ['ækses] *n.* **a)** *(admission)* **gain ~:** Einlaß finden; **b)** *(opportunity to use or approach)* Zugang, *der* **(to** zu).
accessible [ək'sesɪbl] *adj.* **a)** *(reachable)* erreichbar; **b)** *(available, understandable)* zugänglich **(to** für)
accession [ək'seʃn] *n.* Amtsantritt, *der;* **~ [to the throne]** Thronbesteigung, *die*
accessory [ək'sesərɪ] *n.* **a) accessories** *pl.* Zubehör, *das;* **b)** *(dress article)* Accessoire, *das*
accident ['æksɪdənt] *n.* **a)** Unfall, *der;* **b)** *(chance)* Zufall, *der;* **by ~:** zufällig; **c)** *(mistake)* Versehen, *das;* **by ~:** versehentlich. **accidental** [æksɪ'dentl] *adj. (chance)* zufällig; *(unintended)* unbeabsichtigt. **acci'dentally** *adv. (by chance)* zufällig; *(by mistake)* versehentlich
acclaim [ə'kleɪm] *v. t.* feiern
acclimatize [ə'klaɪmətaɪz] *v. t.* **get** *or* **become ~d** sich akklimatisieren
accolade ['ækəleɪd] *n. (praise)* **~[s]** Lob, *das*
accommodate [ə'kɒmədeɪt] *v. t.* **a)** unterbringen; *(hold)* Platz bieten **(+ *Dat.*);** **b)** *(oblige)* gefällig sein

(+ *Dat.*). **accommodating** [ə'kɒ-mədeıtıŋ] *adj.* zuvorkommend. **accommodation** [əkɒmə'deıʃn] *n.* Unterkunft, *die*

accompaniment [ə'kʌmpənımənt] *n.* Begleitung, *die*

accompanist [ə'kʌmpənıst] *n.* Begleiter, *der*/Begleiterin, *die*

accompany [ə'kʌmpənı] *v.t.* begleiten

accomplice [ə'kʌmplıs] *n.* Komplize, *der*/Komplizin, *die*

accomplish [ə'kʌmplıʃ] *v.t.* vollbringen ⟨*Tat*⟩; erfüllen ⟨*Aufgabe*⟩. **accomplished** [ə'kʌmplıʃt] *adj.* fähig; **he is an ~ speaker/dancer** er ist ein erfahrener Redner/vollendeter Tänzer. **ac'complishment** *n.* **a)** *(completion)* Vollendung, *die;* **b)** *(achievement)* Leistung, *die; (skill)* Fähigkeit, *die*

accord [ə'kɔ:d] **1.** *n.* Übereinstimmung, *die;* **of one's own ~:** aus eigenem Antrieb; **with one ~:** geschlossen. **2.** *v.t.* **~ sb. sth.** jmdm. etw. gewähren. **accordance** [ə'kɔ:dəns] *n.* **in ~ with** in Übereinstimmung mit. **ac'cording** *adv.* **~ to** nach; **~ to him** nach seiner Aussage. **ac'cordingly** *adv. (as appropriate)* entsprechend; *(therefore)* folglich

accordion [ə'kɔ:dıən] *n.* Akkordeon, *das*

accost [ə'kɒst] *v.t.* ansprechen

account [ə'kaʊnt] *n.* **a)** *(Finance)* Rechnung, *die; (at bank, shop)* Konto, *das;* **b)** *(consideration)* **take ~ of sth., take sth. into ~:** etw. berücksichtigen; **take no ~ of sth./sb.** etw./jmdn. unberücksichtigt lassen; **don't change your plans on my ~:** ändert nicht meinetwegen eure Pläne; **on ~ of** wegen; **on no ~:** auf [gar] keinen Fall; **c)** *(report)* Bericht, *der;* **d) call sb. to ~:** jmdn. zur Rechenschaft ziehen. **ac'count for** *v.t.* Rechenschaft ablegen über (+*Akk.*); *(explain)* erklären

accountable [ə'kaʊntəbl] *adj.* verantwortlich

accountancy [ə'kaʊntənsı] *n.* Buchhaltung, *die*

accountant [ə'kaʊntənt] *n.* [Bilanz]buchhalter, *der*/-halterin, *die*

ac'count number *n.* Kontonummer, *die*

accrue [ə'kru:] *v.i.* ⟨*Zinsen:*⟩ auflaufen; **~ to sb.** ⟨*Reichtümer, Einnahmen:*⟩ jmdm. zufließen

accumulate [ə'kju:mjʊleıt] **1.** *v.t.*

sammeln. **2.** *v.i.* ⟨*Menge, Staub:*⟩ sich ansammeln; ⟨*Geld:*⟩ sich anhäufen. **accumulation** [əkju:mjʊ'leıʃn] *n.* [An]sammeln, *das; (being accumulated)* Anhäufung, *die*

accuracy ['ækjʊrəsı] *n.* Genauigkeit, *die*

accurate ['ækjʊrət] *adj.,* '**accurately** *adv.* genau; *(correct[ly])* richtig

accusation [ækju:'zeıʃn] *n.* Anschuldigung, *die; (Law)* Anklage, *die*

accusative [ə'kju:zətıv] *adj. & n.* ~ [case] Akkusativ, *der*

accuse [ə'kju:z] *v.t.* beschuldigen; *(Law)* anklagen (**of** wegen + *Gen.*)

accustom [ə'kʌstəm] *v.t.* gewöhnen (**to** an + *Akk.*); **grow/be ~ed to sth.** sich an etw. *(Akk.)* gewöhnen/an etw. *(Akk.)* gewöhnt sein. **accustomed** [ə'kʌstəmd] *attrib. adj.* gewohnt; üblich

ace [eıs] *n.* As, *das*

ache [eık] **1.** *v.i.* schmerzen; weh tun. **2.** *n.* Schmerz, *der*

achieve [ə'tʃi:v] *v.t.* zustande bringen; erreichen ⟨*Ziel, Standard*⟩. **a'chievement** *n.* **a)** *see* **achieve:** Zustandebringen, *das;* Erreichen, *das;* **b)** *(thing accomplished)* Leistung, *die*

acid ['æsıd] **1.** *adj.* sauer. **2.** *n.* Säure, *die.* **acidic** [ə'sıdık] *adj.* säuerlich. **acidity** [ə'sıdıtı] *n.* Säure, *die*

acid: ~ 'rain *n.* saurer Regen; ~ **test** *n. (fig.)* Feuerprobe, *die*

acknowledge [ək'nɒlıdʒ] *v.t.* **a)** zugeben ⟨*Tatsache, Fehler, Schuld*⟩; **b)** sich erkenntlich zeigen für ⟨*Dienste, Bemühungen*⟩; erwidern ⟨*Gruß*⟩; **c)** bestätigen ⟨*Empfang, Bewerbung*⟩; **~ a letter** den Empfang eines Briefes bestätigen. **acknowledg[e]ment** [ək'nɒlıdʒmənt] *n.* **a)** *(admission)* Eingeständnis, *das;* **b)** *(thanks)* Dank, *der* (**of** für); **c)** *(of letter)* Bestätigung [des Empfangs]

acne ['æknı] *n.* Akne, *die*

acorn ['eıkɔ:n] *n.* Eichel, *die*

acoustic [ə'ku:stık] *adj.* akustisch. **a'coustics** *n. pl.* Akustik, *die*

acquaint [ə'kweınt] *v.t.* **be ~ed with sb.** mit jmdm. bekannt sein. **acquaintance** [ə'kweıntəns] *n.* **a)** ~ **with sb.** Bekanntschaft mit jmdm.; **make sb.'s ~:** jmds. Bekanntschaft machen; **b)** *(person)* Bekannte, *der/die*

acquiesce [ækwı'es] *v.i.* einwilligen (**in** in + *Akk.*)

acquire [ə'kwaıə(r)] *v.t.* sich *(Dat.)* anschaffen ⟨*Gegenstände*⟩; erwerben

⟨*Besitz, Kenntnisse*⟩. **acquisition** [ækwɪ'zɪʃn] *n.* Erwerb, *der;* *(thing)* Anschaffung, *die.* **acquisitive** [ə'kwɪzɪtɪv] *adj.* raffsüchtig

acquit [ə'kwɪt] *v. t.,* -tt- freisprechen. **acquittal** [ə'kwɪtl] *n.* Freispruch, *der*

acre ['eɪkə(r)] *n.* Acre, *der*

acrid ['ækrɪd] *adj.* beißend ⟨*Geruch, Rauch*⟩; bitter ⟨*Geschmack*⟩

acrimonious [ækrɪ'məʊnɪəs] *adj.* bitter; erbittert ⟨*Streit*⟩

acrobat ['ækrəbæt] *n.* Akrobat, *der*/Akrobatin, *die.* **acrobatic** [ækrə'bætɪk] *adj.* akrobatisch. **acrobatics** [ækrə'bætɪks] *n.* Akrobatik, *die*

acronym ['ækrənɪm] *n.* Akronym, *das*

across [ə'krɒs] **1.** *adv.* *(from one side to the other)* darüber; *(from here to there)* hinüber; **be 9 miles** ~: 9 Meilen breit sein. **2.** *prep.* über *(+ Akk.);* *(on the other side of)* auf der anderen Seite *(+ Gen.)*

act [ækt] **1.** *n.* **a)** *(deed)* Tat, *die;* **b)** *(Theatre)* Akt, *der;* **c)** *(pretence)* Theater, *das;* **put on an** ~: Theater spielen; **d)** *(Law)* Gesetz, *das.* **2.** *v. t.* spielen ⟨*Stück*⟩. **3.** *v. i.* **a)** *(perform actions)* handeln; **b)** *(behave)* sich verhalten; ~ **as** fungieren als; **c)** *(perform play)* spielen; **d)** *(have effect)* ~ **on sth.** auf etw. *(Akk.)* wirken. '**acting 1.** *n.* *(Theatre etc.)* die Schauspielerei. **2.** *adj.* *(temporary)* stellvertretend

action ['ækʃn] *n.* **a)** *(doing sth.)* Handeln, *das;* **take** ~: Schritte *od.* etwas unternehmen; **put a plan into** ~: einen Plan in die Tat umsetzen; **put sth. out of** ~: etw. außer Betrieb setzen; **b)** *(act)* Tat, *die;* **c)** *(legal process)* [Gerichts]verfahren, *das;* **d) die in** ~: im Kampf fallen. **action 'replay** *n.* Wiederholung [in Zeitlupe]

activate ['æktɪveɪt] *v. t.* **a)** in Gang setzen; **b)** *(Chem., Phys.)* aktivieren

active ['æktɪv] *adj.,* '**actively** *adv.* aktiv

activist ['æktɪvɪst] *n.* Aktivist, *der*/Aktivistin, *die*

activity [æk'tɪvɪtɪ] *n.* Aktivität, *die*

actor ['æktə(r)] *n.* Schauspieler, *der*

actress ['æktrɪs] *n.* Schauspielerin, *die*

actual ['æktʃʊəl] *adj.* eigentlich; wirklich ⟨*Name*⟩. '**actually** *adv.* *(in fact)* eigentlich; *(by the way)* übrigens; *(believe it or not)* sogar

acumen ['ækjʊmen] *n.* Scharfsinn, *der;* **business** ~: Geschäftssinn, *der*

acupuncture ['ækjʊpʌnktʃə(r)] *n.* Akupunktur, *die*

acute [ə'kju:t] *adj.* **a)** spitz ⟨*Winkel*⟩; **b)** *(critical; Med.)* akut

AD *abbr.* **Anno Domini** n. Chr.

ad [æd] *n.* *(coll.)* Annonce, *die*

adamant ['ædəmənt] *adj.* unnachgiebig; **be** ~ **that** ...: darauf bestehen, daß ...

adapt [ə'dæpt] *v. t.* **a)** anpassen (**to** *Dat.*); ~ **oneself to sth.** sich an etw. *(Akk.)* gewöhnen; **b)** bearbeiten ⟨*Text, Theaterstück*⟩. **adaptable** [ə'dæptəbl] *adj.* anpassungsfähig. **adaptation** [ædəp'teɪʃn] *n.* **a)** Anpassung, *die;* **b)** *(version)* Adap[ta]tion, *die;* *(of story, text)* Bearbeitung, *die.* **adapter, adaptor** [ə'dæptə(r)] *n.* Adapter, *der*

add [æd] **1.** *v. t.* hinzufügen (**to** *Dat.*); ~ **two and two** zwei und zwei zusammenzählen. **2.** *v. i.* ~ **to** vergrößern ⟨*Schwierigkeiten, Einkommen*⟩. **add** '**up 1.** *v. i.* ~ **up to sth.** *(fig.)* auf etw. *(Akk.)* hinauslaufen. **2.** *v. t.* zusammenzählen

adder ['ædə(r)] *n.* Viper, *die*

addict 1. [ə'dɪkt] *v. t.* **be** ~**ed** süchtig sein (**to** nach). **2.** ['ædɪkt] *n.* Süchtige, *der/die.* **addiction** [ə'dɪkʃn] *n.* Sucht, *die* (**to** nach). **addictive** [ə'dɪktɪv] *adj.* **be** ~: süchtig machen

addition [ə'dɪʃn] *n.* **a)** Hinzufügen, *das; (adding up)* Addieren, *das; (process)* Addition, *die;* **in** ~: außerdem; **in** ~ **to** zusätzlich zu; **b)** *(thing added)* Ergänzung, *die* (**to** zu). **additional** [ə'dɪʃənl] *adj.* zusätzlich

additive ['ædɪtɪv] *n.* Zusatz, *der*

address [ə'dres] **1.** *v. t.* **a)** *(mark with* ~*)* adressieren (**to** an *+ Akk.*); **b)** *(speak to)* anreden; sprechen zu ⟨*Zuhörern*⟩. **2.** *n.* **a)** *(on letter)* Adresse, *die;* **b)** *(speech)* Ansprache, *die.* **addressee** [ædre'si:] *n.* Adressat, *der*/Adressatin, *die*

adept ['ædept] *adj.* geschickt (**in, at** in + *Dat.*)

adequate ['ædɪkwət] *adj.* **a)** angemessen (**to** *Dat.*); *(suitable)* passend; **b)** *(sufficient)* ausreichend. '**adequately** *adv.* **a)** *(sufficiently)* ausreichend; **b)** *(suitably)* angemessen ⟨*gekleidet, qualifiziert usw.*⟩

adhere [əd'hɪə(r)] *v. i.* haften, *(by glue)* kleben (**to** an + *Dat.*). **adhesion** [əd'hi:ʒn] *n.* Haften, *das.* **adhesive** [əd'hi:sɪv] **1.** *adj.* gummiert ⟨*Briefmarke*⟩; Klebe⟨*band*⟩. **2.** *n.* Klebstoff, *der*

adjacent [ə'dʒeɪsənt] *adj.* angrenzend; ~ **to** neben *(position: + Dat.; direction: + Akk.)*

adjective ['ædʒɪktɪv] *n.* Adjektiv, *das*
adjoin [ə'dʒɔɪn] *v.t.* grenzen an (+ *Akk.*)
adjourn [ə'dʒɜːn] **1.** *v.t. (break off)* unterbrechen; *(put off)* aufschieben. **2.** *v.i.* sich vertagen; ~ **for lunch/half an hour** eine Mittagspause/halbstündige Pause einlegen. **a'djournment** *n. (of court)* Vertagung, *die; (of meeting)* Unterbrechung, *die*
adjudicate [ə'dʒuːdɪkeɪt] *v.i. (in court, tribunal)* das Urteil fällen; *(in contest)* entscheiden
adjust [ə'dʒʌst] **1.** *v.t.* einstellen; ~ **sth. [to sth.]** etw. [an etw. *(Akk.)*] anpassen. **2.** *v.i.* ⟨*Person:*⟩ sich anpassen (**to** an + *Akk.*). **adjustable** [ə'dʒʌstəbl] *adj.* einstellbar; verstellbar ⟨*Gerät*⟩. **a'djustment** *n.* Einstellung, *die; (to situation etc.)* Anpassung, *die*
ad-lib [æd'lɪb] **1.** *adj.* improvisiert. **2.** *v.i.,* **-bb-** improvisieren
administer [æd'mɪnɪstə(r)] *v.t.* **a)** *(manage)* verwalten; **b)** leisten ⟨*Hilfe*⟩; verabreichen ⟨*Medikamente*⟩. **administration** [ədmɪnɪ'streɪʃn] *n.* Verwaltung, *die.* **administrative** [əd'mɪnɪstrətɪv] *adj.* Verwaltungs-. **administrator** [əd'mɪnɪstreɪtə(r)] *n.* Administrator, *der;* Verwalter, *der*
admirable ['ædmərəbl] *adj.* bewundernswert
admiral ['ædmərəl] *n.* Admiral, *der*
admiration [ædmə'reɪʃn] *n.* Bewunderung, *die* (**of, for** für)
admire [əd'maɪə(r)] *v.t.* bewundern
admirer [əd'maɪərə(r)] *n.* Bewunderer, *der*/Bewunderin, *die*
admission [əd'mɪʃn] *n.* **a)** *(entry)* Zutritt, *der;* **b)** *(charge)* Eintritt, *der;* **c)** *(confession)* Eingeständnis, *das*
admit [əd'mɪt] *v.t.,* **-tt-: a)** *(let in)* hinein-/hereinlassen; **b)** *(acknowledge)* zugeben. **admittance** [əd'mɪtəns] *n.* Zutritt, *der.* **admittedly** [əd'mɪtɪdlɪ] *adv.* zugegeben[ermaßen]
admonish [əd'mɒnɪʃ] *v.t.* ermahnen
ado [ə'duː] *n.* **without more** ~: ohne weiteres Aufheben
adolescence [ædə'lesns] *n.* die Zeit des Erwachsenenwerdens. **adolescent** [ædə'lesnt] **1.** *n.* Heranwachsende, *der/die.* **2.** *adj.* heranwachsend
adopt [ə'dɒpt] *v.t.* **a)** adoptieren; **b)** *(take over)* annehmen ⟨*Glaube, Kultur*⟩; **c)** *(take up)* übernehmen ⟨*Methode*⟩; einnehmen ⟨*Standpunkt, Haltung*⟩. **adoption** [ə'dɒpʃn] *n.* **a)** Adoption, *die;* **b)** *(taking over)* Annahme,

die; c) *(taking up)* Übernahme, *die; (of point of view)* Einnahme, *die*
adorable [ə'dɔːrəbl] *adj.* bezaubernd
adoration [ædə'reɪʃn] *n.* Verehrung, *die*
adore [ə'dɔː(r)] *v.t.* verehren
adorn [ə'dɔːn] *v.t.* schmücken. **a'dornment** *n.* Verzierung, *die;* ~s Schmuck, *der*
adrenalin [ə'drenəlɪn] *n.* Adrenalin, *das*
Adriatic [eɪdrɪ'ætɪk] *pr. n.* ~ [**Sea**] Adriatisches Meer
adrift [ə'drɪft] *adj.* **be** ~: treiben
adroit [ə'drɔɪt] *adj.* geschickt
adulation [ædjʊ'leɪʃn] *n.* Vergötterung, *die*
adult ['ædʌlt, ə'dʌlt] **1.** *adj.* erwachsen. **2.** *n.* Erwachsene, *der/die*
adulterate [ə'dʌltəreɪt] *v.t.* verunreinigen
adultery [ə'dʌltərɪ] *n.* Ehebruch, *der*
advance [əd'vɑːns] **1.** *v.t.* **a)** *(also Mil.)* vorrücken lassen; **b)** *(put forward)* vorbringen ⟨*Plan, Meinung*⟩; **c)** *(further)* fördern; **d)** *(pay before due date)* vorschießen; leihen ⟨*Bank:*⟩. **2.** *v.i.* **a)** *(also Mil.)* vorrücken; ⟨*Prozession:*⟩ sich vorwärts bewegen; **b)** *(fig.: make progress)* vorankommen. **3.** *n.* **a)** Vorrücken, *das; (fig.: progress)* Fortschritt, *der;* **b)** *usu. in pl. (personal approach)* Annäherungsversuch, *der;* **c)** *(on salary)* Vorschuß, *der;* **d) in** ~: im voraus. **advanced** [əd'vɑːnst] *adj.* fortgeschritten
advantage [əd'vɑːntɪdʒ] *n.* Vorteil, *der;* **take** ~ **of sb.** jmdn. ausnutzen; **be to one's** ~: für jmdn. von Vorteil sein; **turn sth. to [one's]** ~: etw. ausnutzen. **advantageous** [ædvən'teɪdʒəs] *adj.* vorteilhaft
advent ['ædvent] *n.* Beginn, *der;* **A~:** Advent, *der*
adventure [əd'ventʃə(r)] *n.* Abenteuer, *das.* **adventurous** [əd'ventʃərəs] *adj.* abenteuerlustig
adverb ['ædvɜːb] *n.* Adverb, *das*
adversary ['ædvəsərɪ] *n. (enemy)* Widersacher, *der*/Widersacherin, *die; (opponent)* Kontrahent, *der*/Kontrahentin, *die*
adverse ['ædvɜːs] *adj.* **a)** *(unfavourable)* ungünstig; **b)** *(contrary)* widrig ⟨*Wind, Umstände*⟩. **adversity** [əd'vɜːsɪtɪ] *n.* **a)** *no pl.* Not, *die;* **b)** *usu. in pl.* Widrigkeit, *die*
advert ['ædvɜːt] *(Brit. coll.) see* **advertisement**

advertise ['ædvətaız] 1. *v. t.* werben für; *(by small ad)* inserieren; ausschreiben ⟨*Stelle*⟩. 2. *v. i.* werben; *(in newspaper)* inserieren; annoncieren. **advertisement** [əd'vɜːtısmənt] *n.* Anzeige, *die;* TV ~: Fernsehspot, *der.* **advertiser** ['ædvətaızə(r)] *n. (in newspaper)* Inserent, *der/*Inserentin, *die.* **advertising** ['ædvətaızıŋ] *n.* Werbung, *die; attrib.* Werbe-

advice [əd'vaıs] *n.* Rat, *der;* **take sb.'s** ~: jmds. Rat *(Dat.)* folgen

advisable [əd'vaızəbl] *adj.* ratsam

advise [əd'vaız] *v. t.* beraten; ~ **sth.** zu etw. raten; *(inform)* unterrichten (**of** über + *Akk.*). **adviser, advisor** [əd-'vaızə(r)] *n.* Berater, *der/*Beraterin, *die.* **advisory** [əd'vaızərı] *adj.* beratend

advocate 1. ['ædvəkət] *n. (of a cause)* Befürworter, *der/*Befürworterin, *die; (Law)* [Rechts]anwalt, *der/*-anwältin, *die.* 2. ['ædvəkeıt] *v. t.* befürworten

aerial ['eərıəl] 1. *adj.* Luft-. 2. *n.* Antenne, *die*

aero- [eərəʊ] *in comb.* Aero-

aerody'namic *adj.* aerodynamisch

aeronautics [eərə'nɔːtıks] *n.* Aeronautik, *die*

aeroplane ['eərəpleın] *n. (Brit.)* Flugzeug, *das*

aerosol ['eərəsɒl] *n. (spray)* Spray, *der od. das; (container)* ~ [spray] Spraydose, *die*

aesthetic [iːs'θetık] *adj.* ästhetisch

afar [ə'fɑː] *adv.* **from** ~: aus der Ferne

affable ['æfəbl] *adj.* freundlich

affair [ə'feə(r)] *n.* **a)** *(concern)* Angelegenheit, *die;* **b)** *in pl. (business)* Geschäfte *Pl.;* **c)** *(love* ~*)* Affäre, *die*

affect [ə'fekt] *v. t.* **a)** sich auswirken auf (+ *Akk.*); **b)** *(emotionally)* betroffen machen

affectation [æfek'teıʃn] *n. (studied display)* Verstellung, *die; (artificiality)* Affektiertheit, *die*

affected [ə'fektıd] *adj.* affektiert; gekünstelt ⟨*Sprache, Stil*⟩

affection [ə'fekʃn] *n.* Zuneigung, *die.* **affectionate** [ə'fekʃənət] *adj.* anhänglich; liebevoll ⟨*Umarmung*⟩. **af'fectionately** *adv.* liebevoll

affiliate [ə'fılıeıt] *v. t.* **be** ~**d to sth.** an etw. *(Akk.)* angegliedert sein

affinity [ə'fınıtı] *n.* **a)** *(relationship)* Verwandtschaft, *die* (**to** mit); **b)** *(liking)* Neigung, *die* (**for** zu); **feel an** ~ **to** *or* **for sb./sth.** sich zu jmdm./etw. hingezogen fühlen

affirm [ə'fɜːm] *v. t. (assert)* bekräftigen ⟨*Absicht*⟩; beteuern ⟨*Unschuld*⟩; *(state as a fact)* bestätigen. **affirmation** [æfə'meıʃn] *n. (of intention)* Bekräftigung, *die; (of fact)* Bestätigung, *die.* **affirmative** [ə'fɜːmətıv] 1. *adj.* affirmativ; bejahend ⟨*Antwort*⟩. 2. *n.* **answer in the** ~: bejahend antworten

afflict [ə'flıkt] *v. t. (physically)* plagen; *(mentally)* quälen; peinigen; **be** ~**ed with sth.** von etw. befallen sein. **affliction** [ə'flıkʃn] *n.* Leiden, *das*

affluence ['æflʊəns] *n.* Reichtum, *der.* **affluent** ['æflʊənt] *adj.* reich

afford [ə'fɔːd] *v. t.* **a)** sich *(Dat.)* leisten; **b)** *(provide)* bieten; gewähren ⟨*Schutz*⟩

affray [ə'freı] *n.* Schlägerei, *die*

affront [ə'frʌnt] 1. *v. t.* beleidigen. 2. *n.* Beleidigung, *die*

afield [ə'fiːld] *adv.* **far** ~ *(direction)* weit hinaus; *(place)* weit draußen

afloat [ə'fləʊt] *pred. adj.* **a)** *(floating)* über Wasser; flott ⟨*Schiff*⟩; **b)** *(at sea)* auf See; **be** ~: auf dem Meer treiben

afoot [ə'fʊt] *pred. adj.* im Gange

aforementioned [ə'fɔː'menʃnd], **aforesaid** [ə'fɔːsed] *adjs.* obenerwähnt *od.* -genannt

afraid [ə'freıd] *adj.* **be** ~ [**of sb./sth.**] [vor jmdm./etw.] Angst haben; **be** ~ **to do sth.** Angst davor haben, etw. zu tun; **I'm** ~ **so/not** ich fürchte ja/nein

afresh [ə'freʃ] *adv.* von neuem

Africa ['æfrıkə] *pr. n.* Afrika *(das).* **African** ['æfrıkən] 1. *adj.* afrikanisch. 2. *n.* Afrikaner, *der/*Afrikanerin, *die*

after ['ɑːftə(r)] 1. *adv.* **a)** *(later)* danach; **b)** *(behind)* hinterher. 2. *prep.* **a)** *(in time)* nach; **two days** ~: zwei Tage danach; **b)** *(behind)* hinter (+ *Dat.*); **c) ask** ~ **sb./sth.** nach jmdm./etw. fragen; **d)** ~ **all** schließlich. 3. *conj.* nachdem. **'after-care** *n. (Med.)* Nachbehandlung, *die.* **'after-effect** *n.* Nachwirkung, *die*

aftermath ['ɑːftəmæθ, 'ɑːftəmɑːθ] *n.* Nachwirkungen *Pl.*

after: ~**'noon** *n.* Nachmittag, *der;* **this/tomorrow** ~: heute/morgen nachmittag; **in the** ~: am Nachmittag; *(regularly)* nachmittags; ~**shave** *n.* After-shave, *das;* ~**thought** *n.* nachträglicher Einfall

afterwards ['ɑːftəwədz] *adv.* danach

again [ə'gen, ə'geın] *adv.* wieder; *(one more time)* noch einmal; ~ **and** ~, **time and** [**time**] ~: immer wieder; **back** ~: wieder zurück

against [ə'genst, ə'geɪnst] *prep.* gegen

age [eɪdʒ] **1.** *n.* **a)** Alter, *das;* **what ~ are you?** wie alt bist du?; **at the ~ of** im Alter von; **come of ~:** volljährig werden; **be under ~:** zu jung sein; **b)** *(great period)* Zeitalter, *das;* **~s** *(coll.: a long time)* eine Ewigkeit. **2.** *v. t.* altern lassen. **3.** *v. i.* altern. **aged** *adj.* **a)** [eɪdʒd] **be ~ five** fünf Jahre alt sein; **a boy ~ five** ein fünfjähriger Junge; **b)** ['eɪdʒɪd] *(elderly)* bejahrt

age: ~-group *n.* Altersgruppe, *die;* **~ limit** *n.* Altersgrenze, *die*

agency ['eɪdʒənsɪ] *n. (business establishment)* Geschäftsstelle, *die; (news/ advertising ~)* Agentur, *die*

agenda [ə'dʒendə] *n.* Tagesordnung, *die*

agent ['eɪdʒənt] *n.* Vertreter, *der/*Vertreterin, *die; (spy)* Agent, *der/*Agentin, *die*

aggravate ['ægrəveɪt] *v. t.* **a)** *(make worse)* verschlimmern; **b)** *(annoy)* aufregen; ärgern. **aggravating** ['ægrəveɪtɪŋ] *adj.* ärgerlich. **aggravation** [ægrə'veɪʃn] *n.* **a)** Verschlimmerung, *die;* **b)** *(annoyance)* Ärger, *der*

aggregate ['ægrɪgət] **1.** *n.* Gesamtmenge, *die.* **2.** *adj.* gesamt

aggression [ə'greʃn] *n.* Aggression, *die*

aggressive [ə'gresɪv] *adj.,* **ag'gressively** *adv.* aggressiv. **ag'gressiveness** *n.* Aggressivität, *die*

aggressor [ə'gresə(r)] *n.* Aggressor, *der*

aggrieved [ə'griːvd] *v. t. (resentful)* verärgert; *(offended)* gekränkt

aghast [ə'gɑːst] *pred. adj.* bestürzt

agile ['ædʒaɪl] *adj.* beweglich; flink ⟨*Bewegung*⟩. **agility** [ə'dʒɪlɪtɪ] *n.* Beweglichkeit, *die; (of movement)* Flinkheit, *die*

agitate ['ædʒɪteɪt] **1.** *v. t.* **a)** *(shake)* schütteln; **b)** *(disturb)* erregen. **2.** *v. i.* agitieren. **agitation** [ædʒɪ'teɪʃn] *n.* **a)** *(shaking)* Schütteln, *das;* **b)** *(emotional)* Erregung, *die.* **agitator** ['ædʒɪteɪtə(r)] *n.* Agitator, *der*

agnostic [æg'nɒstɪk] *n.* Agnostiker, *der/*Agnostikerin, *die*

ago [ə'gəʊ] *adv.* **ten years ~:** vor zehn Jahren; **|not| long ~:** vor [nicht] langer Zeit

agog [ə'gɒg] *pred. adj.* gespannt

agonize ['ægənaɪz] *v. i.* **~ over sth.** sich *(Dat.)* den Kopf über etw. *(Akk.)* zermartern

agony ['ægənɪ] *n.* Todesqualen *Pl.*

agree [ə'griː] **1.** *v. i.* **a)** *(consent)* einverstanden sein (**to, with** mit); **b)** *(hold similar opinion)* einer Meinung sein; **they ~d |with me|** sie waren derselben Meinung [wie ich]; **c)** *(reach similar opinion)* **~ on sth.** sich über etw. *(Akk.)* einigen; **d)** *(harmonize)* übereinstimmen; **e)** **~ with sb.** *(suit)* jmdm. bekommen. **2.** *v. t.* vereinbaren. **agreeable** [ə'griːəbl] *adj.* **a)** *(pleasing)* angenehm; **b)** **be ~ |to sth.|** [mit etw.] einverstanden sein. **agreeably** [ə'griːəblɪ] *adv.* angenehm. **agreed** [ə'griːd] *adj.* einig; vereinbart ⟨*Summe, Zeit*⟩. **a'greement** *n.* Übereinstimmung, *die;* **be in ~ |about sth.|** sich *(Dat.)* [über etw. *(Akk.)*] einig sein

agricultural [ægrɪ'kʌltʃərl] *adj.* landwirtschaftlich

agriculture ['ægrɪkʌltʃə(r)] *n.* Landwirtschaft, *die*

aground [ə'graʊnd] *adj.* **go** *or* **run ~:** auf Grund laufen

ahead [ə'hed] *adv.* voraus; **~ of** vor (+ *Dat.*); **be ~ of the others** *(fig.)* den anderen voraus sein

aid [eɪd] **1.** *v. t.* **a)** **~ sb. |to do sth.|** jmdm. helfen[, etw. zu tun]; **~ed by** unterstützt von; **b)** *(promote)* fördern. **2.** *n.* **a)** *(help)* Hilfe, *die;* **with the ~ of sth./sb.** mit Hilfe einer Sache *(Gen.)/*mit jmds. Hilfe; **in ~ of sth.** zugunsten von jmdm./etw.; **b)** *(source of help)* Hilfsmittel, *das* (**to** für)

aide [eɪd] *n.* Berater, *der/*Beraterin, *die*

Aids [eɪdz] *n.* Aids *(das)*

ailment ['eɪlmənt] *n.* Gebrechen, *das*

aim [eɪm] **1.** *v. t.* ausrichten ⟨*Schußwaffe, Rakete*⟩; **~ sth. at sb./sth.** etw. auf jmdn./etw. richten. **2.** *v. i.* **a)** zielen (**at** auf + *Akk.*); **b)** **~ to do sth.** beabsichtigen, etw. zu tun; **~ at** *or* **for sth.** *(fig.)* etwas anstreben. **3.** *n.* Ziel, *das;* **take ~ |at sth./sb.|** [auf etw./jmdn.] zielen. **'aimless** *adj.,* **'aimlessly** *adv.* ziellos

air [eə(r)] **1.** *n.* **a)** Luft, *die;* **be/go on the ~:** senden; ⟨*Programm:*⟩ gesendet werden; **by ~:** mit dem Flugzeug; *(by ~ mail)* mit Luftpost; **b)** *(facial expression)* Miene, *die;* **c)** **put on ~s** sich aufspielen. **2.** *v. t.* *(ventilate)* lüften; *(make public)* [öffentlich] darlegen

air: ~-bed *n.* Luftmatratze, *die;* **~borne** *adj.* **be ~borne** sich in der Luft befinden; **~-conditioned** *adj.* klimatisiert; **~-conditioning** *n.* Klimaanlage, *die;* **~craft** *n., pl. same*

Flugzeug, *das;* **~craft-carrier** *n.*
Flugzeugträger, *der;* ~ **fare** *n.* Flug-
preis, *der;* **~field** *n.* Flugplatz, *der;* ~
force *n.* Luftwaffe, *die;* **~gun** *n.*
Luftgewehr, *das;* ~ **hostess** *n.* Stewardeß, *die;* ~ **letter** *n.* Aerogramm,
das; **~line** *n.* Fluggesellschaft, *die;* ~
mail *n.* Luftpost, *die;* by ~ **mail** mit
Luftpost; **~man** ['əmən] *n., pl.* **~men**
[~mən] Flieger, *der;* **~plane** *n.*
(Amer.) Flugzeug, *das;* **~port** *n.*
Flughafen, *der;* ~ **raid** *n.* Luftangriff,
der; **~-raid shelter** *n.* Luftschutzraum, *der;* **~ship** *n.* Luftschiff, *das;*
~sick *adj.* luftkrank; **~tight** *adj.*
luftdicht; **~-traffic controller** *n.*
Fluglotse, *der*

'airy *adj.* luftig ‹Büro, Zimmer›
aisle [aɪl] *n.* Gang, *der;* (of church) Sei-
tenschiff, *das*
ajar [ə'dʒɑː(r)] *adj.* be ~: einen Spalt-
breit offenstehen
akin [ə'kɪn] *adj.* be ~ to sth. einer Sache *(Dat.)* ähnlich sein
alarm [ə'lɑːm] **1.** *n.* **a)** Alarm, *der;* give
or raise the ~: Alarm schlagen; **b)**
(fear) Angst, *die.* **2.** *v. t.* aufschrecken.
a'larm clock *n.* Wecker, *der*
alas [ə'læs] *int.* ach
albatross ['ælbətrɒs] *n.* Albatros, *der*
album ['ælbəm] *n.* Album, *das*
alcohol ['ælkəhɒl] *n.* Alkohol, *der.* **alcoholic** [ælkə'hɒlɪk] **1.** *adj.* alkoholisch. **2.** *n.* Alkoholiker, *der*/Alkoholi-
kerin, *die.* **alcoholism** ['ælkəhɒlɪzm]
n. Alkoholismus, *der*
alcove ['ælkəʊv] *n.* Alkoven, *der*
ale [eɪl] *n.* Ale, *das*
alert [ə'lɜːt] **1.** *adj.* wachsam. **2.** *n.*
Alarmbereitschaft, *die;* on the ~: auf
der Hut. **3.** *v. t.* alarmieren; ~ sb. [to
sth.] jmdn. [vor etw. *(Dat.)*] warnen
'A level *n. (Brit. Sch.)* ≈ Abitur, *das*
algebra ['ældʒɪbrə] *n.* Algebra, *die*
Algeria [æl'dʒɪərɪə] *pr. n.* Algerien
(das)
alias ['eɪlɪəs] **1.** *adv.* alias. **2.** *n.* ange-
nommener Name
alibi ['ælɪbaɪ] *n.* Alibi, *das*
alien ['eɪlɪən] **1.** *adj.* **a)** *(strange)*
fremd; **b)** *(foreign)* ausländisch. **2.** *n.*
a) *(from another world)* Außerirdi-
sche, *der/die;* **b)** *(Admin.: foreigner)*
Ausländer, *der*/Ausländerin, *die.*
alienate ['eɪlɪəneɪt] *v. t.* befremden.
alienation [eɪlɪə'neɪʃn] *n.* Entfremdung, *die*
'alight [ə'laɪt] *v. i.* **a)** aussteigen (from
aus); **b)** ‹Vogel:› sich niedersetzen

²alight *adj.* be/catch ~: brennen; set
sth. ~: etw. in Brand setzen
align [ə'laɪn] *v. t.* **a)** *(place in a line)*
ausrichten; **b)** *(bring into line)* in eine
Linie bringen. **a'lignment** *n.* Aus-
richtung, *die;* out of ~: nicht richtig
ausgerichtet
alike [ə'laɪk] *pred. adj.* ähnlich; *(indis-
tinguishable)* gleich
alimony ['ælɪmənɪ] *n.* Unterhaltszah-
lung, *die*
alive [ə'laɪv] *pred. adj.* **a)** lebendig; **b)**
(aware) be ~ to sth. sich *(Dat.)* einer
Sache *(Gen.)* bewußt sein; **c)** *(swarm-
ing)* be ~ with wimmeln von
alkali ['ælkəlaɪ] *n., pl.* **~s** *or* **~es** Alkali,
das
all [ɔːl] **1.** *attrib. adj.* **a)** *(entire extent or
quantity of)* ganz; ~ **day** den ganzen
Tag; ~ **my money** all mein Geld; mein
ganzes Geld; **b)** *(entire number of)* alle; ~ **the books** alle Bücher; ~ **my
books** all[e] meine Bücher; ~ **the
others** alle anderen; **c)** *(any whatever)*
jeglicher/jegliche/jegliches; **d)** *(greatest possible)* **in** ~ **innocence** in aller
Unschuld. **2.** *n.* **a)** *(~ persons)* alle; ~
of us wir alle; **the happiest of** ~: der/
die Glücklichste unter *od.* von allen;
b) *(every bit)* ~ of it alles; ~ **of the
money** das ganze Geld; **c)** ~ of *(coll.:
as much as)* be ~ of seven feet tall gut
sieben Fuß groß sein; **d)** *(~ things)* alles; ~ **I need is the money** ich brauche
nur das Geld; **that is** ~: das ist alles;
the most beautiful of ~: der/die/das
Schönste von allen; **most of** ~: am
meisten; **it was** ~ **but impossible** es war
fast unmöglich; **it's** ~ **the same to me**
es ist mir ganz egal; **can I help you at
**~? kann ich Ihnen irgendwie behilf-
lich sein?; **she has no talent at** ~: sie
hat überhaupt kein Talent; **nothing at**
~: gar nichts; **not at** ~ **happy/well**
überhaupt nicht glücklich/gesund;
not at ~! überhaupt nicht!; *(acknow-
ledging thanks)* gern geschehen!; **if at**
~: wenn überhaupt; **in** ~: insgesamt;
e) *(Sport)* **two [goals]** ~: zwei zu zwei;
(Tennis) **thirty** ~: dreißig beide. **3.**
adv. ganz; ~ **but fast;** ~ **the better/
worse [for that]** um so besser/schlim-
mer; ~ **at once** *(suddenly)* plötzlich; **be**
~ **'in** *(exhausted)* total erledigt sein
(ugs.); **sth. is** ~ **right** etw. ist in Ordnung; *(tolerable)* etw. ist ganz gut; **I'm**
~ **right** mir geht es ganz gut; **yes,** ~
right ja, gut; **it's** ~ **right by me** das ist
mir recht

allay [ə'leɪ] *v. t.* zerstreuen ⟨*Besorgnis, Befürchtungen*⟩

all-'clear *n.* Entwarnung, *die*

allegation [ælı'geɪʃn] *n.* Behauptung, *die*

allege [ə'ledʒ] *v. t.* behaupten. **alleged** [ə'ledʒd] *adj.*, **allegedly** [ə'ledʒɪdlı] *adv.* angeblich

allegiance [ə'li:dʒəns] *n.* Loyalität, *die* (to gegenüber)

allegory ['ælıgərı] *n.* Allegorie, *die*

allergic [ə'lɜ:dʒɪk] *adj.* allergisch (to gegen)

allergy ['ælədʒı] *n.* Allergie, *die*

alleviate [ə'li:vɪeɪt] *v. t.* abschwächen

alley ['ælı] *n.* [schmale] Gasse

alliance [ə'laɪəns] *n.* Bündnis, *das; (league)* Allianz, *die*

allied ['ælaɪd] *adj.* be ~ to or with sb./ sth. mit jmdm./etw. verbündet sein

alligator ['ælıgeɪtə(r)] *n.* Alligator, *der*

'all-in *adj.* Pauschal-

allocate ['æləkeɪt] *v. t.* zuweisen, zuteilen (to *Dat.*). **allocation** [ælə'keɪʃl] *n.* Zuweisung, *die; (ration)* Zuteilung, *die*

allot [ə'lɒt] *v. t.*, **-tt-**: ~ sth. to sb. jmdm. etw. zuteilen. **al'lotment** *n.* (*Brit.: plot of land*) ≈ Schrebergarten, *der*

allow [ə'laʊ] **1.** *v. t.* erlauben; zulassen; ~ sb. to do sth. jmdm. erlauben, etw. zu tun; be ~ed to do sth. etw. tun dürfen. **2.** *v. i.* ~ for sth. etw. berücksichtigen. **allowance** [ə'laʊəns] *n.* **a)** Zuteilung, *die; (for special expenses)* Zuschuß, *der;* **b)** make ~s for sth./sb. etw./jmdn. berücksichtigen

alloy ['ælɔı] *n.* Legierung, *die*

all: **~-round** *adj.* Allround-; **~-'rounder** *n.* Allroundtalent, *das;* **~-time** *adj.* **~-time record** absoluter Rekord

allude [ə'lu:d] *v. i.* ~ to sich beziehen auf (+ *Akk.*); *(indirectly)* anspielen auf (+ *Akk.*). **allusion** [ə'lu:ʒn] *n.* Hinweis, *der; (indirect)* Anspielung, *die*

ally ['ælaı] *n.* Verbündete, *der/die;* **the Allies** die Alliierten

almighty [ɔ:l'maɪtı] *adj.* allmächtig; **the A~:** der Allmächtige

almond ['ɑ:mənd] *n.* Mandel, *die*

almost ['ɔ:lməʊst] *adv.* fast; beinahe

alms [ɑ:mz] *n.* Almosen, *das*

alone [ə'ləʊn] **1.** *pred. adj.* allein; alleine (*ugs.*). **2.** *adv.* allein

along [ə'lɒŋ] **1.** *prep.* entlang *(position:* + *Dat.; direction:* + *Akk.*). **2.** *adv.*

weiter; **I'll be ~ shortly** ich komme gleich; **all ~:** die ganze Zeit [über].

along'side 1. *adv.* daneben. **2.** *prep.* neben *(position:* + *Dat.; direction:* + *Akk.*)

aloof [ə'lu:f] **1.** *adv.* abseits; **hold ~ from sb.** sich von jmdm. fernhalten. **2.** *adj.* distanziert

aloud [ə'laʊd] *adv.* laut; **read [sth.] ~:** [etw.] vorlesen

alphabet ['ælfəbet] *n.* Alphabet, *das.* **alphabetical** [ælfə'betɪkl] *adj.*, **alpha'betically** *adv.* alphabetisch

alpine ['ælpaın] *adj.* alpin

Alps [ælps] *pr. n. pl.* **the ~:** die Alpen

already [ɔ:l'redı] *adv.* schon

Alsation [æl'seɪʃn] *n.* [deutscher] Schäferhund

also ['ɔ:lsəʊ] *adv.* auch; *(moreover)* außerdem

altar ['ɔ:ltə(r), 'ɒltə(r)] *n.* Altar, *der*

alter ['ɔ:ltə(r), 'ɒltə(r)] **1.** *v. t.* ändern. **2.** *v. i.* sich verändern. **alteration** [ɔ:ltə'reɪʃn, ɒltə'reɪʃn] *n.* Änderung, *die*

alternate 1. [ɔ:l'tɜ:nət] *adj.* sich abwechselnd. **2.** ['ɔ:ltəneɪt] *v. t.* abwechseln lassen. **3.** ['ɔ:ltəneɪt] *v. i.* sich abwechseln. **al'ternately** *adv.* abwechselnd

alternative [ɔ:l'tɜ:nətɪv] **1.** *adj.* alternativ; Alternativ-. **2.** *n.* **a)** *(choice)* Alternative, *die;* **b)** *(possibility)* Möglichkeit, *die.* **al'ternatively** *adv.* oder aber; **or ~:** oder aber auch

although [ɔ:l'ðəʊ] *conj.* obwohl

altitude ['æltɪtju:d] *n.* Höhe, *die*

altogether [ɔ:ltə'geðə(r)] *adv.* völlig; *(on the whole)* im großen und ganzen; *(in total)* insgesamt; **not ~ [true/convincing]** nicht ganz [wahr/überzeugend]

altruistic [æltrʊ'ıstık] *adj.* altruistisch

aluminium [æljʊ'mınıəm] *(Brit.),* **aluminum** [ə'lu:mınəm] *(Amer.) ns.* Aluminium, *das*

always ['ɔ:lweız] *adv.* immer; *(repeatedly)* ständig

AM *abbr.* **amplitude modulation** AM

am *see* **be**

a.m. [eɪ'em] *adv.* vormittags; **[at] one/ four ~:** [um] ein/vier Uhr früh

amalgamate 1. [ə'mælgəmeɪt] *v. t.* vereinigen. **2.** *v. i.* sich vereinigen; ⟨*Firmen:*⟩ fusionieren. **amalgamation** [əmælgə'meɪʃn] *n.* Vereinigung, *die; (of firms)* Fusion, *die*

amass [ə'mæs] *v. t.* anhäufen

amateur ['æmətə(r)] *n.* Amateur, *der; attrib.* Amateur-; Laien-. **amateur-**

ish ['æmətərıʃ] *adj.* laienhaft; amateurhaft

amaze [ə'meız] *v. t.* verblüffen; verwundern. **a'mazement** *n.* Verblüffung, *die;* Verwunderung, *die.* **amazing** [ə'meızıŋ] *adj. (remarkable)* erstaunlich; *(astonishing)* verblüffend

Amazon ['æməzən] *pr. n.* the ~: der Amazonas

ambassador [æm'bæsədə(r)] *n.* Botschafter, *der/*Botschafterin, *die*

amber ['æmbə(r)] **1.** *n.* **a)** Bernstein, *der;* **b)** *(traffic light)* Gelb, *das.* **2.** *adj.* Bernstein-; *(colour)* bernsteinfarben; gelb ⟨*Verkehrslicht*⟩

ambiguity [æmbı'gjuːıtı] *n.* Zweideutigkeit, *die*

ambiguous [æm'bıgjʊəs] *adj.* zweideutig

ambition [æm'bıʃn] *n.* Ehrgeiz, *der; (aspiration)* Ambition, *die.* **ambitious** [æm'bıʃəs] *adj.* ehrgeizig

ambivalent [æm'bıvələnt] *adj.* ambivalent

amble ['æmbl] *v. i.* schlendern

ambulance ['æmbjʊləns] *n.* Krankenwagen, *der;* Ambulanz, *die*

ambush ['æmbʊʃ] **1.** *n.* Hinterhalt, *der;* lie in ~: im Hinterhalt liegen. **2.** *v. t.* [aus dem Hinterhalt] überfallen

amen [ɑː'men, eı'men] **1.** *int.* amen. **2.** *n.* Amen, *das*

amenable [ə'miːnəbl] *adj.* zugänglich, aufgeschlossen (**to** *Dat.*)

amend [ə'mend] *v. t.* berichtigen; abändern ⟨*Gesetzentwurf, Antrag*⟩. **a'mendment** *n. (to motion)* Abänderungsantrag, *der; (to bill)* Änderungsantrag, *der*

amends [ə'mendz] *n. pl.* make ~ |to sb.| es [bei jmdm.] wiedergutmachen; make ~ for sth. etw. wiedergutmachen

amenity [ə'miːnıtı] *n., usu. in pl.* amenities *(of town)* kulturelle und Freizeiteinrichtungen

America [ə'merıkə] *pr. n.* Amerika *(das).* **American** [ə'merıkən] **1.** *adj.* amerikanisch; **sb. is** ~: jmd. ist Amerikaner/Amerikanerin. **2.** *n. (person)* Amerikaner, *der/*Amerikanerin, *die.* **Americanize** [ə'merıkənaız] *v. t.* amerikanisieren

amiable ['eımıəbl] *adj.* umgänglich

amicable ['æmıkəbl] *adj.* freundschaftlich; gütlich ⟨*Einigung*⟩. **amicably** ['æmıkəblı] *adv.* in [aller] Freundschaft

amid[st] [ə'mıd(st)] *prep.* inmitten; *(fig.: during)* bei

amiss [ə'mıs] **1.** *pred. adj.* verkehrt; **is anything** ~? stimmt irgend etwas nicht? **2.** *adv.* **take sth.** ~: etw. übelnehmen

ammonia [ə'məʊnıə] *n.* Ammoniak, *das*

ammunition [æmjʊ'nıʃn] *n.* Munition, *die*

amnesia [æm'niːzıə] Amnesie, *die*

amnesty ['æmnıstı] *n.* Amnestie, *die*

amok [ə'mɒk] *adv.* run ~: Amok laufen

among[st] [ə'mʌŋ(st)] *prep.* unter (+ *Dat.*); ~ **other things** unter anderem; **they often quarrel** ~ **themselves** sie streiten oft miteinander

amoral [eı'mɒrl] *adj.* amoralisch

amorphous [ə'mɔːfəs] *adj.* formlos; amorph ⟨*Masse*⟩

amount [ə'maʊnt] **1.** *v. i.* ~ **to sth.** sich auf etw. *(Akk.)* belaufen; *(fig.)* etw. bedeuten. **2.** *n.* **a)** *(total)* Betrag, *der;* Summe, *die;* **b)** *(quantity)* Menge, *die*

amp [æmp] *n.* Ampere, *das*

amphibian [æm'fıbıən] **1.** *adj.* amphibisch. **2.** *n.* Amphibie, *die.* **amphibious** [æm'fıbıəs] *adj.* amphibisch

amphitheatre ['æmfıθıətə(r)] *n.* Amphitheater, *das*

ample ['æmpl] *adj.* **a)** *(spacious)* weitläufig ⟨*Garten, Räume*⟩; reichhaltig ⟨*Mahl*⟩; **b)** *(enough)* ~ **room/food** reichlich Platz/zu essen

amplifier ['æmplıfaıə(r)] *n.* Verstärker, *der*

amplify ['æmplıfaı] *v. t.* verstärken; *(enlarge on)* weiter ausführen

amputate ['æmpjʊteıt] *v. t.* amputieren. **amputation** [æmpjʊ'teıʃn] *n.* Amputation, *die*

amuse [ə'mjuːz] *v. t.* **a)** *(interest)* unterhalten; ~ **oneself by doing sth.** sich *(Dat.)* die Zeit damit vertreiben, etw. zu tun; **b)** *(make laugh or smile)* amüsieren. **a'musement** *n.* Belustigung, *die;* ~ **arcade** Spielhalle, *die.* **amusing** [ə'mjuːzıŋ] *adj.* amüsant

an [ən, *stressed* æn] *indef. art. see also* ²**a:** ein/eine/ein

anaemia [ə'niːmıə] *n.* Blutarmut, *die;* Anämie, *die.* **anaemic** [ə'niːmık] *adj.* blutarm; anämisch

anaesthetic [ænıs'θetık] *n.* Anästhetikum, *das;* **general** ~: Narkosemittel, *das;* **local** ~: Lokalanästhetikum, *das*

anagram ['ænəgræm] *n.* Anagramm, *das*

analogy [ə'nælədʒı] *n.* Analogie, *die*

analyse ['ænəlaız] *v. t.* analysieren.

analysis [ə'næləsıs] *n., pl.* **analyses**
[ə'næləsi:z] Analyse, *die.* **analyst**
['ænəlıst] *n.* **a)** *(Psych.)* Analytiker,
*der/*Analytikerin, *die;* **b)** *(Econ.,
Polit., etc.)* Experte, *der.* **analytic**
[ænə'lıtık], **analytical** [ænə'lıtıkl] *adj.*
analytisch. **analyze** *(Amer.) see* **analyse**
anarchist ['ænəkıst] *n.* Anarchist,
*der/*Anarchistin, *die*
anarchy ['ænəkı] *n.* Anarchie, *die*
anatomical [ænə'tɒmıkl] *adj.* anatomisch
anatomy [ə'nætəmı] *n.* Anatomie, *die*
ancestor ['ænsestə(r)] *n.* Vorfahr, *der.*
ancestry ['ænsestrı] *n.* Abstammung, *die*
anchor ['æŋkə(r)] **1.** *n.* Anker, *der.* **2.**
v.t. verankern. **3.** *v.i.* ankern. **anchorage** ['æŋkərıdʒ] *n.* Ankerplatz,
der
anchovy ['æntʃəvı] *n.* Sardelle, *die*
ancient ['eınʃənt] *adj.* alt; historisch
⟨*Gebäude usw.*⟩; *(of antiquity)* antik
and [ənd, *stressed* ænd] *conj.* und; **for
weeks ~ weeks** wochenlang; **better ~
better** immer besser
anecdote ['ænıkdəʊt] *n.* Anekdote,
die
anemia, anemic *(Amer.) see* **anaem-**
angel ['eındʒl] *n.* Engel, *der.* **angelic**
[æn'dʒelık] *adj.* engelhaft
anger ['æŋgə(r)] **1.** *n.* Zorn, *der* (**at**
über + *Akk.*); *(fury)* Wut, *die* (**at** über
+ *Akk.*). **2.** *v.t.* verärgern; *(infuriate)*
wütend machen
¹**angle** ['æŋgl] *n.* **a)** *(Geom.)* Winkel,
der; **at an ~ of 60°** im Winkel von 60°;
at an ~: schief; **b)** *(fig.)* Gesichtspunkt, *der*
²**angle** *v.i.* angeln; *(fig.)* **~ for sth.** sich
um etw. bemühen. **angler** ['æŋglə(r)]
n. Angler, *der/*Anglerin, *die*
Anglican ['æŋglıkən] **1.** *adj.* anglikanisch. **2.** *n.* Anglikaner, *der/*Anglika-
nerin, *die*
Anglo- [æŋgləʊ] *in comb.* anglo-/
Anglo-. **Anglo-Saxon** [~'sæksn] **1.**
n. Angelsachse, *der/*Angelsächsin,
die; (language) Angelsächsisch, *das.*
2. *adj.* angelsächsisch
angrily ['æŋgrılı] *adv.* verärgert;
(stronger) zornig
angry ['æŋgrı] *adj.* böse; verärgert
⟨*Person, Stimme, Geste*⟩; *(stronger)*
zornig; wütend; **be ~ at** *or* **about sth.**
wegen etw. böse sein; **be ~ with** *or* **at
sb.** mit jmdm. *od.* auf jmdn. böse sein;
get ~: böse werden

anguish ['æŋgwıʃ] *n.* Qualen *Pl.*
angular ['æŋgjʊlə(r)] *adj.* eckig ⟨*Gebäude, Struktur*⟩; kantig ⟨*Gesicht*⟩
animal ['ænıməl] **1.** *n.* Tier, *das.* **2.**
adj. tierisch
animate 1. ['ænımeıt] *v.t.* beleben. **2.**
['ænımət] *adj.* beseelt ⟨*Leben, Körper*⟩; belebt ⟨*Objekt, Welt*⟩. **ani-
mated** ['ænımeıtıd] *adj.* lebhaft ⟨*Diskussion, Gebärde*⟩; **~ cartoon** Zeichentrickfilm, *der.* **animation** [ænı-
'meıʃn] *n.* **a)** Lebhaftigkeit, *die;* **b)**
(Cinemat.) Animation, *die*
animosity [ænı'mɒsıtı] *n.* Feindseligkeit, *die*
aniseed ['ænısi:d] *n.* Anis[samen], *der*
ankle ['æŋkl] *n.* Fußgelenk, *das*
annex 1. [ə'neks] *v.t.* annektieren
⟨*Land, Territorium*⟩. **2.** ['æneks] *n.* Anbau, *der.* **annexe** *see* **annex 2**
annihilate [ə'naıleıt] *v.t.* vernichten.
annihilation [ənaıı'leıʃn] *n.* Vernichtung, *die*
anniversary [ænı'vɜːsərı] *n.* Jahres-
tag, *der;* **wedding ~:** Hochzeitstag, *der*
annotate ['ænəteıt] *v.t.* kommentie-
ren
announce [ə'naʊns] *v.t.* bekanntgeben; ansagen ⟨*Programm*⟩; *(over
Tannoy etc.)* durchsagen; *(in newspaper)* anzeigen ⟨*Heirat usw.*⟩. **an-
'nouncement** *n.* Bekanntgabe, *die;
(over Tannoy etc.)* Durchsage, *die; (in
newspaper)* Anzeige, *die.* **an'nouncer**
n. Ansager, *der/*Ansagerin, *die*
annoy [ə'nɔı] *v.t.* **a)** ärgern; **b)** *(harass)*
schikanieren. **annoyance** [ə'nɔıəns]
n. Verärgerung, *die; (nuisance)* Plage,
die. **annoyed** [ə'nɔıd] *adj.* **be ~ [at** *or*
with sb./sth.] ärgerlich [auf *od.* über
jmdn./über etw.] sein; **he got very ~:**
er hat sich darüber sehr geärgert. **an-
'noying** *adj.* ärgerlich; lästig ⟨*Gewohnheit, Person*⟩
annual ['ænjʊəl] **1.** *adj.* **a)** *(reckoned by
the year)* Jahres-; **~ rainfall** jährliche
Regenmenge; **b)** *(recurring yearly)*
[all]jährlich ⟨*Ereignis, Feier*⟩; Jahres-
⟨*bericht, -hauptversammlung*⟩. **2.** *n.* **a)**
Jahrbuch, *das; (of comic etc.)* Jahres-
album, *das;* **b)** *(plant)* einjährige
Pflanze. **'annually** *adv.* jährlich
annul [ə'nʌl] *v.t., -ll-* annullieren; auflösen ⟨*Vertrag*⟩
anonymous [ə'nɒnıməs] *adj.* anonym
anorak ['ænəræk] *n.* Anorak, *der*
anorexia [ænə'reksıə] *n.* Anorexie, *die*
(Med.); Magersucht, *die (volkst.)*
another [ə'nʌðə(r)] **1.** *pron.* **a)** *(an*

additional one) noch einer/eine/eins;
ein weiterer/eine weitere/ein weiteres; b) *(counterpart)* wieder einer/ei-
ne/eins; c) *(a different one)* ein ande-
rer/eine andere/ein anderes. 2. *adj.* a)
(additional) noch ein/eine; ein weite-
rer/eine weitere/ein weiteres; **after ~
six weeks** nach weiteren sechs Wochen; b) *(different)* ein anderer/eine
andere/ein anderes
answer ['ɑ:nsə(r)] 1. *n.* a) *(reply)* Antwort, *die* (to auf + *Akk.*); b) *(to problem)* Lösung, *die* (to *Gen.*); *(to calculation)* Ergebnis, *das.* 2. *v. i.* a) beantworten ⟨*Brief, Frage*⟩; antworten auf
(+ *Akk.*) ⟨*Frage, Hilferuf, Einladung,
Inserat*⟩; eingehen auf (+ *Akk.*)
⟨*Angebot, Vorschlag*⟩; sich stellen zu
⟨*Beschuldigung*⟩; erhören ⟨*Gebet*⟩; erfüllen ⟨*Bitte, Wunsch*⟩; **~ sb.** jmdm.
antworten; b) **~ the door/bell** an die
Tür gehen. 3. *v. i.* a) *(reply)* antworten;
~ to sth. sich zu etw. äußern; b) *(be responsible)* **~ for sth.** für etw. die Verantwortung übernehmen; c) **~ to a description** einer Beschreibung *(Dat.)*
entsprechen. **answerable** ['ɑ:nsə-
rəbl] *adj.* verantwortlich (for für; to
Dat.). '**answering machine** *n.* An-
rufbeantworter, *der*
ant [ænt] *n.* Ameise, *die*
antagonism [æn'tægənɪzm] *n.* Feindseligkeit, *die* (towards, against gegenüber). **antagonist** [æn'tægənɪst] *n.*
Gegner, *der*/Gegnerin, *die.* **anta-
gonistic** [æntægə'nɪstɪk] *adj.* feindlich. **antagonize** [æn'tægənaɪz] *v. t.*
~ sb. sich *(Dat.)* jmdn. zum Feind machen
antarctic [ænt'ɑ:ktɪk] 1. *adj.* antarktisch. 2. *n.* **the A~:** die Antarktis
antelope ['æntɪləʊp] *n.* Antilope, *die*
antenna [æn'tenə] *n.* a) *pl.* **~e** [æn-
'teni:] *(Zool.)* Fühler, *der*; b) *pl.* **~s**
(Amer.: aerial) Antenne, *die*
anthem ['ænθəm] *n.* Chorgesang, *der*
anthology [æn'θɒlədʒɪ] *n.* Antholo-
gie, *die*
anthropology [ænθrə'pɒlədʒɪ] *n.* An-
thropologie, *die*
anti- [æntɪ] *pref.* anti-/Anti-
anti-'aircraft *adj.* *(Mil.)* Flugab-
wehr-; **~ gun** Flak, *die*
antibiotic [æntɪbaɪ'ɒtɪk] *n.* Antibiotikum, *das*
antic ['æntɪk] *n.* *(trick)* Mätzchen, *das*
(ugs.); (of clown) Possen, *der*
anticipate [æn'tɪsɪpeɪt] *v. t.* a) *(expect)*
erwarten; *(foresee)* voraussehen; **~**

trouble mit Ärger rechnen; b) *(consider before due time)* vorwegnehmen.
anticipation [æntɪsɪ'peɪʃn] *n.* Erwartung, *die*
anti'climax *n.* Abstieg, *der*
anti'clockwise *adv., adj.* gegen den
Uhrzeigersinn
anti'cyclone *n.* Hochdruckgebiet,
das
antidote ['æntɪdəʊt] *n.* Gegenmittel,
das (for, against, to gegen)
'**antifreeze** *n.* Frostschutzmittel, *das*
antiquated ['æntɪkweɪtɪd] *adj.* antiquiert; veraltet
antique [æn'ti:k] 1. *adj.* antik ⟨*Möbel,
Schmuck usw.*⟩. 2. *n.* Antiquität, *die;*
~ shop Antiquitätenladen, *der*
antiquity [æn'tɪkwɪtɪ] *n.* Altertum,
das; Antike, *die*
anti'septic 1. *adj.* antiseptisch. 2. *n.*
Antiseptikum, *das*
anti'social *adj.* asozial
antithesis [æn'tɪθəsɪs] *n., pl.* **anti-
theses** [æn'tɪθəsi:z] Gegenstück, *das*
(of, to zu)
antler ['æntlə(r)] *n.* Geweihsprosse,
die; |pair of| **~s** Geweih, *das*
anvil ['ænvɪl] *n.* Amboß, *der*
anxiety [æŋ'zaɪətɪ] *n.* Angst, *die; (concern about future)* Sorge, *die* (about
wegen)
anxious ['æŋkʃəs] *adj.* a) *(troubled)*
besorgt (about um); b) *(eager)* sehnlich; **be ~ for sth.** sich nach etw. sehnen. '**anxiously** *adv.* a) besorgt; b)
(eagerly) sehnsüchtig
any ['enɪ] 1. *adj.* a) *(some)* |irgend|ein/
eine; **not ~:** kein/keine; **have you ~
wool/wine?** haben Sie Wolle/Wein?;
b) *(one)* ein/eine; c) *(all, every)* jeder/
jede/jedes; |at| **~ time** jederzeit; d)
(whichever) jeder/jede/jedes [beliebi-
ge]; **choose ~ |one| book/~ books you
like** suchen Sie sich *(Dat.)* irgendein
Buch/irgendwelche Bücher aus. 2.
pron. a) *(some)* in condit., interrog., or
neg. sentence (replacing sing. n.) einer/
eine/ein[e]s; *(replacing collect. n.)* wel-
cher/welche/welches; *(replacing pl.
n.)* welche; **not ~:** keiner/keine/
kein[e]s/Pl. keine; **without ~:** ohne; b)
(no matter which) irgendeiner/irgend-
eine/irgendein[e]s/irgendwelche Pl. 3.
adv. **do you feel ~ better today?** fühlen
Sie sich heute [etwas] besser?; **if it gets
~ colder** wenn es noch kälter wird; **I
can't wait ~ longer** ich kann nicht
[mehr] länger warten
'**anybody** *n. & pron.* a) *(whoever)* je-

der; **b)** *(somebody)* [irgend]jemand; *after neg.* niemand

'anyhow *adv.* **a)** *see* **anyway; b)** *(haphazardly)* irgendwie

'anyone *see* **anybody**

'anything 1. *n. & pron.* **a)** *(whatever thing)* was [immer]; alles, was; **b)** *(something)* irgend etwas; *after neg.* nichts; **c)** *(a thing of any kind)* alles. **2.** *adv.* not ~ **like as ... as** keineswegs so ... wie

'anyway *adv.* **a)** *(in any case, besides)* sowieso; **b)** *(at any rate)* jedenfalls

'anywhere *adv.* **a)** *(in any place) (wherever)* überall, wo; wo [immer]; *(somewhere)* irgendwo; **not ~ near as ... as** *(coll.)* nicht annähernd so ... wie; **b)** *(to any place) (wherever)* wohin [auch immer]; *(somewhere)* irgendwohin

apart [ə'pɑːt] *adv.* **a)** *(separately)* getrennt; ~ **from ...:** außer ...; **b)** *(into pieces)* auseinander

apartheid [ə'pɑːteɪt] *n.* Apartheid, *die*

apartment [ə'pɑːtmənt] *n.* **a)** *(room)* Apartment, *das;* **b)** *(Amer.: flat)* Wohnung, *die*

apathetic [æpə'θetɪk] *adj.* apathisch *(about* gegenüber*)*

apathy ['æpəθɪ] *n.* Apathie, *die* **(about** gegenüber**)**

ape [eɪp] **1.** *n.* [Menschen]affe, *der.* **2.** *v. t.* nachahmen

aperitif [əperɪ'tiːf] *n.* Aperitif, *der*

aperture ['æpətʃə(r)] *n.* Öffnung, *die*

apex ['eɪpeks] *n.* Spitze, *die*

aphrodisiac [æfrə'dɪzɪæk] *n.* Aphrodisiakum, *das*

apiece [ə'piːs] *adv.* je; **they cost a penny ~:** sie kosten einen Penny das Stück

apologetic [əpɒlə'dʒetɪk] *adj.* entschuldigend; **be ~:** sich entschuldigen

apologize [ə'pɒlədʒaɪz] *v. i.* sich entschuldigen **(to** bei**)**

apology [ə'pɒlədʒɪ] *n.* Entschuldigung, *die;* **make an ~:** sich entschuldigen **(to** bei**)**

apoplectic [æpə'plektɪk] *adj.* apoplektisch; ~ **fit** Schlaganfall, *der*

apostle [ə'pɒsl] *n.* Apostel, *der*

apostrophe [ə'pɒstrəfɪ] *n.* Apostroph, *der;* Auslassungszeichen, *das*

appal *(Amer.:* **appall)** [ə'pɔːl] *v. t.,* **-ll-** entsetzen. **ap'palling** *adj.* entsetzlich

apparatus [æpə'reɪtəs] *n. (equipment)* Gerät, *das; (gymnastic ~)* Geräte *Pl.; (machinery, lit. or fig.)* Apparat, *der;* **a piece of ~:** ein Gerät

apparent [ə'pærənt] *adj.* **a)** *(clear)* offensichtlich; offenbar *(Bedeutung, Wahrheit);* **b)** *(seeming)* scheinbar.

ap'parently *adv.* **a)** *(clearly)* offensichtlich; **b)** *(seemingly)* scheinbar

apparition [æpə'rɪʃn] *n.* [Geister]erscheinung, *die*

appeal [ə'piːl] **1.** *v. i.* **a)** *(Law etc.)* Einspruch einlegen; **b)** *(make earnest request)* ~ **to sb. for sth./to do sth.** jmdn. um etw. ersuchen/jmdn. ersuchen, etw. zu tun; **c)** *(address oneself)* ~ **to sb./sth.** an jmdn./etw. appellieren; **d)** *(be attractive)* ~ **to sb.** jmdm. zusagen. **2.** *n.* **a)** *(Law etc.)* Einspruch, *der* **(to** bei**);** *(to higher court)* Berufung, *die* **(to** bei**); b)** *(request)* Appell, *der;* **an ~ to sb. for sth.** eine Bitte an jmdn. um etw.; **c)** *(attraction)* Reiz, *der.* **ap'pealing** *adj.* **a)** *(imploring)* flehend; **b)** *(attractive)* ansprechend; verlockend *(Idee)*

appear [ə'pɪə(r)] *v. i.* **a)** *(become visible, arrive)* erscheinen; *(Licht, Mond:)* auftauchen; *(present oneself)* auftreten; **b)** *(occur)* vorkommen; **c)** *(seem)* ~ [to be] ...: scheinen ... [zu sein]. **appearance** [ə'pɪərəns] *n.* **a)** *(becoming visible)* Auftauchen, *das; (arrival)* Erscheinen, *das; (of performer etc.)* Auftritt, *der;* **b)** *(look)* Äußere, *das;* **to all ~s** allem Anschein nach; **c)** *(semblance)* Anschein, *der;* **d)** *(occurrence)* Vorkommen, *das*

appease [ə'piːz] *v. t.* besänftigen; *(Polit.)* beschwichtigen

append [ə'pend] *v. t.* anhängen **(to** an + *Akk.*); *(add)* anfügen **(+** *Dat.*). **appendage** [ə'pendɪdʒ] *n.* Anhängsel, *das; (addition)* Anhang, *der*

appendicitis [əpendɪ'saɪtɪs] *n.* Blinddarmentzündung, *die*

appendix [ə'pendɪks] *n., pl.* **appendices** [ə'pendɪsiːz] *or* **-es a)** Anhang, *der* **(to** zu**); b)** *(Anat.)* Blinddarm, *der*

appetite ['æpɪtaɪt] *n.* **a)** Appetit, *der* **(for** auf + *Akk.*); **b)** *(fig.)* Verlangen, *das* **(for** nach**). appetizer** ['æpɪtaɪzə(r)] *n.* Appetitanreger, *der.* **appetizing** ['æpɪtaɪzɪŋ] *adj.* appetitlich

applaud [ə'plɔːd] **1.** *v. i.* applaudieren; [Beifall] klatschen. **2.** *v. t.* applaudieren **(+** *Dat.*). **applause** [ə'plɔːz] *n.* Beifall, *der;* Applaus, *der*

apple ['æpl] *n.* Apfel, *der*

appliance [ə'plaɪəns] *n.* Gerät, *das*

applicable [ə'plɪkəbl] *adj.* **a)** anwendbar **(to** auf + *Akk.*); **b)** *(appropriate)* geeignet; zutreffend *(Fragebogenteil)*

applicant ['æplıkənt] *n.* Bewerber, *der*/Bewerberin, *die* (for um); *(claimant)* Antragsteller, *der*/-stellerin, *die*
application [æplı'keıʃn] *n.* **a)** *(request)* Bewerbung, *die* (for um); *(for passport, licence, etc.)* Antrag, *der* (for auf + *Akk.*); ~ **form** Antragsformular, *das;* **b)** *(putting)* Auftragen, *das* (to auf + *Akk.*); **c)** *(use)* Anwendung, *die*
apply [ə'plaı] **1.** *v.t.* **a)** auftragen ⟨*Creme, Farbe*⟩ (to auf + *Akk.*); **b)** *(make use of)* anwenden. **2.** *v.i.* **a)** *(have relevance)* zutreffen (to auf + *Akk.*); **b)** ~ |to sb.| for sth. [jmdn.] um etw. bitten; *(for passport etc.)* [bei jmdm.] etw. beantragen; *(for job)* sich [bei jmdm.] um etw. bewerben
appoint [ə'pɔınt] *v.t.* **a)** *(fix)* bestimmen; festlegen ⟨*Zeitpunkt, Ort*⟩; **b)** *(to job)* einstellen; *(to office)* ernennen.
ap'pointment *n.* **a)** *(to job)* Einstellung, *die; (to office)* Ernennung, *die* (as zum/zur); **b)** *(job)* Stelle, *die;* **c)** *(arrangement)* Termin, *der;* **make an ~ with sb.** sich *(Dat.)* von jmdm. einen Termin geben lassen; **by ~:** nach Anmeldung
appreciable [ə'priːʃəbl] *adj.* **a)** *(perceptible)* nennenswert ⟨*Unterschied, Einfluß*⟩; spürbar ⟨*Veränderung, Wirkung*⟩; merklich ⟨*Verringerung, Anstieg*⟩; **b)** *(considerable)* beträchtlich. **appreciably** [ə'priːʃəblı] *adv.* **a)** *(perceptibly)* spürbar ⟨*verändern*⟩; merklich ⟨*sich unterscheiden*⟩; **b)** *(considerably)* beträchtlich
appreciate [ə'priːʃıeıt] **1.** *v.t.* **a)** *([correctly] estimate)* [richtig] einschätzen; *(understand)* verstehen; *(be aware of)* sich *(Dat.)* bewußt sein (+ *Gen.*); **b)** *(be grateful for)* schätzen; *(enjoy)* genießen. **2.** *v.i.* im Wert steigen. **appreciation** [əpriːʃı'eıʃn] *n.* **a)** *([correct] estimation)* [richtige] Einschätzung; *(understanding)* Verständnis, *das* (of für); *(awareness)* Bewußtsein, *das;* **b)** *(gratefulness)* Dankbarkeit, *die; (enjoyment)* Gefallen, *das* (of an + *Dat.*). **appreciative** [ə'priːʃətıv] *adj.* *(grateful)* dankbar (of für); *(approving)* anerkennend
apprehend [æprı'hend] *v.t.* **a)** *(arrest)* festnehmen; **b)** *(understand)* erfassen. **apprehension** [æprı'henʃn] *n.* Besorgnis, *die.* **apprehensive** [æprı'hensıv] *adj.* besorgt
apprentice [ə'prentıs] *n.* Lehrling, *der* (to bei). **ap'prenticeship** *n.*

(training) Lehre, *die; (learning period)* Lehrzeit, *die*
approach [ə'prəutʃ] **1.** *v.i.* sich nähern; *(in time)* nahen. **2.** *v.t.* **a)** *(come near to)* sich nähern (+ *Dat.*); **b)** *(approximate to)* nahekommen (+ *Dat.*); **c)** *(appeal to)* sich wenden an (+ *Akk.*). **3.** *n.* **a)** [Heran]nahen, *das;* **b)** *(approximation)* Annäherung, *die* (to an + *Akk.*); **c)** *(appeal)* Herantreten, *das* (to an + *Akk.*); **d)** *(access)* Zugang, *der; (road)* Zufahrtsstraße, *die.* **approachable** [ə'prəutʃəbl] *adj.* **a)** *(friendly)* umgänglich; **b)** *(accessible)* zugänglich
appropriate **1.** [ə'prəuprıət] *adj.* geeignet (to, for für). **2.** [ə'prəuprıeıt] *v.t.* sich *(Dat.)* aneignen. **appropriately** [ə'prəuprıətlı] *adv.* gebührend; passend ⟨*gekleidet, genannt*⟩
approval [ə'pruːvl] *n.* **a)** *(sanctioning)* Genehmigung, *die; (of proposal)* Billigung, *die; (agreement)* Zustimmung, *die;* **b)** **on** ~ *(Commerc.)* zur Probe
approve [ə'pruːv] **1.** *v.t.* **a)** *(sanction)* genehmigen ⟨*Plan, Projekt*⟩; billigen ⟨*Vorschlag*⟩; **b)** *(find good)* gutheißen. **2.** *v.i.* ~ **of** billigen; zustimmen (+ *Dat.*) ⟨*Plan*⟩. **approving** [ə'pruːvıŋ] *adj.* zustimmend ⟨*Worte*⟩; anerkennend ⟨*Blicke*⟩
approximate [ə'prɒksımət] *adj.* ungefähr *attr.* **ap'proximately** *adv.* ungefähr. **approximation** [əprɒksı'meıʃn] *n.* **a)** Annäherung, *die* (to an + *Dat.*); **b)** *(estimate)* Annäherungswert, *der*
Apr. *abbr.* **April** Apr.
apricot ['eıprıkɒt] *n.* Aprikose, *die*
April ['eıprəl] *n.* April, *der;* ~ **fool** April[s]narr, *der; see also* **August**
apron ['eıprən] *n.* Schürze, *die*
apt [æpt] *adj.* **a)** *(suitable)* passend; treffend ⟨*Bemerkung*⟩; **b)** **be** ~ **to do sth.** dazu neigen, etw. zu tun
aptitude ['æptıtjuːd] *n.* Begabung, *die*
'aptly *adv.* passend
aqualung ['ækwəlʌŋ] *n.* Tauchgerät, *das*
aquarium [ə'kweərıəm] *n., pl.* ~s *or* **aquaria** [ə'kweərıə] Aquarium, *das*
Aquarius [ə'kweərıəs] *n.* der Wassermann
aquatic [ə'kwætık] *adj.* aquatisch; Wasser-; ~ **plant** Wasserpflanze, *die*
aqueduct ['ækwıdʌkt] *n.* Aquädukt, *der od. das*
Arab ['ærəb] **1.** *adj.* arabisch. **2.** *n.* Araber, *der*/Araberin, *die*

Arabian [ə'reɪbɪən] 1. *adj.* arabisch. 2. *n.* Araber, *der*/Araberin, *die*
Arabic ['ærəbɪk] 1. *adj.* arabisch. 2. *n.* Arabisch, *das; see also* **English 2 a**
arbitrary ['ɑːbɪtrərɪ] *adj.* willkürlich
arbitrate ['ɑːbɪtreɪt] 1. *v. t.* schlichten ⟨*Streit*⟩. 2. *v. i.* ~ [upon sth.] [in einer Sache] vermitteln. **arbitration** [ɑːbɪ-'treɪʃn] *n.* Vermittlung, *die; (in industry)* Schlichtung, *die;* **arbitrator** ['ɑːbɪtreɪtə(r)] *n.* Vermittler, *der; (in industry)* Schlichter, *der*
arc [ɑːk] *n.* [Kreis]bogen, *der*
arcade [ɑː'keɪd] *n.* Arkade, *die*
arch [ɑːtʃ] 1. *n.* Bogen, *der; (of foot)* Wölbung, *die.* 2. *v. t.* beugen ⟨*Rücken*⟩; ~ its back ⟨*Katze:*⟩ einen Buckel machen
arch- *pref.* Erz-
archaeological [ɑːkɪə'lɒdʒɪkl] *adj.* archäologisch
archaeologist [ɑːkɪ'ɒlədʒɪst] *n.* Archäologe, *der*/Archäologin, *die*
archaeology [ɑːkɪ'ɒlədʒɪ] *n.* Archäologie, *die*
archaic [ɑː'keɪɪk] *adj.* veraltet
arch'bishop *n.* Erzbischof, *der*
archeology *etc. (Amer.) see* **archaeology** *etc.*
archery ['ɑːtʃərɪ] *n.* Bogenschießen, *das*
archetype ['ɑːkɪtaɪp] *n. (original)* Urfassung, *die; (typical specimen)* Prototyp, *der*
architect ['ɑːkɪtekt] *n.* Architekt, *der*/Architektin, *die*
architectural [ɑːkɪ'tektʃərl] *adj.* architektonisch
architecture ['ɑːkɪtektʃə(r)] *n.* Architektur, *die*
archive ['ɑːkaɪv] 1. *n., usu. in pl.* Archiv, *das.* 2. *v. t.* archivieren
arctic ['ɑːktɪk] 1. *adj.* arktisch; A~ Circle nördlicher Polarkreis; A~ Ocean Nordpolarmeer, *das.* 2. *n.* the A~: die Arktis
ardent ['ɑːdənt] *adj.* leidenschaftlich; brennend ⟨*Wunsch*⟩; *(eager)* begeistert
ardor *(Amer.),* **ardour** *(Brit.)* ['ɑːdə(r)] *n.* Leidenschaft, *die*
arduous ['ɑːdjʊəs] *adj.* anstrengend
are *see* **be**
area ['eərɪə] *n.* a) *(surface measure)* Fläche, *die;* Flächeninhalt, *der;* b) *(region)* Gelände, *das; (of wood, marsh, desert)* Gebiet, *das; (of city, country)* Gegend, *die;* **parking/picnic** ~: Park-/Picknickplatz, *der;* c) *(subject field)* Gebiet, *das*

arena [ə'riːnə] *n.* Arena, *die*
aren't [ɑːnt] *(coll.)* = **are not;** *see* **be**
Argentina [ɑːdʒən'tiːnə] *pr. n.* Argentinien *(das).* **Argentinian** [ɑːdʒən-'tɪnɪən] 1. *adj.* argentinisch. 2. *n.* Argentinier, *der*/Argentinierin, *die*
arguable ['ɑːgjʊəbl] *adj. (questionable)* fragwürdig. **arguably** ['ɑːgjʊəblɪ] *adv.* möglicherweise
argue ['ɑːgjuː] 1. *v. t.* a) *(maintain)* ~ **that** ...: die Ansicht vertreten, daß ...; b) *(with reasoning)* darlegen ⟨*Grund, Standpunkt*⟩. 2. *v. i.* ~ **with sb.** sich mit jmdm. streiten; ~ **for/against sth.** für/gegen etw. eintreten; ~ **about sth.** sich über/um etw. *(Akk.)* streiten. **argument** ['ɑːgjʊmənt] *n.* a) *(reason)* Begründung, *die;* ~s **for/against sth.** Argumente für/gegen etw.; b) *(reasoning process)* Argumentieren, *das;* c) *(disagreement, quarrel)* Auseinandersetzung, *die.* **argumentative** [ɑːgjʊ-'mentətɪv] *adj.* widerspruchsfreudig
arid ['ærɪd] *adj.* trocken
Aries ['eəriːz] *n.* der Widder
arise [ə'raɪz] *v. i., arose* [ə'rəʊz], *arisen* [ə'rɪzn] a) *(originate)* entstehen; b) *(present itself)* auftreten; ⟨*Gelegenheit:*⟩ sich bieten; c) *(result)* ~ **from** *or* **out of sth.** von etw. herrühren
aristocracy [ærɪ'stɒkrəsɪ] *n.* Aristokratie, *die*
aristocrat ['ærɪstəkræt] *n.* Aristokrat, *der*/Aristokratin, *die.* **aristocratic** [ærɪstə'krætɪk] *adj.* aristokratisch
arithmetic [ə'rɪθmətɪk] *n.* Arithmetik, *die*
¹arm [ɑːm] *n.* Arm, *der*
²arm 1. *n.* a) *usu. in pl. (weapon)* Waffe, *die;* up in ~s *(fig.)* in Harnisch (about wegen); b) *in pl. (heraldic device)* Wappen, *das.* 2. *v. t.* bewaffnen
armada [ɑː'mɑːdə] *n.* Armada, *die*
arm: ~**band** *n.* Armbinde, *die;* ~**chair** *n.* Sessel, *der*
armed [ɑːmd] *adj.* bewaffnet; ~ **forces** Streitkräfte *Pl.*
armistice ['ɑːmɪstɪs] *n.* Waffenstillstand, *der*
armor *(Amer.),* **armour** *(Brit.)* ['ɑːmə(r)] *n.* a) *(Hist.)* Rüstung, *die;* b) *(steel plates)* Panzerung, *die*
'armpit *n.* Achselhöhle, *die*
army ['ɑːmɪ] *n.* Heer, *das;* **join the** ~: zum Militär gehen
aroma [ə'rəʊmə] *n.* Duft, *der.* **aromatic** [ærə'mætɪk] *adj.* aromatisch
arose *see* **arise**
around [ə'raʊnd] 1. *adv.* a) *(on every*

side) |**all**| ~: überall; **b)** *(round)* herum; **c)** *(in various places)* **ask/look** ~: herumfragen/sich umsehen. **2.** *prep.* **a)** um [... herum]; **b)** *(approximately)* ~ 3 o'clock gegen 3 Uhr; **sth.** |**costing**| ~ £2 etw. für ungefähr 2 Pfund

arouse [ə'raʊz] *v. t.* **a)** *(awake)* |auf]wecken; **b)** *(excite)* erregen; erwecken ⟨*Interesse, Begeisterung*⟩; ~ **suspicion** Verdacht erregen

arrange [ə'reɪndʒ] **1.** *v. t.* **a)** *(order)* anordnen; **b)** *(settle, agree)* ausmachen, vereinbaren ⟨*Termin*⟩; planen ⟨*Urlaub*⟩; **they ~d to meet the following day** sie verabredeten sich für den nächsten Tag. **2.** *v. i. (plan)* sorgen (**for** für). **ar'rangement** *n.* **a)** *(ordering, order)* Anordnung, *die;* **b)** *(settling, agreement)* Vereinbarung, *die;* **c)** *in pl. (plans)* Vorkehrungen; **make ~s** Vorkehrungen treffen

arrears [ə'rɪəz] *n. pl.* Schulden *Pl.;* **be in** ~ **with sth.** mit etw. im Rückstand sein

arrest [ə'rest] **1.** *v. t.* **a)** verhaften, *(temporarily)* festnehmen ⟨*Person*⟩; **b)** *(stop)* aufhalten. **2.** *n.* Verhaftung, *die;* **under** ~: festgenommen

arrival [ə'raɪvl] *n.* Ankunft, *die;* **new ~s** Neuankömmlinge

arrive [ə'raɪv] *v. i.* **a)** ankommen; ~ **at a conclusion/an agreement** zu einem Schluß/einer Einigung kommen; **b)** ⟨*Stunde, Tag, Augenblick:*⟩ kommen

arrogance ['ærəgəns] *n.* Arroganz, *die*

arrogant ['ærəgənt] *adj.* arrogant

arrow ['ærəʊ] *n.* Pfeil, *der*

arse [ɑːs] *n. (coarse)* Arsch, *der (derb)*

arsenal ['ɑːsənl] *n.* Waffenlager, *das*

arsenic ['ɑːsənɪk] *n.* **a)** Arsenik, *das;* **b)** *(element)* Arsen, *das*

arson ['ɑːsn] *n.* Brandstiftung, *die.* **arsonist** ['ɑːsənɪst] *n.* Brandstifter, *der/* Brandstifterin, *die*

art [ɑːt] *n.* **a)** Kunst, *die;* **works of** ~: Kunstwerke *Pl.;* ~ **college** *or* **school** Kunsthochschule, *die;* ~**s and crafts** Kunsthandwerk, *das;* **b)** *in pl. (branch of study)* Geisteswissenschaften

artery ['ɑːtəri] *n. (Anat.)* Schlagader, *die;* Arterie, *die (bes. fachspr.)*

artful ['ɑːtfl] *adj.* schlau

'**art gallery** *n.* Kunstgalerie, *die*

arthritic [ɑːˈθrɪtɪk] *adj.* arthritisch.

arthritis [ɑːˈθraɪtɪs] *n.* Arthritis, *die (fachspr.);* Gelenkentzündung, *die*

artichoke ['ɑːtɪtʃəʊk] *n.* |**globe**| ~: Artischocke, *die*

article ['ɑːtɪkl] *n.* **a)** *(in magazine,*

newspaper; Ling.) Artikel, *der;* **b)** **an** ~ **of furniture/clothing** ein Möbel-/Kleidungsstück; **an** ~ **of value** ein Wertgegenstand

articulate [ɑːˈtɪkjʊlət] *adj.* redegewandt; **be** ~**/not very** ~: sich gut/nicht sehr gut ausdrücken [können]

articulated [ɑːˈtɪkjʊleɪtɪd] *adj.* ~ 'lorry Sattelzug, *der*

artificial [ɑːtɪˈfɪʃl] *adj.* **a)** künstlich; Kunst-; *(not real)* unecht; ~ **limb** Prothese, *die;* **b)** *(affected)* gekünstelt

artificial: ~ **insemi'nation** *n.* künstliche Besamung; ~ **in'telligence** *n.* künstliche Intelligenz; ~ **respi'ration** *n.* künstliche Beatmung

artillery [ɑːˈtɪləri] *n.* Artillerie, *die*

artisan ['ɑːtɪzn, ɑːtɪˈzæn] *n.* [Kunst]handwerker, *der*

artist ['ɑːtɪst] *n.* Künstler, *der/*Künstlerin, *die*

artiste [ɑːˈtiːst] *n.* Artist, *der/*Artistin, *die*

artistic [ɑːˈtɪstɪk] *adj.* **a)** *(of art)* Kunst-; künstlerisch; **b)** *(naturally skilled in art)* künstlerisch veranlagt

'**artless** *adj.* arglos

as [əz, *stressed* æz] **1.** *adv., conj.* **a)** **he is as tall as I am** er ist so groß wie ich; **as quickly as you can/as possible** so schnell du kannst/wie möglich; **b)** *(though)* **small as he was** obwohl er klein war; **c)** *(however much)* **try as he might/would, he could not concentrate** sosehr er sich auch bemühte, er konnte sich nicht konzentrieren; **d)** *expr. manner* wie; **as you may already have heard,** ...: wie Sie vielleicht schon gehört haben, ...; **as it were** sozusagen; **e)** *expr. time* als; während; **as we climbed the stairs** als wir die Treppe hinaufgingen; **as we were talking** während wir uns unterhielten; **f)** *expr. reason* da. **2.** *prep.* **a)** *(in the function of)* als; **as an artist** als Künstler; **speaking as a mother** ...: als Mutter ...; **b)** *(like)* wie; **c)** **the same as** ...: der-/die/dasselbe wie ...; **such as** wie zum Beispiel. **3.** **as for** ...: was ... angeht *od.* betrifft; **as** |**it**| **is** wie die Dinge liegen; **the place is untidy enough as it is** es ist hier [so] schon unordentlich genug; **as of** ... *(Amer.)* von ... an; **as to** hinsichtlich (+ *Gen.*); **as yet** bis jetzt; noch

asbestos [æzˈbestɒs] *n.* Asbest, *der*

ascend [əˈsend] **1.** *v. i.* **a)** *(go up)* hinaufsteigen; *(climb up)* hinaufklettern; *(by vehicle)* hinauffahren; **b)** *(rise)* aufsteigen; ⟨*Hubschrauber:*⟩ höher-

steigen; **c)** *(slope upwards)* ⟨*Hügel,
Straße:*⟩ ansteigen. **2.** *v. t.* **a)** *(go up)*
hinaufsteigen ⟨*Treppe, Leiter, Berg*⟩;
b) ~ **the throne** den Thron besteigen

A'scension Day *n.* Himmelfahrtstag,
der

ascent [ə'sent] *n.* Aufstieg, *der*

ascertain [æsə'teɪn] *v. t.* feststellen;
ermitteln ⟨*Fakten, Daten*⟩

ascribe [ə'skraɪb] *v. t.* zuschreiben (**to**
Dat.)

¹ash [æʃ] *n. (tree)* Esche, *die*

²ash *n. (from fire etc.)* Asche, *die*

ashamed [ə'ʃeɪmd] *adj.* beschämt; **be
~:** sich schämen (**of** wegen)

ashen ['æʃn] *adj.* aschfahl ⟨*Gesicht*⟩

ashore [ə'ʃɔ:(r)] *adv.* an Land

'ash-tray *n.* Aschenbecher, *der*

Ash 'Wednesday *n.* Aschermitt-
woch, *der*

Asia ['eɪʃə] *pr. n.* Asien *(das).* **Asian**
['eɪʃən] **1.** *adj.* asiatisch. **2.** *n.* Asiat,
der/Asiatin, *die*

aside [ə'saɪd] *adv.* beiseite; zur Seite

ask [ɑ:sk] **1.** *v. t.* **a)** fragen; ~ **sb.** |**sth.**|
jmdn. [nach etw.] fragen; **b)** *(seek to
obtain)* ~ **sth.** um etw. bitten; **how
much are you ~ing for that car?** wieviel verlangen Sie für das Auto?; ~ **sb.
to do sth.** jmdn. [darum] bitten, etw. zu
tun; **c)** *(invite)* einladen. **2.** *v. i.* ~ **after
sb./sth.** nach jmdm./etw. fragen; ~
for sth./sb. etw./jmdn. verlangen

askance [ə'skæns, ə'skɑ:ns] *adv.* **look
~ at sb.** jmdn. befremdet ansehen

askew [ə'skju:] *adv., pred. adj.* schief

asleep [ə'sli:p] *pred. adj.* schlafend;
be/lie ~: schlafen; **fall ~:** einschlafen

asparagus [ə'spærəgəs] *n.* Spargel,
der

aspect ['æspekt] *n.* Aspekt, *der*

aspersion [ə'spɜ:ʃn] *n.* **cast ~s on sb./
sth.** jmdn./etw in den Schmutz ziehen

asphalt ['æsfælt] *n.* Asphalt, *der*

asphyxiate [æs'fɪksɪeɪt] *v. t. & i.* ersticken

aspiration [æspə'reɪʃn] *n.* Streben,
das

aspire [ə'spaɪə(r)] *v. i.* ~ **to** or **after sth.**
nach etw. streben

aspirin ['æspərɪn] *n.* Aspirin Ⓦ, *das;*
Kopfschmerztablette, *die*

ass [æs] *n.* Esel, *der*

assailant [ə'seɪlənt] *n.* Angreifer, *der*/
Angreiferin, *die*

assassin [ə'sæsɪn] *n.* Mörder, *der*/
Mörderin, *die*. **assassinate** [ə'sæsɪ-
neɪt] *v. t.* ermorden; **be ~d** einem Attentat zum Opfer fallen. **assassina-**

tion [əsæsɪ'neɪʃn] *n.* Mord, *der* (**of** an
+ *Dat.*); ~ **attempt** Attentat, *das* (**on**
auf + *Akk.*)

assault [ə'sɔ:lt] **1.** *n.* Angriff, *der;* *(fig.)*
Anschlag, *der.* **2.** *v. t.* angreifen

assemble [ə'sembl] **1.** *v. t.* **a)** zusammentragen; zusammenrufen ⟨*Men-
schen*⟩; **b)** *(fit together)* zusammenbauen. **2.** *v. i.* sich versammeln. **assembly** [ə'semblɪ] *n.* **a)** *(meeting)*
Versammlung, *die;* *(in school)* Mor-
genandacht, *die;* **b)** *(fitting together)*
Zusammenbau, *der.* **as'sembly line**
n. Fließband, *das*

assent [ə'sent] **1.** *v. i.* zustimmen (**to**
Dat.). **2.** *n.* Zustimmung, *die*

assert [ə'sɜ:t] *v. t.* **a)** geltend machen;
~ **oneself** sich durchsetzen; **b)** *(declare)* behaupten; beteuern ⟨*Un-
schuld*⟩. **assertion** [ə'sɜ:ʃn] *n.* **a)** Gel-
tendmachen, *das;* **b)** *(declaration)* Behauptung, *die.* **assertive** [ə'sɜ:tɪv]
adj. energisch ⟨*Person*⟩; bestimmt
⟨*Ton, Verhalten*⟩

assess [ə'ses] *v. t.* einschätzen; festsetzen ⟨*Steuer*⟩ (**at** auf + *Akk.*). **as-
'sessment** *n.* **a)** Einschätzung, *die;*
b) *(tax to be paid)* Steuerbescheid, *der*

asset ['æset] *n.* **a)** Vermögenswert,
der; **b)** *(useful quality)* Vorzug, *der* (**to**
für); *(person)* Stütze, *die;* *(thing)* Hilfe,
die

assiduous [ə'sɪdjʊəs] *adj.* **a)** *(diligent)*
eifrig; **b)** *(conscientious)* gewissenhaft

assign [ə'saɪn] *v. t.* **a)** *(allot)* zuweisen
(**to** *Dat.*); **b)** *(appoint)* zuteilen; ~ **sb.
to do sth.** jmdn. damit betrauen, etw.
zu tun. **as'signment** *n.* **a)** *(allotment)*
Zuweisung, *die;* *(appointment)* Zuteilung, *die;* **b)** *(task)* Aufgabe, *die*

assimilate [ə'sɪmɪleɪt] *v. t.* angleichen
(**to, with** an + *Akk.*). **assimilation**
[əsɪmɪ'leɪʃn] *n.* Angleichung, *die* (**to,
with** an + *Akk.*)

assist [ə'sɪst] **1.** *v. t.* helfen (+ *Dat.*). **2.**
v. i. helfen; ~ **with sth./in doing sth.**
bei etw. helfen/helfen, etw. zu tun.
assistance [ə'sɪstəns] *n.* Hilfe, *die.*
assistant [ə'sɪstənt] *n.* *(helper)* Helfer, *der*/Helferin, *die;* *(subordinate)*
Mitarbeiter, *der*/Mitarbeiterin, *die;*
(of professor, artist) Assistent, *der*/As-
sistentin, *die;* *(in shop)* Verkäufer,
der/Verkäuferin, *die*

associate 1. [ə'səʊʃɪət, ə'səʊsɪət] *n.*
(partner) Partner, *der*/Partnerin, *die;*
(colleague) Kollege, *der*/Kollegin,
die. **2.** [ə'səʊʃɪeɪt, ə'səʊsɪeɪt] *v. t.* in
Verbindung bringen; **be ~d in** Verbin-

dung stehen. **3.** [ə'səυʃɪeɪt, ə'səυsɪeɪt]
v. i. ~ **with sb.** mit jmdm. Umgang haben. **association** [əsəυsɪ'eɪʃn] *n.* **a)**
(organization) Vereinigung, *die;* **b)**
(mental connection) Assoziation, *die;*
c) *(connection)* Verbindung, *die*
assorted [ə'sɔ:tɪd] *adj.* gemischt
assortment [ə'sɔ:tmənt] *n.* Sortiment,
das; **a good ~ of hats [to choose from]**
eine gute Auswahl an Hüten
assume [ə'sju:m] *v. t.* **a)** voraussetzen;
assuming that ...: vorausgesetzt,
daß ...; **b)** *(undertake)* übernehmen
⟨*Amt, Pflichten*⟩; **c)** *(take on)* annehmen ⟨*Namen, Rolle*⟩. **assumption**
[ə'sʌmpʃn] *n.* Annahme, *die;* **going on
the ~ that ...:** vorausgesetzt, daß ...
assurance [ə'ʃυərəns] *n.* **a)** Zusiche-
rung, *die;* **b)** *(self-confidence)* Selbstsicherheit, *die*
assure [ə'ʃυə(r)] *v. t.* **a)** versichern
(+ *Dat.*); **b)** *(convince)* ~ **sb./oneself**
jmdn./sich überzeugen; **c)** *(make certain or safe)* gewährleisten. **assured**
[ə'ʃυəd] *adj.* gewährleistet ⟨*Erfolg*⟩; **be
~ of sth.** sich *(Dat.)* einer Sache *(Gen.)*
sicher sein
asterisk ['æstərɪsk] *n.* Sternchen, *das*
astern [ə'stɜ:n] *adv. (Naut., Aeronaut.)*
achtern; *(towards the rear)* achteraus
asteroid ['æstərɔɪd] *n.* Asteroid, *der*
asthma ['æsmə] *n.* Asthma, *das.*
asthmatic [æs'mætɪk] **1.** *adj.*
asthmatisch. **2.** *n.* Asthmatiker,
*der/*Asthmatikerin, *die*
astonish [ə'stɒnɪʃ] *v. t.* erstaunen.
a'stonishing *adj.* erstaunlich.
a'stonishment *n.* Erstaunen, *das*
astound [ə'staυnd] *v. t.* verblüffen.
a'stounding *adj.* erstaunlich
astray [ə'streɪ] *adv.* sth. **goes ~** *(is mislaid)* etw. wird verlegt; *(is lost)* etw.
geht verloren; **go/lead ~** *(fig.)* in die
Irre gehen/führen
astride [ə'straɪd] **1.** *adv.* rittlings ⟨*sitzen*⟩. **2.** *prep.* rittlings auf (+ *Dat.*)
astringent [ə'strɪndʒənt] *adj.* scharf
astrologer [ə'strɒlədʒə(r)] *n.* Astrologe, *der/*Astrologin, *die*
astrological [æstrə'lɒdʒɪkl] *adj.*
astrologisch
astrology [ə'strɒlədʒɪ] *n.* Astrologie,
die
astronaut ['æstrənɔ:t] *n.* Astronaut,
*der/*Astronautin, *die*
astronomer [ə'strɒnəmə(r)] *n.* Astronom, *der/*Astronomin, *die*
astronomical [æstrə'nɒmɪkl] *adj.*
astronomisch

astronomy [ə'strɒnəmɪ] *n.* Astronomie, *die*
astute [ə'stju:t] *adj.* scharfsinnig
asylum [ə'saɪləm] *n.* Asyl, *das*
at [ət, *stressed* æt] *prep.* **a)** *expr. place*
an (+ *Dat.*); **at the station** am Bahnhof; **at the baker's/butcher's/grocer's**
beim Bäcker/Fleischer/Kaufmann; **at
the chemist's** in der Apotheke/Droge-
rie; **at the supermarket** im Supermarkt; **at the party** auf the Party; **at
the office/hotel** im Büro/Hotel; **at
Dover** in Dover; **b)** *expr. time* **at
Christmas** [zu *od.* an] Weihnachten;
at six o'clock um sechs Uhr; **at midnight** um Mitternacht; **at midday** am
Mittag; **at [the age of] 40** mit 40; im Alter von 40; **at this/the moment** in die-
sem/im Augenblick *od.* Moment; **c)**
expr. price **at £2.50 [each]** zu *od.* für
[je] 2,50 Pfund; **d)** *expr. speed* **at 30
m. p. h.** *etc.* mit dreißig Meilen pro
Stunde *usw.;* **e)** **at that** *(at that point)*
dabei; *(at that provocation)* darauf-
hin; *(moreover)* noch dazu.
ate *see* **eat**
atheism ['eɪθɪɪzm] *n.* Atheismus, *der.*
atheist ['eɪθɪɪst] *n.* Atheist, *der/*At-
heistin, *die*
Athens ['æθɪnz] *pr. n.* Athen *(das)*
athlete ['æθli:t] *n.* Athlet, *der/*Athle-
tin, *die; (runner, jumper)* Leichtathlet,
*der/*Leichtathletin, *die.* **athletic** [æθ-
'letɪk] *adj.* sportlich. **ath'letics** [æθ-
'letɪks] *n.* Leichtathletik, *die*
Atlantic [ət'læntɪk] **1.** *adj.* atlantisch;
~ **Ocean** Atlantischer Ozean. **2.** *pr. n.*
Atlantik, *der*
atlas ['ætləs] *n.* Atlas, *der*
atmosphere ['ætməsfɪə(r)] *n.* Atmosphäre, *die.* **atmospheric** [ætməs-
'ferɪk] *adj.* atmosphärisch
atom ['ætəm] *n.* Atom, *das.* '**atom
bomb** *n.* Atombombe, *die*
atomic [ə'tɒmɪk] *adj.* Atom-
atomizer ['ætəmaɪzə(r)] *n.* Zerstäuber,
der
atone [ə'təυn] *v. i.* es wiedergutmachen; ~ **for sth.** etw. wiedergutmachen. **a'tonement** *n.* Buße, *die*
atrocious [ə'trəυʃəs] *adj.* grauenhaft;
scheußlich ⟨*Wetter, Benehmen*⟩.
a'trociously *adv.* grauenhaft;
scheußlich ⟨*sich benehmen*⟩. **atrocity**
[ə'trɒsɪtɪ] *n.* **a)** *(wickedness)* Grauen-
haftigkeit, *die;* **b)** *(deed)* Greueltat, *die*
attach [ə'tætʃ] *v. t.* **a)** *(fasten)* befestigen (to an + *Dat.*); **please find ~ed a
copy of the letter** beigeheftet ist eine

31 **August**

Kopie des Briefes; **b)** *(fig.)* ~ **import- ance to sth.** einer Sache *(Dat.)* Gewicht beimessen
attaché [əˈtæʃeɪ] *n.* Attaché, *der.* **at- 'taché case** *n.* Diplomatenkoffer, *der*
attached [əˈtætʃt] *adj. (emotionally)* be ~ **to sb./sth.** an jmdm./etw. hängen
at'tachment *n.* **a)** *(act or means of fastening)* Befestigung, *die;* **b)** *(affection)* Anhänglichkeit, *die* (**to an +** *Akk.*); **c)** *(accessory)* Zusatzgerät, *das*
attack [əˈtæk] **1.** *v. t.* **a)** angreifen; *(ambush, raid)* überfallen; *(fig.: criticize)* attackieren; **b)** *(affect)* ⟨*Krankheit:*⟩ befallen. **2.** *v. i.* angreifen. **3.** *n.* Angriff, *der; (ambush)* Überfall, *der; (fig.: criticism)* Attacke, *die; (of illness)* Anfall, *der.* **at'tacker** *n.* Angreifer, *der/*Angreiferin, *die*
attain [əˈteɪn] *v. t.* erreichen. **at'tain- ment** *n.* Verwirklichung, *die*
attempt [əˈtempt] **1.** *v. t.* versuchen. **2.** *n.* Versuch, *der*
attend [əˈtend] **1.** *v. i.* **a)** *(give care and thought)* aufpassen; *(apply oneself)* ~ **to sth.** *(deal with sth.)* sich um etw. kümmern; **b)** *(be present)* anwesend sein (**at** bei). **2.** *v. t.* **a)** *(be present at)* teilnehmen an (+ *Dat.*); *(go regularly to)* besuchen; **b)** *(wait on)* bedienen (+ *Dat.*); **c)** ⟨*Arzt:*⟩ behandeln. **at- tendance** [əˈtendəns] *n.* Anwesenheit, *die; (number of people)* Teilnehmerzahl, *die.* **attendant** [əˈtendənt] *n.* **a)** |lavatory| ~: Toilettenmann, *der/*-frau, *die;* |cloakroom| ~: Garderobenmann, *der/*-frau, *die;* museum ~: Museumswärter, *der/*-wärterin, *die;* **b)** *(member of entourage)* Begleiter, *der/*Begleiterin, *die*
attention [əˈtenʃn] **1.** *n.* **a)** Aufmerksamkeit, *die;* **attract** |sb.'s| ~: |jmdn.| auf sich *(Akk.)* aufmerksam machen; **pay** ~ **to sb./sth.** jmdn./etw. beachten; **pay** ~! gib acht!; paß auf!; **hold sb.'s** ~: jmds. Interesse wachhalten; ~ **Miss Jones** *(on letter)* zu Händen [von] Miss Jones; **b)** *(Mil.)* **stand to** ~: stillstehen. **2.** *int.* **a)** Achtung; **b)** *(Mil.)* stillgestanden
attentive [əˈtentɪv] *adj.* aufmerksam
attic [ˈætɪk] *n. (room)* Dachboden, *der; (habitable)* Dachkammer, *die*
attire [əˈtaɪə(r)] *n.* Kleidung, *die*
attitude [ˈætɪtjuːd] *n.* **a)** Haltung, *die;* **b)** *(mental ~)* Einstellung, *die*
attorney [əˈtɜːnɪ] *n.* **a)** Bevollmächtigte, *der/die;* **power of** ~: Vollmacht,

die; **b)** *(Amer.: lawyer)* [Rechts]anwalt, *der/*-anwältin, *die*
attract [əˈtrækt] *v. t.* **a)** *(draw)* anziehen; **auf sich** *(Akk.)* ziehen ⟨*Interesse, Blick, Kritik*⟩; **b)** *(arouse pleasure in)* anziehend wirken auf (+ *Akk.*); **c)** *(arouse interest in)* reizen (**about** an + *Dat.*). **attraction** [əˈtrækʃn] *n.* **a)** Anziehung, *die; (force, lit. or fig.)* Anziehung[skraft], *die;* **b)** *(fig.: thing that attracts)* Attraktion, *die; (charm)* Verlockung, *die;* Reiz, *der.* **attractive** [əˈtræktɪv] *adj.* **a)** anziehend; **b)** *(fig.)* attraktiv; reizvoll ⟨*Vorschlag, Möglichkeit, Idee*⟩
attribute 1. [ˈætrɪbjuːt] *n.* Eigenschaft, *die.* **2.** [əˈtrɪbjuːt] *v. t.* zuschreiben (**to** *Dat.*). **attributive** [əˈtrɪbjʊtɪv] *adj. (Ling.)* attributiv
aubergine [ˈəʊbəʒiːn] *n.* Aubergine, *die*
auburn [ˈɔːbən] *adj.* rötlichbraun
auction [ˈɔːkʃn] **1.** *n.* Versteigerung, *die.* **2.** *v. t.* versteigern. **auctioneer** [ˌɔːkʃəˈnɪə(r)] *n.* Auktionator, *der/* Auktionatorin, *die*
audacious [ɔːˈdeɪʃəs] *adj.* **a)** *(daring)* kühn; verwegen; **b)** *(impudent)* dreist. **audacity** [ɔːˈdæsɪtɪ] *n.* **a)** *(daringness)* Kühnheit, *die;* Verwegenheit, *die;* **b)** *(impudence)* Dreistigkeit, *die*
audible [ˈɔːdɪbl] *adj.* hörbar
audience [ˈɔːdɪəns] *n.* **a)** Publikum, *das;* **b)** *(formal interview)* Audienz, *die* (**with** bei)
audio [ˈɔːdɪəʊ] *adj.* Ton-. **'audio typist** *n.* Phonotypist, *der/*-typistin, *die.* **audio'visual** *adj.* audiovisuell
audit [ˈɔːdɪt] **1.** *n.* ~ |of the accounts| Rechnungsprüfung, *die.* **2.** *v. t.* prüfen
audition [ɔːˈdɪʃn] **1.** *n. (singing)* Vorsingen, *das; (dancing)* Vortanzen, *das; (acting)* Vorsprechen, *das.* **2.** *v. i. (sing)* vorsingen; *(dance)* vortanzen; *(act)* vorsprechen. **3.** *v. t.* vorsingen/ vortanzen/vorsprechen lassen
auditor [ˈɔːdɪtə(r)] *n.* Buchprüfer, *der/*-prüferin, *die*
auditorium [ˌɔːdɪˈtɔːrɪəm] *n.* Zuschauerraum, *der*
Aug. *abbr.* **August** Aug.
augment [ɔːgˈment] *v. t.* verbessern ⟨*Einkommen*⟩; aufstocken ⟨*Fonds*⟩
augur [ˈɔːgə(r)] **1.** *v. t.* bedeuten; versprechen ⟨*Erfolg*⟩. **2.** *v. i.* ~ **well/ill for sth./sb.** ein gutes/schlechtes Zeichen für etw./jmdn. sein
August [ˈɔːgəst] *n.* August, *der;* **in** ~: im August; **last/next** ~: letzten/näch-

sten August; **the first of/on the first of**
~: der erste/am ersten August
aunt [ɑːnt] *n.* Tante, *die*
auntie, aunty ['ɑːntɪ] *n. (coll.)* Tänt-
chen, *das; (with name)* Tante, *die*
au pair [əʊ 'peə(r)] *n.* Au-pair-Mäd-
chen, *das*
aura ['ɔːrə] *n.* Aura, *die*
auspices ['ɔːspɪsɪs] *n. pl.* **under the** ~
of sb./sth. unter jmds./einer Sache
Schirmherrschaft
auspicious [ɔː'spɪʃəs] *adj.* günstig;
vielversprechend ⟨*Anfang*⟩
austere [ɒ'stɪə(r)] *adj.* **a)** *(strict, stern)*
streng; **b)** *(severely simple)* karg. **aus-**
terity [ɒ'sterɪtɪ] *n.* **a)** *(strictness)*
Strenge, *die;* **b)** *(severe simplicity)*
Kargheit, *die;* **c)** *(lack of luxuries)*
wirtschaftliche Einschränkung
Australia [ɒ'streɪlɪə] *pr. n.* Australien
(das). **Australian** [ɒ'streɪlɪən] **1.** *adj.*
australisch. **2.** *n.* Australier, *der/*Au-
stralierin, *die*
Austria ['ɒstrɪə] *pr. n.* Österreich
(das). **Austrian** ['ɒstrɪən] **1.** *adj.*
österreichisch. **2.** *n.* Österreicher,
*der/*Österreicherin, *die*
authentic [ɔː'θentɪk] *adj.* authentisch.
authenticity [ɔːθen'tɪsɪtɪ] *n.* Authen-
tizität, *die*
author ['ɔːθə(r)] *n.* Autor, *der/*Autorin, *die; (profession)* Schriftsteller,
*der/*Schriftstellerin, *die*
authoritarian [ɔːθɒrɪ'teərɪən] **1.** *adj.*
autoritär. **2.** *n.* autoritäre Person
authoritative [ɔː'θɒrɪtətɪv] *adj.* maß-
gebend; zuverlässig ⟨*Bericht, Informa-*
tion⟩
authority [ɔː'θɒrɪtɪ] *n.* **a)** Autorität,
die; **in** ~: verantwortlich; **b) the au-**
thorities die Behörde[n]
authorization [ɔːθəraɪ'zeɪʃn] *n.* Genehmigung, *die*
authorize ['ɔːθəraɪz] *v. t.* **a)** ermächtigen; bevollmächtigen; **b)** *(sanction)*
genehmigen
auto ['ɔːtəʊ] *n., pl.* ~**s** *(Amer. coll.)* Auto, *das*
auto- [ɔːtəʊ] *in comb.* auto-/Auto-
autobio'graphical *adj.* autobiogra-
phisch
autobi'ography *n.* Autobiographie,
die
autocratic [ɔːtə'krætɪk] *adj.* autokra-
tisch
autograph ['ɔːtəgrɑːf] **1.** *n.* Auto-
gramm, *das.* **2.** *v. t.* signieren
automate ['ɔːtəmeɪt] *v. t.* automatisieren

automatic [ɔːtə'mætɪk] **1.** *adj.* automatisch. **2.** *n. (weapon)* automatische
Waffe; *(vehicle)* Fahrzeug mit Auto-
matikgetriebe. **automatically** [ɔːtə-
'mætɪkəlɪ] *adv.* automatisch
automation [ɔːtə'meɪʃn] *n.* Automation, *die*
automobile ['ɔːtəməbiːl] *n. (Amer.)*
Auto, *das*
autonomous [ɔː'tɒnəməs] *adj.* auto-
nom. **autonomy** [ɔː'tɒnəmɪ] *n.* Auto-
nomie, *die*
autopsy ['ɔːtɒpsɪ] *n.* Autopsie, *die*
autumn ['ɔːtəm] *n.* Herbst, *der;* **in [the]**
~: im Herbst. **autumnal** [ɔː'tʌmnl]
adj. herbstlich
auxiliary [ɔːg'zɪljərɪ] **1.** *adj.* Hilfs-. **2.**
n. **a)** Hilfskraft, *die;* **b)** *(Ling.)* Hilfsverb, *das*
avail [ə'veɪl] **1.** *n.* **be of no** ~: nichts
nützen; **to no** ~: vergebens. **2.** *v. refl.*
~ **oneself of sth.** von etw. Gebrauch
machen
available [ə'veɪləbl] *adj.* **a)** *(at one's*
disposal) verfügbar; **b)** *(obtainable)*
erhältlich; lieferbar ⟨*Waren*⟩
avalanche ['ævəlɑːnʃ] *n.* Lawine, *die*
avarice ['ævərɪs] *n.* Geldgier, *die;*
Habsucht, *die.* **avaricious** [ævə'rɪ-
ʃəs] *adj.* geldgierig; habsüchtig
avenge [ə'vendʒ] *v. t.* rächen
avenue ['ævənjuː] *n.* Allee, *die; (fig.)*
Weg, *der* (to zu)
average ['ævərɪdʒ] **1.** *n.* Durchschnitt,
der; **on** ~: im Durchschnitt; durchschnittlich. **2.** *adj.* durchschnittlich. **3.**
v. t. **a)** *(find the* ~ *of)* den Durchschnitt ermitteln von; **b)** *(amount on* ~
to) durchschnittlich betragen. **4.** *v. i.*
~ **out at** im Durchschnitt betragen
averse [ə'vɜːs] *adj.* **be** ~ **to sth.** einer
Sache *(Dat.)* abgeneigt sein. **aver-**
sion [ə'vɜːʃn] *n.* Abneigung, *die* (to
gegen)
avert [ə'vɜːt] *v. t.* abwenden; verhüten
⟨*Unfall*⟩
aviary ['eɪvɪərɪ] *n.* Vogelhaus, *das*
aviation [eɪvɪ'eɪʃn] *n.* Luftfahrt, *die*
avid ['ævɪd] *adj. (enthusiastic)* begeistert; **be** ~ **for sth.** *(eager, greedy)* begierig auf etw. *(Akk.)* sein
avocado [ævə'kɑːdəʊ] *n., pl.* ~**s:** ~
[**pear**] Avocado[birne], *die*
avoid [ə'vɔɪd] *v. t.* **a)** meiden ⟨*Ort*⟩; ~ **a**
cyclist einem Radfahrer ausweichen;
~ **the boss when he's in a temper** geh
dem Chef aus dem Weg, wenn er
schlechte Laune hat; **b)** *(refrain from,*
escape) vermeiden. **avoidable** [ə'vɔɪ-

dəbl] *adj.* vermeidbar. **avoidance**
[ə'vɔɪdəns] *n.* Vermeidung, *die*
await [ə'weɪt] *v. t.* erwarten
awake [ə'weɪk] **1.** *v. i.,* awoke [ə'wəʊk],
awoken [ə'wəʊkn] erwachen. **2.** *v. t.*
awoke, awoken wecken. **3.** *pred. adj.*
wach; **wide** ~: hellwach
awaken [ə'weɪkn] *v. t. & i. (esp. fig.)*
see awake 1, 2
award [ə'wɔːd] **1.** *v. t.* verleihen ⟨*Preis,
Auszeichnung*⟩; zusprechen ⟨*Sorge-
recht, Entschädigung*⟩; gewähren
⟨*Zahlung, Gehaltserhöhung*⟩. **2.** *n.
(prize)* Auszeichnung, *die*
aware [ə'weə(r)] *adj.* be ~ of sth. sich
(Dat.) einer Sache *(Gen.)* bewußt
sein; **be ~ that ...:** sich *(Dat.)* [dessen]
bewußt sein, daß ... **a'wareness** *n.*
Bewußtsein, *das*
awash [ə'wɒʃ] *adj.* be ~ *(flooded)* unter Wasser stehen
away [ə'weɪ] **1.** *adv.* **a)** *(at a distance)*
entfernt; **play** ~ *(Sport)* auswärts spielen; **b)** *(to a distance)* weg; fort; **c)** *(absent)* nicht da. **2.** *adj. (Sport)* auswärts
präd.; Auswärts-
awe [ɔː] *n.* Ehrfurcht, *die* (of vor +
Dat.)
awful ['ɔːfl] *adj.,* **'awfully** *adv.*
furchtbar
awkward ['ɔːkwəd] *adj.* **a)** *(difficult to
use)* ungünstig; **be ~ to use** unhand-
lich sein; **b)** *(clumsy)* unbeholfen; **c)**
(embarrassing) peinlich; **d)** *(difficult)*
schwierig; ungünstig ⟨*Zeitpunkt*⟩
awning ['ɔːnɪŋ] *n. (on house)* Markise,
die; (of tent) Vordach, *das*
awoke, awoken see awake
awry [ə'raɪ] *adv.* schief; **go** ~ *(fig.)*
schiefgehen *(ugs.);* ⟨*Plan:*⟩ fehlschlagen
axe [æks] *n.* Axt, *die;* Beil, *das*
axis ['æksɪs] *n., pl.* axes ['æksiːz] Achse,
die
axle ['æksl] *n.* Achse, *die*

B

B, b [biː] *n.* B, b, *das*
BA *abbr.* **Bachelor of Arts**
babble ['bæbl] *v. i.* **a)** *(talk incoher-
ently)* stammeln; **b)** *(talk foolishly)*

[dumm] schwatzen; **c)** ⟨*Bach:*⟩ plätschern
baboon [bə'buːn] *n.* Pavian, *der*
baby ['beɪbɪ] *n.* **a)** Baby, *das;* have a
~/be going to have a ~: ein Kind bekommen; **b)** *(childish person)* be a ~:
sich wie ein kleines Kind benehmen.
'baby-carriage *n. (Amer.)* Kinderwagen, *der*
'babyish *adj.* kindlich ⟨*Aussehen*⟩;
kindisch ⟨*Benehmen, Person*⟩
baby: ~**-minder** *n.* Tagesmutter, *die;*
~**-sit** *v. i., forms as* sit 1 babysitten
(ugs.); auf das Kind/die Kinder aufpassen; ~**-sitter** *n.* Babysitter, *der*
bachelor ['bætʃələ(r)] *n.* **a)** Junggeselle, *der;* **b)** *(Univ.)* B~ of Arts/Science
Bakkalaureus der philosophischen
Fakultät/der Naturwissenschaften
back [bæk] **1.** *n.* **a)** *(of person, animal)*
Rücken, *der; (of house, cheque)* Rück-
seite, *die; (of vehicle)* Heck, *das; (inside car)* Rücksitz, *der;* **stand ~ to ~:**
Rücken an Rücken stehen; ~ **to front**
verkehrt rum; **turn one's ~ on sb.**
jmdm. den Rücken zuwenden; *(fig.)*
jmdn. im Stich lassen; **turn one's ~ on
sth.** *(fig.)* sich um etw. nicht kümmern; **get** *or* **put sb.'s ~ up** *(fig.)* jmdn.
wütend machen; **be glad to see the ~
of sb./sth.** *(fig.)* froh sein, jmdn./etw.
nicht mehr sehen zu müssen; **have
one's ~ to the wall** *(fig.)* mit dem
Rücken zur Wand stehen; **put one's ~
into sth.** *(fig.)* sich für etw. mit allen
Kräften einsetzen; **with the ~ of one's
hand** mit dem Handrücken; **at the ~
[of the book]** hinten [im Buch]; **b)**
(Sport: player) Verteidiger, *der.* **2.** *adj.*
hinter... **3.** *adv.* zurück; **two miles ~:**
vor zwei Meilen; ~ **and forth** hin und
her; **there and** ~: hin und zurück; **a
week/month** ~: vor einer Woche/vor
einem Monat. **4.** *v. t.* **a)** *(assist)* unterstützen; **b)** *(bet on)* wetten od. setzen
auf (+ *Akk.*); **c)** zurücksetzen [mit]
⟨*Fahrzeug*⟩. **5.** *v. i.* zurücksetzen; ~
into/out of sth. rückwärts in etw.
(Akk.)/aus etw. fahren; ~ **on to sth.**
hinten an etw. *(Akk.)* grenzen. **back
'down** *v. i.* nachgeben. **back 'out**
v. i. rückwärts herausfahren; ~ **out of
sth.** *(fig.)* von etw. zurücktreten.
back 'up *v. t.* unterstützen; unter-
mauern ⟨*Anspruch, These*⟩
back: ~**ache** *n.* Rückenschmerzen
Pl.; ~**-bencher** [bæk'bentʃə(r)] *n.
(Brit. Parl.)* [einfacher] Abgeordneter/
[einfache] Abgeordnete; ~**bone** *n.*

Rückgrat, *das;* ~**chat** *n. (coll.)* [freche] Widerrede; ~**date** *v. t.* zurückdatieren (**to auf** + *Akk.*); ~ '**door** *n.* Hintertür, *die*

'**backer** *n.* Geldgeber, *der*

back: ~-'**fire** *v. i.* knallen; *(fig.)* fehlschlagen; **it** ~**fired on me/him** *etc.* der Schuß ging nach hinten los *(ugs.);* ~**ground** *n.* Hintergrund, *der; (social status)* Herkunft, *die;* ~**hand** *(Tennis etc.)* 1. *adj.* Rückhand-; 2. *n.* Rückhand, *die;* ~-'**handed** *adj.* **a)** *(Tennis etc.)* Rückhand-; **b)** *(fig.)* indirekt; zweifelhaft ⟨*Kompliment*⟩; ~'**hander** *n. (sl.: bribe)* Schmiergeld, *das*

'**backing** *n. (support)* Unterstützung, *die*

back: ~**lash** *n. (fig.)* Gegenreaktion, *die;* ~**log** *n.* Rückstand, *der;* ~**number** *n.* alte Nummer; ~**pedal** *v. i.* die Pedale rückwärts treten; ~ '**seat** *n.* Rücksitz, *der;* ~**side** *n.* Hinterteil, *das (ugs.);* ~'**stage** *adv.* go ~stage hinter die Bühne gehen; ~ **street** *n.* kleine Seitenstraße; ~**stroke** *n.* Rückenschwimmen, *das*

backward ['bækwəd] 1. *adj.* **a)** rückwärts gerichtet; Rückwärts-; **b)** *(reluctant, shy)* zurückhaltend; **c)** *(underdeveloped)* rückständig ⟨*Land, Region*⟩. 2. *adv. see* **backwards**

backwards ['bækwədz] *adv.* **a)** nach hinten; **the child fell** |**over**| ~ **into the water** das Kind fiel rückwärts ins Wasser; **bend** *or* **lean over** ~ **to do sth.** *(fig. coll.)* sich zerreißen, um etw. zu tun *(ugs.);* **b)** *(oppositely to normal direction)* rückwärts; ~ **and forwards** hin und her

back: ~**water** *n. (fig.)* Kaff, *das (ugs.);* ~ '**yard** *n.* Hinterhof, *der*

bacon ['beɪkn] *n.* [Frühstücks]speck, *der*

bacterium [bæk'tɪərɪəm] *n., pl.* **bacteria** [bæk'tɪərɪə] Bakterie, *die*

bad [bæd] *adj.,* **worse** [wɜːs], **worst** [wɜːst] **a)** schlecht; *(rotten)* schlecht, verdorben ⟨*Fleisch, Fisch, Essen*⟩; faul ⟨*Ei, Apfel*⟩; **not** ~ *(coll.)* nicht schlecht; nicht übel; **b)** *(naughty)* ungezogen, böse ⟨*Kind, Hund*⟩; **c)** *(offensive)* |*use*| ~ **language** Kraftausdrücke [benutzen]; **d)** *(regretful)* **feel** ~ **about sth.** etw. bedauern; **I feel** ~ **about him** ich habe seinetwegen ein schlechtes Gewissen; **e)** *(serious)* schlimm ⟨*Sturz, Krise*⟩; schwer ⟨*Fehler, Krankheit, Unfall*⟩; **f)** *(Commerc.)* **a** ~ **debt** eine uneinbringliche Schuld

bade *see* **bid 1 b**

badge [bædʒ] *n.* Abzeichen, *das*

badger ['bædʒə(r)] *n.* Dachs, *der*

'**badly** *adv.,* **worse** [wɜːs], **worst** [wɜːst] **a)** schlecht; **b)** schwer ⟨*verletzt, beschädigt*⟩; **c)** *(urgently)* dringend

bad-mannered [bæd'mænəd] *adj.* **be** ~: schlechte Manieren haben

badminton ['bædmɪntən] *n.* Federball, *der; (als Sport)* Badminton, *das*

bad-tempered [bæd'tempəd] *adj.* griesgrämig

baffle ['bæfl] *v. t.* ~ **sb.** jmdm. unverständlich sein. **baffling** ['bæflɪŋ] *adj.* rätselhaft

bag [bæg] 1. *n.* Tasche, *die; (sack)* Sack, *der; (hand*~*)* Handtasche, *die; (plastic* ~*)* Beutel, *der; (small paper* ~*)* Tüte, *die;* ~**s of** *(sl.: large amount)* jede Menge. 2. *v. t.,* -**gg**-: **a)** in Säcke/Beutel/Tüten füllen; **b)** *(claim possession of)* sich *(Dat.)* schnappen *(ugs.)*

baggage ['bægɪdʒ] *n.* Gepäck, *das.* '**baggage reclaim** *n.* Gepäckausgabe, *die*

baggy ['bægɪ] *adj.* weit [geschnitten] ⟨*Kleid, Hose*⟩; *(through long use)* ausgebeult ⟨*Hose*⟩

'**bagpipe**[**s**] *n.* Dudelsack, *der*

Bahamas [bə'hɑːməz] *pr. n. pl.* **the** ~: die Bahamas

[1]'**bail** [beɪl] 1. *n.* Kaution, *die;* **be** |**out**| **on** ~: gegen Kaution auf freiem Fuß sein. 2. *v. t.* ~ **sb. out** jmdn. gegen Kaution freibekommen; *(fig.)* jmdm. aus der Klemme helfen *(ugs.)*

[2]**bail** *v. t. (scoop)* ~ |**out**| ausschöpfen. '**bail out** *v. i.* ⟨*Pilot:*⟩ abspringen

bailiff ['beɪlɪf] *n.* ≈ Gerichtsvollzieher, *der*

bait [beɪt] 1. *v. t.* mit einem Köder versehen. 2. *n.* Köder, *der*

bake [beɪk] *v. t. & i.* backen. '**baker** *n.* Bäcker, *der.* **bakery** ['beɪkərɪ] *n.* Bäckerei, *die*

baking: ~-**powder** *n.* Backpulver, *das;* ~-**tin** *n.* Backform, *die;* ~-**tray** *n.* Kuchenblech, *das*

balance ['bæləns] 1. *n.* **a)** *(instrument)* Waage, *die;* **b)** *(fig.)* **be** *or* **hang in the** ~: in der Schwebe sein; **c)** *(steady position)* Gleichgewicht, *das;* **keep/lose one's** ~: das Gleichgewicht halten/verlieren; *(fig.)* sein Gleichgewicht bewahren/verlieren; **strike a** ~ **between** *(fig.)* den Mittelweg finden zwischen (+ *Dat.*); **d)** *(Bookk.: difference)* Bilanz, *die; (state of bank account)* Kontostand, *der;* **on** ~ *(fig.)* al-

les in allem; ~ **sheet** Bilanz, *die;* **e)**
(Econ.) ~ **of payments** Zahlungsbi-
lanz, *die;* **f)** *(remainder)* Rest, *der.* **2.**
v. t. **a)** *(weigh up)* abwägen; **b)** *(bring
into or keep in ~)* balancieren; aus-
wuchten ⟨*Rad*⟩; **c)** *(equal, neutralize)*
ausgleichen; ~ **each other, be ~d** sich
(Dat.) die Waage halten. '**balanced**
adj. ausgewogen; ausgeglichen ⟨*Person, Team, Gemüt*⟩
balcony ['bælkənɪ] *n.* Balkon, *der*
bald [bɔːld] *adj.* kahl ⟨*Kopf*⟩; kahlköp-
fig, glatzköpfig ⟨*Person*⟩
bale [beɪl] *n.* Ballen, *der*
balk [bɔːk] **1.** *v. t.* they were ~ed in
their plan ihr Plan wurde blockiert. **2.**
v. i. sich sträuben (**at** gegen)
Balkan ['bɔːlkn] **1.** *adj.* Balkan-. **2.** *n.
pl.* **the ~s** der Balkan
¹**ball** [bɔːl] *n.* **a)** Ball, *der;* *(Billiards etc.,
Croquet)* Kugel, *die;* **be on the ~** *(coll.:
be alert)* auf Zack sein *(ugs.);* **b)** *(of
wool, string, fluff, etc.)* Knäuel, *das*
²**ball** *n.* *(dance)* Ball, *der*
ballad ['bæləd] *n.* Ballade, *die*
ballast ['bæləst] *n.* Ballast, *der*
ball-'bearing *n.* Kugellager, *das*
ballerina [bælə'riːnə] *n.* Ballerina, *die*
ballet ['bæleɪ] *n.* Ballett, *das;* ~ **dancer**
Balletttänzer, *der/*Balletttänzerin, *die*
balloon [bə'luːn] *n.* **a)** Ballon, *der;*
hot-air ~: Heißluftballon, *der;* **b)**
(toy) Luftballon, *der*
ballot ['bælət] *n.* Abstimmung, *die;*
|secret| ~: geheime Wahl
ball: ~**-pen,** ~**-point 'pen** *ns.* Kugelschreiber, *der;* ~**room** *n.* Tanzsaal,
der
balm [bɑːm] *n.* Balsam, *der*
balmy ['bɑːmɪ] *adj.* *(mild)* mild
Baltic ['bɔːltɪk] **1.** *pr. n.* Ostsee, *die.* **2.**
adj. ~ **Sea** Ostsee, *die*
balustrade [bælə'streɪd] *n.* Balustrade, *die*
bamboo [bæm'buː] *n.* Bambus, *der*
ban [bæn] **1.** *v. t.,* **-nn-** verbieten; ~ **sb.
from doing sth.** jmdm. verbieten, etw.
zu tun. **2.** *n.* Verbot, *das*
banal [bə'nɑːl] *adj.* banal
banana [bə'nɑːnə] *n.* Banane, *die*
band [bænd] **1.** *n.* **a)** Band, *das;* **a ~ of
light/colour** ein Streifen Licht/Farbe;
b) *(range of values)* Bandbreite, *die;* **c)**
(organized group) Gruppe, *die;* *(of rob-
bers, outlaws, etc.)* Bande, *die;* **d)**
(Mus.) [Musik]kapelle, *die;* *(pop
group, jazz ~)* Band, *die.* **2.** *v. i.* ~
together |with sb.| sich [mit jmdm.] zu-
sammenschließen

bandage ['bændɪdʒ] **1.** *n.* Verband,
der; *(as support)* Bandage, *die.* **2.** *v. t.*
verbinden; bandagieren ⟨*[verstauch-
tes] Gelenk usw.*⟩
bandit ['bændɪt] *n.* Bandit, *der*
band: ~**stand** *n.* Musiktribüne, *die;*
~**wagon** *n.* **climb** *or* **jump on |to| the
~wagon** *(fig.)* auf den fahrenden Zug
aufspringen *(fig.)*
¹**bandy** ['bændɪ] *v. t.* **they were ~ing
words/insults** sie stritten sich/be-
schimpften sich gegenseitig
²**bandy** *adj.* krumm; **he is ~-legged** er
hat O-Beine *(ugs.)*
bang [bæŋ] **1.** *v. t.* knallen *(ugs.);*
schlagen; zuknallen *(ugs.)* ⟨*Tür, Fenster, Deckel*⟩; ~ **one's head on sth.** mit
dem Kopf an etw. *(Akk.)* knallen
(ugs.). **2.** *v. i.* *(strike)* ~ |**against sth.**|
[gegen etw.] knallen *(ugs.);* ~ **shut**
⟨*Tür:*⟩ zuknallen *(ugs.).* **3.** *n.* **a)** *(blow)*
Schlag, *der;* **b)** *(noise)* Knall, *der.* **4.**
adv. **go** ~ ⟨*Gewehr, Feuerwerkskörper:*⟩ krachen
'**banger** *n.* *(sl.)* **a)** *(sausage)* Würstchen, *das;* **b)** *(firework)* Kracher, *der*
(ugs.); **c)** *(car)* Klapperkiste, *die (ugs.)*
bangle ['bæŋgl] *n.* Armreif, *der*
banish ['bænɪʃ] *v. t.* verbannen (**from**
aus)
banister ['bænɪstə(r)] *n.* [Treppen]ge-
länder, *das*
banjo ['bændʒəʊ] *n., pl.* ~**s** *or* ~**es**
Banjo, *das*
¹**bank** [bæŋk] *n.* **a)** *(slope)* Böschung,
die; **b)** *(of river)* Ufer, *das*
²**bank** **1.** *n.* *(Finance)* Bank, *die.* **2.** *v. i.*
~ **at/with ...:** ein Konto haben bei ...;
~ **on sth.** *(fig.)* auf etw. *(Akk.)* zählen.
3. *v. t.* zur Bank bringen
bank: ~ **account** *n.* Bankkonto, *das;*
~ **card** *n.* Scheckkarte, *die;* ~ **clerk**
n. Bankangestellte, *der/die*
'**banker** *n.* Bankier, *der*
bank 'holiday *n.* *(Brit.)* Feiertag, *der*
'**banking** *n.* Bankwesen, *das*
bank: ~ **manager** *n.* Zweigstellenlei-
ter/-leiterin [einer/der Bank]; ~**note**
n. Banknote, *die*
bankrupt ['bæŋkrʌpt] **1.** *n.* Bankrot-
teur, *der.* **2.** *adj.* **go** ~: Bankrott machen. **3.** *v. t.* bankrott machen. **bankruptcy** ['bæŋkrʌptsɪ] *n.* Konkurs,
der; Bankrott, *der*
banner ['bænə(r)] *n.* Banner, *das;* *(on
two poles)* Spruchband, *das*
banns [bænz] *n. pl.* Aufgebot, *das*
banquet ['bæŋkwɪt] *n.* Bankett, *das*
baptism ['bæptɪzm] *n.* Taufe, *die*

Baptist ['bæptıst] *n.* Baptist, *der*/Baptistin, *die*

baptize [bæp'taız] *v.t.* taufen

bar [bɑ:(r)] 1. *n.* **a)** Stange, *die; (shorter, thinner also)* Stab, *der; (of cage, prison)* Gitterstab, *der;* **a ~ of soap** ein Stück Seife; **a ~ of chocolate** eine Tafel Schokolade; **b)** *(for refreshment)* Bar, *die; (counter)* Theke, *die.* 2. *v.t.,* **-rr-: a)** *(fasten)* verriegeln; **b) ~ sb.'s way** jmdm. den Weg versperren; **c)** *(prohibit, hinder)* verbieten; **~ sb. from doing sth.** jmdn. daran hindern, etw. zu tun. 3. *prep.* abgesehen von; **~ none** ohne Einschränkung

barb [bɑ:b] *n.* Widerhaken, *der*

barbarian [bɑ:'beərıən] *n.* Barbar, *der*

barbaric [bɑ:'bærık] *adj.* barbarisch

barbarity [bɑ:'bærıtı] *n.* Grausamkeit, *die*

barbecue ['bɑ:bıkju:] 1. *n.* **a)** *(party)* Grillparty, *die;* **b)** *(food)* Grillgericht, *das.* 2. *v.t.* grillen

barbed wire [bɑ:bd 'waıə(r)] *n.* Stacheldraht, *der*

barber ['bɑ:bə(r)] *n.* [Herren]friseur, *der*

'**bar code** *n.* Strichcode, *der*

bare [beə(r)] 1. *adj.* nackt; *(leafless, unfurnished)* kahl; *(empty)* leer; äußerst ⟨*Notwendige*⟩; **do sth. with one's ~ hands** etw. mit den bloßen Händen tun. 2. *v.t.* entblößen ⟨*Kopf, Arm, Bein*⟩; blecken ⟨*Zähne*⟩. '**barefaced** *adj. (fig.)* unverhüllt. '**barefoot** 1. *adj.* barfüßig. 2. *adv.* barfuß

barely ['beəlı] *adv.* kaum; knapp ⟨*vermeiden, entkommen*⟩

bargain ['bɑ:gın] 1. *n.* **a)** *(agreement)* Abmachung, *die;* **into the ~:** darüber hinaus; **b)** *(thing offered cheap)* günstiges Angebot; *(thing acquired cheaply)* guter Kauf. 2. *v.i.* **a)** *(discuss)* handeln; **b) ~ for** *or* **on sth.** *(expect sth.)* mit etw. rechnen

barge [bɑ:dʒ] 1. *n.* Kahn, *der.* 2. *v.i.* **~ into sb.** jmdn. anrempeln; **~ in** *(intrude)* hineinplatzen/hereinplatzen *(ugs.)*

baritone ['bærıtəʊn] 1. *n.* Bariton, *der.* 2. *adj.* Bariton-

'**bark** [bɑ:k] *n. (of tree)* Rinde, *die*

²**bark** 1. *n. (of dog)* Bellen, *das.* 2. *v.i.* bellen; **be ~ing up the wrong tree** auf dem Holzweg sein

barley ['bɑ:lı] *n.* Gerste, *die*

bar: ~maid *n. (Brit.)* Bardame, *die;* **~man** ['bɑ:mən] *n., pl.* **~men** ['bɑ:mən] Barmann, *der*

barmy ['bɑ:mı] *adj. (sl.: crazy)* bescheuert *(salopp)*

barn [bɑ:n] *n. (Brit.: for grain etc.)* Scheune, *die; (Amer.: for animals)* Stall, *der*

barnacle ['bɑ:nəkl] *n.* Rankenfüßer, *der*

barometer [bə'rɒmıtə(r)] *n.* Barometer, *das*

baron ['bærn] *n.* Baron, *der;* Freiherr, *der;* **baroness** ['bærənıs] *n.* Baronin, *die;* Freifrau, *die*

baroque [bə'rɒk, bə'rəʊk] 1. *n.* Barock, *das.* 2. *adj.* barock

barracks ['bærəks] *n. pl.* Kaserne, *die*

barrage ['bærɑ:ʒ] *n. (Mil.)* Sperrfeuer, *das;* **a ~ of questions** ein Bombardement von Fragen

barrel ['bærl] *n.* **a)** Faß, *das;* **b)** *(of gun)* Lauf, *der*

barren ['bærn] *adj.* unfruchtbar

barricade [bærı'keıd] 1. *n.* Barrikade, *die.* 2. *v.t.* verbarrikadieren

barrier ['bærıə(r)] *n.* Barriere, *die; (at level crossing etc.)* Schranke, *die*

barring ['bɑ:rıŋ] *prep.* außer im Falle (+ *Gen.*)

barrister ['bærıstə(r)] *n. (Brit.)* ~|-at-law| Barrister, *der;* ≈ [Rechts]anwalt/-anwältin vor höheren Gerichten

barrow ['bærəʊ] *n.* **a)** Karre, *die;* Karren, *der;* **b)** *see* **wheelbarrow**

barter ['bɑ:tə(r)] 1. *v.t.* [ein]tauschen; **~ sth. for sth.** [else] etw. für *od.* gegen etw. [anderes] [ein]tauschen. 2. *v.i.* Tauschhandel treiben. 3. *n.* Tauschhandel, *der*

base [beıs] 1. *n.* **a)** *(of lamp, mountain)* Fuß, *der; (of cupboard, statue)* Sockel, *der; (fig.: support)* Basis, *die;* **b)** *(Mil.)* Basis, *die;* Stützpunkt, *der.* 2. *v.t.* **a)** **be ~d on sth.** sich auf etw. *(Akk.)* gründen; **~ sth. on sth.** etw. auf etw. *(Dat.)* aufbauen; **b)** *in pass.* **be ~d in Paris** *(permanently)* in Paris sitzen; *(temporarily)* in Paris sein

'**baseball** *n.* Baseball, *der*

basement ['beısmənt] *n.* Untergeschoß, *das;* **a ~ flat** eine Kellerwohnung

bash [bæʃ] *v.t. (heftig)* schlagen

bashful ['bæʃfl] *adj.* schüchtern

basic ['beısık] *adj.* grundlegend; Grund⟨*prinzip, -bestandteil, -lohn, -gehalt usw.*⟩; Haupt⟨*problem, -grund, -sache*⟩; **be ~ to sth.** wesentlich für etw. sein. **basically** ['beısıkəlı] *adv.* im Grunde; grundsätzlich ⟨*übereinstimmen*⟩; *(mainly)* hauptsächlich

basil ['bæzıl] *n.* Basilikum, *das*

basin ['beɪsn] *n.* **a)** Becken, *das;* (wash-~) Waschbecken, *das;* (bowl) Schüssel, *die;* **b)** (of river) Becken, *das*

basis ['beɪsɪs] *n., pl.* **bases** ['beɪsiːz] Basis, *die;* Grundlage, *die*

bask [bɑːsk] *v. i.* sich [wohlig] wärmen

basket ['bɑːskɪt] *n.* Korb, *der.* '**basketball** *n.* Basketball, *der*

Basle [bɑːl] *pr. n.* Basel *(das)*

bass [beɪs] **1.** *n.* **a)** Baß, *der;* **b)** (coll.) (double-~) [Kontra]baß, *der;* (~ guitar) Baß, *der.* **2.** *adj.* Baß-. **bass guitar** *n.* Baßgitarre, *die*

bassoon [bə'suːn] *n.* Fagott, *das*

bastard ['bɑːstəd] **1.** *adj.* unehelich. **2.** *n.* **a)** uneheliches Kind; **b)** (coll. derog.: person) Schweinehund, *der (derb)*

baste ['beɪst] *v. t.* [mit Fett] begießen

bastion ['bæstɪən] *n.* Bastei, *die*

¹bat [bæt] *n.* (Zool.) Fledermaus, *die*

²bat 1. *n.* (Sport) Schlagholz, *das;* (for table-tennis) Schläger, *der;* do sth. off one's own ~ (fig.) etw. auf eigene Faust tun. **2.** *v. t.,* -tt- schlagen

³bat *v. t.* not ~ an eyelid nicht mit der Wimper zucken

batch [bætʃ] *n.* **a)** (of loaves) Schub, *der;* **b)** (of people) Gruppe, *die;* (of books, papers) Stapel, *der*

bated ['beɪtɪd] *v. t.* with ~ breath mit angehaltenem Atem

bath [bɑːθ] **1.** *n., pl.* ~s [bɑːðz] **a)** Bad, *das;* have or take a ~: ein Bad nehmen; **b)** (tub) Badewanne, *die;* room with ~: Zimmer mit Bad; **c)** usu. in pl. (building) Bad, *das.* **2.** *v. t. & i.* baden. '**bath cubes** *n. pl.* Badesalz, *das*

bathe [beɪð] *v. t. & i.* baden. **bather** ['beɪðə(r)] *n.* Badende, *der/die.* '**bathing** ['beɪðɪŋ] *n.* Baden, *das.* '**bathing-costume**, '**bathing-suit** *ns.* Badeanzug, *der*

bath: ~**mat** *n.* Bademette, *die;* ~**room** *n.* Badezimmer, *das;* ~ **salts** *n. pl.* Badesalz, *das;* ~**towel** *n.* Badetuch, *das;* ~**tub** *see* **bath 1 b**

baton ['bætn] *n.* **a)** (truncheon) Schlagstock, *der;* **b)** (Mus.) Taktstock, *der*

batsman ['bætsmən] *n., pl.* **batsmen** ['bætsmən] Schlagmann, *der*

battalion [bə'tæljən] *n.* Bataillon, *das*

¹batter ['bætə(r)] *v. t.* (strike) einschlagen auf (+ Akk.)

²batter *n.* (Cookery) [Back]teig, *der*

battery ['bætərɪ] *n.* Batterie, *die*

battery: ~ **charger** *n.* Batterieladegerät, *das;* ~ '**farming** *n.* Batteriehaltung, *die;* ~ '**hen** *n.* Batteriehuhn, *das*

battle ['bætl] **1.** *n.* Schlacht, *die;* (fig.) Kampf, *der.* **2.** *v. i.* kämpfen

battle: ~**axe** *n.* (coll.: woman) Schreckschraube, *die (ugs.);* ~**field,** ~**ground** *ns.* Schlachtfeld, *das*

battlements ['bætlmənts] *n. pl.* Zinnen *Pl.*

'**battleship** *n.* Schlachtschiff, *das*

batty ['bætɪ] *adj.* (sl.) bekloppt (salopp)

bauble ['bɔːbl] *n.* Flitter, *der*

baulk *see* **balk**

Bavaria [bə'veərɪə] *pr. n.* Bayern *(das).* **Bavarian** [bə'veərɪən] **1.** *adj.* bay[e]risch. **2.** *n.* Bayer, *der/*Bayerin, *die*

bawdy ['bɔːdɪ] *adj.* zweideutig; (stronger) obszön

¹bay [beɪ] *n.* (of sea) Bucht, *die*

²bay *n.* **a)** (space in room) Erker, *der;* **b)** |parking-|~: Stellplatz, *der*

³bay *n.* hold or keep sb./sth. at ~: sich (Dat.) jmdn./etw. vom Leib halten

bayonet ['beɪənɪt] *n.* Bajonett, *das*

bay 'window *n.* Erkerfenster, *das*

bazaar [bə'zɑː(r)] *n.* Basar, *der*

BBC *abbr.* **British Broadcasting Corporation** BBC, *die*

BC *abbr.* **before Christ** v. Chr.

be [biː] *v., pres. t.* **I am** [əm, *stressed* æm], **he is** [ɪz], **we are** [ə(r), *stressed* ɑː(r)]; *p. t.* **I was** [wəz, *stressed* wɒz], **we were** [wə(r), *stressed* wɜː(r)]; *pres. p.* **being** ['biːɪŋ]; *p. p.* **been** [bɪn, *stressed* biːn] **1.** *copula* **a)** sein; **she is a mother/an Italian/a teacher** sie ist Mutter/Italienerin/Lehrerin; **be sensible!** sei vernünftig!; **be ill/unwell** krank sein/sich nicht wohl fühlen; **I am well** es geht mir gut; **I am hot** mir ist heiß; **I am freezing** mich friert es; **how are you/is she?** wie geht's (ugs.)/geht es ihr?; **it is the 5th today** heute haben wir den Fünften; **who's that?** wer ist das?; **if I were you** an deiner Stelle; **it's hers** ist ihrs; **b)** (cost) kosten; **how much are the eggs?** was kosten die Eier?; **two times three is six, two threes are six** zweimal drei ist od. sind sechs; **c)** (constitute) bilden. **2.** *v. i.* **a)** (exist) [vorhanden] sein; **there is/are ...:** es gibt ...; **for the time being** vorläufig; **be that as it may** wie dem auch sei; **b)** (remain) bleiben; **I shan't be a moment** ich komme sofort; **let it be** laß es sein; **let him/her be** laß ihn/sie in Ruhe; **c)** (happen) stattfinden; sein; **d)** (go, come) **be off with you!** geh/geht!; **I'm off home** ich gehe jetzt nach Hause; **she's from Australia** sie stammt od. ist aus Australien; **e)** (go or come *on visit)* sein; **have you [ever] been to London?** bist du schon einmal in London gewesen?; **has anyone been?** ist jemand dagewesen? **3.** *v. aux.* **a)** *forming passive* werden; **the child was found** das Kind wurde gefunden; **German is spoken here** hier wird Deutsch gesprochen; **b)** *forming continuous tenses, active* **he is reading** er liest [gerade]; **I am leaving tomorrow** ich reise morgen [ab]; **the train was departing when I got there** der Zug fuhr gerade ab, als ich ankam; **c)** *forming continuous tenses, passive* **the house is/was being built** das Haus wird/wurde [gerade] gebaut; **d)** *expr. arrangement, obligation* **be to** sollen; **I am to go/to inform you** ich soll gehen/Sie unterrichten; **e)** *expr. destiny* **they were never to meet again** sie sollten sich nie wieder treffen; **f)** *expr. condition* **if I were to tell you that ...:** wenn ich dir sagen würde, daß ... **4. bride-/husband-to-be** zukünftige Braut/zukünftiger Ehemann

beach [biːtʃ] *n.* Strand, *der;* **on the ~:** am Strand. **'beach wear** *n.* Strandkleidung, *die*

beacon ['biːkn] *n.* Leuchtfeuer, *das;* *(Naut.)* Leuchtbake, *die*

bead [biːd] *n.* Perle, *die;* ~s Perlen *Pl.;* Perlenkette, *die;* ~s **of dew/sweat** Tau-/Schweißtropfen

beak [biːk] *n.* Schnabel, *der*

beaker ['biːkə(r)] *n.* Becher, *der*

beam [biːm] **1.** *n.* **a)** *(timber etc.)* Balken, *der;* **b)** *(ray etc.)* [Licht]strahl, *der.* **2.** *v. i.* **a)** *(shine)* strahlen; glänzen; **b)** *(smile)* strahlen; ~ **at sb.** jmdn. anstrahlen

bean [biːn] *n.* Bohne, *die;* **full of ~s** *(fig. coll.)* putzmunter *(ugs.)*

¹bear [beə(r)] *n.* Bär, *der*

²bear 1. *v. t.,* **bore** [bɔː(r)], **borne** [bɔːn] **a)** tragen; aufweisen ⟨Spuren, Ähnlichkeit⟩; tragen, führen ⟨Namen, Titel⟩; ~ **some/little relation to sth.** einen gewissen/wenig Bezug zu etw. haben; **b)** *(endure, tolerate)* ertragen ⟨Schmerz, Kummer⟩; *with neg.* ertragen, aushalten ⟨Schmerz⟩; ausstehen ⟨Geruch, Lärm⟩; **c)** *(be fit for)* vertragen; **it will not ~ scrutiny** es hält einer Überprüfung nicht stand; **it does not ~ thinking about** daran darf man gar nicht denken; **d)** *(give birth to)* gebären ⟨Kind, Junges⟩. **2.** *v. i.,* **bore, borne:** ~ **left** ⟨Person:⟩ sich links halten; **the path ~s to the left** der Weg führt nach

links. **bear 'out** *v. t. (fig.)* bestätigen ⟨Bericht, Erklärung⟩; ~ **sb. out** jmdm. recht geben. **'bear with** *v. t.* Nachsicht haben mit

bearable ['beərəbl] *adj.* erträglich

beard [bɪəd] *n.* Bart, *der.* **'bearded** *adj.* bärtig. **be ~:** einen Bart haben

'bearer *n. (carrier)* Träger, *der/*Trägerin, *die; (of message, cheque)* Überbringer, *der/*Überbringerin, *die*

'bearing *n.* **a)** *(behaviour)* Verhalten, *das;* **b)** *(relation)* Bezug, *der;* **have some/no ~ on sth.** relevant/irrelevant für etw. sein; **c)** *(Mech. Engin.)* Lager, *das;* **d)** *(compass ~)* Position, *die;* **take a compass ~:** den Kompaßkurs feststellen; **get one's ~s** sich orientieren; *(fig.)* sich zurechtfinden

beast [biːst] *n.* Tier, *das; (fig.: brutal person)* Bestie, *die.* **'beastly** *adj., adv. (coll.)* scheußlich

beat [biːt] **1.** *v. t.,* **beat, beaten** ['biːtn] schlagen; klopfen ⟨Teppich⟩; *(surpass)* brechen ⟨Rekord⟩; **hard to ~:** schwer zu schlagen; **it ~s me how/why ...:** es ist mir ein Rätsel wie/warum ...; ~ **time** den Takt schlagen; ~ **it!** *(sl.)* hau ab! *(ugs.); see also* **beaten 2. 2.** *v. i.* **beat, beaten** schlagen **(on auf +** *Akk.);* ⟨Regen, Hagel:⟩ prasseln **(against gegen). 3.** *n.* **a)** *(stroke, throbbing)* Schlagen, *das; (Mus.) (rhythm)* Takt, *der; (single ~)* Schlag, *der;* **b)** *(of policeman)* Runde, *die.* **beat 'off** *v. t.* abwehren ⟨Angriff⟩. **beat 'up** *v. t.* zusammenschlagen ⟨Person⟩

beaten ['biːtn] **1.** *see* **beat 1, 2. 2.** *adj.* **a) off the ~ track** weit abgelegen; **b)** gehämmert ⟨Silber, Gold⟩

'beating *n.* **a)** *(punishment)* **a ~:** Schläge *Pl.;* Prügel *Pl.;* **b)** *(defeat)* Niederlage, *die;* **c) take some/a lot of ~:** nicht leicht zu übertreffen sein

'beat-up *adj. (sl.)* ramponiert *(ugs.)*

beautiful ['bjuːtɪfl] *adj.* schön; wunderschön ⟨Augen, Aussicht, Morgen⟩

beautify ['bjuːtɪfaɪ] *v. t.* verschönen

beauty ['bjuːtɪ] *n.* **1.** Schönheit, *die; (beautiful feature)* Schöne, *das;* **the ~ of it** das Schöne daran

beauty: ~ **parlour** *see* ~ **salon;** ~ **queen** *n.* Schönheitskönigin, *die;* ~ **salon** *n.* Kosmetiksalon, *der;* ~ **spot** *n.* Schönheitsfleck, *der; (place)* schönes Fleckchen [Erde]

beaver ['biːvə(r)] *n.* Biber, *der*

became *see* **become**

because [bɪ'kɒz] **1.** *conj.* weil. **2.** *adv.* ~ **of** wegen (+ *Gen.*)

beckon ['bekn] *v. t. & i.* winken (**to** sb. jmdm.); *(fig.)* locken

become [bɪ'kʌm] **1.** *copula,* **became** [bɪ'keɪm], **become** werden; ~ **a politician** Politiker werden; ~ **a nuisance/ rule** zu einer Plage/zur Regel werden. **2.** *v. i.,* **became, become** werden; **what has** ~ **of him?** was ist aus ihm geworden? **3.** *v. t.,* **became, become** *(suit)* ~ sb. jmdm. stehen

becoming [bɪ'kʌmɪŋ] *adj.* **a)** *(fitting)* schicklich *(geh.);* **b)** *(flattering)* vorteilhaft ⟨ *Hut, Kleid, Frisur* ⟩

bed [bed] *n.* **a)** Bett, *das; (without bedstead)* Lager, *das;* **in** ~: im Bett; ~ **and breakfast** Zimmer mit Frühstück; **get out of/into** ~: aufstehen/ins Bett gehen; **go to** ~: ins Bett gehen; **put** sb. **to** ~: jmdn. ins Bett bringen; **b)** *(flat base)* Unterlage, *die; (of machine)* Bett, *das;* **c)** *(in garden)* Beet, *das;* **d)** *(of sea, lake)* Grund, *der; (of river)* Bett, *das.* '**bedclothes** *n. pl.* Bettzeug, *das.* **bedding** ['bedɪŋ] *n.* Matratze und Bettzeug

bedlam ['bedləm] *n., no indef. art.* Tumult, *der*

'**bedpan** *n.* Bettpfanne, *die*

bedraggled [bɪ'drægld] *adj. (soaked)* durchnäßt; *(with mud)* verdreckt

bed: ~**ridden** *adj.* bettlägerig; ~**room** *n.* Schlafzimmer, *das;* ~**side** *n.* Seite des Bettes, *die;* ~**side table/ lamp** Nachttisch, *der*/Nachttischlampe, *die;* ~-'**sit,** ~-'**sitter** *ns. (coll.)* Wohnschlafzimmer, *das;* ~**spread** *n.* Tagesdecke, *die;* ~**stead** *n.* Bettgestell, *das;* ~**time** *n.* Schlafenszeit, *die;* **at** ~**time** vor dem Zubettgehen; **a** ~**time story** eine Gutenachtgeschichte

bee [biː] *n.* Biene, *die*

beech [biːtʃ] *n.* Buche, *die*

beef [biːf] **1.** *n.* **a)** Rindfleisch, *das;* **b)** *(coll.: muscles)* Muskeln. **2.** *v. t.* ~ **up** stärken. **beefburger** ['biːfbɜːɡə(r)] *n.* Beefburger, *der*

bee: ~**hive** *n.* Bienenstock, *der;* ~-**keeper** *n.* Imker, *der*/Imkerin, *die;* ~-**keeping** *n.* Imkerei, *die;* ~-**line** *n.* **make a** ~-**line for** sth./sb. schnurstracks auf etw./jmdn. zustürzen

been *see* **be**

beer [bɪə(r)] *n.* Bier, *das*

beet [biːt] *n.* Rübe, *die*

beetle ['biːtl] *n.* Käfer, *der*

'**beetroot** *n.* rote Beete *od.* Rübe

before [bɪ'fɔː(r)] **1.** *adv.* **a)** *(of time)* vorher; *(already)* schon; **the day** ~:

am Tag zuvor; **never** ~: noch nie; **b)** *(ahead in position)* vor[aus]. **2.** *prep. (of time; position)* vor (+ *Dat.*); *(direction)* vor (+ *Akk.*); **the day** ~ **yesterday** vorgestern; ~ **now/then** früher/vorher; ~ **Christ** vor Christus; ~ **leaving,** **he phoned** bevor er wegging, rief er an. **3.** *conj.* bevor. **be'forehand** *adv.* vorher; *(in anticipation)* im voraus

beg [beg] **1.** *v. t.,* -**gg**-: **a)** betteln um; **b)** *(ask earnestly for)* ~ sth. um etw. bitten. **2.** *v. i.,* -**gg**- betteln (**for** um)

began *see* **begin**

beggar ['beɡə(r)] *n.* **a)** Bettler, *der*/Bettlerin, *die;* **b)** *(coll.)* **poor** ~: armer Teufel

begin [bɪ'ɡɪn] **1.** *v. t.,* -**nn**-, **began** [bɪ'ɡæn], **begun** [bɪ'ɡʌn] ~ sth. [mit] etw. beginnen; ~ **doing** *or* **to do** sth. anfangen *od.* beginnen, etw. zu tun. **2.** *v. i.,* -**nn**-, **began, begun** anfangen; ~ [up]on sth. etw. anfangen. **be'ginner** *n.* Anfänger, *der*/Anfängerin, *die.* **be'ginning** *n.* Anfang, *der;* **at** *or* **in the** ~: am Anfang; **at the** ~ **of February/the month** Anfang Februar/des Monats; **from the** ~: von Anfang an

begrudge [bɪ'ɡrʌdʒ] *v. t.* ~ sb. sth. jmdm. etw. mißgönnen; ~ **doing** sth. etw. ungern tun

begun *see* **begin**

behalf [bɪ'hɑːf] *n.* **on** *or (Amer.)* **in** ~ **of** sb./sth. für jmdn./etw.; *(more formally)* im Namen von jmdm./etw.

behave [bɪ'heɪv] **1.** *v. i.* sich verhalten; sich benehmen; **well-/ill-** *or* **badly** ~d brav/ungezogen. **2.** *v. refl.* ~ **oneself** sich benehmen. **behaviour** [bɪ'heɪvjə(r)] *n.* Verhalten, *das*

behead [bɪ'hed] *v. t.* enthaupten

behind [bɪ'haɪnd] **1.** *adv.* hinten; *(further back)* **be miles** ~: kilometerweit zurückliegen; **stay** ~: dableiben; **leave** sb./sth. ~: jmdn./etw. zurücklassen; **fall** ~: zurückbleiben; *(fig.)* in Rückstand geraten; **be/get** ~ **with one's payments/rent** mit seinen Zahlungen/der Miete im Rückstand sein/in Rückstand geraten. **2.** *prep.* **a)** hinter (+ *Dat.*); **one** ~ **the other** hintereinander; **b)** *(towards rear of)* hinter (+ *Akk.*)

being ['biːɪŋ] *n.* **a)** *(existence)* Dasein, *das;* **in** ~: bestehend; **come into** ~: entstehen; **b)** *(person etc.)* Wesen, *das*

belated [bɪ'leɪtɪd] *adj.,* **be'latedly** *adv.* verspätet

belch [beltʃ] **1.** *v. i.* heftig aufstoßen; rülpsen *(ugs.).* **2.** *n.* Rülpser, *der (ugs.)*

belfry ['belfrɪ] *n.* Glockenturm, *der*
Belgian ['beldʒən] 1. *n.* Belgier, *der*/Belgierin, *die.* 2. *adj.* belgisch
Belgium ['beldʒəm] *pr. n.* Belgien *(das)*
belie [bɪ'laɪ] *v. t.,* **belying** [bɪ'laɪŋ] hinwegtäuschen über ⟨*Tatsachen, wahren Zustand*⟩; nicht erfüllen ⟨*Versprechen*⟩; nicht entsprechen ⟨*Vorstellung (Dat.)*⟩
belief [bɪ'li:f] *n.* **a)** Glaube, *der* (in an + *Akk.*); **in the ~ that ...**: in der Überzeugung, daß ...; **b)** *(Relig.)* Glaube[n], *der*
believable [bɪ'li:vəbl] *adj.* glaubhaft
believe [bɪ'li:v] 1. *v. i.* glauben (in an + *Dat.*); *(have faith)* glauben (in an + *Akk.*) ⟨*Gott, Himmel usw.*⟩; **I ~ so/not** ich glaube schon/nicht. 2. *v. t.* glauben; **~ sb.** jmdm. glauben; **I don't ~ you** das glaube ich dir nicht; **make ~ that ...**: so tun, als ob ...
Belisha beacon [bəli:ʃə 'bi:kn] *n.* *(Brit.)* gelbes Blinklicht an Zebrastreifen
belittle [bɪ'lɪtl] *v. t.* herabsetzen
bell [bel] *n.* Glocke, *die;* (door~) Klingel, *die*
belligerent [bɪ'lɪdʒərənt] *adj.* kriegführend ⟨*Nation*⟩; streitlustig ⟨*Person*⟩
bellow ['beləʊ] 1. *v. i.* brüllen. 2. *v. t.* ~ |out| brüllen ⟨*Befehl*⟩
bellows ['beləʊz] *n. pl.* Blasebalg, *der*
belly ['belɪ] *n.* Bauch, *der.* '**bellyache** *n.* Bauchschmerzen *Pl.*
belong [bɪ'lɒŋ] *v. i.* ~ **to sb./sth.** jmdm./zu etw. gehören; ~ **to a club** einem Verein angehören; **where does this ~?** wo gehört das hin? **be'longings** *n. pl.* Habe, *die;* Sachen *Pl.*
beloved [bɪ'lʌvɪd] 1. *adj.* geliebt. 2. *n.* Geliebte, *der/die*
below [bɪ'ləʊ] 1. *adv.* **a)** *(position)* unten; *(lower down)* darunter; **from ~:** von unten [herauf]; **b)** *(direction)* nach unten; hinunter. 2. *prep.* unter *(position: + Dat.; direction: + Akk.)*
belt [belt] *n.* Gürtel, *der;* *(for tools, weapons, ammunition)* Gurt, *der;* *(of trees)* Streifen, *der.* **belt 'up** *v. i.* *(Brit. sl.)* die Klappe halten *(salopp)*
bemused [bɪ'mju:zd] *adj.* verwirrt
bench [bentʃ] *n.* Bank, *die;* *(worktable)* Werkbank, *die*
bend [bend] 1. *n.* Beuge, *die;* *(in road)* Kurve, *die.* 2. *v. t.,* **bent** [bent] biegen; beugen ⟨*Arm, Knie*⟩; anwinkeln ⟨*Bein*⟩. 3. *v. i.,* **bent** sich biegen; *(bow)* sich bücken. **bend 'down** *v. i.* sich

bücken. **bend 'over** *v. i.* sich nach vorn beugen
beneath [bɪ'ni:θ] *prep.* **a)** *(unworthy of)* ~ **sb.,** ~ **sb.'s dignity** unter jmds. Würde *(Dat.);* **b)** *(arch./literary: under)* unter *(+ Dat.)*
benefactor ['benɪfæktə(r)] *n.* Wohltäter, *der;* *(patron)* Gönner, *der*
beneficial [benɪ'fɪʃl] *adj.* nützlich; vorteilhaft ⟨*Einfluß*⟩
benefit ['benɪfɪt] 1. *n.* **a)** Vorteil, *der;* **be of ~ to sb./sth.** jmdm./einer Sache von Nutzen sein; **have the ~ of** den Vorteil (+ *Gen.*) haben; **with the ~ of** mit Hilfe (+ *Gen.*); **for sb.'s ~:** in jmds. Interesse *(Dat.);* **b)** *(allowance)* Beihilfe, *die;* **unemployment ~:** Arbeitslosenunterstützung, *die.* 2. *v. t.* nützen *(+ Dat.).* 3. *v. i.* ~ **by/from sth.** von etw. profitieren
benevolent [bɪ'nevələnt] *adj.* **a)** gütig; **b)** wohltätig ⟨*Institution, Verein*⟩
benign [bɪ'naɪn] *adj.* gütig; *(Med.)* gutartig
bent [bent] 1. *see* bend 2, 3. 2. *n.* *(liking)* Neigung, *die* (for zu). 3. **a)** *adj.* krumm; **b)** *(Brit. sl.: corrupt)* link *(salopp)*
bequeath [bɪ'kwi:ð] *v. t.* ~ **sth. to sb.** jmdm. etw. hinterlassen. **bequest** [bɪ'kwest] *n.* Legat, *das* (**to** an + *Akk.*)
bereaved [bɪ'ri:vd] *n.* **the ~:** der/die Hinterbliebene/die Hinterbliebenen
beret ['bereɪ] *n.* Baskenmütze, *die*
Berlin [bɜ:'lɪn] *pr. n.* Berlin *(das)*
Berne [bɜ:n] *pr. n.* Bern *(das)*
berry ['berɪ] *n.* Beere, *die*
berserk [bə'sɜ:k] *adj.* rasend; **go ~:** durchdrehen *(ugs.)*
berth [bɜ:θ] *n.* *(for ship)* Liegeplatz, *der;* *(sleeping-place)* *(in ship)* Koje, *die;* *(in train)* Schlafwagenbett, *das*
beside [bɪ'saɪd] *prep.* **a)** neben (+ *Dat.*); ~ **the sea/lake** am Meer/ See; **b)** **be ~ the point** nichts damit zu tun haben; **c)** ~ **oneself** außer sich
besides [bɪ'saɪdz] 1. *adv.* außerdem. 2. *prep.* außer
besiege [bɪ'si:dʒ] *v. t.* belagern
best [best] 1. *adj.* best...; **the ~ part of an hour** fast eine ganze Stunde. 2. *adv.* am besten. 3. *n.* **the ~:** der/die/das Beste; **do one's ~:** sein bestes tun; **make the ~ of it** das Beste daraus machen; **at ~:** bestenfalls. **best 'man** *n.* Trauzeuge, *der* *(des Bräutigams).* **best 'seller** *n.* Bestseller, *der*
bet [bet] 1. *v. t. & i.,* **-tt-,** *or* **~ted** wetten; **I ~ him £10** ich habe mit ihm um

10 Pfund gewettet; ~ **on** sth. auf etw.
(Akk.) setzen. **2.** *n.* Wette, *die; (fig.
coll.)* Tip, *der*

betray [bɪ'treɪ] *v. t.* verraten (**to** an
+ *Akk.*). **betrayal** [bɪ'treɪəl] *n.* Verrat, *der*

better ['betə(r)] **1.** *adj.* besser; ~ **and**
~: immer besser; **be much** ~ *(re-
covered)* sich viel besser fühlen; **get** ~
(recover) gesund werden; **the** ~ **part
of** sth. der größte Teil einer Sache
(Gen.). **2.** *adv.* besser; ~ 'off *(financially)* besser gestellt; **be** ~ **off without**
sb./**sth.** ohne jmdn./etw. besser dran
sein; **I'd** ~ **be off** now ich gehe jetzt
besser. **3.** *n.* **get the** ~ **of** sb./**sth.**
jmdn./etw. unterkriegen *(ugs.);* **a
change for the** ~: eine vorteilhafte
Veränderung. **4.** *v. t.* übertreffen

'**betting shop** *n.* Wettbüro, *das*

between [bɪ'twiːn] **1.** *prep.* **a)** [in] ~:
zwischen *(position:* + *Dat.; direction:*
+ *Akk.*); **b)** *(amongst)* unter
(+ *Dat.*); ~ **ourselves,** ~ **you and me**
unter uns *(Dat.)* gesagt; **c)** ~ **them/us**
(by joint action of) gemeinsam; ~ **us**
we had 40p wir hatten zusammen 40
Pence. **2.** *adv.* [in] ~: dazwischen; *(in
time)* zwischendurch

beverage ['bevərɪdʒ] *n.* Getränk, *das*

beware [bɪ'weə(r)] *v. t. & i.; only in
imper. and inf.* ~ [of] sb./**sth.** sich vor
jmdm./etw. in acht nehmen; ~ **of
doing** sth. sich davor hüten, etw. zu
tun; '~ **of the dog**" „Vorsicht, bissiger
Hund!"

bewilder [bɪ'wɪldə(r)] *v. t.* verwirren.
be'wilderment *n.* Verwirrung, *die*

bewitch [bɪ'wɪtʃ] *v. t.* verzaubern;
(fig.) bezaubern

beyond [bɪ'jɒnd] **1.** *adv.* **a)** *(in space)*
jenseits; *(on other side of wall, moun-
tain range, etc.)* dahinter; **b)** *(in time)*
darüber hinaus; **c)** *(in addition)* außerdem. **2.** *prep.* **a)** *(at far side of)* jenseits
(+ *Gen.*); **b)** *(later than)* nach; **c)** *(out
of reach or comprehension or range)*
über ... (+ *Akk.*) hinaus

bias ['baɪəs] **1.** *n.* Voreingenommen-
heit, *die.* **2.** *v. t.,* **-s-** *or* **-ss-** beeinflussen; **be** ~**ed in favour of/against** sth./
sb. für etw./jmdn. eingestellt sein/ge-
gen etw./jmdn. voreingenommen sein

bib [bɪb] *n.* Lätzchen, *das*

Bible ['baɪbl] *n.* Bibel, *die.* **biblical**
['bɪblɪkl] *adj.* biblisch

bibliography [bɪblɪ'ɒgrəfɪ] *n.* Biblio-
graphie, *die*

biceps ['baɪseps] *n.* Bizeps, *der*

bicker ['bɪkə(r)] *v. i.* sich zanken

bicycle ['baɪsɪkl] **1.** *n.* Fahrrad, *das;
attrib.* Fahrrad-; ~ **clip** Hosenklam-
mer, *die.* **2.** *v. i.* radfahren

bid [bɪd] **1.** *v. t.* **a)** **-dd-, bid** *(at auction)*
bieten; **b)** **-dd-, bade** [bæd, beɪd] *or*
bid, bidden ['bɪdn] *or* **bid:** ~ sb. **wel-
come/goodbye** jmdn. willkommen hei-
ßen/sich von jmdm. verabschieden. **2.**
v. i., **-dd-, bid** **a)** werben (**for** um); **b)**
(at auction) bieten. **3.** *n.* **a)** *(at auction)*
Gebot, *das;* **b)** *(attempt)* Versuch, *der*

bidden *see* **bid** 1

'**bidder** *n.* Bieter, *der*/Bieterin, *die*

bide ['baɪd] *v. t.* ~ **one's time** den richtigen Augenblick abwarten

bifocal [baɪ'fəʊkl] **1.** *adj.* Bifokal-. **2.**
n. in pl. Bifokalgläser *Pl.*

big [bɪg] *adj.* groß

bigamy ['bɪgəmɪ] *n.* Bigamie, *die*

big-'headed *adj. (coll.)* eingebildet

bigoted ['bɪgətɪd] *adj.* eifernd

big: ~ **toe** *n.* große Zehe; ~ '**top** *n.*
Zirkuszelt, *das;* ~ '**wheel** *n. (at fair)*
Riesenrad, *das*

bike [baɪk] *(coll.)* **1.** *n. (bicycle)* Rad,
das; (motor cycle) Maschine, *die.* **2.**
v. i. radfahren/[mit dem] Motorrad
fahren

bikini [bɪ'kiːnɪ] *n.* Bikini, *der*

bilingual [baɪ'lɪŋgwəl] *adj.* zweispra-
chig

bilious ['bɪljəs] *adj. (Med.)* Gallen-; ~
attack Gallenanfall, *der*

¹**bill** [bɪl] *n. (of bird)* Schnabel, *der*

²**bill** *n.* **a)** *(Parl.)* Gesetzentwurf, *der;* **b)**
(note of charges) Rechnung, *die; could
we have the* ~ **please?** wir möchten
zahlen; **c)** *(poster)* '[stick] no ~s' „[Pla-
kate] ankleben verboten"

'**billboard** *n.* Reklametafel, *die*

billet ['bɪlɪt] **1.** *n.* Quartier, *das.* **2.** *v. t.*
einquartieren (**with, on** bei)

'**billfold** *n. (Amer.)* Brieftasche, *die*

billiards ['bɪljədz] *n.* Billard[spiel], *das*

billion ['bɪljən] *n.* **a)** *(thousand million)*
Milliarde, *die;* **b)** *(Brit.: million million)* Billion, *die*

billy-goat ['bɪlɪgəʊt] *n.* Ziegenbock,
der

bin [bɪn] *n.* Behälter, *der; (for bread)*
Brotkasten, *der; (for rubbish)* Müllei-
mer, *der*

binary ['baɪnərɪ] *adj.* binär

bind [baɪnd] *v. t.,* **bound** [baʊnd] **a)** fesseln ⟨Person, Tier⟩; *(bandage)* wickeln
⟨Glied, Baum⟩; verbinden ⟨Wunde⟩
(**with** mit); **b)** *(fasten together)* zusam-
menbinden; **c)** binden ⟨Buch⟩; **d)** **be**

bound up with sth. *(fig.)* eng mit etw. verbunden sein; **e) be bound to do sth.** *(required)* verpflichtet sein, etw. zu tun; *(certain)* etw. ganz bestimmt tun; **it is bound to rain** es wird bestimmt regnen. **'binder** *n. (for papers)* Hefter, *der; (for magazines)* Mappe, *die.* **'binding** **1.** *adj.* bindend ⟨*Vertrag, Abkommen*⟩ (on für). **2.** *n. (of book)* Einband, *der*

bingo ['bɪŋgəʊ] *n.* Bingo, *das*

binoculars [bɪ'nɒkjʊləz] *n. pl.* [a pair of] ~: Fernglas, *das*

biodegradable [baɪəʊdɪ'greɪdəbl] *adj.* biologisch abbaubar

biographer [baɪ'ɒgrəfə(r)] *n.* Biograph, *der*/Biographin, *die*

biographical [baɪə'græfɪkl] *adj.* biographisch

biography [baɪ'ɒgrəfɪ] *n.* Biographie, *die*

biological [baɪə'lɒdʒɪkl] *adj.* biologisch

biologist [baɪ'ɒlədʒɪst] *n.* Biologe, *der*/Biologin, *die*

biology [baɪ'ɒlədʒɪ] *n.* Biologie, *die*

biotechnology [baɪəʊtek'nɒlədʒɪ] *n.* Biotechnologie, *die*

birch [bɜːtʃ] *n.* Birke, *die*

bird [bɜːd] *n.* Vogel, *der*

bird: ~ **cage** *n.* Vogelkäfig, *der;* ~'**s-eye** '**view** *n.* Vogelperspektive, *die;* ~'**s nest** *n.* Vogelnest, *das*

Biro, (P) ['baɪrəʊ] *n., pl.* ~**s** Kugelschreiber, *der;* Kuli, *der (ugs.)*

birth [bɜːθ] *n.* **a)** Geburt, *die;* **give** ~ ⟨*Frau:*⟩ entbinden; ⟨*Tier:*⟩ jungen; werfen; **give** ~ **to a child** ein Kind zur Welt bringen; **b)** *(of movement, fashion, etc.)* Aufkommen, *das*

birth: ~ **certificate** *n.* Geburtsurkunde, *die;* ~ **control** *n.* Geburtenkontrolle, *die;* ~**day** *n.* Geburtstag, *der; attrib.* Geburtstags-; ~**place** *n.* Geburtsort, *der*

biscuit ['bɪskɪt] *n. (Brit.)* Keks, *der*

bisect [baɪ'sekt] *v. t.* halbieren

bishop ['bɪʃəp] *n.* **a)** *(Eccl.)* Bischof, *der;* **b)** *(Chess)* Läufer, *der*

¹bit [bɪt] *n.* **a)** *(for horse)* Gebiß, *das;* **b)** *(of drill)* [Bohr]einsatz, *der*

²bit *n. (piece)* Stück, *das;* **not a** *or* **one** ~ *(not at all)* überhaupt nicht; **a** ~ **tired/too early** ein bißchen müde/zu früh; **be a** ~ **of a coward/bully** ein ziemlicher Feigling sein/den starken Mann markieren *(ugs.)*

³bit *n. (Computing)* Bit, *das*

⁴bit *see* bite 1, 2

bitch [bɪtʃ] *n.* **a)** *(dog)* Hündin, *die;* **b)** *(sl. derog.: woman)* Miststück, *das (derb)*

bite [baɪt] **1.** *v. t.,* **bit** [bɪt], **bitten** ['bɪtn] beißen; ⟨*Moskito usw.:*⟩ stechen. **2.** *v. i.,* **bit, bitten** beißen/stechen; *(take bait)* anbeißen. **3.** *n.* Biß, *der; (piece)* Bissen, *der; (wound)* Bißwunde, *die; (by mosquito etc.)* Stich, *der.* **bite** '**off** *v. t.* abbeißen

biting ['baɪtɪŋ] *adj.* beißend

bitten *see* bite 1, 2

bitter ['bɪtə(r)] *adj.* bitter. '**bitterly** *adv.* bitterlich ⟨*weinen, sich beschweren*⟩; ~ **cold** bitterkalt. '**bitterness** *n.* Bitterkeit, *die*

bizarre [bɪ'zɑː(r)] *adj.* bizarr

black [blæk] **1.** *adj.* **a)** schwarz; ~ **and blue** *(fig.)* grün und blau; **in** ~ **and white** *(fig.)* schwarz auf weiß; **in the** ~ *(in credit)* in den schwarzen Zahlen; **b) B**~ *(dark-skinned)* schwarz. **2.** *n.* **a)** Schwarz, *das;* **b) B**~ *(person)* Schwarze, *der/die.* **3.** *v. t.* bestreiken ⟨*Betrieb*⟩; boykottieren ⟨*Arbeit*⟩. **black** '**out** **1.** *v. t.* verdunkeln. **2.** *v. i.* das Bewußtsein verlieren

black: ~**berry** ['blækbərɪ] *n.* Brombeere, *die;* ~**bird** *n.* Amsel, *die;* ~**board** *n.* [Wand]tafel, *die;* ~'**currant** *n.* schwarze Johannisbeere

blacken ['blækn] *v. t.* schwärzen; verfinstern ⟨*Himmel*⟩

black: ~ '**eye** *n.* blaues Auge; **B**~ '**Forest** *pr. n.* Schwarzwald, *der;* ~ '**ice** *n.* Glatteis, *das;* ~**leg** *n. (Brit.)* Streikbrecher, *der*/-brecherin, *die;* ~ **list** *n.* schwarze Liste; ~**list** *v. t.* auf die schwarze Liste setzen; ~**mail** **1.** *v. t.* erpressen; **2.** *n.* Erpressung, *die;* ~ **market** *n.* schwarzer Markt

'**blackness** *n.* Schwärze, *die; (darkness)* Finsternis, *die*

black: ~-**out** *n.* **a)** Verdunkelung, *die; (Theatre, Radio)* Blackout, *der;* **b)** *(Med.)* **have a** ~-**out** das Bewußtsein verlieren; **B**~ '**Sea** *pr. n.* Schwarze Meer, *das;* ~**smith** ['blæksmɪθ] *n.* Schmied, *der;* ~ **spot** *n.* Gefahrenstelle, *die*

bladder ['blædə(r)] *n.* Blase, *die*

blade [bleɪd] *n.* **a)** *(of sword, knife, razor, etc.)* Klinge, *die; (of saw, oar, propeller)* Blatt, *das;* **b)** *(of grass)* Spreite, *die*

blame [bleɪm] **1.** *v. t.* ~ **sb.** [for sth.] jmdm. die Schuld [an etw. *(Dat.)*] geben; **be to** ~ [for sth.] an etw. *(Dat.)* schuld sein; ~ **sth.** [for sth.] etw. [für

etw.] verantwortlich machen. 2. *n.*
Schuld, *die*. '**blameless** *adj.* untadelig

blancmange [bləˈmɒnʒ] *n.* Flammeri,
der

bland [blænd] *adj.* mild; *(suave)* verbindlich

blank [blæŋk] 1. *adj.* **a)** leer; kahl
⟨*Wand, Fläche*⟩; **b)** *(empty)* frei. 2. *n.*
a) *(space)* Lücke, *die;* **b)** *(cartridge)*
Platzpatrone, *die;* **c) draw a ~:** kein
Glück haben. **blank 'cheque** *n.*
Blankoscheck, *der; (fig.)* Blankovoll-
macht, *die*

blanket ['blæŋkɪt] *n.* Decke, *die;* **wet
'~** *(fig.)* Trauerkloß, *der (ugs.)*

blare ['bleə(r)] 1. *v. i.* ⟨*Lautsprecher:*⟩
plärren; ⟨*Trompete:*⟩ schmettern. 2.
v. t. **~ |out|** [hinaus]plärren ⟨*Worte*⟩;
[hinaus]schmettern ⟨*Melodie*⟩

blasé ['blɑːzeɪ] *adj.* blasiert

blasphemous ['blæsfəməs] *adj.* lä-
sterlich

blasphemy ['blæsfəmɪ] *n.* Blasphemie, *die*

blast [blɑːst] 1. *n.* **a) a ~ |of wind|** ein
Windstoß; **b)** *(of horn)* Tuten, *das.* 2.
v. t. (blow up) sprengen. **blast 'off** *v. i.*
abheben

'**blasted** *adj. (damned)* verdammt *(salopp)*

'**blast-off** *n.* Abheben, *das*

blatant ['bleɪtənt] *adj.* **a)** *(flagrant)*
eklatant; **b)** *(unashamed)* unverhohlen; unverfroren ⟨*Lüge*⟩

blaze [bleɪz] 1. *n.* Feuer, *das.* 2. *v. i.*
brennen; lodern *(geh.)*

blazer ['bleɪzə(r)] *n.* Blazer, *der*

bleach [bliːtʃ] 1. *v. t.* bleichen. 2. *n.*
Bleichmittel, *das*

bleak ['bliːk] *adj.* **a)** öde ⟨*Landschaft
usw.*⟩; **b)** *(unpromising)* düster

bleat [bliːt] *v. i.* ⟨*Schaf:*⟩ blöken;
⟨*Ziege:*⟩ meckern

bled *see* **bleed**

bleed [bliːd] *v. i.,* **bled** [bled] bluten

bleeper ['bliːpə(r)] *n.* Kleinempfän-
ger, *der*

blemish ['blemɪʃ] *n.* Fleck, *der*

blend [blend] 1. *v. t.* mischen. 2. *v. i.*
sich mischen lassen. 3. *n.* Mischung,
die. '**blender** *n.* Mixer, *der*

bless [bles] *v. t.* segnen; **~ you!** *(after
sb. sneezes)* Gesundheit! **blessed**
['blesɪd] *adj.* **a)** *(revered)* heilig; **b)**
(cursed) verdammt *(salopp).* '**blessing** *n.* Segen, *der*

blew *see* ¹**blow**

blight [blaɪt] *n. (fig.)* Fluch, *der*

blind [blaɪnd] 1. *adj.* blind; **~ in one
eye** auf einem Auge blind. 2. *adv.*
blindlings. 3. *n.* Jalousie, *die; (made of
cloth)* Rouleau, *das; (of shop)* Markise, *die.* 4. *v. t.* blenden. '**blindfold** 1.
v. t. die Augen verbinden (+ *Dat.*). 2.
adj. mit verbundenen Augen *nachgestellt.* '**blinding** *adj.* blendend.
'**blindly** *adv.* [wie] blind; *(fig.)* blindlings. '**blindness** *n.* Blindheit, *die*

blink [blɪŋk] *v. i.* **a)** blinzeln; **b)** *(shine
intermittently)* blinken

'**blinkers** *n. pl.* Scheuklappen *Pl.*

bliss [blɪs] *n.* [Glück]seligkeit, *die.*
blissful ['blɪsfl] *adj.* [glück]selig

blister ['blɪstə(r)] 1. *n.* Blase, *die.* 2.
v. i. ⟨*Haut:*⟩ Blasen bekommen; ⟨*Anstrich:*⟩ Blasen werfen

blizzard ['blɪzəd] *n.* Schneesturm, *der*

blob [blɒb] *n. (drop)* Tropfen, *der;*
(small mass) Klacks, *der (ugs.)*

block [blɒk] 1. *n.* **a)** Klotz, *der; (for
chopping on)* Hackklotz, *der; (of concrete or stone, building-stone)* Block,
der; **b)** *(building)* [Häuser]block, *der;*
~ of flats/offices Wohnblock, *der/*Bü-
rohaus, *das.* 2. *v. t.* versperren ⟨*Tür,
Straße, Durchgang, Sicht*⟩; verstopfen
⟨*Pfeife, Abfluß*⟩; verhindern ⟨*Fortschritt*⟩. **block 'up** *v. t.* verstopfen;
versperren ⟨*Eingang*⟩

blockade [blɒˈkeɪd] 1. *n.* Blockade,
die. 2. *v. t.* blockieren

blockage ['blɒkɪdʒ] *n.* Block, *der; (of
pipe, gutter)* Verstopfung, *die*

block: ~ 'booking *n.* Gruppenbu-
chung, *die;* **~ 'capital** *n.* Blockbuch-
stabe, *der;* **~head** *n.* Dummkopf,
der; **~ 'letters** *n. pl.* Blockschrift, *die*

bloke [bləʊk] *n. (Brit. coll.)* Typ, *der*
(ugs.)

blonde [blɒnd] 1. *adj.* blond. 2. *n.*
Blondine, *die*

blood [blʌd] *n.* Blut, *das*

blood: ~ donor *n.* Blutspender, *der/*
-spenderin, *die;* **~ group** *n.* Blut-
gruppe, *die;* **~hound** *n.* Bluthund,
der; **~ pressure** *n.* Blutdruck, *der;*
~shed *n.* Blutvergießen, *das;* **~shot**
adj. blutunterlaufen; **~-stained** *adj.*
blutbefleckt; **~stream** *n.* Blutstrom,
der; **~ test** *n.* Blutprobe, *die;*
~thirsty *adj.* blutrünstig; **~ transfusion** *n.* Bluttransfusion, *die;*
~-vessel *n.* Blutgefäß, *das*

'**bloody** 1. *adj.* **a)** *(running with
blood)* blutend; **b)** *(sl.: damned)* verdammt *(salopp).* 2. *adv. (sl.: damned)*
verdammt *(salopp)*

bloom [blu:m] 1. *n.* Blüte, *die;* be in ~:
in Blüte stehen. 2. *v. i.* blühen

blossom ['blɒsəm] 1. *n. (flower)* Blüte,
die; (mass) Blütenmeer, *das (geh.).* 2.
v. i. blühen; ⟨*Mensch:*⟩ aufblühen

blot [blɒt] 1. *n. (of ink)* Tintenklecks,
der; (stain) Fleck, *der.* 2. *v. t.,* -tt- ab-
löschen ⟨*Tinte, Papier*⟩. **blot 'out** *v. t.,*
(fig.) auslöschen

blotchy ['blɒtʃɪ] *adj.* fleckig

'blotting-paper *n.* Löschpapier, *das*

blouse [blaʊz] *n.* Bluse, *die*

¹blow [bləʊ] 1. *v. i.,* blew [blu:], blown
[bləʊn] ⟨*Wind:*⟩ wehen; ⟨*Sturm:*⟩ blasen. 2. *v. t.,* blew, blown: a) machen
⟨*Wind:*⟩ wehen; machen ⟨*Seifen-
blase*⟩; ~ sb. a kiss jmdm. eine Kuß-
hand zuwerfen; b) ~ one's nose sich
(Dat.) die Nase putzen; c) ~ sth. to
pieces etw. in die Luft sprengen.
blow 'out 1. *v. t.* ausblasen. 2. *v. i.*
ausgeblasen werden. **blow 'over** 1.
v. i. umgeblasen werden; ⟨*Streit,
Sturm:*⟩ sich legen. 2. *v. t.* umblasen.
blow 'up 1. *v. t.* a) *(shatter)* in die
Luft] sprengen; b) aufblasen ⟨*Ballon*⟩;
aufpumpen ⟨*Reifen*⟩; c) *(coll.: exaggerate)* hochspielen. 2. *v. i. (explode)*
explodieren

²blow *n.* a) Schlag, *der; (with axe)*
Hieb, *der;* come to ~s handgreiflich
werden; b) *(disaster)* [schwerer]
Schlag. **'blow-dry** *v. t.* fönen. **'blow-
lamp** *n.* Lötlampe, *die*

blown *see* **¹blow**

blubber ['blʌbə(r)] *n.* Walspeck, *der*

blue [blu:] 1. *adj.* blau. 2. *n.* a) Blau,
das; b) have the ~s deprimiert sein; c)
(Mus.) the ~s der Blues; d) out of the
~: aus heiterem Himmel

blue: ~bell *n.* Glockenblume, *die;*
~bottle *n.* Schmeißfliege, *die;*
~-collar *adj.* ~-collar worker Arbeiter, *der*/Arbeiterin, *die;* ~ 'jeans *n.*
pl. Blue jeans *Pl.;* ~print *n. (fig.)*
Entwurf, *der*

bluff [blʌf] 1. *n.* Bluff, *der (ugs.);* call
sb.'s ~: es darauf ankommen lassen
(ugs.). 2. *v. i. & t.* bluffen *(ugs.)*

blunder ['blʌndə(r)] 1. *n.* [schwerer]
Fehler. 2. *v. i.* a) *(make mistake)* einen
[schweren] Fehler machen; b) *(move
blindly)* tappen

blunt [blʌnt] 1. *adj.* a) stumpf; b) *(out-
spoken)* direkt; glatt *(ugs.)* ⟨*Ablehnung*⟩. 2. *v. t.* ~ [the edge of] stumpf
machen. **'bluntly** *adv.* direkt; glatt
⟨*ablehnen*⟩

blur [blɜ:(r)] 1. *v. t.,* -rr-: a) verwischen;

b) *(become indistinct)* verschwimmen;
his vision was ~red er sah alles verschwommen. 2. *n. (smear)* Fleck, *der;*
(dim image) verschwommener Fleck

blurt [blɜ:t] *v. t.* ~ out herausplatzen
mit *(ugs.)*

blush [blʌʃ] 1. *v. i.* rot werden. 2. *n.*
Rotwerden, *das*

bluster ['blʌstə(r)] *v. i.* sich aufplu-
stern *(ugs.)*

blustery ['blʌstərɪ] *adj.* stürmisch

boar [bɔː(r)] *n.* [wild] ~: Keiler, *der*

board [bɔːd] 1. *n.* a) Brett, *das;*
(black~) Tafel, *die; (notice-~)*
Schwarzes Brett; above ~ *(fig.)* korrekt; b) *(Commerc.)* [of directors]
Vorstand, *der; (supervisory ~)* Aufsichtsrat, *der;* c) *(Naut., Aeronaut.)* on
~: an Bord; d) ~ and lodging Unterkunft und Verpflegung; full ~: Voll-
pension, *die.* 2. *v. t.* ~ the ship/plane
an Bord des Schiffes/Flugzeuges gehen; ~ the train/bus in den Zug/Bus
einsteigen

'boarder *n. (Sch.)* Internatsschüler,
der/-schülerin, *die*

'board game *n.* Brettspiel, *das*

boarding: ~-house *n.* Pension, *die;*
~ pass *n.* Bordkarte, *die;* ~-school
n. Internat, *das*

board: ~ meeting *n.* Vorstandssit-
zung, *die;* ~room *n.* Sitzungssaal, *der*

boast [bəʊst] *v. i.* prahlen. **boastful**
['bəʊstfl] *adj.* prahlerisch

boat [bəʊt] *n.* Boot, *das*

¹bob [bɒb] *v. i.,* -bb-: ~ [up and down]
sich auf und nieder bewegen

²bob *n. (~-sled)* Bob, *der*

bobbin ['bɒbɪn] *n.* Spule, *die*

bob: ~-sled, ~-sleigh *ns.* Bobschlit-
ten, *der*

bodice ['bɒdɪs] *n.* Mieder, *das; (part of
dress)* Oberteil, *das*

bodily ['bɒdɪlɪ] *adj.* körperlich; ~
needs leibliche Bedürfnisse

body ['bɒdɪ] *n.* a) Körper, *der;* b)
(corpse) Leiche, *die;* c) *(group)* Gruppe, *die; (with particular function)* Organ, *das.* **'bodyguard** *n. (single)*
Leibwächter, *der; (group)* Leibwache,
die. **'bodywork** *n.* Karosserie, *die*

bog [bɒg] 1. *n.* Moor, *das; (marsh,
swamp)* Sumpf, *der.* 2. *v. t.,* -gg-: be/
get ~ged down *(fig.)* sich verzettelt ha-
ben/sich verzetteln

boggle ['bɒgl] *v. i. (coll.)* the mind ~s
da kann man nur [noch] staunen

bogus ['bəʊgəs] *adj.* falsch

¹boil [bɔɪl] 1. *v. i. & t.* kochen. 2. *n.*

come to/go off the ~: zu kochen anfangen/aufhören; **bring to the ~**: zum Kochen bringen. **boil 'down** *v. i.* **~ down to sth.** *(fig.)* auf etw. hinauslaufen. **boil 'over** *v. i.* überkochen
²**boil** *n. (Med.)* Furunkel, *der*
'**boiler** *n.* Kessel, *der*
'**boiling-point** *n.* Siedepunkt, *der*
boisterous ['bɔɪstərəs] *adj.* ausgelassen
bold [bəʊld] *adj.* **a)** *(courageous)* mutig; *(daring)* kühn; **b)** auffallend ⟨*Farbe, Muster*⟩. '**boldly** *adv. (courageously)* mutig; *(daringly)* kühn
Bolivia [bə'lɪvɪə] *pr. n.* Bolivien *(das)*
bollard ['bɒlɑ:d] *n. (Brit.)* Poller, *der*
bolster ['bəʊlstə(r)] **1.** *n. (pillow)* Nackenrolle, *die.* **2.** *v. t. (fig.)* stärken
bolt [bəʊlt] **1.** *n.* **a)** *(on door or window)* Riegel, *der; (on gun)* Kammerverschluß, *der;* **b)** *(metal pin)* Schraube, *die; (without thread)* Bolzen, *der.* **2.** *v. i.* davonlaufen; ⟨*Pferd:*⟩ durchgehen; ⟨*Fuchs, Kaninchen:*⟩ flüchten. **3.** *v. t.* **a)** verriegeln ⟨*Tür, Fenster*⟩; **b)** *(fasten with ~s)* verschrauben/mit Bolzen verbinden; **c)** **~ |down|** hinunterschlingen ⟨*Essen*⟩. **4.** *adv.* **~ upright** kerzengerade
bomb [bɒm] **1.** *n.* Bombe, *die.* **2.** *v. t.* bombardieren
bombard [bɒm'bɑ:d] *v. t.* beschießen. **bom'bardment** *n.* Beschuß, *der*
bombastic [bɒm'bæstɪk] *adj.* bombastisch
bomber ['bɒmə(r)] *n. (Air Force)* Bomber, *der (ugs.)*
'**bomb-shell** *n.* Bombe, *die; (fig.)* Sensation, *die*
bond [bɒnd] *n.* **a)** Band, *das; in pl. (shackles)* Fesseln; **b)** *(adhesion)* Verbindung, *die;* **c)** *(Commerc.)* Anleihe, *die*
bone [bəʊn] **1.** *n.* Knochen, *der; (of fish)* Gräte, *die.* **2.** *v. t.* den/die Knochen herauslösen aus; entgräten ⟨*Fisch*⟩. **bone 'dry** *adj.* knochentrocken *(ugs.).* **bone 'idle** *adj.* stinkfaul *(salopp)*
bonfire ['bɒnfaɪə(r)] *n.* Freudenfeuer, *das; (for rubbish)* Feuer, *das*
bonnet ['bɒnɪt] *n.* **a)** *(woman's)* Haube, *die; (child's)* Häubchen, *das;* **b)** *(Brit. Motor Veh.)* Motorhaube, *die*
bonus ['bəʊnəs] *n.* zusätzliche Leistung; *(to shareholders)* Bonus, *der;* **Christmas ~**: Weihnachtsgratifikation, *die*
bony ['bəʊnɪ] *adj.* **a)** Knochen-; *(like*

bone) knochenartig; **b)** *(skinny)* knochendürr *(ugs.);* spindeldürr
boo [bu:] **1.** *int. to surprise sb.* huh; *expr. disapproval, contempt* buh. **2.** *n.* Buh, *das (ugs.).* **3.** *v. t.* ausbuhen *(ugs.).* **4.** *v. i.* buhen *(ugs.)*
booby ['bu:bɪ] *n.* Trottel, *der (ugs.).* '**booby prize** *n.* Preis für den schlechtesten Teilnehmer an einem Wettbewerb. '**booby trap** *n.* **a)** Falle, mit der man jmdm. einen Streich spielen will; **b)** *(Mil.)* versteckte Sprengladung
book [bʊk] **1.** *n.* Buch, *das; (for accounts)* Rechnungsbuch, *das; (for exercises)* [Schreib]heft, *das.* **2.** *v. t.* buchen ⟨*Reise, Flug, Platz |im Flugzeug|*⟩; [vor]bestellen ⟨*Eintrittskarte, Tisch, Zimmer, Platz |im Theater|*⟩. **3.** *v. i.* buchen. **book 'in 1.** *v. i.* sich eintragen. **2.** *v. t.* eintragen. **book 'up** *v. i. & t.* buchen; **be ~ed up** ⟨*Hotel usw.:*⟩ ausgebucht sein
book: ~case *n.* Bücherschrank, *der;* **~ends** *n. pl.* Buchstützen
'**booking office** *n.* [Fahrkarten]schalter, *der*
book: ~keeper *n.* Buchhalter, *der/*-halterin, *die;* **~keeping** *n.* Buchführung, *die;* Buchhaltung, *die*
booklet ['bʊklɪt] *n.* Broschüre, *die*
book: ~maker *n. (in betting)* Buchmacher, *der;* **~mark** *n.* Lesezeichen, *das;* **~seller** *n.* Buchhändler, *der/*-händlerin, *die;* **~shelf** *n.* Bücherbord, *das; ~shop* *n.* Buchhandlung, *die; ~stall* *n.* Bücherstand, *der;* **~store** *n. (Amer.)* Buchhandlung, *die; ~ token* *n.* Büchergutschein, *der; ~worm* *n.* Bücherwurm, *der*
¹**boom** [bu:m] *n.* **a)** *(for camera or microphone)* Ausleger, *der;* **b)** *(Naut.)* Baum, *der*
²**boom 1.** *v. i.* **a)** dröhnen; **b)** ⟨*Geschäft, Verkauf, Gebiet:*⟩ sich sprunghaft entwickeln. **2.** *n.* **a)** Dröhnen, *das;* **b)** *(in business or economy)* Boom, *der*
boomerang ['bu:məræŋ] *n.* Bumerang, *der*
boon [bu:n] *n.* Segen, *der* **(to für)**
boorish ['bʊərɪʃ] *adj.* rüpelhaft
boost [bu:st] **1.** *v. t.* in die Höhe treiben ⟨*Preis, Wert*⟩; stärken ⟨*Selbstvertrauen, Moral*⟩. **2.** *n.* Auftrieb, *der*
boot [bu:t] **1.** *n.* **a)** Stiefel, *der;* **give sb. the ~** *(fig. coll.)* jmdn. rausschmeißen *(ugs.);* **b)** *(Brit.: of car)* Kofferraum, *der.* **2.** *v. t. (coll.: kick)* kicken *(ugs.)*
booth [bu:ð] *n.* **a)** Bude, *die;* **b)** *(telephone ~)* Zelle, *die*

'**bootleg** *adj.* schwarz verkauft/gebrannt

booze [buːz] *(coll.)* 1. *v. i.* saufen *(derb).* 2. *n.* Alkohol, *der*

border ['bɔːdə(r)] 1. *n.* **a)** Rand, *der; (of table-cloth, handkerchief)* Bordüre, *die;* **b)** *(of country)* Grenze, *die;* **c)** *(flower-bed)* Rabatte, *die.* 2. *attrib. adj.* Grenz⟨*stadt, -streit*⟩. 3. *v. t.* **a)** *(adjoin)* [an]grenzen an (+ *Akk.*); **b)** *(put a ~ to, act as ~ to)* umranden; einfassen. 4. *v. i.* ~ **on a)** *see* 3 **a**; **b)** *(resemble)* grenzen an (+ *Akk.*). '**borderline** 1. *n.* Grenzlinie, *die.* 2. *adj.* **be ~:** auf der Grenze liegen; **a ~ case/candidate** ein Grenzfall

'**bore** [bɔː(r)] 1. *v. t.* bohren. 2. *n. (of firearm)* Kaliber, *das*

²**bore** 1. *n.* **a)** **it's a real ~:** es ist wirklich ärgerlich; **what a ~!** wie ärgerlich!; **b)** *(person)* Langweiler, *der (ugs.).* 2. *v. t.* langweilen; **be ~d** sich langweilen

³**bore** *see* ²**bear**

boredom ['bɔːdəm] *n.* Langeweile, *die*

'**borehole** *n.* Bohrloch, *das*

boring ['bɔːrɪŋ] *adj.* langweilig

born [bɔːn] 1. **be ~:** geboren werden. 2. *adj.* geboren; **be a ~ orator** der geborene Redner sein

borne *see* ²**bear**

borough ['bʌrə] *n. (town)* Stadt, *die; (village)* Gemeinde, *die*

borrow ['bɒrəʊ] *v. t.* leihen **(from von, bei)**; *(from library)* entleihen. '**borrower** *n. (from bank)* Kreditnehmer, *der; (from library)* Entleiher, *der*

bosom ['bʊzəm] *n.* Brust, *die*

boss [bɒs] 1. *n. (coll.)* Boß, *der (ugs.);* Chef, *der.* 2. *v. t.* ~ [**about** *or* **around**] herumkommandieren *(ugs.).* '**bossy** *adj. (coll.)* herrisch

botanical [bə'tænɪkl] *adj.* botanisch

botanist ['bɒtənɪst] *n.* Botaniker, *der/*Botanikerin, *die*

botany ['bɒtənɪ] *n.* Botanik, *die*

botch [bɒtʃ] 1. *v. t.* pfuschen bei *(ugs.).* 2. *v. i.* pfuschen *(ugs.).* **botch 'up** *v. t. (bungle)* verpfuschen *(ugs.)*

both [bəʊθ] 1. *adj.* beide; ~ [**the**] **brothers** beide Brüder. 2. *pron.* beide; ~ [**of them**] **are dead** beide sind tot; ~ **of you/them are ...:** ihr seid/sie sind beide ... 3. *adv.* ~ **A and B** sowohl A als [auch] B; **he and I were ~ there** er und ich waren beide da

bother ['bɒðə(r)] 1. *v. t.* **a)** **I can't ~ed** ich habe keine Lust; **b)** *(annoy)* lästig sein (+ *Dat.*); ⟨*Lärm, Licht:*⟩

stören; ⟨*Schmerz, Zahn:*⟩ zu schaffen machen (+ *Dat.*); **I'm sorry to ~ you, but ...:** es tut mir leid, wenn ich Sie störe, aber ...; **c)** *(worry)* Sorgen machen (+ *Dat.*); ⟨*Problem, Frage:*⟩ beschäftigen. 2. *v. i.* **don't ~ to do it** Sie brauchen es nicht zu tun; **you needn't/shouldn't have ~ed** das wäre nicht nötig gewesen; **don't ~!** nicht nötig! 3. *n.* **a)** *(trouble)* Ärger, *der;* **b)** *(effort)* Mühe, *die.* 4. *int. (coll.)* wie ärgerlich!

bottle ['bɒtl] 1. *n.* Flasche, *die;* **a ~ of beer** eine Flasche Bier. 2. *v. t.* **a)** *(put into ~s)* in Flaschen [ab]füllen; **b)** *(preserve in jars)* einmachen. **bottle 'up** *v. t.* **a)** *(conceal)* in sich *(Dat.)* aufstauen; **b)** *(trap)* einschließen

bottle: ~ **bank** *n.* Altglasbehälter, *der;* ~**-neck** *n. (fig.)* Flaschenhals, *der (ugs.);* ~**-opener** *n.* Flaschenöffner, *der;* ~**-top** *n.* Flaschenverschluß, *der*

bottom ['bɒtəm] 1. *n.* **a)** unteres Ende; *(of cup, glass, box)* Boden, *der; (of valley, well, shaft)* Sohle, *die; (of hill, cliff, stairs)* Fuß, *der;* **b)** *(buttocks)* Hinterteil, *das;* **c)** *(of sea, lake)* Grund, *der;* **d)** *(farthest point)* **at the ~ of the garden/street** hinten im Garten/am Ende der Straße; **e)** *(underside)* Unterseite, *die;* **f)** *(fig.)* **start at the ~:** ganz unten anfangen; **be ~ of the class** der/die Letzte in der Klasse sein. 2. *adj.* **a)** *(lowest)* unterst...; *(lower)* unter...; **b)** *(fig.: last)* letzt... '**bottomless** *adj.* bodenlos; unendlich tief ⟨*Meer, Ozean*⟩

bough [baʊ] *n.* Ast, *der*

bought *see* **buy** 1

boulder ['bəʊldə(r)] *n.* Felsbrocken, *der*

boulevard ['buːləvɑːd] *n.* Boulevard, *der*

bounce [baʊns] 1. *v. i.* **a)** springen; **b)** *(coll.)* ⟨*Scheck:*⟩ platzen *(ugs.).* 2. *v. t.* aufspringen lassen ⟨*Ball*⟩. 3. *n.* Aufprall, *der.* '**bouncer** *n. (coll.)* Rausschmeißer, *der (ugs.).* **bouncing** ['baʊnsɪŋ] *adj.* stramm ⟨*Baby*⟩. **bouncy** ['baʊnsɪ] *adj.* gut springend ⟨*Ball*⟩; *(fig.: lively)* munter

'**bound** [baʊnd] 1. *n., usu. in pl. (limit)* Grenze, *die;* **within the ~s of possibility** im Bereich des Möglichen; **sth. is out of ~s** jmdm. den Zutritt zu etw. ist [für jmdn.] verboten. 2. *v. t.* **be ~ed by sth.** durch etw. begrenzt werden

²**bound** 1. *v. i.* hüpfen. 2. *n.* Satz, *der*

³bound *pred. adj.* **be ~ for home/ Frankfurt** auf dem Heimweg/nach Frankfurt unterwegs sein; **homeward ~:** auf dem Weg nach Hause

⁴bound *see* **bind**

boundary ['baʊndərɪ] *n.* Grenze, *die*

'boundless *adj.* grenzenlos

bounty ['baʊntɪ] *n.* Kopfgeld, *das*

bouquet [bʊ'keɪ] *n.* [Blumen]strauß, *der*

bourgeois ['bʊəʒwɑː] **1.** *n., pl. same* Bürger, *der*/Bürgerin, *die.* **2.** *adj.* bürgerlich

bout [baʊt] *n.* **a)** *(contest)* Wettkampf, *der;* **b)** *(fit)* Anfall, *der*

boutique [buː'tiːk] *n.* Boutique, *die*

¹bow [bəʊ] **a)** *(curve, weapon, Mus.)* Bogen, *der;* **b)** *(knot, ribbon)* Schleife, *die*

²bow [baʊ] **1.** *v. i.* **a)** ~ |to sb.| sich [vor jmdm.] verbeugen; **b)** *(submit)* sich beugen (**to** *Dat.*). **2.** *n.* Verbeugung, *die*

³bow [baʊ] *n. (Naut.)* Bug, *der*

bowel ['baʊəl] *n. (Anat.)* ~**s** *pl., (Med.)* ~: Darm, *der*

¹bowl [bəʊl] *n. (basin)* Schüssel, *die; (shallower)* Schale, *die; (of spoon)* Schöpfteil, *der; (of pipe)* Kopf, *der*

²bowl 1. *n.* **a)** *(ball)* Kugel, *die;* **b)** *in pl. (game)* Bowls, *das.* **2.** *v. i.* **a)** *(play* ~s) Bowls spielen; **b)** *(Cricket)* werfen

bow-legged ['bəʊlegɪd] O-beinig *(ugs.)*

¹bowler ['bəʊlə(r)] *n. (Cricket)* Werfer, *der*

²bowler *n.* ~ |hat| Bowler, *der*

'bowling *n.* |ten-pin| ~: Bowling, *das;* **go** ~: bowlen gehen. **'bowling-alley** *n.* Bowlingbahn, *die.* **'bowling-green** *n.* Rasenfläche für Bowls

bow [bəʊ]: ~**-tie** *n.* Fliege, *die;* ~**-window** *n.* Erkerfenster, *das*

¹box [bɒks] *n.* Kasten, *der; (bigger)* Kiste, *die; (of cardboard)* Schachtel, *die.*

²box 1. *n.* **he gave him a ~ on the ear|s|** er gab ihm eine Ohrfeige. **2.** *v. t.* **a) he ~ed his ears** *or* **him round the ears** er ohrfeigte ihn; **b)** *(Sport)* ~ **sb.** gegen jmdn. boxen. **3.** *v. i.* boxen. **'boxer** *n.* Boxer, *der.* **'boxing** *n.* Boxen, *das*

boxing: B~ Day *n.* zweiter Weihnachtsfeiertag; ~**-glove** *n.* Boxhandschuh, *der;* ~**-match** *n.* Boxkampf, *der;* ~**-ring** *n.* Boxring, *der*

box: ~ **number** *n. (at newspaper office)* Chiffre, *die; (at post office)* Postfach, *das;* ~**-office** *n.* Kasse, *die;* ~**-room** *n. (Brit.)* Abstellraum, *der*

boy [bɔɪ] *n.* Junge, *der*

boycott ['bɔɪkɒt] **1.** *v. t.* boykottieren. **2.** *n.* Boykott, *der*

'boy-friend *n.* Freund, *der*

'boyish *adj.* jungenhaft

bra [brɑː] *n.* BH, *der (ugs.)*

brace [breɪs] **1.** *n.* **a)** *(connecting piece)* Klammer, *die; (strut)* Strebe, *die; (Dent.)* [Zahn]spange, *die;* **b)** *in pl. (trouser-straps)* Hosenträger. **2.** *v. refl.* ~ **oneself for sth.** sich auf etw. *(Akk.)* vorbereiten

bracelet ['breɪslɪt] *n.* Armband, *das*

bracing ['breɪsɪŋ] *adj.* belebend

bracken ['brækn] *n.* [Adler]farn, *der*

bracket ['brækɪt] **1.** *n.* **a)** *(support)* Konsole, *die;* **b)** *(mark)* Klammer, *die.* **2.** *v. t.* einklammern

brag [bræg] *v. i. & t.,* -gg- prahlen (**about** mit)

braid [breɪd] **1.** *n.* **a)** *(plait)* Flechte, *die (geh.);* Zopf, *der;* **b)** *(woven band)* Borte, *die; (on uniform)* Litze, *die.* **2.** *v. t.* flechten

Braille [breɪl] *n.* Blindenschrift, *die*

brain [breɪn] *n.* Gehirn, *das*

brain: ~**-child** *n. (coll.)* Geistesprodukt, *das;* ~**less** *adj.* hirnlos; ~**wash** *v. t.* einer Gehirnwäsche unterziehen; ~**wave** *n. (coll.: inspiration)* genialer Einfall

'brainy *adj.* intelligent

brake [breɪk] **1.** *n.* Bremse, *die.* **2.** *v. t. & i.* bremsen; **braking distance** Bremsweg, *der.* **'brake light** *n.* Bremslicht, *das*

bramble ['bræmbl] *n.* Dornenstrauch, *der*

bran [bræn] *n.* Kleie, *die*

branch [brɑːntʃ] **1.** *n.* **a)** *(bough)* Ast, *der; (twig)* Zweig, *der;* **b)** *(of artery, antlers)* Ast, *der;* **c)** *(office)* Zweigstelle, *die; (shop)* Filiale, *die.* **2.** *v. i.* sich verzweigen. **branch 'off** *v. i.* abzweigen. **branch 'out** *v. i. (fig.)* ~ **out into sth.** sich auch mit etw. befassen

'branch line *n.* Nebenstrecke, *die*

brand [brænd] *n.* **a)** *(trade mark)* Markenzeichen, *das; (goods of particular make)* Marke, *die;* **b)** *(mark)* Brandmal, *das*

brandish ['brændɪʃ] *v. t.* schwenken; schwingen ⟨*Waffe*⟩

brand: ~ **name** *n.* Markenname, *der;* ~**'new** *adj.* nagelneu *(ugs.)*

brandy ['brændɪ] *n.* Weinbrand, *der*

brash [bræʃ] *adj.* dreist

brass [brɑːs] *n.* Messing, *das; attrib.* Messing-; **the ~** *(Mus.)* das Blech; ~

player *(Mus.)* Blechbläser, *der;* **get down to ~ tacks** zur Sache kommen.
brass band *n.* Blaskapelle, *die*
brassière ['bræzjə(r)] *n.* Büstenhalter, *der*
brat [bræt] *n.* Balg, *das od. der (ugs.)*
bravado [brə'vɑːdəʊ] *n.* **do sth. out of ~:** so waghalsig sein, etw. zu tun
brave [breɪv] **1.** *adj.* tapfer. **2.** *n.* [indianischer] Krieger. **3.** *v.t.* trotzen *(+ Dat.).* '**bravely** *adv.* tapfer.
bravery ['breɪvərɪ] *n.* Tapferkeit, *die*
bravo [brɑːˈvəʊ] *int.* bravo
brawl [brɔːl] **1.** *v.i.* sich schlagen. **2.** *n.* Schlägerei, *die*
brawny ['brɔːnɪ] *adj.* muskulös
bray [breɪ] **1.** Iah, *das.* **2.** *v.i. ⟨Esel:⟩* iahen
brazen ['breɪzn] **1.** *adj.* dreist; *(shameless)* schamlos. **2.** *v.t.* **~ [out]** trotzen *(+ Dat.);* **~ it out** *(deny guilt)* es abstreiten; *(not admit guilt)* es nicht zugeben
brazier ['breɪzɪə(r)] *n.* Kohlenbecken, *das*
Brazil [brə'zɪl] *pr. n.* Brasilien *(das).* **Bra'zil nut** *n.* Paranuß, *die*
breach [briːtʃ] **1.** *n.* **a)** *(violation)* Verstoß, *der* **(of gegen);** **~ of faith/duty** Vertrauensbruch, *der/*Pflichtverletzung, *die;* **b)** *(of relations)* Bruch, *der;* **c)** *(gap)* Bresche, *die; (fig.)* Riß, *der.* **2.** *v.t.* durchbrechen
bread [bred] *n.* Brot, *das;* **a piece of ~ and butter** ein Butterbrot
bread: ~-bin *n.* Brotkasten, *der;* **~-board** *n.* [Brot]brett, *das;* **~crumb** *n.* Brotkrume, *die;* **~crumbs** *(coating)* Paniermehl, *das;* **~-knife** *n.* Brotmesser, *das;* **~-line** *n.* **be** *or* **live on/below the ~line** gerade noch/nicht einmal mehr das Notwendigste zum Leben haben
breadth [bredθ] *n.* Breite, *die*
'**bread-winner** *n.* Ernährer, *der/*Ernährerin, *die*
break [breɪk] **1.** *v.t.,* **broke** [brəʊk], **broken** ['brəʊkn] **a)** brechen; *(so as to damage)* zerbrechen; kaputtmachen *(ugs.);* zerreißen *⟨Seil⟩; (fig.: interrupt)* unterbrechen; brechen *⟨Bann, Zauber, Schweigen⟩;* **the TV/my watch is broken** der Fernseher/meine Uhr ist kaputt *(ugs.);* **~ the habit** es sich *(Dat.)* abgewöhnen; **b)** *(fracture)* sich *(Dat.)* brechen *⟨Arm, Bein usw.⟩;* **c)** brechen *⟨Vertrag, Versprechen⟩;* verstoßen gegen *⟨Regel, Gesetz⟩;* **d)** *(surpass)* brechen *⟨Rekord⟩;* **e)** *(cushion)*

auffangen *⟨Schlag, jmds. Fall⟩.* **2.** *v.i.,* **broke, broken a)** kaputtgehen *(ugs.);* *⟨Faden, Seil:⟩* [zer]reißen; *⟨Glas, Tasse, Teller:⟩* zerbrechen; *⟨Eis:⟩* brechen; **~ in two/in pieces** durchbrechen/zerbrechen; **b)** **~ into** einbrechen in *(+ Akk.) ⟨Haus⟩;* aufbrechen *⟨Auto, Safe⟩;* **~ into laughter/tears** in Gelächter/Tränen ausbrechen; **~ into a trot/run** zu traben/laufen anfangen; **c)** *(escape)* **~ out of prison** aus dem Gefängnis ausbrechen; **~ free** *or* **loose** sich losreißen; **d)** *⟨Welle:⟩* sich brechen **(on/against** an *+ Dat.);* **e)** *⟨Tag:⟩* anbrechen; *⟨Sturm:⟩* losbrechen; **f) sb's voice is ~ing** jmd. kommt in den Stimmbruch. **3.** *n.* **a)** Bruch, *der; (of rope)* Reißen, *das;* **a ~ with sb./sth.** ein Bruch mit jmdm./etw.; **b)** *(gap)* Lücke, *die; (broken place)* Sprung, *der;* **c)** *(dash)* **they made a sudden ~:** sie stürmten plötzlich davon; **d)** *(interruption)* Unterbrechung, *die; (pause, holiday)* Pause, *die;* **take** *or* **have a ~:** Pause machen; **e)** *(coll.: chance)* Chance, *die.* **break 'down 1.** *v.i.* zusammenbrechen; *⟨Verhandlungen:⟩* scheitern; *⟨Auto:⟩* eine Panne haben. **2.** *v.t.* **a)** aufbrechen *⟨Tür⟩;* brechen *⟨Widerstand⟩;* niederreißen *⟨Barriere, Schranke⟩;* **b)** *(analyse)* aufgliedern. **break 'in 1.** *v.i. (into building etc.)* einbrechen. **2.** *v.t.* **a)** zureiten *⟨Pferd⟩;* **b)** einlaufen *⟨Schuhe⟩;* **c)** **~ the door in** die Tür aufbrechen. '**break into** *see* **~ 2b. break 'off 1.** *v.t.* abbrechen; abreißen *⟨Faden⟩;* auflösen *⟨Verlobung⟩.* **2.** *v.i.* **a)** abbrechen; **b)** *(cease)* aufhören. **break 'out** *v.i.* ausbrechen; **~ out in spots/a rash** Pickel/einen Ausschlag bekommen. **break 'up 1.** *v.t.* **a)** *(~ into pieces)* zerkleinern; ausschlachten *⟨Auto⟩;* aufbrechen *⟨Erde⟩;* **b)** *(disband)* auflösen. **2.** *v.i.* **a)** *(~ into pieces, lit. or fig.)* zerbrechen; **b)** *(disband)* sich auflösen; *⟨Schule:⟩* schließen; *⟨Schüler, Lehrer:⟩* in die Ferien gehen; **c)** **~ up [with sb.]** sich [von jmdm.] trennen
breakable ['breɪkəbl] **1.** *adj.* zerbrechlich. **2.** *n.* **~s** zerbrechliche Dinge
breakage ['breɪkɪdʒ] *n.* Zerbrechen, *das;* **~s must be paid for** zerbrochene Ware muß bezahlt werden
'**breakdown** *n.* **a)** *(of vehicle)* Panne, *die; (in machine)* Störung, *die;* **~ truck/van** Abschleppwagen, *der;* **b)** *(Med.)* Zusammenbruch, *der;* **c)** *(analysis)* Aufschlüsselung, *die*

'**breaker** *n.* **a)** *(wave)* Brecher, *der;* **b)** ~'s |yard| Autoverwertung, *die*
breakfast ['brekfəst] **1.** *n.* Frühstück, *das;* for ~: zum Frühstück. **2.** *v.i.* frühstücken. '**breakfast cereal** *n.* ≈ Frühstücksflocken *Pl.* **breakfast 'television** *n.* Frühstücksfernsehen, *das*
'**break-in** *n.* Einbruch, *der*
'**breaking** *n.* ~ **and entering** *(Law)* Einbruch, *der*
break: ~neck *adj.* halsbrecherisch; **~through** *n.* Durchbruch, *der;* **~-up** *n.* Auflösung, *die; (of relationship)* Bruch, *der;* **~water** *n.* Wellenbrecher, *der*
breast [brest] *n.* Brust, *die*
breast: ~bone *n.* Brustbein, *das;* **~-feed** *v.t. & i.* stillen; **~-stroke** *n.* Brustschwimmen, *das*
breath [breθ] *n.* **a)** Atem, *der;* **get one's ~ back** wieder zu Atem kommen; **hold one's ~:** den Atem anhalten; **be out of ~:** außer Atem sein; **say sth. under one's ~:** etw. vor sich *(Akk.)* hin murmeln; **b)** *(one respiration)* Atemzug, *der.* **Breathalyser** *(Brit.),* **Breathalyzer** (P) ['breθəlaɪzə(r)] *n.* Alcotest-Röhrchen ⓦ, *das;* ~ **test** Alcotest ⓦ, *der*
breathe [bri:ð] **1.** *v.i.* atmen; ~ **in** einatmen; ~ **out** ausatmen. **2.** *v.t.* **a)** ~ |in/out| ein-/ausatmen; **b)** *(utter)* hauchen. '**breather** ['bri:ðə(r)] *n.* Verschnaufpause, *die*
'**breathless** *adj.* atemlos (**with** vor + *Dat.*)
'**breath-taking** *adj.* atemberaubend
bred *see* **breed 1, 2**
breeches ['brɪtʃɪz] *n. pl.* |pair of| ~: [Knie]bundhose, *die;* |riding-|~: Reithose, *die*
breed [bri:d] **1.** *v.t.,* bred [bred] **a)** *(cause)* erzeugen; **b)** züchten ⟨*Tiere, Pflanzen*⟩. **2.** *v.i.,* bred sich vermehren. **3.** *n. (of animals)* Rasse, *die.* '**breeding** *n.* |good| ~: gute Erziehung
breeze [bri:z] *n.* Brise, *die.* **breezy** ['bri:zɪ] *adj.* windig
brevity ['brevɪtɪ] *n.* Kürze, *die*
brew [bru:] **1.** *v.t.* brauen ⟨*Bier*⟩; ~ |up| kochen ⟨*Kaffee, Tee usw.*⟩. **2.** *v.i.* **a)** ⟨*Bier:*⟩ gären; ⟨*Kaffee, Tee:*⟩ ziehen; **b)** ⟨*Unwetter:*⟩ sich zusammenbrauen. **3.** *n. (brewed beer/tea)* Bier, *das/*Tee, *der.* '**brewer** *n.* Brauer, *der; (firm)* Brauerei, *die.* **brewery** ['bru:ərɪ] *n.* Brauerei, *die*

bribe [braɪb] **1.** *n.* Bestechung, *die.* **2.** *v.t.* bestechen; ~ **sb. to do/into doing sth.** jmdn. bestechen, damit er etw. tut. **bribery** ['braɪbərɪ] *n.* Bestechung, *die*
brick [brɪk] **1.** *n.* Ziegelstein, *der; (toy)* Bauklötzchen, *das.* **2.** *adj.* Ziegelstein-. '**bricklayer** *n.* Maurer, *der.* '**bricklaying** *n.* Mauern, *das*
bridal ['braɪdl] *adj.* Braut-
bride [braɪd] *n.* Braut, *die.* '**bridegroom** *n.* Bräutigam, *der.* **bridesmaid** ['braɪdzmeɪd] *n.* Brautjungfer, *die*
¹**bridge** [brɪdʒ] **1.** *n.* **a)** Brücke, *die;* **b)** *(Naut.)* [Kommando]brücke, *die;* **c)** *(of nose)* Nasenbein, *das;* **d)** *(of spectacles)* Steg, *der.* **2.** *v.t.* eine Brücke bauen über (+ *Akk.*)
²**bridge** *n. (Cards)* Bridge, *das*
bridle ['braɪdl] *n.* Zaum, *der.* '**bridle path** *n.* Reitweg, *der*
¹**brief** [bri:f] *adj.* **a)** kurz; gering ⟨*Verspätung*⟩; **b)** *(concise)* knapp; **in ~, to be ~:** kurz gesagt
²**brief 1.** *n. (instructions)* Instruktionen *Pl.; (Law: case)* Mandat, *das.* **2.** *v.t.* Instruktionen geben (+ *Dat.*); *(inform)* unterrichten. '**briefcase** *n.* Aktentasche, *die.* '**briefing** *n.* Briefing, *das; (of reporters)* Unterrichtung, *die*
'**briefly** *adv.* **a)** kurz; **b)** *(concisely)* knapp; kurz
briefs [bri:fs] *n. pl.* |pair of| ~: Slip, *der*
brigade [brɪ'geɪd] *n. (Mil.)* Brigade, *die.* **brigadier** [brɪgə'dɪə(r)] *n.* Brigadegeneral, *der*
bright [braɪt] *adj.* **a)** hell; grell ⟨*Scheinwerfer[licht], Sonnenlicht*⟩; strahlend ⟨*Sonnenschein, Augen, Tag*⟩; leuchtend ⟨*Farbe, Blume*⟩; ~ **intervals/ periods** Aufheiterungen *Pl.;* **b)** *(cheerful)* fröhlich; **c)** *(clever)* intelligent.
brighten ['braɪtn] **1.** *v.t.* ~ |up| aufhellen. **2.** *v.i.* **the weather** *or* **it is ~ing** |up| es klärt sich auf. '**brightly** *adv.* **a)** hell; **b)** *(cheerfully)* fröhlich. '**brightness** *n. see* **bright: a)** Helligkeit, *die;* Grelle, *die;* Strahlen, *das;* Leuchtkraft, *die;* **b)** Fröhlichkeit, *die;* **c)** Intelligenz, *die*
brilliance ['brɪlɪəns] *n. see* **brilliant: a)** Helligkeit, *die;* Leuchten, *das;* **b)** Genialität, *die;* Glanz, *der*
brilliant ['brɪlɪənt] *adj.* **a)** hell ⟨*Licht*⟩; leuchtend ⟨*Farbe*⟩; **b)** genial ⟨*Mensch, Gedanke, Leistung*⟩; glänzend ⟨*Verstand, Aufführung, Idee*⟩
brim [brɪm] **1.** *n.* Rand, *der; (of hat)* [Hut]krempe, *die.* **2.** *v.i.,* **-mm-:** be

~**ming with sth.** randvoll mit etw. sein.
brim-'full *pred. adj.* randvoll (**with** mit)
brine [braɪn] *n.* Salzwasser, *das*
bring [brɪŋ] *v. t.*, **brought** [brɔːt] **a)** bringen; *(as a present or favour)* mitbringen; ~ **sth. with one** etw. mitbringen; **b)** ~ **sb. to do sth.** jmdn. dazu bringen, etw. zu tun; **I could not ~ myself to do it** ich konnte es nicht über mich bringen, es zu tun. **bring a'bout** *v. t.* verursachen. **bring 'back** *v. t.* **a)** *(return)* zurückbringen; *(from a journey)* mitbringen; **b)** *(recall)* in Erinnerung bringen; **c)** *(restore, reintroduce)* wieder einführen. **bring 'down** *v. t.* **a)** herunterbringen; **b)** *(kill, wound)* zur Strecke bringen; **c)** senken ⟨*Preise, Inflationsrate, Fieber*⟩. **bring 'forward** *v. t.* **a)** nach vorne bringen; **b)** vorbringen ⟨*Argument*⟩; zur Sprache bringen ⟨*Fall, Angelegenheit*⟩; **c)** vorverlegen ⟨*Termin*⟩ (**to** auf + *Akk.*). **bring 'in** *v. t.* hereinbringen; einbringen ⟨*Gesetzesvorlage, Verdienst, Summe*⟩. **bring 'off** *v. t.* *(conduct successfully)* zustande bringen. **bring 'on** *v. t.* **a)** *(cause)* verursachen; **b)** *(Sport)* einsetzen. **bring 'out** *v. t.* **a)** herausbringen; **b)** hervorheben ⟨*Unterschied*⟩; **c)** einführen ⟨*Produkt*⟩; herausbringen ⟨*Buch, Zeitschrift*⟩. **bring 'up** *v. t.* **a)** heraufbringen; **b)** *(educate)* erziehen; *(rear)* aufziehen; **c)** zur Sprache bringen ⟨*Angelegenheit, Thema, Problem*⟩
brink ['brɪŋk] *n.* Rand, *der;* **be on the ~ of doing sth.** nahe daran sein, etw. zu tun
brisk [brɪsk] *adj.* flott ⟨*Gang*⟩; forsch ⟨*Person, Art*⟩; frisch ⟨*Wind*⟩; *(fig.)* rege ⟨*Handel, Nachfrage*⟩; lebhaft ⟨*Geschäft*⟩. **'briskly** *adv.* flott
bristle ['brɪsl] **1.** *n.* Borste, *die.* **2.** *v. i.* **a)** ~ |ʊp| ⟨*Haare:*⟩ sich sträuben; **b)** ~ **with** *(fig.)* starren vor (+ *Dat.*).
bristly ['brɪslɪ] *adj.* borstig
Britain ['brɪtn] *pr. n.* Großbritannien *(das)*
British ['brɪtɪʃ] **1.** *adj.* britisch; **he/she is ~:** er ist Brite/sie ist Britin. **2.** *n. pl.* **the ~:** die Briten. **British 'Isles** *pr. n. pl.* Britische Inseln
Briton ['brɪtn] *n.* Brite, *der*/Britin, *die*
Brittany ['brɪtənɪ] *pr. n.* Bretagne, *die*
brittle ['brɪtl] *adj.* spröde ⟨*Material*⟩
broach [brəʊtʃ] *v. t.* anschneiden ⟨*Thema*⟩
broad [brɔːd] *adj.* **a)** breit; *(extensive)* weit ⟨*Ebene, Land*⟩; ausgedehnt

⟨*Fläche*⟩; **b)** *(explicit)* klar ⟨*Hinweis*⟩; breit ⟨*Lächeln*⟩; **c)** *(main)* grob; *(generalized)* allgemein; **d)** stark ⟨*Akzent*⟩.
broad 'bean *n.* Saubohne, *die*
broadcast ['brɔːdkɑːst] **1.** *n.* Sendung, *die; (live)* Übertragung, *die.* **2.** *v. t.* **broadcast** senden; übertragen ⟨*Livesendung*⟩. **3.** *v. i.* **broadcast** senden. **'broadcasting** *n.* Senden, *das; (live)* Übertragen, *das;* **work in ~:** beim Funk arbeiten
broaden ['brɔːdn] **1.** *v. t.* **a)** verbreitern; **b)** ausweiten ⟨*Diskussion*⟩. **2.** *v. i.* sich verbreitern; *(fig.)* sich erweitern
'broadly *adv.* **a)** deutlich ⟨*hinweisen*⟩; breit ⟨*grinsen, lächeln*⟩; **b)** *(in general)* allgemein ⟨*beschreiben*⟩; ~ **speaking** allgemein gesagt
broad: ~-'minded *adj.* tolerant; ~side *n.* Breitseite, *die*
brocade [brə'keɪd] *n.* Brokat, *der*
broccoli ['brɒkəlɪ] *n.* Brokkoli, *der*
brochure ['brəʊʃə(r)] *n.* Broschüre, *die;* Prospekt, *der*
broil ['brɔɪl] *v. t.* *(esp. Amer.)* grillen
broke [brəʊk] **1.** *see* **break** 1, 2. **2.** *pred. adj. (coll.)* pleite *(ugs.)*
broken ['brəʊkn] **1.** *see* **break** 1, 2. **2.** *adj.* **a)** zerbrochen; gebrochen ⟨*Bein, Hals*⟩; verletzt ⟨*Haut*⟩; abgebrochen ⟨*Zahn*⟩; gerissen ⟨*Seil*⟩; kaputt *(ugs.)* ⟨*Uhr, Fernsehen, Fenster*⟩; ~ **glass** Glasscherben; **b)** *(imperfect)* gebrochen; **in ~ English** in gebrochenem Englisch; **c)** *(fig.)* ruiniert ⟨*Ehe*⟩; gebrochen ⟨*Mensch, Herz*⟩. **'broken-down** *adj.* baufällig ⟨*Gebäude*⟩; kaputt *(ugs.)* ⟨*Wagen*⟩. **broken-'hearted** *adj.* untröstlich
broker ['brəʊkə(r)] *n.* Makler, *der*
brolly ['brɒlɪ] *n. (Brit. coll.)* [Regen]schirm, *der*
bronchitis [brɒŋ'kaɪtɪs] *n.* Bronchitis, *die*
bronze [brɒnz] **1.** *n.* Bronze, *die.* **2.** *attrib. adj.* Bronze-; *(coloured like ~)* bronzefarben
brooch [brəʊtʃ] *n.* Brosche, *die*
brood [bruːd] **1.** *n.* Brut, *die.* **2.** *v. i.* [vor sich *(Akk.)* hin] brüten
brook [brʊk] *n.* Bach, *der*
broom [bruːm] *n.* **a)** Besen, *der;* **b)** *(Bot.)* Ginster, *der.* **'broom-cupboard** *n.* Besenschrank, *der.* **'broomstick** *n.* Besenstiel, *der*
broth [brɒθ] *n.* Brühe, *die*
brothel ['brɒθl] *n.* Bordell, *das*
brother ['brʌðə(r)] *n.* Bruder, *der;* **my ~s and sisters** meine Geschwister.

'**brotherhood** n. (organization) Bruderschaft, die. '**brother-in-law** n., pl. brothers-in-law Schwager, der
brought see bring
brow [braʊ] n. a) (eye~) Braue, die; b) (forehead) Stirn, die; c) (of hill) Kuppe, die
'**browbeat** v.t., forms as **beat** 1 einschüchtern
brown [braʊn] 1. adj. braun. 2. n. Braun, das. **brown 'bread** n. ≈ Mischbrot, das
Brownie ['braʊnı] n. Wichtel, die
brown 'paper n. Packpapier, das
browse [braʊz] v.i. (in shop) sich umsehen; (read) blättern (**through** in + Dat.)
bruise [bru:z] 1. n. a) (Med.) blauer Fleck; b) (on fruit) Druckstelle, die. 2. v.t. quetschen 〈Obst, Pflanzen〉; ~ oneself/one's leg sich stoßen/sich am Bein stoßen
brunette [bru:'net] 1. n. Brünette, die. 2. adj. brünett
brunt [brʌnt] n. bear the ~ of the attack/financial cuts von dem Angriff/von den Einsparungen am meisten betroffen sein
brush [brʌʃ] 1. n. a) Bürste, die; (for sweeping) Besen, der; (with short handle) Handfeger, der; (for painting or writing) Pinsel, der; b) (skirmish) Zusammenstoß, der; c) (light touch) flüchtige Berührung. 2. v.t. a) kehren; fegen; abbürsten 〈Kleidung〉; ~ one's teeth/hair sich (Dat.) die Zähne putzen/die Haare bürsten; b) (touch in passing) streifen. 3. v.i. ~ past sb./sth. jmdn./etw. streifen. **brush 'up** v.t. & i. ~ up [on] auffrischen 〈Kenntnisse usw.〉
brusque [brʌsk] adj., '**brusquely** adv. schroff
Brussels ['brʌslz] pr. n. Brüssel (das). **Brussels 'sprouts** n. pl. Rosenkohl, der
brutal ['bru:tl] adj. brutal. **brutality** [bru:'tælıtı] n. Brutalität, die. **brutally** ['bru:təlı] adv. brutal
brute [bru:t] 1. n. a) (animal) Bestie, die; b) (person) Rohling, der. 2. attrib. adj. by ~ force mit roher Gewalt
B.Sc. abbr. **Bachelor of Science**
BST abbr. **British Summer Time** Britische Sommerzeit
bubble ['bʌbl] 1. n. Blase, die; (small) Perle, die. 2. v.i. 〈Wasser, Schlamm, Lava:〉 Blasen bilden. '**bubble bath** n. Schaumbad, das

'**buck** [bʌk] n. (deer, chamois) Bock, der; (rabbit, hare) Rammler, der
²**buck** n. pass the ~ to sb. jmdm. die Verantwortung aufhalsen
³**buck** (coll.) 1. v.i. ~ '**up a)** (make haste) sich ranhalten (ugs.); b) (cheer up) ~ up! Kopf hoch! 2. v.t. ~ one's ideas up (coll.) sich zusammenreißen
⁴**buck** n. (Amer. sl.) Dollar, der
bucket ['bʌkıt] n. Eimer, der
buckle ['bʌkl] 1. n. Schnalle, die. 2. v.t. a) zuschnallen; ~ sth. on/up etw. anschnallen/festschnallen; b) verbiegen 〈Stoßstange, Rad〉. 3. v.i. 〈Rad, Metallplatte:〉 [sich] verbiegen
bud [bʌd] 1. n. Knospe, die; come into ~/be in ~: Knospen treiben. 2. v.i., -dd- Knospen treiben
Buddhism ['bʊdızm] n. Buddhismus, der. **Buddhist** ['bʊdıst] 1. n. Buddhist, der/Buddhistin, die. 2. adj. buddhistisch
budge [bʌdʒ] 1. v.i. sich rühren; 〈Gegenstand:〉 sich bewegen. 2. v.t. bewegen
budgerigar ['bʌdʒərıgɑ:(r)] n. Wellensittich, der
budget ['bʌdʒıt] 1. n. Etat, der; Haushalt[splan], der. 2. v.i. ~ for sth. etw. [im Etat] einplanen
budgie ['bʌdʒı] n. (coll.) Wellensittich, der
buff [bʌf] 1. adj. gelbbraun. 2. n. (coll.: enthusiast) Fan, der (ugs.)
buffalo ['bʌfələʊ] n., pl. ~es or same Büffel, der
buffer ['bʌfə(r)] n. Prellbock, der; (on vehicle; also fig.) Puffer, der
buffet ['bʊfeı] n. Büfett, das. '**buffet car** n. Büfettwagen, der
bug [bʌg] n. (also coll.: microphone) Wanze, die
buggy ['bʌgı] n. (pushchair) Sportwagen, der
bugle ['bju:gl] n. Bügelhorn, das
build [bıld] 1. v.t., built [bılt] bauen; (fig.) aufbauen 〈System, Gesellschaft, Zukunft〉. 2. v.i., built bauen. 3. n. Körperbau, der. **build 'in** v.t. einbauen. **build 'on** aufbauen auf (+ Dat.); bebauen 〈Gebiet〉. **build 'up 1.** v.t. aufhäufen 〈Reserven, Mittel〉; kräftigen 〈Personen, Körper〉; steigern 〈Produktion, Kapazität〉; stärken 〈[Selbst]vertrauen〉; aufbauen 〈Firma, Geschäft〉. 2. v.i. 〈Spannung, Druck:〉 zunehmen; 〈Schlange, Rückstau:〉 sich bilden; 〈Verkehr:〉 sich verdichten
'**builder** n. Bauunternehmer, der

'**building** *n.* **a)** Bau, *der;* **b)** *(structure)* Gebäude, *das.* '**building-site** *n.* Baustelle, *die.* '**building society** *n.* *(Brit.)* Bausparkasse, *die*

built *see* **build 1, 2**

built: ~**-in** *adj.* **a)** eingebaut; Einbau-⟨*schrank, küche usw.*⟩*;* **b)** *(fig.: instinctive)* angeboren; ~**-up** *adj.* bebaut; ~**-up area** Wohngebiet, *das; (Motor Veh.)* geschlossene Ortschaft

bulb [bʌlb] *n.* **a)** *(Bot., Hort.)* Zwiebel, *die;* **b)** *(of lamp)* [Glüh]birne, *die*

Bulgaria [bʌl'geərɪə] *pr. n.* Bulgarien *(das).* **Bulgarian** [bʌl'geərɪən] **1.** *adj.* bulgarisch. **2.** *n.* **a)** *(person)* Bulgare, *der/*Bulgarin, *die;* **b)** *(language)* Bulgarisch, *das; see also* **English 2 a**

bulge [bʌldʒ] **1.** *n.* Ausbeulung, *die;* ausgebeulte Stelle. **2.** *v. i.* sich wölben

bulk [bʌlk] *n.* **a)** *(large quantity)* **in** ~**:** in großen Mengen; **b)** *(large shape)* massige Gestalt; **c)** *(size)* Größe, *die;* **d)** *(greater part)* der größte Teil; *(of population, votes)* Mehrheit, *die.* '**bulky** *adj.* sperrig ⟨*Gegenstand*⟩*;* massig ⟨*Gestalt, Körper*⟩

bull [bʊl] *n.* Bulle, *der; (esp. for bullfight)* Stier, *der*

'**bulldog** *n.* Bulldogge, *die*

'**bulldozer** ['bʊldəʊzə(r)] *n.* Planierraupe, *die*

bullet ['bʊlɪt] *n.* Kugel, *die*

bulletin ['bʊlɪtɪn] *n.* Bulletin, *das*

'**bulletproof** *adj.* kugelsicher

'**bullfight** *n.* Stierkampf, *der*

bullion ['bʊljən] *n.* **gold** ~**:** Goldbarren *Pl.*

bullock ['bʊlək] *n.* Ochse, *der*

bull: ~**ring** *n.* Stierkampfarena, *die;* ~'**s-eye** *n.* *(of target)* Schwarze, *das*

bully ['bʊlɪ] **1.** *n.* *(schoolboy etc.)* ≈ Rabauke, *der; (boss)* Tyrann, *der.* **2.** *v. t.* schikanieren; *(frighten)* einschüchtern

¹**bum** [bʌm] *n.* *(Brit. sl.)* Hintern, *der (ugs.)*

²**bum** *n.* *(Amer. sl.: tramp)* Penner, *der (salopp)*

bumble-bee ['bʌmblbi:] *n.* Hummel, *die*

bump [bʌmp] **1.** *n.* **a)** *(sound)* Bums, *der; (impact)* Stoß, *der;* **b)** *(swelling)* Beule, *die;* **c)** *(hump)* Buckel, *der (ugs.).* **2.** *adv.* bums. **3.** *v. t.* anstoßen. '**bump into** *v. t.* **a)** stoßen an (+ *Akk.*)*;* **b)** *(meet by chance)* zufällig [wieder]treffen

'**bumper 1.** *n.* Stoßstange, *die.* **2.** *attrib. adj.* Rekord⟨*ernte, -jahr*⟩

'**bumpy** *adj.* holp[e]rig ⟨*Straße, Fahrt, Fahrzeug*⟩*;* uneben ⟨*Fläche*⟩*;* unruhig ⟨*Flug*⟩

bun [bʌn] *n.* süßes Brötchen; *(currant* ~*)* Korinthenbrötchen, *das*

bunch [bʌntʃ] *n.* **a)** *(of flowers)* Strauß, *der; (of grapes, bananas)* Traube, *die; (of parsley, radishes)* Bund, *das;* ~ **of flowers/grapes** Blumenstrauß, *der/* Traube, *die;* **a** ~ **of keys** ein Schlüsselbund; **b)** *(lot)* Anzahl, *die;* **the best** *or* **pick of the** ~**:** der/die/das Beste [von allen]; **c)** *(of people)* Haufen, *der (ugs.)*

bundle ['bʌndl] *n.* Bündel, *das; (of papers)* Packen, *der*

bung [bʌŋ] **1.** *n.* Spund, *der.* **2.** *v. t. (sl.)* schmeißen *(ugs.).* **bung** '**up** *v. i.* **be/ get** ~**ed up** verstopft sein/verstopfen

bungalow ['bʌŋgələʊ] *n.* Bungalow, *der*

bungle ['bʌŋgl] *v. t.* stümpern bei

bunk [bʌŋk] *n.* *(in ship, lorry)* Koje, *die; (in sleeping-car)* Bett, *das; (~-bed)* Etagenbett, *das*

bunker ['bʌŋkə(r)] *n.* Bunker, *der*

bunny ['bʌnɪ] *n.* Häschen, *das*

buoy [bɔɪ] *n.* Boje, *die*

buoyancy ['bɔɪənsɪ] *n.* Auftrieb, *der*

buoyant ['bɔɪənt] *adj.* schwimmend; **be** ~**:** schwimmen

burden ['bɜ:dn] **1.** *n.* Last, *die;* **become a** ~ *(fig.)* zur Last werden. **2.** *v. t.* belasten *(with* mit*)*

bureau ['bjʊərəʊ, bjʊə'rəʊ] *n.* **a)** *(Brit.: writing-desk)* Sekretär, *der;* **b)** *(office)* Büro, *das*

bureaucracy [bjʊə'rɒkrəsɪ] *n.* Bürokratie, *die.* **bureaucrat** ['bjʊərəkræt] *n.* Bürokrat, *der/*Bürokratin, *die.* **bureaucratic** [bjʊərə'krætɪk] *adj.* bürokratisch

burglar ['bɜ:glə(r)] *n.* Einbrecher, *der.* '**burglar alarm** *n.* Alarmanlage, *die*

burglary ['bɜ:glərɪ] *n.* Einbruch, *der*

burgle ['bɜ:gl] *v. t.* einbrechen in (+ *Akk.*)*;* **the shop/he was** ~**d** in dem Laden/bei ihm wurde eingebrochen

burial ['berɪəl] *n.* Begräbnis, *das*

burly ['bɜ:lɪ] *adj.* stämmig

Burma ['bɜ:mə] *pr. n.* Birma *(das)*

burn [bɜ:n] **1.** *n.* *(on the skin)* Verbrennung, *die; (on material)* Brandfleck, *der.* **2.** *v. t.,* ~**t** [bɜ:nt] *or* ~**ed a)** verbrennen; ~ **oneself/one's hand** sich verbrennen/sich *(Dat.)* die Hand verbrennen; ~ **a hole in sth.** ein Loch in etw. *(Akk.)* brennen; **b)** als Brennstoff verwenden ⟨*Gas, Öl usw.*⟩*;* heizen mit ⟨*Kohle, Holz, Torf*⟩*;* **c)** *(spoil)*

anbrennen lassen ⟨*Fleisch, Kuchen*⟩;
be ~**t** angebrannt sein. 3. *v. i.*, ~**t** *or*
~**ed** brennen; ~ **to death** verbrennen;
she ~**s easily** sie bekommt leicht einen
Sonnenbrand. **burn 'down** *v. t. & i.*
niederbrennen
'**burner** *n.* Brenner, *der*
'**burning** *adj.* glühend ⟨*Leidenschaft,
Haß, Wunsch*⟩; brennend ⟨*Wunsch,
Frage, Problem*⟩
burnt *see* burn 2, 3
burp [bɜ:p] *(coll.)* 1. *n.* Rülpser, *der*
(ugs.). 2. *v. i.* rülpsen *(ugs.)*
burrow ['bʌrəʊ] 1. *n.* Bau, *der.* 2. *v. i.*
[sich *(Dat.)*] einen Gang graben
burst [bɜ:st] 1. *n.* **a)** *(split)* Bruch, *der;*
b) *(of firing)* Salve, *die;* **c)** *(fig.)* **a)** ~ **of
applause/cheering** ein Beifallsaus-
bruch/Beifallsrufe *Pl.* 2. *v. t.*, **burst**
zum Platzen bringen; platzen lassen
⟨*Luftballon*⟩; ~ **pipe** Rohrbruch, *der.*
3. *v. i.*, **burst a)** platzen; ⟨*Bombe:*⟩ explodieren; ⟨*Damm:*⟩ brechen; ⟨*Flußufer:*⟩ überschwemmt werden; ⟨*Furunkel, Geschwür:*⟩ aufgehen; **b) be**
~**ing with sth.** zum Bersten voll sein
mit etw.; **be** ~**ing with pride/impa-
tience/excitement** vor Stolz/Ungeduld
platzen/vor Aufregung außer sich
sein. '**burst into** *v. t.* **a)** eindringen
in; **b)** ~ **into tears/laughter** in Tränen/
Gelächter ausbrechen; ~ **into flames**
in Brand geraten. **burst 'out** *v. i.* **a)**
herausstürzen; **b)** *(exclaim)* losplat-
zen; **c)** ~ **out laughing/crying** in La-
chen/Tränen ausbrechen
bury ['berɪ] *v. t.* **a)** begraben; **b)** *(hide)*
vergraben; ~ **one's face in one's hands**
das Gesicht in den Händen vergra-
ben; **c)** ~ **one's teeth in sth.** seine Zähne in etw. *(Akk.)* graben
bus [bʌs] *n.* Bus, *der*
bus: ~**-conductor** *n.* Busschaffner,
der; ~**-driver** *n.* Busfahrer, *der;*
~ **fare** *n.* [Bus]fahrpreis, *der*
bush [bʊʃ] *n.* **a)** Busch, *der;* **b)** *(shrubs)*
Gebüsch, *das.* '**bushy** *adj.* buschig
busily ['bɪzɪlɪ] *adj.* eifrig
business ['bɪznɪs] *n.* **a)** *(trading operation)* Geschäft, *das; (company, firm)*
Betrieb, *der; (large)* Unternehmen,
das; **b)** *(buying and selling)* Geschäfte
Pl.; **c)** *(task, province)* Aufgabe, *die;*
mind your own ~! kümmere dich um
deine [eigenen] Angelegenheiten!; **d)**
(difficult matter) Problem, *das*
business: ~ **letter** *n.* Geschäftsbrief,
der; ~**-like** *adj.* geschäftsmäßig
⟨*Art*⟩; geschäftstüchtig ⟨*Person*⟩;

~**man** *n.* Geschäftsmann, *der;* ~
school *n.* kaufmännische Fachschu-
le; ~**woman** *n.* Geschäftsfrau, *die*
busker ['bʌskə(r)] *n.* Straßenmusi-
kant, *der*
bus: ~**-route** *n.* Buslinie, *die;* ~
shelter *n.* Wartehäuschen, *das;*
~**-station** *n.* Omnibusbahnhof, *der;*
~**-stop** *n.* Bushaltestelle, *die*
¹**bust** [bʌst] *n.* **a)** *(sculpture)* Büste, *die;*
b) ~ |**measurement**| Oberweite, *die*
²**bust** *(coll.)* 1. *adj.* kaputt *(ugs.).* 2.
v. t., ~**ed** *or* **bust** *(break)* kaputtmachen
(ugs.); ~ **sth. open** etw. aufbrechen. 3.
v. i., ~**ed** *or* **bust** kaputtgehen *(ugs.)*
'**bus-ticket** *n.* Busfahrkarte, *die*
bustle ['bʌsl] 1. *v. i.* ~ **about** geschäftig
hin und her eilen. 2. *n.* Betrieb, *der.*
bustling ['bʌslɪŋ] *adj.* belebt ⟨*Straße,
Stadt, Markt usw.*⟩; rege ⟨*Tätigkeit*⟩
busy ['bɪzɪ] 1. *adj.* **a)** beschäftigt (**at,
with** mit); arbeitsreich ⟨*Leben*⟩; ziemlich hektisch ⟨*Zeit*⟩; **I'm** ~ **now** ich
habe jetzt zu tun; **he was** ~ **packing** er
war mit Packen beschäftigt; **b)** *(Amer.
Teleph.)* besetzt. 2. *v. refl.* ~ **oneself**
sich beschäftigen (**with** mit). '**busy-
body** *n.* G[e]schaftlhuber, *der*
but 1. [bət, *stressed* bʌt] *conj.* aber; *cor-
recting after a negative* sondern; **not
that book** ~ **this one** nicht das Buch,
sondern dieses. 2. [bət] *prep.* außer
(+ *Dat.*); **the next/last** ~ **one** der/die/
das übernächste/vorletzte
butcher ['bʊtʃə(r)] 1. *n.* Fleischer, *der.*
2. *v. t. (murder)* niedermetzeln
butler ['bʌtlə(r)] *n.* Butler, *der*
¹**butt** [bʌt] *n.* **a)** *(of rifle)* Kolben, *der;*
b) *(of cigarette, cigar)* Stummel, *der*
²**butt** *n. (object of teasing or ridicule)*
Zielscheibe, *die*
³**butt** 1. *n. (push) (by person)*
[Kopf]stoß, *der; (by animal)* Stoß [mit
den Hörnern]. 2. *v. t. & i.* mit dem
Kopf/den Hörnern stoßen. **butt 'in**
v. i. dazwischenreden
butter ['bʌtə(r)] 1. *n.* Butter, *die.* 2.
v. t. buttern
butter: ~**-bean** *n.* Mondbohne, *die;*
~**cup** *n.* Butterblume, *die;* ~**fly** *n.* **a)**
Schmetterling, *der;* **b)** ~ |**stroke**| Del-
phinstil, *der*
buttock ['bʌtək] *n.* Hinterbacke, *die;*
Gesäßhälfte, *die;* ~**s** Gesäß, *das*
button ['bʌtn] 1. *n.* Knopf, *der.* 2. *v. t.*
~ |**up**| zuknöpfen. **buttonhole** 1. *n.*
a) Knopfloch, *das;* **b)** *(flower)* Knopf-
lochblume, *die.* 2. *v. t.* zu fassen kriegen *(ugs.)*

buttress ['bʌtrɪs] *n. (Archit.)* Mauer-
stütze, *die*
buxom ['bʌksəm] *adj.* drall
buy [baɪ] **1.** *v. t.,* **bought** [bɔːt] kaufen;
~ **sb./oneself sth.** jmdm./sich etw.
kaufen. **2.** *n.* [Ein]kauf, *der;* **be a good**
~: preiswert sein. **buy 'up** *v. t.* auf-
kaufen
'buyer *n.* Käufer, *der*/Käuferin, *die*
buzz [bʌz] **1.** *n.* Summen, *das.* **2.** *v. i.*
summen. **buzz 'off** *v. i. (sl.)* abhauen
(salopp)
'buzzer *n.* Summer, *der*
by [baɪ] **1.** *prep.* **a)** *(near, beside)* an
(+ *Dat.*); bei; *(next to)* neben; ~ **the**
window/river am Fenster/Fluß; **b)** *(to*
position beside) zu; **c)** *(about, in the*
possession of) bei; **d)** **[all]** **by herself/**
himself *etc.* [ganz] allein[e]; **e)** *(along)*
entlang; *(via)* über (+ *Akk.*); **f)** *(pas-*
sing) vorbei an (+ *Dat.*); **g)** *(during)*
bei; **by day/night** bei Tag/Nacht; **h)**
(through the agency of) von; **written**
by ...: geschrieben von ...; **i)** *(through*
the means of) durch; **by bus/ship** *etc.*
mit dem Bus/Schiff *usw.;* **by air/sea**
mit dem Flugzeug/Schiff; **j)** *(not later*
than) bis; **by now/this time** inzwischen; **k)** *indicating unit* pro; **by the**
minute/hour pro Minute/Stunde; **day**
by day/month by month Tag für Tag/
Monat für Monat; **10 ft. by 20 ft.** 10
[Fuß] mal 20 Fuß; **l)** *indicating*
amount **one by one** einzeln; **two by**
two/three by three zu zweit/dritt; **m)**
indicating factor durch; **8 divided by 2**
is 4 8 geteilt durch 2 ist 4; **n)** *indicating*
extent um; **wider by a foot** um einen
Fuß breiter; **o)** *(according to)* nach. **2.**
adv. **a)** *(past)* vorbei; **b)** *(near)* **close/**
near by in der Nähe; **c) by and large** im
großen und ganzen
bye[-bye] ['baɪ(baɪ)] *int. (coll.)* tschüs
(ugs.)
bye-law *see* **by-law**
'by-election *n.* Nachwahl, *die*
bygone ['baɪgɒn] *adj.* vergangen
'by-law *n. (esp. Brit.)* Verordnung, *die*
'bypass 1. *n.* Umgehungsstraße, *die.*
2. *v. t.* **a) the road ~es the town** die
Straße führt um die Stadt herum; **b)**
(fig.) übergehen
'by-product *n.* Nebenprodukt, *das*
'by-road *n.* Nebenstraße, *die*
bystander ['baɪstændə(r)] *n.* Zuschauer, *der*/Zuschauerin, *die*
byte ['baɪt] *n. (Computing)* Byte, *das*
'byway *n.* Seitenweg, *der*
'byword *n.* Inbegriff, *der* **(for** *Gen.*)

C

C, c [siː] *n.* C, c, *das*
C. *abbr.* **a) Celsius** C; **b) Centigrade** C
cab [kæb] *n.* **a)** *(taxi)* Taxi, *das;* **b)** *(of*
lorry, truck) Fahrerhaus, *das;* *(of*
train) Führerstand, *der*
cabaret ['kæbəreɪ] *n.* Varieté, *das;*
(satirical) Kabarett, *das*
cabbage ['kæbɪdʒ] *n.* Kohl, *der;* **red/**
white ~: Rot-/Weißkohl, *der*
cabin ['kæbɪn] *n.* *(in ship)* *(for passen-*
gers) Kabine, *die;* *(for crew)* Kajüte,
die; *(in aircraft)* Kabine, *die*
cabinet ['kæbɪnɪt] *n.* **a)** Schrank, *der;*
(in bathroom, for medicines) Schränkchen, *das;* **[display]** ~: Vitrine, *die;* **b)**
the C~ *(Polit.)* das Kabinett; **C~ Min-**
ister Minister, *der*
cable ['keɪbl] **1.** *n.* **a)** *(rope)* Kabel, *das;*
(of ~-car etc.) Seil, *das;* **b)** *(Electr.,*
Teleph.) Kabel, *das;* **c)** *(message)* Kabel, *das.* **2.** *v. t.* kabeln ⟨*Mitteilung,*
Nachricht⟩. **'cable-car** *n.* Drahtseil-
bahn, *die.* **cable 'television** *n.* Ka-
belfernsehen, *das*
cache [kæʃ] *n.* geheimes [Waffen-/
Proviant-]lager
cackle ['kækl] **1.** *n.* **a)** *(of hen)*
Gackern, *das;* **b)** *(laughter)* [meckern-
des] Gelächter. **2.** *v. i.* **a)** ⟨*Henne:*⟩
gackern; **b)** *(laugh)* meckernd lachen
cactus ['kæktəs] *n., pl.* **cacti** ['kæktaɪ]
or ~**es** Kaktus, *der*
caddie ['kædɪ] *n. (Golf)* Caddie, *der*
caddy ['kædɪ] *n.* Dose, *die*
cadet [kə'det] *n.* Offiziersschüler, *der;*
naval/police ~: Marinekadett/Anwär-
ter für den Polizeidienst
cadge [kædʒ] *v. t.* (sich *(Dat.)*) erbet-
teln
café, cafe ['kæfeɪ] *n.* Lokal, *das;* *(tea-*
room) Café, *das*
cafeteria [kæfɪ'tɪərɪə] *n.* Cafeteria, *die*
caffeine ['kæfiːn] *n.* Koffein, *das*
cage [keɪdʒ] **1.** *n.* **a)** Käfig, *der;* **b)** *(of*
lift) Fahrkabine, *die.* **2.** *v. t.* einsperren
cagey ['keɪdʒɪ] *adj. (coll.)* zugeknöpft

(ugs.); **be ~ about sth.** mit etw. hinterm Berg halten *(ugs.)*

Cairo ['kaɪərəʊ] *pr. n.* Kairo *(das)*

cajole [kə'dʒəʊl] *v. t.* **~ sb. into sth./ doing sth.** jmdn. etw. einreden/jmdm. einreden, etw. zu tun

cake [keɪk] **1.** *n.* Kuchen, *der;* **a ~ of soap** ein Riegel *od.* Stück Seife. **2.** *v. t.* verkrusten; **~d with dirt/blood** schmutz-/blutverkrustet

calamity [kə'læmɪtɪ] *n.* Unheil, *das*

calcium ['kælsɪəm] *n.* Kalzium, *das*

calculate ['kælkjʊleɪt] **1.** *v. t.* **a)** berechnen; *(by estimating)* ausrechnen; **b) be ~d to do sth.** darauf abzielen, etw. zu tun. **2.** *v. i.* **~ on doing sth.** damit rechnen, etw. zu tun. **'calculated** *adj.* kalkuliert ⟨*Risiko*⟩; vorsätzlich ⟨*Handlung*⟩. **calculation** [kælkjʊ-'leɪʃn] *n.* **a)** *(result)* Rechnung, *die;* **he is out in his ~s** er hat sich verrechnet; **b)** *(calculating)* Berechnung, *die.* **calculator** ['kælkjʊleɪtə(r)] *n.* Rechner, *der*

calculus ['kælkjʊləs] *n.* **differential/ integral ~:** Differential-/Integralrechnung, *die*

calendar ['kælɪndə(r)] *n.* Kalender, *der; attrib.* Kalender-

¹calf [kɑːf] *n., pl.* **calves** Kalb, *das*

²calf *n., pl.* **calves** *(Anat.)* Wade, *die*

calibre *(Brit./ Amer.:* **caliber)** ['kælɪbə(r)] *n.* Kaliber, *das*

calico ['kælɪkəʊ] *n.* Kattun, *der*

California [kælɪ'fɔːnɪə] *pr. n.* Kalifornien *(das)*

caliper *see* **calliper**

call [kɔːl] **1.** *v. i.* **a)** rufen; **~ to sb.** jmdm. etwas zurufen; **~ ǀoutǀ for help** um Hilfe rufen; **b)** *(pay brief visit)* ǀkurzǀ besuchen (**at** *Akk.*); **~ on sb.** jmdn. besuchen; **~ round** vorbeikommen *(ugs.);* **~ at a port/station** einen Hafen anlaufen/an einem Bahnhof halten; **c)** *(Teleph.)* **who is ~ing, please?** wer spricht da, bitte?; **thank you for ~ing** vielen Dank für Ihren Anruf! **2.** *v. t.* **a)** rufen; aufrufen ⟨*Namen, Nummer*⟩; **b)** *(cry to, summon)* rufen; *(to a duty, to do sth.)* aufrufen; **c)** *(by radio/telephone)* rufen/ anrufen; *(initially)* Kontakt aufnehmen mit; **d)** *(rouse)* wecken; **e)** einberufen ⟨*Konferenz*⟩; ausrufen ⟨*Streik*⟩; **f)** *(name)* nennen; **he is ~ed Bob** er heißt Bob; **what is it ~ed in English?** wie heißt das auf englisch? **3.** *n.* **a)** Ruf, *der;* **a ~ for help** ein Hilferuf; **be on ~:** Bereitschaftsdienst haben; **b)**

(visit) Besuch, *der;* **make** *or* **pay a ~ on sb., make** *or* **pay sb. a ~:** jmdn. besuchen; **c)** *(telephone ~)* Anruf, *der;* **give sb. a ~:** jmdn. anrufen; **make a ~:** telefonieren; **d)** *(invitation, summons)* Aufruf, *der;* **e)** *(need, occasion)* Anlaß, *der.* **call 'back 1.** *v. t.* zurückrufen. **2.** *v. i.* zurückrufen; *(come back)* zurückkommen. **'call for** *v. t.* **a)** *(send for, order)* bestellen; **b)** *(collect)* abholen; **c)** *(require, demand)* erfordern; **this ~s for a celebration** das muß gefeiert werden. **call 'in 1.** *v. i.* vorbeikommen *(ugs.)* (**on** bei). **2.** *v. t.* zu Rate ziehen ⟨*Fachmann usw.*⟩. **call 'off** *v. t.* absagen ⟨*Treffen, Verabredung*⟩; rückgängig machen ⟨*Geschäft*⟩; lösen ⟨*Verlobung*⟩; *(end)* abbrechen ⟨*Streik*⟩. **'call on** *v. t.* **a)** *see* **~ 1b; b)** *see* **~ ǀupǀon. call 'out 1.** *v. t.* alarmieren ⟨*Truppen*⟩; zum Streik aufrufen ⟨*Arbeitnehmer*⟩. **2.** *v. i. see* **~ 1 a. call 'up** *v. t.* **a)** *(by telephone)* anrufen; **b)** *(Mil.)* einberufen. **'call ǀupǀon** *v. t.* **~ upon sb.'s generosity** an jmds. Großzügigkeit *(Akk.)* appellieren; **~ ǀupǀon sb. to do sth.** jmdn. auffordern, etw. zu tun **'call-box** *n.* Telefonzelle, *die*

'caller *n.* *(visitor)* Besucher, *der/* Besucherin, *die; (on telephone)* Anrufer, *der/* Anruferin, *die*

'call-girl *n.* Callgirl, *das*

'calling *n.* Beruf, *der*

calliper ['kælɪpə(r)] *n.* **a)** ǀa pair ofǀ **~s** Tasterzirkel, *der;* **b)** *(Med.)* Beinschiene, *die*

callous ['kæləs] *adj.* gefühllos; herzlos ⟨*Handlung, Verhalten*⟩

'call-up *n.* *(Mil.)* Einberufung, *die*

calm [kɑːm] **1.** *n.* *(stillness)* Stille, *die; (serenity)* Ruhe, *die.* **2.** *adj.* ruhig. **3.** *v. t.* **~ sb. ǀdownǀ** jmdn. beruhigen. **4.** *v. i.* **~ ǀdownǀ** sich beruhigen. **'calmly** *adv.* ruhig; gelassen. **'calmness** *n.* Ruhe, *die; (of water)* Stille, *die*

Calor gas, (P) ['kælə gæs] *n.* Butangas, *das*

calorie ['kælərɪ] *n.* Kalorie, *die*

calves *pl. of* **¹,²calf**

camber ['kæmbə(r)] *n.* Wölbung, *die*

came *see* **come**

camel ['kæml] *n.* Kamel, *das*

camera ['kæmərə] *n.* Kamera, *die.* **'cameraman** *n.* Kameramann, *der*

camouflage ['kæməflɑːʒ] **1.** *n.* Tarnung, *die.* **2.** *v. t.* tarnen

camp [kæmp] **1.** *n.* Lager, *das.* **2.** *v. i.* **~ ǀoutǀ** campen; *(in tent)* zelten; **go ~ing** Campen/Zelten fahren/gehen

campaign [kæm'peɪn] **1.** *n.* **a)** *(Mil.)* Feldzug, *der;* **b)** *(organized action)* Kampagne, *die;* **publicity** ~ : Werbekampagne, *die.* **2.** *v. i.* ~ **for/against** **sth.** sich für etw. einsetzen/gegen etw. etwas unternehmen; **be** ~**ing** ⟨*Politiker:*⟩ im Wahlkampf stehen

'**camp-bed** *n.* Campingliege, *die*

'**camper** *n. (person)* Camper, *der/* Camperin, *die*

'**camping** *n.* Camping, *das; (in tent)* Zelten, *das.* '**camping-ground** *(Amer.),* '**camping site** *ns.* Campingplatz, *der*

'**campsite** *n.* Campingplatz, *der*

campus ['kæmpəs] *n.* Campus, *der*

¹**can** [kæn] **1.** *n.* **a)** *(milk* ~*, watering-*~*)* Kanne, *die; (for oil, petrol)* Kanister, *der; (Amer.: for refuse)* Eimer, *der;* **b)** *(for preserving)* [Konserven]dose, *die;* **a** ~ **of tomatoes/beer** eine Dose Tomaten/Bier. **2.** *v. t.,* **-nn-** konservieren

²**can** [kən, *stressed* kæn] *v. aux., only in pres.* **can,** *neg.* **cannot** ['kænət], *(coll.)* **can't** [kɑːnt], *past* **could** [kʊd], *neg. (coll.)* **couldn't** ['kʊdnt] können; *(have right, be permitted)* dürfen; können; **I can't do that** das kann ich nicht; *(it would be wrong)* das kann ich nicht tun; **you can't smoke here** hier dürfen Sie nicht rauchen; **could you ring me tomorrow?** könnten Sie mich morgen anrufen?; **I could have killed him** ich hätte ihn umbringen können; [**that**] **could be** |so| das könnte *od.* kann sein

Canada ['kænədə] *pr. n.* Kanada *(das).* **Canadian** [kə'neɪdɪən] **1.** *adj.* kanadisch. **2.** *n.* Kanadier, *der/*Kanadierin, *die*

canal [kə'næl] *n.* Kanal, *der*

canary [kə'neərɪ] *n.* Kanarienvogel, *der*

Ca'nary Islands *pr. n. pl.* Kanarische Inseln *Pl.*

cancel ['kænsl] **1.** *v. t.,* *(Brit.)* **-ll-** absagen ⟨*Besuch, Urlaub, Reise, Sportveranstaltung*⟩; ausfallen lassen ⟨*Veranstaltung, Vorlesung, Zug, Bus*⟩; fallenlassen ⟨*Pläne*⟩; rückgängig machen ⟨*Einladung, Vertrag*⟩; zurücknehmen ⟨*Befehl*⟩; stornieren ⟨*Bestellung, Auftrag*⟩; kündigen ⟨*Abonnement*⟩; abbestellen ⟨*Zeitung*⟩. **2.** *v. i., (Brit.)* **-ll-:** ~ |**out**| sich [gegenseitig] aufheben. **cancellation** [kænsə'leɪʃn] *n. see* **cancel** 1: Absage, *die;* Ausfall, *der;* Fallenlassen, *das;* Rückgängigmachen, *das;* Zurücknahme, *die;* Stornierung, *die;* Kündigung, *die;* Abbestellung, *die*

cancer ['kænsə(r)] *n.* **a)** *(Med.)* Krebs, *der;* **b)** **C~** *(Astrol., Astron.)* der Krebs

candelabra [kændɪ'lɑːbrə] *n.* Leuchter, *der*

candid ['kændɪd] *adj.* offen; ehrlich ⟨*Ansicht, Bericht*⟩

candidate ['kændɪdət, 'kændɪdeɪt] *n.* Kandidat, *der/*Kandidatin, *die*

candle ['kændl] *n.* Kerze, *die*

candle: ~**-light** *n.* Kerzenlicht, *das;* ~**stick** *n.* Kerzenhalter, *der; (elaborate)* Leuchter, *der;* ~**wick** *n. (material)* Frottierplüsch, *der*

candour *(Brit., Amer.:* **candor)** ['kændə(r)] *n. see* **candid:** Offenheit, *die;* Ehrlichkeit, *die*

candy ['kændɪ] *n. (Amer.) (sweets)* Süßigkeiten *Pl.; (sweet)* Bonbon, *das od. der.* '**candyfloss** ['kændɪflɒs] *n.* Zuckerwatte, *die*

cane [keɪn] **1.** *n.* **a)** *(stem)* Rohr, *das; (of raspberry, blackberry)* Sproß, *der;* **b)** *(material)* Rohr, *das;* **c)** *(stick)* [Rohr]stock, *der.* **2.** *v. t.* [mit dem Stock] schlagen

canine ['keɪnaɪn] *adj.* **a)** *(of dog[s])* Hunde-; **b)** ~ **tooth** Eckzahn, *der*

canister ['kænɪstə(r)] *n.* Büchse, *die; (for petrol, oil, etc.)* Kanister, *der*

cannabis ['kænəbɪs] *n. (hashish)* Haschisch, *das; (marijuana)* Marihuana, *das*

canned [kænd] *adj.* Dosen-; in Dosen *nachgestellt;* ~ **meat/fruit** Fleisch-/ Obstkonserven *Pl.;* ~ **beer** Dosenbier; ~ **food** [Lebensmittel]konserven *Pl.;* ~ **music** Musikkonserve, *die*

cannibal ['kænɪbl] *n.* Kannibale, *der/*Kannibalin, *die.* **cannibalism** ['kænɪbəlɪzm] *n.* Kannibalismus, *der*

cannon ['kænən] **1.** *n.* Kanone, *die.* **2.** *v. i. (Brit.)* ~ **into sb./sth.** mit etw./ jmdm. zusammenprallen. '**cannonball** *n.* Kanonenkugel, *die*

cannot *see* ²**can**

canny ['kænɪ] *adj. (shrewd)* schlau

canoe [kə'nuː] *n.* Paddelboot, *das; (Indian* ~*, Sport)* Kanu, *das.* **canoeist** [kə'nuːɪst] *n.* Paddelbootfahrer, *der/* -fahrerin, *die*

canon ['kænən] *n.* **a)** *(general law, criterion)* Grundregel, *die;* **b)** *(Eccl.: person)* Kanoniker, *der*

canonize ['kænənaɪz] *v. t.* kanonisieren ⟨*Heiligen*⟩; heiligsprechen ⟨*Märtyrer*⟩

'**can-opener** *n.* Dosenöffner, *der*

canopy ['kænəpɪ] *n.* Baldachin, *der; (over entrance)* Vordach, *das*

can't [kɑ:nt] *(coll.)* = **cannot**; *see* ²**can**
cantankerous [kæn'tæŋkərəs] *adj.* streitsüchtig
canteen [kæn'ti:n] *n.* Kantine, *die*
canter ['kæntə(r)] **1.** *n.* Handgalopp, *der.* **2.** *v.i.* leicht galoppieren
canvas ['kænvəs] *n.* Leinwand, *die*
canvass ['kænvəs] **1.** *v.t.* Wahlwerbung treiben in ⟨*einem Wahlkreis, Gebiet*⟩; Wahlwerbung treiben bei ⟨*Wählern, Bürgern*⟩. **2.** *v.i.* werben (**on behalf of** für); ~ **for votes** um Stimmen werben. '**canvasser** *n. (for votes)* Wahlhelfer, *der/*-helferin, *die*
canyon ['kænjən] *n.* Cañon, *der*
cap [kæp] **1.** *n.* **a)** Mütze, *die; (nurse's, servant's)* Haube, *die; (with peak)* Schirmmütze, *die; (skull-~)* Kappe, *die;* **b)** *(of bottle, jar)* [Verschluß]kappe, *die; (petrol ~, radiator-~)* Deckel, *der.* **2.** *v.t.,* -**pp-:** **a)** verschließen ⟨*Flasche*⟩; zudecken ⟨*Bohrloch*⟩; mit einer Schutzkappe versehen ⟨*Zahn*⟩; **b)** *(fig.)* überbieten; **to ~ it all** obendrein
capability [keɪpə'bɪlɪtɪ] *n.* Fähigkeit, *die*
capable ['keɪpəbl] *adj.* **a)** be ~ **of sth.** ⟨*Person*⟩ zu etw. imstande sein; **b)** *(gifted, able)* fähig
capacity [kə'pæsɪtɪ] *n.* **a)** Fassungsvermögen, *das;* **the machine is working to** ~: die Maschine ist voll ausgelastet; **a seating** ~ **of 300** 300 Sitzplätze; **b)** *(measure)* Rauminhalt, *der;* Volumen, *das;* **measure of** ~: Hohlmaß, *das;* **c)** *(position)* Eigenschaft, *die;* **in his** ~ **as ...:** in seiner Eigenschaft als ...
¹**cape** [keɪp] *n. (garment)* Umhang, *der;* Cape, *das*
²**cape** *n. (Geog.)* Kap, *das;* **the C~ |of Good Hope|** das Kap der guten Hoffnung; **C~ Town** Kapstadt *(das)*
caper ['keɪpə(r)] *v.i.* ~ |**about**| [herum]tollen
capital ['kæpɪtl] **1.** *attrib. adj.* **a)** Todes⟨*strafe, -urteil*⟩; Kapital⟨*verbrechen*⟩; **b)** groß, Groß⟨*buchstabe*⟩; **c)** *(principal)* Haupt⟨*stadt*⟩. **2.** *n.* **a)** *(letter)* Großbuchstabe, *der;* **b)** *(city, town)* Hauptstadt, *die;* **c)** *(stock, wealth)* Kapital, *das*
capitalism ['kæpɪtəlɪzm] *n.* Kapitalismus, *der.* **capitalist** ['kæpɪtəlɪst] **1.** *n.* Kapitalist, *der/*Kapitalistin, *die.* **2.** *adj.* kapitalistisch
capitalize ['kæpɪtəlaɪz] **1.** *v.t.* groß schreiben ⟨*Buchstaben, Wort*⟩. **2.** *v.i.* ~ **on sth.** aus etw. Kapital schlagen *(ugs.)*

capital 'punishment *n.* Todesstrafe, *die*
capitulate [kə'pɪtjʊleɪt] *v.i.* kapitulieren. **capitulation** [kəpɪtjʊ'leɪʃn] *n.* Kapitulation, *die*
capricious [kə'prɪʃəs] *adj.* launisch
Capricorn ['kæprɪkɔ:n] *n.* der Steinbock
capsize [kæp'saɪz] **1.** *v.t.* zum Kentern bringen. **2.** *v.i.* kentern
capsule ['kæpsju:l] *n.* Kapsel, *die*
captain ['kæptɪn] **1.** *n.* Kapitän, *der; (Army)* Hauptmann, *der.* **2.** *v.t.* ~ **a team** Kapitän einer Mannschaft sein
caption ['kæpʃn] *n. (heading)* Überschrift, *die; (under photograph, drawing)* Bildunterschrift, *die; (Cinemat., Telev.)* Untertitel, *der*
captivate ['kæptɪveɪt] *v.t.* fesseln. **captivating** ['kæptɪveɪtɪŋ] *adj.* bezaubernd; einnehmend ⟨*Lächeln*⟩
captive ['kæptɪv] **1.** *adj.* gefangen; **be taken** ~: gefangengenommen werden. **2.** *n.* Gefangener, *der/*Gefangene, *die.* **captivity** [kæp'tɪvɪtɪ] *n.* Gefangenschaft, *die;* **be held in** ~: gefangengehalten werden
captor ['kæptə(r)] *n.* **his** ~: der, der/die, die ihn gefangennahm
capture ['kæptʃə(r)] **1.** *n.* **a)** *(of thief etc.)* Festnahme, *die; (of town)* Einnahme, *die;* **b)** *(thing, person)* Fang, *der.* **2.** *v.t.* festnehmen ⟨*Person*⟩; [ein]fangen ⟨*Tier*⟩; einnehmen ⟨*Stadt*⟩; gefangennehmen ⟨*Phantasie*⟩
car [kɑ:(r)] *n.* Auto, *das;* Wagen, *der;* **by** ~: mit dem Auto
carafe [kə'ræf] *n.* Karaffe, *die*
caramel ['kærəmel] *n.* Karamel, *der; (toffee)* Karamelbonbon, *das*
carat ['kærət] *n.* Karat, *das;* **a 22-~ gold ring** ein 22karätiger Goldring
caravan ['kærəvæn] *n. (Brit.)* Wohnwagen, *der.* '**caravan site** *n.* Campingplatz für Wohnwagen
carbohydrate [kɑ:bəʊ'haɪdreɪt] *n.* Kohlenhydrat, *das*
carbon ['kɑ:bən] *n.* Kohlenstoff, *der*
carbon: ~ '**copy** *n.* Durchschlag, *der;* ~ **dioxide** [~ daɪ'ɒksaɪd] *n.* Kohlendioxid, *das;* ~ **paper** *n.* Kohlepapier, *das*
carburettor *(Amer.:* **carburetor**) [kɑ:bə'retə(r)] *n.* Vergaser, *der*
carcass *(Brit. also:* **carcase**) ['kɑ:kəs] *n.* Kadaver, *der*
'**car crash** *n.* Autounfall, *der*
card [kɑ:d] *n.* Karte, *die;* **play ~s** Karten spielen

card: ~board n. Pappe, die; **~board box** n. [Papp]karton, der; (smaller) [Papp]schachtel, die; **~ game** n. Kartenspiel, das

cardigan ['kɑːdɪgən] n. Strickjacke, die

cardinal ['kɑːdɪnl] **1.** adj. grundlegend ⟨Frage, Doktrin, Pflicht⟩; Kardinal⟨fehler, -problem⟩; Haupt⟨punkt, -merkmal⟩. **2.** n. (Eccl.) Kardinal, der. **cardinal 'number** n. Kardinalzahl, die. **cardinal 'sin** n. Todsünde, die

care [keə(r)] **1.** n. **a)** (anxiety) Sorge, die; **b)** (pains) Sorgfalt, die; **c)** (caution) Vorsicht, die; **take ~**: aufpassen; **d) medical ~**: ärztliche Betreuung; **e)** (charge) Obhut, die (geh.); **put sb. in ~/take sb. into ~**: jmdn. in Pflege geben/nehmen; **~ of** (on letter) bei; **take ~ of sb./sth.** (ensure safety of) auf jmdn./etw. aufpassen; (attend to) sich um jmdn./etw. kümmern. **2.** v. i. **~ for sb./sth.** (look after) sich um jmdn./etw. kümmern; (like) jmdn./etw. mögen; **~ to do sth.** etw. tun mögen; **I don't ~** [whether/how/what etc.] es ist mir gleich[, ob/wie/was usw.]

career [kə'rɪə(r)] **1.** n. Beruf, der. **2.** v. i. rasen; ⟨Pferd, Reiter:⟩ galoppieren

carefree adj. sorgenfrei

careful ['keəfl] adj. (thorough) sorgfältig; (cautious) vorsichtig; |be| **~!** Vorsicht!; **be ~ of sb./sth.** (be cautious of) sich vor jmdm./etw. in acht nehmen; **be ~ with sb./sth.** vorsichtig mit jmdm./etw. umgehen. **'carefully** adv. (thoroughly) sorgfältig; (attentively) aufmerksam; (cautiously) vorsichtig

careless ['keəlɪs] adj. **a)** (inattentive) unaufmerksam; (thoughtless) gedankenlos; leichtsinnig ⟨Fahrer⟩; nachlässig ⟨Arbeiter, Arbeit⟩; gedankenlos ⟨Bemerkung, Handlung⟩; unachtsam ⟨Fahren⟩; **b)** (nonchalant) ungezwungen. **'carelessly** adv. (without care) nachlässig; (thoughtlessly) gedankenlos. **'carelessness** n. (lack of care) Nachlässigkeit, die; (thoughtlessness) Gedankenlosigkeit, die

caress [kə'res] **1.** n. Liebkosung, die. **2.** v. t. liebkosen

'caretaker n. Hausmeister, der/-meisterin, die

'car ferry n. Autofähre, die

cargo ['kɑːgəʊ] n. Fracht, die. **'cargo boat, 'cargo ship** ns. Frachter, der

Caribbean [kærɪ'biːən] **1.** n. **the ~**: die Karibik. **2.** adj. karibisch

caricature ['kærɪkətjʊə(r)] **1.** n. Karikatur, die. **2.** v. t. karikieren

carnage ['kɑːnɪdʒ] n. Gemetzel, das

carnal ['kɑːnl] adj. sinnlich

carnation [kɑː'neɪʃn] n. [Garten]nelke, die

carnet ['kɑːneɪ] n. (of motorist) Triptyk, das; |camping| **~**: Ausweis für Camper

carnival ['kɑːnɪvl] n. Volksfest, das

carnivorous [kɑː'nɪvərəs] adj. fleischfressend

carol ['kærl] n. |Christmas| **~**: Weihnachtslied, das

carp [kɑːp] n., pl. same Karpfen, der

'car-park n. Parkplatz, der; (building) Parkhaus, das

carpenter ['kɑːpɪntə(r)] n. Zimmermann, der; (for furniture) Tischler, der/Tischlerin, die. **carpentry** ['kɑːpɪntrɪ] n. Zimmerhandwerk, das; (in furniture) Tischlerhandwerk, das

carpet ['kɑːpɪt] n. Teppich, der. **'carpet-slipper** n. Hausschuh, der. **'carpet-sweeper** n. Teppichkehrer, der

'car-port n. Einstellplatz, der

carriage ['kærɪdʒ] n. **a)** (horse-drawn) Kutsche, die; **b)** (Railw.) Wagen, der. **'carriageway** n. Fahrbahn, die

carrier ['kærɪə(r)] n. **a)** (bearer) Träger, der; **b)** (firm) Transportunternehmen, das. **'carrier-bag** n. Tragetasche, die. **'carrier pigeon** n. Brieftaube, die

carrot ['kærət] n. Möhre, die

carry ['kærɪ] v. t. **a)** tragen; (emphasizing destination) bringen; **b)** (possess) besitzen ⟨Autorität, Gewicht⟩. **carry a'way** v. t. forttragen; **be** or **get carried away** sich hinreißen lassen. **carry 'on 1.** v. t. fortführen; **~ on |doing sth.|** weiterhin etw. tun. **2.** v. i. weitermachen. **carry 'out** v. t. durchführen; ausführen ⟨Anweisung, Auftrag⟩; vornehmen ⟨Verbesserungen⟩

'carry-cot n. Babytragetasche, die

cart [kɑːt] **1.** n. Wagen, der. **2.** v. t. (sl.) schleppen

cartilage ['kɑːtɪlɪdʒ] n. Knorpel, der

carton ['kɑːtn] n. [Papp]karton, der; (of drink) Tüte, die; (of cream, yoghurt) Becher, der

cartoon [kɑː'tuːn] n. humoristische Zeichnung; (satirical) Karikatur, die; (film) Zeichentrickfilm, der

cartridge ['kɑːtrɪdʒ] n. **a)** (for gun) Patrone, die; **b)** (of film; cassette) Kassette, die

'**cart-wheel** *n.* *(Gymnastics)* Rad, *das;* **turn** *or* **do** ~s radschlagen
carve [kɑ:v] **1.** *v. t.* **a)** tranchieren ⟨*Fleisch, Braten, Hähnchen*⟩; **b)** *(from wood)* schnitzen; *(from stone)* meißeln. **2.** *v. i.* ~ **in wood/stone** in Holz schnitzen/in Stein meißeln. **carving** ['kɑ:vɪŋ] *n.* *(in or from wood)* Schnitzerei, *die; (in or from stone)* Skulptur, *die.* '**carving-knife** *n.* Tranchiermesser, *das*
'**car wash** *n.* Waschanlage, *die*
cascade [kæs'keɪd] *n.* Kaskade, *die*
¹**case** [keɪs] *n.* **a)** *(instance, matter, set of arguments)* Fall, *der;* **it is |not| the ~ that ...:** es trifft [nicht] zu, daß ...; **in ~ ...:** falls ...; **|just| in ~:** für alle Fälle; **in ~ of emergency** im Notfall; **in any ~:** jedenfalls; **in that ~:** in diesem Fall; **b)** *(Med., Police, Soc. Serv., etc.)* Fall, *der;* **c)** *(Law)* Fall, *der; (action)* Verfahren, *das;* **d)** *(Ling.)* Fall, *der;* Kasus, *der (fachspr.)*
²**case** *n.* **a)** Koffer, *der; (brief-~)* [Akten]tasche, *die;* **b)** *(for spectacles, cigarettes)* Etui, *das;* **c)** *(crate)* Kiste, *die;* **d)** |display-|~: Schaukasten, *der*
cash [kæʃ] **1.** *n.* Bargeld, *das;* **pay |in|** ~, **pay** ~ **down** bar zahlen. **2.** *v. t.* einlösen ⟨*Scheck*⟩
cash: ~ **and** '**carry** *n.* cash and carry; *(store)* Cash-and-carry-Laden, *der;* ~**card** *n.* Geldautomatenkarte, *die;* ~ **desk** *n. (Brit.)* Kasse, *die;* ~ **dispenser** *n.* Geldautomat, *der*
cashier [kæ'ʃɪə(r)] *n.* Kassierer, *der/*Kassiererin, *die*
cash: ~**point** *n.* Geldautomat, *der;* ~ **register** *n.* [Registrier]kasse, *die*
casino [kə'si:nəʊ] *n.* Kasino, *das*
cask [kɑ:sk] *n.* Faß, *das*
casket ['kɑ:skɪt] *n.* **a)** Kästchen, *das;* **b)** *(Amer.: coffin)* Sarg, *der*
casserole ['kæsərəʊl] *n.* Schmortopf, *der*
cassette [kə'set, kæ'set] *n.* Kassette, *die.* **cas'sette-deck** *n.* Kassettendeck, *das.* **cas'sette recorder** *n.* Kassettenrecorder, *der*
cast [kɑ:st] **1.** *v. t.,* **cast** **a)** werfen; **b)** *(shape, form)* gießen; **c)** abgeben ⟨*Stimme*⟩. **2.** *n.* **a)** *(Med.)* Gipsverband, *der;* **b)** *(actors)* Besetzung, *die.* **cast** a'**side** *v. t.* beiseite schieben ⟨*Vorschlag*⟩; vergessen ⟨*Sorgen*⟩; fallenlassen ⟨*Hemmungen*⟩. **cast** '**off** *v. i. & t. (Naut.)* losmachen
castanets [kæstə'nets] *n. pl.* Kastagnetten Pl.

'**castaway** *n.* Schiffbrüchige, *der/die*
caste [kɑ:st] *n.* Kaste, *die*
cast '**iron** *n.* Gußeisen, *das*
castle ['kɑ:sl] *n.* Burg, *die; (mansion)* Schloß, *das*
'**cast-offs** *n. pl.* abgelegte Sachen
castor ['kɑ:stə(r)] *n. (wheel)* Rolle, *die*
castor: ~ '**oil** *n.* Rizinusöl, *das;* ~ **sugar** *n.* Raffinade, *die*
castrate [kæ'streɪt] *v. t.* kastrieren. **castration** [kæ'streɪʃn] *n.* Kastration, *die*
casual ['kæʒjʊəl] *adj.* ungezwungen; leger ⟨*Kleidung*⟩; beiläufig ⟨*Bemerkung*⟩; flüchtig ⟨*Bekannter, Bekanntschaft, Blick*⟩; unbekümmert ⟨*Haltung, Einstellung*⟩. '**casually** *adv.* ungezwungen; beiläufig ⟨*bemerken*⟩; flüchtig ⟨*anschauen*⟩; leger ⟨*sich kleiden*⟩
casualty ['kæʒjʊəltɪ] *n.* **a)** *(injured person)* Verletzte, *der/die; (in battle)* Verwundete, *der/die; (dead person)* Tote, *der/die;* **b)** *(hospital department)* Unfallstation, *die*
cat [kæt] *n.* Katze, *die*
catalogue *(Amer.:* **catalog)** ['kætəlɒg] **1.** *n.* Katalog, *der.* **2.** *v. t.* katalogisieren
catalyst ['kætəlɪst] *n.* Katalysator, *der.* **catalytic** [kætə'lɪtɪk] *adj.* ~ **converter** Katalysator, *der*
catapult ['kætəpʌlt] **1.** *n.* Katapult, *das.* **2.** *v. t.* katapultieren
cataract ['kætərækt] *n.* **a)** Katarakt, *der;* **b)** *(Med.)* grauer Star
catarrh [ka'tɑ:(r)] *n.* Katarrh, *der*
catastrophe [kə'tæstrəfɪ] *n.* Katastrophe, *die.* **catastrophic** [kætə'strɒfɪk] *adj.* katastrophal
catch [kætʃ] **1.** *v. t.,* **caught** [kɔ:t] **a)** fangen; ~ **hold of sb./sth.** jmdn./etw. festhalten; *(to stop oneself falling)* sich an jmdm./etw. festhalten; **get sth. caught** *or* ~ **sth. on/in sth.** mit etw. an/in etw. *(Dat.)* hängenbleiben; ~ **one's finger in the door** sich *(Dat.)* den Finger in der Tür einklemmen; **b)** *(travel by)* nehmen; *(be in time for)* [noch] erreichen; **c)** *(surprise)* ~ **sb. doing sth.** jmdn. [dabei] erwischen, wie er etw. tut *(ugs.);* **d)** *(become infected with)* sich *(Dat.)* zuziehen; ~ **sth. from sb.** sich bei jmdm. mit etw. anstecken; ~ **a cold** sich erkälten; ~ **it** *(fig. coll.)* etwas kriegen *(ugs.);* **e)** ~ **sb.'s attention/ interest** jmds. Aufmerksamkeit erregen/jmds. Interesse wecken. **2.** *v. i.,* **caught** **a)** *(begin to burn)* [anfangen zu]

brennen; **b)** *(become hooked up)* hängenbleiben; ⟨*Haar, Faden:*⟩ sich verfangen. **3.** *n.* **a)** *(of ball)* **make a ~:** fangen; **b)** *(amount caught, lit. or fig.)* Fang, *der;* **c)** *(difficulty)* Haken, *der* **(in an + *Dat.*);** **d)** *(of door)* Schnapper, *der.* **catch** 'on *v. i. (coll.)* **a)** *(become popular)* [gut] ankommen *(ugs.);* **b)** *(understand)* kapieren *(ugs.).* **catch** 'up **1.** *v. t.* **~ sb.** up jmdn. einholen. **2.** *v. i.* **~ up** gleichziehen; **~ up on sth.** etw. nachholen
'catching *adj.* ansteckend
'catchy *adj.* eingängig
categorical [kætɪ'gɒrɪkl] *adj.* kategorisch
category ['kætɪgərɪ] *n.* Kategorie, *die*
cater ['keɪtə(r)] *v. i.* **~ for sb./sth.** für jmdn./etw. [die] Speisen und Getränke liefern; *(fig.)* auf jmdn./etw. eingestellt sein. **'caterer** *n.* Lieferant von Speisen und Getränken. **'catering** *n.* **a)** *(trade)* Gastronomie, *die;* **b)** *(service)* Lieferung von Speisen und Getränken
caterpillar ['kætəpɪlə(r)] *n.* Raupe, *die*
cathedral [kə'θiːdrl] *n.* Dom, *der*
Catherine wheel ['kæθrɪn wiːl] *n.* Feuerrad, *das*
Catholic ['kæθəlɪk] **1.** *adj.* katholisch. **2.** *n.* Katholik, *der*/Katholikin, *die.* **Catholicism** [kə'θɒlɪsɪzm] *n.* Katholizismus, *der*
catkin ['kætkɪn] *n. (Bot.)* Kätzchen, *das*
'Cat's-eye, (P) *n. (Brit.: on road)* Bodenrückstrahler, *der*
cattle ['kætl] *n. pl.* Rinder *Pl.*
caught see catch 1, 2
cauldron ['kɔːldrən] *n.* Kessel, *der*
cauliflower ['kɒlɪflaʊə(r)] *n.* Blumenkohl, *der*
cause [kɔːz] **1.** *n.* **a)** Ursache, *die (of* für *od. Gen.);* *(person)* Verursacher, *der*/Verursacherin, *die;* **be the ~ of sth.** etw. verursachen; **b)** *(reason)* Grund, *der;* **~ for sth.** Grund zu etw.; **c)** *(object of support)* Sache, *die;* [in] a **good ~:** [für] eine gute Sache. **2.** *v. t.* verursachen; erregen ⟨*Aufsehen, Ärgernis*⟩; hervorrufen ⟨*Unruhe, Verwirrung*⟩; **~ sb. worry/pain** jmdm. Sorge/Schmerzen bereiten; **~ sb. to do sth.** jmdn. veranlassen, etw. zu tun
causeway ['kɔːzweɪ] *n.* Damm, *der*
caustic ['kɔːstɪk] *adj.* ätzend; *(fig.)* bissig; beißend ⟨*Spott*⟩
caution ['kɔːʃn] **1.** *n.* **a)** Vorsicht, *die;* **b)** *(warning)* Warnung, *die.* **2.** *v. t.*

(warn) warnen; *(warn and reprove)* verwarnen **(for wegen)**
cautious ['kɔːʃəs] *adj.,* **'cautiously** *adv.* vorsichtig
cavalry ['kævəlrɪ] *n.* Kavallerie, *die*
cave [keɪv] *n.* Höhle, *die.* **cave** 'in *v. i.* einbrechen
'caveman *n.* Höhlenbewohner, *der*
cavern ['kævən] *n.* Höhle, *die.* **cavernous** ['kævənəs] *adj.* höhlenartig
caviar[e] ['kævɪɑː(r)] *n.* Kaviar, *der*
cavity ['kævɪtɪ] *n.* Hohlraum, *der; (in tooth)* Loch, *das*
CB *abbr.* **citizen's band** CB
cc [siː'siː] *abbr.* **cubic centimetre(s)** cm³
CD *abbr.* **compact disc** CD
cease [siːs] **1.** *v. i.* aufhören. **2.** *v. t.* **a)** *(stop)* aufhören; **b)** *(end)* aufhören mit; einstellen ⟨*Bemühungen*⟩. **'cease-fire** *n.* Waffenruhe, *die*
cedar ['siːdə(r)] *n.* Zeder, *die*
ceiling ['siːlɪŋ] *n.* **a)** Decke, *die;* **b)** *(upper limit)* Maximum, *das*
celebrate ['selɪbreɪt] *v. t. & i.* feiern. **'celebrated** *adj.* berühmt. **celebration** [selɪ'breɪʃn] *n.* Feier, *die.* **celebrity** [sɪ'lebrɪtɪ] *n.* Berühmtheit, *die*
celery ['selərɪ] *n.* Sellerie, *der od. die*
celibate ['selɪbət] *adj.* zölibatär *(Rel.);* ehelos
cell [sel] *n.* Zelle, *die*
cellar ['selə(r)] *n.* Keller, *der*
cellist ['tʃelɪst] *n.* Cellist, *der*/Cellistin, *die*
cello ['tʃeləʊ] *n., pl.* **~s** Cello, *das*
Cellophane, (P) ['seləfeɪn] *n.* Cellophan ⓦ, *das*
Celsius ['selsɪəs] *adj.* Celsius
cement [sɪ'ment] **1.** *n.* Zement, *der.* **2.** *v. t.* zementieren; *(stick together)* zusammenkleben. **ce'ment-mixer** *n.* Betonmischmaschine, *die*
cemetery ['semɪtərɪ] *n.* Friedhof, *der*
censor ['sensə(r)] **1.** *n.* Zensor, *der.* **2.** *v. t.* zensieren. **'censorship** *n.* Zensur, *die*
censure ['senʃə(r)] *v. t.* tadeln
census ['sensəs] *n.* Volkszählung, *die*
cent [sent] *n.* Cent, *der*
centenary [sen'tiːnərɪ] *adj. & n.* **~ |celebrations]** Hundertjahrfeier, *die*
center *(Amer.)* see centre
centigrade ['sentɪgreɪd] see Celsius
centimetre *(Brit.; Amer.:* **centimeter)** ['sentɪmiːtə(r)] *n.* Zentimeter, *der*
centipede ['sentɪpiːd] *n.* Tausendfüßler, *der*
central ['sentrl] *adj.* zentral

Central: ~ **A'merica** *pr. n.* Mittel-
amerika *(das);* ~ **'Europe** *pr. n.* Mit-
teleuropa *(das);* ~ **Euro'pean** *adj.*
mitteleuropäisch; **c~ 'heating** *n.*
Zentralheizung, *die*
centralize ['sentrəlaız] *v. t.* zentrali-
sieren
central reser'vation *n. (Brit.)* Mittelstreifen, *der*
centre ['sentə(r)] *(Brit.)* **1.** *n.* **a)** Mitte,
die; (of circle) Mittelpunkt, *der;* **b)** *(of
area, city)* Zentrum, *das.* **2.** *adj.* mittler... **3.** *v. i.* ~ **on sth.** sich auf etw.
(Akk.) konzentrieren; ~ **|a|round sth.**
sich um etw. drehen. **4.** *v. t.* **a)** in der
Mitte anbringen; **b)** *(concentrate)* be
~**d |a|round sth.** etw. zum Mittelpunkt
haben; ~ **sth. on sth.** etw. auf etw.
(Akk.) konzentrieren. **centre-'forward** *n.* Mittelstürmer, *der*
centrifugal [sentrɪ'fjuːgl] *adj.* ~ **force**
Zentrifugalkraft, *die;* Fliehkraft, *die*
century ['sentʃərɪ] *n. (hundred-year
period from a year ..00)* Jahrhundert,
das; (hundred years) hundert Jahre
ceramic [sɪ'ræmɪk] *adj.* keramisch
cereal ['sɪərɪəl] *n.* Getreide, *das;
(breakfast dish)* Getreideflocken *Pl.*
ceremonial [serɪ'məʊnɪəl] **1.** *adj.* feierlich; *(prescribed for ceremony)* zeremoniell. **2.** *n.* Zeremoniell, *das*
ceremony ['serɪmənɪ] *n.* Feier, *die;
(formal act)* Zeremonie, *die*
certain ['sɜːtn, 'sɜːtɪn] *adj.* **a)** *(settled,
definite)* bestimmt; **b) be** ~ **to do sth.**
etw. bestimmt tun; **c)** *(confident, sure
to happen)* sicher; **d)** *(indisputable)* unbestreitbar; **e) a** ~ **Mr Smith** ein gewisser Herr Smith; **to a** ~ **extent** in gewisser Weise. **'certainly** *adv.* **a)** *(admittedly)* sicher[lich]; *(definitely)* bestimmt; **b)** *(in answer)* [aber] sicher;
|most| ~ **'not!** auf [gar] keinen Fall!
certainty ['sɜːtntɪ, 'sɜːtɪntɪ] *n.* **a) be a**
~**:** sicher sein; **b)** *(absolute conviction)*
Gewißheit, *die*
certificate [sə'tɪfɪkət] *n.* Urkunde,
die; (of action performed) Schein, *der*
certify ['sɜːtɪfaɪ] *v. t.* bescheinigen; bestätigen; **this is to** ~ **that ...:** hiermit
wird bescheinigt *od.* bestätigt, daß ...
cf. *abbr.* **compare** vgl.
chafe [tʃeɪf] *v. t.* wund scheuern
chaff [tʃɑːf] *n.* Spreu, *die*
chaffinch ['tʃæfɪntʃ] *n.* Buchfink, *der*
chagrin ['ʃægrɪn] *n.* Kummer, *der*
chain [tʃeɪn] **1.** *n.* Kette, *die;* ~ **of
shops/hotels** Laden-/Hotelkette, *die.*
2. *v. t.* [an]ketten **(to an +** *Akk.***)**

chain: ~ **re'action** *n.* Kettenreakti-
on, *die;* ~**-saw** *n.* Kettensäge, *die;*
~**-smoker** *n.* Kettenraucher, *der/*
-raucherin, *die;* ~ **store** Kettenladen,
der
chair [tʃeə(r)] **1.** *n.* **a)** Stuhl, *der;
(arm~, easy ~)* Sessel, *der;* **b)** *(profes-
sorship)* Lehrstuhl, *der;* **c)** *(at meeting)*
Vorsitz, *der.* **2.** *v. t.* den Vorsitz haben
bei
chair: ~**-back** *n.* Rückenlehne, *die;*
~**-lift** *n.* Sessellift, *der;* ~**man** ['tʃeə-
mən] *n., pl.* ~**men** ['tʃeəmən] Vorsitzende, *der/die*
chalet ['ʃæleɪ] *n.* Chalet, *das*
chalk [tʃɔːk] **1.** *n.* Kreide, *die.* **2.** *v. t.*
mit Kreide schreiben/malen *usw.*
challenge ['tʃælɪndʒ] **1.** *n.* Herausforderung, *die.* **2.** *v. t.* **a)** *(to contest etc.)*
herausfordern; **b)** *(fig.)* auffordern;
(question) in Frage stellen. **'chal-
lenger** *n.* Herausforderer, *der/*Her-
ausforderin, *die.* **challenging** ['tʃæ-
lɪndʒɪŋ] *adj.* herausfordernd; fesselnd
⟨*Problem*⟩; anspruchsvoll ⟨*Arbeit*⟩
chamber ['tʃeɪmbə(r)] *n.* Kammer, *die*
chamber: ~**maid** *n.* Zimmermäd-
chen, *das;* ~ **music** *n.* Kammermu-
sik, *die;* ~**-pot** *n.* Nachttopf, *der*
chameleon [kə'miːljən] *n.* Chamäle-
on
chamois ['ʃæmwɑː] *n.* **a)** Gemse, *die;*
b) ['ʃæmɪ] ~**|-leather|** Chamois[leder],
das
champagne [ʃæm'peɪn] *n.* Sekt, *der;
(from Champagne)* Champagner, *der*
champion ['tʃæmpɪən] **1.** *n.* **a)** *(defender)* Verfechter, *der/*Verfechterin,
die; **b)** *(Sport)* Meister, *der/*Meisterin,
die. **2.** *v. t.* verfechten ⟨*Sache*⟩; sich
einsetzen für ⟨*Person*⟩. **'championship** *n.* Meisterschaft, *die*
chance [tʃɑːns] **1.** *n.* **a)** *(fortune, trick
of fate)* Zufall, *der; attrib.* zufällig; ~
encounter Zufallsbegegnung, *die;*
game of ~**:** Glücksspiel, *das;* **by** ~**:** zufällig; **take a** ~**:** es riskieren; **the** ~**s
are that ...:** es ist wahrscheinlich,
daß ...; **by |any|** ~**, by some** ~ **or other**
zufällig; **b)** *(opportunity, possibility)*
Chance, *die;* **get a/the** ~ **to do sth.** ei-
ne/die Gelegenheit haben, etw. zu
tun. **2.** *v. t.* riskieren
chancellor ['tʃɑːnsələ(r)] *n.* Kanzler,
der; **C~ of the Exchequer** *(Brit.)*
Schatzkanzler, *der*
chandelier [ʃændə'lɪə(r)] *n.* Kron-
leuchter, *der*
change [tʃeɪndʒ] **1.** *n.* **a)** Veränderu-

rung, *die;* Änderung, *die; (of job, sur-roundings, government, etc.)* Wechsel, *der;* b) *(for the sake of variety)* Abwechslung, *die;* for a ~: zur Abwechslung; c) *(money)* Wechselgeld, *das;* [loose *or* small] ~: Kleingeld, *das;* [here is] 15 marks ~: 15 Mark zurück; keep the ~: [es] stimmt so. 2. *v. t.* a) *(switch)* wechseln; auswechseln ⟨*Glühbirne, Batterie*⟩; ~ one's clothes sich umziehen; ~ one's address/name seine Anschrift/seinen Namen ändern; ~ trains/buses umsteigen; b) *(transform)* verwandeln (into *in* + *Akk.*); *(alter)* ändern; c) *(exchange)* eintauschen (for *für*); wechseln ⟨*Geld*⟩. 3. *v. i.* a) *(alter)* sich ändern; ⟨*Person, Land:*⟩ sich verändern; b) *(into something else)* sich verwandeln; c) *(put on other clothes)* sich umziehen.

change 'over *v. i.* ~ over from sth. to sth. von etw. zu etw. übergehen

changeable ['tʃeɪndʒəbl] *adj.* veränderlich

'changing room *n. (Brit.)* Umkleideraum, *der*

channel ['tʃænl] 1. *n. (also Telev., Radio)* Kanal, *der;* the C~ *(Brit.)* der [Ärmel]kanal. 2. *v. t. (fig.)* lenken. 'Channel Islands *pr. n. pl.* Kanalinseln *Pl.*

chant [tʃɑːnt] 1. *v. t.* skandieren; *(Eccl.)* singen. 2. *v. i.* Sprechchöre anstimmen; *(Eccl.)* singen. 3. *n.* Sprechchor, *der; (Eccl.)* Gesang, *der*

chaos ['keɪɒs] *n.* Chaos, *das.* chaotic [keɪ'ɒtɪk] *adj.* chaotisch

¹chap [tʃæp] *n. (Brit. coll.)* Bursche, *der;* Kerl, *der*

²chap *v. t.,* -pp- aufplatzen lassen

chapel ['tʃæpl] *n.* Kapelle, *die*

chaperon ['ʃæpərəʊn] 1. *n.* Anstandsdame, *die.* 2. *v. t.* beaufsichtigen

chaplain ['tʃæplɪn] *n.* Kaplan, *der*

chapter ['tʃæptə(r)] *n.* Kapitel, *das*

char [tʃɑː(r)] *v. t. & i.,* -rr- verkohlen

character ['kærɪktə(r)] *n.* a) Charakter, *der;* b) *(in novel etc.)* Figur, *die;* c) *(coll.: extraordinary person)* Original, *das;* d) *(symbol)* Zeichen, *das.* characteristic [kærɪktə'rɪstɪk] 1. *adj.* charakteristisch (of *für*). 2. *n.* charakteristisches Merkmal. characterize ['kærɪktəraɪz] *v. t.* charakterisieren

charade [ʃə'rɑːd] *n.* Scharade, *die; (fig.)* Farce, *die*

charcoal ['tʃɑːkəʊl] *n.* Holzkohle, *die*

charge [tʃɑːdʒ] 1. *n.* a) *(price)* Preis, *der; (for services)* Gebühr, *die;* b) be in

~ of sth. für etw. die Verantwortung haben; take ~: die Verantwortung übernehmen; c) *(Law: accusation)* Anklage, *die;* d) *(attack)* Angriff, *der;* e) *(of explosives, electricity)* Ladung, *die.* 2. *v. t.* a) ~ sb. sth., ~ sth. to sb. jmdm. etw. berechnen; b) *(Law: accuse)* anklagen (with *wegen*); c) *(Electr.)* [auf]laden ⟨*Batterie*⟩; d) *(rush at)* angreifen. 3. *v. i.* a) *(attack)* angreifen; b) *(coll.: hurry)* sausen

charitable ['tʃærɪtəbl] *adj.* a) wohltätig; b) *(lenient)* großzügig

charity ['tʃærɪtɪ] *n.* a) Wohltätigkeit, *die;* b) *(organization)* wohltätige Organisation

charlady ['tʃɑːleɪdɪ] *n. (Brit.)* Putzfrau, *die*

charlatan ['ʃɑːlətən] *n.* Scharlatan, *der*

charm [tʃɑːm] 1. *n.* a) *(act)* Zauber, *der;* b) *(talisman)* Talisman, *der;* c) *(attractiveness)* Reiz, *der; (of person)* Charme, *der.* 2. *v. t.* bezaubern. 'charming *adj.* bezaubernd

chart [tʃɑːt] 1. *n.* a) *(map)* Karte, *die;* b) *(graph etc.)* Schaubild, *das;* c) the ~s die Hitliste. 2. *v. t. (fig.: describe)* schildern

charter ['tʃɑːtə(r)] 1. *n.* a) Charta, *die;* b) on ~ gechartert. 2. *v. t.* chartern ⟨*Schiff, Flugzeug*⟩. chartered accountant *n. (Brit.)* Wirtschaftsprüfer, *der/*-prüferin, *die*

'charter flight *n.* Charterflug, *der*

charwoman ['tʃɑːwʊmən] *n.* Putzfrau, *die*

chase [tʃeɪs] 1. *n.* Verfolgungsjagd, *die.* 2. *v. t. (pursue)* jagen; ~ sth. *(fig.)* einer Sache *(Dat.)* nachjagen. 3. *v. i.* ~ after sb./sth. hinter jmdm./etw. herjagen. chase 'up *v. t. (coll.)* ausfindig machen

chasm ['kæzm] *n.* Kluft, *die*

chassis ['ʃæsɪ] *n., pl. same* ['ʃæsɪz] Chassis, *das;* Fahrgestell, *das*

chaste [tʃeɪst] *adj.* keusch

chastening ['tʃeɪsənɪŋ] *adj.* ernüchternd

chastise [tʃæ'staɪz] *v. t.* züchtigen

chastity ['tʃæstɪtɪ] *n.* Keuschheit, *die*

chat [tʃæt] 1. *n.* Schwätzchen, *das.* 2. *v. i.,* -tt- plaudern; ~ with *or* to sb. about sth. mit jmdm. von etw. plaudern. chat 'up *v. t. (Brit. coll.)* anmachen *(ugs.)*

'chat show *n.* Talk-Show, *die*

chattels ['tʃætəlz] *n. pl.* bewegliche Habe *(geh.)*

chatter ['tʃætə(r)] **1.** *v. i.* **a)** schwatzen; **b)** ⟨*Zähne:*⟩ klappern. **2.** *n.* Schwatzen, *das.* '**chatterbox** *n.* Quasselstrippe, *die (ugs.)*

chatty ['tʃætɪ] *adj.* gesprächig

chauffeur ['ʃəʊfə(r)] **1.** *n.* Fahrer, *der;* Chauffeur, *der.* **2.** *v. t.* fahren

chauvinist ['ʃəʊvɪnɪst] *n.* Chauvinist, *der*/Chauvinistin, *die.* **chauvinistic** [ʃəʊvɪˈnɪstɪk] *adj.* chauvinistisch

cheap [tʃiːp] *adj., adv.* billig. **cheapen** ['tʃiːpn] *v. t. (fig.)* herabsetzen. '**cheaply** *adv.* billig

cheat [tʃiːt] **1.** *n.* Schwindler, *der*/Schwindlerin, *die.* **2.** *v. t. & i.* betrügen

¹**check** [tʃek] **1.** *n.* **a)** Kontrolle, *die;* **make/keep a ~ on** kontrollieren; **b)** *(Amer.: bill)* Rechnung, *die.* **2.** *v. t.* **a)** *(restrain)* unter Kontrolle halten; **b)** *(examine)* nachprüfen; kontrollieren ⟨*Fahrkarte*⟩; **c)** *(stop)* aufhalten. **3.** *v. i.* **~ on sth.** etw. überprüfen; **~ with sb.** bei jmdm. nachfragen. **check 'in** *v. t. & i. (at airport)* einchecken. **check 'out 1.** *v. t.* überprüfen. **2.** *v. i.* abreisen. **check 'up** *v. i.* **~ up [on]** überprüfen

²**check** *n. (pattern)* Karo, *das*

checkers ['tʃekəz] *(Amer.) see* **draughts**

check: ~-in *n.* Abfertigung, *die;* **~-list** *n.* Checkliste, *die;* **~-mate 1.** *n.* [Schach]matt, *das;* **2.** *int.* [schach]matt; **~-out [desk]** *n.* Kasse, *die;* **~-point** *n.* Kontrollpunkt, *der;* **~-up** *n. (Med.)* Untersuchung, *die*

cheek [tʃiːk] *n.* **a)** Backe, *die;* Wange, *die (geh.);* **b)** *(impertinence)* Frechheit, *die.* '**cheekily** *adv.,* '**cheeky** *adj.* frech

cheep [tʃiːp] **1.** *v. i.* piep[s]en. **2.** *n.* Piep[s]en, *das*

cheer [tʃɪə(r)] **1.** *n.* **a)** *(applause)* Beifallsruf, *der;* **b)** *in pl. (Brit. coll.)* prost! **2.** *v. t.* **a)** *(applaud)* **~ sth./sb.** etw. bejubeln/jmdm. zujubeln; **b)** *(gladden)* aufmuntern. **3.** *v. i.* jubeln. **cheer 'on** *v. t.* anfeuern ⟨*Sportler*⟩. **cheer 'up 1.** *v. t.* aufheitern. **2.** *v. i.* bessere Laune bekommen; **~ up!** Kopf hoch!

cheerful [[ˈtʃɪəfl] *adj. (in good spirits)* fröhlich; *(bright, pleasant)* heiter. '**cheerfully** *adv.* vergnügt

'**cheering 1.** *adj.* fröhlich stimmend. **2.** *n.* Jubeln, *das*

cheerio [tʃɪərɪˈəʊ] *int. (Brit. coll.)* tschüs *(ugs.)*

'**cheery** *adj.* fröhlich

cheese [tʃiːz] *n.* Käse, *der.* '**cheeseboard** *n.* Käseplatte, *die.* '**cheesecake** *n.* Käsetorte, *die*

cheetah ['tʃiːtə] *n.* Gepard, *der*

chef [ʃef] *n.* Küchenchef, *der; (as profession)* Koch, *der*

chemical ['kemɪkl] **1.** *adj.* chemisch. **2.** *n.* Chemikalie, *die*

chemist ['kemɪst] *n.* **a)** *(scientist)* Chemiker, *der*/Chemikerin, *die;* **b)** *(Brit.: pharmacist)* Drogist, *der*/Drogistin, *die;* **~'s [shop]**Drogerie, *die.* **chemistry** ['kemɪstrɪ] *n.* Chemie, *die*

cheque [tʃek] *n.* Scheck, *der;* **pay by ~:** mit [einem] Scheck bezahlen. '**cheque-book** *n.* Scheckbuch, *das.* '**cheque card** *n.* Scheckkarte, *die*

cherish ['tʃerɪʃ] *v. t.* hegen ⟨*Hoffnung, Gefühl*⟩; in Ehren halten ⟨*[Erinnerungs]gegenstand*⟩

cherry ['tʃerɪ] *n.* Kirsche, *die*

chess [tʃes] *n., no art.* das Schach[spiel]

chess: ~-board *n.* Schachbrett, *das;* **~-man** *n.* Schachfigur, *die;* **~-player** *n.* Schachspieler, *der*/-spielerin, *die*

chest [tʃest] *n.* **a)** Kiste, *die;* **b)** *(Anat.)* Brust, *die;* **get sth. off one's ~** *(fig. coll.)* sich *(Dat.)* etw. von der Seele reden; **c)** **~ [measurement]** Brustumfang, *der*

chestnut ['tʃesnʌt] **1.** *n.* **a)** Kastanie, *die;* **b)** *(colour)* Kastanienbraun, *das.* **2.** *adj. (colour)* **~[-brown]** kastanienbraun. '**chestnut-tree** *n.* Kastanie, *die*

chest of 'drawers *n.* Kommode, *die*

chew [tʃuː] *v. t. & i.* kauen. '**chewing-gum** *n.* Kaugummi, *der od. das*

chic [ʃiːk] *adj.* schick; elegant

chick [tʃɪk] *n.* **a)** Küken, *das;* **b)** *(sl.: young woman)* Biene, *die (ugs.)*

chicken ['tʃɪkɪn] **1.** *n.* **a)** Huhn, *das; (grilled, roasted)* Hähnchen, *das;* **b)** *(coll.: coward)* Angsthase, *der.* **2.** *adj. (coll.)* feig[e]. **3.** *v. i.* **~ out** *(sl.)* kneifen '**chicken-pox** [~pɒks] *n.* Windpocken *Pl.*

chicory ['tʃɪkərɪ] *n. (plant)* Chicorée, *der od. die; (for coffee)* Zichorie, *die*

chief [tʃiːf] **1.** *n.* **a)** Oberhaupt, *das; (of tribe)* Häuptling, *der;* **b)** *(of department)* Leiter, *der;* **~ of police** Polizeipräsident, *der.* **2.** *adj., usu. attrib.* **a)** Haupt-; **b)** *(leading)* führend. '**chiefly** *adv.* hauptsächlich

chieftain ['tʃiːftən] *n.* Stammesführer, *der*

chilblain ['tʃɪlbleɪn] n. Frostbeule, die
child [tʃaɪld] n., pl. ~ren ['tʃɪldrən] Kind, das. **'childbirth** n. Geburt, die. **'childhood** n. Kindheit, die
childish ['tʃaɪldɪʃ] adj., **'childishly** adv. kindisch. **'childishness** n. (behaviour) kindisches Benehmen
child: ~less adj. kinderlos; ~like adj. kindlich; ~-minder ['~maɪndə(r)] n. (Brit.) Tagesmutter, die
children pl. of **child**
'child's play n. (fig.) ein Kinderspiel
Chile ['tʃɪlɪ] n. Chile (das)
chill [tʃɪl] 1. n. Kühle, die; (illness) Erkältung, die. 2. v. t. kühlen
chilli ['tʃɪlɪ] n., pl. ~es Chili, der
'chilly adj. kühl; **I am rather** ~: mir ist ziemlich kühl ·
chime [tʃaɪm] 1. n. Geläute, das. 2. v. i. läuten; ⟨Turmuhr:⟩ schlagen
chimney ['tʃɪmnɪ] n. Schornstein, der. **'chimney-sweep** n. Schornsteinfeger, der
chimpanzee [tʃɪmpən'ziː] n. Schimpanse, der
chin [tʃɪn] n. Kinn, das
China ['tʃaɪnə] pr. n. China (das)
china n. Porzellan, das; (crockery) Geschirr, das
Chinese [tʃaɪ'niːz] 1. adj. chinesisch. 2. n. a) pl. same (person) Chinese, der/Chinesin, die; b) (language) Chinesisch, das; see also **English 2 a**
chink n. (gap) Spalt, der
chip [tʃɪp] 1. n. a) Splitter, der; b) in pl. (Brit.: potato~s) Pommes frites Pl.; c) (Gambling) Chip, der. 2. v. t., -pp- anschlagen. **chip 'in** (coll.) 1. v. i. a) (interrupt) sich einmischen; b) (contribute money) etwas beisteuern. 2. v. t. (contribute) beisteuern
'chipboard n. Spanplatte, die
chipmunk ['tʃɪpmʌŋk] n. Chipmunk, das
chiropodist [kɪ'rɒpədɪst] n. Fußpfleger, der/-pflegerin, die
chiropody [kɪ'rɒpədɪ] n. Fußpflege, die
chirp [tʃɜːp] 1. v. i. zwitschern; ⟨Grille:⟩ zirpen. 2. n. Zwitschern, das; Zirpen, das
chisel ['tʃɪzl] 1. n. Meißel, der; (for wood) Stemmeisen, das. 2. v. t., (Brit.) -ll- meißeln; (in wood) hauen
chit [tʃɪt] n. Notiz, die
chit-chat ['tʃɪttʃæt] n. Plauderei, die
chivalrous ['ʃɪvlrəs] adj. ritterlich. **chivalry** ['ʃɪvlrɪ] n. Ritterlichkeit, die
chives [tʃaɪvz] n. Schnittlauch, der

chloride ['klɔːraɪd] n. Chlorid, das
chlorine ['klɔːriːn] n. Chlor, das
chock [tʃɒk] n. Bremsklotz, der. **'chock-a-block** pred adj. vollgepfropft
chocolate ['tʃɒklət] n. Schokolade, die
choice [tʃɔɪs] 1. n. a) Wahl, die; **from** ~: freiwillig; b) (variety) Auswahl, die. 2. adj. ausgewählt
choir [kwaɪə(r)] n. Chor, der. **'choirboy** n. Chorknabe, der
choke [tʃəʊk] 1. v. t. a) ersticken; b) (block up) verstopfen. 2. v. i. (temporarily) keine Luft [mehr] bekommen; (permanently) ersticken (**on an** + Dat.). 3. n. (Motor Veh.) Choke, der
cholera ['kɒlərə] n. Cholera, die
cholesterol [kə'lestərɒl] n. Cholesterin, das
choose [tʃuːz] 1. v. t., **chose** [tʃəʊz], **chosen** ['tʃəʊzn] a) wählen; b) (decide) ~/~ **not to do sth.** sich dafür/dagegen entscheiden, etw. zu tun. 2. v. i., **chose, chosen** wählen (**between** zwischen); ~ **from sth.** aus etw./(from several) unter etw. (Dat.) [aus]wählen. **choos[e]y** ['tʃuːzɪ] adj. wählerisch
chop [tʃɒp] 1. n. a) Hieb, der; b) (of meat) Kotelett, das; c) **get the** ~ (coll.: be dismissed) rausgeworfen werden (ugs.). 2. v. t., -pp- hacken ⟨Holz⟩; kleinschneiden ⟨Fleisch, Gemüse⟩. **'chopper** n. (axe) Beil, das; (cleaver) Hackbeil, das
'choppy adj. bewegt
choral ['kɔːrl] adj. Chor-
chord [kɔːd] n. (Mus.) Akkord, der
chore [tʃɔː(r)] n. [lästige] Routinearbeit
chortle ['tʃɔːtl] 1. v. i. vor Lachen glucksen. 2. n. Glucksen, das
chorus ['kɔːrəs] n. a) Chor, der; b) (of song) Chorus, der
chose, chosen see **choose**
chow [tʃaʊ] n. (Amer. sl.: food) Futter, das (salopp)
Christ [kraɪst] n. Christus (der)
christen ['krɪsn] v. t. taufen. **'christening** n. Taufe, die
Christian ['krɪstjən] 1. adj. christlich. 2. n. Christ, der/Christin, die. **Christianity** [krɪstɪ'ænɪtɪ] n. das Christentum
'Christian name n. Vorname, der
Christmas ['krɪsməs] n. Weihnachten, das od. Pl.; **merry** or **happy** ~: frohe od. fröhliche Weihnachten; **at** ~: [zu] Weihnachten

Christmas: ~ '**Day** *n.* erster Weihnachtsfeiertag; ~ '**Eve** *n.* Heiligabend, *der;* ~ **tree** *n.* Weihnachtsbaum, *der*

chrome [krəʊm], **chromium** ['krəʊmɪəm] *ns.* Chrom, *das.* '**chromium-plated** *adj.* verchromt

chronic ['krɒnɪk] *adj.* chronisch

chronicle ['krɒnɪkl] *n.* Chronik, *die*

chronological [krɒnə'lɒdʒɪkl] *adj.* chronologisch

chrysalis ['krɪsəlɪs] *n., pl.* ~es Puppe, *die*

chrysanthemum [krɪ'sænθɪməm] *n.* Chrysantheme, *die*

chubby ['tʃʌbɪ] *adj.* pummelig

chuck [tʃʌk] *v. t. (coll.)* schmeißen *(ugs.).* **chuck 'away, chuck 'out** *v. t. (coll.)* wegschmeißen *(ugs.)*

chuckle ['tʃʌkl] **1.** *v. i.* leise [vor sich hin] lachen (**at** über + *Akk.*). **2.** *n.* leises, glucksendes Lachen

chug [tʃʌg] *v. i.,* -gg- tuckern

chum [tʃʌm] *n. (coll.)* Kumpel, *der (salopp)*

chunk [tʃʌŋk] *n.* dickes Stück. '**chunky** *adj.* **a)** *(small and sturdy)* stämmig; **b)** dick *(Pullover)*

church [tʃɜːtʃ] *n.* Kirche, *die;* go to ~: in die Kirche gehen; **the C~ of England** die Kirche von England. '**churchyard** *n.* Friedhof, *der (bei einer Kirche)*

churlish ['tʃɜːlɪʃ] *adj. (ill-bred)* ungehobelt; *(surly)* griesgrämig

churn [tʃɜːn] *n. (Brit.)* Butterfaß, *das.* **churn 'out** *v. t.* massenweise produzieren *(ugs.)*

chute [ʃuːt] *n.* Schütte, *die; (for persons)* Rutsche, *die*

CIA *abbr. (Amer.)* **Central Intelligence Agency** CIA, *der od. die*

CID *abbr. (Brit.)* **Criminal Investigation Department** C.I.D.; **the** ~: die Kripo

cider ['saɪdə(r)] *n.* ≈ Apfelwein, *der*

cigar [sɪ'gɑː(r)] *n.* Zigarre, *die*

cigarette [sɪgə'ret] *n.* Zigarette, *die*

cigarette: ~-**end** *n.* Zigarettenstummel, *der;* ~-**lighter** *n.* Feuerzeug, *das;* ~-**packet** *n.* Zigarettenschachtel, *die*

cinders ['sɪndəz] *n. pl.* Asche, *die*

cine ['sɪnɪ]: ~ **camera** *n.* Filmkamera, *die;* ~ **film** *n.* Schmalfilm, *der*

cinema ['sɪnɪmə] *n.* Kino, *das;* go to the ~: ins Kino gehen

cinnamon ['sɪnəmən] *n.* Zimt, *der*

cipher ['saɪfə(r)] *n.* Geheimschrift, *die;* **in** ~: chiffriert

circle ['sɜːkl] **1.** *n.* Kreis, *der.* **2.** *v. i.* kreisen. **3.** *v. t.* umkreisen

circuit ['sɜːkɪt] *n.* **a)** *(Electr.)* Schaltung, *die;* **b)** *(Motor-racing)* Rundkurs, *der*

circular ['sɜːkjʊlə(r)] **1.** *adj. (round)* kreisförmig. **2.** *n.* Rundschreiben, *das*

circulate ['sɜːkjʊleɪt] **1.** *v. i.* zirkulieren; ⟨*Personen, Wein usw.:*⟩ herumgehen *(ugs.).* **2.** *v. t.* in Umlauf setzen; herumgehen lassen ⟨*Buch, Bericht*⟩ (**around** in + *Dat.*). **circulation** [sɜːkjʊ'leɪʃn] *n.* **a)** *(Physiol.)* Kreislauf, *der;* **poor** ~: Kreislaufstörungen *Pl.;* **b)** *(copies sold)* verkaufte Auflage

circumcise ['sɜːkəmsaɪz] *v. t.* beschneiden

circumference [sə'kʌmfərəns] *n.* Umfang, *der*

circumstances ['sɜːkəmstənsɪz] *n. pl.* Umstände; **in** *or* **under the** ~: unter diesen·Umständen; **under no** ~: unter keinen Umständen

circus ['sɜːkəs] *n.* Zirkus, *der*

CIS *abbr.* **Commonwealth of Independent States** GUS

cissy ['sɪsɪ] *see* **sissy**

cistern ['sɪstən] *n.* Wasserkasten, *der; (in roof)* Wasserbehälter, *der*

citation [saɪ'teɪʃn] *n.* Zitat, *das*

cite [saɪt] *v. t. (quote)* zitieren; anführen ⟨*Beispiel*⟩

citizen ['sɪtɪzən] *n.* **a)** *(of town, city)* Bürger, *der*/Bürgerin, *die;* **b)** *(of state)* [Staats]bürger, *der*/-bürgerin, *die.* '**citizenship** *n.* Staatsbürgerschaft, *die*

citrus ['sɪtrəs] *n.* ~ |**fruit**| Zitrusfrucht, *die*

city ['sɪtɪ] *n.* [Groß]stadt, *die.* **city 'centre** *n.* Stadtzentrum, *das*

civic ['sɪvɪk] *adj.* [staats]bürgerlich; ~ **centre** Verwaltungszentrum der Stadt

civil ['sɪvl] *adj.* **a)** *(not military)* zivil; **b)** *(polite, obliging)* höflich; **c)** *(Law)* Zivil-. **civil engi'neer** *n.* Bauingenieur, *der*/-ingenieurin, *die.* **civil engi'neering** *n.* Hoch- und Tiefbau, *der*

civilian [sɪ'vɪljən] **1.** *n.* Zivilist, *der.* **2.** *adj.* Zivil-

civility [sɪ'vɪlɪtɪ] *n.* Höflichkeit, *die*

civilization [sɪvɪlaɪ'zeɪʃn] *n.* Zivilisation, *die*

civilized ['sɪvɪlaɪzd] *adj.* zivilisiert

civil: ~ '**law** *n.* Zivilrecht, *das;* ~ '**rights** *n. pl.* Bürgerrechte *Pl.;* ~ '**servant** *n.* ≈ Staatsbeamte, *der*/-beamtin, *die;* C~ '**Service** *n.* öffentlicher Dienst; ~ '**war** *n.* Bürgerkrieg, *der*

clad [klæd] *adj. (arch./literary)* gekleidet (**in** in + *Akk.*)

claim [kleɪm] **1.** *v. t.* **a)** beanspruchen ⟨*Thron, Gebiete*⟩; fordern ⟨*Lohnerhöhung, Schadenersatz*⟩; beantragen ⟨*Sozialhilfe usw.*⟩; **b)** *(assert)* behaupten. **2.** *v. i. (Insurance)* Ansprüche geltend machen. **3.** *n.* Anspruch, *der* (**to** auf + *Akk.*); **lay** ~ **to** sth. auf etw. *(Akk.)* Anspruch erheben. **claimant** ['kleɪmənt] *n.* Antragsteller, *der*/-stellerin, *die*

clairvoyant [kleə'vɔɪənt] **1.** *n.* Hellseher, *der*/Hellseherin, *die.* **2.** *adj.* hellseherisch

clam [klæm] **1.** *n.* Klaffmuschel, *die.* **2.** *v. i.*, **-mm-:** ~ **up** *(coll.)* den Mund nicht [mehr] aufmachen

clamber ['klæmbə(r)] *v. i.* klettern

clammy ['klæmɪ] *adj.* feucht; kalt und schweißig ⟨*Haut*⟩; klamm ⟨*Kleidung*⟩

clamour *(Brit.; Amer.:* **clamor**) ['klæmə(r)] **1.** *n. (noise, shouting)* Lärm, *der;* lautes Geschrei. **2.** *v. i.* ~ **for** sth. nach etw. schreien

clamp [klæmp] **1.** *n.* Klammer, *die; (Woodw.)* Schraubzwinge, *die.* **2.** *v. t.* klemmen; einspannen ⟨*Werkstück*⟩. **3.** *v. i. (fig.)* ~ **down on** sb./sth. gegen jmdn./etw. rigoros vorgehen

clan [klæn] *n.* Sippe, *die; (of Scottish Highlanders)* Clan, *der*

clandestine [klæn'destɪn] *adj.* heimlich

clang [klæŋ] **1.** *n. (of bell)* Läuten, *das; (of hammer)* Klingen, *das.* **2.** *v. i.* ⟨*Glocke:*⟩läuten; ⟨*Hammer:*⟩klingen

clap [klæp] **1.** *n. a)* Klatschen, *das;* ~ **of thunder** Donnerschlag, *der.* **2.** *v. i.*, **-pp-** klatschen. **3.** *v. t.*, **-pp-:** ~ **one's hands** in die Hände klatschen; ~ sth. etw. beklatschen; ~ **sb.** jmdm. Beifall klatschen. **'clapping** *n.* Applaus, *der*

claret ['klærət] **1.** *n.* roter Bordeauxwein. **2.** *adj.* weinrot

clarification [klærɪfɪ'keɪʃn] *n.* Klarstellung, *die*

clarify ['klærɪfaɪ] *v. t.* klären ⟨*Situation usw.*⟩; *(by explanation)* klarstellen; erläutern ⟨*Bedeutung, Aussage*⟩

clarinet [klærɪ'net] *n.* Klarinette, *die*

clarity ['klærɪtɪ] *n.* Klarheit, *die*

clash [klæʃ] **1.** *v. i. a)* scheppern *(ugs.);* **b)** *(meet in conflict)* zusammenstoßen; **c)** *(disagree)* sich streiten; **d)** ⟨*Interesse, Ereignis:*⟩ kollidieren, ⟨*Farbe:*⟩ sich beißen *(ugs.)* (**with** mit). **2.** *v. t.* gegeneinanderschlagen. **3.** *n. a)*

(of cymbals) Dröhnen, *das;* **b)** *(meeting in conflict)* Zusammenstoß, *der;* **c)** *(disagreement)* Auseinandersetzung, *die;* **d)** *(of personalities, colours)* Unverträglichkeit, *die; (of events)* Überschneiden, *das*

clasp [klɑːsp] **1.** *n.* Verschluß, *der.* **2.** *v. t.* umklammern

class [klɑːs] **1.** *n.* Klasse, *die; (in society)* Gesellschaftsschicht, *die; (Sch.: lesson)* Stunde, *die.* **2.** *v. t.* einstufen (**as** als). **'class-conscious** *adj.* klassenbewußt

classic ['klæsɪk] **1.** *adj.* klassisch. **2.** *n.* Klassiker, *der;* ~**s** Altphilologie, *die*

classical ['klæsɪkl] *adj.* klassisch

classification [klæsɪfɪ'keɪʃn] *n.* Klassifikation, *die*

classified ['klæsɪfaɪd] *adj. a) (secret)* geheim; **b)** ~ **advertisement** Kleinanzeige, *die*

classify ['klæsɪfaɪ] *v. t.* klassifizieren

class: ~**-mate** *n.* Klassenkamerad, *der*/-kameradin, *die;* ~**-room** *n.* Klassenzimmer, *das*

'classy *adj. (coll.)* klasse

clatter ['klætə(r)] **1.** *n.* Klappern, *das.* **2.** *v. i. a)* klappern; **b)** *(move or fall with a* ~) poltern

clause [klɔːz] *n. a)* Klausel, *die;* **b)** *(Ling.)* Teilsatz, *der;* |**subordinate**| ~**:** Nebensatz, *der*

claustrophobia [klɒstrə'fəʊbɪə] *n.* Klaustrophobie, *die.* **claustrophobic** [klɒstrə'fəʊbɪk] *adj.* beengend ⟨*Ort*⟩

claw [klɔː] **1.** *n.* Kralle, *die; (of crab etc.)* Schere, *die.* **2.** *v. t.* kratzen

clay [kleɪ] *n.* Lehm, *der; (for pottery)* Ton, *der*

clean [kliːn] **1.** *adj.* sauber; frisch ⟨*Wäsche, Hemd*⟩. **2.** *adv.* glatt. **3.** *v. t.* saubermachen; putzen ⟨*Zimmer, Schuh*⟩; reinigen ⟨*Teppich, Kleidung, Wunde*⟩; ~ **one's teeth** sich *(Dat.)* die Zähne putzen. **4.** *n.* **give** sth. **a** ~**:** etw. putzen. **clean 'out** *v. t. a)* saubermachen; *(sl.)* ~ **sb. out** *(take all sb.'s money)* jmdn. [total] schröpfen *(ugs.).* **clean 'up 1.** *v. t. a)* aufräumen; **b)** *(fig.)* säubern. **2.** *v. i.* aufräumen

'cleaner *n. a)* Raumpfleger, *der*/-pflegerin, *die; (woman also)* Putzfrau, *die;* **b)** *usu. in pl.* (**dry-**~) Reinigung, *die;* **take** sth. **to the** ~**'s** etw. in die Reinigung bringe

cleanliness ['klenlɪnɪs] *n.* Reinlichkeit, *die*

cleanly ['kliːnlɪ] *adv.* sauber

cleanse [klenz] *v.t.* [gründlich] reinigen. **'cleanser** *n.* Reinigungsmittel, *das*

'clean-shaven *adj.* glattrasiert

clear [klɪə(r)] **1.** *adj.* **a)** klar; scharf ⟨*Bild*⟩; **make oneself ~:** sich deutlich [genug] ausdrücken; **make it ~** [to sb.] **that ...:** [jmdm.] klar und deutlich sagen, daß ...; **b)** *(complete)* **three ~ days** volle drei Tage; **c)** *(unobstructed)* frei; **keep sth. ~** *(not block)* etw. frei halten. **2.** *adv.* **keep ~ of sth./sb.** etw./jmdn. meiden; **please stand** *or* **keep ~ of the door** bitte von der Tür zurücktreten. **3.** *v.t.* **a)** räumen ⟨*Straße*⟩; abräumen ⟨*Schreibtisch*⟩; freimachen ⟨*Abfluß, Kanal*⟩; **~ a space for sb./sth.** für jmdn./etw. Platz machen; **b)** *(empty)* räumen; leeren ⟨*Briefkasten*⟩; **c)** *(remove)* wegräumen; beheben ⟨*Verstopfung*⟩; **d)** *(show to be innocent)* freisprechen; **e)** *(get permission for)* ~ **sth. with sb.** etw. von jmdm. genehmigen lassen. **4.** *v.i.* **a)** ⟨*Wetter, Himmel:*⟩ sich aufheitern; **b)** *(disperse)* sich verziehen. **5.** *n.* **we're in the ~** *(free of suspicion)* auf uns fällt kein Verdacht; *(free of trouble)* wir haben es geschafft. **clear 'off** *v.i.* abhauen *(salopp)*. **clear 'out 1.** *v.t.* ausräumen. **2.** *v.i.* *(coll.)* verschwinden. **clear 'up 1.** *v.t.* **a)** wegräumen ⟨*Abfall*⟩; aufräumen ⟨*Platz, Sachen*⟩; **b)** *(explain)* klären. **2.** *v.i.* **a)** aufräumen; **b)** ⟨*Wetter:*⟩ sich aufhellen

clearance ['klɪərəns] *n.* **a)** *(of obstruction)* Beseitigung, *die;* **b)** *(clear space)* Spielraum, *der*

'clear cut *adj.* klar umrissen; klar ⟨*Abgrenzung, Ergebnis*⟩

'clearing *n.* Lichtung, *die*

'clearly *adv.* **a)** *(distinctly)* klar; deutlich ⟨*sprechen*⟩; **b)** *(manifestly, unambiguously)* eindeutig; klar ⟨*denken*⟩

'clearway *n.* *(Brit.)* Straße mit Halteverbot

cleaver ['kliːvə(r)] *n.* Hackbeil, *das*

clef [klef] *n.* Notenschlüssel, *der*

cleft [kleft] *n.* Spalte, *die*

clench [klentʃ] *v.t.* zusammenpressen; ~ **one's fist** *or* **fingers** die Faust ballen; ~ **one's teeth** die Zähne zusammenbeißen

clergy ['klɜːdʒɪ] *n. pl.* Geistlichkeit, *die;* Klerus, *der.* **clergyman** ['klɜːdʒɪmən] *n., pl.* ~**men** ['klɜːdʒɪmən] Geistliche, *der*

clerical ['klerɪkl] *adj.* Büro⟨*arbeit, -personal*⟩; ~ **error** Schreibfehler, *der*

clerk [klɑːk] *n.* *(in bank)* Bankangestellte, *der/die;* *(in office)* Büroangestellte, *der/die*

clever ['klevə(r)] *adj.* **a)** klug; **b)** *(skilful)* geschickt; **c)** *(ingenious)* geistreich ⟨*Idee, Argument*⟩; **d)** *(smart, cunning)* clever. **'cleverly** *adv.* **a)** klug; **b)** *(skilfully)* geschickt

cliché ['kliːʃeɪ] *n.* Klischee, *das*

click [klɪk] **1.** *n.* Klicken, *das.* **2.** *v.i.* klicken

client ['klaɪənt] *n.* **a)** Klient, *der*/Klientin, *die;* **b)** *(customer)* Kunde, *der*/Kundin, *die*

clientele [kliːɒn'tel] *n.* *(of shop)* Kundschaft, *die*

cliff [klɪf] *n.* Kliff, *das.* **'cliff-hanger** *n.* Thriller, *der*

climate ['klaɪmət] *n.* Klima, *das*

climax ['klaɪmæks] *n.* Höhepunkt, *der*

climb [klaɪm] **1.** *v.t.* hinaufsteigen; klettern auf ⟨*Baum*⟩; ⟨*Auto:*⟩ hinaufkommen ⟨*Hügel*⟩. **2.** *v.i.* **a)** klettern (**up** auf + *Akk.*); **b)** ⟨*Flugzeug, Sonne:*⟩ aufsteigen. **3.** *n.* Aufstieg, *der.* **climb 'down** *v.i.* **a)** hinunterklettern; **b)** *(fig.)* nachgeben

'climb-down *n.* Rückzieher, *der (ugs.)*

climber ['klaɪmə(r)] *n.* Bergsteiger, *der*

clinch [klɪntʃ] **1.** *v.t.* zum Abschluß bringen; perfekt machen *(ugs.)* ⟨*Geschäft*⟩. **2.** *n.* *(Boxing)* Clinch, *der*

cling [klɪŋ] *v.i.,* **clung** [klʌŋ] sich klammern (**to an** + *Akk.*). **'cling film** *n.* Klarsichtfolie, *die*

clinic ['klɪnɪk] *n.* Klinik, *die.* **clinical** ['klɪnɪkl] *adj.* **a)** *(Med.)* klinisch; **b)** *(dispassionate)* nüchtern

clink [klɪŋk] **1.** *n.* *(of glasses)* Klirren, *das;* *(of coins)* Klimpern, *das.* **2.** *v.i.* ⟨*Flaschen:*⟩ klirren; ⟨*Münzen:*⟩ klimpern. **3.** *v.t.* klirren mit ⟨*Glas*⟩; klimpern mit ⟨*Kleingeld*⟩

¹clip [klɪp] **1.** *n.* Klammer, *die;* *(for paper)* Büroklammer, *die.* **2.** *v.t.,* **-pp-** klammern (**[on]** to an + *Akk.*)

²clip *v.t.,* **-pp-** *(cut)* schneiden ⟨*Fingernägel, Haar, Hecke*⟩; stutzen ⟨*Flügel*⟩

clique [kliːk] *n.* Clique, *die*

cloak [kləʊk] **1.** *n.* Umhang, *der.* **2.** *v.t.* [ein]hüllen. **'cloakroom** *n.* Garderobe, *die;* *(Brit. euphem.: lavatory)* Toilette, *die*

clock [klɒk] **1.** *n.* **a)** Uhr, *die;* [**work**] **against the ~:** gegen die Zeit [arbeiten]; **round the ~:** rund um die Uhr; **b)** *(coll.) (speedometer)* Tacho, *der (ugs.); (milometer)* ≈ Kilometerzähler, *der.* **2.** *v.t.* ~ [**up**] zu verzeichnen haben

⟨*Erfolg*⟩; erreichen ⟨*Geschwindigkeit*⟩.
clock 'in, clock 'on *v. i.* [bei Arbeitsantritt] stechen. **clock 'off,**
clock 'out *v. i.* [bei Arbeitsschluß]
stechen
'**clockwise** *adv., adj.* im Uhrzeigersinn
'**clockwork** *n.* Uhrwerk, *das;* **a ~ car.**
ein Aufziehauto; **as regular as ~** *(fig.)*
absolut regelmäßig
clog [klɒg] **1.** *n.* Clog, *der; (traditional)*
Holzschuh, *der.* **2.** *v. t.,* **-gg-: ~** |up|
verstopfen
cloister ['klɔɪstə(r)] *n.* Kreuzgang, *der*
clone [kləʊn] **1.** *n.* Klon, *der.* **2.** *v. t.*
klonen
close 1. [kləʊs] *adj.* **a)** *(in space)* dicht;
nahe; **be ~ to sth.** nahe bei *od.* an etw.
(Dat.) sein; **at ~ quarters** aus der Nähe betrachtet; **b)** *(in time)* nahe **(to an**
+ *Dat.*); **c)** eng ⟨*Freund, Zusammenarbeit*⟩; nahe ⟨*Verwandte, Bekanntschaft*⟩; **d)** eingehend ⟨*Untersuchung,
Prüfung usw.*⟩; **e)** hart ⟨*Wett[kampf],
Spiel*⟩; knapp ⟨*Ergebnis*⟩; **that was a ~**
call *or* **shave** *(coll.)* das war knapp! **2.**
[kləʊs] *adv.* nah[e]; **~ by** in der Nähe;
~ to sb./sth. nahe bei jmdm./etw. **3.**
[kləʊz] *v. t.* **a)** *(shut)* schließen; zuziehen ⟨*Vorhang*⟩; schließen ⟨*Laden,
Fabrik*⟩; sperren ⟨*Straße*⟩; **b)** *(conclude)* schließen ⟨*Diskussion, Versammlung*⟩. **4.** [kləʊz] *v. i.* **a)** *(shut)*
sich schließen; **b)** ⟨*Laden, Fabrik:*⟩
schließen, *(ugs.)* zumachen. **5.** [kləʊz]
n. Ende, *das;* Schluß, *der;* **come** *or*
draw to a ~: zu Ende gehen; **bring** *or*
draw sth. to a ~: etw. zu Ende bringen.
close [kləʊz] '**down 1.** *v. t.* schließen; stillegen ⟨*Werk*⟩. **2.** *v. i.* geschlossen werden; ⟨*Werk:*⟩ stillgelegt werden. **close 'in** *v. i.* ⟨*Nacht, Dunkelheit:*⟩ hereinbrechen; ⟨*Tage:*⟩ kürzer
werden; **~ in on** umzingeln. **close**
'**off** *v. t.* [ab]sperren
closed [kləʊzd] *adj.* geschlossen;
we're ~: wir haben geschlossen.
'**closed-circuit** *adj.* **~ television** interne Fernsehanlage
close-down ['kləʊzdaʊn] *n. (Radio,
Telev.)* Sendeschluß, *der*
closed 'shop *n.* Closed Shop, *der*
closely ['kləʊslɪ] *adv.* **a)** dicht; **b)**
(intimately) eng; **c)** genau ⟨*befragen,
prüfen*⟩; streng ⟨*bewachen*⟩
closet ['klɒzɪt] *n. (Amer.: cupboard)*
Schrank, *der*
close-up ['kləʊsʌp] *n.* **~** |picture/shot|
Nahaufnahme, *die*

closing ['kləʊzɪŋ]: **~ date** *n. (for competition)* Einsendeschluß, *der; (to take
part)* Meldefrist, *die;* **~-time** *n. (of
pub)* Polizeistunde, *die*
closure ['kləʊzə(r)] *n.* Schließung, *die;
(of road)* Sperrung, *die*
clot [klɒt] **1.** *n.* **a)** *(blood)* Gerinnsel,
das; **b)** *(Brit. sl.: stupid person)* Trottel,
der. **2.** *v. i.,* **-tt-** ⟨*Blut:*⟩ gerinnen
cloth [klɒθ] *n., pl.* **~s** [klɒθs] **a)** Stoff,
der; Tuch, *das;* **b)** *(dish-~)* Spültuch,
das; (table-~) [Tisch]decke, *die*
clothe [kləʊð] *v. t.* kleiden
clothes [kləʊðz] *n. pl.* Kleider *Pl.;* **put
one's ~ on** sich anziehen; **take one's**
~ off sich ausziehen
'**clothes: ~-brush** *n.* Kleiderbürste,
die; **~-line** *n.* Wäscheleine, *die;*
~-peg *(Brit.),* **~-pin** *(Amer.) ns.* Wäscheklammer, *die*
clothing ['kləʊðɪŋ] *n.* Kleidung, *die*
clotted cream [klɒtɪd 'kri:m] *n. sehr
fetter Rahm*
cloud [klaʊd] *n.* **a)** Wolke, *die;* **every ~
has a silver lining** *(prov.)* es hat alles
sein Gutes; **b)** **~ of dust/smoke**
Staub-/Rauchwolke, *die.* **cloud**
'**over** *v. i.* sich bewölken
'**cloudburst** *n.* Wolkenbruch, *der*
'**cloudless** *adj.* wolkenlos
'**cloudy** *adj.* bewölkt ⟨*Himmel*⟩; trübe
⟨*Wetter, Flüssigkeit, Glas*⟩
clout [klaʊt] *(coll.)* **1.** *n.* Schlag, *der.* **2.**
v. t. hauen *(ugs.)*
[1]**clove** [kləʊv] *n.* **~** |of garlic| [Knoblauch]zehe, *die*
[2]**clove** *n. (spice)* [Gewürz]nelke, *die*
clover ['kləʊvə(r)] *n.* Klee, *der.*
'**cloverleaf** *n.* Kleeblatt, *das*
clown [klaʊn] **1.** *n.* Clown, *der.* **2.** *v. i.*
~ |about *or* around| den Clown spielen
cloying ['klɔɪɪŋ] *adj.* süßlich
club [klʌb] **1.** *n.* **a)** *(weapon)* Keule,
die; (golf-~) Schläger, *der;* **b)** *(association)* Klub, *der;* Verein, *der;* **c)**
(Cards) Kreuz, *das;* **~s are trumps**
Kreuz ist Trumpf; **the ace/seven of ~s**
das Kreuzas/die Kreuzsieben. **2.** *v. t.,*
-bb- *(beat)* prügeln; *(with ~)* knüppeln. **3.** *v. i.,* **-bb-: ~ together** *(to buy
something)* zusammenlegen
cluck [klʌk] **1.** *n.* Gackern, *das.* **2.** *v. i.*
gackern
clue [klu:] *n.* Anhaltspunkt, *der; (in
criminal investigation)* Spur, *die;* **not
have a ~:** keine Ahnung haben. '**clueless** *adj. (coll.)* unbedarft *(ugs.)*
clump [klʌmp] *n.* Gruppe, *die; (of
grass)* Büschel, *das*

clumsy ['klʌmzı] *adj.* schwerfällig, unbeholfen ⟨*Person, Bewegung*⟩; plump ⟨*Form, Figur, Nachahmung*⟩

clung *see* **cling**

cluster ['klʌstə(r)] 1. *n. (of grapes, berries)* Traube, *die; (of fruit, flowers)* Büschel, *das; (of stars, huts)* Haufen, *der.* 2. *v. i.* ~ [a]round sb./sth. sich um jmdn./etw. scharen *od.* drängen

clutch [klʌtʃ] 1. *v. t.* umklammern. 2. *v. i.* ~ at sth. nach etw. greifen; *(fig.)* sich an etw. *(Akk.)* klammern. 3. *n.* a) in pl. *(fig.: control)* Klauen; b) *(Motor Veh.)* Kupplung, *die*

clutter ['klʌtə(r)] 1. *n.* Durcheinander, *das.* 2. *v. t.* ~ [up] the table/room überall auf dem Tisch/im Zimmer herumliegen

cm. *abbr.* **centimetre[s]** cm

Co. *abbr.* a) **company** Co.; b) **county**

c/o *abbr.* **care of** bei; c/o

coach [kəʊtʃ] 1. *n.* a) *(horse-drawn)* Kutsche, *die;* b) *(Railw.)* Wagen, *der;* c) *(bus)* [Reise]bus, *der;* by ~: mit dem Bus; d) *(Sport)* Trainer, *der*/Trainerin, *die.* 2. *v. t.* trainieren. '**coach station** *n.* Busbahnhof, *der.* '**coach tour** *n.* Rundreise [im Omnibus]

coagulate [kəʊ'ægjʊleıt] 1. *v. t.* gerinnen lassen. 2. *v. i.* gerinnen

coal [kəʊl] *n.* Kohle, *die.* '**coalfield** *n.* Kohlenrevier, *das*

coalition [kəʊə'lıʃn] *n. (Polit.)* Koalition, *die*

coal: ~**-mine** *n.* [Kohlen]bergwerk, *das;* ~**-miner** *n.* [im Kohlenbergbau tätiger] Grubenarbeiter; ~**-mining** *n.* Kohlenbergbau, *der*

coarse [kɔ:s] *adj.* a) *(in texture)* grob; b) *(unrefined, obscene)* derb

coast [kəʊst] 1. *n.* Küste, *die.* 2. *v. i.* im Freilauf fahren. **coastal** ['kəʊstl] *adj.* Küsten-. '**coaster** *n.* a) *(mat)* Untersetzer, *der;* b) *(ship)* Küstenmotorschiff, *das*

coast: ~**guard** *n.* Küstenwache, -wacht, *die;* ~**line** *n.* Küste, *die*

coat [kəʊt] 1. *n.* a) Mantel, *der;* b) *(layer)* Schicht, *die; (of paint)* Anstrich, *der;* c) *(animal's hair, fur, etc.)* Fell, *das.* 2. *v. t.* überziehen; *(with paint)* streichen

'**coat-hanger** *n.* Kleiderbügel, *der*

'**coating** *n.* Schicht, *die*

coat of arms *n.* Wappen, *das*

coax [kəʊks] *v. t.* überreden

cobble ['kɒbl] *n.* Pflasterstein, *der*

cobbler ['kɒblə(r)] *n.* Schuster, *der*

'**cobble-stone** *see* **cobble**

cobra ['kɒbrə] *n.* Kobra, *die*

cobweb ['kɒbweb] *n.* Spinnengewebe, *das;* Spinnennetz, *das*

cocaine [kə'keın] *n.* Kokain, *das*

cock [kɒk] 1. *n.* Hahn, *der.* 2. *v. t.* spitzen ⟨*Ohren*⟩; ~ a/the gun den Hahn spannen. **cock-a-hoop** [kɒkə'hu:p] *adj.* überschwenglich

cockatoo [kɒkə'tu:] *n.* Kakadu, *der*

cockerel ['kɒkərəl] *n.* junger Hahn

cock-eyed ['kɒkaıd] *adj.* a) *(crooked)* schief; b) *(absurd)* verrückt

cockle ['kɒkl] *n.* Herzmuschel, *die*

cockney ['kɒknı] 1. *adj.* Cockney-. 2. *n.* Cockney, *der*

'**cockpit** *n.* Cockpit, *das*

cockroach ['kɒkrəʊtʃ] *n.* [Küchen-, Haus-]schabe, *die*

cocktail ['kɒkteıl] *n.* Cocktail, *der.* '**cocktail cabinet** *n.* Hausbar, *die.* '**cocktail party** *n.* Cocktailparty, *die*

cocoa ['kəʊkəʊ] *n.* Kakao, *der*

coconut ['kəʊkənʌt] *n.* Kokosnuß, *die*

cocoon [kə'ku:n] *(Zool.)* Kokon, *der*

cod [kɒd] *n., pl. same* Kabeljau, *der*

COD *abbr.* **cash on delivery,** *(Amer.)* **collect on delivery** p. Nachn.

code [kəʊd] 1. *n.* a) *(statutes etc.)* Gesetzbuch, *das;* ~s of behaviour Verhaltensnormen; b) *(system of signals)* Code, *der;* be in ~: verschlüsselt sein. 2. *v. t.* chiffrieren; verschlüsseln.

'**code-name** *n.* Deckname, *der.*

'**code-word** *n.* Kennwort, *das*

cod-liver 'oil *n.* Lebertran, *der*

co-driver ['kəʊdraıvə(r)] *n.* Beifahrer, *der*/-fahrerin, *die*

coed ['kəʊed] *(esp. Amer. coll.)* 1. *n.* Studentin, *die.* 2. *adj.* ~ school gemischte Schule

coeducational [kəʊedjʊ'keıʃənl] *adj.* koedukativ; Koedukations-

coerce [kəʊ'ɜ:s] *v. t.* zwingen; ~ sb. into sth. jmdn. zu etw. zwingen. **coercion** [kəʊ'ɜ:ʃn] *n.* Zwang, *der*

coexist [kəʊıg'zıst] *v. i.* koexistieren. **coexistence** [kəʊıg'zıstəns] *n.* Koexistenz, *die*

C. of E. [si:əv'i:] *abbr.* **Church of England**

coffee ['kɒfı] *n.* Kaffee, *der;* three black/white ~s drei [Tassen] Kaffee ohne/mit Milch

coffee: ~ **bar** *n.* Café, *das;* ~**-bean** *n.* Kaffeebohne, *die;* ~**-break** *n.* Kaffeepause, *die;* ~**-cup** *n.* Kaffeetasse, *die;* ~**-pot** *n.* Kaffeekanne, *die;* ~ **shop** *n.* Kaffeestube, *die;* ~**-table** *n.* Couchtisch, *der*

coffin ['kɒfɪn] *n.* Sarg, *der*

cog [kɒg] *n. (Mech.)* Zahn, *der*

cogent ['kəʊdʒənt] *adj.* überzeugend ⟨*Argument*⟩; zwingend ⟨*Grund*⟩

cognac ['kɒnjæk] *n.* Cognac, *der* Ⓦ

cog: ~-railway *n.* Zahnradbahn, *die;* **~-wheel** *n.* Zahnrad, *das*

cohere [kəʊ'hɪə(r)] *v. i.* zusammenhalten. **coherent** [kəʊ'hɪərənt] *adj.* zusammenhängend

coil [kɔɪl] **1.** *v. t.* aufwickeln; *(twist)* aufdrehen. **2.** *v. i.* **~ round sth.** etw. umschlingen. **3.** *n.* **a)** **~s of rope/wire** aufgerollte Seile *Pl.*/aufgerollter Draht; **b)** *(single turn)* Windung, *die;* **c)** *(Electr.)* Spule, *die*

coin [kɔɪn] **1.** *n.* Münze, *die.* **2.** *v. t.* prägen ⟨*Wort, Redewendung*⟩

coincide [kəʊɪn'saɪd] *v. i.* **a)** *(in time)* zusammenfallen; **b)** *(agree)* übereinstimmen (**with** mit). **coincidence** [kəʊ'ɪnsɪdəns] *n.* Zufall, *der.* **coincidental** [kəʊɪnsɪ'dentl] *adj.* zufällig

coke [kəʊk] *n.* Koks, *der*

colander ['kʌləndə(r)] *n.* Sieb, *das*

cold [kəʊld] **1.** *adj.* **a)** kalt; **I feel ~:** mir ist kalt; **b)** *(fig.)* [betont] kühl ⟨*Person, Aufnahme, Begrüßung*⟩. **2.** *adv.* kalt. **3.** *n.* **a)** Kälte, *die;* **b)** *(illness)* Erkältung, *die;* **~ [in the head]** Schnupfen, *der.* **cold-blooded** ['kəʊldblʌdɪd] *adj.* **a)** wechselwarm ⟨*Tier*⟩; **b)** kaltblütig ⟨*Person, Mord*⟩

'**coldly** *adv.* [betont] kühl

coleslaw ['kəʊlslɔː] *n.* Krautsalat, *der*

collaborate [kə'læbəreɪt] *v. i.* **a)** zusammenarbeiten; **~ [with sb.] on sth.** zusammen [mit jmdm.] an etw. *(Dat.)* arbeiten; **b)** *(with enemy)* kollaborieren. **collaboration** [kəlæbə'reɪʃn] *n.* Zusammenarbeit, *die; (with enemy)* Kollaboration, *die.* **collaborator** [kə'læbəreɪtə(r)] *n.* Mitarbeiter, *der*/-arbeiterin, *die; (with enemy)* Kollaborateur, *der*/Kollaborateurin, *die*

collage ['kɒlɑːʒ] *n.* Collage, *die*

collapse [kə'læps] **1.** *n.* **a)** *(of person)* Zusammenbruch, *der;* **b)** *(of structure)* Einsturz, *der;* **c)** *(of negotiations)* Scheitern, *das; (of company)* Zusammenbruch, *der.* **2.** *v. i.* **a)** ⟨*Person:*⟩ zusammenbrechen; **b)** ⟨*Stuhl:*⟩ zusammenbrechen; ⟨*Gebäude:*⟩ einstürzen; **c)** ⟨*Verhandlungen:*⟩ scheitern; ⟨*Unternehmen:*⟩ zusammenbrechen; **d)** *(fold down)* ⟨*Regenschirm, Fahrrad, Tisch:*⟩ sich zusammenklappen lassen. **collapsible** [kə'læpsɪbl] *adj.* Klapp- ⟨*stuhl, -tisch, -fahrrad*⟩

collar ['kɒlə(r)] **1.** *n.* **a)** Kragen, *der;* **b)** *(for dog)* [Hunde]halsband, *das.* **2.** *v. t.* schnappen *(ugs.).* '**collar-bone** *n.* Schlüsselbein, *das*

colleague ['kɒliːg] *n.* Kollege, *der*/Kollegin, *die*

collect [kə'lekt] **1.** *v. i.* sich versammeln; ⟨*Staub, Müll usw.:*⟩ sich ansammeln. **2.** *v. t.* sammeln; aufsammeln ⟨*Müll, leere Flaschen usw.*⟩; *(coll.: fetch)* abholen ⟨*Menschen, Dinge*⟩; **~ one's wits/thoughts** seine Gedanken sammeln. **col'lected** *adj.* **a)** *(gathered)* gesammelt; **b)** *(calm)* gesammelt; gelassen. **collection** [kə'lekʃn] *n.* **a)** *(collecting)* Sammeln, *das; (coll.: of goods, persons)* Abholen, *das;* **b)** *(amount of money collected)* Sammlung, *die; (in church)* Kollekte, *die;* **c)** *(from post-box)* Leerung, *die;* **d)** *(of stamps etc.)* Sammlung, *die.* **collective** [kə'lektɪv] *adj.* kollektiv *nicht präd.* **collective 'bargaining** *n.* Tarifverhandlungen *Pl.*

collector [kə'lektə(r)] *n.* **a)** *(of stamps etc.)* Sammler, *der*/Sammlerin, *die;* **b)** *(of taxes)* Einnehmer, *der*/Einnehmerin, *die.* **col'lector's item, col'lector's piece** *ns.* Sammlerstück, *das*

college ['kɒlɪdʒ] *n.* **a)** *(esp. Brit. Univ.)* College, *das;* **b)** *(place of further education)* Fach[hoch]schule, *die;* **go to ~** *(esp. Amer.)* studieren

collide [kə'laɪd] *v. i.* zusammenstoßen (**with** mit)

collie ['kɒlɪ] *n.* Collie, *der*

colliery ['kɒljərɪ] *n.* Kohlengrube, *die*

collision [kə'lɪʒn] *n.* Zusammenstoß, *der;* **on a ~ course** *(lit. or fig.)* auf Kollisionskurs

colloquial [kə'ləʊkwɪəl] *adj.* umgangssprachlich

collusion [kə'luːʒn] *n.* geheime Absprache

Cologne [kə'ləʊn] **1.** *pr. n.* Köln *(das).* **2.** *attrib. adj.* Kölner

cologne *see* eau-de-Cologne

Colombia [kə'lɒmbɪə] *pr. n.* Kolumbien *(das)*

colon ['kəʊlən] *n.* Doppelpunkt, *der*

colonel [kɜːnl] *n.* Oberst, *der*

colonial [kə'ləʊnɪəl] *adj.* Kolonial-; kolonial

colonize ['kɒlənaɪz] *v. t.* kolonisieren

colony ['kɒlənɪ] *n.* Kolonie, *die*

color *etc. (Amer.) see* colour *etc.*

colossal [kə'lɒsl] *adj.* ungeheuer; gewaltig ⟨*Bauwerk*⟩

colour ['kʌlə(r)] *(Brit.)* **1.** *n.* Farbe,

die; **what** ~ **is it?** welche Farbe hat es?; **change** ~: die Farbe ändern; **he is off** ~: ihm ist nicht gut. **2.** *v. t.* **a)** *(give* ~ *to)* Farbe geben (+ *Dat.*); **b)** *(paint)* malen; **c)** *(stain, dye)* färben. **3.** *v. i.* ~ [up] erröten. '**colour-blind** *adj.* farbenblind

coloured ['kʌləd] *(Brit.)* **1.** *adj.* **a)** farbig; **b)** *(of non-white descent)* farbig; ~ **people** Farbige *Pl.* **2.** *n.* Farbige, *der/die*

'**colour film** *n.* Farbfilm, *der*

colourful ['kʌləfl] *adj. (Brit.)* bunt; anschaulich ⟨*Sprache, Stil, Bericht*⟩

'**colouring** *n. (Brit.)* **a)** *(colours)* Farben *Pl.;* **b)** ~ [**matter**] *(in food etc.)* Farbstoff, *der*

'**colourless** *adj. (Brit.)* farblos

colour: ~ **photograph** *n.* Farbaufnahme, *die;* ~ **scheme** *n.* Farb[en]zusammenstellung, *die;* ~ **supplement** *n.* Farbbeilage, *die;* ~ **television** *n.* Farbfernsehen, *das; (set)* Farbfernsehgerät, *das;* ~ **transparency** *n.* Farbdia, *das*

colt [kəult] *n.* [Hengst]fohlen, *das*

column ['kɒləm] *n.* **a)** Säule, *die;* **b)** *(of page)* Spalte, *die; sports* ~: Sportteil, *der.* **columnist** ['kɒləmɪst] *n.* Kolumnist, *der/*Kolumnistin, *die*

coma ['kəumə] *n.* Koma, *das;* **in a** ~: im Koma

comb [kəum] **1.** *n.* Kamm, *der.* **2.** *v. t.* **a)** kämmen; ~ **sb.'s/one's hair** jmdm./ sich die Haare kämmen; **b)** *(search)* durchkämmen

combat ['kɒmbæt] **1.** *n.* Kampf, *der.* **2.** *v. t.* bekämpfen. **combatant** ['kɒmbətənt] *n.* Kombattant, *der*

combination [kɒmbɪ'neɪʃn] *n.* Kombination, *die.* **combi'nation lock** *n.* Kombinationsschloß, *das*

combine 1. [kəm'baɪn] *v. t.* zusammenfügen (**into** zu); verbinden ⟨*Substanzen*⟩. **2.** *v. i. (join together)* ⟨*Stoffe:*⟩ sich verbinden. **3.** ['kɒmbaɪn] *n.* ~ [**harvester**] Mähdrescher, *der*

combustion [kəm'bʌstʃn] *n.* Verbrennung, *die*

come [kʌm] *v. i., came* [keɪm], *come* [kʌm] kommen; ~ **here!** komm [mal] her!; [**I'm**] **coming!** [ich] komme schon!; **the train came into the station** der Zug fuhr in den Bahnhof ein; **Christmas is coming** bald ist Weihnachten; **the handle has** ~ **loose** der Griff ist lose; **nothing came of it** es ist nichts daraus geworden. **come a'bout** *v. i.* passieren. **come across**

1. [--'-] *v. i. (be understood)* verstanden werden. **2.** ['---] *v. t.* begegnen (+ *Dat.*). **come a'long** *v. i. (coll.)* **a)** *(hurry up)* ~ **along!** komm/kommt!; **b)** *(make progress)* ~ **along nicely** gute Fortschritte machen; **c)** *(to place)* mitkommen (**with** mit). **come 'back** *v. i.* zurückkommen. **come by 1.** ['--] *v. t. (obtain)* bekommen. **2.** [-'-] *v. i.* vorbeikommen. **come 'down** *v. i.* **a)** *(fall)* ⟨*Schnee, Regen, Preis:*⟩ fallen; **b)** *(~ lower)* herunterkommen; **c)** *(land)* [not]landen; *(crash)* abstürzen. **come 'in** *v. i. (enter)* hereinkommen; ~ **in!** herein! '**come into** *v. t.* **a)** *(enter)* hereinkommen in (+ *Akk.*); **b)** *(inherit)* erben. **come off 1.** [-'-] *v. i.* **a)** ⟨*Griff, Knopf:*⟩ abgehen; *(be removable)* sich abnehmen lassen; **b)** *(succeed)* ⟨*Pläne, Versuche:*⟩ Erfolg haben; **c)** *(take place)* stattfinden. **2.** ['--] *v. t.* ~ **off a horse/bike** vom Pferd/Fahrrad fallen; ~ '**off it!** *(coll.)* nun mach mal halblang! *(ugs.).* **come on 1.** [-'-] *v. i.* **a)** *(continue coming, follow)* kommen; ~ **on!** komm, komm/kommt, kommt!; *(encouraging)* na, komm; **b)** *(make progress)* ~ **on very well** gute Fortschritte machen. **2.** ['--] *v. t. see* ~ **upon. come 'out** *v. i.* **a)** herauskommen; **b)** *(fig.)* ⟨*Sonne, Wahrheit, Buch:*⟩ herauskommen; **c)** ~ **out with** herausrücken mit *(ugs.).* **come 'over 1.** *v. i.* herüberkommen. **2.** *v. t. (coll.)* kommen über (+ *Akk.*). **come 'round** *v. i.* **a)** *(visit)* vorbeischauen; **b)** *(recover)* wieder zu sich kommen. **come 'through 1.** *v. i.* durchkommen. **2.** *v. t. (survive)* überleben. **come to 1.** ['--] *v. t. (amount to)* ⟨*Rechnung, Kosten:*⟩ sich belaufen auf (+ *Akk.*). **2.** [-'-] *v. i.* wieder zu sich kommen. '**come under** *v. t.* **a)** *(be classed as or among)* kommen unter (+ *Akk.*); **b)** *(be subject to)* kommen unter (+ *Akk.*). **come 'up** *v. i.* **a)** *(~ higher)* hochkommen; **b)** ~ **up to sb.** *(approach for talk)* auf jmdn. zukommen; **c)** *(present itself)* sich ergeben; **d)** ~ **up to** *(reach)* reichen bis an (+ *Akk.*); entsprechen (+ *Dat.*) ⟨*Erwartungen*⟩; **e)** ~ **up against sth.** *(fig.)* auf etw. *(Akk.)* stoßen; **f)** ~ **up with** vorbringen ⟨*Vorschlag*⟩; wissen ⟨*Lösung, Antwort*⟩. '**come upon** *v. t. (meet by chance)* begegnen (+ *Dat.*). '**come-back** *n. (to profession etc.)* Comeback, *das*

comedian [kə'miːdɪən] *n.* Komiker,

der. **comedienne** [kəmi:dɪ'en] *n.* Komikerin, *die*

'**come-down** *n.* Abstieg, *der*

comedy ['kɒmɪdɪ] **a)** *n.* Lustspiel, *das;* Komödie, *die;* **b)** *(humour)* Witz, *der;* Witzigkeit, *die*

comet ['kɒmɪt] *n.* Komet, *der*

comeuppance [kʌm'ʌpəns] *n.* **get one's ~:** die Quittung kriegen *(fig.)*

comfort ['kʌmfət] **1.** *n.* **a)** *(consolation)* Trost, *der;* **b)** *(physical well-being)* Behaglichkeit, *die;* **c)** *in pl.* Komfort, *der.* **2.** *v. t.* trösten. **comfortable** ['kʌmfətəbl] *adj.* **a)** bequem ⟨*Bett, Schuhe*⟩; komfortabel ⟨*Haus, Zimmer*⟩; **a ~ victory** ein leichter Sieg; **b)** *(at ease)* **be/feel ~:** sich wohl fühlen. **comfortably** ['kʌmfətəblɪ] *adv.* bequem; leicht *(gewinnen)*

'**comfort station** *n.* *(Amer.)* öffentliche Toilette

comfy ['kʌmfɪ] *adj. (coll.)* bequem; gemütlich ⟨*Haus, Zimmer*⟩

comic ['kɒmɪk] **1.** *adj.* komisch. **2.** *n.* **a)** *(comedian)* Komiker, *der*/Komikerin, *die;* **b)** *(periodical)* Comic-Heft, *das.* **comical** ['kɒmɪkl] *adj.* komisch

coming ['kʌmɪŋ] **1.** *adj.* **in the ~ week** kommende Woche. **2.** *n.* **~s and goings** das Kommen und Gehen

comma ['kɒmə] *n.* Komma, *das*

command [kə'mɑ:nd] **1.** *v. t.* **a)** *(order)* befehlen (**sb.** jmdm.); **b)** *(be in ~ of)* befehligen ⟨*Schiff, Armee*⟩; **c)** verfügen über (+ *Akk.*) ⟨*Gelder, Wortschatz*⟩. **2.** *n.* **a)** Kommando, *das;* *(in writing)* Befehl, *der;* **have/take ~ of** das Kommando über (+ *Akk.*) ... haben/übernehmen; **b)** *(mastery, possession)* Beherrschung, *die*

commandeer [kɒmən'dɪə(r)] *v. t.* requirieren

com'mander *n.* Führer, *der*

com'manding *adj.* **a)** gebieterisch ⟨*Erscheinung, Stimme*⟩; imposant ⟨*Gestalt*⟩; **b)** beherrschend ⟨*Ausblick, Lage*⟩. **commanding** '**officer** *n.* Befehlshaber, *der*/Befehlshaberin, *die*

com'mandment *n.* Gebot, *das*

commemorate [kə'meməreɪt] *v. t.* gedenken (+ *Gen.*). **commemoration** [kəmemə'reɪʃn] *n.* Gedenken, *das;* **in ~ of** zum Gedenken an (+ *Akk.*)

commence [kə'mens] *v. t. & i.* beginnen. **com'mencement** *n.* Beginn, *der*

commend [kə'mend] *v. t. (praise)* loben. **commendable** [kə'mendəbl] *adj.* lobenswert; löblich. **commen-**

dation [kɒmen'deɪʃn] *n. (praise)* Lob, *das;* *(official)* Belobigung, *die;* *(award)* Auszeichnung, *die*

comment ['kɒment] **1.** *n.* Bemerkung, *die* (**on** über + *Akk.*); *(note)* Anmerkung, *die* (**on** über + *Akk.*); **no ~!** *(coll.)* kein Kommentar! **2.** *v. i.* **~ on sth.** über etw. *(Akk.)* Bemerkungen machen; **he ~ed that ...:** er bemerkte, daß ... **commentary** ['kɒməntərɪ] *n.* **a)** Kommentar, *der* (**on** zu); **b)** *(Radio, Telev.)* **[live** *or* **running] ~:** Live-Reportage, *die.* **commentator** ['kɒmənteɪtə(r)] *n.* Kommentator, *der*/Kommentatorin, *die;* *(Sport)* Reporter, *der*/Reporterin, *die*

commerce ['kɒmɜ:s] *n.* Handel, *der*

commercial [kə'mɜ:ʃl] **1.** *adj.* Handels-; kaufmännisch ⟨*Ausbildung*⟩. **2.** *n.* Werbespot, *der.* **commercialism** [kə'mɜ:ʃəlɪzm] *n.* Kommerzialismus, *der.* **commercialize** [kə'mɜ:ʃəlaɪz] *v. t.* kommerzialisieren

commercial: ~ 'television *n.* Werbefernsehen, *das;* **~ 'vehicle** *n.* Nutzfahrzeug, *das*

commiserate [kə'mɪzəreɪt] *v. i.* **~ with sb.** jmdm. sein Mitgefühl aussprechen (**on** zu)

commission [kə'mɪʃn] **1.** *n.* **a)** *(official body)* Kommission, *die;* **b)** *(instruction, piece of work)* Auftrag, *der;* **c)** *(Mil.)* Ernennungsurkunde, *die;* **d)** *(pay of agent)* Provision, *die;* **e) in/out of ~** ⟨*Auto, Maschine*⟩ in/außer Betrieb. **2.** *v. t.* beauftragen ⟨*Künstler*⟩; in Auftrag geben ⟨*Gemälde usw.*⟩

commissionaire [kəmɪʃə'neə(r)] *n.* *(esp. Brit.)* Portier, *der*

commissioner [kə'mɪʃənə(r)] *n. (of police)* Präsident, *der*

commit [kə'mɪt] *v. t.,* **-tt-:** **a)** begehen ⟨*Verbrechen, Fehler, Ehebruch*⟩; **b)** *(pledge, bind)* **~ oneself/sb. to doing sth.** sich/jmdn. verpflichten, etw. zu tun; **c)** *(entrust)* anvertrauen (**to** *Dat.*); **d) ~ sb. for trial** jmdn. dem Gericht überstellen. **com'mitment** *n.* Verpflichtung (**to** gegenüber). **com'mitted** *adj.* engagiert

committee [kə'mɪtɪ] *n.* Ausschuß, *der*

commodity [kə'mɒdɪtɪ] *n.* **a)** **household ~:** Haushaltsartikel, *der;* **b)** *(St. Exch.)* **[vertretbare] Ware;** *(raw material)* Rohstoff, *der*

common ['kɒmən] **1.** *adj.* **a)** *(belonging to all)* gemeinsam; **b)** *(public)* öffentlich; **c)** *(usual)* gewöhnlich; *(frequent)* häufig; allgemein verbreitet

⟨*Sitte, Redensart*⟩; **d)** *(vulgar)* ordinär.
2. *n.* **a)** *(land)* Gemeindeland, *das;* **b)**
have sth./nothing/a lot in ~ [with sb.]
etw./nichts/viel [mit jmdm.] gemein[sam] haben. **'commoner** *n.*
Bürgerliche *der/die*
'**common-law** *adj.* **she's his ~ wife** sie
lebt mit ihm in eheähnlicher Gemeinschaft
'**commonly** *adv.* im allgemeinen
common: C~ 'Market *n.* gemeinsa-
mer Markt; **~place 1.** *n.* Gemeinplatz, *der;* **2.** *adj.* alltäglich
Commons ['kɒmənz] *n. pl.* **the [House
of] ~:** das Unterhaus
common: ~ 'sense *n.* gesunder
Menschenverstand; **~wealth** *n.* **the
[British] C~wealth** das Commonwealth
commotion [kə'məʊʃn] *n.* Tumult,
der
communal ['kɒmjʊnl] *adj.* **a)** *(of or for
the community)* gemeindlich; **b)** *(for
common use)* gemeinsam
commune ['kɒmjuːn] *n.* Kommune,
die
communicate [kə'mjuːnɪkeɪt] **1.** *v. t.*
übertragen ⟨*Krankheit*⟩; übermitteln
⟨*Informationen*⟩; vermitteln ⟨*Gefühle,
Ideen*⟩. **2.** *v. i.* **~ with sb.** mit jmdm.
kommunizieren. **communication**
[kəmjuːnɪ'keɪʃn] *n.* **a)** *(of information)*
Übermittlung, *die;* **b)** *(message)* Mitteilung, *die* (**to an** + *Akk.*). **communi'cation-cord** *n.* Notbremse.
die. **communi'cations satellite** *n.*
Nachrichtensatellit, *der*
communicative [kə'mjuːnɪkətɪv] *adj.*
gesprächig
Communion [kə'mjuːnɪən] *n.* **[Holy] ~**
(Protestant Ch.) das [heilige] Abend-
mahl; *(RC Ch.)* die [heilige] Kommunion
communiqué [kə'mjuːnɪkeɪ] *n.* Kom-
muniqué, *das*
communism ['kɒmjʊnɪzm] *n.* Kommunismus, *der;* **C~:** der Kommunismus. **Communist, communist**
['kɒmjʊnɪst] **1.** *n.* Kommunist,
*der/*Kommunistin, *die.* **2.** *adj.* kommunistisch
community [kə'mjuːnɪtɪ] *n.* **a)** *(organized body)* Gemeinwesen, *das;* **the
Jewish ~:** die jüdische Gemeinde; **b)**
no pl. (public) Öffentlichkeit, *die.*
com'munity centre *n.* Gemeinde-
zentrum, *das*
commute [kə'mjuːt] **1.** *v. t.* umwan-
deln ⟨*Strafe*⟩ (**to in** + *Akk.*). **2.** *v. i.*

pendeln. **com'muter** *n.* Pendler,
*der/*Pendlerin, *die*
¹**compact** [kəm'pækt] *adj.* kompakt
²**compact** ['kɒmpækt] *n.* Puderdose
[mit Puder(stein)]
compact 'disc *n.* Compact Disc, *die*
companion [kəm'pænjən] *n.* Begleiter, *der/*Begleiterin, *die.* **com'pan-
ionship** *n.* Gesellschaft, *die*
company ['kʌmpənɪ] *n.* **a)** *(persons as-
sembled, companionship)* Gesell-
schaft, *die;* **expect ~:** Besuch *od.* Gäste erwarten; **keep sb. ~:** jmdm. Gesellschaft leisten; **b)** *(firm)* Gesellschaft, *die;* **~ car** Firmenwagen, *der;*
c) *(of actors)* Truppe, *die;* Ensemble,
das; **d)** *(Mil.)* Kompanie, *die*
comparable ['kɒmpərəbl] *adj.* ver-
gleichbar (**to, with** mit)
comparative [kəm'pærətɪv] **1.** *adj.* **a)**
(relative) relativ; **in ~ comfort** relativ
komfortabel; **b)** *(Ling.)* komparativ
(fachspr.); **a ~ adjective/adverb** ein
Adjektiv/Adverb im Komparativ. **2.**
n. *(Ling.)* Komparativ, *der.* **com-
'paratively** *adv.* verhältnismäßig
compare [kəm'peə(r)] **1.** *v. t.* vergleichen (**to, with** mit); **~d with** *or* **to sb./
sth.** verglichen mit *od.* im Vergleich
zu jmdm./etw. **2.** *v. i.* sich vergleichen
lassen. **comparison** [kəm'pærɪsn] *n.*
Vergleich, *der;* **in** *or* **by ~ [with sb./
sth.]** im Vergleich [zu jmdm./etw.]
compartment [kəm'pɑːtmənt] *n. (in
drawer, desk, etc.)* Fach, *das; (of railway carriage)* Abteil, *das*
compass ['kʌmpəs] *n.* **a)** *in pl.* **[a pair
of] ~es** ein Zirkel; **b)** *(for navigating)*
Kompaß, *der*
compassion [kəm'pæʃn] *n.* Mitgefühl, *das* (**for** mit). **compassionate**
[kəm'pæʃənət] *adj.* mitfühlend; **on ~
grounds** aus persönlichen Gründen;
(for family reasons) aus familiären
Gründen
compatible [kəm'pætɪbl] *adj.* vereinbar; zueinander passend ⟨*Personen*⟩;
(Computing) kompatibel
compel [kəm'pel] *v. t.,* **-ll-** zwingen
compendium [kəm'pendɪəm] *n.*
Kompendium, *das*
compensate ['kɒmpenseɪt] **1.** *v. i.* **~
for sth.** etw. ersetzen. **2.** *v. t.* **~ sb. for
sth.** jmdn. für etw. entschädigen.
compensation [kɒmpen'seɪʃn] *n.*
Ersatz, *der; (for damages, injuries,
etc.)* Schaden[s]ersatz, *der*
compère ['kɒmpeə(r)] *n. (Brit.)* Con-
férencier, *der*

compete [kəm'pi:t] *v. i.* konkurrieren
(**for** um); *(Sport)* kämpfen
competence ['kɒmpɪtəns] *n.* Fähigkeiten *Pl.*
competent ['kɒmpɪtənt] *adj.* fähig;
not ~ to do sth. nicht kompetent, etw.
zu tun. '**competently** *adv.* kompetent
competition [kɒmpɪ'tɪʃn] *n.* **a)** *(contest)* Wettbewerb, *der; (in magazine
etc.)* Preisausschreiben, *das;* **b)** *(those
competing)* Konkurrenz, *die*
competitive [kəm'petɪtɪv] *adj.* wett-
bewerbsfähig ⟨*Preis, Unternehmen*⟩; ~
sports Leistungssport, *der*
competitor [kəm'petɪtə(r)] *n.* Konkurrent, *der*/Konkurrentin, *die; (in
contest, race)* Teilnehmer, *der*/-neh-
merin, *die*
compile [kəm'paɪl] *v. t.* zusammen-
stellen
complacency [kəm'pleɪsənsɪ] *n.*
Selbstzufriedenheit, *die*
complacent [kəm'pleɪsənt] *adj.*
selbstzufrieden
complain [kəm'pleɪn] *v. i.* sich beklagen (**about, at** über + *Akk.*); ~ **of sth.**
über etw. klagen. *(Akk.)* **complaint**
[kəm'pleɪnt] *n.* **a)** Beschwerde, *die;* **b)**
(ailment) Leiden, *das*
complement 1. ['kɒmplɪmənt] *n.* **a)**
(what completes) Vervollständigung,
die; **b)** *(full number)* **a |full| ~:** die vol-
le Zahl; *(of people)* die volle Stärke. **2.**
['kɒmplɪment] *v. t.* ergänzen. **com-
plementary** [kɒmplɪ'mentərɪ] *adj.* **a)**
(completing) ergänzend; **b)** *(completing each other)* einander ergänzend
complete [kəm'pli:t] **1.** *adj.* **a)** vollständig; *(in number)* vollzählig; **b)**
(finished) fertig; **c)** *(absolute)* völlig
⟨*Idiot*⟩; absolut ⟨*Katastrophe*⟩; total,
(ugs.) blutig ⟨*Anfänger*⟩. **2.** *v. t.* **a)** *(finish)* beenden; fertigstellen ⟨*Gebäude,
Arbeit*⟩; **b)** ausfüllen ⟨*Formular*⟩.
com'pletely *adv.* völlig; absolut ⟨*erfolgreich*⟩. **completion** [kəm'pli:ʃn]
n. Beendigung, *die; (of building, work)*
Fertigstellung, *die*
complex ['kɒmpleks] **1.** *adj.* kompliziert. **2.** *n.* Komplex, *der*
complexion [kəm'plekʃn] *n.* Gesichtsfarbe, *die; (fig.)* Gesicht, *das*
complexity [kəm'pleksɪtɪ] *n.* Kompliziertheit, *die*
complicate ['kɒmplɪkeɪt] *v. t.* komplizieren. '**complicated** *adj.* kompliziert. **complication** [kɒmplɪ'keɪʃn]
n. Komplikation, *die*

complicity [kəm'plɪsɪtɪ] *n.* Mittäter-
schaft, *die* (**in** bei)
compliment **1.** ['kɒmplɪmənt] *n.*
Kompliment, *das; in pl. (formal greetings)* Grüße *Pl.;* **pay sb. a ~:** jmdm. ein
Kompliment machen. **2.** ['kɒmplɪ-
ment] *v. t.* ~ **sb. on sth.** jmdm. Kom-
plimente wegen etw. machen. **com-
plimentary** [kɒmplɪ'mentərɪ] *adj.* **a)**
schmeichelhaft; **b)** *(free)* Frei-
comply [kəm'plaɪ] *v. i.* ~ **with sth.** sich
nach etw. richten; **he refused to ~:** er
wollte sich nicht danach richten
component [kəm'pəʊnənt] **1.** *n.* Bestandteil, *der.* **2.** *adj.* **a ~ part** ein Bestandteil
compose [kəm'pəʊz] *v. t.* **a)** bilden;
be ~d of sich zusammensetzen aus; **b)**
verfassen ⟨*Rede, Gedicht*⟩; abfassen
⟨*Brief*⟩; **c)** *(Mus.)* komponieren.
com'poser *n.* Komponist, *der*/Kom-
ponistin, *die.* **composition** [kɒmpə-
'zɪʃn] *n.* **a)** *(constitution) (of soil etc.)*
Zusammensetzung, *die; (of picture)*
Aufbau, *der;* **b)** *(essay)* Aufsatz, *der;*
(Mus.) Komposition, *die*
compost ['kɒmpɒst] *n.* Kompost, *der.*
'**compost heap** *n.* Komposthaufen,
der
composure [kəm'pəʊʒə(r)] *n.* Gleich-
mut, *der*
¹**compound** **1.** ['kɒmpaʊnd] *adj.* **a)**
zusammengesetzt; **b)** *(Med.)* ~ **fracture** komplizierter Bruch. **2.**
['kɒmpaʊnd] *n.* **a)** *(mixture)* Mischung, *die;* **b)** *(Ling.)* Kompositum,
das; **c)** *(Chem.)* Verbindung, *die.* **3.**
['kɒmpaʊnd] *v. t.* verschlimmern
⟨*Schwierigkeiten, Verletzung usw.*⟩
²**compound** ['kɒmpaʊnd] *n.* umzäun-
tes Gelände
compound 'interest *n.* Zinseszinsen
Pl.

comprehend [kɒmprɪ'hend] *v. t.* verstehen. **comprehensible** [kɒmprɪ-
'hensɪbl] *adj.* verständlich. **comprehension** [kɒmprɪ'henʃn] *n.* Verständnis, *das*
comprehensive [kɒmprɪ'hensɪv] **1.**
adj. **a)** umfassend; **b)** ~ **school** Gesamtschule, *die;* **c)** *(insurance)* Voll-
kasko-. **2.** *n.* Gesamtschule, *die*
compress **1.** [kəm'pres] *v. t.* **a)**
(squeeze) zusammenpressen (**into** zu);
b) komprimieren ⟨*Luft, Gas, Bericht*⟩.
2. ['kɒmpres] *n.* Kompresse, *die.*
compression [kəm'preʃn] *n.* Kom-
pression, *die.* **compressor** [kəm-
'presə(r)] *n.* Kompressor, *der*

comprise [kəm'praɪz] *v.t. (include)* umfassen; *(consist of)* bestehen aus
compromise ['kɒmprəmaɪz] **1.** *n.* Kompromiß, *der.* **2.** *v.i.* Kompromisse/einen Kompromiß schließen. **3.** *v.t.* kompromittieren
compulsion [kəm'pʌlʃn] *n.* Zwang, *der;* **be under no ~ to do sth.** keineswegs etw. tun müssen. **compulsive** [kəm'pʌlsɪv] *adj.* **a)** zwanghaft; **he is a ~ gambler** er ist dem Spiel verfallen; **b) this book is ~ reading** von diesem Buch kann man sich nicht losreißen. **compulsory** [kəm'pʌlsərɪ] *adj.* obligatorisch
compunction [kəm'pʌŋkʃn] *n.* Schuldgefühle
computer [kəm'pju:tə(r)] *n.* Computer, *der*
computer: ~-aided, ~-assisted *adjs.* computergestützt; **~ program** *n.* Programm, *das;* **~ programmer** *n.* Programmierer, *der*/Programmiererin, *die;* **~ programming** *n.* Programmieren, *das;* **~ terminal** *n.* Terminal, *das*
computing [kəm'pju:tɪŋ] *n.* EDV, *die;* elektronische Datenverarbeitung
comrade ['kɒmreɪd, 'kɒmrɪd] *n.* Kamerad, *der*/Kameradin, *die.* **'comradeship** *n.* Kameradschaft, *die*
con [kɒn] *(coll.)* **1.** *n.* Schwindel, *der.* **2.** *v.t., -nn-* reinlegen *(ugs.);* **~ sb. into sth.** jmdm. etw. aufschwatzen *(ugs.)*
concave ['kɒnkeɪv] *adj.* konkav
conceal [kən'si:l] *v.t.* verbergen (**from** vor + *Dat.*). **con'cealment** *n.* Verbergen, *das*
concede [kən'si:d] *v.t.* zugeben
conceit [kən'si:t] *n.* Einbildung, *die.* **con'ceited** *adj.* eingebildet
conceivable [kən'si:vəbl] *adj.* vorstellbar; **it is scarcely ~ that ...:** man kann sich *(Dat.)* kaum vorstellen, daß ... **conceivably** [kən'si:vəblɪ] *adj.* möglicherweise; **he cannot ~ have done it** er kann es unmöglich getan haben
conceive [kən'si:v] **1.** *v.t.* **a)** empfangen ⟨*Kind*⟩; **b)** *(form in mind)* sich *(Dat.)* vorstellen; haben ⟨*Idee, Plan*⟩. **2.** *v.i.* **a)** *(become pregnant)* empfangen; **b) ~ of sth.** sich *(Dat.)* etw. vorstellen
concentrate ['kɒnsəntreɪt] **1.** *v.t.* konzentrieren. **2.** *v.i.* sich konzentrieren (**on** auf + *Akk.*). **'concentrated** *adj.* konzentriert. **concentration** [kɒnsən'treɪʃn] *n.* Konzentration, *die*

concentric [kən'sentrɪk] *adj.* konzentrisch
concept ['kɒnsept] *n.* Begriff, *der;* *(idea)* Vorstellung, *die.* **conception** [kən'sepʃn] **a)** Vorstellung, *die* (**of** von); **b)** *(of child)* Empfängnis, *die*
concern [kən'sɜ:n] **1.** *v.t.* **a)** *(affect)* betreffen; **so far as ... is ~ed** was ... betrifft; **'to whom it may ~'** ≈ „Bestätigung"; *(on certificate, testimonial)* ≈ „Zeugnis"; **b)** *(interest)* **~ oneself with** *or* **about sth.** sich mit etw. befassen; **c)** *(trouble)* beunruhigen. **2.** *n.* **a)** *(anxiety)* Besorgnis, *die;* *(interest)* Interesse, *das;* **b)** *(matter)* Angelegenheit, *die;* **d)** *(firm)* Unternehmen, *das.* **con'cerned** *adj.* **a)** *(involved)* betroffen; *(interested)* interessiert; **as** *or* **so far as I'm ~:** was mich betrifft; **b)** *(troubled)* besorgt. **con'cerning** *prep.* bezüglich
concert ['kɒnsət] *n.* Konzert, *das*
concerted [kən'sɜ:tɪd] *adj.* vereint
concert: ~-goer *n.* Konzertbesucher, *der*/-besucherin, *die;* **~-hall** *n.* Konzertsaal, *der*
concertina [kɒnsə'ti:nə] *n.* Konzertina, *die*
concerto [kən'tʃeətəʊ] *n.* Konzert, *das*
concession [kən'seʃn] *n.* Konzession, *die.* **concessionary** [kən'seʃənərɪ] *adj.* Konzessions-; **~ rate/fare** ermäßigter Tarif
conciliatory [kən'sɪljətərɪ] *adj.* versöhnlich
concise [kən'saɪs] *adj.* kurz und prägnant; knapp, konzis ⟨*Stil*⟩
conclude [kən'klu:d] **1.** *v.t.* **a)** *(end)* beschließen; **b)** *(infer)* schließen (**from** aus); **c)** *(reach decision)* beschließen. **2.** *v.i.* *(end)* schließen. **concluding** [kən'klu:dɪŋ] *adj.* abschließend. **conclusion** [kən'klu:ʒn] *n.* **a)** *(end)* Abschluß, *der;* **in ~:** zum Abschluß; **b)** *(result)* Ausgang, *der;* **c)** *(inference)* Schluß, *der;* **draw** *or* **reach a ~:** zu einem Schluß kommen. **conclusive** [kən'klu:sɪv] *adj.,* **con'clusively** *adv.* schlüssig
concoct [kən'kɒkt] *v.t.* zubereiten; zusammenbrauen ⟨*Trank*⟩. **concoction** [kən'kɒkʃn] *n.* Gebräu, *das*
concourse ['kɒnkɔ:s] *n.* Halle, *die;* **station ~:** Bahnhofshalle, *die*
concrete ['kɒnkri:t] **1.** *adj.* konkret. **2.** *n.* Beton, *der; attrib.* Beton-; **aus Beton** *präd.* **'concrete-mixer** *n.* Betonmischer, *der*

concur [kən'kɜ:(r)] *v. i.*, **-rr-**: ~ |with sb.| |in sth.| |jmdm.| [in etw. *(Dat.)*] zustimmen. **concurrent** [kən'kʌrənt] *adj.*, **con'currently** *adv.* gleichzeitig

concussion [kən'kʌʃn] *n.* Gehirnerschütterung, *die*

condemn [kən'dem] *v. t.* **a)** *(censure)* verdammen; **b)** *(Law: sentence)* verurteilen (**to** zu); **c)** für unbewohnbar erklären 〈*Gebäude*〉. **condemnation** [kɒndem'neɪʃn] *n.* Verdammung, *die*

condensation [kɒnden'seɪʃn] *n.* **a)** *(condensing)* Kondensation, *die;* **b)** *(water)* Kondenswasser, *das*

condense [kən'dens] **1.** *v. t.* **a)** komprimieren; ~**d milk** Kondensmilch, *die;* **b)** *(Phys., Chem.)* kondensieren. **2.** *v. i.* kondensieren

condescend [kɒndɪ'send] *v. i.* ~ **to do sth.** sich dazu herablassen, etw. zu tun. **conde'scending** *adj.* herablassend

condition [kən'dɪʃn] *n.* **a)** *(stipulation)* [Vor]bedingung, *die;* **on** |the| ~ **that ...**: unter der Voraussetzung, daß ...; **b)** *in pl. (circumstances)* Umstände *Pl.;* **weather/living** ~**s** Witterungs-/Wohnverhältnisse; **working** ~**s** Arbeitsbedingungen; **c)** *(of athlete etc.)* Form, *die;* *(of thing)* Zustand, *der;* *(of patient)* Verfassung, *die;* **d)** *Med.)* Leiden, *das.* **conditional** [kən'dɪʃənl] *adj.* **a)** bedingt; **be** ~ |up|on **sth.** von etw. abhängen; **b)** *(Ling.)* Konditional-

con'ditioner *n.* Frisiermittel, *das*

condolence [kən'dəʊləns] *n.* Anteilnahme, die; **letter of** ~: Beileidsbrief, *der*

condom ['kɒndɒm] *n.* Kondom, *das od. der*

condominium ['kɒndə'mɪnɪəm] *n. (Amer.)* Appartementhaus [mit Eigentumswohnungen]

condone [kən'dəʊn] *v. t.* hinwegsehen über (+ *Akk.*); *(approve)* billigen

conducive [kən'dju:sɪv] *adj.* **be** ~ **to sth.** einer Sache *(Dat.)* förderlich sein

conduct 1. ['kɒndʌkt] *n.* **a)** *(behaviour)* Verhalten, *das;* **b)** *(way of* ~*ing)* Führung, *die.* **2.** [kən'dʌkt] *v. t.* **a)** führen; **b)** *(Mus.)* dirigieren; **c)** *(Phys.)* leiten; **d)** ~**ed tour** Führung, *die.* **conduction** [kən'dʌkʃn] *n. (Phys.)* Leitung, *die.* **conductor** [kən'dʌktə(r)] *n.* **a)** *(Mus.)* Dirigent, *der*/Dirigentin, *die;* **b)** *(of bus, tram)* Schaffner, *der.* **conductress** [kən'dʌktrɪs] *n.* Schaffnerin, *die*

cone [kəʊn] *n.* **a)** Kegel, *der; (traffic* ~*)* Leitkegel, *der;* **b)** *(Bot.)* Zapfen, *der;* **c)** **ice-cream** ~: Eistüte, *die*

confectioner [kən'fekʃənə(r)] *n.* ~**'s** |shop| Süßwarengeschäft, *das.* **con'fectionery** *n.* Süßwaren *Pl.*

confederation [kən'fedə'reɪʃn] *n.* [Staaten]bund, *der*

confer [kən'fɜ:(r)] **1.** *v. t.*, **-rr-**: ~ **sth.** |up|on sb. jmdm. etw. verleihen. **2.** *v. i.*, **-rr-**: ~ **with sb.** sich mit jmdm. beraten

conference ['kɒnfərəns] *n.* **a)** Konferenz, *die;* **b)** **be in** ~: in einer Besprechung sein. **'conference-room** *n.* Konferenzraum, *der*

confess [kən'fes] **1.** *v. t.* **a)** gestehen; **b)** *(Eccl.)* beichten. **2.** *v. i.* **a)** ~ **to sth.** etw. gestehen; **b)** *(Eccl.)* beichten (**to** sb. jmdm.). **confession** [kən'feʃn] *n.* **a)** Geständnis, *das;* **b)** *(Eccl.: of sins etc.)* Beichte, *die*

confetti [kən'fetɪ] *n.* Konfetti, *das*

confide [kən'faɪd] **1.** *v. i.* ~ **in sb.** sich jmdm. anvertrauen. **2.** *v. t.* ~ **sth. to sb.** jmdm. etw. anvertrauen

confidence ['kɒnfɪdəns] *n.* **a)** *(firm trust)* Vertrauen, *das;* **have** ~ **in sb./ sth.** Vertrauen zu jmdm./etw. haben; **have** |absolute| ~ **that ...**: |absolut| sicher sein, daß ...; **b)** *(assured expectation)* Gewißheit, *die;* **c)** *(self-reliance)* Selbstvertrauen, *das;* **d)** **in** ~: im Vertrauen; **this is in** |strict| ~: das ist [streng] vertraulich. **'confidence trick** *n. (Brit.)* Trickbetrug, *der*

confident ['kɒnfɪdənt] *adj.* **a)** zuversichtlich (**about** in bezug auf + *Akk.*); **be** ~ **that ...**: sicher sein, daß ... ; **b)** *(self-assured)* selbstbewußt

confidential [kɒnfɪ'denʃl] *adj.* vertraulich. **confidentiality** [kɒnfɪdenʃɪ'ælɪtɪ] *n.* Vertraulichkeit, *die.* **confi'dentially** *adv.* vertraulich

'confidently *adv.* zuversichtlich

confine [kən'faɪn] *v. t.* **a)** einsperren; **be** ~**d to bed/the house** ans Bett/Haus gefesselt sein; **b)** *(fig.)* ~ **oneself to doing sth.** sich darauf beschränken, etw. zu tun. **con'fined** *adj.* begrenzt. **con'finement** *n. (imprisonment)* Einsperrung, *die.* **confines** ['kɒnfaɪnz] *n. pl.* Grenzen

confirm [kən'fɜ:m] *v. t.* bestätigen. **confirmation** [kɒnfə'meɪʃn] *n.* **a)** Bestätigung, *die;* **b)** *(Protestant Ch.)* Konfirmation, *die;(RC Ch.)* Firmung, *die.* **con'firmed** *adj.* eingefleischt 〈*Junggeselle*〉; überzeugt 〈*Vegetarier*〉

confiscate ['kɒnfɪskeɪt] *v. t.* beschlagnahmen. **confiscation** [kɒnfɪsˈkeɪʃn] *n.* Beschlagnahme, *die*

conflict 1. [ˈkɒnflɪkt] *n.* **a)** *(fight)* Kampf, *der;* **b)** *(clashing)* Konflikt, *der.* 2. [kənˈflɪkt] *v.i. (be incompatible)* sich *(Dat.)* widersprechen; ~ **with** sth. einer Sache *(Dat.)* widersprechen. **conˈflicting** *adj.* widersprüchlich

conform [kənˈfɔːm] *v.i.* **a)** entsprechen (**to** *Dat.*); **b)** *(comply)* sich einfügen; ~ **to** *or* **with** sth./**with** sb. sich nach etw./jmdm. richten. **conformist** [kənˈfɔːmɪst] *n.* Konformist, *der*/Konformistin, *die.* **conformity** [kənˈfɔːmɪtɪ] *n.* Übereinstimmung, *die* (**with, to** mit)

confound [kənˈfaʊnd] *v.t.* **a)** *(defeat)* vereiteln; **b)** *(confuse)* verwirren. **conˈfounded** *adj. (coll. derog.)* verdammt

confront [kənˈfrʌnt] *v.t.* **a)** gegenüberstellen; ~ **sb. with** sth./**sb.** jmdn. mit etw./[mit] jmdm. konfrontieren; **b)** *(stand facing)* gegenüberstehen (+ *Dat.*). **confrontation** [kɒnfrənˈteɪʃn] *n.* Konfrontation, *die*

confuse [kənˈfjuːz] *v.t.* **a)** *(disorder)* durcheinanderbringen; **b)** *(mix up mentally)* verwechseln; **c)** *(perplex)* verwirren. **conˈfused** *adj.* konfus; wirr ⟨*Gedanken, Gerüchte*⟩; verworren ⟨*Lage, Situation*⟩. **confusing** [kənˈfjuːzɪŋ] *adj.* verwirrend. **confusion** [kənˈfjuːʒn] *n.* **a)** Verwirrung, *die; (mixing up)* Verwechslung, *die;* **b)** *(embarrassment)* Verlegenheit, *die*

congeal [kənˈdʒiːl] *v.i.* gerinnen

conger [ˈkɒŋɡə(r)] *n.* ~ [eel] Seeaal, *der*

congested [kənˈdʒestɪd] *adj.* verstopft ⟨*Straße, Nase*⟩. **congestion** [kənˈdʒestʃn] *n. (of traffic)* Stauung, *die;* **nasal** ~: verstopfte Nase

conglomerate [kənˈlɒmərət] *n. (Commerc.)* Großkonzern, *der.* **conglomeration** [kənɡlɒməˈreɪʃn] *n.* Anhäufung, *die*

congratulate [kənˈɡrætjʊleɪt] *v.t.* gratulieren (+ *Dat.*); ~ **sb./oneself on** sth. jmdm./sich zu etw. gratulieren. **congratulations** [kənɡrætjʊˈleɪʃnz] 1. *int.* ~! herzlichen Glückwunsch! (**on** zu). 2. *n. pl.* Glückwünsche *Pl.*

congregate [ˈkɒŋɡrɪɡeɪt] *v.i.* sich versammeln. **congregation** [kɒŋɡrɪˈɡeɪʃn] *n. (Eccl.)* Gemeinde, *die*

congress [ˈkɒŋɡres] *n.* Kongreß, *der;* **C~** *(Amer.)* der Kongreß. **congressional** [kənˈɡreʃənl] *adj.* Kongreß-

conical [ˈkɒnɪkl] *adj.* kegelförmig

conifer [ˈkɒnɪfə(r)] *n.* Nadelbaum, *der*

conjecture [kənˈdʒektʃə(r)] 1. *n.* Vermutung, *die.* 2. *v.t.* vermuten. 3. *v.i.* Vermutungen anstellen

conjugate [ˈkɒndʒʊɡeɪt] *v.t. (Ling.)* konjugieren. **conjugation** [kɒndʒʊˈɡeɪʃn] *n. (Ling.)* Konjugation, *die*

conjunction [kənˈdʒʌŋkʃn] *n.* **a)** Verbindung, *die;* **in** ~ **with** in Verbindung mit; **b)** *(Ling.)* Konjunktion, *die*

conjure [ˈkʌndʒə(r)] *v.i.* zaubern; **conjuring trick** Zaubertrick, *der.* **conjure ˈup** *v.t.* heraufbeschwören

conjurer, conjuror [ˈkʌndʒərə(r)] *n.* Zauberkünstler, *der*/-künstlerin, *die*

connect [kəˈnekt] 1. *v.t.* verbinden (**to, with** mit). 2. *v.i.* ~ **with** sth. mit etw. zusammenhängen. **conˈnected** *adj.* zusammenhängend. **connection,** *(Brit.)* **connexion** [kəˈnekʃn] *n.* **a)** *(act, state)* Verbindung, *die;* **b)** *(fig.: of ideas)* Zusammenhang, *der;* **in** ~ **with** im Zusammenhang mit; **c)** *(train, bus, etc.)* Anschluß, *der*

connoisseur [kɒnəˈsɜː(r)] *n.* Kenner, *der*

connotation [kɒnəˈteɪʃn] *n.* Assoziation, *die*

conquer [ˈkɒŋkə(r)] *v.t.* besiegen; erobern ⟨*Land*⟩. **conqueror** [ˈkɒŋkərə(r)] *n. (of a country)* Eroberer, *der*

conquest [ˈkɒŋkwest] *n.* Eroberung, *die*

conscience [ˈkɒnʃəns] *n.* Gewissen, *das;* **have a clear/guilty** ~: ein gutes/schlechtes Gewissen haben

conscientious [kɒnʃɪˈenʃəs] *adj.* pflichtbewußt; *(meticulous)* gewissenhaft; ~ **objector** Wehrdienstverweigerer [aus Gewissensgründen]. **consciˈentiously** *adv.* pflichtbewußt; *(meticulously)* gewissenhaft

conscious [ˈkɒnʃəs] *adj.* **a)** **he is not** ~ **of it** es ist ihm nicht bewußt; **b)** *pred. (awake)* bei Bewußtsein *präd.;* **c)** *(realized by doer)* bewußt ⟨*Versuch, Bemühung*⟩. **consciousness** [ˈkɒnʃəsnɪs] *n.* Bewußtsein, *das*

conscript 1. [kənˈskrɪpt] *v.t.* einberufen. 2. [ˈkɒnskrɪpt] *n.* Einberufene, *der/die.* **conscription** [kənˈskrɪpʃn] *n.* Wehrpflicht, *die*

consecrate [ˈkɒnsɪkreɪt] *v.t.* weihen

consecutive [kənˈsekjʊtɪv] *adj.* aufeinanderfolgend ⟨*Monate, Jahre*⟩; fortlaufend ⟨*Zahlen*⟩. **conˈsecutively** *adj.* hintereinander

consensus [kənˈsensəs] *n.* Einigkeit, *die*

consent [kən'sent] **1.** *v. i.* zustimmen. **2.** *n. (agreement)* Zustimmung, *die* (**to** zu); **by common** *or* **general** ~: nach allgemeiner Auffassung

consequence ['kɒnsɪkwəns] *n.* **a)** *(result)* Folge, *die;* **in** ~: folglich; **as a** ~: infolgedessen; **b)** *(importance)* Bedeutung, *die*. **consequent** ['kɒnsɪkwənt] *adj.* daraus folgend. '**consequently** *adv.* infolgedessen

conservation [kɒnsə'veɪʃn] *n.* Erhaltung, *die;* **wildlife** ~: Schutz wildlebender Tierarten. **conservationist** [kɒnsə'veɪʃənɪst] *n.* Naturschützer, *der/*-schützerin, *die*

conservative [kən'sɜːvətɪv] **1.** *adj.* **a)** konservativ; **b)** vorsichtig ⟨*Schätzung⟩;* **c)** C~ *(Brit. Polit.)* konservativ; **the** C~ **Party** die Konservative Partei. **2.** *n.* C~ *(Brit. Polit.)* Konservative, *der/die*. **con'servatively** *adv.* vorsichtig ⟨*geschätzt⟩*

conservatory [kən'sɜːvətərɪ] *n.* Wintergarten, *der*

conserve [kən'sɜːv] *v. t.* erhalten; schonen ⟨*Kräfte⟩*

consider [kən'sɪdə(r)] *v. t.* **a)** *(think about)* ~ **sth.** an etw. *(Akk.)* denken; **he's** ~**ing emigrating** er denkt daran, auszuwandern; **b)** *(reflect on)* sich *(Dat.)* überlegen; **c)** *(regard as)* halten für; **all things** ~**ed** alles in allem. **considerable** [kən'sɪdərəbl] *adj.,* **con'siderably** *adv.* erheblich. **con'siderate** [kən'sɪdərət] *adj.* rücksichtsvoll; *(thoughtfully kind)* entgegenkommend. **consideration** [kənsɪdə'reɪʃn] *n.* **a)** Überlegung, *die;* **take sth. into** ~: etw. berücksichtigen; **the matter is under** ~: die Angelegenheit wird geprüft; **b)** *(thoughtfulness)* Rücksichtnahme, *die*. **con'sidering** *prep.* ~ **sth.** wenn man etw. bedenkt; ~ |**that**| ...: wenn man bedenkt, daß ...

consign [kən'saɪn] *v. t.* anvertrauen (**to** *Dat.*). **con'signment** *n. (Commerc.)* Sendung, *die; (large)* Ladung, *die*

consist [kən'sɪst] *v. i.* ~ **of** bestehen aus. **consistency** [kən'sɪstənsɪ] *n.* **a)** *(density)* Konsistenz, *die;* **b)** *(being consistent)* Konsequenz, *die*

consistent [kən'sɪstənt] *adj.* **a)** *(compatible* [miteinander] vereinbar; **b)** *(uniform)* gleichbleibend ⟨*Qualität⟩;* **c)** *(unchanging)* konsequent

consolation [kɒnsə'leɪʃn] *n.* Trost, *der*. **conso'lation prize** *n.* Trostpreis, *der*

console [kən'səʊl] *v. t.* trösten

consolidate [kən'sɒlɪdeɪt] *v. t.* festigen

consonant ['kɒnsənənt] *n.* Konsonant, *der*

consort [kən'sɔːt] *v. i.* verkehren (**with** mit)

consortium [kən'sɔːtɪəm] *n., pl.* **consortia** [kən'sɔːtɪə] Konsortium, *das*

conspicuous [kən'spɪkjʊəs] *adj.* **a)** *(visible)* unübersehbar; **b)** *(obvious)* auffallend

conspiracy [kən'spɪrəsɪ] *n. (conspiring)* Verschwörung, *die; (plot)* Komplott, *das*

conspire [kən'spaɪə(r)] *v. i.* sich verschwören

constable ['kʌnstəbl, 'kɒnstəbl] *n. (Brit.)* Polizist, *der/*Polizistin, *die*. **constabulary** [kən'stæbjʊlərɪ] *n.* Polizei, *die*

constant ['kɒnstənt] *adj.* **a)** *(unceasing)* ständig; **b)** *(unchanging)* gleichbleibend. '**constantly** *adv.* **a)** *(unceasingly)* ständig; **b)** *(unchangingly)* konstant

constellation [kɒnstə'leɪʃn] *n.* Sternbild, *das*

consternation [kɒnstə'neɪʃn] *n.* Bestürzung, *die*

constipated ['kɒnstɪpeɪtɪd] *adj.* **be** ~: an Verstopfung leiden. **constipation** [kɒnstɪ'peɪʃn] *n.* Verstopfung, *die*

constituency [kən'stɪtjʊənsɪ] *n.* Wahlkreis, *der*

constituent [kən'stɪtjʊənt] *n.* **a)** *(part)* Bestandteil, *der;* **b)** *(Polit.)* Wähler, *der/*Wählerin, *die*

constitute ['kɒnstɪtjuːt] *v. t.* **a)** *(form, be)* sein; ~ **a threat to** eine Gefahr sein für; **b)** *(make up)* bilden. **constitution** [kɒnstɪ'tjuːʃn] *n.* **a)** *(of person)* Konstitution, *die;* **b)** *(of state)* Verfassung, *die*. **constitutional** [kɒnstɪ'tjuːʃənl] *adj. (of constitution)* der Verfassung *nachgestellt; (in harmony with constitution)* verfassungsmäßig

constrain [kən'streɪn] *v. t.* zwingen. **constraint** [kən'streɪnt] *n. (limitation)* Einschränkung, *die*

constrict [kən'strɪkt] *v. t.* verengen. **constriction** [kən'strɪkʃn] *n.* Verengung, *die*

construct [kən'strʌkt] *v. t.* bauen; *(fig.)* erstellen *(Plan).* **construction** [kən'strʌkʃn] *n.* **a)** *(constructing)* Bau, *der;* **be under** ~: im Bau sein; **b)** *(thing constructed)* Bauwerk, *das*. **con-**

structive [kən'strʌktɪv] *adj.* konstruktiv

consul ['kɒnsl] *n.* Konsul, *der.* **consulate** ['kɒnsjʊlət] *n.* Konsulat, *das*

consult [kən'sʌlt] *v.t.* konsultieren ⟨*Arzt, Fachmann*⟩; ~ **a book** in einem Buch nachsehen. **consultant** [kən-'sʌltənt] *n.* Berater, *der*/Beraterin, *die; (Med.)* Chefarzt, *der*/-ärztin, *die.* **consultation** [kɒnsəl'teɪʃn] *n.* Beratung, *die*

consume [kən'sju:m] *v.t.* verbrauchen; *(eat, drink)* konsumieren. **con-'sumer** *n.* Verbraucher, *der*/Verbraucherin, *die.* **con'sumer goods** *n. pl.* Konsumgüter

consumption [kən'sʌmpʃn] *n.* Verbrauch, *der* (**of** an + *Dat.*); *(eating or drinking)* Verzehr, *der* (**of** von)

cont. *abbr.* **continued** Forts.

contact 1. ['kɒntækt] *n.* Berührung, *die; (fig.)* Kontakt, *der;* **be in ~ with sth.** etw. berühren; **be in ~ with sb.** *(fig.)* mit jmdm. Kontakt haben. **2.** ['kɒntækt, kən'tækt] *v.t.* sich in Verbindung setzen mit. '**contact lens** *n.* Kontaktlinse, *die*

contagious [kən'teɪdʒəs] *adj.* ansteckend

contain [kən'teɪn] *v.t.* **a)** *(hold, include)* enthalten; **b)** *(prevent from spreading)* aufhalten. **con'tainer** *n.* Behälter, *der; (cargo ~)* Container, *der;* **cardboard/wooden ~:** Pappkarton, *der*/Holzkiste, *die*

contaminate [kən'tæmɪneɪt] *v.t.* verunreinigen; *(with radioactivity)* verseuchen. **contamination** [kəntæmɪ-'neɪʃn] *n.* Verunreinigung, *die; (with radioactivity)* Verseuchung, *die*

contemplate ['kɒntəmpleɪt] *v.t.* **a)** betrachten; *(mentally)* nachdenken über (+ *Akk.*); **b)** *(expect)* rechnen mit; *(consider)* ~ **sth./doing sth.** an etw. *(Akk.)* denken/daran denken, etw. zu tun. **contemplation** [kɒntəm'pleɪʃn] *n.* Betrachtung, *die; (mental)* Nachdenken, *das* (**of** über + *Akk.*)

contemporary [kən'tempərəri] **1.** *adj.* zeitgenössisch. **2.** *n.* Zeitgenosse, *der*/-genossin, *die*

contempt [kən'tempt] *n.* Verachtung, *die* (**of, for** für). **contemptible** [kən-'temptɪbl] *adj.* verachtenswert. **contemptuous** [kən'temptjʊəs] *adj.* verächtlich

contend [kən'tend] *v.i.* **be able/have to ~ with** fertigwerden können/müssen mit. **con'tender** *n.* Bewerber, *der*/Bewerberin, *die*

¹**content** ['kɒntent] *n.* **a)** *in pl.* Inhalt, *der;* |**table of**| ~**s** Inhaltsverzeichnis, *das;* **b)** *(amount contained)* Gehalt, *der* (**of** an + *Dat.*)

²**content** [kən'tent] **1.** *pred. adj.* zufrieden. **2.** *v.t.* zufriedenstellen; ~ **oneself with sth./sb.** sich mit etw./jmdm. zufriedengeben. **con'tented** *adj.*, **con-'tentedly** *adv.* zufrieden

contention [kən'tenʃn] *n.* **a)** Streit, *der;* **b)** *(point asserted)* Behauptung, *die.* **contentious** [kən'tenʃəs] *adj.* strittig ⟨*Punkt, Thema*⟩

con'tentment *n.* Zufriedenheit, *die*

contest 1. ['kɒntest] *n.* Wettbewerb, *der.* **2.** [kən'test] *v.t.* **a)** bestreiten; in Frage stellen ⟨*Behauptung*⟩; **b)** *(Brit.: compete for)* kandidieren für. **contestant** [kən'testənt] *n. (competitor)* Teilnehmer, *der*/Teilnehmerin, *die*

context ['kɒntekst] *n.* Kontext, *der;* **in/out of ~:** im/ohne Kontext; **in this ~:** in diesem Zusammenhang

continent ['kɒntɪnənt] *n.* Kontinent, *der;* **the C~:** das europäische Festland. **continental** [kɒntɪ'nentl] *adj.* **a)** kontinental; **b)** C~ *(mainland European)* kontinental[europäisch]. **continental 'breakfast** *n.* kontinentales Frühstück. **continental 'quilt** *n. (Brit.)* [Stepp]federbett, *das*

contingent [kən'tɪndʒənt] *n.* Kontingent, *das*

continual [kən'tɪnjʊəl] *adj.*, **con-'tinually** *adv. (frequent[ly])* ständig; *(without stopping)* unaufhörlich

continuation [kəntɪnjʊ'eɪʃn] *n.* Fortsetzung, *die*

continue [kən'tɪnju:] **1.** *v.t.* fortsetzen; '~**d on page 2**' „Fortsetzung auf S. 2"; ~ **doing** *or* **to do sth.** etw. weiter tun; **it** ~**d to rain** es regnete weiter. **2.** *v.i. (persist)* ⟨*Wetter, Zustand, Krise usw.:*⟩ andauern; *(persist in doing sth.)* nicht aufhören; ~ **with sth.** mit etw. fortfahren. **continuity** [kɒntɪ'nju:ɪtɪ] *n.* Kontinuität, *die.* **continuous** [kən'tɪnjʊəs] *adj.* **a)** ununterbrochen; anhaltend ⟨*Regen, Sonnenschein*⟩; ständig ⟨*Kritik, Streit*⟩; durchgezogen ⟨*Linie*⟩; **b)** *(Ling.)* ~ |**form**| Verlaufsform, *die.* **con'tinuously** *adv.* ununterbrochen; ständig ⟨*sich ändern*⟩

contort [kən'tɔ:t] *v.t.* verdrehen. **contortion** [kən'tɔ:ʃn] *n.* Verdrehung, *die*

contour ['kɒntʊə(r)] Kontur, *die;* ~ **map** Höhenlinienkarte, *die*

contraband ['kɒntrəbænd] *n.*
Schmuggelware, *die*

contraception [kɒntrə'sepʃn] *n.*
Empfängnisverhütung, *die.* **contraceptive** [kɒntrə'septɪv] 1. *adj.* empfängnisverhütend. 2. *n.* Verhütungsmittel, *das*

contract 1. ['kɒntrækt] *n.* Vertrag, *der; ~ of employment* Arbeitsvertrag, *der;* **be under ~ to do sth.** vertraglich verpflichtet sein, etw. zu tun. 2. [kən-'trækt] *v. i. (Med.)* sich *(Dat.)* zuziehen. 3. *v. i.* **a)** *~ to do sth.* sich vertraglich verpflichten, etw. zu tun; **b)** *(become smaller, be drawn together)* sich zusammenziehen. **contraction** [kən'trækʃn] *n.* Kontraktion, *die.*

contractor [kən'træktə(r)] *n.* Auftragnehmer, *der/*-nehmerin, *die*

contradict [kɒntrə'dɪkt] *v. t.* widersprechen (+ *Dat.*). **contradiction** [kɒntrə'dɪkʃn] *n.* Widerspruch, *der;* **in ~ to sb./sth.** im Widerspruch zu jmdm./etw. **contradictory** [kɒntrə-'dɪktərɪ] *adj.* widersprüchlich

contralto [kən'træltəʊ] *n., pl.* ~s Alt, *der*

contraption [kən'træpʃn] *n. (coll.)* [komisches] Gerät

contrary ['kɒntrərɪ] 1. *adj.* **a)** entgegengesetzt; **be ~ to sth.** im Gegensatz zu etw. stehen; **b)** [kən'treərɪ] *(coll.: perverse)* widerspenstig. 2. *n.* **the ~:** das Gegenteil; **on the ~:** im Gegenteil. 3. *adv.* **~ to sth.** entgegen einer Sache

contrast 1. [kən'trɑːst] *v. t.* gegenüberstellen. 2. ['kɒntrɑːst] *n.* Kontrast, *der* (with zu); **in ~, ...:** im Gegensatz dazu, ...; [be] **in ~ with sth.** im Gegensatz zu etw. [stehen]. **con'trasting** *adj.* gegensätzlich

contravene [kɒntrə'viːn] *v. t.* verstoßen gegen. **contravention** [kɒntrə-'venʃn] *n.* Verstoß, *der* (of gegen)

contribute [kən'trɪbjuːt] 1. *v. t.* **~ sth.** [to *or* towards sth.] etw. [zu etw.] beitragen. 2. *v. i.* **~ to charity** für karitative Zwecke spenden; **~ to the success of sth.** zum Erfolg einer Sache *(Gen.)* beitragen. **contribution** [kɒntrɪ-'bjuːʃn] *n.* Beitrag, *der; (for charity)* Spende, *die* (to für); **make a ~:** einen Beitrag leisten; *(to charity)* etwas spenden. **contributor** [kən'trɪbjʊtə(r)] *n. (to encyclopaedia etc.)* Mitarbeiter, *der/*Mitarbeiterin, *die*

contrite ['kɒntraɪt] *adj.* zerknirscht

contrive [kən'traɪv] *v. t.* **~ to do sth.** es fertigbringen, etw. zu tun

control [kən'trəʊl] 1. *n.* **a)** Kontrolle, *die* (of über + *Akk.*); **keep ~ of sth.** etw. unter Kontrolle halten; **be in ~** [of sth.] die Kontrolle [über etw. *(Akk.)*] haben; [go *or* get] **out of ~:** außer Kontrolle [geraten]; [get sth.] **under ~:** [etw.] unter Kontrolle [bringen]; **b)** *(device)* Regler, *der;* **~s** Schalttafel, *die.* 2. *v. t.,* **-ll-** kontrollieren; lenken ⟨*Auto*⟩; zügeln ⟨*Zorn*⟩; regeln ⟨*Verkehr*⟩. **con'trol centre** *n.* Kontrollzentrum, *das.* **con'trol desk** *n.* Schaltpult, *das*

con'troller *n. (director)* Leiter, *der/*Leiterin, *die*

control: ~ panel *n.* Schalttafel, *die;* **~ room** *n.* Kontrollraum, *der;* **~ tower** *n.* Kontrollturm, *der*

controversial [kɒntrə'vɜːʃl] *adj.* umstritten

controversy ['kɒntrəvɜːsɪ, kən'trɒvəsɪ] *n.* Auseinandersetzung, *die*

convalesce [kɒnvə'les] *v. i.* genesen. **convalescence** [kɒnvə'lesəns] *n.* Genesung, *die*

convection [kən'vekʃn] *n. (Phys., Meteorol.)* Konvektion, *die*

convector [kən'vektə(r)] *n.* Konvektor, *der*

convene [kən'viːn] 1. *v. t.* einberufen. 2. *v. i.* zusammenkommen

convenience [kən'viːnɪəns] *n.* **a)** for sb.'s ~ zu jmds. Bequemlichkeit; **at your ~:** wann es Ihnen paßt; **b)** *(toilet)* [public] **~:** [öffentliche] Toilette. **con'venience food** *n.* Fertignahrung, *die*

convenient [kən'viːnɪənt] *adj.* günstig; *(useful)* praktisch; **would it be ~ to** *or* **for you?** würde es Ihnen passen? **con'veniently** *adv.* **a)** günstig ⟨*gelegen, angebracht*⟩; **b)** *(opportunely)* angenehmerweise

convent ['kɒnvənt] *n.* Kloster, *das*

convention [kən'venʃn] *n.* **a)** Brauch, *der;* **b)** *(assembly)* Konferenz, *die;* **c)** *(agreement)* Konvention, *die.* **conventional** [kən'venʃənl] *adj.* konventionell

converge [kən'vɜːdʒ] *v. i.* **~ [on each other]** aufeinander zulaufen

conversant [kən'vɜːsənt] *pred. adj.* vertraut (with mit)

conversation [kɒnvə'seɪʃn] *n.* Unterhaltung, *die;* **have a ~:** ein Gespräch führen. **conversational** [kɒnvə'seɪʃənl] *adj.* **~ English** gesprochenes Englisch

¹converse [kən'vɜːs] *v. i. (formal)* ~

cork

|with sb.| |about *or* on sth.| sich [mit jmdm.] [über etw. *(Akk.)*] unterhalten ²**converse** ['kɒnvɜ:s] **1.** *adj.* entgegengesetzt; umgekehrt ‹*Fall, Situation*›. **2.** *n.* Gegenteil, *das.* **conversely** [kən'vɜ:slɪ] *adj.* umgekehrt

conversion [kən'vɜ:ʃn] *n.* **a)** Umwandlung, *die* (**into** in + *Akk.*); **b)** *(adaptation)* Umbau, *der;* **c)** *(of person)* Bekehrung, *die* (**to** zu)

convert [kən'vɜ:t] **1.** *v. t.* umwandeln (**into** in + *Akk.*); ~ **sb.** |**to sth.**| jmdn. [zu etw.] bekehren. **2.** [kən'vɜ:t] *v. i.* ~ **into sth.** sich in etw. *(Akk.)* umwandeln lassen. **3.** ['kɒnvɜ:t] *n.* Konvertit, *der*/Konvertitin, *die.* **convertible** [kən'vɜ:tɪbl] **1.** *adj.* be ~ **into sth.** sich in etw. *(Akk.)* umwandeln lassen. **2.** *n.* Kabrio[lett], *das*

convex ['kɒnveks] *adj.* konvex

convey [kən'veɪ] *v. t.* befördern. **conveyance** [kən'veɪəns] *n.* **a)** *(transportation)* Beförderung, *die;* **b)** *(formal: vehicle)* Beförderungsmittel, *das.* **con'veyancing** *n.* *(Law)* ~ |**of property**| [Eigentums]übertragung, *die.* **con'veyor** [kən'veɪə(r)] *n.* ~ |**belt**| Fließband, *das*

convict **1.** ['kɒnvɪkt] *n.* Strafgefangene, *der/die.* **2.** [kən'vɪkt] *v. t.* verurteilen. **conviction** [kən'vɪkʃn] *n.* **a)** *(Law)* Verurteilung, *die* (**for** wegen); **b)** *(belief)* Überzeugung, *die*

convince [kən'vɪns] *v. t.* überzeugen; ~ **sb. that ...**: jmdn. davon überzeugen, daß ...; **be ~d that ...**: davon überzeugt sein, daß ... **convincing** [kən'vɪnsɪŋ] *adj.*, **con'vincingly** *adv.* überzeugend

convivial [kən'vɪvɪəl] *adj.* fröhlich

convoluted ['kɒnvəlu:tɪd] *adj.* *(complex)* kompliziert

convoy ['kɒnvɔɪ] *n.* Konvoi, *der;* in ~: im Konvoi

convulse [kən'vʌls] *v. t.* be ~d **with** sich krümmen vor (+ *Dat.*). **convulsions** [kən'vʌlʃnz] *n. pl.* Krämpfe

coo [ku:] *v. i.* gurren

cook [kʊk] **1.** *n.* Koch, *der*/Köchin, *die.* **2.** *v. t.* kochen ‹*Mahlzeit*›; *(fry, roast)* braten; *(boil)* kochen. **3.** *v. i.* kochen. **cook 'up** *v. t.* erfinden ‹*Geschichte*›

'**cookbook** *n.* *(Amer.)* Kochbuch, *das*

'**cooker** *n.* *(Brit.)* Herd, *der*

cookery ['kʊkərɪ] *n.* Kochen, *das.* '**cookery book** *n.* *(Brit.)* Kochbuch, *das*

cookie ['kʊkɪ] *n.* *(Amer.)* Keks, *der*

'**cooking** *n.* Kochen, *das.* '**cooking apple** *n.* Kochapfel, *der.* '**cooking utensil** *n.* Küchengerät, *das*

cool [ku:l] **1.** *adj.* **a)** kühl; **store in a** ~ **place** kühl aufbewahren; **b)** *(unemotional, unfriendly)* kühl; *(calm)* ruhig. **2.** *n.* Kühle, *die.* **3.** *v. i.* abkühlen. **4.** *v. t.* kühlen; *(from high temperature)* abkühlen. **cool 'down, cool 'off** *v. i. & t.* abkühlen

coolly ['ku:llɪ] *adv.* *(calmly)* ruhig; *(unemotionally)* kühl

coop [ku:p] **1.** *n.* *(for poultry)* Hühnerstall, *der.* **2.** *v. t.* ~ **up** einpferchen

co-operate [kəʊ'ɒpəreɪt] *v. i.* mitarbeiten (**in** bei); *(with each other)* zusammenarbeiten (**in** bei). **co-operation** [kəʊɒpə'reɪʃn] *n.* Zusammenarbeit, *die.* **co-operative** [kəʊ'ɒpərətɪv] **1.** *adj.* kooperativ; *(helpful)* hilfsbereit. **2.** *n.* Genossenschaft, *die*

co-ordinate [kəʊ'ɔ:dɪneɪt] *v. t.* koordinieren. **co-ordination** [kəʊɔ:dɪ-'neɪʃn] *n.* Koordination, *die*

cop [kɒp] *n.* *(sl.: police officer)* Bulle, *der (salopp)*

cope [kəʊp] *v. i.* ~ **with sb./sth.** mit jmdm./etw. fertig werden

Copenhagen [kəʊpn'heɪgn] *pr. n.* Kopenhagen *(das)*

copier ['kɒpɪə(r)] *n.* *(machine)* Kopiergerät, *das*

co-pilot ['kəʊpaɪlət] *n.* Kopilot, *der*/Kopilotin, *die*

copious ['kəʊpɪəs] *adj.* reichhaltig

¹**copper** ['kɒpə(r)] *n.* Kupfer, *das*

²**copper** *(Brit. sl.) see* cop

coppice ['kɒpɪs], **copse** [kɒps] *ns.* Wäldchen, *das*

copulate ['kɒpjʊleɪt] *v. i.* kopulieren

copy ['kɒpɪ] **1.** *n.* **a)** *(reproduction)* Kopie, *die;* **b)** *(specimen)* Exemplar, *das.* **2.** *v. t. & i.* kopieren; *(transcribe)* abschreiben. '**copyright** *n.* Urheberrecht, *das*

coral ['kɒrl] *n.* Koralle, *die*

cord [kɔ:d] *n.* **a)** Kordel, *die;* **b)** *(cloth)* Cord, *der;* **c)** *in pl. (trousers)* |**pair of**| ~**s** Cordhose, *die*

cordial ['kɔ:dɪəl] **1.** *adj.* herzlich. **2.** *n.* *(drink)* Sirup, *der.* '**cordially** *adv.* herzlich

cordon ['kɔ:dn] **1.** *n.* Kordon, *der.* **2.** *v. t.* ~ |**off**| absperren

corduroy ['kɔ:dərɔɪ, 'kɔ:djʊrɔɪ] *n.* Cordsamt, *der*

core [kɔ:(r)] **1.** *n.* *(of fruit)* Kerngehäuse, *das.* **2.** *v. t.* entkernen

cork [kɔ:k] **1.** *n.* **a)** *(bark)* Kork, *der;* **b)**

(bottle-stopper) Korken, *der.* **2.** *v. t.* zukorken. '**corkscrew** *n.* Korkenzieher, *der*

¹**corn** [kɔ:n] *n.* Getreide, *das*

²**corn** *n. (on foot)* Hühnerauge, *das*

corned beef [kɔ:nd 'bi:f] *n.* Corned beef, *das*

corner ['kɔ:nə(r)] **1.** *n.* **a)** Ecke, *die; (curve)* Kurve, *die;* **on the ~:** an der Ecke/in der Kurve; **b)** *(of mouth, eye)* Winkel, *der.* **2.** *v. t. (fig.)* in die Enge treiben. **3.** *v. i.* die Kurve nehmen. '**corner kick** *n. (Footb.)* Eckball, *der.* '**cornerstone** *n. (fig.)* Eckpfeiler, *der*

cornet ['kɔ:nɪt] *n.* **a)** *(Brit.: for icecream)* [Eis]tüte, *die;* **b)** *(Mus.)* Kornett, *das*

corn: ~flakes *n. pl.* Corn-flakes *Pl.;* **~flour** *(Brit.),* **~starch** *(Amer.) ns.* Maismehl, *das*

'**corny** *adj. (coll.: trite)* abgedroschen

coronation [kɒrə'neɪʃn] *n.* Krönung, *die*

coroner ['kɒrənə(r)] *n.* Coroner, *der; Beamter, der gewaltsame od. unnatürliche Todesfälle untersucht*

coronet ['kɒrənet] *n.* Krone, *die*

¹**corporal** ['kɔ:pərl] *adj.* körperlich

²**corporal** *n.* ≈ Hauptgefreite, *der*

corporation [kɔ:pə'reɪʃn] *n.* Stadtverwaltung, *die*

corps [kɔ:(r)] *n., pl. same* [kɔ:z] Korps, *das*

corpse [kɔ:ps] *n.* Leiche, *die*

corpulent ['kɔ:pjʊlənt] *adj.* korpulent

correct [kə'rekt] **1.** *v. t.* korrigieren. **2.** *adj.* korrekt; **that is ~:** das stimmt. **correction** [kə'rekʃn] *n.* Korrektur, *die.* **cor'rectly** *adv.* korrekt

correspond [kɒrɪ'spɒnd] *v. i.* **a)** ~ |to each other| einander entsprechen; ~ **to sth.** einer Sache *(Dat.)* entsprechen; **b)** *(communicate)* ~ **with sb.** mit jmdm. korrespondieren. **correspondence** [kɒrɪ'spɒndəns] *n.* **a)** *(with, to mit)* Übereinstimmung, *die;* **b)** *(communication)* Briefwechsel, *der.* **correspondent** [kɒrɪ'spɒndənt] *n. (reporter)* Korrespondent, *der/*Korrespondentin, *die.* **corre'sponding** *adj.* entsprechend **(to** *Dat.*). **corre'spondingly** *adv.* entsprechend

corridor ['kɒrɪdɔ:(r)] *n.* **a)** Flur, *der;* **b)** *(Railw.)* [Seiten]gang, *der*

corroborate [kə'rɒbəreɪt] *v. t.* bestätigen

corrode [kə'rəʊd] **1.** *v. t.* zerfressen. **2.** *v. i.* zerfressen werden. **corrosion** [kə'rəʊʒn] *n.* Korrosion, *die*

corrugated ['kɒrəgeɪtɪd] *adj.* ~ **cardboard** Wellpappe, *die;* ~ **iron** Wellblech, *das*

corrupt [kə'rʌpt] **1.** *adj. (depraved)* verdorben *(geh.); (influenced by bribery)* korrupt. **2.** *v. t. (deprave)* korrumpieren; *(bribe)* bestechen. **corruption** [kə'rʌpʃn] *n. (moral deterioration)* Verdorbenheit, *die (geh.); (corrupt practices)* Korruption, *die*

corset ['kɔ:sɪt] *n.* Korsett, *das*

Corsica ['kɔ:sɪkə] *pr. n.* Korsika *(das)*

cortège [kɔ:'teɪʒ] *n.* Trauerzug, *der*

cosh [kɒʃ] *(Brit. coll.)* **1.** *n.* Totschläger, *der.* **2.** *v. t.* niederknüppeln

cosmetic [kɒz'metɪk] **1.** *adj.* kosmetisch. **2.** *n.* Kosmetikum, *das*

cosmic ['kɒzmɪk] *adj.* kosmisch

cosmonaut ['kɒzmənɔ:t] *n.* Kosmonaut, *der/*Kosmonautin, *die*

cosmopolitan [kɒzmə'pɒlɪtən] *adj.* kosmopolitisch

cosmos ['kɒzmɒs] *n.* Kosmos, *der*

cosset ['kɒsɪt] *v. t.* [ver]hätscheln

cost [kɒst] **1.** *n.* **a)** Kosten *Pl.;* **b)** *(fig.)* Preis, *der;* **at all ~s, at any ~:** um jeden Preis. **2.** *v. t.* **a)** *p.t., p.p.* cost *(lit. or fig.)* kosten; **how much does it ~?** was kostet es?; **b)** *p.t., p.p.* **costed** *(Commerc.: fix price of)* ~ **sth.** den Preis für etw. kalkulieren. '**cost-effective** *adj.* rentabel

'**costly** *adj.* teuer

cost: ~ of 'living *n.* Lebenshaltungskosten *Pl.;* ~ **price** *n.* Selbstkostenpreis, *der*

costume ['kɒstju:m] *n.* Kleidermode, *die; (theatrical ~)* Kostüm, *das*

cosy ['kəʊzɪ] *adj.* gemütlich

cot [kɒt] *n.* Kinderbett, *das*

cottage ['kɒtɪdʒ] *n.* Cottage, *das*

cottage: ~ 'cheese *n.* Hüttenkäse, *der;* ~ **industry** *n.* Heimarbeit, *die;* ~ **'pie** *n.* mit Kartoffelbrei überbackenes Hackfleisch

cotton ['kɒtn] **1.** *n.* Baumwolle, *die; (thread)* Baumwollgarn, *das.* **2.** *attrib. adj.* Baumwoll-. **3.** *v. i.* ~ **'on** *(coll.)* kapieren *(ugs.).* **cotton 'wool** *n.* Watte, *die*

couch [kaʊtʃ] *n.* Couch, *die*

couchette [ku:'ʃet] *n. (Railw.)* Liegesitz, *der*

cough [kɒf] **1.** *n.* Husten, *der.* **2.** *v. i.* husten. '**cough mixture** *n.* Hustensaft, *der*

could *see* ²**can**

couldn't ['kʊdnt] *(coll.)* = could not; *see* ²**can**

council ['kaʊnsl] *n.* Rat, *der;* **local ~:** Gemeinderat, *der;* **city/town ~:** Stadtrat, *der.* '**council flat** *n.* Sozialwohnung, *die.* '**council house** *n.* Haus des sozialen Wohnungsbaus
councillor ['kaʊnsələ(r)] *n.* Ratsmitglied, *das*
'**council tax** *n. (Brit.)* Gemeindesteuer, *die*
counsel ['kaʊnsl] **1.** *n.* **a)** Rat[schlag], *der;* **b)** *pl. same (Law)* Rechtsanwalt, *der/*-anwältin, *die.* **2.** *v. t., (Brit.)* -**ll**beraten. **counsellor,** *(Amer.)* **counselor** ['kaʊnsələ(r)] *n.* Berater, *der/*Beraterin, *die*
¹**count** [kaʊnt] **1.** *n.* Zählen, *das;* **keep ~ |of sth.|** [etw.] zählen; **lose ~:** sich verzählen. **2.** *v. t.* **a)** zählen; **b)** *(include)* mitzählen; **not ~ing** abgesehen von; **c)** *(consider)* halten für; **~ oneself lucky** sich glücklich schätzen können. **3.** *v. i.* **a)** zählen; **~ |up| to ten** bis zehn zählen; **b)** *(be included)* zählen. '**count on** *v. t.* **~ on sb./sth.** sich auf jmdn./etw. verlassen. **count 'up** *v. t.* zusammenzählen
²**count** *n. (nobleman)* Graf, *der*
'**countdown** *n.* Countdown, *der od. das*
countenance ['kaʊntɪnəns] **1.** *n. (literary: face)* Antlitz, *das.* **2.** *v. t. (formal: approve)* gutheißen
¹**counter** ['kaʊntə(r)] *n.* **a)** *(in shop)* Ladentisch, *der; (in cafeteria)* Büfett, *das; (in bank)* Schalter, *der;* **b)** *(for games)* Spielmarke, *die*
²**counter** **1.** *adj.* Gegen-. **2.** *v. t.* **a)** *(oppose)* begegnen (+ *Dat.*); **b)** *(act against)* kontern. **3.** *adv.* **go ~ to** zuwiderlaufen (+ *Dat.*)
counter: ~'**act** *v. t.* entgegenwirken (+ *Dat.*); ~**attack** *n.* Gegenangriff, *der;* ~**balance** *v. t. (fig.)* ausgleichen; ~-'**espionage** *n.* Spionageabwehr, *die*
counterfeit ['kaʊntəfɪt] **1.** *adj.* gefälscht; ~ **money** Falschgeld, *das.* **2.** *v. t.* fälschen. '**counterfeiter** *n.* Fälscher, *der/*Fälscherin, *die*
counter: ~**foil** *n.* Kontrollabschnitt, *der;* ~**part** *n.* Gegenstück, *das* (of zu); ~-**pro'ductive** *adj.* sth. is ~-**productive** etw. bewirkt das Gegenteil des Gewünschten; ~**sign** *v. t.* gegenzeichnen
countess ['kaʊntɪs] *n.* Gräfin, *die*
'**countless** *adj.* zahllos
country ['kʌntrɪ] *n.* **a)** Land, *das;* sb's |**home**| ~: jmds. Heimat; **b)** *(~ side)*

Landschaft, *die;* **in the ~:** auf dem Land. **countryman** ['kʌntrɪmən] *n., pl.* **countrymen** ['kʌntrɪmən] Landsmann, *der.* '**countryside** *n.* **a)** *(rural areas)* Land, *das;* **b)** *(rural scenery)* Landschaft, *die*
county ['kaʊntɪ] *n. (Brit.)* Grafschaft, *die*
coup [ku:] *n.* **a)** Coup, *der;* **b)** *see* **coup d'état. coup d'état** [ku: deɪ'ta:] *n.* Staatsstreich, *der*
coupé ['ku:peɪ] *n.* Coupé, *das*
couple [kʌpl] *n.* **1.** **a)** *(pair)* Paar, *das; (married)* [Ehe]paar, *das;* **b)** **a ~ |of|** *(a few)* ein paar; *(two)* zwei. **2.** *v. t.* koppeln
coupon ['ku:pɒn] *n.* **a)** *(for rations)* Marke, *die;* **b)** *(in advertisement)* Coupon, *der*
courage ['kʌrɪdʒ] *n.* Mut, *der.* **courageous** [kə'reɪdʒəs] *adj.,* **cou'rageously** *adv.* mutig
courgette [kʊə'ʒet] *n. (Brit.)* Zucchino, *der*
courier ['kʊrɪə(r)] *n.* **a)** *(Tourism)* Reiseleiter, *der/*-leiterin, *die;* **b)** *(messenger)* Kurier, *der*
course [kɔ:s] *n.* **a)** *(of ship, plane)* Kurs, *der;* **~ |of action|** Vorgehensweise, *die;* **b)** **of ~:** natürlich; **c)** **in due ~:** zu gegebener Zeit; **in the ~ of the day/his life** im Lauf[e] des Tages/seines Lebens; **d)** *(of meal)* Gang, *der;* **e)** *(Sport)* Kurs, *der;* |**golf**|-~: [Golf]platz, *der;* **f)** *(Educ.)* Kurs[us], *der;* **g)** *(Med.)* **a ~ of treatment** eine Kur
court [kɔ:t] **1.** *n.* **a)** Hof, *der;* **b)** *(Tennis, Squash)* Platz, *der;* **c)** *(Law)* Gericht, *das.* **2.** *v. t.* **~ sb.** jmdn. umwerben
courteous ['kɜ:tɪəs] *adj.* höflich.
courtesy ['kɜ:təsɪ] *n.* Höflichkeit, *die*
court: ~-**house** *n. (Law)* Gerichtsgebäude, *das;* ~ '**martial** *n., pl.* ~**s martial** *(Mil.)* Kriegsgericht, *das;* ~**yard** *n.* Hof, *der*
cousin ['kʌzn] *n.* |**first**| ~: Cousin, *der/*Cousine, *die*
cove [kəʊv] *n. (Geog.)* [kleine] Bucht
covenant ['kʌvənənt] *n.* formelle Übereinkunft
cover ['kʌvə(r)] **1.** *n.* **a)** *(piece of cloth)* Decke, *die; (of cushion, bed)* Bezug, *der; (lid)* Deckel, *der; (of hole, engine, typewriter, etc.)* Abdeckung, *die;* **b)** *(of book)* Einband, *der; (of magazine)* Umschlag, *der;* **c)** |**send sth.**| **under separate ~:** [etw.] mit getrennter Post [schicken]; **d) take ~ |from sth.|** Schutz

[vor etw. *(Dat.)*] suchen; **under ~** *(from rain)* überdacht. **2.** *v. t.* **a)** bedecken; beziehen ⟨*Sessel, Kisses*⟩; zudecken ⟨*Pfanne*⟩; **the roses are ~ed with greenfly** die Rosen sind voller Blattläuse; **b)** *(include)* abdecken; **c)** *(Journ.)* berichten über (+ *Akk.*); **d)** decken ⟨*Kosten*⟩. **cover 'up** *v. t.* **1.** zudecken; *(fig.)* vertuschen. **2.** *v. i.* **~ up for sb.** jmdn. decken

coverage ['kʌvərɪdʒ] *n. (Journ.)* Berichterstattung, *die*

'**cover charge** *n.* [Preis für das] Gedeck

'**covering** *n.* Decke, *die;(of chair, bed)* Bezug, *der.* '**covering letter** *n.* Begleitbrief, *der*

covert ['kʌvət] *adj.* versteckt

'**cover-up** *n.* Verschleierung, *die*

covet ['kʌvɪt] *v. t.* begehren *(geh.).* **covetous** ['kʌvɪtəs] *adj.* begehrlich *(geh.)*

cow [kaʊ] *n.* Kuh, *die*

coward ['kaʊəd] *n.* Feigling, *der.* **cowardice** ['kaʊədɪs] *n.* Feigheit, *die.* '**cowardly** *adj.* feig[e]

'**cowboy** *n.* Cowboy, *der*

cower ['kaʊə(r)] *v. i.* sich ducken

cow: ~-shed *n.* Kuhstall, *der;* **~slip** *n.* Schlüsselblume, *die*

coy [kɔɪ] *adj.* gespielt schüchtern

cozy *(Amer.) see* **cosy**

crab [kræb] *n.* Krabbe, *die.* '**crab-apple** *n.* Holzapfel, *der*

crack [kræk] **1.** *n.* **a)** *(noise)* Krachen, *das;* **b)** *(in china etc.)* Sprung, *der; (in rock)* Spalte, *die; (chink)* Spalt, *der; c)* *(coll.: try)* **have a ~ at sth./doing sth.** versuchen, etw. zu tun. **2.** *attrib. adj. (coll.)* erstklassig. **3.** *v. t.* **a)** knacken ⟨*Nuß, Problem, Kode*⟩; **b)** *(make a ~ in)* anschlagen ⟨*Porzellan usw.*⟩; **c) ~ a joke** einen Witz machen; **d) ~ a whip** mit einer Peitsche knallen. **4.** *v. i.* ⟨*Porzellan usw.*:⟩ einen Sprung/Sprünge bekommen. **crack 'down** *v. i. (coll.)* **~ down [on sb./sth.]** [gegen jmdn./etw.] [hart] vorgehen. **crack 'up** *v. i. (coll.)* ⟨*Person:*⟩ zusammenbrechen

cracked [krækt] *adj.* gesprungen ⟨*Porzellan usw.*⟩; rissig ⟨*Verputz*⟩

cracker ['krækə(r)] *n.* **a)** |Christmas| ~ ≈ Knallbonbon, *der od. das;* **b)** *(biscuit)* Cracker, *der.* '**crackers** *pred. adj. (Brit. coll.)* übergeschnappt *(ugs.)*

crackle ['krækl] **1.** *v. i.* knistern; ⟨*Feuer:*⟩ prasseln. **2.** *n.* Knistern, *das*

cradle ['kreɪdl] **1.** *n.* Wiege, *die.* **2.** *v. t.* wiegen

craft [krɑːft] *n.* **a)** *(trade)* Handwerk, *das; (art)* Kunsthandwerk, *das;* **b)** *pl. same (boat)* Boot, *das.* **craftsman** ['krɑːftsmən] *n., pl.* **craftsmen** ['krɑːftsmən] Handwerker, *der.* '**crafty** *adj.* listig

crag [kræg] *n.* Felsspitze, *die.* '**craggy** *adj.* **a)** felsig; **b)** zerfurcht ⟨*Gesicht*⟩

cram [kræm] **1.** *v. t.,* **-mm-** *(overfill)* vollstopfen *(ugs.); (force)* stopfen. **2.** *v. i.,* **-mm-** *(for exam)* büffeln *(ugs.)*

cramp [kræmp] **1.** *n. (Med.)* Krampf, *der.* **2.** *v. t.* einengen

cranberry ['krænbəri] *n.* Preiselbeere, *die*

crane [kreɪn] **1.** *n.* Kran, *der.* **2.** *v. t.* **~ one's neck** den Hals recken

'**crank** [kræŋk] *n. (Mech. Engin.)* [Hand]kurbel, *die*

²**crank** *n.* Irre, *der/die (salopp)*

'**crankshaft** *n. (Mech. Engin.)* Kurbelwelle, *die*

'**cranky** *adj. (eccentric)* schrullig

cranny ['krænɪ] *n.* Ritze, *die*

crash [kræʃ] **1.** *n.* **a)** *(noise)* Krachen, *das;* **b)** *(collision)* Zusammenstoß, *der;* **have a ~:** einen Unfall haben. **2.** *v. i.* **a)** *(make a noise, go noisily)* krachen; **b)** *(have a collision)* einen Unfall haben; ⟨*Flugzeug, Flieger:*⟩ abstürzen; **~ into sth.** gegen etw. krachen. **3.** *v. t.* **a)** *(smash)* schmettern; **b)** *(cause to have collision)* einen Unfall haben mit

crash: ~ barrier *n.* Leitplanke, *die;* **~ course** *n.* Intensivkurs, *der;* **~-helmet** *n.* Sturzhelm, *der*

crass [kræs] *adj.* kraß

crate [kreɪt] *n.* Kiste, *die*

crater ['kreɪtə(r)] *n.* Krater, *der*

cravat [krə'væt] *n.* Krawatte, *die*

crave [kreɪv] *v. t.* **a)** *(beg)* erbitten; **b)** *(long for)* sich sehnen nach. '**craving** *n.* Verlangen, *das* **(for** nach)

crawl [krɔːl] **1.** *v. i.* **a)** kriechen; ⟨*Baby, Insekt:*⟩ krabbeln; **b)** *(coll.)* **~ to sb.** vor jmdm. kriechen. **2.** *n.* **a) go at a ~:** im Schneckentempo fahren; **b)** *(swimming-stroke)* Kraulen, *das.* '**crawler lane** *n.* Kriechspur, *die*

crayfish ['kreɪfɪʃ] *n., pl. same* Flußkrebs, *der*

crayon ['kreɪən] *n.* |coloured| ~: Buntstift, *der; (wax)* Wachsmalstift, *der*

craze [kreɪz] *n.* Begeisterung, *die*

crazy ['kreɪzɪ] *adj.* verrückt; **be ~ about sb./sth.** *(coll.)* nach jmdm./etw. verrückt sein *(ugs.)*

creak [kriːk] **1.** *n.* Knarren, *das.* **2.** *v. i.* knarren

cream [kri:m] **1.** *n.* **a)** Sahne, *die;* **b)** *(dessert, cosmetic)* Creme, *die.* **2.** *adj.* ~-[-coloured] creme[farben]. **cream 'cheese** *n.* ≈ Frischkäse, *der*

'creamy *adj. (with cream)* sahnig; *(like cream)* cremig

crease [kri:s] **1.** *n. (pressed)* Bügelfalte, *die; (accidental)* Falte, *die.* **2.** *v. t. (press)* eine Falte bügeln in (+ *Akk.*); *(accidentally)* zerknittern. **3.** *v. i.* Falten bekommen; knittern. **'crease-resistant** *adj.* knitterfrei

create [kri:'eɪt] *v. t.* schaffen; verursachen ⟨*Verwirrung*⟩; machen ⟨*Eindruck*⟩. **creation** [kri:'eɪʃn] *n.* Schaffung, *die; (of the world)* Schöpfung, *die (geh.).* **creative** [kri:'eɪtɪv] *adj.* kreativ. **creator** [kri:'eɪtə(r)] *n.* Schöpfer, *der*/Schöpferin, *die*

creature ['kri:tʃə(r)] *n.* Geschöpf, *das*

crèche [kreʃ] *n.* [Kinder]krippe, *die*

credentials [krɪ'denʃlz] *n. pl.* Zeugnis, *das*

credibility [kredɪ'bɪlɪtɪ] *n.* Glaubwürdigkeit, *die*

credible ['kredɪbl] *adj.* glaubwürdig

credit ['kredɪt] **1.** *n.* **a)** *(honour)* Ehre, *die;* **take the ~ for sth.** die Anerkennung für etw. einstecken; **b)** *(Commerc.)* Kredit, *der.* **2.** *v. t.* **a)** glauben; **b)** *(Finance)* gutschreiben. **creditable** ['kredɪtəbl] *adj.* anerkennenswert

'credit card *n.* Kreditkarte, *die*

creditor ['kredɪtə(r)] *n.* Gläubiger, *der*/Gläubigerin, *die*

creed [kri:d] *n.* Glaubensbekenntnis, *das*

creek [kri:k] *n.* **a)** *(Brit.: of coast)* [kleine] Bucht; **b)** *(of river)* [kurzer] Flußarm

creep [kri:p] **1.** *v. i.,* **crept** [krept] kriechen; *(move timidly, slowly, stealthily)* schleichen. **2.** *n.* **a)** *(sl.: person)* Fiesling, *der (salopp);* **b)** *(coll.)* **give sb. the ~s** jmdn. nicht [ganz] geheuer sein. **'creeper** *n.* Kletterpflanze, *die.* **'creepy** *adj.* unheimlich

cremate [krɪ'meɪt] *v. t.* einäschern. **cremation** [krɪ'meɪʃn] *n.* Einäscherung, *die.* **crematorium** [kremə'tɔ:rɪəm] *n.* Krematorium, *das*

creosote ['kri:əsəʊt] *n.* Kreosot, *das*

crept *see* **creep 1**

crescent ['kresənt] *n.* Mondsichel, *die*

cress [kres] *n.* Kresse, *die*

crest [krest] *n.* Kamm, *der.* **'crestfallen** *adj.* niedergeschlagen

Crete [kri:t] *pr. n.* Kreta *(das)*

cretin ['kretɪn] *n. (coll.)* Trottel, *der*

crevasse [krɪ'væs] *n.* Gletscherspalte, *die*

crevice ['krevɪs] *n.* Spalt, *der*

crew [kru:] *n.* Besatzung, *die.* **'crew-cut** *n.* Bürstenschnitt, *der*

crib [krɪb] **1.** *n.* Krippe, *die.* **2.** *v. t.,* -bb- *(coll.)* abkupfern *(salopp)*

crick [krɪk] *n.* **a** ~ **[in one's neck/back]** ein steifer Hals/Rücken

¹cricket ['krɪkɪt] *n.* Kricket, *das*

²cricket *n. (Zool.)* Grille, *die*

'cricket bat *n.* Schlagholz, *das*

'cricketer *n.* Kricketspieler, *der*/-spielerin, *die*

cried *see* **cry**

crime [kraɪm] *n.* **a)** Verbrechen, *das;* **b)** *collect.* **a wave of ~:** eine Welle von Straftaten; ~ **doesn't pay** Verbrechen lohnen sich nicht

criminal ['krɪmɪnl] **1.** *adj.* kriminell; strafbar; ~ **act** *or* **deed**/**offence** Straftat, *die.* **2.** *n.* Kriminelle, *der/die*

crimson ['krɪmzn] **1.** *adj.* purpurrot. **2.** *n.* Purpurrot, *das*

cringe [krɪndʒ] *v. i.* zusammenzucken

crinkle ['krɪŋkl] **1.** *n.* Knitterfalte, *die.* **2.** *v. t.* zerknittern. **3.** *v. i.* knittern

cripple ['krɪpl] **1.** *n.* Krüppel, *der.* **2.** *v. t.* zum Krüppel machen; *(fig.)* lähmen. **crippled** ['krɪpld] *adj.* verkrüppelt

crisis ['kraɪsɪs] *n., pl.* **crises** ['kraɪsi:z] Krise, *die*

crisp [krɪsp] **1.** *adj.* knusprig. **2. a)** *n. usu. in pl. (Brit.: potato* ~) [Kartoffel]chip, *der;* **be burned to a** ~: verbrannt sein. **'crispbread** *n.* Knäckebrot, *das*

'crispy *adj.* knusprig

criss-cross ['krɪskrɒs] **1.** *adj.* ~ **pattern** Muster aus gekreuzten Linien. **2.** *adv.* kreuz und quer. **3.** *v. t.* wiederholt schneiden

criterion [kraɪ'tɪərɪən] *n., pl.* **criteria** [kraɪ'tɪərɪə] Kriterium, *das*

critic ['krɪtɪk] *n.* Kritiker, *der*/Kritikerin, *die.* **critical** ['krɪtɪkl] *adj.* kritisch; **be** ~ **of sb./sth.** jmdn./etw. kritisieren. **critically** ['krɪtɪkəlɪ] *adv.* kritisch; ~ **ill** ernstlich krank

criticism ['krɪtɪsɪzm] *n.* Kritik, *die* (of an + *Dat.*)

criticize ['krɪtɪsaɪz] *v. t.* kritisieren (**for** wegen)

croak [krəʊk] **1.** *n. (of frog)* Quaken, *das; (of person)* Krächzen, *das.* **2.** *v. i.* ⟨*Frosch:*⟩ quaken; ⟨*Person:*⟩ krächzen. **3.** *v. t.* krächzen

crochet ['krəʊʃeɪ] **1.** *n.* Häkelarbeit, *die;* ~ **hook** Häkelhaken, *der.* **2.** *v.t.* häkeln

crock [krɒk] *n. (coll.)* |old| ~ *(person)* altes Wrack, *das (fig.); (vehicle)* |alte| Klapperkiste *(ugs.)*

crockery ['krɒkərɪ] *n.* Geschirr, *das*

crocodile ['krɒkədaɪl] *n.* Krokodil, *das*

crocus ['krəʊkəs] *n.* Krokus, *der*

crony ['krəʊnɪ] *n.* Kumpel, *der (ugs.)*

crook [krʊk] *n.* **a)** *(coll.: rogue)* Gauner, *der;* **b)** *(shepherd's)* Hirtenstab, *der*

crooked ['krʊkɪd] *adj.* krumm; *(fig.: dishonest)* betrügerisch

crop [krɒp] *n.* **1.** [Feld]frucht, *die; (season's yield)* Ernte, *die.* **2.** *v.t.* stutzen ⟨*Haare usw.*⟩. **crop 'up** *v.i.* auftauchen

'cropper *n. (coll.)* **come a** ~: einen Sturz bauen *(ugs.)*

croquet ['krəʊkeɪ] *n.* Krocket[spiel], *das*

croquette [krə'ket] *n.* Krokette, *die*

cross [krɒs] **1.** *n.* **a)** Kreuz, *das;* **b)** *(mixture)* Mischung, *die* (**between** aus). **2.** *v.t.* **a)** [über]kreuzen; ~ **one's arms/legs** die Arme verschränken/die Beine übereinanderschlagen; **keep one's fingers** ~**ed** |**for sb.**| *(fig.)* |jmdm.| die *od.* den Daumen drücken; **b)** *(go across)* kreuzen; überqueren ⟨*Straße, Gebirge*⟩; durchqueren ⟨*Land, Zimmer*⟩; ~ **sb.'s mind** *(fig.)* jmdm. einfallen; **c)** *(Brit.)* **a** ~**ed cheque** ein Verrechnungsscheck; **d)** ~ **oneself** sich bekreuzigen. **3.** *v.i.* aneinander vorbeigehen; ~ |**in the post**| ⟨*Briefe:*⟩ sich kreuzen. **4.** *adj.* verärgert; **sb. will be** ~: jmd. wird ärgerlich *od.* böse werden; **be** ~ **with sb.** böse auf jmdn. sein.

cross 'out *v.t.* ausstreichen. **cross 'over** *v.t.* überqueren; *abs.* hinübergehen

cross: ~**bar** *n.* **a)** [Fahrrad]stange, *die;* **b)** *(Sport)* Querlatte, *die;* ~**-check 1.** *n.* Gegenprobe, *die;* **2.** *v.t.* |nochmals| nachprüfen; nachkontrollieren; ~**-country 1.** *adj.* Querfeldein-; **2.** *adv.* querfeldein; ~**-examination** *n.* Kreuzverhör, *das;* ~**-examine** *v.t.* ins Kreuzverhör nehmen; ~**-eyed** ['krɒsaɪd] *adj.* |nach innen| schielend; **be** ~**-eyed** schielen; ~**-fire** *n.* Kreuzfeuer, *das*

'crossing *n.* **a)** *(act)* Überquerung, *die;* **b)** *(pedestrian* ~*)* Überweg, *der*

'crossly *adv.* verärgert

cross: ~ **'purposes** *n. pl.* **talk at** ~

purposes aneinander vorbeireden; ~**-reference** *n.* Querverweis, *der;* ~**roads** *n. sing.* Kreuzung, *die; (fig.)* Wendepunkt, *der;* ~**-section** *n.* Querschnitt, *der;* ~**word** *n.* ~**word** |**puzzle**| Kreuzworträtsel, *das*

crotchet ['krɒtʃɪt] *n. (Brit. Mus.)* Viertelnote, *die*

crouch [kraʊtʃ] *v.i.* [sich zusammen]kauern

crow [krəʊ] *n.* Krähe, *die;* **as the** ~ **flies** Luftlinie

'crowbar *n.* Brechstange, *die*

crowd [kraʊd] **1.** *n.* [Menschen]menge, *die.* **2.** *vt.* füllen. **3.** *v.i.* sich sammeln. **'crowded** *adj.* überfüllt

crown [kraʊn] **1.** *n.* Krone, *die.* **2.** *v.t.* **a)** krönen; **b)** überkronen ⟨*Zahn*⟩

crucial ['kru:ʃl] *adj.* entscheidend (**to** für)

crucifix ['kru:sɪfɪks] *n.* Kruzifix, *das.*

crucifixion [kru:sɪ'fɪkʃn] *n.* Kreuzigung, *die*

crucify ['kru:sɪfaɪ] *v.t.* kreuzigen

crude [kru:d] *adj.* **a)** roh; ~ **oil** Rohöl, *das;* **b)** *(fig.)* grob ⟨*Entwurf, Worte*⟩

cruel ['kru:əl] *adj.* grausam. **cruelty** ['kru:əltɪ] *n.* Grausamkeit, *die*

cruise [kru:z] **1.** *v.i. (at random)* ⟨*Fahrzeug, Fahrer:*⟩ herumfahren. **2.** *n.* Kreuzfahrt, *die.* **'cruise missile** *n.* Marschflugkörper, *der.* **'cruiser** *n.* Kreuzer, *der*

crumb [krʌm] *n.* Krümel, *der*

crumble ['krʌmbl] **1.** *v.t.* zerkrümeln ⟨*Keks, Kuchen*⟩. **2.** *v.i.* ⟨*Mauer:*⟩ zusammenfallen. **crumbly** ['krʌmblɪ] *adj.* krümelig ⟨*Keks, Kuchen*⟩; bröckelig ⟨*Gestein*⟩

crumpet ['krʌmpɪt] *n. weiches Hefeküchlein zum Toasten*

crumple ['krʌmpl] **1.** *v.t.* **a)** *(crush)* zerdrücken; **b)** *(wrinkle)* zerknittern. **2.** *v.i.* knittern

crunch [krʌntʃ] **1.** *v.t.* [geräuschvoll] knabbern ⟨*Keks*⟩. **2.** *v.i.* ⟨*Schnee, Kies:*⟩ knirschen. **3.** *n.* Knirschen, *das; when it comes to the* ~: wenn es hart auf hart geht. **'crunchy** *adj.* knusprig

crusade [kru:'seɪd] **1.** *n. (Hist.; also fig.)* Kreuzzug, *der.* **2.** *v.i. (fig.)* zu Felde gehen. **cru'sader** *n. (Hist.)* Kreuzfahrer, *der*

crush [krʌʃ] **1.** *v.t.* **a)** quetschen; **b)** *(powder)* zerstampfen; **c)** *(fig.)* niederschlagen. **2.** *n. (crowd)* Gedränge, *das*

crust [krʌst] *n.* Kruste, *die.* **'crusty** *adj.* knusprig

crutch [krʌtʃ] *n.* Krücke, *die;* **go about on ~es** an Krücken gehen

crux [krʌks] *n.* **the ~ of the matter** der springende Punkt bei der Sache

cry [kraɪ] **1.** *n. (of grief)* Schrei, *der; (of words)* Schreien, *das;* **a far ~ from ...** *(fig.)* etwas ganz anderes als ... **2.** *v. i.* **a)** rufen; *(loudly)* schreien; **b)** *(weep)* weinen (**over** wegen). **cry 'off** *v. i.* absagen. **cry 'out** *v. i.* aufschreien

'**crying** *adj.* **it's a ~ shame** es ist eine wahre Schande

crypt [krɪpt] *n.* Krypta, *die*

cryptic ['krɪptɪk] *adj.* geheimnisvoll

crystal ['krɪstl] **1.** *n.* **a)** Kristall, *der;* **b)** *(glass)* Bleikristall, *das.* **2.** *adj. (made of ~ glass)* kristallen. **crystallize** ['krɪstəlaɪz] *v. i.* kristallisieren; *(fig.)* feste Form annehmen

cub [kʌb] *n.* **a)** Junge, *das; (of wolf, fox, dog)* Welpe, *der;* **b)** **Cub** *see* **Cub Scout**

Cuba ['kju:bə] *n.* Kuba *(das)*

cubby[-hole] ['kʌbɪ(həʊl)] *n.* Kämmerchen, *das*

cube [kju:b] *n.* Würfel, *der.* **cubic** ['kju:bɪk] *adj.* **a)** würfelförmig; **b)** Kubik⟨*meter usw.*⟩

cubicle ['kju:bɪkl] *n.* Kabine, *die*

'**Cub Scout** *n.* Wölfling, *der*

cuckoo ['kʊku:] *n.* Kuckuck, *der.* '**cuckoo clock** *n.* Kuckucksuhr, *die*

cucumber ['kju:kʌmbə(r)] *n.* [Salat]gurke, *die*

cuddle ['kʌdl] **1.** *n.* enge Umarmung. **2.** *v. t.* schmusen mit; hätscheln ⟨*kleines Kind*⟩. **3.** *v. i.* schmusen

cuddly ['kʌdlɪ] *adj.* zum Schmusen nachgestellt. **cuddly 'toy** *n.* Plüschtier, *das*

cudgel ['kʌdʒl] *n.* Knüppel, *der*

¹**cue** [kju:] *n. (Billiards etc.)* Queue, *das*

²**cue** *n. (Theatre)* Stichwort, *das*

¹**cuff** [kʌf] *n.* **a)** Manschette, *die;* **off the ~** *(fig.)* aus dem Stegreif; **b)** *(Amer.: trouser turn-up)* [Hosen]aufschlag, *der*

²**cuff** **1.** *v. t.* **~ sb.** jmdm. einen Klaps geben. **2.** *n.* Klaps, *der*

'**cuff-link** *n.* Manschettenknopf, *der*

cul-de-sac ['kʌldəsæk] *n.* Sackgasse, *die*

culinary ['kʌlɪnərɪ] *adj.* kulinarisch

culminate ['kʌlmɪneɪt] *v. i.* gipfeln; **~ in sth.** in etw. *(Dat.)* seinen Höchststand erreichen. **culmination** [kʌlmɪ'neɪʃn] *n.* Höhepunkt, *der*

culottes [kju:'lɒts] *n. pl.* Hosenrock, *der*

culprit ['kʌlprɪt] *n.* Täter, *der*/Täterin, *die*

cult [kʌlt] *n.* Kult, *der*

cultivate ['kʌltɪveɪt] *v. t.* kultivieren *(auch fig.);* bestellen ⟨*Acker, Land*⟩; anbauen ⟨*Pflanzen*⟩. **cultivation** [kʌltɪ'veɪʃn] *n. see* **cultivate:** Kultivierung, *die;* Bestellen *das;* Anbau, *der*

culture ['kʌltʃə(r)] *n.* Kultur, *die.* '**cultured** *adj.* kultiviert

cumbersome ['kʌmbəsəm] *adj.* hinderlich ⟨*Kleider*⟩; sperrig ⟨*Pakete*⟩; schwerfällig ⟨*Arbeitsweise*⟩

cunning ['kʌnɪŋ] **1.** *n.* Schläue, *die.* **2.** *adj.* schlau

cup [kʌp] *n.* **a)** Tasse, *die;* **b)** *(prize, competition)* Pokal, *der;* **c)** *(~ful)* Tasse, *die;* **a ~ of coffee/tea** eine Tasse Kaffee/Tee

cupboard ['kʌbəd] *n.* Schrank, *der*

'**Cup Final** *n.* Pokalendspiel, *das*

cupful ['kʌpfl] *n.* Tasse, *die;* **a ~ of water** eine Tasse Wasser

curable ['kjʊərəbl] *adj.* heilbar

curate ['kjʊərət] *n.* Kurat, *der*

curator [kjʊə'reɪtə(r)] *n. (of museum)* Direktor, *der*/Direktorin, *die*

curb [kɜ:b] *v. t.* zügeln

curdle ['kɜ:dl] *v. i.* gerinnen

cure [kjʊə(r)] **1.** *n.* [Heil]mittel, *das* (**for** gegen); *(fig.)* Mittel, *das.* **2.** *v. t.* **a)** heilen; **b)** [ein]pökeln ⟨*Fleisch*⟩

curfew ['kɜ:fju:] *n.* Ausgangssperre, *die*

curiosity [kjʊərɪ'ɒsɪtɪ] *n.* **a)** Neugier[de], *die;* **b)** *(object)* Wunderding, *das*

curious ['kjʊərɪəs] *adj.* **a)** *(inquisitive)* neugierig; **b)** *(strange, odd)* seltsam

curl [kɜ:l] **1.** *n.* Locke, *die.* **2.** *v. t.* locken. **3.** *v. i.* **a)** sich locken; **b)** ⟨*Straße, Fluß:*⟩ sich winden. '**curler** *n.* Lockenwickler, *der.* '**curly** *adj.* lockig

currant ['kʌrənt] *n.* Korinthe, *die*

currency ['kʌrənsɪ] *n. (money)* Währung, *die;* **foreign currencies** Devisen

current ['kʌrənt] **1.** *adj.* **a)** verbreitet ⟨*Meinung*⟩; gebräuchlich ⟨*Wort*⟩; **b)** laufend ⟨*Jahr, Monat*⟩; **c)** *(the present)* aktuell ⟨*Ereignis, Mode*⟩; Tages⟨*politik, -preis*⟩; **~ affairs** Tagespolitik, *die.* **2.** *n.* **a)** *(of water, air)* Strömung, *die;* **b)** *(Electr.)* Strom, *der.* '**current account** *n.* Girokonto, *das*

'**currently** *adv.* zur Zeit

curriculum [kə'rɪkjʊləm] *n.* Lehrplan, *der.* **curriculum vitae** [~ 'vi:taɪ] *n.* Lebenslauf, *der*

¹curry ['kʌrɪ] *n.* Curry[gericht], *das*

²curry *v. t.* ~ **favour |with sb.|** sich [bei jmdm.] einschmeicheln

curse [kɜːs] 1. *n.* Fluch, *der.* 2. *v. t.* verfluchen. 3. *v. i.* fluchen

cursory ['kɜːsərɪ] *adj.* flüchtig

curt [kɜːt] *adj.* kurz angebunden; kurz und schroff ⟨*Brief*⟩

curtain ['kɜːtən] *n.* Vorhang, *der;* **draw** *or* **pull the** ~**s** *(open)* die Vorhänge aufziehen; *(close)* die Vorhänge zuziehen

curtsy ['kɜːtsɪ] 1. *n.* Knicks, *der.* 2. *v. i.* einen Knicks machen (**to** vor + *Dat.)*

curve [kɜːv] 1. *v. t.* krümmen. 2. *v. i.* ⟨*Straße, Fluß:*⟩ eine Biegung machen. 3. *n.* Kurve, *die*

cushion ['kʊʃn] 1. *n.* Kissen, *das.* 2. *v. t.* dämpfen ⟨*Aufprall, Stoß*⟩

cushy ['kʊʃɪ] *adj. (coll.)* bequem

custard ['kʌstəd] *n.* ≈ Vanillesoße, *die*

custodian [kʌs'təʊdɪən] *n. (of museum)* Wächter, *der*/Wächterin, *die; (of valuables)* Hüter, *der*/Hüterin, *die*

custody ['kʌstədɪ] *n.* **a)** *(care)* Obhut, *die;* **b)** *(imprisonment)* |**be**| **in** ~: in Haft [sein]

custom ['kʌstəm] *n.* **a)** Brauch, *der;* **b)** *in pl. (duty on imports)* Zoll, *der.* '**customs officer** *n.* Zollbeamter, *der*/-beamtin, *die.* **customary** ['kʌstəmərɪ] *adj.* üblich

customer ['kʌstəmə(r)] *n.* Kunde, *der*/Kundin, *die*

cut [kʌt] 1. *v. t.,* -tt-, **cut a)** schneiden; durchschneiden ⟨*Seil*⟩; ~ **one's leg** sich *(Dat. od. Akk.)* ins Bein schneiden; **b)** abschneiden ⟨*Scheibe*⟩; schneiden ⟨*Hecke*⟩; mähen ⟨*Getreide, Gras*⟩; ~ **one's nails** sich *(Dat.)* die Nägel schneiden; **c)** *(reduce)* senken ⟨*Preise*⟩; kürzen ⟨*Lohn*⟩; **d)** ~ **sth. short** *(interrupt)* etw. abbrechen. 2. *v. i.,* -tt-, **cut a)** ⟨*Messer:*⟩ schneiden; **b)** ~ **through** *or* **across the field/park** [quer] über das Feld/durch den Park gehen. 3. *n.* **a)** *(act of cutting)* Schnitt, *der;* **b)** *(stroke, blow) (with knife)* Schnitt, *der; (with sword, whip)* Hieb, *der;* **c)** *(reduction)* Kürzung, *die; (in prices)* Senkung, *die; (in services)* Verringerung, *die;* **d)** *(of meat)* Stück, *das.* **cut a'way** *v. t.* abschneiden. **cut 'back** *v. t.* **a)** *(reduce)* einschränken; **b)** *(prune)* stutzen. **cut 'down** 1. *v. t.* **a)** fällen ⟨*Baum*⟩; **b)** *(reduce)* einschränken. 2. *v. i.* ~ **down on sth.** etw. einschränken. **cut 'off** *v. t.* abschnei-

den; unterbrechen ⟨*Telefongespräch, Sprecher*⟩. **cut 'out** 1. *v. t.* **a)** ausschneiden (of aus); **b)** **be** ~ **out for** geeignet sein zu. 2. *v. i.* ⟨*Motor:*⟩ aussetzen. **cut 'up** *v. t.* zerschneiden

cutlery ['kʌtlərɪ] *n.* Besteck, *das*

cutlet ['kʌtlɪt] *n.* Kotelett, *das*

'**cut-price** *adj.* herabgesetzt

'**cutting** 1. *adj.* beißend ⟨*Bemerkung, Antwort*⟩. 2. *n. (from newspaper)* Ausschnitt, *der*

c. v. *abbr.* **curriculum vitae**

cycle ['saɪkl] 1. *n.* **a)** *(recurrent period)* Zyklus, *der;* **b)** *(bicycle)* Rad, *das.* 2. *v. i.* radfahren. **cyclist** ['saɪklɪst] *n.* Radfahrer, *der*/-fahrerin, *die*

cylinder ['sɪlɪndə(r)] *n.* Zylinder, *der.* **cylindrical** [sɪ'lɪndrɪkl] *adj.* zylindrisch

cymbals ['sɪmblz] *n. pl.* Becken *Pl.*

cynic ['sɪnɪk] *n.* Zyniker, *der.* **cynical** ['sɪnɪkl] *adj.* zynisch; bissig ⟨*Bemerkung, Worte*⟩. **cynicism** ['sɪnɪsɪzm] *n.* Zynismus, *der*

Cyprus ['saɪprəs] *pr. n.* Zypern *(das)*

Czech [tʃek] 1. *adj.* tschechisch. 2. *n.* **a)** *(language)* Tschechisch, *das;* **b)** *(person)* Tscheche, *der*/Tschechin, *die*

Czechoslovakia [tʃekəʊslə'vækɪə] *pr.n. (Hist.)* die Tschechoslowakei. **Czechoslovakian** [tʃekəʊslə'vækɪən] *(Hist.)* 1. *adj.* tschechoslowakisch. 2. *n.* Tschechoslowake, *der*/Tschechoslowakin, *die*

Czech Republic *pr. n.* Tschechische Republik; Tschechien *(das)*

D

D, d [diː] *n.* D, d, *das*

dab [dæb] 1. *n.* Tupfer, *der.* 2. *v. t.,* -bb- abtupfen; ~ **sth. on** *or* **against sth.** etw. auf etw. *(Akk.)* tupfen

dabble ['dæbl] *v. i.* ~ **in sth.** sich in etw. *(Dat.)* versuchen

dachshund ['dækshʊnd] *n.* Dackel, *der*

dad [dæd] *n. (coll.)* Vater, *der*

daddy ['dædɪ] *n. (coll.)* Vati, *der (fam.).* **daddy-'long-legs** *n.* Schnake, *die*

daffodil ['dæfədɪl] *n.* Osterglocke, *die*

daft [dɑːft] *adj.* doof *(ugs.)*
dagger ['dægə(r)] *n.* Dolch, *der*
daily ['deɪlɪ] 1. *adj.* täglich; ~ |news|-
paper Tageszeitung, *die.* 2. *adv.* täglich. 3. *n.* Tageszeitung, *die*
dainty ['deɪntɪ] *adj.* zierlich; anmutig
⟨*Bewegung, Person*⟩; zart ⟨*Gesichts-
züge*⟩
dairy ['deərɪ] *n.* a) Molkerei, *die;* b)
(shop) Milchladen, *der*
dais ['deɪs] *n.* Podium, *das*
daisy ['deɪzɪ] *n.* Gänseblümchen, *das*
dam [dæm] 1. *n.* [Stau]damm, *der.* 2.
v.t., **-mm-:** a) ~ |up| sth. etw. ab-
blocken; b) aufstauen ⟨*Fluß*⟩
damage ['dæmɪdʒ] 1. *n.* Schaden, *der.*
2. *v.t.* beschädigen. **damaging** ['dæ-
mɪdʒɪŋ] *adj.* schädlich (**to** für)
damn [dæm] 1. *v.t.* verdammen. 2.
adj., adv., int. (coll.) verdammt *(ugs.).*
3. *n.* **he doesn't give** *or* **care a** ~: ihm
ist es völlig wurscht *(ugs.)*
damp [dæmp] 1. *adj.* feucht. 2. *v.t. see*
dampen. 3. *n.* Feuchtigkeit, *die*
dampen ['dæmpn] *v.t.* befeuchten;
(fig.) dämpfen ⟨*Begeisterung, Eifer*⟩
'**dampness** *n.* Feuchtigkeit, *die*
dance [dɑːns] 1. *v.i.&t.* tanzen. 2. *n.*
a) Tanz; b) *(party)* Tanzveranstal-
tung, *die; (private)* Tanzparty, *die.*
'**dance-hall** *n.* Tanzsaal, *der*
'**dancer** *n.* Tänzer, *der/*Tänzerin, *die*
dandelion ['dændɪlaɪən] *n.* Löwen-
zahn, *der*
dandruff ['dændrʌf] *n.* [Kopf]schup-
pen *Pl.*
Dane [deɪn] *n.* Däne, *der/*Dänin, *die*
danger ['deɪndʒə(r)] *n.* Gefahr, *die;*
in/out of ~: in/außer Gefahr. **dangerous** ['deɪndʒərəs] *adj.,* '**dangerously** *adv.* gefährlich
dangle ['dæŋgl] 1. *v.i.* baumeln (**from**
an + *Dat.*). 2. *v.t.* baumeln lassen
Danish ['deɪnɪʃ] 1. *adj.* dänisch; **sb. is**
~: jmd. ist Däne/Dänin. 2. *n.* Dä-
nisch, *das; see also* **English 2 a**
dank [dæŋk] *adj.* feucht
Danube ['dænjuːb] *pr. n.* Donau, *die*
dare [deə(r)] 1. *v.t.* a) [es] wagen; ~ **to
do sth.** [es] wagen, etw. zu tun; b)
(challenge) ~ **sb. to do sth.** jmdn. aufstacheln, etw. zu tun; **I** ~ **you!** trau
dich! 2. *n.* Mutprobe, *die.* **daring**
['deərɪŋ] *adj.* kühn
dark [dɑːk] 1. *adj.* dunkel; *(dark-
haired)* dunkelhaarig; ~**-blue/-brown**
dunkelblau/-braun; ~ **glasses** dunkle
Brille. 2. *n.* a) Dunkel, *das;* **in the** ~:
im Dunkeln; **keep sb. in the** ~ *(fig.)*

jmdn. im dunkeln lassen; b) *no art.
(nightfall)* Einbruch der Dunkelheit.
darken ['dɑːkn] *v.t.* verdunkeln.
'**darkness** *n.* Dunkelheit, *die*
'**dark-room** *n.* Dunkelkammer, *die*
darling ['dɑːlɪŋ] *n.* Liebling, *der*
darn [dɑːn] *v.t.* stopfen
dart [dɑːt] 1. *n.* a) *(missile)* Pfeil, *der;*
b) *(Sport)* Wurfpfeil, *der;* ~**s** *sing.
(game)* Darts, *das.* 2. *v.i.* sausen.
'**dartboard** *n.* Dartscheibe, *die*
dash [dæʃ] 1. *v.i.* sausen. 2. *v.t.
(fling)* schleudern. 3. *n.* a) **make a**
~: rasen *(ugs.)* (**for** zu); b) *(horizontal
stroke)* Gedankenstrich, *der;* c) *(small
amount)* Schuß, *der*
'**dashboard** *n.* Armaturenbrett, *das*
data ['deɪtə, 'dɑːtə] *n.* Daten *Pl.* **data**
'**processing** *n.* Datenverarbeitung,
die
¹**date** [deɪt] *n. (Bot.)* Dattel, *die*
²**date** 1. *n.* a) Datum, *das; (on coin etc.)*
Jahreszahl, *die;* ~ **of birth** Geburtsda-
tum, *das;* **be out of** ~: altmodisch
sein; **to** ~: bis heute; b) *(coll.: appointment)* Verabredung, *die;* **have/make a**
~ **with sb.** mit jmdm. verabredet sein/
sich mit jmdm. verabreden. 2. *v.t.* a)
datieren; b) *(coll.: make seem old)* alt
machen. 3. *v.i.* ~ **back to/**~ **from**
stammen aus. **dated** ['deɪtɪd] *adj.* altmodisch. '**date-line** *n.* Datumsgren-
ze, *die*
dative ['deɪtɪv] *adj. & n.* ~ |case| Dativ,
der
daub [dɔːb] *v.t. (smear)* beschmieren;
(put crudely) schmieren
daughter ['dɔːtə(r)] *n.* Tochter, *die.*
'**daughter-in-law** *n., pl.* **daughters-
in-law** Schwiegertochter, *die*
daunt [dɔːnt] *v.t.* entmutigen
dawdle ['dɔːdl] *v.i.* bummeln *(ugs.)*
dawn [dɔːn] 1. *v.i.* dämmern; **sth.** ~**s**
|up|on **sb.** etw. dämmert jmdm. 2. *n.*
[Morgen]dämmerung, *die;* **at** ~: im
Morgengrauen
day [deɪ] *n.* Tag, *der;* **all** ~ |long| den
ganzen Tag [lang]; **for two** ~**s** zwei Tage [lang]; **the** ~ **before yesterday/after
tomorrow** vorgestern/übermorgen; ~
after ~: Tag für Tag; ~ **out** tagaus,
tagein; **in the** ~**s when** ...: zu der
Zeit, als ...; **these** ~**s** heutzutage; **in
those** ~**s** damals
day: ~**break** *n.* Tagesanbruch, *der;*
~**-dream** 1. *n.* Tagtraum, *der;* 2. *v.i.*
träumen; ~**light** *n.* Tageslicht, *das;*
in broad ~**light** am hellichten Tag[e];
~**-re'turn** *n.* Tagesrückfahrkarte,

die; ~**time** *n.* Tag, *der;* ~**-to-**~ *adj.*
[tag]täglich; ~ **trip** *n.* Tagesausflug,
der

daze ['deɪz] *v.t.* benommen machen.
dazed ['deɪzd] *adj.* benommen
dazzle ['dæzl] *v.t.* blenden
DC *abbr.* direct current GS
dead [ded] **1.** *adj.* **a)** tot; **b)** plötzlich
⟨*Halt*⟩; genau ⟨*Mitte*⟩; **c)** *(numb)* taub.
2. *adv.* völlig; ~ **straight** schnurgera-
de; ~ **easy/slow** kinderleicht/ganz
langsam; ~ **on time** auf die Minute; ~
tired todmüde

deaden ['dedn] *v.t.* dämpfen; betäuben ⟨*Schmerz*⟩

dead: ~ '**end** *n.* Sackgasse, *die;* ~
'**heat** *n.* totes Rennen; ~**line** *n.* [letz-
ter] Termin; ~**lock** *n.* völliger Stillstand

deadly ['dedlɪ] *adj.* tödlich; *(fig. coll.:
boring)* todlangweilig

Dead 'Sea *pr. n.* Tote Meer, *das*
deaf [def] *adj.* taub; ~ **and dumb** taub-
stumm. **deafen** ['defn] *v.t.* ~ **sb.** bei
jmdm. zur Taubheit führen; **I was** ~**ed
by the noise** *(fig.)* ich war von dem
Lärm wie betäubt. '**deafening** *adj.*
ohrenbetäubend. '**deafness** *n.* Taubheit, *die*

'**deal** [diːl] **1.** *v. t.,* dealt [delt] **a)** *(Cards)*
austeilen; **b)** ~ **sb.** a blow jmdm. einen
Schlag versetzen. **2.** *v.i.,* dealt **a)** *(do
business)* ~ **in sth.** mit etw. handeln;
b) ~ **with sth.** *(occupy oneself)* sich mit
etw. befassen; *(manage)* mit etw.
fertig werden; *(be about)* von etw.
handeln; ~ **with sb.** mit jmdm. fertig
werden. **3.** *n. (coll.: arrangement)* Geschäft, *das.* **deal 'out** *v.t.* verteilen
²**deal** *n.* **a great** *or* **good** ~: viel; *(often)*
ziemlich viel; **a great** *or* **good** ~ **of** viel
'**dealer** *n.* **a)** Händler, *der;* **b)** *(Cards)*
Geber, *der;* **he's the** ~: er gibt
'**dealings** *n. pl.* **have** ~ **with sb.** mit
jmdm. zu tun haben
dealt *see* '**deal 1, 2**
dean [diːn] *n. (Eccl.)* Dechant, *der*
dear [dɪə(r)] **1.** *adj.* **a)** lieb; **sb./sth. is** ~
to sb.['s **heart]** jmd. liebt jmdn./etw.;
(beginning letter) **D~ Sir/Madam** Sehr
geehrter Herr/Sehr verehrte gnädige
Frau; **D~ Mr Jones/Mrs Jones** Sehr
geehrter Herr Jones/Sehr verehrte
Frau Jones; **D~ Malcolm/Emily** Lieber Malcolm/Liebe Emily; **b)** *(expensive)* teuer. **2.** *int.* ~, ~!, ~ **me!,** oh ~!
[ach] du liebe *od.* meine Güte!
'**dearly** *adv.* **a)** von ganzem Herzen;
b) *(at high price)* teuer

dearth [dɜːθ] *n.* Mangel, *der* (of an
+ *Dat.*)

death [deθ] *n.* **a)** Tod, *der;* ... **to** ~: zu
Tode ...; **bleed to** ~: verbluten; **b)** *(instance)* Todesfall, *der*

death: ~ **penalty** *n.* Todesstrafe, *die;*
~ **sentence** *n.* Todesurteil, *das;*
~**-trap** *n.* lebensgefährliche Sache
debatable [dɪ'beɪtəbl] *adj. (questionable)* fraglich
debate [dɪ'beɪt] *n.* Debatte, *die*
debit ['debɪt] **1.** *n.* Soll, *das.* **2.** *v. t.* belasten ⟨*Konto*⟩
debris ['debriː] *n.* Trümmer *Pl.*
debt [det] *n.* Schuld, *die;* **be in** ~:
Schulden haben; **get into** ~: in Schulden geraten. **debtor** ['detə(r)] *n.*
Schuldner, *der/*Schuldnerin, *die*
début *(Amer.:* **debut)** ['deɪbuː, 'deɪ-
bjuː] *n.* Debüt, *das*
Dec. *abbr.* December Dez.
decade ['dekeɪd] *n.* Jahrzehnt, *das*
decadent ['dekədənt] *adj.* dekadent
decanter [dɪ'kæntə(r)] *n.* Karaffe, *die*
decay [dɪ'keɪ] **1.** *v.i.* verrotten; ⟨*Gebäude:*⟩ zerfallen; ⟨*Zahn:*⟩ faul werden. **2.** *n.* Verrotten, *das;* *(of building)*
Zerfall, *der;* *(of tooth)* Fäule, *die*
deceased [dɪ'siːst] **1.** *adj* verstorben.
2. *n.* Verstorbene, *der/die*
deceit [dɪ'siːt] *n.* Täuschung, *die.* **deceitful** [dɪ'siːtfl] *adj.* falsch ⟨*Person,
Art*⟩; hinterlistig ⟨*Trick*⟩
deceive [dɪ'siːv] *v.t.* täuschen; *(be unfaithful to)* betrügen
December [dɪ'sembə(r)] *n.* Dezember, *der; see also* **August**
decency ['diːsənsɪ] *n.* Anstand, *der*
decent ['diːsənt] *adj.* anständig
deception [dɪ'sepʃn] *n.* Betrug, *der;*
(being deceived) Täuschung, *die.* **deceptive** [dɪ'septɪv] *adj.* trügerisch
decibel ['desɪbel] *n.* Dezibel, *das*
decide [dɪ'saɪd] **1.** *v. t.* **a)** *(settle, judge)*
entscheiden über (+ *Akk.*); **b)** *(re-
solve)* ~ **that** ...: beschließen, daß ...; ~
to do sth. sich entschließen, etw. zu
tun. **2.** *v. i.* sich entscheiden (**in favour
of** zugunsten von, **against** gegen). **de-
'cided** *adj.,* **de'cidedly** *adv.* entschieden
deciduous [dɪ'sɪdjʊəs] *adj.* ~ **tree**
≈ Laubbaum, *der*
decimal ['desɪml] **1.** *n.* Dezimalbruch,
der. **2.** *adj.* Dezimal-; ~ '**point** Komma, *das*
decimate ['desɪmeɪt] *v.t.* dezimieren
decipher [dɪ'saɪfə(r)] *v.t.* entziffern
decision [dɪ'sɪʒn] *n.* Entscheidung,

die. **decisive** [dɪ'saɪsɪv] *adj.* entscheidend

deck [dek] *n.* Deck, *das;* on ~: an Deck; below ~[s] unter Deck. **'deckchair** *n.* Liegestuhl, *der*

declaration [deklə'reɪʃn] *n.* Erklärung, *die*

declare [dɪ'kleə(r)] *v. t.* erklären; kundtun *(geh.)* ⟨*Wunsch, Absicht*⟩; ~ **sth./sb.** |**to be**| **sth.** etw./jmdn. für etw. erklären

declension [dɪ'klenʃn] *n.* Deklination, *die*

decline [dɪ'klaɪn] **1.** *v. i.* nachlassen; ⟨*Anzahl:*⟩ sinken. **2.** *v. t.* **a)** ablehnen; **b)** *(Ling.)* deklinieren. **3.** *n. see* 1: Nachlassen, *das*/Sinken, *das* (in *Gen.*); **be on the** ~: nachlassen/sinken

decode [di:'kəʊd] *v. t.* entziffern

decompose [di:kəm'pəʊz] *v. i.* sich zersetzen

décor ['deɪkɔ:(r)] *n.* Ausstattung, *die*

decorate ['dekəreɪt] *v. t.* **a)** schmücken ⟨*Raum, Straße, Baum*⟩; verzieren ⟨*Kuchen, Kleid*⟩; *(paint)* streichen; *(wallpaper)* tapezieren; **b)** *(award medal etc. to)* auszeichnen.
decoration [dekə'reɪʃn] *n.* **a)** Schmücken, *das;* *(with paint)* Streichen, *das;* *(with wallpaper)* Tapezieren, *das;* **b)** *(adornment)* Schmuck, *der;* **c)** *(medal etc.)* Auszeichnung, *die.* **decorative** ['dekərətɪv] *adj.* dekorativ.
decorator ['dekəreɪtə(r)] *n.* Maler, *der; (paper-hanger)* Tapezierer, *der*

decorum [dɪ'kɔ:rəm] *n.* Schicklichkeit, *die (geh.)*

decoy ['di:kɔɪ] *n.* Lockvogel, *der*

decrease 1. [dɪ'kri:s] *v. i.* abnehmen; ⟨*Stärke:*⟩ nachlassen. **2.** [dɪ'kri:s] *v. t.* [ver]mindern ⟨*Wert, Lärm*⟩; schmälern ⟨*Popularität, Macht*⟩. **3.** ['di:kri:s] *n.* Rückgang, *der; (in weight)* Abnahme, *die; (in strength)* Nachlassen, *das; (in value, noise)* Minderung, *die*

decree [dɪ'kri:] **1.** *n.* Dekret, *das;* Erlaß, *der.* **2.** *v. t.* verfügen

decrepit [dɪ'krepɪt] *adj.* altersschwach; *(dilapidated)* heruntergekommen

dedicate ['dedɪkeɪt] *v. t.* ~ **sth. to sb.** jmdm. etw. widmen. **'dedicated** *adj.* **a)** *(devoted)* **be** ~ **to sth./sb.** nur für etw./jmdn. leben; **b)** *(to vocation)* hingebungsvoll; **a** ~ **teacher** ein Lehrer mit Leib und Seele. **dedication** [dedɪ'keɪʃn] *n.* **a)** Widmung, *die* (**to** *Dat.*); **b)** *(devotion)* Hingabe, *die*

deduce [dɪ'dju:s] *v. t.* ~ **sth.** |**from sth.**| etw. [aus etw.] schließen

deduct [dɪ'dʌkt] *v. t.* ~ **sth.** |**from sth.**| etw. [von etw.] abziehen. **deduction** [dɪ'dʌkʃn] *n.* **a)** *(deducting)* Abzug, *der;* **b)** *(deducing, thing deduced)* Ableitung, *die;* **c)** *(amount)* Abzüge *Pl.*

deed [di:d] *n.* **a)** Tat, *die;* **b)** *(Law)* Urkunde, *die*

deem [di:m] *v. t.* erachten für

deep [di:p] **1.** *adj. (lit. or fig.)* tief; tiefgründig ⟨*Bemerkung*⟩; **water ten feet** ~: drei Meter tiefes Wasser; **take a** ~ **breath** tief Atem holen; **be** ~ **in thought** in Gedanken versunken sein. **2.** *adv.* tief. **'deepen 1.** *v. t.* vertiefen. **2.** *v. i.* sich vertiefen. **deep-'freeze** *v. t.* tiefgefrieren. **'deeply** *adv. (lit. or fig.)* tief; äußerst ⟨*interessiert, dankbar*⟩

deer [dɪə(r)] *n., pl. same* Hirsch, *der; (roe~)* Reh, *das*

deface [dɪ'feɪs] *v. t.* verunstalten

defamation [defə'meɪʃn] *n.* Diffamierung, *die.* **defamatory** [dɪ'fæmətərɪ] *adj.* diffamierend

default [dɪ'fɔ:lt, dɪ'fɒlt] **1.** *n.* **lose/go by** ~: durch Abwesenheit verlieren/nicht zur Geltung kommen; **win by** ~: durch Nichterscheinen des Gegners gewinnen. **2.** *v. i.* ~ **on one's payments/ debts** seinen Zahlungsverpflichtungen nicht nachkommen

defeat [dɪ'fi:t] **1.** *v. t.* besiegen. **2.** *n.* *(being* ~*ed)* Niederlage, *die; (*~*ing)* Sieg, *der* (**of** über + *Akk.*). **de'featist** *adj.* defätistisch

defect 1. ['di:fekt] *n.* **a)** *(lack)* Mangel, *der;* **b)** *(shortcoming)* Fehler, *der.* **2.** [dɪ'fekt] *v. i.* überlaufen (**to** zu). **defection** [dɪ'fekʃn] *n.* Flucht, *die.* **defective** [dɪ'fektɪv] *adj.* defekt ⟨*Maschine*⟩; fehlerhaft ⟨*Material, Arbeiten, Methode*⟩. **defector** [dɪ'fektə(r)] *n.* Überläufer, *der/*-läuferin, *die*

defence [dɪ'fens] *n. (Brit.)* Verteidigung, *die; (means of* ~*)* Schutz, *der.* **de'fenceless** *adj.* wehrlos

defend [dɪ'fend] *v. t.* verteidigen. **de'fendant** *n. (Law) (accused)* Angeklagte, *der/die; (sued)* Beklagte, *der/die.* **de'fender** *n.* Verteidiger, *der*

defense *etc. (Amer.) see* **defence** *etc.*

defensive [dɪ'fensɪv] **1.** *adj.* defensiv. **2.** *n.* **be on the** ~: in der Defensive sein

¹defer [dɪ'fɜ:(r)] *v. t.,* **-rr-** aufschieben

²defer *v. i.,* **-rr-** : ~ |**to sb.**| sich |jmdm.| beugen. **deference** ['defərəns] *n.* Respekt, *der;* in ~ to sb./sth. aus Achtung vor jmdm./etw. **deferential** [defə'renʃl] *adj.* respektvoll

defiance [dɪ'faɪəns] *n.* Trotz, *der;* in ~ of sb./sth. jmdm./einer Sache zum Trotz

defiant [dɪ'faɪənt] *adj.,* **de'fiantly** *adv.* trotzig

deficiency [dɪ'fɪʃənsɪ] *n.* Mangel, *der* **deficient** [dɪ'fɪʃənt] *adj.* unzulänglich; sb./sth. is ~ in sth. jmdm./einer Sache mangelt es an etw. *(Dat.)*

deficit ['defɪsɪt] *n.* Defizit, *das* (of an + *Dat.*)

defile [dɪ'faɪl] *v.t.* verpesten ⟨*Luft*⟩; beflecken ⟨*Reinheit, Unschuld*⟩

define [dɪ'faɪn] *v.t.* definieren

definite ['defɪnɪt] *adj.* bestimmt; eindeutig ⟨*Antwort, Entscheidung, Beschluß, Verbesserung*⟩; klar umrissen ⟨*Ziel, Plan*⟩; klar ⟨*Vorstellung*⟩; genau ⟨*Zeitpunkt*⟩. '**definitely 1.** *adv.* bestimmt; eindeutig ⟨*festlegen, größer sein, verbessert*⟩; endgültig ⟨*entscheiden*⟩. **2.** *int. (coll.)* na, klar *(ugs.)*

definition [defɪ'nɪʃn] *n.* Definition, *die; (Telev., Phot.)* Schärfe, *die*

definitive [dɪ'fɪnɪtɪv] *adj.* endgültig ⟨*Beschluß, Antwort, Urteil*⟩; *(authoritative)* maßgeblich

deflate [dɪ'fleɪt] *v.t.* die Luft ablassen aus; *(fig.)* ernüchtern. **deflation** [dɪ'fleɪʃn] *n. (Econ.)* Deflation, *die*

deflect [dɪ'flekt] *v.t.* brechen ⟨*Licht*⟩; ~ sb./sth. [from sb./sth.] jmdn./etw. [von jmdm./einer Sache] ablenken

deform [dɪ'fɔːm] *v.t.* deformieren. **deformed** [dɪ'fɔːmd] *adj.* entstellt ⟨*Gesicht*⟩; verunstaltet ⟨*Person, Körperteil*⟩. **deformity** [dɪ'fɔːmɪtɪ] *n. (malformation)* Verunstaltung, *die*

defraud [dɪ'frɔːd] *v.t.* ~ sb. [of sth.] jmdn. [um etw.] betrügen

defray [dɪ'freɪ] *v.t.* bestreiten

defrost [diːˈfrɒst] *v.t.* auftauen ⟨*Speisen*⟩; abtauen ⟨*Kühlschrank*⟩

deft [deft] *adj.,* '**deftly** *adv.* sicher und geschickt

defunct [dɪ'fʌŋkt] *adj.* defekt ⟨*Maschine*⟩; veraltet ⟨*Gesetz*⟩

defuse [diːˈfjuːz] *v.t.* entschärfen

defy [dɪ'faɪ] *v.t.* a) *(resist openly)* ~ sb. jmdm. trotzen; b) *(refuse to obey)* ~ sb./sth. sich jmdm./einer Sache widersetzen

degenerate [dɪ'dʒenəreɪt] *v.i.* ~ [into sth.] [zu etw.] verkommen

degradation [degrə'deɪʃn] *n.* Erniedrigung, *die*

degrade [dɪ'greɪd] *v.t.* erniedrigen

degree [dɪ'griː] *n.* a) Grad, *der;* 20 ~s 20 Grad; b) *(academic rank)* [akademischer] Grad

de-ice [diːˈaɪs] *v.t.* enteisen

deign [deɪn] *v.t.* ~ to do sth. sich [dazu] herablassen, etw. zu tun

deity ['diːɪtɪ] *n.* Gottheit, *die*

dejected [dɪ'dʒektɪd] *adj.* niedergeschlagen. **dejection** [dɪ'dʒekʃn] *n.* Niedergeschlagenheit, *die*

delay [dɪ'leɪ] **1.** *v.t. (make late)* aufhalten; verzögern ⟨*Ankunft, Abfahrt*⟩; the train has been ~ed der Zug hat Verspätung. **2.** *v.i.* warten. **3.** *n.* a) Verzögerung, *die* (to bei); b) *(Transport)* Verspätung, *die*

delectable [dɪ'lektəbl] *adj.* köstlich

delegate 1. ['delɪgət] *n.* Delegierte, *der/die.* **2.** ['delɪgeɪt] *v.t.* delegieren (to an + *Akk.*). **delegation** [delɪ'geɪʃn] *n.* Delegation, *die*

delete [dɪ'liːt] *v.t.* streichen (from in + *Dat.*); *(Computing)* löschen. **deletion** [dɪ'liːʃn] *n.* Streichung, *die; (Computing)* Löschung, *die*

deliberate [dɪ'lɪbərət] *adj.* a) *(intentional)* absichtlich; bewußt ⟨*Lüge, Irreführung*⟩; b) *(fully considered)* wohlüberlegt. **de'liberately** *adv.* absichtlich. **deliberation** [dɪlɪbə'reɪʃn] *n.* Überlegung, *die; (discussion)* Beratung, *die*

delicacy ['delɪkəsɪ] *n.* a) *(tactfulness and care)* Feingefühl, *das;* b) *(food)* Delikatesse, *die*

delicate ['delɪkət] *adj.* zart; *(requiring careful handling)* empfindlich; delikat ⟨*Frage, Angelegenheit*⟩

delicatessen [delɪkə'tesən] *n.* Feinkostgeschäft, *das*

delicious [dɪ'lɪʃəs] *adj.* köstlich

delight [dɪ'laɪt] **1.** *v.t.* erfreuen. **2.** *v.i.* sb. ~s in doing sth. es macht jmdm. Freude, etw. zu tun. **3.** *n.* Freude, *die* (at über + *Akk.;* in an + *Dat.*). **de'lighted** *adj.* be ~ ⟨*Person:*⟩ hocherfreut sein; be ~ by or with sth. sich über etw. *(Akk.)* freuen. **delightful** [dɪ'laɪtfl] *adj.* wunderbar; köstlich ⟨*Geschmack*⟩; reizend ⟨*Person, Landschaft*⟩. **de'lightfully** *adv.* wunderbar

delinquent [dɪ'lɪŋkwənt] **1.** *n.* Randalierer, *der.* **2.** *adj.* kriminell

delirious [dɪ'lɪrɪəs] *adj.* be ~: im Delirium sein; be ~ [with sth.] *(fig.)* außer sich [vor etw. *(Dat.)*] sein

delirium [dɪ'lɪrɪəm] *n.* Delirium, *das*

deplorable

deliver [dɪ'lɪvə(r)] *v.t.* **a)** bringen; liefern ⟨*Ware*⟩; zustellen ⟨*Post, Telegramm*⟩; überbringen ⟨*Botschaft*⟩; **b)** halten ⟨*Rede*⟩. **delivery** [dɪ'lɪvərɪ] *n.* Lieferung, *die; (of letters, parcels)* Zustellung, *die.* **de'livery van** *n.* Lieferwagen, *der*

delta ['deltə] *n.* Delta, *das*

delude [dɪ'lju:d] *v.t.* täuschen

deluge ['delju:dʒ] **1.** *n.* sintflutartiger Regen. **2.** *v.t.* überschwemmen

delusion [dɪ'lju:ʒn] *n.* Illusion, *die*

de luxe [də'lʌks] *adj.* Luxus-

demand [dɪ'mɑ:nd] **1.** *n.* Forderung, *die* (for nach); *(for commodity)* Nachfrage, *die;* **sth./sb. is in ~:** etw. ist gefragt/jmd. ist begehrt. **2.** *v.t.* verlangen (of, from von); fordern ⟨*Recht*⟩. **de'manding** *adj.* anspruchsvoll

demented [dɪ'mentɪd] *adj.* wahnsinnig

de'mobilize *v.t.* demobilisieren ⟨*Armee, Kriegsschiff*⟩; aus dem Kriegsdienst entlassen ⟨*Soldat*⟩

democracy [dɪ'mɒkrəsɪ] *n.* Demokratie, *die.* **Democrat** ['deməkræt] *n. (Amer. Polit.)* Demokrat, *der/*Demokratin, *die.* **democratic** [demə'krætɪk] *adj.,* **democratically** [demə'krætɪkəlɪ] *adv.* demokratisch

demolish [dɪ'mɒlɪʃ] *v.t.* abreißen. **demolition** [demə'lɪʃn] *n.* Abriß, *der;* ~ **work** Abbruchsarbeit, *die*

demon ['di:mən] *n.* Dämon, *der*

demonstrate ['demənstreɪt] **1.** *v.t.* zeigen; *(be proof of)* zeigen; beweisen. **2.** *v.i.* demonstrieren. **demonstration** [demən'streɪʃn] *n. (also Pol. etc.)* Demonstration, *die; (proof)* Beweis, *der.* **demonstrative** [də'mɒnstrətɪv] *adj.* **a)** offen ⟨*Person*⟩; **b)** *(Ling.)* Demonstrativ-. **demonstrator** ['demənstreɪtə(r)] *n. (Pol. etc.)* Demonstrant, *der/*Demonstrantin, *die*

demoralize [dɪ'mɒrəlaɪz] *v.t.* demoralisieren

demote [di:'məʊt] *v.t.* degradieren (**to** zu). **demotion** [di:'məʊʃn] *n.* Degradierung, *die* (**to** zu)

demur [dɪ'mɜ:(r)] *v.i.,* **-rr-** Einwände erheben

demure [dɪ'mjʊə(r)] *adj.* betont zurückhaltend

den [den] *n.* Höhle, *die*

denial [dɪ'naɪəl] *n. (refusal)* Verweigerung, *die; (of request)* Ablehnung, *die*

denim ['denɪm] *n.* Denim ⓦ, *der;* Jeansstoff, *der;* ~ **jacket** Jeansjacke, *die;* ~**s** Bluejeans *Pl.*

Denmark ['denmɑ:k] *pr.n.* Dänemark *(das)*

denomination [dɪnɒmɪ'neɪʃn] *n. (Relig.)* Konfession, *die*

denote [dɪ'nəʊt] *v.t.* bezeichnen

denounce [dɪ'naʊns] *v.t.* denunzieren; *(accuse publicly)* beschuldigen

dense [dens] *adj.* **a)** dicht; massiv ⟨*Körper*⟩; **b)** *(stupid)* dumm. **'densely** *adv.* dicht; ~ **packed** dichtgedrängt. **density** ['densɪtɪ] *n.* Dichte, *die*

dent [dent] **1.** *n.* Beule, *die.* **2.** *v.t.* einbeulen

dental ['dentl] *adj.* Zahn-. **dental floss** ['dentl flɒs] *n.* Zahnseide, *die*

dentist ['dentɪst] *n.* Zahnarzt, *der/*-ärztin, *die.* **dentistry** ['dentɪstrɪ] *n.* Zahnheilkunde, *die*

denture ['dentʃə(r)] *n.* ~|s| Zahnprothese, *die*

denunciation [dɪnʌnsɪ'eɪʃn] *n.* Denunziation, *die; (public accusation)* Beschuldigung, *die*

deny [dɪ'naɪ] *v.t. (declare untrue)* bestreiten; *(refuse)* ~ **sb. sth.** jmdm. etw. verweigern; ~ **sb.'s request** jmdm. seine Bitte abschlagen

deodorant [di:'əʊdərənt] **1.** *adj.* deodorierend. **2.** *n.* Deodorant, *das*

depart [dɪ'pɑ:t] *v.i.* **a)** *(go away)* weggehen; **b)** *(set out, leave)* abfahren; *(on one's journey)* abreisen; **c)** *(fig.: deviate)* abweichen (**from** von)

department [dɪ'pɑ:tmənt] *n.* Abteilung, *die; (government ~)* Ministerium, *das; (of university)* Seminar, *das.* **de'partment store** *n.* Kaufhaus, *das*

departure [dɪ'pɑ:tʃə(r)] *n.* **a)** Abreise, *die; (of train, bus, ship)* Abfahrt, *die; (of aircraft)* Abflug, *der;* **b)** *(deviation)* ~ **from sth.** Abweichen von etw. **de'parture lounge** *n.* Abflughalle, *die*

depend [dɪ'pend] *v.i.* **a)** ~ |up|on abhängen von; **it/that** ~**s** es kommt drauf an; **b)** *(rely, trust)* ~ |up|on sich verlassen auf (+ *Akk.*); *(have to rely on)* angewiesen sein auf (+ *Akk.*). **dependable** [dɪ'pendəbl] *adj.* zuverlässig. **dependant** [dɪ'pendənt] *n.* Abhängige, *der/die.* **dependence** [dɪ'pendəns] *n.* Abhängigkeit, *die.* **dependent** [dɪ'pendənt] **1.** *n. see* **dependant. 2.** *adj.* abhängig

depict [dɪ'pɪkt] *v.t.* darstellen

deplete [dɪ'pli:t] *v.t.* erheblich verringern

deplorable [dɪ'plɔ:rəbl] *adj.* beklagenswert

deplore [dɪ'plɔ:(r)] *v. t.* **a)** *(disapprove of)* verurteilen; **b)** *(regret)* beklagen

deploy [dɪ'plɔɪ] *v. t.* einsetzen

deport [dɪ'pɔ:t] *v. t.* ausweisen. **deportation** [di:pɔ:'teɪʃn] *n.* Ausweisung, *die*

depose [dɪ'pəʊz] *v. t.* absetzen

deposit [dɪ'pɒzɪt] **1.** *n.* **a)** *(in bank)* Depot, *das;* *(credit)* Guthaben, *das;* *(Brit.: at interest)* Sparguthaben, *das;* **b)** *(first instalment)* Anzahlung, *die;* **put down a ~ on sth.** eine Anzahlung für etw. leisten; **c)** *(on bottle)* Pfand, *das.* **2.** *v. t.* **a)** *(lay down)* ablegen; abstellen ⟨*etw. Senkrechtes*⟩; **b)** *(in bank)* deponieren. **de'posit account** *n.* *(Brit.)* Sparkonto, *das*

depot ['depəʊ] *n.* Depot, *das*

depraved [dɪ'preɪvd] *adj.* verdorben. **depravity** [dɪ'prævɪtɪ] *n.* Verdorbenheit, *die*

depreciate [dɪ'pri:ʃeɪt] *v. i.* an Wert verlieren. **depreciation** [dɪpri:ʃɪ'eɪʃn] *n.* Wertverlust, *der*

depress [dɪ'pres] *v. t.* **a)** *(deject)* deprimieren; **b)** *(push down)* herunterdrücken. **depressed** [dɪ'prest] *adj.* deprimiert. **de'pressing** *adj.,* **de'pressingly** *adv.* deprimierend. **depression** [dɪ'preʃn] *n.* **a)** Depression, *die;* **b)** *(sunk place)* Vertiefung, *die;* **c)** *(Meteorol.)* Tief[druckgebiet], *das;* **d)** *(Econ.)* Wirtschaftskrise, *die*

deprivation [deprɪ'veɪʃn] *n.* Entbehrung, *die*

deprive [dɪ'praɪv] *v. t.* **~ sb. of sth.** jmdm. etw. nehmen; *(prevent from having)* jmdm. etw. vorenthalten. **deprived** [dɪ'praɪvd] *adj.* benachteiligt ⟨*Kind, Familie usw.*⟩

depth [depθ] *n.* **a)** Tiefe, *die;* **in ~:** gründlich; **in the ~s of winter** im tiefsten Winter. **'depth-charge** *n.* Wasserbombe, *die*

deputation [depjʊ'teɪʃn] *n.* Abordnung, *die*

deputize ['depjʊtaɪz] *v. i.* **~ for sb.** jmdn. vertreten

deputy ['depjʊtɪ] *n.* [Stell]vertreter, *der*/-vertreterin, *die; attrib.* stellvertretend

derail [dɪ'reɪl] *v. t.* **be ~ed** entgleisen. **de'railment** *n.* Entgleisung, *die*

deranged [dɪ'reɪndʒd] *adj.* [mentally] **~:** geistesgestört

derelict ['derɪlɪkt] **1.** *adj.* verlassen und verfallen. **2.** *n.* Ausgestoßene, *der/die*

deride [dɪ'raɪd] *v. t.* sich lustig machen

über (+ *Akk.*). **derision** [dɪ'rɪʒn] *n.* Spott, *der.* **derisive** [dɪ'raɪsɪv] *adj.* *(ironical)* spöttisch; *(scoffing)* verächtlich. **derisory** [dɪ'raɪzərɪ] *adj. (ridiculously inadequate)* lächerlich

derivation [derɪ'veɪʃn] *n.* Ableitung, *die*

derivative [dɪ'rɪvətɪv] **1.** *adj.* abgeleitet; *(lacking originality)* nachahmend. **2.** *n.* Ableitung, *die*

derive [dɪ'raɪv] **1.** *v. t.* **~ sth. from sth.** etw. aus etw. gewinnen; **~ pleasure from sth.** Freude an etw. *(Dat.)* haben. **2.** *v. i.* **~ from** beruhen auf (+ *Dat.*)

derogatory [dɪ'rɒgətərɪ] *adj.* abfällig

derrick ['derɪk] *n.* [Derrick]kran, *der*

derv [dɜ:v] *n.* Diesel[kraftstoff], *der*

descend [dɪ'send] **1.** *v. i.* **a)** *(go down)* hinuntergehen / -steigen / -klettern / -fahren; *(come down)* herunterkommen; ⟨*Fallschirm, Flugzeug:*⟩ niedergehen; **b)** *(slope downwards)* abfallen; **c)** **~ on sb.** jmdn. überfallen. **2.** *v. t.* *(go/come down)* hinunter- / heruntergehen / -steigen / -klettern / -fahren.

descendant [dɪ'sendənt] *n.* Nachkomme, *der.* **de'scended** *adj.* **be ~ from sb.** von jmdm. abstammen. **descent** [dɪ'sent] *n.* **a)** Abstieg, *der;* *(of parachute, plane)* Niedergehen, *das;* **b)** *(lineage)* Herkunft, *die*

describe [dɪ'skraɪb] *v. t.* beschreiben. **description** [dɪ'skrɪpʃn] *n.* **a)** Beschreibung, *die;* **b)** *(sort, class)* Art, *die.* **descriptive** [dɪ'skrɪptɪv] *adj.* beschreibend; *(vivid)* anschaulich; **a purely ~ report** ein reiner Tatsachenbericht

desecrate ['desɪkreɪt] *v. t.* entweihen

¹desert ['dezət] *n.* Wüste, *die*

²desert [dɪ'zɜ:t] **1.** *v. t.* verlassen. **2.** *v. i.* ⟨*Soldat:*⟩ desertieren. **de'serted** *adj.* verlassen. **de'serter** *n.* Deserteur, *der.* **desertion** [dɪ'zɜ:ʃn] *n.* Desertion, *die*

desert 'island [dezət 'aɪlənd] *n.* einsame Insel

deserts [dɪ'zɜ:ts] *n. pl.* **get one's [just] ~:** das bekommen, was man verdient hat

deserve [dɪ'zɜ:v] *v. t.* verdienen. **deserving** [dɪ'zɜ:vɪŋ] *adj.* verdienstvoll; **a ~ cause** ein guter Zweck

design [dɪ'zaɪn] **1.** *n.* Entwurf, *der;* *(pattern)* Muster, *das;* *(established form of machine, engine, etc.)* Bauweise, *die;* *(general idea, construction)* Konstruktion, *die.* **2.** *v. t.* entwerfen; **be ~ed to do sth.** etw. tun sollen

designate ['dezɪgneɪt] *v.t.* **a)** bezeichnen; **b)** *(appoint)* designieren *(geh.).*
designation [dezɪg'neɪʃn] *n.* Bezeichnung, *die*
'**designer** *n.* Designer, *der/* Designerin, *die; (of machines)* Konstrukteur, *der/*Konstrukteurin, *die; attrib.* Modell⟨-*kleidung, -jeans*⟩
desirability [dɪzaɪərə'bɪlɪtɪ] *n.* Wunschbarkeit, *die*
desirable [dɪ'zaɪərəbl] *adj.* wünschenswert
desire [dɪ'zaɪə(r)] **1.** *n.* Wunsch, *der* (for nach); *(longing)* Sehnsucht, *die* (for nach). **2.** *v.t.* sich *(Dat.)* wünschen; *(long for)* sich sehnen nach
desist [dɪ'zɪst] *v.i. (literary)* einhalten *(geh.);* ~ **from sth.** von etw. ablassen *(geh.)*
desk [desk] *n.* **a)** Schreibtisch, *der; (in school)* Tisch, *der;* **b)** *(cash* ~*)* Kasse, *die; (reception* ~*)* Rezeption, *die*
desolate ['desələt] *adj.* trostlos.
desolation [desə'leɪʃn] *n.* Trostlosigkeit, *die*
despair [dɪ'speə(r)] **1.** *n.* Verzweiflung, *die;* **be the** ~ **of sb.** jmdn. zur Verzweiflung bringen. **2.** *v.i.* verzweifeln. **desperate** ['despərət] *adj.* verzweifelt; extrem ⟨*Maßnahmen*⟩; **be** ~ **for sth.** etw. dringend brauchen. **desperation** [despə'reɪʃn] *n.* Verzweiflung, *die*
despicable [dɪ'spɪkəbl] *adj.* verabscheuungswürdig
despise [dɪ'spaɪz] *v.t.* verachten
despite [dɪ'spaɪt] *prep.* trotz
despondent [dɪ'spɒndənt] *adj.* bedrückt
despot ['despɒt] *n.* Despot, *der*
dessert [dɪ'zɜ:t] *n.* Nachtisch, *der.*
des'sert spoon *n.* Dessertlöffel, *der*
destination [destɪ'neɪʃn] *n.* Reiseziel, *das; (of goods)* Bestimmungsort, *der; (of train, bus)* Zielort, *der*
destine ['destɪn] *v.t.* bestimmen; **be** ~**d to do sth.** dazu bestimmt sein, etw. zu tun
destiny ['destɪnɪ] *n.* Schicksal, *das*
destitute ['destɪtju:t] *adj.* mittellos
destroy [dɪ'strɔɪ] *v.t.* zerstören.
de'stroyer *n. (also Naut.)* Zerstörer, *der.* **destruction** [dɪ'strʌkʃn] *n.* Zerstörung, *die.* **destructive** [dɪ'strʌktɪv] *adj.* zerstörerisch; verheerend ⟨*Sturm, Feuer*⟩
detach [dɪ'tætʃ] *v.t.* entfernen; abnehmen ⟨*wieder zu Befestigendes*⟩; herausnehmen ⟨*innen Befindliches*⟩.

detachable [dɪ'tætʃəbl] *adj.* abnehmbar. **detached** [dɪ'tætʃt] *adj.* **a)** *(impartial)* unvoreingenommen; *(unemotional)* unbeteiligt; **b) a** ~ **house** ein Einzelhaus. **de'tachment** *n.* **a)** *see* **detach**: Entfernen, *das;* Abnehmen, *das;* Herausnehmen, *das;* **b)** *(Mil.)* Abteilung, *die*
detail ['di:teɪl] **1.** *n.* Einzelheit, *die;* Detail, *das;* **in** ~: Punkt für Punkt; **go into** ~|s| ins Detail gehen. **2.** *v.t.* **a)** einzeln ausführen; **b)** *(Mil.)* abkommandieren. **detailed** ['di:teɪld] *adj.* detailliert; eingehend ⟨*Studie*⟩
detain [dɪ'teɪn] *v.t.* **a)** festhalten; *(take into confinement)* verhaften; **b)** *(delay)* aufhalten. **detainee** [di:teɪ'ni:] *n.* Verhaftete, *der/die*
detect [dɪ'tekt] *v.t.* entdecken; wahrnehmen ⟨*Bewegung*⟩; aufdecken ⟨*Irrtum, Verbrechen*⟩. **detection** [dɪ'tekʃn] *n.* Entdeckung, *die; (of error, crime)* Aufdeckung, *die.* **detective** [dɪ'tektɪv] *n.* Detektiv, *der; private* ~: Privatdetektiv, *der;* ~ **work** Ermittlungsarbeit, *die;* ~ **story** Detektivgeschichte, *die.* **detector** [dɪ'tektə(r)] *n.* Detektor, *der*
detention [dɪ'tenʃn] *n.* **a)** Festnahme, *die; (confinement)* Haft, *die;* **b)** *(Sch.)* Nachsitzen, *das*
deter [dɪ'tɜ:(r)] *v.t.,* -rr- abschrecken
detergent [dɪ'tɜ:dʒənt] *n.* Waschmittel, *das*
deteriorate [dɪ'tɪərɪəreɪt] *v.i.* sich verschlechtern; ⟨*Haus:*⟩ verfallen. **deterioration** [dɪtɪərɪə'reɪʃn] *n. see* **deteriorate**: Verschlechterung, *die;* Verfall, *der*
determination [dɪtɜ:mɪ'neɪʃn] *n.* Entschlossenheit, *die*
determine [dɪ'tɜ:mɪn] *v.t.* **a)** *(decide)* beschließen; **b)** *(be a decisive factor for)* bestimmen; **c)** *(ascertain)* feststellen. **determined** [dɪ'tɜ:mɪnd] *adj.* **a) be** ~ **to do sth.** etw. unbedingt tun wollen; **b)** *(resolute)* entschlossen
deterrent [dɪ'terənt] *n.* Abschreckungsmittel, *das* (**to** für)
detest [dɪ'test] *v.t.* verabscheuen. **detestable** [dɪ'testəbl] *adj.* verabscheuenswert
detonate ['detəneɪt] **1.** *v.t.* zünden. **2.** *v.i.* detonieren. **detonation** [detə'neɪʃn] *n.* Detonation, *die.* **detonator** ['detəneɪtə(r)] *n.* Sprengkapsel, *die*
detour ['di:tʊə(r)] *n.* Umweg, *der; (diversion)* Umleitung, *die*

detract [dɪ'trækt] *v. i.* ~ **from** sth. etw. beeinträchtigen

detriment ['detrɪmənt] *n.* **to the** ~ **of** sth. zum Nachteil einer Sache *(Gen.).* **detrimental** [detrɪ'mentl] *adj.* schädlich; **be** ~ **to** sth. einer Sache *(Dat.)* schaden

deuce [djuːs] *n. (Tennis)* Einstand, *der*

devaluation [diːvæljuːˈeɪʃn] *n.* Abwertung, *die*

devalue [diːˈvæljuː] *v. t.* abwerten

devastate ['devəsteɪt] *v. t.* verwüsten; *(fig.)* niederschmettern. **devastating** ['devəsteɪtɪŋ] *adj.* verheerend; *(fig.)* niederschmetternd. **devastation** [devə'steɪʃn] *n.* Verwüstung, *die*

develop [dɪ'veləp] **1.** *v. t.* entwickeln; erschließen *(natürliche Ressourcen);* bekommen *(Krankheit, Fieber, Lust);* ~ **a taste for** sth. Geschmack an etw. *(Akk.)* finden. **2.** *v. i.* sich entwickeln **(from** aus; **into** zu). **developer** *n.* **a)** *(Photog.)* Entwickler, *der;* **b)** *(of land)* Bauunternehmer, *der*

developing country *n.* Entwicklungsland, *das*

development *n.* Entwicklung, *die* **(from** aus; **into** zu); *(of natural resources etc.)* Erschließung, *die*

deviant ['diːvɪənt] *adj.* abweichend

deviate ['diːvɪeɪt] *v. i.* abweichen. **deviation** [diːvɪ'eɪʃn] *n.* Abweichung, *die*

device [dɪ'vaɪs] *n.* Gerät, *das; (as part of* sth.*)* Vorrichtung, *die;* **leave** sb. **to his own** ~s jmdn. sich *(Dat.)* selbst überlassen

devil ['devl] *n.* Teufel, *der;* **the D**~: der Teufel. **devilish** *adj.* teuflisch

devious ['diːvɪəs] *adj.* **a)** *(winding)* verschlungen; ~ **route** Umweg, *der;* **b)** *(unscrupulous, insincere)* hinterhältig

devise [dɪ'vaɪz] *v. t.* entwerfen; schmieden *(Pläne)*

devoid [dɪ'vɔɪd] *adj.* ~ **of** sth. *(lacking)* ohne etw.; *(free from)* frei von etw.

devolution [diːvə'luːʃn] *n. (Polit.)* Dezentralisierung, *die*

devote [dɪ'vəʊt] *v. t.* widmen **(to** *Dat.*). **devoted** *adj.* treu; aufrichtig *(Freundschaft, Liebe, Verehrung);* **be** ~ **to** sb. jmdn. innig lieben. **devotion** [dɪ'vəʊʃn] *n.* ~ **to** sb./sth. Hingabe an jmdn./etw.

devour [dɪ'vaʊə(r)] *v. t.* verschlingen

devout [dɪ'vaʊt] *adj.* fromm

dew [djuː] *n.* Tau, *der*

dexterity [dek'sterɪtɪ] *n.* Geschicklichkeit, *die*

dextrous ['dekstrəs] *adj.* geschickt

diabetes [daɪə'biːtiːz] *n.* Zuckerkrankheit, *die.* **diabetic** [daɪə'betɪk] **1.** *adj.* zuckerkrank *(Person).* **2.** *n.* Diabetiker, *der/*Diabetikerin, *die*

diabolical [daɪə'bɒlɪkl] *adj.* teuflisch

diagnose ['daɪəg'nəʊz] *v. t.* diagnostizieren; feststellen *(Fehler).* **diagnosis** [daɪəg'nəʊsɪs] *n., pl.* **diagnoses** [daɪəg'nəʊsiːz] Diagnose, *die;* **make a** ~: eine Diagnose stellen

diagonal [daɪ'ægənl] **1.** *adj.* diagonal. **2.** *n.* Diagonale, *die.* **diagonally** *adv.* diagonal

diagram ['daɪəgræm] *n.* Diagramm, *das*

dial ['daɪəl] **1.** *n. (of clock or watch)* Zifferblatt, *das; (of gauge, meter, etc.)* Skala, *die; (Teleph.)* Wählscheibe, *die.* **2.** *v. t. & i., (Brit.)* **-ll-** *(Teleph.)* wählen; ~ **direct** selbst wählen; *(dial extension)* durchwählen

dialect ['daɪəlekt] *n.* Dialekt, *der*

dialling *(Amer.:* **dialing**): ~ **code** *n.* Vorwahl, *die;* ~ **tone** Wählton, *der*

dialogue ['daɪəlɒg] *n.* Dialog, *der*

dial tone *n. (Amer.)* Wählton, *der*

diameter [daɪ'æmɪtə(r)] *n.* Durchmesser, *der.* **diametrical** [daɪə'metrɪkl] *adj.,* **diametrically** *adv.* diametral

diamond ['daɪəmənd] *n.* **a)** Diamant, *der;* **b)** *(figure)* Raute, *die;* **c)** *(Cards)* Karo, *das; see also* **club I c**

diaper ['daɪəpə(r)] *n. (Amer.)* Windel, *die*

diaphragm ['daɪəfræm] *n.* Diaphragma, *das*

diarrhoea *(Amer.:* **diarrhea**) [daɪə'rɪə] *n.* Durchfall, *der*

diary ['daɪərɪ] *n.* **a)** Tagebuch, *das;* **b)** *(for appointments)* Terminkalender, *der*

dice [daɪs] **1.** *n.* Würfel, *der.* **2.** *v. t. (Cooking)* würfeln

dicey ['daɪsɪ] *adj. (sl.)* riskant

dictate [dɪk'teɪt] *v. t. & i.* diktieren; *(prescribe)* vorschreiben; ~ **to** Vorschriften machen (+ *Dat.*). **dictation** [dɪk'teɪʃn] *n.* Diktat, *das.* **dictator** [dɪk'teɪtə(r)] *n.* Diktator, *der.* **dictatorial** [dɪktə'tɔːrɪəl] *adj.* diktatorisch. **dictatorship** *n.* Diktatur, *die*

dictionary ['dɪkʃənərɪ] *n.* Wörterbuch, *das*

did *see* **do**

diddle ['dɪdl] *v. t. (sl.)* übers Ohr hauen *(ugs.)*

didn't ['dɪdnt] *(coll.)* = **did not;** *see* **do**

die [daɪ] *v. i.,* **dying** ['daɪɪŋ] sterben **(of,**

from an + *Dat.*); ⟨*Tier, Pflanze:*⟩ eingehen; **be dying to do sth.** darauf brennen, etw. zu tun; **be dying for sth.** etw. unbedingt brauchen. **die 'down** *v.i.* ⟨*Sturm, Wind, Protest:*⟩ sich legen; ⟨*Flammen:*⟩ kleiner werden; ⟨*Feuer:*⟩ herunterbrennen; ⟨*Lärm:*⟩ leiser werden. **die 'out** *v.i.* aussterben

'die-hard *n.* Ewiggestrige, *der/die*

diesel ['di:zl] *n.* ~ **|engine|** Diesel[motor], *der;* ~ **|fuel|** Diesel[kraftstoff], *der*

diet ['daɪət] **1.** *n.* Diät, *die;* **be/go on a** ~: eine Schlankheitskur machen. **2.** *v.i.* eine Schlankheitskur machen

differ ['dɪfə(r)] *v.i. (be different)* sich unterscheiden

difference ['dɪfərəns] *n.* **a)** Unterschied, *der;* **make no** ~ **|to sb.|** [jmdm.] nichts ausmachen; **it makes a** ~: es ist ein *od. (ugs.)* macht einen Unterschied; **b)** *(disagreement)* Meinungsverschiedenheit, *die*

different ['dɪfərənt] *adj.* verschieden; *(pred. also)* anders; *(attrib. also)* ander...; **be** ~ **from** *or (esp. Brit.)* **to** *or (Amer.)* **than** ...: anders sein als ...

differentiate [dɪfəˈrenʃɪeɪt] *v.t. & i.* unterscheiden (**between** zwischen + *Dat.*)

'differently *adv.* anders (**from**, *esp. Brit.* **to** als)

difficult ['dɪfɪkəlt] *adj.* schwierig. **'difficulty** *n.* Schwierigkeit, *die;* **with |great|** ~: [sehr] mühsam; **get into difficulties** in Schwierigkeiten kommen

diffident ['dɪfɪdənt] *adj.* zaghaft; *(modest)* zurückhaltend

diffuse 1. [dɪˈfju:z] *v.t.* verbreiten. **2.** *v.i.* sich ausbreiten (**through** in + *Dat.*). **3.** [dɪˈfju:s] *adj.* diffus

dig [dɪg] **1.** *v.i., -gg-, dug* [dʌg] graben (**for** nach). **2.** *v.t., -gg-, dug* graben; umgraben ⟨*Erde, Garten*⟩. **dig 'out** *v.t.* ausgraben. **dig 'up** *v.t.* ausgraben; umgraben ⟨*Garten*⟩; aufreißen ⟨*Straße*⟩

digest [dɪˈdʒest, daɪˈdʒest] *v.t.* verdauen. **digestion** [dɪˈdʒestʃn, daɪˈdʒestʃn] *n.* Verdauung, *die*

'digger *n.* Bagger, *der*

digit ['dɪdʒɪt] *n.* Ziffer, *die*

digital ['dɪdʒɪtl] *adj.* Digital-

dignified ['dɪgnɪfaɪd] *adj.* würdig; *(stately)* würdevoll

dignify ['dɪgnɪfaɪ] *v.t.* Würde verleihen (+ *Dat.*)

dignitary ['dɪgnɪtərɪ] *n.* Würdenträger, *der;* **dignitaries** *(prominent people)* Honoratioren

dignity ['dɪgnɪtɪ] *n.* Würde, *die*

digress [daɪˈgres] *v.i.* abschweifen. **digression** [daɪˈgreʃn] *n.* Abschweifung, *die*

dike [daɪk] *n.* Deich, *der*

dilapidated [dɪˈlæpɪdeɪtɪd] *adj.* verfallen ⟨*Gebäude*⟩; verwahrlost ⟨*Erscheinung*⟩

dilate [daɪˈleɪt] **1.** *v.i.* sich weiten. **2.** *v.t.* ausdehnen

dilemma [dɪˈlemə, daɪˈlemə] *n.* Dilemma, *das*

diligence ['dɪlɪdʒəns] *n.* Fleiß, *der*

diligent ['dɪlɪdʒənt] *adj.,* **'diligently** *adv.* fleißig

dilute 1. [daɪˈlju:t, ˈdaɪlju:t] *adj.* verdünnt. **2.** [daɪˈlju:t] *v.t.* verdünnen

dim [dɪm] **1.** *adj.* **a)** schwach ⟨*Licht, Flackern*⟩; dunkel ⟨*Zimmer*⟩; verschwommen ⟨*Gestalt*⟩; **b)** *(vague)* verschwommen; **c)** *(coll.: stupid)* beschränkt. **2.** *v.i.* schwächer werden

dime [daɪm] *n. (Amer. coll.)* Zehncentstück, *das*

dimension [dɪˈmenʃn, daɪˈmenʃn] *n.* Dimension, *die;* ~**s** *(measurements)* Abmessungen; Maße

diminish [dɪˈmɪnɪʃ] **1.** *v.i.* nachlassen; ⟨*Vorräte, Einfluß:*⟩ abnehmen; ⟨*Wert, Ansehen:*⟩ geringer werden. **2.** *v.t.* verringern; schmälern ⟨*Ansehen, Ruf*⟩

dimple ['dɪmpl] *n.* Grübchen, *das*

dim: ~-**wit** *n. (coll.)* Dummkopf, *der (ugs.);* ~-**witted** ['dɪmwɪtɪd] *adj. (coll.)* dusselig *(salopp)*

din [dɪn] *n.* Lärm, *der*

dine [daɪn] *v.i.* [zu Mittag/zu Abend] essen. **'diner** *n.* Gast, *der*

dinghy ['dɪŋgɪ, 'dɪŋɪ] *n.* Ding[h]i, *das; (inflatable)* Schlauchboot, *das*

dingy ['dɪndʒɪ] *adj.* schmuddelig

dining ['daɪnɪŋ]: ~-**car** *n.* Speisewagen, *der;* ~-**room** *n.* Eßzimmer, *das; (in hotel etc.)* Speisesaal, *der*

dinner ['dɪnə(r)] *n. (at midday)* Mittagessen, *das; (in the evening)* Abendessen, *das; (formal)* Diner, *das.* **'dinner-table** *n.* Eßtisch, *der.* **'dinner-time** *n.* Essenszeit, *die;* **at** ~-**time** zur Essenszeit; *(12–2 p.m.)* mittags

dinosaur ['daɪnəsɔ:(r)] *n.* Dinosaurier, *der*

dint [dɪnt] *n.* **by** ~ **of** durch; **by** ~ **of doing sth.** indem jmd. etw. tut

dip [dɪp] **1.** *v.t., -pp-:* **a)** [ein]tauchen (**in** in + *Akk.*); **b)** ~ **one's headlights** abblenden. **2.** *v.i.* sinken; *(incline)* abfallen. **3.** *n.* **a)** *(in road)* Senke, *die;* **b)** *(coll.: bathe)* [kurzes] Bad

diphtheria [dɪfˈθɪərɪə] *n.* Diphtherie, *die*

diphthong [ˈdɪfθɒŋ] *n.* Diphthong, *der*

diploma [dɪˈpləʊmə] *n.* Diplom, *das*

diplomacy [dɪˈpləʊməsɪ] *n.* Diplomatie, *die*

diplomat [ˈdɪpləmæt] *n.* Diplomat, *der*/Diplomatin, *die*

diplomatic [dɪpləˈmætɪk] *adj.,* **diplo-**
'**matically** *adv.* diplomatisch

dire [ˈdaɪə(r)] *adj.* furchtbar

direct [dɪˈrekt, daɪˈrekt] 1. *v. t.* a) *(turn)* richten (to[wards] auf + *Akk.*); ~ sb. to a place jmdn. den Weg zu einem Ort weisen; b) *(control)* leiten; regeln ⟨*Verkehr*⟩; c) *(order)* anweisen; d) *(Theatre, Cinemat., etc.)* Regie führen bei. 2. *adj.* direkt; durchgehend ⟨*Zug*⟩; unmittelbar ⟨*Ursache, Auswirkung, Erfahrung, Verantwortung*⟩; genau ⟨*Gegenteil*⟩; direkt ⟨*Widerspruch*⟩; diametral ⟨*Gegensatz*⟩; ~ speech direkte Rede. 3. *adv.* direkt. **direct** '**current** *n.* Gleichstrom, *der.* **diroct** '**hit** *n.* Volltreffer, *der*

direction [daɪˈrekʃn] *n.* a) Richtung, *die;* in the ~ of London in Richtung London; b) *(guidance)* Führung, *die;* c) *usu. in pl. (order)* Anordnung, *die;* ~s [for use] Gebrauchsanweisung, *die*

di'rectly *adv.* a) direkt; unmittelbar ⟨*folgen, verantwortlich sein*⟩; b) *(exactly)* genau; c) *(at once)* umgehend; d) *(shortly)* gleich

di'rect object *n.* direktes Objekt

director [daɪˈrektə(r)] *n.* a) *(Commerc.)* Direktor, *der*/Direktorin, *die;* board of ~s Aufsichtsrat, *der;* b) *(Theatre, Cinemat., etc.)* Regisseur, *der*/Regisseurin, *die*

directory [daɪˈrektərɪ] *n. (telephone* ~*)* Telefonbuch, *das; (of tradesmen etc.)* Branchenverzeichnis, *das;* ~ **enquiries** *(Brit.),* ~ **information** *(Amer.)* [Fernsprech]auskunft, *die*

dirt [dɜːt] *n.* Schmutz, *der;* ~ **cheap** spottbillig. '**dirty** 1. *adj.* schmutzig; get sth. ~: etw. schmutzig machen. 2. *v. t.* schmutzig machen

disa'bility *n.* Behinderung, *die*

disabled [dɪsˈeɪbld] *adj.* behindert

disad'vantage *n.* Nachteil, *der;* at a ~: im Nachteil

disa'gree *v. i.* anderer Meinung sein; ~ with sb./sth. mit jmdm./etw. nicht übereinstimmen; ~ [with sb.] about or over sth. sich [mit jmdm.] über etw. *(Akk.)* nicht einig sein. **dis-**

a'**greeable** *adj.* unangenehm. **dis-**
a'**greement** *n.* a) *(difference of opinion)* Uneinigkeit, *die;* be in ~ with sb./sth. mit jmdm./etw. nicht übereinstimmen; b) *(quarrel)* Meinungsverschiedenheit, *die;* c) *(discrepancy)* Diskrepanz, *die*

disal'low *v. t.* verbieten; *(Sport)* nicht geben ⟨*Tor*⟩

disap'pear *v. i.* verschwinden; ⟨*Brauch, Tierart:*⟩ aussterben. **dis-**
ap'**pearance** *n.* Verschwinden, *das*

disap'point *v. t.* enttäuschen. **dis-**
ap'**pointed** *adj.* enttäuscht. **dis-**
ap'**pointing** *adj.* enttäuschend. **dis-**
ap'**pointment** *n.* Enttäuschung, *die*

disap'proval *n.* Mißbilligung, *die*

disap'prove *v. i.* dagegen sein; ~ of sb./sth. jmdn. ablehnen/etw. mißbilligen

dis'arm *v. t.* entwaffnen. **disarma-**
ment [dɪsˈɑːməmənt] *n.* Abrüstung, *die*

disarray [dɪsəˈreɪ] *n.* Unordnung, *die;* in ~: in Unordnung

disaster [dɪˈzɑːstə(r)] *n.* Katastrophe, *die;* ~ **area** Katastrophengebiet, *das.* **disastrous** [dɪˈzɑːstrəs] *adj.* katastrophal; verhängnisvoll ⟨*Irrtum, Entscheidung, Politik*⟩

dis'band 1. *v. t.* auflösen. 2. *v. i.* sich auflösen

disbe'lief *n.* Unglaube, *der;* in ~: ungläubig

disbe'lieve *v. t.* ~ sb./sth. jmdm./etw. nicht glauben

disc [dɪsk] *n.* Scheibe, *die; (record)* Platte, *die;* **floppy** ~: Floppy disk, *die;* **hard** ~ *(fixed)* Festplatte, *die*

discard [dɪsˈkɑːd] *v. t.* wegwerfen; fallenlassen ⟨*Vorschlag, Idee*⟩

discern [dɪˈsɜːn] *v. t.* wahrnehmen. **discernible** [dɪˈsɜːnɪbl] *adj.* erkennbar. **di'scerning** *adj.* kritisch

discharge 1. [dɪsˈtʃɑːdʒ] *v. t.* a) entlassen (**from** aus); freisprechen ⟨*Angeklagte*⟩; b) ablassen ⟨*Flüssigkeit, Gas*⟩. 2. [ˈdɪstʃɑːdʒ] *n.* a) Entlassung, *die* (**from** aus); *(of defendant)* Freispruch, *der;* b) *(emission)* Ausfluß, *der*

disciple [dɪˈsaɪpl] *n.* a) *(Relig.)* Jünger, *der;* b) *(follower)* Anhänger, *der*/Anhängerin, *die*

disciplinary [dɪsɪˈplɪnərɪ] *adj.* disziplinarisch; ~ **action** Disziplinarmaßnahmen

discipline [ˈdɪsɪplɪn] 1. *n.* Disziplin, *die.* 2. *v. t.* disziplinieren; *(punish)* bestrafen

'**disc jockey** n. Diskjockey, *der*

dis'claim v. t. abstreiten

disclose [dɪs'kləʊz] v. t. enthüllen; bekanntgeben ⟨*Information, Nachricht*⟩.

dis'closure n. Enthüllung, *die; (of information, news)* Bekanntgabe, *die*

disco ['dɪskəʊ] n., *pl.* ~s *(coll.)* Disko, *die*

dis'colour *(Brit.; Amer.:* **discolor)** v. t. verfärben

dis'comfort n. **a)** *no pl. (slight pain)* Beschwerden *Pl.;* **b)** *(hardship)* Unannehmlichkeit, *die*

disconcert [dɪskɒn'sɜːt] v. t. irritieren

discon'nect v. t. abtrennen; abstellen ⟨*Telefon*⟩

disconsolate [dɪs'kɒnsələt] *adj.* **a)** *(unhappy)* unglücklich; **b)** *(inconsolable)* untröstlich

discon'tent n. Unzufriedenheit, *die.* **discon'tented** *adj.* unzufrieden

discon'tinue v. t. einstellen

discord ['dɪskɔːd] n. **a)** Zwietracht, *die;* **b)** *(Mus.)* Dissonanz, *die.* **discordant** [dɪs'kɔːdənt] *adj.* **a)** *(conflicting)* gegensätzlich; **b)** **a** ~ **note** ein Mißton

discothèque ['dɪskətek] n. Diskothek, *die*

discount **1.** ['dɪskaʊnt] n. *(Commerc.)* Rabatt, *der* (**on** auf + *Akk.*). **2.** [dɪ'skaʊnt] v. t. *(disbelieve)* unberücksichtigt lassen

discourage [dɪ'skʌrɪdʒ] v. t. **a)** entmutigen; **b)** *(advise against)* abraten. **di'scouragement** n. **a)** Entmutigung, *die;* **b)** *(depression)* Mutlosigkeit, *die.* **discouraging** [dɪ'skʌrɪdʒɪŋ] *adj.* entmutigend

dis'courteous *adj.* unhöflich. **dis'courtesy** n. Unhöflichkeit, *die*

discover [dɪ'skʌvə(r)] v. t. **a)** entdecken; *(by search)* herausfinden. **di'scovery** n. Entdeckung, *die*

dis'credit **1.** n. Mißkredit, *der;* **bring** ~ **on sb./sth., bring sb./sth. into** ~: jmdn./etw. in Mißkredit bringen. **2.** v. t. in Mißkredit bringen

discreet [dɪ'skriːt] *adj.,* **di'screetly** *adv.* diskret

discrepancy [dɪ'skrepənsɪ] n. Diskrepanz, *die*

discretion [dɪ'skreʃn] n. *(prudence)* Umsicht, *die*

discriminate [dɪ'skrɪmɪneɪt] v. i. **a)** unterscheiden; **b)** ~ **against/in favour of sb.** jmdn. diskriminieren/bevorzugen. **discrimination** [dɪskrɪmɪ'neɪʃn] n. **a)** Unterscheidung, *die;* **b)** Diskri-

minierung, *die* (**against** *Gen.*); ~ **in favour of** Bevorzugung (+ *Gen.*)

discus ['dɪskəs] n. Diskus, *der*

discuss [dɪ'skʌs] v. t. besprechen; *(debate)* diskutieren über (+ *Akk.*). **discussion** [dɪ'skʌʃn] n. Gespräch, *das; (debate)* Diskussion, *die*

disdain [dɪs'deɪn] **1.** n. Verachtung, *die.* **2.** v. t. verachten; ~ **to do sth.** zu stolz sein, etw. zu tun. **disdainful** [dɪs'deɪnfl] *adj.* verächtlich

disease [dɪ'ziːz] n. Krankheit, *die.* **diseased** [dɪ'ziːzd] *adj.* krank

disem'bark v. i. von Bord gehen

disen'chant v. t. ernüchtern; **he became** ~**ed with her/it** sie/es hat ihn desillusioniert

disen'gage v. t. lösen (**from** aus, von); ~ **the clutch** auskuppeln

disen'tangle v. t. entwirren; *(extricate)* befreien (**from** aus)

dis'figure v. t. entstellen

disgrace [dɪs'greɪs] n. **1.** Schande, *die* (**to** für). **2.** v. t. Schande machen (+ *Dat.*); ~ **oneself** sich blamieren. **dis'graceful** [dɪs'greɪsfl] *adj.* skandalös; **it's** ~: es ist ein Skandal

disgruntled [dɪs'grʌntld] *adj.* verstimmt

disguise [dɪs'gaɪz] **1.** v. t. verkleiden ⟨*Person*⟩; verstellen ⟨*Stimme*⟩; tarnen ⟨*Gegenstand*⟩. **2.** n. Verkleidung, *die*

disgust [dɪs'gʌst] **1.** n. *(nausea)* Ekel, *der* (**at** vor + *Dat.*); *(revulsion)* Abscheu, *der* (**at** vor + *Dat.*); *(indignation)* Empörung, *die* (**at** über + *Akk.*). **2.** v. t. anwidern; *(fill with nausea)* ekeln; *(fill with indignation)* empören. **dis'gusted** *adj.* angewidert; *(nauseated)* angeekelt; *(indignant)* empört. **dis'gusting** *adj.* widerlich

dish [dɪʃ] n. **a)** Schale, *die; (deeper)* Schüssel, *die;* ~**es** *(crockery)* Geschirr, *das;* **wash** or *(coll.)* **do the** ~**es** Geschirr spülen; **b)** *(type of food)* Gericht, *das.* **dish 'out** v. t. **a)** austeilen ⟨*Essen*⟩; **b)** *(coll.: distribute)* verteilen. **dish 'up** v. t. auftragen

'**dishcloth** n. Spültuch, *das*

dis'hearten v. t. entmutigen

dishevelled *(Amer.:* **disheveled)** [dɪ'ʃevld] *adj.* zerzaust ⟨*Haar*⟩; ungepflegt ⟨*Erscheinung*⟩

dis'honest *adj.,* **dis'honestly** *adv.* unehrlich. **dis'honesty** n. Unehrlichkeit, *die*

dis'honour **1.** n. Unehre, *die.* **2.** v. t. beleidigen. **dishonourable** [dɪs'ɒnərəbl] *adj.* unehrenhaft '**dishwasher** *n*. Geschirrspülmaschine, *die*

disil'lusion 1. *v. t.* ernüchtern. 2. *n.* Desillusion, *die* (**with** über + *Akk.*).
disil'lusionment *n*. Desillusionierung, *die*

disin'fect *v. t.* desinfizieren. **disinfectant** [dısın'fektənt] 1. *adj.* desinfizierend. 2. *n*. Desinfektionsmittel, *das*

dis'integrate *v. i.* zerfallen. **disintegration** [dısıntı'greıʃn] *n*. Zerfall, *der*

dis'interested *adj.* **a)** *(impartial)* unvoreingenommen; **b)** *(coll.: uninterested)* desinteressiert

disjointed [dıs'dʒɔıntıd] *adj.* unzusammenhängend

disk *see* disc

diskette [dı'sket] *n*. Diskette, *die*

dis'like 1. *v. t.* nicht mögen; ~ **doing sth.** etw. ungern tun. 2. *n*. Abneigung, *die* (**of, for** gegen); **take a ~ to sb./sth.** eine Abneigung gegen jmdn./etw. empfinden

dislocate ['dısləkeıt] *v. t.* ausrenken; auskugeln ⟨*Schulter, Hüfte*⟩

dis'lodge *v. t.* entfernen (**from** aus)

dis'loyal *adj.* illoyal (**to** gegenüber). **dis'loyalty** *n*. Illoyalität, *die* (**to** gegenüber)

dismal ['dızməl] *adj.* trist

dis'mantle [dıs'mæntl] *v. t.* demontieren; abbauen ⟨*Schuppen, Gerüst*⟩

dismay [dıs'meı] 1. *v. t.* bestürzen. 2. *n*. Bestürzung, *die* (**at** über + *Akk.*)

dismiss [dıs'mıs] *v. t.* entlassen; *(reject)* ablehnen. **dismissal** [dıs'mısl] *n*. Entlassung, *die*

dis'mount *v. i.* absteigen

diso'bedience *n*. Ungehorsam, *der*

diso'bedient *adj.* ungehorsam

diso'bey *v. t.* nicht gehorchen (+ *Dat.*); nicht befolgen ⟨*Befehl*⟩

dis'order *n*. **a)** Durcheinander, *das;* **b)** *(Med.)* Störung, *die*. **dis'orderly** *adj. (untidy)* unordentlich; ~ **conduct** ungebührliches Benehmen

dis'organized *adj.* chaotisch

dis'orientated, dis'oriented *adj.* desorientiert

dis'own *v. t.* verleugnen

disparage [dı'spærıdʒ] *v. t.* herabsetzen. **disparaging** [dı'spærıdʒıŋ] *adj.* abschätzig

disparity [dı'spærıtı] *n*. Ungleichheit, *die*

dispatch [dı'spætʃ] 1. *v. t.* **a)** schicken; **b)** *(kill)* töten. 2. *n*. Bericht, *der*

dispel [dı'spel] *v. t.,* **-ll-** vertreiben; zerstreuen ⟨*Besorgnis, Befürchtung*⟩

dispensable [dı'spensəbl] *adj.* entbehrlich

dispensary [dı'spensərı] *n*. Apotheke, *die*

dispense [dı'spens] *v. i.* ~ **with** verzichten auf (+ *Akk.*)

dispersal [dı'spɜːsl] *n*. Zerstreuung, *die*

disperse [dı'spɜːs] 1. *v. t.* zerstreuen. 2. *v. i.* sich zerstreuen

dispirited [dı'spırıtıd] *adj.* entmutigt

dis'place *v. t.* verschieben; *(supplant)* ersetzen

display [dı'spleı] 1. *v. t.* zeigen; ausstellen ⟨*Waren*⟩. 2. *n*. Ausstellung, *die; (of goods)* Auslage, *die; (ostentatious show)* Zurschaustellung, *die*

dis'please *v. t.* ~ **sb.** jmds. Mißfallen erregen. **dis'pleasure** *n*. Mißfallen, *das*

disposable [dı'spəʊzəbl] *adj.* Wegwerf-

disposal [dı'spəʊzl] *n*. Beseitigung, *die;* **have sth./sb. at one's ~:** etw./ jmdn. zur Verfügung haben; **be at sb.'s ~:** jmdm. zur Verfügung stehen

dispose [dı'spəʊz] *v. t.* ~ **sb. to sth.** jmdn. zu etw. veranlassen; ~ **sb. to do sth.** jmdn. dazu veranlassen, etw. zu tun. **di'spose of** *v. t.* beseitigen; *(settle)* erledigen

disposed [dı'spəʊzd] *adj.* **be ~ to do sth.** dazu neigen, etw. zu tun; **be well ~ towards sb./sth.** jmdm. wohl gesinnt sein/einer Sache *(Dat.)* positiv gegenüberstehen. **disposition** [dıspə'zıʃn] *n*. Veranlagung, *die; (nature)* Art, *die*

dis'prove *v. t.* widerlegen

dispute [dı'spjuːt] 1. *n*. Streit, *der* (**over** um). 2. *v. t.* **a)** *(discuss)* sich streiten über (+ *Akk.*); **b)** *(oppose)* bestreiten

disqualifi'cation *n*. Ausschluß, *der; (Sport)* Disqualifikation, *die*

dis'qualify *v. t.* ausschließen (**from** von); *(Sport)* disqualifizieren

disre'gard 1. *v. t.* ignorieren. 2. *n*. Mißachtung, *die* (**of, for** *Gen.*); *(of wishes, feelings)* Gleichgültigkeit, *die* (**for, of** gegenüber)

dis'reputable *adj.* verrufen

disrepute [dısrı'pjuːt] *n*. Verruf, *der;* **bring sb./sth. into ~:** jmdn./etw. in Verruf bringen

disre'spect *n*. Mißachtung, *die;* **show ~ for sb./sth.** keine Achtung vor jmdm./etw. haben. **disre'spectful** *adj.* respektlos

disrupt [dɪs'rʌpt] *v. t.* stören. **disruption** [dɪs'rʌpʃn] *n.* Störung, *die.* **disruptive** [dɪs'rʌptɪv] *adj.* störend

dissatis'faction *n.* Unzufriedenheit, *die*

dis'satisfied *adj.* unzufrieden

dissect [dɪ'sekt] *v. t.* sezieren

dissent [dɪ'sent] **1.** *v. i.* **a)** *(refuse to assent)* nicht zustimmen; ~ **from sth.** mit etw. nicht übereinstimmen; **b)** *(disagree)* ~ **from sth.** von etw. abweichen. **2.** *n.* Ablehnung, *die; (from majority)* Abweichung, *die*

dissertation [dɪsə'teɪʃn] *n.* Dissertation, *die*

dis'service *n.* **do sb. a ~:** jmdm. einen schlechten Dienst erweisen

dissident ['dɪsɪdənt] *n.* Dissident, *der*/Dissidentin, *die*

dis'similar *adj.* unähnlich (**to** *Dat.*)

dissociate [dɪ'səʊʃieɪt] *v. t.* trennen; ~ **oneself** sich distanzieren (**from** von)

dissolve [dɪ'zɒlv] **1.** *v. t.* auflösen. **2.** *v. i.* sich auflösen

dissuade [dɪ'sweɪd] *v. t.* abbringen (**from** von)

distance ['dɪstəns] *n.* **a)** Entfernung, *die* (**from** zu); **b)** *(way to cover)* Strecke, *die;* **from a ~:** von weitem; **in/into the ~:** in der/die Ferne

distant ['dɪstənt] *adj.* **a)** fern; entfernt ⟨*Ähnlichkeit, Verwandtschaft, Verwandte*⟩; **b)** *(reserved)* distanziert

dis'taste *n.* Abneigung, *die* (**for** gegen). **dis'tasteful** *adj.* unangenehm

distend [dɪ'stend] *v. t.* erweitern

distil, *(Amer.)* **distill** [dɪ'stɪl] *v. t.* destillieren; brennen ⟨*Branntwein*⟩. **distillation** [dɪstɪ'leɪʃn] *n.* Destillation, *die.* **distillery** [dɪ'stɪlərɪ] *n.* Brennerei, *die*

distinct [dɪ'stɪŋkt] *adj.* deutlich; *(different)* verschieden. **distinction** [dɪ'stɪŋkʃn] *n.* Unterschied, *der.* **distinctive** [dɪ'stɪŋktɪv] *adj.* unverwechselbar. **dis'tinctly** *adv.* deutlich

distinguish [dɪ'stɪŋgwɪʃ] **1.** *v. t.* **a)** *(make out)* erkennen; **b)** *(differentiate)* unterscheiden; **c)** *(characterize)* kennzeichnen; **d)** ~ **oneself** [**by sth.**] sich [durch etw.] hervortun. **2.** *v. i.* unterscheiden; ~ **between** auseinanderhalten. **distinguished** [dɪ'stɪŋgwɪʃt] *adj.* angesehen; glänzend ⟨*Laufbahn*⟩; vornehm ⟨*Aussehen*⟩

distort [dɪ'stɔːt] *v. t.* verzerren; *(fig.)* verdrehen. **distortion** [dɪ'stɔːʃn] *n.* Verzerrung, *die; (fig.)* Verdrehung, *die*

distract [dɪ'strækt] *v. t.* ablenken; ~

sb.|'s **attention from sth.**] jmdn. [von etw.] ablenken. **di'stracted** *adj.* von Sinnen *nachgestellt; (mentally far away)* abwesend. **distraction** [dɪ'strækʃn] *n.* **a)** *(diversion)* Ablenkung, *die; (interruption)* Störung, *die;* **b)** **drive sb. to ~:** jmdn. zum Wahnsinn treiben

distraught [dɪ'strɔːt] *adj.* aufgelöst (**with** vor + *Dat.*); verstört ⟨*Blick*⟩

distress [dɪ'stres] **1.** *n.* **a)** Kummer, *der* (**at** über + *Akk.*); **b)** *(pain)* Qualen *Pl.;* **c)** **an aircraft/ship in ~:** ein Flugzeug in Not/ein Schiff in Seenot. **2.** *v. t.* nahegehen (+ *Dat.*). **di'stressing** *adj.* erschütternd. **di'stress signal** *n.* Notsignal, *das*

distribute [dɪ'strɪbjuːt] *v. t.* verteilen (**to an** + *Akk.;* **among** unter + *Akk.*); *(Commerc.)* vertreiben. **distribution** [dɪstrɪ'bjuːʃn] *n.* Verteilung, *die; (Commerc.)* Vertrieb, *der.* **distributor** [dɪ'strɪbjʊtə(r)] *n.* Verteiler, *der*/Verteilerin, *die; (Commerc.)* Vertreiber, *der*

district ['dɪstrɪkt] *n.* Gegend, *die; (Admin.)* Bezirk, *der.* **district 'nurse** *n. (Brit.)* Gemeindeschwester, *die*

dis'trust [dɪs'trʌst] **1.** *n.* Mißtrauen, *das* (**of** gegen). **2.** *v. t.* mißtrauen (+ *Dat.*)

disturb [dɪ'stɜːb] *v. t.* **a)** stören; **'do not ~!'** „bitte nicht stören!"; **b)** *(worry)* beunruhigen. **disturbance** [dɪ'stɜː-bəns] *n.* Störung, *die;* **political ~s** politische Unruhen. **disturbed** [dɪ'stɜːbd] *adj.* besorgt; [**mentally**] ~: geistig gestört

disuse [dɪs'juːs] *n.* **fall into ~:** außer Gebrauch kommen

disused [dɪs'juːzd] *adj.* stillgelegt; leerstehend ⟨*Gebäude*⟩

ditch [dɪtʃ] **1.** *n.* Graben, *der.* **2.** *v. t. (sl.)* sausenlassen ⟨*Plan*⟩; sitzenlassen ⟨*Familie, Freund*⟩

dither ['dɪðə(r)] *v. i.* schwanken

ditto ['dɪtəʊ] *n., pl.* ~**s** ebenso; ditto; ~ **marks** Unterführungszeichen, *das*

divan [dɪ'væn] *n.* [Polster]liege, *die*

dive [daɪv] **1.** *v. i.,* dived *or (Amer.)* **dove** [dəʊv] **a)** einen Kopfsprung machen; *(when already in water)* tauchen; **b)** ⟨*Vogel, Flugzeug usw.*⟩ einen Sturzflug machen. **2.** *n.* **a)** Kopfsprung, *der; (of bird, aircraft, etc.)* Sturzflug, *der;* **b)** *(coll.: place)* Spelunke, *die.* **'diver** *n.* **a)** *(Sport)* Kunstspringer, *der*/-springerin, *die;* **b)** *(as profession)* Taucher, *der*/Taucherin, *die*

diverge [daɪ'vɜːdʒ] *v. i.* auseinandergehen. **divergent** [daɪ'vɜːdʒənt] *adj.* auseinandergehend

diverse [daɪ'vɜːs] *adj.* verschieden

diversion [daɪ'vɜːʃn] *n.* **a)** Ablenkung, *die;* **create a ~:** ein Ablenkungsmanöver durchführen; **b)** *(Brit.: alternative route)* Umleitung, *die*

diversity [daɪ'vɜːsɪtɪ] *n.* Vielfalt, *die*

divert [daɪ'vɜːt] *v. t.* umleiten ⟨Verkehr, Fluß⟩; ablenken ⟨Aufmerksamkeit⟩

divide [dɪ'vaɪd] **1.** *v. t.* **a)** teilen; **~ sth. in two** etw. [in zwei Teile] zerteilen; **b)** *(distribute)* aufteilen **(among/between** unter + *Akk. od. Dat.);* **c)** *(Math.)* dividieren *(fachspr.),* teilen **(by** durch). **2.** *v. i.* sich teilen; **~ |from sth.|** von etw. abzweigen. **divide 'out** *v. t.* aufteilen **(among/between** unter + *Akk. od. Dat.);* *(distribute)* verteilen an (+ *Akk.*). **divide 'up** *v. t.* aufteilen

dividend ['dɪvɪdend] *n.* Dividende, *die*

dividers [dɪ'vaɪdəz] *n. pl.* Stechzirkel, *der*

divine [dɪ'vaɪn] *adj.* göttlich

diving ['daɪvɪŋ] *n.* Kunstspringen, *das.* **'diving-board** *n.* Sprungbrett, *das.* **'diving-suit** *n.* Taucheranzug, *der*

divinity [dɪ'vɪnɪtɪ] *n.* **a)** Göttlichkeit, *die;* **b)** *(god)* Gottheit, *die*

divisible [dɪ'vɪzɪbl] *adj.* teilbar **(by** durch)

division [dɪ'vɪʒn] *n.* **a)** Teilung, *die;* **b)** *(Math.)* Dividieren, *das;* **c)** *(section, part)* Abteilung, *die;* **d)** *(group)* Gruppe, *die;* **e)** *(Mil. etc.)* Division, *die;* **f)** *(Footb. etc.)* Liga, *die;* Spielklasse, *die; (in British football)* Division, *die*

divorce [dɪ'vɔːs] **1.** *n.* [Ehe]scheidung, *die.* **2.** *v. t.* **~ one's husband/wife** sich von seinem Mann/seiner Frau scheiden lassen. **divorced** [dɪ'vɔːst] *adj.* geschieden; **get ~:** sich scheiden lassen

divulge [daɪ'vʌldʒ] *v. t.* preisgeben

DIY *abbr.* **do-it-yourself**

dizzy ['dɪzɪ] *adj.* schwind[e]lig; **I feel ~:** mir ist schwindlig

do [də, *stressed* duː] **1.** *v. t., neg. coll.* **don't** [dəʊnt], *pres. t.* **he does** [dʌz], *neg. (coll.)* **doesn't** ['dʌznt], *p. t.* **did** [dɪd], *neg. (coll.)* **didn't** ['dɪdnt], *pres. p.* **doing** ['duːɪŋ], *p. p.* **done** [dʌn] **a)** machen ⟨Hausaufgaben, Hausarbeit, Examen, Handstand⟩; erfüllen ⟨Pflicht⟩; verrichten ⟨Arbeit⟩; vorführen ⟨Trick, Nummer, Tanz⟩; durchführen ⟨Test⟩; machen ⟨Übersetzung, Kopie, Bett⟩; schaffen ⟨Pensum⟩; *(clean)* putzen;

(arrange) [zurecht]machen ⟨Haare⟩; schminken ⟨Lippen, Augen, Gesicht⟩; machen *(ugs.)* ⟨Nägel⟩; *(cut)* schneiden ⟨Nägel⟩; *(paint)* machen *(ugs.)* ⟨Zimmer⟩; streichen ⟨Haus, Möbel⟩; *(repair)* in Ordnung bringen; **do the shopping / washing-up / cleaning** einkaufen [gehen]/abwaschen/saubermachen; **what can I do for you?** *(in shop)* was darf's sein?; **do sth. about sth./sb.** etw. gegen etw./jmdn. unternehmen; **b)** *(cook)* braten; **well done** durch[gebraten]; **c)** *(solve)* lösen ⟨Problem, Rätsel⟩; machen ⟨Puzzle, Kreuzworträtsel⟩; **d)** *(sl.: swindle)* reinlegen *(ugs.);* **do sb. out of sth.** jmdn. um etw. bringen; **e)** *(satisfy)* zusagen (+ *Dat.*). **2.** *v. i., forms as* **1: a)** *(act)* tun; **do as they do** mach es wie sie; **b)** *(fare)* **how are you doing?** wie geht's dir?; **c)** *(get on)* vorankommen; *(in exams)* abschneiden; **do well/badly at school** gut/schlecht in der Schule sein; **d) how do you do?** *(formal)* guten Tag/Morgen/Abend!; **e)** *(serve purpose)* es tun; *(suffice)* [aus]reichen; *(be suitable)* gehen; **that won't do** das geht nicht; **that will do!** jetzt aber genug! **3.** *v. substitute, forms as* **1: you mustn't act as he does** du darfst nicht so wie er handeln; **You went to Paris, didn't you? – Yes, I did** Du warst doch in Paris, nicht wahr? – Ja[, stimmt]; **come in, do!** komm doch herein! **4.** *v. aux. forms as* **1: I do love Greece** Griechenland gefällt mir wirklich gut; **little did he know that ...:** er hatte keine Ahnung, daß ...; **do you know him?** kennst du ihn?; **what does he want?** was will er?; **I don't** *or* **do not wish to take part** ich möchte nicht teilnehmen; **don't be so noisy!** seid [doch] nicht so laut! **5.** *n.* [duː], *pl.* **do's** *or* **dos** [duːz] *(Brit. coll.)* Feier, *die;* Fete, *die (ugs.).* **do a'way with** *v. t.* abschaffen. **'do for** *v. t. (coll.)* **do for sb.** jmdn. fertigmachen *(ugs.);* **be done for** erledigt sein. **do 'in** *v. t. (sl.)* kaltmachen *(salopp).* **do 'up** *v. t.* **a)** *(fasten)* zumachen; binden ⟨Schnürsenkel, Fliege⟩; **b)** *(wrap)* einpacken. **'do with** *v. t.* **I could do with ...:** ich brauche ... **'do without** *v. t.* **do without sth.** auf etw. *(Akk.)* verzichten

docile ['dəʊsaɪl] *adj.* sanft; *(submissive)* unterwürfig

¹dock [dɒk] **1.** *n.* **a)** Dock, *das;* **b)** *usu. in pl. (area)* Hafen, *der.* **2.** *v. t.* [ein]docken. **3.** *v. i.* anlegen

dote

²**dock** *n.* *(in lawcourt)* Anklagebank, *die;* **stand/be in the ~:** ≈ auf der Anklagebank sitzen

'**docker** *n.* Hafenarbeiter, *der*

'**dockyard** *n.* Schiffswerft, *die*

doctor ['dɒktə(r)] **1.** *n.* **a)** Arzt, *der*/Ärztin, *die; as address* Herr/Frau Doktor; **b)** *(holder of degree)* Doktor, *der.* **2.** *v. t.* *(coll.)* verfälschen

doctrine ['dɒktrɪn] *n.* Lehre, *die*

document ['dɒkjʊmənt] *n.* Dokument, *das;* Urkunde, *die*

documentary [dɒkjʊ'mentərɪ] **1.** *adj.* dokumentarisch. **2.** *n. (film)* Dokumentarfilm, *der*

dodge [dɒdʒ] **1.** *v. i.* ausweichen. **2.** *v. t.* ausweichen (+ *Dat.*) ⟨*Schlag, Hindernis usw.*⟩; entkommen (+ *Dat.*) ⟨*Polizei, Verfolger*⟩. **3.** *n. (trick)* Trick, *der*

dodgems ['dɒdʒəmz] *n. pl.* [Auto]skooterbahn, *die;* **have a ride/go on the ~:** Autoskooter fahren

dodgy ['dɒdʒɪ] *adj. (Brit. coll.) (unreliable)* unsicher; *(risky)* gewagt

doe [dəʊ] *n. (deer)* Damtier, *das; (rabbit)* [Kaninchen]weibchen, *das*

does [dʌz] *see* **do**

doesn't ['dʌznt] *(coll.)* = **does not**; *see* **do**

dog [dɒg] **1.** *n.* Hund, *der.* **2.** *v. t.,* -gg- verfolgen; *(fig.)* heimsuchen

dog: ~-**biscuit** *n.* Hundekuchen, *der;* ~-**collar** *n.* [Hunde]halsband, *das; (joc.: clerical collar)* Kollar, *das;* ~-**eared** *adj.* **a** ~-**eared book** ein Buch mit Eselsohren

dogged ['dɒgɪd] *adj.* hartnäckig ⟨*Weigerung, Verurteilung*⟩; zäh ⟨*Durchhaltevermögen, Ausdauer*⟩

dogma ['dɒgmə] *n.* Dogma, *das.* **dogmatic** [dɒg'mætɪk] *adj.* dogmatisch

doing ['duːɪŋ] *n.* Tun, *das*

do-it-yourself [duːɪtjə'self] **1.** *adj.* Do-it-yourself-. **2.** *n.* Heimwerken, *das*

doldrums ['dɒldrəmz] *n. pl.* **in the ~** *(in low spirits)* niedergeschlagen; *(Econ.)* in einer Flaute

dole [dəʊl] **1.** *n. (coll.)* **the ~:** Stempelgeld, *das (ugs.);* **be/go on the ~:** stempeln gehen *(ugs.).* **2.** *v. t.* ~ **out** [in kleinen Mengen] verteilen

doll [dɒl] *n.* Puppe, *die*

dollar ['dɒlə(r)] *n.* Dollar, *der*

dollop ['dɒləp] *n. (coll.)* Klacks, *der (ugs.)*

'**doll's house** *n.* Puppenhaus, *das*

dolphin ['dɒlfɪn] *n.* Delphin, *der*

domain [də'meɪn] *n.* Gebiet, *das*

dome [dəʊm] *n.* Kuppel, *die*

domestic [də'mestɪk] *adj.* **a)** *(household)* häuslich; *(family)* familiär ⟨*Angelegenheit, Reibereien*⟩; **b)** *(Econ.)* inländisch; Binnen-; **c)** ~ **animal/cat** Haustier, *das*/-katze, *die*

domesticated [də'mestɪkeɪtɪd] *adj.* gezähmt ⟨*Tier*⟩; *(fig.)* häuslich

dominant ['dɒmɪnənt] *adj.* vorherrschend

dominate ['dɒmɪneɪt] *v. t.* beherrschen. **domination** [dɒmɪ'neɪʃn] *n.* [Vor]herrschaft, *die* (**over** über + *Akk.*)

domineering [dɒmɪ'nɪərɪŋ] *adj.* herrisch

domino ['dɒmɪnəʊ] *n.* Domino[stein], *der;* ~**es** *sing. (game)* Domino[spiel], *das;* **play** ~**es** Domino spielen

'**don** [dɒn] *v. t. (Liter.)* anlegen *(geh.)*

²**don** *n. (Univ.)* Dozent, *der*

donate [dəʊ'neɪt] *v. t.* spenden; *(on large scale)* stiften. **donation** [də'neɪʃn] *n.* Spende, *die* (**to** für); *(large-scale)* Stiftung, *die*

done [dʌn] *see* **do**

donkey ['dɒŋkɪ] *n.* Esel, *der*

donor ['dəʊnə(r)] *n.* Spender, *der*/Spenderin, *die*

don't [dəʊnt] *(coll.)* = **do not**; *see* **do**

doodle ['duːdl] *v. i.* [herum]kritzeln

doom [duːm] *n.* **1.** Verhängnis, *das.* **2.** *v. t.* verurteilen; **be ~ed** verloren sein; **be ~ed to fail** *or* **failure** zum Scheitern verurteilt sein

door [dɔː(r)] *n.* Tür, *die; (of castle, barn)* Tor, *das; out of* ~**s** im Freien; **go out of** ~**s** nach draußen gehen

door: ~**bell** *n.* Türklingel, *die;* ~-**handle** *n.* Türklinke, *die;* ~**mat** *n.* Fußmatte, *die;* ~-**step** *n.* Türstufe, *die;* **on one's/the** ~**step** *(fig.)* vor jmds. Tür; ~**way** *n.* Eingang, *der*

dope [dəʊp] **1.** *n.* **a)** *(sl.: narcotic)* Stoff, *der (salopp);* **b)** *(coll.: fool)* Dussel, *der.* **2.** *v. t.* dopen ⟨*Pferd, Athleten*⟩

dormant ['dɔːmənt] *adj.* ruhend ⟨*Tier, Pflanze*⟩; untätig ⟨*Vulkan*⟩

dormitory ['dɔːmɪtərɪ] *n.* Schlafsaal, *der*

dormouse ['dɔːmaʊs] *n., pl.* **dormice** ['dɔːmaɪs] Haselmaus, *die*

dose [dəʊs] **1.** *n.* Dosis, *die.* **2.** *v. t.* ~ **sb. with sth.** jmdm. etw. geben

dot [dɒt] *n.* Punkt, *der;* **on the ~:** auf den Punkt genau

dote [dəʊt] *v. i.* ~ **on sb./sth.** jmdn./etw. abgöttisch lieben

dotted ['dɒtɪd] *adj.* gepunktet
dotty ['dɒtɪ] *adj. (coll.) (silly)* dümmlich; *(feeble-minded)* vertrottelt *(ugs.);*
(absurd) blödsinnig *(ugs.)*
double ['dʌbl] **1.** *adj.* doppelt; ~ **bed/
room** Doppelbett, *das/*-zimmer, *das;*
be ~ the height/width/length doppelt
so hoch/breit/lang sein. **2.** *adv.* doppelt. **3.** *n.* **a)** Doppelte, *das;* **b)** *(twice
as much)* doppelt soviel; *(twice as
many)* doppelt so viele; **c)** *(person)*
Doppelgänger, *der/*-gängerin, *die;* **d)**
in pl. (Tennis etc.) Doppel, *das;* **e)** **at
the ~** *(Mil.)* im Laufschritt; *(fig.)* ganz
schnell. **4.** *v.t.* verdoppeln. **5.** *v.i.* sich
verdoppeln. **double 'back** *v.i.* kehrtmachen *(ugs.).* **double 'up** krümmen
(**with** vor + *Dat.*)
double: ~'**bass** *n.* Kontrabaß, *der;*
~'**check** *v.t. (verify twice)* zweimal
kontrollieren; *(verify in two ways)*
zweifach überprüfen; ~ '**chin** *n.*
Doppelkinn, *das;* ~'**cross** *v.t.* ein
Doppelspiel treiben mit; ~-**decker**
n. [dʌbl'dekə(r)] *n.* Doppeldeckerbus,
der; ~ '**glazing** *n.* Doppelverglasung,
die; ~-'**jointed** *adj.* sehr gelenkig
doubly ['dʌblɪ] *adv.* doppelt
doubt [daʊt] **1.** *n.* Zweifel, *der (*about,
as to, of an + *Dat.*); ~|**s|** |**about** *or* as
to sth./as to whether ...| *(as to future)*
Ungewißheit, *(as to fact)* Unsicherheit
[über etw. *(Akk.)*/darüber, ob ...];
there's no ~ that ...: es besteht kein
Zweifel daran, daß ...; ~|**s|** *(hesita-
tions)* Bedenken *Pl.* (**about** gegen); **no**
~ *(certainly)* gewiß; *(probably)* sicherlich. **2.** *v.i.* zweifeln. **3.** *v.t.* zweifeln
an (+ *Dat.*); **I don't ~ that** *or* **it** ich bezweifle das nicht; **I ~ whether** *or* **if** *or*
that ...: ich bezweifle, daß ... **doubtful** ['daʊtfl] *adj.* skeptisch *(Wesen);*
unglâubig *(Blick)*
dough [daʊ] *n.* **a)** Teig, *der;* **b)** *(sl.:
money)* Knete, *die (salopp).* '**dough-
nut** *n.* [Berliner] Pfannkuchen, *der*
douse [daʊs] *v.t.* übergießen; *(extinguish)* ausmachen
'**dove** [dʌv] *n.* Taube, *die*
²**dove** [dəʊv] *see* dive 1
dowdy ['daʊdɪ] *adj.* unansehnlich;
(shabby) schäbig
'**down** [daʊn] *n. (feathers)* Daunen *Pl.*
²**down** **1.** *adv.* **a)** *(to lower place)* her-
unter/hinunter; *(in lift)* abwärts; **b)** *(in
lower place, downstairs)* unten; ~
there/here da/hier unten; **the next
floor** ~: ein Stockwerk tiefer; **be ~
with an illness** eine Krankheit haben;

be three points/games ~: mit drei
Punkten/Spielen zurückliegen. **2.**
prep. herunter/hinunter; **lower** ~ **the
river** weiter unten am Fluß; **walk** ~ **the
hill/road** den Berg/die Straße heruntergehen; **fall** ~ **the stairs/steps** die
Treppe/Stufen herunterstürzen; **fall**
~ **a hole/ditch** in ein Loch/ einen Graben fallen; **go** ~ **the pub** in die Kneipe
gehen; **live just** ~ **the road** ein Stück
weiter unten in der Straße wohnen; **be**
~ **the pub/town** in der Kneipe/Stadt
sein; **I've got coffee |all|** ~ **my skirt**
mein ganzer Rock ist voll Kaffee. **3.**
v.t. (coll.) schlucken *(ugs.) (Getränk);*
~ **tools** die Arbeit niederlegen
down: ~-**and**-'**out** *n.* Stadtstreicher,
der/-streicherin, *die;* ~**cast** *adj.* niedergeschlagen; ~**fall** *n.* Untergang,
der; ~-'**hearted** *adj.* niedergeschlagen; ~'**hill** *adv.* bergab; ~ **payment**
n. Anzahlung, *die;* ~**pour** *n.* Regen-
guß, *der;* ~**right** *adj.* ausgemacht;
glatt *(Lüge);* ~**stairs 1.** [-'-] *adv.* die
Treppe hinunter *(gehen, fallen, kommen);* unten *(wohnen, sein);* **2.** ['--]
adj. im Erdgeschoß *nachgestellt;*
~'**stream** *adv.* flußabwärts; ~-**to**-
'**earth** *adj.* sachlich; ~**town** *adv.* im/
(direction) ins Stadtzentrum; ~**trodden** *adj.* unterdrückt; ~ '**under** *adv.*
(coll.) in/*(to)* nach Australien/Neu-
seeland
downward ['daʊnwəd] **1.** *adj.* nach
unten gerichtet. **2.** *adv.* abwärts *(sich
bewegen);* nach unten *(sehen, gehen).*
downwards ['daʊnwədz] *see* **downward 2**
dowry ['daʊrɪ] *n.* Aussteuer, *die*
doze [dəʊz] **1.** *v.i.* dösen *(ugs.).* **2.** *n.*
Nickerchen, *das (ugs.).* **doze 'off** *v.i.*
eindösen *(ugs.)*
dozen ['dʌzn] *n.* **a)** Dutzend, *das;* **half
a** ~: sechs; **b)** *in pl. (coll.: many)* Dut-
zende *Pl.*
Dr *abbr.* **doctor** Dr.
drab [dræb] *adj.* langweilig; trostlos
(Landschaft); eintönig *(Leben)*
draft [drɑːft] **1.** *n.* **a)** *(of speech)* Konzept, *das;* *(of treaty, bill)* Entwurf, *der;*
b) *(Amer.) see* draught. **2.** *v.t.* entwerfen. **drafty** *(Amer.) see* draughty
drag [dræg] **1.** *v.t.,* -gg- schleppen. **2.**
v.i., -gg- schleifen; *(fig.: pass slowly)*
sich [hin]schleppen. **3.** *n. (sl.)* **in** ~: in
Frauenkleidung. **drag 'on** *v.i.* sich
[da]hin schleppen
dragon ['drægn] *n.* Drache, *der.* '**dra-
gonfly** *n.* Libelle, *die*

drain [dreın] 1. *n.* Abflußrohr, *das;*
(underground) Kanalisationsrohr,
das; *(grating at roadside)* Gully, *der;*
go down the ~ *(fig. coll.)* für die Katz
sein *(ugs.).* 2. *v.t.* **a)** trockenlegen
⟨Teich⟩; entwässern ⟨Land⟩; ableiten
⟨Wasser⟩; **b)** *(Cookery)* abgießen
⟨Wasser, Gemüse⟩; **c)** austrinken
⟨Glas⟩. 3. *v.i.* ⟨Flüssigkeit:⟩ ablaufen;
⟨Geschirr, Gemüse:⟩ abtropfen. **drainage** ['dreınıdȝ] *n.* Kanalisation, *die.*
'draining-board (*Brit.; Amer.:*
'drainboard) *n.* Abtropfbrett, *das.*
'drainpipe *n.* Regen[abfall]rohr, *das*
drake [dreık] *n.* Enterich, *der*
drama ['drɑːmə] *n.* Drama, *das.* **dramatic** [drə'mætık] *adj.* dramatisch.
dramatist ['dræmətıst] *n.* Dramatiker, *der*/Dramatikerin, *die.* **dramatize** ['dræmətaız] *v.t.* dramatisie-
ren
drank *see* **drink** 2
drape [dreıp] 1. *v.t.* drapieren. 2. *n.*
(Amer.: curtain) Vorhang, *der.*
'draper *n.* *(Brit.)* Textilkaufmann,
der; **~'s |shop|** Textilgeschäft, *das*
drastic ['dræstık] *adj.* drastisch
draught [drɑːft] *n.* [Luft]zug, *der;*
there's a ~: es zieht
'draughtboard *n.* *(Brit.)* Damebrett,
das
'draughts *n.* *(Brit.)* Damespiel, *das*
'draughtsman [~men] *n., pl.*
draughtsmen [~mən] Zeichner,
der/Zeichnerin, *die*
'draughty *adj.* zugig
draw [drɔː] 1. *v.t.,* **drew** [druː], **drawn**
[drɔːn] **a)** *(pull)* ziehen; **~ the curtains/
blinds** *(close)* die Vorhänge zuziehen/
die Jalousien herunterlassen; **~ sth.
towards one** etw. zu sich heranziehen;
b) *(attract)* anlocken; **be ~n to sb.** von
jmdm. angezogen werden; **c)** *(take
out)* herausziehen; schöpfen ⟨Was-
ser⟩; **~ money from the bank** Geld bei
der Bank holen/abheben; **d)** beziehen
⟨Gehalt, Rente, Arbeitslosenunterstüt-
zung⟩; **e)** ziehen ⟨Strich⟩; zeichnen
⟨geometrische Figur, Bild⟩; **f)** ziehen
⟨Parallele, Vergleich⟩; herausstellen
⟨Unterschied⟩. 2. *v.i.* **drew, drawn:** **~ to
an end** zu Ende gehen. 3. *n.* **a)** *(raffle)*
Tombola, *die;* **b)** *[[result of] drawn
game]* Unentschieden, *das.* **draw
'back** 1. *v.t.* zurückziehen. 2. *v.i.* zu-
rückweichen. **draw 'in** *v.i.* einfahren; ⟨Tage:⟩ kürzer werden. **draw
'out** *v.i.* abfahren; ⟨Tage:⟩ länger
werden. **draw 'up** 1. *v.t.* **a)** aufsetzen

⟨Vertrag⟩; aufstellen ⟨Liste⟩; **b)** *(pull
closer)* heranziehen. 2. *v.i.* [an]halten
draw: ~back *n.* Nachteil, *der;*
~bridge *n.* Zugbrücke, *die*
drawer [drɔː(r), 'drɔːə(r)] *n.* Schublade, *die*
'drawing *n.* *(sketch)* Zeichnung, *die*
drawing: ~board *n.* Zeichenbrett,
das; **~pin** *n.* *(Brit.)* Reißzwecke, *die;*
~room *n.* Salon, *der*
drawl [drɔːl] 1. *v.i.* gedehnt sprechen.
2. *n.* gedehntes Sprechen
drawn *see* **draw** 1, 2
dread [dred] 1. *v.t.* sich sehr fürchten
vor (+ *Dat.*); **the ~ed day/moment** der
gefürchtete Tag/Augenblick. 2. *n.*
Angst, *die.* **dreadful** ['dredfl] *adj.*
schrecklich; *(coll.: very bad)* fürchterlich; **I feel ~** *(unwell)* ich fühle mich
scheußlich *(ugs.).* **'dreadfully** *adv.*
schrecklich; *(coll.: very badly)* fürchterlich
dream [driːm] 1. *n.* Traum, *der;* **have a
~ about sb./sth.** von jmdm./etw. träumen. 2. *v.i. & t.* **dreamt** [dremt] *or*
dreamed träumen
dreary ['drıərı] *adj.* trostlos
dredge [dredȝ] *v.t.* ausbaggern.
'dredger *n.* Bagger, *der*
dregs [dregz] *n. pl.* [Boden]satz, *der*
drench [drentʃ] *v.t.* durchnässen
dress [dres] 1. *n.* Kleid, *das;* *(clothing)*
Kleidung, *die.* 2. *v.t.* **a)** anziehen; **be
well ~ed** gut gekleidet sein; **get ~ed**
sich anziehen; **b)** verbinden ⟨Wunde⟩.
3. *v.i.* sich anziehen. **dress 'up** *v.i.*
sich feinmachen
'dresser *n.* **a)** Anrichte, *die;* **b)** *(Amer.)*
see **dressing-table**
'dressing *n.* **a)** *no pl.* Anziehen, *das;*
b) *(Cookery)* Dressing, *das;* **c)** *(Med.)*
Verband, *der*
dressing: ~gown *n.* Bademantel,
der; **~room** *n.* *(Sport)* Umkleideraum, *der;* *(for actor)* Garderobe, *die;*
~table *n.* Frisierkommode, *die*
dress: ~maker *n.* Damenschneider,
der/-schneiderin, *die;* **~making** *n.*
Damenschneiderei, *die;* **~ rehearsal**
n. Generalprobe, *die*
drew *see* **draw** 1, 2
dribble ['drıbl] *v.i.* **a)** *(slobber)* sabbern; **b)** *(Sport)* dribbeln
dried [draıd] *adj.* getrocknet; **~ fruit|s|**
Dörrobst, *das;* **~ milk** Trockenmilch,
die
drier ['draıə(r)] *n.* *(for hair)* Trocken-
haube, *die;* *(hand-held)* Fön Ⓦ, *der;*
(for laundry) [Wäsche]trockner, *der*

drift [drɪft] 1. *n.* **a)** *(of snow or sand)* Verwehung, *die;* **b)** *(gist)* **get** *or* **catch the ~ of** sth. etw im wesentlichen verstehen. 2. *v. i.* **a)** treiben; ⟨*Wolke:*⟩ ziehen; **b)** ⟨*Sand, Schnee:*⟩ zusammengeweht werden. '**driftwood** *n.* Treibholz, *das*

drill [drɪl] 1. *n.* **a)** *(tool)* Bohrer, *der;* **b)** *(Mil.: training)* Drill, *der.* 2. *v. t. & i.* bohren **(for** nach)

drink [drɪŋk] 1. *n.* Getränk, *das; (alcoholic)* Glas, *das; (not with food)* Drink, *der;* **have a ~:** [etwas] trinken; *(alcoholic)* ein Glas trinken. 2. *v. t. & i.* **drank** [dræŋk], **drunk** [drʌŋk] trinken. **drinkable** ['drɪŋkəbl] *adj.* trinkbar. '**drinking-water** *n.* Trinkwasser, *das*

drip [drɪp] 1. *n.* **a)** Tropfen, *das;* **b)** *(coll.: feeble person)* Schlappschwanz, *der (salopp).* 2. *v. i.,* **-pp-** tropfen; **be ~ping with water/moisture** triefend naß sein. '**drip-dry** *adj.* bügelfrei

'**dripping** *n. (Cookery)* Schmalz, *das*

drive [draɪv] 1. *n.* **a)** Fahrt, *die;* **b)** *(private road)* Zufahrt, *die; (entrance) (to small building)* Einfahrt, *die; (to large building)* Auffahrt, *die;* **c)** *(energy)* Tatkraft, *die;* **d)** *(Psych.)* Trieb, *der;* **e)** *(Motor Veh.)* **left-hand/right-hand ~:** Links-/Rechtssteuerung, *die.* 2. *v. t.,* **drove** [drəʊv], **driven** ['drɪvn] **a)** fahren; **b)** treiben ⟨*Tier*⟩; *(compel to move)* vertreiben **(out of, from** aus); **d)** *(fig.)* **~ sb. to** sth. jmdn. zu etw. treiben; **~ sb. to do** sth. *or* **into doing** sth. jmdn. dazu treiben, etw. zu tun; **e)** *(power)* antreiben. 3. *v. i.,* **drove, driven a)** fahren; **can you ~?** kannst du Auto fahren?; **b)** *(go by car)* mit dem [eigenen] Auto fahren. '**drive at** *v. t. (fig.)* hinauswollen auf (+ *Akk.*); **what are you driving at?** worauf wollen Sie hinaus? **drive a'way** 1. *v. i.* wegfahren. 2. *v. t.* **a)** wegfahren; **b)** *(chase away)* vertreiben. **drive 'off** *see* **drive away. drive 'on** *v. i.* weiterfahren. **drive 'up** *v. i.* vorfahren **(to** vor + *Dat.*)

'**drive-in** *adj.* Drive-in-; **~ cinema** *or (Amer.)* **movie |theater|** Autokino, *das*

drivel ['drɪvl] *n.* Gefasel, *das (ugs.);* **talk ~:** faseln *(ugs.)*

driven *see* **drive** 2, 3

driver ['draɪvə(r)] *n.* Fahrer, *der/*Fahrerin, *die; (of locomotive)* Führer, *der/*Führerin, *die;* **~s license** *(Amer.)* Führerschein, *der*

driving ['draɪvɪŋ] 1. *n.* Fahren, *das.* 2. *adj.* peitschend ⟨*Regen*⟩

driving: ~-instructor *n.* Fahrlehrer, *der/*-lehrerin, *die;* **~-lesson** *n.* Fahrstunde, *die;* **~-licence** *n.* Führerschein, *der;* **~-school** *n.* Fahrschule, *die;* **~-test** *n.* Fahrprüfung, *die*

drizzle ['drɪzl] 1. *n.* Nieseln, *das.* 2. *v. i.* **it's drizzling** es nieselt

drone [drəʊn] 1. *v. i.* **a)** ⟨*Biene:*⟩ summen; ⟨*Maschine:*⟩ brummen; **b)** ⟨*Rezitator:*⟩ leiern. 2. *n. see* 1: Summen, *das;* Brummen, *das;* Geleier, *das*

drool [druːl] *v. i.* **~ over** eine kindische Freude haben an (+ *Dat.*)

droop [druːp] *v. i.* herunterhängen; ⟨*Blume:*⟩ den Kopf hängen lassen

drop [drɒp] 1. *n.* **a)** Tropfen, *der;* **in ~s** tropfenweise; **b)** *(decrease)* Rückgang, *der.* 2. *v. i.,* **-pp-: a)** *(fall) (accidentally)* [herunter]fallen; *(deliberately)* sich [hinunter]fallen lassen; **b)** *(in amount etc.)* sinken; ⟨*Preis, Wert:*⟩ sinken, fallen; ⟨*Wind:*⟩ sich legen; ⟨*Stimme:*⟩ sich senken. 3. *v. t.,* **-pp-: a)** fallen lassen; abwerfen ⟨*Bomben, Nachschub*⟩; **b)** *(discontinue, abandon)* fallenlassen; **c)** *(omit)* auslassen. **drop 'by, drop 'in** *v. i.* vorbeikommen. **drop 'off** 1. *v. i.* **a)** *(fall off)* abfallen; **b)** *(fall asleep)* einnicken. 2. *v. t.* absetzen ⟨*Fahrgast*⟩. **drop 'out** *v. i.* **a)** herausfallen **(of** aus); **b)** *(withdraw)* aussteigen *(ugs.)* **(of** aus); *(beforehand)* seine Teilnahme absagen

'**drop-out** *n.* Aussteiger, *der/*Aussteigerin, *die*

drought [draʊt] *n.* Dürre, *die*

drove *see* **drive** 2, 3

drown [draʊn] 1. *v. i.* ertrinken. 2. *v. t.* ertränken; **be ~ed** ertrinken

drowsy ['draʊzɪ] *adj.* schläfrig; *(on just waking)* verschlafen

drudgery ['drʌdʒərɪ] *n.* Schufterei, *die*

drug [drʌg] 1. *n.* **a)** *(Med.)* [Arznei]mittel, *das;* **b)** *(narcotic)* Droge, *die;* **be on ~s** Rauschgift nehmen. 2. *v. t.,* **-gg-** betäuben ⟨*Person*⟩; **~ sb.'s food/drink** jmds. Essen/Getränk (*Dat.*) ein Betäubungsmittel beimischen

drug: ~ addict *n.* Drogensüchtige, *der/die;* **~ addiction** *n.* Drogensucht, *die;* **~-store** *n. (Amer.)* Drugstore, *der*

drum [drʌm] 1. *n.* **a)** Trommel, *die;* **b)** *in pl. (in jazz or pop)* Schlagzeug, *das;* **c)** *(container)* Faß, *das.* 2. *v. i.* trommeln. **drum 'up** *v. i.* auftreiben

'**drummer** *n.* Schlagzeuger, *der*

'**drumstick** *n.* **a)** Trommelschlegel, *der;* **b)** *(Cookery)* Keule, *die*

drunk [drʌŋk] **1.** *adj.* be ~: betrunken sein; get ~: betrunken werden (**on** von); *(intentionally)* sich betrinken (**on** mit). **2.** *n.* Betrunkene, *der/die*

drunkard ['drʌŋkəd] *n.* Trinker, *der/* Trinkerin, *die*

drunken ['drʌŋkn] *attrib. adj.* betrunken; *(habitually)* ständig betrunken; ~ **driving** Trunkenheit am Steuer.

'**drunkenness** *n.* Betrunkenheit, *die; (habitual)* Trunksucht, *die*

dry [draɪ] **1.** *adj.* trocken; trocken, *(very ~)* herb ⟨*Wein*⟩; ausgetrocknet ⟨*Flußbett*⟩; get *or* become ~: trocknen. **2.** *v.t.* **a)** trocknen ⟨*Haare, Wäsche*⟩; abtrocknen ⟨*Geschirr, Baby*⟩; ~ oneself sich abtrocknen; ~ one's eyes *or* tears/hands sich *(Dat.)* die Tränen abwischen/die Hände abtrocknen; **b)** *(preserve)* trocknen; dörren ⟨*Obst, Fleisch*⟩. **3.** *v.i.* trocknen. **dry 'out** *v.t. & i.* trocknen. **dry 'up 1.** *v.t.* abtrocknen. **2.** *v.i.* **a)** *(~ the dishes)* abtrocknen; **b)** ⟨*Brunnen, Quelle:*⟩ versiegen; ⟨*Fluß, Teich:*⟩ austrocknen

dry: ~-'**clean** *v.t.* chemisch reinigen; ~-'**cleaner's** *n.* chemische Reinigung; ~-'**cleaning** *n.* chemische Reinigung

'**dryer** *see* **drier**

'**dryness** *n.* Trockenheit, *die*

dual ['djuːəl] *adj.* doppelt. **dual 'carriageway** *n. (Brit.)* Straße mit Mittelstreifen. **dual-'purpose** *adj.* zweifach verwendbar

dubious ['djuːbɪəs] *adj. (doubting)* unschlüssig; *(suspicious)* zweifelhaft

duchess ['dʌtʃɪs] *n.* Herzogin, *die*

duck [dʌk] **1.** *n.* Ente, *die.* **2.** *v.i.* sich [schnell] ducken. **3.** *v.t.* ~ one's head den Kopf einziehen

duckling ['dʌklɪŋ] *n.* Entenküken, *das*

duct [dʌkt] *n.* Rohr, *das; (for air)* Ventil, *das*

dud [dʌd] **1.** *n. (useless thing)* Niete, *die (ugs.); (counterfeit)* Fälschung, *die.* **2.** *adj.* mies *(ugs.);* schlecht; *(fake)* gefälscht; geplatzt ⟨*Scheck*⟩

due [djuː] **1.** *adj.* **a)** *(owed)* geschuldet; zustehend ⟨*Eigentum, Recht usw.*⟩; there's sth. ~ to me, I've got sth. ~: mir steht etw. zu; **b)** *(immediately payable)* fällig; **c)** *(that it is proper to give or use)* gebührend; angemessen ⟨*Belohnung*⟩; be ~ to sb. jmdm. gebühren; **with all** ~ **respect** bei allem gebotenen Respekt; **d)** *(attributable)* the mistake was ~ to negligence der Fehler war durch Nachlässigkeit verursacht; it's ~ to

her that we missed the train ihretwegen verpaßten wir den Zug; **e)** *(scheduled, expected);* be ~ to do sth. etw. tun sollen; be ~ [to arrive] ankommen sollen; **f)** *(likely to get, deserving)* be ~ for sth. etw. verdienen. **2.** *adv.* **a)** ~ north genau nach Norden; **b)** ~ to auf Grund (+ *Gen.*); aufgrund (+ *Gen.*). **3.** *n.* **a)** give sb. his ~: jmdm. Gerechtigkeit widerfahren lassen; **b)** ~s *(fees)* Gebühren *Pl.*

duel ['djuːəl] *n.* Duell, *das*

duet [djuː'et] *n. (for voices)* Duett, *das; (instrumental)* Duo, *das*

duffle ['dʌfl]: ~ **bag** *n.* Matchbeutel, *der;* ~ **coat** *n.* Dufflecoat, *der*

dug *see* **dig**

duke [djuːk] *n.* Herzog, *der*

dull [dʌl] **1.** *adj.* **a)** *(stupid)* beschränkt; *(slow to understand)* begriffsstutzig; **b)** *(boring)* langweilig; **c)** *(gloomy)* trübe ⟨*Wetter, Tag*⟩. **2.** *v.t.* abstumpfen ⟨*Geist, Sinne, Verstand*⟩

duly ['djuːlɪ] *adv.* ordnungsgemäß

dumb [dʌm] *adj.* **a)** stumm; **b)** *(coll.: stupid)* doof *(ugs.)*

dumbfounded [dʌm'faʊndɪd] *adj.* sprachlos

dummy ['dʌmɪ] *n.* **a)** *(of tailor)* Schneiderpuppe, *die; (in shop)* Schaufensterpuppe, *die; (of ventriloquist)* Puppe, *die; (stupid person)* Dummkopf, *der (ugs.);* **like a stuffed** ~: wie ein Ölgötze *(ugs.);* **b)** *(imitation)* Attrappe, *die;* **c)** *(esp. Brit.: for baby)* Schnuller, *der*

dump [dʌmp] **1.** *n.* **a)** *(place)* Müllkippe, *die; (heap)* Müllhaufen, *der; (permanent)* Müllhalde, *die;* **b)** *(Mil.)* Depot, *das;* **c)** *(coll.: town)* Kaff, *das (ugs.).* **2.** *v.t. (dispose of)* werfen; *(deposit)* abladen ⟨*Sand, Müll usw.*⟩; *(leave)* lassen; *(place)* abstellen

dumpling ['dʌmplɪŋ] *n.* Kloß, *der*

dumps *n. pl.* be *or* feel down in the ~: ganz down sein *(ugs.)*

dunce [dʌns] *n.* Null, *die (ugs.)*

dune [djuːn] *n.* Düne, *die*

dung [dʌŋ] *n.* Dung, *der*

dungarees [dʌŋɡə'riːz] *n. pl.* Latzhose, *die*

dungeon ['dʌndʒən] *n.* Kerker, *der*

dunk [dʌŋk] *v.t.* tunken

dupe [djuːp] **1.** *v.t.* übertölpeln. **2.** *n.* Dumme, *der/die*

duplex ['djuːpleks] *adj. (esp. Amer.) (two-storey)* zweistöckig ⟨*Wohnung*⟩; *(two-family)* Zweifamilien⟨*haus*⟩

duplicate 1. ['djuːplɪkət] *adj.* **a)** *(identical)* Zweit-; **b)** *(twofold)* doppelt. **2.** *n.*

Kopie, *die; (second copy of letter/document/key)* Duplikat, *das;* in ~: in doppelter Ausfertigung. 3. ['dju:plɪkeɪt] *v. t.* a) *(make a copy of, make in ~)* ~ sth. eine zweite Anfertigung von etw. machen; b) *(on machine)* vervielfältigen; c) *(do twice)* noch einmal tun

durable ['djʊərəbl] *adj.* haltbar; dauerhaft *⟨Friede, Freundschaft usw.⟩*

duration [djʊə'reɪʃn] *n.* Dauer, *die*

duress [djʊə'res] *n.* Zwang, *der*

during ['djʊərɪŋ] *prep.* während; *(at a point in)* in (+ *Dat.*)

dusk [dʌsk] *n.* Einbruch der Dunkelheit

dust [dʌst] 1. *n.* Staub, *der.* 2. *v. t.* abstauben *⟨Möbel⟩;* ~ a room/ house in einem Zimmer/Haus Staub wischen. 3. *v. i.* Staub wischen. 'dustbin *n.* *(Brit.)* Mülltonne, *die.* 'dustcart *(Brit.)* Müllwagen, *der*

'duster *n.* Staubtuch, *das*

dust: ~-jacket *n.* Schutzumschlag, *der;* ~man [~mən] *n., pl.* ~men [~mən] *(Brit.)* Müllmann, *der;* ~pan *n.* Kehrschaufel, *die*

'dusty *adj.* staubig; verstaubt *⟨Bücher, Möbel⟩*

Dutch [dʌtʃ] 1. *adj.* holländisch; sb. is ~: jmd. ist Holländer/Holländerin. 2. *n.* a) *(language)* Holländisch, *das; see also* English 2 a; b) the ~ *pl.* die Holländer

Dutch: ~ 'courage *n.* angetrunkener Mut; ~man [~mən] *n., pl.* ~men [~mən] Holländer, *der;* ~woman *n.* Holländerin, *die*

dutiful ['dju:tɪfl] *adj.* pflichtbewußt

duty ['dju:tɪ] *n.* a) Pflicht, *die; (task)* Aufgabe, *die;* be on ~: Dienst haben; off ~: nicht im Dienst; be off ~: keinen Dienst haben; *⟨ab ... Uhr⟩* dienstfrei sein; b) *(tax)* Zoll, *der;* pay ~ on sth. Zoll für etw. bezahlen. 'duty-free *adj.* zollfrei

duvet ['du:veɪ] *n.* Federbett, *das*

dwarf [dwɔːf] *n., pl.* ~s *or* dwarves ['dwɔːvz] Zwerg, *der/*Zwergin, *die*

dwell [dwel] *v. i.,* dwelt [dwelt] *(literary)* wohnen. 'dwell [up]on *v. t. (in discussion)* sich ausführlich befassen mit; *(in thought)* in Gedanken verweilen bei

'dwelling *n.* Wohnung, *die*

dwelt *see* dwell

dwindle ['dwɪndl] *v. i.* ~ [away] abnehmen; *⟨Unterstützung, Interesse:⟩* nachlassen; *⟨Vorräte:⟩* schrumpfen

dye [daɪ] 1. *n.* Färbemittel, *das.* 2. *v. t.,* ~ing ['daɪɪŋ] färben

dying ['daɪɪŋ] *adj.* sterbend; absterbend *⟨Baum⟩*

dyke *see* dike

dynamic [daɪ'næmɪk] *adj.* dynamisch. **dynamism** ['daɪnəmɪzm] *n.* Dynamik, *die*

dynamite ['daɪnəmaɪt] *n.* Dynamit, *das*

dynamo ['daɪnəməʊ] *n.* Dynamo, *der; (in car)* Lichtmaschine, *die*

dynasty ['dɪnəstɪ] *n.* Dynastie, *die*

dysentry ['dɪsəntrɪ] *n.* Ruhr, *die*

E

E, e [iː] *n.* E, e, *das*

E. *abbr.* a) east O; b) eastern ö.

each [iːtʃ] 1. *adj.* jeder/jede/jedes; they cost *or* are a pound ~: sie kosten ein Pfund pro Stück. 2. *pron.* a) jeder/jede/jedes; b) ~ other sich

eager ['iːgə(r)] *adj.* eifrig; be ~ to do sth. etw. unbedingt tun wollen. 'eagerly *adv.* eifrig; gespannt *⟨warten⟩*

eagle ['iːgl] *n.* Adler, *der*

¹ear [ɪə(r)] *n.* Ohr, *das*

²ear *n. (Bot.)* Ähre, *die*

ear: ~ache *n.* Ohrenschmerzen *Pl.;* ~-drum *n.* Trommelfell, *das*

earl [ɜːl] *n.* Graf, *der*

'ear lobe *n.* Ohrläppchen, *das*

early ['ɜːlɪ] 1. *adj.* früh. 2. *adv.* früh; I am a bit ~: ich bin etwas zu früh gekommen; ~ next week Anfang der nächsten Woche; ~ in June Anfang Juni; from ~ in the morning till late at night von früh [morgens] bis spät [nachts]; ~ on schon früh

ear: ~mark *v. t.* vorsehen; ~-muffs *n. pl.* Ohrenschützer, *Pl.*

earn [ɜːn] *v. t.* verdienen; *(bring in as income or interest)* einbringen

earnest ['ɜːnɪst] 1. *adj.* ernsthaft. 2. *n.* in ~: mit vollem Ernst

earnings ['ɜːnɪŋz] *n. pl.* Verdienst, *der; (of business etc.)* Ertrag, *der*

ear: ~phones *n. pl.* Kopfhörer, *der;*

~-**plug** n. Ohropax, das ⓦ; ~-**ring** n. Ohrring, der; ~**shot** n. out of/within ~ shot außer/in Hörweite

earth [ɜ:θ] 1. n. (also Brit. Electr.) Erde, die; how/what etc. on ~ ...? wie/was usw. in aller Welt ...? 2. v. t. (Brit. Electr.) erden

earthenware ['ɜ:θnweə(r)] 1. n. Tonwaren Pl. 2. adj. Ton-

earth: ~**quake** n. Erdbeben, das; ~**worm** n. Regenwurm, der

'**earthy** adj. a) erdig; b) (coarse) derb

earwig ['ɪəwɪg] n. Ohrwurm, der

ease [i:z] 1. n. a) set sb. at ~: jmdn. beruhigen; at [one's] ~: entspannt; be or feel at [one's] ~: sich wohl fühlen; [stand] at ~! (Mil.) rührt euch!; b) with ~ (without difficulty) mit Leichtigkeit. 2. v. t. lindern ⟨Schmerz, Kummer⟩; entspannen ⟨Lage⟩; verringern ⟨Belastung, Druck, Spannung⟩. 3. v. i. nachlassen

easel ['i:zl] n. Staffelei, die

easily ['i:zɪlɪ] adv. leicht

easiness ['i:zɪnɪs] n. Leichtigkeit, die

east [i:st] 1. n. a) Osten, der; in/to[wards]/from the ~: im/nach/von Osten; to the ~ of östlich von; b) usu. E~ (Geog., Polit.) Osten, der. 2. adj. östlich; Ost⟨küste, -wind, -grenze⟩. 3. adv. nach Osten; ~ of östlich von. '**East Ber'lin** pr. n. (Hist.) Ostberlin, das. '**eastbound** adj. ⟨Zug, Verkehr usw.⟩ in Richtung Osten

Easter ['i:stə(r)] n. Ostern, das od. Pl. '**Easter egg** n. Osterei, das

easterly ['i:stəlɪ] adj. östlich; ⟨Wind⟩ aus östlichen Richtungen

eastern ['i:stən] adj. östlich; Ost⟨grenze, -hälfte, -seite⟩; ~ Germany Ostdeutschland, das. **Eastern 'Europe** pr. n. Osteuropa, das

Easter 'Sunday n. Ostersonntag, der

East: ~ '**German** (Hist.) 1. adj. ostdeutsch; 2. n. Ostdeutsche, der/die; ~ '**Germany** pr. n. (Hist.) Ostdeutschland (das)

eastward(s) ['i:stwəd(z)] adv. ostwärts

easy ['i:zɪ] 1. adj. a) leicht; on ~ terms auf Raten ⟨kaufen⟩; b) sorglos ⟨Leben, Zeit⟩; c) (free from constraint) ungezwungen. 2. adv. leicht; **easier said than done** leichter gesagt als getan; take it ~! (calm down!) beruhige dich! '**easy chair** n. Sessel, der. **easy-'going** adj. gelassen; (lax) nachlässig

eat [i:t] v. t. & i., **ate** [et, eɪt], **eaten** ['i:tn] essen; ⟨Tier:⟩ fressen. **eat a'way** v. t. ⟨Rost, Säure:⟩ zerfressen. **eat 'out** v. i. essen gehen. **eat 'up** v. t. aufessen; ⟨Tier:⟩ auffressen

eaten see eat

eau-de-Cologne [əʊdəkə'ləʊn] n. Kölnisch Wasser, das

eaves [i:vz] n. pl. Dachgesims, das. '**eavesdrop** v. i. lauschen; ~ on belauschen. '**eavesdropper** n. Lauscher, der/Lauscherin, die

ebb [eb] 1. n. Ebbe, die; be at a low ~ (fig.) ⟨Person, Stimmung, Moral:⟩ auf dem Nullpunkt sein. 2. v. i. zurückgehen; ~ away (fig.) dahinschwinden. '**ebb-tide** n. Ebbe, die

ebony ['ebənɪ] n. Ebenholz, das

EC abbr. European Community EG

eccentric [ik'sentrɪk] 1. adj. exzentrisch. 2. n. Exzentriker, der/Exzentrikerin, die. **eccentricity** [eksen'trɪsɪtɪ] n. Exzentrizität, die

ecclesiastical [ɪkli:zɪ'æstɪkl] adj. kirchlich; geistlich ⟨Musik⟩

echo ['ekəʊ] 1. n. Echo, das. 2. v. t. zurückwerfen; (fig.: repeat) wiederholen

éclair [eɪ'kleə(r)] n. Eclair, das

eclipse [ɪ'klɪps] n. (Astron.) Finsternis, die; ~ of the sun Sonnenfinsternis, die

ecological [ikə'lɒdʒɪkl] adj. ökologisch

ecology [ɪ'kɒlədʒɪ] n. Ökologie, die

economic [i:kə'nɒmɪk] adj. a) Wirtschafts⟨politik, -abkommen, -system⟩; wirtschaftlich ⟨Entwicklung, Zusammenbruch⟩; b) (giving adequate return) wirtschaftlich

economical [i:kə'nɒmɪkl] adj. wirtschaftlich; sparsam ⟨Person⟩; be ~ with sth. mit etw. haushalten. **eco'nomically** adv. wirtschaftlich; (not wastefully) sparsam

economics [i:kə'nɒmɪks] n. Wirtschaftswissenschaft, die (meist Pl.)

economist [ɪ'kɒnəmɪst] n. Wirtschaftswissenschaftler, der/-wissenschaftlerin, die

economize [ɪ'kɒnəmaɪz] v. i. sparen; ~ on sth. etw. sparen

economy [ɪ'kɒnəmɪ] n. a) (frugality) Sparsamkeit, die; b) (instance) Einsparung, die; make economies zu Sparmaßnahmen greifen; c) (of country etc.) Wirtschaft, die. e'conomy size n. Haushaltspackung, die

ecstasy ['ekstəsɪ] n. Ekstase, die. **ec-static** [ɪk'stætɪk] adj. ekstatisch

ECU, ecu ['eɪkju:] abbr. European currency unit Ecu, der od. die

eddy ['edɪ] n. Strudel, der

edge [edʒ] 1. *n.* a) *(of knife, razor, weapon)* Schneide, *die;* on ~ *(fig.)* nervös *od.* gereizt (**about** wegen); b) *(of solid, bed, table)* Kante, *die; (of sheet of paper, road, forest, cliff)* Rand, *der.* 2. *v. i.* sich schieben

edgy ['edʒɪ] *adj.* nervös

edible ['edɪbl] *adj.* eßbar

edict ['i:dɪkt] *n.* Erlaß, *der*

edit ['edɪt] *v. t.* herausgeben ⟨*Zeitung*⟩; redigieren ⟨*Buch, Artikel, Manuskript*⟩. **edition** [ɪ'dɪʃn] *n.* Ausgabe, *die.* **editor** ['edɪtə(r)] *n.* Redakteur, *der*/Redakteurin, *die; (of particular work)* Bearbeiter, *der*/Bearbeiterin, *die; (of newspaper)* Herausgeber, *der*/-geberin, *die.* **editorial** [edɪ-'tɔːrɪəl] 1. *n.* Leitartikel, *der.* 2. *adj.* redaktionell

educate ['edjʊkeɪt] *v. t.* a) *(bring up)* erziehen; *(train mind and character of)* bilden; b) *(provide schooling for)* **he was ~d at ...:** er hat seine Ausbildung in ... erhalten. **educated** ['edjʊkeɪtɪd] *adj.* gebildet. **education** [edjʊ'keɪʃn] *n.* Erziehung, *die; (system)* Erziehungswesen, *das.* **educational** [edjʊ'keɪʃənl] *adj.* pädagogisch; Lehr-⟨*film, -spiele, -anstalt*⟩; Erziehungs-⟨*methoden, -arbeit*⟩

EEC *abbr.* European Economic Community EWG

eerie ['ɪərɪ] *adj.* unheimlich

eel [i:l] *n.* Aal, *der*

effect [ɪ'fekt] *n.* a) Wirkung, *die* (**on** auf + *Akk.*); **the ~s of** sth. **on** sth. die Auswirkungen einer Sache *(Gen.)* auf etw. *(Akk.);* **take ~:** die erwünschte Wirkung erzielen; **in ~:** in Wirklichkeit; b) **come into ~:** gültig werden; ⟨*Gesetz:*⟩ in Kraft treten; **put** sth. **into ~:** in Kraft setzen ⟨*Gesetz*⟩; verwirklichen ⟨*Plan*⟩; **with ~ from 2 November/Monday** mit Wirkung vom 2. November/ von Montag

effective [ɪ'fektɪv] *adj.* a) wirksam ⟨*Mittel, Maßnahmen*⟩; **be ~** ⟨*Arzneimittel:*⟩ wirken; b) *(in operation)* gültig; ~ **from/as of** mit Wirkung vom. **effectively** *adv. (in fact)* effektiv; *(with effect)* wirkungsvoll

effectual [ɪ'fektjʊəl] *adj.* wirksam

effeminate [ɪ'femɪnət] *adj.* unmännlich

effervescent [efə'vesənt] *adj.* sprudelnd; *(fig.)* übersprudelnd

efficiency [ɪ'fɪʃənsɪ] *n. (of person)* Fähigkeit, *die;* Tüchtigkeit, *die; (of machine, factory, engine)* Leistungsfähig-

keit, *die; (of organization, method)* gutes Funktionieren

efficient [ɪ'fɪʃənt] *adj.* fähig ⟨*Person*⟩; tüchtig ⟨*Arbeiter, Sekretärin*⟩; leistungsfähig ⟨*Maschine, Motor, Fabrik*⟩; gut funktionierend ⟨*Methode, Organisation*⟩. **efficiently** *adv.* gut

effigy ['efɪdʒɪ] *n.* Bildnis, *das*

effluent ['eflʊənt] Abwässer *Pl.*

effort ['efət] *n.* a) Anstrengung, *die;* Mühe, *die;* **make an/every ~** *(physically)* sich anstrengen; *(mentally)* sich bemühen; b) *(attempt)* Versuch, *der.* '**effortless** *adj.* mühelos

effrontery [ɪ'frʌntərɪ] *n.* Dreistigkeit, *die;* **have the ~ to do** sth. die Stirn besitzen, etw. zu tun

effusive [ɪ'fjuːsɪv] *adj.* überschwenglich; exaltiert *(geh.)* ⟨*Person*⟩

e.g. [iː'dʒiː] *abbr.* **for example** z. B.

egg [eg] *n.* Ei, *das.* **egg 'on** *v. t.* anstacheln

egg: ~-**cup** *n.* Eierbecher, *der;* ~-**shell** *n.* Eierschale, *die;* ~-**timer** *n.* Eieruhr, *die;* ~-**white** *n.* Eiweiß, *das;* ~ **yolk** *n.* Eigelb, *das*

ego ['egəʊ, 'iːgəʊ] *n., pl.* ~**s** a) *(Psych.)* Ego, *das;* b) *(self-esteem)* Selbstbewußtsein, *das*

Egypt ['iːdʒɪpt] *pr. n.* Ägypten *(das).* **Egyptian** [ɪ'dʒɪpʃn] 1. *adj.* ägyptisch. 2. *n. (person)* Ägypter, *der*/Ägypterin, *die*

eiderdown ['aɪdədaʊn] *n.* Federbett, *das*

eight [eɪt] 1. *adj.* acht; **at ~:** um acht; **half past ~:** halb neun; ~ **thirty** acht Uhr dreißig; ~ **ten/fifty** zehn nach acht/vor neun; *(esp. in timetable)* acht Uhr zehn/fünfzig; ~-**year-old boy** achtjähriger Junge; **an ~-year-old** ein Achtjähriger/eine Achtjährige; **at [the age of]** ~, **aged** ~: mit acht Jahren; ~ **times** achtmal. 2. *n.* Acht, *die;* **the first/last** ~: die ersten/letzten acht; **there were ~ of us present** wir waren [zu] acht

eighteen [eɪ'tiːn] 1. *adj.* achtzehn. 2. *n.* Achtzehn, *die; See also* **eight**. **eighteenth** [eɪ'tiːnθ] 1. *adj.* achtzehnt... 2. *n. (fraction)* Achtzehntel, *das. See also* **eighth**

eighth [eɪtθ] 1. *adj.* acht...; **be/come ~:** achter sein/als achter ankommen; ~-**largest** achtgrößt... 2. *n. (in sequence)* achte, *der/die/das; (in rank)* Achte, *der/die/das; (fraction)* Achtel, *das;* **the ~ of May** der achte Mai

eightieth ['eɪtɪɪθ] *adj.* achtzigst...

eighty ['eɪtɪ] **1.** *adj.* achtzig. **2.** *n.* Achtzig, *die;* **the eighties** *(years)* die achtziger Jahre; **be in one's eighties** in den Achtzigern sein. *See also* **eight**

Eire ['eərə] *pr. n.* Irland, *das;* Eire, *das*

either ['aɪðə(r), 'iːðə(r)] **1.** *adj.* **a)** *(each)* **at ~ end of the table** an beiden Enden des Tisches; **b)** *(one or other)* [irgend]ein ... [von beiden]; **take ~ one** nimm einen/eine/eins von [den] beiden. **2.** *pron.* **a)** *(each)* beide *Pl.;* **I can't cope with ~:** ich kann mit keinem von beiden fertig werden; **b)** *(one or other)* einer/eine/ein[e]s [von beiden]. **3.** *adv.* auch [nicht]; **'I don't like that ~:** ich mag es auch nicht. **4.** *conj.* **~ ... or ...:** entweder ... oder ...; *(after negation)* weder ... noch ...

eject ['dʒekt] **1.** *v. t.* **a)** *(from hall, meeting)* hinauswerfen **(from** aus); **b)** ⟨*Gerät:*⟩ auswerfen; ⟨*Person:*⟩ herausholen ⟨*Kassette*⟩. **2.** *v. i.* sich hinauskatapultieren. **ejector seat** [ɪ'dʒektə siːt] *n.* Schleudersitz, *der*

eke out [iːk 'aʊt] *v. t.* strecken

elaborate 1. [ɪ'læbərət] *adj.* kompliziert; kunstvoll [gearbeitet] ⟨*Arrangement, Verzierung*⟩. **2.** [ɪ'læbəreɪt] *v. i.* mehr ins Detail gehen; **~ on** näher ausführen

elapse [ɪ'læps] *v. i.* ⟨*Zeit:*⟩ vergehen

elastic [ɪ'læstɪk] **1.** *adj.* elastisch. **2.** *n.* **(~ band)** Gummiband, *das.* **elastic 'band** *n.* Gummiband, *das*

elated [ɪ'leɪtɪd] *adj.* freudig erregt; **be or feel ~:** in Hochstimmung sein. **elation** [ɪ'leɪʃn] *n.* freudige Erregung

elbow ['elbəʊ] **1.** *n.* Ell[en]bogen, *der.* **2.** *v. t.* **~ sb. aside** jmdn. mit dem Ellenbogen zur Seite stoßen. **'elbow room** *n.* Ell[en]bogenfreiheit, *die*

¹elder ['eldə(r)] **1.** *attrib. adj.* älter... **2.** *n.* **a)** *(senior)* Ältere, *der/die;* **b)** *(village ~, church ~)* Älteste, *der/die*

²elder *n. (Bot.)* Holunder, *der.* **'elderberry** *n.* Holunderbeere, *die*

elderly ['eldəlɪ] **1.** *adj.* älter. **2.** *n. pl.* **the ~:** ältere Menschen

eldest ['eldɪst] *adj.* ältest...

elect [ɪ'lekt] **1.** *adj. postpos.* gewählt; **the President ~:** der designierte Präsident. **2.** *v. t.* wählen; **~ sb. chairman** jmdn. zum Vorsitzenden wählen. **election** [ɪ'lekʃn] *n.* Wahl, *die;* **general ~:** allgemeine Wahlen. **e'lection campaign** *n.* Wahlkampagne, *die*

electioneer [ɪlekʃə'nɪə(r)] *v. i.* be/go ~ing Wahlkampf machen

elector [ɪ'lektə(r)] *n.* Wähler, *der*/ Wählerin, *die.* **electoral** [ɪ'lektərl] *adj.* Wahl-. **electorate** [ɪ'lektərət] *n.* Wähler *Pl.*

electric [ɪ'lektrɪk] *adj.* elektrisch; Elektro⟨*kabel, -motor, -herd, -kessel*⟩; Strom⟨*versorgung*⟩; *(fig.)* spannungsgeladen ⟨*Atmosphäre*⟩. **electrical** [ɪ'lektrɪkl] *adj.* elektrisch; Elektro⟨*abteilung, -handel, -geräte*⟩

electric: ~ 'blanket *n.* Heizdecke, *die;* **~ 'fire** *n.* [elektrischer] Heizofen

electrician [ɪlek'trɪʃn] *n.* Elektriker, *der*/Elektrikerin, *die.* **electricity** [ɪlek'trɪsɪtɪ] *n.* Elektrizität, *die*

electric 'shock *n.* Stromschlag, *der*

electrify [ɪ'lektrɪfaɪ] *v. t.* elektrifizieren; *(fig.)* elektrisieren

electrocute [ɪ'lektrəkjuːt] *v. t.* durch Stromschlag töten

electrode [ɪ'lektrəʊd] *n.* Elektrode, *die*

electron [ɪ'lektrɒn] *n.* Elektron, *das*

electronic [ɪlek'trɒnɪk] *adj.* elektronisch. **electronics** [ɪlek'trɒnɪks] *n.* Elektronik, *die*

elegance ['elɪgəns] *n.* Eleganz, *die*

elegant ['elɪgənt] *adj.* elegant

element ['elɪmənt] *n.* **a)** Element, *das;* **b)** *(Electr.)* Heizelement, *das;* **c)** **~s** *(rudiments)* Grundlagen *Pl.* **elementary** [elɪ'mentərɪ] *adj.* elementar; grundlegend ⟨*Fakten, Wissen*⟩; Grundschul⟨*bildung*⟩; Grund⟨*kurs, -ausbildung, -kenntnisse*⟩

elephant ['elɪfənt] *n.* Elefant, *der*

elevate ['elɪveɪt] *v. t.* [empor]heben. **elevation** [elɪ'veɪʃn] *n.* **a)** *(height)* Höhe, *die;* **b)** *(Archit.)* Aufriß, *der*

elevator ['elɪveɪtə(r)] *n. (Amer.)* Aufzug, *der;* Fahrstuhl, *der*

eleven [ɪ'levn] **1.** *adj.* elf. **2.** *n. (also Sport)* Elf, *die. See also* **eight**

elevenses [ɪ'levnzɪz] *n. sing. or pl. (Brit. coll.)* ≈ zweites Frühstück [gegen elf Uhr]

eleventh [ɪ'levnθ] **1.** *adj.* elft...; **at the ~ hour** in letzter Minute. **2.** *n. (fraction)* Elftel, *das. See also* **eighth**

elf [elf] *n., pl.* **elves** [elvz] Elf, *der*/ Elfe, *die*

elicit [ɪ'lɪsɪt] *v. t.* entlocken **(from** *Dat.*); gewinnen ⟨*Unterstützung*⟩

eligible ['elɪdʒɪbl] *adj.* **be ~ for sth.** *(fit)* für etw. geeignet sein; *(entitled)* zu etw. berechtigt sein

eliminate [ɪ'lɪmɪneɪt] *v. t.* **a)** *(remove)* beseitigen; ausschließen ⟨*Möglich-*

keit⟩; b) (exclude) ausschließen; **be ~d**
(Sport) ausscheiden. **elimination**
[ɪlɪmɪ'neɪʃn] *n.* **a)** *(removal)* Beseitigung, *die;* **process of ~:** Ausleseverf-
fahren, *das;* **b)** *(exclusion)* Ausschluß,
der; (Sport) Ausscheiden, *das*
élite [eɪ'liːt] *n.* Elite, *die*
ellipse [ɪ'lɪps] *n.* Ellipse, *die.* **ellipt-**
ical [ɪ'lɪptɪkl] *adj.* elliptisch
elm [elm] *n.* Ulme, *die*
elongated ['iːlɒŋgeɪtɪd] *adj.* langge-
streckt
elope [ɪ'ləʊp] *v. i.* durchbrennen *(ugs.)*
eloquence ['eləkwəns] *n.* Beredtheit,
die. **eloquent** ['eləkwənt] *adj.* beredt
⟨*Person*⟩; gewandt ⟨*Stil, Redner*⟩
else [els] *adv.* **a)** *(besides)* sonst [noch];
somebody/something ~: [noch] je-
mand anders/noch etwas; **everybody/**
everything ~: alle anderen/alles andere; **who/what/when/how ~?** wer/was/
wann/wie sonst noch?; **why ~?** wa-
rum sonst?; **b)** *(instead)* ander...; **sb.**
~'s hat der Hut von jmd. anders; **any-**
body/anything ~? [irgend] jemand an-
ders/etwas anderes?; **somebody/some-**
thing ~: jemand anders/etwas anderes; **everybody/everything ~:** alle an-
deren/alles andere; **c)** *(otherwise)*
sonst; **or ~:** oder aber; **do it or ~ ...!**
tun Sie es, sonst ...! '**elsewhere** *adv.*
woanders
elude [ɪ'luːd] *v.t. (avoid)* ausweichen
(+ *Dat.*); *(escape from)* entkommen
(+*Dat.*). **elusive** [ɪ'luːsɪv] *adj.*
schwer zu erreichen ⟨*Person*⟩; schwer
zu fassen ⟨*Straftäter*⟩; schwer defi-
nierbar ⟨*Begriff, Sinn*⟩
elves *pl. of* **elf**
emaciated [ɪ'meɪsɪeɪtɪd] *adj.* abge-
zehrt
emancipated [ɪ'mænsɪpeɪtɪd] *adj.*
emanzipiert: **become ~:** sich emanzipieren
emancipation [ɪmænsɪ'peɪʃn] *n.*
Emanzipation, *die*
embalm [ɪm'bɑːm] *v. t.* einbalsamie-
ren
embankment [ɪm'bæŋkmənt] *n.*
Damm, *der*
embargo [ɪm'bɑːgəʊ] *n., pl.* **~es** Embargo, *das*
embark [ɪm'bɑːk] *v. i.* **a)** sich einschif-
fen **(for** nach**);** **b)** **~ [up]on sth.** etw. in
Angriff nehmen. **embarkation** [emba-
'keɪʃn] *n.* Einschiffung, *die*
embarrass [ɪm'bærəs] *v. t.* in Verlegenheit bringen. **embarrassed** [ɪm-
'bærəst] *adj.* verlegen; **feel ~:** verlegen

sein. **em'barrassing** *adj.* peinlich.
em'barrassment *n.* Verlegenheit,
die
embassy ['embəsɪ] *n.* Botschaft, *die*
embellish [ɪm'belɪʃ] *v. t.* beschönigen
⟨*Wahrheit*⟩; ausschmücken ⟨*Ge-*
schichte, Bericht⟩
embers ['embəz] *n. pl.* Glut, *die*
embezzle [ɪm'bezl] *v. t.* unterschlagen
embitter [ɪm'bɪtə(r)] *v. t.* verbittern
emblem ['embləm] *n.* Emblem, *das*
embody [ɪm'bɒdɪ] *v. t.* verkörpern
embrace [ɪm'breɪs] **1.** *v. t.* umarmen;
(fig.: accept, adopt) annehmen. **2.** *v. i.*
sich umarmen. **3.** *n.* Umarmung, *die*
embroider [ɪm'brɔɪdə(r)] *v. t.* sticken
⟨*Muster*⟩; besticken ⟨*Tuch, Kleid*⟩;
(fig.) ausschmücken. **embroidery**
[ɪm'brɔɪdərɪ] *n.* Stickerei, *die*
embroil [ɪm'brɔɪl] *v. t.* **become/be ~ed**
in sth. in etw. *(Akk.)* verwickelt wer-
den/sein
embryo ['embrɪəʊ] *n.* Embryo, *der*
emerald ['emərəld] **1.** *n.* Smaragd,
der. **2.** *adj.* smaragdgrün
emerge [ɪ'mɜːdʒ] *v. i.* auftauchen
(from aus, **from behind** hinter
+ *Dat.*); ⟨*Wahrheit:*⟩ an den Tag
kommen; **it ~s that ...:** es stellt sich
heraus, daß ...
emergency [ɪ'mɜːdʒənsɪ] **1.** *n.* Notfall, *der;* **in an** *or* **in case of ~:** im Notfall. **2.** *adj.* Notfall-
emigrant ['emɪgrənt] *n.* Auswanderer,
der/Auswanderin, *die*
emigrate ['emɪgreɪt] *v. i.* auswandern
(to nach, **from** aus**).** **emigration**
[emɪ'greɪʃn] *n.* Auswanderung **(to**
nach, **from** aus**)**
eminence ['emɪnəns] *n.* hohes Ansehen
eminent ['emɪnənt] *adj.* bedeutend;
herausragend
emission [ɪ'mɪʃn] *n.* Emission, *die*
(fachspr.); (process also) Abgabe, *die*
emit [ɪ'mɪt] *v. t.,* -tt- abgeben, emittie-
ren *(fachspr.)* ⟨*Wärme, Strahlung*
usw.⟩; ausstoßen ⟨*Rauch*⟩
emotion [ɪ'məʊʃn] *n.* Gefühl, *das.*
emotional [ɪ'məʊʃənl] *adj.* emotional; Gemüts⟨*zustand, -störung*⟩; gefühlvoll ⟨*Stimme*⟩. **e'motionally**
adv. emotional; gefühlvoll ⟨*spre-*
chen⟩; **~ disturbed** seelisch gestört
emotive [ɪ'məʊtɪv] *adj.* emotional
emperor ['empərə(r)] *n.* Kaiser, *der*
emphasis ['emfəsɪs] *n., pl.* **emphases**
['emfəsiːz] Betonung, *die;* **lay** *or* **place**
or **put ~ on sth.** etw. betonen

emphasize ['emfəsaɪz] *v. t.* betonen
emphatic [ɪm'fætɪk] *adj.* nachdrücklich; demonstrativ ⟨*Ablehnung*⟩; **be ~ that ...**: darauf bestehen, daß ... **em'phatically** *adv.* nachdrücklich
empire ['empaɪə(r)] *n.* Reich, *das*
employ [ɪm'plɔɪ] *v. t.* a) *(take on)* einstellen; *(have working for one)* beschäftigen; **be ~ed by a company** bei einer Firma arbeiten; b) *(use)* einsetzen (for, in, on für); anwenden ⟨*Methode, List*⟩ (for, in, on bei). **employee** (*Amer.:* **employe**) [emplɔɪ-'iː, em'plɔɪiː] *n.* Angestellte, *der/die.* **employer** [ɪm'plɔɪə(r)] *n.* Arbeitgeber, *der/-geberin, die.* **employment** [ɪm'plɔɪmənt] *n.* a) *(work)* Arbeit, *die;* b) *(regular trade or profession)* Beschäftigung, *die.* **em'ployment agency** *n.* Stellenvermittlung, *die*
empower [ɪm'paʊə(r)] *v. t.* *(authorize)* ermächtigen; *(enable)* befähigen
empress ['emprɪs] *n.* Kaiserin, *die*
emptiness ['emptɪnɪs] *n.* Leere, *die*
empty ['emptɪ] 1. *adj.* leer; frei ⟨*Sitz, Parkplatz*⟩. 2. *v. t.* leeren; *(pour)* schütten (over über + *Akk.*). 3. *v. i.* sich leeren. '**empty-handed** *adj.* mit leeren Händen
EMS *abbr.* **European Monetary System** EWS
emulate ['emjʊleɪt] *v. t.* nacheifern (+ *Dat.*)
emulsion [ɪ'mʌlʃn] *n.* Emulsion, *die*
enable [ɪ'neɪbl] *v. t.* **~ sb. to do sth.** es jmdm. ermöglichen, etw. zu tun
enamel [ɪ'næml] 1. *n.* Email, *das.* 2. *v. t., (Brit.)* **-ll-** emaillieren
enchant [ɪn'tʃɑːnt] *v. t.* verzaubern; *(delight)* entzücken. **en'chanted** *adj.* verzaubert. **en'chanting** *adj.* entzückend. **en'chantment** *n.* Verzauberung, *die; (fig.)* Zauber, *der*
encircle [ɪn'sɜːkl] *v. t.* umgeben
encl. *abbr.* **enclosed, enclosure[s]** Anl.
enclave ['enkleɪv] *n.* Enklave, *die*
enclose [ɪn'kləʊz] *v. t.* a) *(surround)* umgeben; *(shut up or in)* einschließen; b) *(with letter)* beilegen (with, in *Dat.*); **please find ~d** anbei erhalten Sie. **enclosure** [ɪn'kləʊʒə(r)] *n.* a) *(in zoo)* Gehege, *das;* b) *(with letter)* Anlage, *die*
encore ['ɒŋkɔː(r)] 1. *int.* Zugabe. 2. *n.* Zugabe, *die*
encounter [ɪn'kaʊntə(r)] 1. *v. t. (as adversary)* treffen auf (+ *Akk.*); *(by chance)* begegnen (+ *Dat.*); stoßen auf (+ *Akk.*) ⟨*Problem, Widerstand*

usw.⟩. 2. *n. (chance meeting)* Begegnung, *die*
encourage [ɪn'kʌrɪdʒ] *v. t.* ermutigen; *(promote)* fördern. **encouragement** *n.* Ermutigung, *die* (**from** durch)
encroach [ɪn'krəʊtʃ] *v. i.* **~ on** eindringen in (+ *Akk.*); in Anspruch nehmen ⟨*Zeit*⟩
encumber [ɪn'kʌmbə(r)] *v. t.* belasten. **encumbrance** [ɪn'kʌmbrəns] *n.* Belastung, *die*
encyclopaedia [ɪnsaɪklə'piːdɪə] *n.* Lexikon, *das;* Enzyklopädie, *die.* **encyclopaedic** [ɪnsaɪklə'piːdɪk] *adj.* enzyklopädisch
end [end] 1. *n.* a) Ende, *das; (of nose, hair, finger)* Spitze, *die;* **from ~ to ~:** von einem Ende zum anderen; **at the ~ of 1987/March** Ende 1987/März; **in the ~:** schließlich; **come to an ~:** ein Ende nehmen; **be at an ~:** zu Ende sein; b) *(of box, packet, etc.)* Schmalseite, *die; (top/bottom surface)* Ober-/Unterseite, *die;* **on ~:** hochkant; **make ~s meet** *(fig.)* zurechtkommen; **no ~ of** *(coll.)* unendlich viel/viele; c) *(remnant)* Rest, *der; (of cigarette)* Stummel, *der;* d) *(purpose, object)* Ziel, *das;* **~ in itself** Selbstzweck, *der.* 2. *v. t.* beenden. 3. *v. i.* enden. **end 'up** *v. i.* enden; **~ up in** *(coll.)* landen in (+ *Dat.*); **~ up [as] a teacher** *(coll.)* schließlich Lehrer werden
endanger [ɪn'deɪndʒə(r)] *v. t.* gefährden
endear [ɪn'dɪə(r)] *v. t.* **~ sb./sth./oneself to sb.** jmdn./etw./sich bei jmdm. beliebt machen. **en'dearing** *adj.* reizend; gewinnend ⟨*Lächeln, Art*⟩
endeavour (*Brit.; Amer.:* **endeavor**) [ɪn'devə(r)] 1. *v. i.* **~ to do sth.** sich bemühen, etw. zu tun. 2. *n.* Bemühung, *die; (attempt)* Versuch, *der*
'**ending** *n.* Schluß, *der; (of word)* Endung, *die*
endive ['endaɪv] *n.* Endivie, *die*
'**endless** *adj.* endlos. '**endlessly** *adv.* unaufhörlich ⟨*streiten, schwatzen*⟩
endorse [ɪn'dɔːs] *v. t.* a) indossieren ⟨*Scheck*⟩; b) beipflichten (+ *Dat.*) ⟨*Meinung*⟩; billigen ⟨*Entscheidung, Handlung*⟩; unterstützen ⟨*Vorschlag*⟩; c) *(Brit. Law)* einen Strafvermerk machen auf (+ *Akk. od. Dat.*). **en'dorsement** *n.* a) *(of cheque)* Indossament, *das;* b) *(support)* Billigung, *die; (of proposal)* Unterstützung, *die;* c) *(Brit. Law)* Strafvermerk, *der*
endow [ɪn'daʊ] *v. t.* [über Stiftungen/

eine Stiftung] finanzieren; stiften ⟨*Preis, Lehrstuhl*⟩; **be ~ed with charm/a talent for music** Charme/musikalisches Talent besitzen

endurable [ɪn'djʊərəbl] *adj.* erträglich

endurance [ɪn'djʊərəns] *n.* Ausdauer, *die*

endure [ɪn'djʊə(r)] *v. t.* ertragen

enema ['enəmə] *n.* Einlauf, *der*

enemy ['enəmɪ] **1.** *n.* Feind, *der* (**of, to** *Gen.*). **2.** *adj.* feindlich

energetic [enə'dʒetɪk] *adj.* energiegeladen; *(active)* tatkräftig

energy ['enədʒɪ] *n.* Energie, *die*

enforce [ɪn'fɔːs] *v. t.* durchsetzen; sorgen für ⟨*Disziplin*⟩; **~d** erzwungen ⟨*Schweigen*⟩; unfreiwillig ⟨*Untätigkeit*⟩

engage [ɪn'geɪdʒ] **1.** *v. t.* **a)** *(hire)* einstellen ⟨*Arbeiter*⟩; engagieren ⟨*Sänger*⟩; **b)** wecken ⟨*Interesse*⟩; auf sich *(Akk.)* ziehen ⟨*Aufmerksamkeit*⟩; **c) ~ the clutch/first gear** einkuppeln/den ersten Gang einlegen. **2.** *v. i.* **~ in sth.** sich an etw. *(Dat.)* beteiligen; **~ in politics** sich politisch engagieren. **engaged** [ɪn'geɪdʒd] *adj.* **a) be ~** [**to be married**] [**to sb.**] [mit jmdm.] verlobt sein; **get ~** [**to be married**] [**to sb.**] sich [mit jmdm.] verloben; **b) be ~ in sth./in doing sth.** mit etw. beschäftigt sein/damit beschäftigt sein, etw. zu tun; **be otherwise ~:** etwas anderes vorhaben; **c)** besetzt ⟨*Toilette, [Telefon]anschluß, Nummer*⟩; **~ signal** *or* **tone** *(Brit.)* Besetztzeichen, *das*. **en'gagement** *n.* **a)** *(to be married)* Verlobung, *die* (**to** mit); **b)** *(appointment)* Verabredung, *die.* **en'gagement ring** *n.* Verlobungsring, *der*

engaging [ɪn'geɪdʒɪŋ] *adj.* bezaubernd; einnehmend ⟨*Persönlichkeit, Art*⟩

engine ['endʒɪn] *n.* **a)** Motor, *der; (rocket/jet ~)* Triebwerk, *das;* **b)** *(locomotive)* Lok[omotive], *die.* **'engine driver** *n.* Lok[omotiv]führer, *der*

engineer [endʒɪ'nɪə(r)] **1.** *n.* **a)** Ingenieur, *der*/Ingenieurin, *die; (service ~, installation ~)* Techniker, *der*/Technikerin, *die;* **b)** *(Amer.: engine-driver)* Lok[omotiv]führer, *der.* **2.** *v. t.* arrangieren. **engi'neering** *n.* Technik, *die*

England ['ɪŋglənd] *pr. n.* England *(das)*

English ['ɪŋglɪʃ] **1.** *adj.* englisch; **he/she is ~:** er ist Engländer/sie ist Engländerin. **2.** *n.* **a)** Englisch, *das;* **say sth. in ~:** etw. auf englisch sagen; **I**

cannot *or* **do not speak ~:** ich spreche kein Englisch; **translate into/from** |**the**| **~:** ins Englische/aus dem Englischen übersetzen; **b)** *pl.* **the ~:** die Engländer

English: ~ 'Channel *pr. n.* **the ~ Channel** der [Ärmel]kanal; **~man** [~mən] *n., pl.* **~men** [~mən] Engländer, *der;* **~woman** *n.* Engländerin, *die*

engrave [ɪn'greɪv] *v. t.* gravieren; eingravieren ⟨*Namen, Figur usw.*⟩. **engraving** [ɪn'greɪvɪŋ] *n.* Stich, *der; (from wood)* Holzschnitt, *der*

engross [ɪn'grəʊs] *v. t.* fesseln; **be ~ed in sth.** in etw. *(Akk.)* vertieft sein; **become** *or* **get ~ed in sth.** sich in etw. *(Akk.)* vertiefen

engulf [ɪn'gʌlf] *v. t.* verschlingen

enhance [ɪn'hɑːns] *v. t.* erhöhen ⟨*Wert, Aussichten, Schönheit*⟩; verstärken ⟨*Wirkung*⟩; heben ⟨*Aussehen*⟩

enigma [ɪ'nɪgmə] *n.* Rätsel, *das.* **enigmatic** [enɪg'mætɪk] *adj.* rätselhaft

enjoy [ɪn'dʒɔɪ] **1.** *v. t.* **a) I ~ed the book/work** das Buch/die Arbeit hat mir gefallen; **he ~s reading/travelling** er liest/reist gern; **b)** genießen ⟨*Rechte, Privilegien, Vorteile*⟩. **2.** *v. refl.* sich amüsieren. **enjoyable** [ɪn'dʒɔɪəbl] *adj.* schön; angenehm ⟨*Empfindung, Arbeit*⟩; unterhaltsam ⟨*Buch, Film, Stück*⟩. **en'joyment** *n.* Vergnügen, *das* (**of an** + *Dat.*)

enlarge [ɪn'lɑːdʒ] **1.** *v. t.* vergrößern; verbreitern ⟨*Straße, Durchgang*⟩. **2.** *v. i.* **~** |**up**|**on sth.** etw. weiter ausführen. **en'largement** *n.* Vergrößerung, *die; (making wider)* Verbreiterung, *die*

enlighten [ɪn'laɪtn] *v. t.* aufklären (**on, as to** über + *Akk.*). **en'lightenment** *n.* Aufklärung, *die*

enlist [ɪn'lɪst] **1.** *v. t.* *(obtain)* gewinnen. **2.** *v. i.* **~** |**for the army/navy**| in die Armee/Marine eintreten; **~** |**as a soldier**| Soldat werden

enliven [ɪn'laɪvn] *v. t.* beleben

enmity ['enmɪtɪ] *n.* Feindschaft, *die*

enormous [ɪ'nɔːməs] *adj.* enorm; riesig, gewaltig ⟨*Figur, Tier, Menge*⟩. **e'normously** *adv.* enorm

enough [ɪ'nʌf] **1.** *adj.* genug; **there's ~ room** es ist Platz genug. **2.** *n.* genug; **be ~ to do sth.** genügen, etw. zu tun; **have had ~** |**of sb./sth.**| genug [von jmdm./etw.] haben; **I've had ~!** jetzt reicht's mir aber! **3.** *adv.* genug; **oddly/funnily ~:** merkwürdiger-/*(ugs.)* komischerweise

enquire, enquiry *see* **inquir-**
enrage [ın'reıdʒ] *v. t.* wütend machen;
be ~d by sth. über etw. *(Akk.)* wütend
werden
enrich [ın'rıtʃ] *v. t.* reich machen;
(fig.) bereichern
enrol *(Amer.:* **enroll)** [ın'rəʊl] **1.** *v. i.*
-ll- sich einschreiben; **~ for a course**
sich zu einem Kurs anmelden. **2.** *v. t.*
einschreiben. **en'rolment** *(Amer.:*
en'rollment) *n.* Einschreibung, *die*
en route [ɑ̃ 'ruːt] *adv.* unterwegs; **~ to**
Scotland/for Edinburgh auf dem Weg
nach Schottland/Edinburgh
ensign ['ensaın, 'ensn] *n.* Hoheitszei-
chen, *das*
enslave [ın'sleıv] *v. t.* versklaven
ensue [ın'sjuː] *v. i.* folgen **(from, on**
aus); **the discussion which ~d** die an-
schließende Diskussion
ensure [ın'ʃʊə(r)] *v. t.* **~ that ...** *(see to*
it that) gewährleisten, daß ...; **~ sth.**
etw. gewährleisten
entail [ın'teıl] *v. t.* mit sich bringen;
sth. ~s doing sth. etw. bedeutet, daß
man etw. tun muß
entangle [ın'tæŋgl] *v. t.* sich verfangen lassen; **get** *or* **become ~d in** *or*
with sth. sich in etw. *(Dat.)* verfangen
enter ['entə(r)] **1.** *v. i.* **a)** hineingehen;
⟨*Fahrzeug:*⟩ hineinfahren; *(come in)*
hereinkommen; *(into room)* eintreten;
b) *(register as competitor)* sich zur
Teilnahme anmelden **(for an** + *Dat.).*
2. *v. t.* **a)** [hinein]gehen in (+ *Akk.*);
⟨*Fahrzeug:*⟩ [hinein]fahren in
(+ *Akk.*); betreten ⟨*Gebäude, Zim-*
mer⟩; einlaufen in (+ *Akk.*) ⟨*Hafen*⟩;
einreisen in (+ *Akk.*) ⟨*Land*⟩; *(come*
into) [herein]kommen in (+ *Akk.*); **b)**
teilnehmen an (+ *Dat.*) ⟨*Rennen,*
Wettbewerb⟩; **c)** *(in book etc.)* eintragen **(in in** + *Akk.*). **'enter into** *v. t.*
aufnehmen ⟨*Verhandlungen*⟩; einge-
hen ⟨*Verpflichtung*⟩; schließen ⟨*Ver-*
trag⟩. **'enter [up]on** *v. t.* beginnen
enterprise ['entəpraız] *n.* **a)** *(under-*
taking) Unternehmen, *das;* **free/pri-**
vate ~: freies/privates Unternehmer-
tum; **b)** *(enterprising spirit)* Unterneh-
mungsgeist, *der.* **enterprising** ['en-
təpraızıŋ] *adj.* unternehmungslustig
entertain [entə'teın] *v. t.* **a)** *(amuse)*
unterhalten; **b)** *(receive as guest)* bewirten; **c)** haben ⟨*Vorstellung*⟩; hegen
(geh.) ⟨*Gefühl, Verdacht, Zweifel*⟩;
(consider) in Erwägung ziehen.
enter'tainer *n.* Unterhalter, *der/*Un-
terhalterin, *die.* **enter'taining** *adj.*

unterhaltsam. **enter'tainment** *n.* **a)**
(amusement) Unterhaltung, *die;* **b)**
(performance, show) Veranstaltung,
die
enthral *(Amer.:* **enthrall)** [ın'θrɔːl]
v. t., **-ll-** gefangennehmen *(fig.)*
enthuse [ın'θjuːz] *(coll.)* **1.** *v. i.* in Begeisterung ausbrechen **(about** über
+ *Akk.*). **2.** *v. t.* begeistern
enthusiasm [ın'θjuːzıæzm] *n.* Begeisterung, *die.* **enthusiast** [ın'θjuːzı-
æst] *n.* Enthusiast, *der; (for sports)*
Fan, *der;* **a DIY ~:** ein begeisterter
Heimwerker. **enthusiastic** [ınθjuː-
zı'æstık] *adj.* begeistert; **not be very ~**
about doing sth. keine große Lust
haben, etw. zu tun
entice [ın'taıs] *v. t.* locken **(into in** +
Akk.); **~ sb. into doing** *or* **to do sth.**
jmdn. dazu verleiten, etw. zu tun
entire [ın'taıə(r)] *adj.* **a)** *(whole)* ganz;
b) *(intact)* vollständig. **en'tirely** *adv.*
a) *(wholly)* völlig; **b)** *(solely)* ganz ⟨*für*
sich behalten⟩; voll ⟨*verantwortlich*
sein⟩; **it's up to you ~:** es liegt ganz bei
dir. **entirety** [ın'taıərətı] *n.* **in its ~:** in
seiner/ihrer Gesamtheit
entitle [ın'taıtl] *v. t.* **a)** berechtigen **(to**
zu); **~ sb. to do sth.** jmdm. das Recht
geben, etw. zu tun; **be ~d to** |**claim**|
sth. Anspruch auf etw. *(Akk.)* haben;
be ~d to do sth. das Recht haben, etw.
zu tun
entourage [ɒntʊ'rɑːʒ] *n.* Gefolge, *das*
entrails ['entreılz] *n. pl.* Eingeweide
Pl.
¹entrance [ın'trɑːns] *v. t.* hinreißen
²entrance ['entrəns] *n. (way in)* Eingang, *der* **(to** *Gen. od.* zu); *(for*
vehicles) Einfahrt, *die.* **'entrance fee**
n. Eintrittsgeld, *das*
entrant ['entrənt] *n. (for competition,*
race, etc.) Teilnehmer, *der/*Teilneh-
merin, *die* **(for** *Gen.,* an + *Dat.*)
entreat [ın'triːt] *v. t.* anflehen. **en-**
'treaty *n.* flehentliche Bitte
entrepreneur [ɒntrəprə'nɜː(r)] *n.* Unternehmer, *der/*Unternehmerin, *die*
entrust [ın'trʌst] *v. t.* **~ sb. with sth.**
jmdm. etw. anvertrauen; **~ sb./sth. to**
sb./sth. jmdn./etw. einer Sache anvertrauen; **~ a task to sb.** jmdn.
mit einer Aufgabe betrauen
entry ['entrı] *n.* **a)** Eintritt, *der* **(into in**
+ *Akk.*); *(into country)* Einreise, *die;*
'no ~' *(for people)* „Zutritt verboten";
(for vehicles) „Einfahrt verboten"; **b)**
(way in) Eingang, *der; (for vehicle)*
Einfahrt, *die;* **c)** *(registration, item)*

Eintragung, *die* (**in, into** in + *Akk. od. Dat.*); *(in dictionary, encyclopaedia)* Eintrag, *der*

entry: ~ **fee** *n.* Eintrittsgeld, *das;* ~ **form** *n.* Anmeldeformular, *das;* ~ **visa** *n.* Einreisevisum, *das*

envelop [ɪn'veləp] *v. t.* [ein]hüllen (**in** in + *Akk.*); **be ~ed in flames** ganz von Flammen umgeben sein

envelope ['envələʊp, 'ɒnvələʊp] *n.* [Brief]umschlag, *der*

enviable ['enviəbl] *adj.* beneidenswert

envious ['enviəs] *adj.* neidisch (**of** auf + *Akk.*)

environment [ɪn'vaiərənmənt] *n.* Umwelt, *die; (surrounding objects, region)* Umgebung, *die.* **environmental** [ɪnvaiərən'mentl] *adj.* Umwelt-. **environ'mentalist** *n.* Umweltschützer, *der/*-schützerin, *die.* **environ'mentally** *adv.* ~ **friendly** umweltfreundlich

envisage [ɪn'vɪzɪdʒ] *v. t.* sich *(Dat.)* vorstellen

envoy ['envɔɪ] *n.* Gesandte, *der/*Gesandtin, *die*

envy ['envɪ] **1.** *n.* Neid, *der;* **you'll be the ~ of all your friends** werden dich alle deine Freunde werden dich beneiden. **2.** *v. t.* beneiden; ~ **sb. sth.** jmdn. um etw. beneiden

enzyme ['enzaɪm] *n.* Enzym, *das*

ephemeral [ɪ'femərl] *adj.* kurzlebig

epic ['epɪk] **1.** *adj.* episch. **2.** *n.* Epos, *das*

epidemic [epɪ'demɪk] **1.** *adj.* epidemisch. **2.** *n.* Epidemie, *die*

epilepsy ['epɪlepsɪ] *n.* Epilepsie, *die.* **epileptic** [epɪ'leptɪk] **1.** *adj.* epileptisch; epileptischer Anfall. **2.** *n.* Epileptiker, *der/*Epileptikerin, *die*

episode ['epɪsəʊd] *n.* **a)** Episode, *die;* **b)** *(of serial)* Folge, *die*

epitaph ['epɪtɑːf] *n.* Grab[in]schrift, *die*

epitome [ɪ'pɪtəmɪ] *n.* Inbegriff, *der.* **epitomize** [ɪ'pɪtəmaɪz] *v. t.* ~ **sth.** der Inbegriff einer Sache *(Gen.)* sein

epoch ['iːpɒk] *n.* Epoche, *die.* **'epoch-making** *adj.* epochemachend

equal ['iːkwl] **1.** *adj.* **a)** gleich; ~ **in** or **of** ~ **height/size/importance** *etc.* gleich hoch/groß/wichtig *usw.;* **b)** **be ~ to sth./sb.** *(strong, clever, etc. enough)* einer Sache/jmdm. gewachsen sein. **2.** *n.* Gleichgestellte, *der/die;* **have no ~:** nicht seines-/ihresgleichen haben. **3.** *v. t., (Brit.)* **-ll-:** ~ **sb.** es

jmdm. gleich tun; **three times four ~s twelve** drei mal vier ist [gleich] zwölf.

equality [ɪ'kwɒlɪtɪ] *n.* Gleichheit, *die; (equal rights)* Gleichberechtigung, *die.* **equalize** ['iːkwəlaɪz] *v. i. (Sport)* den Ausgleich[streffer] erzielen. **'equalizer** *n. (Sport)* Ausgleich[streffer], *der.* **'equally** *adv.* gleich; *(just as)* ebenso; in gleiche Teile ⟨*aufteilen*⟩; gleichmäßig ⟨*verteilen*⟩. **equal oppor'tunity** *n.* Chancengleichheit, *die.* **'equals sign** *n. (Math.)* Gleichheitszeichen, *das*

equanimity [ekwə'nɪmɪtɪ] *n.* Gelassenheit, *die*

equate [ɪ'kweɪt] *v. t.* gleichsetzen (**with** mit). **equation** [ɪ'kweɪʒn] *n. (Math.)* Gleichung, *die*

equator [ɪ'kweɪtə(r)] *n.* Äquator, *der*

equilibrium [iːkwɪ'lɪbrɪəm] *n., pl.* **equilibria** [iːkwɪ'lɪbrɪə] *or* **~s** Gleichgewicht, *das*

equinox ['ekwɪnɒks] *n.* Tagundnachtgleiche, *die*

equip [ɪ'kwɪp] *v. t.,* **-pp-** ausrüsten ⟨*Fahrzeug, Armee*⟩; ausstatten ⟨*Küche*⟩; **fully ~ped** komplett ausgerüstet/ausgestattet; ~ **sb./oneself with sth.**] jmdn./sich [mit etw.] ausrüsten. **e'quipment** *n.* Ausrüstung, *die; (of kitchen, laboratory)* Ausstattung, *die; (needed for activity)* Geräte

equivalent [ɪ'kwɪvələnt] **1.** *adj.* gleichwertig; **be ~ to sth.** einer Sache *(Dat.)* entsprechen. **2.** *n.* **a)** *(thing, person)* Pendant, *das;* Gegenstück, *das* (**of** zu); **b) be ~ of sth.** *(have same result)* einer Sache *(Dat.)* entsprechen

equivocal [ɪ'kwɪvəkl] *adj.* zweideutig

era ['ɪərə] *n.* Ära, *die*

eradicate [ɪ'rædɪkeɪt] *v. t.* ausrotten

erase [ɪ'reɪz] *v. t.* auslöschen; *(with rubber, knife)* ausradieren; *(from tape, also Computing)* löschen. **e'raser** *n.* |pencil] ~: Radiergummi, *der*

erect [ɪ'rekt] **1.** *adj.* aufrecht. **2.** *v. t.* errichten; aufstellen ⟨*Standbild, Mast, Verkehrsschild, Gerüst, Zelt*⟩. **erection** [ɪ'rekʃn] *n.* **a)** *see* **erect 2:** Errichtung, *die;* Aufstellen, *das;* **b)** *(Physiol.)* Erektion, *die*

ermine ['ɜːmɪn] *n.* Hermelin, *der*

erode [ɪ'rəʊd] *v. t.* **a)** ⟨*Säure, Rost:*⟩ angreifen; ⟨*Wasser:*⟩ auswaschen; ⟨*Wind:*⟩ verwittern lassen; **b)** *(fig.)* unterminieren. **erosion** [ɪ'rəʊʒn] *n.* **a)** *see* **erode a:** Angreifen, *das;* Auswaschung, *die;* Verwitterung, *die;* **b)** *(fig.)* Unterminierung, *die*

ethical

erotic [ɪ'rɒtɪk] *adj.* erotisch
err [ɜ:(r)] *v. i.* sich irren
errand ['erənd] *n.* Botengang, *der;*
(shopping) Besorgung, *die;* **go on** *or*
run an ~: einen Botengang/eine Besorgung machen. **'errand boy** *n.*
Laufbursche, *der*
erratic [ɪ'rætɪk] *adj.* unregelmäßig;
sprunghaft ⟨*Wesen, Person, Art*⟩; launenhaft ⟨*Verhalten*⟩
erroneous [ɪ'rəʊnɪəs] *adj.* falsch; irrig
⟨*Schlußfolgerung, Annahme*⟩
error ['erə(r)] *n. (mistake)* Fehler, *der;*
(wrong opinion) Irrtum, *der;* **in** ~: irrtümlich[erweise]
erudite ['eru:daɪt] *adj.* gelehrt
erupt [ɪ'rʌpt] *v. i.* ausbrechen. **eruption** [ɪ'rʌpʃn] *n.* Ausbruch, *der*
escalate ['eskəleɪt] *v. i.* sich ausweiten
(into zu); ⟨*Preise, Kosten:*⟩ [ständig]
steigen. **escalator** ['eskəleɪtə(r)] *n.*
Rolltreppe, *die*
escapade [eskə'peɪd] *n.* Eskapade,
die (geh.)
escape [ɪ'skeɪp] **1.** *n.* Flucht, *die* **(from**
aus); **have a narrow** ~: gerade noch
einmal davonkommen. **2.** *v. i.* **a)** fliehen **(from** aus); *(successfully)* entkommen **(from** *Dat.*); **b)** ⟨*Gas:*⟩ ausströmen; ⟨*Flüssigkeit:*⟩ auslaufen. **3.** *v. t.*
a) entkommen (+ *Dat.*) ⟨*Verfolger,
Feind*⟩; entgehen (+ *Dat.*) ⟨*Bestrafung, Gefangennahme, Tod*⟩; ver-
schont bleiben von ⟨*Zerstörung, Auswirkungen*⟩; **b)** *(not be remembered by)*
entfallen sein (+ *Dat.*). **e'scape
route** *n.* Fluchtweg, *der*
escapism [ɪ'skeɪpɪzm] *n.* Realitäts-
flucht, *die*
escort 1. ['eskɔ:t] *n.* **a)** Begleitung, *die;*
(Mil.) Eskorte, *die;* **b)** *(hired companion)* Begleiter, *der/*Begleiterin, *die.* **2.**
[ɪ'skɔ:t] *v. t.* begleiten; *(lead)* führen;
(Mil.) eskortieren
Eskimo ['eskɪməʊ] **1.** *adj.* Eskimo-.
2. *n., pl.* ~s *or same* Eskimo, *der/*Eski-
mofrau, *die;* **the** ~[**s**] die Eskimos
esoteric [esəʊ'terɪk] *adj.* esoterisch
especial [ɪ'speʃl] *attrib. adj.* [ganz] besonder... **especially** [ɪ'speʃəlɪ] *adv.*
besonders
espionage ['espɪənɑ:ʒ] *n.* Spionage,
die
espresso [e'spresəʊ] *n., pl.* ~s *(coffee)*
Espresso, *der.* **e'spresso bar** *n.* Es-
pressobar, *die*
Esq. [ɪ'skwaɪə(r)] *abbr.* **Esquire** ≈ Hr.;
(on letter) ≈ Hrn.; **Jim Smith,** ~: Hr./
Hrn. Jim Smith

essay ['eseɪ] *n.* Essay, *der;* Aufsatz,
der (bes. Schulw.)
essence ['esəns] *n.* **a)** Wesen, *das;*
(gist) Wesentliche, *das;* **in** ~: im Wesentlichen; **b)** *(Cookery)* Essenz, *die*
essential [ɪ'senʃl] **1.** *adj.* **a)** *(fundamental)* wesentlich; **b)** *(indispensable)* unentbehrlich; lebensnotwen-
dig ⟨*Versorgungseinrichtungen, Güter*⟩; unabdingbar ⟨*Qualifikation, Voraussetzung*⟩; **it is** ~ **that ...:** es ist unbedingt notwendig, daß ... **2.** *n. pl.* **the**
~**s** *(fundamentals)* das Wesentliche;
(items) das Notwendigste. **es'sen-
tially** *adv.* im Grunde
establish [ɪ'stæblɪʃ] *v. t.* **a)** schaffen
⟨*Einrichtung, Präzedenzfall*⟩; gründen
⟨*Organisation, Institut*⟩; errichten
⟨*Geschäft, System*⟩; **b)** *(secure acceptance for)* etablieren; **become** ~**ed** sich
einbürgern; **c)** *(prove)* beweisen; **d)**
(discover) feststellen. **established**
[ɪ'stæblɪʃt] *adj.* bestehend ⟨*Ordnung*⟩;
etabliert ⟨*Schriftsteller*⟩; *(accepted)* üblich; fest ⟨*Brauch*⟩; feststehend ⟨*Tatsache*⟩; **become** ~: sich durchsetzen.
e'stablishment *n.* **a)** *(setting up,
foundation)* Gründung, *die;* **b)** |busi-
ness| ~: Unternehmen, *das*
estate [ɪ'steɪt] *n.* **a)** *(landed property)*
Gut, *das;* **b)** *(Brit.: housing* ~)
[Wohn]siedlung, *die;* **c)** *(of deceased
person)* Erbmasse, *die.* **e'state
agent** *n. (Brit.)* Grundstücksmakler,
der; **e'state car** *n. (Brit.)* Kombiwagen, *der*
esteem [ɪ'sti:m] **1.** *n.* Wertschätzung,
die (geh.) **(for** *Gen.,* für). **2.** *v. t.* schätzen; **highly** ~**ed** hochgeschätzt
estimate 1. ['estɪmət] *n.* **a)** Schätzung,
die; **at a rough** ~: grob geschätzt; **b)**
(Commerc.) Kostenvoranschlag, *der.*
2. ['estɪmeɪt] *v. t.* schätzen **(at** auf +
Akk.). **estimation** [estɪ'meɪʃn] *n.*
Schätzung, *die;* **in sb.'s** ~: nach jmds.
Schätzung
estuary ['estjʊərɪ] *n.* [Trichter]mün-
dung, *die*
etc. *abbr.* et cetera usw.
etch [etʃ] *v. t.* ätzen **(on** auf + *Akk.*);
(on metal also) ⟨*bes. Künstler:*⟩ radieren; *(fig.)* einprägen **(in, on** *Dat.*).
'etching *n. (Art)* Radierung, *die*
eternal [ɪ'tɜ:nl] *adj.,* **e'ternally** *adv.*
ewig
eternity [ɪ'tɜ:nɪtɪ] *n.* Ewigkeit, *die*
ether ['i:θə(r)] *n.* Äther, *der.* **ethereal**
[ɪ'θɪərɪəl] *adj.* ätherisch
ethical ['eθɪkl] *adj.* ethisch

ethics ['eθɪks] *n.* **a)** Moral, *die; (moral philosophy)* Ethik, *die;* **b)** *usu. constr. as pl. (moral code)* Ethik, *die (geh.)*

Ethiopia [i:θɪ'əupɪə] *pr. n.* Äthiopien *(das)*

ethnic ['eθnɪk] *adj.* ethnisch

etiquette ['etɪket] *n.* Etikette, *die*

etymology [etɪ'mɒlədʒɪ] *n.* Etymologie, *die*

eulogy ['ju:lədʒɪ] *n.* Lobrede, *die*

euphemism ['ju:fəmɪzm] *n.* Euphemismus, *der.* **euphemistic** [ju:fə'mɪstɪk] *adj.* verhüllend

euphoria [ju:'fɔ:rɪə] *n.* Euphorie, *die (geh.)*

Euro- ['juərəu] *in comb.* euro-/Euro-. **'Eurocheque** *n.* Euroscheck, *der*

Europe ['juərəp] *pr. n.* Europa *(das).* **European** [juərə'pi:ən] **1.** *adj.* europäisch; ~ |**Economic**| **Community** Europäische [Wirtschafts]gemeinschaft. **2.** *n.* Europäer, *der*/Europäerin, *die*

euthanasia [ju:θə'neɪzɪə] *n.* Euthanasie, *die*

evacuate [ɪ'vækjueɪt] *v. t.* evakuieren **(from** aus). **evacuation** [ɪvækjʊ'eɪʃn] *n.* Evakuierung, *die* **(from** aus)

evade [ɪ'veɪd] *v. t.* ausweichen (+ *Dat.*) ⟨*Angriff, Angreifer, Schlag, Problem, Frage*⟩; sich entziehen (+ *Dat.*) ⟨*Verhaftung, Verantwortung*⟩; entkommen (+ *Dat.*) ⟨*Verfolger, Verfolgung*⟩; hinterziehen ⟨*Steuern*⟩; ~ **doing** sth. vermeiden, etw. zu tun

evaluate [ɪ'væljueɪt] *v. t.* einschätzen; bewerten ⟨*Daten*⟩

evangelical [i:væn'dʒelɪkl] *adj.* missionarisch *(fig.); (Protestant)* evangelikal. **evangelist** [ɪ'vændʒəlɪst] *n.* Evangelist, *der*

evaporate [ɪ'væpəreɪt] **1.** *v. i.* verdunsten. **2.** *v. t.* verdunsten lassen. **evaporated 'milk** *n.* Kondensmilch, *die* **evaporation** [ɪvæpə'reɪʃn] *n.* Verdunstung, *die*

evasion [ɪ'veɪʒn] *n.* Umgehung, *die; (of responsibility, question)* Ausweichen, *das* **(of** vor + *Dat.*); **tax** ~: Steuerhinterziehung, *die.* **evasive** [ɪ'veɪsɪv] *adj.* **a)** be/**become** ~: ausweichen; **b)** ausweichend ⟨*Antwort*⟩

eve [i:v] *n.* Vorabend, *der* **(of** *Gen.*); *(day)* Vortag, *der* **(of** *Gen.*)

even ['i:vn] **1.** *adj.* **a)** eben ⟨*Boden, Fläche*⟩; gleich hoch ⟨*Stapel, Stuhl-, Tischbein*⟩; **be of** ~ **height/length** gleich hoch/lang sein; **b)** gerade ⟨*Zahl, Seite, Hausnummer*⟩; **c)** be *or*

get ~ **with sb.** *(quits)* es jmdm. heimzahlen; **break** ~: die Kosten decken. **2.** *adv.* sogar; selbst; sogar noch ⟨*weniger, schlimmer usw.*⟩; ~ **if** selbst wenn; ~ **so** [aber] trotzdem; **not** *or* **never** ~ ...: [noch] nicht einmal ... **even 'up** *v. t.* ausgleichen

evening ['i:vnɪŋ] *n.* Abend, *der;* **this/tomorrow** ~: heute/morgen abend; **in the** ~: am Abend; *(regularly)* abends. **'evening class** *n.* Abendkurs, *der.* **'evening dress** *n.* Abendkleidung, *die*

'evenly *adv.* gleichmäßig

'even-numbered *adj.* gerade

event [ɪ'vent] *n.* **a)** **in the** ~ **of his dying** *or* **death** im Falle seines Todes; **in the** ~: letztes Endes; **in the** ~ **of rain** bei Regenwetter; **b)** *(occurrence)* Ereignis, *das.* **e'ventful** *adj.* ereignisreich

eventual [ɪ'ventjuəl] *adj.* **predict sb.'s** ~ **downfall** vorhersagen, daß jmd. schließlich zu Fall kommen wird; **the career of Napoleon and his** ~ **defeat** der Aufstieg Napoleons und schließlich seine Niederlage. **eventuality** [ɪventjʊ'ælɪtɪ] *n.* Eventualität, *die.* **e'ventually** *adv.* schließlich

ever ['evə(r)] *adv.* **a)** *(always)* immer; **for** ~: für immer; ewig ⟨*lieben, dasein, leben*⟩; ~ **since** |**then**| seit [dieser Zeit]; **b)** *(at any time)* je[mals]; **hardly** ~: so gut wie nie; **c)** *in comb. with compar. adj. or adv.* noch; ~~**increasing** ständig zunehmend; **d)** *(coll.)* **what** ~ **does he want?** was will er nur?; **why** ~ **not?** warum denn nicht? **'evergreen 1.** *adj.* immergrün. **2.** *n.* immergrüne Pflanze. **ever'lasting** *adj.* **a)** *(eternal)* immerwährend; ewig ⟨*Leben*⟩; unvergänglich ⟨*Ruhm, Ehre*⟩; **b)** *(incessant)* endlos

every ['evrɪ] *adj.* **a)** jeder/jede/jedes; ~ **one** jeder/jede/jedes [einzelne]; **your** ~ **wish** all[e] deine Wünsche; **she comes** ~ **day** sie kommt jeden Tag; ~ **three/few days** alle drei/paar Tage; ~ **other** (~ **second, almost** ~) jeder/jede/jedes zweite; **b)** *(the greatest possible)* all ⟨*Respekt, Aussicht*⟩

every: ~**body** *n. & pron.* jeder; ~**body else** alle anderen; ~**day** *attrib. adj.* alltäglich; Alltags⟨*kleidung, -sprache*⟩; **in** ~**day life** im Alltag; ~**one** *see* ~**body;** ~**place** *(Amer.) see* ~**where;** ~**thing** *n. & pron.* alles; ~**where** *adv.* überall; ~**where you go/look** wohin man auch geht/sieht

evict [ɪ'vɪkt] *v. t.* ~ **sb.** |**from his home**|

jmdn. zur Räumung [seiner Wohnung] zwingen. **eviction** [ɪ'vɪkʃn] n. Zwangsräumung, die; **the ~ of the tenant** die zwangsweise Vertreibung des Mieters

evidence ['evɪdəns] n. **a)** Beweis, der; (indication) Anzeichen, das; **be ~ of sth.** etw. beweisen; **b)** (Law) Beweismaterial, das; **give ~:** aussagen

evident ['evɪdənt] adj. offensichtlich; **be ~ to sb.** jmdm. klar sein; **it soon became ~ that ...:** es stellte sich bald heraus, daß ... '**evidently** adv. offensichtlich

evil ['i:vl, 'i:vɪl] **1.** adj. böse; schlecht 〈Charakter, Einfluß, System〉. **2.** n. **a)** Böse, das; **b)** (bad thing) Übel, das

evocative [ɪ'vɒkətɪv] adj. **be ~ of sth.** etw. heraufbeschwören

evoke [ɪ'vəʊk] v. t. heraufbeschwören; hervorrufen 〈Bewunderung, Überra­schung〉; erregen 〈Interesse〉

evolution [i:və'lu:ʃn] n. Entwicklung, die; (Biol.) Evolution, die

evolve [ɪ'vɒlv] **1.** v. i. sich entwickeln (**from** aus, **into** zu). **2.** v. t. entwickeln

ewe [ju:] n. Mutterschaf, das

ex- pref. Ex-〈Freundin, Präsident, Champion〉; Alt〈[bundes]kanzler〉

exacerbate [ek'sæsəbeɪt] v. t. verschärfen 〈Lage〉; verschlechtern 〈Zu­stand〉

exact [ɪg'zækt] **1.** adj. genau. **2.** v. t. fordern; erheben 〈Gebühr〉. **exacting** [ɪg'zæktɪŋ] n. anspruchsvoll; hoch 〈Anforderung〉. **exactitude** [ɪg'zæktɪtju:d] Genauigkeit, die. **exactly** [ɪg'zæktlɪ] adv. genau; **not ~** (coll. iron.) nicht gerade. **exactness** [ɪg'zæktnɪs] n. Genauigkeit, die

exaggerate [ɪg'zædʒəreɪt] v. t. übertreiben. **exaggeration** [ɪgzædʒə'reɪʃn] n. Übertreibung, die

exam [ɪg'zæm] (coll.) see **examination b**

examination [ɪgzæmɪ'neɪʃn] n. **a)** (inspection; Med.) Untersuchung, die; **b)** (Sch. etc.) Prüfung, die; (final ~ at university) Examen, das

examine [ɪg'zæmɪn] v. t. **a)** (inspect; Med.) untersuchen (**for** auf + Akk.); prüfen 〈Dokument, Gewissen〉; kontrollieren 〈Ausweis, Gepäck〉; **b)** (Sch. etc.) prüfen (**in** in + Dat.); **c)** (Law) verhören. **examiner** [ɪg'zæmɪnə(r)] n. Prüfer, der/Prüferin, die

example [ɪg'zɑ:mpl] n. Beispiel, das; **for ~:** zum Beispiel; **make an ~ of sb.** ein Exempel an jmdm. statuieren

exasperate [ɪg'zæspəreɪt] v. t. (irritate) verärgern; (infuriate) zur Verzweiflung bringen. **exasperation** [ɪg'zæspəreɪʃn] n. see **exasperate:** Ärger, der/Verzweiflung, die (**with** über + Akk.); **in ~:** verärgert/verzweifelt

excavate ['ekskəveɪt] v. t. **a)** ausschachten; (with machine) ausbaggern; **b)** (Archaeol.) ausgraben. **excavation** [ekskə'veɪʃn] n. **a)** Ausschachtung, die; (with machine) Ausbaggerung, die; **b)** (Archaeol.) Ausgrabung, die. **excavator** ['ekskəveɪtə(r)] n. Bagger, der

exceed [ɪk'si:d] v. t. **a)** (be greater than) übertreffen (**in** an + Dat.); 〈Kosten, Summe, Anzahl:〉 übersteigen (**by** um); **b)** (go beyond) überschreiten; hinausgehen über (+ Akk.) 〈Auftrag, Befehl〉. **ex'ceedingly** adv. äußerst; ausgesprochen 〈häßlich, dumm〉

excel [ɪk'sel] **1.** v. t., **-ll-** übertreffen; **~ oneself** (lit. or iron.) sich selbst übertreffen. **2.** v. i., **-ll-** sich hervortun (**at, in** in + Dat.)

excellence ['eksələns] n. hervorragende Qualität. **excellent** ['eksələnt] adj. hervorragend

except [ɪk'sept] **1.** prep. **~** [(coll.) for] außer (+ Dat.); **~ for** (in all respects other than) abgesehen von. **2.** v. t. ausnehmen (**from** bei); **~ed** ausgenommen. **ex'cepting** prep. außer (+ Dat.). **exception** [ɪk'sepʃn] n. Ausnahme, die; **take ~ to** Anstoß nehmen an (+ Dat.). **exceptional** [ɪk'sepʃnl] adj. außergewöhnlich. **ex'ceptionally** adv. **a)** (as an exception) ausnahmsweise; **b)** (remarkably) ungewöhnlich

excerpt ['eksɜ:pt] n. Auszug, der (**from** aus)

excess [ɪk'ses] n. **a)** Übermaß, das (of an + Dat.); **eat/drink to ~:** übermäßig essen/trinken; **b)** esp. in pl. (overindulgence) Exzeß, der; **c) be in ~ of sth.** etw. übersteigen; **d)** (surplus) Überschuß, der

excess ['ekses] **~ 'baggage** n. Mehrgepäck, das; **~ 'fare** n. Mehrpreis, der; **pay the ~ fare** nachlösen

excessive [ɪk'sesɪv] adj. übermäßig; übertrieben 〈Forderung, Lob, An­sprüche〉; unmäßig 〈Esser, Trinker〉. **ex'cessively** adv. übertrieben; unmäßig 〈essen, trinken〉

exchange [ɪks'tʃeɪndʒ] **1.** v. t. **a)** tauschen 〈Plätze, Ringe, Küsse〉; umtauschen 〈Geld〉; wechseln 〈Blicke, Worte〉; **~ insults** sich beleidigen; **b)**

(give in place of another) eintauschen **(for** für, gegen); umtauschen *⟨gekaufte⟩ Ware⟩* **(for** gegen). **2.** *n.* **a)** Tausch, *der;* **in ~:** dafür; **in ~ for sth.** für etw.; **b)** *(of money)* Umtausch, *der;* **~ rate, rate of ~:** Wechselkurs, *der;* **c)** *(Teleph.)* Fernmeldeamt, *das*

exchequer [ɪks'tʃekə(r)] *n. (Brit.)* Schatzamt, *das*

excise ['eksaɪz] *n.* Verbrauchsteuer, *die;* **Customs and E~** *(Brit.)* Amt für Zölle und Verbrauchsteuer

excitable [ek'saɪtəbl] *adj.* leicht erregbar

excite [ɪk'saɪt] *v. t.* **a)** *(thrill)* begeistern; **b)** *(agitate)* aufregen. **ex'cited** *adj.* aufgeregt **(at** über + *Akk.);* **get ~:** sich aufregen. **ex'citement** *n.* Aufregung, *die; (enthusiasm)* Begeisterung, *die.* **exciting** [ɪk'saɪtɪŋ] *adj.* aufregend; *(full of suspense)* spannend

exclaim [ɪk'skleɪm] **1.** *v. t.* ausrufen. **2.** *v. i.* aufschreien. **exclamation** [eksklə'meɪʃn] *n.* Ausruf, *der.* **excla'mation mark,** *(Amer.)* **excla'mation point** *ns.* Ausrufezeichen, *das*

exclude [ɪk'sklu:d] *v. t.* ausschließen. **excluding** [ɪk'sklu:dɪŋ] *prep.* **~ drinks/VAT** Getränke ausgenommen/ ohne Mehrwertsteuer. **exclusion** [ɪk'sklu:ʒn] *n.* Ausschluß, *der.* **exclusive** [ɪk'sklu:sɪv] *adj.* **a)** alleinig *⟨Besitzer, Kontrolle⟩;* Allein⟨eigentum⟩; *(Journ.)* Exklusiv⟨bericht, -interview⟩; **b)** *(select)* exklusiv; **c) ~ of** ohne. **ex'clusively** *adv.* ausschließlich

excrement ['ekskrɪmənt] *n.* Kot, *der (geh.)*

excrete [ɪk'skri:t] *v. t.* ausscheiden

excruciating [ɪk'skru:'ʃɪeɪtɪŋ] *adj.* unerträglich

excursion [ɪk'skɜ:ʃn] *n.* Ausflug, *der*

excusable [ɪk'skju:zəbl] *adj.* entschuldbar; verzeihlich

excuse 1. [ɪk'skju:z] *v. t.* **a)** entschuldigen; **~ oneself** sich entschuldigen; **~ me** Entschuldigung; **b)** *(release, exempt)* befreien **(from** von). **2.** [ɪk'skju:s] *n.* Entschuldigung, *die*

ex-di'rectory *adj. (Brit. Teleph.)* Geheim⟨nummer, -anschluß⟩; **be ~:** nicht im Telefonbuch stehen

execute ['eksɪkju:t] *v. t.* **a)** hinrichten; **b)** *(put into effect)* ausführen. **execution** [eksɪ'kju:ʃn] *n.* **a)** Hinrichtung, *die;* **b)** *(putting into effect)* Ausführung, *die.* **exe'cutioner** *n.* Scharfrichter, *der*

executive [ɪg'zekjʊtɪv] **1.** *n.* leitender Angestellter/leitende Angestellte. **2.** *adj.* leitend *⟨Stellung, Funktion⟩*

executor [ɪg'zekjʊtə(r)] *n. (Law)* Testamentsvollstrecker, *der*

exemplary [ɪg'zemplərɪ] *adj.* **a)** *(model)* vorbildlich; **b)** *(deterrent)* exemplarisch

exemplify [ɪg'zemplɪfaɪ] *v. t.* veranschaulichen

exempt [ɪg'zempt] **1.** *adj.* |be| **~ |from sth.|** |von etw.| befreit |sein|. **2.** *v. t.* befreien. **exemption** [ɪg'zempʃn] *n.* Befreiung, *die*

exercise ['eksəsaɪz] **1.** *n.* **a)** Übung, *die;* **b)** *no pl. (physical exertion)* Bewegung, *die;* **take ~:** sich *(Dat.)* Bewegung schaffen. **2.** *v. t.* ausüben *⟨Recht, Macht, Einfluß⟩;* walten lassen *⟨Vorsicht⟩.* **3.** *v. i.* sich *(Dat.)* Bewegung schaffen. **'exercise book** *n.* [Schul]heft, *das*

exert [ɪg'zɜ:t] **1.** *v. t.* aufbieten *⟨Kraft⟩;* ausüben *⟨Einfluß, Druck⟩.* **2.** *v. refl.* sich anstrengen. **exertion** [ɪg'zɜ:ʃn] *n.* **a)** *(of strength, force)* Aufwendung, *die; (of influence, pressure)* Ausübung, *die;* **b)** *(effort)* Anstrengung, *die*

exhale [eks'heɪl] *v. t. & i.* ausatmen

exhaust [ɪg'zɔ:st] **1.** *v. t.* erschöpfen; erschöpfend behandeln *⟨Thema⟩.* **2.** *n. (Motor Veh.)* Auspuff, *der; (gases)* Auspuffgase *Pl.* **ex'hausted** *adj.* erschöpft. **ex'hausting** *adj.* anstrengend. **exhaustion** [ɪg'zɔ:stʃn] *n.* Erschöpfung, *die.* **exhaustive** [ɪg'zɔ:stɪv] *adj.* umfassend. **ex'haust-pipe** *n.* Auspuffrohr, *das*

exhibit [ɪg'zɪbɪt] **1.** *v. t.* ausstellen; zeigen *⟨Mut, Symptome, Angst usw.⟩.* **2.** *n.* Ausstellungsstück, *das.* **exhibition** [eksɪ'bɪʃn] *n.* Ausstellung, *die;* **make an ~ of oneself** sich unmöglich aufführen. **exhibitor** [ɪg'zɪbɪtə(r)] *n.* Aussteller, *der/*Ausstellerin, *die*

exhilarated [ɪg'zɪləreɪtɪd] *adj.* belebt. **exhilarating** [ɪg'zɪləreɪtɪŋ] *adj.* belebend. **exhilaration** [ɪgzɪlə'reɪʃn] *n.* |feeling of| **~:** Hochgefühl, *das*

exhort [ɪg'zɔ:t] *v. t.* ermahnen

exile ['eksaɪl] **1.** *n.* **a)** Exil, *das;* **in/into ~:** im/ins Exil; **b)** *(person)* Verbannte, *der/die.* **2.** *v. t.* verbannen

exist [ɪg'zɪst] *v. i.* existieren; *⟨Zweifel, Gefahr, Problem, Einrichtung:⟩* bestehen; **~ on sth.** von etw. leben. **existence** [ɪg'zɪstəns] *n.* Existenz, *die; (mode of living)* Dasein, *das;* **be in/ come into ~:** existieren/entstehen

exit ['eksɪt] *n. (way out)* Ausgang, *der* (**from** aus); *(for vehicle)* Ausfahrt, *die.* '**exit visa** *n.* Ausreisevisum, *das*
exonerate [ɪg'zɒnəreɪt] *v. t.* entlasten
exorbitant [ɪg'zɔ:bɪtənt] *adj.* [maßlos] überhöht
exorcize ['eksɔ:saɪz] *v. t.* austreiben
exotic [ɪg'zɒtɪk] *adj.* exotisch
expand [ɪk'spænd] **1.** *v. i.* **a)** sich ausdehnen; *(Commerc.)* expandieren; **b)** ~ **on** weiter ausführen. **2.** *v. t.* ausdehnen; *(Commerc.)* erweitern
expanse [ɪk'spæns] *n.* [weite] Fläche
expansion [ɪk'spænʃn] *n.* Ausdehnung, *die; (Commerc.)* Expansion, *die*
expect [ɪk'spekt] *v. t.* **a)** erwarten; ~ **to do sth.** damit rechnen, etw. zu tun; ~ **sb. to do sth.** damit rechnen, daß jmd. etw. tut; *(require)* von jmdm. erwarten, daß er etw. tut; **b)** *(coll.: think, suppose)* glauben; **I** ~ **so** ich glaube schon. **expectancy** [ɪk'spektənsɪ] *n.* Erwartung, *die.* **expectant** [ɪk'spektənt] *adj.* erwartungsvoll; ~ **mother** werdende Mutter. **ex'pectantly** *adv.* erwartungsvoll; gespannt ⟨*warten*⟩. **expectation** [ekspek'teɪʃn] *n.* Erwartung, *die*
expedient [ɪk'spi:dɪənt] **1.** *adj.* angebracht. **2.** *n.* Mittel, *das*
expedition [ekspɪ'dɪʃn] *n.* Expedition, *die*
expel [ɪk'spel] *v. t.,* **-ll-** ausweisen (**from** aus); ~ **sb. from school** jmdn. von der Schule verweisen
expend [ɪk'spend] *v. t.* **a)** aufwenden (**up|on** für); **b)** *(use up)* aufbrauchen (**up|on** für). **expendable** [ɪk'spendəbl] *adj.* entbehrlich; **be** ~; geopfert werden können
expenditure [ɪk'spendɪtʃə(r)] *n.* **a)** *(amount spent)* Ausgaben *Pl.* (**on** für); **b)** *(spending)* Ausgabe, *die*
expense [ɪk'spens] *n.* **a)** Kosten *Pl.;* **at sb.'s** ~: auf jmds. Kosten *(Akk.);* **at one's own** ~: auf eigene Kosten; **b)** *usu. in pl. (Commerc. etc.: amount spent [and repaid])* Spesen *Pl.;* **c)** *(fig.)* |**be**| **at the** ~ **of sth.** auf Kosten von etw. [gehen]. **ex'pense account** *n.* Spesenabrechnung, *die;* **put sth. on one's** ~: etw. als Spesen abrechnen.
expensive [ɪk'spensɪv] *adj.,* **ex'pensively** *adv.* teuer
experience [ɪk'spɪərɪəns] **1.** *n.* Erfahrung, *die; (event)* Erlebnis, *das.* **2.** *v. t.* erleben; haben ⟨*Schwierigkeiten*⟩: verspüren ⟨*Kälte, Schmerz, Gefühl*⟩. **ex'perienced** *adj.* erfahren

experiment 1. [ɪk'sperɪmənt] *n.* **a)** Experiment, *das,* Versuch, *der* (**on an** + *Dat.*); **b)** *(fig.)* Experiment, *das.* **2.** [ɪk'sperɪment] *v. i.* Versuche anstellen (**on an** + *Dat.*). **experimental** [ɪksperɪ'mentl] *adj.* experimentell; Experimentier⟨*theater, -kino*⟩
expert ['ekspɜ:t] **1.** *adj.* ausgezeichnet; **be** ~ **in** *or* **at sth.** Fachmann *od.* Experte für etw. sein; **be** ~ **in** *or* **at doing sth.** etw. ausgezeichnet können. **2.** *n.* Fachmann, *der;* Experte, *der*/Expertin, *die;* **be an** ~ **in** *or* **at/on sth.** Fachmann *od.* Experte in etw. *(Dat.)*/für etw. sein. **expertise** [ekspɜ:'ti:z] *n.* Fachkenntnisse; *(skill)* Können, *das*
expire [ɪk'spaɪə(r)] *v. i.* ablaufen. **expiry** [ɪk'spaɪərɪ] *n.* Ablauf, *der*
explain [ɪk'spleɪn] **1.** *v. t., also abs.* erklären. **2.** *v. refl., often abs.* **please** ~ |**yourself**| bitte erklären Sie mir das. **explain a'way** *v. t.* eine [plausible] Erklärung finden für
explanation [eksplə'neɪʃn] *n.* Erklärung, *die;* **need** ~: einer Erklärung *(Gen.)* bedürfen
explanatory [ɪk'splænətərɪ] *adj.* erklärend; erläuternd ⟨*Bemerkung*⟩
explicable [ɪk'splɪkəbl] *adj.* erklärbar
explicit [ɪk'splɪsɪt] *adj.* klar; ausdrücklich ⟨*Zustimmung, Erwähnung*⟩. **ex'plicitly** *adv.* ausdrücklich; deutlich ⟨*beschreiben, ausdrücken*⟩
explode [ɪk'spləʊd] **1.** *v. i.* explodieren. **2.** *v. t.* zur Explosion bringen
exploit 1. ['eksplɔɪt] *n.* Heldentat, *die.* **2.** [ɪk'splɔɪt] *v. t.* ausbeuten ⟨*Arbeiter usw.*⟩; ausnutzen ⟨*Gutmütigkeit, Freund, Unwissenheit*⟩. **exploitation** [eksplɔɪ'teɪʃn] *n. see* **exploit** 2: Ausbeutung, *die;* Ausnutzung, *die*
exploration [eksplə'reɪʃn] *n.* Erforschung, *die; (fig.)* Untersuchung, *die*
exploratory [ɪk'splɒrətərɪ] *adj.* Forschungs-
explore [ɪk'splɔ:(r)] *v. t.* erforschen; *(fig.)* untersuchen. **ex'plorer** *n.* Entdeckungsreisende, *der/die*
explosion [ɪk'spləʊʒn] *n.* Explosion, *die.* **explosive** [ɪk'spləʊzɪv] **1.** *adj.* explosiv. **2.** *n.* Sprengstoff, *der*
export 1. [ɪk'spɔ:t, 'ekspɔ:t] *v. t.* exportieren; ausführen. **2.** ['ekspɔ:t] *n.* Export, *der.* **ex'porter** *n.* Exporteur, *der*
expose [ɪk'spəʊz] *v. t.* **a)** *(uncover)* freilegen; entblößen ⟨*Haut, Körper*⟩; **b)** offenbaren ⟨*Schwäche*⟩; aufdecken ⟨*Mißstände, Verbrechen*⟩; entlarven ⟨*Täter, Spion*⟩; **c)** *(subject)* ~ **to sth.** ei-

ner Sache *(Dat.)* aussetzen; **d)** *(Photog.)* belichten. **exposed** [ɪk-ˈspəʊzd] *adj. (unprotected)* ungeschützt; ~ **position** exponierte Stellung. **exposure** [ɪkˈspəʊʒə(r)] *n.* **a)** *(to cold etc.)* **die of/suffer from** ~: an Unterkühlung *(Dat.)* sterben/leiden; **b)** *(Photog.) (exposing time)* Belichtung, *die; (picture)* Aufnahme, *die.* **ex'posure meter** *n.* Belichtungsmesser, *der*

expound [ɪkˈspaʊnd] *v. t.* darlegen

express [ɪkˈspres] **1.** *v. t.* ausdrücken; äußern ⟨*Meinung, Wunsch, Dank, Bedauern*⟩; ~ **oneself** sich ausdrücken. **2.** *attrib. adj.* **a)** Eil⟨*brief, -bote usw.*⟩; Schnell⟨*paket, -sendung*⟩; **b)** ausdrücklich ⟨*Wunsch, Absicht*⟩. **3.** *adv.* als Eilsache ⟨*senden*⟩. **4.** *n. (train)* Schnellzug, *der.* **expression** [ɪkˈspreʃn] *n.* Ausdruck, *der.* **expressive** [ɪkˈspresɪv] *adj.* ausdrucksvoll

express: ~ **'train** *n.* D-Zug, *der;* ~**way** *n. (Amer.)* Schnellstraße, *die* **ex'pressly** *adv.* ausdrücklich

expulsion [ɪkˈspʌlʃn] *n.* Ausweisung, *die* (**from** aus); *(from school)* Verweisung, *die* (**from** von)

exquisite [ˈekskwɪzɪt, ɪkˈskwɪzɪt] *adj.* erlesen. **ex'quisitely** *adv.* vorzüglich; kunstvoll ⟨*verziert, geschnitzt*⟩

extend [ɪkˈstend] **1.** *v. t.* verlängern; ausstrecken ⟨*Arm, Bein, Hand*⟩; ausziehen ⟨*Leiter, Teleskop*⟩; verlängern lassen ⟨*Leihbuch, Visum*⟩; ausdehnen ⟨*Einfluß, Macht*⟩; vergrößern ⟨*Haus, Geschäft, Fabrik*⟩; gewähren ⟨*[Gast]freundschaft, Hilfe, Kredit*⟩ (**to** *Dat.*); ~ **the time limit** den Termin hinausschieben. **2.** *v. i.* sich erstrecken; **the season ~s from November to March** die Saison geht von November bis März

extension [ɪkˈstenʃn] *n.* **a)** Verlängerung, *die;* **b)** *(part of house)* Anbau, *der;* **c)** *(telephone)* Nebenanschluß, *der; (number)* Apparat, *der.* **extensive** [ɪkˈstensɪv] *adj.* ausgedehnt; umfangreich ⟨*Reparatur, Wissen, Nachforschungen*⟩; beträchtlich ⟨*Schäden*⟩; weitreichend ⟨*Änderungen*⟩. **ex'tensively** *adv.* beträchtlich ⟨*ändern, beschädigen*⟩; ausführlich ⟨*berichten, schreiben*⟩

extent [ɪkˈstent] *n.* Ausdehnung, *die; (scope)* Umfang, *der; (of damage)* Ausmaß, *das;* **to what ~?** inwieweit?

exterior [ɪkˈstɪərɪə(r)] **1.** *adj.* äußer...;

Außen⟨*fläche, -wand*⟩. **2.** *n.* Äußere, *das; (of house)* Außenwände *Pl.*

exterminate [ɪkˈstɜːmɪneɪt] *v. t.* ausrotten; vertilgen ⟨*Ungeziefer*⟩. **extermination** [ɪkstɜːmɪˈneɪʃn] *n.* Ausrottung, *die; (of pests)* Vertilgung, *die*

external [ɪkˈstɜːnl] *adj.* äußer...; Außen⟨*fläche, -abmessungen*⟩; **purely** ~: rein äußerlich; **for** ~ **use only** nur äußerlich anzuwenden

extinct [ɪkˈstɪŋkt] *adj.* erloschen ⟨*Vulkan*⟩; ausgestorben ⟨*Art, Rasse, Gattung*⟩. **extinction** [ɪkˈstɪŋkʃn] *n.* Aussterben, *das*

extinguish [ɪkˈstɪŋgwɪʃ] *v. t.* löschen. **ex'tinguisher** *n.* Feuerlöscher, *der*

extol [ɪkˈstɒl] *v. t.,* **-ll-** rühmen; preisen

extort [ɪkˈstɔːt] *v. t.* erpressen (**out of** von). **extortion** [ɪkˈstɔːʃn] *n.* Erpressung, *die.* **extortionate** [ɪkˈstɔːʃənət] *adj.* Wucher⟨*preis, -zinsen usw.*⟩; maßlos überzogen ⟨*Forderung*⟩

extra [ˈekstrə] **1.** *adj.* zusätzlich; Mehr⟨*arbeit, -kosten, -ausgaben*⟩; Sonder⟨*bus, -zug*⟩. **2.** *adv.* **a)** *(more than usually)* besonders; extra ⟨*lang, stark, fein*⟩; **b)** *(additionally)* extra; **packing and postage** ~: zuzüglich Verpackung und Porto. **3.** *n.* **a)** *(added to services, salary, etc.)* zusätzliche Leistung; **b)** *(in play, film, etc.)* Statist, *der*/Statistin, *die*

extract **1.** [ˈekstrækt] *n.* **a)** Extrakt, *der (fachspr. auch: das);* **b)** *(from book, music, etc.)* Auszug, *der.* **2.** [ɪkˈstrækt] *v. t.* ziehen ⟨*Zahn*⟩; herausziehen ⟨*Dorn, Splitter usw.*⟩. **extraction** [ɪkˈstrækʃn] *n. (of tooth)* Extraktion, *die; (of thorn, splinter, etc.)* Herausziehen, *das.* **ex'tractor fan** *n.* Entlüfter, *der*

extradite [ˈekstrədaɪt] *v. t.* ausliefern. **extradition** [ekstrəˈdɪʃn] *n.* Auslieferung, *die*

extraordinary [ɪkˈstrɔːdɪnərɪ] *adj.* außergewöhnlich; merkwürdig ⟨*Benehmen*⟩; **how** ~! wie seltsam!

extravagance [ɪkˈstrævəgəns] *n.* **a)** Extravaganz, *die;* **b)** *(extravagant thing)* Luxus, *der*

extravagant [ɪkˈstrævəgənt] *adj.* verschwenderisch; aufwendig ⟨*Lebensstil*⟩; teuer ⟨*Geschmack*⟩

extreme [ɪkˈstriːm] **1.** *adj.* **a)** äußerst... ⟨*Spitze, Rand, Ende*⟩; extrem ⟨*Gegensätze, Hitze, Kälte*⟩; höchst... ⟨*Gefahr*⟩; äußerst... ⟨*Notfall, Höflichkeit, Bescheidenheit*⟩; stärkst... ⟨*Schmerzen*⟩; größt... ⟨*Wichtigkeit*⟩; **at the ~ edge/left** ganz am Rand/ganz links; **b)**

(not moderate) extrem; drastisch ⟨*Maßnahme*⟩. **2.** *n.* Extrem, *das;* go to ~s vor nichts zurückschrecken; go from one ~ to the other von einem Extrem ins andere fallen. **ex'tremely** *adv.* äußerst. **extremist** [ık'striːmıst] *n.* Extremist, *der*/Extremistin, *die; attrib.* extremistisch. **extremity** [ık-'stremıtı] *n.* äußerstes Ende

extricate ['ekstrıkeıt] *v. t.* ~ sth. from sth. etw. aus etw. herausziehen; ~ oneself/sb. from sth. sich/jmdn. aus etw. befreien

extrovert ['ekstrəvɜːt] **1.** *n.* extrovertierter Mensch; **be an** ~: extrovertiert sein. **2.** *adj.* extrovertiert

exuberant [ıg'zjuːbərənt] *adj.* **be** ~: sich überschwenglich freuen

exude [ıg'zjuːd] *v. t.* absondern; *(fig.)* ausstrahlen

exult [ıg'zʌlt] *v. i.* jubeln (**in, at, over** über + *Akk.*)

eye [aı] **1.** *n.* **a)** Auge, *das;* keep an ~ on sb./sth. auf jmdn./etw. aufpassen; see ~ to ~: einer Meinung sein; with one's ~s shut *(fig.)* blind; *(easily)* im Schlaf; **be up to one's** ~s in work/debt bis über beide Ohren in Arbeit/Schulden stecken *(ugs.);* **b)** *(of needle)* Öhr, *das; (metal loop)* Öse, *die.* **2.** *v. t.,* beäugen; ~ sb. up and down jmdn. von oben bis unten mustern

eye: ~**ball** *n.* Augapfel, *der;* ~**brow** *n.* Augenbraue, *die;* ~**lash** *n.* Augenwimper, *die;* ~**-level** *n.* Augenhöhe, *die; attrib.* in Augenhöhe *nachgestellt;* **at** ~**level** in Augenhöhe; ~**lid** *n.* Augenlid, *das;* ~**-shadow** *n.* Lidschatten, *der;* ~**sight** *n.* Sehkraft, *die;* **have good** ~sight gute Augen haben; **his** ~sight is poor er hat schlechte Augen; ~**sore** *n.* Schandfleck, *der;* ~**witness** *n.* Augenzeuge, *der*/-zeugin, *die*

F

F, f [ef] *n.* F, f, *das*

fable ['feıbl] *n.* Fabel, *die; (myth, lie)* Märchen, *das*

fabric ['fæbrık] *n.* Gewebe, *das*

fabricate ['fæbrıkeıt] *v. t. (invent)* erfinden. **fabrication** [fæbrıkeıʃn] *n.* Erfindung, *die*

fabulous ['fæbjʊləs] *adj.* **a)** sagenhaft; **b)** *(coll.: marvellous)* fabelhaft *(ugs.)*

face [feıs] **1.** *n.* **a)** Gesicht, *das;* lie ~ down|ward| ⟨*Person/Buch:*⟩ auf dem Bauch/Gesicht liegen; **make** *or* **pull a** ~/~s Grimassen schneiden; **on the** ~ of it dem Anschein nach; **in the** ~ of sth. trotz etw. *(Gen.);* **b)** *(of mountain, cliff)* Wand, *die; (of clock, watch)* Zifferblatt, *das; (of dice)* Seite, *die; (of coin, playing-card)* Vorderseite, *die.* **2.** *v. t.* **a)** sich wenden zu; |stand| **facing one another** sich *(Dat.)* gegenüber [stehen]; **b)** *(fig.)* ins Auge sehen (+ *Dat.*) ⟨*Tod, Vorstellung*⟩; stehen vor (+ *Dat.*) ⟨*Ruin, Entscheidung*⟩; ~ **the facts** den Tatsachen ins Gesicht sehen; **be** ~**d with sth.** sich einer Sache *(Dat.)* gegenübersehen; **c)** *(coll.: bear)* verkraften. **3.** *v. i. (in train etc.)* ~ **forwards/backwards** ⟨*Person:*⟩ in/entgegen Fahrtrichtung sitzen. **face 'up to** *v. t.* ins Auge sehen (+ *Dat.*); sich abfinden mit ⟨*Möglichkeit*⟩

face: ~**-cream** *n.* Gesichtscreme, *die;* ~**-flannel** *n. (Brit.)* Waschlappen, *der;* ~**-lift** *n.* **a)** Facelifting, *das;* **have** *or* **get a** ~-lift sich liften lassen; **b)** *(fig.)* Verschönerung, *die*

facet ['fæsıt] *n.* Facette, *die; (fig.)* Aspekt, *der*

facetious [fə'siːʃəs] *adj.* [gewollt] witzig

face: ~**-to-**~: persönlich ⟨*Gespräch, Treffen*⟩; ~ **value** *n.* Nennwert, *der;* **accept sth. at** |its| ~ **value** *(fig.)* etw. für bare Münze nehmen

facial ['feıʃl] *adj.* Gesichts-

facile ['fæsaıl] *adj.* nichtssagend

facilities [fə'sılıtız] *n. pl.* Einrichtungen; **cooking/washing** ~: Koch-/Waschgelegenheit, *die;* **sports** ~: Sportanlagen; **shopping** ~: Einkaufsmöglichkeiten

facsimile [fæk'sımılı] *n.* **a)** Faksimile, *das;* **b)** *see* fax 1

fact [fækt] *n.* Tatsache, *die;* ~s and figures Fakten und Zahlen; the ~ remains that ...: Tatsache bleibt: ...; the true ~s of the case *or* matter der wahre Sachverhalt; know for a ~ that ...: genau wissen, daß ...; in ~: tatsächlich

faction ['fækʃn] *n.* Splittergruppe, *die*

factor ['fæktə(r)] *n.* Faktor, *der*

factory ['fæktərı] *n.* Fabrik, *die.* **'factory farm** *n.* Agrarfabrik, *die*

factual ['fæktjʊəl] *adj.* sachlich
faculty ['fækəltı] *n.* **a)** Fähigkeit, *die;* **mental** ~: geistige Kraft; **b)** *(Univ.)* Fakultät, *die*
fad [fæd] *n.* Marotte, *die*
fade [feɪd] *v. i.* **a)** ⟨*Blätter, Blumen:*⟩ [ver]welken; **b)** ~ |in colour| [ver]bleichen; **the light** ~**d** es dunkelte; **c)** ⟨*Laut:*⟩ verklingen; **d)** *(fig.)* verblassen; ⟨*Schönheit:*⟩ verblühen; ⟨*Hoffnung:*⟩ schwinden; **e)** *(blend)* übergehen (into in + *Akk.*). **fade aʹway** *v. i.* schwinden; ⟨*Laut:*⟩ verklingen (into in + *Dat.*)
faded ['feɪdɪd] *adj.* welk ⟨*Blume, Blatt, Laub*⟩; verblichen ⟨*Stoff, Farbe*⟩
fag [fæg] *n.* **a)** *(Brit. coll.)* Schinderei, *die (ugs.);* **b)** *(sl.: cigarette)* Stäbchen, *das (ugs.)*
fail [feɪl] **1.** *v. i.* **a)** scheitern; *(in examination)* nicht bestehen (in in + *Dat.*); **b)** *(become weaker)*⟨*Augenlicht, Gehör, Stärke:*⟩ nachlassen; **c)** *(break down, stop)* ⟨*Versorgung:*⟩ zusammenbrechen; ⟨*Motor:*⟩ aussetzen; ⟨*Batterie, Pumpe:*⟩ ausfallen; ⟨*Bremse:*⟩ versagen. **2.** *v. t.* **a)** ~ **to do sth.** *(not succeed in doing)* etw. nicht tun [können]; ~ **to achieve one's purpose/aim** seine Absicht/sein Ziel verfehlen; **b)** *(be unsuccessful in)* nicht bestehen ⟨*Prüfung*⟩; **c)** *(reject)* durchfallen lassen *(ugs.)* ⟨*Prüfling*⟩; **d)** ~ **to do sth.** *(not do)* etw. nicht tun; *(neglect to do)* [es] versäumen, etw. zu tun; **not** ~ **to do sth.** etw. tun; **e)** **words** ~ **me** mir fehlen die Worte; **his courage** ~**ed him** ihn verließ der Mut. **3.** *n.* **without** ~: auf jeden Fall. **ʹfailing 1.** *n.* Schwäche, *die.* **2.** *prep.* ~ **that** andernfalls. **failure** ['feɪljə(r)] *n.* **a)** *(omission, neglect)* Versäumnis, *das;* **b)** *(lack of success)* Scheitern, *das;* **end in** ~: scheitern; **c)** *(person or thing)* Versager, *der;* **our plan/attempt was a** ~: unser Plan/Versuch war fehlgeschlagen
faint [feɪnt] **1.** *adj.* **a)** matt ⟨*Licht, Farbe, Stimme, Lächeln*⟩; schwach ⟨*Geruch, Duft*⟩; leise ⟨*Flüstern, Geräusch, Stimme*⟩; entfernt ⟨*Ähnlichkeit*⟩; undeutlich ⟨*Umriß, Linie, Spur, Fotokopie*⟩; **b)** *(giddy, weak)* matt; **she felt** ~: ihr war schwindelig. **2.** *v. i.* ohnmächtig werden (**from** vor + *Dat.*). **3.** *n.* Ohnmacht, *die.* **ʹfaintly** *adv.* schwach; entfernt ⟨*sich ähneln*⟩
¹fair [feə(r)] *n. (fun-~)* Jahrmarkt, *der;* *(exhibition)* Messe, *die;* **book/trade** ~: Buch-/Handelsmesse, *die*

²fair 1. *adj.* **a)** *(just)* gerecht; begründet ⟨*Beschwerde, Annahme*⟩; fair ⟨*Spiel, Kampf, Prozeß, Preis, Beurteilung, Handel*⟩; ~ **play** Fairneß, *die;* **b)** *(not bad, pretty good)* ganz gut ⟨*Bilanz, Anzahl, Chance*⟩; ziemlich ⟨*Maß, Geschwindigkeit*⟩; **c)** *(blond)* blond ⟨*Haar, Person*⟩; *(light)* hell ⟨*Haut*⟩; *(~-skinned)* hellhäutig ⟨*Person*⟩; schön ⟨*Wetter, Tag*⟩. **ʹfair-haired 1.** *adj.* blond. **2.** *adv.* fair ⟨*kämpfen, spielen*⟩. **ʹfairly** *adv.* **a)** fair ⟨*kämpfen, spielen*⟩; gerecht ⟨*bestrafen, beurteilen, behandeln*⟩; **b)** *(rather)* ziemlich. **ʹfairness** *n.* Gerechtigkeit, *die;* **in all** ~ |to **sb.**| um fair [gegen jmdn.] zu sein
fairy ['feərı] *n.* Fee, *die*
fairy: ~ **ʹgodmother** *n.* gute Fee; ~ **story,** ~**-tale** *ns.* Märchen, *das*
faith [feɪθ] *n.* **a)** *(reliance, trust)* Vertrauen, *das* (in zu); **have** ~ **in oneself** Selbstvertrauen haben; **in good** ~: in gutem Glauben; **b)** *(religious belief)* Glaube, *der.* **faithful** ['feɪθfl] *adj.* **a)** treu (to *Dat.*); **b)** *(conscientious)* pflichtbewußt; [ge]treu ⟨*Diener*⟩; **c)** *(accurate)* [wahrheits]getreu; originalgetreu ⟨*Wiedergabe, Kopie*⟩. **ʹfaithfully** *adv.* **a)** treu ⟨*dienen*⟩; pflichtbewußt ⟨*überbringen, zustellen*⟩; hoch und heilig ⟨*versprechen*⟩; **b)** *(accurately)* wahrheitsgetreu ⟨*erzählen*⟩; originalgetreu ⟨*wiedergeben*⟩; genau ⟨*befolgen*⟩; **c) yours** ~: hochachtungsvoll
fake [feɪk] **1.** *adj.* unecht; gefälscht ⟨*Dokument, Banknote, Münze*⟩. **2.** *n.* **a)** Imitation, *die;* *(painting)* Fälschung, *die;* **b)** *(person)* Schwindler, *der/*Schwindlerin, *die.* **3.** *v. t.* fälschen ⟨*Unterschrift*⟩; vortäuschen ⟨*Krankheit, Unfall*⟩
falcon ['fɔːlkn] *n.* Falke, *der*
fall [fɔːl] **1.** *n.* **a)** Fallen, *das;* *(of person)* Sturz, *der;* ~ **of snow/rain** Schnee-/Regenfall, *der;* **have a** ~: stürzen; **b)** *(collapse, defeat)* Fall, *der;* *(of dynasty, empire)* Untergang, *der;* **c)** *(decrease)* Rückgang, *der;* **d)** *(Amer.: autumn)* Herbst, *der.* **2.** *v. i.,* **fell** [fel], ~**en** ['fɔːln] **a)** fallen; ⟨*Baum:*⟩ umstürzen; ⟨*Pferd:*⟩ stürzen; ~ **off sth.,** ~ **down from sth.** von etw. [herunter]fallen; ~ **down |into| sth.** in etw. *(Akk.)* [hinein]fallen; ~ **to the ground** auf den Boden fallen; ~ **down the stairs** *or* **downstairs** die Treppe herunter-/hinunterfallen; **b)** ⟨*Nacht, Dunkelheit:*⟩ hereinbrechen; ⟨*Abend:*⟩ anbrechen; **c)** ⟨*Blätter:*⟩ [ab]fallen; **d)** *(sink)* sinken;

⟨*Barometer:*⟩ fallen; ⟨*Absatz, Verkauf:*⟩ zurückgehen; ~ **by 10 per cent/ from 10[°C] to 0[°C]** um 10%/von 10[°C] auf 0[°C] sinken; **e)** *(be killed)* ⟨*Soldat:*⟩ fallen; **f)** *(collapse)* einstürzen; ~ **to pieces,** ~ **apart** auseinanderfallen; **g)** *(occur)* fallen (on auf + *Akk.*). **fall 'back** *v.i.* zurückweichen. **fall 'back on** *v.t.* zurückgreifen auf (+ *Akk.*). **fall 'down** *v.i.* **a)** *see* **fall 2 a;** **b)** ⟨*Brücke, Gebäude:*⟩ einstürzen. **'fall for** *v.t. (coll.)* ~ **for sb.** sich in jmdn. verknallen *(ugs.):* ~ **for sth.** auf etw. *(Akk.)* hereinfallen *(ugs.).* **fall 'in** *v.i.* **a)** hineinfallen; **b)** *(Mil.)* antreten; ~ **in!** angetreten!; **c)** ⟨*Gebäude, Wand usw.:*⟩ einstürzen. **fall 'off** *v.i.* **a)** herunterfallen; **b)** *(diminish)* nachlassen. **fall 'out** *v.i.* **a)** ⟨*Haare, Federn*⟩ ausfallen; **b)** *(quarrel)* ~ **out** |with sb.| sich [mit jmdm.] streiten. **fall 'over** *v.i.* umfallen; ⟨*Person:*⟩ [hin]fallen. **fall 'through** *v.i. (fig.)* ins Wasser fallen *(ugs.)*

fallacy ['fæləsɪ] *n.* Irrtum, *der*
fallen *see* **fall 2**
fallible ['fælɪbl] *adj.* nicht unfehlbar; fehlbar ⟨*Person*⟩
'fall-out *n.* radioaktiver Niederschlag
fallow ['fæləʊ] *adj.* brachliegend; ~ **ground/land** Brache, *die*/Brachland, *das;* **lie ~:** brachliegen
false [fɔːls, fɒls] *adj.* falsch; gefälscht ⟨*Urkunde, Dokument*⟩; künstlich ⟨*Wimpern*⟩; **under a ~ name** unter falschem Namen. **'falsely** *adv.* falsch; fälschlich[erweise] ⟨*annehmen, glauben, behaupten, beschuldigen*⟩
false: ~ **a'larm** *n.* blinder Alarm; ~ **'start** *n.* Fehlstart, *der;* ~ **'teeth** *n. pl.* [künstliches] Gebiß
falsify ['fɔːlsɪfaɪ] *v.t. (alter)* fälschen; *(misrepresent)* verfälschen ⟨*Tatsachen, Wahrheit*⟩
falter ['fɔːltə(r)] *v.i.* stocken
fame [feɪm] *n.* Ruhm, *der*
familiar [fə'mɪljə(r)] *adj.* **a)** vertraut; bekannt ⟨*Gesicht, Name, Lied*⟩; **he looks ~:** er kommt mir bekannt vor; **b)** *(informal)* ungezwungen ⟨*Sprache, Art*⟩. **familiarity** [fəmɪlɪ'ærɪtɪ] *n.* Vertrautheit, *die.* **familiarize** [fə'mɪljəraɪz] *v.t.* vertraut machen (**with** mit)
family ['fæmlɪ] *n.* Familie, *die*
family: ~ **name** *n.* Familienname, *der;* ~ **'planning** *n.* Familienplanung, *die;* ~ **'tree** *n.* Stammbaum, *der*
famine ['fæmɪn] *n.* Hungersnot, *die*

famished ['fæmɪʃt] *adj.* ausgehungert; **I'm absolutely ~** *(coll.)* ich sterbe vor Hunger *(ugs.)*
famous ['feɪməs] *adj.* berühmt
¹fan [fæn] **1.** *n.* Fächer, *der; (apparatus)* Ventilator, *der.* **2.** *v.t.,* **-nn-** fächeln ⟨*Gesicht*⟩; anfachen ⟨*Feuer*⟩; ~ **oneself/sb.** sich/jmdm. Luft zufächeln. **fan 'out** *v.i.* fächern; ⟨*Soldaten:*⟩ ausfächern
²fan *n. (devotee)* Fan, *der*
fanatic [fə'nætɪk] *n.* Fanatiker, *der*/Fanatikerin, *die.* **fanatical** [fə'nætɪkl] *adj.* fanatisch. **fanaticism** [fə'nætɪsɪzm] *n.* Fanatismus, *der*
'fan belt *n.* Keilriemen, *der*
fanciful ['fænsɪfl] *adj.* überspannt ⟨*Vorstellung, Gedanke*⟩; phantastisch ⟨*Gemälde, Design*⟩
'fan club *n.* Fanklub, *der*
fancy ['fænsɪ] **1.** *n.* **a)** *(taste, inclination)* **he has taken a ~ to a new car/her** ein neues Auto/sie hat es ihm angetan; **take** *or* **catch sb.'s ~:** jmdm. gefallen; **b)** *(whim)* Laune, *die;* **tickle sb.'s ~:** jmdn. reizen. **2.** *attrib. adj.* kunstvoll ⟨*Arbeit, Muster*⟩; fein[st] ⟨*Kuchen, Spitzen*⟩. **3.** *v.t.* **a)** *(imagine)* sich *(Dat.)* einbilden; ~ **that!** *(coll.)* sieh mal einer an!; **b)** *(suppose)* glauben; **c)** *(wish to have)* mögen; **what do you ~ for dinner?** was hättest du gern zum Abendessen? **fancy 'dress** *n.* [Masken]kostüm, *das;* **in ~:** kostümiert; **fancy-dress party** Kostümfest, *das;* **fancy-dress ball** Maskenball, *der*
fanfare ['fænfeə(r)] *n.* Fanfare, *die*
fang [fæŋ] *n.* Reißzahn, *der; (of snake)* Giftzahn, *der*
fan: ~ **heater** *n.* Heizlüfter, *der;* ~ **light** *n.* Oberlicht, *das;* ~ **mail** *n.* Fanpost, *die*
fantastic [fæn'tæstɪk] *adj.* **a)** *(grotesque, quaint)* bizarr; **b)** *(coll.: excellent)* phantastisch *(ugs.)*
fantasy ['fæntəzɪ] *n.* Phantasie, *die; (mental image)* Phantasiegebilde, *das*
far [fɑː(r)] **1.** *adv.* weit; ~ **above/below** hoch über/tief unter (+ *Dat.*); hoch oben/tief unten; **as** ~ **as Munich/the church** bis [nach] München/bis zur Kirche; ~ **and wide** weit und breit; **from** ~ **and wide** von fern und nah; ~ **too much** viel zu; ~ **longer/better** weit[aus] länger/besser; **as** ~ **as I remember/know** soweit ich mich erinnere/weiß; **go so** ~ **as to do sth.** so weit gehen und etw. tun; **so** ~ *(until now)* bisher; **so** ~ **so good** so weit, so gut; **by ~:** bei wei-

tem; ~ **from easy/good** alles andere
als leicht/gut. **2.** *adj.* **a)** *(remote)* weit
entfernt; *(in time)* fern; **in the ~ distance** in weiter Ferne; **b)** *(more
remote)* weiter entfernt; **the ~ bank of
the river/side of the road** das andere
Flußufer/die andere Straßenseite; **the
~ door/wall** *etc.* die hintere Tür/
Wand *usw.*

farce [fɑ:s] *n.* Farce, *die.* **farcical**
[ˈfɑ:sɪkl] *adj. (absurd)* farcenhaft

fare [feə(r)] *n.* **a)** *(price)* Fahrpreis, *der;
(money)* Fahrgeld, *das;* **what** *or* **how
much is the ~?** was kostet die Fahrt?;
b) *(food)* Kost, *die*

Far: ~ **'East** *n.* **the ~ East** der Ferne
Osten; ~ **'Eastern** *adj.* fernöstlich;
des Fernen Ostens *nachgestellt*

farewell [feəˈwel] **1.** *int.* leb[e] wohl
(veralt.). **2.** *n. attrib.* ~ **speech/gift** Ab-
schiedsrede, *die/*-geschenk, *das*

far-'fetched *adj.* weit hergeholt

farm [fɑ:m] **1.** *n.* [Bauern]hof, *der;
(larger)* Gut, *das;* ~ **animals** Nutzvieh,
das. **2.** *v.t.* bebauen ⟨*Land*⟩. **3.** *v.i.*
Landwirtschaft treiben. **'farmer** *n.*
Landwirt, *der/*-wirtin, *die*

'farmhouse *n.* Bauernhaus, *das;
(larger)* Gutshaus, *das*

'farming *n.* Landwirtschaft, *die*

farm: ~ **land** *n.* Acker- und Weide-
land, *das;* ~ **yard** *n.* Hof, *der*

far: ~ **'reaching** *adj.* weitreichend;
~ **-sighted** *adj.* **a)** *(fig.)* weitblickend; **b)** *(Amer.: long-sighted)*
weitsichtig

fart [fɑ:t] *(coarse)* **1.** *v.i.* furzen *(derb).*
2. *n.* Furz, *der (derb)*

farther [ˈfɑ:ðə(r)] *see* **further 1 a, 2**

farthest [ˈfɑ:ðɪst] *see* **furthest**

fascinate [ˈfæsɪneɪt] *v.t.* fesseln; bezaubern. **fascination** [fæsɪˈneɪʃn] *n.*
Zauber, *der;* **have a ~ for sb.** einen be-
sonderen Reiz auf jmdn. ausüben

Fascism [ˈfæʃɪzm] *n.* Faschismus, *der.*
Fascist [ˈfæʃɪst] **1.** *n.* Faschist,
*der/*Faschistin, *die.* **2.** *adj.* faschistisch

fashion [ˈfæʃn] **1.** *n.* **a)** Mode, *die;* **b)**
(manner) Art [und Weise]; **talk/be-
have in a peculiar ~:** merkwürdig
sprechen/sich merkwürdig verhalten.
2. *v.t.* formen **(out of, from** aus; [in]to
zu). **fashionable** [ˈfæʃənəbl] *adj.*
modisch; vornehm ⟨*Hotel, Restaurant*⟩; Mode⟨*farbe, -autor*⟩. **fashionably** [ˈfæʃənəblɪ] *adv.* modisch

¹fast [fɑ:st] **1.** *v.i.* fasten. **2.** *n.* Fasten,
das

²fast 1. *adj.* **a)** *(fixed, attached)* fest;
make [the boat] ~: das Boot festmachen; **hard and ~:** fest; bindend
⟨*Regel*⟩; klar ⟨*Entscheidung*⟩; **b)**
(rapid) schnell; ~ **train** Schnellzug,
der; D-Zug, *der;* **c) be [ten minutes] ~**
⟨*Uhr:*⟩ [zehn Minuten] vorgehen. **2.**
adv. **a) be ~ asleep** fest schlafen;
(when one should be awake) fest einge-
schlafen sein; **b)** *(quickly)* schnell

fasten [ˈfɑ:sn] *v.t.* befestigen **(on,** to
an + *Dat.*); zumachen ⟨*Kleid,
Spange, Jacke*⟩; [ab]schließen ⟨*Tür*⟩;
anstecken ⟨*Brosche*⟩ **(to an** + *Akk.*); ~
one's seat-belt sich anschnallen. **'fastener, 'fastening** *ns.* Verschluß, *der*

fastidious [fæˈstɪdɪəs] *adj.* wählerisch; *(hard to please)* heikel

'fast lane *n.* Überholspur, *die;* **life in
the ~** *(fig.)* Leben auf vollen Touren
(ugs.)

fat [fæt] **1.** *adj.* dick; rund ⟨*Wangen,
Gesicht*⟩. **2.** *n.* Fett, *das*

fatal [ˈfeɪtl] *adj.* **a)** *(disastrous)* verheerend **(to** für); **it would be ~:** das wäre
das Ende; **b)** *(deadly)* tödlich ⟨*Unfall,
Verletzung*⟩. **fatality** [fəˈtælɪtɪ] *n.* To-
desopfer, *das.* **fatally** *adv.* tödlich;
be ~ ill todkrank sein

fate [feɪt] *n.* Schicksal, *das*

'fat-head *n.* Dummkopf, *der (ugs.)*

father [ˈfɑ:ðə(r)] *n.* Vater, *der.* **Father
'Christmas** *n.* der Weihnachtsmann.
father-in-law *n., pl.* ~ **s-in-law**
Schwiegervater, *der.* **'fatherly** *adj.*
väterlich

fathom [ˈfæðəm] **1.** *n. (Naut.)* Faden,
der. **2.** *v.t. (comprehend)* verstehen; ~
sb./sth. out jmdn./etw. ergründen

fatigue [fəˈti:g] **1.** *n.* Ermüdung, *die.*
2. *v.t.* ermüden

'fatness *n.* Dicke, *die*

fatten [ˈfætn] *v.t.* herausfüttern ⟨*Person*⟩; mästen ⟨*Tier*⟩. **'fattening** *adj.*
be ~: dick machen

fatty [ˈfætɪ] *adj.* fett ⟨*Fleisch, Soße*⟩;
fetthaltig ⟨*Speise, Nahrungsmittel*⟩

faucet [ˈfɔ:sɪt] *n. (Amer.)* Wasserhahn,
der

fault [fɔ:lt, fɒlt] *n.* **a)** Fehler, *der;* **b)**
(responsibility) Schuld, *die;* **it's your
~:** du bist schuld; **it isn't my ~:** ich
habe keine Schuld; **be at ~:** im Unrecht sein; **c)** *(in machinery; also
Electr.)* Defekt, *der.* **'faultless** *adj.*
einwandfrei. **'faulty** *adj.* fehlerhaft;
defekt ⟨*Gerät, usw.*⟩

fauna [ˈfɔ:nə] *n., pl.* ~ **e** [ˈfɔ:ni:] *or* ~ **s**
Fauna, *die*

favor etc. (Amer.) see **favour** etc.
favour ['feɪvə(r)] **1.** n. **a)** Gunst, die; **b)** (kindness) Gefallen, der; **ask sb. a ~**, **ask a ~ of sb.** jmdn. um einen Gefallen bitten; **do sb. a ~**, **do a ~ for sb.** jmdm. einen Gefallen tun; **as a ~:** aus Gefälligkeit; **c) be in ~ of sth.** für etw. sein. **2.** v. t. bevorzugen
favourable ['feɪvərəbl] adj. (Brit.) **a)** günstig ⟨Eindruck, Licht⟩; gewogen ⟨Haltung, Einstellung⟩; freundlich ⟨Erwähnung⟩; positiv ⟨Bericht[erstattung], Bemerkung⟩; **b)** (helpful) günstig (to für) ⟨Wetter, Wind, Umstand⟩.
favourably ['feɪvərəbli] adv. (Brit.) wohlwollend; **be ~ disposed towards sb./sth.** jmdm./einer Sache positiv gegenüberstehen
favourite ['feɪvərɪt] (Brit.) **1.** adj. Lieblings-. **2.** n. **a)** Liebling, der; (food/country etc.) Lieblingsessen, das/-land, das usw.; **this/he is my ~:** das/ihn mag ich am liebsten; **b)** (Sport) Favorit, der/Favoritin, die.
favouritism ['feɪvərɪtɪzm] n. (Brit.) Begünstigung, die; (when selecting sb. for a post etc.) Günstlingswirtschaft, die
fawn [fɔːn] **1.** n. **a)** (colour) Rehbraun, das; **b)** (young deer) [Dam]kitz, das. **2.** adj. rehfarben
fax [fæks] **1.** n. [Tele]fax, das. **2.** v. t. faxen. **'fax machine** n. Faxgerät, das
FBI abbr. (Amer.) Federal Bureau of Investigation FBI, das
fear [fɪə(r)] **1.** n. Angst, die (of vor + Dat.); (instance) Befürchtung, die; **~ of death** or **dying/heights** Todes-/Höhenangst, die; **~ of doing sth.** Angst davor, etw. zu tun; **in ~:** angstvoll; **no ~!** (coll.) keine Bange! (ugs.). **2.** v. t. **a)** **~ sb./sth.** vor jmdm./etw. Angst haben; **~ to do** or **doing sth.** Angst haben, etw. zu tun; **b)** (be worried about) befürchten; **~ |that ...|** fürchten[, daß ...]. **fearful** ['fɪəfl] adj. **a)** (terrible) furchtbar; **b)** (frightened) ängstlich; **be ~ of sth./sb.** vor etw./jmdm. Angst haben. **'fearless** adj., **'fearlessly** adv. furchtlos
feasibility [fiːzɪ'bɪlɪtɪ] n. Durchführbarkeit, die
feasible ['fiːzɪbl] adj. durchführbar
feast [fiːst] **1.** n. **a)** (Relig.) Fest, das; **b)** (banquet) Festessen, das. **2.** v. i. schlemmen; **~ on sth.** sich an etw. (Dat.) gütlich tun
feat [fiːt] n. Meisterleistung, die
feather ['feðə(r)] n. Feder, die.

'featherweight n. (Boxing) Federgewicht, das
feature ['fiːtʃə(r)] **1.** n. **a)** usu. in pl. (of face) Gesichtszug, der; **b)** (characteristic) [charakteristisches] Merkmal; **be a ~ of sth.** charakteristisch für etw. sein; **c)** (Journ.) Feature, das; **d)** (Cinemat.) **~ |film|** Hauptfilm, der. **2.** v. t. vorrangig vorstellen; (in film) in der Hauptrolle zeigen. **3.** v. i. vorkommen; **~ in** (be important) eine bedeutende Rolle haben bei
Feb. abbr. **February** Febr.
February ['februərɪ] n. Februar, der (see also **August**): Februar, der
fed [fed] **1.** see **feed** 1, 2. **2.** pred. adj. (sl.) **be/get ~ up with sb./sth.** jmdn./ etw. satt haben/kriegen (ugs.); **I'm ~ up** Ich hab' die Nase voll (ugs.)
federal ['fedərl] adj. Bundes-; föderativ ⟨System⟩. **federation** [fedə'reɪʃn] n. Föderation, die
fee [fiː] n. Gebühr, die; (of doctor, lawyer, etc.) Honorar, das
feeble ['fiːbl] adj. schwach; wenig überzeugend ⟨Entschuldigung⟩; zaghaft ⟨Versuch⟩; lahm (ugs.) ⟨Witz⟩
feed [fiːd] **1.** v. t., **fed** [fed] **a)** füttern; **~ sb./an animal with sth.** jmdm. etw. zu essen/einem Tier [etw.] zu fressen geben; **b)** (provide food for) ernähren (on, with mit). **2.** v. i., **fed** ⟨Tier:⟩ fressen (from aus); ⟨Person:⟩ essen (off von); **~ on sth.** ⟨Tier:⟩ etw. fressen. **3.** n. **a)** (for baby) Mahlzeit, die; **b)** (fodder) Futter, das. **'feedback** n. Reaktion, die
feel [fiːl] **1.** v. t., **felt** [felt] **a)** (explore by touch) befühlen; **b)** (perceive by touch) fühlen; (become aware of) bemerken; (have sensation of) spüren; **c)** (experience) empfinden; verspüren ⟨Drang⟩; **~ the cold/heat** unter der Kälte/Hitze leiden; **~ |that| ...:** das Gefühl haben, daß ...; (think) glauben, daß ... **2.** v. i., **felt** **a)** **~ |about| in sth. |for sth.|** in etw. (Dat.) [nach etw.] [herum]suchen; **b)** (be conscious that one is) sich ... fühlen; **~ angry/sure/disappointed** böse/ sicher/enttäuscht sein; **~ like sth./ doing sth.** auf etw. (Akk.) Lust haben/ Lust haben, etw. zu tun; **c)** (be consciously perceived as) sich ... anfühlen. **'feel for** v. t. **~ for sb.** mit jmdm. Mitleid haben
feeler n. Fühler, der. **'feeling** n. **a)** Gefühl, das; (sense of touch) |sense of| **~:** Tastsinn, der; **hurt sb.'s ~s** jmdn. verletzen; **b)** (opinion) Ansicht, die
feet pl. of **foot**

feign [feın] *v. t.* vortäuschen; ~ **to do sth.** vorgeben, etw. zu tun

¹**fell** *see* **fall 2**

²**fell** [fel] *v. t.* fällen ‹*Baum*›

³**fell** *adj.* **in one ~ swoop** auf einen Schlag

fellow ['feləʊ] **1.** *n.* **a)** *(comrade)* Kamerad, *der;* **b)** *(Brit. Univ.)* Fellow, *der;* **c)** *(of academy or society)* Mitglied, *das;* **d)** *(coll.: man, boy)* Kerl, *der (ugs.).* **2.** *attrib. adj.* Mit-; ~ **man** *or* **human being** Mitmensch, *der*

¹**felt** [felt] *n.* Filz, *der*

²**felt** *see* **feel**

felt[-tipped] 'pen *n.* Filzstift, *der*

female ['fi:meıl] **1.** *adj.* weiblich; Frauen‹*stimme, -chor, -verein*›. **2.** *n.* Frau, *die; (foetus, child)* Mädchen, *das; (animal)* Weibchen, *das*

feminine ['femının] *adj.* weiblich; Frauen‹*angelegenheit, -leiden*›; *(womanly)* feminin. **feminist** ['femınıst] **1.** *adj.* feministisch; Feministen‹*bewegung, -gruppe*›. **2.** *n.* Feministin, *die*/Feminist, *der*

fence [fens] **1.** *n.* Zaun, *der.* **2.** *v. i. (Sport)* fechten. **3.** *v. t.* ~ **[in]** einzäunen. '**fencer** *n.* Fechter, *der*/Fechterin, *die.* **fencing** ['fensıŋ] *n. (Sport)* Fechten, *das*

fend [fend] *v. i.* ~ **for oneself** für sich selbst sorgen; *(in hostile surroundings)* sich allein durchschlagen. **fend 'off** *v. t.* abwehren

fender ['fendə(r)] *n.* **a)** *(for fire)* Kaminschutz, *der;* **b)** *(Amer.) (car bumper)* Stoßstange, *die; (car mudguard)* Kotflügel, *der*

ferment [fə'ment] **1.** *v. i.* gären. **2.** *v. t.* zur Gärung bringen. **fermentation** [fɜ:men'teıʃn] *n.* Gärung, *die*

fern [fɜ:n] *n.* Farnkraut, *das*

ferocious [fə'rəʊʃəs] *adj.* wild. **ferocity** [fə'rɒsıtı] *n.* Wildheit, *die*

ferret ['ferıt] *n.* Frettchen, *das*

ferry ['ferı] **1.** *n.* Fähre, *die; (service)* Fährverbindung, *die.* **2.** *v. t. (in boat)* ~ **|across** *or* **over|** übersetzen

fertile ['fɜ:taıl] *adj. (fruitful)* fruchtbar; *(capable of developing)* befruchtet. **fertility** [fɜ:'tılıtı] *n.* Fruchtbarkeit, *die.* **fertilize** ['fɜ:tılaız] *v. t.* befruchten. '**fertilizer** *n.* Dünger, *der*

fervent ['fɜ:vənt] *adj.* leidenschaftlich; inbrünstig ‹*Gebet, Wunsch, Hoffnung*›. **fervour** *(Brit.;* **fervor** *Amer.)* ['fɜ:və(r)] *n.* Leidenschaftlichkeit, *die*

fester ['festə(r)] *v. i.* eitern

festival ['festıvl] *n.* **a)** *(feast day)* Fest, *das;* **b)** *(of music etc.)* Festival, *das*

festive ['festıv] *adj.* festlich; fröhlich; **the ~ season** die Weihnachtszeit. **festivity** [fe'stıvıtı] *n.* **a)** *(gaiety)* Feststimmung, *die;* **b)** *(celebration)* Feier, *die;* **festivities** Feierlichkeiten *Pl.*

festoon [fe'stu:n] **1.** *n.* Girlande, *die.* **2.** *v. t.* schmücken (**with** mit)

fetch [fetʃ] *v. t.* **a)** holen; *(collect)* abholen (**from** von); ~ **sb. sth.,** ~ **sth. for sb.** jmdm. etw. holen; **b)** *(be sold for)* erzielen ‹*Preis*›. '**fetching** *adj.* einnehmend

fête [feıt] *n.* [Wohltätigkeits]basar, *der*

fetish ['fetıʃ] *n.* Fetisch, *der.* **fetishism** ['fetıʃızm] *n.* Fetischismus, *der.* **fetishist** ['fetıʃıst] *n.* Fetischist, *der*/Fetischistin, *die*

fetter ['fetə(r)] *v. t.* fesseln

feud [fju:d] *n.* Fehde, *die*

feudal ['fju:dl] *adj.* Feudal-; feudalistisch; ~ **system** System Feudalsystem, *das*

fever ['fi:və(r)] *n.* **a)** *(high temperature)* Fieber, *das;* **have a |high| ~:** [hohes] Fieber haben; **b)** *(disease)* Fieberkrankheit, *die.* '**feverish** *adj.* **a)** *(Med.)* fiebrig; **be ~:** Fieber haben; **b)** *(excited)* fiebrig

few [fju:] **1.** *adj.* **a)** *(not many)* wenige; *abs.* nur wenige; **with very ~ exceptions** mit ganz wenigen Ausnahmen; **his ~ belongings** seine paar Habseligkeiten; **a ~ ...:** wenige ...; **b)** *(some)* wenige; **a ~ ...:** ein paar ...; **a ~ more ...:** noch ein paar ... **2.** *n.* **a)** *(not many)* wenige; **a ~:** wenige; **just a ~ of you/her friends** nur ein paar von euch/ihrer Freunde; **b)** *(some)* **with a ~ of our friends** mit einigen unserer Freunde; **quite a ~:** ziemlich viele

fiancé [fı'ɑ̃seı] *n.* Verlobte, *der*

fiancée [fı'ɑ̃seı] *n.* Verlobte, *die*

fiasco [fı'æskəʊ] *n., pl.* ~s Fiasko, *das*

fib [fıb] **1.** *n.* Flunkerei, *die (ugs.);* **tell ~s** flunkern *(ugs.).* **2.** *v. i.,* **-bb-** flunkern *(ugs.)*

fibre *(Brit.; Amer.:* **fiber**) ['faıbə(r)] *n.* **a)** Faser, *die;* **b)** *(material)* [Faser]gewebe, *das.* '**fibreglass** *n. (plastic)* glasfaserverstärkter Kunststoff

fiche [fi:ʃ] *n., pl.* same *or* ~s Mikrofiche, *das od. der*

fickle ['fıkl] *adj.* unberechenbar

fiction ['fıkʃn] *n.* erzählende Literatur; **a ~/~s** eine Erfindung. **fictional** ['fıkʃənl] *adj.* erfunden ‹*Geschichte*›; fiktiv ‹*Figur*›

fictitious [fɪk'tɪʃəs] *adj.* fingiert; falsch ⟨*Name, Identität*⟩

fiddle ['fɪdl] **1.** *n.* **a)** *(Mus.) (coll./ derog.)* Fiedel, *die; (violin for traditional music)* Geige, *die;* |**as**| **fit as a ~:** kerngesund; **b)** *(sl.: swindle)* Gaunerei, *die.* **2.** *v. t. (sl.)* frisieren *(ugs.)* ⟨*Bücher, Rechnungen*⟩. **3.** *v. i.* herumspielen (with mit). **fiddler** ['fɪdlə(r)] *n.* Geiger, *der*/Geigerin, *die*

fiddly ['fɪdlɪ] *adj. (coll.)* knifflig

fidelity [fɪ'delɪtɪ] *n.* Treue, *die* (to zu)

fidget ['fɪdʒɪt] **1.** *v. i.* ~ |**about**| herumrutschen. **2.** *n. (person)* Zappelphilipp, *der (ugs.).* **'fidgety** *adj.* unruhig; zappelig ⟨*Kind*⟩

field [fiːld] *n.* **a)** Feld, *das;* **b)** *(for game)* Platz, *der;* [Spiel]feld, *das;* **c)** *(subject area)* [Fach]gebiet, *das;* in the ~ **of medicine** auf dem Gebiet der Medizin; **that is outside my ~:** das fällt nicht in mein Fach

field: ~**-day** *n.* **have a ~-day** seinen großen Tag haben; ~ **events** *n. pl.* technische Disziplinen; ~**-glasses** *n. pl.* Feldstecher, *der;* **F~ 'Marshal** *n. (Brit. Mil.)* Feldmarschall, *der;* ~ **mouse** *n.* Brandmaus, *die*

fiend [fiːnd] *n.* **a)** *(wicked person)* Scheusal, *das;* **b)** *(evil spirit)* böser Geist. **'fiendish** *adj.* **a)** teuflisch; **b)** *(very awkward)* höllisch

fierce ['fɪəs] *adj.* wild; erbittert ⟨*Widerstand, Kampf*⟩; scharf ⟨*Kritik*⟩. **'fiercely** *adv.* heftig ⟨*angreifen, Widerstand leisten*⟩; wütend ⟨*brüllen*⟩; aufs heftigste ⟨*kritisieren, bekämpfen*⟩

fiery ['faɪərɪ] *adj.* glühend; *(looking like fire)* feurig; *(blazing red)* feuerrot

fifteen [fɪf'tiːn] **1.** *adj.* fünfzehn. **2.** *n.* Fünfzehn, *die. See also* **eight. fifteenth** [fɪf'tiːnθ] **1.** *adj.* fünfzehnt... **2.** *n. (fraction)* Fünfzehntel, *das. See also* **eighth**

fifth [fɪfθ] **1.** *adj.* fünft... **2.** *n. (in sequence)* fünfte, *der/die/das; (in rank)* Fünfte, *der/die/das; (fraction)* Fünftel, *das. See also* **eighth**

fiftieth ['fɪftɪɪθ] *adj.* fünfzigst...

fifty ['fɪftɪ] **1.** *adj.* fünfzig. **2.** *n.* Fünfzig, *die. See also* **eight; eighty** 2

fig [fɪg] *n.* Feige, *die*

fig. *abbr.* **figure** Abb.

fight [faɪt] **1.** *v. i.,* fought [fɔːt] **a)** kämpfen; *(with fists)* sich schlagen; **b)** *(squabble)* [sich] streiten (**about** wegen). **2.** *v. t.,* fought **a)** ~ **sb./sth.** gegen jmdn./etw. kämpfen; *(using fists)* ~ **sb.** sich mit jmdm. schlagen; **b)** *(seek* ↗

to overcome) bekämpfen; *(resist)* ~ **sb./sth.** gegen jmdn./etw. ankämpfen; **c)** ~ **a battle** einen Kampf austragen; **d)** kandidieren bei ⟨*Wahl*⟩. **3.** *n.* Kampf, *der* (**for** um). **'fight against** *v. t.* kämpfen gegen; ankämpfen gegen ⟨*Wellen, Wind*⟩. **fight 'back 1.** *v. i.* zurückschlagen. **2.** *v. t. (suppress)* zurückhalten. **fight 'off** *v. t.* abwehren. **'fight with** *v. t.* **a)** kämpfen mit; **b)** *(squabble with)* [sich] streiten mit

'fighter *n.* Kämpfer, *der*/Kämpferin, *die; (aircraft)* Kampfflugzeug, *das*

'fighting *n.* Kämpfe

figment ['fɪgmənt] *n.* **a** ~ **of one's** or **the imagination** pure Einbildung

'fig-tree *n.* Feigenbaum, *der*

figurative ['fɪgərətɪv] *adj.* übertragen

figure ['fɪgə(r)] **1.** *n.* **a)** *(shape)* Form, *die;* **b)** *(carving, sculpture, one's bodily shape)* Figur, *die;* **c)** *(illustration)* Abbildung, *die;* **d)** *(person as seen)* Gestalt, *die; (literary ~)* Figur, *die;* **e)** *(numerical symbol)* Ziffer, *die; (number)* Zahl, *die; (amount of money)* Betrag, *der;* **f)** ~ **of speech** Redewendung, *die.* **2.** *v. i.* **a)** vorkommen; **b)** **that ~s** *(coll.)* das kann gut sein. **figure 'out** *v. t.* **a)** *(by arithmetic)* ausrechnen; **b)** *(understand)* verstehen

filament ['fɪləmənt] *n.* **a)** Faden, *der;* **b)** *(Electr.)* Glühfaden, *der*

filch ['fɪltʃ] *v. t.* stibitzen *(ugs.)*

¹file [faɪl] **1.** *n.* Feile, *die.* **2.** *v. t.* feilen ⟨*Fingernägel*⟩; mit der Feile bearbeiten ⟨*Holz, Eisen*⟩

²file 1. *n.* **a)** *(holder)* Ordner, *der; (box)* Kassette, *die;* **b)** *(papers)* Ablage, *die; (cards)* Kartei, *die.* **2.** *v. t.* **a)** [in die Kartei] einordnen/[in die Akten] aufnehmen; **b)** einreichen ⟨*Antrag*⟩

³file 1. *n. (Mil. etc.)* Reihe, *die;* |**in**| **single** or **Indian ~:** [im] Gänsemarsch. **2.** *v. i.* ~ |**in/out**| in einer Reihe [hinein-/hinaus]gehen

filigree ['fɪlɪgriː] *n.* Filigran, *das*

'filing-cabinet *n.* Aktenschrank, *der*

filings ['faɪlɪŋz] *n. pl.* Späne

fill [fɪl] **1.** *v. t.* **a)** füllen; besetzen ⟨*Sitzplätze*⟩; *(fig.)* ausfüllen ⟨*Gedanken, Zeit*⟩; *(pervade)* erfüllen; ~**ed** with voller ⟨*Reue, Bewunderung, Neid usw.*⟩; **b)** *(appoint sb. to)* besetzen ⟨*Posten*⟩. **2.** *v. i.* ~ |**with sth.**| sich [mit etw.] füllen. **3.** *n.* **eat/drink one's ~:** sich satt essen/trinken. **fill 'in 1.** *v. t.* **a)** füllen; zuschütten ⟨*Erdloch*⟩; **b)** *(complete)* ausfüllen; **c)** ~ **sb. in** |**on sth.**| *(coll.)* jmdn. [über etw. *(Akk.)*] ins ↗

Bild setzen. **2.** *v. i.* ~ **in for sb.** für jmdn. einspringen. **fill 'out** *v. t.* ausfüllen. **fill 'up** *v. t.* **a)** füllen (with mit); **b)** *(put petrol into)* tanken

fillet ['fɪlɪt] **1.** *n.* Filet, *das.* **2.** *v. t.* entgräten ‹*Fisch*›

'filling *n.* **a)** *(for teeth)* Füllung, *die;* **b)** *(for pancakes etc.)* Füllung, *die; (for sandwiches etc.)* Belag, *der; (for spreading)* Aufstrich, *der.* **'filling station** *n.* Tankstelle, *die*

filly ['fɪlɪ] *n.* junge Stute

film [fɪlm] **1.** *n.* **a)** Film, *der;* **b)** *(thin layer)* Schicht, *die.* **2.** *v. t.* filmen; drehen ‹*Kinofilm, Szene*›. **'film script** *n.* Drehbuch, *das.* **'film star** *n.* Filmstar, *der*

Filofax, (P) ['faɪləʊfæks] *n.* ≈ Terminplaner, *der*

filter ['fɪltə(r)] **1.** *n.* Filter, *der.* **2.** *v. t.* filtern. **filter 'through** *v. t.* durchsickern

'filter-tip *n.* **a)** Filter, *der;* **b)** ~ |cigarette| Filterzigarette, *die*

filth [fɪlθ] *n.* Dreck, *der.* **'filthy** *adj.* schmutzig

fin [fɪn] *n.* Flosse, *die*

final ['faɪnl] **1.** *adj.* letzt...; End‹*spiel, -stadium, -stufe, -ergebnis*›; endgültig ‹*Entscheidung*›. **2.** *n.* **a)** *(Sport etc.)* Finale, *das;* **b)** ~s *pl.* *(university examination)* Examen, *das*

finale [fɪ'nɑ:lɪ] *n.* Finale, *das*

finalist ['faɪnəlɪst] *n.* Teilnehmer/Teilnehmerin in der Endausscheidung; *(Sport)* Finalist, *der*/Finalistin, *die*

finalize ['faɪnəlaɪz] *v. t.* [endgültig] beschließen; *(complete)* zum Abschluß bringen

finally ['faɪnəlɪ] *adv.* **a)** *(in the end)* schließlich; *(expressing impatience etc.)* endlich; **b)** *(in conclusion)* abschließend; **c)** *(conclusively)* entschieden ‹*sagen*›

finance [faɪ'næns, 'faɪnæns] **1.** *n.* **a)** *in pl. (resources)* Finanzen *Pl.; (management of money)* Geldwesen, *das;* **c)** *(support)* Geldmittel *Pl.* **2.** *v. t.* finanzieren. **financial** [faɪ'nænʃl] *adj.* finanziell; Finanz‹*mittel, -experte, -lage*›; ~ **year** Geschäftsjahr, *das.* **financially** *adv.* finanziell. **financier** [faɪ'nænsɪə(r)] *n.* Finanzexperte, *der*/-expertin, *die*

finch [fɪntʃ] *n.* Fink[envogel], *der*

find [faɪnd] **1.** *v. t., found* [faʊnd] finden; *(come across unexpectedly)* entdecken; auftreiben ‹*Geld, Gegenstand*›; aufbringen ‹*Kraft, Energie*›;

want to ~: suchen; ~ **that** ...: herausfinden, daß ...; ~ **sth. necessary** etw. für nötig erachten; ~ **sth./sb. to be** ...: herausfinden, daß etw./jmd. ... ist/war; **you will** ~ |**that**| ...: Sie werden sehen, daß ... **2.** *n.* Fund, *der.* **find 'out** *v. t.* herausfinden

'finder *n.* Finder, *der*/Finderin, *die*

'findings *n. pl.* Ergebnisse

¹fine [faɪn] **1.** *n.* Geldstrafe, *die.* **2.** *v. t.* mit einer Geldstrafe belegen

²fine *adj.* **a)** hochwertig ‹*Qualität, Lebensmittel*›; fein ‹*Gewebe, Spitze*›; edel ‹*Holz, Wein*›; **b)** *(delicate)* fein; zart ‹*Porzellan*›; *(thin)* hauchdünn; **cut** *or* **run it** ~: knapp kalkulieren; **c)** *(in small particles)* [hauch]fein ‹*Sand, Staub*›; ~ **rain** Nieselregen, *der;* **d)** *(sharp)* scharf ‹*Spitze, Klinge*›; spitz ‹*Nadel, Schreibfeder*›; **e)** *(excellent)* ausgezeichnet ‹*Sänger, Schauspieler*›; **f)** *(satisfactory)* schön; **that's** ~ **by** *or* **with me** ja, ist mir recht; **g)** *(in good health or state)* gut; **feel** ~: sich wohl fühlen; **h)** schön ‹*Wetter*›. **fine 'arts** *n. pl.* schöne Künste

finery ['faɪnərɪ] *n.* Pracht, *die; (garments etc.)* Staat, *der*

finger ['fɪŋgə(r)] **1.** *n.* Finger, *der.* **2.** *v. t.* berühren; *(meddle with)* befingern

finger: ~-**mark** *n.* Fingerabdruck, *der;* ~**nail** *n.* Fingernagel, *der;* ~**print** *n.* Fingerabdruck, *der;* ~**tip** *n.* Fingerspitze, *die;* **have sth. at one's** ~**tips** *(fig.)* etw. im kleinen Finger haben *(ugs.)*

finish ['fɪnɪʃ] **1.** *v. t.* **a)** beenden ‹*Unterhaltung*›; erledigen ‹*Arbeit*›; abschließen ‹*Kurs, Ausbildung*›; **have** ~**ed sth.** etw. fertig haben; ~ **writing/reading sth.** etw. zu Ende schreiben/lesen; **b)** aufessen ‹*Mahlzeit*›; auslesen ‹*Buch, Zeitung*›; austrinken ‹*Flasche, Glas*›. **2.** *v. i.* **a)** aufhören; **have you** ~**ed?** sind Sie fertig?; **when does the concert** ~? wann ist das Konzert aus?; **b)** *(in race)* das Ziel erreichen. **3.** *n.* **a)** Ende, *das;* **b)** *(~ing line)* Ziel, *das.* **finish 'off** *v. t.* abschließen

'finishing post *n.* Zielpfosten, *der*

finite ['faɪnaɪt] *adj.* begrenzt

Finland ['fɪnlənd] *pr. n.* Finnland *(das)*

Finn [fɪn] *n.* Finne, *der*/Finnin, *die*

Finnish ['fɪnɪʃ] **1.** *adj.* finnisch. **2.** *n.* Finnisch, *das; see also* **English 2 a**

fiord [fɪ'ɔ:d] *n.* Fjord, *der*

fir [fɜ:(r)] *n.* Tanne, *die*

fire ['faɪə(r)] **1.** *n.* **a)** Feuer, *das;* **be on**

~: brennen; **catch** ~: Feuer fangen; ⟨*Wald, Gebäude:*⟩ in Brand geraten; **set** ~ **to** sth. etw. anzünden; **b)** *(in grate)* [offenes] Feuer; *(electric or gas* ~*)* Heizofen, *der;* **light the** ~: den Ofen anstecken; *(in grate)* das [Kamin]feuer anmachen; **c)** *(destructive burning)* Brand, *der;* **d)** *(of guns)* **come/be under** ~: unter Beschuß geraten/beschossen werden. **2.** *v. t.* **a)** abschießen ⟨*Gewehr*⟩; abfeuern ⟨*Kanone*⟩; abgeben ⟨*Schuß*⟩; ~ **one's gun/pistol/rifle at** sb. auf jmdn. schießen; **two shots were** ~**d** es fielen zwei Schüsse; ~ **questions at** sb. jmdn. mit Fragen bombardieren; **b)** *(coll.: dismiss)* feuern *(ugs.)*. **3.** *v. i.* feuern; ~ **at/on** schießen auf (+ *Akk.*); ~! Feuer!

fire: ~**-alarm** *n.* Feuermelder, *der;* ~**arm** *n.* Schußwaffe, *die;* ~ **brigade** *(Brit.),* ~ **department** *(Amer.)* *ns.* Feuerwehr, *die;* ~**-drill** *n.* Probe[feuer]alarm, *der;* ~**-engine** *n.* Löschfahrzeug, *das;* ~**-escape** *n.* *(staircase)* Feuertreppe, *die;* ~ **extinguisher** *n.* Feuerlöscher, *der;* ~ **hazard** *n.* Brandrisiko, *das;* ~**man** ['faɪəmən] *n., pl.* ~**men** [~mən] Feuerwehrmann, *der;* ~**place** *n.* Kamin, *der;* ~**side** *n.* **at** *or* **by the** ~**side** am Kamin; ~ **station** *n.* Feuerwache, *die;* ~**wood** *n.* Brennholz, *das;* ~**work** *n.* Feuerwerkskörper, *der;* ~**works** *(display)* Feuerwerk, *das*

¹**firm** [fɜːm] *n.* Firma, *die*

²**firm** *adj.* **a)** fest; stabil ⟨*Konstruktion, Stuhl*⟩; **b)** *(resolute, strict)* bestimmt.

'**firmly** *adv.* **a)** fest; **b)** *(resolutely, strictly)* bestimmt

first [fɜːst] **1.** *adj.* erst...; **he was** ~ **to arrive** er kam als erster an. **2.** *adv.* **a)** *(before anyone else)* zuerst; als erster/erste ⟨*sprechen, ankommen*⟩; *(before anything else)* an erster Stelle ⟨*stehen, kommen*⟩; ~ **come** ~ **served** wer zuerst kommt, mahlt zuerst (Spr.); **b)** *(beforehand)* vorher; *(for the* ~ *time)* zum ersten Mal; **d)** ~ **of all** zuerst; *(in importance)* vor allem. **3.** *n.* **a) the** ~ *(in sequence)* der/die/das erste; *(in rank)* der/die/das Erste; **b) at** ~: zuerst; **from the** ~: von Anfang an

first: ~ '**aid** *n.* erste Hilfe; ~**-aid box/kit** Verbandkasten, *der*/Erste-Hilfe-Ausrüstung, *die;* ~**-class 1.** ['-'] *adj.* **a)** erster Klasse ⟨*Fahrkarte, Abteil, Post, Brief usw.*⟩; **b)** *(excellent)* erstklassig; **2.** [-'-] *adv.* erster Klasse ⟨*reisen*⟩

'**firstly** *adv.* zunächst [einmal]; *(followed by 'secondly')* erstens

first: ~ **name** *n.* Vorname, *der;* ~**-rate** *adj.* erstklassig; ~ **school** *n.* *(Brit.)* ≈ Grundschule, *die*

'**fir tree** *n.* Tanne, *die*

fish [fɪʃ] **1.** *n.* Fisch, *der.* **2.** *v. i.* fischen; *(with rod)* angeln; **go** ~**ing** fischen/angeln gehen. **fish 'out** *v. t.* *(coll.)* herausfischen *(ugs.)*

fisherman ['fɪʃəmən] *n., pl.* **fishermen** ['fɪʃəmən] Fischer, *der;* *(angler)* Angler, *der*

fish: ~ '**finger** *n.* Fischstäbchen, *das;* ~**-hook** *n.* Angelhaken, *der*

'**fishing** *n.* Fischen, *das;* *(with rod)* Angeln, *das*

fishing: ~ **boat** *n.* Fischerboot, *das;* ~**-net** *n.* Fischernetz, *das;* ~**-rod** *n.* Angelrute, *die*

fish: ~**monger** ['fɪʃmʌŋgə(r)] *n.* *(Brit.)* Fischhändler, *der/*-händlerin, *die;* ~ **shop** *n.* Fischgeschäft, *das*

'**fishy** *adj.* **a)** fischartig; Fisch⟨*geschmack, -geruch*⟩; **b)** *(coll.: suspicious)* verdächtig

fist [fɪst] *n.* Faust, *die*

¹**fit** [fɪt] *n.* Anfall, *der;* *(fig.)* [plötzliche] Anwandlung; **be in** ~**s of laughter** sich vor Lachen biegen; **in a** ~ **of** ...: in einem Anfall von ...

²**fit 1.** *adj.* **a)** *(suitable)* geeignet; ~ **to eat** eßbar; **b)** *(worthy)* würdig; wert; **c)** *(proper)* richtig; **see** *or* **think** ~ [**to do** sth.] es für richtig halten[, etw. zu tun]; **d)** *(healthy)* fit *(ugs.)*; **keep** ~: sich fit halten. **2.** *n.* Paßform, *die;* **it is a good/bad** ~: es sitzt *od.* paßt gut/nicht gut. **3.** *v. t.,* **-tt-: a)** ⟨*Kleider:*⟩ passen (+ *Dat.*); ⟨*Deckel, Bezug:*⟩ passen auf (+ *Akk.*); **b)** *(put into place)* anbringen (**to** an + *Dat. od. Akk.*); einbauen ⟨*Motor, Ersatzteil*⟩. **4.** *v. i.,* -tt- passen. **fit 'in 1.** *v. t.* unterbringen. **2.** *v. i.* **a)** ⟨*Person:*⟩ sich anpassen (**with** an + *Akk.*); **b)** *(be in accordance with)* ~ **in with** sth. mit etw. übereinstimmen

fitful ['fɪtfl] *adj.* unbeständig; unruhig ⟨*Schlaf*⟩; launisch ⟨*Brise*⟩

'**fitment** *n.* Einrichtung, *die*

'**fitness** *n.* **a)** *(physical)* Fitneß, *die;* **b)** *(suitability)* Eignung, *die*

'**fitted** *adj.* **a)** *(suited)* geeignet (**for** für, zu); **b)** *(shaped)* tailliert ⟨*Kleider*⟩; Einbau⟨*küche, schrank*⟩; ~ **carpet** Teppichboden, *der*

'**fitter** *n.* Monteur, *der;* *(of pipes)* Installateur, *der;* *(of machines)* Maschinenschlosser, *der* '**fitting 1.** *adj. (appropriate)* passend; *(becoming)* schicklich *(geh.)* ‹*Benehmen*›. **2.** *n.* **a)** *usu. in pl. (fixture)* Anschluß, *der;* ~s *(furniture)* Ausstattung, *die;* **b)** *(Brit.: size)* Größe, *die*

five [faɪv] **1.** *adj.* fünf. **2.** *n.* Fünf, *die. See also* **eight. fiver** ['faɪvə(r)] *n. (Brit. coll.)* Fünfpfundschein, *der*

fix [fɪks] **1.** *v. t.* **a)** befestigen; **b)** festsetzen ‹*Termin, Preis, Grenze*›; *(agree on)* ausmachen; **c)** *(repair)* reparieren; **d)** *(arrange)* arrangieren. **2.** *n. (coll.: predicament)* Klemme, *die (ugs.);* **be in a** ~: in der Klemme sitzen. **fix 'up** *v. t.* **a)** *(arrange)* arrangieren; festsetzen ‹*Termin, Treffpunkt*›; **b)** *(provide)* versorgen; ~ **sb. up with sth.** jmdm. etw. verschaffen. **fixture** ['fɪkstʃə(r)] *n.* **a)** *(furnishing)* eingebautes Teil; **b)** *(Sport)* Veranstaltung, *die*

fizz [fɪz] *v. i.* [zischend] sprudeln

fizzle ['fɪzl] *v. i.* zischen. **fizzle 'out** *v. i.* ‹*Kampagne:*› im Sande verlaufen

fizzy ['fɪzɪ] *adj.* sprudelnd; ~ **lemonade** Brause[limonade], *die*

flabbergast ['flæbəgɑːst] *v. t.* umhauen *(ugs.)*

flabby ['flæbɪ] *adj.* schlaff

¹**flag** [flæg] *n.* Fahne, *die; (national* ~, *on ship)* Flagge, *die*

²**flag** *v. i.,* **-gg-** ‹*Person:*› abbauen; ‹*Kraft, Begeisterung usw.:*› nachlassen

flagon ['flægn] *n.* Kanne, *die*

'**flag-pole** *n.* Flaggenmast, *der*

flagrant ['fleɪgrənt] *adj.* eklatant; flagrant ‹*Verstoß*›

'**flagstone** *n.* Steinplatte, *die*

flair [fleə(r)] *n.* Gespür, *das; (special ability)* Talent, *das*

flake [fleɪk] **1.** *n.* Flocke, *die; (of dry skin)* Schuppe, *die.* **2.** *v. i.* abblättern. **flaky** ['fleɪkɪ] *adj.* blättrig ‹*Kruste*›; ~ **pastry** Blätterteig, *der*

flamboyant [flæm'bɔɪənt] *adj.* extravagant

flame [fleɪm] *n.* Flamme, *die;* **be in ~s** in Flammen stehen

flan [flæn] *n.* [fruit] ~: [Obst]torte, *die*

flank [flæŋk] *n.* Seite, *die; (of animal; also Mil.)* Flanke, *die*

flannel ['flænl] *n.* **a)** *(fabric)* Flanell, *der;* **b)** *(Brit.: for washing)* Waschlappen, *der*

flap [flæp] **1.** *v. t.,* **-pp-:** ~ **its wings** mit den Flügeln schlagen. **2.** *v. i.,* **-pp-** ‹*Flügel:*› schlagen; ‹*Segel, Fahne, Vorhang:*› flattern. **3.** *n.* **a)** Klappe, *die; (envelope-seal, of shoe)* Lasche, *die;* **b)** *(fig. coll.)* **in a** ~: furchtbar aufgeregt

flare [fleə(r)] **1.** *v. i.* flackern; *(fig.)* ausbrechen; **tempers ~d** die Gemüter erhitzten sich. **2.** *n.* Leuchtsignal, *das.* **flare 'up** *v. i.* **a)** aufflackern; **b)** *(break out)* [wieder] ausbrechen

flash [flæʃ] **1.** *n.* Aufleuchten, *das; (as signal)* Lichtsignal, *das;* ~ **of lightning** Blitz, *der;* **in a** ~: *(quickly)* im Nu. **2.** *v. t.* **a)** aufleuchten lassen; ~ **one's headlights** die Lichthupe betätigen; ~ **sb. a smile/glance** jmdm. ein Lächeln/ einen Blick zuwerfen; **b)** *(display briefly)* kurz zeigen. **3.** *v. i.* aufleuchten; ~ **by or past** ‹*Zeit, Ferien:*› wie im Fluge vergehen

flash: ~**back** *n.* Rückblende, *die* (**to** auf + *Akk.*); ~ **bulb** *n.* Blitzbirnchen, *das;* ~**-cube** *n.* Blitzwürfel, *der;* ~**-gun** *n.* Blitzgerät, *das;* ~**light** *n.* **a)** *(for signals)* Blinklicht, *das;* **b)** *(Amer.: torch)* Taschenlampe, *die*

'**flashy** *adj.* auffällig

flask [flɑːsk] *n.* **a)** *see* **Thermos; b)** *(for wine, oil)* [bauchige] Flasche; **c)** *(Chem.)* Kolben, *der*

¹**flat** [flæt] *n. (Brit.)* Wohnung, *die*

²**flat 1.** *adj.* **a)** flach; eben ‹*Fläche*›; platt ‹*Nase, Reifen*›; **b)** *(downright)* glatt *(ugs.)* ‹*Absage, Weigerung, Widerspruch*›; **c)** ‹*Mus.*› [um einen Halbton] erniedrigt ‹*Note*›; **d)** schal, abgestanden ‹*Bier, Sekt*›; **e)** leer ‹*Batterie*›. **2.** *adv.* ‹*Mus.*› zu tief

flat: ~ '**feet** *n. pl.* Plattfüße; ~**-'fish** *n.* Plattfisch, *der;* ~**-'footed** *adj.* plattfüßig

'**flatly** *adv.* rundweg

flatten ['flætn] **1.** *v. t.* flach drücken ‹*Schachtel*›; dem Erdboden gleichmachen ‹*Stadt, Gebäude*›. **2.** *v. refl.* ~ **oneself against sth.** sich flach gegen etw. drücken

flatter ['flætə(r)] *v. t.* schmeicheln (+ *Dat.*). '**flattering** *adj.* schmeichelhaft. '**flattery** *n.* Schmeichelei, *die*

flat 'tyre *n.* Reifenpanne, *die*

flaunt [flɔːnt] *v. t.* zur Schau stellen

flavor *etc. (Amer.) see* **flavour** *etc.*

flavour ['fleɪvə(r)] *(Brit.)* **1.** *n.* **a)** Geschmack, *der;* **b)** *(fig.)* Anflug, *der.* **2.** *v. t.* abschmecken. '**flavouring** *n. (Brit.)* Aroma, *das*

flaw [flɔː] *n.* Fehler, *der; (imperfection)* Makel, *der; (in workmanship or goods)* Mangel, *der*

flax [flæks] *n.* Flachs, *der*

flea [fliː] *n.* Floh, *der.* '**flea market** *n. (coll.)* Flohmarkt, *der*

fled *see* **flee**

flee [fli:] 1. *v.i.*, **fled** [fled] fliehen; ~
from sth./sb. aus etw./vor jmdm.
flüchten. 2. *v.t.*, **fled** fliehen aus
fleece [fli:s] 1. *n.* [Schaf]fell, *das.* 2.
v.t. (fig.) ausplündern. **fleecy** ['fli:sı]
adj. flauschig
fleet [fli:t] *n.* Flotte, *die*
fleeting ['fli:tıŋ] *adj.* flüchtig
flesh [fleʃ] *n.* Fleisch, *das; (of fruit,
plant)* [Frucht]fleisch, *das.* '**fleshy**
adj. fett; fleischig ⟨*Hände*⟩
flew *see* ²**fly** 1, 2
¹**flex** [fleks] *n. (Brit. Electr.)* Kabel, *das*
²**flex** *v.t.* beugen ⟨*Arm, Knie*⟩; ~ **one's
muscles** seine Muskeln spielen lassen
flexible ['fleksıbl] *adj.* **a)** biegsam;
elastisch; **b)** *(fig.)* flexibel
flick [flık] *v.t.* schnippen; anknipsen
⟨*Schalter*⟩; verspritzen ⟨*Tinte*⟩. '**flick
through** *v.t.* durchblättern
flicker ['flıkə(r)] 1. *v.i.* flackern;
⟨*Fernsehapparat:*⟩ flimmern. 2. *n.*
Flackern, *das; (of TV)* Flimmern, *das.*
¹**flight** [flaıt] *n.* **a)** Flug, *der;* **b)** ~ [of
stairs *or* steps] Treppe, *die*
²**flight** *n. (fleeing)* Flucht, *die;* **take** ~:
die Flucht ergreifen; **put to** ~: in die
Flucht schlagen
'**flight attendant** *n.* Flugbegleiter,
der/-begleiterin, *die*
flimsy ['flımzı] *adj.* **a)** dünn; nicht sehr
haltbar ⟨*Verpackung*⟩; **b)** *(fig.)* faden-
scheinig ⟨*Entschuldigung, Argument*⟩
flinch [flıntʃ] *v.i.* zurückschrecken
(from vor + *Dat.*); *(wince)* zusammenzucken
fling [flıŋ] 1. *n.* **have a** *or* **one's** ~: sich
ausleben. 2. *v.t.*, **flung** [flʌŋ] werfen;
~ **oneself into sth.** *(fig.)* sich in etw.
(Akk.) stürzen
flint [flınt] *n.* Feuerstein, *der*
flip [flıp] *v.t.*, -**pp-** schnipsen; ~ [over]
(turn over) umdrehen. '**flip through**
v.t. durchblättern
flippant ['flıpənt] *adj.* leichtfertig
flipper ['flıpə(r)] *n.* Flosse, *die*
flirt [flɜ:t] *v.i.* flirten. **flirtation**
[flɜ:'teıʃn] *n.* Flirt, *der*
flit [flıt] *v.i.* huschen
float [fləʊt] 1. *v.i.* treiben; *(in air)*
schweben. 2. *n. (for carnival)* Festwa-
gen, *der.* 3. *v.t. (set afloat)* flott machen; *(fig.)* lancieren ⟨*Plan, Idee*⟩.
floating '**voter** *n.* Wechselwähler,
der/-wählerin, *die*
flock [flɒk] 1. *n.* **a)** Herde, *die; (of
birds)* Schwarm, *der;* **b)** *(of people)*
Schar, *die.* 2. *v.i.* strömen; ~ **round
sb.** sich um jmdn. scharen

flog [flɒg] *v.t.*, -**gg-: a)** auspeitschen;
b) *(Brit. sl.: sell)* verscheuern *(salopp)*
flood [flʌd] 1. *n.* Überschwemmung,
die; **the F**~ *(Bibl.)* die Sintflut. 2. *v.t.*
⟨*Fluß:*⟩ über die Ufer treten; *(fig.)*
strömen. 3. *v.t.* überschwemmen.
'**floodlight** 1. *n.* Scheinwerfer, *der.*
2. *v.t.*, **floodlit** ['flʌdlıt] anstrahlen
floor [flɔ:(r)] 1. *n.* **a)** Boden, *der;* **b)**
(storey) Stockwerk, *das;* **first** ~
(Amer.) Erdgeschoß, *das;* **first** ~
(Brit.), **second** ~ *(Amer.)* erster Stock;
ground ~: Erdgeschoß, *das;* Parterre,
das. 2. *v.t.* **a)** *(confound)* überfordern;
b) *(knock down)* zu Boden schlagen
floor: ~**board** *n.* Dielenbrett, *das;*
~-**cloth** *n. (Brit.)* Scheuertuch, *das;*
~-**polish** *n.* Bohnerwachs, *das;*
~ **show** *n.* ≈ Unterhaltungspro-
gramm, *das*
flop [flɒp] 1. *v.i.*, -**pp-: a)** plumpsen; **b)**
(coll.: fail) fehlschlagen; ⟨*Theater-
stück, Show:*⟩ durchfallen. 2. *n. (coll.:
failure)* Reinfall, *der (ugs.)*
floppy ['flɒpı] *adj.* weich und biegsam
flora ['flɔ:rə] *n.* Flora, *die*
floral ['flɔ:rl, 'flɒrl] *adj.* geblümt
⟨*Kleid, Stoff*⟩; Blumen⟨*muster*⟩
Florence ['flɒrəns] *pr. n.* Florenz *(das)*
florid ['flɒrıd] *adj.* blumig ⟨*Stil, Redeweise*⟩; gerötet ⟨*Teint*⟩
florist ['flɒrıst] *n.* Florist, *der/*Floristin, *die*
flotsam ['flɒtsəm] *n.* ~ [and jetsam]
Treibgut, *das*
flounder ['flaʊndə(r)] *v.i.* taumeln
flour ['flaʊə(r)] *n.* Mehl, *das*
flourish ['flʌrıʃ] 1. *v.i.* gedeihen; ⟨*Geschäft:*⟩ florieren, gutgehen. 2. *v.t.*
schwingen. 3. *n.* **do sth. with a** ~: etw.
schwungvoll tun
flout [flaʊt] *v.t.* mißachten
flow [fləʊ] 1. *v.i.* fließen; ⟨*Körner,
Sand:*⟩ rinnen, rieseln; ⟨*Gas:*⟩ strömen. 2. *n.* **a)** Fließen, *das;* ~ **of water/
people** Wasser-/Menschenstrom, *der;*
~ **of information** Informationsfluß,
der; **b)** *(of tide, river)* Flut, *die*
flower ['flaʊə(r)] 1. *n. (blossom)* Blüte,
die; (plant) Blume, *die;* **come into** ~:
zu blühen beginnen. 2. *v.i.* blühen.
'**flower-bed** *n.* Blumenbeet, *das.*
'**flower-pot** *n.* Blumentopf, *der*
'**flowery** *adj.* geblümt ⟨*Stoff, Muster*⟩;
(fig.) blumig ⟨*Sprache*⟩
'**flowing** *adj.* fließend; wallend
⟨*Haar*⟩
flown *see* ²**fly** 1, 2
flu [flu:] *n. (coll.)* Grippe, *die*

fluctuate ['flʌktjʊeit] v.i. schwanken. **fluctuation** [flʌktjʊ'eiʃn] n. Schwankung, die

fluency ['fluːənsi] n. Gewandtheit, die; (spoken) Redegewandtheit, die

fluent ['fluːənt] adj. gewandt ⟨Stil, Redeweise, Redner, Schreiber⟩; be ~ in Russian, speak ~ Russian fließend Russisch sprechen

fluff [flʌf] n. Flusen; Fusseln

fluffy ['flʌfi] adj. [flaum]weich ⟨Kissen, Küken⟩; flauschig ⟨Spielzeug, Decke⟩

fluid ['fluːid] 1. n. Flüssigkeit, die. 2. adj. flüssig

fluke [fluːk] n. (piece of luck) Glücksfall, der

flung see **fling 2**

fluorescent [flʊəˈresənt] adj. fluoreszierend. **fluorescent 'light** n. Leuchtstofflampe, die

fluoride ['fluːəraid] n. Fluorid, das; **fluoride toothpaste** fluorhaltige Zahnpasta

flurry ['flʌri] n. **a)** Aufregung, die; **b)** (of rain/snow) [Regen-/Schnee]schauer, der

¹flush [flʌʃ] 1. v.i. rot werden. 2. v.t ausspülen ⟨Becken⟩; ~ the toilet or lavatory spülen. 3. n. Rotwerden, das

²flush adj. (level) bündig; be ~ with sth. mit etw. bündig abschließen

fluster ['flʌstə(r)] v.t. aus der Fassung bringen. **flustered** ['flʌstəd] adj. nervös

flute [fluːt] n. Flöte, die

flutter ['flʌtə(r)] 1. v.i. flattern. 2. v.t. flattern mit ⟨Flügel⟩

flux [flʌks] n. in a state of ~: im Fluß

¹fly [flai] n. Fliege, die

²fly 1. v.i., **flew** [fluː], **flown** [fləʊn] **a)** fliegen; ~ **away** or **off** wegfliegen; **b)** (fig.) ~ |by or past| wie im Fluge vergehen; **c)** ⟨Fahne:⟩ gehißt sein. 2. v.t., **flew, flown** fliegen ⟨Flugzeug, Fracht, Einsatz usw.⟩; fliegen über (+ Akk.) ⟨Strecke⟩. 3. n. in sing. or pl. (on trousers) Hosenschlitz, der. **fly 'in** v.i. [mit dem Flugzeug] eintreffen (from aus). **fly 'out** v.i. abfliegen (of von)

flying ['flaiiŋ]: ~ '**saucer** n. fliegende Untertasse; ~ '**start** n. (Sport) fliegender Start; ~ '**visit** n. Stippvisite, die (ugs.)

fly: ~**leaf** n. Vorsatzblatt, das; ~**over** n. (Brit.) [Straßen]überführung, die

foal [fəʊl] n. Fohlen, das

foam [fəʊm] 1. n. Schaum, der. 2. v.i. schäumen. **foam 'rubber** n. Schaumgummi, der

fob [fɒb] v.t., -bb-: ~ sb. off with sth. jmdn. mit etw. abspeisen (ugs.)

focus ['fəʊkəs] 1. n., pl. ~es or **foci** ['fəʊsai] Brennpunkt, der; out of/in ~: unscharf/scharf eingestellt; unscharf/scharf ⟨Foto, Film usw.⟩; (fig.) be the ~ of attention im Brennpunkt des Interesses stehen. 2. v.t., -s- or -ss- einstellen (on auf + Akk.); bündeln ⟨Licht, Strahlen⟩. 3. v.i., -s- or -ss- (fig.) sich konzentrieren (on auf + Akk.)

fodder ['fɒdə(r)] n. [Vieh]futter, das

foe [fəʊ] n. (poet./rhet.) Feind, der

foetus ['fiːtəs] n. Fötus, der

fog [fɒg] n. Nebel, der. '**fog-light** n. (Motor Veh.) Nebelscheinwerfer, der

foggy ['fɒgi] adj. neblig

fogy ['fəʊgi] n. |old| ~: [alter] Opa (salopp)/[alte] Oma (salopp)

foible ['fɔibl] n. Eigenheit, die

¹foil [fɔil] n. Folie, die

²foil v.t. vereiteln

foist [fɔist] v.t. ~ |off| on to sb. jmdn. andrehen (ugs.); auf jmdn. abwälzen ⟨Probleme, Verantwortung⟩

fold [fəʊld] 1. v.t. [zusammen]falten; ~ one's arms die Arme verschränken. 2. v.i. **a)** (become ~ed) sich zusammenfalten; **b)** (be able to be ~ed) sich falten lassen. 3. n. Falte, die; (line made by ~ing) Kniff, der. **fold 'up** v.t. zusammenfalten ⟨Laken⟩; zusammenklappen ⟨Stuhl⟩

'**folder** n. Mappe, die

foliage ['fəʊliidʒ] n. Blätter Pl.; (of tree also) Laub, das

folk [fəʊk] n. **a)** Volk, das; **b)** in pl. ~|s| (people) Leute Pl.

folk: ~**-dance** n. Volkstanz, der; ~**lore** [~lɔː(r)] n. Folklore, die; ~**-music** n. Volksmusik, die; ~**-song** Volkslied, das; (modern) Folksong, der

follow ['fɒləʊ] 1. v.t. **a)** folgen (+ Dat.); **b)** entlanggehen/-fahren ⟨Straße usw.⟩; **c)** (come after) folgen auf (+ Akk.); **d)** (result from) die Folge sein von; **e)** (treat or take as guide) sich orientieren an (+ Dat.); **f)** folgen (+ Dat.) ⟨Prinzip, Instinkt, Trend⟩; verfolgen ⟨Politik⟩; befolgen ⟨Regel, Vorschrift, Rat, Warnung⟩; sich halten an (+ Akk.) ⟨Konventionen, Diät⟩; **g)** (grasp meaning of) folgen (+ Dat.); do you ~ me? verstehst du, was ich meine? 2. v.i. **a)** (go, come) ~ after sb./sth. jmdm./einer Sache folgen; **b)** (come next in order or time) folgen; as ~s wie folgt; **c)** ~ from sth.

(result) die Folge von etw. sein; *(be deducible)* aus etw. folgen. **follow 'on** *v. i. (continue)* ~ **on from sth.** die Fortsetzung von etw. sein. **follow 'up** *v. t.* a) ausbauen ⟨*Erfolg, Sieg*⟩; b) nachgehen (+ *Dat.*) ⟨*Hinweis*⟩

'follower *n.* Anhänger, *der*/Anhängerin, *die*

'following 1. *adj.* folgend; **the ~:** folgendes. 2. *prep.* nach. 3. *n.* Anhängerschaft, *die*

folly ['fɒlɪ] *n.* Torheit, *die (geh.)*

fond [fɒnd] *adj.* liebevoll; lieb ⟨*Erinnerung*⟩; **be ~ of sb.** jmdn. mögen; **be ~ of doing sth.** etw. gern tun

fondle ['fɒndl] *v. t.* streicheln

'fondness *n.* Liebe, *die;* ~ **for sth.** Vorliebe für etw.

font [fɒnt] *n.* Taufstein, *der*

food [fu:d] *n.* a) Nahrung, *die; (for animals)* Futter, *das;* b) *(as commodity)* Lebensmittel *Pl.;* c) *(in solid form)* Essen, *das;* d) *(particular kind)* Nahrungsmittel, *das;* Kost, *die.* **'food poisoning** *n.* Lebensmittelvergiftung, *die.* **'food processor** *n.* Küchenmaschine, *die*

fool [fu:l] 1. *n.* Dummkopf, *der (ugs.).* 2. *v. t.* ~ **sb. into doing sth.** jmdn. [durch Tricks] dazu bringen, etw. zu tun. **fool a'bout, fool a'round** *v. i.* Unsinn machen

foolhardy ['fu:lhɑːdɪ] *adj.* tollkühn

'foolish *adj.* töricht; verrückt *(ugs.)* ⟨*Idee, Vorschlag*⟩

'foolproof *adj. (infallible)* absolut sicher

foot [fʊt] 1. *n., pl.* **feet** [fi:t] a) Fuß, *der;* **on ~:** zu Fuß; **put one's ~ in it** *(fig. coll.)* ins Fettnäpfchen treten *(ugs.);* b) *(far end)* unteres Ende; *(of bed)* Fußende, *das;* c) *(measure)* Fuß, *der (30,48 cm).* 2. *v. t.* ~ **the bill** die Rechnung bezahlen

football ['fʊtbɔːl] *n. (game, ball)* Fußball, *der.* **'football boot** *n.* Fußballschuh, *der.* **'footballer** *n.* Fußballspieler, *der/-*spielerin, *die.* **'football pools** *n. pl.* **the ~:** das Fußballtoto

foot: ~**-brake** *n.* Fußbremse, *die;* ~**-bridge** *n.* Fußgängerbrücke, *die;* ~**hold** *n.* Halt, *der*

'footing *n.* a) *(fig.)* **be on an equal ~** |**with sb.**| [jmdm.] gleichgestellt sein; b) *(foothold)* Halt, *der*

foot: ~**note** *n.* Fußnote, *die;* ~**path** *n.* Fußweg, *der;* ~**print** *n.* Fußabdruck, *der;* ~**step** *n.* Schritt, *der;* **follow in sb.'s ~steps** *(fig.)* in jmds. Fuß-

stapfen *(Akk.)* treten; ~**wear** *n.* Schuhe *Pl.*

for [fə(r), *stressed* fɔː(r)] 1. *prep.* a) für; **what is it ~?** wofür ist das?; **reason ~ living** Grund zu leben; **a request ~ help** eine Bitte um Hilfe; **study ~ a university degree** auf einen Hochschulabschluß hin studieren; **take sb. ~ a walk** mit jmdm. einen Spaziergang machen; **be '~ doing sth.** *(in favour)* dafür sein, etw. zu tun; **cheque/bill ~ £5** Scheck/Rechnung über 5 Pfund; b) *(on account of, as penalty of)* wegen; **were it not ~ you/ your help** ohne dich/deine Hilfe; ~ **fear of** aus Angst vor (+ *Dat.*); c) *(in spite of)* ~ **all …:** trotz …; ~ **all that, …:** trotzdem …; d) ~ **all I know/care …:** möglicherweise/ was mich betrifft, …; ~ **one thing, …:** zunächst einmal …; e) *(during)* **stay ~ a week** eine Woche bleiben; **we've/we haven't been here ~ three years** wir sind seit drei Jahren hier/nicht mehr hier gewesen; f) **walk ~ 20 miles** 20 Meilen gehen. 2. *conj.* denn

forage ['fɒrɪdʒ] 1. *n.* Futter, *das.* 2. *v. i.* ~ **for sth.** auf der Suche nach etw. sein

forbad, forbade *see* forbid

forbid [fə'bɪd] *v. t.,* -dd-, **forbad** [fə-'bæd] *or* **forbade** [fə'bæd, fə'beɪd], **forbidden** [fə'bɪdn] ~ **sb. to do sth.** jmdm. verbieten, etw. zu tun; ~ |**sb.**| **sth.** [jmdm.] etw. verbieten; **it is ~den |to do sth.|** es ist verboten[, etw. zu tun]. **forbidden** *see* forbid. **for'bidding** *adj.* furchteinflößend

force [fɔːs] 1. *n.* a) *(strength, power)* Stärke, *die; (of explosion, storm)* Wucht, *die; (Phys.; physical strength)* Kraft, *die;* **in ~:** mit einem großen Aufgebot; b) *(validity)* Kraft, *die;* **in ~:** in Kraft; **come into ~** ⟨*Gesetz usw.*:⟩ in Kraft treten; c) *(violence)* Gewalt, *die;* **by ~:** gewaltsam; d) *(group) (of workers)* Kolonne, *die;* Trupp, *der; (of police)* Einheit, *die; (Mil.)* Armee, *die;* **the ~s** die Armee; **be in the ~s** beim Militär sein. 2. *v. t.* a) zwingen; ~ **sth.** |**up|on sb.** jmdm. etw. aufzwingen; b) ~ |**open**| aufbrechen; ~ **one's way in** sich *(Dat.)* mit Gewalt Zutritt verschaffen. **forced** [fɔːst] *adj.* a) *(contrived, unnatural)* gezwungen; b) *(compelled by force)* erzwungen; Zwangs⟨*arbeit*⟩. **forced 'landing** *n.* Notlandung, *die.* **'force-feed** *v. t.* zwangsernähren. **forceful** ['fɔːsfl] *adj.* stark ⟨*Persönlichkeit, Charakter*⟩;

energisch ⟨*Person, Art*⟩; eindrucksvoll
⟨*Sprache*⟩

forceps ['fɔ:seps] *n., pl. same* |pair of|
~: Zange, *die*

forcible ['fɔ:sɪbl] *adj.*, **forcibly** ['fɔ:sɪ-
blɪ] *adv.* gewaltsam

ford [fɔ:d] **1.** *n.* Furt, *die.* **2.** *v.t.* durch-
queren; *(wade through)* durchwaten

fore [fɔ:(r)] **1.** *adj., esp. in comb.* vorder...; Vorder⟨*teil, -front usw.*⟩. **2.** *n.* to
the ~: im Vordergrund

'**forearm** *n.* Unterarm, *der*

foreboding [fɔ:'bəʊdɪŋ] *n.* Vorahnung, *die*

'**forecast 1.** *v.t.,* **forecast** *or* **forecasted**
vorhersagen. **2.** *n.* Voraussage, *die*

'**forecourt** *n.* Vorhof, *der*

'**forefather** *n., usu. in pl.* Vorfahr, *der*

'**forefinger** *n.* Zeigefinger, *der*

'**forefront** *n.* |be| in the ~ of in vorder-
ster Linie (+ *Gen.*) [stehen]

'**foregone** *adj.* be a ~ conclusion von
vornherein feststehen; *(be certain)* so
gut wie sicher sein

'**foreground** *n.* Vordergrund, *der*

forehead ['fɒrɪd, 'fɔ:hed] *n.* Stirn, *die*

foreign ['fɒrɪn] *adj.* **a)** *(from abroad)*
ausländisch; Fremd⟨*kapital, -spra-
che*⟩; he is ~: er ist Ausländer; **b)**
(abroad) fremd; ~ country Ausland,
das; Außen⟨*politik, -handel*⟩; **c)** *(from
outside)* fremd; ~ body *or* substance
Fremdkörper, *der.* '**foreigner** *n.*
Ausländer, *der*/Ausländerin, *die*

foreign: ~ ex'change *n.* Devisen
Pl.; F~ Office *n. (Brit. Hist./coll.)*
Außenministerium, *das;* F~ 'Secret-
ary *n. (Brit.)* Außenminister, *der*

foreman ['fɔ:mən] *n., pl.* **foremen**
['fɔ:mən] Vorarbeiter, *der*

foremost ['fɔ:məʊst, 'fɔ:məst] **1.** *adj.*
a) vorderst...; **b)** *(fig.)* führend. **2.** *adv.*
first and ~: zunächst einmal

'**forename** *n.* Vorname, *der*

'**forerunner** *n.* Vorläufer, *der*/Vorläu-
ferin, *die*

foresaw *see* foresee

foresee [fɔ:'si:] *v.t., forms as* see voraussehen. **foreseeable** [fɔ:'si:əbl]
adj. vorhersehbar; in the ~ future in
nächster Zukunft

foreseen *see* foresee

'**foresight** *n.* Weitblick, *der*

foreskin *n. (Anat.)* Vorhaut, *die*

forest ['fɒrɪst] *n.* Wald, *der; (commercially exploited)* Forst, *der*

fore'stall *v.t.* zuvorkommen (+ *Dat.*)

forestry ['fɒrɪstrɪ] *n.* Forstwirtschaft,
die

'**foretaste** *n.* Vorgeschmack, *der*

fore'tell *v.t.,* fore'told voraussagen

forever [fə'revə(r)] *adv. (constantly)*
ständig

fore'warn *v.t.* vorwarnen

'**foreword** *n.* Vorwort, *das*

forfeit ['fɔ:fɪt] **1.** *v.t.* verlieren; verwir-
ken *(geh.)* ⟨*Recht, jmds. Gunst*⟩. **2.** *n.*
Strafe, *die; (games)* Pfand, *das*

forgave *see* forgive

¹**forge** [fɔ:dʒ] **1.** *n.* **a)** *(workshop)*
Schmiede, *die;* **b)** *(blacksmith's
hearth)* Esse, *die.* **2.** *v.t.* **a)** schmieden
(into zu); **b)** *(fig.)* schmieden ⟨*Plan*⟩;
schließen ⟨*Vereinbarung, Freundschaft*⟩; **c)** *(counterfeit)* fälschen

²**forge** *v.i.* ~ ahead |das Tempo| be-
schleunigen; *(fig.)* Fortschritte machen

'**forger** *n.* Fälscher, *der*/Fälscherin,
die

forgery ['fɔ:dʒərɪ] *n.* Fälschung, *die*

forget [fə'get] **1.** *v.t.,* -tt-, forgot [fə-
'gɒt], forgotten [fə'gɒtn] vergessen; *(~
learned ability)* verlernen. **2.** *v.i.,* -tt-,
forgot, forgotten es vergessen; ~
about sth. etw. vergessen; ~ about it!
(coll.) schon gut! **forgetful** [fə'getfl]
adj. vergeßlich. **for'getfulness** *n.*
Vergeßlichkeit, *die.* **for'get-me-not**
n. (Bot.) Vergißmeinnicht, *das*

forgive [fə'gɪv] *v.t.,* forgave [fə'geɪv],
forgiven [fə'gɪvn] verzeihen; vergeben
⟨*Sünden*⟩; ~ sb. |sth. *or* for sth.| jmdm.
[etw.] verzeihen. **for'giveness** *n.*
Verzeihung, *die; (of sins)* Vergebung,
die

forgo [fɔ:'gəʊ] *v.t., forms as* go verzichten auf (+ *Akk.*)

forgone *see* forgo

forgot, forgotten *see* forget

fork [fɔ:k] **1.** *n.* **a)** Gabel, *die; knives
and ~s* Besteck, *das;* **b)** *(in road)* Gabelung, *die; (one branch)* Abzweigung,
die. **2.** *v.i. (divide)* sich gabeln; *(turn)*
abbiegen; ~ left links abbiegen. **fork
'out** *v.i. (sl.)* blechen *(ugs.)*

'**fork-lift truck** *n.* Gabelstapler, *der*

forlorn [fə'lɔ:n] *adj.* **a)** *(desperate)* verzweifelt; **b)** *(forsaken)* verlassen

form [fɔ:m] **1.** *n.* **a)** *(shape, type, style)*
Form, *die;* take ~: Gestalt annehmen;
b) *(printed sheet)* Formular, *das;* **c)**
(Brit. Sch.) Klasse, *die;* **d)** *(bench)*
Bank, *die;* **e)** *(Sport: physical condition)* Form, *die; (fig.)* true to ~: wie
üblich. **2.** *v.t.* **a)** bilden; **b)** *(shape)*
formen, gestalten (into zu); **c)** sich
(Dat.) bilden ⟨*Meinung, Urteil*⟩; ge-

winnen 〈*Eindruck*〉; fassen 〈*Plan*〉; entwickeln 〈*Vorliebe, Gewohnheit*〉; schließen 〈*Freundschaft*〉; **d)** *(set up)* bilden 〈*Regierung*〉; gründen 〈*Bund, Firma, Partei*〉. **3.** *v. i.* sich bilden; 〈*Idee:*〉 Gestalt annehmen

formal ['fɔːml] *adj.* formell; förmlich 〈*Person, Art, Einladung, Begrüßung*〉; *(official)* offiziell; **a** ~ **'yes'/'no'** eine bindende Zusage/endgültige Absage.

formality [fɔːˈmælɪtɪ] *n.* **a)** *(require-ment)* Formalität, *die;* **b)** *(being formal)* Förmlichkeit, *die*

format ['fɔːmæt] *n.* Format, *das*

formation [fɔːˈmeɪʃn] *n.* **a)** *see* **form** 2 a, d: Bildung, *die;* Gründung, *die;* **b)** *(Mil., Aeronaut.)* Formation, *die*

former ['fɔːmə(r)] *attrib. adj.* ehema-lig; **in ~ times** früher; **the ~ :** der/die/das erstere; *pl.* die ersteren. **'for-merly** *adv.* früher

formidable ['fɔːmɪdəbl] *adj.* gewaltig; gefährlich 〈*Herausforderung, Gegner*〉

formula ['fɔːmjʊlə] *n.* Formel, *die.*
formulate ['fɔːmjʊleɪt] *v. t.* formulie-ren; *(devise)* entwickeln

forsake [fəˈseɪk] *v. t.,* **forsook** [fəˈsʊk], ~**n** [fəˈseɪkn] **a)** *(give up)* verzichten auf (+ *Akk.*); **b)** *(desert)* verlassen. **for'saken** *adj.* verlassen

fort [fɔːt] *n. (Mil.)* Fort, *das*

forte ['fɔːteɪ] *n.* Stärke, *die*

forth [fɔːθ] *adv.* **and so ~:** und so wei-ter; *see also* **back** 3

forthcoming ['---, -'--] *adj.* **a)** *(ap-proaching)* bevorstehend; in Kürze er-scheinend 〈*Buch usw.*〉; **b)** *pred.* **be ~** 〈*Geld, Antwort:*〉 kommen; 〈*Hilfe:*〉 ge-leistet werden; **not be ~:** ausbleiben; **c)** *(responsive)* mitteilsam 〈*Person*〉

'forthright *adj.* direkt

forth'with *adv.* unverzüglich

fortieth ['fɔːtɪɪθ] *adj.* vierzigst ...

fortify ['fɔːtɪfaɪ] *v. t.* **a)** *(Mil.)* befesti-gen; **b)** *(strengthen)* stärken

fortitude ['fɔːtɪtjuːd] *n.* innere Stärke

fortnight ['fɔːtnaɪt] *n.* vierzehn Tage

fortress ['fɔːtrɪs] *n.* Festung, *die*

fortuitous [fɔːˈtjuːɪtəs] *adj.,* **for'tuit-ously** *adv.* zufällig

fortunate ['fɔːtʃənət] *adj.* glücklich.
'fortunately *adv.* glücklicherweise

fortune ['fɔːtʃən, 'fɔːtʃuːn] *n.* **a)** *(wealth)* Vermögen, *das;* **b)** *(luck)* Schicksal, *das;* **bad/good ~:** Pech/ Glück, *das.* **'fortune-teller** *n.* Wahr-sager, *der*/Wahrsagerin, *die*

forty ['fɔːtɪ] **1.** *adj.* vierzig; **have ~ 'winks** ein Nickerchen machen *(ugs.).*

2. *n.* Vierzig, *die. See also* **eight; eighty** 2

forum ['fɔːrəm] *n.* Forum, *das*

forward ['fɔːwəd] **1.** *adv.* **a)** *(in direc-tion faced)* vorwärts; **b)** *(to the front)* nach vorn; vor〈*laufen, -rücken, -schieben*〉; **c)** *(closer)* heran; **he came ~ to greet me** er kam auf mich zu, um mich zu begrüßen; **d) come ~** 〈*Zeuge, Helfer:*〉 sich melden. **2.** *adj.* **a)** *(dir-ected ahead)* vorwärts gerichtet; **b)** *(at or to the front)* Vorder-; vorder... **3.** *n.* *(Sport)* Stürmer, *der*/Stürmerin, *die.* **4.** *v. t. (send on)* nachschicken 〈*Post*〉 (to an + *Akk.*)

forwards ['fɔːwədz] *see* **forward** 1 a, b

forwent *see* **forgo**

fossil ['fɒsɪl] *n.* Fossil, *das*

foster ['fɒstə(r)] **1.** *v. t.* **a)** fördern; pflegen 〈*Freundschaft*〉; **b)** in Pflege haben 〈*Kind*〉. **2.** *adj.* ~-: Pflege〈*kind, -eltern; -sohn usw.*〉

fought *see* **fight** 1, 2

foul [faʊl] **1.** *adj.* **a)** abscheulich 〈*Ge-ruch, Geschmack*〉; **b)** *(polluted)* ver-schmutzt 〈*Wasser, Luft*〉; *(putrid)* fau-lig 〈*Wasser*〉; stickig 〈*Luft*〉; **c)** *(sl.: awful)* scheußlich *(ugs.);* anstößig 〈*Sprache*〉. **2.** *n. (Sport)* Foul, *das.* **3.** *v. t.* **a)** beschmutzen; verpesten 〈*Luft*〉; **b)** *(Sport)* foulen. **'foul-smelling** *adj.* übelriechend

¹found [faʊnd] *v. t.* **a)** *(establish)* grün-den; stiften 〈*Krankenhaus, Kloster*〉; begründen 〈*Wissenschaft, Religion*〉; **b)** *(fig.: base)* begründen; **be ~ed [up]-on sth.** [sich] auf etw. *(Akk.)* gründen

²found *see* **find** 1

foundation [faʊnˈdeɪʃn] *n.* **a)** Grün-dung, *die; (of hospital, monastery)* Stiftung, *die;* **b)** *usu. in pl.* ~[s] *(lit. or fig.)* Fundament, *das;* **be without ~** *(fig.)* unbegründet sein. **foun'dation stone** *n.* Grundstein, *der*

¹'founder *n.* Gründer, *der*/Gründerin, *die; (of hospital)* Stifter, *der*/Stifterin, *die*

²'founder *v. i.* **a)** 〈*Schiff:*〉 sinken; **b)** *(fig.: fail)* sich zerschlagen

fountain ['faʊntɪn] *n.* Fontäne, *die; (structure)* Springbrunnen, *der; (fig.)* Quelle, *die.* **'fountain-pen** *n.* Füllfe-derhalter, *der*

four [fɔː(r)] **1.** *adj.* vier. **2.** *n.* Vier, *die;* **on all ~s** auf allen vieren *(ugs.). See also* **eight. 'four-poster** *n.* ~ **[bed]** Himmelbett, *das.* **foursome** ['fɔːsəm] *n.* Quartett, *das;* **go in** *or* **as a ~:** zu viert gehen

fourteen [fɔː'tiːn] 1. *adj.* vierzehn. 2. *n.* Vierzehn, *die. See also* **eight.**
fourteenth [fɔː'tiːnθ] 1. *adj.* vierzehnt... 2. *n. (fraction)* Vierzehntel, *das. See also* **eighth**
fourth [fɔːθ] 1. *adj.* viert... 2. *n. (in sequence)* vierte, *der/die/das; (in rank)* Vierte, *der/die/das; (fraction)* Viertel, *das. See also* **eighth.** '**fourthly** *adv.* viertens
fowl [faʊl] *n.* Haushuhn, *das; (collectively)* Geflügel, *das*
fox [fɒks] 1. *n.* Fuchs, *der.* 2. *v.t.* verwirren
foyer ['fɔɪeɪ] *n.* Foyer, *das*
fraction ['frækʃn] *n.* **a)** *(Math.)* Bruch, *der;* **b)** *(small part)* Bruchteil, *der*
fracture ['fræktʃə(r)] 1. *n.* Bruch, *der.* 2. *v.t.* brechen
fragile ['frædʒaɪl] *adj.* zerbrechlich
fragment ['frægmənt] *n.* Bruchstück, *das.* **fragmentary** ['frægməntərɪ] *adj.* bruchstückhaft
fragrance ['freɪgrəns] *n.* Duft, *der.* **fragrant** ['freɪgrənt] *adj.* duftend
frail [freɪl] *adj.* zerbrechlich; gebrechlich ⟨*Greis, Greisin*⟩
frame [freɪm] 1. *n.* **a)** *(of vehicle)* Rahmen, *der; (of bed)* Gestell, *das;* **b)** *(border)* Rahmen, *der;* |spectacle| ~s [Brillen]gestell, *das.* 2. *v.t.* **a)** rahmen; **b)** formulieren ⟨*Frage, Antwort*⟩; **c)** *(sl.: incriminate)* ~ sb. jmdm. etwas anhängen *(ugs.).* '**frame-up** *n. (coll.)* abgekartetes Spiel *(ugs.).* '**framework** *n.* Gerüst, *das*
franc [fræŋk] *n.* Franc, *der; (Swiss)* Franken, *der*
France [frɑːns] *pr. n.* Frankreich *(das)*
franchise ['fræntʃaɪz] *n.* **a)** Stimmrecht, *das;* **b)** *(Commerc.)* Lizenz, *die*
¹**frank** *adj.* offen; freimütig ⟨*Geständnis, Äußerung*⟩; **be ~ with sb.** zu jmdm. offen sein
²**frank** *v.t. (Post)* frankieren
frankfurter ['fræŋkfɜːtə(r)] *(Amer.:* **frankfurt** ['fræŋkfɜːt]) *n.* Frankfurter [Würstchen]
'**frankly** *adv.* offen; *(honestly)* offen gesagt
frantic ['fræntɪk] *adj.* **a)** verzweifelt ⟨*Hilferufe, Gestikulieren*⟩; **be ~ with fear/rage** *etc.* außer sich *(Dat.)* sein vor Angst/Wut *usw.;* **b)** hektisch ⟨*Aktivität, Suche*⟩. **frantically** ['fræntɪkəlɪ], '**franticly** *adv.* verzweifelt
fraternize ['frætənaɪz] *v.i.* ~ |with sb.| sich verbrüdern [mit jmdm.]
fraud [frɔːd] *n.* **a)** *no pl.* Betrug, *der;* **b)**

(trick) Schwindel, *der;* **c)** *(person)* Betrüger, *der/*Betrügerin, *die.* **fraudulent** ['frɔːdjʊlənt] *adj.* betrügerisch
fraught [frɔːt] *adj.* **be ~ with danger** voller Gefahren sein
¹**fray** [freɪ] *n.* [Kampf]getümmel, *das;* **enter** *or* **join the ~:** sich in den Kampf stürzen
²**fray** *v.i.* [sich] durchscheuern; ⟨*Hosenbein, Teppich, Seilende:*⟩ ausfransen; **our nerves/tempers began to ~** *(fig.)* wir verloren langsam die Nerven/unsere Gemüter erhitzten sich
freak [friːk] *n.* **a)** Mißgeburt, *die; attrib.* ungewöhnlich ⟨*Wetter, Ereignis*⟩; **b)** *(sl.: fanatic)* Freak, *der*
freckle ['frekl] *n.* Sommersprosse, *die.* '**freckled** *adj.* sommersprossig
free [friː] 1. *adj.,* **freer** ['friːə(r)], **freest** ['friːɪst] **a)** frei; **get ~:** freikommen; **set ~:** freilassen; **~ of charge/cost** gebührenfrei/kostenlos; **sb. is ~ to do sth.** es steht jmdm. frei, etw. zu tun; **~ time** Freizeit, *die;* **he's ~ in the mornings** er hat morgens Zeit; **b)** *(without payment)* kostenlos; frei ⟨*Unterkunft, Verpflegung*⟩; Frei⟨*karte, -exemplar*⟩; Gratis⟨*probe*⟩; '**admission ~**' „Eintritt frei"; **for ~** *(coll.)* umsonst. 2. *adv.* gratis; umsonst. 3. *v.t. (set at liberty)* freilassen; *(disentangle)* befreien (**of, from** von); **~ sb./oneself from** jmdn./sich befreien aus ⟨*Gefängnis, Sklaverei*⟩. **freedom** ['friːdəm] *n.* Freiheit, *die*
free: **~ 'gift** *n.* Gratisgabe, *die;* **~hold** 1. *n.* Besitzrecht, *das;* 2. *adj.* Eigentums-; **~lance** 1. *n.* freier Mitarbeiter/freie Mitarbeiterin; 2. *adj.* freiberuflich
'**freely** *adv. (willingly)* großzügig; freimütig ⟨*eingestehen*⟩; *(without restriction)* frei; *(frankly)* offen
free: **F~mason** *n.* Freimaurer, *der;* **~-range** *adj.* freilaufend ⟨*Huhn*⟩; **~-range eggs** Eier von freilaufenden Hühnern; **~ speech** *n.* Redefreiheit; **~way** *n. (Amer.)* Autobahn, *die;* **~-wheel** *v.i.* im Freilauf fahren
freeze [friːz] 1. *v.i.,* **froze** [frəʊz], **frozen** ['frəʊzn] **a)** frieren; *(become covered with ice)* zufrieren; ⟨*Straße:*⟩ vereisen; ⟨*Flüssigkeit:*⟩ gefrieren; ⟨*Rohr, Schloß:*⟩ einfrieren; **b)** *(become rigid)* steif frieren. 2. *v.t.,* **froze, frozen a)** *(preserve)* tiefkühlen; **b)** einfrieren ⟨*Kredit, Löhne, Preise usw.*⟩. '**freezer** *n.* Tiefkühltruhe, *die;* |upright| **~:** Tiefkühlschrank, *der;* **~ com-**

partment Tiefkühlfach, *das.* **freezing**
['fri:zɪŋ] 1. *adj. (lit. or fig.)* frostig; **it's**
~: es ist eiskalt. 2. *n.* **above/below** ~:
über/unter dem/den Gefrierpunkt
freight [freɪt] *n.* Fracht, *die.*
'**freighter** *n.* Frachter, *der*
French [frentʃ] 1. *adj.* französisch; **he/**
she is ~: er ist Franzose/sie ist Französin. 2. *n.* **a)** *(language)* Französisch,
das; see also **English 2 a**; **b)** the ~ *pl.*
die Franzosen
French: ~ '**bean** *n. (Brit.)* Gartenboh-
ne, *die;* ~ '**dressing** *n.* Vinaigrette,
die; ~ '**fries** *n. pl.* Pommes frites *Pl.*
~**man** ['frentʃmən] *n., pl.* ~**men**
['frentʃmən] Franzose, *der;* ~ '**win-**
dow *n.* französisches Fenster;
~**woman** *n.* Französin, *die*
frenzied ['frenzɪd] *adj.* rasend
frenzy ['frenzɪ] *n.* Wahnsinn, *der;*
(fury) Raserei, *die*
frequency ['fri:kwənsɪ] *n.* **a)** Häufigkeit, *die;* **b)** *(Phys.)* Frequenz, *die*
frequent 1. ['fri:kwənt] *adj.* **a)** häufig;
become less ~: seltener werden; **b)**
(habitual) eifrig. 2. [fri:'kwent] *v. t.*
häufig besuchen 〈*Café, Klub, usw.*〉.
frequently ['fri:kwəntlɪ] *adv.* häufig
fresco *n. pl.* ~**es** *or* ~**s** Fresko, *das*
fresh [freʃ] *adj.* frisch; neu 〈*Beweise,
Anstrich, Mut, Energie*〉; ~ **supplies**
Nachschub, *der* (of an + *Dat.*); **make**
a ~ **start** noch einmal von vorne anfangen; *(fig.)* neu beginnen
freshen ['freʃn] *v. i.* auffrischen.
freshen '**up** *v. i.* sich auffrischen
'**freshly** *adv.* frisch
'**freshness** *n.* Frische, *die*
fresh '**water** *n.* Süßwasser, *das*
fret [fret] *v. i.,* -tt- sich *(Dat.)* Sorgen
machen. **fretful** ['fretfl] *adj.* verdrießlich; quengelig *(ugs.)*
'**fretsaw** *n.* Laubsäge, *die*
Fri. *abbr.* **Friday** Fr.
friar ['fraɪə(r)] *n.* Ordensbruder, *der*
friction ['frɪkʃn] *n.* Reibung, *die*
Friday ['fraɪdeɪ, 'fraɪdɪ] *n.* Freitag, *der;*
on ~: [am] Freitag; **on a** ~, **on** ~**s** freitags; ~ **13 August** Freitag, der 13. August; *(at top of letter etc.)* Freitag, den
13. August; **next/last** ~: [am] näch-
sten/letzten Freitag; **Good** ~: Karfrei-
tag, *der*
fridge [frɪdʒ] *n. (Brit. coll.)* Kühlschrank, *der*
fried *see* '**fry**
friend [frend] *n.* **a)** Freund, *der/*
Freundin, *die;* **be** ~**s with sb.** mit
jmdm. befreundet sein; **make** ~**s |with**

sb.| [mit jmdm.] Freundschaft schlie-
ßen. **friendliness** ['frendlɪnɪs] *n.*
Freundlichkeit, *die.* '**friendly 1.** *adj.*
freundlich (**to** zu); freundschaftlich
〈*Rat, Beziehungen, Wettkampf*〉. **2.**
n. (Sport) Freundschaftsspiel, *das.*
'**friendship** *n.* Freundschaft, *die*
frigate ['frɪgət] *n. (Naut.)* Fregatte, *die*
fright [fraɪt] *n.* Schreck, *der;* **take** ~:
erschrecken. **frighten** ['fraɪtn] *v. t.*
〈*Explosion, Schuß:*〉 erschrecken; 〈*Gedanke, Drohung:*〉 angst machen
(+ *Dat.*); **be** ~**ed at** *or* **by sth.** vor etw.
(Dat.) erschrecken. '**frightful** *adj.,*
'**frightfully** *adv.* furchtbar
frigid ['frɪdʒɪd] *adj.* frostig; *(sexually)*
frigid[e]
frill [frɪl] *n.* **a)** Rüsche, *die;* **b)** *in pl.*
(embellishments) Beiwerk, *das.* '**frilly**
adj. mit Rüschen besetzt; Rüschen-
〈*kleid, -bluse*〉
fringe [frɪndʒ] *n.* **a)** Fransenkante, *die*
(**on an** + *Dat.*); **b)** *(hair)* [Pony]fran-
sen *(ugs.);* **c)** *(edge)* Rand, *der*
frisk [frɪsk] 1. *v. i.* [about] [herum]
springen. 2. *v. t. (coll.)* filzen *(ugs.).*
'**frisky** *adj.* munter
'**fritter** ['frɪtə(r)] *n.* **apple** *etc.* ~**s** Apfel-
stücke *usw.* in Pfannkuchenteig
²**fritter** *v. t.* ~ **away** vergeuden
frivolity [frɪ'vɒlɪtɪ] *n.* Oberflächlich-
keit, *die*
frivolous ['frɪvələs] *adj.* **a)** frivol; **b)**
(trifling) belanglos
frizzy ['frɪzɪ] *adj.* kraus
fro [frəʊ] *adv. see* **to 2**
frock [frɒk] *n.* Kleid, *das*
frog [frɒg] *n.* Frosch, *der.* **frogman**
['frɒgmən] *n., pl.* ~**men** ['frɒgmən]
Froschmann, *der.* '**frog-spawn** *n.*
Froschlaich, *der*
frolic ['frɒlɪk] *v. i.,* -ck-: ~ [about *or*
around] [herum]springen
from [frəm, *stressed* frɒm] *prep.* von;
(~ *within; expr. origin)* aus; ~ **Paris**
aus Paris; ~ **Paris to Munich** von Paris
nach München; **be a mile** ~ **sth.** eine
Meile von etw. entfernt sein; **where do**
you come ~? **where are you** ~? woher
kommen Sie?; **painted** ~ **life** nach
dem Leben gemalt; **weak** ~ **hunger**
schwach vor Hunger; ~ **the year 1972**
seit 1972; ~ |**the age of**| **18** ab 18 Jahre;
~ **4 to 6 eggs** 4 bis 6 Eier
front [frʌnt] **1.** *n.* **a)** Vorderseite, *die;*
(of house) Vorderfront, *die;* **in** *or* **at**
the ~ |**of sth.**| vorn [in etw. *position:*
Dat., movement: Akk.]; **to the** ~: nach
vorn; **in** ~: vorn[e]; **be in** ~ **of sth./sb.**

vor etw./jmdm. sein; **b)** *(Mil.)* Front,
die; **c)** *(at seaside)* Strandpromenade,
die; **d)** *(Meteorol.)* Front, *die;* **e)** *(bluff)*
Fassade, *die.* **2.** *adj.* vorder...; Vorder-
⟨*rad, -zimmer, -zahn*⟩; ~ **garden** Vor-
garten, *der;* ~ **row** erste Reihe.
frontal ['frʌntl] *adj.* Frontal-. **front
'door** *n. (of flat)* Wohnungstür, *die;*
(of house) Haustür, *die*
frontier ['frʌntɪə(r)] *n.* Grenze, *die*
front 'page *n.* Titelseite, *die*
frost [frɒst] **1.** *n.* Frost, *der;* **ten de-**
grees of ~ *(Brit.)* zehn Grad minus. **2.**
v. t. **~ed glass** Mattglas, *das.* **'frost-**
bite *n.* Erfrierung, *die.* **'frosting** *n.*
(esp. Amer.) Glasur, *die.* **'frosty** *adj.*
frostig
froth [frɒθ] **1.** *n.* Schaum, *der.* **2.** *v. i.*
schäumen. **'frothy** *adj.* schaumig
frown [fraʊn] **1.** *v. i.* die Stirn runzeln
(⟨up⟩on über + *Akk.*). **2.** *n.* Stirnrun-
zeln, *das*
froze *see* **freeze**
frozen ['frəʊzn] **1.** *see* **freeze. 2.** *adj.* **a)**
zugefroren ⟨*Fluß, See*⟩; eingefroren
⟨*Wasserleitung*⟩; **I'm ~** *(fig.)* ich bin
eiskalt; **b)** *(to preserve)* tiefgekühlt; ~
food Tiefkühlkost, *die*
frugal ['fru:gl] *adj.* genügsam ⟨*Lebens-*
weise, Mensch⟩; frugal ⟨*Mahl*⟩
fruit [fru:t] *n.* Frucht, *die; collect.* Obst,
das
fruitful ['fru:tfl] *adj.* fruchtbar
'fruit juice *n.* Obstsaft, *der*
'fruitless *adj.* nutzlos ⟨*Versuch, Ge-*
spräch⟩; fruchtlos ⟨*Verhandlung,*
Suche⟩
fruit: ~ machine *n. (Brit.)* Spielautomat, *der;* ~ **'salad** *n.* Obstsalat, *der*
'fruity *adj.* fruchtig ⟨*Geschmack,*
Wein⟩
frustrate [frʌ'streɪt] *v. t.* vereiteln
⟨*Plan, Versuch*⟩; zunichte machen
⟨*Hoffnung, Bemühungen*⟩. **'frus-**
trated *adj.* frustriert. **frustration**
[frʌ'streɪʃn] *n.* Frustration, *die*
¹fry [fraɪ] *v. t. & i.* braten; **fried egg**
Spiegelei, *das*
²fry *n. (fishes)* Brut, *die;* **small ~** *(fig.)*
unbedeutende Leute
'frying-pan *n.* Bratpfanne, *die*
ft. *abbr.* **feet, foot** ft.
fuck [fʌk] *(coarse)* **1.** *v. t. & i.* ficken
(vulg.). **2.** *n.* Fick, *der (vulg.)*
fuddy-duddy ['fʌdɪdʌdɪ] *(sl.)* **1.** *adj.*
verkalkt *(ugs.).* **2.** *n.* Fossil, *das (fig.)*
fudge [fʌdʒ] *n.* Karamelbonbon, *der*
od. das
fuel ['fju:əl] *n.* Brennstoff, *der; (for*

vehicle) Kraftstoff, *der; (for ship, air-*
craft) Treibstoff, *der*
fugitive ['fju:dʒɪtɪv] *n.* Flüchtige, *der/*
die
fugue [fju:g] *n. (Mus.)* Fuge, *die*
fulfil *(Amer.:* **fulfill)** [fʊl'fɪl] *v. t.,* **-ll-**
erfüllen; halten ⟨*Versprechen*⟩. **ful'fil-**
ment *(Amer.:* **ful'fillment)** *n.* Erfüllung, *die*
full [fʊl] **1.** *adj.* **a)** voll; satt ⟨*Person*⟩; ~
of voller; **be ~ up** *(coll.)* voll [besetzt]
sein; ⟨*Behälter:*⟩ randvoll sein; ⟨*Flug:*⟩
völlig ausgebucht sein; **I'm ~** [up]
(coll.) ich bin voll [bis obenhin] *(ugs.);*
be ~ of oneself sehr von sich einge-
nommen sein; **b)** ausführlich ⟨*Bericht,*
Beschreibung⟩; erfüllt ⟨*Leben*⟩; ganz
⟨*Stunde, Jahr, Monat, Seite*⟩; voll
⟨*Name, Bezahlung, Verständnis*⟩; ~
details alle Einzelheiten; **at ~ speed**
mit Höchstgeschwindigkeit; **c)** voll
⟨*Gesicht*⟩; füllig ⟨*Figur*⟩; weit ⟨*Rock*⟩.
2. *n.* **in ~:** vollständig. **3.** *adv. (exactly)*
genau
full: ~ back *n.* Verteidiger, *der/*Verteidigerin, *die;* **~-length** *adj.* lang
⟨*Kleid*⟩; ~ **'moon** *n.* Vollmond, *der;*
~-scale *adj.* **a)** in Originalgröße; **b)**
großangelegt ⟨*Untersuchung, Suchak-*
tion⟩; ~ **'stop** *n.* Punkt, *der;* **~-time**
adj. ganztägig; ganztags⟨*arbeit*⟩
fully ['fʊlɪ] *adv.* voll [und ganz]; reich
⟨*belohnt*⟩; ausführlich ⟨*erklären*⟩
fulsome ['fʊlsəm] *adj.* übertrieben
fumble ['fʌmbl] *v. i.* ~ **at** *or* **with** [her-
um]fingern an (+ *Dat.*); ~ **in one's**
pockets for sth. in seinen Taschen
nach etw. kramen *(ugs.)*
fume [fju:m] **1.** *n. in pl.* **~s** Dämpfe. **2.**
v. i. vor Wut schäumen
fumigate ['fju:mɪgeɪt] *v. t.* ausräu-
chern
fun [fʌn] *n.* Spaß, *der;* **have ~!** viel
Spaß!; **make ~ of sb.** sich über jmdn.
lustig machen; **for ~, for the ~ of it**
zum Spaß
function ['fʌŋkʃn] **1.** *n.* Aufgabe, *die;*
Funktion, *die; (formal event)* Veranstaltung, *die.* **2.** *v. i.* ⟨*Maschine, Sy-*
stem:⟩ funktionieren; ~ **as** fungieren
als; *(serve as)* dienen als. **functional**
['fʌŋkʃənl] *adj.* **a)** *(useful)* funktionell;
b) *(working)* funktionsfähig
fund [fʌnd] **1.** *n.* **a)** *(money)* Fonds,
der; **b)** *(fig.: stock)* Fundus, *der (of*
von, an + *Dat.*). **2.** *v. t.* finanzieren
fundamental [fʌndə'mentl] *adj.*
grundlegend (**to** für); elementar ⟨*Be-*
dürfnisse⟩. **fundamentally** [fʌndə-

'mentəlı] *adv.* grundlegend; von Grund auf ⟨*verschieden, ehrlich*⟩

funeral ['fju:nərl] *n.* Beerdigung, *die.* ~ **director** Bestattungsunternehmer, *der;* ~ **service** Trauerfeier, *die*

'**fun-fair** *n. (Brit.)* Jahrmarkt, *der*

fungus ['fʌŋgəs] *n., pl.* **fungi** ['fʌŋgaɪ, 'fʌndʒaɪ] *or* **-es** Pilz, *der*

funicular [fju:'nɪkjʊlə(r)] *adj. & n.* ~ |**railway**| [Stand]seilbahn, *die*

funnel ['fʌnl] *n.* Trichter, *der; (of ship etc.)* Schornstein, *der*

funnily ['fʌnɪlɪ] *adv.* komisch; ~ **enough** komischerweise

funny ['fʌnɪ] *adj.* **a)** komisch; lustig; witzig ⟨*Mensch, Einfall*⟩; **b)** *(strange)* komisch. '**funny-bone** *n.* Musikantenknochen, *der*

fur [fɜ:(r)] *n.* **a)** Fell, *das; (garment)* Pelz, *der;* ~ **coat** Pelzmantel, *der;* **b)** *(in kettle)* Kesselstein, *der*

furious ['fjʊərɪəs] *adj.* wütend; heftig ⟨*Streit*⟩; wild ⟨*Tanz, Tempo, Kampf*⟩; **be** ~ **with sb.** wütend auf jmdn. sein. '**furiously** *adv.* wütend; wild ⟨*kämpfen*⟩: wie wild *(ugs.)* arbeiten

furl [fɜ:l] *v.t.* einrollen ⟨*Segel, Flagge*⟩

furnace ['fɜ:nɪs] *n.* Ofen, *der*

furnish ['fɜ:nɪʃ] *v.t.* **a)** möblieren; **b)** *(supply)* liefern; ~ **sb. with sth.** jmdm. etw. liefern. '**furnishings** *n. pl.* Einrichtungsgegenstände

furniture ['fɜ:nɪtʃə(r)] *n.* Möbel *Pl.;* **piece of** ~: Möbel[stück], *das*

furrow ['fʌrəʊ] *n.* Furche, *die*

furry ['fɜ:rɪ] *adj.* haarig; ~ **animal** *(toy)* Plüschtier, *das*

further ['fɜ:ðə(r)] **1.** *adj.* **a)** *(in space)* weiter entfernt; **b)** *(additional)* weiter... **2.** *adv.* weiter. **3.** *v.t.* fördern. **further'more** *adv.* außerdem. '**furthermost** *adj.* äußerst ...

furthest ['fɜ:ðɪst] **1.** *adj.* am weitesten entfernt. **2.** *adv.* am weitesten ⟨*springen, laufen*⟩; am weitesten entfernt ⟨*sein, wohnen*⟩

furtive ['fɜ:tɪv] *adj.,* **furtively** *adv.* verstohlen

fury ['fjʊərɪ] *n.* Wut, *die; (of sea, battle)* Wüten, *das*

¹**fuse** [fju:z] **1.** *v.t. (blend)* verschmelzen (**into** zu). **2.** *v.i.* ~ **together** miteinander verschmelzen

²**fuse** *n.* |time-|~: *(Zeit|zünder, der; (cord)* Zündschnur, *die*

³**fuse** *(Electr.)* **1.** *n.* Sicherung, *die.* **2.** *v.i.* **the lights have** ~**d** die Sicherung ist durchgebrannt. '**fuse box** *n.* Sicherungskasten, *der*

fuselage ['fju:zəlɑ:ʒ] *n.* [Flugzeug]rumpf, *der*

fusion ['fju:ʒn] *n.* **a)** Verschmelzung, *die;* **b)** *(Phys.)* Fusion, *die*

fuss [fʌs] **1.** *n.* Theater, *das (ugs.);* **make a** ~ |**about sth.**| einen Wirbel |um etw.| machen. **2.** *v.i.* Wirbel machen; *(get agitated)* sich [unnötig] aufregen. '**fussy** *adj. (fastidious)* eigen; penibel; **I'm not** ~ *(I don't mind)* ich bin nicht wählerisch

futile ['fju:taɪl] *adj.* vergeblich

future ['fju:tʃə(r)] **1.** *adj.* [zu]künftig; **at some** ~ **date** zu einem späteren Zeitpunkt. **2.** *n.* **a)** Zukunft, *die;* **in** ~: in Zukunft; künftig; **b)** *(Ling.)* Futur, *das;* Zukunft, *die.* **futuristic** [fju:tʃə'rɪstɪk] *adj.* futuristisch

fuze [fju:z] *see* ²**fuse**

fuzzy ['fʌzɪ] *adj.* **a)** *(frizzy)* kraus; **b)** *(blurred)* verschwommen

G

G, g [dʒi:] *n.* G, g, *das*

gab [gæb] *n. (coll.)* **have the gift of the** ~: reden können

gabble ['gæbl] *v.i.* brabbeln *(ugs.)*

gable ['geɪbl] *n.* Giebel, *der*

gad [gæd] *v.i.,* **-dd-** *(coll.)* ~ **about** herumziehen

gadget ['gædʒɪt] *n.* Gerät, *das*

Gaelic ['geɪlɪk, 'gælɪk] **1.** *adj.* gälisch. **2.** *n.* Gälisch, *das*

gaffe [gæf] *n.* Fauxpas, *der*

gag [gæg] **1.** *n.* **a)** Knebel, *der;* **b)** *(joke)* Gag, *der.* **2.** *v.t.,* **-gg-** knebeln

gaiety ['geɪətɪ] *n.* Fröhlichkeit, *die*

gaily ['geɪlɪ] *adv.* fröhlich; in leuchtenden Farben ⟨*bemalt, geschmückt*⟩

gain [geɪn] **1.** *n.* **a)** Gewinn, *der;* **b)** *(increase)* Zunahme, *die* (**in** an + *Dat.*). **2.** *v.t.* **a)** gewinnen; finden ⟨*Zugang, Zutritt*⟩; erwerben ⟨*Wissen, Ruf*⟩; erlangen ⟨*Freiheit*⟩; erzielen ⟨*Vorteil, Punkte*⟩; verdienen ⟨*Lebensunterhalt, Geldsumme*⟩; ~ **weight/five pounds** |**in weight**| zunehmen/fünf Pfund zunehmen; ~ **speed** schneller werden; **b)** ⟨*Uhr:*⟩ vorgehen um. **3.** *v.i.* **a)** ~ **by**

sth. von etw. profitieren; b) ⟨Uhr:⟩ vorgehen

gait [geɪt] n. Gang, der

gala ['gɑːlə, 'geɪlə] n. Festveranstaltung, die; attrib. Gala⟨abend, -vorstellung⟩; swimming ~: Schwimmfest, das

galaxy ['gæləksɪ] n. Galaxie, die

gale [geɪl] n. Sturm, der

gall [gɔːl] n. (sl.) Unverschämtheit, die

gallant ['gælənt] adj. (brave) tapfer; (chivalrous) ritterlich. **gallantry** ['gæləntrɪ] n. (bravery) Tapferkeit, die

gall-bladder n. Gallenblase, die

gallery ['gælərɪ] n. a) Galerie, die; b) (Theatre) dritter Rang

galley ['gælɪ] n. a) (ship's kitchen) Kombüse, die; b) (Hist.) Galeere, die

gallivant ['gælɪvænt] v.i. (coll.) herumziehen (ugs.)

gallon ['gælən] n. Gallone, die

gallop ['gæləp] 1. n. Galopp, der. 2. v.i. ⟨Pferd, Reiter:⟩ galoppieren

gallows ['gæləʊz] n. sing. Galgen, der

galore [gə'lɔː(r)] adv. im Überfluß; in Hülle und Fülle

galvanize ['gælvənaɪz] v.t. wachrütteln; ~ sb. into action jmdn. veranlassen, sofort aktiv zu werden

gambit ['gæmbɪt] n. Gambit, das

gamble ['gæmbl] v.i. a) [um Geld] spielen; b) (fig.) spekulieren; ~ on sth. sich auf etw. (Akk.) verlassen. **gambler** ['gæmblə(r)] n. Glücksspieler, der

'game [geɪm] n. a) Spiel, das; (of [table-]tennis, chess, cards, cricket) Partie, die; b) (fig.: scheme) Vorhaben, das; c) in pl. (athletic contests) Spiele; (in school) (sports) Sport, der; (athletics) Leichtathletik, die; d) (Hunting, Cookery) Wild, das

²game adj. mutig; be ~ to do sth. bereit sein, etw. zu tun

'gamekeeper n. Wildheger, der

gammon ['gæmən] n. Räucherschinken, der

gamut ['gæmət] n. Skala, die

gander ['gændə(r)] n. Gänserich, der

gang [gæŋ] 1. n. Bande, die; (of workmen, prisoners) Trupp, der. 2. v.i. ~ up against or on (coll.) sich verbünden gegen

gangling ['gæŋglɪŋ] schlaksig (ugs.)

gangster ['gæŋstə(r)] n. Gangster, der

'gangway n. Gangway, die; (Brit.: between seats) Gang, der

gaol [dʒeɪl] see jail

gap [gæp] n. a) Lücke, die; b) (in time) Pause, die; c) (divergence) Kluft, die

gape [geɪp] v.i. a) den Mund aufsperren; ⟨Loch, Abgrund, Wunde:⟩ klaffen; b) (stare) Mund und Nase aufsperren (ugs.); ~ at sb./sth. jmdn./ etw. mit offenem Mund anstarren

garage ['gærɪdʒ] n. Garage, die; (selling petrol) Tankstelle, die; (for repairing cars) [Kfz-]Werkstatt, die

garb [gɑːb] n. Tracht, die

garbage ['gɑːbɪdʒ] n. a) Abfall, der; Müll, der; b) (coll.: nonsense) Quatsch, der (salopp). **'garbage can** n. (Amer.) Mülltonne, die

garble ['gɑːbl] v.t. verstümmeln

garden ['gɑːdn] n. Garten, der. **'garden centre** n. Gartencenter, das. **gardener** ['gɑːdnə(r)] n. Gärtner, der/Gärtnerin, die. **gardening** ['gɑːdnɪŋ] n. Gartenarbeit, die

gargle ['gɑːgl] v.i. gurgeln

garish ['geərɪʃ] adj. grell ⟨Farbe, Licht⟩; knallbunt ⟨Kleidung⟩

garland ['gɑːlənd] n. Girlande, die

garlic ['gɑːlɪk] n. Knoblauch, der

garment ['gɑːmənt] n. Kleidungsstück, das; ~s pl. (clothes) Kleidung, die; Kleider

garnish ['gɑːnɪʃ] 1. v.t. garnieren. 2. n. Garnierung, die

garret ['gærɪt] n. Dachkammer, die

garrison ['gærɪsn] n. Garnison, die

garter ['gɑːtə(r)] n. Strumpfband, das

gas [gæs] 1. n. a) pl. ~es ['gæsɪz] Gas, das; b) (Amer. coll.: petrol) Benzin, das. 2. v.t., -ss- mit Gas vergiften. **gas 'cooker** n. (Brit.) Gasherd, der. **gas 'fire** n. Gasofen, der

gash [gæʃ] 1. n. Schnittwunde, die. 2. v.t. aufritzen ⟨Haut⟩; ~ one's finger sich (Dat. od. Akk.) in den Finger schneiden

gas: ~ mask n. Gasmaske, die; ~ **meter** n. Gaszähler, der

gasoline (gasolene) ['gæsəliːn] n. (Amer.) Benzin, das

gasometer [gæ'sɒmɪtə(r)] n. Gasometer, der

gasp [gɑːsp] 1. v.i. nach Luft schnappen (with vor); he was ~ing for air er rang nach Luft. 2. v.t. ~ out hervorstoßen. 3. n. Keuchen, das

'gas station n. (Amer.) Tankstelle, die

gastronomy [gæ'strɒnəmɪ] n. Gastronomie, die

'gasworks n. sing. Gaswerk, das

gate [geɪt] n. Tor, das; (barrier) Sperre, die; (to field etc.) Gatter, das; (of level crossing) [Bahn]schranke, die; (in airport) Flugsteig, der

gateau ['gætəʊ] *n., pl.* ~s *or* ~x ['gætəʊz] Torte, *die*

gate: ~**crasher** ['geɪtkræʃə(r)] *n.* ungeladener Gast; ~**way** *n.* Tor, *das*

gather ['gæðə(r)] 1. *v. t.* **a)** sammeln; zusammentragen ⟨*Informationen*⟩; pflücken ⟨*Obst, Blumen*⟩; **b)** *(infer, deduce)* schließen (**from** aus); **c)** ~ **speed/force** schneller/stärker werden. 2. *v. i.* sich versammeln; ⟨*Wolken:*⟩ sich zusammenziehen. '**gathering** *n.* Versammlung, *die*

gaudy ['gɔːdɪ] *adj.* protzig; grell ⟨*Farben*⟩

gauge [geɪdʒ] *n.* 1. **a)** *(measure)* Maß, *das;* **b)** *(instrument)* Meßgerät, *das.* 2. *v. t.* messen; *(fig.)* beurteilen

gaunt [gɔːnt] *adj.* hager

gauntlet ['gɔːntlɪt] *n.* Stulpenhandschuh, *der*

gauze [gɔːz] *n.* Gaze, *die*

gave *see* **give** 1, 2

gay [geɪ] 1. *adj.* **a)** fröhlich; *(brightcoloured)* farbenfroh; **b)** *(coll.: homosexual)* schwul *(ugs.);* Schwulen⟨*lokal*⟩. 2. *n. (coll.)* Schwule, *der (ugs.)*

gaze [geɪz] *v. i.* blicken; *(fixedly)* starren; ~ **at sb./sth.** jmdn./etw. anstarren

GB *abbr.* **Great Britain** GB

GCSE *abbr. (Brit.)* **General Certificate of Secondary Education**

gear [gɪə(r)] 1. *n.* **a)** *(Motor Veh.)* Gang, *der;* **top/bottom** ~ *(Brit.)* der höchste/erste Gang; **change** *or* **shift** ~: schalten; **put the car into** ~: einen Gang einlegen; **out of** ~: im Leerlauf; **b)** *(coll.: clothes)* Aufmachung, *die;* **c)** *(equipment)* Gerät, *das;* Ausrüstung, *die.* 2. *v. t.* ausrichten (**to** auf + *Akk.*). '**gearbox** *n.* Getriebekasten, *der.* '**gear-lever,** *(Amer.)* '**gear-shift** *ns.* Schalthebel, *der*

geese *pl. of* **goose**

geezer ['giːzə(r)] *(sl.: old man)* Opa, *der (ugs.)*

gel [dʒel] *n.* Gel, *das*

gelatin ['dʒelətɪn], *(Brit.)* **gelatine** ['dʒelətiːn] *n.* Gelatine, *die*

gelignite ['dʒelɪgnaɪt] *n.* Gelatinedynamit, *das*

gem [dʒem] *n.* Edelstein, *der*

Gemini ['dʒemɪnaɪ, 'dʒemɪnɪ] *n.* Zwillinge *Pl.*

gender ['dʒendə(r)] *n. (Ling.)* [grammatisches] Geschlecht

gene [dʒiːn] *n. (Biol.)* Gen, *das*

general ['dʒenrl] 1. *adj.* allgemein; weitverbreitet ⟨*Ansicht*⟩; *(true of [nearly] all cases)* allgemeingültig; ungefähr ⟨*Vorstellung, Beschreibung usw.*⟩; **the** ~ **public** weite Kreise der Bevölkerung; **in** ~ **use** allgemein verbreitet; **as a** ~ **rule, in** ~: im allgemeinen. 2. *n. (Mil.)* General, *der.* **general election** *see* **election**

generalization [dʒenrəlaɪ'zeɪʃn] *n.* Verallgemeinerung, *die*

generalize ['dʒenrəlaɪz] 1. *v. t.* verallgemeinern. 2. *v. i.* ~ **about sth.** [etw.] verallgemeinern

generally ['dʒenrəlɪ] *adv.* **a)** allgemein; ~ **available** überall erhältlich; ~ **speaking** im allgemeinen; **b)** *(usually)* im allgemeinen

general practitioner *n. (Med.)* Arzt/Ärztin für Allgemeinmedizin

generate ['dʒenəreɪt] *v. t.* erzeugen (**from** aus); *(result in)* führen zu. **generation** [dʒenə'reɪʃn] *n.* **a)** Generation, *die;* **b)** *(production)* Erzeugung, *die.* **generator** ['dʒenəreɪtə(r)] *n.* Generator, *der*

generosity [dʒenə'rɒsɪtɪ] *n.* Großzügigkeit, *die*

generous ['dʒenərəs] *adj.* großzügig; reichlich ⟨*Vorrat, Portion*⟩. '**generously** *adv.* großzügig

genetic [dʒɪ'netɪk] *adj.* genetisch. **genetics** [dʒɪ'netɪks] *n.* Genetik, *die*

Geneva [dʒɪ'niːvə] 1. *pr. n.* Genf *(das).* 2. *attrib. adj.* Genfer

genial ['dʒiːnɪəl] *adj.* freundlich

genitals ['dʒenɪtlz] *n. pl.* Geschlechtsorgane

genitive ['dʒenɪtɪv] *adj. & n.* ~ [**case**] Genitiv, *der*

genius ['dʒiːnɪəs] *n.* **a)** *(person)* Genie, *das;* **b)** *(ability)* Talent, *das*

genre ['ʒɑ̃rə] *n.* Genre, *das*

gent [dʒent] *n.* **a)** *(coll./joc.)* Gent, *der (iron.);* **b) the G**~**s** *(Brit. coll.)* die Herrentoilette

genteel [dʒen'tiːl] *adj.* vornehm

gentle ['dʒentl] *adj.,* ~**r** ['dʒentlə(r)], ~**st** ['dʒentlɪst] sanft; liebenswürdig ⟨*Person, Verhalten*⟩; leicht, schwach ⟨*Brise*⟩; leise ⟨*Geräusch*⟩; gemächlich ⟨*Spaziergang, Tempo*⟩; mäßig ⟨*Hitze*⟩

gentleman ['dʒentlmən] *n., pl.* **gentlemen** ['dʒentlmən] Herr, *der; (well-mannered)* Gentleman, *der;* **Ladies and Gentlemen!** meine Damen und Herren!

'**gentleness** *n.* Sanftheit, *die; (of nature)* Sanftmütigkeit, *die*

gently ['dʒentlɪ] *adv. (tenderly)* zart; zärtlich; *(mildly)* sanft; *(carefully)* behutsam; *(quietly, softly)* leise

genuine ['dʒenjʊin] *adj.* **a)** *(real)* echt;
b) *(true)* aufrichtig; wahr ⟨*Grund,
Not*⟩. '**genuinely** *adv.* wirklich
genus ['dʒi:nəs, 'dʒenəs] *n., pl.* **genera**
['dʒenərə] *(Biol.)* Gattung, *die*
geographical [dʒi:ə'græfıkl] *adj.* geographisch
geography [dʒı'ɒgrəfı] *n.* Geographie, *die;* Erdkunde, *die (Schulw.)*
geological [dʒi:ə'lɒdʒıkl] *adj.* geologisch
geologist [dʒı'ɒlədʒıst] *n.* Geologe,
*der/*Geologin, *die*
geology [dʒı'ɒlədʒı] *n.* Geologie, *die*
geometric [dʒi:ə'metrık], **geomet-
rical** [dʒi:ə'metrıkl] *adj.* geometrisch
geometry [dʒı'ɒmıtrı] *n.* Geometrie,
die
geranium [dʒə'reınıəm] *n.* Geranie,
die; Pelargonie, *die*
geriatric [dʒerı'ætrık] *adj.* geriatrisch
germ [dʒɜ:m] *n.* Keim, *der*
German ['dʒɜ:mən] **1.** *adj.* deutsch;
he/she is ~: er ist Deutscher/sie ist
Deutsche. **2.** *n.* **a)** *(person)* Deutsche,
der/die; **b)** *(language)* Deutsch, *das;
see also* **English 2 a**
German Democratic Re'public *pr.
n. (Hist.)* Deutsche Demokratische
Republik
Germanic [dʒɜ:'mænık] *adj.* germanisch
German 'measles *n.* Röteln *Pl.*
Germany ['dʒɜ:mənı] *pr. n.* Deutschland *(das);* **Federal Republic of ~:**
Bundesrepublik Deutschland, *die*
germinate ['dʒɜ:mıneıt] *v. i.* keimen
gesticulate [dʒe'stıkjʊleıt] *v. i.* gestikulieren. **gesticulation** [dʒestıkjʊ-
'leıʃn] *n.* Gesten *Pl.*
gesture ['dʒestʃə(r)] *n.* Geste, *die*
get [get] **1.** *v. t.,* -tt-, got [gɒt], got *or
(Amer.)* gotten ['gɒtn] **a)** *(obtain, receive)* bekommen; kriegen *(ugs.);* sich
(Dat.) besorgen ⟨*Visum, Genehmigung*⟩; sich *(Dat.)* beschaffen ⟨*Geld*⟩;
(find) finden ⟨*Zeit*⟩; *(fetch)* holen;
(buy) kaufen; **where did you ~ that?**
wo hast du das her?; **~ sb. a job/taxi,
~ a job/taxi for sb.** jmdm. einen Job
verschaffen/ein Taxi besorgen; **~ oneself sth.** sich *(Dat.)* etw. zulegen; **b) ~
the bus** *etc. (be in time for, catch)* den
Bus *usw.* erreichen *od. (ugs.)* kriegen;
(travel by) den Bus *usw.* nehmen; **c)**
(prepare) machen *(ugs.),* zubereiten
⟨*Essen*⟩; **d)** *(win)* bekommen; finden
⟨*Anerkennung*⟩; erzielen ⟨*Tor, Punkt,
Treffer*⟩; gewinnen ⟨*Spiel, Preis, Be-*

lohnung⟩; **~ permission** die Erlaubnis
erhalten; **e)** finden ⟨*Schlaf, Ruhe*⟩; bekommen ⟨*Einfall, Vorstellung, Gefühl,
Kopfschmerzen, Grippe*⟩; gewinnen
⟨*Eindruck*⟩; **f) have got** *(coll.: have)* haben; **have got a cold** eine Erkältung
haben; **have got to do sth.** etw. tun
müssen; **g)** *(succeed in placing, bringing, etc.)* bringen; kriegen *(ugs.);* **~ a
message to sb.** jmdm. eine Nachricht
zukommen lassen; **~ things going** *or*
started die Dinge in Gang bringen; **h)
~ everything packed/prepared** alles
[ein]packen/vorbereiten; **~ sth. ready/
done** etw. fertig machen; **~ one's feet
wet** nasse Füße kriegen; **~ one's hands
dirty** sich *(Dat.)* die Hände schmutzig
machen; **~ one's hair cut** sich die Haare schneiden lassen; **~ sb. to do sth.**
(induce) jmdn. dazu bringen, etw. zu
tun; **i) ~ sb. [on the telephone]** jmdn.
[telefonisch] erreichen; **j)** *(coll.)
(understand)* kapieren *(ugs.); (hear)*
mitkriegen *(ugs.).* **2.** *v. i.,* -tt-, got, got
or (Amer.) gotten **a)** *(succeed in coming
or going)* kommen; **~ to London before dark** London vor Einbruch der
Dunkelheit erreichen; **b)** *(come to be)*
~ working sich an die Arbeit machen;
~ going *or* **started** *(leave)* losgehen;
(become lively or operative) in
Schwung kommen; **~ going on** *or* **with
sth.** mit etw. anfangen; **c) ~ to know
sb.** jmdn. kennenlernen; **d)** *(become)*
werden; **~ ready/washed** sich fertig-
machen/waschen; **~ frightened/hun-
gry** Angst/Hunger kriegen. **get
a'bout** *v. i.* **a)** *(travel)* herumkommen;
b) ⟨*Gerücht:*⟩ sich verbreiten. '**get at**
v. t. **a)** herankommen an (+ *Akk.*); **b)**
(find out) [he]rausfinden ⟨*Wahrheit
usw.*⟩; **what are you getting at?** worauf
wollen Sie hinaus? **get a'way** *v. i.* **a)**
(leave) wegkommen; **b)** *(escape)* entkommen. **get 'back 1.** *v. i.* zurückkommen; **~ back home** nach Hause
kommen. **2.** *v. i. (recover)* zurückbekommen; **~ one's own back** *(sl.)* sich
rächen. **get 'by** *v. i.* **a)** vorbeikommen; **b)** *(coll.: manage)* über die Runden kommen *(ugs.).* **get 'down 1.**
v. i. hinunter-/heruntersteigen; **~
down to sth.** *(start)* sich an etw. *(Akk.)*
machen. **2.** *v. t.* **a) ~ sb./sth. down**
jmdn./etw. hinunter-/herunterbrin-
gen; **b)** *(coll.: depress)* fertigmachen
(ugs.). **get 'in** *v. i. (into bus etc.)* einsteigen; *(arrive)* ankommen. **2.** *v. t.
(fetch)* reinholen. **get 'off 1.** *v. i.* **a)**

(alight) aussteigen; *(dismount)* absteigen; b) *(leave)* [weg]gehen; c) *(escape punishment)* davonkommen. **2.** *v. t.* a) *(remove)* ausziehen ⟨Kleidung usw.⟩; entfernen ⟨Fleck usw.⟩; abbekommen ⟨Deckel usw.⟩; b) aussteigen aus; absteigen von ⟨Fahrrad⟩; c) ~ off the subject vom Thema abkommen. **get 'on** *v. i.* a) *(mount)* aufsteigen; *(enter vehicle)* einsteigen; b) *(make progress)* vorankommen; he's ~ting on well es geht ihm gut; c) *(manage)* zurechtkommen. **get 'on with** *v. t.* a) weitermachen mit; b) ~ on [well] with sb. mit jmdm. [gut] auskommen. **get 'out 1.** *v. i.* a) rausgehen/rausfahren (of aus); b) *(alight)* aussteigen; c) *(escape)* ausbrechen (of aus); *(fig.)* herauskommen; ~ out of *(avoid)* herumkommen um *(ugs.)*. **2.** *v. t.* a) *(cause to leave)* rausbringen; b) *(withdraw)* abheben ⟨Geld⟩ (of von). **get 'over** *v. t.* a) *(cross)* gehen über (+ Akk.); *(climb)* klettern über (+ Akk.); b) *(recover from)* überwinden; hinwegkommen über (+ Akk.). **get 'round** *v. i.* ~ round to doing sth. dazu kommen, etw. zu tun. **get 'through** *v. i.* durchkommen. **get 'up** *v. i.* aufstehen. **get 'up to** *v. t.* ~ up to mischief etwas anstellen

get: ~away *n.* Flucht, *die;* attrib. Flucht⟨plan, -wagen⟩ make one's ~-away entkommen; ~-up *n. (coll.)* Aufmachung, *die*

geyser ['gi:zə(r)] *n.* a) *(spring)* Geysir, *der;* b) *(Brit.)* Durchlauferhitzer; ent-

ghastly ['gɑ:stlɪ] *adj.* grauenvoll; entsetzlich ⟨Verletzungen⟩; schrecklich ⟨Fehler⟩

gherkin ['gɜ:kɪn] *n.* Essiggurke, *die*

ghetto ['getəʊ] *n., pl.* ~s Getto, *das*

ghost [gəʊst] *n.* Geist, *der;* Gespenst, *das.* **ghostly** *adj.* gespenstisch

giant ['dʒaɪənt] **1.** *n.* Riese, *der.* **2.** *attrib. adj.* riesig

gibberish ['dʒɪbərɪʃ] *n.* Kauderwelsch, *das*

gibe [dʒaɪb] *n.* Stichelei, *die*

giblets ['dʒɪblɪts] *n. pl.* [Geflügel]klein, *das*

giddiness ['gɪdɪnɪs] *n.* Schwindel, *der*

giddy ['gɪdɪ] *adj.* schwind[e]lig

gift [gɪft] *n.* a) Geschenk, *das;* make sb. a ~ of sth., make a ~ of sth. to sb. jmdm. etw. schenken; a ~ box/pack eine Geschenkpackung; b) *(talent)* Begabung, *die;* have a ~ for languages/mathematics sprachbegabt/mathema-

tisch begabt sein. **'gifted** *adj.* begabt (in, at für). **'gift-wrap** *v. t.* als Geschenk einpacken

gigantic [dʒaɪ'gæntɪk] *adj.* gigantisch; riesig; enorm ⟨Verbesserung, Appetit⟩

giggle ['gɪgl] **1.** *n.* Kichern, *das.* **2.** *v. i.* kichern

gild [gɪld] *v. t.* vergolden

gill [gɪl] *n.* Kieme, *die*

gilt [gɪlt] **1.** *n.* Goldauflage, *die;* *(paint)* Goldfarbe, *die.* **2.** *adj.* vergoldet

gimmick ['gɪmɪk] *n. (coll.)* Gag, *der*

gin [dʒɪn] *n.* Gin, *der*

ginger ['dʒɪndʒə(r)] *n.* a) Ingwer, *der;* b) *(colour)* Rötlichgelb, *das.* **ginger 'beer** *n.* Ingwerbier, *das.* **'gingerbread** *n.* Pfefferkuchen, *der*

gingerly ['dʒɪndʒəlɪ] *adv.* vorsichtig

gipsy *see* gypsy

giraffe [dʒɪ'rɑ:f] *n.* Giraffe, *die*

girder ['gɜ:də(r)] *n.* Träger, *der*

girdle ['gɜ:dl] *n.* Hüfthalter, *der*

girl [gɜ:l] *n.* Mädchen, *das;* *(teenager)* junges Mädchen, *die.* **'girl-friend** *n.* Freundin, *die.* **'girlish** *adj.* mädchenhaft

giro ['dʒaɪərəʊ] *n.* a) Giro, *das;* attrib. Giro-; **bank ~:** Giroverkehr, *der;* b) *(coll.: cheque)* Scheck, *der*

girth [gɜ:θ] *n.* a) Umfang, *der;* b) *(for horse)* Bauchgurt, *der*

gismo ['gɪzməʊ] *n. (sl.)* Ding, *das (ugs.)*

gist [dʒɪst] *n.* Wesentliche, *das;* *(of tale, question, etc.)* Kern, *der*

give [gɪv] **1.** *v. t.,* gave [geɪv], given ['gɪvn] a) geben (to Dat.); b) *(as gift)* schenken; ~ sb. sth., ~ sth. to sb. jmdm. etw. schenken; ~ and take *(fig.)* Kompromisse eingehen; c) *(assign)* aufgeben ⟨Hausaufgaben usw.⟩; *(grant, award, offer, allow to have)* geben; verleihen ⟨Preis, Titel usw.⟩; lassen ⟨Wahl, Zeit⟩; verleihen ⟨Gewicht, Nachdruck⟩; bereiten, machen ⟨Freude, Mühe, Kummer⟩; bieten ⟨Schutz⟩; leisten ⟨Hilfe⟩; gewähren ⟨Unterstützung⟩; **be ~n sth.** etw. bekommen; **~n that** *(because)* da; *(if)* wenn; ~ sb. hope jmdm. Hoffnung machen; d) *(tell)* angeben ⟨Namen, Anschrift, Alter, Grund⟩; nennen ⟨Einzelheiten⟩; geben ⟨Rat, Befehl, Anweisung, Antwort⟩; fällen ⟨Urteil, Entscheidung⟩; sagen ⟨Meinung⟩; bekanntgeben ⟨Nachricht⟩; ~ him my best wishes richte ihm meine besten Wünsche aus; e) *(perform, sing, etc.)* geben ⟨Vorstellung, Konzert⟩; halten

⟨Vortrag, Seminar⟩; **f)** *(produce)* geben ⟨Licht, Milch⟩; ergeben ⟨Zahlen, Resultat⟩; **g)** *(make, show)* geben ⟨Zeichen, Stoß, Tritt⟩; machen ⟨Satz, Ruck⟩; ausstoßen ⟨Schrei, Seufzer, Pfiff⟩; ~ **sb. a |friendly| look** jmdm. einen [freundlichen] Blick zuwerfen; **h)** *(inflict)* versetzen ⟨Schlag, Stoß⟩; **sth. ~s me a headache** von etw. bekomme ich Kopfschmerzen; **i)** geben ⟨Party, Essen usw.⟩. **2.** *v.i.,* **gave, given** *(yield)* nachgeben; ⟨Knie:⟩ weich werden; ⟨Bett:⟩ federn. **3.** *n.* Nachgiebigkeit, *die;* *(elasticity)* Elastizität, *die.* **give a'way** *v.t.* **a)** verschenken; **b)** *(in marriage)* dem Bräutigam zuführen; **c)** *(betray)* verraten. **give 'back** *v.t.* zurückgeben. **give in 1.** ['--] *v.t.* abgeben. **2.** [-'-] *v.i.* nachgeben **(to** *Dat.)*. **give 'off** *v.t.* ausströmen ⟨Geruch⟩; aussenden ⟨Strahlen⟩. **give 'up 1.** *v.i.* aufgeben. **2.** *v.t.* aufgeben; widmen ⟨Zeit⟩; ~ **sth. up** *(abandon habit)* sich *(Dat.)* etw. abgewöhnen; ~ **oneself up** sich stellen. **give 'way** *v.i.* **a)** *(yield)* nachgeben; **b)** *(in traffic)* ~ **way |to traffic from the right|** [dem Rechtsverkehr] die Vorfahrt lassen; **'G~ Way** „Vorfahrt beachten"; **c)** *(collapse)* einstürzen

given *see* **give 1, 2**
gizmo *see* **gismo**
glacier ['glæsɪə(r)] *n.* Gletscher, *der*
glad [glæd] *adj.* froh; **be ~ of sth.** über etw. *(Akk.)* froh sein; für etw. dankbar sein. **gladden** ['glædn] *v.t.* erfreuen
glade [gleɪd] *n.* Lichtung, *die*
'gladly *adv.* gern
glamor *(Amer.) see* **glamour**
glamorous ['glæmərəs] *adj.* glanzvoll; glamourös ⟨Filmstar⟩
glamour ['glæmə(r)] *n.* Glanz, *der; (of person)* Ausstrahlung, *die*
glance [glɑːns] **1.** *n.* Blick, *der.* **2.** *v.i.* blicken; ~ **at sb./sth.** jmdn./etw. anblicken; ~ **at one's watch** auf seine Uhr blicken; ~ **at the newspaper** *etc.* einen Blick in die Zeitung *usw.* werfen; ~ **round |the room|** sich [im Zimmer] umsehen
gland [glænd] *n.* Drüse, *die.* **glandular** ['glændjʊlə(r)] *adj.* Drüsen-
glare [gleə(r)] **1.** *n.* **a)** grelles Licht; **b)** *(hostile look)* feindseliger Blick; **with a ~:** feindselig. **2.** *v.i.* *(glower)* [finster] starren; ~ **at sb./sth.** jmdn./etw. anstarren. **glaring** ['gleərɪŋ] *adj.* grell; *(fig.: conspicuous)* schreiend; grob ⟨Fehler⟩; kraß ⟨Gegensatz⟩

glass [glɑːs] *n.* **a)** *(substance)* Glas, *das;* **pieces of/broken ~:** Glasscherben *Pl.; (smaller)* Glassplitter *Pl.;* **b)** *(drinking ~)* Glas, *das;* **a ~ of milk** ein Glas Milch; **c)** *(pane)* [Glas]scheibe, *die;* **d)** in *pl. (spectacles)* |**a pair of**| ~**es** eine Brille. **'glassy** *adj.* gläsern
glaze [gleɪz] **1.** *n.* Glasur, *die.* **2.** *v.t.* **a)** glasieren; **b)** *(fit with glass)* verglasen. **glazier** ['gleɪzɪə(r)] *n.* Glaser, *der*
gleam [gliːm] **1.** *n.* Schein, *der; (fainter)* Schimmer, *der;* ~ **of hope** Hoffnungsschimmer, *der.* **2.** *v.i.* ⟨Licht:⟩ scheinen; ⟨Fußboden, Stiefel:⟩ glänzen; ⟨Zähne:⟩ blitzen; ⟨Augen:⟩ leuchten. **'gleaming** *adj.* glänzend
glean [gliːn] *v.t.* zusammentragen ⟨Informationen usw.⟩; ~ **sth. from sth.** einer Sache *(Dat.)* etw. entnehmen
glee [gliː] *n.* Freude, *die; (gloating joy)* Schadenfreude, *die.* **gleeful** ['gliːfl] *adj.* freudig; *(gloating)* schadenfroh
glen [glen] *n.* [schmales] Tal
glib [glɪb] *adj.* aalglatt ⟨Person⟩; leicht dahingesagt ⟨Antwort⟩
glide [glaɪd] *v.i.* gleiten; *(through the air)* schweben. **'glider** *n.* Segelflugzeug, *das*
glimmer ['glɪmə(r)] **1.** *n.* Schimmer, *der* (of von); *(of fire)* Glimmen, *das.* **2.** *v.i.* glimmen
glimpse [glɪmps] **1.** *n.* [kurzer] Blick; **catch** *or* **have** *or* **get a ~ of sb./sth.** jmdn./etw. [kurz] zu sehen bekommen. **2.** *v.t.* flüchtig sehen
glint [glɪnt] **1.** *n.* Schimmer, *der.* **2.** *v.i.* blinken; glitzern
glisten ['glɪsn] *v.i.* glitzern
glitter ['glɪtə(r)] **1.** *v.i.* glitzern; ⟨Juwelen, Sterne:⟩ funkeln. **2.** *n.* Glitzern, *das; (of diamonds)* Funkeln, *das*
gloat [gləʊt] *v.i.* ~ **over sth.** sich hämisch über etw. *(Akk.)* freuen
global ['gləʊbl] *adj.* weltweit; ~ **warming** globaler Temperaturanstieg
globe [gləʊb] *n.* **a)** Kugel, *die;* **b)** Globus, *der;* **c)** *(world)* **the ~:** der Globus; der Erdball
gloom [gluːm] *n.* **a)** *(darkness)* Dunkel, *das (geh.);* **b)** *(despondency)* düstere Stimmung. **'gloomy** *adj.* **a)** düster; finster; **b)** *(depressing)* düster; *(depressed)* trübsinnig ⟨Person⟩
glorify ['glɔːrɪfaɪ] *v.t.* verherrlichen; **a glorified messenger-boy** ein besserer Botenjunge
glorious ['glɔːrɪəs] *adj.* **a)** *(illustrious)* ruhmreich ⟨Held, Sieg⟩; **b)** *(delightful)* wunderschön; herrlich

glory ['glɔ:rɪ] **1.** *n.* **a)** *(splendour)* Schönheit, *die; (majesty)* Herrlichkeit, *die;* **b)** *(fame)* Ruhm, *der.* **2.** *v. i.* ~ **in** sth. *(be proud of)* sich einer Sache *(Gen.)* rühmen

gloss [glɒs] *n.* Glanz, *der;* ~ **paint** Lackfarbe, *die.* '**gloss over** *v. t.* bemänteln; beschönigen ⟨*Fehler*⟩

glossary ['glɒsərɪ] *n.* Glossar, *das*

'**glossy** *adj.* glänzend

glove [glʌv] *n.* Handschuh, *der.* '**glove compartment** *n.* Handschuhfach, *das*

glow [gləʊ] *v. i.* **a)** glühen; ⟨*Lampe, Leuchtfarbe:*⟩ schimmern, leuchten; **b)** *(fig.) (with warmth or pride)* ⟨*Gesicht, Wangen:*⟩ glühen (**with** vor + *Dat.*); *(with health or vigour)* strotzen (**with** vor + *Dat.*)

glower ['glaʊə(r)] *v. i.* finster dreinblicken; ~ **at** sb. jmdn. finster anstarren

'**glowing** *adj.* glühend; begeistert ⟨*Bericht*⟩

'**glow-worm** *n.* Glühwürmchen, *das*

glucose ['glu:kəʊz] *n.* Glucose, *die*

glue [glu:] **1.** *n.* Klebstoff, *der.* **2.** *v. t.* kleben; ~ **sth. to** sth. etw. an etw. *(Dat.)* an- *od.* festkleben

glum [glʌm] *adj.* verdrießlich

glut [glʌt] *n.* Überangebot, *das* (**of** an, von + *Dat.*)

glutton ['glʌtən] *n.* Vielfraß, *der (ugs.);* **a** ~ **for punishment** *(iron.)* ein Masochist *(fig.).* **gluttony** ['glʌtənɪ] *n.* Gefräßigkeit, *die*

glycerine ['glɪsəri:n] *(Amer.:* **glycerin** ['glɪsərɪn]) *n.* Glyzerin, *das*

GMT *abbr.* **Greenwich Mean Time** GMT; WEZ

gnarled [nɑ:ld] *adj.* knorrig; knotig ⟨*Hand*⟩

gnash [næʃ] *v. t.* ~ **one's teeth** mit den Zähnen knirschen

gnat [næt] *n.* [Stech]mücke, *die*

gnaw [nɔ:] **1.** *v. i.* ~ [**away**] **at** sth. an etw. *(Dat.)* nagen. **2.** *v. t.* nagen an (+ *Dat.*); abnagen ⟨*Knochen*⟩

gnome [nəʊm] *n.* Gnom, *der*

go [gəʊ] **1.** *v. i., pres.* **he goes** [gəʊz], *p. t.* **went** [went], *pres. p.* **going** ['gəʊɪŋ], *p. p.* **gone** [gɒn] **a)** gehen; ⟨*Fahrzeug:*⟩ fahren; ⟨*Flugzeug:*⟩ fliegen; ⟨*Vierfüßer:*⟩ laufen; *(on horseback etc.)* reiten; *(in lift)* fahren; *(on outward journey)* weg-, abfahren; *(travel regularly)* ⟨*Verkehrsmittel:*⟩ verkehren (**from** ... **to** zwischen + *Dat.* ... und); **go by bicycle/car/bus/train** *or* **rail/boat** *or* **sea**

or **ship** mit dem [Fahr]rad/Auto/Bus/Zug/Schiff fahren; **go by plane** *or* **air** fliegen; **go on foot** zu Fuß gehen; laufen *(ugs.);* **go on a journey** verreisen; **have far to go** es weit haben; **go to the toilet/cinema/a museum** auf die Toilette/ins Kino/ins Museum gehen; **go to the doctor['s]** *etc.* zum Arzt *usw.* gehen; **go bathing** baden gehen; **go cycling** radfahren; **go to see sb.** jmdn. aufsuchen; **go and see whether** ...: nachsehen [gehen], ob ...; **I'll go!** ich geh schon!; *(answer phone)* ich geh ran *od.* nehme ab; *(answer door)* ich mache auf; **b)** *(start)* losgehen; *(in vehicle)* losfahren; **c)** *(pass, circulate)* gehen; **a shiver went up** *or* **down my spine** ein Schauer lief mir über den Rücken; **go to** *(be given to)* ⟨*Preis, Gelder, Job:*⟩ gehen an (+ *Akk.*); ⟨*Titel, Besitz:*⟩ übergehen auf (+ *Akk.*); **go towards** *(be of benefit to)* zugute kommen (+ *Dat.*); **d)** *(act, function effectively)* gehen; ⟨*Mechanismus, Maschine:*⟩ laufen; **keep going** *(in movement)* weitergehen/-fahren; *(in activity)* weitermachen; *(not fail)* sich aufrecht halten; **keep sth. going** etw. in Gang halten; **make sth. go, get/set sth. going** etw. in Gang bringen; **e) go to work** zur Arbeit gehen; **go to school** in die Schule gehen; **go to a comprehensive school** auf eine Gesamtschule gehen; **f)** *(depart)* gehen; ⟨*Bus, Zug:*⟩ [ab]fahren; ⟨*Post:*⟩ rausgehen *(ugs.);* **g)** *(cease to function)* kaputtgehen; ⟨*Sicherung:*⟩ durchbrennen; *(break)* brechen; ⟨*Seil usw.:*⟩ reißen; **h)** *(disappear)* weggehen; ⟨*Mantel, Hut, Fleck:*⟩ verschwinden; ⟨*Geruch, Rauch:*⟩ sich verziehen; ⟨*Geld, Zeit:*⟩ draufgehen *(ugs.)* (**in, on** für); **i)** *(still remaining)* **have sth.** [**still**] **to go** [noch] etw. übrig haben; **one week** *etc.* **to go to** ...: noch eine Woche *usw.* bis ...; **there's hours to go** es dauert noch Stunden; **j)** *(be sold)* weggehen *(ugs.);* verkauft werden; **going! going! gone!** zum ersten! zum zweiten! zum dritten!; **go to sb.** an jmdn. gehen; **k)** *(run)* ⟨*Grenze, Straße usw.:*⟩ verlaufen, ⟨*Weg:*⟩ gehen; führen; *(extend)* reichen; **as** *or* **so far as he/it goes** soweit; **l)** *(turn out, progress)* ⟨*Projekt, Interview, Abend:*⟩ verlaufen; **how did your holiday go?** wie war Ihr Urlaub?; **things have been going well/badly** in der letzten Zeit läuft alles gut/schief; **m)** *(be, have form or nature)* sein;

⟨*Sprichwort, Gedicht, Titel:*⟩ lauten; **that's the way it goes** so ist es nun mal; **go hungry** hungern; **go without food/ water** es ohne Essen/Wasser aushalten; **n)** *(become)* werden; **the tyre has gone flat** der Reifen ist platt; **o)** *(have usual place)* kommen; *(belong)* gehören; **where does the box go?** wo kommt *od.* gehört die Kiste hin?; **p)** *(fit)* passen; **go in|to|** sth. in etw. *(Akk.)* gehen *od.* [hinein]passen; **go through** sth. durch etw. [hindurch]gehen; **q)** *(match)* passen (**with** zu); **r)** ⟨*Turmuhr, Gong:*⟩ schlagen; ⟨*Glocke:*⟩ läuten; **s)** *(coll.: be acceptable or permitted)* erlaubt sein; **it/that goes without saying** es/das ist doch selbstverständlich. *See also* **going** 2. **2.** *n., pl.* **goes** [gəʊz] *(coll.)* **a)** *(attempt, try)* Versuch, *der;* *(chance)* Gelegenheit, *die;* **have a go** es versuchen; **let me have a go/can I have a go?** laß mich [auch ein]mal/kann ich [auch ein]mal? *(ugs.);* **it's 'my go** ich bin an der Reihe *od.* dran; **at one go** auf einmal; **at the first go** auf Anhieb; **b)** *(vigorous activity)* **it's all go** es ist alles eine einzige Hetzerei *(ugs.);* **be on the go** auf Trab sein *(ugs.);* **c)** *(success)* **make a go of** sth. mit etw. Erfolg haben. **go a'head** *v. i.* **a)** *(in advance)* vorausgehen (**of** *Dat.*); **b)** *(proceed)* weitermachen; *(make progress)* ⟨*Arbeit:*⟩ fortschreiten, vorangehen. **go a'way** *v. i.* weggehen; *(on holiday or business)* verreisen. **go 'back** *v. i.* zurückgehen/-fahren; *(restart)* ⟨*Schule, Fabrik:*⟩ wieder anfangen; *(fig.)* zurückgehen; **go back to the beginning** noch mal von vorne anfangen. **go by 1.** ['--] *v. t.* **go by** sth. sich nach etw. richten; *(adhere to)* sich an etw. *(Akk.)* halten. **2.** [-'-] *v. i.* ⟨*Zeit:*⟩ vergehen. **go 'down** *v. i.* hinuntergehen/-fahren; ⟨*Sonne:*⟩ untergehen; ⟨*Schiff:*⟩ untergehen; *(fall to ground)* ⟨*Flugzeug usw.:*⟩ abstürzen. **'go for** *v. t.* **go for** sb./sth. *(go to fetch)* jmdn./etw. holen; *(apply to)* für jmdn./etw. gelten; *(like)* jmdn./etw. gut finden. **go 'in** *v. i.* hineingehen; reingehen *(ugs.)*. **go 'off 1.** *v. i.* **a)** **go off with** sb./sth. sich mit jmdm./etw. auf- und davonmachen *(ugs.);* **b)** ⟨*Alarm, Schußwaffe:*⟩ losgehen; ⟨*Wecker:*⟩ klingeln; ⟨*Bombe:*⟩ hochgehen; **c)** *(turn bad)* schlecht werden; **d)** ⟨*Strom:*⟩ ausfallen. **2.** *v. t.* *(begin to dislike)* **go off** sth. von etw. abkommen. **go 'on** *v. i.* **a)** weitergehen/-fahren; **b)** *(continue)* weiterma-

chen; **c)** *(happen)* passieren. **go 'out** *v. i.* ausgehen; **go out to work/for a meal** arbeiten/essen gehen. **go over 1.** [-'--] *v. i.* hinübergehen. **2.** ['---, -'--] *v. t.* *(re-examine)* durchgehen. **go 'round** *v. i.* **a)** *(coll.)* **go round and** *or* **to see** sb. bei jmdm. vorbeigehen *(ugs.);* **b)** *(look round)* sich umschauen; **c)** *(suffice)* reichen; langen *(ugs.);* **d)** *(spin)* sich drehen. **go through 1.** [-'-] *v. i.* ⟨*Ernennung:*⟩ durchkommen; ⟨*Antrag:*⟩ durchgehen. **2.** ['--] **a)** *(rehearse)* durchgehen; **b)** *(examine)* durchsehen; **c)** *(endure)* durchmachen. **go 'under** *v. i.* untergehen; *(fig.: fail)* eingehen. **go 'up** *v. i.* **a)** hinaufgehen/-fahren; ⟨*Ballon:*⟩ aufsteigen; *(Theatre)* ⟨*Vorhang:*⟩ aufgehen; ⟨*Lichter:*⟩ angehen; **b)** *(increase)* ⟨*Zahl:*⟩ wachsen; ⟨*Preis, Wert, Niveau:*⟩ steigen; *(in price)* ⟨*Ware:*⟩ teurer werden. **go without 1.** ['---] *v. t.* verzichten auf (+ *Akk.*). **2.** [-'-] *v. i.* verzichten

goad [gəʊd] *v. t.* ~ sb. into sth./doing sth. jmdn. zu etw. anstacheln/dazu anstacheln, etw. zu tun

'go-ahead 1. *adj.* unternehmungslustig; *(progressive)* fortschrittlich. **2.** *n.* **give sb./sth. the ~:** jmdm./einer Sache grünes Licht geben

goal [gəʊl] *n.* **a)** *(aim)* Ziel, *das;* **b)** *(Footb., Hockey)* Tor, *das;* **score/kick a ~:** einen Treffer erzielen. **'goalkeeper** *n.* Torwart, *der*

goat [gəʊt] *n.* Ziege, *die*

gobble ['gɒbl] **1.** *v. t.* ~ [down *or* up] hinunterschlingen. **2.** *v. i.* schlingen

'go-between *n.* Vermittler, *der*/Vermittlerin, *die*

goblet ['gɒblɪt] *n.* Kelchglas, *das*

goblin ['gɒblɪn] *n.* Kobold, *der*

god [gɒd] *n.* **a)** Gott, *der;* **b)** God *(Theol.)* Gott. **'godchild** *n.* Patenkind, *das.* **'god-daughter** *n.* Patentochter, *die*

goddess ['gɒdɪs] *n.* Göttin, *die*

god: ~father *n.* Pate, *der;* **G~forsaken** *adj.* gottverlassen; **~mother** *n.* Patentante, *die;* **~send** *n.* Gottesgabe, *die;* **be a ~send to sb.** für jmdn. ein Geschenk des Himmels sein; **~son** *n.* Patensohn, *der*

goggles ['gɒglz] *n. pl.* Schutzbrille, *die*

going ['gəʊɪŋ] **1.** *n.* *(progress)* Vorankommen, *das;* **while the ~ is good** solange es noch geht. **2.** *adj.* **a)** *(available)* erhältlich; **there is sth. ~:** es gibt etw.; **b)** **be ~ to do sth.** etw. tun [wer-

den/wollen]; **I was** ~ **to say** ich wollte
sagen; **it's** ~ **to snow** es wird schneien;
a ~ **concern** eine gesunde Firma
goings-'on *n. pl.* Ereignisse
gold [gəʊld] **1.** *n.* Gold, *das.* **2.** *attrib.*
adj. golden; Gold⟨münze, -kette *usw.*⟩
golden ['gəʊldn] *adj.* golden. **golden
'wedding** *n.* goldene Hochzeit
gold: ~**fish** *n.* Goldfisch, *der;* ~
'**medal** *n.* Goldmedaille, *die;*
~-**mine** *n.* Goldmine, *die; (fig.)*
Goldgrube, *die;* ~-'**plated** *adj.* vergoldet; ~**smith** *n.* Goldschmied,
der/-schmiedin, *die*
golf [gɒlf] *n.* Golf, *das*
golf: ~ **ball** *n.* Golfball, *der;* ~-**club**
n. **a)** *(implement)* Golfschläger, *der;*
b) *(association)* Golfclub, *der;*
~-**course** *n.* Golfplatz, *der*
'**golfer** *n.* Golfer, *der/*Golferin, *die*
gondola ['gɒndələ] *n.* Gondel, *die*
gone [gɒn] **1.** *see* **go 1. 2.** *pred. adj.* **a)**
(away) weg; **it's time you were** ~ : es ist
od. wird Zeit, daß du gehst; **b)** *(of
time: after)* nach; **it's** ~ **ten o'clock** es
ist zehn Uhr vorbei
gong [gɒŋ] *n.* Gong, *der*
good [gʊd] **1.** *adj.,* **better** ['betə(r)], **best**
[best] **a)** gut; günstig ⟨Gelegenheit,
Angebot⟩; ausreichend ⟨Vorrat⟩; ausgiebig ⟨Mahl⟩; **as** ~ **as** so gut wie; **his**
~ **eye/leg** sein gesundes Auge/Bein;
in ~ **time** frühzeitig; **all in** ~ **time** alles
zu seiner Zeit; **be** ~ **at sth.** in etw.
(Dat.) gut sein; **too** ~ **to be true** zu
schön, um wahr zu sein; **apples are** ~
for you Äpfel sind gesund; **be too
much of a** ~ **thing** zuviel des Guten
sein; ~ **times** eine schöne Zeit; **feel** ~ :
sich wohl fühlen; **take a** ~ **look round**
sich gründlich umsehen; **give sb. a** ~
beating/scolding jmdn. tüchtig ver-
prügeln/ausschimpfen; ~ **afternoon/
day** guten Tag!; ~ **evening/morning**
guten Abend/Morgen!; ~ **night** gute
Nacht!; **b)** *(enjoyable)* schön ⟨Leben,
Urlaub, Wochenende⟩; **the** ~ **life** das
angenehme[, sorglose] Leben; **have a**
~ **time!** viel Spaß!; **have a** ~ **journey!**
gute Reise!; **c)** *(well-behaved)* gut;
brav; **be** ~!, **be a** ~ **girl/boy!** sei brav
od. lieb!; [**as**] ~ **as gold** ganz artig *od.*
brav; **d)** *(virtuous)* rechtschaffen;
(kind) nett; gut ⟨Absicht, Wünsche,
Benehmen, Tat⟩; **be** ~ **to sb.** gut zu
jmdm. sein; **would you be so** ~ **as to** *or*
~ **enough to do that?** wären Sie so
freundlich *od.* nett, das zu tun?; **that/
it is** ~ **of you** das/es ist nett *od.* lieb

von dir; **e)** *(commendable)* gut; ~ **for
'you** *etc. (coll.)* bravo!; **f)** *(attractive)*
schön; gut ⟨Figur⟩; **look** ~ : gut aussehen; **g)** *(considerable)* [recht] ansehnlich ⟨Menschenmenge⟩; ganz schön,
ziemlich *(ugs.)* ⟨Entfernung, Strecke⟩;
gut ⟨Preis, Erlös⟩; **h) make** ~ *(succeed)*
erfolgreich sein; *(compensate for)* wiedergutmachen; *(indemnify)* ersetzen.
2. *n.* **a)** *(use)* Nutzen, *der;* **be some** ~ **to
sb./sth.** jmdm./einer Sache nützen; **be
no** ~ **to sb./sth.** für jmdn./etw. nicht zu
gebrauchen sein; **it is no/not much** ~
doing sth. es hat keinen/kaum einen
Sinn, etw. zu tun; **what's the** ~ **of ...?**,
what ~ **is ...?** was nützt ...?; **b)** *(benefit)*
for your/his *etc.* **own** ~ : zu deinem/
seinem *usw.* Besten; **do no/little** ~ :
nichts/wenig helfen *od.* nützen; **do
sb./sth.** ~ : jmdm./einer Sache nützen;
⟨Ruhe, Erholung:⟩ jmdm./einer Sache
guttun; ⟨Arznei:⟩ jmdm./einer Sache
helfen; **c)** *(goodness)* Gute, *das;* **be up
to no** ~ : nichts Gutes im Sinn haben;
d) for ~ *(finally)* ein für allemal; *(permanently)* für immer; **e)** *in pl. (wares
etc.)* Waren; *(belongings)* Habe, *die;*
(Brit. Railw.) Fracht, *die; attrib.* Güter-
⟨wagen, -zug⟩
good: ~'**bye** *(Amer.:* ~'**by)** *int.* auf
Wiedersehen!; *(on telephone)* auf
Wiederhören!; ~-**for-nothing 1.**
adj. nichtsnutzig; **2.** *n.* Taugenichts,
der; ~-'**looking** *adj.* gutaussehend
'**goodness 1.** *n.* Güte, *die.* **2.** *int.* [my]
~! meine Güte! *(ugs.)*
good'will *n.* guter Wille; *attrib.*
Goodwill⟨botschaft, -reise *usw.*⟩
'**goody** *n. (coll.: hero)* Gute, *der/die*
gooey ['guːɪ] *adj.,* **gooier** ['guːɪə(r)],
gooiest ['guːɪɪst] *(coll.)* klebrig
goose [guːs] *n., pl.* **geese** [giːs] Gans,
die
gooseberry ['gʊzbərɪ] *n.* Stachelbee-
re, *die*
'**goose:** ~-**pimples** *n. pl.* **have** ~-
pimples eine Gänsehaut haben
¹**gore** [gɔː(r)] *v.t.* [mit den Hörnern]
aufspießen *od.* durchbohren
²**gore** *n.* Blut, *das*
gorge [gɔːdʒ] **1.** *n.* Schlucht, *die.* **2.**
v.i. & refl. ~ [oneself] sich vollstopfen
(ugs.) **(on** mit)
gorgeous ['gɔːdʒəs] *adj.* prächtig;
hinreißend ⟨Frau, Mann, Lächeln⟩
gorilla [gəˈrɪlə] *n.* Gorilla, *der*
gormless ['gɔːmlɪs] *adj. (Brit. coll.)*
dämlich *(ugs.)*
gorse [gɔːs] *n.* Stechginster, *der*

gory ['gɔːrɪ] *adj.* *(fig.)* blutrünstig
gosh [gɒʃ] *int. (coll.)* Gott!
'**go-slow** *n. (Brit.)* Bummelstreik, *der*
gospel ['gɒspl] *n.* Evangelium, *das*
gossamer ['gɒsəmə(r)] *n.* Altweibersommer, *der; attrib.* hauchdünn
gossip ['gɒsɪp] **1.** *n.* **a)** *(talk)* Klatsch, *der (ugs.);* **b)** *(person)* Klatschbase, *die (ugs.).* **2.** *v.i.* klatschen *(ugs.)*
got *see* **get**
Gothic ['gɒθɪk] *adj.* gotisch
gotten *see* **get**
gouge [gaʊdʒ] *v.t.* aushöhlen
goulash ['guːlæʃ] *n.* Gulasch, *das od. der*
gourmet ['gʊəmeɪ] *n.* Gourmet, *der*
gout [gaʊt] *n.* Gicht, *die*
govern ['gʌvn] **1.** *v.t.* **a)** regieren ⟨*Land, Volk*⟩; verwalten ⟨*Provinz*⟩; **b)** *(dictate)* bestimmen. **2.** *v.i.* regieren
governess ['gʌvənɪs] *n.* Gouvernante, *die (veraltet);* Hauslehrerin, *die*
government ['gʌvnmənt] *n.* Regierung, *die; attrib.* Regierungs-
governor ['gʌvənə(r)] *n.* **a)** *(of province etc.)* Gouverneur, *der;* **b)** *(of institution)* Direktor, *der/*Direktorin, *die;* **[board of]** ~s Vorstand, *der;* **c)** *(sl.: employer)* Boß, *der (ugs.)*
gown [gaʊn] *n.* **a)** [elegantes] Kleid; **b)** *(official or uniform robe)* Talar, *der*
GP *abbr.* **general practitioner**
grab [græb] **1.** *v.t.,* **-bb-** greifen nach; *(seize)* packen; ~ **the chance** die Gelegenheit ergreifen; ~ **hold of sb./sth.** sich *(Dat.)* jmdn./etw. schnappen *(ugs.).* **2.** *v.i.,* **-bb-:** ~ **at** sth. nach etw. greifen. **3.** *n.* **make a** ~ **at** or **for sb./ sth.** nach jmdn./etw. greifen
grace [greɪs] *n.* **a)** *(charm)* Anmut, *die (geh.);* **b)** *(decency)* **have the** ~ **to do** sth. so anständig sein und etw. tun; **c)** *(delay)* Frist, *die;* **give sb. a day's** ~**:** jmdm. einen Tag Aufschub gewähren; **d)** *(prayers)* **say** ~**:** das Tischgebet sprechen. **graceful** ['greɪsfl] *adj.* elegant; graziös ⟨*Bewegung, Eleganz*⟩
gracious ['greɪʃəs] **1.** *adj.* **a)** liebenswürdig; **b)** *(merciful)* gnädig. **2.** *int.* **good** ~! [ach] du meine Güte!
grade [greɪd] **1.** *n.* **a)** Rang, *der; (Mil.)* Dienstgrad, *der;* **b)** *(position)* Stufe, *die;* **c)** *(Amer. Sch.: class)* Klasse, *die;* **d)** *(Sch., Univ.: mark)* Note, *die;* Zensur, *die.* **2.** *v.t.* **a)** einstufen ⟨*Schüler*⟩; [nach Größe/Qualität] sortieren ⟨*Eier, Kartoffeln*⟩; **b)** *(mark)* benoten
gradient ['greɪdɪənt] *n. (ascent)* Steigung, *die; (descent)* Gefälle, *das*

gradual ['grædʒʊəl] *adj.,* '**gradually** *adv.* allmählich
graduate 1. ['grædʒʊət] *n.* Graduierte, *der/die; (who has left university)* Akademiker, *der/*Akademikerin, *die;* **university** ~**:** Hochschulabsolvent, *der/*-absolventin, *die.* **2.** ['grædʒʊeɪt] *v.i.* einen akademischen Grad/Titel erwerben; *(Amer. Sch.)* die [Schul]abschlußprüfung bestehen **(from an + Dat.)**
graffiti [grə'fiːtiː] *n. sing. or pl.* Graffiti *Pl.*
graft [grɑːft] **1.** *n.* **a)** *(Bot.)* Edelreis, *das;* **b)** *(Med.) (operation)* Transplantation, *die; (thing* ~*ed)* Transplantat, *das;* **c)** *(Brit. sl.: work)* Plackerei, *die (ugs.).* **2.** *v.t.* **a)** *(Bot.)* pfropfen; **b)** *(Med.)* transplantieren. **3.** *v.i. (Brit. sl.)* schuften *(ugs.)*
grain [greɪn] *n.* **a)** Korn, *das; collect.* Getreide, *das;* **b)** *(particle)* Korn, *das;* **c)** *(in wood)* Maserung, *die; (in paper)* Faser, *die; (in leather)* Narbung, *die;* **go against the** ~ **[for sb.]** *(fig.)* jmdm. gegen den Strich gehen *(ugs.).* '**grainy** *adj.* körnig; gemasert ⟨*Holz*⟩; genarbt ⟨*Leder*⟩
gram [græm] *n.* Gramm, *das*
grammar ['græmə(r)] *n.* Grammatik, *die.* '**grammar book** *n.* Grammatik, *die.* '**grammar school** *n. (Brit.)* ≈ Gymnasium, *das*
grammatical [grə'mætɪkl] *adj.* **a)** grammat[ikal]isch richtig *od.* korrekt; **b)** *(of grammar)* grammatisch. **grammatically** [grə'mætɪkəlɪ] *adv.* grammati[kal]isch ⟨*richtig, falsch*⟩
gramme *see* **gram**
gramophone ['græməfəʊn] *n.* Plattenspieler, *der*
granary ['grænərɪ] *n.* Getreidesilo, *der od. das;* Kornspeicher, *der*
grand [grænd] *adj.* **a)** *(most or very important)* groß; ~ **finale** großes Finale; **b)** *(splendid)* grandios; **c)** *(coll.: excellent)* großartig
grand: ~**child** *n.* Enkel, *der/*Enkelin, *die;* Enkelkind, *das;* ~~**dad[dy]** ['grændæd(ɪ)] *n. (coll./child lang.);* Opa, *der (Kinderspr./ugs.);* ~~**daughter** *n.* Enkelin, *die*
grandeur ['grændʒə(r), 'grændjə(r)] *n.* Erhabenheit, *die*
'**grandfather** *n.* Großvater, *der;* ~ **clock** *n.* Standuhr, *die*
grandiose ['grændɪəʊs] *adj.* grandios; *(pompous)* bombastisch
grand: ~**ma** *n. (coll./child lang.)* Oma,

die (Kinderspr./ugs.); ~**mother** *n.*
Großmutter, *die;* ~**pa** *n. (coll./child
lang.)* Opa, *der (Kinderspr./ugs.);*
~**parent** *n. (male)* Großvater, *der;
(female)* Großmutter, *die;* ~**parents**
Großeltern *Pl.;* ~ **pi'ano** *n.* [Kon-
zert]flügel, *der;* ~**son** *n.* Enkel, *der;*
~**stand** *n.* [Haupt]tribüne, *die*

granite ['grænɪt] *n.* Granit, *der*
granny ['grænɪ] *n. (coll./child lang.)*
Oma, *die (Kinderspr./ugs.)*

grant [grɑːnt] **1.** *v. t.* **a)** erfüllen
⟨*Wunsch*⟩; stattgeben (+ *Dat.*) ⟨*Gesuch*⟩; **b)** *(concede, give)* gewähren;
geben ⟨*Zeit*⟩; bewilligen ⟨*Geldmittel*⟩;
zugestehen ⟨*Recht*⟩; erteilen ⟨*Erlaubnis*⟩; **c)** *(in argument)* zugeben; **take
sb./sth. for** ~**ed** sich *(Dat.)* jmds. sicher sein/etw. für selbstverständlich
halten. **2.** *n.* Zuschuß, *der; (financial
aid [to student])* [Studien]beihilfe, *die;
(scholarship)* Stipendium, *das*

granulated sugar [grænjʊleɪtɪd 'ʃʊg-
ə(r)] *n.* Kristallzucker, *der*

granule ['grænjuːl] *n.* Körnchen, *das*
grape [greɪp] *n.* Weintraube, *die;* **a
bunch of** ~**s** eine Traube

'**grapefruit** *n., pl. same* Grapefruit,
die

graph [grɑːf] *n.* graphische Darstellung; ~ **paper** Diagrammpapier, *das*
graphic ['græfɪk] *adj.* **a)** graphisch; **b)**
(vivid) plastisch; anschaulich. **graphically** ['græfɪkəlɪ] *adv.* **a)** *(vividly)* plastisch; **b)** *(using graphics)* graphisch.
graphics ['græfɪks] *n. (use of dia-
grams)* graphische Darstellung; **computer** ~: Computergraphik, *die*
grapple ['græpl] *v. i.* handgemein werden; ~ **with** *(fig.)* sich auseinanderset-
zen mit

grasp [grɑːsp] **1.** *v. i.* ~ **at** ergreifen;
sich stürzen auf (+ *Akk.*) ⟨*Angebot*⟩.
2. *v. t.* **a)** *(seize)* ergreifen; **b)** *(hold
firmly)* festhalten; **c)** *(understand)* verstehen; erfassen ⟨*Bedeutung*⟩. **3.** *n.* **a)**
(firm hold) Griff, *der;* **b)** *(mental* ~*)*
have a good ~ **of sth.** etw. gut beherrschen. '**grasping** *adj.* habgierig

grass [grɑːs] *n.* **a)** Gras, *das;* **b)** *(lawn)*
Rasen, *der;* **c)** *(Brit. sl.: police informer)* Spitzel, *der.* '**grasshopper**
n. Grashüpfer, *der.* '**grass-root[s]**
attrib. adj. (Polit.) Basis-

'**grate** [greɪt] *n.* Rost, *der; (recess)* Kamin, *der*

²**grate** *v. t.* **a)** reiben; *(less finely)* ras-
peln; **b)** *(grind)* ~ **one's teeth** mit den
Zähnen knirschen

grateful ['greɪtfl] *adj.* dankbar (**to**
Dat.). '**gratefully** *adv.* dankbar
'**grater** *n.* Reibe, *die;* Raspel, *die*
gratify ['grætɪfaɪ] *v. t.* freuen; **be grati-
fied by** *or* **with** *or* **at sth.** über etw.
(Akk.) erfreut sein. '**gratifying** *adj.*
erfreulich

grating ['greɪtɪŋ] *n.* Gitter, *das*
gratitude ['grætɪtjuːd] *n.* Dankbarkeit, *die* (**to** gegenüber)

gratuitous [grə'tjuːɪtəs] *adj. (motive-
less)* grundlos

gratuity [grə'tjuːɪtɪ] *n.* Trinkgeld, *das*
'**grave** [greɪv] *n.* Grab, *das*
²**grave** *adj.* **a)** *(important, solemn)*
ernst; **b)** *(serious)* schwer ⟨*Fehler, Irrtum*⟩; ernst ⟨*Situation, Lage*⟩; groß
⟨*Gefahr*⟩; schlimm ⟨*Nachricht*⟩
'**grave-digger** *n.* Totengräber, *der*
gravel ['grævl] *n.* Kies, *der*
grave: ~**stone** *n.* Grabstein, *der;*
~**yard** *n.* Friedhof, *der*
gravity ['grævɪtɪ] *n.* **a)** *(of mistake, offence)* Schwere, *die; (of situation)*
Ernst, *der;* **b)** *(Phys., Astron.)* Gravitation, *die;* Schwerkraft, *die*
gravy ['greɪvɪ] *n.* **a)** *(juices)* Bratensaft,
der; **b)** *(dressing)* [Braten]soße, *die*
gray etc. *(Amer.) see* **grey** etc.
'**graze** [greɪz] *v. i.* grasen; weiden
²**graze** **1.** *n.* Schürfwunde, *die.* **2.** *v. t.*
a) *(touch lightly)* streifen; **b)** *(scrape)*
abschürfen ⟨*Haut*⟩; zerkratzen ⟨*Oberfläche*⟩
grease [griːs] **1.** *n.* Fett, *das; (lubricant)* Schmierfett, *das.* **2.** *v. t.* einfet-
ten; *(lubricate)* schmieren. '**grease-
proof** *adj.* fettdicht; ~ **paper** Perga-
ment- *od.* Butterbrotpapier, *das*
greasy ['griːsɪ] *adj.* fettig; fett ⟨*Essen*⟩;
(lubricated) geschmiert; *(dirty with
lubricant)* schmierig
great [greɪt] *adj.* **a)** groß; **a** ~ **many**
sehr viele; sehr gut ⟨*Freund*⟩; *(impressive; coll.: splendid)* großartig; **be
a** ~ **one for sth.** etw. sehr gern tun; **b)**
Groß⟨*onkel, -tante, -neffe, -nichte*⟩;
Ur⟨*großmutter, -großvater, -enkel, -en-
kelin*⟩. **Great 'Britain** *pr. n.* Großbritannien *(das).* '**greatly** *adv.* sehr;
höchst ⟨*verärgert*⟩; stark ⟨*beeinflußt*⟩;
bedeutend ⟨*verbessert*⟩. '**greatness**
n. Größe, *die*
Greece [griːs] *pr. n.* Griechenland
(das)
greed [griːd] *n.* Gier, *die* (**for** nach);
(gluttony) Gefräßigkeit, *die.* '**greedy**
adj. gierig; *(gluttonous)* gefräßig
Greek [griːk] **1.** *adj.* griechisch; **sb. is**

~: jmd. ist Grieche/Griechin. **2.** *n.* **a)** *(person)* Grieche, *der*/Griechin, *die;* **b)** *(language)* Griechisch, *das; see also* **English 2a**

green [gri:n] **1.** *adj.* **a)** grün; **b)** *(environmentally safe)* ökologisch; .**c)** *(gullible)* naiv; *(inexperienced)* grün; **d)** *(Polit.)* G~: grün; **the G~s** die Grü-, nen. **2.** *n.* **a)** *(colour)* Grün, *das;* **b)** *(piece of land)* Grünfläche, *die;* **village** ~: Dorfanger, *der;* **c)** *in pl.* *(~ vegetables)* Grüngemüse, *das.* '**green belt** *n.* Grüngürtel, *der.* **green 'card** *n.* *(Motor Veh.)* grüne Karte

greenery ['gri:nəri] *n.* Grün, *das*

green: ~**fly** *n. (Brit.)* grüne Blattlaus; ~**gage** ['gri:ngeidʒ] *n.* Reineclaude, *die;* ~**grocer** *n. (Brit.)* Obst- und Gemüsehändler, *der*/-händlerin, *die;* ~**house** *n.* Gewächshaus, *das;* ~**house effect** Treibhauseffekt, *der*

Greenland ['gri:nlənd] *pr. n.* Grönland *(das)*

'**Green Party** *n. (Polit.)* die Grünen

greet [gri:t] *v. t.* begrüßen; *(in passing)* grüßen; *(receive)* empfangen. '**greeting** *n.* Begrüßung, *die;* *(in passing)* Gruß, *der;* *(words)* Grußformel, *die.* '**greetings card** *n.* Grußkarte, *die;* *(for birthday)* Glückwunschkarte, *die*

gregarious [gri'geəriəs] *adj.* gesellig

grenade [gri'neid] *n.* Granate, *die*

grew *see* **grow**

grey [grei] **1.** *adj.* grau. **2.** *n.* Grau, *das.* '**greyhound** *n.* Windhund, *der*

grid [grid] *n.* **a)** *(grating)* Rost, *der;* **b)** *(of lines)* Gitter[netz], *das;* **c)** *(for supply)* Versorgungsnetz, *das*

grief [gri:f] *n.* Kummer, *der* (over, at über + *Akk.*, um); *(at loss of sb.)* Trauer, *die* (for um); **come to ~** *(fail)* scheitern

grievance ['gri:vəns] *n.* *(complaint)* Beschwerde, *die;* *(grudge)* Groll, *der*

grieve [gri:v] **1.** *v. t.* betrüben; bekümmern. **2.** *v. i.* trauern (for um)

grievous ['gri:vəs] *adj.* schwer ⟨*Verwundung, Krankheit*⟩

'**grill** [gril] **1.** *v. t. (cook)* grillen; *(fig.: question)* in die Mangel nehmen *(ugs.).* **2.** *n.* **a)** **mixed** ~: gemischte Grillplatte; **b)** *(on cooker)* Grill, *der*

grille (²**grill**) *(Motor Veh.)* [Kühler]grill, *der*

grim [grim] *adj.* *(stern)* streng; grimmig ⟨*Lächeln, Schweigen*⟩; *(unrelenting)* erbittert ⟨*Widerstand, Kampf*⟩; *(ghastly)* grauenvoll ⟨*Aufgabe, Nachricht*⟩; trostlos ⟨*Aussichten*⟩

grimace [gri'meis] **1.** *n.* Grimasse, *die.* **2.** *v. i.* Grimassen schneiden; **~ with pain** vor Schmerz das Gesicht verziehen

grime [graim] *n.* Schmutz, *der.* **grimy** ['graimi] *adj.* schmutzig

grin [grin] **1.** *n.* Grinsen, *das.* **2.** *v. i.,* -**nn-** grinsen; **~ at sb.** jmdn. angrinsen

grind [graind] **1.** *v. t.,* **ground** [graund] **a)** ~ [up] zermahlen; mahlen ⟨*Kaffee, Pfeffer, Getreide*⟩; **b)** *(sharpen)* schleifen ⟨*Schere, Messer*⟩; schärfen ⟨*Klinge*⟩; **c)** *(rub harshly)* zerquetschen; ~ **one's teeth** mit den Zähnen knirschen. **2.** *v. i.,* **ground:** ~ **to a halt** ⟨*Fahrzeug:*⟩ quietschend zum Stehen kommen; *(fig.)* ⟨*Verkehr:*⟩ zum Erliegen kommen. **3.** *n.* *(coll.)* Plackerei, *die (ugs.).* '**grinder** *n.* Schleifmaschine, *die;* *(coffee-~ etc.)* Mühle, *die.* '**grindstone** *n.* Schleifstein, *der*

grip [grip] **1.** *n.* **a)** *(firm hold)* Halt, *der;* *(fig.: power)* Umklammerung, *die;* **have a ~ on sth.** etw. festhalten; *(fig.)* etwas im Griff haben; **loosen one's ~:** loslassen; **lose one's ~** *(fig.)* nachlassen; **b)** *(strength or way of ~ping)* Griff, *der.* **2.** *v. t.,* -**pp-** [fest] halten; ⟨*Reifen:*⟩ greifen; *(fig.)* fesseln ⟨*Publikum, Aufmerksamkeit*⟩. **3.** *v. i.,* -**pp-** ⟨*Räder, Bremsen usw.:*⟩ greifen

gripe [graip] *v. i.* *(sl.)* meckern *(ugs.)* (about über + *Akk.*)

gripping ['gripiŋ] *adj. (fig.)* packend

grisly ['grizli] *adj.* grausig

gristle ['grisl] *n.* Knorpel, *der*

grit [grit] **1.** *n.* **a)** Sand, *der;* **b)** *(coll.: courage)* Schneid, *der (ugs.).* **2.** *v. t.,* -**tt-:** **a)** streuen ⟨*Straßen*⟩; **b)** ~ **one's teeth** die Zähne zusammenbeißen *(ugs.)*

groan [grəun] **1.** *n.* Stöhnen, *das;* *(of thing)* Achzen, *das.* **2.** *v. i.* [auf]stöhnen **(at** bei); ⟨*Tisch, Planken:*⟩ ächzen. **3.** *v. t.* stöhnen

grocer ['grəusə(r)] *n.* Lebensmittelhändler, *der*/-händlerin, *die.* **grocery** ['grəusəri] *n.* **a)** *in pl.* *(goods)* Lebensmittel *Pl.;* **b)** ~ **[store]** Lebensmittelgeschäft, *das*

groggy ['grogi] *adj.* groggy präd. *(ugs.)*

groin [grɔin] *n.* Leistengegend, *die*

groom [gru:m, grʊm] **1.** *n.* **a)** *(stableboy)* Stallbursche, *der;* **b)** *(bride~)* Bräutigam, *der.* **2.** *v. t.* striegeln ⟨*Pferd*⟩; *(fig.)* vorbereiten **(for** auf + *Akk.*)

groove [gru:v] *n.* Rille, *die*

grope [grəup] *v. i.* tasten **(for** nach)

¹**gross** [grəʊs] *adj.* **a)** *(flagrant)* grob ⟨*Fahrlässigkeit, Fehler*⟩; **b)** *(obese)* fett; **c)** *(total)* Brutto-

²**gross** *n., pl. same* Gros, *das*

'**grossly** *adj. (flagrantly)* äußerst; grob ⟨*übertreiben*⟩

grotesque [grəʊ'tesk] *adj.* grotesk

grotto ['grɒtəʊ] *n., pl.* ~es *or* ~s Grotte, *die*

grotty ['grɒtɪ] *adj. (Brit. sl.)* mies *(ugs.)*

¹**ground** [graʊnd] 1. *n.* **a)** Boden, *der;* get off the ~ *(coll.)* konkrete Gestalt annehmen; **b)** |sports| ~: Sportplatz, *der;* **c)** *in pl. (attached to house)* Anlage, *die;* **d)** *(reason)* Grund, *der;* on the ~|s| of auf Grund (+ *Gen.*); on the ~|s| that ...: unter Berufung auf die Tatsache, daß ...; **e)** *in pl. (sediment)* Satz, *der.* 2. *v. t. (Aeronaut.)* am Boden festhalten

²**ground** 1. *see* grind 1, 2. 2. *adj.* gemahlen ⟨*Kaffee, Getreide*⟩

ground 'floor *see* floor 1 b

'**grounding** *n.* Grundkenntnisse *Pl.*

'**groundless** *adj.* unbegründet

ground: ~**sheet** *n.* Bodenplane, *die;* ~**sman** ['graʊndzmən] *n., pl.* -smen ['graʊndzmən] *(Sport)* Platzwart, *der;* ~**work** *n.* Vorarbeiten *Pl.*

group [gru:p] 1. *n.* Gruppe, *die.* 2. *v. t.* gruppieren

¹**grouse** [graʊs] *n., pl. same* Rauhfußhuhn, *das;* |red| ~ *(Brit.)* Schottisches Moorschneehuhn

²**grouse** *v. i. (coll.)* meckern *(ugs.)*

grove [grəʊv] *n.* Wäldchen, *das*

grovel ['grɒvl] *v. i., (Brit.)* -ll- *(fig.)* katzbuckeln

grow [grəʊ] 1. *v. i.,* grew [gru:], grown [grəʊn] **a)** wachsen; ~ out of *or* from sth. sich aus etw. entwickeln; *(from sth. abstract)* von etw. herrühren; ~ in gewinnen an (+ *Dat.*) ⟨*Größe, Bedeutung*⟩; **b)** *(become)* werden; ~ apart *(fig.)* sich auseinanderleben; ~ to love/hate sb./sth. jmdn./etw. liebenlernen/hassenlernen; ~ to like sb./sth. nach und nach Gefallen an jmdm./ etw. finden. 2. *v. t.,* grew, grown ziehen; *(on a large scale)* anpflanzen; züchten ⟨*Blumen*⟩. ~ up **a)** aufwachsen; *(become adult)* erwachsen werden; **b)** ⟨*Legende:*⟩ entstehen

growl [graʊl] 1. *n.* Knurren, *das;* *(of bear)* Brummen, *das.* 2. *v. i.* knurren; ⟨*Bär:*⟩ |böse| brummen

grown [grəʊn] 1. *see* grow. 2. *adj.* erwachsen. '**grown-up** 1. *n.* Erwachsene, *der/die.* 2. *adj.* erwachsen

growth [grəʊθ] *n.* **a)** Wachstum, *das* (of, in *Gen.*); *(increase)* Zunahme, *die* (of, in *Gen.*); **b)** *(Med.)* Gewächs, *das*

grub [grʌb] *n.* **a)** Larve, *die;* *(maggot)* Made, *die;* **b)** *(sl.: food)* Fressen, *das (salopp)*

grubby ['grʌbɪ] *adj.* schmudd[e]lig *(ugs.)*

grudge [grʌdʒ] 1. *v. t.* ~ sb. sth. jmdm. etw. mißgönnen; ~ doing sth. etw. ungern tun. 2. *n.* Groll, *der;* bear sb. a. ~ *or* a ~ against sb. jmdm. gegenüber nachtragend sein. **grudging** ['grʌdʒɪŋ] *adj.* widerwillig; widerwillig gewährt ⟨*Zuschuß*⟩. '**grudgingly** *adv.* wiederwillig

gruelling (*Amer.:* **grueling**) ['gru:ə-lɪŋ] *adj.* aufreibend; strapaziös ⟨*Reise*⟩

gruesome ['gru:səm] *adj.* grausig

gruff [grʌf] *adj.* barsch; rauh ⟨*Stimme*⟩

grumble ['grʌmbl] *v. i.* murren; ~ about *or* over sth. sich über etw. *(Akk.)* beklagen

grumpy ['grʌmpɪ] *adj.* unleidlich

grunt [grʌnt] 1. *n.* Grunzen, *das.* 2. *v. i.* grunzen

guarantee [gærən'ti:] 1. *v. t.* **a)** garantieren für; |eine| Garantie geben auf (+ *Akk.*); the clock is ~d for a year die Uhr hat ein Jahr Garantie; **b)** *(promise)* garantieren *(ugs.);* *(ensure)* bürgen für ⟨*Qualität*⟩. 2. *n.* **a)** *(Commerc. etc.)* Garantie, *die;* *(document)* Garantieschein, *der;* **b)** *(coll.: promise)* Garantie, *die (ugs.);* give sb. a ~ that ...: jmdm. garantieren, daß ...

guard [gɑ:d] 1. *n.* **a)** *(guardsman)* Wachtposten, *der;* *(group of soldiers)* Wache, *die;* be on ~: Wache haben; be on |one's| ~ *(lit. or fig.)* sich hüten; **b)** *(Brit. Railw.)* [Zug]schaffner, *der/* -schaffnerin, *die;* **c)** *(Amer.: prison warder)* [Gefängnis]wärter, *der/*-wärterin, *die;* **d)** *(safety device)* Schutz, *der.* 2. *v. t.* bewachen; hüten ⟨*Geheimnis*⟩; schützen ⟨*Leben*⟩ beschützen ⟨*Prominenten*⟩. '**guard against** *v. t.* sich hüten vor (+ *Dat.*); vorbeugen (+ *Dat.*) ⟨*Krankheit, Irrtum*⟩

'**guarded** *adj.* zurückhaltend

guardian ['gɑ:dɪən] *n.* **a)** Hüter, *der;* Wächter, *der;* **b)** *(Law)* Vormund, *der*

guerrilla [gə'rɪlə] *n.* Guerillakämpfer, *der/*-kämpferin, *die; attrib.* Guerilla-

guess [ges] 1. *v. t.* **a)** *(estimate)* schätzen; *(surmise)* raten; *(surmise correctly)* erraten; raten ⟨*Rätsel*⟩; ~ what! *(coll.)* stell dir vor!; **b)** *(esp. Amer.:*

suppose) I ~: ich glaube. **2.** *v. i. (estimate)* schätzen; *(make assumption)* vermuten; *(surmise correctly)* es erraten; ~ **at sth.** etw. schätzen; **keep sb.** ~**ing** *(coll.)* jmdn. im unklaren lassen. **3.** *n.* Schätzung, *die;* **make** *or* **have a** ~: schätzen. **'guesswork** *n.* **be** ~ : eine Vermutung sein

guest [gest] *n.* Gast, *der.* **'guest-house** *n.* Pension, *die*

guffaw [gʌ'fɔ:] **1.** *n.* brüllendes Gelächter. **2.** *v. i.* brüllend lachen

guidance ['gaɪdəns] *n. (leadership)* Führung, *die; (by teacher etc.)* [An]leitung, *die;* **b)** *(advice)* Rat, *der*

guide [gaɪd] **1.** *n.* **a)** Führer, *der*/Führerin, *die; (Tourism)* [Fremden]führer, *der*/-führerin, *die;* **b)** *(indicator)* **be a** [good] ~ **to sth.** ein [guter] Anhaltspunkt für etw. sein; **be no** ~ **to sth.** keine Rückschlüsse auf etw. *(Akk.)* zulassen; **c)** *(Brit.)* [Girl] **G~**: Pfadfinderin, *die;* **d)** *(handbook)* Handbuch, *das;* **e)** *(for tourists)* [Reise]führer, *der.* **2.** *v. t.* führen; *(fig.)* bestimmen ⟨*Handeln, Urteil*⟩; **be** ~**d by sth./sb.** sich von etw./jmdm. leiten lassen. **'guidebook** *n.* [Reise]führer, *der.* **guided 'missile** *n.* Lenkflugkörper, *der.* **'guide-dog** *n.* Blinden[führ]hund, *der.* **guided 'tour** *n.* Führung, *die* (of durch). **'guideline** *n.* Richtlinie, *die*

guild [gɪld] *n.* **a)** Verein, *der;* **b)** *(Hist.)* Gilde, *die;* Zunft, *die*

guile [gaɪl] *n.* Hinterlist, *die*

guillotine ['gɪləti:n] *n.* Guillotine, *die*

guilt [gɪlt] *n.* **a)** Schuld, *die* (of, for an + *Dat.*); **b)** *(guilty feeling)* Schuldgefühle *Pl.* **'guilty** *adj.* **a)** schuldig; **be** ~ **of murder** des Mordes schuldig sein; **find sb.** ~**/not** ~ [of sth.] jmdn. [an etw. *(Dat.)*] schuldig sprechen/[von etw.] freisprechen; **feel** ~ *(coll.)* ein schlechtes Gewissen haben; **b)** schuldbewußt ⟨*Miene, Blick, Verhalten*⟩; schlecht ⟨*Gewissen*⟩

guinea-pig ['gɪnɪpɪg] *n.* Meerschweinchen, *das; (fig.)* Versuchskaninchen, *das (ugs.)*

guise [gaɪz] *n.* Gestalt, *die;* **in the** ~ **of** in Gestalt (+ *Gen.*)

guitar [gɪ'tɑ:(r)] *n.* Gitarre, *die.* **guitarist** [gɪ'tɑ:rɪst] *n.* Gitarrist, *der*/Gitarristin, *die*

gulf [gʌlf] *n.* **a)** *(Geog.)* Golf, *der;* **b)** *(wide gap)* Kluft, *die*

gull [gʌl] *n.* Möwe, *die*

gullet ['gʌlɪt] *n.* **a)** Speiseröhre, *die;* **b)** *(throat)* Kehle, *die*

gullible ['gʌlɪbl] *adj.* leichtgläubig

gully ['gʌlɪ] *n. (artificial channel)* Abzugsrinne, *die; (drain)* Gully, *der*

gulp [gʌlp] **1.** *v. t.* hinunterschlingen; hinuntergießen ⟨*Getränk*⟩. **2.** *n.* **a)** Schlucken, *das;* **b)** *(large mouthful of drink)* kräftiger Schluck. **gulp 'down** *v. t.* hinunterschlingen; hinuntergießen ⟨*Getränk*⟩

¹gum [gʌm] *n. (Anat.)* ~[s] Zahnfleisch, *das*

²gum 1. *n.* **a)** Gummi, *das; (glue)* Klebstoff, *der;* **b)** *(Amer.)* see **chewing-gum.** **2.** *v. t.,* **-mm-: a)** *(smear with* ~*)* mit Klebstoff bestreichen; gummieren ⟨*Briefmarken, Etiketten usw.*⟩; **b)** *(fasten with* ~*)* kleben. **'gumboot** *n.* Gummistiefel, *der*

gumption ['gʌmpʃn] *n. (coll.)* Grips, *der*

gun [gʌn] *n.* Schußwaffe, *die; (rifle)* Gewehr, *das; (pistol)* Pistole, *die; (revolver)* Revolver, *der.* **gun 'down** *v. t.* niederschießen

gun: ~**-fire** *n.* Geschützfeuer, *das;* ~**man** [gʌnmən] *n., pl.* ~**men** ['gʌnmən] bewaffneter Mann

gun: ~**powder** *n.* Schießpulver, *das;* ~**shot** *n.* Schuß, *der*

gurgle ['gɜ:gl] **1.** *n.* Gluckern, *das; (of brook)* Plätschern, *das.* **2.** *v. i.* gluckern; ⟨*Bach:*⟩ plätschern; ⟨*Baby:*⟩ lallen; *(with delight)* glucksen

gush [gʌʃ] **1.** *n.* Schwall, *der.* **2.** *v. i.* **a)** strömen; ~ **out** herausströmen; **b)** *(fig.: enthuse)* schwärmen

gust [gʌst] *n.* ~ [of wind] Bö[e], *die*

gusto ['gʌstəʊ] *n.* Genuß, *der; (vitality)* Schwung, *der*

'gusty *adj.* böig

gut [gʌt] **1.** *n.* **a)** *(material)* Darm, *der;* **b)** *in pl. (bowels)* Eingeweide *Pl.;* Gedärme *Pl.;* **c)** *in pl. (coll.: courage)* Schneid, *der (ugs.).* **2.** *v. t.,* **-tt-: a)** *(remove* ~ *of)* ausnehmen; **b)** *(remove fittings from)* ausräumen; **the house was** ~**ted** [by fire] das Haus brannte aus

gutter ['gʌtə(r)] *n. (below edge of roof)* Dachrinne, *die; (at side of street)* Rinnstein, *der;* Gosse, *die*

guttural ['gʌtərl] *adj.* guttural; kehlig

guy [gaɪ] *n.* **a)** *(sl.: man)* Typ, *der (ugs.);* **b)** *in pl. (Amer.: everyone)* [listen,] you ~**s!** [hört mal,] Kinder! *(ugs.)*

guzzle ['gʌzl] **1.** *v. t. (eat)* hinunterschlingen; *(drink)* hinuntergießen. **2.** *v. i.* schlingen

gym [dʒɪm] *n.* *(coll.)* **a)** *(gymnasium)* Turnhalle, *die;* **b)** *(gymnastics)* Turnen, *das*

gymnasium *n.* [dʒɪm'neɪzɪəm] *n., pl.* ~s *or* **gymnasia** [dʒɪm'neɪzɪə] Turnhalle, *die*

gymnast ['dʒɪmnæst] *n.* Turner, *der/*Turnerin, *die*

gymnastic [dʒɪm'næstɪk] *adj.* turnerisch ⟨*Können*⟩; ~ **equipment** Turngeräte. **gymnastics** [dʒɪm'næstɪks] *n.* Gymnastik, *die; (esp. with apparatus)* Tu.nen, *das*

'gym-slip *n.* Trägerrock, *der*

gynaecologist [gaɪnɪ'kɒlədʒɪst] *n.* Frauenarzt, *der/*Frauenärztin, *die*

gynaecology [gaɪnɪ'kɒlədʒɪ] *n.* Gynäkologie, *die*

gypsy, Gypsy ['dʒɪpsɪ] *n.* Zigeuner, *der/*Zigeunerin, *die*

gyrate [dʒaɪə'reɪt] *v. i.* sich drehen

H

¹H, h [eɪtʃ] *n.* H, h, *das*

haberdashery ['hæbədæʃərɪ] *n.* *(goods)* Kurzwaren *Pl.; (Amer.: menswear)* Herrenmoden *Pl.*

habit ['hæbɪt] *n.* **a)** Gewohnheit, *die;* **good/bad** ~: gute/schlechte [An]gewohnheit; **get** *or* **fall into a** *or* **the** ~ **of doing sth.** [es] sich *(Dat.)* angewöhnen, etw. zu tun; **b)** *(coll.: addiction)* Süchtigkeit, *die*

habitable ['hæbɪtəbl] *adj.* bewohnbar

habitat ['hæbɪtæt] *n.* Habitat, *das*

habitation [hæbɪ'teɪʃn] *n.* **fit/unfit for human** ~: bewohnbar/unbewohnbar

habitual [hə'bɪtjʊəl] *adj.* **a)** gewohnt; **b)** *(given to habit)* gewohnheitsmäßig; Gewohnheits⟨*trinker*⟩. **ha'bitually** *adv. (regularly)* regelmäßig

¹hack [hæk] *v. t.* hacken ⟨*Holz*⟩; ~ **sth. to bits** *or* **pieces** etw. in Stücke hacken. **hack 'off** *v. t.* abhacken. **hack 'out** *v. t.* heraushauen **(from aus)**

²hack *n. (derog.: writer)* Schreiberling, *der*

hackneyed ['hæknɪd] *adj.* abgegriffen; abgedroschen *(ugs.)*

'hack-saw *n.* [Metall]bügelsäge, *die*

had *see* **have**

haddock ['hædək] *n., pl. same* Schellfisch, *der*

hadn't ['hædnt] *(coll.)* = **had not**; *see* **have**

haemorrhage ['hemərɪdʒ] *n.* Blutung, *die*

haemorrhoid ['hemərɔɪd] *n.* Hämorrhoide, *die*

hag [hæg] *n.* [alte] Hexe

haggard ['hægəd] *adj.* ausgezehrt; *(with worry)* abgehärmt

haggle ['hægl] *v. i.* sich zanken **(over, about** wegen); *(over price)* feilschen **(over, about** um)

Hague [heɪg] *pr. n.* **The** ~: Den Haag *(das)*

¹hail [heɪl] **1.** *n.* Hagel, *der.* **2.** *v. i.* **it** ~s *or* **is** ~**ing** es hagelt; ~ **down** *(fig.)* niederprasseln **(on** auf + *Akk.)*

²hail *v. t.* **a)** *(call out to)* anrufen; *(signal to)* anhalten ⟨*Taxi*⟩; **b)** *(acclaim)* zujubeln (+ *Dat.*); bejubeln **(as** als)

'hailstone *n.* Hagelkorn, *das*

hair [heə(r)] *n.* **a)** *(one strand)* Haar, *das;* **b)** *collect.* Haar, *das;* Haare *Pl.; attrib.* Haar-; **have** *or* **get one's** ~ **done** sich *(Dat.)* das Haar *od.* die Haare machen lassen *(ugs.)*

hair: ~**brush** *n.* Haarbürste, *die;* ~**-conditioner** *n.* Frisiermittel, *das;* ~**cut** *n.* **a)** *(act)* Haareschneiden, *das;* **go for/need a** ~**cut** zum Friseur gehen/müssen; **get/have a** ~**cut** sich *(Dat.)* die Haare schneiden lassen; **b)** *(style)* Haarschnitt, *der;* ~**-do** *n. (style)* Frisur, *die;* ~**dresser** *n.* Friseur, *der/*Friseuse, *die;* **go to the** ~**dresser's** zum Friseur gehen; ~**pin** *n.* Haarnadel, *die;* ~**pin 'bend** *n.* Haarnadelkurve, *die;* ~**-raising** ['heəreɪzɪŋ] *adj.* haarsträubend; ~**-style** *n.* Frisur, *die*

'hairy *adj.* **a)** behaart; flauschig ⟨*Pullover, Teppich*⟩; **b)** *(sl.: difficult)* haarig

hale [heɪl] *adj.* ~ **and hearty** gesund und munter

half [hɑːf] **1.** *n., pl.* **halves** [hɑːvz] **a)** Hälfte, *die;* ~ **[of sth.]** die Hälfte [von etw.]; ~ **of Europe** halb Europa; **one and a** ~ **hours, one hour and a** ~: anderthalb *od.* eineinhalb Stunden; **divide sth. in** ~ *or* **into halves** etw. halbieren; **she is three and a** ~: sie ist dreieinhalb; **b)** *(Footb. etc.: period)* Halbzeit, *die.* **2.** *adj.* halb; ~ **the house/books/time** die Hälfte des Hauses/der Bücher/der Zeit; ~ **an hour** ei-

ne halbe Stunde. **3.** *adv.* **a)** zur Hälfte;
halb ⟨*schließen, aufessen, fertig, voll,
geöffnet*⟩*; (almost)* fast ⟨*ersticken, tot
sein*⟩*; ~* **as much/many** halb so viel/
viele; **only ~ hear what ...**: nur zum
Teil hören, was ...; **b)** *~* **past** *or (coll.)*
~ **one/two/three** *etc.* halb zwei/drei/
vier *usw.; ~* **past twelve** halb eins

half: ~-caste *n.* Mischling, *der;*
~-'hearted *adj.* halbherzig; **~-'hour**
n. halbe Stunde; **~-'mast** *n.* **be
|flown| at ~-mast** auf Halbmast ste-
hen; **~-note** *n.. (Amer. Mus.)* halbe
Note; **~-'price 1.** *n.* halber Preis; **2.**
adj. zum halben Preis *nachgestellt;* **3.**
adv. zum halben Preis; **~-'term** *n.*
(Brit.) (holiday) **~-term |holiday/
break|** Ferien in der Mitte des Trime-
sters; **~-'time** *n. (Sport)* Halbzeit,
die; **~-'way 1.** *adj.* **~-way point** Mitte,
die; **2.** *adv.* die Hälfte des Weges ⟨*begleiten, fahren*⟩

hall [hɔ:l] *n.* **a)** Saal, *der; (building)*
Halle, *die;* **b)** *(entrance ~)* Flur, *der*

'hallmark *n.* [Feingehalts]stempel,
der; (fig.) Kennzeichen, *das*

hallo [hə'ləʊ] *int.* **a)** *(to call attention)*
hallo; **b)** *(Brit.) see* **hello**

Hallowe'en [hæləʊ'i:n] *n.* Hallo-
ween, *das; Abend vor Allerheiligen*

hallucination [həlu:sɪ'neɪʃn] *n.* Halluzination, *die*

'hallway *n.* Flur, *der*

halo ['heɪləʊ] *n.. pl.* **~es** Heiligen-
schein, *der*

halt [hɔlt, hɒlt] **1.** *n.* **a)** Pause, *die; (interruption)* Unterbrechung, *die;* **call a
~ to sth.** mit etw. Schluß machen; **b)**
(Brit. Railw.) Haltepunkt, *der.* **2.** *v. i.*
a) stehenbleiben; ⟨*Fahrer:*⟩ anhalten;
(for a rest) eine Pause machen; *(esp.
Mil.)* haltmachen; **~, who goes there?**
(Mil.) halt, wer da?; **b)** *(end)* eingestellt werden. **3.** *v. t.* anhalten; einstellen ⟨*Projekt*⟩. **'halting** *adj.* schleppend; zögernd ⟨*Antwort*⟩

halve [hɑ:v] *v. t.* halbieren

halves *pl. of* **half**

ham [hæm] *n.* Schinken, *der*

hamburger ['hæmbɜ:gə(r)] *n.* Hack-
steak, *das; (in roll)* Hamburger, *der*

hamlet ['hæmlɪt] *n.* Weiler, *der*

hammer ['hæmə(r)] **1.** *n.* Hammer,
der. **2.** *v. t.* hämmern. **3.** *v. i.* hämmern
(at an + *Dat.*). **hammer 'out** *v. t.*
ausklopfen ⟨*Delle, Beule*⟩*; (fig.: devise)* ausarbeiten

hammock ['hæmək] *n.* Hängematte,
die

'hamper ['hæmpə(r)] *n.* [Deckel]korb,
der

²hamper *v. t.* behindern

hamster ['hæmstə(r)] *n.* Hamster, *der*

hand [hænd] **1.** *n.* **a)** Hand, *die;* **by ~**
(manually) mit der *od.* von Hand; **give**
or lend |sb.| a ~ |with *or* **in sth.|** [jmdm.]
[bei etw.] helfen; **b)** *(share)* **have a ~ in**
sth. bei etw. seine Hände im Spiel ha-
ben; **c)** *(worker)* Arbeiter, *der; (Naut.:
seaman)* Matrose, *der;* **d)** *(of clock or
watch)* Zeiger, *der;* **e)** **at ~**: in der Nä-
he; **on the one ~ ..., |but| on the other
|~| ...**: einerseits ..., andererseits ...; **f)**
(Cards) Karte, *die.* **2.** *v. t.* geben;
⟨*Überbringer:*⟩ übergeben ⟨*Sendung,
Lieferung*⟩. **hand 'in** *v. t.* abgeben **(to,
at** bei); einreichen ⟨*Petition*⟩. **hand
'out** *v. t.* austeilen. **hand 'over** *v. t.*
übergeben **(to** *Dat.*)

hand: ~-bag *n.* Handtasche, *die;*
~-baggage *n.* Handgepäck, *das;*
~-book *n.* Handbuch, *das;* **~-brake**
n. Handbremse, *die;* **~-cuff 1.** *n., usu.
in pl.* Handschelle, *die;* **2.** *v. t.* **~-cuff**
sb. jmdm. Handschellen anlegen

handful ['hændfʊl] *n.* Handvoll, *die;*
be a ~ *(fig. coll.)* einen ständig auf
Trab halten *(ugs.)*

handicap ['hændɪkæp] **1.** *n.* **a)** *(Sport,
also fig.)* Handikap, *das;* **b)** *(physical)*
Behinderung, *die.* **2.** *v. t.,* **-pp-** benachteiligen. **handicapped** ['hændɪ-
kæpt] *adj.* **|mentally/physically| ~**:
[geistig/körperlich] behindert

handicraft ['hændɪkrɑ:ft] *n.* [Kunst]-
handwerk, *das; (needlework, knitting,
etc.)* Handarbeit, *die*

handiwork ['hændɪwɜ:k] *n.* hand-
werkliche Arbeit; **it's all his own ~**:
das hat er selbst gemacht

handkerchief ['hæŋkətʃɪf] *n., pl.* **~s**
or **handkerchieves** ['hæŋkətʃi:vz] Taschentuch, *das*

handle ['hændl] **1.** *n.* Griff, *der; (of
door)* Klinke, *die; (of axe, brush,
comb, broom, saucepan)* Stiel, *der; (of
cup, jug)* Henkel, *der.* **2.** *v. t.* **a)** *(touch,
feel)* anfassen; **b)** *(control)* handhaben
⟨*Fahrzeug, Flugzeug*⟩; **c)** *(deal/cope
with)* umgehen/fertigwerden mit.
'handlebars *n. pl.* Lenkstange, *die*

hand: ~-luggage *n.* Handgepäck,
das; **~-made** *adj.* handgearbeitet;
~-shake *n.* Händedruck, *der*

handsome ['hænsəm] *adj.* gutaussehend

hand: ~-stand *n.* Handstand, *der;*
~-writing *n.* [Hand]schrift, *die*

handy ['hændɪ] *adj.* greifbar; **keep/ have sth. ~:** etw. greifbar haben.
'**handyman** *n.* Handwerker, *der;* |home| ~: Heimwerker, *der*
hang [hæŋ] **1.** *v.t.* **a)** *p.t., p.p.* hung [hʌŋ] hängen; aufhängen ‹*Bild, Gardinen*›; ankleben ‹*Tapete*›; **b)** *p.t., p.p.* hanged *(execute)* hängen (for wegen); ~ **oneself** sich erhängen. **2.** *v.i.,* hung **a)** hängen; ‹*Kleid usw.:*› fallen; **b)** *(be executed)* hängen. **3.** *n.* **get the ~ of sth.** *(coll.)* mit etw. klarkommen *(ugs.).* **hang a'bout, hang a'round** *v.i.* **a)** *(loiter)* herumlungern *(salopp);* **b)** *(coll.: wait)* warten. **hang 'on** *v.i.* **a)** sich festhalten (to an + *Dat.*); **b)** *(sl.: wait)* warten; **c)** ~ **on to** *(coll.: keep)* behalten. **hang 'out 1.** *v.t.* aufhängen ‹*Wäsche*›. **2.** *v.i.* **a)** her?aushängen; **b)** *(sl.) (live)* wohnen; *(be often present)* sich herumtreiben *(ugs.).* **hang 'up** *v.t.* **1.** aufhängen. **2.** *v.i. (Teleph.)* auflegen
hangar ['hæŋə(r)] *n.* Hangar, *der*
'**hanger** *n.* Bügel, *der*
'**hang-glider** *n.* Drachen, *der*
'**hanging** *n. (execution)* Hinrichtung [durch den Strang]
hang: ~**man** [hæŋmən] *n., pl.* ~**men** [hæŋmən] Henker, *der;* ~**over** *n.* Kater, *der (ugs.);* ~**up** *n. (sl.)* Macke, *die (ugs.)*
hanker ['hæŋkə(r)] *v.i.* ~ **after** ein heftiges Verlangen haben nach
hanky ['hæŋkɪ] *n. (coll.)* Taschentuch, *das*
Hanover ['hænəʊvə(r)] *pr. n.* Hannover *(das)*
haphazard [hæp'hæzəd] *adj.,* **hap?'hazardly** *adv.* willkürlich
happen ['hæpn] *v.i.* geschehen; ‹*Vorhergesagtes:*› eintreffen; ~ **to do.** jmdm. passieren; ~ **to do sth./be sb.** zufällig etw. tun/jmd. sein; **as it ~s** *or* **it so ~s I have ...:** zufällig habe ich ...
'**happening** *n.* Ereignis, *das*
happily ['hæpɪlɪ] *adv.* **a)** glücklich ‹*lächeln*›; vergnügt ‹*spielen, lachen*›; **b)** *(gladly)* mit Vergnügen
happiness ['hæpɪnɪs] *n. see* **happy a:** Glück, *das;* Heiterkeit, *die;* Zufriedenheit, *die*
happy ['hæpɪ] *adj.* **a)** *(joyful)* glücklich; heiter ‹*Bild, Veranlagung*›; erfreulich ‹*Erinnerung, Szene*›; froh ‹*Ereignis*›; **b)** *(contented)* zufrieden; **be ~ to do sth.** *(glad)* etw. gern tun.
happy-go-'lucky *adj.* sorglos
harass ['hærəs] *v.t.* schikanieren.

'**harassment** *n.* Schikanierung, *die;* **sexual ~:** [sexuelle] Belästigung
harbour *(Brit.; Amer.:* **harbor)** ['hɑːbə(r)] **1.** *n.* Hafen, *der;* **in ~:** im Hafen. **2.** *v.t.* Unterschlupf gewähren (+ *Dat.*) ‹*Verbrecher, Flüchtling*›; hegen *(geh.)* ‹*Groll, Verdacht*›
hard [hɑːd] **1.** *adj.* **a)** hart; fest ‹*Gelee*›; stark ‹*Regen*›; streng ‹*Frost, Winter*›; gesichert ‹*Beweis, Daten*›; **b)** *(difficult)* schwer; **this is ~ to believe** das ist kaum zu glauben; **do sth. the ~ way** es sich *(Dat.)* bei etw. unnötig schwermachen; **c)** *(strenuous)* hart; **d)** *(vigorous)* kräftig ‹*Schlag, Stoß, Tritt*›; **e)** *(harsh)* hart. **2.** *adv.* **a)** *(strenuously)* hart ‹*arbeiten, trainieren*›; fleißig ‹*studieren, üben*›; genau ‹*überlegen*›; gut ‹*aufpassen, zuhören*›; **try ~:** sich sehr bemühen; **b)** *(vigorously)* heftig; fest ‹*schlagen, drücken, klopfen*›; **c)** *(severely)* hart; **be ~ up** knapp bei Kasse sein *(ugs.);* **feel ~ done by** sich schlecht behandelt fühlen
hard: ~**back** *n.* gebundene Ausgabe; ~**board** *n.* Hartfaserplatte, *die;* ~**-boiled** *adj.* **a)** hartgekocht ‹*Ei*›; **b)** *(tough)* hartgesotten
harden ['hɑːdn] **1.** *v.t.* härten; *(fig.)* abhärten (**to** gegen). **2.** *v.i.* hart werden; *(become confirmed)* sich verhärten. **hardened** ['hɑːdnd] *adj.* abgehärtet (**to** gegen); hartgesotten ‹*Verbrecher*›
hard: ~**-headed** *adj.* nüchtern; ~**-hearted** *adj.* hartherzig (**towards** gegenüber)
hardly ['hɑːdlɪ] *adv.* kaum; ~ **anyone** *or* **anybody/anything** fast niemand/ nichts; ~ **ever** so gut wie nie; ~ **at all** fast überhaupt nicht
'**hardness** *n.* Härte, *die*
'**hardship** *n.* **a)** Not, *die;* Elend, *das;* **b)** *(instance)* Notlage, *die*
hard: ~ '**shoulder** *n. (Brit.)* Standspur, *die;* ~**ware** *n.* **a)** *(goods)* Eisenwaren *Pl.; attrib.* Eisenwaren‹*geschäft*›; **b)** *(Computing)* Hardware, *die;* ~**-wearing** *adj.* strapazierfähig; ~**-working** *adj.* fleißig
hardy ['hɑːdɪ] *adj.* abgehärtet; zäh ‹*Rasse*›; winterhart ‹*Pflanze*›
hare [heə(r)] *n.* Hase, *der*
hark [hɑːk] *v.i.* |*just*| ~ **at him** hör ihn dir/hört ihn euch nur an!; ~ **back to** zurückkommen auf (+ *Akk.*)
harm [hɑːm] **1.** *n.* Schaden, *der;* **do sb. ~, do ~ to sb.** jmdm. schaden. **2.** *v.t.* etwas [zuleide] tun (+ *Dat.*); schaden

(+ *Dat.*) ⟨*Beziehungen, Land, Ruf*⟩.
harmful ['hɑːmfl] *adj.* schädlich (**to**
für). '**harmless** *adj.* harmlos
harmonica [hɑːˈmɒnɪkə] *n.* Mundharmonika, *die*
harmonious [hɑːˈməʊnɪəs] *adj.* harmonisch
harmonize ['hɑːmənaɪz] 1. *v. t.* aufeinander abstimmen. 2. *v. i.* harmonieren (**with** mit)
harmony ['hɑːmənɪ] *n.* Harmonie,
die; **be in** ~: harmonieren
harness ['hɑːnɪs] 1. *n.* Geschirr, *das.*
2. *v. t.* anschirren; *(fig.)* nutzen
harp [hɑːp] 1. *n.* Harfe, *die.* 2. *v. i.* ~ **on**
[about] sth. immer wieder von etw. re-
den; *(critically)* auf etw. *(Dat.)* herum-
reiten *(salopp)*
harpoon [hɑːˈpuːn] *n.* Harpune, *die*
harrowing ['hærəʊɪŋ] *adj.* entsetzlich; grauenhaft ⟨*Anblick, Geschichte*⟩
harsh [hɑːʃ] *adj.* **a)** rauh ⟨*Gewebe,
Klima*⟩; schrill ⟨*Ton, Stimme*⟩; grell
⟨*Licht*⟩; hart ⟨*Bedingungen, Leben*⟩; **b)**
(excessively severe) [sehr] hart; [äu-
ßerst] streng ⟨*Disziplin*⟩; rücksichtslos
⟨*Tyrann, Herrscher, Politik*⟩. '**harshly**
adv. [sehr] hart
harvest ['hɑːvɪst] 1. *n.* Ernte, *die.* 2.
v. t. ernten
has *see* **have**
hash [hæʃ] *n.* **a)** *(Cookery)* Haschee,
das; **b) make a ~ of** sth. *(coll.)* etw.
verpfuschen *(ugs.)*
hasn't ['hæznt] = **has not**; *see* **have**
hassle ['hæsl] *(coll.)* 1. *n.* Ärger, *der.* 2.
v. t. schikanieren
haste [heɪst] *n.* Eile, *die; (rush)* Hast,
die; **make ~:** sich beeilen
hasten ['heɪsn] 1. *v. t.* beschleunigen.
2. *v. i.* eilen
hastily ['heɪstɪlɪ] *adv. (hurriedly)* eilig;
(rashly) übereilt
hasty ['heɪstɪ] *adj.* eilig; flüchtig
⟨*Skizze, Blick*⟩; *(rash)* übereilt
hat [hæt] *n.* Hut, *der*
¹**hatch** [hætʃ] *n.* Luke, *die; (serving~)*
Durchreiche, *die*
²**hatch** 1. *v. t.* ausbrüten. 2. *v. i.*
[aus]schlüpfen. **hatch 'out** 1. *v. i.*
ausschlüpfen. 2. *v. t.* ausbrüten
'**hatchback** *n. (car)* Schräghheckli-
mousine, *die*
hatchet ['hætʃɪt] *n.* Beil, *das;* **bury the
~** *(fig.)* das Kriegsbeil begraben
hate [heɪt] 1. *n.* Haß, *der.* 2. *v. t.* hassen; **I ~ to say this** *(coll.)* ich sage das
nicht gern. **hateful** ['heɪtfl] *adj.* abscheulich

hatred ['heɪtrɪd] *n.* Haß, *der*
haughty ['hɔːtɪ] *adj.* hochmütig
haul [hɔːl] 1. *v. i. & t.* ziehen. 2. *n.* **a)**
Ziehen, *das;* **b)** *(catch)* Fang, *der;*
(fig.) Beute, *die.* **haulage** ['hɔːlɪdʒ] *n.*
Transport, *der*
haunch [hɔːntʃ] *n.* **sit on one's/its ~es**
auf seinem Hinterteil sitzen
haunt [hɔːnt] *v. t.* ~ **a house/castle** in
einem Haus/Schloß spuken; **a ~ed
house** ein Haus, in dem es spukt.
'**haunting** *adj.* sehnsüchtig
have 1. [hæv] *v. t., pres.* **he has** [hæz],
p. t. & p. p. **had** [hæd] haben; *(obtain)*
bekommen; *(take)* nehmen; bekom-
men ⟨*Kind*⟩; ~ **breakfast/dinner/lunch**
frühstücken/zu Abend/zu Mittag essen; ~ **a cup of tea** eine Tasse Tee trinken; ~ **sb. to stay** jmdn. zu Besuch haben; **you've had it now** *(coll.)* jetzt ist es
aus *(ugs.);* ~ **a game of football** Fußball spielen. 2. [həv, əv, *stressed* hæv]
v. aux., **he has** [həz, əz, *stressed* hæd],
had [həd, əd, *stressed* hæd] **I ~/I had
read** ich habe/hatte gelesen; **I ~/I had
gone** ich bin/war gegangen; **if I had
known ...:** wenn ich gewußt hätte ...; ~
sth. made etw. machen lassen; ~ **to**
müssen. **have 'on** *v. t. (wear)* tragen; **b)** *(Brit. coll.: deceive)* ~ **sb. on**
jmdn. auf den Arm nehmen *(ugs.).*
have 'out *v. t.* **a)** ~ **a tooth/one's tonsils out** sich *(Dat.)* einen Zahn ziehen
lassen/sich *(Dat.)* die Mandeln herausnehmen lassen; **b)** ~ **it out with sb.**
mit jmdm. offen sprechen
haven ['heɪvn] *n.* geschützte Anlegestelle, *die; (fig.)* Zufluchtsort, *der*
haven't ['hævnt] = **have not**; *see* **have**
haversack ['hævəsæk] *n.* Brotbeutel,
der
havoc ['hævək] *n.* **a)** *(devastation)* Verwüstungen; **cause** *or* **wreak ~:** Verwüstungen anrichten; **b)** *(confusion)*
Chaos; **play ~ with** sth. etw. völlig
durcheinanderbringen
¹**hawk** [hɔːk] *n.* Falke, *der*
²**hawk** *v. t.* hausieren mit. '**hawker** *n.*
Hausierer, *der*/Hausiererin, *die*
hay [heɪ] *n.* Heu, *das*
hay: ~ **fever** *n.* Heuschnupfen, *der;*
~**stack** *n.* Heuschober, *der (südd.);*
Heudieme, *die (nordd.);* ~**wire** *adj.*
(coll.) **go ~wire** ⟨*Instrument:*⟩ verrückt
spielen *(ugs.)*
hazard ['hæzəd] 1. *n.* Gefahr, *die.* 2.
v. t. ~ **a guess** mit Raten probieren.
hazardous ['hæzədəs] *adj.* gefährlich

haze [heɪz] *n.* Dunst[schleier], *der*
hazelnut ['heɪzlnʌt] *n.* Haselnuß, *die*
hazy ['heɪzɪ] *adj.* dunstig; *(fig.)* vage
he [hɪ, *stressed* hiː] *pron.* er
head [hed] **1.** *n.* **a)** Kopf, *der;* ~ **first**
mit dem Kopf voran; ~ **over heels**
kopfüber; **keep/lose one's** ~: einen
klaren Kopf behalten/den Kopf verlieren; **in one's** ~: im Kopf; **enter sb.'s**
~: jmdm. in den Sinn kommen; **use**
your ~: gebrauch deinen Verstand; **a**
or per ~: pro Kopf; **b)** *in pl. (on coin)*
~s Kopf; ~s **or tails?** Kopf oder
Zahl?; **c)** *(leader)* Leiter, *der/*Leiterin,
die; **d)** *(on beer)* Blume, *die.* **2.** *attrib.*
adj. ~ **waiter** Oberkellner, *der;* ~ **of-**
fice Hauptverwaltung, *die.* **3.** *v.t.* **a)**
(stand at top of) anführen ⟨*Liste*⟩;
(lead) leiten; führen ⟨*Bewegung*⟩; **b)**
(Football) köpfen. **4.** *v.i.* steuern; ~
for London ⟨*Flugzeug, Schiff:*⟩ Kurs
auf London nehmen; ⟨*Auto:*⟩ in Richtung London fahren; **you're** ~**ing for**
trouble du wirst Ärger bekommen.
'**headache** *n.* Kopfschmerzen *Pl.*
'**header** *n. (Footb.)* Kopfball, *der*
'**headgear** *n.* Kopfbedeckung, *die*
'**heading** *n.* Überschrift, *die*
head: ~**lamp** *n.* Scheinwerfer, *der;*
~**land** *n.* Landspitze, *die;* ~**light** *n.*
Scheinwerfer, *der;* ~**line** *n.* Schlagzeile, *die;* ~**long** *adv.* kopfüber;
~'**master** *n.* Schulleiter, *der;* ~'**mis-**
tress *n.* Schulleiterin, *die;* ~-**on 1.**
['--] *adj.* frontal; Frontal⟨*zusammen-*
stoß⟩; **2.** [-'-] *adv.* frontal; ~-**phones**
n. pl. Kopfhörer, *der;* ~'**quarters** *n.*
sing. or pl. Hauptquartier, *das;*
~-**rest** *n.* Kopfstütze, *die;* ~**room** *n.*
[lichte] Höhe, *die;* ~**strong** *adj.* eigensinnig; ~**way** *n.* **make** ~**way** Fortschritte machen; ~ **wind** *n.* Gegen-
wind, *der*
heady ['hedɪ] *adj.* berauschend
heal [hiːl] **1.** *v.t.* heilen. **2.** *v.i.* ~ [up]
[ver]heilen
health [helθ] *n.* Gesundheit, *die;* **in**
good/very good ~: bei guter/bester
Gesundheit; **good** *or* **your** ~! auf deine Gesundheit!
health: ~ **centre** *n.* Poliklinik, *die;* ~
food *n.* Reformhauskost, *die;* ~-**food**
shop Reformhaus, *das;* ~ **service** *n.*
Gesundheitsdienst, *der*
healthy ['helθɪ] *adj.* gesund
heap [hiːp] **1.** *n.* Haufen, *der;* ~s **of**
(coll.) jede Menge *(ugs.).* **2.** *v.t.* aufhäufen
hear [hɪə(r)] **1.** *v.t.,* **heard** [hɜːd] **a)** hö-

ren; **b)** *(understand)* verstehen. **2.** *v.i.,*
heard: ~ **about sb./sth.** von jmdm./
etw. [etwas] hören; **he wouldn't** ~ **of it**
er wollte nichts davon hören. **3.** *int.*
H~! **H**~! bravo!; richtig! **hear 'out**
v.t. ausreden lassen
heard *see* **hear 1, 2**
'**hearing** *n.* Gehör, *das;* **be hard of** ~:
schwerhörig sein. '**hearing-aid** *n.*
Hörgerät, *das*
hearsay ['hɪəseɪ] *n.* Gerücht, *das;* **it's**
only ~: es ist nur ein Gerücht
hearse [hɜːs] *n.* Leichenwagen, *der*
heart [hɑːt] *n. (also Cards)* Herz, *das;*
by ~: auswendig; **at** ~: im Grunde
seines/ihres Herzens; **take/lose** ~:
Mut schöpfen/verlieren; **my** ~ **sank**
mein Mut sank; **the** ~ **of the matter**
der wahre Kern der Sache; *see also*
club 1 c
heart: ~ **attack** *n.* Herzanfall, *der;*
(fatal) Herzschlag, *der;* ~**beat** *n.*
Herzschlag, *der;* ~-**breaking** *adj.*
herzzerreißend; ~-**broken** *adj.* **she**
was ~-**broken** ihr Herz war gebrochen; ~**burn** *n.* Sodbrennen, *das*
hearten ['hɑːtn] *v.t.* ermutigen.
'**heartening** *adj.* ermutigend
heart: ~ **failure** *n.* Herzversagen,
das; ~**felt** *adj.* tiefempfunden ⟨*Bei-*
leid⟩; aufrichtig ⟨*Dankbarkeit*⟩
hearth [hɑːθ] *n.* Platz vor dem Kamin.
'**hearth-rug** *n.* Kaminvorleger, *der*
heartily ['hɑːtɪlɪ] *adv.* von Herzen; **eat**
~: tüchtig essen
'**heartless** *adj.* herzlos
hearty ['hɑːtɪ] *adj.* herzlich; ungeteilt
⟨*Zustimmung*⟩; herzhaft ⟨*Mahlzeit*⟩
heat [hiːt] **1.** *n.* **a)** *(hotness)* Hitze, *die;*
b) *(Phys.)* Wärme, *die;* **c)** *(Sport)* Vor-
lauf, *der.* **2.** *v.t.* heizen. **heat 'up** *v.t.*
heiß machen
'**heated** *adj. (angry)* hitzig
'**heater** *n.* Ofen, *der; (for water)* Boiler,
der
heath [hiːθ] *n.* Heide, *die*
heathen ['hiːðn] **1.** *adj.* heidnisch. **2.**
n. Heide, *der/*Heidin, *die*
heather ['heðə(r)] *n.* Heidekraut, *das*
'**heating** *n.* Heizung, *die*
heat: ~-**stroke** *n.* Hitzschlag, *der;*
~**wave** *n.* Hitzewelle, *die*
heave [hiːv] **1.** *v.t.* **a)** heben; **b)** *(coll.:*
throw) schmeißen *(ugs.);* **c)** ~ **a sigh**
aufseufzen. **2.** *v.i. (pull)* ziehen. **3.** *n.*
Zug, *der*
heaven ['hevn] *n.* Himmel, *der;* **in** ~:
im Himmel; **for H**~'**s sake!** um Gottes
willen! '**heavenly** *adj.* himmlisch

heavily ['hevɪlɪ] *adj.* schwer; *(to a great extent)* stark; schwer ⟨*bewaffnet*⟩; tief ⟨*schlafen*⟩; dicht ⟨*bevölkert*⟩; **smoke/drink** ~: ein starker Raucher/Trinker sein; **it rained/snowed** ~: es regnete/schneite stark

heavy ['hevɪ] *adj.* schwer; unmäßig ⟨*Trinken, Rauchen*⟩; **a** ~ **smoker/drinker** ein starker Raucher/Trinker; **be a** ~ **sleeper** sehr fest schlafen

heavy: ~**-duty** *adj.* strapazierfähig ⟨*Kleidung, Material*⟩; schwer ⟨*Werkzeug, Maschine*⟩; ~ '**goods vehicle** *n. (Brit.)* Schwerlastwagen, *der;* ~**weight** *n.* Schwergewicht, *das*

Hebrew ['hi:bru:] **1.** *adj.* hebräisch. **2.** *n. (language)* Hebräisch, *das*

heckle ['hekl] *v. t.* Zwischenrufe unterbrechen. **heckler** ['heklə(r)] *n.* Zwischenrufer, *der*

hectic ['hektɪk] *adj.* hektisch

he'd [hɪd, *stressed* hi:d] **a)** = **he had; b)** = **he would**

hedge [hedʒ] **1.** *n.* Hecke, *die.* **2.** *v. t.* ~ **one's bets** *(fig.)* nicht alles auf eine Karte setzen. **3.** *v. i.* sich nicht festlegen

hedgehog ['hedʒhɒg] *n.* Igel, *der*

'**hedgerow** *n.* Hecke, *die* [als Feldbegrenzung]

heed [hi:d] **1.** *v. t.* beachten; beherzigen ⟨*Rat, Lektion*⟩; ~ **the danger/risk** sich *(Dat.)* der Gefahr/des Risikos bewußt sein. **2.** *n.* **give** *or* **pay** ~ **to, take** ~ **of** Beachtung schenken (+ *Dat.*). '**heedless** *adj.* unachtsam; **be** ~ **of** sth. auf etw. *(Akk.)* nicht achten

heel [hi:l] *n.* Ferse, *die; (of shoe)* Absatz, *der;* **Achilles'** ~ *(fig.)* Achillesferse, *die;* **down at** ~ *(fig.)* heruntergekommen; **take to one's** ~**s** Fersengeld geben *(ugs.)*

hefty ['heftɪ] *adj.* kräftig; *(heavy)* schwer

height [haɪt] *n.* **a)** Höhe, *die; (of person, animal, building)* Größe, *die;* **b)** *(fig.: highest point)* Höhepunkt, *der.* **heighten** ['haɪtn] *v. t.* aufstocken; *(fig.)* verstärken.

heir [eə(r)] *n.* Erbe, *der*/Erbin, *die.* **heiress** ['eərɪs] *n.* Erbin, *die*

heirloom ['eəlu:m] *n.* Erbstück, *das*

held *see* ²**hold** 1, 2

helicopter ['helɪkɒptə(r)] *n.* Hubschrauber, *der*

heliport ['helɪpɔ:t] *n.* Heliport, *der*

helium ['hi:lɪəm] *n.* Helium, *das*

hell [hel] *n.* **a)** Hölle, *die;* **b)** *(coll.)* [oh] ~! verdammter Mist! *(ugs.);* **what the**

~! ach, zum Teufel! *(ugs.);* **run like** ~: wie der Teufel rennen *(ugs.)*

he'll [hɪl, *stressed* hi:l] = **he will**

hello [hə'ləʊ, he'ləʊ] *int. (greeting)* hallo; *(surprise)* holla

hell's 'angel *n.* Rocker, *der*

helm [helm] *n. (Naut.)* Ruder, *das*

helmet ['helmɪt] *n.* Helm, *der*

help [help] **1.** *v. t.* **a)** ~ **sb.** [**to do sth.**] jmdm. helfen[, etw. zu tun]; **can I** ~ **you?** *(in shop)* was möchten Sie bitte?; **b)** *(serve)* ~ **oneself** sich bedienen; ~ **oneself to sth.** sich *(Dat.)* etw. nehmen; *(coll.: steal)* etw. mitgehen lassen *(ugs.);* **c)** *(avoid)* **if I/you can** ~ **it** wenn es irgend zu vermeiden ist; *(remedy)* **I can't** ~ **it** ich kann nichts dafür *(ugs.);* **it can't be** ~**ed** es läßt sich nicht ändern; **d)** *(refrain from)* **I can't** ~ **thinking** *or* **can't** ~ **but think that ...**: ich kann mir nicht helfen, ich glaube, ...; **I can't** ~ **laughing** ich muß einfach lachen. **2.** *n.* Hilfe, *die;* **with the** ~ **of ...**: mit Hilfe ... (+ *Gen.*); **be of |some|/no/much** ~ **to sb.** jmdm. eine gewisse/keine/eine große Hilfe sein.

help 'out 1. *v. i.* aushelfen. **2.** *v. t.* ~ **sb. out** jmdm. helfen

'**helper** *n.* Helfer, *der*/Helferin, *die*

helpful ['helpfl] *adj. (willing)* hilfsbereit; *(useful)* hilfreich; nützlich

'**helping 1.** *adj.* **lend |sb.| a** ~ **hand |with sth.|** *(fig.)* [jmdm.] [bei etw.] helfen. **2.** *n.* Portion, *die*

'**helpless** *adj.,* '**helplessly** *adv.* hilflos

helter-skelter [heltə'skeltə(r)] *n.* [spiralförmige] Rutschbahn

hem [hem] **1.** *n.* Saum, *der.* **2.** *v. t.,* **-mm-** säumen. **hem 'in** *v. t.* einschließen; **feel** ~**med in** sich eingeengt fühlen

hemisphere ['hemɪsfɪə(r)] *n.* Halbkugel, *die*

'**hem-line** *n.* Saum, *der*

hemp [hemp] *n.* Hanf, *der*

hen [hen] *n.* Huhn, *das;* Henne, *die*

hence [hens] *adv. (therefore)* daher. **hence'forth** *adv.* von nun an

henchman ['hentʃmən] *n., pl.* **henchmen** ['hentʃmən] Handlanger, *der*

henpecked ['henpekt] *adj.* **a** ~ **husband** ein Pantoffelheld, *der (ugs.);* **be** ~: unter dem Pantoffel stehen *(ugs.)*

¹**her** [hə(r), *stressed* hɜ:(r)] *pron.* sie; *as indirect object* ihr; **it was** ~: sie war's

²**her** *poss. pron. attr.* ihr

herald ['herəld] **1.** *n.* Herold, *der.* **2.** *v. t.* ankündigen. **heraldic** [he'rældɪk]

adj. heraldisch. **heraldry** ['herəldrı] *n.* Heraldik, *die*
herb [hɜːb] *n.* Kraut, *das.* **herbaceous** [hɜːˈbeıʃəs] *adj.* krautartig; ~ **border** Staudenrabatte, *die.* **herbal** ['hɜːbl] *attrib. adj.* Kräuter
herd [hɜːd] **1.** *n.* Herde, *die; (of wild animals)* Rudel, *das.* **2.** *v.t.* **a)** treiben; ~ **people together** Menschen zusammenpferchen; **b)** *(tend)* hüten
here [hıə(r)] **1.** *adv.* **a)** *(in or at this place)* hier; **down/in/up** ~: hier unten/drin/oben; ~ **you are** *(coll.: giving sth.)* hier; **b)** *(to this place)* hierher; **in|to|** ~: hierherein; **come/bring** ~: [hier]herkommen/-bringen. **2.** *int. (attracting attention)* he. **here'by** *adv. (formal)* hiermit
hereditary [hıˈredıtərı] *adj.* **a)** erblich ⟨*Titel, Amt*⟩; **b)** *(Biol.)* angeboren
heresy ['herısı] *n.* Ketzerei, *die*
heretic ['herıtık] *n.* Ketzer, *der/*Ketzerin, *die*
here'with *adv.* in der Anlage
heritage ['herıtıdʒ] *n.* Erbe, *das*
hermetic [hɜːˈmetık] *adj.* luftdicht. **hermetically** [hɜːˈmetıkəlı] *adv.* hermetisch
hermit ['hɜːmıt] *n.* Einsiedler, *der/* Einsiedlerin, *die*
hernia ['hɜːnıə] *n.* Bruch, *der*
hero ['hıərəʊ] *n., pl.* ~es Held, *der.* **heroic** [hıˈrəʊık] *adj.* heldenhaft
heroin ['herəʊın] *n.* Heroin, *das*
heroine ['herəʊın] *n.* Heldin, *die*
heroism ['herəʊızm] *n.* Heldentum, *das*
heron ['hern] *n.* Reiher, *der*
herring ['herıŋ] *n.* Hering, *der*
hers [hɜːz] *poss. pron. pred.* ihrer/ihre/ihres; **the book is** ~: das Buch gehört ihr
her'self *pron.* **a)** *emphat.* selbst; **[all] by** ~: [ganz] allein[e]; **b)** *refl.* sich; allein[e] ⟨*tun, wählen*⟩; **younger than/as heavy as** ~: jünger als/so schwer wie sie selbst
he's [hız, *stressed* hiːz] **a)** = **he is; b)** = **he has**
hesitant ['hezıtənt] *adj.* zögernd ⟨*Reaktion*⟩; stockend ⟨*Rede*⟩
hesitate ['hezıteıt] *v.i.* zögern; *(falter)* ins Stocken geraten; ~ **to do sth.** Bedenken haben, etw. zu tun. **hesitation** [hezıˈteıʃn] *n.* **a)** *(indecision)* Unentschlossenheit, *die;* **without** ~: ohne zu zögern; **b)** *(instance of faltering)* Unsicherheit, *die;* **c)** *(reluctance)* Bedenken *Pl.*

heterosexual [hetərəʊˈseksjʊəl] **1.** *adj.* heterosexuell. **2.** *n.* Heterosexuelle, *der/die*
het up [het 'ʌp] *adj.* aufgeregt
hew [hjuː] *v.t., p.p.* **hewn** [hjuːn] *or* **hewed** [hjuːd] hacken ⟨*Holz*⟩; losschlagen ⟨*Kohle, Gestein*⟩
hewn *see* **hew**
hexagon ['heksəgən] *n.* Sechseck, *das*
hey [heı] *int.* he; ~ **presto!** simsalabim!
heyday ['heıdeı] *n.* Blütezeit, *die*
HGV *abbr. (Brit.)* **heavy goods vehicle**
hi [haı] *int.* hallo *(ugs.)*
hiatus [haıˈeıtəs] *n.* Unterbrechung, *die*
hibernate ['haıbəneıt] *v.i.* Winterschlaf halten. **hibernation** [haıbəˈneıʃn] *n.* Winterschlaf, *der*
hiccup ['hıkʌp] **1.** *n.* **a)** Schluckauf, *der;* **have/get |the|** ~s den Schluckauf haben/bekommen; **b)** *(fig.: stoppage)* Störung, *die.* **2.** *v.i.* schlucksen *(ugs.)*
hid *see* ¹**hide**
hidden *see* ¹**hide**
¹**hide** [haıd] **1.** *v.t.,* **hid** [hıd], **hidden** ['hıdn] **a)** verstecken ⟨*Gegenstand, Person usw.*⟩ **(from** vor + *Dat.);* verbergen ⟨*Gefühle, Sinn usw.*⟩ **(from** vor + *Dat.);* verheimlichen ⟨*Tatsache, Absicht usw.*⟩ **(from** *Dat.);* **b)** *(obscure)* verdecken. **2.** *v.i.,* **hid, hidden** sich verstecken **(from** vor + *Dat.)*
²**hide** *n.* Haut, *die; (of furry animal)* Fell, *das; (dressed)* Leder, *das*
hide-and-'seek *n.* Versteckspiel, *das;* **play** ~: Verstecken spielen
hideous ['hıdıəs] *adj.* scheußlich
'**hide-out** *n.* Versteck, *das*
¹**hiding** ['haıdıŋ] *n.* **go into** ~: sich verstecken; *(to avoid police, public attention)* untertauchen; **be in** ~: sich versteckt halten; *(to avoid police, public attention)* untergetaucht sein
²**hiding** *n. (coll.: beating)* Tracht Prügel; **give sb. a |good|** ~: jmdm. eine [ordentliche] Tracht Prügel verpassen *(ugs.)*
'**hiding-place** *n.* Versteck, *das*
hierarchy ['haıərɑːkı] *n.* Hierarchie, *die*
hi-fi ['haıfaı] *(coll.)* **1.** *adj.* Hi-Fi-. **2.** *n.* Hi-Fi-Anlage, *die*
high [haı] **1.** *adj.* **a)** hoch; groß ⟨*Höhe*⟩; stark ⟨*Wind*⟩; **b)** *(coll.: on a drug)* high *(ugs.);* **c)** **it's** ~ **time you left** es ist höchste Zeit, daß du gehst. **2.** *adv.* hoch; **search** *or* **look** ~ **and low** überall suchen. **3.** *n.* **a)** *(~est level/figure)* Höchststand, *der;* **b)** *(Met*

eorol.) Hoch, *das.* **'highbrow** *(coll.)*
1. *n.* Intellektuelle, *der/die.* **2.** *adj.* intellektuell ⟨*Person, Gerede usw.*⟩;
hochgestochen *(abwertend)* ⟨*Person,
Musik, Literatur usw.*⟩. **'high chair** *n.*
Hochstuhl, *der*
higher edu'cation *n.* Hochschulbildung, *die*
high: ~-'**handed** *adj.* selbstherrlich;
~-**heeled** [haɪ'hiːld] *adj.* ⟨*Schuhe*⟩ mit
hohen Absätzen; ~ **jump** *n.* Hochsprung, *der;* ~**land** ['haɪlənd] *n.*
Hochland, *das;* ~**light 1.** *n.* **a)** Höhepunkt, *der;* **b)** *(bright area)* Licht, *das;*
2. *v. t.,* ~**lighted** ein Schlaglicht werfen auf (+ *Akk.*) ⟨*Probleme usw.*⟩
'highly *adv.* sehr; hoch⟨*interessant,
-angesehen, -bezahlt, -gebildet*⟩; leicht
⟨*entzündlich*⟩; stark ⟨*gewürzt*⟩; **think** ~
of sb./sth. eine hohe Meinung von
jmdm./etw. haben; **speak** ~ **of sb./sth.**
jmdn./etw. sehr loben. **highlystrung** ['haɪlɪstrʌŋ] *adj.* übererregbar
Highness ['haɪnɪs] *n.* **His/her** *etc.* ~:
Seine/Ihre *usw.* Hoheit
high: ~-**pitched** ['haɪpɪtʃt] *adj.* hoch
⟨*Ton, Stimme*⟩; ~ '**pressure** *n.* **a)**
(Meteorol.) Hochdruck, *der;* **b)** *(Mech.
Engin.)* Überdruck, *der;* ~-**rise** *adj.*
~-**rise building** Hochhaus, *das;* ~-**rise
block of flats/office block** Wohn-/
Bürohochhaus, *das;* ~ **school** *n.*
≈ Oberschule, *die;* ~ **season** *n.*
Hochsaison, *die;* ~**way** *n.* öffentliche Straße
hijack ['haɪdʒæk] *v. t.* entführen. **'hijacker** *n.* Entführer, *der;* *(of aircraft)*
Hijacker, *der*
hike [haɪk] *n.* Wanderung, *die.* **'hiker**
n. Wanderer, *der*/Wanderin, *die*
hilarious [hɪ'leərɪəs] *adj.* urkomisch
hill [hɪl] *n.* Hügel, *der;* *(higher)* Berg,
der; *(slope)* Hang, *der*
hill: ~-**billy** ['hɪlbɪlɪ] *n. (Amer.)* Hinterwäldler, *der*/Hinterwäldlerin, *die;*
~**side** *n.* Hang, *der;* ~**top** *n.*
[Berg]gipfel, *der*
'hilly *adj.* hüg[e]lig
hilt [hɪlt] *n.* Griff, *der;* **[up] to the** ~
(fig.) voll und ganz
him [ɪm, *stressed* hɪm] *pron.* ihn; *as indirect object* ihm; **it was** ~: er war's
Himalayas [hɪmə'leɪəz] *pr. n. pl.* Himalaya, *der*
him'self *pron.* **a)** *emphat.* selbst; **b)**
refl. sich. *See also* **herself**
hind [haɪnd] *adj.* hinter...; ~ **legs** Hinterbeine
hinder ['hɪndə(r)] *v. t. (impede)* behin

dern; *(delay)* verzögern ⟨*Vollendung
einer Arbeit, Vorgang*⟩; aufhalten ⟨*Person*⟩; ~ **sb. from doing sth.** jmdn. daran hindern, etw. zu tun
'hindquarters *n. pl.* Hinterteil, *das*
hindrance ['hɪndrəns] *n.* Hindernis,
das (**to** für)
'hindsight *n.* **with |the benefit of|** ~:
im nachhinein
Hindu ['hɪndu:, hɪn'du:] **1.** *n.* Hindu,
der. **2.** *adj.* hinduistisch; Hindu⟨*gott,
-tempel*⟩
hinge [hɪndʒ] **1.** *n.* Scharnier, *das.* **2.**
v. t. mit Scharnieren versehen. **3.** *v. i.*
(depend) abhängen (**|up|on** von)
hint [hɪnt] **1.** *n.* **a)** *(suggestion)* Wink,
der; **b)** *(slight trace)* Spur, *die* (**of** von);
the ~/**no** ~ **of a smile** der Anflug/nicht
die Spur eines Lächelns. **c)** *(information)* Tip, *der* (**on** für). **2.** *v. i.* ~ **at** andeuten
hip [hɪp] *n.* Hüfte, *die*
hippie ['hɪpɪ] *n. (coll.)* Hippie, *der*
hippopotamus [hɪpə'pɒtəməs] *n.*
Nilpferd, *das*
hippy *see* **hippie**
hire [haɪə(r)] **1.** *n.* Mieten, *das;* **be on** ~
|to sb.| [an jmdn.] vermietet sein; **for**
~: zu vermieten. **2.** *v. t.* **a)** *(employ)*
anwerben; engagieren ⟨*Anwalt, Berater usw.*⟩; **b)** *(obtain use of)* mieten;
~ **sth. from sb.** etw. bei jmdm. mieten;
c) *(grant use of)* ~ **|out|** vermieten; ~
sth. |out| to sb. etw. jmdm. *od.* an
jmdn. vermieten. **'hire-car** *n.* Mietwagen, *der.* **hire-'purchase** *n. (Brit.)*
Ratenkauf, *der; attrib.* Raten-; **pay
for/buy sth. on** ~: etw. in Raten bezahlen/auf Raten kaufen
his [ɪz, *stressed* hɪz] *poss. pron.* **a)** *attrib.* sein; **b)** *pred.* seiner/seine/sein[e]s; *see also* **hers**
hiss [hɪs] **1.** *n.* Zischen, *das.* **2.** *v. i.* zischen
historian [hɪ'stɔːrɪən] *n.* Historiker,
der/Historikerin, *die*
historic [hɪ'stɒrɪk] *adj.* historisch.
historical [hɪ'stɒrɪkl] *adj.* historisch;
geschichtlich ⟨*Belege, Hintergrund*⟩
history ['hɪstərɪ] *n.* Geschichte, *die*
hit [hɪt] **1.** *v. t.,* -**tt**-, **hit** schlagen; *(with
missile)* treffen; ⟨*Geschoß, Ball usw.:*⟩
treffen; ⟨*Fahrzeug:*⟩ prallen gegen;
⟨*Schiff:*⟩ laufen gegen; ~ **one's head on
sth.** mit dem Kopf gegen etw. stoßen;
~ **it off with sb.** gut mit jmdm. auskommen. **2.** *v. i.,* -**tt**-, **hit** schlagen. **3.**
n. **a)** *(blow)* Schlag, *der;* *(shot or bomb
striking target)* Treffer, *der;* **b)** *(suc

cess) Erfolg, *der;* *(in entertainment)*
Schlager, *der;* Hit, *der (ugs.).* **hit**
'**back** *v. t. & i.* zurückschlagen. '**hit**
[**up**]**on** *v. t.* kommen auf (+ *Akk.*)
⟨*Idee*⟩; finden ⟨*richtige Antwort, Methode*⟩

hitch [hɪtʃ] **1.** *v. t.* **a)** binden ⟨*Seil*⟩
(**round** um + *Akk.*); [an]koppeln ⟨*Anhänger usw.*⟩ (**to** an + *Akk.*); spannen
⟨*Zugtier usw.*⟩ (**to** vor + *Akk.*); **b)** ~ **a**
lift *or* **ride** *(coll.)* per Anhalter fahren.
2. *n. (problem)* Problem, *das.* **hitch**
'**up** *v. t.* hochheben ⟨*Rock*⟩

'**hitch-hike** *v. i.* per Anhalter fahren.
'**hitch-hiker** *n.* Anhalter, *der*/Anhal-
terin, *die*

'**hit parade** *n.* Hitparade, *die*

HIV *abbr.* **human immuno-deficiency**
virus HIV

hive [haɪv] *n.* [Bienen]stock, *der*

HMS *abbr. (Brit.)* **Her/His Majesty's**
Ship H.M.S.

hoard [hɔːd] **1.** *n.* Vorrat, *der.* **2.** *v. t.* ~
|**up**| horten; hamstern ⟨*Lebensmittel*⟩

hoarding ['hɔːdɪŋ] *n. (fence)* Bauzaun,
der; (Brit.: for advertisements) Rekla-
mewand, *die*

hoar-frost ['hɔːfrɒst] *n.* [Rauh]reif,
der

hoarse [hɔːs] *adj.* heiser

hoax [həʊks] **1.** *v. t.* anführen *(ugs.);*
foppen. **2.** *n. (deception)* Schwindel,
der; (practical joke) Streich, *der; (false*
alarm) blinder Alarm

hob [hɒb] *n.* [Koch]platte, *die*

hobble ['hɒbl] *v. i.* ~ |**about**| [her-
um]humpeln

hobby ['hɒbɪ] *n.* Hobby, *das.* '**hobby-**
horse *n.* Steckenpferd, *das*

hobnailed ['hɒbneɪld] *adj.* Nagel-
⟨*schuh, -stiefel*⟩

hobo ['həʊbəʊ] *n., pl.* **-es** *(Amer.)*
Landstreicher, *der*/-streicherin, *die*

hockey ['hɒkɪ] *n.* Hockey, *das.*
'**hockey-stick** *n.* Hockeyschläger,
der

hoe [həʊ] **1.** *n.* Hacke, *die.* **2.** *v. t. & i.*
hacken

hog [hɒg] **1.** *n.* [Mast]schwein. **2.** *v. t.,*
-gg- *(coll.)* mit Beschlag belegen

hoist [hɔɪst] **1.** *v. t.* hochziehen, hissen
⟨*Flagge usw.*⟩; hieven ⟨*Last*⟩; setzen
⟨*Segel*⟩. **2.** *n.* [Lasten]aufzug, *der*

¹**hold** [həʊld] *n. (of ship)* Laderaum,
der; (of aircraft) Frachtraum, *der*

²**hold** **1.** *v. t.,* **held** [held] **a)** halten;
(carry) tragen; *(keep fast)* festhalten;
~ **the door open for sb.** jmdm. die Tür
aufhalten; ~ **sth. in place** etw. halten;

b) *(contain)* enthalten; *(be able to contain)* fassen ⟨*Liter, Personen usw.*⟩; **c)**
(possess) besitzen; haben; **d)** *(keep*
possession of) halten ⟨*Stützpunkt,*
Stadt, Stellung⟩; ~ **the line** *(Teleph.)*
am Apparat bleiben; ~ **one's own** sich
behaupten; **e)** *(cause to take place)*
stattfinden lassen; abhalten ⟨*Veranstaltung, Konferenz, Gottesdienst, Sitzung*⟩; veranstalten ⟨*Festival, Auktion*⟩; austragen ⟨*Meisterschaften*⟩;
führen ⟨*Unterhaltung, Gespräch*⟩;
durchführen ⟨*Untersuchung*⟩; halten
⟨*Vortrag, Rede*⟩; **f)** *(think, believe)* ~ **a**
view *or* **an opinion** eine Ansicht haben
(**on** über + *Akk.*); ~ **that ...:** der Ansicht sein, daß ...; ~ **oneself respons-**
ible for sth. sich für etw. verantwortlich fühlen; ~ **sth. against sb.** jmdm.
etw. vorwerfen. **2.** *v. i.,* **held** halten;
⟨*Wetter:*⟩ sich halten. **3.** *n.* **a)** *(grasp)*
Griff, *der;* **grab** *or* **seize** ~ **of sth.** etw.
ergreifen; **get** *or* **lay** *or* **take** ~ **of sth.**
etw. fassen *od.* packen; **keep** ~ **of sth.**
etw. festhalten; **get** ~ **of sth.** *(fig.)* etw.
auftreiben; **get** ~ **of sb.** *(fig.)* jmdn. erreichen; **b)** *(influence)* Einfluß, *der*
(**on, over** auf + *Akk.*); **c)** *(Sport)* Griff,
der. **hold** '**back** **1.** *v. t.* zurückhalten.
2. *v. i.* zögern. **hold** '**on** **1.** *v. t.*
[fest]halten. **2.** *v. i.* **a)** sich festhalten;
~ **on to** sich festhalten an (+ *Dat.*);
(keep) behalten; **b)** *(coll.: wait)* warten. **hold** '**out** **1.** *v. t.* ausstrecken
⟨*Hand, Arm usw.*⟩: hinhalten ⟨*Tasse,*
Teller⟩. **2.** *v. i. (resist)* sich halten.
hold '**up** *v. t.* **a)** *(raise)* hochhalten;
heben ⟨*Hand, Kopf*⟩; **b)** *(delay)* aufhalten; **c)** *(rob)* überfallen. '**hold**
with *v. t.* **not** ~ **with sth.** etw. ablehnen

'**holdall** *n.* Reisetasche, *die*

'**holder** *n.* **a)** *(of post, title)* Inhaber,
der/Inhaberin, *die;* **b)** ⟨*Zigaretten*⟩-
spitze, *die;* ⟨*Papier-, Zahnputzglas*⟩-
halter, *der*

'**hold-up** *n.* **a)** *(robbery)* [Raub]über-
fall, *der;* **b)** *(delay)* Verzögerung, *die*

hole [həʊl] *n.* Loch, *das; (of fox,*
badger, rabbit) Bau, *der;* **pick** ~**s in**
(fig.) zerpflücken *(ugs.)*

holiday ['hɒlɪdeɪ] *n.* **a)** [arbeits]freier
Tag; *(public* ~*)* Feiertag, *der;* **b)** *in*
sing. or pl. (Brit.: vacation) Urlaub,
der; (Sch.) [Schul]ferien *Pl.* '**holiday-**
maker *n.* Urlauber, *der*/Urlauberin,
die

Holland ['hɒlənd] *pr. n.* Holland *(das)*

hollow ['hɒləʊ] **1.** *adj.* hohl; eingefallen ⟨Wangen, Schläfen⟩; (fig.) leer ⟨Versprechen⟩. **2.** n. [Boden]senke, die. **3.** v. t. ~ out aushöhlen

holly ['hɒlɪ] n. Stechpalme, die

hologram ['hɒləgræm] n. Hologramm, der

holster ['həʊlstə(r)] n. [Pistolen]halfter, die od. das

holy ['həʊlɪ] adj. heilig

Holy: ~ 'Ghost see ~ Spirit; ~ **Land** n. the ~ **Land** das Heilige Land; ~ 'Spirit n. Heiliger Geist

homage ['hɒmɪdʒ] n. Huldigung, die (to an + Akk.); **pay** or **do** ~ **to sb./sth.** jmdm./einer Sache huldigen

home [həʊm] **1.** n. a) Heim, das; (flat) Wohnung, die; (house) Haus, das; (household) [Eltern]haus, das; (native country) Heimat, die; **at** ~: zu Hause; **be/feel at** ~ (fig.) sich wohl fühlen; **make yourself at** ~: fühl dich wie zu Hause; b) (institution) Heim, das. **2.** adj. a) Haus-; b) (Sport) Heim-. **3.** adv. nach Hause

home: ~ **address** n. Privatanschrift, die; ~ **com'puter** n. Heimcomputer, der; ~**-grown** adj. selbstgezogen; ~**land** n. Heimat, die

'homeless 1. adj. obdachlos. **2.** n. the ~: die Obdachlosen. **'homelessness** n. Obdachlosigkeit, die

homely ['həʊmlɪ] adj. wohnlich ⟨Zimmer usw.⟩; behaglich ⟨Atmosphäre⟩

home: ~**-made** adj. selbstgemacht; selbstgebacken ⟨Brot⟩; hausgemacht ⟨Lebensmittel⟩; **H~ Office** n. (Brit.) Innenministerium, das; **H~ 'Secretary** n. (Brit.) Innenminister, der; ~**sick** adj. heimwehkrank; **become/be** ~**sick** Heimweh bekommen/haben; ~ **'town** n. Heimatstadt, die; ~**work** n. (Sch.) Hausaufgaben Pl.; **piece of** ~**work** Hausaufgabe, die

homicide ['hɒmɪsaɪd] n. Tötung, die; (manslaughter) Totschlag, der

homosexual [hɒʊməʊ'seksjʊəl] **1.** adj. homosexuell. **2.** n. Homosexuelle, der/die

hone [həʊn] v. t. wetzen

honest ['ɒnɪst] adj. ehrlich. **'honestly** adv. ehrlich; redlich ⟨handeln⟩; ~! ehrlich!; (annoyed) also wirklich! **honesty** ['ɒnɪstɪ] n. Ehrlichkeit, die

honey ['hʌnɪ] n. Honig, der. **'honeycomb** n. Honigwabe, die. **'honeymoon** n. Flitterwochen Pl.; (journey) Hochzeitsreise, die

honk [hɒŋk] **1.** v. i. ⟨Fahrzeug, Fahrer:⟩ hupen. **2.** n. Hupen, das

honor, honorable (Amer.) see honour, honourable

honorary ['ɒnərərɪ] adj. Ehren⟨mitglied, -präsident, -doktor, -bürger⟩

honour ['ɒnə(r)] (Brit.) **1.** n. a) Ehre, die; b) (distinction) Auszeichnung, die. **2.** v. t. ehren; (Commerc.) honorieren. **honourable** ['ɒnərəbl] adj. (Brit.) ehrenwert (geh.)

hood [hʊd] n. a) Kapuze, die; b) (Amer. Motor Veh.) Motorhaube, die; c) (of pram) Verdeck, das

hoodlum ['hu:dləm] n. Rowdy, der

hoodwink ['hʊdwɪŋk] v. t. hinters Licht führen

hoof [hu:f] n., pl. ~s or **hooves** [hu:vz] Huf, der

hook [hʊk] **1.** n. Haken, der; **by** ~ **or by crook** mit allen Mitteln. **2.** v. t. a) (grasp) mit Haken/mit einem Haken greifen; b) (fasten) mit Haken/mit einem Haken befestigen (to an + Dat.); c) **be** ~**ed** [on sth.] (addicted) [von etw.] abhängig sein; (harmlessly) auf etw. stehen (ugs.). **hook 'up** v. t. festhaken (to an + Akk.)

hooligan ['hu:lɪgən] n. Rowdy, der. **hooliganism** ['hu:lɪgənɪzm] n. Rowdytum, das

hoop [hu:p] n. Reifen, der

hooray [hʊ'reɪ] int. hurra

hoot [hu:t] **1.** v. i. a) (call out) johlen; b) ⟨Eule:⟩ schreien; c) ⟨Fahrzeug, Fahrer:⟩ hupen. **2.** n. a) (shout) ~s of derision verächtliches Gejohle; b) (of owl) Schrei, der; c) (of vehicle) Hupen, das. **'hooter** n. (Brit.: siren) Sirene, die

hoover ['hu:və(r)] (Brit.) **1.** n. a) **H~ (P)** [Hoover]staubsauger, der; b) (made by any company) Staubsauger, der. **2.** v. t. staubsaugen

hooves pl. of **hoof**

¹hop [hɒp] n. a) (plant) Hopfen, der; b) in pl. (Brewing) Hopfen, der

²hop 1. v. i., **-pp-:** a) hüpfen; ⟨Hase:⟩ hoppeln; b) (fig. coll.) ~ **out of bed** aus dem Bett springen; ~ **into the car/on** [to] **the bus/train** sich ins Auto/in den Bus/Zug schwingen (ugs.). **2.** v. t., **-pp-** (Brit. sl.) ~ **it** sich verziehen (ugs.). **3.** n. a) Hüpfer, der; b) (Brit. coll.) **catch sb. on the** ~: jmdn. überraschen

hope [həʊp] **1.** n. Hoffnung, die; **sb.'s** ~[s] **of sth.** jmds. Hoffnung auf etw. (Akk.); **raise sb.'s** ~s jmdm. Hoffnung machen. **2.** v. i. & t. hoffen (for auf + Akk.); **I** ~ **so/not** hoffentlich/hoffentlich nicht; ~ **for the best** das Beste hoffen. **hopeful** ['həʊpfl] *adj.* **a)** zuversichtlich; **be ~ of sth./of doing sth.** auf etw. *(Akk.)* hoffen/voller Hoffnung sein, etw. zu tun; **b)** *(promising)* vielversprechend. '**hopefully** *adv.* **a)** *(expectantly)* voller Hoffnung; **b)** *(coll.: it is hoped that)* hoffentlich. '**hopeless** *adj.* **a)** hoffnungslos; **b)** *(inadequate)* miserabel. '**hopelessly** *adv.* **a)** hoffnungslos; **b)** *(inadequately)* miserabel

hopscotch ['hɒpskɒtʃ] *n.* Himmel-und-Hölle-Spiel, *das*

horde [hɔːd] *n.* Horde, *die*

horizon [həˈraɪzn] *n.* Horizont, *der;* **on the ~:** am Horizont

horizontal [hɒrɪˈzɒntl] *adj.* horizontal; waagerecht. **horiˈzontally** *adv.* horizontal; *(flat)* waagerecht

hormone ['hɔːməʊn] *n.* Hormon, *das*

horn [hɔːn] *n.* Horn, *das; (of vehicle)* Hupe, *die*

hornet ['hɔːnɪt] *n.* Hornisse, *die*

'**horny** *adj. (hard)* hornig

horoscope ['hɒrəskəʊp] *n.* Horoskop, *das*

horrible ['hɒrɪbl] *adj.* grauenhaft; grausig ⟨*Monster*⟩; grauenvoll ⟨*Verbrechen, Alptraum*⟩

horrid ['hɒrɪd] *adj.* scheußlich

horrific [həˈrɪfɪk] *adj.* schrecklich

horrify ['hɒrɪfaɪ] *v. t.* mit Schrecken erfüllen; **be horrified** *(shocked, scandalized)* entsetzt sein (**at, by** über + *Akk.*). '**horrifying** *adj.* grauenhaft

horror ['hɒrə(r)] **1.** *n.* Entsetzen, *das* (**at** über + *Akk.*); *(repugnance)* Grausen, *das; (horrifying thing)* Greuel, *der.* **2.** *attrib. adj.* Horror-. '**horror-stricken**, '**horror-struck** *adjs.* von Entsetzen gepackt

hors-d'œuvre [ɔːˈdɜːvr] *n.* Hors-d'œuvre, *das;* ≈ Vorspeise, *die*

horse [hɔːs] *n.* Pferd, *die*

horse: ~**back** *n.* **on** ~**back** zu Pferd; ~**man** ['hɔːsmən] *n., pl.* ~**men** ['hɔːsmən] *(skilled) rider)* [guter] Reiter; ~**play** *n.* Balgerei, *die;* ~**power** *n., pl. same (Mech.)* Pferdestärke, *die;* ~**racing** *n.* Pferderennsport, *der;* ~**radish** *n.* Meerrettich, *der;* ~**shoe** *n.* Hufeisen, *das*

horticulture ['hɔːtɪkʌltʃə(r)] *n.* Gartenbau, *der*

hose [həʊz], '**hose-pipe** *ns.* Schlauch, *der*

hospice ['hɒspɪs] *n. (Brit.: for the terminally ill)* Sterbeklinik, *die*

hospitable [hɒˈspɪtəbl] *adj.* gastfreundlich ⟨*Person, Wesensart*⟩; **be ~ to sb.** jmdn. gastfreundlich aufnehmen

hospital ['hɒspɪtl] *n.* Krankenhaus, *das;* **in ~** *(Brit.),* **in the ~** *(Amer.)* im Krankenhaus

hospitality [hɒspɪˈtælɪtɪ] *n.* Gastfreundschaft, *die*

'**host** [həʊst] *n. (large number)* Menge, *die;* **a ~ of people/children** eine Menge Leute/eine Schar von Kindern

²**host** *n.* Gastgeber, *der/*-geberin, *die*

hostage ['hɒstɪdʒ] *n.* Geisel, *die*

hostel ['hɒstl] *n. (Brit.)* Wohnheim, *das*

hostess ['həʊstɪs] *n.* Gastgeberin, *die; (in night-club)* Animierdame, *die*

hostile ['hɒstaɪl] *adj.* **a)** feindlich; **b)** *(unfriendly)* feindselig (**to|wards|** gegenüber); **be ~ to sth.** etw. ablehnen.

hostility [hɒˈstɪlɪtɪ] *n.* Feindseligkeit, *die*

hot [hɒt] *adj.* **a)** heiß; warm ⟨*Mahlzeit, Essen*⟩; **I am/feel ~:** mir ist heiß; **b)** *(pungent)* scharf ⟨*Gewürz, Senf usw.*⟩; scharf gewürzt ⟨*Essen*⟩; **c)** *(recent)* noch warm ⟨*Nachrichten*⟩; **d)** *(sl.: illegally obtained)* heiß ⟨*Ware, Geld*⟩.

hot 'air *n. (sl.)* leeres Gerede *(ugs.).*

'**hotbed** *n. (Hort.)* Mistbeet, *das; (fig.: of vice, corruption)* Brutstätte, *die* (of für)

'**hot dog** *n. (coll.)* Hot dog, *der od. das*

hotel [həʊˈtel] *n.* Hotel, *das.* **ho'tel room** *n.* Hotelzimmer, *das*

hot: ~**house** *n.* Treibhaus, *das; ~* **line** *n. (Polit.)* heißer Draht

'**hotly** *adv.* heftig

hot: ~**plate** *n.* Kochplatte, *die; (to keep food ~)* Warmhalteplatte, *die; ~* **'water bottle** *n.* Wärmflasche, *die*

hound [haʊnd] **1.** *n.* Jagdhund, *der.* **2.** *v. t.* verfolgen

hour ['aʊə(r)] *n.* **a)** Stunde, *die;* **half an ~:** eine halbe Stunde; **an ~ and a half** anderthalb Stunden; **be paid by the ~:** stundenweise bezahlt werden; **the 24-~ clock** die Vierundzwanzigstundenuhr; **b)** *(time o'clock)* Zeit, *die;* **the small ~s |of the morning|** die frühen Morgenstunden; **0100/0200/1700/1800 ~s** *(on 24-~ clock)* 1.00/2.00/17.00/18.00 Uhr. '**hourly** *adj., adv.* stündlich; **be paid ~:** stundenweise bezahlt werden

house 1. [haʊs] *n., pl.* ~**s** ['haʊzɪz] Haus, *das;* **to/at my ~:** zu mir |nach Hause|/bei mir |zu Hause|. **2.** [haʊz]

v. t. **a)** ein Heim geben (+ *Dat.*); **b)**
(keep, store) unterbringen. **house-**
boat ['haʊsbəʊt] *n.* Hausboot, *das*
household ['haʊshəʊld] *n.* Haushalt,
der; attrib. Haushalts-. **'house-**
holder *n.* Wohnungsinhaber, *der/*
-inhaberin, *die*
house [haʊs]: **~keeper** *n.* Haushälte-
rin, *die;* **~keeping** *n.* Hauswirt-
schaft, *die;* **~plant** *n.* Zimmerpflan-
ze, *die;* **~-trained** *adj. (Brit.)* stuben-
rein ⟨*Hund, Katze*⟩; **~-warming** *n.*
~-warming [party] Einzugsfeier, *die;*
~wife *n.* Hausfrau, *die;* **~work** *n.*
Hausarbeit, *die*
housing ['haʊzɪŋ] *n. (dwellings)* Woh-
nungen; *(provision of dwellings)* Woh-
nungsbeschaffung, *die.* **'housing es-**
tate *n. (Brit.)* Wohnsiedlung, *die*
hovel ['hɒvl] *n.* [armselige] Hütte
hover ['hɒvə(r)] *v. i.* **a)** schweben; **b)**
(linger) sich herumdrücken *(ugs.).*
'hovercraft *n., pl. same* Hovercraft,
das; Luftkissenfahrzeug, *das.* **'hover**
mower *n.* Luftkissenmäher, *der*
how [haʊ] *adv.* wie; **learn ~ to ride a**
bike/swim radfahren/schwimmen lernen; **~ 'are you?** wie geht es dir?;
(greeting) guten Morgen/Tag/
Abend!; **~ do you 'do?** *(formal)* guten
Morgen/Tag/Abend!; **~ much?** wieviel?; **~ many?** wieviel?; wie viele?
however [haʊ'evə(r)] *adv.* **a)** wie ...
auch; **b)** *(nevertheless)* jedoch; aber
howl [haʊl] **1.** *n. (of animal)* Heulen,
das; (of distress) Schrei, *der;* **~s of**
laughter brüllendes Gelächter. **2.** *v. i.*
⟨*Tier, Wind:*⟩ heulen; *(with distress)*
schreien. **3.** *v. t.* [hinaus]schreien
howler ['haʊlə(r)] *n. (coll.: blunder)*
Schnitzer, *der (ugs.)*
HP *abbr. (Brit.)* **hire-purchase**
HQ *abbr.* **headquarters** HQ
hub [hʌb] *n.* [Rad]nabe, *die; (fig.)* Mittelpunkt, *der*
hubbub ['hʌbʌb] *n.* Lärm, *der;* **a ~ of**
voices ein Stimmengewirr
'hub-cap *n.* Radkappe, *die*
huddle ['hʌdl] *v. i.* sich drängen; **~**
together sich zusammendrängen.
huddle 'up *v. i. (nestle up)* sich zu-
sammenkauern; *(crowd together)* sich
[zusammen]drängen
'hue [hju:] *n.* Farbton, *der*
²hue *n.* **~ and cry** lautes Geschrei;
(protest) Gezeter, *das*
huff [hʌf] **1.** *v. i.* **~ and puff** schnaufen
und keuchen. **2.** *n.* **in a ~:** beleidigt
hug [hʌg] **1.** *n.* Umarmung, *die;* **give**

sb. a ~: jmdn. umarmen. **2.** *v. t.,* **-gg-**
umarmen
huge [hju:dʒ] *adj.* riesig; gewaltig ⟨*Un-*
terschied, Verbesserung, Interesse⟩
hulking ['hʌlkɪŋ] *adj. (coll.)* **~ great**
klobig
hull [hʌl] *n. (Naut.)* Schiffskörper, *der*
hum [hʌm] **1.** *v. i.,* **-mm-: a)** summen;
⟨*Maschine:*⟩ brummen; **b) ~ and haw**
(coll.) herumdrucksen *(ugs.).* **2.** *v. t.,*
-mm- summen. **3.** *n.* **a)** Summen, *das;*
(of machinery) Brummen, *das;* **b)** *(of*
voices, conversation) Gemurmel, *das;*
(of traffic) Brausen, *das*
human ['hju:mən] **1.** *adj.* menschlich;
the ~ race die menschliche Rasse. **2.**
n. Mensch, *der.* **human 'being** *n.*
Mensch, *der*
humane [hju:'meɪn] *adj.* human
humanitarian [hju:mænɪ'teərɪən] *adj.*
humanitär
humanity [hju:'mænɪtɪ] *n.* **a)** *(man-*
kind) Menschheit, *die; (people col-*
lectively) Menschen; **b)** *(being hu-*
mane) Humanität, *die*
humble ['hʌmbl] **1.** *adj.* **a)** demütig; **b)**
(modest) bescheiden; **c)** *(low-ranking)*
einfach; niedrig ⟨*Status, Rang usw.*⟩.
2. *v. t.* **a)** demütigen; **~ oneself** sich
demütigen *od.* erniedrigen; **b)** *(defeat*
decisively) [vernichtend] schlagen.
humbly ['hʌmblɪ] *adv.* demütig
humdrum ['hʌmdrʌm] *adj.* alltäglich;
eintönig ⟨*Leben*⟩
humid ['hju:mɪd] *adj.* feucht. **hu-**
midity [hju:'mɪdɪtɪ] *n.* Feuchtigkeit,
die
humiliate [hju:'mɪlɪeɪt] *v. t.* demütigen. **humiliation** [hju:mɪlɪ'eɪʃn] *n.*
Demütigung, *die*
humility [hju:'mɪlɪtɪ] *n.* Demut, *die*
humor *(Amer.) see* **humour**
humorous ['hju:mərəs] *adj.* lustig, komisch ⟨*Geschichte, Name, Situation*⟩;
witzig ⟨*Bemerkung*⟩
humour ['hju:mə(r)] *(Brit.)* **1.** *n.* **a)**
Humor, *der; (mood)* Laune, *die;* **sense of ~:** Sinn für
Humor; **b)** *(mood)* Laune, *die.* **2.** *v. t.*
~ sb. jmdm. seinen Willen lassen
hump [hʌmp] **1.** *n.* **a)** *(of person)*
Buckel, *der; (of animal)* Höcker, *der;*
b) *(mound)* Hügel, *der.* **2.** *v. t. (Brit.*
sl.: carry) schleppen. **humpback**
'bridge *n.* gewölbte Brücke
'hunch [hʌntʃ] *v. t.* **~ [up]** hochziehen
²hunch *n. (feeling)* Gefühl, *das*
'hunchback *n. (back)* Buckel, *der;*
(person) Bucklige, *der/die;* **be a ~:** einen Buckel haben

hundred ['hʌndrəd] **1.** *adj.* hundert; **a**
or one ~: [ein]hundert; **two/several** ~:
zweihundert/mehrere hundert; **a** *or*
one ~ **and one** [ein]hundert[und]eins.
2. *n.* **a)** *(number)* hundert; **a** *or* **one/**
two ~: [ein]hundert/zweihundert; **b)**
(written figure; group) Hundert, *das;*
c) *(indefinite amount)* ~s Hunderte.
See also **eight. hundredth** ['hʌnd-
rədθ] **1.** *adj.* hundertst...; **a** ~ **part** ein
Hundertstel. **2.** *n. (fraction)* Hundertstel, *das; (in sequence)* hundertste,
der/die/das; (in rank) Hundertste, *der/*
die/das. 'hundredweight *n., pl.*
same *(Brit.)* 50,8 kg; ≈ Zentner, *der*
hung *see* **hang 1, 2**
Hungarian [hʌŋ'geərɪən] **1.** *adj.* ungarisch; **sb. is** ~: jmd. ist Ungar/Unga-
rin. **2.** *n.* **a)** *(person)* Ungar, *der/*Unga-
rin, *die;* **b)** *(language)* Ungarisch, *das;*
see also **English 2 a**
Hungary ['hʌŋgərɪ] *pr. n.* Ungarn *(das)*
hunger ['hʌŋgə(r)] **1.** *n.* Hunger, *der.*
2. *v.i.* ~ **after** *or* **for sb./sth.** [heftiges]
Verlangen nach jmdm./etw. haben.
'hunger-strike *n.* Hungerstreik,
der; **go on** ~: in den Hungerstreik treten
hungry ['hʌŋgrɪ] *adj.* hungrig; **be** ~:
Hunger haben; **go** ~: hungern
hunk [hʌŋk] *n.* [großes] Stück
hunt [hʌnt] **1.** *n.* Jagd, *die; (search)* Suche, *die.* **2.** *v.t.* jagen; *(search for)*
Jagd machen auf (+ *Akk.*) ⟨*Mörder*
usw.⟩. **3.** *v.i.* jagen; **go ~ing** auf die
Jagd gehen; ~ **after** *or* **for** Jagd machen auf (+ *Akk.*); *(seek)* suchen
'hunter *n.* Jäger, *der*
'hunting *n.* die Jagd **(of** auf + *Akk.*);
(searching) Suche, *die* **(for** nach)
hurdle ['hɜːdl] *n.* Hürde, *die*
hurl [hɜːl] *v.t.* werfen; *(violently)*
schleudern; ~ **insults at sb.** jmdm. Beleidigungen ins Gesicht schleudern
hurrah [hʊ'rɑː], **hurray** [hʊ'reɪ] *int.*
hurra
hurricane ['hʌrɪkən] *n.* Orkan, *der*
hurried ['hʌrɪd] *adj.* eilig; überstürzt
⟨*Abreise*⟩; in Eile ausgeführt ⟨*Arbeit*⟩
hurry ['hʌrɪ] **1.** *n.* Eile, *die;* **in a** ~: eilig; **be in a** ~: es eilig haben; **there's no**
~: es eilt nicht. **2.** *v.t.* antreiben ⟨*Per-*
son⟩; hinunterschlingen ⟨*Essen*⟩; ~
one's work seine Arbeit in zu großer
Eile erledigen. **3.** *v.i.* sich beeilen; *(to*
or from place) eilen. **hurry 'up 1.** *v.i.*
sich beeilen. **2.** *v.t.* antreiben
hurt [hɜːt] **1.** *v.t.,* **hurt a)** weh tun
(+ *Dat.*); *(injure)* verletzen; ~ **oneself**

sich *(Dat.)* weh tun; *(injure oneself)*
sich verletzen; ~ **one's arm/back** sich
(Dat.) am Arm/Rücken weh tun; *(in-*
jure) sich *(Dat.)* den Arm/am Rücken
verletzen; **b)** *(damage, be detrimental*
to) schaden (+ *Dat.*); **c)** *(upset)* verletzen ⟨*Person, Stolz*⟩. **2.** *v.i.,* **hurt a)**
weh tun; **b)** *(cause damage, be det-*
rimental) schaden. **3.** *adj.* gekränkt
⟨*Tonfall, Miene*⟩. **4.** *n. (emotional pain)*
Schmerz, *der.* **hurtful** ['hɜːtfl] *adj.*
verletzend
hurtle ['hɜːtl] *v.i.* rasen *(ugs.)*
husband ['hʌzbənd] *n.* Ehemann, *der;*
my/your/her ~: mein/dein/ihr Mann;
~ **and wife** Mann und Frau
hush [hʌʃ] **1.** *n. (silence)* Schweigen,
das; (stillness) Stille, *die.* **2.** *v.t.*
(silence) zum Schweigen bringen;
(still) beruhigen. **3.** *v.i.* still sein; ~!
still! **hush 'up** *v.t.* vertuschen
husk [hʌsk] *n.* Spelze, *die*
¹**husky** ['hʌskɪ] *adj.* heiser
²**husky** *n.* Eskimohund, *der*
hustle ['hʌsl] **1.** *v.t.* drängen **(into** zu).
2. *n.* ~ **and bustle** geschäftiges Treiben
hut [hʌt] *n.* Hütte, *die*
hutch [hʌtʃ] *n.* Stall, *der*
hyacinth ['haɪəsɪnθ] *n.* Hyazinthe, *die*
hybrid ['haɪbrɪd] **1.** *n.* Hybride, *die od.*
der **(between** aus); *(fig.: mixture)* Mischung, *die.* **2.** *adj.* hybrid ⟨*Züchtung*⟩
hydrangea [haɪ'dreɪndʒə] *n.* Hortensie, *die*
hydrant ['haɪdrənt] *n.* Hydrant, *der*
hydraulic [haɪ'drɔːlɪk] *adj.* hydraulisch
hydrochloric acid [haɪdrəklɔːrɪk
'æsɪd] *n.* Salzsäure, *die*
hydroelectric [haɪdrəʊɪ'lektrɪk] *adj.*
hydroelektrisch; ~ **power station** Was-
serkraftwerk, *das*
hydrofoil ['haɪdrəfɔɪl] *n.* Tragflächen-
boot, *das*
hydrogen ['haɪdrədʒən] *n.* Wasser-
stoff, *der.* 'hydrogen bomb *n.* Was-
serstoffbombe, *die*
hyena [haɪ'iːnə] *n.* Hyäne, *die*
hygiene ['haɪdʒiːn] *n.* Hygiene, *die.*
hygienic [haɪ'dʒiːnɪk] *adj.* hygienisch
hymn [hɪm] *n.* Hymne, *die; (sung in*
service) Kirchenlied, *das.* 'hymn-
book *n.* Gesangbuch, *das*
hypermarket ['haɪpəmɑːkɪt] *n. (Brit.)*
Verbrauchermarkt, *der*
hyphen ['haɪfn] **1.** *n.* Bindestrich, *der.*
2. *v.t.* mit Bindestrich schreiben

hyphenate ['haɪfəneɪt] *see* **hyphen** 2
hypnosis [hɪp'nəʊsɪs] *n., pl.* **hypnoses** [hɪp'nəʊsiːz] Hypnose, *die; (act, process)* Hypnotisierung, *die;* **under ~:** in Hypnose *(Dat.).* **hypnotic** [hɪp'nɒtɪk] *adj.* hypnotisch. **hypnotism** ['hɪpnətɪzm] *n.* Hypnotik, *die; (act)* Hypnotisieren, *das.* **hypnotist** ['hɪpnətɪst] *n.* Hypnotiseur, *der*/Hypnotiseuse, *die.* **hypnotize** ['hɪpnətaɪz] *v. t.* hypnotisieren
hypochondria [haɪpə'kɒndrɪə] *n.* Hypochondrie, *die.* **hypochondriac** [haɪpə'kɒndrɪæk] *n.* Hypochonder, *der*
hypocrisy [hɪ'pɒkrɪsɪ] *n.* Heuchelei, *die.* **hypocrite** ['hɪpəkrɪt] *n.* Heuchler, *der*/Heuchlerin, *die.* **hypocritical** [hɪpə'krɪtɪkl] *adj.* heuchlerisch
hypodermic [haɪpə'dɜːmɪk] *adj. & n.* **~ |syringe|** Injektionsspritze, *die*
hypotenuse [haɪ'pɒtənjuːz] *n.* Hypotenuse, *die*
hypothesis [haɪ'pɒθɪsɪs] *n., pl.* **hypotheses** [haɪ'pɒθɪsiːz] Hypothese, *die.* **hypothetical** [haɪpə'θetɪkl] *adj.* hypothetisch
hysteria [hɪ'stɪərɪə] *n.* Hysterie, *die.* **hysterical** [hɪ'sterɪkl] *adj.* hysterisch. **hysterics** [hɪ'sterɪks] *n. pl. (laughter)* hysterischer Lachanfall; *(crying)* hysterischer Weinkrampf; **have ~:** hysterisch lachen/weinen

I

¹**I, i** [aɪ] *n.* I, i, *das*
²**I** *pron.* ich
ice [aɪs] **1.** *n.* **a)** Eis, *das;* **feel/be like ~** *(be very cold)* eiskalt sein; **b)** *(~cream)* [Speise]eis, *das;* **an ~/two ~s** ein/zwei Eis. **2.** *v. t.* glasieren ⟨*Kuchen*⟩. **ice 'over, ice 'up** *v. i.* ⟨*Gewässer:*⟩ zufrieren
'ice age *n.* Eiszeit, *die*
iceberg ['aɪsbɜːg] *n.* Eisberg, *der*
ice: ~box *n. (Amer.)* Kühlschrank, *der;* **~-cold** *adj.* eiskalt; **~-'cream** *n.* Eis, *das;* Eiscreme, *die;* **one ~-cream/two/too many ~-creams** ein/

zwei/zuviel Eis; **~-cube** *n.* Eiswürfel, *die;* **~ 'hockey** *n.* Eishockey, *das*
Iceland ['aɪslənd] *pr. n.* Island *(das).*
Icelandic [aɪs'lændɪk] **1.** *adj.* isländisch. **2.** *n.* Isländisch, *das; see also* **English 2 a**
ice: ~ 'lolly *n.* Eis am Stiel; **~-rink** *n.* Eisbahn, *die;* **~-skate 1.** *n.* Schlittschuh, *der;* **2.** *v. i.* Schlittschuh laufen; **~-skating** *n.* Schlittschuhlaufen, *das*
icicle ['aɪsɪkl] *n.* Eiszapfen, *der*
icing ['aɪsɪŋ] *n.* Zuckerguß, *der.* **'icing sugar** *n. (Brit.)* Puderzucker, *der*
icon ['aɪkɒn] *n.* Ikone, *die*
icy ['aɪsɪ] *adj.* **a)** vereist ⟨*Berge, Landschaft, Straße*⟩; eisreich ⟨*Region, Land*⟩; **in ~ conditions** bei Eis; **b)** *(very cold)* eiskalt; eisig; *(fig.)* frostig
I'd [aɪd] **a) = I had; b) = I would**
idea [aɪ'dɪə] *n.* Idee, *die;* Gedanke, *der; (mental picture)* Vorstellung, *die; (vague notion)* Ahnung, *die;* **have you any ~ |of| how ...?** weißt du ungefähr, wie ...?; **have no ~ |of| where ...:** keine Ahnung haben, wo ...; **not have the slightest** *or* **faintest ~:** nicht die leiseste Ahnung haben
ideal [aɪ'dɪəl] **1.** *adj.* ideal; vollendet ⟨*Ehemann, Gastgeber*⟩; vollkommen ⟨*Welt*⟩. **2.** *n.* Ideal, *das.* **idealism** [aɪ'dɪəlɪzm] *n.* Idealismus, *der.* **idealist** [aɪ'dɪəlɪst] *n.* Idealist, *der*/Idealistin, *die.* **idealistic** [aɪdɪə'lɪstɪk] *adj.* idealistisch. **idealize** [aɪ'dɪəlaɪz] *v. t.* idealisieren. **ideally** [aɪ'dɪəlɪ] *adv.* ideal; **~, ...:** idealerweise *od.* im Idealfall ...
identical [aɪ'dentɪkl] *adj.* identisch; **be ~:** sich *(Dat.)* völlig gleichen; **~ twins** eineiige Zwillinge
identification [aɪdentɪfɪ'keɪʃn] *n.* Identifizierung, *die; (of plants, animals)* Bestimmung, *die*
identify [aɪ'dentɪfaɪ] *v. t.* identifizieren; bestimmen ⟨*Pflanze, Tier*⟩
identity [aɪ'dentɪtɪ] *n.* Identität, *die;* **proof of ~:** Identitätsnachweis, *der;* **|case of| mistaken ~:** [Personen]verwechslung, *die.* **i'dentity card** *n.* [Personal]ausweis, *der*
idiocy ['ɪdɪəsɪ] *n.* Idiotie, *die*
idiom ['ɪdɪəm] *n.* [Rede]wendung, *die.* **idiomatic** [ɪdɪə'mætɪk] *adj.* idiomatisch
idiosyncrasy [ɪdɪə'sɪŋkrəsɪ] *n.* Eigentümlichkeit, *die.* **idiosyncratic** [ɪdɪəsɪŋ'krætɪk] *adj.* eigenwillig
idiot ['ɪdɪət] *n.* Idiot, *der (ugs.).* **idiotic** [ɪdɪ'ɒtɪk] *adj.* idiotisch *(ugs.)*

idle ['aɪdl] **1.** *adj.* **a)** *(lazy)* faul; **b)** *(not in use)* außer Betrieb *nachgestellt;* **be ~** ⟨*Maschinen, Fabrik:*⟩ stillstehen; **c)** bloß ⟨*Neugier, Spekulation*⟩; leer ⟨*Geschwätz*⟩. **2.** *v. i.* ⟨*Motor:*⟩ leerlaufen. **idle a'way** *v. t.* vertun

'idleness *n.* Faulheit, *die*

idol ['aɪdl] *n.* Idol, *das.* **idolize** ['aɪdəlaɪz] *v. t.* vergöttern

idyllic [ɪ'dɪlɪk] *adj.* idyllisch

i.e. [aɪ'iː] *abbr.* that is d. h.; i. e.

if [ɪf] *conj.* **a)** wenn; **if anyone should ask ...:** falls jemand fragt, ...; **if I knew what to do ...:** wenn ich wüßte, was ich tun soll ...; **if I were you** an deiner Stelle; **if so/not** wenn ja/nein *od.* nicht; **if then/that/at all** wenn überhaupt; **as if** als ob; **if I only knew, if only I knew!** wenn ich das nur wüßte!; **if it isn't Ronnie!** das ist doch Ronnie!; **b)** *(whenever)* [immer] wenn; **c)** *(whether)* ob; **d)** *(though)* auch *od.* selbst wenn; **e)** *(despite being)* wenn auch

igloo ['ɪgluː] *n.* Iglu, *der od. das*

ignite [ɪg'naɪt] **1.** *v. t.* anzünden. **2.** *v. i.* sich entzünden. **ignition** [ɪg'nɪʃn] *n.* **a)** *(igniting)* Zünden, *das;* **b)** *(Motor Veh.)* Zündung, *die;* **~ key** Zündschlüssel, *der*

ignorance ['ɪgnərəns] *n.* Unwissenheit, *die;* **keep sb. in ~ of sth.** jmdn. in Unkenntnis über etw. *(Akk.)* lassen

ignorant ['ɪgnərənt] *adj.* unwissend; **be ~ of sth.** *(uninformed)* über etw. *(Akk.)* nicht informiert sein

ignore [ɪg'nɔː(r)] *v. t.* ignorieren; nicht befolgen ⟨*Befehl, Rat*⟩; übergehen ⟨*Frage, Bemerkung*⟩

ill [ɪl] **1.** *adj.,* **worse** [wɜːs], **worst** [wɜːst] krank; **fall ~:** krank werden. **2.** *adv.* **be ~ at ease** sich unwohl fühlen. **3.** *n.* Übel, *das*

I'll [aɪl] **a)** = **I shall;** **b)** = **I will**

'ill-advised *adj.* unklug

illegal [ɪ'liːgl] *adj.,* **il'legally** *adv.* illegal

illegible [ɪ'ledʒɪbl] *adj.* unleserlich

illegitimate [ɪlɪ'dʒɪtɪmət] *adj.* unehelich ⟨*Kind*⟩

ill 'health *n.* schwache Gesundheit

illicit [ɪ'lɪsɪt] *adj.* unerlaubt ⟨*Beziehung, [Geschlechts]verkehr*⟩; Schwarz- ⟨*handel, -verkauf, -arbeit*⟩

'ill-informed *adj.* schlecht informiert; auf Unkenntnis beruhend ⟨*Bemerkung, Urteil*⟩

illiteracy [ɪ'lɪtərəsɪ] *n.* Analphabetentum, *das*

illiterate [ɪ'lɪtərət] *adj.* des Lesens und

Schreibens unkundig; analphabetisch ⟨*Bevölkerung*⟩

illness ['ɪlnɪs] *n.* Krankheit, *die*

illogical [ɪ'lɒdʒɪkl] *adj.* unlogisch

ill-'treat *v. t.* mißhandeln. **ill-'treatment** *n.* Mißhandlung, *die*

illuminate [ɪ'luːmɪneɪt] *v. t.* beleuchten. **illuminating** [ɪ'luːmɪneɪtɪŋ] *adj.* aufschlußreich. **illumination** [ɪluː-mɪ'neɪʃn] *n.* Beleuchtung, *die*

illusion [ɪ'luːʒn] *n.* Illusion, *die;* **be under the ~ that ...:** sich *(Dat.)* einbilden, daß ... **illusory** [ɪ'luːsərɪ] *adj.* illusorisch

illustrate ['ɪləstreɪt] *v. t.* **a)** *(serve as example of)* veranschaulichen; **b)** illustrieren ⟨*Buch, Erklärung*⟩. **illustration** [ɪlə'streɪʃn] *n.* **a)** *(example)* Beispiel, *das* **(of** für); **b)** *(picture)* Abbildung, *die*

ill 'will *n.* Böswilligkeit, *die*

I'm [aɪm] = **I am**

image ['ɪmɪdʒ] *n.* **a)** Bildnis, *das (geh.);* **b)** *(Optics)* Bild, *das;* **c)** |public| **~:** Image, *das*

imaginable [ɪ'mædʒɪnəbl] *adj.* **the best solution ~:** die denkbar beste Lösung

imaginary [ɪ'mædʒɪnərɪ] *adj.* imaginär *(geh.);* eingebildet ⟨*Krankheit*⟩

imagination [ɪmædʒɪ'neɪʃn] *n.* **a)** Phantasie, *die;* **b)** *(fancy)* Einbildung, *die*

imaginative [ɪ'mædʒɪnətɪv] *adj.* phantasievoll; *(showing imagination)* einfallsreich

imagine [ɪ'mædʒɪn] *v. t.* **a)** sich *(Dat.)* vorstellen; **b)** *(coll.: suppose)* glauben; **c)** *(get the impression)* **~ that ...:** sich *(Dat.)* einbilden[, daß ...]

imbalance [ɪm'bæləns] *n.* Unausgeglichenheit, *die*

imbecile ['ɪmbɪsiːl] *n.* Idiot, *der (ugs.)*

imitate ['ɪmɪteɪt] *v. t.* nachahmen. **imitation** [ɪmɪ'teɪʃn] *n* **a)** Nachahmung, *die;* **b)** *(counterfeit)* Imitation, *die*

immaculate [ɪ'mækjʊlət] *adj. (spotless)* makellos; *(faultless)* tadellos

immaterial [ɪmə'tɪərɪəl] *adj.* unerheblich

immature [ɪmə'tjʊə(r)] *adj.* unreif; noch nicht voll entwickelt ⟨*Lebewesen*⟩. **immaturity** [ɪmə'tjʊərɪtɪ] *n.* Unreife, *die*

immediate [ɪ'miːdjət] *adj.* **a)** unmittelbar; *(nearest)* nächst... ⟨*Nachbar[schaft], Umgebung, Zukunft*⟩; engst... ⟨*Familie*⟩; **b)** *(occurring at once)* prompt; unverzüglich ⟨*Han-*

deln, Maßnahmen⟩; umgehend ⟨*Antwort*⟩. **im'mediately 1.** *adv.* **a)** unmittelbar; **b)** *(without delay)* sofort. **2.** *conj. (coll.)* sobald

immemorial [ımı'mɔːrɪəl] *adj.* **from time ~:** seit undenklichen Zeiten

immense [ı'mens] *adj.* **a)** ungeheuer; **b)** *(coll.: great)* enorm. **im'mensely** *adv.* **a)** ungeheuer; **b)** *(coll.: very much)* unheimlich *(ugs.)*

immerse [ı'mɜːs] *v. t.* [ein]tauchen; **be ~d in thought/one's work** in Gedanken versunken/in seine Arbeit vertieft sein. **immersion** [ı'mɜːʃn] *n.* Eintauchen, *das.* **im'mersion heater** *n.* Heißwasserbereiter, *der*

immigrant ['ımıgrənt] **1.** *n.* Einwanderer, *der*/Einwanderin, *die.* **2.** *adj.* Einwanderer-; ~ **workers** ausländische Arbeitnehmer

immigration [ımı'greıʃn] *n.* Einwanderung *die* (**into** nach, **from** aus); *attrib.* Einwanderungs⟨*kontrolle, -gesetz*⟩; ~ **officer** Beamter/Beamtin der Einwanderungsbehörde

imminent ['ımınənt] *adj.* unmittelbar bevorstehend; drohend ⟨*Gefahr*⟩; **be ~:** unmittelbar bevorstehen/drohen

immobile [ı'məʊbaıl] *adj. (immovable)* unbeweglich. **immobilize** [ı'məʊbəlaız] *v. t.* verankern; *(fig.)* lähmen

immodest [ı'mɒdıst] *adj.* unbescheiden; *(improper)* unanständig

immoral [ı'mɒrəl] *adj.* unmoralisch; *(in sexual matters)* sittenlos. **immorality** [ımə'rælıtı] *n.* Unmoral, *die; (in sexual matters)* Sittenlosigkeit, *die*

immortal [ı'mɔːtl] *adj.* unsterblich. **immortality** [ımɔː'tælıtı] *n.* Unsterblichkeit, *die.* **immortalize** [ı'mɔːtəlaız] *v. t.* unsterblich machen

immovable [ı'muːvəbl] *adj.* unbeweglich; **be ~:** sich nicht bewegen lassen

immune [ı'mjuːn] *adj.* **a)** *(exempt)* sicher (**from** vor + *Dat.*); **b)** *(not susceptible)* unempfindlich (**to** gegen); **c)** *(Med.)* immun (**to** gegen). **immunity** [ı'mjuːnıtı] *n.* **a) diplomatic ~:** diplomatische Immunität; **b)** *(Med.)* Immunität, *die.* **immunize** ['ımjʊnaız] *v. t.* immunisieren

imp [ımp] *n.* **a)** Kobold, *der;* **b)** *(coll.: child)* Racker, *der (fam.)*

impact ['ımpækt] *n.* **a)** Aufprall, *der* (**on, against** auf + *Akk.*); *(collision)* Zusammenprall, *der;* **b)** *(fig.)* Wirkung, *die*

impair [ım'peə(r)] *v. t.* beeinträchtigen; schaden (+ *Dat.*) ⟨*Gesundheit*⟩

impale [ım'peıl] *v. t.* aufspießen

impart [ım'pɑːt] *v. t.* **a)** *(give)* [ab]geben (**to an** + *Akk.*); **b)** *(communicate)* kundtun *(geh.)* (**to** *Dat.*); vermitteln ⟨*Kenntnisse*⟩ (**to** *Dat.*)

impartial [ım'pɑːʃl] *adj.* unparteiisch; gerecht ⟨*Entscheidung, Urteil*⟩

impassable [ım'pɑːsəbl] *adj.* unpassierbar (**to** für); *(to vehicles)* unbefahrbar (**to** für)

impasse ['æmpɑːs] *n.* Sackgasse, *die*

impassive [ım'pæsıv] *adj.* ausdruckslos

impatience [ım'peıʃəns] *n.* Ungeduld, *die* (**at** über + *Akk.*)

impatient [ım'peıʃənt] *adj.* ungeduldig; ~ **at sth./with sb.** ungeduldig über etw. *(Akk.)*/mit jmdm. **im'patiently** *adv.* ungeduldig

impeccable [ım'pekəbl] *adj.* makellos; tadellos ⟨*Manieren*⟩

impede [ım'piːd] *v. t.* behindern. **impediment** [ım'pedımənt] *n.* **a)** Hindernis, *das* (**to** für); **b)** *(speech defect)* Sprachfehler, *der*

impel [ım'pel] *v. t.,* **-ll-** treiben; **feel ~led to do sth.** sich genötigt *od.* gezwungen fühlen, etw. zu tun

impending [ım'pendıŋ] *adj.* bevorstehend

impenetrable [ım'penıtrəbl] *adj.* undurchdringlich (**by, to** für)

imperative [ım'perətıv] **1.** *adj.* dringend erforderlich. **2.** *n. (Ling.)* Imperativ, *der*

imperceptible [ımpə'septıbl] *adj.* nicht wahrnehmbar; *(very slight or gradual)* unmerklich

imperfect [ım'pɜːfıkt] **1.** *adj.* **a)** *(incomplete)* unvollständig; **b)** *(faulty)* mangelhaft. **2.** *n. (Ling.)* Imperfekt, *das.* **imperfection** [ımpə'fekʃn] *n.* **a)** *(incompleteness)* Unvollständigkeit, *die;* **b)** *(fault)* Mangel, *der.* **im'perfectly** *adv.* **a)** *(incompletely)* unvollständig; **b)** *(faultily)* fehlerhaft

imperial [ım'pıərıəl] *adj.* kaiserlich. **imperialism** [ım'pıərıəlızm] *n.* Imperialismus, *der*

imperil [ım'perıl] *v. t.,* *(Brit.)* **-ll-** gefährden

imperious [ım'pıərıəs] *adj.* herrisch

impersonal [ım'pɜːsənl] *adj.* unpersönlich

impersonate [ım'pɜːsəneıt] *v. t.* sich ausgeben als; *(to entertain)* imitieren; nachahmen. **impersonator** [ım'pɜːsəneıtə(r)] *n. (entertainer)* Imitator, *der*/Imitatorin, *die*

impertinence [ɪm'pɜːtɪnəns] *n.* Unverschämtheit, *die*

impertinent [ɪm'pɜːtɪnənt] *adj.* unverschämt

imperturbable [ɪmpə'tɜːbəbl] *adj.* gelassen; **be completely ~:** durch nichts zu erschüttern sein

impervious [ɪm'pɜːvɪəs] *adj.* undurchlässig; **be ~ to sth.** *(fig.)* unempfänglich für etw. sein

impetuous [ɪm'petjʊəs] *adj.* unüberlegt; impulsiv ⟨*Person*⟩

impetus ['ɪmpɪtəs] *n.* **a)** Kraft, *die;* **b)** *(fig.)* Motivation, *die*

impinge [ɪm'pɪndʒ] *v.i.* **~ on sth.** auf etw. *(Akk.)* Einfluß nehmen

'**impish** *adj.* lausbübisch

implacable [ɪm'plækəbl] *adj.* unversöhnlich; erbittert ⟨*Gegner*⟩

implausible [ɪm'plɔːzɪbl] *adj.* unglaubwürdig

implement 1. ['ɪmplɪmənt] *n.* Gerät, *das.* 2. ['ɪmplɪment] *v.t.* [in die Tat] umsetzen ⟨*Politik, Plan usw.*⟩

implicate ['ɪmplɪkeɪt] *v.t.* belasten; **be ~d in a scandal** in einen Skandal verwickelt sein. **implication** [ɪmplɪ'keɪʃn] *n.* Implikation, *die;* **by ~:** implizit

implicit [ɪm'plɪsɪt] *adj.* **a)** *(implied)* implizit *(geh.);* unausgesprochen ⟨*Drohung, Zweifel*⟩; **b)** *(resting on authority)* unbedingt; blind ⟨*Vertrauen*⟩

implore [ɪm'plɔː(r)] *v.t.* anflehen **(for** um)

imply [ɪm'plaɪ] *v.t.* **a)** implizieren *(geh.); (say indirectly)* hindeuten auf (+ *Akk.*); **b)** *(insinuate)* unterstellen

impolite [ɪmpə'laɪt] *adj.* unhöflich

import 1. [ɪm'pɔːt] *v.t.* importieren, einführen ⟨*Waren*⟩ **(from** aus, **into** nach). 2. ['ɪmpɔːt] *n.* **a)** *(process)* Import, *der;* **b)** *(article)* Importgut, *das*

importance [ɪm'pɔːtəns] *n.* Wichtigkeit, *die* **(to** für); *(significance)* Bedeutung, *die;* **be of ~:** wichtig sein; **full of one's own ~:** von seiner eigenen Wichtigkeit überzeugt

important [ɪm'pɔːtənt] *adj.* wichtig **(to** für); *(significant)* bedeutend

im'porter *n.* Importeur, *der*

impose [ɪm'pəʊz] *v.t.* auferlegen *(geh.)* ⟨*Bürde, Verpflichtung*⟩ **(up]on** *Dat.*); erheben ⟨*Steuer*⟩ **(on** auf + *Akk.*); verhängen ⟨*Kriegsrecht*⟩; anordnen ⟨*Rationierung*⟩. **im'pose on** *v.t.* ausnutzen ⟨*Gutmütigkeit, Toleranz usw.*⟩; **~ on sb.** sich jmdm. aufdrängen

imposing [ɪm'pəʊzɪŋ] *adj.* imposant

imposition [ɪmpə'zɪʃn] *n.* **a)** Auferlegung, *die; (of tax)* Erhebung, *die;* **b)** *(unreasonable demand)* Zumutung, *die*

impossibility [ɪmpɒsɪ'bɪlɪtɪ] *n.* Unmöglichkeit, *die*

impossible [ɪm'pɒsɪbl] *adj.*, **impossibly** [ɪm'pɒsɪblɪ] *adv.* unmöglich

impostor [ɪm'pɒstə(r)] *n.* Hochstapler, *der/*-staplerin, *die; (swindler)* Betrüger, *der/*Betrügerin, *die*

impound [ɪm'paʊnd] *v.t.* beschlagnahmen

impoverished [ɪm'pɒvərɪʃt] *adj.* **be/become ~:** verarmt sein/verarmen

impracticable [ɪm'præktɪkəbl] *adj.* undurchführbar

impractical [ɪm'præktɪkl] *adj.* **a)** *(unpractical)* unpraktisch; **b)** *see* **impracticable**

imprecise [ɪmprɪ'saɪs] *adj.* ungenau

impregnable [ɪm'pregnəbl] *adj.* uneinnehmbar ⟨*Festung, Bollwerk*⟩; *(fig.)* unanfechtbar ⟨*Ruf, Stellung*⟩

impregnate ['ɪmpregneɪt] *v.t.* imprägnieren

impress [ɪm'pres] *v.t.* beeindrucken; *abs.* Eindruck machen; **be ~ed by** *or* **with sth.** von etw. beeindruckt sein. **im'press [up]on** *v.t.* einschärfen (+ *Dat.*); **~ sth. [up]on sb.'s memory** jmdm. etw. einschärfen. **impression** [ɪm'preʃn] *n.* **a)** Eindruck, *der;* **form an ~ of sb.** sich *(Dat.)* ein Bild von jmdm. machen; **b)** *(impersonation)* **do an ~ of sb.** jmdn. imitieren; **do ~s** andere Leute imitieren. **impressionist** [ɪm'preʃənɪst] *n.* Impressionist, *der/* Impressionistin, *die*

impressive [ɪm'presɪv] *adj.* beeindruckend; imponierend

imprint 1. ['ɪmprɪnt] *n.* Abdruck, *der; (fig.)* Stempel, *der.* 2. [ɪm'prɪnt] *v.t.* aufdrucken; *(fig.)* einprägen **(on** *Dat.*)

imprison [ɪm'prɪzn] *v.t.* in Haft nehmen; **be ~ed** sich in Haft befinden. **im'prisonment** *n.* Haft, *die;* **a long term of ~:** eine lange Haftstrafe

improbable [ɪm'prɒbəbl] *adj.* unwahrscheinlich

impromptu [ɪm'prɒmptjuː] 1. *adj.* improvisiert; **an ~ speech** eine Stegreifrede. 2. *adv.* aus dem Stegreif

improper [ɪm'prɒpə(r)] *adj.* **a)** *(wrong)* unrichtig; **b)** *(unseemly)* unpassend; *(indecent)* unanständig. **im'properly** *adv. see* **improper:** unrichtig; unpassend; unanständig

improvable [ɪm'pru:vəbl] *adj.* verbesserungsfähig

improve [ɪm'pru:v] **1.** *v. i.* besser werden; ⟨*Person, Wetter:*⟩ sich bessern. **2.** *v. t.* verbessern. **3.** *v. refl.* ~ **oneself** sich weiterbilden. **im'prove [up]on** *v. t.* überbieten ⟨*Rekord, Angebot*⟩; verbessern ⟨*Leistung*⟩. **improvement** [ɪm'pru:vmənt] *n.* Verbesserung, *die* (**on, over** gegenüber); **make** ~**s to sth.** Verbesserungen an etw. *(Dat.)* vornehmen

improvise ['ɪmprəvaɪz] *v. t.* improvisieren

impudence ['ɪmpjʊdəns] *n.* Unverschämtheit, *die; (brazenness)* Dreistigkeit, *die*

impudent ['ɪmpjʊdənt] *adj.,* **impudently** *adv.* unverschämt; *(brazen[ly])* dreist

impulse ['ɪmpʌls] *n.* Impuls, *der;* **on [an]** ~: impulsiv. **impulsive** [ɪm'pʌlsɪv] *adj.* impulsiv

impunity [ɪm'pju:nɪtɪ] *v. t.* **with** ~: ungestraft

impure [ɪm'pjʊə(r)] *adj.* unrein. **impurity** [ɪm'pjʊərɪtɪ] *n.* Unreinheit, *die; (foreign body)* Fremdstoff, *der*

impute [ɪm'pju:t] *v. t.* zuschreiben (**to** *Dat.*)

in [ɪn] **1.** *prep. (position; also fig.)* in (+ *Dat.*); *(into)* in (+ *Akk.*); **in this heat** bei dieser Hitze; **two feet in diameter** mit einem Durchmesser von zwei Fuß; **there are three feet in a yard** ein Yard hat drei Fuß; **draw in crayon/ ink** mit Kreide/Tinte zeichnen; **pay in pounds/dollars** in Pfund/Dollars bezahlen; **in fog/rain** *etc.* bei Nebel/Regen *usw.;* **in the 20th century** im 20. Jahrhundert; **4 o'clock in the morning/ afternoon** 4 Uhr morgens/abends; **in 1990** [im Jahre] 1990; **in three minutes/ years** in drei Minuten/Jahren; **in doing this, he ...;** indem er das tut/tat, er ...; **in that ...;** insofern als. **2.** *adv.* **a)** *(inside)* hinein⟨*gehen usw.*⟩; herein⟨*kommen usw.*⟩; **b)** *(at home, work, etc.)* **be in** dasein; **c) have it in for sb.** es auf jmdn. abgesehen haben *(ugs.);* **sb. is in for sth.** *(about to undergo)* jmdm. steht etw. bevor. **3.** *adj. (coll.: in fashion)* in *(ugs.).* **4.** *n.* **know the ins and outs of sth.** sich in einer Sache genau auskennen

ina'bility *n.* Unfähigkeit, *die*

inaccessible [ɪnək'sesɪbl] *adj.* unzugänglich

in'accuracy *n.* **a)** *(incorrectness)* Unrichtigkeit, *die;* **b)** *(imprecision)* Ungenauigkeit, *die*

in'accurate *adj.* **a)** *(incorrect)* unrichtig; **b)** *(imprecise)* ungenau

in'active *adj.* untätig. **inac'tivity** *n.* Untätigkeit, *die*

in'adequate *adj.* unzulänglich; *(incompetent)* ungeeignet; **feel** ~: sich überfordert fühlen

inadvertent [ɪnəd'vɜ:tənt] *adj.,* **inad'vertently** *adv.* versehentlich

inad'visable *adj.* nicht ratsam

inane [ɪn'eɪn] *adj.* dümmlich

in'animate *adj.* unbelebt

inap'plicable *adj.* nicht zutreffend

inap'propriate *adj.* unpassend

in'apt *adj.* unpassend

inar'ticulate *adj.* **a) she's rather/very** ~: sie kann sich ziemlich/sehr schlecht ausdrücken; **b)** *(indistinct)* unverständlich

inat'tentive *adj.* unaufmerksam (**to** gegenüber)

in'audible *adj.* unhörbar

inau'spicious *adj. (ominous)* unheilvoll; *(unlucky)* unglücklich

'inborn *adj.* angeboren (**in** *Dat.*)

'in-built *adj.* jmdm./einer Sache eigen

incalculable [ɪn'kælkjʊləbl] *adj. (very great)* unermeßlich

in'capable *adj.* **a) be** ~ **of doing sth.** außerstande sein, etw. zu tun; **be** ~ **of sth.** zu etw. unfähig sein; **b) be** ~ **of** nicht zulassen ⟨*Beweis, Messung usw.*⟩

incapacitate [ɪnkə'pæsɪteɪt] *v. t.* unfähig machen

incarcerate [ɪn'kɑ:səreɪt] *v. t.* einkerkern *(geh.)*

incendiary [ɪn'sendɪərɪ] *adj. & n.* ~ **device** Brandsatz, *der;* ~ [**bomb**] Brandbombe, *die*

'incense ['ɪnsens] *n.* Weihrauch, *der*

'incense [ɪn'sens] *v. t.* erzürnen

incentive [ɪn'sentɪv] *n.* Anreiz, *der*

incessant [ɪn'sesənt] *adj.,* **in'cessantly** *adv.* unablässig

incest ['ɪnsest] *n.* Inzest, *der.* **incestuous** [ɪn'sestjʊəs] *adj.* inzestuös

inch [ɪntʃ] **1.** *n.* Inch, *der;* Zoll, *der (veralt.).* **2.** *v. t. & i.* ~ [**one's way**] **forward** sich Zoll für Zoll vorwärtsbewegen

incident ['ɪnsɪdənt] *n.* **a)** *(notable event)* Vorfall, *der;* **b)** *(clash)* Zwischenfall, *der*

incidental [ɪnsɪ'dentl] *adj.* beiläufig ⟨*Bemerkung*⟩; Neben⟨*ausgaben, -einnahmen*⟩. **incidentally** [ɪnsɪ'dentəlɪ] *adv.* nebenbei [bemerkt]

incinerate [ɪn'sɪnəreɪt] *v. t.* verbrennen. **incinerator** [ɪn'sɪnəreɪtə(r)] *n.* Verbrennungsofen, *der*

incision [ɪn'sɪʒn] *n.* Einschnitt, *der*

incisive [ɪn'saɪsɪv] *adj.* schneidend ⟨*Ton*⟩; scharf ⟨*Verstand*⟩; scharfsinnig ⟨*Kritik, Frage, Bemerkung, Argument*⟩

incite [ɪn'saɪt] *v. t.* anstiften; aufstacheln ⟨*Massen, Volk*⟩. **in'citement** *n.* Anstiftung, *die*/Aufstachelung, *die*

inclination [ɪŋklɪ'neɪʃn] *n.* Neigung, *die*

incline 1. [ɪn'klaɪn] *v. t.* a) *(bend)* neigen; b) *(dispose)* veranlassen. 2. *v. i. (be disposed)* neigen (to|wards| zu). 3. ['ɪnklaɪn] *n.* Steigung, *die.* **inclined** [ɪn'klaɪnd] *adj.* geneigt; **they are ~ to be slow** sie neigen zur Langsamkeit; **if you feel |so| ~**: wenn Sie Lust dazu haben

include [ɪn'kluːd] *v. t.* einschließen; *(contain)* enthalten; **~d in the price** im Preis inbegriffen. **including** [ɪn'kluːdɪŋ] *prep.* einschließlich (+ *Gen.*); **~ VAT** inklusive Mehrwertsteuer. **inclusion** [ɪn'kluːʒn] *n.* Aufnahme, *die.* **inclusive** [ɪn'kluːsɪv] *adj.* einschließlich; **be ~ of sth.** etw. einschließen; **from 2 to 6 January ~**: vom 2. bis einschließlich 6. Januar; **cost £50 ~**: 50 Pfund kosten, alles inbegriffen

incognito [ɪnkɒg'niːtəʊ] *adj., adv.* inkognito

inco'herent *adj.* zusammenhanglos

income ['ɪnkəm] *n.* Einkommen, *das.* **'income tax** *n.* Einkommensteuer, *die;* *(on wages, salary)* Lohnsteuer, *die*

'incoming *adj.* ankommend; landend ⟨*Flugzeug*⟩; einfahrend ⟨*Zug*⟩; eingehend ⟨*Telefongespräch, Auftrag*⟩

in'comparable *adj.* unvergleichlich

incom'patible *adj.* unvereinbar; **be ~** ⟨*Menschen*⟩ nicht zueinander passen

in'competence [ɪn'kɒmpɪtəns] *n.* Unfähigkeit, *die;* Unvermögen, *das*

in'competent *adj.* unfähig

incom'plete *adj.* unvollständig

incompre'hensible *adj.* unbegreiflich; unverständlich ⟨*Rede, Argument*⟩

incon'ceivable *adj.* unvorstellbar

incon'clusive *adj.* ergebnislos; nicht schlüssig ⟨*Beweis, Argument*⟩

incongruous [ɪn'kɒŋgruəs] *adj.* unpassend

inconsequential [ɪnkɒnsɪ'kwenʃl] *adj.* belanglos

incon'siderate *adj.* rücksichtslos

incon'sistency *n. see* **inconsistent**: Widersprüchlichkeit, *die;* Inkonsequenz, *die;* Unbeständigkeit, *die*

incon'sistent *adj.* widersprüchlich; *(illogical)* inkonsequent; *(irregular)* unbeständig

inconsolable [ɪnkən'səʊləbl] *adj.* untröstlich

incon'spicuous *adj.* unauffällig

incontinence [ɪn'kɒntɪnəns] *n. (Med.)* Inkontinenz, *die*

incontinent [ɪn'kɒntɪnənt] *adj. (Med.)* inkontinent; **be ~**: an Inkontinenz leiden

incontrovertible [ɪnkɒntrə'vɜːtəbl] *adj.* unbestreitbar; unwiderlegbar ⟨*Beweis*⟩

incon'venience 1. *n.* Unannehmlichkeiten (to für); **put sb. to a lot of ~**: jmdm. große Unannehmlichkeiten bereiten. 2. *v. t.* Unannehmlichkeiten bereiten (+ *Dat.*); *(disturb)* stören

incon'venient *adj.* unbequem; ungünstig ⟨*Lage, Standort*⟩; **come at an ~ time** zu ungelegener Zeit kommen; **be ~ for sb.** jmdm. nicht passen

incorporate [ɪn'kɔːpəreɪt] *v. t.* aufnehmen (in|to|, **with** in + *Akk.*)

incor'rect *adj.* a) unrichtig; **be ~**: nicht stimmen; **it is ~ to say that ...**: es stimmt nicht, daß ...; b) *(improper)* inkorrekt. **incor'rectly** *adv.* a) unrichtigerweise; falsch ⟨beantworten, aussprechen⟩; b) *(improperly)* inkorrekt

increase 1. [ɪn'kriːs] *v. i.* zunehmen; ⟨*Lärm:*⟩ größer werden; ⟨*Preise, Nachfrage:*⟩ steigen; **~ in weight/size/price** schwerer/größer/teurer werden. 2. *v. t.* a) *(make greater)* erhöhen; b) *(intensify)* verstärken. 3. ['ɪnkriːs] *n.* Zunahme, *die* (in *Gen.*); **be on the ~**: ständig zunehmen. **increasing** [ɪn'kriːsɪŋ] *adj.* steigend; **an ~ number of people** mehr und mehr Menschen. **in'creasingly** *adv.* in zunehmendem Maße; **become ~ apparent** immer deutlicher werden

in'credible *adj. (also coll.: remarkable)* unglaublich. **in'credibly** *adv. (also coll.: remarkably)* unglaublich

incredulous [ɪn'kredjʊləs] *adj.* ungläubig

incriminate [ɪn'krɪmɪneɪt] *v. t.* belasten

incubate ['ɪŋkjʊbeɪt] *v. t.* bebrüten; *(to hatching)* ausbrüten. **incubation** [ɪŋkjʊ'beɪʃn] *n.* Bebrütung, *die.* **incubator** [ɪŋkjʊ'beɪtə(r)] *n.* Inkubator, *der;* *(for babies also)* Brutkasten, *der*

incur [ɪn'kɜ:(r)] *v. t.*, **-rr-** sich *(Dat.)* zuziehen ⟨*Unwillen, Ärger*⟩; ~ **debts/expenses/risks** Schulden machen/Ausgaben haben/Risiken eingehen

in'curable *adj.* unheilbar

incursion [ɪn'kɜ:ʃn] *n.* Eindringen, *das; (by sudden attack)* Einfall, *der*

indebted [ɪn'detɪd] *pred. adj.* be |**much**| ~ **to sb. for sth.** jmdm. für etw. [sehr] zu Dank verpflichtet sein

in'decency *n.* Unanständigkeit, *die*

in'decent *adj.,* **in'decently** *adv.* unanständig

inde'cision *n.* Unentschlossenheit, *die*

inde'cisive *adj.* **a)** ergebnislos ⟨*Streit, Diskussion*⟩; nichtssagend ⟨*Ergebnis*⟩; **b)** *(hesitating)* unentschlossen

indeed [ɪn'di:d] *adv.* **a)** in der Tat; **thank you very much** ~: haben Sie vielen herzlichen Dank; ~ **it** is in der Tat; **b)** *(in fact)* ja sogar; ~, **he can** ...: ja, er kann sogar ...; **c)** *(admittedly)* zugegebenermaßen

in'definite *adj.* **a)** *(vague)* unbestimmt; **b)** *(unlimited)* unbegrenzt. **in'definitely** *adv.* **a)** *(vaguely)* unbestimmt; **b)** *(unlimitedly)* unbegrenzt; auf unbestimmte Zeit ⟨*verschieben*⟩

indelible [ɪn'delɪbl] *adj.* unauslöschlich; ~ **ink** Wäschetinte, *die*

indemnify [ɪn'demnɪfaɪ] *v. t.* absichern (**against** gegen); *(compensate)* entschädigen. **indemnity** [ɪn'demnɪtɪ] *n.* Absicherung, *die; (compensation)* Entschädigung, *die*

inde'pendence *n.* Unabhängigkeit, *die*

inde'pendent *adj.,* **inde'pendently** *adv.* unabhängig (**of** von)

indescribable [ɪndɪ'skraɪbəbl] *adj.* unbeschreiblich

indestructible [ɪndɪ'strʌktɪbl] *adj.* unzerstörbar

indeterminate [ɪndɪ'tɜ:mɪnət] *adj.* unbestimmt; unklar ⟨*Konzept*⟩

index ['ɪndeks] **1.** *n.* Register, *das.* **2.** *v. t.* mit einem Register versehen. **'index finger** *n.* Zeigefinger, *der*

India ['ɪndɪə] *n.* Indien *(das).* **Indian** ['ɪndɪən] **1.** *adj.* **a)** indisch; **b)** |*American*| ~: indianisch. **2.** *n.* **a)** Inder, *der*/Inderin, *die;* **b)** |*American*| ~: Indianer, *der*/Indianerin, *die.* **Indian 'Ocean** *pr. n.* Indischer Ozean

indicate ['ɪndɪkeɪt] **1.** *v. t.* **a)** *(be a sign of)* erkennen lassen; **b)** *(state briefly)* andeuten; **c)** *(mark, point out)* anzeigen; **d)** *(suggest, make evident)* zum Ausdruck bringen (**to** gegenüber). **2.**

v. i. (Motor Veh.) blinken. **indication** [ɪndɪ'keɪʃn] *n.* [An]zeichen, *das* (**of** *Gen.,* für). **indicative** [ɪn'dɪkətɪv] **1.** *adj.* **a)** be ~ **of sth.** auf etw. *(Akk.)* schließen lassen; **b)** *(Ling.)* indikativisch. **2.** *n. (Ling.)* Indikativ, *der.* **indicator** ['ɪndɪkeɪtə(r)] *n. (on vehicle)* Blinker, *der*

indict [ɪn'daɪt] *v. t.* anklagen (**for,** on **a charge of** *Gen.*)

in'difference *n.* Gleichgültigkeit, *die* (**to**|**wards**| gegenüber)

in'different *adj.* **a)** gleichgültig; **b)** *(not good)* mittelmäßig

indi'gestion *n.* Magenverstimmung, *die; (chronic)* Verdauungsstörungen

indignant [ɪn'dɪgnənt] *adj.* entrüstet (**at, over, about** über + *Akk.*); indigniert ⟨*Blick, Geste*⟩. **in'dignantly** *adv.* entrüstet; indigniert. **indignation** [ɪndɪg'neɪʃn] *n.* Entrüstung, *die* (**about, at, against, over** über + *Akk.*)

in'dignity *n.* Demütigung, *die*

indigo ['ɪndɪgəʊ] **1.** *adj.* ~ |**blue**| indigoblau. **2.** *n.* ~ |**blue**| Indigoblau, *das*

indi'rect *adj.* indirekt; ~ **speech** indirekte Rede. **indi'rectly** *adv.* indirekt. **indirect 'object** *n.* indirektes Objekt; *(in German)* Dativobjekt, *das*

indi'screet *adj.* indiskret. **indi'scretion** *n.* Indiskretion, *die*

indiscriminate [ɪndɪ'skrɪmɪnət] *adj.* unkritisch

indi'spensable *adj.* unentbehrlich (**to** für); unabdingbar ⟨*Voraussetzung*⟩

indisputable [ɪndɪ'spju:təbl] *adj.,* **indisputably** [ɪndɪ'spju:təblɪ] *adv.* unbestreitbar

indi'stinct *adj.,* **indi'stinctly** *adv.* undeutlich

indi'stinguishable *adj.* nicht unterscheidbar

individual [ɪndɪ'vɪdjʊəl] **1.** *adj.* **a)** einzeln; **b)** *(distinctive, characteristic)* individuell. **2.** *n.* einzelne, *der/die.* **indi'vidually** *adv.* einzeln

indi'visible *adj.* unteilbar

indoctrinate [ɪn'dɒktrɪneɪt] *v. t.* indoktrinieren

indolence ['ɪndələns] *n.* Trägheit, *die*

indolent ['ɪndələnt] *adj.* träge

indomitable [ɪn'dɒmɪtəbl] *adj.* unbeugsam

Indonesia [ɪndə'ni:ʃə] *pr. n.* Indonesien *(das)*

'indoor *adj.* ~ **swimming-pool/sports** Hallenbad, *das*/-sport, *der;* ~ **plants** Zimmerpflanzen; ~ **games** Spiele im Haus; *(Sport)* Hallenspiele

indoors [ɪn'dɔːz] *adv.* drinnen; im
Haus; **go/come ~**: nach drinnen ge-
hen/kommen
induce [ɪn'djuːs] *v. t.* **~ sb. to do sth.**
jmdn. dazu bringen, etw. zu tun. **in-
'ducement** *n. (incentive)* Anreiz, *der*
indulge [ɪn'dʌldʒ] **1.** *v. t.* **a)** nachgeben
(+ *Dat.*) ⟨*Wunsch, Verlangen, Ver-
lockung*⟩; frönen *(geh.)* (+ *Dat.*)
⟨*Leidenschaft*⟩; **b)** *(please)* verwöhnen. **2.** *v. i.* **~ in** frönen *(geh.)* (+ *Dat.*)
⟨*Leidenschaft*⟩. **indulgence** [ɪn'dʌl-
dʒəns] *n.* **a)** Nachsicht, *die; (humour-
ing)* Nachgiebigkeit, *die* (**with** gegenüber); *(thing indulged in)* Luxus, *der.*
indulgent [ɪn'dʌldʒənt] *adj.* nach-
sichtig (**with, to|wards|** gegenüber)
industrial [ɪn'dʌstrɪəl] *adj.* industriell;
Arbeits⟨*unfall, -medizin, -psychologie*⟩
industrial: ~ 'action *n.* Arbeits-
kampfmaßnahmen; **take ~ action:** in
den Ausstand treten; **~ dispute** *n.*
Arbeitskonflikt, *der;* **~ estate** *n.* In-
dustriegebiet, *das*
industrialize [ɪn'dʌstrɪəlaɪz] *v. t.* industrialisieren
industrious [ɪn'dʌstrɪəs] *adj.* fleißig;
(busy) emsig
industry ['ɪndəstrɪ] *n.* **a)** Industrie,
die; **b)** *see* **industrious:** Fleiß, *der;*
Emsigkeit, *die*
in'edible *adj.* ungenießbar
ineffective *adj.* unwirksam; fruchtlos ⟨*Anstrengung, Versuch*⟩
ineffectual [ɪnɪ'fektjʊəl] *adj.* unwirksam; fruchtlos ⟨*Versuch, Bemühung*⟩;
· ineffizient ⟨*Methode, Person*⟩
inefficiency *n.* Leistungsschwäche,
die; (of organization, method) schlechtes Funktionieren
inefficient *adj.* leistungsschwach;
schlecht funktionierend ⟨*Organisation, Methode*⟩
in'elegant *adj.* unelegant
in'eligible *adj.* ungeeignet; **be ~ for**
nicht in Frage kommen für ⟨*Beförderung, Position*⟩; nicht berechtigt sein
zu ⟨*Leistungen des Staats usw.*⟩
inept [ɪ'nept] *adj.* unbeholfen
ine'quality *n.* Ungleichheit, *die*
inert [ɪ'nɜːt] *adj.* **a)** reglos; *(sluggish)*
träge; **b)** *(Chem.)* inert; **~ gas** Edelgas,
das. **inertia** [ɪ'nɜːʃə] *n.* Trägheit, *die*
inescapable [ɪnɪ'skeɪpəbl] *adj.* un-
ausweichlich
ines'sential *adj.* unwesentlich; *(dispensable)* entbehrlich
inevitable [ɪn'evɪtəbl] *adj.* unvermeidlich; unabwendbar ⟨*Ereignis, Krieg,*

Schicksal⟩; zwangsläufig ⟨*Ergebnis,
Folge*⟩. **inevitably** [ɪn'evɪtəblɪ] *adv.*
zwangsläufig
ine'xact *adj.* ungenau
inex'cusable *adj.* unverzeihlich
inexhaustible [ɪnɪg'zɔːstɪbl] *adj.* unerschöpflich; unverwüstlich ⟨*Person*⟩
inexorable [ɪn'eksərəbl] *adj.* unerbittlich
inex'pensive *adj.* preisgünstig
inex'perience *n.* Unerfahrenheit,
die. **inex'perienced** *adj.* unerfahren; **~ in sth.** wenig vertraut mit etw.
inex'plicable *adj.* unerklärlich
in'fallible *adj.* unfehlbar
infamous ['ɪnfəməs] *adj.* berüchtigt
infancy ['ɪnfənsɪ] *n.* frühe Kindheit;
be in its ~ *(fig.)* noch in den Anfängen
stecken
infant ['ɪnfənt] *n.* kleines Kind. **infantile** ['ɪnfəntaɪl] *adj.* kindlich;
(childish) kindisch
infantry ['ɪnfəntrɪ] *n.* Infanterie, *die*
'infant school *n. (Brit.)* ≈ Vorschule,
die
infatuated [ɪn'fætjʊeɪtɪd] *adj.* **be ~
with sb.** in jmdn. vernarrt sein
infect [ɪn'fekt] *v. t.* anstecken; infizieren; **the wound became ~ed** die Wunde
entzündete sich. **infection** [ɪn'fekʃn]
n. Infektion, *die;* **throat/ear/eye
~:** Hals-/Ohren-/Augenentzündung,
die. **infectious** [ɪn'fekʃəs] *adj.* ansteckend; **be ~** ⟨*Person*⟩ eine an-
steckende Krankheit haben
infer [ɪn'fɜː(r)] *v. t.,* **-rr-** schließen
(**from** aus); ziehen ⟨*Schlußfolgerung*⟩.
inference ['ɪnfərəns] *n.* [Schluß]fol-
gerung, *die*
inferior [ɪn'fɪərɪə(r)] **1.** *adj. (of lower
quality)* minderwertig ⟨*Ware*⟩; min-
der... ⟨*Qualität*⟩; unterlegen ⟨*Gegner*⟩;
~ to sth. schlechter als etw.; **feel ~:**
Minderwertigkeitsgefühle haben. **2.**
n. Untergebene, *der/die.* **inferiority**
[ɪnfɪərɪ'ɒrɪtɪ] *n.* Minderwertigkeit, *die/*
Unterlegenheit, *die.* **inferi'ority
complex** *n.* Minderwertigkeitskom-
plex, *der*
infernal [ɪn'fɜːnl] *adj.* **a)** *(of hell)* höllisch; **b)** *(coll.)* verdammt *(salopp)*
inferno [ɪn'fɜːnəʊ] *n.* Inferno, *das*
in'fertile *adj.* unfruchtbar. **infer-
'tility** *n.* Unfruchtbarkeit, *die*
infest [ɪn'fest] *v. t.* ⟨*Ungeziefer:*⟩ befallen; ⟨*Unkraut:*⟩ überwuchern; **~ed
with** befallen/überwuchert von
infidelity [ɪnfɪ'delɪtɪ] *n.* Untreue, *die*
(**to** gegenüber)

infiltrate ['ınfıltreıt] *v. t.* **a)** infiltrieren; unterwandern ⟨*Partei, Organisation*⟩; **b)** einschleusen ⟨*Agenten*⟩

infinite ['ınfınıt] *adj.* **a)** *(endless)* unendlich; **b)** *(very great)* ungeheuer

infinitive [ın'fınıtıv] *n. (Ling.)* Infinitiv, *der*

infinity [ın'fınıtı] *n.* Unendlichkeit, *die*

infirm [ın'fɜ:m] *adj.* gebrechlich. **infirmity** [ın'fɜ:mıtı] *n.* Gebrechlichkeit, *die; (malady)* Gebrechen, *das*

inflamed [ın'fleımd] *adj. (Med.)* **be/become** ~: entzündet sein/sich entzünden

inflammable [ın'flæməbl] *adj.* feuergefährlich

inflammation [ınflə'meıʃn] *n. (Med.)* Entzündung, *die*

inflammatory [ın'flæmətərı] *adj.* aufrührerisch; **an ~ speech** eine Hetzrede

inflatable [ın'fleıtəbl] *adj.* aufblasbar; ~ **dinghy** Schlauchboot, *das*

inflate [ın'fleıt] *v. t.* aufblasen; *(with pump)* aufpumpen

inflation [ın'fleıʃn] *n. (Econ.)* Inflation, *die*

in'flexible *adj.* **a)** *(stiff)* unbiegsam; **b)** *(obstinate)* [geistig] unbeweglich

inflict [ın'flıkt] *v. t.* zufügen ⟨*Leid, Schmerzen*⟩, beibringen ⟨*Wunde*⟩, versetzen ⟨*Schlag*⟩ **(on** *Dat.*)

influence ['ınflʊəns] **1.** *n.* Einfluß, *der;* **be a good/bad ~ [on sb.]** einen guten/schlechten Einfluß [auf jmdn.] ausüben. **2.** *v. t.* beeinflussen. **influential** [ınflʊ'enʃl] *adj.* einflußreich

influenza [ınflʊ'enzə] *n.* Grippe, *die*

influx ['ınflʌks] *n.* Zustrom, *der*

inform [ın'fɔ:m] **1.** *n.* informieren **(of, about** über + *Akk.*); **keep sb. ~ed** jmdn. auf dem laufenden halten. **2.** *v. i.* ~ **against** *or* **on sb.** jmdn. denunzieren **(to** bei)

in'formal *adj.* **a)** zwanglos; **b)** *(unofficial)* informell. **infor'mality** *n.* Zwanglosigkeit, *die*

informant [ın'fɔ:mənt] *n.* Informant, *der*/Informantin, *die*

information [ınfə'meıʃn] *n.* Informationen *Pl.;* **give ~ on sth.** Auskunft über etw. *(Akk.)* erteilen; **piece** *or* **bit of ~:** Information, *die;* ~ **centre** Auskunftsbüro, *das*

informative [ın'fɔ:mətıv] *adj.* informativ; **not very ~:** nicht sehr aufschlußreich ⟨*Dokument, Schriftstück*⟩

informed [ın'fɔ:md] *adj.* informiert

in'former *n.* Denunziant, *der*/Denunziantin, *die*

infra-red [ınfrə'red] *adj.* infrarot

in'frequent *adj.*, **in'frequently** *adv.* selten

infringe [ın'frındʒ] *v. t. & i.* ~ **[on]** verstoßen gegen. **in'fringement** *n.* Verstoß, *der* **(of** gegen)

infuriate [ın'fjʊərıeıt] *v. t.* wütend machen; **be ~d** wütend sein **(by** über + *Akk.*). **infuriating** [ın'fjʊərıeıtıŋ] *adj.* ärgerlich

ingenious [ın'dʒi:nıəs] *adj.* einfallsreich; genial ⟨*Methode, Idee*⟩; raffiniert ⟨*Spielzeug, Maschine*⟩. **ingenuity** [ındʒı'nju:ıtı] *n.* Genialität, *die*

ingot ['ıŋgət] *n.* Ingot, *der*

ingratiate [ın'greıʃıeıt] *v. refl.* ~ **oneself with sb.** sich bei jmdm. einschmeicheln

in'gratitude *n.* Undankbarkeit, *die* **(to|wards|** gegenüber)

ingredient [ın'gri:dıənt] *n.* Zutat, *die*

ingrowing ['ıngrəʊıŋ] *adj.* eingewachsen ⟨*Zehennagel usw.*⟩

inhabit [ın'hæbıt] *v. t.* bewohnen. **inhabitable** [ın'hæbıtəbl] *adj.* bewohnbar. **inhabitant** [ın'hæbıtənt] *n.* Bewohner, *der*/Bewohnerin, *die*

inhale [ın'heıl] *v. t. & i.* einatmen; inhalieren *(ugs.)*⟨*Zigarettenrauch usw.*⟩

inherit [ın'herıt] *v. t.* erben. **inheritance** [ın'herıtəns] *n.* Erbe, *das; (inheriting)* Erbschaft, *die*

inhibit [ın'hıbıt] *v. t.* hemmen. **in'hibited** *adj.* gehemmt. **inhibition** [ınhı'bıʃn] *n.* Hemmung, *die*

inho'spitable *adj.* ungastlich ⟨*Person, Verhalten*⟩; unwirtlich ⟨*Gegend, Klima*⟩

in'human *adj.* unmenschlich

initial [ı'nıʃl] **1.** *adj.* anfänglich; Anfangs⟨*stadium, -schwierigkeiten*⟩. **2.** *n. esp. in pl.* Initiale, *die.* **3.** *v. t., (Brit.)* **-ll-** abzeichnen ⟨*Scheck, Quittung*⟩; paraphieren ⟨*Vertrag, Abkommen usw.*⟩. **i'nitially** *adv.* anfangs; am Anfang

initiate [ı'nıʃıeıt] *v. t.* **a)** *(introduce)* einführen **(into** in + *Akk.*); *(into knowledge, mystery)* einweihen **(into** in + *Akk.*); **b)** *(begin)* einleiten. **initiation** [ınıʃı'eıʃn] *n.* **a)** *(introduction)* Einführung, *die; (into knowledge, mystery)* Einweihung, *die*

initiative [ı'nıʃətıv] *n.* Initiative, *die;* **lack ~:** keine Initiative haben

inject [ın'dʒekt] *v. t.* [ein]spritzen; injizieren *(Med.)*. **injection** [ın'dʒekʃn] *n.* Spritze, *die;* Injektion, *die*

injure ['ındʒə(r)] *v. t.* **a)** verletzen; **his**

leg was ~d er wurde/*(state)* war am Bein verletzt; **b)** *(impair)* schaden (+ *Dat.*). **injured** ['ɪndʒəd] *adj.* verletzt; verwundet ⟨*Soldat*⟩. **injury** ['ɪndʒərɪ] *n.* Verletzung, *die* (**to** *Gen.*)

in'justice *n.* Ungerechtigkeit, *die*

ink [ɪŋk] *n.* Tinte, *die*

inkling ['ɪŋklɪŋ] *n.* Ahnung, *die;* **have an ~ of** sth. etw. ahnen

inland ['ɪnlənd, 'ɪnlænd] *adj.* Binnen-; binnenländisch. **Inland 'Revenue** *n.* *(Brit.)* ≈ Finanzamt, *das*

'in-laws *n pl. (coll.)* Schwiegereltern

inlet ['ɪnlət] *n.* [schmale] Bucht

'inmate *n.* Insasse, *der*/Insassin, *die*

inn [ɪn] *n. (hotel)* Gasthof, *der; (pub)* Wirtshaus, *das*

innate [ɪ'neɪt] *adj.* angeboren

inner ['ɪnə(r)] *adj.* inner...; Innen⟨*hof, -tür, -fläche, -seite usw.*⟩; **~ tube** Schlauch, *der.* **innermost** ['ɪnəməʊst] *adj.* innerst...

innocence ['ɪnəsəns] *n.* **a)** Unschuld, *die;* **b)** *(naïvity)* Naivität, *die*

innocent ['ɪnəsənt] *adj.* **a)** unschuldig (**of** an + *Dat.*); **b)** *(naïve)* naiv

innocuous [ɪ'nɒkjʊəs] *adj.* harmlos

innovation [ɪnə'veɪʃn] *n.* Innovation, *die; (thing, change)* Neuerung, *die*

innumerable [ɪ'njuːmərəbl] *adj.* unzählig

inoculate [ɪ'nɒkjʊleɪt] *v. t.* impfen. **inoculation** [ɪnɒkjʊ'leɪʃn] *n.* Impfung, *die*

inof'fensive *adj.* harmlos

in'opportune *adj.* unpassend; unangebracht ⟨*Bemerkung*⟩

inordinate [ɪ'nɔːdɪnət] *adj.* unmäßig; ungeheuer ⟨*Menge*⟩

inor'ganic *adj.* anorganisch

'in-patient *n.* stationär behandelter Patient/behandelte Patientin

'input *n.* Input, *der od. das*

inquest ['ɪŋkwest] *n.* gerichtliche Untersuchung der Todesursache

inquire [ɪn'kwaɪə(r)] **1.** *v. i.* sich erkundigen (**about,** after **nach, of** bei); **~ into** untersuchen. **2.** *v. t.* sich erkundigen nach ⟨*Weg, Namen*⟩. **inquiry** [ɪn-'kwaɪrɪ] *n.* **a)** *(question)* Erkundigung, *die* (**into** über + *Akk.*); **make inquiries** Erkundigungen einziehen; **b)** *(investigation)* Untersuchung, *die*

inquisitive [ɪn'kwɪzɪtɪv] *adj.* neugierig

'inroad *n.* Eingriff, *der* (**on, into** in + *Akk.*); **make ~s into** sb.'s **savings** jmds. Ersparnisse angreifen

in'sane *adj.* geisteskrank

in'sanitary *adj.* unhygienisch

in'sanity *n.* Geisteskrankheit, *die*

insatiable [ɪn'seɪʃəbl] *adj.* unersättlich; unstillbar ⟨*Verlangen*⟩

inscribe [ɪn'skraɪb] *v. t.* schreiben; *(on stone, rock)* einmeißeln; mit einer Inschrift versehen ⟨*Denkmal, Grabstein*⟩. **inscription** [ɪn'skrɪpʃn] *n.* Inschrift, *die; (on coin)* Aufschrift, *die*

inscrutable [ɪn'skruːtəbl] *adj.* unergründlich; undurchdringlich ⟨*Miene*⟩

insect ['ɪnsekt] *n.* Insekt, *das.* **insecticide** [ɪn'sektɪsaɪd] *n.* Insektizid, *das.* **'insect repellent** *n.* Insektenschutzmittel, *das*

inse'cure *adj.* unsicher. **inse'curity** *n.* Unsicherheit, *die*

in'sensitive *adj.* **a)** gefühllos ⟨*Person, Art*⟩; *(unappreciative)* unempfänglich (**to** für); **b)** *(physically)* unempfindlich (**to** gegen)

in'separable *adj.* untrennbar; *(fig.)* unzertrennlich

insert [ɪn'sɜːt] *v. t.* einlegen ⟨*Film*⟩; einwerfen ⟨*Münze*⟩; hineinstecken ⟨*Schlüssel*⟩; einstechen ⟨*Nadel*⟩. **insertion** [ɪn'sɜːʃn] *n. see* **insert:** Einlegen, *das;* Einwerfen, *das;* Hineinstecken, *das;* Einstechen, *das*

inside 1. [-'-, '--] *n.* **a)** *(internal side)* Innenseite, *die;* **on the ~:** innen; **to/from the ~:** nach/von innen; **b)** *(inner part)* Innere, *das.* **2.** ['--] *adj.* inner...; Innen⟨*wand, -einrichtung, -ansicht*⟩; *(fig.)* intern. **3.** [-'-] *adv. (on or in the ~)* innen; *(to the ~)* nach innen hinein/herein; *(indoors)* drinnen; **come ~:** hereinkommen; **take a look ~:** hineinsehen; **go ~:** [ins Haus] hineingehen; **turn a jacket ~ out** eine Jacke nach links wenden; **know** sth. **~ out** etw. in- und auswendig kennen. **4.** [-'-] *prep. (position)* in (+ *Dat.*); *(direction)* in (+ *Akk.*) hinein

insidious [ɪn'sɪdɪəs] *adj.* heimtückisch

'insight *n. (discernment)* Verständnis, *das;* **gain an ~ into** sth. Einblick in etw. *(Akk.)* gewinnen

insig'nificant *adj.* unbedeutend; geringfügig ⟨*Summe*⟩

insin'cere *adj.* unaufrichtig. **insin-'cerity** *n.* Unaufrichtigkeit, *die*

insinuate [ɪn'sɪnjʊeɪt] *v. t.* andeuten (**to** sb. jmdm. gegenüber). **insinuation** [ɪnsɪnjʊ'eɪʃn] *n.* Anspielung, *die* (**about** auf + *Akk.*)

insipid [ɪn'sɪpɪd] *adj.* fade

insist [ɪn'sɪst] *v. i.* bestehen (**[up]on** auf + *Dat.*); **~ on doing** sth./**on** sb.'s **doing** sth. darauf bestehen, etw. zu tun/daß jmd. etw. tut; **if you** ~: wenn du darauf bestehst. **insistence** [ın-'sıstəns] *n*. Bestehen, *das* (**on** auf + *Dat*.). **insistent** [ın'sıstənt] *adj*. **be** ~ **that ...**: darauf bestehen, daß ...

insolence ['ınsələns] *n*. Unverschämtheit, *die;* Frechheit, *die*

insolent ['ınsələnt] *adj*., **insolently** *adv*. unverschämt; frech

in'soluble *adj*. **a)** *(esp. Chem.)* unlöslich; **b)** *(not solvable)* unlösbar

in'solvent *adj*. zahlungsunfähig

insomnia [ın'sɒmnıə] *n*. Schlaflosigkeit, *die*. **insomniac** [ın'sɒmnıæk] *n*. **be an** ~: an Schlaflosigkeit leiden

inspect [ın'spekt] *v. t*. prüfend betrachten; *(examine officially)* überprüfen; kontrollieren ⟨*Räumlichkeiten*⟩. **inspection** [ın'spekʃn] *n*. Überprüfung, *die; (of premises)* Kontrolle, *die;* Inspektion, *die;* **on** [**closer**] ~: bei näherer Betrachtung. **inspector** [ın-'spektə(r)] *n*. **a)** *(on bus, train, etc.)* Kontrolleur, *der*/Kontrolleurin, *die;* **b)** *(Brit.)* ≈ Polizeiinspektor, *der*

inspiration [ınspə'reıʃn] *n*. Inspiration, *die (geh.)*

inspire [ın'spaıə(r)] *v. t*. **a)** inspirieren *(geh.)* ⟨*Person*⟩; **b)** *(instil)* einflößen (**in** *Dat*.). **inspiring** [ın'spaıərıŋ] *adj*. inspirierend *(geh.)*

insta'bility *n*. Instabilität, *die; (of person)* Labilität, *die*

install [ın'stɔːl] *v. t*. installieren; einbauen ⟨*Badezimmer*⟩; anschließen ⟨*Telefon, Herd*⟩; ~ **oneself** sich installieren. **installation** [ınstə'leıʃn] *n*. **a)** Installation, *die; (of bathroom)* Einbau, *der; (of telephone, cooker)* Anschluß, *der;* **b)** *(apparatus etc. installed)* Anlage, *die*

instalment *(Amer.:* **installment)** [ın'stɔːlmənt] *n*. **a)** *(part-payment)* Rate, *die;* **pay by** *or* **in** ~**s** in Raten zahlen; **b)** *(of serial, novel)* Fortsetzung, *die; (Radio, Telev.)* Folge, *die*

instance ['ınstəns] *n*. *(example)* Beispiel, *das* (**of** für); **for** ~: zum Beispiel; **in many** ~**s** *(cases)* in vielen Fällen; **in the first** ~: zunächst einmal

instant ['ınstənt] **1.** *adj*. unmittelbar; sofortig ⟨*Wirkung, Linderung, Ergebnis*⟩; ~ **coffee/tea** Pulverkaffee/Instanttee, *der;* ~ **potatoes** fertiger Kartoffelbrei. **2.** *n*. Augenblick, *der;* **at that very** ~: genau in dem Augenblick; **come here this** ~: komm sofort her; **in an** ~: augenblicklich. **instantaneous** [ınstən'teınıəs] *adj*. unmittel-

bar; **his reaction was** ~: er reagierte sofort. '**instantly** *adv*. sofort

instead [ın'sted] *adv*. statt dessen; ~ **of doing sth.** [an]statt etw. zu tun; ~ **of sth.** anstelle einer Sache *(Gen.);* **I will go** ~ **of you** ich gehe an deiner Stelle

'**instep** *n*. *(of foot)* Spann, *der;* Fußrücken, *der; (of shoe)* Blatt, *das*

instigate ['ınstıgeıt] *v. t*. anstiften (**to** zu); initiieren *(geh.)* ⟨*Reformen, Projekt usw.*⟩. **instigation** [ınstı'geıʃn] *n*. Anstiftung, *die; (of reforms, project, etc.)* Initiierung, *die;* **at sb.'s** ~: auf jmds. Betreiben *(Akk.)*

instil *(Amer.:* **instill)** [ın'stıl] *v. t.,* **-ll-** einflößen (**in** *Dat*.); beibringen ⟨*gutes Benehmen, Wissen*⟩ (**in** *Dat*.)

instinct ['ınstıŋkt] *n*. Instinkt, *der*. **instinctive** [ın'stıŋktıv] *adj*., **in'stinctively** *adv*. instinktiv

institute ['ınstıtjuːt] **1.** *n*. Institut, *das*. **2.** *v. t*. einführen; einleiten ⟨*Suche, Verfahren*⟩; anstrengen ⟨*Prozeß*⟩

institution [ınstı'tjuːʃn] *n*. Institution, *die; (home)* Heim, *das;* Anstalt, *die*

instruct [ın'strʌkt] *v. t*. **a)** *(teach)* unterrichten ⟨*Klasse, Fach*⟩; **b)** *(direct, command)* anweisen. **instruction** [ın'strʌkʃn] *n*. **a)** *(teaching)* Unterricht, *der;* **b)** *esp. in pl. (direction, order)* Anweisung, *die;* ~ **manual/**~**s for use** Gebrauchsanleitung, *die*. **instructive** [ın'strʌktıv] *adj*. aufschlußreich; lehrreich ⟨*Erfahrung, Buch*⟩. **instructor** [ın'strʌktə(r)] *n*. Lehrer, *der*/Lehrerin, *die; (Mil.)* Ausbilder, *der*

instrument ['ınstrʊmənt] *n*. Instrument, *das*. **instrumental** [ınstrə-'mentl] *adj*. **a)** *(Mus.)* Instrumental-; **b)** *(helpful)* dienlich (**to** *Dat*.); **he was** ~ **in finding me a job** er hat mir zu einer Stelle verholfen

insufferable [ın'sʌfərəbl] *adj*. *(unbearably arrogant)* unausstehlich

insufficient *adj*. nicht genügend; unzulänglich ⟨*Beweise*⟩; unzureichend ⟨*Versorgung, Beleuchtung*⟩. **insufficiently** *adv*. ungenügend

insulate ['ınsjʊleıt] *v. t*. isolieren (**against, from** gegen); **insulating tape** Isolierband, *das*. **insulation** [ınsjʊ-'leıʃn] *n*. Isolierung, *die*

insulin ['ınsjʊlın] *n*. Insulin, *das*

insult 1. ['ınsʌlt] *n*. Beleidigung, *die* (**to** *Gen.*). **2.** [ın'sʌlt] *v. t*. beleidigen. **insulting** [ın'sʌltıŋ] *adj*. beleidigend

insuperable [ın'suːpərəbl] *adj*. unüberwindlich

insurance [ɪn'ʃʊərəns] *n.* Versicherung, *die; (fig.)* Sicherheit, *die;* take out ~ against/on sth. eine Versicherung gegen etw. abschließen/etw. versichern lassen; travel ~ : Reisegepäck- und -unfallversicherung, *die.* in'surance policy *n.* Versicherungspolice, *die*

insure [ɪn'ʃʊə(r)] *v. t.* versichern ⟨*Person*⟩; versichern lassen ⟨*Gepäck, Gemälde usw.*⟩; ~ |oneself| against sth. [sich] gegen etw. versichern

insurmountable [ɪnsə'maʊntəbl] *adj.* unüberwindlich

intact [ɪn'tækt] *adj.* a) *(entire)* unbeschädigt; intakt ⟨*Uhr, Maschine usw.*⟩; b) *(unimpaired)* unversehrt

'intake *n.* a) *(action)* Aufnahme, *die;* b) *(persons, things)* Neuzugänge; *(amount)* aufgenommene Menge

in'tangible *adj.* nicht greifbar; *(mentally)* unbestimmbar

integral ['ɪntɪgrl] *adj.* a) wesentlich ⟨*Bestandteil*⟩; b) *(whole)* vollständig

integrate ['ɪntɪgreɪt] *v. t.* integrieren (into in + *Akk.*). **integration** [ɪntɪ'greɪʃn] *n.* Integration, *die* (into in + *Akk.*)

integrity [ɪn'tegrɪtɪ] *n.* Redlichkeit, *die*

intellect ['ɪntəlekt] *n.* Verstand, *der;* Intellekt, *der.* **intellectual** [ɪntə'lektjʊəl] 1. *adj.* intellektuell; geistig anspruchsvoll ⟨*Person, Publikum*⟩. 2. *n.* Intellektuelle, *der/die*

intelligence [ɪn'telɪdʒəns] *n.* a) Intelligenz, *die;* b) *(information)* Informationen *Pl.;* c) *military ~ (organization)* militärischer Geheimdienst. **intelligent** [ɪn'telɪdʒənt] *adj.* intelligent

intelligible [ɪn'telɪdʒɪbl] *adj.* verständlich (to für)

intend [ɪn'tend] *v. t.* beabsichtigen; it was ~ed as a joke das sollte ein Witz sein. **in'tended** *adj.* beabsichtigt ⟨*Wirkung*⟩; be ~ for sb./sth. für jmdn./ etw. gedacht sein

intense [ɪn'tens] *adj.* a) intensiv; groß ⟨*Hitze, Belastung, Interesse*⟩; stark ⟨*Schmerzen*⟩; b) *(earnest)* ernst. **in'tensely** *adv.* äußerst; intensiv ⟨*studieren, fühlen*⟩

intensify [ɪn'tensɪfaɪ] 1. *v. t.* intensivieren. 2. *v. i.* zunehmen

intensity [ɪn'tensɪtɪ] *n. see* intense a: Intensität, *die;* Größe, *die;* Stärke, *die*

intensive [ɪn'tensɪv] *adj.* intensiv; intensiv⟨*kurs*⟩; be in ~ care auf der Intensivstation sein. **in'tensively** *adv.* intensiv

intent [ɪn'tent] 1. *n.* Absicht, *die;* to all ~s and purposes im Grunde. 2. *adj.* be ~ on achieving sth. etw. unbedingt erreichen wollen

intention [ɪn'tenʃn] *n.* Absicht, *die.* **intentional** [ɪn'tenʃənl] *adj.,* **in'tentionally** *adv.* absichtlich

in'tently *adv.* aufmerksam

interact [ɪntər'ækt] *v. i.* interagieren. **interaction** [ɪntər'ækʃn] *n.* Interaktion, *die*

intercede [ɪntə'si:d] *v. i.* sich einsetzen (with bei; for, on behalf of für)

intercept [ɪntə'sept] *v. t.* abfangen

interchange 1. ['ɪntətʃeɪndʒ] *n.* a) Austausch, *der;* b) *(road junction)* [Autobahn]kreuz, *das.* 2. [ɪntə'tʃeɪndʒ] *v. t.* austauschen. **interchangeable** [ɪntə'tʃeɪndʒəbl] *adj.* austauschbar

inter-city [ɪntə'sɪtɪ] *adj.* Intercity-; ~ train Intercity[-Zug], *der*

intercom ['ɪntəkɒm] *n. (coll.)* Gegensprechanlage, *die*

interconnect [ɪntəkə'nekt] 1. *v. t.* miteinander verbinden. 2. *v. i.* miteinander in Zusammenhang stehen

intercourse ['ɪntəkɔ:s] *n. (sexual)* [Geschlechts]verkehr, *der*

interest ['ɪntrəst] 1. *n.* a) Interesse, *das;* take *or* have an ~ in sb./sth. sich für jmdn./etw. interessieren; |just| for *or* out of ~ : [nur] interessehalber; with ~ : interessiert; act in one's own/sb.'s ~|s| im eigenen/in jmds. Interesse handeln; be of ~ : interessant sein (to für); b) *(Finance)* Zinsen *Pl.* 2. *v. t.* interessieren; be ~ed sich interessieren (in für). **'interesting** *adj.* interessant

interfere [ɪntə'fɪə(r)] *v. i.* sich einmischen (in in + *Akk.*); ~ with sth. sich ⟨*Dat.*⟩ an etw. ⟨*Dat.*⟩ zu schaffen machen. **interference** [ɪntə'fɪərəns] *n.* a) *(interfering)* Einmischung, *die;* b) *(Radio, Telev.)* Störung, *die*

interim ['ɪntərɪm] 1. *n.* in the ~ : in der Zwischenzeit. 2. *adj.* vorläufig

interior [ɪn'tɪərɪə(r)] 1. *adj.* inner...; Innen⟨*fläche, -wand*⟩. 2. *n.* Innere, *das*

interject [ɪntə'dʒekt] *v. t.* einwerfen. **interjection** [ɪntə'dʒekʃn] *n.* Ausruf, *der*

interloper ['ɪntələʊpə(r)] *n.* Eindringling, *der*

interlude ['ɪntəlu:d] *n.* Pause, *die; (music)* Zwischenspiel, *das*

intermediate [ɪntə'mi:djət] *adj.* Zwischen-

interminable [ɪn'tɜ:mɪnəbl] *adj.* endlos

intermission [ıntə'mıʃn] *n.* Pause, *die*
intermittent [ıntə'mıtənt] *adj.* in Abständen auftretend. **inter'mittently**
adv. in Abständen
intern [ın'tɜ:n] *v. t.* gefangenhalten
internal [ın'tɜ:nl] *adj.* inner...; Innen-
⟨*fläche, -abmessungen*⟩. **internally**
[ın'tɜ:nəlı] *adv.* innerlich
international [ıntə'næʃənl] **1.** *adj.* international. **2.** *n.* **a)** *(Sport) (contest)*
Länderspiel, *das; (participant)* Nationalspieler, *der/*-spielerin, *die.* **inter'nationally** *adv.* international
in'ternment *n.* Internierung, *die*
interplay ['ıntəpleı] *n.* Zusammenspiel, *das*
interpret [ın'tɜ:prıt] **1.** *v. t.* **a)** interpretieren; deuten ⟨*Traum, Zeichen*⟩; **b)**
(between languages) dolmetschen. **2.**
v. i. dolmetschen. **interpretation**
[ıntɜ:prı'teıʃn] *n.* Interpretation, *die;*
(of dream, symptoms) Deutung, *die.*
in'terpreter *n.* Dolmetscher, *der/*
Dolmetscherin, *die*
interrogate [ın'terəgeıt] *v. t.* verhören; ausfragen ⟨*Freund, Kind usw.*⟩.
interrogation [ınterə'geıʃn] *n.* Verhör, *das*
interrogative [ıntə'rɒgətıv] *adj.*
(Ling.) Interrogativ-
interrupt [ıntə'rʌpt] **1.** *v. t.* unterbrechen; **don't ~ me when I'm busy** stör
mich nicht, wenn ich zu tun habe. **2.**
v. i. unterbrechen; stören. **interruption** [ıntə'rʌpʃn] *n.* Unterbrechung,
die; Störung, *die*
intersect [ıntə'sekt] *v. i.* **a)** ⟨*Straßen:*⟩
sich kreuzen; **b)** *(Geom.)* sich schneiden. **intersection** [ıntə'sekʃn] *n.* **a)**
(road junction) Kreuzung, *die;* **b)**
(Geom.) Schnittpunkt, *der*
intersperse [ıntə'spɜ:s] *v. t.* **be ~d**
with durchsetzt sein mit
interval ['ıntəvl] *n.* **a)** [Zeit]abstand,
der; **at ~s** in Abständen; **b)** *(break;*
also Brit. Theatre etc.) Pause, *die;*
sunny ~s Aufheiterungen *Pl.*
intervene [ıntə'vi:n] *v. i.* **a)** [vermittelnd] eingreifen (**in** in + *Akk.*); **b) the**
intervening years die dazwischenliegenden Jahre. **intervention** [ıntə-
'venʃn] *n.* Eingreifen, *das*
interview ['ıntəvju:] **1.** *n.* **a)** *(for job)*
Vorstellungsgespräch, *das;* **b)** *(Journ.,*
Radio, Telev.) Interview, *das.* **2.** *v. t.*
ein Vorstellungsgespräch führen mit;
interviewen ⟨*Politiker, Filmstar usw.*⟩.
'interviewer *n.* Interviewer, *der/*Interviewerin, *die*

intestine [ın'testın] *n.* Darm, *der*
intimacy ['ıntıməsı] *n.* **a)** Vertrautheit,
die; **b)** *(sexual)* Intimität, *die*
intimate 1. ['ıntımət] *adj.* **a)** eng
⟨*Freund, Verhältnis*⟩; genau, *(geh.)* intim ⟨*Kenntnis*⟩; **b)** *(sexually)* intim. **2.**
['ıntımeıt] *v. t. (imply)* andeuten. **intimately** ['ıntımətlı] *adv.* genau-
[estens] ⟨*kennen*⟩; eng ⟨*verbinden*⟩
intimidate [ın'tımıdeıt] *v. t.* einschüchtern. **intimidation** [ıntımı-
'deıʃn] *n.* Einschüchterung, *die*
into [*before vowel* 'ıntʊ, *before consonant* 'ıntə] *prep.* in (+ *Akk.*); *(against)*
gegen; **I went out ~ the street** ich ging
auf die Straße hinaus; **translate sth. ~**
English etw. ins Englische übersetzen
in'tolerable *adj.* unerträglich
in'tolerance *n.* Intoleranz, *die*
in'tolerant *adj.* intolerant (**of** gegenüber)
intonation [ıntə'neıʃn] *n.* Intonation,
die
intoxicate [ın'tɒksıkeıt] *v. t.* betrunken machen. **intoxication** [ıntɒksı-
'keıʃn] *n.* Rausch, *der*
intractable [ın'træktəbl] *adj.* hartnäckig ⟨*Problem*⟩
intransigent [ın'trænsıdʒənt] *adj.* unnachgiebig
in'transitive *adj. (Ling.)* intransitiv
'in-tray *n.* Eingangskorb, *der*
intrepid [ın'trepıd] *adj.* unerschrocken
intricacy ['ıntrıkəsı] *n.* Kompliziertheit, *die*
intricate ['ıntrıkət] *adj.* kompliziert
intrigue [ın'tri:g] *v. t.* faszinieren. **intriguing** [ın'tri:gıŋ] *adj.* faszinierend
intrinsic [ın'trınsık] *adj.* innewohnend; inner...; **~ value** innerer Wert
introduce [ıntrə'dju:s] *v. t.* einführen;
~ oneself/sb. [**to sb.**] sich/jmdn.
[jmdm.] vorstellen. **introduction** [ıntrə'dʌkʃn] *n.* Einführen, *das;* Einführung, *die; (to person)* Vorstellung, *die;*
(to book) Einleitung, *die.* **introductory** [ıntrə'dʌktərı] *adj.* einleitend;
Einführungs⟨*kurs, -vortrag*⟩
introspective [ıntrə'spektıv] *adj.* in
sich *(Akk.)* gerichtet
introvert ['ıntrəvɜ:t] **1.** *n.* Introvertierte, *der/die;* **be an ~:** introvertiert sein.
2. *adj.* introvertiert
intrude [ın'tru:d] *v. i.* stören. **in'truder** *n.* Eindringling, *der.* **intrusion** [ın'tru:ʒn] *n.* Störung, *die.* **intrusive** [ın'tru:sıv] *adj.* aufdringlich
intuition [ıntju:'ıʃn] *n.* Intuition, *die*

intuitive [ɪr.ˈtjuːɪtɪv] *adj.,* **inˈtuitively** *adv.* intuitiv

inundate [ˈɪnəndeɪt] *v. t.* überschwemmen

inure [ɪˈnjʊə(r)] *v. t.* gewöhnen (**to** an + *Akk.*)

invade [ɪnˈveɪd] *v. t.* einfallen in (+ *Akk.*). **inˈvader** *n.* Angreifer, *der*

¹invalid [ˈɪnvəlɪd] (*Brit.*) **1.** *n.* Kranke, *der/die; (disabled)* Körperbehinderte, *der/die.* **2.** *adj.* körperbehindert

²invalid [ɪnˈvælɪd] *adj.* nicht schlüssig ⟨*Argument, Theorie*⟩; ungültig ⟨*Fahrkarte, Garantie, Vertrag*⟩. **invalidate** [ɪnˈvælɪdeɪt] *v. t.* aufheben; widerlegen ⟨*Theorie, These*⟩

inˈvaluable *adj.* unersetzlich ⟨*Person*⟩; unschätzbar ⟨*Dienst, Hilfe*⟩; außerordentlich wichtig ⟨*Rolle*⟩

inˈvariable *adj.* unveränderlich. **invariably** [ɪnˈveərɪəblɪ] *adv.* immer; ausnahmslos ⟨*falsch, richtig*⟩

invasion [ɪnˈveɪʒn] *n.* Invasion, *die*

invective [ɪnˈvektɪv] *n.* Beschimpfungen *Pl.*

invent [ɪnˈvent] *v. t.* erfinden. **invention** [ɪnˈvenʃn] *n.* Erfindung, *die.* **inventive** [ɪnˈventɪv] *adj.* **a)** schöpferisch ⟨*Person, Begabung*⟩; **b)** *(original)* originell. **inventor** [ɪnˈventə(r)] *n.* Erfinder, *der*/Erfinderin, *die*

inventory [ˈɪnvəntərɪ] *n.* Bestandsliste, *die;* **make** *or* **take an ~ of sth.** von etw. ein Inventar aufstellen

inverse [ˈɪnvɜːs] *adj.* umgekehrt

invert [ɪnˈvɜːt] *v. t.* umstülpen

inˈvertebrate *n.* wirbelloses Tier

inverted ˈcommas *n. pl.* (*Brit.*) Anführungszeichen *Pl.*

invest [ɪnˈvest] *v. t.* **a)** *(Finance)* anlegen (**in** in + *Dat.*); investieren (**in** in + *Dat. od. Akk.*); **b)** *(fig.)* investieren; **~ sb. with sth.** jmdm. etw. übertragen; **~ sth. with sth.** einer Sache *(Dat.)* etw. verleihen

investigate [ɪnˈvestɪgeɪt] *v. t.* untersuchen. **investigation** [ɪnvestɪˈgeɪʃn] *n.* Untersuchung, *die.* **investigator** [ɪnˈvestɪgeɪtə(r)] *n.* |private| **~:** [Privat]detektiv, *der*/-detektivin, *die*

inˈvestment *n.* Investition, *die; (money invested)* angelegtes Geld; **be a good ~** *(fig.)* sich bezahlt machen. **investor** [ɪnˈvestə(r)] *n.* [Kapital]anleger, *der*/-anlegerin, *die*

inveterate [ɪnˈvetərət] *adj.* eingefleischt ⟨*Trinker, Raucher*⟩; unverbesserlich ⟨*Lügner*⟩

invigorate [ɪnˈvɪgəreɪt] *v. t.* stärken;

(physically) kräftigen. **invigorating** [ɪnˈvɪgəreɪtɪŋ] *adj.* kräftigend ⟨*Getränk, Klima*⟩

invincible [ɪnˈvɪnsɪbl] *adj.* unbesiegbar

inˈvisible *adj.* unsichtbar

invitation [ɪnvɪˈteɪʃn] *n.* Einladung, *die;* **at sb.'s ~:** auf jmds. Einladung *(Akk.)*

invite [ɪnˈvaɪt] *v. t.* **a)** *(request to come)* einladen; **b)** *(request to do sth.)* auffordern; **c)** *(bring on)* herausfordern ⟨*Kritik, Verhängnis*⟩. **inviting** [ɪnˈvaɪtɪŋ] *adj.* einladend; verlockend ⟨*Gedanke, Vorstellung*⟩

invoice [ˈɪnvɔɪs] **1.** *n. (bill)* Rechnung, *die.* **2.** *v. t.* **~ sb.** jmdm. eine Rechnung schicken; **~ sb. for sth.** jmdm. etw. in Rechnung stellen

invoke [ɪnˈvəʊk] *v. t.* anrufen

inˈvoluntarily *adv.,* **inˈvoluntary** *adj.* unwillkürlich

involve [ɪnˈvɒlv] *v. t.* **a)** *(implicate)* verwickeln; **b)** **become** *or* **get ~d in a fight** in eine Schlägerei verwickelt werden; **get ~d with sb.** sich mit jmdm. einlassen; **c)** *(entail)* mit sich bringen. **involved** [ɪnˈvɒlvd] *adj.* verwickelt; *(complicated)* kompliziert

invulnerable [ɪnˈvʌlnərəbl] *adj.* unverwundbar; *(fig.)* unantastbar

inward [ˈɪnwəd] **1.** *adj.* inner... **2.** *adv.* einwärts ⟨*gerichtet, gebogen*⟩; **open ~:** nach innen öffnen. **ˈinwardly** *adv.* im Inneren; innerlich. **inwards** [ˈɪnwədz] *see* **inward 2**

iodine [ˈaɪədiːn] *n.* Jod, *das*

ion [ˈaɪən] *n.* Ion, *das*

iota [aɪˈəʊtə] *n.* **not one** *or* **an ~:** nicht ein Jota *(geh.)*

IOU [aɪəʊˈjuː] *n.* Schuldschein, *der*

Iran [ɪˈrɑːn] *pr. n.* Iran, *der od. (das)*

Iraq [ɪˈrɑːk] *pr. n.* Irak, *der od. (das)*

irate [aɪˈreɪt] *adj.* wütend

Ireland [ˈaɪələnd] *pr. n.* Irland *(das)*

iris [ˈaɪərɪs] *n. (Bot., Anat.)* Iris, *die*

Irish [ˈaɪərɪʃ] **1.** *adj.* irisch; **sb. is ~:** jmd. ist Ire/Irin. **2.** *n.* **a)** *(language)* Irisch, *das; see also* **English 2 a; b)** *constr. as pl.* **the ~:** die Iren

Irish: ~man [ˈaɪərɪʃmən] *n., pl.* **~men** [ˈaɪərɪʃmən] Ire, *der;* **~ Reˈpublic** *pr. n.* Irische Republik; **~ ˈSea** *pr. n.* Irische See; **~woman** *n.* Irin, *die*

irk [ɜːk] *v. t.* ärgern. **irksome** [ˈɜːksəm] *adj.* lästig

iron [ˈaɪən] **1.** *n.* **a)** *(metal)* Eisen, *das;* **b)** *(for smoothing)* Bügeleisen, *das.* **2.** *attrib. adj.* eisern; Eisen⟨*platte usw.*⟩.

3. *v. t. & i.* bügeln. **iron 'out** *v. t.* herausbügeln; *(fig.)* aus dem Weg räumen

Iron 'Curtain *n.* *(Hist.)* Eiserner Vorhang

ironic [aɪ'rɒnɪk], **ironical** [aɪ'rɒnɪkl] *adj.* ironisch

ironing ['aɪənɪŋ] *n.* Bügeln, *das;* *(items)* Bügelwäsche, *die;* **do the ~:** bügeln. **'ironing-board** *n.* Bügelbrett, *das*

ironmonger ['aɪənmʌŋgə(r)] *n.* *(Brit.)* Eisenwarenhändler, *der/*-händlerin, *die*

irony ['aɪrənɪ] *n.* Ironie, *die;* **the ~ was that …:** die Ironie lag darin, daß …

irradiate [ɪ'reɪdɪeɪt] *v. t.* bestrahlen

irrational [ɪ'ræʃənl] *adj.* irrational

irreconcilable [ɪ'rekənsaɪləbl] *adj.* *(incompatible)* unvereinbar

irrefutable [ɪrɪ'fjuːtəbl] *adj.* unwiderlegbar

irregular [ɪ'regjʊlə(r)] *adj.* unregelmäßig; unkorrekt ⟨*Verhalten, Handlung usw.*⟩. **irregularity** [ɪregjʊ'lærɪtɪ] *n.* *see* **irregular:** Unregelmäßigkeit, *die;* Unkorrektheit, *die*

irrelevant [ɪ'relɪvənt] *adj.* belanglos; irrelevant *(geh.)*

irreparable [ɪ'repərəbl] *adj.* nicht wiedergutzumachend *nicht präd.;* irreparabel *(geh., Med.)*

irreplaceable [ɪrɪ'pleɪsəbl] *adj.* unersetzlich

irrepressible [ɪrɪ'presɪbl] *adj.* nicht zu unterdrücken *nicht präd.;* **she is ~:** sie ist nicht unterzukriegen *(ugs.)*

irreproachable [ɪrɪ'prəʊtʃəbl] *adj.* untadelig

irresistible [ɪrɪ'zɪstɪbl] *adj.* unwiderstehlich; bestechend ⟨*Argument*⟩

irresolute [ɪ'rezəluːt] *adj.* unentschlossen

irrespective [ɪrɪ'spektɪv] *adj.* **~ of** ungeachtet (+ *Gen.*)

irresponsible [ɪrɪ'spɒnsɪbl] *adj.* verantwortungslos ⟨*Person*⟩; unverantwortlich ⟨*Benehmen*⟩

irretrievable [ɪrɪ'triːvəbl] *adj.* nicht mehr wiederzubekommen *nicht attr.*

irreverent [ɪ'revərənt] *adj.* respektlos

irreversible [ɪrɪ'vɜːsɪbl], **irrevocable** [ɪ'revəkəbl] *adjs.* unwiderruflich

irrigate ['ɪrɪgeɪt] *v. t.* bewässern. **irrigation** [ɪrɪ'geɪʃn] *n.* Bewässerung, *die*

irritable ['ɪrɪtəbl] *adj.* *(quick to anger)* reizbar; *(temporarily)* gereizt

irritant ['ɪrɪtənt] *n.* Reizstoff, *der*

irritate ['ɪrɪteɪt] *v. t.* **a)** ärgern; **get ~d** ärgerlich werden; **be ~d by sth.** sich über etw. *(Akk.)* ärgern; **b)** *(Med.)* reizen. **irritating** ['ɪrɪteɪtɪŋ] *adj.* lästig. **irritation** [ɪrɪ'teɪʃn] *n.* **a)** Ärger, *der;* **b)** *(Med.)* Reizung, *die*

is *see* **be**

Islam ['ɪzlɑːm] *n.* Islam, *der*

island ['aɪlənd] *n.* Insel, *die.* **'islander** *n.* Inselbewohner, *der/*-bewohnerin, *die*

isle [aɪl] *n.* Insel, *die*

isn't ['ɪznt] *(coll.)* = **is not;** *see* **be**

isolate ['aɪsəleɪt] *v. t.* isolieren. **isolated** ['aɪsəleɪtɪd] *adj.* **a)** *(single)* einzeln; ~ **cases/instances** Einzelfälle; **b)** *(remote)* abgelegen. **isolation** [aɪsə'leɪʃn] *n.* **a)** *(act)* Isolierung, *die;* **b)** *(state)* Isolation, *die*

Israel ['ɪzreɪl] *pr. n.* Israel *(das).* **Israeli** [ɪz'reɪlɪ] **1.** *adj.* israelisch. **2.** *n.* Israeli, *der/die*

issue ['ɪʃuː, 'ɪsjuː] **1.** *n.* **a)** *(point in question)* Frage, *die;* **make an ~ of sth.** etw. aufbauschen; **evade** *or* **dodge the ~:** ausweichen; **b)** *(of magazine etc.)* Ausgabe, *die;* **c)** *(result, outcome)* Ergebnis, *das.* **2.** *v. t.* **a)** *(give out)* ausgeben; ausstellen ⟨*Paß*⟩; erteilen ⟨*Lizenz, Befehl*⟩; ~ **sb. with sth.** etw. an jmdn. austeilen; **b)** *(publish)* herausgeben ⟨*Publikation*⟩

it [ɪt] *pron.* **a)** es; **I can't cope with it any more** ich halte das nicht mehr länger aus; **what is it?** was ist los?; **b)** *(the thing, animal, young child previously mentioned)* er/sie/es; *as direct obj.* ihn/sie/es; *as indirect obj.* ihm/ihr/ihm; **c)** *(the person in question)* **who is it?** wer ist da?; **it was the children** es waren die Kinder; **is it you, Dad?** bist du es, Vater?

Italian [ɪ'tæljən] **1.** *adj.* italienisch; **sb. is ~:** jmd. ist Italiener/Italienerin. **2.** *n.* **a)** *(person)* Italiener, *der/*Italienerin, *die;* **b)** *(language)* Italienisch, *das; see also* **English 2 a**

italic [ɪ'tælɪk] **1.** *adj.* kursiv. **2.** *n.* *in pl.* Kursivschrift, *die;* **in ~s** kursiv

Italy ['ɪtəlɪ] *pr. n.* Italien *(das)*

itch [ɪtʃ] **1.** *n.* Juckreiz, *der;* **I have an ~:** es juckt mich. **2.** *v. i.* **a)** einen Juckreiz haben; **it ~es** es juckt; **b)** ~ *or* **be ~ing to do sth.** darauf brennen, etw. zu tun. **'itchy** *adj.* kratzig; **be ~:** ⟨*Körperteil:*⟩ jucken

it'd ['ɪtəd] *(coll.)* **a)** = **it had; b)** = **it would**

item ['aɪtəm] *n.* **a)** Ding, *das;* Sache, *die; (in shop, catalogue)* Artikel, *der;*

(on radio, TV) Nummer, *die;* ~ **of
clothing** Kleidungsstück, *das;* **b)** ~ |of
news| Nachricht, *die.* **itemize** ['aɪtə-
maɪz] *v.t.* einzeln aufführen

itinerary [aɪ'tɪnərərɪ] *n.* Reiseroute,
die

it'll [ɪtl] *(coll.)* = it will

its [ɪts] *poss. pron. attrib.* sein/ihr/sein

it's [ɪts] **a)** = it is; **b)** = it has

itself [ɪt'self] *pron.* **a)** *emphat.* selbst;
b) *refl.* sich

I've [aɪv] = I have

ivory ['aɪvərɪ] *n.* Elfenbein, *das; attrib.*
elfenbeinern; Elfenbein-

ivy ['aɪvɪ] *n.* Efeu, *der*

J

J, j [dʒeɪ] *n.* J, j, *das*

jab [dʒæb] **1.** *v.t.,* **-bb-** stoßen. **2.** *n.* **a)**
Stoß, *der; (with needle)* Stich, *der;* **b)**
(Brit. coll.: injection) Spritze, *die*

jabber ['dʒæbə(r)] *v.i.* plappern *(ugs.)*

jack [dʒæk] *n.* **a)** *(for car)* Wagenhe-
ber, *der;* **b)** *(Cards)* Bube, *der*

jackal ['dʒækl] *n.* Schakal, *der*

jackdaw ['dʒækdɔː] *n.* Dohle, *die*

jacket ['dʒækɪt] *n.* **a)** Jacke, *die; (of
suit)* Jackett, *das; sports* ~: Sakko,
der; **b)** *(of book)* Schutzumschlag, *der;*
c) ~ **potatoes** in der Schale gebackene
Kartoffeln

'jackpot *n.* Jackpot, *der;* **hit the** ~
(fig.) das große Los ziehen

jaded ['dʒeɪdɪd] *adj.* abgespannt

jagged ['dʒægɪd] *adj.* gezackt

jaguar ['dʒægjʊə(r)] *n.* Jaguar, *der*

jail [dʒeɪl] **1.** *n.* Gefängnis, *das.* **2.** *v.t.*
ins Gefängnis bringen. **'jailbreak** *n.*
Gefängnisausbruch, *der.* **jailer,
jailor** ['dʒeɪlə(r)] *n.* Gefängniswärter,
*der/-*wärterin, *die*

'jam [dʒæm] **1.** *v.t.,* **-mm-:** **a)** *(between
two surfaces)* einklemmen; **b)** *(make
immovable)* blockieren; *(fig.)* lähmen.
2. *v.i.,* **-mm-:** **a)** *(become wedged)* sich
verklemmen; **b)** ⟨*Maschine:*⟩ klem-
men. **3.** *n.* **a)** *(crush, stoppage)*
Blockierung, *die;* **b)** *(coll.: dilemma)*
be in a ~: in der Klemme stecken

(ugs.). **jam 'on** *v.t.* ~ **the brakes |full|
on** [voll] auf die Bremse steigen *(ugs.)*

²jam *n.* Marmelade, *die*

Jamaica [dʒə'meɪkə] *pr. n.* Jamaika
(das)

Jan. *abbr.* **January** Jan.

jangle ['dʒæŋgl] **1.** *v.i.* klimpern;
⟨*Klingel:*⟩ bimmeln. **2.** *v.t.* rasseln mit

janitor ['dʒænɪtə(r)] *n.* Hausmeister,
der

January ['dʒænjʊərɪ] *n.* Januar, *der;
see also* **August**

Japan [dʒə'pæn] *n.* Japan *(das).* **Jap-
anese** [dʒæpə'niːz] **1.** *adj.* japanisch.
2. *n., pl. same* **a)** *(person)* Japaner,
*der/*Japanerin, *die;* **b)** *(language)* Japanisch, *das; see also* **English 2 a**

'jar [dʒɑː(r)] **1.** *v.i.,* **-rr-** quietschen;
(fig.) ~ **on sb./sb.'s nerves** jmdm. auf
die Nerven gehen. **2.** *v.t.,* **-rr-** erschüttern

²jar *n.* Topf, *der; (glass* ~*)* Glas, *das*

jargon ['dʒɑːgən] *n.* Jargon, *der*

jasmin[e] ['dʒæsmɪn] *n.* Jasmin, *der*

jaundice ['dʒɔːndɪs] *n. (Med.)* Gelb-
sucht, *die.* **jaundiced** ['dʒɔːndɪst] *adj.
(fig.)* verbittert

jaunt [dʒɔːnt] *n.* Ausflug, *der*

javelin ['dʒævlɪn] *n.* **a)** Speer, *der;* **b)**
(Sport: event) Speerwerfen, *das*

jaw [dʒɔː] *n.* Kiefer, *der.* **'jawbone** *n.*
Kieferknochen, *der*

jay [dʒeɪ] *n.* Eichelhäher, *der*

jazz [dʒæz] **1.** *n.* Jazz, *der; attrib.* Jazz-.
2. *v.t.* ~ **up** aufpeppen *(ugs.)*

jealous ['dʒeləs] *adj.* eifersüchtig **(of**
auf + *Akk.*). **'jealousy** *n.* Eifersucht,
die

jeans [dʒiːnz] *n. pl.* Jeans *Pl.*

jeer [dʒɪə(r)] *v.i.* höhnen *(geh.);* ~ **at**
sb. jmdn. verhöhnen

jelly ['dʒelɪ] *n.* Gelee, *das; (dessert)*
Götterspeise, *die.* **'jellyfish** *n.* Qualle, *die*

jeopardize ['dʒepədaɪz] *v.t.* gefährden

jeopardy ['dʒepədɪ] *n.* **in** ~: in Gefahr; gefährdet

jerk [dʒɜːk] **1.** *n.* Ruck, *der.* **2.** *v.t.* reißen an (+ *Dat.*). **3.** *v.i.* zucken

jersey ['dʒɜːzɪ] *n.* Pullover, *der;
(Sport)* Trikot, *das*

jest [dʒest] **1.** *n.* Scherz, *der;* **in** ~: im
Scherz. **2.** *v.i.* scherzen

Jesus ['dʒiːzəs] *pr. n.* Jesus *(der)*

jet [dʒet] *n.* **a)** *(stream)* Strahl, *der;* **b)**
(nozzle) Düse, *die;* **c)** *(aircraft)* Düsen-
flugzeug, *das;* Jet, *der*

jet: ~**-black** *adj.* pechschwarz; ~ **en-**

gine n. Düsentriebwerk, das; ~ **lag** n. Jet-travel-Syndrom, das; ~- **propelled** adj. düsengetrieben
jetsam ['dʒetsəm] n. see **flotsam**
'**jet-set** n. Jet-set, der
jettison ['dʒetɪsən] v.t. über Bord werfen; (discard) wegwerfen
jetty ['dʒetɪ] n. Landungsbrücke, die
Jew [dʒuː] n. Jude, der/Jüdin, die
jewel ['dʒuːəl] n. Juwel, das od. der. **jeweller** (Amer.: **jeweler**) ['dʒuːələ(r)] n. Juwelier, der. **jewellery** (Brit.), **jewelry** ['dʒuːəlrɪ] n. Schmuck, der
Jewish ['dʒuːɪʃ] adj. jüdisch
jib [dʒɪb] v.i., -bb- sich sträuben (**at** gegen)
jibe see **gibe**
jiffy ['dʒɪfɪ] n. (coll.) **in a ~:** sofort
jig [dʒɪg] n. Jig, die
'**jigsaw** n. ~ |**puzzle**| Puzzle, das
jilt [dʒɪlt] v.t. sitzenlassen (ugs.)
jingle ['dʒɪŋgl] 1. n. (Commerc.) Werbespruch, der. 2. v.i. klimpern; ⟨Glöckchen:⟩ bimmeln. 3. v.t. klimpern mit ⟨Münzen, Schlüsseln⟩
jinx [dʒɪŋks] (coll.) 1. n. Fluch, der. 2. v.t. verhexen
jitters ['dʒɪtəz] n. pl. (coll.) großes Zittern. **jittery** ['dʒɪtərɪ] adj. (coll.) (nervous) nervös; (frightened) verängstigt
job [dʒɒb] n. **a)** (piece of work) Arbeit, die; **I have a ~ for you** ich habe eine Aufgabe für dich; **b)** (employment) Stelle, die; Job, der (ugs.). '**job-centre** n. (Brit.) Arbeitsvermittlungsstelle, die. '**jobless** adj. arbeitslos
jockey ['dʒɒkɪ] n. Jockei, der
jocular ['dʒɒkjʊlə(r)] adj. lustig
jodhpurs ['dʒɒdpəz] n. pl. Reithose, die
jog [dʒɒg] 1. v.t., -gg-: **a)** (shake) rütteln; **b)** (nudge) [an]stoßen; **c)** ~ **sb.'s memory** jmds. Gedächtnis (Dat.) auf die Sprünge helfen. 2. v.i., -gg-: **a)** (up and down) auf und ab hüpfen; **b)** (trot) ⟨Pferd:⟩ [dahin]trotten; **c)** (Sport) joggen. 3. n. **go for a ~:** joggen gehen. '**jogging** n. Jogging, das
join [dʒɔɪn] 1. v.t. **a)** (connect) verbinden (**to** mit); **b)** (come into company of) sich gesellen zu; **c)** eintreten in (+ Akk.) ⟨Armee, Firma, Verein, Partei⟩. 2. v.i. ⟨Straßen:⟩ zusammenlaufen. **join in** 1. [-'-] v.i. mitmachen (**with** bei). 2. ['--] v.t. mitmachen bei. **join up** 1. v.i. (Mil.) einrücken. 2. v.t. miteinander verbinden
'**joiner** n. Tischler, der/Tischlerin, die

joint [dʒɔɪnt] 1. n. **a)** (Building) Fuge, die; **b)** (Anat.) Gelenk, das; **c) a ~** |**of meat**| ein Stück Fleisch; (for roasting) ein Braten; **d)** (sl.: place) Laden, der. 2. adj. **a)** (of two or more) gemeinsam; **b)** Mit⟨autor, -erbe, -besitzer⟩. '**jointly** adv. gemeinsam
joist [dʒɔɪst] n. (Building) Deckenbalken, der; (steel) [Decken]träger, der
joke [dʒəʊk] 1. n. Witz, der; Scherz, der. 2. v.i. scherzen, Witze machen (**about** über + Akk.); **joking apart** Scherz beiseite! '**joker** n. **a)** Spaßvogel, der; **b)** (Cards) Joker, der
jollity ['dʒɒlɪtɪ] n. Fröhlichkeit, die; (merry-making) Festlichkeit, die
jolly ['dʒɒlɪ] 1. adj. fröhlich. 2. adv. (Brit. coll.) ganz schön (ugs.); ~ **good!** ausgezeichnet!
jolt [dʒəʊlt] 1. v.t. ⟨Fahrzeug:⟩ durchrütteln. 2. v.i. ⟨Fahrzeug:⟩ holpern. 3. n. **a)** (jerk) Stoß, der; Ruck, der; **b)** (fig.: shock) Schock, der
Jordan ['dʒɔːdn] pr.n. Jordanien (das)
jostle ['dʒɒsl] 1. v.i. ~ |**against each other**| aneinanderstoßen. 2. v.t. stoßen
jot [dʒɒt] n. |**not**| **a ~:** [k]ein bißchen. **jot 'down** v.t. [rasch] aufschreiben
jotter ['dʒɒtə(r)] n. Notizblock, der
journal ['dʒɜːnl] n. Zeitschrift, die
journalism ['dʒɜːnəlɪzm] n. Journalismus, der. **journalist** ['dʒɜːnəlɪst] n. Journalist, der/Journalistin, die
journey ['dʒɜːnɪ] n. **a)** Reise, die; **b)** (of vehicle) Fahrt, die
jovial ['dʒəʊvɪəl] adj. herzlich ⟨Gruß⟩; fröhlich ⟨Person⟩
joy [dʒɔɪ] n. Freude, die. **joyful** ['dʒɔɪfl] adj. froh[gestimmt] ⟨Person⟩; freudig ⟨Blick, Ereignis, Gesang⟩. **joyride** n. (coll.) Spritztour, die
JP abbr. Justice of the Peace
jubilant ['dʒuːbɪlənt] adj. jubelnd; **be** ~ ⟨Person:⟩ frohlocken. **jubilation** [dʒuːbɪ'leɪʃn] n. Jubel, der
jubilee ['dʒuːbɪliː] n. Jubiläum, das
judge [dʒʌdʒ] 1. n. **a)** Richter, der/Richterin, die; **b)** (in contest) Preisrichter, der/-richterin, die; **c)** (fig.: critic) Kenner, der/Kennerin, die. 2. v.t. **a)** (sentence) richten (geh.); **b)** (form opinion about) [be]urteilen. '**judg[e]ment** n. **a)** Urteil, das; **b)** (critical faculty) Urteilsvermögen, das
judicial [dʒuː'dɪʃl] adj. gerichtlich
judicious [dʒuː'dɪʃəs] adj. klarblickend
judo ['dʒuːdəʊ] n. Judo, das

jug [dʒʌg] *n.* Krug, *der; (with lid, water-~)* Kanne, *die*

juggernaut ['dʒʌgənɔːt] *n. (Brit.: lorry)* schwerer Brummer *(ugs.)*

juggle ['dʒʌgl] *v. i.* jonglieren. **juggler** ['dʒʌglə(r)] *n.* Jongleur, *der/*Jongleuse, *die*

juice [dʒuːs] *n.* Saft, *der.* **juicy** ['dʒuː-sɪ] *adj.* saftig

juke-box ['dʒuːkbɒks] *n.* Jukebox, *die;* Musikbox, *die*

Jul. *abbr.* July Jul.

July [dʒʊ'laɪ] *n.* Juli, *der; see also* August

jumble ['dʒʌmbl] **1.** *v. t.* ~ up durcheinanderbringen. **2.** *n.* Durcheinander, *das.* 'jumble sale *n. (Brit.)* Trödelmarkt, *der*

jumbo jet [dʒʌmbəʊ 'dʒet] *n.* Jumbo-Jet, *der*

jump [dʒʌmp] **1.** *n.* **a)** Sprung, *der;* **b)** *(in prices)* sprunghafter Anstieg. **2.** *v. i.* **a)** springen; ~ for joy einen Freudensprung machen; **b)** ~ to conclusions voreilige Schlüsse ziehen. **3.** *v. t.* **a)** überspringen; **b)** ~ the queue *(Brit.)* sich vordrängeln. **jump a'bout, jump a'round** *v. i.* herumspringen *(ugs.).* 'jump at *v. t. (fig.)* sofort zugreifen bei ⟨*Angebot, Gelegenheit*⟩ 'jumper *n.* Pullover, *der*

jumpy ['dʒʌmpɪ] *adj.* nervös

Jun. *abbr.* June Jun.

junction ['dʒʌŋkʃn] *n.* **a)** *(of railway lines, roads)* ≈ Einmündung, *die;* **b)** *(crossroads)* Kreuzung, *die*

juncture ['dʒʌŋktʃə(r)] *n.* at this ~: zu diesem Zeitpunkt

June [dʒuːn] *n.* Juni, *der; see also* August

jungle ['dʒʌŋgl] *n.* Dschungel, *der*

junior ['dʒuːnɪə(r)] *adj.* **a)** *(in age)* jünger; ~ team *(Sport)* Juniorenmannschaft, *die;* **b)** *(in rank)* rangniedriger ⟨*Person*⟩; niedriger ⟨*Rang*⟩. 'junior school *n. (Brit.)* Grundschule, *die*

junk [dʒʌŋk] *n.* Trödel, *der (ugs.); (trash)* Ramsch, *der (ugs.).* 'junk food *n.* minderwertige Kost. 'junk shop *n.* Trödelladen, *der (ugs.)*

Jupiter ['dʒuːpɪtə(r)] *pr. n. (Astron.)* Jupiter, *der*

jurisdiction [dʒʊərɪs'dɪkʃn] *n.* Gerichtsbarkeit, *die*

juror ['dʒʊərə(r)] *n.* Geschworene, *der/ die*

jury ['dʒʊərɪ] *n.* **a)** *(in court)* the ~: die Geschworenen; **b)** *(in competition)* Jury, *die*

just [dʒʌst] **1.** *adj. (morally right)* gerecht. **2.** *adv.* **a)** *(exactly)* genau; ~ then/enough gerade da/genug; ~ as *(exactly as)* genauso wie; *(when)* gerade, als; ~ as you like *or* please ganz wie Sie wünschen/du magst; ~ as good *etc.* genauso gut *usw.;* **b)** *(barely)* gerade [eben]; *(with little time to spare)* gerade noch; *(no more than)* nur; ~ under £10 nicht ganz zehn Pfund; **c)** *(at this moment)* gerade; not ~ now im Moment nicht; **d)** *(coll.) (simply)* einfach; *(only)* nur; *esp. with imper.* mal [eben]; ~ look at that! guck dir das mal an!; ~ a moment einen Moment mal; ~ in case für alle Fälle

justice ['dʒʌstɪs] *n.* **a)** Gerechtigkeit, *die;* **b)** *(magistrate)* Schiedsrichter, *der/*-richterin, *die;* J~ of the Peace Friedensrichter, *der/*-richterin, *die*

justifiable [dʒʌstɪ'faɪəbl] *adj.* berechtigt. **justifiably** [dʒʌstɪ'faɪəblɪ] *adv.* zu Recht

justification [dʒʌstɪfɪ'keɪʃn] *n.* Rechtfertigung, *die*

justify ['dʒʌstɪfaɪ] *v. t.* rechtfertigen; be justified in doing sth. etw. zu Recht tun

jut [dʒʌt] *v. i., -tt-:* ~ [out] [her]vorragen; herausragen

juvenile ['dʒuːvənaɪl] **1.** *adj.* **a)** jugendlich; **b)** *(immature)* kindisch. **2.** *n.* Jugendliche, *der/die.* **juvenile delinquency** [~ dɪ'lɪŋkwənsɪ] *n.* Jugendkriminalität, *die.* **juvenile delinquent** [~ dɪ'lɪŋkwənt] *n.* jugendlicher Straftäter/jugendliche Straftäterin

juxtapose [dʒʌkstə'pəʊz] *v. t.* nebeneinanderstellen (with, to und). **juxtaposition** [dʒʌkstəpə'zɪʃn] *n.* Nebeneinanderstellung, *die*

K

K, k [keɪ] *n.* K, k, *das*

kaleidoscope [kə'laɪdəskəʊp] *n.* Kaleidoskop, *das*

kangaroo [kæŋgə'ruː] *n.* Känguruh, *das*

karate [kɔ'rɑːtɪ] *n.* Karate, *das*
keel [kiːl] *n. (Naut.)* Kiel, *der*
keen [kiːn] *adj.* **a)** *(sharp)* scharf; **b)**
(cold) schneidend ⟨*Wind, Kälte*⟩; **c)**
(eager) begeistert ⟨*Fußballfan, Sportler*⟩; lebhaft ⟨*Interesse*⟩; **be ~ to do
sth.** darauf erpicht sein, etw. zu tun;
d) *(sensitive)* scharf ⟨*Augen*⟩; fein
⟨*Sinne*⟩. **'keenly** *adv.* **a)** *(sharply)*
scharf; **b)** *(eagerly)* eifrig; brennend
⟨*interessiert sein*⟩; **c)** *(acutely)* **be ~
aware of sth.** sich *(Dat.)* einer Sache
(Gen.) voll bewußt sein
keep [kiːp] **1.** *v. t.*, **kept** [kept] **a)** halten
⟨*Versprechen, Schwur, Sabbat, Fa-
sten*⟩; einhalten ⟨*Verabredung, Vereinbarung*⟩; begehen, feiern ⟨*Fest*⟩;
b) *(have charge of)* aufbewahren; **c)**
(retain) behalten; *(not lose or destroy)*
aufheben ⟨*Quittung, Rechnung*⟩; **d)**
halten ⟨*Bienen, Hund usw*⟩; **e)** führen
⟨*Tagebuch, Geschäft, Ware*⟩; **f)** *(support)* versorgen ⟨*Familie*⟩; **g)** *(detain)*
festhalten; **~ sb. waiting** jmdn. warten
lassen; **what kept you?** wo bleibst du
denn?; **h)** *(reserve)* aufheben. **2.** *v. i.*,
kept a) *(remain)* bleiben; **are you ~ing
well?** geht's dir gut?; **b) ~ [to the] left/
right** sich links/rechts halten; **~ doing
sth.** *(repeatedly)* etw. immer wieder
tun; **~ talking/working** *etc.* **until ...:**
weiterreden/-arbeiten *usw.*, bis ...; **c)**
(remain good)⟨*Lebensmittel:*⟩ sich halten. **3.** *n.* **a)** *(maintenance)* Unterhalt,
der; **b) for ~s** *(coll.)* auf Dauer; **c)**
(Hist.: tower) Bergfried, *der.* **keep
'back 1.** *v. i.* zurückbleiben. **2.** *v. t.* **a)**
(restrain) zurückhalten ⟨*Menschen-
menge, Tränen*⟩; **b)** *(withhold)* verschweigen ⟨*Informationen, Tatsachen*⟩ **(from** *Dat.*). **keep 'down 1.**
v. i. unten bleiben. **2.** *v. t.* **a)** niedrig
halten ⟨*Steuern, Preise usw.*⟩; **keep
one's weight down** nicht zunehmen; **b)
keep your voice down!** rede nicht so
laut! **keep 'off 1.** *v. i.* ⟨*Person:*⟩ wegbleiben. **2.** *v. t.* fernhalten; **'keep off
the grass'** „Betreten des Rasens verboten". **keep 'out 1.** *v. i.* **'keep out'** „Zutritt verboten". **2.** *v. t.* nicht hereinlas-
sen. **keep 'up 1.** *v. i.* **keep up with sb./
sth.** mit jmdm./etw. Schritt halten. **2.**
v. t. aufrechterhalten ⟨*Freundschaft,
jmds. Moral*⟩; **keep one's strength up**
sich bei Kräften halten; **keep it up!**
weiter so!
keep-'fit *n.* Fitneßtraining, *das*
'keeping *n.* **be in ~ with sth.** einer Sache *(Dat.)* entsprechen

'keepsake *n.* Andenken, *das*
keg [keg] *n.* [kleines] Faß
kennel ['kenl] *n.* Hundehütte, *die*
Kenya ['kenjə] *pr. n.* Kenia *(das)*
kept *see* **keep 1, 2**
kerb [kɜːb], **'kerbstone** *ns. (Brit.)*
Bordstein, *der*
kernel ['kɜːnl] *n.* Kern, *der*
ketchup ['ketʃʌp] *n.* Ketchup, *der od.
das*
kettle ['ketl] *n.* [Wasser]kessel, *der*
key [kiː] *n.* **a)** Schlüssel, *der;* **b)** *(on
piano, typewriter, etc.)* Taste, *die;* **c)**
(Mus.) Tonart, *die*
key: ~board *n. (of piano etc.)* Klavia-
tur, *die; (of typewriter etc.)* Tastatur,
die; **~hole** *n.* Schlüsselloch, *das;*
~ring *n.* Schlüsselring, *der*
kg. *abbr.* **kilogram[s]** kg
khaki ['kɑːkɪ] **1.** *adj.* khakifarben. **2.** *n.*
(cloth) Khaki, *der*
kick [kɪk] **1.** *n.* **a)** [Fuß]tritt, *der;*
(Footb.) Schuß, *der;* **give sb. a ~:**
jmdm. einen Tritt geben; **b)** *(coll.:
thrill)* **do sth. for ~s** etw. zum Spaß
tun; **he gets a ~ out of it** er hat Spaß
daran. **2.** *v. i.* treten; ⟨*Pferd:*⟩ ausschlagen. **3.** *v. t.* einen Tritt geben
(+ Dat.) ⟨*Person, Hund*⟩; treten gegen ⟨*Gegenstand*⟩; kicken *(ugs.),*
schießen ⟨*Ball*⟩. **kick a'bout, kick
a'round** *v. t.* [in der Gegend] herum-
kicken *(ugs.).* **kick 'off** *v. i. (Footb.)*
anstoßen. **kick 'up** *v. t. (coll.)* **~ up a
fuss/row** Krach schlagen/anfangen
(ugs.)
kid [kɪd] **1.** *n.* **a)** *(young goat)* Kitz, *das;*
b) *(coll.: child)* Kind, *das.* **2.** *v. t.,* **-dd-**
(coll.) auf den Arm nehmen *(ugs.);* **~
oneself** sich *(Dat.)* was vormachen
kidnap ['kɪdnæp] *v. t., (Brit.)* **-pp-** entführen. **'kidnapper** *n.* Entführer,
*der/*Entführerin, *die*
kidney ['kɪdnɪ] *n.* Niere, *die.* **'kidney
machine** *n.* künstliche Niere
kill [kɪl] *v. t.* **a)** töten; *(deliberately)* um-
bringen; **be ~ed in action** im Kampf
fallen; **be ~ed in a car crash** bei einem
Autounfall ums Leben kommen; **b) ~
time** die Zeit totschlagen. **'killer** *n.*
Mörder, *der/*Mörderin, *die.* **'killing**
n. **a)** Töten, *das;* **b) make a ~** *(coll.:
great profit)* einen [Mords]reibach machen *(ugs.).* **'killjoy** *n.* Spielverder-
ber, *der/*-verderberin, *die*
kiln [kɪln] *n.* Brennofen, *der*
kilo ['kiːləʊ] *n., pl.* **~s** Kilo, *das*
kilogram, kilogramme ['kɪləgræm]
n. Kilogramm, *das*

kilometre (*Brit.; Amer.:* **kilometer**) ['kɪləmi:tə(r) (*Brit.*), kɪ'lɒmɪtə(r)] *n.* Kilometer, *der*

kilowatt *n.* ['kɪləwɒt] Kilowatt, *das*

kilt [kɪlt] *n.* Kilt, *der*

kin [kɪn] *n.* Verwandte

¹kind [kaɪnd] *n.* **a)** *(class, sort)* Art, *die;* **several ~s of apples** mehrere Sorten Äpfel; **all ~s of things/excuses** alles mögliche/alle möglichen Ausreden; **no ... of any ~:** keinerlei ...; **what ~ is it?** was für einer/eine/eins ist es?; **what ~ of [a] tree is this?** was für ein Baum ist das?; **b)** *(implying vagueness)* **a ~ of ...:** [so] eine Art ...; **~ of cute** *(coll.)* irgendwie niedlich *(ugs.)*

²kind *adj.* liebenswürdig; *(showing friendliness)* freundlich; **be ~ to animals** gut zu Tieren sein; **how ~!** wie nett [von ihm/Ihnen *usw.*]!

kindergarten ['kɪndəgɑːtn] *n.* Kindergarten, *der*

kindle ['kɪndl] *(fig.)* wecken

kindly ['kaɪndlɪ] **1.** *adv.* **a)** freundlich; nett; **b)** *in polite request etc.* freundlicherweise; **thank you ~:** herzlichen Dank. **2.** *adj.* freundlich; nett; *(kindhearted)* gütig

'**kindness** *n.* **a)** *no pl. (kind nature)* Freundlichkeit, *die;* **b) do sb. a ~** *(kind act)* jmdm. eine Gefälligkeit erweisen

kindred ['kɪndrɪd] *adj.* verwandt; **~ 'spirit** Gleichgesinnte, *der/die*

king [kɪŋ] *n.* König, *der.* **kingdom** ['kɪŋdəm] *n.* Königreich, *das*

'**kingfisher** *n.* Eisvogel, *der*

'**king-size[d]** *adj.* extragroß; King-size-⟨*Zigarette*⟩

kink [kɪŋk] *n. (in pipe, wire, etc.)* Knick, *der; (in hair, wool)* Welle, *die*

'**kinky** *adj. (coll.)* spleenig; *(sexually)* abartig

kiosk ['kiːɒsk] *n.* **a)** Kiosk, *der;* **b)** *(telephone booth)* [Telefon]zelle, *die*

kip [kɪp] *n. (Brit. sl.: sleep)* **have a/get some ~:** eine Runde pennen *(salopp)*

kipper ['kɪpə(r)] *n.* Kipper, *der*

kiss [kɪs] **1.** *n.* Kuß, *der.* **2.** *v.t.* küssen; **~ sb. good night/goodbye** jmdm. einen Gutenacht-/Abschiedskuß geben. **3.** *v.i.* **they ~ed** sie küßten sich

kit [kɪt] *n.* **a)** *(Brit.: set of items)* Set, *das;* **b)** *(Brit.: clothing etc.)* **sports ~:** Sportzeug, *das;* **riding-/skiing-~:** Reit-/Skiausrüstung, *die.* '**kitbag** *n.* Tornister, *der*

kitchen ['kɪtʃɪn] *n.* Küche, *die; attrib.* Küchen-. **kitchen 'sink** *n.* [Küchen]ausguß, *der*

kite [kaɪt] *n.* Drachen, *der*

kith [kɪθ] *n.* **~ and kin** Freunde und Verwandte

kitten ['kɪtn] *n.* Kätzchen, *das*

kitty ['kɪtɪ] *n. (money)* Kasse, *die*

kleptomania [kleptə'meɪnɪə] *n.* Kleptomanie, *die.* **kleptomaniac** [kleptə'meɪnɪæk] *n.* Kleptomane, *der/*Kleptomanin, *die*

km. *abbr.* **kilometre[s]** km

knack [næk] *n.* Talent, *das;* **get the ~ [of doing sth.]** den Bogen rauskriegen [, wie man etw. macht] *(ugs.);* **have lost the ~:** es nicht mehr zustande bringen

knapsack ['næpsæk] *n.* Rucksack, *der; (Mil.)* Tornister, *der*

knead [niːd] *v.t.* kneten

knee [niː] *n.* Knie, *das*

knee: ~cap *n.* Kniescheibe, *die;* **~-deep** *adj.* knietief; **~-high** *adj.* kniehoch; **~-jerk reaction** *n. (fig.)* automatische Reaktion; **~-joint** *n.* Kniegelenk, *das*

kneel [niːl] *v.i.,* **knelt** [nelt] *or (esp. Amer.)* **kneeled** knien; **~ down** niederknien

knelt *see* **kneel**

knew *see* **know**

knickers ['nɪkəz] *n. pl. (Brit.)* [Damen]schlüpfer, *der*

knife [naɪf] **1.** *n., pl.* **knives** [naɪvz] Messer, *das.* **2.** *v.t. (stab)* einstechen auf (+ *Akk.*); *(kill)* erstechen

knight [naɪt] *n.* **a)** *(Hist.)* Ritter, *der;* **b)** *(Chess)* Springer, *der.* '**knighthood** *n.* Ritterwürde, *die*

knit [nɪt] *v.t.,* **-tt-** stricken; **~ one's brow** die Stirn runzeln. '**knitting** *n.* Stricken, *das; (work being knitted)* Strickarbeit, *die.* '**knitting needle** *n.* Stricknadel, *die.* '**knitwear** *n.* Strickwaren *Pl.*

knives *pl. of* **knife** 1

knob [nɒb] *n.* **a)** *(on door, walking-stick, etc.)* Knauf, *der;* **b)** *(control on radio etc.)* Knopf, *der;* **c)** *(of butter)* Klümpchen, *das*

knock [nɒk] **1.** *v.t.* **a)** *(strike) (lightly)* klopfen an (+ *Akk.*); *(forcefully)* schlagen gegen *od.* an (+ *Akk.*); **~ a hole in sth.** ein Loch in etw. (+ *Akk.*) schlagen; **b)** *(sl.: criticize)* herziehen über (+ *Akk.*) *(ugs.).* **2.** *v.i.* klopfen (**at** an + *Akk.*). **3.** *n.* Klopfen, *das.* **knock 'down** *v.t.* **a)** *(in car)* umfahren; **b)** *(demolish)* abreißen. **knock 'off 1.** *v.t.* **a)** **~ off work** *(coll.: leave)* Feierabend machen; **b)** *(deduct)* **~ five pounds off the price** es fünf Pfund billiger machen; **c)** *(coll.: do quickly)* aus dem Ärmel schütteln *(ugs.);* **d)** *(sl.: steal)* klauen *(salopp).* **2.** *v. i. (coll.)* Feierabend machen. **knock 'out** *v. t.* **a)** *(make unconscious)* bewußtlos umfallen lassen; **b)** *(Boxing)* k. o. schlagen; **c)** *(sl.: exhaust)* kaputtmachen *(ugs.).* **knock 'over** *v. t.* umstoßen; ⟨*Fahrer, Fahrzeug:*⟩ umfahren ⟨*Person*⟩

'**knock-down** *adj.* ~ **prices** Schleuderpreise

'**knocker** *n.* [Tür]klopfer, *der*

knock: ~-**kneed** ['nɒkni:d] *adj.* X-beinig ⟨*Person*⟩; ~-**out** *n. (Boxing)* K.-o.-Schlag, *der*

knot [nɒt] **1.** *n.* Knoten, *der.* **2.** *v. t.,* -**tt**- knoten ⟨*Seil, Faden usw.*⟩

'**knotty** *adj. (fig.: puzzling)* verwickelt

know [nəʊ] *v. t.,* **knew** [nju:], **known** [nəʊn] **a)** *(recognize)* erkennen (**by** an + *Dat.,* **for** als + *Akk.*); **b)** *(be able to distinguish)* ~ **sth. from sth.** etw. von etw. unterscheiden können; **c)** *(be aware of)* wissen; **d)** *(have understanding of)* können ⟨*ABC, Einmaleins, Deutsch usw.*⟩; ~ **how to mend fuses** wissen, wie man Sicherungen repariert; ~ **how to drive a car** Auto fahren können; **e)** kennen ⟨*Person*⟩. '**know-all** *n.* Neunmalkluge, *der/die.* '**know-how** *n.* praktisches Wissen

'**knowing** *adj.* **a)** wissend ⟨*Blick, Lächeln*⟩; **b)** *(cunning)* verschlagen. '**knowingly** *adv.* **a)** *(intentionally)* wissentlich; **b)** vielsagend ⟨*lächeln, anblicken*⟩

knowledge ['nɒlɪdʒ] *n.* **a)** *(familiarity)* Kenntnisse (**of** in + *Dat.*); **b)** *(awareness)* Wissen, *das;* **have no** ~ **of sth.** nichts von etw. wissen; keine Kenntnis von etw. haben *(geh.);* **c)** |**a**| ~ **of languages/French** Sprach-/Französischkenntnisse *Pl.* **knowledgeable** ['nɒlɪdʒəbl] *adj.* **be** ~ **about** *or* **on sth.** viel über etw. *(Akk.)* wissen

known [nəʊn] **1.** *see* **know. 2.** *adj.* bekannt

knuckle ['nʌkl] *n.* [Finger]knöchel, *der*

Korea [kə'rɪə] *pr. n.* Korea *(das)*

kosher ['kəʊʃə(r)] *adj.* koscher

kudos ['kju:dɒs] *n. (coll.)* Prestige, *das*

kW *abbr.* **kilowatt|s|** kW

L

L, l [el] *n.* L, l, *das*

£ *abbr.* **pound|s|** £; **cost £5** 5 £ *od.* Pfund kosten

l. *abbr.* **litre|s|** l

lab [læb] *n. (coll.)* Labor, *das*

label ['leɪbl] **1.** *n.* Schildchen, *das; (on bottles, in clothes)* Etikett, *das; (tied/stuck to an object)* Anhänger/Aufkleber, *der.* **2.** *v. t., (Brit.)* -**ll**-: **a)** etikettieren; auszeichnen ⟨*Waren*⟩; *(write on)* beschriften; **b)** *(fig.)* ~ **sb./sth. |as| sth.** jmdn./etw. als etw. etikettieren

labor *(Amer.) see* **labour**

laboratory [lə'bɒrətərɪ] *n.* Labor[atorium], *das*

labored, laborer *(Amer.) see* **labour-**

laborious [lə'bɔ:rɪəs] *adj.* mühsam. **la'boriously** *adv.* mühevoll

labour ['leɪbə(r)] *(Brit.)* **1.** *n.* **a)** Arbeit, *die;* **b)** *(workers)* Arbeiterschaft, *die;* **immigrant** ~: ausländische Arbeitskräfte; **c)** **L**~, **the** ~ **Party** *(Polit.)* die Labour Party; **d)** *(childbirth)* Wehen *Pl.;* **be in** ~: in den Wehen liegen. **2.** *v. i.* hart arbeiten (**at, on** an + *Dat.*). **3.** *v. t.* ~ **the point** sich lange darüber verbreiten

laboured ['leɪbəd] *adj. (Brit.)* mühsam; schwerfällig ⟨*Stil*⟩; **his breathing was** ~: er atmete schwer

'**labourer** *n. (Brit.)* Arbeiter, *der*/Arbeiterin, *die*

'**labour-saving** *adj.* arbeit[s]sparend

labyrinth ['læbərɪnθ] *n.* Labyrinth, *das*

lace [leɪs] **1.** *n.* **a)** *(for shoe)* Schnürsenkel, *der;* **b)** *(fabric)* Spitze, *die; attrib.* Spitzen-. **2.** *v. t.* ~ |**up**| [zu]schnüren

lacerate ['læsəreɪt] *v. t.* aufreißen

'**lace-up 1.** *attrib. adj.* Schnür-. **2.** *n.* Schnürschuh/-stiefel, *der*

lack [læk] **1.** *n.* Mangel, *der* (**of** an + *Dat.*). **2.** *v. t.* **sb./sth.** ~**s sth.** jmdm./einer Sache fehlt es an etw. *(Dat.)*

lackey ['lækɪ] *n.* Lakai, *der*

'**lacking** *adj.* **be** ~: fehlen

laconic [lə'kɒnɪk] *adj.* lakonisch

lacquer ['lækə(r)] *n.* Lack, *der*
lacrosse [lə'krɒs] *n.* Lacrosse, *das*
lacy ['leɪsɪ] *adj.* Spitzen-
lad [læd] *n.* Junge, *der*
ladder ['lædə(r)] 1. *n.* **a)** Leiter, *die;* **b)** *(Brit.: in tights etc.)* Laufmasche, *die.* 2. *v.i. (Brit.)* Laufmaschen/eine Laufmasche bekommen. 3. *v.t. (Brit.)* Laufmaschen/eine Laufmasche machen in (+ *Akk.*)
laden ['leɪdn] beladen (**with** mit)
ladle ['leɪdl] *n.* Schöpfkelle, *die*
lady ['leɪdɪ] *n.* **a)** Dame, *die;* **~-in-waiting** *(Brit.)* Hofdame, *die;* **b)** '**Ladies**' *(WC)* „Damen"; **c)** *as form of address* **Ladies** meine Damen; **d)** *(Brit.) as title* L**~**: Lady
lady: ~bird, *(Amer.)* **~bug** *ns.* Marienkäfer, *der;* **~like** *adj.* damenhaft
¹lag [læg] *v.i.,* **-gg-:** ~ [**behind**] zurückbleiben; *(fig.)* im Rückstand sein
²lag *v.t.,* **-gg-** *(insulate)* isolieren
lager ['lɑːgə(r)] *n.* Lagerbier, *das*
lagging *n.* Isolierung, *die*
lagoon [lə'guːn] *n.* Lagune, *die*
laid *see* **²lay**
'**laid-back** *adj. (coll.)* gelassen
lain *see* **²lie**
lair [leə] *n. (of wild animal)* Unterschlupf, *der; (of pirates, bandits)* Schlupfwinkel, *der*
lake [leɪk] *n.* See, *der*
lamb [læm] *n.* **a)** Lamm, *das;* **b)** *(meat)* Lamm[fleisch], *das.* **lamb 'chop** *n.* Lammkotelett, *das.* **lamb's-wool** *n.* Lambswool, *die*
lame [leɪm] *adj.,* **'lamely** *adv.* lahm
lament [lə'ment] 1. *n.* Klage, *die* (**for** um). 2. *v.t.* ~ **that ...:** beklagen, daß ... 3. *v.i.* klagen *(geh.);* ~ **over sth.** etw. beklagen *(geh.)*. **lamentable** ['læməntəbl] *adj.* beklagenswert
laminated ['læmɪneɪtɪd] *adj.* lamelliert; ~ **glass** Verbundglas, *das*
lamp [læmp] *n.* Lampe, *die; (in street)* [Straßen]laterne, *die.* '**lamppost** *n.* Laternenpfahl, *der.* '**lampshade** *n.* Lampenschirm, *der*
lance [lɑːns] 1. *n.* Lanze, *die.* 2. *v.t. (Med.)* mit der Lanzette öffnen
lance-'corporal *n.* Obergefreite, *der*
land [lænd] 1. *n.* Land, *das;* **have or own ~:** Grundbesitz haben. 2. *v.t.* **a)** *(set ashore)* [an]landen; **b)** *(Aeronaut.)* landen; **c)** ~ **oneself in trouble** sich in Schwierigkeiten bringen; ~ **sb. with sth.,** ~ **sth. on sb.** jmdm. etw. aufhalsen *(ugs.)*. 3. *v.i.* **a)** ⟨*Boot usw.:*⟩ anlegen, landen; ⟨*Passagier:*⟩ aussteigen

(**from** aus); **we ~ed at Dieppe** wir gingen in Dieppe an Land; **b)** *(Aeronaut.)* landen; **c)** ~ **on one's feet** *(fig.)* [wieder] auf die Füße fallen. '**landed** *adj.* ~ **gentry/aristrocracy** Landadel, *der.*
'**landing** *n.* **a)** *(of ship, aircraft)* Landung, *die;* **b)** *(on stairs)* Treppenabsatz, *der; (passage)* Treppenflur, *der.* '**landing-card** *n.* Landekarte, *die.* '**landing-stage** *n.* Landesteg, *der*
land: ~lady *n.* **a)** *(of rented property)* Vermieterin, *die;* **b)** *(of public house)* [Gast]wirtin, *die;* **~-locked** *adj.* vom Land eingeschlossen ⟨*Bucht, Hafen*⟩; ⟨*Staat*⟩ ohne Zugang zum Meer; **~lord** *n.* **a)** *(of rented property)* Vermieter, *der;* **b)** *(of public house)* [Gast]wirt, *der;* **~mark** *n.* **a)** Orientierungspunkt, *der;* **b)** *(fig.)* Markstein, *der;* **~owner** *n.* Grundbesitzer, *der/*-besitzerin, *die;* **~scape** ['lændskeɪp] *n.* Landschaft, *die;* **~slide** *n.* Erdrutsch, *der*
lane [leɪn] *n.* **a)** *(in the country)* Landsträßchen, *das;* Weg, *der;* **b)** *(in town)* Gasse, *die;* **c)** *(part of road)* [Fahr]spur, *die;* '**get in ~**' „bitte einordnen"; **d)** *(Sport)* Bahn, *die*
language ['læŋgwɪdʒ] *n.* Sprache, *die; (style)* Ausdrucksweise, *die*
languid ['læŋgwɪd] *adj.* träge
languish ['læŋgwɪʃ] *v.i.* **a)** *(lose vitality)* ermatten *(geh.);* **b)** ~ **under sth.** unter etw. *(Dat.)* schmachten *(geh.)*
lank [læŋk] *adj.* **a)** hager; **b)** glatt herabhängend ⟨*Haar*⟩
lanky ['læŋkɪ] *adj.* schlaksig *(ugs.)*
lantern ['læntən] *n.* Laterne, *die*
¹lap [læp] *n. (part of body)* Schoß, *der*
²lap *n. (Sport)* Runde, *die*
³lap 1. *v.i.,* **-pp-** schlecken. 2. *v.t.,* **-pp-:** ~ [**up**] [auf]schlecken. **lap 'up** *v.t. (fig.)* schlucken
lapel [lə'pel] *n.* Revers, *das*
Lapland ['læplænd] *pr. n.* Lappland *(das)*
lapse [læps] 1. *n.* **a)** *(interval)* **a/the ~ of ...:** eine/die Zeitspanne von ...; **b)** *(mistake)* Fehler, *der;* ~ **of memory** Gedächtnislücke, *die.* 2. *v.i.* **a)** ⟨*Vertrag, usw.:*⟩ ungültig werden; **b)** ~ **into** verfallen in (+ *Akk.*)
larceny ['lɑːsənɪ] *n.* Diebstahl, *der*
lard [lɑːd] *n.* Schweineschmalz, *das*
larder ['lɑːdə(r)] *n.* Speisekammer, *die*
large [lɑːdʒ] 1. *adj.* groß. 2. *n.* **at ~** *(not in prison etc.)* auf freiem Fuß. 3. *adv. see* **by 2 d.** '**largely** *adv.* weitgehend
'**large-size[d]** *adj.* groß

¹lark [lɑːk] *n. (Ornith.)* Lerche, *die*

²lark *(coll.)* 1. *n.* Jux, *der (ugs.).* 2. *v. i.* ~ |**about** *or* **around**| herumalbern *(ugs.)*

larva ['lɑːvə] *n., pl.* ~**e** ['lɑːviː] Larve, *die*

laryngitis [lærɪn'dʒaɪtɪs] *n.* Kehlkopf-entzündung, *die*

larynx ['lærɪŋks] *n.* Kehlkopf, *der*

lascivious [lə'sɪvɪəs] *adj.* lüstern *(geh.)*

laser ['leɪzə(r)] *n.* Laser, *der.* '**laser beam** *n.* Laserstrahl, *der*

lash [læʃ] 1. *n.* **a)** *(stroke)* [Peit-schen]hieb, *der;* **b)** *(on eyelid)* Wim-per, *die.* 2. *v. i.* ⟨*Welle, Regen:*⟩ peit-schen (**against** gegen, **on** auf + *Akk.*). 3. *v. t.* **a)** *(fasten)* festbinden (**to** an + *Dat.*); **b)** *(as punishment)* auspeit-schen. **lash 'down** 1. *v. t.* festbinden. 2. *v. i.* ⟨*Regen:*⟩ niederprasseln. **lash 'out** *v. i.* **a)** *(hit out)* um sich schlagen; ~ **out at sb.** nach jmdm. schlagen; **b)** ~ **out on sth.** *(coll.: spend freely)* sich *(Dat.)* etw. leisten

lashings ['læʃɪŋz] *n. pl.* ~ **of sth.** Un-mengen von etw.

lass [læs] *n.* Mädchen, *das*

lasso [lə'suː] Lasso, *das*

¹last [lɑːst] 1. *adj.* letzt...; **be** ~ **to arrive** als letzter/letzte ankommen; ~ **night** gestern nacht. 2. *adv.* **a)** [ganz] zuletzt; als letzter/letzte ⟨*sprechen, ankom-men*⟩; **b)** *(on ~ previous occasion)* das letzte Mal; zuletzt. 3. *n.* **a)** *(person or thing)* letzter...; **b)** **at** |**long**| ~: endlich

²last *v. i.* **a)** *(continue)* dauern; ⟨*Wetter, Ärger:*⟩ anhalten; **b)** *(suffice)* reichen

last-ditch *adj.* ~ **attempt** letzter ver-zweifelter Versuch

'**lasting** *adj.* bleibend; dauerhaft ⟨*Be-ziehung*⟩; nachhaltig ⟨*Eindruck, Wir-kung*⟩

'**lastly** *adv.* schließlich

latch [lætʃ] *n.* Riegel, *der;* **on the** ~: nur eingeklinkt. **latch 'on to** *v. t. (coll.: understand)* kapieren *(ugs.)*

late [leɪt] 1. *adj.* **a)** spät; **am I** ~? kom-me ich zu spät?; **be** ~ **for the train** den Zug verpassen; **the train is** |**an hour**| ~: der Zug hat [eine Stunde] Verspätung; ~ **shift** Spätschicht, *die;* ~ **summer** Spätsommer, *der;* **b)** *(dead)* verstor-ben; **c)** *(former)* ehemalig. *See also* **later** 1; **latest**. 2. *adv.* **a)** *(after proper time)* verspätet; **b)** *(at/till a ~ hour)* spät; **be up** ~: bis spät in die Nacht aufbleiben; **work** ~ **at the office** [abends] lange im Büro arbeiten; |**a bit**| ~ **in the day** *(fig. coll.)* reichlich

spät. 3. *n.* **of** ~: in letzter Zeit.

latecomer ['leɪtkʌmə(r)] *n.* Zuspät-kommende, *der/die.* '**lately** *adv.* in letzter Zeit. '**lateness** *n.* **a)** *(delay)* Verspätung, *die;* **b) the** ~ **of the per-formance** der späte Beginn der Vor-stellung

latent ['leɪtənt] *adj.* latent

later ['leɪtə(r)] 1. *adv.* ~ |**on**| später. 2. *adj.* später; *(more recent)* neuer

lateral ['lætərl] *adj.* seitlich (**to** von); ~ **thinking** Querdenken, *das*

latest ['leɪtɪst] *adj.* **a)** *(modern)* neu[e]st...; **b)** *(most recent)* letzt...; **c) at** |**the**| ~/**the very** ~: spätestens/aller-spätestens

lathe [leɪð] *n.* Drehbank, *die*

lather ['lɑːðə(r)] 1. *n.* [Seifen]schaum, *der.* 2. *v. t.* einschäumen

Latin ['lætɪn] 1. *adj.* lateinisch. 2. *n.* Latein, *das; see also* **English** 2 a. **Latin A'merica** *pr. n.* Lateinamerika *(das).* **Latin-A'merican** *adj.* latein-amerikanisch

latitude ['lætɪtjuːd] *n.* **a)** *(freedom)* Freiheit, *die;* **b)** *(Geog.)* Breite, *die*

latrine [lə'triːn] *n.* Latrine, *die*

latter ['lætə(r)] *attrib. adj.* letzter...; **the** ~: der/die/das letztere; *pl.* die letzte-ren. '**latterly** *adv.* in letzter Zeit

lattice ['lætɪs] *n.* Gitter, *das*

laudable ['lɔːdəbl] *adj.* lobenswert

laugh [lɑːf] 1. *n.* Lachen, *das; (continu-ous)* Gelächter, *das.* 2. *v. i.* lachen; ~ **out loud** laut auflachen; ~ **at sb./sth.** über jmdn./etw. lachen; *(jeer)* jmdn. auslachen/etw. verlachen. **laugh 'off** *v. t.* mit einem Lachen abtun

laughable ['lɑːfəbl] *adj.* lachhaft; lä-cherlich

'**laughing** *n.* **be no** ~ **matter** nicht zum Lachen sein. '**laughing-gas** *n.* Lach-gas, *das.* '**laughing-stock** *n.* **make sb. a** ~, **make a** ~ **of sb.** jmdn. zum Ge-spött machen

laughter ['lɑːftə(r)] *n.* Lachen, *das; (continuous)* Gelächter, *das*

launch [lɔːntʃ] *v. t.* **a)** zu Wasser lassen ⟨*Boot*⟩; vom Stapel lassen ⟨*neues Schiff*⟩; abschießen ⟨*Harpune, Tor-pedo*⟩; schleudern ⟨*Speer*⟩; **b)** *(fig.)* auf den Markt bringen ⟨*Produkt*⟩; vorstellen ⟨*Buch, Schallplatte, Sänger*⟩; ~ **an attack** einen Angriff durchführen. '**launching pad**, **launch pad** *ns.* [Raketen]abschuß-rampe, *die*

launder ['lɔːndə(r)] *v. t.* waschen und bügeln. **launderette** [lɔːndə'ret],

laundrette [lɔːn'dret], *(Amer.)*
laundromat ['lɔːndrəmæt] *ns.*
Waschsalon, *der.* **laundry** ['lɔːndrɪ]
n. **a)** *(place)* Wäscherei, *die;* **b)** *(clothes
etc.)* Wäsche, *die*
lava ['lɑːvə] *n.* Lava, *die*
lavatory ['lævətərɪ] *n.* Toilette, *die*
lavender ['lævɪndə(r)] *n.* Lavendel,
der
lavish ['lævɪʃ] **1.** *adj.* großzügig. **2.** *v. t.*
~ sth. on sb. jmdn. mit· etw. überhäu-
fen
law [lɔː] *n.* **a)** Gesetz, *das;* **break the ~:**
gegen das Gesetz verstoßen; **take the
~ into one's own hands** sich *(Dat.)*
selbst Recht verschaffen; **~ and order**
Ruhe und Ordnung; **b)** *(of game)* Regel, *die;* **c)** *(as subject)* Jura *o. Art.*
law: ~**-abiding** ['lɔːəbaɪdɪŋ] *adj.* ge-
setzestreu; ~**court** *n.* Gerichtsgebäude, *das;* *(room)* Gerichtssaal, *der;*
~**ful** ['lɔːfl] *adj.* rechtmäßig ⟨*Besitzer,
Erbe*⟩; legal, gesetzmäßig ⟨*Vorgehen,
Maßnahme*⟩; ~**less** *adj.* gesetzlos
lawn [lɔːn] *n.* Rasen, *der.* '**lawnmower** *n.* Rasenmäher, *der*
'**law suit** *n.* Prozeß, *der*
lawyer ['lɔːjə(r)] *n.* Rechtsanwalt,
*der/*Rechtsanwältin, *die*
lax [læks] *adj.* lax
laxative ['læksətɪv] *n.* Abführmittel,
das
laxity ['læksɪtɪ], '**laxness** *ns.* Laxheit,
die
¹**lay** [leɪ] *adj.* Laien-
²**lay** *v. t.,* **laid** [leɪd] **a)** legen ⟨*Teppichboden, Rohr, Kabel*⟩; **b)** *(impose)* auferlegen ⟨*Verantwortung, Verpflichtung*⟩ (**on** *Dat.*); verhängen ⟨*Strafe*⟩
(**on** über + *Akk.*); **c)** ~ **the table** den
Tisch decken; **d)** *(Biol.)* legen ⟨*Ei*⟩.
lay a'side *v. t.* beiseite legen. **lay 'by**
v. t. beiseite legen. **lay 'down** *v. t.* **a)**
hinlegen; **b)** festlegen ⟨*Regeln, Bedingungen*⟩. **lay 'off 1.** *v. t.* *(from work)*
vorübergehend entlassen. **2.** *v. i. (coll.:
stop)* aufhören. **lay 'out** *v. t.* **a)**
(spread out) ausbreiten; **b)** anlegen
⟨*Garten*⟩. **lay 'up** *v. t.* **a)** *(store)* lagern;
b) I was laid up in bed for a week ich
mußte eine Woche mein Bett hüten
³**lay** *see* ²**lie**
lay: ~**about** *n.* *(Brit.)* Gammler, *der*
(ugs.); ~**-by** *n.,* pl. ~**-bys** *(Brit.)* Park-
bucht, *die;* Haltebucht, *die*
layer ['leɪə(r)] *n.* Schicht, *die*
layette [leɪ'et] *n.* **[baby's]** ~ **:** Babyaus-
stattung, *die*
lay: ~**man** ['leɪmən] *n.,* pl. ~**men** ['leɪ-

mən] Laie, *der;* ~**out** *n.* *(of garden,
park)* Anlage, *die;* *(of book, advertisement, etc.)* Layout, *das*
laze [leɪz] *v. i.* faulenzen; ~ **around** *or*
about herumfaulenzen *(ugs.)*
lazily ['leɪzɪlɪ] *adv.* faul
laziness ['leɪzɪnɪs] *n.* Faulheit, *die*
lazy ['leɪzɪ] *adj.* faul. '**lazy-bones** *n.
sing.* Faulpelz, *der*
lb. *abbr.* **pound|s|** ≈ Pfd.
¹**lead** [led] **1.** *n.* **a)** *(metal)* Blei, *das;* **b)**
(in pencil) [Bleistift]mine, *die.* **2.** *attrib.
adj.* Blei-
²**lead** [liːd] **1.** *v. t.,* **led** [led] **a)** führen; ~
sb. to do sth. *(fig.)* jmdn. dazu bringen,
etw. zu tun; **b)** *(fig.: influence)* ~ **sb. to
do sth.** jmdn. veranlassen, etw. zu tun;
be easily led sich leicht beeinflussen
lassen; **he led me to believe that ...:** er
machte mich glauben, daß ...; **c)** *(be
first in)* anführen; **d)** *(direct)* anführen
⟨*Bewegung, Abordnung*⟩; leiten ⟨*Diskussion, Orchester*⟩. **2.** *v. i.,* **led a)**
⟨*Straße usw., Tür:*⟩ führen; **b)** *(be first)*
führen; *(go in front)* vorangehen. **3.** *n.*
a) *(precedent)* Beispiel, *das;* *(clue)* Anhaltspunkt, *der;* **follow sb.'s ~:** jmds.
Beispiel *(Dat.)* folgen; **b)** *(first place)*
Führung, *die;* **be in the ~:** in Führung
liegen; **c)** *(distance ahead)* Vorsprung,
der; **d)** *(leash)* Leine, *die;* **on a ~:** an
der Leine; **e)** *(Electr.)* Kabel, *das;* **f)**
(Theatre) Hauptrolle, *die.* **lead
a'way** *v. t.* abführen ⟨*Gefangenen,
Verbrecher*⟩. **lead 'off 1.** *v. t.* abführen. **2.** *v. i.* beginnen. **lead 'on 1.** *v. t.*
~ **sb. on** *(entice)* jmdn. reizen; *(deceive)* jmdn. auf den Leim führen. **2.**
v. i. ~ **on to the next topic** *etc.* zum
nächsten Thema *usw.* führen. **lead
'up to** *v. t.* schließlich führen zu
'**leader** *n.* **a)** Führer, *der/*Führerin,
die; *(of political party)* Vorsitzende,
der/die; *(of expedition)* Leiter,
*der/*Leiterin, *die;* **b)** *(Brit. Journ.)*
Leitartikel, *der.* '**leadership** *n.* Führung, *die*
lead-free ['ledfriː] *adj.* bleifrei
leading ['liːdɪŋ] *adj.* führend
leading: ~ '**lady** *n.* Hauptdarstelle-
rin, *die;* ~ '**man** *n.* Hauptdarsteller,
der; ~ '**question** *n.* Suggestivfrage,
die; ~ **role** *n.* Hauptrolle, *die;* *(fig.)*
führende Rolle
lead [led]: ~-'**pencil** *n.* Bleistift, *der;*
~-'**poisoning** *n.* Bleivergiftung, *die*
leaf [liːf] *n.,* pl. **leaves** [liːvz] Blatt, *das;*
(of table) Platte *die.* **leaf 'through**
v. t. durchblättern

leaflet ['li:flɪt] *n.* [Hand]zettel, *der;*
(advertising) Reklamezettel, *der; (po-*
litical) Flugblatt, *das*
'leafy *adj.* belaubt
league [li:g] *n.* **a)** *(agreement)* Bündnis, *das;* be in ~ with sb. mit jmdm. im
Bunde sein; **b)** *(Sport)* Liga, *die*
leak [li:k] **1.** *n.* **a)** *(hole)* Leck, *das; (in*
roof, tent; also fig.) undichte Stelle; **b)**
(escaping gas) durch ein Leck austre-
tendes Gas. **2.** *v. i.* **a)** *(escape)* austre-
ten (from aus); **b)** ⟨Faß, Tank, Schiff:⟩
lecken; ⟨Rohr, Leitung, Dach:⟩ undicht sein; ⟨Gefäß, Füller:⟩ auslaufen;
c) *(fig.)* ~ |out| durchsickern. **3.** *v. t.* ~
sth. to sb. jmdm. etw. zuspielen. **leak-**
age ['li:kɪdʒ] *n.* Auslaufen, *das; (of*
fluid, gas) Ausströmen, *das; (fig.: of*
information) Durchsickern, *das.*
'leaky *adj.* undicht; leck ⟨*Boot*⟩
¹lean [li:n] **1.** *adj.* mager. **2.** *n. (meat)*
Magere, *das*
²lean 1. *v. i.,* **leaned** [li:nd, lent] *or*
(Brit.) **leant** [lent] **a)** sich beugen; ~
against the door sich gegen die Tür
lehnen; ~ **down/forward** sich herab-/
vorbeugen; ~ **back** sich zurücklehnen; **b)** *(support oneself)* ~ **against/on**
sth. sich gegen/an etw. *(Akk.)* lehnen;
c) *(be supported)* lehnen (against an +
Dat.); **d)** *(fig.)* ~ |up|on sb. *(rely)* auf
jmdn. bauen; ~ to|wards| sth. *(tend)* zu
etw. neigen. **2.** *v. t.,* **leaned** *or (Brit.)*
leant lehnen (**against** gegen *od.* an +
Akk.). **lean 'over** *v. i.* sich hinüber-
beugen
'leaning *n.* Neigung, *die*
leant *see* **²lean**
leap [li:p] **1.** *v. i.,* **leaped** [li:pt, lept] *or*
leapt [lept] **a)** springen; ⟨Herz:⟩ hüp-
fen; **b)** *(fig.)* ~ **at the chance** die Gelegenheit beim Schopf packen. **2.** *v. t.,*
leaped *or* **leapt** überspringen. **3.** *n.*
Sprung, *der;* with *or* in one ~: mit einem Satz; by ~s and bounds *(fig.)* mit
Riesenschritten. **'leap-frog 1.** *n.*
Bockspringen, *das.* **2.** *v. i.,* **-gg-** Bockspringen machen
leapt *see* **leap** 1, 2
'leap year *n.* Schaltjahr, *das*
learn [lɜ:n] **1.** *v. t.,* **learned** [lɜ:nd, lɜ:nt]
or **learnt** [lɜ:nt] **a)** lernen; ~ **to swim**
schwimmen lernen; **b)** *(find out)* er-
fahren. **2.** *v. i.,* **learned** *or* **learnt a)** lernen; ~ **about sth.** etwas über etw.
(Akk.) lernen; **b)** *(get to know)* erfahren (of von). **learned** ['lɜ:nɪd] *adj.* gelehrt. **'learner** *n. (beginner)* Anfän-
ger, *der/*Anfängerin, *die;* ~ |driver|

Fahrschüler, *der/*-schülerin, *die.*
'learning *n. (of person)* Gelehrsamkeit, *die*
learnt *see* **learn**
lease [li:s] **1.** *n. (of land, business*
premises) Pachtvertrag, *der; (of house,*
flat, office) Mietvertrag, *der.* **2.** *v. t.* **a)**
(grant ~ on) verpachten ⟨*Grundstück,*
Geschäft, Rechte⟩; vermieten ⟨*Haus,*
Wohnung, Büro⟩; **b)** *(take ~ on)* pachten ⟨*Grundstück, Geschäft*⟩; mieten
⟨*Haus, Wohnung, Büro*⟩. **'leasehold**
n. see **lease** 2: **have the** ~ **of** *or* **on sth.**
etw. gepachtet/gemietet haben
leash [li:ʃ] *n.* Leine, *die*
least [li:st] **1.** *adj. (smallest)* kleinst...;
(in quantity) wenigst...; *(in status)* geringst... **2.** *n.* Geringste, *das;* the ~ I
can do das mindeste, was ich tun
kann; at ~: mindestens; *(anyway)* we-
nigstens; at the |very| ~: [aller]minde-
stens; not |in| the ~: nicht im gering-
sten. **3.** *adv.* am wenigsten
leather ['leðə(r)] **1.** *n.* Leder, *das.* **2.**
adj. ledern; Leder⟨jacke, -mantel⟩.
'leather goods *n.* Lederwaren *Pl.*
'leathery *adj.* ledern
¹leave [li:v] *n.* **a)** *(permission)* Erlaubnis, *die;* **b)** *(from duty or work)* Urlaub,
der; ~ |of absence| Urlaub, *der;* **c)** take
one's ~ sich verabschieden
²leave *v. t.,* **left** [left] **a)** *(make or let re-*
main) hinterlassen; ~ **sb. to do sth.** es
jmdm. überlassen, etw. zu tun; *(in*
will) ~ **sb. sth.,** ~ **sth. to sb.** jmdm. etw.
hinterlassen; **b)** *(refrain from doing,*
using, etc.) stehenlassen ⟨*Abwasch,*
Essen⟩; **c)** *(in given state)* lassen; ~ **sb.**
alone *(allow to be alone)* jmdn. allein
lassen; *(stop bothering)* jmdn. in Ruhe
lassen; **d)** *(refer, entrust)* ~ **sth. to sb.'**
sth. etw. jmdm./einer Sache überlas-
sen; **e)** *(go away from, quit, desert)* verlassen; ~ **home at 6 a.m.** um 6 Uhr
früh von zu Hause weggehen/-fahren;
~ **Bonn at 6 p.m.** *(by car, in train)* um
18 Uhr von Bonn abfahren; *(by plane)*
um 18 Uhr in Bonn abfliegen; *abs.* the
train ~**s at 8.30 a.m.** der Zug fährt *od.*
geht um 8.30 Uhr; ~ **on the 8 a.m.**
train/flight mit dem Acht-Uhr-Zug
fahren/der Acht-Uhr-Maschine flie-
gen. **leave a'side** *v. t.* beiseite lassen.
leave be'hind *v. t.* zurücklassen; *(by*
mistake) vergessen; liegenlassen.
leave 'off *v. t. (stop)* aufhören mit;
abs. aufhören. **leave 'out** *v. t.* auslassen. **leave 'over** *v. t.* **be left over** übrig
[geblieben] sein

leaves *pl. of* **leaf**
Lebanon ['lebənən] *pr. n.* |the| ~: [der] Libanon
lecherous ['letʃərəs] *adj.* lüstern *(geh.)*
lecture ['lektʃə(r)] **1. a)** *n.* Vortrag, *der; (Univ.)* Vorlesung, *die;* **b)** *(reprimand)* Strafpredigt, *die (ugs.).* **2.** *v. i.* ~ |to sb.| |on sth.| [vor jmdm.] einen Vortrag/*(Univ.)* eine Vorlesung [über etw. *(Akk.)*] halten. **3.** *v. t. (scold)* ~ sb. jmdm. eine Strafpredigt halten. '**lecturer** *n.* Vortragende, *der/die;* **senior** ~: Dozent, *der/*Dozentin, *die*
led *see* ²**lead 1, 2**
ledge [ledʒ] *n.* Sims, *der od. das; (of rock)* Vorsprung, *der*
ledger ['ledʒə(r)] *n. (Commerc.)* Hauptbuch, *das*
lee [liː] *n.* **a)** *(shelter)* Schutz, *der;* **b)** ~ |side| *(Naut.)* Leeseite, *die*
leech [liːtʃ] *n.* [Blut]egel, *der*
leek [liːk] *n.* Stange Porree *od.* Lauch; ~s Porree, *der;* Lauch, *der*
leer [lɪə(r)] **1.** *n.* anzüglicher/spöttischer Blick. **2.** *v. i.* ~ **at** sb. jmdm. einen anzüglichen/spöttischen [Seiten]blick zuwerfen
leeward ['liːwəd] **1.** *adj.* **to/on the** ~ **side of the ship** nach/in Lee. **2.** *n.* Leeseite, *die;* **to** ~: leewärts
'**leeway** *n.* **a)** *(Naut.)* Leeweg, *der;* Abdrift, *die;* **b)** *(fig.)* Spielraum, *der*
¹**left** *see* ²**leave**
²**left** [left] **1.** *adj.* **a)** link...; **on the** ~ **side** auf der linken Seite; links; **b)** **L~** *(Polit.)* link... **2.** *adv.* nach links. **3.** *n.* **a)** *(~-hand side)* linke Seite; **on** *or* **to the** ~ |of sb./sth.| links [von jmdm./etw.]; **b)** *(Polit.)* **the L~**: die Linke
left: ~-**hand** *adj.* link...; ~-'**handed 1.** *adj.* linkshändig; *(Werkzeug)* für Linkshänder; **be** ~-**handed** Linkshänder/Linkshänderin sein; **2.** *adv.* linkshändig; ~-'**luggage [office]** *n. (Brit. Railw.)* Gepäckaufbewahrung, *die;* ~-**overs** *n. pl.* Reste; ~ '**wing** *n.* linker Flügel; ~-**wing** *adj. (Polit.)* linksgerichtet; Links⟨*extremist, -intellektueller*⟩; ~-'**winger** *n.* **a)** *(Sport)* Linksaußen, *der;* **b)** *(Polit.)* Angehöriger/Angehörige des linken Flügels
leg [leg] *n.* **a)** Bein, *das;* **pull sb.'s** ~ *(fig.)* jmdn. auf den Arm nehmen *(ugs.);* **stretch one's** ~s sich *(Dat.)* die Beine vertreten; **b)** ~ **of lamb** Lammkeule, *die;* **c)** *(of journey)* Etappe, *die*
legacy ['legəsɪ] *n.* Vermächtnis, *das (Rechtsspr.);* Erbschaft, *die*

legal ['liːgl] *adj.* **a)** *(concerning the law)* juristisch; Rechts⟨*beratung, -streit, -experte, -schutz*⟩; gesetzlich ⟨*Vertreter*⟩; rechtlich ⟨*Gründe, Stellung*⟩; Gerichts⟨*kosten*⟩; **b)** *(required by law)* gesetzlich ⟨*Verpflichtung*⟩; gesetzlich verankert ⟨*Recht*⟩; **c)** *(lawful)* legal; rechtsgültig ⟨*Vertrag, Testament*⟩.
legality [lɪ'gælɪtɪ] *n.* Legalität, *die.*
legalize ['liːgəlaɪz] *v. t.* legalisieren
legend ['ledʒənd] *n.* Sage, *die; (unfounded belief)* Legende, *die.* **legendary** ['ledʒəndərɪ] *adj.* legendär
legibility [ledʒɪ'bɪlɪtɪ] *n.* Leserlichkeit, *die*
legible ['ledʒɪbl] *adj.* leserlich; **easily/scarcely** ~: leicht/kaum lesbar
legion ['liːdʒn] *n.* Legion, *die*
legislate ['ledʒɪsleɪt] *v. i.* Gesetze verabschieden. **legislation** [ledʒɪs'leɪʃn] *n.* **a)** *(laws)* Gesetze; **b)** *(legislating)* Gesetzgebung, *die.* **legislative** ['ledʒɪslətɪv] *adj.* gesetzgebend. **legislator** ['ledʒɪsleɪtə(r)] *n.* Gesetzgeber, *der.* **legislature** ['ledʒɪsleɪtʃə(r)] *n.* Legislative, *die*
legitimate [lɪ'dʒɪtɪmət] *adj.* **a)** *(lawful)* legitim; rechtmäßig ⟨*Besitzer, Regierung*⟩; **b)** *(valid)* berechtigt; **c)** ehelich ⟨*Kind*⟩
leisure ['leʒə(r)] *n.* Freizeit, *die;* attrib. Freizeit-. '**leisurely** *adj.* gemächlich
lemon ['lemən] *n.* Zitrone, *die.* **lemonade** [lemə'neɪd] *n.* [Zitronen]limonade, *die*
lend [lend] *v. t.,* **lent** [lent] leihen; ~ **sth. to sb.** jmdm. etw. leihen. '**lender** *n.* Verleiher, *der/*Verleiherin, *die*
length [leŋθ, leŋkθ] *n.* **a)** *(also of time)* Länge, *die;* **be six feet in** ~: sechs Fuß lang sein; **a short** ~ **of time** kurze Zeit; **b)** **at** ~ **a)** *(for a long time)* lange; *(eventually)* schließlich; **at |great|** ~ *(in great detail)* lang und breit; **at some** ~: ziemlich ausführlich; **c)** **go to any/great** ~s alles nur/alles Erdenkliche tun; **d)** *(piece of material)* Länge, *die;* Stück, *das.* **lengthen** ['leŋθən] **1.** *v. i.* länger werden. **2.** *v. t.* verlängern; länger machen ⟨*Kleid*⟩. **lengthways** ['leŋθweɪz] *adv.* der Länge nach; längs. '**lengthy** *adj.* überlang
lenient ['liːnɪənt] *adj.* nachsichtig
lens [lenz] *n.* Linse, *die*
Lent [lent] *n.* Fastenzeit, *die*
lent *see* **lend**
lentil ['lentl] *n.* Linse, *die*
Leo ['liːəʊ] *n., pl.* ~s der Löwe
leopard ['lepəd] *n.* Leopard, *der*

leotard ['li:ətɑ:d] *n.* Turnanzug, *der*
leper ['lepə(r)] *n.* Leprakranke, *der/die*
leprosy ['leprəsı] *n.* Lepra, *die*
lesbian ['lezbıən] **1.** *n.* Lesbierin, *die.*
2. *adj.* lesbisch
less [les] **1.** *adj.* weniger; **of ~ value/
importance** weniger wertvoll/wichtig.
2. *adv.* weniger; **~ and ~:** immer we-
niger; **~ and ~ |often|** immer seltener.
3. *n.* weniger. **4.** *prep. (deducting)* ten
~ three zehn weniger drei. **lessen**
['lesn] **1.** *v. t.* verringern. **2.** *v. i.* sich
verringern. **lesser** ['lesə(r)] *attrib.*
adj. geringer...
lesson ['lesn] *n.* **a)** *(class)* [Unter-
richts]stunde, *die;* **b)** *(example, warning)* Lehre, *die;* **c)** *(Eccl.)* Lesung, *die*
let [let] **1.** *v. t.,* -tt-, **let a)** *(allow to)* lassen; **~ sb. do sth.** jmdn. etw. tun las-
sen; **~ alone** *(far less)* geschweige
denn; **b)** *(cause to)* **~ sb. know** jmdn.
wissen lassen; **c)** *(Brit.: rent out)* vermieten. **2.** *v. aux.,* -tt-, **let** lassen; **Let's
go to the cinema. − Yes, ~'s/No, ~'s
not** Komm/Kommt, wir gehen ins Kino. − Ja, gut/Nein, lieber nicht; **~
them come in** sie sollen hereinkom-
men. **let 'down** *v. t.* **a)** *(lower)* herun-
ter-/hinunterlassen; **b)** *(Dressm.)* auslassen; **c)** *(disappoint, fail)* im Stich
lassen. **let 'in** *v. t.* **a)** *(admit)* herein-/
hineinlassen; **b) ~ oneself in for sth.**
sich auf etw. *(Akk.)* einlassen; **c) ~ sb.
in on a secret/plan** *etc.* jmdn. in ein
Geheimnis/einen Plan *usw.* einwei-
hen. **'let into** *v. t.* **a)** *(admit into)* lassen in (+ *Akk.*); **b)** *(fig.: acquaint
with)* **~ sb. into a secret** jmdn. in ein
Geheimnis einweihen. **let 'off** *v. t.* **a)**
(excuse) laufenlassen *(ugs.);* **~ sb. off
sth.** jmdm. etw. erlassen; **b)** *(allow to
alight)* aussteigen lassen; **c)** abbren-
nen ⟨Feuerwerk⟩. **let 'on** *(sl.)* **1.** *v. i.*
don't ~ on! nichts verraten! **2.** *v. t.* **sb.
~ on to me that ...:** man hat mir gesteckt, daß ... *(ugs.).* **let 'out** *v. t.* **a) ~
sb./an animal out** jmdn./ein Tier her-
aus-/hinauslassen; **b)** ausstoßen
⟨Schrei⟩; **~ out a groan** aufstöhnen; **c)**
verraten ⟨Geheimnis⟩; **d)** *(Dressm.)*
auslassen; **e)** *(Brit.: rent out)* vermieten. **let 'through** *v. t.* durchlassen.
let 'up *v. i. (coll.)* nachlassen
'let-down *n.* Enttäuschung, *die*
lethal ['li:θl] *adj.* tödlich
lethargic [lı'θɑ:dʒık] *adj.* träge; *(apathetic)* lethargisch
lethargy ['leθədʒı] *n.* Trägheit, *die;
(apathy)* Lethargie, *die*

letter ['letə(r)] **a)** Brief, *der* (**to an**
+ *Akk.*); **b)** *(of alphabet)* Buchstabe,
der. **'letter bomb** *n.* Briefbombe,
die. **'letter-box** *n.* Briefkasten, *der*
'lettering *n.* Typographie, *die*
lettuce ['letıs] *n.* [Kopf]salat, *der*
leukaemia, *(Amer.)* **leukemia**
[lu:'ki:mıə] *n.* Leukämie, *die*
level ['levl] **1.** *n.* **a)** Höhe, *die; (storey)*
Etage, *die;* **b)** *(fig.: steady state)* Ni-
veau, *das;* **be on a ~ |with sb./sth.|** auf
dem gleichen Niveau sein [wie jmd./
etw.]. **2.** *adj.* **a)** waagerecht; eben
⟨Boden, Land⟩; **b)** *(on a ~)* **be ~ |with
sth./sb.|** auf gleicher Höhe [mit etw./
jmdm.] sein; **c)** *(fig.)* **keep a ~ head** einen kühlen Kopf bewahren; **do one's
~ best** *(coll.)* sein möglichstes tun. **3.**
v. t., (Brit.) -ll-: **a)** *(make ~)* ebnen; **b)**
(aim) richten ⟨Blick, Gewehr⟩ (**at** auf
+ *Akk.*); *(fig.)* richten ⟨Kritik *usw.*⟩
(**at** gegen). **level 'crossing** *n. (Brit.
Railw.)* [schienengleicher] Bahnüber-
gang. **level-'headed** *adj.* besonnen
lever ['li:və(r)] **1.** *n.* Hebel, *der.* **2.** *v. t.*
~ sth. open etw. aufhebeln. **leverage**
['li:vərıdʒ] *n.* Hebelwirkung, *die*
levity ['levıtı] *n. (frivolity)* Unernst, *der*
levy ['levı] **1.** *n. (tax)* Steuer, *die.* **2.** *v. t.*
erheben
lewd [lju:d] geil; anzüglich ⟨Geste⟩;
schlüpfrig ⟨Witz⟩
liability [laıə'bılıtı] *n.* **a)** Haftung, *die;*
b) *(handicap)* Belastung, *die* (**to** für)
liable ['laıəbl] *pred. adj.* **a)** *(legally
bound)* **be ~ for sth.** für etw. haftbar
sein *od.* haften; **b)** *(prone)* **be ~ to sth.**
⟨Person:⟩ zu etw. neigen; **be ~ to do
sth.** ⟨Sache:⟩ leicht etw. tun; ⟨Person:⟩
dazu neigen, etw. zu tun
liaise [lı'eız] *v. i. (coll.)* eine Verbindung herstellen; **~ on a project** bei einem Projekt zusammenarbeiten. **li-
aison** [lı'eızən] *n. (co-operation)* Zusammenarbeit, *die*
liar ['laıə(r)] *n.* Lügner, *der*/Lügnerin,
die
libel ['laıbl] **1.** *n.* Verleumdung, *die.* **2.**
v. t., (Brit.) -ll- verleumden. **libellous**
(Amer.: libelous) ['laıbələs] *adj.* verleumderisch
liberal ['lıbərl] **1.** *adj.* **a)** großzügig; **b)**
(Polit.) liberal; **the L~ Democrats**
(Brit.) die Liberaldemokraten. **2.** *n.*
L~ *(Polit.)* Liberale, *der/die*
liberate ['lıbəreıt] *v. t.* befreien (**from**
aus). **liberation** [lıbə'reıʃn] *n.* Befreiung, *die.* **liberator** ['lıbəreıtə(r)] *n.*
Befreier, *der*/Befreierin, *die*

liberty ['lɪbətɪ] *n.* Freiheit, *die;* **take the ~ of doing sth.** sich *(Dat.)* die Freiheit nehmen, etw. zu tun; **take liberties with sb.** sich *(Dat.)* Freiheiten gegen jmdn. herausnehmen *(ugs.)*

Libra ['li:brə] *n.* Waage, *die*

librarian [laɪ'breərɪən] *n.* Bibliothekar, *der*/Bibliothekarin, *die*

library ['laɪbrərɪ] *n.* Bibliothek, *die;* **public ~:** öffentliche Bücherei. **'library book** *n.* Buch aus der Bibliothek

Libya ['lɪbɪə] *pr. n.* Libyen *(das)*

lice *pl. of* **louse**

licence ['laɪsəns] **1.** *n.* [behördliche] Genehmigung; Lizenz, *die;* [driving-] **~:** Führerschein, *der.* **2.** *v. t. see* **license 1**

license ['laɪsəns] **1.** *v. t.* ermächtigen; **get a car ~d** ≈ die Kfz-Steuer für ein Auto bezahlen. **2.** *n. (Amer.) see* **licence 1**

licentious [laɪ'senʃəs] *adj.* zügellos ⟨*Person*⟩; unzüchtig ⟨*Benehmen*⟩

lichen ['laɪkn, 'lɪtʃn] *n.* Flechte, *die*

lick [lɪk] **1.** *v. t.* **a)** lecken; **b)** *(sl.: beat)* verdreschen *(ugs.).* **2.** *n.* Lecken, *das.* **lick 'off** *v. t.* ablecken

lid [lɪd] *n.* **a)** Deckel, *der;* **b)** *(eyelid)* Lid, *das*

lido ['li:dəʊ] *n., pl.* **~s** Freibad, *das*

¹lie [laɪ] **1.** *n.* Lüge, *die;* **tell ~s/a ~:** lügen. **2.** *v. i.,* **lying** ['laɪɪŋ] lügen; **~ to sb.** jmdn. be- *od.* anlügen

²lie *v. i.,* **lying** ['laɪɪŋ], **lay** [leɪ], **lain** [leɪn] **a)** liegen; *(assume horizontal position)* sich legen; **b) ~ idle** ⟨*Maschine, Fabrik:*⟩ stillstehen. **lie a'bout,** **lie a'round** *v. i.* herumliegen *(ugs.).* **lie 'back** *v. i.* sich zurücklegen; *(sitting)* sich zurücklehnen. **lie 'down** *v. i.* sich hinlegen

lie-detector ['laɪdɪ'tektə(r)] *n.* Lügendetektor, *der*

'lie-in *n. (coll.)* **have a ~:** [sich] ausschlafen

lieu [lju:] *n.* **in ~ of sth.** anstelle einer Sache *(Gen.);* **get holiday in ~:** statt dessen Urlaub bekommen

lieutenant [lef'tenənt] *n. (Army)* Oberleutnant, *der*

life [laɪf] *n., pl.* **lives** [laɪvz] Leben, *das;* **for ~:** lebenslänglich ⟨*inhaftiert*⟩; **true to ~:** wahrheitsgetreu

life: ~belt *n.* Rettungsring, *der;* **~boat** *n.* Rettungsboot, *das;* **~buoy** *n.* Rettungsring, *der;* **~ cycle** *n.* Lebenszyklus, *der;* **~-guard** *n.* Rettungsschwimmer, *der*/-schwimmerin,

die; **~-insurance** *n.* Lebensversicherung, *die;* **~-jacket** *n.* Schwimmweste, *die;* **~-less** *adj.* leblos; *(fig.)* farblos; **~-like** *adj.* lebensecht; **~-line** *n.* Rettungsleine, *die; (fig.)* Rettungsanker, *der;* **~-long** *adj.* lebenslang; **~-saving** *n.* Rettungsschwimmen, *das; attrib.* Rettungs-; **~ sentence** *n.* lebenslängliche Freiheitsstrafe; **~-size, ~-sized** *adj.* lebensgroß; **in Lebensgröße** *nachgestellt;* **~-style** *n.* Lebensstil, *der;* **~-time** *n.* Lebenszeit, *die;* **during my ~time** während meines Lebens; **the chance of a ~time** eine einmalige Gelegenheit

lift [lɪft] **1.** *v. t.* heben; *(fig.)* erheben ⟨*Gemüt, Geist*⟩. **2.** *n.* **a)** *(in vehicle)* **get a ~:** mitgenommen werden; **give sb. a ~:** jmdn. mitnehmen; **b)** *(Brit.: elevator)* Aufzug, *der.* **3.** *v. i.* ⟨*Nebel:*⟩ sich auflösen. **'lift off** *v. t. & i.* abheben. **lift 'up** *v. t.* hochheben; heben ⟨*Kopf*⟩ **'lift-off** *n.* Abheben, *das*

ligament ['lɪgəmənt] *n.* Band, *das*

¹light [laɪt] **1.** *n.* **a)** Licht, *das;* **~ of day** Tageslicht, *das;* **b)** *(lamp)* Licht, *das; (fitting)* Lampe, *die;* **c)** *(signal to traffic)* Ampel, *die;* **d)** *(to ignite)* **have you got a ~?** haben Sie Feuer? **set ~ to sth.** etw. anzünden; **e) bring sth. to ~:** etw. ans [Tages]licht bringen; **throw** *or* **shed ~ [up]on sth.** Licht in etw. *(Akk.)* bringen; **f)** *(aspect)* **in that ~:** aus dieser Sicht; **seen in this ~:** so gesehen; **in the ~ of** angesichts (+ *Gen.*); **show sb. in a bad ~:** ein schlechtes Licht auf jmdn. werfen. **2.** *adj.* hell; **~-blue/-brown** *etc.* hellblau/-braun *usw.* **3.** *v. t.,* **lit** [lɪt] *or* **lighted a)** *(ignite)* anzünden; **b)** *(illuminate)* erhellen. **light 'up 1.** *v. i.* **a)** *(become lit)* erleuchtet werden; **b)** *(become bright)* aufleuchten (with vor). **2.** *v. t.* **a)** *(illuminate)* erleuchten; **b)** anzünden ⟨*Zigarette*⟩

²light 1. *adj.* leicht; *(mild)* mild ⟨*Strafe*⟩. **2.** *adv.* **travel ~:** mit wenig *od.* leichtem Gepäck reisen

'light-bulb *n.* Glühbirne, *die*

'lighted *adj.* brennend ⟨*Kerze, Zigarette*⟩; angezündet ⟨*Streichholz*⟩

¹lighten ['laɪtn] *v. t. (make less heavy, difficult)* leichter machen

²lighten 1. *v. t. (make brighter)* aufhellen; heller machen ⟨*Raum*⟩. **2.** *v. i.* sich aufhellen

'lighter *n.* Feuerzeug, *das*

light: ~-'headed *adj.* leicht benommen; **~-'hearted** *adj.* **a)** *(humorous)* unbeschwert; **b)** *(optimistic)* unbekümmert; **~house** *n*. Leuchtturm, *der*

'**lighting** *n*. Beleuchtung, *die*

'**lightly** *adv*. **a)** leicht; **b)** *(without serious consideration)* leichtfertig; **c)** *(cheerfully)* leichthin; **not treat sth. ~:** etw. nicht auf die leichte Schulter nehmen; **d) get off ~:** glimpflich davonkommen

'**lightness** *n*. *(of weight; also fig.)* Leichtigkeit, *die*

²**lightness** *n*. *(of colour)* Helligkeit, *die*

lightning ['laɪtnɪŋ] *n*. Blitz, *der;* **flash of ~:** Blitz, *der.* '**lightning-conductor** *n*. Blitzableiter, *der*

'**lightweight 1.** *adj*. leicht. **2.** *n*. Leichtgewicht, *das*

¹**like** [laɪk] **1.** *adj*. **a)** *(resembling)* wie; **your dress is ~ mine** dein Kleid ist so ähnlich wie meins; **in a case ~ that** in so einem Fall; **what is sb./sth. ~?** wie ist jmd./etw.?; **b)** *(characteristic of)* typisch für ⟨*dich, ihn usw.*⟩; **c)** *(similar)* ähnlich. **2.** *prep*. *(in the manner of)* wie; [just] **~ that** [einfach] so. **3.** *n*. **a)** *(equal)* **his/her ~:** seines-/ihresgleichen; **b)** *(similar things)* **the ~:** so etwas; **and the ~:** und dergleichen

²**like 1.** *v. t*. *(be fond of, wish for)* mögen; **~ vegetables** Gemüse mögen; gern Gemüse essen; **~ doing sth.** etw. gern tun; **would you ~ a drink?** möchtest du etwas trinken?; **would you ~ me to do it?** möchtest du, daß ich es tue?; **how do you ~ it?** wie gefällt es dir?; **if you ~** *expr. assent* wenn du willst. **2.** *n., in pl.* **~s and dislikes** Vorlieben und Abneigungen. **likeable** ['laɪkəbl] *adj*. nett; sympathisch

likelihood ['laɪklɪhʊd] *n*. Wahrscheinlichkeit, *die*

likely ['laɪklɪ] **1.** *adj*. wahrscheinlich; **there are ~ to be [traffic] hold-ups** man muß mit [Verkehrs]staus rechnen; **they are [not] ~ to come** sie werden wahrscheinlich [nicht] kommen; **is it ~ to rain tomorrow?** wird es morgen wohl regnen?; **this is not ~ to happen** es ist unwahrscheinlich, daß das geschieht. **2.** *adv*. wahrscheinlich; **as ~ as not** höchstwahrscheinlich; **not ~!** *(coll.)* auf keinen Fall!

'**like-minded** *adj*. gleichgesinnt

liken ['laɪkn] *v. t*. **~ sth./sb. to sth./sb.** etw./jmdn. mit etw./jmdm. vergleichen

'**likeness** *n*. Ähnlichkeit, *die* (to mit)

likewise ['laɪkwaɪz] *adv*. ebenso

liking ['laɪkɪŋ] *n*. Vorliebe, *die;* **take a ~ to sb./sth.** an jmdm./etw. Gefallen finden; **sth. is [not] to sb.'s ~:** etw. ist [nicht] nach jmds. Geschmack

lilac ['laɪlək] *n*. **a)** *(Bot.)* Flieder, *der;* **b)** *(colour)* Zartlila, *das*

lily ['lɪlɪ] *n*. Lilie, *die*

limb [lɪm] *n*. **a)** *(Anat.)* Glied, *das;* **b) be out on a ~** *(fig.)* exponiert sein

limber up [lɪmbər 'ʌp] *v. i*. *(loosen up)* die Muskeln lockern

¹**lime** [laɪm] *n*. [quick]**~:** [ungelöschter] Kalk

²**lime** *n*. *(fruit)* Limone, *die*

³**lime** *see* **lime-tree**

'**limelight** *n*. **be in the ~:** im Rampenlicht [der Öffentlichkeit] stehen

limerick ['lɪmərɪk] *n*. Limerick, *der*

'**lime-tree** *n*. Linde, *die*

limit ['lɪmɪt] **1.** *n*. **a)** Grenze, *die;* **set or put a ~ on sth.** etw. begrenzen; **be over the ~** ⟨*Autofahrer:*⟩ zu viele Promille haben; **lower/upper ~:** Untergrenze/Höchstgrenze, *die;* **without ~:** unbegrenzt; **within ~s** inerhalb gewisser Grenzen; **b)** *(coll.)* **this is the ~!** das ist [doch] die Höhe!; **he/she is the [very] ~:** er/sie ist [einfach] unmöglich. **2.** *v. t*. begrenzen (**to** auf + *Akk.*); einschränken ⟨*Freiheit*⟩. **limitation** [lɪmɪ'teɪʃn] *n*. Beschränkung, *die*.

'**limited** *adj*. **a)** *(restricted)* begrenzt; **b)** *(intellectually narrow)* beschränkt.

'**limitless** *adj*. grenzenlos

limousine ['lɪmʊziːn] *n*. Limousine, *die*

¹**limp** [lɪmp] **1.** *v. i*. hinken. **2.** *n*. Hinken, *das*

²**limp** *adj*. schlaff. '**limply** *adv*. schlaff; *(weakly)* schwach

limpet ['lɪmpɪt] *n*. *(Zool.)* Napfschnecke, *die*

limpid ['lɪmpɪd] *adj*. klar

linctus ['lɪŋktəs] *n*. Hustensaft, *der*

¹**line** [laɪn] **1.** *n*. **a)** *(string, cord, rope, etc.)* Leine, *die;* **b)** *(telephone cable)* Leitung, *die;* **c)** *(long mark; also Math., Phys.)* Linie, *die;* **d)** *(row, series)* Reihe, *die; (Amer.: queue)* Schlange, *die;* **bring sb. into ~:** dafür sorgen, daß jmd. nicht aus der Reihe tanzt *(ugs.);* **e)** *(row of words on a page)* Zeile, *die;* **f)** *(wrinkle)* Falte, *die;* **g)** *(direction, course)* Richtung, *die;* **on the ~s of** nach Art (+ *Gen.*); **be on the right/wrong ~s** in die richtige/falsche Richtung gehen; **along or on the same ~s** in der gleichen Richtung; **h)** *(Railw.)* Bahnlinie, *die; (track)* Gleis, *das;* **i)** *(field of activity)*

Branche, *die;* **j)** *(Commerc.: product)*
Artikel, *der;* Linie, *die (fachspr.).* **2.**
v. t. **a)** linieren ⟨*Papier*⟩; **a ~d face** ein
faltiges Gesicht; **b)** säumen *(geh.)*
⟨*Straße, Strecke*⟩. **line 'up 1.** *v. t.* antreten lassen ⟨*Gefangene, Soldaten
usw.*⟩; [in einer Reihe] aufstellen
⟨*Gegenstände*⟩. **2.** *v. i.* ⟨*Gefangene,
Soldaten:*⟩ antreten; *(queue up)* sich
anstellen

²**line** *v. t.* füttern ⟨*Kleidungsstück*⟩;
ausschlagen ⟨*Schublade usw.*⟩

lineage ['lɪnɪɪdʒ] *n.* Abstammung, *die*

linear ['lɪnɪə(r)] *adj.* linear

linen ['lɪnɪn] **1.** *n.* **a)** Leinen, *das;* **b)**
(shirts, sheets, etc.) Wäsche, *die.* **2.**
adj. Leinen⟨*faden, -bluse*⟩; Lein⟨*tuch*⟩

liner ['laɪnə(r)] Linienschiff, *das*

'**line-up** *n.* Aufstellung, *die*

linger ['lɪŋgə(r)] *v. i.* verweilen *(geh.);*
bleiben

lingerie ['læʒərɪ] *n.* [women's] ~: Da-
menunterwäsche, *die*

lingo ['lɪŋgəʊ] *n. (coll.)* Sprache, *die*

linguist ['lɪŋgwɪst] *n.* Sprachkundige,
der/die

linguistic [lɪŋ'gwɪstɪk] *adj. (of ~s)* lin-
guistisch; *(of language)* sprachlich.
linguistics [lɪŋ'gwɪstɪks] *n.* Lingui-
stik, *die*

lining ['laɪnɪŋ] *n. (of clothes)* Futter,
das; (of objects, machines, etc.) Aus-
kleidung, *die*

link [lɪŋk] **1.** *n.* **a)** *(of chain)* Glied, *das;*
b) *(connection)* Verbindung, *die.* **2.**
v. t. verbinden; ~ **arms** sich unterha-
ken. **link 'up** *v. t.* miteinander verbinden

links [lɪŋks] *n.* [golf] ~: Golfplatz, *der*

lino ['laɪnəʊ] *n., pl.* ~s Linoleum, *das*

linseed ['lɪnsiːd] *n.* Leinsamen, *der.*
linseed 'oil *n.* Leinöl, *das*

lint [lɪnt] *n.* Mull, *der*

lintel ['lɪntl] *n. (Archit.)* Sturz, *der*

lion ['laɪən] *n.* Löwe, *der.* **lioness**
['laɪənɪs] *n.* Löwin, *die*

lip [lɪp] *n.* **a)** Lippe, *die;* **lower/upper ~:**
Unter-/Oberlippe, *die;* **b)** *(of cup)*
[Gieß]rand, *der; (of jug)* Schnabel, *der.*
lip: ~-**read** *v. i.* von den Lippen lesen;
~-**reading** *n.* Lippenlesen, *das;*
~-**service** *n.* **pay ~-service to sth.** ein
Lippenbekenntnis zu etw. ablegen;
~**stick** *n.* Lippenstift, *der*

liquefy ['lɪkwɪfaɪ] **1.** *v. t.* verflüssigen.
2. *v. i.* sich verflüssigen

liqueur [lɪ'kjʊə(r)] *n.* Likör, *der*

liquid ['lɪkwɪd] **1.** *adj.* flüssig. **2.** *n.*
Flüssigkeit, *die*

liquidate ['lɪkwɪdeɪt] *v. t. (Commerc.)*
liquidieren. **liquidation** [lɪkwɪ'deɪʃn]
n. (Commerc.) Liquidation, *die*

liquidize ['lɪkwɪdaɪz] *v. t.* auflösen;
(Cookery) [im Mixer] pürieren.
'**liquidizer** *n.* Mixer, *der*

liquor ['lɪkə(r)] *n. (drink)* Alkohol, *der*

liquorice ['lɪkərɪs] *n.* Lakritze, *die*

Lisbon ['lɪzbən] *pr. n.* Lissabon *(das)*

lisp [lɪsp] **1.** *v. i. & t.* lispeln. **2.** *n.* Lispeln, *das*

'**list** [lɪst] **1.** *n.* Liste, *die.* **2.** *v. t.* aufführen; auflisten; *(verbally)* aufzählen

²**list** *v. i. (Naut.)* Schlagseite haben

listen ['lɪsn] *v. i.* zuhören; ~ **to music/
the radio** Musik/Radio hören; **they
~ed to his words** sie hörten ihm zu.
listener ['lɪsnə(r)] *n.* Zuhörer,
*der/*Zuhörerin, *die; (to radio)* Hörer,
*der/*Hörerin, *die*

listless ['lɪstlɪs] *adj.* lustlos

lit *see* ¹**light 3**

litany ['lɪtənɪ] *n.* Litanei, *die*

liter *(Amer.) see* **litre**

literacy ['lɪtərəsɪ] *n.* Lese- und
Schreibfertigkeit, *die*

literal ['lɪtərl] *adj.* **a)** wörtlich; **b)** *(not
exaggerated)* buchstäblich. **literally**
['lɪtərəlɪ] *adv.* **a)** wörtlich; **b)** *(actually)*
buchstäblich; **c)** *(coll.: with some exaggeration)* geradezu

literary ['lɪtərərɪ] *adj.* literarisch

literate ['lɪtərət] *adj.* des Lesens und
Schreibens kundig; *(educated)* gebildet

literature ['lɪtrətʃə(r)] *n.* Literatur, *die*

lithe [laɪð] *adj.* geschmeidig

litigation [lɪtɪ'geɪʃn] *n.* Rechtsstreit,
der

litre ['liːtə(r)] *n. (Brit.)* Liter, *der od. das*

litter ['lɪtə(r)] **1.** *n.* **a)** *(rubbish)* Abfall,
der; **b)** *(of animals)* Wurf, *der.* **2.** *v. t.*
verstreuen. '**litter-basket** *n.* Abfall-
korb, *der.* '**litter-bin** Abfalleimer, *der*

little ['lɪtl] **1.** *adj.,* ~**r** ['lɪtlə(r)], ~**st** ['lɪt-
lɪst] (*Note: it is more common to use the
compar. and superl. forms* **smaller,
smallest**) **a)** klein; **a ~ way** ein kurzes
Stück; **after a ~ while** nach kurzer
Zeit; **b)** *(not much)* wenig; **there is very
~ tea left** es ist kaum noch Tee da; **a
~ ...** *(a small quantity of)* etwas ...; ein
bißchen ... **2.** *n.* wenig; **a ~** *(a small
quantity)* etwas; *(somewhat)* ein wenig; ~ **by ~:** nach und nach

liturgy ['lɪtədʒɪ] *n.* Liturgie, *die*

¹**live** [laɪv] **1.** *adj.* **a)** *attrib. (alive)* lebend; **b)** *(Radio, Telev.)* ~ **perform-
ance** Live-Aufführung, *die;* ~ **broad-**

cast Live-Sendung, *die;* c) *(Electr.)* stromführend. **2.** *adv. (Radio, Telev.)* live 〈*übertragen usw.*〉

²live [lɪv] **1.** *v. i.* **a)** leben; **b)** *(make permanent home)* wohnen; leben. **2.** *v. t.* leben. **live 'down** *v. t.* Gras wachsen lassen über (+ *Akk.*); **he will never be able to ~ it down** das wird ihm ewig anhängen. **live on 1.** ['--] *v. t.* leben von. **2.** [-'-] *v. i.* weiterleben. **live 'up to** *v. t.* gerecht werden (+ *Dat.*)

livelihood ['laɪvlɪhʊd] *n.* Lebensunterhalt, *der*

liveliness ['laɪvlɪnɪs] *n.* Lebhaftigkeit, *die*

lively ['laɪvlɪ] *adj.* lebhaft; lebendig 〈*Schilderung*〉; rege 〈*Handel*〉

liven up [laɪvn 'ʌp] **1.** *v. t.* Leben bringen in (+ *Akk.*). **2.** *v. i.* 〈*Person:*〉 aufleben

liver ['lɪvə(r)] *n.* Leber, *die*

livery ['lɪvərɪ] *n.* Livree, *die*

lives *pl. of* **life**

livestock ['laɪvstɒk] *n. pl.* Vieh, *das*

livid ['lɪvɪd] *adj. (Brit. coll.)* fuchtig *(ugs.)*

living ['lɪvɪŋ] **1.** *n.* **a)** Leben, *das;* **b) make a ~:** seinen Lebensunterhalt verdienen; **c) the ~:** die Lebenden. **2.** *adj.* lebend; **within ~ memory** seit Menschengedenken. **'living-room** *n.* Wohnzimmer, *das*

lizard ['lɪzəd] *n.* Eidechse, *die*

llama ['lɑːmə] *n.* Lama, *das*

load [ləʊd] **1.** *n. (burden, weight; also fig.)* Last, *die; (amount carried)* Ladung, *die.* **2.** *v. t.* **a)** *(put ~ on)* beladen; *(put as load)* ~ sb. with work *(fig.)* jmdm. Arbeit auftragen; **b)** laden 〈*Gewehr*〉; ~ **a camera** einen Film [in einen Fotoapparat] einlegen. **load 'up** *v. i.* laden (with *Akk.*)

'loaded *adj.* **a** ~ **question** eine suggestive Frage; **be** ~ *(sl.: rich)* [schwer] Kohle haben *(salopp)*

¹loaf [ləʊf] *n., pl.* **loaves** [ləʊvz] Brot, *das;* [Brot]laib, *der;* **a** ~ **of bread** ein Laib Brot

²loaf *v. i.* ~ **round town/the house** in der Stadt/zu Hause herumlungern *(ugs.)*

loan [ləʊn] **1.** *n.* **a)** *(thing lent)* Leihgabe, *die;* **be out on** ~: ausgeliehen sein; **have sth. on** ~ **[from sb.]** etw. [von jmdm.] geliehen haben; **b)** *(money lent)* Darlehen, *das.* **2.** *v. t.* ~ **sth. to sb.** jmdm. etw. leihen

loath [ləʊθ] *pred. adj.* **be** ~ **to do sth.** etw. ungern tun

loathe [ləʊð] *v. t.* verabscheuen.

loathing ['ləʊðɪŋ] *n.* Abscheu, *der* (of, for vor + *Dat.*). **loathsome** ['ləʊðsəm] *adj.* abscheulich; widerlich

loaves *pl. of* **¹loaf**

lobby ['lɒbɪ] *n.* **a)** *(pressure group)* Lobby, *die;* **b)** *(of hotel)* Eingangshalle, *die; (of theatre)* Foyer, *das*

lobe [ləʊb] *n. (ear~)* Ohrläppchen, *das*

lobster ['lɒbstə(r)] *n.* Hummer, *der*

local ['ləʊkl] **1.** *adj.* lokal *(bes. Zeitungsw.);* Kommunal〈*wahl, -abgaben*〉; *(of this area)* hiesig; *(of that area)* dortig; ortsansässig 〈*Firma, Familie*〉; 〈*Wein, Produkt, Spezialität*〉 [aus] der Gegend; **she's a ~ girl** sie ist von hier/dort. **2.** *n.* **a)** *(person)* Einheimische, *der/die;* **b)** *(Brit. coll.: pub)* [Stamm]kneipe, *die*

local: ~ anaes'thetic *n.* Lokalanästhetikum, *das;* ~ **au'thority** *n. (Brit.)* Kommunalverwaltung, *die;* ~ **call** *n. (Teleph.)* Ortsgespräch, *das;* ~ **'government** *n.* Kommunalverwaltung, *die*

locality [ləʊ'kælɪtɪ] *n.* Ort, *der*

'locally *adv.* im/am Ort

locate [ləʊ'keɪt] *v. t.* **a) be ~d** liegen; **b)** *(determine position of)* ausfindig machen. **location** [ləʊ'keɪʃn] *n.* **a)** Lage, *die;* **b)** *(Cinemat.)* **be on ~:** bei Außenaufnahmen sein

loch [lɒx, lɒk] *n. (Scot.)* See, *der*

¹lock [lɒk] *n. (of hair)* [Haar]strähne, *die*

²lock 1. *n.* **a)** *(of door etc.)* Schloß, *das;* **b)** *(on canal etc.)* Schleuse, *die.* **2.** *v. t.* zuschließen. **3.** *v. i.* 〈*Tür, Kasten usw.:*〉 sich zuschließen lassen. **lock a'way** *v. t.* einschließen; einsperren 〈*Person*〉. **lock 'in** *v. t.* einschließen; *(deliberately)* einsperren. **lock 'out** *v. t.* aussperren (of aus); ~ **oneself out** sich aussperren. **lock 'up 1.** *v. i.* abschließen. **2.** *v. t.* **a)** abschließen 〈*Haus, Tür*〉; **b)** *(imprison)* einsperren

locker ['lɒkə(r)] *n.* Schließfach, *das*

locket ['lɒkɪt] *n.* Medaillon, *das*

lock: ~jaw *n. (Med.)* Kieferklemme, *die;* ~**-out** *n.* Aussperrung, *die;* ~**smith** *n.* Schlosser, *der*

locomotive [ləʊkə'məʊtɪv] *n.* Lokomotive, *die*

locust ['ləʊkəst] *n.* Heuschrecke, *die*

lodge [lɒdʒ] **1.** *n.* **a)** *(cottage)* Pförtner-/Gärtnerhaus, *das;* **b)** *(porter's room)* [Pförtner]loge, *die.* **2.** *v. t.* **a)** einlegen 〈*Beschwerde, Protest usw.*〉; **b)** einreichen 〈*Klage*〉. **3.** *v. i.* [zur Miete] wohnen. **'lodger** *n.* Untermieter, *der*/Untermieterin, *die*. **lodging** ['lɒdʒɪŋ] *n*. [möbliertes] Zimmer

loft [lɒft] *n*. *(attic)* [Dach]boden, *der* **lofty** ['lɒftɪ] *adj*. **a)** *(exalted)* hoch; **b)** *(haughty)* hochmütig

log [lɒg] *n*. **a)** *(timber)* [geschlagener] Baumstamm; *(as firewood)* [Holz]scheit, *das*; **b)** ~[-book] *(Naut.)* Logbuch, *das*. **log 'cabin** *n*. Blockhütte, *die*. **log-'fire** *n*. Holzfeuer, *das*

loggerheads ['lɒgəhedz] *n. pl.* **be at ~ with sb.** mit jmdm. im Clinch liegen

logic ['lɒdʒɪk] *n*. Logik, *die*. **logical** ['lɒdʒɪkl] *adj*. logisch; **she has a ~ mind** sie denkt logisch. **logically** ['lɒdʒɪkəlɪ] *adv*. logisch

logo ['ləʊgəʊ] *n., pl.* ~s Signet, *das*

loin [lɔɪn] *n*. Lende, *die*. **'loincloth** *n*. Lendenschurz, *der*

loiter ['lɔɪtə(r)] *v. i.* trödeln; *(linger suspiciously)* herumlungern

loll [lɒl] *v. i.* sich lümmeln *(ugs.)*

lollipop ['lɒlɪpɒp] *n*. Lutscher, *der*

London ['lʌndən] **1.** *pr. n.* London *(das)*. **2.** *attrib. adj.* Londoner. **'Londoner** *pr. n.* Londoner, *der*/Londonerin, *die*

lone [ləʊn] *attrib. adj.* einsam. **loneliness** ['ləʊnlɪnɪs] *n*. Einsamkeit, *die* **lonely** ['ləʊnlɪ] *adj*. einsam

loner ['ləʊnə(r)] *n*. Einzelgänger, *der*/-gängerin, *die*

lonesome ['ləʊnsəm] *adj*. einsam

¹long [lɒŋ] **1.** *adj.*, ~er ['lɒŋgə(r)], ~est ['lɒŋgɪst] **a)** lang; weit ⟨*Reise, Weg*⟩; **b)** *(elongated)* länglich; schmal; **c) in the '~ run** auf die Dauer. **2.** *n*. (~ *interval*) **take ~:** lange dauern; **for ~:** lange; *(since ~ ago)* seit langem; **before ~:** bald. **3.** *adv.*, ~er, ~est **a)** lang[e]; **as or so ~ as** solange; **you should have finished ~ before now** du hättest schon längst fertig sein sollen; **much ~er** viel länger; **b) as or so ~ as** *(provided that)* solange; wenn

²long *v. i.* **~ for sb./sth.** sich nach jmdm./etw. sehnen; **~ to do sth.** sich danach sehnen, etw. zu tun

long-distance 1. ['---] *adj*. Fern⟨*gespräch, -verkehr usw.*⟩; Langstrecken⟨*läufer, -flug usw.*⟩. **2.** [-'--] *adv.* **phone ~:** ein Ferngespräch führen

longevity [lɒn'dʒevɪtɪ] *n*. Langlebigkeit, *die*

'longhand *n*. Langschrift, *die*

'longing 1. *n*. Sehnsucht, *die*. **2.** *adj*. sehnsüchtig. **'longingly** *adv.* sehnsüchtig

longitude ['lɒŋgɪtjuːd] *n*. Länge, *die*

long: ~ jump *n*. *(Brit. Sport)* Weitsprung, *der;* **~-lived** ['lɒŋlɪvd] *adj*. langlebig; **~-playing 'record** *n*. Langspielplatte, *die;* **~-range** *adj*. **a)** Langstrecken⟨*flugzeug, -rakete usw.*⟩; **b)** *(relating to time)* langfristig; **~-sighted** [lɒŋ'saɪtɪd] *adj*. weitsichtig; *(fig.)* weitblickend; **~-sleeved** ['lɒŋsliːvd] *adj*. langärmelig; **~-standing** *attrib. adj.* seit langem bestehend; alt ⟨*Schulden, Streit*⟩; **~-suffering** *adj*. schwer geprüft; **~-term** *adj*. langfristig; **~ wave** *n*. *(Radio)* Langwelle, *die;* **~-winded** [lɒŋ'wɪndɪd] *adj*. langatmig

loo [luː] *n*. *(Brit. coll.)* Klo, *das (ugs.)*

look [lʊk] **1.** *v. i.* **a)** sehen; gucken *(ugs.)*; **b)** *(search)* nachsehen; **c)** *(face)* zugewandt sein (to[wards] *Dat.*); **d)** *(appear)* aussehen; **~ well/ill** gut/schlecht aussehen. **2.** *n*. **a)** Blick, *der;* **have or take a ~ at sb./sth.** sich *(Dat.)* jmdn./etw. ansehen; **b)** *(appearance)* Aussehen, *das*. **look 'after** *v. t. (care for)* sorgen für. **look a'head** *v. i. (fig.)* an die Zukunft denken. **'look at** *v. t.* **a)** *(regard)* ansehen; **b)** *(consider)* betrachten. **look 'back** *v. i.* **a)** sich umsehen; **b) ~ back on** *or* **to sth.** an etw. *(Akk.)* zurückdenken. **look 'down [up]on** *v. t.* **a)** herunter-/hinuntersehen auf (+ *Akk.*); **b)** *(fig.: despise)* herabsehen auf (+ *Akk.*). **'look for** *v. t.* **a)** *(seek)* suchen nach; **b)** *(expect)* erwarten. **look 'out** *v. i.* **a)** hinaus-/heraussehen (of aus); **b)** *(take care)* aufpassen; **c) ~ out on sth.** ⟨*Zimmer, Wohnung usw.*⟩ zu etw. hin liegen. **look 'out for** *v. t. (be prepared for)* achten auf (+ *Akk.*); *(keep watching for)* Ausschau halten nach ⟨*Arbeit, Gelegenheit, Sammelobjekt usw.*⟩. **look 'over** *v. t.* **a)** sehen über (+ *Akk.*); **b)** *(survey)* sich *(Dat.)* ansehen ⟨*Haus*⟩. **look 'round** *v. i.* sich umsehen. **'look through** *v. t.* **a)** ~ **through sth.** durch etw. [hindurch] sehen; **b)** *(inspect)* durchsehen ⟨*Papiere*⟩. **'look to** *v. t.* *(rely on)* ~ **to sb./sth. for sth.** etw. von jmdm./etw. erwarten. **look 'up 1.** *v. i.* **a)** aufblicken; **b)** *(improve)* besser werden. **2.** *v. t.* nachschlagen ⟨*Wort*⟩; heraussuchen ⟨*Telefonnummer, Zugverbindung usw.*⟩. **look 'up to** *v. t.* ~ **up to sb.** zu jmdm. aufsehen

'look-alike *n*. Doppelgänger, *der*/-gängerin, *die*

looker-'on *n*. Zuschauer, *der*/Zuschauerin, *die*

'looking-glass *n.* Spiegel, *der*

'look-out *n., pl.* ~s **a)** *(observation post)* Ausguck, *der;* **b)** *(person)* Wache, *die;* **c)** *(Brit. fig.)* **that's a bad ~:** das sind schlechte Aussichten; **that's his ~:** das ist sein Problem; **d) keep a ~ |for sb./sth.|** [nach etw./jmdm.] Ausschau halten

'loom [lu:m] *n. (Weaving)* Webstuhl, *der*

²loom *v.i.* auftauchen

loop [lu:p] **1.** *n.* **a)** Schleife, *die;* **b)** *(cord)* Schlaufe, *die.* **2.** *v.t.* zu einer Schlaufe formen. **'loophole** *n. (fig.)* Lücke, *die*

loose [lu:s] *adj.* **a)** *(not firm)* locker ⟨*Zahn, Schraube, Knopf*⟩; **b)** *(not fixed)* lose ⟨*Knopf, Buchseite, Brett, Stein*⟩; offen ⟨*Haar*⟩; **c) be at a ~ end** *(fig.)* nichts zu tun haben; **d)** *(inexact)* ungenau. **'loose-fitting** *adj.* bequem geschnitten. **'loose-leaf** *adj.* Loseblatt-; ~ **file** Ringbuch, *das*

'loosely *adv.* locker; lose ⟨*zusammenhängen*⟩; frei ⟨*übersetzen*⟩

loosen ['lu:sn] *v.t.* lockern. **loosen 'up** *v.i.* sich auflockern; *(relax)* auftauen

'looseness *n.* Lockerheit, *die*

loot [lu:t] **1.** *v.t.* plündern. **2.** *n.* Beute, *die.* **'looter** *n.* Plünderer, *der*

lop [lɒp] *v.t.* ~ **sth. |off** *or* **away|** etw. abbauen *od.* abhacken

lopsided [lɒp'saɪdɪd] *adj.* schief

lord [lɔ:d] **1.** *n.* **a)** *(master)* Herr, *der;* **b)** **L~** *(Relig.)* Herr, *der;* **c)** *(Brit.: as title)* Lord, *der;* **the House of L~s** *(Brit.)* das Oberhaus. **2.** *int. (coll.)* Gott; **oh/good L~!** du lieber Himmel! **'lordship** *n.* Lordschaft, *die*

lore [lɔ:(r)] *n.* Überlieferung, *die*

lorry ['lɒrɪ] *n. (Brit.)* Lastwagen, *der;* Lkw, *der.* **'lorry-driver** *n. (Brit.)* Lastwagenfahrer, *der;* Lkw-Fahrer, *der*

lose [lu:z] **1.** *v.t.,* lost [lɒst] **a)** verlieren; ~ **one's way** sich verlaufen/verfahren; **b)** ⟨*Uhr:*⟩ nachgehen; **c)** *(waste)* vertun ⟨*Zeit*⟩; *(miss)* versäumen ⟨*Gelegenheit*⟩; **d)** ~ **weight** abnehmen. **2.** *v.i.,* lost **a)** *(in match, contest)* verlieren; **b)** ⟨*Uhr:*⟩ nachgehen. **'loser** *n.* Verlierer, *der/*Verliererin, *die*

loss [lɒs] *n.* **a)** Verlust, *der* (of *Gen.*); **sell at a ~:** mit Verlust verkaufen; **b) be at a ~:** nicht [mehr] weiterwissen; **be at a ~ for words** um Worte verlegen sein; **be at a ~ what to do** nicht wissen, was zu tun ist

lost [lɒst] **1.** *see* **lose. 2.** *adj.* **a)** verloren; **get ~** ⟨*Person:*⟩ sich verlaufen/verfahren; **get ~!** *(sl.)* verdufte! *(salopp);* ~ **cause** aussichtslose Sache; **b)** *(wasted)* vertan ⟨*Zeit*⟩; *(missed)* versäumt ⟨*Gelegenheit*⟩

lot [lɒt] *n.* **a)** *(destiny)* Los, *das;* **b)** *(set of persons)* Haufen, *der;* **the ~:** [sie] alle; **c)** *(set of things)* Menge, *die;* **the ~:** alle/alles; **d)** *(coll.: large quantity)* ~s *or* **a ~ of money** *etc.* viel *od.* eine Menge Geld *usw.;* **sing** *etc.* **a ~:** viel singen *usw.;* **like sth. a ~:** etw. sehr mögen; **have ~s to do** viel zu tun haben; **e)** *(for choosing)* Los, *das;* **draw/cast/throw ~s |for sth.|** um etw. losen

lotion ['ləʊʃn] *n.* Lotion, *die*

lottery ['lɒtərɪ] *n.* Lotterie, *die*

loud [laʊd] **1.** *adj.* **a)** laut; lautstark ⟨*Protest, Kritik*⟩; **b)** *(flashy, conspicuous)* aufdringlich; grell ⟨*Farbe*⟩. **2.** *adv.* laut; **laugh out ~:** laut auflachen; **say sth. out ~:** etw. aussprechen. **loud 'hailer** *n.* Megaphon, *das*

'loudly *adv.* laut

'loudness *n.* Lautstärke, *die*

loud'speaker *n.* Lautsprecher, *der*

lounge [laʊndʒ] **1.** *v.i.* ~ **|about** *or* **around|** *(faul)* herumliegen/-sitzen/ -stehen. **2.** *n.* **a)** *(in hotel)* [Hotel]halle, *die;* *(at airport)* Wartehalle, *die;* **b)** *(sitting-room)* Wohnzimmer, *das*

louse [laʊs] *n., pl.* **lice** [laɪs] Laus, *die*

lousy ['laʊzɪ] *adj. (sl.)* **a)** *(disgusting)* ekelhaft; **b)** *(very poor)* lausig *(ugs.);* **feel ~:** sich mies *(ugs.)* fühlen

lout [laʊt] *n.* Rüpel, *der;* Flegel, *der*

louver, louvre ['lu:və(r)] *n.* ~ **window** Jalousiefenster, *das;* ~ **door** Jalousietür, *die*

lovable ['lʌvəbl] *adj.* liebenswert

love [lʌv] **1.** *n.* **a)** Liebe, *die* (of, for zu); **in** ~ **|with|** verliebt [in (+ *Akk.*)]; **fall in** ~ **|with|** sich verlieben [in (+ *Akk.*)]; **for ~:** aus Liebe; ~ **from Beth** *(in letter)* herzliche Grüße von Beth; **send one's** ~ **to sb.** jmdn. grüßen lassen; **b)** *(sweetheart)* Geliebte, *der/ die;* **|my|** ~ *(coll.: form of address)* [mein] Liebling *od.* Schatz; **c)** *(Tennis)* **fifteen/thirty** ~ fünfzehn/dreißig null. **2.** *v.t.* **a)** lieben; **our/their ~d ones** unsere/ihre Lieben; **b)** *(like)* **I'd ~ a cigarette** ich hätte sehr gerne eine Zigarette; ~ **to do** *or* ~ **doing sth.** etw. gern tun

love: ~ **affair** *n.* Liebesverhältnis, *das;* **~-letter** *n.* Liebesbrief, *der;* **~-life** *n.* Liebesleben, *das*

loveliness ['lʌvlinis] *n.* Schönheit, *die*

lovely ['lʌvli] *adj.* [wunder]schön; herrlich ⟨*Tag, Essen*⟩

lover ['lʌvə(r)] *n.* **a)** Liebhaber, *der;* Geliebte, *der; (woman)* Geliebte, *die;* **be ~s** ein Liebespaar sein; **b)** *(person who likes sth.)* Freund, *der*/Freundin, *die*

love: ~sick *adj.* an Liebeskummer leidend; liebeskrank *(geh.);* **~-song** *n.* Liebeslied, *das;* **~-story** *n.* Liebesgeschichte, *die*

loving ['lʌviŋ] *adj.* **a)** *(affectionate)* liebend; **b)** *(expressing love)* liebevoll. **'lovingly** *adv.* liebevoll

low [ləʊ] **1.** *adj.* **a)** niedrig; tief ausgeschnitten ⟨*Kleid*⟩; tief ⟨*Ausschnitt*⟩; tiefliegend ⟨*Grund*⟩; **b)** *(of humble rank)* nieder...; niedrig; **c)** *(inferior)* niedrig; gering ⟨*Intelligenz, Bildung*⟩; **d)** *(in pitch)* tief; *(in loudness)* leise. **2.** *adv.* **a)** *(to a ~ position)* tief; **b)** *(not loudly)* leise; **c) lie ~** *(hide)* untertauchen. **'lowbrow** *adj. (coll.)* schlicht ⟨*Person*⟩; [geistig] anspruchslos ⟨*Buch, Programm*⟩. **'low-cut** *adj.* [tief] ausgeschnitten ⟨*Kleid*⟩

'lower ['ləʊə(r)] *v.t.* **a)** herab-/hinablassen; **b)** senken ⟨*Blick*⟩; auslassen ⟨*Saum*⟩; senken ⟨*Preis, Miete, Zins usw.*⟩; **~ one's voice** leiser sprechen

²lower **1.** *compar. adj.* unter...; Unter- ⟨*grenze-, arm, -lippe usw.*⟩. **2.** *compar. adv.* tiefer

low: ~-fat *adj.* fettarm; **~-grade** *adj.* minderwertig; **~land** ['ləʊlənd] *n.* Tiefland, *das*

lowly ['ləʊli] *adj. (modest)* bescheiden

low: ~-lying *adj.* tiefliegend; **~ point** *n.* Tiefpunkt, *der;* **~ pressure** *n. (Meteorol.)* Tiefdruck, *der*

loyal ['lɔɪəl] *adj.* treu. **loyalty** ['lɔɪəlti] *n.* Treue, *die*

lozenge ['lɒzɪndʒ] *n.* Pastille, *die*

LP *abbr.* **long-playing record** LP, *die*

Ltd. *abbr.* **Limited** GmbH

lubricant ['lu:brɪkənt] *n.* Schmiermittel, *das*

lubricate ['lu:brɪkeɪt] *v.t.* schmieren. **lubrication** [lu:brɪ'keɪʃn] *n.* Schmierung, *die; attrib.* Schmier⟨*system, -vorrichtung*⟩

lucid ['lu:sɪd] *adj.* klar. **lucidity** [lu:-'sɪdɪti] *n.* Klarheit, *die*

luck [lʌk] *n.* Glück, *das;* **good ~:** Glück, *das;* **bad** *or* **hard ~:** Pech, *das;* **good ~!** viel Glück!; **be in/out of ~:** Glück/kein Glück haben; **no such ~:** schön wär's. **luckily** ['lʌkɪli] *adv.*

glücklicherweise. **lucky** ['lʌkɪ] *adj.* **a)** glücklich; **be ~:** Glück haben; **b)** *(bringing good luck)* Glücks⟨*zahl, -tag usw.*⟩; **~ charm** Glücksbringer, *der*

lucrative ['lu:krətɪv] *adj.* einträglich; lukrativ

ludicrous ['lu:dɪkrəs] *adj.* lächerlich; lachhaft ⟨*Angebot, Ausrede*⟩

lug [lʌg] *v.t.,* **-gg-** *(drag)* schleppen

luggage ['lʌgɪdʒ] *n.* Gepäck, *das.* **'luggage-locker** *n.* [Gepäck]-schließfach, *das.* **'luggage-rack** *n.* Gepäckablage, *die*

lugubrious [lu:'gu:brɪəs] *adj. (mournful)* kummervoll; *(dismal)* düster

lukewarm ['lu:kwɔ:m] *adj.* lauwarm

lull [lʌl] **1.** *v.t.* **a)** *(soothe)* lullen; **b)** *(fig.)* einlullen; **~ sb. into a false sense of security** jmdn. in einer trügerischen Sicherheit wiegen. **2.** *n.* Pause, *die*

lullaby ['lʌləbaɪ] *n.* Schlaflied, *das*

lumbago [lʌm'beɪgəʊ] *n., pl.* **~s** *(Med.)* Hexenschuß, *der*

lumber ['lʌmbə(r)] **1.** *n.* **a)** *(furniture)* Gerümpel, *das;* **b)** *(useless material)* Kram, *der (ugs.);* **c)** *(Amer.: timber)* [Bau]holz, *das.* **2.** *v.t.* **~ sb. with sth./ sb.** jmdm. etw./jmdn. aufhalsen *(ugs.)*

'lumbering *adj.* schwerfällig

lumberjack ['lʌmbədʒæk] *n. (Amer.)* Holzfäller, *der*

luminous ['lu:mɪnəs] *adj.* [hell] leuchtend; Leucht⟨*anzeige, -zeiger usw.*⟩

lump [lʌmp] **1.** *n.* **a)** Klumpen, *der; (of sugar, butter, etc.)* Stück, *das; (of wood)* Klotz, *der; (of dough)* Kloß, *der; (of bread)* Brocken, *der;* **b)** *(swelling)* Beule, *die.* **2.** *v.t.* **~ sth. with sth.** etw. und etw. zusammentun. **lump 'sum** *n.* Pauschalsumme, *die*

'lumpy *adj.* klumpig ⟨*Brei*⟩; ⟨*Kissen, Matratze*⟩ mit klumpiger Füllung

lunacy ['lu:nəsi] *n.* Wahnsinn, *der*

lunar ['lu:nə(r)] *adj.* Mond-

lunatic ['lu:nətɪk] **1.** *adj.* wahnsinnig. **2.** *n.* Wahnsinnige, *der/die;* Irre, *der/ die.* **'lunatic asylum** *n. (Hist.)* Irrenanstalt, *die (veralt., ugs.)*

lunch [lʌntʃ] **1.** *n.* Mittagessen, *das;* **have** *or* **eat [one's] ~:** zu Mittag essen. **2.** *v.i.* zu Mittag essen

luncheon voucher ['lʌntʃn vaʊtʃə(r)] *n. (Brit.)* Essenmarke, *die*

lunch: ~-hour *n.* Mittagspause, *die;* **~-time** *n.* Mittagszeit, *die;* **at ~-time** mittags

lung [lʌŋ] *n. (right or left)* Lungenflügel, *der;* **~s** Lunge, *die.* **'lung cancer** *n.* Lungenkrebs, *der*

lunge [lʌndʒ] **1.** *n.* Sprung nach vorn. **2.** *v. i.* ~ **at sb. with a knife** jmdn. mit einem Messer angreifen

¹lurch [lɜːtʃ] *n.* **leave sb. in the ~:** jmdn. im Stich lassen

²lurch 1. *n.* Rucken, *das.* **2.** *v. i.* rucken; ⟨*Betrunkener:*⟩ torkeln

lure [ljʊə(r), lʊə(r)] **1.** *v. t.* locken. **2.** *n.* Lockmittel, *das*

lurid ['ljʊərɪd, 'lʊərɪd] *adj.* **a)** *(in colour)* grell; **b)** *(sensational)* reißerisch

lurk [lɜːk] *v. i.* lauern

luscious ['lʌʃəs] *adj.* köstlich [süß]; saftig [süß] ⟨*Obst*⟩

lush [lʌʃ] *adj.* saftig ⟨*Wiese*⟩; grün ⟨*Tal*⟩; üppig ⟨*Vegetation*⟩

lust [lʌst] **1.** *n.* **a)** *(sexual)* Sinnenlust, *die;* **b)** *(strong desire)* Gier, *die* (for nach). **2.** *v. i.* ~ **after** [lustvoll] begehren *(geh.).* **lustful** ['lʌstfl] *adj.* lüstern *(geh.)*

lustily ['lʌstɪlɪ] *adv.* kräftig; aus voller Kehle ⟨*rufen, singen*⟩

lustre ['lʌstə(r)] *n. (Brit.)* **a)** Schimmer, *der;* **b)** *(fig.: splendour)* Glanz, *der*

lusty ['lʌstɪ] *adj.* kräftig

Luxembourg, Luxemburg ['lʌksəmbɜːg] *pr. n.* Luxemburg *(das)*

luxuriant [lʌg'zjʊərɪənt] *adj.* üppig

luxuriate [lʌg'zjʊərɪeɪt] *v. i.* ~ **in** sich aalen in (+ *Dat.*)

luxurious [lʌg'zjʊərɪəs] *adj.* luxuriös

luxury ['lʌkʃərɪ] *n.* **a)** Luxus, *der;* **b)** *(article)* Luxusgegenstand, *der;* **luxuries** Luxus, *der*

LW *abbr. (Radio)* **long wave** LW

lying ['laɪɪŋ] *adj.* verlogen ⟨*Person*⟩. *See also* ¹**lie 2**

lynch [lɪntʃ] *v. t.* lynchen

lyric ['lɪrɪk] **1.** *adj.* lyrisch; ~ **poetry** Lyrik, *die.* **2.** *n.* **in** *pl. (of song)* Text, *der.* **lyrical** ['lɪrɪkl] *adj.* **a)** lyrisch; **b)** *(coll.: enthusiastic)* gefühlvoll

M

M, m [em] *n.* M, m, *das*

m. *abbr.* **a)** masculine m.; **b)** metre[s] m; **c)** million[s] Mill.; **d)** minute[s] Min.

MA *abbr.* **Master of Arts** M. A.

mac [mæk] *n. (Brit. coll.)* Regenmantel, *der*

macaroni [mækə'rəʊnɪ] *n.* Makkaroni *Pl.*

machine [mə'ʃiːn] *n.* Maschine, *die.* **ma'chine-gun** *n.* Maschinengewehr, *das*

machinery [mə'ʃiːnərɪ] *n.* **a)** *(machines)* Maschinen *Pl.;* **b)** *(mechanism)* Mechanismus, *der*

machine: ~ **tool** *n.* Werkzeugmaschine, *die;* **~-washable** *adj.* waschmaschinenfest

machinist [mə'ʃiːnɪst] *n.* Maschinist, *der*/Maschinistin, *die;* |**sewing-**|~: [Maschinen]näherin, *die*/-näher, *der*

macho ['mætʃəʊ] *adj.* Macho-; **he is** ~: er ist ein Macho

mackerel ['mækərl] *n., pl. same or* ~**s** Makrele, *die*

mackintosh ['mækɪntɒʃ] *n.* Regenmantel, *der*

mad [mæd] *adj.* **a)** *(insane)* geisteskrank; **b)** *(frenzied)* wahnsinnig; **drive sb. mad** jmdn. um den Verstand bringen; **c)** *(foolish)* verrückt *(ugs.);* **d)** *(very enthusiastic)* **be** ~ **about** *or* **on sb./sth.** auf jmdn./etw. wild sein *(ugs.);* **e)** *(coll.: annoyed)* ~ |**with** *or* **at sb.**| sauer [auf jmdn.] *(ugs.);* **f)** *(with rabies)* toll[wütig]; |**run** *etc.*| **like** ~: wie wild [laufen *usw.*]

madam ['mædəm] *n.* gnädige Frau; **Dear M~** *(in letter)* Sehr verehrte gnädige Frau

madden ['mædn] *v. t. (irritate)* [ver]ärgern. **maddening** ['mædənɪŋ] *adj. (irritating)* [äußerst] ärgerlich

made *see* **make 1**

'madly *adv. (coll.)* wahnsinnig *(ugs.)*

madman ['mædmən] *n., pl.* **madmen** ['mædmən] *n.* Wahnsinnige, *der*

'madness *n.* Wahnsinn, *der*

magazine [mægə'ziːn] *n.* **a)** Zeitschrift, *die;* **b)** *(of firearm)* Magazin, *das*

maggot ['mægət] *n.* Made, *die*

magic ['mædʒɪk] **1.** *n.* **a)** Magie, *die;* **work like** ~: wie ein Wunder wirken; **b)** *(conjuring)* Zauberei, *die.* **2.** *adj.* **a)** magisch; Zauber⟨*trank, -baum*⟩; **b)** *(fig.)* wunderbar. **magical** ['mædʒɪkl] *adj.* zauberhaft. **magician** [mə'dʒɪʃn] *n.* Magier, *der*/Magierin, *die; (conjurer)* Zauberer, *der*/Zauberin, *die*

magistrate ['mædʒɪstreɪt] *n.* Friedensrichter, *der*/-richterin, *die*

magnanimity [mægnə'nɪmɪtɪ] *n.* Großmut, *die*

make

magnanimous [mæg'nænıməs] *adj.*
großmütig (**towards** gegen)
magnate ['mægneıt] *n.* Magnat,
der/Magnatin, *die*
magnesium [mæg'ni:zıəm] *n.* Magnesium, *das*
magnet ['mægnıt] *n.* Magnet, *der.*
magnetic [mæg'netık] *adj.* magne-
tisch. **magnetic 'tape** *n.* Magnet-
band, *der*
magnetism ['mægnıtızm] *n.* **a)** *(force,
lit. or fig.)* Magnetismus, *der;* **b)** *(fig.:
charm)* Anziehungskraft, *die*
magnetize ['mægnıtaız] *v.t.* magneti-
sieren
magnification [mægnıfı'keıʃn] *n.*
Vergrößerung, *die*
magnificence [mæg'nıfısəns] *n.*
Pracht, *die; (beauty)* Herrlichkeit, *die;
(lavishness)* Üppigkeit, *die*
magnificent [mæg'nıfısənt] *adj.* **a)**
prächtig; herrlich ‹*Garten, Kunstwerk,
Wetter*›; *(lavish)* üppig ‹*Mahl*›; **b)**
(coll.: excellent) fabelhaft *(ugs.)*
magnify ['mægnıfaı] *v.t.* **a)** vergrößern; **b)** *(exaggerate)* aufbauschen.
'**magnifying glass** *n.* Lupe, *die*
magnitude ['mægnıtjuːd] *n.* **a)** *(size)*
Größe, *die;* **b)** *(importance)* Wichtigkeit, *die*
magpie ['mægpaı] *n.* Elster, *die*
mahogany [mə'hɒgənı] *n.* Mahagoni[holz], *das; attrib.* Mahagoni-
maid [meıd] *n.* Dienstmädchen, *das*
maiden ['meıdn] **1.** *n.* Jungfrau, *die.* **2.**
adj. **a)** *(unmarried)* unverheiratet; **b)**
(first) ~ **voyage/speech** Jungfernfahrt/
-rede, *die.* '**maiden name** *n.* Mäd-
chenname, *der*
mail [meıl] **1.** *n. see* ²post 1. **2.** *v.t.* abschicken
mail: ~**bag** *n.* Postsack, *der;* ~**box** *n.*
(Amer.) Briefkasten, *der;* ~**ing list** *n.*
Adressenliste, *die;* ~**man** *n. (Amer.)*
Briefträger, *der;* ~ **order** *n.* Bestellung per Post
maim [meım] *v.t.* verstümmeln
main [meın] **1.** *n.* **a)** *(channel, pipe)*
Hauptleitung, *die;* ~s *(Electr.)* Strom-
netz, *das;* **b)** **in the** ~: im großen und
ganzen. **2.** *attrib. adj.* Haupt-; **the** ~
thing is that …: die Hauptsache ist,
daß … **mainland** ['meınlənd] *n.* Festland, *das*
'**mainly** *adv.* hauptsächlich
main: ~**stay** *n.* [wichtigste] Stütze; ~
street [*Brit.* -'-, *Amer.* '--] *n.* Haupt-
straße, *die*
maintain [meın'teın] *v.t.* **a)** *(keep up)*

aufrechterhalten; **b)** *(provide for)* ~ **sb.**
für jmds. Unterhalt aufkommen; **c)**
(preserve) instand halten; warten ‹*Maschine*›; **d)** ~ **that …:** behaupten,
daß … **maintenance** ['meıntənəns]
n. **a)** *(keeping up)* Aufrechterhaltung,
die; **b)** *(preservation)* Instandhaltung,
die; (of machinery) Wartung, *die;* **c)**
(Law: money paid to support sb.) Unterhalt, *der*
maison[n]ette [meızə'net] *n.* [zwei-
stöckige] Wohnung
maize [meız] *n.* Mais, *der*
majestic [mə'dʒestık] *adj.,* **majestically** [mə'dʒestıkəlı] *adv.* majestätisch
majesty ['mædʒıstı] *n.* Majestät, *die
(geh.);* **Your/Her** *etc.* **M~:** Eure/Seine
usw. Majestät
major ['meıdʒə(r)] **1.** *adj.* **a)** *attrib.
(greater)* größer…; **b)** *attrib. (important)* bedeutend…; *(serious)* schwer; ~
road Hauptverkehrsstraße, *die;* **c)**
(Mus.) Dur-; C ~: C-Dur. **2.** *n. (Mil.)*
Major, *der.* **3.** *v.i. (Amer. Univ.)* ~ **in
sth.** etw. als Hauptfach haben
Majorca [mə'jɔːkə] *pr. n.* Mallorca
(das)
majority [mə'dʒɒrıtı] *n.* Mehrheit,
die; **be in the** ~: in der Mehrzahl sein
make [meık] **1.** *v.t.,* **made** [meıd] **a)**
machen (**of** aus); bauen ‹*Straße,
Flugzeug*›; anlegen ‹*Teich, Weg usw.*›;
zimmern ‹*Tisch, Regal*›; basteln
‹*Spielzeug, Vogelhäuschen usw.*›; nähen ‹*Kleider*›; *(manufacture)* herstellen; *(prepare)* zubereiten ‹*Mahlzeit*›;
machen, kochen ‹*Kaffee, Tee*›;
backen ‹*Brot, Kuchen*›; **b)** *(establish,
enact)* treffen ‹*Unterscheidung, Über-
einkommen*›; ziehen ‹*Vergleich*›; erlassen ‹*Gesetz*›; aufstellen ‹*Regeln,
Behauptung*›; stellen ‹*Forderung*›; geben ‹*Bericht*›; vornehmen ‹*Zahlung*›;
erheben ‹*Protest, Beschwerde*›; **c)**
(cause to be or become) ~ **happy/
known** *etc.* glücklich/bekannt *usw.*
machen; ~ **sb. captain** jmdn. zum Kapitän machen; **d)** ~ **sb. do sth.** *(cause)*
jmdn. dazu bringen, etw. zu tun;
(compel) jmdn. zwingen, etw. zu tun;
be made to do sth. etw. tun müssen; **e)**
(earn) machen ‹*Profit, Verlust*›; verdienen ‹*Lebensunterhalt*›; **f)** **what do
you** ~ **of him?** was hältst du von ihm?;
g) *(arrive at)* erreichen; **make it** *(succeed in arriving)* es schaffen; **h)** ~ '**do**
vorliebnehmen; ~ '**do with/without
sth.** mit/ohne etw. auskommen. **2.** *n.*

(brand) Marke, *die.* 'make for *v.t.*
zusteuern auf (+ *Akk.*). make 'off
v.i. sich davonmachen. make 'off
with *v.t.* ~ off with sb./sth. sich mit
jmdm./etw. [auf und] davonmachen.
make 'out 1. *v.t.* a) *(write)* ausstellen; b) *(claim)* behaupten; c) *(manage
to see or hear)* ausmachen; *(manage to
read)* entziffern; d) *(pretend)* vorgeben. 2. *v.i.* *(coll.)* zurechtkommen (at
bei). make 'over *v.t.* überschreiben.
make 'up 1. *v.t.* a) *(assemble)* zusam-
menstellen; b) *(invent)* erfinden; c)
(constitute) bilden; be made up of ...:
bestehen aus ...; d) *(apply cosmetics to)*
schminken; ~ up one's face sich
schminken. 2. *v.i.* *(be reconciled)* sich
wieder vertragen. make 'up for *v.t.*
wiedergutmachen; ~ up for lost time
Versäumtes nachholen
'make-believe 1. *n.* it's only ~: das
ist bloß Phantasie. 2. *adj.* nicht echt
'maker *n.* *(manufacturer)* Hersteller,
der
make: ~shift *adj.* behelfsmäßig;
~-up *n.* *(Cosmetics)* Make-up, *das*
making ['meɪkɪŋ] *n.* in the ~: im Entstehen; have the ~s of a leader das
Zeug zum Führer haben *(ugs.)*
maladjusted [mælə'dʒʌstɪd] *adj.* ver-
haltensgestört
malady ['mælədɪ] *n.* Leiden, *das*
malaise [mə'leɪz] *n.* Unbehagen, *das*
malaria [mə'leərɪə] *n.* Malaria, *die*
Malaysia [mə'leɪzɪə] *pr. n.* Malaysia
(das)
male [meɪl] 1. *adj.* männlich; Männer-
‹*stimme, -chor, -verein*›; ~ doctor/
nurse Arzt, *der*/Krankenpfleger, *der.*
2. *n.* *(person)* Mann, *der; (animal)*
Männchen, *das*
malevolence [mə'levələns] *n.* Boshaftigkeit, *die*
malevolent [mə'levələnt] *adj.* boshaft
malfunction [mæl'fʌŋkʃn] 1. *n.* Störung, *die; (Med.)* Funktionsstörung,
die. 2. *v.i.* nicht richtig funktionieren
malice ['mælɪs] *n.* Bosheit, *die.* malicious [mə'lɪʃəs] *adj.* böse
malign [mə'laɪn] *v.t.* verleumden
malignant [mə'lɪgnənt] *adj.* bösartig
malinger [mə'lɪŋgə(r)] *v.i.* simulieren.
ma'lingerer *n.* Simulant, *der*/Simu-
lantin, *die*
malleable ['mælɪəbl] *adj.* formbar
mallet ['mælɪt] *n.* Holzhammer, *der*
malnutrition [mælnjuː'trɪʃn] *n.* Un-
terernährung, *die*
malt [mɔːlt] *n.* Malz, *das*

Malta ['mɔːltə] *pr. n.* Malta *(das)*
maltreat [mæl'triːt] *v.t.* mißhandeln.
mal'treatment *n.* Mißhandlung, *die*
mammal ['mæml] *n.* Säugetier, *das*
mammoth ['mæməθ] 1. *n.* Mammut,
das. 2. *adj.* Mammut-; gigantisch
‹*Vorhaben*›
man [mæn] 1. *n.* a) *pl.* men [men]
Mann, *der;* b) *(human race)* der
Mensch. 2. *v.t.,* -nn- bemannen
‹*Schiff*›; besetzen ‹*Büro, Stelle usw.*›;
bedienen ‹*Telefon, Geschütz*›
manacle ['mænəkl] 1. *n., usu. in pl.*
[Hand]fessel, *die.* 2. *v.t.* Handfesseln
anlegen (+ *Dat.*)
manage ['mænɪdʒ] 1. *v.t.* a) leiten
‹*Geschäft*›; b) *(Sport)* betreuen
‹*Mannschaft*›; c) *(cope with)* schaffen;
d) ~ to do sth. es fertigbringen, etw. zu
tun; he ~d to do it es gelang ihm, es zu
tun. 2. *v.i.* zurechtkommen; ~ without
sth. ohne etw. auskommen; I can ~:
es geht. manageable ['mænɪdʒəbl]
adj. leicht frisierbar ‹*Haar*›; fügsam
‹*Person, Tier*›; überschaubar ‹*Größe,
Menge*›. 'management *n.* a) *(of a
business)* Leitung, *die;* b) *(managers)*
the ~: die Geschäftsleitung. 'manager *n.* *(of shop or bank)* Filialleiter,
der/-leiterin, *die; (of football team)*
[Chef]trainer, *der*/-trainerin, *die; (of
restaurant, shop, hotel)* Geschäftsführ-
rer, *der*/-führerin, *die.* manageress
[mænɪdʒə'res] *n.* Geschäftsführerin,
die. managing ['mænɪdʒɪŋ] *adj.* ~
director Geschäftsführer, *der*/-führe-
rin, *die*
¹mandarin ['mændərɪn] *n.* ~ [orange]
Mandarine, *die*
²mandarin *n.* *(bureaucrat)* Bürokrat,
der/Bürokratin, *die*
mandarine ['mændəriːn] *see* ¹mandarin
mandate ['mændeɪt] *n.* Mandat, *das*
mandatory ['mændətərɪ] *adj.* obligatorisch
mandolin[e] [mændə'lɪn] *n.* Mando-
line, *die*
mane [meɪn] *n.* Mähne, *die*
maneuver[able] *(Amer.)* *see* man-
œuvr-
manful ['mænfl] *adj.,* manfully
['mænfəlɪ] *adv.* mannhaft
manger ['meɪndʒə(r)] *n.* Krippe, *die*
mangle ['mæŋgl] *v.t.* verstümmeln
‹*Person*›; demolieren ‹*Sache*›
mangy ['meɪndʒɪ] *adj.* a) *(Vet. Med.)*
räudig; b) *(shabby)* schäbig
man: ~handle *v.t.* a) von Hand be-

wegen ⟨*Gegenstand*⟩; **b)** grob behandeln ⟨*Person*⟩; **~hole** *n.* Mannloch, *das*

'**manhood** *n.* Mannesalter, *das*

man: ~-hour *n.* Arbeitsstunde, *die;* **~-hunt** *n.* Verbrecherjagd, *die*

mania ['meɪnɪə] *n.* Manie, *die*

manicure ['mænɪkjʊə(r)] **1.** *n.* Maniküre, *die.* **2.** *v. t.* maniküren

manifest ['mænɪfest] **1.** *adj.* offenkundig. **2.** *v. t. (reveal)* offenbaren. '**manifestly** *adv.* offenkundig

manifesto [mænɪ'festəʊ] *n., pl.* **~s** Manifest, *das*

manifold ['mænɪfəʊld] *adj. (literary)* mannigfaltig *(geh.)*

manipulate [mə'nɪpjʊleɪt] *v. t.* **a)** manipulieren; **b)** *(handle)* handhaben. **manipulation** [mənɪpjʊ'leɪʃn] *n.* **a)** Manipulation, *die;* **b)** *(handling)* Handhabung, *die*

mankind [mæn'kaɪnd] *n.* Menschheit, *die*

manly ['mænlɪ] *adj.* männlich

'**man-made** *adj.* künstlich; *(synthetic)* Kunst⟨*faser, -stoff*⟩

manned [mænd] *adj.* bemannt

manner ['mænə(r)] *n.* **a)** Art, *die;* Weise, *die;* **in this ~:** auf diese Art und Weise; **b)** *(general behaviour)* Art, *die;* **c)** *in pl.* Manieren *Pl.* **mannerism** ['mænərɪzm] *n.* Eigenart, *die*

manœuvrable [mə'nu:vrəbl] *adj. (Brit.)* manövrierfähig

manœuvre [mə'nu:və(r)] *(Brit.)* **1.** *n.* Manöver, *das.* **2.** *v. t. & i.* manövrieren

manor ['mænə(r)] *n.* **a)** *(land)* [Land]gut, *das;* **b)** *see* **manor-house.** '**manor-house.** Herrenhaus, *das*

'**manpower** *n.* Arbeitskräfte *Pl.*

mansion ['mænʃn] *n.* Herrenhaus, *das*

manslaughter ['mænslɔ:tə(r)] *n.* Totschlag, *der*

mantelpiece ['mæntlpi:s] *n.* Kaminsims, *der od. das*

mantle ['mæntl] *n.* Umhang, *der*

manual ['mænjʊəl] **1.** *adj.* **a)** manuell; **~ work** Handarbeit; **b)** *(not automatic)* handbetrieben; ⟨*Bedienung, Schaltung*⟩ von Hand. **2.** *n.* Handbuch, *das*

manufacture [mænjʊ'fæktʃə(r)] **1.** *n.* Herstellung, *die.* **2.** *v. t.* herstellen. **manu'facturer** *n.* Hersteller, *der*

manure [mə'njʊə(r)] **1.** *n.* Dung, *der.* **2.** *v. t.* düngen

manuscript ['mænjʊskrɪpt] *n.* Manuskript, *das*

many ['menɪ] **1.** *adj.* viele; **how ~**

people/books? wie viele *od.* wieviel Leute/Bücher? **2.** *n.* viele [Leute]; **~ of us** viele von uns; **a good/great ~:** eine Menge

map [mæp] **1.** *n.* [Land]karte, *die; (street plan)* Stadtplan, *der.* **2.** *v. t.,* **-pp-** kartographieren. **~ 'out** *v. t.* im einzelnen festlegen

maple ['meɪpl] *n.* Ahorn, *der*

mar [mɑ:(r)] *v. t.* verderben

marathon ['mærəθən] *n.* **a)** Marathon[lauf], *der;* **b)** *(fig.)* Marathon, *das*

marauder [mə'rɔ:də(r)] *n.* Plünderer, *der*

marble ['mɑ:bl] *n.* **a)** *(stone)* Marmor, *der;* **b)** *(toy)* Murmel, *die;* [game of] **~s** Murmelspiel, *das*

March [mɑ:tʃ] *n.* März, *der; see also* August

march 1. *n.* Marsch, *der;* [protest] **~:** Protestmarsch, *der.* **2.** *v. i.* marschieren. **march 'off 1.** *v. i.* losmarschieren. **2.** *v. t.* abführen. **march 'past** *v. i.* vorbeimarschieren

'**marcher** *n.* [protest] **~:** Demonstrant, *der*/Demonstrantin, *die*

mare [meə(r)] *n.* Stute, *die*

margarine [mɑ:dʒə'ri:n], *(coll.)* **marge** [mɑ:dʒ] *ns.* Margarine, *die*

margin ['mɑ:dʒɪn] *n.* **a)** *(of page)* Rand, *der;* **b)** *(extra amount)* Spielraum, *der;* [profit] **~:** [Gewinn]spanne, *die;* **by a narrow ~:** knapp. **marginal** ['mɑ:dʒɪnl] *adj.,* '**marginally** *adv.* unwesentlich

marigold ['mærɪɡəʊld] *n.* Ringelblume, *die*

marijuana [mærɪjʊ'ɑ:nə] *n.* Marihuana, *das*

marina [mə'ri:nə] *n.* Jachthafen, *der*

marinade [mærɪ'neɪd] **1.** *n.* Marinade, *die.* **2.** *v. t.* marinieren

marine [mə'ri:n] **1.** *adj.* Meeres-; See⟨*versicherung, -recht usw.*⟩; Schiffs⟨*ausrüstung, -turbine usw.*⟩. **2.** *n. (person)* Marineinfanterist, *der.* **mariner** ['mærɪnə(r)] *n.* Seemann, *der*

marionette [mærɪə'net] *n.* Marionette, *die*

marital ['mærɪtl] *adj.* ehelich; **~ status** Familienstand, *der*

maritime ['mærɪtaɪm] *adj.* See-

¹**mark** [mɑ:k] **1.** *n.* **a)** *(trace)* Spur, *die; (stain etc.)* Fleck, *der; (scratch)* Kratzer, *der;* **b)** *(sign)* Zeichen, *das;* **c)** *(Sch.)* Note, *die;* **d)** *(target)* Ziel, *das.* **2.** *v. t.* **a)** *(dirty)* schmutzig machen; *(scratch)* zerkratzen; **b)** *(put distinguishing ~ on)* kennzeichnen, markie-

ren (**with** mit); **c**) *(Sch.) (correct)* korrigieren; *(grade)* benoten; **d**) ~ **time** auf der Stelle treten. **mark 'off** *v. t.* abgrenzen (**from** von, gegen). **mark 'out** *v. t.* markieren

²**mark** *n. (monetary unit)* Mark, *die*

marked [mɑːkt] *adj.,* **markedly** ['mɑːkɪdlɪ] *adv.* deutlich

'**marker** *n.* Markierung, *die.* '**marker pen** *n.* Markierstift, *der*

market ['mɑːkɪt] **1.** *n.* Markt, *der.* **2.** *v. t.* vermarkten. '**marketing** *n.* Marketing, *das.* '**market-place** *n.* Marktplatz, *der; (fig.)* Markt, *der*

'**marking** *n.* **a**) Markierung, *die;* **b**) *(on animal)* Zeichnung, *die*

marksman ['mɑːksmən] *n., pl.* **marksmen** ['mɑːksmən] Scharfschütze, *der*

marmalade ['mɑːməleɪd] *n.* |orange| ~: Orangenmarmelade, *die*

¹**maroon** [mə'ruːn] **1.** *adj.* kastanienbraun. **2.** *n.* Kastanienbraun, *das*

²**maroon** *v. t.* **a**) *(Naut.: put ashore)* aussetzen; **b**) ⟨*Flut, Hochwasser:*⟩ von der Außenwelt abschneiden

marquee [mɑːˈkiː] *n.* Festzelt, *das*

marquess, marquis ['mɑːkwɪs] *n.* Marquis, *der*

marriage ['mærɪdʒ] *n.* **a**) Ehe, *die* (**to** mit); **b**) *(wedding)* Hochzeit, *die*

married ['mærɪd] *adj.* **a**) verheiratet; ~ **couple** Ehepaar, *das;* **b**) *(marital)* Ehe⟨*leben, -name*⟩

marrow ['mærəʊ] *n.* **a**) |vegetable| ~: Speisekürbis, *der;* **b**) *(Anat.)* [Knochen]mark, *das*

marry ['mærɪ] **1.** *v. t.* **a**) heiraten; **b**) *(join)* trauen; **they were** *or* **got/have got married** sie haben geheiratet. **2.** *v. i.* heiraten

Mars [mɑːz] *pr. n. (Astron.)* Mars, *der*

marsh [mɑːʃ] *n.* Sumpf, *der*

marshal ['mɑːʃl] **1.** *n.* **a**) *(officer in army)* Marschall, *der;* **b**) *(Sport)* Ordner, *der.* **2.** *v. t., (Brit.)* **-ll-** aufstellen ⟨*Truppen*⟩; ordnen ⟨*Fakten*⟩. '**marshalling yard** *n.* Rangierbahnhof, *der*

marshmallow [mɑːʃ'mæləʊ] *n. (sweet)* ≈ Mohrenkopf, *der*

'**marshy** *adj.* sumpfig

marsupial [mɑːˈsjuːpɪəl] *n.* Beuteltier, *das*

martial ['mɑːʃl] *adj.* kriegerisch. **martial 'law** *n.* Kriegsrecht, *das*

martyr ['mɑːtə(r)] **1.** *n.* Märtyrer, *der*/Märtyrerin, *die.* **2.** *v. t.* **be ~ed** den Märtyrertod sterben

marvel ['mɑːvl] **1.** *n.* Wunder, *das.* **2.**

v. i., (Brit.) **-ll-** *(literary)* ~ **at sth.** über etw. *(Akk.)* staunen. **marvellous** ['mɑːvələs] *adj.,* '**marvellously** *adv.* wunderbar

marvelous[ly] *(Amer.) see* **marvellous|ly|**

Marxism ['mɑːksɪzm] *n.* Marxismus, *der.* **Marxist** ['mɑːksɪst] **1.** *n.* Marxist, *der*/Marxistin, *die.* **2.** *adj.* marxistisch

marzipan ['mɑːzɪpæn] *n.* Marzipan, *das*

mascara [mæˈskɑːrə] *n.* Mascara, *das*

mascot ['mæskɒt] *n.* Maskottchen, *das*

masculine ['mæskjʊlɪn] *adj.* männlich. **masculinity** [mæskjuˈlɪnɪtɪ] *n.* Männlichkeit, *die*

mash [mæʃ] **1.** *n.* **a**) Brei, *der;* **b**) *(Brit. coll.: ~ed potatoes)* Kartoffelbrei, *der.* **2.** *v. t.* zerdrücken; **~ed potatoes** Kartoffelbrei, *der*

mask [mɑːsk] **1.** *n.* Maske, *die.* **2.** *v. t.* maskieren

masochism ['mæsəkɪzm] *n.* Masochismus, *der.* **masochist** ['mæsəkɪst] *n.* Masochist, *der*/Masochistin, *die.* **masochistic** [mæsəˈkɪstɪk] *adj.* masochistisch

mason ['meɪsn] *n.* **a**) Steinmetz, *der;* **b**) **M~** *(Free~)* [Frei]maurer, *der.* **Masonic** [məˈsɒnɪk] *adj.* [frei]maurerisch; ~ **lodge** [Frei]maurerloge, *die.* **masonry** ['meɪsnrɪ] *n.* Mauerwerk, *das*

masquerade [mæskəˈreɪd, mɑːskəˈreɪd] **1.** *n.* Maskerade, *die.* **2.** *v. i.* ~ **as sb./sth.** sich als jmd./etw. ausgeben

¹**mass** [mæs] *n. (Eccl.)* Messe, *die*

²**mass** [mæs] **1.** *n.* **a**) Masse, *die;* **b**) **a** ~ **of ...:** eine Unmenge von ... **2.** *v. t.* anhäufen. **3.** *v. i.* sich ansammeln; ⟨*Truppen:*⟩ sich massieren

massacre ['mæsəkə(r)] **1.** *n.* Massaker, *das.* **2.** *v. t.* massakrieren

massage ['mæsɑːʒ] **1.** *n.* Massage, *die.* **2.** *v. t.* massieren

massive ['mæsɪv] *adj.* massiv; gewaltig ⟨*Aufgabe*⟩; enorm ⟨*Schulden*⟩

mass: ~ '**media** *n. pl.* Massenmedien *Pl.;* ~-**pro'duced** *adj.* serienmäßig produziert; ~ **pro'duction** *n.* Massenproduktion, *die*

mast [mɑːst] *n.* Mast, *der*

master ['mɑːstə(r)] **1.** *n.* **a**) Herr, *der;* **b**) *(of dog)* Herrchen, *das; (of ship)* Kapitän, *der;* **c**) *(Sch.: teacher)* Lehrer, *der;* **d**) *(expert, great artist)* Meister, *der* (**at** in + *Dat.*); **e**) **M~ of**

Arts/Science Magister Artium/rerum naturalium. **2.** *adj.* Haupt-. **3.** *v.t. (learn)* erlernen; **have ~ed a language** eine Sprache beherrschen. **masterful** ['mɑ:stəfl] *adj. (masterly)* meisterhaft

'**master-key** *n.* Hauptschlüssel, *der* **masterly** ['mɑ:stəlɪ] *adj.* meisterhaft **master:** **~mind** **1.** *n.* führender Kopf; **2.** *v.t.* **~mind the plot** der Kopf des Komplotts sein; **~piece** *n. (work of art)* Meisterwerk, *das;* **~-stroke** *n.* Meisterstück, *das;* **~ switch** *n.* Hauptschalter, *der*

mastery ['mɑ:stərɪ] *n.* **a)** *(skill)* Meisterschaft, *die;* **b)** *(knowledge)* Beherrschung, *die* **(of** *Gen.***)**

masturbate ['mæstəbeɪt] *v.i. & t.* masturbieren. **masturbation** [mæstə-'beɪʃn] *n.* Masturbation, *die*

mat [mæt] *n.* **a)** Matte, *die;* **b)** *(to protect table etc.)* Untersetzer, *der*

¹match [mætʃ] **1.** *n.* **a)** **be no ~ for sb.** sich mit jmdm. nicht messen können; **meet one's ~:** seinen Meister finden; **b)** **be a [good** *etc.***] ~ for sth.** [gut *usw.*] zu etw. passen; **c)** *(Sport)* Spiel, *das; (Boxing)* Kampf, *der.* **2.** *v.t.* **a)** *(equal)* **~ sb. at chess** es mit jmdm. im Schach aufnehmen [können]; **b)** *(harmonize with)* passen zu; **a handbag and ~ing shoes** eine Handtasche und [dazu] passende Schuhe; **~ each other** zueinander passen. **3.** *v.i.* zusammenpassen

²match *n.* *(~stick)* Streichholz, *das*

'**matchless** *adj.* unvergleichlich

'**matchstick** *n.* Streichholz, *das*

¹mate [meɪt] **1.** *n.* **a)** Kumpel, *der (ugs.);* **b)** *(Naut.)* ≈ Kapitänleutnant, *der;* **c)** *(workman's assistant)* Gehilfe, *der;* **d)** *(Zool.) (male)* Männchen, *das; (female)* Weibchen, *das.* **2.** *v.i.* sich paaren. **3.** *v.t.* paaren ⟨*Tiere*⟩

²mate *(Chess) see* **checkmate**

material [mə'tɪərɪəl] **1.** *adj.* **a)** materiell; **b)** *(relevant)* wesentlich. **2.** *n.* **a)** **~[s]** Material, *das;* **building/writing ~s** Bau-/Schreibmaterial, *das;* **b)** *(cloth)* Stoff, *der.* **materialism** [mə'tɪərɪəlɪzm] *n.* Materialismus, *der.* **materialistic** [mətɪərɪə'lɪstɪk] *adj.* materialistisch. **materialize** [mə'tɪərɪəlaɪz] *v.i.* ⟨*Plan, Idee:*⟩ sich verwirklichen; ⟨*Treffen:*⟩ zustande kommen

maternal [mə'tɜ:nl] *adj.* mütterlich; Mutter⟨*instinkt*⟩

maternity [mə'tɜ:nɪtɪ] *n.* Mutterschaft, *die.* **ma'ternity dress** *n.*

Umstandskleid, *das.* **ma'ternity hospital** *n.* Entbindungsheim, *das*

matey ['meɪtɪ] *adj.,* **matier** ['meɪtɪə(r)], **matiest** ['meɪtɪɪst] *(Brit. coll.)* kameradschaftlich

math [mæθ] *(Amer. coll.) see* **maths**

mathematical [mæθɪ'mætɪkl] *adj.,* **mathematically** [mæθɪ'mætɪkəlɪ] *adv.* mathematisch

mathematician [mæθɪmə'tɪʃn] *n.* Mathematiker, *der*/Mathematikerin, *die*

mathematics [mæθɪ'mætɪks] *n.* Mathematik, *die*

maths [mæθs] *n. (Brit. coll.)* Mathe, *die (Schülerspr.)*

matinée ['mætɪneɪ] *n.* Nachmittagsvorstellung, *die*

matrices *pl. of* **matrix**

matriculate [mə'trɪkjʊleɪt] **1.** *v.t.* immatrikulieren (**in** an + *Dat.*). **2.** *v.i.* sich immatrikulieren. **matriculation** [mɛtrɪkjʊ'leɪʃn] *n.* Immatrikulation, *die*

matrimonial [mætrɪ'məʊnɪəl] *adj.* Ehe-

matrimony ['mætrɪmənɪ] *n.* Ehestand, *der*

matrix ['meɪtrɪks] *n., pl.* **matrices** ['meɪtrɪsi:z] *or* **~es** Matrix, *die*

matron ['meɪtrən] *n. (in school)* ≈ Hausmutter, *die; (in hospital)* Oberschwester, *die*

matt [mæt] *adj.* matt

'**matted** *adj.* verfilzt

matter ['mætə(r)] **1.** *n.* **a)** *(affair)* Angelegenheit, *die;* **~s** die Dinge; **money ~s** Geldangelegenheiten; **b)** **it's a ~ of taste** das ist Geschmackssache; **[only] a ~ of time** [nur noch] eine Frage der Zeit; **c) what's the ~?** was ist [los]?; **d)** *(physical material)* Materie, *die.* **2.** *v.i.* etwas ausmachen; **what does it ~?** was macht das schon?; **[it] doesn't ~:** [das] macht nichts *(ugs.).* '**matter-of-fact** *adj.* sachlich

mattress ['mætrɪs] *n.* Matratze, *die*

mature [mə'tjʊə(r)] **1.** *adj.* reif; ausgereift ⟨*Stil, Käse, Portwein, Sherry*⟩. **2.** *v.t.* reifen lassen. **3.** *v.i.* reifen. **maturity** [mə'tjʊərɪtɪ] *n.* Reife, *die*

Maundy Thursday [mɔ:ndɪ 'θɜ:zdɪ] *n.* Gründonnerstag, *der*

mausoleum [mɔ:sə'li:əm] *n.* Mausoleum, *das*

mauve [məʊv] *adj.* mauve

mawkish ['mɔ:kɪʃ] *adj.* rührselig

max. *abbr.* **maximum** *(adj.)* max., *(n.)* Max.

maxim ['mæksɪm] *n.* Maxime, *die*
maximum ['mæksɪməm] **1.** *n., pl.*
maxima ['mæksɪmə] Maximum, *das.*
2. *adj.* maximal; Maximal-; ~ **speed/**
temperature Höchstgeschwindigkeit,
die/-temperatur, *die*
May [meɪ] *n.* Mai, *der; see also* **August**
may *v. aux., only in pres.* **may,** *neg.*
(coll.) **mayn't** [meɪnt], *past* **might**
[maɪt], *neg. (coll.)* **mightn't** ['maɪtnt] **a)**
expr. possibility können; it ~ **be true**
das kann stimmen; **I** ~ **be wrong** vielleicht irre ich mich; **it** ~ **not be**
possible das wird vielleicht nicht möglich sein; **he** ~ **have missed his train**
vielleicht hat er seinen Zug verpaßt; **it**
~ *or* **might rain** es könnte regnen; **we**
~ *or* **might as well go** wir könnten eigentlich ebensogut [auch] gehen; **b)**
expr. permission dürfen; **c)** *expr. wish*
mögen; ~ **the best man win!** auf daß
der Beste gewinnt!
maybe ['meɪbi:, 'meɪbɪ] *adv.* vielleicht
mayn't [meɪnt] *(coll.)* **= may not;** *see*
may
mayonnaise [meɪə'neɪz] *n.* Mayonnaise, *die*
mayor [meə(r)] *n.* Bürgermeister, *der*
mayoress ['meərɪs] *n. (woman mayor)*
Bürgermeisterin, *die; (mayor's wife)*
[Ehe]frau des Bürgermeisters
maze [meɪz] *n.* Labyrinth, *das*
me [mɪ, *stressed* mi:] *pron.* mich; *as in-*
direct object mir; **who, me?** wer, ich?;
not me ich nicht; **it's me** ich bin's
meadow ['medəʊ] *n.* Wiese, *die*
meagre ['mi:gə(r)] *adj.* dürftig
meal [mi:l] *n.* Mahlzeit, *die;* **go out for**
a ~: essen gehen. **'mealtime** *n.* Essenszeit, *die*
¹mean [mi:n] *n.* **a)** Mittelweg, *der;* **b)**
(Math.) Mittelwert, *der*
²mean *adj.* **a)** *(miserly)* geizig; **b)** *(un-*
kind) gemein; **c)** *(shabby)* schäbig
³mean *v. t.,* **meant** [ment] **a)** *(intend)*
beabsichtigen; ~ **to do sth.** etw. tun
wollen; **b)** *(design, destine)* **be ~t to do**
sth. etw. tun sollen; **c)** *(intend to con-*
vey) meinen; **I [really]** ~ **it** ich meine
das ernst; **what do you** ~ **by that?** was
hast du damit gemeint?; **d)** *(signify)*
bedeuten
meander [mɪ'ændə(r)] *v. i.* **a)** *(Fluß:)*
sich winden; **b)** *(Person:)* schlendern
'meaning *n.* Bedeutung, *die; (of text*
etc., life) Sinn, *der.* **meaningful**
['mi:nɪŋfl] *adj.* bedeutungsvoll ⟨*Blick,*
Ergebnis⟩; sinnvoll ⟨*Aufgabe, Ge-*
spräch⟩. **'meaningless** *adj.* ⟨*Wort,*

Gespräch:⟩ ohne Sinn; sinnlos ⟨*Aktivi-*
tät⟩
means [mi:nz] *n.* **a)** Möglichkeit, *die;*
[Art und] Weise; **by this** ~: hierdurch;
~ **of transport** Transportmittel, *das;* **b)**
pl. (resources) Mittel *Pl.;* **live within/**
beyond one's ~: seinen Verhältnissen
entsprechend/über seine Verhältnisse
leben; **c) by all** ~! selbstverständlich!;
by no [manner of] ~: ganz und gar
nicht; **by** ~ **of** durch; mit [Hilfe von]
'means test *n.* Überprüfung der Be-
dürftigkeit
meant *see* **³mean**
mean: ~**time** *n.* **in the** ~**time** inzwischen; ~**time,** ~**while** *advs.* inzwischen
measles ['mi:zlz] *n.* Masern *Pl.*
measly ['mi:zlɪ] *adj. (coll.)* pop[e]lig
(ugs.)
measurable ['meʒərəbl] *adj.* meßbar
measure ['meʒə(r)] **1.** *n.* **a)** Maß, *das;*
for good ~: sicherheitshalber; *(as an*
extra) zusätzlich; **made to** ~: maßgeschneidert; **b)** *(degree)* **in some/large**
~: in gewisser Hinsicht/ in hohem
Maße; **c)** *(for measuring)* Maß, *das;* **d)**
(step) Maßnahme, *die;* **take** ~**s** Maßnahmen treffen. **2.** *v. t.* ausmessen
⟨*Größe, Menge usw.*⟩; ausmessen
⟨*Raum*⟩. **3.** *v. i.* messen. **measure 'up**
to *v. t.* entsprechen (+ *Dat.*)
'measured ['meʒəd] *adj.* gemessen
⟨*Schritt, Worte*⟩
'measurement *n.* **a)** Messung, *die;* **b)**
(dimension) Maß, *das*
meat [mi:t] *n.* Fleisch, *das.* **'meaty**
adj. **a)** fleischig; **b)** *(fig.)* gehaltvoll
mechanic [mɪ'kænɪk] *n.* Mechaniker,
*der/*Mechanikerin, *die*
mechanical [mɪ'kænɪkl] *adj.,*
me'chanically *adv.* mechanisch.
mechanical 'pencil *n. (Amer.)*
Drehbleistift, *der*
me'chanics *n.* **a)** Mechanik, *die;* **b)**
pl. (mechanism) Mechanismus, *der*
mechanism ['mekənɪzm] *n.* Mechanismus, *der*
mechanization [mekənaɪ'zeɪʃn] *n.*
Mechanisierung, *die*
mechanize ['mekənaɪz] *v. t.* mechani-
sieren
medal ['medl] *n.* Medaille, *die; (dec-*
oration) Orden, *der*
medallion [mɪ'dæljən] *n.* [große] Medaille
medallist ['medəlɪst] *n.* Medaillenge-
winner, *der/*-gewinnerin, *die*
meddle ['medl] *v. i.* ~ **with sth.** sich

(Dat.) an etw. *(Dat.)* zu schaffen machen; ~ **in sth.** sich in etw. *(Akk.)* einmischen

media ['mi:dɪə] *see* **mass media; medium** 1

mediaeval *see* **medieval**

mediate ['mi:dɪeɪt] *v. i.* vermitteln.

mediator ['mi:dɪeɪtə(r)] *n.* Vermittler, *der/*Vermittlerin, *die*

medical ['medɪkl] *adj.* medizinisch; ärztlich ‹*Behandlung, Untersuchung*›

medical: ~ certificate *n.* Attest, *das; ~* **school** *n.* medizinische Hochschule; ~ **student** *n.* Medizinstudent, *der/*-studentin *die*

medicated ['medɪkeɪtɪd] *adj.* medizinisch

medication [medɪ'keɪʃn] *n. (medicine)* Medikament, *das*

medicinal [mɪ'dɪsɪnl] *adj.* medizinisch

medicine ['medsən, 'medɪsɪn] *n.* **a)** *(science)* Medizin, *die;* **b)** *(preparation)* Medikament, *das*

medieval [medɪ'i:vl] *adj.* mittelalterlich

mediocre [mi:dɪ'əʊkə(r)] *adj.* mittelmäßig. **mediocrity** [mi:dɪ'ɒkrɪtɪ] *n.* Mittelmäßigkeit, *die*

meditate ['medɪteɪt] *v. i.* nachdenken, *(esp. Relig.)* meditieren (**[up]on** über + *Akk.*). **meditation** [medɪ'teɪʃn] *n.* **a)** *(act)* Nachdenken, *das;* **b)** *(Relig.)* Meditation, *die*

Mediterranean [medɪtə'reɪnɪən] *pr. n.* the ~: das Mittelmeer

medium ['mi:dɪəm] **1.** *n., pl.* **media** ['mi:dɪə] *or* ~**s a)** *(substance)* Medium, *das;* **b)** *(means)* Mittel, *das;* **by** *or* **through the** ~ **of** durch; **c)** *pl.* ~**s** *(Spiritualism)* Medium, *das;* **d)** in *pl.* **media** *(mass media)* Medien *Pl.* **2.** *adj.* mittler ...; medium *nur präd.* ‹*Steak*›.

'**medium-size[d]** *adj.* mittelgroß

medley ['medlɪ] *n.* **a)** buntes Gemisch; **b)** *(Mus.)* Potpourri, *das*

meek [mi:k] *adj.* **a)** *(humble)* sanftmütig; **b)** *(submissive)* zu nachgiebig

meet [mi:t] **1.** *v. t.,* met [met] **a)** treffen; *(collect)* abholen; **b)** *(make the acquaintance of)* kennenlernen; **pleased to** ~ **you** [sehr] angenehm; **c)** *(experience)* stoßen auf (+ *Akk.*) ‹*Widerstand, Problem*›; **d)** *(satisfy)* entsprechen (+ *Dat.*) ‹*Wunsch, Bedürfnis, Kritik*›; **e)** *(pay)* decken ‹*Kosten*›; bezahlen ‹*Rechnung*›. **2.** *v. i.,* **met a)** *(by chance)* sich *(Dat.)* begegnen; *(by arrangement)* sich treffen; **we've met before** wir kennen uns bereits; **b)** ‹*Komi-*

tee, Ausschuß usw.:› tagen. **meet 'up** *v. i.* sich treffen; ~ **up with sb.** *(coll.)* sich treffen. '**meet with** *v. t.* **a)** begegnen (+ *Dat.*); **b)** *(experience)* haben ‹*Erfolg, Unfall*›; stoßen auf (+ *Akk.*) ‹*Widerstand*›

'**meeting** *n.* **a)** Begegnung, *die; (by arrangement)* Treffen, *das;* **b)** *(assembly)* Versammlung, *die; (of committee etc.)* Sitzung, *die*

megalomania [megələ'meɪnɪə] *n.* Größenwahn, *der*

megaphone ['megəfəʊn] *n.* Megaphon, *das*

melancholic [melən'kɒlɪk] *adj.* melancholisch

melancholy ['melənkəlɪ] **1.** *n.* Melancholie, *die.* **2.** *adj.* melancholisch

mellow ['meləʊ] **1.** *adj.* **a)** *(softened by age or experience)* abgeklärt; **b)** *(ripe, well-matured)* reif. **2.** *v. i.* reifen

melodic [mɪ'lɒdɪk], **melodious** [mɪ'ləʊdɪəs] *adjs.,* **me'lodiously** *adv.* melodisch

melodrama ['melədrɑ:mə] *n.* Melodrama, *das.* **melodramatic** [melədrə'mætɪk] *adj.* melodramatisch

melody ['melədɪ] *n.* Melodie, *die*

melon ['melən] *n.* Melone, *die*

melt [melt] **1.** *v. i.* schmelzen. **2.** *v. t.* schmelzen; zerlassen ‹*Butter*›. **melt a'way** *v. i.* [weg]schmelzen. **melt 'down 1.** *v. i.* schmelzen. **2.** *v. t.* einschmelzen

melting: ~-point *n.* Schmelzpunkt, *der; ~-***pot** *n. (fig.)* Schmelztiegel, *der*

member ['membə(r)] *n.* **a)** Mitglied, *das;* **be a** ~: Mitglied sein; ~ **of a/the family** Familienangehörige, *der/die;* **b)** M~ [**of Parliament**] *(Brit.)* Abgeordnete [des Unterhauses], *der/die.*

'**membership** *n.* **a)** Mitgliedschaft, *die* (**of** in + *Dat.*); **b)** *(number of members)* Mitgliederzahl, *die;* **c)** *(members)* Mitglieder *Pl.*

membrane ['membreɪn] *n. (Biol.)* Membran, *die*

memento [mɪ'mentəʊ] *n., pl.* ~**es** *or* ~**s** Andenken, *das* (**of** an + *Akk.*)

memo ['meməʊ] *n., pl.* ~**s** *(coll.) see* **memorandum**

memoirs ['memwɑ:z] *n. pl.* Memoiren *Pl.*

memorable ['memərəbl] *adj.* denkwürdig ‹*Ereignis, Tag*›; unvergeßlich ‹*Film, Buch, Aufführung*›

memorandum [memə'rændəm] *n., pl.* **memoranda** [memə'rændə] *or* ~**s** Mitteilung, *die*

memorial [mɪˈmɔːrɪəl] **1.** *adj.* Gedenk-. **2.** *n.* Denkmal, *das* (to für)
memorize [ˈmeməraɪz] *v.t.* sich *(Dat.)* merken *od.* einprägen; *(learn by heart)* auswendig lernen
memory [ˈmemərɪ] *n.* **a)** Gedächtnis, *das;* **b)** *(thing remembered, act of remembering)* Erinnerung, *die* (of an + *Akk.*); **from ~:** aus dem Gedächtnis; **in ~ of** zur Erinnerung an (+ *Akk.*); **c)** *(Computing)* Speicher, *der*
men *pl. of* **man**
menace [ˈmenɪs] **1.** *v.t.* bedrohen. **2.** *n.* Plage, *die.* **ˈmenacing** [ˈmenəsɪŋ] *adj.* drohend
mend [mend] **1.** *v.t.* reparieren; ausbessern ⟨*Kleidung*⟩; kleben ⟨*Glas, Porzellan*⟩. **2.** *v.i.* ⟨*Knochen, Bein usw.*:⟩ heilen. **3.** *n.* **be on the ~:** auf dem Wege der Besserung sein
ˈmenfolk *n. pl.* Männer
menial [ˈmiːnɪəl] *adj.* niedrig; untergeordnet ⟨*Aufgabe*⟩
meningitis [menɪnˈdʒaɪtɪs] *n.* Hirnhautentzündung, *die*
menopause [ˈmenəpɔːz] *n.* Wechseljahre *Pl.*
menstruate [ˈmenstrʊeɪt] *v.i.* menstruieren. **menstruation** [menstrʊˈeɪʃn] *n.* Menstruation, *die*
menswear [ˈmenzweə(r)] *n.* Herrenbekleidung, *die*
mental [ˈmentl] *adj.* **a)** *(of the mind)* geistig; Geistes⟨*zustand, -störung*⟩; **b)** *(Brit. coll.: mad)* verrückt *(salopp)*
mental: ~ aˈrithmetic *n.* Kopfrechnen, *das;* **~ ˈhospital** *n.* Nervenklinik, *die (ugs.);* **~ ˈillness** *n.* Geisteskrankheit, *die*
mentality [menˈtælɪtɪ] *n.* Mentalität, *die*
ˈmentally *adv.* geistig
mention [ˈmenʃn] **1.** *n.* Erwähnung, *die.* **2.** *v.t.* erwähnen (**to** gegenüber); **don't ~ it** keine Ursache
menu [ˈmenjuː] *n.* [Speise]karte, *die*
mercenary [ˈmɜːsɪnərɪ] **1.** *adj.* gewinnsüchtig. **2.** *n.* Söldner, *der*
merchandise [ˈmɜːtʃəndaɪz] *n.* [Handels]ware, *die*
merchant [ˈmɜːtʃənt] *n.* Kaufmann, *der.* **merchant ˈbank** *n.* Handelsbank, *die.* **merchant ˈnavy** *n. (Brit.)* Handelsmarine, *die*
merciful [ˈmɜːsɪfl] *adj.* gnädig. **mercifully** [ˈmɜːsɪfəlɪ] *adv. (fortunately)* glücklicherweise
merciless [ˈmɜːsɪlɪs] *adj.,* **ˈmercilessly** *adv.* gnadenlos

mercury [ˈmɜːkjʊrɪ] **1.** *n.* Quecksilber, *das.* **2.** *pr. n.* **M~** *(Astron.)* Merkur, *der*
mercy [ˈmɜːsɪ] *n.* Erbarmen, *das* (**on** mit); **show sb. [no] ~:** mit jmdm. [kein] Erbarmen haben; **be at the ~ of sb./sth.** jmdm./einer Sache [auf Gedeih und Verderb] ausgeliefert sein
mere [mɪə(r)] *adj.,* **ˈmerely** *adv.* bloß
merge [mɜːdʒ] **1.** *v.t.* **a)** *(combine)* zusammenschließen; **b)** *(blend gradually)* verschmelzen (**with** mit). **2.** *v.i.* **a)** *(combine)* fusionieren (**with** mit); **b)** ⟨*Straße:*⟩ zusammenlaufen (**with** mit).
merger [ˈmɜːdʒə(r)] *n.* Fusion, *die*
meringue [məˈræŋ] *n.* Meringe, *die;* Baiser, *das*
merit [ˈmerɪt] **1.** *n.* **a)** *(worth)* Verdienst, *das;* **b)** *(good feature)* Vorzug, *der.* **2.** *v.t.* verdienen
mermaid [ˈmɜːmeɪd] *n.* Nixe, *die*
merrily [ˈmerɪlɪ] *adv.* munter
merriment [ˈmerɪmənt] *n.* Fröhlichkeit, *die*
merry [ˈmerɪ] *adj.* fröhlich; **~ Christmas!** frohe *od.* fröhliche Weihnachten! **ˈmerry-go-round** *n.* Karussell, *das.* **ˈmerry-making** *n.* Feiern, *das*
mesh [meʃ] *n.* **a)** Masche, *die;* **b)** *(netting; also fig.: network)* Geflecht, *das;* **wire ~:** Maschendraht, *der*
mesmerize [ˈmezməraɪz] *v.t.* faszinieren
mess [mes] *n.* **a)** *(dirty/untidy state)* **[be] a ~** *or* **in a ~:** schmutzig/unaufgeräumt [sein]; **what a ~!** was für ein Dreck *(ugs.)*/Durcheinander!; **b)** *(bad state)* **be [in] a ~:** sich in einem schlimmen Zustand befinden; ⟨*Person:*⟩ schlimm dran sein; **get into a ~:** in Schwierigkeiten geraten; **make a ~ of** verpfuschen *(ugs.)* ⟨*Arbeit, Leben*⟩; **c)** *(Mil.)* Kasino, *das.* **mess aˈbout, mess aˈround 1.** *v.i. (potter)* herumwerken; *(fool about)* herumalbern. **2.** *v.t.* **~ sb. about** *or* **around** mit jmdm. nach Belieben umspringen. **mess ˈup** *v.t.* **a)** *(make dirty)* schmutzig machen; *(make untidy)* in Unordnung bringen; **b)** *(bungle)* **~ it/things up** Mist bauen *(ugs.)*
message [ˈmesɪdʒ] *n.* Nachricht, *die;* **give sb. a ~:** jmdm. etwas ausrichten
messenger [ˈmesɪndʒə(r)] *n.* Bote, *der*/Botin, *die*
Messiah [mɪˈsaɪə] *n.* Messias, *der*
Messrs [ˈmesəz] *n. pl.* **a)** *(in name of firm)* ≈ Fa.; **b)** *pl. of* **Mr**; *(in list of names)* **~ A and B** die Herren A und B

'**messy** *adj. (dirty)* schmutzig; *(untidy)* unordentlich

met *see* **meet**

metabolism [mɪ'tæbəlɪzm] *n.* Stoffwechsel, *der*

metal ['metl] **1.** *n.* Metall, *das.* **2.** *adj.* Metall-. **metallic** [mɪ'tælɪk] *adj.* metallisch; **have a ~ taste** nach Metall schmecken. **metallurgy** [mɪ'tælədʒɪ] *n.* Metallurgie, *die*

metamorphosis [metə'mɔːfəsɪs] *n., pl.* **metamorphoses** [metə'mɔːfəsiːz] Metamorphose, *die*

metaphor ['metəfə(r)] *n.* Metapher, *die.* **metaphorical** [metə'fɒrɪkl] *adj..* **metaphorically** [metə'fɒrɪkəlɪ] *adv.* metaphorisch

meteor ['miːtɪə(r)] *n.* Meteor, *der.* **meteoric** [miːtɪ'ɒrɪk] *adj. (fig.)* kometenhaft

meteorological [miːtɪərə'lɒdʒɪkl] *adj.* meteorologisch ⟨*Instrument*⟩; Wetter⟨*ballon, -bericht*⟩

meteorologist [miːtɪə'rɒlədʒɪst] *n.* Meteorologe, *der*/Meteorologin, *die*

meteorology [miːtɪə'rɒlədʒɪ] *n.* Meteorologie, *die*

¹**meter** ['miːtə(r)] *n.* **a)** Zähler, *der; (for coins)* Münzzähler, *der;* **b)** *(parking-~)* Parkuhr, *die*

²**meter** *(Amer.) see* ¹, ²**metre**

method ['meθəd] *n.* Methode, *die.* **methodical** [mɪ'θɒdɪkl] *adj..* **me-'thodically** *adv.* systematisch

Methodist ['meθədɪst] *n.* Methodist, *der*/Methodistin, *die*

meths [meθs] *n. (Brit. coll.)* [Brenn]spiritus, *der*

methylated spirit[s] [meθɪleɪtɪd 'spɪrɪt(s)] *n. [pl.]* Brennspiritus, *der*

meticulous [mɪ'tɪkjʊləs] *adj..* **me-'ticulously** *adv. (scrupulous[ly])* sorgfältig; *(over-scrupulous[ly])* übergenau

¹**metre** ['miːtə] *n. (Brit.: poetic rhythm)* Metrum, *das*

²**metre** *n. (Brit.: unit)* Meter, *der od. das.* **metric** ['metrɪk] *adj.* metrisch; **~ system** metrisches System. **metrication** [metrɪ'keɪʃn] *n.* Umstellung auf das metrische System

metronome ['metrənəʊm] *n.* Metronom, *das*

metropolis [mɪ'trɒpəlɪs] *n.* Metropole, *die.* **metropolitan** [metrə'pɒlɪtən] *adj.* ~ **New York** der Großraum New York; ~ **London** Großlondon *(das)*

Mexican ['meksɪkən] **1.** *adj.* mexikanisch. **2.** *n.* Mexikaner, *der*/Mexikanerin, *die*

Mexico ['meksɪkəʊ] *pr. n.* Mexiko *(das)*

miaow [mɪ'aʊ] **1.** *v. i.* miauen. **2.** *n.* Miauen, *das*

mice *pl. of* **mouse**

microbe ['maɪkrəʊb] *n.* Mikrobe, *die*

micro ['maɪkrəʊ]: **~chip** *n.* Mikrochip, *der;* **~computer** *n.* Mikrocomputer, *der;* **~fiche** *n.* Mikrofiche, *das od. der;* **~film 1.** *n.* Mikrofilm, *der;* **2.** *v. t.* auf Mikrofilm aufnehmen

microphone ['maɪkrəfəʊn] *n.* Mikrophon, *das*

microprocessor [maɪkrəʊ'prəʊsesə(r)] *n.* Mikroprozessor, *der*

microscope ['maɪkrəskəʊp] *n.* Mikroskop, *das.* **microscopic** [maɪkrə'skɒpɪk] *adj.* mikroskopisch; *(fig.: very small)* winzig

'**microwave** *n.* Mikrowelle, *die;* ~ **[oven]** Mikrowellenherd, *der*

mid- [mɪd] *in comb.* **in ~-air** in der Luft; **in ~-sentence** mitten im Satz; **~-July** Mitte Juli; **the ~-60s** die Mitte der sechziger Jahre; **a man in his ~-fifties** ein Mittfünfziger; **be in one's ~-thirties** Mitte Dreißig sein

midday ['mɪdeɪ, mɪd'deɪ] *n.* **a)** *(noon)* zwölf Uhr; **b)** *(middle of day)* Mittag, *der; attrib.* Mittags-

middle ['mɪdl] **1.** *attrib. adj.* mittler... **2.** *n.* **a)** Mitte, *die;* **in the ~ of the forest/night** mitten im Wald/in der Nacht; **b)** *(waist)* Taille, *die*

middle: ~ '**age** *n.* mittleres [Lebens]alter; **~-aged** ['mɪdleɪdʒd] *adj.* mittleren Alters *nachgestellt;* **M~ 'Ages** *n. pl.* **the M~ Ages** das Mittelalter; ~ '**class** *n.* Mittelstand, *der;* **~-class** *adj.* bürgerlich; **M~ 'East** *pr. n.* **the M~ East** der Nahe [und Mittlere] Osten; **M~ 'Eastern** *adj.* nahöstlich

middling ['mɪdlɪŋ] *adj.* mittelmäßig

midge [mɪdʒ] *n.* Stechmücke, *die*

midget ['mɪdʒɪt] **1.** *n.* Liliputaner, *der*/Liliputanerin, *die.* **2.** *adj.* winzig

Midlands ['mɪdləndz] *n. pl.* **the ~** *(Brit.)* Mittelengland

'**midnight** *n.* Mitternacht, *die*

'**midpoint** *n.* Mitte, *die*

midriff ['mɪdrɪf] *n.* Bauch, *der*

midst [mɪdst] *n.* **in the ~ of sth.** mitten in einer Sache; **in our/their/your ~:** in unserer/ihrer/eurer Mitte

midsummer ['--, -'--] *n.* die [Zeit der] Sommersonnenwende

midway ['--, -'--] *adv.* auf halbem Weg[e] ⟨*sich treffen, sich befinden*⟩

'**midwife** *n., pl.* '**midwives** Hebamme, *die*

mid'winter *n.* die [Zeit der] Wintersonnenwende

'**might** [maɪt] *see* may

²**might** *n.* **a)** *(force)* Gewalt, *die;* **b)** *(power)* Macht, *die*

mightn't ['maɪtnt] *(coll.)* = might not; *see* may

mighty ['maɪtɪ] **1.** *adj.* mächtig. **2.** *adv. (coll.)* verdammt *(ugs.)*

migraine ['miːgreɪn] *n.* Migräne, *die*

migrant ['maɪgrənt] *n.* **a)** Auswanderer, *der/*Auswanderin, *die;* **b)** *(bird)* Zugvogel, *der*

migrate [maɪ'greɪt] *v. i.* **a)** *(to a town)* abwandern; *(to another country)* auswandern; **b)** ⟨*Vogel:*⟩ fortziehen. **mi-gration** [maɪ'greɪʃn] *n.* **a)** *(to a town)* Abwandern, *das; (to another country)* Auswandern, *das;* **b)** *(of birds)* Zug, *der*

mike [maɪk] *n. (coll.)* Mikro, *das*

Milan [mɪ'læn] *pr. n.* Mailand *(das)*

mild [maɪld] *adj.* mild; sanft ⟨*Person*⟩

mildew ['mɪldjuː] *n.* **a)** Schimmel, *der;* **b)** *(on plant)* Mehltau, *der*

'**mildly** *adv.* **a)** *(gently)* mild[e]; **b)** *(slightly)* ein bißchen; **c) to put it ~ :** gelinde gesagt

mile [maɪl] *n.* **a)** Meile, *die;* **b)** *(fig. coll.)* ~s **better/too big** tausendmal besser/viel zu groß; **be ~s ahead of sb.** jmdm. weit voraus sein. **mileage** ['maɪlɪdʒ] *n.* [Anzahl der] Meilen; **a low ~ :** ein niedriger Meilenstand.

'**milestone** *n.* Meilenstein, *der*

militant ['mɪlɪtənt] **1.** *adj.* militant. **2.** *n.* Militante, *der/die*

military ['mɪlɪtərɪ] **1.** *adj.* militärisch; Militär⟨*regierung, -akademie, -uniform, -parade*⟩; **~ service** Militärdienst, *der.* **2.** *n.* **the ~ :** das Militär

militate ['mɪlɪteɪt] *v. i.* **~ against/in favour of sth.** [deutlich] gegen/für etw. sprechen

militia [mɪ'lɪʃə] *n.* Miliz, *die*

milk [mɪlk] **1.** *n.* Milch, *die.* **2.** *v. t.* melken

milk: ~ 'chocolate *n.* Milchschokolade, *die;* **~ jug** *n.* Milchkännchen, *das;* **~man** ['mɪlkmən] *n., pl.* **~men** ['mɪlkmən] Milchmann, *der;* **~ shake** *n.* Milchshake, *der;* **~-tooth** *n.* Milchzahn, *der*

'**milky** *adj.* milchig. **Milky 'Way** *n.* Milchstraße, *die*

mill [mɪl] **1.** *n.* **a)** Mühle, *die;* **b)** *(factory)* Fabrik, *die.* **2.** *v. t.* **a)** mahlen ⟨*Ge-*

treide⟩; **b)** fräsen ⟨*Metallgegenstand*⟩.

mill a'bout *(Brit.),* **mill a'round** *v. i.* durcheinanderlaufen

'**miller** *n.* Müller, *der*

millet ['mɪlɪt] *n.* Hirse, *die*

milligram ['mɪlɪgræm] *n.* Milligramm, *das*

millilitre *(Brit.; Amer.:* **milliliter)** ['mɪlɪliːtə(r)] *n.* Milliliter, *der od. das*

millimetre *(Brit.; Amer.:* **millimeter)** ['mɪlɪmiːtə(r)] *n.* Millimeter, *der*

milliner ['mɪlɪnə(r)] *n.* Modist, *der/*Modistin, *die.* '**millinery** *n.* Hutmacherei, *die*

million ['mɪljən] **1.** *adj.* **a** *or* one/two **~ :** eine Million/zwei Millionen; **half a ~ :** eine halbe Million. **2.** *n.* **a)** Million, *die;* **b)** *(indefinite amount)* ~s **of people** eine Unmenge Leute. **mil-lionaire** [mɪljə'neə(r)] *n.* Millionär, *der/*Millionärin, *die.* **millionth** ['mɪljənθ] **1.** *adj.* millionst... **2.** *n. (fraction)* Millionstel, *das*

'**millstone** *n.* Mühlstein, *der*

mime [maɪm] **1.** *n.* **a)** *(performance)* Pantomime, *die;* **b)** *(art)* Pantomimik, *die.* **2.** *v. i.* pantomimisch agieren. **3.** *v. t.* pantomimisch darstellen

mimic ['mɪmɪk] **1.** *n.* Imitator, *der.* **2.** *v. t.,* -ck- nachahmen

min. *abbr.* **a)** minute[s] Min.; **b) mini-mum** *(adj.)* mind., *(n.)* Min.

mince [mɪns] **1.** *n.* Hackfleisch, *das.* **2.** *v. t.* durch den [Fleisch]wolf drehen ⟨*Fleisch*⟩. '**mincemeat** *n.* **a)** Hackfleisch, *das;* **b)** *(sweet)* süße Pastetenfüllung aus Obst, Rosinen, Gewürzen, Nierenfett usw. **mince 'pie** *n.* mit „mincemeat b" gefüllte Pastete

'**mincer** *n.* Fleischwolf, *der*

mind [maɪnd] **1.** *n.* **a)** Geist, *der;* **b)** *(remembrance)* **bear** *or* **keep sth. in ~ :** an etw. *(Akk.)* denken; **have [got] sb./sth. in ~ :** an jmdn./etw. denken; **c)** *(opinion)* **give sb. a piece of one's ~ :** jmdm. gründlich die Meinung sagen; **to my ~ :** meiner Meinung *od.* Ansicht nach; **change one's ~ :** seine Meinung ändern; **I have a good ~ to do that** ich hätte große Lust, das zu tun; **make up one's ~, make one's ~ up** sich entscheiden; **d)** *([normal] mental powers)* Verstand, *der;* **be out of one's ~ :** den Verstand verloren haben; **e) frame of ~ :** [seelische] Verfassung. **2.** *v. t.* **a) I can't afford a bicycle, never ~ a car** ich kann mir kein Fahrrad leisten, geschweige denn ein Auto; **b)** *usu. neg.*

or interrog. (object to) **would you ~ opening the door?** würdest du bitte die Tür öffnen?; **I wouldn't ~ a walk** ich hätte nichts gegen einen Spaziergang; **c)** *(take care)* **~ you don't go too near the cliff-edge!** paß auf, daß du nicht zu nah an den Klippenrand gehst!; **~ how you go!** paß auf! **d)** *(have charge of)* aufpassen auf (+ *Akk.*). **3.** *v. i.* **a)** **~!** Vorsicht!; Achtung!; **b)** *(care, object)* **do you ~ if I smoke?** stört es Sie, wenn ich rauche?; **c) never ~** *(it's not important)* macht nichts. **mind 'out** *v. i.* aufpassen **(for** auf + *Akk.*); **~ out!** Vorsicht!

'minded *adj.* **mechanically ~:** technisch veranlagt; **not politically ~:** unpolitisch

mindful ['maɪndfl] *adj.* **be ~ of sth.** etw. berücksichtigen

'mindless *adj.* geistlos ⟨*Person*⟩; sinnlos ⟨*Gewalt*⟩

¹mine [maɪn] *n.* **a)** Bergwerk, *das;* **b)** *(explosive)* Mine, *die*

²mine *poss. pron. pred.* meiner/meine/mein[e]s; *see also* **hers**

'minefield *n.* Minenfeld, *das*

'miner *n.* Bergmann, *der*

mineral ['mɪnərl] **1.** *adj.* mineralisch; Mineral⟨*salz, -quelle*⟩. **2.** *n.* **a)** Mineral, *das;* **b)** *(Brit.: soft drink)* Erfrischungsgetränk, *das.* **'mineral water** *n.* Mineralwasser, *das*

minesweeper ['maɪnswiːpə(r)] *n.* Minensuchboot, *das*

mingle ['mɪŋgl] **1.** *v. t.* [ver]mischen. **2.** *v. i.* sich [ver]mischen **(with** mit)

mini ['mɪnɪ] *n. (coll.)* **a)** *(car)* M~, **(P)** Mini, *der;* **b)** *(skirt)* Mini, *der (ugs.)*

mini- ['mɪnɪ] *in comb.* Mini-; Klein-⟨*bus, -wagen, -taxi*⟩

miniature ['mɪnɪtʃə(r)] **1.** *n. (picture)* Miniatur, *die.* **2.** *adj.* Miniatur-

mini-: ~bus *n.* Kleinbus, *der;* **~cab** *n.* Minicar, *das*

minim ['mɪnɪm] *n. (Brit. Mus.)* halbe Note

minimal ['mɪnɪml] *adj.* minimal

minimize ['mɪnɪmaɪz] *v. t.* **a)** *(reduce)* auf ein Mindestmaß reduzieren; **b)** *(understate)* bagatellisieren

minimum ['mɪnɪməm] **1.** *n., pl.* **minima** ['mɪnɪmə] Minimum, *das* **(of** an + *Dat.*). **2.** *attrib. adj.* Mindest-

mining ['maɪnɪŋ] *n.* Bergbau, *der; attrib.* Bergbau-. **'mining industry** *n.* Bergbau, *der.* **'mining town** *n.* Bergbaustadt, *die*

minion ['mɪnjən] *n.* Lakai, *der*

minister ['mɪnɪstə(r)] **1.** *n.* **a)** *(Polit.)* Minister, *der/*Ministerin, *die;* **b)** *(Eccl.)* Geistliche, *der/die;* Pfarrer, *der/*Pfarrerin, *die.* **2.** *v. i.* **~ to sb.** sich um jmdn. kümmern. **ministerial** [mɪnɪ'stɪərɪəl] *adj. (Polit.)* Minister-; ministeriell. **ministry** ['mɪnɪstrɪ] *n.* **a)** *(Polit.)* Ministerium, *das;* **b)** *(Eccl.)* geistliches Amt

mink [mɪŋk] *n.* Nerz, *der*

minnow ['mɪnəʊ] *n.* Elritze, *die*

minor ['maɪnə(r)] **1.** *adj.* **a)** *(lesser)* kleiner...; **b)** *(unimportant)* weniger bedeutend; *(not serious)* leicht; **~ road** kleine Straße; **c)** *(Mus.)* Moll-; **A ~:** a-Moll. **2.** *n.* Minderjährige, *der/die.* **minority** [maɪ'nɒrɪtɪ, mɪ'nɒrɪtɪ] *n.* Minderheit, *die;* **in the ~:** in der Minderheit

minstrel ['mɪnstrl] *n.* fahrender Sänger

¹mint [mɪnt] **1.** *n. (place)* Münzanstalt, *die.* **2.** *adj.* funkelnagelneu *(ugs.);* **in ~ condition** in tadellosem Zustand. **3.** *v. t.* prägen

²mint *n.* **a)** *(plant)* Minze, *die;* **b)** *(peppermint)* Pfefferminz, *das; attrib.* Pfefferminz-

minuet [mɪnjʊ'et] *n.* Menuett, *das*

minus ['maɪnəs] *prep.* minus; weniger; *(without)* abzüglich (+ *Gen.*)

minuscule ['mɪnəskjuːl] *adj.* winzig

¹minute ['mɪnɪt] *n.* **a)** Minute, *die; (moment)* Moment, *der;* **b) ~s** *(of meeting)* Protokoll, *das;* **take the ~s of a meeting** bei einer Sitzung [das] Protokoll führen

²minute [maɪ'njuːt] *adj. (tiny)* winzig

miracle ['mɪrəkl] *n.* Wunder, *das.* **miraculous** [mɪ'rækjʊləs] *adj.* wunderbar

mirage ['mɪrɑːʒ] *n.* Fata Morgana, *die*

mirror ['mɪrə(r)] **1.** *n.* Spiegel, *der.* **2.** *v. t.* [wider]spiegeln

misadventure [mɪsəd'ventʃə(r)] *n.* Mißgeschick, *das*

misapprehension [mɪsæprɪ'henʃn] *n.* Mißverständnis, *das;* **be under a ~:** einem Irrtum unterliegen

misbehave [mɪsbɪ'heɪv] *v. i. & refl.* sich schlecht benehmen. **misbehaviour** *(Amer.:* **misbehavior)** [mɪsbɪ-'heɪvjə(r)] *n.* schlechtes Benehmen

miscalculate [mɪs'kælkjʊleɪt] **1.** *v. t.* falsch berechnen; *(misjudge)* falsch einschätzen. **2.** *v. i.* sich verrechnen. **miscalculation** [mɪskælkjʊ'leɪʃn] *n.* Rechenfehler, *der; (misjudgement)* Fehleinschätzung, *die*

miscarriage [mıs'kærıdʒ] *n.* **a)** Fehlgeburt, *die;* **b)** ~ **of justice** Justizirrtum, *das*

miscellaneous [mısə'leınıəs] *adj.* **a)** [kunter]bunt; **b)** *with pl. n.* verschieden. **miscellany** [mı'selənı] *n.* [buntes] Sammlung; [buntes] Gemisch

mischief ['mıstʃıf] *n.* **a)** Unfug, *der;* **get up to ~:** etwas anstellen; **b)** *(harm)* Schaden, *der.* **mischievous** ['mıstʃıvəs] *adj.* spitzbübisch; schelmisch

misconception [mıskən'sepʃn] *n.* falsche Vorstellung (**about** von); **be |labouring| under a ~ about sth.** sich *(Dat.)* eine falsche Vorstellung von etw. machen

misconduct [mıs'kɒndʌkt] *n.* unkorrektes Verhalten

misconstrue [mıskən'stru:] *v.t.* mißverstehen

miscount [mıs'kaʊnt] **1.** *v.i.* sich verzählen. **2.** *v.t.* falsch zählen

misdeed [mıs'di:d] *n.* Missetat, *die (veralt., scherzh.)*

misdemeanour *(Amer.:* **misdemeanor)** [mısdı'mi:nə(r)] *n.* Missetat, *die (veralt., scherzh.)*

misdirect [mısdı'rekt, mısdaı'rekt] *v.t.* falsch adressieren ⟨*Brief*⟩; in die falsche Richtung schicken ⟨*Person*⟩

miser ['maızə(r)] *n.* Geizhals, *der*

miserable ['mızərəbl] *adj.* **a)** unglücklich; **feel ~:** sich elend fühlen; **b)** trist ⟨*Wetter, Urlaub*⟩. **miserably** ['mızərəblı] *adv.* unglücklich; jämmerlich ⟨*versagen*⟩; ~ **poor** bettelarm

miserly ['maızəlı] *adj.* geizig

misery ['mızərı] *n.* **a)** Elend, *das;* **b)** *(coll.: discontented person)* ~|-guts| Miesepeter, *der (ugs.)*

misfire [mıs'faıə(r)] *v.i.* **a)** ⟨*Motor:*⟩ Fehlzündungen haben; **b)** ⟨*Plan, Versuch:*⟩ fehlschlagen; ⟨*Streich, Witz:*⟩ danebengehen

misfit ['mısfıt] *n.* Außenseiter, *der/* Außenseiterin, *die*

misfortune [mıs'fɔ:tʃu:n] *n.* Mißgeschick, *das*

misgiving [mıs'gıvıŋ] *n.* ~|s| Bedenken *Pl.*

misguided [mıs'gaıdıd] *adj.* töricht

mishandle [mıs'hændl] *v.t.* falsch behandeln

mishap ['mıshæp] *n.* Mißgeschick, *das*

mishear [mıs'hıə(r)] **1.** *v.i.,* **misheard** [mıs'hɜ:d] sich verhören. **2.** *v.t.,* **misheard** falsch verstehen

mishit 1. ['mıshıt] *n.* Fehlschlag, *der.*

2. [mıs'hıt] *v.t.,* **-tt-, mishit** verschlagen

mishmash ['mıʃmæʃ] *n.* Mischmasch, *der (ugs.)* (**of** aus)

misinform [mısın'fɔ:m] *v.t.* falsch informieren

misinterpret [mısın'tɜ:prıt] *v.t. (make wrong inference from)* falsch deuten; mißdeuten. **misinterpretation** [mısıntɜ:prı'teıʃn] *n.* **be open to ~:** leicht mißdeutet werden können

misjudge [mıs'dʒʌdʒ] *v.t.* falsch einschätzen; falsch beurteilen ⟨*Person*⟩. **misjudgement, misjudgment** [mıs'dʒʌdʒmənt] *n.* Fehleinschätzung, *die; (of person)* falsche Beurteilung

mislay [mıs'leı] *v.t.,* **mislaid** [mıs'leıd] verlegen

mislead [mıs'li:d] *v.t.,* **misled** [mıs'led] irreführen. **mis'leading** *adj.* irreführend

mismanage [mıs'mænıdʒ] *v.t.* schlecht abwickeln ⟨*Geschäft, Projekt*⟩. **mismanagement** [mıs'mænıdʒmənt] *n.* schlechte Abwicklung

misnomer [mıs'nəʊmə(r)] *n.* unzutreffende Bezeichnung

misplace [mıs'pleıs] *v.t.* an den falschen Platz stellen/legen/setzen *usw.*

misprint 1. ['mısprınt] *n.* Druckfehler, *der.* **2.** [mıs'prınt] *v.t.* verdrucken

mispronounce [mısprə'naʊns] *v.t.* falsch aussprechen

misread [mıs'ri:d] *v.t.,* **misread** [mıs'red] falsch lesen

misrepresent [mısreprı'zent] *v.t.* falsch darstellen. **misrepresentation** [mısreprızen'teıʃn] *n.* falsche Darstellung

Miss [mıs] *n. (unmarried woman)* Frau; Fräulein *(veralt.); (girl)* Fräulein

miss 1. *n.* Fehlschlag, *der; (shot)* Fehlschuß, *der; (throw)* Fehlwurf, *der.* **2.** *v.t.* **a)** *(fail to hit)* verfehlen; **b)** *(let slip)* verpassen; ~ **an opportunity** sich *(Dat.)* eine Gelegenheit entgehen lassen; **c)** *(fail to catch)* verpassen ⟨*Zug*⟩; **d)** *(fail to take part in)* versäumen; ~ **school** in der Schule fehlen; **e)** *(fail to see)* übersehen; *(fail to hear)* nicht mitbekommen; **f)** *(feel the absence of)* vermissen; **she ~es him** er fehlt ihr. **3.** *v.i. (not hit sth.)* nicht treffen. **miss 'out 1.** *v.t.* weglassen. **2.** *v.i.* ~ **out on sth.** *(coll.)* sich *(Dat.)* etw. entgehen lassen

misshapen [mıs'ʃeıpn] *adj.* mißgebildet

missile ['mɪsaɪl] n. a) (thrown) [Wurf]geschoß, das; b) (Mil.) Rakete, die. '**missile base**, '**missile site** ns. Raketenbasis, die

'**missing** adj. fehlend; be ~: fehlen; ⟨Person:⟩ (Mil. etc.) vermißt werden; (not present) fehlen; ~ **person** Vermißte, der/die

mission ['mɪʃn] n. a) Mission, die; b) (planned operation) Einsatz, der. **missionary** ['mɪʃənərɪ] n. Missionar, der/Missionarin, die

misspell [mɪs'spel] v. t., forms as ¹**spell** falsch schreiben

mist [mɪst] n. (fog) Nebel, der; (haze) Dunst, der; (on windscreen etc.) Beschlag, der. **mist 'up** v. i. [sich] beschlagen

mistake [mɪ'steɪk] 1. n. Fehler, der; by ~: versehentlich. 2. v. t., forms as **take** 1: a) falsch verstehen; b) ~ x for y x mit y verwechseln. **mistaken** [mɪ'steɪkn] adj. be ~: sich täuschen; a case of ~ identity eine Verwechslung. **mi'stakenly** adv. irrtümlicherweise

mistletoe ['mɪsltəʊ] n. Mistel, die

mistook see **mistake** 2

mistress ['mɪstrɪs] n. a) (Brit. Sch.: teacher) Lehrerin, die; b) (lover) Geliebte, die

mistrust [mɪs'trʌst] 1. v. t. mißtrauen (+ Dat.). 2. n. Mißtrauen, das (of gegenüber + Dat.). **mistrustful** [mɪs-'trʌstfl] adj. mißtrauisch (of gegenüber)

'**misty** adj. dunstig

misunderstand [mɪsʌndə'stænd] v. t., forms as **understand** mißverstehen. **misunder'standing** n. Mißverständnis, das

misuse 1. [mɪs'juːz] v. t. mißbrauchen. 2. [mɪs'juːs] n. Mißbrauch, der

mite [maɪt] n. a) (Zool.) Milbe, die; b) (small child) Würmchen, das (fam.); **poor little** ~: armes Kleines

miter (Amer.) see **mitre**

mitigate ['mɪtɪgeɪt] v. t. a) (reduce) lindern; b) (make less severe) mildern; **mitigating circumstances** mildernde Umstände

mitre ['maɪtə(r)] n. (Brit. Eccl.) Mitra, die

mitten ['mɪtn] n. Fausthandschuh, der

mix [mɪks] 1. v. t. [ver]mischen; verrühren ⟨Zutaten⟩. 2. v. i. a) (become ~ed) sich vermischen; b) (be sociable, participate) Umgang mit anderen [Menschen] haben; ~ **with** Umgang haben mit; ~ **well** kontaktfreudig sein. 3. n.

(coll.) Mischung, die; |**cake-**|~: Backmischung, die. **mix 'up** v. t. a) vermischen; b) (muddle) durcheinanderbringen; (confuse) verwechseln; c) **be/get ~ed up in sth.** in etw. (Akk.) verwickelt sein/werden

mixed [mɪkst] adj. a) gemischt; b) (diverse) unterschiedlich. **mixed 'grill** n. Mixed grill, der. **mixed 'up** adj. (coll.) verwirrt ⟨Person⟩; **be/feel very** ~: völlig durcheinander sein

'**mixer** n. (for food) Mixer, der

mixture ['mɪkstʃə(r)] n. a) Mischung, die (of aus); b) (Med.) Mixtur, die

'**mix-up** n. Durcheinander, das; (misunderstanding) Mißverständnis, das

mm. abbr. millimetre|s| mm

moan [məʊn] 1. n. a) Stöhnen, das; b) **have a** ~ (complain) jammern. 2. v. i. a) stöhnen (**with** vor + Dat.); b) (complain) jammern (**about** über + Akk.). 3. v. t. stöhnen

moat [məʊt] n. |**castle**| ~: Burggraben, der

mob [mɒb] 1. n. a) (rabble) Mob, der; b) (sl.: group) Peter **and his** ~: Peter und seine ganze Blase (salopp). 2. v. t., -**bb-** belagern (ugs.) ⟨Star⟩

mobile ['məʊbaɪl] 1. adj. beweglich; (on wheels) fahrbar. 2. n. Mobile, die. **mobile 'home** n. transportable Wohneinheit. **mobile 'phone** n. Mobiltelefon, das

mobility [mə'bɪlɪtɪ] n. Beweglichkeit, die

mobilization [məʊbɪlaɪ'zeɪʃn] n. Mobilisierung, die

mobilize ['məʊbɪlaɪz] v. t. mobilisieren

moccasin ['mɒkəsɪn] n. Mokassin, der

mocha ['mɒkə] n. Mokka, der

mock [mɒk] 1. v. t. sich lustig machen über (+ Akk.). 2. v. i. sich lustig machen (**at** über + Akk.). 3. adj. Schein-⟨kampf, -angriff, -ehe⟩. **mockery** ['mɒkərɪ] n. Spott, der; **make a** ~ **of** sth. etw. zur Farce machen

'**mock-up** n. Modell [in Originalgröße]

mode [məʊd] n. a) Art [und Weise], die; b) (fashion) Mode, die

model ['mɒdl] 1. n. a) Modell, das; b) (example to be imitated) Vorbild, das; c) (Art) Modell, das; (Fashion) Mannequin, das; (male) Dressman, der. 2. adj. a) (exemplary) Muster-; b) (miniature) Modell-. 3. v. t., (Brit.) -**ll**-: a) modellieren; ~ **sth. after** or |**up**|**on** sth. etw. einer Sache (Dat.) nachbilden; b)

(Fashion) vorführen. **4.** *v.i. (Fashion)* als Mannequin/Dressman arbeiten; *(Art)* Modell stehen/sitzen

modem ['məʊdem *n.* Modem, *der*

moderate 1. ['mɒdərət] *adj.* **a)** gemäßigt ‹*Ansichten*›; maßvoll ‹*Trinker, Forderungen*›; **b)** mittler... ‹*Größe, Menge, Wert*›; *(reasonable)* angemessen ‹*Preis, Summe*›. **2.** ['mɒdərət] *n.* Gemäßigte, *der/die.* **3.** ['mɒdəreɪt] *v.t.* mäßigen. **4.** ['mɒdəreɪt] *v.i.* nachlassen. **moderately** ['mɒdərətlɪ] *adv.* einigermaßen; mäßig ‹*begeistert, groß, begabt*›. **moderation** [mɒdə'reɪ ʃn] *n.* Mäßigkeit, *die;* **in ~:** mit Maßen

modern ['mɒdn] *adj.* modern; heutig ‹*Zeit[alter], Welt, Mensch*›; **~ languages** neuere Sprachen. **modernize** ['mɒdənaɪz] *v.t.* modernisieren

modest ['mɒdɪst] *adj.* bescheiden; einfach ‹*Haus, Kleidung*›. '**modestly** *adv.* bescheiden. '**modesty** *n.* Bescheidenheit, *die*

modification [mɒdɪfɪ'keɪʃn] *n.* [Ab]änderung, *die*

modify ['mɒdɪfaɪ] *v.t.* [ab]ändern

modulate ['mɒdjʊleɪt] *v.t.&i.* modulieren. **modulation** [mɒdjʊ'leɪʃn] *n.* Modulation, *die*

module ['mɒdju:l] *n.* **a)** Bauelement, *das;* **b)** *(Astronaut.)* **command ~:** Kommandoeinheit, *die*

mohair ['məʊheə(r)] *n.* Mohair, *der*

moist [mɔɪst] *adj.* feucht (**with** von). **moisten** ['mɔɪsn] *v.t.* anfeuchten. **moisture** ['mɔɪstʃə(r)] *n.* Feuchtigkeit, *die.* **moisturizer** ['mɔɪstʃəraɪzə(r)], **moisturizing cream** ['mɔɪstʃəraɪzɪŋ kri:m] *ns.* Feuchtigkeitscreme, *die*

molar ['məʊlə(r)] *n.* Backenzahn, *der*

molasses [mə'læsɪz] *n.* Melasse, *die*

mold *(Amer.) see* [1,2]**mould**

molder, molding, moldy *(Amer.) see* **mould-**

[1]mole [məʊl] *n. (on skin)* Leberfleck, *der*

[2]mole *n. (animal)* Maulwurf, *der*

molecular [mə'lekjʊlə(r)] *adj.* molekular

molecule ['mɒlɪkju:l] *n.* Molekül, *das*

'molehill *n.* Maulwurfshügel, *der*

molest [mə'lest] *v.t.* belästigen

mollify ['mɒlɪfaɪ] *v.t.* besänftigen

mollusc, *(Amer.)* **mollusk** ['mɒləsk] *n.* Weichtier, *das*

mollycoddle ['mɒlɪkɒdl] *v.t.* [ver]hätscheln

molt *(Amer.) see* **moult**

molten ['məʊltn] *adj.* geschmolzen

mom [mɒm] *(Amer. coll.) see* [2]**mum**

moment ['məʊmənt] *n.* Augenblick, *der;* **at any ~,** *(coll.)* **any ~:** jeden Augenblick; **one** *or* **just a** *or* **wait a ~!** einen Augenblick!; **in a ~** *(very soon)* sofort; **at the ~:** im Augenblick; **the ~ of truth** die Stunde der Wahrheit. **momentarily** ['məʊməntərɪlɪ] *adv.* einen Augenblick lang. **momentary** ['məʊməntərɪ] *adj.* kurz

momentous [mə'mentəs] *adj. (important)* bedeutsam; *(of consequence)* folgenschwer

momentum [mə'mentəm] *n.* Schwung, *der*

Mon. *abbr.* **Monday** Mo.

monarch ['mɒnək] *n.* Monarch, *der/*Monarchin, *die.* '**monarchy** *n.* Monarchie, *die*

monastery ['mɒnəstrɪ] *n.* Kloster, *das.* **monastic** [mə'næstɪk] *adj.* mönchisch

Monday ['mʌndeɪ, 'mʌndɪ] *n.* Montag, *der; see also* **Friday**

monetary ['mʌnɪtərɪ] *adj.* **a)** *(of currency)* monetär; **Währungs**‹*politik, -system*›; **b)** *(of money)* finanziell

money ['mʌnɪ] *n.* Geld, *das;* **make ~** ‹*Person:*› [viel] Geld verdienen; ‹*Geschäft:*› etwas einbringen; **for 'my ~:** wenn man mich fragt

money: ~-bag *n.* Geldsack, *der;* **~-box** *n.* Sparbüchse, *die;* **~-making** *adj.* gewinnbringend; **~ order** *n.* Postanweisung, *die*

Mongolia [mɒŋ'gəʊlɪə] *pr. n.* Mongolei, *die.* **Mongolian** [mɒŋ'gəʊlɪən] **1.** *adj.* mongolisch. **2.** *n. (person)* Mongole, *der/*Mongolin, *die*

mongrel ['mʌŋgrəl] *n.* ~ [**dog**] Promenadenmischung, *die*

monitor ['mɒnɪtə(r)] **1.** *n.* **a)** *(Sch.)* Aufsichtsschüler, *der/*-schülerin, *die;* **b)** *(Med., Telev., etc.)* Monitor, *der.* **2.** *v.t.* beobachten ‹*Wetter, Flugzeug*›; abhören ‹*Sendung, Telefongespräch*›

monk [mʌŋk] *n.* Mönch, *der*

monkey ['mʌŋkɪ] *n.* Affe, *der*

monkey: ~ business *n. (coll.: mischief)* Schabernack, *der;* **~-nut** *n.* Erdnuß, *die;* **~-wrench** *n.* Universalschraubenschlüssel, *der*

mono ['mɒnəʊ] *adj.* Mono‹*platte[nspieler], -wiedergabe*›

monocle ['mɒnəkl] *n.* Monokel, *das*

monologue *(Amer.:* **monolog)** ['mɒnəlɒg] *n.* Monolog, *der*

monopolize [mə'nɒpəlaɪz] *v.t.*

(Econ.) monopolisieren; *(fig.)* mit Beschlag belegen; ~ **the conversation** den/die anderen nicht zu Wort kommen lassen

monopoly [mə'nɒpəlɪ] *n.* **a)** *(Econ.)* Monopol, *das* (of auf + *Dat.*); **b)** *(exclusive possession)* alleiniger Besitz

monotone ['mɒnətəʊn] *n.* gleichbleibender Ton. **monotonous** [mə'nɒtənəs] *adj.,* **mo'notonously** *adv.* eintönig. **monotony** [mə'nɒtənɪ] *n.* Eintönigkeit, *die*

monsoon [mɒn'su:n] *n.* Monsun, *der*

monster ['mɒnstə(r)] *n.* **a)** *(creature)* Ungeheuer, *das; (huge thing)* Ungetüm, *das;* **b)** *(inhuman person)* Unmensch, *der.* **monstrosity** [mɒn-'strɒsɪtɪ] *n.* **a)** *(outrageous thing)* Ungeheuerlichkeit, *die;* **b)** *(hideous building etc.)* Ungetüm, *das.* **monstrous** ['mɒnstrəs] *adj.* **a)** *(huge)* riesig; **b)** *(outrageous)* ungeheuerlich; **c)** *(atrocious)* scheußlich

month [mʌnθ] *n.* Monat, *der;* **for a ~/~s** einen Monat [lang]/monatelang. **'monthly 1.** *adj.* monatlich; Monats- ⟨*einkommen, -gehalt*⟩. **2.** *adv.* einmal im Monat. **3.** *n.* Monatsschrift, *die*

monument ['mɒnjʊmənt] *n.* Denkmal, *das.* **monumental** [mɒnjʊ-'mentl] *adj.* **a)** *(massive)* monumental; **b)** gewaltig ⟨*Mißerfolg, Irrtum*⟩

moo [mu:] **1.** *n.* Muhen, *das.* **2.** *v.i.* muhen

mooch [mu:tʃ] *v.i. (sl.)* ~ **about** *or* **around/along** herumschleichen *(ugs.)*/ zockeln *(ugs.)*

mood [mu:d] *n.* **a)** Stimmung, *die;* **be in a good/bad ~:** [bei] guter/schlechter Laune sein; **I'm not in the ~:** ich hab' keine Lust dazu; **b)** *(bad ~)* Verstimmung, *die;* **c)** *(subject to moods)* launenhaft. **'moody** *adj.* **a)** *(sullen)* mißmutig; **b)** *(subject to moods)* launenhaft

moon [mu:n] *n.* Mond, *der*

moon: **~beam** *n.* Mondstrahl, *der;* **~light 1.** *n.* Mondlicht, *das;* Mondschein, *der;* **2.** *v.i. (coll.)* nebenberuflich abends arbeiten; **~lit** *adj.* mondbeschienen *(geh.)*

¹moor [mʊə(r), mɔ:(r)] *n. (Geog.)* [Hoch]moor, *das*

²moor *v.t. & i.* festmachen; vertäuen. **'mooring** *n.* ~[s] Anlegestelle, *die*

moose [mu:s] *n., pl. same* Amerikanischer Elch

moot [mu:t] **1.** *adj.* umstritten; offen ⟨*Frage*⟩; strittig ⟨*Punkt*⟩. **2.** *v.t.* erörtern ⟨*Frage, Punkt*⟩

mop [mɒp] **1.** *n.* **a)** Mop, *der;* **b)** ~ **|of hair|** Wuschelkopf, *der.* **2.** *v.t.,* **-pp-** moppen ⟨*Fußboden*⟩; *(wipe)* abwischen ⟨*Träne, Schweiß, Stirn*⟩. **mop 'up** *v.t.* aufwischen

mope [məʊp] *v.i.* Trübsal blasen

moped ['məʊped] *n.* Moped, *das*

moral ['mɒrl] **1.** *adj.* **a)** moralisch; sittlich ⟨*Wert*⟩; Moral⟨*begriff, -prinzip*⟩; **b)** *(virtuous)* moralisch ⟨*Leben, Person*⟩. **2.** *n.* **a)** Moral, *die;* **b)** *in pl. (habits)* Moral, *die*

morale [mə'rɑ:l] Moral, *die;* **low/high ~:** schlechte/gute Moral

morality [mə'rælɪtɪ] *n.* Moral, *die*

morbid ['mɔ:bɪd] *adj.* krankhaft; morbid *(geh.)* ⟨*Faszination, Neigung*⟩

more [mɔ:(r)] **1.** *adj.* mehr; **any** *or* **some ~** *(apples, books, etc.)* noch welche; **any** *or* **some ~** *(tea, paper, etc.)* noch etwas; **any** *or* **some ~ apples/tea** noch Äpfel/Tee; **I haven't any ~ |apples/tea|** ich habe keine [Apfel]/keinen [Tee] mehr; **~ and ~:** immer mehr. **2.** *n.* mehr; **~ and ~:** immer mehr; **six or ~:** mindestens sechs. **3.** *adv.* **a)** mehr; **~ interesting** interessanter; **b)** *(nearer, rather)* eher; **c)** *(again)* wieder; **no ~, not any ~:** nicht mehr; **once ~:** noch einmal; **d)** **~ and ~:** immer mehr; **~ and ~ absurd** immer absurder; **e)** **~ or less** *(fairly)* mehr oder weniger; *(approximately)* annähernd. **more'over** *adv.* und außerdem

morgue [mɔ:g] *see* **mortuary**

morning ['mɔ:nɪŋ] *n.* Morgen, *der; (not afternoon)* Vormittag, *der; attrib.* morgendlich; Morgen-; **this ~:** heute morgen; **tomorrow ~,** *(coll.)* **in the ~:** morgen früh; **|early| in the ~:** am [frühen] Morgen; *(regularly)* [früh] morgens

Moroccan [mə'rɒkən] **1.** *adj.* marokkanisch. **2.** *n.* Marokkaner, *der*/Marokkanerin, *die*

Morocco [mə'rɒkəʊ] *pr. n.* Marokko *(das)*

moron ['mɔ:rɒn] *n. (coll.)* Schwachkopf, *der (ugs.)*

Morse [code] [mɔ:s ('kəʊd)] *n.* Morsealphabet, *das*

mortal ['mɔ:tl] **1.** *adj.* **a)** sterblich; **b)** *(fatal)* tödlich **(to** für.) **2.** *n.* Sterbliche, *der/die.* **mortality** [mɔ:'tælɪtɪ] *n.* **a)** Sterblichkeit, *die;* **b)** ~ **|rate|** Sterblichkeitsrate, *die.* **'mortally** *adv.* tödlich

mortar ['mɔ:tə(r)] *n.* Mörtel, *der*

mortgage ['mɔ:gɪdʒ] **1.** *n.* Hypothek,

die. **2.** *v. t.* mit einer Hypothek belasten

mortuary ['mɔːtjʊərɪ] *n.* Leichenschauhaus, *das*

mosaic [məʊ'zeɪk] *n.* Mosaik, *das*

Moscow ['mɒskəʊ] *pr. n.* Moskau *(das)*

Moselle [məʊ'zel] *pr. n.* Mosel, *die*

Moslem ['mɒzləm] *see* **Muslim**

mosque [mɒsk] *n.* Moschee, *die*

mosquito [mɒs'kiːtəʊ] *n., pl.* **~es** Stechmücke, *die; (in tropics)* Moskito, *der*

moss [mɒs] *n.* Moos, *das.* **'mossy** *adj.* moosig

most [məʊst] **1.** *adj. (in number, majority of)* die meisten; *(in amount)* meist...; **make the ~ mistakes/the ~ noise** die meisten Fehler/den größten Lärm machen; **for the ~ part** größtenteils. **2.** *n.* **a)** *(greatest amount)* **the ~ it will cost is £10** es wird höchstens zehn Pfund kosten; **pay the ~:** am meisten bezahlen; **b)** *(greater part)* **~ of the girls** die meisten Mädchen; **~ of his friends** die meisten seiner Freunde; **~ of the poem** der größte Teil des Gedichts; **~ of the time** die meiste Zeit; **c)** *(on ~ occasions)* meistens. **3.** *adv.* **a)** am meisten; **the ~ interesting book** das interessanteste Buch; **~ often** am häufigsten; **b)** *(exceedingly)* äußerst. **'mostly** *adv. (most of the time)* meistens; *(mainly)* größtenteils

MOT *see* **MOT test**

motel [məʊ'tel] *n.* Motel, *das*

moth [mɒθ] *n.* Nachtfalter, *der; (in clothes)* Motte, *die.* **'mothball** *n.* Mottenkugel, *die.* **'moth-eaten** *adj.* von Motten zerfressen

mother ['mʌðə(r)] **1.** *n.* Mutter, *die.* **2.** *v. t. (over-protect)* bemuttern. **'motherhood** *n.* Mutterschaft, *die*

mother: ~-in-law *n., pl.* **~s-in-law** Schwiegermutter, *die;* **~land** *n.* Vaterland, *das*

motherly ['mʌðəlɪ] *adj.* mütterlich; **~ love** Mutterliebe, *die*

mother: ~-of-'pearl *n.* Perlmutt, *das;* **M~'s Day** *n.* Muttertag, *der;* **~ 'tongue** *n.* Muttersprache, *die.* **'moth-proof** *adj.* mottenfest

motif [məʊ'tiːf] *n.* Motiv, *das*

motion ['məʊʃn] **1.** *n.* **a)** Bewegung, *die;* **b)** *(proposal)* Antrag, *der.* **2.** *v. t. & i.* **~ [to] sb. to do sth.** jmdm. bedeuten *(geh.)*, etw. zu tun. **motionless** *adj.* bewegungslos

motivate ['məʊtɪveɪt] *v. t.* motivieren.

motivation [məʊtɪ'veɪʃn] *n.* Motivation, *die*

motive ['məʊtɪv] *n.* Beweggrund, *der;* **the ~ for the crime** das Tatmotiv

motley ['mɒtlɪ] *adj.* buntgemischt

motor ['məʊtə(r)] **1.** *n.* **a)** Motor, *der;* **b)** *(Brit.: ~ car)* Auto, *das.* **2.** *adj.* Motor⟨mäher, -jacht usw.⟩. **3.** *v. i. (Brit.)* [mit dem Auto] fahren

motor: ~bike *n. (coll.)* Motorrad, *das;* **~ boat** *n.* Motorboot, *das;* **~ car** *n. (Brit.)* Kraftfahrzeug, *das;* **~ cycle** *n.* Motorrad, *das*

'motoring *n. (Brit.)* Autofahren, *das.* **'motorist** *n.* Autofahrer, *der/*-fahrerin, *die*

motorize ['məʊtəraɪz] *v. t.* motorisieren

motor: ~racing *n.* Autorennsport, *der;* **~ vehicle** *n.* Kraftfahrzeug, *das;* **~way** *n. (Brit.)* Autobahn, *die*

MOT test *n. (Brit.)* ≈ TÜV, *der*

mottled ['mɒtld] *adj.* gesprenkelt

motto ['mɒtəʊ] *n., pl.* **~es** Motto, *das*

'mould [məʊld] **1.** *n. (hollow container)* Form, *die.* **2.** *v. t.* formen **(out of, from aus)**

'mould *n. (Bot.)* Schimmel, *der*

moulder ['məʊldə(r)] *v. i.* **~ [away]** [ver]modern

'moulding *n.* **a)** Formteil, *das* **(of, in aus)**; *(Archit.)* Zierleiste, *die;* **b)** *(wooden)* Leiste, *die*

'mouldy *adj.* schimmlig; **go ~:** schimmeln

moult [məʊlt] *v. i.* ⟨Vogel:⟩ sich mausern; ⟨Hund, Katze:⟩ sich haaren

mound [maʊnd] *n.* **a)** *(of earth)* Hügel, *der;* **b)** *(heap)* Haufen, *der*

mount [maʊnt] **1.** *n.* **a)** **M~ Vesuvius/Everest** der Vesuv/der Mount Everest; **b)** *(animal)* Reittier, *das; (horse)* Pferd, *das;* **c)** *(of picture, photograph)* Passepartout, *das;* **d)** *(for gem)* Fassung, *die.* **2.** *v. t.* **a)** hinaufsteigen ⟨Treppe⟩; steigen auf (+ Akk.) ⟨Plattform, Reittier, Fahrzeug⟩; **b)** aufziehen ⟨Bild⟩; einfassen ⟨Edelstein usw.⟩; **c)** inszenieren ⟨Stück, Oper⟩; organisieren ⟨Ausstellung⟩; durchführen ⟨Angriff, Operation⟩. **3.** *v. i.* **~ [up]** *(increase)* steigen **(to auf + Akk.)**

mountain ['maʊntɪn] *n.* Berg, *der;* **in the ~s** im Gebirge. **mountaineer** [maʊntɪ'nɪə(r)] *n.* Bergsteiger, *der/* Bergsteigerin, *die.* **mountai'neering** *n.* Bergsteigen, *das.* **mountainous** ['maʊntɪnəs] *adj.* **a)** gebirgig; **b)** *(huge)* riesig

mourn [mɔ:n] **1.** *v. i.* trauern; ~ **for** *or* **over** trauern um ⟨*Toten*⟩. **2.** *v. t.* betrauern. 'mourner *n.* Trauernde, *der/die*. **mournful** ['mɔ:nfl] *adj.* klagend ⟨*Stimme, Ton, Schrei*⟩; trauervoll *(geh.)* ⟨*Person*⟩. 'mourning *n.* Trauer, *die;* **be in/go into** ~: Trauer tragen/anlegen

mouse [maʊs] *n., pl.* **mice** [maɪs] Maus, *die.* 'mouse trap *n.* Mausefalle, *die*

mousse [mu:s] *n.* Mousse, *die*

moustache [mə'sta:ʃ] *n.* Schnurrbart, *der*

mousy ['maʊsɪ] *adj.* **a)** mattbraun ⟨*Haar*⟩; **b)** *(timid)* scheu

mouth 1. [maʊθ] *n.* **a)** *(of person)* Mund, *der; (of animal)* Maul, *das;* **with one's** ~ **open/full** mit offenem/vollem Mund; **b)** *(harbour entrance)* [Hafen]einfahrt, *die; (of tunnel, cave)* Eingang, *der; (of river)* Mündung, *die.* **2.** [maʊð] *v. t.* mit Lippenbewegungen sagen. **mouthful** ['maʊθfʊl] *n.* Mundvoll, *der*

mouth: ~**organ** *n.* Mundharmonika, *die;* ~**piece** *n.* **a)** Mundstück, *das;* **b)** *(fig.)* Sprachrohr, *das*

movable ['mu:vəbl] *adj.* beweglich

move [mu:v] **1.** *n.* **a)** *(change of home)* Umzug, *der;* **b)** *(action taken)* Schritt, *der; (Footb. etc.)* Spielzug, *der;* **c)** *(turn in game)* Zug, *der;* **make a** ~: ziehen; **it's your** ~: du bist am Zug; **d) be on the** ~ ⟨*Person:*⟩ unterwegs sein; **e) make a** ~ *(do sth.)* etwas tun; *(coll.: leave)* losziehen *(ugs.);* **f) get a** ~ **on** *(coll.)* einen Zahn zulegen *(ugs.);* **get a** ~ **on!** *(coll.)* [mach] Tempo! *(ugs.).* **2.** *v. t.* **a)** *(change position of)* bewegen; wegräumen ⟨*Hindernis, Schutt*⟩; *(transport)* befördern; ~ **sth. to a new position** etw. an einen neuen Platz bringen; **b)** *(in game)* ziehen; **c)** *(affect)* bewegen; ~ **sb. to tears** jmdn. zu Tränen rühren; **be ~d by sth.** über etw. *(Akk.)* gerührt sein; **d)** *(prompt)* ~ **sb. to do sth.** jmdn. dazu bewegen, etw. zu tun; **e)** *(propose)* beantragen. **3.** *v. i.* **a)** sich bewegen; *(in vehicle)* fahren; **b)** *(in games)* ziehen; **c)** *(do sth.)* handeln; **d)** *(change home)* umziehen **(to** nach); ~ **into a flat** in eine Wohnung einziehen; ~ **out of a flat** aus einer Wohnung ausziehen; ~ **to London** nach London ziehen; **e)** *(change posture or state)* sich bewegen; **don't** ~! keine Bewegung! **move a'bout 1.** *v. i.* zu-

gange sein; *(travel)* unterwegs sein. **2.** *v. t.* herumräumen. **move a'long 1.** *v. i.* **a)** gehen/fahren; **b)** ~ **along, please!** gehen/fahren Sie bitte weiter! **2.** *v. t.* zum Weitergehen/-fahren auffordern. **move 'in 1.** *v. i.* **a)** *(to home etc.)* einziehen; **b)** ~ **in on** ⟨*Truppen, Polizeikräfte:*⟩ vorrücken gegen. **2.** *v. t.* hineinbringen. **move 'off** *v. i.* sich in Bewegung setzen. **move 'on 1.** *v. i.* weitergehen/-fahren; ~ **on to another question** *(fig.)* zu einer anderen Frage übergehen. **2.** *v. t.* zum Weitergehen/-fahren auffordern. **move 'out** *v. t.* ausziehen (of aus). **move 'over** *v. i.* rücken. **move 'up** *v. i.* **a)** rücken; **b)** *(in queue, hierarchy)* aufrücken

'movement *n.* **a)** Bewegung, *die; (trend, tendency)* Tendenz, *die* **(towards** zu); **b)** *in pl.* Aktivitäten *Pl.;* **c)** *(Mus.)* Satz, *der*

movie ['mu:vɪ] *n. (Amer. coll.)* Film, *der;* **the** ~**s** der Film; **go to the** ~**s** ins Kino gehen

moving ['mu:vɪŋ] *adj.* **a)** beweglich; **b)** *(affecting)* ergreifend

mow [məʊ] *v. t., p.p.* **mown** [məʊn] *or* **mowed** [məʊd] mähen. **mow 'down** *v. t. (shoot)* niedermähen ⟨*Menschen*⟩

'mower *n.* Rasenmäher, *der*

mown *see* **mow**

MP *abbr.* **Member of Parliament**

m.p.g. *abbr.* **miles per gallon**

m.p.h. *abbr.* **miles per hour**

Mr ['mɪstə(r)] *n.* Herr; *(in an address)* Herrn

Mrs ['mɪsɪz] *n.* Frau

Ms [mɪz] *n.* Frau

Mt. *abbr.* **Mount**

much [mʌtʃ] **1.** *adj., more* [mɔ:(r)], *most* [məʊst] viel; **too** ~: zuviel *indekl.* **2.** *n.* vieles; ~ **of the day** der Großteil des Tages; **not be** ~ **to look at** nicht sehr ansehnlich sein. **3.** *adv., more, most* **a)** viel ⟨*besser, schöner usw.*⟩; ~ **more lively/attractive** viel lebhafter/attraktiver; **b)** mit Abstand ⟨*der/die/das beste, klügste usw.*⟩; **c)** *(greatly)* sehr ⟨*lieben, genießen usw.*⟩; *(for* ~ *of the time)* viel ⟨*lesen, spielen usw.*⟩; *(often)* oft ⟨*sehen, besuchen usw.*⟩; **d)** [**pretty** *or* **very**] ~ **the same** fast [genau] der-/die-/dasselbe

muck [mʌk] *n.* **a)** *(coll.: something disgusting)* Dreck, *der (ugs.);* **b)** *(coll.: nonsense)* Mist, *der (ugs.).* **muck a'bout, muck a'round** *(Brit. sl.) v. i.* **a)** herumalbern *(ugs.);* **b)** *(tinker)* her-

umfummeln (**with** an + *Dat.*). **muck
'in** *v. i. (coll.)* mit anpacken (**with** bei).
muck 'up *v.t.* **a)** *(Brit. coll.: bungle)*
vermurksen *(ugs.);* **b)** *(make dirty)*
dreckig machen *(ugs.);* **c)** *(coll.: spoil)*
vermasseln *(salopp)*
'**mucky** *adj.* dreckig *(ugs.)*
mucus ['mju:kəs] *n.* Schleim, *der*
mud [mʌd] *n.* Schlamm, *der*
muddle ['mʌdl] **1.** *n.* Durcheinander,
das. **2.** *v. t.* ~ |up| durcheinanderbrin-
gen; ~ **up** *(mix up)* verwechseln (**with**
mit). **muddle a'long, muddle 'on**
v. i. vor sich *(Akk.)* hin wursteln
(ugs.). **muddle 'through** *v. i.* sich
durchwursteln *(ugs.)*
muddy ['mʌdɪ] *adj.* schlammig; **get** *or*
become ~: verschlammen
'**mudguard** *n.* Schutzblech, *das; (of
car)* Kotflügel, *der*
¹**muff** [mʌf] *n.* Muff, *der*
²**muff** *v.t.* verpatzen *(ugs.)*
muffle ['mʌfl] *v.t.* **a)** *(envelop)* ~ |up|
einhüllen; **b)** dämpfen ⟨*Geräusch*⟩.
'**muffler** *n.* **a)** *(wrap, scarf)* Schal,
der; **b)** *(Amer. Motor Veh.)* Schall-
dämpfer, *der*
mug [mʌg] **1.** *n.* **a)** Becher, *der (meist
mit Henkel); (for beer etc.)* Krug, *der;*
b) *(sl.: face, mouth)* Visage, *die (salopp).* **c)** *(Brit. sl.: gullible person)* Trottel, *der (ugs.).* **2.** *v. t.,* -gg- *(rob)* überfallen und berauben. '**mugger** *n.*
Straßenräuber, *der/*-räuberin, *die.*
'**mugging** *n.* Straßenraub, *der*
muggy ['mʌgɪ] *adj.* schwül
mule [mju:l] *n.* Maultier, *das*
multicoloured (*Brit., Amer.:* **multi-
colored**) ['mʌltɪkʌləd] *adj.* mehrfar-
big; bunt ⟨*Stoff, Kleid*⟩
multinational [mʌltɪ'næʃənl] **1.** *adj.*
multinational. **2.** *n.* multinationaler
Konzern, *der;* Multi, *der (ugs.)*
multiple ['mʌltɪpl] *adj.* mehrfach.
multiple-'choice *adj.* Multiple-
choice-⟨*Test, Frage*⟩. **multiple 'store**
n. (Brit.: shop) Kettenladen, *der*
multiplication [mʌltɪplɪ'keɪʃn] *n.*
Multiplikation, *die*
multiply ['mʌltɪplaɪ] **1.** *v. t.* multiplizieren, malnehmen (**by** mit). **2.** *v. i.*
sich vermehren
multi-storey ['mʌltɪstɔ:rɪ] *adj.* mehr-
stöckig; ~ **car park/block of flats**
Parkhaus/Wohnhochhaus, *das*
multitude ['mʌltɪtju:d] *n. (crowd)*
Menge, *die; (great number)* Vielzahl,
die
¹**mum** [mʌm] *(coll.)* **1.** *int.* ~'**s the word**

nicht weitersagen! **2.** *adj.* **keep** ~: den
Mund halten *(ugs.)*
²**mum** *n. (Brit. coll.: mother)* Mama, *die
(fam.)*
mumble ['mʌmbl] *v. i. & t.* nuscheln
(ugs.)
mumps [mʌmps] *n.* Mumps, *der*
munch [mʌntʃ] *v. t. & i.* ~ |one's food|
mampfen *(salopp)*
mundane [mʌn'deɪn] *adj.* **a)** *(dull)* banal; **b)** *(worldly)* weltlich
Munich ['mju:nɪk] *pr. n.* München
(das)
municipal [mju:'nɪsɪpl] *adj.* kommunal; Kommunal⟨*politik, -verwaltung*⟩
mural ['mjʊərl] *n.* Wandbild, *das*
murder ['mɜ:də(r)] **1.** *n.* Mord, *der* (**of**
an + *Dat.*). **2.** *v. t.* ermorden. '**murderer** *n.* Mörder, *der/*Mörderin, *die.*
murderess ['mɜ:dərɪs] *n.* Mörderin,
die. **murderous** ['mɜ:dərəs] *adj.* tödlich; Mord⟨*absicht, -drohung*⟩*;* mörderisch *(ugs.)* ⟨*Kampf*⟩
murk [mɜ:k] *n.* Dunkelheit, *die.*
'**murky** *adj.* **a)** *(dark)* düster; **b)**
(dirty) schmutzig-trüb ⟨*Wasser*⟩
murmur ['mɜ:mə(r)] **1.** *n.* **a)** *(subdued
sound)* Rauschen, *das;* **b)** *(expression
of discontent)* Murren, *das;* **c)** *(soft
speech)* Murmeln, *das.* **2.** *v. t.* murmeln. **3.** *v. i.* ⟨*Person:*⟩ murmeln; *(complain)* murren
muscle ['mʌsl] *n.* Muskel, *der.* **muscular** ['mʌskjʊlə(r)] *adj.* **a)** *(Anat.)*
Muskel-; **b)** *(strong)* muskulös
muse [mju:z] *(literary) v. i.* [nach]sin-
nen *(geh.)* (**on, over** über + *Akk.*)
museum [mju:'zi:əm] *n.* Museum, *das*
mush [mʌʃ] *n.* Brei, *der*
mushroom ['mʌʃrʊm, 'mʌʃru:m] **1.** *n.*
Pilz, *der; (cultivated)* Champignon,
der. **2.** *v. i.* wie Pilze aus dem Boden
schießen
'**mushy** *adj.* breiig
music ['mju:zɪk] *n.* **a)** Musik, *die;*
piece of ~: Musikstück, *das;* **set sth. to**
~: etw. vertonen; **b)** *(score)* Noten *Pl.*
musical ['mju:zɪkl] **1.** *adj.* musikalisch; Musik⟨*instrument, -verständnis,
-notation, -abend*⟩. **2.** *n.* Musical, *das*
Muslim ['mʊslɪm, 'mʌzlɪm] **1.** *adj.*
moslemisch. **2.** *n.* Moslem, *der/*Mos-
lime, *die*
muslin ['mʌzlɪn] *n.* Musselin, *der*
mussel ['mʌsl] *n.* Muschel, *die*
must [məst, *stressed* mʌst] **1.** *v. aux.,
only in pres., neg. (coll.)* **mustn't**
['mʌsnt] müssen; *with neg.* dürfen. **2.**
n. (coll.) Muß, *das*

mustache *see* moustache
mustard ['mʌstəd] *n.* Senf, *der*
muster ['mʌstə(r)] **1.** *n.* pass ~: akzeptabel sein. **2.** *v. t.* versammeln; *(Mil., Naut.)* [zum Appell] antreten lassen; *(fig.)* zusammennehmen ⟨*Kraft, Mut, Verstand*⟩. **3.** *v. i.* sich [ver]sammeln.
muster 'up *v. t.* aufbringen
mustn't ['mʌsnt] *(coll.)* = must not; *see* must 1
musty ['mʌstɪ] *adj.* muffig
mutant ['mjuːtənt] **1.** *adj.* mutiert. **2.** *n.* Mutante, *die*
mutation [mjuː'teɪʃn] *n.* Mutation, *die*
mute [mjuːt] **1.** *adj.* stumm. **2.** *n.* Stumme, *der/die.* '**muted** *adj.* gedämpft
mutilate ['mjuːtɪleɪt] *v. t.* verstümmeln. **mutilation** [mjuːtɪ'leɪʃn] *n.* Verstümmelung, *die*
mutinous ['mjuːtɪnəs] *adj.* meuternd
mutiny ['mjuːtɪnɪ] **1.** *n.* Meuterei, *die.* **2.** *v. i.* meutern
mutter ['mʌtə(r)] *v. i. & t.* murmeln. '**muttering** *n.* Gemurmel, *das*
mutton ['mʌtn] *n.* Hammelfleisch, *das*
mutual ['mjuːtjʊəl] *adj.* **a)** gegenseitig; **b)** *(coll.: shared)* gemeinsam. '**mutually** *adv.* **a)** gegenseitig; **be ~ exclusive** sich [gegenseitig] ausschließen; **b)** *(in common)* gemeinsam
muzzle ['mʌzl] **1.** *n.* **a)** *(of dog)* Schnauze, *die; (of horse, cattle)* Maul, *das;* **b)** *(of gun)* Mündung, *die;* **c)** *(put over animal's mouth)* Maulkorb, *der.* **2.** *v. t.* **a)** einen Maulkorb anlegen (+ *Dat.*) ⟨*Hund*⟩; **b)** *(fig.)* mundtot machen *(ugs.)* (+ *Dat.*)
MW *abbr. (Radio)* **medium wave** MW
my [maɪ] *poss. pron. attrib.* mein; my|, my|!, |my| **oh my!** [ach du] **meine Güte!** *(ugs.)*
myself [maɪ'self] *pron.* **a)** *emphat.* selbst; **I thought so ~**: das habe ich auch gedacht; **b)** *refl.* mich/mir. *See also* herself
mysterious [mɪ'stɪərɪəs] *adj.* rätselhaft; geheimnisvoll ⟨*Fremder, Orient*⟩. **my'steriously** *adv.* auf rätselhafte Weise; geheimnisvoll ⟨*lächeln usw.*⟩
mystery ['mɪstərɪ] *n.* **a)** Rätsel, *das;* **b)** *(secrecy)* Geheimnis, *das.* '**mystery tour** *n.* Fahrt ins Blaue *(ugs.)*
mystic ['mɪstɪk] **1.** *adj.* mystisch. **2.** *n.* Mystiker, *der*/Mystikerin, *die.* **mystical** ['mɪstɪkl] *adj.* mystisch
mystify ['mɪstɪfaɪ] *v. t.* verwirren
myth [mɪθ] *n.* Mythos, *der.* **mythical** ['mɪθɪkl] *adj.* **a)** *(based on myth)* my-

thisch; **b)** *(invented)* fiktiv. **mythological** [mɪθə'lɒdʒɪkl] *adj.* mythologisch. **mythology** [mɪ'θɒlədʒɪ] *n.* Mythologie, *die*

N

N, n [en] *n.* N, n, *das*
N. *abbr.* **a) north** N; **b) northern** n.
NAAFI ['næfɪ] *abbr. (Brit.)* **Navy, Army and Air Force Institutes** Kaufhaus für Angehörige der britischen Truppen
nab [næb] *v. t.*, **-bb-** *(sl.)* **a)** *(arrest)* schnappen *(ugs.);* **b)** *(seize)* sich *(Dat.)* schnappen
nag [næg] *v. i. & t.* **-gg-**: ~ |at| sb. an jmdm. herumnörgeln; ~ |at| sb. to do sth. jmdm. zusetzen *(ugs.)*, daß er etw. tut. '**nagging 1.** *adj. (persistent)* quälend; bohrend ⟨*Schmerz*⟩. **2.** *n.* Genörgel, *das*
nail [neɪl] **1.** *n.* Nagel, *der;* **hit the ~ on the head** *(fig.)* den Nagel auf den Kopf treffen *(ugs.).* **2.** *v. t.* nageln (**to** an + *Akk.*). **nail 'down** *v. t.* festnageln; zunageln ⟨*Kiste*⟩
nail: **~-brush** *n.* Nagelbürste, *die;* **~-clippers** *n. pl.* |pair of| ~-clippers Nagelknipser, *der;* **~-file** *n.* Nagelfeile, *die;* ~ **polish** *n.* Nagellack, *der;* **~-polish remover** Nagellackentferner, *der;* **~-scissors** *n. pl.* |pair of| ~-scissors Nagelschere, *die;* ~ **varnish** *(Brit.) see* ~ polish
naïve, naive [naɪ'iːv] *adj.*, **na'ïvely, na'ively** *adv.* naiv
naked ['neɪkɪd] *adj.* nackt; **visible to** *or* **with the ~ eye** mit bloßem Auge zu erkennen. '**nakedness** *n.* Nacktheit, *die*
name [neɪm] **1.** *n.* **a)** Name, *der;* **what's your ~/the ~ of this place?** wie heißt du/dieser Ort?; **my ~ is Jack** ich heiße Jack; **last ~**: Nachname, *der;* **by ~**: namentlich ⟨*erwähnen, aufrufen usw.*⟩; **know sb. by ~**: jmdn. mit Namen kennen; **b)** *(reputation)* Ruf, *der;* **make a ~ for oneself** sich *(Dat.)* einen Namen machen; **c) call sb. ~s** jmdn. beschimpfen. **2.** *v. t.* **a)** *(give ~ to)* ei-

nen Namen geben (+ *Dat.*); ~ **sb.**
John jmdn. John nennen; ~ **sb./sth.**
after *or (Amer.)* **for sb.** jmdn./etw.
nach jmdm. benennen; **be ~d John**
John heißen; **a man ~d Smith** ein
Mann namens Smith; **b)** *(call by right*
~) benennen; **c)** *(nominate)* ~ **sb. [as]**
sth. jmdn. zu etw. ernennen. **'name-**
less *adj.* namenlos. **'namely** *adv.*
nämlich. **'namesake** *n.* Namensvet-
ter, *der/*-schwester, *die*
nanny ['nænɪ] *n. (Brit.)* Kindermäd-
chen, *das.* **'nanny-goat** *n.* Ziege, *die*
nap [næp] **1.** *n.* Nickerchen, *das*
(fam.); **have a ~:** ein Nickerchen hal-
ten. **2.** *v.i.,* **-pp-** dösen *(ugs.);* **catch sb.**
~ping *(fig.)* jmdn. überrumpeln
nape [neɪp] *n.* ~ **|of the neck|** Nacken,
der; Genick, *das*
napkin ['næpkɪn] *n.* Serviette, *die*
Naples ['neɪplz] *pr. n.* Neapel *(das)*
nappy ['næpɪ] *n. (Brit.)* Windel, *die*
narcissus [nɑː'sɪsəs] *n., pl.* **narcissi**
[nɑː'sɪsaɪ] *or* **~es** Narzisse, *die*
narcotic [nɑː'kɒtɪk] **1.** *n.* **a)** *(drug)*
Rauschgift, *das;* **b)** *(active ingredient)*
Betäubungsmittel, *das.* **2.** *adj.* **a)** nar-
kotisch; ~ **drug** Rauschgift, *das;* **b)**
(causing drowsiness) einschläfernd
narrate [nə'reɪt] *v.t.* erzählen; kom-
mentieren ⟨*Film*⟩. **narration** [nə-
'reɪʃn] *n.* Erzählung, *die.* **narrative**
['nærətɪv] **1.** *n.* Erzählung, *die.* **2.** *adj.*
erzählend. **narrator** [nə'reɪtə(r)] *n.*
Erzähler, *der/*Erzählerin, *die*
narrow ['nærəʊ] **1.** *adj.* **a)** schmal;
schmal geschnitten ⟨*Rock, Hose,*
Ärmel usw.⟩; eng ⟨*Tal, Gasse*⟩; **b)**
(limited) eng; begrenzt ⟨*Auswahl*⟩; **c)**
knapp ⟨*Sieg, Mehrheit*⟩; **have a ~ es-**
cape mit knapper Not entkommen
(from *Dat.*); **d)** *(not tolerant)* engstirnig. **2.** *v.i.* sich verschmälern; ⟨*Tal:*⟩
sich verengen. **3.** *v.t.* verschmälern;
(fig.) einengen. **narrow 'down** *v.t.*
einengen **(to** auf + *Akk.*)
narrow-'minded *adj.* engstirnig
nasal ['neɪzl] *adj.* **a)** *(Anat.)* Nasen-; **b)**
näselnd; **speak in a ~ voice** näseln
nastily ['nɑːstɪlɪ] *adv.* **a)** *(unpleasantly)*
scheußlich; **b)** *(ill-naturedly)* gemein;
behave ~: häßlich sein
nasty ['nɑːstɪ] *adj.* **a)** *(unpleasant)*
scheußlich ⟨*Geruch, Geschmack*⟩; gemein ⟨*Trick, Person*⟩; häßlich ⟨*Ange-*
wohnheit⟩; **that was a ~ thing to say/**
do das war gemein; **b)** *(ill-natured)* böse; **be ~ to sb.** häßlich zu jmdm. sein;
c) *(serious)* übel; schlimm ⟨*Krankheit,*

Husten, Verletzung⟩; **she had a ~ fall**
sie ist übel gefallen
nation ['neɪʃn] *n.* Nation, *die; (people)*
Volk, *das.* **national** ['næʃənl] **1.** *adj.*
national; National⟨*flagge, -held,*
-theater, -gericht, -charakter⟩; Staats-
⟨*sicherheit, -religion*⟩; überregional
⟨*Rundfunkstation, Zeitung*⟩; landesweit ⟨*Streik*⟩. **2.** *n. (citizen)* Staatsbürger, *der/*-bürgerin, *die; foreign* ~:
Ausländer, *der/*Ausländerin, *die*
national: ~ **'anthem** *n.* National-
hymne, *die;* ~ **'costume** *n.* National-
tracht, *die;* **N~ 'Health [Service]** *n.*
(Brit.) staatlicher Gesundheitsdienst;
N~ Health doctor/patient/spectacles
≈ Kassenarzt, *der/*-patient, *der/*-bril-
le, *die;* **N~ In'surance** *n. (Brit.)* Sozi-
alversicherung, *die*
nationalism ['næʃənəlɪzm] *n.* Nationalismus, *der.* **nationalist** ['næʃənə-
lɪst] **1.** *n.* Nationalist, *der/*Nationali-
stin, *die.* **2.** *adj.* nationalistisch
nationality [næʃə'nælɪtɪ] *n.* Staatsangehörigkeit, *die;* **what's his ~?** welche
Staatsangehörigkeit hat er?
nationalization [næʃənəlaɪ'zeɪʃn] *n.*
Verstaatlichung, *die*
nationalize ['næʃənəlaɪz] *v.t.* ver-
staatlichen
'nationally *adv.* landesweit
native ['neɪtɪv] **1.** *n.* **a)** *(of specified*
place) **a ~ of Britain** ein gebürtiger
Brite/eine gebürtige Britin; **b)** *(person*
born in a place) Eingeborene, *der/die;*
c) *(local inhabitant)* Einheimische,
der/die. **2.** *adj.* eingeboren; einheimisch ⟨*Pflanze, Tier*⟩; ~ **inhabitant**
Eingeborene/Einheimische, *der/die;*
~ **land** Geburts- *od.* Heimatland, *das;*
~ **language** Muttersprache, *die*
nativity [nə'tɪvɪtɪ] *n.* **the N~ |of Christ|**
die Geburt Christi. **na'tivity play** *n.*
Krippenspiel, *das*
NATO, Nato ['neɪtəʊ] *abbr.* North Atlantic Treaty Organization NATO, *die*
natter ['nætə(r)] *(Brit. coll.)* **1.** *v.i.*
quatschen *(ugs.).* **2.** *n.* **have a ~:** quatschen *(ugs.)*
natural ['nætʃrəl] *adj.* natürlich; Na-
tur⟨*zustand, -seide, -gewalt*⟩. **natural**
'gas *n.* Erdgas, *das.* **natural 'his-**
tory *n.* Naturkunde, *die*
naturalism ['nætʃrəlɪzm] *n.* Naturalismus, *der*
naturalist ['nætʃrəlɪst] *n.* Naturfor-
scher, *der/*-forscherin, *die*
naturalization [nætʃrəlaɪ'zeɪʃn] *n.*
Einbürgerung, *die*

naturalize ['nætʃrəlaɪz] *v. t.* einbürgern

'**naturally** *adv.* **a)** *(by nature)* von Natur aus *⟨blaß, fleißig usw.⟩; (in a true-to-life way)* naturgetreu; **b)** *(of course)* natürlich

'**naturalness** *n.* Natürlichkeit, *die*

nature ['neɪtʃə(r)] *n.* **a)** Natur, *die;* **b)** *(essential qualities)* Beschaffenheit, *die;* **in the ~ of things** naturgemäß; **c)** *(kind)* Art, *die;* **things of this ~:** derartiges; **d)** *(character)* Wesen, *das;* **be proud/friendly** *etc.* **by ~:** ein stolzes/freundliches *usw.* Wesen haben. '**nature reserve** *n.* Naturschutzgebiet, *das.* '**nature study** *n.* Naturkunde, *die.* '**nature trail** *n.* Naturlehrpfad, *der*

naught [nɔːt] *n. (arch./dial.)* **come to ~:** zunichte werden

naughtily ['nɔːtɪlɪ] *adv.* ungezogen

naughtiness ['nɔːtɪnɪs] *n.* Ungezogenheit, *die*

naughty ['nɔːtɪ] *adj.* ungezogen; **you ~ boy/dog** du böser Junge/Hund

nausea ['nɔːzɪə] *n.* Übelkeit, *die.* **nauseate** ['nɔːzɪeɪt] *v. t. (disgust)* anwidern. '**nauseating** *adj. (disgusting)* widerlich. **nauseous** ['nɔːzɪəs] *adj.* **sb. is** *or* **feels ~:** jmdm. ist übel

nautical ['nɔːtɪkl] *adj.* nautisch. **nautical 'mile** *n.* Seemeile, *die*

naval ['neɪvl] *adj.* Marine-; See-⟨*schlacht, -macht, -streitkräfte*⟩; **~ ship** Kriegsschiff, *das*

nave [neɪv] *n.* [Mittel]schiff, *das*

navel ['neɪvl] *n.* Nabel, *der*

navigate ['nævɪgeɪt] *v. t.* **a)** navigieren ⟨*Schiff, Flugzeug*⟩; **b)** befahren ⟨*Fluß usw.*⟩. **navigation** [nævɪ'geɪʃn] *n.* Navigation, *die.* **navigator** ['nævɪgeɪtə(r)] *n.* Navigator, *der*/Navigatorin, *die*

navy ['neɪvɪ] *n.* **a)** [Kriegs]marine, *die;* **b)** *see* **navy blue. navy 'blue** *n.* Marineblau, *das.* '**navy-blue** *adj.* marineblau

Nazi ['nɑːtsɪ] **1.** *n.* Nazi, *der.* **2.** *adj.* nazistisch; Nazi-

NB *abbr.* **nota bene** NB

NCO *abbr.* **non-commissioned officer** Uffz.

NE *abbr.* **north-east** NO

near [nɪə(r)] **1.** *adv.* nah[e]; **stand/live |quite| ~:** [ganz] in der Nähe stehen/wohnen; **come** *or* **draw ~/~er** ⟨*Tag, Zeitpunkt:*⟩ nahen/näherrücken; **get ~er together** näher zusammenrücken; **~ at hand** in Reichweite *(Dat.); ⟨Ort⟩*

ganz in der Nähe; **~ to = 2. 2. *prep.* a)** *(position)* nahe an/bei *(+ Dat.); (fig.)* in der Nähe *(+ Gen.);* **keep ~ me** halte dich in meiner Nähe; **it's ~ here** es ist hier in der Nähe; **b)** *(motion)* nahe an *(+ Akk.); (fig.)* in der Nähe *(+ Gen.);* **don't come ~ me** komm mir nicht zu nahe. **3.** *adj.* **a)** *(in space or time)* nahe; **in the ~ future** in nächster Zukunft; **the ~est man** der am nächsten stehende Mann; **b)** *(in nature)* **£30 or ~/~est offer** 30 Pfund oder nächstbestes Angebot; **~ escape** Entkommen mit knapper Not; **that was a ~ miss/thing!** das war knapp! **4.** *v. t.* sich nähern *(+ Dat.);* **the building is ~ing completion** das Gebäude steht kurz vor seiner Vollendung. **5.** *v. i.* ⟨*Zeitpunkt:*⟩ näherrücken. '**nearby** *adj.* nahe gelegen

'**nearly** *adv.* fast; **be ~ in tears** den Tränen nahe sein; **it is ~ six o'clock** es ist kurz vor sechs Uhr; **are you ~ ready?** bist du bald fertig?

'**nearness** *n.* Nähe, *die*

'**near-sighted** *adj. (Amer.)* kurzsichtig

neat [niːt] *adj.* **a)** *(tidy)* ordentlich; **b)** *(undiluted)* pur; **c)** *(smart)* gepflegt ⟨*Erscheinung, Kleidung*⟩; **d)** *(deft)* geschickt. '**neatly** *adv. see* **neat a, c, d:** ordentlich; gepflegt; geschickt. '**neatness** *n. see* **neat a, c, d:** Ordentlichkeit, *die;* Gepflegtheit, *die;* Geschicktheit, *die*

necessarily [nesɪ'serɪlɪ] *adv.* zwangsläufig; **it is not ~ true** es muß nicht [unbedingt] stimmen

necessary ['nesɪsərɪ] **1.** *adj.* nötig; notwendig; **do everything ~:** das Nötige *od.* Notwendige tun. **2.** *n.* **the necessaries of life** das Lebensnotwendige

necessitate [nɪ'sesɪteɪt] *v. t.* erforderlich machen

necessity [nɪ'sesɪtɪ] *n.* **a)** *(need, necessary thing)* Notwendigkeit, *die;* **do sth. out of** *or* **from ~:** etw. notgedrungen tun; **of ~:** notwendigerweise; **b)** *(want)* Not, *der*

neck [nek] *n.* **a)** Hals, *der;* **be a pain in the ~** *(coll.)* jmdm. auf die Nerven gehen *(ugs.);* **break one's ~** *(fig. coll.)* sich den Hals brechen; **~ and ~:** Kopf an Kopf; **b)** *(of garment)* Kragen, *der*

neck: **~lace** ['neklɪs] *n.* [Hals]kette, *die; (with jewels)* Kollier, *das;* **~line** *n.* [Hals]ausschnitt, *der;* **~tie** *n.* Krawatte, *die*

nectar ['nektə(r)] *n.* Nektar, *der*
née (*Amer.:* **nee**) [neɪ] *adj.* geborene
need [niːd] 1. *n.* a) Notwendigkeit, *die*
(for, of *Gen.*); *(demand)* Bedarf, *der*
(for, of an + *Dat.*); **as the ~ arises**
nach Bedarf; **if ~ be** nötigenfalls;
there's no ~ for that [das ist] nicht nötig; **there's no ~ to do sth.** es ist nicht
nötig, etw. zu tun; **be in ~ of sth.** etw.
brauchen; **there's no ~ for you to come**
du brauchst nicht zu kommen; b) *no
pl. (emergency)* Not, *die;* **in case of ~:**
im Notfall; c) *(thing)* Bedürfnis, *das.*
2. *v. t.* a) *(require)* brauchen; **sth. that
urgently ~s doing** etw., was dringend
gemacht werden muß; **it ~s a coat of
paint** es muß gestrichen werden; b)
expr. necessity müssen; **I ~ to do it** ich
muß es tun; **it ~s/doesn't ~ to be done**
es muß getan werden/es braucht nicht
getan zu werden; c) *pres.* **he ~,** *neg.* **~
not** *or (coll.)* **~n't** ['niːdnt] *expr. desirability* müssen; *with neg.* brauchen zu
needle ['niːdl] 1. *n.* Nadel, *die.* 2. *v. t.
(coll.)* nerven *(ugs.)*
needless ['niːdlɪs] *adj.* unnötig; **~ to
add** *or* **say, ...:** überflüssig zu sagen,
daß ... '**needlessly** *adv.* unnötig
'**needlework** *n.* Handarbeit, *die;* **do
~:** handarbeiten
needn't ['niːdnt] *(coll.)* = need not;
see need 2 c
'**needy** *adj.* notleidend; bedürftig
negation [nɪ'geɪʃn] *n.* Verneinung, *die*
negative ['negətɪv] 1. *adj.* negativ. 2.
n. a) *(Photog.)* Negativ, *das;* b) *(~
statement)* negative Aussage; *(answer)* Nein, *das.* '**negatively** *adv.*
negativ
neglect [nɪ'glekt] 1. *v. t.* vernachlässigen; **she ~ed to write** sie hat es versäumt zu schreiben. 2. *n.* Vernachlässigung, *die;* **be in a state of ~** *(Gebäude:)* verwahrlost sein. **neglectful**
[nɪ'glektfl] *adj.* gleichgültig (of gegenüber); **be ~ of** sich nicht kümmern um
negligence ['neglɪdʒəns] *n.* Nachlässigkeit, *die; (Law, Insurance, etc.)*
Fahrlässigkeit, *die*
negligent ['neglɪdʒənt] *adj.* nachlässig; **be ~ about sth.** sich um etw. nicht
kümmern
negligible ['neglɪdʒɪbl] *adj.* unerheblich
negotiable [nɪ'gəʊʃəbl] *adj.* a) ver-
handlungsfähig *(Forderung, Bedingungen);* b) passierbar *(Straße, Fluß)*
negotiate [nɪ'gəʊʃɪeɪt] 1. *v. i.* verhandeln (for, on, about über + *Akk.*). 2.

v. t. a) *(arrange)* aushandeln; b) überwinden *(Hindernis);* passieren
(Straße, Fluß); nehmen *(Kurve).*
negotiation [nɪgəʊʃɪ'eɪʃn] *n.* Verhandlung, *die.* **negotiator** [nɪ'gəʊ-
ʃɪeɪtə(r)] *n.* Unterhändler, *der/*-händ-
lerin, *die*
Negress ['niːgrɪs] *n.* Negerin, *die*
Negro ['niːgrəʊ] 1. *n., pl.* **~es** Neger,
der. 2. *adj.* Neger-
neigh [neɪ] 1. *v. i.* wiehern. 2. *n.* Wiehern, *das*
neighbor *etc. (Amer.) see* **neighbour**
etc.
neighbour ['neɪbə(r)] 1. *n.* Nachbar,
*der/*Nachbarin, *die;* **my next-door ~s**
meine Nachbarn von nebenan. 2. *v. t.
& i.* **~ [upon]** grenzen an (+ *Akk.*).
'**neighbourhood** *n. (district)* Gegend, *die; (neighbours)* Nachbarschaft, *die;* **[somewhere] in the ~ of
£100** [so] um [die] 100 Pfund. '**neighbouring** *adj.* Nachbar-; angrenzend
(Felder)
neither ['naɪðə(r), niː'ðə(r)] 1. *adj.* kei-
ner/keine/keins der beiden. 2. *pron.*
keiner/keine/keins von *od.* der beiden. 3. *adv. (also not)* auch nicht; **~
am I,** *(sl.)* **me ~:** ich auch nicht. 4.
conj. (not either) weder; **~ ... nor ...:**
weder ... noch ...
neon ['niːɒn] *n.* Neon, *das*
neon: ~ 'light *n.* Neonlampe, *die;* **~
'sign** *n.* Neonreklame, *die*
nephew ['nevjuː, 'nefjuː] *n.* Neffe, *der*
nepotism ['nepətɪzm] *n.* Vetternwirt-
schaft, *die*
Neptune ['neptjuːn] *pr. n. (Astron.)*
Neptun, *der*
nerve [nɜːv] *n.* Nerv, *der;* **get on sb.'s
~s** jmdm. auf die Nerven gehen
(ugs.); **lose one's ~:** die Nerven verlieren; **what [a] ~!** [so eine] Frechheit!
'**nerve gas** *n.* Nervengas, *das.*
'**nerve-racking** *adj.* nervenaufrei-
bend
nervous ['nɜːvəs] *adj.* a) *(Anat., Med.)*
Nerven-; **~ breakdown** Nervenzusam-
menbruch, *der;* b) *(having delicate
nerves)* nervös; **be a ~ wreck** mit den
Nerven völlig am Ende sein; c) *(Brit.:
timid)* **be ~ of** *or* **about** Angst haben
vor (+ *Dat.*); **be a ~ person** ängstlich
sein. '**nervously** *adv.* nervös. '**nervousness** *n.* Ängstlichkeit, *die*
nervy ['nɜːvɪ] *adj.* a) nervös; b) *(Amer.
coll.:* impudent*)* unverschämt
nest 1. *n.* Nest, *das.* 2. *v. i.* nisten.
'**nest-egg** *n. (fig.)* Notgroschen, *der*

nestle ['nesl] *v. i.* **a)** sich schmiegen
(**to, up against** an + *Akk.*); **b)** *(lie half
hidden)* eingebettet sein

¹**net** [net] **1.** *n.* Netz, *das.* **2.** *v. t.,* -tt-
[mit einem Netz] fangen

²**net** *adj.* **a)** netto; Netto⟨*einkommen,
-[verkaufs]preis usw.*⟩; ~ **weight** Netto-
gewicht, *das;* **b)** *(ultimate)* End-
⟨*ergebnis, -effekt*⟩

net: ~**ball** *n.* Netzball, *der.* ~ '**curtain** *n.* Store, *der*

Netherlands ['neðələndz] *pr. n. sing.
or pl.* Niederlande *Pl.*

nett *see* ²**net a**

'**netting** *n.* *([piece of] net)* Netz, *das;*
wire ~: Maschendraht, *der*

nettle ['netl] *n.* Nessel, *die*

'**network** *n.* Netz, *das*

neuralgia [njʊəˈrældʒə] *n.* Neuralgie,
die

neurosis [njʊəˈrəʊsɪs] *n., pl.* **neuroses**
[njʊəˈrəʊsiːz] Neurose, *die.* **neurotic**
[njʊəˈrɒtɪk] *adj.* **a)** nervenkrank; **b)**
(coll.) neurotisch

neuter ['njuːtə(r)] *adj.* sächlich

neutral ['njuːtrl] **1.** *adj.* neutral. **2.** *n.*
(~ *gear)* Leerlauf, *der.* **neutrality**
[njuːˈtrælɪtɪ] *n.* Neutralität, *die*

neutralize ['njuːtrəlaɪz] *v. t.* neutrali-
sieren

neutron ['njuːtrɒn] *n.* Neutron, *das*

never ['nevə(r)] *adv.* **a)** nie; ~**-ending**
endlos; **b)** *(coll.)* **you** ~ **believed that,
did you?** du hast das doch wohl nicht
geglaubt?; **well, I ~ [did]!** [na] so was!
neverthe'**less** *adv.* trotzdem

new [njuː] *adj.* neu

new: ~**-born** *adj.* neugeboren;
~**comer** ['njuːkʌmə(r)] *n.* Neuan-
kömmling, *der;* ~**fangled** ['njuː-
fæŋgld] *adj.* neumodisch; ~**-found**
adj. neu; ~**-laid** *adj.* frisch [gelegt]
'**newly** *adv.* *(recently)* neu; ~ **married**
seit kurzem verheiratet. '**newly-wed**
n. Jungverheiratete, *der/die*

new '**moon** *n.* Neumond, *der*

'**newness** *n.* Neuheit, *die*

news [njuːz] *n., no pl.* **a)** Nachricht,
die; **be in the** ~: Schlagzeilen machen;
good/bad ~: schlechte/gute Nachrichten; **b)** *(Radio, Telev.)* Nachrichten *Pl.*

news: ~**agent** *n.* Zeitungshändler,
der/-händlerin, *die;* ~ **bulletin** *n.*
Nachrichten *Pl.* ~**caster** *n.*
Nachrichtensprecher, *der/*-sprecherin,
die; ~**flash** *n.* Kurzmeldung, *die;* ~
'**headline** *n.* Schlagzeile, *die;*
~**letter** *n.* Rundschreiben, *das;*

~**paper** ['njuːspeɪpə(r)] *n.* **a)** Zeitung,
die; **b)** *(material)* Zeitungspapier, *das;*
~**reader** *n.* Nachrichtensprecher,
der/-sprecherin, *die;* ~**reel** *n.* Wo-
chenschau, *die;* ~-**sheet** *n.* Informa-
tionsblatt, *das;* ~ **summary** *n.* Kurz-
nachrichten *Pl.;* ~**worthy** *adj.* [für
die Medien] interessant

newt [njuːt] *n.* [Wasser]molch, *der*

New: new '**year** *n.* Neujahr, *das;*
over the new year über Neujahr; **a
Happy ~ Year** ein glückliches *od.* gutes neues Jahr. ~ '**Year's** *(Amer.),* ~
Year's '**Day** *ns.* Neujahrstag, *der;* ~
Year's '**Eve** *n.* Silvester, *der od. das;*
~ **Zealand** [~ 'ziːlənd] *pr. n.* Neuseeland *(das);* ~ '**Zealander** *n.* Neuseeländer, *der/*-länderin, *die*

next [nekst] **1.** *adj.* nächst...; **the ~ but
one** der/die/das übernächste; ~ **to**
(fig.: almost) fast; nahezu; |**the**| ~ **time**
das nächste Mal; **the ~ best** der/die/
das nächstbeste; **am I ~?** komme ich
jetzt dran? **2.** *adv.* *(in the ~ place)* als
nächstes; *(on the ~ occasion)* das
nächste Mal; **it's my turn ~:** ich komme als nächster dran; **sit/stand ~ to
sb.** neben jmdm. stehen/sitzen; **place
sth. ~ to sb./sth.** etw. neben jmdn./
etw. stellen. **3.** *n.* **a) the week after ~:**
[die] übernächste Woche; **b)** *(person)*
~ **of kin** nächster/nächste Angehörige; ~, **please!** der nächste, bitte!
'**next-door** *adj.* gleich nebenan
nachgestellt

NHS *abbr. (Brit.)* National Health Service

nib [nɪb] *n.* Feder, *die*

nibble ['nɪbl] *v. t. & i.* knabbern (**at, on**
an + *Dat.*)

nice [naɪs] *adj.* nett; angenehm
⟨*Stimme*⟩; schön ⟨*Wetter*⟩; *(iron.: dis-
graceful, difficult)* schön; ~ |**and**|
warm/fast schön warm/schnell;
~**-looking** hübsch. '**nicely** *adv. (coll.)*
a) *(well)* nett; gut ⟨*arbeiten, sich benehmen, plaziert sein*⟩; **b)** *(all right)* gut;
that will do ~: das reicht völlig.
niceties ['naɪsɪtɪz] *n. pl.* Feinheiten
niche [nɪtʃ, niːʃ] *n.* **a)** *(in wall)* Nische,
die; **b)** *(fig.: suitable place)* Platz, *der*

nick *n.* **a)** *(notch)* Kerbe, *die;* **b)** *(sl.:
prison)* Knast, *der (salopp);* **c)** *(Brit.:
police station)* Wache, *die;* **d) in good/
poor** ~ *(coll.)* gut/nicht gut im Schuß
(ugs.); **e) in the** ~ **of time** gerade noch
rechtzeitig. **2.** *v. t.* **a)** einkerben; **b)**
(Brit. sl.: arrest) einlochen *(salopp);* **c)**
(Brit. sl.: steal) klauen *(salopp)*

nickel ['nɪkl] *n.* **a)** Nickel, *das;* **b)** *(Amer. coll.: coin)* Fünfcentstück, *das*

nickname ['nɪkneɪm] *n.* Spitzname, *der; (affectionate)* Koseform, *die*

nicotine ['nɪkəti:n] *n.* Nikotin, *das*

niece [ni:s] *n.* Nichte, *die*

Nigeria [naɪ'dʒɪərɪə] *pr. n.* Nigeria *(das)*

niggardly ['nɪgədlɪ] *adj.* knaus[e]rig *(ugs.)*

niggling ['nɪglɪŋ] *adj.* **a)** *(petty)* belanglos; **b)** *(trivial)* nichtssagend; **c)** *(nagging)* nagend

night [naɪt] *n.* Nacht, *die; (evening)* Abend, *der;* **the following ~:** die Nacht/der Abend darauf; **the previous ~:** die vorausgegangene Nacht/der vorausgegangene Abend; **on Sunday ~:** Sonntag nacht/[am] Sonntag abend; **for the ~:** über Nacht; **at ~:** nachts/abends; **late at ~:** spätabends

night: **~cap** *n. (drink)* Schlaftrunk, *der;* **~club** *n.* Nachtklub, *der;* **~-dress** *n.* Nachthemd, *das;* **~fall** *n.* Einbruch der Dunkelheit

nightie ['naɪtɪ] *n. (coll.)* Nachthemd, *das*

nightingale ['naɪtɪŋgeɪl] *n.* Nachtigall, *die*

'**night-life** *n.* Nachtleben, *das*

nightly ['naɪtlɪ] **1.** *adj. (happening every night/evening)* allnächtlich/allabendlich. **2.** *adv. (every night)* jede Nacht; *(every evening)* jeden Abend

night: **~mare** *n.* Alptraum, *der;* **~ school** *n.* Abendschule, *die;* **~ shift** *n.* Nachtschicht, *die;* **~-time** *n.* Nacht, *die;* **in the** *or* **at ~-time** nachts; **~-'watchman** *n.* Nachtwächter, *der*

nil [nɪl] *n.* null

Nile [naɪl] *pr. n.* Nil, *der*

nimble ['nɪmbl] *adj.,* **nimbly** ['nɪmblɪ] *adv.* flink

nine [naɪn] **1.** *adj.* neun. **2.** *n.* Neun, *die. See also* **eight**

nineteen [naɪn'ti:n] **1.** *adj.* neunzehn. **2.** *n.* Neunzehn, *die. See also* **eight**.

nineteenth [naɪn'ti:nθ] **1.** *adj.* neunzehnt... **2.** *n. (fraction)* Neunzehntel, *das. See also* **eighth**

ninetieth ['naɪntɪɪθ] *adj.* neunzigst...

ninety ['naɪntɪ] **1.** *adj.* neunzig. **2.** *n.* Neunzig, *die. See also* **eight; eighty** 2

ninth [naɪnθ] **1.** *adj.* neunt... **2.** *n. (in sequence)* neunte, *der/die/das; (in rank)* Neunte, *der/die/das; (fraction)* Neuntel, *das. See also* **eighth**

nip **1.** *v. t.,* **-pp-** zwicken. **2.** *v. i.,* **-pp-** *(Brit. sl.)* **~ in** hinein-/hereinflitzen

(ugs.); **~ out** hinaus-/herausflitzen *(ugs.).* **3.** *n. (pinch, squeeze)* Kniff, *der; (bite)* Biß, *der.* '**nipper** *n. (Brit. coll.: child)* Balg, *das (ugs.)*

nipple ['nɪpl] *n.* **a)** Brustwarze, *die;* **b)** *(of feeding-bottle)* Sauger, *der*

nitric acid ['naɪtrɪk æsɪd] *n.* Salpetersäure, *die*

nitrogen ['naɪtrədʒən] *n.* Stickstoff, *der*

nitwit ['nɪtwɪt] *n. (coll.)* Trottel, *der (ugs.)*

no [nəʊ] **1.** *adj.* kein. **2.** *adv.* **a)** *(by no amount)* nicht; **no less [than]** nicht weniger [als]; **no more wine?** keinen Wein mehr?; **b)** *(as answer)* nein. **3.** *n., pl.* **noes** [nəʊz] Nein, *das*

No. *abbr.* **number** Nr.

Noah's ark [nəʊəz 'ɑːk] *n.* die Arche Noah

nobility [nə'bɪlɪtɪ] *n.* Adel, *der;* **many of the ~:** viele Adlige

noble ['nəʊbl] **1.** *adj.* ad[e]lig; edel ⟨*Gedanken, Gefühle*⟩. **2.** *n.* Adlige, *der/die.* **nobleman** ['nəʊblmən] *n., pl.* **noblemen** ['nəʊblmən] Adlige, *der*

nobly ['nəʊblɪ] *adv.* **a)** edel[gesinnt]; **b)** *(generously)* edelmütig *(geh.)*

nobody ['nəʊbədɪ] *n. & pron.* niemand; keiner; *(person of no importance)* Niemand, *der*

nocturnal [nɒk'tɜːnl] *adj.* nächtlich; **~ animal/bird** Nachttier, *das/*-vogel, *der*

nod [nɒd] **1.** *v. i.,* **-dd-** nicken. **2.** *v. t.,* **-dd-:** **~ one's head [in greeting]** [zum Gruß] mit dem Kopf nicken. **3.** *n.* [Kopf]nicken, *das.* **nod 'off** *v. i.* einnicken *(ugs.)*

noise [nɔɪz] *n.* Geräusch, *das; (loud, harsh, unwanted)* Lärm, *der.* '**noiseless** *adj.,* '**noiselessly** *adv.* lautlos.

noisily ['nɔɪzɪlɪ] *adv.,* **noisy** ['nɔɪzɪ] *adj.* laut

nomad ['nəʊmæd] *n.* Nomade, *der.* **nomadic** [nəʊ'mædɪk] *adj.* nomadisch; **~ tribe** Nomadenstamm, *der*

'**no man's land** *n.* Niemandsland, *das*

nominal ['nɒmɪnl] *adj.* nominell; äußerst niedrig ⟨*Preis, Miete*⟩

nominate ['nɒmɪneɪt] *v. t.* **a)** *(propose)* nominieren; **b)** *(appoint)* ernennen. **nomination** [nɒmɪ'neɪʃn] *n. see* **nominate:** Nominierung, *die;* Ernennung, *die*

nominative ['nɒmɪnətɪv] *adj. & n.* **~ [case]** Nominativ, *der*

nominee [nɒmɪ'ni:] *n. (candidate)* Kandidat, *der/*Kandidatin, *die*

non- [nɒn] *pref.* nicht-

nonchalant ['nɒnʃələnt] *adj.* unbekümmert

non-commissioned 'officer *n.* Unteroffizier, *der*

non-committal [nɒnkə'mɪtl] *adj.* unverbindlich; **he was** ~: er hat sich nicht klar geäußert

nondescript ['nɒndɪskrɪpt] *adj.* unscheinbar; undefinierbar ⟨*Farbe*⟩

none [nʌn] **1.** *pron.* kein...; ~ **of them** keiner/keine/keines von ihnen; ~ **of this** nichts davon. **2.** *adv.* keineswegs; **I'm** ~ **the wiser now** jetzt bin ich um nichts klüger; ~ **the less** nichtsdestoweniger

nonentity [nɒ'nentɪtɪ] *n.* Nichts, *das*

non-existent [nɒnɪg'zɪstənt] *adj.* nicht vorhanden

non-'fiction *n.* Sachliteratur, *die*

non-'iron *adj.* bügelfrei

non-'member *n.* Nichtmitglied, *das*

nonplus [nɒn'plʌs] *v. t.*, **-ss-** verblüffen

nonsense ['nɒnsəns] **1.** *n.* Unsinn, *der.* **2.** *int.* Unsinn. **nonsensical** [nɒn'sensɪkl] *adj.* unsinnig

non-'smoker *n.* **a)** *(person)* Nichtraucher, *der*/-raucherin, *die;* **b)** *(train compartment)* Nichtraucherabteil, *das*

non-'stick *adj.* ~ **frying-pan** *etc.* Bratpfanne *usw.* mit Antihaftbeschichtung

non-stop 1. ['--] *adj.* durchgehend ⟨*Zug, Busverbindung*⟩; Nonstop⟨*flug, -revue*⟩. **2.** [-'-] *adv.* ohne Unterbrechung ⟨*tanzen, reden, reisen, senden*⟩; nonstop ⟨*fliegen, tanzen, fahren*⟩

noodle ['nu:dl] *n., usu. pl.* Nudel, *die*

nook [nʊk] *n.* Winkel, *der;* Ecke, *die*

noon [nu:n] *n.* Mittag, *der;* zwölf Uhr [mittags]; **at/before** ~: um/vor zwölf [Uhr mittags]

'no one *pron. see* **nobody**

noose [nu:s] *n.* Schlinge, *die*

nor [nə(r), *stressed* nɔ:(r)] *conj.* noch; **neither/not** ... ~ ...: weder ... noch ...

norm [nɔ:m] *n.* Norm, *die*

normal ['nɔ:ml] **1.** *adj.* normal. **2.** *n.* **a)** *(~ value)* Normalwert, *der;* **b)** *(usual state)* normaler Stand; **everything is back to** *or* **has returned to** ~: es hat sich wieder alles normalisiert. **normality** [nɔ:'mælɪtɪ] Normalität, *die.* **'normally** *adv.* **a)** *(in normal way)* normal; **b)** *(ordinarily)* normalerweise

north [nɔ:θ] **1.** *n.* **a)** Norden, *der;* **in/ to|wards|/from the** ~: im/nach/von Norden; **to the** ~ **of** nördlich von; **b)**

usu. N~ *(Geog., Polit.)* Norden, *der.* **2.** *adj.* nördlich; Nord⟨*wind, -küste, -grenze*⟩. **3.** *adv.* nach Norden; ~ **of** nördlich von

north: N~ 'Africa *pr. n.* Nordafrika *(das);* **N~ A'merica** *pr. n.* Nordamerika *(das);* **N~ A'merican 1.** *adj.* nordamerikanisch; **2.** *n.* Nordamerikaner, *der*/-amerikanerin, *die;* ~**bound** *adj.* ⟨*Zug, Verkehr usw.*⟩ in Richtung Norden; ~-'**east 1.** *n.* Nordosten, *der;* **2.** *adj.* nordöstlich; Nordost⟨*wind, -küste*⟩; **3.** *adv.* nordostwärts; nach Nordosten; ~-'**eastern** *adj.* nordöstlich

northerly ['nɔ:ðəlɪ] *adj.* nördlich; ⟨*Wind*⟩ aus nördlichen Richtungen

northern ['nɔ:ðən] *adj.* nördlich; Nord⟨*grenze, -hälfte, -seite*⟩. **Northern 'Ireland** *pr. n.* Nordirland *(das)*

North: ~ '**Germany** *pr. n.* Norddeutschland *(das);* ~ '**Pole** *pr. n.* Nordpol, *der;* ~ '**Sea** *pr. n.* Nordsee, *die*

northward[s] ['nɔ:θwəd(z)] *adv.* nordwärts

north: ~-'**west 1.** *n.* Nordwesten, *der;* **2.** *adj.* nordwestlich; Nordwest⟨*wind, -küste*⟩; **3.** *adv.* nordwestwärts; nach Nordwesten; ~-'**western** *adj.* nordwestlich

Norway ['nɔ:weɪ] *pr. n.* Norwegen *(das).* **Norwegian** [nɔ:'wi:dʒn] **1.** *adj.* norwegisch; **sb. is** ~: jmd. ist Norweger/Norwegerin. **2.** *n.* **a)** *(person)* Norweger, *der*/Norwegerin, *die;* **b)** *(language)* Norwegisch, *das; see also* **English 2 a**

Nos. *abbr.* **numbers** Nrn.

nose [nəʊz] **1.** *n.* Nase, *die.* **2.** *v. t.* ~ **one's way** sich *(Dat.)* vorsichtig seinen Weg bahnen. **3.** *v. i.* sich vorsichtig bewegen. **nose a'bout, nose a'round** *v. i. (coll.)* herumschnüffeln *(ugs.)*

nose: ~**bleed** *n.* Nasenbluten, *das;* ~**dive 1.** *n.* Sturzflug, *der;* **2.** *v. i.* im Sturzflug hinuntergehen

nosey *see* **nosy**

nostalgia [nɒ'stældʒə] *n.* Nostalgie, *die;* ~ **for sth.** Sehnsucht nach etw. **nostalgic** [nɒ'stældʒɪk] *adj.* nostalgisch

nostril ['nɒstrɪl] *n.* Nasenloch, *das; (of horse)* Nüster, *die*

nosy ['nəʊzɪ] *adj. (sl.)* neugierig

not [nɒt] *adv.* nicht; **he is** ~ **a doctor** er ist kein Arzt; ~ **at all** überhaupt nicht; ~ ... **but** ...: nicht ..., sondern ...; ~ **a thing** gar nichts

notable ['nəʊtəbl] *adj.* bemerkenswert; **be ~ for sth.** für etw. bekannt sein. **notably** ['nəʊtəblı] *adv.* besonders

notation [nəʊ'teıʃn] *n.* Notierung, *die*

notch [nɒtʃ] **1.** *n.* Kerbe, *die.* **2.** *v. t.* kerben. **notch 'up** *v. t.* erreichen

note [nəʊt] **1.** *n.* **a)** *(Mus.) (sign)* Note, *die; (key of piano)* Taste, *die; (sound)* Ton, *der;* **b)** *(jotting)* Notiz, *die;* **take** *or* **make ~s** sich *(Dat.)* Notizen machen; **take** *or* **make a ~ of sth.** sich *(Dat.)* etw. notieren; **c)** *(comment, footnote)* Anmerkung, *die;* **d)** *(short letter)* [kurzer] Brief; **e)** *(importance)* **a person/something of ~:** eine bedeutende Persönlichkeit/etwas Bedeutendes; **be of ~:** bedeutend sein. **2.** *v. t.* **a)** *(pay attention to)* beachten; **b)** *(notice)* bemerken; **c)** *(write)* **~ |down|** [sich *(Dat.)*] notieren. **'notebook** *n.* Notizbuch, *das*

'noted *adj.* bekannt (**for** für, wegen). **note: ~pad** *n.* Notizblock, *der;* **~paper** *n.* Briefpapier, *das;* **~worthy** *adj.* bemerkenswert

nothing ['nʌθıŋ] *n.* nichts; **~ interesting** nichts Interessantes; **~ much** nichts Besonderes; **~ more than** nur; **~ more, ~ less** nicht mehr, nicht weniger; **next to ~:** so gut wie nichts; **have |got|** *or* **be ~ to do with sb./sth.** *(not concern)* nichts zu tun haben mit jmdm./etw.; **have ~ to do with sb.** *(avoid)* jmdm. aus dem Weg gehen

notice ['nəʊtıs] **1.** *n.* **a)** Anschlag, *der; (in newspaper)* Anzeige, *die;* **b)** *(warning)* **at short/a moment's ~:** kurzfristig/von einem Augenblick zum andern; **c)** *(formal notification)* Ankündigung, *die;* **until further ~:** bis auf weiteres; **d)** *(ending an agreement)* Kündigung, *die;* **give sb. a month's ~:** jmdm. mit einer Frist von einem Monat kündigen; **hand in one's ~, give ~** *(Brit.),* **give one's ~** *(Amer.)* kündigen; **e)** *(attention)* **bring sb./sth. to sb.'s ~:** jmdn. auf jmdn./etw. aufmerksam machen; **take no ~ of sb./sth.** *(disregard)* keine Notiz von jmdm./etw. nehmen; **take no ~:** sich nicht darum kümmern. **2.** *v. t.* bemerken. **noticeable** ['nəʊtısəbl] *adj.* wahrnehmbar ⟨*Fleck, Schaden, Geruch*⟩; merklich ⟨*Verbesserung*⟩; spürbar ⟨*Mangel*⟩. **'notice-board** *n.* *(Brit.)* Anschlagbrett, *das;* Schwarzes Brett

notification [nəʊtıfı'keıʃn] *n.* Mitteilung, *die* (**of sth.** über etw. *[Akk.]*)

notify ['nəʊtıfaı] *v. t.* **a)** *(make known)* ankündigen; **b)** *(inform)* benachrichtigen (**of** über + *Akk.*)

notion ['nəʊʃn] *n.* Vorstellung, *die;* **not have the faintest/least ~ of how/what** *etc.* nicht die blasseste/geringste Ahnung haben, wie/was *usw.*

notoriety [nəʊtə'raıətı] *n.* traurige Berühmtheit

notorious [nə'tɔːrıəs] *adj.* berüchtigt (**for** wegen); notorisch ⟨*Lügner*⟩

nougat ['nuːgɑː] *n.* Nougat, *das od. der*

nought [nɔːt] *n.* Null, *die*

noun [naʊn] *n. (Ling.)* Substantiv, *das*

nourish ['nʌrıʃ] *v. t.* ernähren (**on** mit). **'nourishing** *adj.* nahrhaft. **'nourishment** *n.* Nahrung, *die*

Nov. *abbr.* November Nov.

novel ['nɒvl] **1.** *n.* Roman, *der.* **2.** *adj.* neuartig. **novelist** ['nɒvəlıst] *n.* Romanautor, *der*/-autorin, *die*

novelty ['nɒvltı] *n.* **a)** **be a/no ~:** etwas/nichts Neues sein; **b)** *(newness)* Neuheit, *die;* **c)** *(gadget)* Überraschung, *die*

November [nə'vembə(r)] *n.* November, *der; see also* **August**

novice ['nɒvıs] *n.* Anfänger, *der*/Anfängerin, *die*

now [naʊ] **1.** *adv.* jetzt; *(nowadays)* heutzutage; *(immediately)* [jetzt] sofort; **just ~** *(very recently)* gerade eben; **|every| ~ and then** *or* **again** hin und wieder; **well ~:** also; **~, ~:** na, na; **~ then** na *(ugs.).* **2.** *conj.* **~ |that|...:** jetzt, wo... **3.** *n.* **before ~:** früher; **by ~:** inzwischen; **a week from ~:** [heute] in einer Woche. **nowadays** ['naʊədeız] *adv.* heutzutage

nowhere ['nəʊweə(r)] *adv.* nirgends; nirgendwo; *(to no place)* nirgendwohin

nozzle ['nɒzl] *n.* Düse, *die*

nuance ['njuːɑ̃s] *n.* Nuance, *die*

nuclear ['njuːklıə(r)] *adj.* Atom-; Kern⟨*explosion*⟩; atomar ⟨*Antrieb, Gefechtskopf, Wettrüsten, Abrüstung*⟩; nuklear ⟨*Abschreckung, Sprengkörper*⟩; atomgetrieben ⟨*Unterseeboot*⟩

nucleus ['njuːklıəs] *n., pl.* **nuclei** ['njuːklıaı] Kern, *der*

nude [njuːd] **1.** *adj.* nackt. **2.** *n.* **a)** *(figure)* Akt, *der;* **b)** **in the ~:** nackt

nudge [nʌdʒ] **1.** *v. t.* anstoßen. **2.** *n.* Stoß, *der.*

nudism ['njuːdızm] *n.* Nudismus, *der;* Freikörperkultur, *die.* **nudist** ['njuːdıst] *n.* Nudist, *der*/Nudistin, *die; at-*

trib. Nudisten-. **nudity** ['nju:dɪtɪ] *n.*
Nacktheit, *die*
nugget ['nʌgɪt] *n.* Klumpen, *der; (of
gold)* Goldklumpen, *der; (fig.)* ~s *of
wisdom* goldene Weisheiten
nuisance ['nju:səns] *n.* Ärgernis, *das;*
what a ~! so etwas Dummes!
null [nʌl] *adj.* ~ **and void** null und nichtig
numb [nʌm] **1.** *adj.* gefühllos, taub
(**with** vor + *Dat.*); *(without emotion)*
benommen. **2.** *v. t.* betäuben
number ['nʌmbə(r)] **1.** *n.* **a)** *(in series)*
Nummer, *die;* **you've got the wrong** ~
(Teleph.) Sie sind falsch verbunden;
dial a wrong ~: sich verwählen *(ugs.);*
b) *(esp. Math.: numeral)* Zahl, *die;* **c)**
(sum, total, quantity) [An]zahl, *die;* **a**
~ **of people/things** einige Leute/Din-
ge; **a** ~ **of times** mehrmals. **2.** *v. t.* **a)**
(assign ~ *to)* numerieren; **b)** *(amount
to, comprise)* zählen; **c)** *(include)* zählen (**among, with** zu); **d)** **sb.'s days are**
~**ed** jmds. Tage sind gezählt. '**number-plate** *n.* Nummernschild, *das*
numeral ['nju:mərl] *n.* Ziffer, *die*
numerate [nju:mərət] *adj.* **be** ~: rechnen können
numerical [nju:'merɪkl] *adj.* nume-
risch; Zahlen⟨*wert, -folge*⟩; zahlenmäßig ⟨*Stärke, Überlegenheit*⟩
numerous ['nju:mərəs] *adj.* zahlreich
nun [nʌn] *n.* Nonne, *die*
nurse [nɜ:s] **1.** *n.* Krankenschwester,
die; |**male**] ~: Krankenpfleger, *der.* **2.**
v. t. **a)** pflegen ⟨*Kranke*⟩; **b)** *(fig.)* hegen *(geh.)* ⟨*Gefühl, Groll*⟩
nursery ['nɜ:sərɪ] *n.* **a)** *(room)* Kinder-
zimmer, *das;* **b)** *(crèche)* Kindertages-
stätte, *die;* **c)** *see* **nursery school; d)**
(for plants) Gärtnerei, *die.* '**nursery
rhyme** *n.* Kinderreim, *der.* '**nursery
school** *n.* Kindergarten, *der*
nursing ['nɜ:sɪŋ] *n.* Krankenpflege,
die; attrib. Pflege⟨*personal, -beruf*⟩.
'**nursing home** *n.* Pflegeheim, *das*
nurture ['nɜ:tʃə(r)] *v. t. (rear)* aufziehen; *(fig.)* nähren
nut [nʌt] *n.* **a)** Nuß, *die;* **b)** *(Mech.
Engin.)* [Schrauben]mutter, *die;* **c)**
(crazy person) Verrückte, *der/die
(ugs.).* '**nut-case** *n. (sl.)* Verrückte,
der/die (ugs.). '**nutcrackers** *n. pl.*
Nußknacker, *der*
nutmeg ['nʌtmeg] *n.* Muskat, *der*
nutrient ['nju:trɪənt] *n.* Nährstoff, *der*
nutrition [nju:'trɪʃn] *n.* Ernährung,
die; (food) Nahrung, *die.* **nutritious**
[nju:'trɪʃəs] *adj.* nahrhaft

'**nutshell** *n.* Nußschale, *die;* **in a** ~
(fig.) in aller Kürze
nutty ['nʌtɪ] *adj.* **a)** *(in taste)* nussig; **b)**
(sl.: crazy) verrückt *(ugs.)*
nuzzle ['nʌzl] *v. i.* sich kuscheln (**up to,
against** an + *Akk.*)
NW *abbr.* **north-west** NW
nylon ['naɪlɒn] *n.* **a)** Nylon, *das; attrib.* Nylon-; **b)** *in pl. (stockings)* Ny-
lonstrümpfe
nymph [nɪmf] *n.* Nymphe, *die*

O

O, o [əʊ] *n.* O, o, *das*
oaf [əʊf] *n.* Stoffel, *der (ugs.)*
oak [əʊk] *n.* Eiche, *die*
OAP *abbr. (Brit.)* **old-age pensioner**
Rentner, *der*/Rentnerin, *die*
oar [ɔ:(r)] *n.* Ruder, *das*
oasis [əʊ'eɪsɪs] *n., pl.* **oases** [əʊ'eɪsi:z]
Oase, *die*
oat [əʊt] *n.* ~s Hafer, *der*
oath [əʊθ] *n.* **a)** Eid, *der;* Schwur, *der;*
b) *(swear-word)* Fluch, *der*
obedience [ə'bi:dɪəns] *n.* Gehorsam,
der
obedient [ə'bi:dɪənt] *adj.* gehorsam;
be ~ **to sb./sth.** jmdm./einer Sache gehorchen. **o'bediently** *adv.* gehorsam
obelisk ['ɒbəlɪsk] *n.* Obelisk, *der*
obese [əʊ'bi:s] *adj.* fettleibig.
obesity [əʊ'bi:sɪtɪ] *n.* Fettleibigkeit,
die
obey [əʊ'beɪ] **1.** *v. t.* gehorchen
(+ *Dat.*); sich halten an (+ *Akk.*)
⟨*Vorschrift, Regel*⟩; befolgen ⟨*Befehl*⟩.
2. *v. i.* gehorchen
obituary [ə'bɪtjʊərɪ] *n.* Nachruf, *der*
(**to, of** auf + *Akk.*)
object 1. ['ɒbdʒɪkt] *n.* **a)** *(thing)* Gegenstand, *der;* **b)** *(purpose)* Ziel, *das;*
c) *(obstacle)* **money/time** *etc.* **is no** ~:
Geld/Zeit *usw.* spielt keine Rolle; **d)**
(Ling.) Objekt, *das.* **2.** [əb'dʒekt] *v. i.*
a) Einwände/einen Einwand erheben
(**to** gegen); **b)** *(have objection or dislike)* etwas dagegen haben; ~ **to sb./
sth.** etwas gegen jmdn./etw. haben. **3.**
v. t. einwenden. **objection** [əb-

'dʒekʃn] *n.* **a)** Einwand, *der;* **raise** *or* **make an ~ [to sth.]** einen Einwand [gegen etw.] erheben; **b)** *(dislike)* Abneigung, *die;* **have an/no ~ to sb./sth.** etw./nichts gegen jmdn./etw. haben; **have no ~s** nichts dagegen haben. **objectionable** [əb'dʒekʃənəbl] *adj.* unangenehm ⟨*Anblick, Geruch*⟩; anstößig ⟨*Bemerkung, Wort, Benehmen*⟩

objective ['əb'dʒektɪv] **1.** *adj.* objektiv. **2.** *n.* *(goal)* Ziel, *das.* **ob'jectively** *adv.* objektiv. **objectivity** [ɒbdʒek'tɪvɪtɪ] *n.* Objektivität, *die*

obligation [ɒblɪ'geɪʃn] *n.* Verpflichtung, *die;* **be under an ~ to sb.** jmdm. verpflichtet sein; **without ~:** unverbindlich

obligatory [ə'blɪgətərɪ] *adj.* obligatorisch; **it has become ~ to ...:** es ist jetzt Pflicht, zu ...

oblige [ə'blaɪdʒ] *v. t.* **a)** *(be binding on)* **~ sb. to do sth.** jmdm. vorschreiben, etw. zu tun; **b)** *(compel)* zwingen; **be ~d to do sth.** gezwungen sein, etw. zu tun; **feel ~d to do sth.** sich verpflichtet fühlen, etw. zu tun; **c)** *(be kind to)* **~ sb. by doing sth.** jmdm. den Gefallen tun und etw. tun; **d)** *(grateful)* **be much/greatly ~d to sb. [for sth.]** jmdm. [für etw.] sehr verbunden sein; **much ~d!** besten Dank! **obliging** [ə'blaɪdʒɪŋ] *adj.* entgegenkommend

oblique [ə'bliːk] *adj.* schief ⟨*Gerade, Winkel*⟩; *(fig.)* indirekt

obliterate [ə'blɪtəreɪt] *v. t.* auslöschen

oblivion [ə'blɪvɪən] *n.* Vergessenheit, *die;* **sink** *or* **fall into ~:** in Vergessenheit geraten

oblivious [ə'blɪvɪəs] *adj.* **be ~ to** *or* **of sth.** sich *(Dat.)* einer Sache *(Gen.)* nicht bewußt sein

oblong ['ɒblɒŋ] **1.** *adj.* rechteckig. **2.** *n.* Rechteck, *das*

obnoxious [əb'nɒkʃəs] *adj.* widerlich

oboe ['əʊbəʊ] *n.* Oboe, *die*

obscene [əb'siːn] *adj.* obszön. **ob'scenity** [əb'senɪtɪ] *n.* Obszönität, *die*

obscure [əb'skjʊə(r)] **1.** *adj.* **a)** *(unexplained)* dunkel; **b)** *(hard to understand)* schwer verständlich ⟨*Argument, Dichtung, Autor, Stil*⟩; **c)** *(unknown)* unbekannt. **2.** *v. t.* **a)** *(make indistinct)* verdunkeln; versperren ⟨*Aussicht*⟩; **b)** *(make unintelligible)* unverständlich machen

obsequious [əb'siːkwɪəs] *adj.* unterwürfig

observance [əb'zɜːvəns] *n.* Einhaltung, *die*

observant [əb'zɜːvənt] *adj.* aufmerksam

observation [ɒbzə'veɪʃn] *n.* **a)** Beobachtung, *die;* **be [kept] under ~:** beobachtet werden; *(by police)* überwacht werden; **b)** *(remark)* Bemerkung, *die* (**on** über + *Akk.*)

observatory [əb'zɜːvətərɪ] *n.* *(Astron.)* Sternwarte, *die*

observe [əb'zɜːv] *v. t.* **a)** *(watch)* beobachten; *(perceive)* bemerken; **b)** *(abide by, keep)* einhalten; **c)** *(say)* bemerken. **ob'server** *n.* Beobachter, *der*/Beobachterin, *die*

obsess [əb'ses] *v. t.* **~ sb.** von jmdm. Besitz ergreifen *(fig.);* **be/become ~ed with** *or* **by sb./sth.** von jmdm./etw. besessen sein/werden. **obsession** [əb'seʃn] *n.* Zwangsvorstellung, *die.* **obsessive** [əb'sesɪv] *adj.* zwanghaft; **be ~ about sth.** von etw. besessen sein

obsolete ['ɒbsəliːt] *adj.* veraltet

obstacle ['ɒbstəkl] *n.* Hindernis, *das* (**to** für)

obstinacy ['ɒbstɪnəsɪ] *n. see* **obstinate:** Starrsinn, *der;* Hartnäckigkeit, *die*

obstinate ['ɒbstɪnət] *adj.* starrsinnig; *(adhering to particular course of action)* hartnäckig

obstruct [əb'strʌkt] *v. t.* **a)** *(block)* blockieren; behindern ⟨*Verkehr*⟩; **~ sb.'s view** jmdm. die Sicht versperren; **b)** *(fig.: impede; also Sport)* behindern. **obstruction** [əb'strʌkʃn] *n.* Blockierung, *die; (of progress; also Sport)* Behinderung, *die.* **obstructive** [əb'strʌktɪv] *adj.* hinderlich; obstruktiv ⟨*Politik, Taktik*⟩; **be ~** ⟨*Person:*⟩ sich querlegen *(ugs.)*

obtain [əb'teɪn] *v. t.* bekommen; erzielen ⟨*Resultat, Wirkung*⟩. **obtainable** [əb'teɪnəbl] *adj.* erhältlich

obtrusive [əb'truːsɪv] *adj.* aufdringlich; *(conspicuous)* auffällig

obtuse [əb'tjuːs] *adj.* **a)** stumpf ⟨*Winkel*⟩; **b)** *(stupid)* begriffsstutzig

obvious ['ɒbvɪəs] *adj.* offenkundig; *(easily seen)* augenfällig; **be ~ [to sb.] that ...:** [jmdm.] klar sein, daß ... '**obviously** *adv.* offenkundig; sichtlich ⟨*enttäuschen, überraschen usw.*⟩

occasion [ə'keɪʒn] **1.** *n.* **a)** Gelegenheit, *die;* **rise to the ~:** sich der Situation gewachsen zeigen; **on several ~s** bei mehreren Gelegenheiten; **on ~[s]** gelegentlich; **b)** *(special occurrence)* Anlaß, *der;* **it was quite an ~:** es war ein Ereignis; **c)** *(reason)* Grund, *der*

(for zu). **2.** *v. t.* verursachen. **occa-sional** [ə'keɪʒənl] *adj.* gelegentlich; vereinzelt ⟨*Regenschauer*⟩. **oc'ca-sionally** *adv.* gelegentlich; |only| **very ~:** gelegentlich einmal

occult [ɒ'kʌlt, 'ɒkʌlt] *adj.* okkult; **the ~:** das Okkulte

occupant ['ɒkjʊpənt] *n.* Bewohner, *der*/Bewohnerin, *die;* (*of car, bus, etc.*) Insasse, *der*/Insassin, *die*

occupation [ɒkjʊ'peɪʃn] *n.* **a)** *(Mil.)* Besetzung, *die;* (*period*) Besatzungs-zeit, *die;* **b)** (*activity*) Beschäftigung, *die;* **c)** *(profession)* Beruf, *der.* **occu-pational** [ɒkjʊ'peɪʃənl] *adj.* Berufs-⟨*beratung, -risiko*⟩; **~ therapy** Beschäf-tigungstherapie, *die*

occupier ['ɒkjʊpaɪə(r)] *n.* *(Brit.)* Besit-zer, *der*/Besitzerin, *die;* (*tenant*) Be-wohner, *der*/Bewohnerin, *die*

occupy ['ɒkjʊpaɪ] *v. t.* **a)** *(Mil.; as demonstration)* besetzen; **b)** *(live in)* bewohnen; **c)** *(take up, fill)* einneh-men; belegen ⟨*Zimmer*⟩; in Anspruch nehmen ⟨*Zeit, Aufmerksamkeit*⟩; **d)** *(busy, employ)* beschäftigen

occur [ə'kɜː(r)] *v. i.,* **-rr-:** **a)** *(be met with)* vorkommen; ⟨*Gelegenheit:*⟩ sich bieten; ⟨*Problem:*⟩ auftreten; **b)** *(hap-pen)* ⟨*Veränderung:*⟩ eintreten; ⟨*Un-fall, Vorfall:*⟩ sich ereignen; **c) ~ to sb.** *(be thought of)* jmdm. in den Sinn kommen; ⟨*Idee:*⟩ jmdm. kommen. **occurrence** [ə'kʌrəns] *n.* **a)** *(incid-ent)* Ereignis, *das;* Begebenheit, *die;* **b)** *(occurring)* Vorkommen, *das*

ocean ['əʊʃn] *n.* Ozean, *der;* Meer, *das*

o'clock [ə'klɒk] *adv.* **it is two/six ~:** es ist zwei/sechs Uhr; **at two/six ~:** um zwei/sechs Uhr; **six ~** *attrib.* Sechs-Uhr-⟨*Zug, Maschine, Nachrichten*⟩

Oct. *abbr.* October Okt.

octagon ['ɒktəgən] *n.* Achteck, *das*

octane ['ɒkteɪn] *n.* Oktan, *das*

octave ['ɒktɪv] *n.* Oktave, *die*

October [ɒk'təʊbə(r)] *n.* Oktober, *der; see also* **August**

octopus ['ɒktəpəs] *n.* Tintenfisch, *der*

odd [ɒd] *adj.* **a)** *(surplus, spare)* übrig ⟨*Stück, Silbergeld*⟩; **£25 and a few ~ pence** 25 Pfund und ein paar Pence; **b)** *(occasional)* gelegentlich; **~ job/~-job man** Gelegenheitsarbeit, *die*/-arbeiter, *der;* **c)** *(one of pair or group)* einzeln; **~ socks** nicht zusam-mengehörende Socken; **be the ~ man out** ⟨*Gegenstand:*⟩ nicht dazu passen; **d)** *(uneven)* ungerade ⟨*Zahl, Seite, Hausnummer*⟩; **e)** *(plus something)*

forty ~: über vierzig; **twelve pounds ~:** etwas mehr als zwölf Pfund; **f)** *(strange, eccentric)* seltsam. **oddity** ['ɒdɪtɪ] *n.* *(object, event)* Kuriosität, *die.* **'oddly** *adv.* seltsam; **~ enough** seltsamerweise. **'odd-numbered** *adj.* ungerade

odds [ɒdz] *n. pl.* **a)** *(Betting)* Odds *Pl.;* **b)** |the| **~ are that she did it** wahr-scheinlich hat sie es getan; **the ~ are against/in favour of sb./sth.** jmds. Aussichten/die Aussichten für etw. sind gering/gut; **c) ~ and ends** Klei-nigkeiten; *(of food)* Reste; **d) be at ~ with sb. over sth.** mit jmdm. in etw. *(Dat.)* uneinig sein; **e) it makes no/ little ~** |whether ...| es ist völlig/ziem-lich gleichgültig[, ob ...]

odious ['əʊdɪəs] *adj.* widerwärtig

odor *etc.* *(Amer.) see* **odour** *etc.*

odour ['əʊdə(r)] *n.* Geruch, *der.* **'odourless** *adj.* geruchlos

of [əv, *stressed* ɒv] *prep.* von; *indicating material, substance* aus; **articles of clothing** Kleidungsstücke; **a friend of mine** ein Freund von mir; **where's that pencil of mine?** wo ist mein Bleistift?; **it was clever of you to do that** es war klug von dir, das zu tun; **the approval of sb.** jmds. Zustimmung; **the works of Shakespeare** Shakespeares Werke; **be made of ...:** aus ... [hergestellt] sein; **the fifth of January** der fünfte Januar; **his love of his father** seine Liebe zu sei-nem Vater; **person of extreme views** Mensch mit extremen Ansichten; **a boy of 14 years** ein vierzehnjähriger Junge; **the five of us** wir fünf

off [ɒf] **1.** *adv.* **a)** *(away)* **be a few miles ~:** wenige Meilen entfernt sein; **the lake is not far ~:** der See ist nicht weit [weg]; **I'm ~ now** jetzt geht's jetzt; **~ we go!** los geht's!; **b)** *(not on or attached or supported)* ab; **get the lid ~:** den Deckel abbekommen; **c) be ~** *(switched or turned ~)* ⟨*Wasser, Gas, Strom:*⟩ abgestellt sein; **the light/radio** *etc.* **is ~:** das Licht/Radio *usw.* ist aus; **d) the meat** *etc.* **is ~:** das Fleisch *usw.* ist schlecht [geworden]; **e) be ~** *(cancelled)* abgesagt sein; ⟨*Verlo-bung:*⟩ [auf]gelöst sein; **~ and on** im-mer und wieder *(ugs.);* **f)** *(not at work)* frei; **on my day ~:** an meinem freien Tag; **have a week ~:** eine Woche Ur-laub bekommen; **g)** *(no longer avail-able)* |the| **soup** *etc.* **is ~:** es gibt keine Suppe *usw.* mehr; **h)** *(situated as re-gards money etc.)* **he is badly** *etc.* **~:** er ist schlecht *usw.* gestellt. **2.** *prep.* von; **be ~ school/work** in der Schule/am Arbeitsplatz fehlen; **be ~ one's food** keinen Appetit haben; **just ~ the square** ganz in der Nähe des Platzes

offal ['ɒfl] *n.* Innereien *Pl.*

offence [ə'fens] *n. (Brit.)* **a)** *(hurting of sb.'s feelings)* Kränkung, *die;* **I meant no ~:** ich wollte Sie/ihn *usw.* nicht kränken; **b)** *(annoyance)* **give ~:** Mißfallen erregen; **take ~:** verärgert sein; **c)** *(crime)* Straftat, *die;* **criminal ~:** strafbare Handlung

offend [ə'fend] **1.** *v. i.* verstoßen **(against** gegen). **2.** *v. t.* **~ sb.** bei jmdm. Anstoß erregen; *(hurt feelings of)* jmdn. kränken. **offender** *n.* Straffällige, *der/die*

offense *(Amer.) see* offence

offensive [ə'fensɪv] **1.** *adj.* **a)** *(aggressive)* offensiv; Angriffs(waffe); **b)** *(giving offence)* ungehörig; *(indecent)* anstößig. **2.** *n.* Offensive, *die;* **take the** or **go on the ~:** in die *od.* zur Offensive übergehen

offer ['ɒfə(r)] **1.** *v. t.* anbieten; vorbringen ⟨*Entschuldigung*⟩; bieten ⟨*Chance*⟩; aussprechen ⟨*Beileid*⟩; **~ to help** seine Hilfe anbieten; **~ resistance** Widerstand leisten. **2.** *n.* Angebot, *das;* [**have/be**] **on ~:** im Angebot [haben/sein]

offhand 1. *adv.* **a)** *(without preparation)* auf Anhieb ⟨*sagen, wissen*⟩; spontan ⟨*beschließen, entscheiden*⟩; **b)** *(casually)* leichthin. **2.** *adj.* **a)** *(without preparation)* spontan; **b)** *(casual)* beiläufig; **be ~ with sb.** zu jmdm. kurz angebunden sein

office ['ɒfɪs] *n.* **a)** Büro, *das;* **b)** *(branch)* Zweigstelle, *die;* **c)** *(position)* Amt, *das;* **hold ~:** amtieren. '**office hours** *n. pl.* Dienststunden *Pl.*

officer ['ɒfɪsə(r)] *n.* **a)** *(Army etc.)* Offizier, *der;* **b)** *(official)* Beamte, *der*/Beamtin, *die;* **c)** *(constable)* Polizeibeamte, *der*/-beamtin, *die*

official [ə'fɪʃl] **1.** *adj.* offiziell; amtlich ⟨*Verlautbarung*⟩; regulär ⟨*Streik*⟩. **2.** *n.* Beamte, *der*/Beamtin, *die;* (*party, union,* or *sports* ~) Funktionär, *der*/Funktionärin, *die.* **officially** *adv.* offiziell

officious [ə'fɪʃəs] *adj.* übereifrig

offing ['ɒfɪŋ] *n.* **be in the ~:** bevorstehen; ⟨*Gewitter:*⟩ aufziehen

off: ~-licence *n. (Brit.)* ≈ Wein- und Spirituosenladen, *der;* **~-load** *v. t.* abladen; **~-putting** ['ɒfpʊtɪŋ] *adj.*

(Brit. coll.) abstoßend; **~set** ['--, -'-] *v. t., forms as* **set:** ausgleichen; **~shore** *adj.* küstennah; **~'side** *adj.* Abseits-; **be ~-side** abseits sein; **~spring** *n., pl. same* Nachkommenschaft, *die; (of animal)* Junge *Pl.*

often ['ɒfn, 'ɒftn] *adv.* oft; **every so ~:** gelegentlich

oh [əʊ] *int.* oh; *expr. pain* au

oil [ɔɪl] **1.** *n.* Öl, *das.* **2.** *v. t.* ölen

oil: ~field *n.* Ölfeld, *das;* **~-painting** *n.* Ölgemälde, *das;* **~ refinery** *n.* [Erd]ölraffinerie, *die;* **~ rig** *see* ¹rig 1; **~skins** *n. pl.* Ölzeug, *das;* **~-slick** *n.* Ölteppich, *der;* **~-tanker** *n.* Öltanker, *der;* **~ well** *n.* Ölquelle, *die*

oily ['ɔɪlɪ] *adj.* ölig; ölverschmiert ⟨*Gesicht, Hände*⟩

ointment ['ɔɪntmənt] *n.* Salbe, *die*

OK [əʊ'keɪ] *(coll.)* **1.** *adj.* in Ordnung; okay *(ugs.).* **2.** *adv.* gut. **3.** *int.* okay *(ugs.).* **4.** *v. t. (approve)* zustimmen (+ *Dat.*); **be OK'd by sb.** von jmdm. das Okay bekommen *(ugs.)*

okay [əʊ'keɪ] *see* OK

old [əʊld] *adj.* alt; **be [more than] 30 years ~:** [über] 30 Jahre alt sein

old: ~ 'age *n.* [fortgeschrittenes] Alter; **~-age** *attrib. adj.* Alters(rente, -ruhegeld); **~-age pensioner** Rentner, *der*/Rentnerin, *die;* **~-fashioned** [əʊld'fæʃnd] *adj.* altmodisch

olive ['ɒlɪv] *n.* Olive, *die.* **olive 'oil** *n.* Olivenöl, *das*

Olympic [ə'lɪmpɪk] *adj.* olympisch; **~ Games** Olympische Spiele

omelette (omelet) ['ɒmlɪt] *n.* Omelett, *das*

omen ['əʊmən] *n.* Vorzeichen, *das*

ominous ['ɒmɪnəs] *adj. (of evil omen)* ominös; *(worrying)* beunruhigend

omission [ə'mɪʃn] *n.* Auslassung, *die; (failure to act)* Unterlassung, *die*

omit [ə'mɪt] *v. t., -tt-* weglassen; **~ to do sth.** es versäumen, etw. zu tun

on [ɒn] **1.** *prep.* auf *(position:* + *Dat.; direction:* + *Akk.); (attached to)* an (+ *Dat./Akk.); (concerning, about)* über (+ *Akk.); in expressions of time* an ⟨*einem Abend, Tag usw.*⟩; **write sth. on the wall** etw. an die Wand schreiben; **be hanging on the wall** an der Wand hängen; **have sth. on one** etw. bei sich haben; **on the bus/train** im Bus/Zug; *(by bus/train)* mit dem Bus/Zug; **on Oxford 56767** unter der Nummer Oxford 56767; **on Sundays** sonntags; **on [his] arrival** bei seiner

Ankunft; **on entering the room** ...: beim Betreten des Zimmers ...; **it's just on 9** es ist fast 9 Uhr; **the drinks are on me** *(coll.)* die Getränke gehen auf mich. **2.** *adv.* **with/without a hat/coat on** mit/ohne Hut/Mantel; **have a hat on** einen Hut aufhaben; **on and on** immer weiter; **speak/wait/work** *etc.* **on** weiterreden/-warten/-arbeiten *usw.;* **from now on** von jetzt an; **the light/ radio** *etc.* **is on** das Licht/Radio *usw.* ist an; **is Sunday's picnic on?** findet das Picknick am Sonntag statt?; **what's on at the cinema?** was läuft im Kino?; **on and off** immer mal wieder *(ugs.);* **on to, onto** auf (+ *Akk.*)

once [wʌns] **1.** *adv.* **a)** einmal; ~ **a week/month/year** einmal die Woche/ im Monat/im Jahr; ~ **again** *or* **more** noch einmal; ~ **[and] for all** ein für allemal; **never/not** ~: nicht ein einziges Mal; **b)** *(multiplied by one)* ein mal; **c)** *(formerly)* früher einmal; ~ **upon a time there lived a king** es war einmal ein König; **d) at** ~ *(immediately)* sofort; *(at the same time)* gleichzeitig; **all at** ~ *(suddenly)* plötzlich; *(simultaneously)* alle[s] zugleich. **2.** *conj.* wenn; *(with past tense)* als. **3.** *n.* [just *or* only] **this** ~: [nur] dieses eine Mal

'**oncoming** *adj.* entgegenkommend ⟨*Fahrzeug, Verkehr*⟩

one [wʌn] **1.** *adj.* ein; *see also* **eight 1;** *(single, only)* einzig; **no/not** ~: kein; **the** ~ **thing** das einzige; **at** ~ **time** einmal; ~ **morning/night** eines Morgens/ Nachts. **2.** *n.* **a)** eins; **b)** *(number, symbol)* Eins, *die;* **c)** *(unit)* in ~**s** einzeln. **3.** *pron.* **a)** ein... *(of* + *Gen.*); **big** ~**s and little** ~**s** große und kleine; **the older/younger** ~: der/die/das ältere/ jüngere; **this** ~: dieser/diese/dieses [da]; **that** ~: der/die/das [da]; **which** ~? welcher/welche/welches?; **which** ~**s?** welche?; ~ **by** ~: einzeln; **love/ hate** ~ **another** sich lieben/hassen; **be kind to** ~ **another** nett zueinander sein; **b)** *(people in general; coll.: I, we)* man; *as indirect object* einem; *as direct object* einen; ~'**s** sein

one: ~'**self** *pron.* **a)** *emphat.* selbst; **be** ~**self** man selbst sein; **b)** *refl.* sich; *see also* **herself;** ~**-sided** *adj.* einseitig; ~**-way** *adj.* **a)** in einer Richtung nachgestellt; Einbahn⟨*straße, -verkehr*⟩; **b)** einfach ⟨*Fahrpreis, Flug*⟩

onion ['ʌnjən] *n.* Zwiebel, *die*

'**onlooker** *n.* Zuschauer, *der*/Zuschauerin, *die*

only ['əʊnlı] **1.** *attrib. adj.* einzig...; **the** ~ **person** der/die einzige; **an** ~ **child** ein Einzelkind. **2.** *adv.* nur; **we had been waiting** ~ **5 minutes when** ...: wir hatten erst 5 Minuten gewartet, als ...; **it's** ~/~ **just 6 o'clock** es ist erst 6 Uhr/ gerade erst 6 Uhr vorbei; **he** ~ **just made it** er hat es gerade noch geschafft; ~ **if** nur [dann]..., wenn; ~ **the other day/week** erst neulich

'**onset** *n.* *(of winter)* Einbruch, *der;* *(of disease)* Ausbruch, *der*

onslaught ['ɒnslɔːt] *n.* [heftige] Attacke *(fig.)*

onus ['əʊnəs] *n.* **the** ~ **is on him to do it** es ist seine Sache, es zu tun

onward[s] ['ɒnwədz] *adv.* *(in space)* vorwärts; **from X** ~: von X an; **from that day** ~: von diesem Tag an

ooze [uːz] **1.** *v. i.* sickern **(from** aus). **2.** *v. t.* triefen von *od.* vor (+ *Dat.*); *(fig.)* ausstrahlen

opaque [əʊ'peık] *adj.* lichtundurchlässig; opak *(fachspr.)*

open ['əʊpn] **1.** *adj.* **a)** offen; *(not blocked or obstructed)* frei; *(available)* frei ⟨*Stelle*⟩; **in the** ~ **air** im Freien; **be** ~ ⟨*Laden, Museum, Bank usw.:*⟩ geöffnet sein; **have an** ~ **mind about** *or* **on sth.** einer Sache gegenüber aufgeschlossen sein; **b)** unverhohlen ⟨*Bewunderung, Haß, Verachtung*⟩; **c)** *(frank, communicative)* offen ⟨*Wesen, Streit, Abstimmung, Regierungsstil*⟩; *(not secret)* öffentlich ⟨*Wahl*⟩; **d)** geöffnet ⟨*Regenschirm*⟩; aufgeblüht ⟨*Blume, Knospe*⟩; aufgeschlagen ⟨*Zeitung, Landkarte*⟩. **2.** *n.* **in the** ~ *(outdoors)* unter freiem Himmel; **[out] in the** ~ *(fig.)* öffentlich bekannt. **3.** *v. t.* **a)** öffnen; **b)** eröffnen ⟨*Konferenz, Diskussion, Laden*⟩; beginnen ⟨*Verhandlungen, Spiel*⟩; **c)** *(unfold, spread out)* aufschlagen ⟨*Zeitung, Landkarte*⟩; öffnen ⟨*Schirm*⟩. **4.** *v. i.* **a)** sich öffnen; ~ **into/on to sth.** zu etw. führen; **b)** *(become* ~ *to customers)* öffnen; *(start trading etc.)* eröffnet werden; **c)** *(start)* beginnen; ⟨*Ausstellung:*⟩ eröffnet werden; ⟨*Theaterstück:*⟩ Premiere haben. **open** '**up 1.** *v. t.* öffnen; *(establish)* eröffnen. **2.** *v. i.* sich öffnen; ⟨*Filiale:*⟩ eröffnet werden; ⟨*Firma:*⟩ sich niederlassen

'**open-air** *attrib. adj.* Openair⟨*konzert*⟩; ~ **[swimming-]pool** Freibad, *das*

'**opener** *n.* Öffner, *der*

'**opening 1.** *n.* **a)** Öffnen, *das; (becoming open)* Sichöffnen, *das; (of exhibi-*

tion, new centre) Eröffnen, *das;* **b)** *(establishment, ceremony)* Eröffnung, die; **c)** *(initial part)* Anfang, *der;* **d)** *(gap, aperture)* Öffnung, *die;* **e)** *(opportunity)* Möglichkeit, *die; (vacancy)* freie Stelle. **2.** *adj.* einleitend. **'opening hours** *n. pl.* Öffnungszeiten *Pl.*
'openly *adv.* **a)** *(publicly)* in der Öffentlichkeit; öffentlich ⟨*zugeben, verurteilen*⟩; **b)** *(frankly)* offen
open: ~-'**minded** *adj.* aufgeschlossen; ~-'**plan** *adj.* ~-**plan office** Großraumbüro, *das;* ~ '**sandwich** *n.* belegtes Brot
opera ['ɒpərə] *n.* Oper, *die*
opera: ~-**glasses** *n. pl.* Opernglas, *das;* ~-**house** *n.* Opernhaus, *das;* ~-**singer** *n.* Opernsänger, *der/*-sängerin, *die*
operate ['ɒpəreɪt] **1.** *v. i.* **a)** *(be in action)* in Betrieb sein; ⟨*Bus, Zug usw.:*⟩ verkehren; **b)** *(function)* arbeiten; **the torch** ~**s on batteries** die Taschenlampe arbeitet mit Batterien; **c)** ~ **|on sb.|** *(Med.)* [jmdn.] operieren. **2.** *v. t.* bedienen ⟨*Maschine*⟩; unterhalten ⟨*Busverbindung, Telefondienst*⟩; betätigen ⟨*Hebel, Bremse*⟩. '**operating-theatre** *n. (Brit. Med.)* Operationssaal, *der*
operation [ɒpə'reɪʃn] *n.* **a)** *(causing to work) (of machine)* Bedienung, *die; (of bus service, telephone service, etc.)* Unterhaltung, *die; (of lever, brake)* Betätigung, *die;* **b) come into** ~ ⟨*Gesetz, Gebühr usw.:*⟩ in Kraft treten; **be in/out of** ~ ⟨*Maschine, Gerät usw.:*⟩ in/außer Betrieb sein; **c)** *(Med.)* Operation, *die;* **have an** ~: operiert werden
operational [ɒpə'reɪʃənl] *adj. (esp. Mil.: ready to function)* einsatzbereit
operative ['ɒpərətɪv] *adj.* **become** ~ ⟨*Gesetz:*⟩ in Kraft treten; **the scheme is** ~: das Programm läuft
operator ['ɒpəreɪtə(r)] *n.* [Maschinen]bediener, *der/*-bedienerin, *die; (Teleph.) (at exchange)* Vermittlung, *die; (at switchboard)* Telefonist, *der/* Telefonistin, *die*
opinion [ə'pɪnjən] *n.* Meinung, *die* (**on** über + *Akk.,* zu); **have a high/low** ~ **of sb.** eine/keine hohe Meinung von jmdm. haben; **in my** ~: meiner Meinung nach. **opinionated** [ə'pɪnjəneɪtɪd] *adj.* rechthaberisch
opium ['əʊpɪəm] *n.* Opium, *das*
opponent [ə'pəʊnənt] *n.* Gegner, *der/* Gegnerin, *die*
opportune ['ɒpətjuːn] *adj.* **a)** *(favour-*

able) günstig; **b)** *(well-timed)* zur rechten Zeit *nachgestellt.* **opportunism** [ɒpə'tjuːnɪzm] *n.* Opportunismus, *der*
opportunist [ɒpə'tjuːnɪst] *n.* Opportunist, *der/*Opportunistin, *die*
opportunity [ɒpə'tjuːnɪtɪ] *n.* Gelegenheit, *die*
oppose [ə'pəʊz] **1.** *v. t.* sich wenden gegen. **2.** *v. i.* **the opposing team** die gegnerische Mannschaft. **opposed** [ə'pəʊzd] *adj.* **as** ~ **to** im Gegensatz zu; **be** ~ **to sth.** ⟨*Personen:*⟩ gegen etw. sein
opposite ['ɒpəzɪt] **1.** *adj.* gegenüberliegend ⟨*Straßenseite, Ufer*⟩; entgegengesetzt ⟨*Ende, Weg, Richtung*⟩; **the** ~ **sex** das andere Geschlecht. **2.** *n.* Gegenteil, *das* (**of** von). **3.** *adv.* gegenüber. **4.** *prep.* gegenüber
opposition [ɒpə'zɪʃn] *n.* **a)** Opposition, *die; (resistance)* Widerstand, *der* (**to** gegen); **in** ~ **to** entgegen; **b)** *(Brit. Polit.)* **the O**~: die Opposition
oppress [ə'pres] *v. t.* unterdrücken; *(fig.)* ⟨*Gefühl:*⟩ bedrücken. **oppression** [ə'preʃn] *n.* Unterdrückung, *die.*
oppressive [ə'presɪv] *adj.* repressiv; *(fig.)* bedrückend ⟨*Ängste, Atmosphäre*⟩; *(hot and close)* drückend ⟨*Wetter, Klima, Tag*⟩
opt [ɒpt] *v. i.* sich entscheiden (**for** für); ~ **to do sth.** sich dafür entscheiden, etw. zu tun; ~ **out** nicht mitmachen/*(stop taking part)* nicht länger mitmachen (**of** bei)
optical ['ɒptɪkl] *adj.* optisch
optician [ɒp'tɪʃn] *n.* Optiker, *der/*Optikerin, *die*
optima *pl. of* **optimum**
optimism ['ɒptɪmɪzm] *n.* Optimismus, *der.* **optimist** ['ɒptɪmɪst] *n.* Optimist, *der/*Optimistin, *die.* **optimistic** [ɒptɪ'mɪstɪk] *adj.* optimistisch
optimum ['ɒptɪməm] **1.** *n., pl.* **optima** ['ɒptɪmə] Optimum, *das.* **2.** *adj.* optimal
option ['ɒpʃn] *n. (choice)* Wahl, *die; (thing)* Wahlmöglichkeit, *die.* **optional** ['ɒpʃənl] *adj.* nicht zwingend; ~ **subject** Wahlfach, *das*
opulence ['ɒpjʊləns] *n.* Wohlstand, *der*
opulent ['ɒpjʊlənt] *adj.* wohlhabend; feudal ⟨*Auto, Haus usw.*⟩
or [ə(r), *stressed* ɔ:(r)] *conj.* **a)** oder; **he cannot read or write** er kann weder lesen noch schreiben; **without food or water** ohne Essen und Wasser; **15 or 20 minutes** 15 bis 20 Minuten; **in a day**

or two in ein, zwei Tagen; **b)** *introducing explanation* das heißt; **or rather** beziehungsweise

oracle ['ɒrəkl] *n.* Orakel, *das*

oral ['ɔːrl] *adj.* mündlich; *(Med.)* oral

orange ['ɒrɪndʒ] **1.** *n.* **a)** *(fruit)* Orange, *die;* Apfelsine, *die;* **b)** *(colour)* Orange, *das.* **2.** *adj.* orange[farben]

orator ['ɒrətə(r)] *n.* Redner, *der*/Rednerin, *die*

oratory ['ɒrətərɪ] *n.* Redekunst, *die*

orbit ['ɔːbɪt] **1.** *n.* *(Astron.)* [Umlauf]bahn, *die.* **2.** *v. i.* kreisen. **3.** *v. t.* umkreisen. **orbital** ['ɔːbɪtl] *adj.* ~ **road** Ringstraße, *die*

orchard ['ɔːtʃəd] *n.* Obstgarten, *der; (commercial)* Obstplantage, *die*

orchestra ['ɔːkɪstrə] *n.* Orchester, *das.* **orchestral** [ɔːˈkestrl] *adj.* Orchester-

orchid ['ɔːkɪd] *n.* Orchidee, *die*

ordain [ɔːˈdeɪn] *v. t.* **a)** *(Eccl.)* ordinieren; **b)** *(decree)* verfügen

ordeal [ɔːˈdiːl] *n.* Qual, *die*

order ['ɔːdə(r)] **1.** *n.* **a)** *(sequence)* Reihenfolge, *die;* **out of** ~: durcheinander; **b)** *(regular arrangement, normal state)* Ordnung, *die;* **be/not be in** ~: in Ordnung/nicht in Ordnung sein *(ugs.);* **be out of/in** ~ *(not in/in working condition)* nicht funktionieren/funktionieren; **'out of** ~' „außer Betrieb"; **in good/bad** ~: in gutem/schlechtem Zustand; **c)** *(command)* Anweisung, *die; (Mil.)* Befehl, *der;* **d) in** ~ **to do sth.** um etw. zu tun; **e)** *(Commerc.)* Auftrag, *der* (**for** über + *Akk.*); *(to waiter,* ~*ed goods)* Bestellung, *die;* **f) keep** ~: Ordnung [be]wahren; *see also* **law** b; **g)** *(religious* ~*)* Orden, *der.* **2.** *v. t.* **a)** *(command)* befehlen; ⟨*Richter:*⟩ verfügen; ~ **sb. to do sth.** jmdn. anweisen/ *(Milit.)* jmdm. befehlen, etw. zu tun; **b)** *(Commerc.)* bestellen (**from** bei); **c)** *(arrange)* ordnen

orderly ['ɔːdəlɪ] **1.** *adj.* friedlich; diszipliniert ⟨*Menge*⟩; *(methodical)* methodisch; *(tidy)* ordentlich. **2.** *n.* **a)** *(Mil.)* [Offiziers]bursche, *der;* **b) medical** ~: ≈ Krankenpflegehelfer, *der*

ordinal ['ɔːdɪnl] *adj. & n.* ~ |**number**| Ordinalzahl, *die*

ordinary ['ɔːdɪnərɪ] *adj. (normal)* normal ⟨*Gebrauch*⟩; üblich ⟨*Verfahren*⟩; *(not exceptional)* gewöhnlich

ordination [ɔːdɪˈneɪʃn] *n. (Eccl.)* Ordination, *die;* Ordinierung, *die*

ore [ɔː(r)] *n.* Erz, *das*

organ ['ɔːgən] *n.* **a)** *(Mus.)* Orgel, *die;* **b)** *(Biol.)* Organ, *das*

organic [ɔːˈgænɪk] *adj.* organisch; biologisch-dynamisch ⟨*Ackerbau*⟩; biodynamisch ⟨*Nahrungsmittel*⟩

organism ['ɔːgənɪzm] *n.* Organismus, *der*

organist ['ɔːgənɪst] *n.* Organist, *der*/Organistin, *die*

organization [ɔːgənaɪˈzeɪʃn] *n.* Organisation, *die;* ~ **of time/work** Zeit-/Arbeitseinteilung, *die*

organize ['ɔːgənaɪz] *v. t.* organisieren; einteilen ⟨*Arbeit, Zeit*⟩; veranstalten ⟨*Konferenz, Festival*⟩; ~ **into groups** in Gruppen einteilen. '**organizer** *n.* Organisator, *der*/Organisatorin, *die; (of event, festival)* Veranstalter, *der*/Veranstalterin, *die*

orgasm ['ɔːgæzm] *n.* Orgasmus, *der*

orgy ['ɔːdʒɪ] *n.* Orgie, *die*

orient 1. ['ɔːrɪənt] *n.* **the O**~: der Orient. **2.** ['ɒrɪent] *v. t.* ausrichten (**towards** nach); ~ **oneself** sich orientieren

oriental [ɒrɪˈentl] **1.** *adj.* orientalisch. **2.** *n.* Asiat, *der*/Asiatin, *die*

orientate ['ɒrɪənteɪt] *see* **orient** 2. **orientation** [ɒrɪənˈteɪʃn] *n.* Orientierung, *die*

orienteering [ɒrɪənˈtɪərɪŋ] *n. (Brit.)* Orientierungsrennen, *das*

orifice ['ɒrɪfɪs] *n.* Öffnung, *die*

origin ['ɒrɪdʒɪn] *n. (derivation)* Herkunft, *die; (beginnings)* Anfänge *Pl.; (source)* Ursprung, *der;* **country of** ~: Herkunftsland, *das;* **have its** ~ **in sth.** seinen Ursprung in etw. *(Dat.)* haben. **original** [əˈrɪdʒɪnl] **1.** *adj.* ursprünglich; Ur⟨*text, -fassung*⟩; eigenständig ⟨*Forschung*⟩; *(inventive)* originell; **an** ~ **painting** ein Original. **2.** *n.* Original, *das.* **originality** [ərɪdʒɪˈnælɪtɪ] *n.* Originalität, *die.* **originally** [əˈrɪdʒɪnəlɪ] *adv.* **a)** ursprünglich; **b)** originell ⟨*schreiben usw.*⟩. **originate** [əˈrɪdʒɪneɪt] *v. i.* ~ **from** entstehen aus; ~ **in** seinen Ursprung haben in (+ *Dat.*)

ornament ['ɔːnəmənt] *n.* Ziergegenstand, *der.* **ornamental** [ɔːnəˈmentl] *adj.* dekorativ; Zier⟨*pflanze, -naht usw.*⟩

ornate [ɔːˈneɪt] *adj.* reich verziert; prunkvoll ⟨*Dekoration*⟩

ornithology [ɔːnɪˈθɒlədʒɪ] *n.* Ornithologie, *die*

orphan ['ɔːfn] **1.** *n.* Waise, *die.* **2.** *v. t.* **be** ~**ed** [zur] Waise werden. **orphanage** ['ɔːfənɪdʒ] *n.* Waisenhaus, *das*

orthodox [ˈɔːθədɒks] *adj.* orthodox
oscillate [ˈɒsɪleɪt] *v.i.* schwingen. **oscillation** [ɒsɪˈleɪʃn] *n.* Schwingen,
das; (single ~) Schwingung, *die*
ostensible [ɒˈstensɪbl] *adj.* vorge-
schoben. **ostensibly** [ɒˈstensɪblɪ]
adv. vorgeblich
ostentatious [ɒstenˈteɪʃəs] *adj.*
prunkhaft ⟨*Kleidung, Schmuck*⟩;
prahlerisch ⟨*Art*⟩
osteopath [ˈɒstɪəpæθ] *n.* Spezialist
für Knochenleiden
ostrich [ˈɒstrɪtʃ] *n.* Strauß, *der*
other [ˈʌðə(r)] 1. *adj.* a) *(not the same)*
ander...; the ~ two/three *etc. (the remaining)* die beiden/drei *usw.* anderen; the ~ one der/die/das andere;
some ~ time ein andermal; b) *(further)*
one ~ thing noch eins; some/six ~
people noch ein paar/noch sechs [an-
dere *od.* weitere] Leute; no ~ questions keine weiteren Fragen; c) ~ than
(different from) anders als; *(except)*
außer; d) the ~ day/evening neulich/
neulich abends. 2. *n.* anderer/andere/
anderes; there are six ~s es sind noch
sechs andere da; any ~: irgendein an-
derer/-eine andere/-ein anderes; not
any ~: kein anderer/keine andere/
kein anderes; one after the ~: einer/
eine/eins nach dem/der/dem anderen. 3. *adv.* anders; ~ than that, ...:
abgesehen davon, ...
otherwise [ˈʌðəwaɪz] 1. *adv.* a) *(in a
different way)* anders; b) *(or else)* an-
derenfalls; c) *(in other respects)* im
übrigen. 2. *pred. adj.* anders
otter [ˈɒtə(r)] *n.* [Fisch]otter, *der*
ouch [aʊtʃ] *int.* autsch
ought [ɔːt] *v. aux. only in pres. and past
ought, neg. (coll.)* **oughtn't** [ˈɔːtnt] I ~
to do/have done it *expr. moral duty* ich
müßte es tun/hätte es tun müssen;
expr. desirability ich sollte es tun/hät-
te es tun sollen; ~ not *or* ~n't you to
have left by now? müßtest du nicht
schon weg sein?; one ~ not to do it
man sollte es nicht tun; he ~ to be
hanged/in hospital er gehört an den
Galgen/ins Krankenhaus; that ~ to be
enough das dürfte reichen; he ~ to win
er müßte [eigentlich] gewinnen
oughtn't [ˈɔːtnt] *(coll.)* **= ought not**
ounce [aʊns] *n. (measure)* Unze, *die*
our [ˈaʊə(r)] *poss. pron. attrib.* unser
ours [ˈaʊəz] *poss. pron. pred.* unserer/
unsere/unseres; *see also* **hers**
ourselves [aʊəˈselvz] *pron.* a) *emphat.*
selbst; b) *refl.* uns. *See also* **herself**

oust [aʊst] *v.t.* verdrängen; ~ sb. from
his job/from power jmdn. von seinem
Arbeitsplatz vertreiben/jmdn. entmachten
out [aʊt] *adv.* a) *(away from place)* ~
here/there hier/da draußen; be ~ in
the garden draußen im Garten sein;
what's it like ~? wie ist es draußen?;
go ~ shopping *etc.* einkaufen *usw.* gehen; be ~ *(not at home, not in one's office, etc.)* nicht dasein; she was ~ all
night sie war eine/die ganze Nacht
weg; have a day ~ in London einen
Tag in London verbringen; row ~
to ...: hinaus-/herausrudern zu ...; be
~ at sea auf See sein; b) *(Sport,
Games)* be ~ ⟨*Ball:*⟩ aus *od.* im Aus
sein; ⟨*Mitspieler:*⟩ ausscheiden;
⟨*Schlagmann:*⟩ aus[geschlagen] sein;
not ~: nicht aus; c) be ~ *(asleep)* weg
sein *(ugs.); (unconscious)* bewußtlos
sein; d) *(no longer burning)* aus[gegan-
gen]; e) *(in error)* be 3% ~ in one's cal-
culations sich um 3% verrechnet haben; this is £5 ~: das stimmt um 5
Pfund nicht; f) *(not in fashion)* passé
(ugs.); out *(ugs.);* g) say it ~ loud es
laut sagen; ~ with it! heraus mit der
Sprache; their secret is ~: ihr Geheimnis ist bekannt geworden; [the]
truth will ~: die Wahrheit wird an den
Tag kommen; the sun/moon is ~: die
Sonne/der Mond scheint; the third
volume is just ~: der dritte Band ist so-
eben erschienen; the roses are ~: die
Rosen blühen; h) be ~ for sth./to do
sth. auf etw. *(Akk.)* aussein/darauf
aussein, etw. zu tun; be ~ for trouble
Streit suchen; i) *(to or at an end)* before the day/month was ~: am selben
Tag/vor Ende des Monats. *See also*
out of

out: ~'bid *v.t.,* ~bid überbieten;
~**board** *adj.* ~board motor Außen-
bordmotor, *der;* ~**break** *n.* Ausbruch, *der;* at the ~break of war bei
Kriegsausbruch; an ~break of flu eine
Grippeepidemie; ~**building** *n.* Nebengebäude, *das;* ~**burst** *n.* Ausbruch, *der;* an ~burst of weeping/
laughter ein Weinkrampf/Lachanfall;
an ~burst of temper ein Wutanfall;
~**cast** *n.* Ausgestoßene, *der/die;* a social ~cast ein Geächteter/eine Geäch-
tete; ~**come** *n.* Ergebnis, *das;* Resultat, *das;* ~**cry** *n.* [Aufschrei der] Empörung; ~'**dated** *adj.* überholt; ~'**do**
v.t. überbieten (in an + *Dat.*);
~**door** *adj.* ~door shoes/things Stra-

ßenschuhe/-kleidung, *die;* ~**door games/pursuits** Spiele/Beschäftigungen im Freien; ~**door swimming-pool** Freibad, *das;* ~'**doors 1.** *adv.* draußen; **go** ~**doors** nach draußen gehen; **2.** *n.* **the |great|** ~**doors** die freie Natur
outer ['aʊtə(r)] *adj.* äußer...; Außen‹fläche, -seite, -wand, -tür›. **outer 'space** *n.* Weltraum, *der*
out: ~**fit** *n.* **a)** *(clothes)* Kleider *Pl.;* **b)** *(equipment)* Ausrüstung, *die;* **c)** *(coll.: organization)* Laden, *der (ugs.);* ~**going 1.** *adj.* **a)** [aus dem Amt] scheidend ‹*Regierung, Präsident*›; **b)** *(friendly)* kontaktfreudig ‹*Person*›; **2.** *n., in pl.* ~**s** *(expenditure)* Ausgaben *Pl.;* ~'**grow** *v. t., forms as* **grow** herauswachsen aus ‹*Kleider*›; *(leave behind)* entwachsen (+ *Dat.*); ~**house** *n.* Nebengebäude, *das*
'**outing** *n.* Ausflug, *der*
out: ~**landish** [aʊt'lændɪʃ] *adj.* ausgefallen; ~**law 1.** *n.* Bandit, *der*/Banditin, *die;* **2.** *v. t.* verbieten; ~**lay** *n.* Ausgaben *Pl.* (**on** für); ~**let** ['aʊtlet, 'aʊtlɪt] *n.* **a)** Ablauf, -fluß, *der;* **b)** *(fig.)* Ventil, *das;* ~**line 1.** *n.* **a)** *in sing. or pl.* Umriß, *der;* **b)** *(short account)* Grundriß, *der; (of topic)* Übersicht, *die* (**of** über + *Akk.*); **2.** *v. t. (describe)* umreißen; ~**live** [aʊt'lɪv] *v. t.* überleben; ~**look** *n.* **a)** *(view)* Aussicht, *die* (**over** über + *Akk.,* **on to** auf + *Akk.*); *(fig.; Meteorol.)* Aussichten *Pl.;* **b)** *(mental attitude)* Einstellung, *die* (**on** zu); ~**lying** *adj.* entlegen; ~**moded** [aʊt'məʊdɪd] *adj.* antiquiert; ~'**number** *v. t.* zahlenmäßig überlegen sein (+ *Dat.*)
out of *prep.* **a)** *(from within)* aus; **go** ~ **the door** zur Tür hinausgehen; **b)** *(not within)* **be** ~ **the country** im Ausland sein; **be** ~ **town/the room** nicht in der Stadt/im Zimmer sein; **feel** ~ **it** *or* **things** sich ausgeschlossen fühlen; **c)** *(from among)* **one** ~ **every three smokers** jeder dritte Raucher; **58** ~ **every 100** 58 von hundert; **d)** *(beyond range of)* außer ‹*Reich-/Hörweite, Sicht, Kontrolle*›; **e)** *(from)* aus; **get money** ~ **sb.** Geld aus jmdm. herausholen; **do well** ~ **sb./sth.** von jmdm./ etw. profitieren; **f)** aus ‹*Mitleid, Furcht, Neugier usw.*›; **g)** *(without)* ~ **money** ohne Geld; **we're** ~ **tea** wir haben keinen Tee mehr; **h)** *(away from)* von ... entfernt; **ten miles** ~ **London** 10 Meilen außerhalb von London
out: ~**-of-'date** *attrib. adj.* veraltet;

(expired) ungültig ‹*Karte*›; ~-**patient** *n.* ambulanter Patient/ambulante Patientin; ~**-patients|' department|** Poliklinik, *die;* ~'**play** *v. t. (Sport)* besser spielen als; ~**post** *n.* Außenposten, *der; (of civilization etc.; also Mil.)* Vorposten, *der;* ~**put** *n.* Produktion, *die; (of liquid, electricity, etc.)* Leistung, *die; (Computing)* Ausgabe, *die*
outrage 1. ['aʊtreɪdʒ] *n.* **a)** *(deed)* Verbrechen, *das; (during war)* Greueltat, *die; (against decency)* grober Verstoß; **b)** *(strong resentment)* Empörung, *die* (**at** gegen). **2.** [aʊt'reɪdʒ] *v. t.* empören.
outrageous [aʊt'reɪdʒəs] *adj.* unverschämt; unverschämt hoch ‹*Preis*›; unerhört ‹*Frechheit, Skandal*›
out: ~**right 1.** [-'-] *adv.* **a)** ganz, komplett ‹*kaufen, verkaufen*›; **b)** *(openly)* freiheraus ‹*erzählen, sagen, lachen*›; **2.** ['--] *adj.* ausgemacht ‹*Unehrlichkeit*›; glatt *(ugs.)* ‹*Ablehnung, Absage, Lüge*›; klar ‹*Sieg, Niederlage, Sieger*›; ~**set** *n.* Anfang, *der;* **at the** ~**set** zu Anfang; **from the** ~**set** von Anfang an
outside 1. [-'-, '--] *n.* **a)** Außenseite, *die;* **on the** ~: außen; **to/from the** ~: nach/von außen; **b)** *(external appearance)* Äußere, *das;* **c)** **at the |very|** ~ *(coll.)* äußerstenfalls; höchstens. **2.** ['--] *adj.* **a)** äußer...; Außen‹*wand, -antenne, -kajüte, -toilette, -durchmesser*›; ~ **lane** Überholspur, *die;* **have only an** ~ **chance** nur eine sehr geringe Chance haben. **3.** [-'-] *adv. (on the* ~) draußen; *(to the* ~) nach draußen. **4.** [-'-] *prep.* **a)** *(position)* außerhalb (+ *Gen.*); ~ **the door** vor der Tür; **b)** *(to the* ~ *of)* aus ... hinaus; **go** ~ **the house** nach draußen gehen. **out'sider** *n. (Sport; also fig.)* Außenseiter, *der*
out: ~**size** *adj.* überdimensional; ~**size clothes** Kleidung in Übergröße; **the** ~**skirts of the town** die Außenbezirke der Stadt; ~'**spoken** *adj.* freimütig; **be** ~ **about sth.** sich freimütig über etw. äußern; ~-'**standing** *adj.* **a)** *(exceptional)* hervorragend; überragend ‹*Bedeutung*›; außergewöhnlich ‹*Person, Mut, Fähigkeit*›; **b)** *(not yet settled)* ausstehend ‹*Schuld, Geldsumme*›; unbezahlt ‹*Rechnung*›; ungelöst ‹*Problem*›; ~'**standingly** *adv.* außergewöhnlich; ~'**stretched** *adj.* ausgestreckt; *(spread out)* ausgebreitet; ~'**strip** *v. t. (pass in running)* überholen; *(in competition)* überflügeln;

~-**tray** n. Ablage für Ausgänge;
~'**vote** v. t. überstimmen
outward ['aʊtwəd] 1. adj. a) (external,
apparent) [rein] äußerlich; äußere ⟨Er-
scheinung, Bedingung⟩; b) Hin⟨reise,
-fracht⟩. 2. adv. nach außen ⟨auf-
gehen, richten⟩. '**outwardly** adv.
nach außen hin ⟨Gefühle zeigen⟩; öffentlich ⟨Loyalität erklären⟩. '**outwards** see outward 2
out: ~'**weigh** v. t. schwerer wiegen
als; überwiegen ⟨Nachteile⟩; ~'**wit**
v. t., -tt- überlisten
oval ['əʊvl] 1. adj. oval. 2. n. Oval, das
ovation [əʊ'veɪʃn] n. Ovation, die; a
standing ~: stehende Ovationen
oven ['ʌvn] n. [Back]ofen, der
oven: ~-**glove** n. Topfhandschuh,
der; ~-**proof** adj. feuerfest;
~-**ready** adj. backfertig ⟨Pommes
frites, Pastete⟩; bratfertig ⟨Geflügel⟩
over ['əʊvə(r)] 1. adv. a) (outward and
downward) hinüber; **climb/look/jump**
~: hinüber- od. (ugs.) rüberklettern/
-sehen/-springen; b) (so as to cover
surface) **board/cover** ~: zunageln/
-decken; c) (across a space) hinüber;
(towards speaker) herüber; **he swam** ~
to us/the other side er schwamm zu
uns herüber/hinüber zur anderen Seite; ~ **here/there** (direction) hier her-
über/dort hinüber; (location) hier/
dort; |come in, please,| ~ (Radio) über-
nehmen Sie bitte; ~ **and out** (Radio)
Ende; d) (in excess etc.) **children of 12
and** ~: Kinder im Alter von zwölf Jahren und darüber; **be** [left] ~: übrig[ge-
blieben] sein; e) (from beginning to
end) von Anfang bis Ende; **say sth.
twice** ~: etw. zweimal sagen; |all| ~
again, (Amer.) ~: noch einmal [ganz
von vorn]; ~ **and** ~ [again] immer wieder; f) (at an end) vorbei; vorüber; **be**
~: vorbei sein; ⟨Aufführung:⟩ zu Ende
sein; **get sth.** ~ **with** etw. hinter sich
(Akk.) bringen; **be** ~ **and done with** erledigt sein; g) **all** ~ (completely finished) aus [und vorbei]; **I ache all** ~:
mir tut alles weh; **be shaking all** ~: am
ganzen Körper zittern. 2. prep. a)
(above, on, round about) über (position: + Dat.; direction: + Akk.);
(across) über (+ Akk.); **look** ~ **a wall**
über eine Mauer sehen; **fall** ~ **a cliff**
von einem Felsen stürzen; **the pub** ~
the road die Wirtschaft gegenüber; **hit
sb.** ~ **the head** jmdm. auf den Kopf
schlagen; ~ **the page** auf der nächsten
Seite; b) (in or across every part of)

[überall] in (+ Dat.); (to and fro upon)
über (+ Akk.); (all through) durch;
all ~ (in or on all parts of) überall in
(+ Dat.); **travel all** ~ **the country** das
ganze Land bereisen; **all** ~ **Spain** in
ganz Spanien; **all** ~ **the world** in der
ganzen Welt; c) (on account of) wegen; d) (engaged with) bei; **take
trouble** ~ **sth.** sich (Dat.) mit etw. Mühe geben; **be a long time** ~ **sth.** lange
für etw. brauchen; ~ **work/dinner** bei
der Arbeit/beim Essen; e) (superior to,
in charge of) über (+ Akk.); **have com-
mand/authority** ~ **sb.** Befehlsgewalt
über jmdn./Weisungsbefugnis gegenüber jmdm. haben; **be** ~ **sb.** (in rank)
über jmdm. stehen; f) (beyond, more
than) über (+ Akk.); ~ **and above** zusätzlich zu; g) (throughout, during)
über (+ Akk.); ~ **the weekend/sum-
mer** übers Wochenende/den Sommer
über; ~ **the past years** in den letzten
Jahren
over: ~**all** 1. n. (Brit.: garment) Ar-
beitskittel, der; 2. adj. a) Gesamt-
⟨breite, -einsparung, -abmessung⟩;
have an ~**all majority** die absolute
Mehrheit haben; b) (general) allgemein; 3. ['---, --'-] adv. a) (in all parts)
insgesamt; b) (taken as a whole) im
großen und ganzen; ~'**awe** v. t. Ehrfurcht einflößen (+ Dat.); ~'**balance** v. i. das Gleichgewicht verlieren; ~'**bearing** adj. herrisch;
~**board** adv. über Bord; **fall** ~**board**
über Bord gehen; ~**cast** adj. trübe;
bewölkt ⟨Himmel⟩; ~'**charge** v. t. a)
(beyond reasonable price) zuviel abver-
langen (+ Dat.); b) (beyond right
price) zuviel berechnen (+ Dat.);
~**coat** n. Mantel, der; ~'**come** v. t.,
forms as **come:** a) überwinden; bezwingen ⟨Feind⟩; ⟨Dämpfe:⟩ betäuben; b) **he was** ~**come by grief/with
emotion** Kummer/Rührung überwäl-
tigte ihn; ~'**cooked** adj. verkocht;
~'**crowded** adj. überfüllt; ~'**do** v. t.
(carry to excess) übertreiben; ~**do it** or
things (work too hard) sich übernehmen; ~'**done** adj. a) (exaggerated)
übertrieben; b) (~-cooked) verkocht;
verbraten ⟨Fleisch⟩; ~**dose** n. Über-
dosis, die; ~'**draft** n. Kontoüberzie-
hung, die; **have an** ~**draft of £50** sein
Konto um 50 Pfund überzogen ha-
ben; ~'**draw** v. t., forms as **draw** 1
überziehen ⟨Konto⟩; ~'**drawn** adj.
überzogen ⟨Konto⟩; **I am** ~**drawn** [at
the bank] mein Konto ist überzogen;

~drive *n.* Schongang, *der;* ~'**due** *adj.* überfällig; **the train is 15 minutes ~due** der Zug hat schon 15 Minuten Verspätung; ~'**eat** *v. i., forms as* **eat** zuviel essen; **~estimate 1.** [~'estɪmeɪt] *v. t.* überschätzen; **2.** [~'estɪmət] *n.* zu hohe Schätzung; **~'fill** *v. t.* zu voll machen; **~flow 1.** [--'-] *v. t.* laufen über (+ *Akk.*) ⟨*Rand*⟩; *(flow over brim of)* überlaufen aus; **~flow its banks** ⟨*Fluß:*⟩ über die Ufer treten; **2.** [--'-] *v. i.* überlaufen; **3.** ['---] *n.* **~flow** |pipe| Überlauf, *der;* ~'**full** *adj.* zu voll; übervoll; ~**grown** *adj.* überwachsen (**with** von); **~hang 1.** [--'-] *v. t.,* **~hung** [əʊvəˈhʌŋ] ⟨*Felsen, Stockwerk:*⟩ hinausragen über (+ *Akk.*); **2.** ['---] *n.* Überhang, *der;* ~'**hanging** *adj.* überhängend; **~haul 1.** [--'-] *v. t.* überholen; überprüfen ⟨*System*⟩; **2.** ['---] *n.* Überholung, *die;* **~head 1.** [--'-] *adv.* über mir/ihm/uns *usw.;* **2.** ['---] *adj.* **~head wires** Hochleitung, *die;* **3.** ['---] *n.* **~heads,** *(Amer.)* **~head** *(Commerc.)* Gemeinkosten *Pl.;* ~'**hear** *v. t., forms as* **hear** 1 *(accidentally)* zufällig [mit]hören; *(intentionally)* belauschen; ~'**heat** *v. i.* zu heiß werden; ⟨*Maschine, Lager:*⟩ heißlaufen

overjoyed [əʊvəˈdʒɔɪd] *adj.* überglücklich (**at** über + *Akk.*).

over: ~lap 1. [--'-] *v. t.* überlappen; **2.** [--'-] *v. i.* ⟨*Flächen, Dachziegel:*⟩ sich überlappen; ⟨*Aufgaben:*⟩ sich überschneiden; **3.** *n.* Überlappung, *die;* ~'**leaf** *adv.* auf der Rückseite; ~**load** *v. t.* überladen; ~'**look** *v. t.* **a)** ⟨*Hotel, Zimmer, Haus:*⟩ Aussicht bieten auf (+ *Akk.*); **b)** *(ignore, not see)* übersehen; *(allow to go unpunished)* hinwegsehen über (+ *Akk.*)

'**overly** *adv.* allzu

over: ~night 1. [--'-] *adv. (also fig.: suddenly)* über Nacht; **stay ~ night** übernachten; **2.** ['---] *adj.* **~night stay** Übernachtung, *die;* **be an ~night success** *(fig.)* über Nacht Erfolg haben; ~'**pay** *v. t., forms as* **pay** 2 überbezahlen; ~'**power** *v. t.* überwältigen; ~'**powering** *adj.* überwältigend; durchdringend ⟨*Geruch*⟩; ~~'**priced** *adj.* zu teuer; ~'**rate** *v. t.* überschätzen; ~~**re'act** *v. i.* unangemessen heftig reagieren (**to** auf + *Akk.*); ~~**re'action** *n.* Überreaktion, *die* (**to** auf + *Akk.*); ~'**ride** *v. t. forms as* **ride** 3 sich hinwegsetzen über (+ *Akk.*); ~**ripe** *adj.* überreif; ~'**rule** *v. t.* auf-

heben ⟨*Entscheidung*⟩; zurückweisen ⟨*Einwand, Argument*⟩; **~rule sb.** jmds. Vorschlag ablehnen; ~'**run** *v. t., forms as* **run 3: be ~run with** überlaufen sein von ⟨*Touristen*⟩; überwuchert sein von ⟨*Unkraut*⟩; **~seas 1.** [--'-] *adv.* in Übersee ⟨*leben, sein*⟩; nach Übersee ⟨*gehen*⟩; **2.** ['---] *adj.* Übersee-; ~'**see** *v. t., forms as* **see** 1 überwachen; *(manage)* leiten ⟨*Abteilung*⟩; ~'**shadow** *v. t.* überschatten; ~'**shoot** *v. t., forms as* **shoot** 1 hinausschießen über (+ *Akk.*); ~**shoot** |the runway| ⟨*Pilot, Flugzeug:*⟩ zu weit kommen; ~**sight** *n.* Versehen, *das;* ~'**sleep** *v. i., forms as* **sleep** 2 verschlafen; ~'**spend** *v. i., forms as* **spend** zuviel [Geld] ausgeben; ~**statement** *n.* Übertreibung, *die;* ~'**step** *v. t.* überschreiten

overt [əʊˈvɜːt] *adj.* unverhohlen

over: ~'**take** *v. t.* überholen; '**no ~taking'** *(Brit.)* „Überholen verboten"; ~'**throw 1.** [--'-] *v. t., forms as* **throw** 1 stürzen; **2.** ['---] *n.* Sturz, *der;* ~**time 1.** *n.* Überstunden; **2.** *adv.* **work ~time** Überstunden machen; ~**tone** *n. (fig.)* Unterton, *der*

overture ['əʊvətjʊə(r)] *n. (Mus.)* Ouvertüre, *die*

over: ~'**turn 1.** *v. t.* umstoßen; **2.** *v. i.* ⟨*Auto, Boot:*⟩ umkippen; ⟨*Boot:*⟩ kentern; ~**use** ⟨əʊˈjuːz⟩ *v. t.* zu oft verwenden; ~**weight** *adj.* übergewichtig ⟨*Person*⟩; **be ~weight** Übergewicht haben

overwhelm [əʊvəˈwelm] *v. t.* überwältigen. **over'whelming** *adj.* überwältigend

over: ~'**work 1.** *v. t.* mit Arbeit überlasten; **2.** *v. i.* sich überarbeiten; ~'**wrought** *adj.* überreizt

owe [əʊ] *v. t.,* **owing** ['əʊɪŋ] schulden; ~ **sb. sth.,** ~ **sth. to sb.** jmdm. etw. schulden; *(fig.)* jmdm. etw. verdanken.

owing ['əʊɪŋ] *pred. adj.* ausstehend; **be ~:** ausstehen. '**owing to** *prep.* wegen

owl [aʊl] *n.* Eule, *die*

own [əʊn] **1.** *adj.* eigen; **be sb.'s ~** |property| jmdm. selbst gehören; **a house/ideas of one's ~:** ein eigenes Haus/eigene Ideen; **on one's/its ~:** allein. **2.** *v. t.* besitzen; **be ~ed by sb.** jmdm. gehören. **own 'up** *v. i.* gestehen; ~ **up to sth.** etw. zugeben

'**owner** *n.* Besitzer, *der/*Besitzerin, *die; (of shop, hotel, firm, etc.)* Inhaber, *der/*Inhaberin, *die.* '**ownership** *n.* Besitz, *der*

ox [ɒks] n., pl. oxen ['ɒksn] Ochse, der
oxygen ['ɒksɪdʒən] n. Sauerstoff, der
oyster ['ɔɪstə(r)] n. Auster, die
oz. abbr. ounce|s|
ozone ['əʊʒəʊn] n. Ozon, das.
'ozone-friendly adj. ozonsicher;
(not using (CFCs) FCKW-frei. 'ozone
layer n. Ozonschicht, die

P

P, p [pi:] n. P, p, das
p. abbr. a) page S.; b) (Brit.) penny/
pence p
pace [peɪs] 1. n. a) (step) Schritt, der;
b) (speed) Tempo, das; keep ~ with
Schritt halten mit. 2. v.i. ~ up and
down auf und ab gehen. 3. v.t. auf-
und abgehen in (+ Dat.)
'pacemaker n. (Sport, Med.) Schritt-
macher, der
Pacific [pə'sɪfɪk] 1. adj. (Geog.) ~
Ocean Pazifischer od. Stiller Ozean.
2. n. the ~: der Pazifik
pacifier ['pæsɪfaɪə(r)] n. (Amer.:
dummy) Schnuller, der
pacifism ['pæsɪfɪzm] n. Pazifismus,
der. pacifist ['pæsɪfɪst] 1. n. Pazifist,
der/Pazifistin, die. 2. adj. pazifistisch
pacify ['pæsɪfaɪ] v.t. besänftigen
pack [pæk] 1. n. a) (bundle) Bündel,
das; (Mil.) Tornister, der; (rucksack)
Rucksack, der; b) (derog.: lot) (people)
Bande, die; a ~ of lies/nonsense ein
Sack voll Lügen/eine Menge Unsinn;
c) (Brit.) ~ |of cards| [Karten]spiel,
das; d) (wolves, wild dogs) Rudel, das;
(hounds) Meute, die; e) (packet)
Packung, die. 2. v.t. a) einpacken;
(fill) packen; ~ one's bags seine Koffer packen; b) (cram) vollstopfen
(ugs.); c) (wrap) verpacken (in in +
Dat. od. Akk.). 3. v.i packen; send sb.
~ing (fig.) jmdn. rausschmeißen
(ugs.). pack 'up 1. v.t. zusammen-
packen (Sachen, Werkzeug); packen
(Paket). 2. v.i. (coll.: stop) aufhören
package ['pækɪdʒ] 1. n. Paket, das. 2.
v.t. verpacken
package: ~ deal n. Paket, das; ~

holiday, ~ tour ns. Pauschalreise,
die
packed [pækt] adj. a) gepackt; ~
lunch Lunchpaket, das; b) (crowded)
[über]voll; ~ out gerammelt voll (ugs.)
packet ['pækɪt] n. Päckchen, das;
(box) Schachtel, die; a ~ of cigarettes
ein Päckchen/eine Schachtel Zigaretten
'packing n. (material) Verpackungs-
material, das; postage and ~: Porto
und Verpackung. 'packing-case n.
[Pack]kiste, die
pact [pækt] n. Pakt, der
¹pad [pæd] 1. n. Polster, das; (block of
paper) Block, der. 2. v.t., -dd- polstern (Jacke, Schulter). pad 'out v.t.
(fig.) auswalzen
²pad v.i., -dd- tappen
padding ['pædɪŋ] n. Polsterung, die;
(fig.) Füllsel, das
¹paddle ['pædl] 1. n. [Stech]paddel,
das. 2. v.t. & i. paddeln
²paddle 1. v.i. (with feet) planschen.
2. n. have a/go for a ~: ein bißchen planschen/planschen gehen.
paddling-pool ['pædlɪŋpu:l] n.
Planschbecken, das
paddock ['pædək] n. Koppel, die
'padlock 1. n. Vorhängeschloß, das.
2. v.t. [mit einem Vorhängeschloß]
verschließen
pagan ['peɪgən] 1. n. Heide, der/Hei-
din, die. 2. adj. heidnisch
¹page [peɪdʒ] n. (boy) Page, der
²page n. (of book etc.) Seite, die
pageant ['pædʒənt] n. (spectacle)
Schauspiel, das. pageantry ['pæ-
dʒəntri] n. Prunk, der
paid [peɪd] 1. see pay 2, 3. 2. adj. a) bezahlt (Urlaub, Arbeit); b) put ~ to
(Brit. coll.) zunichte machen; kurzen
Prozeß machen mit (ugs.) (Person)
pail [peɪl] n. Eimer, der
pain [peɪn] n. a) (suffering) Schmerzen; (mental ~) Qualen; be in ~:
Schmerzen haben; b) (instance)
Schmerz, der; I have a ~ in my knee/
stomach mein Knie/Magen tut weh; c)
in pl. (trouble taken) Mühe, die; take
~s sich (Dat.) Mühe geben (over mit,
bei). painful ['peɪnfl] adj. a) schmerzhaft; be ~ (Körperteil:) weh tun; b)
(distressing) schmerzlich (Gedanke,
Erinnerung); traurig (Pflicht). 'pain-
killer n. schmerzstillendes Mittel.
'painless adj. schmerzlos; (fig.) un-
problematisch. painstaking ['peɪnz-
teɪkɪŋ] adj. gewissenhaft

paint [peint] **1.** *n.* Farbe, *die; (on car)* Lack, *der.* **2.** *v. t. (cover, colour)* [an]streichen; *(make picture of, make by ~ing)* malen; bemalen ⟨*Wand, Vase, Decke*⟩. **'paintbox** *n.* Malkasten, *der;* **~brush** *n.* Pinsel, *der*

'painter *n.* Maler, *der/*Malerin, *die*

'painting *n. (art)* Malerei, *die; (picture)* Gemälde, *das;* Bild, *das*

pair [peə(r)] **1.** *n.* Paar, *das;* **a ~ of gloves/socks/shoes** *etc.* ein Paar Handschuhe/Socken/Schuhe *usw.;* **in ~s** paarweise; **a ~ of trousers/jeans** eine Hose/Jeans. **2.** *v. t.* paaren. **pair 'off** *v. i.* Zweiergruppen bilden

pajamas [pə'dʒɑːməz] *(Amer.) see* **pyjamas**

Pakistan [pɑːkɪ'stɑːn] *pr. n.* Pakistan *(das).* **Pakistani** [pɑːkɪ'stɑːnɪ] **1.** *adj.* pakistanisch. **2.** *n.* Pakistani, *der/die*

pal [pæl] *n. (coll.)* Kumpel, *der (ugs.)*

palace ['pælɪs] *n.* Palast, *der*

palate ['pælət] *n.* Gaumen, *der*

palatial [pə'leɪʃl] *adj.* palaststartig

¹pale [peɪl] *adj.* blaß, *(nearly white)* bleich ⟨*Gesichtsfarbe, Haut, Gesicht*⟩; blaß ⟨*Farbe*⟩; fahl ⟨*Licht*⟩; **go ~:** blaß/ bleich werden; *(fig.)* **~ imitation** schlechte Nachahmung

²pale *n.* **beyond the ~:** unmöglich

Palestine ['pælɪstaɪn] *pr. n.* Palästina *(das).* **Palestinian** [pælɪ'stɪnɪən] **1.** *adj.* palästinensisch. **2.** *n.* Palästinenser, *der/*Palästinenserin, *die*

palette ['pælɪt] *n.* Palette, *die*

¹pall [pɔːl] *n.* **a)** *(over coffin)* Sargtuch, *das;* **b)** *(fig.)* Schleier, *der*

²pall *v. i.* **~ [on sb.]** [jmdm.] langweilig werden

pallor ['pælə(r)] *n.* Blässe, *die*

¹palm [pɑːm] *n. (tree)* Palme, *die*

²palm *n.* Handteller, *der.* **palm 'off** *v. t.* **~ sth. off on sb., ~ sb. off with sth.** jmdm. etw. andrehen *(ugs.)*

palmistry ['pɑːmɪstrɪ] *n.* Handlesekunst, *die*

palm: P~ 'Sunday *n.* Palmsonntag, *der;* **~-tree** *n.* Palme, *die*

paltry ['pɔːltrɪ, 'pɒltrɪ] *adj.* schäbig

pamper ['pæmpə(r)] *v. t.* verhätscheln; **~ oneself** sich verwöhnen

pamphlet ['pæmflɪt] *n. (leaflet)* Prospekt, *der; (booklet)* Broschüre, *die*

pan [pæn] *n.* [Koch]topf, *der; (for frying)* Pfanne, *die*

panacea [pænə'sɪə] *n.* Allheilmittel, *das*

Panama [pænə'mɑː] *pr. n.* Panama *(das);* **~ Ca'nal** Panamakanal, *der*

'pancake *n.* Pfannkuchen, *der*

panda ['pændə] *n.* Panda, *der*

pandemonium [pændɪ'məʊnɪəm] *n.* Chaos, *das; (uproar)* Tumult, *der*

pander ['pændə(r)] *v. i.* **~ to** allzu sehr entgegenkommen (+ *Dat.*)

pane [peɪn] *n.* Scheibe, *die*

panel ['pænl] *n.* **a)** Paneel, *das;* **b)** *(esp. Telev., Radio, etc.) (quiz team)* Rateteam, *das; (in public discussion)* Podium, *das*

pang [pæŋ] *n. (of pain)* Stich, *der;* **feel ~s of conscience/guilt** Gewissensbisse haben; **~[s] of hunger** quälender Hunger

panic ['pænɪk] **1.** *n.* Panik, *die;* **hit the ~ button** *(fig. coll.)* Alarm schlagen; *(~)* durchdrehen *(ugs.).* **2.** *v. i.,* **-ck-** in Panik *(Akk.)* geraten; **don't ~!** nur keine Panik! **'panic-stricken, 'panic-struck** *adjs.* von Panik erfaßt

panorama [pænə'rɑːmə] *n.* Panorama, *das*

pansy ['pænzɪ] *n.* Stiefmütterchen, *das*

pant [pænt] *v. i.* keuchen; ⟨*Hund:*⟩ hecheln

panther ['pænθə(r)] *n.* Panther, *der*

panties ['pæntɪz] *n. pl. (coll.)* **[pair of] ~:** Schlüpfer, *der*

pantomime ['pæntəmaɪm] *n. (Brit.) Märchenspiel im Varietéstil, das um Weihnachten aufgeführt wird*

pantry ['pæntrɪ] *n.* Speisekammer, *die*

pants [pænts] *n. pl.* **a)** *(esp. Amer. coll.: trousers)* **[pair of] ~:** Hose, *die;* **b)** *(Brit. coll.: underpants)* Unterhose, *die*

paper ['peɪpə(r)] **1.** *n.* **a)** *(material)* Papier, *das;* **b)** *in pl. (documents)* Unterlagen *Pl.; (to prove identity etc.)* Papiere *Pl.;* **c)** *(in examination) (Univ.)* Klausur, *die; (Sch.)* Arbeit, *die;* **d)** *(newspaper)* Zeitung, *die;* **e)** *(learned article)* Referat, *das.* **2.** *adj.* aus Papier *nachgestellt;* Papier⟨*mütze, -taschentuch*⟩. **3.** *v. t.* tapezieren

paper: ~back 1. *n.* Paperback, *das;* **2.** *adj.* **~back book** Paperback, *das;* **~ 'bag** *n.* Papiertüte, *die;* **~-clip** *n.* Büroklammer, *die; (larger)* Aktenklammer, *die;* **~weight** *n.* Briefbeschwerer, *der;* **~work** *n.* Schreibarbeit, *die*

par [pɑː(r)] *n.* **feel below ~:** nicht ganz auf dem Posten sein *(ugs.);* **be on a ~ with sb./sth.** jmdm./einer Sache gleichkommen

parable ['pærəbl] *n.* Gleichnis, *das*

parachute ['pærəʃuːt] **1.** *n.* Fallschirm, *der.* **2.** *v. i.* ⟨*Truppen:*⟩ abspringen (**into** über + *Dat.*)

parade [pə'reɪd] 1. *n.* **a)** *(display)* Zurschaustellung, *die;* **b)** *(Mil.)* Appell, *der;* **c)** *(procession)* Umzug, *der; (of troops)* Parade, *die.* **2.** *v. t.* zur Schau stellen. **3.** *v. i.* paradieren
paradise ['pærədaɪs] *n.* Paradies, *das*
paradox ['pærədɒks] *n.* Paradox[on], *das.* **paradoxical** [pærə'dɒksɪkl] *adj.* paradox
paraffin ['pærəfɪn] *n.* Paraffin, *das; (Brit.: fuel)* Petroleum, *das*
paragon ['pærəgən] Muster, *das* (of an + *Dat.*); ~ of virtue Tugendheld, *der*
paragraph ['pærəgrɑːf] *n.* Absatz, *der*
parallel ['pærəlel] **1.** *adj.* parallel; *(fig.: similar)* vergleichbar; ~ **bars** Barren, *der.* **2.** *n.* Parallele, *die;* ~ |of **latitude**| Breitenkreis, *der*
paralyse ['pærəlaɪz] *v. t.* lähmen; *(fig.)* lahmlegen 〈*Verkehr, Industrie*〉. **paralysis** [pə'rælɪsɪs] *n.* Lähmung, *die*
paralyze *(Amer.) see* **paralyse**
paramount ['pærəmaʊnt] *adj.* größt... 〈*Wichtigkeit*〉; Haupt〈*überlegung*〉; be ~: Vorrang haben
paranoia [pærə'nɔɪə] *n.* Paranoia, *die (Med.); (tendency)* Verfolgungswahn, *der.* **paranoid** ['pærənɔɪd] *adj.* be ~ 〈*Person:*〉 an Verfolgungswahn leiden
parapet ['pærəpɪt] *n.* Brüstung, *die*
paraphernalia [pærəfə'neɪlɪə] *n. sing.* Apparat, *der*
paraphrase ['pærəfreɪz] **1.** *n.* Umschreibung, *die.* **2.** *v. t.* umschreiben
parasite ['pærəsaɪt] *n.* Schmarotzer, *der.* **parasitic** [pærə'sɪtɪk] *adj.* **a)** *(Biol.)* parasitisch; **b)** *(fig.)* schmarotzerhaft
parasol ['pærəsɒl] *n.* Sonnenschirm, *der*
paratroops ['pærətruːps] *n. pl.* Fallschirmjäger *Pl.*
parcel ['pɑːsl] *n.* Paket, *das*
parched [pɑːtʃt] *adj.* ausgedörrt; trocken 〈*Lippen*〉
parchment ['pɑːtʃmənt] *n.* Pergament, *das*
pardon ['pɑːdn] **1.** *n.* Verzeihung, *die;* beg sb.'s ~: jmdn. um Entschuldigung bitten; **I beg your** ~: entschuldigen Sie bitte. **2.** *v. t.* **a)** ~ **sb.** |for| **sth.** jmdm. etw. verzeihen; **b)** *(excuse)* entschuldigen. **pardonable** ['pɑːdənəbl] *adj.* verzeihlich
pare [peə(r)] *v. t. (trim)* schneiden; *(peel)* schälen
parent ['peərənt] *n.* Elternteil, *der;* ~s Eltern *Pl.*

parenthesis [pə'renθɪsɪs] *n., pl.* **parentheses** [pə'renθɪsiːz] *(bracket)* runde Klammer
Paris ['pærɪs] *pr. n.* Paris *(das)*
parish ['pærɪʃ] *n.* Gemeinde, *die.* **parishioner** [pə'rɪʃənə(r)] *n.* Gemeinde[mit]glied, *das*
park [pɑːk] **1.** *n.* Park, *der.* **2.** *v. i.* parken. **3.** *v. t.* abstellen; parken 〈*Kfz*〉; a ~ed **car** ein parkendes Auto. 'parking *n.* Parken, *das;* 'No ~' „Parken verboten"
parking: ~-light *n.* Parkleuchte, *die;* ~-lot *n. (Amer.)* Parkplatz, *der;* ~-meter *n.* Parkuhr, *die;* ~-space *n.* **a)** *no pl.* Parkraum, *der;* **b)** *(single space)* Parkplatz, *der;* ~-ticket *n.* Strafzettel [für falsches Parken]
parliament ['pɑːləmənt] *n.* Parlament, *das;* |Houses of| P~ *(Brit.)* Parlament, *das.* **parliamentary** [pɑːlə'mentərɪ] *adj.* parlamentarisch; Parlaments〈*geschäfte, -wahlen, -reform*〉
parlour *(Brit.; Amer.:* **parlor)** ['pɑːlə(r)] *n. (dated)* Wohnzimmer, *das*
parochial [pə'rəʊkɪəl] *adj.* krähwinklig
parody ['pærədɪ] **1.** *n.* Parodie, *die* (of auf + *Akk.*). **2.** *v. t.* parodieren
parole [pə'rəʊl] *n.* bedingter Straferlaß *(Rechtsw.);* on ~: auf Bewährung
parquet ['pɑːkɪ, 'pɑːkeɪ] *n.* ~ |floor/flooring| Parkett, *das*
parrot ['pærət] *n.* Papagei, *der*
parry ['pærɪ] *v. t.* abwehren 〈*Faustschlag*〉; *(Fencing; also fig.)* parieren
parsley ['pɑːslɪ] *n.* Petersilie, *die*
parsnip ['pɑːsnɪp] *n.* Gemeiner Pastinak, *der*
parson ['pɑːsn] *n.* Pfarrer, *der*
part [pɑːt] **1.** *n.* **a)** Teil, *der;* **the greater** ~: der größte Teil; der Großteil; **for the most** ~: größtenteils; **in** ~: teilweise; **in large** ~: groß[en]teils; **in** ~s zum Teil; **b)** *(of machine)* [Einzel]teil, *das;* **c)** *(share)* Anteil, *der;* **d)** *(Theatre)* Rolle, *die;* **e)** *(Mus.)* Part, *der;* Stimme, *die;* **f)** *usu. in pl. (region)* Gegend, *die; (of continent, world)* Teil, *der;* **g)** *(side)* Partei, *die;* **take sb.'s** ~: jmds. *od.* für jmdn. Partei ergreifen; **h) take** |no| ~ |in sth.| sich [an etw. *(Dat.)*] [nicht] beteiligen; **i) take sth. in good** ~: etw. nicht übelnehmen. **2.** *adv.* teils. **3.** *v. i.* **a)** *(divide into* ~s*)* teilen; scheiteln 〈*Haar*〉; **b)** *(separate)* trennen. **4.** *v. i.* 〈*Seil, Tau, Kette:*〉 reißen; 〈*Wege, Personen:*〉 sich trennen; ~ **with** sich trennen von 〈*Besitz, Geld*〉

partial ['pɑːʃl] *adj.* **a)** *(biased)* voreingenommen; **b) be/not be ~ to sth.** eine
Schwäche/keine besondere Vorliebe
für etw. haben; **c)** partiell ⟨*Lähmung,
Sonnenfinsternis*⟩; **a ~ success** ein
Teilerfolg. '**partially** *adv.* teilweise
participant [pɑːˈtɪsɪpənt] *n.* Beteilig-
te, *der/die* (**in an +** *Dat.*)
participate [pɑːˈtɪsɪpeɪt] *v.i.* sich beteiligen (**in an +** *Dat.*); *(in arranged
event)* teilnehmen (**in an +** *Dat.*).
participation [pɑːtɪsɪˈpeɪʃn] *n.* Beteiligung, *die* (**in an +** *Dat.*); *(in arranged event)* Teilnahme, *die* (**in bei,
an +** *Dat.*)
participle ['pɑːtɪsɪpl] *n.* Partizip, *das*
particle ['pɑːtɪkl] *n.* Teilchen, *das*
particular [pəˈtɪkjʊlə(r)] **1.** *adj.* **a)** besonder...; **here in ~:** besonders hier;
nothing/anything [**in**] **~:** nichts/irgend
etwas Besonderes; **b)** *(fastidious)* genau; **I am not ~:** es ist mir gleich; **be ~
about sth.** es mit etw. genau nehmen.
2. *n., in pl.* Einzelheiten; Details; *(of
person)* Personalien *Pl.* **par'ticularly**
adv. besonders
'**parting 1.** *n.* **a)** [*final*] **~:** Abschied,
der; **b)** *(Brit.: in hair)* Scheitel, *der.* **2.**
attrib. adj. Abschieds-
partisan ['pɑːtɪzæn] *n.* Partisan,
der/Partisanin, *die*
partition [pɑːˈtɪʃn] **1.** *n.* **a)** *(Polit.)* Teilung, *die;* **b)** *(room-divider)* Trenn-
wand, *die.* **2.** *v.t.* **a)** *(divide)* aufteilen
⟨*Land, Zimmer*⟩; **b)** *(Polit.)* teilen
⟨*Land*⟩. **partition 'off** *v.t.* abteilen
'**partly** *adv.* zum Teil; teilweise
partner ['pɑːtnə(r)] *n.* Partner,
der/Partnerin, *die.* '**partnership** *n.*
Partnerschaft, *die;* **business ~:** [Perso-
nen]gesellschaft, *die*
partridge ['pɑːtrɪdʒ] *n., pl. same or ~s*
Rebhuhn, *das*
part-time 1. ['--] *adj.* Teilzeit⟨*arbeit,
-arbeiter*⟩. **2.** [-'-] *adv.* stundenweise,
halbtags ⟨*arbeiten, studieren*⟩
party ['pɑːtɪ] *n.* **a)** *(Polit., Law)* Partei,
die; attrib. Partei-; **b)** *(group)* Gruppe,
die; **c)** *(social gathering)* Party, *die*
pass [pɑːs] **1.** *n.* **a)** *(passing of an examination)* bestandene Prüfung; '**~'**
(mark) Ausreichend, *das;* **get a ~ in**
maths die Mathematikprüfung bestehen; **b)** *(written permission)* Ausweis,
der; **c)** *(Footb.)* Paß, *der (fachspr.);*
Ballabgabe, *die;* **d)** *(in mountains)*
Paß, *der.* **2.** *v.i.* **a)** *(go by)* ⟨*Fußgänger:*⟩ vorbeigehen; ⟨*Fahrer,
Fahrzeug:*⟩ vorbeifahren; ⟨*Zeit, Se-*

kunde:⟩ vergehen; *(by chance)* ⟨*Person,
Fahrzeug:*⟩ vorbeikommen; **b)** *(come
to an end)* vorbeigehen; ⟨*Gewitter, Unwetter:*⟩ vorüberziehen; **c)** *(be accepted)* durchgehen (**as als, for** für); **d)**
(in exam) bestehen. **3.** *v.t.* **a)** ⟨*Fußgänger:*⟩ vorbeigehen an (**+** *Dat.*);
⟨*Fahrer, Fahrzeug:*⟩ vorbeifahren an
(**+** *Dat.*); *(by chance)* ⟨*Person,
Fahrzeug:*⟩ vorbeikommen an
(**+** *Dat.*); **b)** *(overtake)* vorbeifahren
an (**+** *Dat.*); **c)** bestehen ⟨*Prüfung*⟩; **d)**
(approve) verabschieden ⟨*Gesetzent-
wurf*⟩; annehmen ⟨*Vorschlag*⟩; bestehen lassen ⟨*Prüfungskandidaten*⟩; **e)**
(Footb. etc.) abgeben (**to an +** *Akk.*);
f) *(spend)* verbringen ⟨*Leben, Zeit,
Tag*⟩; **g)** *(hand)* **~ sb. sth.** jmdm. etw.
reichen *od.* geben; **h)** fällen ⟨*Urteil*⟩;
machen ⟨*Bemerkung*⟩; **i) ~ water** Wasser lassen. **pass a'way** *v.i.* *(euphem.)*
die Augen schließen *(verhüll.).* **pass
'off** *v.t.* **~ sth. off as sth.** etw. als etw.
ausgeben. **pass 'on** *v.t.* weitergeben
(**to an +** *Akk.*). **pass 'out** *v.i.* ohnmächtig werden. **pass 'up** *v.t.* entgehen lassen ⟨*Gelegenheit*⟩; ablehnen
⟨*Angebot*⟩
passable ['pɑːsəbl] *adj.* **a)** *(acceptable)* passabel; **b)** befahrbar ⟨*Straße*⟩
passage ['pæsɪdʒ] *n.* **a)** *(voyage)*
Überfahrt, *die;* **b)** *(way)* Durchgang,
der; (corridor) Korridor, *der;* **c)** *(part
of book etc.)* Textstelle, *die; (Mus.)*
Stelle, *die*
passenger ['pæsɪndʒə(r)] *n.* Passagier, *der; (on train)* Reisende, *der/die;
(on bus, in taxi)* Fahrgast, *der; (in car,
on motor cycle)* Mitfahrer, *der*/Mit-
fahrerin, *die; (in front seat of car)* Beifahrer, *der*/Beifahrerin, *die.* '**passenger seat** *n.* Beifahrersitz, *der*
passer-by [pɑːsəˈbaɪ] *n.* Passant, *der*/
Passantin, *die*
'**passing 1.** *n.* *(of time, years)* Lauf,
der; **in ~:** beiläufig ⟨*bemerken usw.*⟩.
2. *adj.* **a)** vorbeifahrend ⟨*Zug, Auto*⟩;
vorbeikommend ⟨*Person*⟩; **b)** flüchtig
⟨*Blick*⟩; vorübergehend ⟨*Mode, Interesse*⟩; flüchtig ⟨*Bekanntschaft*⟩
passion ['pæʃn] *n.* Leidenschaft, *die;
(enthusiasm)* leidenschaftliche Begeisterung; **he has a ~ for steam engines**
Dampfloks sind seine Leidenschaft.
passionate ['pæʃənət] *adj.* leidenschaftlich; heftig ⟨*Verlangen*⟩
passive ['pæsɪv] **1.** *adj.* **a)** passiv; **b)**
(Ling.) Passiv-. **2.** *n.* *(Ling.)* Passiv,
das

pass: ~port *n.* **a)** [Reise]paß, *der; attrib.* Paß-; **b)** *(fig.)* Schlüssel, *der* (**to** zu); **~word** *n.* **a)** Parole, *die;* Losung, *die;* **b)** *(Computing)* Paßwort, *das*

past [pɑːst] **1.** *adj.* **a)** *pred. (over)* vorbei; **b)** *attrib. (previous)* früher; vergangen; ehemalig ⟨*Präsident, Vorsitzende usw.*⟩; **c)** *attrib. (just gone by)* letzt...; vergangen; **in the ~ few days** während der letzten Tage; **d)** *(Ling.)* **~ tense** Vergangenheit, *die.* **2.** *n.* Vergangenheit, *die;* **in the ~:** früher; in der Vergangenheit ⟨*leben*⟩; **be a thing of the ~:** der Vergangenheit angehören. **3.** *prep. (in time)* nach; *(in place)* hinter (+ *Dat.*); **half ~ three** halb vier; **five |minutes| ~ two** fünf [Minuten] nach zwei; **gaze/walk ~ sb./sth.** an jmdm./etw. vorbeiblicken/vorbeigehen; **~ repair** nicht mehr zu reparieren. **4.** *adv.* vorbei; **hurry ~:** vorübereilen

pasta ['pæstə] *n.* Nudeln *Pl.*

paste [peɪst] **1.** *n.* **a)** Brei, *der;* **b)** *(glue)* Kleister, *der;* **c)** *(of meat, fish, etc.)* Paste, *die.* **2.** *v. t.* kleben; **~ sth. into sth.** etw. in etw. *(Akk.)* einkleben

pastel ['pæstl] **1.** *n. (crayon)* Pastellstift, *der.* **2.** *adj.* pastellfarben; Pastell⟨*farben, -töne, -zeichnung*⟩

pasteurize ['pɑːstʃəraɪz] *v. t.* pasteurisieren

pastille ['pæstɪl] *n.* Pastille, *die*

pastime ['pɑːstaɪm] *n.* Zeitvertreib, *der; (person's specific ~)* Hobby, *das*

pastor ['pɑːstə(r)] *n.* Pfarrer, *der/*Pfarrerin, *die;* Pastor, *der/*Pastorin, *die*

pastoral ['pɑːstərl] *adj.* Weide-; ländlich ⟨*Reiz, Idylle, Umgebung*⟩

pastry ['peɪstrɪ] *n.* Teig, *der; (article of food)* Gebäckstück, *das;* **pastries** *collect.* [Fein]gebäck, *das*

pasture ['pɑːstʃə(r)] *n.* Weide, *die*

pasty ['pæstɪ] *n.* Pastete, *die*

¹pat [pæt] **1.** *n.* **a)** *(tap)* Klaps, *der;* **b)** *(of butter)* Stückchen, *das.* **2.** *v. t.,* **-tt-** leicht klopfen auf (+ *Akk.*); tätscheln, *(once)* einen Klaps geben (+ *Dat.*) ⟨*Person, Hund, Pferd*⟩; **~ sb. on the arm/head** jmdm. den Arm/Kopf tätscheln

²pat *adv.* **have sth. off ~:** etw. parat haben

patch [pætʃ] **1.** *n.* **a)** Stelle, *die;* **fog ~es** Nebelfelder; **b)** *(on worn garment)* Flicken, *der;* **be not a ~ on sth.** *(fig. coll.)* nichts gegen etw. sein. **2.** *v. t.* flicken. **patch 'up** *v. t.* reparieren; *(fig.)* beilegen ⟨*Streit*⟩

patchy ['pætʃɪ] *adj.* uneinheitlich ⟨*Qualität*⟩; ungleichmäßig ⟨*Arbeit*⟩; sehr lückenhaft ⟨*Wissen*⟩

pâté ['pæteɪ] *n.* Pastete, *die*

patent ['peɪtənt, 'pætənt] **1.** *adj. (obvious)* offenkundig. **2.** *n.* Patent, *das.* **3.** *v. t.* patentieren lassen. **patent 'leather** *n.* Lackleder, *das;* **~ shoes** Lackschuhe. '**patently** *adv.* offenkundig; **~ obvious** ganz offenkundig

paternal [pə'tɜːnl] *adj.* väterlich

path [pɑːθ] *n.* Weg, *der; (line of motion)* Bahn, *die*

pathetic [pə'θetɪk] *adj.* **a)** *(pitiful)* mitleiderregend; **b)** *(contemptible)* armselig ⟨*Entschuldigung*⟩; erbärmlich ⟨*Person, Leistung*⟩

'**pathway** *n.* Weg, *der*

patience ['peɪʃəns] *n.* Geduld, *die*

patient ['peɪʃənt] **1.** *adj.* geduldig. **2.** *n.* Patient, *der/*Patientin, *die.* '**patiently** *adv.* geduldig

patio ['pætɪəʊ] *n., pl.* **~s** Veranda, *die;* Terrasse, *die*

patriot ['peɪtrɪət] *n.* Patriot, *der/*Patriotin, *die.* **patriotic** [peɪtrɪ'ɒtɪk] *adj.* patriotisch. **patriotism** ['peɪtrɪətɪzm] *n.* Patriotismus, *der*

patrol [pə'trəʊl] **1.** *n. (Police)* Streife, *die; (Mil.)* Patrouille, *die;* **be on ~:** patrouillieren. **2.** *v. i.,* **-ll-** patrouillieren; ⟨*Polizei:*⟩ Streife laufen/fahren. **3.** *v. t.,* **-ll-** patrouillieren durch (+ *Akk.*); abpatrouillieren ⟨*Straßen, Gegend, Lager*⟩; patrouillieren vor (+ *Dat.*) ⟨*Küste, Grenze*⟩; ⟨*Polizei:*⟩ Streife laufen/fahren in (+ *Dat.*) ⟨*Straßen, Stadtteil*⟩. **pa'trol boat** *n.* Patrouillenboot, *das.* **pa'trol car** *n.* Streifenwagen, *der*

patron ['peɪtrən] *n.* **a)** Gönner, *der/*Gönnerin, *die; (of institution, campaign)* Schirmherr, *der/*Schirmherrin, *die;* **b)** *(customer) (of shop)* Kunde, *der/*Kundin, *die; (of restaurant, hotel)* Gast, *der; (of theatre, cinema)* Besucher, *der/*Besucherin, *die;* **c)** **~ |saint|** Schutzheilige, *der/die.* **patronage** ['pætrənɪdʒ] *n.* Gönnerschaft, *die; (for campaign, institution)* Schirmherrschaft, *die*

patronize ['pætrənaɪz] *v. t.* **a)** *(frequent)* besuchen; **b)** *(condescend to)* **~ sb.** jmdn. herablassend behandeln. **patronizing** ['pætrənaɪzɪŋ] *adj.* gönnerhaft; herablassend

patter ['pætə(r)] **1.** *n. (of rain)* Prasseln, *das; (of feet)* Trappeln, *das.* **2.** *v. i.* ⟨*Regen:*⟩ prasseln

pattern ['pætən] *n.* Muster, *das;* *(model)* Vorlage, *die;* *(for sewing)* Schnittmuster, *das;* *(for knitting)* Strickmuster, *das*

paunch [pɔːntʃ] *n.* Bauch, *der*

pauper ['pɔːpə(r)] *n.* Arme, *der/die*

pause [pɔːz] **1.** *n.* Pause, *die.* **2.** *v. i.* eine Pause machen; ⟨*Redner:*⟩ innehalten; *(hesitate)* zögern

pave [peɪv] *v. t.* befestigen; *(with stones)* pflastern; ~ **the way for sth.** *(fig.)* einer Sache *(Dat.)* den Weg ebnen. '**pavement** *n.* **a)** *(Brit.: footway)* Bürgersteig, *der;* **b)** *(Amer.: roadway)* Fahrbahn, *die*

pavilion [pə'vɪljən] *n.* Pavillon, *der;* *(Brit. Sport)* Klubhaus, *das*

paw [pɔː] *n.* Pfote, *die; (of bear, lion, tiger)* Pranke, *die*

¹**pawn** [pɔːn] *n.* *(Chess)* Bauer, *der;* *(fig.)* Schachfigur, *die*

²**pawn** **1.** *n.* Pfand, *das;* **in** ~: verpfändet. **2.** *v. t.* verpfänden. '**pawnbroker** *n.* Pfandleiher, *der/*-leiherin, *die.* '**pawnshop** *n.* Leihhaus, *das*

pay [peɪ] **1.** *n.* *(wages)* Lohn, *der;* *(salary)* Gehalt, *das;* **be in the** ~ **of sb./ sth.** für jmdn./etw. arbeiten. **2.** *v. t.,* **paid** [peɪd] bezahlen; zahlen ⟨*Geld*⟩; ~ **sb. to do sth.** jmdn. dafür bezahlen, daß er etw. tut; ~ **sb. £10** jmdm. 10 Pfund zahlen. **3.** *v. i.,* **paid a)** zahlen; ~ **for sth./sb.** etw./für jmdn. bezahlen; **sth.** ~**s for itself** etw. macht sich bezahlt; **b)** *(be profitable)* sich lohnen; ⟨*Geschäft:*⟩ rentabel sein; **it** ~**s to be careful** es lohnt sich, vorsichtig zu sein. *See also* **paid. pay** '**back** *v. t.* zurückzahlen; **I'll** ~ **you back later** ich gebe dir das Geld später zurück. **pay** '**in** *v. t.* einzahlen. **pay** '**off** *v. t.* auszahlen ⟨*Arbeiter*⟩; abbezahlen ⟨*Schulden*⟩; ablösen ⟨*Hypothek*⟩; befriedigen ⟨*Gläubiger*⟩. **pay** '**out** *v. t.* auszahlen; *(spend)* ausgeben. **pay** '**up** *v. i.* zahlen

payable ['peɪəbl] *adj.* zahlbar; **be** ~ **to sb.** an jmdn. zu zahlen sein; **make a cheque** ~ **to the Post Office/to sb.** einen Scheck auf die Post/auf jmds. Namen ausstellen

payee [peɪ'iː] *n.* Zahlungsempfänger, *der/*-empfängerin, *die*

'**payment** *n.* **a)** *(of sum, bill, debt, fine)* Bezahlung, *die; (of interest, instalment, tax, fee)* Zahlung, *die;* **in** ~ [**for sth.**] als Bezahlung [für etw.]; **b)** *(amount)* Zahlung, *die*

pay: ~-**packet** *n.* *(Brit.)* Lohntüte,

die; ~ **phone** *n.* Münzfernsprecher, *der;* ~-**rise** *n.* Lohn-/Gehaltserhöhung, *die;* ~-**roll** *n.* Lohnliste, *die;* **be on sb.'s** ~**roll** für jmdn. arbeiten; ~-**slip** *n.* Lohnstreifen, *der/*Gehaltszettel, *der;* ~ **station** *n.* *(Amer.) see* ~ **phone**

PC *abbr.* **a)** *(Brit.)* **police constable** Wachtm.; **b) personal computer** PC

PE *abbr.* **physical education**

pea [piː] *n.* Erbse, *die*

peace [piːs] *n.* Frieden, *der; (tranquillity)* Ruhe, *die;* ~ **of mind** Seelenfrieden, *der.* **peaceable** ['piːsəbl] *adj.* friedfertig; *(calm)* friedlich. **peaceful** ['piːsfl] *adj.* friedlich; friedfertig ⟨*Person, Volk*⟩. '**peacefully** *adv.* friedlich; **die** ~: sanft entschlafen

'**peacetime** *n.* Friedenszeiten *Pl.*

peach [piːtʃ] *n.* Pfirsich, *der*

'**peacock** *n.* Pfau, *der*

peak [piːk] **1.** *n.* **a)** *(of cap)* Schirm, *der;* **b)** *(of mountain)* Gipfel, *der; (fig.)* Höhepunkt, *der.* **2.** *attrib. adj.* Höchst-, Spitzen⟨*preise, -werte*⟩; ~-**hour traffic** Stoßverkehr, *der.* **peaked** [piːkt] *adj.* ~ **cap** Schirmmütze, *die*

peal [piːl] *n.* Läuten, *das;* ~ **of bells** Glockenläuten, *das;* **a** ~/~**s of laughter** schallendes Gelächter

peanut ['piːnʌt] *n.* Erdnuß, *die;* ~ **butter** Erdnußbutter, *die;* ~**s** *(coll.: little money)* ein paar Kröten *(salopp)*

pear [peə(r)] *n.* Birne, *die*

pearl [pɜːl] *n.* Perle, *die*

'**pear-tree** *n.* Birnbaum, *der*

peasant ['pezənt] *n.* [armer] Bauer, *der;* Landarbeiter, *der*

peat [piːt] *n.* Torf, *der*

pebble ['pebl] *n.* Kiesel[stein], *der*

peck [pek] **1.** *v. t.* hacken; picken ⟨*Körner*⟩. **2.** *v. i.* picken (**at** nach); ~ **at one's food** in seinem Essen herumstochern. **3.** *n.* *(kiss)* flüchtiger Kuß. '**pecking order** *n.* Hackordnung, *die*

peckish ['pekɪʃ] *adj.* *(coll.)* **feel/get** ~: Hunger haben/bekommen

peculiar [pɪ'kjuːlɪə(r)] *adj.* **a)** *(strange)* seltsam; **I feel [slightly]** ~: mir ist [etwas] komisch; **b)** *(especial)* besonder...; **c)** *(belonging exclusively)* eigentümlich (**to** *Dat.*). **peculiarity** [pɪkjuːlɪ'ærɪtɪ] *n.* **a)** *(odd trait)* Eigentümlichkeit, *die;* **b)** *(distinguishing characteristic)* [charakteristisches] Merkmal. **pe'culiarly** *adv.* **a)** *(strangely)* seltsam; **b)** *(especially)* besonders

pedal ['pedl] **1.** *n.* Pedal, *das.* **2.** *v. i.,*

(Brit.) **-ll-** in die Pedale treten.
'**pedal-bin** *n.* Treteimer, *der*
pedant ['pedǝnt] *n.* Pedant, *der*/Pedantin, *die.* **pedantic** [pɪ'dæntɪk] *adj.* pedantisch
peddle ['pedl] *v. t.* auf der Straße verkaufen; *(door to door)* hausieren mit
pedestal ['pedɪstl] *n.* Sockel, *der*
pedestrian [pɪ'destrɪǝn] **1.** *adj. (uninspired)* trocken; langweilig. **2.** *n.* Fußgänger, *der*/-gängerin, *die.* **pedestrian 'crossing** *n.* Fußgängerüberweg, *der*
pedigree ['pedɪgri:] **1.** *n.* Stammbaum, *der.* **2.** *adj.* mit Stammbaum *nachgestellt*
pedlar ['pedlǝ(r)] *n.* Straßenhändler, *der*/-händlerin, *die; (door to door)* Hausierer, *der*/Hausiererin, *die*
pee [pi:] *(coll.)* **1.** *v. i.* pinkeln *(salopp);* Pipi machen *(Kinderspr.).* **2.** *n.* **a) have a ~:** pinkeln *(salopp);* **b)** *(urine)* Pipi, *das (Kinderspr.)*
peek [pi:k] *see* ²**peep**
peel [pi:l] **1.** *v. t.* schälen. **2.** *v. i.* ⟨*Person, Haut:*⟩ sich schälen; ⟨*Farbe:*⟩ abblättern. **3.** *n.* Schale, *die.* '**peelings** *n. pl.* Schalen
¹**peep** [pi:p] **1.** *v. i.* ⟨*Maus, Vogel:*⟩ piep[s]en. **2.** *n.* Piepsen, *das; (coll.: remark etc.)* Piep[s], *der*
²**peep** **1.** *v. i.* gucken *(ugs.); (furtively)* verstohlen gucken *(ugs.).* **2.** *n.* kurzer/ verstohlener Blick. '**peep-hole** *n.* Guckloch, *das.* **peeping 'Tom** *n.* Spanner, *der (ugs.)*
¹**peer** [pɪǝ(r)] *n.* Peer, *der; (equal)* Gleichgestellte, *der/die*
²**peer** *v. i.* forschend schauen; *(with difficulty)* angestrengt schauen; **~ at sth./sb.** [sich *(Dat.)*] etw. genau ansehen/jmdn. forschend ansehen; *(with difficulty)* [sich *(Dat.)*] etw./jmdn. angestrengt ansehen
peerage ['pɪǝrɪdʒ] *n.* Peerswürde, *die*
peevish ['pi:vɪʃ] *adj.* nörgelig
peg [peg] *n. (for holding together)* Stift, *der; (for tying things to)* Pflock, *der; (for hanging things on)* Haken, *der; (clothes-~)* Wäscheklammer, *die; (tent-~)* Hering, *der;* **off the ~** *(Brit.: ready-made)* von der Stange *(ugs.)*
pejorative [pɪ'dʒɒrǝtɪv] *adj.,* **pe'joratively** *adv.* abwertend
pelican ['pelɪkǝn] *n.* Pelikan, *der.* '**pelican crossing** *n. (Brit.)* Ampelübergang, *der*
pellet ['pelɪt] *n.* Kügelchen, *das*
pelmet ['pelmɪt] *n.* Blende, *die*

¹**pelt** [pelt] *n.* Fell, *das*
²**pelt** **1.** *v. t.* **~ sb. with sth.** jmdn. mit etw. bewerfen. **2.** *v. i.* **a) it was ~ing down [with rain]** es goß wie aus Kübeln *(ugs.);* **b)** *(run fast)* rasen *(ugs.)*
pelvis ['pelvɪs] *n., pl.* **pelves** ['pelvi:z] *or* **~es** *(Anat.)* Becken, *das*
¹**pen** [pen] **1.** *n. (enclosure)* Pferch, *der.* **2.** *v. t.,* **-nn-:** **~ sb. in a corner** jmdn. in eine Ecke drängen. **pen 'in** *v. t.* einpferchen
²**pen** **1.** *n.* Federhalter, *der; (fountain-~)* Füller, *der; (ball-~)* Kugelschreiber, *der; (felt-tip ~)* Filzstift, *der.* **2.** *v. t.,* **-nn-** schreiben
penal ['pi:nl] *adj.* Straf-
penalize ['pi:nǝlaɪz] *v. t.* bestrafen; *(Sport)* eine Strafe verhängen gegen
penalty ['penltɪ] *n.* **a)** Strafe, *die;* **pay the ~/the ~ for** *or* **of sth.** dafür/für etw. büßen [müssen]; **b)** *(Footb.)* Elfmeter, *der*
penance ['penǝns] *n.* Buße, *die;* **act of ~:** Bußwerk, *das;* **do ~:** Buße tun
pence *see* **penny**
pencil ['pensɪl] **1.** *n.* Bleistift, *der;* **red/coloured ~:** Rot-/Buntstift, *der.* **2.** *v. t., (Brit.)* **-ll-** mit einem Bleistift/ Farbstift schreiben. '**pencil-case** *n.* Griffelkasten, *der; (of soft material)* Federmäppchen, *das.* '**pencil-sharpener** *n.* Bleistiftspitzer, *der*
pendant ['pendǝnt] *n.* Anhänger, *der*
pending ['pendɪŋ] **1.** *adj.* unentschieden ⟨*Angelegenheit, Sache*⟩; schwebend ⟨*Verfahren*⟩. **2.** *prep.* **~ his return** bis zu seiner Rückkehr
pendulum ['pendjʊlǝm] *n.* Pendel, *das*
penetrate ['penɪtreɪt] *v. t.* eindringen in (+ *Akk.*); *(pass through)* durchdringen. **penetrating** ['penɪtreɪtɪŋ] *adj.* durchdringend. **penetration** [penɪ'treɪʃn] *n.* Eindringen, *das* (**of** in + *Akk.*); *(passing through)* Durchdringen, *das*
'**pen-friend** *n.* Brieffreund, *der*/ -freundin, *die*
penguin ['peŋgwɪn] *n.* Pinguin, *der*
penicillin [penɪ'sɪlɪn] *n.* Penizillin, *das*
peninsula [pɪ'nɪnsjʊlǝ] *n.* Halbinsel, *die*
penis ['pi:nɪs] *n.* Penis, *der*
penitence ['penɪtǝns] *n.* Reue, *die*
penitent ['penɪtǝnt] *adj.* reuevoll *(geh.);* reuig *(geh.)* ⟨*Sünder*⟩
penitentiary [penɪ'tenʃǝrɪ] *n. (Amer.)* Straf[vollzugs]anstalt, *die*
'**penknife** *n.* Taschenmesser, *das*

pennant ['penənt] *n.* Wimpel, *der; (on official car etc.)* Ständer, *der*

penniless ['penɪlɪs] *adj.* mittellos

penny ['penɪ] *n., pl. usu.* **pennies** ['penɪz] *(for separate coins),* **pence** [pens] *(for sum of money)* Penny, *der;* **fifty pence** fünfzig Pence; **two/fifty pence [piece]** Zwei-/Fünfzigpencestück, *das*

pension ['penʃn] *n.* Rente, *die; (payment to retired civil servant also)* Pension, *die;* **be on a ~:** eine Rente beziehen; **widow's ~:** Witwenrente, *die.* **pension 'off** *v. t.* berenten *(Amtsspr.);* auf Rente setzen *(ugs.);* pensionieren ⟨*Lehrer, Beamten*⟩

'**pensioner** *n.* Rentner, *der*/Rentnerin, *die; (retired civil servant)* Pensionär, *der*/Pensionärin, *die*

pensive ['pensɪv] *adj.* nachdenklich

pentagon ['pentəgən] *n.* Fünfeck, *das*

pent: ~**house** *n.* Penthaus, *das;* ~**-up** *adj.* angestaut ⟨*Ärger, Wut*⟩; unterdrückt ⟨*Sehnsucht, Gefühle*⟩

penultimate [pe'nʌltɪmət] *adj.* vorletzt...

people ['piːpl] *n.* **a)** *constr. as pl.* Leute *Pl.;* Menschen; *(as opposed to animals)* Menschen *Pl.;* **city/country ~** *(inhabitants)* Stadt-/Landbewohner; **local ~:** Einheimische; **working ~:** arbeitende Menschen; **coloured/white ~:** Farbige/Weiße; **~ say ...:** man sagt ...; **a crowd of ~:** eine Menschenmenge; **b)** *(nation)* Volk, *das*

pepper ['pepə(r)] *n.* **a)** Pfeffer, *der;* **b)** *(vegetable)* Paprikaschote, *die;* **red/green ~:** roter/grüner Paprika. **2.** *v. t.* **a)** pfeffern; **b)** *(pelt)* bombardieren *(ugs.)*

pepper: ~**corn** *n.* Pfefferkorn, *das;* ~**mint** *n.* *(sweet)* Pfefferminz, *das;* ~**-pot** *n.* Pfefferstreuer, *der*

per [pə(r), *stressed* pɜː(r)] *prep.* pro

perceive [pə'siːv] *v. t.* wahrnehmen; *(with the mind)* spüren; ~**d** vermeintlich ⟨*Bedrohung, Gefahr, Wert*⟩

per cent (*Brit.; Amer.:* **percent**) [pə'sent] **1.** *adv.* **ninety ~ effective** zu 90 Prozent wirksam. **2.** *adj.* **a 5 ~ increase** ein Zuwachs von 5 Prozent. **3.** *n.* **a)** Prozent, *das;* **b)** *see* **percentage**

percentage [pə'sentɪdʒ] *n.* Prozentsatz, *der*

perceptible [pə'septɪbl] *adj.* wahrnehmbar

perception [pə'sepʃn] *n.* *(act)* Wahrnehmung, *die; (result)* Erkenntnis, *die; (faculty)* Wahrnehmungsvermögen, *das*

perceptive [pə'septɪv] *adj.* einfühlsam ⟨*Person, Bemerkung*⟩

perch [pɜːtʃ] **1.** *n.* Sitzstange, *die.* **2.** *v. i.* **a)** sich niederlassen; **b)** *(be supported)* sitzen. **3.** *v. t.* setzen/stellen/legen

percolate ['pɜːkəleɪt] *v. i.* [durch]sickern. **percolator** ['pɜːkəleɪtə(r)] *n.* Kaffeemaschine, *die*

percussion [pə'kʌʃn] *n.* *(Mus.)* Schlagzeug, *das;* ~ **instrument** Schlaginstrument, *das*

perennial [pə'renjəl] **1.** *adj.* **a)** *(Bot.)* ausdauernd; **b)** immer wieder auftretend ⟨*Problem*⟩. **2.** *n.* *(Bot.)* ausdauernde Pflanze

perfect 1. ['pɜːfɪkt] *adj.* vollkommen; perfekt ⟨*Englisch, Timing*⟩; tadellos ⟨*Zustand*⟩; *(coll.: unmitigated)* absolut; **a ~ stranger** ein völlig Fremder. **2.** [pə'fekt] *v. t.* vervollkommnen. **perfection** [pə'fekʃn] *n.* Perfektion, *die;* **to ~:** perfekt. **perfectionism** [pə'fekʃənɪzm] *n.* Perfektionismus, *der.* **perfectionist** [pə'fekʃənɪst] *n.* Perfektionist, *der*/Perfektionistin, *die.* '**perfectly** *adv.* **a)** *(completely)* vollkommen; **be ~ entitled to do sth.** durchaus berechtigt sein, etw. zu tun; **b)** *(faultlessly)* perfekt; tadellos ⟨*sich verhalten*⟩

perforate ['pɜːfəreɪt] *v. t.* perforieren; *(make opening into)* durchlöchern. **perforation** [pɜːfə'reɪʃn] *n.* **a)** *(hole)* Loch, *das;* **b)** *in pl.* ~**s** Perforation, *die; (in sheets of stamps)* Zähnung, *die*

perform [pə'fɔːm] **1.** *v. t.* ausführen ⟨*Arbeit, Operation*⟩; erfüllen ⟨*Pflicht, Aufgabe*⟩; vollbringen ⟨*[Helden]tat, Leistung*⟩; ausfüllen ⟨*Funktion*⟩; vollbringen ⟨*Wunder*⟩; anstellen ⟨*Berechnungen*⟩; durchführen ⟨*Experiment, Sektion*⟩; vorführen ⟨*Trick*⟩; aufführen ⟨*Theaterstück, Scharade*⟩; vortragen ⟨*Lied, Sonate usw.*⟩. **2.** *v. i.* eine Vorführung geben; *(sing)* singen; *(play)* spielen. **performance** [pə'fɔːməns] *n.* **a)** *(of duty, task)* Erfüllung, *die;* **b)** *[notable] achievement; Motor Veh.)* Leistung, *die;* **c)** *(at theatre, cinema, etc.)* Vorstellung, *die;* **her ~ as Desdemona** ihre Darstellung der Desdemona; **the ~ of a play/opera** die Aufführung eines Theaterstücks/einer Oper. **per'former** *n.* Künstler, *der*/Künstlerin, *die.* **per'forming** *attrib. adj.* dressiert ⟨*Tier*⟩

perfume ['pɜːfjuːm] *n.* Duft, *der; (fluid)* Parfüm, *das*

perfunctory [pə'fʌŋktərɪ] *adj.* ober-flächlich ⟨*Arbeit, Überprüfung*⟩; flüchtig ⟨*Erkundigung, Bemerkung*⟩
perhaps [pə'hæps] *adv.* vielleicht
peril ['perl] *n.* Gefahr, *die.* **perilous** ['perələs] *adj.* gefahrvoll; **be** ~: gefährlich sein
perimeter [pə'rɪmɪtə(r)] *n.* [äußere] Begrenzung; Grenze, *die*
period ['pɪərɪəd] **1.** *n.* **a)** *(of history or life)* Periode, *die;* Zeit, *die; (any portion of time)* Zeitraum, *der;* **the Classical/Romantic** ~: die Klassik/Romantik; **b)** *(Sch.)* Stunde, *die;* **chemistry/English** ~: Chemie-/Englischstunde, *die;* **c)** *(menstruation)* Periode, *die;* **d)** *(punctuation mark)* Punkt, *der.* **2.** *adj.* zeitgenössisch ⟨*Tracht, Kostüm*⟩; antik ⟨*Möbel*⟩. **periodic** [pɪərɪ-'ɒdɪk] *adj.* regelmäßig; *(intermittent)* gelegentlich. **periodical** [pɪərɪ'ɒdɪkl] **1.** *adj.* see **periodic. 2.** *n.* Zeitschrift, *die;* **weekly/monthly** ~: Wochenzeitschrift/Monatsschrift, *die.* **peri'odically** *adv.* regelmäßig; *(intermittently)* gelegentlich
peripheral [pə'rɪfərl] *adj.* peripher *(geh.);* Rand⟨*problem, -erscheinung*⟩
periphery [pə'rɪfərɪ] *n.* Peripherie, *die*
periscope ['perɪskəʊp] *n.* Periskop, *das*
perish ['perɪʃ] *v.i.* **a)** *(die)* umkommen; **b)** *(rot)* verderben; ⟨*Gummi:*⟩ altern. **perishable** ['perɪʃəbl] *adj.* [leicht] verderblich
'**perishing** *(coll.)* **1.** *adj.* mörderisch ⟨*Kälte*⟩; **it's/I'm** ~: es ist bitterkalt/ich komme um vor Kälte *(ugs.).* **2.** *adv.* mörderisch ⟨*kalt*⟩
perjury ['pɜːdʒərɪ] *n.* Meineid, *der;* **commit** ~: einen Meineid leisten
¹**perk** [pɜːk] *(coll.)* **1.** *v.i.* ~ **up** munter werden. **2.** *v.t.* ~ **up** aufmuntern
²**perk** *n. (Brit. coll.)* [Sonder]vergünstigung, *die*
perky ['pɜːkɪ] *adj.* lebhaft; munter
perm [pɜːm] **1.** *n.* Dauerwelle, *die.* **2.** *v.t.* **have one's hair** ~**ed** sich *(Dat.)* eine Dauerwelle machen lassen
permanence ['pɜːmənəns] *n.* Dauerhaftigkeit, *die*
permanent ['pɜːmənənt] *adj.* fest ⟨*Sitz, Bestandteil, Mitglied*⟩; ständig ⟨*Wohnsitz, Adresse, Kampf*⟩; Dauer⟨*stellung, -visum*⟩; bleibend ⟨*Schaden*⟩. '**permanently** *adv.* dauernd; auf Dauer ⟨*verhindern, bleiben*⟩
permeable ['pɜːmɪəbl] *adj.* durchlässig; **be** ~ **to sth.** etw. durchlassen

permeate ['pɜːmɪeɪt] **1.** *v.t.* dringen durch; **be** ~**d with** *or* **by sth.** *(fig.)* von etw. durchdrungen sein. **2.** *v.i.* ~ **through sth.** etw. durchdringen
permissible [pə'mɪsɪbl] *adj.* zulässig; **be** ~ **to** *or* **for sb.** jmdm. erlaubt sein
permission [pə'mɪʃn] *n.* Erlaubnis, *die; (given by official body)* Genehmigung, *die;* **give sb.** ~ **to do sth.** jmdm. erlauben, etw. zu tun
permissive [pə'mɪsɪv] *adj.* **the** ~ **society** die permissive Gesellschaft
permit 1. [pə'mɪt] *v.t.,* -**tt**- zulassen ⟨*Berufung, Einspruch usw.*⟩; ~ **sb. sth.** jmdm. etw. erlauben; **sb. is** ~**ted to do sth.** es ist jmdm. erlaubt, etw. zu tun. **2.** *v.i.,* -**tt**- es zulassen. **3.** ['pɜːmɪt] *n.* Genehmigung, *die*
pernicious [pə'nɪʃəs] *adj.* verderblich; bösartig ⟨*Krankheit*⟩
perpendicular [pɜːpən'dɪkjʊlə(r)] *adj.* senkrecht
perpetrate ['pɜːpɪtreɪt] *v.t.* begehen; verüben ⟨*Greuel*⟩
perpetual [pə'petjʊəl] *adj.* **a)** *(eternal)* ewig; **b)** *(continuous; coll.: repeated)* ständig. **per'petually** *adv.* **a)** *(eternally)* ewig; **b)** *(continuously; coll.: repeatedly)* ständig
perpetuate [pə'petjʊeɪt] *v.t.* aufrechterhalten
perplex [pə'pleks] *v.t.* verwirren. **perplexed** [pə'plekst] *adj.* verwirrt; *(puzzled)* ratlos. **perplexity** [pə'pleksɪtɪ] *n.* Verwirrung, *die; (puzzlement)* Ratlosigkeit, *die*
persecute ['pɜːsɪkjuːt] *v.t.* verfolgen. **persecution** [pɜːsɪ'kjuːʃn] *n.* Verfolgung, *die*
perseverance [pɜːsɪ'vɪərəns] *n.* Beharrlichkeit, *die;* Ausdauer, *die*
persevere [pɜːsɪ'vɪə(r)] *v.i.* ausharren; ~ **with** *or* **at** *or* **in sth.** bei etw. dabeibleiben
Persian ['pɜːʃn] *adj.* persisch; Perser⟨*katze, -teppich*⟩
persist [pə'sɪst] *v.i.* **a)** nicht nachgeben; ~ **in doing sth.** etw. weiterhin [beharrlich] tun; **b)** *(continue to exist)* anhalten. **persistence** [pə'sɪstəns] Hartnäckigkeit, *die.* **persistent** [pə-'sɪstənt] *adj.* **a)** hartnäckig; **b)** *(constantly repeated)* dauernd; hartnäckig ⟨*Gerüchte*⟩. **per'sistently** *adv.* hartnäckig
person ['pɜːsn] *n.* Mensch, *der;* **in** ~: persönlich; selbst
personal ['pɜːsənl] *adj.* persönlich; Privat⟨*angelegenheit, -leben*⟩; ~ **com-**

puter Personalcomputer, *der;* ~ **stereo** Walkman, *der;* ~ **hygiene** Körperpflege, *die.* **personal as'sistant** *n.*persönlicher Referent/persönliche Referentin
personality [pɜːsə'nælɪtɪ] *n.* Persönlichkeit, *die*
'**personally** *adv.* persönlich
personification [pəsɒnɪfɪ'keɪʃn] *n.* Verkörperung, *die*
personify [pə'sɒnɪfaɪ] *v. t.* verkörpern; **be kindness personified** die Freundlichkeit in Person sein
personnel [pɜːsə'nel] *n.* Belegschaft, *die; (of shop, restaurant, etc.)* Personal, *das; attrib.* Personal-
perspective [pə'spektɪv] *n.* Perspektive, *die; (fig.)* Blickwinkel, *der*
perspiration [pɜːspɪ'reɪʃn] *n.* Schweiß, *der*
perspire [pə'spaɪə(r)] *v. i.* schwitzen
persuade [pə'sweɪd] *v. t.* **a)** *(convince)* überzeugen **(of** von); ~ **oneself |that|** ... : sich *(Dat.)* einreden, daß ...; **b)** *(induce)* überreden. **persuasion** [pə'sweɪʒn] *n.* Überzeugung, *die;* **it didn't take much** ~: es brauchte nicht viel Überredungskunst. **persuasive** [pə'sweɪsɪv] *adj.,* **per'suasively** *adv.* überzeugend
pert [pɜːt] *adj.* keck
pertinent ['pɜːtɪnənt] *adj.* relevant **(to** für)
perturb [pə'tɜːb] *v. t.* beunruhigen
Peru [pə'ruː] *pr. n.* Peru *(das).* **Peruvian** [pə'ruːvɪən] **1.** *adj.* peruanisch. **2.** *n.* Peruaner, *der*/Peruanerin, *die*
pervade [pə'veɪd] *v. t.* durchdringen. **pervasive** [pə'veɪsɪv] *adj.* durchdringend *(Geruch, Kälte);* weit verbreitet *(Ansicht);* sich ausbreitend *(Gefühl)*
perverse [pə'vɜːs] *adj.* starrköpfig
perversion [pə'vɜːʃn] *n.* **a)** *(sexual)* Perversion, *die;* **b)** ~ **of justice** Rechtsbeugung, *die.* **pervert 1.** [pə'vɜːt] *v. t. (morally)* verderben. **2.** ['pɜːvɜːt] *n.* perverser Mensch. **perverted** [pə'vɜːtɪd] *adj. (sexually)* pervers
pessimism ['pesɪmɪzm] *n.* Pessimismus, *der.* **pessimist** ['pesɪmɪst] *n.* Pessimist, *der*/Pessimistin, *die.* **pessimistic** [pesɪ'mɪstɪk] *adj.* pessimistisch
pest [pest] *n. (thing)* Ärgernis, *das; (person)* Nervensäge, *die (ugs.); (animal)* Schädling, *der*
pester ['pestə(r)] *v. t.* belästigen; nerven *(ugs.);* ~ **sb. for sth.** jmdm. wegen etw. in den Ohren liegen

pesticide ['pestɪsaɪd] *n.* Pestizid, *das*
pet [pet] **1.** *n.* **a)** *(animal)* Haustier, *das;* **b)** *(as term of endearment)* Schatz, *der.* **2.** *adj. (favourite)* Lieblings-. **3.** *v. i.,* **-tt-** knutschen *(ugs.)*
petal ['petl] *n.* Blütenblatt, *das*
peter ['piːtə(r)] *v. i.* ~ **out** [allmählich] zu Ende gehen; *(Weg:)* sich verlieren
petite [pə'tiːt] *adj.* zierlich
petition [pə'tɪʃn] **1.** *n.* Petition, *die;* Eingabe, *die.* **2.** *v. t.* eine Eingabe richten an **(+** *Akk.)*
petrify ['petrɪfaɪ] *v. t.* **be petrified with fear/shock** starr vor Angst/Schrecken sein
petrol ['petrl] *n. (Brit.)* Benzin, *das*
petroleum [pɪ'trəʊlɪəm] *n.* Erdöl, *das.* **petrol:** ~-**pump** *n. (Brit.)* Zapfsäule, *die;* ~-**station** *n. (Brit.)* Tankstelle, *die;* ~-**tank** *n. (Brit.)* Benzintank, *der;* ~-**tanker** *n. (Brit.)* Benzintankwagen, *der*
'**pet shop** *n.* Tierhandlung, *die*
petticoat ['petɪkəʊt] *n.* Unterrock, *der*
petty ['petɪ] *adj.* kleinlich *(Vorschrift, Einwand);* belanglos *(Detail, Sorgen)*
petulant ['petjʊlənt] *adj.* bockig
pew [pjuː] *n. (Eccl.)* Kirchenbank, *die*
pewter ['pjuːtə(r)] *n.* Pewter, *der*
phantom ['fæntəm] *n.* Phantom, *das*
pharmacist ['fɑːməsɪst] *n.* Apotheker, *der*/Apothekerin, *die*
pharmacy ['fɑːməsɪ] *n. (dispensary)* Apotheke, *die*
phase [feɪz] *n.* Phase, *die.* **phase 'in** *v. t.* stufenweise einführen. **phase 'out** *v. t.* allmählich abschaffen *(Verfahrensweise, Methode); (stop producing)* [langsam] auslaufen lassen
Ph.D. [piːeɪtʃ'diː] *abbr.* **Doctor of Philosophy** Dr. phil.
pheasant ['feznt] *n.* Fasan, *der*
phenomenal [fɪ'nɒmɪnl] *adj.* phänomenal
phenomenon [fɪ'nɒmɪnən] *n., pl.* **phenomena** [fɪ'nɒmɪnə] Phänomen, *das*
phew [fjuː] *int.* puh
Philippines ['fɪlɪpiːnz] *pr. n. pl.* Philippinen *Pl.*
philistine ['fɪlɪstaɪn] *n.* Banause, *der*/Banausin, *die*
philosopher [fɪ'lɒsəfə(r)] *n.* Philosoph, *der*/Philosophin, *die*
philosophical [fɪlə'sɒfɪkl] *adj.* **a)** philosophisch; **b)** *(resigned)* abgeklärt
philosophy [fɪ'lɒsəfɪ] *n.* Philosophie, *die*
phlegm [flem] *n.* Schleim, *der*
phobia ['fəʊbɪə] *n.* Phobie, *die*

phone [fəʊn] *(coll.)* **1.** *n.* Telefon, *das;* by ~: telefonisch; **be on the** ~: Telefon haben; *(be phoning)* telefonieren. **2.** *v. t. & i.* anrufen. **phone 'back** *v. t. & i.* zurückrufen; *(make further call)* wieder anrufen. **phone 'up** *v. t. & i.* anrufen

phone: ~ **book** *n.* Telefonbuch, *das;* ~ **box** *n.* Telefonzelle, *die;* ~ **call** *n.* Anruf, *der;* ~ **card** *n.* Telefonkarte, *die;* ~ **number** *n.* Telefonnummer, *die*

phonetic [fə'netɪk] *adj.* phonetisch. **phonetics** [fə'netɪks] *n.* Phonetik, *die*

phoney ['fəʊnɪ] *adj. (coll.) (sham)* falsch; gefälscht ‹*Brief, Dokument*›

phonograph ['fəʊnəɡrɑːf] *n. (Amer.)* Plattenspieler, *der*

phony *see* **phoney**

phosphorus ['fɒsfərəs] *n.* Phosphor, *der*

photo ['fəʊtəʊ] *n., pl.* ~**s** Foto, *das*

photo: ~**copier** *n.* Fotokopiergerät, *das;* ~**copy 1.** *n.* Fotokopie, *die;* **2.** *v. t.* fotokopieren

photogenic [fəʊtə'dʒiːnɪk] *adj.* fotogen

photograph ['fəʊtəɡrɑːf] **1.** *n.* Fotografie, *die;* Foto, *das;* **take a** ~ |**of sb./ sth.|** [jmdn./etw.] fotografieren. **2.** *v. t. & i.* fotografieren. **photographer** [fə'tɒɡrəfə(r)] *n.* Fotograf, *der*/Fotografin, *die*. **photographic** [fəʊtə'ɡræfɪk] *adj.* fotografisch; Foto‹*ausrüstung, -apparat, -ausstellung*›. **photography** [fə'tɒɡrəfɪ] *n.* Fotografie, *die*

phrase [freɪz] **1.** *n.* [Rede]wendung, *die.* **2.** *v. t.* formulieren. **'phrasebook** *n.* Sprachführer, *der*

physical ['fɪzɪkl] *adj.* **a)** physisch ‹*Gewalt*›; dinglich ‹*Welt, Universum*›; **b)** *(of physics)* physikalisch; **c)** *(bodily)* körperlich. **physical edu'cation** *n. (Sch.)* Sport, *der.* **'physically** *adv. (relating to the body)* körperlich

physician [fɪ'zɪʃn] *n.* Arzt, *der*/Ärztin, *die*

physicist ['fɪzɪsɪst] *n.* Physiker, *der*/ Physikerin, *die*

physics ['fɪzɪks] *n.* Physik, *die*

physiology [fɪzɪ'ɒlədʒɪ] *n.* Physiologie, *die*

physiotherapy [fɪzɪəʊ'θerəpɪ] *n.* Physiotherapie, *die*

physique [fɪ'ziːk] *n.* Körperbau, *der*

pianist ['piːənɪst] *n.* Pianist, *der*/Pianistin, *die*

piano [pɪ'ænəʊ] *n., pl.* ~**s** *(upright)* Klavier, *das; (grand)* Flügel, *der.* **piano-ac'cordion** *n.* Akkordeon, *das*

¹pick [pɪk] *n. (tool)* Spitzhacke, *die*

²pick 1. *n.* **a)** *(choice)* Wahl, *die;* **take your** ~: du hast die Wahl; **b)** *(best part)* Elite, *die;* **the** ~ **of the fruit** die besten Früchte. **2.** *v. t.* **a)** pflücken ‹*Blumen, Äpfel usw.*›; lesen ‹*Trauben*›; **b)** *(select)* auswählen; ~ **one's way** sich *(Dat.)* vorsichtig [s]einen Weg suchen; **c)** ~ **one's nose** in der Nase bohren; **d)** ~ **sb.'s pocket** jmdn. bestehlen; **he had his pocket** ~**ed** er wurde von einem Taschendieb bestohlen; **e)** ~ **a lock** ein Schloß knacken *(salopp).* **3.** *v. i.* ~ **and choose** wählerisch sein. **'pick at** *v. t.* herumstochern in *(+ Dat.)* ‹*Essen*›. **'pick on** *v. t. (victimize)* es abgesehen haben auf *(+ Akk.).* **pick 'out** *v. t.* **a)** *(choose)* auswählen; *(for oneself)* sich *(Dat.)* aussuchen; **b)** *(distinguish)* entdecken ‹*Detail, jmds. Gesicht in der Menge*›. **pick up 1.** [**'--**] *v. t.* **a)** [in die Hand] nehmen; hochnehmen ‹*Baby*›; *(after dropping)* aufheben; aufnehmen ‹*Masche*›; ~ **up the telephone** den [Telefon]hörer abnehmen; **b)** *(collect)* mitnehmen; *(by arrangement)* abholen **(at, from** von); *(obtain)* holen; **c)** *(become infected by)* sich *(Dat.)* holen *(ugs.)* ‹*Virus, Grippe*›; **d)** ‹*Bus, Autofahrer:*› mitnehmen; **e)** *(rescue from the sea)* [aus Seenot] bergen; **f)** empfangen ‹*Signal, Funkspruch usw.*›; **g)** *(coll.: make acquaintance of)* aufreißen *(ugs.).* **2.** [**-'-**] *v. i.* **a)** sich bessern; **b)** ‹*Wind:*› auffrischen

'pickaxe *(Amer.:* **'pickax)** *see* **¹pick**

picket ['pɪkɪt] **1.** *n.* Streikposten, *der.* **2.** *v. i.* Streikposten stehen. **3.** *v. t.* Streikposten stellen vor *(+ Dat.).* **'picket-line** *n.* Streikpostenkette, *die*

pickle ['pɪkl] **1.** *n., usu. in pl. (food)* [Mixed] Pickles *Pl.* **2.** *v. t.* einlegen ‹*Gurken, Zwiebeln, Eier*›; marinieren ‹*Hering*›

pick: ~**-me-up** *n.* Stärkungsmittel, *das;* ~**pocket** *n.* Taschendieb, *der*/-diebin, *die;* ~**-up** *n.* **a)** ~ |**truck**| Kleinlastwagen, *der;* **b)** *(of record-player, guitar)* Tonabnehmer, *der*

picnic ['pɪknɪk] **1.** *n.* Picknick, *das;* **go for** *or* **on/have a** ~: ein Picknick machen. **2.** *v. i.,* -ck- picknicken; Picknick machen. **'picnic site** *n.* Picknickplatz, *der*

pictorial [pɪk'tɔːrɪəl] *adj.* illustriert ⟨*Bericht, Zeitschrift*⟩; bildlich ⟨*Darstellung*⟩

picture ['pɪktʃə(r)] 1. *n.* **a)** Bild, *das;* get the ~ *(coll.)* verstehen[, worum es geht]; put sb. in the ~: jmdn. ins Bild setzen; **b)** *(film)* Film, *der;* **c)** *in pl. (Brit.: cinema)* Kino, *das;* go to the ~s ins Kino gehen; what's on at the ~s? was läuft im Kino? 2. *v. t.* ~ [to oneself] sich *(Dat.)* vorstellen. '**picture-book** *n.* Bilderbuch, *das.* **picture** 'postcard *n.* Ansichtskarte, *die*

picturesque [pɪktʃə'resk] *adj.* malerisch

pidgin ['pɪdʒɪn] *n.* Pidgin, *das.* **pidgin** 'English *n.* Pidgin-Englisch, *das*

pie [paɪ] *n. (of meat, fish, etc.)* Pastete, *die; (of fruit etc.)* ≈ Obstkuchen, *der*

piece [piːs] 1. *n.* **a)** Stück, *das; (of broken glass or pottery)* Scherbe, *die; (of jigsaw puzzle, crashed aircraft, etc.)* Teil, *der; (Amer.: distance)* [kleines] Stück; **a** ~ **of meat/cake** ein Stück Fleisch/Kuchen; ~ **of furniture/luggage** Möbel-/Gepäckstück, *das;* **a three-~ suite** eine dreiteilige Sitzgarnitur; ~ **of luck** Glücksfall, *der;* ~ **of news/gossip/information** Nachricht, *die*/Klatsch, *der*/Information, *die;* **b)** *(Chess)* Figur, *die;* **c)** *(coin)* gold ~: Goldstück, *das;* **a 10p** ~: ein 10-Pence-Stück; **d)** *(literary or musical composition)* Stück, *das;* ~ **of music** Musikstück, *das.* 2. *v. t.* ~ **to**'**gether** zusammenfügen **(from** aus)

piece: ~meal *adv., adj.* stückweise; ~-**work** *n.* Akkordarbeit, *die*

pier [pɪə(r)] *n. (at seaside)* Pier, *der*

pierce [pɪəs] *v. t. (prick)* durchstechen; *(penetrate)* [ein]dringen in (+ *Akk.*) ⟨*Körper, Fleisch, Herz*⟩; ~ **a hole in sth.** ein Loch in etw. *(Akk.)* stechen.

piercing ['pɪəsɪŋ] *adj.* durchdringend ⟨*Stimme, Schrei, Blick*⟩

piety ['paɪətɪ] *n.* Frömmigkeit, *die*

pig [pɪg] *n.* **a)** Schwein, *das;* ~s might fly *(iron.)* da müßte schon ein Wunder geschehen; **b)** *(coll.: greedy person)* Vielfraß, *der (ugs.)*

pigeon ['pɪdʒɪn] *n.* Taube, *die.* '**pigeon-hole** *n.* [Ablage]fach, *das; (for letters)* Postfach, *das*

piggy ['pɪgɪ] : ~**back** *n.* **give sb. a** ~**back** jmdn. huckepack nehmen; ~ **bank** *n.* Sparschwein[chen], *das*

pig'**headed** *adj.* dickschädelig *(ugs.)*

pigment ['pɪgmənt] *n.* Pigment, *das*

pig: ~**sty** *n. (lit. or fig.)* Schweinestall, *der;* ~**tail** *n. (plaited)* Zopf, *der;* ~**tails** *(at either side of head)* Rattenschwänzchen *Pl. (ugs.)*

pike [paɪk] *n., pl. same* Hecht, *der*

pilchard ['pɪltʃəd] *n.* Sardine, *die*

¹**pile** [paɪl] 1. *n.* **a)** *(of dishes, plates)* Stapel, *der; (of paper, books, letters)* Stoß, *der; (of clothes)* Haufen, *der;* **b)** *(coll.: large quantity)* Haufen, *der (ugs.).* 2. *v. t.* **a)** *(load)* [voll] beladen; **b)** *(heap up)* aufstapeln ⟨*Holz, Steine*⟩; aufhäufen ⟨*Abfall, Schnee*⟩. **pile** '**in** *v. i. (seen from outside)* hineindrängen; *(seen from inside)* hereindrängen. '**pile into** *v. t.* sich zwängen in (+ *Akk.*) ⟨*Auto, Zimmer, Zugabteil*⟩. **pile** '**on** 1. *v. i. see* pile in. 2. *v. t. (fig.)* ~ **on the pressure** Druck machen. '**pile on to** *v. t.* drängen in (+ *Akk.*) ⟨*Bus usw.*⟩. **pile** '**out** *v. i.* nach draußen drängen. **pile** '**up** 1. *v. i.* **a)** ⟨*Waren, Post, Arbeit, Schnee:*⟩ sich auftürmen; ⟨*Verkehr:*⟩ sich stauen; **b)** *(crash)* aufeinander auffahren. 2. *v. t.* aufstapeln ⟨*Steine, Bücher usw.*⟩; aufhäufen ⟨*Abfall, Schnee*⟩

²**pile** *n. (of fabric etc.)* Flor, *der*

³**pile** *n. (stake)* Pfahl, *der.* '**pile-driver** *n.* [Pfahl]ramme, *die*

piles [paɪlz] *n. pl. (Med.)* Hämorrhoiden *Pl.*

'**pile-up** *n.* Massenkarambolage, *die*

pilfer ['pɪlfə(r)] *v. t.* stehlen

pilgrim ['pɪlgrɪm] *n.* Pilger, *der*/Pilgerin, *die.* **pilgrimage** ['pɪlgrɪmɪdʒ] *n.* Pilgerfahrt, *die*

pill [pɪl] *n.* **a)** Tablette, *die;* Pille, *die (ugs.);* **b)** *(coll.: contraceptive)* the ~ or P~: die Pille *(ugs.);* be on the ~: die Pille nehmen *(ugs.)*

pillage ['pɪlɪdʒ] *v. t.* [aus]plündern

pillar ['pɪlə(r)] *n.* Säule, *die.* '**pillarbox** *n. (Brit.)* Briefkasten, *der*

pillion ['pɪljən] *n.* Beifahrersitz, *der;* **ride** ~: als Beifahrer/Beifahrerin mitfahren

pillow ['pɪləʊ] *n.* [Kopf]kissen, *das.* '**pillowcase,** '**pillowslip** *ns.* [Kopf]kissenbezug, *der*

pilot ['paɪlət] 1. *n.* **a)** *(Aeronaut.)* Pilot, *der*/Pilotin, *die;* **b)** *(Naut.)* Lotse, *der.* 2. *adj.* Pilot⟨*programm, -studie, -projekt usw.*⟩. 3. *v. t.* **a)** *(Aeronaut.)* fliegen; **b)** *(Naut.; fig.)* lotsen

'**pilot-light** *n.* Zündflamme, *die*

pimp [pɪmp] *n.* Zuhälter, *der*

pimple ['pɪmpl] *n.* Pickel, *der*

pin 1. *n.* **a)** Stecknadel, *die;* ~**s and needles** *(fig.)* Kribbeln, *das;* **b)** *(peg)*

Stift, *der;* c) *(Electr.)* **a two-/three-~ plug** ein zwei-/dreipoliger Stecker. **2.** *v.t.,* **-nn-: a)** nageln ⟨*Knochen, Bein*⟩; **~ a badge to one's lapel** sich *(Dat.)* ein Abzeichen ans· Revers stecken; **b)** *(fig.)* **~ one's hopes on sb./sth.** seine [ganze] Hoffnung auf jmdn./etw. setzen; **~ the blame for sth. on sb.** jmdm. die Schuld an etw. *(Dat.)* zuschieben; **c) ~ sb. against the wall** jmdn. an die Wand drängen. **pin 'down** *v.t.* **a)** *(fig.)* festnageln **(to** *or* **on auf +** *Akk.*); **b)** *(trap)*· festhalten. **pin 'up** *v.t.* aufhängen ⟨*Bild, Foto*⟩; anschlagen ⟨*Bekanntmachung, Liste*⟩; aufstecken ⟨*Haar*⟩; heften ⟨*Saum*⟩

pinafore ['pɪnəfɔː(r)] *n.* Schürze, *die (mit Oberteil)*

pincers ['pɪnsəz] *n. pl.* **a)** |**pair of**| **~:** Beißzange, *die;* **b)** *(of crab etc.)* Schere, *die*

pinch [pɪntʃ] **1.** *n.* **a)** *(squeezing)* Kniff, *der;* **give sb. a ~ on the arm/cheek** jmdn. *od.* jmdm. in den Arm/die Backe kneifen; **b)** *(fig.)* **feel the ~:** knapp bei Kasse sein *(ugs.);* **at a ~:** zur Not; **c)** *(small amount)* Prise, *die.* **2.** *v.t.* **a)** kneifen; **~ sb.'s cheek/bottom** jmdn. in die Wange/den Hintern *(ugs.)* kneifen; **b)** *(coll.: steal)* klauen *(salopp)*

'pincushion *n.* Nadelkissen, *das*

¹pine [paɪn] *n. (tree)* Kiefer, *die*

²pine *v.i.* sich [vor Kummer] verzehren *(geh.).* **pine a'way** *v.i.* dahinkümmern

pineapple ['paɪnæpl] *n.* Ananas, *die*

'pine-tree *n.* Kiefer, *die*

ping-pong *(Amer.:* **Ping-Pong,** P) ['pɪŋpɒŋ] *n.* Tischtennis, *das*

pink [pɪŋk] **1.** *n.* Pink, *das;* Rosa, *das.* **2.** *adj.* pinkfarben; rosa

pinkie ['pɪŋkɪ] *n. (Amer., Scot.)* kleiner Finger

'pin-money *n.* Taschengeld, *das*

pinnacle ['pɪnəkl] *n.* Gipfel, *der; (fig.)* Höhepunkt, *der*

'pin-point *v.t.* genau festlegen

pint [paɪnt] *n.* Pint, *das;* ≈ halber Liter

'pin-up *(coll.) n.* Pin-up-Girl, *das; (picture) (of beautiful girl)* Pin-up[-Foto], *das; (of sports, film or pop star)* Starfoto, *das*

pioneer [paɪə'nɪə(r)] **1.** *n.* Pionier, *der.* **2.** *v.t.* Pionierarbeit leisten für

pious ['paɪəs] *adj.* fromm

pip [pɪp] *n. (seed)* Kern, *der*

pipe [paɪp] **1.** *n.* **a)** *(tube)* Rohr, *das;* **b)**

(Mus.) Pfeife, *die;* **c)** |**tobacco-**|**~:** [Tabaks]pfeife, *die.* **2.** *v.t.* [durch ein Rohr/durch Rohre] leiten. **pipe 'down** *v.i. (coll.)* ruhig sein. **pipe 'up** *v.i. (coll.)* etwas sagen

'pipeline *n.* Pipeline, *die;* **in the ~** *(fig.)* in Vorbereitung

piper ['paɪpə(r)] *n.* Pfeifer, *der*/Pfeiferin, *die; (bagpiper)* Dudelsackspieler, *der*/-spielerin, *die*

piping hot ['paɪpɪŋ hɒt] *adj.* kochendheiß

piquant ['piːkənt] *adj.* pikant

pique [piːk] *n.* **in a** |**fit of**|**~:** verstimmt

piracy ['paɪrəsɪ] *n.* Seeräuberei, *die*

pirate ['paɪrət] *n.* **a)** Pirat, *der;* Seeräuber, *der;* **b)** *(Radio)* **~ radio station** Piratensender, *der*

Pisces ['paɪsiːz] *n.* Fische Pl.

piss [pɪs] *(coarse)* **1.** *n.* **a)** *(urine)* Pisse, *die (derb);* **b)** **have a/go for a ~:** pissen/pissen gehen *(derb).* **2.** *v.i.* pissen *(derb)*

pistol ['pɪstl] *n.* Pistole, *die*

piston ['pɪstən] *n.* Kolben, *der*

pit [pɪt] **1.** *n. (hole, mine)* Grube, *die; (natural)* Vertiefung, *die.* **2.** *v.t.,* **-tt-:** **~ one's wits/skill** *etc.* **against sth.** seinen Verstand/sein Können *usw.* an etw. *(Dat.)* messen

¹pitch [pɪtʃ] **1.** *n.* **a)** *(Brit.: usual place)* [Stand]platz, *der; (Sport: playing-area)* Feld, *das;* Platz, *der;* **b)** *(Mus.)* Tonhöhe, *die;* **c)** *(slope)* Neigung, *die.* **2.** *v.t.* **a)** *(erect)* aufschlagen; **~ camp** ein/das Lager aufschlagen; **b)** *(throw)* werfen. **3.** *v.i.* stürzen; ⟨*Schiff:*⟩ stampfen; **~ forward** vornüberstürzen

²pitch *n. (substance)* Pech, *das.* **pitch-'black** *adj.* pechschwarz; stockdunkel *(ugs.)* ⟨*Nacht*⟩. **pitch-'dark** *adj.* stockdunkel *(ugs.)*

pitcher ['pɪtʃə(r)] *n.* [Henkel]krug, *der*

'pitchfork *n.* Heugabel, *die*

'pitfall *n.* Fallstrick, *der*

pith [pɪθ] *n.* **a)** *(of orange etc.)* weiße Haut; **b)** *(fig.)* Kern, *der.* **'pithy** *adj. (fig.)* prägnant

pitiable ['pɪtɪəbl], **pitiful** ['pɪtɪfl] *adjs.* **a)** mitleiderregend; **b)** *(contemptible)* jämmerlich

'pitiless *adj.* unbarmherzig

pittance ['pɪtəns] *n.* Hungerlohn, *der*

pity ['pɪtɪ] **1.** *n.* Mitleid, *das;* **feel ~ for sb.** Mitgefühl für jmdn. empfinden; **have/take ~ on sb.** Erbarmen mit jmdm. haben; |**what a**| **~!** |**wie**| **schade! 2.** *v.t.* bemitleiden; **I ~ you** du tust mir leid

pivot ['pɪvət] 1. *n.* [Dreh]zapfen, *der.* 2. *v. i.* sich drehen

pixie ['pɪksɪ] *n.* Kobold, *der*

pizza ['pi:tsə] *n.* Pizza, *die*

placard ['plæka:d] *n.* Plakat, *das*

placate [plə'keɪt] *v. t.* beschwichtigen

place [pleɪs] 1. *n.* **a)** Ort, *der;* (*spot*) Stelle, *die;* **a [good] ~ to park/to stop** ein [guter] Platz zum Parken/eine [gute] Stelle zum Halten; **do you know a good/cheap ~ to eat?** weißt du, wo man gut/billig essen kann?; **~ of worship** Andachtsort, *der;* **all over the ~:** überall; *(coll.: in a mess)* ganz durcheinander *(ugs.);* **b)** *(rank, position)* Stellung, *die;* **put sb. in his ~:** jmdn. in seine Schranken weisen; **c)** *(country, town)* Ort, *der;* **~ of birth** Geburtsort, *der;* **'go ~s** *(coll.: fig.)* es [im Leben] zu was bringen *(ugs.);* **d)** *(coll.: premises)* Bude, *die (ugs.);* **she is at his ~:** sie ist bei ihm; **e)** *(seat etc.)* [Sitz]platz, *der;* **change ~s [with sb.]** [mit jmdm.] die Plätze tauschen; *(fig.)* [mit jmdm.] tauschen; **f)** *(step, stage)* **in the first ~:** zuerst; **why didn't you say so in the first ~?** warum hast du das nicht gleich gesagt?; **g)** *(space ~)* Platz, *der;* **everything fell into ~** *(fig.)* alles wurde klar; **out of ~:** nicht am richtigen Platz; *(several things)* in Unordnung; **h)** *(position in competition)* Platz, *der.* 2. *v. t.* **a)** *(vertically)* stellen; *(horizontally)* legen; **b)** *in p.p. (situated)* gelegen; **c)** *(find situation or home for)* unterbringen **(with** bei); **d)** *(class)* einordnen; einstufen; **be ~d second in the race** im Rennen den zweiten Platz belegen

placid ['plæsɪd] *adj.* ruhig

plagiarism ['pleɪdʒərɪzm] *n.* Plagiat, *das.* **plagiarize** ['pleɪdʒəraɪz] *v. t.* plagiieren

plague [pleɪg] 1. *n.* **a)** *(esp. Hist.: epidemic)* Seuche, *die;* **the ~** *(bubonic)* die Pest; **b)** *(infestation)* **~ of rats** Rattenplage, *die.* 2. *v. t.* plagen; **~d with** *or* **by sth.** von etw. geplagt

plaice [pleɪs] *n., pl. same* Scholle, *die*

plain [pleɪn] 1. *adj.* **a)** *(clear)* klar; *(obvious)* offensichtlich; **b)** *(frank)* offen; schlicht ⟨*Wahrheit*⟩; **be ~ sailing** *(fig.)* [ganz] einfach sein; **c)** *(unsophisticated)* einfach; schlicht ⟨*Kleidung*⟩; unliniert ⟨*Papier*⟩; ⟨*Stoff*⟩ ohne Muster; **d)** wenig attraktiv ⟨*Mädchen*⟩. 2. *adv.* **a)** *(clearly)* deutlich; **b)** *(simply)* einfach. 3. *n.* Ebene, *die.* **plain 'chocolate** *n.* halbbittere Schokolade. **plain 'clothes** *n. pl.* **in ~:** in Zivil

plainly *adv.* **a)** *(clearly)* deutlich; **b)** *(obviously)* offensichtlich; *(undoubtedly)* eindeutig; **c)** *(frankly)* offen; **d)** *(simply)* schlicht

plaintiff ['pleɪntɪf] *n.* Kläger, *der/*Klägerin, *die*

plaintive ['pleɪntɪv] *adj.* klagend

plait [plæt] 1. *n.* Zopf, *der.* 2. *v. t.* flechten

plan [plæn] 1. *n.* Plan, *der;* **[go] according to ~:** nach Plan [gehen]; planmäßig [verlaufen]. 2. *v. t.,* **-nn-** planen; *(design)* entwerfen. 3. *v. i.,* **-nn-** planen

¹plane [pleɪn] *n.* **~[-tree]** Platane, *die*

²plane 1. *n. (tool)* Hobel, *der.* 2. *v. t.* hobeln

³plane *n.* **a)** *(Geom.: fig.)* Ebene, *die;* **b)** *(aircraft)* Flugzeug, *das;* Maschine, *die (ugs.)*

planet ['plænɪt] *n.* Planet, *der*

plank [plæŋk] *n.* Brett, *das;* *(thicker)* Bohle, *die;* *(on ship)* Planke, *die*

plankton ['plæŋktən] *n.* Plankton, *das*

planner *n.* Planer, *der/*Planerin, *die*

planning *n.* Planen, *das;* Planung, *die*

plant [pla:nt] 1. *n.* **a)** *(Bot.)* Pflanze, *die;* **b)** *no indef. art. (machinery)* Maschinen; **c)** *(factory)* Fabrik, *die;* Werk, *das.* 2. *v. t.* **a)** pflanzen; **b)** *(sl.: conceal)* anbringen ⟨*Wanze*⟩; legen ⟨*Bombe*⟩; **~ sth. on sb.** jmdm. etw. unterschieben. **plantation** [pla:n'teɪʃn] *n.* Plantage, *die*

plaque [pla:k, plæk] *n.* **a)** Platte, *die;* *(commemorating sb.)* [Gedenk]tafel, *die;* **b)** *(Dent.)* Plaque, *die*

plaster ['pla:stə(r)] 1. *n.* **a)** *(for walls etc.)* [Ver]putz, *der;* **b)** **~ |of Paris|** Gips, *der;* **c)** *see* **sticking-plaster.** 2. *v. t.* **a)** verputzen ⟨*Wand*⟩; **b)** *(daub)* **~ sth. on sth.** etw. dick auf etw. *(Akk.)* auftragen. **plastered** ['pla:stəd] *adj.* *(sl.: drunk)* voll *(salopp).* **plasterer** *n.* Gipser, *der*

plastic ['plæstɪk] 1. *n.* Plastik, *das;* Kunststoff, *der.* 2. *adj.* aus Plastik *od.* Kunststoff *nachgestellt;* **~ bag** Plastiktüte, *die;* **~ surgery** plastische Chirurgie

Plasticine, (P) ['plæstɪsi:n] *n.* Plastilin, *das*

plate [pleɪt] 1. *n.* **a)** Teller, *der;* *(serving ~)* Platte, *die;* **b)** *(metal ~ with name etc.)* Schild, *das;* **c)** *(for printing)* Platte, *die;* *(illustration)* [Bild]tafel, *die.* 2. *v. t.* **~ sth. [with gold/silver]** etw. vergolden/versilbern

plateau ['plætəʊ] *n., pl.* **~x** ['plætəʊz] *or* **~s** Hochebene, *die;* Plateau, *das*

plate 'glass n. Flachglas, das
platform ['plætfɔ:m] n. **a)** (Brit. Railw.) Bahnsteig, der; ~ 4 Gleis 4; **b)** (stage) Podium, das
platinum ['plætɪnəm] n. Platin, das
platitude ['plætɪtju:d] n. Platitüde, die (geh.); Gemeinplatz, der
platoon [plə'tu:n] n. (Mil.) Zug, der
plausible ['plɔ:zɪbl] adj. plausibel; einleuchtend
play [pleɪ] **1.** n. **a)** (Theatre) [Theater]stück, das; **television** ~: Fernsehspiel, das; **b)** (recreation) Spielen, das; Spiel, das; ~ **on words** Wortspiel, das; **c)** (Sport) Spiel, das; **d) come into** ~, **be brought** or **called into** ~: ins Spiel kommen. **2.** v.i. **a)** spielen; ~ **safe** sichergehen; ~ **for time** Zeit gewinnen wollen; **b)** (Mus.) spielen (**on** auf + Dat.). **3.** v.t. (also Sport, Theatre, Cards, Mus.) spielen; abspielen ⟨Schallplatte, Tonband⟩; schlagen ⟨Ball⟩; spielen gegen ⟨Mannschaft, Gegner⟩; ~ **the violin** etc. Geige usw. spielen; ~ **a trick/joke on sb.** jmdn. hereinlegen (ugs.)/jmdm. einen Streich spielen; ~ **one's cards right** (fig.) es richtig anfassen (fig.). **play a'bout, play a'round** v.i. spielen; **stop** ~**ing about** or **around** hör doch auf mit dem Unsinn! **play a'long** v.i. mitspielen. **play 'back** v.t. abspielen ⟨Tonband⟩. **play 'down** v.t. herunterspielen. **play 'up 1.** v.i. (coll.) ⟨Kinder:⟩ nichts als Ärger machen. **2.** v.t. (coll.: annoy) ärgern
'playboy n. Playboy, der
'player n. Spieler, der/Spielerin, die
playful ['pleɪfl] adj. spielerisch; (frolicsome) verspielt
play: ~ground n. Spielplatz, der; (Sch.) Schulhof, der; ~ **group** n. Spielgruppe, die
playing: ~-card n. Spielkarte, die; ~-**field** n. Sportplatz, der
play: ~mate n. Spielkamerad, der/Spielkameradin, die; ~-**off** n. Entscheidungsspiel, das; ~-**pen** Laufgitter, das; ~-**thing** n. Spielzeug, das; ~**wright** ['pleɪraɪt] n. Dramatiker, der/Dramatikerin, die
PLC, plc abbr. (Brit.) **public limited company** ≈ GmbH
plea [pli:] n. Appell, der (**for** zu)
plead [pli:d] **1.** v.i. **a)** inständig bitten (**for** um); (imploringly) flehen (**for** um); ~ **with sb. for sth.** jmdn. inständig um etw. bitten; **b)** (Law; also fig.) plädieren. **2.** v.t. **a)** inständig bitten;

(imploringly) flehen; **b)** (Law) ~ **guilty/not guilty** sich schuldig/nicht schuldig bekennen. **'pleading** adj. flehend
pleasant ['plezənt] adj. angenehm
please [pli:z] **1.** v.t. gefallen (+ Dat.); ~ **oneself** tun, was man will; ~ **yourself** ganz wie du willst. **2.** v.i. **I come and go as I** ~: ich komme und gehe, wie es mir gefällt; **if you** ~: bitte schön. **3.** int. bitte; ~ **do!** aber bitte od. gern! **pleased** [pli:zd] adj. (satisfied) zufrieden (**by** mit); (happy) erfreut (**by** über + Akk.); **be** ~ **at** or **about sth.** sich über etw. (Akk.) freuen. **pleasing** ['pli:zɪŋ] adj. gefällig
pleasure ['pleʒə(r)] n. (joy) Freude, die; (enjoyment) Vergnügen, das; **have the** ~ **of doing sth.** das Vergnügen haben, etw. zu tun; **with** ~: mit Vergnügen
pleat [pli:t] n. Falte, die. **'pleated** adj. gefältelt; Falten⟨rock⟩
pledge [pledʒ] **1.** n. Versprechen, das. **2.** v.t. versprechen; geloben ⟨Treue⟩
plentiful ['plentɪfl] adj. reichlich; **be** ~: reichlich vorhanden sein
plenty ['plentɪ] n. ~ **of** viel; eine Menge; (coll.: enough) genug
pleurisy ['plʊərɪsɪ] n. Pleuritis, die; Brustfellentzündung, die
pliable ['plaɪəbl] adj. biegsam
plied see **ply**
pliers ['plaɪəz] n. pl. [**pair of**] ~: Zange, die
plight [plaɪt] n. Notlage, die
plimsoll ['plɪmsl] n. (Brit.) Turnschuh, der
plinth [plɪnθ] n. Sockel, der
plod [plɒd] v.i., -dd- trotten. **plod 'on** v.i. (fig.) sich weiterkämpfen
plonk [plɒŋk] n. (sl.) [billiger] Wein
plot [plɒt] **1.** n. **a)** (conspiracy) Verschwörung, die; **b)** (of play, novel) Handlung, die; **c)** (of ground) Stück Land. **2.** v.t., -tt-: **a)** [heimlich] planen; **b)** (mark on map) einzeichnen. **3.** v.i., -tt-: ~ **against sb.** sich gegen jmdn. verschwören. **'plotter** n. Verschwörer, der/Verschwörerin, die
plough [plaʊ] **1.** n. Pflug, der. **2.** v.t. pflügen. **plough 'back** v.t. (Finance) reinvestieren
plow (Amer./arch.) see **plough**
ploy [plɔɪ] n. Trick, der
pluck [plʌk] **1.** v.t. **a)** pflücken ⟨Obst⟩; ~ [**out**] auszupfen ⟨Federn, Haare⟩; **b)** (pull at) zupfen an (+ Dat.); **c)** (strip of feathers) rupfen. **2.** v.i. ~ **at sth.** an

etw. *(Dat.)* zupfen. **3.** *n.* Mut, *der.*
pluck 'up *v. t.* ~ **up |one's| courage** all
seinen Mut zusammennehmen
pluckily ['plʌkılı] *adv.,* '**plucky** *adj.*
tapfer
plug [plʌg] **1.** *n.* **a)** *(filling hole)* Pfropfen, *der; (in cask)* Spund, *der; (for
basin etc.)* Stöpsel, *der;* **b)** *(Electr.)*
Stecker, *der.* **2.** *v. t.,* **-gg-: a)** ~ **|up|** zu-
stopfen ⟨*Loch usw.*⟩; **b)** *(coll.: advertise)* Schleichwerbung machen für.
plug 'in *v. t.* anschließen
'**plug-hole** *n.* Abfluß, *der.*
plum [plʌm] *n.* **a)** Pflaume, *die;* **b)**
(fig.) Leckerbissen, *der;* **a** ~ **job** ein
Traumjob *(ugs.)*
plumage ['plu:mıdʒ] *n.* Gefieder, *das*
¹**plumb** [plʌm] **1.** *v. t.* [aus]loten. **2.**
adv. **a)** lotrecht; **b)** *(fig.)* genau
²**plumb** *v. t.* ~ **in** fest anschließen.
plumber ['plʌmə(r)] *n.* Klempner,
der. **plumbing** ['plʌmıŋ] *n.* **a)**
Klempnerarbeiten *Pl.;* **b)** *(waterpipes)*
Wasserleitungen *Pl.*
'**plumb-line** *n.* Lot, *das*
plume [plu:m] *n.* Feder, *die; (ornamental bunch)* Federbusch, *der*
plummet ['plʌmıt] *v. i.* stürzen
plump [plʌmp] *adj.* mollig; rundlich.
'**plump for** *v. t.* sich entscheiden für
plunder ['plʌndə(r)] **1.** *v. t.* [aus]plün-
dern ⟨*Gebäude, Gebiet*⟩. **2.** *n.* Plünde-
rung, *die; (booty)* Beute, *die*
plunge [plʌndʒ] **1.** *v. t.* stecken; *(into
liquid)* tauchen. **2.** *v. i.* **a)** ~ **into sth.** in
etw. *(Akk.)* stürzen; **b)** ⟨*Straße usw.:*⟩
steil abfallen. **3.** *n.* Sprung, *der;* **take
the** ~ *(fig. coll.)* den Sprung wagen
plural ['plʊərl] **1.** *adj.* pluralisch; Plu-
ral-; ~ **noun** Substantiv im Plural. **2.**
n. Mehrzahl, *die;* Plural, *der*
plus [plʌs] **1.** *prep.* plus (+ *Dat.*). **2.** *n.*
(advantage) Pluspunkt, *der*
plush [plʌʃ] **1.** *n.* Plüsch, *der.* **2.** *adj.*
(coll.) feudal *(ugs.)*
Pluto ['plu:təʊ] *pr. n. (Astron.)* Pluto,
der
ply [plaı] **1.** *v. t.* **a)** *(use)* gebrauchen; **b)**
nachgehen (+ *Dat.*) ⟨*Handwerk, Ar-
beit*⟩; **c)** *(supply)* ~ **sb. with sth.** jmdn.
mit etw. versorgen; **d)** *(assail)* überhäufen. **2.** *v. i.* ~ **between** zwischen
⟨*Orten*⟩ [hin- und her]pendeln
'**plywood** *n.* Sperrholz, *das*
p.m. [pi:'em] *adv.* nachmittags; **one** ~:
ein Uhr mittags
pneumatic [nju:'mætık] *adj.* pneuma-
tisch. **pneumatic 'drill** *n.* Preßluft-
bohrer, *der*

pneumonia [nju:'məʊnıə] *n.* Lungen-
entzündung, *die*
PO *abbr.* **a) postal order** PA; **b) Post
Office** PA
¹**poach** [pəʊtʃ] *v. t.* **a)** *(catch illegally)*
wildern; illegal fangen ⟨*Fische*⟩; **b)**
stehlen, *(ugs.)* klauen ⟨*Idee*⟩
²**poach** *v. t. (Cookery)* pochieren ⟨*Ei*⟩;
dünsten ⟨*Fisch, Fleisch, Gemüse*⟩
'**poacher** *n.* Wilderer, *der*
pocket ['pɒkıt] **1.** *n.* **a)** Tasche, *die;* **b)**
(fig.) **be in** ~: Geld verdient haben; **be
out of** ~: draufgelegt haben. **2.** *adj.*
Taschen⟨*rechner, -uhr, -ausgabe*⟩. **3.**
v. t. **a)** einstecken; **b)** *(steal)* in die eigene Tasche stecken *(ugs.).* '**pocket-
book** *n. (wallet)* Brieftasche, *die;
(notebook)* Notizbuch, *das.* '**pocket-
money** *n.* Taschengeld, *das*
'**pock-marked** *adj.* **a)** pockennarbig
⟨*Gesicht, Haut*⟩; **b) a wall** ~ **with bul-
lets** eine mit Einschüssen übersäte
Wand
pod [pɒd] *n.* Hülse, *die; (of pea)* Schote, *die*
podgy ['pɒdʒı] *adj.* dicklich
poem ['pəʊım] *n.* Gedicht, *das*
poet ['pəʊıt] *n.* Dichter, *der.* **poetic**
[pəʊ'etık] *adj.* dichterisch
poetry ['pəʊıtrı] *n.* [Vers]dichtung,
die; Lyrik, *die*
poignant ['pɔınjənt] *adj.* tief ⟨*Bedauern, Trauer*⟩; ergreifend ⟨*Anblick*⟩
point [pɔınt] **1.** *n.* **a)** *(tiny mark, dot)*
Punkt, *der;* **b)** *(of tool, pencil, etc.)*
Spitze, *die;* **c)** *(single item; unit of scor-
ing)* Punkt, *der;* **d)** *(stage, degree)* **up
to a** ~: bis zu einem gewissen Grad;
he gave up at this ~: an diesem Punkt
gab er auf; **e)** *(moment)* Zeitpunkt,
der; **be on the** ~ **of doing sth.** etw. gerade tun wollen; **f)** *(distinctive trait)* Seite, *die;* **best/strong** ~: starke Seite;
Stärke, *die;* **g)** *(thing to be discussed)*
come to *or* **get to the** ~: zum Thema
kommen; **be beside the** ~: keine Rolle
spielen; **make a** ~ **of doing sth.** [gro-
ßen] Wert darauf legen, etw. zu tun;
h) *(of story, joke, remark)* Pointe, *die;*
i) *(purpose)* Zweck, *der;* Sinn, *der;* **j)**
(precise place, spot) Punkt, *der;* Stelle,
die; ~ **of view** *(fig.)* Standpunkt, *der;*
k) *(Brit.)* **|power** *or* **electric|** ~: Steck-
dose, *die;* **l)** *usu in pl. (Brit. Railw.)*
Weiche, *die.* **2.** *v. i.* **a)** zeigen, weisen
(to, at auf + *Akk.*); **b)** ~ **towards** *or* **to**
(fig.) [hin]deuten auf (+ *Akk.*). **3.** *v. t.*
richten ⟨*Waffe, Kamera*⟩ **(at** auf +
Akk.); ~ **one's finger at sth./sb.** mit

dem Finger auf etw./jmdn. zeigen.
point 'out *v.t.* hinweisen auf
(+ *Akk.*); ~ sth./sb. out to sb. jmdn.
auf etw./jmdn. hinweisen
point-'blank 1. *adj. (lit. or fig.)* direkt;
glatt ‹*Weigerung*›; ~ **range** kürzeste
Entfernung. **2.** *adv. (at very close
range)* aus kürzester Entfernung
'**pointed** *adj.* **a)** spitz; **b)** *(fig.)* unmißverständlich
'**pointer** *n.* **a)** Zeiger, *der; (rod)* Zeige-
stock, *der;* **b)** *(coll.: indication)* Hinweis, *der* (to auf + *Akk.*)
'**pointless** *adj.* sinnlos; belanglos
‹*Bemerkung, Geschichte*›
poise [pɔɪz] *n. (composure)* Haltung,
die; (self-confidence) Selbstvertrauen,
das. **poised** [pɔɪzd] *adj.* selbstsicher
poison ['pɔɪzn] **1.** *n.* Gift, *das.* **2.** *v.t.*
vergiften. '**poisoning** *n.* Vergiftung,
die. **poisonous** ['pɔɪzənəs] *adj.* giftig
poke 1. *v.t.* **a)** ~ **sth.** |**with sth.|** [mit
etw.] gegen etw. stoßen; ~ **sth. into
sth.** etw. in etw. *(Akk.)* stoßen; ~ **the
fire** das Feuer schüren; **b)** stecken
‹*Kopf*›. **2.** *v.i.* **a)** [herum]stochern (**at,
in, among** in + *Dat.*); **b)** *(pry)* schnüffeln *(ugs.).* **3.** *n.* **a)** *(thrust)* Stoß, *der;*
give sb. a ~ |**in the ribs|** jmdm. einen
[Rippen]stoß versetzen; **give the fire a**
~: das Feuer [an]schüren. **poke
a'bout, poke a'round** *v.i.* herumschnüffeln *(ugs.)*
'**poker** *n.* Schüreisen, *das*
²'**poker** *n. (Cards)* Poker, *das od. der*
'**poker-faced** *adj.* mit unbewegter
Miene *nachgestellt*
poky ['pəʊkɪ] *adj.* winzig
Poland ['pəʊlənd] *pr. n.* Polen *(das)*
polar ['pəʊlə(r)] *adj.* polar ‹*Kaltluft,
Gewässer*›; Polar‹*eis, -gebiet, -fuchs*›.
polar 'bear *n.* Eisbär, *der*
Pole [pəʊl] *n.* Pole, *der*/Polin, *die*
'**pole** *n. (support)* Stange, *die;* **drive sb.
up the** ~ *(Brit. sl.)* jmdn. zum Wahnsinn treiben *(ugs.)*
²**pole** *n. (Astron., Geog., Magn.,
Electr., fig.)* Pol, *der.* '**pole-star** *n.*
Polarstern, *der*
'**pole-vault** *n.* Stabhochsprung, *der*
police [pə'li:s] **1.** *n. pl.* Polizei, *die;
(members)* Polizisten *Pl.; attrib.* Poli-
zei-. **2.** *v.t.* [polizeilich] überwachen
‹*Fußballspiel*›; kontrollieren ‹*Gebiet*›
police: ~ **force** *n.* the ~ force die Polizei; ~**man** [pə'li:smən] *n., pl.* **-men**
[pə'li:smən] Polizist, *der;* ~ **station**
n. Polizeirevier, *das;* ~**woman** *n.*
Polizistin, *die*

'**policy** ['pɒlɪsɪ] *n.* Politik, *die*
²'**policy** *n. (Insurance)* Police, *die*
polio ['pəʊlɪəʊ] *n., no art.* Polio, *die;*
[spinale] Kinderlähmung
Polish ['pəʊlɪʃ] **1.** *adj.* polnisch; **sb. is**
~: jmd. ist Pole/Polin. **2.** *n.* Polnisch,
das; see also **English 2 a**
polish ['pɒlɪʃ] **1.** *v.t.* **a)** polieren; bohnern ‹*Fußboden*›; putzen ‹*Schuhe*›; **b)**
(fig.) ausfeilen ‹*Text, Theorie, Stil*›. **2.**
n. **a)** *(smoothness)* Glanz, *der;* **b)** *(substance)* Politur, *die;* **c)** *(fig.)* Schliff,
der. **polish 'off** *v.t. (coll.)* **a)** *(consume)* verdrücken *(ugs.);* **b)** *(complete
quickly)* durchziehen *(ugs.).* **polish
'up** *v.t.* **a)** polieren; **b)** ausfeilen
‹*Stil*›; aufpolieren ‹*Kenntnisse*›
polite [pə'laɪt] *adj.,* ~**r** [pə'laɪtə(r)], ~**st**
[pə'laɪtɪst] höflich. **po'liteness** *n.*
Höflichkeit, *die*
political [pə'lɪtɪkl] *adj.* politisch
politician [pɒlɪ'tɪʃn] *n.* Politiker,
der/Politikerin, *die*
politics ['pɒlɪtɪks] *n.* Politik, *die; (of
individual)* politische Einstellung
polka ['pɒlkə, 'pəʊlkə] *n.* Polka, *die.*
'**polka dot** *n.* [großer] Tupfen
poll [pəʊl] **1.** *n.* **a)** *(voting)* Abstimmung, *die; (to elect sb.)* Wahl, *die;* **go
to the** ~**s** zur Wahl gehen; **b)** *(opinion
~)* Umfrage, *die.* **2.** *v.t.* **a)** *(take vote[s]
of)* abstimmen/wählen lassen; **b)**
(take opinion of) befragen
pollen ['pɒlən] *n.* Pollen, *der;* Blüten-
staub, *der.* '**pollen count** *n.* Pollen-
menge, *die*
'**polling-booth** *n.* Wahlkabine, *die*
'**poll-tax** *n.* Kopfsteuer, *die*
pollutant [pə'lu:tənt] *n.* [Um-
welt]schadstoff, *der*
pollute [pə'lu:t] *v.t.* verschmutzen
‹*Luft, Boden, Wasser*›. **pollution** [pə-
'lu:ʃn] *n.* [Umwelt]verschmutzung, *die*
polo ['pəʊləʊ] *n.* Polo, *das.* '**polo-
neck** *n.* Rollkragen, *der*
polyester [pɒlɪ'estə(r)] *n.* Polyester,
der
polystyrene [pɒlɪ'staɪri:n] *n.* Polysty-
rol, *das;* ~ **foam** Styropor Ⓦ, *das*
polytechnic [pɒlɪ'teknɪk] *n. (Brit.)* ≈
technische Hochschule
polythene ['pɒlɪθi:n] *n.* Polyäthylen,
das; ~ **bag** Plastikbeutel, *der*
pomegranate ['pɒmɪɡrænɪt] *n.* Gra-
natapfel, *der*
'**pommel-horse** *n.* Seitpferd, *das*
pomp [pɒmp] *n.* Pomp, *der*
pom-pom ['pɒmpɒm] *n.* Pompon,
der; ~ **hat** Pudelmütze, *die*

pompous ['pɒmpəs] *adj.* großspurig; gespreizt ⟨*Sprache*⟩
pond [pɒnd] *n.* Teich, *der*
ponder ['pɒndə(r)] **1.** *v.t.* nachdenken über (+ *Akk.*) ⟨*Frage, Ereignis*⟩; abwägen ⟨*Vorteile, Worte*⟩. **2.** *v.i.* nachdenken (**over, on** über + *Akk.*)
ponderous ['pɒndərəs] *adj.* schwer
pong [pɒŋ] *(Brit. coll.)* **1.** *n.* Mief, *der (ugs.).* **2.** *v.i.* miefen *(ugs.)*
pony ['pəʊnɪ] *n.* Pony, *das.* '**ponytail** *n.* Pferdeschwanz, *der.* **ponytrekking** ['pəʊnɪtrekɪŋ] *n. (Brit.)* Ponyreiten, *das*
poodle ['puːdl] *n.* Pudel, *der*
¹**pool** [puːl] *n.* **a)** Tümpel, *der;* **b)** *(temporary)* Lache, *die;* ~ **of blood** Blutlache, *die;* **c)** *(swimming-~)* Schwimmbecken, *das; (public)* Schwimmbad, *das; (in house or garden)* Pool, *der*
²**pool 1.** *n.* **a)** *(Gambling)* [gemeinsame Spiel]kasse; **the ~s** *(Brit.)* das Toto; **b)** *(common supply)* Topf, *der;* **a** ~ **of experience** ein Erfahrungsschatz; **c)** *(game)* Pool[billard], *das.* **2.** *v.t.* zusammenlegen ⟨*Geld, Ersparnisse*⟩; bündeln ⟨*Anstrengungen*⟩
poor [pʊə(r)] **1.** *adj.* **a)** arm; **b)** *(inadequate)* schlecht; schwach ⟨*Spiel, Gesundheit, Leistung, Rede*⟩; dürftig ⟨*Kleidung, Essen, Unterkunft*⟩; **of** ~ **quality** minderer Qualität; **c)** *(paltry)* schwach ⟨*Trost*⟩; schlecht ⟨*Aussichten*⟩; **d)** *(unfortunate)* arm *(auch iron.);* **e)** karg ⟨*Boden*⟩; **f)** *(deficient)* arm (**in an** + *Dat.*); ~ **in vitamins** vitaminarm. **2.** *n. pl.* **the** ~: die Armen. **poorly** ['pʊəlɪ] *adv., pred. adj.* schlecht
¹**pop** [pɒp] **1.** *v.i.,* **-pp-:** **a)** *(make sound)* knallen; **b)** *(coll.: go quickly)* **let's** ~ **round to Fred's** komm, wir gehen kurz bei Fred vorbei *(ugs.).* **2.** *v.t.,* **-pp-:** **a)** *(coll.: put)* ~ **the meat in the fridge** das Fleisch in den Kühlschrank tun; **b)** platzen ⟨*Luftballon*⟩. **3.** *n.* **a)** Knall, *der;* Knallen, *das;* **b)** *(coll.: drink)* Brause, *die (ugs.).* **4.** *adv.* **go** ~: knallen. **pop 'out** *v.i.* hervorschießen; ~ **out to the shops** schnell einkaufen gehen
²**pop** *(coll.)* **1.** *n.* Popmusik, *die;* Pop, *der.* **2.** *adj.* Pop⟨*star, -musik usw.*⟩
'**popcorn** *n.* Popcorn, *das*
pope [pəʊp] *n.* Papst, *der/*Päpstin, *die*
poplar ['pɒplə(r)] *n.* Pappel, *die*
popper ['pɒpə(r)] *n. (Brit. coll.)* Druckknopf, *der*
poppy ['pɒpɪ] *n.* Mohn, *der*
popular ['pɒpjʊlə(r)] *adj.* **a)** *(well liked)* beliebt; populär ⟨*Entscheidung, Maßnahme*⟩; **b)** verbreitet ⟨*Aberglaube, Irrtum, Meinung*⟩; allgemein ⟨*Wahl, Unterstützung*⟩. **popularity** [pɒpjʊ'lærɪtɪ] *n.* Beliebtheit, *die; (of decision, measure)* Popularität, *die.*
popularize ['pɒpjʊləraɪz] *v.t.* **a)** *(make popular)* populär machen; **b)** *(make understandable)* breiteren Kreisen zugänglich machen. '**popularly** *adv.* allgemein
populate ['pɒpjʊleɪt] *v.t.* bevölkern; bewohnen ⟨*Insel*⟩. **population** [pɒpjʊ'leɪʃn] *n.* Bevölkerung, *die;* **Britain has a** ~ **of 56 million** Großbritannien hat 56 Millionen Einwohner
porcelain ['pɔːslɪn] *n.* Porzellan, *das*
porch [pɔːtʃ] *n.* Vordach, *das; (with side walls)* Vorbau, *der; (enclosed)* Windfang, *der*
porcupine ['pɔːkjʊpaɪn] *n.* Stachelschwein, *das*
¹**pore** [pɔː(r)] *n.* Pore, *die*
²**pore** *v.i.* ~ **over sth.** etw. [genau] studieren
pork [pɔːk] *n.* Schweinefleisch, *das; attrib.* Schweine-. **pork 'chop** *n.* Schweinekotelett, *das.* **pork 'pie** *n.* Schweinepastete, *die*
porn [pɔːn] *n. (coll.)* Pornographie, *die;* Pornos *(ugs.)*
pornographic [pɔːnə'græfɪk] *adj.* pornographisch; Porno- *(ugs.)*
pornography [pɔː'nɒgrəfɪ] *n.* Pornographie, *die*
porous ['pɔːrəs] *adj.* porös
porridge ['pɒrɪdʒ] *n.* [Hafer]brei, *der*
¹**port** [pɔːt] **1.** *n.* **a)** Hafen, *der;* **b)** *(Naut., Aeronaut.: left side)* Backbord, *das.* **2.** *adj. (Naut., Aeronaut.: left)* Backbord-; backbordseitig
²**port** *n. (wine)* Portwein, *der*
portable ['pɔːtəbl] *adj.* tragbar
¹**porter** ['pɔːtə(r)] *n. (Brit.: doorman)* Pförtner, *der; (of hotel)* Portier, *der*
²**porter** *n.* [Gepäck]träger, *der/*-trägerin, *die; (in hotel)* Hausdiener, *der*
portfolio [pɔːt'fəʊlɪəʊ] *n. pl.* ~**s** **a)** *(Polit.)* Geschäftsbereich, *der;* **b)** *(case, contents)* Mappe, *die*
porthole ['pɔːthəʊl] *n. (Naut.)* Seitenfenster, *das; (round)* Bullauge, *das*
portion ['pɔːʃn] *n.* **a)** *(part)* Teil, *der; (of ticket)* Abschnitt, *der;* **b)** *(of food)* Portion, *die*
portly ['pɔːtlɪ] *adj.* beleibt
portrait ['pɔːtrɪt] *n.* Porträt, *das*
portray [pɔː'treɪ] *v.t.* darstellen; *(make likeness of)* porträtieren

Portugal ['pɔːtjʊgl] *pr. n.* Portugal *(das).* **Portuguese** [pɔːtjʊˈgiːz] **1.** *adj.* portugiesisch; **sb. is** ~: jmd. ist Portugiese/Portugiesin. **2.** *n., pl. same* **a)** *(person)* Portugiese, *der*/Portugiesin, *die·* **b)** *(language)* Portugiesisch, *das; see also* **English 2 a**

pose [pəʊz] **1.** *v. t.* aufwerfen ⟨*Frage, Problem*⟩; darstellen ⟨*Bedrohung*⟩; mit sich bringen ⟨*Schwierigkeiten*⟩. **2.** *v. i.* **a)** *(assume attitude)* posieren; *(fig.)* sich geziert benehmen; **b)** ~ **as** sich geben als. **3.** *n.* Pose, *die;* **strike a** ~: eine Pose einnehmen. **poser** ['pəʊzə(r)] *n. (question)* knifflige Frage

posh [pɒʃ] *adj. (coll.)* vornehm; nobel *(spött.);* stinkvornehm *(salopp)*

position [pəˈzɪʃn] **1.** *n.* **a)** *(place occupied)* Platz, *der; (of player in team, of plane, ship, etc.)* Position, *die; (of hands of clock, words, stars)* Stellung, *die; (of building)* Lage, *die;* **be in/out of** ~: an seinem Platz/nicht an seinem Platz sein; **b)** *(Mil.)* Stellung, *die;* **c)** *(fig.: mental attitude)* Standpunkt, *der;* **d)** *(fig.: situation)* **be in a good** ~ **[financially]** [finanziell] gut gestellt sein; **be in a** ~ **of strength** eine starke Position haben; **e)** *(rank)* Stellung, *die;* **f)** *(job)* Stelle, *die;* **g)** *(posture)* Haltung, *die.* **2.** *v. t.* plazieren; postieren ⟨*Polizisten, Wachen*⟩; ~ **oneself** sich stellen/*(sit)* setzen

positive ['pɒzɪtɪv] *adj.* **a)** *(also Math.)* positiv; konstruktiv ⟨*Vorschlag*⟩; *(definite)* eindeutig; *(convinced)* sicher; **I'm** ~ **of it** ich bin [mir] [dessen] ganz sicher; **b)** *(Electr.)* positiv ⟨*Elektrode, Ladung*⟩; Plus⟨*platte, -leiter*⟩; **c)** *as intensifier (coll.)* echt

possess [pəˈzes] *v. t.* besitzen; *(as faculty or quality)* haben; ⟨*Furcht usw.*⟩ ergreifen; **what** ~**ed you?** *(coll.)* was ist in dich gefahren? **possessed** [pəˈzest] *adj.* besessen. **possession** [pəˈzeʃn] *n.* **a)** *(thing possessed)* Besitz, *der;* **some of my** ~**s** einige meiner Sachen; **b)** *in pl. (property)* Besitz, *der;* **c)** *(possessing)* Besitz, *der;* **be in** ~ **of sth.** im Besitz einer Sache *(Gen.)* sein; **take** ~ **of** in Besitz nehmen; beziehen ⟨*Haus, Wohnung*⟩. **possessive** [pəˈzesɪv] *adj.* **a)** besitzergreifend; **be** ~ **about sth./sb.** etw. eifersüchtig hüten/ an jmdn. Besitzansprüche stellen; **b)** *(Ling.)* possessiv. **possessor** [pəˈzesə(r)] *n.* Besitzer, *der*/Besitzerin, *die*

possibility [pɒsɪˈbɪlɪtɪ] *n.* Möglichkeit, *die*

possible ['pɒsɪbl] *adj.* möglich; *(lihely)* [gut] möglich; **if** ~: wenn möglich; **as ... as** ~: so ... wie möglich; **möglichst ... possibly** ['pɒsɪblɪ] *adv.* **a) as often as I** ~ **can** so oft ich irgend kann; **I cannot** ~ **commit myself** ich kann mich unmöglich festlegen; **b)** *(perhaps)* möglicherweise

¹**post** [pəʊst] *n.* **a)** *(as support)* Pfosten, *der;* **b)** *(stake)* Pfahl, *der;* **c)** *(starting/finishing* ~*)* Start-/Zielpfosten, *der*

²**post 1.** *n.* **a)** *(Brit.: one dispatch/delivery of letters)* Postausgang, *der*/Post[zustellung], *die;* **by return of** ~: postwendend; **b)** *no indef. art. (Brit.: official conveying)* Post, *die;* **by** ~: mit der Post; per Post; **c)** *(*~ *office)* Post, *die.* **2.** *v. t.* **a)** abschicken; **b)** *(fig. coll.)* **keep sb.** ~**ed** jmdn. auf dem laufenden halten

³**post 1.** *n.* **a)** *(job)* Stelle, *die;* Posten, *der;* **b)** *(Mil.; also fig.)* Posten, *der.* **2.** *v. t.* postieren; aufstellen

postage ['pəʊstɪdʒ] *n.* Porto, *das*

postal ['pəʊstl] *adj.* Post-; postalisch ⟨*Aufgabe, Einrichtung*⟩; *(by post)* per Post *nachgestellt.* '**postal order** *n.* ≈ Postanweisung, *die*

post: ~**box** *n. (Brit.)* Briefkasten, *der;* ~**card** *n.* Postkarte, *die;* ~**code** *n. (Brit.)* Postleitzahl, *die;* ~**ˈdate** *v. t. (give later date to)* vordatieren

poster ['pəʊstə(r)] *n.* Plakat, *das*

posterior [pɒˈstɪərɪə(r)] *n. (joc.)* Hinterteil, *das (ugs.)*

posterity [pɒˈsterɪtɪ] *n., no art.* Nachwelt, *die*

posthumous ['pɒstjʊməs] *adj.* postum

post: ~**man** ['pəʊstmən], *pl.* ~**men** ['pəʊstmən] *n.* Briefträger, *der;* ~**mark 1.** *n.* Poststempel, *der;* **2.** *v. t.* abstempeln

post-mortem [pəʊstˈmɔːtəm] *n.* Obduktion, *die*

post office *n.* **a)** *(organization)* **the P~ Office** die Post; **b)** *(place)* Postamt, *das;* Post, *die*

postpone [pəˈspəʊn] *v. t.* verschieben; *(for an indefinite period)* aufschieben. **postˈponement** *n.* Verschiebung, *die*/Aufschub, *der*

postscript ['pəʊskrɪpt] *n.* Nachschrift, *die; (fig.)* Nachtrag, *der*

posture ['pɒstʃə(r)] *n.* [Körper]haltung, *die*

'**post-war** *adj.* Nachkriegs-; der Nachkriegszeit *nachgestellt*

posy ['pəʊzɪ] *n.* Sträußchen, *das*

pot [pɒt] **1.** *n.* **a)** [Koch]topf, *der;* go to ~ *(coll.)* den Bach runtergehen *(ugs.);* **b)** *(container, contents)* Topf, *der; (tea-pot, coffee-pot)* Kanne, *die;* **c)** *(coll.: large sum)* **a** ~ of/~s of massenweise. **2.** *v.t.* ~ [up] eintopfen ⟨*Pflanze*⟩

potassium [pə'tæsıəm] *n.* Kalium, *das*

potato [pə'teıtəʊ] *n., pl.* ~es Kartoffel, *die*

potent ['pəʊtənt] *adj.* [hoch]wirksam ⟨*Droge*⟩; stark ⟨*Schnaps usw.*⟩; schlag-kräftig ⟨*Waffe*⟩

potential [pə'tenʃl] **1.** *adj.* potentiell *(geh.)*; möglich. **2.** *n.* Potential, *das (geh.)*; Möglichkeiten

'**pot-hole** *n.* **a)** Schlagloch, *das;* **b)** *(cave)* [tiefe] Höhle. '**pot-holer** *n.* Höhlenforscher, *der/*-forscherin, *die*

'**pot-shot** *n.* take **a** ~ [at sb./sth.] aufs Geratewohl [auf jmdn./etw.] schießen

'**potted** *adj.* **a)** *(planted)* Topf-; **b)** *(abridged)* kurzgefaßt

¹**potter** *n.* Töpfer, *der/*Töpferin, *die*

²**potter** *v.i.* ~ [about] [he]rumwerkeln *(ugs.)*

pottery ['pɒtərı] *n.* **a)** Töpferware, *die;* **b)** *(workshop, craft)* Töpferei, *die*

¹**potty** ['pɒtı] *adj. (Brit. sl.)* verrückt *(ugs.)* **(about, on** nach)

²**potty** *n. (Brit. coll.)* Töpfchen, *das*

pouch [paʊtʃ] *n.* Beutel, *der*

pouffe [pu:f] *n.* Sitzpolster, *das*

poultry ['pəʊltrı] *n.* Geflügel, *das*

pounce [paʊns] *v.i.* **a)** sich auf sein Opfer stürzen; ⟨*Raubvogel:*⟩ herabsto-ßen auf (+ *Akk.*); **b)** *(fig.)* ~ [up]on/at sich stürzen auf (+ *Akk.*)

¹**pound** [paʊnd] *n.* **a)** *(unit of weight)* [britisches] Pfund *(453,6 Gramm);* two ~[s] of apples 2 Pfund Äpfel; **b)** *(unit of currency)* Pfund, *das*

²**pound** *n. (enclosure)* Pferch, *der; (for stray dogs)* Zwinger, *der; (for cars)* Ab-stellplatz, *der*

³**pound 1.** *v.t. (crush)* zerstoßen. **2.** *v.i.* **a)** *(make one's way heavily)* stampfen; **b)** ⟨*Herz:*⟩ heftig schlagen

pour [pɔ:(r)] **1.** *v.t.* gießen; *(into cup, glass)* einschenken. **2.** *v.i.* **a)** *(flow)* strömen; ⟨*Rauch:*⟩ hervorquellen **(from** aus); ~ **[with rain]** in Strömen regnen; **b)** *(fig.)* strömen; ~ **in** her-ein-/hineinströmen; ~ **out** heraus-/hinausströmen. **pour** 'down *v.i.* it's ~ing down es gießt [in Strömen] *(ugs.)*

pout [paʊt] **1.** *v.i.* einen Schmollmund machen. **2.** *v.t.* aufwerfen ⟨*Lippen*⟩

poverty ['pɒvətı] *n.* Armut, *die*

powder ['paʊdə(r)] **1.** *n.* **a)** Pulver, *das;* **b)** *(cosmetic)* Puder, *der.* **2.** *v.t.* **a)** pudern; **b)** *(reduce to* ~*)* pulverisie-ren; ~**ed milk** Milchpulver, *das.* '**powdery** *adj.* pulv[e]rig

power ['paʊə(r)] **1.** *n.* **a)** *(ability)* Kraft, *die;* **do all in one's** ~ **to help sb.** alles in seiner Macht Stehende tun, um jmdm. zu helfen; **b)** *(faculty)* Fä-higkeit, *die;* **c)** *(strength, intensity)* Kraft, *die; (of blow)* Wucht, *die;* **d)** *(authority, political* ~*)* Macht, *die* **(over** über + *Akk.*); **come into** ~: an die Macht kommen; **e)** *(authorization)* Vollmacht, *die;* **f)** *(State)* Macht, *die;* **g)** *(Math.)* Potenz, *die;* **h)** *(Mech., Electr.)* Kraft, *die; (electric current)* Strom, *der.* **2.** *v.t.* ⟨*Treibstoff, Strom:*⟩ antreiben; ⟨*Batterie:*⟩ mit Energie ver-sorgen. **powerful** ['paʊəfl] *adj.* **a)** *(strong)* stark; kräftig ⟨*Tritt, Schlag, Tier*⟩; heftig ⟨*Gefühl, Empfindung*⟩; hell, strahlend ⟨*Licht*⟩; **b)** mächtig ⟨*Clique, Person, Herrscher*⟩. '**power-less** *adj.* machtlos. '**power station** *n.* Kraftwerk, *das*

p.p. [pi:'pi:] *abbr.* by proxy pp[a].

pp. *abbr.* pages

practicable ['præktıkəbl] *adj.* durch-führbar ⟨*Projekt, Plan*⟩

practical ['præktıkl] *adj.* **a)** praktisch; praktisch veranlagt ⟨*Person*⟩; **b)** *(vir-tual)* tatsächlich; **c)** *(feasible)* mög-lich. **practical 'joke** *n.* Streich, *der*

'**practically** *adv.* praktisch; *(almost)* so gut wie; praktisch *(ugs.)*

¹**practice** ['præktıs] *n.* **a)** *(repeated exercise)* Übung, *die;* **be out of** ~: au-ßer Übung sein; **b)** *(session)* Übungen *Pl.;* **piano** ~: Klavierüben, *das;* **c)** *(of doctor, lawyer, etc.)* Praxis, *die;* **d)** *(ac-tion)* **put sth. into** ~: etw. in die Praxis umsetzen; **e)** *(custom)* Gewohnheit, *die;* **regular** ~: Brauch, *der*

²**practice, practiced, practicing** *(Amer.)* see **practis-**

practise ['præktıs] **1.** *v.t.* **a)** *(apply)* anwenden; praktizieren; **b)** ausüben ⟨*Beruf, Religion*⟩; **c)** trainieren in (+ *Dat.*) ⟨*Sportart*⟩; ~ **the piano/flute** Klavier/Flöte üben. **2.** *v.i.* üben. **practised** ['præktıst] *adj.* geübt. **practising** ['præktısıŋ] *adj.* prakti-zierend ⟨*Arzt, Katholik usw.*⟩

pragmatic [præg'mætık] *adj.* pragma-tisch

Prague [prɑ:g] *pr. n.* Prag *(das)*

prairie ['preərı] *n.* Grassteppe, *die; (in North America)* Prärie, *die*

praise [preɪz] 1. *v.t.* loben; *(more strongly)* rühmen. 2. *n.* Lob, *das.* **'praiseworthy** *adj.* lobenswert

pram [præm] *n. (Brit.)* Kinderwagen, *der*

prance [prɑːns] *v.i.* a) ⟨*Pferd:*⟩ tänzeln; b) *(fig.)* stolzieren; ~ **about** *or* **around** herumhüpfen

prank [præŋk] *n.* Streich, *der*

prattle ['prætl] 1. *v.i.* plappern *(ugs.).* 2. *n.* Geplapper, *das (ugs.).*

prawn [prɔːn] *n.* Garnele, *die*

pray [preɪ] *v.i.* beten **(for um). prayer** [preə(r)] *n.* a) Gebet, *das;* b) *no art. (praying)* Beten, *das*

preach [priːtʃ] 1. *v.i.* predigen **(to zu,** vor + *Dat.;* **on** über + *Akk.).* 2. *v.t.* halten ⟨*Predigt*⟩; predigen ⟨*Evangelium, Botschaft*⟩. **'preacher** *n.* Prediger, *der*/Predigerin, *die*

precarious [prɪ'keərɪəs] *adj.* a) *(uncertain)* labil; prekär; **make a ~ living** eine unsichere Existenz haben; b) *(insecure, dangerous)* gefährlich

precaution [prɪ'kɔːʃn] *n.* Vorsichts-, Schutzmaßnahme, *die;* **as a ~:** vorsichtshalber

precede [prɪ'siːd] *v.t. (in order or time)* vorangehen (+ *Dat.).* **precedence** ['presɪdəns] *n.* Priorität, *die (geh.),* Vorrang, *der* **(over** vor + *Dat.).* **precedent** ['presɪdənt] *n.* Präzedenzfall, *der*

precinct ['priːsɪŋkt] *n.* a) ⟨pedestrian⟩ ~: Fußgängerzone, *die;* b) *(Amer.: district)* Bezirk, *der*

precious ['preʃəs] 1. *adj.* a) kostbar ⟨*Schmuckstück, Zeit*⟩; b) *(beloved)* lieb; c) *(affected)* affektiert. 2. *adv. (coll.)* herzlich ⟨*wenig, wenige*⟩

precipice ['presɪpɪs] *n.* Abgrund, *der*

precipitate 1. [prɪ'sɪpɪtət] *adj.* eilig ⟨*Flucht*⟩; übereilt ⟨*Entschluß*⟩. 2. [prɪ'sɪpɪteɪt] *v.t. (hasten)* beschleunigen; *(trigger)* auslösen

precipitation [prɪsɪpɪ'teɪʃn] *n. (Meteorol.)* Niederschlag, *der*

precipitous [prɪ'sɪpɪtəs] *adj.* a) *(steep)* sehr steil; b) *see* precipitate 1

précis ['preɪsiː] *n., pl. same* [preɪsiːz] Zusammenfassung, *die*

precise [prɪ'saɪs] *adj.* genau; präzise; fein ⟨*Instrument*⟩; förmlich ⟨*Art*⟩; **be |more|** ~: sich präzise[r] ausdrücken. **pre'cisely** *adv.* genau. **precision** [prɪ'sɪʒn] *n.* Genauigkeit, *die*

preclude [prɪ'kluːd] *v.t.* ausschließen

precocious [prɪ'kəʊʃəs] *adj.* frühreif ⟨*Kind*⟩; altklug ⟨*Äußerung*⟩

preconceived [priːkən'siːvd] *adj.* vorgefaßt ⟨*Ansicht, Vorstellung*⟩. **preconception** [priːkən'sepʃn] *n.* vorgefaßte Meinung **(of** über + *Akk.)*

precondition [priːkən'dɪʃn] *n.* Vorbedingung, *die* **(of** für)

precursor [priː'kɜːsə(r)] *n.* Wegbereiter, *der*/-bereiterin, *die*

predator ['predətə(r)] *n.* Raubtier, *das;* *(fish)* Raubfisch, *der.* **'predatory** *adj.* räuberisch; ~ **animal** Raubtier, *das*

predecessor ['priːdɪsesə(r)] *n.* Vorgänger, *der*/-gängerin, *die*

predestine [priː'destɪn] *v.t.* von vornherein bestimmen **(to zu)**

predicament [prɪ'dɪkəmənt] *n.* Dilemma, *das*

predicate ['predɪkət] *n. (Ling.)* Prädikat, *das.* **predicative** [prɪ'dɪkətɪv] *adj. (Ling.)* prädikativ

predict [prɪ'dɪkt] *v.t.* voraus-, vorhersagen; vorhersehen ⟨*Folgen*⟩. **predictable** [prɪ'dɪktəbl] *adj.* voraussagbar; vorhersehbar ⟨*Ereignis, Reaktion*⟩; berechenbar ⟨*Person*⟩. **prediction** [prɪ'dɪkʃn] *n.* Vorhersage, *die*

predominance [prɪ'dɒmɪnəns] *n.* a) *(control)* Vorherrschaft, *die* **(over** über + *Akk.);* b) *(majority)* Überzahl, *die* **(of** von)

predominant [prɪ'dɒmɪnənt] *adj. (having more power)* dominierend; *(prevailing)* vorherrschend

predominate [prɪ'dɒmɪneɪt] *v.i. (be more powerful)* dominierend sein; *(be more important)* vorherrschen

pre-eminent [priː'emɪnənt] *adj.* herausragend

pre-empt [priː'empt] *v.t.* zuvorkommen (+ *Dat.)*

preen [priːn] *v.t.* putzen ⟨*Federn*⟩

prefab ['priːfæb] *n. (coll.)* Fertighaus, *das.* **prefabricated** [priː'fæbrɪkeɪtɪd] *adj.* vorgefertigt

preface ['prefəs] 1. *n.* Vorwort, *das* **(to** Gen.). 2. *v.t. (introduce)* einleiten

prefect ['priːfekt] *n. (Sch.)* die Aufsicht führender älterer Schüler/führende ältere Schülerin

prefer [prɪ'fɜː(r)] *v.t.,* -rr- vorziehen; ~ **to do sth.** etw. lieber tun; ~ **sth. to sth.** etw. einer Sache *(Dat.)* vorziehen. **preferable** ['prefərəbl] *adj.* vorzuziehen *präd.;* vorzuziehend *attr.;* besser **(to** als). **preferably** ['prefərəblɪ] *adv.* am besten; *(as best liked)* am liebsten; **Wine or beer?** – **Wine,** ~! Wein oder Bier? – Lieber Wein! **preference**

['prefərəns] *n.* **a)** *(greater liking)* Vorliebe, *die;* **for ~** *see* **preferably; have a ~ for sth. |over sth.|** etw. [einer Sache *(Dat.)*] vorziehen; **do sth. in ~ to sth.** else etw. lieber als etw. anderes tun; **b)** *(thing preferred)* **what are your ~s?** was wäre dir am liebsten?; **c) give ~ to sb.** jmdn. bevorzugen. **preferential** [prefə'renʃl] *adj.* bevorzugt ⟨*Behandlung*⟩

prefix ['pri:fɪks] *n.* Präfix, *das*

pregnancy ['pregnənsɪ] *n. (of woman)* Schwangerschaft, *die; (of animal)* Trächtigkeit, *die*

pregnant ['pregnənt] *adj.* schwanger ⟨*Frau*⟩; trächtig ⟨*Tier*⟩

prehistoric [pri:hɪ'stɒrɪk] *adj.* prähistorisch. **prehistory** [pri:'hɪstərɪ] Vorgeschichte, *die*

prejudge [pri:'dʒʌdʒ] *v.t.* vorschnell urteilen über (+ *Akk.*)

prejudice ['predʒʊdɪs] **1.** *n.* Vorurteil, *das.* **2.** *v.t.* beeinflussen. **prejudiced** ['predʒʊdɪst] *adj.* voreingenommen (**about** gegenüber, **against** gegen)

preliminary [prɪ'lɪmɪnərɪ] **1.** *adj.* Vor-; vorbereitend ⟨*Forschung, Maßnahme*⟩. **2.** *n., usu. in pl.* **preliminaries** Präliminarien *Pl.;* **as a ~ to sth.** als Vorbereitung auf etw. *(Akk.)*

prelude ['prelju:d] *n.* **a)** *(introduction)* Anfang, *der* (**to** *Gen.*); **b)** *(Theatre, Mus.)* Vorspiel, *das*

premature ['premətjʊə(r)] *adj.* **a)** *(hasty)* übereilt; **b)** *(early)* vorzeitig ⟨*Altern, Ankunft*⟩; verfrüht ⟨*Bericht, Eile*⟩; **~ baby** Frühgeburt, *die.* **prematurely** *adv. (early)* vorzeitig; zu früh ⟨*geboren werden*⟩; *(hastily)* übereilt

premeditated [pri:'medɪteɪtɪd] *adj.* vorsätzlich

premier ['premɪə(r)] *n.* Premier[minister], *der*/Premierministerin, *die*

première ['premɪeə(r)] *n.* Premiere, *die;* Erstaufführung, *die*

premise ['premɪs] *n.* **a) ~s** *pl. (building)* Gebäude, *das; (buildings and land)* Gelände, *das; (rooms)* Räumlichkeiten *Pl.;* **b)** *see* **premiss**

premiss ['premɪs] *n.* Prämisse, *die*

premium ['pri:mɪəm] *n.* Prämie, *die;* **be at a ~** *(fig.)* sehr gefragt sein. **Premium Bond** *n. (Brit.)* Prämienanleihe, *die;* Losanleihe, *die*

premonition [premə'nɪʃn] *n.* Vorahnung, *die*

preoccupation [prɪɒkjʊ'peɪʃn] *n.* Sorge, *die* (**with** um)

preoccupied [prɪ'ɒkjʊpaɪd] *adj. (lost in thought)* gedankenverloren; *(concerned)* besorgt (**with** um)

pre-'packed *adj.* abgepackt

preparation [prepə'reɪʃn] *n.* Vorbereitung, *die; ~s pl.* Vorbereitungen *Pl.* (**for** für). **preparatory** [prɪ'pærətərɪ] **1.** *adj.* vorbereitend ⟨*Maßnahme, Schritt*⟩; **~ work** Vorarbeiten *Pl.* **2.** *adv.* **~ to sth.** vor etw. *(Dat.)*

prepare [prɪ'peə(r)] **1.** *v.t.* **a)** vorbereiten; ausarbeiten ⟨*Plan, Rede*⟩; vorbereiten ⟨*Person*⟩ (**for** auf + *Akk.*); **be ~d to do sth.** *(be willing)* bereit sein, etw. zu tun; **b)** herstellen ⟨*Chemikalie usw.*⟩; zubereiten ⟨*Essen*⟩. **2.** *v.i.* sich vorbereiten (**for** auf + *Akk.*)

prepaid [pri:'peɪd] *adj.* **~ envelope** frankierter Umschlag

preponderance [prɪ'pɒndərəns] *n.* Überlegenheit, *die* (**over** über + *Akk.*)

preposition [prepə'zɪʃn] *n. (Ling.)* Präposition, *die*

prepossessing [pri:pə'zesɪŋ] *adj.* einnehmend

preposterous [prɪ'pɒstərəs] *adj.* absurd; grotesk ⟨*Äußeres, Kleidung*⟩

prerequisite [pri:'rekwɪzɪt] **1.** *n.* [Grund]voraussetzung, *die.* **2.** *adj.* unbedingt erforderlich

prerogative [prɪ'rɒgətɪv] *n.* Privileg, *das;* Vorrecht, *das*

Presbyterian [prezbɪ'tɪərɪən] **1.** *adj.* presbyterianisch. **2.** *n.* Presbyterianer, *der*/Presbyterianerin, *die*

prescribe [prɪ'skraɪb] *v.t.* **a)** *(impose)* vorschreiben; **b)** *(Med.; also fig.)* verschreiben. **prescription** [prɪ'skrɪpʃn] *n.* **a)** Vorschreiben, *das;* **b)** *(Med.)* Rezept, *das*

presence ['prezəns] *n.* **a)** *(of person)* Anwesenheit, *die; (of things)* Vorhandensein, *das;* **in the ~ of** in Anwesenheit (+ *Gen.*); **b) ~ of mind** Geistesgegenwart, *die*

¹present ['prezənt] **1.** *adj.* **a)** anwesend (**at** bei); **all those ~:** alle Anwesenden; **b)** *(existing now)* gegenwärtig; jetzig ⟨*Bischof, Chef usw.*⟩; **c)** *(Ling.)* **~ tense** Präsens, *das;* Gegenwart, *die.* **2.** *n.* **a) the ~:** die Gegenwart; **at ~:** zur Zeit; **for the ~:** vorläufig; **b)** *(Ling.)* Präsens, *das;* Gegenwart, *die*

²present 1. ['prezənt] *n. (gift)* Geschenk, *das.* **2.** [prɪ'zent] *v.t.* **a)** schenken; überreichen ⟨*Preis, Medaille, Geschenk*⟩; **~ sth. to sb.** *or* **sb. with sth.** jmdm. etw. schenken/überreichen; **~**

sb. with difficulties/a problem jmdn.
vor Schwierigkeiten/ein Problem stellen; b) überreichen ⟨Gesuch⟩ (to bei);
vorlegen ⟨Scheck, Bericht, Rechnung⟩
(to Dat.); ~ one's case seinen Fall darlegen; c) (exhibit) zeigen; bereiten
⟨Schwierigkeit⟩; d) (introduce) vorstellen (to Dat.); vorlegen ⟨Abhandlung⟩;
moderieren ⟨Sendung⟩. 3. v. refl.
⟨Problem:⟩ auftreten; ⟨Möglichkeit:⟩
sich ergeben; ~ oneself for an interview zu einem Gespräch erscheinen.
presentable [prɪ'zentəbl] adj. ansehnlich; I'm not ~: ich kann mich
nicht so zeigen. **presentation** [prez-
ən'teɪʃn] n. a) (giving) Schenkung, die;
(of prize, medal) Überreichung, die; b)
(ceremony) Verleihung, die; c) (of petition) Überreichung, die; (of cheque, report, account) Vorlage, die; (of case)
Darlegung, die
present-'day adj. heutig
presenter [prɪ'zentə(r)] n. (Radio,
Telev.) Moderator, der/Moderatorin,
die
presentiment [prɪ'zentɪmənt] n. Vorahnung, die
presently ['prezəntlɪ] adv. bald;
(Amer., Scot.: now) zur Zeit
preservation [prezə'veɪʃn] n. Erhaltung, die; (of leather, wood, etc.) Konservierung, die. **preservative** [prɪ-
'zɜːvətɪv] n. Konservierungsmittel, das
preserve [prɪ'zɜːv] 1. n. a) in sing. or
pl. (fruit) Eingemachte, das; b) (fig.:
special sphere) Domäne, die (geh.); c)
wildlife/game ~: Tierschutzgebiet,
das/Wildpark, der. 2. v. t. a) (keep
safe) schützen (from + Dat.); b)
bewahren ⟨Brauch⟩; wahren ⟨An-
schein, Reputation⟩; c) (keep from decay) konservieren; einmachen ⟨Obst,
Gemüse⟩; d) (protect) hegen ⟨Tierart,
Wald⟩
preside [prɪ'zaɪd] v. i. präsidieren, vor-
sitzen (over Dat.); (at meeting etc.)
den Vorsitz haben (at bei)
presidency ['prezɪdənsɪ] n. a) Präsi-
dentschaft, die; b) (of society) Vorsitz,
der
president ['prezɪdənt] n. a) Präsident,
der/Präsidentin, die; b) (of society)
Vorsitzende, der/die. **presidential**
[prezɪ'denʃl] adj. Präsidenten-
¹press [pres] 1. n. a) (newspapers etc.)
Presse, die; attrib. Presse-; b) see
printing-press; c) (for flattening, com-
pressing, etc.) Presse, die. 2. v. t. a)
drücken; drücken auf (+ Akk.) ⟨Klin-

gel, Knopf⟩; treten auf (+ Akk.)
⟨Gas-, Brems-, Kupplungspedal usw.⟩;
b) (urge) drängen ⟨Person⟩; (force)
aufdrängen (|up|on Dat.); nachdrück-
lich vorbringen ⟨Forderung, Argu-
ment⟩; he did not ~ the point er ließ
die Sache auf sich beruhen; c) (compress) pressen; auspressen ⟨Orangen,
Saft⟩; keltern ⟨Trauben, Äpfel⟩; d)
(iron) bügeln; e) be ~ed for time/
money zu wenig Zeit/Geld haben. 3.
v. i. a) (exert pressure) drücken; b) (be
urgent) drängen; c) (make demand) ~
for sth. auf etw. (Akk.) drängen.
press a'head, press 'on v. i. (continue) [zügig] weitermachen; (continue
travelling) [zügig] weitergehen/-fah-
ren; ~ on with one's work sich mit der
Arbeit ranhalten (ugs.)
²press v. t. ~ into service/use in Dienst
nehmen; einsetzen
press conference n. Pressekonfe-
renz, die
'pressing adj. (urgent) dringend
press: ~ release n. Presseinformati-
on, die; ~-up n. Liegestütz, der
pressure ['preʃə(r)] 1. n. Druck, der; ~
put ~ on sb. jmdn. unter Druck setzen; atmospheric ~: Luftdruck, der. 2.
v. t. unter Druck setzen ⟨Person⟩; ~
sb. into doing sth. jmdn. [dazu] drängen, etw. zu tun. **'pressure-cooker**
n. Schnellkochtopf, der. **'pressure
group** n. Pressure-group, die
pressurize ['preʃəraɪz] v. t. a) see
pressure 2; b) ~d cabin Druckkabine,
die
prestige [pre'stiːʒ] n. Prestige, das.
prestigious [pre'stɪdʒəs] adj. angesehen
presumably [prɪ'zjuːməblɪ] adv. vermutlich
presume [prɪ'zjuːm] 1. v. t. a) ~ to do
sth. sich (Dat.) anmaßen, etw. zu tun;
(take the liberty) sich (Dat.) erlauben,
etw. zu tun; b) (suppose) annehmen. 2.
v. i. |up|on sth. etw. ausnützen. **pre-
sumption** [prɪ'zʌmpʃn] n. a) (arrogance) Anmaßung, die; b) (assumption)
Annahme, die. **presumptuous** [prɪ-
'zʌmptjʊəs] adj. anmaßend
presuppose [priːsə'pəʊz] v. t. voraussetzen
pretence [prɪ'tens] n. (Brit.) a) (pretext) Vorwand, der; b) no art. (make-
believe, insincere behaviour) Verstellung, die; it is all or just a ~: das ist alles nicht echt
pretend [prɪ'tend] 1. v. t. a) vorgeben;

she ~ed to be asleep sie tat, als ob sie schlief[e]; **b)** *(imagine in play)* ~ **to be sth.** so tun, als ob man etw. sei. **2.** *v. i.* sich verstellen; **she's only ~ing** sie tut nur so

pretense *(Amer.) see* **pretence**

pretension [prɪ'tenʃn] *n.* **a)** Anspruch, *der* **(to** auf + *Akk.*); **b)** *(pretentiousness)* Überheblichkeit, *die.* **pretentious** [prɪ'tenʃəs] *adj.* hochgestochen; wichtigtuerisch ⟨*Person*⟩; *(ostentatious)* großspurig

pretext ['pri:tekst] *n.* Vorwand, *der;* [up]on *or* **under the** ~ **of doing sth.** unter dem Vorwand, etw. tun zu wollen

prettily ['prɪtɪlɪ] *adv.* hübsch; sehr schön ⟨*singen, tanzen*⟩

pretty ['prɪtɪ] **1.** *adj. (also iron.)* hübsch. **2.** *adv.* ziemlich; **I am** ~ **well** es geht mir ganz gut

prevail [prɪ'veɪl] *v. i.* **a)** die Oberhand gewinnen **(against, over** über + *Akk.*); ~ [up]on **sb. to do sth.** jmdn. dazu bewegen, etw. zu tun; **b)** *(predominate)* ⟨*Zustand, Bedingung:*⟩ vorherrschen; **c)** *(be current)* herrschen

prevalence ['prevələns] *n.* Vorherrschen, *das*

prevalent ['prevələnt] *adj.* **a)** *(existing)* herrschend; weit verbreitet ⟨*Krankheit*⟩; **b)** *(predominant)* vorherrschend

prevent [prɪ'vent] *v. t. (hinder)* verhindern; *(forestall)* vorbeugen; ~ **sb. from doing sth.,** ~ **sb.'s doing sth.,** *(coll.)* ~ **sb. doing sth.** jmdn. daran hindern, etw. zu tun. **prevention** [prɪ'venʃn] *n.* Verhinderung, *die;* *(forestalling)* Vorbeugung, *die.* **preventive** [prɪ'ventɪv] *adj.* vorbeugend; Präventiv⟨*maßnahme*⟩

preview ['pri:vju:] *n. (of film, play)* Voraufführung, *die;* *(of exhibition)* Vernissage, *die (geh.)*

previous ['pri:vɪəs] **1.** *adj.* **a)** früher ⟨*Anstellung, Gelegenheit*⟩; vorherig ⟨*Abend*⟩; vorig ⟨*Besitzer, Wohnsitz*⟩; **the** ~ **page** die Seite davor; **b)** *(prior)* ~ **to** vor (+ *Dat.*). **2.** *adv.* ~ **to** vor (+ *Dat.*). '**previously** *adv.* vorher

pre-war ['pri:wɔː(r)] *adj.* Vorkriegs-

prey [preɪ] **1.** *n., pl. same* **a)** *(animal[s])* Beute, *die;* **beast/bird of** ~: Raubtier, *das/*-vogel, *der;* **b)** *(victim)* Opfer, *das.* **2.** *v. i.* ~ [up]on ⟨*Raubtier, Raubvogel:*⟩ schlagen; *(plunder)* ausplündern ⟨*Person*⟩; Jagd machen auf (+ *Akk.*); ~ [up]on **sb.'s mind** jmdm. keine Ruhe lassen

price [praɪs] *n. (lit. or fig.)* Preis, *der;* **at a** ~ **of** zum Preis von; **what is the** ~ **of this?** was kostet das?; **at/not at any** ~: um jeden/keinen Preis. '**priceless** *adj.* **a)** *(invaluable)* unbezahlbar; **b)** *(coll.: amusing)* köstlich

price: ~**-list** *n.* Preisliste, *die;* ~**-rise** *n.* Preisanstieg, *der;* ~**-tag** *n.* Preisschild, *das*

prick [prɪk] **1.** *v. t.* stechen; stechen in ⟨*Ballon*⟩; aufstechen ⟨*Blase*⟩. **2.** *v. i.* stechen. **3.** *n.* Stich, *der.* '**prick up** *v. t.* aufrichten ⟨*Ohren*⟩; ~ **up one's/its ears** die Ohren spitzen

prickle ['prɪkl] **1.** *n.* **a)** Dorn, *der;* **b)** *(Zool., Bot.)* Stachel, *der.* **2.** *v. i.* kratzen. **prickly** ['prɪklɪ] *adj.* dornig; stachelig; *(fig.)* empfindlich

pride [praɪd] **1.** *n.* **a)** Stolz, *der;* *(arrogance)* Hochmut, *der;* **take** [a] ~ **in sb./ sth.** auf jmdn./etw. stolz sein; **sb's** ~ **and joy** jmds. ganzer Stolz; **b)** *(of lions)* Rudel, *das.* **2.** *v. refl.* ~ **oneself** [up]on **sth.** auf etw. *(Akk.)* stolz sein

pried *see* **pry**

priest [pri:st] *n.* Priester, *der.* '**priesthood** *n.* geistliches Amt

prim [prɪm] *adj.* spröde; *(prudish)* zimperlich

primarily ['praɪmərɪlɪ] *adv.* in erster Linie

primary ['praɪmərɪ] **1.** *adj.* **a)** *(first)* primär *(geh.);* grundlegend; **b)** *(chief)* Haupt⟨*rolle, -ziel, -zweck*⟩. **2.** *n.* *(Amer.: election)* Vorwahl, *die.* '**primary school** *n.* Grundschule, *die*

primate ['praɪmeɪt] *n.* **a)** *(Eccl.)* Primas, *der;* **b)** *(Zool.)* Primat, *der*

¹**prime** [praɪm] **1.** *n.* Höhepunkt, *der;* **be in one's** ~: in den besten Jahren sein. **2.** *adj.* **a)** Haupt-; hauptsächlich; **b)** *(excellent)* erstklassig; vortrefflich ⟨*Beispiel*⟩

²**prime** *v. t.* **a)** *(equip)* vorbereiten; ~ **sb. with information/advice** jmdn. instruieren/jmdm. Ratschläge erteilen; **b)** grundieren ⟨*Wand, Decke*⟩; **c)** schärfen ⟨*Sprengkörper*⟩

prime: ~ '**minister** *n.* Premierminister, *der/*-ministerin, *die;* ~ '**number** *n. (Math.)* Primzahl, *die*

'**primer** *n.* **a)** *(explosive)* Zündvorrichtung, *die;* **b)** *(paint)* Grundierlack, *der*

primeval [praɪ'mi:vl] *adj.* urzeitlich; Ur⟨*zeiten, -wälder*⟩

primitive ['prɪmɪtɪv] *adj.* primitiv; *(prehistoric)* urzeitlich ⟨*Mensch*⟩

primrose ['prɪmrəʊz] *n.* gelbe Schlüsselblume

Primus, (P) ['praɪməs] *n.* ~ |stove| Primuskocher, *der*

prince [prɪns] *n.* Prinz, *der.* '**princely** *adj.* fürstlich

princess [prɪn'ses] *n.* Prinzessin, *die; (wife of prince)* Fürstin, *die*

principal ['prɪnsɪpl] **1.** *adj.* Haupt-; *(most important)* wichtigst... **2.** *n. (of college)* Rektor, *der*/Rektorin, *die*

principality [prɪnsɪ'pælɪtɪ] *n.* Fürstentum, *das*

'**principally** *adv.* in erster Linie

principle ['prɪnsɪpl] *n.* Prinzip, *das;* on the ~ that ...: nach dem Grundsatz, daß ...; in ~: im Prinzip; do sth. on ~ *or* as a matter of ~: etw. prinzipiell *od.* aus Prinzip tun

print [prɪnt] **1.** *n.* **a)** *(impression)* Abdruck, *der; (finger~)* Fingerabdruck, *der;* **b)** *(~ed lettering)* Gedruckte, *das; (type-face)* Druck, *der;* **c)** be in/out of ~ 〈*Buch:*〉 erhältlich/vergriffen sein; **d)** *(~ed picture or design)* Druck, *der;* **e)** *(Photog.)* Abzug, *der.* **2.** *v.t.* **a)** drucken 〈*Buch, Zeitschrift usw.*〉; **b)** *(write)* in Druckschrift schreiben. **print 'out** *v.t. (Computing)* ausdrucken

'**printed** *adj.* **a)** gedruckt; **b)** *(published)* veröffentlicht. '**printed matter** *n. (Post)* Drucksachen *Pl.*

'**printer** *n.* **a)** *(worker)* Drucker, *der*/Druckerin, *die; (firm)* Druckerei, *die;* **b)** *(Computing)* Drucker, *der*

'**printing** *n.* **a)** Drucken, *das;* **b)** *(writing like print)* Druckschrift, *die;* **c)** *(edition)* Auflage, *die.* '**printing-press** *n.* Druckerpresse, *die*

'**printout** *n. (Computing)* Ausdruck, *der*

prior ['praɪə(r)] **1.** *adj.* vorherig 〈*Warnung, Zustimmung usw.*〉; früher 〈*Verabredung*〉; Vor〈*geschichte, -kenntnis*〉. **2.** *adv.* ~ to vor (+ *Dat.*); ~ to doing sth. bevor man etw. tut/tat; ~ to that vorher. **priority** [praɪ'ɒrɪtɪ] *n.* **a)** *(precedence)* Vorrang, *der; attrib.* vorrangig; have *or* take ~: Vorrang haben (over vor + *Dat.*); have ~ *(on road)* Vorfahrt haben; give ~ to sb./sth. jmdm./einer Sache den Vorrang geben; give top ~ to sth. einer Sache *(Dat.)* höchste Priorität einräumen; **b)** *(matter)* vordringliche Angelegenheit

prism ['prɪzm] *n.* Prisma, *das*

prison ['prɪzn] *n.* **a)** Gefängnis, *das; attrib.* Gefängnis-; **b)** *(custody)* Haft, *die;* in ~: im Gefängnis; go to ~: ins Gefängnis gehen. '**prisoner** *n.* Gefangene, *der/die;* take sb. ~: jmdn. gefangennehmen

pristine ['prɪstiːn] *adj.* unberührt; in ~ condition in tadellosem Zustand

privacy ['prɪvəsɪ] *n.* Privatsphäre, *die; (being undisturbed)* Ungestörtheit, *die;* invasion of ~: Eindringen in die Privatsphäre; in the strictest ~: unter strengster Geheimhaltung

private ['praɪvət] **1.** *adj.* **a)** *(outside State system)* privat; Privat〈*schule, -industrie, -klinik usw.*〉; **b)** persönlich 〈*Dinge, Meinung, Interesse*〉; nichtöffentlich 〈*Versammlung, Sitzung*〉; privat 〈*Telefongespräch, Vereinbarung*〉; Privat〈*strand, -parkplatz, -leben*〉; geheim 〈*Verhandlung, Geschäft*〉; persönlich 〈*Gründe*〉; *(confidential)* vertraulich. **2.** *n.* **a)** *(Brit. Mil.)* einfacher Soldat; **b)** in ~: privat; in kleinem Kreis 〈*feiern*〉; *(confidentially)* ganz im Vertrauen. '**privately** *adv.* privat 〈*erziehen, zugeben*〉; vertraulich 〈*jmdn. sprechen*〉; insgeheim 〈*denken, glauben*〉; ~ owned in Privatbesitz

privation [praɪ'veɪʃn] *n.* Not, *die;* suffer many ~s viele Entbehrungen erleiden

privatize ['praɪvətaɪz] *v.t.* privatisieren

privet ['prɪvɪt] *n.* Liguster, *der*

privilege ['prɪvɪlɪdʒ] *n. (right, immunity)* Privileg, *das; (special benefit)* Sonderrecht, *das; (honour)* Ehre, *die.* '**privileged** *adj.* privilegiert

privy ['prɪvɪ] *adj.* be ~ to sth. in etw. *(Akk.)* eingeweiht sein

'**prize** [praɪz] **1.** *n.* **a)** *(reward, money)* Preis, *der;* win *or* take first ~: den ersten Preis gewinnen; **b)** *(in lottery)* Gewinn, *der.* **2.** *v.t.* ~ sth. |highly| etw. hoch schätzen

²**prize** *v.t.* ~ |open| aufstemmen

prize: ~**-giving** *n.* Preisverleihung, *die;* ~**-money** *n.* Geldpreis, *der; (Sport)* Preisgeld, *das;* ~**-winner** *n.* Preisträger, *der*/-trägerin, *die; (in lottery)* Gewinner, *der*/Gewinnerin, *die*

pro [prəʊ] *n. in pl.* the ~s and cons das Pro und Kontra

probability [prɒbə'bɪlɪtɪ] *n.* Wahrscheinlichkeit, *die;* in all ~: aller Wahrscheinlichkeit nach

probable ['prɒbəbl] *adj.* wahrscheinlich; highly ~: höchstwahrscheinlich

probably ['prɒbəblɪ] *adv.* wahrscheinlich

probation [prə'beɪʃn] *n.* **a)** Probezeit, *die;* **b)** *(Law)* Bewährung, *die;* on ~:

auf Bewährung. **probationary** [prə-'beɪʃənərɪ] *adj.* Probe-; ~ **period** Probezeit, *die*

probe [prəʊb] **1.** *n.* **a)** Untersuchung, *die* (**into** *Gen.*); **b)** (*Med., Astron.*) Sonde, *die.* **2.** *v. t.* untersuchen

problem ['prɒbləm] *n.* Problem, *das;* (*puzzle*) Rätsel, *das;* **what's the ~?** (*coll.*) wo fehlt's denn?; **the ~ about** *or* **with sb./sth.** das Problem mit jmdm./ bei etw. **problematic** [prɒblə'mætɪk], **problematical** [prɒblə'mætɪkl] *adj.* problematisch

procedure [prə'siːdjə(r)] *n.* Verfahren, *das*

proceed [prə'siːd] *v. i.* (*formal*) **a)** (*on foot*) gehen; (*as or by vehicle*) fahren; (*after interruption*) weitergehen/-fahren; **b)** (*begin and carry on*) beginnen; (*after interruption*) fortfahren; ~ **in** *or* **with sth.** (*begin*) [mit] etw. beginnen; (*continue*) etw. fortsetzen; **c)** (*be under way*) ⟨*Verfahren:*⟩ laufen; (*be continued after interruption*) fortgesetzt werden. **pro'ceedings** *n. pl.* **a)** (*events*) Vorgänge; **b)** (*Law*) Verfahren, *das;* **legal** ~: Gerichtsverfahren, *das;* **start/take [legal]** ~: gerichtlich vorgehen (**against** gegen)

proceeds ['prəʊsiːdz] *n. pl.* Erlös, *der* (**from** aus)

¹**process** ['nrəʊses] **1.** *n.* **a)** (*of time or history*) Lauf, *der;* **he learnt a lot in the** ~: er lernte eine Menge dabei; **be in the ~ of doing sth.** gerade etw. tun; **b)** (*proceeding, natural operation*) Vorgang, *der;* **c)** (*method*) Verfahren, *das.* **2.** *v. t.* verarbeiten ⟨*Rohstoff, Signal*⟩; bearbeiten ⟨*Antrag, Akte*⟩; (*Photog.*) entwickeln ⟨*Film*⟩

²**process** [prə'ses] *v. i.* ziehen. **procession** [prə'seʃn] *n.* Zug, *der;* (*religious*) Prozession, *die;* (*festive*) Umzug, *der;* **go/march in** ~: ziehen

proclaim [prə'kleɪm] *v. t.* erklären ⟨*Absicht*⟩; geltend machen ⟨*Recht, Anspruch*⟩; verkünden ⟨*Amnestie*⟩; ausrufen ⟨*Republik*⟩. **proclamation** [prɒklə'meɪʃn] *n.* **a)** (*proclaiming*) Verkündung, *die;* **b)** (*notice*) Bekanntmachung, *die;* (*decree*) Erlaß, *der*

procure [prə'kjʊə(r)] *v. t.* beschaffen

prod [prɒd] **1.** *v. t.,* **-dd-** (*poke*) stupsen (*ugs.*); stoßen mit ⟨*Stock, Finger usw.*⟩; ~ **sb.** **gently** jmdn. anstupsen. **2.** *n.* Stupser, *der;* **give sb. a ~:** jmdm. einen Stupser geben

prodigal ['prɒdɪgl] *adj.* verschwenderisch; ~ **son** verlorener Sohn

prodigious [prə'dɪdʒəs] *adj.* ungeheuer

prodigy ['prɒdɪdʒɪ] *n.* [außergewöhnliches] Talent; **child** ~: Wunderkind, *das*

produce 1. ['prɒdjuːs] *n.* Produkte *Pl.;* Erzeugnisse *Pl.* **2.** [prə'djuːs] *v. t.* **a)** vorzeigen ⟨*Paß, Fahrkarte*⟩; **b)** produzieren ⟨*Show, Film*⟩; inszenieren ⟨*Theaterstück, Hörspiel*⟩; herausgeben ⟨*Schallplatte, Buch*⟩; **c)** (*manufacture*) herstellen; (*in nature; Agric.*) produzieren; **d)** (*cause*) hervorrufen; bewirken ⟨*Änderung*⟩; **e)** (*bring into being*) erzeugen; führen zu ⟨*Situation*⟩; **f)** (*yield*) geben ⟨*Milch*⟩; legen ⟨*Eier*⟩; **g)** ⟨*Baum, Blume:*⟩ tragen ⟨*Früchte, Blüten*⟩; entwickeln ⟨*Triebe*⟩; bilden ⟨*Keime*⟩. **producer** [prə'djuːsə(r)] *n.* **a)** (*Cinemat., Theatre, Radio, Telev.*) Produzent, *der*/Produzentin, *die;* **b)** (*Brit. Theatre/Radio/Telev.*) Regisseur, *der*/Regisseurin, *die*

product ['prɒdʌkt] *n.* **a)** Produkt, *das;* (*of industrial process*) Erzeugnis, *das;* (*of art or intellect*) Werk, *das;* **b)** (*result*) Folge, *die;* **c)** (*Math.*) Produkt, *das* (**of** aus)

production [prə'dʌkʃn] *n.* **a)** (*Cinemat.*) Produktion, *die;* (*Theatre*) Inszenierung, *die;* (*of record, book*) Herausgabe, *die;* **b)** (*making*) Produktion, *die;* (*manufacturing*) Herstellung, *die;* (*thing produced*) Produkt, *das;* (*thing created*) Werk, *das;* **c)** (*yielding*) Produktion, *die;* (*yield*) Ertrag, *der.* **pro'duction line** *n.* Fertigungsstraße, *die*

productive [prə'dʌktɪv] *adj.* leistungsfähig ⟨*Betrieb, Bauernhof*⟩; fruchtbar ⟨*Gespräch, Verhandlungen*⟩. **productivity** [prɒdʌk'tɪvɪtɪ] *n.* Produktivität, *die*

Prof. [prɒf] *abbr.* Professor Prof.

profane [prə'feɪn] *adj.* **a)** (*irreligious*) gotteslästerlich; **b)** (*secular*) weltlich; **c)** (*irreverent*) respektlos ⟨*Bemerkung*⟩; profan ⟨*Sprache*⟩

profess [prə'fes] *v. t.* **a)** (*declare openly*) bekunden ⟨*Vorliebe, Abneigung*⟩; ~ **to be/do sth.** erklären, etw. zu sein/tun; **b)** (*claim*) vorgeben; ~ **to be/do sth.** behaupten, etw. zu sein/tun

profession [prə'feʃn] *n.* **a)** Beruf, *der;* **be a pilot by** ~: von Beruf Pilot sein; **b)** (*body of people*) Berufsstand, *der.* **professional** [prə'feʃənl] **1.** *adj.* **a)** Berufs⟨*ausbildung, -leben*⟩; beruflich ⟨*Qualifikation*⟩; **b)** (*worthy of profes-*

sion) (in technical expertise) fachmännisch; *(in attitude)* professionell; *(in experience)* routiniert; c) ~ **people** Angehörige hochqualifizierter Berufe; d) *(by profession)* gelernt; *(not amateur)* Berufs‹musiker, -sportler›; Profi‹sportler›; e) *(paid)* Profi‹sport, -boxen›. **2.** *n. (trained person)* Fachmann, *der*/Fachfrau, *die; (nonamateur; also Sport)* Profi, *der*

professor [prə'fesə(r)] *n.* **a)** *(Univ.)* Professor, *der*/Professorin, *die* (of für); **b)** *(Amer.: teacher at university)* Dozent, *der*/Dozentin, *die*

proficiency [prə'fiʃənsi] *n.* Können, *das*

proficient [prə'fiʃənt] *adj.* fähig; gut ‹Pianist, Reiter usw.›; geschickt ‹Radfahrer, Handwerker›; **be ~ at** *or* **in maths** viel von Mathematik verstehen

profile ['prəʊfail] *n.* **a)** *(side aspect)* Profil, *das;* **b)** *(biographical sketch)* Porträt, *das;* **c)** *(fig.)* **keep a low ~:** sich zurückhalten

profit ['prɒfit] *n.* Gewinn, *der;* Profit, *der;* **make a ~ from** *or* **out of sth.** mit etw. Geld verdienen; **make [a few pence] ~ on sth.** [ein paar Pfennige] an etw. *(Dat.)* verdienen. **'profit by** *v. t.* profitieren von; Nutzen ziehen aus ‹Fehler, Erfahrung›. **'profit from** *v. t.* profitieren von

profitable ['prɒfitəbl] *adj.* rentabel; einträglich; *(fruitful)* nützlich

profiteer [prɒfi'tiə(r)] **1.** *n.* Profitmacher, *der*/-macherin, *die.* **2.** *v. i.* sich bereichern. **profi'teering** *n.* Wucher, *der*

profligate ['prɒfligət] *adj.* verschwenderisch; **be ~ of** *or* **with sth.** verschwenderisch umgehen mit etw.

profound [prə'faʊnd] *adj.* tief; nachhaltig ‹Wirkung, Einfluß›; tiefgreifend ‹Wandel, Veränderung›; tiefempfunden ‹Beileid, Mitgefühl›; tiefsitzend ‹Mißtrauen›

program ['prəʊgræm] **1.** *n.* **a)** *(Amer.)* see **programme 1;** **b)** *(Computing)* Programm, *das.* **2.** *v. t.,* **-mm-** *(Computing)* programmieren

programme ['prəʊgræm] *n.* **a)** *([notice of] events)* Programm, *das;* **b)** *(Radio, Telev.)* Sendung, *die;* **c)** *(plan, instructions for machine)* Programm, *das*

progress 1. ['prəʊgres] *n.* **a)** *no pl., no indef. art. (onward movement)* [Vorwärts]bewegung, *die; (advance)* Fortschritt, *der;* **make ~:** vorankommen; ‹Student, Patient:› Fortschritte ma-

chen; **in ~:** im Gange. **2.** [prə'gres] *v. i.* **a)** *(move forward)* vorankommen; **b)** *(be carried on, develop)* Fortschritte machen. **progression** [prə'greʃn] *n.* **a)** *(development)* Fortschritt, *der;* **b)** *(succession)* Folge, *die.* **progressive** [prə'gresiv] *adj.* **a)** fortschreitend ‹Verbesserung, Verschlechterung›; schrittweise ‹Reform›; allmählich ‹Veränderung›; **b)** *(favouring reform; in culture)* fortschrittlich; progressiv. **pro'gressively** *adv.* immer ‹schlechter, weiter›

prohibit [prə'hibit] *v. t. (forbid)* verbieten; **~ sb.'s doing sth., ~ sb. from doing sth.** jmdm. verbieten, etw. zu tun. **prohibition** [prəʊhi'biʃn, prəʊi-'biʃn] *n.* Verbot, *das.* **prohibitive** [prə'hibitiv] *adj.* unerschwinglich ‹Preis, Miete›; untragbar ‹Kosten›

project 1. [prə'dʒekt] *v. t.* werfen ‹Schein›; senden ‹Strahl›; *(Cinemat.)* projizieren. **2.** [prə'dʒekt] *v. i. (jut out)* ‹Felsen:› vorspringen; ‹Zähne, Brauen:› vorstehen. **3.** ['prɒdʒekt] *n.* Projekt, *das*

projectile [prə'dʒektail] *n.* Geschoß, *das*

projection [prə'dʒekʃn] *n.* **a)** *(protruding thing)* Vorsprung, *der;* **b)** *(estimate)* Hochrechnung, *die; (forecast)* Voraussage, *die*

projector [prə'dʒektə(r)] *n.* Projektor, *der*

proliferate [prə'lifəreit] *v. i. (increase)* sich ausbreiten. **proliferation** [prəlifə'reiʃn] *n.* starke Zunahme

prolific [prə'lifik] *adj.* **a)** *(fertile)* fruchtbar; **b)** *(productive)* produktiv

prologue *(Amer.:* **prolog)** ['prəʊlɒg] *n.* Prolog, *der* **(to** zu)

prolong [prə'lɒŋ] *v. t.* verlängern. **prolonged** [prə'lɒŋd] *adj.* lang; lang anhaltend ‹Beifall›

promenade [prɒmə'nɑːd] *n.* Promenade, *die*

prominence ['prɒminəns] *n.* **a)** *(conspicuousness)* Auffälligkeit, *die;* **b)** *(distinction)* Bekanntheit, *die*

prominent ['prɒminənt] *adj.* **a)** *(conspicuous)* auffallend; **b)** *(foremost)* herausragend; **he was ~ in politics** er war ein prominenter Politiker; **c)** *(projecting)* vorspringend; vorstehend ‹Backenknochen, Brauen›

promiscuity [prɒmi'skjuːiti] *n.* Promiskuität, *die (geh.)*

promiscuous [prə'miskjʊəs] *adj.* promiskuitiv *(geh.);* **a ~ man** ein Mann, der häufig die Partnerin wechselt

promise ['prɒmɪs] 1. *n.* **a)** Versprechen, *das;* **sb.'s ~s** jmds. Versprechungen; **give** *or* **make a ~ |to sb.|** [jmdm.] ein Versprechen geben; **give** *or* **make a ~ |to sb.| to do sth.** [jmdm.] versprechen, etw. zu tun; **b)** *(fig.: reason for expectation)* Hoffnung, *die;* **a painter of** *or* **with ~:** ein vielversprechender Maler. **2.** *v.t.* **a)** versprechen; **~ sth. to sb., ~ sb. sth.** jmdm. etw. versprechen; **b)** *(fig.: give reason for expectation of)* verheißen *(geh.);* **~ sb. sth.** jmdm. etw. in Aussicht stellen. **3.** *v.i.* **~ well** *or* **favourably** vielversprechend sein; **I can't ~:** ich kann es nicht versprechen. **promising** ['prɒmɪsɪŋ] *adj.* vielversprechend

promote [prə'məʊt] *v.t.* **a)** *(to more senior job)* befördern; **b)** *(encourage)* fördern; **c)** *(publicize)* Werbung machen für; **d)** *(Footb.)* **be ~d** aufsteigen. **pro'moter** *n.* Veranstalter, *der*/Veranstalterin, *die.* **promotion** [prə'məʊʃn] *n.* **a)** Beförderung, *die;* **win** *or* **gain ~:** befördert werden; **b)** *(furtherance)* Förderung, *die;* **c)** *(publicization)* Werbung, *die;* *(instance)* Werbekampagne, *die;* **d)** *(Footb.)* Aufstieg, *der.* **promotional** [prə'məʊʃənl] *adj.* Werbe⟨*kampagne, -broschüre usw.*⟩

prompt [prɒmpt] 1. *adj.* **a)** *(ready to act)* bereitwillig; **be ~ in doing sth.** *or* **to do sth.** unverzüglich tun; **b)** *(done readily)* sofortig; **her ~ answer** ihre prompte Antwort; **take ~ action** sofort handeln; **c)** *(punctual)* pünktlich. **2.** *adv.* pünktlich; **at 6 o'clock ~:** Punkt 6 Uhr. **3.** *v.t.* **a)** *(incite)* veranlassen; **b)** *(supply with words)* soufflieren (+ *Dat.*); *(give suggestion to)* weiterhelfen (+ *Dat.*); **c)** hervorrufen ⟨*Kritik*⟩; provozieren ⟨*Antwort*⟩. **'promptly** *adv.* **a)** *(quickly)* prompt; **b)** *(punctually)* pünktlich

prone [prəʊn] *adj. (liable)* **be ~ to** anfällig sein für ⟨*Krankheiten*⟩; **be ~ to do sth.** dazu neigen, etw. zu tun

prong [prɒŋ] *n. (of fork)* Zinke, *die*

pronoun ['prəʊnaʊn] *n. (Ling.)* Pronomen, *das;* Fürwort, *das*

pronounce [prə'naʊns] 1. *v.t.* **a)** *(declare)* verkünden; **~ sb./sth. |to be| sth.** jmdn./etw. für etw. erklären; **~ sb. fit for work** jmdn. für arbeitsfähig erklären; **b)** aussprechen ⟨*Wort, Buchstaben usw.*⟩. **2.** *v.i.* **~ on sth.** zu etw. Stellung nehmen; **~ for** *or* **in favour of/against sth.** sich für/gegen etw. aussprechen. **pronounced** [prə-

'naʊnst] *adj. (marked)* ausgeprägt. **pro'nouncement** *n.* Erklärung, *die;* **make a ~ |about sth.|** eine Erklärung [zu etw.] abgeben

pronunciation [prənʌnsɪ'eɪʃn] *n.* Aussprache, *die;* **what is the ~ of this word?** wie wird dieses Wort ausgesprochen?

proof [pruːf] 1. *n.* **a)** *(fact, evidence)* Beweis, *der;* **b)** *no indef. art. (Law)* Beweismaterial, *das;* **c)** *(proving)* **in ~ of** zum Beweis (+ *Gen.*); **d)** *no art. (standard of strength)* Proof *o. Art.;* **100° ~ (Brit.), 128° ~ (Amer.)** 64 Vol.-% Alkohol; **e)** *(Printing)* Abzug, *der.* **2.** *adj.* **a)** **be ~ against sth.** unempfindlich gegen etw. sein; *(fig.)* gegen etw. immun sein; **b)** *in comb.* ⟨*kugel-, einbruch-, idioten*⟩sicher; ⟨*schall-, wasser*⟩dicht; **flame-~:** nicht brennbar

'proof-read *v.t.* Korrektur lesen. **'proof-reader** *n.* Korrektor, *der*/Korrektorin, *die*

prop [prɒp] 1. *n.* Stütze, *die;* *(Mining)* Strebe, *die.* **2.** *v.t.,* **-pp-** stützen; **the ladder was ~ped against the house** die Leiter war gegen das Haus gelehnt. **prop 'up** *v.t.* stützen; *(fig.)* vor dem Konkurs bewahren ⟨*Firma*⟩; stützen ⟨*Regierung*⟩

propaganda [prɒpə'gændə] *n.* Propaganda, *die*

propagate ['prɒpəgeɪt] 1. *v.t.* **a)** *(Hort., Agric.)* vermehren **(from, by** durch); **b)** *(spread)* verbreiten. **2.** *v.i.* **a)** *(Bot.)* sich vermehren; **b)** *(spread)* sich ausbreiten. **propagation** [prɒpə'geɪʃn] *n.* **a)** *(Hort., Agric.)* Züchtung, *die;* **b)** *(Bot.)* Vermehrung, *die;* **c)** *(spreading)* Verbreitung, *die*

propel [prə'pel] *v.t.,* **-ll-** antreiben. **pro'peller** *n.* Propeller, *der.* **pro'pelling 'pencil** *n. (Brit.)* Drehbleistift, *der*

propensity [prə'pensɪtɪ] *n.* **have a ~ to do sth.** *or* **for doing sth.** dazu neigen, etw. zu tun

proper ['prɒpə(r)] *adj.* **a)** *(accurate)* richtig; zutreffend ⟨*Beschreibung*⟩; eigentlich ⟨*Wortbedeutung*⟩; *postpos. (strictly so called)* im engeren Sinn *nachgestellt;* **in London ~:** in London selbst; **c)** *(genuine)* echt; richtig ⟨*Wirbelsturm, Schauspieler*⟩; **d)** *(satisfactory)* richtig; zufriedenstellend ⟨*Antwort*⟩; **e)** *(suitable)* angemessen; *(morally fitting)* gebührend; **do sth. the ~ way** etw. richtig machen; **f)** *attrib.*

(coll.: thorough) richtig. **'properly**
adv. richtig; *(rightly)* zu Recht; ~
speaking genaugenommen
proper: ~ **'name,** ~ **'noun** *ns. (Ling.)*
Eigenname, *der*
property ['propəti] *n.* **a)** *(posses-*
sion[s]) Eigentum, *das;* **b)** *(estate)* Besitz, *der;* Immobilie, *die (fachspr.);* **c)**
(attribute) Eigenschaft, *die; (effect,*
special power) Wirkung, *die*
prophecy ['profɪsɪ] *n. (prediction)* Vorhersage, *die; (prophetic utterance)* Pro-
phezeiung, *die*
prophesy ['profɪsaɪ] *v. t. (predict)* vorhersagen; *(fig.)* prophezeien ⟨*Un-*
glück⟩; *(as fortune-teller)* weissagen
prophet ['profɪt] *n.* Prophet, *der.* **pro-**
phetic [prə'fetɪk] *adj.* prophetisch
proportion [prə'pɔːʃn] **1.** *n.* **a)** *(por-*
tion) Teil, *der;* **b)** *(ratio)* Verhältnis,
das; **the** ~ **of sth. to sth.** das Verhältnis
von etw. zu etw.; **c)** *(correct relation;*
Math.) Proportion, *die;* **be in** ~ |**to** *or*
with sth.] im richtigen Verhältnis [zu
od. mit etw.] stehen; **keep things in** ~
(fig.) die Dinge im richtigen Licht se-
hen; **be out of** ~/**all** *or* **any** ~ |**to** *or*
with sth.] in keinem/keinerlei Verhältnis zu etw. stehen; **d)** *in pl. (size)* Dimension, *die.* **2.** *v. t.* proportionieren.
proportional [prə'pɔːʃənl] *adj.* **a)** *(in*
proportion) entsprechend; **be** ~ **to sth.**
einer Sache *(Dat.)* entsprechen; **b)**
(Math.) **be directly/indirectly** ~ **to sth.**
einer Sache *(Dat.)* direkt/umgekehrt
proportional sein. **proportionate**
[prə'pɔːʃənət] *see* **proportional a**
proposal [prə'pəʊzl] *n.* Vorschlag,
der; (offer) Angebot, *das;* ~ |**of mar-**
riage| [Heirats]antrag, *der*
propose [prə'pəʊz] **1.** *v. t.* **a)** vorschlagen; ~ **sth. to sb.** jmdm. etw. vorschla-
gen; ~ **marriage** |**to sb.**] [jmdm.] einen
Heiratsantrag machen; **b)** *(nominate)*
~ **sb. as/for sth.** jmdn. als/für etw.
vorschlagen; **c)** *(intend)* ~ **doing** *or* **to**
do sth. beabsichtigen, etw. zu tun. **2.**
v. i. (offer marriage) ~ |**to sb.**] jmdm.
einen Heiratsantrag machen. **pro-**
position [propə'zɪʃn] *n.* **a)** *(proposal)*
Vorschlag, *der;* **make** *or* **put a** ~ **to sb.**
jmdm. einen Vorschlag machen; **b)**
(statement; Logic) Aussage, *die*
propound [prə'paʊnd] *v. t.* darlegen
proprietary [prə'praɪətərɪ] *adj.* ~
name *or* **term** Markenname, *der*
proprietor [prə'praɪətə(r)] *n.* Inhaber,
*der/*Inhaberin, *die*
propriety [prə'praɪətɪ] *n.* Anstand,

der; **breach of** ~: Verstoß gegen die
guten Sitten
propulsion [prə'pʌlʃn] *n.* Antrieb, *der*
prosaic [prə'zeɪɪk] *adj.* prosaisch
(geh.); nüchtern
proscribe [prə'skraɪb] *v. t.* verbieten
prose [prəʊz] *n.* Prosa, *die; attrib.* Pro-
sa⟨*werk, -stil*⟩
prosecute ['prosɪkjuːt] **1.** *v. t.* strafrechtlich verfolgen; ~ **sb. for sth.**/
doing sth. jmdn. wegen etw. strafrechtlich verfolgen/jmdn. strafrechtlich verfolgen, weil er etw. tut/getan
hat. **2.** *v. i.* Anzeige erstatten. **pro-**
secution [prosɪ'kjuːʃn] *n. (bringing to*
trial) [strafrechtliche] Verfolgung;
(court procedure) Anklage, *die; (pro-*
secuting party) Anklage[vertretung],
die; **the** ~: die Anklage. **prosecutor**
['prosɪkjuːtə(r)] *n.* Ankläger, *der/*An-
klägerin, *die;* **public** ~ ≈ General-
staatsanwalt, *der/*-anwältin, *die*
prospect 1. ['prospekt] *n.* **a)** *(expecta-*
tion) Erwartung, *die* ⟨of hinsichtlich⟩;
|**at the**] ~ **of sth.**/**doing sth.** [bei der]
Aussicht auf etw.*(Akk.)*/[darauf], etw.
zu tun; **b)** *in pl. (hope of success)* Zu-
kunftsaussichten; **a man with** |**good**] ~s
ein Mann mit Zukunft; **sb.'s** ~**s of**
sth./**doing sth.** jmds. Chancen auf etw.
(Akk.)/darauf, etw. zu tun; **the** ~**s for**
sb./**sth.** die Aussichten für jmdn./etw.
2. [prə'spekt] *v. i.* nach Bodenschätzen
suchen. **prospective** [prə'spektɪv]
adj. voraussichtlich; zukünftig ⟨*Erbe,*
Braut⟩; potentiell ⟨*Käufer, Kandi-*
dat⟩. **prospector** [prə'spektə(r)] *n.*
Prospektor, *der; (for gold)* Goldsu-
cher, *der*
prospectus [prə'spektəs] *n.* Prospekt,
der; (Brit. Univ.) Studienführer, *der*
prosper ['prospə(r)] *v. i.* gedeihen;
⟨*Geschäft:*⟩ florieren; ⟨*Berufstätiger:*⟩
Erfolg haben. **prosperity** [pro'sperɪ-
tɪ] *n.* Wohlstand, *der.* **prosperous**
['prospərəs] *adj.* wohlhabend; florie-
rend ⟨*Unternehmen*⟩
prostitute ['prostɪtjuːt] *n.* Prostituierte, *die.* **prostitution** [prostɪ'tjuːʃn] *n.*
Prostitution, *die*
prostrate 1. ['prostreɪt] *adj.* [auf dem
Bauch] ausgestreckt. **2.** [pro'streɪt] *v.*
refl. ~ **oneself** |**at sth.**/**before sb.**| sich
[vor etw./jmdm.] niederwerfen
protagonist [prəʊ'tægənɪst] *n. (Lit.)*
Protagonist, *der/*Protagonistin, *die*
protect [prə'tekt] *v. t.* **a)** schützen
(**from** vor + *Dat.,* **against** gegen); **b)**
(preserve) unter [Natur]schutz stellen

⟨*Pflanze, Tier*⟩. **protection** [prə-'tekʃn] *n*. Schutz, *der* (from vor + *Dat.*, **against** gegen). **protective** [prə'tektɪv] *adj*. schützend; Schutz-⟨hülle, -anstrich, -vorrichtung, -maske⟩; **be ~ towards sb.** fürsorglich gegenüber jmdm. sein

protein ['prəʊtiːn] *n*. Protein, *das (fachspr.)*; Eiweiß, *das*

protest 1. ['prəʊtest] *n*. **a)** Beschwerde, *die;* **make** *or* **lodge a ~ |against sb./ sth.|** eine Beschwerde [gegen jmdn./ etw.] einreichen; **b)** *(gesture of disapproval)* ~|s| Protest, *der;* **under ~** : unter Protest; **in ~ |against sth.|** aus Protest [gegen etw.]; **c)** *no art. (dissent)* Protest, *der*. **2.** [prə'test] *v.t. (affirm)* beteuern. **3.** [prə'test] *v.i.* protestieren **(about** gegen); *(make written or formal* ~*)* Protest einlegen **(to** bei)

Protestant ['prɒtɪstənt] **1.** *n*. Protestant, *der/*Protestantin, *die*. **2.** *adj*. protestantisch; evangelisch

pro'tester *n*. Protestierende, *der/die; (at demonstration)* Demonstrant, *der/* Demonstrantin, *die*

protocol ['prəʊtəkɒl] *n*. Protokoll, *das*

proton ['prəʊtɒn] *n*. Proton, *das*

prototype ['prəʊtətaɪp] *n*. Prototyp, *der*

protract [prə'trækt] *v.t.* verlängern.

protractor [prə'træktə(r)] *n. (Geom.)* Winkelmesser, *der*

protrude [prə'truːd] *v.i.* herausragen **(from** aus); ⟨*Zähne*⟩ vorstehen

proud [praʊd] **1.** *adj*. **a)** stolz; **~ to do sth.** *or* **to be doing sth.** stolz darauf, etw. zu tun; **~ of sb./sth./doing sth.** stolz auf jmdn./etw./darauf, etw. zu tun; **b)** *(arrogant)* hochmütig. **2.** *adv. (Brit. coll.)* **do sb. ~** : jmdn. verwöhnen. **'proudly** *adv*. **a)** stolz; **b)** *(arrogantly)* hochmütig

prove [pruːv] **1.** *v.t., p.p.* ~**d** *or* **proven** ['pruːvn] beweisen; nachweisen ⟨*Identität*⟩; **~ one's ability** sein Können unter Beweis stellen; **~ sb. right/ wrong** ⟨*Ereignis:*⟩ jmdm. recht/unrecht geben; **be ~d wrong** *or* **to be false** ⟨ *Theorie:*⟩ widerlegt werden; **~ one's/sb.'s case** *or* **point** beweisen, daß man recht hat/jmdm. recht geben. **2.** *v. refl., p. p.* **proved** *or* **proven:** **~ oneself** sich bewähren. **3.** *v. i., p. p.* **proved** *or* **proven:** **~ |to be|** sich erweisen als

proven *see* **prove**

proverb ['prɒvɜːb] *n*. Sprichwort, *das*.

proverbial [prə'vɜːbɪəl] *adj*. sprichwörtlich

provide [prə'vaɪd] *v.t.* **a)** besorgen; liefern ⟨*Beweis*⟩; bereitstellen ⟨*Dienst, Geld*⟩; **~ a home/a car for sb.** jmdm. Unterkunft/ein Auto [zur Verfügung] stellen; **b)** ⟨*Vertrag, Gesetz:*⟩ vorsehen.

pro'vide for *v.t.* **a)** *(make provision for)* vorsorgen für; ⟨*Plan, Gesetz:*⟩ vorsehen; **b)** *(maintain)* sorgen für, versorgen ⟨*Familie, Kind*⟩. **pro'vided** *conj*. **~ |that| ...**: vorausgesetzt, [daß] ...

providence ['prɒvɪdəns] *n*. **a)** |divine| **~**: die [göttliche] Vorsehung; **b)** **P~** *(God)* der Himmel

province ['prɒvɪns] *n*. **a)** Provinz, *die;* **b)** **the ~s** *(regions outside capital)* die Provinz; **c)** *(sphere of action)* [Tätigkeits]bereich, *der; (area of responsibility)* Zuständigkeitsbereich, *der*.

provincial [prə'vɪnʃl] *adj*. Provinz-

provision [prə'vɪʒn] *n*. **a)** *(providing)* Bereitstellung, *die;* **make ~ for** vorsorgen *od:* Vorsorge treffen für ⟨*Notfall*⟩; **b)** **~s** *pl. (food)* Lebensmittel

provisional [prə'vɪʒənl] *adj.*. **provisionally** [prə'vɪʒənəlɪ] *adv*. vorläufig; provisorisch

proviso [prə'vaɪzəʊ] *n., pl.* **~s** Vorbehalt, *der*

provocation [prɒvə'keɪʃn] *n*. Provokation, *die*

provocative [prə'vɒkətɪv] *adj*. provozierend; *(sexually)* aufreizend

provoke [prə'vəʊk] *v.t.* **a)** provozieren ⟨*Person*⟩; reizen ⟨*Person, Tier*⟩; **~ sb. into doing sth.** jmdn. so sehr provozieren, daß er etw. tut; **b)** *(give rise to)* hervorrufen; erregen

prow [praʊ] *n. (Naut.)* Bug, *der*

prowl [praʊl] **1.** *v.i.* streifen. **2.** *v.t.* durchstreifen. **3.** *n*. **be on the ~**: auf einem Streifzug sein

proximity [prɒk'sɪmɪtɪ] *n*. Nähe, *die*

proxy ['prɒksɪ] *n*. **by ~**: durch einen Bevollmächtigten/eine Bevollmächtigte

prude [pruːd] *n*. prüder Mensch

prudence ['pruːdəns] *n*. Besonnenheit, *die*

prudent ['pruːdənt] *adj*. **a)** *(careful)* besonnen; **b)** *(circumspect)* vorsichtig

prudish ['pruːdɪʃ] *adj*. prüde

¹prune [pruːn] *n*. Backpflaume, *die*

²prune *v.t.* **a)** *(trim)* [be]schneiden; **b)** *(fig.)* reduzieren

pry [praɪ] *v.i.* neugierig sein. **'pry into** *v.t.* seine Nase stecken in (+ *Akk.*) *(ugs.)* ⟨*Angelegenheit*⟩

PS *abbr*. **postscript** PS

psalm [sɑːm] *n*. Psalm, *der*

pseudonym ['sju:dənɪm] *n.* Pseudonym, *das*

psychiatric [saɪkɪ'ætrɪk] *adj.* psychiatrisch

psychiatrist [saɪ'kaɪətrɪst] *n.* Psychiater, *der*/Psychiaterin, *die*

psychiatry [saɪ'kaɪətrɪ] *n.* Psychiatrie, *die*

psychic ['saɪkɪk] *adj.* **be ~:** übernatürliche Fähigkeiten haben

psychoanalyse [saɪkəʊænəlaɪz] *v.t.* psychoanalysieren. **psychoa'nalysis** *n.* Psychoanalyse, *die.* **psycho'analyst** *n.* Psychoanalytiker, *der*/-analytikerin, *die*

psychological [saɪkə'lɒdʒɪkl] *adj.* psychologisch; psychisch ⟨*Problem*⟩

psychologist [saɪ'kɒlədʒɪst] *n.* Psychologe, *der*/Psychologin, *die*

psychology [saɪ'kɒlədʒɪ] *n.* Psychologie, *die*

psychopath ['saɪkəpæθ] *n.* Psychopath, *der*/Psychopathin, *die*

PTO *abbr.* **please turn over** b.w.

pub [pʌb] *n. (Brit. coll.)* Kneipe, *die (ugs.)*

puberty ['pju:bətɪ] *n., no art.* Pubertät, *die*

public ['pʌblɪk] **1.** *adj.* öffentlich; **make sth. ~:** etw. bekannt machen. **2.** *n., sing. or pl.* **a)** *(the people)* Öffentlichkeit, *die;* **b)** *(section of community)* Publikum, *das;* **c) in ~:** öffentlich

publican ['pʌblɪkən] *n. (Brit.)* [Gast]wirt, *der*/-wirtin, *die*

publication [pʌblɪ'keɪʃn] *n.* Veröffentlichung, *die*

public: ~ con'venience *n.* öffentliche Toilette; **~ 'holiday** *n.* gesetzlicher Feiertag; **~ 'house** *n. (Brit.)* Gastwirtschaft, *die;* Gaststätte, *die*

publicity [pʌb'lɪsɪtɪ] *n.* Publicity, *die; (advertising)* Werbung, *die;* **~ campaign** Werbekampagne, *die*

publicize ['pʌblɪsaɪz] *v.t.* publik machen ⟨*Ungerechtigkeit*⟩; werben für, Reklame machen für ⟨*Produkt*⟩

public 'library *n.* öffentliche Bücherei

'publicly *adv.* öffentlich; **~ owned** staatseigen

public: ~ re'lations *n., sing. or pl.* Public Relations *Pl.;* **~ school** *n.* **a)** *(Brit.)* Privatschule, *die;* **b)** *(Scot., Amer.)* staatliche *od.* öffentliche Schule; **~ 'transport** *n.* öffentlicher Personenverkehr

publish ['pʌblɪʃ] *v.t.* ⟨*Verlag:*⟩ verlegen ⟨*Buch, Zeitschrift, Musik usw.*⟩;

⟨*Autor:*⟩ veröffentlichen ⟨*Text*⟩. **'publisher** *n.* Verleger, *der*/Verlegerin, *die;* **~|s|** *(company)* Verlag, *der.* **'publishing** *n., no art.* Verlagswesen, *das*

puck [pʌk] *n. (Ice Hockey)* Puck, *der*

pucker ['pʌkə(r)] **1.** *v.t.* **~ |up|** runzeln ⟨*Brauen, Stirn*⟩; kräuseln ⟨*Lippen*⟩. **2.** *v.i.* **~ |up|** ⟨*Stoff:*⟩ sich kräuseln

pudding ['pʊdɪŋ] *n.* **a)** Pudding, *der;* **b)** *(dessert)* süße Nachspeise

puddle ['pʌdl] *n.* Pfütze, *die*

puerile ['pjʊəraɪl] *adj.* kindisch

puff [pʌf] **1.** *n.* **a)** Stoß, *der;* **~ of breath/wind** Atem-/Windstoß, *der;* **b)** **~ of smoke** Rauchstoß, *der;* **c)** *(pastry)* Blätterteigteilchen, *das.* **2.** *v.i.* **a)** **~ |and blow|** schnaufen [und keuchen]; **b)** *(~ cigarette smoke etc.)* paffen *(ugs.)* **(at an + Dat.);** **c)** ⟨*Person:*⟩ keuchen; ⟨*Zug, Lokomotive*⟩ schnaufend fahren. **3.** *v.t.* blasen ⟨*Rauch*⟩; stäuben ⟨*Puder*⟩. **puff 'out** *v.t.* **a)** bauschen ⟨*Segel*⟩; **b)** *(put out of breath)* außer Atem bringen ⟨*Person*⟩; **be ~ed |out|** außer Atem sein

puff 'pastry *n.* Blätterteig, *der*

puffy ['pʌfɪ] *adj.* verschwollen

pugnacious [pʌg'neɪʃəs] *adj.* kampflustig

pull [pʊl] **1.** *v.t.* **a)** *(draw, tug)* ziehen an (+ *Dat.*); ziehen ⟨*Hebel*⟩; **~ sb.'s or sb. by the hair/ears/sleeve** jmdn. an den Haaren/Ohren/am Ärmel ziehen; **~ sth. over one's ears/head** sich *(Dat.)* etw. über die Ohren/den Kopf ziehen; **~ to pieces** in Stücke reißen; *(fig.)* zerpflücken ⟨*Argument usw.*⟩; **b)** *(extract)* [her]ausziehen; [heraus]ziehen ⟨*Zahn*⟩; **c)** *(strain)* sich *(Dat.)* zerren ⟨*Muskel*⟩. **2.** *v.i.* **a)** ziehen; **'P~'** „Ziehen"; **b)** **~ |to the left/right|** ⟨*Auto, Boot:*⟩ [nach links/rechts] ziehen; **c)** *(pluck)* **~ at** ziehen an (+ *Dat.*); **~ at sb.'s sleeve** jmdn. am Ärmel ziehen. **3.** *n.* **a)** Zug, *der;* **b)** *(influence)* Einfluß, *der* **(with auf + Akk.,** bei). **pull a'part** *v.t.* **a)** *(take to pieces)* auseinandernehmen; **b)** *(fig.: criticize)* zerpflücken; verreißen ⟨*Buch, [literarisches] Werk*⟩. **pull 'down** *v.t.* **a)** herunterziehen; *(demolish)* abreißen. **pull 'in 1.** *v.t.* hereinziehen. **2.** *v.i.* **a)** ⟨*Zug:*⟩ einfahren; **b)** *(move to side of road)* an die Seite fahren; *(stop)* anhalten. **pull 'off** *v.t.* **a)** *(remove)* abziehen; *(violently)* abreißen; **b)** *(accomplish)* an Land ziehen *(ugs.).* **pull 'out 1.** *v.t.* herausziehen. **2.** *v.i.* **a)** *(depart)* abfahren; **b)**

(away from roadside) ausscheren. **pull 'through** *v.i.* ⟨*Patient:*⟩ durchkommen. **pull to'gether** *v. refl.* sich zusammennehmen. **pull 'up** 1. *v.t.* **a)** hochziehen; **b)** [he]rausziehen ⟨*Unkraut, Pflanze*⟩; **c)** *(reprimand)* zurechtweisen. 2. *v.i. (stop)* anhalten.

pulley ['pʊlɪ] *n.* Rolle, *die*

pullover ['pʊləʊvə(r)] *n.* Pullover, *der*

pulp [pʌlp] 1. *n.* Brei, *der.* 2. *v.t.* zerdrücken ⟨*Rübe*⟩; einstampfen ⟨*Druckerzeugnis*⟩

pulpit ['pʊlpɪt] *n.* Kanzel, *die*

pulsate [pʌl'seɪt] *v.i.* pulsieren

¹pulse [pʌls] *n.* Puls, *der; (single beat)* Pulsschlag, *der*

²pulse *n. (Cookery)* Hülsenfrucht, *die*

pulverize ['pʌlvəraɪz] *v.t.* pulverisieren

puma ['pjuːmə] *n.* Puma, *der*

pumice ['pʌmɪs] *n.* ~-[-stone] Bimsstein, *der*

pummel ['pʌml] *v.t., (Brit)* -ll- einschlagen auf (+ *Akk.*)

pump [pʌmp] 1. *n.* Pumpe, *die.* 2. *v.i.* pumpen. 3. *v.t.* pumpen; ~ **sth.** dry etw. leerpumpen; ~ **sb. for information** Auskünfte aus jmdm. herausholen; ~ **up** aufpumpen

pumpkin ['pʌmpkɪn] *n.* Kürbis, *der*

pun [pʌn] *n.* Wortspiel, *das*

¹punch 1. *v.t.* **a)** *(with fist)* boxen; **b)** *(pierce)* lochen; ~ **a hole** ein Loch stanzen; ~ **a hole/holes in sth.** etw. lochen. 2. *n.* **a)** *(blow)* Faustschlag, *der;* **b)** *(for making holes) (in leather, tickets)* Lochzange, *die; (in paper)* Locher, *der*

²punch *n. (drink)* Punsch, *der*

punch: ~ **line** *n.* Pointe, *die;* ~-**up** *n. (Brit. coll.)* Prügelei, *die*

punctual ['pʌŋktjʊəl] *adj.* pünktlich. **punctuality** [pʌŋktjʊ'ælɪtɪ] *n.* Pünktlichkeit, *die.* '**punctually** *adv.* pünktlich

punctuate [pʌŋktjʊəɪt] *v.t.* mit Satzzeichen versehen. **punctuation** [pʌŋktjʊ'eɪʃn] *n.* Zeichensetzung, *die.* **punctu'ation mark** *n.* Satzzeichen, *das*

puncture ['pʌŋktʃə(r)] 1. *n.* **a)** *(flat tyre)* Reifenpanne, *die;* **b)** *(hole)* Loch, *das.* 2. *v.t.* durchstechen; **be ~d** ⟨*Reifen:*⟩ platt sein

pundit ['pʌndɪt] *n.* Experte, *der/*Expertin, *die*

pungent ['pʌndʒənt] *adj.* beißend, ätzend ⟨*Rauch*⟩; scharf ⟨*Soße*⟩; stechend riechend ⟨*Gas*⟩

punish ['pʌnɪʃ] *v.t.* bestrafen. **punishable** ['pʌnɪʃəbl] *adj.* strafbar. '**punishment** *n.* **a)** *(punishing)* Bestrafung, *die;* **b)** *(penalty)* Strafe, *die*

punitive ['pjuːnɪtɪv] *adj.* **a)** *(penal)* Straf-; **b)** *(severe)* [allzu] rigoros

punk [pʌŋk] *n.* **a)** *(Amer. sl.: worthless person)* Dreckskerl, *der (salopp);* **b)** *(admirer of ~ rock)* Punk, *der; (performer)* Punk[rock]er, *der/*-[rock]erin, *die;* **c)** *(music)* Punkrock, *der*

punt [pʌnt] *n.* Stechkahn, *der*

puny ['pjuːnɪ] *adj.* **a)** *(undersized)* zu klein ⟨*Baby, Junge*⟩; **b)** *(feeble)* gering ⟨*Kraft*⟩; schwach ⟨*Waffe, Person*⟩

pup [pʌp] *n.* Welpe, *der*

pupa ['pjuːpə] *n., pl.* ~-e ['pjuːpiː] Puppe, *die.* **pupate** [pjuː'peɪt] *v.i.* sich verpuppen

pupil ['pjuːpɪl] *n.* **a)** Schüler, *der/*Schülerin, *die;* **b)** *(Anat.)* Pupille, *die*

puppet ['pʌpɪt] *n.* Puppe, *die; (marionette; also fig.)* Marionette, *die*

puppy ['pʌpɪ] *n.* Hundejunge, *das;* Welpe, *der*

purchase ['pɜːtʃəs] 1. *n.* **a)** Kauf, *der;* **make a ~:** etwas kaufen; **b)** *(hold)* Halt, *der; (leverage)* Hebelwirkung, *die.* 2. *v.t.* kaufen. '**purchaser** *n.* Käufer, *der/*Käuferin, *die*

pure [pjʊə(r)] *adj.* rein

purée ['pjʊəreɪ] *n.* Püree, *das*

'**purely** *adv.* **a)** *(solely)* rein; **b)** *(merely)* lediglich

purgatory ['pɜːgətərɪ] *n.* **it was ~** *(fig.)* es war eine Strafe

purge [pɜːdʒ] 1. *v.t.* **a)** *(cleanse)* reinigen (**of** von); **b)** *(remove)* entfernen; **c)** *(rid)* säubern ⟨*Partei*⟩ (**of** von). 2. *n.* Säuberung[saktion], *die*

purification [pjʊərɪfɪ'keɪʃn] *n.* Reinigung, *die*

purify ['pjʊərɪfaɪ] *v.t.* reinigen

purist ['pjʊərɪst] *n.* Purist, *der/*Puristin, *die*

puritan, (Hist.) Puritan ['pjʊərɪtn] *n.* Puritaner, *der/*Puritanerin, *die.* **puritanical** [pjʊərɪ'tænɪkl] *adj.* puritanisch

purity ['pjʊərɪtɪ] *n.* Reinheit, *die*

purl [pɜːl] 1. *n.* linke Masche. 2. *v.t.* ~ **three [stitches]** drei linke Maschen stricken

purple ['pɜːpl] 1. *adj.* lila; violett. 2. *n.* Lila, *das;* Violett, *das*

purport [pə'pɔːt] *v.t.* ~ **to do sth.** *(profess)* [von sich] behaupten, etw. zu tun; *(be intended to seem)* den Anschein erwecken sollen, etw. zu tun

purpose ['pɜ:pəs] *n.* **a)** *(object)* Zweck, *der;* *(intention)* Absicht, *die;* **what is the ~ of doing that?** was hat es für einen Zweck, das zu tun?; **on ~:** mit Absicht; absichtlich; **b)** *(effect)* **to no ~:** ohne Erfolg; **to some/good ~:** mit einigem/gutem Erfolg; **c)** *(determination)* Entschlossenheit, *die.* **purposeful** ['pɜ:pəsfl] *adj.* zielstrebig; *(with specific aim)* entschlossen. **purposely** *adv.* absichtlich

purr [pɜ:(r)] **1.** *v.i.* schnurren. **2.** *n.* Schnurren, *das*

purse [pɜ:s] **1.** *n.* Portemonnaie, *das.* **2.** *v.t.* kräuseln ⟨*Lippen*⟩

purser ['pɜ:sə(r)] *n.* Zahlmeister, *der/* -meisterin, *die*

pursue [pə'sju:] *v.t.* **a)** *(chase)* verfolgen; **b)** *(look into)* nachgehen (+ *Dat.*); **c)** *(engage in)* betreiben. **pursuer** [pə'sju:ə(r)] *n.* Verfolger, *der/*Verfolgerin, *die.* **pursuit** [pə-'sju:t] *n.* **a)** Verfolgung, *die; (of knowledge, truth, etc.)* Streben, *das* (of nach); **in ~ of** auf der Jagd nach ⟨*Wild, Dieb usw.*⟩; **in** Ausführung (+ *Gen.*) ⟨*Beschäftigung*⟩; **with the police in |full| ~:** mit der Polizei [dicht] auf den Fersen; **b)** *(pastime)* Beschäftigung, *die*

pus [pʌs] *n.* Eiter, *der*

push [pʊʃ] **1.** *v.t.* **a)** schieben; *(make fall)* stoßen; drücken gegen ⟨*Tür*⟩; **~ one's way through/into/on to** *etc.* sth. sich *(Dat.)* einen Weg durch/in/auf usw. etw. *(Akk.)* bahnen; **b)** *(fig.: impel)* drängen; **c)** *(tax)* **~ sb. |hard|** jmdn. [stark] fordern; **be ~ed for sth.** *(coll.: find it difficult to provide sth.)* mit etw. knapp sein; **be ~ed for money** *or* **cash** knapp bei Kasse sein *(ugs.);* **d)** *(sell illegally, esp. drugs)* pushen *(Drogenjargon).* **2.** *v.i.* **a)** schieben; *(in queue)* drängeln; *(at door)* drücken; **~ and shove** schubsen und drängeln; **b)** *(make demands)* **~ for sth.** etw. fordern; **c)** *(make one's way)* **he ~ed between us** er drängte sich zwischen uns; **~ through the crowd** sich durch die Menge drängeln. **3.** *n.* **a)** Stoß, *der;* **give sth. a ~:** etw. schieben; **b)** *(effort)* Anstrengung *Pl.;* (*Mil.: attack)* Vorstoß, *der;* **c)** *(crisis)* **when it comes to the ~,** *(Amer. coll.)* **when ~ comes to shove** wenn es ernst wird; **d)** *(Brit. sl.: dismissal)* **get the ~:** rausfliegen *(ugs.).* **push aˈhead** *v.i.* **~ ahead with sth.** etw. vorantreiben. **push ˈin** *v.i.* sich hineindrängen. **push ˈoff** *v.i.* **a)** *(Boating)* abstoßen; **b)** *(sl.: leave)* abhauen *(salopp).* **push ˈon 1.** *v.i. (with plans etc.)* weitermachen. **2.** *v.t.* draufdrücken ⟨*Deckel usw.*⟩. **push ˈup** *v.t.* hochschieben; *(fig.)* hochtreiben

push: **~-button** *n.* [Druck]knopf, *der;* Drucktaste; **~-chair** *n. (Brit.)* Sportwagen, *der;* **~-over** *n. (coll.)* Kinderspiel, *das*

pushy ['pʊʃi] *adj. (coll.)* [übermäßig] ehrgeizig ⟨*Person*⟩

pussy ['pʊsi] *n. (child lang.: cat)* Miezekatze, *die (fam.)*

put [pʊt] **1.** *v.t.,* **-tt-, put a)** *(place)* tun; *(vertically)* stellen; *(horizontally)* legen; **~ plates on the table** Teller auf den Tisch stellen; **~ a stamp on the letter** eine Briefmarke auf den Brief kleben; **~ the letter in an envelope/the letter-box** den Brief in einen Umschlag/in den Briefkasten stecken; **~ sth. in one's pocket** etw. in die Tasche stecken; **~ petrol in the tank** Benzin in den Tank füllen; **~ the car in|to| the garage** das Auto in die Garage stellen; **~ the plug in the socket** den Stecker in die Steckdose stecken; **~ one's hands over one's eyes** sich *(Dat.)* die Hände auf die Augen legen; **where shall I ~ it?** wo soll ich es hintun *(ugs.)*/-stellen/-legen *usw.*?; *(fig.)* **be ~ in a difficult position** in eine schwierige Lage geraten; **~ sb. on to sth.** jmdn. auf etw. *(Akk.)* hinweisen; **~ sb. to work** jmdn. arbeiten lassen; **~ sb. on antibiotics** jmdn. auf Antibiotika setzen; **~ oneself in sb.'s place** *or* **situation** sich in jmds. Lage *(Akk.)* versetzen; **b)** *(submit)* unterbreiten ⟨*Vorschlag, Plan*⟩ (to *Dat.*); **c)** *(express)* ausdrücken; **let's ~ it like this: ...:** sagen wir so: ...; **~ sth. into English** *etc.* etw. ins Englische *usw.* übertragen; **~ sth. into words** etw. in Worte fassen; **d)** *(write)* schreiben; **~ one's name on the list** seinen Namen auf die Liste setzen; **~ sth. on the bill** etw. auf die Rechnung setzen; **e)** *(stake)* setzen (on auf + *Akk.*); **f)** *(estimate)* **~ sb./sth. at** jmdn./etw. schätzen auf (+ *Akk.*). **2.** *v.i.* **-tt-, put** *(Naut.)* **~ |out| to sea** in See stechen. **put aˈcross** *v.t.* **a)** *(communicate)* vermitteln (to *Dat.*); **b)** *(make acceptable)* ankommen mit. **put aˈway** *v.t.* **a)** wegräumen; reinstellen ⟨*Auto*⟩; *(in file)* abheften; **b)** *(save)* beiseite legen; **c)** *(coll.) (eat)* verdrücken *(ugs.);* *(drink)* runterkippen *(ugs.);* **d)** *(coll.:*

confine) einsperren *(ugs.).* **put 'back** *v. t.* **a)** ~ **the book back** das Buch zurücktun; **b)** ~ **the clock back** die Uhr zurückstellen; **c)** *(postpone)* verschieben. **put 'down** *v. t.* **a)** *(set down) (vertically)* hinstellen; *(horizontally)* hinlegen; auflegen ⟨*Hörer*⟩; **b)** *(suppress)* niederwerfen; **c)** *(humiliate)* herabsetzen; **d)** *(kill)* töten; **e)** *(write)* notieren; **f)** *(attribute)* ~ **sth. down to sth.** etw. auf etw. *(Akk.)* zurückführen. **put 'forward** *v. t.* **a)** *(propose)* aufwarten mit; **b)** *(nominate)* vorschlagen; **c)** ~ **the clock forward** die Uhr vorstellen. **put 'in 1.** *v. t.* **a)** *(install)* einbauen; **b)** *(submit)* stellen ⟨*Forderung*⟩; einreichen ⟨*Bewerbung*⟩; **c)** *(devote)* aufwenden ⟨*Mühe*⟩; *(perform)* einlegen ⟨*Sonderschicht, Überstunden*⟩. **2.** *v. i.* ~ **in for** sich bewerben um ⟨*Stellung*⟩; beantragen ⟨*Urlaub*⟩. **put 'off** *v. t.* **a)** *(postpone)* verschieben **(until** auf + *Akk.*); *(postpone engagement with)* vertrösten **(until** auf + *Akk.*); **b)** *(switch off)* ausmachen; **c)** *(repel)* abstoßen; ~ **sb. off sth.** jmdm. etw. verleiden; **d)** *(distract)* stören; **e)** *(dissuade)* ~ **sb. off doing sth.** jmdn. davon abbringen, etw. zu tun. **put 'on** *v. t.* **a)** anziehen ⟨*Kleidung, Hose usw.*⟩; aufsetzen ⟨*Hut, Brille*⟩; draufsetzen ⟨*Deckel*⟩; ~ **it on** *(coll.)* [nur] Schau machen *(ugs.)*; **b)** anmachen ⟨*Radio, Licht*⟩; aufsetzen ⟨*Wasser, Kessel*⟩; **c)** *(gain)* ~ **on weight** zunehmen; **d)** *(stage)* spielen ⟨*Stück*⟩; zeigen ⟨*Film*⟩. **put 'out** *v. t.* **a)** rausbringen; **b)** ausmachen ⟨*Licht*⟩; löschen ⟨*Feuer*⟩; **c)** *(inconvenience)* in Verlegenheit bringen. **put 'through** *v. t.* **a)** *(carry out)* durchführen ⟨*Plan, Programm*⟩; **b)** *(Teleph.)* verbinden **(to** mit). **put 'up 1.** *v. t.* **a)** heben ⟨*Hand*⟩; errichten ⟨*Gebäude, Denkmal*⟩; aufstellen ⟨*Gerüst*⟩; **b)** *(display)* aushängen; **c)** hochnehmen ⟨*Fäuste*⟩; leisten ⟨*Widerstand, Gegenwehr*⟩; **d)** *(propose)* vorschlagen; *(nominate)* aufstellen; **e)** *(incite)* ~ **sb. up to sth.** jmdn. zu etw. anstiften; **f)** *(accommodate)* unterbringen; **g)** *(increase)* [he]raufsetzen ⟨*Preis, Miete*⟩. **2.** *v. i. (lodge)* übernachten. **put 'up with** *v. t.* sich *(Dat.)* bieten lassen ⟨*Beleidigung, Benehmen*⟩; sich abfinden mit ⟨*Lärm, Elend*⟩; sich abgeben mit ⟨*Person*⟩
putrefy ['pju:trɪfaɪ] *v. i.* sich zersetzen
putrid ['pju:trɪd] *adj. (rotten)* faul; ~ **smell** Fäulnisgeruch, *der*

putt [pʌt] *(Golf)* **1.** *v. i. & t.* putten. **2.** *n.* Putt, *der.* **'putter** *n.* Putter, *der*
putty ['pʌtɪ] *n.* Kitt, *der*
'put-up *adj.* **a** ~ **job** ein abgekartetes Spiel *(ugs.)*
puzzle ['pʌzl] **1.** *n. (problem, enigma)* Rätsel, *das; (toy)* Geduldsspiel, *das.* **2.** *v. t.* rätselhaft *od.* ein Rätsel sein *(+ Dat.).* **3.** *v. i.* ~ **over** *or* **about sth.** sich *(Dat.)* über etw. den Kopf zerbrechen. **puzzled** ['pʌzld] *adj.* ratlos. **puzzling** ['pʌzlɪŋ] *adj.* rätselhaft
PVC *abbr.* **polyvinyl chloride** PVC, *das*
pygmy ['pɪgmɪ] *n.* Pygmäe, *der*
pyjamas [pɪ'dʒɑ:məz] *n. pl.* [**pair of**] ~: Schlafanzug, *der*
pylon ['paɪlən] *n.* Mast, *der*
pyramid ['pɪrəmɪd] *n.* Pyramide, *die*
Pyrenees [pɪrə'ni:z] *pr. n. pl.* **the** ~: die Pyrenäen
python ['paɪθən] *n.* Python, *die*

Q

Q, q [kju:] *n.* Q, q, *das*
quack [kwæk] **1.** *v. i.* ⟨*Ente:*⟩ quaken. **2.** *n.* Quaken, *das*
quadrangle ['kwɒdræŋgl] *n.* [viereckiger] Innenhof
quadruped ['kwɒdruped] *n.* Vierfüßler, *der*
quadruple ['kwɒdrupl] **1.** *adj.* vierfach. **2.** *v. t.* vervierfachen. **3.** *v. i.* sich vervierfachen
quagmire ['kwægmaɪə(r)] *n.* Sumpf, *der;* Morast, *der*
¹quail [kweɪl] *n. (Ornith.)* Wachtel, *die*
²quail *v. i.* ⟨*Person:*⟩ [ver]zagen
quaint [kweɪnt] *adj.* drollig ⟨*Häuschen, Einrichtung*⟩; malerisch ⟨*Ort*⟩; *(odd)* kurios ⟨*Bräuche, Anblick*⟩
quake [kweɪk] **1.** *n. (coll.)* [Erd]beben, *das.* **2.** *v. i.* beben; ~ **with fear** vor Angst zittern
Quaker ['kweɪkə(r)] *n.* Quäker, *der/* Quäkerin, *die*
qualification [kwɒlɪfɪ'keɪʃn] *n.* **a)** Qualifikation, *die; (condition)* Voraussetzung, *die;* **b)** *(limitation)* Vorbehalt, *der;* **without** ~: vorbehaltlos

qualified ['kwɒlɪfaɪd] *adj.* **a)** qualifiziert; *(by training)* ausgebildet; **b)** *(restricted)* nicht uneingeschränkt; **a ~ success** kein voller Erfolg; **~ acceptance** bedingte Annahme

qualify ['kwɒlɪfaɪ] **1.** *v. t.* **a)** *(make competent)* berechtigen **(for** zu); **b)** *(modify)* einschränken. **2.** *v. i.* **a)** **~ in law/medicine** seinen [Studien]abschluß in Jura/Medizin machen; **~ as a doctor/lawyer** sein Examen als Arzt/Anwalt machen; **b)** *(fulfil a condition)* in Frage kommen **(for** für); **c)** *(Sport)* sich qualifizieren

quality ['kwɒlɪtɪ] **1.** *n.* **a)** Qualität, *die;* **b)** *(characteristic)* Eigenschaft, *die.* **2.** *adj.* Qualitäts-

qualm [kwɑːm] *n.* Bedenken, *das* **(over, about** gegen)

quandary ['kwɒndərɪ] *n.* Dilemma, *das*

quantity ['kwɒntɪtɪ] *n.* **a)** Quantität, *die;* **b)** *(amount, sum)* Menge, *die*

quarantine ['kwɒrəntiːn] *n.* Quarantäne, *die;* **be in ~:** unter Quarantäne stehen

quarrel ['kwɒrl] **1.** *n.* **a)** Streit, *der;* **have/pick a ~ with** sb. [**about/over** sth.] sich mit jmdm. [über etw. *(Akk.)*] streiten/Streit anfangen; **b)** *(cause of complaint)* Einwand, *der* **(with** gegen). **2.** *v. i., (Brit.)* **-ll-** [sich] streiten **(over um, about** über + *Akk.*); **~ with each other** [sich] [miteinander] streiten; *(fall out)* sich [zer]streiten **(over um, about** über + *Akk.*). **quarrelsome** ['kwɒrlsəm] *adj.* streitsüchtig

¹quarry ['kwɒrɪ] *n.* Steinbruch, *der*

²quarry *n. (prey)* Beute, *die*

quart [kwɔːt] *n.* Quart, *das*

quarter ['kwɔːtə(r)] **1.** *n.* **a)** Viertel, *das;* **a** or **one ~ of** ein Viertel (+ *Gen.*); **a ~ of a mile/an hour** eine Viertelmeile/-stunde; **b)** *(of year)* Quartal, *das;* Vierteljahr, *das;* **c)** [**a]** **~ to/past six** Viertel vor/nach sechs; **d)** *(direction)* Richtung, *die;* **e)** *(area of town)* [Stadt]viertel, *das;* **f)** **~s** *pl. (lodgings)* Quartier, *das (bes. Milit.);* Unterkunft, *die;* **g)** *(Amer. coin)* Vierteldollar, *der.* **2.** *v. t.* **a)** *(divide)* vierteln; **b)** *(lodge)* einquartieren ⟨Soldaten⟩. **quarter-'final** *n.* Viertelfinale, *das.* **quarterly 1.** *adj.* vierteljährlich. **2.** *n.* Vierteljahr[e]sschrift, *die*

quartet [kwɔː'tet] *n.* Quartett, *das*

quartz [kwɔːts] *n.* Quarz, *der*

quash [kwɒʃ] *v. t.* **a)** *(annul)* aufheben; **b)** *(suppress)* niederschlagen

quaver ['kweɪvə(r)] **1.** *n. (Brit. Mus.)* Achtelnote, *die.* **2.** *v. i. (vibrate)* zittern

quay [kiː], **'quayside** *ns.* Kai, *der*

queasy ['kwiːzɪ] *adj.* unwohl

queen [kwiːn] *n.* **a)** Königin, *die;* **b)** *(Chess, Cards)* Dame, *die.* **queen 'mother** *n.* Königinmutter, *die*

queer [kwɪə(r)] **1.** *adj.* **a)** *(strange)* sonderbar; *(eccentric)* verschroben; **b)** *(shady)* merkwürdig; **c)** *(out of sorts)* unwohl; **d)** *(sl. derog.: homosexual)* schwul *(ugs.).* **2.** *n. (sl. derog.: homosexual)* Schwule, *der (ugs.)*

quell [kwel] *v. t. (literary)* niederschlagen ⟨Aufstand⟩; zügeln ⟨Furcht⟩

quench [kwentʃ] *v. t.* löschen

query ['kwɪərɪ] **1.** *n.* Frage, *die.* **2.** *v. t.* in Frage stellen ⟨Anweisung, Glaubwürdigkeit⟩; beanstanden ⟨Rechnung⟩

quest [kwest] *n.* Suche, *die* **(for** nach)

question ['kwestʃn] **1.** *n.* **a)** Frage, *die;* **ask** sb. **a ~:** jmdm. eine Frage stellen; **b)** *(doubt, objection)* Zweifel, *der* **(about an** + *Dat.);* **there is no ~ about** sth. es besteht kein Zweifel an etw. *(Dat.);* **beyond all** or **without ~:** ohne Frage; **c)** *(problem, concern)* Frage, *die;* sth./it **is only a ~ of time** etw./es ist [nur] eine Frage der Zeit; **it is [only] a ~ of doing** sth. es geht [nur] darum, etw. zu tun; **the person/thing in ~:** die fragliche Person/Sache; sth./it **is out of the ~:** etw./es ist ausgeschlossen. **2.** *v. t.* **a)** befragen; ⟨Polizei, Gericht usw.:⟩ vernehmen; **b)** *(throw doubt upon, raise objections to)* bezweifeln. **questionable** ['kwestʃənəbl] *adj.* fragwürdig. '**question mark** *n.* Fragezeichen, *das*

questionnaire [kwestʃə'neə(r)] *n.* Fragebogen, *der*

queue [kjuː] **1.** *n.* Schlange, *die.* **join the ~:** sich anstellen. **2.** *v. i.* **~ [up]** Schlange stehen

quibble ['kwɪbl] **1.** *n.* Spitzfindigkeit, *die.* **2.** *v. i.* streiten

quiche [kiːʃ] *n.* Quiche, *die*

quick [kwɪk] **1.** *adj.* schnell; kurz ⟨Rede, Pause⟩; flüchtig ⟨Kuß, Blick⟩; **be ~!** mach schnell! *(ugs.);* **be ~ to do** sth. etw. schnell tun; **a ~ temper** ein aufbrausendes Wesen. **2.** *adv.* schnell. **3.** *n.* empfindliches Fleisch; **be cut to the ~** *(fig.)* tief getroffen sein. **quicken** ['kwɪkn] **1.** *v. t.* beschleunigen. **2.** *v. i.* sich beschleunigen. '**quickly** *adv.* schnell. '**quickness** *n.* **a)** *(speed)* Schnelligkeit, *die;* **b)** *(~ of perception)* Schärfe, *die*

quick: ~**sand** *n.* Treibsand, *der;*
~-**tempered** [~'tempəd] *adj.* hitzig;
be ~-**tempered** leicht aufbrausen;
~-**witted** *adj.* geistesgegenwärtig
quid [kwɪd] *n., pl. same (Brit. sl.)*
Pfund, *das*
quiet ['kwaɪət] **1.** *adj.,* ~**er** ['kwaɪə-
tə(r)], ~**est** ['kwaɪətɪst] **a)** *(silent)* still;
(not loud) leise; **keep** ~ **about sth.** *(fig.)*
etw. geheimhalten; **b)** *(peaceful, not
busy)* ruhig; **c)** *(not overt)* versteckt;
on the ~: still und heimlich. **2.** *n.* Ruhe, *die; (silence, stillness)* Stille, *die.*
quieten ['kwaɪətn] *v.t.* beruhigen.
quieten '**down** *v.i.* sich beruhigen
'**quietly** *adv.* **a)** *(silently)* still; *(not
loudly)* leise; **b)** *(peacefully)* ruhig
'**quietness** *n. (absence of noise)* Stille,
die; (peacefulness) Ruhe, *die*
quill [kwɪl] *n. (feather)* Kielfeder, *die;
(of porcupine)* Stachel, *der*
quilt [kwɪlt] **1.** *n.* Schlafdecke, *die.* **2.**
v.t. wattieren
quince [kwɪns] *n.* Quitte, *die*
quintet [kwɪn'tet] *n.* Quintett, *das*
quip [kwɪp] **1.** *n.* Witzelei, *die.* **2.** *v.i.,*
-**pp-** witzeln (**at** über + *Akk.*)
quirk [kwɜ:k] *n.* Marotte, *die;* **a** ~ **of
fate** eine Laune des Schicksals
quit [kwɪt] *v.t.,* -**tt-,** *(Amer.)* quit *(give
up)* aufgeben; *(stop)* aufhören mit; ~
doing sth. aufhören, etw. zu tun; **they
were given notice to** ~ |**the flat**| ihnen
wurde [die Wohnung] gekündigt
quite [kwaɪt] *adv.* **a)** *(entirely)* ganz;
völlig; fest *(entschlossen);* ~ |**so**|! [ja,]
genau!; **b)** *(to some extent)* ziemlich;
ganz ⟨*gern*⟩; ~ **a few** ziemlich viele
quits [kwɪts] *pred. adj.* **be** ~ |**with sb.**|
[mit jmdm.] quitt sein *(ugs.)*
¹**quiver** ['kwɪvə(r)] *v.i.* zittern (**with** vor
+ *Dat.*); ⟨*Stimme, Lippen:*⟩ beben
(geh.); ⟨*Lid:*⟩ zucken
²**quiver** *n. (for arrows)* Köcher, *der*
quiz [kwɪz] **1.** *n., pl.* ~**zes** Quiz, *das.* **2.**
v.t., -**zz-** ausfragen (**about** sth. nach
etw., **about** sb. über jmdn.). **quizzical**
['kwɪzɪkl] *adj.* fragend
quoit [kɔɪt] *n.* [Gummi]ring, *der*
quorum ['kwɔ:rəm] *n.* Quorum, *das*
quota ['kwəʊtə] *n.* **a)** *(share)* Anteil,
der; **b)** *(goods to be produced)* Produk-
tionsmindestquote, *die;* **c)** *(maximum
number)* Höchstquote, *die*
quotation [kwəʊ'teɪʃn] *n.* **a)** Zitieren,
das; (passage) Zitat, *das;* **b)** *(estimate)*
Kosten[vor]anschlag, *der.* **quo'ta-
tion-marks** *n. pl.* Anführungszeichen *Pl.*

quote [kwəʊt] **1.** *v.t. also abs.* zitieren
(**from** aus); zitieren aus ⟨*Buch, Text*⟩;
(mention) anführen; nennen ⟨*Preis*⟩. **2.**
n. (coll.) **a)** *(passage)* Zitat, *das;* **b)** *(estimate)* Kosten[vor]anschlag, *der;* **c)**
usu. in pl. (quotation-mark) Anführungszeichen, *das*

R

R, r [ɑ:(r)] *n.* R, r, *das*
R. *abbr.* **River** Fl.
rabbi ['ræbaɪ] *n.* Rabbi[ner], *der; (as
title)* Rabbi, *der*
rabbit ['ræbɪt] *n.* Kaninchen, *das*
rabbit: ~-**burrow** *n.* Kaninchenbau,
der; ~-**hutch** *n. (also fig.)* Kanin-
chenstall, *der;* ~-**warren** *n.* Kanin-
chengehege, *das; (fig.)* Labyrinth, *das*
rabble ['ræbl] *n.* Mob, *der*
rabid ['ræbɪd] *adj.* **a)** tollwütig; **b)** *(extreme)* fanatisch
rabies ['reɪbi:z] *n.* Tollwut, *die*
¹**race** [reɪs] **1.** *n.* Rennen, *das; (fig.)* **a** ~
against time ein Wettlauf mit der Zeit.
2. *v.i.* **a)** *(in swimming, running, etc.)*
um die Wette schwimmen/laufen
usw. (**with, against** mit); **b)** ⟨*Motor:*⟩
durchdrehen; ⟨*Puls:*⟩ jagen; **c)** *(rush)*
sich sehr beeilen; ~ **after** sb. jmdn.
hinterherhetzen. **3.** *v.t.* um die Wette
schwimmen/laufen *usw.* mit
²**race** *n. (Anthrop., Biol.)* Rasse, *die;*
the human ~: die Menschheit
race: ~-**course** *n.* Rennbahn, *die;*
~-**horse** *n.* Rennpferd, *das;* ~-**track**
n. Rennbahn, *die*
racial ['reɪʃl] *adj.* Rassen⟨*diskriminierung, -konflikt, -gleichheit*⟩; rassisch
⟨*Gruppe, Minderheit*⟩. **racialism** ['reɪ-
ʃəlɪzm] *n.* Rassismus, *der.* **racialist**
['reɪʃəlɪst] **1.** *n.* Rassist, *der*/Rassistin,
die. **2.** *adj.* rassistisch
racing ['reɪsɪŋ] *n.* Rennsport, *der; (with
horses)* Pferdesport, *der.* '**racing-car**
n. Rennwagen, *der.* '**racing driver**
n. Rennfahrer, *der*/-fahrerin, *die*
racism ['reɪsɪzm] *n.* Rassismus, *der.*
racist ['reɪsɪst] **1.** *n.* Rassist, *der*/Ras-
sistin, *die.* **2.** *adj.* rassistisch

rack [ræk] **1.** *n. (for luggage)* Ablage, *die; (for toast, plates)* Ständer, *der; (on bicycle, motor cycle)* Gepäckträger, *der.* **2.** *v. t.* ~ **one's brain|s|** *(fig.)* sich *(Dat.)* den Kopf zerbrechen *(ugs.)*

¹**racket** ['rækɪt] *n.* Schläger, *der*

²**racket** *n.* **a)** *(disturbance)* Lärm, *der;* Krach, *der;* **b)** *(scheme)* Schwindelgeschäft, *das (ugs.).* **racketeer** [rækɪ-'tɪə(r)] *n.* Ganove, *der; (profiteer)* Wucherer, *der*

racoon [rə'ku:n] *n.* Waschbär, *der*

racy ['reɪsɪ] *adj.* flott *(ugs.)* ⟨*Stil*⟩

radar ['reɪdɑ:(r)] *n.* Radar, *das od. der*

radiant ['reɪdɪənt] *adj.* strahlend; fröhlich ⟨*Stimmung*⟩; **be** ~: strahlen (with *vor* + *Dat.*)

radiate ['reɪdɪeɪt] **1.** *v. i.* **a)** ⟨*Hitze, Wärme:*⟩ ausstrahlen; ⟨*Schein, Wellen:*⟩ ausgehen (**from** von); **b)** *(from central point)* strahlenförmig ausgehen (**from** von). **2.** *v. t.* ausstrahlen ⟨*Licht, Wärme; Glück, Liebe*⟩; aussenden ⟨*Strahlen, Wellen*⟩. **radiation** [reɪdɪ'eɪʃn] *n. (of energy)* Emission, *die; (of signals)* Ausstrahlung, *die; (energy transmitted)* Strahlung, *die.* **radiator** ['reɪdɪeɪtə(r)] *n.* **a)** *(for heating)* Heizkörper, *der;* **b)** *(Motor Veh.)* Kühler, *der*

radical ['rædɪkl] *adj.* **1. a)** *(thorough; also Polit.)* radikal; drastisch ⟨*Maßnahme*⟩; **b)** *(progressive)* radikal; **c)** *(fundamental)* grundlegend. **2.** *n. (Polit.)* Radikale, *der/die*

radio ['reɪdɪəʊ] **1.** *n., pl.* ~**s a)** *no indef. art.* Funk, *der; (for private communication)* Sprechfunk, *der;* **b)** *no indef. art. (Broadcasting)* Rundfunk, *der;* **on the** ~: im Radio; **c)** *(apparatus)* Radio, *das.* **2.** *attrib. adj. (Broadcasting)* Rundfunk-; Radio⟨*welle, -teleskop*⟩; Funk⟨*mast, -turm, -taxi*⟩. **3.** *v. t.* funken

radio: ~'**active** *adj.* radioaktiv; ~**ac'tivity** *n.* Radioaktivität, *die;* ~**con'trolled** *adj.* funkgesteuert

radish ['rædɪʃ] *n.* Rettich, *der; (small, red)* Radieschen, *das*

radius ['reɪdɪəs] *n., pl.* **radii** ['reɪdɪaɪ] *or* ~**es** *(Math.)* Radius, *der; (fig.)* Umkreis, *der*

RAF [ɑ:reɪ'ef, *(coll.)* ræf] *abbr.* **Royal Air Force**

raffle ['ræfl] **1.** *n.* Tombola, *die;* ~ **ticket** Los, *das.* **2.** *v. t.* ~ |**off**| verlosen

raft [rɑ:ft] *n.* Floß, *das*

rafter ['rɑ:ftə(r)] *n.* Sparren, *der*

¹**rag** [ræg] *n.* **a)** [Stoff]fetzen, *der;* **b)**

(old and torn clothes) Lumpen *Pl.;* **c)** *(derog.: newspaper)* Käseblatt, *das (salopp)*

²**rag** *v. t.,* -**gg**- *(tease)* aufziehen

rag: ~-**bag** *n. (fig.)* Sammelsurium, *das;* ~ **doll** *n.* Stoffpuppe, *die*

rage [reɪdʒ] **1.** *n.* **a)** *(violent anger)* Wut, *die; (fit of anger)* Wutausbruch, *der;* **b) sth. is |all| the** ~: etw. ist [ganz] groß in Mode. **2.** *v. i.* **a)** *(rave)* toben; ~ **at** *or* **against sth./sb.** gegen etw./ jmdn. wüten; **b)** *(be violent, unchecked)* toben; ⟨*Krankheit:*⟩ wüten

ragged ['rægɪd] *adj.* zerrissen

raid [reɪd] **1.** *n.* Einfall, *der;* Überfall, *der; (Mil.)* Überraschungsangriff, *der; (by police)* Razzia, *die* (**on** in + *Dat.*). **2.** *v. t.* ⟨*Polizei:*⟩ eine Razzia machen auf (+ *Akk.*); ⟨*Räuber, Soldaten:*⟩ überfallen. '**raider** *n.* Räuber, *der/* Räuberin, *die*

rail [reɪl] *n.* **a)** Stange, *die; (on ship)* Reling, *die; (as protection against contact)* Barriere, *die;* **b)** *(Railw.: of track)* Schiene, *die;* **c)** *(~way)* [Eisen]bahn, *die; attrib.* Bahn-; **by** ~: mit der Bahn

railing ['reɪlɪŋ] *n. (round park)* Zaun, *der; (on staircase)* Geländer, *das*

'**railroad** *(Amer.),* '**railway** *ns.* **a)** *(track)* Bahnlinie, *die;* Bahnstrecke, *die;* **b)** *(system)* [Eisen]bahn, *die*

railway: ~ **carriage** *n.* Eisenbahnwagen, *der;* ~ **engine** *n.* Lokomotive, *die;* ~ **line** *n.* [Eisen]bahnlinie, *die;* ~ **station** *n.* Bahnhof, *der*

rain [reɪn] **1.** *n.* **a)** Regen, *der;* **b)** *(fig.: of arrows, blows, etc.)* Hagel, *der.* **2.** *v. i. impers.* **it is** ~**ing** es regnet. **3.** *v. t.* hageln lassen ⟨*Schläge, Hiebe*⟩

rain: ~**bow** ['reɪnbəʊ] *n.* Regenbogen, *der;* ~**check** *n. (Amer. fig.)* **take a** ~**check on sth.** auf etw. *(Akk.)* später wieder zurückkommen; ~**coat** *n.* Regenmantel, *der;* ~**fall** *n.* Niederschlag, *der;* ~**proof** *adj.* regendicht; ~**water** *n.* Regenwasser, *das*

'**rainy** *adj.* regnerisch ⟨*Tag, Wetter*⟩; regenreich ⟨*Gebiet, Sommer*⟩; ~ **season** Regenzeit, *die;* **keep sth. for a** ~ **day** *(fig.)* sich *(Dat.)* etw. für schlechte Zeiten aufheben

raise [reɪz] *v. t.* **a)** *(lift up)* heben; erhöhen ⟨*Temperatur, Miete, Gehalt*⟩; hochziehen ⟨*Fahne*⟩; aufziehen ⟨*Vorhang*⟩; hochheben ⟨*Arm*⟩; ~ **one's glass to sb.** das Glas auf jmdn. erheben; **b)** *(set upright)* aufrichten; erheben ⟨*Banner*⟩; ~ **sb.'s spirits** jmds. Stimmung heben; **c)** erheben ⟨*Forde-*

rungen, Einwände); aufwerfen
(Frage); zur Sprache bringen *(Thema,
Problem);* **d)** aufziehen *(Vieh,
[Haus]tiere);* großziehen *(Familie,
Kinder);* **e)** aufbringen *(Geld, Betrag);*
f) aufheben *(Belagerung, Blockade,
Embargo, Verbot)*
raisin ['reizn] *n.* Rosine, *die*
rake [reik] **1.** *n.* Rechen, *der;* Harke,
die. **2.** *v.t.* **a)** harken; **b)** ~ **the fire** die
Asche entfernen; **c)** *(with eyes, shots)*
bestreichen. **rake 'in** *v.t. (coll.)* schef-
feln *(ugs.).* **rake 'up** *v.t.* zusammen-
harken; *(fig.)* wieder ausgraben
'**rake-off** *n. (coll.)* [Gewinn]anteil, *der*
rakish ['reikiʃ] *adj.* flott; keß
rally ['ræli] **1.** *v.i. (regain health)* sich
wieder [ein wenig] erholen. **2.** *v.t.* **a)**
(reassemble) wieder zusammenrufen;
b) einigen *(Partei, Kräfte);* sammeln
(Anhänger). **3.** *n.* **a)** *(mass meeting)*
Versammlung, *die;* **b)** |motor| ~: Ral-
lye, *die;* **c)** *(Tennis)* Ballwechsel, *der*
ram [ræm] **1.** *n. (Zool.)* Schafbock, *der;*
Widder, *der.* **2.** *v.t.,* **-mm-: a)** *(force)*
stopfen; ~ **a post into the ground** einen
Pfosten in die Erde rammen; ~ **sth.
home to sb.** jmdm. etw. deutlich vor
Augen führen; **b)** *(collide with)* rammen
ramble ['ræmbl] **1.** *n.* |nature| ~: Wan-
derung, *die.* **2.** *v.i.* **a)** *(walk)* umherstreifen **(through, in** in + *Dat.);* **b)** *(in
talk)* zusammenhangloses Zeug re-
den; **keep rambling on about sth.** sich
endlos über etw. *(Akk.)* auslassen.
rambler ['ræmblə(r)] *n.* Wanderer,
*der/*Wanderin, *die.* **rambling** ['ræm-
bliŋ] **1.** *n.* Wandern, *das.* **2.** *adj.* **a)** *(irregularly arranged)* verschachtelt;
verwinkelt *(Straßen);* **b)** *(incoherent)*
unzusammenhängend *(Erklärung);* **c)**
~ **rose** Kletterrose, *die*
ramp [ræmp] *n.* Rampe, *die*
rampage 1. ['ræmpeidʒ] *n.* Randale,
die (ugs.); **be/go on the** ~ *(coll.)* randalieren. **2.** [ræm'peidʒ] *v.i.* randalieren
rampant ['ræmpənt] *adj.* zügellos *(Gewalt, Rassismus);* steil ansteigend *(Inflation);* üppig *(Wachstum)*
rampart ['ræmpɑːt] *n.* Wehrgang, *der*
'**ramshackle** ['ræmʃækl] *adj.* klapprig *(Auto);*
verkommen *(Gebäude)*
ran *see* run 2, 3
ranch [rɑːntʃ] *n.* Ranch, *die*
rancid ['rænsid] *adj.* ranzig
rancour *(Brit.; Amer.:* **rancor)** ['ræŋ-
kə(r)] *n.* [tiefe] Verbitterung
random ['rændəm] **1.** *n.* **at** ~: wahllos;

willkürlich; *(aimlessly)* ziellos; **choose
at** ~: aufs Geratewohl wählen. **2.** *adj.*
willkürlich
randy ['rændi] *adj.* geil; scharf *(ugs.)*
rang *see* ²ring 2, 3
range [reindʒ] **1.** *n.* **a)** ~ **of mountains**
Bergkette, *die;* **b)** *(of subjects)* Palette,
die; (of knowledge, voice) Umfang,
der; **c)** *(of missile etc.)* Reichweite,
die; **at a** ~ **of 200 metres** auf eine Entfernung von 200 Metern; **d)** *(series, selection)* Kollektion, *die;* **e)** *(stove)*
Herd, *der.* **2.** *v.i. (Preise, Temperaturen:)* schwanken, sich bewegen
(from ... to zwischen [+ *Dat.*] ... **und)**
'**ranger** *n.* Förster, *der/*Försterin, *die*
'**rank** [ræŋk] **1.** *n.* **a)** *(position in hierarchy)* Rang, *der; (Mil. also)* Dienst-
grad, *der;* **b)** *(social position)* [soziale]
Stellung; **c)** *(row)* Reihe, *die;* **the** ~
and file *(fig.)* die breite Masse; **the** ~**s**
(enlisted men) die Mannschaften und
Unteroffiziere. **2.** *v.t.* ~ **among** zählen
zu. **3.** *v.i.* ~ **among** zählen zu
²**rank** *adj.* **a)** kraß *(Außenseiter);* **b)** ~
weeds [wild]wucherndes Unkraut
ransack ['rænsæk] *v.t.* **a)** *(search)*
durchsuchen **(for** nach**); b)** *(pillage)*
plündern
ransom ['rænsəm] *n.* ~ |money| Löse-
geld, *das;* **hold to** ~: als Geisel festhalten
rant [rænt] *v.i.* ~ |and rave| wettern
(ugs.) **(about** über + *Akk.*)
rap [ræp] **1.** *n.* [energisches] Klopfen.
2. *v.t.,* **-pp-** klopfen. **3.** *v.i.,* **-pp-** klopfen **(on an** + *Akk.*)
'**rape** [reip] **1.** *n.* Vergewaltigung, *die.*
2. *v.t.* vergewaltigen
²**rape** *n. (Bot., Agric.)* Raps, *der*
rapid ['ræpid] **1.** *adj.* schnell *(Bewegung, Wachstum, Puls);* rasch *(Fortschritt, Ausbreitung).* **2.** *n. in pl.*
Stromschnellen. **rapidity** [rə'piditi]
n. Schnelligkeit, *die.* '**rapidly** *adv.*
schnell
rapist ['reipist] *n.* Vergewaltiger, *der*
rapport [rə'pɔː(r)] *n.* [harmonisches]
Verhältnis
rapt [ræpt] *adj.* gespannt *(Miene)*
rapture ['ræptʃə(r)] *n.* |state of| ~:
Verzückung, *die.* **rapturous**
['ræptʃərəs] *adj.* begeistert
'**rare** [reə(r)] *adj.,* '**rarely** *adv.* selten
²**rare** *adj. (Cookery)* englisch gebraten
rarity ['reəriti] *n.* Seltenheit, *die*
'**rash** [ræʃ] *n.* [Haut]ausschlag, *der*
²**rash** *adj.* voreilig *(Urteil, Entscheidung);* überstürzt *(Versprechung)*

rasher ['ræʃə(r)] n. Speckscheibe, die
'**rashly** adv. voreilig
rasp [rɑːsp] n. (tool) Raspel, die
raspberry ['rɑːzbərɪ] n. Himbeere, die
rat [ræt] n. **a)** Ratte, die; **smell a ~** (fig.) Lunte riechen (ugs.); **b)** (coll. derog.. person) Ratte, die (derb)
rate [reɪt] **1.** n. **a)** (proportion) Rate, die; **b)** (tariff) Satz, der; **~** |**of pay**| Lohnsatz, der; **c)** (speed) Geschwindigkeit, die; Tempo, das; **d)** (Brit.: levy) |**local** or **council**| ~**s** Gemeindeabgaben; **e)** (coll.) **at any ~** (at least) zumindest; wenigstens; (whatever happens) auf jeden Fall; **at this ~ we won't get any work done** so kriegen wir gar nichts fertig (ugs.). **2.** v. t. **a)** einschätzen (Intelligenz, Leistung); **b)** (consider) betrachten; rechnen (**among** zu). **3.** v. i. **~ as** gelten als
rather ['rɑːðə(r)] adv. **a)** (by preference) lieber; **b)** (somewhat) ziemlich; **I ~ think that ...**: ich bin ziemlich sicher, daß ...; **c)** (more truly) vielmehr; **or ~**: beziehungsweise
ratification [rætɪfɪ'keɪʃn] n. Ratifizierung, die
ratify ['rætɪfaɪ] v. t. ratifizieren
rating ['reɪtɪŋ] n. **a)** (estimated standing) Einschätzung, die; **b)** (Radio, Telev.) |**popularity**| **~**: Einschaltquote, die; **c)** (Brit. Navy) Matrose, der
ratio ['reɪʃɪəʊ] n., pl. **~s** Verhältnis, das
ration ['ræʃn] **1.** n. **~**|**s**| Ration, die (of an + Dat.). **2.** v. t. rationieren (Benzin, Zucker usw.)
rational ['ræʃənl] adj. (having reason) rational (Wesen); (sensible) vernünftig (Person, Art usw.)
rationalize ['ræʃənəlaɪz] v. t. rationalisieren
'**rat race** n. erbarmungsloser Konkurrenzkampf
rattle ['rætl] **1.** v. i. **a)** (Fenster:) klappern; (Flaschen:) klirren; (Kette:) rasseln; **b)** (Zug, Bus:) rattern. **2.** v. t. **a)** klappern mit (Würfel, Geschirr); klirren lassen (Fenster[scheiben]); rasseln mit (Kette); **b)** (sl.: disconcert) **~ sb.**, **get sb. ~d** jmdn. durcheinanderbringen. **3.** n. **a)** (of baby) Rassel, die; **b)** (sound) Klappern, das. **rattle** '**off** v. t. (coll.) herunterrasseln (ugs.)
'**rattlesnake** n. Klapperschlange, die
raucous ['rɔːkəs] adj. rauh
ravage ['rævɪdʒ] **1.** v. t. heimsuchen (Gebiet, Stadt). **2.** n. in pl. verheerende Wirkung
rave [reɪv] **1.** v. i. **a)** (talk wildly) irrere-

den; **b)** (speak admiringly) schwärmen (**about** von). **2.** attrib. adj. (coll.) begeistert (Kritik)
raven ['reɪvn] n. Rabe, der
ravenous ['rævənəs] adj. **I'm ~**: ich habe einen Bärenhunger (ugs.)
ravine [rə'viːn] n. Schlucht, die
raving ['reɪvɪŋ] **1.** adj. irreredend (Idiot). **2.** adv. **be ~ mad** völlig verrückt sein (ugs.)
ravish ['rævɪʃ] v. t. (charm) entzücken. '**ravishing** adj. bildschön (Anblick, Person); hinreißend (Schönheit)
raw [rɔː] adj. **a)** (uncooked) roh; **b)** (inexperienced) unerfahren; **c)** (stripped of skin) blutig (Fleisch); offen (Wunde); **d)** (chilly) naßkalt. **raw** ma'**terial** n. Rohstoff, der
ray [reɪ] n. Strahl, der; **~ of sunshine/light** Sonnen-/Lichtstrahl, der
raze [reɪz] v. t. **~ to the ground** dem Erdboden gleichmachen
razor ['reɪzə(r)] n. Rasiermesser, das; |**electric**| **~**: [elektrischer] Rasierapparat. '**razor-blade** n. Rasierklinge, die
RC abbr. **Roman Catholic** r.-k.; röm.-kath.
Rd. abbr. **road** Str.
RE abbr. (Brit.) **Religious Education** Religionslehre, die
re [riː] prep. (Commerc.) betreffs
reach [riːtʃ] **1.** v. t. **a)** (arrive at) erreichen; ankommen in (+ Dat.) (Stadt, Land); erzielen (Übereinstimmung); kommen zu (Entscheidung; Ausgang, Eingang); **you can ~ her at this number** du kannst sie unter dieser Nummer erreichen; **b)** (extend to) (Straße:) führen bis zu; (Leiter, Haar:) reichen bis zu. **2.** v. i. **a)** (stretch out hand) **~ for sth.** nach etw. greifen; **~ across the table** über den Tisch langen; **~ be long/tall enough)** sth. **will/won't ~**: etw. ist/ist nicht lang genug; **I can't ~**: ich komme nicht daran; **c)** (go as far as) (Wasser, Gebäude, Besitz:) reichen (|**up**| **to** bis [hinauf] zu). **3.** n. Reichweite, die; **be within easy ~**: leicht erreichbar sein; **be out of ~**: nicht erreichbar sein. **reach** '**out** v. i. die Hand ausstrecken (**for** nach)
react [rɪ'ækt] v. i. reagieren (**to** auf + Akk.). **reaction** [rɪ'ækʃn] n. Reaktion, die (**to** auf + Akk.)
reactionary [rɪ'ækʃənərɪ] (Polit.) **1.** adj. reaktionär. **2.** n. Reaktionär, der/Reaktionärin, die
reactor [rɪ'æktə(r)] n. |**nuclear**| **~**: Kernreaktor, der

read [ri:d] **1.** *v. t.*, **read** [red] **a)** lesen; ~ sb. sth., ~ sth. to sb. jmdm. etwas vorlesen; ~ **the gas meter** das Gas ablesen; **b)** *(interpret)* deuten; ~ **between the lines** zwischen den Zeilen lesen; **c)** *(study)* studieren. **2.** *v. i.*, **read a)** lesen; ~ **to sb.** jmdm. vorlesen; **b)** *(convey meaning)* lauten; **the contract ~s as follows** der Vertrag hat folgenden Wortlaut. **read 'out** *v. t.* laut vorlesen. **read 'over, read 'through** *v. t.* durchlesen. **read 'up** *v. t.* sich informieren (**on** über + *Akk.*)

readable ['ri:dəbl] *adj.* **a)** *(pleasant to read)* lesenswert; **b)** *(legible)* leserlich

reader *n.* **a)** Leser, *der*/Leserin, *die;* **b)** *(book)* Lesebuch, *das*

readership *n.* Leserschaft, *die*

readily ['redɪlɪ] *adv.* **a)** *(willingly)* bereitwillig; **b)** *(easily)* ohne weiteres

readiness ['redɪnɪs] *n.* Bereitschaft, *die;* **be in** ~: bereit sein (**for** für)

reading *n.* **a)** Lesen, *das;* **b)** *(figure shown)* Anzeige, *die;* **c)** *(recital)* Lesung, *die* (**from** aus); **d)** *(Parl.)* Lesung, *die.* **'reading-lamp, 'reading-light** *ns.* Leselampe, *die.* **'reading-matter** *n.* Lesestoff, *der;* Lektüre, *die*

ready ['redɪ] **1.** *adj.* **a)** *(prepared)* fertig; **be ~ to do sth.** bereit sein, etw. zu tun; **get ~:** sich fertigmachen; **b)** *(willing)* bereit; **c)** *(within reach)* griffbereit. **2.** *adv.* fertig. **3.** *n.* **at the ~** ⟨Schußwaffe⟩ im Anschlag

ready: ~ **'cash** *see* ~ **money;** ~-**'made** *adj.* **a)** Konfektions⟨anzug, -kleidung⟩; **b)** *(fig.)* vorgefertigt; ~ **'money** *n.* Bargeld, *das*

real [rɪəl] *adj.* **a)** *(actually existing)* real ⟨Ereignis, Lebewesen⟩; wirklich ⟨Macht⟩; **b)** *(genuine)* echt ⟨Interesse, Gold, Seide⟩; **c)** *(complete)* total (*ugs.*) ⟨Desaster, Enttäuschung⟩; **d)** *(true)* wahr ⟨Grund, Name, Glück⟩; echt ⟨Mitleid, Sieg⟩; **the ~ thing** der/die/das Echte; **be for ~** *(sl.)* echt sein. **'real estate** *n.* Immobilien *Pl.*

realism ['rɪəlɪzm] *n.* Realismus, *der*

realist *n.* Realist, *der*/Realistin, *die*

realistic [rɪə'lɪstɪk] *adj.* realistisch

reality [rɪ'ælɪtɪ] *n.* Realität, *die*

realization [rɪəlaɪ'zeɪʃn] *n.* Erkenntnis, *die*

realize ['rɪəlaɪz] *v. t.* **a)** *(be aware of)* bemerken; erkennen ⟨Fehler⟩; **I didn't ~** *(abs.)* ich habe es nicht gewußt; ~ |**that**|...: merken, daß ...; **b)** *(make happen)* verwirklichen; **c)** erbringen ⟨Summe, Preis⟩

really ['rɪəlɪ] *adv.* wirklich; **not** ~: eigentlich nicht; |**well,**| ~! [also] so was!

realm [relm] *n.* Königreich, *das*

realtor ['ri:əltə(r)] *(Amer.)* Grundstücksmakler, *der*

reap [ri:p] *v. t.* *(cut)* schneiden ⟨Getreide⟩; *(gather in)* einfahren ⟨Getreide, Ernte⟩

reappear [ri:ə'pɪə(r)] *v. i.* wieder auftauchen; *(come back)* [wieder] zurückkommen

¹rear [rɪə(r)] **1.** *n.* **a)** *(back part)* hinterer Teil; **b)** *(back)* Rückseite, *die;* **c)** *(Mil.)* Rücken, *der.* **2.** *adj.* hinter...; ~ **axle** Hinterachse, *die*

²rear 1. *v. t.* großziehen ⟨Kind, Familie⟩; halten ⟨Vieh⟩. **2.** *v. i.* ⟨Pferd:⟩ sich aufbäumen

rear: ~**guard** *n.* *(Mil.)* Nachhut, *die;* ~-**light** *n.* Rücklicht, *das*

rearm [ri:'ɑ:m] *v. i. & t.* wiederaufrüsten

rearrange [ri:ə'reɪndʒ] *v. t.* umräumen ⟨Möbel⟩; verlegen ⟨Spiel⟩ (**for** auf + *Akk.*); ändern ⟨Programm⟩

rear-view 'mirror *n.* Rückspiegel, *der*

reason ['ri:zn] **1.** *n.* **a)** *(cause)* Grund, *der;* **have no ~ to complain** sich nicht beklagen können; **for that |very| ~:** aus [eben] diesem Grund; **b)** *(power to understand; sense)* Vernunft, *die; (power to think)* Verstand, *der;* **in** *or* **within** ~: innerhalb eines vernünftigen Rahmens. **2.** *v. i.* **a)** schlußfolgern (**from** aus); **b)** ~ **with** diskutieren mit (**about, on** über + *Akk.*); **you can't ~ with her** mit ihr kann man nicht vernünftig reden. **3.** *v. t.* schlußfolgern

reasonable ['ri:zənəbl] *adj.* **a)** vernünftig; **b)** *(inexpensive)* günstig. **reasonably** ['ri:zənəblɪ] *adv.* **a)** *(within reason)* vernünftig; **b)** *(fairly)* ganz ⟨gut⟩; ziemlich ⟨gesund⟩

reassurance [ri:ə'ʃʊərəns] *n.* **a)** *(calming)* **give sb.** ~: jmdn. beruhigen; **b)** *(confirmation)* Bestätigung, *die*

reassure [ri:ə'ʃʊə(r)] *v. t.* beruhigen; ~ **sb. about his health.** jmdm. versichern, daß er gesund ist. **reassuring** [ri:ə'ʃʊərɪŋ] *adj.* beruhigend

rebate ['ri:beɪt] *n.* **a)** *(refund)* Rückzahlung, *die;* **b)** *(discount)* Preisnachlaß, *der* (**on** auf + *Akk.*)

rebel 1. ['rebl] *n.* Rebell, *der*/Rebellin, *die.* **2.** *attrib. adj.* Rebellen-. **3.** [rɪ'bel] *v. i.*, **-ll-** rebellieren. **rebellion** [rɪ'beljən] *n.* Rebellion, *die.* **rebellious** [rɪ'beljəs] *adj.* rebellisch

rebound 1. [rɪ'baʊnd] *v. i.* **a)** *(spring back)* abprallen (**from** von); **b)** *(fig.)* zurückfallen (**upon** auf + *Akk.*). **2.** ['ri:baʊnd] *n.* Abprall, *der*

rebuff [rɪ'bʌf] **1.** *n.* [schroffe] Ab·weisung. **2.** *v. t.* [schroff] zurückweisen

rebuild [ri:'bɪld] *v. t.*, **rebuilt** [ri:'bɪlt] wieder aufbauen

rebuke [rɪ'bju:k] **1.** *v. t.* tadeln, rügen (**for** wegen). **2.** *n.* Rüge, *die*

recall 1. [rɪ'kɔ:l] *v. t.* **a)** *(remember)* sich erinnern an (+ *Akk.*); **b)** *(serve as reminder of)* erinnern an (+ *Akk.*); **c)** abberufen ‹*Botschafter*›. **2.** [rɪ'kɔ:l, 'ri:kɔ:l] *n.* **a)** |powers of| ~: Gedächtnis, *das;* **b) beyond** ~: unwiderruflich

recant [rɪ'kænt] *v. i.* [öffentlich] widerrufen

recap ['ri:kæp] *v. t. & i.,* **-pp-** *(coll.)* rekapitulieren

recapitulate [ri:kə'pɪtjʊleɪt] *v. t. & i.* rekapitulieren

recapture [ri:'kæptʃə(r)] *v. t.* wieder ergreifen ‹*Gefangenen*›; wieder einfangen ‹*Tier*›

recede [ri'si:d] *v. i.* ‹*Hochwasser, Flut:*› zurückgehen; ~ **|into the distance|** in der Ferne verschwinden. **receding** [rɪ'si:dɪŋ] *adj.* fliehend ‹*Kinn, Stirn*›

receipt [rɪ'si:t] *n.* **a)** *(receiving)* Empfang, *der;* **b)** *(written acknowledgement)* Quittung, *die;* **c)** in *pl. (amount received)* Einnahmen (**from** aus)

receive [rɪ'si:v] *v. t.* **a)** *(get)* erhalten; beziehen ‹*Gehalt, Rente*›; **b)** *(accept)* entgegennehmen ‹*Bukett, Lieferung*›; **c)** *(entertain)* empfangen ‹*Gast*›. **re**·'**ceiver** *n.* **a)** Empfänger, *der*/Empfängerin, *die;* **b)** *(Teleph.)* [Telefon]hörer, *der;* **c)** *(of stolen goods)* Hehler, *der*/Hehlerin, *die*

recent ['ri:sənt] *adj.* jüngst ‹*Ereignisse, Vergangenheit usw.*›; **the** ~ **closure of the factory** die kürzlich erfolgte Schließung der Fabrik. '**recently** *adv. (a short time ago)* vor kurzem; *(in the recent past)* in der letzten Zeit

receptacle [rɪ'septəkl] *n.* Behälter, *der;* Gefäß, *das*

reception [rɪ'sepʃn] *n.* **a)** *(welcome)* Aufnahme, *die;* **b)** *(party)* Empfang, *der;* **c)** *(Brit.: foyer)* die Rezeption. **re**·'**ceptionist** *n. (in hotel)* Empfangschef, *der*/-dame, *die; (at doctor's)* Sprechstundenhilfe, *die.* **re**·'**ception desk** *n.* Rezeption, *die*

receptive [rɪ'septɪv] *adj.* aufgeschlossen, empfänglich (**to** für)

recess [rɪ'ses, 'ri:ses] *n.* **a)** *(alcove)* Ni-

sche, *die;* **b)** *(Brit. Parl.; Amer.: short vacation)* Ferien *Pl.; (Amer. Sch.; between classes)* Pause, *die*

recharge [ri:'tʃɑ:dʒ] *v. t.* aufladen ‹*Batterie*›

recipe ['resɪpɪ] *n.* Rezept, *das*

recipient [rɪ'sɪpɪənt] *n.* Empfänger, *der*/Empfängerin, *die*

reciprocal [rɪ'sɪprəkl] *adj.* gegenseitig ‹*Abkommen, Zuneigung*›

reciprocate [rɪ'sɪprəkeɪt] *v. t.* erwidern

recital [rɪ'saɪtl] *n. (performance)* [Solisten]konzert, *das; (of literature also)* Rezitation, *die*

recitation [resɪ'teɪʃn] *n.* Rezitation, *die*

recite [rɪ'saɪt] *v. t.* **a)** rezitieren ‹*Gedicht*›; **b)** *(list)* aufzählen

reckless ['reklɪs] *adj.* unbesonnen; rücksichtslos ‹*Fahrweise*›; ~ **of the dangers/consequences** ungeachtet der Gefahren/Folgen

reckon ['rekn] *v. t.* **a)** *(work out)* ausrechnen ‹*Kosten*›; bestimmen ‹*Position*›; **b)** *(consider)* halten (**as** für); **c)** *(estimate)* schätzen. '**reckon on** *v. t.* **a)** *(rely on)* zählen auf (+ *Akk.*); **b)** *(expect)* rechnen mit. '**reckon with** *v. i.* rechnen mit

reckoning *n.* Berechnung, *die;* **by my** ~: nach meiner Rechnung

reclaim [rɪ'kleɪm] *v. t.* **a)** zurückbekommen ‹*Steuern*›; **b)** urbar machen ‹*Land*›

recline [rɪ'klaɪn] *v. i.* liegen; **reclining seat** Liegesitz, *der*

recluse [rɪ'klu:s] *n.* Einsiedler, *der*/Einsiedlerin, *die*

recognition [rekəg'nɪʃn] *n.* **a)** Wiedererkennen, *das;* **be beyond all** ~: nicht wiederzuerkennen sein; **b)** *(acknowledgement)* Anerkennung, *die;* **in** ~ **of** als Anerkennung für

recognize ['rekəgnaɪz] *v. t.* **a)** *(know again)* wiedererkennen (**by** an + *Dat.,* **from** durch); **b)** *(acknowledge)* erkennen; anerkennen ‹*Gültigkeit, Land*›; **be** ~**d as** gelten als

recoil 1. [rɪ'kɔɪl] *v. i.* zurückfahren. **2.** ['ri:kɔɪl, rɪ'kɔɪl] *n.* Rückstoß, *der*

recollect [rekə'lekt] **1.** *v. t.* sich erinnern an (+ *Akk.*). **2.** *v. i.* sich erinnern. **recollection** [rekə'lekʃn] *n.* Erinnerung, *die*

recommend [rekə'mend] *v. t.* empfehlen. **recommendation** [rekəmen'deɪʃn] *n.* Empfehlung, *die;* **on sb.'s** ~: auf jmds. Empfehlung *(Akk.)*

recompense ['rekəmpens] 1. v. t. entschädigen. 2. n. Entschädigung, die
reconcile ['rekənsaɪl] v. t. a) (restore to friendship) versöhnen; b) ~ oneself to sth.: sich mit etw. versöhnen
reconnaissance [rɪ'kɒnɪsəns] n. (Mil.) Aufklärung, die
reconnoitre (Brit.; Amer.: **reconnoiter**) [rekə'nɔɪtə(r)] v. i. auf Erkundung [aus]gehen
reconsider [ri:kən'sɪdə(r)] v. t. [noch einmal] überdenken
reconstruct [ri:kən'strʌkt] v. t. wieder aufbauen; (fig.) rekonstruieren. **reconstruction** [ri:kən'strʌkʃn] n. Wiederaufbau, der; (thing reconstructed) Rekonstruktion, die
record 1. [rɪ'kɔːd] v. t. a) aufzeichnen; ~ a new LP eine neue LP aufnehmen; b) (register officially) dokumentieren; protokollieren (Verhandlung). 2. ['rekɔːd] n. a) be on ~ (Prozeß, Verhandlung, Besprechung:) protokolliert sein; **have sth. on ~:** etw. dokumentiert haben; b) (report) Protokoll, das; c) (document) Dokument, das; [strictly] off the ~: [ganz] inoffiziell; d) (for ~-player) [Schall]platte, die; e) **have a** [criminal/police] ~: vorbestraft sein; f) (Sport) Rekord, der
recorded [rɪ'kɔːdɪd] adj. aufgezeichnet (Konzert, Rede); ~ **music** Musikaufnahmen. **recorded de'livery** n. (Brit. Post.) eingeschriebene Sendung (ohne Versicherung)
recorder [rɪ'kɔːdə(r)] n. (Mus.) Blockflöte, die
recording [rɪ'kɔːdɪŋ] n. a) (process) Aufzeichnung, die; b) (what is recorded) Aufnahme, die. **re'cording studio** n. Tonstudio, das
record ['rekɔːd]: ~**-player** n. Plattenspieler, der; ~ **token** n. [Schall]plattengutschein, der
re-count 1. [ri:'kaʊnt] v. t. [noch einmal] nachzählen. 2. ['ri:kaʊnt] n. Nachzählung, die
recoup [rɪ'kuːp] v. t. [wieder] hereinbekommen ([Geld]einsatz)
recourse [rɪ'kɔːs] n. **have ~ to sb./sth.** bei jmdm./zu etw. Zuflucht nehmen
recover [rɪ'kʌvə(r)] 1. v. t. zurückbekommen. 2. v. i. ~ **from sth.** sich von etw. [wieder] erholen; **be** [fully] ~ed [völlig] wiederhergestellt sein. **re'covery** [rɪ'kʌvərɪ] n. Erholung, die; **make a quick/good ~:** sich schnell/gut erholen
recreation [rekrɪ'eɪʃn] n. Freizeitbe-

schäftigung, die; Hobby, das. **recreational** [rekrɪ'eɪʃnl] adj. Freizeit-
recruit [rɪ'kruːt] 1. n. a) (Mil.) Rekrut, der; b) (new member) neues Mitglied. 2. v. t. (Mil.: enlist) anwerben; (into party etc.) werben (Mitglied); einstellen (neuen Mitarbeiter). **re'cruitment** n. (Mil.) Anwerbung, die; (of new staff) Neueinstellung, die; ~ **of members** Mitgliederwerbung, die
rectangle ['rektæŋgl] n. Rechteck, das. **rectangular** [rek'tæŋgjʊlə(r)] adj. rechteckig
rector ['rektə(r)] n. a) Pfarrer, der; b) (Univ.) Rektor, der/Rektorin, die. **rectory** ['rektərɪ] n. Pfarrhaus, das
recuperate [rɪ'kjuːpəreɪt] v. i. sich erholen. **recuperation** [rɪkjuːpə'reɪʃn] n. Erholung, die
recur [rɪ'kɜː(r)] v. i., **-rr-** sich wiederholen; (Krankheit:) wiederkehren; (Symptom:) wieder auftreten. **recurrence** [rɪ'kʌrəns] n. Wiederholung, die; (of illness, thought, feeling) Wiederkehr, die; (of symptom) Wiederauftreten, das. **recurrent** [rɪ'kʌrənt] adj. immer wiederkehrend
recycle [riː'saɪkl] v. t. wiederverwerten. **recycling** [riː'saɪklɪŋ] n. Recycling, das
red [red] 1. adj. rot. 2. n. Rot, das. **Red 'Cross** n. Rotes Kreuz. **red'currant** [rote] Johannisbeere
redden ['redn] v. i. (Gesicht, Himmel:) sich röten; (Person:) rot werden
reddish ['redɪʃ] adj. rötlich
redecorate [riː'dekəreɪt] v. t. renovieren; (with wallpaper) neu tapezieren; (with paint) neu streichen
redeem [rɪ'diːm] v. t. a) [wieder] einlösen (Pfand); einlösen (Gutschein, Coupon); b) (save) retten. **redemption** [rɪ'dempʃn] n. (from sin) Erlösung, die
redeploy [riːdɪ'plɔɪ] v. t. woanders einsetzen (Arbeitskräfte)
red: ~**-'handed** adj. **catch sb.** ~**-handed** jmdn. auf frischer Tat ertappen; ~ **'herring** n. (fig.) Ablenkungsmanöver, das; ~**-hot** adj. [rot]glühend; **Red 'Indian** (Brit.) 1. n. Indianer, der/Indianerin, die; 2. adj. Indianer-
redirect [riːdaɪ'rekt] v. t. nachsenden (Post, Brief usw.); umleiten (Verkehr)
rediscover [riːdɪ'skʌvə(r)] v. t. wiederentdecken
red: ~**-'letter day** n. großer Tag; ~ **'light** n. rotes Warnlicht; (traffic-

light) rote Ampel; **drive through a ~ light** bei rot über die Ampel fahren; **~-'light district** *n.* Strich, *der (salopp)*

redo [ri:'du:] *v. t. forms as* **do** noch einmal machen ⟨*Bett, Hausaufgabe*⟩; *neu* frisieren ⟨*Haare*⟩

redouble [ri:'dʌbl] *v. t.* verdoppeln

redress [rɪ'dres] **1.** *n.* Entschädigung, *die.* **2.** *v. t.* wiedergutmachen; **~ the balance** das Gleichgewicht wiederherstellen

red 'tape *n. (fig.)* [unnötige] Bürokratie

reduce [rɪ'dju:s] *v. t.* **a)** senken ⟨*Preis, Gebühr, Fieber, Aufwendungen, Blutdruck usw.*⟩; reduzieren ⟨*Geschwindigkeit, Gewicht*⟩; **at ~d prices** zu herabgesetzten Preisen; **b)** **~ to silence/tears** verstummen lassen/zum Weinen bringen. **reduction** [rɪ'dʌkʃn] *n. (in price, costs, speed, etc.)* Senkung, *die* (**in** *Gen.*); **~ in wages/weight** Lohnsenkung, *die*/Gewichtsabnahme, *die*

redundancy [rɪ'dʌndənsɪ] *n. (Brit.)* Arbeitslosigkeit, *die;* **redundancies** Entlassungen

redundant [rɪ'dʌndənt] *adj. (Brit.)* arbeitslos; **be made ~:** den Arbeitsplatz verlieren; **make ~:** entlassen

red 'wine *n.* Rotwein, *der*

reed [ri:d] *n.* Schilf[rohr], *das*

reef [ri:f] *n.* Riff, *das*

'reef-knot *n.* Kreuzknoten, *der*

reek [ri:k] *v. i.* stinken **(of** nach)

reel [ri:l] **1.** *n.* ⟨*Garn-, Angel*⟩rolle, *die;* ⟨*Film-, Tonband*⟩spule, *die.* **2.** *v. i.* **a)** *(be in a whirl)* sich drehen; **b)** *(sway)* torkeln

refectory [rɪ'fektərɪ] *n.* Mensa, *die*

refer [rɪ'fɜ:(r)] **1.** *v. i.,* **-rr-: a) ~** *to (allude to)* sich beziehen auf (+ *Akk.*) ⟨*Buch, Person usw.*⟩; *(speak of)* sprechen von ⟨*Person, Problem usw.*⟩; **b) ~ to** *(apply to, relate to)* betreffen; **c) ~ to** *(consult, cite as proof)* nachsehen in (+ *Dat.*). **2.** *v. t.,* **-rr-: ~ sb./sth. to sb./ sth.** jmdn./etw. an jmdn./auf etw. *(Akk.)* verweisen

referee [refə'ri:] *(Sport)* **1.** *n. (umpire)* Schiedsrichter, *der/*-richterin, *die; (Boxing)* Ringrichter, *der.* **2.** *v. t.* als Schiedsrichter/-richterin leiten

reference ['refrəns] *n.* **a)** *(allusion)* Hinweis, *der* **(to** auf + *Akk.*); **make no ~ to sth.** etw. nicht ansprechen; **b)** *(testimonial)* Zeugnis, *das*

referendum [refə'rendəm] *n.* Volksentscheid, *der*

refill 1. [ri:'fɪl] *v. t.* nachfüllen; **~ the glasses** nachschenken. **2.** ['ri:fɪl] *n. (for ball-pen)* Ersatzmine, *die*

refine [rɪ'faɪn] *v. t.* **a)** *(purify)* raffinieren; **b)** *(make cultured)* kultivieren; **c)** *(improve)* verbessern; verfeinern ⟨*Stil, Technik*⟩. **refined** [rɪ'faɪnd] *adj.* kultiviert. **re'finement** *n.* Kultiviertheit, *die; (improvement)* Verbesserung, *die.* **refinery** [rɪ'faɪnərɪ] *n.* Raffinerie, *die*

reflect [rɪ'flekt] *v. t.* **a)** reflektieren; **b)** *(fig.)* widerspiegeln ⟨*Ansichten*⟩; **c)** *(contemplate)* nachdenken über (+ *Akk.*); **~ what/how ...:** überlegen, was/wie ... **re'flect [up]on** *v. t.* **a)** *(consider)* nachdenken über (+ *Akk.*); **b) ~ badly [up]on sb./sth.** auf jmdn./ etw. ein schlechtes Licht werfen. **reflection** [rɪ'flekʃn] *n.* **a)** Reflexion, *die; (by surface of water)* Spiegelung, *die;* **b)** *(image)* Spiegelbild, *das;* **c)** *(consideration)* Nachdenken, *das* (**upon** über + *Akk.*); **on ~:** bei weiterem Nachdenken. **reflective** [rɪ'flektɪv] *adj.* **a)** reflektierend; **b)** *(thoughtful)* nachdenklich. **reflector** [rɪ'flektə(r)] *n.* Rückstrahler, *der*

reflex ['ri:fleks] **1.** *n.* Reflex, *der.* **2.** *adj.* **~ action** Reflexhandlung, *die*

reflexive [ri'fleksɪv] *adj. (Ling.)* reflexiv

reform [rɪ'fɔ:m] **1.** *v. t. (make better)* bessern ⟨*Person*⟩; reformieren ⟨*Institution*⟩. **2.** *n.* Reform, *die* (**in** *Gen.*). **reformation** [refə'meɪʃn] *n. (of character)* Wandlung, *die;* **the R~** *(Hist.)* die Reformation. **re'former** *n.* [political] **~:** Reformpolitiker, *der/*Reformpolitikerin, *die*

refract [rɪ'frækt] *v. t. (Phys.)* brechen

'refrain [rɪ'freɪn] *n.* Refrain, *der*

'refrain *v. i.* **~ from doing sth.** es unterlassen, etw. zu tun

refresh [rɪ'freʃ] *v. t.* erfrischen. **re'freshing** *adj.* erfrischend; wohltuend ⟨*Abwechslung*⟩. **re'freshment** *n.* Erfrischung, *die*

refrigerate [rɪ'frɪdʒəreɪt] *v. t.* **a)** kühl lagern ⟨*Lebensmittel*⟩; **b)** *(chill)* kühlen; *(freeze)* einfrieren. **refrigeration** [rɪfrɪdʒə'reɪʃn] *n.* kühle Lagerung; *(chilling)* Kühlung, *die; (freezing)* Einfrieren, *das.* **refrigerator** [rɪ'frɪdʒəreɪtə(r)] *n.* Kühlschrank, *der*

refuel [ri:'fju:əl], *(Brit.)* **-ll-: 1.** *v. t.* auftanken. **2.** *v. i.* [auf]tanken

refuge ['refju:dʒ] *n.* Zuflucht, *die;* **take ~ in** Schutz *od.* Zuflucht suchen in (+ *Dat.*) **(from** vor + *Dat.*)

refugee [refjʊ'dʒi:] *n.* Flüchtling, *der*
refund 1. [ri:'fʌnd] *v. t. (pay back)* zurückzahlen ⟨*Geld*⟩; erstatten ⟨*Kosten*⟩. 2. ['ri:fʌnd] *n.* Rückzahlung, *die; (of expenses)* [Rück]erstattung, *die*
refusal [rɪ'fju:zl] *n.* Ablehnung, *die; (after a period of time)* Absage, *die;* ~ **to do sth.** Weigerung, etw. zu tun
¹refuse [rɪ'fju:z] 1. *v. t.* ablehnen; verweigern ⟨*Zutritt, Einreise, Erlaubnis*⟩; ~ **sb. admittance/entry/permission** jmdm. den Zutritt/die Einreise/die Erlaubnis verweigern; ~ **to do sth.** sich weigern, etw. zu tun. 2. *v. i.* ablehnen; *(after request)* sich weigern
²refuse ['refju:s] *n.* Abfall, *der*
refuse ['refju:s]: ~ **collection** *n.* Müllabfuhr, *die;* ~ **collector** *n.* Müllwerker, *der;* ~ **disposal** *n.* Abfallbeseitigung, *die*
refute [rɪ'fju:t] *v. t.* widerlegen
regain [rɪ'geɪn] *v. t.* zurückgewinnen ⟨*Zuversicht, Vertrauen, Augenlicht*⟩; ~ **one's strength** wieder zu Kräften kommen
regal ['ri:gl] *adj.* majestätisch
regalia [rɪ'geɪlɪə] *n. pl. (of royalty)* Krönungsinsignien
regard [rɪ'gɑ:d] 1. *v. t.* **a)** *(look at)* betrachten; **b)** *(give heed to)* beachten; **c)** *(fig.: look upon, contemplate)* betrachten; ~ **sb. as a friend/fool/genius** jmdn. als Freund betrachten/für einen Dummkopf/ein Genie halten; **be** ~**ed as** gelten als; **d)** *(concern, have relation to)* betreffen; **as** ~**s sb./sth.,** ~**ing sb./sth.** was jmdn./etw. angeht *od.* betrifft. 2. *n.* **a)** *(attention)* **pay** *or* **have** ~ **to sth.** jmdm./etw. Beachtung schenken; **without** ~ **to** ohne Rücksicht auf (+ *Akk.*); **b)** *(esteem)* Achtung, *die;* **hold sb./sth. in high** ~**:** jmdn./etw. sehr schätzen; **c)** *in pl.* Grüße; **give her my** ~**s** grüße sie von mir; **with kind[est]** ~**s** mit herzlich[st]en Grüßen. **re'gardless** *adj.* ohne Rücksicht **(of** auf + *Akk.*)
regatta [rɪ'gætə] *n.* Regatta, *die*
regenerate [rɪ'dʒenəreɪt] *v. t.* erneuern
regime, régime [reɪ'ʒi:m] *n.* [Regierungs]system, *das*
regiment ['redʒɪmənt, 'redʒmənt] *n.* Regiment, *das.* **regimental** [redʒɪ'mentl] *adj.* Regiments-
region ['ri:dʒn] *n.* **a)** *(area)* Gebiet, *das;* **b)** *(administrative division)* Bezirk, *der;* **in the** ~ **of** *(fig.)* ungefähr. **regional** ['ri:dʒənl] *adj.* regional

register ['redʒɪstə(r)] 1. *n.* Register, *das; (at school)* Klassenbuch, *das.* 2. *v. t.* **a)** *(enter)* registrieren; *(cause to be entered)* registrieren lassen; anmelden ⟨*Auto, Patent*⟩; *(at airport)* einchecken ⟨*Gepäck*⟩; *(at hotel)* sich ins Fremdenbuch eintragen; ~ **with the police** sich polizeilich anmelden; **b)** *(enrol)* anmelden; *(Univ.)* sich einschreiben; **c)** zum Ausdruck bringen ⟨*Überraschung*⟩; ~ **a protest** Protest anmelden. **registered** ['redʒɪstəd] *adj.* eingetragen ⟨*Firma*⟩; eingeschrieben ⟨*Student, Brief*⟩; ~ **trade mark** eingetragenes Warenzeichen; **by** ~ **post** per Einschreiben
registrar ['redʒɪstrɑ:(r), redʒɪ'strɑ:(r)] *n.* Standesbeamte, *der/*-beamtin, *die*
registration [redʒɪ'streɪʃn] *n.* Registrierung, *die; (enrolment)* Anmeldung, *die; (of students)* Einschreibung, *die.* **regi'stration document** *n.* *(Brit.)* Kraftfahrzeugbrief, *der.* **regi'stration number** *n.* amtliches Kennzeichen
registry ['redʒɪstrɪ] *n.* ~ **[office]** Standesamt, *das*
regret [rɪ'gret] 1. *v. t.,* -tt- bedauern; **I** ~ **to say that ...:** ich muß leider sagen, daß ... 2. *n.* Bedauern, *das;* **have no** ~**s** nichts bereuen. **regretfully** [rɪ'gretfəlɪ] *adv.* mit Bedauern. **regrettable** [rɪ'gretəbl] *adj.* bedauerlich. **regrettably** [rɪ'gretəblɪ] *adv.* bedauerlicherweise
regroup [ri:'gru:p] 1. *v. t.* umgruppieren. 2. *v. i.* **a)** *(form new group)* sich neu gruppieren; **b)** *(Mil.)* sich neu formieren
regular ['regjʊlə(r)] 1. *adj.* regelmäßig; geregelt ⟨*Arbeit*⟩; fest ⟨*Anstellung*⟩; ~ **customer** Stammkunde, *der/*-kundin, *die;* ~ **army** reguläre Armee. 2. *n. (coll.:* ~ *customer)* Stammkunde, *der/*-kundin, *die; (in pub)* Stammgast, *der.* **regularity** [regjʊ'lærɪtɪ] *n.* Regelmäßigkeit, *die.* '**regularly** *adv.* regelmäßig
regulate ['regjʊleɪt] *v. t. (control)* regeln; *(restrict)* begrenzen; *(adjust)* regulieren. **regulation** [regjʊ'leɪʃn] *n.* **a)** *see* **regulate:** Regelung, *die;* Begrenzung, *die;* Regulierung, *die;* **b)** *(rule)* Vorschrift, *die*
rehabilitate [ri:hə'bɪlɪteɪt] *v. t.* rehabilitieren; ~ **[back into society]** wieder [in die Gesellschaft] eingliedern
rehash 1. [ri:'hæʃ] *v. t.* aufwärmen. 2. ['ri:hæʃ] *n.* Aufguß, *der*

rehearsal [rɪˈhɜ:sl] *n*. Probe, *die*. **rehearse** [rɪˈhɜ:s] *v. t*. proben
reign [reɪn] **1.** *n*. Herrschaft, *die*. **2.** *v. i*. herrschen (**over** über + *Akk*.)
rein [reɪn] *n*. Zügel, *der*
reincarnation [ri:ɪnkɑ:ˈneɪʃn] *n*. *(Relig.)* Reinkarnation, *die*
reindeer [ˈreɪndɪə(r)] *n., pl. same* Ren[tier], *das*
reinforce [ri:ɪnˈfɔ:s] *v. t*. verstärken; **~d concrete** Stahlbeton, *der*. **reinˈforcement** *n*. Verstärkung, *die;* **~|s|** *(additional men etc.)* Verstärkung, *die*
reinstate [ri:ɪnˈsteɪt] *v. t*. *(in job)* wieder einstellen
reinvigorate [ri:ɪnˈvɪɡəreɪt] *v. t*. neu beleben; **feel ~d** sich gestärkt fühlen
reiterate [ri:ˈɪtəreɪt] *v. t*. wiederholen
reject 1. [rɪˈdʒekt] *v. t*. ablehnen; zurückweisen ⟨*Bitte, Annäherungsversuch*⟩. **2.** [ˈri:dʒekt] *(thing)* Ausschuß, *der*. **rejection** [rɪˈdʒekʃn] *n*. Ablehnung, *die*/Zurückweisung, *die*
rejoice [rɪˈdʒɔɪs] *v. i*. sich freuen (**over, at** über + *Akk*.)
¹rejoin [rɪˈdʒɔɪn] *v. t*. *(reply)* erwidern (**to** auf + *Akk*.)
²rejoin [ri:ˈdʒɔɪn] *v. t*. wieder eintreten in (+ *Akk*.) ⟨*Partei, Verein*⟩
rejoinder [rɪˈdʒɔɪndə(r)] *n*. Erwiderung, *die* (**to** auf + *Akk*.)
rejuvenate [rɪˈdʒu:vəneɪt] *v. t*. verjüngen
rekindle [ri:ˈkɪndl] *v. t*. wieder anfachen; wieder aufleben lassen ⟨*Verlangen, Hoffnungen*⟩
relapse [rɪˈlæps] **1.** *v. i*. ⟨*Kranker:*⟩ einen Rückfall bekommen. **2.** *n*. Rückfall, *der*
relate [rɪˈleɪt] **1.** *v. t*. **a)** erzählen ⟨*Geschichte*⟩; erzählen von ⟨*Abenteuer*⟩; **b)** *(bring into relation)* in Zusammenhang bringen (**to, with** mit). **2.** *v. i*. **a)** **~ to** *(have reference)* in Zusammenhang stehen mit; betreffen ⟨*Person*⟩; **b)** **~ to** *(feel involved with)* eine Beziehung haben zu. **reˈlated** *adj*. verwandt (**to** mit). **relation** [rɪˈleɪʃn] *n*. **a)** *(connection)* Beziehung, *die*, Zusammenhang, *der* (**of** ... **and** zwischen ... und); **in** *or* **with ~ to** in bezug auf (+ *Akk*.); **b)** *in pl. (dealings)* Verhältnis, *das* (**with** zu); **c)** *(relative)* Verwandte, *der/die*. **reˈlationship** *n*. **a)** *(mutual tie)* Beziehung, *die* (**with** zu); **b)** *(kinship)* Verwandtschaftsverhältnis, *das;* **c)** *(connection)* Beziehung, *die; (between cause and effect)* Zusammenhang, *der;* **d)** *(sexual)* Verhältnis, *das*

relative [ˈrelətɪv] **1.** *n*. Verwandte, *der/die*. **2.** *adj*. relativ. **ˈrelatively** *adv*. relativ; verhältnismäßig. **relative ˈpronoun** *n*. *(Ling.)* Relativpronomen, *das*
relax [rɪˈlæks] **1.** *v. t*. **a)** entspannen ⟨*Muskel, Körper[teil]*⟩; lockern ⟨*Griff*⟩; **b)** *(make less strict)* lockern ⟨*Gesetz, Disziplin*⟩. **2.** *v. i*. sich entspannen. **relaxation** [ri:lækˈseɪʃn] *n*. Entspannung, *die;* **for ~:** zur Entspannung. **relaxed** [rɪˈlækst] *adj*. entspannt, gelöst ⟨*Atmosphäre, Person*⟩. **reˈlaxing** *adj*. entspannend
relay 1. [ˈri:leɪ] *n*. **a)** *(race)* Staffel, *die;* **b)** *(gang)* Schicht, *die;* **work in ~s** schichtweise arbeiten; **c)** *(Electr.)* Relais, *das*. **2.** [ri:ˈleɪ] *v. t*. **a)** weiterleiten; **b)** *(Radio, Telev.)* übertragen. **ˈrelay race** *n*. Staffellauf, *der; (Swimming)* Staffelschwimmen, *das*
release [rɪˈli:s] **1.** *v. t*. **a)** *(free)* freilassen ⟨*Tier, Häftling, Sklaven*⟩; *(from jail)* entlassen (**from** aus); **b)** *(let go)* loslassen; lösen ⟨*Handbremse*⟩; **c)** *(make known)* veröffentlichen ⟨*Erklärung, Nachricht*⟩; *(issue)* herausbringen ⟨*Film, Schallplatte*⟩. **2.** *n*. **a)** *see* **1 a:** Freilassung, *die;* Entlassung, *die;* **b)** *(of published item)* Veröffentlichung, *die;* **c)** *(handle, lever, button)* Auslöser, *der*
relegate [ˈrelɪɡeɪt] *v. t*. **a)** **~ sb. to the position of ...:** jmdn. zu ... degradieren; **b)** *(Sport)* absteigen lassen; **be ~d** absteigen (**to** in + *Akk*.). **relegation** [relɪˈɡeɪʃn] *n*. *(Sport)* Abstieg, *der*
relent [rɪˈlent] *v. i*. nachgeben. **reˈlentless** *adj*., **reˈlentlessly** *adv*. unerbittlich
relevance [ˈrelɪvəns] *n*. Relevanz, *die* (**to** für)
relevant [ˈrelɪvənt] *adj*. relevant (**to** für); wichtig ⟨*Information*⟩
reliability [rɪlaɪəˈbɪlɪtɪ] *n*. Zuverlässigkeit, *die*
reliable [rɪˈlaɪəbl] *adj*., **reliably** [rɪˈlaɪəblɪ] *adv*. zuverlässig
reliance [rɪˈlaɪəns] *n*. Abhängigkeit, *die* (**on** von)
reliant [rɪˈlaɪənt] *adj*. **be ~ on sb./sth.** auf jmdn./etw. angewiesen sein
¹relief [rɪˈli:f] *n*. **a)** Erleichterung, *die;* **give |sb.| ~ |from pain|** [jmdm.] [Schmerz]linderung verschaffen; **what a ~!, that's a ~!** da bin ich aber erleichtert!; **b)** *(assistance)* Hilfe, *die*
²relief *n*. *(Art)* Relief, *das*
relief: ~ bus *n*. Entlastungsbus, *der;*

(as replacement) Ersatzbus, *der;* ~ **map** *n.* Reliefkarte, *die;* ~ **road** *n.* Entlastungsstraße, *die*

relieve [rɪ'li:v] *v. t.* **a)** erleichtern; unterbrechen *⟨Eintönigkeit⟩;* abbauen *⟨Anspannung⟩;* stillen *⟨Schmerzen⟩;* I **am** *or* **feel ~d to hear that** ...: es erleichtert mich zu hören, daß ...; **b)** ablösen *⟨Wache, Truppen⟩*

religion [rɪ'lɪdʒn] *n.* Religion, *die*

religious [rɪ'lɪdʒəs] *adj.* religiös; Religions*⟨freiheit, -unterricht⟩.* **re'ligiously** *adv. (conscientiously)* gewissenhaft

relinquish [rɪ'lɪŋkwɪʃ] *v. t.* **a)** *(give up)* aufgeben; **b)** ~ **one's hold** *or* **grip on sb./sth.** jmdn./etw. loslassen

relish ['relɪʃ] **1.** *n.* **a)** *(liking)* Vorliebe, *die;* **do sth. with [great]** ~: etw. mit [großem] Genuß tun; **b)** *(condiment)* Relish, *das.* **2.** *v. t.* genießen

relive [ri:'lɪv] *n.* noch einmal durchleben

reload [ri:'ləʊd] *v. t.* nachladen *⟨Schußwaffe⟩*

reluctance [rɪ'lʌktəns] *n.* Widerwille, *der;* **have a [great]** ~ **to do sth.** etw. nur mit Widerwillen tun

reluctant [rɪ'lʌktənt] *adj.* unwillig; **be** ~ **to do sth.** etw. nur ungern tun. **re'luctantly** *adv.* nur ungern

rely [rɪ'laɪ] *v. i. (have trust)* sich verlassen/*(be dependent)* angewiesen sein (**[up]on** auf + *Akk.*)

remain [rɪ'meɪn] *v. i.* **a)** *(be left over)* übrigbleiben; **b)** *(stay)* bleiben; ~ **behind** noch dableiben; **c)** *(continue to be)* bleiben; **it** ~**s to be seen** es wird sich zeigen. **remainder** [rɪ'meɪndə(r)] *n.* Rest, *der.* **re'maining** *adj.* restlich. **re'mains** *n. pl.* **a)** Reste; **b)** *(human)* sterbliche [Über]reste *(verhüll.)*

remand [rɪ'mɑ:nd] **1.** *v. t.* ~ **sb. [in custody]** jmdn. in Untersuchungshaft behalten. **2.** *n.* **on** ~: in Untersuchungshaft

remark [rɪ'mɑ:k] **1.** *v. t.* bemerken (**to** gegenüber). **2.** *v. i.* eine Bemerkung machen (**[up]on** zu, über + *Akk.*). **3.** *n.* Bemerkung, *die* (**on** über + *Akk.*)

remarkable [rɪ'mɑ:kəbl] *adj.* **a)** *(notable)* bemerkenswert; **b)** *(extraordinary)* außergewöhnlich. **remarkably** [rɪ'mɑ:kəblɪ] *adv.* **a)** *(notably)* bemerkenswert; **b)** *(exceptionally)* außergewöhnlich

remarry [ri:'mærɪ] *v. i. & t.* wieder heiraten

remedy ['remɪdɪ] **1.** *n.* [Heil]mittel,

das (**for** gegen). **2.** *v. t.* beheben *⟨Problem⟩;* retten *⟨Situation⟩*

remember [rɪ'membə(r)] *v. t.* **a)** sich erinnern an (+ *Akk.*); I ~**ed to bring the book** ich habe daran gedacht, das Buch mitzubringen; **an evening to** ~: ein unvergeßlicher Abend; **b)** *(convey greetings)* ~ **me to them** grüße sie von mir. **remembrance** [rɪ'membrəns] *n.* Gedenken, *das;* **in** ~ **of sb.** zu jmds. Gedächtnis

remind [rɪ'maɪnd] *v. t.* erinnern (**of** an + *Akk.*); ~ **sb. to do sth.** jmdn. daran erinnern, etw. zu tun; **that** ~**s me,** ...: dabei fällt mir ein, ... **re'minder** *n.* Erinnerung, *die* (**of** an + *Akk.*); *(letter)* Mahnung, *die;* Mahnbrief, *der*

reminisce [remɪ'nɪs] *v. i.* sich in Erinnerungen *(Dat.)* ergehen (**about** an + *Akk.*). **reminiscences** [remɪ'nɪsənsɪz] *n. pl.* Erinnerungen; *(memoirs)* [Lebens]erinnerungen *Pl.* **reminiscent** [remɪ'nɪsnt] *adj.* **be** ~ **of sth.** an etw. *(Akk.)* erinnern

remiss [rɪ'mɪs] *adj.* nachlässig (**of** von)

remission [rɪ'mɪʃn] *n.* **a)** *(of debt, punishment)* Erlaß, *der;* **b)** *(of prison sentence)* Straferlaß, *der*

remit [rɪ'mɪt] *v. t.,* -tt- *(send)* überweisen *⟨Geld⟩.* **remittance** [rɪ'mɪtəns] *n.* Überweisung, *die*

remnant ['remnənt] *n.* Rest, *der*

remonstrate ['remənstreɪt] *v. i.* protestieren (**against** gegen); ~ **with sb.** jmdm. Vorenthaltungen machen (**about, on** wegen)

remorse [rɪ'mɔ:s] *n.* Reue, *die* (**for, about** über + *Akk.*). **re'morseful** [rɪ'mɔ:sfl] *adj.* reumütig. **re'morseless** *adj.* unerbittlich

remote [rɪ'məʊt] *adj.,* ~**r** [rɪ'məʊtə(r)], ~**st** [rɪ'məʊtɪst] *adj.* **a)** fern *⟨Vergangenheit, Zukunft, Zeit⟩;* abgelegen *⟨Ort, Gebiet⟩;* ~ **from** weit entfernt von; **b)** *(slight)* gering *⟨Chance⟩.* **remote con'trol** *n. (of vehicle)* Fernlenkung, *die; (for TV set)* Fernbedienung, *die.* **remote-con'trol[led]** *adj.* ferngelenkt; fernbedient *⟨Anlage⟩*

re'motely *adv.* entfernt *⟨verwandt⟩;* **they are not** ~ **alike** sie haben nicht die entfernteste Ähnlichkeit

removable [rɪ'mu:vəbl] *adj.* abnehmbar; entfernbar *⟨Trennwand⟩;* herausnehmbar *⟨Futter⟩*

removal [rɪ'mu:vl] *n.* **a)** Entfernung, *die; (of obstacle, problem)* Beseitigung, *die;* **b)** *(transfer of furniture)* Umzug, *der*

removal: ~ **firm** n. Spedition, die; ~ **man** n. Möbelpacker, der; ~ **van** n. Möbelwagen, der

remove [rɪ'muːv] v. t. entfernen; beseitigen ⟨Spur, Hindernis⟩; (take off) abnehmen; ausziehen ⟨Kleidungsstück⟩; ~ **a book from the shelf** ein Buch vom Regal nehmen. **re'mover** n. **a)** (of paint/varnish/hair/rust) Farb- / Lack- / Haar- / Rostentferner, der; **b)** (man) Möbelpacker, der; [firm of] ~s Spedition[sfirma], die

remunerate [rɪ'mjuːnəreɪt] v. t. bezahlen. **remuneration** [rɪmjuːnə-'reɪʃn] n. Bezahlung, die

Renaissance [rə'neɪsəns, rɪ'neɪsəns] n. (Hist.) Renaissance, die

rename [riː'neɪm] v. t. umbenennen

render ['rendə(r)] v. t. **a)** (make) machen; **b)** erweisen ⟨Dienst⟩; **c)** (translate) übersetzen (by mit). **'rendering** n. (translation) Übersetzung, die

rendezvous ['rɒndeɪvuː] n., pl. same ['rɒndeɪvuːz] **a)** (meeting-place) Treffpunkt, der; **b)** (meeting) Verabredung, die

renegade ['renɪgeɪd] **1.** n. Abtrünnige, der/die. **2.** adj. abtrünnig

renew [rɪ'njuː] v. t. erneuern; fortsetzen ⟨Angriff, Bemühungen⟩; (extend) erneuern ⟨Vertrag, Ausweis usw.⟩; ~ **a library book** ⟨Bibliothekar/Benutzer:⟩ ein Buch [aus der Bücherei] verlängern/verlängern lassen. **renewal** [rɪ-'njuːəl] n. Erneuerung, die

renounce [rɪ'naʊns] v. t. verzichten auf (+ Akk.); verstoßen ⟨Person⟩; ~ **the devil/one's faith** dem Teufel/seinem Glauben abschwören

renovate ['renəveɪt] v. t. renovieren ⟨Gebäude⟩; restaurieren ⟨Möbel usw.⟩. **renovation** [renə'veɪʃn] n. Renovierung, die/Restaurierung, die

renown [rɪ'naʊn] n. Renommee, das. **renowned** [rɪ'naʊnd] adj. berühmt (for wegen, für)

rent [rent] **1.** n. (for house etc.) Miete, die; (for land) Pacht, die. **2.** v. t. **a)** (use) mieten ⟨Haus, Wohnung usw.⟩; pachten ⟨Land⟩; mieten ⟨Auto⟩; **b)** (let) vermieten ⟨Haus, Auto usw.⟩ (to Dat., an + Akk.); verpachten ⟨Land⟩ (to Dat., an + Akk.). **rent 'out** v. t. see rent 2 b

rental ['rentl] n. Miete, die

renunciation [rɪnʌnsɪ'eɪʃn] n. see renounce: Verzicht, der; Verstoßung, die

reopen [riː'əʊpn] **1.** v. t. wieder öffnen; wieder aufmachen; wiedereröffnen

⟨Geschäft, Lokal usw.⟩; wiederaufnehmen ⟨Diskussion, Verhandlung⟩. **2.** v. i. ⟨Geschäft, Lokal usw.:⟩ wieder öffnen

reorder [riː'ɔːdə(r)] v. t. **a)** (Commerc.) nachbestellen ⟨Ware⟩; **b)** (rearrange) umordnen

reorganization [riːɔːgənaɪ'zeɪʃn] n. Umorganisation, die; (of time, work) Neueinteilung, die

reorganize [riː'ɔːgənaɪz] v. t. umorganisieren; neu einteilen ⟨Zeit, Arbeit⟩

rep [rep] n. (coll.: representative) Vertreter, der/Vertreterin, die

repaid see repay

repair [rɪ'peə(r)] **1.** v. t. (mend) reparieren; ausbessern ⟨Kleidung, Straße⟩. **2.** n. Reparatur, die; **be in good/bad** ~: in gutem/schlechtem Zustand sein. **re'pair man** n. Mechaniker, der; (in house) Handwerker, der. **re'pair shop** n. Reparaturwerkstatt, die

repatriate [riː'pætrɪeɪt] v. t. repatriieren. **repatriation** [riːpætrɪ'eɪʃn] n. Repatriierung, die

repay [riː'peɪ] v. t., repaid [riː'peɪd] zurückzahlen ⟨Schulden usw.⟩; erwidern ⟨Besuch, Gruß, Freundlichkeit⟩; ~ **sb. for sth.** jmdm. etw. vergelten. **re'payment** n. Rückzahlung, die

repeal [rɪ'piːl] **1.** v. t. aufheben ⟨Gesetz, Erlaß usw.⟩. **2.** n. Aufhebung, die

repeat [rɪ'piːt] **1.** n. Wiederholung, die. **2.** v. t. wiederholen; **please** ~ **after me: ...:** sprich/sprecht/sprechen Sie mir bitte nach: ... **re'peated** adj. wiederholt; (several) mehrere; **make** ~ **efforts to ...:** wiederholt od. mehrfach versuchen, ...zu... **re'peatedly** adv. mehrmals

repel [rɪ'pel] v. t., -ll-: **a)** (drive back) abwehren; **b)** (be repulsive to) abstoßen. **repellent** [rɪ'pelənt] adj. abstoßend

repent [rɪ'pent] v. i. bereuen (of Akk.). **repentance** [rɪ'pentəns] n. Reue, die. **repentant** [rɪ'pentənt] adj. reuig

repercussion [riːpə'kʌʃn] n., usu. in pl. Auswirkung, die ([up]on auf + Akk.)

repertoire ['repətwɑː(r)] n. Repertoire, das

repertory ['repətərɪ] n. (Theatre) Repertoiretheater, das. **'repertory company** n. Repertoiretheater, das

repetition [repɪ'tɪʃn] n. Wiederholung, die

repetitious [repɪ'tɪʃəs] adj. sich immer wiederholend attr.

repetitive [rɪ'petɪtɪv] adj. eintönig
rephrase [ri:'freɪz] v. t. umformulieren; **I'll ~ that** ich will es anders ausdrücken
replace [rɪ'pleɪs] v. t. **a)** (vertically) zurückstellen; (horizontally) zurücklegen; **b)** (take place of) ersetzen; **~ A with** or **by B** A durch B ersetzen; **c)** (exchange) austauschen, auswechseln ⟨Maschinen[teile] usw.⟩. **re'placement** n. **a)** see replace **a**: Zurückstellen, das; Zurücklegen, das; **b)** (provision of substitute for) Ersatz, der; attrib. Ersatz-; **c)** (substitute) Ersatz, der; **~ [part]** Ersatzteil, das
replay 1. [ri:'pleɪ] v. t. wiederholen ⟨Spiel⟩; nochmals abspielen ⟨Tonband usw.⟩. **2.** ['ri:pleɪ] n. Wiederholung, die; (match) Wiederholungsspiel, das
replenish [rɪ'plenɪʃ] v. t. auffüllen
replica ['replɪkə] n. Nachbildung, die
reply [rɪ'plaɪ] **1.** v. i. **~ |to sb./sth.|** [jmdm./auf etw. (Akk.)] antworten. **2.** v. t. **~ that ...**: antworten, daß ... **3.** n. Antwort, die (to auf + Akk.)
report [rɪ'pɔːt] **1.** v. t. **a)** (relate) berichten/(in writing) einen Bericht schreiben über (+ Akk.); (state formally also) melden; **b)** (name to authorities) melden (to Dat.); (for prosecution) anzeigen (to bei). **2.** v. i. **a)** Bericht erstatten (**on** über + Akk.); berichten (**on** über + Akk.); **b)** (present oneself) sich melden (to bei). **3.** n. **a)** (account) Bericht, der (**on, about** über + Akk.); **b)** (Sch.) Zeugnis, das; **c)** (of gun) Knall, der. **reportedly** [rɪ'pɔːtɪdlɪ] adv. wie verlautet. **reported 'speech** n. indirekte Rede. **re'porter** n. Reporter, der/Reporterin, die
repossess [ri:pə'zes] v. t. wieder in Besitz nehmen
reprehensible [reprɪ'hensɪbl] adj. tadelnswert
represent [reprɪ'zent] v. t. **a)** darstellen (**as** als); **b)** (act for) vertreten. **representation** [reprɪzen'teɪʃn] n. **a)** (depicting, image) Darstellung, die; **b)** (acting for sb.) Vertretung, die; **c)** **make ~s to sb.** bei jmdm. Protest einlegen. **representative** [reprɪ'zentətɪv] **1.** n. **a)** (Commerc.) Vertreter, der/Vertreterin, die; **b)** R~ (Amer. Polit.) Abgeordneter/Abgeordnete. **2.** adj. (typical) repräsentativ (**of** für)
repress [rɪ'pres] v. t. unterdrücken. **repression** [rɪ'preʃn] n. Unterdrückung, die. **repressive** [rɪ'presɪv] adj. repressiv

reprieve [rɪ'priːv] **1.** v. t. **~ sb.** (postpone execution) jmdm. Strafaufschub gewähren; (remit execution) jmdn. begnadigen. **2.** n. Strafaufschub, der (of für)/Begnadigung, die; (fig.) Gnadenfrist, die
reprimand ['reprɪmɑːnd] **1.** n. Tadel, der. **2.** v. t. tadeln
reprint 1. [ri:'prɪnt] v. t. wieder abdrucken. **2.** ['ri:prɪnt] n. Nachdruck, der
reprisal [rɪ'praɪzl] n. Vergeltungsakt, der (**for** gegen)
reproach [rɪ'prəʊtʃ] **1.** v. t. **~ sb.** jmdm. Vorwürfe machen. **2.** n. Vorwurf, der. **reproachful** [rɪ'prəʊtʃfl] adv. vorwurfsvoll
reproduce [ri:prə'djuːs] **1.** v. t. wiedergeben. **2.** v. i. (multiply) sich fortpflanzen. **reproduction** [ri:prə'dʌkʃn] n. **a)** Wiedergabe, die; **b)** (producing offspring) Fortpflanzung, die; **c)** (copy) Reproduktion, die
reprove [rɪ'pruːv] v. t. tadeln
reptile ['reptaɪl] n. Reptil, das
republic [rɪ'pʌblɪk] n. Republik, die. **republican** [rɪ'pʌblɪkən] **1.** adj. republikanisch. **2.** n. R~ (Amer. Polit.) Republikaner, der/Republikanerin, die
repudiate [rɪ'pjuːdɪeɪt] v. t. zurückweisen
repugnance [rɪ'pʌgnəns] n. Abscheu, der (to|wards| vor + Dat.)
repugnant [rɪ'pʌgnənt] adj. widerlich (to Dat.)
repulse [rɪ'pʌls] v. t. abwehren
repulsion [rɪ'pʌlʃn] n. (disgust) Widerwille, der (towards gegen)
repulsive [rɪ'pʌlsɪv] adj. abstoßend
reputable ['repjʊtəbl] adj. angesehen ⟨Person, Beruf, Zeitung usw.⟩; anständig ⟨Verhalten⟩; seriös ⟨Firma⟩
reputation [repjʊ'teɪʃn] n. **a)** Ruf, der; **have a ~ for** or **of doing/being sth.** in dem Ruf stehen, etw. zu tun/sein; **b)** (good name) Name, der
repute [rɪ'pjuːt] **1.** v. t. in pass. **be ~d |to be|** als etw. gelten; **she is ~d to have/make ...**: man sagt, daß sie ... hat/macht. **2.** n. Ruf, der. **reputed** [rɪ'pjuːtɪd] adj., **re'putedly** adv. angeblich
request [rɪ'kwest] **1.** v. t. bitten; **~ sth. of** or **from sb.** jmdn. um etw. bitten. **2.** n. Bitte, die (for um); **at sb.'s ~:** auf jmds. Bitte (Akk.) [hin]. **re'quest stop** n. (Brit.) Bedarfshaltestelle, die
require [rɪ'kwaɪə(r)] v. t. **a)** (need) brauchen; **b)** (order, demand) verlan-

gen (of von); **be ~d to do sth.** etw. tun
müssen. **re'quirement** *n.* **a)** *(need)*
Bedarf, *der;* **b)** *(condition)* Erfordernis, *das*

requisite ['rekwɪzɪt] **1.** *adj.* notwendig
(to, for für). **2.** *n. in pl.* **toilet/travel ~s**
Toiletten-/Reiseartikel *Pl.*

requisition [rekwɪ'zɪʃn] **1.** *n. (order for
sth.)* Anforderung, *die* (for Gen.). **2.**
v. t. anfordern

rescind [rɪ'sɪnd] *v. t.* für ungültig erklären

rescue ['reskju:] **1.** *v. t.* retten **(from
aus). 2.** *n.* Rettung, *die; attrib.* Rettungs‹*dienst, -mannschaft*›; **go/come
to the/sb.'s ~:** jmdm. zu Hilfe kommen. **rescuer** ['reskju:ə(r)] *n.* Retter,
der/Retterin, *die*

research [rɪ'sɜːtʃ, 'riːsɜːtʃ] **1.** *n.* Forschung, *die* **(into, on** über + *Akk.*); ~
work Recherchen *Pl.* **2.** *v. i.* forschen;
~ into sth. etw. erforschen. **researcher** [-'--, '---] *n.* Forscher, *der*/
Forscherin, *die*

resell [riː'sel] *v. t., resold* [riː'səʊld]
weiterverkaufen **(to an** + *Akk.*)

resemblance [rɪ'zembləns] *n.* Ähnlichkeit, *die* **(to** mit)

resemble [rɪ'zembl] *v. t.* ähneln, gleichen (+ *Dat.*)

resent [rɪ'zent] *v. t.* übelnehmen. **resentful** [rɪ'zentfl] *adj.* übelnehmerisch, nachtragend ‹*Person, Art*›; **be ~
of** *or* **feel ~ about sth.** etw. übelnehmen. **re'sentment** *n.* Groll, *der
(geh.);* **feel ~ towards** *or* **against sb.** einen Groll auf jmdn. haben

reservation [rezə'veɪʃn] *n.* **a)** Reservierung, *die;* **have a ~ [for a room]** ein
Zimmer reserviert haben; **b)** *(doubt)*
Vorbehalt, *der* **(about** gegen); Bedenken **(about** bezüglich + *Gen.*); **without ~:** ohne Vorbehalt

reserve [rɪ'zɜːv] **1.** *v. t.* reservieren lassen ‹*Zimmer, Tisch, Platz*›*; (set aside)*
reservieren; **~ the right to do sth.** sich
(Dat.) [das Recht] vorbehalten, etw.
zu tun. **2.** *n.* **a)** *(extra amount)* Reserve, *die* **(of an** + *Dat.*) **have/hold** *or*
keep sth. in ~: etw. in Reserve haben/
halten; **b)** *(place set apart)* Reservat,
das; **c)** *(Sport)* Reservespieler,
der/-spielerin, *die;* **the R~s** die Reserve; **d)** *(reticence)* Zurückhaltung, *die.*
reserved [rɪ'zɜːvd] *adj. (reticent)* reserviert

reservoir ['rezəvwɑː(r)] *n. ([artificial]
lake)* Reservoir, *das*

reshape [riː'ʃeɪp] *v. t.* umgestalten

reshuffle [riː'ʃʌfl] **1.** *v. t.* **a)** umbilden
‹*Kabinett*›; **b)** *(Cards)* neu mischen. **2.**
n. Umbildung, *die*

reside [rɪ'zaɪd] *v. i. (formal)* wohnen;
wohnhaft sein *(Amtsspr.).* **residence**
['rezɪdəns] *n.* **a)** *(abode)* Wohnsitz,
der; (of ambassador etc.) Residenz,
die; **b)** *(stay)* Aufenthalt, *der.*
'residence permit *n.* Aufenthaltsgenehmigung, *die.* **resident** ['rezɪdənt] **1.** *adj.* wohnhaft; **be ~ in England** sein Wohnsitz in England haben.
2. *n. (inhabitant)* Bewohner, *der*/Bewohnerin, *die; (at hotel)* Hotelgast,
der. **residential** [rezɪ'denʃl] *adj.*
Wohn‹*gebiet, -siedlung, -straße*›; **~
hotel** Hotel für Dauergäste

residue ['rezɪdjuː] *n.* **a)** Rest, *der;* **b)**
(Chem.) Rückstand, *der*

resign [rɪ'zaɪn] **1.** *v. t.* zurücktreten von
‹*Amt*›. **2.** *v. refl.* **~ oneself to sth./to
doing sth.** sich mit etw. abfinden/sich
damit abfinden, etw. zu tun. **3.** *v. i.*
‹*Arbeitnehmer:*› kündigen; ‹*Regierungsbeamter:*› zurücktreten **(from**
von). **resignation** [rezɪg'neɪʃn] *n.* **a)**
see **resign 3:** Kündigung, *die;* Rücktritt, *der;* **tender one's ~:** seine Kündigung/seinen Rücktritt einreichen; **b)**
(being resigned) Resignation, *die;* **with
~:** resigniert. **resigned** [rɪ'zaɪnd] *adj.*
resigniert; **be ~ to sth.** sich mit etw.
abgefunden haben

resilience [rɪ'zɪlɪəns] *n.* **a)** Elastizität,
die; **b)** *(fig.)* Unverwüstlichkeit, *die*

resilient [rɪ'zɪlɪənt] *adj.* elastisch;
(fig.) unverwüstlich

resin ['rezɪn] *n.* Harz, *das*

resist [rɪ'zɪst] **1.** *v. t.* **a)** standhalten
(+ *Dat.*) ‹*Frost, Hitze, Feuchtigkeit
usw.*›; **b)** *(oppose)* sich widersetzen
(+ *Dat.*); widerstehen (+ *Dat.*) ‹*Versuchung*›. **2.** *v. i. see* **1 b:** sich widersetzen; widerstehen. **resistance** [rɪ'zɪstəns] *n.* Widerstand, *der* **(to** gegen).
resistant [rɪ'zɪstənt] *adj.* **a)** *(opposed)*
be ~ to sich widersetzen (+ *Dat.*); **b)**
(having power to resist) widerstandsfähig **(to** gegen)

resold *see* **resell**

resolute ['rezəluːt] *adj.* resolut, energisch ‹*Person*›; entschlossen ‹*Tat*›

resolution [rezə'luːʃn] *n.* **a)** *(firmness)*
Entschlossenheit, *die;* **b)** *(decision)*
Entschließung, *die; (Polit. also)* Resolution, *die;* **c)** *(resolve)* Vorsatz, *der;*
make a ~: einen Vorsatz fassen

resolve [rɪ'zɒlv] **1.** *v. t.* **a)** lösen ‹*Problem, Rätsel*›; ausräumen ‹*Schwierig-*

keit⟩; **b)** *(decide)* beschließen; **c)** *(settle)* beilegen ⟨*Streit*⟩; regeln ⟨*Angelegenheit*⟩. **2.** *n.* **a)** Vorsatz, *der;* **b)** *(resoluteness)* Entschlossenheit, *die.* **resolved** [rɪ'zɒlvd] *adj.* ~ |to do sth.| entschlossen[, etw. zu tun]

resonant ['rezənənt] *adj.* hallend ⟨*Ton, Klang*⟩

resort [rɪ'zɔːt] **1.** *n.* **a)** *(place)* Aufenthalt[sort], *der;* |holiday| ~: Ferienort, *der;* ski ~: Skiurlaubsort, *der;* seaside ~: Seebad, *das;* **b)** *(recourse)* as a last ~: als letzter Ausweg. **2.** *v.i.* ~ to sth./ sb. zu etw. greifen/sich an jmdn. wenden (for um)

resound [rɪ'zaʊnd] *v.i.* widerhallen. **re'sounding** *adj.* hallend ⟨*Lärm*⟩; überwältigend ⟨*Sieg, Erfolg*⟩

resource [rɪ'sɔːs, rɪ'zɔːs] *n. usu. in pl. (stock)* Mittel *Pl.;* Ressource, *die.* **resourceful** [rɪ'sɔːsfl, rɪ'zɔːsfl] *adj.* findig ⟨*Person*⟩

respect [rɪ'spekt] **1.** *n.* **a)** *(esteem)* Respekt, *der,* Achtung, *die* (for vor + *Dat.*); show ~ for sb./sth. Respekt vor jmdm./etw. zeigen; **b)** *(aspect)* Hinsicht, *die;* in some ~s in mancher Hinsicht; **c)** with ~ to ...: in bezug auf ... *(Akk.);* was ... [an]betrifft. **2.** *v.t.* respektieren; achten. **respectable** [rɪ'spektəbl] *adj.* angesehen ⟨*Bürger usw.*⟩; ehrenwert ⟨*Motive*⟩; *(decent)* ehrbar *(geh.)* ⟨*Leute, Kaufmann*⟩; anständig, respektabel ⟨*Beschäftigung usw.*⟩. **respectful** [rɪ'spektfl] *adj.* respektvoll (to|wards| gegenüber). **re-'spectfully** *adv.* respektvoll

respective [rɪ'spektɪv] *adj.* jeweilig. **re'spectively** *adv.* beziehungsweise

respiration [respɪ'reɪʃn] *n.* Atmung, *die*

respite ['respaɪt] *n.* Ruhepause, *die;* *(delay)* Aufschub, *der;* without ~: ohne Pause

resplendent [rɪ'splendənt] *adj.* prächtig

respond [rɪ'spɒnd] **1.** *v.i.* **a)** *(answer)* antworten (to auf + *Akk.*); **b)** *(react)* reagieren (to auf + *Akk.*); ⟨*Patient, Bremsen:*⟩ ansprechen (to auf + *Akk.*). **2.** *v.t.* antworten; erwidern

response [rɪ'spɒns] *n.* **a)** *(answer)* Antwort, *die* (to auf + *Akk.*); in ~ |to| als Antwort [auf (+ *Akk.*)]; **b)** *(reaction)* Reaktion, *die*

responsibility [rɪspɒnsɪ'bɪlɪtɪ] *n.* **a)** *(being responsible)* Verantwortung, *die;* **b)** *(duty)* Verpflichtung, *die*

responsible [rɪ'spɒnsɪbl] *adj.* **a)** ver-

antwortlich; be ~ to sb. jmdm. gegenüber verantwortlich sein (for für); **b)** *(trustworthy)* verantwortungsvoll. **responsibly** [rɪ'spɒnsɪblɪ] *adv.* verantwortungsbewußt

responsive [rɪ'spɒnsɪv] *adj.* aufgeschlossen ⟨*Person*⟩; be ~ to sth. auf etw. *(Akk.)* reagieren

¹**rest** [rest] **1.** *v.i.* ruhen; ~ on ruhen auf (+ *Dat.*); ~ from sth. sich von etw. ausruhen; ~ assured that ...: seien Sie versichert, daß ...; ~ with sb. ⟨*Verantwortung:*⟩ bei jmdm. liegen. **2.** *v.t.* **a)** ~ sth. against etw. an etw. *(Akk.)* lehnen; **b)** ausruhen ⟨*Augen*⟩. **3.** *n.* **a)** *(repose)* Ruhe, *die;* **b)** *(break, relaxation)* Ruhe[pause], *die;* Erholung, *die* (from von); take a ~: sich ausruhen (from von); **c)** *(pause)* have a ~: [eine] Pause machen; ~ period [Ruhe]pause, *die*

²**rest** *n.* the ~: der Rest; we'll do the ~: alles Übrige erledigen wir

restaurant ['restərɔ̃, 'restərɒnt] *n.* Restaurant, *das*

rested ['restɪd] *adj.* ausgeruht

restful ['restfl] *adj.* ruhig ⟨*Tag, Woche*⟩

restive ['restɪv] *adj.* unruhig

restless ['restlɪs] *adj.* unruhig ⟨*Nacht, Schlaf, Bewegung*⟩; ruhelos ⟨*Person*⟩

restoration [restə'reɪʃn] *n.* **a)** *(of peace, health)* Wiederherstellung, *die; (of work of art, building)* Restaurierung, *die;* **b)** the R~ *(Brit. Hist.)* die Restauration

restore [rɪ'stɔː(r)] *v.t.* **a)** *(give back)* zurückgeben; **b)** restaurieren ⟨*Bauwerk, Kunstwerk usw.*⟩; ~ sb. to health jmdn. wiederherstellen; **c)** wiederherstellen ⟨*Ordnung, Ruhe*⟩

restrain [rɪ'streɪn] *v.t.* zurückhalten ⟨*Gefühl, Lachen, Person*⟩; bändigen ⟨*unartiges Kind, Tier*⟩; ~ sb./oneself from doing sth. jmdn. davon abhalten/ sich zurückhalten, etw. zu tun. **restrained** [rɪ'streɪnd] *adj.* zurückhaltend ⟨*Wesen, Kritik*⟩; beherrscht ⟨*Reaktion, Worte*⟩. **restraint** [rɪ'streɪnt] *n.* **a)** *(restriction)* Einschränkung, *die;* **b)** *(reserve)* Zurückhaltung, *die;* **c)** *(self-control)* Selbstbeherrschung, *die*

restrict [rɪ'strɪkt] *v.t.* beschränken (to auf + *Akk.*). **re'stricted** *adj.* beschränkt. **restriction** [rɪ'strɪkʃn] *n.* Beschränkung, *die* (on *Gen.*). **restrictive** [rɪ'strɪktɪv] *adj.* restriktiv

'rest room *n. (esp. Amer.)* Toilette, *die*

result [rɪ'zʌlt] **1.** *v.i.* **a)** *(follow)* ~ from sth. die Folge einer Sache *(Gen.)* sein;

b) *(end)* ~ **in sth.** in etw. *(Dat.)* resultieren. **2.** *n.* Ergebnis, *das;* **be the ~ of sth.** die Folge einer Sache *(Gen.)* sein; **as a ~ |of this|** infolgedessen. **re'sultant** [rɪ'zʌltənt] *attrib. adj.* daraus resultierend

resume [rɪ'zju:m] *v. t.* wiederaufnehmen; fortsetzen ⟨*Reise*⟩

résumé ['rezʊmeɪ] *n.* Zusammenfassung, *die*

resumption [rɪ'zʌmpʃn] *n.* Wiederaufnahme, *die*

resurrection [rezə'rekʃn] *n.* *(Relig.)* Auferstehung, *die*

resuscitate [rɪ'sʌsɪteɪt] *v. t.* wiederbeleben

retail ['ri:teɪl] **1.** *adj.* Einzel⟨*handel*⟩; Einzelhandels⟨*geschäft,* -*preis*⟩. **2.** *adv.* **buy/sell** ~: en détail kaufen/verkaufen. **'retailer** *n.* Einzelhändler, *der/*-händlerin, *die.* **retail 'price index** *n.* *(Brit.)* Preisindex des Einzelhandels

retain [rɪ'teɪn] *v. t.* behalten; ein-, zurückbehalten ⟨*Gelder*⟩

retaliate [rɪ'tælɪeɪt] *v. i.* Vergeltung üben (**against an** + *Dat.*). **retaliation** [rɪtælɪ'eɪʃn] *n.* Vergeltung, *die;* **in ~ for** als Vergeltung für

retarded [rɪ'tɑ:dɪd] *adj.* |**mentally**| ~: [geistig] zurückgeblieben

retch [retʃ] *v. i.* würgen

retentive [rɪ'tentɪv] *adj.* gut ⟨*Gedächtnis*⟩

rethink [ri:'θɪŋk] *v. t.,* rethought [ri:'θɔ:t] noch einmal überdenken

reticence ['retɪsəns] *n.* Zurückhaltung, *die*

reticent ['retɪsənt] *adj.* zurückhaltend (**on, about** in bezug auf + *Akk.*)

retina ['retɪnə] *n.* Netzhaut, *die*

retinue ['retɪnju:] *n.* Gefolge, *das*

retire [rɪ'taɪə(r)] *v. i.* **a)** ⟨*Angestellter, Arbeiter:*⟩ in Rente *(Akk.)* gehen; ⟨*Beamter, Militär:*⟩ in Pension *od.* den Ruhestand gehen; **b)** *(withdraw)* sich zurückziehen (**to** in + *Akk.*). **retired** [rɪ'taɪəd] *adj.* aus dem Berufsleben ausgeschieden; ⟨*Beamter, Soldat*⟩ im Ruhestand, pensioniert. **re'tirement** *n.* Ruhestand, *der*

retiring [rɪ'taɪərɪŋ] *adj.* *(shy)* zurückhaltend

retort [rɪ'tɔ:t] **1.** *n.* Entgegnung, *die* (**to** auf + *Akk.*). **2.** *v. t.* entgegnen

retrace [rɪ'treɪs] *v. t.* zurückverfolgen; ~ **one's steps** denselben Weg noch einmal zurückgehen

retract [rɪ'trækt] *v. t.* zurücknehmen

retrain [ri:'treɪn] **1.** *v. i.* [sich] umschulen [lassen]. **2.** *v. t.* umschulen

retreat [rɪ'tri:t] **1.** *n.* **a)** *(withdrawal)* Rückzug, *der;* **beat a ~** *(fig.)* das Feld räumen; **b)** *(place)* Zufluchtsort, *der.* **2.** *v. i.* sich zurückziehen

retribution [retrɪ'bju:ʃn] *n.* Vergeltung, *die*

retrieval [rɪ'tri:vl] *n.* **a)** *(of situation)* Rettung, *die;* **beyond** *or* **past** ~: hoffnungslos; **b)** *(rescue)* Rettung, *die; (from wreckage)* Bergung, *die*

retrieve [rɪ'tri:v] *v. t.* **a)** *(rescue)* retten (**from** aus); *(from wreckage)* bergen (**from** aus); **b)** *(recover)* zurückholen ⟨*Brief*⟩; wiederholen ⟨*Ball*⟩; wiederbekommen ⟨*Geld*⟩; **c)** *(Computing)* wiederauffinden ⟨*Informationen*⟩; **d)** ⟨*Hund:*⟩ apportieren; **e)** retten ⟨*Situation*⟩. **re'triever** *n.* Apportierhund, *der; (breed)* Retriever, *der*

return [rɪ'tɜ:n] **1.** *v. i.* *(come back)* zurückkommen; *(go back)* zurückgehen; *(by vehicle)* zurückfahren. **2.** *v. t.* **a)** *(bring back)* zurückbringen; zurückgeben ⟨*geliehenen/gestohlenen Gegenstand*⟩; ~**ed with thanks** mit Dank zurück; **b)** erwidern ⟨*Besuch, Gruß, Liebe*⟩; sich revanchieren für *(ugs.)* ⟨*Freundlichkeit, Gefallen*⟩; **c)** *(elect)* wählen ⟨*Kandidaten*⟩; **d)** ~ **a verdict of guilty/not guilty** ⟨*Geschworene:*⟩ auf „schuldig"/„nicht schuldig" erkennen. **3.** *n.* **a)** Rückkehr, *die;* **many happy ~s |of the day|!** herzlichen Glückwunsch [zum Geburtstag]!; **b)** **by ~ |of post|** postwendend; **c)** *(ticket)* Rückfahrkarte, *die; (for flight)* Rückflugschein, *der;* **d)** ~|**s**| *(proceeds)* Gewinn, *der* (**on, from** aus); **e)** *(bringing back)* Zurückbringen, *das; (of property, goods, book)* Rückgabe, *die* (**to** an + *Akk.*); **receive/get sth. in ~ |for sth.|** etw. [für etw.] bekommen

return: ~ **'fare** *n.* Preis für eine Rückfahrkarte/*(for flight)* einen Rückflugschein; ~ **'flight** *n.* Rückflug, *der;* ~ **'journey** *n.* Rückreise, *die;* Rückfahrt, *die;* ~ **'match** *n.* Rückspiel, *das;* ~ **'ticket** *n.* *(Brit.)* Rückfahrkarte, *die; (for flight)* Rückflugschein, *der*

retype [ri:'taɪp] *v. t.* neu tippen

reunion [ri:'ju:njən] *n.* *(gathering)* Treffen, *das*

reunite [ri:jʊ'naɪt] *v. t.* wieder zusammenführen

reuse 1. [ri:'ju:z] *v. t.* wiederverwenden. **2.** [ri:'ju:s] *n.* Wiederverwendung, *die*

rev [rev] *(coll.)* **1.** *n., usu. in pl.* Umdrehung, *die.* **2.** *v. i.,* -vv- hochtourig laufen. **3.** *v. t.,* -vv- aufheulen lassen. **rev 'up** *v. t.* aufheulen lassen

Rev. ['revərənd, *(coll.)* rev] *abbr.* Reverend Rev.

reveal [rɪ'vi:l] *v. t.* enthüllen *(geh.);* **be** ~**ed** ⟨*Wahrheit:*⟩ ans Licht kommen. **re'vealing** *adj.* aufschlußreich

revel ['revl] *v. i., (Brit.)* -ll- genießen (**in** *Akk.*); ~ **in doing sth.** es [richtig] genießen, etw. zu tun

revelation [revə'leɪʃn] *n.* **a)** Enthüllung, *die (geh.); be* **a** ~: einem die Augen öffnen; **b)** *(Relig.)* Offenbarung, *die*

revelry ['revlrɪ] *n.* Feiern, *das*

revenge [rɪ'vendʒ] **1.** *v. t.* rächen ⟨*Person, Tat*⟩. **2.** *n. (action)* Rache, *die;* **take** ~ *or* **have one's** ~ |**on sb.**| |**for sth.**| Rache [an jmdm.] [für etw.] nehmen; **in** ~ **for sth.** als Rache für etw.

revenue ['revənju:] *n.* ~|**s**| Einnahmen

revere [rɪ'vɪə(r)] *v. t.* verehren. **reverence** ['revərəns] *n.* Ehrfurcht, *die* **Reverend** ['revərənd] *adj.* the ~ **John Wilson** Hochwürden John Wilson

reverent ['revərənt] *adj.* ehrfürchtig

reverie ['revərɪ] *n.* Träumerei, *die*

reversal [rɪ'vɜ:sl] *n.* Umkehrung, *die*

reverse [rɪ'vɜ:s] **1.** *adj.* entgegengesetzt ⟨*Richtung*⟩; Rück⟨*seite*⟩; umgekehrt ⟨*Reihenfolge*⟩. **2.** *n.* **a)** *(contrary)* Gegenteil, *das;* **b)** *(Motor Veh.)* Rückwärtsgang, *der;* **put the car into** ~**, go into** ~: den Rückwärtsgang einlegen. **3.** *v. t.* **a)** umkehren ⟨*Reihenfolge*⟩; ~ **the charge|s|** *(Brit.)* ein R-Gespräch anmelden; **b)** zurücksetzen ⟨*Fahrzeug*⟩. **4.** *v. i.* zurücksetzen; rückwärts fahren. **reverse 'gear** *n. (Motor Veh.)* Rückwärtsgang, *der; see also* **gear 1 a**

reversible [rɪ'vɜ:sɪbl] *adj.* beidseitig tragbar ⟨*Kleidungsstück*⟩; Wende-⟨*mantel, -jacke*⟩

re'versing light *n.* Rückfahrscheinwerfer, *der*

revert [rɪ'vɜ:t] *v. i.* ~ **to** zurückkommen auf (+ *Akk.*) ⟨*Thema, Frage*⟩; ~ **to savagery** in den Zustand der Wildheit zurückfallen

review [rɪ'vju:] **1.** *n.* **a)** *(survey)* Überblick, *der* (**of** über + *Akk.*); **b)** *(re-examination)* [nochmalige] Überprüfung; **c)** *(of book, play, etc.)* Kritik, *die;* Rezension, *die.* **2.** *v. t.* **a)** *(survey)* untersuchen; prüfen; **b)** *(re-examine)* überprüfen; **c)** *(Mil.)* inspizieren; **d)**

(write a criticism of) rezensieren. **re-'viewer** *n.* Rezensent, *der*/Rezensentin, *die*

revile [rɪ'vaɪl] *v. t.* schmähen *(geh.)*

revise [rɪ'vaɪz] *v. t.* **a)** *(check over)* durchsehen ⟨*Manuskript*⟩; **b)** *(for exam)* wiederholen; *abs.* lernen. **revision** [rɪ'vɪʒn] *n.* **a)** *(checking over)* Durchsicht, *die;* **b)** *(amended version)* revidierte Fassung; **c)** *(for exam)* Wiederholung, *die*

revisit [ri:'vɪzɪt] *v. t.* wieder besuchen

revitalize [ri:'vaɪtəlaɪz] *v. t.* neu beleben

revival [rɪ'vaɪvl] *n.* Neubelebung, *die*

revive [rɪ'vaɪv] **1.** *v. i. (come back to consciousness)* wieder zu sich kommen; *(be reinvigorated)* zu neuem Leben erwachen. **2.** *v. t.* **a)** *(restore to consciousness)* wiederbeleben; *(reinvigorate)* wieder zu Kräften kommen lassen; **b)** wieder wecken ⟨*Lebensgeister, Interesse*⟩

revoke [rɪ'vəʊk] *v. t.* aufheben ⟨*Entscheidung*⟩; widerrufen ⟨*Befehl*⟩; widerrufen ⟨*Erlaubnis, Genehmigung*⟩

revolt [rɪ'vəʊlt] **1.** *v. i.* revoltieren (**against** gegen). **2.** *v. t.* mit Abscheu erfüllen. **3.** *n.* Revolte, *die (auch fig.);* Aufstand, *der.* **re'volting** *adj.* abscheulich; *(coll.: unpleasant)* widerlich

revolution [revə'lu:ʃn] *n.* Revolution, *die.* **revolutionary** [revə'lu:ʃənərɪ] **1.** *adj.* revolutionär. **2.** *n.* Revolutionär, *der*/Revolutionärin, *die*

revolve [rɪ'vɒlv] **1.** *v. t.* drehen. **2.** *v. i.* sich drehen (**round, about, on** um)

revolver [rɪ'vɒlvə(r)] *n.* [Trommel]revolver, *der*

revolving [rɪ'vɒlvɪŋ] *attrib. adj.* Dreh⟨*bühne, -tür*⟩

revue [rɪ'vju:] *n.* Kabarett, *das; (musical show)* Revue, *die*

revulsion [rɪ'vʌlʃn] *n.* Abscheu, *der* (**at** vor + *Dat.,* gegen)

reward [rɪ'wɔ:d] **1.** *n.* Belohnung, *die.* **2.** *v. t.* belohnen. **re'warding** *adj.* lohnend; **be** ~/**financially** ~: sich lohnen/einträglich sein

rewind [ri:'waɪnd] *v. t.,* **rewound** [ri:'waʊnd] **a)** wieder aufziehen ⟨*Uhr*⟩; **b)** zurückspulen ⟨*Film, Band*⟩

reword [ri:'wɜ:d] *v. t.* umformulieren

rewrite [ri:'raɪt] *v. t.,* **rewrote** [ri:'rəʊt], **rewritten** [ri:'rɪtn] noch einmal [neu] schreiben; *(write differently)* umschreiben

rhetoric ['retərɪk] *n.* |**art of**| ~: Rede-

kunst, *die;* Rhetorik, *die.* **rhetorical**
[rɪ'tɒrɪkl] *adj.* rhetorisch
rheumatic [ru:'mætɪk] *adj.* rheuma-
tisch
rheumatism ['ru:mətɪzm] *n.* Rheuma-
tismus, *der;* Rheuma, *das (ugs.)*
Rhine [raɪn] *pr. n.* Rhein, *der*
rhino ['raɪnəʊ] *n., pl.* **same** *or* **~s** *(coll.),*
rhinoceros [raɪ'nɒsərəs] *n., pl. same*
or **~es** Nashorn, *das;* Rhinozeros, *das*
rhododendron [rəʊdə'dendrən] *n.*
Rhododendron, *der*
rhubarb ['ru:bɑ:b] *n.* Rhabarber, *der*
rhyme [raɪm] **1.** *n.* Reim, *der;* **without**
~ or reason ohne Sinn und Verstand.
2. *v. i.* sich reimen (**with** auf + *Akk.*)
rhythm ['rɪðm] *n.* Rhythmus, *der.*
rhythmic ['rɪðmɪk], **rhythmical**
['rɪðmɪkl] *adj.* rhythmisch
rib [rɪb] **1.** *n.* Rippe, *die.* **2.** *v. t.,* **-bb-**
(coll.) aufziehen *(ugs.)*
ribald ['rɪbəld] *adj.* zotig
ribbon ['rɪbn] *n.* Band, *das; (on type-*
writer) [Farb]band, *das*
rice [raɪs] *n.* Reis, *der.* **rice 'pudding**
n. Milchreis, *der.* **'rice wine** *n.* Reis-
wein, *der*
rich [rɪtʃ] **1.** *adj.* **a)** reich (**in** an +
Dat.); *(fertile)* fruchtbar ⟨*Land,*
Boden⟩; **b)** *(splendid)* prachtvoll; **c)**
(containing much fat, oil, eggs, etc.) gehaltvoll; **d)** *(deep, full)* voll[tönend]
⟨*Stimme*⟩; voll ⟨*Ton*⟩; satt ⟨*Farbe,*
Farbton⟩. **2.** *n. pl.* **the ~:** die Reichen;
~ and poor Arm und Reich. **riches**
['rɪtʃɪz] *n. pl.* Reichtum, *der.* **'richly**
adv. **a)** *(splendidly)* reich; üppig ⟨*aus-*
gestattet⟩; prächtig ⟨*gekleidet*⟩; **b)**
(fully) voll und ganz; **~ deserved** wohl-
verdient. **'richness** *n.* **a)** *(of food)*
Reichhaltigkeit, *die;* **b)** *(of voice)* voller Klang; *(of colour)* Sattheit, *die*
rickets ['rɪkɪts] *n.* Rachitis, *die*
rickety ['rɪkɪtɪ] *adj.* wack[e]lig
ricochet ['rɪkəʃeɪ] **1.** *n.* **a)** Abprallen,
das; **b)** *(hit)* Abpraller, *der.* **2.** *v. i.,*
~ed ['rɪkəʃeɪd] abprallen (**off** von)
rid [rɪd] *v. t.,* **-dd-, rid: ~ sth. of sth.** etw.
von etw. befreien; **~ oneself of sb./sth.**
sich von jmdm./etw. befreien; **be ~ of**
sb./sth. jmdn./etw. los sein *(ugs.);* **get**
~ of sb./sth. jmdn./etw. loswerden
riddance ['rɪdəns] *n.* **good ~!** Gott sei
Dank ist er/es *usw.* weg!
ridden *see* ride 2, 3
¹riddle ['rɪdl] *n.* Rätsel, *das*
²riddle *v. t.* durchlöchern; **~d with bul-**
lets von Kugeln durchsiebt
ride [raɪd] **1.** *n. (on horseback)* [Aus]ritt,

der; (in vehicle, at fair) Fahrt, die; **~ in**
a train/coach Zug-/Busfahrt, *die;* **go**
for a ~: ausreiten; **go for a [bi]cycle ~:**
radfahren; **go for a ~ [in the car]** [mit
dem Auto] wegfahren; **take sb. for a ~**
(fig. sl.: deceive) jmdn. reinlegen
(ugs.). **2.** *v. i.,* **rode** [rəʊd], **ridden** ['rɪdn]
(on horse) reiten; *(on bicycle, in*
vehicle) fahren; **~ to town on one's**
bike/in one's car/on the train mit dem
Rad/Auto/Zug in die Stadt fahren. **3.**
v. t., **rode, ridden** reiten ⟨*Pferd usw.*⟩;
fahren mit ⟨*Fahrrad*⟩. **ride a'way,**
ride 'off *v. i.* wegreiten/-fahren
'rider *n.* **a)** Reiter, *der/*Reiterin, *die; (of*
cycle) Fahrer, *der/*Fahrerin, *die;* **b)**
(addition) Zusatz, *der*
ridge [rɪdʒ] *n.* **a)** *(of roof)* First, *der;* **b)**
(long hilltop) Grat, *der;* Kamm, *der;* **c)**
(Meteorol.) **~ [of high pressure]** langge-
strecktes Hoch
ridicule ['rɪdɪkju:l] **1.** *n.* Spott, *der.* **2.**
v. t. verspotten
ridiculous [rɪ'dɪkjʊləs] *adj.* lächerlich
riding ['raɪdɪŋ] *n.* Reiten, *das.* **'riding**
lesson *n.* Reitstunde, *die.* **'riding-**
school *n.* Reitschule, *die*
rife [raɪf] *pred. adj.* weit verbreitet
riff-raff ['rɪfræf] *n.* Gesindel, *das*
rifle ['raɪfl] **1.** *n.* Gewehr, *das.* **2.** *v. t.*
durchwühlen. **3.** *v. i.* **~ through sth.**
etw. durchwühlen
rift [rɪft] *n.* Unstimmigkeit, *die*
¹rig [rɪg] *n. (for oil-well)* [Öl]förderturm,
der; (off shore) Förderinsel, *die.* **rig**
'out *v. t.* ausstaffieren. **rig 'up** *v. t.*
aufbauen
²rig *v. t.,* **-gg-** manipulieren ⟨*[Wahl]-*
ergebnis⟩; fälschen ⟨*Wahl*⟩
rigging ['rɪgɪŋ] *n.* Takelung, *die*
right [raɪt] **1.** *adj.* **a)** *(just, morally*
good, sound) richtig; **b)** *(correct, true)*
richtig; **you're [quite] ~:** du hast [völ-
lig] recht; **be ~ in sth.** recht mit etw.
haben; **is that clock ~?** geht die Uhr
da richtig?; **put** *or* **set ~:** richtigstellen
⟨*Irrtum, Behauptung*⟩; wiedergutma-
chen ⟨*Unrecht*⟩; berichtigen ⟨*Fehler*⟩;
richtig stellen ⟨*Uhr*⟩; **put** *or* **set sb. ~:**
jmdn. berichtigen; **that's ~:** ja[wohl];
so ist es; is that ~? stimmt das?; *(in-*
deed?) aha!; **[am I] ~?** nicht [wahr]?;
c) *(preferable, most suitable)* richtig;
recht; **do sth. the ~ way** etw. richtig
machen; **d)** *(opposite of left)* recht...;
on the ~ side rechts; **e)** R~ *(Polit.)*
recht... **2.** *v. t.* aus der Welt schaffen
⟨*Unrecht*⟩. **3.** *n.* **a)** *(fair claim, author-*
ity) Recht, *das;* **have a/no ~ to sth.**

ein/kein Anrecht *od.* Recht auf etw. *(Akk.)* haben; **in one's own ~:** aus eigenem Recht; **~ of way** Vorfahrtsrecht, *das;* **have ~ of way** Vorfahrt haben; **b)** *(what is just)* Recht, *das;* by **~|s|** von Rechts wegen; **in the ~:** im Recht; **c)** *(~-hand side)* rechte Seite; **on** *or* **to the ~ |of sb./sth.|** rechts [von jmdm./etw.]; **d)** *(Polit.)* **the R~:** die Rechte. **4.** *adv.* **a)** *(correctly)* richtig; **b)** *(to the ~-hand side)* nach rechts; **c)** *(completely)* ganz; **d)** *(exactly)* genau; **~ 'now** im Moment; jetzt sofort *(handeln);* **e)** *(straight)* direkt

'**right angle** *n.* rechter Winkel; **at ~s to sth.** rechtwinklig zu etw.

righteous ['raɪtʃəs] *adj.* rechtschaffen

rightful ['raɪtfl] *adj.* rechtmäßig *(Besitzer, Herrscher)*

right: ~-hand *adj.* recht...; **~-'handed 1.** *adj.* rechtshändig; *(Werkzeug)* für Rechtshänder; **be ~-handed** *(Person:)* Rechtshänder/Rechtshänderin sein; **2.** *adv.* rechtshändig; **~-hand 'man** *n.* rechte Hand

'**rightly** *adv.* zu Recht

right: ~-'minded *adj.* gerecht denkend; **~ 'wing** *n.* rechter Flügel; **~-wing** *adj.* *(Polit.)* rechtsgerichtet; Rechts*(extremist, -intellektueller)*; **~-winger** *n.* **a)** *(Sport)* Rechtsaußen, *der;* **b)** *(Polit.)* Rechte, *der/die*

rigid ['rɪdʒɪd] *adj.* **a)** starr; *(stiff)* steif; **b)** *(strict)* streng; unbeugsam *(System).* **rigidity** [rɪ'dʒɪtɪ] *n. see* **rigid:** Starrheit, *die;* Steifheit, *die;* Strenge, *die*

rigmarole ['rɪgmərəʊl] *n.* **a)** *(talk)* langatmiges Geschwafel *(ugs.);* **b)** *(procedure)* Zirkus, *der*

rigor ['rɪgə(r)] *(Amer.) see* **rigour**

rigor mortis [rɪgə 'mɔːtɪs] *n.* Totenstarre, *die*

rigorous ['rɪgərəs] *adj.* streng

rigour ['rɪgə(r)] *n. (Brit.)* Strenge, *die*

rile [raɪl] *v. t. (coll.)* ärgern

rim [rɪm] *n.* Rand, *der;* *(of wheel)* Felge, *die*

rind [raɪnd] *n. (of fruit)* Schale, *die;* *(of cheese)* Rinde, *die;* *(of bacon)* Schwarte, *die*

¹**ring** [rɪŋ] **1.** *n.* **a)** Ring, *der;* **b)** *(Boxing)* Ring, *der;* *(in circus)* Manege, *die.* **2.** *v. t. (surround)* umringen; einkreisen *(Wort usw.).*

²**ring 1.** *n.* **a)** *(act of sounding bell)* Läuten, *das;* Klingeln, *das;* **b)** *(Brit. coll.: telephone call)* Anruf, *der;* **give sb. a**

~: jmdn. anrufen; **c)** *(fig.: impression)* **have the ~ of truth |about it|** glaubhaft klingen. **2.** *v. i.,* **rang** [ræŋ], **rung** [rʌŋ] **a)** *(sound clearly)* [er]schallen; *(Hammer:)* [er]dröhnen; **b)** *(be sounded)* *(Glocke, Klingel, Telefon:)* läuten; *(Wecker, Telefon, Kasse:)* klingeln; **the doorbell rang** es klingelte; **c)** *(~ bell)* läuten (for nach); **d)** *(Brit.: make telephone call)* anrufen. **3.** *v. t.,* **rang, rung a)** läuten *(Glocke);* **~ the |door|bell** läuten; klingeln; **it ~s a bell** *(fig. coll.)* es kommt mir [irgendwie] bekannt vor; **b)** *(Brit.: telephone)* anrufen. **ring 'back** *(Brit.) v. t. & i.* **a)** *(again)* wieder anrufen; **b)** *(in return)* zurückrufen. **ring 'off** *v. i. (Brit.)* auflegen. **ring 'out** *v. i.* ertönen

ring: ~ binder *n.* Ringbuch, *das;* **~-finger** *n.* Ringfinger, *der*

ringing ['rɪŋɪŋ] *n.* Läuten, *das;* *(Brit. Teleph:)* **~ tone** Freiton, *der*

'**ringleader** *n.* Anführer, *der/*Anführerin, *die*

ringlet ['rɪŋlɪt] *n.* [Ringel]löckchen, *das*

'**ring road** *n.* Ringstraße, *die*

rink [rɪŋk] *n. (for ice-skating)* Eisbahn, *die;* *(for roller-skating)* Rollschuhbahn, *die*

rinse [rɪns] **1.** *v. t.* **a)** *(wash out)* ausspülen *(Mund, Gefäß usw.);* **b)** [aus]spülen *(Wäsche usw.);* abspülen *(Hände, Geschirr).* **2.** *n.* Spülen, *das;* **give sth. a |good/quick| ~:** etw. [gut/schnell] ausspülen/abspülen/spülen. **rinse 'out** *v. t.* ausspülen

riot ['raɪət] **1.** *n.* Aufruhr, *der;* ~s Unruhen *Pl.;* **run ~:** randalieren. **2.** *v. i.* randalieren. '**rioter** *n.* Randalierer, *der.* **riotous** ['raɪətəs] *adj.* **a)** *(gewalttätig;* **b)** *(unrestrained)* wild

rip [rɪp] **1.** *n.* Riß, *der.* **2.** *v. t.,* -pp- zerreißen; **~ open** aufreißen. **rip 'off** *v. t.* **a)** *(remove from)* reißen von; *(remove)* abreißen; **b)** *(sl.: defraud)* übers Ohr hauen *(ugs.).* **rip 'out** *v. t.* herausreißen *(of aus)*

RIP *abbr.* **rest in peace** R.I.P.

'**rip-cord** *n.* Reißleine, *die*

ripe [raɪp] *adj.* reif **(for zu). ripen** ['raɪpn] **1.** *v. t.* zur Reife bringen. **2.** *v. i.* reifen. '**ripeness** *n.* Reife, *die*

'**rip-off** *n. (sl.)* Nepp, *der (ugs.)*

riposte [rɪ'pɒst] **1.** *n. (retort)* [rasche] Entgegnung. **2.** *v. i.* [rasch] antworten

ripple ['rɪpl] **1.** *n.* kleine Welle. **2.** *v. i.* *(See:)* sich kräuseln; *(Welle:)* plätschern. **3.** *v. t.* kräuseln

rise [raiz] **1.** *n.* **a)** *(advancement)* Aufstieg, *der;* **b)** *(in value, price, cost)* Steigerung, *die;* *(in population, temperature)* Zunahme, *die;* **c)** *(Brit.)* |pay| ~ *(in wages)* Lohnerhöhung, *die;* *(in salary)* Gehaltserhöhung, *die;* **d)** *(hill)* Anhöhe, *die;* **e)** give ~ to führen zu; Anlaß geben zu ⟨*Spekulation*⟩. **2.** *v.i.,* **rose** [rəuz], **risen** ['rizn] **a)** *(go up)* aufsteigen; **b)** ⟨*Sonne, Mond:*⟩ aufgehen; **c)** *(increase, reach higher level)* steigen; **d)** *(advance)* ⟨*Person:*⟩ aufsteigen; **e)** ⟨*Teig, Kuchen:*⟩ aufgehen; **f)** *(Theatre)* ⟨*Vorhang:*⟩ aufgehen; **g)** ⟨*Fluß:*⟩ entspringen. **rise up** *v.i.* **a)** ~ up |in revolt| aufbegehren *(geh.);* **b)** ⟨*Berg:*⟩ aufragen

risen *see* **rise 2**

riser *n.* **early ~:** Frühaufsteher, *der/*Frühaufsteherin, *die*

rising ['raiziŋ] **1.** *n. (of sun, moon, etc.)* Aufgang, *der.* **2.** *adj.* **a)** aufgehend ⟨*Sonne, Mond usw.*⟩; **b)** steigend ⟨*Kosten, Temperatur, Wasser, Flut*⟩; **c)** *(sloping upwards)* ansteigend

risk [risk] **1.** *n.* Gefahr, *die; (chance taken)* Risiko, *das;* **at one's own ~:** auf eigene Gefahr *od.* eigenes Risiko; **take the ~ of doing sth.** es riskieren, etw. zu tun; **be at ~** ⟨*Zukunft, Plan:*⟩ gefährdet sein. **2.** *v.t.* riskieren; **I'll ~ it** ich lasse es darauf ankommen. **risky** *adj.* gefährlich; gewagt ⟨*Experiment, Projekt*⟩

risqué ['risкei] *adj.* gewagt

rissole ['risəul] *n.* Rissole, *die*

rite [rait] *n.* Ritus, *der*

ritual ['ritʃʊəl] **1.** *adj.* rituell; Ritual-⟨*mord, -tötung*⟩. **2.** *n.* Ritual, *das*

rival ['raivl] **1.** *n. (competitor)* Rivale, *der/*Rivalin, *die;* **business ~s** Konkurrenten. **2.** *v.t., (Brit.)* -ll- nicht nachstehen (+ *Dat.*). **rivalry** ['raivlri] *n.* Rivalität, *die (geh.)*

river ['rivə(r)] *n.* Fluß, *der.* **river-bed** *n.* Flußbett, *das.* **riverside 1.** *n.* Flußufer, *das.* **2.** *attrib. adj.* am Fluß gelegen; am Fluß *nachgestellt*

rivet ['rivit] **1.** *n.* Niete, *die.* **2.** *v.t.* **a)** |ver|nieten; **b)** *(fig.)* fesseln. **riveting** *adj.* fesselnd

RN *abbr. (Brit.)* **Royal Navy** Königl. Mar.

road [rəud] *n.* Straße, *die;* **across or over the ~** |from us| [bei uns] gegenüber; **by ~** *(by car/bus/lorry)* per Auto/Bus/Lkw; **be on the ~:** auf Reisen *od.* unterwegs sein; ⟨*Theaterensemble usw.:*⟩ auf Tournee *od.* Tour sein

road: **~ accident** *n.* Verkehrsunfall, *der;* **~-block** *n.* Straßensperre, *die;* **~-hog** *n.* Verkehrsrowdy, *der;* **~-map** *n.* Straßenkarte, *die* **~ safety** *n.* Verkehrssicherheit, *die;* ~ **sense** *n.* Gespür für Verkehrssituationen; **~side** *n.* Straßenrand, *der;* **at or by/along the ~side** am Straßenrand; **~ sign** *n.* Verkehrszeichen, *das;* Straßenschild, *das (ugs.);* **~-sweeper** *n.* Straßenkehrer, *der/*-kehrerin, *die;* **~-user** *n.* Verkehrsteilnehmer, *der/*-teilnehmerin, *die;* **~-way** *n.* Fahrbahn, *die;* **~works** *n. pl.* Straßenbauarbeiten *Pl.;* **~worthy** *adj.* fahrtüchtig

roam [rəum] **1.** *v.i.* umherstreifen. **2.** *v.t.* streifen durch

roar [rɔ:(r)] **1.** *n. (of wild beast)* Gebrüll, *das; (of applause)* Tosen, *das; (of engine, traffic)* Dröhnen, *das;* **~s/a ~ |of laughter|** dröhnendes Gelächter. **2.** *v.i.* brüllen (with vor + *Dat.*); ⟨*Motor:*⟩ dröhnen. **roaring** *adj.* **a)** bullernd *(ugs.)* ⟨*Feuer*⟩; **b)** **a ~ success** ein Bombenerfolg; **do a ~ trade** ein Bombengeschäft machen

roast [rəust] **1.** *v.t.* braten; rösten ⟨*Kaffeebohnen, Kastanien*⟩. **2.** *attrib. adj.* gebraten ⟨*Fleisch, Ente usw.*⟩; Brat⟨*hähnchen, -kartoffeln*⟩; Röst⟨*kastanien*⟩; ~ **beef** *(sirloin)* Roastbeef, *das.* **3.** *n.* Braten, *der*

rob [rɒb] *v.t.,* -bb- ausrauben ⟨*Bank, Safe, Kasse*⟩; berauben ⟨*Person*⟩. **robber** ['rɒbə(r)] *n.* Räuber, *der/*Räuberin, *die.* **robbery** ['rɒbəri] *n.* Raub, *der;* **robberies** Raubüberfälle

robe [rəub] *n.* Gewand, *das (geh.); (of judge, vicar)* Talar, *der*

robin ['rɒbin] *n.* ~ |redbreast| Rotkehlchen, *das*

robot ['rəubɒt] *n.* Roboter, *der*

robust [rəu'bʌst] *adj.* robust

¹rock [rɒk] *n.* **a)** *(piece of ~)* Fels, *der;* **b)** *(large ~, hill)* Felsen, *der;* **c)** *(substance)* Fels, *der; (esp. Geol.)* Gestein, *das;* **d)** *(boulder)* Felsbrocken, *der; (Amer.: stone)* Stein, *der;* **e)** **stick of ~:** Zuckerstange, *die;* **f)** **be on the ~s** *(fig. coll.)* ⟨*Ehe, Firma:*⟩ kaputt sein *(ugs.)*

²rock 1. *v.t.* wiegen; *(in cradle)* schaukeln. **2.** *v.i.* **a)** schaukeln; **b)** *(sway)* schwanken. **3.** *n. (Mus.)* Rock, *der; attrib.* Rock-; ~ **and** *or* **'n' roll** |music| Rock and Roll, *der*

rock: **~-bottom** *(coll.)* **1.** *adj.* **~-bottom prices** Schleuderpreise *(ugs.);* **2.** *n.* **reach** *or* **touch ~-bottom** ⟨*Handel,*

Preis:) in den Keller fallen *(ugs.);* **her spirits reached ~-bottom** ihre Stimmung war auf dem Tiefpunkt; **~-climbing** n. [Fels]klettern, *das*
rockery ['rɒkərɪ] n. Steingarten, *der*
rocket ['rɒkɪt] **1.** n. Rakete, *die.* **2.** v. i. ⟨*Preise:*⟩ in die Höhe schnellen
rocking: ~-chair n. Schaukelstuhl, *der;* **~-horse** n. Schaukelpferd, *das*
'rocky *adj.* **a)** felsig; **b)** *(coll.: unsteady)* wackelig *(ugs.)*
rod [rɒd] n. Stange, *die; (for punishing)* Rute, *die; (for fishing)* [Angel]rute, *die*
rode *see* **ride 2, 3**
rodent ['rəʊdənt] n. Nagetier, *das*
'roe [rəʊ] n. *(of fish)* |**hard**| ~: Rogen, *der;* |**soft**| ~: Milch, *die*
²roe n. ~ |**deer**| Reh, *das*
rogue [rəʊg] n. Gauner, *der*
role, rôle [rəʊl] n. Rolle, *die*
'roll [rəʊl] n. **a)** Rolle, *die; (of cloth etc.)* Ballen, *der;* ~ **of film** Rolle Film; **b)** |**bread**| ~: Brötchen, *das*
²roll 1. n. *(of drum)* Wirbel, *der.* **2.** v. t. **a)** rollen; *(between surfaces)* drehen; **b)** *(shape by ~ing)* rollen; drehen ⟨Zigarette⟩; **c)** walzen ⟨Rasen, Metall usw.⟩; ausrollen ⟨Teig⟩. **3.** v. i. **a)** rollen; **b)** ⟨Maschine:⟩ laufen; **get sth. ~ing** *(fig.)* etw. ins Rollen bringen; **c) be ~ing in money** *or* **in it** *(coll.)* im Geld schwimmen *(ugs.).* **roll a'bout** v. i. herumrollen; ⟨*Schiff:*⟩ schlingern; ⟨*Kind, Hund:*⟩ sich wälzen. **roll 'back** v. t. zurückrollen. **roll 'by** v. i. ⟨*Zeit:*⟩ vergehen. **roll 'in** v. i. *(coll.)* ⟨*Briefe, Geldbeträge:*⟩ eingehen. **roll 'out** v. t. ausrollen ⟨*Teig, Teppich*⟩. **roll 'over** v. i. ⟨*Person:*⟩ sich umdrehen, *(to make room)* sich zur Seite rollen. **roll 'up 1.** v. t. aufrollen ⟨*Teppich*⟩; zusammenrollen ⟨*Landkarte, Dokument usw.*⟩; hochkrempeln ⟨*Ärmel*⟩. **2.** v. i. *(coll.: arrive)* aufkreuzen *(salopp)*
'roll-call n. Ausrufen aller Namen; *(Mil.)* Zählappell, *der*
'roller n. **a)** Rolle, *die; (for lawn, road, etc.)* Walze, *die;* **b)** *(for hair)* Lockenwickler, *der*
roller: ~ blind n. Rouleau, *das;* **~-coaster** n. Achterbahn, *die;* **~-skate 1.** n. Rollschuh, *der;* **2.** v. i. Rollschuh laufen; **~-skating** n. Rollschuhlaufen, *das*
'rolling *adj.* wellig ⟨*Gelände*⟩; ~ **hills** sanfte Hügel
rolling: ~-pin n. Teigrolle, *die;* **~-stock** n. *(Brit. Railw.)* Fahrzeugbestand, *der*

ROM [rɒm] *abbr. (Computing)* **read only memory** ROM
Roman ['rəʊmən] **1.** n. Römer, *der/* Römerin, *die.* **2.** *adj.* römisch.
Roman 'Catholic 1. *adj.* römisch-katholisch. **2.** n. Katholik, *der/*Katholikin, *die;* **sb. is a ~:** jmd. ist römisch-katholisch
romance [rə'mæns] n. **a)** *(love affair)* Romanze, *die;* **b)** *(love-story)* [romantische] Liebesgeschichte
Romania [rəʊ'meɪnɪə] *pr. n.* Rumänien *(das).* **Romanian** [rəʊ'meɪnɪən] **1.** *adj.* rumänisch. **2.** n. **a)** *(person)* Rumäne, *der/*Rumänin, *die;* **b)** *(language)* Rumänisch, *das; see also* **English 2a**
Roman 'numeral n. römische Ziffer
romantic [rəʊ'mæntɪk] *adj.* romantisch
romanticism [rəʊ'mæntɪsɪzm] n. *(Lit., Art., Mus.)* Romantik, *die*
Romany ['rəʊmənɪ] **1. a)** *(person)* Rom, *der;* **b)** *(language)* Romani, *das.* **2.** *adj.* Roma-; *(Ling.)* Romani-
Rome [rəʊm] *pr. n.* Rom *(das)*
romp [rɒmp] **1.** v. i. **a)** [herum]tollen; **b)** ~ **home** *or* **in** *(coll.: win easily)* spielend gewinnen. **2.** n. Tollerei, *die*
rompers ['rɒmpəz] n. pl. Spielhöschen, *das*
roof [ru:f] **1.** n. **a)** Dach, *das;* **b)** ~ **of the mouth** Gaumen, *der.* **2.** v. t. bedachen. **'roofing** n. *(material)* Deckung, *die*
roof: ~-rack n. Dachgepäckträger, *der;* **~-top** n. Dach, *das*
'rook [rʊk] n. *(Ornith.)* Saatkrähe, *die*
²rook n. *(Chess)* Turm, *der*
room [ru:m, rʊm] n. **a)** *(in building)* Zimmer, *das; (for function)* Saal, *der;* **b)** *(space)* Platz, *der;* **make ~** [for sb./ sth.] [jmdm./einer Sache] Platz machen; **there is still ~ for improvement in his work** seine Arbeit ist noch verbesserungsfähig
room: ~-mate n. Zimmergenosse, *der/*-genossin, *die;* ~ **service** n. Zimmerservice, *der;* ~ **temperature** n. Zimmertemperatur, *die*
roomy ['ru:mɪ] *adj.* geräumig
roost [ru:st] **1.** n. [Sitz]stange, *die.* **2.** v. i. ⟨*Vogel:*⟩ sich [zum Schlafen] niederlassen
'root [ru:t] **1.** n. Wurzel, *die;* **put down ~s/take** ~: Wurzeln schlagen. **2.** v. i. ⟨*Pflanze:*⟩ wurzeln. **3.** v. t. **stand ~ed to the spot** wie angewurzelt dastehen.
root 'out v. t. ausrotten

²root *v. i* **a)** *(turn up ground)* wühlen (for nach); **b)** *(coll.)* ~ **for** *(cheer)* anfeuern

rope [rəʊp] **1.** *n.* **a)** *(cord)* Seil, *das;* **b)** **know the** ~s sich auskennen. **2.** *v. t.* festbinden. **rope 'in** *v. t. (fig.)* einspannen *(ugs.)*

rope-'ladder *n.* Strickleiter, *die*

rosary ['rəʊzərɪ] *n.* Rosenkranz, *der*

¹rose [rəʊz] *n.* **a)** *(plant, flower)* Rose, *die;* **b)** *(colour)* Rosa, *das*

²rose *see* **rise 2**

rosé [rəʊ'zeɪ, 'rəʊzeɪ] *n.* Rosé, *der*

rose: ~**-bed** *n.* Rosenbeet, *das;* ~**-bud** *n.* Rosenknospe, *die;* ~**-bush** *n.* Rosenstrauch, *der*

rosemary ['rəʊzmərɪ] *n.* Rosmarin, *der*

'rose petal *n.* Rosen[blüten]blatt, *das*

rosette [rəʊ'zet] *n.* Rosette, *die*

roster ['rɒstə(r)] *n.* Dienstplan, *der*

rostrum ['rɒstrəm] *n., pl.* **rostra** ['rɒstrə] *or* ~**s** Podium, *das*

rosy ['rəʊzɪ] *adj.* rosig

rot [rɒt] **1.** *n.* **a)** *see* **2:** Verrottung, *die;* Fäulnis, *die; (fig.: deterioration)* Verfall, *der;* **stop the** ~ *(fig.)* dem Verfall Einhalt gebieten; **b)** *(sl.: nonsense)* Quark, *der (salopp).* **2.** *v. i.,* -tt- verrotten; ⟨*Fleisch, Gemüse, Obst:*⟩ verfaulen. **3.** *v. t.,* -tt- verrotten lassen; verfaulen lassen ⟨*Fleisch, Gemüse, Obst*⟩; zerstören ⟨*Zähne*⟩

rota ['rəʊtə] *n. (Brit.) (order of rotation)* Turnus, *der; (list)* Arbeitsplan, *der*

rotary ['rəʊtərɪ] *adj.* rotierend

rotate [rəʊ'teɪt] **1.** *v. i. (revolve)* rotieren; sich drehen. **2.** *v. t.* in Rotation versetzen. **rotation** [rəʊ'teɪʃn] *n.* **a)** Rotation, *die,* Drehung, *die* (**about** um); **b)** *(succession)* turnusmäßiger Wechsel; **in** *or* **by** ~: im Turnus

rote [rəʊt] *n.* **by** ~: auswendig

rotten ['rɒtn] *adj.,* ~**er** ['rɒtənə(r)], ~**est** ['rɒtənɪst] **a)** *(decayed)* verrottet; verfault ⟨*Obst, Gemüse*⟩; faul ⟨*Ei, Holz, Zähne*⟩; ~ **to the core** *(fig.)* verdorben bis ins Mark; **b)** *(corrupt)* verdorben; **c)** *(sl.: bad)* mies *(ugs.)*

rotund [rəʊ'tʌnd] *adj.* **a)** *(round)* rund; **b)** *(plump)* rundlich

rouble ['ruːbl] *n.* Rubel, *der*

rouge [ruːʒ] *n.* Rouge, *das*

rough [rʌf] **1.** *adj.* **a)** *(coarse, uneven)* rauh; holp[e]rig ⟨*Straße usw.*⟩; uneben ⟨*Gelände*⟩; unruhig ⟨*Überfahrt*⟩; **b)** *(violent)* grob ⟨*Person, Worte, Behandlung*⟩; **c)** *(trying)* hart; **this is** ~ **on him** das ist hart für ihn; **sth. is** ~ **going**

etw. ist nicht einfach; **d)** *(approximate)* grob ⟨*Skizze, Schätzung*⟩; vag ⟨*Vorstellung*⟩; ~ **paper/notebook** Konzeptpapier, *das*/Kladde, *die;* **e)** *(coll.: ill)* angeschlagen *(ugs.).* **2.** *n.* **[be] in** ~: [sich] im Rohzustand [befinden]. **3.** *adv.* rauh ⟨*spielen*⟩; **sleep** ~: im Freien schlafen. **4.** *v. t.* ~ **it** primitiv leben. **rough 'out** *v. t.* grob entwerfen. **rough 'up** *v. t. (sl.)* anrempeln *(ugs.)*

roughage ['rʌfɪdʒ] *n.* Ballaststoffe *Pl.*

rough: ~**-and-ready** *adj.* provisorisch; ~**-and-'tumble** *n.* [milde] Rauferei; ~ **copy,** ~ **draft** *ns.* grobe Skizze; grober Entwurf

roughen ['rʌfn] *v. t.* aufrauhen

'roughly *adv.* **a)** *(violently)* roh; grob; **b)** *(crudely)* leidlich; grob ⟨*skizzieren, bearbeiten, bauen*⟩; **c)** *(approximately)* ungefähr; grob ⟨*geschätzt*⟩

'roughness *n.* **a)** Rauheit, *die; (unevenness)* Unebenheit, *die;* **b)** *(violence)* Roheit, *die*

'roughshod *adj.* **ride** ~ **over sb./sth.** jmdn./etw. mit Füßen treten

roulette [ruː'let] *n.* Roulette, *das*

round [raʊnd] **1.** *adj.* rund; **in** ~ **figures** rund gerechnet. **2.** *n.* **a)** *(recurring series)* Serie, *die;* ~ **of talks/negotiations** Gesprächs-/Verhandlungsrunde, *die;* **the daily** ~: der Alltag; **b)** *(of ammunition)* Ladung, *die;* **50** ~s **[of ammunition]** 50 Schuß Munition; **c)** *(of game or contest)* Runde, *die;* **d)** *(burst)* ~ **of applause** Beifallssturm, *der;* **e)** ~ **[of drinks]** Runde, *die;* **f)** *(regular calls)* Runde, *die;* Tour, *die;* **go [on]** *or* **make one's** ~s seine Runden machen; **g) a** ~ **of toast/sandwiches** eine Scheibe Toast/eine Portion Sandwiches. **3.** *adv.* **a) all the year** ~: das ganze Jahr hindurch; **the third time** ~: beim dritten Mal; **have a look** ~: sich umsehen; **ask sb.** ~ **[for a drink]** jmdn. [zu einem Gläschen zu sich] einladen; **b)** *(by indirect way)* herum; **walk** ~: außen herum gehen; **c)** *(here)* hier; *(there)* dort; **I'll go** ~ **tomorrow** ich gehe morgen hin. **4.** *prep.* **a)** um [... herum]; **travel** ~ **England** durch England reisen; **run** ~ **the streets** durch die Straßen rennen; **walk** ~ **and** ~ **sth.** immer wieder um etw. herumgehen; **b)** *(in various directions from)* um [... herum]; rund um ⟨*einen Ort*⟩. **5.** *v. t.* ~ **a bend** eine Kurve fahren/gehen/kommen *usw.* **round 'off** *v. t.* abrunden. **round 'up** *v. t.* verhaften ⟨*Verdächtige*⟩; zusammentreiben ⟨*Vieh*⟩

round: ~ **a'bout** *adv. (on all sides)* ringsum; **~about** 1. *n.* **a)** *(Brit.: merry-go-round)* Karussell, *das;* **b)** *(Brit.: road junction)* Kreisverkehr, *der.* 2. *adj.* umständlich

rounders ['raʊndəz] *n. sing. (Brit.)* Rounders, *das*

round: ~ **'number** *n.* runde Zahl; **~-shouldered** [raʊnd'ʃəʊldəd] *adj.* 〈*Person*〉 mit einem Rundrücken; ~ 'trip *n.* Rundreise, *die*

rouse [raʊz] *v. t.* wecken (**from** aus)

rousing ['raʊzɪŋ] *adj.* mitreißend 〈*Lied*〉; leidenschaftlich 〈*Rede*〉

rout [raʊt] 1. *n.* [wilde] Flucht; *(defeat)* verheerende Niederlage. 2. *v. t.* aufreiben 〈*Feind, Truppen*〉; vernichtend schlagen 〈*Gegner*〉

route [ruːt] *n.* Route, *die;* Weg, *der*

routine [ruː'tiːn] 1. *n.* **a)** Routine, *die;* **b)** *(coll.: set speech)* Platte, *die (ugs.);* **c)** *(Theatre)* Nummer, *die; (Dancing, Skating)* Figur, *die.* 2. *adj.* routinemäßig; Routine〈*arbeit*〉

roux [ruː] *n.* Mehlschwitze, *die*

¹row [raʊ] 1. 〈*coll.*〉 *n.* **a)** *(noise)* Krach, *der;* **make a** ~: Krach machen; **b)** *(quarrel)* Krach, *der (ugs.);* **have/start a** ~: Krach haben/anfangen *(ugs.).* 2. *v. i* sich streiten

²row [rəʊ] *n.* Reihe, *die;* **in a** ~: in einer Reihe

³row [rəʊ] *v. i. & t. (with oars)* rudern

rowan ['rəʊən] *n.* ~[-tree] Eberesche, *die*

row-boat ['rəʊbəʊt] *n. (Amer.)* Ruderboot, *das*

rowdy ['raʊdɪ] 1. *adj.* rowdyhaft; **the party was** ~: auf der Party ging es laut zu. 2. *n.* Krawallmacher, *der*

rowing-boat ['rəʊɪŋbəʊt] *n. (Brit.)* Ruderboot, *das*

royal ['rɔɪəl] *adj.* königlich

royal: **R~** **'Air Force** *n. (Brit.)* Königliche Luftwaffe; ~ **'blue** *n. (Brit.)* Königsblau, *das;* ~ **'family** *n.* königliche Familie; **R~** **'Navy** *n. (Brit.)* Königliche Kriegsmarine

royalty ['rɔɪəltɪ] *n.* **a)** *(payment)* Tantieme, *die* (**on** für); **b)** *collect. (royal persons)* Mitglieder des Königshauses

RSPCA *abbr. (Brit.)* **Royal Society for the Prevention of Cruelty to Animals** britischer Tierschutzverein

rub [rʌb] 1. *v. t.,* **-bb-** reiben (**on, against** an + *Dat.*); *(to remove dirt etc.)* abreiben; *(to dry)* trockenreiben; ~ **sth. off sth.** etw. von etw. reiben. 2. *v. i.,* **-bb-** reiben (**[up]on, against** an +

Dat.). 3. *n.* **give it a** ~: reib es ab; **there's the** ~ *(fig.)* da liegt der Haken [dabei] *(ugs.).* **rub 'down** *v. t.* abreiben. **rub 'in** *v. t.* einreiben; **there's no need to** *or* **don't** ~ **it in** *(fig.)* reib es mir nicht [dauernd] unter die Nase. **rub 'off** *v. t.* wegreiben; wegwischen. **rub 'out** 1. *v. t.* ausreiben; *(using eraser)* ausradieren. 2. *v. i.* sich ausreiben/sich ausradieren lassen

rubber ['rʌbə(r)] *n.* **a)** Gummi, *das od. der;* **b)** *(eraser)* Radiergummi, *der*

rubber: ~ **'band** *n.* Gummiband, *das;* ~ **plant** *n.* Gummibaum, *der;* ~ **'stamp** *n.* Gummistempel, *der;* **~-stamp** *v. t. (fig.)* absegnen *(ugs.)*

rubbish ['rʌbɪʃ] 1. *n.* **a)** *(refuse)* Abfall, *der;* (*to be collected and dumped)* Müll, *der;* **b)** *(worthless material)* Plunder, *der (ugs.);* **be** ~: nichts taugen; **c)** *(nonsense)* Quatsch, *der (ugs.).* 2. *int.* Quatsch *(ugs.).* **'rubbish-bin** *n.* Abfall-/Mülleimer, *der.* **'rubbish dump** *n.* Müllkippe, *die*

rubble ['rʌbl] *n.* Trümmer *Pl.*

ruby ['ruːbɪ] *n.* Rubin, *der*

rucksack ['rʌksæk, 'rʊksæk] *n.* Rucksack, *der*

rudder ['rʌdə(r)] *n.* Ruder, *das*

ruddy ['rʌdɪ] *adj.* **a)** *(reddish)* rötlich; **b)** *(Brit. sl.: bloody)* verdammt *(salopp)*

rude [ruːd] *adj.* **a)** unhöflich; *(stronger)* rüde; **be** ~ **to sb.** zu jmdm. grob unhöflich sein/jmdn. rüde behandeln; **b)** *(abrupt)* unsanft; ~ **awakening** böses Erwachen. **'rudely** *adv.* **a)** *(impolitely)* unhöflich; rüde; **b)** *(abruptly)* jäh *(geh.).* **'rudeness** *n. (bad manners)* ungehöriges Benehmen

rudimentary [ruːdɪ'mentərɪ] elementar; primitiv 〈*Gebäude*〉

rudiments ['ruːdɪmənts] *n. pl.* Grundlagen *Pl.*

rueful ['ruːfl] *adj.* reumütig

ruffian ['rʌfɪən] *n.* Rohling, *der*

ruffle ['rʌfl] *v. t.* **a)** kräuseln; ~ **sb.'s hair** jmdm. durch die Haare fahren; **b)** *(upset)* aus der Fassung bringen

rug [rʌg] *n.* [kleiner, dicker] Teppich

Rugby ['rʌgbɪ] *n.* Rugby, *das*

rugged ['rʌgɪd] *adj.* **a)** *(uneven)* zerklüftet; unwegsam 〈*Land*〉; zerfurcht 〈*Gesicht*〉; **b)** *(sturdy)* robust

ruin ['ruːɪn] 1. *n.* **a)** *in sing. or pl. (remains)* Ruine, *die;* **in ~s** in Trümmern; **b)** *(downfall)* Ruin, *der.* 2. *v. t.* ruinieren; verderben 〈*Urlaub, Abend*〉; **~ed** *(reduced to ruins)* verfal-

len; **a ~ed castle/church** eine Burg-/
Kirchenruine. **ruinous** ['ru:ɪnəs] *adj.*
ruinös

rule [ru:l] **1.** *n.* **a)** Regel, *die;* **the ~s of
the game** die Spielregeln; **be against
the ~s** regelwidrig sein; *(fig.)* gegen
die Spielregeln verstoßen; **as a ~:** in
der Regel; **~ of thumb** Faustregel, *die;*
b) *no pl. (government)* Herrschaft, *die*
(over über + *Akk.*). **2.** *v. t.* **a)** *(control)*
beherrschen; **b)** *(be the ruler of)* regieren; ⟨*Monarch, Diktator usw.*:⟩ herrschen über (+ *Akk.*). **3.** *v. i.* **a)** *(govern)* herrschen; **b)** *(decide)* entscheiden (**against** gegen; **in favour of** für).
rule 'out *v. t.* ausschließen; *(prevent)*
unmöglich machen
ruled [ru:ld] *adj.* liniert ⟨*Papier*⟩
ruler ['ru:lə(r)] *n.* **a)** *(person)* Herrscher, *der*/Herrscherin, *die;* **b)** *(for
measuring)* Lineal, *das*
ruling ['ru:lɪŋ] **1.** *adj.* herrschend
⟨*Klasse*⟩; regierend ⟨*Partei*⟩. **2.** *n.* Entscheidung, *die*
rum [rʌm] *n.* Rum, *der*
Rumania *etc.* [ru:'meɪnɪə] *see* **Romania** *etc.*
rumble ['rʌmbl] **1.** *n.* Grollen, *das.* **2.**
v. i. **a)** grollen; ⟨*Magen:*⟩ knurren; **b)**
⟨*Fahrzeug:*⟩ rumpeln *(ugs.)*
ruminate ['ru:mɪneɪt] *v. i.* ~ **on** *or* **over**
sth. über etw. *(Akk.)* grübeln
rummage ['rʌmɪdʒ] *v. i.* wühlen; ~
through sth. etw. durchwühlen *(ugs.)*
rummy ['rʌmɪ] *n.* Rommé, *das*
rumour *(Brit.; Amer.:* **rumor)**
['ru:mə(r)] **1.** *n.* Gerücht, *das;* **there is
a ~ that ...:** es geht das Gerücht, daß ...
2. *v. t.* **it is ~ed that ...:** es geht das Gerücht, daß ...

rump [rʌmp] *n.* **a)** *(buttocks)* Hinterteil, *das (ugs.);* **b)** *(remnant)* Rest, *der*
rumple ['rʌmpl] *v. t.* **a)** *(crease)* zerknittern; **b)** *(tousle)* zerzausen
'rump steak *n.* Rumpsteak, *das*
rumpus ['rʌmpəs] *n. (coll.)* Krach, *der
(ugs.);* **kick up** *or* **make a ~:** einen
Spektakel veranstalten *(ugs.)*
run [rʌn] **1.** *n.* **a)** Lauf, *der;* **on the ~:**
auf der Flucht; **b)** *(trip in vehicle)*
Fahrt, *die; (for pleasure)* Ausflug, *der;*
c) *(continuous stretch)* Länge, *die;* **d)**
(spell) **she has had a long ~ of success**
sie war lange [Zeit] erfolgreich; **have a
long ~** ⟨*Stück, Show:*⟩ viele Auffüh-
rungen erleben; **e)** *(succession)* Serie,
die; (Cards) Sequenz, *die;* **a ~ of vic-
tories** eine Siegesserie; **f)** *(use)* **have
the ~ of sth.** etw. zu seiner freien Ver-

fügung haben; **g)** *(enclosure)* Auslauf,
der; **h)** *(in stocking etc.)* Laufmasche,
die. **2.** *v. i.,* **-nn-, ran** [ræn], **run a)** laufen; ~ **for the bus** laufen, um den Bus
zu kriegen *(ugs.);* ~ **to help sb.** jmdm.
zu Hilfe eilen; **b)** *(roll, slide)* laufen;
⟨*Ball, Kugel:*⟩ rollen, laufen; ⟨*Schlitten, [Schiebe]tür:*⟩ gleiten; **c)** ⟨*Rad,
Maschine:*⟩ laufen; **d)** *(operate on a
schedule)* fahren; ~ **between two places**
⟨*Zug, Bus:*⟩ zwischen zwei Orten verkehren; **e)** *(flow)* laufen; ⟨*Fluß:*⟩ fließen; ⟨*Augen:*⟩ tränen; **his nose was
~ning** ihm lief die Nase; **f)** ⟨*Vertrag,
Theaterstück:*⟩ laufen; **g)** *(have wording)* lauten; ⟨*Geschichte:*⟩ gehen *(fig.);*
h) ⟨*Butter, Eis:*⟩ zerlaufen; ⟨*Farben:*⟩
auslaufen; **i)** *(in election)* kandidieren.
3. *v. t.,* **-nn-, ran, run a)** laufen lassen;
(drive) fahren; ~ **one's hand/fingers
through/along** *or* **over sth.** mit der
Hand/den Fingern durch etw. fahren/
über etw. *(Akk.)* streichen; ~ **an** *or*
one's eye along *or* **down** *or* **over sth.**
(fig.) etw. überfliegen; **b)** *(cause to
flow)* [ein]laufen lassen; ~ **a bath** ein
Bad einlaufen lassen; **c)** *(organize,
manage)* führen, leiten ⟨*Geschäft
usw.*⟩; veranstalten ⟨*Wettbewerb*⟩; **d)**
(operate) bedienen ⟨*Maschine*⟩; verkehren lassen ⟨*Verkehrsmittel*⟩; einsetzen ⟨*Sonderbus, -zug*⟩; laufen lassen ⟨*Motor*⟩; **e)** *(own and use)* sich
⟨*Dat.*⟩ halten ⟨*Auto*⟩; **f)** ~ **sb. into town**
etc. jmdn. in die Stadt *usw.* fahren.
run a'cross *v. t.* ~ **across sb./sth.**
jmdn. treffen/auf etw. *(Akk.)* stoßen.
run a'way *v. i.* **a)** *(flee)* weglaufen;
fortlaufen; **b)** *(abscond)* ~ **away [from
home]** [von zu Hause] weglaufen. **run
'down 1.** *v. t.* **a)** *(collide with)* überfahren; **b)** *(criticize)* heruntermachen
(ugs.); **c)** *(reduce)* abbauen. **2.** *v. i.* **a)**
hin-/herunterlaufen; **b)** *(decline)* sich
verringern; **c)** ⟨*Uhr, Spielzeug:*⟩ ablaufen; ⟨*Batterie*⟩ leer werden. **'run into**
v. t. **a)** ~ **into a tree** gegen einen Baum
fahren; **b)** *(meet)* ~ **into sb.** jmdm. in
die Arme laufen *(ugs.);* **c)** stoßen auf
(+ *Akk.*) ⟨*Schwierigkeiten, Widerstand
usw.*:⟩; **d)** *(amount to)* ~ **into thousands**
in die Tausende gehen. **run 'off 1.** *v. i.*
weglaufen. **2.** *v. t.* abziehen ⟨*Kopien*⟩.
run 'out *v. i.* **a)** hin-/herauslaufen; **b)**
⟨*Vorräte, Bestände:*⟩ zu Ende gehen.
run 'out of *v. t.* **sb. ~s out of sth.**
jmdm. geht etw. aus; **I'm ~ning out of
patience** meine Geduld geht zu Ende.
run 'over 1. ['---] *v. t. (knock down)*

überfahren. **2.** [-'--] *v.i.* überlaufen. 'run **through** *v.t.* durchspielen ⟨*Theaterstück*⟩. 'run **to** *v.t.* **a)** *(amount to)* sich belaufen auf ⟨*Akk.*⟩; **b)** *(be sufficient for)* **sth. will ~ to sth.** etw. reicht für etw. **run 'up 1.** *v.i.* hinlaufen; **come ~ning up** hingelaufen kommen. **2.** *v.t.* **a)** rasch nähen ⟨*Kleidungsstück*⟩; **b)** zusammenkommen lassen ⟨*Schulden, Rechnung*⟩. **run 'up against** *v.t.* stoßen auf (+ *Akk.*) ⟨*Probleme, Widerstand usw.*⟩

run: **~away 1.** *n.* Ausreißer, *der*/Ausreißerin, *die* (*ugs.*); **2.** *attrib. adj.* durchgegangen ⟨*Pferd*⟩; außer Kontrolle geraten ⟨*Fahrzeug, Preise*⟩; galoppierend ⟨*Inflation*⟩; **~-down 1.** ['--] *n.* *(coll.: briefing)* Übersicht, *die* (on über + *Akk.*); **2.** [-'-] *adj.* *(tired)* mitgenommen

¹rung [rʌŋ] *n.* Sprosse, *die*
²rung see **²ring** 2, 3

'runner *n.* **a)** Läufer, *der*/Läuferin, *die;* **b)** *(Bot.)* Ausläufer, *der;* **c)** *(on sledge)* Kufe, *die.* 'runner **bean** *n.* *(Brit.)* Stangenbohne, *die.* **runner-'up** *n.* Zweite, *der/die;* **the runners-up** die Plazierten

'running **1.** *n.* **a)** *(management)* Leitung, *die;* **b)** *(action)* Laufen, *das;* **in/ out of the ~:** im/aus dem Rennen. **2.** *adj. (in succession)* hintereinander; **win for the third year ~:** schon drei Jahre hintereinander gewinnen. **running 'commentary** *n.* *(Broadcasting; also fig.)* Live-Kommentar, *der*
runny ['rʌnɪ] *adj.* **a)** laufend ⟨*Nase*⟩; **b)** zu dünn ⟨*Farbe, Marmelade*⟩
run: -of-the-'mill *adj.* ganz gewöhnlich; **~-up** *n.* **a) during** *or* **in the ~-up to an event** im Vorfeld eines Ereignisses; **b)** *(Sport)* Anlauf, *der;* **~way** *n.* *(for take-off)* Startbahn, *die; (for landing)* Landebahn, *die*
rupture ['rʌptʃə(r)] **1.** *n.* Bruch, *der.* **2.** *v.t.* **~ oneself** sich *(Dat.)* einen Bruch zuziehen
rural ['rʊərl] *adj.* ländlich
ruse [ruːz] *n.* List, *die*
¹rush [rʌʃ] *n.* *(Bot.)* Binse, *die*
²rush 1. *n.* **a)** *(hurry)* Eile, *die;* **what's all the ~?** wozu diese Hast?; **be in a [great] ~:** in [großer] Eile sein; **b)** *(period of great activity)* Hochbetrieb, *der; (~-hour)* Stoßzeit, *die;* **c) make a ~ for sth.** sich auf etw. *(Akk.)* stürzen. **2.** *v.t.* **a) ~ sb./sth. somewhere** jmdn./ etw. auf schnellstem Wege irgendwohin bringen; **be ~ed** *(have to hurry)* in

Eile sein; **~ sb. into doing sth.** jmdn. dazu drängen, etw. zu tun; **b)** *(perform quickly)* auf die Schnelle erledigen; **~ it zu schnell machen. 3.** *v.i.* **a)** *(move quickly)* eilen; ⟨*Hund, Pferd:*⟩ laufen; **~ to help sb.** jmdm. zu Hilfe eilen; **b)** *(hurry unduly)* sich zu sehr beeilen; **don't ~!** nur keine Eile! **rush a'bout, rush a'round** *v.i.* herumhetzen
rush-hour *n.* Stoßzeit, *die*
rusk [rʌsk] *n.* Zwieback, *der*
Russia ['rʌʃə] *pr. n.* Rußland *(das).*
Russian ['rʌʃn] **1.** *adj.* russisch; **sb. is ~:** jmd. ist Russe/Russin. **2.** *n.* **a)** *(person)* Russe, *der/*Russin, *die;* **b)** *(language)* Russisch, *das; see also* **English 2 a**
rust [rʌst] **1.** *n.* Rost, *der.* **2.** *v.i.* rosten
rustic ['rʌstɪk] *adj.* **a)** ländlich; **b)** rustikal ⟨*Mobiliar*⟩
rustle ['rʌsl] **1.** *n.* Rascheln, *das.* **2.** *v.i.* rascheln. **3.** *v.t.* **a)** rascheln lassen; **b)** *(Amer.: steal)* stehlen. **rustle 'up** *v.t.* zusammenzaubern ⟨*Mahlzeit*⟩
rust-proof *adj.* rostfrei
rusty *adj.* rostig
rut [rʌt] *n.* Spurrille, *die;* **be in a ~** *(fig.)* aus dem [Alltags]trott nicht mehr herauskommen
ruthless ['ruːθlɪs] *adj.* rücksichtslos
rye [raɪ] *n.* Roggen, *der*

S

S, s [es] *n.* S, s, *das*
S. *abbr.* **a)** south S; **b)** southern s.
sabbath ['sæbəθ] *n.* Sabbath, *der*
sabbatical [səˈbætɪkl] **1.** *adj.* **~ term/ year** Forschungssemester/-jahr, *das.* **2.** *n.* Forschungsurlaub, *der*
sabotage ['sæbətɑːʒ] **1.** *n.* Sabotage, *die.* **2.** *v.t.* einen Sabotageakt verüben auf (+ *Akk.*); *(fig.)* sabotieren
saccharin ['sækərɪn] *n.* Saccharin, *das*
sachet ['sæʃeɪ] *n.* Beutel, *der; (cushion-shaped)* Kissen, *das*
sack [sæk] **1.** *n.* **a)** Sack, *der;* **b)** *(coll.: dismissal)* Rausschmiß, *der (ugs.);* **get the ~:** rausgeschmissen werden *(ugs.);* **give sb. the ~:** jmdn. raus-

schmeißen *(ugs.).* **2.** *v. t. (coll.)* rausschmeißen *(ugs.)* **(for** wegen)
sacrament ['sækrəmənt] *n.* Sakrament, *das*
sacred ['seıkrıd] *adj.* heilig
sacrifice ['sækrıfaıs] **1.** *n.* Opfer, *das.*
2. *v. t.* opfern
sacrilege [sækrılıdʒ] *n.* |**act of**| ~ : Sa-
krileg, *das*
sad [sæd] *adj.* traurig **(at, about** über
+ *Akk.);* schmerzlich ⟨*Tod, Verlust⟩;*
feel ~ : traurig sein. **sadden** ['sædn]
v. t. traurig stimmen
saddle ['sædl] **1.** *n.* Sattel, *der.* **2.** *v. t.*
a) satteln ⟨*Pferd usw.⟩;* **b)** *(fig.)* ~ **sb.**
with sth. jmdm. etw. aufbürden *(geh.).*
'**saddle-bag** *n.* Satteltasche, *die*
sadism ['seıdızm] *n.* Sadismus, *der.*
sadist ['seıdıst] *n.* Sadist, *der/*Sadistin, *die.* **sadistic** [sə'dıstık] *adj.,* **sa-**
'**distically** *adv.* sadistisch
'**sadly** *adv.* **a)** *(with sorrow)* traurig; **b)**
(unfortunately) leider
'**sadness** *n.* Traurigkeit, *die*
safari [sə'fɑ:rı] *n.* Safari, *die;* **on** ~ : auf
Safari
safe [seıf] **1.** *n.* Safe, *der;* Geld-
schrank, *der.* **2.** *adj.* **a)** *(out of danger)*
sicher **(from** vor + *Dat.);* **he's** ~ : er ist
in Sicherheit; ~ **and sound** sicher und
wohlbehalten; **b)** *(free from danger)*
ungefährlich; sicher ⟨*Ort, Hafen⟩;*
wish sb. a ~ **journey** jmdm. eine gute
Reise wünschen; **to be on the** ~ **side**
zur Sicherheit; **c)** *(reliable)* sicher
⟨*Methode, Investition⟩.* '**safeguard 1.**
n. Schutz, *der.* **2.** *v. t.* schützen.
'**safely** *adv.* sicher; **did the parcel ar-**
rive ~ **?** ist das Paket heil angekom-
men? **safety** ['seıftı] *n.* Sicherheit, *die*
safety: ~-**belt** *n.* Sicherheitsgurt,
der; ~**helmet** *n.* Schutzhelm, *der;* ~
margin *n.* Spielraum, *der;* ~-**pin** *n.*
Sicherheitsnadel, *die;* ~-**valve** *n.* Si-
cherheitsventil, *das; (fig.)* Ventil, *das*
sag [sæg] *v. i.,* -**gg**- durchhängen;
(sink) sich senken
saga ['sɑ:gə] *n.* **a)** *(story of adventure)*
Heldenepos, *das; (medieval narrative)*
Saga, *die;* **b)** *(coll.: long involved story)*
[ganzer] Roman *(fig.)*
¹**sage** [seıdʒ] *n. (Bot.)* Salbei, *der od.*
die
²**sage 1.** *adj.* weis. **2.** *n.* Weise, *der*
Sagittarius [sædʒı'teərıəs] *n.* der
Schütze
Sahara [sə'hɑ:rə] *pr. n.* **the** ~ |**Desert**|
die [Wüste] Sahara
said *see* **say** 1

sail [seıl] **1.** *n.* **a)** Segelfahrt, *die;* **b)**
(piece of canvas) Segel, *das.* **2.** *v. i.* **a)**
(travel on water) fahren; *(in sailing*
boat) segeln; **b)** *(start voyage)* auslaufen **(for** nach). **3.** *v. t.* **a)** steuern ⟨*Boot,*
Schiff⟩; segeln mit ⟨*Segeljacht,*
-*schiff⟩;* **b)** durchfahren/⟨*Segelschiff:⟩*
durchsegeln ⟨*Meer⟩*
sail: ~**board** *n.* Surfbrett, *das (zum*
Windsurfen); ~-**boarding** *n.* Windsurfen, *das;* ~**boat** *n. (Amer.)* Segelboot, *das*
'**sailing** *n.* Segeln, *das.* '**sailing boat**
n. Segelboot, *das.* '**sailing ship** *n.*
Segelschiff, *das*
sailor ['seılə(r)] *n.* Seemann, *der; (in*
navy) Matrose, *der*
saint 1. [sənt] *adj.* **S**~ **Michael** der heilige Michael; Sankt Michael. **2.** [seınt]
n. Heilige, *der/die.* '**saintly** ['seıntlı]
adj. heilig
sake [seık] *n.* **for the** ~ **of** um ... *(Gen.)*
willen; **for my** *etc.* ~ : um meinetwil-
len *usw.;* mir *usw.* zuliebe
salad ['sæləd] *n.* Salat, *der.* '**salad**
cream *n.* ≈ Mayonnaise, *die.* '**salad**
dressing *n.* Salatsoße, *die*
salary ['sælərı] *n.* Gehalt, *das*
sale [seıl] *n.* **a)** Verkauf, *der; (at re-*
duced prices) Ausverkauf, *der;* |up| **for**
~ : zu verkaufen; **b)** ~**s** *(amount sold)*
Verkaufszahlen *Pl.* **(of** für); Absatz,
der; **c)** |**jumble** *or* **rummage**| ~ : [Wohl-
tätigkeits]basar, *der*
salesman ['seılzmən] *n., pl.* ~**men**
['seılzmən] Verkäufer, *der.* '**sales-**
manship *n.* Kunst des Verkaufens
'**saleswoman** *n.* Verkäuferin, *die*
salient ['seılıənt] *adj.* auffallend
saliva [sə'laıvə] *n.* Speichel, *der*
sallow ['sæləʊ] *adj.* blaßgelb
salmon ['sæmən] *n.* Lachs, *der*
saloon [sə'lu:n] *n.* **a)** *(Brit.)* ~ |**bar**| *se-*
parater Teil eines Pubs mit mehr Kom-
fort; **b)** *(Brit.)* ~ |**car**| Limousine, *die*
salt [sɔ:lt, sɒlt] **1.** *n.* |**common**| ~ :
[Koch]salz, *das.* **2.** *adj. (containing or*
tasting of ~) salzig; *(preserved with* ~)
gepökelt ⟨*Fleisch⟩;* gesalzen ⟨*Butter⟩.*
3. *v. t.* **a)** salzen; **b)** *(cure)* [ein]pökeln;
c) ~ **the roads** Salz auf die Straßen
streuen. '**salt-cellar** *n.* Salzstreuer,
der. **salt 'water** *n.* Salzwasser, *das*
'**salty** *adj.* salzig
salute [sə'lu:t] **1.** *v. t.* grüßen. **2.** *v. i.*
(Mil., Navy) [militärisch] grüßen. **3.** *n.*
Salut, *der;* militärischer Gruß
salvage ['sælvıdʒ] **1.** *n.* Bergung, *die.*
2. *v. t.* bergen

salvation [sæl'veɪʃn] n. Erlösung, die.
Salvation 'Army n. Heilsarmee, die
salvo ['sælvəʊ] n. Salve, die
Samaritan [sə'mærɪtən] n. **good** ~:
[barmherziger] Samariter; **the ~s** (organization) ≈ die Telefonseelsorge
same [seɪm] **1.** adj. **the** ~: der/die/das
gleiche; **the** ~ |**thing|** (identical) der-/
die-/dasselbe. **2.** adv. **all** or **just the** ~:
trotzdem
sample ['sɑːmpl] **1.** n. (example) [Muster]beispiel, das; (specimen) Probe,
die; |**commercial|** ~: Muster, das. **2.**
v. t. probieren
sanctify ['sæŋktɪfaɪ] v. t. heiligen
sanctimonious [sæŋktɪ'məʊnɪəs] adj.
scheinheilig
sanction ['sæŋkʃn] **1.** n. Sanktion,
die. **2.** v. t. sanktionieren
sanctity ['sæŋktɪtɪ] n. Heiligkeit, die
sanctuary ['sæŋktʃʊərɪ] n. **a)** (holy
place) Heiligtum, das; **b)** (refuge) Zufluchtsort, der; **c)** (for animals) Naturschutzgebiet, das
sand [sænd] **1.** n. Sand, der. **2.** v. t. ~
sth. |**down|** etw. [ab]schmirgeln
sandal ['sændl] n. Sandale, die
sand: ~**bag 1.** n. Sandsack, der; **2.**
v. t. mit Sandsäcken schützen;
~**bank** n. Sandbank, die; ~**castle**
n. Sandburg, die; ~**paper 1.** n. Sandpapier, das; **2.** v. t. [mit Sandpapier]
[ab]schmirgeln; ~**pit** n. Sandkasten,
der; ~**stone** n. Sandstein, der
sandwich ['sænwɪdʒ] **1.** n. Sandwich,
der od. das; ≈ [zusammengeklapptes]
belegtes Brot; **cheese** ~: Käsebrot,
das. **2.** v. t. einschieben (between zwischen + Akk.; into in + Akk.)
'**sandy** adj. **a)** sandig; Sand(boden,
-strand); **b)** rotblond (Haar)
sane [seɪn] adj. **a)** geistig gesund; **b)**
(sensible) vernünftig
sang see sing
sanitary ['sænɪtərɪ] adj. sanitär (Verhältnisse, Anlagen). '**sanitary napkin** (Amer.), '**sanitary towel** (Brit.)
ns. Damenbinde, die
sanitation [sænɪ'teɪʃn] n. Kanalisation und Abfallbeseitigung
sanity ['sænɪtɪ] n. geistige Gesundheit; **lose one's** ~: den Verstand verlieren
sank see sink 2, 3
Santa Claus ['sæntə klɔːz] n. der
Weihnachtsmann
sap [sæp] **1.** n. Saft, der. **2.** v. t., -**pp**-
zehren an (+ Dat.)
sapling ['sæplɪŋ] n. junger Baum

sarcasm ['sɑːkæzm] n. Sarkasmus,
der. **sarcastic** [sɑ'kæstɪk] adj. sarkastisch
sardine [sɑː'diːn] n. Sardine, die
Sardinia [sɑː'dɪnɪə] pr. n. Sardinien
(das)
sardonic [sɑː'dɒnɪk] adj. höhnisch;
sardonisch (Lächeln)
sash [sæʃ] n. Schärpe, die
sat see sit
Sat. abbr. **Saturday** Sa.
Satan ['seɪtən] pr. n. Satan, der. **satanic** [sə'tænɪk] adj. satanisch
satchel ['sætʃl] n. [Schul]ranzen, der
satellite ['sætəlaɪt] n. Satellit, der
satellite: ~ '**broadcasting** n. Satellitenfunk, der; ~-**dish** n. Satellitenschüssel, die; ~ '**television** n. Satellitenfernsehen, das
satin ['sætɪn] n. Satin, der
satire ['sætaɪə(r)] n. Satire, die (on auf
+ Akk.). **satirical** [sə'tɪrɪkl] adj. satirisch
satisfaction [sætɪs'fækʃn] n. Befriedigung, die (at, with über + Akk.);
meet with sb.'s |complete| ~: jmdn. [in
jeder Weise] zufriedenstellen
satisfactory [sætɪs'fæktərɪ] adj. zufriedenstellend
satisfy ['sætɪsfaɪ] v. t. **a)** befriedigen;
zufriedenstellen (Kunden); stillen
(Hunger, Durst); **b)** (convince) ~ **sb.**
|**of sth.|** jmdn. [von etw.] überzeugen.
'**satisfying** adj. befriedigend; sättigend (Gericht, Speise)
saturate ['sætʃəreɪt] v. t. durchnässen;
[mit Feuchtigkeit durch]tränken
(Boden, Erde). **saturated** ['sætʃəreɪtɪd] adj. durchnäßt. **saturation** [sætʃə'reɪʃn] n. Durchnässung, die
Saturday ['sætədeɪ, 'sætədɪ] n. Sonnabend, der; Samstag, der; see also **Friday**
Saturn ['sætən] pr. n. (Astron.) Saturn,
der
sauce [sɔːs] n. **a)** Soße, die; **b)** (impudence) Frechheit, die. **saucepan**
['sɔːspən] n. Kochtopf, der; (with
straight handle) Kasserolle, die
saucer ['sɔːsə(r)] n. Untertasse, die
saucy ['sɔːsɪ] adj. **a)** (rude) frech; **b)**
(pert, jaunty) keck
Saudi Arabia [saʊdɪ ə'reɪbɪə] pr. n.
Saudi-Arabien (das)
sauna ['sɔːnə, 'saʊnə] n. Sauna, die
saunter ['sɔːntə(r)] v. i. schlendern
sausage ['sɒsɪdʒ] n. Wurst, die. **sausage 'roll** n. Blätterteig mit Wurstfüllung

savage ['sævɪdʒ] 1. *adj.* a) *(uncivilized)* primitiv; wild ‹*Volksstamm*›; unzivilisiert ‹*Land*›; b) *(fierce)* brutal; wild ‹*Tier*›. 2. *n.* Wilde, *der/die (veralt.)*.
savagery ['sævɪdʒrɪ] *n.* Brutalität, *die*
save [seɪv] 1. *v.t.* a) *(rescue)* retten (**from** vor + *Dat.*); ~ **oneself from falling** sich [beim Hinfallen] fangen; b) *(put aside)* aufheben; sparen ‹*Geld*›; sammeln ‹*Briefmarken usw.*›; *(conserve)* sparsam umgehen mit; c) *(make unnecessary)* sparen ‹*Geld, Zeit, Energie*›; ~ **sb./oneself sth.** jmdm./sich etw. ersparen; d) *(Sport)* abwehren ‹*Schuß, Ball*›. 2. *v.i.* sparen (**on** *Akk.*). 3. *n. (Sport)* Abwehr, *die*.
save up 1. *v.t.* sparen. 2. *v.i.* sparen (**for** für, auf + *Akk.*)
'saver *n.* Sparer, *der*/Sparerin, *die*
saving ['seɪvɪŋ] 1. *n. in pl.* Ersparnisse *Pl.* 2. *adj.* ‹*kosten-, benzin*›sparend
savings: ~ **account** *n.* Sparkonto, *das;* ~ **bank** *n.* Sparkasse, *die*
saviour ['seɪvjə(r)] *n.* a) Retter, *der*/Retterin, *die;* b) *(Relig.)* **the S~:** der Heiland
savor *etc. (Amer.) see* **savour** *etc.*
savour ['seɪvə(r)] *(Brit.)* 1. *n. (flavour)* Geschmack, *der.* 2. *v.t.* genießen
savoury ['seɪvərɪ] *(Brit.)* 1. *adj.* a) pikant; salzig; b) *(appetizing)* appetitanregend. 2. *n.* [pikantes] Häppchen
'saw [sɔː] 1. *n.* Säge, *die.* 2. *v.t., p.p.* **sawn** [sɔːn] *or* **sawed** [zɛr]sägen; ~ **in half** in der Mitte durchsägen. 3. *v.i., p.p.* **sawn** *or* **sawed** sägen; ~ **through sth.** etw. durchsägen
²saw *see* **see**
'sawdust *n.* Sägemehl, *das*
sawn *see* **'saw** 2, 3
saxophone ['sæksəfəʊn] *n.* Saxophon, *das*
say [seɪ] 1. *v.t. pres. t.* **he says** [sez], *p.t. & p.p.* **said** [sed] a) sagen; **that is to ~:** das heißt; **do as** *or* **what I ~:** tun Sie, was ich sage; **when all is said and done** letzten Endes; **go without ~ing** sich von selbst verstehen; **she is said to be clever/to have done it** man sagt, sie sei klug/habe es getan; b) *(recite)* sprechen ‹*Gebet, Text*›; c) *(have specified wording or reading)* sagen; ‹*Zeitung:*› schreiben; ‹*Uhr:*› zeigen ‹*Uhrzeit*›; **what does it ~ here?** was steht hier? 2. *n.* **have a** *or* **some ~:** ein Mitspracherecht haben (**in** bei); **have one's ~:** nichts zu sagen haben; **have one's ~:** seine Meinung sagen. **'saying** *n.* Redensart, *die*

scab [skæb] *n.* [Wund]schorf, *der*
scaffold ['skæfəld] *n.* Schafott, *das*
'scaffolding *n.* Gerüst, *das*
scald [skɔːld, skɒld] 1. *n.* Verbrühung, *die.* 2. *v.t.* verbrühen
'scale [skeɪl] *n.* a) *(of fish, reptile, etc.)* Schuppe, *die;* b) *(in kettle etc.)* Kesselstein, *der; (on teeth)* Zahnstein, *der*
²scale *n.* a) *in sing. or pl. (weighing-instrument)* ~[s] Waage, *die;* b) *(dish of balance)* Waagschale, *die*
³scale 1. *n.* a) *(series of degrees)* Skala, *die;* b) *(Mus.)* Tonleiter, *die;* c) *(dimensions)* Ausmaß, *das;* **be on a small ~:** bescheidenen Umfang haben; d) *(ratio of reduction)* Maßstab, *der;* **what is the ~ of the map?** welchen Maßstab hat diese Karte?; e) *(indication) (on map)* Maßstab, *der; (on thermometer)* [Anzeige]skala, *die.* 2. *v.t.* ersteigen ‹*Mauer, Leiter, Gipfel*›.
scale down *v.t.* [entsprechend] drosseln ‹*Produktion*›; Abstriche machen bei ‹*Planungen*›
scalp [skælp] *n.* Kopfhaut, *die*
scalpel ['skælpl] *n.* Skalpell, *das*
scam [skæm] *n. (Amer. sl.)* Masche, *die (ugs.)*
scamper ['skæmpə(r)] *v.i.* ‹*Person:*› flitzen; ‹*Tier:*› huschen
scampi ['skæmpɪ] *n. pl.* Scampi *Pl.*
scan [skæn] 1. *v.t., -nn-:* a) *(search thoroughly)* absuchen (**for** nach); b) *(look over cursorily)* flüchtig ansehen; überfliegen ‹*Zeitung, Liste usw.*› (**for** auf der Suche nach); c) *(Med.)* szintigraphisch untersuchen. 2. *v.i., -nn-* ‹*Vers[zeile]:*› das richtige Versmaß haben. 3. *n. (Med.)* szintigraphische Untersuchung, *die*
scandal ['skændl] *n.* a) Skandal, *der* (**about/of** um); *(story)* Skandalgeschichte, *die;* b) *(outrage)* Empörung, *die;* c) *(gossip)* Klatsch, *der (ugs.).*
scandalize ['skændəlaɪz] *v.t.* schockieren. **scandalous** ['skændələs] *adj.* skandalös; schockierend ‹*Bemerkung*›
Scandinavia [skændɪ'neɪvɪə] *pr. n.* Skandinavien *(das)*
scant [skænt] *adj.* wenig. **scanty** ['skæntɪ] *adj.* spärlich; knapp ‹*Bikini*›
scapegoat ['skeɪpgəʊt] *n.* Sündenbock, *der;* **make sb. a ~:** jmdn. zum Sündenbock machen
scar [skɑː(r)] 1. *n.* Narbe, *die.* 2. *v.t., -rr-:* ~ **sb./sb.'s face** bei jmdm./in jmds. Gesicht *(Dat.)* Narben hinterlassen

scarce [skeəs] adj. a) (insufficient) knapp; b) (rare) selten; **make oneself ~** (coll.) sich aus dem Staub machen (ugs.). 'scarcely adv. kaum. **scarcity** ['skeəsɪtɪ] n. Knappheit, die (of an + Dat.)

scare [skeə(r)] 1. n. a) (sensation of fear) Schreck[en], der; **give sb. a ~**: jmdm. einen Schreck[en] einjagen; b) (general alarm) [allgemeine] Hysterie; **bomb ~**: Bombendrohung, die. 2. v. t. (frighten) Angst machen (+ Dat.); (startle) erschrecken. **scare a'way, scare 'off** v. t. verscheuchen

'**scarecrow** n. Vogelscheuche, die

scared [skeəd] adj. **be ~ of sb./sth.** vor jmdm./etw. Angst haben; **be ~ of doing/to do sth.** sich nicht [ge]trauen, etw. zu tun

scarf [skɑːf] n., pl. ~s or **scarves** [skɑːvz] Schal, der; (square) Halstuch, das; (worn over hair) Kopftuch, das

scarlet ['skɑːlɪt] 1. n. Scharlach, der. 2. adj. scharlachrot. **scarlet 'fever** n. Scharlach, der

scarves see scarf

scary ['skeərɪ] adj. furchterregend ⟨Anblick⟩; schaurig ⟨Film, Geschichte⟩

scatter ['skætə(r)] 1. v. t. a) vertreiben; auseinandertreiben ⟨Menge⟩; b) (distribute irregularly) verstreuen. 2. v. i. sich auflösen; ⟨Menge:⟩ sich zerstreuen; (in fear) auseinanderstieben. **scattered** ['skætəd] adj. verstreut; vereinzelt ⟨Regenschauer⟩

scavenge ['skævɪndʒ] v. i. **~ for sth.** nach etw. suchen. '**scavenger** n. (animal) Aasfresser, der; (fig. derog.: person) Aasgeier, der (ugs.)

scene [siːn] n. a) (place of event) Schauplatz, der; **~ of the crime** Tatort, der; b) (division of act) Auftritt, der; c) (view) Anblick, der; d) **behind the ~s** hinter den Kulissen. **scenery** ['siːnərɪ] n. a) Landschaft, die; b) (Theatre) Bühnenbild, das. **scenic** ['siːnɪk] adj. landschaftlich schön

scent [sent] 1. n. a) (smell) Duft, der; b) (Hunting; also fig.: trail) Fährte, die; **be on the ~ of sb./sth.** (fig.) jmdm./einer Sache auf der Spur sein; c) (Brit.: perfume) Parfüm, das. 2. v. t. wittern

sceptic ['skeptɪk] n. Skeptiker, der/Skeptikerin, die. **sceptical** ['skeptɪkl] adj. skeptisch; **be ~ about** or **of sb./sth.** jmdm./einer Sache skeptisch gegenüberstehen. **scepticism** ['skeptɪsɪzm] n. Skepsis, die

schedule ['ʃedjuːl] 1. n. a) (list) Tabelle, die; (for event) Programm, das; b) (of work) Zeitplan, der; c) **on ~**: plangemäß. 2. v. t. zeitlich planen. '**scheduled flight** n. Linienflug, der

scheme [skiːm] n. a) (arrangement) Anordnung, die; b) (plan) Programm, das; (project) Projekt, das; c) (dishonest plan) Intrige, die

schizophrenia [skɪtsə'friːnɪə] n. Schizophrenie, die. **schizophrenic** [skɪtsə'frenɪk, skɪtsə'friːnɪk] adj. schizophren

scholar ['skɒlə(r)] n. Gelehrte, der/die. '**scholarly** adj. wissenschaftlich; gelehrt ⟨Person⟩. '**scholarship** n. a) (award) Stipendium, das; b) (scholarly work) Gelehrsamkeit, die

school [skuːl] n. Schule, die; (Amer.: college) Hochschule, die; **be at** or **in ~**: in der Schule sein; (attend ~) zur Schule gehen; **go to ~**: zur Schule gehen; **~ holidays/exchange** Schulferien Pl./Schüleraustausch, der

school: ~boy n. Schüler, der; **~girl** n. Schülerin, die; **~master** n. Lehrer, der; **~mistress** n. Lehrerin, die; **~teacher** n. Lehrer, der/Lehrerin, die

sciatica [saɪ'ætɪkə] n. Ischias, die

science ['saɪəns] n. Wissenschaft, die. **science 'fiction** n. Science-fiction, die. **scientific** [saɪən'tɪfɪk] adj. wissenschaftlich. **scientist** ['saɪəntɪst] n. Wissenschaftler, der/Wissenschaftlerin, die

scintillating ['sɪntɪleɪtɪŋ] adj. (fig.) geistsprühend

scissors ['sɪzəz] n. pl. [pair of] **~**: Schere, die

¹**scoff** [skɒf] v. i. (mock) spotten; **~ at** sich lustig machen über (+ Akk.)

²**scoff** v. t. (sl.: eat greedily) verschlingen

scold [skəʊld] v. t. ausschimpfen (for wegen); **she ~ed him for being late** sie schimpfte ihn aus, weil er zu spät kam

scone [skɒn, skəʊn] n. weicher, oft zum Tee gegessener kleiner Kuchen

scoop [skuːp] 1. n. a) Schaufel, die; (for ice-cream etc.) Portionierer, der; b) (Journ.) Knüller, der (ugs.). 2. v. t. schaufeln ⟨Kohlen, Zucker⟩; schöpfen ⟨Flüssigkeit⟩. **scoop 'out** v. t. a) (hollow out) aushöhlen; schaufeln ⟨Loch, Graben⟩; b) [her]ausschöpfen ⟨Flüssigkeit⟩; auslöffeln ⟨Fruchtfleisch⟩; (with a knife) herausschneiden ⟨Gehäuse, Fruchtfleisch⟩. **scoop 'up** v. t.

schöpfen ⟨*Flüssigkeit, Suppe*⟩; schaufeln ⟨*Erde*⟩

scooter ['sku:tə(r)] *n.* **a)** *(toy)* Roller, *der;* **b)** |motor| ~: [Motor]roller, *der*

scope [skəʊp] *n.* **a)** Bereich, *der; (of discussion etc.)* Rahmen, *der;* **b)** *(opportunity)* Entfaltungsmöglichkeiten *Pl.*

scorch [skɔ:tʃ] *v.t.* versengen. 'scorching *adj.* glühend heiß

score [skɔ:(r)] **1.** *n.* **a)** *(points)* [Spiel]stand, *der; (made by one player)* Punktzahl, *die;* keep |the| ~: zählen; **b)** *(Mus.)* Partitur, *die; (Cinemat.)* [Film]musik, *die;* **c)** *pl. same or* ~s *(group of 20)* zwanzig; **d)** *in pl. (great numbers)* ~s |and ~s| of zig *(ugs.);* Dutzende [von]; **e) on that** ~: was das betrifft; **f) pay off** *or* **settle an old** ~ *(fig.)* eine alte Rechnung begleichen. **2.** *v.t.* erzielen ⟨*Erfolg, Punkt usw.*⟩; ~ **a goal** ein Tor schießen. **3.** *v.i.* **a)** *(make* ~*)* Punkte/einen Punkt erzielen; *(*~ *goal/goals)* ein Tor/Tore schießen/werfen; **b)** *(keep* ~*)* aufschreiben. 'score-board *n.* Anzeigetafel, *die.* 'scorer *n.* **a)** *(recorder)* Anschreiber, *der*/Anschreiberin, *die;* **b)** *(Footb.)* Torschütze, *der*/-schützin, *die*

scorn [skɔ:n] **1.** *n.* Verachtung, *die.* **2.** *v.t.* verachten; in den Wind schlagen ⟨*Rat*⟩; ausschlagen ⟨*Angebot*⟩. **scornful** ['skɔ:nfl] *adj.* verächtlich ⟨*Lächeln, Blick*⟩; **be** ~ **of sth.** für etw. nur Verachtung haben

Scorpio ['skɔ:pɪəʊ] *n.* der Skorpion

scorpion ['skɔ:pɪən] *n.* Skorpion, *der*

Scot [skɒt] *n.* Schotte, *der*/Schottin, *die*

Scotch [skɒtʃ] **1.** *adj. see* **Scottish. 2.** *n.* Scotch, *der;* schottischer Whisky

scotch *v.t.* den Boden entziehen (+ *Dat.*) ⟨*Gerücht*⟩; zunichte machen ⟨*Plan*⟩

Scotch: ~ **'egg** *n.* hartgekochtes Ei in *Wurstbrät;* ~ **'whisky** *n.* schottischer Whisky

scot-'free *adj.* |get off/go| ~: ungeschoren [davonkommen *od.* bleiben]

Scotland ['skɒtlənd] *pr. n.* Schottland *(das)*

Scots [skɒts] **1.** *adj. (esp. Scot.)* schottisch; **sb. is** ~: jmd. ist Schotte/Schottin. **2.** *n. (dialect)* Schottisch, *das.*

Scotsman ['skɒtsmən] *n., pl.* **Scotsmen** ['skɒtsmən] Schotte, *der.* 'Scotswoman *n.* Schottin, *die*

Scottish ['skɒtɪʃ] *adj.* schottisch; **sb. is** ~: jmd. ist Schotte/Schottin

scoundrel ['skaʊndrl] *n.* Schuft, *der*

'scour [skaʊə(r)] *v.t. (search)* durchkämmen **(for** nach**)**

²scour *v.t.* scheuern ⟨*Topf, Metall*⟩. 'scourer *n.* Topfreiniger, *der*

scourge [skɜ:dʒ] *n.* Geißel, *die*

scout [skaʊt] **1.** *n.* **a)** |Boy| **S**~: Pfadfinder, *der;* **b)** *(Mil.)* Späher, *der.* **2.** *v.i.* ~ **for** Ausschau halten nach

scowl [skaʊl] **1.** *v.i.* ein mürrisches Gesicht machen. **2.** *n.* mürrischer [Gesichts]ausdruck

scram [skræm] *v.i.,* **-mm-** *(sl.)* abhauen *(salopp)*

scramble ['skræmbl] **1.** *v.i.* **a)** *(clamber)* klettern; ~ **through a hedge** sich durch eine Hecke zwängen; **b)** *(move hastily)* rennen *(ugs.);* ~ **for sth.** um etw. rangeln. **2.** *v.t. (Teleph., Radio)* verschlüsseln. **scrambled 'egg** *n.* Rührei, *das*

'scrap [skræp] **1.** *n.* **a)** *(of paper)* Fetzen, *der; (of food)* Bissen, *der;* **b)** *in pl. (odds and ends) (of food)* Reste *Pl.;* **c)** *(smallest amount)* **not a** ~ **of** kein bißchen; *(of sympathy, truth also)* nicht ein Fünkchen; **not a** ~ **of evidence** nicht die Spur eines Beweises; **d)** ~ |metal| Schrott, *der;* ~ **iron** Alteisen, *das.* **2.** *v.t.,* **-pp-** wegwerfen; *(send for* ~*)* verschrotten; *(fig.)* aufgeben

²scrap *(coll.)* **1.** *n. (fight)* Rauferei, *die.* **2.** *v.i.,* **-pp-** sich raufen

'scrap-book *n.* [Sammel]album, *das*

scrape [skreɪp] **1.** *v.t.* **a)** *(make smooth)* schaben ⟨*Häute, Möhren, Kartoffeln usw.*⟩; abziehen ⟨*Holz*⟩; *(damage)* verschrammen ⟨*Fußboden, Auto*⟩; **b)** *(remove)* [ab]kratzen ⟨*Farbe, Schmutz, Rost*⟩ **(off, from** von**)**; **c)** *(draw along)* schleifen; **d)** ~ **together** *(raise)* zusammenkratzen *(ugs.);* (save up) zusammensparen. **2.** *v.i.* **a)** *(move with sound)* schleifen; **b)** *(emit scraping noise)* ein schabendes Geräusch machen; **c)** *(rub)* streifen **(against,** over *Akk.*). **3.** *n.* **a)** *(act, sound)* Kratzen, *das* **(against** an + *Dat.*); **b)** *(predicament)* Schwulitäten *Pl. (ugs.).* **scrape 'by** *v.i. (fig.)* sich über Wasser halten **(on** mit**). scrape 'out** *v.t.* **a)** *(excavate)* buddeln *(ugs.);* **b)** *(clean)* auskratzen. **scrape through 1.** ['--] *v.t.* sich zwängen durch; *(fig.)* mit Hängen und Würgen kommen durch ⟨*Prüfung*⟩. **2.** [-'-] *v.i.* sich durchzwängen; *(fig.: in examination)* mit Hängen und Würgen durchkommen '**scraper** n. (for shoes) Kratzeisen, das; (grid) Abtreter, der; (tool, kitchen utensil) Schaber, der; (for removing ice from car windows) [Eis]kratzer, der **scrap: ~-heap** n. Schutthaufen, der; ~ '**paper** n. Schmierpapier, das **scrappy** ['skræpɪ] adj. lückenhaft '**scrap-yard** n. Schrottplatz, der **scratch** [skrætʃ] 1. v. t. a) (score surface of) zerkratzen; b) (get scratch[es] on) ~ oneself/one's hands etc. sich schrammen/ sich (Dat.) die Hände usw. zerkratzen; c) (scrape without marking) kratzen; kratzen an (+ Dat.) ⟨Insektenstich usw.⟩; ~ oneself/one's arm sich kratzen/sich (Dat.) den Arm od. am Arm kratzen. 2. v. i. kratzen; (~ oneself) sich kratzen. 3. n. a) (mark, wound) Kratzer, der (ugs.); Schramme, die; b) (sound) Kratzen, das; c) have a [good] ~: sich [ordentlich] kratzen; d) start from ~: bei Null anfangen (ugs.); be up to ~ ⟨Arbeit, Leistung:⟩ nichts zu wünschen übriglassen; ⟨Person:⟩ den Anforderungen genügen. **scratch a'bout, scratch a'round** v. i. scharren; (fig.: search) suchen (for nach). **scratch 'out** v. t. auskratzen ⟨Auge⟩

scrawl [skrɔːl] 1. v. t. hinkritzeln. 2. v. i. kritzeln. 3. n. Gekritzel, das; (handwriting) Klaue, die (salopp) **scrawny** ['skrɔːnɪ] adj. hager; dürr **scream** [skriːm] 1. v. i. schreien (with vor + Dat.). 2. v. t. schreien. 3. n. Schrei, der; (of jet engine) Heulen, das; ~s of pain Schmerzensschreie **screech** [skriːtʃ] 1. v. i. & t. kreischen. 2. n. Kreischen, das **screen** [skriːn] 1. n. a) (partition) Trennwand, die; (piece of furniture) Wandschirm, der; b) (of trees, persons, fog) Wand, die; c) (Cinemat.) Leinwand, die; [TV] ~: Bildschirm, der. 2. v. t. a) (shelter) schützen (from vor + Dat.); (conceal) verdecken; b) vorführen ⟨Film⟩; c) (for disease) untersuchen. '**screenplay** n. Drehbuch, das **screw** [skruː] 1. n. Schraube, die. 2. v. t. schrauben (to an + Akk.); ~ together zusammenschrauben; ~ down festschrauben. **screw 'up** v. t. a) (crumple up) zusammenknüllen ⟨Blatt Papier⟩; b) verziehen ⟨Gesicht⟩; zusammenkneifen ⟨Augen, Mund⟩; c) (sl.: bungle) vermurksen (salopp); ~ it/ things up Mist bauen (salopp) **screw: ~-cap** n. Schraubverschluß,

der; ~-**driver** n. Schraubenzieher, der; ~-**top** see ~-**cap** **screwy** ['skruːɪ] adj. (sl.) spinnig (ugs.) **scribble** ['skrɪbl] 1. v. t. hinkritzeln. 2. v. i. kritzeln. 3. n. Gekritzel, das **script** [skrɪpt] n. a) (handwriting) Handschrift, die; b) (of play) Regiebuch, das; (of film) [Dreh]buch, das; c) (for broadcaster) Manuskript, das **scripture** ['skrɪptʃə(r)] n. a) [Holy] S~, the [Holy] S~s die [Heilige] Schrift; b) (Sch.) Religion, die '**script-writer** n. (of film) Drehbuchautor, der/-autorin, die **scroll** [skrəʊl] n. (roll) Rolle, die **scrounge** ['skraʊndʒ] (coll.) 1. v. t. schnorren (ugs.) (off, from von). 2. v. i. schnorren (ugs.) (from bei). '**scrounger** n. (coll.) Schnorrer, der/ Schnorrerin, die (ugs.) ¹**scrub** [skrʌb] 1. v. t., -bb-: a) schrubben (ugs.); scheuern; b) (coll.: cancel) zurücknehmen ⟨Befehl⟩; sausenlassen (ugs.) ⟨Plan⟩. 2. v. i., -bb- schrubben (ugs.); scheuern. 3. n. give sth. a ~: etw. schrubben (ugs.) od. scheuern ²**scrub** n. (brushwood) Buschwerk, das; (area) Buschland, das ¹**scruff** [skrʌf] n. by the ~ of the neck beim Genick ²**scruff** n. (Brit. coll.) (man) vergammelter Typ (ugs.); (woman, girl) Schlampe, die. '**scruffy** adj. vergammelt (ugs.) **scrum** [skrʌm] n. Gedränge, das **scruple** ['skruːpl] n. Skrupel, der; have no ~s about doing sth. keine Skrupel haben, etw. zu tun **scrupulous** ['skruːpjʊləs] adj. gewissenhaft ⟨Person⟩; unbedingt ⟨Ehrlichkeit⟩; peinlich ⟨Sorgfalt⟩ **scrutinize** ['skruːtɪnaɪz] v. t. [genau] untersuchen ⟨[Forschungs]gegenstand⟩; [über]prüfen ⟨Rechnung, Paß, Fahrkarte⟩; mustern ⟨Person⟩ **scrutiny** ['skruːtɪnɪ] n. a) (critical gaze) musternder Blick; b) (examination) (of recruit) Musterung, die; (of bill, passport, ticket) [Über]prüfung, die **scuff** [skʌf] 1. v. t. streifen; verschrammen ⟨Schuhe, Fußboden⟩. 2. n. Schramme, die **scuffle** ['skʌfl] 1. n. Handgreiflichkeiten Pl. 2. v. i. handgreiflich werden (with gegen) **scullery** ['skʌlərɪ] n. Spülküche, die **sculptor** ['skʌlptə(r)] n. Bildhauer, der/-hauerin, die **sculpture** ['skʌlptʃə(r)] n. a) (art)

Bildhauerei, *die;* **b)** *(piece of work)* Skulptur, *die;* Plastik, *die; (pieces collectively)* Skulpturen
scum [skʌm] *n.* **a)** Schmutzschicht, *die; (film)* Schmutzfilm, *der;* **b)** *(fig. derog.)* Abschaum, *der*
scurry ['skʌrɪ] *v.i.* huschen
¹scuttle ['skʌtl] *n.* Kohlenfüller, *der*
²scuttle *(Naut.) v.t.* versenken
³scuttle *v.i.* rennen; flitzen *(ugs.);* ⟨*Maus, Krabbe:*⟩ huschen
scythe [saɪð] *n.* Sense, *die*
SE *abbr.* **south-east** SO
sea [siː] *n.* **a)** Meer, *das;* **the ~:** das Meer; **the See; by ~:** mit dem Schiff; **by the ~:** am Meer; **at ~:** auf See *(Dat.);* **be all at ~** *(fig.)* nicht mehr weiter wissen; **put** |out| **to ~:** in See *(Akk.)* gehen; **b)** *(specific tract of water)* Meer, *das*
sea: ~ 'air *n.* Seeluft, *die;* **~-'bed** *n.* Meeresboden, *der;* **~-gull** *n.* [See]möwe, *die*
¹seal [siːl] *n. (Zool.)* Robbe, *die;* |**common**| **~:** [Gemeiner] Seehund
²seal **1.** *n. (wax etc., stamp, impression)* Siegel, *das.* **2.** *v.t.* **a)** *(stamp, affix ~ to)* siegeln ⟨*Dokument*⟩; *(fasten with ~)* verplomben ⟨*Tür, Stromzähler*⟩; **b)** *(close securely)* abdichten ⟨*Behälter, Rohr usw.*⟩; zukleben ⟨*Umschlag, Paket*⟩; **c)** *(stop up)* verschließen; abdichten ⟨*Leck*⟩; verschmieren ⟨*Riß*⟩. **seal 'off** *v.t.* abriegeln
sea: ~-legs *n. pl.* Seebeine *Pl. (Seemannsspr.);* **get** or **find one's ~-legs** sich *(Dat.)* Seebeine wachsen lassen; **~-level** *n.* Meeresspiegel, *der*
'sealing-wax *n.* Siegellack, *der*
'sea-lion *n.* Seelöwe, *der*
seam [siːm] *n.* **a)** Naht, *die;* **b)** *(of coal)* Flöz, *das*
seaman ['siːmən] *n., pl.* **seamen** ['siːmən] Matrose, *der*
'sea mist *n.* Küstennebel, *der*
'seamless *adj.* nahtlos
'seamy *adj.* **the ~ side |of life etc.|** *(fig.)* die Schattenseite[n] [des Lebens *usw.*]
seance ['seɪəns], **séance** ['seɪãs] *n.* Séance, *die*
sea: ~-plane *n.* Wasserflugzeug, *das;* **~-port** *n.* Seehafen, *der*
sear ['sɪə(r)] *v.t.* versengen
search [sɜːtʃ] **1.** *v.t.* durchsuchen **(for** nach); absuchen ⟨*Gebiet, Fläche*⟩ **(for** nach); *(fig.: probe)* erforschen ⟨*Herz, Gewissen*⟩; suchen in (+ *Dat.*) ⟨*Gedächtnis*⟩ **(for** nach). **2.** *v.i.* suchen **(for** nach). **3.** *n.* Suche, *die* **(for** nach);

(of building, room, etc.) Durchsuchung, *die;* **in ~ of sb./sth.** auf der Suche nach jmdm./etw. **'searching** *adj.* prüfend, forschend ⟨*Blick*⟩; bohrend ⟨*Frage*⟩
search: ~-light *n.* Suchscheinwerfer, *der;* **~-party** *n.* Suchtrupp, *der;* **~-warrant** *n.* Durchsuchungsbefehl, *der*
sea: ~-shore *n.* [Meeres]küste, *die; (beach)* Strand, *der;* **~-sick** *adj.* seekrank; **~-sickness** *n.* Seekrankheit, *die;* **~-side** *n.* [Meeres]küste, *die;* **by/to/at the ~-side** am/ans/am Meer; **~-side town** Seestadt, *die*
season ['siːzn] **1.** *n.* **a)** Jahreszeit, *die;* **nesting ~:** Nistzeit, *die;* **b)** *(period of social activity)* |**opera/football**| **~:** [Opern-/Fußball]saison, *die;* **holiday** or *(Amer.)* **vacation ~:** Urlaubszeit, *die;* **tourist ~:** Reisezeit, *die;* **c)** raspberries are **in/out of** or **not in ~:** jetzt ist die/nicht die Saison *od.* Zeit für Himbeeren; **be in ~** *(on heat)* brünstig sein; **d)** *see* **season-ticket. 2.** *v.t.* würzen ⟨*Fleisch, Rede*⟩. **seasonable** ['siːzənəbl] *adj.* der Jahreszeit gemäß.
'seasoned *adj. (fig.)* erfahren. **'seasoning** *n.* Gewürze *Pl.;* Würze, *die.*
'season-ticket *n.* Dauerkarte, *die*
seat [siːt] **1.** *n.* **a)** Sitzgelegenheit, *die; (in vehicle, cinema, etc.)* Sitz, *der; (of toilet)* [Klosett]brille, *die (ugs.);* **b)** *(place)* Platz, *der; (in vehicle)* [Sitz]platz, *der;* **have** or **take a ~:** sich [hin]setzen; **c)** *(part of chair)* Sitzfläche, *die;* **d)** *(buttocks)* Gesäß, *das; (part of clothing)* Gesäßpartie, *die; (of trousers)* Sitz, *der.* **2.** *v.t.* **a)** *(cause to sit)* setzen; ⟨*Platzanweiser:*⟩ einen Platz anweisen (+ *Dat.*); **~ oneself** sich setzen; **b)** *(have ~s for)* Sitzplätze bieten (+ *Dat.*); **~ 500 people** 500 Sitzplätze haben. **'seat-belt** *n.* Sicherheitsgurt, *der.* **'seated** *adj.* sitzend; **remain ~:** sitzen bleiben. **'seating** *n.* Sitzplätze; *attrib.* Sitz⟨*ordnung, -plan*⟩.
sea: ~-urchin *n.* Seeigel, *der;* **~-wall** *n.* Strandmauer, *die;* **~-water** *n.* Meerwasser, *das;* **~-weed** *n.* [See]tang, *der;* **~-worthy** *adj.* seetüchtig
secluded [sɪ'kluːdɪd] *adj. (hidden)* versteckt; *(isolated)* abgelegen; zurückgezogen ⟨*Leben*⟩. **seclusion** [sɪ'kluːʒn] *n. (remoteness)* Abgelegenheit, *die; (privacy)* Zurückgezogenheit, *die*
'second ['sekənd] **1.** *adj.* zweit...; **~**

largest/highest *etc.* zweitgrößt.../ -höchst... *usw.;* **come/be** ~ : zweiter/ zweite werden/sein. **2.** *n.* **a)** *(unit of time or angle)* Sekunde, *die;* **b)** *(coll.: moment)* Sekunde, *die (ugs.);* **wait a few** ~**s** einen Moment warten; **in a** ~ *(immediately)* sofort *(ugs.); (very quickly)* im Nu *(ugs.);* **just a** ~**!** *(coll.)* einen Moment!; **c) the** ~ *(in sequence)* der/die/das Zweite; **d)** *in pl. (helping of food)* zweite Portion. **3.** *v. t. (support)* unterstützen

²**second** [sɪ'kɒnd] *v. t. (transfer)* vorübergehend versetzen

secondary ['sekəndərɪ] *adj. (of less importance)* zweitrangig; Neben-⟨*sache*⟩; **be** ~ **to sth.** einer Sache *(Dat.)* untergeordnet sein. '**secondary school** *n.* höhere Schule

second: ~-**best 1.** ['---] *adj.* zweitbest...; **2.** [--'-] *n.* Zweitbeste, *der/die/ das;* ~-**class 1.** ['---] *adj. (of lower class)* zweiter Klasse *nachgestellt;* Zweite[r]-Klasse-⟨*Fahrkarte, Abteil, Post, Brief usw.*⟩; ~-**class stamp** Briefmarke für einen Zweiter-Klasse-Brief; **2.** [--'-] *adv.* zweiter Klasse *(fahren);* ~ '**floor** *see* floor 1 b; ~ **hand** *n.* Sekundenzeiger, *der;* ~-**hand 1.** ['---] *adj.* **a)** gebraucht ⟨*Kleidung, Auto usw.*⟩; *anti-*quarisch ⟨*Buch*⟩; **b)** *(selling used goods)* Gebrauchtwaren-; Second-hand⟨*laden*⟩; **c)** ⟨*Nachrichten, Bericht*⟩ aus zweiter Hand; **2.** [--'-] *adv.* aus zweiter Hand

'**secondly** *adv.* zweitens

second: ~ **name** *n.* Nachname, *der;* ~-'**rate** *adj.* zweitklassig; ~ '**thoughts** *n. pl.* **have** ~ **thoughts** es sich *(Dat.)* anders überlegen (**about** mit); **we've had** ~ **thoughts about buying it** wir wollen es nun doch nicht kaufen; **but on** ~ **thoughts ...:** wenn ich's mir [noch mal] überlege, ...

secrecy ['siːkrɪsɪ] *n.* **a)** *(keeping of secret)* Geheimhaltung, *die;* **b)** *(secretiveness)* Heimlichtuerei, *die;* **c) in** ~**:** im geheimen

secret ['siːkrɪt] **1.** *adj.* geheim; Geheim⟨*fach, -tür, -abkommen, -kode*⟩; heimlich ⟨*Trinker, Liebhaber*⟩; **keep sth.** ~**:** etw. geheimhalten (**from** vor + *Dat.*). **2.** *n.* **a)** Geheimnis, *das;* **make no** ~ **of sth.** kein Geheimnis aus etw. machen; *(fig.)* keinen Hehl aus etw. machen; **keep** ~**s/ a** ~**:** schweigen *(fig.);* **b) in** ~**:** im geheimen. **se-cret 'agent** *n.* Geheimagent, *der/* -agentin, *die*

secretarial [sekrə'teərɪəl] *adj.* Sekretärinnen⟨*kursus, -tätigkeit*⟩; ⟨*Arbeit*⟩ als Sekretärin

secretary ['sekrətərɪ] *n.* Sekretär, *der/*Sekretärin, *die*

secretive ['siːkrɪtɪv] *adj.* verschlossen ⟨*Person*⟩: **be** ~**:** geheimnisvoll tun (**about** mit)

'**secretly** *adv.* heimlich; insgeheim ⟨*etw. glauben*⟩

sect [sekt] *n.* Sekte, *die*

section ['sekʃn] *n.* **a)** *(part cut off)* Abschnitt, *der;* Stück, *das; (part of divided whole)* Teil, *der;* **b)** *(of firm)* Abteilung, *die; (of organization)* Sektion, *die;* **c)** *(of chapter, book)* Abschnitt, *der; (of statute etc.)* Paragraph, *der*

sector ['sektə(r)] *n.* Sektor, *der*

secular ['sekjʊlə(r)] *adj.* weltlich

secure [sɪ'kjʊə(r)] **1.** *adj.* sicher; *(firmly fastened)* fest; ~ **against burglars** gegen Einbruch geschützt. **2.** *v. t.* **a)** sichern (**for** *Dat.*); beschaffen ⟨*Auftrag*⟩ (**for** *Dat.*); *(for oneself)* sich ⟨*Dat.*⟩ sichern; **b)** *(fasten)* sichern. **se-**'**curely** *adv. (firmly)* fest ⟨*verriegeln, zumachen*⟩; sicher ⟨*befestigen, untergebracht sein*⟩. **security** [sɪ'kjʊərɪtɪ] *n.* **a)** Sicherheit, *die;* ~ **|measures|** Sicherheitsmaßnahmen; **b)** *(Finance)* **securities** *pl.* Wertpapiere

security: ~ **forces** *n. pl.* Sicherheitskräfte *Pl.;* ~ **guard** *n.* Wächter, *der/* Wächterin, *die;* ~ **risk** *n.* Sicherheitsrisiko, *das*

sedan [sɪ'dæn] *n. (Amer. Motor Veh.)* Limousine, *die*

sedate [sɪ'deɪt] **1.** *adj.* bedächtig; gesetzt ⟨*alte Dame*⟩; gemächlich ⟨*Tempo, Leben*⟩. **2.** *v. t.* sedieren. **sedation** [sɪ'deɪʃn] *n.* Sedation, *die;* **be under** ~**:** sediert sein. **sedative** ['sedətɪv] **1.** *n.* Beruhigungsmittel, *das.* **2.** *adj.* sedativ

sedentary ['sedəntərɪ] *adj.* sitzend

sediment ['sedɪmənt] *n.* Ablagerung, *die; (of tea, coffee, etc.)* Bodensatz, *der*

seduce [sɪ'djuːs] *v. t.* verführen. **se-duction** [sɪ'dʌkʃn] *n.* Verführung, *die.* **seductive** [sɪ'dʌktɪv] *adj.* verführerisch; verlockend ⟨*Angebot*⟩

see [siː] **1.** *v. t.,* **saw** [sɔː]**, seen** [siːn] **a)** sehen; **I can** ~ **it's hard for you** ich verstehe, daß es nicht leicht für dich ist; **I** ~ **what you mean** ich verstehe[, was du meinst]; **b)** *(meet [with])* sehen; treffen; *(meet socially)* sich treffen mit; **I'll** ~ **you there/at five** wir sehen uns dort/um fünf; ~ you!, [I'll] be ~ing you! *(coll.)* bis bald! *(ugs.);* c) *(speak to)* sprechen ⟨Person⟩ **(about** wegen); *(visit)* gehen zu ⟨Arzt, Anwalt usw.⟩; *(receive)* empfangen; d) *(find out)* feststellen; *(by looking)* nachsehen; e) *(make sure)* ~ |**that**| ...: darauf achten, daß ...; f) *(imagine)* sich *(Dat.)* vorstellen; g) *(escort)* begleiten. 2. *v. i.,* **saw, seen a)** sehen; b) *(make sure)* nachsehen; c) **I** ~: ich verstehe; **you** ~: weißt du/wißt ihr/wissen Sie. '**see about** *v. t.* sich kümmern um. **see 'off** *v. t.* **a)** *(say goodbye to)* verabschieden; b) *(chase away)* vertreiben. **see 'out** *v. t. (escort)* hinausbegleiten **(of** aus); ~ **oneself out** allein hinausfinden. **see through** *v. t.* **a)** ['--] hindurchsehen durch; *(fig.)* durchschauen; b) [-'-] *(not abandon)* zu Ende bringen. '**see to** *v. t.* sich kümmern um

seed [si:d] **1.** *n.* **a)** Samen, *der; (of grape etc.)* Kern, *der;* b) *no pl., no indef. art. (~s collectively)* Samen[körner] *Pl.; (as collected for sowing)* Saatgut, *das; (for birds)* Körner *Pl.;* **go** *or* **run to** ~: Samen bilden; *(fig.)* herunterkommen *(ugs.);* c) *(Sport)* gesetzter Spieler/gesetzte Spielerin. **2.** *v. t.* **a)** *(place ~s in)* besäen; b) *(Sport)* setzen ⟨Spieler⟩; **be ~ed number one** als Nummer eins gesetzt werden/sein. '**seedless** *adj.* kernlos

seedling ['si:dlıŋ] *n.* Sämling, *der*

'**seedy** *adj.* **a)** *(coll.: unwell)* **feel** ~: sich [leicht] angeschlagen fühlen; b) *(shabby)* schäbig, *(ugs.)* vergammelt ⟨Aussehen⟩; heruntergekommen ⟨Stadtteil⟩; c) *(disreputable)* zweifelhaft

'**seeing** *conj.* ~ |that| ...: da ...; wo ... *(ugs.)*

seek [si:k] *v. t.,* **sought** [sɔ:t] suchen; anstreben ⟨Posten, Amt⟩; sich bemühen um ⟨Anerkennung, Interview, Einstellung⟩; *(try to reach)* aufsuchen

seem [si:m] *v. i.* scheinen; **you** ~ **tired** du wirkst müde; **she** ~**s nice** sie scheint nett zu sein. '**seeming** *adj.* scheinbar. '**seemingly** *adv.* **a)** *(evidently)* offensichtlich; b) *(to outward appearance)* scheinbar

seemly ['si:mlı] *adj.* schicklich

seen *see* **see**

seep [si:p] *v. i.* ~ |away| [ab]sickern

'**see-saw** *n.* Wippe, *die*

seethe [si:ð] *v. i.* **a)** ~ |with anger/inwardly| vor Wut/innerlich schäumen; b) ⟨Straßen usw.:⟩ wimmeln **(with** von)

'**see-through** *adj.* durchsichtig

segment ['segmənt] *n. (of orange, pineapple, etc.)* Scheibe, *die*

segregate ['segrɪgeɪt] *v. t.* trennen; *(racially)* absondern. **segregation** [segrɪ'geɪʃn] *n.* Trennung, *die;* |racial| ~: Rassentrennung, *die*

seismic ['saɪzmɪk] *adj.* seismisch

seize [si:z] **1.** *v. t.* **a)** ergreifen; ~ **power** die Macht ergreifen; ~ **sb. by the arm/collar** jmdn. am Arm/Kragen packen; ~ **the opportunity** |to do sth.| die Gelegenheit ergreifen [und etw. tun]; ~ **any/a** *or* **the chance** |to do sth.| jede/die Gelegenheit nutzen[, um etw. zu tun]; **be ~d with remorse/panic** von Gewissensbissen geplagt/von Panik ergriffen werden; b) *(capture)* gefangennehmen ⟨Person⟩; kapern ⟨Schiff⟩; mit Gewalt übernehmen ⟨Flugzeug, Gebäude⟩; einnehmen ⟨Festung, Brücke⟩; c) *(confiscate)* beschlagnahmen. **2.** *v. i. see* ~ **up.** '**seize on** *v. t.* sich *(Dat.)* vornehmen ⟨Einzelheit, Aspekt, Schwachpunkt⟩; aufgreifen ⟨Idee, Vorschlag⟩. **seize 'up** *v. i.* sich festfressen

seizure ['si:ʒə(r)] *n.* **a)** *see* **seize 1 b, c:** Gefangennahme, *die;* Kapern, *das;* Übernahme, *die;* Einnahme, *die;* Beschlagnahme, *die;* b) *(Med.)* Anfall, *der*

seldom ['seldəm] *adv.* selten

select [sɪ'lekt] **1.** *adj.* ausgewählt. **2.** *v. t.* auswählen. **selection** [sɪ'lekʃn] *n.* **a)** *(what is selected [from])* Auswahl, *die* **(of** an + *Dat.,* **from** aus); b) *(act of choosing)* [Aus]wahl, *die.* **selective** [sɪ'lektɪv] *adj. (using selection)* selektiv; *(careful in one's choice)* wählerisch

self [self] *n., pl.* **selves** [selvz] Selbst, *das (geh.);* Ich, *das*

self- *in comb.* selbst-/Selbst-

self: ~-ad'dressed *adj.* **~-addressed envelope** adressierter Rückumschlag; **~-ad'hesive** *adj.* selbstklebend; **~-ap'pointed** *adj.* selbsternannt; **~-as'surance** *n.* Selbstsicherheit, *die;* **~-as'sured** *adj.* selbstsicher; **~-'catering 1.** *adj.* mit Selbstversorgung *nachgestellt;* **2.** *n.* Selbstversorgung, *die;* **~-'centred** *adj.* egozentrisch; **~-'confidence** *n.* Selbstbewußtsein, *das;* **~-'confident** *adj.* selbstbewußt; **~-'conscious** *adj.* unsicher; **~-'consciousness** *n.* Unsicherheit, *die;* **~-con'tained** *adj.* abgeschlossen ⟨Wohnung⟩; **~-con'trol** *n.* Selbstbeherrschung, *die;* ~-

con'trolled adj. voller Selbstbeherrschung nachgestellt; ~-**de'ception** n. Selbsttäuschung, die; ~-**de'fence** n. Notwehr, die; in ~-**defence** aus Notwehr; ~-**drive** adj. ~-**drive hire** [company] Autovermietung, die; ~-**drive vehicle** Mietwagen, der; ~-**em-'ployed** adj. selbständig; ~-'**evid-ent** adj. offenkundig; ~-**ex'planat-ory** adj. ohne weiteres verständlich; be ~-**explanatory** für sich selbst sprechen; ~-'**help** n. Selbsthilfe, die; ~-**im'portant** adj. eingebildet; ~-**in'dulgent** adj. maßlos; ~-'**inter-est** n. Eigeninteresse, das

'**selfish** adj., '**selfishly** adv. selbstsüchtig. '**selfishness** n. Selbstsucht, die

self: ~-'**pity** n. Selbstmitleid, das; ~-'**portrait** n. Selbstporträt, das; ~-**pos'sessed** adj. selbstbeherrscht; ~-'**raising flour** n. (Brit.) mit Backpulver versetztes Mehl; ~-**re'spect** n. Selbstachtung, die; ~-**re'specting** adj. no ~-respecting person ...: niemand, der etwas auf sich hält, ...; ~-'**righteous** adj. selbstgerecht; ~-'**sacrifice** n. Selbstaufopferung, die; ~-'**satisfied** adj. selbstzufrieden; (smug) selbstgefällig; ~-'**ser-vice** n. Selbstbedienung, die; attrib. Selbstbedienungs-; ~-**sufficient** adj. unabhängig; selbständig ⟨Person⟩; ~-'**willed** adj. eigenwillig

sell [sel] 1. v.t., **sold** [səʊld] ~ **sth. to sb.**, ~ **sb. sth.** jmdm. etw. verkaufen; **be sold out** ausverkauft sein. 2. v.i., **sold** sich verkaufen; ⟨Person:⟩ verkaufen. **sell 'off** v.t. verkaufen. **sell 'out** 1. v.t. a) ausverkaufen; b) (coll.: betray) verpfeifen (ugs.). 2. v.i. **we have** or **are sold out** wir sind ausverkauft

'**sell-by date** n. ≈ Mindesthaltbarkeitsdatum, das

'**seller** n. a) Verkäufer, der/Verkäuferin, die; b) (product) **be a good/slow ~:** sich gut/nur langsam verkaufen

Sellotape, (P) ['seləteɪp] n. ≈ Tesafilm, der Ⓦ

'**sellotape** v.t. mit Tesafilm kleben

'**sell-out** n. **be a ~:** ausverkauft sein; (coll.: betrayal) Verrat sein

selves pl. of **self**

semaphore ['seməfɔ:(r)] 1. n. (system) Winken, das. 2. v.i. ~ **to sb.** jmdm. ein Winksignal übermitteln

semblance ['sembləns] n. Anschein, der

semen ['si:mən] n. Samen, der

semi- [semɪ] pref. halb-/Halb-

semi: ~**breve** n. (Brit. Mus.) ganze Note; ~**circle** n. Halbkreis, der; ~'**circular** adj. halbkreisförmig; ~**colon** n. Semikolon, das; ~-**de'tached** adj. & n. ~-**detached** [house] Doppelhaushälfte, die; ~'**final** n. Halbfinale, das

seminar ['semɪnɑ:(r)] n. Seminar, das

'**semitone** n. (Mus.) Halbton, der

semolina [semə'li:nə] n. Grieß, der

senate ['senət] n. Senat, der. **senator** ['senətə(r)] n. Senator, der

send [send] v.t., **sent** [sent] schicken; senden (geh.). **send a'way** 1. v.t. wegschicken. 2. v.i. ~ **away** [**to sb.**] for **sth.** etw. [bei jmdm.] anfordern. **send 'back** v.t. zurückschicken. '**send for** v.t. a) (tell to come) holen lassen; rufen ⟨Polizei, Arzt usw.⟩; b) (order from elsewhere) anfordern. **send 'off** v.t. 1. a) (dispatch) abschicken ⟨Sache⟩; b) (Sport) vom Platz stellen. 2. v.i. see **send away** 2. **send 'up** v.t. (Brit. coll.: parody) parodieren

'**sender** n. Absender, der

'**send-off** n. Verabschiedung, die

senile ['si:naɪl] adj. senil. **senility** [sɪ'nɪlɪtɪ] n. Senilität, die

senior ['si:nɪə(r)] 1. adj. a) (older) älter; b) höher ⟨Rang, Beamter, Stellung⟩; leitend ⟨Angestellter, Stellung⟩. 2. n. (older) Ältere, der/die; (of higher rank) Vorgesetzte, der/die. **senior 'citizen** n. Senior, der/Seniorin, die. **seniority** [si:nɪ'ɒrɪtɪ] n. (greater length of service) höheres Dienstalter; (higher rank) höherer Rang

sensation [sen'seɪʃn] n. a) (feeling) Gefühl, das; b) (person, event, etc.) Sensation, die. **sensational** [sen'seɪʃənl] adj. sensationell

sense [sens] 1. n. a) (faculty) Sinn, der; ~ **of smell/touch/taste** Geruchs-/Tast-/Geschmackssinn, der; **come to one's ~s** das Bewußtsein wiedererlangen; b) in pl. (normal state of mind) Verstand, der; **have taken leave of one's ~s** den Verstand verloren haben; c) (consciousness) Gefühl, das; ~ **of responsibility/guilt** Verantwortungs-/Schuldgefühl, das; d) (practical wisdom) Verstand, der; **sound** or **good ~:** [gesunder Menschen]verstand; **not have the ~ to do sth.** nicht so schlau sein, etw. zu tun; **there is no ~ in doing that** es hat keinen Sinn, das zu tun; e) (meaning) Sinn, der; (of word) Bedeutung, die; **make ~:** einen

Sinn ergeben; **in a** *or* **one ~:** in gewisser Hinsicht; **make ~ of sth.** etw. verstehen. **2.** *v. t.* spüren. **'senseless** *adj.* **a)** *(unconscious)* bewußtlos; **b)** *(purposeless)* sinnlos

sensible ['sensɪbl] *adj.* **a)** *(reasonable)* vernünftig; **b)** *(practical)* zweckmäßig. **sensibly** ['sensɪblɪ] *adv.* **a)** *(reasonably)* vernünftig; **b)** *(practically)* zweckmäßig

sensitive ['sensɪtɪv] *adj.* empfindlich; **be ~ to sth.** empfindlich auf etw. *(Akk.)* reagieren. **sensitivity** [sensɪ-'tɪvɪtɪ] *n.* Empfindlichkeit, *die*

sensory ['sensərɪ] *adj.* Sinnes-

sensual ['sensjʊəl] *adj.* sinnlich

sensuous ['sensjʊəs] *adj.* sinnlich

sent *see* **send**

sentence ['sentəns] **1.** *n.* **a)** *(Law)* [Straf]urteil, *das;* **b)** *(Ling.)* Satz, *der.* **2.** *v. t.* verurteilen **(to** zu)

sentiment ['sentɪmənt] *n.* **a)** Gefühl, *das;* **b)** *(sentimentality)* Sentimentalität, *die;* **c)** *(opinion)* Gedanke, *der.* **sentimental** [sentɪ'mentl] *adj.* sentimental. **sentimentality** [sentɪmen-'tælɪtɪ] *n.* Sentimentalität, *die*

sentry ['sentrɪ] *n.* Wache, *die*

separable ['sepərəbl] *adj.* trennbar

separate 1. ['sepərət] *adj.* verschieden ⟨*Fragen, Probleme, Gelegenheiten*⟩; gesondert ⟨*Teil*⟩; separat ⟨*Eingang, Toilette, Blatt Papier, Abteil*⟩; *(one's own, individual)* eigen ⟨*Zimmer, Identität, Organisation*⟩; **keep two things ~:** zwei Dinge auseinanderhalten. **2.** ['sepəreɪt] *v. t.* trennen; **they are ~d** *(no longer live together)* sie leben getrennt. **3.** *v. i.* **a)** *(disperse)* sich trennen; **b)** ⟨*Ehepaar:*⟩ sich trennen. **separately** ['sepərətlɪ] *adv.* getrennt. **separation** [sepə'reɪʃn] *n.* Trennung, *die*

Sept. *abbr.* September Sept.

September [sep'tembə(r)] *n.* September, *der; see also* **August**

septic ['septɪk] *adj.* septisch; **go ~:** eitrig werden

sequel ['siːkwl] *n.* **a)** *(consequence, result)* Folge, *die* **(to** von); **b)** *(continuation)* Fortsetzung, *die*

sequence ['siːkwəns] *n.* **a)** Reihenfolge, *die;* **b)** *(part of film)* Sequenz, *die*

sequin ['siːkwɪn] *n.* Paillette, *die*

serenade [serə'neɪd] **1.** *n.* Ständchen, *das.* **2.** *v. t.* **~ sb.** jmdm. ein Ständchen bringen

serene [sɪ'riːn] *adj.* gelassen. **serenity** [sɪ'renɪtɪ] *n.* Gelassenheit, *die*

sergeant ['saːdʒənt] *n. (Mil.)* Unterof-

fizier, *der; (police officer)* ≈ Polizeimeister, *der.* **sergeant-'major** *n.* ≈ [Ober]stabsfeldwebel, *der*

serial ['sɪərɪəl] *n.* Fortsetzungsgeschichte, *die; (Radio, Telev.)* Serie, *die.* **serialize** ['sɪərɪəlaɪz] *v. t.* in Fortsetzungen veröffentlichen; *(Radio, Telev.)* in Fortsetzungen senden

series ['sɪərɪːz, 'sɪərɪz] *n., pl. same* **a)** *(sequence)* Reihe, *die; (of events, misfortunes)* Folge, *die;* **b)** *(set of successive issues)* Serie, *die;* **radio/TV ~:** Hörfunkreihe/Fernsehserie, *die;* **c)** *(set of books)* Reihe, *die*

serious ['sɪərɪəs] *adj.* **a)** *(earnest)* ernst; **b)** *(important, grave)* ernst ⟨*Angelegenheit, Lage, Problem, Zustand*⟩; ernsthaft ⟨*Frage, Einwand, Kandidat*⟩; schwer ⟨*Krankheit, Unfall, Fehler, Niederlage*⟩; ernstzunehmend ⟨*Rivale*⟩; ernstlich ⟨*Gefahr, Bedrohung*⟩; bedenklich ⟨*Mangel*⟩. **'seriously** *adv.* **a)** *(earnestly)* ernst; **take sth./sb. ~:** etw./jmdn. ernst nehmen; **b)** *(severely)* ernstlich; schwer ⟨*verletzt*⟩. **'seriousness** *n.* Ernst, *der;* **in all ~:** ganz im Ernst

sermon ['sɜːmən] *n.* Predigt, *die*

serrated [se'reɪtɪd] *adj.* gezackt; **~ knife** Sägemesser, *das*

serum ['sɪərəm] *n.* Serum, *das*

servant ['sɜːvənt] *n.* Diener, *der/*Dienerin, *die*

serve [sɜːv] **1.** *v. t.* **a)** *(work for)* dienen (+ *Dat.*); **b)** *(be useful to)* dienlich sein (+ *Dat.*); **c)** *(meet needs of)* nutzen (+ *Dat.*); **~ a/no purpose** einen Zweck erfüllen/keinen Zweck haben; **d)** durchlaufen ⟨*Lehre*⟩; verbüßen ⟨*Haftstrafe*⟩; **e)** *(dish up)* servieren; *(pour out)* einschenken **(to** *Dat.*); **f)** **~[s]** *or* **it ~s him right!** *(coll.)* [das] geschieht ihm recht! **2.** *v. i.* **a)** dienen; **~ as chairman** das Amt des Vorsitzenden innehaben; **~ as a Member of Parliament** Mitglied des Parlaments sein; **~ on a jury** Geschworener/Geschworene sein; **b)** *(be of use)* **~ to do sth.** dazu dienen, etw. zu tun; **~ to show sth.** etw. zeigen; **~ for** *or* **as** dienen als; **c)** *(Sport)* aufschlagen. **3.** *n. see* **service 1 g. serve 'up** *v. t.* **a)** servieren; **b)** *(offer for consideration)* auftischen *(ugs.)*

service ['sɜːvɪs] **1.** *n.* **a)** Dienst, *der;* **do sb. a ~:** jmdm. einen guten Dienst erweisen; **b)** *(Eccl.)* Gottesdienst, *der;* **c)** *(attending to customer)* Service, *der; (in shop, garage, etc.)* Bedienung, *die,*

d) *(system of transport)* Verbindung, *die;* **there is no |bus| ~ on Sundays** Sonntags verkehren keine Busse; **e)** *(provision of maintenance)* |after-sale| ~: Kundendienst, *der;* **take one's car in for a ~:** sein Auto zur Inspektion bringen; **f)** *(operation)* Betrieb, *der;* **out of ~:** außer Betrieb; **g)** *(Sport)* Aufschlag, *der;* **whose ~ is it?** wer hat Aufschlag?; **h)** *(crockery set)* Service, *das;* **i)** *(assistance)* **can I be of ~ |to you|?** kann ich Ihnen behilflich sein?; **I'm at your ~:** ich stehe zu Ihren Diensten; **j)** *(Mil.)* the |armed *or* fighting| ~s die Streitkräfte; **in the ~s** beim Militär; **k)** |motorway| ~s [Autobahn]-raststätte, *die.* **2.** *v. t.* warten ⟨*Wagen, Waschmaschine, Heizung*⟩. **serviceable** ['sɜːvɪsəbl] *adj.* **a)** *(useful)* nützlich; **b)** *(durable)* haltbar

service: **~ area** *n.* Raststätte, *die;* **~ charge** *n.* Bedienungsgeld, *das;* **~ industry** *n.* Dienstleistungsbetrieb, *der;* **~ man** ['sɜːvɪsmən] *n., pl.* **~men** ['sɜːvɪsmən] Militärangehörige, *der;* **~ station** *n.* Tankstelle, *die*

serviette [sɜːvɪ'et] *n. (Brit.)* Serviette, *die*

servile ['sɜːvaɪl] *adj.* unterwürfig

serving ['sɜːvɪŋ] *n.* Portion, *die.* **'serving spoon** *n.* Vorlegelöffel, *der*

session ['seʃn] *n. (meeting)* Sitzung, *die;* **be in ~:** tagen

set [set] **1.** *v. t.,* **-tt-, set a)** *(put) (horizontally)* legen; *(vertically)* stellen; **~ sb. ashore** jmdn. an Land setzen; **~ sth./things right** *or* **in order** etw./die Dinge in Ordnung bringen; **b)** *(apply)* setzen; **~ a match to sth.** ein Streichholz an etw. *(Akk.)* halten; *see also* **fire 1 a; 'light 1 d; c)** *(adjust)* einstellen *(at auf + Akk.);* aufstellen ⟨*Falle*⟩; stellen ⟨*Uhr*⟩; **~ the alarm for 5.30 a.m.** den Wecker auf 5.30 Uhr stellen; **d)** **be ~** ⟨*Buch, Film:*⟩ spielen; **e)** *(specify)* festlegen ⟨*Bedingungen*⟩; festsetzen ⟨*Termin, Ort usw.*⟩ *(for auf + Akk.);* **~ limits** Grenzen setzen; **f)** **~ sb. thinking that ...:** jmdn. auf den Gedanken bringen, daß ...; **g)** *(put forward)* stellen ⟨*Frage, Aufgabe*⟩; aufgeben ⟨*Hausaufgabe*⟩; aufstellen ⟨*Rekord*⟩; *(compose)* zusammenstellen ⟨*Rätsel, Fragen*⟩; **~ sb. an example, ~ an example to sb.** jmdm. ein Beispiel geben; **~ sb. a task/problem** jmdm. eine Aufgabe stellen/jmdn. vor ein Problem stellen; **~ |sb./oneself| a target** [jmdm./sich] ein Ziel setzen; **h)** *(Med.:*

put into place) [ein]richten; einrenken ⟨*verrenktes Gelenk*⟩; **i)** legen ⟨*Haare*⟩; **j)** decken ⟨*Tisch*⟩; auflegen ⟨*Gedeck*⟩; **k)** fassen ⟨*Edelstein*⟩. **2.** *v. i.,* **-tt-, set a)** *(solidify)* fest werden; **b)** *(go down)* ⟨*Sonne, Mond:*⟩ untergehen. **3.** *n.* **a)** *(group)* Satz, *der;* **~ |of two|** Paar, *das;* **a ~ of chairs** eine Sitzgruppe; **b)** *(radio, TV)* Gerät, *das;* **c)** *(Tennis)* Satz, *der;* **d)** *(of hair)* Legen, *das;* **e)** *(Theatre: scenery)* Bühnenbild, *das; (area of performance) (of film)* Drehort, *der; (of play)* Bühne, *die;* **f)** *(of people)* Kreis, *der;* **g)** *(Math.)* Menge, *die.* **4.** *adj.* **a)** *(fixed)* ⟨*Absichten, Zielvorstellungen, Zeitpunkt*⟩; **be ~ in one's ways** *or* **habits** in seinen Gewohnheiten festgefahren sein; **~ meal** *or* **menu** Menü, *das;* **b)** vorgeschrieben ⟨*Buch, Lektüre*⟩; **c)** *(ready)* **be |all| ~ for sth.** zu etw. bereit sein; **be |all| ~ to do sth.** bereit sein, etw. zu tun; **d)** *(determined)* **be ~ on sth./doing sth.** zu etw. entschlossen sein/entschlossen sein, etw. zu tun. **'set about** *v. t.* **~ about sth.** sich an etw. *(Akk.)* machen; **~ about doing sth.** sich daranmachen, etw. zu tun. **set a'side** *v. t.* **a)** beiseite legen; **b)** aufheben ⟨*Urteil, Entscheidung*⟩. **set 'back** *v. t.* **a)** aufhalten ⟨*Entwicklung*⟩; zurückwerfen ⟨*Projekt, Programm*⟩; **b)** *(coll.: cost)* kosten ⟨*Person*⟩; **c)** *(place at a distance)* zurücksetzen. **set 'down** *v. t.* **a)** absetzen ⟨*Fahrgast*⟩; **b)** *(record)* niederschreiben. **set 'off 1.** *v. i. (begin journey)* aufbrechen; *(start to move)* loslaufen; ⟨*Fahrzeug:*⟩ losfahren. **2.** *v. t.* **a)** *(cause to explode)* explodieren lassen; abbrennen ⟨*Feuerwerk*⟩; **b)** auslösen ⟨*Reaktion, Alarmanlage*⟩. **set 'out 1.** *v. i.* **a)** *(begin journey)* aufbrechen *(for nach/zu);* **b)** **~ out to do sth.** sich *(Dat.)* vornehmen, etw. zu tun. **2.** *v. t.* darlegen. **set 'up 1.** *v. t.* **a)** errichten ⟨*Straßensperre, Denkmal*⟩; aufbauen ⟨*Zelt, Klapptisch*⟩; **b)** *(establish)* gründen ⟨*Firma, Organisation*⟩; einrichten ⟨*Büro*⟩. **2.** *v. i.* **~ up in business** ein Geschäft aufmachen

'set-back *n.* Rückschlag, *der*

settee [se'tiː] *n.* Sofa, *das*

'setting *n.* **a)** *(Mus.)* Vertonung, *die;* **b)** *(surroundings)* Rahmen, *der; (of novel etc.)* Schauplatz, *der*

settle ['setl] **1.** *v. t.* **a)** *(horizontally)* [sorgfältig] legen; *(vertically)* [sorgfältig] stellen; *(at an angle)* [sorgfältig] lehnen; **b)** *(determine, resolve)* sich ei nigen auf 〈*Preis*〉; beilegen 〈*Streit, Konflikt, Meinungsverschiedenheit*〉; ausräumen 〈*Zweifel*〉; entscheiden 〈*Frage, Spiel*〉; c) bezahlen 〈*Rechnung, Betrag*〉; erfüllen 〈*Forderung, Anspruch*〉; ausgleichen 〈*Konto*〉. 2. *v.i.* **a)** *(become established)* sich niederlassen; *(as colonist)* sich ansiedeln; **b)** *(pay)* abrechnen; **c)** *(in chair, in front of fire, etc.)* sich niederlassen; *(to work etc.)* sich konzentrieren **(to auf +** **Akk.**); *(into way of life, retirement, etc.)* sich gewöhnen **(into an +** *Akk.*); **d)** *(subside)* 〈*Haus, Fundament, Boden:*〉 sich senken; **e)** 〈*Schnee:*〉 liegenbleiben. **settle 'down 1.** *v.i.* **a)** *(make oneself comfortable)* sich niederlassen **(in in +** *Dat.*); **b)** *(in town or house)* heimisch werden. **2.** *v.t.* **a)** ~ **oneself down** sich [gemütlich] hinsetzen; **b)** *(calm down)* beruhigen. **'settle for** *v.t.* *(agree to)* sich zufriedengeben mit. **settle 'in** *v.i.* *(in new home)* sich einleben. **'settle on** *v.t.* *(decide on)* sich entscheiden für. **settle 'up** *v.i.* abrechnen; ~ **up with the waiter** beim Kellner bezahlen

'settlement *n.* **a)** *(of argument, conflict, dispute, differences)* Beilegung, *die; (of question)* Klärung, *die; (of bill, account)* Bezahlung, *die; (of court case)* Vergleich, *der;* **b)** *(colony)* Siedlung, *die*

settler ['setlə(r)] *n.* Siedler, *der/*Siedlerin, *die*

set: ~**-to** *n., pl.* ~**-tos: have a** ~**-to** Streit haben; *(with fists)* sich prügeln; ~**-up** *n.* System, *das*

seven ['sevn] **1.** *adj.* sieben. **2.** *n.* Sieben, *die. See also* **eight**

seventeen [sevn'ti:n] **1.** *adj.* siebzehn. **2.** *n.* Siebzehn, *die. See also* **eight.**

seventeenth [sevn'ti:nθ] **1.** *adj.* siebzehnt... **2.** *n. (fraction)* Siebzehntel, *das. See also* **eighth**

seventh ['sevnθ] **1.** *adj.* sieb[en]t... **2.** *n. (in sequence)* sieb[en]te, *der/die/das; (in rank)* Sieb[en]te, *der/die/das; (fraction)* Sieb[en]tel, *das. See also* **eighth**

seventieth ['sevntɪɪθ] *adj.* siebzigst...

seventy ['sevntɪ] **1.** *adj.* siebzig. **2.** *n.* Siebzig, *die. See also* **eight; eighty 2**

sever ['sevə(r)] *v.t.* **a)** *(cut)* durchtrennen; *(fig.)* abbrechen 〈*Beziehungen*〉; **b)** *(separate)* abtrennen; *(with axe etc.)* abhacken

several ['sevrl] **1.** *adv.* mehrere; einige; ~ **times** mehrmals. **2.** *pron.* einige;

~ **of us** einige von uns; ~ **of the buildings** einige *od.* mehrere [der] Gebäude

severe [sɪ'vɪə(r)] *adj.,* ~**r** [sɪ'vɪərə(r)], ~**st** [sɪ'vɪərɪst] hart 〈*Urteil, Strafe, Kritik, Test, Prüfung*〉; streng 〈*Frost, Stil, Schönheit*〉; schwer 〈*Dürre, Verlust, Behinderung, Verletzung, Krankheit*〉; rauh 〈*Wetter*〉; heftig 〈*Anfall, Schmerz*〉; bedrohlich 〈*Mangel, Knappheit*〉; stark 〈*Blutung*〉. **se-'verely** *adv.* hart; schwer 〈*verletzt, behindert*〉. **severity** [sɪ'verɪtɪ] *n.* Strenge, *die; (of drought, shortage)* großes Ausmaß; *(of criticism)* Schärfe, *die*

sew [səʊ] *v.t. & i., p.p.* **sewn** [səʊn] *or* **sewed** [səʊd] nähen. **sew 'on** *v.t.* annähen 〈*Knopf*〉; aufnähen 〈*Abzeichen, Band*〉. **sew 'up** *v.t.* nähen 〈*Saum, Naht, Wunde*〉

sewer ['sju:ə(r), 'su:ə(r)] *n. (tunnel)* Abwasserkanal, *der; (pipe)* Abwasserleitung, *die*

'sewing *n.* Näharbeit, *die.* **'sewing-machine** *n.* Nähmaschine, *die*

sewn *see* **sew**

sex [seks] *n.* **a)** Geschlecht, *das;* **b)** *(sexuality; coll.: intercourse)* Sex, *der (ugs.);* **have** ~ **with sb.** *(coll.)* mit jmdm. schlafen

sexism ['seksɪzm] *n.* Sexismus, *der*

sexist ['seksɪst] *adj.* sexistisch

'sex maniac *n.* Triebverbrecher, *der*

sexual ['seksʊəl] *adj.* sexuell. **sexual 'intercourse** *n.* Geschlechtsverkehr, *der.* **sexuality** [seksʊ'ælɪtɪ] *n.* Sexualität, *die*

'sexy *adj.* sexy *(ugs.)*

shabbily ['ʃæbɪlɪ] *adv.,* **shabby** ['ʃæbɪ] *adj.* schäbig

shack [ʃæk] *n.* [armselige] Hütte

shackle ['ʃækl] **1.** *n., usu. in pl.* Fessel, *die.* **2.** *v.t.* anketten **(to an +** *Akk.*)

shade [ʃeɪd] **1.** *n.* **a)** Schatten, *der;* **b)** *(colour)* Ton, *der; (fig.)* Schattierung, *die;* **c)** *(lamp~)* [Lampen]schirm, *der.* **2.** *v.t.* **a)** *(screen)* beschatten; **b)** *(darken with lines)* ~ **[in]** [ab]schattieren. **3.** *v.i.* übergehen **(into in +** *Akk.*)

shadow ['ʃædəʊ] **1.** *n.* Schatten, *der.* **2.** *v.t. (follow)* beschatten. **'shadowy** *adj. (indistinct)* schattenhaft

shady ['ʃeɪdɪ] *adj.* **a)** schattig; **b)** *(disreputable)* zwielichtig

shaft [ʃɑ:ft] *n.* **a)** *(of tool, golf club)* Schaft, *der;* **b)** *(Mech. Engin.)* Welle, *die;* **c)** *(of mine, lift)* Schacht, *der;* **d)** *(of light, lightning)* Strahl, *der*

shaggy ['ʃægɪ] *adj.* zottelig

shake [ʃeɪk] **1.** *n.* Schütteln, *das;* **give**

sb./sth. a ~: jmdn./etw. schütteln. 2.
v. t., **shook** [ʃʊk], **shaken** ['ʃeɪkn] a)
(move violently) schütteln; ~ **one's**
fist/a stick at sb. jmdm. mit der Faust/
einem Stock drohen; ~ **hands** sich
(Dat.) die Hand geben; b) *(cause to*
tremble) erschüttern ⟨*Gebäude usw.*⟩;
~ **one's head** den Kopf schütteln; c)
(shock) erschüttern. 3. *v. i.,* **shook,**
shaken wackeln; ⟨*Boden, Stimme:*⟩ beben; ⟨*Hand:*⟩ zittern. **shake 'off** *v. t.*
abschütteln. **shake 'up** *v. t.* a) *(upset,*
shock) einen Schrecken einjagen
(+ *Dat.*); b) *(coll.: reorganize)* um-
krempeln *(ugs.)*

shaken *see* **shake** 2, 3

shaky ['ʃeɪkɪ] *adj.* wack[e]lig ⟨*Möbel-*
stück, Leiter⟩; zittrig ⟨*Hand, Stimme,*
Greis⟩; **feel** ~: sich zittrig fühlen

shall [ʃl, *stressed* ʃæl] *v. aux. only in*
pres. **shall,** *neg. (coll.)* **shan't** [ʃɑːnt],
past **should** [ʃəd, *stressed* ʃʊd], *neg.*
(coll.) **shouldn't** [ʃʊdnt] a) *expr. simple*
future werden; b) **should** *expr. condi-*
tional würde/würdest/würden/wür-
det; **I should have been killed if I had**
let go ich wäre getötet worden, wenn
ich losgelassen hätte; **if we should be**
defeated falls wir unterliegen [sollten];
c) *expr. will or intention* **what** ~ **we do?**
was sollen wir tun?; **let's go in,** ~ **we?**
gehen wir doch hinein, oder?; **we**
should be safe by now jetzt dürften wir
in Sicherheit sein; **he shouldn't do**
things like that! er sollte so etwas
nicht tun!

shallot [ʃə'lɒt] *n.* Schalotte, *die*

shallow ['ʃæləʊ] *adj.* seicht ⟨*Wasser,*
Fluß⟩; flach ⟨*Schüssel, Teller, Was-*
ser⟩; *(fig.)* flach ⟨*Person*⟩

sham [ʃæm] 1. *adj.* unecht; imitiert
⟨*Leder, Holz, Pelz*⟩. 2. *n. (pretence)*
Heuchelei, *die; (person)* Heuchler,
der/Heuchlerin, *die*. 3. *v. t.,* **-mm-** vortäuschen. 4. *v. i.,* **-mm-** simulieren

shambles ['ʃæmblz] *n. (coll.)* Chaos,
das; **the room was a** ~: das Zimmer
glich einem Schlachtfeld

shame [ʃeɪm] *n.* a) Scham, *die;* b)
(state of disgrace) Schande, *die;* **put**
sb./sth. to ~: jmdn. beschämen/etw.
in den Schatten stellen; c) **what a** ~!
wie schade! **'shamefaced** *adj.* betreten. **shameful** ['ʃeɪmfl] *adj.* beschämend. **'shameless** *adj.* schamlos

shampoo [ʃæm'puː] 1. *v. t.* schampo-
nieren. 2. *n.* Shampoo[n], *das*

shamrock ['ʃæmrɒk] *n.* Klee, *der*

shandy ['ʃændɪ] *n.* Bier mit Limonade

shan't [ʃɑːnt] *(coll.)* = **shall not**

'shanty ['ʃæntɪ] *n. (hut)* [armselige]
Hütte

²shanty *n. (song)* Shanty, *das*

'shanty town *n.* Elendsviertel, *das*

shape [ʃeɪp] 1. *v. t.* formen; bearbeiten
⟨*Holz, Stein*⟩ (into zu). 2. *n.* Form, *die;*
take ~: Gestalt annehmen. **shape**
'up *v. i.* sich entwickeln

'shapeless *adj.* formlos; unförmig
⟨*Kleid, Person*⟩

shapely ['ʃeɪplɪ] *adj.* wohlgeformt
⟨*Beine, Busen*⟩; gut ⟨*Figur*⟩

share [ʃeə(r)] 1. *n.* a) *(portion)* Teil, *der*
od. das; |**fair**| ~: Anteil, *der;* **fair** ~s
gerechte Teile; **do more than one's**
|**fair**| ~ **of the work** mehr als seinen
Teil zur Arbeit beitragen. b) *(Com-*
merc.) Aktie, *die*. 2. *v. t.* teilen; gemeinsam tragen ⟨*Verantwortung*⟩. 3.
v. i. ~ **in** teilnehmen an (+ *Dat.*); beteiligt sein an (+ *Dat.*) ⟨*Gewinn*⟩; teilen ⟨*Freude, Erfahrung*⟩. **share 'out**
v. t. aufteilen (**among** unter + *Akk.*)

share: ~**holder** *n.* Aktionär, *der*/
Aktionärin, *die;* ~**out** *n.* Aufteilung,
die

shark [ʃɑːk] *n.* Hai[fisch], *der*

sharp [ʃɑːp] 1. *adj.* a) scharf; spitz
⟨*Nadel, Bleistift, Gipfel, Winkel*⟩;
deutlich ⟨*Unterscheidung*⟩; sauer
⟨*Apfel*⟩; herb ⟨*Wein*⟩; *(shrill, piercing)*
schrill ⟨*Schrei, Pfiff*⟩; heftig ⟨*Schmerz,*
Krampf, Kampf⟩; begabt ⟨*Schüler,*
Student⟩; b) *(derog.: dishonest)* gerissen; c) *(Mus.)* [um einen Halbton] er-
höht ⟨*Note*⟩. 2. *adv.* a) *(punctually)* **at**
six o'clock ~: Punkt sechs Uhr; b)
turn ~ **right/left** scharf nach rechts/
links abbiegen; c) **look** ~! halt dich
ran! *(ugs.);* d) *(Mus.)* zu hoch ⟨*singen,*
spielen⟩. **sharpen** ['ʃɑːpn] *v. t.* schärfen; [an]spitzen ⟨*Bleistift*⟩. **'sharp-**
ener *n. (for pencils)* Spitzer, *der*
(ugs.). **'sharp-eyed** *adj.* scharfäu-
gig; **be** ~: scharfe Augen haben.
'sharply *adv.* scharf; in scharfem
Ton ⟨*antworten*⟩. **'sharpness** *n.*
Schärfe, *die; (fineness of point)* Spitz-
heit, *die*

shatter ['ʃætə(r)] 1. *v. t.* zertrümmern;
zerbrechen ⟨*Glas, Fenster*⟩; zerschlagen ⟨*Hoffnungen*⟩. 2. *v. i.* zerbrechen.
shattered ['ʃætəd] *adj.* a) zerbrochen ⟨*Glas, Fenster*⟩; *(fig.)* zerstört
⟨*Hoffnungen*⟩; zerrüttet ⟨*Nerven*⟩; b)
(coll.: greatly upset) **she was** ~ **by the**
news die Nachricht hat sie schwer mitgenommen; **I'm** ~! ich bin ganz er-

schüttert!; *(Brit. coll.: exhausted)* ich bin kaputt! *(ugs.)*. '**shattering** *adj.* verheerend ⟨*Wirkung*⟩; vernichtend ⟨*Schlag, Niederlage*⟩

shave [ʃeɪv] **1.** *v. t.* rasieren; abrasieren ⟨*Haare*⟩. **2.** *v. i.* sich rasieren. **3.** *n.* Rasur, *die;* **have a ~:** sich rasieren. **shave 'off** *v. t.* abrasieren

'**shaven** ['ʃeɪvn] *adj.* rasiert; [kahl]geschoren ⟨*Kopf*⟩

'**shaver** *n.* Rasierapparat, *der.* '**shaver point** *n.* Anschluß für den Rasierapparat

shaving ['ʃeɪvɪŋ] *n.* **a)** Rasieren, *das;* **b)** *in pl. (of wood, metal, etc.)* Späne **shaving:** **~-brush** *n.* Rasierpinsel, *der;* **~-cream** *n.* Rasiercreme, *die;* **~-foam** *n.* Rasierschaum, *der*

shawl [ʃɔːl] *n.* Schultertuch, *das*

she [ʃɪ, *stressed* ʃiː] *pron.* sie

sheaf [ʃiːf] *n., pl.* **sheaves** [ʃiːvz] *(of corn etc.)* Garbe, *die; (of paper, arrows, etc.)* Bündel, *das*

shear [ʃɪə(r)] *v. t., p.p.* **shorn** [ʃɔːn] *or* **sheared** *(clip)* scheren. **shears** [ʃɪəz] *n. pl.* |**pair of**| ~: Schere, *die;* **garden ~:** Gartenschere, *die*

sheath [ʃiːθ] *n., pl.* **~s** [ʃiːðz, ʃiːθs] **a)** *(for knife, sword, etc.)* Scheide, *die;* **b)** *(condom)* Gummischutz, *der*

sheaves *pl. of* **sheaf**

¹**shed** [ʃed] *v. t.,* **-dd-,** **shed a)** verlieren; abwerfen ⟨*Laub, Geweih*⟩; **b)** vergießen ⟨*Blut, Tränen*⟩; **c)** verbreiten ⟨*Licht*⟩

²**shed** *n.* Schuppen, *der*

she'd [ʃɪd, *stressed* ʃiːd] **a)** = **she had; b)** = **she would**

sheen [ʃiːn] *n.* Glanz, *der*

sheep [ʃiːp] *n., pl.* same Schaf, *das.* '**sheep-dog** *n.* Hütehund, *der*

sheepish ['ʃiːpɪʃ] *adj.* verlegen '**sheepskin** *n.* Schaffell, *das*

sheer [ʃɪə(r)] *adj.* **a)** rein; blank ⟨*Unsinn, Gewalt*⟩; **by ~ chance** rein zufällig; **b)** schroff ⟨*Felsen, Abfall*⟩

sheet [ʃiːt] *n.* **a)** Laken, *das;* **b)** *(of thin metal or plastic)* Folie, *die; (of iron, tin)* Blech, *das; (of glass)* Platte, *die; (of paper)* Bogen, *der;* Blatt, *das;* **c)** ⟨*Eis-, Nebel*⟩decke, *die*

sheik[h] [ʃeɪk, ʃiːk] *n.* Scheich, *der*

shelf [ʃelf] *n., pl.* **shelves** [ʃelvz] Brett, *das;* **shelves** *(set)* Regal, *das.* '**shelf-life** *n.* Lagerfähigkeit, *die*

shell [ʃel] **1.** *n.* **a)** Schale, *die; (of snail)* Haus, *das; (of turtle, tortoise)* Panzer, *der; (on beach)* Muschel, *die;* **b)** *(Mil.) (bomb)* Granate, *die.* **2.** *v. t.* **a)** *(take*

out of ~) schälen; **b)** *(Mil.)* [mit Artillerie] beschießen. **shell 'out** *v. t. & i. (sl.)* blechen *(ugs.)* **(on** für)

she'll [ʃɪl, *stressed* ʃiːl] = **she will**

'**shellfish** *n., pl.* same **a)** Schal[en]tier, *das; (oyster, clam)* Muschel, *die; (crustacean)* Krebstier, *das;* **b)** *in pl. (Gastr.)* Meeresfrüchte *Pl.*

shelter ['ʃeltə(r)] **1.** *n.* **a)** *(shield)* Schutz, *der* (**against** vor + *Dat.,* gegen); **bomb** *or* **air-raid ~:** Luftschutzraum, *der;* **get under ~:** sich unterstellen; **b)** *no pl. (place of safety)* Zuflucht, *die.* **2.** *v. t.* schützen **(from** vor + *Dat.)*; Unterschlupf gewähren (+ *Dat.*) ⟨*Flüchtling*⟩. **3.** *v. i.* Schutz suchen **(from** vor + *Dat.*). '**sheltered** *adj.* geschützt; behütet ⟨*Leben*⟩

shelve [ʃelv] **1.** *v. t. (defer)* auf Eis legen *(ugs.).* **2.** *v. i. (slope)* abfallen

shelves *pl. of* **shelf**

'**shelving** *n.* Regale *Pl.*

shepherd ['ʃepəd] **1.** *n.* Schäfer, *der.* **2.** *v. t.* führen. '**shepherdess** *n.* Schäferin, *die*

shepherd: **~'s 'crook** *n.* Schäferstock, *der;* **~'s 'pie** *n. Auflauf aus Hackfleisch mit einer Schicht Kartoffelbrei darüber*

sherry ['ʃerɪ] *n.* Sherry, *der*

she's [ʃɪz, *stressed* ʃiːz] **a)** = **she is; b)** = **she has**

shield [ʃiːld] **1.** *n.* Schild, *der.* **2.** *v. t.* schützen **(from** vor + *Dat.)*

shift [ʃɪft] **1.** *v. t.* **a)** *(move)* umstellen ⟨*Möbel*⟩; wegnehmen ⟨*Arm, Hand, Fuß*⟩; wegräumen ⟨*Schutt*⟩; entfernen ⟨*Schmutz, Fleck*⟩; **~ the responsibility/ blame on to sb.** die Verantwortung/ Schuld auf jmdn. schieben; **b)** *(Amer. Motor Veh.)* **~ gears** schalten. **2.** *v. i.* **a)** ⟨*Wind:*⟩ drehen **(to** nach); ⟨*Ladung:*⟩ verrutschen; **b)** *(sl.: move quickly)* rasen. **3.** *n.* **a) a ~ in emphasis** eine Verlagerung des Akzents; **a ~ in public opinion** ein Umschwung der öffentlichen Meinung; **b)** *(for work)* Schicht, *die;* **eight-hour/late ~:** Achtstunden-/ Spätschicht, *die;* **do** *or* **work the late ~:** Spätschicht haben. '**shift work** *n.* Schichtarbeit, *die*

shifty ['ʃɪftɪ] *adj.* verschlagen

shilling ['ʃɪlɪŋ] *n. (Hist.)* Shilling, *der*

shilly-shally ['ʃɪlɪʃælɪ] *v. i.* zaudern; **stop ~ing!** entschließ dich endlich!

shimmer ['ʃɪmə(r)] **1.** *v. i.* schimmern. **2.** *n.* Schimmer, *der*

shin [ʃɪn] **1.** *n.* Schienbein, *das.* **2.** *v. i.,* **-nn-:** **~ up/down a tree** *etc.* einen

Baum *usw.* hinauf-/hinunterklettern.
'**shin-bone** *n.* Schienbein, *das*
shine [ʃaɪn] **1.** *v.i.,* **shone** [ʃɒn]
⟨*Lampe, Licht, Stern:*⟩ leuchten;
⟨*Sonne, Mond:*⟩ scheinen; *(reflect
light)* glänzen. **2.** *v.t.,* **shone:** ~ **a light
on sth./in sb.'s eyes** etw. anleuchten/
jmdm. in die Augen leuchten. **3.** *n.*
Glanz, *der*
shingle ['ʃɪŋgl] *n.* *(pebbles)* Kies, *der*
'**shingles** *n.* *(Med.)* Gürtelrose, *die*
shin: ~-**guard,** ~-**pad** *ns.* Schien-
beinschutz, *der*
shiny ['ʃaɪnɪ] *adj.* glänzend
ship [ʃɪp] **1.** *n.* Schiff, *das.* **2.** *v.t.,* -**pp**-
(transport by sea) verschiffen; *(send
by road, train, or air)* verschicken
⟨*Waren*⟩. '**shipbuilding** *n.* Schiffbau,
der
'**shipment** *n.* **a)** Versand, *der;* *(by sea)*
Verschiffung, *die;* **b)** *(amount)* Sendung, *die*
'**shipowner** *n.* Schiffseigentümer,
der/-eigentümerin, *die;* *(of several
ships)* Reeder, *der/*Reederin, *die*
'**shipper** *n.* Spediteur, *der/*Spediteu-
rin, *die;* *(company)* Spedition, *die*
'**shipping** *n.* **a)** *(ships)* Schiffe; *(traffic)* Schiffahrt, *die;* **b)** *(transporting)*
Versand, *der*
ship: ~**shape** *adj.* in bester Ordnung;
~**wreck 1.** *n.* Schiffbruch, *der.* **2.** *v.t.*
be ~**wrecked** Schiffbruch erleiden;
~**yard** *n.* [Schiffs]werft, *die*
shirk [ʃɜ:k] *v.t.* sich drücken vor
(+ *Dat.*). '**shirker** *n.* Drückeberger,
der (ugs.)
shirt [ʃɜ:t] *n.* |**man's**| ~: [Herren- *od.*
Ober]hemd, *das;* |**woman's**| ~: Hemd-
bluse, *die.* '**shirt-sleeve** *n.* Hemds-
ärmel, *der;* **in** ~**s** in Hemdsärmeln
shit [ʃɪt] *(coarse)* **1.** *v.i.,* -**tt**-, **shitted** *or*
shit scheißen *(derb).* **2.** *n.* **a)** Scheiße,
die (derb); **have** *(Brit.)* or *(Amer.)* **take
a** ~: scheißen *(derb);* **b)** *(person)*
Scheißkerl, *der (derb);* **c)** *(nonsense)*
Scheiß, *der (salopp)*
shiver ['ʃɪvə(r)] **1.** *v.i.* zittern (**with** vor
+ *Dat.*). **2.** *n.* Schau[d]er, *der (geh.)*
shoal [ʃəʊl] *n.* *(of fish)* Schwarm, *der*
shock [ʃɒk] **1.** *n.* **a)** Schock, *der;* **give
sb. a** ~: jmdm. einen Schock verset-
zen; **b)** *(violent impact)* Erschütterung,
die (**of** durch); **c)** *(Electr.)* Schlag, *der;*
d) *(Med.)* Schock, *der.* **2.** *v.t.* ~ **sb.**
|**deeply**| ein [schwerer] Schock für
jmdn. sein; *(scandalize)* jmdn.
schockieren. '**shock absorber** *n.*
Stoßdämpfer, *der*

'**shocking** *adj.* **a)** schockierend; **b)**
(coll.: very bad) fürchterlich *(ugs.)*
'**shock-proof** *adj.* stoßfest
shod *see* **shoe** 2
shoddy ['ʃɒdɪ] *adj.* schäbig; minderwertig ⟨*Arbeit, Stoff, Artikel*⟩
shoe [ʃu:] **1.** *n.* Schuh, *der;* *(of horse)*
[Huf]eisen, *das;* **put oneself into sb.'s**
~**s** *(fig.)* sich in jmds. Lage *(Akk.)* versetzen. **2.** *v.t.,* ~**ing, shod** [ʃɒd] beschlagen ⟨*Pferd*⟩
shoe: ~**horn** *n.* Schuhlöffel, *der;*
~-**lace** *n.* Schnürsenkel, *der;*
~**maker** *n.* Schuhmacher, *der;*
~-**polish** *n.* Schuhcreme, *die;*
~-**shop** *n.* Schuhgeschäft, *das;*
~**string** *n.* **on a** ~**string** *(coll.)* mit
ganz wenig Geld
shone *see* **shine** 1, 2
shoo [ʃu:] **1.** *int.* sch. **2.** *v.t.* scheuchen; ~ **away** fortscheuchen
shook *see* **shake** 2, 3
shoot [ʃu:t] **1.** *v.i.* **a)** schießen (**at** auf + *Akk.*); **b)** *(move rapidly)*
schießen *(ugs.).* **2.** *v.t.,* **shot a)**
(wound) anschießen; *(kill)* erschießen; *(hunt)* schießen; ~ **sb. dead**
jmdn. erschießen; **b)** schießen mit
⟨*Bogen, Munition, Pistole*⟩; abschießen *(Pfeil, Kugel)* (**at** auf + *Akk.*); **c)**
(Cinemat.) drehen ⟨*Film, Szene*⟩. **3.** *n.*
(Bot.) Trieb, *der.* **shoot** '**down** *v.t.*
niederschießen ⟨*Person*⟩; abschie-
ßen ⟨*Flugzeug*⟩. **shoot** '**out** *v.i.* hervorschießen. **shoot** '**up** *v.i.* in die Höhe
schießen; ⟨*Preise, Kosten, Temperatur:*⟩ in die Höhe schnellen
shooting: ~-**range** *n.* Schießstand,
der; ~ '**star** *n.* Sternschnuppe, *die*
'**shoot-out** *n.* Schießerei, *die*
shop [ʃɒp] **1.** *n.* Laden, *der;* Geschäft,
das; **go to the** ~**s** einkaufen gehen;
talk ~: fachsimpeln *(ugs.).* **2.** *v.i.,*
-**pp**- einkaufen; **go** ~**ping** einkaufen
gehen. **shop a**'**round** *v.i.* sich umsehen (**for** nach)
shop: ~ **assistant** *n.* *(Brit.)* Verkäufer, *der/*Verkäuferin, *die;* ~**keeper**
n. Ladenbesitzer, *der/*-besitzerin, *die;*
~-**lifter** *n.* Ladendieb, *der/*-diebin,
die; ~-**lifting** *n.* Ladendiebstahl,
der; ~**owner** *see* ~**keeper**
'**shopper** *n.* Käufer, *der/*Käuferin, *die*
'**shopping** *n.* **a)** Einkaufen, *das;* **do
the/one's** ~: einkaufen/[seine] Ein-
käufe machen; **b)** *(items bought)* Ein-
käufe *Pl.*
shopping: ~-**bag** *n.* Einkaufstasche,
die; ~-**basket** *n.* Einkaufskorb, *der;*

~ **centre** *n.* Einkaufszentrum, *das;*
~-**list** *n.* Einkaufszettel, *der;* ~ **mall**
[~ mæl] *n.* Einkaufszentrum, *das;* ~
street *n.* Geschäftsstraße, *die;* ~
trolley *n.* Einkaufswagen, *der*
shop: ~-**soiled** *adj. (Brit.) (slightly
damaged)* leicht beschädigt; *(slightly
dirty)* angeschmutzt; ~ '**window** *n.*
Schaufenster, *das*
shore [ʃɔː(r)] *n.* Ufer, *das; (beach)*
Strand, *der.* **shore 'up** *v. t.* abstützen
⟨*Mauer, Haus*⟩; *(fig.)* stützen
shorn *see* **shear**
short [ʃɔːt] **1.** *adj.* **a)** kurz; **in a ~ time**
or **while** *(soon)* bald; **in Kürze; a ~
time** *or* **while ago/later** vor kurzem/
kurze Zeit später; **in ~, ...:** kurz, ...; **b)**
klein ⟨*Person, Wuchs*⟩; **c)** *(deficient,
scanty)* knapp; **go ~ |of sth.|** [an etw.
(Dat.)] Mangel leiden; **sb. is ~ of sth.**
jmdm. fehlt es an etw. *(Dat.);* **time is
getting/is ~:** die Zeit wird/ist knapp;
be in ~ supply knapp sein; **be ~ |of
cash|** knapp [bei Kasse] sein *(ugs.).* **2.**
adv. **a)** *(abruptly)* plötzlich; **stop ~:**
plötzlich abbrechen; **stop sb. ~:**
jmdm. ins Wort fallen; **b) stop ~ of
doing sth.** davor zurückschrecken,
etw. zu tun. **shortage** [ˈʃɔːtɪdʒ] *n.*
Mangel, *der* **(of an +** *Dat.);* ~ **of
fruit/teachers** Obstknappheit, *die/*
Lehrermangel, *der*
short: ~-**bread** *n.* Shortbread, *das;*
Keks aus Butterteig; ~ '**circuit** *n.*
(Electr.) Kurzschluß, *der;* ~-**coming**
n., usu. in pl. Unzulänglichkeit, *die;* ~
'**cut** *n.* Abkürzung, *die;* **take a ~ cut**
den Weg abkürzen
shorten [ˈʃɔːtn] **1.** *v. i.* kürzer werden.
2. *v. t.* kürzen; verkürzen ⟨*Besuch,
Wartezeit*⟩
short: ~-**hand** *n.* Stenographie, *die;*
~-**hand typist** Stenotypist, *der/*-typi-
stin, *die;* ~ **list** *n. (Brit.)* engere Auswahl; **be on/put sb. on the ~ list** in der
engeren Auswahl sein/jmdn. in die
engere Auswahl nehmen; ~-**list** *v. t.*
in die engere Auswahl nehmen;
~-**lived** *adj.* kurzlebig
'**shortly** *adv.* in Kürze; gleich *(ugs.);* ~
before/after sth. kurz vor/nach etw.
'**short-range** *adj.* **a)** Kurzstrecken-
⟨*flugzeug, -rakete usw.*⟩; **b)** *(relating to
time)* kurzfristig
shorts [ʃɔːts] *n. pl.* **a)** *(trousers)* kurze
Hose[n]; Shorts *Pl.;* **b)** *(Amer.: underpants)* Unterhose, *die*
short: ~-'**sighted** *adj.* kurzsichtig;
~-**sleeved** ['~sliːvd] *adj.* kurzärm[e]-

lig; ~-**staffed** [~ˈstaːft] *adj.* **be |very|**
~-**staffed** [viel] zu wenig Personal haben; ~ '**story** *n.* Kurzgeschichte, *die;*
~-**term** *adj.* kurzfristig; *(provisional)*
vorläufig ⟨*Lösung*⟩; ~ **wave** *n.*
(Radio) Kurzwelle, *die*
shot [ʃɒt] **1.** *n.* **a)** Schuß, *der;* **fire a ~:**
einen Schuß abgeben **(at auf +** *Akk.);*
like a ~ *(fig.)* wie der Blitz *(ugs.);* **I'd
do it like a ~:** ich würde es auf der
Stelle tun; **b)** *(Athletics)* **put the ~:** die
Kugel stoßen; **|putting| the ~:** Kugel-
stoßen, *das;* **c)** *(Sport: stroke, kick,
throw)* Schuß, *der;* **d)** *(Photog.)* Aufnahme, *die; (Cinemat.)* Einstellung,
die. **2.** *see* **shoot** 1, 2. **3.** *adj.* **be/get ~
of** *(sl.)* los sein/loswerden. '**shotgun**
n. Schrotflinte, *die*
should *see* **shall**
shoulder [ˈʃəʊldə(r)] **1.** *n.* Schulter,
die. **2.** *v. t.* schultern; *(fig.)* übernehmen
shoulder: ~-**bag** *n.* Umhängetasche,
die; ~-**blade** *n.* Schulterblatt, *das;*
~-**strap** *n. (on garment)* Schulter-
klappe, *die; (on bag)* Tragriemen, *der*
shouldn't [ˈʃʊdnt] *(coll.)* = **should
not;** *see* **shall**
shout [ʃaʊt] **1.** *n.* Ruf, *der; (inarticu-
late)* Schrei, *der.* **2.** *v. i. & t.* schreien.
shout 'down *v. t.* niederschreien.
shout 'out 1. *v. i.* aufschreien. **2.** *v. t.*
[laut] rufen
'**shouting** *n.* Geschrei, *das*
shove [ʃʌv] **1.** *n.* Stoß, *der.* **2.** *v. t.* stoßen; schubsen *(ugs.); (coll.: put)* tun.
shove a'way *v. t. (coll.)* wegschub-
sen *(ugs.).* **shove 'off** *v. i. (sl.: leave)*
abschieben *(ugs.)*
shovel [ˈʃʌvl] **1.** *n.* Schaufel, *die.* **2.**
v. t., (Brit.) -**ll-** schaufeln
show [ʃəʊ] **1.** *n.* **a)** *(entertainment, performance)* Show, *die; (Theatre)* Vorstellung, *die; (Radio, Telev.)* [Unter-
haltungs]sendung, *die;* **b)** *(exhibition)*
Ausstellung, *die;* Schau, *die;* **put sth.
on ~:** etw. ausstellen; **be on ~:** ausge-
stellt sein; **c)** *(appearance)* Anschein,
der; **be for ~:** reine Angeberei sein
(ugs.). **2.** *v. t., p.p.* **shown** [ʃəʊn] **a)**
zeigen; vorzeigen ⟨*Paß, Fahrschein
usw.*⟩; ~ **sb. sth., ~ sth. to sb.** jmdm.
etw. zeigen; **b)** beweisen ⟨*Mut, Urteilsvermögen usw.*⟩; ~ **sb. that ...:** jmdm.
beweisen, daß ...; ~ **|sb.| kindness/
mercy** freundlich [zu jmdm.] sein/Er-
barmen [mit jmdm.] haben; **c)** ⟨*Thermometer, Uhr usw.*⟩ anzeigen; **d)** *(exhibit in a show)* ausstellen; zeigen

⟨*Film*⟩. **3.** *v. i., p. p.* **shown a)** *(be visible)* sichtbar *od.* zu sehen sein; *(come into sight)* sich zeigen; **b)** *(be ~n)* ⟨*Film*:⟩ laufen. **show 'in** *v. t.* hinein-/hereinführen. **show 'off** *v. i.* angeben *(ugs.);* prahlen. **show 'out** *v. t.* hinausführen. **show 'round** *v. t.* herumführen. **show 'through** *v. i.* durchscheinen. **show 'up 1.** *v. t.* **a)** *(make visible)* [deutlich] sichtbar machen; **b)** *(coll.: embarrass)* blamieren. **2.** *v. i.* **a)** *(be visible)* [deutlich] zu sehen sein; **b)** *(coll.: arrive)* sich blicken lassen *(ugs.)*

'**show-down** *n. (fig.)* Kraftprobe, *die;* have a ~ |with sb.| sich |mit jmdm.| auseinandersetzen

shower ['ʃaʊə(r)] **1.** *n.* **a)** Schauer, *der;* ~ of rain/hail Regen-/Hagelschauer, *der;* **b)** *(for washing)* Dusche, *die;* have *or* take a |cold/quick| ~: [kalt/schnell] duschen. **2.** *v. t. (lavish)* ~ sth. |up|on sb., ~ sb. with sth. jmdn. mit etw. überhäufen. **3.** *v. i. (have a ~)* duschen

shower: ~**-curtain** *n.* Duschvorhang, *der;* ~ **gel** *n.* Duschgel, *das;* ~**-proof** *adj.* [bedingt] regendicht

'**showery** *adj.* it is ~: es gibt immer wieder leichte Schauer; a ~ **day** ein Tag mit Schauerwetter

'**show-jumping** *n.* Springreiten, *das*

shown *see* show 2, 3

show: ~**-off** *n. (coll.)* Angeber, *der/* Angeberin, *die;* ~**-piece** *n. (of exhibition, collection)* Schaustück, *das; (highlight)* Paradestück, *das;* ~**room** *n.* Ausstellungsraum, *der*

'**showy** *adj.* protzig *(ugs.)*

shrank *see* shrink

shred [ʃred] **1.** *n.* Fetzen, *der; (fig.)* Spur, *die;* tear sth. to ~s etw. zerfetzen; *(fig.)* etw. zerpflücken. **2.** *v. t.,* -dd- [im Reißwolf] zerkleinern

shrew [ʃruː] *n. (Zool.)* Spitzmaus, *die*

shrewd [ʃruːd] *adj.* klug; genau ⟨*[Ein]schätzung*⟩

shriek [ʃriːk] **1.** *n.* [Auf]schrei, *der.* **2.** *v. i.* [auf]schreien. **3.** *v. t.* schreien

shrift [ʃrɪft] *n.* give sb. short ~: jmdn. kurz abfertigen *(ugs.);* get short ~ kurz abgefertigt werden *(ugs.)*

shrill [ʃrɪl] *adj.* schrill

shrimp [ʃrɪmp] *n.* Garnele, *die*

shrine [ʃraɪn] *n. (tomb)* Grab, *das*

shrink [ʃrɪŋk] **1.** *v. i.,* **shrank** [ʃræŋk], **shrunk** [ʃrʌŋk] **a)** schrumpfen; ⟨*Kleidung, Stoff:*⟩ einlaufen; ⟨*Metall, Holz:*⟩ sich zusammenziehen; **b)** *(recoil)* ~ from sb./sth. vor jmdm. zu-

rückweichen/vor etw. *(Dat.)* zurückschrecken; ~ **from doing** sth. sich scheuen, etw. zu tun. **2.** *v. t.,* **shrank,** **shrunk** einlaufen lassen ⟨*Textilien*⟩

shrivel ['ʃrɪvl] *v. i., (Brit.)* -ll-: ~ |up| verschrumpeln; ⟨*Pflanze, Blume:*⟩ welk werden

shroud [ʃraʊd] **1.** *n.* Leichentuch, *das.* **2.** *v. t.* ~ sth. in sth. etw. in etw. *(Akk.)* hüllen

Shrove [ʃrəʊv] '**Tuesday** *n.* Fastnachtsdienstag, *der*

shrub [ʃrʌb] *n.* Strauch, *der*

shrug [ʃrʌg] **1.** *v. t. & i.,* -gg-: ~ |one's shoulders| die Achseln zucken. **2.** *n.* ~ |of one's *or* the shoulders| Achselzucken, *das.* **shrug 'off** *v. t.* in den Wind schlagen

shrunk *see* shrink

shrunken ['ʃrʌŋkn] *adj.* verhutzelt *(ugs.)* ⟨*Person*⟩; schrump[e]lig ⟨*Apfel*⟩

shudder ['ʃʌdə(r)] **1.** *v. i.* zittern (with vor + *Dat.*). **2.** *n.* Zittern, *das*

shuffle ['ʃʌfl] **1.** *n.* **a)** Schlurfen, *das;* walk with a ~: schlurfen; **b)** *(Cards)* Mischen, *das;* give the cards a |good| ~: die Karten [gut] mischen. **2.** *v. t.* **a)** *(Cards)* mischen; **b)** ~ one's feet von einem Fuß auf den anderen treten

shun [ʃʌn] *v. t.,* -nn- meiden

shunt [ʃʌnt] *v. t. (Railw.)* rangieren

shush [ʃʊʃ] *int.* still

shut [ʃʌt] **1.** *v. t.,* -tt-, **shut** zumachen; schließen; zusammenklappen ⟨*Klappmesser, Fächer*⟩; ~ one's finger in the door sich *(Dat.)* den Finger in der Tür einklemmen. **2.** *v. i.,* -tt-, **shut** schließen; ⟨*Blüte:*⟩ sich schließen. **shut 'down 1.** *v. t.* **a)** schließen, zumachen ⟨*Deckel*⟩; **b)** stillegen ⟨*Fabrik*⟩; abschalten ⟨*Kernreaktor*⟩. **2.** *v. i.* ⟨*Laden, Fabrik:*⟩ geschlossen werden. **shut 'out** *v. t.* aussperren. **shut 'up 1.** *v. t.* abschließen; einsperren ⟨*Tier, Person*⟩. **2.** *v. i. (coll.: be quiet)* den Mund halten

shutter ['ʃʌtə(r)] *n.* **a)** [Fenster]laden, *der;* **b)** *(Photog.)* Verschluß, *der;* ~ **release** Auslöser, *der;* ~ **speed** Verschlußzeit, *die*

shuttle ['ʃʌtl] **1.** *n. (in loom)* Schiffchen, *das.* **2.** *v. i.* pendeln. '**shuttlecock** *n.* Federball, *der.* '**shuttle service** *n.* Pendelverkehr, *der*

shy [ʃaɪ] *adj.,* ~**er** *or* **shier** ['ʃaɪə(r)], ~**est** *or* **shiest** ['ʃaɪɪst] scheu *(diffident)* schüchtern. **shy a'way** *v. i.* ~ away from sth./doing sth. etw. scheuen/sich scheuen, etw. zu tun

'**shyness** *n.* Scheuheit, *die;* *(diffidence)* Schüchternheit, *die*
Siamese [saɪə'mi:z]: ~ '**cat** *n.* Siamkatze, *die;* ~ '**twins** *n. pl.* siamesische Zwillinge
Siberia [saɪ'bɪərɪə] *pr. n.* Siberien *(das)*
Sicily ['sɪsɪlɪ] *pr. n.* Sizilien *(das)*
sick [sɪk] *adj.* **a)** *(ill)* krank; **be off** ~: krank [gemeldet] sein; **b)** *(Brit.: vomiting or about to vomit)* **be** ~: sich erbrechen; **I'm going to be** ~: ich muß mich erbrechen; **sb. gets/feels** ~: jmdm. wird/ist [es] übel *od.* schlecht; **be/get** ~ **of sb./sth.** *(fig.)* jmdn./etw. satt haben/allmählich satt haben; **make sb.** ~ *(disgust)* jmdn. anekeln. '**sicken** ['sɪkn] **1.** *v. i.* **be** ~**ing for sth.** *(Brit.)* krank werden; etw. ausbrüten *(ugs.).* **2.** *v. t. (disgust)* anwidern. '**sickening** *adj.* ekelerregend, widerlich ⟨*Anblick, Geruch*⟩
sickle ['sɪkl] *n.* Sichel, *die*
'**sick-leave** *n.* Urlaub wegen Krankheit; **be on** ~ ≈ krank geschrieben sein
sickly ['sɪklɪ] *adj.* kränklich
'**sickness** *n.* Krankheit, *die; (nausea)* Übelkeit, *die*
sick: ~**-pay** *n.* Entgeltfortzahlung im Krankheitsfalle; *(paid by insurance)* Krankengeld, *das;* ~**-room** *n.* Krankenzimmer, *das*
side [saɪd] **1.** *n.* **a)** Seite, *die;* ~ **of beef** Rinderhälfte, *die;* ~ **of bacon** Speckseite, *die;* **walk/stand** ~ **by** ~: nebeneinander gehen/stehen; **work/fight** ~ **by** ~ [**with sb.**] Seite an Seite [mit jmdm.] arbeiten/kämpfen; **live** ~ **by** ~ [**with sb.**] **in** [jmds.] unmittelbarer Nachbarschaft leben; **to one** ~: zur Seite; **on one** ~: an der Seite; **on the** ~ *(as* ~*line)* nebenbei; **take** ~**s** [**with/against sb.**] [für/gegen] jmdn. Partei ergreifen; **b)** *(Sport: team)* Mannschaft, *die.* **2.** *v. i.* ~ **with sb.** sich auf jmds. Seite *(Akk.)* stellen. **3.** *adj.* Seiten-
side: ~**board** *n.* Anrichte, *die;* ~**-car** *n.* Beiwagen, *der;* ~**-dish** *n.* Beilage, *die;* ~**-door** *n.* Seitentür, *die;* ~**-effect** *n.* Nebenwirkung, *die;* ~**-entrance** *n.* Seiteneingang, *der;* ~**-exit** *n.* Seitenausgang, *der;* ~**light** *n.* Begrenzungsleuchte, *die;* **drive on** ~**lights** mit Standlicht fahren; ~**line** *n. (occupation)* Nebenbeschäftigung, *die;* ~**-road** *n.* Seitenstraße, *die;* ~**-show** *n.* Nebenattraktion, *die;* ~**-step 1.** *n.* Schritt zur Seite; **2.** *v. t.*

ausweichen (+ *Dat.*); ~**-street** *n.* Seitenstraße, *die;* ~**track** *v. t.* **get** ~**tracked** abgelenkt werden; ~**walk** *n. (Amer.)* Bürgersteig, *der;* ~**ways** ['saɪdweɪz] **1.** *adv.* **look at sb./sth.** ~**ways** jmdn./etw. von der Seite ansehen; **2.** *adj.* seitlich
siding ['saɪdɪŋ] *n.* Abstellgleis, *das*
sidle ['saɪdl] *v. i.* schleichen [up to zu]
siege [si:dʒ] *n.* Belagerung, *die; (by police)* Umstellung, *die;* **lay** ~ **to sth.** etw. belagern
sieve [sɪv] **1.** *n.* Sieb, *das.* **2.** *v. t.* sieben
sift [sɪft] *v. t.* sieben; ~ **sth. from sth.** etw. von etw. trennen. **sift 'out** *v. t.* aussieben
sigh [saɪ] **1.** *n.* Seufzer, *der;* **breathe** *or* **give** *or* **heave a** ~: einen Seufzer ausstoßen; ~ **of relief/contentment** Seufzer der Erleichterung/Zufriedenheit. **2.** *v. i.* seufzen; ~ **with relief/despair** erleichtert/verzweifelt seufzen
sight [saɪt] **1.** *n.* **a)** *(faculty)* Sehvermögen, *das;* **know sb. by** ~: jmdn. vom Sehen kennen; **b)** *(act of seeing; spectacle)* Anblick, *der;* **catch/lose** ~ **of sb./sth.** jmdn./etw. erblicken/aus dem Auge verlieren; **at first** ~: auf den ersten Blick; **c)** *in pl.* ~**s** *(places of interest)* Sehenswürdigkeiten; **see the** ~**s** die Sehenswürdigkeiten ansehen; **d)** *(range)* Sichtweite, *die;* **in** ~: in Sicht; **within** *or* **in** ~ **of sb./sth.** *(able to see)* in jmds. Sichtweite *(Dat.)/*in Sichtweite einer Sache; **out of** ~: außer Sicht; **e)** *(of gun)* Visier, *das;* **set/have** [**set**] **one's** ~**s on sth.** *(fig.)* etw. anpeilen. **2.** *v. t.* sichten ⟨*Land, Schiff, Flugzeug*⟩; sehen ⟨*Entflohenen, Vermißten*⟩. '**sightseeing** *n.* **go** ~: Besichtigungen machen. **sightseer** ['saɪtsi:ə(r)] *n.* Tourist *(der die Sehenswürdigkeiten besichtigt)*
sign [saɪn] **1.** *n.* **a)** *(symbol, signal, indication)* Zeichen, *das; (of future event)* Anzeichen, *das;* **as a** ~ **of** als Zeichen (+ *Gen.*); **b)** *(Astrol.)* ~ [**of the zodiac**] Sternzeichen, *das;* **c)** *(notice; on shop etc.)* Schild, *das.* **2.** *v. t. & i.* unterschreiben; ~ **one's name** [mit seinem Namen] unterschreiben. **sign 'on** *v. i. (as unemployed)* sich arbeitslos melden. **sign 'up** *v. i.* sich [vertraglich] verpflichten (**with** bei); *(for course)* sich einschreiben
signal ['sɪgnl] **1.** *n.* Signal, *das;* **a** ~ **for sth./to sb.** ein Zeichen zu etw./für jmdn. **2.** *v. i., (Brit.)* **-ll-** signalisieren; Signale geben; ⟨*Kraftfahrer:*⟩ blinken;

(with hand) anzeigen; ~ **to sb. |to do sth.|** jmdm. ein Zeichen geben|, etw. zu tun]. '**signal-box** *n.* Stellwerk, *das* **signature** ['sɪgnətʃə(r)] *n.* Unterschrift, *die; (on painting)* Signatur, *die.* '**signature tune** *n.* Erkennungsmelodie, *die* '**signboard** *n.* Schild, *das* **signet-ring** ['sɪgnɪt rɪŋ] *n.* Siegelring, *der* **significance** [sɪg'nɪfɪkəns] *n.* Bedeutung, *die;* **be of |no|** ~: [nicht] von Bedeutung sein **significant** [sɪg'nɪfɪkənt] *adj.* **a)** *(noteworthy, important)* bedeutend; **b)** *(full of meaning)* bedeutsam. **sig'nificantly** *adv.* **a)** *(meaningfully)* bedeutungsvoll; ~ **|enough|** bedeutsamerweise; **b)** *(notably)* bedeutend **signify** ['sɪgnɪfaɪ] *v. t.* bedeuten '**signpost** *n.* Wegweiser, *der* **silence** ['saɪləns] **1.** *n.* Schweigen, *das; (keeping a secret)* Verschwiegenheit, *die; (stillness)* Stille, *die;* **there was** ~: es herrschte Schweigen/Stille; **in** ~: schweigend. **2.** *v. t.* zum Schweigen bringen; *(fig.)* ersticken ⟨*Proteste*⟩; mundtot machen ⟨*Gegner*⟩. '**silencer** *n. (Arms; Brit. Motor Veh.)* Schalldämpfer, *der* **silent** ['saɪlənt] *adj.* stumm; *(noiseless)* unhörbar; *(still)* still; **be** ~ *(say nothing)* schweigen; ~ **film** Stummfilm, *der.* '**silently** *adv.* schweigend; stumm ⟨*weinen, beten*⟩; *(noiselessly)* lautlos **silhouette** [sɪlʊ'et] **1.** *n.* **a)** *(picture)* Schattenriß, *der;* **b)** *(appearance against the light)* Silhouette, *die.* **2.** *v. t.* **be** ~**d against sth.** sich als Silhouette gegen etw. abheben **silicon** ['sɪlɪkən] *n.* Silicium, *das;* ~ **chip** Siliciumchip, *der* **silk** [sɪlk] **1.** *n.* Seide, *die.* **2.** *attrib. adj.* seiden; Seiden-. '**silkworm** *n.* Seidenraupe, *die.* '**silky** *adj.* seidig **sill** [sɪl] *n. (of door)* [Tür]schwelle, *die; (of window)* Fensterbank, *die* **silly** ['sɪlɪ] *adj.* dumm; *(imprudent, unwise)* töricht; *(childish)* albern **silo** ['saɪləʊ] *n., pl.* ~**s** Silo, *der* **silt** [sɪlt] *n.* Schlamm, *der;* Schlick, *der* **silver** ['sɪlvə(r)] **1.** *n.* Silber, *das.* **2.** *attrib. adj.* silbern; Silber⟨*pokal, -münze*⟩ **silver:** ~ '**medal** *n.* Silbermedaille, *die;* ~ '**paper** *n.* Silberpapier, *das;* ~**-plated** *adj.* versilbert; ~ '**wedding** *n.* Silberhochzeit, *die*

similar ['sɪmɪlə(r)] *adj.* ähnlich **(to** *Dat.*). **similarity** [sɪmɪ'lærɪtɪ] *n.* Ähnlichkeit, *die* **(to** mit). '**similarly** *adv.* ähnlich; *(in exactly the same way)* ebenso **simile** ['sɪmɪlɪ] *n.* Vergleich, *der* **simmer** ['sɪmə(r)] **1.** *v. i.* ⟨*Flüssigkeit:*⟩ sieden. **2.** *v. t.* köcheln lassen. **simmer 'down** *v. i.* sich abregen *(ugs.)* **simple** ['sɪmpl] *adj.* einfach; *(unsophisticated, not elaborate)* schlicht ⟨*Mobiliar, Schönheit, Kunstwerk, Kleidung*⟩; **it was a** ~ **misunderstanding** es war [ganz] einfach ein Mißverständnis. '**simple-minded** *adj.* **a)** *(unsophisticated)* schlicht; **b)** *(unintelligent)* beschränkt. **simpleton** ['sɪmpltən] *n.* Einfaltspinsel, *der (ugs.).* **simplicity** [sɪm'plɪsɪtɪ] *n.* Einfachheit, *die; (unpretentiousness, lack of sophistication)* Schlichtheit, *die.* **simplification** [sɪmplɪfɪ'keɪʃn] *n.* Vereinfachung, *die.* **simplify** ['sɪmplɪfaɪ] *v. t.* vereinfachen. **simplistic** [sɪm'plɪstɪk] *adj.* [all]zu simpel. **simply** ['sɪmplɪ] *adv.* einfach; *(in an unsophisticated manner)* schlicht; *(merely)* nur; **it** ~ **isn't true** es ist einfach nicht wahr; **I was** ~ **trying to help** ich wollte nur helfen **simulate** ['sɪmjʊleɪt] *v. t.* **a)** *(feign)* vortäuschen; **b)** simulieren ⟨*Bedingungen, Wetter usw.*⟩ **simultaneous** [sɪml'teɪnɪəs] *adj.,* **simul'taneously** *adv.* gleichzeitig **sin** [sɪn] **1.** *n.* Sünde, *die.* **2.** *v. i.,* **-nn-** sündigen **since** [sɪns] **1.** *adv.* seitdem. **2.** *prep.* seit; ~ **seeing you ...:** seit ich dich gesehen habe; ~ **then/that time** inzwischen. **3.** *conj.* **a)** seit; **it is a long time/ so long/not so long** ~ **...:** es ist lange/so lange/gar nicht lange her, daß ...; **b)** *(seeing that, as)* da **sincere** [sɪn'sɪə(r)] *adj.,* ~**r** [sɪn'sɪərə(r)], ~**st** [sɪn'sɪərɪst] aufrichtig; herzlich ⟨*Grüße, Glückwünsche usw.*⟩. **sin'cerely** *adv.* aufrichtig; **yours** ~: mit freundlichen Grüßen. **sincerity** [sɪn'serɪtɪ] *n.* Aufrichtigkeit, *die* **sinew** ['sɪnju:] *n.* Sehne, *die* **sinful** ['sɪnfl] *adj.* sündig; *(reprehensible)* sündhaft; **it is** ~ **to ...:** es ist eine Sünde, ... zu ... **sing** [sɪŋ] *v. i. & t.,* **sang** [sæŋ], **sung** [sʌŋ] singen. **sing 'up** *v. i.* lauter singen **singe** [sɪndʒ] *v. t. & i.,* ~**ing** versengen **singer** ['sɪŋə(r)] *n.* Sänger, *der*/Sängerin, *die*

single ['sɪŋgl] 1. *adj.* **a)** einfach; *(sole)* einzig; *(separate, individual, isolated)* einzeln; **not a ~ one** kein einziger/keine einzige/kein einziges; **every ~ one** jeder/jede/jedes einzelne; **every ~ day** jeden Tag; **~ ticket** *(Brit.)* einfache Fahrkarte; **b)** *(for one person)* Einzel-⟨bett, -zimmer⟩; **c)** *(unmarried)* ledig; **a ~ man/woman** ein Lediger/eine Ledige; **~ people** Ledige. 2. *n.* **a)** *(Brit.: ticket)* einfache Fahrkarte; |**a** ~/**two** ~**s to Manchester, please** einmal/zweimal einfach nach Manchester, bitte; **b)** *(record)* Single, *die;* **c)** in *pl. (Tennis etc.)* Einzel, *das.* **single 'out** *v. t.* **~ sb./sth. out as/for sth.** jmdn./etw. als/für etw. auswählen

single: **~-decker** 1. *n.* **be a ~-decker** ⟨*Bus, Straßenbahn:*⟩ nur ein Deck haben; 2. *adj.* **~-decker bus/tram** Bus/Straßenbahn mit [nur] einem Deck; **~ [European] market** *n.* [europäischer] Binnenmarkt; **~-'handed** *adv.* allein; **~-minded** *adj.* zielstrebig

singlet ['sɪŋglɪt] *n. (Brit.) (vest)* Unterhemd, *das; (Sport)* Trikot, *das*

singly ['sɪŋglɪ] *adv.* einzeln

singular ['sɪŋgjʊlə(r)] 1. *adj.* **a)** *(Ling.)* singularisch; Singular-; **~ noun** Substantiv im Singular; **b)** *(extraordinary)* einmalig. 2. *n. (Ling.)* Einzahl, *die;* Singular, *der.* **'singularly** *adv. (extraordinarily)* außerordentlich

sinister ['sɪnɪstə(r)] *adj.* finster; *(of evil omen)* unheilverkündend

sink [sɪŋk] 1. *n.* Spülbecken, *das.* 2. *v. i.*, **sank** [sæŋk] *or* **sunk** [sʌŋk], **sunk** sinken. 3. *v. t.*, **sank** *or* **sunk**, **sunk a)** versenken ⟨*Schiff*⟩; **b)** niederbringen ⟨*Schacht*⟩. **sink 'in** *v. i. (fig.)* jmdm. ins Bewußtsein dringen; ⟨*Warnung, Lektion:*⟩ verstanden werden

'sinner *n.* Sünder, *der/*Sünderin, *die*

sinus ['saɪnəs] *n.* Nebenhöhle, *die*

sip [sɪp] 1. *v. t.*, **-pp-:** ~ |up| schlürfen. 2. *v. i.*, **-pp-:** ~ **at/from sth.** an etw. *(Dat.)* nippen. 3. *n.* Schlückchen, *das*

siphon ['saɪfn] 1. *n.* Siphon, *der.* 2. *v. t.* [durch einen Saugheber] laufen lassen

sir [sɜː(r)] *n.* **a)** *(formal address)* der Herr; *(to teacher)* Herr Meier/Schmidt *usw.;* **b)** *(in letter)* **Dear Sir** Sehr geehrter Herr; **Dear Sirs** Sehr geehrte [Damen und] Herren; **Dear Sir or Madam** Sehr geehrte Dame/Sehr geehrter Herr; **c)** **Sir** [sə(r)] *(title of knight etc.)* Sir

siren ['saɪrən] *n.* Sirene, *die*

sirloin ['sɜːlɔɪn] *n.* **a)** *(Brit.)* Roastbeef, *das;* ~ **steak** Rumpsteak, *das;* **b)** *(Amer.)* Rumpsteak, *das*

sissy ['sɪsɪ] 1. *n.* Waschlappen, *der.* 2. *adj.* feige

sister ['sɪstə(r)] *n.* **a)** Schwester, *die;* **b)** *(Brit.: nurse)* Oberschwester, *die.* **'sister-in-law** *n., pl.* **sisters-in-law** Schwägerin, *die*

sit [sɪt] 1. *v. i.*, **-tt-**, **sat** [sæt] **a)** *(become seated)* sich setzen; ~ **on** *or* **in a chair/in an armchair** sich auf einen Stuhl/in einen Sessel setzen; **b)** *(be seated)* sitzen. 2. *v. t.*, **-tt-**, **sat a)** setzen; **b)** *(Brit.)* machen ⟨*Prüfung*⟩. **sit 'back** *v. i.* sich zurücklehnen; *(fig.)* sich im Sessel zurücklehnen. **sit 'down** *v. i.* **a)** *(become seated)* sich setzen (on/in auf/in + *Akk.*); **b)** *(be seated)* sitzen. **sit 'up 1.** *v. i.* **a)** *(rise)* sich aufsetzen; **b)** *(be sitting erect)* [aufrecht] sitzen; **c)** *(stay up)* aufbleiben. 2. *v. t.* aufsetzen

site [saɪt] 1. *n.* **a)** *(land)* Grundstück, *das;* **b)** *(location)* Sitz, *der; (of new factory etc.)* Standort, *der.* 2. *v. t.* stationieren ⟨*Raketen*⟩; ~ **a factory in London** London als Standort einer Fabrik wählen; **be ~d** gelegen sein

'sitting *n.* Sitzung, *die;* **the first ~** |**for lunch**| der erste Schub [zum Mittagessen]

situate ['sɪtjʊeɪt] *v. t.* legen. **'situated** *adj.* gelegen; **be ~:** liegen. **situation** [sɪtjʊ'eɪʃn] *n.* **a)** *(location)* Lage, *die;* **b)** *(circumstances)* Situation, *die;* **c)** *(job)* Stelle, *die*

six [sɪks] 1. *adj.* sechs. 2. *n.* Sechs, *die. See also* **eight**

sixteen [sɪks'tiːn] 1. *adj.* sechzehn. 2. *n.* Sechzehn, *die. See also* **eight**. **sixteenth** [sɪks'tiːnθ] 1. *adj.* sechzehnt... 2. *n. (fraction)* Sechzehntel, *das. See also* **eighth**

sixth [sɪksθ] 1. *adj.* sechst... 2. *n. (in sequence)* sechste, *der/die/das; (in rank)* Sechste, *der/die/das; (fraction)* Sechstel, *das. See also* **eighth**

sixtieth ['sɪkstɪɪθ] *adj.* sechzigst...

sixty ['sɪkstɪ] 1. *adj.* sechzig. 2. *n.* Sechzig, *die. See also* **eight**; **eighty 2**

size [saɪz] *n.* Größe, *die;* (*in format, das;* **be twice the ~ of sth.** zweimal so groß wie etw. sein; **a ~ 8 dress** ein Kleid [in] Größe 8; **be ~ 8** ⟨*Person:*⟩ Größe 8 haben. **size 'up** *v. t.* taxieren ⟨*Lage*⟩

sizeable ['saɪzəbl] *adj.* ziemlich groß; beträchtlich ⟨*Summe, Einfluß*⟩

sizzle ['sɪzl] *v. i.* zischen

skate 1. *n. (ice-~)* Schlittschuh, *der;*
(roller-~) Rollschuh, *der.* **2.** *v.i.*
(ice-~) Schlittschuh laufen; *(roller-~)*
Rollschuh laufen. **'skateboard 1.** *n.*
Skateboard, *das;* Rollerbrett, *das.* **2.**
v.i. Skateboard fahren. **'skater** *n.*
(ice~) Eisläufer, *der/*Eisläuferin, *die;*
(roller~) Rollschuhläufer, *der/*-läufe-
rin, *die.* **skating** ['skeitiŋ] *n. (ice~)*
Schlittschuhlaufen, *das; (roller~)*
Rollschuhlaufen, *das.* **'skating rink**
n. (ice) Eisbahn, *die; (for roller-*
skating) Rollschuhbahn, *die*
skeleton ['skelitn] *n.* Skelett, *das.*
'skeleton key *n.* Dietrich, *der.*
'skeleton staff *n.* Minimalbeset-
zung, *die*
skeptic *etc. (Amer.) see* **sceptic** *etc.*
sketch [sketʃ] **1.** *n.* **a)** *(drawing)* Skizze, *die.* **b)** *(play)* Sketch, *der.* **2.** *v.t.*
skizzieren. **'sketch-book** *n.* Skiz-
zenbuch, *das.* **'sketch map** *n.* Faust-
skizze, *die*
'sketchy *adj.* skizzenhaft; lückenhaft
⟨*Informationen, Bericht*⟩
skew [skju:] **1.** *adj.* schräg. **2.** *n.* **on the**
~: schief
skewer ['skju:ə(r)] **1.** *n.* Bratspieß,
der. **2.** *v.t.* aufspießen
ski [ski:] **1.** *n.* **a)** Ski, *der;* **b)** *(on vehicle)*
Kufe, *die.* **2.** *v.i.* Ski laufen *od.* fah-
ren. **'ski boot** *n.* Skistiefel, *der.* **'ski-**
lift *n.* Skilift, *der*
skid [skid] **1.** *v.i., -dd-* schlittern; *(from*
one side to the other; spinning round)
schleudern. **2.** *n.* Schlittern/Schleu-
dern, *das.* **'skid marks** *n. pl.* Schleu-
derspur, *die*
skier ['ski:ə(r)] *n.* Skiläufer, *der/*-läu-
ferin, *die*
skiing ['ski:iŋ] *n.* Skilaufen, *das;*
(Sport) Skisport, *der*
skilful ['skilfl] *adj.* geschickt; gewandt
⟨*Redner*⟩; gut ⟨*Beobachter, Lehrer*⟩
skill [skil] *n.* **a)** *(expertness)* Geschick,
das; (of artist) Können, *das;* **b)** *(tech-*
nique) Fertigkeit, *die; (of weaving,*
bricklaying) Technik, *die.* **skilled**
['skild] *adj.* **a)** *see* **skilful; b)** qualifiziert ⟨*Arbeit, Tätigkeit*⟩; **~ trade** Aus-
bildungsberuf, *der;* **c)** *(trained)* ausgebildet. **'skillful** *(Amer.) see* **skilful**
skim [skim] *v.t., -mm-:* **a)** *(remove)* abschöpfen; **b)** abrahmen ⟨*Milch*⟩; **c)** *see*
~ through. skim 'off *v.t.* abschöpfen.
'skim through *v.t.* überfliegen
⟨*Buch, Zeitung*⟩
skimmed 'milk *n.* entrahmte Milch
skimp [skimp] **1.** *v.t.* sparen an

(+ Dat.). **2.** *v.i.* sparen **(with, on** an
+ Dat.). **'skimpy** *adj.* winzig ⟨*Ba-*
deanzug⟩; spärlich ⟨*Wissen*⟩
skin [skin] **1.** *n.* **a)** Haut, *die;* **b)** *(fur)*
Fell, *das;* **c)** *(peel)* Schale, *die.* **2.** *v.t.,*
-nn- häuten; schälen ⟨*Frucht*⟩
skin: **~ cream** *n.* Hautcreme, *die;*
~-'deep *adj. (fig.)* oberflächlich;
~-diver *n.* Taucher, *der/*Taucherin,
die; **~flint** *n.* Geizhals, *der;* **~head**
n. (Brit.) Skinhead, *der*
skinny ['skini] *adj.* mager
'skin-tight *adj.* hauteng
¹skip [skip] **1.** *v.i., -pp-:* **a)** hüpfen; **b)**
(with skipping-rope) seilspringen. **2.**
v.t., -pp- (omit) überspringen; **~**
breakfast/lunch das Frühstück/Mit-
tagessen auslassen. **3.** *n.* Hüpfer, *der*
²skip *n. (Building)* Container, *der*
ski: **~ pass** *n.* Skipaß, *der;* **~ pole** *n.*
Skistock, *der*
skipper ['skipə(r)] *n.* Kapitän, *der*
'skipping-rope *(Brit.),* **'skip-rope**
(Amer.) ns. Sprungseil, *das*
'ski-resort *n.* Skiurlaubsort, *der*
skirmish ['skɜ:miʃ] *n. (Mil.)* **a)** Ge-
fecht, *das;* **b)** *(argument)* Auseinandersetzung, *die*
skirt [skɜ:t] **1.** *n.* Rock, *der.* **2.** *v.t.* herumgehen um. **skirt 'round** *v.t.* her-
umgehen um; *(fig.)* umgehen
'skirting *n.* **~[-board]** *(Brit.)* Fußleiste,
die
ski: **~-run** *n.* Skihang, *der; (prepared)*
[Ski]piste, *die;* **~-stick** *n.* Skistock,
der
skittle ['skitl] *n.* **a)** Kegel, *der;* **b)** **~s**
sing. (game) Kegeln, *das*
skive [skaiv] *v.i. (Brit. sl.)* sich
drücken *(ugs.).* **skive 'off** *(Brit. sl.)* **1.**
v.i. sich verdrücken *(ugs.).* **2.** *v.t.*
schwänzen *(ugs.)*
skulk [skʌlk] *v.i.* lauern
skull [skʌl] *n.* Schädel, *der*
skunk [skʌŋk] *n.* Stinktier, *das*
sky [skai] *n.* Himmel, *der;* **in the ~:** am
Himmel
sky: **~-high 1.** *adj.* himmelhoch;
astronomisch *(ugs.)* ⟨*Preise usw.*⟩; **2.**
adv. **go ~-high** ⟨*Preise usw.*:⟩ in astro-
nomische Höhen klettern *(ugs.);*
~light *n.* Dachfenster, *das;*
~scraper *n.* Wolkenkratzer, *der*
slab [slæb] *n.* **a)** *(flat stone etc.)* Platte,
die; **b)** *(thick slice)* [dicke] Scheibe; *(of*
cake) [dickes] Stück; *(of chocolate, tof-*
fee) Tafel, *die*
slack [slæk] **1.** *adj.* **a)** *(lax)* nachlässig;
schlampig *(ugs.);* **b)** *(loose)* schlaff;

locker ⟨*Verband*⟩. **2.** *n.* **take in** *or* **up the ~:** das Seil/die Schnur *usw.* straffen. **3.** *v.i.* (*coll.*) bummeln *(ugs.)*

slacken ['slækn] **1.** *v.i.* **a)** *(loosen)* sich lockern; **b)** *(diminish)* nachlassen; ⟨*Geschwindigkeit:*⟩ sich verringern. **2.** *v.t.* **a)** *(loosen)* lockern; **b)** *(diminish)* verringern

slacks [slæks] *n. pl.* |pair of| ~: lange Hose; Slacks *Pl. (Mode)*

slag [slæg] *n.* Schlacke, *die*

slain *see* **slay**

slake [sleɪk] *v.t.* stillen

slam [slæm] **1.** *v.t.,* **-mm-: a)** *(shut)* zuschlagen; **b)** *(put violently)* knallen *(ugs.)*. **2.** *v.i.,* **-mm-** zuschlagen

slander ['slɑːndə(r)] **1.** *n.* Verleumdung, *die* (on *Gen.*). **2.** *v.t.* verleumden. **slanderous** ['slɑːndərəs] *adj.* verleumderisch

slang [slæŋ] *n.* Slang, *der;* ⟨*Theater-, Soldaten-, Juristen*⟩jargon, *der; attrib.* Slang⟨*wort, -ausdruck*⟩

slant [slɑːnt] **1.** *v.i.* ⟨*Fläche:*⟩ sich neigen; ⟨*Linie:*⟩ schräg verlaufen. **2.** *v.t.* **a)** abschrägen; **b)** *(fig.: bias)* [so] hinbiegen *(ugs.)* ⟨*Meldung, Bemerkung*⟩. **3.** *n.* Schräge, *die;* **on the** *or* **a ~:** schräg

slap [slæp] **1.** *v.t.,* **-pp-: a)** schlagen; **b)** *(put)* knallen *(ugs.)*. **2.** *v.i.,* **-pp-** schlagen; klatschen. **3.** *n.* Schlag, *der.* **4.** *adv.* voll; **~ in the middle** genau in der Mitte. **'slapdash** *adj.* schludrig *(ugs.)*. **'slap-up** *attrib. adj. (sl.)* ⟨*Essen*⟩ mit allen Schikanen *(ugs.)*

slash [slæʃ] **1.** *v.t.* **a)** aufschlitzen; **b)** *(fig.)* [drastisch] reduzieren; [drastisch] kürzen ⟨*Gehalt, Umfang*⟩. **2.** *n.* **a)** *(slit)* Schlitz, *der;* **b)** *(~ing stroke)* Hieb, *der*

slat [slæt] *n.* Latte, *die*

slate [sleɪt] **1.** *n.* **a)** *(Geol.)* Schiefer, *der;* **b)** *(Building)* Schieferplatte, *die.* **2.** *v.t.* *(Brit. coll.: criticize)* in der Luft zerreißen *(ugs.)*

slaughter ['slɔːtə(r)] **1.** *n.* Schlachten, *das; (massacre)* Gemetzel, *das.* **2.** *v.t.* schlachten; *(massacre)* abschlachten

slave [sleɪv] **1.** *n.* Sklave, *der*/Sklavin, *die.* **2.** *v.i.* ~ |away| schuften *(ugs.);* sich abplagen **(at** mit). **'slave-driver** *n. (fig.)* Sklaventreiber, *der*/-treiberin, *die.* **slavery** ['sleɪvərɪ] *n.* Sklaverei, *die.* **slavish** ['sleɪvɪʃ] *adj.* sklavisch

slay [sleɪ] *v.t.,* **slew** [sluː], **slain** [sleɪn] *(literary)* ermorden

sleazy ['sliːzɪ] *adj.* schäbig; *(disreputable)* anrüchig

sled [sled], **sledge** [sledʒ] *ns.* Schlitten, *der.* **'sledge-hammer** *n.* Vorschlaghammer, *der*

sleek [sliːk] *adj. (glossy)* seidig

sleep [sliːp] **1.** *n.* Schlaf, *der;* **get/go to ~:** einschlafen; **put to ~:** einschläfern ⟨*Tier*⟩. **2.** *v.i.,* **slept** [slept] schlafen. **3.** *v.t.* **slept: the hotel ~s 80** das Hotel hat 80 Betten. **'sleeper** *n.* **a) be a heavy/light ~:** einen tiefen/leichten Schlaf haben; **b)** *(Brit. Railw.: support)* Schwelle, *die;* **c)** *(Railw.)(coach)* Schlafwagen, *der; (train)* |night| ~: Nachtzug mit Schlafwagen

sleeping: ~-bag *n.* Schlafsack, *der;* **~-car** *n.* Schlafwagen, *der;* **~-pill, ~-tablet** *ns.* Schlaftablette, *die*

sleep: ~less *adj.* schlaflos; **~-walk** *v.i.* schlafwandeln; **~-walker** *n.* Schlafwandler, *der*/-wandlerin, *die*

'sleepy *adj.* schläfrig

sleet [sliːt] **1.** *n.* Schneeregen, *der.* **2.** *v.i. impers.* **it is ~ing** es gibt Schneeregen

sleeve [sliːv] *n.* **a)** Ärmel, *der; (fig.)* **have sth. up one's ~:** etw. in petto haben *(ugs.);* **roll up one's ~s** die Ärmel hochkrempeln *(ugs.);* **b)** *(for record)* Hülle, *die.* **'sleeveless** *adj.* ärmellos

sleigh [sleɪ] *n.* Schlitten, *der*

sleight [slaɪt] **of 'hand** *n.* Fingerfertigkeit, *die*

slender ['slendə(r)] *adj.* **a)** *(slim)* schlank; schmal ⟨*Buch, Band*⟩; **b)** gering ⟨*Chance, Mittel, Hoffnung*⟩

slept *see* **sleep 2, 3**

sleuth [sluːθ] *n.* Detektiv, *der*

¹slew [sluː] *v.i. & t.* schwenken

²slew *see* **slay**

slice [slaɪs] **1.** *n.* Scheibe, *die; (of apple, melon, peach, cake, pie)* Stück, *das;* **a ~ of cake** ein Stück Kuchen. **2.** *v.t.* in Scheiben schneiden; in Stücke schneiden ⟨*Bohnen, Apfel, Kuchen usw.*⟩; **~d bread** Schnittbrot, *das*

slick [slɪk] **1.** *adj. (coll.)* **a)** *(dexterous)* professionell; **b)** *(pretentiously dexterous)* clever *(ugs.)*. **2.** *n.* |oil-|~: Ölteppich, *der*

slid *see* **slide 1, 2**

slide [slaɪd] **1.** *v.i.,* **slid** [slɪd] rutschen; ⟨*Kolben, Schublade, Feder:*⟩ gleiten. **2.** *v.t.,* **slid** schieben. **3.** *n.* **a)** *(children's ~)* Rutschbahn, *die;* **b)** *(Photog.)* Dia[positiv], *das.* **'sliding** ['slaɪdɪŋ] **door** *n.* Schiebetür, *die*

slight [slaɪt] **1.** *adj.* leicht; schwach ⟨*Hoffnung, Aussichten, Wirkung*⟩; **not in the ~est** nicht im geringsten. **2.** *n.*

Verunglimpfung, die (on Gen.); (lack of courtesy) Affront, der (on gegen).

'**slightly** adv. ein bißchen; leicht ⟨verletzen, riechen nach, gewürzt sein, ansteigen⟩; flüchtig ⟨jmdn. kennen⟩; oberflächlich ⟨etw. kennen⟩

slim [slɪm] 1. adj. schlank; schmal ⟨Band, Buch⟩; schwach ⟨Aussicht, Hoffnung⟩; gering ⟨Gewinn, Chancen⟩. 2. v.i. abnehmen

slime [slaɪm] n. Schleim, der. **slimy** ['slaɪmɪ] adj. schleimig

sling [slɪŋ] 1. n. (Med.) Schlinge, die. 2. v.t., **slung** [slʌŋ] (coll.: throw) schmeißen (ugs.). **sling 'out** v.t. (coll.) wegschmeißen (ugs.); ~ **sb. out** jmdn. rausschmeißen (ugs.)

slink [slɪŋk] v.i., **slunk** [slʌŋk] schleichen. **slink a'way, slink 'off** v.i. davonschleichen

slip [slɪp] 1. v.i., -pp-: a) (slide) rutschen; ⟨Messer:⟩ abrutschen; (and fall) ausrutschen; b) (escape) schlüpfen; c) (go) ~ **to the butcher's etc.** [rasch] zum Fleischer usw. rüberspringen (ugs.). 2. v.t., -pp-: a) stecken; ~ **the dress over one's head** das Kleid über den Kopf streifen; b) ~ **sb.'s mind** or **memory** jmdm. entfallen. 3. n. a) (fall) **after his** ~: nachdem er ausgerutscht [und gestürzt] war; b) (mistake) Versehen, das; ~ **of the tongue** Versprecher, der; c) (underwear) Unterrock, der; d) (piece of paper) Zettel, der; e) **give sb. the** ~: jmdm. entwischen (ugs.). **slip a'way** v.i. a) ⟨Person:⟩ sich fortschleichen; b) ⟨Zeit:⟩ verfliegen. **slip 'down** v.i. runterrutschen (ugs.). **slip 'in** v.i. ⟨Person:⟩ sich hineinschleichen. '**slip into** v.t. schlüpfen in (+ Akk.) ⟨Kleidungsstück⟩. **slip 'off** 1. v.i. a) runterrutschen (ugs.); b) see **slip away** a. 2. v.t. abstreifen ⟨Schmuck, Handschuh⟩; schlüpfen aus ⟨Kleid, Schuh⟩. **slip 'on** v.t. überstreifen ⟨Handschuh, Ring⟩; schlüpfen in (+ Akk.) ⟨Kleid, Schuh⟩. **slip 'out** v.i. ⟨Person:⟩ sich hinausschleichen. **slip 'over** v.i. (fall) ausrutschen. **slip 'up** v.i. (coll.) einen Schnitzer machen (ugs.)

slipped [slɪpt] '**disc** n. Bandscheibenvorfall, der

'**slipper** n. Hausschuh, der

slippery ['slɪpərɪ] adj. schlüpfrig

slip: ~-**road** n. (Brit.) (to motorway) Auffahrt, die; (from motorway) Ausfahrt, die; ~**shod** adj. schludrig (ugs.); ~-**up** n. (coll.) Schnitzer, der

slit [slɪt] 1. n. Schlitz, der. 2. v.t., -tt-, slit aufschlitzen; ~ **sb.'s throat** jmdm. die Kehle durchschneiden

slither ['slɪðə(r)] v.i. rutschen

sliver ['slɪvə(r)] n. Splitter, der

slobber ['slɒbə(r)] v.i. sabbern (ugs.)

slog [slɒg] 1. v.t., -gg- (in boxing, fight) voll treffen. 2. v.i., -gg- (work) schuften (ugs.). 3. n. a) (hit) wuchtiger Schlag; b) (work) Plackerei, die (ugs.)

slogan ['sləʊgən] n. Slogan, der; (advertising ~) Werbeslogan, der

slop [slɒp] 1. v.i. schwappen (out of, from aus). 2. v.t. schwappen; (intentionally) kippen. **slop 'over** v.i. überschwappen

slope [sləʊp] 1. n. a) (slant) Neigung, die; b) (slanting ground) Hang, der. 2. v.i. (slant) sich neigen; ⟨Boden, Garten:⟩ abschüssig sein; ~ **downwards/upwards** ⟨Straße:⟩ abfallen/ansteigen. **slope a'way** v.i. abfallen. **slope 'off** v.i. (sl.) sich verdrücken (ugs.)

sloppy ['slɒpɪ] adj. schludrig (ugs.)

slosh [slɒʃ] adj. 1. v.i. platschen (ugs.); ⟨Flüssigkeit:⟩ schwappen. 2. v.t. (coll.: pour clumsily) schwappen

slot [slɒt] 1. n. a) (hole) Schlitz, der; b) (groove) Nut, die. 2. v.t., -tt-: ~ **sth. into place/sth.** etw. einfügen/in etw. (Akk.) einfügen. **slot 'in** 1. v.t. einfügen. 2. v.i. sich einfügen

sloth [sləʊθ] n. a) (lethargy) Trägheit, die; b) (Zool.) Faultier, das

'**slot-machine** n. Automat, der; (for gambling) Spielautomat, der

slouch [slaʊtʃ] v.i. sich schlecht halten

slovenly ['slʌvnlɪ] adj. schlampig (ugs.)

slow [sləʊ] 1. adj. langsam; langwierig ⟨Arbeit⟩; **be |ten minutes|** ~ ⟨Uhr:⟩ [zehn Minuten] nachgehen. 2. adv. langsam. 3. v.i. langsamer werden; ~ **to a halt** anhalten. **slow 'down, slow 'up** v.i. langsamer werden

'**slowcoach** n. Trödler, der/Trödlerin, die (ugs.)

'**slowly** adv. langsam

slow 'motion n. **in** ~: in Zeitlupe

slowness n. Langsamkeit, die

sludge [slʌdʒ] n. Schlamm, der

slug [slʌg] n. Nacktschnecke, die

sluggish ['slʌgɪʃ] adj. träge; schleppend ⟨Nachfrage⟩

sluice [slu:s] 1. n. Schütz, das. 2. v.t. ~ |**down**| abspritzen

slum [slʌm] n. Slum, der; (single house or apartment) Elendsquartier, das

slumber ['slʌmbə(r)] *(poet./rhet.)* **1.** *n.* ~|s| Schlummer, *der (geh.).* **2.** *v.i.* schlummern *(geh.)*

slump [slʌmp] **1.** *n.* Sturz, *der (fig.); (in demand, investment, sales)* starker Rückgang (**in** *Gen.*); *(economic depression)* Depression, *die.* **2.** *v.i.* **a)** *(Commerc.)* stark zurückgehen; ⟨*Preise, Kurse:*⟩ stürzen; **b)** *(collapse)* ⟨*Person:*⟩ fallen; **~ed in a chair** in einem Sessel zusammengesunken

slung *see* **sling** 2

slunk *see* **slink**

slur [slɜ:(r)] **1.** *v.t., -rr-:* **~ one's words/ speech** undeutlich sprechen. **2.** *n.* Beleidigung, *die* (**on** für)

slurp [slɜ:p] *(coll.)* **1.** *v.t.* ~ |up| schlürfen. **2.** *n.* Schlürfen, *das*

slush [slʌʃ] *n.* Schneematsch, *der.* **'slushy** *adj.* **a)** matschig; **b)** *(sloppy)* sentimental

slut [slʌt] *n.* Schlampe, *die (ugs.)*

sly [slaɪ] **1.** *adj.* schlau; gerissen *(ugs.)* ⟨*Geschäftsmann, Trick*⟩; verschlagen ⟨*Blick*⟩. **2.** *n.* **on the ~:** heimlich

'smack [smæk] **1.** *n.* **a)** *(sound)* Klatsch, *der;* **b)** *(blow)* Schlag, *der;* (on child's bottom) Klaps, *der (ugs.).* **2.** *v.t.* **a)** [mit der flachen Hand] schlagen; **b)** ~ **one's lips** [mit den Lippen] schmatzen. **3.** *adv. (coll.)* direkt

²smack *v.i.* ~ **of** schmecken nach; *(fig.)* riechen nach *(ugs.)*

small [smɔ:l] **1.** *adj.* klein; gering ⟨*Wirkung, Appetit, Fähigkeit*⟩; schmal ⟨*Taille*⟩; dünn ⟨*Stimme*⟩; **make sb. feel ~:** jmdn. beschämen. **2.** *n.* ~ **of the back** Kreuz, *das.* **3.** *adv.* klein

small: ~ **ad** *n. (coll.)* Kleinanzeige, *die;* ~ **'change** *n.* Kleingeld, *das;* ~**holding** *n.* landwirtschaftlicher Kleinbetrieb; ~**'minded** *adj.* kleinlich; ~**pox** *n.* Pocken *Pl.;* ~ **talk** *n.* leichte Unterhaltung; *(at parties)* Smalltalk, *der;* **make ~ talk |with sb.|** [mit jmdm.] Konversation machen

smarmy ['smɑ:mɪ] *adj. (coll.)* kriecherisch

smart [smɑ:t] **1.** *adj.* **a)** *(clever)* clever; *(ingenious)* raffiniert; **b)** *(neat)* schick; schön ⟨*Haus, Garten, Auto*⟩; **c)** *attrib. (fashionable)* elegant; smart. **2.** *v.i.* schmerzen. **smart alec[k]** [smɑ:t 'ælɪk] *n. (coll.)* Besserwisser, *der.* **smarten** ['smɑ:tn] *v.t.* herrichten; ~ **oneself |up|** auf sein Äußeres achten. **'smartly** *adv.* **a)** *(cleverly)* clever; **b)** *(neatly)* schmuck ⟨*|an|gestrichen*⟩; smart, flott ⟨*gekleidet, geschnitten*⟩

smash [smæʃ] **1.** *v.t.* **a)** zerschlagen; **b)** ~ **sb. in the face/mouth** jmdm. [hart] ins Gesicht/auf den Mund schlagen; **c)** *(Tennis etc.)* schmettern. **2.** *v.i.* **a)** zerbrechen; **b)** *(crash)* krachen (**into** gegen). **3.** *n.* **a)** *(sound)* Krachen, *das;* **b)** *see* **smash-up; c)** *(Tennis)* Schmetterball, *der.* **smash 'in** *v.t.* zerschmettern; einschlagen ⟨*Tür, Schädel*⟩. **smash 'up** *v.t.* zertrümmern

smash-and-'grab [raid] *n. (coll.)* Schaufenstereinbruch, *der*

'smashing *adj. (coll.)* toll *(ugs.)*

'smash-up *n.* schwerer Zusammenstoß

smattering ['smætərɪŋ] *n.* |**have**| **a ~ of German** etc. ein paar Brocken Deutsch *usw.* [können]

smear [smɪə(r)] **1.** *v.t.* **a)** *(daub)* beschmieren; *(put on or over)* schmieren; **b)** *(smudge)* verwischen; **c)** *(fig.)* in den Schmutz ziehen. **2.** *n.* **a)** *(blotch)* [Schmutz]fleck, *der;* **b)** *(fig.)* Beschmutzung, *die* (**on** Gen.)

smell [smel] **1.** *n.* **a)** **have a good/bad sense of ~:** einen guten/schlechten Geruchssinn haben; **b)** *(odour)* Geruch, *der* (**of** nach); *(pleasant also)* Duft, *der* (**of** nach); **a ~ of burning/ gas** ein Brand-/Gasgeruch; **c)** *(stink)* Gestank, *der.* **2.** *v.t., smelt* [smelt] *or* **smelled** [smeld] **a)** *(perceive)* riechen; **b)** *(inhale ~ of)* riechen an (+ *Dat.*). **3.** *v.i., smelt or smelled* **a)** *(emit ~)* riechen; *(pleasantly also)* duften; **b)** ~ **of sth.** *(lit. or fig.)* nach etw. riechen; **c)** *(stink)* riechen. **'smelly** *adj.* stinkend; **be ~:** stinken

smelt *see* **smell** 2, 3

smile [smaɪl] **1.** *n.* Lächeln, *das;* **give sb. a ~:** jmdn. anlächeln. **2.** *v.i.* lächeln; ~ **at sb./sth.** jmdn. anlächeln/ über etw. *(Akk.)* lächeln

smirk [smɜ:k] **1.** *v.t.* grinsen. **2.** *n.* Grinsen, *das*

smith [smɪθ] *n.* Schmied, *der*

smithereens [smɪðə'ri:nz] *n. pl.* **blow/ smash sth. to ~:** etw. in tausend Stücke sprengen/schlagen

smock [smɒk] *n.* Kittel, *der*

smog [smɒg] *n.* Smog, *der*

smoke [sməʊk] **1.** *n.* Rauch, *der.* **2.** *v.i. & t.* rauchen. **smoked** [sməʊkt] *adj. (Cookery)* geräuchert

smoke: ~ **detector** *n.* Rauchmelder, *der;* ~**less** *adj.* rauchlos; rauchfrei ⟨*Zone*⟩

'smoker *n.* **a)** Raucher, *der/*Raucherin, *die;* **b)** *(Railw.)* Raucherabteil, *das*

'**smoke-screen** n. [künstliche] Nebelwand; *(fig.)* Vernebelung *die* (**for** *Gen.*)

smoking ['sməʊkɪŋ] n. **a)** Rauchen, *das;* '**no ~**' „Rauchen verboten"; **b)** *(seating area)* [**do you want to sit in**] ~ or **non-~**? möchten Sie für Raucher oder Nichtraucher?

smoky ['sməʊkɪ] adj. *(emitting smoke)* rauchend; *(smoke-filled)* verräuchert

smooth [smu:ð] **1.** adj. **a)** *(even)* glatt; eben ⟨*Straße, Weg*⟩; **b)** *(mild)* weich; **c)** *(not jerky)* geschmeidig ⟨*Bewegung*⟩; ruhig ⟨*Fahrt, Flug*⟩; weich ⟨*Landung*⟩; **d)** *(without problems)* reibungslos. **2.** v.t. glätten. '**smoothly** adv. **a)** *(evenly)* glatt; **b)** *(not jerkily)* geschmeidig ⟨*sich bewegen*⟩; weich ⟨*landen*⟩; reibungslos ⟨*funktionieren*⟩

smother ['smʌðə(r)] v.t. ersticken; *(fig.)* unterdrücken ⟨*Gähnen*⟩; ersticken ⟨*Gelächter, Schreie*⟩

smoulder ['sməʊldə(r)] v.i. schwelen; **she was ~ing with rage** Zorn schwelte in ihr

smudge [smʌdʒ] **1.** v.t. verwischen. **2.** v.i. schmieren. **3.** n. Fleck, *der*

smug [smʌg] adj. selbstgefällig

smuggle ['smʌgl] v.t. schmuggeln. **smuggle 'in** v.t. einschmuggeln; hinein-/hereinschmuggeln ⟨*Person*⟩. **smuggle 'out** v.t. hinaus-/herausschmuggeln

smuggler ['smʌglə(r)] n. Schmuggler, *der*/Schmugglerin, *die*

smuggling ['smʌglɪŋ] n. Schmuggel, *der*

smutty ['smʌtɪ] adj. *(lewd)* schmutzig

snack [snæk] n. Imbiß, *der.* '**snackbar** n. Schnellimbiß, *der*

snag [snæg] n. *(problem)* Haken, *der;* **what's the ~?** wo klemmt es? *(ugs.)*

snail [sneɪl] n. Schnecke, *die;* **at** [**a**] **~'s pace** im Schneckentempo *(ugs.)*

snake [sneɪk] n. Schlange, *die*

snap [snæp] **1.** v.t., **-pp-: a)** *(break)* zerbrechen; **~ sth. in two** *or* **in half** etw. in zwei Stücke brechen; **b) ~ one's fingers** mit den Fingern schnalzen; **c) ~ sth. home** *or* **into place** etw. einschnappen lassen; **~ shut** zuschnappen lassen ⟨*Portemonnaie, Schloß*⟩; zuklappen ⟨*Buch, Etui*⟩; **~ sth. open** etw. aufschnappen lassen; **d)** *(take photograph of)* knipsen; **e)** *(say sharply)* bellen. **2.** v.i., **-pp-: a)** *(break)* brechen; **b)** *(fig.: give way under strain)* ausrasten *(ugs.);* **my patience**

has finally ~ped nun ist mir der Geduldsfaden aber gerissen. **3.** n. *(Photog.)* Schnappschuß, *der.* '**snap at** v.t. *(speak sharply to)* anfauchen *(ugs.).* **snap 'off** v.t. & i. abbrechen. **snap 'up** v.t. *(fig. coll.)* [sich *(Dat.)*] schnappen *(ugs.)*

'**snapshot** n. Schnappschuß, *der*

snare [sneə(r)] **1.** n. Schlinge, *die.* **2.** v.t. [mit einer Schlinge] fangen

¹**snarl** [snɑ:l] **1.** v.i. knurren. **2.** n. Knurren, *das*

²**snarl** n. *(tangle)* Knoten, *der.* **snarl 'up** v.t. *(bring to a halt)* zum Erliegen bringen; **get ~ed up in the traffic** im Verkehr steckenbleiben

'**snarl-up** n. Stau, *der*

snatch [snætʃ] **1.** v.t. **a)** *(grab)* schnappen; ~ **sth. from sb.** jmdm. etw. wegreißen; ~ **some sleep** ein bißchen schlafen; **b)** *(steal)* klauen *(ugs.).* **2.** v.i. einfach zugreifen. **3.** n. **~es of talk/conversation** Gesprächsfetzen *Pl.*

sneak [sni:k] **1.** v.t. schmuggeln; ~ **a look at** schielen nach. **2.** v.i. **a)** schleichen; **b)** *(Brit. Sch. sl.: tell tales)* petzen *(Schülerspr.).* **3.** n. *(Brit. Sch. sl.)* Petzer, *der (Schülerspr.)*

sneer [snɪə(r)] v.i. höhnisch lächeln/grinsen. '**sneer at** v.t. höhnisch anlächeln/angrinsen; *(scorn)* verhöhnen

sneeze [sni:z] **1.** v.i. niesen. **2.** n. Niesen, *das*

sniff [snɪf] **1.** n. Schnuppern, *das; (with running nose, while crying)* Schniefen, *das.* **2.** v.i. schniefen; *(to detect a smell)* schnuppern. **3.** v.t. riechen od. schnuppern an (+ *Dat.*). '**sniff at** v.t. **a)** *see* **sniff 3; b)** *(show contempt for)* die Nase rümpfen über

snigger ['snɪgə(r)] **1.** v.i. *(boshaft)* kichern. **2.** n. *(boshaftes)* Kichern

snip [snɪp] **1.** v.t., **-pp-** schnippeln *(ugs.),* schneiden ⟨*Loch*⟩; schnippeln *(ugs.)* od. schneiden an (+ *Dat.*) ⟨*Tuch, Haaren, Hecke*⟩; *(cut off)* abschnippeln *(ugs.);* abschneiden. **2.** n. *(cut)* Schnitt, *der;* Schnipser, *der (ugs.)*

snipe [snaɪp] v.i. ~ **at** aus dem Hinterhalt beschießen. '**sniper** n. Heckenschütze, *der*

snippet ['snɪpɪt] n. *(of information in newspaper)* Notiz, *die; (of conversation)* Gesprächsfetzen, *der;* **useful ~s of information** nützliche Hinweise

snivel ['snɪvl] v.i., *(Brit.)* **-ll-** schniefen

snob [snɒb] n. Snob, *der.* **snobbery** ['snɒbərɪ] n. Snobismus, *der.* **snobbish** ['snɒbɪʃ] adj. snobistisch

snooker ['snu:kə(r)] *n.* Snooker, *das*
snoop [snu:p] *v.i.* schnüffeln *(ugs.)*
snooty ['snu:tı] *adj. (coll.)* hochnäsig *(ugs.)*
snooze [snu:z] *(coll.)* **1.** *v.i.* dösen *(ugs.).* **2.** *n.* Nickerchen, *das (fam.)*
snore [snɔ:(r)] **1.** *v.i.* schnarchen. **2.** *n.* Schnarcher, *der (ugs.); ~s* Schnarchen, *das*
snorkel ['snɔ:kl] *n.* Schnorchel, *der*
snort [snɔ:t] *v.i.* schnauben (**with, in** vor + *Dat.*)
snot [snɒt] *n. (sl.)* Rotz, *der (derb).*
snotty *adj.* rotznäsig *(salopp); ~* **child/nose** Rotznase, *die (salopp)*
snout [snaʊt] *n.* Schnauze, *die; (of pig)* Rüssel, *der*
snow [snəʊ] **1.** *n.* Schnee, *der.* **2.** *v.i. impers.* it *~s/is ~ing* es schneit. **snow 'in** *v.t.* they are *~ed in* sie sind eingeschneit. **snow 'under** *v.t.* be *~ed* **under** *(with work)* erdrückt werden; *(with gifts, mail)* überschüttet werden
snow: *~***ball 1.** *n.* Schneeball, *der;* **2.** *v.i. (fig.)* lawinenartig zunehmen; *~***bound** *adj.* eingeschneit; *~***-drift** *n.* Schneewehe, *die; ~***drop** *n.* Schneeglöckchen, *das; ~***fall** *n.* Schneefall, *der; ~***flake** *n.* Schneeflocke, *die; ~***man** *n.* Schneemann, *der; ~***-plough** *n.* Schneepflug, *der; ~***storm** *n.* Schneesturm, *der*
'snowy *adj.* schneereich *(Gegend);* schneebedeckt *(Berge)*
snub [snʌb] **1.** *v.t., -bb-:* **a)** *(rebuff)* brüskieren; **b)** *(reject)* ablehnen. **2.** *n.* Abfuhr, *die*
snub-'nosed *adj.* stupsnasig
¹snuff [snʌf] *n.* Schnupftabak, *der;* **take a pinch of** *~:* eine Prise schnupfen
²snuff *v.t. ~* **|out|** löschen *(Kerze)*
snuffle ['snʌfl] *v.i.* schnüffeln
snug [snʌg] *adj.* gemütlich; behaglich; **be a** *~* **fit** genau passen
snuggle ['snʌgl] *v.i. ~* **up to sb.** sich an jmdn. kuscheln; *~* **together** sich aneinanderkuscheln; *~* **up** *or* **down in bed** sich ins Bett kuscheln
so [səʊ] **1.** *adv.* so; **as winter draws near, so it gets darker** je näher der Winter rückt, desto dunkler wird es; **so ... as so ...** wie; **so far** bis hierher; *(until now)* bisher; *(to such a distance)* so weit; **so much the better** um so besser; **so long!** bis dann! *(ugs.);* **and so on |and so forth|** und so weiter |und so fort|; **so as to** um ... zu; **so |that|** damit; **I'm so glad/tired!** ich bin ja so froh/

müde!; **It's a rainbow! – So it is!** Es ist ein Regenbogen! – Ja, wirklich!; **'You suggested it. – So I did** Du hast es vorgeschlagen. – Das stimmt; **is that so?** so? *(ugs.);* wirklich?; **so am/have/would/could/will/do** I ich auch. **2.** *pron.* **he suggested that I take the train, and if I had done so, ...:** er riet mir, den Zug zu nehmen, und wenn ich es getan hätte, ...; **I'm afraid so** leider ja; **I told you so** ich habe es dir [doch] gesagt; **a week or so** etwa eine Woche; **very much so** in der Tat. **3.** *conj. (therefore)* daher; **so there you 'are!** ich habe also recht!; **so 'there!** |und| fertig!; **so?** na und?; **so you see ...:** du siehst also ...; **so where have you been?** wo warst du denn?
soak [səʊk] **1.** *v.t.* **a)** einweichen ⟨Wäsche in Lauge⟩; eintauchen ⟨Brot in Milch⟩; **b)** *(wet)* naß machen. **2.** *v.i.* **a)** *(steep)* put sth. in sth. to *~:* etw. in etw. *(Dat.)* einweichen; **b)** *(drain)* ⟨Feuchtigkeit, Nässe:⟩ sickern. **'soaking** *adj. & adv.* |**wet**| völlig durchnäßt
'so-and-so *n., pl. ~'s* **a)** *(person not named)* |Herr/Frau| Soundso; **b)** *(coll.: disliked person)* Biest, *das (ugs.)*
soap [səʊp] *n.* Seife, *die;* **with** *~* **and water** mit Wasser und Seife
soap: *~* **opera** *n.* Seifenoper, *die (ugs.); ~* **powder** *n.* Seifenpulver, *das; ~***suds** *n. pl.* Seifenschaum, *der*
'soapy *adj.* seifig; *~* **water** Seifenlauge, *die*
soar [sɔ:(r)] *v.i.* aufsteigen; *(fig.)* ⟨Preise, Kosten usw.:⟩ in die Höhe schießen *(ugs.)*
sob [sɒb] **1.** *v.i., -bb-* schluchzen (**with** vor + *Dat.*). **2.** *n.* Schluchzer, *der*
sober ['səʊbə(r)] *adj.* **a)** *(not drunk)* nüchtern; **b)** *(serious)* ernst. **sober 'up 1.** *v.i.* nüchtern werden. **2.** *v.t.* ausnüchtern
'sobering *adj.* ernüchternd
so-called ['səʊkɔ:ld] *adj.* sogenannt; *(alleged)* angeblich
soccer ['sɒkə(r)] *n.* Fußball, *der*
sociable ['səʊʃəbl] *adj.* gesellig
social ['səʊʃl] *adj.* **a)** sozial; gesellschaftlich; **b)** *(of ~ life)* gesellschaftlich; gesellig ⟨Abend, Beisammensein⟩
socialism ['səʊʃəlızm] *n.* Sozialismus, *der.* **socialist** ['səʊʃəlɪst] **1.** *n.* Sozialist, *der*/Sozialistin, *die.* **2.** *adj.* sozialistisch
socialize ['səʊʃəlaɪz] *v.i.* geselligen Umgang pflegen; *~* **with sb.** *(chat)* sich mit jmdm. unterhalten

'**socially** *adv.* **meet** ~ : sich privat treffen; ~ **deprived** sozial benachteiligt
social: ~ **se'curity** *n.* **a)** *(Brit.: benefit)* Sozialhilfe, *die;* **b)** *(system)* soziale
Sicherheit; ~ '**service** *n.* staatliche
Sozialleistung; ~ **work** *n.* Sozialarbeit, *die;* ~ **worker** *n.* Sozialarbeiter,
der/-arbeiterin, *die*
society [sə'saɪətɪ] *n.* **a)** Gesellschaft,
die; **high** ~: High-Society, *die;* **b)**
(club, association) Verein, *der*
sociologist [səʊsɪ'ɒlədʒɪst] *n.* Soziologe, *der/*Soziologin, *die*
sociology [səʊsɪ'ɒlədʒɪ] *n.* Soziologie,
die
'**sock** [sɒk] *n.* Socke, *die*
²**sock** *v. t. (coll.: hit)* hauen *(ugs.)*
socket ['sɒkɪt] *n.* **a)** *(Anat.) (of eye)*
Höhle, *die;* *(of joint)* Pfanne, *die;* **b)**
(Electr.) Steckdose, *die*
soda ['səʊdə] *n.* Soda, *das.* '**soda
water** *n.* Soda[wasser], *das*
sodden ['sɒdn] *adj.* durchnäßt (**with**
von)
sodium ['səʊdɪəm] *n.* Natrium, *das*
sofa ['səʊfə] *n.* Sofa, *das*
soft [sɒft] *adj.* weich; *(quiet)* leise;
(gentle) sanft; **have a** ~ **spot for sb.** eine Vorliebe für jmdn. haben. '**softboiled** *adj.* weichgekocht 〈*Ei*〉. '**soft
drink** *n.* alkoholfreies Getränk
soften ['sɒfn] **1.** *v. i.* weicher werden.
2. *v. t.* aufweichen 〈*Boden*〉; enthärten
〈*Wasser*〉; mildern 〈*Farbe*〉
'**softly** *adv. (quietly)* leise; *(gently)*
sanft
soft: ~ **toy** *n.* Stofftier, *das;* ~**ware**
n. (Computing) Software, *die*
soggy ['sɒgɪ] *adj.* aufgeweicht
'**soil** [sɔɪl] *n.* Erde, *die;* Boden, *der*
²**soil** *v. t.* beschmutzen
solace ['sɒləs] *n.* Trost, *der;* **take** *or*
find ~ **in sth.** Trost in etw. *(Dat.)* finden
solar ['səʊlə(r)] *adj.* Sonnen-
sold *see* **sell**
solder ['səʊldə(r)] **1.** *n.* Lot, *das.* **2.** *v. t.*
löten
soldier ['səʊldʒə(r)] *n.* Soldat, *der*
'**sole** [səʊl] *n. (of foot/shoe)* Sohle, *die*
²**sole** *adj.* einzig; alleinig 〈*Verantwortung, Recht*〉; Allein〈*erbe, -eigentümer*〉. '**solely** *adv.* einzig und allein
solemn ['sɒləm] *adj.* feierlich; ernst
〈*Anlaß, Gespräch*〉
solicitor [sə'lɪsɪtə(r)] *n. (Brit.: lawyer)*
Rechtsanwalt, *der/*-anwältin, *die*
solid ['sɒlɪd] **1.** *adj.* **a)** *(rigid)* fest; **b)**
(of the same substance all through)

massiv; **c)** *(well-built)* stabil; solide gebaut 〈*Haus, Mauer usw.*〉; **d)** *(complete)* ganz; **a good** ~ **meal** eine kräftige Mahlzeit. **2.** *n.* fester Körper
solidarity [sɒlɪ'dærɪtɪ] *n.* Solidarität,
die
solidify [sə'lɪdɪfaɪ] *v. i* fest werden
solitary ['sɒlɪtərɪ] *adj.* **a)** einsam; ~
confinement Einzelhaft, *die;* **b)** *(sole)*
einzig
solitude ['sɒlɪtjuːd] *n.* Einsamkeit, *die*
solo ['səʊləʊ] **1.** *n., pl.* ~**s** *(Mus.)* Solo,
das. **2.** *adj.* **a)** *(Mus.)* Solo-; **b)** ~ **flight**
Alleinflug, *der.* **3.** *adv.* **a)** *(Mus.)* solo;
b) go/fly ~ *(Aeronaut.)* einen Alleinflug machen. **soloist** ['səʊləʊɪst] *n.*
(Mus.) Solist, *der/*Solistin, *die*
solstice ['sɒlstɪs] *n.* Sonnenwende, *die*
soluble ['sɒljʊbl] *adj.* **a)** *(esp. Chem.)*
löslich; **b)** *(solvable)* lösbar
solution [sə'luːʃn] *n.* **a)** *(esp. Chem.)*
Lösung, *die;* **b)** *[result of] solving]* Lösung, *die* (**to** Gen.); **find a** ~ **to sth.** eine Lösung für etw. finden; etw. lösen
solvable ['sɒlvəbl] *adj.* lösbar
solve [sɒlv] *v. t.* lösen
solvent ['sɒlvənt] **1.** *adj.* **a)** *(esp.
Chem.)* lösend; **b)** *(Finance)* solvent.
2. *n. (esp. Chem.)* Lösungsmittel, *das*
sombre *(Amer.:* **somber)** ['sɒmbə(r)]
adj. dunkel; düster 〈*Stimmung, Atmosphäre*〉
some [səm, *stressed* sʌm] **1.** *adj.* **a)**
(one or other) [irgend]ein; ~ **day** eines
Tages; **b)** *(a considerable quantity of)*
einig...; **c)** *(a small quantity of)* ein
bißchen; **would you like** ~ **wine/cherries?** möchten Sie [etwas] Wein/[ein
paar] Kirschen?; **do** ~ **shopping/reading** einkaufen/lesen; **d)** *(to a certain
extent)* ~ **guide** eine gewisse Orientierungshilfe. **2.** *pron.* einig...; **would you
like** ~? möchtest du etwas/*(plural)*
welche?; ~ ..., **others** ...: manche ...,
andere ...
somebody ['sʌmbədɪ] *n. & pron.* jemand; ~ **or other** irgend jemand
'**somehow** *adv.* ~ [**or other**] irgendwie
someone ['sʌmwʌn] *see* **somebody**
somersault ['sʌməsɔːlt] *n.* Purzelbaum, *der (ugs.);* Salto, *der (Sport);*
turn a ~: einen Purzelbaum schlagen
*(ugs.)/*einen Salto springen
'**something** *n. & pron.* etwas; ~ **new**
etwas Neues; ~ **or other** irgend etwas;
see ~ **of sb.** jmdn. sehen
'**sometime** **1.** *adj.* ehemalig. **2.** *adv.*
irgendwann
'**sometimes** *adv.* manchmal

'**somewhat** *adv.* ziemlich

'**somewhere 1.** *adv.* **a)** *(in a place)* irgendwo; **b)** *(to a place)* irgendwohin. **2.** *n.* look for ~ to stay sich nach einer Unterkunft umsehen

son [sʌn] *n.* Sohn, *der*

sonata [sə'nɑ:tə] *n.* Sonate, *die*

song [sɒŋ] *n.* **a)** Lied, *das;* **b)** *(bird cry)* Gesang, *der*

'**son-in-law** *n., pl.* **sons-in-law** Schwiegersohn, *der*

soon [su:n] *adv.* **a)** bald; *(quickly)* schnell; **b)** *(early)* früh; **none too** ~: keinen Augenblick zu früh; **~er or later** früher oder später; **c) we'll set off as ~ as he arrives** sobald er ankommt, machen wir uns auf den Weg; **as ~ as possible** so bald wie möglich; **d)** *(willingly)* **just as ~ |as ...|** genauso gern [wie ...]; **she would ~er die than ...**: sie würde lieber sterben, als ...

soot [sʊt] *n.* Ruß, *der*

soothe [su:ð] *v. t.* **a)** *(calm)* beruhigen; **b)** lindern ⟨*Schmerz*⟩

'**sooty** *adj.* verrußt; rußig

sophisticated [sə'fɪstɪkeɪtɪd] *adj.* **a)** *(cultured)* kultiviert; **b)** *(elaborate, complex)* hochentwickelt; subtil ⟨*Argument, System*⟩

soporific [sɒpə'rɪfɪk] *adj.* einschläfernd

sopping ['sɒpɪŋ] *adj. & adv.* ~ |wet| völlig durchnäßt

soppy ['sɒpɪ] *adj.* *(Brit. coll.)* rührselig; sentimental ⟨*Person*⟩

soprano [sə'prɑ:nəʊ] *n.* Sopran, *der; (female also)* Sopranistin, *die*

sordid ['sɔ:dɪd] *adj.* dreckig; unerfreulich ⟨*Detail, Geschichte*⟩

sore [sɔ:(r)] **1.** *adj.* weh; *(inflamed or injured)* wund; **a ~ throat** Halsschmerzen *Pl.;* **sb. has a ~ back/foot** *etc.* jmdm. tut der Rücken/Fuß *usw.* weh. **2.** *n.* wunde Stelle. '**sorely** *adv.* sehr; dringend ⟨*nötig*⟩; ~ **tempted** stark versucht

sorrow ['sɒrəʊ] *n.* Kummer, *der*

sorry ['sɒrɪ] *adj.* **a) sb. is ~ that ...**: es tut jmdm. leid, daß ...; **sb. is ~ about sth.** jmdm. tut etwas leid; **I am** *or* **feel ~ for him** er tut mir leid; **sb. is** *or* **feels ~ for sth.** jmd. bedauert etw.; ~! Entschuldigung!; ~? wie bitte?; **I'm ~ to say** leider; **you'll be ~!** das wird dir noch leid tun; **b)** *(wretched)* traurig

sort [sɔ:t] **1.** *n.* **a)** Art, *die; (type)* Sorte, *die;* **a new ~ of bicycle** ein neuartiges Fahrrad; **all ~s of ...**: alle möglichen ...; **there are all ~s of things to do**

es gibt alles mögliche *od.* allerlei zu tun; ~ **of** *(coll.: more or. less)* mehr oder weniger; **nothing of the ~**: nichts dergleichen; **b) be out of ~s** nicht in Form sein. **2.** *v. t.* sortieren. **sort 'out** *v. t.* **a)** *(settle)* klären; schlichten ⟨*Streit*⟩; beenden ⟨*Verwirrung*⟩; **b)** *(select)* aussuchen

'**sort code** *n.* Bankleitzahl, *die*

sortie ['sɔ:tɪ] *n.* Ausfall, *der; (flight)* Einsatz, *der*

SOS *n.* SOS, *das*

'**so so, 'so-so** *adj., adv.* so lala *(ugs.)*

soufflé ['su:fleɪ] *n.* Soufflé, *das*

sought *see* **seek**

soul [səʊl] *n.* Seele, *die;* **not a ~**: keine Menschenseele

'**soul-destroying** *adj.* **a)** *(boring)* nervtötend; **b)** *(depressing)* deprimierend

'**soulful** ['səʊlfl] *adj.* gefühlvoll; *(sad)* schwermütig

soul: ~ **mate** *n.* Seelenverwandte, *der/die;* ~**-searching** *n.* Gewissenskampf, *der*

¹**sound** [saʊnd] **1.** *adj.* **a)** *(healthy)* gesund; intakt ⟨*Gebäude, Mauerwerk*⟩; **of ~ mind** im Vollbesitz der geistigen Kräfte; **b)** *(well-founded)* vernünftig ⟨*Argument, Rat*⟩; klug ⟨*Wahl*⟩; **it makes ~ sense** es ist sehr vernünftig; **c)** *(Finance: secure)* gesund, solide ⟨*Basis*⟩; klug ⟨*Investition*⟩. **2.** *adv.* fest, tief ⟨*schlafen*⟩

²**sound 1.** *n.* **a)** *(Phys.)* Schall, *der;* **b)** *(noise)* Laut, *der; (of wind, sea, car, footsteps, breaking glass or twigs)* Geräusch, *das; (of voices, laughter, bell)* Klang, *der;* **do sth. without a ~**: etw. lautlos tun; **c)** *(Radio, Telev., Cinemat.)* Ton, *der;* **d)** *(fig.: impression)* **I like the ~ of your plan** ich finde, Ihr Plan hört sich gut an; **I don't like the ~ of this** das hört sich nicht gut an. **2.** *v. i.* klingen; **it ~s as if .../like ...**: es klingt, als .../wie ...; **that ~s a good idea to me** ich finde, die Idee hört sich gut an; **that ~s odd to me** das hört sich seltsam an, finde ich; ~**s good to me!** klingt gut! *(ugs.).* **3.** *v. t.* **a)** ertönen lassen; **b)** *(utter)* ~ **a note of caution** zur Vorsicht mahnen. **sound 'off** *v. i.* tönen *(ugs.),* schwadronieren **(on, about,** von). **sound 'out** *v. i.* ausfragen ⟨*Person*⟩; ~ **sb. out on sth.** bei jmdm. wegen etw. vorfühlen

sound: ~ **barrier** *n.* Schallmauer, *die;* ~ **effect** *n.* Geräuscheffekt, *der*

'**sounding-board** *n.* **a)** *(Mus.)* Decke,

die; **b)** *(fig.: trial audience)* ≈ Testgruppe, *die*

'soundless *adj.* lautlos

'soundly *adv.* **a)** *(solidly)* stabil, solide ⟨*bauen*⟩; **b)** *(deeply)* tief, fest ⟨*schlafen*⟩; **c)** *(thoroughly)* ordentlich *(ugs.)* ⟨*verhauen*⟩; vernichtend ⟨*schlagen, besiegen*⟩

sound: ~**-proof 1.** *adj.* schalldicht; **2.** *v. t.* schalldicht machen; ~**-track** *n.* Soundtrack, *der;* ~**-wave** *n.* Schallwelle, *die*

soup [su:p] *n.* Suppe, *die;* **be/land in the** ~ *(fig. sl.)* in der Patsche sitzen/ landen *(ugs.)*

soup: ~**-plate** *n.* Suppenteller, *der;* ~**-spoon** *n.* Suppenlöffel, *der*

sour ['saʊə(r)] *adj.* **a)** sauer; **b)** *(morose)* griesgrämig; säuerlich ⟨*Blick*⟩; **c)** *(unpleasant)* bitter

source [sɔ:s] *n.* Quelle, *die;* ~ **of income/infection** Einkommensquelle, *die/*Infektionsherd, *der;* **at** ~: an der Quelle

south [saʊθ] **1.** *n.* **a)** Süden, *der;* **in/ to|wards|/from the** ~: im/nach/von Süden; **to the** ~ **of** südlich von; **b)** *usu.* **S~** *(Geog., Polit.)* Süden, *der.* **2.** *adj.* südlich; Süd⟨*küste, -wind, -grenze*⟩. **3.** *adv.* nach Süden; ~ **of** südlich von

South: ~ **'Africa** *pr. n.* Südafrika *(das);* ~ **'African** *adj.* südafrikanisch; ~ **A'merica** *pr. n.* Südamerika *(das);* ~ **A'merican** *adj.* südamerikanisch; **s~-bound** *adj.* ⟨*Zug, Verkehr usw.*⟩ in Richtung Süden; **s~-'east 1.** *n.* Südosten, *der;* **2.** *adj.* südöstlich; Südost⟨*wind, -küste*⟩; **3.** *adv.* südostwärts; nach Südosten; **s~-'eastern** *adj.* südöstlich

southerly ['sʌðəlɪ] *adj.* südlich; ⟨*Wind*⟩ aus südlichen Richtungen

southern ['sʌðən] *adj.* südlich; Süd⟨*grenze, -hälfte, -seite*⟩

South: ~ **'Germany** *pr. n.* Süddeutschland *(das);* ~ **'Pole** *pr. n.* Südpol, *der*

southward[s] ['saʊθwəd(s)] *adv.* südwärts

south: ~**-'west 1.** *n.* Südwesten, *der;* **2.** *adj.* südwestlich; Südwest⟨*wind, -küste*⟩; **3.** *adv.* südwestwärts; nach Südwesten; ~**-'western** *adj.* südwestlich

souvenir [su:və'nɪə(r)] *n.* Souvenir, *das (of aus)*

sovereign ['sɒvrɪn] *n.* *(ruler)* Souverän, *der.* **sovereignty** ['sɒvrɪntɪ] *n.* Souveränität, *die*

Soviet ['səʊvɪət, 'sɒvɪət] *adj. (Hist.)* sowjetisch; Sowjet⟨*bürger, -literatur*⟩

Soviet 'Union *pr. n. (Hist.)* Sowjetunion, *die*

¹sow [səʊ] *v. t., p. p.* **sown** [səʊn] *or* **sowed** [səʊd] **a)** *(plant)* [aus]säen; **b)** einsäen ⟨*Feld, Boden*⟩

²sow [saʊ] *n. (female pig)* Sau, *die*

sown *see* **¹sow**

soya [bean] ['sɔɪə (bi:n)] *n.* Sojabohne, *die*

spa [spɑ:] *n.* **a)** *(place)* Bad, *das;* Badeort, *der;* **b)** *(spring)* Mineralquelle, *die*

space [speɪs] *n.* **a)** Raum, *der;* **b)** *(interval between points)* Platz, *der;* **clear a** ~: Platz schaffen; **c) the wide open** ~**s** das weite, flache Land; **d)** *(Astron.)* Weltraum, *der;* **e)** *(blank between words)* Zwischenraum, *der;* **f)** *(interval of time)* Zeitraum, *der;* **in the** ~ **of a minute/an hour** innerhalb einer Minute/Stunde; **in a short** ~ **of time he was back** nach kurzer Zeit war er zurück.

space 'out *v. t.* verteilen

space: ~ **age** *n.* [Welt]raumzeitalter, *das;* ~**-bar** *n.* Leertaste, *die;* ~**-craft** *n.* Raumfahrzeug, *das;* ~**-saving** *adj.* platzsparend; ~**-ship** *n.* Raumschiff, *das;* ~**-suit** *n.* Raumanzug, *der;* ~ **travel** *n.* Raumfahrt, *die*

spacious ['speɪʃəs] *adj.* geräumig

spade [speɪd] *n.* **a)** Spaten, *der;* **b)** *(Cards)* Pik, *das; see also* **club 1 c**

spaghetti [spə'getɪ] *n.* Spaghetti *Pl.*

Spain [speɪn] *pr. n.* Spanien *(das)*

span [spæn] **1.** *n.* **a)** Spanne, *die;* Zeitspanne, *die;* **b)** *(of bridge)* Spannweite, *die.* **2.** *v. t.,* **-nn-** überspannen ⟨*Fluß*⟩; umfassen ⟨*Zeitraum*⟩

Spaniard ['spænjəd] *n.* Spanier, *der/* Spanierin, *die*

Spanish ['spænɪʃ] **1.** *adj.* spanisch; **sb. is** ~: jmd. ist Spanier/Spanierin. **2.** *n.* **a)** *(language)* Spanisch, *das; see also* **English 2 a; b) the** ~ *pl.* die Spanier

spank [spæŋk] **1.** *n.* ≈ Klaps, *der (ugs.).* **2.** *v. t.* ~ **sb.** jmdm. den Hintern versohlen *(ugs.)*

spanner ['spænə(r)] *n. (Brit.)* Schraubenschlüssel, *der*

spar [spɑ:(r)] *v. i.,* **-rr-: a)** *(Boxing)* sparren; **b)** *(fig.: argue)* [sich] zanken

spare [speə(r)] **1.** *adj.* **a)** *(not in use)* übrig; ~ **time/moment** Freizeit, *die/*freier Augenblick; **there is one** ~ **seat** ein Platz ist noch frei; **b)** *(for use when needed)* zusätzlich; Extra⟨*bett, -tasse*⟩; ~ **room** Gästezimmer, *das.* **2.** *n.* Ersatzteil, *das/*-reifen, *der usw.* **3.**

v. t. **a)** entbehren; **we arrived with ten minutes to** ~: wir kamen zehn Minuten früher an; **b)** *(not inflict on)* ~ **sb. sth.** jmdm. etw. ersparen; **c)** *(not hurt)* [ver]schonen; **d)** *(fail to use)* **not** ~ **any expense/pains** *or* **efforts** keine Kosten/Mühe scheuen; **no expense** ~**d** an nichts gespart

spare: ~ '**part** *n.* Ersatzteil, *das;* ~ '**tyre** *n.* Reserve-, Ersatzreifen, *der;* ~ '**wheel** *n.* Ersatzrad, *das*

sparing ['speərɪŋ] *adj.* sparsam

spark [spɑːk] 1. *n.* **a)** Funke, *der;* *(fig.)* **a** ~ **of generosity/decency** ein Funke[n] Großzügigkeit/Anstand; **b) a bright** ~ *(person, also iron.)* ein schlauer Kopf. 2. *v. t.* ~ |**off**| zünden; *(fig.)* auslösen

sparkle ['spɑːkl] 1. *v. i.* **a)** ⟨*Diamant:*⟩ glitzern; ⟨*Augen:*⟩ funkeln; **b)** *(be lively)* sprühen (**with** vor + *Dat.*). 2. *n.* Funkeln, *das.* **sparkling** ['spɑːklɪŋ] *adj.* glitzernd ⟨*Diamant*⟩; funkelnd ⟨*Augen*⟩. **sparkling** '**wine** *n.* Schaumwein, *der*

'**spark-plug** *n.* Zündkerze, *die*

sparrow ['spærəʊ] *n.* Spatz, *der*

sparse [spɑːs] *adj.* spärlich; dünn ⟨*Besiedlung*⟩

spasm ['spæzm] *n.* Krampf, *der*

spasmodic [spæz'mɒdɪk] *adj.* **a)** *(marked by spasms)* krampfartig; **b)** *(intermittent)* sporadisch

spastic ['spæstɪk] 1. *n.* Spastiker, *der/* Spastikerin, *die.* 2. *adj.* spastisch

spat *see* **spit** 1, 2

spate [speɪt] *n.* **a) the river is in |full|** ~: der Fluß führt Hochwasser; **b)** *(fig.)* **a** ~ **of sth.** eine Flut von etw.; **a** ~ **of burglaries** eine Einbruchsserie

spatial ['speɪʃl] *adj.* räumlich

spatter ['spætə(r)] *v. t.* spritzen; ~ **sb./sth. with sth.** jmdn./etw. mit etw. bespritzen

spatula ['spætjʊlə] *n.* Spachtel, *die*

spawn [spɔːn] 1. *v. t. (fig.)* hervorbringen. 2. *v. i. (Zool.)* laichen. 3. *n. (Zool.)* Laich, *der*

speak [spiːk] 1. *v. i.,* **spoke** [spəʊk], **spoken** ['spəʊkn] **a)** sprechen; ~ |**with sb.**| **on** *or* **about sth.** [mit jmdm.] über etw. *(Akk.)* sprechen; ~ **for/against sth.** sich für/gegen etw. aussprechen; **b)** *(on telephone)* **Is Mr Grant there?** – **S**~**ing!** Ist Mister Grant da? – Am Apparat!; **who is** ~**ing, please?** wer ist am Apparat, bitte? 2. *v. t.,* **spoke, spoken** sprechen ⟨*Satz, Wort, Sprache*⟩; sagen ⟨*Wahrheit*⟩; ~ **one's mind** sagen, was man denkt. '**speak**

for *v. t.* sprechen für; **sth. is spoken for** *(reserved)* etw. ist schon vergeben. '**speak of** *v. t.* sprechen von; ~**ing of Mary** da wir gerade von Mary sprechen; **nothing to** ~ **of** nichts Besonderes. '**speak to** *v. t.* sprechen *od.* reden mit. **speak** '**up** *v. i.* lauter sprechen

'**speaker** *n.* **a)** *(in public)* Redner, *der/*Rednerin, *die;* **b)** *(of a language)* Sprecher *der/*Sprecherin, *die;* **be a** '**French** ~: Französisch sprechen; **c)** *(loudspeaker)* Lautsprecher, *der*

'**speaking** 1. *n.* Sprechen, *das;* ~ **clock** *(Brit.)* telefonische Zeitansage. 2. *adv.* **strictly/generally** ~: genaugenommen/im allgemeinen

spear [spɪə(r)] *n.* Speer, *der.* '**spearhead** 1. *n. (fig.)* Speerspitze, *die.* 2. *v. t. (fig.)* anführen. '**spearmint** *n.* Grüne Minze; ~ **chewing-gum** Pfefferminzkaugummi, *der od. das*

special ['speʃl] *adj.* speziell; besonder...; **nobody** ~: niemand Besonderer. **special de'livery** *n. (Post)* Eilzustellung, *die*

specialist ['speʃəlɪst] *n.* **a)** Spezialist, *der/*Spezialistin, *die* (**in** für); **b)** *(Med.)* Facharzt, *der/*-ärztin, *die*

speciality [speʃɪ'ælɪtɪ] *n.* Spezialität, *die*

specialize ['speʃəlaɪz] *v. i.* sich spezialisieren (**in** auf + *Akk.*)

'**specially** *adv.* **a)** speziell; **make sth.** ~: etw. speziell *od.* extra anfertigen; **b)** *(especially)* besonders

special '**offer** *n.* Sonderangebot, *das;* **on** ~: im Sonderangebot

specialty ['speʃltɪ] *(esp. Amer.) see* **speciality**

species ['spiːʃiːz] *n., pl. same* Art, *die*

specific [spɪ'sɪfɪk] *adj.* bestimmt; ~~could you be more ~?~~ kannst du dich genauer ausdrücken? **specifically** [spɪ'sɪfɪkəlɪ] *adv.* ausdrücklich; eigens; extra *(ugs.)*

specification [spesɪfɪ'keɪʃn] *n., often pl. (details)* technische Daten; *(for building)* Baubeschreibung, *die*

specify ['spesɪfaɪ] *v. t.* ausdrücklich sagen; **unless otherwise specified** wenn nicht anders angegeben

specimen ['spesɪmən] *n.* **a)** *(example)* Exemplar, *das;* **b)** *(sample)* Probe, *die*

speck [spek] *n.* **a)** *(spot)* Fleck, *der;* **b)** *(particle)* Teilchen, *das;* ~ **of soot/dust** Rußflocke, *die/*Staubkörnchen, *das*

specs [speks] *n. pl. (coll.: spectacles)* Brille, *die*

spectacle ['spektəkl] *n.* **a)** *in pl.* |pair of] ~s Brille, *die;* **b)** *(public show)* Spektakel, *das;* **c)** *(object of attention)* Anblick, *der.* 'spectacle case *n.* Brillenetui, *das*

spectacular [spek'tækjʊlə(r)] *adj.* spektakulär

spectator [spek'teɪtə(r)] *n.* Zuschauer, *der/*Zuschauerin, *die*

specter *(Amer.) see* spectre

spectra *pl. of* spectrum

spectre ['spektə(r)] *n. (Brit.)* **a)** *(ghost)* Gespenst, *das;* **b)** *(fig.)* Schreckgespenst, *das*

spectrum ['spektrəm] *n., pl.* **spectra** ['spektrə] Spektrum, *das*

speculate ['spekjʊleɪt] *v.i.* spekulieren (**about, on** über + *Akk.*). **speculation** [spekjʊ'leɪʃn] *n.* Spekulation, *die* (**over** über + *Akk.*). **speculative** ['spekjʊlətɪv] *adj.* spekulativ. **speculator** ['spekjʊleɪtə(r)] *n.* Spekulant, *der/*Spekulantin, *die*

sped *see* speed 2

speech [spi:tʃ] *n.* **a)** *(public address)* Rede, *die;* **make** *or* **deliver** *or* **give a** ~: eine Rede halten; **b)** *(faculty or manner of speaking)* Sprache, *die.* 'speechless *adj.* sprachlos (**with** vor + *Dat.*)

speed [spi:d] **1.** *n.* Geschwindigkeit, *die;* Schnelligkeit, *die;* **at a** ~ **of** ...: mit einer Geschwindigkeit von ... **2.** *v.i.* **a)** *p.t. & p.p.* **sped** [sped] *or* **speeded** schnell fahren; rasen *(ugs.);* **b)** *p.t. & p.p.* **speeded** *(go too fast)* zu schnell fahren; rasen *(ugs.).* 'speedboat *n.* Rennboot, *das* 'speeding *n.* Geschwindigkeitsüberschreitung, *die* 'speed limit *n.* Geschwindigkeitsbeschränkung, *die*

speedometer [spi:'dɒmɪtə(r)] *n.* Tachometer, *der od. das*

'speedy *adj.* schnell; umgehend, prompt *(Antwort)*

¹spell [spel] **1.** *v.t.,* **spelt** [spelt] *(Brit.)* *or* **spelled a)** schreiben; *(aloud)* buchstabieren; **b)** *(fig.: mean)* bedeuten. **2.** *v.i.,* **spelt** *(Brit.) or* **spelled** *(say)* buchstabieren; *(write)* richtig schreiben

²spell *n. (period)* Weile, *die;* **a cold** ~: eine Kälteperiode

³spell *n.* **a)** *(magic charm)* Zauberspruch, *der;* **cast a** ~ **on sb.** jmdn. verzaubern; **b)** *(fascination)* Zauber, *der;* **break the** ~: den Bann brechen. 'spellbound *adj.* verzaubert

'spelling *n.* Rechtschreibung, *die*

spelt *see* ¹spell

spend [spend] *v.t.,* **spent** [spent] **a)** *(pay out)* ausgeben; ~ **a penny** *(fig. coll.)* mal verschwinden *(ugs.);* **b)** verbringen *(Zeit).* 'spendthrift *n.* Verschwender, *der/*Verschwenderin, *die*

spent 1. *see* spend. **2.** *adj.* **a)** *(used up)* verbraucht; **b)** *(drained of energy)* erschöpft

sperm ['spɜːm] *n. pl* ~s *or same (Biol.)* Sperma, *der*

spew [spju:] *v.t.* spucken

sphere [sfɪə(r)] *n.* **a)** *(field of action)* Bereich, *der;* Sphäre, *die (geh.);* **b)** *(Geom.)* Kugel, *die.* **spherical** ['sferɪkl] *adj.* kugelförmig

spice [spaɪs] **1.** *n.* Gewürz, *das; (fig.)* Würze, *die.* **2.** *v.t.* würzen. **spicy** ['spaɪsɪ] *adj.* pikant; würzig

spider ['spaɪdə(r)] *n.* Spinne, *die*

spike [spaɪk] *n.* Stachel, *der.* **spiky** ['spaɪkɪ] *adj.* stachelig

spill [spɪl] **1.** *v. t.,* **spilt** [spɪlt] *or* **spilled** verschütten *(Flüssigkeit);* ~ **sth. on** 3th. etw. auf etw. *(Akk.)* schütten; ~ **the beans** aus der Schule plaudern. **2.** *v.i.,* **spilt** *or* **spilled** überlaufen

spilt *see* spill

spin [spɪn] **1.** *v.t.,* **-nn-, spun** [spʌn] **a)** spinnen; ~ **yarn** Garn spinnen; **b)** *(in washing-machine etc.)* schleudern. **2.** *v.i.,* **-nn-, spun** sich drehen; **my head is** ~**ning** *(fig.)* mir schwirrt der Kopf. **spin 'out** *v.t. (prolong)* in die Länge ziehen

spinach ['spɪnɪdʒ] *n.* Spinat, *der*

spinal ['spaɪnl] *adj.* Wirbelsäulen-; Rückgrat[s]-. **spinal 'column** *n.* Wirbelsäule, *die.* **spinal 'cord** *n.* Rückenmark, *das*

spindle ['spɪndl] *n.* Spindel, *die.* **spindly** ['spɪndlɪ] *adj.* spindeldürr

spin-'drier *n.* Wäscheschleuder, *die*

spin-'dry *v.t.* schleudern

spine [spaɪn] *n.* **a)** *(backbone)* Wirbelsäule, die; **b)** *(Bot., Zool.)* Stachel, *der.* 'spineless *adj. (fig.)* rückgratlos

'spin-off *n.* Nebenprodukt, *das*

spinster ['spɪnstə(r)] *n.* ledige Frau

spiny ['spaɪnɪ] *adj.* stachelig

spiral ['spaɪrl] **1.** *adj.* spiralförmig. **2.** *n.* Spirale, *die.* **3.** *v.i., (Brit.)* **-ll-** *(Weg:)* sich hochwinden; *(Kosten:)* in die Höhe klettern; *(Rauch:)* in einer Spirale aufsteigen. **spiral 'staircase** *n.* Wendeltreppe, *die*

spire [spaɪə(r)] *n.* Turmspitze, *die*

spirit ['spɪrɪt] *n.* **a)** *in pl. (distilled liquor)* Spirituosen *Pl.;* **b)** *(mental atti-*

tude) Geisteshaltung, *die;* **in the right/ wrong** ~: mit der richtigen/falschen Einstellung; **take sth. in the wrong** ~: etw. falsch auffassen; **c)** *(courage)* Mut, *der;* **d)** *(mental tendency)* Geist, *der;* **high** ~s gehobene Stimmung; **in poor** *or* **low** ~s niedergedrückt. **'spirited** *adj.* beherzt

'spirit-level *n.* Wasserwaage, *die*

spiritual ['spɪrɪtʃʊəl] *adj.* spirituell *(geh.)*

spit [spɪt] **1.** *v. i.,* -tt-, spat [spæt] *or* spit spucken. **2.** *v. t.,* -tt-, spat *or* spit spucken. **3.** *n.* Spucke, *die.* **spit 'out** *v. t.* ausspucken

spite [spaɪt] **1.** *n.* **a)** Boshaftigkeit, *die;* **b) in** ~ **of** trotz; **in** ~ **of oneself** obwohl man es eigentlich nicht will. **2.** *v. t.* ärgern. **spiteful** ['spaɪtfl] *adj.* gehässig

spittle ['spɪtl] *n.* Spucke, *die*

splash [splæʃ] **1.** *v. t.* spritzen; ~ **sth. on |to|** *or* **over sb./sth.** jmdn./etw. mit etw. bespritzen. **2.** *v. i.* **a)** spritzen; **b)** *(in water)* platschen *(ugs.).* **3.** *n.* **a)** *(liquid)* Spritzer, *der;* **b)** *(noise)* Plätschern, *das*

splendid ['splendɪd] *adj. (excellent)* großartig; *(magnificent)* prächtig

splendour *(Brit.; Amer.:* **splendor)** ['splendə(r)] *n.* Pracht, *die*

splint [splɪnt] *n.* Schiene, *die*

splinter ['splɪntə(r)] *n.* Splitter, *der*

split [splɪt] **1.** *n.* **a)** *(tear)* Riß, *der;* **b)** *(division into parts)* [Auf]teilung, *die;* *(fig.)* Spaltung, *die.* **2.** *adj.* gespalten; **be** ~ **on a question** [sich *(Dat.)*] in einer Frage uneins sein. **3.** *v. t.,* -tt-, split **a)** *(tear)* zerreißen; **b)** *(divide)* teilen. **4.** *v. i.,* -tt-, split **a)** ⟨Holz:⟩ splittern; ⟨Stoff, Seil:⟩ reißen; ~ **apart** zersplittern; **b)** *(divide into parts)* sich teilen. **split 'up 1.** *v. t.* aufteilen. **2.** *v. i. (coll.)* sich trennen; ~ **up with sb.** sich von jmdm. trennen

splutter ['splʌtə(r)] *v. i.* ⟨Person:⟩ prusten; ⟨Motor:⟩ stottern

spoil [spɔɪl] **1.** *v. t.,* spoilt [spɔɪlt] *or* spoiled **a)** *(impair)* verderben; **b)** *(pamper)* verwöhnen; **be** ~t **for choice** die Qual der Wahl haben. **2.** *v. i.,* spoilt *or* spoiled **a)** verderben; **b) be** ~ing **for a fight** Streit suchen. **3.** *n.* ~|s *pl.|* Beute, *die.* **'spoilsport** *n.* Spielverderber, *der/*-verderberin, *die*

spoilt *see* spoil 1, 2

¹spoke [spəʊk] *n.* Speiche, *die*

²spoke, spoken *see* speak

spokesman ['spəʊksmən] *n., pl.* spokesmen ['spəʊksmən] Sprecher, *der*

sponge [spʌndʒ] **1.** *n.* Schwamm, *der.* **2.** *v. t.* mit einem Schwamm waschen. **'sponge on** *v. t.* ~ **on sb.** bei *od.* von jmdm. schnorren *(ugs.)*

sponge: ~**-bag** *n. (Brit.)* Kulturbeutel, *der;* ~**-cake** *n.* Biskuitkuchen, *der*

sponger ['spʌndʒə(r)] *n.* Schmarotzer, *der/*Schmarotzerin, *die*

spongy ['spʌndʒɪ] *adj.* schwammig

sponsor ['spɒnsə(r)] **1.** *n.* Sponsor, *der.* **2.** *v. t.* **a)** sponsern; **b)** *(Polit.)* ~ **sb.** jmds. Kandidatur unterstützen

spontaneous [spɒn'teɪnɪəs] *adj.* spontan

spooky ['spuːkɪ] *adj.* gespenstisch

spool [spuːl] *n.* Spule, *die*

spoon [spuːn] *n.* **a)** Löffel, *der;* **b)** *(amount) see* spoonful. **spoonful** ['spuːnfʊl] *n.* **a** ~ **of sugar** ein Löffel [voll] Zucker

sporadic [spə'rædɪk] *adj.* sporadisch

spore [spɔː(r)] *n.* Spore, *die*

sport [spɔːt] **1.** *n.* **a)** Sport, *der;* ~s Sportarten; **water/indoor** ~: Wasser-/ Hallensport, *der;* **b)** *(fun)* Spaß, *der;* **c) be a |real|** ~ *(coll.)* ein prima Kerl sein *(ugs.);* **be a** ~! sei kein Spielverderber! **2.** *v. t.* stolz tragen. **'sporting** *adj.* **a)** sportlich; **b) give sb. a** ~ **chance** jmdm. eine [faire] Chance geben

sports: ~ **car** *n.* Sportwagen, *der;* ~ **jacket** *n.* sportlicher Sakko; ~**man** ['spɔːtsmən] *n., pl.* ~**men** ['spɔːtsmən] Sportler, *der;* ~**manship** ['spɔːtsmənʃɪp] *n. (fairness)* [sportliche] Fairneß; ~**wear** *n.* Sport[be]kleidung, *die;* ~**woman** *n.* Sportlerin, *die*

'sporty *adj.* sportlich

spot [spɒt] **1.** *n.* **a)** *(precise place)* Stelle, *die;* **on this** ~: an dieser Stelle; **be in a tight** ~ *(fig. coll.)* in der Klemme sitzen *(ugs.);* **put sb. on the** ~ *(fig. coll.)* jmdn. in Verlegenheit bringen; **b)** *(suitable area)* Platz, *der;* **c)** *(dot)* Tupfen, *der;* **d)** *(stain)* ~ |of blood/grease/ ink| [Blut-/Fett-/Tinten]fleck, *der;* **e)** *(Brit. coll.: small amount)* **do a** ~ **of work/sewing** ein bißchen arbeiten/nähen; **f)** *(drop)* **a** ~ **or a few** ~s **of rain** ein paar Regentropfen; **g)** *(Med.)* Pickel, *der.* **2.** *v. t.,* -tt- *(detect)* entdecken; erkennen ⟨Gefahr⟩

spot: ~ '**check** *n.* Stichprobe, *die;* ~**less** *adj.* fleckenlos; **her house is absolutely** ~ *(fig.)* ihr Haus ist makellos sauber; ~**light** *n.* Scheinwerfer, *der;* **be in the** ~**light** *(fig.)* im Rampenlicht stehen

spotted ['spɒtɪd] *adj.* gepunktet
spotty *adj. (pimply)* picklig
spouse [spaʊs] *n.* [Ehe]gatte, *der*/-gattin, *die*
spout [spaʊt] **1.** *n.* Schnabel, *der; (of tap)* Ausflußrohr, *das.* **2.** *v.i. (gush)* schießen **(from** aus)
sprain [spreɪn] **1.** *v.t.* verstauchen. **2.** *n.* Verstauchung, *die*
sprang *see* spring 2, 3
sprawl [sprɔ:l] *v.i.* **a)** sich ausstrecken; *(fall)* der Länge nach hinfallen; **b)** *(straggle)* sich ausbreiten
¹spray [spreɪ] *(bouquet)* Strauß, *der*
²spray 1. *v.t.* spritzen; sprühen 〈*Parfüm*〉; besprühen 〈*Haar, Pflanze*〉. **2.** *n.* **a)** *(drops)* Sprühnebel, *der;* **b)** *(liquid)* Spray, *der od. das*
spread [spred] **1.** *v.t.* spread **a)** ausbreiten 〈*Tuch, Landkarte*〉 **(on** auf + *Dat.*); streichen 〈*Butter, Farbe, Marmelade*〉; **b)** *(extend range of)* verbreiten; **c)** *(distribute)* verteilen. **2.** *v.i.,* spread sich ausbreiten. **3.** *n.* **a)** Verbreitung, *die; (of city, poverty)* Ausbreitung, *die;* **b)** *(coll.: meal)* Festessen, *das;* **c)** *(paste)* Brotaufstrich, *der.*
spread 'out 1. *v.t.* ausbreiten. **2.** *v.i.* sich verteilen
spree [spri:] *n.* go on a shopping ~: ganz groß einkaufen gehen
sprig [sprɪg] *n.* Zweig, *der*
sprightly ['spraɪtlɪ] *adj.* munter
spring [sprɪŋ] **1.** *n.* **a)** *(season)* Frühling, *der;* in [the] ~: im Frühling *od.* Frühjahr; **b)** *(water)* Quelle, *die;* **c)** *(Mech.)* Feder, *die;* **d)** *(jump)* Sprung, *der.* **2.** *v.i.,* sprang [spræŋ] *or (Amer.)* sprung [sprʌŋ], sprung **a)** *(jump)* springen; ~ **to life** *(fig.)* [plötzlich] zum Leben erwachen; **b)** *(arise)* entspringen **(from** *Dat.*). **3.** *v.t.,* sprang *or (Amer.)* sprung, sprung: ~ **sth. on sb.** jmdn. mit etw. überfallen
spring: ~board *n.* Sprungbrett, *das;* ~-'clean **1.** *n.* Frühjahrsputz, *der;* **2.** *v.t.* Frühjahrsputz machen; ~ 'onion *n.* Frühlingszwiebel, *die;* ~time *n.* Frühling, *der*
sprinkle ['sprɪŋkl] *v.t.* streuen; sprengen 〈*Flüssigkeit*〉. **sprinkler** ['sprɪŋklə(r)] *n. (Hort.)* Sprinkler, *der*
sprint [sprɪnt] **1.** *v.t. & i.* rennen; sprinten *(bes. Sport).* **2.** *n.* Sprint, *der*
sprout [spraʊt] **1.** *n.* **a)** Brussels ~s Rosenkohl, *der;* **b)** *(Bot.)* Trieb, *der.* **2.** *v.i.* sprießen *(geh.)*
spruce [spru:s] **1.** *adj.* gepflegt. **2.** *n.* Fichte, *die*

sprung [sprʌŋ] **1.** *see* spring 2, 3. **2.** *attrib. adj.* gefedert
spud [spʌd] *n. (sl.)* Kartoffel, *die*
spun *see* spin
spur [spɜ:(r)] **1.** *n.* Sporn, *der; (fig.)* Ansporn, *der;* **on the** ~ **of the moment** ganz spontan. **2.** *v.t.,* **-rr-** *(fig.)* anspornen
spurious ['spjʊərɪəs] *adj.* gespielt 〈*Interesse*〉; zweifelhaft 〈*Anspruch*〉
spurn [spɜ:n] *v.t.* zurückweisen
¹spurt [spɜ:t] *n.* Spurt, *der;* **put on a** ~: einen Spurt einlegen
²spurt 1. *v.i.* ~ **out** [from *or* of] herausspritzen [aus]. **2.** *n.* Strahl, *der*
spy [spaɪ] **1.** *n.* Spion, *der*/Spionin, *die.* **2.** *v.i.* spionieren; ~ **on sb.** jmdm. nachspionieren
squabble ['skwɒbl] **1.** *n.* Streit, *der.* **2.** *v.i.* sich zanken **(over, about** wegen)
squad [skwɒd] *n.* **a)** *(Mil.)* Gruppe, *die;* **b)** *(group)* Mannschaft, *die*
squadron ['skwɒdrən] *n.* **a)** *(Navy)* Geschwader, *das;* **b)** *(Air Force)* Staffel, *die*
squalid ['skwɒlɪd] *adj.* **a)** *(dirty)* schmutzig; **b)** *(poor)* schäbig
squall [skwɔ:l] *n. (gust)* Bö, *die*
squalor ['skwɒlə(r)] *n.* Schmutz, *der*
squander ['skwɒndə(r)] *v.t.* vergeuden
square [skweə(r)] **1.** *n.* **a)** *(Geom.)* Quadrat, *das;* **b)** *(open area)* Platz, *der.* **2.** *adj.* **a)** quadratisch; **b)** **a** ~ **foot/mile** ein Quadratfuß/eine Quadratmeile. **3.** *v.t.* **a)** *(Math.)* quadrieren; **b)** ~ **it with sb.** es mit jmdm. klären. **4.** *v.i. (agree)* übereinstimmen.
square 'up *v.i. (settle up)* abrechnen
square 'root *n.* Quadratwurzel, *die*
squash [skwɒʃ] **1.** *v.t. (crush)* zerquetschen; ~ **sth. flat** etw. platt drücken. **2.** *n.* **a)** Fruchtsaftgetränk, *das;* **b)** *(Sport)* Squash, *das*
squat [skwɒt] *v.i.,* **-tt-:** **a)** *(crouch)* hocken; **b)** ~ **in a house** ein Haus besetzen. **'squatter** *n.* Hausbesetzer, *der*/-besetzerin, *die*
squawk [skwɔ:k] *v.i.* 〈*Krähe:*〉 krähen; 〈*Huhn:*〉 kreischen
squeak [skwi:k] **1.** *n.* **a)** *(of animal)* Quieken, *das;* **b)** *(of brakes, hinge, etc.)* Quietschen, *das.* **2.** *v.i.* **a)** 〈*Tier:*〉 quieken; **b)** 〈*Scharnier, Tür, Bremse, Schuh usw.:*〉 quietschen
squeal [skwi:l] **1.** *v.i.* **a)** ~ **with pain/in fear** 〈*Person:*〉 vor Schmerz/Angst aufschreien; 〈*Tier:*〉 vor Schmerz/Angst laut quieken; **b)** 〈*Bremsen, Räder:*〉

kreischen; ‹*Reifen:*› quietschen. **2.** *n.*
Kreischen, *das;* *(of tyres)* Quietschen,
das; (of animal) Quieken, *das*
squeamish ['skwi:mıʃ] *adj.* **be ~:**
zartbesaitet sein
squeeze [skwi:z] **1.** *n.* Druck, *der;* **give
sth. a small ~:** etw. [leicht] drücken. **2.**
v. t. **a)** *(press)* drücken; drücken auf
(+ Akk.) ‹*Tube, Plastikflasche*›; *(to get
juice)* auspressen; **b)** *(extract)* drücken
(out of aus); **~ out sth.** etw. heraus-
drücken; **c)** *(force)* zwängen
squelch [skweltʃ] *v. i.* quatschen *(ugs.)*
squid [skwıd] *n.* Kalmar, *der*
squiggle ['skwıgl] *n.* Schnörkel, *der*
squint [skwınt] **1.** *n.* Schielen, *das.* **2.**
v. i. **a)** *(Med.)* schielen; **b)** *(with half-
closed eyes)* blinzeln
squire ['skwaıə(r)] *n.* ≈ Gutsherr, *der*
squirm [skwɜ:m] *v. i.* sich winden
(with vor + *Dat.*)
squirrel ['skwırl] *n.* Eichhörnchen, *das*
squirt [skwɜ:t] **1.** *v. t.* spritzen; sprühen ‹*Spray, Puder*›; **~ sth. at sb.** jmdn.
mit etw. bespritzen/besprühen. **2.** *v. i.*
spritzen. **3.** *n.* Spritzer, *der*
St *abbr.* **Saint** St.
St. *abbr.* **Street** Str.
st. *abbr. (Brit.: unit of weight)* **stone**
stab [stæb] **1.** *v. t.,* **-bb-** stechen; **~ sb.
in the chest** jmdm. in die Brust ste-
chen. **2.** *v. i.,* **-bb-** stechen. **3.** *n.* **a)**
Stich, *der;* **b)** *(coll.: attempt)* **make** or
have a ~ [at it] [es] probieren
stability [stə'bılıtı] *n.* Stabilität, *die*
stabilize ['steıbılaız] **1.** *v. t.* stabilisieren. **2.** *v. i.* sich stabilisieren
¹**stable** ['steıbl] *adj.* stabil; gefestigt
‹*Person*›
²**stable** *n.* Stall, *der*
stack [stæk] **1.** *n.* **a)** *(pile)* Stoß, *der;*
Stapel, *der;* **b)** *(coll.: large amount)*
Haufen, *der (ugs.);* **c)** |chimney-|**~:**
Schornstein, *der.* **2.** *v. t.* **~** |up|
[auf]stapeln
stadium ['steıdıəm] *n.* Stadion, *das*
staff [sta:f] **1.** *n.* **a)** *(stick)* Stock, *der;*
b) *(personnel)* Personal, *das; (of
school)* Lehrkollegium, *das.* **2.** *v. t.* mit
Personal ausstatten. **'staff-room** *n.
(Sch.)* Lehrerzimmer, *das*
stag [stæg] *n.* Hirsch, *der*
stage [steıdʒ] **1.** *n.* **a)** *(Theatre)* Bühne,
die; **b)** *(part of process)* Stadium, *das;*
at this ~: in diesem Stadium; **do sth.
by ~s** etw. abschnittsweise tun; **in the
final ~s** in der Schlußphase; **c)** *(distance)* Etappe, *die.* **2.** *v. t.* **a)** *(present)*
inszenieren; **b)** *(arrange)* veranstalten

stage: **~-coach** *n.* Postkutsche, *die;*
~ door *n.* Bühneneingang, *der;* **~
fright** *n.* Lampenfieber, *das;*
~-manage *v. t. (fig.)* veranstalten
stagger ['stægə(r)] **1.** *v. i.* schwanken.
2. *v. t. (astonish)* die Sprache verschlagen (+ *Dat.*)
stagnant ['stægnənt] *adj.* **a)** stehend
‹*Gewässer*›; **b)** *(Econ.)* stagnierend
stagnate [stæg'neıt] *v. i.* **a)** ‹*Wasser:*›
abstehen; **b)** ‹*Wirtschaft, Geschäft:*›
stagnieren; ‹*Person:*› abstumpfen.
stagnation [stæg'neıʃn] *n.* **a)** *(of
water)* Stehen, *das;* **b)** *(Econ.)* Stagnation, *die*
staid [steıd] *adj.* gesetzt
stain [steın] **1.** *v. t.* **a)** verfärben; *(make
~s on)* Flecken hinterlassen auf
(+ *Dat.*); **b)** *(colour)* beizen ‹*Holz*›. **2.**
n. Fleck, *der.* **stained 'glass** *n.* far-
biges Glas; **~ 'window** Fenster mit
Glasmalerei
'stainless *adj.* fleckenlos. **stainless
'steel** *n.* Edelstahl, *der*
stair [steə(r)] *n. (step)* [Treppen]stufe,
die; **~s** Treppe, *die.* **'staircase** *n.*
Treppenhaus, *das*
stake [steık] *n.* **a)** *(pointed stick)* Pfahl,
der; **b)** *(wager)* Einsatz, *der;* **be at ~:**
auf dem Spiel stehen
stale [steıl] *adj.* alt; muffig; abgestanden ‹*Luft*›; alt[backen] ‹*Brot*›; schal
‹*Bier, Wein usw.*›
'stalemate *n.* Patt, *das*
¹**stalk** [stɔ:k] *v. t.* sich heranpirschen
an (+ *Akk.*)
²**stalk** *n. (Bot.) (main stem)* Stengel,
der; (of leaf, flower, fruit) Stiel, *der*
stall [stɔ:l] **1.** *n.* **a)** Stand, *der;* **b)** *(Brit.
Theatre)* **~s** Parkett, *das.* **2.** *v. t.* ab-
würgen *(ugs.)* ‹*Motor*›. **3.** *v. i.* ‹*Motor:*›
stehenbleiben
stallion ['stæljən] *n.* Hengst, *der*
stalwart ['stɔ:lwət] *adj. (determined)*
entschieden; *(loyal)* treu
stamina ['stæmınə] *n.* Ausdauer, *die*
stammer ['stæmə(r)] **1.** *v. i.* stottern. **2.**
v. t. stammeln. **3.** *n.* Stottern, *das*
stamp [stæmp] **1.** *v. t.* **a)** *(impress, imprint sth. on)* [ab]stempeln; **b)** **~ one's
foot** mit dem Fuß stampfen; **c)** *(put
postage ~ on)* frankieren; **~ed ad-
dressed envelope** frankierter Rückumschlag; **d)** **become** or **be ~ed on sb.'s
memory** or **mind** sich jmdm. fest einprägen. **2.** *v. i.* aufstampfen. **3.** *n.* Marke, *die; (postage ~)* Briefmarke, *die;
(instrument for ~ing)* Stempel, *der.*
'stamp on *v. t.* **a)** zertreten ‹*Insekt*›;

~ **on sb's foot** jmdm. auf den Fuß treten; **b)** *(suppress)* durchgreifen gegen.
stamp '**out** *v.t.* [aus]stanzen; *(fig.)* ausmerzen
stamp: ~ **album** *n.* Briefmarkenalbum, *das;* ~-**collecting** *n.* Briefmarkensammeln, *das*
stampede [stæm'pi:d] *n.* Stampede, *die*
stand [stænd] **1.** *v.i.,* stood [stʊd] **a)** stehen; **b) my offer/promise still** ~s mein Angebot/Versprechen gilt nach wie vor; **as it** ~s, **as things** ~: wie die Dinge [jetzt] liegen; **I'd like to know where I** ~ *(fig.)* ich möchte wissen, wo ich dran bin; **c)** *(be candidate)* kandidieren; **d)** |not| ~ **in sb.'s way** *(fig.)* jmdm. [keine] Steine in den Weg legen; **e)** *(be likely)* ~ **to win** *or* **gain/lose** sth. etw. gewinnen/verlieren können. **2.** *v.t.,* stood **a)** *(set in position)* stellen; **b)** *(endure)* ertragen; **I cannot** ~ |the **sight of**| **him/her** ich kann ihn/sie nicht ausstehen; **he can't** ~ **the pressure/strain** er ist dem Druck/den Strapazen nicht gewachsen; **I can't** ~ **it any longer!** ich halte es nicht mehr aus!; **c)** *(buy)* ~ **sb. sth.** jmdm. etw. ausgeben. **3.** *n.* **a)** *(support)* Ständer, *der;* **b)** *(stall; at exhibition)* Stand, *der;* **c)** *(raised structure)* Tribüne, *die.*
stand a'**bout, stand a**'**round** *v.i.* herumstehen. **stand a**'**side** *v.i.* zur Seite treten. '**stand between** *v.t.* sth. ~s **between sb. and sth.** *(fig.)* etw. steht jmdm. bei etw. im Wege. **stand by 1.** [-'-] *v.i.* **a)** *(be near)* daneben stehen; **b)** *(be ready)* sich zur Verfügung halten. **2.** ['--] *v.t.* **a)** *(support)* ~ **by sb./ one another** jmdm./sich [gegenseitig] beistehen; **b)** *(adhere to)* ~ **by sth.** zu etw. stehen. '**stand for** *v.t.* **a)** *(signify)* bedeuten; **b)** *(coll.: tolerate)* sich *(Dat.)* bieten lassen. **stand** '**in** *v.i.* aushelfen; ~ **in for sb.** für jmdn. einspringen. **stand** '**out** *v.i.* *(be prominent)* herausragen; ~ **out a mile** *(fig.)* nicht zu übersehen sein. '**stand over** *v.t.* beaufsichtigen. **stand** '**up** *v.i.* **a)** aufstehen; ~ **up straight** sich aufrecht hinstellen; **b)** ~ **up well** |**in comparison with sb./sth.**| [im Vergleich zu jmdm./ etw.] gut abschneiden; ~ **up for sb./ sth.** für jmdn./etw. Partei ergreifen; ~ **up to sb.** sich jmdm. entgegenstellen
standard ['stændəd] **1.** *n.* **a)** Maßstab, *der;* **safety** ~s Sicherheitsnormen; **above/below/up to** ~: überdurchschnittlich [gut]/unter dem Durch-

schnitt/der Norm entsprechend; **b)** *(degree)* Niveau, *das;* ~ **of living** Lebensstandard, *der;* **c)** ~s *(morals)* Prinzipien; **d)** *(flag)* Standarte, *die.* **2.** *adj.* Standard-; **b)** ~ **practice** allgemein üblich sein. **standardize** ['stændədaɪz] *v.t.* standardisieren
'**standard lamp** *n.* Stehlampe, *die*
stand: ~-**by 1.** *n.* **be on** ~-**by** einsatzbereit sein; **2.** *adj.* Ersatz-; ~-**in 1.** *n.* Ersatz, *der;* **2.** *adj.* Ersatz-
'**standing 1.** *n.* **a)** *(repute)* Ansehen, *das;* **b)** *(duration)* **of long/short** ~: von langer/kurzer Dauer. **2.** *adj.* **a)** *(erect)* stehend; **b)** fest ⟨*Regel, Brauch*⟩
standing: ~ '**order** *n.* Dauerauftrag, *der;* ~ **o**'**vation** *n.* stürmischer Beifall; ~-**room** *n.* Stehplätze
stand: ~-**pipe** *n.* Standrohr, *das;* ~**point** *n.* *(fig.)* Standpunkt, *der;* ~**still** *n.* Stillstand, *der;* **be at a** ~**still** stillstehen; **come to a** ~**still** zum Stehen kommen
stank *see* **stink 1**
staple ['steɪpl] **1.** *n.* [Heft]klammer, *die.* **2.** *v.t.* heften (**on to** an + *Akk.*). **stapler** ['steɪplə(r)] *n.* [Draht]hefter, *der*
star [stɑ:(r)] **1.** *n.* **a)** Stern, *der;* **b)** *(prominent person)* Star, *der.* **2.** *v.i.* ~ **in a film** in einem Film die Hauptrolle spielen
starboard ['stɑ:bəd] *n.* Steuerbord, *das*
starch [stɑ:tʃ] *n.* Stärke, *die*
stardom ['stɑ:dəm] *n.* Starruhm, *der*
stare [steə(r)] *v.i.* starren; ~ **at sb./sth.** jmdn./etw. anstarren
'**starfish** *n.* Seestern, *der*
stark [stɑ:k] **1.** *adj.* scharf ⟨*Kontrast, Umriß*⟩. **2.** *adv.* völlig; ~ **naked** splitternackt *(ugs.)*
starling ['stɑ:lɪŋ] *n.* Star, *der*
starry ['stɑ:rɪ] *adj.* sternklar
start [stɑ:t] **1.** *v.i.* **a)** *(begin)* anfangen; ~ **on sth.** etw. beginnen; **b)** *(set out)* aufbrechen; **c)** *(begin to function)* anlaufen; ⟨*Auto, Motor usw.:*⟩ anspringen. **2.** *v.t.* **a)** *(begin)* beginnen [mit]; ~ **doing** *or* **to do sth.** [damit] anfangen, etw. zu tun; **b)** *(cause)* auslösen; anfangen ⟨*Streit, Schlägerei*⟩; legen/*(accidentally)* verursachen ⟨*Brand*⟩; **c)** *(set up)* ins Leben rufen ⟨*Organisation, Projekt*⟩; **d)** *(switch on)* einschalten; anlassen ⟨*Motor, Auto*⟩. **3.** *n.* **a)** Anfang, *der;* Beginn, *der;* *(of race)* Start, *der;* **from the** ~: von Anfang an; **from** ~ **to finish** von Anfang bis Ende;

make a ~: anfangen (on mit); *(on journey)* aufbrechen; **b)** *(Sport: ~ing place)* Start, *der.* '**starter** *n.* **a)** *(food)* Vorspeise, *die;* **b)** *(Sport)* Starter, *der*

startle ['staːtl] *v. t.* erschrecken; **be ~d by** sth. über etw. *(Akk.)* erschrecken.

startling ['staːtlıŋ] *adj.* erstaunlich

starvation [staː'veıʃn] *n.* Verhungern, *das*

starve [staːv] *v. i.* ~ [**to death**] verhungern

state [steıt] **1.** *n.* **a)** *(condition)* Zustand, *der;* **b)** *(nation)* Staat, *der;* **c)** be in a ~: aufgeregt sein; **d)** lie in ~: aufgebahrt sein. **2.** *v. t. (express)* erklären; angeben ⟨*Alter usw.*⟩

stately ['steıtlı] *adj.* majestätisch; stattlich ⟨*Körperbau, Gebäude*⟩. **stately 'home** *n.* Herrensitz, *der*

'**statement** *n.* **a)** *(stating, account)* Aussage, *die; (declaration)* Erklärung, *die;* **b)** |bank| ~: Kontoauszug, *der*

statesman ['steıtsmən] *n., pl.* **statesmen** ['steıtsmən] Staatsmann, *der*

static ['stætık] *adj.* statisch

station ['steıʃn] **1.** *n.* **a)** *see* **railway-station;** **b)** *(status)* Rang, *der.* **2.** *v. t.* aufstellen ⟨*Wache*⟩

stationary ['steıʃənərı] *adj.* stehend; **be ~:** stehen

stationer ['steıʃənə(r)] *n.* **~'s** |shop| Schreibwarengeschäft, *das.* **stationery** ['steıʃənərı] *n.* **a)** *(writing materials)* Schreibwaren *Pl.;* **b)** *(writing-paper)* Briefpapier, *das*

'**station-wagon** *n. (Amer.)* Kombiwagen, *der*

statistical [stə'tıstıkl] *attrib. adj.,* **statistically** [stə'tıstıkəlı] *adv.* statistisch

statistics [stə'tıstıks] *n.* Statistik, *die*

statue ['stætʃuː, 'stætjuː] *n.* Statue, *die*

stature ['stætʃə(r)] *n.* Statur, *die; (fig.)* Format, *das*

status ['steıtəs] *n.* Rang, *der; social* ~: [gesellschaftlicher] Status. '**status symbol** *n.* Statussymbol, *das*

statute ['stætjuːt] *n.* Gesetz, *das.* **statutory** ['stætjʊtərı] *adj.* gesetzlich

staunch [stɔːntʃ] *adj.* treu ⟨*Freund*⟩; überzeugt ⟨*Katholik usw.*⟩

stave [steıv] *v. t.* ~ '**off** abwenden; stillen ⟨*Hunger*⟩

stay [steı] **1.** *n.* Aufenthalt, *der; (visit)* Besuch, *der;* **come/go for a short ~ with** sb. jmdn. kurz besuchen. **2.** *v. i.* bleiben; ~ **put** *(coll.)* ⟨*Person:*⟩ bleiben[, wo man ist]; ~ **the night in a hotel** die Nacht in einem Hotel ver-

bringen. **3.** *v. t.* ~ **the course** *(fig.)* durchhalten. **stay a'way** *v. i.* wegbleiben. **stay be'hind** *v. i.* zurückbleiben. **stay 'in** zu Hause bleiben. **stay 'out** *v. i.* **a)** *(not go home)* wegbleiben *(ugs.);* **b)** *(remain outside)* draußen bleiben. **stay 'up** *v. i.* aufbleiben

stead [sted] *n.* **a)** **in** sb.'s ~: an jmds. Stelle *(Dat.);* **b)** **stand** sb. **in good ~:** jmdm. zustatten kommen

steadfast ['stedfaːst] *adj.* standhaft; zuverlässig ⟨*Freund*⟩

steadily ['stedılı] *adv.* **a)** *(stably)* fest; **b)** *(continuously)* stetig

steady ['stedı] **1.** *adj.* **a)** *(stable)* stabil; *(not wobbling)* standfest; **b)** *(still)* ruhig; **c)** *(regular, constant)* stetig; gleichmäßig ⟨*Arbeit, Tempo*⟩; gleichbleibend ⟨*Preis, Lohn*⟩; gleichbleibend ⟨*Temperatur*⟩; **we had ~ rain/drizzle** wir hatten Dauerregen/es nieselte [bei uns] ständig; **d) a ~ job** eine feste Stelle; **a ~ boy-friend** ein fester Freund. **2.** *v. t.* festhalten ⟨*Leiter*⟩; beruhigen ⟨*Nerven*⟩

steak [steık] *n.* Steak, *das*

steal [stiːl] **1.** *v. t.,* **stole** [stəʊl], **stolen** ['stəʊln] stehlen *(from Dat.).* **2.** *v. i.,* **stole, stolen a)** stehlen; ~ **from** sb. jmdn. bestehlen; **b)** ~ **in/out** sich hinein-/hinausstehlen

stealth [stelθ] *n.* Heimlichkeit, *die;* **by ~:** heimlich. **stealthy** ['stelθı] *adj.* heimlich

steam [stiːm] **1.** *n.* Dampf, *der;* **let off ~** *(fig.)* Dampf ablassen *(ugs.);* **run out of ~** *(fig.)* den Schwung verlieren; **under one's own ~** *(fig.)* aus eigener Kraft. **2.** *v. t. (Cookery)* dämpfen; dünsten. **3.** *v. i.* dämpfen; **~ing hot** dampfend heiß. **steam 'up** *v. i.* beschlagen

'**steam engine** *n.* Dampflok[omotive], *die*

'**steamer** *n.* Dämpfer, *der*

'**steamroller** *n.* Dampfwalze, *die*

'**steam train** *n.* Dampfzug, *der*

'**steamy** *adj.* dunstig; beschlagen ⟨*Glas*⟩

steel [stiːl] **1.** *n.* Stahl, *der.* **2.** *attrib. adj.* stählern; Stahl⟨*helm, -block, -platte*⟩. **3.** *v. t.* ~ **oneself for/against** sth. sich für/gegen etw. wappnen *(geh.);* ~ **oneself to do** sth. allen Mut zusammennehmen, um etw. zu tun.

'**steelworks** *n. sing. or pl.* Stahlwerk, *das*

¹**steep** [stiːp] *adj.* **a)** steil; **b)** *(coll.: ex-*

cessive) happig *(ugs.); the* **bill is [a bit]**
~: die Rechnung ist [ziemlich] gesal-
zen *(ugs.)*

²steep *v. t. (soak)* einweichen

steeple ['sti:pl] *n.* Kirchturm, *der*

steer [stɪə(r)] **1.** *v. t.* steuern; lenken. **2.**
v. i. steuern; ~ **clear of sb./sth.** *(fig.
coll.)* jmdm./einer Sache aus dem
Weg[e] gehen. **'steering** *n. (Motor
Veh.)* Lenkung, *die.* **'steering-
wheel** *n.* Lenkrad, *das*

¹stem [stem] **1.** *n.* **a)** *(Bot.)* Stiel, *der;*
b) *(Ling.)* Stamm, *der.* **2.** *v. i.,* **-mm-:** ~
from sth. auf etw. *(Akk.)* zurückzufüh-
ren sein

²stem *v. t.,* **-mm-** *(check, dam up)* aufhalten; eindämmen ⟨*Flut⟩;* stillen
⟨*Blutung⟩*

stench [stentʃ] *n.* Gestank, *der*

stencil ['stensl] *n.* Schablone, *die; (for
duplicating)* Matritze, *die*

step [step] **1.** *n.* **a)** Schritt, *der;* **take a**
~ **back/forwards** einen Schritt zurück-
treten/nach vorn treten; **b)** *(stair)* Stufe, *die;* **a flight of** ~s eine Treppe;
[**pair of]** ~s *(ladder)* Stehleiter, *die;* **c)**
be in ~: im Schritt sein; *(with music)*
im Takt sein; **d) take** ~s **to do sth.**
Schritte unternehmen, um etw. zu
tun; **e)** *(stage)* ~ **by** ~: Schritt für
Schritt; **what is the next** ~? wie geht es
weiter?; **f)** *(grade)* Stufe, *die.* **2.** *v. i.,*
-pp- treten; ~ **inside** eintreten; ~ **into**
sb's shoes *(fig.)* an jmds. Stelle *(Akk.)*
treten; ~ **over sb./sth.** über jmdn./etw.
steigen. **step 'back** *v. i.* zurücktreten.
step 'in *v. i.* **a)** eintreten; **b)** *(fig.)
(take sb.'s place)* einspringen; *(intervene)* eingreifen. **step 'up 1.** *v. i.
(ascend)* hinaufsteigen. **2.** *v. t.* erhöhen;
verstärken ⟨*Anstrengungen⟩*

step: ~**child** *n.* Stiefkind, *das;*
~**daughter** *n.* Stieftochter, *die;*
~**father** *n.* Stiefvater, *der;* ~-**ladder**
n. Stehleiter, *die;* ~**mother** *n.* Stief-
mutter, *die*

'stepping-stone *n.* Trittstein, *der;*
(fig.) Sprungbrett, das *(to* für)

stereo ['sterɪəʊ] **1.** *n.* Stereo, *das;
(equipment)* Stereoanlage, *die.* **2.** *adj.*
stereo; Stereo⟨*aufnahme, -platte⟩*

stereophonic [sterɪə'fɒnɪk] *adj.* ste-
reophon

stereotype ['sterɪətaɪp] **1.** *n.* Stereotyp, *das.* **2.** *v. t.* in ein Klischee zwängen; ~**d** stereotyp

sterile ['steraɪl] *adj.* steril

sterilize ['sterɪlaɪz] *v. t.* sterilisieren

sterling ['stɜ:lɪŋ] **1.** *n.* Sterling, *der;* in
~: in Pfund [Sterling]. **2.** *attrib. adj.* **a)**
~ **silver** Sterlingsilber, *das;* **b)** *(fig.)*
gediegen

¹stern [stɜ:n] *adj.* streng; ernst ⟨*War-
nung⟩*

²stern *n. (Naut.)* Heck, *das*

'sternly *adv.* streng

steroid ['sterɔɪd] *n.* Steroid, *das*

stethoscope ['steθəskəʊp] *n.* Stethoskop, *das*

stew [stju:] **1.** *n.* Eintopf, *der.* **2.** *v. t.*
schmoren [lassen]

steward ['stju:əd] *n.* **a)** *(on ship, plane)*
Steward, *der;* **b)** *(at public meeting
etc.)* Ordner, *der.* **'stewardess** *n.*
Stewardeß, *die*

stick [stɪk] **1.** *v. t.,* **stuck** [stʌk] **a)** *(thrust
point of)* stecken; ~ **sth. in|to] sth.** mit
etw. in etw. *(Akk.)* stechen; **b)** *(coll.:
put)* stecken; ~ **a picture on the wall/a
vase on the shelf** ein Bild an die Wand
hängen/eine Vase aufs Regal stellen;
~ **sth. in the kitchen** etw. in die Küche
tun *(ugs.);* **c)** *(with glue etc.)* kleben; **d)**
the car is stuck in the mud das Auto ist
im Schlamm steckengeblieben; **the
door is stuck** die Tür klemmt [fest]. **2.**
v. i., **stuck a)** *(be fixed by point)*
stecken; **b)** *(adhere)* kleben; ~ **to sth.**
an etw. *(Dat.)* kleben; **c)** *(become immobile)* ⟨*Auto, Räder:⟩* steckenbleiben; ⟨*Schublade, Tür, Griff, Bremse:⟩*
klemmen; ⟨*Schlüssel:⟩* feststecken. **3.**
n. Stock, *der;* **a** ~ **of chalk** ein Stück
Kreide; **a** ~ **of celery/rhubarb** eine
Stange Sellerie/Rhabarber. **stick
a'bout, stick a'round** *v. i. (coll.)* dableiben; *(wait)* warten. **'stick by** *v. t.
(fig.)* stehen zu. **stick 'on** *v. t. (glue
on)* aufkleben. **stick 'out 1.** *v. t.* **a)**
herausstrecken ⟨*Zunge⟩;* **b)**~ **it out**
(coll.) durchhalten. **2.** *v. i.* **a)** ⟨*Bauch:⟩*
vorstehen; **his ears** ~ **out** er hat abste-
hende Ohren; **b)** *(fig.: be obvious)* sich
abheben; ~ **out a mile** *(sl.)* [klar] auf
der Hand liegen; ~ **out like a sore
thumb** *(coll.)* ins Auge springen.
'stick to *v. t.* **a)** *(be faithful to)* halten
⟨*Versprechen⟩;* bleiben bei ⟨*Entschei-
dung⟩;* **b)** ~ **to the point** beim Thema
bleiben. **stick 'up 1.** *v. t.* **a)** *(coll.)* anschlagen ⟨*Poster⟩;* ~ **up one's hand** die
Hand heben; **b)** *(seal)* zukleben. **2.**
v. i. ~ **up for sb./sth.** für jmdn./etw.
eintreten; ~ **up for yourself!** setz dich
zur Wehr!

'sticker *n.* Aufkleber, *der*

'sticking-plaster *n.* Heftpflaster, *das*

'sticky *adj.* **a)** klebrig; ~ **label** Aufkle-

ber, *der;* b) *(humid)* schwül ⟨*Klima, Luft*⟩
stiff [stɪf] *adj.* **a)** *(rigid)* steif; hart ⟨*Bürste, Stock*⟩; **be frozen** ~ : steif vor Kälte sein; b) *(intense, severe)* hartnäckig; c) *(formal)* steif; d) *(difficult)* hart ⟨*Test*⟩; schwer ⟨*Frage, Prüfung*⟩; e) *(coll.)* **be bored/scared** ~ : sich zu Tode langweilen/eine wahnsinnige Angst haben *(ugs.).* **stiffen** ['stɪfn] 1. *v. t.* steif machen. 2. *v. i.* steifer werden; ⟨*Person:*⟩ erstarren. **'stiffness** *n.* Steifheit, *die*
stifle ['staɪfl] 1. *v. t.* ersticken; *(fig.)* unterdrücken. 2. *v. i.* ersticken. **stifling** ['staɪflɪŋ] *adj.* stickig; drückend ⟨*Hitze*⟩
stigma ['stɪɡmə] *n.* Stigma, *das (geh.)*
stile [staɪl] *n.* Zauntritt, *der*
stiletto [stɪ'letəʊ] *n.* ~ [heel] Stöckelabsatz, *der*
¹still [stɪl] 1. *pred. adj.* still; **be** ~ : [still] stehen; **hold sth.** ~ : etw. ruhig halten; **keep** *or* **stay** ~ : stillhalten; **stand** ~ : stillstehen. 2. *adv.* **a)** *(without change)* noch; *expr. surprise or annoyance* immer noch; b) *(nevertheless)* trotzdem; c) *with comparative (even)* noch
²still *n.* Destillierapparat, *der*
still: ~**born** *adj.* totgeboren; ~ '**life** *n.* *(Art)* Stilleben, *das*
stilt [stɪlt] *n.* Stelze, *die.* **'stilted** *adj.* gestelzt
stimulant ['stɪmjʊlənt] *n.* Stimulans, *das*
stimulate ['stɪmjʊleɪt] *v. t.* anregen. **stimulation** [stɪmjʊ'leɪʃn] *n.* Anregung, *die*
stimulus ['stɪmjʊləs] *n., pl.* **stimuli** ['stɪmjʊlaɪ] Ansporn, *der*
sting [stɪŋ] 1. *n.* **a)** *(wounding)* Stich, *der;* *(by jellyfish, nettles)* Verbrennung, *die;* b) *(from ointment, wind)* Brennen, *das.* 2. *v. t.,* **stung** [stʌŋ] stechen. 3. *v. i.,* **stung** brennen. **'stinging-nettle** *n.* Brennessel, *die*
stingy ['stɪndʒɪ] *adj.* geizig; knaus[e]rig *(ugs.)*
stink [stɪŋk] 1. *v. i.,* **stank** [stæŋk] *or* **stunk** [stʌŋk], **stunk** stinken (**of** nach). 2. *n.* Gestank, *der*
stint [stɪnt] 1. *v. i.* ~ **on sth.** an etw. *(Dat.)* sparen. 2. *n.* [Arbeits]pensum, *das*
stipulate ['stɪpjʊleɪt] *v. t.* *(demand)* fordern; *(lay down)* festlegen. **stipulation** [stɪpjʊ'leɪʃn] *n.* *(condition)* Bedingung, *die*
stir [stɜː(r)] 1. *v. t.,* **-rr-:** a) *(mix)* rüh-

ren; umrühren ⟨*Tee, Kaffee*⟩; b) *(move)* bewegen. 2. *v. i.,* **-rr-** *(move)* sich rühren. 3. *n.* Aufregung, *die.* **stir 'in** *v. t.* einrühren. **stir 'up** *v. t.* a) *(disturb)* aufrühren; b) *(fig.: arouse)* wecken ⟨*Interesse, Leidenschaft*⟩
stirring ['stɜːrɪŋ] *adj.* bewegend ⟨*Musik, Poesie*⟩; mitreißend ⟨*Rede*⟩
stirrup ['stɪrəp] *n.* Steigbügel, *der*
stitch [stɪtʃ] 1. *n.* **a)** *(Sewing)* Stich, *der;* *(Knitting)* Masche, *die;* b) *(pain)* **have a** ~ : Seitenstechen haben. 2. *v. t.* nähen
stoat [stəʊt] *n.* Hermelin, *das*
stock [stɒk] 1. *n.* **a)** *(origin, family, breed)* Abstammung, *die;* b) *(supply, store)* Vorrat, *der;* *(in shop etc.)* Warenbestand, *der;* **be in/out of** ~ ⟨*Ware:*⟩ vorrätig/nicht vorrätig sein; **have sth. in** ~ : etw. auf Lager haben; **take** ~ **of sth.** *(fig.)* über etw. *(Akk.)* Bilanz ziehen; c) *(Cookery)* Brühe, *die.* 2. *v. t.* **a)** *(supply with* ~) beliefern; b) *(Commerc.: keep in* ~*)* auf Lager haben. 3. *attrib. adj.* Standard-
stock: ~**broker** Effektenmakler, *der*/-maklerin, *die;* ~ **cube** *n.* Brühwürfel, *der;* ~ **exchange** *n.* Börse, *die*
stocking ['stɒkɪŋ] *n.* Strumpf, *der*
'stockist *n.* Fachhändler, *der*/-händlerin, *die*
stock: ~**-market** *n.* a) Börse, *die;* b) *(trading)* Börsengeschäft, *das;* ~**pile** 1. *n.* Vorrat, *der;* *(weapons)* Arsenal, *das;* 2. *v. t.* horten; anhäufen ⟨*Waffen*⟩; ~'**still** *pred. adj.* bewegungslos; ~**-taking** *n.* Inventur, *die*
stocky ['stɒkɪ] *adj.* stämmig
stodgy ['stɒdʒɪ] *adj.* pappig
stoical ['stəʊɪkl] *adj.* stoisch
stoke [stəʊk] *v. t.* heizen ⟨*Ofen, Kessel*⟩; unterhalten ⟨*Feuer*⟩
stole *see* steal
stolen ['stəʊln] 1. *see* steal. 2. *attrib. adj.* heimlich ⟨*Vergnügen, Kuß*⟩
stolid ['stɒlɪd] *adj.* stur *(ugs.)*
stomach ['stʌmək] 1. *n.* **a)** Magen, *der;* b) *(abdomen)* Bauch, *der.* 2. *v. t.* *(fig.: tolerate)* ausstehen. **'stomach-ache** *n.* Magenschmerzen *Pl.* **'stomach upset** *n.* Magenverstimmung, *die*
stone [stəʊn] 1. *n.* **a)** Stein, *der;* **a** ~'**s throw [away]** *(fig.)* nur einen Steinwurf weit entfernt; b) *(Brit.: weight unit)* Gewicht *von 6,35 kg.* 2. *adj.* steinern; Stein⟨*mauer, -brücke*⟩. 3. *v. t.* mit Steinen bewerfen

stone: S~ Age *n.* Steinzeit, *die;* **~-cold** *adj.* eiskalt; **~-'deaf** *adj.* stocktaub *(ugs.)*

stony ['stəʊnɪ] *adj.* steinig

stood *see* **stand** 1, 2

stool [stu:l] *n.* Hocker, *der*

stoop [stu:p] **1.** *v.i.* ~ |**down**| sich bücken. **2.** *n.* **walk with a** ~: gebeugt gehen

stop [stɒp] **1.** *v.t.,* **-pp-:** **a)** anhalten ⟨*Person, Fahrzeug*⟩; aufhalten ⟨*Fortschritt, Verkehr, Feind*⟩; **b)** *(not let continue)* unterbrechen ⟨*Redner, Spiel, Gespräch*⟩; beenden ⟨*Krieg, Arbeit*⟩; stoppen ⟨*Produktion, Uhr*⟩; einstellen ⟨*Zahlung, Lieferung*⟩; ~ **that**! hör damit auf!; ~ **smoking/crying** aufhören zu rauchen/weinen; **c)** *(not let happen)* verhindern ⟨*Verbrechen, Unfall*⟩; ~ **sth. |from| happening** verhindern, daß etw. geschieht; **d)** *(switch off)* abstellen ⟨*Maschine*⟩; **e)** *(block up)* zustopfen ⟨*Loch*⟩; verschließen ⟨*Wasserhahn, Flasche*⟩; **f)** ~ **a cheque** einen Scheck sperren lassen. **2.** *v.i.,* **-pp-:** **a)** *(not extend further)* aufhören; ⟨*Zahlungen, Lieferungen:*⟩ eingestellt werden; **b)** *(not move further)* ⟨*Fahrzeug, Fahrer:*⟩ halten; ⟨*Maschine, Motor:*⟩ stillstehen; ⟨*Uhr, Fußgänger, Herz:*⟩ stehenbleiben. **3.** *n.* **a)** *(halt)* Halt, *der;* **bring to a** ~: zum Stehen bringen ⟨*Fahrzeug*⟩; zum Erliegen bringen ⟨*Verkehr*⟩; unterbrechen ⟨*Arbeit*⟩; **come to a** ~: stehenbleiben; ⟨*Fahrzeug:*⟩ zum Stehen kommen; ⟨*Arbeit, Verkehr:*⟩ zum Erliegen kommen; **put a** ~ **to** abstellen ⟨*Mißstände, Unsinn*⟩; **b)** *(place)* Haltestelle, *die.* **stop 'by** *v.i.* *(Amer.)* vorbeischauen *(ugs.).* **stop 'out** *v.i.* *(coll.)* draußen bleiben. **stop 'over** *v.i.* übernachten (**at** bei). **stop 'up** **1.** *v.t.* zustopfen ⟨*Loch, Öffnung*⟩. **2.** *v.i.* *(coll.)* see **stay up**

stop: **~-gap** *n.* Notlösung, *die;* **~-light** *n.* *(traffic-light)* rotes Licht; **~over** *n.* Stopover, *der*

stoppage ['stɒpɪdʒ] *n.* **a)** *(halt)* Stillstand, *der;* *(strike)* Streik, *der;* **b)** *(deduction)* Abzug, *der*

stopper ['stɒpə(r)] *n.* Stöpsel, *der*

stop: **~-press** *n.* letzte Meldung/ Meldungen; ~ **sign** *n.* Stoppschild, *das;* **~watch** *n.* Stoppuhr, *die*

storage ['stɔːrɪdʒ] *n.* Lagerung, *die; (of films, books, documents)* Aufbewahrung, *die; (of data, water, electricity)* Speicherung, *die.* '**storage**

heater *n.* [Nacht]speicherofen, *der.* '**storage tank** *n.* Sammelbehälter, *der*

store [stɔː(r)] **1.** *n.* **a)** *(Amer.: shop)* Laden, *der;* **b)** *(Brit.: large general shop)* Kaufhaus, *das;* **c)** *(warehouse)* Lager, *das;* **put sth. in** ~: etw. einlagern; **d)** *(stock)* Vorrat, *der* (**of an** + *Dat.*); **be or lie in** ~ **for sb.** jmdn. erwarten; **e)** **set |great|** ~ **by** *or* **on sth.** [großen] Wert auf etw. *(Akk.)* legen. **2.** *v.t.* einlagern; speichern ⟨*Getreide, Energie, Wissen, Daten*⟩. **store 'up** *v.t.* speichern; ~ **up provisions** sich *(Dat.)* Vorräte anlegen

store: **~house** *n.* Lager[haus], *das;* **~-room** *n.* Lagerraum, *der*

storey ['stɔːrɪ] *n.* Stockwerk, *das*

stork [stɔːk] *n.* Storch, *der*

storm [stɔːm] **1.** *n.* Unwetter, *das; (thunder~)* Gewitter, *das.* **2.** *v.t. & i.* stürmen. '**stormy** *adj.* stürmisch

¹story ['stɔːrɪ] *n.* **a)** Geschichte, *die;* **b)** *(news item)* Bericht, *der;* **c)** *(coll.: lie)* Märchen, *das*

²story *(Amer.)* see **storey**

stout [staʊt] *adj.* **a)** *(strong)* fest; **b)** *(fat)* beleibt

stove [stəʊv] *n.* Ofen, *der; (for cooking)* Herd, *der*

stow [stəʊ] *v.t.* verstauen (**into** in + *Dat.*). **stow a'way** **1.** *v.t.* verwahren. **2.** *v.i.* als blinder Passagier reisen

straddle ['strædl] *v.t.* ~ **a fence/chair** rittlings auf einem Zaun/Stuhl sitzen

straggle ['strægl] *v.i.* ~ |**along**| **behind the others** den anderen hinterherzockeln *(ugs.).* **straggler** ['stræglə(r)] *n.* Nachzügler, *der*

straight [streɪt] **1.** *adj.* **a)** gerade; glatt ⟨*Haar*⟩; **in a** ~ **line** in gerader Linie; **b)** *(undiluted)* **drink whisky** ~: Whisky pur trinken; **c)** *(direct)* direkt ⟨*Blick, Schuß, Weg*⟩; **be** ~ **with sb.** zu jmdm. offen sein; **get sth.** ~ *(fig.)* etw. genau verstehen; **put** *or* **set the record** ~: die Sache richtigstellen. **2.** *adv.* **a)** gerade; **b)** *(directly)* geradewegs; ~ **after** sofort nach; **come** ~ **to the point** direkt zur Sache kommen; **look sb.** ~ **in the eye** jmdm. direkt in die Augen blicken; ~ **ahead** *or* **on** immer geradeaus; **c)** *(frankly)* aufrichtig; **d)** *(clearly)* klar ⟨*sehen, denken*⟩. **straight a'way** *adv.* *(coll.)* sofort

straighten ['streɪtn] **1.** *v.t.* **a)** geradeziehen ⟨*Teppich*⟩; glätten ⟨*Kleidung, Haare*⟩; **b)** *(put in order)* aufräumen. **2.** *v.i.* gerade werden. **straighten**

'**out 1.** *v. t.* **a)** geradebiegen; glätten 〈*Decke, Teppich*〉; **b)** *(clear up)* klären. **2.** *v. i.* gerade werden. **straighten** '**up 1.** *v. t. see* tidy up. **2.** *v. i.* sich aufrichten

straight'forward *adj.* **a)** *(frank)* freimütig; schlicht 〈*Stil, Sprache, Bericht*〉; klar 〈*Anweisung, Vorstellungen*〉; **b)** *(simple)* einfach

strain [streɪn] **1.** *n.* **a)** *(pull)* Belastung, *die; (on rope)* Spannung, *die;* **b)** *(tension)* Streß, *der;* **be under |a great deal of|** ~: unter großem Streß stehen; **c)** *(person, thing)* **be a** ~ **on sb./sth.** jmdn./etw. belasten; **d)** *(muscular injury)* Zerrung, *die.* **2.** *v. t.* **a)** *(overexert)* überanstrengen; zerren 〈*Muskel*〉; **b)** *(stretch tightly)* [fest] spannen; **c)** *(filter)* durchseihen; seihen **(through** durch). **3.** *v. i. (strive intensely)* sich anstrengen. **strained** [streɪnd] *adj.* gezwungen 〈*Lächeln*〉; ~ **relations** gespannte Beziehungen

'**strainer** *n.* Sieb, *das*

strait [streɪt] *n.* **a)** *in sing. or pl. (Geog.)* Meerenge, *die;* **b)** *usu. in pl. (distress, difficulty)* Schwierigkeiten. '**straitjacket** *n.* Zwangsjacke, *die.* **strait-laced** [streɪt'leɪst] *adj.* puritanisch

'**strand** [strænd] *n. (thread)* Faden, *der; (of beads)* Kette, *die; (of hair)* Strähne, *die; (of rope)* Strang, *der*

²**strand** *v. t. (leave behind)* trocken setzen; **be |left|** ~**ed** *(fig.)* seinem Schicksal überlassen sein

strange [streɪndʒ] *adj. (peculiar)* seltsam; sonderbar; ~ **to say** seltsamerweise; **feel** ~: sich komisch fühlen. **stranger** ['streɪndʒə(r)] *n.* Fremde, *der/die;* **he is a** ~ **here/to the town** er ist hier/in der Stadt fremd

strangle ['stræŋgl] *v. t.* erwürgen. '**stranglehold** *n.* Würgegriff, *der.* **strangulation** [stræŋgjʊ'leɪʃn] *n.* Erwürgen, *das*

strap [stræp] **1.** *n.* **a)** *(leather)* Riemen, *der; (textile)* Band, *das; (shoulder-~)* Träger, *der; (for watch)* Armband, *das;* **b)** *(to grasp in vehicle)* Halteriemen, *der.* **2.** *v. t.,* **-pp-:** ~ **|into position|/down** festschnallen; ~ **oneself in** sich anschnallen. '**strapless** *adj.* trägerlos

'**strapping** ['stræpɪŋ] *adj.* stramm

strata *pl. of* **stratum**

strategic [strə'tiːdʒɪk] *adj.* strategisch **strategist** ['strætɪdʒɪst] *n.* Stratege, *der/*Strategin, *die* **strategy** ['strætɪdʒɪ] *n.* Strategie, *die*

stratosphere ['strætəsfɪə(r)] *n.* Stratosphäre, *die*

stratum ['strɑːtəm] *n., pl.* **strata** ['strɑːtə] Schicht, *die*

straw [strɔː] *n.* **a)** *no pl.* Stroh, *das;* **b)** *(single stalk)* Strohhalm, *der;* **that's the last** *or* **final** ~: jetzt reicht's aber; **c) |drinking-|**~: Strohhalm, *der*

strawberry ['strɔːbərɪ] *n.* Erdbeere, *die*

stray [streɪ] **1.** *v. i.* **a)** *(wander)* streunen; **b)** *(deviate)* abweichen **(from** von). **2.** *n. (animal)* streunendes Tier. **3.** *adj.* **a)** streunend; **b)** *(occasional)* vereinzelt

streak [striːk] *n.* Streifen, *der; (in hair)* Strähne, *die;* **have a jealous/cruel** ~: zur Eifersucht/Grausamkeit neigen. '**streaky** *adj.* streifig; ~ **bacon** durchwachsener Speck

stream [striːm] **1.** *n. (of water)* Wasserlauf, *der; (brook)* Bach, *der.* **2.** *v. i.* strömen; 〈*Sonnenlicht:*〉 fluten. '**streamline** *v. t.* [eine] Stromlinienform geben (+ *Dat.*); **be** ~**lined** eine Stromlinienform haben

street [striːt] *n.* Straße, *die;* **in the** ~: auf der Straße; **in** *(Brit.) or* **on ... Street** in der ...straße

street: ~**car** *n. (Amer.)* Straßenbahn, *die;* ~-**lamp** *n.* Straßenlaterne, *die;* ~-**lighting** *n.* Straßenbeleuchtung, *die;* ~-**map** *n.* Stadtplan, *der;* ~-**market** *n.* Markt, *der;* ~-**plan** *n.* Stadtplan, *der;* ~-**wise** *adj. (coll.)* **be** ~-**wise** wissen, wo es langgeht

strength [streŋθ] *n. (power)* Kraft, *die; (strong point, force, intensity, amount of ingredient)* Stärke, *die; (of poison, medicine)* Wirksamkeit, *die;* **not know one's own** ~: nicht wissen, wie stark man ist; **give sb.** ~: jmdn. stärken; **go from** ~ **to** ~: immer erfolgreicher werden; **on the** ~ **of sth./that** auf Grund einer Sache *(Gen.)/*dessen; **in full** ~: in voller Stärke; **the police were there in** ~: ein starkes Polizeiaufgebot war da. **strengthen** ['streŋθən] *v. t.* stärken; *(reinforce, intensify)* verstärken

strenuous ['strenjʊəs] *adj.* **a)** *(energetic)* energisch; gewaltig 〈*Anstrengung*〉; **b)** *(requiring exertion)* anstrengend

stress [stres] **1.** *n.* **a)** *(strain)* Streß, *der;* **be under** ~: unter Streß *(Dat.)* stehen; **b)** *(emphasis)* Betonung, *die.* **2.** *v. t. (emphasize)* betonen

stretch [stretʃ] **1.** *v. t.* **a)** *(lengthen)* strecken 〈*Arm, Hand*〉; recken 〈*Hals*〉;

dehnen *(Gummiband)*; *(tighten)* spannen; **b)** *(widen)* dehnen. **2. a)** *v.i. (extend in length)* sich dehnen; **b)** ~ **to sth.** *(be sufficient for)* für etw. reichen. **3.** *v. refl.* sich strecken. **4.** *n.* **a) have a** ~: sich strecken; **b) at a** ~ *(fig.)* wenn es sein muß; **c)** *(expanse)* Abschnitt, *der;* **a** ~ **of road** ein Stück Straße; **d)** *(period)* **a four-hour** ~: eine [Zeit]spanne von vier Stunden; **at a** ~: ohne Unterbrechung. **5.** *adj.* Stretch- *(hose, -gewebe)*
stretcher ['stretʃə(r)] *n.* [Trag]bahre, *die*
strew [stru:] *v.t., p.p.* **strewed** [stru:d] *or* **strewn** [stru:n] streuen
stricken ['strɪkn] *adj. (afflicted)* heimgesucht; havariert *(Schiff)*; **be** ~ **with fear/grief** angsterfüllt/gramgebeugt
strict [strɪkt] *adj.* **a)** *(firm)* streng; **in** ~ **confidence** streng vertraulich; **b)** *(precise)* streng. **'strictly** *adv.* streng; ~ |speaking| strenggenommen
stride [straɪd] **1.** *n.* Schritt, *der;* **put sb. off his** ~ *(fig.)* jmdn. aus dem Konzept bringen; **take sth. in one's** ~ *(fig.)* mit etw. gut fertig werden. **2.** *v.i.,* **strode** [strəʊd], **stridden** ['strɪdn] [mit großen Schritten] gehen
strident ['straɪdənt] *adj.* schrill
strife [straɪf] *n.* Streit, *der*
strike [straɪk] **1.** *n. (Industry)* Streik, *der;* Ausstand, *der;* **be on/go |out| or come out on** ~: in den Streik getreten sein/in den Streik treten. **2.** *v.t.,* **struck** [strʌk] **a)** *(hit)* schlagen; *(Schlag, Geschoß:)* treffen; *(Blitz:)* [ein]schlagen in (+ *Akk.*); **b)** *(delete)* streichen (**from, off** aus); **c)** *(ignite)* anzünden *(Streichholz)*; **d)** *(chime)* schlagen; **e)** *(impress)* beeindrucken; ~ **sb. as |being| silly** jmdm. dumm erscheinen; **it** ~**s sb. that** ...: es scheint jmdm., daß ...; **f)** *(occur to)* einfallen (+ *Dat.*). **3.** *v.i.,* **struck a)** *(deliver a blow)* zuschlagen; *(Blitz:)* einschlagen; *(Unheil, Katastrophe:)* hereinbrechen *(geh.)*; *(hit)* schlagen (**against** gegen, |up|on auf + *Akk.*); **b)** *(ignite)* zünden; **c)** *(chime)* schlagen; **d)** *(Industry)* streiken. **strike 'back** *v.i.* zurückschlagen. **strike 'off** *v.t.* (~ *off list)* streichen *(Namen)*; *(from professional body)* die Zulassung entziehen (+ *Dat.*). **'strike up** *v.t.* beginnen *(Unterhaltung)*; schließen *(Freundschaft)*
'strike pay *n.* Streikgeld, *das*
'striker *n.* Streikende, *der/die*

striking ['straɪkɪŋ] *adj.* auffallend; erstaunlich *(Ähnlichkeit)*; schlagend *(Beispiel)*
string [strɪŋ] **1.** *n.* **a)** *(thin cord)* Schnur, *die;* *(to tie up parcels etc. also)* Bindfaden, *der;* **pull |a few or some|** ~**s** *(fig.)* seine Beziehungen spielen lassen; **with no** ~**s attached** ohne Bedingung[en]; **b)** *(of bow)* Sehne, *die;* *(of racket, musical instrument)* Saite, *die.* **2.** *v.t.,* **strung** [strʌŋ] *(thread)* auffädeln. **string a'long** *v.t. (deceive)* an der Nase herumführen *(ugs.).* **string to'gether** *v.t.* auffädeln; miteinander verknüpfen *(Wörter)*. **string 'up** *v.t.* aufhängen
string 'bag *n.* [Einkaufs]netz, *das*
stringent ['strɪndʒənt] *adj.* streng
'strip [strɪp] **1.** *v.t.,* **-pp-** ausziehen *(Person)*. **2.** *v.i.,* **-pp-** sich ausziehen
'strip *n. (narrow piece)* Streifen, *der*
stripe · [straɪp] *n.* Streifen, *der.*
striped [straɪpt] *adj.* gestreift
strip: ~ **light** *n.* Neonröhre, *die;* ~ **lighting** *n.* Neonbeleuchtung, *die*
stripper ['strɪpə(r)] *n.* Stripper, *der/* Stripperin, *die (ugs.)*
stripy ['straɪpɪ] *adj.* gestreift; Streifen- *(muster)*
strive [straɪv] *v.i.,* **strove** [strəʊv], **striven** ['strɪvn] sich bemühen; ~ **after** *or* **for sth.** nach etw. streben
strode *see* stride 2
'stroke [strəʊk] *n.* **a)** *(act of striking)* Schlag, *der;* **b)** *(Med.)* Schlaganfall, *der;* **c)** *(sudden impact)* ~ **of lightning** Blitzschlag, *der;* ~ **of |good| luck** Glücksfall, *der;* **d)** **at a** *or* **one** ~: auf einen Schlag; **not do a** ~ |of work| keinen [Hand]schlag tun; ~ **of genius** genialer Einfall, *der;* **e)** *(in swimming)* Zug, *der;* **f)** *(of clock)* Schlag, *der;* **on the** ~ **of nine** Punkt neun [Uhr]
'stroke **1.** *v.t.* streicheln. **2.** *n.* **give sb./sth. a** ~: jmdn./etw. streicheln
stroll [strəʊl] **1.** *v.i.* spazierengehen. **2.** *n.* **go for a** ~: einen Spaziergang machen
strong [strɒŋ] *adj.,* ~**er** ['strɒŋgə(r)], ~**est** ['strɒŋgɪst] stark; fest *(Fundament, Schuhe)*; robust *(Konstitution, Magen)*; kräftig *(Arme, Muskeln, Tritt, Zähne)*; leistungsfähig *(Wirtschaft)*; gut, handfest *(Grund, Beispiel, Argument)*; glühend *(Anhänger)*; kräftig *(Geruch, Geschmack, Stimme)*; **there is a** ~ **possibility that** ...: es ist sehr wahrscheinlich, daß ...; **take** ~ **measures/action** energisch vorgehen.

'**stronghold** *n.* Festung, *die; (fig.)* Hochburg, *die.* **strong 'language** *n.* derbe Ausdrucksweise

'**strongly** *adv.* stark; solide ⟨*gearbeitet*⟩; energisch ⟨*protestieren, bestreiten*⟩; nachdrücklich ⟨*unterstützen*⟩; dringend ⟨*raten*⟩; fest ⟨*glauben*⟩

strong: ~**man** *n.* Muskelmann, *der (ugs.);* ~-'**minded** *adj.* willensstark; ~-**room** *n.* Tresorraum, *der*

strove *see* **strive**

struck *see* **strike 2, 3**

structural ['strʌktʃərl] *adj.* baulich

structure ['strʌktʃə(r)] *n.* **a)** Struktur, *die;* **b)** *(something constructed)* Konstruktion, *die; (building)* Bauwerk, *das*

struggle ['strʌgl] **1.** *v. i.* kämpfen; ~ **to do sth.** sich abmühen, etw. zu tun; ~ **against** *or* **with sb./sth.** mit jmdm./ etw. *od.* gegen jmdn./etw. kämpfen; ~ **with sth.** *(try to cope)* mit etw. kämpfen. **2.** *n.* Kampf, *der*

strum [strʌm] **1.** *v. i.,* -**mm**- klimpern *(ugs.)* **(on** auf + *Dat.*). **2.** *v. t.,* -**mm**- klimpern *(ugs.)* auf (+ *Dat.*)

strung *see* **string 2**

'**strut** [strʌt] **1.** *v. i.,* -**tt**- stolzieren. **2.** *n.* stolzierender Gang

²**strut** *n. (support)* Strebe, *die*

stub [stʌb] **1.** *n.* **a)** *(remaining portion)* Stummel, *der; (of cigarette)* Kippe, *die;* **b)** *(counterfoil)* Abschnitt, *der.* **2.** *v. t.,* -**bb**-: **a)** ~ **one's toe** [**against** *or* **on sth.**] sich *(Dat.)* den Zeh [an etw. *(Dat.)*] stoßen; **b)** ausdrücken ⟨*Zigarette*⟩. **stub 'out** *v. t.* ausdrücken

stubble ['stʌbl] *n.* Stoppeln *Pl.*

stubborn ['stʌbən] *adj.* **a)** *(obstinate)* starrköpfig; störrisch ⟨*Tier, Gesicht, Haltung*⟩; **b)** *(resolute)* hartnäckig. '**stubbornness** *n. see* **stubborn:** Starrköpfigkeit, *die;* Hartnäckigkeit, *die*

stuck *see* **stick 1, 2**

'**stuck up** *adj. (conceited)* eingebildet

'**student** ['stju:dənt] *n.* Student, *der/* Studentin, *die; (in school or training establishment)* Schüler, *der/*Schülerin, *die;* **be a** ~ **of sth.** etw. studieren

studio ['stju:dɪəʊ] *n., pl.* ~**s a)** *(workroom)* Atelier, *das;* **b)** *(Cinemat., Radio, Telev.)* Studio, *das*

studious ['stju:dɪəs] *adj.* lerneifrig

study ['stʌdɪ] **1.** *n.* **a)** Studium, *das;* **b)** *(room)* Arbeitszimmer, *das.* **2.** *v. t.* studieren; sich *(Dat.)* [sorgfältig] durchlesen ⟨*Prüfungsfragen, Bericht*⟩

stuff [stʌf] **1.** *n. (material[s])* Zeug, *das (ugs.).* **2.** *v. t.* **a)** stopfen; zustopfen

⟨*Loch, Ohren*⟩; *(Cookery)* füllen; ~ **sth. with** *or* **full of sth.** etw. mit etw. vollstopfen *(ugs.);* **b)** *(sl.)* ~ **him!** zum Teufel mit ihm! '**stuffing** *n.* **a)** *(material)* Füllmaterial, *das;* **b)** *(Cookery)* Füllung, *die*

stuffy ['stʌfɪ] *adj.* stickig

stumble ['stʌmbl] *v. i.* stolpern (**over** über + *Akk.*). **stumbling-block** ['stʌmblɪŋblɒk] *n.* Stolperstein, *der*

stump [stʌmp] **1.** *n. (of tree, branch, tooth)* Stumpf, *der; (of cigar, pencil)* Stummel, *der.* **2.** *v. t.* verwirren; **be** ~**ed** ratlos sein. '**stumpy** *adj.* gedrungen; ~ **tail** Stummelschwanz, *der*

stun [stʌn] *v. t.,* -**nn**- *(knock senseless)* betäuben; **be** ~**ned** *at or* **by sth.** *(fig.)* von etw. wie betäubt sein

stung *see* **sting 2, 3**

stunk *see* **stink 1**

'**stunt** [stʌnt] *v. t.* hemmen

²**stunt** *n.* halsbrecherisches Kunststück; *(Cinemat.)* Stunt, *der*

stupendous [stju:'pendəs] *adj.* gewaltig

stupid ['stju:pɪd] *adj.* dumm; *(ridiculous)* lächerlich; **it would be** ~ **to do sth.** es wäre töricht, etw. zu tun. **stupidity** [stu:'pɪdɪtɪ] *n.* Dummheit, *die.* '**stupidly** *adv.* dumm

stupor ['stju:pə(r)] *n.* Benommenheit, *die;* **in a drunken** ~: sinnlos betrunken

sturdy ['stɜ:dɪ] *adj.* kräftig; stämmig ⟨*Beine, Arme*⟩

stutter ['stʌtə(r)] **1.** *v. i.* stottern. **2.** *n.* Stottern, *das*

'**sty** [staɪ] *see* **pigsty**

²**sty, stye** [staɪ] *n. (Med.)* Gerstenkorn, *das*

style [staɪl] *n.* Stil, *der;* **dress in the latest** ~: sich nach der neuesten Mode kleiden; [**hair-/**~-: Frisur, *die*

styli *pl. of* **stylus**

stylish ['staɪlɪʃ] *adj.* stilvoll; elegant ⟨*Kleidung, Auto, Person*⟩

stylist ['staɪlɪst] *n. (hair-*~) Haarstilist, *der/*-stilistin, *die*

stylus ['staɪləs] *n., pl.* **styli** ['staɪlaɪ] *or* ~**es** [Abtast]nadel, *die*

suave [swɑ:v] *adj.* gewandt

sub- [sʌb] *pref.* unter-; sub-

sub'conscious *(Psych.)* **1.** *adj.* unterbewußt. **2.** *n.* Unterbewußtsein, *das*

'**subcontract** *v. t.* an einen Subunternehmer vergeben

subdivide ['---, --'-] *v. t.* unterteilen

subdue [səb'dju:] *v. t.* bändigen ⟨*Kind, Tier*⟩; dämpfen ⟨*Zorn, Lärm, Licht*⟩. **subdued** [səb'dju:d] *adj.* gedämpft

subject 1. ['sʌbdʒɪkt] *n.* **a)** Staatsbürger, *der/*-bürgerin, *die; (to monarch)* Untertan, *der/*Untertanin, *die;* **b)** *(topic)* Thema, *das; (of study)* Fach, *das;* **change the ~:** das Thema wechseln. **2.** ['sʌbdʒɪkt] *adj.* **be ~ to sth.** von etw. abhängen. **3.** [səb'dʒekt] *v. t.* unterwerfen (to *Dat.*); *(expose)* **~ sb./ sth. to sth.** jmdn./etw. einer Sache *(Dat.)* aussetzen

subjective [səb'dʒektɪv] *adj.* subjektiv

subjugate ['sʌbdʒʊgeɪt] *v. t.* unterjochen (to unter + *Akk.*)

subjunctive [səb'dʒʌŋktɪv] *(Ling.) n.* Konjunktiv, *der*

sub'let *v. t., -tt-, sublet* untervermieten

sublime [sə'blaɪm] *adj.* erhaben

submarine [sʌbmə'ri:n] *n.* Unterseeboot, *das;* U-Boot, *das*

submerge [səb'mɜ:dʒ] *v. t.* **a)** **~ sth. [in the water]** etw. eintauchen; **b)** *(flood)* ⟨*Wasser:*⟩ überschwemmen; **be ~d in water** unter Wasser stehen

submission [səb'mɪʃn] *n.* **a)** *(surrender, meekness)* Unterwerfung, *die;* **b)** *(presentation)* Einreichung, *die* (to bei)

submissive [səb'mɪsɪv] *adj.* gehorsam

submit [səb'mɪt] *v. t., -tt- (present)* einreichen; vorbringen ⟨*Vorschlag*⟩; **~ sth. to sb.** jmdm. etw. vorlegen

subordinate 1. [sə'bɔ:dɪnət] *adj.* untergeordnet. **2.** [sə'bɔ:dɪnət] *n.* Untergebene, *der/die.* **3.** [sə'bɔ:dɪneɪt] *v. t.* unterordnen (to *Dat.*)

subscribe [səb'skraɪb] *v. i.* **a)** *(support)* **~ to sth.** sich einer Sache *(Dat.)* anschließen; **b)** *(make contribution)* **~ to sth.** eine Spende für etw. zusichern.

sub'scriber *n. (to newspaper etc.)* Abonnent, *der/*Abonnentin, *die* (to *Gen.*). **subscription** [səb'skrɪpʃn] *n. (membership fee)* Mitgliedsbeitrag, *der* (to für); *(to newspaper etc.)* Abonnement, *das*

subsequent ['sʌbsɪkwənt] *adj.* folgend; später ⟨*Gelegenheit*⟩

subservient [səb'sɜ:vɪənt] *adj.* untergeordnet (to *Dat.*); *(servile)* unterwürfig

subside [səb'saɪd] *v. i.* **a)** *(sink lower)* ⟨*Flut, Fluß:*⟩ sinken; ⟨*Boden, Haus:*⟩ sich senken; **b)** *(abate)* nachlassen

subsidiary [səb'sɪdɪərɪ] **1.** *adj.* untergeordnet ⟨*Funktion, Stellung*⟩; Neben⟨*fach, -aspekt*⟩. **2.** *n. (Commerc.)* Tochtergesellschaft, *die*

subsidize ['sʌbsɪdaɪz] *v. t.* subventio-

nieren. **subsidy** ['sʌbsɪdɪ] *n.* Subvention, *die*

subsist [səb'sɪst] *v. i.* **~ on sth.** von etw. leben. **subsistence** [səb'sɪstəns] *n.* [Über]leben, *das*

substance ['sʌbstəns] *n.* **a)** Stoff, *der;* **b)** *(solidity)* Substanz, *die;* **c)** *(content)* Inhalt, *der*

sub'standard *adj.* unzulänglich

substantial [səb'stænʃl] *adj.* **a)** *(considerable)* beträchtlich; **b)** gehaltvoll ⟨*Essen*⟩; **c)** *(solid)* solide ⟨*Möbel, Haus*⟩; wesentlich ⟨*Unterschied*⟩. **sub'stantially** *adv.* **a)** *(considerably)* wesentlich; **b)** *(solidly)* solide; **c)** *(essentially)* im wesentlichen

substitute ['sʌbstɪtju:t] **1.** *n.* **~|s** *pl.|* Ersatz, *der.* **2.** *v. t.* **~ A for B** B durch A ersetzen. **substitution** [sʌbstɪ'tju:ʃn] *n.* Ersetzung, *die*

'subtitle *n.* Untertitel, *der*

subtle ['sʌtl] *adj.* subtil *(geh.);* zart ⟨*Duft, Parfüm, Hinweis*⟩; fein ⟨*Geschmack, Unterschied, Humor*⟩

subtract [səb'trækt] *v. t.* abziehen. **subtraction** [səb'trækʃn] *n.* Subtraktion, *die*

suburb ['sʌbɜ:b] *n.* Vorort, *der.* **suburban** [sə'bɜ:bən] *adj.* Vorort-; ⟨*Leben, Haus*⟩ am Stadtrand

subversive [səb'vɜ:sɪv] *adj.* subversiv

'subway *n.* **a)** *(passage)* Unterführung, *die;* **b)** *(Amer.: railway)* Untergrundbahn, *die;* U-Bahn, *die*

succeed [sək'si:d] *v. i.* **a)** Erfolg haben; **sb. ~s in sth.** jmdm. gelingt etw.; jmd. schafft etw.; **sb. ~s in doing sth.** es gelingt jmdm., etw. zu tun; jmd. schafft es, etw. zu tun; **~ in business/ college** geschäftlich/im Studium erfolgreich sein; **I did not ~ in doing it** ich habe es nicht geschafft; **b)** *(come next)* die Nachfolge antreten

success [sək'ses] *n.* Erfolg, *der;* **make a ~ of sth.** bei etw. Erfolg haben. **successful** [sək'sesfl] *adj.* erfolgreich; **be ~ in sth./doing sth.** Erfolg bei etw. haben/dabei haben, etw. zu tun. **suc'cessfully** *adv.* erfolgreich

succession [sək'seʃn] *n.* **a)** Folge, *die;* **in ~:** hintereinander; **b)** *(series)* Serie, *die;* **c)** *(to throne)* Erbfolge, *die*

successive [sək'sesɪv] *adj.* aufeinanderfolgend. **suc'cessively** *adv.* hintereinander

successor [sək'sesə(r)] *n.* Nachfolger, *der/*Nachfolgerin, *die*

succinct [sək'sɪŋkt] *adj.* **a)** *(terse)* knapp; **b)** *(clear)* prägnant

succulent ['sʌkjʊlənt] *adj.* saftig
succumb [sə'kʌm] *v. i.* unterliegen; ~
to sth. einer Sache *(Dat.)* erliegen
such [sʌtʃ] **1.** *adj.* **a)** *(of that kind)*
solch...; ~ **a person** ein solcher
Mensch; ~ **a book** ein solches Buch;
~ **people** solche Leute; ~ **things** so etwas; **I said no** ~ **thing** ich habe nichts
dergleichen gesagt; **there is no** ~ **bird**
einen solchen Vogel gibt es nicht; **or**
some ~ **thing** oder so etwas; **you'll do**
no ~ **thing** das wirst du nicht tun; **ex-**
periences ~ **as these** solche Erfahrun-
gen; **b)** *(so great)* solch...; derartig;
I got ~ **a fright that ...**: ich bekam
einen derartigen *od. (ugs.)* so einen
Schrecken, daß ...; ~ **was the force of**
the explosion that ...: die Explosion
war so stark, daß ...; **to** ~ **an extent**
dermaßen; **c)** *with adj.* so; ~ **a big**
house ein so großes Haus; ~ **a long**
time so lange. **2.** *pron.* **as** ~: als sol-
cher/solche/solches; *(strictly speak-*
ing) im Grunde genommen; an sich;
~ **as** wie [zum Beispiel]; ~ **is life** so ist
das Leben. **such-and-such** ['sʌtʃən-
sʌtʃ] *adj.* **at** ~ **a time** um die und die
Zeit. **'suchlike** *pron.* derlei
suck [sʌk] *v. t.* saugen **(out of** aus); lutschen ⟨*Bonbon*⟩. **suck 'up 1.** *v. t.* aufsaugen. **2.** *v. i.* ~ **up to sb.** *(sl.)* jmdm.
in den Hintern kriechen *(salopp)*
'sucker *n.* **a)** *(suction pad)* Saugfuß,
der; (Zool.) Saugnapf, *der;* **b)** *(sl.:*
dupe) Dumme, *der/die*
suckle ['sʌkl] *v. t.* säugen
suction ['sʌkʃn] *n.* Saugwirkung, *die*
Sudan [su:'dɑ:n] *pr. n.* **[the]** ~: [der]
Sudan
sudden ['sʌdn] **1.** *adj.* **a)** *(unexpected)*
plötzlich; **b)** *(abrupt)* jäh ⟨*Abgrund,*
Übergang, Ruck⟩; **there was a** ~ **bend**
in the road plötzlich machte die Straße eine Biegung. **2.** *n.* **all of a** ~:
plötzlich. **'suddenly** *adv.* plötzlich.
'suddenness *n.* Plötzlichkeit, *die*
suds [sʌdz] *n.* **[soap-]**~: [Seifen]lauge,
die; (froth) Schaum, *der*
sue [su:] **1.** *v. t.* verklagen **(for** auf +
Akk.). **2.** *v. i.* klagen **(for** auf + *Akk.*)
suede [sweɪd] *n.* Wildleder, *das*
suet ['su:ɪt] *n.* Talg, *der*
Suez ['sʊɪz, 'sju:ɪz] *pr. n.* Suez *(das);* ~
Canal Suez-Kanal, *der*
suffer ['sʌfə(r)] **1.** *v. t.* erleiden; durchmachen ⟨*Schweres, Kummer*⟩; dulden
⟨*Unverschämtheit*⟩. **2.** *v. i.* leiden. **'suf-**
fer from *v. t.* leiden unter (+ *Dat.*);
leiden an (+ *Dat.*) ⟨*Krankheit*⟩

sufferance ['sʌfərəns] *n.* Duldung,
die; **he remains here on** ~ **only** er ist
hier bloß geduldet
'suffering *n.* Leiden, *das*
suffice [sə'faɪs] **1.** *v. i.* genügen; ~ **it to**
say ...: nur soviel sei gesagt: ... **2.** *v. t.*
genügen (+ *Dat.*)
sufficiency [sə'fɪʃənsɪ] *n.* Zulänglich-
keit, *die*
sufficient [sə'fɪʃənt] *adj.* genug; ~
money/food genug Geld/genug zu essen; **be** ~: genügen; ~ **reason** Grund
genug; **have you had** ~? *(food, drink)*
haben Sie schon genug? **suffi-**
ciently *adv.* genug; *(adequately)* ausreichend; ~ **large** groß genug; **a** ~
large number eine genügend große
Zahl
suffix ['sʌfɪks] *n.* Nachsilbe, *die*
suffocate ['sʌfəkeɪt] **1.** *v. t.* ersticken;
he was ~**d by the smoke** der Rauch er-
stickte ihn. **2.** *v. i.* ersticken. **suffoca-**
tion [sʌfə'keɪʃn] *n.* Erstickung, *die;* **a**
feeling of ~: das Gefühl, zu ersticken
sugar ['ʃʊɡə(r)] **1.** *n.* Zucker, *der;* **two**
~**s, please** *(lumps)* zwei Stück Zucker,
bitte; *(spoonfuls)* zwei Löffel Zucker,
bitte. **2.** *v. t.* zuckern
sugar: ~ **basin** *see* ~**-bowl;** ~**-beet**
n. Zuckerrübe, *die;* ~**-bowl** *n.*
Zuckerschale, *die; (covered)* Zucker-
dose, *die;* ~**-cane** *n.* Zuckerrohr,
das; ~**-coated** *adj.* gezuckert; mit
Zucker überzogen ⟨*Dragee usw.*⟩;
~**-lump** *n.* Zuckerstück, *das; (when*
counted) Stück Zucker
'sugary *adj.* süß; *(fig.)* süßlich
suggest [sə'dʒest] *v. t.* **a)** *(propose)*
vorschlagen; ~ **sth. to sb.** jmdm. etw.
vorschlagen; **he** ~**ed going to the**
cinema er schlug vor, ins Kino zu ge-
hen; **b)** *(assert)* **are you trying to** ~ **that**
he is lying wollen Sie damit sagen, daß
er lügt?; **c)** *(make one think of)* sugge-
rieren; ⟨*Symptome, Tatsachen:*⟩
schließen lassen auf (+ *Akk.*). **sug-**
gestion [sə'dʒestʃn] *n.* **a)** Vorschlag,
der; **at** *or* **on sb.'s** ~: auf jmds. Vorschlag *(Akk.);* **b)** *(insinuation)* Andeu-
tungen *Pl.;* **c)** *(fig.: trace)* Spur, *die.*
suggestive [sə'dʒestɪv] *adj.* **a) be** ~
of sth. auf etw. *(Akk.)* schließen lassen; **b)** *(indecent)* anzüglich
suicidal [su:ɪ'saɪdl] *adj.* selbstmörde-
risch; **I felt** *or* **was quite** ~: ich hätte
mich am liebsten gleich umgebracht
suicide ['su:ɪsaɪd] *n.* Selbstmord, *der.*
'suicide attempt *n.* Selbstmordver-
such, *der*

suit [su:t] **1.** *n.* **a)** *(for men)* Anzug, *der;* *(for women))* Kostüm, *das;* **b)** *(Law)* ~ |at law| Prozeß, *der;* **c)** *(Cards)* Farbe, *die;* **follow** ~ *(fig.)* das Gleiche tun. **2.** *v. t.* **a)** anpassen (**to** *Dat.*); **b)** be ~ed |to sth./one another| [zu etw./zueinander] passen; **c)** *(satisfy needs of)* passen (+ *Dat.*); **will Monday** ~ **you?** paßt Ihnen Montag?; **does the climate** ~ **you?** bekommt Ihnen das Klima?; **d)** *(go well with)* passen zu; **does this hat** ~ **me?** steht mir dieser Hut?; **black** ~s **her** Schwarz steht ihr gut. **3.** *v. refl.* ~ oneself tun, was man will; ~ yourself! [ganz] wie du willst!

suitability [su:tə'bılıtı] *n.* Eignung, *die* (for für)

suitable ['su:təbl] *adj.* geeignet; angemessen ⟨*Kleidung*⟩; *(convenient)* passend; **Monday is the most** ~ **day** |for me| Montag paßt [mir] am besten. **suitably** ['su:təblı] *adv.* angemessen; entsprechend ⟨*gekleidet*⟩

'**suitcase** *n.* Koffer, *der*

suite [swi:t] *n.* **a)** *(of furniture)* Garnitur, *die;* **three-piece** ~: Polstergarnitur, *die;* **b)** *(of rooms)* Suite, *die*

suitor ['su:tə(r)] *n.* Freier, *der*

sulfur, sulfuric *(Amer.)* see **sulph-**

sulk [sʌlk] *v. i.* schmollen. '**sulky** *adj.* schmollend; eingeschnappt *(ugs.)*

sullen ['sʌlən] *adj.* mürrisch

sulphur ['sʌlfə(r)] *n.* Schwefel, *der.* **sulphuric** [sʌl'fjʊərık] *adj.* ~ **acid** Schwefelsäure, *die*

sultan ['sʌltən] *n.* Sultan, *der*

sultana [sʌl'tɑ:nə] *n.* Sultanine, *die*

sultry ['sʌltrı] *adj.* schwül

sum [sʌm] *n.* **a)** Summe, *die* (**of** aus); ~ |total| Ergebnis, *das;* **b)** *(Arithmetic)* Rechenaufgabe, *die;* **do** ~s *(coll.)* rechnen; **she is good at** ~s *(coll.)* sie kann gut rechnen. **sum 'up 1.** *v. t.* **a)** zusammenfassen; **b)** *(Brit.: assess)* einschätzen. **2.** *v. i.* ein Fazit ziehen

summarily ['sʌmərılı] *adv.* summarisch; ~ **dismissed** fristlos entlassen

summarize ['sʌməraız] *v. t.* zusammenfassen

summary ['sʌmərı] **1.** *adj.* summarisch; fristlos ⟨*Entlassung*⟩. **2.** *n.* Zusammenfassung, *die*

summer ['sʌmə(r)] *n.* Sommer, *der;* **in** |the| ~: im Sommer. '**summer-house** *n.* [Garten]laube, *die.* '**summertime** *n.* Sommer, *der.* '**summery** *adj.* sommerlich

summing 'up *n.* Zusammenfassung, *die*

summit ['sʌmıt] *n.* Gipfel, *der*

summon ['sʌmən] *v. t.* **a)** rufen (**to** zu); holen ⟨*Hilfe*⟩; **b)** *(Law)* vorladen. **summon 'up** *v. t.* aufbringen

summons ['sʌmənz] *n.* Vorladung, *die*

sump [sʌmp] *n.* Ölwanne, *die*

sumptuous ['sʌmptjʊəs] *adj.* üppig; luxuriös ⟨*Möbel, Kleidung*⟩

sun [sʌn] **1.** *n.* Sonne, *die;* **catch the** ~ *(be in sunny position)* viel Sonne abbekommen; *(get ~burnt)* einen Sonnenbrand bekommen. **2.** *v. refl.,* -**nn**- sich sonnen

Sun. *abbr.* **Sunday** So.

sun: ~**bathe** *v. i.* sonnenbaden; ~**bathing** *n.* Sonnenbaden, *das;* ~**beam** *n.* Sonnenstrahl, *der;* ~**bed** *n.* (with UV lamp) Sonnenbank, *die;* (in garden) Gartenliege, *die;* ~**burn** *n.* Sonnenbrand, *der;* ~**burnt** *adj.* **be/get** ~**burnt** einen Sonnenbrand haben/bekommen

sundae ['sʌndeı] *n.* |ice-cream| ~: Eisbecher, *der*

Sunday ['sʌndeı, 'sʌndı] *n.* Sonntag, *der; see also* **Friday**

'**sundial** *n.* Sonnenuhr, *die*

sundry ['sʌndrı] **1.** *adj.* verschieden. **2.** *n. in pl.* Verschiedenes

'**sunflower** *n.* Sonnenblume, *die*

sung *see* **sing**

sun: ~-**glasses** *n. pl.* Sonnenbrille, *die;* ~-**hat** *n.* Sonnenhut, *der*

sunk *see* **sink** 2, 3

sun: ~-**lamp** *n.* Höhensonne, *die;* ~**lit** *adj.* sonnenbeschienen; ~**light** *n.* Sonnenlicht, *das*

sunny ['sʌnı] *adj.* sonnig; ~ **intervals** Aufheiterungen

sun: ~**rise** *n.* Sonnenaufgang, *der;* ~-**roof** *n.* (Motor Veh.) Schiebedach, *das;* ~**set** *n.* Sonnenuntergang, *der;* ~**shade** *n.* Sonnenschirm, *der;* ~**shine** *n.* Sonnenschein, *der;* ~**stroke** *n.* Sonnenstich, *der;* ~-**tan** *n.* [Sonnen]bräune, *die;* **get a** ~-**tan** braun werden; ~-**tan lotion** *n.* Sonnencreme, *die;* ~-**tanned** *adj.* braun[gebrannt]; ~-**tan oil** *n.* Sonnenöl, *das*

super ['su:pə(r)] *adj. (coll.)* super *(ugs.)*

superb [su:'pɜ:b] *adj.* einzigartig; erstklassig ⟨*Essen*⟩

supercilious [su:pə'sılıəs] *adj.* hochnäsig

superficial [su:pə'fıʃl] *adj.* oberflächlich

superfluous [sʊ'pɜ:flʊəs] *adj.* überflüssig

super: ~**glue** n. Sekundenkleber, der; ~**human** adj. übermenschlich
superintendent [su:pərın'tendənt] n. (Brit. Police) Kommissar, der/Kommissarin, die
superior [su:'pıərıə(r)] 1. adj. a) (of higher quality) besonders gut ⟨Restaurant, Qualität, Stoff⟩; überlegen ⟨Technik, Intelligenz⟩; he thinks he is ~ to us er hält sich für besser als wir; b) (having higher rank) höher...; be ~ to sb. einen höheren Rang als jmd. haben. 2. n. Vorgesetzte, der/die. **superiority** [su:pıərı'ɒrıtı] n. Überlegenheit, die (to über + Akk.)
superlative [su:'pɜ:lətıv] 1. adj. a) unübertrefflich; b) (Ling.) **a** ~ **adjective/ adverb** ein Adjektiv/Adverb im Superlativ. 2. n. (Ling.) Superlativ, der
super: ~**market** n. Supermarkt, der; ~'**natural** adj. übernatürlich; ~**power** n. (Polit.) Supermacht, die
supersede [su:pə'si:d] v.t. ablösen (by durch)
supersonic [su:pə'sɒnık] adj. Überschall-
superstition [su:pə'stıʃn] n. Aberglaube, der. **superstitious** [su:pə-'stıʃəs] adj. abergläubisch
supervise ['su:pəvaız] v.t. beaufsichtigen. **supervision** [su:pə'vıʒn] n. Aufsicht, die. **supervisor** ['su:pəvaı-zə(r)] n. Aufseher, der/Aufseherin, die
supper ['sʌpə(r)] n. Abendessen, das; have [one's] ~: zu Abend essen. '**supper-time** n. Abendbrotzeit, die; it's ~: es ist Zeit zum Abendessen
supplant [sə'plɑ:nt] v.t. ablösen, ersetzen (by durch)
supple ['sʌpl] adj. geschmeidig
supplement ['sʌplımənt] 1. n. a) Ergänzung, die (to + Gen.); (addition) Zusatz, der; b) (of book) Nachtrag, der; c) (to fare) Zuschlag, der. 2. v.t. ergänzen. **supplementary** [sʌplı-'mentərı] adj. zusätzlich; ~ **fare/ charge** Zuschlag, der
supplier [sə'plaıə(r)] n. (Commerc.) Lieferant, der/Lieferantin, die
supply [sə'plaı] 1. v.t. liefern ⟨Waren usw.⟩; beliefern ⟨Kunden, Geschäft⟩; ~ **sth. to sb.,** ~ **sb. with sth.** jmdn. mit etw. versorgen/(Commerc.) beliefern. 2. n. Vorräte Pl.; **military/medical supplies** militärischer/medizinischer Nachschub; ~ **and demand** (Econ.) Angebot und Nachfrage
support [sə'pɔ:t] 1. v.t. a) (hold up) stützen ⟨Mauer, Verletzten⟩; (bear

weight of) tragen; b) unterstützen ⟨Politik, Verein⟩; (Footb.) ~ **Spurs** Spurs-Fan sein; c) (provide for) ernähren ⟨Familie, sich selbst⟩; d) (speak in favour of) befürworten. 2. n. a) Unterstützung, die; **in** ~: zur Unterstützung; **speak in** ~ **of sb./sth.** jmdn. unterstützen/etw. befürworten; b) (money) Unterhalt, der; c) (sb./sth. that ~s) Stütze, die. **sup'porter** n. Anhänger, der/Anhängerin, die; **football** ~: Fußballfan, der. **sup'porting** adj. (Cinemat., Theatre) ~ **role** Nebenrolle, die; ~ **actor/actress** Schauspieler/-spielerin in einer Nebenrolle; ~ **film** Vorfilm, der. **supportive** [sə-'pɔ:tıv] adj. hilfreich; **be very** ~ [**to sb.**] [jmdm.] eine große Hilfe od. Stütze sein
suppose [sə'pəʊz] v.t. a) (assume) annehmen; ~ **or supposing [that] he ...:** angenommen, [daß] er ...; b) (presume) vermuten; **I** ~ **so** (doubtfully) ja, vermutlich; (more confidently) ich glaube schon; c) **be** ~**d to do/be sth.** (be generally believed to do/be sth.) etw. tun/ sein sollen; d) (allow) **you are not** ~**d to do that** das darfst du nicht; **I'm not** ~**d to be here** ich dürfte eigentlich gar nicht hier sein. **supposedly** [sə'pəʊ-zıdlı] adv. angeblich
supposition [sʌpə'zıʃn] n. Annahme, die; Vermutung, die
suppress [sə'pres] v.t. unterdrücken. **suppression** [sə'preʃn] n. Unterdrückung, die
supremacy [su:'preməsı] n. a) (supreme authority) Souveränität, die; b) (superiority) Überlegenheit, die
supreme [su:'pri:m] adj. höchst...
surcharge ['sɜ:tʃɑ:dʒ] n. Zuschlag, der
sure [ʃʊə(r)] 1. adj. sicher; **be** ~ **of sth.** sich (Dat.) einer Sache (Gen.) sicher sein; ~ **of oneself** selbstsicher; **don't be too** ~: da wäre ich mir nicht so sicher; **there is** ~ **to be a garage** es gibt bestimmt eine Tankstelle; **don't worry, it's** ~ **to turn out well** keine Sorge, es wird schon alles gutgehen; **for** ~ (coll.) auf jeden Fall; **make** ~ [**of sth.**] sich [einer Sache] vergewissern; **make** or **be** ~ **you do it, be** ~ **to do it** (do not fail to do it) sieh zu, daß du es tust; (do not forget) vergiß nicht, es zu tun; **a** ~ **winner** ein todsicherer Tip (ugs.). 2. adv. ~ **enough** tatsächlich. 3. int. ~!, ~ **thing!** (Amer.) na klar! (ugs.). **sure-footed** ['ʃʊəfʊtıd] adj. trittsi-

cher. **'surely 1.** *adv.* **a)** *as sentence-modifier* doch; ~ **we've met before?** wir kennen uns doch, oder?; **b)** *(steadily)* sicher; **slowly but** ~: langsam, aber sicher; **c)** *(certainly)* sicherlich. **2.** *int. (Amer.)* natürlich

surf [sɜ:f] *n.* Brandung, *die*

surface ['sɜ:fɪs] **1.** *n.* Oberfläche, *die;* **outer** ~: Außenfläche, *die;* **the earth's** ~: die Erdoberfläche; **on the** ~: an der Oberfläche; *(fig.)* oberflächlich betrachtet. **2.** *v.i.* auftauchen; *(fig.)* hochkommen. **'surface area** *n.* Oberfläche, *die.* **'surface mail** *n.* gewöhnliche Post

'surfboard *n.* Surfbrett, *das*

surfeit ['sɜ:fɪt] *n.* Übermaß, *das*

'surfer *n.* Surfer, *der/*Surferin, *die*

'surfing *n.* Surfen, *das*

surge [sɜ:dʒ] *v.i.* ⟨*Wellen:*⟩ branden; **the crowd ~d forward** die Menschenmenge drängte sich nach vorn

surgeon ['sɜ:dʒən] *n.* Chirurg, *der/*Chirurgin, *die*

surgery ['sɜ:dʒərɪ] *n.* **a)** Chirurgie, *die;* **undergo** ~: sich einer Operation *(Dat.)* unterziehen; **b)** *(Brit.: place)* Praxis, *die;* **doctor's/dental** ~: Arzt-/Zahnarztpraxis, *die;* **c)** *(Brit.: time)* Sprechstunde, *die*

surgical ['sɜ:dʒɪkl] *adj.* chirurgisch; ~ **treatment** Operation, *die/*Operationen

surly ['sɜ:lɪ] *adj.* mürrisch

surmise [sə'maɪz] **1.** *n.* Vermutung, *die.* **2.** *v.t.* mutmaßen

surmount [sə'maʊnt] *v.t.* überwinden

surname ['sɜ:neɪm] *n.* Nachname, *der;* Zuname, *der*

surpass [sə'pɑ:s] *v.t.* übertreffen; ~ **oneself** sich selbst übertreffen

surplus ['sɜ:pləs] **1.** *n.* Überschuß, *der* (of an + *Dat.*). **2.** *adj.* überschüssig; **be** ~ **to sb.'s requirements** von jmdm. nicht benötigt werden

surprise [sə'praɪz] **1.** *n.* **a)** Überraschung, *die;* **take sb. by** ~: jmdn. überrumpeln; **to my great** ~, **much to my** ~: zu meiner großen Überraschung; **it came as a** ~ **to us** es war für uns eine Überraschung; **b)** *attrib.* überraschend, unerwartet ⟨*Besuch*⟩; **a** ~ **attack** ein Überraschungsangriff. **2.** *v.t.* überraschen; überrumpeln ⟨*Feind*⟩; **I shouldn't be ~d if** ...: es würde mich nicht wundern, wenn ...; **be ~d at sb./sth.** sich über jmdn./etw. wundern. **surprising** [sə'praɪzɪŋ] *adj.* überraschend

surreal [sə'rɪəl] *adj.* surrealistisch

surrealism [sə'rɪəlɪzm] *n.* Surrealismus, *der*

surrender [sə'rendə(r)] **1.** *n. (to enemy)* Kapitulation, *die; (of possession)* Aufgabe, *die.* **2.** *v.i.* kapitulieren. **3.** *v.t.* aufgeben

surreptitious [sʌrəp'tɪʃəs] *adj.* heimlich; verstohlen ⟨*Blick*⟩

surrogate ['sʌrəgət] *n.* Ersatz, *der*

surround [sə'raʊnd] *v.t.* **a)** *(come or be all round)* umringen; ⟨*Truppen, Heer:*⟩ umzingeln ⟨*Stadt, Feind*⟩; **b)** *(encircle)* umgeben; **be ~ed by or with sth.** von etw. umgeben sein. **sur'rounding** *adj.* umliegend; **the** ~ **countryside** die [Landschaft in der] Umgebung. **sur'roundings** *n. pl.* Umgebung, *die*

surveillance [sə'veɪləns] *n.* Überwachung, *die;* **be under** ~: überwacht werden

survey 1. [sə'veɪ] *v.t.* betrachten; überblicken ⟨*Landschaft*⟩; inspizieren ⟨*Gebäude*⟩; bewerten ⟨*Situation*⟩. **2.** ['sɜ:veɪ] *n.* Überblick, *der* (of über + *Akk.*); *(poll)* Umfrage, *die; (Surv.)* Vermessung, *die.* **surveyor** [sə'veɪə(r)] *n. (of building)* Gutachter, *der/*Gutachterin, *die; (of land)* Landvermesser, *der/*-vermesserin, *die*

survival [sə'vaɪvl] *n.* Überleben, *das;* **fight for** ~: Existenzkampf, *der*

survive [sə'vaɪv] **1.** *v.t.* überleben. **2.** *v.i.* ⟨*Person:*⟩ überleben; ⟨*Schriften, Traditionen:*⟩ erhalten bleiben. **survivor** [sə'vaɪvə(r)] *n.* Überlebende, *der/die*

susceptible [sə'septɪbl] *adj.* empfänglich **(to** für); *(to illness)* anfällig **(to** für)

suspect 1. [sə'spekt] *v.t.* **a)** *(imagine to be likely)* vermuten; ~ **the worst** das Schlimmste befürchten; ~ **sb. to be sth.,** ~ **that sb. is sth.** glauben *od.* vermuten, daß jmd. etw. ist; **b)** *(mentally accuse)* verdächtigen; ~ **sb. of sth./of doing sth.** jmdn. einer Sache verdächtigen/jmdn. verdächtigen, etw. zu tun. **2.** ['sʌspekt] *adj.* fragwürdig; verdächtig ⟨*Stoff, Paket*⟩. **3.** ['sʌspekt] *n.* Verdächtige, *der/die*

suspend [sə'spend] *v.t.* **a)** *(hang up)* [auf]hängen; **b)** *(stop)* suspendieren; **c)** *(from work)* ausschließen **(from** von); sperren ⟨*Sportler*⟩. **suspended 'sentence** *n. (Law)* Strafe mit Bewährung

suspender belt [sə'spendə belt] *n. (Brit.)* Strumpfbandgürtel, *der*

suspenders [sə'spendəz] *n. pl.* **a)**
(Brit.: for stockings) Strumpfbänder;
b) *(Amer.: for trousers)* Hosenträger
suspense [sə'spens] *n.* Spannung,
die; **keep sb. in ~** : jmdn. auf die Folter
spannen. **suspension** [sə'spenʃn] *n.*
(Motor Veh.) Federung, *die.* **su'spen-
sion bridge** *n.* Hängebrücke, *die*
suspicion [sə'spɪʃn] *n.* **a)** *(uneasy feeling)* Mißtrauen, *das (of* gegenüber);
(unconfirmed belief) Verdacht, *der;*
have a ~ that ... : den Verdacht haben,
daß ...; **b)** *(suspecting)* Verdacht, *der
(of* auf *+ Akk.*); **on ~ of murder** wegen Mordverdachts; **be under ~** : ver-
dächtigt werden
suspicious [sə'spɪʃəs] *adj.* **a)** *(tending
to suspect)* mißtrauisch *(of* gegenüber); **be ~ of sb./sth.** jmdm./einer
Sache mißtrauen; **b)** *(arousing suspicion)* verdächtig
sustain [sə'steɪn] *v.t.* **a)** *(support)* tragen *(Gewicht); (fig.)* aufrechterhalten;
b) erleiden *(Verlust, Verletzung)*
sustenance ['sʌstɪnəns] *n.* Nahrung,
die
SW *abbr.* **a) south-west** SW; **b)** *(Radio)*
short wave KW
swab [swɒb] *n. (Med.: pad)* Tupfer,
der
swagger ['swægə(r)] *v.i.* großspurig
stolzieren
¹swallow ['swɒləʊ] **1.** *v.t.* schlucken;
(by mistake) verschlucken. **2.** *v.i.*
schlucken. **3.** *n.* Schluck, *der.* **swallow 'up** *v.t.* verschlucken
²swallow *n.* Schwalbe, *die*
swam *see* swim 1
swamp [swɒmp] **1.** *n.* Sumpf, *der.* **2.**
v.t. überschwemmen. **'swampy** *adj.*
sumpfig
swan [swɒn] *n.* Schwan, *der*
swap [swɒp] **1.** *v.t.,* -pp- tauschen (for
gegen). **2.** *v.i.,* -pp- tauschen. **3.** *n.*
Tausch, *der*
swarm [swɔːm] **1.** *n.* Schwarm, *der.*
2. *v.i.* schwärmen; *(teem)* wimmeln
(with von)
swarthy ['swɔːðɪ] *adj.* dunkel
swastika ['swɒstɪkə] *n.* Hakenkreuz,
das
swat [swɒt] *v.t.,* -tt- totschlagen
sway [sweɪ] **1.** *v.i.* [hin und her]
schwanken; *(gently)* sich wiegen. **2.**
v.t. **a)** wiegen; **b)** *(influence)* beeinflussen. **3.** *n. (fig.)* Herrschaft, *die;*
hold ~ over sb. über jmdn. herrschen
swear [sweə(r)] **1.** *v.t.,* swore [swɔː(r)],
sworn [swɔːn] schwören *(Eid usw.).* **2.**

v.i., swore, sworn **a)** fluchen; **b)** ~ **to**
sth. etw. beschwören. **'swear at** *v.t.*
beschimpfen. **'swear by** *v.t. (coll.)*
schwören auf *(+ Akk.)*
swear-word *n.* Kraftausdruck, *der*
sweat [swet] **1.** *n.* Schweiß, *der.* **2.** *v.i.*
schwitzen
sweater ['swetə(r)] *n.* Pullover, *der*
'sweaty *adj.* schweißig
Swede [swiːd] *n.* Schwede, *der/*
Schwedin, *die*
swede *n.* Kohlrübe, *die*
Sweden ['swiːdn] *pr. n.* Schweden
(das)
Swedish ['swiːdɪʃ] **1.** *adj.* schwedisch; **sb. is ~** : jmd. ist Schwede/
Schwedin. **2.** *n.* Schwedisch, *das; see
also* **English 2 a**
sweep [swiːp] **1.** *v.t.,* swept [swept] **a)**
fegen; kehren; **b)** ~ **the country**
(Epidemie, Mode:) das Land überrol-
len. **2.** *v.i.,* swept **a)** fegen; kehren; **b)**
(go fast) (Person, Auto:) rauschen;
(Wind usw.:) fegen. **3.** *n.* **a) give sth. a**
~ : etw. fegen *od.* kehren; **b)** *(curve)*
Bogen, *der.* **sweep 'up** *v.t.* zusam-
menfegen; zusammenkehren
'sweeping *adj.* pauschal; weitreichend *(Einsparung);* umwälzend *(Veränderung)*
sweet [swiːt] **1.** *adj.* süß; reizend
(Wesen, Gesicht, Mädchen); **have a ~
tooth** gern Süßes mögen; **how ~ of
you!** wie nett *od.* lieb von dir! **2.** *n.*
(Brit.) **a)** *(candy)* Bonbon, *das od. der;*
b) *(dessert)* Nachtisch, *der.* **sweet-
and-'sour** *attrib. adj.* süßsauer.
'sweet corn *n.* Zuckermais, *der*
sweeten ['swiːtn] *v.t.* süßen. **'sweetener** *n.* Süßstoff, *der*
'sweetheart *n.* Schatz, *der*
'sweetness *n.* Süße, *die*
sweet: ~ 'pea *n.* Wicke, *die;* **~-shop**
n. (Brit.) Süßwarengeschäft, *das*
swell [swel] **1.** *v.t.,* swelled, swollen
['swəʊlən] *or* swelled anschwellen lassen. **2.** *v.i.,* swelled, swollen *or* swelled
a) *(expand) (Körperteil:)* anschwellen;
(Segel:) sich blähen; *(Material:)* auf-
quellen; **b)** *(Anzahl:)* zunehmen.
'swelling *n.* Schwellung, *die*
swelter ['sweltə(r)] *v.i.* ~**ing** glühend
heiß *(Tag, Wetter);* ~**ing heat** Bruthit-
ze, *die*
swept *see* sweep 1, 2
swerve [swɜːv] **1.** *v.i.* einen Bogen
machen; ~ **to the right/left** nach
rechts/links [aus]schwenken. **2.** *n.* Bogen, *der*

swift [swɪft] 1. *adj.* schnell. 2. *n.* Mauersegler, *der.* '**swiftly** *adv.* schnell

swig [swɪg] *(coll.)* Schluck, *der*

swill [swɪl] *v. t.* ~ |out| [aus]spülen

swim [swɪm] 1. *v. i.,* **-mm-,** **swam** [swæm], **swum** [swʌm] schwimmen; my head was ~ming mir war schwindelig. 2. *n.* have a/go for a ~: schwimmen/schwimmen gehen. '**swimmer** *n.* Schwimmer, *der*/Schwimmerin, *die;* be a good/poor ~: gut/schlecht schwimmen können. '**swimming** *n.* Schwimmen, *das*

swimming: ~-**baths** *n. pl.* Schwimmbad, *das;* ~-**costume** *n.* Badeanzug, *der;* ~-**pool** *n.* Schwimmbecken, *das; (building)* Schwimmbad, *das;* ~-**trunks** *n. pl.* Badehose, *die*

'**swim-suit** *n.* Badeanzug, *der*

swindle ['swɪndl] 1. *v. t.* betrügen; ~ sb. out of sth. jmdn. um etw. betrügen. 2. *n.* Schwindel, *der;* Betrug, *der.* **swindler** ['swɪndlə(r)] *n.* Schwindler, *der*/Schwindlerin, *die*

swine [swaɪn] *n.* Schwein, *das*

swing [swɪŋ] 1. *n.* **a)** Schaukel, *die;* **b)** (~*ing*) Schaukeln, *das;* in full ~ *(fig.)* in vollem Gang[e]. 2. *v. i.,* **swung** [swʌŋ] **a)** schwingen; *(in wind)* schaukeln; **b)** *(go in sweeping curve)* schwenken. 3. *v. t.,* **swung** schwingen. **swing-**'**door** *n.* Pendeltür, *die*

swipe [swaɪp] *(coll.)* *v. t.* **a)** *(hit)* knallen *(ugs.);* **b)** *(sl.: steal)* klauen *(ugs.)*

swirl [swɜ:l] 1. *v. i.* wirbeln. 2. *v. t.* umherwirbeln. 3. *n.* Spirale, *die*

swish [swɪʃ] 1. *v. i.* zischen. 2. *n.* Zischen, *das.* 3. *adj. (coll.)* schick *(ugs.)*

Swiss [swɪs] 1. *adj.* Schweizer; schweizerisch; sb. is ~: jmd. ist Schweizer/Schweizerin. 2. *n.* Schweizer, *der*/Schweizerin, *die;* the ~ *pl.* die Schweizer. **Swiss** '**roll** *n.* Biskuitrolle, *die*

switch [swɪtʃ] 1. *n.* **a)** *(esp. Electr.)* Schalter, *der;* **b)** *(change)* Wechsel, *der.* 2. *v. t.* **a)** *(change)* ~ sth. |over| to sth. etw. auf etw. *(Akk.)* umstellen *od. (Electr.)* umschalten; **b)** *(exchange)* tauschen. 3. *v. i.* wechseln; ~ |over| to sth. auf etw. *(Akk.)* umstellen *od. (Electr.)* umschalten. **switch** '**off** *v. t. & i.* ausschalten; *(also fig. coll.)* abschalten. **switch** '**on** 1. *v. t.* einschalten; anschalten. 2. *v. i.* sich anschalten

switch: ~**back** *n.* Achterbahn, *die;* ~**board** *n.* [Telefon]zentrale, *die*

Switzerland ['swɪtsələnd] *pr. n.* die Schweiz

swivel ['swɪvl] 1. *v. i.,* **-ll-** sich drehen. 2. *v. t.,* **-ll-** drehen. '**swivel chair** *n.* Drehstuhl, *der*

swollen ['swəʊlən] 1. *see* **swell.** 2. *adj.* geschwollen; angeschwollen ⟨*Fluß*⟩

swoon [swu:n] *(literary)* *v. i.* ohnmächtig werden

swoop [swu:p] 1. *n.* **a)** Sturzflug, *der;* **b)** *(coll.: raid)* Razzia, *die.* 2. *v. i.* herabstoßen; ~ on sb. sich auf jmdn. stürzen

sword [sɔ:d] *n.* Schwert, *das.* '**swordfish** *n.* Schwertfisch, *der*

swore, sworn *see* **swear**

swot [swɒt] *(Brit. coll.)* 1. *n.* Streber, *der*/Streberin, *die.* 2. *v. i.,* **-tt-** büffeln *(ugs.)*

swum *see* **swim** 1

swung *see* **swing** 2, 3

sycamore ['sɪkəmɔ:(r)] *n.* Bergahorn, *der*

sycophant ['sɪkəfænt] *n.* Kriecher, *der*

syllable ['sɪləbl] *n.* Silbe, *die*

syllabus ['sɪləbəs] *n.* Lehrplan, *der; (for exam)* Studienplan, *der*

symbol ['sɪmbl] *n.* Symbol, *das* (of für)

symbolic [sɪm'bɒlɪk], **symbolical** [sɪm'bɒlɪkl] *adj.* symbolisch. **symbolism** ['sɪmbəlɪzm] *n.* Symbolik, *die.* **symbolize** ['sɪmbəlaɪz] *v. t.* symbolisieren

symmetrical [sɪ'metrɪkl] *adj.* symmetrisch

symmetry ['sɪmɪtrɪ] *n.* Symmetrie, *die*

sympathetic [sɪmpə'θetɪk] *adj.* mitfühlend

sympathize ['sɪmpəθaɪz] *v. i.* **a)** ~ with sb. mit jmdm. |mit|fühlen; **b)** ~ with *(understand)* Verständnis haben für

sympathy ['sɪmpəθɪ] *n.* Mitgefühl, *das;* in deepest ~: mit aufrichtigem Beileid

symphonic [sɪm'fɒnɪk] *adj.* sinfonisch

symphony ['sɪmfənɪ] *n.* Sinfonie, *die*

symptom ['sɪmptəm] *n.* Symptom, *das.* **symptomatic** [sɪmptə'mætɪk] *adj.* symptomatisch (of für)

synagogue *(Amer.:* **synagog)** ['sɪnəgɒg] *n.* Synagoge, *die*

synchromesh ['sɪŋkrəmeʃ] *n. (Motor Veh.)* Synchrongetriebe, *das*

synchronize ['sɪŋkrənaɪz] *v. t.* synchronisieren; gleichstellen ⟨*Uhren*⟩

syndicate ['sɪndɪkət] *n.* Syndikat, *das*

syndrome ['sındrəʊm] *n.* Syndrom, *das*

synonym ['sınənım] *n.* Synonym, *das.*

synonymous [sı'nɒnıməs] *adj.* **a)** *(Ling.)* synonym (**with** mit); **b)** ~ **with** *(fig.)* gleichbedeutend mit

synopsis [sı'nɒpsıs] *n., pl.* **synopses** [sı'nɒpsi:z] Inhaltsangabe, *die*

syntactic [sın'tæktık] *adj.* syntaktisch

syntax ['sıntæks] *n.* Syntax, *die*

synthesis ['sınθısıs] *n., pl.* **syntheses** ['sınθısi:z] Synthese, *die*

synthesize ['sınθısaız] *v. t.* zur Synthese bringen; *(Chem.)* synthetisieren.
synthesizer ['sınθısaızə(r)] *n. (Mus.)* Synthesizer, *der*

synthetic [sın'θetık] *adj.* synthetisch

syphilis ['sıfılıs] *n.* Syphilis, *die*

syphon *see* **siphon**

Syria ['sırıə] *pr. n.* Syrien *(das)*

syringe [sı'rındʒ] **1.** *n.* Spritze, *die.* **2.** *v. t.* spritzen; ausspritzen ⟨*Ohr*⟩

syrup ['sırəp] *n.* Sirup, *der*

system ['sıstəm] *n.* System, *das.* **systematic** [sıstə'mætık] *adj.*, **systematically** [sıstə'mætıkəlı] *adv.* systematisch. **systematize** ['sıstəmətaız] *v. t.* systematisieren. **'systems analyst** *n.* Systemanalytiker, *der/* -analytikerin, *die*

T

T, t [ti:] *n.* T, t, *das;* **to a T** ganz genau; **T-junction** Einmündung, *die;* **T-bone steak** T-bone-Steak, *das;* **T-shirt** T-shirt, *das*

ta [tɑ:] *int. (Brit. coll.)* danke

tab [tæb] *n.* **a)** *(projecting flap)* Zunge, *die; (on clothing)* Etikett, *das; (with name)* Namensschild, *das;* **b) pick up the** ~ *(Amer. coll.)* die Zeche bezahlen; **c) keep** ~s *or* **a** ~ **on** *(watch)* [genau] beobachten

tabby ['tæbı] *n.* ~ |**cat**| Tigerkatze, *die*

table ['teıbl] **1.** *n.* **a)** Tisch, *der;* **b)** *(list)* Tabelle, *die;* ~ **of contents** Inhaltsverzeichnis, *das.* **2.** *v. t.* einbringen

tableau ['tæbləʊ] *n., pl.* ~x ['tæbləʊz] Tableau, *das*

table: ~-**cloth** *n.* Tischdecke, *die;* ~ **manners** *n. pl.* Tischmanieren *Pl.;* ~-**mat** *n.* Set, *das;* ~ **salt** *n.* Tafelsalz, *das;* ~**spoon** *n.* Servierlöffel, *der;* ~**spoonful** *n.* ≈ Eßlöffel[voll], *der*

tablet ['tæblıt] *n.* **a)** Tablette, *die;* **b)** *(of soap)* Stück, *das*

table: ~ **tennis** *n.* Tischtennis, *das;* ~ **tennis bat** Tischtennisschläger, *der;* ~ **wine** *n.* Tischwein, *der*

tabloid ['tæblɔıd] *n.* Boulevardzeitung, *die*

taboo, tabu [tə'bu:] **1.** *n.* Tabu, *das.* **2.** *adj.* Tabu⟨*wort*⟩; **be** ~: tabu sein

tabulate ['tæbjʊleıt] *v. t.* tabellarisch darstellen. **tabulator** ['tæbjʊleıtə(r)] *n.* Tabulator, *der*

tacit ['tæsıt] *adj.*, **'tacitly** *adv.* stillschweigend

taciturn ['tæsıtɜ:n] *adj.* schweigsam; wortkarg

tack [tæk] **1.** *n.* **a)** *(nail)* kleiner Nagel; **b)** *(stitch)* Heftstich, *der;* **c)** *(Naut., also fig.)* Kurs, *der.* **2.** *v. t.* **a)** *(nail)* festnageln; **b)** *(stitch)* heften. **3.** *v. i. (Naut.)* kreuzen

tackle ['tækl] **1.** *v. t.* **a)** angehen ⟨*Problem usw.*⟩; ~ **sb. about/on/over sth.** jmdn. auf etw. *(Akk.)* ansprechen; *(ask for sth.)* jmdn. um etw. angehen; **b)** *(Sport)* angreifen ⟨*Spieler*⟩; *(Amer. Footb.; Rugby)* fassen. **2.** *n.* **a)** *(equipment)* Ausrüstung, *die;* **b)** *(Sport)* Angriff, *der; (sliding* ~) Tackling, *das; (Amer. Footb.; Rugby)* Fassen und Halten

tacky ['tækı] *adj.* klebrig

tact [tækt] *n.* Takt, *der;* **he has no** ~: er hat kein Taktgefühl. **tactful** ['tæktfl] *adj.*, **'tactfully** *adv.* taktvoll

tactical ['tæktıkl] *adj.* taktisch

tactics ['tæktıks] *n. pl.* Taktik, *die*

'tactless *adj.*, **'tactlessly** *adv.* taktlos

tadpole ['tædpəʊl] *n.* Kaulquappe, *die*

¹tag [tæg] *n.* Schild, *das.* **tag a'long** *v. i.* mitkommen

²tag *n. (game)* Fangen, *das*

tail [teıl] **1.** *n.* **a)** Schwanz, *der;* **b)** *in pl. (on coin)* ~s |**it is**| Zahl. **2.** *v. t. (sl.: follow)* beschatten. **tail 'back** *v. i.* sich stauen. **tail 'off** *v. i.* **a)** zurückgehen; **b)** *(into silence)* verstummen

tail: ~-**back** *n. (Brit.)* Rückstau, *der;* ~-**end** *n.* Ende, *das;* ~-**gate** *n. (Motor Veh.)* Heckklappe, *die;* ~-**light** *n.* Rücklicht, *das*

tailor ['teılə(r)] *n.* Schneider, *der/*

Schneiderin, *die.* '**tailor-made** *adj.*
maßgeschneidert

'**tail wind** *n.* Rückenwind, *der*
taint [teɪnt] *v. t.* verderben; **be ~ed with**
sth. mit etw. behaftet sein *(geh.)*
Taiwan [taɪˈwɑːn] *pr. n.* Taiwan *(das)*
take [teɪk] **1.** *v. t.,* took [tʊk], **taken**
['teɪkn] **a)** *(get hold of, grasp, seize)*
nehmen; **b)** *(capture)* einnehmen
⟨*Stadt, Festung*⟩; **c)** *(gain, earn)* ⟨*Laden:*⟩
einbringen; ⟨*Person:*⟩ einnehmen;
⟨*Film, Stück:*⟩ einspielen; *(win)* gewinnen ⟨*Satz, Spiel, Preis, Titel*⟩; **d)** *(~*
away with one) mitnehmen; *(steal)*
mitnehmen *(verhüll.); ~* **place** stattfinden; *(spontaneously)* sich ereignen;
⟨*Wandlung:*⟩ sich vollziehen; **e)** *(avail*
oneself of, use) nehmen; machen
⟨*Pause, Ferien, Nickerchen*⟩; **~ the op-**
portunity to do/of doing sth. die Gelegenheit dazu benutzen, etw. zu tun; **f)**
(carry, guide, convey) bringen; **~ sb. to**
visit sb. jmdn. zu Besuch bei jmdm.
mitnehmen; **~ home** mit nach Hause
nehmen; *(earn)* nach Hause bringen
⟨*Geld*⟩; *(accompany)* nach Hause bringen; **g)** *(remove)* nehmen; *(deduct)* abziehen; **~ sth./sb. from sb.** jmdm.
etw./jmdm. wegnehmen; **h)** *(make)*
machen ⟨*Foto, Kopie*⟩; *(photograph)*
aufnehmen; aufnehmen ⟨*Brief,*
Diktat⟩; machen ⟨*Prüfung, Sprung,*
Spaziergang, Reise⟩; ablegen ⟨*Ge-*
lübde, Eid⟩; treffen ⟨*Entscheidung*⟩; **i)**
(conduct) halten ⟨*Gottesdienst, Unter-*
richt⟩; **Ms X ~s us for maths** in Mathe
haben wir Frau X; **j)** *(eat, drink)* nehmen ⟨*Zucker, Milch, Tabletten, Über-*
dosis⟩; trinken ⟨*Tee, Kaffee, Kognak*
usw.⟩; **k)** *(need, require)* brauchen
⟨*Platz, Zeit*⟩; haben ⟨*Objekt, Plural-s*⟩;
gebraucht werden mit ⟨*Kasus*⟩; **sth.**
~s an hour/a year/all day etw. dauert
eine Stunde/ein Jahr/einen ganzen
Tag; **l)** *(ascertain and record)* notieren
⟨*Namen, Adresse, Autonummer usw.*⟩;
fühlen ⟨*Puls*⟩; messen ⟨*Temperatur,*
Größe usw.⟩; **m)** *(assume)* **~ it** [**that**]**...:**
annehmen, daß ...; **~ sb./sth. for/to be**
sth. jmdm./etw. für etw. halten; **n)**
(react to) aufnehmen; **~ sth. well/**
badly etw. gut/nur schwer verkraften;
~ sth. calmly *or* **coolly** etw. gelassen
[auf]nehmen; **o)** *(accept)* annehmen;
p) *(adopt, choose)* ergreifen ⟨*Maß-*
nahmen⟩; unternehmen ⟨*Schritte*⟩; **~**
the wrong road die falsche Straße nehmen; **q) be ~n ill** krank werden; **r) ~**

sth. **to bits** *or* **pieces** etw. auseinander-
nehmen. **2.** *v. i.,* took, **taken a)** ⟨*Trans-*
plantat:⟩ vom Körper angenommen
werden; ⟨*Sämling, Pflanze:*⟩ angehen;
b) *(detract)* **~ from sth.** etw. schmälern. '**take after** *v. t. (resemble)*
jmdm. ähnlich sein; *(~ as one's*
example) es jmdm. gleichtun. **take**
a'**way** *v. t.* **a)** *(remove)* wegnehmen;
(to a distance) mitnehmen; **~ sth.**
away from sb. jmdm. etw. abnehmen;
to ~ away ⟨*Pizza, Snack usw.*⟩ zum
Mitnehmen; **b)** *(Math.: deduct)* abziehen. **take** a'**way from** *v. t.* schmälern. **take** '**back** *v. t.* zurücknehmen;
(return) zurückbringen. **take** '**down**
v. t. **a)** *(carry or lead down)* hinunter-
bringen; **b)** abnehmen ⟨*Bild, Ankündi-*
gung, Weihnachtsschmuck⟩; herunter-
ziehen ⟨*Hose*⟩; **~ sth. down from a**
shelf etw. von einem Regal herunter-
nehmen; **c)** *(write down)* aufnehmen.
take '**in** *v. t.* **a)** hineinbringen; *(bring*
indoors) hereinholen; **b)** enger ma-
chen ⟨*Kleidungsstück*⟩; **c)** *(under-*
stand) begreifen; **d)** *(cheat)* hereinlegen *(ugs.); (deceive)* täuschen. **take**
'**off 1.** *v. t.* **a)** abnehmen ⟨*Deckel, Hut,*
Tischtuch, Verband⟩; abziehen ⟨*Kis-*
senbezug⟩; ausziehen ⟨*Schuhe, Hand-*
schuhe⟩; ablegen ⟨*Mantel, Schmuck*⟩;
b) *(deduct)* abziehen; **~ sth. off sth.**
etw. von etw. abziehen; **c) ~ a day** *etc.*
off sich *(Dat.)* einen Tag *usw.* frei
nehmen *(ugs.);* **d)** *(mimic)* nachahmen. **2.** *v. i. (Aeronaut.)* starten. **take**
'**on** *v. t.* **a)** *(undertake)* übernehmen;
auf sich *(Akk.)* nehmen ⟨*Bürde*⟩; **b)**
(employ) einstellen; **c)** *(as opponent)* es
aufnehmen mit; *(Sport: meet)* antre-
ten gegen. **take** '**out** *v. t.* **a)** *(remove)*
herausnehmen; ausziehen ⟨*Zahn*⟩; **~**
sth. out of sth. etw. aus etw. [heraus]neh-
men; **b)** *(withdraw)* abheben ⟨*Geld*⟩;
c) *(go out with)* **~ sb. out** mit jmdm.
ausgehen; **~ sb. out to** *or* **for lunch**
jmdn. zum Mittagessen einladen; **d)**
(get issued) abschließen ⟨*Versiche-*
rung⟩; ausleihen ⟨*Bücher*⟩; **~ out a**
subscription to sth. etw. abonnieren;
e) ~ it out on sb. seine Wut an jmdm.
auslassen. **take** '**over 1.** *v. t.* übernehmen. **2.** *v. i.* übernehmen; ⟨*Man-*
ager, Firmenleiter:⟩ die Geschäfte
übernehmen; ⟨*Regierung, Präsident:*⟩
die Amtsgeschäfte übernehmen; **~**
over from sb. jmdn. ersetzen; *(tempor-*
arily) jmdn. vertreten. '**take to** *v. t.* **a)**
(get into habit of) **~ to doing sth.** es

sich *(Dat.)* angewöhnen, etw. zu tun;
b) *(like)* sich hingezogen fühlen zu
⟨*Person*⟩; sich erwärmen für ⟨*Sache*⟩.
take 'up 1. *v. t.* **a)** *(lift up)* hochheben; *(pick up)* aufheben; herausreißen
⟨*Dielen*⟩; aufreißen ⟨*Straße*⟩; **b)** *(carry
or lead up)* hinaufbringen; **c)** in Anspruch nehmen ⟨*Zeit*⟩; brauchen/*(un-
desirably)* wegnehmen ⟨*Platz*⟩; **d)**
(start) ergreifen ⟨*Beruf*⟩; anfangen
⟨*Tennis, Schach, Gitarre usw.*⟩; aufnehmen ⟨*Arbeit, Kampf*⟩; antreten
⟨*Stelle*⟩; ~ **up a hobby** sich *(Dat.)* ein
Hobby zulegen; **e)** *(pursue further)* ~
sth. up with sb. sich in einer Sache an
jmdn. wenden. **2.** *v. i.* ~ **up with sb.**
(coll.) sich mit jmdm. einlassen
'take-away *n. (meal)* Essen zum Mitnehmen; *(restaurant)* Restaurant mit
Straßenverkauf
taken *see* **take**
take: ~**-off** *n.* **a)** *(Aeronaut.)* Start,
der; **b)** *(coll.: caricature)* Parodie, *die;*
~**-over** *n.* Übernahme, *die*
takings ['teɪkɪŋz] *n. pl.* Einnahmen
talcum ['tælkəm] *n.* ~ |**powder**| Kör-
perpuder, *der*
tale [teɪl] *n.* Erzählung, *die;* Geschichte, *die* (**of** von, **about** über + *Akk.*)
talent ['tælənt] *n.* Talent, *das;* **have**
|**great/no** *etc.*] ~ |**for sth.**| [viel/kein
usw.] Talent [zu *od.* für etw.] haben.
'talented *adj.* talentiert
talk [tɔ:k] **1.** *n.* **a)** *(discussion)* Ge-
spräch, *das;* **have a** ~ |**with sb.**| |**about
sth.**| [mit jmdm.] [über etw. *(Akk.)*]
sprechen; **have** *or* **hold** ~**s** |**with sb.**|
[mit jmdm.] Gespräche führen; **b)**
(speech, lecture) Vortrag, *der.* **2.** *v. i.*
sprechen **(with, to** mit); *(lecture)* sprechen; *(converse)* sich unterhalten;
(have ~*s)* Gespräche führen; *(gossip)*
reden; ~ **on the phone** telefonieren. **3.**
v. t. reden; ~ **sb. into/out of sth.** jmdn.
zu etw. überreden/jmdm. etw. ausre-
den. **talk 'over** *v. t.* besprechen. **talk
'round** *v. t.* ~ **sb. round** jmdn. überreden
talkative ['tɔ:kətɪv] *adj.* gesprächig
talking: ~ **point** *n.* Gesprächsthema,
das; ~**-to** *n. (coll.)* Standpauke, *die*
(ugs.)
tall [tɔ:l] *adj.* hoch; groß ⟨*Person,
Tier*⟩; **that's a** ~ **order** das ist ziemlich
viel verlangt; ~ **story** unglaubliche
Geschichte
tally ['tælɪ] **1.** *n.* **keep a** ~ **of sth.** über
etw. *(Akk.)* Buch führen. **2.** *v. i.* übereinstimmen

talon ['tælən] *n.* Klaue, *die*
tambourine [tæmbə'ri:n] *n.* Tambu-
rin, *das*
tame [teɪm] **1.** *adj.* zahm; *(fig.: spir-
itless)* lahm *(ugs.).* **2.** *v. t.* zähmen
tamper ['tæmpə(r)] *v. i.* ~ **with** sich
(Dat.) zu schaffen machen an
(+ *Dat.*)
tampon ['tæmpon] *n.* Tampon, *der*
tan [tæn] **1.** *v. t.,* -**nn-** gerben ⟨*Tierhaut,
Fell*⟩. **2.** *v. i.,* -**nn-** braun werden. **3.** *n.*
a) *(colour)* Gelbbraun, *das;* **b)** *(sun-*~*)*
Bräune, *die;* **have/get a** ~ **:** braun sein/
werden. **4.** *adj.* gelbbraun
tandem ['tændəm] *n.* ~ |**bicycle**| Tan-
dem, *das*
tang [tæŋ] *n. (taste)* Geschmack, *der;*
(smell) Geruch, *der*
tangent ['tændʒənt] *n.* Tangente, *die;*
go off at a ~ *(fig.)* plötzlich vom Thema abschweifen
tangible ['tændʒɪbl] *adj.* greifbar;
spürbar ⟨*Unterschied, Verbesserung*⟩;
handfest ⟨*Beweis*⟩
tangle ['tæŋgl] **1.** *n.* Gewirr, *das; (in
hair)* Verfilzung, *die.* **2.** *v. t.* verheddern *(ugs.);* verfilzen ⟨*Haar*⟩. **tangle
'up** *v. t.* verheddern *(ugs.)*
tango ['tæŋgəʊ] *n., pl.* ~**s** Tango, *der*
tank [tæŋk] *n.* **a)** Tank, *der;* **b)** *(Mil.)*
Panzer, *der*
tankard ['tæŋkəd] *n.* Krug, *der*
tanker ['tæŋkə(r)] *n. (ship)* Tanker,
der; (vehicle) Tank[last]wagen, *der*
tanned [tænd] *adj.* braungebrannt
tantalize ['tæntəlaɪz] *v. t.* reizen. **tan-
talizing** ['tæntəlaɪzɪŋ] *adj.* verlockend
tantamount ['tæntəmaʊnt] *adj.* **be** ~
to sth. gleichbedeutend mit etw. sein
tantrum ['tæntrəm] *n.* Wutanfall, *der;*
(of child) Trotzanfall, *der;* **throw a** ~ **:**
einen Wutanfall/Trotzanfall bekom-
men
¹tap [tæp] **1.** *n.* Hahn, *der;* **hot/
cold**[-**water**] ~ **:** Warm-/Kaltwasser-
hahn, *der;* **be on** ~ *(fig.)* zur Verfügung stehen. **2.** *v. t.,* -**pp-: a)** erschließen ⟨*Reserven, Markt*⟩; **b)** *(Teleph.)*
abhören; anzapfen *(ugs.)*
²tap 1. *v. t.,* -**pp-** klopfen an (+ *Akk.*);
(on upper surface) klopfen auf
(+ *Akk.*). **2.** *v. i.,* -**pp-: ~ at/on sth.** an
etw. *(Akk.)* klopfen; *(on upper surface)*
auf etw. *(Akk.)* klopfen. **3.** *n.* Klopfen,
das. **'tap-dance 1.** *n.* Step[tanz], *der.*
2. *v. i.* steptanzen; steppen
tape [teɪp] **1.** *n.* **a)** Band, *das;* **adhesive**
or (coll.) **sticky** ~ **:** Klebeband, *das;* **b)**

(for recording) [Ton]band, *das* (of mit); **make a ~ of sth.** etw. auf Band aufnehmen. 2. *v. t.* **a)** *(record on ~)* [auf Band] aufnehmen; **b)** *(bind with ~)* [mit Klebeband] zukleben; **c)** **have got sb./sth. ~d** *(sl.)* jmdn. durchschaut haben/etw. im Griff haben

tape: ~ cassette *n.* Tonbandkassette, *die;* **~ deck** *n.* Tapedeck, *das;* **~-measure** *n.* Bandmaß, *das*

taper ['teɪpə(r)] 1. *v. i.* sich verjüngen; **~ [to a point]** spitz zulaufen. 2. *n.* |wax| ~: Wachsstock, *der*

tape: ~ recorder *n.* Tonbandgerät, *das;* **~ recording** *n.* Tonbandaufnahme, *die*

tapestry ['tæpɪstrɪ] *n.* Gobelingewebe, *das; (wall-hanging)* Bildteppich, *der*

'**tapeworm** *n.* Bandwurm, *der*

'**tap-water** *n.* Leitungswasser, *das*

tar [tɑː(r)] 1. *n.* Teer, *der.* 2. *v. t.,* -rr- teeren

target ['tɑːgɪt] *n.* **a)** Ziel, *das;* **hit/miss the/its ~:** [das Ziel] treffen/das Ziel verfehlen; **b)** *(Sport)* Zielscheibe, *die*

tariff ['tærɪf] *n.* **a)** *(tax)* Zoll, *der;* **b)** *(list of charges)* Tarif, *der*

tarnish ['tɑːnɪʃ] 1. *v. t.* stumpf werden lassen ⟨Metall⟩; *(fig.)* beflecken ⟨Ruf⟩. 2. *v. i.* stumpf werden

tarpaulin [tɑːˈpɔːlɪn] *n.* Persenning, *die*

¹**tart** [tɑːt] *adj.* herb; sauer ⟨Obst⟩; *(fig.)* scharfzüngig

²**tart** *n.* **a)** *(Brit.) (filled pie)* ≈ Obstkuchen, *der; (small pastry)* Obsttörtchen, *das;* **b)** *(sl.: prostitute)* Nutte, *die (salopp).* **tart 'up** *v. t. (Brit. coll.)* **~ oneself up, get ~ed up** sich auftakeln *(ugs.)*

tartan ['tɑːtən] 1. *n.* Schotten[stoff], *der.* 2. *adj.* Schotten⟨rock, -jacke⟩

tartar ['tɑːtə(r)] *n.* Zahnstein, *der*

tartar sauce ['tɑːtə 'sɔːs] *n.* Remouladе[nsoße], *die*

task [tɑːsk] *n.* Aufgabe, *die;* **take sb. to ~:** jmdm. eine Lektion erteilen. '**task force** *n.* Sonderkommando, *das*

tassel ['tæsl] *n.* Quaste, *die*

taste [teɪst] 1. *v. t.* **a)** schmecken; *(try a little)* probieren; **b)** *(recognize flavour of)* [heraus]schmecken. 2. *v. i.* schmecken (**of** nach); **not ~ of anything** nach nichts schmecken. 3. *n.* **a)** *(flavour)* Geschmack, *der;* |sense of| ~: Geschmack[ssinn], *der;* **b)** *(discernment)* Geschmack, *der;* **c)** *(sample)* Kostprobe, *die.* **tasteful** ['teɪstfl]

adj., '**tastefully** *adv.* geschmackvoll.

'**tasteless** *adj.* geschmacklos. **tasty** ['teɪstɪ] *adj.* lecker

tat [tæt] *n. see* ²**tit**

tattered ['tætəd] *adj.* zerlumpt ⟨Kleidung⟩; zerfleddert ⟨Buch⟩. **tatters** ['tætəz] *n. pl.* Fetzen; **be in ~:** in Fetzen sein; *(fig.)* ruiniert sein

tattoo [təˈtuː] 1. *v. t.* tätowieren. 2. *n.* Tätowierung, *die*

tatty ['tætɪ] *adj. (coll.)* schäbig

taught *see* **teach**

taunt [tɔːnt] 1. *v. t.* verspotten (**about** wegen). 2. *n.* spöttische Bemerkung

Taurus ['tɔːrəs] *n.* der Stier

taut [tɔːt] *adj.* straff ⟨Seil, Kabel⟩; gespannt ⟨Muskel⟩

tavern ['tævən] *n.* Schenke, *die*

tawny ['tɔːnɪ] *adj.* gelbbraun

tax [tæks] 1. *n.* Steuer, *die.* 2. *v. t.* **a)** besteuern; versteuern ⟨Einkommen⟩; **b)** *(fig.)* strapazieren ⟨Kräfte, Geduld⟩.

taxable ['tæksəbl] *adj.* steuerpflichtig. **taxation** [tækˈseɪʃn] *n.* Besteuerung, *die; (taxes payable)* Steuern. '**tax-free** *adj.* steuerfrei

taxi ['tæksɪ] 1. *n.* Taxi, *das.* 2. *v. i.,* **~ing** *or* **taxying** ⟨Flugzeug:⟩ rollen. '**taxi-driver** *n.* Taxifahrer, *der/*-fahrerin, *die*

'**tax inspector** *n.* Steuerinspektor, *der/*-inspektorin, *die*

taxi: ~-rank *(Brit.),* **~ stand** *(Amer.)* *ns.* Taxistand, *der*

tax: ~-payer *n.* Steuerzahler, *der/* -zahlerin, *die;* **~ return** *n.* Steuererklärung, *die*

tea [tiː] *n.* **a)** Tee, *der;* **b)** *(meal)* |high| ~: Abendessen, *das.* '**tea-bag** *n.* Teebeutel, *der.* '**tea-break** *n. (Brit.)* Teepause, *die*

teach [tiːtʃ] 1. *v. t.,* **taught** [tɔːt] unterrichten; *(at university)* lehren; **~ sb./ oneself/an animal sth.** jmdm./sich/einem Tier etw. beibringen; **~ sb. to ride** jmdm. das Reiten beibringen. 2. *v. i.,* **taught** unterrichten. '**teacher** *n.* Lehrer, *der/*Lehrerin, *die*

tea: ~-cloth *n.* Geschirrtuch, *das;* **~cup** *n.* Teetasse, *die*

teak [tiːk] *n.* Teak[holz], *das*

'**tea-leaf** *n.* Teeblatt, *die*

team [tiːm] *n.* Team, *das; (Sport also)* Mannschaft, *die.* **team 'up** *v. i.* sich zusammentun *(ugs.)*

'**team-work** *n.* Teamarbeit, *die*

'**teapot** *n.* Teekanne, *die*

¹**tear** [teə(r)] 1. *n.* Riß, *der.* 2. *v. t.,* **tore** [tɔː(r)], **torn** [tɔːn] **a)** *(rip)* zerreißen;

(pull apart) auseinanderreißen; *(damage)* aufreißen; ~ **open** aufreißen ⟨ *Brief, Paket* ⟩; **b)** ~ **sth. out of sb.'s hands** jmdm. etw. aus der Hand reißen. **3.** *v. i.,* **tore, torn a)** *(rip)* [zer]reißen; **b)** *(move hurriedly)* rasen *(ugs.).* **tear a'way** *v. t.* wegreißen; ~ **oneself away** *(fig.)* sich losreißen. **tear 'up** *v. t.* zerreißen

²**tear** [tɪə(r)] *n.* Träne, *die.* **tearful** ['tɪəfl] *adj.* weinend

tear [tɪə(r)]: ~**-drop** *n.* Träne, *die;* ~**-gas** *n.* Tränengas, *das*

tease [tiːz] **1.** *v. t.* necken (**about** wegen); aufziehen *(ugs.)* (**about** mit). **2.** *v. i.* seine Späße machen

tea: ~**-shop** *n. (Brit.)* ≈ Café, *das;* ~**spoon** *n.* Teelöffel, *der;* ~**-strainer** *n.* Teesieb, *das*

teat [tiːt] *n.* **a)** Zitze, *die;* **b)** *(of rubber or plastic)* Sauger, *der*

tea: ~**-time** *n.* Teezeit, *die;* ~**towel** *n.* Geschirrtuch, *das*

technical ['teknɪkl] *adj.* technisch ⟨ *Problem, Daten, Fortschritt* ⟩; Fach⟨ *kenntnis, -sprache, -begriff, -wörterbuch* ⟩; ~ **term** Fachbegriff, *der;* Fachausdruck, *der.* **technicality** [teknɪ'kælɪtɪ] *n.* technisches Detail

technician [tek'nɪʃn] *n.* Techniker, *der/* Technikerin, *die*

technique [tek'niːk] *n.* Technik, *die;* *(procedure)* Methode, *die*

technological [teknə'lɒdʒɪkl] *adj.* technisch; technologisch

technology [tek'nɒlədʒɪ] *n.* Technik, *die; (application of science)* Technologie, *die*

teddy ['tedɪ] *n.* ~ **|bear|** Teddy[bär], *der*

tedious ['tiːdɪəs] *adj.* langwierig ⟨ *Reise, Arbeit* ⟩; *(uninteresting)* langweilig

tee [tiː] *(Golf)* Tee, *das*

teem [tiːm] *v. i.* wimmeln (**with** von)

teenage[d] ['tiːneɪdʒ(d)] *attrib. adj.* im Teenageralter *nachgestellt.* **teenager** ['tiːneɪdʒə(r)] *n.* Teenager, *der; (loosely)* Jugendliche, *der/die*

teens [tiːnz] *n. pl.* Teenagerjahre

teeter ['tiːtə(r)] *v. i.* wanken; ~ **on the edge of sth.** schwankend am Rande einer Sache *(Gen.)* stehen

teeth *pl. of* tooth

teething troubles ['tiːðɪŋ trʌblz] *n. pl.* **have** ~ *(fig.)* Anfangsschwierigkeiten haben

teetotal [tiː'təʊtl] *adj.* abstinent lebend. **teetotaller** [tiː'təʊtələ(r)] *n.* Abstinenzler, *der/* Abstinenzlerin, *die*

telecommunications [telɪkəmjuːnɪ'keɪʃnz] *n. pl.* Fernmelde- *od.* Nachrichtentechnik, *die*

telegram ['telɪgræm] *n.* Telegramm, *das*

telegraph ['telɪɡrɑːf] *n.* Telegraf, *der;* ~ **pole** Telegrafenmast, *der*

telepathy [tɪ'lepəθɪ] *n.* Telepathie, *die*

telephone ['telɪfəʊn] **1.** *n.* Telefon, *das; attrib.* Telefon-; **answer the** ~: Anrufe entgegennehmen; *(on one occasion)* ans Telefon gehen; *(speak)* sich melden; **be on the** ~: Telefon haben; *(be speaking)* telefonieren (**to** mit). **2.** *v. t.* anrufen. **3.** *v. i.* anrufen; ~ **for a taxi** nach einem Taxi telefonieren

telephone: ~ **book** *n.* Telefonbuch, *das;* ~ **booth,** *(Brit.)* ~**-box** *ns.* Telefonzelle, *die;* ~ **call** *n.* Telefongespräch, *das;* ~ **directory** *n.* Telefonverzeichnis, *das;* ~ **exchange** *n.* Fernmeldeamt, *das;* ~ **number** *n.* Telefonnummer, *die;* ~ **operator** *n.* Telegrafist, *der/* Telegrafistin, *die*

telephoto [telɪ'fəʊtəʊ] *adj. (Photog.)* ~ **lens** Teleobjektiv, *das*

teleprinter ['telɪprɪntə(r)] *n.* Fernschreiber, *der*

telescope ['telɪskəʊp] *n.* Teleskop, *das;* Fernrohr, *das.* **telescopic** [telɪ'skɒpɪk] *adj. (collapsible)* ausziehbar; Teleskop⟨ *antenne* ⟩

televise ['telɪvaɪz] *v. t.* im Fernsehen senden *od.* übertragen

television ['telɪvɪʒn, telɪ'vɪʒn] *n.* **a)** *no art.* das Fernsehen; **on** ~: im Fernsehen; **watch** ~: fernsehen; **b)** *(~ set)* Fernsehapparat, *der;* Fernseher, *der (ugs.)*

television: ~ **channel** *n.* [Fernseh]kanal, *der;* ~ **programme** *n.* Fernsehsendung, *die;* ~ **set** *n.* Fernsehgerät, *das*

Telex, telex ['teleks] **1.** *n.* Telex, *das.* **2.** *v. t.* ein Telex schicken (+ *Dat.*); telexen ⟨ *Nachricht* ⟩

tell [tel] **1.** *v. t.,* **told** [təʊld] **a)** *(relate)* erzählen; *(make known)* sagen ⟨ *Name, Adresse* ⟩; anvertrauen ⟨ *Geheimnis* ⟩; ~ **sb. sth.** *or* **sth. to sb.** jmdm. etw. erzählen/sagen/anvertrauen; ~ **sb. the way to the station** jmdm. den Weg zum Bahnhof beschreiben; ~ **sb. the time** jmdm. die Uhrzeit sagen; ~ **tales** *(lie)* Lügengeschichten erzählen; *(gossip)* tratschen *(ugs.);* **b)** *(instruct)* sagen; ~ **sb. |not| to do sth.** jmdm. sagen, er soll[e] etw. [nicht] tun; **c)** *(determine)*

feststellen; *(see, recognize)* erkennen
(by an + *Dat.*); *(with reference to the
future)* [vorher]sagen; d) *(distinguish)*
unterscheiden; e) **all told** insgesamt.
2. *v.i.*, **told a)** *(determine)* **how can you
~?** wie kann man das feststellen *od.*
wissen?; **you never can ~:** man kann
nie wissen; b) *(give information)* erzählen (**of**, **about** von); c) *(reveal secret)* es verraten; **time will ~:** das wird
sich zeigen; d) *(produce an effect)* sich
auswirken. **tell a'part** *v.t.* auseinanderhalten. **tell 'off** *v.t. (coll.)* ~ **sb. off**
[for sth.] jmdn. [für *od.* wegen etw.]
ausschimpfen

teller ['telə(r)] *n.* **a)** *(in bank)* see
cashier; b) *(counting votes)* Stimmen-
zähler, *der/*-zählerin, *die*

telly ['telı] *n. (Brit. coll.)* Fernseher, *der
(ugs.)*

temp [temp] *n. (Brit. coll.)* Zeitarbeits-
kraft, *die*

temper ['tempə(r)] **1.** *n.* **a)** Naturell,
das; **be in a good/bad ~:** gute/schlech-
te Laune haben; **keep/lose one's ~:**
sich beherrschen/die Beherrschung
verlieren; b) *(anger)* **fit of ~:** Wutanfall, *der;* **have a ~:** jähzornig sein. **2.**
v.t. mäßigen; mildern ⟨*Kritik*⟩

temperament ['temprəmənt] *n. (nature)* Veranlagung, *die;* Natur, *die;
(disposition)* Temperament, *das.*
temperamental [temprə'mentl] *adj.*
launenhaft

temperate ['tempərət] *adj.* gemäßigt
temperature ['temprıtʃə(r)] *n.* Temperatur, *die;* **have** *or* **run a ~** *(coll.)*
Temperatur *od.* Fieber haben

template ['templıt] *n.* Schablone, *die*
¹temple ['templ] *n.* Tempel, *der*
²temple *n. (Anat.)* Schläfe, *die*

tempo ['tempəʊ] *n., pl.* **~s** *or* **tempi**
['tempi:] Tempo, *das*

temporary ['tempərərı] *adj.* vorübergehend; provisorisch ⟨*Gebäude, Büro*⟩

tempt [tempt] *v.t.* **a)** **~ sb. to do sth.**
jmdn. geneigt machen, etw. zu tun; **be
~ed to do sth.** versucht sein, etw. zu
tun; **~ sb. out** jmdn. hinauslocken; b)
(provoke) herausfordern; **~ fate** das
Schicksal herausfordern. **tempta-
tion** [temp'teıʃn] *n.* **a)** *no pl. (attract-
ing)* Verlockung, *die; (being attracted)*
Versuchung, *die;* b) *(thing)* Verlok-
kung, *die.* **'tempting** *adj.* verlockend

ten [ten] **1.** *adj.* zehn. **2.** *n.* Zehn, *die.
See also* **eight**

tenable ['tenəbl] *adj.* haltbar ⟨*Theorie*⟩; vertretbar ⟨*Standpunkt*⟩

tenacious [tı'neıʃəs] *adj.* hartnäckig.
tenacity [tı'næsıtı] *n.* Hartnäckigkeit, *die*

tenant ['tenənt] *n. (of flat, residential
building)* Mieter, *der/*Mieterin, *die;
(of farm, shop)* Pächter, *der/*Pächterin, *die*

¹tend [tend] *v.i.* **~ to do sth.** dazu neigen *od.* tendieren, etw. zu tun; **~ to
sth.** zu etw. neigen; **he ~s to get upset
if ...:** er regt sich leicht auf, wenn ...

²tend *v.t.* sich kümmern um; hüten
⟨*Schafe*⟩; bedienen ⟨*Maschine*⟩

tendency ['tendənsı] *n. (inclination)*
Tendenz, *die;* **have a ~ to do sth.** dazu
neigen, etw. zu tun

¹tender ['tendə(r)] *adj.* **a)** *(not tough)*
zart; b) *(loving)* zärtlich; c) *(sensitive)*
empfindlich

²tender **1.** *v.t.* **a)** *(present)* einreichen
⟨*Rücktritt*⟩; vorbringen ⟨*Entschuldi-
gung*⟩; b) *(offer as payment)* anbieten.
2. *n.* Angebot, *das*

'tenderly *adv. (gently)* behutsam; *(lovingly)* zärtlich

'tenderness *n. see* **¹tender:** Zartheit,
die; Zärtlichkeit, *die;* Empfindlichkeit, *die*

tendon ['tendən] *n. (Anat.)* Sehne, *die*
tenement ['tenımənt] *n.* Mietshaus,
das

tenet ['tenıt] *n.* Grundsatz, *der*
tenner ['tenə(r)] *n. (Brit. coll.)* Zehn-
pfundschein, *der*

tennis ['tenıs] *n.* Tennis, *das*
tennis: **~-ball** *n.* Tennisball, *der;*
~-court *n. (for lawn ~)* Tennisplatz,
der; (indoor) Tennishalle, *die;*
~-racket *n.* Tennisschläger, *der*

tenor ['tenə(r)] *n. (Mus.)* Tenor, *der*
¹tense [tens] *n. (Ling.)* Zeit, *die*
²tense **1.** *adj.* gespannt. **2.** *v.i.* **sb. ~s**
jmds. Muskeln spannen sich an. **3.**
v.t. anspannen. **tension** ['tenʃn] *n.* **a)**
Spannung, *die;* b) *(mental strain)* An-
spannung, *die*

tent [tent] *n.* Zelt, *das*
tentacle ['tentəkl] *n.* Tentakel, *der od.
das*

tentative ['tentətıv] *adj.* **a)** *(not definite)* vorläufig; b) *(hesitant)* zaghaft
tenterhooks ['tentəhʊks] *n. pl.* **be on
~:** [wie] auf glühenden Kohlen sitzen
tenth [tenθ] **1.** *adj.* zehnt... **2.** *n. (in sequence)* zehnte, *der/die/das; (in rank)*
Zehnte, *der/die/das; (fraction)* Zehntel, *das. See also* **eighth**

'tent-peg *n.* Zeltpflock, *der*
tenuous ['tenjʊəs] *adj.* dünn ⟨*Atmo-*

sphäre); dürftig (*Argument*); unbegründet (*Anspruch*)

tepid ['tepɪd] *adj.* lauwarm

term [tɜ:m] **1.** *n.* **a)** [Fach]begriff, *der;* **b)** *in pl. (conditions)* Bedingungen; **come to ~s with sth.** mit etw. zurechtkommen; *(resign oneself to sth.)* sich mit etw. abfinden; **c)** *in pl. (charges)* Konditionen; **d) in the short/long/medium ~:** kurz-/lang-/mittelfristig; **e)** *(Sch.)* Halbjahr, *das; (Univ.: one of two/three divisions per year)* Semester, *das*/Trimester, *das;* **f)** *(limited period)* Zeitraum, *der;* ~ |of office| Amtszeit, *die;* **g)** *in pl. (mode of expression)* Worte; **h)** *in pl. (relations)* **be on good/bad ~s with sb.** jit jmdm. auf gutem/schlechtem Fuß stehen. **2.** *v. t.* nennen

terminal ['tɜ:mɪnl] **1.** *n.* **a)** *(for train or bus)* Bahnhof, *der; (for airline passengers)* Terminal, *der od. das;* **b)** *(Teleph., Computing)* Terminal, *das.* **2.** *adj. (Med.)* unheilbar

terminate ['tɜ:mɪneɪt] *v. t.* **a)** beenden; lösen (*Vertrag*); **b)** *(Med.)* unterbrechen (*Schwangerschaft*). **termination** [tɜ:mɪ'neɪʃn] *n.* **a)** *no pl.* Beendigung, *die; (of lease)* Ablauf, *der;* **b)** *(Med.)* Schwangerschaftsabbruch, *der*

termini *pl. of* **terminus**

terminology [tɜ:mɪ'nɒlədʒɪ] *n.* Terminologie, *die*

terminus ['tɜ:mɪnəs] *n., pl.* **~es** *or* **termini** ['tɜ:mɪnaɪ] Endstation, *die*

terrace ['terəs, 'terɪs] *n.* Häuserreihe, *die.* **terraced house** ['terəst haʊs], 'terist haʊs] *n.* Reihenhaus, *das*

terrain [te'reɪn] *n.* Gelände, *das*

terrible ['terɪbl] *adj.* **a)** *(coll.: very great or bad)* schrecklich *(ugs.);* **b)** *(coll.: incompetent)* schlecht; **c)** *(causing terror)* furchtbar. **terribly** ['terɪblɪ] *adv.* **a)** *(coll.: very)* unheimlich *(ugs.);* **b)** *(coll.: appallingly)* furchtbar *(ugs.);* **c)** *(coll.: incompetently)* schlecht; **d)** *(fearfully)* auf erschreckende Weise

terrier ['terɪə(r)] *n.* Terrier, *der*

terrific [tə'rɪfɪk] *adj. (coll.)* **a)** *(great, intense)* irrsinnig *(ugs.);* **b)** *(magnificent)* sagenhaft *(ugs.);* **c)** *(highly expert)* klasse *(ugs.)*

terrify ['terɪfaɪ] *v. t.* **a)** angst machen (+ *Dat.*); **be terrified that ...:** Angst haben, daß ...; **b)** *(scare)* Angst einjagen (+ *Dat.*). **'terrifying** *adj.* entsetzlich (*Erlebnis, Buch*); furchterregend (*Anblick*); beängstigend (*Geschwindigkeit*)

territorial [terɪ'tɔ:rɪəl] *adj.* territorial;

Gebiets(*anspruch usw.*). **territory** ['terɪtrɪ] *n.* Gebiet, *das*

terror ['terə(r)] *n.* [panische] Angst; Schrecken, *der.* **terrorism** ['terərɪzm] *n.* Terrorismus, *der; (terrorist acts)* Terror, *der.* **'terrorist** *n.* Terrorist, *der*/Terroristin, *die.* **terrorize** ['terəraɪz] *v. t.* **a)** *(frighten)* in [Angst und] Schrecken versetzen; **b)** *(coerce)* terrorisieren

terse [tɜ:s] *adj.* **a)** *(concise)* kurz und bündig; **b)** *(curt)* knapp

test [test] **1.** *n.* **a)** *(Sch.)* Klassenarbeit, *die; (Univ.)* Klausur, *die;* **put sb./sth. to the ~:** jmdn./etw. erproben; **b)** *(analysis)* Test, *der.* **2.** *v. t.* untersuchen (*Wasser, Augen*); testen (*Gehör, Augen*); prüfen (*Schüler*); ~ **sb. for Aids** jmdn. auf Aids untersuchen. **'test out** *v. t.* ausprobieren (*Produkte*) (**on** an + *Dat.*); erproben (*Theorie, Idee*)

Testament ['testəmənt] *n.* **Old/New ~** *(Bibl.)* Altes/Neues Testament

testicle ['testɪkl] *n.* Testikel, *der (fachspr.);* Hoden, *der*

testify ['testɪfaɪ] **1.** *v. i.* **a)** ~ **to sth.** etw. bezeugen; **b)** *(Law)* ~ **against sb.** gegen jmdn. aussagen. **2.** *v. t.* bestätigen

testimonial [testɪ'məʊnɪəl] Zeugnis, *das;* Referenz, *die*

testimony ['testɪmənɪ] *n.* Aussage, *die*

'test-tube *n.* Reagenzglas, *das*

testy ['testɪ] *adj.* leicht reizbar (*Person*); gereizt (*Antwort*)

tetanus ['tetənəs] *n.* Tetanus, *der*

tetchy ['tetʃɪ] *adj.* leicht reizbar; gereizt

tether ['teðə(r)] **1.** *n.* **be at the end of one's ~:** am Ende [seiner Kraft] sein. **2.** *v. t.* anbinden (**to** an + *Dat. od. Akk.*)

text [tekst] *n.* Text, *der.* **'textbook** *n.* Lehrbuch, *das*

textile ['tekstaɪl] *n.* Stoff, *der;* ~**s** Textilien *Pl.*

texture ['tekstʃə(r)] *n.* Beschaffenheit, *die; (of fabric)* Struktur, *die*

Thai [taɪ] **1.** *adj.* thailändisch. **2.** *n.* **a)** *pl. same or* ~**s** Thai, *der/die;* **b)** *(language)* Thai, *das.* **Thailand** ['taɪlænd] *pr. n.* Thailand *(das)*

Thames [temz] *pr. n.* Themse, *die*

than [ðən, *stressed* ðæn] *conj.* als; **I know you better ~** [I do] **him** ich kenne dich besser als ihn

thank [θæŋk] *v. t.* ~ **sb.** [for sth.] jmdm. [für etw.] danken; ~ **God** *or* **goodness** *or* **heaven**[s] Gott sei Dank; [I] ~ **you**

danke; **no,** ~ **you** nein, danke; **yes,** ~ **you** ja, bitte; ~ **you very much** vielen herzlichen Dank. **thankful** [ˈθæŋkfl] *adj.* dankbar. '**thankless** *adj.* undankbar. **thanks** [θæŋks] *n.pl.* **a)** *(gratitude)* Dank, *der;* ~ **to** *(with the help of)* dank; *(on account of the bad influence of)* wegen; **b)** *(formula expr. gratitude)* danke; **no,** ~: nein, danke; **yes,** ~: ja, bitte; **many** ~ *(coll.)* vielen Dank. '**thank-you** *n. (coll.)* Dankeschön, *das*

that 1. [ðæt] *adj., pl.* **those** [ðəʊz] **a)** dieser/diese/dieses; **b)** *(coupled or contrasted with 'this')* der/die/das. **2.** [ðæt] *pron., pl.* **those a)** der/die/das; **what bird is** ~**?** was für ein Vogel ist das?; **like** ~: so; **|just| like** ~ *(without effort, thought)* einfach so; ~**'s right!** gut *od.* recht so; *(iron.)* nur so weiter!; ~ **will do** das reicht; **b)** *(Brit.)* **who is** ~**?** wer ist da?; *(on telephone)* wer ist am Apparat? **3.** [ðət] *rel. pron., pl.* **same** der/die/das; **everyone** ~ **I know** jeder, den ich kenne; **this is all |the money|** ~ **I have** das ist alles [Geld], was ich habe. **4.** [ðæt] *adv. (coll.)* so. **5.** [ðət] *rel. adv.* der/die/das; **the day** ~ **I first met her** der Tag, an dem ich sie zum ersten Mal sah. **6.** [ðət, *stressed* ðæt] *conj.* daß; **|in order|** ~: damit

thatch [θætʃ] *n. (of straw)* Strohdach, *das; (of reeds)* Schilfdach, *das; (roofing)* Dachbedeckung, *die.* **thatched** [θætʃt] *adj.* stroh-/schilfgedeckt

thaw [θɔ:] **1.** *n.* Tauwetter, *das.* **2.** *v.i.* **a)** tauen; **b)** *(melt)* auftauen. **3.** *v.t.* auftauen. **thaw 'out** *see* **thaw 2, 3**

the [*before vowel* ðɪ, *before consonant* ðə, *when stressed* ði:] **1.** *def. art.* der/die/das. **2.** *adv.* ~ **more I practise** ~ **better I play** je mehr ich übe, desto *od.* um so besser spiele ich; **so much** ~ **worse for sb./sth.** um so schlimmer für jmdn./etw.

theatre *(Amer.:* **theater)** [ˈθɪətə(r)] *n.* **a)** Theater, *das;* **b)** *(lecture* ~*)* Hörsaal, *der;* **c)** *(Brit. Med.) see* **operating theatre. theatrical** [θɪˈætrɪkl] *adj.* **a)** schauspielerisch; **b)** *(showy)* theatralisch

theft [θeft] *n.* Diebstahl, *der*

their [ðeə(r)] *poss. pron. attrib.* ihr

theirs [ðeəz] *poss. pron. pred.* ihrer/ihre/ihres

them [ðəm, *stressed* ðem] *pron.* sie; *(as indirect object)* ihnen; *see also* ¹**her**

theme [θi:m] *n.* Thema, *das*

themselves [ðəmˈselvz] *pron.* **a)** em-

phat. selbst; **b)** *refl.* sich ⟨*waschen usw.*⟩; sich selbst ⟨*die Schuld geben, regieren*⟩. *See also* **herself**

then [ðen] **1.** *adv.* **a)** *(at that time)* damals; ~ **and there** auf der Stelle; **b)** *(after that)* dann; ~ **|again|** *(and also)* außerdem; **but** ~ *(after all)* aber schließlich; **c)** *(in that case)* dann; **but** ~ **again** aber andererseits. **2.** *n.* **before** ~: vorher; davor; **since** ~: seitdem. **3.** *adj.* damalig

theological [θɪːəˈlɒdʒɪkl] *adj.* theologisch; Theologie⟨*student*⟩

theology [θɪˈɒlədʒɪ] *n.* Theologie, *die*

theoretical [θɪəˈretɪkl] *adj.* theoretisch

theory [ˈθɪərɪ] *n.* Theorie, *die;* **in** ~: theoretisch

therapeutic [θerəˈpju:tɪk] *adj.* therapeutisch

therapist [ˈθerəpɪst] *n.* Therapeut, *der*/Therapeutin, *die*

therapy [ˈθerəpɪ] *n.* Therapie, *die*

there [ðeə(r)] **1.** *adv.* **a)** *(in/at that place)* da; dort; *(fairly close)* da; **be down/in/up** ~: da unten/drin/oben sein; **b)** *(calling attention)* **hello** *or* **hi** ~**!** hallo!; **you** ~**!** Sie da!; **c)** *(in that respect)* da; **so** ~: und damit basta *(ugs.);* **d)** *(to that place)* dahin, dorthin ⟨*gehen, fahren, rücken*⟩*;* **down/up** ~: dort hinunter/hinauf; **e)** [ðə(r), *stressed* ðeə(r)] **was** ~ **anything in it?** war da irgendwas drin?; ~ **was once as** war einmal; ~ **is enough food** es gibt genug zu essen. **2.** *int.* ~, ~: na, na *(ugs.);* ~ **|you are|!** da, siehst du! **3.** *n.* da; dort; **near** ~: da *od.* dort in der Nähe. **thereabouts** [ˈðeərəbaʊts] *adv.* **a)** da [in der Nähe]; **b)** *(near that number)* ungefähr. **therefore** [ˈðeəfɔ:(r)] *adv.* deshalb; also

thermal [ˈθɜ:ml] *adj.* thermisch; ~ **underwear** kälteisolierende Unterwäsche

thermometer [θəˈmɒmɪtə(r)] *n.* Thermometer, *das*

Thermos, thermos, (P) [ˈθɜ:məs] *n.* ~ **|flask/jug/bottle|** Thermosflasche, *die* Ⓦ

thermostat [ˈθɜ:məstæt] *n.* Thermostat, *der*

these *pl. of* **this**

thesis [ˈθi:sɪs] *n., pl.* **theses** [ˈθi:si:z] **a)** *(proposition)* These, *die;* **b)** *(dissertation)* Dissertation, *die* (**on** über + *Akk.*)

they [ðeɪ] *pron.* **a)** sie; **b)** *(people in general)* man

they'd [ðeɪd] **a)** = they would; **b)** = they had

they'll [ðeɪl] = they will

they're [ðeə(r)] = they are

they've [ðeɪv] = they have

thick [θɪk] **1.** *adj.* **a)** dick; **a rope two inches ~, a two-inch ~ rope** ein zwei Zoll starkes *od.* dickes Seil; **b)** *(dense)* dicht ⟨*Haar, Nebel, Wolken usw.*⟩; **c)** *(filled)* **~ with** voll von; **d)** dickflüssig ⟨*Sahne*⟩; dick ⟨*Suppe, Schlamm, Kleister*⟩; **e)** *(stupid)* dumm. **2.** *n.* **in the ~ of** mitten in (+ *Dat.*). **thick 'ear** *n.* **give sb. a ~** *(Brit. sl.)* jmdm. ein paar hinter die Ohren geben *(ugs.)*

thicken ['θɪkn] **1.** *v.t.* dicker machen; eindicken ⟨*Sauce*⟩. **2.** *v.i.* **a)** dicker werden; **b)** ⟨*Nebel:*⟩ dichter werden; **c) the plot ~s** die Sache wird kompliziert

'thickly *adv.* **a)** *(in a thick layer)* dick; **b)** *(densely)* dicht

'thickness *n.* **a)** Dicke, *die;* **be two metres in ~:** zwei Meter dick sein; **b)** *(denseness)* Dichte, *die*

thick: ~-set *adj.* gedrungen; **~skinned** *adj. (fig.)* dickfellig *(ugs.)*

thief [θiːf] *n., pl.* **thieves** [θiːvz] Dieb, *der*/Diebin, *die*

thieve [θiːv] *v.i.* stehlen

thieves *pl. of* **thief**

thigh [θaɪ] *n.* Oberschenkel, *der*

thimble ['θɪmbl] *n.* Fingerhut, *der*

thin [θɪn] **1.** *adj.* **a)** dünn; **a tall, ~ man** ein großer, hagerer Mann; **b)** *(sparse)* dünn, schütter ⟨*Haar*⟩. **2.** *adv.* dünn. **3.** *v.t.,* **-nn-: a)** dünner machen; **b)** *(dilute)* verdünnen. **thin 'out** *v.i.* ⟨*Menschenmenge:*⟩ sich verlaufen; ⟨*Verkehr:*⟩ abnehmen

thing [θɪŋ] *n.* **a)** Sache, *die;* Ding, *das;* **what's that ~ in your hand?** was hast du da in der Hand?; **be a rare ~:** etwas Seltenes sein; **b)** *(action)* **it was the right ~ to do** es war das einzig Richtige; **that was a foolish/friendly ~ to do** das war eine große Dummheit/ das war sehr freundlich; **c)** *(fact)* [Tat]sache, *die;* **it's a strange ~ that ...:** es ist seltsam, daß ...; **the best/worst ~ about her** das Beste/Schlimmste an ihr; **d)** *(idea)* **say the first ~ that comes into one's head** das sagen, was einem gerade so einfällt; **what a ~ to say!** wie kann man nur so etwas sagen!; **e)** *(task)* **she has a reputation for getting ~s done** sie ist für ihre Tatkraft bekannt; **a big ~ to undertake** ein großes Unterfangen; **f)** *(affair)* Sache, *die;* Angelegenheit, *die;* **g)** *(circumstance)*

take ~s too seriously alles zu ernst nehmen; **how are ~s?** wie geht's [dir]?; **h)** *(individual, creature)* Ding, *das;* **i)** *in pl. (personal belongings, clothes)* Sachen; **j)** *(product of work)* Sache, *die;* **the latest ~:** der letzte Schrei; **k)** *(what is important or proper)* das Richtige; **the ~ is ...** *(question)* die Frage ist ...

think [θɪŋk] **1.** *v.t.,* **thought** [θɔːt] **a)** *(consider)* meinen; **we ~ |that| he will come** wir denken *od.* glauben, daß er kommt; **what do you ~?** was meinst du? **do you really ~ so?** findest du wirklich?; **what do you ~ of him/it?** was hältst du von ihm/davon?; **..., don't you ~?** ..., findest *od.* meinst du nicht auch?; **I ~ so/not** ich glaube schon/nicht; **I ~ I'll try** ich glaube, ich werde es versuchen; **b)** *(imagine)* sich *(Dat.)* vorstellen. **2.** *v.i.,* **thought** [nach]denken; **I need time to ~:** ich muß es mir erst überlegen; **I've been ~ing** ich habe nachgedacht; **~ twice** es sich *(Dat.)* zweimal überlegen. **'think of** *v.t.* **a)** denken an (+ *Akk.*); **he ~s of everything** er denkt einfach an alles; **b)** *(have as idea)* **we'll ~ of something** wir werden uns etwas einfallen lassen; **can you ~ of anyone who ...?** fällt dir jemand ein, der ...?; **c)** *(remember)* sich erinnern an (+ *Akk.*); **I just can't ~ of her name** ich komme einfach nicht auf ihren Namen; **d)** **~ little/nothing of sb./sth.** *(consider contemptible)* wenig/nichts von jmdm./ etw. halten. **think 'over** *v.t.* sich *(Dat.)* überlegen. **think 'through** *v.t.* [gründlich] durchdenken. **think 'up** *v.t. (coll.)* sich *(Dat.)* ausdenken

'thinker *n.* Denker, *der*/Denkerin, *die*

third [θɜːd] **1.** *adj.* dritt... **2.** *n. (in sequence)* dritte, *der/die/das;* *(in rank)* Dritte, *der/die/das;* *(fraction)* Drittel, *das. See also* **eighth.** **'thirdly** *adv.* drittens

'third-rate *adj.* drittklassig

Third 'World *n.* dritte Welt

thirst [θɜːst] **1.** *n.* Durst, *der;* **die of ~:** verdursten. **2.** *v.i.* **~ for revenge/ knowledge** nach Rache/Wissen dürsten *(geh.).* **'thirsty** *adj.* durstig; **be ~:** Durst haben

thirteen [θɜː'tiːn] **1.** *adj.* dreizehn. **2.** *n.* Dreizehn, *die. See also* **eight. thirteenth** [θɜː'tiːnθ] *adj.* dreizehnt... *See also* **eighth**

thirtieth ['θɜːtɪɪθ] **1.** *adj.* dreißigst... **2.** *n. (fraction)* Dreißigstel, *das. See also* **eighth**

thirty ['θɜ:tɪ] 1. *adj.* dreißig. 2. *n.* Dreißig, *die. See also* **eight; eighty 2**
this [ðɪs] 1. *adj., pl.* **these** [ði:z] dieser/
diese/dieses; *(with less emphasis)* der/
die/das; **at ~ time** zu dieser Zeit; **by ~
time** inzwischen; mittlerweile; **these
days** heut[zutag]e; **before ~ time** vorher; zuvor; **all ~ week** die[se] ganze
Woche; **~ morning/evening** *etc.* heute
morgen/abend *usw.;* **these last three
weeks** die letzten drei Wochen; **~
Monday** *(to come)* nächsten Montag.
2. *pron., pl.* **these a) what's ~?** was ist
[denn] das?; **fold it like ~!** falte es so!;
b) *(the present)* **before ~:** bis jetzt; **c)**
(Brit. Teleph.: person speaking) **~ is
Andy** hier [spricht *od.* ist] Andy;
(Amer. Teleph.) **who did you say ~ was?**
wer ist am apparat?; **d) ~ and that** dies
und das
thistle ['θɪsl] *n.* Distel, *die*
thorn [θɔ:n] *n.* **a)** *(part of plant)* Dorn,
der; **b)** *(plant)* Dornenstrauch, *der.*
'thorny *adj.* **a)** dornig; **b)** *(fig.)* heikel
thorough ['θʌrə] *adj.* gründlich
thorough: ~bred *n.* reinrassiges
Tier; *(horse)* Rassepferd, *das;* **~fare**
n. Durchfahrtsstraße, *die;* **'no ~fare'**
„Durchfahrt verboten"; *(on foot)*
„kein Durchgang"
'thoroughly *adv.* gründlich ⟨unter-
suchen⟩; gehörig ⟨erschöpft⟩; so richtig ⟨genießen⟩; zutiefst ⟨beschämt⟩; total ⟨verdorben, verwöhnt⟩; **be ~ fed up
with sth.** *(sl.)* von etw. die Nase gestrichen voll haben *(ugs.).* **'thoroughness** *n.* Gründlichkeit, *die*
those *see* **that 1, 2**
though [ðəʊ] 1. *(conj.)* **a)** *(despite the
fact that)* obwohl; **late ~ it was** obwohl es so spät war; **the car, ~ powerful, is also economical** der Wagen ist
zwar stark, aber [zugleich] auch wirtschaftlich; **b)** *(but nevertheless)* aber; **a
slow ~ certain method** eine langsame,
aber *od.* wenn auch sichere Methode;
c) *(even if)* [even] **~:** auch wenn; **d)**
(and yet) **~ you never know** obwohl
man nie weiß. 2. *adv. (coll.)* trotzdem
thought [θɔ:t] 1. *see* **think.** 2. *n.* **a)** no
pl. Denken, *das;* **b)** no *pl., no art. (reflection)* Überlegung, *die;* Nachdenken, *das;* **c)** *(consideration)* Rücksicht,
die (**for** auf + *Akk.*); **d)** *(idea, conception)* Gedanke, *der;* **it's the ~ that
counts** der gute Wille zählt; **give up all
~[s] of sth.** sich *(Dat.)* etw. aus dem
Kopf schlagen. **thoughtful** ['θɔ:tfl]
adj. **a)** nachdenklich; **b)** *(considerate)*

rücksichtsvoll; *(helpful)* aufmerksam.
'thoughtfully *adv.* **a)** nachdenklich;
b) *(considerately)* rücksichtsvollerwei-
se. **'thoughtless** *adj.* **a)** gedankenlos; **b)** *(inconsiderate)* rücksichtslos.
'thoughtlessly *adv.* **a)** gedankenlos; **b)** *(inconsiderately)* aus Rück-
sichtslosigkeit
thousand ['θaʊznd] 1. *adj.* **a)** tausend; **a** *or* **one ~:** eintausend; **two/sev-
eral ~:** zweitausend/mehrere tau-
send; **a** *or* **one ~ and one** [ein]tau-
send[und]eins; **b) a ~** [**and one**] *(fig.:
innumerable)* tausend *(ugs.).* 2. *n.* **a)**
(number) tausend; **a** *or* **one/two ~:**
ein-/zweitausend; **b)** *(written figure;
group)* Tausend, *das;* **c)** *(indefinite
amount)* **~s** Tausende. **thousandth**
['θaʊzndθ] 1. *adj.* tausendst... 2. *n.*
(fraction) Tausendstel, *das; (in sequence)* Tausendste, *der/die/das*
thrash [θræʃ] *v.t.* **a)** verprügeln; **b)**
(defeat) vernichtend ~ schlagen.
thrash 'out *v.t.* ausdiskutieren
thread [θred] 1. *n.* **a)** Faden, *der;* **b)** *(of
screw)* Gewinde, *das.* 2. *v.t.* **a)** einfädeln; auffädeln ⟨Perlen⟩; **b) ~ one's
way through sth.** sich durch etw.
schlängeln. **'threadbare** *adj.* abgenutzt; abgetragen ⟨Kleidung⟩; *(fig.)*
abgedroschen ⟨Argument⟩
threat [θret] *n.* Drohung, *die.*
threaten ['θretn] *v.t.* **a)** bedrohen; **~
sb. with sth.** jmdm. etw. androhen; **b)
~ to do sth.** damit drohen, etw. zu tun;
c) drohen mit ⟨Gewalt, Rache *usw.*⟩.
threatening ['θretnɪŋ] *adj.* drohend
three [θri:] 1. *adj.* drei. 2. *n.* Drei, *die.*
See also **eight**
three: ~-dimensional [θri:dɪ'men-
ʃnl] *adj.* dreidimensional; **~fold**
adj., adv. dreifach; **a ~fold increase**
ein Anstieg auf das Dreifache;
~-quarters 1. *n.* **a)** drei Viertel *pl.*
(**of** + *Gen.*); **~-quarters of an hour** eine Dreiviertelstunde; 2. *adv.* dreiviertel ⟨voll⟩; **~some** ['θri:səm] *n.* Drei-
gespann, *das;* Trio, *das*
thresh [θreʃ] *v.t.* dreschen
threshold ['θreʃəʊld] *n.* Schwelle, *die*
threw *see* **throw 1**
thrift [θrɪft] *n.* Sparsamkeit, *die.*
'thrifty *adj.* sparsam
thrill [θrɪl] 1. *v.t.* **a)** *(excite)* faszinieren; **b)** *(delight)* begeistern. 2. *n.* **a)** Erregung, *die;* **b)** *(exciting experience)*
aufregendes Erlebnis. **'thriller** *n.*
Thriller, *der.* **'thrilling** *adj.* aufregend; spannend ⟨Buch, Film⟩

thrive [θraɪv] *v. i.,* **thrived** *or* **throve** [θrəʊv], **thrived** *or* **thriven** ['θrɪvn] **a)** ⟨*Pflanze:*⟩ wachsen und gedeihen; **b)** *(prosper)* aufblühen **(on** bei)

throat [θrəʊt] *n.* Hals, *der; (esp. inside)* Kehle, *die;* **a |sore| ~:** Halsschmerzen

throb [θrɒb] **1.** *v. i.,* **-bb-** pochen; ⟨*Motor:*⟩ dröhnen. **2.** *n.* Pochen, *das; (of engine)* Dröhnen, *das*

throes [θrəʊz] *n. pl.* Qual, *die;* **be in the ~ of** sth. *(fig.)* mitten in etw. *(Dat.)* stecken *(ugs.)*

thrombosis [θrɒm'bəʊsɪs] *n., pl.* **thromboses** [θrɒm'bəʊsiːz] Thrombose, *die*

throne [θrəʊn] *n.* Thron, *der*

throng [θrɒŋ] *n.* [Menschen]menge, *die*

throttle ['θrɒtl] *v. t.* erdrosseln

through [θruː] **1.** *prep.* **a)** durch; **b)** *(Amer.: up to and including)* bis [einschließlich]; **c)** *(by reason of)* durch; infolge von ⟨*Vernachlässigung, Einflüssen*⟩. **2.** *adv.* **a)** let sb. **~:** jmdn. durchlassen; **b)** *(Teleph.)* **be ~:** durch sein *(ugs.);* **be ~ to** sb. mit jmdm. verbunden sein. **3.** *attrib. adj.* durchgehend ⟨*Zug*⟩. **through'out 1.** *prep.* **~ the war/period** den ganzen Krieg/die ganze Zeit hindurch; **~ the country** im ganzen Land. **2.** *adv. (entirely)* ganz; *(always)* stets; die ganze Zeit [hindurch]

throve *see* **thrive**

throw [θrəʊ] **1.** *v. t.,* **threw** [θruː], **thrown** [θrəʊn] **a)** werfen; **~ sth. to** sb. jmdm. etw. zuwerfen; **~ sth. at** sb. etw. nach jmdm. werfen; **b)** *(bring to the ground)* zu Boden werfen; abwerfen ⟨*Reiter*⟩; **c)** *(coll.: disconcert)* ⟨*Frage:*⟩ aus der Fassung bringen. **2.** *n.* Wurf, *der.* **throw a'way** *v. t.* **a)** wegwerfen; **b)** *(lose by neglect)* verschenken ⟨*Vorteil, Spiel usw.*⟩. **throw 'up 1.** *v. t.* **a)** hochwerfen ⟨*Arme, Hände*⟩; **b)** *(produce)* hervorbringen ⟨*Ideen usw.*⟩. **2.** *v. i. (coll.)* brechen *(ugs.)*

'throw-away *adj.* **a)** Wegwerf-; Einweg-; **b)** beiläufig ⟨*Bemerkung*⟩

thrown *see* **throw** 1

thrush [θrʌʃ] *n. (Ornith.)* Drossel, *die*

thrust [θrʌst] **1.** *v. t.,* **thrust** stoßen; **~ aside** *(fig.)* beiseite schieben. **2.** *n.* Stoß, *der*

thud [θʌd] *n.* dumpfer Schlag

thug [θʌg] *n.* Schläger, *der*

thumb [θʌm] **1.** *n.* Daumen, *der;* **get the ~s up** ⟨*Person, Projekt:*⟩ akzeptiert

werden; **be under** sb.'s **~:** unter jmds. Fuchtel stehen. **2.** *v. t.* **~ a lift** per Anhalter fahren. **'thumb through** *v. t.* durchblättern

thumb: ~ index *n.* Daumenregister, *das;* **~tack** *n. (Amer.)* Reißzwecke, *die*

thump [θʌmp] **1.** *v. t.* [mit Wucht] schlagen. **2.** *v. i.* **a)** hämmern **(at, on** gegen); **b)** ⟨*Herz:*⟩ heftig pochen. **3.** *n. (blow)* Schlag, *der; (sound)* Bums, *der (ugs.);* dumpfer Schlag

thunder ['θʌndə(r)] **1.** *n.* Donner, *der.* **2.** *v. i.* donnern. **'thunderclap** *n.* Donnerschlag, *der.* **'thunderstorm** *n.* Gewitter, *das.* **'thundery** *adj.* gewittrig

Thurs. *abbr.* **Thursday** Do.

Thursday ['θɜːzdeɪ, 'θɜːzdɪ] *n.* Donnerstag, *der; see also* **Friday**

thus [ðʌs] *adv.* so

thwart [θwɔːt] *v. t.* durchkreuzen ⟨*Pläne*⟩; vereiteln ⟨*Versuch*⟩; **~ sb.** jmdm. einen Strich durch die Rechnung machen

thyme [taɪm] *n.* Thymian, *der*

thyroid ['θaɪrɔɪd] *n.* Schilddrüse, *die*

tiara [tɪ'ɑːrə] *n.* Diadem, *das*

tick [tɪk] **1.** *v. i.* ticken. **2.** *v. t.* **a)** mit einem Häkchen versehen; **b)** *see* **~ off a. 3.** *n.* **a)** *(of clock etc.)* Ticken, *das;* **b)** *(mark)* Häkchen, *das.* **tick 'off** *v. t.* **a)** *(cross off)* abhaken; **b)** *(coll.: reprimand)* rüffeln *(ugs.)*

ticket ['tɪkɪt] *n.* Karte, *die; (for bus, train)* Fahrschein, *der; (for aeroplane)* Flugschein, *der; (for lottery, raffle)* Los, *das; (for library)* Ausweis, *der;* **price ~:** Preisschild, *das.* **'ticket-collector** *n. (on train)* Schaffner, *der/*Schaffnerin, *die; (on station)* Fahrkartenkontrolleur, *der/*-kontrolleurin, *die.* **'ticket-office** *n.* Fahrkartenschalter, *der; (for advance booking)* Kartenvorverkaufsstelle, *die*

tickle ['tɪkl] **1.** *v. t.* kitzeln. **2.** *v. i.* kitzeln. **ticklish** ['tɪklɪʃ] *adj.* kitzlig

tidal ['taɪdl] *adj.* Gezeiten-. **'tidal wave** *n.* Flutwelle, *die*

tiddly-winks ['tɪdlɪwɪŋks] *n. sing. (game)* Flohhüpfen, *das*

tide [taɪd] **1.** *n.* Tide, *die (nordd.);* **high ~:** Flut, *die;* **low ~:** Ebbe, *die;* **the ~s** die Gezeiten; **the ~ is in/out** es ist Flut/Ebbe. **2.** *v. t.* **~ sb. over** jmdm. über die Runden helfen *(ugs.)*

tidiness ['taɪdɪnɪs] *n.* Ordentlichkeit, *die*

tidy ['taɪdɪ] **1.** *adj.* ordentlich; aufge-

räumt ⟨*Zimmer, Schreibtisch*⟩. **2.** *v.t.*
aufräumen; ~ **oneself** sich zurechtma-
chen. **tidy 'up** *v.i.* aufräumen
tie [taɪ] **1.** *v.t.,* **tying** ['taɪɪŋ] binden (**to**
an + *Akk.,* **into** zu); ~ **a knot** einen
Knoten machen; *(Sport)* ~ **the match**
unentschieden spielen. **2.** *v.i.,* **tying a)**
(be fastened) **it ~s at the back** es wird
hinten gebunden; **b)** *(have equal
scores)* ~ **for second place** mit gleicher
Punktzahl den zweiten Platz errei-
chen. **3.** *n.* **a)** Krawatte, *die;* **b)** *(bond)*
Band, *das; (restriction)* Bindung, *die;*
c) *(equality of scores)* Punktgleichheit,
die; **d)** *(Sport: match)* Begegnung, *die.*
tie 'in *v.i.* ~ **in with sth.** zu etw. passen. **tie 'up** *v.t.* **a)** festbinden; ~ **up a
parcel** ein Paket verschnüren; **b)** *(keep
busy)* beschäftigen
tier [tɪə(r)] *n.* **a)** Rang, *der;* **b)** *(unit)*
Stufe, *die*
tiger ['taɪɡə(r)] *n.* Tiger, *der*
tight [taɪt] **1.** *adj.* **a)** *(firm)* fest; fest angezogen ⟨*Schraube, Mutter*⟩; festsit-
zend ⟨*Deckel*⟩; **b)** *(close-fitting)* eng
⟨*Kleid, Schuh usw.*⟩; **c)** *(impermeable)*
~ **seal/joint** dichter Verschluß/dichte
Fuge; **d)** *(taut)* straff; **e)** *(difficult to
negotiate)* **a** ~ **corner** eine enge Kurve;
be in a ~ **corner** *(fig.)* in der Klemme
sein *(ugs.);* **f)** *(strict)* streng ⟨*Kontrolle,
Disziplin*⟩; **g)** *(coll.: stingy)* knauserig
(ugs.); **h)** *(coll.: drunk)* voll *(salopp).* **2.**
adv. fest; **hold** ~! halt dich fest! **3.** *n.
in pl.* **a)** *(Brit.)* |**pair of**| ~s Strumpfho-
se, *die;* **b)** *(of dancer etc.)* Trikothose,
die. **tighten** ['taɪtn] **1.** *v.t.* **a)** |fest| an-
ziehen ⟨*Knoten, Schraube*⟩; straffzie-
hen ⟨*Seil*⟩; **b)** verschärfen ⟨*Kontrolle*⟩.
2. *v.i.* sich spannen. **tight-fisted**
[taɪt'fɪstɪd] *adj.* geizig. **'tightrope** *n.*
Drahtseil, *das*
tile [taɪl] **1.** *n. (on roof)* Ziegel, *der; (on
floor, wall)* Fliese, *die;* Kachel, *die.* **2.**
v.t. [mit Ziegeln] decken ⟨*Dach*⟩; flie-
sen ⟨*Wand, Fußboden*⟩; kacheln
⟨*Wand*⟩
¹till [tɪl] **1.** *prep.* bis; *(followed by article
+ noun)* bis zu; **not** |...| ~: erst. **2.**
conj. bis
²till *n.* Kasse, *die*
tilt [tɪlt] **1.** *v.i.* kippen. **2.** *v.t.* kippen;
neigen ⟨*Kopf*⟩. **3.** *n.* **a)** Schräglage,
die; **a 45°** ~: eine Neigung von 45°; **b)**
|at| **full** ~: mit voller Wucht
timber ['tɪmbə(r)] *n.* [Bau]holz, *das*
time [taɪm] **1.** *n.* **a)** Zeit, *die;* **in |the
course of|** ~, **as** ~ **goes on/went on** mit
der Zeit; im Laufe der Zeit; **in** ~, **with**

~ *(sooner or later)* mit der Zeit; **in
|good|** ~ *(not late)* rechtzeitig; **all the**
or this ~: die ganze Zeit; *(without
ceasing)* ständig; **a short** ~ **ago** vor
kurzem; ~ **off** *or* **out** freie Zeit; **in 'no**
~: im Handumdrehen; **in a**
week's/year's ~: in einer Woche/in einem Jahr; **harvest/Christmas** ~: Ern-
te-/Weihnachtszeit, *die;* **on** ~ *(punctually)* pünktlich; **ahead of** ~: zu früh
⟨*ankommen*⟩; vorzeitig ⟨*fertig werden*⟩; **have a good** ~: sich amüsieren;
Spaß haben *(ugs.);* **b)** *(occasion)* Mal,
das; **for the first** ~: zum ersten Mal;
at ~s gelegentlich; ~ **and again,** ~
after ~: immer [und immer] wieder; **at
one** ~, **at |one and| the same** ~ *(simulta-
neously)* gleichzeitig; **one at a** ~: einzeln; **two at a** ~: jeweils zwei; **c)** *(point
in day etc.)* [Uhr]zeit, *die;* **tell the** ~:
die Uhr lesen; **what** ~ **is it?, what is the
~?** wie spät ist es?; **by this/that** ~: in-
zwischen; **by the** ~ |**that**| **we arrived** bis
wir hinkamen; **d)** *(multiplication)* mal;
three ~s **four** drei mal vier; **e)** *(Mus.)*
Takt, *der;* **in** ~: im Takt. **2.** *v.t.* **a)** zeitlich abstimmen; **be well** ~d zur richti-
gen Zeit kommen; **b)** *(set to operate at
correct* ~*)* einstellen; **c)** *(measure* ~
taken by) stoppen
time: ~ **bomb** *n.* Zeitbombe, *die;*
~**-lag** *n.* zeitliche Verzögerung;
~**-limit** *n.* Frist, *die*
timely ['taɪmlɪ] *adj.* rechtzeitig
time: ~**-scale** *n.* Zeitskala, *die;*
~**-switch** *n.* Zeitschalter, *der;*
~**-table** *n.* **a)** *(scheme of work)* Zeitplan, *der; (Educ.)* Stundenplan, *der;*
b) *(Transport)* Fahrplan, *der;* ~**-zone**
n. Zeitzone, *die*
timid ['tɪmɪd] *adj.* **a)** scheu ⟨*Tier*⟩; **b)**
zaghaft ⟨*Mensch*⟩; *(shy)* schüchtern
timing ['taɪmɪŋ] *n.* **a) that was perfect
~!** du kommst gerade im richtigen
Augenblick!; **b)** *(Theatre, Sport)*
Timing, *das*
tin [tɪn] **1.** *n.* **a)** *(metal)* Zinn, *das;*
~**|-plate|** Weißblech, *das;* **b)** *(Brit.: for
preserving)* [Konserven]dose, *die.* **2.**
v.t., **-nn-** *(Brit.)* zu Konserven verarbeiten. **tin 'foil** *n.* Stanniol, *das;* Alufolie, *die*
tinge [tɪndʒ] **1.** *v.t.,* ~**ing** ['tɪndʒɪŋ] tönen. **2.** *n.* [leichte] Färbung; *(fig.)*
Hauch, *der*
tingle ['tɪŋɡl] *v.i.* kribbeln
tinker ['tɪŋkə(r)] **1.** *n.* Kesselflicker,
der. **2.** *v.i.* ~ **with sth.** an etw. *(Dat.)*
herumbasteln *(ugs.)*

tinkle ['tɪŋkl] **1.** *n.* Klingeln, *das.* **2.**
v.i. klingeln
tinned [tɪnd] *adj. (Brit.)* Dosen-
tin: ~-**opener** *n. (Brit.)* Dosenöffner,
der. ~**pot** *attrib. adj. (derog.)* schäbig
tinsel ['tɪnsl] *n.* Lametta, *die*
tint [tɪnt] **1.** *n.* Farbton, *der.* **2.** *v.t.* tönen; kolorieren ⟨*Zeichnung*⟩
tiny ['taɪnɪ] *adj.* winzig
¹tip [tɪp] *n. (end, point)* Spitze, *die*
²tip 1. *v.i.,* -pp- *(lean, fall)* kippen; ~
over umkippen. **2.** *v.t.,* -pp-: **a)** *(make
tilt)* kippen; **b)** *(make overturn)* umkippen; *(Brit.: discharge)* kippen; **c)**
voraussagen ⟨*Sieger*⟩; ~ **sb. to win** auf
jmds. Sieg tippen; **d)** *(reward)* ~ **sb.**
jmdm. Trinkgeld geben. **3.** *n.* **a)**
(money) Trinkgeld, *das;* **b)** *(special information)* Hinweis, *der;* Tip, *der
(ugs.);* **c)** *(Brit.)* Müllkippe, *die.* **tip
'off** *v.t.* ~ **sb. off** jmdm. einen Hinweis *od. (ugs.)* Tip geben
'tip-off *n.* Hinweis, *der*
tipsy ['tɪpsɪ] *adj. (coll.)* angeheitert; beschwipst *(ugs.)*
tip: ~**toe 1.** *v.i.* auf Zehenspitzen ge-
hen; **2.** *n.* **on** ~**toe|s|** auf Zehenspit-
zen; ~**top** *adj.* tipptopp *(ugs.)*
¹tire ['taɪə(r)] *(Amer.) see* **tyre**
²tire 1. *v.t.* ermüden. **2.** *v.i.* müde werden; ermüden; ~ **of sth./doing sth.** einer Sache *(Gen.)* überdrüssig werden.
tire 'out *v.t.* erschöpfen; ~ **oneself
out doing sth.** etw. bis zur Erschöpfung tun
tired ['taɪəd] *adj.* **a)** *(weary)* müde; **b)**
(fed up) **be** ~ **of sth./doing sth.** etw.
satt haben/es satt haben etw. zu tun.
'tireless *adj.* unermüdlich. **tiresome** ['taɪəsəm] *adj.* **a)** *(wearisome)*
mühsam; **b)** *(annoying)* lästig. **tiring**
['taɪərɪŋ] *adj.* ermüdend
tissue ['tɪʃuː, 'tɪsjuː] *n.* **a)** Gewebe,
das; **b)** |**paper**| ~: Papiertuch, *das;
(handkerchief)* Papiertaschentuch,
das; **c)** ~ |**paper**| Seidenpapier, *das*
¹tit [tɪt] *n. (Ornith.)* Meise, *die*
²tit *n.* it's ~ **for tat** wie du mir, so ich
dir
'titb.‹ *n.* **a)** *(food)* Häppchen, *das
(ugs.);* **b)** *(piece of news)* Neuigkeit, *die*
title ['taɪtl] *n.* Titel, *der.* **'title-role** *n.*
Titelrolle, *die*
tittle-tattle ['tɪtltætl] *n.* Klatsch, *der
(ugs.)*
to 1. [*before vowel* tʊ, *before consonant*
tə, *stressed* tuː] *prep.* **a)** *(in the direction
of and reaching)* zu; *(with name of
place)* nach; **go to work/to the theatre**

zur Arbeit/ins Theater gehen; **to
France** nach Frankreich; **b)** *(as far as)*
bis zu; **from London to Edinburgh** von
London [bis] nach Edinburgh; **increase from 10 % to 20 %** von 10 % auf
20 % steigen; **c)** *introducing relationship or indirect object* **to sb./sth.**
jmdm./einer Sache *(Dat.);* **lend/ex-
plain** *etc.* **sth. to sb.** jmdm. etw. leihen/
erklären *usw.;* **speak to sb.** mit jmdm.
sprechen; **that's all there is to it** mehr
ist nicht dazu zu sagen; **what's that to
you?** was geht das dich an?; **to me** *(in
my opinion)* meiner Meinung nach; **14
miles to the gallon** 14 Meilen auf eine
Gallone; **d)** *(until)* bis; **to the end** bis
zum Ende; **to this day** bis heute; **five
|minutes| to eight** fünf [Minuten] vor
acht; **e)** *with infinitive of a verb* zu;
expr. purpose, or after **too** um [...] zu;
want to know wissen wollen; **do sth. to
annoy sb.** etw. tun, um jmdn. zu ärgern; **too hot to drink** zu heiß zum
Trinken; **he must have phoned but
forgot to** er hätte angerufen, aber er
vergaß es. **2.** [tuː] *adv.* **to and fro** hin
und her
toad [təʊd] *n. (also fig. derog.)* Kröte,
die
'toadstool *n.* Giftpilz, *der*
toast [təʊst] **1.** *n.* **a)** *no pl.* Toast, *der;* **a
piece of** ~: eine Scheibe Toast; **b)** *(call
to drink)* Toast, *der;* **drink a** ~ **to sb./
sth.** auf jmdn./etw. trinken. **2.** *v.t.* **a)**
rösten; toasten ⟨*Brot*⟩; **b)** *(drink to)*
trinken auf (+ *Akk.*). **'toaster** *n.*
Toaster, *der*
tobacco [tə'bækəʊ] *n., pl.* ~**s** Tabak,
der. **tobacconist** [tə'bækənɪst] *n.*
Tabak[waren]händler, *der*/-**händlerin,** *die*
toboggan [tə'bɒgən] **1.** *n.* Schlitten,
der. **2.** *v.i.* Schlitten fahren
today [tə'deɪ] **1.** *n.* heute; ~**'s newspaper** die Zeitung von heute. **2.** *adv.*
heute
toddler ['tɒdlə(r)] *n.* ≈ Kleinkind, *das*
to-do [tə'duː] *n.* Getue, *das (ugs.)*
toe [təʊ] **1.** *n.* Zeh, *der;* Zehe, *die; (of
footwear)* Spitze, *die.* **2.** *v.t.,* ~**ing**
(fig.) ~ **the line** *or (Amer.)* **mark** sich
einordnen. **'toe-nail** *n.* Zeh[en]nagel,
der
toffee ['tɒfɪ] *n.* Karamel, *der; (Brit.:
piece)* Toffee, *das;* Sahnebonbon, *das*
together [tə'geðə(r)] *adv.* **a)** *(in or into
company)* zusammen; **b)** *(simultaneously)* gleichzeitig; **c)** *(one with
another)* miteinander

toil [tɔɪl] 1. *v.i.* schwer arbeiten. 2. *n.* [harte] Arbeit

toilet ['tɔɪlɪt] *n.* Toilette, *die.* '**toilet-bag** *n.* Kulturbeutel, *der.* '**toilet-paper** *n.* Toilettenpapier, *das*

toiletries ['tɔɪlɪtrɪz] *n. pl.* Körperpflegemittel; Toilettenartikel

toilet: ~-roll *n.* Rolle Toilettenpapier; **~ water** *n.* Toilettenwasser, *das;* Eau de Toilette, *das*

token ['təʊkn] 1. *n.* **a)** *(voucher)* Gutschein, *der;* **b)** *(counter, disc)* Marke, *die;* **c)** *(sign)* Zeichen, *das.* 2. *attrib. adj.* symbolisch ⟨*Preis*⟩

Tokyo ['təʊkjəʊ] *pr. n.* Tokio *(das)*

told *see* **tell**

tolerable ['tɒlərəbl] *adj.* **a)** *(endurable)* erträglich (**to, for** für); **b)** *(fairly good)* leidlich; annehmbar. **tolerance** ['tɒlərəns] *n.* Toleranz, *die.* **tolerant** ['tɒlərənt] *adj.* tolerant (**of, towards** gegen[über]). **tolerate** ['tɒləreɪt] *v.t.* dulden; *(bear)* ertragen ⟨*Schmerzen*⟩. **toleration** [tɒlə'reɪʃn] *n.* Tolerierung, *die (geh.)*

¹**toll** [təʊl] *n.* **a)** Gebühr, *die;* **b)** *(damage etc.)* Aufwand, *der;* **take its ~ of sth.** einen Tribut an etw. *(Dat.)* fordern *(fig.)*

²**toll** *v.i.* ⟨*Glocke:*⟩ läuten

'**toll-bridge** *n.* gebührenpflichtige Brücke

tom [tɒm] *n. (cat)* Kater, *der*

tomato [tə'mɑːtəʊ] *n., pl.* ~**es** Tomate, *die.* **to'mato juice** *n.* Tomatensaft, *der.* **tomato 'purée** *n.* Tomatenmark, *das*

tomb [tuːm] *n.* Grab, *das; (monument)* Grabmal, *das*

'**tomboy** *n.* Wildfang, *der*

'**tombstone** *n.* Grabstein, *der*

'**tom-cat** *n.* Kater, *der*

tome [təʊm] *n.* dicker Band; Wälzer, *der (ugs.)*

tomfoolery [tɒm'fuːlərɪ] *n.* Blödsinn, *der (ugs.)*

tomorrow [tə'mɒrəʊ] 1. *n.* morgen; **~ morning/afternoon/evening/night** morgen früh *od.* vormittag/nachmittag/abend/nacht; **~'s newspaper** die morgige Zeitung. 2. *adv.* morgen; **see you ~!** *(coll.)* bis morgen!; **the day after ~:** übermorgen

ton [tʌn] *n.* Tonne, *die*

tone [təʊn] 1. *n.* **a)** *(sound)* Klang, *der; (Teleph.)* Ton, *der;* **b)** *(style of speaking)* Ton, *der;* **c)** *(tint, shade)* [Farb]ton, *der;* **d)** *(fig.: character)* **lower/raise the ~ of sth.** das Niveau einer Sache *(Gen.)* senken/erhöhen; **set the ~:** den Ton angeben. 2. *v.t.* tönen; abtönen ⟨*Farbe*⟩. **tone 'down** *v.t.* [ab]dämpfen ⟨*Farbe*⟩; *(fig.)* mäßigen ⟨*Sprache*⟩

tongs [tɒŋz] *n.pl.* |**pair of**| ~: Zange, *die*

tongue [tʌŋ] *n.* Zunge, *die;* **bite one's ~** *(lit. or fig.)* sich auf die Zunge beißen; **find one's ~:** seine Sprache wiederfinden; **hold one's ~:** stillschweigen; **he made the remark ~ in cheek** *(fig.)* er meinte die Bemerkung nicht ernst. '**tongue-twister** *n.* Zungenbrecher, *der (ugs.)*

tonic ['tɒnɪk] 1. *n.* **a)** *(Med.)* Tonikum, *das;* **b)** *(fig.: invigorating influence)* Wohltat, *die (geh.);* **c)** *(~ water)* Tonic, *das.* 2. *attrib. adj.* kräftigend; *(fig.)* wohltuend ⟨*Wirkung*⟩. '**tonic water** *n.* Tonic[wasser], *das*

tonight [tə'naɪt] 1. *n.* **a)** *(this evening)* heute abend; ~**'s performance** die heutige [Abend]vorstellung; **b)** *(this or the coming night)* heute nacht. 2. *adv.* **a)** *(this evening)* heute abend; **b)** *(during this or the coming night)* heute nacht; |**I'll**| **see you ~!** bis heute abend!

tonne [tʌn] *n.* [metrische] Tonne

tonsil ['tɒnsl] *n.* [Gaumen]mandel, *die;* **have one's ~s out** sich *(Dat.)* die Mandeln herausnehmen lassen. **tonsillitis** [tɒnsə'laɪtɪs] *n.* Mandelentzündung, *die*

too [tuː] *adv.* **a)** *(excessively)* zu; ~ **difficult a task** eine zu schwierige Aufgabe; **b)** *(also)* auch; **c)** *(coll.: very)* besonders; **not ~ pleased** nicht gerade erfreut

took *see* **take**

tool [tuːl] *n.* Werkzeug, *das; (garden ~)* Gerät, *das;* |**set of**| ~**s** Werkzeug, *das.* '**tool box** *n.* Werkzeugkasten, *der.* '**tool kit** *n.* Werkzeug, *das*

toot [tuːt] 1. *v.i. (on car etc. horn)* hupen. 2. *n.* Tuten, *das*

tooth [tuːθ] *n., pl.* **teeth** [tiːθ] **a)** Zahn, *der;* **b)** *(of rake, fork, comb)* Zinke, *die; (of cog-wheel, saw)* Zahn, *der*

tooth: ~ache *n.* Zahnschmerzen *Pl.;* **~-brush** *n.* Zahnbürste, *die;* ~**paste** *n.* Zahnpasta, *die;* ~**pick** *n.* Zahnstocher, *der*

¹**top** [tɒp] 1. *n.* **a)** *(highest part)* Spitze, *die; (of table)* Platte, *die; (~ end)* oberes Ende; *(of tree)* Wipfel, *der; (~ floor)* oberstes Stockwerk; *(rim of glass)* Rand, *der;* **on ~ of one another**

aufeinander; **on ~ of** sth. *(fig.: in addition)* zusätzlich zu etw.; **from ~ to bottom** von oben bis unten; **at the ~:** oben; **at the ~ of the building/hill/pile/stairs** oben im Gebäude/[oben] auf dem Hügel/[oben] auf dem Stapel/oben an der Treppe; **b)** *(highest rank)* Spitze, *die;* **~ of the table** *(Sport)* Tabellenspitze, *die;* **be [at the] ~ of the class** der/die Klassenbeste sein; **c)** *(upper surface)* Oberfläche, *die; (of cupboard, chest)* Oberseite, *die;* **on ~ of** sth. [oben] auf etw. *(position: Dat.; direction: Akk.);* **d)** *(folding roof)* Verdeck, *das;* **e)** *(upper deck of bus)* Oberdeck, *das;* **f)** *(cap of pen)* [Verschluß]kappe, *die;* **g)** *(upper garment)* Oberteil, *das;* **h)** *(lid)* Deckel, *der; (of bottle)* Stöpsel, *der.* **2.** *adj.* oberst...; höchst... ⟨*Ton, Preis*⟩; **~ end** oberes Ende; **the ~ pupil** der beste Schüler; **~ speed** Spitzen- *od.* Höchstgeschwindigkeit, *die.* **3.** *v. t.* **a)** *(be taller than)* überragen; **b)** *(surpass)* übertreffen. **top 'up** *(Brit. coll.) v. t.* auffüllen ⟨*Tank, Flasche, Glas*⟩

²**top** *n. (toy)* Kreisel, *der*

top: ~ 'hat *n.* Zylinder[hut], *der;* **~-heavy** *adj.* oberlastig

topic ['tɒpɪk] *n.* Thema, *das.* **topical** ['tɒpɪkl] *adj.* aktuell

'**topless** *adj.* **a ~ dress/swimsuit** ein busenfreies Kleid/ein Oben-ohne-Badeanzug

topmost ['tɒpməʊst, 'tɒpməst] *adj.* oberst...; höchst... ⟨*Gipfel, Note*⟩

topple ['tɒpl] **1.** *v. i.* fallen. **2.** *v. t.* stürzen. **topple 'down** *v. i.* hinab-/herabfallen. **topple 'over** *v. i.* umfallen

top 'secret *adj.* streng geheim

topsy-turvy [tɒpsɪ'tɜ:vɪ] *adv.* verkehrtrum *(ugs.);* **turn** sth. **~:** etw. auf den Kopf stellen *(ugs.)*

torch [tɔ:tʃ] *n. (Brit.)* Taschenlampe, *die*

tore, torn *see* ¹**tear** 2, 3

tornado [tɔ:'neɪdəʊ] *n., pl.* **~es** Wirbelsturm, *der; (in North America)* Tornado, *der*

torpedo [tɔ:'pi:dəʊ] **1.** *n., pl.* **~es** Torpedo, *der.* **2.** *v. t.* torpedieren

torrent ['tɒrənt] *n.* reißender Bach; *(fig.)* Flut, *die.* **torrential** [tə'renʃl] *adj.* wolkenbruchartig ⟨*Regen*⟩

torso ['tɔ:səʊ] *n., pl.* **~s** Rumpf, *der;* **bare ~:** nackter Oberkörper

tortoise ['tɔ:təs] *n.* Schildkröte, *die.* **tortoiseshell** ['tɔ:təsʃel] *n.* Schildpatt, *das*

tortuous ['tɔ:tjʊəs] *adj.* verschlungen; *(fig.)* umständlich

torture ['tɔ:tʃə(r)] **1.** *n.* Folter, *die.* **2.** *v. t.* foltern; *(fig.)* quälen

toss [tɒs] **1.** *v. t.* **a)** *(throw upwards)* hochwerfen; **~ a pancake** einen Pfannkuchen [durch Hochwerfen] wenden; **b)** *(throw casually)* werfen; schmeißen *(ugs.);* **c) ~ a coin** eine Münze werfen; **d)** *(Cookery: mix)* wenden; mischen ⟨*Salat*⟩. **2,** *v. i.* **a) ~ and turn** sich [schlaflos] im Bett wälzen; **b)** ⟨*Schiff:*⟩ hin und her geworfen werden; **c)** *(~ coin)* eine Münze werfen; **~ for** sth. mit einer Münze um etw. losen. **3.** *n.* **a) ~ of a coin** Hochwerfen einer Münze; **b)** *(throw)* Wurf, *der.* **toss 'up** *v. i.* eine Münze werfen; **~ up for** sth. mit einer Münze um etw. losen

¹**tot** [tɒt] *n. (coll.)* **a)** kleines Kind; **b)** *(of liquor)* Gläschen, *das*

²**tot** *(coll.) v. t.,* **-tt-: ~ 'up** zusammenziehen *(ugs.)*

total ['təʊtl] **1.** *adj.* **a)** gesamt; Gesamt- ⟨*gewicht, -wert, usw.*⟩; **b)** *(absolute)* völlig *nicht präd.;* **a ~ beginner** ein absoluter Anfänger. **2.** *n. (number)* Gesamtzahl, *die; (amount)* Gesamtbetrag, *der; (result of addition)* Summe, *die;* **a ~ of 200** insgesamt 200; **in ~:** insgesamt. **3.** *v. t., (Brit.)* **-ll-: a)** addieren, zusammenzählen ⟨*Zahlen*⟩; **b)** *(amount to)* [insgesamt] betragen

totalitarian [təʊtælɪ'teərɪən] *adj.* totalitär

'**totally** *adv.* völlig

totter ['tɒtə(r)] *v. i.* wanken; taumeln

touch [tʌtʃ] **1.** *v. t.* **a)** berühren; **b)** *(harm)* anrühren; **c)** *(fig.: rival)* **~** sth. an etw. *(Akk.)* heranreichen; **d)** *(affect emotionally)* rühren. **2.** *v. i.* sich berühren; **don't ~!** nicht anfassen! **3.** *n.* **a)** Berührung, *die;* **b)** *no art. (faculty)* [sense of] **~:** Tastsinn, *der;* **c)** *(small amount)* **a ~ of salt/pepper** *etc.* eine Spur Salz/Pfeffer *usw.;* **a ~ of irony** *etc.* ein Anflug von Ironie *usw.;* **d)** *(fig.)* Detail, *das;* **e)** *(communication)* **be in/out of ~ [with** sb.**]** [mit jmdm.] Kontakt/keinen Kontakt haben; **get in ~:** mit jmdm. Kontakt aufnehmen. **touch 'down** *v. i.* ⟨*Flugzeug:*⟩ landen. **touch on** *v. t. (mention)* ansprechen. **touch 'up** *v. t. (improve)* ausbessern **'touch: ~-and-go** *adj.* **it is ~-and-go [whether...]** es steht auf des Messers Schneide [, ob...]; **~down** *n. (Aeronaut.)* Landung, *die*

'touching *adj.* rührend. **touchy** ['tʌtʃɪ] *adj.* empfindlich; heikel ⟨*Thema*⟩
tough [tʌf] *adj.* **a)** fest ⟨*Material, Stoff*⟩; zäh ⟨*Fleisch; fachspr.*: *Werkstoff, Metall*⟩; widerstandsfähig ⟨*Belag, Glas, Haut*⟩; strapazierfähig ⟨*Kleidung*⟩; **b)** *(hardy)* zäh ⟨*Person*⟩; **c)** *(difficult)* schwierig; **d)** *(severe, harsh)* hart; **e)** *(coll.)* ~ **luck** Pech, *das*.
toughen ['tʌfn] *v.t.* ~ |up| abhärten ⟨*Person*⟩; verschärfen ⟨*Gesetz*⟩
tour [tʊə(r)] **1.** *n.* **a)** [Rund]reise, *die;* Tour, *die (ugs.);* **b)** *(Theatre, Sport)* Tournee, *die;* **c)** *(of house etc.)* Besichtigung, *die;* **d)** ~ |of duty| Dienstzeit, *die.* **2.** *v.i.* **a)** ~/go ~ing in *or* through **a** country eine Reise *od. (ugs.)* Tour durch ein Land machen; **b)** *(Theatre, Sport)* eine Tournee machen. **3.** *v.t.* **a)** besichtigen ⟨*Stadt, Gebäude*⟩; ~ **a** **country/region** eine Reise *od. (ugs.)* Tour durch ein Land/Gebiet machen; **b)** *(Theatre, Sport)* ~ **a country/the provinces** eine Tournee durch das Land/die Provinz machen
tourism ['tʊərɪzm] *n.* **a)** Tourismus, *der;* **b)** *(operation of tours)* Touristik, *die.* **tourist** ['tʊərɪst] **1.** *n.* Tourist, *der/*Touristin, *die.* **2.** *attrib. adj.* Touristen-. **tourist** infor'mation **centre,** 'tourist office *ns.* Fremdenverkehrsbüro, *das*
tournament ['tʊənəmənt] *n. (Hist.; Sport)* Turnier, *das*
'tour operator *n.* Reiseveranstalter, *der/*-veranstalterin, *die*
tousle ['taʊzl] *v.t.* zerzausen
tout [taʊt] **1.** *v.i.* ~ **for customers** Kunden anreißen *(ugs.) od.* werben. **2.** *n.* Anreißer, *der/*Anreißerin, *die (ugs.);* **ticket** ~: Kartenschwarzhändler, *der/*-händlerin, *die*
tow [təʊ] **1.** *v.t.* schleppen; ziehen ⟨*Anhänger, Wasserskiläufer*⟩. **2.** *n.* Schleppen, *das;* **give a car a** ~: einen Wagen schleppen; **on** ~: im Schlepp[tau]. **tow a'way** *v.t.* abschleppen
toward [tə'wɔːd], **towards** [tə'wɔːdz] *prep.* **a)** *(in direction of)* ~ **sb./sth.** auf jmdn./etw. zu; **turn** ~ **sb.** sich zu jmdm. umdrehen; **b)** *(in relation to)* gegenüber; **feel sth.** ~ **sb.** jmdm. gegenüber etw. empfinden; **c)** *(for)* **a contribution** ~ **sth.** ein Beitrag zu etw.; **proposals** ~ **solving a problem** Vorschläge zur Lösung eines Problems; **d)** *(near)* gegen; ~ **the end of May** [gegen] Ende Mai

towel ['taʊəl] *n.* Handtuch, *das*
tower ['taʊə(r)] **1.** *n.* Turm, *der.* **2.** *v.i.* in die Höhe ragen. 'tower above *v.t.* ~ **above sb./sth.** jmdn./etw. überragen
'tower block *n.* Hochhaus, *das*
'towering *attrib. adj.* hoch aufragend; *(fig.)* herausragend ⟨*Leistung*⟩
town [taʊn] *n.* Stadt, *die;* **the** ~ **of Cambridge** die Stadt Cambridge; **in** |the| ~: in der Stadt; **the** ~ *(people)* die Stadt; **be in/out of** ~: in der Stadt/nicht in der Stadt sein
town: ~ 'centre *n.* Stadtmitte, *die;* Stadtzentrum, *das;* ~ 'hall *n.* Rathaus, *das;* ~ 'planning *n.* Stadtplanung, *die*
tow: ~-path *n.* Leinpfad, *der;* ~-rope *n.* Abschleppseil, *das*
toxic ['tɒksɪk] *adj.* giftig
toy [tɔɪ] **1.** *n.* Spielzeug, *das;* ~s Spielzeug, *das.* **2.** *adj.* Spielzeug-. **3.** *v.i.* ~ **with the idea of doing sth.** mit dem Gedanken spielen, etw. zu tun. 'toyshop *n.* Spielwarengeschäft, *das*
trace [treɪs] **1.** *v.t.* **a)** *(copy)* durchpausen; abpausen; **b)** zeichnen ⟨*Linie*⟩; **c)** *(follow track of)* folgen (+ *Dat.*); verfolgen; **d)** *(find)* finden. **2.** *n.* Spur, *die.* 'tracing paper ['treɪsɪŋ peɪpə(r)] *n.* Pauspapier, *das*
track [træk] **1.** *n.* **a)** Spur, *die; (of wild animal)* Fährte, *die;* ~s *(footprints)* [Fuß]spuren; *(of animal also)* Fährte, *die;* **keep** ~ **of sb./sth.** jmdn./etw. im Auge behalten; **b)** *(path)* Weg, *der; (footpath)* Pfad, *der;* **c)** *(Sport)* Bahn, *die;* **cycling/greyhound** ~: Radrennbahn, *die/*Windhundrennbahn, *die;* **d)** *(Railw.)* Gleis, *das;* **e)** *(course taken)* Route, *die; (of rocket, satellite)* Bahn, *die.* **2.** *v.t.* ~ **an animal** die Spur/Fährte eines Tieres verfolgen; **the police** ~ed **him** |to Paris| die Polizei folgte seiner Spur [bis nach Paris]. **track 'down** *v.t.* aufspüren
track: ~ **events** *n. pl.* Laufwettbewerbe; ~ **suit** *n.* Trainingsanzug, *der*
¹**tract** [trækt] *n. (area)* Gebiet, *das*
²**tract** *n. (pamphlet)* [Flug]schrift, *die*
tractor ['træktə(r)] *n.* Traktor, *der*
trade [treɪd] **1.** *n.* **a)** *(line of business)* Gewerbe, *das; he's a* **butcher/lawyer** *etc.* **by** ~: er ist von Beruf Metzger/Rechtsanwalt *usw.;* **b)** *no indef. art (commerce)* Handel, *der;* **c)** *(craft)* Handwerk, *das.* **2.** *v.i. (buy and sell)* Handel treiben. **3.** *v.t.* tauschen; austauschen ⟨*Waren, Grüße*⟩; sich *(Dat.)*

sagen ⟨*Beleidigungen*⟩; ~ sth. for sth. etw. gegen etw. tauschen. **trade 'in** *v. t.* in Zahlung geben
'trade mark *n.* Warenzeichen, *das;* leave one's ~ on sth. *(fig.)* einer Sache *(Dat.)* seinen Stempel aufdrücken
'trader *n.* Händler, *der/*Händlerin, *die*
trade: ~ **'union** *n.* Gewerkschaft, *die; attrib.* Gewerkschafts-; ~-'**unionist** *n.* Gewerkschaft[l]er, *der/*Gewerkschaft[l]erin, *die*
trading ['treɪdɪŋ] *n.* Handel, *der.* '**trading estate** *n. (Brit.)* Gewerbegebiet, *das.* '**trading stamp** *n.* Rabattmarke, *die*
tradition [trə'dɪʃn] *n.* Tradition, *die.*
traditional [trə'dɪʃənl] *adj.* traditionell; herkömmlich ⟨*Erziehung, Methode*⟩. **tra'ditionally** *adv.* traditionell
traffic ['træfɪk] **1.** *n.* **a)** *no indef. art.* Verkehr, *der;* **b)** *(trade)* Handel, *der.* **2.** *v. i.,* **-ck-:** ~ **in** sth. mit etw. handeln
traffic: ~ **circle** *n. (Amer.)* Kreisverkehr, *der;* ~ **jam** *n.* [Verkehrs]stau, *der;* ~ **lights** *n. pl.* [Verkehrs]ampel, *die;* ~ **sign** *n.* Verkehrszeichen, *das;* ~ **signals** *see* ~ **lights;** ~ **warden** *n. (Brit.)* Hilfspolizist, *der;* (woman) Hilfspolizistin, *die;* Politesse, *die*
tragedy ['trædʒɪdɪ] *n.* Tragödie, *die.* **tragic** ['trædʒɪk] *adj.* tragisch
trail [treɪl] **1.** *n.* **a)** Spur, *die;* ~ **of** smoke/dust Rauch-/Staubfahne, *die;* **b)** *(Hunting)* Spur, *die;* Fährte, *die;* **c)** *(path)* Pfad, *der;* Weg, *der.* **2.** *v. t.* **a)** *(pursue)* verfolgen; **b)** *(drag)* ~ **sth.** [after *or* behind one] etw. hinter sich *(Dat.)* herziehen. **3.** *v. i.* **a)** *(be dragged)* schleifen; **b)** *(lag)* hinterhertrotten; **c)** ⟨*Pflanze:*⟩ kriechen
trailer ['treɪlə(r)] *n.* **a)** Anhänger, *der;* *(Amer.: caravan)* Wohnanhänger, *der;* **b)** *(Cinemat., Telev.)* Trailer, *der*
train [treɪn] **1.** *v. t.* **a)** ausbilden (**in** in + *Dat.*); erziehen ⟨*Kind*⟩; abrichten ⟨*Hund*⟩; dressieren ⟨*Tier*⟩; **b)** *(Sport)* trainieren; **c)** *(Hort.)* ziehen. **2.** *v. i.* **a)** eine Ausbildung machen; **he is ~ing as** *or* **to be a doctor/engineer** er macht eine Arzt-/Ingenieursausbildung; **b)** *(Sport)* trainieren. **3.** *n.* **a)** *(Railw.)* Zug, *der;* **on the** ~**:** im Zug; **b)** *(of skirt etc.)* Schleppe, *die;* **c)** ~ **of thought** Gedankengang, *der.* '**train-driver** *n.* Lokomotivführer, *der/*-führerin, *die*
trained [treɪnd] *adj.* ausgebildet ⟨*Arbeiter, Lehrer, Arzt, Stimme*⟩; abgerichtet ⟨*Hund*⟩; dressiert ⟨*Tier*⟩; geschult ⟨*Geist, Auge, Ohr*⟩

trainee [treɪ'ni:] *n.* Auszubildende, *der/die*
'**trainer** *n.* [Konditions]trainer, *der/*-trainerin, *die*
'**train fare** *n.* Fahrpreis, *der*
'**training** *n.* **a)** Ausbildung, *die;* **b)** *(Sport)* Training, *das*
train: ~ **journey** *n.* Bahnfahrt, *die;* *(long)* Bahnreise, *die;* ~ **set** *n.* [Modell]eisenbahn, *die;* ~ **station** *n.* *(Amer.)* Bahnhof, *der*
trait [treɪt] *n.* Eigenschaft, *die*
traitor ['treɪtə(r)] *n.* Verräter, *der/*Verräterin, *die*
tram [træm] *n. (Brit.)* Straßenbahn, *die;* ~**lines** Straßenbahnschienen
tramp [træmp] **1.** *n.* Landstreicher, *der/*-streicherin, *die; (in city)* Stadtstreicher, *der/*-streicherin, *die.* **2.** *v. i.* **a)** *(tread heavily)* trampeln; **b)** *(walk)* marschieren
trample ['træmpl] **1.** *v. t.* zertrampeln. **2.** *v. i.* trampeln. '**trample on** *v. t.* herumtrampeln auf (+ *Dat.*)
trampoline ['træmpəli:n] *n.* Trampolin, *das*
trance [trɑ:ns] *n.* Trance, *die;* **be in a** ~**:** in Trance sein
tranquil ['træŋkwɪl] *adj.* ruhig. **tranquillity** [træŋ'kwɪlɪtɪ] Ruhe, *die.*
tranquillizer ['træŋkwɪlaɪzə(r)] *n.* Beruhigungsmittel, *das*
transact [træn'zækt] *v. t.* ~ **business** Geschäfte tätigen. **transaction** [træn'zækʃn] *n.* Geschäft, *das; (financial)* Transaktion, *die*
transcend [træn'send] *v. t.* übersteigen
transcript ['trænskrɪpt] *n.* Abschrift, *die; (of trial)* Protokoll, *das*
transfer **1.** [træns'fɜ:(r)] *v. t.,* **-rr-: a)** *(move)* verlegen (**to** nach); überweisen ⟨*Geld*⟩ (**to** auf + *Akk.*); übertragen ⟨*Befugnis, Macht*⟩ (**to** *Dat.*); **b)** übereignen ⟨*Gegenstand, Grundbesitz*⟩ (**to** *Dat.*); **c)** versetzen ⟨*Arbeiter, Angestellte*⟩; *(Footb.)* transferieren. **2.** [træns'fɜ:(r)] *v. i.,* **-rr-: a)** *(when travelling)* umsteigen; **b)** *(change job etc.)* wechseln. **3.** ['trænsfɜ:(r)] *n.* **a)** *(moving)* Verlegung, *die; (of powers)* Übertragung, *die* (**to** an + *Akk.*); *(of money)* Überweisung, *die;* **b)** *(of employee etc.)* Versetzung, *die; (Footb.)* Transfer, *der;* **c)** *(picture)* Abziehbild, *das.* **transferable** [træns'fɜ:rəbl] *adj.* übertragbar
transform [træns'fɔ:m] *v. t.* verwandeln. **transformation** [trænsfə-

'meıʃn] *n.* Verwandlung, *die.* **trans-'former** *n. (Electr.)* Transformator, *der*
transfusion [træns'fju:ʒn] *n. (Med.)* Transfusion, *die*
transient ['trænzıənt] *adj.* kurzlebig; vergänglich
transistor [træn'zıstə(r)] *n.* Transistor, *der*
transit ['trænsıt] *n.* **in ~:** auf der Durchreise; ⟨*Waren*⟩ auf dem Transport; **passengers in ~:** Transitreisende
transition [træn'sıʒn, træn'zıʃn] *n.* Übergang, *der;* Wechsel, *der*
transitive ['trænsıtıv] *adj. (Ling.)* transitiv
transitory ['trænsıtərı] *adj.* vergänglich; *(fleeting)* flüchtig
translate [træns'leıt] *v. t.* übersetzen.
translation [træns'leıʃn] *n.* Übersetzung, *die.* **translator** [træns'leıtə(r)] *n.* Übersetzer, *der/*Übersetzerin, *die*
translucent [træns'lu:sənt] *adj.* durchscheinend
transmission [træns'mıʃn] *n.* **a)** Übertragung, *die;* **b)** *(Motor Veh.)* Antrieb, *der; (gearbox)* Getriebe, *das*
transmit [træns'mıt] *v. t.,* **-tt-: a)** *(pass on)* übersenden; übertragen; **b)** durchlassen ⟨*Licht*⟩; leiten ⟨*Wärme*⟩. **trans'mitter** *n.* Sender, *der*
transparency [træns'pærənsı] *n.* **a)** Durchsichtigkeit, *die;* **b)** *(Photog.)* Transparent, *das; (slide)* Dia, *das*
transparent [træns'pærənt] *adj.* durchsichtig
transpire [træn'spaıə(r)] *v. i.* sich herausstellen; *(coll.: happen)* passieren
transplant 1. [træns'plɑ:nt] *v. t.* **a)** verpflanzen ⟨*Organ*⟩; **b)** *(plant in another place)* umpflanzen. **2.** ['trænsplɑ:nt] *n. (Med.)* Transplantation, *die;* Verpflanzung, *die*
transport 1. [træns'pɔ:t] *v. t.* transportieren; befördern. **2.** ['trænspɔ:t] *n.* **a)** Transport, *der;* Beförderung, *die; attrib.* Beförderungs-; **b)** *(means of conveyance)* Verkehrsmittel, *das;* **be without ~:** kein [eigenes] Fahrzeug haben
transpose [træns'pəʊz] *v. t.* vertauschen; umstellen
transvestite [træns'vestaıt] *n.* Transvestit, *der*

trap [træp] **1.** *n.* **a)** Falle, *die;* **set** *or* **lay a ~ for an animal** eine Falle für ein Tier legen *od.* aufstellen; **set** *or* **lay a ~ for sb.** *(fig.)* jmdm. eine Falle stellen; **fall into a/sb.'s ~** *(fig.)* in die/ jmdm. in die Falle gehen; **b)** *(sl.: mouth)* Klappe, *die (salopp).* **2.** *v. t.,*

-pp-: a) [in *od.* mit einer Falle] fangen ⟨*Tier*⟩; *(fig.)* in eine Falle locken ⟨*Person*⟩; **be ~ped** *(fig.)* in eine Falle gehen/in der Falle sitzen; **be ~ped in a cave/by the tide** in einer Höhle festsitzen/von der Flut abgeschnitten sein; **b)** *(confine)* einschließen; einklemmen ⟨*Körperteil*⟩. **trap'door** *n.* Falltür, *die*
trapeze [trə'pi:z] *n.* Trapez, *das*
trash [træʃ] *n., no indef. art.* **a)** *(rubbish)* Abfall, *der;* **b)** *(badly made thing)* Mist, *der (ugs.); (bad literature)* Schund, *der (ugs.)*
trauma ['trɔ:mə] *n., pl.* **~ta** ['trɔ:mətə] *or* **~s** Trauma, *das.* **traumatic** [trɔ:'mætık] *adj.* traumatisch
travel ['trævl] **1.** *n.* Reisen, *das; attrib.* Reise-. **2.** *v. i., (Brit.)* **-ll-** reisen; *(go in vehicle)* fahren. **3.** *v. t., (Brit.)* **-ll-** zurücklegen ⟨*Strecke, Entfernung*⟩; benutzen ⟨*Weg, Straße*⟩; **we had ~led 10 miles** wir waren 10 Meilen gefahren. **'travel agency** *n.* Reisebüro, *das.* **'travel agent** *n.* Reisebürokaufmann, *der/*-kauffrau, *die*
traveler, traveling *(Amer.) see* **travell-**
traveller ['trævlə(r)] *n. (Brit.)* **a)** Reisende, *der/die;* **b)** *in pl. (gypsies etc.)* fahrendes Volk. **'traveller's cheque** *n.* Reisescheck, *der*
travelling ['trævlıŋ] *attrib. adj. (Brit.)* Wander⟨*zirkus, -ausstellung*⟩
trawler ['trɔ:lə(r)] *n.* [Fisch]trawler, *der*
tray [treı] *n.* Tablett, *das; (for correspondence)* Ablageschachtel, *die*
treacherous ['tretʃərəs] *adj.* **a)** treulos ⟨*Person*⟩; **b)** *(deceptive)* tückisch.
treachery ['tretʃərı] *n.* Verrat, *der*
treacle ['tri:kl] *n. (Brit.)* Sirup, *der*
tread [tred] **1.** *n.* **a)** *(of tyre, boot, etc.)* Lauffläche, *die;* **2 millimetres of ~ on a tyre** 2 Millimeter Profil auf einem Reifen; **b)** *(sound of walking)* Schritt, *der.* **2.** *v. i.,* **trod** [trɒd], **trodden** ['trɒdn] *or* **trod** treten **(in/on** in/auf + *Akk.*); *(walk)* gehen. **3.** *v. t.* **trod, trodden** *or* **trod** treten auf (+ *Akk.*); stampfen ⟨*Weintrauben*⟩
treason ['tri:zn] *n.* **[high] ~:** Hochverrat, *der*
treasure ['treʒə(r)] **1.** *n.* Schatz, *der;* Kostbarkeit, *die;* **art ~s** Kunstschätze. **2.** *v. t.* in Ehren halten. **'treasure-hunt** *n.* Schatzsuche, *die*
treasurer ['treʒərə(r)] *n.* Kassenwart, *der/*-wartin, *die.* **treasury** ['treʒərı] *n.* **the T~:** das Finanzministerium

treat [tri:t] 1. *n.* **a)** [besonderes] Vergnügen; **b)** *(entertainment) Vergnügen, für dessen Kosten jmd. anderes aufkommt;* **lay on a special ~ for sb.** jmdm. etwas Besonderes bieten. 2. *v. t.* **a)** behandeln; ~ **sth. as a joke etw.** als Witz nehmen; ~ **sth. with contempt** für etw. nur Verachtung haben; **b)** *(Med.)* behandeln; ~ **sb. for sth.** jmdn. wegen etw. behandeln; *(before confirmation of diagnosis)* jmdn. auf etw. *(Akk.)* behandeln; **c)** klären ⟨Abwässer⟩; **d)** *(provide with at own expense)* einladen; ~ **sb. to sth.** jmdm. etw. spendieren; ~ **oneself to a new hat** sich *(Dat.)* einen neuen Hut leisten
treatise ['tri:tɪs, 'tri:tɪz] *n.* Abhandlung, *die*
'**treatment** *n.* Behandlung, *die*
treaty ['tri:tɪ] *n.* [Staats]vertrag, *der*
treble ['trebl] 1. *adj.* **a)** dreifach; **b)** *(Brit. Mus.)* ~ **voice** Sopranstimme, *die.* 2. *n.* **a)** *(~ quantity)* Dreifache, *das;* **b)** *(Mus.)* **he is a ~:** er singt Sopran. 3. *v. t.* verdreifachen. 4. *v. i.* sich verdreifachen. '**treble clef** *n.* *(Mus.)* Violinschlüssel, *der*
tree [tri:] *n.* Baum, *der*
trek [trek] 1. *v. i.,* **-kk-** ziehen (**across** durch). 2. *n.* [schwierige] Reise
trellis ['trelɪs] *n.* Gitter, *das; (for plants)* Spalier, *das*
tremble ['trembl] *v. i.* zittern (**with** vor + *Dat.*)
tremendous [trɪ'mendəs] *adj.* gewaltig; *(coll.: wonderful)* großartig
tremor ['tremə(r)] *n.* **a)** Zittern, *das;* **b)** [earth] ~: leichtes Erdbeben
trench [trentʃ] *n.* Graben, *der; (Mil.)* Schützengraben, *der*
trend [trend] *n.* **a)** Trend, *der;* **upward** ~: steigende Tendenz; **b)** [fashion] Mode, *die;* [Mode]trend, *der.* '**trendy** *adj. (Brit. coll.)* modisch; Schickimicki⟨kneipe⟩ *(ugs.)*
trepidation [trepɪ'deɪʃn] *n.* Beklommenheit, *die*
trespass ['trespəs] *v. i.* ~ **on** unerlaubt betreten ⟨Grundstück⟩. '**trespasser** *n.* Unbefugte, *der/die*
trial ['traɪəl] *n.* **a)** *(Law)* [Gerichts]verfahren, *das;* **be on ~** [for murder] [wegen Mordes] angeklagt sein; **b)** *(testing)* Test, *der;* **employ sb. on ~:** jmdn. probeweise einstellen; [by] ~ **and error** [durch] Ausprobieren; **c)** *(trouble)* Problem, *das;* **d)** *(Sport) (competition)* Prüfung, *die; (for selection)* Testspiel, *das*

triangle ['traɪæŋgl] *n.* **a)** Dreieck, *das;* **b)** *(Mus.)* Triangel, *das od. der.* **triangular** [traɪ'æŋgjʊlə(r)] *adj.* dreieckig
tribe [traɪb] *n.* Stamm, *der*
tribulation [trɪbjʊ'leɪʃn] *n.* Kummer, *der*
tribunal [traɪ'bju:nl] *n.* Schiedsgericht, *das*
tributary ['trɪbjʊtərɪ] *n.* Nebenfluß, *der*
tribute ['trɪbju:t] *n.* Tribut, *der* (**to an** + *Akk.*); **pay ~ to sb./sth.** jmdm./einer Sache den schuldigen Tribut zollen *(geh.)*
trice [traɪs] *n.* **in a ~:** im Handumdrehen
trick [trɪk] 1. *n.* **a)** Trick, *der;* **it was all a ~:** das war [alles] nur Bluff; **b)** *(feat of skill etc.)* Kunststück, *das;* **that should do the ~** *(coll.)* damit dürfte es klappen *(ugs.);* **c)** *(knack)* **get** *or* **find the ~** [of doing sth.] den Dreh finden[, wie man etw. tut]; **d)** *(prank)* Streich, *der;* **play a ~ on sb.** jmdm. einen Streich spielen; **e)** *(Cards)* Stich, *der.* 2. *v. t.* täuschen; hereinlegen; ~ **sb. out of/into sth.** jmdm. etw. ablisten. 3. *adj.* ~ **photograph** Trickaufnahme, *die;* ~ **question** Fangfrage, *die.*
trickery ['trɪkərɪ] *n.* [Hinter]list, *die*
trickle ['trɪkl] *v. i.* rinnen; *(in drops)* tröpfeln
trickster ['trɪkstə(r)] *n.* Schwindler, *der*/Schwindlerin, *die*
'**tricky** *adj.* verzwickt *(ugs.)*
tricycle ['traɪsɪkl] *n.* Dreirad, *das*
tried *see* **try** 2, 3
trifle ['traɪfl] *n.* **a)** *(Brit. Gastron.)* Trifle, *das;* **b)** *(thing of slight value)* Kleinigkeit, *die.* **trifling** ['traɪflɪŋ] *adj.* unbedeutend ⟨Angelegenheit⟩; gering ⟨Wert⟩
trigger ['trɪgə(r)] 1. *n.* **a)** *(of gun)* Abzug, *der; (of machine)* Drücker, *der;* **b)** *(fig.)* Auslöser, *der.* 2. *v. t.* ~ [off] auslösen
trigonometry [trɪgə'nɒmɪtrɪ] *n.* Trigonometrie, *die*
trim [trɪm] 1. *v. t.,* **-mm-:** **a)** schneiden ⟨Hecke⟩; [nach]schneiden ⟨Haar⟩; beschneiden ⟨Papier, Hecke, Budget⟩; **b)** *(ornament)* besetzen (**with** mit). 2. *adj.* proper; gepflegt ⟨Garten⟩. 3. *n.* **a)** **be in ~** *(healthy)* in Form *od.* fit sein; **b)** *(cut)* Nachschneiden, *das.* '**trimming** *n.* **a)** *(decorations)* Verzierung, *die;* **b)** *in pl. (coll.: accompaniments)* Beilagen; **with all the ~s** mit allem Drum und Dran *(ugs.)*

Trinity ['trınıtı] *n. (Theol.)* **the |Holy| ~ :** die Heilige Dreieinigkeit

trinket ['trıŋkıt] *n.* kleines, billiges Schmuckstück

trio ['tri:əʊ] *n., pl.* ~s Trio, *das*

trip [trıp] **1.** *n.* **a)** Reise, *die; (shorter)* Ausflug, *der;* **b)** *(coll.: drug-induced hallucinations)* Trip, *der.* **2.** *v. i.,* -pp- stolpern (**on** über + *Akk.*). **trip 'up 1.** *v. i.* **a)** stolpern; **b)** *(fig.)* einen Fehler machen. **2.** *v. t.* **a)** stolpern lassen; **b)** *(fig.)* aufs Glatteis führen *(fig.)*

tripe [traıp] *n.* **a)** Kaldaunen *Pl.;* **b)** *(sl.: rubbish)* Quatsch, *der (ugs.)*

triple ['trıpl] **1.** *adj.* **a)** *(threefold)* drei- fach; **b)** *(three times greater than)* ~ **the** ...: der/die/das dreifache ... **2.** *n.* Dreifache, *das.* **3.** *v. i.* sich verdreifa- chen. **4.** *v. t.* verdreifachen

triplet ['trıplıt] *n.* Drilling, *der*

triplicate ['trıplıkət] *n.* **in** ~ : in dreifa- cher Ausfertigung

tripod ['traıpɒd] *n.* Dreibein, *das*

'tripper *n. (Brit.)* Ausflügler, *der/*Aus- flüglerin, *die*

trite [traıt] *adj.* banal

triumph ['traıəmf, 'traıʌmf] **1.** *n.* Tri- umph, *der* (**over** über + *Akk.*). **2.** *v. i.* triumphieren (**over** über + *Akk.*). **triumphant** [traı'ʌmfənt] *adj.* **a)** siegreich; **b)** triumphierend ⟨*Blick*⟩

trivial ['trıvıəl] *adj.* belanglos. **tri- viality** [trıvı'ælıtı] *n.* Belanglosigkeit, *die*

trod, trodden *see* tread 2, 3

trolley ['trɒlı] *n.* **a)** *(for serving food)* Servierwagen, *der;* **b)** |**supermarket**| ~ : Einkaufswagen, *der*

trombone [trɒm'bəʊn] *n.* Posaune, *die*

troop [tru:p] **1.** *n.* **a)** *in pl.* Truppen; **b)** *(fig.)* Schar, *die.* **2.** *v. i.* ~ **in/out** hin- ein-/hinausströmen

trophy ['trəʊfı] *n.* Trophäe, *die*

tropic ['trɒpık] *n.* **the** T~s *(Geog.)* die Tropen; **the** ~ **of Cancer/Capricorn** *(Astron., Geog.)* der Wendekreis des Krebses./Steinbocks. **tropical** ['trɒ- pıkl] *adj.* tropisch; Tropen⟨*krankheit, -kleidung*⟩

trot [trɒt] **1.** *n. (coll.)* **on the** ~ : hinter- einander; **be on the** ~ : auf Trab sein *(ugs.).* **2.** *v. i.,* -tt- traben

trouble ['trʌbl] **1.** *n.* **a)** Ärger, *der;* Schwierigkeiten *Pl.;* **there'll be ~ |if ...|** es wird Ärger geben, [wenn ...]; **what's the ~?** was ist denn?; **b) engine/brake** ~ : Probleme mit dem Motor/der Bremse; **suffer from heart/liver** ~ :

Probleme mit dem Herz/der Leber haben; **c)** *(inconvenience)* Mühe, *die;* **take a lot of** ~ : sich *(Dat.)* sehr viel Mühe geben; **it's more ~ than it's worth** es lohnt sich nicht; **d)** *in sing. or pl. (unrest)* Unruhen. **2.** *v. t.* **a)** *(agit- ate)* beunruhigen; **don't let it ~ you** mach dir deswegen keine Sorgen; **b)** *(inconvenience)* stören. **3.** *v. i. (make an effort)* sich bemühen. **troubled** ['trʌbld] *adj.* **a)** *(worried)* besorgt; **b)** *(restless)* unruhig. '**trouble-maker** *n.* Unruhestifter *der/*-stifterin, *die.* **troublesome** ['trʌblsəm] *adj.* schwierig; lästig ⟨*Krankheit*⟩

trough [trɒf] *n.* Trog, *der*

troupe [tru:p] *n.* Truppe, *die*

trousers ['traʊzəz] *n. pl.* |**pair of**| ~ : Hose, *die*

'**trouser suit** *n. (Brit.)* Hosenanzug, *der*

trousseau ['tru:səʊ] *n., pl.* ~s *or* ~x ['tru:səʊz] Aussteuer, *die*

trout [traʊt] *n., pl. same* Forelle, *die*

trowel ['traʊəl] *n.* Kelle, *die; (Hort.)* Pflanzkelle, *die*

truant ['tru:ənt] *n.* **play** ~ : |die Schule] schwänzen *(ugs.)*

truce [tru:s] *n.* Waffenstillstand, *der*

truck [trʌk] *n.* **a)** Last[kraft]wagen, *der;* Lkw, *der;* **b)** *(Brit. Railw.)* offener Güterwagen

truculent ['trʌkjʊlənt] *adj.* aufsässig

trudge [trʌdʒ] *v. i.* trotten; *(through snow etc.)* stapfen

true [tru:] *adj.,* ~**r** ['tru:ə(r)], ~**st** ['tru:ıst] **a)** wahr; wahrheitsgetreu ⟨*Bericht*⟩; richtig ⟨*Vorteil*⟩; *(rightly so called)* eigentlich; echt, wahr ⟨*Freund*⟩; **is it ~ that ...?** stimmt es, daß ...?; ~ **to life** lebensecht; **b)** *(loyal)* treu

truffle ['trʌfl] *n.* Trüffel, *die od. (ugs.) der*

truism ['tru:ızm] *n.* Binsenweisheit, *die*

truly ['tru:lı] *adv.* **a)** wirklich; **b)** *(ac- curately)* zutreffend; **yours** ~ : mit freundlichen Grüßen

trump [trʌmp] *(Cards)* **1.** *n.* Trumpf, *der.* **2.** *v. t.* übertrumpfen. '**trump up** *v. t. (coll.)* konstruieren

trumpet ['trʌmpıt] *n.* Trompete, *die.* '**trumpeter** *n.* Trompeter, *der/*Trom- peterin, *die*

truncheon ['trʌntʃn] *n.* Schlagstock, *der*

trundle ['trʌndl] *v. t. & i.* rollen

trunk [trʌŋk] *n.* **a)** ⟨*of elephant etc.*)

Rüssel, *der;* **b)** *(large box)* Schrank-koffer, *der;* **c)** *(of tree)* Stamm, *der;* **d)** *(of body)* Rumpf, *der;* **e)** *(Amer.: of car)* Kofferraum, *der;* **f)** *in pl. (Brit.)* |swimming| ~s Badehose, *die*

truss [trʌs] *n. (Med.)* Bruchband, *das*

trust [trʌst] **1.** *n.* **a)** Vertrauen, *das;* **place** *or* **put one's** ~ **in sb./sth.** sein Vertrauen auf *od.* in jmdn./etw. setzen; **take sth. on** ~: etw. einfach glauben; **b)** *(organization managed by trustees)* Treuhandgesellschaft, *die;* |charitable| ~: Stiftung, *die; (association of companies)* Trust, *der;* **c)** *(Law)* **hold in** ~: treuhänderisch verwalten. **2.** *v.t. (rely on)* trauen (+ *Dat.*); vertrauen (+ *Dat.*) ⟨*Person*⟩; ~ **sb. with sth.** jmdm. etw. anvertrauen. **3.** *v.i.* **a)** ~ **to** sich verlassen auf (+ *Akk.*); **b)** *(believe)* ~ **in sb./sth.** auf jmdn./etw. vertrauen. **trustee** [trʌˈstiː] *n.* Treuhänder, *der*/Treuhänderin, *die.* **trustful** [ˈtrʌstfl], **trusting** *adjs.* vertrauensvoll. **ˈtrust-worthy** *adj.* vertrauenswürdig

truth [truːθ] *n., pl.* ~s [truːðz, truːθs] Wahrheit, *die;* **tell the** |whole| ~: die [ganze] Wahrheit sagen. **truthful** [ˈtruːθfl] *adj.* ehrlich

try [traɪ] **1.** *n.* Versuch, *der;* **have a** ~ **at sth./doing sth.** etw. versuchen/versuchen, zu tun; **give it a** ~, **have a** ~: es versuchen. **2.** *v.t.* **a)** *(attempt)* versuchen; **b)** *(test usefulness of)* probieren; **c)** *(test)* auf die Probe stellen ⟨*Fähigkeit, Kraft, Geduld*⟩; **d)** *(Law.: take to trial)* ~ **a case** einen Fall verhandeln; ~ **sb.** |for sth.| jmdn. [wegen einer Sache] vor Gericht stellen. **3.** *v.i.* es versuchen; ~ **hard/harder** sich *(Dat.)* viel/mehr Mühe geben. **try 'on** *v.t.* anprobieren ⟨*Kleidungsstück*⟩. **try 'out** *v.t.* ausprobieren

ˈtrying *adj.* **a)** *(testing)* schwierig; **b)** *(difficult to endure)* anstrengend

T-shirt *n.* T-Shirt, *das*

tub [tʌb] *n.* Kübel, *der; (for ice-cream etc.)* Becher, *der*

tuba [ˈtjuːbə] *n. (Mus.)* Tuba, *die*

tubby [ˈtʌbɪ] *adj.* rundlich

tube [tjuːb] *n.* **a)** *(for conveying liquids etc.)* Rohr, *das;* **b)** *(small cylinder)* Tube, *die; (for sweets, tablets)* Röhrchen, *das;* **c)** *(Anat., Zool.)* Röhre, *die;* **d)** *(of TV etc.)* Röhre, *die; (Brit. coll.: underground railway)* U-Bahn, *die*

tuber [ˈtjuːbə(r)] *n. (Bot.)* Knolle, *die*

tuberculosis [tjuːbɜːkjʊˈləʊsɪs] *n.* Tuberkulose, *die*

tube: ~ **station** *n. (Brit. coll.)* U-Bahnhof, *der;* ~ **train** *n. (Brit. coll.)* U-bahn-Zug, *der*

tubing [ˈtjuːbɪŋ] *n.* Rohre *Pl.*

tubular [ˈtjuːbjʊlə(r)] *adj.* rohrförmig

tuck [tʌk] **1.** *v.t.* stecken. **2.** *n. (in fabric) (for decoration)* Biese, *die; (to tighten)* Abnäher, *der.* **tuck 'in 1.** *v.t.* hineinstecken. **2.** *v.i. (coll.)* zulangen *(ugs.).* **tuck 'up** *v.t.* **a)** hochkrempeln ⟨*Ärmel, Hose*⟩; hochnehmen ⟨*Rock*⟩; **b)** *(cover snugly)* zudecken

Tue., Tues. *abbrs.* **Tuesday** Di.

Tuesday [ˈtjuːzdeɪ, ˈtjuːzdɪ] *n.* Dienstag, *der; see also* **Friday**

tuft [tʌft] *n.* Büschel, *das*

tug [tʌg] **1.** *n.* **a)** Ruck, *der;* ~ **of war** Tauziehen, *das;* **b)** ~ |boat| Schlepper, *der.* **2.** *v.t., -gg-* ziehen. **3.** *v.i., -gg-* zerren (**at an** + *Dat.*)

tuition [tjuːˈɪʃn] *n.* Unterricht, *der*

tulip [ˈtjuːlɪp] *n.* Tulpe, *die*

tumble [ˈtʌmbl] **1.** *v.i.* stürzen; fallen. **2.** *n.* Sturz, *der.* **ˈtumble-drier** *n.* Wäschetrockner, *der.* **ˈtumble-dry** *v.t.* im Automaten trocknen

tumbler [ˈtʌmblə(r)] *n. (short)* Whiskyglas, *das; (long)* Wasserglas, *das*

tummy [ˈtʌmɪ] *n. (child lang./coll.)* Bäuchlein, *das.* **ˈtummy-ache** *n. (child lang./coll.)* Bauchweh, *das*

tumour *(Brit.; Amer.:* **tumor)** [ˈtjuːmə(r)] *n.* Tumor, *der*

tumult [ˈtjuːmʌlt] *n.* Tumult, *der*

tuna [ˈtjuːnə] *n., pl. same or* ~s Thunfisch, *der*

tune [tjuːn] **1.** *n.* **a)** *(melody)* Melodie, *die;* **change one's** ~ *(fig.)* sein Verhalten ändern; **call the** ~: den Ton angeben; **b)** *(correct pitch)* **sing in/out of** ~: richtig/falsch singen; **be in/out of** ~ ⟨*Instrument*⟩ richtig gestimmt/verstimmt sein. **2.** *v.t.* **a)** *(Mus.: put in* ~*)* stimmen; **b)** *(Radio, Telev.)* einstellen (**to auf** + *Akk.*); **c)** einstellen ⟨*Motor, Vergaser*⟩. **tune 'in** *(Radio, Telev.)* ~ **to a station** einen Sender einstellen

tuneful [ˈtjuːnfl] *adj.* melodisch

tunic [ˈtjuːnɪk] *n. (of soldier)* Uniformjacke, *die; (of schoolgirl)* Kittel, *der*

ˈtuning-fork [ˈtjuːnɪŋfɔːk] *n.* Stimmgabel, *die*

Tunisia [tjuːˈnɪzɪə] *pr. n.* Tunesien *(das)*

tunnel [ˈtʌnl] **1.** *n.* Tunnel, *der; (dug by animal)* Gang, *der.* **2.** *v.i., (Brit.)* **-ll-** einen Tunnel graben

turban [ˈtɜːbən] *n.* Turban, *der*

turbine [ˈtɜːbaɪn] *n.* Turbine, *die*

turbulence ['tɜ:bjʊləns] *n.* **a)** Aufgewühltheit, *die; (fig.)* Aufruhr, *der;* **b)** *(Phys.)* Turbulenz, *die*

turbulent ['tɜ:bjʊlənt] *adj.* **a)** aufgewühlt; **b)** *(Phys.)* turbulent

tureen [tjʊə'ri:n] *n.* Terrine, *die*

turf [tɜ:f] *n., pl.* **~s** *or* **turves** [tɜ:vz] **a)** *no pl.* Rasen, *der;* **b)** *(segment)* Rasenstück, *das.* **turf 'out** *v.t. (sl.)* rausschmeißen *(ugs.)*

Turk [tɜ:k] *n.* Türke, *der*/Türkin, *die*

Turkey ['tɜ:kɪ] *pr. n.* die Türkei

turkey *n.* Truthahn, *der*/Truthenne, *die; (esp. as food)* Puter, *der*/Pute, *die*

Turkish ['tɜ:kɪʃ] **1.** *adj.* türkisch; **sb. is ~:** jmd. ist Türke/Türkin. **2.** *n.* Türkisch, *das; see also* **English 2 a**

turmoil ['tɜ:mɔɪl] *n.* Aufruhr, *der*

turn [tɜ:n] **1.** *n.* **a) it is sb.'s ~ to do sth.** jmd. ist an der Reihe, etw. zu tun; **it's your ~ |next|** du bist als nächster/nächste dran *(ugs.) od.* an der Reihe; **out of ~:** außer der Reihe; *(fig.)* an der falschen Stelle ⟨*lachen*⟩; **take |it in|** **~s** sich abwechseln; **b)** *(rotary motion)* Drehung, *die;* **c)** *(change of direction)* Wende, *die;* **take a ~ to the right/left, do** *or* **take a right/left ~:** nach rechts/links abbiegen; *(fig.)* **take a favourable ~** sich zum Guten wenden; **the ~ of the year/century** die Jahres-/Jahrhundertwende; **d)** *(bend)* Kurve, *die; (corner)* Ecke, *die;* **e)** *(short performance)* Nummer, *die;* **f)** *(service)* **do sb. a good ~:** jmdm. einen guten Dienst erweisen; **g)** *(coll.: fright)* **give sb. quite a ~:** jmdm. einen gehörigen Schrekken einjagen *(ugs.).* **2.** *v.t.* **a)** *(make revolve)* drehen; **b)** *(reverse)* umdrehen; wenden ⟨*Pfannkuchen, Auto, Heu*⟩; **~ sth. upside down** *or* **on its head** *(lit. or fig.)* etw. auf den Kopf stellen; **~ the page** umblättern; **c)** *(give new direction to)* drehen, wenden ⟨*Kopf*⟩; **~ a hose/gun on sb./sth.** einen Schlauch/ein Gewehr auf jmdn./etw. richten; **~ one's attention/mind to sth.** sich/seine Gedanken einer Sache *(Dat.)* zuwenden; **d)** **~ sb. loose on sb./sth.** jmdn. auf jmdn./etw. loslassen; **e)** *(cause to become)* verwandeln; **~ the lights |down| low** das Licht dämpfen; **~ a play/book into a film** ein Theaterstück/Buch verfilmen; **f)** *(shape in lathe)* drechseln ⟨*Holz*⟩; drehen ⟨*Metall*⟩; **g)** *(make)* ⟨*Pirouette*⟩; schlagen ⟨*Purzelbaum*⟩. **3.** *v.i.* **a)** *(revolve)* sich drehen; **b)** *(reverse direction)* ⟨*Person:*⟩ sich herumdrehen; ⟨*Auto:*⟩ wenden;

c) *(take new direction)* sich wenden; *(~ round)* sich umdrehen; **~ to the left/right** nach links/rechts abbiegen; **d)** *(become)* werden; **~ |in|to sth.** zu etw. werden; *(be transformed)* sich verwandeln *(Akk.)* verwandeln; **e)** *(become sour)* ⟨*Milch:*⟩ sauer werden. **turn a'way 1.** *v.i.* sich abwenden. **2.** *v.t.* **a)** *(avert)* abwenden; **b)** *(send away)* wegschikken. **turn 'down 1.** *v.t.* **a)** herunterschlagen ⟨*Kragen*⟩; **b)** niedriger stellen ⟨*Heizung*⟩; herunterdrehen ⟨*Gas*⟩; leiser stellen ⟨*Ton, Radio, Fernseher*⟩; **c)** *(reject)* ablehnen; abweisen ⟨*Kandidaten usw.*⟩. **turn 'in 1.** *v.t.* **a)** nach innen drehen; **b)** *(hand in)* abgeben. **2.** *v.i.* **a)** *(enter)* einbiegen; **b)** *(coll.: go to bed)* in die Falle gehen *(salopp).* **turn 'off 1.** *v.t.* abschalten; abstellen ⟨*Wasser, Gas*⟩; zudrehen ⟨*Wasserhahn*⟩. **2.** *v.i.* abbiegen. **turn on** *v.t.* **a)** [-'-] anschalten; aufdrehen ⟨*Wasserhahn, Gas*⟩; **b)** ['--] *(attack)* angreifen. **turn 'out 1.** *v.t.* **a)** *(expel)* hinauswerfen *(ugs.);* **b)** *(switch off)* ausschalten; abdrehen ⟨*Gas*⟩; **c)** *(produce)* produzieren; **d)** *(Brit.) (empty)* ausräumen; leeren; *(get rid of)* wegwerfen. **2.** *v.i.* **a)** *(prove to be)* **sb./sth. ~s out to be sth.** jmd./etw. stellt sich als jmd./etw. heraus; **everything ~ed out well/all right in the end** alles endete gut; **b)** *(appear)* ⟨*Fans usw.:*⟩ erscheinen. **turn 'over 1.** *v.t.* umdrehen. **2.** *v.i.* **a)** *(tip over)* umkippen; ⟨*Boot:*⟩ kentern; ⟨*Auto, Flugzeug:*⟩ sich überschlagen; **b)** *(from one side to the other)* sich umdrehen; **c)** *(~ a page)* weiterblättern. **turn 'round** *v.i.* sich umdrehen. **'turn to** *v.t. (fig.)* **~ to sb.** sich an jmdn. wenden; **~ to sb. for help/advice** bei jmdm. Hilfe/Rat suchen; **~ to drink** sich in den Alkohol flüchten. **turn 'up 1.** *v.i.* **a)** ⟨*Person:*⟩ erscheinen; **b)** *(present itself)* auftauchen; ⟨*Gelegenheit:*⟩ sich bieten. **2.** *v.t.* **a)** hochschlagen ⟨*Kragen*⟩; **b)** lauter stellen ⟨*Ton, Radio, Fernseher*⟩; aufdrehen ⟨*Heizung, Gas*⟩; heller machen ⟨*Licht*⟩

'turning *n.* Abzweigung, *die.* **'turning-point** *n.* Wendepunkt, *der*

turnip ['tɜ:nɪp] *n.* Kohlrübe, *die*

turn: **~-out** *n. (of people)* Beteiligung, *die* (for an + *Dat.*); **~over** *n.* **a)** *(Commerc.)* Umsatz, *der; (of stock)* Umschlag, *der;* **b)** *(of staff)* Fluktuation, *die;* **~pike** *n. (Amer.)* gebührenpflichtige Autobahn; **~stile** *n.* Drehkreuz, *das;* **~table** *n.* Plattenteller, *der;* **~-up** *n. (Brit. Fashion)* Aufschlag, *der*

turpentine ['tɜ:pntaɪn] *n.* Terpentin, *das*

turquoise ['tɜ:kwɔɪz] 1. *n.* a) Türkis, *der;* b) *(colour)* Türkis, *das.* 2. *adj.* türkis[farben]

turret ['tʌrɪt] *n.* Türmchen, *das*

turtle ['tɜ:tl] *n.* a) Meeresschildkröte, *die;* b) *(Amer.: freshwater reptile)* Wasserschildkröte, *die*

turves *see* turf b·

tusk [tʌsk] *n.* Stoßzahn, *der*

tussle ['tʌsl] 1. *n.* Gerangel, *das (ugs.).* 2. *v. i.* sich balgen

tutor ['tju:tə(r)] *n.* |private| ~: [Privat]lehrer, *der*/-lehrerin, *die*

tuxedo [tʌk'si:dəʊ] *n., pl.* ~s *or* ~es *(Amer.)* Smoking, *der*

TV [ti:'vi:] *n.* a) Fernsehen, *das;* b) *(television set)* Fernseher, *der (ugs.)*

twaddle ['twɒdl] *n.* Gewäsch, *das (ugs.)*

twang [twæŋ] 1. *v. t.* zupfen ⟨Saite⟩. 2. *n.* |nasal| ~: Näseln, *das*

tweed [twi:d] *n.* Tweed, *der*

tweezers ['twi:zəz] *n. pl.* |pair of| ~: Pinzette, *die*

twelfth [twelfθ] 1. *adj.* zwölft... 2. *n. (fraction)* Zwölftel, *das. See also* eighth

twelve [twelv] 1. *adj.* zwölf. 2. *n.* Zwölf, *die. See also* eight

twentieth ['twentɪθ] 1. *adj.* zwanzigst... 2. *n. (fraction)* Zwanzigstel, *das. See also* eighth

twenty ['twentɪ] 1. *adj.* zwanzig. 2. *n.* Zwanzig, *die. See also* eight; eighty 2

twice [twaɪs] *adv.* a) zweimal; b) *(doubly)* doppelt

twiddle ['twɪdl] *v. t.* herumdrehen an (+ *Dat.) (ugs.)*

¹**twig** [twɪg] *n.* Zweig, *der*

²**twig** *(coll.)* 1. *v. t.,* -gg- kapieren *(ugs.).* 2. *v. i.,* -gg- *es* kapieren *(ugs.)*

twilight ['twaɪlaɪt] *n.* a) *(evening light)* Dämmerlicht, *das;* b) *(period of half-light)* Dämmerung, *die*

twin [twɪn] 1. *attrib. adj.* a) Zwillings-; b) *(forming a pair)* Doppel-. 2. *n.* Zwilling, *der.* **twin 'beds** *n. pl.* zwei Einzelbetten

twine [twaɪn] 1. *n.* Bindfaden, *der.* 2. *v. i.* sich winden (**about, around** um)

twinge [twɪndʒ] *n.* Stechen, *das;* ~|s| **of conscience** *(fig.)* Gewissensbisse

twinkle ['twɪŋkl] 1. *v. i.* funkeln (**with** vor + *Dat.).* 2. *n.* Funkeln, *das*

twinkling ['twɪŋklɪŋ] *n.* **in a** ~, **in the** ~ **of an eye** im Handumdrehen

'**twin town** *n. (Brit.)* Partnerstadt, *die*

twirl [twɜ:l] 1. *v. t.* [schnell] drehen. 2. *v. i.* wirbeln (**around** über + *Akk.)*

twist [twɪst] 1. *v. t.* a) verdrehen ⟨Worte, Bedeutung⟩; ~ **one's ankle** sich *(Dat.)* den Knöchel verrenken; ~ **sb.'s arm** jmdm. den Arm umdrehen; *(fig.)* jmdm. [die] Daumenschrauben anlegen; b) *(rotate)* drehen. 2. *v. i.* sich winden. 3. *n.* a) *(motion)* Drehung, *die;* b) *(unexpected occurrence)* überraschende Wendung

twit [twɪt] *n. (Brit. sl.)* Trottel, *der (ugs.)*

twitch [twɪtʃ] 1. *v. i.* ⟨Mund, Lippe:⟩ zucken. 2. *n.* Zucken, *das*

twitter ['twɪtə(r)] 1. *n.* Zwitschern, *das.* 2. *v. i.* zwitschern

two [tu:] 1. *adj.* zwei. 2. *n.* Zwei, *die. See also* eight

two: **~-faced** ['tu:feɪst] *adj. (fig.)* falsch; **~-fold** *adj., adv.* zweifach; **a ~-fold increase** ein Anstieg auf das Doppelte; **~-piece** 1. *n.* Zweiteiler, *der;* 2. *adj.* zweiteilig; **~some** ['tu:səm] *n.* Paar, *das;* **~-way** *adj.* **a)** zweibahnig *(Verkehrsw.);* '**~-way traffic ahead'** „Achtung Gegenverkehr"; **b)** **~-way mirror** Einwegspiegel, *der*

tycoon [taɪ'ku:n] *n.* Magnat, *der*

tying *see* tie 1, 2

type [taɪp] 1. *n.* a) Art, *die; (person)* Typ, *der;* **what ~ of car ...?** was für ein Auto ...?; b) *(Printing)* Drucktype, *die.* 2. *v. t.* [mit der Maschine] schreiben; tippen *(ugs.).* 3. *v. i.* maschineschreiben. **type 'out** *v. t.* [mit der Schreibmaschine] abschreiben; abtippen *(ugs.)*

'**typewriter** *n.* Schreibmaschine, *die.* '**typewritten** *adj.* maschine[n]geschrieben

typhoid ['taɪfɔɪd] *n.* ~ Typhus, *der*

typhoon [taɪ'fu:n] *n.* Taifun, *der*

typical ['tɪpɪkl] *adj.* typisch (**of** für)

typify ['tɪpɪfaɪ] *v. t.* ~ **sth.** als typisches Beispiel für etw. dienen

typing ['taɪpɪŋ] *n.* Maschineschreiben, *das*

typist ['taɪpɪst] *n.* Schreibkraft, *die*

tyrannical [tɪ'rænɪkl] *adj.* tyrannisch

tyranny ['tɪrənɪ] *n.* Tyrannei, *die*

tyrant ['taɪərənt] *n.* Tyrann, *der*

tyre ['taɪə(r)] *n.* Reifen, *der*

U

U, u [ju:] *n.* U, u, *das*
ubiquitous [ju:'bɪkwɪtəs] *adj.* allgegenwärtig
udder ['ʌdə(r)] *n.* Euter, *das*
ugliness ['ʌglɪnɪs] *n.* Häßlichkeit, *die*
ugly ['ʌglɪ] *adj.* **a)** häßlich; **b)** *(nasty)* übel 〈*Wunde, Laune usw.*〉
UK *abbr.* United Kingdom
Ukraine [ju:'kreɪn] *pr. n.* Ukraine, *die*
ulcer ['ʌlsə(r)] *n.* Geschwür, *das*
ulterior [ʌl'tɪərɪə(r)] *adj.* hintergründig; ~ **motive** Hintergedanke, *der*
ultimate ['ʌltɪmət] **1.** *attrib. adj.* **a)** *(final)* letzt...; *(eventual)* endgültig 〈*Sieg*〉; **b)** *(fundamental)* tiefst... **2.** *n.* the ~ **in** comfort/luxury der Gipfel an Bequemlichkeit/Luxus. '**ultimately** *adv.* **a)** *(in the end)* schließlich; **b)** *(in the last analysis)* letzten Endes
ultimatum [ʌltɪ'meɪtəm] *n., pl.* ~s *or* **ultimata** [ʌltɪ'meɪtə] Ultimatum, *das*
ultra'violet *adj. (Phys.)* ultraviolett; UV-〈*Lampe, Filter*〉
umbilical cord [ʌm'bɪlɪkl kɔ:d] *n.* Nabelschnur, *die*
umbrage ['ʌmbrɪdʒ] *n.* take ~ [at sth.] [an etw. (+ *Dat.*)] Anstoß nehmen
umbrella [ʌm'brelə] *n.* [Regen]schirm, *der*
umpire ['ʌmpaɪə(r)] *n.* Schiedsrichter, *der*/-richterin, *die*
umpteen [ʌmp'ti:n] *adj. (coll.)* zig *(ugs.)*; x *(ugs.)*
unabashed [ʌnə'bæʃt] *adj.* ungeniert
unable [ʌn'eɪbl] *pred. adj.* be ~ to do sth. etw. nicht tun können
unabridged [ʌnə'brɪdʒd] *adj.* ungekürzt
unac'ceptable *adj.* unannehmbar
unac'countable *adj.* unerklärlich. **unaccountably** [ʌnə'kaʊntəblɪ] *adv.* unerklärlicherweise
unac'customed *adj.* ungewohnt; be ~ to sth. etw. *(Akk.)* nicht gewöhnt sein
unadulterated [ʌnə'dʌltəreɪtɪd] *adj.* **a)** *(pure)* unverfälscht; **b)** *(utter)* völlig

unaided [ʌn'eɪdɪd] *adj.* ohne fremde Hilfe
unanimity [ju:nə'nɪmɪtɪ] *n.* Einmütigkeit, *die*
unanimous [ju:'nænɪməs] *adj.* einstimmig; be ~ in doing sth. etw. einmütig tun
unarmed [ʌn'ɑ:md] *adj.* unbewaffnet; ~ **combat** Kampf ohne Waffen
unassuming [ʌnə'sju:mɪŋ] *adj.* bescheiden
unattached [ʌnə'tætʃt] *adj.* **a)** nicht befestigt; **b)** *(without a partner)* ungebunden
unat'tended *adj.* **a)** ~ to *(not dealt with)* unerledigt; nicht bedient 〈*Kunde*〉; nicht behandelt 〈*Patient*〉; **b)** *(not supervised)* unbewacht 〈*Parkplatz, Gepäck*〉
unat'tractive *adj.* unattraktiv
unauthorized [ʌn'ɔ:θəraɪzd] *adj.* unbefugt; no entry for ~ persons Zutritt für Unbefugte verboten
una'vailable *adj.* nicht erhältlich 〈*Ware*〉; be ~ for comment zur Stellungnahme nicht zur Verfügung stehen
una'voidable *adj.* unvermeidlich
unaware [ʌnə'weə(r)] *adj.* be ~ of sth. sich *(Dat.)* einer Sache *(Gen.)* nicht bewußt sein. **unawares** [ʌnə'weəz] *adv.* catch sb. ~: jmdn. überraschen
unbalanced [ʌn'bælənst] *adj.* **a)** unausgewogen; **b)** *(mentally ~)* unausgeglichen
un'bearable *adj.,* **unbearably** [ʌn'beərəblɪ] *adv.* unerträglich
unbeatable [ʌn'bi:təbl] *adj.* unschlagbar *(ugs.)*
un'beaten *adj.* **a)** ungeschlagen; **b)** *(not surpassed)* unerreicht; ungebrochen 〈*Rekord*〉
unbe'lievable *adj.* **a)** unglaublich; **b)** *(tremendous)* unwahrscheinlich
unbiased, unbiassed [ʌn'baɪəst] *adj.* unvoreingenommen
unblemished [ʌn'blemɪʃt] *adj.* makellos 〈*Haut, Ruf*〉
un'block *v. t.* frei machen
un'bolt *v. t.* aufriegeln 〈*Tür*〉
unborn [ʌn'bɔ:n, *attrib.* 'ʌnbɔ:n] *adj.* ungeboren
un'breakable *adj.* unzerbrechlich
unburden [ʌn'bɜ:dn] *v. t.* ~ oneself sein Herz ausschütten
un'button *v. t.* aufknöpfen
uncalled-for [ʌn'kɔ:ldfɔ:(r)] *adj.* unangebracht
uncanny [ʌn'kænɪ] *adj.* unheimlich

uncaring [ʌnˈkeərɪŋ] *adj.* gleichgültig
unceasing [ʌnˈsiːsɪŋ] *adj.* unaufhörlich
unceremonious [ʌnserɪˈməʊnɪəs] *adj.* a) *(informal)* formlos; b) *(abrupt)* brüsk. **unceˈmoniously** *adv.* ohne Umschweife
unˈcertain *adj.* a) *(not sure)* be ~ |whether ...| sich *(Dat.)* nicht sicher sein[, ob ...]; b) *(not clear)* ungewiß ⟨Ergebnis, Zukunft⟩; of ~ age/origin unbestimmten Alters/unbestimmter Herkunft; c) *(ambiguous)* vage; in no ~ terms ganz eindeutig. **uncertainty** [ʌnˈsɜːtntɪ] *n.* a) Ungewißheit, *die;* b) *(hesitation)* Unsicherheit, *die*
unchanged [ʌnˈtʃeɪndʒd] *adj.* unverändert
unˈcharitable *adj.* **uncharitably** [ʌnˈtʃærɪtəblɪ] *adv.* lieblos
unˈcivil *adj.* unhöflich
uncle [ˈʌŋkl] *n.* Onkel, *der*
unˈcomfortable *adj.* a) unbequem; b) *(feeling discomfort)* be ~ : sich unbehaglich fühlen; c) *(uneasy, disconcerting)* unangenehm; peinlich ⟨Stille⟩. **unˈcomfortably** *adv.* unbequem; be ~ aware of sth. sich *(Dat.)* einer Sache peinlich bewußt sein
unˈcommon *adj.* ungewöhnlich
uncompliˈmentary *adj.* wenig schmeichelhaft
uncompromising [ʌnˈkɒmprəmaɪzɪŋ] *adj.* kompromißlos
unconˈditional *adj.* bedingungslos ⟨Kapitulation⟩; kategorisch ⟨Ablehnung⟩; ⟨Versprechen⟩ ohne Vorbehalte
unˈconscious 1. *adj.* a) *(Med.)* bewußtlos; b) *(unaware)* be ~ of sth. sich einer Sache *(Gen.)* nicht bewußt sein; c) *(not intended; Psych.)* unbewußt. 2. *n.* Unbewußte, *das.* **unˈconsciously** *adv.* unbewußt
unconˈventional *adj.,* **unconˈventionally** *adv.* unkonventionell
uncoˈoperative *adj.* unkooperativ; *(unhelpful)* wenig hilfsbereit
unˈcork *v. t.* entkorken
uncouth [ʌnˈkuːθ] *adj.* ungehobelt ⟨Person, Benehmen⟩; grob ⟨Bemerkung⟩
unˈcover *v. t.* aufdecken
undaunted [ʌnˈdɔːntɪd] *adj.* unverzagt
undecided [ʌndɪˈsaɪdɪd] *adj.* a) *(not settled)* nicht entschieden; b) *(hesitant)* unentschlossen
undeniably [ʌndɪˈnaɪəblɪ] *adv.* unbestreitbar

under [ˈʌndə(r)] 1. *prep.* a) *(underneath, below)* unter *(position:* + *Dat.; motion:* + *Akk.);* from ~ the table/bed unter dem Tisch/Bett hervor; b) *(undergoing)* ~ treatment in Behandlung; ~ repair in Reparatur; ~ construction im Bau; c) *(in conditions of)* bei ⟨Streß, hohen Temperaturen usw.⟩; d) *(subject to)* unter (+ *Dat.)*; ~ the terms of the contract nach den Bestimmungen des Vertrags; e) *(with the use of)* unter (+ *Dat.)*; ~ an assumed name unter falschem Namen; f) *(less than)* unter (+ *Dat.)*. 2. *adv.* a) *(in or to a lower or subordinate position)* darunter; b) *(in/into a state of unconsciousness)* be ~/put sb. ~ : in Narkose liegen/jmdn. in Narkose versetzen
under: ~**carriage** *n.* Fahrwerk, *das;* ~**clothes** *n. pl.,* ~**clothing** *see* underwear; ~**cover** *adj. (disguised)* getarnt; *(secret)* verdeckt; ~**cover agent** Geheimagent, *der;* ~**current** *n.* Unterströmung, *die; (fig.)* Unterton, *der;* ~ˈ**cut** *v. t.,* ~**cut** unterbieten; ~**dog** *n.* a) *(in fight)* Unterlegene, *der/die;* b) *(fig.)* Benachteiligte, *der/die;* ~ˈ**done** *adj.* halbgar; ~**estimate** [ʌndərˈestɪmeɪt] 1. *v. t.* unterschätzen; 2. [ʌndərˈestɪmət] *n.* Unterschätzung, *die;* ~ˈ**fed** *adj.* unterernährt; ~**foot** *adv.* am Boden; be trampled ~**foot** mit Füßen zertrampelt werden; ~ˈ**go** *v. t.,* forms as go 1 durchmachen; ~**go treatment** sich einer Behandlung unterziehen; ~**go a change** sich verändern; ~ˈ**graduate** *n.* ~**graduate |student|** Student/Studentin vor der ersten Prüfung; ~**ground** 1. |--ˈ-| *adv.* a) unter der Erde; *(Mining)* unter Tage; b) *(fig.) (in hiding)* im Untergrund; *(into hiding)* in den Untergrund; 2. |ˈ--| *adj.* unterirdisch ⟨Höhle, See⟩; ~**ground railway** Untergrundbahn, *die;* U-Bahn, *die;* ~**ground car-park** Tiefgarage, *die;* 3. *n. (railway)* U-Bahn, *die;* ~ **station/train** U-Bahnhof, *der/*U-Bahn-Zug, *der;* ~**growth** *n.* Unterholz, *das;* ~**hand,** ~**handed** *adj.* a) *(secret)* heimlich; b) *(crafty)* hinterhältig; ~**lay** *n.* Unterlage, *die;* ~ˈ**lie** *v. t.,* forms as ²lie: ~**lie sth.** *(fig.)* einer Sache *(Dat.)* zugrundeliegen; ~**lying cause** eigentliche Ursache; ~ˈ**line** *v. t.* unterstreichen
underling [ˈʌndəlɪŋ] *n.* Untergebene, *der/die*
under: ~ˈ**lying** *see* underlie; ~ˈ**mine**

v. t. **a)** unterhöhlen; **b)** *(fig.)* untergraben; unterminieren ⟨*Autorität*⟩

underneath [ʌndəˈniːθ] **1.** *prep.* unter *(position:* + *Dat.; motion:* + *Akk.).* **2.** *adv.* darunter

under: ~**'paid** *adj.* unterbezahlt; ~**pants** *n. pl.* Unterhose, *die;* ~**pass** *n.* Unterführung, *die;* ~'**play** *v. t.* herunterspielen; ~'**privileged** *adj.* unterprivilegiert; ~'**rate** *v. t.* unterschätzen; ~**seal** *n.* Unterbodenschutz, *der*

understand [ʌndəˈstænd] **1.** *v. t.,* **understood** [ʌndəˈstʊd] **a)** verstehen; **make oneself understood** sich verständlich machen; **b)** *(have heard)* gehört haben; **c)** *(take as implied)* **it was understood that ...:** es wurde allgemein angenommen, daß ... **2.** *v. i.,* **understood a)** verstehen; **b)** *(gather, hear)* **if I** ~ **correctly** wenn ich mich nicht irre; **he is, I** ~**, no longer here** er ist, wie ich höre, nicht mehr hier.

understandably [ʌndəˈstændəblɪ] *adv.* verständlicherweise. **under-**'**standing 1.** *adj.* verständnisvoll. **2.** *n.* **a)** *(agreement)* Verständigung, *die;* **reach an** ~ **with sb.** sich mit jmdm. verständigen; **on the** ~ **that ...:** unter der Voraussetzung, daß ...; **b)** *(intelligence)* Verstand, *der;* **c)** *(insight)* Verständnis, *das* *(of,* for für)

under: ~**statement** *n.* Untertreibung, *die;* ~**study** *n.* Ersatzspieler, *der/*-spielerin, *die;* ~'**take** *v. t., forms as* **take** 1 unternehmen; ~**take a task** eine Aufgabe übernehmen; ~**take to do sth.** sich verpflichten, etw. zu tun; ~**taker** *n.* Leichenbestatter, *der/*-bestatterin, *die;* ~'**taking** *n.* **a)** *(task)* Aufgabe, *die;* **b)** *(pledge)* Versprechen, *das;* ~**tone** *n.* **in** ~**tones** *or* **an** ~**tone** mit gedämpfter Stimme; ~**tone of criticism** kritischer Unterton; ~**tow** *n.* Unterströmung, *die;* ~'**value** *v. t.* unterbewerten; ~**water 1.** ['----] *attrib. adj.* Unterwasser-; **2.** [--'--] *adv.* unter Wasser; ~**wear** *n.* Unterwäsche, *die;* ~'**weight** *adj.* untergewichtig; ~**world** *n.* Unterwelt, *die*

unde'sirable *adj.* unerwünscht; **it is** ~ **that ...:** es ist nicht wünschenswert, daß ...

undeveloped [ʌndɪˈveləpt] *adj.* **a)** *(immature)* nicht voll ausgebildet; **b)** *(not built on)* nicht bebaut

undies ['ʌndɪz] *n. pl. (coll.)* Unterwäsche, *die*

un'dignified *adj.* blamabel

undo [ʌnˈduː] *v. t.,* **undoes** [ʌnˈdʌz], **un-**doing [ʌnˈduːɪŋ], **undid** [ʌnˈdɪd], **undone** [ʌnˈdʌn] *(unfasten)* aufmachen

un'done *adj.* **a)** *(not accomplished)* unerledigt; **b)** *(not fastened)* offen

undoubted [ʌnˈdaʊtɪd] *adj.* unzweifelhaft. **un'doubtedly** *adv.* zweifellos

un'dress 1. *v. t.* ausziehen; **get** ~**ed** sich ausziehen **2.** *v. i.* sich ausziehen

un'due *attrib. adj.* übertrieben; übermäßig

undulating ['ʌndjʊleɪtɪŋ] *adj.* Wellen⟨*linie*⟩; ~ **country** sanfte Hügellandschaft

unduly [ʌnˈdjuːlɪ] *adv.* übermäßig

undying [ʌnˈdaɪɪŋ] *adj.* ewig; unsterblich ⟨*Ruhm*⟩

unearth [ʌnˈɜːθ] *v. t.* **a)** ausgraben; **b)** *(fig.: discover)* aufdecken

unearthly [ʌnˈɜːθlɪ] *adj.* unheimlich; **at an** ~ **hour** in aller Herrgottsfrühe

un'easy *adj.* **a)** *(anxious)* besorgt; **he felt** ~: ihm war unbehaglich zumute; **b)** *(restless)* unruhig

uneatable [ʌnˈiːtəbl] *adj.* ungenießbar

uneco'nomic *adj.* unrentabel. **uneco'nomical** *adj.* ~ [**to run**] unwirtschaftlich

unemployed [ʌnɪmˈplɔɪd] **1.** *adj.* arbeitslos. **2.** *n. pl.* **the** ~: die Arbeitslosen. **unem'ployment** *n.* Arbeitslosigkeit, *die.* **unem'ployment benefit** *n.* Arbeitslosengeld, *das*

un'ending *adj.* endlos

un'equal *adj.* unterschiedlich; ungleich ⟨*Kampf*⟩; **be** ~ **to sth.** einer Sache *(Dat.)* nicht gewachsen sein. **un-equalled** *(Amer.:* **unequaled)** [ʌnˈiːkwld] *adj.* unerreicht

une'quivocal *adj.* eindeutig

unerring [ʌnˈɜːrɪŋ] *adj.* unfehlbar

un'ethical *adj.* unmoralisch

un'even *adj.* **a)** *(not smooth)* uneben; **b)** *(not uniform)* ungleichmäßig; **c)** *(odd)* ungerade ⟨*Zahl*⟩. **un'evenly** *adv.* ungleichmäßig

unex'pected *adj.* unerwartet

un'fair *adj.* unfair; ungerecht. **un-**'**fairly** *adv.* **a)** *(unjustly)* ungerecht; unfair ⟨*spielen*⟩; **b)** *(unreasonably)* zu Unrecht. **un'fairness** *n.* Ungerechtigkeit, *die*

un'faithful *adj.* untreu

unfa'miliar *adj.* **a)** *(strange)* unbekannt; ungewohnt ⟨*Arbeit*⟩; **be** ~ **with sth.** sich mit etw. nicht auskennen

un'fasten *v. t.* **a)** öffnen; **b)** *(detach)* lösen

un'favourable *adj.* ungünstig. **un'favourably** *adv.* ungünstig; **be ~ disposed towards sb./sth.** jmdm./etw. gegenüber ablehnend eingestellt sein
un'feeling *adj.* gefühllos
unfinished [ʌnˈfɪnɪʃt] *adj.* unvollendet ⟨*Werk*⟩; unerledigt ⟨*Arbeit*⟩
un'fit *adj.* **a)** ungeeignet; **b)** *(not physically fit)* nicht fit *(ugs.)*; **~ for military service** [wehrdienst]untauglich
un'flattering *adj.* wenig schmeichelhaft
un'flinching *adj.* unerschrocken
un'fold **1.** *v. t.* entfalten; ausbreiten ⟨*Zeitung, Landkarte*⟩. **2.** *v. i.* sich entfalten; *(develop)* sich entwickeln
unfore'seen *adj.* unvorhergesehen
unforgettable [ʌnfəˈgetəbl] *adj.* unvergeßlich
un'fortunate *adj.* unglücklich. **un'fortunately** *adv.* leider
un'founded *adj.* *(fig.)* unbegründet
un'freeze *v. t. & i.,* **unfroze** [ʌnˈfrəʊz], **unfrozen** [ʌnˈfrəʊzn] auftauen
un'friendly *adj.* unfreundlich; feindlich ⟨*Staat*⟩
un'furl **1.** *v. t.* aufrollen; losmachen ⟨*Segel*⟩. **2.** *v. i.* sich aufrollen
un'furnished *adj.* unmöbliert
ungainly [ʌnˈgeɪnlɪ] *adj.* unbeholfen
ungram'matical *adj.* ungrammatisch
un'grateful *adj.* undankbar
un'happily *adv.* **a)** unglücklich; **b)** *(unfortunately)* leider
un'happiness *n.* Bekümmertheit, *die*
un'happy *adj.* unglücklich; *(not content)* unzufrieden (**about** with); **be or feel ~ about doing sth.** Bedenken haben, etw. zu tun
un'harmed *adj.* unbeschädigt; *(uninjured)* unverletzt
un'healthy *adj.* ungesund
un'helpful *adj.* wenig hilfsbereit ⟨*Person*⟩; ⟨*Bemerkung, Kritik*⟩ die einem nicht weiterhilft
un'hook *v. t.* vom Haken nehmen; aufhaken ⟨*Kleid*⟩
un'hurt *adj.* unverletzt
unhy'gienic *adj.* unhygienisch
unicorn [ˈjuːnɪkɔːn] *n.* Einhorn, *das*
uni'dentified *adj.* nicht identifiziert; **~ flying object** unbekanntes Flugobjekt
unification [juːnɪfɪˈkeɪʃn] *n.* Einigung, *die*
uniform [ˈjuːnɪfɔːm] **1.** *adj.* einheitlich; **be ~ in shape/size** die gleiche Form/Größe haben. **2.** *n.* Uniform, *die;* **in/out of ~:** in/ohne Uniform.

uniformity [juːnɪˈfɔːmɪtɪ] *n.* Einheitlichkeit, *die.* **'uniformly** *adv.* einheitlich
unify [ˈjuːnɪfaɪ] *v. t.* einigen
unilateral [juːnɪˈlætərl] *adj.* einseitig
uni'maginable *adj.* unvorstellbar
uni'maginative *adj.* phantasielos
unim'portant *adj.* unwichtig; bedeutungslos
unin'habitable *adj.* unbewohnbar
unin'habited *adj.* unbewohnt
un'injured *adj.* unverletzt
uninspiring [ʌnɪnˈspaɪərɪŋ] *adj.* langweilig
unin'telligent *adj.* nicht intelligent
unin'telligible *adj.* unverständlich
unin'tended *adj.* unbeabsichtigt
unin'tentional *adj.,* **unin'tentionally** *adv.* unabsichtlich
un'interested *adj.* desinteressiert (**in** an + *Dat.*)
union [ˈjuːnɪən] *n.* **a)** *(trade ~)* Gewerkschaft, *die;* **b)** *(Polit.)* Union, *die.* **Union 'Jack** *n.* *(Brit.)* Union Jack, *der*
unique [juːˈniːk] *adj.* einzigartig
unison [ˈjuːnɪsən] *n.* Unisono, *das;* **in ~:** einstimmig; **act in ~** *(fig.)* vereint handeln
unit [ˈjuːnɪt] *n.* **a)** *(also Mil., Math.)* Einheit, *die;* **~ of length/monetary ~:** Längen-/Währungseinheit, *die;* **b)** *(piece of furniture)* Element, *das;* **kitchen ~:** Küchenelement, *das*
unite [juːˈnaɪt] **1.** *v. t.* vereinigen; einen, einigen ⟨*Partei, Mitglieder*⟩. **2.** *v. i.* sich vereinigen. **u'nited** *adj.* **a)** *(harmonious)* einig; **b)** *(combined)* gemeinsam
United: ~ 'Kingdom *pr. n.* Vereinigtes Königreich [Großbritannien und Nordirland]; **~ 'Nations** *pr. n. sing.* Vereinte Nationen *Pl.;* **~ States [of A'merica]** *pr. n. sing.* Vereinigte Staaten [von Amerika]
unity [ˈjuːnɪtɪ] *n.* Einheit, *die*
universal [juːnɪˈvɜːsl] *adj.,* **uni'versally** *adv.* allgemein
universe [ˈjuːnɪvɜːs] *n.* Universum, *das*
university [juːnɪˈvɜːsɪtɪ] *n.* Universität, *die; attrib.* Universitäts-
un'just *adj.* ungerecht
unkempt [ʌnˈkempt] *adj.* ungepflegt
un'kind *adj.,* **un'kindly** *adv.* unfreundlich. **un'kindness** *n.* Unfreundlichkeit, *die*
un'known **1.** *adj.* unbekannt. **2.** *adv.* **~ to sb.** ohne daß jmd. davon weiß/wußte

un'lawful *adj.* ungesetzlich
unless [ən'les] *conj.* es sei denn; wenn ... nicht
un'like 1. *adj.* nicht ähnlich. **2.** *prep.* be ~ **sb./sth.** jmdm./einer Sache nicht ähnlich sein; ~ **him, ...**: im Gegensatz zu ihm ...
un'likely *adj.* unwahrscheinlich; **be ~ to do sth.** etw. wahrscheinlich nicht tun
un'limited *adj.* unbegrenzt
un'load *v.t.* entladen ⟨*Lastwagen, Waggon*⟩; löschen ⟨*Schiff, Schiffsladung*⟩; ausladen ⟨*Gepäck*⟩
un'lock *v.t.* aufschließen
un'lucky *adj.* **a)** unglücklich; *(not successful)* glücklos; **be [very] ~:** [großes] Pech haben; **b)** *(bringing bad luck)* **an ~ number** eine Unglückszahl; **be ~:** Unglück bringen
un'manned *adj.* unbemannt
un'married *adj.* unverheiratet; ledig
un'mask *v.t. (fig.)* entlarven
unmi'stakable *adj.* deutlich; unverwechselbar ⟨*Handschrift, Stimme*⟩. **unmistakably** [ʌnmɪ'stəɪkəblɪ] *adv.* unverkennbar
un'mitigated *adj.* vollkommen; **be an ~ disaster** *(coll.)* eine einzige Katastrophe sein
un'natural *adj.*, **un'naturally** *adv.* unnatürlich; *(abnormal)* nicht normal
un'necessarily *adv.*, **un'necessary** *adj.* unnötig
unof'ficial *adj.*, **unof'ficially** *adv.* inoffiziell
un'pack *v.t. & i.* auspacken
un'paid *adj.* unbezahlt; nicht bezahlt; ~ **for** nicht bezahlt
unpalatable [ʌn'pælətəbl] *adj.* ungenießbar
un'paralleled *adj.* beispiellos
un'pardonable *adj.* unverzeihlich
un'pleasant *adj.*, **un'pleasantly** *adv.* unangenehm. **un'pleasantness** *n. (bad feeling)* Verstimmung, die
un'plug *v.t.*, **-gg-:** ~ **a lamp** den Stecker einer Lampe herausziehen
un'popular *adj.* unbeliebt ⟨*Lehrer, Regierung usw.*⟩, unpopulär ⟨*Maßnahme, Politik*⟩ **(with** bei)
un'precedented *adj.* beispiellos
unpre'dictable *adj.* unberechenbar
unpre'pared *adj.* unvorbereitet
unprepos'sessing *adj.* wenig attraktiv
unpre'tentious *adj.* einfach ⟨*Wein, Stil, Haus*⟩; bescheiden ⟨*Person*⟩

unprincipled [ʌn'prɪnsɪpld] *adj.* skrupellos
unprintable [ʌn'prɪntəbl] *adj.* nicht druckreif
unpro'ductive *adj.* fruchtlos ⟨*Diskussion, Nachforschung*⟩; unproduktiv ⟨*Zeit, Arbeit*⟩
unpro'fessional *adj. (contrary to standards)* standeswidrig
un'profitable *adj.* unrentabel
un'promising *adj.* nicht sehr vielversprechend
un'qualified *adj.* **a)** unqualifiziert; **b)** *(absolute)* uneingeschränkt; voll ⟨*Erfolg*⟩
un'questionable *adj.* unbezweifelbar ⟨*Tatsache*⟩; unbestreitbar ⟨*Recht, Ehrlichkeit*⟩. **unquestionably** [ʌn'kwestʃənəblɪ] *adv.* ohne Frage
unravel [ʌn'rævl] **1.** *v.t., (Brit.)* **-ll-** entwirren; *(undo)* aufziehen; *(fig.)* ~ **a mystery/the truth** ein Geheimnis enträtseln/die Wahrheit aufdecken. **2.** *v.i., (Brit.)* **-ll-** sich aufziehen
un'real *adj.* unwirklich
unrea'listic *adj.* unrealistisch
un'reasonable *adj.* unvernünftig; übertrieben ⟨*Ansprüche, Forderung, Preis, Kosten*⟩
unrecognizable [ʌn'rekəgnaɪzəbl] *adj.* **be [absolutely** *or* **quite] ~:** [überhaupt] nicht wiederzuerkennen sein
unre'lated *adj.* **be ~:** nicht miteinander zusammenhängen; *(by family)* nicht verwandt sein
unre'liable *adj.* unzuverlässig
unrequited [ʌnrɪ'kwaɪtɪd] *adj.* unerwidert
unreservedly [ʌnrɪ'zɜːvɪdlɪ] *adv.* uneingeschränkt
un'rest *n.* Unruhen *Pl.*
un'ripe *adj.* unreif
un'rivalled *(Amer.:* **un'rivaled)** *adj.* unübertroffen
un'roll 1. *v.t.* aufrollen. **2.** *v.i.* sich aufrollen
unruly [ʌn'ruːlɪ] *adj.* ungebärdig
un'safe *adj.* nicht sicher; **feel ~:** sich unsicher fühlen
un'said *adj.* ungesagt
un'salted *adj.* ungesalzen
unsatis'factory *adj.* unbefriedigend
un'savoury *(Amer.:* **un'savory)** *adj.* unangenehm; zweifelhaft ⟨*Angelegenheit*⟩; unerfreulich ⟨*Einzelheiten*⟩
unscathed [ʌn'skeɪðd] *adj.* unversehrt
un'screw 1. *v.t.* abschrauben. **2.** *v.i.* sich abschrauben lassen

un'scrupulous *adj.* skrupellos
un'seemly *adj.* unschicklich
unself'conscious *adj.* unbefangen
un'selfish *adj.* selbstlos. un'selfish-
ress *n.* Selbstlosigkeit, *die*
un'settled *adj. (changeable)* wechselhaft; *(fig.)* ruhelos ⟨*Leben*⟩; unruhig
⟨*Zeit, Land*⟩
un'settling *adj.* störend
unshak[e]able [ʌn'ʃeɪkəbl] *adj.* un-
erschütterlich
un'shaven *adj.* unrasiert
un'sightly *adj.* unschön
un'skilled *adj.* ungelernt ⟨*Arbeiter*⟩
un'sociable *adj.* ungesellig
unso'phisticated *adj.* einfach
un'sound *adj.* a) *(diseased)* nicht gesund; krank; b) baufällig ⟨*Gebäude*⟩;
c) *(ill-founded)* wenig stichhaltig;
nicht vertretbar ⟨*Ansicht, Methode*⟩;
d) of ~ mind unzurechnungsfähig
unspeakable [ʌn'spiːkəbl] *adj.* unbeschreiblich; *(very bad)* unsäglich
un'stable *adj.* nicht stabil; |mentally/
emotionally| ~: [psychisch] labil
un'steadily *adv.* unsicher
un'steady *adj.* unsicher; wackelig
⟨*Leiter, Tisch*⟩
un'stuck *adj.* come ~: sich lösen; *(fig.
coll.: fail)* ⟨*Person:*⟩ baden gehen *(ugs.)*
(over mit)
unsuc'cessful *adj.* erfolglos; be ~:
keinen Erfolg haben. unsuc'cessfully *adv.* erfolglos
un'suitable *adj.* ungeeignet
unsu'specting *adj.* nichtsahnend
un'sweetened *adj.* ungesüßt
unsympa'thetic *adj.* wenig mitfühlend; be ~: kein Mitgefühl zeigen
unthinkable [ʌn'θɪŋkəbl] *adj.* unvorstellbar
un'tidily *adv.* unordentlich
un'tidiness *n. see* untidy: Ungepflegt-
heit, *die;* Unaufgeräumtheit, *die*
un'tidy *adj.* ungepflegt ⟨*Äußeres, Person, Garten*⟩; unaufgeräumt ⟨*Zimmer*⟩
un'tie *v. t.,* un'tying aufknüpfen ⟨*Seil,
Paket*⟩; aufbinden ⟨*Knoten*⟩; losbin-
den ⟨*Pferd, Boot*⟩
until [ən'tɪl] 1. *prep.* bis; ~ |the| evening
bis zum Abend; ~ then bis dahin; not
~ |Christmas/the summer| erst [Weih-
nachten/im Sommer]. 2. *conj.* bis
un'timely *adj.* a) ungelegen; b) *(premature)* vorzeitig
un'tiring *adj.* unermüdlich
un'told *adj.* unbeschreiblich; unermeßlich ⟨*Reichtümer, Anzahl*⟩
untoward [ʌntə'wɔːd, ʌn'təʊəd] *adj.*

ungünstig; nothing ~ happened es gab
keine Schwierigkeiten
untranslatable [ʌntræns'leɪtəbl] *adj.*
unübersetzbar
un'true *adj.* unwahr; that's ~: das ist
nicht wahr
un'trustworthy *adj.* unzuverlässig
un'truth *n.* Unwahrheit, *die*
¹unused [ʌn'juːzd] *adj. (new, fresh)* unbenutzt; *(not utilized)* ungenutzt
²unused [ʌn'juːst] *adj. (unaccustomed)*
be ~ to sth./doing sth. etw. *(Akk.)*
nicht gewohnt sein/nicht gewohnt
sein, etw. zu tun
un'usual *adj.,* un'usually *adv.* ungewöhnlich
un'veil *v. t.* enthüllen; *(fig.)* vorstellen
⟨*Produkt*⟩; enthüllen ⟨*Plan*⟩
un'versed *adj.* nicht bewandert (in in
+ *Dat.*)
un'wanted *adj.* unerwünscht
un'warranted *adj.* ungerechtfertigt
un'welcome *adj.* unwillkommen
un'well *adj.* unwohl; look ~: nicht
wohl *od.* gut aussehen; he feels ~
(poorly) er fühlt sich nicht wohl
unwieldy [ʌn'wiːldɪ] *adj.* sperrig
un'willing *adj.* widerwillig; be ~ to do
sth. etw. nicht tun wollen. un'willingly *adv.* widerwillig
unwind [ʌn'waɪnd] 1. *v. t.,* unwound
[ʌn'waʊnd] abwickeln. 2. *v. i.,* unwound a) sich abwickeln; b) *(coll.:
relax)* sich entspannen
un'wise *adj.* unklug
unwitting [ʌn'wɪtɪŋ] *adj.,* un'wittingly *adv.* unwissentlich
un'workable *adj.* undurchführbar
⟨*Plan*⟩
un'worthy *adj.* unwürdig; be ~ of sth.
einer Sache *(Gen.)* nicht würdig sein;
be ~ of sb./sth. ⟨*Verhalten:*⟩ einer Per-
son/Sache *(Gen.)* unwürdig sein
un'wrap *v. t.,* -pp- auswickeln
un'written *adj.* ungeschrieben
un'zip *v. t.,* -pp-: ~ a dress/bag *etc.* den
Reißverschluß eines Kleides/einer
Tasche *usw.* öffnen
up [ʌp] 1. *adv.* a) *(to higher place)* nach
oben; *(in lift)* aufwärts; the bird flew
up to the roof der Vogel flog aufs
Dach [hinauf]; up into the air in die
Luft [hinauf]; up here/there hier her-
auf/dort hinauf; higher/a little way up
höher/ein kurzes Stück hinauf; come
on up! komm [hier/weiter] herauf!;
b) *(to upstairs)* herauf/hinauf; nach
oben; c) *(in higher place, upstairs)*
oben; up here/there hier/da oben; the

next floor up ein Stockwerk höher; **d)** *(out of bed)* **be up** aufsein; **e)** *(in price, value, amount)* **prices have gone up/are up** die Preise sind gestiegen; **butter is up [by ...]** Butter ist [...] teurer; **f)** *(as far as)* **up to sth.** bis zu etw.; **up to here/ there** bis hier[hin]/bis dorthin; **g) [not] be/feel up to sth.** *(capable of sth.)* einer Sache *(Dat.)* [nicht] gewachsen sein/ sich einer Sache *(Dat.)* [nicht] gewachsen fühlen; **[not] be/feel up to doing sth.** [nicht] in der Lage sein/sich [nicht] in der Lage fühlen, etw. zu tun; **h) be up to sth.** *(doing)* etw. anstellen *(ugs.);* **it is [not] up to sb. to do sth.** *(sb.'s duty)* es ist [nicht] jmds. Sache, etw. zu tun; **i) be three points/games up** mit drei Punkten/Spielen vorn liegen; **j) walk up and down** auf und ab gehen; **k) time is up** die Zeit ist abgelaufen. **2.** *prep.* herauf/hinauf; **walk up the hill/road** den Berg/die Straße hinaufgehen; **walk up and down the platform** auf dem Bahnsteig auf und ab gehen; **further up the ladder/coast** weiter oben auf der Leiter/an der Küste; **live just up the road** ein Stück weiter oben in der Straße wohnen. **3.** *adj.* *(coll.: amiss)* **what's up?** was ist los? *(ugs.);* **something is up** irgendwas ist los *(ugs.).* **4.** *v. t.,* **-pp-** *(coll.: increase)* erhöhen
'upbringing *n.* Erziehung, *die*
up'date *v. t.* auf den aktuellen Stand bringen
up'grade *v. t.* **a)** aufwerten *⟨Stellung⟩;* **b)** *(improve)* verbessern
upheaval [ʌp'hiːvl] *n.* Aufruhr, *der; (disturbance)* Durcheinander, *das*
up'hill **1.** *adj.* *(fig.)* **an ~ task/struggle** eine mühselige Aufgabe/ein harter Kampf. **2.** *adv.* bergauf
uphold *v. t.,* **upheld** unterstützen; wahren *⟨Tradition⟩*
upholster [ʌp'həʊlstə(r)] *v. t.* polstern.
up'holsterer *n.* Polsterer, *der/*Polsterin, *die.* **up'holstery** *n.* **a)** *(craft)* Polster[er]handwerk, *das;* **b)** *(padding)* Polsterung, *die*
'upkeep *n.* Unterhalt, *der*
'up-market *adj.* exklusiv
upon [ə'pɒn] *prep.* auf *(direction:* + *Akk.; position:* + *Dat.)*
upper ['ʌpə(r)] **1.** *compar. adj.* ober...; Ober*⟨grenze, -lippe, -arm usw.⟩;* **~ circle** oberer Rang; **~ class[es]** Oberschicht, *die;* **have/get/gain the ~ hand** die Oberhand haben/gewinnen/erhalten. **2.** *n.* Oberteil, *das.* **upper 'deck**

n. Oberdeck, *das.* **'uppermost 1.** *adj.* oberst... **2.** *adv.* ganz oben
'upright 1. *adj.* aufrecht. **2.** *n.* seitliche Leiste
'uprising *n.* Aufstand, *der*
'uproar *n.* Aufruhr, *der*
up'root *v. t.* [her]ausreißen; *⟨Sturm:⟩* entwurzeln
upset 1. [ʌp'set] *v. t.,* **-tt-,** **upset a)** *(overturn)* umkippen; *(accidentally)* umstoßen *⟨Tasse, Milch usw.⟩;* **b)** *(distress)* erschüttern; *(make angry)* aufregen; **don't let it ~ you** nimm es nicht so schwer; **c)** *(make ill)* **sth. ~s sb.** etw. bekommt jmdm. nicht; **d)** durcheinanderbringen *⟨Plan⟩.* **2.** *v. i.,* **-tt-,** **upset** umkippen. **3.** *adj.* *(distressed)* bestürzt; *(agitated)* aufgeregt; **get ~ [about/over sth.]** sich [über etw. *(Akk.)*] aufregen. **4.** ['ʌpset] *n.* **a)** *(agitation)* Aufregung, *die; (annoyance)* Verärgerung, *die;* **b) stomach ~:** Magenverstimmung, *die;* **c)** *(upheaval)* Aufruhr, *der.* **up'setting** *adj.* erschütternd; *(sad)* traurig; *(annoying)* ärgerlich
'upshot *n.* Ergebnis, *das*
upside 'down 1. *adv.* verkehrt herum; **turn sth. ~:** etw. auf den Kopf stellen. **2.** *adj.* auf dem Kopf stehend *⟨Bild⟩;* **be ~:** auf dem Kopf stehen
upstairs 1. [-'-] *adv.* nach oben *⟨gehen, kommen⟩;* oben *⟨sein, wohnen⟩.* **2.** ['--] *adj.* im Obergeschoß *nachgestellt*
'upstart *n.* Emporkömmling, *der*
'up'stream *adv.* flußaufwärts
'uptake *n.* **be quick/slow on the ~** *(coll.)* schnell begreifen/schwer von Begriff sein *(ugs.)*
uptight [-'-, '--] *adj.* *(coll.: tense)* nervös *(about* wegen*)*
up to 'date *adj.* **be/keep ~:** auf dem neusten Stand sein/bleiben; **bring sth. ~:** etw. auf den neusten Stand bringen. **up-to-'date** *attrib. adj. (current)* aktuell; *(modern)* modern
'upturn *n.* Aufschwung, *der (in Gen.)*
upward ['ʌpwəd] **1.** *adj.* nach oben gerichtet. **2.** *adv.* aufwärts *⟨sich bewegen⟩;* nach oben *⟨sehen, gehen⟩.* **upwards** ['ʌpwədz] *adv.* **a)** *see* **upward 2; b) ~ of** über *(+ Akk.)*
uranium [jʊə'reɪnɪəm] *n.* Uran, *das*
Uranus ['jʊərənəs, jʊə'reɪnəs] *pr. n. (Astron.)* Uranus, *der*
urban ['ɜːbn] *adj.* städtisch; Stadt*⟨gebiet, -bevölkerung, -planung⟩*
urchin ['ɜːtʃɪn] *n.* Strolch, *der*
urge [ɜːdʒ] **1.** *v. t.* **~ sb. to do sth.** jmdn. drängen, etw. zu tun. **2.** *n.* Trieb, *der.*

urge ˈon *v.t.* antreiben; *(encourage)* anfeuern
urgency [ˈɜːdʒənsɪ] *n.* Dringlichkeit, *die*
urgent [ˈɜːdʒənt] *adj.* dringend; *(to be dealt with immediately)* eilig; **be in ~ need of sth.** etw. dringend brauchen.
ˈ**urgently** *adv.* dringend; *(immediately)* eilig
urinate [ˈjʊərɪneɪt] *v.i.* urinieren
urine [ˈjʊərɪn] *n.* Urin, *der;* Harn, *der*
urn [ɜːn] *n.* **a) tea/coffee ~:** Tee-/Kaffeemaschine, *die;* **b)** *(vessel)* Urne, *die*
Uruguay [ˈjʊərəgwaɪ] *pr. n.* Uruguay *(das)*
US *abbr.* United States USA
us [əs, *stressed* ʌs] *pron.* uns; **it's us** wir sind's *(ugs.)*
USA *abbr.* United States of America USA
usage [ˈjuːzɪdʒ, ˈjuːsɪdʒ] *n.* **a)** Brauch, *der;* **b)** *(Ling.)* Sprachgebrauch, *der*
use 1. [juːs] *n.* **a)** Gebrauch, *der; (of dictionary, calculator, room)* Benutzung, *die; (of word, pesticide, spice)* Verwendung, *die;* |**not**| **be in ~:** [nicht] in Gebrauch sein; **be no longer in ~:** nicht mehr verwendet werden; **make ~ of sb./sth.** jmdn./etw. gebrauchen; *(exploit)* ausnutzen; **make good ~ of, turn** *or* **put to good ~:** gut nutzen ⟨*Zeit, Talent, Geld*⟩; **put sth. to ~:** etw. verwenden; **b)** *(usefulness)* Nutzen, *der;* **is it of |any| ~?** ist das |irgendwie| von Nutzen?; **be |of| no ~ |to sb.|** |jmdm.| nicht nützen; **it's no ~ |doing that|** es hat keinen Sinn[, das zu tun]; **c)** *(purpose)* Verwendung, *die;* **have/find a ~ for sth./sb.** für etw./jmdn. Verwendung haben/finden; **have no/not much ~ for sth./sb.** etw./jmdn. nicht/kaum brauchen. **2.** [juːz] *v.t.* **a)** benutzen; nutzen ⟨*Gelegenheit*⟩; anwenden ⟨*Gewalt*⟩; in Anspruch nehmen ⟨*Firma, Dienstleistung*⟩; nutzen ⟨*Zeit, Gelegenheit*⟩; verwenden ⟨*Kraftstoff, Butter, Wort*⟩; **b) ~d to** [ˈjuːst tə]: **I ~d to live in London** früher habe ich in London gelebt. **use ˈup** *v.t.* aufbrauchen; verbrauchen ⟨*Geld, Energie*⟩
used 1. *adj.* **a)** [juːzd] gebraucht; gestempelt ⟨*Briefmarke*⟩; **~ car** Gebrauchtwagen, *der;* **b)** [juːst] **~ to sth.** [an] etw. *(Akk.)* gewöhnt. **2.** [juːst] *see* **use 2 b**
useful [ˈjuːsfl] *adj.* nützlich; praktisch ⟨*Werkzeug*⟩; hilfreich ⟨*Rat, Idee*⟩.
ˈ**usefulness** *n.* Nützlichkeit, *die*
ˈ**useless** *adj.* unbrauchbar ⟨*Werkzeug,*

Rat, Idee⟩; nutzlos ⟨*Wissen, Information, Protest, Anstrengung, Kampf*⟩; zwecklos ⟨*Widerstand, Protest*⟩
ˈ**user** *n.* Benutzer, *der/*Benutzerin, *die.*
ˈ**user-friendly** *adj.* benutzerfreundlich
usher [ˈʌʃə(r)] **1.** *n.* *(in court)* Gerichtsdiener, *der; (at cinema, church)* Platzanweiser, *der.* **2.** *v.t.* führen. **usher ˈin** *v.t.* hineinführen; *(fig.)* einläuten
usherette [ʌʃəˈret] *n.* Platzanweiserin, *die*
USSR *abbr. (Hist.)* Union of Soviet Socialist Republics UdSSR, *die*
usual [ˈjuːʒʊəl] *adj.* üblich. **usually** [ˈjuːʒʊəlɪ] *adv.* gewöhnlich
usurp [juːˈzɜːp] *v.t.* sich *(Dat.)* widerrechtlich aneignen
utensil [juːˈtensɪl] *n.* Utensil, *das;* **writing ~s** Schreibutensilien; **kitchen ~s** Küchengeräte
uterus [ˈjuːtərəs] *n.* Gebärmutter, *die*
utility [juːˈtɪlɪtɪ] *n.* **a)** Nutzen, *der;* **b)** |**public**| **~:** öffentlicher Versorgungsbetrieb. **uˈtility room** *n.* Raum, *in den [größere] Haushaltsgeräte (z. B. Waschmaschine) installiert sind*
utilize [ˈjuːtɪlaɪz] *v.t.* nutzen
utmost [ˈʌtməʊst] **1.** *adj.* äußerst...; größt... ⟨*Höflichkeit, Eleganz, Einfachheit, Geschwindigkeit*⟩. **2.** *n.* Äußerste, *das;* **do** *or* **try one's ~ to do sth.** mit allen Mitteln versuchen, etw. zu tun
¹**utter** [ˈʌtə(r)] *adj.* völlig; vollkommen; **~ fool** Vollidiot, *der (ugs.)*
²**utter** *v.t.* **a)** von sich geben ⟨*Schrei, Seufzer*⟩; **b)** *(say)* sagen. **utterance** [ˈʌtərəns] *n.* Worte *Pl.*
ˈ**utterly** *adv.* völlig; vollkommen; äußerst ⟨*dumm, lächerlich*⟩
ˈ**U-turn** *n.* Wende [um 180°]; *(fig.)* Kehrtwendung, *die;* **make a ~:** wenden; **'No ~s'** „Wenden verboten"

V

¹**V, v** [viː] *n.* V, v, *das*
²**V** *abbr.* volt|s| V
v. *abbr.* versus gg.
vacancy [ˈveɪkənsɪ] *n.* **a)** *(job)* freie

Stelle; b) *(room)* freies Zimmer; **'vacancies'** „Zimmer frei"; **'no vacancies'** „belegt"
vacant ['veikənt] *adj.* **a)** frei; **'situations ~'** „Stellenangebote"; **b)** *(mentally)* leer
vacate [və'keit] *v.t.* räumen
vacation [və'keiʃn] *n.* **a)** *(Brit. Univ.)* Ferien *Pl.;* **b)** *(Amer.) see* holiday b
vaccinate ['væksineit] *v.t.* impfen.
vaccination [væksi'neiʃn] *n.* Impfung, *die;* **have a ~:** geimpft werden
vaccine ['væksi:n] *n.* Impfstoff, *der*
vacuum ['vækjʊəm] **1.** *n.* **a)** Vakuum, *das;* **live in a ~:** im luftleeren Raum leben; **b)** *(coll.: ~ cleaner)* Sauger, *der (ugs.).* **2.** *v.t. & i.* [staub]saugen
vacuum: ~ cleaner *n.* Staubsauger, *der;* **~ flask** *n. (Brit.)* Thermosflasche, *die;* **~-packed** *adj.* vakuumverpackt
vagaries ['veigəriz] *n. pl.* Launen *Pl.*
vagina [və'dʒainə] *n.* Scheide, *die*
vagrant ['veigrənt] *n.* Landstreicher, *der/*Landstreicherin, *die; (in cities)* Stadtstreicher, *der/*Stadtstreicherin, *die*
vague [veig] *adj.* vage; verschwommen ⟨*Form, Umriß*⟩; *(absent-minded)* geistesabwesend; **not have the ~st idea** *or* **notion** nicht die blasseste *od.* leiseste Ahnung haben. **'vaguely** *adv.* vage; entfernt ⟨*bekannt sein, erinnern an*⟩; schwach ⟨*sich erinnern*⟩
vain [vein] *adj.* **a)** *(conceited)* eitel; **b)** *(useless)* leer; vergeblich ⟨*Hoffnung, Versuch*⟩; **in ~:** vergeblich. **'vainly** *adv.* vergebens
vale [veil] *n. (arch./poet.)* Tal, *das*
valentine ['væləntain] *n.* **~** |card| Grußkarte zum Valentinstag
valet ['vælei] *n.* Kammerdiener, *der*
valiant ['væliənt] *adj.,* **'valiantly** *adv.* tapfer
valid ['vælid] *adj.* **a)** *(legally acceptable)* gültig; berechtigt ⟨*Anspruch*⟩; **b)** *(justifiable)* stichhaltig ⟨*Argument*⟩; triftig ⟨*Grund*⟩; begründet ⟨*Einwand, Entschuldigung*⟩. **validate** ['vælideit] *v.t.* rechtskräftig machen. **validity** [və'liditi] *n.* Gültigkeit, *die*
valley ['væli] *n.* Tal, *das*
valour *(Amer.:* **valor)** ['vælə(r)] *n.* Tapferkeit, *die*
valuable ['væljʊəbl] **1.** *adj.* wertvoll; **be ~ to sb.** für jmdn. wertvoll sein. **2.** *n.* **~s** Wertsachen
valuation [væljʊ'eiʃn] *n.* Schätzung, *die*

value ['vælju:] **1.** *n.* Wert, *der;* **be of great/little/some/no ~** |to sb.| [für jmdn.] von großem/geringem/einigem/keinerlei Nutzen sein; **know the ~ of sth.** wissen, was etw. wert ist; **something/nothing of ~:** etwas/nichts Wertvolles. **2.** *v.t.* schätzen. **value added 'tax** *n.* Mehrwertsteuer, *die*
valve [vælv] *n.* **a)** Ventil, *das;* **b)** *(Anat.)* Klappe, *die*
vampire ['væmpaiə(r)] *n.* Vampir, *der*
van [væn] *n.* |delivery| **~:** Lieferwagen, *der*
vandal ['vændl] *n.* Rowdy, *der.* **vandalism** ['vændəlizm] *n.* Wandalismus, *der.* **vandalize** ['vændəlaiz] *v.t.* [mutwillig] beschädigen
vanilla [və'nilə] **1.** *n.* Vanille, *die.* **2.** *adj.* Vanille-
vanish ['væniʃ] *v.i.* verschwinden
vanity ['væniti] *n.* Eitelkeit, *die.* **'vanity bag** *n.* Kosmetiktäschchen, *das*
vantage-point ['vɑ:ntidʒ point] *n.* Aussichtspunkt, *der*
vapour *(Brit.; Amer.:* **vapor)** ['veipə(r)] *n.* Dampf, *der*
variable ['veəriəbl] *adj.* **a)** *(alterable)* veränderbar; **be ~:** verändert werden können; **b)** *(inconsistent)* unbeständig ⟨*Wetter, Wind, Leistung*⟩; wechselhaft ⟨*Wetter, Launen, Qualität*⟩
variance ['veəriəns] *n.* **be at ~** |with sth.| [mit etw.] nicht übereinstimmen
variant ['veəriənt] *n.* Variante, *die*
variation [veəri'eiʃn] *n.* **a)** *(varying)* Veränderung, *die; (difference)* Unterschied, *der;* **b)** *(variant)* Variante, *die (of, on Gen.)*
varicose vein [værikəus 'vein] *n.* Krampfader, *die*
varied ['veərid] *adj.* unterschiedlich; abwechslungsreich ⟨*Diät, Leben*⟩
variety [və'raiəti] *n.* **a)** *(diversity)* Vielfältigkeit, *die; (in diet, routine)* Abwechslung, *die;* **add** *or* **give ~ to sth.** etw. abwechslungsreicher gestalten; **b)** *(assortment)* Auswahl, *die (of an + Dat.,* von); **for a ~ of reasons** aus verschiedenen Gründen; **c)** *(Theatre)* Varieté, *das;* **d)** *(form)* Art, *die; (of fruit, vegetable)* Sorte, *die; (cultivated)* Züchtung, *die*
various ['veəriəs] *adj.* **a)** *pred. (different)* verschieden; unterschiedlich; **b)** *attrib. (several)* verschiedene; **at ~ times** mehrere Male. **'variously** *adv.* unterschiedlich
varnish ['vɑ:niʃ] **1.** *n.* Lasur, *die.* **2.** *v.t.* lasieren

vary ['veərɪ] **1.** *v. t.* verändern; ändern ⟨*Bestimmungen, Programm, Methode, Route*⟩; *(add variety to)* abwechslungsreicher gestalten. **2.** *v. i. (become different)* sich ändern; ⟨*Preis, Qualität:*⟩ schwanken; *(be different)* unterschiedlich sein. **'varying** *adj.* wechselnd; *(different)* unterschiedlich

vase [vɑːz] *n.* Vase, *die*

vast [vɑːst] *adj.* **a)** *(huge)* riesig; weit ⟨*Fläche, Meer*⟩; **b)** *(coll.: great)* enorm; Riesen⟨*menge, -summe*⟩. **'vastly** *adv. (coll.)* enorm; weitaus ⟨*besser*⟩; weit ⟨*überlegen, unterlegen*⟩

VAT [viːeɪ'tiː, væt] *abbr.* **value added tax** MwSt.

vat [væt] *n.* Bottich, *der*

Vatican ['vætɪkən] *pr. n.* Vatikan, *der*

¹vault [vɔːlt, vɒlt] *n.* **a)** *(Archit.)* Gewölbe, *das;* **b)** *(in bank)* Tresorraum, *der;* **c)** *(tomb)* Gruft, *die*

²vault **1.** *v. i.* sich schwingen. **2.** *v. t.* sich schwingen über (+ *Akk.*). **3.** *n.* Sprung, *der*

VD *n.* Geschlechtskrankheit, *die*

VDU *abbr.* **visual display unit**

veal [viːl] *n.* Kalb[fleisch], *das; attrib.* Kalbs-

veer [vɪə(r)] *v. i.* ⟨*Auto:*⟩ ausscheren. **veer a'way, veer 'off** *v. i.* ⟨*Auto:*⟩ ausscheren; ⟨*Fahrer, Straße:*⟩ abbiegen

veg [vedʒ] *n., pl. same (coll.)* Gemüse, *das*

vegetable ['vedʒɪtəbl] *n.* Gemüse, *das;* fresh ~s frisches Gemüse; *attrib.* Gemüse⟨*suppe, -extrakt, -garten*⟩. **'vegetable oil** *n.* Pflanzenöl, *das*

vegetarian [vedʒɪ'teərɪən] **1.** *n.* Vegetarier, *der*/Vegetarierin, *die.* **2.** *adj.* vegetarisch

vegetate ['vedʒɪteɪt] *v. i.* nur noch [dahin]vegetieren. **vegetation** [vedʒɪ'teɪʃn] *n.* Vegetation, *die*

vehement ['viːəmənt] *adj.,* **'vehemently** *adv.* heftig

vehicle ['viːɪkl] *n.* **a)** Fahrzeug, *das;* **b)** *(fig.: medium)* Vehikel, *das*

veil [veɪl] **1.** *n.* Schleier, *der.* **2.** *v. t.* verschleiern

vein [veɪn] *n.* **a)** Vene, *die; (any blood-vessel)* Ader, *die;* **b)** *(fig.: mood)* Stimmung, *die;* **in a similar ~:** vergleichbarer Art

Velcro, (P) ['velkrəʊ] *n.* Klettverschluß, *der* Ⓦ

velocity [vɪ'lɒsɪtɪ] *n.* Geschwindigkeit, *die*

velvet ['velvɪt] **1.** *n.* Samt, *der.* **2.** *adj.* aus Samt *nachgestellt;* Samt-. **'velvety** *adj.* samtig

vendetta [ven'detə] *n.* Hetzkampagne, *die; (feud)* Fehde, *die*

vending-machine ['vendɪŋ məʃiːn] *n.* [Verkaufs]automat, *der*

vendor ['vendə(r)] *n.* Verkäufer, *der*/Verkäuferin, *die*

veneer [vɪ'nɪə(r)] *n.* Furnier, *das*

venerable ['venərəbl] *adj.* ehrwürdig

ve'nereal disease *n. (Med.)* Geschlechtskrankheit, *die*

venetian blind [vɪ'niːʃn blaɪnd] *n.* Jalousie, *die*

Venezuela [venɪ'zweɪlə] *pr. n.* Venezuela *(das)*

vengeance ['vendʒəns] *n.* **a)** Rache, *die;* **take ~ [up]on sb. [for sth.]** sich an jmdm. [für etw.] rächen; **b) with a ~** *(coll.)* gewaltig *(ugs.)*

Venice ['venɪs] *pr. n.* Venedig *(das)*

venison ['venɪsn, 'venɪzn] *n.* Hirsch, *der;* Hirschfleisch, *das; (roe deer)* Reh[fleisch], *das*

venom ['venəm] *n.* Gift, *das.* **venomous** ['venəməs] *adj.* giftig

¹vent [vent] **1.** *n.* **a)** Öffnung, *die;* **b)** *(fig.)* Ventil, *das (fig.);* **give ~ to** Luft machen (+ *Dat.*). **2.** *v. t. (fig.)* Luft machen (+ *Dat.*)

²vent *n. (in garment)* Schlitz, *der*

ventilate ['ventɪleɪt] *v. t.* belüften. **ventilation** [ventɪ'leɪʃn] *n.* Belüftung, *die.* **ventilator** ['ventɪleɪtə(r)] *n.* **a)** Ventilator, *der;* **b)** *(Med.)* Beatmungsgerät, *das*

ventriloquist [ven'trɪləkwɪst] *n.* Bauchredner, *der*/-rednerin, *die*

venture ['ventʃə(r)] **1.** *n.* Unternehmung, *die.* **2.** *v. i.* **a)** *(dare)* wagen; **b)** *(dare to go)* sich wagen. **3.** *v. t.* wagen. **venture 'out** *v. i.* sich hinauswagen

venue ['venjuː] *n. (Sport)* [Austragungs]ort, *der; (Mus., Theatre)* [Veranstaltungs]ort, *der; (meeting-place)* Treffpunkt, *der*

Venus ['viːnəs] *pr. n. (Astron.)* Venus, *die*

veranda[h] [və'rændə] *n.* Veranda, *die*

verb [vɜːb] *n.* Verb, *das.* **verbal** ['vɜːbl] *adj.,* **verbally** ['vɜːbəlɪ] *adv.* **a)** *(relating to words)* sprachlich; **b)** *(or-al[ly])* mündlich

verbatim [və'beɪtɪm] *adj., adv.* [wort]wörtlich

verbose [və'bəʊs] *adj.* weitschweifig ⟨*Roman, Autor*⟩; langatmig ⟨*Rede, Redner*⟩

verdict ['vɜːdɪkt] *n.* Urteil, *das; ~ of guilty/not guilty* Schuld-/Freispruch, *der;* **reach a ~:** zu einem Urteil kommen

verge [vɜːdʒ] *n.* **a)** Rasensaum, *der; (on road)* Bankette, *die;* **b)** *(fig.)* **be on the ~ of war/tears** am Rande des Krieges stehen/den Tränen nahe sein; **be on the ~ of doing sth.** kurz davor stehen, etw. zu tun. '**verge on** *v.t.* [an]grenzen an (+ *Akk.*)

verger ['vɜːdʒə(r)] *n.* Küster, *der*

verification [verɪfɪ'keɪʃn] *n.* **a)** *(check)* Überprüfung, *die;* **b)** *(confirmation)* Bestätigung, *die*

verify ['verɪfaɪ] *v. t.* **a)** *(check)* überprüfen; **b)** *(confirm)* bestätigen

vermin ['vɜːmɪn] *n.* Ungeziefer, *das*

vernacular [və'nækjʊlə(r)] *n.* Landessprache, *die*

versatile ['vɜːsətaɪl] *adj.* vielseitig; *(having many uses)* vielseitig verwendbar. **versatility** [vɜːsə'tɪlɪti] *n.* Vielseitigkeit, *die*

verse [vɜːs] *n.* **a)** *(stanza)* Strophe, *die;* **b)** *(poetry)* Lyrik, *die;* write some ~: einige Verse schreiben; **piece of ~:** Gedicht, *das;* written in ~: in Versform; **c)** *(in Bible)* Vers, *der.* **versed** [vɜːst] *adj.* be |well| ~ in sth. sich in etw. *(Dat.)* [gut] auskennen

version ['vɜːʃn] *n.* Version, *die; (in another language)* Übersetzung, *die; (of vehicle, machine, tool)* Modell, *das*

versus ['vɜːsəs] *prep.* gegen

vertebra ['vɜːtɪbrə] *n., pl.* ~e ['vɜːtɪbriː] Wirbel, *der.* **vertebrate** ['vɜːtɪbrət] *n.* Wirbeltier, *das*

vertical ['vɜːtɪkl] *adj.* senkrecht; **be ~:** senkrecht stehen. **vertically** ['vɜːtɪkəlɪ] *adv.* senkrecht

vertigo ['vɜːtɪgəʊ] *n.* Schwindel, *der*

verve [vɜːv] *n.* Schwung, *der*

very ['verɪ] **1.** *attrib. adj.* **a)** *(precise, exact)* genau; **you're the ~ person I wanted to see** genau dich wollte ich sehen; **at the ~ moment when ...:** im selben Augenblick, als ...; **at the ~ centre** genau in der Mitte; **the ~ thing** genau das Richtige; **b)** *(extreme)* **at the ~ back/front** ganz hinten/vorn; **at the ~ end/beginning** ganz am Ende/Anfang; **from the ~ beginning** von Anfang an; **only a ~ little** nur ein ganz kleines bißchen; **c)** *(mere)* bloß ⟨*Gedanke*⟩; **d)** *(absolute)* absolut ⟨*Minimum, Maximum*⟩; **the ~ most I can offer is ...:** ich kann allerhöchstens ... anbieten; **for the ~ last time** zum allerletzten Mal;

e) *emphat.* **before their ~ eyes** vor ihren Augen. **2.** *adv.* **a)** *(extremely)* sehr; **it's ~ near** es ist ganz in der Nähe; **~ probably** höchstwahrscheinlich; **not ~ much** nicht sehr; **~ little** [nur] sehr wenig ⟨*verstehen, essen*⟩; **thank you** [~,] **~ much** [vielen,] vielen Dank; **b)** *(absolutely)* aller⟨*best..., -letzt..., -leichtest...*⟩; **at the ~ latest** allerspätestens; **c)** *(precisely)* **the ~ same one** genau der-/die-/dasselbe

vessel ['vesl] *n.* **a)** *(receptacle)* Gefäß, *das;* |drinking-|~: Trinkgefäß, *das;* **b)** *(Naut.)* Schiff, *das*

vest [vest] **1.** *n.* **a)** *(Brit.)* Unterhemd, *das;* **b)** *(Amer.: waistcoat)* Weste, *die.* **2.** *v. t.* **~ sb. with sth., ~ sth. in sb.** jmdm. etw. verleihen. '**vested** *adj.* **have a ~ interest in sth.** ein persönliches Interesse an etw. *(Dat.)* haben

vestige ['vestɪdʒ] *n.* Spur, *die;* **not a ~ of truth** kein Fünkchen Wahrheit

vestment ['vestmənt] *n.* [Priester]gewand, *das*

vestry ['vestrɪ] *n.* Sakristei, *die*

vet [vet] **1.** *n.* Tierarzt, *der/*-ärztin, *die.* **2.** *v. t.,* -tt- überprüfen

veteran ['vetərən] *n.* Veteran, *der/*Veteranin, *die.* **veteran 'car** *n.* *(Brit.)* Veteran, *der*

veterinarian [vetərɪ'neərɪən] *n.* *(Amer.)* Tierarzt, *der/*-ärztin, *die*

veterinary ['vetərɪnərɪ] *adj.* tiermedizinisch. **veterinary 'surgeon** *n.* *(Brit.)* Tierarzt, *der/*-ärztin, *die*

veto ['viːtəʊ] **1.** *n., pl.* ~es Veto, *das.* **2.** *v. t.* sein Veto einlegen gegen

vex [veks] *v. t.* [ver]ärgern; *(cause to worry)* beunruhigen; **be ~ed with sb.** sich über jmdn. ärgern. **vexation** [vek'seɪʃn] *n.* Verärgerung, *die.* **vexed** [vekst] *adj.* **a)** verärgert; **b)** ~ **question** vieldiskutierte Frage

VHF *abbr.* **Very High Frequency** UKW

via ['vaɪə] *prep.* über (+ *Akk.*) ⟨*Ort, Sender, Telefon*⟩; durch ⟨*Eingang, Schornstein, Person*⟩; per ⟨*Post*⟩

viability [vaɪə'bɪlɪtɪ] *n.* *(feasibility)* Realisierbarkeit, *die*

viable ['vaɪəbl] *adj.* *(feasible)* realisierbar

viaduct ['vaɪədʌkt] *n.* Viadukt, *das od. der*

vibrant ['vaɪbrənt] *adj.* lebenssprühend ⟨*Atmosphäre*⟩; lebhaft ⟨*Farbe*⟩

vibrate [vaɪ'breɪt] **1.** *v. i.* vibrieren; *(under strong impact)* beben. **2.** *v. t.* vibrieren lassen. **vibration** [vaɪ'breɪʃn] *n.* Vibrieren/Beben, *das*

vicar ['vɪkə(r)] *n.* Pfarrer, *der.* **vicarage** ['vɪkərɪdʒ] *n.* Pfarrhaus, *das*
vicarious [vɪ'keərɪəs] *adj.* nachempfunden
¹vice [vaɪs] *n.* Laster, *das*
²vice *n. (Brit.: tool)* Schraubstock, *der*
vice: ~-'**chairman** *n.* stellvertretender Vorsitzender; ~-'**president** *n.* Vizepräsident, *der/*-präsidentin, *die*
vice versa [vaɪsɪ 'vɜːsə] *adv.* umgekehrt
vicinity [vɪ'sɪnɪtɪ] *n.* Umgebung, *die;* **in the** ~ [**of a place**] in der Nähe [eines Ortes]
vicious ['vɪʃəs] *adj.* **a)** *(malicious)* böse; bösartig ⟨*Tier*⟩; **b)** *(violent)* brutal.
vicious 'circle *n.* Teufelskreis, *der*
'viciously *adv.* **a)** *(maliciously)* boshaft; **b)** *(violently)* brutal
victim ['vɪktɪm] *n.* Opfer, *das; (of sarcasm, abuse)* Zielscheibe, *die (fig.).*
victimization [vɪktɪmaɪ'zeɪʃn] *n.* Schikanierung, *die.* **victimize** ['vɪktɪmaɪz] *v. t.* schikanieren
victor ['vɪktə(r)] *n.* Sieger, *der/*Siegerin, *die*
victorious [vɪk'tɔːrɪəs] *adj.* siegreich
victory ['vɪktərɪ] *n.* Sieg, *der* (**over über** + *Akk.*); *attrib.* Sieges-
video ['vɪdɪəʊ] **1.** *adj.* Video-. **2.** *n., pl.* ~**s** (~ *recorder)* Videorecorder, *der; (~ tape, ~ recording)* Video, *das (ugs.).* **3.** *v. t. see* videotape 2
video: ~ **camera** *n.* Videokamera, *die;* ~ **cas'sette** *n.* Videokassette, *die;* ~ **game** *n.* Videospiel, *das;* ~ '**nasty** *n.* Horrorvideo, *das;* ~ **recorder** *n.* Videorecorder, *der;* ~ **recording** *n.* Videoaufnahme, *die;* ~**tape 1.** *n.* Videoband, *das;* **2.** *v. t.* [auf Videoband *(Akk.)*] aufnehmen
vie [vaɪ] *v. i.,* vying ['vaɪɪŋ] ~ [**with sb.**] for sth. [mit jmdm.] um etw. wetteifern
Vienna [vɪ'enə] **1.** *pr. n.* Wien *(das).* **2.** *attrib. adj.* Wiener. **Viennese** [vɪə'niːz] **1.** *adj.* Wiener. **2.** *n., pl. same* Wiener, *der/*Wienerin, *die*
Vietnam [vɪet'næm] *pr. n.* Vietnam *(das).* **Vietnamese** [vɪetnə'miːz] **1.** *adj.* vietnamesisch. **2.** *n., pl. same* **a)** *(person)* Vietnamese, *der/*Vietnamesin, *die;* **b)** *(language)* Vietnamesisch, *das*
view [vjuː] **1.** *n.* **a)** *(range of vision)* Sicht, *die;* **be out of/in** ~: nicht zu sehen/zu sehen sein; **b)** *(what is seen)* Aussicht, *die;* **c)** *(picture)* Ansicht, *die;* **d)** *(opinion)* Ansicht, *die;* **what is your** ~ **or are your** ~**s on this?** was meinst

du dazu?; **hold** *or* **take the** ~ **that** ...: der Ansicht sein, daß ...; **in my** ~: meiner Ansicht nach; **e) be on** ~: besichtigt werden können; **in** ~ **of sth.** *(fig.)* angesichts einer Sache; **with a** ~ **to doing sth.** in der Absicht, etw. zu tun. **2.** *v. t.* **a)** *(look at)* sich *(Dat.)* ansehen; **b)** *(consider)* betrachten; **c)** *(inspect)* besichtigen. **3.** *v. i. (Telev.)* fernsehen.
'viewer *n.* **a)** *(Telev.)* [Fernseh]zuschauer, *der/-*zuschauerin, *die;* **b)** *(for slides)* Diabetrachter, *der*
view: ~**finder** *n.* Sucher, *der;* ~**point** *n.* Standpunkt, *der*
vigil ['vɪdʒɪl] *n.* Wachen, *das;* **keep** ~: wachen
vigilance ['vɪdʒɪləns] *n.* Wachsamkeit, *die*
vigilant ['vɪdʒɪlənt] *adj.* wachsam
vigor *n. (Amer.) see* vigour
vigorous ['vɪgərəs] *adj.* kräftig; heftig ⟨*Attacke, Protest*⟩; energisch ⟨*Versuch, Anstrengung, Leugnen, Maßnahme*⟩. **'vigorously** *adv.* heftig; kräftig ⟨*schrubben, drücken*⟩
vigour ['vɪgə(r)] *n. (Brit.) (of person)* Vitalität, *die; (of body)* Kraft, *die; (of protest, attack)* Heftigkeit, *die*
vile [vaɪl] *adj.* gemein ⟨*Verleumdung*⟩; vulgär ⟨*Sprache*⟩; *(repulsive)* widerwärtig; *(coll.: very unpleasant)* scheußlich *(ugs.)*
villa ['vɪlə] *n.* **a)** [**holiday**] ~: Ferienhaus, *das;* **b)** [**country**] ~: Landhaus, *das*
village ['vɪlɪdʒ] *n.* Dorf, *das; attrib.* Dorf-. **'villager** *n.* Dorfbewohner, *der/-*bewohnerin, *die*
villain ['vɪlən] *n.* **a)** Verbrecher, *der;* **b)** *(Theatre)* Bösewicht, *der.* **villainous** ['vɪlənəs] *adj.* gemein
vindicate ['vɪndɪkeɪt] *v. t.* **a)** *(justify)* rechtfertigen; **b)** *(clear)* rehabilitieren.
vindication [vɪndɪ'keɪʃn] *n.* **a)** *(justification)* Rechtfertigung, *die;* **b)** *(clearing)* Rehabilitierung, *die*
vindictive [vɪn'dɪktɪv] *adj.* nachtragend
vine [vaɪn] *n.* Weinrebe, *die*
vinegar ['vɪnɪgə(r)] *n.* Essig, *der*
vineyard ['vɪnjɑːd, 'vɪnjəd] *n.* Weinberg, *der*
vintage ['vɪntɪdʒ] **1.** *n.* Jahrgang, *der.* **2.** *adj.* erlesen ⟨*Wein*⟩. **vintage 'car** *n. (Brit.)* Oldtimer, *der*
vinyl ['vaɪnɪl] *n.* Vinyl, *das*
viola [vɪ'əʊlə] *n.* Bratsche, *die*
violate ['vaɪəleɪt] *v. t.* **a)** verletzen; brechen ⟨*Vertrag, Versprechen, Gesetz*⟩;

b) *(profane, rape)* schänden. **violation** [vaɪə'leɪʃn] *n. see* violate: Verletzung, *die;* Bruch, *der;* Schändung, *die*
violence ['vaɪələns] *n.* a) *(force)* Heftigkeit, *die; (of blow)* Wucht, *die;* b) *(brutality)* Gewalt, *die; (at public event)* Gewalttätigkeiten; **resort to** *or* **use ~:** Gewalt anwenden
violent ['vaɪələnt] *adj.* gewalttätig; *(fig.)* heftig; wuchtig ⟨*Schlag, Stoß*⟩; Gewalt⟨*verbrecher, -tat*⟩. **'violently** *adv.* brutal; *(fig.)* heftig
violet ['vaɪələt] 1. *n.* a) Veilchen, *das;* b) *(colour)* Violett, *das.* 2. *adj.* violett
violin [vaɪə'lɪn] *n.* Violine, *die;* Geige, *die.* **vio'linist** *n.* Geiger, *der*/Geigerin, *die*
VIP [viːaɪ'piː] *n.* Prominente, *der*/*die;* **the ~s** die Prominenz
viper ['vaɪpə(r)] *n.* Viper, *die*
virgin ['vɜːdʒɪn] 1. *n.* a) Jungfrau, *die;* b) **the [Blessed] V~ [Mary]** die [Heilige] Jungfrau [Maria]. 2. *adj. (unspoiled)* unberührt. **virginity** [və'dʒɪnɪti] *n.* Unschuld, *die*
Virgo ['vɜːgəʊ] *n., pl.* **~s** die Jungfrau
virile ['vɪraɪl] *adj.* männlich. **virility** [vɪ'rɪlɪti] *n.* Männlichkeit, *die*
virtual ['vɜːtjʊəl] *adj.* **a ~ ...:** so gut wie ein/eine ...; **the traffic came to a ~ standstill** der Verkehr kam praktisch zum Stillstand *(ugs.).* **'virtually** *adv.* so gut wie; praktisch *(ugs.)*
virtue ['vɜːtjuː] *n.* a) *(moral excellence)* Tugend, *die;* b) *(advantage)* Vorteil, *der;* c) **by ~ of** auf Grund (+ *Gen.*)
virtuoso [vɜːtjʊ'əʊzəʊ] *n., pl.* **virtuosi** [vɜːtjʊ'əʊzi:] *or* **~s** Virtuose, *der*/Virtuosin, *die*
virtuous ['vɜːtjʊəs] *adj.* rechtschaffen ⟨*Person*⟩; tugendhaft ⟨*Leben*⟩
virulent ['vɪrʊlənt] *adj.* a) *(Med.)* virulent; starkwirkend ⟨*Gift*⟩; b) *(fig.)* heftig; scharf ⟨*Angriff*⟩
virus ['vaɪərəs] *n.* Virus, *das*
visa ['viːzə] *n.* Visum, *das*
vis-à-vis [viːzaː'viː] *prep. (in relation to)* bezüglich (+ *Gen.*)
viscount ['vaɪkaʊnt] *n.* Viscount, *der*
viscous ['vɪskəs] *adj.* dickflüssig
visibility [vɪzɪ'bɪlɪti] *n.* a) Sichtbarkeit, *die;* b) *(range of vision)* Sicht, *die; (Meteorol.)* Sichtweite, *die*
visible ['vɪzɪbl] *adj.* sichtbar. **'visibly** *adv.* sichtlich
vision ['vɪʒn] *n.* a) *(sight)* Sehkraft, *die;* b) *(dream)* Vision, *die;* c) *usu. pl. (imaginings)* Phantasien; d) *(insight, foresight)* Weitblick, *der*

visit ['vɪzɪt] 1. *v. t.* besuchen; aufsuchen ⟨*Arzt*⟩. 2. *v. i.* einen Besuch/Besuche machen. 3. *n.* Besuch, *der;* **pay** *or* **make a ~ to sb., pay sb. a ~:** jmdm. einen Besuch abstatten *(geh.)*
'visiting: ~ card *n.* Visitenkarte, *die;* **~ hours** *n. pl.* Besuchszeiten
visitor ['vɪzɪtə(r)] *n.* Besucher, *der*/Besucherin, *die; (to hotel)* Gast, *der;* **have ~s/a ~:** Besuch haben
visual ['vɪzjʊəl, 'vɪʒjʊəl] *adj.* visuell; optisch ⟨*Eindruck, Darstellung*⟩. **visual 'aids** *n. pl.* Anschauungsmaterial, *das.* **visual dis'play unit** *n.* Bildschirmgerät, *das*
visualize ['vɪzjʊəlaɪz, 'vɪʒjʊəlaɪz] *v. t.* a) *(imagine)* sich *(Dat.)* vorstellen; b) *(envisage)* voraussehen
'visually *adv.* bildlich
vital ['vaɪtl] *adj.* a) *(essential to life)* lebenswichtig; b) *(essential)* unbedingt notwendig; c) *(crucial)* entscheidend (to für); **it is ~ that you ...:** es ist von entscheidender Bedeutung, daß Sie ...
vitality [vaɪ'tælɪti] *n.* Vitalität, *die.* **'vitally** *adv.* **~ important** von allergrößter Wichtigkeit; *(crucial)* von entscheidender Bedeutung
vitamin ['vɪtəmɪn, 'vaɪtəmɪn] *n.* Vitamin, *das*
vivacious [vɪ'veɪʃəs] *adj.* lebhaft. **vivacity** [vɪ'væsɪti] *n.* Lebhaftigkeit, *die*
vivid ['vɪvɪd] *adj.* lebhaft ⟨*Farbe, Erinnerung*⟩; lebendig ⟨*Schilderung*⟩. **'vividly** *adv.* lebendig ⟨*beschreiben*⟩; **remember sth. ~:** sich lebhaft an etw. *(Akk.)* erinnern
vixen ['vɪksn] *n.* Füchsin, *die*
vocabulary [və'kæbjʊlərɪ] *n.* a) *(list)* Vokabelverzeichnis, *das;* **learn ~:** Vokabeln lernen; b) *(range of language)* Wortschatz, *der*
vocal ['vəʊkl] *adj.* a) *(concerned with voice)* stimmlich; b) lautstark ⟨*Minderheit, Protest*⟩. **'vocal cords** *n. pl.* Stimmbänder
vocalist ['vəʊkəlɪst] *n.* Sänger, *der*/Sängerin, *die*
vocation [və'keɪʃn] *n.* Berufung, *die*
vocational [və'keɪʃənl] *adj.* berufsbezogen. **vocational 'guidance** *n.* Berufsberatung, *die.* **vocational 'training** *n.* berufliche Bildung
vociferous [və'sɪfərəs] *adj.* laut; lautstark ⟨*Forderung, Protest*⟩
vodka ['vɒdkə] *n.* Wodka, *der*
vogue [vəʊg] *n.* Mode, *die;* **be in/come into ~:** in Mode sein/kommen
voice [vɔɪs] 1. *n.* Stimme, *die;* **in a**

firm/loud/soft ~: mit fester/lauter/ sanfter Stimme. **2.** *v. t.* zum Ausdruck bringen

void [vɔɪd] **1.** *adj.* **a)** *(empty)* leer; **b)** *(invalid)* ungültig; **c)** ~ of ohne [jeden/ jedes/jede]. **2.** *n.* Nichts, *das*

volatile ['vɒlətaɪl] *adj.* **a)** *(Chem.)* flüchtig; **b)** *(fig.)* impulsiv; brisant ⟨*Lage*⟩

volcanic [vɒl'kænɪk] *adj.* vulkanisch

volcano [vɒl'keɪnəʊ] *n., pl.* ~es Vulkan, *der*

volition [və'lɪʃn] *n.* Wille, *der;* **of one's own** ~: aus eigenem Willen

volley ['vɒlɪ] *n.* **a)** *(of missiles)* Salve, *die;* **a** ~ **of arrows** ein Hagel von Pfeilen; **b)** *(Tennis)* Volley, *der.* '**volleyball** *n.* Volleyball, *der*

volt [vəʊlt] *n.* Volt, *das.* **voltage** ['vəʊltɪdʒ] *n.* Spannung, *die*

voluble ['vɒljʊbl] *adj.* redselig

volume ['vɒlju:m] *n.* **a)** *(book)* Band, *der;* **b)** *(loudness)* Lautstärke, *die; (of voice)* Volumen, *das; (space)* Rauminhalt, *der; (amount of substance)* Teil, *der.* '**volume control** *n.* Lautstärkeregler, *der*

voluntarily ['vɒləntərɪlɪ] *adv.,* **voluntary** ['vɒləntərɪ] *adj.* freiwillig

volunteer [vɒlən'tɪə(r)] **1.** *n.* Freiwillige, *der/die.* **2.** *v. t.* anbieten ⟨*Hilfe, Dienste*⟩; herausrücken mit ⟨*Informationen*⟩. **3.** *v. i.* sich [freiwillig] melden; ~ **to do** *or* ~ **for the shopping** sich zum Einkaufen bereiterklären

voluptuous [və'lʌptjʊəs] *adj.* üppig

vomit ['vɒmɪt] **1.** *v. t.* erbrechen. **2.** *v. i.* sich übergeben. **3.** *n.* Erbrochene, *das*

voracious [və'reɪʃəs] *adj.* gefräßig ⟨*Person*⟩; unbändig ⟨*Appetit*⟩

vote [vəʊt] **1.** *n.* **a)** *(individual* ~*)* Stimme, *die;* **b)** *(act of voting)* Abstimmung, *die;* **take a** ~ **on sth.** über etw. *(Akk.)* abstimmen; **c)** *(right to* ~*)* Stimmrecht, *das.* **2.** *v. i.* abstimmen; *(in election)* wählen; ~ **for/against** stimmen für/gegen; ~ **to do sth.** beschließen, etw. zu tun; ~ **Labour/Conservative** *etc.* Labour/die Konservativen *usw.* wählen. **3.** *v. t.* ~ **sb. Chairman/President** *etc.* jmdn. zum Vorsitzenden/Präsidenten *usw.* wählen. '**voter** *n.* Wähler, *der*/Wählerin, *die*

vouch [vaʊtʃ] **1.** *v. t.* ~ **that...**: sich dafür verbürgen, daß... **2.** *v. i.* ~ **for sb./ sth.** sich für jmdn./etw. verbürgen

'**voucher** *n.* Gutschein, *der*

vow [vaʊ] **1.** *n.* Gelöbnis, *das; (Relig.)* Gelübde, *das.* **2.** *v. t.* geloben

vowel ['vaʊəl] *n.* Vokal, *der*

voyage ['vɔɪdʒ] **1.** *n.* Reise, *die; (sea* ~*)* Seereise, *die;* **outward/homeward** ~, ~ **out/home** Hin-/Rückreise, *die;* **a** ~ **to the moon** ein Mondflug. **2.** *v. i.* *(literary)* reisen

vulgar ['vʌlgə(r)] *adj.* vulgär; ordinär ⟨*Person, Benehmen, Witz*⟩. **vulgarity** [vʌl'gærɪtɪ] *n.* Vulgarität, *die*

vulnerable ['vʌlnərəbl] *adj.* **a)** *(exposed to danger)* angreifbar; **be** ~ **to sth.** für etw. anfällig sein; **be** ~ **to attack/in a** ~ **position** leicht angreifbar sein; **b)** *(without protection)* schutzlos

vulture ['vʌltʃə(r)] *n.* Geier, *der*

vying *see* **vie**

W

---

¹**W, w** ['dʌblju:] *n.* W, w, *das*

²**W** *abbr.* **watt[s]** W

W. *abbr.* **a) west** W.; **b) western** w.

wad [wɒd] *n.* **a)** Knäuel, *das; (smaller)* Pfropfen, *der;* **b)** *(of papers)* Bündel, *das.* '**wadding** *n.* Futter, *das*

waddle ['wɒdl] **1.** *v. i.* watscheln. **2.** *n.* watschelnder Gang

wade [weɪd] *v. i.* waten. '**wade through** *v. t.* *(fig. coll.)* durchackern *(ugs.)* ⟨*Buch*⟩

wafer ['weɪfə(r)] *n.* Waffel, *die.* '**wafer-thin** *adj.* hauchdünn

¹**waffle** ['wɒfl] *n.* *(Gastr.)* Waffel, *die*

²**waffle** *(Brit. coll.: talk)* **1.** *v. i.* schwafeln *(ugs.).* **2.** *n.* Geschwafel, *das* *(ugs.)*

waft [wɒft, wɑ:ft] **1.** *v. t.* weben. **2.** *v. i.* ziehen

wag [wæg] **1.** *v. t., -gg-* ⟨*Hund:*⟩ wedeln mit ⟨*Schwanz*⟩; ~ **one's finger at sb.** jmdm. mit dem Finger drohen. **2.** *v. i., -gg-* ⟨*Schwanz:*⟩ wedeln

wage [weɪdʒ] **1.** *n. in sing. or pl.* Lohn, *der.* **2.** *v. t.* führen. '**wage increase** *n.* Lohnerhöhung, *die.* '**wage packet** *n.* Lohntüte, *die*

wager ['weɪdʒə(r)] *(dated/formal)* **1.** *n.* Wette, *die;* **lay a** ~ **on sth.** auf etw. *(Akk.)* wetten. **2.** *v. t. & i.* wetten

waggle ['wægl] *(coll.)* **1.** *v. t.* ~ **its tail**

‹*Hund:*› mit dem Schwanz wedeln. **2.** *v.i.* hin und her schlagen

waggon *(Brit.),* **wagon** ['wægən] *n.* Wagen, *der*

wail [weıl] **1.** *v.i.* klagen *(geh.)* (for um); ‹*Kind:*› heulen. **2.** *n.* klagender Schrei; ~s Geheul, *das*

waist [weıst] *n.* Taille, *die;* **tight round the ~:** eng in der Taille. **waistcoat** ['weıskəʊt] *n. (Brit.)* Weste, *die.* '**waistline** *n.* Taille, *die;* **be bad for the ~:** schlecht für die schlanke Linie sein

wait [weıt] **1.** *v.i.* **a)** warten; ~ |for| **an hour** eine Stunde warten; ~ **a moment** Moment mal; **keep sb. ~ing, make sb. ~:** jmdn. warten lassen; **b)** ~ **at table** servieren. **2.** *v.t. (await)* warten auf (+ *Akk.*); ~ **one's turn** warten, bis man drankommt. **3.** *n.* **a) after a long/ short ~:** nach langer/kurzer Wartezeit; **b) lie in ~ for sb./sth.** jmdm./einer Sache auflauern. **wait be'hind** *v.i.* noch hier-/dableiben. '**wait for** *v.t.* warten auf (+ *Akk.*); ~ **for sb. to do sth.** darauf warten, daß jmd. etw. tut; ~ **for the rain to stop** warten, bis der Regen aufhört. '**wait on** *v.t. (serve)* bedienen. **wait 'up** *v.i.* aufbleiben (**for** wegen)

'**waiter** *n.* Kellner, *der;* ~! Herr Ober!

'**waiting:** ~**-list** *n.* Warteliste, *die;* ~**-room** *n.* Wartezimmer, *das; (Railw.)* Warteraum, *der*

waitress ['weıtrıs] *n.* Serviererin, *die;* ~! Fräulein! *(veralt.)*

waive [weıv] *v.t.* verzichten auf (+ *Akk.*)

¹**wake** [weık] **1.** *v.i.,* woke [wəʊk], woken ['wəʊkn] aufwachen. **2.** *v.t.,* woke, woken wecken. **3.** *n. (by corpse)* Totenwache, *die.* **wake 'up** *v.i.* aufwachen; ~ **up to sth.** *(fig.: realize)* etw. erkennen. **2.** *v.t.* **a)** wecken; **b)** *(fig.: enliven)* wachrütteln

²**wake** *n.* Kielwasser, *das;* **in the ~ of sth.** *(fig.)* im Gefolge von etw.

waken ['weıkn] **1.** *v.t.* wecken. **2.** *v.i.* aufwachen

Wales [weılz] *pr.n.* Wales *(das)*

walk [wɔːk] **1.** *v.i.* **a)** laufen; *(not run)* gehen; *(not drive)* zu Fuß gehen; **learn to ~:** laufen lernen; **b)** *(exercise)* gehen. **2.** *v.t.* **a)** *(lead)* führen; ausführen ‹*Hund*›; **b)** *(accompany)* bringen. **3.** *n.* **a)** Spaziergang, *der;* **go |out| for or take or have a ~:** einen Spaziergang machen; **ten minutes' ~ from here** zehn Minuten zu Fuß von hier;

b) *(gait)* Gang, *der;* **c)** *(path)* [Spazier]weg, *der.* **walk a'way with** *v.t. (coll.: win easily)* spielend leicht gewinnen. '**walk into** *v.t. (hit by accident)* laufen gegen ‹*Pfosten, Laternenpfahl*›; ~ **into sb.** mit jmdm. zusammenstoßen; ~ **into a trap** in eine Falle gehen. **walk 'off with** *v.t.* sich davonmachen mit. **walk 'out** *v.i.* **a)** *(leave in protest)* den Saal verlassen; **b)** *(go on strike)* in den Streik treten. **walk 'out of** *v.t. (leave in protest)* aus Protest verlassen. **walk 'out on** *v.t. (coll.)* verlassen

'**walker** *n.* Spaziergänger, *der/*-gängerin, *die; (rambler)* Wanderer, *der/* Wanderin, *die*

walkie-talkie [wɔːkı'tɔːkı] *n.* Walkie-talkie, *das*

'**walking** *n.* [Spazieren]gehen, *das;* **at ~ pace** im Schrittempo; **be within ~ distance** zu Fuß zu erreichen sein

walking: ~ **holiday** *n.* Wanderurlaub, *der;* ~ **shoe** *n.* Wanderschuh, *der;* ~**-stick** *n.* Spazierstock, *der*

walk: ~**-out** *n.* Arbeitsniederlegung, *die;* ~**-over** *n. (fig.: easy victory)* Spaziergang, *der (ugs.)*

wall [wɔːl] *n.* Wand, *die; (freestanding)* Mauer, *die;* **drive sb. up the ~** *(fig. coll.)* jmdn. auf die Palme bringen *(ugs.);* **go to the ~** *(fig.)* an die Wand gedrückt werden. **wall 'up** *v.t.* zumauern

wallet ['wɒlıt] *n.* Brieftasche, *die*

'**wallflower** *n.* Goldlack, *der*

wallop ['wɒləp] *(coll.)* **1.** *v.t.* schlagen. **2.** *n.* Schlag, *der*

wallow ['wɒləʊ] *v.i.* **a)** sich wälzen; **b)** *(fig.)* schwelgen (**in** in + *Dat.*)

wall: ~**-painting** *n.* Wandgemälde, *das;* ~**paper** **1.** *n.* Tapete, *die;* **2.** *v.t.* tapezieren; ~**-to-**~ *adj.* ~**-to-**~ **carpeting** Teppichboden, *der*

walnut ['wɔːlnʌt] *n.* Walnuß, *die*

walrus ['wɔːlrəs] *n.* Walroß, *das*

waltz [wɔːlts, wɒːls] **1.** *n.* Walzer, *der.* **2.** *v.i.* Walzer tanzen

wan [wɒn] *adj.* bleich

wand [wɒnd] *n.* Stab, *der*

wander ['wɒndə(r)] **1.** *v.i. (go aimlessly)* umherirren; *(walk slowly)* bummeln. **2.** *v.t.* wandern durch. **3.** *n. (coll.)* Spaziergang, *der.* **wander a'bout** *v.i.* sich herumtreiben. **wander 'off** *v.i. (stray)* weggehen

wane [weın] *v.i.* abnehmen

wangle ['wæŋgl] *v.t. (coll.)* organisieren *(ugs.)*

want [wɒnt] **1.** *v. t.* **a)** *(desire)* wollen;
~ **to do sth.** etw. tun wollen; **I** ~ **it
done by tonight** ich will, daß es bis
heute abend fertig wird; **b)** *(require,
need)* brauchen; **'W~ed – cook'**
„Koch/Köchin gesucht"; **you're** ~**ed
on the phone** du wirst am Telefon verlangt; **the windows** ~ **painting** die Fenster müßten gestrichen werden; **you** ~
to be |more| careful du solltest vorsich-
tig[er] sein; **c)** ~**ed |by the police|** [poli-
zeilich] gesucht. **2.** *n.* **a)** *(lack)* Mangel, *der* (**of** an + *Dat.*); **for** ~ **of sth.**
aus Mangel an etw. *(Dat.);* **b)** *(need)*
Not, *der;* **c)** *(desire)* Bedürfnis, *das.*
'want for *v. t.* **sb.** ~**s for nothing** *or*
doesn't ~ **for anything** jmdm. fehlt es
an nichts
'wanting *adj.* **be** ~**:** fehlen; **sb./sth. is**
~ **in sth.** jmdm./einer Sache fehlt es
an etw. *(Dat.);* **be found** ~**:** für unzureichend befunden werden
wanton ['wɒntən] *adj.,* **'wantonly**
adv. mutwillig
war [wɔ:(r)] *n.* Krieg, *der;* **between the**
~**s** zwischen den Weltkriegen; **declare**
~**:** den Krieg erklären (**on** *Dat.);* **be at**
~**:** sich im Krieg befinden; **make** ~**:**
Krieg führen (**on** gegen)
warble ['wɔ:bl] *v. t. & i.* trällern
ward [wɔ:d] *n.* **a)** *(in hospital)* Station,
die; **she's in W**~ **3** sie liegt auf Station
3; **b)** *(child)* Mündel, *das od. die;* **c)**
(electoral division) Wahlbezirk, *der.*
ward 'off *v. t.* abwehren
warden ['wɔ:dn] *n.* **a)** *(of hostel)*
Heimleiter, *der/-*leiterin, *die; (of youth
hostel)* Herbergsvater, *der/-*mutter,
die; **b)** *(supervisor)* Aufseher, *der/*Auf-
seherin, *die*
'warder *n. (Brit.)* Wärter, *der*
wardrobe ['wɔ:drəʊb] *n.* **a)** Kleider-
schrank, *der;* **b)** *(clothes)* Garderobe,
die
warehouse ['weəhaʊs] *n.* Lagerhaus,
das; (part of building) Lager, *das*
wares [weəz] *n. pl.* Ware, *die*
warfare ['wɔ:feə(r)] *n.* Krieg, *der*
'warhead *n.* Sprengkopf, *der*
warily ['weərɪlɪ] *adv.* vorsichtig; *(suspiciously)* mißtrauisch
'warlike *adj.* kriegerisch
warm [wɔ:m] **1.** *adj.* **a)** warm; **I am
|very|** ~**:** mir ist [sehr] warm; **b)** *(en-
thusiastic)* herzlich ⟨*Grüße, Dank*⟩. **2.**
v. t. wärmen; **warm machen** ⟨*Flüssigkeit*⟩*;* ~ **one's hands** sich *(Dat.)* die
Hände wärmen. **3.** *v. i.* ~ **to sb./sth.**
(come to like) sich für jmdn./etw. er-

wärmen. **warm 'up 1.** *v. i.* warm werden; ⟨*Sportler:*⟩ sich aufwärmen. **2.**
v. t. aufwärmen ⟨*Speisen*⟩*;* erwärmen
⟨*Raum, Zimmer*⟩
warm: ~**-blooded** ['wɔ:mblʌdɪd] *adj.*
warmblütig; ~**-hearted** ['wɔ:mhɑ:t-
ɪd] *adj.* warmherzig ⟨*Person*⟩
'warmly *adv.* **a)** warm; **b)** *(fig.)* herzlich ⟨*willkommen heißen, gratulieren,
begrüßen, grüßen, danken*⟩
warmonger ['wɔ:mʌŋgə(r)] *n.* Kriegs-
hetzer, *der/-*hetzerin, *die*
warmth [wɔ:mθ] *n.* **a)** Wärme, *die;* **b)**
(fig.) Herzlichkeit, *die*
warn [wɔ:n] *v. t.* **a)** *(inform, give notice)*
warnen (**against, of, about** vor +
Dat.); ~ **sb. that ...:** jmdn. darauf hinweisen, daß ...; ~ **sb. not to do sth.**
jmdn. davor warnen, etw. zu tun; **b)**
(admonish) ermahnen; *(officially)* ab-
mahnen. **'warning 1.** *n.* **a)** *(advance
notice)* Vorwarnung, *die;* **b)** *(lesson)*
let that be a ~ **to you** laß dir das eine
Warnung sein; **c)** *(caution)* Verwarnung, *die; (less official)* Warnung, *die.*
2. *adj.* Warn⟨*schild, -signal usw.*⟩
warp [wɔ:p] **1.** *v. i.* sich verbiegen;
⟨*Holz, Schallplatte:*⟩ sich verziehen. **2.**
v. t. verbiegen; **b)** *(fig.)* **a** ~**ed sense
of humour** ein abartiger Humor
war: ~**-path** *n.* **be on the** ~**-path** *(fig.)*
in Rage sein; ~**plane** *n.* Kampfflug-
zeug, *das*
warrant ['wɒrənt] **1.** *n. (for sb.'s arrest)*
Haftbefehl, *der;* |**search**| ~**:** Durchsu-
chungsbefehl, *der.* **2.** *v. t.* **a)** *(justify)*
rechtfertigen; **b)** *(guarantee)* garantieren. **'warranty** *n.* Garantie, *die*
warrior ['wɒrɪə(r)] *n.* *(esp. literary)*
Krieger, *der (geh.)*
Warsaw ['wɔ:sɔ:] **1.** *pr. n.* Warschau
(das). **2.** *attrib. adj.* Warschauer
'warship *n.* Kriegsschiff, *das*
wart [wɔ:t] *n.* Warze, *die*
'wartime *n.* **a)** Kriegszeit, *die;* **in** *or*
during ~**:** im Krieg; **b)** *attrib.* Kriegs-
⟨*rationierung, -evakuierung usw.*⟩
wary ['weərɪ] *adj.* vorsichtig; *(suspicious)* mißtrauisch (**of** gegenüber); **be**
~ **of sb./sth.** sich vor jmdm./etw. in
acht nehmen
was *see* **be**
wash [wɒʃ] **1.** *v. t.* **a)** waschen; ~ **oneself** sich waschen; ~ **one's hands/face/
hair** sich *(Dat.)* die Hände/das Ge-
sicht/die Haare waschen; ~ **the
clothes** Wäsche waschen; ~ **the dishes**
[Geschirr] spülen; ~ **the floor** den
Fußboden aufwischen; **b)** *(remove)*

waschen ⟨*Fleck*⟩ (out of aus); abwaschen ⟨*Schmutz*⟩ (off von); c) *(carry along)* spülen. 2. *v. i.* a) sich waschen; b) ⟨*Stoff, Kleidungsstück:*⟩ sich waschen lassen. 3. *n.* a) give sb./sth. a |good| ~: jmdn./etw. [gründlich] waschen; b) *(laundering)* Wäsche, *die;* c) *(of ship)* Sog, *der.* wash 'down *v. t.* abspritzen ⟨*Auto, Deck, Hof*⟩. wash 'off 1. *v. t.* ~ sth. off etw. abwaschen. 2. *v. i.* abgehen; *(from fabric etc.)* herausgehen. wash 'out *v. t.* ausscheuern ⟨*Topf*⟩; ausspülen ⟨*Mund*⟩; ~ dirt/ marks out of clothes Schmutz/Flecken aus Kleidern [her]auswaschen. wash 'up 1. *v. t. (Brit.)* ~ the dishes up das Geschirr spülen. 2. *v. i.* spülen

washable ['wɒʃəbl] *adj.* waschbar
'wash-basin *n.* Waschbecken, *das*
'washing *n.* Wäsche, *die;* do the ~: waschen

washing: ~-machine *n.* Waschmaschine, *die;* ~-powder *n.* Waschpulver, *das;* ~-'up *n. (Brit.)* Abwasch, *der;* do the ~-up spülen; ~-'up liquid *n.* Spülmittel, *das*

wasn't ['wɒznt] *(coll.)* = was not; *see* be

wasp *n.* Wespe, *die*

waste [weɪst] 1. *n.* a) *(useless remains)* Abfall, *der;* kitchen ~: Küchenabfälle *Pl.;* b) *(extravagant use)* Verschwendung, *die;* it's a ~ of time/money/energy das ist Zeit-/Geld-/Energieverschwendung. 2. *v. t. (squander)* verschwenden; all his efforts were ~d all seine Mühe war umsonst; don't ~ my time! stehlen Sie mir nicht die Zeit! 3. *adj.* a) ~ material Abfall, *der;* b) lay sth. ~: etw. verwüsten. waste a'way *v. i.* immer mehr abmagern

waste: ~ disposal *n.* Abfallbeseitigung, *die;* ~-disposal unit *n.* Müllzerkleinerer, *der*

wasteful ['weɪstfl] *adj.* a) *(extravagant)* verschwenderisch; b) *(causing waste)* unwirtschaftlich

waste: ~-land *n.* Ödland, *das;* ~ 'paper *n.* Papierabfall, *der;* ~-'paper basket *n.* Papierkorb, *der*

watch [wɒtʃ] 1. *n.* a)|wrist-/pocket-|~: [Armband-/Taschen]uhr, *die;* keep ~: Wache halten; keep |a| ~ for sb./ sth. auf jmdn./etw. achten; c) *(Naut.)* Wache, *die.* 2. *v. i.* ~ for sb./sth. auf jmdn./etw. warten. 3. *v. t.* a) *(observe)* sich *(Dat.)* ansehen ⟨*Sportveranstaltung, Fernsehsendung*⟩; ~ |the| television *or* TV fernsehen; ~ sb. do *or*

doing sth. zusehen, wie jmd. etw. tut; we are being ~ed wir werden beobachtet; b) *(be careful of, look after)* achten auf (+ *Akk.*). watch 'out *v. i.* a) *(be careful)* aufpassen; ~ out! Vorsicht!; b) *(look out)* ~ out for sb./sth. auf jmdn./etw. achten

'watch-dog *n.* Wachhund, *der; (fig.)* |public| ~: *[Leiter/Leiterin einer] Aufsichtsbehörde*

watchful ['wɒtʃfl] *adj.* wachsam

watch: ~-maker *n.* Uhrmacher, *der/* Uhrmacherin, *die;* ~-man ['wɒtʃmən] *n., pl.* ~-men ['wɒtʃmən] Wachmann, *der;* ~-strap *n.* [Uhr]armband, *das;* ~-tower *n.* Wachturm, *der*

water ['wɔːtə(r)] 1. *n.* a) Wasser, *das;* b) *in pl. (part of the sea etc.)* Gewässer *Pl.* 2. *v. t.* a) bewässern ⟨*Land*⟩; wässern ⟨*Pflanzen*⟩; ~ the flowers die Blumen [be]gießen; b) verwässern ⟨*Bier usw.*⟩; c) tränken ⟨*Tier*⟩. 3. *v. i.* ⟨*Augen:*⟩ tränen; my mouth was ~ing mir lief das Wasser im Munde zusammen. water 'down *v. t.* verwässern

water: ~-butt *n.* Regentonne, *die;* ~-colour *n.* a) *(paint)* Wasserfarbe, *die;* b) *(picture)* Aquarell, *das;* ~cress *n.* Brunnenkresse, *die;* ~fall *n.* Wasserfall, *der*

'watering-can *n.* Gießkanne, *die*

water: ~-lily *n.* Seerose, *die;* ~-line *n. (Naut.)* Wasserlinie, *die;* ~-logged ['wɔːtəlɒgd] *adj.* naß ⟨*Boden*⟩; aufgeweicht ⟨*Sportplatz*⟩; ~-main *n.* Hauptwasserleitung, *die;* ~-mark *n.* Wasserzeichen, *das;* ~-melon *n.* Wassermelone, *die;* ~ meter *n.* Wasseruhr, *die;* ~ polo *n.* Wasserball, *der;* ~-proof 1. *adj.* wasserdicht; wasserfest ⟨*Farbe*⟩; 2. *v. t.* wasserdicht machen; imprägnieren ⟨*Stoff*⟩; ~-shed *n. (fig.)* Wendepunkt, *der;* ~-ski 1. *n.* Wasserski, *der;* 2. *v. i.* Wasserski laufen; ~-skiing *n.* Wasserskilaufen, *das;* ~-tight *adj.* wasserdicht; ~-tower *n.* Wasserturm, *der;* ~-way *n.* Wasserstraße, *die*

'watery *adj.* wäßrig

watt [wɒt] *n.* Watt, *das*

wave [weɪv] 1. *n.* a) Welle, *die;* b) *(gesture)* give sb. a ~: jmdm. zuwinken; with a ~ of one's hand mit einem Winken. 2. *v. i.* a) ⟨*Fahne, Flagge, Wimpel:*⟩ wehen; ⟨*Baum, Gras, Korn:*⟩ sich wiegen; b) *(with hand)* winken; ~ at *or* to sb. jmdm. winken. 3. *v. t.* schwenken; schwingen ⟨*Schwert*⟩; ~ one's hand at *or* to sb. jmdm. winken;

~ **goodbye to sb.** jmdm. zum Abschied zuwinken. **wave a'side** *v. t.* **a)** abtun ⟨*Zweifel, Einwand*⟩; **b)** *(signal to move)* ~ **sb. aside** [jmdm.] abwinken
wave: ~**band** *n.* Wellenbereich, *der;* ~**length** *n.* Wellenlänge, *die;* **be on the same** ~**length** |**as sb.**| *(fig.)* die gleiche Wellenlänge [wie jmd.] haben
waver ['weɪvə(r)] *v. i.* schwanken
wavy ['weɪvɪ] *adj.* wellig; ~ **line** Schlangenlinie, *die*
¹wax [wæks] **1.** *n.* **a)** Wachs, *das;* **b)** *(in ear)* Schmalz, *das.* **2.** *v. t.* wachsen
²wax *v. i.* **a)** ⟨*Mond:*⟩ zunehmen; **b)** *(become)* werden
wax: ~**work** *n.* Wachsfigur, *die;* ~**works** *n. sing., pl. same* Wachsfigurenkabinett, *das*
waxy *adj.* wachsweich
way [weɪ] **1.** *n.* **a)** Weg, *der;* **ask the** *or* **one's** ~**:** nach dem Weg fragen; **'W~ In/Out** „Ein-/Ausgang"; **by** ~ **of Switzerland** über die Schweiz; **lead the** ~**:** vorausgehen; **go out of one's** ~**:** einen Umweg machen; *(fig.)* keine Mühe scheuen; **b)** *(method)* Art und Weise, *die;* **do it this** ~**:** mach es so; **c)** *(distance)* Stück, *das;* **it's a long** ~ **off** *or* **a long** ~ **from here** es ist weit weg von hier; **all the** ~**:** den ganzen Weg; **d)** *(direction)* Richtung, *die;* **she went this/that/the other** ~**:** sie ist in diese/die/die andere Richtung gegangen; **stand sth. the right/wrong** ~ **up** etw. richtig/falsch herum stellen; **e)** *(respect)* **in** |**exactly**| **the same** ~**:** [ganz] genauso; **in some** ~**s** in gewisser Hinsicht; **in one** ~**:** auf eine Art; **in every** ~**:** in jeder Hinsicht; **in a** ~**:** auf eine Art; **f)** *(custom)* Art, *die;* **g) get** *or* **have one's** |**own**| ~**, have it one's** |**own**| ~**:** seinen Willen kriegen; **be in sb.'s** *or* **the** ~**:** [jmdm.] im Weg sein; **make** ~ **for sth.** für etw. Platz machen; *(fig.)* einer Sache *(Dat.)* Platz machen; **in a bad** ~**:** schlecht; **either** ~**:** so oder so; **by the** ~**:** übrigens. **2.** *adv.* weit; ~ **back** *(coll.)* vor langer Zeit. **way'lay** *v. t., forms as* ²**lay 1: a)** *(ambush)* überfallen; **b)** *(stop for conversation)* abfangen. **way-'out** *adj. (coll.)* verrückt
WC *abbr.* water-closet WC, *das*
we [wɪ, *stressed* wiː] *pl. pron.* wir
weak [wiːk] *adj.* **a)** schwach; *(easily led)* labil ⟨*Charakter, Person*⟩; **b)** dünn ⟨*Getränk*⟩
weaken ['wiːkn] **1.** *v. t.* schwächen; beeinträchtigen ⟨*Augen*⟩. **2.** *v. i.* ⟨*Entschlossenheit, Kraft:*⟩ nachlassen

weakling ['wiːklɪŋ] *n.* Schwächling, *der*
weakly *adv.* schwach
weakness *n.* Schwäche, *die*
wealth [welθ] *n.* **a)** *(abundance)* Fülle, *die;* **b)** *(riches, being rich)* Reichtum, *der.* **wealthy 1.** *adj.* reich. **2.** *n. pl.* **the** ~**:** die Reichen
wean [wiːn] *v. t.* abstillen; ~ **sb.** |**away**| **from sth.** *(fig.)* jmdm. etw. abgewöhnen
weapon ['wepən] *n.* Waffe, *die*
wear [weə(r)] **1.** *n.* **a)** ~ |**and tear**| Abnutzung, *die;* **b)** *(clothes)* Kleidung, *die.* **2.** *v. t., wore* [wɔː(r)]*, worn* [wɔːn] **a)** *(have on)* tragen ⟨*Schmuck, Brille, Kleidung, Perücke*⟩; **I haven't a thing to** ~**:** ich habe überhaupt nichts anzuziehen; **b)** *(rub)* abtragen ⟨*Kleidungsstück*⟩; abnutzen ⟨*Teppich*⟩; **a** |**badly**| **worn tyre** ein |stark| abgefahrener Reifen. **3.** *v. i., wore, worn* **a)** ⟨*Kleider:*⟩ sich durchscheuern; ⟨*Absätze:*⟩ sich ablaufen; ⟨*Teppich:*⟩ sich abnutzen; **b)** *(endure rubbing)* halten; ~ **well/badly** sich gut/schlecht tragen. **wear a'way 1.** *v. t.* abschleifen. **2.** *v. i.* sich abnutzen. **wear 'down** *v. t. (fig.)* zermürben. **wear 'off** *v. i.* ⟨*Schicht:*⟩ abgehen; ⟨*Wirkung, Schmerz:*⟩ nachlassen. **wear 'out 1.** *v. t.* **a)** aufbrauchen; auftragen ⟨*Kleidungsstück*⟩; **b)** *(fig.: exhaust)* kaputtmachen *(ugs.);* **be worn out** kaputt sein *(ugs.).* **2.** *v. i.* kaputtgehen *(ugs.)*
wearable ['weərəbl] *adj.* **sth. is** |**not**| ~**:** man kann etw. [nicht] anziehen
wearily ['wɪərɪlɪ] *adv.* müde
weary ['wɪərɪ] **1.** *adj.* **a)** *(tired)* müde; **b) be** ~ **of sth.** einer Sache *(Gen.)* überdrüssig sein. **2.** *v. t.* **be wearied by sth.** durch etw. erschöpft sein. **3.** *v. i.* ~ **of sth./sb.** einer Sache/jmds. überdrüssig werden
weasel ['wiːzl] *n.* Wiesel, *das*
weather ['weðə(r)] **1.** *n.* Wetter, *das;* **what's the** ~ **like?** wie ist das Wetter?; **in all** ~**s** bei jedem Wetter; **he is feeling under the** ~ *(fig.)* er ist [zur Zeit] nicht ganz auf dem Posten. **2.** *v. t.* abwettern ⟨*Sturm*⟩; *(fig.)* durchstehen ⟨*schwere Zeit*⟩
weather: ~~**beaten** *adj.* wettergegerbt ⟨*Gesicht*⟩; verwittert ⟨*Felsen, Gebäude*⟩; ~**cock** *n.* Wetterhahn, *der;* ~ **forecast** *n.* Wettervorhersage, *die;* ~**man** *n.* Meteorologe, *der;* ~ **report** *n.* Wetterbericht, *der;* ~~**vane** *n.* Wetterfahne, *die*

¹**weave** [wi:v] **1.** *n.* Bindung, *die.* **2.** *v. t.,* **wove** [wəʊv], **woven** ['wəʊvn] **a)** weben; flechten ⟨*Korb, Kranz*⟩; **b)** *(fig.)* einflechten ⟨*Thema usw.*⟩ (into in + *Akk.*)

²**weave** *v. i. (take intricate course)* sich schlängeln

'**weaver** *n.* Weber, *der*/Weberin, *die*

web [web] *n.* Netz, *das;* spider's ~: Spinnennetz, *das;* **webbed feet** [webd 'fi:t] *n. pl.* Schwimmfüße

we´d [wɪd, *stressed* wi:d] **a)** = **we had; b)** = **we would**

Wed. *abbr.* **Wednesday** Mi.

wedding ['wedɪŋ] *n.* Hochzeit, *die*

wedding: ~ **anniversary** *n.* Hochzeitstag, *der;* ~-**cake** *n.* Hochzeitskuchen, *der;* ~ **day** *n.* Hochzeitstag, *der;* ~ **dress** *n.* Brautkleid, *das;* ~ **present** *n.* Hochzeitsgeschenk, *das;* ~-**ring** *n.* Ehering, *der*

wedge [wedʒ] **1.** *n.* Keil, *der.* **2.** *v. t.* verkeilen; ~ **a door/window open** eine Tür/ein Fenster festklemmen, damit sie/es offen bleibt. '**wedge-shaped** *adj.* keilförmig

wedlock ['wedlɒk] *n.* **born in/out of** ~: ehelich/unehelich geboren

Wednesday ['wenzdeɪ, 'wenzdɪ] *n.* Mittwoch, *der; see also* **Friday**

¹**wee** [wi:] *adj. (child lang./Scot.)* klein

²**wee** *see* **wee-wee**

weed [wi:d] *n.* ~|s| Unkraut, *das.* **2.** *v. t.* jäten. **weed 'out** *v. t. (fig.)* aussieben

'**weed-killer** *n.* Unkrautvertilgungsmittel, *das*

'**weedy** *adj.* spillerig *(ugs.)* ⟨*Person*⟩

week [wi:k] *n.* Woche, *die;* **for several** ~**s** mehrere Wochen lang; **once a** ~, **every** ~: einmal in der Woche; **three times a** ~: dreimal in der Woche; **a two-~ visit** ein zweiwöchiger Besuch; **a** ~ **today/tomorrow** heute/morgen in einer Woche; **a** ~ **on Monday, Monday** ~: Montag in einer Woche. '**weekday** *n.* Wochentag, *der.* **weekend** [-'-, '--] *n.* Wochenende, *das;* **at the** ~: am Wochenende; **go away for the** ~: übers Wochenende wegfahren

weekly ['wi:klɪ] **1.** *adj.* wöchentlich; Wochen⟨*zeitung, -zeitschrift, -lohn*⟩. **2.** *adv.* wöchentlich. **3.** *n. (newspaper)* Wochenzeitung, *die; (magazine)* Wochenzeitschrift, *die*

weep [wi:p] *v. i. & t.,* **wept** [wept] weinen. **weeping 'willow** *n.* Trauerweide, *die*

'**wee-wee** *(coll.)* **1.** *n.* Pipi, *das (ugs.);*

do a ~: Pipi machen *(ugs.).* **2.** *v. i.* Pipi machen *(ugs.)*

weigh [weɪ] *v. t. & i.* wiegen. **weigh 'down** *v. t. (fig.: depress)* niederdrücken. **weigh 'up** *v. t.* abwägen

weight [weɪt] *n.* Gewicht, *das;* **what is your** ~? wieviel wiegen Sie?; **be under/over** ~: zuwenig/zuviel wiegen. '**weighting** *n.* Zulage, *die.* '**weightlessness** *n.* Schwerelosigkeit, *die*

weight: ~-**lifter** *n.* Gewichtheber, *der*/-heberin, *die;* ~-**lifting** *n.* Gewichtheben, *das*

'**weighty** *adj.* **a)** *(heavy)* schwer; **b)** *(important)* gewichtig

weir [wɪə(r)] *n.* Wehr, *das*

weird [wɪəd] *adj. (coll.: odd)* bizarr

welcome ['welkəm] **1.** *int.* willkommen; ~ **home/to England!** willkommen zu Hause/in England! **2.** *n.* **a)** Willkommen, *das;* **b)** *(reception)* Empfang, *der.* **3.** *v. t.* begrüßen. **4.** *adj.* **a)** willkommen; gefällig ⟨*Anblick*⟩; **b)** *pred.* **you are** ~ **to take it** du kannst es gern nehmen; **you're** ~: gern geschehen!

weld [weld] *v. t. (join)* verschweißen; *(repair, make, attach)* schweißen (|on| to an + *Akk.*). **welder** *n.* Schweißer, *der*/Schweißerin, *die*

welfare ['welfeə(r)] *n.* Wohl, *das.* **Welfare 'State** *n.* Wohlfahrtsstaat, *der.* '**welfare work** *n.* Sozialarbeit, *die*

¹**well** [wel] *n.* **a)** Brunnen, *der;* **b)** *see* **oil well; c)** *(stair~)* Treppenloch, *das*

²**well 1.** *int.* ~! meine Güte!; ~, **let's forget that** na ja, lassen wir das; ~, **who was it?** nun *od.* und, wer war's?; **oh** ~|, **never mind|** na ja|, macht nichts|; ~? na? **2.** *adv.,* **better** ['betə(r)|, **best** [best] *gut;* gründlich ⟨*trocknen, schütteln*⟩*;* **the business/patient is doing** ~: das Geschäft geht gut/dem Patienten geht es gut; ~ **done!** großartig!; **he is** ~ **over forty** er ist weit über vierzig; **as** ~ *(in addition)* auch; **A as** ~ **as B:** B und auch [noch] A. **3.** *adj. (in good health)* **How are you feeling now?** – **Quite** ~, **thank you** Wie fühlen Sie sich jetzt? – Ganz gut, danke; **look** ~: gut aussehen; **feel** ~: sich wohl fühlen; **he isn't |very|** ~: es geht ihm nicht [sehr] gut; **get** ~ **soon!** gute Besserung!; **make sb.** ~: jmdn. gesund machen

we´ll [wɪl, *stressed* wi:l] = **we will**

well: ~-**behaved** *see* **behave** 1; ~-**being** *n.* Wohl, *das;* ~-**bred** *adj.*

anständig; ~-**built** adj. ⟨Person:⟩ mit
guter Figur; be ~-**built** eine gute Figur
haben; ~ **done** adj. (Cookery) durch-
gebraten; ~-**dressed** adj. gutgeklei-
det; ~-**educated** adj. gebildet; ~-
heeled adj. (coll.) gutbetucht (ugs.)
wellington ['welɪŋtən] n. ~ |boot|
Gummistiefel, der
well: ~-**known** adj. bekannt; ~
made adj. gut [gearbeitet]; ~-**mannered** adj. ⟨Person⟩ mit guten Manieren; be ~-**mannered** gute Manieren
haben; ~-**meaning** adj. wohlmei-
nend; be ~-**meaning** es gut meinen;
~-**meant** adj. gutgemeint; ~ **off** adj.
wohlhabend; sb. is ~ **off** jmdm. geht
es [finanziell] gut; ~-**read** ['welred]
adj. belesen; ~-**timed** adj. zeitlich
gut gewählt; ~-**to-do** adj. wohlhabend; ~-**wisher** n. Sympathisant,
der/Sympathisantin, die
Welsh [welʃ] 1. adj. walisisch; sb. is
~: jmd. ist Waliser/Waliserin. 2. n. a)
(language) Walisisch, das; see also
English 2 a; b) pl. the ~: die Waliser.
Welshman ['welʃmən] n., pl. ~**men**
['welʃmən] Waliser, der. ~ '**rabbit**, ~
rarebit ['reəbɪt] ns. Käsetoast, der
went see go 1
wept see weep
were see be
we're [wɪə(r)] = we are
weren't (coll.) = were not; see be
west [west] 1. n. a) Westen, der; in/
to|wards|/from the ~: im/nach/von
Westen; to the ~ of westlich von; b)
usu. W~ (Geog., Polit.) Westen, der.
2. adj. westlich; West⟨küste, -wind,
-grenze, -tor⟩. 3. adv. nach Westen; ~
of westlich von
West: ~ **Ber'lin** pr. n. (Hist.) West-
Berlin (das); **w~bound** adj. ⟨Zug,
Verkehr usw.⟩ in Richtung Westen; ~
Country n. (Brit.) Westengland, das;
~ **End** n. (Brit.) Westend, das
westerly ['westəlɪ] adj. westlich;
⟨Wind⟩ aus westlichen Richtungen
western ['westən] 1. adj. westlich;
West⟨grenze, -hälfte, -seite⟩; ~ **Germany** Westdeutschland, das. 2. n.
Western, der. **Western 'Europe** pr.
n. Westeuropa (das)
West: ~ '**German** (Hist.) 1. adj. west-
deutsch; 2. n. Westdeutsche, der/die;
~ '**Germany** pr. n. (Hist.) Westdeutschland (das); ~ '**Indian** 1. adj.
westindisch; 2. n. Westinder, der/-in-
derin, die; ~ '**Indies** pr. n. pl. westin-
dische Inseln

westward[s] ['westwəd(z)] adv.
westwärts
wet [wet] 1. adj. a) naß; b) (rainy) regnerisch; feucht ⟨Klima⟩; c) frisch
⟨Farbe⟩; '~ **paint** „frisch gestrichen";
d) (sl.: feeble) schlapp (ugs.). 2. v. t.,
wet or wetted befeuchten. 3. n. a)
(moisture) Feuchtigkeit, die; b) in the
~: im Regen. '**wetness** n. Nässe, die
'**wet suit** n. Tauchanzug, der
we've [wɪv, stressed wiːv] = we have
whack [wæk] (coll.) 1. v. t. hauen
(ugs.). 2. n. Schlag, der
whale [weɪl] n. a) Wal, der; b) (coll.)
we had a ~ of a |good| time wir haben
uns bombig (ugs.) amüsiert
wharf [wɔːf] n., pl. **wharves** [wɔːvz] or
~s Kai, der
what [wɒt] 1. adj. welch...; ~ **book**?
welches Buch?; ~ **time does it start?**
um wieviel Uhr fängt es an?; ~ **kind
of man is he?** was für ein Mensch ist
er?; ~ **a fool you are!** was für ein
Dummkopf du doch bist!; ~ **cheek/
luck!** was für eine Frechheit/ein
Glück!; **I will give you** ~ **help I can** ich
werde dir helfen, so gut ich kann. 2.
adv. ~ **do I care?** was kümmert's
mich?; ~ **does it matter?** was macht's?
3. pron. was; ~? wie?; was? (ugs.); ~
is your name? wie heißt du/heißen
Sie?; ~ **about...?** (~ will become of...?)
was ist mit ...?; ~ **about a game of
chess?** wie wär's mit einer Partie
Schach?; ~'**s-his/-her/-its-name** wie
heißt er/sie/es noch; ~ **for?** wozu?; ~
is it like? wie ist es?; **so** ~? na und?;
do ~ **I tell you** tu, was ich dir sage
whatever [wɒt'evə(r)] 1. adj. ~ **problems you have** was für Probleme Sie
auch haben; **nothing** ~: absolut
nichts. 2. pron. **do** ~ **you like** mach,
was du willst; ~ **happens, ...**: was auch
geschieht, ...; **or** ~: oder was auch immer; ~ **does he want?** (coll.) was will er
nur?
wheat [wiːt] n. Weizen, der
wheedle ['wiːdl] v. t. ~ **sb. into doing
sth.** jmdm. so lange gut zureden, bis er
etw. tut; ~ **sth. out of sb.** jmdm. etw.
abschwatzen (ugs.)
wheel [wiːl] 1. n. a) Rad, das; |potter's|
~: Töpferscheibe, die; b) (steering ~)
Lenkrad, das; (ship's ~) Steuerrad,
das; **at** or **behind the** ~ (of car) am
Steuer. 2. v. t. (push) schieben. 3. v. i.
a) (turn round) kehrtmachen; b)
(circle) kreisen
wheel: ~**barrow** n. Schubkarre, die;

~chair n. Rollstuhl, der; **~-clamp** n. Parkkralle, die

wheeze [wi:z] v.t. schnaufen

when [wen] **1.** adv. wann; **the time ~ ...:** die Zeit, zu der/(with past tense) als ...; **the day ~ ...:** der Tag, an dem/ (with past tense) als ... **2.** conj. **a)** (at the time that) als; (with present or future tense) wenn; **~ reading [a newspaper]** beim Lesen [einer Zeitung]; **b)** (whereas) **why do you go abroad ~ it's cheaper here?** warum fährst du ins Ausland, wo es doch hier billiger ist? **3.** pron. **by/till ~ ...?;** bis wann ...?; **since ~ ...?** seit wann ...?

whence [wens] adv., conj. (arch./ literary) woher

whenever [wen'evə(r)] **1.** adv. wann immer; **or ~:** oder wann immer; **~ did he do it?** (coll.) wann hat er es nur getan? **2.** conj. jedesmal wenn

where [weə(r)] **1.** adv. **a)** (position) wo; **~ shall we sit?** wohin wollen wir uns setzen?; **b)** (to ~) wohin **2.** conj. wo. **3.** pron. **near/not far from ~ it happened** nahe der Stelle/nicht weit von der Stelle, wo es passiert ist

whereabouts 1. [weərə'bauts] adv. (where) wo; (to where) wohin. **2.** ['weərəbauts] n., sing. or pl. (of thing) Verbleib, der; (of person) Aufenthalt[sort], der

where: ~'as conj. während; **he is very quiet, ~as she is an extrovert** er ist sehr ruhig, sie dagegen ist eher extravertiert; **~'by** adv. mit dem/der/denen; **~upon** [weərə'pɒn] adv. worauf

wherever [weər'evə(r)] **1.** adv. **a)** (position) wo immer; **sit ~ you like** setz dich, wohin du magst; **or ~:** oder wo immer; **b)** (direction) wohin immer; **or ~:** oder wohin immer; **c)** **~ have you been?** (coll.) wo hast du bloß gesteckt? **2.** conj. **a)** (position) überall [da], wo; **~ possible** wo od. wenn [irgend] möglich; **b)** (direction) wohin auch; **~ he went** wohin er auch ging

whet [wet] v.t., **-tt-: a)** (sharpen) wetzen; **b)** (fig.) anregen ⟨Appetit⟩

whether ['weðə(r)] conj. ob; **I don't know ~ to go [or not]** ich weiß nicht, ob ich gehen soll [oder nicht]

which [wɪtʃ] **1.** adj. welch...; **~ one** welcher/welche/welches; **~ ones** welche; **~ way** (how) wie; (in ~ direction) wohin. **2.** pron. **a)** interrog. welcher/ welche/welches; **~ of you?** wer von euch?; **b)** rel. der/die/das; **of ~:** dessen/deren; **after ~:** worauf[hin]

whichever [wɪtʃ'evə(r)] **1.** adj. welcher/welche/welches ... auch. **2.** pron. **a)** welcher/welche/welches ... auch; **b)** (coll.) **~ could it be?** welcher/welche/ welches könnte das nur sein?

whiff [wɪf] n. (puff; fig.: trace) Hauch, der; (smell) leichter Geruch

while [waɪl] **1.** n. Weile, die; **[for] a ~:** eine Weile; **a long ~:** lange; **for a little or short ~:** eine kleine Weile; **be worth sb.'s ~:** sich [für jmdn.] lohnen. **2.** conj. **a)** während; (as long as) solange; **b)** (although) obgleich; **c)** (whereas) während. **while a'way** v.t. **~ away the time** sich (Dat.) die Zeit vertreiben (by, with mit)

whilst [waɪlst] (Brit.) see **while** 2

whim [wɪm] n. Laune, die

whimper ['wɪmpə(r)] **1.** n. **~[s]** Wimmern, das; (of dog etc.) Winseln, das. **2.** v.i. wimmern; ⟨Hund:⟩ winseln

whimsical ['wɪmzɪkl] adj. launenhaft; (odd, fanciful) spleenig

whine [waɪn] **1.** v.i. **a)** heulen; ⟨Hund:⟩ jaulen; **b)** (complain) jammern. **2.** n. **a)** Heulen, das; (of dog) Jaulen, das; **b)** (complaint) **~[s]** Gejammer, das

whip [wɪp] **1.** n. **a)** Peitsche, die; **b)** (Brit. Parl.) Fraktionsgeschäftsführer, der/-führerin, die. **2.** v.t., **-pp-: a)** peitschen; **b)** (Cookery) schlagen; **c)** (move quickly) reißen; **d)** (sl.: steal) klauen (ugs.). **whip 'out** v.t. [blitzschnell] herausziehen. **whip 'up** v.t. **a)** (arouse) anheizen (ugs.); **b)** (coll.: make quickly) schnell hinzaubern ⟨Gericht, Essen⟩

whipped 'cream n. Schlagsahne, die

whirl [wɜ:l] **1.** v.t. [im Kreis] herumwirbeln. **2.** v.i. wirbeln. **3.** n. **a)** Wirbeln, das; **she was od her thoughts were in a ~** (fig.) ihr schwirrte der Kopf; **b)** (bustle) Trubel, der. **whirl 'round 1.** v.t. [im Kreis] herumwirbeln. **2.** v.i. [im Kreis] herumwirbeln; ⟨Rad, Rotor:⟩ wirbeln

whirl: ~pool n. Strudel, der; (bathing pool) Whirlpool, der; **~wind** n. Wirbelwind, der

whirr [wɜ:(r)] **1.** v.i. surren. **2.** n. Surren, das

whisk [wɪsk] **1.** n. (Cookery) Schneebesen, der; (part of mixer) Rührbesen, der. **2.** v.t. **a)** (Cookery) [mit dem Schnee-/Rührbesen] schlagen; **b)** (convey rapidly) in Windeseile bringen. **whisk a'way** v.t. **a)** (remove suddenly) **~ sth. away [from sb.]**

[jmdm.] etw. [plötzlich] wegreißen; **b)** *(convey rapidly)* in Windeseile wegbringen

whisker ['wɪskə(r)] *n.* **a)** ~s *(on man's cheek)* Backenbart, *der;* **b)** *(of cat, mouse, rat)* Schnurrhaar, *das*

whiskey *(Amer., Ir.)*, **whisky** ['wɪskɪ] *n.* Whisky, *der; (American or Irish)* Whiskey, *der*

whisper ['wɪspə(r)] **1.** *v. i.* flüstern; ~ **to sb.** jmdm. etwas zuflüstern. **2.** *v. t.* flüstern; ~ **sth. to sb.** jmdm. etw. zuflüstern. **3.** *n.* **a)** Flüstern, *das;* **in a** ~, **in** ~s im Flüsterton; **b)** *(rumour)* Gerücht, *das*

whistle ['wɪsl] **1.** *v. i.* pfeifen; ~ **at sb.** *(in disapproval)* jmdn. auspfeifen. **2.** *v. t.* pfeifen. **3.** *n.* **a)** *(sound)* Pfiff, *der; (whistling)* Pfeifen, *das;* **b)** *(instrument)* Pfeife, *die;* **blow a/one's** ~: pfeifen

white [waɪt] **1.** *adj.* weiß. **2.** *n.* **a)** *(colour)* Weiß, *das;* **b)** *(of egg)* Eiweiß, *das;* **c)** **W~** *(person)* Weiße, *der/die*

white: ~ **bread** *n.* Weißbrot, *das;* ~ **'coffee** *n. (Brit.)* Kaffee mit Milch; ~-**'collar worker** *n.* Angestellte, *der/die;* **W~ House** *pr. n. (Amer. Polit.)* **the W~ House** das Weiße Haus

whiten ['waɪtn] **1.** *v. t.* weiß machen; weißen ⟨*Wand, Schuhe*⟩. **2.** *v. i.* weiß werden

'whiteness *n.* Weiß, *das*

white: **W~** **'Paper** *n. (Brit.)* öffentliches Diskussionspapier über Vorhaben der Regierung; ~**wash 1.** *n.* [weiße] Tünche; *(fig.)* Schönfärberei, *die;* **2.** *v. t.* [weiß] tünchen; ~ **'wine** *n.* Weißwein, *der*

Whit [wɪt] **'Monday** *n.* Pfingstmontag, *der*

Whitsun ['wɪtsn] *n.* Pfingsten, *das od. Pl.;* **at** ~: zu *od.* an Pfingsten

whittle ['wɪtl]: ~ **a'way** *v. t.* ~ **away sb.'s rights/power** jmdm. nach und nach alle Rechte/Macht nehmen; ~ **'down** *v. t.* allmählich reduzieren ⟨*Anzahl, Gewinn*⟩; verkürzen ⟨*Liste*⟩

whiz, whizz [wɪz] **1.** *v. i.,* **-zz-** zischen. **2.** *n.* Zischen, *das.* **'whiz[z]-kid** *n. (coll.)* Senkrechtstarter, *der*

who [hʊ, *stressed* hu:] *pron.* **a)** *interrog.* wer; *(coll.: whom)* wen; *(coll.: to whom)* wem; **b)** *rel.* der/die/das; *pl.* die; *(coll.: whom)* den/die/das; *(coll.: to whom)* dem/der/denen; **anyone/** **those** ~ ...: wer ...; **everybody** ~ ...: jeder, der ...

whoa [wəʊ] *int.* brr

who'd [hʊd, *stressed* hu:d] **a)** = **who had;** **b)** = **who would**

whoever [hu:'evə(r)] *pron.* **a)** wer [immer]; **b)** *(no matter who)* wer ... auch; **c)** *(coll.)* ~ **could it be?** wer könnte das nur sein?

whole [həʊl] **1.** *adj.* ganz; **the** ~ **lot** [of **them**] [sie] alle. **2.** *n.* Ganze, *das;* **the** ~: das Ganze; **the** ~ **of my money/the village/London** mein ganzes Geld/das ganze Dorf/ganz London; **as a** ~: als Ganzes; **on the** ~: im großen und ganzen

whole: ~-**hearted** [həʊl'hɑːtɪd] *adj.* herzlich ⟨*Dank[barkeit]*⟩; rückhaltlos ⟨*Unterstützung*⟩; ~**meal** *adj.* Vollkorn-; ~ **note** *n. (Amer. Mus.)* ganze Note; ~ **'number** *n.* ganze Zahl; ~**sale 1.** *adj.* **a)** Großhandels-; **b)** *(fig.: on a large scale)* massenhaft; Massen-; **2.** *adv.* **a)** en gros; **b)** *(fig.: on a large scale)* massenweise; ~**saler** ['həʊlseɪlə(r)] *n.* Großhändler, *der/* -händlerin, *die*

wholesome ['həʊlsəm] *adj.* gesund

who'll [hʊl, *stressed* hu:l] = **who will**

wholly ['həʊllɪ] *adv.* völlig

whom [hu:m] *pron.* **a)** *interrog.* wen; *as indirect object* wem; **b)** *rel.* den/die/das; *pl.* die; *as indirect object* dem/der/dem; *pl.* denen

whooping cough ['hu:pɪŋ kɒf] *n.* Keuchhusten, *der*

whopper ['wɒpə(r)] *n. (coll.)* **a)** Riese, *der;* **b)** *(lie)* faustdicke Lüge

whopping ['wɒpɪŋ] *adj. (coll.)* riesig; Riesen- *(ugs.);* faustdick ⟨*Lüge*⟩

whore [hɔː(r)] *n.* Hure, *die*

who's [hu:z] **a)** = **who is;** **b)** = **who has**

whose [hu:z] *pron.* **a)** *interrog.* wessen; ~ **[book] is that?** wem gehört das [Buch]?; **b)** *rel.* dessen/deren/dessen; *pl.* deren

who've [hʊv, *stressed* hu:v] = **who have**

why [waɪ] **1.** *adv.* **a)** *(for what reason)* warum; *(for what purpose)* wozu; ~ **is that?** warum das?; **b)** *(on account of which)* **the reason** ~ **he did it** der Grund, warum er es tat. **2.** *int.* ~, **certainly/of course!** aber sicher!

wick [wɪk] *n.* Docht, *der*

wicked ['wɪkɪd] *adj.* böse. **'wickedness** *n.* Bosheit, *die*

wicker ['wɪkə(r)] *n.* Korbgeflecht, *das; attrib.* Korb⟨*waren, -stuhl*⟩. **'wickerwork** *n.* **a)** *(material)* Korbgeflecht, *das;* **b)** *(articles)* Korbwaren

wicket ['wɪkɪt] *n. (Cricket)* Tor, *das*

wide [waɪd] **1.** *adj.* **a)** *(broad)* breit;
groß ⟨Abstand, Winkel⟩; **three feet ~:**
drei Fuß breit; **b)** *(extensive)* weit;
umfassend ⟨Lektüre, Wissen, Kennt-
nisse⟩; reichhaltig ⟨Auswahl, Sorti-
ment⟩; **c)** *(off target)* **be ~ of sth.** etw.
verfehlen. **2.** *adv.* **a)** ~ **awake** hellwach; **b)** *(off target)* **shoot ~:** dane-
benschießen; **go ~:** das Ziel verfehlen. **wide-angle 'lens** *n.* Weitwin-
kelobjektiv, *das*

'widely *adv.* **a)** *(over a wide area)* weit
⟨verbreitet, gestreut⟩; **b)** *(by many
people)* weithin ⟨bekannt, akzeptiert⟩;
a ~ held view eine weitverbreitete Ansicht; **c)** *(greatly)* erheblich ⟨sich unter-
scheiden⟩

widen ['waɪdn] **1.** *v.t.* verbreitern. **2.**
v.i. sich verbreitern

wide: **~-open** *attrib. adj.*, ~ **'open**
pred. adj. weit geöffnet ⟨Fenster, Tür⟩;
weit aufgerissen ⟨Mund, Augen⟩; **be ~
open** ⟨Fenster, Tür:⟩ weit offenstehen;
~spread *adj.* weitverbreitet *präd.* getrennt geschr.

widow ['wɪdəʊ] *n.* Witwe, *die.* **widowed** ['wɪdəʊd] *adj.* verwitwet. **widower** ['wɪdəʊə(r)] *n.* Witwer, *der*

width [wɪdθ] *n.* Breite, *die; (of garment)* Weite, *die*

wield [wiːld] *v.t.* schwingen; *(fig.)*
ausüben ⟨Macht, Einfluß⟩

wife [waɪf] *n., pl.* **wives** [waɪvz] Frau,
die

wig [wɪg] *n.* Perücke, *die*

wiggle ['wɪgl] *(coll.)* **1.** *v.t.* hin und her
bewegen. **2.** *v.i.* wackeln

wild [waɪld] **1.** *adj.* **a)** wildlebend
⟨Tier⟩; wildwachsend ⟨Pflanze⟩; **b)**
wild ⟨Landschaft⟩; **c)** *(unrestrained)*
wild ⟨Erregung⟩; **run ~** ⟨Pferd, Hund:⟩
frei herumlaufen; ⟨Kind:⟩ herum-
toben; **send** *or* **drive sb. ~:** jmdn. rasend vor Erregung machen; **d)** *(coll.:
very keen)* **be ~ about sb./sth.** wild auf
jmdn./etw. sein. **2.** *n.* **the ~|s|** die
Wildnis; **see an animal in the ~:** ein
Tier in freier Wildbahn sehen

wilderness ['wɪldənɪs] *n.* Wildnis,
die; (desert) Wüste, *die*

wild: **~-'goose chase** *n. (fig.)* aussichtslose Suche; **~life** *n.* die Tier-
und Pflanzenwelt; **~life park/reserve/
sanctuary** Naturpark, *der/*-reservat,
das/-schutzgebiet, *das*

'wildly *adv.* wild; **be ~ excited about
sth.** über etw. *(Akk.)* ganz aus dem
Häuschen sein *(ugs.); ~* **inaccurate**
völlig ungenau

wilful ['wɪlfl] *adj.*, **wilfully** ['wɪlfəlɪ]
adv. **a)** *(deliberate[ly])* vorsätzlich; **b)**
(obstinate[ly]) starrsinnig

¹will [wɪl] *v. aux., only in: pres.* **will,**
neg. (coll.) **won't** ['wəʊnt], *past* **would**
[wʊd], *neg. (coll.)* **wouldn't** ['wʊdnt] **He
won't help me. W~/Would you?** Er
will mir nicht helfen. Bist du bereit?;
the car won't start das Auto springt
nicht an; **~/would you pass the salt,
please?** gibst du bitte mal das Salz rüber?/würdest du bitte mal das Salz rü-
bergeben?; **~ you be quiet!** willst du
wohl ruhig sein!; **he ~ sit there hour
after hour** er pflegt dort stundenlang
zu sitzen; **he '~ insist on doing it** er besteht unbedingt darauf, es zu tun; ~
you have some more cake? möchtest
od. willst du noch etwas Kuchen?; **the
box ~ hold 5 lb. of tea** in die Kiste gehen 5 Pfund Tee; **tomorrow he ~ be in
Oxford** morgen ist er in Oxford; **I
promise I won't do it again** ich verspre-
che, ich mach's nicht noch mal; **if he
tried, he would succeed** wenn er es versuchen würde, würde er es erreichen;
~ you please tidy up würdest du bitte
aufräumen?

²will *n.* **a)** *(faculty)* Wille, *der;* **b)** *(Law:
testament)* Testament, *das;* **c)** *(desire)*
at ~: nach Belieben; **~ to live** Lebens-
wille, *der;* **against one's/sb.'s ~:** gegen
seinen/jmds. Willen

'willing *adj.* willig; **ready and ~:** bereit; **be ~ to do sth.** bereit sein, etw. zu
tun. **'willingly** *adv.* **a)** *(with pleasure)*
gern[e]; **b)** *(voluntarily)* freiwillig.
'willingness *n.* Bereitschaft, *die*

willow ['wɪləʊ] *n.* Weide, *die*

'will-power *n.* Willenskraft, *die*

willy-nilly [wɪlɪ'nɪlɪ] *adv.* wohl oder
übel ⟨etw. tun müssen⟩

wilt [wɪlt] *v.i.* ⟨Pflanze, Blumen:⟩ welk
werden, welken

wily ['waɪlɪ] *adj.* listig; gewieft ⟨Per-
son⟩

wimp [wɪmp] *n. (coll.)* Schlappschwanz, *der (ugs.)*

win [wɪn] **1.** *v.t.,* -nn-, **won** [wʌn] gewinnen; bekommen ⟨Stipendium, Ver-
trag, Recht⟩; **~ sb. sth.** jmdm. etw.
einbringen. **2.** *v.i.,* -nn-, **won** gewinnen. **3.** *n.* Sieg, *der;* **have a ~:** gewinnen. **win 'over, win 'round** *v.t.* bekehren; *(to one's side)* auf seine Seite
bringen; *(convince)* überzeugen. **win
'through** *v.i.* Erfolg haben

wince [wɪns] *v.i.* zusammenzucken (**at**
bei)

winch [wɪntʃ] **1.** *n.* Winde, *die.* **2.** *v. t.* winden; ~ **up** hochwinden

¹wind [wɪnd] **1.** *n.* Wind, *der; (Med.)* Blähungen; **get** ~ **of sth.** *(fig.)* Wind von etw. bekommen; **be in the** ~ *(fig.)* in der Luft liegen; **get/have the** ~ **up** *(sl.)* Manschetten *(ugs.)* kriegen/haben. **2.** *v. t.* **the blow** ~**ed him** der Schlag nahm ihm den Atem

²wind [waɪnd] **1.** *v. i.,* **wound** [waʊnd] **a)** *(curve)* sich winden; *(move)* sich schlängeln; **b)** *(coil)* sich wickeln. **2.** *v. t.,* **wound a)** *(coil)* wickeln; ~ **sth. on** |to| **sth.** etw. auf etw. *(Akk.)* |auf|wickeln; **b)** aufziehen ⟨*Uhr*⟩. **wind 'down** *v. t.* **a)** herunterdrehen ⟨*Autofenster*⟩; **b)** *(fig.: reduce gradually)* einschränken. **wind 'up 1.** *v. t.* **a)** hochdrehen ⟨*Autofenster*⟩; **b)** *(coil)* aufwickeln; **c)** aufziehen ⟨*Uhr*⟩; **d)** *(coll.: annoy deliberately)* auf die Palme bringen *(ugs.);* **e)** beschließen ⟨*Debatte*⟩; **f)** *(Finance, Law)* auflösen. **2.** *v. i.* **a)** *(conclude)* schließen; **b)** *(coll.: end up)* ~ **up in prison/hospital** [zum Schluß] im Gefängnis/Krankenhaus landen *(ugs.)*

wind [wɪnd]: ~**break** *n.* Windschutz, *der;* ~**chill factor** *n.* Wind-chill-Index, *der (Meteor.)*

winder ['waɪndə(r)] *n. (of watch)* Krone, *die; (of clock, toy)* Aufziehschraube, *die*

wind [wɪnd]: ~**fall** *n.* **a)** *(fruit)* ~**falls** Fallobst, *das;* **b)** *(fig.)* warmer Regen *(ugs.);* ~ **farm** *n.* Windpark, *der;* Windfarm, *die;* ~ **instrument** *n. (Mus.)* Blasinstrument, *das;* ~**mill** *n.* Windmühle, *die*

window ['wɪndəʊ] *n.* Fenster, *das; (shop~)* [Schau]fenster, *das;* **break a** ~: eine Fensterscheibe zerbrechen

window: ~-**box** *n.* Blumenkasten, *der;* ~-**cleaner** *n.* Fensterputzer, *der*/-putzerin, *die;* ~-**dressing** *n. (fig.)* Schönfärberei, *die;* ~-**pane** *n.* Fensterscheibe, *die;* ~-**shopping** *n.* Schaufensterbummeln, *das;* **go** ~-**shopping** einen Schaufensterbummel machen; ~-**sill** *n. (inside)* Fensterbank, *die; (outside)* Fenstersims, *der od. das*

wind [wɪnd]: ~**pipe** *n. (Anat.)* Luftröhre, *die;* ~**screen,** *(Amer.)* ~**shield** *ns. (Motor Veh.)* Windschutzscheibe, *die;* ~**screen/**~**shield wiper** Scheibenwischer, *der;* ~**screen/**~**shield washer** Scheibenwaschanlage, *die;* ~**surfer** *n.* Windsurfer, *der;*

~**surfing** *n.* Windsurfen, *das;* ~**swept** *adj.* windgepeitscht; vom Wind zerzaust ⟨*Person, Haare*⟩; ~-**tunnel** *n.* Windkanal, *der*

windward ['wɪndwəd] *adj.* ~ **side** Windseite, *die*

'windy *adj.* windig

wine [waɪn] *n.* Wein, *der*

wine: ~-**bar** *n.* Weinstube, *die;* ~-**cellar** *n.* [Wein]keller, *das;* ~-**glass** *n.* Weinglas, *das;* ~-**list** *n.* Weinkarte, *die;* ~-**tasting** ['waɪnteɪstɪŋ] *n.* Weinprobe, *die*

wing [wɪŋ] *n.* **a)** *(Ornith., Archit., Sport)* Flügel, *der;* **b)** *(Aeronaut.)* Tragfläche, *die;* **c)** *(Brit. Motor. Veh.)* Kotflügel, *der*

wink [wɪŋk] **1.** *v. i.* **a)** blinzeln; *(as signal)* zwinkern; ~ **at sb.** jmdm. zuzwinkern; **b)** *(flash)* blinken. **2.** *n.* **a)** Blinzeln, *das; (signal)* Zwinkern, *das;* **give sb. a** ~: jmdm. zuzwinkern; **b)** **not sleep a** ~: kein Auge zutun

'winner *n.* Sieger, *der*/Siegerin, *die; (of competition or prize)* Gewinner, *der*/Gewinnerin, *die*

'winning *adj.* **a)** *attrib.* siegreich; ~ **number** Gewinnzahl, *die;* **b)** *(charming)* einnehmend; gewinnend ⟨*Lächeln*⟩. **'winning-post** *n.* Zielpfosten, *der.* **'winnings** *n. pl.* Gewinn, *der*

winter ['wɪntə(r)] *n.* Winter, *der;* **in** |the| ~: im Winter. **winter 'sports** *n. pl.* Wintersport, *der*

wintry ['wɪntrɪ] *adj.* winterlich; ~ **shower** Schneegestöber, *das*

wipe [waɪp] **1.** *v. t.* **a)** abwischen; [auf]wischen ⟨*Fußboden*⟩; *(dry)* abtrocknen; ~ **one's mouth/eyes/nose** sich *(Dat.)* den Mund/die Tränen/die Nase abwischen; ~ **one's feet/shoes** [sich *(Dat.)*] die Füße/Schuhe abtreten; **b)** *(get rid of)* [ab]wischen; ~ **one's/sb.'s tears** sich/jmdm. die Tränen abwischen. **2.** *n.* **give sth. a** ~: etw. abwischen. **wipe 'down** *v. t.* abwischen; *(dry)* abtrocknen. **wipe 'off** *v. t.* **a)** *(remove)* wegwischen; löschen ⟨*Bandaufnahme*⟩; **b)** *(pay off)* zurückzahlen ⟨*Schulden*⟩. **wipe 'out** *v. t.* **a)** *(remove)* wegwischen; *(erase)* auslöschen; **b)** *(cancel)* tilgen; zunichte machen ⟨*Vorteil, Gewinn usw.*⟩; **c)** *(destroy)* ausrotten ⟨*Rasse, Tierart, Feinde*⟩; ausmerzen ⟨*Seuche, Korruption*⟩. **wipe 'up** *v. t.* **a)** aufwischen; **b)** *(dry)* abtrocknen

'wiper *n. (Motor Veh.)* Wischer, *der*

wire ['waɪə(r)] **1.** *n.* **a)** Draht, *der;* **b)** *(Electr., Teleph.)* Leitung, *die;* **c)** *(coll.: telegram)* Telegramm, *das.* **2.** *v.t.* **a)** *(fasten)* ~ sth. together etw. mit Draht verbinden; **b)** *(Electr.)* ~ **sth. to sth.** etw. an etw. *(Akk.)* anschließen; ~ **a house** in einem Haus die Stromleitungen legen; **c)** *(coll.: telegraph)* ~ **sb.** jmdm. *od.* an jmdn. telegrafieren. 'wireless *n.* *(Brit.)* Radio, *das.* **wire** 'netting *n.* Maschendraht, *der*

wiring ['waɪərɪŋ] *n.* [elektrische] Leitungen

wisdom ['wɪzdəm] *n.* **a)** Weisheit, *die;* **b)** *(prudence)* Klugheit, *die.* 'wisdom tooth *n.* Weisheitszahn, *der*

wise [waɪz] *adj.* **a)** weise; vernünftig ⟨*Meinung*⟩; **b)** *(prudent)* klug; **c)** be none the ~r kein bißchen klüger als vorher sein. 'wisely *adv.* weise; *(prudently)* klug

wish [wɪʃ] **1.** *v.t.* wünschen; **I ~ I was** *or* **were rich** ich wollte, ich wäre reich; **I ~ to go** ich möchte gehen; ~ **sb. luck/success** etc. jmdm. Glück/Erfolg *usw.* wünschen; ~ **sb. well** jmdm. alles Gute wünschen. **2.** *v.i.* wünschen; ~ **for sth.** sich *(Dat.)* etw. wünschen. **3.** *n.* Wunsch, *der;* **make a** ~: sich *(Dat.)* etwas wünschen; **get** *or* **have one's** ~: seinen Wunsch erfüllt bekommen. **wishful thinking** [wɪʃfl 'θɪŋkɪŋ] *n.* Wunschdenken, *das*

wishy-washy ['wɪʃɪwɒʃɪ] *adj.* labberig *(ugs.); (fig.)* lasch

wisp [wɪsp] *n.* *(of straw)* Büschel, *das;* ~ **of hair** Haarsträhne, *die;* ~ **of cloud/smoke** Wolkenfetzen, *der/* Rauchfahne, *die*

wistful ['wɪstfl] *adj.,* 'wistfully *adv.* wehmütig

wit [wɪt] *n.* **a)** *(humour)* Witz, *der;* **b)** *(intelligence)* Geist, *der;* be **at one's ~'s** *or* ~**s' end** sich *(Dat.)* keinen Rat mehr wissen; **be frightened** *or* **scared out of one's** ~**s** Todesangst haben; **have/keep one's** ~**s about one** auf Draht *(ugs.)* sein/nicht den Kopf verlieren; **c)** *(person)* geistreicher Mensch

witch [wɪtʃ] *n.* Hexe, *die*

witch: ~**craft** *n.* Hexerei, *die;* ~**-doctor** *n.* Medizinmann, *der;* ~**-hunt** *n.* Hexenjagd, *die* (**for** auf + *Akk.*)

with [wɪð] *prep.* mit; **put sth.** ~ **sth.** etw. zu etw. stellen/legen; **have nothing to write** ~: nichts zum Schreiben haben; **I'm not** '~ **you** *(coll.)* ich kom-

me nicht mit; **tremble** ~ **fear** vor Angst zittern; **I have no money** ~ **me** ich habe kein Geld dabei *od.* bei mir; **sleep** ~ **the window open** bei offenem Fenster schlafen

with'draw 1. *v.t., forms as* **draw 1** zurückziehen; abziehen ⟨*Truppen*⟩; ~ **sth. from an account** etw. von einem Konto abheben. **2.** *v.i., forms as* **draw 1** sich zurückziehen. **with'drawal** [wɪð'drɔːəl] *n.* **a)** Zurücknahme, *die; (of troops)* Abzug, *der; (of money)* Abhebung, *die;* **b)** *(from drugs)* Entzug, *der;* ~ **symptoms** Entzugserscheinungen. **with'drawn** *adj.* *(unsociable)* verschlossen

wither ['wɪðə(r)] **1.** *v.t.* verdorren lassen. **2.** *v.i.* [ver]welken. **wither a'way** *v.i.* dahinwelken *(geh.)*

with'hold *v.t., forms as* 2**hold**: ~ **sth. from sb.** jmdm. etw. vorenthalten

within [wɪ'ðɪn] *prep.* innerhalb; **stay/ be** ~ **the law** den Boden des Gesetzes nicht verlassen; ~ **eight miles of sth.** acht Meilen im Umkreis von etw.

without [wɪ'ðaʊt] *prep.* ohne; ~ **doing sth.** ohne etw. zu tun; ~ **his knowing** ohne daß er davon weiß/wußte

with'stand *v.t.,* withstood [wɪθ'stʊd] standhalten (+ *Dat.*); aushalten ⟨*Beanspruchung, hohe Temperaturen*⟩

witness ['wɪtnɪs] **1.** *n.* Zeuge, *der/* Zeugin, *die* (**of,** *to* Gen.). **2.** *v.t.* **a)** *(see)* ~ **sth.** Zeuge/Zeugin einer Sache *(Gen.)* sein; **b)** bestätigen ⟨*Unterschrift*⟩. 'witness-box *(Brit.),* 'witness-stand *(Amer.)* ns. Zeugenstand, *der*

witticism ['wɪtɪsɪzm] *n.* Witzelei, *die*

wittingly ['wɪtɪŋlɪ] *adv.* wissentlich

witty ['wɪtɪ] *adj.* witzig; geistreich ⟨*Person*⟩

wives *pl. of* **wife**

wizard ['wɪzəd] *n.* Zauberer, *der.* **wizardry** ['wɪzədrɪ] *n.* Zauberei, *die*

wizened ['wɪzənd] *adj.* runz[e]lig

wobble ['wɒbl] *v.i.* wackeln. **wobbly** ['wɒblɪ] *adj.* wack[e]lig

woe [wəʊ] *n.* *(arch./literary/joc.)* ~[s] Jammer, *der;* ~ **betide you!** wehe dir!

woke, woken *see* 1**wake 1, 2**

wolf [wʊlf] **1.** *n., pl.* **wolves** [wʊlvz] Wolf, *der.* **2.** *v.t.* ~ **[down]** verschlingen

woman ['wʊmən] *n., pl.* **women** ['wɪmɪn] Frau, *die;* ~ **doctor** Ärztin, *die;* ~ **friend** Freundin, *die.* **womanizer** ['wʊmənaɪzə(r)] *n.* Schürzenjäger, *der.* 'womanly *adj.* fraulich

womb [wu:m] *n.* Gebärmutter, *die*

women *pl. of* **woman**

women: ~**folk** *n. pl.* Frauen; **W~'s 'Lib** *(coll.)*, **W~'s Libe'ration** *ns.* die Frauenbewegung; ~**'s 'rights** *n. pl.* die Rechte der Frau

won *see* **win 1, 2**

wonder ['wʌndə(r)] **1.** *n.* **a)** *(thing)* Wunder, *das;* **b)** *(feeling)* Staunen, *das.* **2.** *adj.* Wunder-. **3.** *v. i.* sich wundern; staunen (**at** über + *Akk.*). **4.** *v. t.* sich fragen; **I ~ what the time is** wieviel Uhr mag es wohl sein?; **I ~ whether I might open the window** dürfte ich vielleicht das Fenster öffnen? **wonderful** ['wʌndəfl] *adj.*, **wonderfully** ['wʌndəfəlɪ] *adv.* wunderbar

won't [wəʊnt] *(coll.)* **=** **will not;** *see* ¹**will**

woo [wu:] *v. t.* **a)** *(literary: court)* ~ **sb.** um jmdn. werben *(geh.);* **b)** umwerben ⟨*Kunden, Wähler*⟩

wood [wʊd] *n.* **a)** Holz, *das;* **touch ~** *(Brit.),* **knock on ~** *(Amer.)* unberufen!; **b)** *(trees)* Wald, *der.* **'woodcut** *n.* Holzschnitt, *der.* **'woodcutter** *n.* Holzfäller, *der*

'wooded *adj.* bewaldet

wooden ['wʊdn] *adj.* **a)** hölzern; Holz-; **b)** *(fig.: stiff)* hölzern

wood: ~**land** ['wʊdlənd] *n.* Waldland, *das;* ~**pecker** *n.* Specht, *der;* ~**wind** *n.* the ~**wind** |section| die Holzbläser; ~**wind instrument** Holzblasinstrument, *das;* ~**work** *n.* **a)** *(craft)* Arbeiten mit Holz; **b)** *(things)* Holzarbeit[en]; ~**worm** *n.* Holzwurm; **it's got ~worm** da ist der Holzwurm drin *(ugs.)*

'woody *adj.* **a)** *(wooded)* waldreich; **b)** *(consisting of wood)* holzig

wool [wʊl] *n.* Wolle, *die;* **attrib.** Woll-. **woollen** *(Amer.:* **woolen)** ['wʊlən] **1.** *adj.* wollen. **2.** *n.* ~**s** Wollsachen *Pl.*

'woolly *adj.* **a)** wollig; Woll⟨*pullover, -mütze*⟩; **b)** *(confused)* verschwommen

word [wɜːd] **1.** *n.* Wort, *das;* ~**s** *(of song or actor)* Text, *der;* **in other ~s** mit anderen Worten; ~ **for ~:** Wort für Wort; **too funny** *etc.* **for ~s** unsagbar komisch *usw.;* **have ~s** einen Wortwechsel haben; **have a ~** |**with sb.**| **about sth.** [mit jmdm.] über etw. *(Akk.)* sprechen; **could I have a ~** |**with you**|**?** kann ich dich mal sprechen?; **say a few ~s** ein paar Worte sprechen; **keep/break one's ~:** sein Wort halten/brechen; **by ~ of mouth** durch mündliche Mitteilung; **send ~ that ...:** Nach-

richt geben, daß ... **2.** *v. t.* formulieren. **'wording** *n.* Formulierung, *die*

word: ~ **order** *n.* Wortstellung, *die;* ~ **processing** *n.* Textverarbeitung, *die;* ~ **processor** *n.* Textverarbeitungssystem, *das*

wore *see* **wear 2, 3**

work [wɜːk] **1.** *n.* **a)** Arbeit, *die;* **at ~** *(engaged in ~ing)* bei der Arbeit; *(fig.: operating)* am Werk; *(at job)* auf der Arbeit; **out of ~:** arbeitslos; **be in ~:** eine Stelle haben; **b)** ~**s** *sing. or pl. (factory)* Werk, *das;* **c)** ~**s** *pl. (~ing parts)* Werk, *das; (operations)* Arbeiten; **d)** *(thing made or achieved)* Werk, *das;* **a ~ of art/literature** ein Kunstwerk/literarisches Werk. **2.** *v. i.* **a)** arbeiten; **b)** *(function effectively)* funktionieren; **make the television ~:** den Fernsehapparat in Ordnung bringen; **c)** *(have an effect)* wirken (**on** auf + *Akk.*); **d)** ~ **loose** sich lockern. **3.** *v. t.* **a)** bedienen ⟨*Maschine*⟩; betätigen ⟨*Bremse*⟩; **b)** *(get labour from)* arbeiten lassen; **c)** ausbeuten ⟨*Steinbruch, Grube*⟩; **d)** *(cause to go gradually)* führen; ~ **one's way up/into sth.** sich hocharbeiten/in etw. hineinarbeiten. **work 'off** *v. t.* **a)** *(get rid of)* loswerden; abreagieren ⟨*Wut*⟩; **b)** abarbeiten ⟨*Schuld*⟩. **'work on** *v. t.* **a)** ~ **on sth.** an etw. *(Dat.)* arbeiten; **b)** *(try to persuade)* ~ **on sb.** jmdn. bearbeiten *(ugs.)*. **work 'out 1.** *v. t.* **a)** *(calculate)* ausrechnen; **b)** *(solve)* lösen; **c)** *(devise)* ausarbeiten. **2.** *v. i.* **a)** **sth. ~s out at £2** etw. ergibt 2 Pfund; **b)** *(have result)* laufen; **things ~ed out |well| in the end** es ist schließlich doch alles gutgegangen. **work 'up 1.** *v. t. (excite)* aufpeitschen ⟨*Menge*⟩; **get ~ed up** sich aufregen. **2.** *v. i.* ~ **up to sth.** ⟨*Musik:*⟩ sich zu etw. steigern; ⟨*Geschichte, Film:*⟩ auf etw. *(Akk.)* zusteuern

workable ['wɜːkəbl] *adj. (feasible)* durchführbar

workaholic [wɜːkə'hɒlɪk] *n. (coll.)* arbeitswütiger Mensch

'worker *n.* Arbeiter, *der*/Arbeiterin, *die*

'workforce *n.* Belegschaft, *die*

'working *adj.* **a)** *(in work)* werktätig; **b)** ~ **model** funktionsfähiges Modell

working: ~ **'class** *n.* Arbeiterklasse, *die;* ~**-class** *adj.* der Arbeiterklasse nachgestellt; **sb. is ~-class** jmd. gehört zur Arbeiterklasse; ~ **clothes** *n. pl.* Arbeitskleidung, *die;* ~ **'day** *n.* **a)** *(portion of day)* Arbeitstag, *der;* **b)**

(day when work is done) Werktag, *der;*
~ 'order *n.* be in |good| ~ order be-
triebsbereit sein; *⟨Auto:⟩* fahrbereit
sein
workman ['wɜːkmən] *n., pl.* ~men
['wɜːkmən] Arbeiter, *der.* 'workmanship *n. (quality)* Kunstfertigkeit, *die*
work: ~-out *n.* [Fitneß]training, *das;*
~shop *n.* a) *(room)* Werkstatt; *die,* b)
(building) Werk, *das*
world [wɜːld] *n.* a) Welt, *die;* in the ~:
auf der Welt; **the tallest building in the**
~: das höchste Gebäude der Welt; **all**
over the ~: in *od.* auf der ganzen
Welt; b) *(vast amount)* **it will do him a**
or **the** ~ **of good** es wird ihm unendlich guttun; **a** ~ **of difference** ein welt-
weiter Unterschied. **world** 'cham-
pion *n.* Weltmeister, *der/*-meisterin,
die. **world-'famous** *adj.* weltbe-
rühmt
'**worldly** *adj.* weltlich; weltlich eingestellt ⟨*Person*⟩
world-wide 1. ['--] *adj.* weltweit *nicht*
präd. **2.** [-'-] *adv.* weltweit
worm [wɜːm] **1.** *n.* Wurm, *der.* **2.** *v.t.*
a) ~ oneself into sb.'s favour sich in
jmds. Gunst *(Akk.)* schleichen; **b)** ~
sth. out of sb. etw. aus jmdm. herausbringen *(ugs.).* 'worm-eaten *adj.*
wurmstichig
worn *see* wear 2, 3
'**worn-out** *adj.* a) abgetragen ⟨*Klei-*
dungsstück⟩; abgenutzt ⟨*Teppich*⟩; b)
erschöpft ⟨*Person*⟩
worried ['wʌrɪd] *adj.* besorgt
worry ['wʌrɪ] **1.** *v.t.* a) beunruhigen;
b) *(bother)* stören. **2.** *v.i.* sich *(Dat.)*
Sorgen machen. '**worrying** *adj.* a)
(causing worry) beunruhigend; b) *(full*
of worry) sorgenvoll ⟨*Zeit, Woche*⟩
worse [wɜːs] **1.** *adj.* schlechter;
schlimmer ⟨*Schmerz, Krankheit,*
Benehmen⟩. **2.** *adv.* schlechter/
schlimmer. **3.** *n.* Schlimmeres.
worsen ['wɜːsn] **1.** *v.t.* verschlechtern. **2.** *v.i.* sich verschlechtern
worship ['wɜːʃɪp] **1.** *v.t., (Brit.)* -pp-:
a) anbeten; b) *(idolize)* abgöttisch verehren. **2.** *v.i., (Brit.)* -pp- am Gottesdienst teilnehmen. **3.** *n.* a) Anbetung,
die; (service) Gottesdienst, *der;* b)
Your/His W~: ≈ Euer/seine Ehren.
'**worshipper** *(Amer.:* **worshiper)**
n. Gottesdienstbesucher, *der/*-besu-
cherin, *die*
worst [wɜːst] **1.** *adj.* schlechtest...;
schlimmst... ⟨*Schmerz, Krankheit,*
Benehmen⟩. **2.** *adv.* am schlechtesten/

schlimmsten. **3.** *n.* a) the ~: der/die/
das Schlimmste; **get** *or* **have the** ~ **of it**
(suffer the most) am meisten zu leiden
haben; **if the** ~ **comes to the** ~: wenn
es zum Schlimmsten kommt; b)
(poorest in quality) Schlechteste, *der/*
die/das
worsted ['wʊstɪd] *n.* Kammgarn, *das*
worth [wɜːθ] **1.** *adj.* wert; **it's** ~ **£80** es
ist 80 Pfund wert; **is it** ~ **hearing/the**
effort? ist es hörenswert/der Mühe
wert?; **is it** ~ **doing?** lohnt es sich?; **it**
isn't ~ **it** es lohnt sich nicht. **2.** *n.*
Wert, *der;* **ten pounds'** ~ **of petrol** Benzin für zehn Pfund. '**worthless** *adj.*
a) *(valueless)* wertlos; b) *(having bad*
qualities) nichtswürdig. '**worth-**
while *adj.* lohnend
worthy ['wɜːðɪ] *adj.* würdig
wouldn't ['wʊdnt] *(coll.)* = would not;
see ¹will
¹**wound** [wuːnd] **1.** *n.* Wunde, *die.* **2.**
v.t. verwunden; *(fig.)* verletzen
²**wound** *see* ²wind
wove, woven *see* ¹weave 2
wrangle ['ræŋgl] **1.** *v.i.* [sich] streiten.
2. *n.* Streit, *der*
wrap [ræp] **1.** *v.t.,* -pp- einwickeln;
(fig.) hüllen; ~ped abgepackt ⟨*Brot*
usw.⟩; ~ **sth. |a|round sth.** etw. um etw.
wickeln. **2.** *n.* Umschlag[e]tuch, *das.*
wrap 'up *v.t.* a) *see* wrap 1; b) *(con-*
clude) abschließen; c) **be** ~ped up in
one's work in seine Arbeit völlig versunken sein
'**wrapper** *n.* a) sweet-/toffee-~|s| Bon-
bonpapier, *das;* b) *(of book)* Schutzumschlag, *der*
'**wrapping** *n.* Verpackung, *die.*
'**wrapping-paper** *n. (strong)* Packpapier, *das; (decorative)* Geschenkpa-
pier, *das*
wrath [rɒθ] *n.* Zorn, *der*
wreak [riːk] *v.t.* a) *(cause)* anrichten;
b) ~ **vengeance on sb.** an jmdm. Rache
nehmen
wreath [riːθ] *n., pl.* **wreaths** [riːðz,
riːθs] Kranz, *der*
wreck [rek] **1.** *n.* a) Wrack, *das;* b) *(de-*
struction of ship) Schiffbruch, *der.* **2.**
v.t. a) *(destroy)* ruinieren; zu Schrott
fahren ⟨*Auto*⟩; **be** ~ed *(shipwrecked)*
Schiffbruch erleiden; b) *(fig.: ruin)*
zerstören; ruinieren ⟨*Gesundheit, Ur-*
laub⟩. **wreckage** ['rekɪdʒ] *n.* Wrack-
teile *Pl.; (fig.)* Trümmer *Pl.*
wren *n.* Zaunkönig, *der*
wrench [rentʃ] **1.** *n.* a) *(tool)* verstell-
barer Schraubenschlüssel; b) *(violent*

twist) Verrenkung, *die;* **c)** *(fig.)* **be a great ~ |for sb.|** sehr schmerzhaft für jmdn. sein. **2.** *v. t.* **a)** reißen; **~ sth. from sb.** jmdm. etw. entreißen; **b) ~ one's ankle** sich *(Dat.)* den Knöchel verrenken

wrest [rest] *v. t.* **~ sth. from sb.** jmdm. etw. entreißen

wrestle ['resl] *v. i.* ringen. **wrestler** ['reslə(r)] *n.* Ringer, *der*/Ringerin, *die.* **wrestling** ['reslıŋ] *n.* Ringen, *das*

wretch [retʃ] *n.* Kreatur, *die*

wretched ['retʃıd] *adj.* **a)** *(miserable)* unglücklich; **b)** *(coll.: damned)* elend; **c)** *(very bad)* erbärmlich

wriggle ['rıgl] **1.** *v. i.* **a)** sich winden; ‹*Fisch:*› zappeln; **b)** *(move)* sich schlängeln. **2.** *v. t.* **~ one's way** sich schlängeln. **3.** *n.* Windung, *die*

wring [rıŋ] *v. t.,* **wrung** [rʌŋ] **a)** wringen; **~ out** auswringen; **b) ~ sb.'s hand** jmdm. fest die Hand drücken; **~ the neck of an animal** einem Tier den Hals umdrehen; **c) ~ sth. from** *or* **out of sb.** *(fig.)* jmdm. etw. abpressen. **wringing 'wet** *adj.* tropfnaß

wrinkle ['rıŋkl] **1.** *n.* Falte, *die; (in paper)* Knick, *der.* **2.** *v. t.* falten. **3.** *v. i.* sich in Falten legen. **wrinkled** ['rıŋkld], **wrinkly** ['rıŋklı] *adjs.* runz[e]lig

wrist [rıst] *n.* Handgelenk, *das.* **'wrist-watch** *n.* Armbanduhr, *die*

writ [rıt] *n. (Law)* Verfügung, *die*

write [raıt] **1.** *v. i.,* **wrote** [rəʊt], **written** ['rıtn] schreiben; **~ to sb./a firm** jmdm./an eine Firma schreiben. **2.** *v. t.,* **wrote, written** schreiben; ausschreiben ‹*Scheck*›; **the written language** die Schriftsprache; **written applications** schriftliche Anträge. **write 'back** *v. i.* zurückschreiben. **write 'down** *v. t.* aufschreiben. **write 'off 1.** *v. t.* **a)** abschreiben ‹*Schulden, Verlust*›; **b)** *(destroy)* zu Schrott fahren. **2.** *v. i.* **~ off for sth.** etw. [schriftlich] anfordern

'write-off *n.* Totalschaden, *der*

writer ['raıtə(r)] *n.* Schriftsteller, *der*/Schriftstellerin, *die; (of letter, article)* Verfasser, *der*/Verfasserin, *die*

'write-up *n. (by critic)* Kritik, *die*

writhe [raıð] *v. i.* sich winden

writing ['raıtıŋ] *n.* **a)** Schreiben, *das;* **put sth. in ~:** etw. schriftlich machen *(ugs.);* **b)** *(handwriting, something written)* Schrift, *die.* **'writing paper** *n.* Schreibpapier, *das*

written *see* **write**

wrong [rɒŋ] **1.** *adj.* **a)** *(morally bad)* unrecht *(geh.); (unfair)* ungerecht; **b)** *(mistaken)* falsch; **be ~** ‹*Person:*› sich irren; **the clock is ~:** die Uhr geht falsch; **c)** *(not suitable)* falsch; **give the ~ answer** eine falsche Antwort geben; **[the] ~ way round** verkehrt herum; **d)** *(out of order)* nicht in Ordnung; **what's ~?** ist etwas nicht in Ordnung? **2.** *adv.* falsch. **3.** *n.* Unrecht, *das;* **do ~:** unrecht tun. **4.** *v. t.* **~ sb.** jmdn. ungerecht behandeln. **wrongful** ['rɒŋfl] *adj.* **a)** *(unfair)* unrecht *(geh.);* **b)** *(unlawful)* rechtswidrig. **'wrongfully** *adv.* **a)** *(unfairly)* unrecht *(geh.)* ‹*handeln*›; zu Unrecht ‹*beschuldigen*›; **b)** *(unlawfully)* rechtswidrig. **'wrongly** *adv.* **a)** falsch; **b)** *(mistakenly)* zu Unrecht; **c)** *see* **wrongfully a**

wrote *see* **write**

wrought iron [rɔːt 'aıən] *n.* Schmiedeeisen, *das; attrib.* schmiedeeisern

wrung *see* **wring**

wry [raı] *adj.,* **~er** *or* **wrier** ['raıə(r)], **~est** *or* **wriest** ['raııst] ironisch ‹*Blick*›; fein ‹*Humor, Witz*›

X

X, x [eks] *n.* X, x, *das*

Xerox, (P), xerox ['zıərɒks] **1.** *n. (copy)* Xerokopie, *die.* **2. xerox** *v. t.* xerokopieren

Xmas ['krısməs, 'eksməs] *n. (coll.)* Weihnachten, *das*

'X-ray 1. *n. (picture)* Röntgenaufnahme, *die.* **2.** *v. t.* röntgen; durchleuchten ‹*Gepäck*›

Y

Y, y [waı] *n.* Y, y, *das*

yacht [jɒt] *n.* **a)** *(for racing)* Segeljacht, *die;* **b)** *(for pleasure)* Jacht, *die.* **'yachting** *n.* Segeln, *das*

Yank [jæŋk] n. (Brit. coll.: American) Ami, der (ugs.)
yank (coll.) 1. v.t. reißen an (+ Dat.). 2. n. Reißen, das
yap [jæp] v.i., -pp- kläffen
¹yard [ja:d] n. (measure) Yard, das
²yard n. a) (attached to building) Hof, der; in the ~: auf dem Hof; b) (for storage) Lager, das
'yardstick n. (fig.) Maßstab, der
yarn [ja:n] n. a) (thread) Garn, das; b) (coll.: story) Geschichte, die
yawn [jɔ:n] 1. n. Gähnen, das. 2. v.i. gähnen. **'yawning** adj. gähnend
year [jɪə(r)] n. a) Jahr, das; for [many] ~s jahrelang; once a ~, every ~: einmal im Jahr; a ten-~-old ein Zehnjähriger/eine Zehnjährige; b) (group of students, vintage of wine) Jahrgang, der. **'yearbook** n. Jahrbuch, das. **'yearly** 1. adj. jährlich; Einjahres-⟨abonnement⟩. 2. adv. jährlich
yearn [jɜ:n] v.i. ~ for or after sth./for sb. sich nach etw./jmdm. sehnen; ~ to do sth. sich danach sehnen, etw. zu tun. **'yearning** n. Sehnsucht, die
yeast [ji:st] n. Hefe, die
yell [jel] 1. n. gellender Schrei. 2. v.t. & i. [gellend] schreien
yellow ['jeləʊ] 1. adj. gelb. 2. n. Gelb, das. **'yellowish** adj. gelblich
yelp [jelp] 1. v.i. jaulen. 2. n. Jaulen, das
yen [jen] n. (coll.: longing) sb. has a ~ to do sth. es drängt jmdn. danach, etw. zu tun
yes [jes] 1. adv. ja; (in contradiction) doch. 2. n., pl. ~es Ja, das
yesterday ['jestədeɪ, 'jestədɪ] 1. n. gestern; the day before ~: vorgestern; ~'s paper die gestrige Zeitung. 2. adv. gestern; the day before ~: vorgestern
yet [jet] 1. adv. a) (still) noch; ~ again noch einmal; b) (hitherto) bisher; his best ~: sein bisher bestes; c) neg. not [just] ~: [jetzt] noch nicht; d) (before all is over) doch noch; he could win ~: er könnte noch gewinnen; e) with compar. (even) noch; f) (nevertheless) doch. 2. conj. doch
yew [ju:] n. ~[-tree] Eibe, die
Yiddish ['jɪdɪʃ] 1. adj. jiddisch. 2. n. Jiddisch, das; see also **English 2 a**
yield [ji:ld] 1. v.t. (give) bringen; hervorbringen ⟨Ernte⟩; abwerfen ⟨Gewinn⟩. 2. v.i. a) sich unterwerfen; b) (give right of way) Vorfahrt gewähren. 3. n. Ertrag, der
yodel ['jəʊdl] v.i. & t., (Brit.) -ll- jodeln

yoga ['jəʊgə] n. Joga, der od. das
yoghurt, yogurt ['jɒgət] n. Joghurt, der od. das
yoke [jəʊk] n. Joch, das
yokel ['jəʊkl] n. [Bauern]tölpel, der
yolk [jəʊk] n. Dotter, der; Eigelb, das
yonder ['jɒndə(r)] (literary) 1. adj. ~ tree jener Baum dort (geh.). 2. adv. dort drüben
you [jʊ, stressed ju:] pron. a) sing./pl. du/ihr; (polite) sing. or pl. Sie; as direct object dich/euch/Sie; as indirect object dir/euch/Ihnen; refl. dich/dir/euch; (polite) sich; it was ~: du warst/ihr wart/Sie waren es; b) (one) man
you'd [jʊd, stressed ju:d] a) = you had; b) = you would
you'll [jʊl, stressed ju:l] a) = you will; b) = you shall
young [jʌŋ] 1. adj., ~er ['jʌŋgə(r)], ~est ['jʌŋgɪst] jung. 2. n. pl. (of animals) Junge; the ~ (~ people) die jungen Leute. **youngster** ['jʌŋstə(r)] n. a) (child) Kleine, der/die/das; b) (young person) Jugendliche, der/die
your [jə(r), stressed jʊə(r), jɔ:(r)] poss. pron. attrib.: sing. dein; pl. euer; (polite) sing. or pl. Ihr
you're [jə(r), stressed jʊə(r), jɔ:(r)] = you are
yours [jʊəz, jɔ:z] poss. pron. pred.: sing. deiner/deine/dein[e]s; pl. eurer/eure/eures; (polite) sing. or pl. Ihrer/Ihre/Ihr[e]s; see also **hers**
yourself [jə'self, jʊə'self, jɔ:'self] pron. a) emphat. selbst; b) refl. dich/dir/ (polite) sich. See also **herself**
yourselves [jə'selvz, jʊə'selvz, jɔ:'selvz] pron. a) emphat. selbst; b) refl. euch/(polite) sich. See also **herself**
youth [ju:θ] n. a) Jugend, die; b) pl. ~s [ju:ðz] (young man) Jugendliche, der. **'youth club** n. Jugendklub, der
youthful ['ju:θfl] adj. jugendlich
'youth hostel n. Jugendherberge, die
you've [jʊv, stressed ju:v] = you have
Yugoslav ['ju:gəslɑ:v] see **Yugoslavian**
Yugoslavia [ju:gə'slɑ:vɪə] pr. n. (Hist.) Jugoslawien (das). **Yugoslavian** [ju:gə'slɑ:vɪən] (Hist.) 1. adj. jugoslawisch. 2. n. Jugoslawe, der/Jugoslawin, die

Z

Z, z [zed, *(Amer.)* ziː] *n.* Z, z, *das*
Zaire [zɑːˈɪə(r)] *pr. n.* Zaire *(das)*
Zambia [ˈzæmbɪə] *pr. n.* Sambia *(das)*
zany [ˈzeɪnɪ] *adj.* irre komisch *(ugs.);*
Wahnsinns⟨*humor, -komiker*⟩
zeal [ziːl] *n.* Eifer, *der.* zealous [ˈzeləs]
adj. eifrig
zebra [ˈzebrə, ˈziːbrə] *n.* Zebra, *das.*
zebra 'crossing *n. (Brit.)* Zebrastreifen, *der*
zenith [ˈzenɪθ] *n.* Zenit, *der*
zero [ˈzɪərəʊ] *n., pl.* ~s Null, *die*
zest [zest] *n. (enthusiasm)* Begeisterung, *die;* ~ for living Lebenslust, *die*
zigzag [ˈzɪgzæg] 1. *adj.* zickzackför-

mig; Zickzack⟨*muster, -anordnung*⟩.
2. *n.* Zickzacklinie, *die*
Zimbabwe [zɪmˈbɑːbwɪ] *pr. n.* Simbabwe *(das)*
zinc [zɪŋk] *n.* Zink, *das*
zip [zɪp] 1. *n.* Reißverschluß, *der.* 2.
v. t., -pp-: ~ |up| sth. den Reißver-
schluß an etw. *(Dat.)* zuziehen
'Zip code *n. (Amer.)* Postleitzahl, *die*
zip-fastener *see* zip 1
zipper [ˈzɪpə(r)] *see* zip 1
zither [ˈzɪðə(r)] *n.* Zither, *die*
zodiac [ˈzəʊdɪæk] *n.* Tierkreis, *der;*
sign of the ~: Tierkreiszeichen, *das*
zombie *(Amer.:* zombi) [ˈzɒmbɪ] *n.*
Zombie, *der*
zone [zəʊn] *n.* Zone, *die*
zoo [zuː] *n.* Zoo, *der*
zoological [zəʊəˈlɒdʒɪkl] *adj.* zoologisch
zoologist [zəʊˈɒlədʒɪst] *n.* Zoologe,
der/Zoologin, *die*
zoology [zəʊˈɒlədʒɪ] *n.* Zoologie, *die*
zoom [zuːm] *v. i.* rauschen. zoom 'in
on *v. t. (Cinemat., Telev.)* zoomen auf
(+ *Akk.*)
'zoom lens *n.* Zoomobjektiv, *das*

A

a, A [a:] *das*; ~, ~ **a)** *(Buchstabe)* a/A; **das A und O** *(fig.)* the essential thing/things *(Gen.* for); **von A bis Z** *(fig. ugs.)* from beginning to end; **b)** *(Musik)* [key of] A

a *Abk.* Ar, Are

à [a] *Präp. mit Nom., Akk. (Kaufmannsspr.)* **zehn Marken à 50 Pfennig** ten stamps at 50 pfennigs each

A *Abk.* Autobahn ≈ M

Aal *der*; ~|e|s, ~e eel; ~ **grün** *(Kochk.)* green eels; stewed eels; **aalen** *refl. V. (ugs.)* stretch out; **aal·glatt** *(abwertend)* **1.** *Adj.* slippery; ~ **sein** be as slippery as an eel; **2.** *adv.* smoothly

Aas *das*; ~es, ~e *od.* **Äser a)** *o. Pl.* carrion *no art.*; **b)** *Pl.* ~e [rotting] carcass; **c)** *Pl.* Äser *(salopp) (abwertend)* swine; *(anerkennend)* devil

ab 1. *Präp. mit Dat.* **a)** from; **ab 1980** as from 1980; **ab Werk** *(Kaufmannsspr.)* ex works; **ab Frankfurt fliegen** fly from Frankfurt; **b)** *([Rang]folge)* from ... on[wards]; **ab 20 DM** from 20 DM [upwards]; **2.** *Adv.* **a)** *(weg)* off; away; **b)** *(ugs.: Aufforderung)* off; away; **ab nach Hause** get off home; **c)** **Gewehr ab!** *(milit. Kommando)* order arms!; **d)** **ab und zu** *od.* **an** now and then

ab|ändern *tr. V.* alter; amend *⟨text⟩*; **Ab·änderung** *die* alteration; *(eines Textes)* amendment

ab|arbeiten *tr. V.* work for *⟨meal⟩*; work off *⟨debt, amount⟩*

ab·artig *Adj.* deviant; abnormal

Abb. *Abk.* Abbildung Fig.

Ab·bau *der* **a)** dismantling; *(von Zelten, Lagern)* striking; **b)** *s.* **abbauen c:** cutback *(Gen.* in); pruning; reduction; **c)** *(Bergbau)* mining; *(von Stein)* quarrying

ab|bauen *tr. V.* **a)** dismantle; strike *⟨tent, camp⟩*; **b)** *(beseitigen)* gradually remove; break down *⟨prejudices, inhibitions⟩*; **c)** *(verringern)* cut back

⟨staff⟩; prune *⟨jobs⟩*; reduce *⟨wages⟩*; **d)** *(Bergbau)* mine; quarry *⟨stone⟩*

ab|beißen 1) *unr. tr. V.* bite off; **2.** *unr. itr. V.* have a bite

ab|bekommen *unr. tr. V.* **a)** get; **b)** **einen Schlag/ein paar Kratzer** ~: get hit/get a few scratches; **etwas** ~ *(getroffen werden)* be hit; *(verletzt werden)* be hurt; **c)** *(los-, herunterbekommen)* get *⟨paint, lid, chain⟩* off

ab|berufen *unr. tr. V.* recall *⟨ambassador, envoy⟩* (**aus, von** from)

ab|bestellen *tr. V.* cancel

ab|bezahlen *tr. V.* pay off

ab|biegen *unr. itr. V.; mit sein* turn off; **links/rechts** ~: turn [off] left/right

Ab·bild *das (eines Menschen)* likeness; *(eines Gegenstandes)* copy; *(fig.)* portrayal; **ab|bilden** *tr. V.* copy; reproduce *⟨object, picture⟩*; depict *⟨person, landscape⟩*; *(fig.)* portray; **Abbildung** *die* illustration

ab|binden *unr. tr. V.* **a)** *(losbinden)* untie; undo; **b)** *(abschnüren)* put a tourniquet on *⟨artery, arm, leg, etc.⟩*; tie *⟨umbilical cord⟩*

ab|blasen *unr. tr. V. (ugs.)* call off

ab|blättern *itr. V.; mit sein* flake off

ab|blenden *itr. V.* dip *(Brit.)* or *(Amer.)* dim one's headlight; **Ab·blend·licht** *das* dipped *(Brit.)* or *(Amer.)* dimmed beam

ab|blitzen *itr. V.; mit sein (ugs.)* **sie ließ alle Verehrer** ~: she gave all her admirers the brush-off

ab|brausen *tr. V.: s.* abduschen

ab|brechen 1. *unr. tr. V.* **a)** break off; break *⟨needle, pencil⟩*; **b)** *(zerlegen)* strike *⟨tent, camp⟩*; **c)** *(abreißen)* demolish, pull down *⟨building⟩*; **d)** *(beenden)* break off *⟨negotiations, [diplomatic] relations, discussion, activity⟩*; *(vorzeitig)* cut short *⟨conversation, holiday, activity⟩*; **2.** *unr. itr. V.* **a)** *mit sein* break [off]; **b)** *(aufhören)* break off

ạb|bremsen 1. *tr. V.* **a)** brake; **b)** retard ⟨*motion*⟩; 2. *itr. V.* brake

ạb|brennen 1. *unr. itr. V.; mit sein* **a)** be burned down; **das Haus ist abgebrannt** the house has burned down; **b)** ⟨*fuse*⟩ burn away; ⟨*candle*⟩ burn down; 2. *unr. tr. V.* **a)** let off ⟨*firework*⟩; **b)** burn down ⟨*building*⟩

ạb|bringen *unr. tr. V.* **jmdn. davon ~, etw. zu tun** dissuade sb. from doing sth. **jmdn. vom Kurs ~:** make sb. change course

ạb|bröckeln *itr. V.; mit sein (auch fig.)* crumble away

Ạb·bruch der a) *o. Pl.* demolition; pulling down; **b)** *(Beendigung)* breaking-off; **c)** **einer Sache** *(Dat.)* **[keinen] ~ tun** do [no] harm to sth.

ạb|buchen *tr. V.* ⟨*bank*⟩ debit (von to); ⟨*creditor*⟩ claim by direct debit (von to)

ạb|bürsten *tr. V.* **a)** brush off; **b)** *(säubern)* brush ⟨*garment*⟩

ạb|büßen *tr. V.* serve [out] ⟨*prison sentence*⟩

Abc [a(:)be(:)'tse:] *das; ~ (auch fig.)* ABC; **Abc-Schütze der** child just starting school

ạb|dampfen *itr. V.; mit sein (ugs.: abfahren)* set off

ạb|danken *itr. V.* ⟨*ruler*⟩ abdicate; ⟨*government, minister*⟩ resign; **Ạbdankung die; ~, ~en** *s.* **abdanken:** abdication; resignation

ạb|decken 1. *tr. V.* **a)** open up; ⟨*gale*⟩ take the roof/roofs off ⟨*house*⟩, take the tiles off ⟨*roof*⟩; **b)** *(herunternehmen, -reißen)* take off; **c)** *(abräumen)* clear ⟨*table*⟩; clear away ⟨*dishes*⟩; **d)** *(schützen)* cover ⟨*person*⟩

ạb|dichten *tr. V.* seal

ạb|drängen *tr. V.* push away

ạb|drehen 1. *tr. V.* **a)** *(ausschalten)* turn off; **den Hahn ~** *(fig.)* turn off the supply; **b)** *(abtrennen)* twist off; 2. *itr. V.; meist mit sein* turn off

Ạb·druck der; *Pl.* **Ạbdrücke** mark; *(Fuß~)* footprint; *(Wachs~)* impression; *(Gips~)* cast; **ạb|drücken** 1. *itr. V.* pull the trigger; shoot; 2. *tr. V.* *(zudrücken)* constrict

ạb|dunkeln *tr. V.* darken ⟨*room*⟩; dim ⟨*light*⟩

ạb|duschen *tr. V.* **sich/jmdn. [warm] ~:** take/give sb. a [hot] shower

ạbend *Adv.* **heute/morgen/gestern ~:** this/tomorrow/yesterday evening; **Ạbend der; ~s, ~e** evening; **guten ~!** good evening; **am [frühen/späten] ~:** [early/late] in the evening; **zu ~ essen**

have dinner; *(allgemeiner)* have one's evening meal; **ein bunter ~:** a social [evening]

Ạbend-: **~an·zug der** evening suit; **~brot das** supper; **~essen das** dinner; **~kasse die** box-office *(open on the evening of the performance)*; **~kleid das** evening dress; **~kurs[us] der** evening class; **~land das;** *o. Pl.* West

ạbendlich *Adj.* evening; ⟨*quiet, coolness*⟩ of the evening

Ạbend-: **~mahl das;** *o. Pl. (Rel.)* Communion; *(N. T.)* Last Supper; **~programm das** evening programmes *pl.;* **~rot das** red glow of the sunset sky

ạbends *Adv.* in the evenings; **um sechs Uhr ~:** at six o'clock in the evening

Ạbend-: **~schule die** night school; **~stern der** evening star; **~stunde die** evening hour; **~vorstellung die** evening performance

Abenteuer das; ~s, ~ a) *(auch fig.)* adventure; **b)** *(Unternehmen)* venture; **c)** *(Liebesaffäre)* affair; **abenteuerlich** *Adj.* **a)** *(riskant)* risky; **b)** *(bizarr)* bizarre; **Abenteuer·roman der** adventure novel; **Abenteurer der; ~s, ~:** adventurer

aber 1. *Konj.* but; 2. *Partikel* **~ ja/ nein!** why, yes/no! **~ natürlich!** but of course!; **du bist ~ groß!** aren't you tall!

Aber·glaube[n] der superstition; **aber·gläubisch** *Adj.* superstitious

abermals *Adv.* once again; once more

Abf. *Abk.* **Abfahrt** dep.

ạb|fahren 1. *unr. itr. V.; mit sein* **a)** *(wegfahren)* leave; **wo fährt der Zug nach Paris ab?** where does the Paris train leave from?; **b)** *(hinunterfahren)* drive down; *(Skisport)* ski down; 2. *unr. tr. V.* **a)** *(abtransportieren)* take away; **b)** *(abnutzen)* wear out; **abgefahrene Reifen** worn tyres; **Ạb·fahrt die a)** departure; **b)** *(Skisport)* descent; *(Strecke)* run; **Abfahrtslauf der** *(Skisport)* downhill [racing]; **Ạbfahrt[s]·zeit die** time of departure; departure time

Ạb·fall der *(Küchen~ o. ä.)* rubbish, *(Amer.)* trash *no indef. art., no pl.;* *(Fleisch~)* offal *no indef. art., no pl.;* *(Industrie~)* waste *no indef. art.; (auf der Straße)* litter *no indef. art., no pl.;* **Ạbfall·eimer der** rubbish bin; trash can *(Amer.); (auf der Straße)* litter bin;

trash can *(Amer.)*; **ạb|fallen** *unr. itr.
V.; mit sein* **a)** fall off; **b)** *(abschüssig
sein)* ⟨*land, road, etc.*⟩ drop away,
slope; **c)** *(übrigbleiben)* be left [over];
für dich wird [dabei] auch etwas ~:
you'll get something out of it too; **d)**
von jmdm. ~: leave sb.; **vom Glauben**
~: desert the faith; **ạb·fällig 1.** *Adj.*
disparaging; **2.** *adv.* **sich** ~ **über jmdn.**
äußern make disparaging remarks
about sb.

ạb|fangen *unr. tr. V.* catch; intercept
⟨*agent, message, aircraft*⟩; **b)** repel
⟨*charge, assault*⟩; ward off ⟨*blow, attack*⟩

ạb|färben *itr. V.* **a)** ⟨*colour, garment,
etc.*⟩ run; **b) auf jmdn./etw.** ~ *(fig.)* rub
off on sb./sth.

ạb|fassen *tr. V.* write ⟨*report, letter,
etc.*⟩; draw up ⟨*will*⟩

ạb|fegen *tr. V.* **a)** brush off; **etw. von
etw.** ~: brush sth. off sth.; **b)** *(säubern)*
etw. ~: brush sth. clean

ạb|fertigen *tr. V.* dispatch ⟨*mail*⟩;
deal with ⟨*applicant*⟩; handle ⟨*passengers*⟩; serve ⟨*customer*⟩; clear ⟨*ship*⟩
for sailing; clear ⟨*aircraft*⟩ for take-
off; clear ⟨*lorry*⟩ for departure

ạb|feuern *tr. V.* fire

ạb|finden 1. *unr. tr. V.* **a)** jmdn. mit
etw. ~: compensate sb. with sth.; **seine
Gläubiger** ~: settle with one's cred-
itors; **2.** *unr. refl. V.* **sich** ~: resign
oneself; **sich** ~ **mit** come to terms
with; learn to live with ⟨*noise, heat*⟩;
Abfindung die; ~, ~**en** settlement;
eine ~ **in Höhe von ... zahlen** make a
settlement of ...

ạb|flauen *itr. V.; mit sein* die down;
subside; ⟨*interest, conversation*⟩ flag;
⟨*business*⟩ become slack; ⟨*noise*⟩ abate

ạb|fliegen *unr. itr. V.; mit sein* leave

ạb|fließen *unr. itr. V.; mit sein* flow
off

Ạb·flug der departure

Ạb·fluß der drain; *(Rohr)* drain-pipe;
(für Abwasser) waste-pipe

ạb|fragen *tr. V.* test; **jmdn.** *od.* **jmdm.
die Vokabeln** ~: test sb. on his/her vocabulary

Abfuhr die; ~, ~**en a)** removal; **b)**
jmdm. **eine** ~ **erteilen** *(fig. ugs.)* rebuff
sb.; **ạb|führen 1.** *tr. V.* **a)** *(nach Fest-
nahme)* take away; **b)** *(zahlen)* pay
out; **c)** *(abbringen)* take away; **2.** *itr. V.
(für Stuhlgang sorgen)* be a laxative;
Abführ·mittel das laxative

ạb|füllen *tr. V. (in Flaschen)* bottle; *(in
Dosen)* can

Ạb·gabe die a) handing in; *(eines
Briefes, Pakets, Telegramms)* delivery;
(eines Gesuchs, Antrags) submission;
b) *(Steuer, Gebühr)* tax; *(auf Produkte)*
duty; **c)** *(Ausstrahlung)* release;
emission; **d)** *(Sport: Abspiel)* pass

Ạb·gang der a) leaving; departure;
(Abfahrt) departure; *(Theater)* exit; **b)**
(jmd., der ausscheidet) departure;
(Schule) leaver; **c)** *(bes. Amtsspr.: Todesfall)* death; **d)** *(Turnen)* dismount

Ạb·gas das exhaust

abgearbeitet *Adj.* work-worn
⟨*hands*⟩

ạb|geben 1. *unr. tr. V.* **a)** *(aushändi-
gen)* hand over; deliver ⟨*letter, parcel,
telegram*⟩; hand in, submit ⟨*application*⟩; hand in ⟨*school work*⟩; **den
Mantel in der Garderobe** ~: leave
one's coat in the cloakroom; **b)** *auch*
itr. jmdm. [etwas] von etw. ~: let sb.
have some of sth.; **c)** *(abfeuern)* fire;
2. *unr. refl. V.* **sich mit jmdm./etw.** ~:
spend time on sb./sth.; *(geringschät-
zig)* waste one's time on sb./sth

ạb·gebrannt *Adj. (ugs.)* broke *(coll.)*

abgebrüht *Adj. (ugs.)* hardened

ạb·gedroschen *Adj. (ugs.)* hackneyed

ạb·gegriffen *Adj.* battered

ạb|gehen *unr. itr. V.; mit sein* **a)** *(sich
entfernen)* leave; *(Theater)* exit; **b)**
(ausscheiden) leave; **c)** *(abfahren)*
⟨*train, ship, bus*⟩ leave, depart; **d)** *(ab-
geschickt werden)* ⟨*message, letter*⟩ be
sent [off]; **e)** *(abzweigen)* branch off; **f)**
(sich lösen) come off

abgehetzt *Adj.* exhausted

ạb·gelegen *Adj.* remote; *(einsam)*
isolated; out-of-the-way ⟨*district*⟩

ạb·geneigt *Adj.* averse *(Dat.* to);
[nicht] ~ **sein, etw. zu tun** [not] be averse
to doing sth.

Ạbgeordnete der/die; *adj. Dekl.*
member [of parliament]; *(z. B. in
Frankreich)* deputy

ạb·gerissen *Adj.* ragged

ạb·geschlagen *Adj. (Sport)* [well]
beaten

ạb·geschlossen *Adj.* secluded

ạb·gesehen *Adv.* ~ **von** apart from; ~
davon, daß ... apart from the fact that ...

ạb·gespannt *Adj.* weary; exhausted

ạb·gestanden *Adj.* flat

ạb·gestorben *Adj.* dead ⟨*branch,
tree*⟩; numb ⟨*fingers, legs, etc.*⟩

ạb·getreten *Adj.* worn down

abgewetzt *Adj.* well-worn; battered
⟨*case etc.*⟩

ab|gewöhnen *tr. V.:* jmdm. etw. ~:
make sb. give up sth.; **sich** *(Dat.)* etw.
~: give up sth.

ab|gießen *unr. tr. V.* pour away ⟨*liquid*⟩; drain ⟨*potatoes*⟩

abgöttisch *Adj.* idolatrous

ab|grenzen *tr. V.* **a)** bound; etw. gegen
od. von etw. ~: separate sth. from sth.;
b) *(unterscheiden)* distinguish

Ab·grund der abyss; chasm; *(Abhang)*
precipice

ab|hacken *tr. V.* chop off; jmdm. die
Hand *usw.* ~: chop sb.'s hand *etc.* off

ab|haken *tr. V.* tick off; check off
(Amer.)

ab|halten *unr. tr. V.* **a)** jmdn./etw. [von
jmdm./etw.] ~: keep sb./sth. off
[sb./sth.]; **b)** jmdn. davon ~, etw. zu tun
stop sb. doing sth.; **c)** *(durchführen)*
hold ⟨*elections, meeting, referendum*⟩

ab|handeln *tr. V.* **a)** jmdm. etw. ~: do a
deal with sb. for sth.; **b)** *(darstellen)*
deal with

abhanden *Adv.* ~ kommen get lost; go
astray; etw. kommt jmdm. ~: sb. loses
sth.

Ab·handlung die treatise (über +
Akk. on)

Ab·hang der slope; incline; **¹ab|hängen**
unr. itr. V. von jmdm./etw. ~: depend on sb./sth.; **²ab|hängen** **1.** *tr. V.*
a) take down; **b)** *(abkuppeln)* uncouple; **c)** *(ugs.)* shake off *(coll.)* ⟨*pursuer, competitor*⟩. **2.** *itr. V.* ⟨*den Hörer
auflegen*⟩ hang up; **abhängig** *Adj.*
dependent (**von** on); *(süchtig)* addicted
(**von** to); von jmdm./etw. ~ sein depend
on sb./sth.; **Abhängigkeit die** ~,
~en dependence; *(Sucht)* addiction

ab|härten *tr. V.* harden

ab|hauen **1.** *unr. tr. V.* **a)** *Prät.* haute ab
knock off; **b)** *Prät.* hieb *(geh.) od.*
haute ab *(mit Schwert, Axt usw.)* chop
off; **2.** *unr. itr. V.; mit sein; Prät.* haute
ab *(salopp)* beat it *(sl.)*

ab|heben **1.** *unr. tr. V.* **a)** lift off ⟨*lid,
cover, etc.*⟩; [den Hörer] ~: answer [the
telephone]; **b)** *(von einem Konto)* withdraw ⟨*money*⟩; **2.** *unr. itr. V.* ⟨*balloon*⟩
rise; ⟨*aircraft, bird*⟩ take off; ⟨*rocket*⟩
lift off; **3.** *unr. refl. V.* stand out (**von**
against)

ab|heften *tr. V.* file

ab|hetzen *refl. V.* rush [around]; *s.
auch* abgehetzt

Ab·hilfe die; *o. Pl.* action to improve
matters; ~ schaffen put things right

ab|holen *tr. V.* collect, pick up ⟨*parcel,
book, tickets, etc.*⟩; pick up ⟨*person*⟩

ab|hören *tr. V.* **a)** jmdm. *od.* jmdn. **Vokabeln** ~: test sb.'s vocabulary [orally];
das Einmaleins ~: ask questions on the
multiplication table; **b)** tap ⟨*telephone
conversation, telephone*⟩; bug *(coll.)*
⟨*conversation, premises*⟩; jmdn. ~: tap
sb.'s telephone

Abi das; ~s, ~s *(Schülerspr.),* **Abitur
das;** ~s, ~e Abitur *(school-leaving examination at grammar school needed
for entry to higher education);* ≈ A
levels *(Brit.);* **Abiturient der;** ~en,
~en *sb. who is taking/has passed the
'Abitur'*

ab|jagen *tr. V.* jmdm. etw. ~: finally
get sth. away from sb.

Abk. *Abk.* Abkürzung abbr.

ab|kaufen *tr. V.* jmdm. etw. ~: buy sth.
from sb.

ab|klopfen *tr. V.* **a)** knock off; **b)** *(säubern)* knock the dirt/snow/crumbs *etc.*
off; **c)** *(untersuchen)* tap

ab|knicken **1.** *tr. V.* snap off; **2.** *itr. V.;
mit sein* snap

ab|kochen *tr. V.* boil

ab|kommen *unr. itr. V.; mit sein* **a)**
vom Weg ~: lose one's way; vom Kurs
~: go off course; von der Fahrbahn
~: leave the road; vom Thema ~: stray
from the topic; **b)** von einem Plan ~:
abandon a plan; **Ab·kommen das;**
~s, ~: agreement; **abkömmlich** *Adj.*
free; available

ab|kratzen **1.** *tr. V.* **a)** *(mit den Fingern)* scratch off; *(mit einem Werkzeug)* scrape off; **b)** *(säubern)* scrape
[clean]; **2.** *itr. V.; mit sein (derb)* snuff it
(sl.)

ab|kriegen *tr. V. (ugs.) s.* abbekommen

ab|kühlen **1.** *tr. V.* cool down; **2.** *itr.,
refl. V.; itr. meist mit sein* cool down;
Ab·kühlung die cooling

ab|kürzen *tr., itr. V.* **a)** *(räumlich)*
shorten; den Weg ~: take a shorter
route; **b)** *(zeitlich)* cut short; **c)** *(kürzer
schreiben)* abbreviate (mit to); **Abkürzung die** **a)** *(Weg)* short cut; **b)** *(Wort)*
abbreviation

ab|laden *unr. tr., itr. V.* unload

ab|lagern *tr. V.* deposit

ab|lassen **1.** *unr. tr. V.* let out (**aus** of);
let off ⟨*steam*⟩; **2.** *unr. itr. V.* **a)** von
jmdm./etw. ~: leave sb./sth. alone; **b)**
von etw. ~ *(etw. aufgeben)* give sth. up

Ab·lauf der **a)** *(Verlauf)* course; *(einer
Veranstaltung)* passing off; **b)** *o. Pl.
(Ende)* nach ~ eines Jahres after a year;
nach ~ einer Frist at the end of a
period of time; **ab|laufen** *unr. itr. V.;*

mit sein **a)** flow away; *(aus einem Behälter)* run out; **b)** *(verlaufen)* pass off; **c)** 〈*alarm clock*〉 run down; 〈*parking meter*〉 expire; **d)** 〈*period, contract, passport*〉 expire

ab|lecken *tr. V.* **a)** lick off; **b)** *(säubern)* lick clean

ab|legen 1. *tr. V.* **a)** lay *or* put down; **b)** *(Bürow.)* file; **c)** stop wearing 〈*clothes*〉; **d)** give up 〈*habit*〉; lose 〈*shyness*〉; **e)** swear 〈*oath*〉; sit 〈*examination*〉; make 〈*confession*〉; 2. *tr., itr. V.* take off; **möchten Sie ~?** would you like to take your coat off?; 3. *itr. V.* |vom Kai| ~: cast off; **Ableger der**; ~s, ~: layer; *(Steckling)* cutting

ab|lehnen *tr. V.* **a)** decline; decline, turn down 〈*money, invitation, position*〉; reject 〈*suggestion, applicant*〉; **b)** *(mißbilligen)* disapprove of; **Ablehnung die**; ~, ~en **a)** rejection; **b)** *(Mißbilligung)* disapproval

ab|leiten *tr. V.* **a)** divert; **b)** *(herleiten)* etw. aus/von etw. ~: derive sth. from sth.; **Ab·leitung die** derivation

ab|lenken *tr. V.* **a)** deflect; **b)** jmdn. von etw. ~: distract sb. from sth.; **c)** *(zerstreuen)* divert; **sich** ~: amuse oneself; **Ab·lenkung die** *s.* **ablenken:** deflection; distraction; diversion

ab|lesen *unr. tr. V.* **a)** read 〈*speech, lecture*〉; **werden Sie frei sprechen oder ~?** will you be talking from notes or reading your speech?; **b)** read 〈*gas meter, thermometer, etc.*〉; check 〈*time, speed, temperature*〉; **c)** *(erkennen)* see

ab|liefern *tr., itr. V.* hand in; deliver 〈*goods*〉

ab|lösen 1. *tr. V.* **a)** etw. |von etw.| ~: get sth. off [sth.]; **b)** jmdn. ~: relieve sb.; **sich** *od.* **einander** ~: take turns; 2. *refl. V.* sich |von etw.| ~: come off [sth.]

Ab·lösung die *(eines Postens)* changing; **ich schicke Ihnen jemanden zur ~:** I'll send someone to relieve you

ab|machen *tr. V.* **a)** *(ugs.)* take off; take down 〈*sign, rope*〉; **b)** *(vereinbaren)* agree; **Abmachung die**; ~, ~en agreement

ab|magern *itr. V.; mit sein* become thin; *(absichtlich)* slim; **Abmagerungs·kur die** reducing diet

ab|marschieren *itr. V.; mit sein* depart; *(Milit.)* march off

ab|melden *tr. V.* **a)** sich/jmdn. ~: report that one/sb. is leaving; **b)** *(Umzug melden)* notify the authorities that one is moving from an address; **c)** ein Auto ~: cancel a car's registration; **Ab·mel-**

dung die a) *(beim Weggehen)* report that one is leaving; **b)** *(beim Umzug)* registration of a move with the authorities at one's old address; **c)** ~ eines Autos cancellation of a car's registration

Ab·messung die *meist Pl.* *(Dimension)* dimension; measurement

ab|montieren *tr. V.* take off 〈*part*〉; dismantle 〈*machine, equipment*〉

ab|mühen *refl. V.* toil; **sie mühte sich mit dem schweren Koffer ab** she struggled with the heavy suitcase

Abnahme die; ~, ~n **a)** *o. Pl.* *(das Entfernen)* removal; **b)** *(Verminderung)* decrease; **ab|nehmen** 1. *unr. tr. V.* **a)** *(entfernen)* take off; take down 〈*picture, curtain, lamp*〉; **b)** jmdm. den Koffer ~: take sb.'s suitcase; jmdm. eine Arbeit ~: save sb. a job; **c)** jmdm. ein Versprechen/einen Eid ~: make sb. give a promise/swear an oath; **d)** *(prüfen)* inspect and approve; test and pass 〈*vehicle*〉; **e)** jmdm. etw. ~ *(wegnehmen)* take sth. off sb.; **f)** *(beim Telefon)* answer 〈*telephone*〉; pick up 〈*receiver*〉; **g)** *(Handarb.)* decrease; **h)** das nehme ich dir/ihm *usw.* nicht ab I won't buy that *(coll.)*; 2. *unr. itr. V.* **a)** *(Gewicht verlieren)* lose weight; **b)** *(sich verringern)* decrease; drop; 〈*attention, interest*〉 flag; 〈*brightness*〉 diminish; **wir haben ~den Mond** there is a waning moon; **c)** *(beim Telefon)* answer the telephone

Ab·neigung die dislike (**gegen** for)

ab|nutzen, *(landsch.:)* **ab|nützen** *tr., refl. V.* wear out; **abgenutzt worn**

Abonnement [abɔnə'mãː] **das**; ~s, ~s subscription (*Gen.* to); **abonnieren** *tr. V.* subscribe to

Ab·ordnung die delegation

ab|passen *tr. V.* **a)** *(abwarten)* wait for; **b)** *(aufhalten)* catch

ab|pausen *tr. V.* trace

ab|pfeifen *(Sport)* 1. *itr. V.* blow the whistle; 2. *tr. V.* [blow the whistle to] stop; **Ab·pfiff der** *(Sport)* final whistle; *(Halbzeit~)* half-time whistle

ab|pflücken *tr. V.* pick

ab|plagen *refl. V.* slave away

ab|prallen *itr. V.; mit sein* rebound; 〈*bullet, missile*〉 ricochet

ab|putzen *tr. V. (ugs.);* **a)** wipe off; **b)** *(säubern)* wipe; **jmdm./sich das Gesicht** ~: clean sb.'s/one's face

ab|quälen *refl. V.* **sich |mit etw.|** ~: struggle [with sth.]

ab|rackern *refl. V. (ugs.)* flog oneself to death *(coll.)*

ab|rasieren *tr. V.* shave off

ab|raten *unr. itr. V.* jmdm. von etw. ~: advise sb. against sth.

ab|räumen *tr. V.* **a)** clear away; **b)** *(leer machen)* clear ⟨*table*⟩

ab|rechnen 1. *itr. V.* cash up; mit jmdm. ~ *(fig.)* call sb. to account; 2. *tr. V.* die Kasse ~: reckon up the till; seine Spesen ~: claim one's expenses; **Ab·rechnung die a)** cashing up *no art.; (Aufstellung)* statement; **b)** *(fig.: Vergeltung)* reckoning

ab|reiben *unr. tr. V.* **a)** rub off; **b)** *(säubern)* rub

Ab·reise die departure **(nach** for); bei meiner ~: when I left/leave; **ab|reisen** *itr. V.; mit sein* leave **(nach** for)

ab|reißen 1. *unr. tr. V.* **a)** tear off; tear down ⟨*poster, notice*⟩; pull off ⟨*button*⟩; **b)** *(niederreißen)* demolish, pull down ⟨*building*⟩; 2. *unr. itr. V.; mit sein* **a)** fly off; ⟨*shoe-lace*⟩ break off; **b)** *(aufhören)* come to an end; ⟨*connection, contact*⟩ be broken off

ab|richten *tr. V.* train

Ab·riß der a) *o. Pl.: s.* abreißen 1 b: demolition; pulling down; **b)** *(knappe Darstellung)* outline

ab|rollen 1. *tr. V.* unwind; 2. *itr. V.; mit sein* unwind [itself]

ab|rücken 1. *tr. V. (wegschieben)* move away; 2. *itr. V.; mit sein* move away

Ab·ruf der: auf ~: on call; *(DV)* in retrievable form; **ab|rufen** *unr. tr. V.* summon; call

ab|runden *tr. V.* **a)** *(auch fig.)* round off; **b)** round ⟨*figure*⟩ up/down **(auf** + Akk. to); etw. nach oben/unten ~: round sth. up/down

abrupt [ap'rʊpt] 1. *Adj.* abrupt; 2. *adv.* abruptly

ab|rüsten *itr., tr. V.* disarm; **Ab·rüstung die;** ~: disarmament

ab|rutschen *itr. V.; mit sein* **a)** slip; **b)** *(nach unten rutschen)* slide down

Abs. *Abk.* **a)** Absender; **b)** Absatz

Ab·sage die *(auf eine Einladung)* refusal; *(auf eine Bewerbung)* rejection; **ab|sagen** 1. *tr. V.* cancel; withdraw ⟨*participation*⟩; 2. *itr. V.* jmdm. ~: tell sb. one cannot come

ab|sägen *tr. V.* saw off

Ab·satz der a) *(am Schuh)* heel; **b)** *(Textunterbrechung)* break; **c)** *(Textabschnitt)* paragraph; **d)** *(Kaufmannsspr.)* sales *pl.*

ab|saufen *unr. itr. V.; mit sein (ugs.)* ⟨*engine, car*⟩ flood

ab|saugen *tr. V.* **a)** suck away; **b)** *(säubern)* hoover *(Brit. coll.)*

ab|schaben *tr. V.* **a)** scrape off; **b)** *(säubern)* scrape [clean]

ab|schaffen *tr. V.* **a)** *(beseitigen)* abolish ⟨*capital punishment, regulation, customs duty, institution*⟩; repeal ⟨*law*⟩; put an end to ⟨*injustice, abuse*⟩; **b)** *(weggeben)* get rid of; **Ab·schaffung die** abolition; ⟨*von Gesetzen*⟩ repeal; ⟨*von Unrecht, Mißstand*⟩ ending

ab|schalten *tr., itr. V.* switch off; shut down ⟨*power-station*⟩

abschätzig 1. *Adj.* derogatory; 2. *adv.* derogatorily

Ab·scheu der; ~s detestation; abhorrence; **abscheulich** 1. *Adj.* **a)** disgusting ⟨*smell, taste*⟩; repulsive ⟨*sight*⟩; **b)** *(verwerflich)* disgraceful ⟨*behaviour*⟩; abominable ⟨*crime*⟩; 2. *adv.* disgracefully

ab|schicken *tr. V.* send [off]

ab|schieben *unr. tr. V.* **a)** push away; **b)** *(abwälzen)* shift ⟨*responsibility, blame*⟩; **c)** *(außer Landes bringen)* deport

Abschied der; ~[e]s, ~e parting **(von** from); farewell **(von** to); ~ nehmen take one's leave **(von** of)

Abschieds-: ~brief der farewell letter; ~geschenk das parting gift; ~gruß der goodbye; farewell

ab|schießen *unr. tr. V.* **a)** shoot down ⟨*aeroplane*⟩; **b)** fire ⟨*arrow*⟩; launch ⟨*spacecraft*⟩; **c)** *(töten)* take

ab|schirmen *tr. V.* **a)** *(schützen)* shield; **b)** *(fernhalten)* screen off ⟨*light, radiation*⟩

ab|schlachten *tr. V.* slaughter

Ab·schlag der a) *(Kaufmannsspr.)* discount; **b)** *(Teilzahlung)* interim payment; *(Vorschuß)* advance; **c)** *(Fußball)* goalkeeper's kick out; **ab|schlagen** 1. *unr. tr. V.* **a)** knock off; *(mit dem Beil, Schwert usw.)* chop off; **b)** *(ablehnen)* refuse; **c)** *(abwehren)* beat off; 2. *unr. itr. V. (Fußball)* kick the ball out

ab|schleifen *unr. tr. V. (von Holz)* sand off; *(von Metall, Glas usw.)* grind off

Abschlepp·dienst der breakdown recovery service; tow[ing] service *(Amer.);* **ab|schleppen** tow away; take ⟨*ship*⟩ in tow; ein Auto zur Werkstatt ~: tow a car to the garage; **Abschlepp·seil das** tow-rope; *(aus Draht)* towing cable

ab|schließen 1. *unr. tr. V.* **a)** *auch itr.*

(zuschließen) lock ⟨*door, gate, cupboard*⟩; lock [up] ⟨*house, flat, room, park*⟩; **b)** *(verschließen)* seal; **etw. luftdicht ~:** seal sth. hermetically; **c)** *(begrenzen)* border; **d)** *(zum Abschluß bringen)* conclude; **e)** *(vereinbaren)* strike ⟨*bargain, deal*⟩; make ⟨*purchase*⟩; enter into ⟨*agreement*⟩; **2.** *unr. itr. V. (aufhören, enden)* end; **~d sagte er ...:** in conclusion he said ...; **Abschluß der** *(Beendigung)* conclusion; end

ab|schmecken *tr. V.* **a)** *(kosten)* taste; try; **b)** *(würzen)* season

ab|schmieren *tr. V. (Technik)* grease

ab|schminken *tr. V.* **jmdn./sich ~:** remove sb.'s/one's make-up

ab|schmirgeln *tr. V.* rub off with emery; *(mit Sandpapier)* sand off

ab|schnallen *tr. V.* unfasten

ab|schneiden 1. *unr. tr. V.* **a)** *(auch fig.: isolieren)* cut off; cut down ⟨*sth. hanging*⟩; **etw. von etw. ~:** cut sth. off sth.; **sich** *(Dat.)* **eine Scheibe Brot ~:** cut oneself a slice of bread; **b)** *(kürzer schneiden)* cut; **c) jmdm. den Weg ~:** take a short cut to get ahead of sb.; **2.** *unr. itr. V.* **bei etw. gut/schlecht ~:** do well/badly in sth.; **Ab · schnitt der a)** *(Kapitel)* section; **b)** *(Zeitspanne)* phase; **d)** *(Teil eines Formulars)* [detachable] portion

ab|schrauben *tr. V.* unscrew [and remove]

ab|schrecken *tr. V.* **a)** deter; **b)** *(fernhalten)* scare off; **c)** *(Kochk.)* pour cold water over; **Abschreckung die; ~, ~en** deterrence

ab|schreiben 1. *unr. tr. V.* **a)** copy out; **etw. bei** *od.* **von jmdm. ~** *(in der Schule)* copy sth. off sb.; *(als Plagiator)* plagiarize sth. from sb.; **b)** *(Wirtsch.)* amortize; **2.** *unr. itr. V.* **bei** *od.* **von jmdm. ~** *(in der Schule)* copy off sb.; *(als Plagiator)* copy from sb.; **Ab · schreibung die** *(Wirtsch.)* amortization; **Ab · schrift die** copy

ab|schürfen *tr. V.* graze

Ab · schuß der a) *(eines Flugzeugs)* shooting down; **b)** *(von Geschossen)* firing; *(eines Raumschiffs)* launching

abschüssig *Adj.* downward sloping ⟨*land*⟩

ab|schütteln *tr. V.* shake off; *(herunterschütteln)* shake down

ab|schwächen 1. *tr. V.* **a)** *(mildern)* tone down ⟨*statement, criticism*⟩; **b)** *(verringern)* lessen ⟨*effect, impression*⟩; cushion ⟨*blow, impact*⟩; **2.** *refl.*

V. ⟨*interest, demand*⟩ wane; **Abschwächung die; ~, ~en a)** *(Milderung)* toning down; **b)** *(eines Aufpralls, Stoßes usw.)* cushioning

ab|schweifen *itr. V.; mit sein* digress; **Abschweifung die; ~, ~en** digression

ab|schwören *unr. itr. V.* **dem Teufel/ seinem Glauben ~:** renounce the Devil/one's faith; **dem Alkohol/Laster ~:** forswear alcohol/vice

absehbar *Adj.* foreseeable; **in ~er Zeit** within the foreseeable future; **ab|sehen 1.** *unr. tr. V.* **a)** *(voraussehen)* predict; foresee ⟨*event*⟩; **b) es auf etw.** *(Akk.)* **abgesehen haben** be after sth.; **er hat es darauf abgesehen, uns zu ärgern** he's out to annoy us; **der Chef hat es auf ihn abgesehen** the boss has got it in for him; **2.** *unr. itr. V.* **a) von etw. ~** *(etw. nicht beachten)* leave aside sth.; *s. auch* **abgesehen; b) von etw. ~** *(auf etw. verzichten)* refrain from sth.

ab|seilen 1. *tr. V.* lower [with a rope]. **2.** *refl. V. (Bergsteigen)* abseil

ab|sein *unr. itr. V.; mit sein (Zusschr. nur im Inf. u. Part.) (abgegangen sein)* have come off

abseits 1. *Präp. mit Gen.* away from; **2.** *Adv.* **a)** far away; **b)** *(Ballspiele)* **~ sein** *od.* **stehen** be offside; **Abseits das; ~, ~: das war ein klares ~:** that was clearly offside

ab|senden *unr. od. regelm. tr. V.* dispatch; **Ab · sender der** sender; *(Anschrift)* sender's address

ab|setzen 1. *tr. V.* **a)** take off ⟨*hat, glasses, etc.*⟩; **b)** *(hinstellen)* put down ⟨*bag, suitcase*⟩; **c)** *(aussteigen lassen)* **jmdn. ~** *(im öffentlichen Verkehr)* put sb. down; let sb. out *(Amer.)*; *(im privaten Verkehr)* drop sb. [off]; **d)** remove ⟨*chancellor, judge*⟩ from office; depose ⟨*king, emperor*⟩; **2.** *refl. V.* **a)** *(sich ablagern)* be deposited; **b)** *(flüchten)* get away

Absetzung die; ~, ~en *s.* **absetzen 1 d:** removal; deposition

ab|sichern 1. *tr. V.* make safe; **2.** *refl. V.* safeguard oneself

Ab · sicht die; ~, ~en intention; **etw. mit ~ tun** do sth. intentionally; **etw. ohne** *od.* **nicht mit ~ tun** do sth. unintentionally; **ab · sichtlich 1.** *Adj.* intentional; deliberate; **2.** *adv.* intentionally; deliberately

ab|sinken *unr. itr. V.; mit sein* sink

absolut *Adj.* absolute; **Absolutismus der; ~** *(hist.)* absolutism *no art.*

Absolvẹnt der; ~en, ~en *(einer Schu-le)* one who has taken the leaving *or* *(Amer.)* final examination; *(einer Aka-demie)* graduate; **absolvịeren** *tr. V.* complete; **Absolvịerung die;** ~: completion

ab·sọnderlich *Adj.* strange; odd; **ạb|sondern** 1. *tr. V.* exude; *(Phy-siol.)* secrete; 2. *refl. V.* isolate oneself

absorbịeren *tr. V.* absorb

ạb|speisen *tr. V.* jmdn. mit etw. ~: fob sb. off with sth.

ạbspenstig *Adj.* jmdm. etw. ~ machen get sb. to part with sth.

ạb|sperren *tr. V.* seal off; close off

Ạb·spiel das *(Ballspiele)* passing; **ạb|spielen** 1. *tr. V.* a) play ⟨record, tape⟩; b) vom Blatt ~: play ⟨piece of music⟩ at sight; c) *(Ballspiele)* pass; 2. *refl. V.* take place

Ạb·sprache die arrangement; eine ~ treffen make an arrangement; **ạb|sprechen** *unr. tr. V.* a) jmdm. etw. ~: deny that sb. has sth.; b) *(vereinbaren)* arrange

ạb|springen *unr. itr. V.; mit sein* jump off; *(herunterspringen)* jump down; vom Fahrrad ~: jump off one's bi-cycle; **Ạb·sprung** der take-off; *(das Herunterspringen)* jump

ạb|spülen 1. *tr. V.* a) wash off; b) *(rei-nigen)* rinse off; **sich** *(Dat.)* **die Hände usw.** ~: rinse one's hands *etc.*; das Geschirr ~ *(bes. südd.)* wash the dishes; 2. *itr. V. (bes. südd.)* wash up

ạb|stammen *itr. V.* be descended (von from); **Ạbstammung die;** ~, ~en descent

Ạb·stand der a) distance; in 20 Meter ~: at a distance of 20 metres; b) *(Un-terschied)* gap

ạb|stauben *tr., itr. V.* dust

Ạbstecher der; ~s, ~: side-trip

ạb|stehen *unr. itr. V.* ⟨hair⟩ stand up; ⟨pigtail[s]⟩ stick out; ~de Ohren pro-truding ears

Ạb·steige die ~, ~n *(ugs. abwertend)* cheap and crummy hotel *(sl.);* **ạb|steigen** *unr. itr. V.; mit sein* a) |vom Pferd/Fahrrad| ~: get off [one's horse/bicycle]; b) *(abwärts gehen)* go down

ạb|stellen *tr. V.* a) put down; b) *(un-terbringen)* put; *(parken)* park; c) *(ausschalten, abdrehen)* turn off; d) *(unterbinden)* put a stop to

Ạbstell-: ~kammer die, ~raum der lumber-room

ạb|stempeln *tr. V.* a) frank ⟨letter⟩;

cancel ⟨stamp⟩; b) *(fig.)* label, brand (zu, als as)

ạb|sterben *unr. itr. V.; mit sein* a) [gradually] die; b) *(gefühllos werden)* go numb

Ạbstieg der; ~|e|s, ~e a) descent; b) *(Niedergang)* decline

ạb|stimmen 1. *itr. V.* vote (über + Akk. on); 2. *tr. V.* etw. mit jmdm. ~: discuss and agree on sth. with sb.; **Ạb·stimmung die** a) vote; während der ~: during the voting; b) *(Abspra-che)* agreement

abstinent [apsti'nɛnt] *Adj.* teetotal; ~ sein be a teetotaller; **Abstinẹnz die;** ~: teetotalism; **Abstinẹnzler der;** ~s, ~: teetotaller

ạb|stoppen 1. *tr. V.* halt; stop; check ⟨advance⟩; 2. *itr. V.* come to a halt; ⟨person⟩ stop

Ạb·stoß der *(Fußball)* goal-kick; **ạb|stoßen** *unr. tr. V.* a) push off; b) *(be schädigen)* chip ⟨crockery, paintwork, plaster⟩; c) *(verkaufen)* sell off; d) *(an-widern)* repel; put off; **ạbstoßend** *Adj.* repulsive

abstrakt [ap'strakt] *Adj.* abstract

ạb|streifen *tr. V.* pull off; strip off ⟨berries⟩; die Asche |von der Zigarette/ Zigarre| ~: remove the ash [from one's cigarette/cigar]

ạb|streiten *unr. tr. V.* deny

Ạb·strich der a) *(Med.)* swab; einen ~ machen take a swab; b) *(Streichung, Kürzung)* cut; ~e machen make cuts (an + Dat. in)

ạb|stumpfen *itr. V.; mit sein* jmd. stumpft ab *(wird unsensibel)* sb.'s mind becomes deadened

Ạb·sturz der fall; *(eines Flugzeugs)* crash; **ạb|stürzen** *itr. V.; mit sein* fall; ⟨aircraft, pilot, passenger⟩ crash

ạb|stützen 1. *refl. V.* support oneself (mit on, an + Dat. against); 2. *tr. V.* support

ạb|suchen *tr. V.* search (nach for)

absụrd *Adj.* absurd

Abszẹß der; Abszẹsses, Abszẹsse a) *(Med.)* abscess; b) *(Geschwür)* ulcer

Abszịsse die; ~, ~en *(Math.)* abscissa

Abt der; ~|e|s, **Ạbte** abbot

Abt. *Abk.* Abteilung

ạb|tasten *tr. V.* etw. ~: feel sth. all over

ạb|tauen 1. *itr. V.; mit sein (eis-/ schneefrei werden)* become clear of ice/snow; ⟨refrigerator⟩ defrost; 2. *tr. V.* melt; thaw; defrost ⟨refrigerator⟩

Abtẹi die; ~, ~en abbey

Abteil das; ~|e|s, ~e compartment; **Ab·teilung** die department; **Abteilungs·leiter** der head of department

ab|tippen tr. V. (ugs.) type out

Äbtissin die; ~, ~nen abbess

ab|tönen tr. V. tint

ab|töten tr. V. destroy ⟨parasites, germs⟩; deaden ⟨nerve, feeling⟩

ab|tragen unr. tr. V. (abnutzen) wear out; **abgetragen** well worn

abträglich Adj. (geh.) einer Sache (Dat.) ~ sein be detrimental to sth.

Ab·transport der s. abtransportieren: taking away; removal; **ab|transportieren** tr. V. take away; remove ⟨dead, injured⟩

ab|treiben 1. unr. tr. V. **a)** carry away; jmdn./ein Schiff vom Kurs ~: drive sb./a ship off course; **b)** abort ⟨foetus⟩; ein Kind ~ lassen have an abortion; 2. unr. itr. V.; mit sein be carried away; ⟨ship⟩ be drives off course; **Abtreibung** die; ~, ~en abortion

ab|trennen tr. V. detach

ab|treten 1. unr. tr. V. **a)** sich (Dat.) die Füße/Schuhe ~: wipe one's feet; **b)** jmdm. etw. ~: let sb. have sth.; 2. unr. itr. V.; mit sein **a)** (Theater) exit; (fig.) make one's exit; **b)** (zurücktreten) step down; ⟨monarch⟩ abdicate; **Abtreter** der; ~s, ~: doormat

ab|trocknen tr. V. dry; sich (Dat.) die Hände/die Tränen ~: dry one's hands/tears

ab|tropfen itr. V.; mit sein drip off

abtrünnig Adj. (einer Partei) renegade; (einer Religion, Sekte) apostate; der Kirche/dem Glauben ~ werden desert the Church/the faith

ab|tun unr. tr. V. dismiss

ab|wägen unr. od. regelm. tr., itr. V. weigh up; **abgewogen** carefully weighted; balanced ⟨judgement⟩

ab|wählen tr. V. vote out; drop ⟨school subject⟩

ab|wandeln tr. V. adapt

ab|wandern itr. V.; mit sein migrate; (in ein anderes Land) emigrate; **Abwanderung** die migration; (in ein anderes Land) emigration

Ab·wandlung die adaptation

ab|warten 1. itr. V. wait; sie warteten ab they awaited events; warte ab! wait and see; (als Drohung) just you wait!; 2. tr. V. wait for

abwärts Adv. downwards; (bergab) downhill; den Fluß ~: downstream

Abwasch der; ~|e|s washing-up (Brit.); washing dishes (Amer.); den ~ machen do the washing-up/wash the dishes; **abwaschbar** Adj. washable; **ab|waschen** 1. unr. tr. V. **a)** wash off; **b)** (reinigen) wash down; wash [up] ⟨dishes⟩; 2. unr. itr. V. wash up (Brit.); wash the dishes (Amer.)

Ab·wasser das; Pl. -wässer sewage

ab|wechseln refl., itr. V. alternate; wir wechselten uns ab we took turns; **abwechselnd** Adv. alternately; **Abwechslung** die; ~, ~en variety; (Wechsel) change; zur ~: for a change

Ab·weg der: auf ~e kommen od. geraten go astray; **abwegig** erroneous; false ⟨suspicion⟩

Ab·wehr die; ~ **a)** repulsion; (von Schlägen) fending off; (Sport) clearance; clearing (Amer.); **b)** (Sport: Hintermannschaft) defence; **ab|wehren** tr. V. **a)** repulse; fend off ⟨blow⟩; (Sport) clear ⟨ball, shot⟩; **b)** avert ⟨danger, consequences⟩

ab|weichen unr. itr. V.; mit sein **a)** deviate; **b)** (sich unterscheiden) differ; **Abweichung** die; ~, ~en **a)** deviation; **b)** (Unterschied) difference

ab|weisen unr. tr. V. turn away; turn down ⟨applicant, suitor⟩; **abweisend** Adj. cold ⟨look, tone of voice⟩; in ~em Ton coldly; **Ab·weisung** die; ~, ~en s. abweisen: turning away; turning down

ab|wenden 1. unr. od. regelm. tr. V. **a)** turn away; **b)** nur regelm. (verhindern) avert. 2. unr. od. regelm. refl. V. turn away

ab|werben unr. tr. V. lure away

ab|werfen 1. unr. tr. V. **a)** drop; throw off ⟨clothing⟩; jettison ⟨ballast⟩; throw ⟨rider⟩; **b)** (ins Spielfeld werfen) throw out ⟨ball⟩; **c)** (einbringen) bring in; 2. unr. itr. V. (Sport) throw the ball out

ab|werten tr., itr. V. devalue; **abwertend** Adj. derogatory ⟨term⟩; **Ab·wertung** die devaluation

abwesend Adj. absent; **Abwesenheit** die; ~ absence

ab|wickeln tr. V. **a)** unwind; **b)** (erledigen) deal with ⟨case⟩; do ⟨business⟩; **Abwicklung** die; ~, ~en s. abwickeln 1 b: dealing (Gen. with); doing

ab|wiegen unr. tr. V. weigh out; weigh ⟨single item⟩

ab|wimmeln tr. V. (ugs.) get rid of

ab|wischen tr. V. **a)** wipe away; **b)** (säubern) wipe

Ab·wurf der a) dropping; *(von Ballast)* jettisoning; b) **beim ~ stolperte der Torwart** the goalkeeper stumbled as he threw the ball out

ab|zahlen *tr. V.* pay off *⟨debt, loan⟩*

ab|zählen *tr. V.* count

Ab·zahlung die paying off; **etw. auf ~ kaufen/verkaufen** buy/sell sth. on easy terms

Ab·zeichen das emblem; *(Ansteck-nadel, Plakette)* badge

ab|zeichnen 1. *tr. V.* a) *(kopieren)* copy; b) *(signieren)* initial; 2. *refl. V.* stand out; *(fig.)* begin to emerge

Abzieh·bild das transfer; **ab|ziehen** 1. *unr. tr. V.* a) pull off; peel off *⟨skin⟩;* strip *⟨bed⟩;* b) *(Fot.)* make a print/prints of; c) *(Milit., auch fig.)* withdraw; d) *(subtrahieren)* subtract; take away; *(abrechnen)* deduct; 2. *unr. itr. V.; mit sein (sich verflüchtigen)* escape; b) *(Milit.)* withdraw; **Ab·zug** der a) *(an einer Schußwaffe)* trigger; b) *(Fot.)* print; c) *(Verminderung)* deduction; **abzüglich** *Präp. mit Gen. (Kaufmannsspr.)* less

ab|zweigen 1. *itr. V.; mit sein* branch off; 2. *tr. V.* put aside; **Abzweigung** die; ~, ~en turn-off; *(Gabelung)* fork

ach *Interj.* a) *(betroffen, mitleidig)* oh [dear]; b) *(bedauernd, unwirsch)* oh; c) *(klagend)* ah; d) *(erstaunt)* oh; ~, **wirklich?** no, really?; ~, **der!** oh, him!; e) ~ **so!** oh, I see; ~ **was** *od.* **wo!** of course not

Achat der; ~[e]s, ~e *(Min.)* agate

Achse die; ~, ~n a) *(Rad~)* axle; b) *(Dreh~, Math., Astron.)* axis

Achsel die; ~, ~n *(Schulter)* shoulder; *(~höhle)* armpit

Achsel-: ~**haare** *Pl.* armpit hair *sing.;* ~**höhle** die armpit

¹**acht** *Kardinalz.* eight; **um ~ [Uhr]** at eight [o'clock]; **um halb ~:** at half past seven; **dreiviertel ~, Viertel vor ~:** [a] quarter to eight; **es steht ~ zu ~/~ zu 2** *(Sport)* the score is eight all/eight to two; ²**acht: sie waren zu ~:** there were eight of them

³**acht: etw. außer ~ lassen** disregard sth.; **sich in ~ nehmen** be careful; **sich vor jmdm./etw. in ~ nehmen** be wary of sb./sth.

acht... *Ordinalz.* eighth; **der ~e** September the eighth of September; **München, [den] 8. Mai 1984** Munich, 8 May 1984; **Acht** die; ~, ~en a) *(Figur)* figure eight; c) *(Verbiegung)* buckle; **mein Rad hat eine ~:** my

wheel is buckled; **Achte** der/die; *adj. Dekl.* eighth

acht-, Acht-: ~**eck** das; ~**s, ~e** octagon; ~**eckig** *Adj.* octagonal; ~**einhalb** *Bruchz.* eight and a half

achtel *Bruchz.* eighth; **Achtel** das *(schweiz. meist* der); ~**s, ~** eighth; **Achtel·note** die *(Musik)* quaver

achten 1. *tr. V.* respect; 2. *itr. V.* **auf etw.** *(Akk.)* ~: pay heed to sth.

achtens *Adv.* eighthly; **Achterbahn** die roller-coaster; **acht·fach** *Verviel-fältigungsz.* eightfold; **die ~fache Menge** eight times the quantity; ~**fach** **vergrößert/verkleinert** magnified/re-duced eight times; **das Achtfache kosten** cost eight times as much

acht|geben *unr. itr. V.* a) **auf jmdn./ etw. ~:** take care of sb./sth.; b) *(vor-sichtig sein)* be careful

acht-: ~**hundert** *Kardinalz.* eight hundred; ~**jährig** *Adj. (8 Jahre alt)* eight-year-old *attrib.;* eight years old *pred.; (8 Jahre dauernd)* eight-year *attrib.;* ~**köpfig** *Adj. ⟨family, commit-tee⟩* of eight

acht·los 1. *Adj.* heedless; 2. *adv.* heedlessly

acht-: ~**mal** *Adv.* eight times; ~**spu-rig** *Adj.* eight-lane *⟨road⟩;* eight-track *⟨cassette⟩;* ~**stellig** *Adj.* eight-figure *attrib.;* ~**stellig sein** have eight fig-ures; ~**stimmig** 1. *Adj.* eight-part *at-trib.;* 2. *adv.* in eight parts; ~**stöckig** *Adj.* eight-storey *attrib.;* ~**tägig** *Adj. (8 Tage alt)* eight-day-old *attrib.; (8 Tage dauernd)* eight-day[-long] *at-trib.;* ~**tausend** *Kardinalz.* eight thousand; ~**teilig** *Adj.* eight-piece *⟨tea-service, tool-set, etc.⟩;* eight-part *⟨series, serial⟩*

Achtung die; ~ a) respect (**vor +** *Dat., Gen.* for); b) ~! watch out!; ~, **fertig, los!** on your marks, get set, go!

acht·zehn *Kardinalz.* eighteen; **18 Uhr 33** 6.33 p.m.; *(auf der 24-Stunden-Uhr)* 1833; **achtzehn·jährig** *Adj. (18 Jahre alt)* eighteen-year-old *at-trib.;* eighteen years old *pred.; (18 Jah-re dauernd)* eighteen-year *attrib.*

achtzig *Kardinalz.* eighty; **mit ~ [km/ h] fahren** drive at *or (coll.)* do eighty [k.p.h.]; **über/etwa ~ [Jahre alt] sein** be over/about eighty [years old]; **mit ~ [Jahren]** *od.* **Achtzig** at eighty [years of age]; **achtzig·jährig** *Adj. (80 Jahre alt)* eighty-year-old *attrib.;* eighty years old *pred.; (80 Jahre dauernd)* eighty-year *attrib.*

ächzen *itr. V.* groan

Acker der; ~s, **Äcker** field; **Ackerbau** der; *o. Pl.* arable farming *no indef. art.*

A. D. *Abk.* Anno Domini AD

ADAC [a:de:a:'tse:] der; ~ *Abk.* Allgemeiner Deutscher Automobilclub

Adams·apfel der *(ugs.)* Adam's apple

adäquat [at|ε'kva:t] *Adj.* ap- propriate *(Dat.* to); suitable *(Dat.* for)

addieren 1. *tr. V.* add [up]; 2. *itr. V.* add; **Addition** die; ~, ~en addition

ade *Interj. (veralt., landsch.)* farewell *(dated);* bye *(coll.)*

Adel der; ~s nobility; **der niedere/hohe** ~: the lesser nobility/the aristocracy; **adelig** s. adlig; **Adelige** s. Adlige; **adeln** *tr. V.* jmdn. ~: give sb. a title; *(in den hohen Adel erheben)* raise sb. to the peerage

Adels-: ~**geschlecht** das noble family; ~**stand** der nobility; *(hoher Adel)* nobility; ~**titel** der title of nobility

Ader die; ~, ~n a) blood-vessel; b) *o. Pl. (Anlage, Begabung)* streak; c) *(Bot., Geol.)* vein; d) *(Elektrot.)* core

adieu [a'djø:] *Interj. (veralt.)* adieu

Adjektiv das; ~s, ~e *(Sprachw.)* adjective

Adjutant der; ~en, ~en adjutant

Adler der; ~s, ~: eagle

adlig *Adj.* noble; ~ sein be a noble [man/woman]; **Adlige** der/die *adj. Dekl.* noble [man/woman]

Admiral der; ~s, ~e *od.* Admiräle admiral

adoptieren *tr. V.* adopt; **Adoption** die; ~, ~en adoption

Adoptiv-: ~**eltern** *Pl.* adoptive parents; ~**kind** das adopted child

Adressat der; ~en, ~en, **Adressatin** die; ~, ~nen addressee; **Adreßbuch** das directory; **Adresse** die; ~, ~n address; **bei jmdm. an die falsche** ~ **kommen** *od.* geraten *(fig. ugs.)* come to the wrong address *(fig.);* **adressieren** *tr. V.* address

adrett 1. *Adj.* smart. 2. *adv.* smartly

Advent [at'vεnt] der; ~s a) Advent; b) *(Adventssonntag)* Sunday in Advent

Advents-: ~**kalender** der Advent calendar; ~**kranz** der *garland of evergreens with four candles for the Sundays in Advent*

Adverb [at'vεrp] das; ~s, ~ien *(Sprachw.)* adverb; **adverbial** *(Sprachw.)* 1. *Adj.* adverbial; 2. *adv.* adverbially

Advokat [atvo'ka:t] der; ~en, ~en *(österr., schweiz., sonst veralt.)* lawyer; advocate *(arch.)*

Aero- [aero- *od.* ε:ro-]: ~**gramm** das air[-mail] letter; ~**sol** das; ~s, ~e aerosol

Affäre die; ~, ~n affair; **sich aus der** ~ **ziehen** *(ugs.)* get out of it

Affe der; ~n, ~n a) monkey; *(Menschen~)* ape; b) *(salopp) (dummer Kerl)* oaf; clot *(Brit. sl.); (Geck)* dandy

Affekt der; ~[e]s, ~e emotion; **im** ~: in the heat of the moment; **affektiert** *(abwertend)* 1. *Adj.* affected; 2. *adv.* affectedly

Affen·theater das *(salopp)* farce

Afghane [af'ga:nə] der; ~n, ~n a) Afghan; b) *(Hund)* Afghan hound; **afghanisch** *Adj.* Afghan; **Afghanistan** [af'ga:nɪsta:n] **(das);** ~s Afghanistan

Afrika·(das); ~s Africa; **Afrikaner** der; ~s, ~African; **afrikanisch** *Adj.* African

After der; ~s, ~: anus

AG [a:'ge:] *Abk.* die; ~, ~s Aktiengesellschaft PLC *(Brit.);* Ltd. *(private company) (Brit.);* Inc. *(Amer.)*

Agent der; ~en, ~en; **Agentin** die; ~, ~nen agent; **Agentur** die; ~, ~en agency

Aggregat das; ~[e]s, ~e *(Technik)* unit; *(Elektrot.)* set; **Aggregat·zustand** der *(Chemie)* state

Aggression die; ~, ~en aggression; **aggressiv** 1. *Adj.* aggressive; 2. *adv.* aggressively; **Aggressivität** die; ~: aggressiveness; **Aggressor** der; ~s, ~en aggressor

Agitation die; ~: agitation; **agitieren** *itr. V.* agitate

Agrar·land das; *Pl.* ~länder agrarian country

Ägypten (das); ~s Egypt; **Ägypter** der; ~s, ~Egyptian; **ägyptisch** *Adj.* Egyptian

ah *Interj. (verwundert)* oh; *(freudig, genießerisch)* ah; *(verstehend)* oh; ah

äh [ε(:)] *Interj.* a) *(angeekelt)* ugh; b) *(stotternd)* er; hum

aha [a'ha(:)] *Interj. (verstehend)* oh[, I see]; *(triumphierend)* aha

Ahn der; ~[e]s, *od.* ~en, ~en *(geh.)*, **Ahne** der; ~n, ~n forebear; ancestor

ähneln *itr. V.* jmdm. ~: resemble *or* be like sb.; **jmdm. sehr/wenig** ~: strongly resemble *or* be very like sb./bear little resemblance to sb.; **einer Sache** *(Dat.)* ~: be similar to sth.; be like sth.; **sich**

(Dat.) ~: resemble one another; be alike

ahnen *tr. V.* a) *(im voraus fühlen)* have a premonition of; b) *(vermuten)* suspect; **das konnte ich doch nicht ~!** I had no way of knowing that

ähnlich 1. *Adj.* similar; **jmdm. ~ sein** be like sb.; **~ wie** like; 2. *adv.* similarly; ⟨*answer, react*⟩ in a similar way; 3. *Präp. mit Dat.* like; **Ähnlichkeit die;** ~, ~en similarity; **mit jmdm. ~ haben** be like sb.

Ahnung die; ~, ~en a) *(Vorgefühl)* premonition; b) *(ugs.: Kenntnisse)* knowledge; **von etw. |viel| ~ haben** know [a lot] about sth.; **keine ~!** [I've] no idea; **ahnungs·los** *Adj. (nichts ahnend)* unsuspecting; *(naiv, unwissend)* naïve

ahoi *Interj. (Seemannsspr.)* ahoy

Ahorn ['a:hɔrn] **der;** ~s, ~e maple

Ähre die; ~, ~n ear

Aids [e:ts] **das;** ~: Aids

Aids-: ~kranke **der/die** person suffering from Aids; ~test **der** Aids test

Akademie die; ~, ~n academy; *(Bergbau, Forst~, Bau~)* school; college; **Akademiker der;** ~s, ~, **Akademikerin die;** ~, ~nen [university/college] graduate; **akademisch** 1. *Adj.* academie; 2. *adv.* academically

Akazie [a'ka:tsiə] **die;** ~, ~n acacia

akklimatisieren *refl. V.* become *or* get acclimatized

Akkord der; ~|e|s, ~e a) *(Musik)* chord; b) *(Wirtsch.) (~arbeit)* piecework; *(~lohn)* piece-work pay *no indef. art., no pl.; (~satz)* piece-rate

Akkordeon das; ~s, ~s accordion

Akku der; ~s, ~s *(ugs.),* **Akkumulator der;** ~s, ~en accumulator *(Brit.);* storage battery

akkurat 1. *Adj.* meticulous; 2. *adv.* meticulously

Akkusativ der; ~s, ~e *(Sprachw.)* accusative [case]; **Akkusativ·objekt das** *(Sprachw.)* accusative *or* direct object

Akne die; ~, ~n *(Med.)* acne

Akrobat der; ~en, ~en acrobat; **Akrobatik die;** ~ acrobatics *pl.;* **akrobatisch** *Adj.* acrobatic

Akt der; ~|e|s, ~e a) *(auch Theater, Zirkus~, Varieté~)* act; b) *(Zeremonie)* ceremony; c) *(Geschlechts~)* sexual act; d) *(bild. Kunst)* nude [picture]; **Akt·bild das** nude [picture]

Akte die; ~, ~n file

Akten-: ~deckel **der** folder; ~kof-

fer der attaché case; ~mappe **die** brief-case; ~ordner **der** file; ~tasche **die** brief-case; ~zeichen **das** reference

Akteur [ak'tø:ɐ̯] **der;** ~s, ~e person involved

Akt·foto das nude photo

Aktie ['aktsiə] **die;** ~, ~n *(Wirtsch.)* share; ~n shares *(Brit.);* stock *(Amer.);* **die ~n fallen/steigen** share *or* stock prices are falling/rising; **Aktien·gesellschaft die** joint-stock company

Aktion die; ~, ~en a) action *no indef. art.; (militärisch)* operation; b) *(Kampagne)* campaign

Aktionär der; ~s, ~e shareholder

aktiv 1. *Adj.* a) active; b) *(Milit.)* serving *attrib.* ⟨*officer, soldier*⟩; 2. *adv.* actively; **Aktiv das;** ~s, ~e *(Sprachw.)* active; **Aktive der/die;** *adj. Dekl. (Sport)* participant; **aktivieren** *tr. V.* mobilize ⟨*party members, group, class, etc.*⟩; **den Kreislauf ~:** stimulate the circulation; **Aktivität die;** ~, ~en activity

Akt·modell das nude model

Aktualität die; ~, ~en a) *(Gegenwartsbezug)* relevance [to the present]; b) *(von Nachrichten usw.)* topicality; **aktuell** *Adj.* topical; *(gegenwärtig)* current; *(neu)* up-to-the-minute; **eine ~e Sendung** *(Ferns., Rundf.)* a [news and] current affairs programme

Akupunktur die; ~, ~en *(Med.)* acupuncture

Akustik die; ~ a) *(Lehre vom Schall)* acoustics *sing., no art.;* b) *(Schallverhältnisse)* acoustics *pl.;* **akustisch** 1. *Adj.* acoustic. 2. *adv.* acoustically

akut *Adj. (auch Med.)* acute; pressing, urgent ⟨*question, issue*⟩

Akzent der; ~|e|s, ~e a) *(Sprachw.) (Betonung)* stress; *(Betonungszeichen)* accent; b) *(Sprachmelodie, Aussprache)* accent

akzeptabel 1. *Adj.* acceptable; 2. *adv.* acceptably; **akzeptieren** *tr. V.* accept

à la [a la] *(Gastr., ugs.)* à la

Alabaster der; ~s, ~: alabaster

à la carte [ala'kart] *(Gastr.)* à la carte

Alarm der; ~|e|s, ~e alarm; *(Flieger~)* air-raid warning; **~ geben/***(fig. ugs.)* **schlagen** raise the alarm; **blinder ~:** false alarm

alarm-, Alarm-: ~anlage **die** alarm system; ~bereit *Adj.* on alert *postpos.;* ~bereitschaft **die** alert

alarmieren *tr. V.* **a)** alarm; **b)** *(zu Hilfe rufen)* call [out] ⟨*doctor, police, fire brigade, etc.*⟩
Alarm-: ~**sirene** die warning siren; ~**stufe** die alert stage
Albaner der; ~s, ~ Albanian; **Albanien** [al'ba:niən] **(das);** ~s Albania; **albanisch** *Adj.* Albanian
Albatros der; ~, ~se *(Zool.)* albatross
Alben *s.* **Album**
albern *Adj.* **a)** silly; **sich** ~ **benehmen** act silly; **b)** *(ugs.: nebensächlich)* silly; stupid; **Albernheit** die; ~, ~en silliness
Albino der; ~s, ~s albino
Album das; ~s, **Alben** album
Alge die; ~, ~n alga
Algebra [*österr.:* al'ge:bra] die; ~: algebra
Algerien [al'ge:riən] **(das);** ~s Algeria; **Algerier** der; ~s, ~: Algerian; **algerisch** *Adj.* Algerian
alias *Adv.* alias
Alibi das; ~s, ~s alibi
Alkohol der; ~s, ~e alcohol; **alkoholfrei** *Adj.* non-alcoholic; **Alkoholiker** der; ~s, ~: alcoholic; **alkoholisch** *Adj.* alcoholic; **Alkoholismus** der; ~: alcoholism *no art.*
all *Indefinitpron. u. unbest. Zahlw.* **1.** *attr. (ganz, gesamt...)* all; ~**es andere/ Weitere/übrige** everything else; ~**es Schöne** everything *or* all that is beautiful; ~**es Gute!** all the best!; **wir/ihr/sie** ~**e** all of us/you/them; ~**e Anwesenden** all those present; ~**e Bewohner der Stadt** all the inhabitants of the town; ~**e Jahre wieder** every year; ~**e fünf Minuten/Meter** every five minutes/ metres; **Bücher** ~**er Art** all kinds of books; **in** ~**er Ruhe** in peace and quiet; **2.** *alleinstehend* **a)** ~**e** all; ~**e, die ...:** all those who ...; **b)** ~**es** *(auf Sachen bezogen)* everything; *(auf Personen bezogen)* everybody; **das** ~**es** all that; **trotz** ~**em** in spite of everything; ~**es in** ~**em** all in all; **vor** ~**em** above all; **das ist** ~**es** that's all *or (coll.)* it; **ist das** ~**es?** is that all *or (coll.)* it?; ~**es mal herhören!** *(ugs.)* listen everybody!; ~**es aussteigen!** *(ugs.)* everyone out!; *(vom Schaffner gesagt)* all change!
All das; ~s *s.* **Weltall**
alle *Adj.; nicht attr.:* ~ **sein** be all gone; ~ **werden** run out
alle·dem *Pron.* **trotz** ~: in spite of *or* despite all that
Allee die; ~, ~n avenue

allein [a'lain] **1.** *Adj.; nicht attr.* **a)** *(für sich)* alone; on one's/its own; by oneself/itself; **ganz** ~: all on one's/its own; **b)** *(einsam)* alone; **2.** *adv. (ohne Hilfe)* by oneself/itself; on one's/its own; **etw.** ~ **tun** do sth. oneself; **von** ~ *(ugs.)* by oneself/itself; **3.** *Adv.* **a)** *(geh.: ausschließlich)* alone; **b)** |**schon**| ~ **der Gedanke/**|**schon**| **der Gedanke** ~: the mere thought [of it]; **alleine** *(ugs.) s.* **allein 1a, 2, 3b; alleinig** *Adj.; nicht präd.* sole
allein-, Allein-: ~**gang** der *(fig.)* independent initiative; **im** ~**gang** off one's own bat; ~**stehend** *Adj.* ⟨*person*⟩ living alone; *(ledig)* single ⟨*person*⟩; ~**stehende der/die;** *adj. Dekl.* person living alone; *(Ledige[r])* single person
alle·mal *Adv.* **a)** *(ugs.)* any time *(coll.);* **was der kann, das kann ich doch** ~: anything he can do, I can do too; **b)** **ein für** ~: once and for all; **allen·falls** *Adv.* **a)** *(höchstens)* at [the] most; **b)** *(bestenfalls)* at best
aller-: ~**dings** *Adv.* **a)** *(einschränkend)* though; **es stimmt** ~**dings, daß ...:** it's true though that ...; **b)** *(zustimmend)* [yes,] certainly; **das war** ~**dings Pech** that was bad luck, to be sure; ~**erst...** *Adj.; nicht präd.* very first; **der/die/das** ~**erste** the very first; **b)** *(best...)* very best
Allergie die; ~, ~n *(Med.)* allergy; **allergisch 1.** *Adj. (Med.)* allergic; **2.** *adv.* **auf etw.** *(Akk.)* ~ **reagieren** have an allergic reaction to sth.
aller-, Aller-: ~**größt...** *Adj.* utmost ⟨*trouble, care, etc.*⟩; biggest ⟨*car, house, town, etc.*⟩ of all; tallest ⟨*person*⟩ of all; **am** ~**größten sein** be [the] biggest/tallest of all; ~**hand** *indekl. unbest. Gattungsz. (ugs.)* **a)** *attr.* all kinds *or* sorts of; **b)** *alleinstehend* all kinds *or* sorts of things; **das ist** ~**hand** *(viel)* that's a lot; **das ist ja** ~**hand!** that's just not on! *(Brit. coll.);* ~**heiligen** das; ~ *(bes. kath. Kirche)* All Saints' Day; ~**herzlichst 1.** *Adj.* warmest ⟨*thanks, greetings, congratulations*⟩; most cordial ⟨*reception, welcome, invitation*⟩; **2.** most warmly; ~**höchst...** **1.** *Adj.* highest ⟨*building, tree, etc.*⟩ of all; **2.** *adv.* **am** ~**höchsten** ⟨*fly, jump, etc.*⟩ the highest of all; ~**höchstens** *Adv.* at the very most
allerlei *indekl. unbest. Gattungsz.: attr.* all kinds *or* sorts of; *alleinstehend* all kinds *or* sorts of things; **Al-**

lerl**e**i das; ~s, ~s *(Gemisch)* potpourri; *(Durcheinander)* jumble
aller-, **A**ller-: ~l**e**tzt... *Adj.; nicht präd.* **a)** very last; **b)** *(ugs. abwertend)* most dreadful *(coll.);* **das ist das A**ller**letzte** that is the absolute limit; ~l**ie**bst... **1)** *Adj.* most favourite; **es wäre mir am ~liebsten** *od.* **das ~liebste, wenn**...: I should like it best of all if ...; **2.** *adv.* **etw. am ~liebsten tun** like doing sth. best of all; ~m**ei**st... **1.** *Indefinitpron. u. unbest. Zahlw.* by far the most *attrib.;* **das ~meiste/am ~meisten** most of all/by far the most; **2.** *Adv.* **am ~meisten** most of all; ~m**i**ndest... *Adj.*slightest; least; **das ~mindeste** the very least; ~n**ä**chst... **1.** *Adj.* very nearest *attrib.; (Reihenfolge ausdrückend)* very next *attrib.;* **2.** *adv.* **am ~nächsten** nearest of all; ~n**eu**[e]st... *Adj.* very latest *attrib.;* **das Allerneu|e|ste** the very latest; ~schl**i**mmst... *Adj.* very worst *attrib.:* ~sch**ö**nst... **1.** *Adj.* most beautiful *attrib.;* loveliest *attrib.; (angenehmst...)* very nicest *attrib.;* **2.** *adv.* **er singt am ~schönsten** his singing is the most beautiful of all; ~s**ei**ts *Adv.* **guten Morgen ~seits!** good morning everyone
Allerw**e**lts-: ~ges**i**cht das nondescript face; ~w**o**rt das hackneyed word
allerw**e**nigst... **1.** *Adj.* lest ... of all; *Pl.* fewest ... of all; **2.** *adv.* **am ~wenigsten** least of all
alle·s**a**mt *Indefinitpron. u. unbest. Zahlw. (ugs.)* all [of you/us/them]; **wir ~:** we all
Alles·kl**e**ber der all-purpose adhesive
all·gem**ei**n **1.** *Adj.* general; universal ⟨*conscription, suffrage*⟩; **im ~en Interesse** in the common interest; **im ~en** in general; **2.** *adv.* **a)** generally; *(ausnahmslos)* universally; **es ist ~ bekannt, daß** ...: it is common knowledge that ...; **b)** *(unverbindlich)* ⟨*write, talk, discuss*⟩ in general terms
Allgem**ei**n-: ~bef**i**nden das *(Med.)* general state of health; ~b**i**ldung die; *o. Pl.* general education
Allgem**ei**nheit die; ~ **a)** generality; **b)** die ~: the general public
Allgem**ei**n-: ~med**i**zin die; *o. Pl.* general medicine; ~w**o**hl das public good
All·h**ei**lmittel das *(auch fig.)* cureall; panacea

Allig**a**tor der; ~s, ~en alligator
Allii**e**rte der; *adj. Dekl.* ally; **die ~n** the Allies
all-: ~j**ä**hrlich **1.** *Adj.* annual; yearly; **2.** *adv.* annually; every year; ~m**ä**chtig *Adj.* all-powerful
all·m**ä**hlich **1.** *Adj.* gradual; **2.** *adv.* gradually; **3.** *Adv.* **wir sollten ~ gehen** it's time we got going
all-, **A**ll-: ~m**o**rgendlich **1.** *Adj.* regular morning; **2.** *adv.* every morning; ~s**ei**tig **1.** *Adj.* general; allround, *(Amer.)* all-around *attrib.;* **2.** *adv.* generally; ~s**ei**ts *Adv.* on all sides; ~t**a**g der **a)** *(Werktag)* weekday; **b)** *o. Pl. (Einerlei)* daily routine; **der graue ~:** the dull routine of everyday life; ~t**ä**glich *Adj.* ordinary ⟨*face, person, appearance, etc.*⟩; everyday ⟨*topic, event, sight*⟩; commonplace ⟨*remark*⟩; **ein nicht ~täglicher Anblick** a sight one doesn't see every day; ~t**a**gs *Adv.* [on] weekdays; ~**zu** *Adv.* all too; **nicht ~zu viele** not too many
allz**u**-: ~fr**ü**h *Adv.* all too early; *(~bald)* all too soon; ~l**a**ng[e] *Adv.* too long; ~**o**ft *Adv.* too often; ~s**e**hr *Adv.* too much; **nicht ~sehr** not too much; ~v**ie**l *Adv.* too much
Alm die; ~, ~en mountain pasture; Alpine pasture; **A**lm·h**ü**tte die Alpine hut
Almosen das; ~s, ~ alms *pl.*
Alp die; ~, ~en *(bes. schweiz.) s.* Alm
Alp**a**ka das; ~s, ~s alpaca
Alpen *Pl.* **die ~:** the Alps
Alpen-: ~r**o**se die rhododendron; ~v**ei**lchen das cyclamen
Alpha das; ~|s|, ~|s| alpha; **A**lphab**e**t das; ~|e|s, ~e alphabet; **a**lphab**e**tisch **1.** *Adj.* alphabetical; **2.** *adv.* alphabetically
Alp·horn das alpenhorn; **a**lp**i**n *Adj.* Alpine; **A**lpin**i**st der; ~en, ~en Alpinist
als *Konj.* **a)** *(zeitlich)* when; **damals, ~:** [in the days] when; **gerade ~:** just as; **b)** *(kausal)* **um so mehr, ~:** all the more since *or* in that; **c)** *Vergleichspartikel* **größer/älter/mehr/weniger ~:** bigger/ older/more/less than; **anders ~ wir sein/leben** be different/live differently from us; **soviel/soweit ~ möglich** as much/as far as possible; **so bald/ schnell ~ möglich** as soon/as quickly as possible; **~ |wenn** *od.* **ob|** *(+ Konjunktiv II)* as if; as though; **~ ob ich das nicht wüßte!** as if I didn't know; **d)**

~ **Rentner/Arzt** as a pensioner/a doctor **sich ~ wahr/Lüge erweisen** prove to be true/a lie

also 1. *Adv.* so; therefore; **2.** *Partikel* **a)** *(das heißt)* that is; **b)** *(nach Unterbrechung)* well [then]; **c)** *(verstärkend)* **na ~!** there you are[, you see]; ~ **schön** well all right then

alt, älter, ältest... *Adj.* **a)** old; ~ **und jung** old and young; **seine ~en Eltern** his aged parents; **wie ~ bist du?** how old are you?; **mein älterer/ältester Bruder** my elder/eldest brother; **b)** *(nicht mehr frisch)* old; ~**es Brot** stale bread; **c)** *(vom letzten Jahr)* old; ~**e Äpfel/Kartoffeln** last year's apples/potatoes; **d)** *(langjährig)* long-standing ⟨*acquaintance*⟩; **e)** *(antik, klassisch)* ancient; **f)** *(vertraut)* old familiar ⟨*streets, sights, etc.*⟩; **ganz der/die ~e sein** be just the same

¹**Alt** der; ~**s,** ~**e** *(Musik)* alto; *(Frauenstimme)* contralto; *(im Chor)* contraltos *pl.*

²**Alt** das; ~**[s],** ~: *top fermented, dark beer*

Altar der; ~**[e]s,** **Altäre** altar

alt-, Alt-: ~**bau·wohnung** die flat *(Brit.)* or *(Amer.)* apartment in an old building; ~**bekannt** *Adj.* well-known; ~**bier** das *s.* ²**Alt**

Alte der/die; *adj. Dekl.* **a)** *(alter Mensch)* old man/woman; *Pl.* old people; **b)** *(salopp) (Vater, Ehemann)* old man *(coll.)*; *(Mutter, Ehefrau)* old woman *(coll.)*; *(Chef)* governor *(sl.)*; *(Chefin)* boss *(coll.)*; **die ~n** *(Eltern)* my/his *etc.* old man and old woman 4(coll.); **c)** *Pl. (Tiereltern)* parents

alt·ehrwürdig *Adj. (geh.)* venerable; time-honoured ⟨*customs*⟩; **Alt·englisch** das Old English

Alter das; ~**s,** ~: age; *(hohes ~)* old age; **im ~:** in one's old age; **im ~ von** at the age of; **älter 1.** *s.* **alt; 2.** *Adj. (nicht mehr jung)* elderly; **altern** *itr. V.; mit sein* age

alters-, Alters-: ~**genosse** der, ~**genossin** die contemporary; ~**gruppe** die age-group; ~**schwach** *Adj.* old and infirm ⟨*person*⟩; old and weak ⟨*animal*⟩; ~**schwäche** die; *o. Pl. (bei Menschen)* [old] age and infirmity; *(bei Tieren)* [old] age and weakness; ~**stufe** die age; ~**unterschied** der age difference; ~**versorgung** die provision for one's old age; *(System)* pension scheme

Altertum das; ~**s** antiquity *no art.*

Älteste der/die; *adj. Dekl.* **a)** *(Dorf~, Vereins~, Kirchen~ usw.)* elder; **b)** *(Sohn, Tochter)* eldest

alt-, Alt-: ~**griechisch** das classical or ancient Greek; ~**hochdeutsch** das Old High German; ~**klug;** ~**kluger,** ~**klugst...** **1.** *Adj.* precocious; **2.** *adv.* precociously; ~**last** die *(Ökologie)* old, improperly disposed of harmful waste; *(fig.)* inherited problem

ältlich *Adj.* rather elderly

alt-, Alt-: ~**modisch 1.** *Adj.* old-fashioned; **2.** *adv.* in an old-fashioned way; ~**rosa** *Adj.* old rose; ~**stadt** die old [part of the] town; ~**waren·händler** der second-hand dealer

Alu das; ~**s** *(ugs.)* aluminium; **Alufolie** die aluminium foil; **Aluminium** das; ~**s** aluminium

am *Präp. + Art.* **a)** = **an dem; b) Frankfurt am Main** Frankfurt on [the] Main; **am Marktplatz** on the market square; **am Meer/Fluß** by the sea/on *or* by the river; **am Anfang/Ende** at the beginning/end; **am 19. November** on 19 November; **am schnellsten laufen** run [the] fastest; **am Verwelken sein** be wilting

Amateur [ama'tø:ɐ̯] der; ~**s,** ~**e** amateur

Amazonas der; ~: Amazon

Amboß der; **Ambosses, Ambosse** anvil

ambulant *(Med.)* **1.** *Adj.* out-patient *attrib.*; **2.** *adv.* **jmdn. ~ behandeln** give sb. out-patient treatment; **Ambulanz** die; ~, ~**en a)** *(in Kliniken)* out-patient[s'] department; **b)** *(Krankenwagen)* ambulance

Ameise die; ~, ~**n** ant

Ameisen-: ~**bär** der ant-eater; ~**haufen** der anthill

amen *Adv.* amen; **Amen** das; ~**s,** ~: Amen

Amerika (das) ~**s** America; **Amerikaner** der; ~**s,** ~ **a)** American; **b)** *(Gebäck) small, flat iced cake*; **Amerikanerin** die; ~, ~**nen** American; **amerikanisch** *Adj.* American

Amino·säure die *(Chemie)* amino acid

Ammann der; ~**[e]s,** **Ammänner** *(schweiz.) (Gemeinde~, Bezirks~)* ≈ mayor; *(Land~)* cantonal president

Amme die; ~, ~**n** wet-nurse

Amnestie [amnɛsˈti:] die; ~, ~**n** amnesty; **amnestieren** *tr. V.* grant an amnesty to

Amöbe die; ~, ~n *(Biol.)* amoeba
Amok der: ~ **laufen** run amok;
Amok·läufer der madman
Ampel die; ~, ~n a) *(Verkehrs~)* traffic lights *pl.*; b) *(für Pflanzen)* hanging flowerpot
Amphibie [am'fi:bɪə] die; ~, ~n *(Zool.)* amphibian; **Amphibien·fahrzeug** das amphibious vehicle
Amphi·theater das amphitheatre
Ampulle die; ~, ~n *(Med.)* ampoule
Amputation die; ~, ~en *(Med.)* amputation; **amputieren** *tr. V.* amputate
Amsel die; ~, ~n blackbird
Amt das; ~|e|s, **Ämter** a) *(Stellung)* post; position; *(hohes politisches od. kirchliches ~)* office; **im ~ sein** be in office; b) *(Aufgabe)* task; job; c) *(Behörde)* office; d) *(Fernsprechvermittlung)* exchange; **amtieren** *itr. V.* a) hold office; b) *(vorübergehend)* act **(als** as); **amtlich** 1. *Adj.* a) official; *(ugs.: sicher)* definite; 2. *adv.* officially; **Amt·mann** der; *Pl.* ...männer od. ...leute, **Amt·männin** die; ~, ~nen senior civil servant
Amts-: ~**arzt** der medical officer; ~**gericht** das local *or* district court; ~**geschäfte** *Pl.* official duties; ~**leitung** die *(Fernspr.)* exchange line
Amulett das; ~|e|s, ~e amulet; charm
amüsant 1. *Adj.* entertaining; 2. *adv.* in an entertaining way; **amüsieren** 1. *refl. V.* a) *(sich vergnügen)* enjoy oneself; **sich mit jmdm. ~:** have fun *or* a good time with sb.; b) *(belustigt sein)* be amused; **sich über jmdn./etw. ~:** find sb./sth. funny; 2. *tr. V.* amuse
an 1. *Präp. mit Dat.* a) *(räumlich)* at; *(auf)* on; **Frankfurt an der Oder** Frankfurt on [the] Oder; **Tür an Tür** next door to one another; **an ... vorbei** past; b) *(zeitlich)* on; **an jedem Sonntag** every Sunday; **an Ostern** *(bes. südd.)* at Easter; c) **arm/reich an Vitaminen** low/rich in vitamins; **jmdn. an etw. erkennen** recognize sb. by sth.; **an etw. leiden** suffer from sth.; **an einer Krankheit sterben** die of a disease; d) **an |und für| sich** actually; 2. *Präp. mit Akk.* a) to; *(auf, gegen)* on; b) **an etw./ jmdn. glauben** believe in sth./sb.; **an etw. denken** think of sth.; **sich an etw. erinnern** remember sth.; 3. *Adv.* a) *(Verkehrsw.)* **Köln an:** 9.15 arriving Cologne 09.15; b) *(ugs.: in Betrieb)* on; **die Waschmaschine/der Fernseher** ist an the washing-machine/television is on; *s. auch* **ansein;** c) *(ugs.: ungefähr)* around; about; **an |die| 20 000 DM** around *or* about 20,000 DM
Analyse die; ~, ~n analysis; **analysieren** *tr. V.* analyse; **analytisch** 1. *Adj.* analytical; 2. *adv.* analytically
Ananas die; ~, ~ od. ~se pineapple
Anarchie die; ~, ~n anarchy; **Anarchist** der; ~en, ~en anarchist
Anatomie die; ~, ~n anatomy; **anatomisch** *Adj.* anatomical
an|bahnen 1. *tr. V.* initiate ⟨negotiations, talks, process, etc.⟩; develop ⟨relationship, connection⟩; 2. *refl. V.* ⟨development⟩ be in the offing; ⟨friendship, relationship⟩ start to develop
an|bändeln *itr. V.* **mit jmdm. ~** *(ugs.)* get off with sb. *(Brit. coll.)*; pick sb. up
An·bau der; *Pl.* **Anbauten** a) *o. Pl.* building; b) *(Gebäude)* extension; c) *o. Pl. (das Anpflanzen)* growing
an|bauen 1. *tr. V.* a) build on; b) *(anpflanzen)* grow; 2. *itr. V. (das Haus vergrößern)* build an extension
an·bei *Adv. (Amtsspr.)* herewith; **Rückporto ~:** return postage enclosed
an|beißen 1. *unr. tr. V.* bite into; take a bite of; 2. *unr. itr. V. (auch fig. ugs.)* bite
an|belangen *tr. V.* **was mich/dies** *usw.* **anbelangt** as far as I am/this matter is *etc.* concerned
an|beten *tr. V. (auch fig.)* worship
An·betracht der: **in ~ einer Sache** *(Gen.)* in view of sth.
an|betreffen *unr. tr. V. s.* **anbelangen**
an|betteln *tr. V.* **jmdn. ~:** beg from sb.; **jmdn. um etw. ~:** beg sb. for sth.
Anbetung die; ~, ~en *(auch fig.)* worship
an|biedern *refl. V.* **sich |bei jmdm.| ~:** curry favour [with sb.]
an|bieten 1. *unr. tr. V.* offer; **jmdm. etw. ~:** offer sb. sth.; 2. *unr. refl. V.* a) offer one's services; **sich ~, etw. zu tun** offer to do sth.; b) *(fig.)* ⟨possibility, solution⟩ suggest itself
an|binden *unr. tr. V.* tie [up] **(an +** *Dat. od. Akk.* to); tie up, moor ⟨boat⟩ **(an +** *Dat. od. Akk.* to); tether ⟨animal⟩ **(an +** *Dat. od. Akk.* to)
an|blasen *unr. tr. V.* a) blow at; b) *(anfachen)* blow on
An·blick der at sight; **an|blicken** *tr. V.* look at
an|blinzeln *tr. V.* a) blink at; b) *(zuzwinkern)* wink at

an|brechen 1. *unr. tr. V.* **a)** crack; **b)** *(öffnen)* open; **c)** *(zu verbrauchen beginnen)* break into ⟨supplies, reserves⟩; **2.** *unr. itr. V.; mit sein (geh.: beginnen)* ⟨dawn, day⟩ break; ⟨age, epoch⟩ dawn

an|brennen 1. *unr. tr. V. (anzünden)* light; **2.** *unr. itr. V.; mit sein* burn

an|bringen *unr. tr. V.* **a)** *(befestigen)* put up ⟨sign, aerial, curtain, plaque⟩ (**an** + *Dat.* on); **b)** *(äußern)* make ⟨request, complaint, comment⟩; **c)** *(zeigen)* demonstrate ⟨knowledge, experience⟩; **d)** *(ugs.: herbeibringen)* bring

An·bruch *der o. Pl. (geh.: Beginn)* dawn[ing]; **der ~ des Tages** daybreak

an|brüllen *tr. V. (ugs.)* bellow at

Andacht die; ~, ~en a) *o. Pl. (Sammlung)* rapt attention; *(im Gebet)* silent worship; **b)** *(Gottesdienst)* prayers *pl.*; **andächtig 1.** *Adj.* rapt; *(ins Gebet versunken)* devout; **2.** *adv.* with rapt attention; *(ins Gebet versunken)* devoutly

an|dauern *itr. V.* ⟨negotiations⟩ continue, go on; ⟨weather, rain⟩ last

andauernd 1. *Adj.* continual; constant; **2.** *adv.* continually; constantly

Anden *Pl.* **die ~:** the Andes

An·denken das; ~s, ~ a) *o. Pl.* memory; **zum ~ an jmdn./etw.** to remind you/us *etc.* of sb./sth.; **b)** *(Erinnerungsstück)* memento; *(Reise~)* souvenir

ander... *Indefinitpron.* **1.** *attr.* **a)** other; **ein ~er/eine ~e/ein ~es** another; **das Kleid gefällt mir nicht, haben Sie noch ~e/ein ~es?** I don't like that dress, do you have any others/another?; **jemand ~er** *od.* **~es** someone else; *(in Fragen)* anyone else; **niemand ~er** *od.* **~es** nobody else; **etwas ~es** something else; *(in Fragen)* anything else; **nichts ~es** nothing else; not anything else; **b)** *(verschieden)* different; **2.** *alleinstehend* **ein ~r/eine ~e:** another [one]; **nicht drängeln, einer nach dem ~n** don't push, one after the other; **ein ~er/eine ~e/ein ~es** another [one]; **ein|e|s nach dem ~|e|n** first things first; **ich will weder das eine noch das ~e** I don't want either; **anderen·falls** *Adv.* otherwise; **anderer·seits** *Adv.* on the other hand; **ander·mal** *Adv.* **ein ~:** another time; **andern·falls** *Adv.* otherwise

ändern 1. *tr. V.* change; alter; alter ⟨garment⟩; change ⟨person⟩; **2.** *refl. V.* change

anders *Adv.* **a)** *(verschieden)* ⟨think,

act, feel, do⟩ differently (**als** from *or esp. Brit.* to); ⟨be, look, sound, taste⟩ different (**als** from *or esp. Brit.* to); **es war alles ganz ~:** it was all quite different; **b)** *(sonst)* else; **niemand ~:** nobody else; **jemand ~:** someone else; *(in Fragen)* anyone else

anders-, Anders-: **~artig** *Adj.* different; **~farbig** *Adj.* different-coloured *attrib.;* **~gläubige der/die** person of a different religion; **~herum** *Adv.* the other way round *or (Amer.)* around; **~herum gehen/fahren** go/drive round *or (Amer.)* around the other way; **~wo** *Adv. (ugs.)* elsewhere; **~woher** *Adv. (ugs.)* from somewhere else; **~wohin** *Adv. (ugs.)* somewhere else

andert·halb *Bruchz.* one and a half; **~ Stunden** an hour and a half

Änderung die; ~, ~en change (*Gen.* in); alteration (*Gen.* to)

anderweitig 1. *Adj.* other; **2.** *adv.* in another way

an|deuten 1. *tr. V.* **a)** *(zu verstehen geben)* hint; **b)** *(nicht vollständig ausführen)* outline; *(kurz erwähnen)* indicate; **2.** *refl. V.* be indicated; **An·deutung die** hint

An·drang der; *o. Pl.* crowd; *(Gedränge)* crush

andre... *s.* **ander...**

an|drehen *tr. V.* **a)** *(einschalten)* turn on; **b) jmdm. etw. ~** *(ugs.)* palm sb. off with sth.

andrer·seits *Adv.* on the other hand

an|drohen *tr. V.* **jmdm. etw. ~:** threaten sb. with sth.; **An·drohung die** threat

an|drücken *tr. V.* press down

an|ecken *itr. V.; mit sein* **bei jmdm. ~** *(fig. ugs.)* rub sb. [up *(Brit.)*] the wrong way

an|eignen *refl. V.* **a)** appropriate; **b)** *(lernen)* acquire; learn

an·einander *Adv.* **~ denken** think of each other *or* one another; **~ vorbeigehen** pass each other *or* one another

aneinander: ~|binden *unr. tr. V.* tie together; **~|legen** *tr. V.* put *or* place next to each other *or* one another; **~|liegen** *unr. itr. V.* lie next to each other

Anekdote die; ~, ~n anecdote

an|ekeln *tr. V.* disgust

Anemone die; ~, ~n anemone

an|erkennen *unr. tr. V.* **a)** recognize ⟨country, record, verdict, qualification, *document*>; acknowledge ⟨*debt*⟩; accept ⟨*demand, bill, conditions, rules*⟩; allow ⟨*claim, goal*⟩; **b)** *(nicht leugnen)* acknowledge; **c)** *(würdigen)* appreciate; respect ⟨*viewpoint, opinion*⟩; **ein ~der Blick** an appreciative look; **an|erkennens·wert** *Adj.* commendable; **Anerkennung die; ~, ~en** *s.* **anerkennen: a)** recognition; acknowledgement; acceptance; allowance; **b)** acknowledgement; **c)** appreciation; respect *(Gen.* for)

an|fachen *tr. V.* fan; *(fig.)* arouse ⟨*anger, curiosity, enthusiasm*⟩; inflame ⟨*passion*⟩; stir up ⟨*hatred*⟩; inspire ⟨*hope*⟩; ferment ⟨*discord, war*⟩

an|fahren 1. *unr. tr. V.* **a)** run into; hit; **b)** *(herbeifahren)* deliver; **c)** *(ansteuern)* stop at ⟨*village etc.*⟩; *(ship)* put in at ⟨*port*⟩; **d)** *(zurechtweisen)* shout at; **2.** *unr. itr. V.; mit sein* **a)** *(starten)* start off; **b) angefahren kommen** come driving/riding up; **An·fahrt die a)** *(das Anfahren)* journey; **b)** *(Weg)* approach

An·fall der attack; *(epileptischer ~, fig.)* fit; **einen ~ bekommen** *od. (ugs.)* **kriegen** have an attack/a fit; **an·fallen 1.** *unr. tr. V.* attack; **2.** *unr. itr V.; mit sein* ⟨*costs*⟩ be incurred; ⟨*interest*⟩ accrue; ⟨*work*⟩ come up; **an·fällig** *Adj.* ⟨*person*⟩ with a delicate constitution; *(machine)* susceptible to faults; **gegen** *od.* **für etw. ~ sein** be susceptible to sth.

An·fang der beginning; start; *(erster Abschnitt)* beginning; **am** *od.* **zu ~:** at first; **von ~ an** from the outset; **~ 1984/der Woche** *usw.* at the beginning of 1984/of the week *etc.;* **an·fangen 1.** *unr. itr. V.* **a)** begin; start; **mit etw. ~:** start [on] sth.; **~, etw. zu tun** start to do sth.; **b)** *(zu sprechen ~)* begin; **von etw. ~:** start on about sth.; **c)** *(eine Stelle antreten)* start; **2.** *unr. tr. V.* **a)** begin; start; *(anbrechen)* start; **b)** *(machen)* do; **An·fänger der; ~s, ~:** beginner; **anfänglich** *Adj.* initial; **anfangs** *Adv.* at first; initially

Anfangs-: ~buchstabe der initial [letter]; **~stadium das** initial stage; **an|fassen 1.** *tr. V.* **a)** *(fassen, halten)* take hold of; **b)** *(berühren)* touch; **c)** **jmdn. ~** *(an der Hand nehmen)* take sb.'s hand; **d)** *(packen)* tackle ⟨*problem, task, etc.*⟩; **e)** *(behandeln)* treat ⟨*person*⟩; **2.** *itr. V.* |**mit**| **~:** lend a hand **anfechtbar** *Adj.: s.* **anfechten a:** disputable; contestable; challengeable;

an|fechten *unr. tr. V.* **a)** dispute ⟨*statement, contract*⟩; contest ⟨*will*⟩; challenge ⟨*decision, law, opinion*⟩; **b)** *(beunruhigen)* trouble

an|fertigen *tr. V.* make

an|feuchten *tr. V.* moisten ⟨*lips, stamp*⟩; dampen ⟨*ironing, cloth, etc.*⟩

an|feuern *tr. V.* spur on

an|flehen *tr. V.* beseech; implore

an|fliegen 1. *unr. itr. V.; mit sein* fly in; **angeflogen kommen** come flying in; **gegen den Wind ~:** fly into the wind; **2.** *unr. tr. V.* fly to ⟨*city, country, airport*⟩; **An·flug der a)** approach; **b)** *(Hauch)* hint; **c)** *(Anwandlung)* fit; **in einem ~ von Großzügigkeit** in a fit of generosity

an|fordern *tr. V.* ask for; order ⟨*goods, materials*⟩; send for ⟨*ambulance*⟩; **An·forderung die a)** *o. Pl.* *(das Anfordern)* request *(Gen.* for); **b)** *(Anspruch)* demand

An·frage die inquiry; *(Parl.)* question; **an|fragen** *itr. V.* inquire; ask

an|freunden *refl. V.* become friends

an|fügen *tr. V.* add

an|fühlen *refl. V.* feel

an|führen *tr. V.* **a)** lead; **b)** *(zitieren)* quote; **c)** *(nennen)* give ⟨*example, reason, details, proof*⟩; **d)** *(ugs.: hereinlegen)* have on *(Brit. coll.);* dupe; **An·führer der** leader; *(Rädelsführer)* ringleader; **An·führung die a)** *(das Zitieren, Zitat)* quotation; **b)** *(Nennung)* giving

Anführungs-: ~strich der, ~zeichen das quotation-mark

An·gabe die a) *(das Mitteilen)* giving; **b)** *(Information)* piece of information; **~n** information *sing.;* **c)** *(Ballspiele)* service; serve; **an|geben 1.** *unr. tr. V.* **a)** give ⟨*reason*⟩; declare ⟨*income, dutiable goods*⟩; name ⟨*witness*⟩; **b)** *(bestimmen)* set ⟨*course, direction*⟩; **den Takt ~:** keep time; **2.** *unr. itr. V.* **a)** *(prahlen)* boast; brag; *(sich angeberisch benehmen)* show off; **b)** *(Ballspiele)* serve; **Angeber der; ~s, ~** braggart; **Angeberei die; ~:** showing-off; **angeblich 1.** *Adj.* alleged; **2.** *adv.* supposedly; allegedly **an·geboren** *Adj.* innate ⟨*characteristic*⟩; congenital ⟨*disease*⟩

An·gebot das a) offer; **b)** *(Wirtsch.)* supply; *(Sortiment)* range

an·gebracht *Adj.* appropriate

an·gegriffen *Adj.* weakened ⟨*health, stomach*⟩; strained ⟨*nerves, voice*⟩

angeheitert *Adj.* tipsy

an|gehen 1. *unr. itr. V.; mit sein* a) *(radio, light, heating)* come on; *(fire)* catch; b) *(anwachsen, wachsen)(plant)* take root; e) **es mag noch ~:** it's [just about] acceptable; f) **gegen etw./jmdn. ~:** fight sth./sb.; 2. *unr. tr. V.* a) *(angreifen)* attack; b) *(in Angriff nehmen)* tackle *(problem, difficulty);* take *(fence, bend);* c) *(bitten)* ask (**um** for); d) *(betreffen)* concern; **das geht dich nichts an** it's none of your business; **angehend** *Adj.* budding; *(zukünftig)* prospective

an|gehören *itr. V.* **jmdm./einer Sache ~:** belong to sb./sth.; **der Regierung/ einer Familie ~:** be a member of the government/a family; **an·gehörig** *Adj.* belonging (*Dat.* to); **Angehörige der/die;** *adj. Dekl.* a) *(Verwandte)* relative; relation; b) *(Mitglied)* member

Angeklagte der/die; *adj. Dekl.* accused; defendant

Angel die; ~, ~n a) fishing-rod; b) *(Tür~, Fenster~ usw.)* hinge; **etw. aus den ~n heben** *(fig.)* turn sth. upside down

An·gelegenheit die matter; *(Aufgabe, Problem)* affair

Angel·haken der fish-hook; **angeln** 1. *tr. V. (zu fangen suchen)* fish for; *(fangen)* catch. 2. *itr. V.* angle; fish; **Angel·rute die** fishing-rod

Angel·sachse der Anglo-Saxon

Angel·schnur die fishing-line

an·gemessen *Adj.* appropriate; reasonable, fair *(price, fee)*

an·genehm 1. *Adj.* pleasant; **~e Reise/Ruhe!** [have a] pleasant journey/ have a good rest; **|sehr| ~!** delighted to meet you; 2. *adv.* pleasantly

an·gesehen *Adj.* respected

angesichts *Präp. mit Gen. (geh.)* a) in the face of; b) *(fig.: in Anbetracht)* in view of

angespannt *Adj.* a) close *(attention);* taut *(nerves);* b) tense *(situation);* tight *(market, economic situation)*

angestellt *Adj.* **bei jmdm. ~ sein** be employed by sb.; work for sb.; **Angestellte der/die;** *adj. Dekl.* [salaried] employee

an·getan *Adj.* **von jmdm./etw. ~ sein** be taken with sb./sth.

an·getrunken *Adj.* [slightly] drunk

an·gewiesen *Adj.* **auf jmdn./etw. ~ sein** have to rely on sb./sth.

an|gewöhnen *tr. V.* **jmdm. etw. ~:** get sb. used to sth.; **jmdm. ~, etw. zu tun** get sb. used to doing sth.; **sich *(Dat.)* etw. ~:** get into the habit of sth.; **|es| sich *(Dat.)* ~, etw. zu tun** get into the habit of doing sth.; **An·gewohnheit die** habit

an|gleichen 1. *unr. tr. V.* **etw. einer Sache *(Dat.)* od. an etw. *(Akk.)* ~:** bring sth. into line with sth.; 2. *unr. refl. V.* **sich jmdm./einer Sache od. an jmdn./etw. ~:** become like sb./sth.; **An·gleichung die: die ~ der Löhne an die Preise** bringing wages into line with prices

Angler der; ~s, ~angler

Anglistik die; ~: English studies *pl.,* no art.

Angola (das); ~s Angola

Angora-: ~katze die angora cat; **~wolle die** angora [wool]

an|greifen 1. *unr. tr. V.* a) *(auch fig.)* attack; b) *(schwächen)* affect *(health, heart, stomach, intestine, voice);* weaken *(person);* 2. *unr. itr. V. (auch fig.)* attack; **An·greifer der** *(auch fig.)* attacker; **An·griff der** a) attack; **zum ~ blasen** *(auch fig.)* sound the attack; b) **etw. in ~ nehmen** tackle sth.

angst *Adj.* **jmdm. ist/wird |es| ~ |und bange|** sb. is/becomes frightened; **Angst die; ~, Ängste** a) *(Furcht)* fear; **~ bekommen** *od. (ugs.)* **kriegen** become frightened; **~ haben** be frightened (**vor** + *Dat.* of); b) *(Sorge)* anxiety; **~ haben** be anxious (**um** about); **keine ~, ich vergesse es schon nicht!** don't worry, I won't forget [it]!; **ängstigen** 1. *tr. V.* frighten; *(beunruhigen)* worry; 2. *refl. V.* be frightened; *(sich sorgen)* worry; **ängstlich** 1. *Adj.* anxious; 2. *adv.* anxiously; **Ängstlichkeit die; ~:** timidity

an|gucken *tr. V. (ugs.)* look at; **sich *(Dat.)* etw./jmdn. ~:** have a look at sth./sb.

an|gurten *tr. V.* strap in; **sich ~:** put on one's seat-belt

an|haben *unr. tr. V.* a) *(ugs.: am Körper tragen)* have on; b) **jmdm./einer Sache etwas ~ können** be able to harm sb./sth.

an|halten 1. *unr. tr. V.* a) stop; b) *(auffordern)* urge; 2. *unr. itr. V.* a) stop; b) *(andauern)* go on; last; **anhaltend** 1. *Adj.* constant; continuous; 2. *adv.* constantly; continuously; **An·halter der** hitch-hiker; **per ~ fahren** hitch[-hike]; **An·halterin die** hitch-hiker; **Anhalts·punkt der** clue (**für** to); *(für eine Vermutung)* grounds *pl.*

an·hand 1. *Präp. mit Gen.* with the help of; 2. *Adv.* ~ von with the help of
An·hang der a) *(Buchw.)* appendix; b) *(Anhängerschaft)* following; c) *(Verwandtschaft)* family; an|hängen 1. *tr. V.* a) hang up (an + *Akk.* on); b) *(ankuppeln)* couple on (an + *Akk.* to); hitch up ⟨*trailer*⟩ (an + *Akk.* to); c) *(anfügen)* add (an + *Akk.* to); 2. *refl. V.* a) hang on (an + *Akk.* to); b) *(ugs.: sich anschließen)* sich |an jmdn. *od.* bei jmdm.| ~: tag along [with sb.] *(coll.)*; An·hänger der a) *(Mensch)* supporter; b) *(Wagen)* trailer; c) *(Schmuckstück)* pendant; d) *(Schildchen)* tag; Anhängerschaft die; ~, ~en supporters *pl.*; anhänglich *Adj.* devoted ⟨*dog, friend*⟩; Anhänglichkeit die; ~: devotion
an|hauchen *tr. V.* breathe on ⟨*mirror, glasses*⟩; blow on ⟨*fingers, hands*⟩
an|häufen *tr. V.* accumulate; Anhäufung die accumulation
an|heben *unr. tr. V.* a) lift [up]; b) *(erhöhen)* raise ⟨*prices, wages, etc.*⟩
an|heften *tr. V.* attach ⟨*label, list*⟩; put up ⟨*sign, notice*⟩
anheim|stellen *(geh.) tr. V.* |es| jmdm. ~, etw. zu tun leave it to sb. to do sth.
An·hieb der: auf ~ *(ugs.)* straight off
an|himmeln *tr. V.* worship
An·höhe die rise
an|hören 1. *tr. V.* listen to; sich *(Dat.)* jmdn./etw. ~: listen to sb./sth.; 2. *refl. V.* sound
animieren *tr. V.* encourage
Anis der; ~|es| aniseed
Ank. *Abk.* Ankunft arr.
An·kauf der purchase; an|kaufen *tr. V.* purchase; buy
Anker der; ~s, ~ anchor; vor ~ gehen/liegen drop anchor/lie at anchor; ~ werfen drop anchor; ankern *itr. V.* a) anchor; b) *(vor Anker liegen)* be anchored; Anker·platz der anchorage
An·klage die a) charge; unter ~ stehen have been charged (wegen with); b) *(~vertretung)* prosecution; Anklage·bank die dock; auf der ~ sitzen *(auch fig.)* be in the dock; an|klagen *tr. V.* a) *(Rechtsw.)* charge *(Gen.,* wegen with); accuse; b) *(geh.: beschuldigen)* accuse; An·kläger der prosecutor
an|klammern 1. *tr. V.* peg *(Brit.)*, pin *(Amer.)* ⟨*clothes, washing*⟩; clip ⟨*sheet etc.*⟩; *(mit Heftklammern)* staple ⟨*sheet etc.*⟩; 2. *refl. V.* sich an jmdn./etw. ~: cling to sb./sth.

An·klang der: |bei jmdm.| ~ finden meet with [sb.'s] approval
an|kleben 1. *tr. V.* stick up ⟨*poster, etc.*⟩; 2. *itr. V.; mit sein* stick
an|kleiden *tr. V. (geh.)* dress; sich ~: dress
an|klopfen *itr. V.* knock
an|knüpfen 1. *tr. V.* a) tie on (an + *Akk.* to); b) *(beginnen)* start up ⟨*conversation*⟩; establish ⟨*relations, business links*⟩; form ⟨*relationship*⟩; 2. *itr. V.* an etw. *(Akk.)* ~: take sth. up; ich knüpfe dort an, wo ... I'll pick up where ...
an|kommen *unr. itr. V.; mit sein* a) *(eintreffen)* arrive; seid ihr gut angekommen? did you arrive safely?; b) |bei jmdm.| |gut| ~ *(fig. ugs.)* go down [very] well [with sb.]; c) gegen jmdn./etw. ~: be able to deal with sb./fight sth.; d) *unpers.* es kommt auf jmdn./etw. an *(jmd./etw. ist ausschlaggebend)* it depends on sb./sth.; es kommt auf etw. *(Akk.)* an *(etw. ist wichtig)* sth. matters *(Dat.* to); es kommt |ganz| darauf *od.* drauf an *(ugs.)* it [all] depends; e) *unpers.* es darauf *od.* drauf ~ lassen *(ugs.)* chance it; es auf etw. *(Akk.)* ~ lassen [be prepared to] risk sth.
an|koppeln 1. *tr. V.* couple ⟨*carriage*⟩ up; hitch ⟨*trailer*⟩ up; dock ⟨*spacecraft*⟩; 2. *itr. V.* ⟨*spacecraft*⟩ dock
an|kreuzen *tr. V.* mark with a cross
an|kündigen 1. *tr. V.* announce; 2. *refl. V.* announce itself; An·kündigung die announcement
Ankunft die; ~, Ankünfte arrival; „~" 'arrivals'
Ankunfts-: ~halle die arrival[s] hall; ~tafel die arrivals board
an|kuppeln *tr. V. s.* ankoppeln 1
an|kurbeln *tr. V.* a) crank [up]; b) *(fig.)* boost ⟨*economy, production, etc.*⟩
Anl. *Abk.* Anlage encl.
an|lächeln *tr. V.* smile at; an|lachen 1. *tr. V.* smile at. 2. *refl. V.* sich *(Dat.)* jmdn. ~ *(ugs.)* get off with sb. *(Brit. coll.)*; pick sb. up
An·lage die a) *o. Pl. (das Anlegen) (einer Kartei)* establishment; *(eines Parks, Gartens usw.)* laying out; *(eines Parkplatzes, Stausees)* construction; b) *(Grün~)* park; *(um ein Schloß usw. herum)* grounds *pl.*; c) *(Einrichtung)* facilities *pl.*; militärische ~n military installations; d) *(Werk)* plant; e) *(Musik~, Lautsprecher~ usw.)* system; f) *(Geld~)* investment; g) *(Konzeption)* conception; *(Struktur)* structure; h)

(Veranlagung) aptitude; *(Neigung)* tendency; **i)** *(Beilage zu einem Brief)* enclosure

Anlaß der; **Anlasses, Anlässe a)** cause (zu for); **etw. zum ~ nehmen, etw. zu tun** take sth. as an opportunity to do sth.; **aus aktuellem ~:** because of current events; **b)** *(Gelegenheit)* occasion

an|lassen 1. *unr. tr. V.* **a)** leave ⟨*light, radio, heating, etc.*⟩ on; leave ⟨*engine*⟩ running; leave ⟨*candle*⟩ burning; **b)** keep ⟨*coat, gloves, etc.*⟩ on; **c)** *(in Gang setzen)* start [up]; **2.** *unr. refl. V.* **sich gut/schlecht ~:** get off to a good/bad start; **Anlasser** der; **~s, ~** starter

an·läßlich *Präp. mit Gen.* on the occasion of

An·lauf der **a)** run-up; **|mehr| ~ nehmen** take [more of] a run-up; **b)** *(Versuch)* attempt; **beim** *od.* **im ersten/ dritten ~:** at the first/third attempt; **an|laufen 1.** *unr. itr. V.; mit sein* **a)** **angelaufen kommen** come running along; *(auf einen zu)* come running up; **b) gegen jmdn./etw. ~:** run at sb./ sth.; **c)** *(Anlauf nehmen)* take a run-up; **d)** *(zu laufen beginnen)* ⟨*engine*⟩ start [up]; *(fig.)* ⟨*film*⟩ open; ⟨*production, campaign, search*⟩ start; **e) rot/ dunkel** *usw.* **~:** go *or* turn red/dark *etc.;* **f)** *(beschlagen)* mist up; **2.** *unr. tr. V.* put in at ⟨*port*⟩

an|legen 1. *tr. V.* **a)** put *or* lay ⟨*domino, card*⟩ [down] **(an** + *Akk.* next to); place, position ⟨*ruler, protractor*⟩ **(an** + *Akk.* on); put ⟨*ladder*⟩ up **(an** + *Akk.* against); **b) die Flügel/Ohren ~:** close its wings/lay its ears back; **die Arme ~:** put one's arms to one's sides; **c)** *(geh.: anziehen, umlegen)* don; **d)** *(schaffen, erstellen)* lay out ⟨*town, garden, plantation, street*⟩; start ⟨*file, album*⟩; compile ⟨*statistics, index*⟩; **e)** *(investieren)* invest; **f)** *(ausgeben)* spend **(für** on); **g) es darauf ~, etw. zu tun be** determined to do sth.; **2.** *itr. V.* **a)** *(landen)* moor; **b)** *(Kartenspiele)* lay a card/cards; **c)** *(Domino)* play [a domino/dominoes]; **d)** *(das Gewehr~)* aim **(auf** + *Akk.* at); **3.** *refl. V.* **sich mit jmdm. ~:** pick an argument with sb.

Anlege-: **~platz** der berth; **~steg** der jetty

an|lehnen 1. *tr. V.* **a)** lean **(an** + *Akk. od. Dat.* against); **b)** leave ⟨*door, window*⟩ slightly open; **2.** *refl. V.* **sich |an jmdn.** *od.* **jmdm./etw./ ~:** lean [on sb./ against sth.]; **Anlehnung** die; **~,**

~en: in ~an *(+ Akk.)* in imitation of; following

Anleihe die; **~, ~n** loan

an|leiten *tr. V.* instruct; **An·leitung** die instructions *pl.*

an|lernen *tr. V.* train

an|liegen *unr. itr. V.* **a)** ⟨*pullover etc.*⟩ fit tightly; **b)** *(ugs.: vorliegen)* be on; **An·liegen das; ~s, ~** *(Bitte)* request; *(Angelegenheit)* matter; **anliegend** *Adj.* **a)** *(angrenzend)* adjacent; **b)** *(beiliegend)* enclosed; **Anlieger** der; **~s, ~:** resident; **„~ frei"** 'except for access'

an|locken *tr. V.* attract ⟨*customers, tourists, etc.*⟩; lure ⟨*bird, animal*⟩

an|lügen *tr. V.* lie to

an|machen *tr. V.* **a)** put ⟨*light, radio, heating*⟩ on; light ⟨*fire*⟩; **b)** mix ⟨*cement, plaster, paint, etc.*⟩; dress ⟨*salad*⟩

an|malen *tr. V.* paint

an|maßen *refl. V.* **sich** *(Dat.)* **etw. ~:** claim sth. [for oneself]; **an·maßend 1.** *Adj.* presumptuous; *(arrogant)* arrogant; **2.** *adv.* presumptuously; *(arrogant)* arrogantly; **Anmaßung** die; **~, ~en** presumption; *(Arroganz)* arrogance

an|melden *tr. V.* **a)** *(als Teilnehmer)* enrol **(zu** for); **sich ~:** enrol **(zu** for); **b)** *(melden, anzeigen)* license ⟨*radio, television*⟩; apply for ⟨*patent*⟩; register ⟨*domicile, car, trade mark*⟩; **sich ~:** register one's new address; **c)** *(ankündigen)* announce; **sind Sie angemeldet?** do you have an appointment?; **sich beim Arzt ~:** make an appointment to see the doctor; **d)** *(geltend machen)* express ⟨*reservation, doubt, wish*⟩; put forward ⟨*demand*⟩; **An·meldung** die **a)** *(zur Teilnahme)* enrolment; **b)** *s.* **anmelden b:** licensing; application *(Gen.* for); registration; **c)** *(Ankündigung)* announcement; *(beim Arzt, Rechtsanwalt usw.)* making an appointment

an|merken *tr. V.* **a) jmdm. seinen Ärger/seine Verlegenheit** *usw.* **~:** notice that sb. is annoyed/embarrassed *etc.;* **man merkt ihm |nicht| an, daß er krank ist** you can|not| tell that he is ill; **sich nichts ~ lassen** not let it show; **b)** *(geh.: bemerken)* note; **Anmerkung** die; **~, ~en a)** *(Fußnote)* note; **b)** *(geh.: Bemerkung)* comment

An·mut die; **~** *(geh.)* grace; **an·mutig** *(geh.)* **1.** *Adj.* graceful ⟨*girl, movement, dance*⟩; charming, delightful

⟨*girl, smile, picture, landscape*⟩; **2.** *adv.* ⟨*move, dance*⟩ gracefully; ⟨*smile, greet*⟩ charmingly

an|nähen *tr. V.* sew on

an|nähern 1. *refl. V.* get closer *(Dat.* to sth); **2.** *tr. V.* bring closer (*Dat.* to);

annähernd 1. *Adv.* almost; *(ungefähr)* approximately; **2.** *adj.* approximate

Annahme die; ~, ~n a) *(das Annehmen)* acceptance; b) *(Vermutung)* assumption; **in der** ~, **daß** ...: on the assumption that...; **annehmbar 1.** *Adj.* a) acceptable; b) *(recht gut)* reasonable; **2.** *adv.* reasonably [well]; **an|nehmen 1.** *unr. tr. V.* a) accept; take; accept ⟨*alms, invitation, condition, help*⟩; take ⟨*food, telephone call*⟩; accept, take up ⟨*offer, challenge*⟩; b) *(Sport)* take ⟨*ball, pass, etc.*⟩; c) *(billigen)* approve; d) *(aufnehmen)* take on ⟨*worker, patient, pupil*⟩; e) *(hinnehmen)* accept ⟨*fate, verdict, punishment*⟩; f) *(adoptieren)* adopt; g) *(haften lassen)* take ⟨*dye, ink*⟩; h) *(sich aneignen)* adopt ⟨*habit, mannerism, name, attitude*⟩; i) *(bekommen)* take on ⟨*look, appearance, form, dimension*⟩; j) *(vermuten, voraussetzen)* assume; **angenommen, |daß|** ...: assuming [that] ...; **2.** *unr. refl. V. (geh.)* **sich jmds./einer Sache** ~: look after sb./sth.; **Annehmlichkeit die;** ~, ~en comfort; *(Vorteil)* advantage

annektieren *tr. V.* annex

Annonce [a'nõːsə] **die;** ~, ~n advertisement; advert *(Brit. coll.);* **annoncieren** *itr. V.* advertise

annullieren *tr. V.* annul

anonym 1. *Adj.* anonymous; **2.** *adv.* anonymously; **Anonymität die;** ~: anonymity

Anorak der; ~s, ~s anorak

an|ordnen *tr. V.* a) *(arrangieren)* arrange; b) *(befehlen)* order; **An·ordnung die** s. **anordnen:** a) arrangement; b) order

an·organisch *Adj.* inorganic

an|packen 1. *tr. V.* a) *(ugs.: anfassen)* grab hold of; b) *(angehen)* tackle; **2.** *itr. V.* |**mit**| ~ *(ugs.: mithelfen)* lend a hand

an|passen 1. *tr. V.* a) *(passend machen)* fit; b) *(abstimmen)* suit *(Dat.* to); **2.** *refl. V.* adapt [oneself] *(Dat.* to); ⟨*animal*⟩ adapt; **Anpassung die;** ~, ~en adaptation (**an** + *Akk.* to); **anpassungs·fähig** *Adj.* adaptable

an|pfeifen 1. *unr. tr. V.* **das Spiel/die zweite Halbzeit** ~: blow the whistle to start the game/the second half; **2.** *unr. itr. V.* blow the whistle; **An·pfiff der** a) *(Sport)* whistle for the start of play; b) *(salopp: Zurechtweisung)* bawling-out *(coll.)*

an|pflanzen *tr. V.* a) plant; b) *(anbauen)* grow

an|pöbeln *tr. V. (ugs.)* abuse

an|prangern *tr. V.* denounce (**als** as)

an|preisen *unr. tr. V.* extol

An·probe die fitting; **an|probieren** *tr. V.* try on

an|rechnen *tr. V.* a) count; b) jmdm. etw. ~ *(in Rechnung stellen)* charge sb. for sth.

An·recht das right; **ein** ~ **auf etw.** *(Akk.)* **haben** be entitled to sth.

An·rede die form of address; **an|reden** *tr. V.* address

an|regen *tr. V.* a) stimulate ⟨*imagination, digestion*⟩; whet ⟨*appetite*⟩; b) *(ermuntern)* prompt; *(vorschlagen)* propose; **anregend** *Adj.* stimulating; **An·regung die** a) s. **anregen** a: stimulation; whetting; b) *(Denkanstoß)* stimulus; c) *(Vorschlag)* proposal

an|reichern 1. *tr. V.* enrich; **2.** *refl. V.* accumulate

An·reise die journey [there/here]; **an|reisen** *itr. V.;* mit sein travel there/here; **mit der Bahn** ~: go/come by train

An·reiz der incentive

an|rempeln *tr. V.* barge into; *(absichtlich)* jostle

Anrichte die; ~, ~n sideboard; **an|richten** *tr. V.* a) arrange ⟨*food*⟩; *(servieren)* serve; b) cause ⟨*disaster, confusion, devastation, etc.*⟩

anrüchig *Adj.* a) disreputable; b) *(unanständig)* indecent

an|rücken *itr. V.;* mit sein ⟨*troops*⟩ advance; ⟨*firemen, police*⟩ move in

An·ruf der call; **Anruf·beantworter der;** ~s, ~: [telephone-]answering machine; **an|rufen** *unr. tr. V.* a) call or shout to ⟨*friend, passer-by*⟩; call ⟨*sleeping person*⟩; b) *(geh.: angehen, bitten)* appeal to ⟨*person, court*⟩ (**um** for); call upon ⟨*God*⟩; c) auch *itr.* *(telefonisch* ~*)* call; **Anrufer der;** ~s, ~: caller

an|rühren *tr. V.* a) touch; b) *(bereiten)* mix

ans *Präp.* + *Art.* a) = **an das;** b) **sich** ~ **Arbeiten machen** set to work

An·sage die announcement; **an|sagen** tr. V. a) announce; b) (Kartenspiele) bid

an|sammeln 1. tr. V. accumulate; amass ⟨riches, treasure⟩; 2. refl. V. accumulate; (fig.) ⟨anger, excitement⟩ build up; **An·sammlung** die a) collection; b) (Auflauf) crowd

ansässig Adj. resident

An·satz der (erstes Zeichen, Beginn) beginnings pl.

an|schaffen tr. V. [sich (Dat.)] etw. ~ get [oneself] sth.; **An·schaffung** die purchase

an|schalten tr. V. switch on

an|schauen tr. V. (bes. südd., österr., schweiz.) s. ansehen; **anschaulich** 1. vivid; 2. adv. vividly; **Anschauung** die; ~, ~en a) (Wahrnehmung) experience; b) (Auffassung) view

An·schein der appearance; **allem** od. **dem ~ nach** to all appearances; **an·scheinend** Adv. apparently

an|schieben unr. tr. V. push ⟨vehicle⟩

an|schießen unr. tr. V. shoot and wound

An·schlag der a) (Bekanntmachung) notice; (Plakat) poster; b) (Attentat) assassination attempt; (auf ein Gebäude, einen Zug o.ä.) attack; c) (Texterfassung) keystroke; **d) mit dem Gewehr im ~:** with rifle/rifles levelled; **an|schlagen** unr. tr. V. put up, ⟨notice, announcement, message⟩ (**an** + Akk. on); b) (beschädigen) chip

an|schließen 1. unr. tr. V. a) connect (**an** + Akk. od. Dat. to); connect up ⟨electrical device⟩; b) (festschließen) lock, secure (**an** + Dat. od. Akk. to); 2. unr. refl. V. sich jmdm./einer Sache ~: join sb./sth.; **An·schluß** der connection; **Anschluß·zug** der connecting train

an|schnallen tr. V. put on ⟨skis, skates⟩; sich ~ (im Auto) put on one's seatbelt; (im Flugzeug) fasten one's seatbelt

an|schrauben tr. V. screw on (**an** + Akk. to)

an|schreien unr. tr. V. shout at

An·schrift die address

Anschuldigung die; ~, ~en accusation

an|schwellen unr. itr. V.; mit sein a) swell [up]; (fig.) swell; ⟨water, river⟩ rise; b) (lauter werden) grow louder; ⟨noise⟩ rise

an|schwemmen tr. V. wash ashore

an|sehen unr. tr. V. a) look at; watch ⟨television programme⟩; see ⟨play, film⟩; **jmdn. groß/böse ~:** stare at sb./give sb. an angry look; **hübsch** usw. **anzusehen sein** be pretty etc. to look at; **sieh |mal| |einer| an!** (ugs.) well, I never! (coll.); b) (erkennen) **man sieht ihm sein Alter nicht an** he does not look his age; **man sieht ihr die Strapazen an** she's showing the strain; c) (zusehen bei) etw. |mit| ~: watch sth.; **das kann man doch nicht |mit| ~:** I/you can't just stand by and watch that; **Ansehen** das; ~s [high] standing; **an·sehnlich** Adj. a) (beträchtlich) considerable; b) (gut aussehend, stattlich) handsome

an|sein unr. itr. V.; mit sein (ugs.)⟨light, gas, etc.⟩ be on

an|setzen tr. V. a) (in die richtige Stellung bringen) position ⟨ladder, jack, drill, saw⟩; b) (anfügen) attach, put on (**an** + Akk. od. Dat. to); c) (festlegen) fix ⟨meeting etc.⟩ (**für, auf** + Akk. for); fix, set ⟨deadline, date, price⟩; d) (veranschlagen) estimate; e) (anrühren) mix

An·sicht die a) (Meinung) opinion; view; **meiner ~ nach** in my opinion or view; b) (Bild) view; **Ansichts·karte** die picture postcard

an|spannen 1. tr. V. a) harness ⟨horse etc.⟩ (**an** + Akk. to); yoke up ⟨oxen⟩ (**an** + Akk. to); hitch up ⟨carriage, cart, etc.⟩ (**an** + Akk. to); b) (anstrengen) strain; **An·spannung** die strain

an|spielen itr. V. **auf jmdn./etw. ~:** allude to sb./sth.; **Anspielung** die; ~, ~en allusion (**auf** + Akk. to); (verächtlich, böse) insinuation (**auf** + Akk. about)

An·sporn der incentive; **an|spornen** tr. V. spur on

An·sprache die speech; address; **an|sprechen** 1. unr. tr. V. a) speak to; b) (gefallen) appeal to; 2. unr. itr. V. (reagieren) respond (**auf** + Akk. to)

an|springen 1. unr. itr. V.; mit sein ⟨car, engine⟩ start; 2. unr. tr. V. jump up at

An·spruch der a) claim; (Forderung) demand; **[keine] Ansprüche stellen** make [no] demands; **in ~ nehmen** take advantage of ⟨offer⟩; exercise ⟨right⟩; take up ⟨time⟩; b) (Anrecht) right

an·spruchs-: ~**los** 1. Adj. a) (genügsam) undemanding; b) (schlicht) unpretentious; 2. adv. a) (genügsam) undemandingly; ⟨live⟩ modestly; b) (schlicht) unpretentiously; ~**voll** 1. Adj. discriminating ⟨reader, audience, *gourmet*); *(schwierig)* demanding; ambitious *(subject)*

an|spucken *tr. V.* spit at

Anstalt die; ~, ~en institution

An·stand der *o. Pl.* decency; **an·ständig 1.** *Adj.* **a)** decent; *(ehrbar)* respectable; **2.** *adv.* decently; *(ordentlich)* properly

an|starren *tr. V.* stare at

an·statt *Konj.* ~ **zu arbeiten/~, daß er arbeitet** instead of working

an|stecken 1. *tr. V.* **a)** pin on *(badge, brooch)*; put on *(ring)*; **b)** *(infizieren, auch fig.)* infect; **2.** *itr. V.* be infectious; **ansteckend** *Adj.* infectious; *(durch Berührung)* contagious; **Ansteckung die; ~, ~en** infection; *(durch Berührung)* contagion

an|stehen *unr. itr. V. (Schlange stehen)* queue [up], *(Amer.)* stand in line **(nach for)**

an·stelle 1. *Präp. mit Gen.* instead of; **2.** *Adv.* ~ **von** instead of

an|stellen 1. *refl. V.* queue [up], *(Amer.)* stand in line **(nach for); 2.** *tr. V.* **a)** *(aufdrehen)* turn on; **b)** *(einschalten)* switch on; **c)** *(einstellen)* employ; **An·stellung die** **a)** *o. Pl.* employment; **b)** *(Stellung)* job

Anstieg der; ~|e|s rise, increase **(+ Gen. in)**

an|stiften *tr. V.* incite; **An·stifter der, An·stifterin die** instigator; **An·stiftung die** incitement

an|stimmen *tr. V.* start singing *(song)*; start playing *(piece of music)*; **ein Geschrei ~:** start shouting

An·stoß der **a)** stimulus **(zu for); den |ersten| ~ zu etw. geben** initiate sth.; **b)** ~ **erregen** cause offence **(bei to); |keinen| ~ an etw.** *(Dat.)* **nehmen** [not] object to sth.; **an|stoßen 1.** *unr. itr. V.* **a)** *mit sein* **an etw.** *(Akk.)* ~**:** bump into sth.; **b)** |**mit den Gläsern|** ~**:** clink glasses; **auf jmdn./etw.** ~**:** drink to sb./sth.; **2.** *unr. tr. V.* **jmdn./etw.** ~**:** give sb./sth. a push; **jmdn. aus Versehen** ~**:** knock into sb. inadvertently; **anstößig 1.** *Adj.* offensive; **2.** *adv.* offensively

an|strahlen *tr. V.* **a)** illuminate; *(mit Scheinwerfer)* floodlight; **b)** *(anblicken)* beam at

an|streben *tr. V. (geh.)* aspire to; *(mit großer Anstrengung)* strive for

an|streichen *unr. tr. V.* **a)** paint; **b)** *(markieren)* mark

an|strengen 1. *refl. V.* make an effort; **sich mehr/sehr** ~**:** make more of an ef-

fort/a great effort; **2.** *tr. V.* strain *(eyes, ears, voice)*; be a strain on *(person)*; **seine Phantasie** ~**:** exercise one's imagination; **anstrengend** *Adj. (körperlich)* strenuous; *(geistig)* demanding; **Anstrengung die; ~, ~en a)** effort; **große ~en machen, etw. zu tun** make every effort to do sth.; **b)** *(Strapaze)* strain

An·strich der paint

An·sturm der rush **(auf + Akk. to);** *(auf Banken, Waren)* run **(auf + Akk. on)**

Antarktika (das); ~s Antarctica; **Antarktis die; ~:** die ~: the Antarctic; **antarktisch** *Adj.* Antarctic

An·teil der share **(an + Dat. of);** ~ **an etw.** *(Dat.)* **nehmen** take an interest in sth.; **An·teilnahme die a)** interest **(an + Dat. in); b)** *(Mitgefühl)* sympathy **(an + Dat. with)**

Antenne die; ~, ~n aerial; antenna *(Amer.)*

anthrazit [antra'tsi:t] *Adj.; nicht attr.* anthracite[-grey]; **anthrazit·grau** *Adj.* anthracite-grey

anti-, Anti- anti-; **Anti·alkoholiker der** teetotaller; **Antibiotikum das; ~s, Antibiotika** *(Med.)* antibiotic

antik *Adj.* **a)** classical; **b)** *(aus vergangenen Zeiten)* antique *(furniture, fittings, etc.)*; **Antike die;** ~ classical antiquity *no art.*

Antilope die; ~, ~n antelope

Antipathie die; ~, ~n antipathy

Antiquariat antiquarian bookshop/department; *(mit neueren gebrauchten Büchern)* second-hand bookshop/department; **Antiquität die; ~, ~en** antique

Antlitz das; ~es, ~e *(dichter., geh.)* countenance *(literary)*; face

Antrag der; ~|e|s, Anträge a) application **(auf + Akk. for); einen ~ stellen** make an application; **b)** *(Formular)* application form

an|treffen *unr. tr. V.* find; *(zufällig)* come across

an|treiben *unr. tr. V.* **a)** drive *(animals, column of prisoners)* on *or* along; *(fig.)* urge; **b)** *(in Bewegung setzen)* drive; power *(ship, aircraft)*

an|treten 1. *unr. itr. V.; mit sein* **a)** form up; *(in Linie)* line up; *(Milit.)* fall in; **b)** *(sich stellen)* meet one's opponent; *(als Mannschaft)* line up; **gegen jmdn.** ~**:** meet sb./line up against sb.; **2.** *unr. tr. V.* **a)** start *(job, apprenticeship)*; take up *(position, appoint-*

ment⟩; set out on ⟨*journey*⟩; begin ⟨*prison sentence*⟩; come into ⟨*inheritance*⟩

An·trieb der drive

An·tritt der: **vor ~ Ihres Urlaubs** before you go on holiday *(Brit.) or (Amer.)* vacation; **vor ~ der Reise** before setting out on the journey

an|tun *unr. tr. V.* **a)** jmdm. **ein Leid ~:** hurt sb.; jmdm. **etwas Böses/ein Unrecht ~:** do sb. harm/an injustice; **b)** jmd./etw. **hat es jmdm. angetan** sb. was taken with sb./sth.; *s. auch* **angetan**

Antwort die; ~, ~en **a)** answer; reply; **er gab mir keine ~:** he didn't answer [me] *or* reply; **b)** *(Reaktion)* response;

antworten *itr. V.* **a)** answer; reply; **auf etw.** *(Akk.)* ~: answer sth.; reply to sth.; jmdm. ~: answer sb.; reply to sb.; **b)** *(reagieren)* respond **(auf** + *Akk.* **to)**

an|vertrauen **1.** *tr. V.* jmdm. etw. ~: entrust sb. with sth.; *(fig.: mitteilen)* confide sth. to sb.; **2.** *refl. V.* sich jmdm./einer Sache ~: put one's trust in sb./sth.; **sich jmdm. ~** *(fig.: sich jmdm. mitteilen)* confide in sb.

an|wachsen *unr. itr. V.; mit sein* **a)** grow on; **b)** *(Wurzeln schlagen)* take root; **c)** *(zunehmen)* grow

Anwalt der; ~[e]s, Anwälte, **Anwältin** die; ~, ~nen **a)** *(Rechts~)* lawyer; solicitor *(Brit.);* attorney *(Amer.); (vor Gericht)* barrister *(Brit.);* attorney[-at-law] *(Amer.);* advocate *(Scot.);* **b)** *(Fürsprecher)* advocate

An·wärter der candidate **(auf** + *Akk.* for); *(Sport)* contender **(auf** + *Akk.* for)

an|weisen *unr. tr. V.* instruct; *s. auch* **angewiesen; An·weisung** die instruction

an|wenden *unr. (auch regelm.) tr. V.* use, employ ⟨*process, trick, method, violence, force*⟩; use ⟨*medicine, money, time*⟩; apply ⟨*rule, paragraph, proverb, etc.*⟩ **(auf** + *Akk.* to); **An·wendung** die *s.* **anwenden**: use; employment; application

An·wesen das property

anwesend *Adj.* present **(bei** at); **die Anwesenden** those present; **Anwesenheit** die; ~: presence

an|widern *tr. V.* nauseate

An·zahl die; ~: number; **eine ganze ~:** a whole lot

an|zahlen *tr. V.* put down ⟨*sum*⟩ as a deposit **(auf** + *Akk.* on); *(bei Ratenzahlung)* make a down payment of

⟨*sum*⟩ **(auf** + *Akk.* on); **An·zahlung** die deposit; *(bei Ratenzahlung)* down payment

An·zeichen das sign; indication

Anzeige die; ~, ~n **a)** *(Straf~)* report; **b)** *(Inserat)* advertisement; **c)** *(eines Instruments)* display; **an|zeigen** *tr. V.* **a)** *(Strafanzeige erstatten)* jmdn./etw. ~: report sb./sth. to the police/the authorities; **b)** *(zeigen)* show; indicate; show ⟨*time, date*⟩; **Anzeigen·teil** der advertisement section *or* pages *pl.*

an|ziehen *unr. tr. V.* **a)** *(auch fig.)* attract; **b)** draw up ⟨*knees, feet, etc.*⟩; **c)** tighten ⟨*rope, wire, screw, knot, belt, etc.*⟩; put on ⟨*handbrake*⟩; **d)** *(ankleiden)* dress; **sich ~:** get dressed; **e)** *(anlegen)* put on ⟨*clothes*⟩; **anziehend** *Adj.* attractive; **An·zug** der **a)** suit; **b)** **im ~ sein** ⟨*storm*⟩ be approaching; ⟨*fever, illness*⟩ be coming on; ⟨*enemy*⟩ be advancing; **anzüglich** **1.** *Adj.* insinuating ⟨*remark, question*⟩; **2.** *adv.* in an insinuating way

an|zünden *tr. V.* light; set fire to ⟨*building etc.*⟩

an|zweifeln *tr. V.* doubt; question

apart **1.** *Adj.* individual *attrib.*; **2.** *adv.* in an individual style

Apartment das; ~s, ~s studio flat *(Brit.);* studio apartment *(Amer.)*

Apathie die; ~, ~n apathy; **apathisch** **1.** *Adj.* apathetic; **2.** *adv.* apathetically

Aperitif [aperi'ti:f] der; ~s, ~s aperitif

Apfel der; ~s, Äpfel apple

Apfel-: ~baum der apple-tree; ~kuchen der apple-cake; *(mit Äpfeln belegt)* apple flan; ~mus das apple purée; ~saft der apple-juice

Apfelsine die; ~, ~n orange

Apfel-: ~strudel der apfelstrudel; ~wein der cider

Apostel der; ~s, ~: apostle

Apotheke die; ~, ~n **a)** chemist's [shop] *(Brit.);* drugstore *(Amer.);* **b)** *(Haus~)* medicine cabinet; *(Reise-, Bord~)* first-aid kit; **Apotheker** der; ~s, ~, **Apothekerin** die; ~, ~nen [dispensing] chemist *(Brit.);* druggist

App. *Abk.* **Apparat** ext.

Apparat der; ~[e]s, ~e **a)** apparatus *no pl.; (Haushaltsgerät)* appliance; *(kleiner)* gadget; **b)** *(Radio~)* radio; *(Fernseh~)* television; *(Foto~)* camera; **c)** *(Telefon)* telephone; *(Nebenstelle)* extension; **d)** *(Personen und Hilfsmittel)* organization; *(Verwaltungs~)* system

Appartement [apartə'mã:, *schweiz.*
auch: -'mɛnt] das; ~s, ~s *(schweiz.*
auch: ~e) **a)** *s.* **Apartment; b)** *(Hotel-
suite)* suite
Appell der; ~s, ~e **a)** appeal (zu for,
an + *Akk.* to); **b)** *(Milit.)* muster; *(An-
wesenheits~)* roll-call; **appellieren**
itr. V. appeal (an + *Akk.* to)
Appetit der; ~|e|s, ~e appetite (auf +
Akk. for); **guten** ~! enjoy your meal!;
appetitlich *Adj.* **a)** appetizing; **b)**
(sauber, ansprechend) attractive and
hygienic; **Appetit·losigkeit die;** ~:
lack of appetite
applaudieren *itr. V.* applaud; **Applaus der;** ~es, ~e applause
Aprikose die; ~, ~n apricot
April der; ~|s|, ~e April; **der** ~: April
Aquädukt der *od.* **das;** ~|e|s, ~e aque-
duct
Aquaplaning das; ~|s| aquaplaning
Aquarell das; ~s, ~e water-colour
[painting]
Aquarium das; ~s, **Aquarien** aquarium
Äquator der; ~s equator
Ar das *od.* **der;** ~s, ~e are
Ära die; ~, **Ären** era
Araber der; ~s, ~ Arab; **Arabien**
[a'ra:biən] **(das);** ~s Arabia; **arabisch** *Adj.* Arabian; Arabic *(language, numeral, literature, etc.)*
Arbeit die; ~, ~en **a)** work *no indef.
art.;* **vor/nach der** ~ *(ugs.)* before/
after work; **b)** *(Produkt, Werk)* work;
c) *(Aufgabe* job; **d)** *(Klassen~)* test;
arbeiten 1. *itr. V.* work; **2.** *tr. V. (herstellen)* make; **Arbeiter der;** ~s, ~:
worker; *(Bau~, Land~)* labourer;
Arbeiter·klasse die working
class[es *pl.*]; **Arbeiterschaft die;** ~:
workers *pl.;* **Arbeit·geber der;** ~s,
~: employer; **Arbeitnehmer der;**
~s, ~: employee
arbeits-, Arbeits-: ~**amt das** job
centre *(Brit.);* ~**bedingungen** *Pl.*
working conditions; ~**fähig** *Adj.* fit
for work *postpos.; (grundsätzlich)* able
to work *postpos.;* ~**gang der** operation; ~**kraft die a)** capacity for work;
b) *(Mensch)* worker; ~**los** *Adj.* unemployed; ~**lose der/die; adj. Dekl.**
unemployed person/man/woman
etc.; **die** ~n **the** unemployed; ~**losigkeit die;** ~: unemployment *no indef.
art.;* ~**markt der** labour market;
~**platz der a)** work-place; **b)** *(~stätte)*
place of work; **c)** *(~verhältnis)* job;
~**scheu** *Adj.* work-shy; ~**tag der**

working day; ~**teilung die** division
of labour; ~**unfähig** *Adj.* unfit for
work *postpos.; (grundsätzlich)* unable
to work *postpos.;* ~**zeit die** working
hours *pl.;* **die tägliche** ~**zeit** the working day
Archäologe der; ~n, ~n archaeologist; **Archäologie die;** ~: archaeology *no art.;* **archäologisch** *Adj.*
archaeological
Arche die; ~, ~n ark; **die** ~ **Noah**
Noah's Ark
Architekt der; ~en, ~en architect;
Architektur die; ~ architecture
Archiv das; ~s, ~e archives *pl.;*
archive
Ären *s.* **Ära**
Arena die; ~, **Arenen** arena; *(Stier-
kampf~, Manege)* ring
arg, ärger, ärgst... *(geh., landsch.)* 1.
Adj. **a)** *(schlimm)* bad; **im** ~en **liegen**
be in a sorry state; **b)** *(unangenehm
groß, stark)* severe ⟨pain, hunger,
shock, disappointment⟩; serious ⟨error,
dilemma⟩; extreme ⟨embarrassment⟩;
gross ⟨exaggeration, injustice⟩; **2.** *adv.*
(äußerst, sehr) extremely
Ärger der; ~s **a)** annoyance; **b)** *(Unannehmlichkeiten)* trouble; ~ **bekommen**
get into trouble; **ärgerlich 1.** *Adj.* **a)**
annoyed; **b)** *(Ärger erregend)* annoying; **2.** *adv.* **a)** with annoyance; **b)**
(Ärger erregend) annoyingly; **ärgern**
1. *tr. V.* **a)** annoy; **b)** *(reizen)* tease; **2.**
refl. V. **sich** |**über jmdn./etw.**| ~: be/get
annoyed [at sb./about sth.]; **Ärgernis**
das; ~ses, ~se annoyance; *(etw. An-
stößiges)* nuisance
arg-, Arg-: ~**listig** *Adj.* deceitful;
(heimtückisch) malicious; ~**los 1.**
Adj. unsuspecting; **2.** *adv.* unsuspect-
ingly; ~**losigkeit die;** ~: unsuspecting nature
ärgst... *s.* **arg**
Argument das; ~|e|s, ~e argument;
Argumentation die; ~, ~en argumentation; **argumentieren** *itr. V.*
argue
Argwohn der; ~|e|s suspicion; **arg-
wöhnisch** *(geh.)* **1.** *Adj.* suspicious;
2. *adv.* suspiciously
Arie ['a:riə] **die;** ~, ~n aria
Aristokrat der; ~en, ~en aristocrat;
Aristokratin die; ~, ~nen aristocrat; **Aristokratie die;** ~, ~n aristocracy; **aristokratisch 1.** *Adj.* aristocratic; **2.** *adv.* aristocratically
arithmetisch 1. *Adj.* arithmetical; **2.**
adv. arithmetically

Arkade die; ~, ~n arcade
Arktis die; ~: Arctic; **arktisch** *Adj.*
Arctic; *(fig.)* arctic
arm, ärmer, ärmst... *Adj.* poor; ~ **und**
reich *(veralt.)* rich and poor [alike]; ~
an Nährstoffen poor in nutrients; **der/**
die Ärmste *od.* **Arme** the poor man/
boy/woman/girl
Arm der; ~|e|s, ~e arm; jmdm. |mit
etw.| unter die ~e greifen help sb. out
[with sth.]; **ein Hemd mit halbem ~**: a
short-sleeved shirt
Armaturen·brett das instrument
panel; *(im Kfz)* dashboard
Arm-: ~**band** das bracelet; *(Uhr~)*
strap; ~**band·uhr** die wrist-watch
Armee die; ~, ~n *(auch fig.)* army
Ärmel der; ~s, ~: sleeve; [sich *(Dat.)*]
etw. aus dem ~ schütteln *(ugs.)* produce sth. just like that
Ärmel·kanal der [English] Channel
ärmer *s.* arm; **ärmlich 1.** *Adj.* cheap
⟨*clothing*⟩; shabby ⟨*flat, office*⟩;
meagre ⟨*meal*⟩. **2.** *adv.* cheaply ⟨*fur-*
nished, dressed⟩
Arm·reif der armlet
arm·selig *Adj.* **a)** miserable; pathetic
⟨*result, figure*⟩; meagre ⟨*meal, food*⟩;
paltry ⟨*return, salary, sum, fee*⟩; **b)**
(abwertend: erbärmlich) miserable;
ärmst... *s.* arm; **Armut** die; ~ poverty
Aroma das; ~s, Aromen *(Duft)* aroma;
(Geschmack) flavour; **aromatisch**
Adj. aromatic; distinctive ⟨*taste*⟩; ~
duften give off an aromatic fragrance
arrangieren [arã'zi:rən] **1.** *tr. V. (geh.,*
Musik) arrange; **2.** *refl. V.* sich ~:
adapt; sich mit jmdm. ~: come to an
accommodation with sb.
Arrest der; ~|e|s, ~e detention
arrogant 1. *Adj.* arrogant; **2.** *adv.* arrogantly; **Arroganz** die; ~ arrogance
Arsch der; ~|e|s, Ärsche *(derb)* **a)** arse
(Brit. coarse); ass *(Amer. sl.);* **leck**
mich am ~! *(fig.)* piss off *(coarse);* **im**
~ **sein** *(fig.)* be buggered *(coarse);* **b)**
(widerlicher Mensch) arse-hole *(Brit.*
coarse); ass-hole *(Amer. sl.);* **Arsch-**
loch das *(derb) s.* Arsch b
Art die; ~, ~en **a)** kind; sort; Bücher
aller ~: all kinds *or* sorts of books;
|so| eine ~ ...: a sort of ...; aus der ~
schlagen not be true to type; *(in einer*
Familie) be different from all the rest
of the family; **b)** *(Biol.)* species; **c)** *o.*
Pl. (Wesen) nature; *(Verhaltensweise)*
way; *(gutes Benehmen)* behaviour; **die**
feine englische ~ *(ugs.)* the proper way

to behave; **d)** *(Weise)* way; **auf diese**
~: in this way; ~ **und Weise** way;
(Kochk.) **nach ~ des Hauses** à la maison; **nach Schweizer ~**: Swiss style
Arterie [ar'te:riə] die; ~, ~n artery
artig *Adj.* well-behaved; **sei ~**: be a
good boy/girl/dog *etc.*
Artikel der; ~s, ~ **a)** article; **b)** *(Ware)*
item
Artillerie die; ~, ~n artillery
Artischocke die; ~, ~n artichoke
Artist der; ~en, ~en [variety/circus]
performer
Arznei die; ~, ~en *(veralt.),* **Arz-**
nei·mittel das medicine
Arzt der; ~es, Ärzte, **Ärztin** die; ~,
~nen doctor; **ärztlich 1.** *Adj.* medical; **auf ~e Verordnung** on doctor's
orders; **2.** *adv.* **sich ~ behandeln lassen**
have medical treatment
As das; ~ses, ~se ace
Asbest der; ~|e|s, ~e asbestos
Asche die; ~, ~n ash[es *pl.*]; *(sterbli-*
che Reste) ashes *pl.*
Aschen-: ~**becher** der ashtray;
~**brödel** das; ~s, ~ *(auch fig.)* Cin-
derella
Ascher·mittwoch der Ash Wednesday
Äser *s.* Aas
Asiat der; ~en, ~en, **Asiatin** die; ~,
~nen Asian; **asiatisch** *Adj.* Asian;
Asien ['a:ziən] (das); ~s Asia
Askese die; ~: asceticism; **Asket**
der; ~en, ~en ascetic; **asketisch 1.**
Adj. ascetic; **2.** *adv.* ascetically
asozial 1. *Adj.* asocial; **2.** *adv.* aso-
cially
Aspekt der; ~|e|s, ~e aspect
Asphalt der; ~|e|s, ~e asphalt
Aspik der *(österr. auch* das); ~s, ~e
aspic
aß *1. u. 3. Pers. Sg. Prät. v.* essen
Assistent der, ~en, ~en, **Assisten-**
tin die; ~, ~nen assistant
Ast der; ~|e|s, Äste branch; sich *(Dat.)*
einen ~ lachen *(ugs.)* split one's sides
[with laughter]
Aster die; ~, ~n aster; *(Herbst~)*
Michaelmas daisy
ästhetisch 1. *Adj.* aesthetic; **2.** *adv.*
aesthetically
Asthma das; ~s asthma
Astrologe der; ~n, ~n astrologer;
Astrologie die; ~: astrology *no art.;*
Astrologin die; ~, ~nen astrologer
Astronaut der; ~en, ~en; **Astro-**
nautin die; ~, ~nen astronaut
Astronom der; ~en, ~en astronomer;

Astronomie die; ~: astronomy *no art.;* **astronomisch** *Adj.* astronomical

Asyl das; ~s, ~e a) asylum; b) *(Obdachlosen~)* hostel; **Asylant** der; ~en, ~en, **Asylantin** die; ~, ~nen person granted [political] asylum; **Asyl·bewerber** der person seeking [political] asylum

Atelier [atə'lie:] das; ~s, ~s studio

Atem der; ~s breath; **außer ~ sein/geraten** be/get out of breath

atem-, Atem-: ~**beraubend** 1. *Adj.* breath-taking; 2. *adv.* breath-takingly; ~**los** 1. *Adj.* breathless; 2. *adv.* breathlessly; ~**pause** die breathing space; ~**zug** der breath

Atheismus der; ~: atheism *no art.;* **Atheist** der; ~en, ~en atheist; **atheistisch** 1. *Adj.* atheistic; 2. *adv.* atheistically

Athen (das); ~s Athens

Äther der; ~s, ~ ether

Äthiopien [ɛ'tio:piən] **(das);** ~s Ethiopia

Athlet der; ~en, ~en a) *(Sportler)* athlete; b) *(ugs.: kräftiger Mann)* muscleman; **athletisch** *Adj.* athletic

Atlanten *s.* ¹**Atlas**

Atlantik der; -s Atlantic; **atlantisch** *Adj.* Atlantic; **der Atlantische Ozean** the Atlantic Ocean

Atlas der; ~ *od.* ~ses, **Atlanten** *od.* ~se atlas

atmen *itr., tr. V.* breathe

Atmosphäre [atmo'sfɛ:rə] die; ~, ~n *(auch fig.)* atmosphere

Atmung die; ~: breathing

Atom das; ~s, ~e atom; **atomar** *Adj.* atomic; *(Atomwaffen betreffend)* nuclear

Atom-: ~**bombe** die atom bomb; ~**energie** die; *o. Pl.* nuclear energy *no indef. art.;* ~**kern** der atomic nucleus; ~**kraft** die; *o. Pl.* nuclear power *no indef. art.;* ~**kraftwerk** das nuclear power-station; ~**krieg** der nuclear war; ~**müll** der nuclear waste; ~**physik** die nuclear physics *sing., no art.;* ~**pilz** der mushroom cloud; ~**reaktor** der nuclear reactor; ~**waffe** die nuclear weapon; ~**waffen·frei** *Adj.* nuclear-free; ~**zeitalter** das; *o. Pl.* nuclear age

Attacke die; ~, ~n *(auch Med.)* attack **(auf** + *Akk.* on)

Attentat das; ~[e]s, ~e assassination attempt; *(erfolgreich)* assassination; **Attentäter** der; ~s, ~, **Attentäterin** die; ~, ~nen would-be assassin; *(erfolgreich)* assassin

Attest das; ~[e]s, ~e medical certificate

Attraktion die; ~, ~en attraction; **attraktiv** 1. *Adj.* attractive; 2. *adv.* attractively; **Attraktivität** die; ~: attractiveness

Attrappe die; ~, ~n dummy

Attribut das; ~[e]s, ~e attribute

ätzen 1. *tr. V.* etch; 2. *itr. V.* corrode; **ätzend** 1. *Adj.* corrosive; *(fig.)* caustic ⟨*wit, remark, criticism*⟩; pungent ⟨*smell*⟩; 2. *adv.* caustically ⟨*ironic, critical*⟩

au *Interj.* a) *(bei Schmerz)* ouch; b) *(bei Überraschung, Begeisterung)* oh

Aubergine [obɛr'ʒi:nə] die; ~, ~n aubergine *(Brit.)*; egg-plant

auch 1. *Adv.* a) as well; too; also; **Klaus war ~ dabei** Klaus was there as well *or* too; Klaus was also there; **Ich gehe jetzt. – Ich ~:** I'm going now – So am I; **Mir ist warm. – Mir ~:** I feel warm – So do I; **das weiß ich ~ nicht** I don't know either; b) *(sogar, selbst)* even; **~ wenn, wenn ~:** even if; 2. *Partikel* a) etwas anderes habe ich **~ nicht erwartet** I never expected anything else; **nun hör aber ~ zu!** now listen!; b) **bist du dir ~ im klaren, was das bedeutet?** are you sure you understand what that means?; **bist du ~ glücklich?** are you truly happy?; **lügst du ~ nicht?** you're not lying, are you?; c) **wo .../wer .../was ...** *usw.* ~: wherever/whoever/whatever *etc. ...;* **wie dem ~ sei** however that may be; d) **mag er ~ noch so klug sein** no matter how clever he is

Audienz die; ~, ~en audience

auf 1. *Präp. mit Dat.* a) on; **~ See** at sea; **~ dem Baum** in the tree; **~ der Erde** on earth; **~ der Welt** in the world; **~ der Straße** in the street; b) at ⟨*post office, town, hall, police station*⟩; **~ seinem Zimmer** *(ugs.)* in his room; **Geld ~ der Bank haben** have money in the bank; **~ der Schule/Uni** at school/university; c) at ⟨*party, wedding*⟩; on ⟨*course, trip, walk, holiday, tour*⟩; 2. *Präp. mit Akk.* a) on; **~ einen Berg steigen** climb up a mountain; **~ die Straße gehen** go [out] into the street; b) **~ die Schule/Uni gehen** go to school/university; **~ einen Lehrgang gehen** go on a course; c) **~ 10 km [Entfernung]** for [a distance of] 10 km; **wir näherten uns der Hütte [bis] ~ 30 m** we approached to within 30 m of the hut; **d)** ~ **Jahre [hinaus]** for years [to come]; **etw.** ~ **nächsten Mittwoch verschieben** postpone sth. until next Wednesday; **die Nacht von Sonntag** ~ **Montag** Sunday night; **das fällt** ~ **einen Montag** it falls on a Monday; **e)** ~ **diese Art und Weise** in this way; ~ **deutsch** in German; ~ **das sorgfältigste** *(geh.)* most carefully; **f)** ~ **Wunsch** on request; ~ **meine Bitte** at my request; ~ **Befehl** on command; **g) ein Teelöffel** ~ **einen Liter Wasser** one teaspoon to one litre of water; ~ **die Sekunde/den Millimeter [genau]** [precise] to the second/ millimetre; ~ **deine Gesundheit!** your health; ~ **bald/morgen!** *(bes. südd.)* see you soon/tomorrow; **3.** *Adv.* **a)** ~**!** *(steh/steht auf!)* up you get!; **b) sie waren längst** ~ **und davon** they had made off long before; **c)** ~**!** *(bes. südd.: los)* come on; ~ **geht's** off we go; ~ **ins Schwimmbad!** come on, off to the swimming-pool!; **d)** ~ **und ab** *(hin und her)* up and down; to and fro; **e) Helm/Hut/Brille** ~**!** helmet/hat/ glasses on!; **f) Fenster/Mund** ~**!** open the window/your mouth!

auf|atmen *itr. V.* breathe a sigh of relief

auf|bahren *tr. V.* lay out; **aufgebahrt sein** lie in state

Auf·bau der; ~[e]s, ~ten **a)** *o. Pl.* building; **b)** *o. Pl. (Struktur)* structure; **c)** *Pl. (Schiffbau)* superstructure *sing.*

auf|bauen *tr. V.* **a)** erect ⟨hut, kiosk, podium⟩; set up ⟨equipment, train set⟩; build ⟨house, bridge⟩; put up ⟨tent⟩; **b)** *(hinstellen, arrangieren)* lay or set out ⟨food, presents, etc.⟩; **c)** *(fig.: schaffen)* build ⟨state, economy, etc.⟩; build up ⟨business, organization, army, spy network⟩; **d)** *(fig.: strukturieren)* structure

auf|bäumen *refl. V.* rear up; **sich gegen jmdn./etw.** ~ *(fig.)* rise up against sb./sth.

auf|bessern *tr. V.* improve; increase ⟨pension, wages, etc.⟩

auf|bewahren *tr. V.* keep; **etw. kühl** ~: store sth. in a cool place; **Auf·bewahrung die** keeping

auf|bieten *unr. tr. V.* exert ⟨strength, energy, will-power, influence, authority⟩; call on ⟨skill, wit, powers of persuasion or eloquence⟩

auf|blasen *unr. tr. V.* blow up; inflate

auf|bleiben *unr. itr. V.; mit sein* **a)** *(geöffnet bleiben)* stay open; **b)** *(nicht zu Bett gehen)* stay up

auf|blenden *itr. V.* switch to full beam

auf|blicken *itr. V.* **a)** look up; *(kurz)* glance up; **b) zu jmdm.** ~ *(fig.)* look up to sb.

auf|blühen *itr. V.; mit sein* **a)** come into bloom; ⟨bud⟩ open; **b)** *(fig.: aufleben)* blossom [out]

auf|brauchen *tr. V.* use up

auf|brechen 1. *unr. tr. V.* break open ⟨lock, safe, box, crate, etc.⟩; break into ⟨car⟩; force [open] ⟨door⟩; **2.** *unr. itr. V.; mit sein* **a)** ⟨bud⟩ open; ⟨ice [sheet], surface, ground⟩ break up; ⟨wound⟩ open; **b)** *(losgehen, -fahren)* set off

auf|bringen *unr. tr. V.* **a)** find; raise ⟨money⟩; *(fig.)* summon [up] ⟨strength, energy, courage⟩; find ⟨patience⟩; **b)** *(kreieren)* start ⟨fashion, custom, rumour⟩; introduce ⟨slogan, theory⟩; **c) jmdn.** ~: make sb. angry; **d) jmdn. gegen jmdn./etw.** ~: set sb. against sb./ sth.

Auf·bruch der departure

auf|brühen *tr. V.* brew [up]

auf|decken *tr. V.* **a)** uncover; **b)** *(Kartenspiele)* show; **c)** *(fig.)* reveal; uncover; *(enthüllen)* expose

auf|drängen *tr. V.* **jmdm. etw.** ~: force sth. on sb.; **2.** *refl. V.* **sich jmdm.** ~: force oneself on sb.

auf|drehen *tr. V.* **a)** unscrew ⟨bottlecap, nut⟩; undo ⟨screw⟩; turn on ⟨tap, gas, water⟩; open ⟨valve, bottle, vice⟩; **b)** *(ugs.)* turn up ⟨radio, record-player, etc.⟩

auf·dringlich 1. *Adj.* pushy *(coll.)* ⟨person⟩; *(fig.)* insistent ⟨music, advertisement⟩; pungent ⟨perfume, smell⟩; loud ⟨colour, wallpaper⟩; **2.** *adv.* ⟨behave⟩ pushily, *(coll.)*; **Aufdringlichkeit die;** ~*s.* **aufdringlich:** pushiness *(coll.)*; insistent manner; pungency

auf·einander *Adv.* on top of one another

aufeinander-: ~**|folgen** *itr. V.; mit sein* follow one another; ~**folgend** successive; ~**|legen 1.** *tr. V.* lay ⟨planks etc.⟩ one on top of the other; **2.** *refl. V.* lie on top of one another; ~**|liegen** *unr. itr. V.* lie on top of each other or one another; ~**|prallen** *itr. V.; mit sein* crash into one another; collide; *(fig.)* ⟨opinions⟩ clash; ~**|treffen** *unr. itr. V.; mit sein (fig.)* meet

Aufenthalt der; ~[e]s, ~e **a)** stay; **b)** *(Fahrtunterbrechung)* stop

Aufenthalts-: ~**erlaubnis die** residence permit; ~**raum der** *(in einer*

Schule o. ä.) common-room *(Brit.); (in einer Jugendherberge)* day-room; *(in einem Betrieb o. ä.)* recreation-room

auf|essen *unr. tr. (auch itr.) V.* eat up

auf|fahren 1. *unr. itr. V.; mit sein* **a) auf ein anderes Fahrzeug ~** *(aufprallen)* drive into the back of another vehicle; **b) auf den Vordermann zu dicht ~**: drive too close to the car in front; **c)** *(vorfahren)* drive up; **d)** *(in Stellung gehen)* move up [into position]; **2.** *unr. tr. V.* **a)** *(in Stellung bringen)* move up; **b)** *(ugs.: auftischen)* serve up; **Auf·fahrt die a)** drive up; **b)** *(Weg)* drive; **c)** *(Autobahn~)* slip-road *(Brit.)*; access road *(Amer.)*; **d)** *(schweiz.) s.* **Himmelfahrt**

auf|fallen *unr. itr. V.; mit sein* stand out; **jmdm. fällt etw. auf** sb. notices sth.; **auffallend 1.** *Adj.* conspicuous; *(eindrucksvoll, bemerkenswert)* striking; **2.** *adv.* conspicuously; *(eindrucksvoll, bemerkenswert)* strikingly; **auf·fällig 1.** *Adj.* conspicuous; garish ⟨*colour*⟩; **2.** *adv.* conspicuously

auf|fangen *unr. tr. V.* **a)** catch; **b)** *(aufnehmen, sammeln)* collect

auf|fassen *tr. V.* grasp; **a) etw. als etw. ~**: regard sth. as sth.; **etw. persönlich/falsch ~**: take sth. personally/misunderstand sth.; **Auf·fassung die** *(Ansicht)* view; *(Begriff)* conception; **der ~ sein, daß ...**: take the view that ...

auffindbar *Adj.* findable; **auf|finden** *unr. tr. V.* find

auf|fordern *tr. V.* **jmdn. ~, etw. zu tun** call upon sb. to do sth.; *(einladen, ermuntern)* ask sb. to do sth.; **jmdn. [zum Tanz] ~**: ask sb. to dance; **Auf·forderung die** request; *(nachdrücklicher)* demand; *(Einladung, Ermunterung)* invitation

auf|fressen *unr. tr. V. (auch fig.)* eat up

auf|führen 1. *tr. V.* **a)** put on ⟨*film*⟩; stage ⟨*play, ballet, opera*⟩; perform ⟨*piece of music*⟩; **b)** *(auflisten)* list; **2.** *refl. V.* behave; **Auf·führung die** performance

Auf·gabe die a) task; **b)** *(fig.: Zweck, Funktion)* function; **c)** *(Schulw.)* *(Übung)* exercise; *(Prüfungs-)* question; *(Haus~) s.* **Haus~; d)** *(Rechen~, Mathematik~)* problem; **e)** *(Kapitulation)* retirement; *(im Schach)* resignation; **jmdn. zur ~ zwingen** force sb. to retire/resign; **f)** *(das Aufgeben a)* giving up; **g)** *(einer Postsendung)* posting *(Brit.)*; mailing *(Amer.)*; *(eines Tele-*

gramms) handing in; *(einer Bestellung, einer Annonce)* placing; **h)** *(von Gepäck)* checking in

Auf·gang der a) *(eines Gestirns)* rising; **b)** *(Treppe)* stairs *pl.*; staircase; stairway; *(in einem Bahnhof, zu einer Galerie, einer Tribüne)* steps *pl.*

auf|geben 1. *unr. tr. V.* **a)** give up; *(Sport)* retire from ⟨*race, competition*⟩; **b)** *(übergeben, übermitteln)* post *(Brit.)*, mail ⟨*letter, parcel*⟩; hand in, *(telefonisch)* phone in ⟨*telegram*⟩; place ⟨*advertisement, order*⟩; check ⟨*luggage, baggage*⟩ in; **c)** *(Schulw.: als Hausaufgabe)* set *(Brit.)*; assign *(Amer.)*; **d)** **jmdm. ein Rätsel ~**: set *(Brit.)* or *(Amer.)* assign sb. a puzzle; **2.** *unr. itr. V.* **a)** give up; *(im Sport)* retire; *(im Schach)* resign

Auf·gebot das a) contingent; **ein gewaltiges ~ an Polizisten/Fahrzeugen/Material** a huge force of police/array of vehicles/materials; **b)** *(zur Heirat)* notice of an/the intended marriage; *(kirchlich)* banns *pl.*

auf|gehen *unr. itr. V.; mit sein* **a)** rise; **b)** *(sich öffnen [lassen])* ⟨*door, parachute, wound*⟩ open; ⟨*stage curtain*⟩ go up; ⟨*knot, button, zip, bandage, shoelace, stitching*⟩ come undone; ⟨*boil, pimple, blister*⟩ burst; ⟨*flower, bud*⟩ open [up]; **c)** *(keimen)* come up; **d)** *(aufgetrieben werden)* ⟨*dough, cake*⟩ rise; **e)** *(Math.)* ⟨*calculation*⟩ work out; ⟨*equation*⟩ come out; **f) etw. geht jmdm. auf** sb. realizes sth.

aufgeklärt *Adj.* enlightened; **~ sein** *(sexualkundlich)* know the facts of life

auf·gelegt *Adj.* **gut/schlecht** *usw.* **~ sein** be in a good/bad *etc.* mood; **zu etw. ~ sein** be in the mood for sth.

auf·gelöst *Adj.* distraught ⟨*person*⟩

aufgeregt 1. *Adj.* excited; *(nervös, beunruhigt)* agitated; **2.** *adv.* exitedly; *(nervös, beunruhigt)* agitatedly

auf·geschlossen *Adj.* open-minded *(gegenüber as regards, about)*; *(interessiert, empfänglich)* receptive *(Dat., für to)*; *(zugänglich)* approachable; **Auf·geschlossenheit die** *s.* **aufgeschlossen:** open-mindedness; receptiveness; approachableness

aufgeweckt *Adj.* bright; **Aufgewecktheit die** **~:** brightness

auf|gießen *unr. tr. V.* make ⟨*coffee, tea*⟩

auf|gliedern *tr. V.* subdivide, break down **(in + Akk.** into); **Auf·gliederung die** subdivision; breakdown

auf|greifen *unr. tr. V.* pick up
auf Grund, aufgrund *s.* Grund c
auf|haben *(ugs.)* **1.** *unr. tr. V.* **a)** *(aufgesetzt haben)* have on; **b)** *(geöffnet haben)* have ⟨zip⟩ undone; have ⟨door, window, jacket, blouse⟩ open; **2.** *unr. itr. V.* ⟨shop, office⟩ be open
auf|halten **1.** *unr. tr. V.* **a)** halt; **b)** *(stören)* hold up; **c)** *(ugs.: geöffnet halten)* hold ⟨sack, door, etc.⟩ open; **die Augen [und Ohren]** ~: keep one's eyes [and ears] open; **2.** *unr. refl. V.* **a)** stay; **b)** **sich mit jmdm./etw.** ~: spend [a long] time on sb./sth.
auf|hängen **1.** *tr. V.* **a)** hang up; hang ⟨picture, curtains⟩; **b)** *(erhängen)* hang; **2.** *refl. V.* hang oneself; **Aufhänger** der; ~s, ~ loop
auf|heben *unr. tr. V.* **a)** pick up; **b)** *(aufbewahren)* keep; **c)** *(abschaffen)* abolish; repeal ⟨law⟩; rescind ⟨order, instruction⟩; cancel ⟨contract⟩; lift ⟨ban, prohibition⟩; **d)** *(ausgleichen)* cancel out; neutralize ⟨effect⟩; **Aufheben das; ~s: viel ~|s|/kein ~ von jmdm./etw. machen** make a great fuss/not make any fuss about sb./sth.
auf|heitern **1.** *tr. V.* cheer up; **2.** *refl. V.* ⟨weather⟩ brighten up
auf|hetzen *tr. V.* incite
auf|holen **1.** *tr. V.* make up ⟨time, delay⟩; pull back ⟨lead⟩; **2.** *itr. V.* catch up; ⟨athlete, competitor⟩ make up ground
auf|horchen *itr. V.* prick up one's ears
auf|hören *itr. V.* stop; **|damit|** ~, **etw. zu tun** stop doing sth.
auf|kaufen *tr. V.* buy up
auf|klappen *tr. V.* open, fold open ⟨chair, table⟩; open [up] ⟨suitcase, trunk⟩; open ⟨book, knife⟩
auf|klären **1.** *tr. V.* **a)** clear up ⟨matter, mystery, question, misunderstanding, error, confusion⟩; solve ⟨crime, problem⟩; explain ⟨event, incident, cause⟩; resolve ⟨contradiction, disagreement⟩; **b)** *(unterrichten)* enlighten; **ein Kind ~** *(sexualkundlich)* tell a child the facts of life; **2.** *refl. V.* **a)** ⟨misunderstanding, mystery⟩ be cleared up; **b)** ⟨weather⟩ brighten [up]; ⟨sky⟩ brighten; **Auf·klärung die** *s.* **aufklären 1: a)** clearing up; solution; explanation; resolution; **b)** enlightenment; **die ~ der Kinder** *(über Sexualität)* telling the children the facts of life
auf|kleben *tr. V.* stick on; *(mit Klei-*

ster) paste on; **Auf·kleber der** sticker
auf|knöpfen *tr. V.* unbutton; undo
auf|kochen **1.** *tr. V.* bring to the boil; **2.** *itr. V. mit sein* come to the boil
auf|kommen *unr. itr. V.; mit sein* **a)** ⟨wind⟩ spring up; ⟨storm, gale⟩ blow up; ⟨fog⟩ come down; ⟨rumour⟩ start; ⟨suspicion, doubt, feeling⟩ arise; ⟨fashion, style, invention⟩ come in; ⟨boredom⟩ set in; ⟨mood, atmosphere⟩ develop; **b)** ~ **für** *(bezahlen)* bear ⟨costs⟩; pay for ⟨damage⟩; pay ⟨expenses⟩; be liable for ⟨debts⟩; stand ⟨loss⟩; **c)** ~ **für** *(Verantwortung tragen für)* be responsible for
auf|krempeln *tr. V.* roll up
auf|laden **1.** *unr. tr. V.* **a)** load (**auf +** *Akk.* on [to]); **b)** **jmdm. etw.** ~ *(ugs.)* load sb. with sth.; *(fig.)* saddle sb. with sth.; **c)** charge [up] ⟨battery⟩; **2.** *unr. refl. V.* ⟨battery⟩ charge
Auf·lage die a) *(Buchw.)* edition; **b)** *(Verpflichtung)* condition
auf|lassen *unr. tr. V. (ugs.)* **a)** leave ⟨door, window, jacket, etc.⟩ open; **b)** keep on ⟨hat, glasses, etc.⟩
auf|lauern *itr. V.* **jmdm.** ~: lie in wait for sb.
Auf·lauf der a) *(Menschen~)* crowd; **b)** *(Speise)* soufflé
auf|leben *itr. V.; mit sein* revive; *(fig.: wieder munter werden)* come to life
auf|legen **1.** *tr. V.* **a)** put on; **den Hörer** ~: put down the receiver; **b)** *(Buchw.)* publish; **2.** *itr. V. (den Hörer ~)* hang up
auf|lehnen *refl. V.* rebel; **Auflehnung die; ~, ~en** rebellion
auf|leuchten *itr. V.; auch mit sein* light up; *(für kurze Zeit)* flash
auf|lockern *tr. V.* **a)** loosen; break up ⟨soil⟩; **b)** *(fig.)* introduce some variety into ⟨landscape, lesson, lecture⟩; relieve ⟨pattern, façade⟩; make ⟨mood, atmosphere, evening⟩ more relaxed; **Auf·lockerung die a)** *s.* **auflockern a:** loosening; breaking up; **b) zur ~ der Stimmung/des Abends** to make the mood/evening more relaxed
auf|lösen **1.** *tr. V.* dissolve; resolve ⟨difficulty, contradiction⟩; solve ⟨puzzle, equation⟩; break off ⟨engagement⟩; cancel ⟨arrangement, contract, agreement⟩; dissolve ⟨organization⟩; **2.** *refl. V.* dissolve (**in +** *Akk.* into); ⟨parliament⟩ dissolve itself; ⟨crowd, demonstration⟩ break up; ⟨fog, mist⟩ lift; *(fig.)* ⟨empire, social order⟩ dis-

integrate; **Auf·lösung die a)** s. **auflösen 1:** dissolving; resolution; solution; breaking off; cancellation; dissolution; **b)** s. **auflösen 2:** dissolving;
breaking up lifting; disintegration
auf|machen 1. tr. V. **a)** open; undo
⟨button, knot⟩; **b)** (ugs.: eröffnen)
open [up] ⟨shop, business, etc.⟩; **2.** itr.
V. **a)** ⟨shop, office, etc.⟩ open; **b)** (ugs.:
die Tür öffnen) open the door; **jmdm.
~:** open the door to sb.; **c)** (ugs.: eröffnet werden) ⟨shop, business⟩ open [up];
Aufmachung die; ~, ~en presentation; (Kleidung) get-up
auf|marschieren itr. V.; mit sein as-
semble; (heranmarschieren) march
up; **Truppen sind an der Grenze auf-
marschiert** troops were deployed
along the border
aufmerksam 1. Adj. **a)** attentive;
sharp ⟨eyes⟩; **jmdn. auf jmdn./etw. ~
machen** draw sb.'s attention to sb./
sth.; **auf jmdn./etw. ~ werden** become
aware of sb./sth.; **~ werden** notice; **b)**
(höflich) attentive; **2.** adv. attentively;
Aufmerksamkeit die; ~, ~en a) o.
Pl. attention; **b)** (Höflichkeit) attent-
iveness; **c)** (Geschenk) small gift
auf|muntern tr. V. **a)** cheer up; **b)** (be-
leben) liven up; **c)** (ermutigen) encourage; **Aufmunterung die; ~** s. **aufmuntern:** cheering up; livening up;
encouragement
Aufnahme die; ~, ~n a) s. **aufnehmen
b:** opening; establishment; taking up;
b) (Empfang) reception; **c)** s. **aufnehmen d:** admission (**in** + Akk. into); **d)**
(Einschließung) inclusion; **e)** (Finanzw.) raising; **f)** (Aufzeichnung) taking down; (von Personalien, eines Dik-
tats) taking [down]; **g)** s. **aufnehmen
k:** taking: photographing; filming; **h)**
(Bild) shot; **i)** (das Aufnehmen auf
Tonträger, das Aufgenommene) recording; **j)** (Anklang) reception; response (Gen. to); **k)** (Einverleibung,
Absorption) absorption
auf|nehmen unr. tr. V. **a)** (aufheben)
pick up; (fig.) take up ⟨idea, theme,
etc.⟩; **es mit jmdm./etw. ~/nicht ~
können** (fig.) be a/no match for sb./
sth.; **b)** (beginnen mit) open ⟨negotiati-
ons, talks⟩; establish ⟨relations, con-
tacts⟩; take up ⟨studies, activity, occu-
pation⟩; start ⟨production, investiga-
tion⟩; **c)** (empfangen) receive; (beherbergen) take in; **d)** (beitreten lassen)
admit (**in** + Akk. to); **e)** (einschließen,
verzeichnen) include; **f)** (erfassen)

take in ⟨impressions, information,
etc.⟩; **g)** (absorbieren) absorb; **h)** (Finanzw.) raise ⟨mortgage, money,
loan⟩; **i)** (reagieren auf) receive; **j)**
(aufschreiben) take down; take [down]
⟨dictation, particulars⟩; **k)** (fotografieren) take ⟨picture⟩; photograph, take a
photograph of ⟨scene, subject⟩; (filmen) film; **l)** (auf Tonträger) record
auf|opfern refl. V. devote oneself sac-
rificingly (**für** to); **aufopfernd 1.**
Adj. self-sacrificing; **2.** adv. self-sacri-
ficingly
auf|passen itr. V. **a)** watch out; (kon-
zentriert sein) pay attention; **paß mal
auf!** (ugs.: hör mal zu!) now listen; **b)**
auf jmdn./etw. ~: keep an eye on sb./
sth.
auf|platzen itr. V.; mit sein burst
open; ⟨seam, cushion⟩ split open;
⟨wound⟩ open up
Auf·prall der; ~[e]s, ~e impact;
auf|prallen itr. V.; mit sein **auf etw.
(Akk.) ~:** hit sth.
Auf·preis der additional charge
auf|pumpen tr. V. pump up
auf|putschen tr. V. stimulate; arouse
⟨passions, urge⟩; **Aufputsch·mittel
das** stimulant
auf|räumen tr., itr. V. clear up
auf·recht 1. Adj. (auch fig.) upright;
2. adv. ⟨walk, sit, hold oneself⟩
straight; **aufrecht|erhalten** unr. tr.
V. maintain; keep up ⟨deception, fiction, contact, custom⟩
auf|regen 1. tr. V. excite; (ärgern)
annoy; irritate; (beunruhigen) agitate;
2. refl. V. get worked up (**über** + Akk.
about); **Auf·regung die** excitement
no pl.; (Beunruhigung) agitation no
pl.; **jmdn. in ~ versetzen** make sb. ex-
cited/agitated
auf|reißen 1. unr. tr. V. **a)** (öffnen)
tear open; wrench open ⟨drawer⟩;
fling open ⟨door, window⟩; **die Augen/
den Mund ~:** open one's eyes/mouth
wide; **b)** (beschädigen) tear open; tear
⟨clothes⟩; break up ⟨road, soil⟩; **2.** itr.
V.; mit sein ⟨clothes⟩ tear; ⟨seam⟩ split;
⟨wound⟩ open; ⟨cloud⟩ break up
auf|reizen tr. V. excite; **auf·reizend
1.** Adj. provocative; **2.** adv. provocat-
ively
auf|richten 1. tr. V. erect; put up; **den
Oberkörper ~:** raise one's upper
body; **jmdn. [wieder] ~** (fig.) give fresh
heart to sb.; **2.** refl. V. stand up
[straight]; **sich an jmdm./etw. [wieder]
~** (fig.) take heart from sb./sth.

auf·richtig 1. *Adj.* sincere; 2. *adv.* sincerely; **Auf·richtigkeit die** sincerity

auf|rücken *itr. V.; mit sein* move up

Auf·ruf der a) call; **b)** *(Appell)* appeal (**an** + *Akk.* to); **auf|rufen** *unr. tr. V.* **a)** call; **b)** jmdn. ~, etw. zu tun call upon sb. to do sth.; **c)** *(Rechtsw.)* appeal for ⟨witnesses⟩

Aufruhr der; ~s, ~e **a)** *(Widerstand)* rebellion; **b)** *o. Pl. (Erregung)* turmoil; **aufrührerisch** *Adj.* inflammatory

Auf·rüstung die armament

aufs *Präp.* + *Art.* = **auf das**

auf|sagen *tr. V.* recite

auf|sammeln *tr. V.* gather up

aufsässig 1. *Adj.* recalcitrant; 2. *adv.* recalcitrantly

Auf·satz der *(Text)* essay

auf|saugen *unr. (auch regelm.) tr. V.* soak up; *(fig.)* absorb

auf|schieben *unr. tr. V.* postpone

Auf·schlag der a) *(Aufprall)* impact; **b)** *(Preis~)* surcharge; **c)** *(Ärmel~)* cuff; *(Hosen~)* turn-up; *(Revers)* lapel; **d)** *(Tennis usw.)* serve

auf|schlagen 1. *unr. itr. V.* **a)** *mit sein* **auf etw.** *(Dat. od. Akk.)* ~: hit sth.; **b)** *(teurer werden)* ⟨price, rent, costs⟩ go up; **c)** *(Tennis usw.)* serve.; 2. *unr. tr. V.* **a)** *(öffnen)* crack ⟨nut, egg⟩ [open]; knock a hole in ⟨ice⟩; **sich** *(Dat.)* **das Knie/den Kopf** ~: cut one's knee/head; **b)** open ⟨book, newspaper, one's eyes⟩; **schlagt S. 15 auf!** turn to page 15; **c)** turn up ⟨collar, sleeve, trouser-leg⟩; **d)** *(aufbauen)* set up ⟨camp⟩; pitch ⟨tent⟩; put up ⟨bed, hut, scaffolding⟩; **e) 5 % auf etw.** *(Akk.)* ~: put 5% on sth.

auf|schließen 1. *unr. tr. V.* unlock; 2. *unr. itr. V.* |jmdm.| ~: unlock the door/gate *etc.* [for sb.]; **Auf·schluß der** information *no pl.*

auf|schneiden 1. *unr. tr. V.* **a)** cut open; **b)** *(zerteilen)* cut; 2. *unr. itr. V.* *(ugs.: prahlen)* boast (mit about); **Auf·schnitt der;** *o. Pl.* [assorted] cold meats *pl./*cheeses *pl.*

auf|schnüren *tr. V.* undo

auf|schrauben *tr. V.* unscrew; unscrew the top of ⟨bottle, jar, etc.⟩

auf|schreiben *unr. tr. V.* write down; [sich *(Dat.)*] etw. ~: make a note of sth.; **Auf·schrift die** inscription

Auf·schub der postponement; **die Sache duldet keinen** ~: the matter brooks no delay

Auf·schwung der upturn *(Gen.* in)

Aufsehen das; ~s stir; |großes| ~ erregen cause a [great] stir; **Auf·seher der** *(im Gefängnis)* warder *(Brit.)*; [prison] guard *(Amer.)*; *(im Park)* park-keeper; *(im Museum, auf dem Parkplatz)* attendant; *(auf einem Gut, Sklaven~)* overseer

auf|sein *unr. itr. V.; mit sein; nur im Inf. und Part. zusammengeschrieben (ugs.)* **a)** be open; **b)** *(nicht im Bett sein)* be up

auf|setzen 1. *tr. V.* **a)** put on; **b)** *(verfassen)* draw up ⟨text⟩; 2. *refl. V.* sit up

Auf·sicht die supervision; *(bei Prüfungen)* invigilation *(Brit.)*; proctoring *(Amer.)*

auf|springen *unr. itr. V.; mit sein* **a)** jump up; **b)** *(hinaufspringen)* jump on (**auf** + *Akk.* to); **c)** *(rissig werden)* crack

Auf·stand der rebellion; **auf·ständisch** *Adj.* rebellious

auf|stehen *unr. itr. V. mit sein* stand up; *(aus dem Liegen)* get up

auf|steigen *unr. itr. V.; mit sein* **a)** *(auf ein Fahrzeug)* get on; **auf etw.** *(Akk.)* ~: get on [to] sth.; **b)** *(bergan steigen)* climb; **c)** *(hochsteigen)* ⟨sap, smoke, mist⟩ rise; **d)** *(beruflich, gesellschaftlich)* rise (**zu** to); **zum Direktor** ~: rise to be manager

auf|stellen 1. *tr. V.* **a)** put up (**auf** + *Akk.* on); set up ⟨skittles⟩; *(postieren)* post; **b)** *(aufrecht hinstellen)* stand up; **c)** *(Sport)* select, pick ⟨team, player⟩; **d)** *(bilden)* put together ⟨team of experts⟩; raise ⟨army⟩; **e)** *(nominieren)* nominate; put up; 2. *refl. V.* position oneself; **Auf·stellung die a)** *s.* **aufstellen 1 a:** putting up; setting up; posting; **b)** *s.* **aufstellen b:** standing up; **c)** *s.* **aufstellen c:** selection; picking; **c)** *s.* **aufstellen d:** putting together; raising; **d)** *(Nominierung)* nomination

Aufstieg der; ~|e|s, ~e **a)** climb; **b)** *s.* **aufsteigen d:** rise

auf|stoßen 1. *unr. tr. V.* push open; 2. *unr. itr. V.* belch; ⟨baby⟩ bring up wind

Auf·strich der spread

auf|stützen 1. *tr. V.* rest ⟨one's arms etc.⟩; 2. *refl. V.* support oneself; **die Arme auf etw.** *(Akk. od. Dat.)* ~: rest one's arms on sth.

auf|suchen *tr. V.* call on; go to ⟨doctor⟩

Auf·takt der *(fig.)* start

auf|tauchen *itr. V.; mit sein* **a)** surface; **b)** *(sichtbar werden)* appear

auf|tauen **1.** *tr. V.* thaw; **2.** *itr. V.; mit sein (auch fig.)* thaw

auf|teilen *tr. V.* **a)** divide [up]; **b)** *(verteilen)* share out

Auftrag der; ~|e|s, **Aufträge** **a)** instructions *pl.;* **in** jmds. ~ *(Dat.)* on sb.'s instructions; *(für jmdn.)* on behalf of sb; **b)** *(Bestellung)* order; *(bei Künstlern, Architekten usw.)* commission; **c)** *(Mission)* task; *(Aufgabe)* job; **auf|tragen** *unr. tr. V.* **a)** jmdm. ~, etw. zu tun instruct sb. to do sth.; **b)** *(aufstreichen)* put on ⟨*paint, make-up, etc.*⟩; **Auftrag·geber** der client

auf|treten *unr. itr. V.; mit sein* **a)** tread; **b)** *(sich benehmen)* behave; **c)** *(eine Vorstellung geben)* appear; **als Zeuge/Kläger** ~: appear as a witness/a plaintiff; **d)** *(auftauchen)* ⟨*problem, difficulty, difference of opinion*⟩ arise; ⟨*symptom, danger, pest*⟩ appear; **Auftreten** das; ~s *(Benehmen)* manner

Auf·trieb der **a)** *(Physik)* ⟨*statischer* ~⟩ buoyancy; *(dynamischer* ~) lift; **b)** *(fig.)* impetus; **das hat ihm** ~/**neuen** ~ **gegeben** that has given him a lift/given him new impetus

Auf·tritt der **a)** *(Vorstellung)* appearance; **b)** *(Theater: das Auftreten)* entrance; *(Szene)* scene

auf|tun *unr. refl. V. (geh.)* open; *(fig.)* open up

auf|wachen *itr. V.; mit sein* wake up, awaken (**aus** from); *(aus Ohnmacht, Narkose)* come round (**aus** from)

auf|wachsen *unr. itr. V.; mit sein* grow up

Auf·wand der; ~|e|s cost; expense

auf|wärmen *tr. V.* heat *or* warm up ⟨*food*⟩; **2.** *refl. V.* warm oneself up

aufwärts *Adv.* upwards

auf|wecken *tr. V.* wake [up]; waken

auf|weichen **1.** *tr. V.* soften; **2.** *itr. V.; mit sein* become soft; soften up

auf·wendig **1.** *Adj.* lavish; *(kostspielig)* costly; expensive; **2.** *adv.* lavishly; *(kostspielig)* expensively

auf|wiegeln *tr. V.* incite; stir up

auf|wirbeln *tr. V.* swirl up

auf|wischen *tr. V.* **a)** wipe *or* mop up; **b)** *(säubern)* wipe ⟨*floor*⟩; *(mit Wasser)* wash ⟨*floor*⟩

auf|zählen *tr. V.* list; **Auf·zählung** die **a)** listing; **b)** *(Liste)* list

auf|zeichnen *tr. V.* **a)** record; **b)** *(zeichnen)* draw; **Auf·zeichnung**

die record; *(Film~, Ton~)* recording; ~en *(Notizen)* notes

auf|ziehen **1.** *unr. tr. V.* **a)** pull open ⟨*drawer*⟩; open, draw [back] ⟨*curtains*⟩; undo ⟨*zip*⟩; **b)** wind up ⟨*clock, toy, etc.*⟩. **2.** *unr. itr. V.; mit sein* come up; ⟨*clouds, storm*⟩ gather

Auf·zucht die raising; rearing

Auf·zug der **a)** *(Lift)* lift *(Brit.)*; elevator *(Amer.)*; **b)** *(abwertend: Aufmachung)* get-up; **c)** *(Theater: Akt)* act

Aug·apfel der eyeball; **Auge** das; ~s, ~n eye; **gute/schlechte** ~n **haben** have good/poor eyesight; **auf einem** ~ **blind** blind in one eye; **da wird er** ~n **machen** *(fig. ugs.)* his eyes will pop out of his head; **ich traute meinen** ~n **nicht** *(ugs.)* I couldn't believe my eyes; **ein** ~ *od.* **beide** ~n **zudrücken** *(fig.)* turn a blind eye; **jmdn./etw. nicht aus den** ~n **lassen** not take one's eyes off sb./sth.; **ins** ~ **gehen** *(fig. ugs.)* end in disaster; **unter vier** ~n *(fig.)* in private

Augen-: ~**arzt** der eye specialist; ~**blick** [*auch:* --'-] der *s.* ¹**Moment**; ~**blicklich** [*auch:* --'--] **1.** *Adj.* **a)** *(sofort)* immediate; **b)** *(gegenwärtig)* present; **2.** *adv.* **a)** *(sofort)* at once; **b)** *(zur Zeit)* at the moment; ~**braue** die eyebrow; ~**lid** das eyelid; ~**zeuge** der eyewitness

August der; ~|e|s *od.* ~, ~e August

Auktion die; ~, ~en auction

Aula die; ~, Aulen *od.* ~s hall

aus **1.** *Präp. mit Dat.* **a)** *(aus dem Inneren von)* out of; **b)** *(Herkunft, Quelle, Ausgangspunkt angebend, auch zeitlich)* from; ~ **Spanien/Köln** *usw.* from Spain/Cologne *etc.*; **c)** ~ **der Mode/Übung sein** be out of fashion/training; **d)** *(Grund, Ursache angebend)* out of; **etw.** ~ **Erfahrung wissen** know sth. from experience; ~ **Versehen** by mistake; **e)** *(bestehend* ~) of; *(hergestellt* ~) made of; ~ **etw. bestehen** consist of sth.; **f)** ~ **ihm ist ein guter Arzt geworden** he made a good doctor; **2.** *Adv.* **a)** *(ugs.: vorbei)* ~ **jetzt!** that's enough; **b)** „~" *(an Lichtschaltern)* 'out'; *(an Geräten)* 'off'; **c)** **vom Fenster/obersten Stockwerk** ~: from the window/top storey; **von mir** ~ *(ugs.)* if you like; **von sich** *(Dat.)* ~: of one's own accord

aus|atmen *itr., tr. V.* breathe out

Aus·bau der; ~|e|s **a)** *(Erweiterung)* extension; **b)** *(Ausgestaltung)* conversion (zu into); **aus|bauen** *tr. V.* **a)** *(demontieren)* remove (**aus** from); **b)** *(erweitern)* extend

Aus·beute die yield; **aus|beuten** tr. V. exploit

aus|bilden tr. V. **a)** train; **b)** (entwickeln) develop; **Aus·bildung** die **a)** training; **b)** (Entwicklung) development

Aus·blick der view (**auf** + Akk. of)

aus|brechen unr. itr. V.; mit sein **a)** break out (**aus** of); (fig.) break free (**aus** from); **b)** jmdm. bricht der Schweiß aus sb. breaks into a sweat; **c)** ⟨volcano⟩ erupt; **d)** (beginnen) break out; ⟨crisis⟩ break; **e)** in Gelächter/Weinen ~: burst out laughing/crying; in Beifall/Tränen ~: burst into applause/tears

aus|breiten 1. tr. V. spread; spread [out] ⟨map, cloth, sheet, etc.⟩; open out ⟨fan, newspaper⟩; (nebeneinanderlegen) spread out; 2. refl. V. spread

Aus·bruch der **a)** (Flucht) escape (**aus** from); **b)** (Beginn) outbreak; **c)** (Gefühls~) outburst; **d)** (eines Vulkans) eruption

aus|brüten tr. V. hatch out; (im Brutkasten) incubate

Aus·dauer die stamina; **aus·dauernd** Adj. with stamina postpos.

aus|dehnen 1. tr. V. **a)** stretch; (fig.) extend (**auf** + Akk. to); (zeitlich) prolong; 2. refl. V. expand; (zeitlich) go on; **Aus·dehnung** die expansion; (fig.) extension; (zeitlich) prolongation

aus|denken unr. refl. V. sich (Dat.) etw. ~: think sth. up

Aus·druck der; ~[e]s, **Ausdrücke** expression; (Terminus) term; etw. zum ~ bringen express sth.; **aus|drücken** 1. tr. V. **a)** (auspressen) squeeze ⟨juice⟩ out; squeeze [out] ⟨lemon, grape, orange, etc.⟩; squeeze out ⟨sponge⟩; squeeze ⟨boil, pimple⟩; **b)** stub out ⟨cigarette⟩; **c)** (mitteilen) express; 2. refl. V. **a)** express oneself; **b)** (offenbar werden) be expressed; **ausdrücklich** [od. -'--] 1. Adj. express attrib. ⟨command, wish, etc.⟩; explicit ⟨reservation⟩; 2. adv. expressly; ⟨mention⟩ explicitly; **ausdrucks·los** 1. Adj. expressionless; 2. adv. expressionlessly; **ausdrucks·voll** 1. Adj. expressive; 2. adv. expressively

aus einander Adv. apart; etw. ~ schreiben write sth. as separate words

auseinander-, Auseinander-: ~|brechen 1. unr. itr. V.; mit sein (auch fig.) break up; 2. unr. tr. V. break ⟨sth.⟩ up; ~|gehen unr. itr. V.; mit sein **a)** part; ⟨crowd⟩ disperse; **b)** (fig.) ⟨opinions, views⟩ differ; ~|halten unr. tr. V. tell ⟨things, people⟩ apart; ~|nehmen unr. tr. V. take ⟨sth.⟩ apart; ~|setzen 1. tr. V. jmdm. etw. ~setzen explain sth. to sb.; 2. refl. V. sich mit jmdm. ~setzen have it out with sb.; sich mit etw. ~setzen concern oneself with sth.; ~setzung die; ~, ~en **a)** (Streit) argument; **b)** (Kampfhandlungen) clash

Aus·fahrt die exit

Aus·fall der **a)** (das Nichtstattfinden) cancellation; **b)** (Einbuße, Verlust) loss; **c)** (eines Motors) failure; (einer Maschine, eines Autos) breakdown; **aus|fallen** unr. itr. V.; mit sein **a)** fall out; **b)** (nicht stattfinden) be cancelled; etw. ~ lassen cancel sth.; **c)** (ausscheiden) drop out; **d)** (nicht mehr funktionieren) ⟨engine, brakes, signal⟩ fail; ⟨machine, car⟩ break down; **e)** (ein bestimmtes Ergebnis zeigen) turn out; **ausfallend** Adj. |gegen jmdn.| ~ sein/werden be/become abusive [towards sb.]; **Ausfall·straße** die main road out of the/a town/city

aus·findig Adv. jmdn./etw. ~ machen find sb./sth.

Aus·flug der outing; **Ausflügler** der; ~s, ~: day-tripper; excursionist (Amer.)

Ausflugs-: ~dampfer der pleasure steamer; ~lokal das restaurant/café catering for [day-]trippers

aus|fragen tr. V. jmdn. ~: question sb., ask sb. questions (**nach, über** + Akk. about)

aus|fransen itr. V.; mit sein fray

Aus·fuhr die; ~, ~en s. Export; **aus|führen** tr. V. **a)** (ausgehen mit) take ⟨person⟩ out; **b)** (spazierenführen) take ⟨person, animal⟩ for a walk; **c)** (exportieren) export; **d)** (durchführen) carry out; (Sport) take ⟨penalty, free kick, corner⟩; **ausführlich** [auch: -'--] 1. Adj. detailed; full; 2. adv. in detail; **Aus·führung** die (Durchführung) carrying out; (Sport) taking

aus|füllen tr. V. **a)** fill; fill in ⟨form, crossword puzzle⟩; **b)** (beanspruchen, einnehmen) take up ⟨space⟩

Aus·gabe die **a)** o. Pl. giving out; (von Essen) serving; **b)** (Geld~) item of expenditure; ~n expenditure sing. (**für** on); **c)** (Edition) edition

Aus·gang der **a)** o. Pl. (Erlaubnis zum Ausgehen) time off; (von Soldaten) leave; **b)** (Tür ins Freie) exit (Gen.

from); **c)** *(Anat.)* outlet; **d)** *(Ende)* end; *(eines Romans, Films usw.)* ending; **e)** *o. Pl. (Ergebnis)* outcome; *(eines Wettbewerbs)* result; **ein Unfall mit tödlichem ~:** an accident with fatal consequences; **Ausgangspunkt der** starting-point

aus|geben *unr. tr. V.* **a)** give out; serve *(food, drinks)*; **b)** *(verbrauchen)* spend *(money)* **(für** on)

ausgebucht *Adj.* booked up

aus·gefallen *Adj.* unusual

ausgeglichen *Adj.* balanced; well-balanced *(person)*; equable *(climate)*

aus|gehen *unr. itr. V.; mit sein* **a)** go out; **b)** *(fast aufgebraucht sein)* run out; **c)** *(enden)* end; **gut/schlecht ~:** turn out well/badly; *(story, film)* end happily/unhappily; **d) von jmdm./etw. ~:** come from sb./sth.; **e) von etw. ~** *(etw. zugrunde legen)* take sth. as one's starting-point; *(etw. annehmen)* assume sth.

aus·gelassen **1.** *Adj.* exuberant *(mood, person)*; lively *(party, celebration)*; *(wild)* boisterous; **2.** *adv.* exuberantly; *(wild)* boisterously

aus·genommen *Konj.* except

ausgeprägt *Adj.* marked

ausgerechnet *Adv.* *(ugs.)* **~ heute/ morgen** today/tomorrow of all days; **~ hier** here of all places; **~ Sie** you of all people

aus·geschlossen *Adj.* **das ist ~:** that is out of the question

aus·geschnitten *Adj.* low-cut *(dress, blouse, etc.)*

aus·gestorben *Adj.* |wie| **~:** deserted

ausgezeichnet [*od.* '--'--] **1.** *Adj.* excellent; outstanding *(expert)*; **2.** *adv.* excellently

ausgiebig **1.** *Adj.* substantial *(meal)*; **2.** *adv. (profit)* handsomely; *(read)* extensively; **von etw. ~ Gebrauch machen** make full use of sth.

aus|gießen *unr. tr. V.* **a)** pour out **(aus** of); **b)** *(leeren)* empty

Ausgleich der; ~|e|s, ~e a) *s.* **ausgleichen a:** evening out; reconciliation; **b)** *(Schadensersatz)* compensation; **als** *od.* **zum ~ für etw.** to make up sth.; **aus|gleichen** *unr. tr. V.* **a)** even out; reconcile *(differences of opinions, contradictions)*; **b)** compensate for *(damage)*; make up for *(misfortune, lack)*; **etw. durch etw. ~:** make up for sth. with sth.; **sich ~:** balance out; *(sich gegenseitig aufheben)* cancel each other out

aus|graben *unr. tr. V.* dig up; *(Archäol.)* excavate; **Aus·grabung die** *(Archäol.)* excavation

aus|halten *unr. tr. V.* stand; bear; endure; withstand *(attack, load, pressure, test, wear and tear)*; **er konnte es zu Hause nicht mehr ~:** he couldn't stand it at home any more; **es ist nicht zum Aushalten** it is unbearable

aus|handeln *tr. V.* negotiate

aus|händigen *tr. V.* hand over

Aus·hang der notice

aus|heben *unr. tr. V.* dig out *(earth etc.)*; dig *(trench, grave, etc.)*

aus|helfen *unr. itr. V.* help out; **jmdm. ~:** help sb. out **(mit, bei** with); **Aus·hilfe die a)** *o. Pl. (das Aushelfen)* help; **b)** *s.* **Aushilfskraft; Aushilfs·kraft die** temporary worker; *(in Läden, Gaststätten)* temporary assistant; *(Sekretärin)* temporary secretary; temp *(coll.)*

aus|holen *itr. V.* |mit dem Arm| **~:** draw back one's arm; *(zum Schlag)* raise one's arm

aus|kennen *unr. refl. V. (an einem Ort usw.)* know one's way around; *(in einem Fach, einer Angelegenheit usw.)* know what's what; **sie kennt sich in dieser Stadt aus** she knows her way around the town; **sich |gut| mit/in etw.** *(Dat.)* **~:** know [a lot] about sth.

Aus·klang der *(geh.)* end; **zum ~ des Festes** to end *or* close the festival

aus|kleiden *tr. V. (geh.)* undress; **sich ~:** undress

aus|klingen *unr. itr. V. mit sein* end

aus|klopfen *tr. V.* **a)** beat out **(aus** + *Dat.* of); **b)** *(säubern)* beat *(carpet)*; knock *(pipe)* out

aus|kochen *tr. V.* boil; *(keimfrei machen)* sterilize *(instruments etc.)* [in boiling water]

aus|kommen *unr. itr. V.; mit sein* **a)** manage **(mit** on); **b) mit jmdm. |gut| ~:** get on [well] with sb.

Auskommen das; ~s livelihood

Auskunft die; ~, Auskünfte a) piece of information; **Auskünfte** information *sing.;* **[jmdm. über etw.** *(Akk.)*] **~ geben** give [sb.] information [about sth.]; **b)** *o. Pl. (Stelle)* information desk/counter/office/centre *etc.;* *(Fernspr.)* directory enquiries *no art.* *(Brit.);* directory information *no art.* *(Amer.)*

aus|lachen *tr. V.* laugh at

aus|laden *unr. tr. V.* unload *(goods etc.)*

Aus·lage die **a)** *Pl. (Unkosten)* expenses; **b)** *(ausgestellte Ware)* item on display; ~n goods on display

Aus·land das; *o. Pl.* foreign countries *pl.;* **im/ins** ~: abroad; **aus dem** ~: from abroad; **Ausländer** der; ~s, ~, **Ausländerin** die; ~, ~nen foreigner; **ausländisch** *Adj.* foreign

Auslands-: ~**aufenthalt** der stay abroad; ~**gespräch** das *(Fernspr.)* international call; ~**korrespondent** der foreign correspondent; ~**reise** die trip abroad

aus|lassen *unr. tr. V.* **a)** *(weglassen)* leave out; **b)** *(versäumen)* miss ⟨*opportunity, chance, etc.*⟩

Auslauf der **a)** *o. Pl.* **keinen/zuwenig ~ haben** have no/too little chance to run around outside; **b)** *(Raum)* space to run around in; **aus|laufen** *unr. itr. V.; mit sein* **a)** run out (**aus** of); **b)** *(leer laufen)* empty; ⟨*egg*⟩ run out; **c)** *(in See stechen)* sail (**nach** for); **d)** *(erlöschen)* ⟨*contract, agreement, etc.*⟩ run out; **Aus·läufer** der **a)** *(Geogr.)* foothill *usu. in pl.;* **b)** *(Met.) (eines Hochs)* ridge; *(eines Tiefs)* trough

aus|legen *tr. V.* **a)** *(hinlegen)* lay out; display ⟨*goods, exhibits*⟩; **b)** etw. mit **Fliesen/Teppichboden** ~: tile/carpet sth.; **c)** *(leihen)* lend; **d)** *(interpretieren)* interpret; **etw. falsch** ~: misinterpret sth.; **Auslegung** die; ~, ~en interpretation

aus|leihen *unr. tr. V. s.* **leihen**

aus|liefern *tr. V.* **jmdm. etw.** *od.* **etw. an jmdn.** ~: hand sth. over to sb.

aus|löschen *tr. V.* **a)** extinguish; **b)** *(beseitigen)* erase ⟨*drawing, writing*⟩

aus|losen *tr. V.* **etw.** ~: draw lots for sth.

aus|lösen *tr. V.* **a)** trigger ⟨*mechanism, device, alarm, etc.*⟩; release ⟨*camera shutter*⟩; **b)** provoke ⟨*discussion, anger, laughter, reaction, outrage, heart attack*⟩; cause ⟨*sorrow, horror, surprise, disappointment, panic, war*⟩; excite, arouse ⟨*interest, enthusiasm*⟩; **Auslöser** der; ~s, ~ *(Fot.)* shutter release

aus|machen *tr. V.* **a)** *(ugs.)* put out ⟨*light, fire, cigarette, candle*⟩; switch off ⟨*television, radio, hi-fi*⟩; turn off ⟨*gas*⟩; **b)** *(vereinbaren)* agree [on]; ~, **daß** ...: agree that ...; **c)** *(auszeichnen, kennzeichnen)* make up; **d)** **wenig/ nichts/viel** ~: make little/no/a great difference; **e) das macht mir nichts aus** I don't mind

Aus·maß das **a)** *(Größe)* size; **b)** *(Grad)* extent

aus|messen *unr. tr. V.* measure up

Aus·nahme die; ~, ~n exception; **mit ~ von** with the exception of; **bei jmdm. eine ~ machen** make an exception in sb.'s case; **Ausnahme·zustand** der state of emergency; **ausnahms·weise** *Adv.* by way of an exception; **Dürfen wir mitkommen? – Ausnahmsweise [ja]** May we come too? – Yes, just this once

aus|nehmen *unr. tr. V.* **a)** gut ⟨*fish, rabbit, chicken*⟩; **b)** *(ausschließen von)* exclude; *(gesondert behandeln)* make an exception of

aus|nutzen, *(bes. südd., österr.)* **aus|nützen** *tr. V.* **a)** take advantage of; **b)** *(ausbeuten)* exploit

aus|packen *tr., itr. V.* unpack; *(auswickeln)* unwrap

aus|pressen *tr. V.* squeeze out ⟨*juice*⟩; squeeze ⟨*orange, lemon*⟩; *(keltern)* press ⟨*grapes etc.*⟩

aus|probieren *tr. V.* try out

Aus·puff der exhaust

aus|radieren *tr. V.* rub out; erase

aus|rauben *tr. V.* rob

aus|räumen **1.** *tr. V.* **a)** clear out (**aus** of); **b)** *(fig.)* clear up; dispel ⟨*prejudice, suspicion, misgivings*⟩; **2.** *itr. V.* clear everything out

aus|rechnen *tr. V.* work out; **das kannst du dir leicht** ~ *(ugs.)* you can easily work that out [for yourself]

Aus·rede die excuse; **aus|reden 1.** *itr. V.* finish [speaking]; **2.** *tr. V.* **jmdm. etw.** ~: talk sb. out of sth.

aus|reichen *itr. V.* be enough *or* sufficient (**zu** for); **ausreichend 1.** *Adj.* sufficient; enough; *(als Note)* fair. **2.** *adv.* sufficiently

aus|reißen 1. *unr. tr. V.* tear out; pull out ⟨*plants, weeds*⟩; **2.** *unr. itr. V.; mit sein* **a)** *(sich lösen)* come off; **b)** *(ugs.: weglaufen)* run away (**Dat.** from)

aus|renken *tr. V.* dislocate

aus|richten *tr. V.* **a)** **jmdm. etw.** ~: tell sb. sth.; **b)** *(einheitlich anordnen)* line up; **c)** *(erreichen)* achieve

aus|rollen *tr. V.* roll out

aus|rotten *tr. V.* eradicate

Aus·ruf der cry; **aus|rufen** *unr. tr. V.* **a)** call out; „**Schön!**" **rief er aus** 'Lovely', he exclaimed; **b)** *(offiziell verkünden)* proclaim; declare ⟨*state of emergency*⟩; **c)** *(zum Kauf anbieten)* cry; **Ausrufe·zeichen** das exclamation mark

aus|ruhen *refl., itr. V.* have a rest; |sich| ein wenig/richtig ~: rest a little/ have a good rest; **ausgeruht sein** be rested

aus|rüsten *tr. V.* equip; **Aus·rüstung die a)** *o. Pl.* equipping; **b)** *(~sgegenstände)* equipment *no pl.*

aus|rutschen *itr. V.; mit sein* slip

Aus·sage die statement; **aus|sagen 1.** *tr. V.* **a)** say; **c)** *(vor Gericht, vor der Polizei)* state; *(unter Eid)* testify; **2.** *itr. V.* make a statement; *(unter Eid)* testify

aus|schalten *tr. V.* **a)** switch *or* turn off; **b)** *(fig.)* eliminate; exclude ⟨emotion, influence⟩; dismiss ⟨doubt, objection⟩; shut out ⟨feeling, thought⟩

Aus·schank der; ~|e|s, serving

Aus·schau die: nach jmdm./etw. ~ halten keep a look-out for sb./sth.; **aus|schauen** *itr. V.* **nach jmdm./etw.** ~ look out for sb./sth.

aus|scheiden 1. *unr. itr. V.; mit sein* **a) aus etw.** ~: leave sth.; **aus dem Amt** ~: leave office; **b)** *(Sport)* be eliminated; **c) diese Möglichkeit/dieser Kandidat scheidet aus** this possibility/candidate has to be ruled out; **2.** *unr. tr. V. (Physiol.)* excrete ⟨waste⟩; eliminate, expel ⟨poison⟩; exude ⟨sweat⟩; **Aus·scheidung die a)** *(Physiol.) s.* **ausscheiden 2:** excretion; elimination; expulsion; exudation; **~en** *(Ausgeschiedenes)* excreta; **b)** *(Sport)* qualifier

aus|schenken *tr. V.* serve

aus|schimpfen *tr. V.* jmdn. ~: tell sb. off

aus|schlafen 1. *unr. itr., refl. V.* have a good sleep; **2.** *unr. tr. V.* **seinen Rausch** ~: sleep off the effects of alcohol

Aus·schlag der a) *(Haut~)* rash; **b)** *(eines Zeigers, einer Waage)* deflection; *(eines Pendels)* swing; **den ~ geben** *(fig.)* tip the scales *(fig.)*; **aus|schlagen 1.** *unr. tr. V.* **a)** knock out; **b)** *(ablehnen)* turn down; **2.** *unr. itr. V.* **a)** ⟨horse⟩ kick; **b)** ⟨needle, pointer⟩ be deflected, swing; **c)** *(sprießen)* come out [in bud]; **aus·schlag·gebend** *Adj.* decisive

aus|schließen *unr. tr. V.* **a)** *(ausstoßen)* expel (aus from); **b)** *(nicht teilnehmen lassen)* exclude (aus from); **c)** *(fig.)* rule out ⟨possibility⟩; **jeden Irrtum** ~: rule out all possibility of error; **e)** *(aussperren)* lock out; **aus·schließlich** [*od.* '-'--, -'--] **1.** *Adj.* ex-

clusive; **2.** *Adv.* exclusively; **3.** *Präp. mit Gen.* excluding; **Aus·schluß der** exclusion (von from); *(aus einer Gemeinschaft)* expulsion (aus from); **unter ~ der Öffentlichkeit** with the public excluded; *(Rechtsw.)* in camera

aus|schmücken *tr. V.* deck out

aus|schneiden *unr. tr. V.* cut out; **Aus·schnitt der a)** *(Zeitungs~)* cutting; clipping; **b)** *(Hals~)* neck; **ein tiefer** ~: a plunging neck-line; **c)** *(Teil)* part; *(eines Textes)* excerpt; *(eines Films)* clip; *(Bild~)* detail

aus|schreiben *unr. tr. V.* **a)** *(nicht abgekürzt schreiben)* etw. ~: write sth. out in full; **b)** *(ausstellen)* make out ⟨cheque, invoice, receipt⟩; **c)** *(bekanntgeben)* call ⟨election, meeting⟩; advertise ⟨flat, job⟩; put ⟨supply order etc.⟩ out to tender; **Aus·schreibung die** *s.* **ausschreiben c:** calling; advertisement; invitation to tender

Ausschreitungen *Pl.* acts of violence

Aus·schuß der committee

aus|schütten *tr. V.* tip out ⟨water, sand, coal, etc.⟩; *(ausleeren)* empty ⟨bucket, bowl, container⟩

ausschweifend 1. *Adj.* wild ⟨imagination, emotion, hope, desire, orgy⟩; extravagant ⟨idea⟩; riotous, wild ⟨enjoyment⟩; dissolute ⟨life, person⟩; **2.** *adv.* ~ leben lead a dissolute life; **Ausschweifung die;** ~, ~en *(im Genießen)* dissolution

aus|sehen *unr. itr. V.* look (wie like); **so siehst du aus!** *(ugs.)* that's what you think!; **Aussehen das;** ~s appearance

aus|sein *unr. itr. V.; mit sein; nur im Inf. und Part. zusammengeschrieben* **a)** ⟨play, film, war⟩ be over; **wann ist die Vorstellung aus?** what time does the performance end?; **die Schule ist aus** school is out; **b)** ⟨fire, candle, etc.⟩ be out; **c)** ⟨radio, light, etc.⟩ be off

außen *Adv.* outside; **die Vase ist ~ bemalt** the vase is painted on the outside; **das Fenster geht nach ~ auf** the window opens outwards; **von ~:** from the outside

außen-, Außen-: ~handel der; *o. Pl.* foreign trade *no art.;* ~minister der Foreign Minister; ~ministerium das Foreign Ministry; ~politik die foreign politics *sing.;* ~politisch **1.** *Adj.* ⟨question⟩ relating to foreign policy; **2.** *adv.* as regards foreign policy; ~seite die outside

Außenseiter der; ~s, ~, **Außenseiterin** die; ~, ~nen outsider
außer 1. *Präp. mit Dat.* **a)** *(abgesehen von)* apart from; aside from *(Amer.)*; **b)** *(außerhalb von)* out of; ~ **sich sein** be beside oneself (**vor** + *Dat.* with); **c)** *(zusätzlich zu)* in addition to; **2.** *Präp. mit Akk.* ~ **sich geraten** become beside oneself (**vor** + *Dat.* with); **3.** *Konj.* except; **äußer...** *Adj.* outer; outside ⟨*pocket*⟩; outlying ⟨*district, area*⟩; external ⟨*injury, form, circumstances, cause, force*⟩; outward ⟨*appearance, similarity, effect, etc.*⟩; foreign ⟨*affairs*⟩
außer·dem [*auch:* --'-] *Adv.* as well; *(überdies)* besides
Äußere das; ~n [outward] appearance
außer-: ~**ehelich 1.** *Adj.* extramarital; illegitimate ⟨*child, birth*⟩; **2.** *adv.* outside marriage; ~**gewöhnlich 1.** *Adj.* **a)** unusual; **b)** *(das Gewohnte übertreffend)* exceptional; **2.** *adv.* **a)** unusually; **b)** *(sehr)* exceptionally; ~**halb** *Präp. mit Gen.* outside
äußerlich 1. *Adj.* external ⟨*use, injury*⟩; outward ⟨*appearance, calm, similarity, etc.*⟩; **2.** *adv.:* s. *Adj.:* externally; outwardly
äußern 1. *tr. V.* express, voice ⟨*opinion, view, criticism, reservations, disapproval, doubt*⟩; express ⟨*wish*⟩; voice ⟨*suspicion*⟩; **2.** *refl. V.* **a) sich über etw.** *(Akk.)* ~: give one's view on sth.; **b)** ⟨*illness*⟩ manifest itself (**in** + *Dat.*, **durch** in)
außer·ordentlich 1. *Adj.* **a)** extraordinary; **b)** *(das Gewohnte übertreffend)* exceptional; **2.** *adv. (sehr)* exceptionally; extremely ⟨*pleased, relieved*⟩
äußerst *Adv.* extremely; **äußerst...** *Adj.* **a)** extreme; **b)** *(letztmöglich)* latest possible ⟨*date, deadline*⟩; *(höchst...)* highest ⟨*price*⟩; *(niedrigst...)* lowest ⟨*price*⟩; **c)** *(schlimmst...)* worst
außerstande *Adv.* ~ **sein, etw. zu tun** *(nicht befähigt)* be unable to do sth.; *(nicht in der Lage)* not be in a position to do sth.
Äußerung die; ~, ~en comment
aus|setzen 1. *tr. V.* **a)** expose *(Dat.* to); **Belastungen ausgesetzt sein** be subject to strains; **b)** *(sich selbst überlassen)* abandon ⟨*baby, animal*⟩; *(auf einer einsamen Insel)* maroon; **c) an jmdm./etw. etwas auszusetzen haben** find fault with sb./sth.; **2.** *itr. V.* **a)** *(aufhören)* stop; ⟨*engine, machine*⟩ cut

out; **b)** *(pausieren)* ⟨*player*⟩ miss a turn; **mit der Arbeit/dem Training |ein paar Wochen|** ~: stop work/training [for a few weeks]
Aus·sicht die **a)** view (**auf** + *Akk.* of); **b)** *(fig.)* prospect; ~ **auf etw.** *(Akk.)* **haben, etw. in** ~ **haben** have the prospect of sth.
aussichts-, Aussichts-: ~**los 1.** *Adj.* hopeless. **2.** *adv.* hopelessly; ~**reich** *Adj.* promising; ~**turm der** look-out tower
aus|sortieren *tr. V.* sort out
aus|spannen *itr. V.* take *or* have a break
aus|sperren 1. *tr. V.* lock out; shut ⟨*animal*⟩ out; **2.** *itr. V.* lock the workforce out; **Aus·sperrung** die lockout
aus|spielen *tr. V.* **a)** *auch itr. (Kartenspiel)* lead; **b) jmdn./etw. gegen jmdn./ etw.** ~: play sb./sth. off against sb./ sth.
Aus·sprache die **a)** pronunciation; **b)** *(Gespräch)* discussion
aus|sprechen 1. *unr. tr. V.* **a)** pronounce; **b)** *(ausdrücken)* express; voice ⟨*suspicion, request*⟩; **2.** *unr. refl. V.* **a) b) sich lobend/mißbilligend** *usw.* **über jmdn./etw.** ~: speak highly/disapprovingly of *etc.* sb./sth.; **c)** *(offen sprechen)* say what's on one's mind; **sich bei jmdm.** ~: have a heart-to-heart talk with sb.; **d)** *(Strittiges klären)* talk things out (**mit** with); **3.** *unr. itr. V. (zu Ende sprechen)* finish [speaking]; **Aus·spruch der** remark
aus|spucken 1. *itr. V.* spit.; **2.** *tr. V.* spit out
aus|spülen *tr. V.* rinse out
Aus·stand der strike
aus|statten ['aʊsʃtatn̩] *tr. V.* provide (**mit** with); *(mit Gerät)* equip; *(mit Möbeln, Teppichen, Gardinen usw.)* furnish; **Ausstattung die; ~, ~en a)** s. **ausstatten** provision; equipping; furnishing; **b)** *(Ausrüstung)* equipment; *(Innen~ eines Autos)* trim; **c)** *(Einrichtung)* furnishings *pl.*
aus|stehen 1. *unr. itr. V.* **noch** ~ ⟨*debt*⟩ be outstanding; ⟨*decision*⟩ be still to be taken; ⟨*solution*⟩ be still to be found; **2.** *unr. tr. V.* **ich kann ihn/ das nicht** ~: I can't stand him/it
aus|steigen *unr. itr. V.; mit sein* get out; *(aus einem Zug, Bus)* get off
aus|stellen *tr. V.* **a)** put on display; display; *(im Museum, auf einer Messe)* exhibit; **b)** *(ausfertigen)* make out

⟨cheque, prescription, receipt, bill⟩; issue ⟨visa, passport, certificate⟩; c) (ugs.: ausschalten) switch off ⟨cooker, radio, heating, engine⟩; **Aus·stel·lung die a)** exhibition; **b)** *s.* ausstellen **b**: making out; issuing

aus|sterben unr. itr. V.; mit sein die out; ⟨species⟩ become extinct

Aus·steuer die trousseau (consisting mainly of household linen)

Ausstieg der: ~|e|s, ~e (Tür) exit

aus|stopfen tr. V. stuff

aus|stoßen unr. tr. V. **a)** expel; give off, emit ⟨gas, fumes, smoke⟩; **b)** give ⟨cry, whistle, laugh, sigh, etc.⟩; let out ⟨cry, scream, yell⟩; utter ⟨curse, threat, etc.⟩

aus|strahlen 1. tr. V. **a)** (auch fig.) radiate; ⟨lamp⟩ give out ⟨light⟩; **b)** (Rundf., Ferns.) broadcast; **2.** itr. V. **a)** radiate; ⟨light⟩ be given out; (fig.) ⟨pain⟩ spread; **b) auf jmdn./etw.** ~ (fig.) communicate itself to sb./influence sth.; **Aus·strahlung die** (fig.) charisma

aus|strecken 1. tr. V. stretch out; put out ⟨feelers⟩; **2.** refl. V. stretch out

aus|streichen unr. tr. V. cross out

aus|strömen itr. V.; mit sein pour out; ⟨gas, steam⟩ escape

aus|suchen tr. V. choose; pick

Aus·tausch der a) exchange; **im** ~ **für** od. **gegen** in exchange for; **b)** (das Ersetzen) replacement (gegen with); **aus|tauschen** tr. V. **a)** exchange (gegen for); **b)** (ersetzen) replace (gegen with); **Austausch·motor der** replacement engine

aus|teilen tr. V. distribute **an** + Akk. to); (aushändigen) hand out ⟨books, post, etc.⟩ (**an** + Akk. to); give ⟨orders⟩; deal [out] ⟨cards⟩; give out ⟨marks, grades⟩; serve ⟨food etc.⟩

Auster die; ~, ~n oyster

aus|tragen unr. tr. V. **a)** deliver ⟨newspapers, post⟩; **b)** ⟨pregnant woman⟩ carry ⟨child⟩ to full term; (nicht abtreiben) have ⟨child⟩; **c)** (ausfechten) settle ⟨conflict, differences⟩; fight out ⟨battle⟩

Australien [aus'tra:liən] (das); ~s Australia; **Australier der;** ~s, ~: Australian; **australisch** Adj. Australian

aus|treiben unr. tr. V. **a)** exorcize, cast out ⟨evil spirit, demon⟩; **b) jmdm. etw.** ~: cure sb. of sth.

aus|treten 1. unr. tr. V. **a)** tread out ⟨spark, cigarette-end⟩; trample out

⟨fire⟩; **b)** (bahnen) tread out ⟨path⟩; **c)** wear out ⟨shoes⟩; **2.** unr. itr. V.; mit sein **a)** (ugs.: zur Toilette gehen) pay a call (coll.); **b) aus etw.** ~ (ausscheiden) leave sth.

aus|trinken tr. V. drink up ⟨drink⟩; finish ⟨glass, cup, etc.⟩

Aus·tritt der leaving

aus|trocknen 1. tr. V. dry out; dry up ⟨river bed, marsh⟩; **2.** itr. V.; mit sein dry out; ⟨river bed, pond, etc.⟩ dry up; ⟨skin, hair⟩ become dry

aus|üben tr. V. practise ⟨art, craft⟩; follow ⟨profession⟩; carry on ⟨trade⟩; do ⟨job⟩; hold ⟨office⟩; wield ⟨power, right, control⟩

Aus·verkauf der sale; **ausverkauft** Adj. sold out

Aus·wahl die a) choice; **b)** (Sortiment) range; **viel/wenig** ~ **haben** have a wide/limited selection (**an** + Dat., **von** of); **aus|wählen** tr. V. choose (**aus** from)

Aus·wanderer der emigrant; **aus|wandern** itr. V.; mit sein emigrate; **Aus·wanderung die** emigration

auswärtig Adj. **a)** non-local; **b)** (das Ausland betreffend) foreign; **auswärts** Adv. **a)** (nach außen) outwards; **b)** (nicht zu Hause) ⟨sleep⟩ away from home; ~**essen** eat out; **c)** (nicht am Ort) in another town; (Sport) away; **Auswärts·spiel das** (Sport) away match

aus|waschen unr. tr. V. wash out

aus|wechseln tr. V. **a)** change (gegen + Akk. for); **b)** (ersetzen) replace (gegen with); (Sport) substitute ⟨player⟩

Aus·weg der way out (**aus** of); **ausweg·los 1.** Adj. hopeless. **2.** adv. hopelessly

aus|weichen unr. itr. V.; mit sein get out of the way (Dat. of); (Platz machen) make way (Dat. for); **einem Schlag/ Angriff** ~: dodge a blow/ evade an attack; **dem Feind** ~: avoid [contact with] the enemy; **einer Frage** ~: evade a question; **eine** ~**de Antwort** an evasive answer

Ausweis der; ~es, ~e card; (Personal~) identity card; **aus|weisen 1.** unr. tr. V. **a)** expel (**aus** from); **b) jmdn. als etw.** ~: show that sb. is/was sth.; **2.** unr. refl. V. prove or establish one's identity [by showing one's papers]; **können Sie sich** ~? do you have any means of identification?; **Aus·weisung die** expulsion (**aus** from)

aus|weiten tr. V. stretch

aus·wendig Adv. etw. ~ können/lernen know/learn sth. [off] by heart

aus|werten tr. V. analyse and evaluate; **Aus·wertung die** analysis and evaluation

aus|wirken refl. V. have an effect (**auf** + Akk. on); **sich günstig ~**: have a favourable effect; **Aus·wirkung die** effect (**auf** + Akk. on)

Aus·wuchs der a) (Wucherung) growth; excrescence (Med., Bot.); **b)** (fig.) unhealthy product; (Exzeß) excess

aus|zahlen 1. tr. V. **a)** pay out ⟨money⟩; **b)** pay off ⟨employee, worker⟩; buy out ⟨business partner⟩; **2.** refl. V. pay

aus|zählen tr. V. **a)** count [up] ⟨votes etc.⟩; **b)** (Boxen) count out

aus|zeichnen tr. V. **a)** (mit einem Preisschild) mark; **b)** (ehren) honour; **Aus·zeichnung die a)** o. Pl. (von Waren) marking; **b)** (Ehrung) honouring; (Orden) decoration; (Preis) award

aus|ziehen 1. unr. tr. V. **a)** pull out ⟨couch⟩; extend ⟨table, tripod, etc.⟩; **b)** (ablegen) take off ⟨clothes⟩; **c)** (entkleiden) undress; **sich ~**: get undressed; **2.** unr. itr. V.; mit sein move out (**aus** of); **Aus·zug der a)** (das Ausziehen) move; **b)** (Bankw.) statement; **c)** (Textpassage) extract

Auto das; ~s, ~s car; automobile (Amer.); ~ **fahren** drive; (mitfahren) go in the car

Auto-: ~**bahn die** motorway (Brit.); expressway (Amer.); ~**biographie** [-----'-] die autobiography; ~**bus der** s. Bus; ~**fähre die** car ferry; ~**fahren** driving; motoring; ~**fahrer der** [car-]driver; ~**fahrt die** drive; ~**gramm** [--'-] das; ~s, ~e autograph; ~**kino das** drive-in cinema

Automat der; ~en, ~en **a)** (Verkaufs~) [vending-] machine; (Spiel~) slot-machine; **b)** (in der Produktion) robot; **Automatik die;** ~, ~en automatic control mechanism; (Getriebe~) automatic transmission; **automatisch** (auch fig.) **1.** Adj. automatic; **2.** adv. automatically; **automatisieren** tr. V. automate; **Automatisierung die;** ~, ~en automation

auto-, Auto-: ~**mobil** [---'-] das; ~s, ~e (geh.) motor car; automobile (Amer.); ~**nom** [--'-] **1.** Adj. autonomous; **2.** adv. autonomously; ~**nomie**

[---'-] **die;** ~, ~n autonomy; ~**nummer die** [car] registration number

Autopsie [autɔ'psi:] **die;** ~, ~n postmortem [examination]

Autor der; ~s, ~en author

Auto-: ~**radio das** car radio; ~**reifen der** car tyre; ~**reisezug der** Motorail train (Brit.); auto train (Amer.)

Autorin die; ~, ~nen authoress; author

autoritär Adj. authoritarian; **Autorität die;** ~, ~en authority

Auto-: ~**schlange die** queue of cars; ~**schlüssel der** car key; ~**stopp der** hitch-hiking; **per** ~**stopp fahren**, ~**stopp machen** hitch-hike; ~**unfall der** car accident; ~**vermietung die** car rental firm; ~**werkstatt die** garage

Avocado [avo'ka:do] **die;** ~, ~s avocado [pear]

Axt die; ~, Äxte axe

Azalee [atsa'le:ə] **die;** ~, ~n azalea

B

b, B [be:] **das;** ~, ~ **a)** (Buchstabe) b/B; **b)** (Musik) [key of] B flat

B Abk. Bundesstraße ≈ A (Brit.)

Baby ['be:bi] **das;** ~s, ~s baby; **Baby·sitter** [-sɪtɐ] **der;** ~s, ~: babysitter

Bach der; ~[e]s, Bäche **a)** stream; brook; **b)** (Rinnsal) stream [of water]

Back·blech das baking-sheet

Back·bord das (Seew., Luftf.) port [side]; **Backe die;** ~, ~n cheek

backen 1. unr. itr. V. bake; **2.** unr. tr. V. **a)** bake; **b)** (bes. südd.) s. **braten**

Backen·zahn der molar

Bäcker der; ~s, ~: baker; **er ist** ~: he is a baker; **zum/beim** ~: to the/at the baker's; **Bäckerei die;** ~, ~en baker's [shop]

Back-: ~**fisch der** fried fish (in breadcrumbs); ~**form die** baking-tin (Brit.); baking-pan (Amer.); ~**hähnchen das**, ~**hendl das** (österr.), ~**huhn das** fried chicken (in breadcrumbs); ~**ofen der** oven; ~**pulver**

das baking-powder; **~stein der** brick; **~waren** *Pl.* bread, cakes, and pastries
Bad das; **~[e]s, Bäder a)** bath; *(das Schwimmen)* swim; *(im Meer o. ä.)* bathe; **ein ~ nehmen** *(geh.)* take a bath; *(schwimmen)* go for a swim; *(im Meer o. ä.)* bathe; **b)** *(Badezimmer)* bathroom; **ein Zimmer mit ~:** a room with [private] bath; **c)** *(Schwimm~)* [swimming-]pool; **d)** *(Heil~)* spa; *(See~)* [seaside] resort
Bade-: **~an·zug** der bathing costume; **~hose die** bathing trunks *pl;* **~mantel der** dressing-gown; bathrobe; **~meister der** swimming-pool attendant; **~mütze die** bathing cap
baden 1. *itr. V.* **a)** have a bath; **b)** *(schwimmen)* bathe; **~ gehen** go for a bathe; 2. *tr. V.* bath ⟨*child, patient, etc.*⟩; bathe ⟨*wound, eye, etc.*⟩
Bäder *s.* Bad
Bade-: **~strand** der bathing-beach; **~tuch** das bath towel; **~wanne die** bath[-tub]; **~wasser das** bath water; **~zimmer** das bathroom
Bagatelle die; ~, ~n trifle
Bagger der; ~s, ~: excavator; *(Schwimm~)* dredger; **Bagger·see der** flooded gravel-pit
Bahn die; ~, ~en **a)** *(Weg)* path; **b)** *(Route)* path; *(eines Geschosses)* trajectory; **c)** *(Sport)* track; *(für Pferderennen)* course *(Brit.);* track *(Amer.);* *(für einzelne Teilnehmer)* lane; *(Kegel~)* alley; *(Bowling~)* lane; **d)** *(Eisen~)* railways *pl.;* railroad *(Amer.);* *(Zug)* train; **jmdn. zur ~ bringen** take sb. to the station; **|mit der| ~ fahren** go by train; **f)** *(Straßen~)* tram; streetcar *(Amer.)*
bahn-, Bahn-: **~brechend** *Adj.* pioneering; **~bus** der railway bus; **~damm** der railway embankment
bahnen *tr. V.* clear ⟨*way, path*⟩; **jmdm./einer Sache einen Weg ~** *(fig.)* pave the way for sb./sth.
Bahn-: **~fahrt die** train journey; **~hof** der [railway *or (Amer.)* railroad] station; **~reise die** train journey; **~schranke die** level-crossing *(Brit.)* *or (Amer.)* grade crossing barrier/gate; **~steig** der; **~[e]s, ~e** [station] platform; **~übergang** der level-crossing *(Brit.);* grade crossing *(Amer.);* **~verbindung die** train connection
Bahre die; ~, ~n **a)** *(Kranken~)* stretcher; **b)** *(Toten~)* bier

Baiser [bɛ'ze:] das; ~s, ~s meringue
Bajonett das; ~[e]s, ~e bayonet
Bakterie [bak'te:riə] die; ~, ~n bacterium
Balance [ba'laŋsə] die; ~, ~n balance; **balancieren** *itr., tr. V.; itr. mit sein* balance
bald *Adv.* **a)** soon; *(leicht, rasch)* quickly; easily; **wird's ~?** get a move on, will you; **bis ~!** see you soon; **b)** *(ugs.: fast)* almost
Baldrian ['baldria:n] der; ~s, ~e valerian
Balkan ['balka:n] der; ~s: **der ~:** the Balkans *pl.;* *(Gebirge)* the Balkan Mountains *pl.* **auf dem ~:** in the Balkans
Balken der; ~s, ~: beam
Balkon [bal'kɔŋ, bal'ko:n] der; ~s, ~s [bal'kɔŋs] *od.* ~e [bal'ko:nə] **a)** balcony; **b)** *(im Theater, Kino)* circle
Ball der; ~[e]s, Bälle **a)** ball; **~ spielen** play ball; **b)** *(Fest)* ball
Ballade die; ~, ~n ballad
Ballast der; ~[e]s, ~e ballast
ballen 1. *tr. V.* clench ⟨*fist*⟩; 2. *refl. V.* ⟨*fist*⟩ clench; **Ballen der;** ~s, ~ **a)** *(Packen)* bale; **b)** *(Hand~, Fuß~)* ball
Ballett das; ~[e]s, ~e ballet
Ball-: **~junge der** ballboy; **~kleid das** ball gown
Ballon [ba'lɔŋ] der; ~s, ~s balloon
Ball-: **~saal der** ballroom; **~spiel das** ball game; **~spielen das;** ~s playing ball *no art.*
Ballungs·gebiet das conurbation
Balsam der; ~s, ~e balsam; *(fig.)* balm
Balte der; ~n, ~n, **Baltin die;** ~, ~nen Balt; **Baltikum das;** ~s Baltic States *pl.;* **baltisch** *Adj.* Baltic
Bambus der; ~ *od.* ~ses, ~se bamboo
banal *Adj.* **a)** banal; **b)** *(gewöhnlich)* commonplace
Banane die; ~, ~n banana
Banause der; ~n, ~n *(abwertend)* philistine
band *1. u. 3. Pers. Sg. Prät. v.* binden
¹Band das; ~[e]s, Bänder **a)** ribbon; *(Haar~, Hut~)* band; *(Schürzen~)* string; **b)** *(Klebe~, Isolier~, Ton~ usw.)* tape; **etw. auf ~** *(Akk.)* **aufnehmen** tape[-record] sth.; **c)** *s.* Förderband; **d)** *s.* Fließband; **e) am laufenden ~** *(ugs.)* nonstop; **f)** *(Anat.)* ligament
²Band der; ~[e]s, Bände ['bɛndə] volume
³Band [bɛnt] die; ~, ~s band; *(Beat~, Rock~ usw.)* group

¹**Bande** die; ~, ~n a) gang; b) *(ugs.: Gruppe)* mob *(sl.)*

²**Bande** die; ~, ~n *(Sport)* [perimeter] barrier; *(mit Reklame)* billboards *pl.; (Billard)* cushion

Bänder s. ¹**Band**

bändigen *tr. V.* tame ⟨*animal*⟩; control ⟨*person, anger, urge*⟩

Bandit der; ~en, ~en bandit

Band·scheibe die [intervertebral] disc

bang, bange; banger, bangst... od. bänger, bängst...: 1. *Adj.* afraid; scared; *(besorgt)* anxious; **mir ist/wurde** ~ [zumute] I am/became scared; 2. *adv.* anxiously; **bangen** *itr. V.* be anxious

¹**Bank** die; ~, **Bänke** bench; *(mit Lehne)* bench seat; *(Kirchen~)* pew; **etw. auf die lange ~ schieben** *(ugs.)* put sth. off

²**Bank** die; ~, ~en bank

¹**Bankett** das; ~[e]s, ~e banquet

²**Bankett** das; ~[e]s, ~e *(an Straßen)* shoulder; *(unbefestigt)* verge

Bankier [baŋ'kie:] der; ~s, ~s banker

Bank-: ~**konto** das bank account; ~**leitzahl** die bank sorting code number; ~**note** die banknote; bill *(Amer.)*; ~**raub** der bank robbery; ~**räuber** der bank robber

bankrott *Adj.* bankrupt; ~ **gehen** go bankrupt; **Bankrott** der; ~[e]s, ~e bankruptcy; ~ **machen** go bankrupt

Bann der; ~[e]s *(fig. geh.)* spell

bar 1. *Adj.* cash; 2. *adv.* in cash

Bar die; ~, ~s bar

Bär der; ~en, ~en bear

Baracke die; ~, ~n hut

Barbar der; ~en, ~en barbarian; **Barbarei** die; ~, ~en a) *(Roheit)* barbarity; b) *(Kulturlosigkeit)* barbarism *no indef. art.;* **barbarisch** 1. *Adj.* a) *(roh)* barbarous; b) *(unzivilisiert)* barbaric; 2. *adv.* a) *(roh)* barbarously; b) *(unzivilisiert)* barbarically

Bar·dame die barmaid

Barett das; ~[e]s, ~e *(eines Geistlichen)* biretta; *(eines Richters, Professors)* cap; *(Baskenmütze)* beret

bar·fuß indekl. *Adj.; nicht attr.* barefooted; ~ **herumlaufen/gehen** run about/go barefoot

barg 1. u. 3. Pers. Sg. Prät. v. **bergen**

Bar-: ~**geld** das cash; ~**hocker** der bar stool

Bariton ['ba(:)ritɔn] der; ~s, ~e baritone

Barkasse die; ~, ~n launch

barmherzig *(geh.)* 1. *Adj.* merciful; 2. *adv.* mercifully; **Barmherzigkeit** die; ~ *(geh.)* mercy

Barock das *od.* der; ~[s] a) baroque; b) *(Zeit)* baroque age

Baro·meter das barometer

Baron der; ~s, ~e baron; *(als Anrede)* [**Herr**] ~: ≈ my lord; **Baronin** die; ~, ~nen baroness; *(als Anrede)* [**Frau**] ~: ≈ my Lady

Barren der; ~s, ~ a) *(Gold~, Silber~ usw.)* bar; b) *(Turngerät)* parallel bars *pl.*

Barriere [ba'riɛ:rə] die; ~, ~n *(auch fig.)* barrier

Barrikade die; ~, ~n barricade

barsch 1. *Adj.* curt; 2. *adv.* curtly

Barsch der; ~[e]s, ~e perch

barst 1. u. 3. Pers. Sg. Prät. v. **bersten**

Bart der; ~[e]s, **Bärte** a) beard; *(Oberlippen~, Schnurr~)* moustache; b) *(von Katzen, Mäusen, Robben)* whiskers *pl.;* c) *(am Schlüssel)* bit; **bärtig** *Adj.* bearded; **Bart·wuchs** der growth of beard

Bar·zahlung die cash payment

Basalt der; ~[e]s, ~e basalt

Basar der; ~s, ~e bazaar

Basis die; ~, **Basen** a) *(Grundlage)* basis; b) *(Math., Archit., Milit.)* base

Baske der; ~n, ~n, **Baskin** die; ~, ~nen Basque

Basken-: ~**land** das Basque region; ~**mütze** die beret

Basket·ball ['ba(:)skət-] der basketball

Baß der; **Basses, Bässe** *(Musik)* a) bass; b) *(Instrument)* double-bass

Bassin [ba'sɛ̃:] das; ~s, ~s *(Schwimm~)* pool; *(im Garten)* pond

Bassist der; ~en, ~en *(Musik)* a) *(Sänger)* bass; b) *(Instrumentalist)* double-bass player; bassist; *(in einer Rockband)* bass guitarist

Bast der; ~[e]s, ~e bast; *(Raffia~)* raffia

basta *Interj. (ugs.)* that's enough; **und damit ~!** and that's that!

Bastelei die; ~, ~en; a) *(Gegenstand)* piece of handicraft work; b) *(ugs.: das Basteln)* handicraft work; **basteln** 1. *tr. V.* make; 2. *itr. V.* make things [with one's hands]

Bastion die; ~, ~en bastion

bat 1. u. 3. Pers. Sg. Prät. v. **bitten**

Bataillon [batal'jo:n] das; ~s, ~e *(Milit.)* battalion

Batik der; ~s, ~en *od.* die; ~, ~en batik

Batist der; ~|e|s, ~e batiste
Batterie die; ~, ~n battery
Batzen der; ~s, ~ *(ugs.)* a) *(Klumpen)* lump; b) *(Menge)* pile *(coll.)*
¹Bau der; ~|e|s, ~ten a) o. Pl. *(Errichtung)* building; **im** ~ **sein** be under construction; b) *(Gebäude)* building; c) **auf dem** ~ **arbeiten** *(Bauarbeiter sein)* be in the building trade; d) o. Pl. *(Struktur)* structure
²Bau der; ~|e|s, ~e *(Kaninchen~)* burrow; hole; *(Fuchs~)* earth
Bau·arbeiten Pl. building work sing.
Bauch der; ~|e|s, Bäuche *(auch fig.: von Schiffen, Flugzeugen)* belly; **bauchig** Adj. bulbous
Bauch-: ~**laden** der vendor's tray; ~**landung** die belly-landing; ~**nabel** der *(ugs.)* belly-button *(coll.)*; ~**redner** der ventriloquist; ~**schmerzen** Pl. stomach-ache sing.; ~**speichel·drüse** die pancreas; ~**tanz** der belly-dance; ~**tänzerin** die belly-dancer; ~**weh das** *(ugs.)* tummy-ache *(coll.)*; stomach-ache
bauen 1. tr. V. build; 2. itr. V. a) build; **wir wollen** ~: we want to build a house; *(bauen lassen)* we want to have a house built; b) **auf jmdn./etw.** ~ *(fig.)* rely on sb./sth.
¹Bauer der; ~n, ~n a) farmer; *(mit niedrigem sozialem Status)* peasant; b) *(Schachfigur)* pawn; c) *(Kartenspiele)* s. Bube
²Bauer das od. der; ~s, ~: [bird-]cage
Bäuerin die; ~, ~nen a) s. ¹Bauer a: [lady] farmer; peasant [woman]; b) *(Frau eines Bauern)* farmer's wife; **bäuerlich** Adj. farming attrib.; *(ländlich)* rural
Bauern-: ~**haus** das farmhouse; ~**hof** der farm
bau-, Bau-: ~**fällig** Adj. ramshackle; unsafe *(roof, ceiling)*; ~**jahr** das year of construction; *(bei Autos)* year of manufacture; ~**kasten** der construction set; *(mit Holzklötzen)* box of bricks; ~**klotz** der building-brick
baulich Adj.; nicht präd. structural
Baum der; ~|e|s, Bäume tree; **Bäumchen** das; ~s, ~ small tree
Bau·meister der *(hist.)* [architect and] master builder
baumeln itr. V. *(ugs.)* dangle **(an +** Dat. from)
Baum-: ~**schule** die tree nursery; ~**stamm** der tree-trunk; ~**stumpf** der tree-stump; ~**wolle** die cotton

Bau·platz der site for building
bäurisch *(abwertend)* 1. Adj. boorish; 2. adv. boorishly
Bau·satz der kit
Bausch der; ~|e|s, ~e od. Bäusche a) *(Watte~)* a wad; b) etw. **in** ~ **und Bogen verwerfen/verdammen** reject/condemn sth. wholesale; **bauschen** 1. tr. V. billow ⟨sail, curtains, etc.⟩; 2. refl. V. ⟨dress, sleeve⟩ puff out; *(ungewollt)* bunch up; *(im Wind)* ⟨curtain, flag, etc.⟩ billow [out]; **bauschig** Adj. puffed ⟨dress⟩; baggy ⟨trousers⟩
bau-, Bau-: ~**sparen** itr. V.; nur Inf. gebr. save with a building society; ~**spar·kasse die** ≈ building society; ~**stein der** a) building stone; b) *(Bestandteil)* element; *(Elektronik, DV)* module; c) *(~klotz)* building-brick; ~**stelle die** building site; *(beim Straßenbau)* road-works pl.
Bauten Pl.: s. Bau
Bau-: ~**unternehmer** der building contractor; ~**weise die** method of construction; ~**werk das** building; *(Brücke, Staudamm)* structure
Bayer der; ~n, ~n Bavarian; **bay[e]risch** Adj. Bavarian; **Bayern (das);** ~s Bavaria
Bazille die; ~, ~n *(ugs.)* s. Bazillus a; **Bazillus** der; ~, Bazillen a) bacillus; b) *(fig.)* cancer
Bd. Abk. Band Vol.
beabsichtigen tr. V. intend
beachten tr. V. a) follow ⟨rule, regulations, instruction⟩; heed, follow ⟨advice⟩; obey ⟨traffic signs⟩; observe ⟨formalities⟩; b) *(berücksichtigen)* take account of; *(achten auf)* pay attention to; **beachtlich** 1. Adj. considerable; 2. adv. considerably; **Beachtung die** a) s. beachten a: following; heeding; obeying; b) *(Berücksichtigung)* consideration; c) *(Aufmerksamkeit)* attention
Beamte der; adj. Dekl. official; *(Staats~)* [permanent] civil servant; *(Kommunal~)* [established] local government officer; *(Polizei~)* [police] officer; **Beamtin die;** ~, ~nen s. Beamte
beängstigend Adj. worrying
beanspruchen tr. V. a) claim; **etw.** ~ **können** be entitled to expect sth.; b) *(ausnutzen)* make use of ⟨person, equipment⟩; take advantage of ⟨hospitality, services⟩; c) *(erfordern)* demand ⟨energy, attention, stamina⟩; take up ⟨time, space, etc.⟩; **Bean-**

spruchung die; ~, ~en demands *pl.*
(*Gen.* on); **die ~ durch den Beruf** the
demands of his/her job
beanstanden *tr. V.* take exception
to; *(sich beklagen über)* complain
about; **Beanstandung** die; ~, ~en
complaint
beantragen *tr. V.* apply for
beantworten *tr. V.* answer; reply to
⟨*letter*⟩; return ⟨*greeting*⟩
bearbeiten *tr. V.* **a)** deal with; handle
⟨*case*⟩; **b)** *(adaptieren)* adapt (**für** for);
Bearbeitung die; ~, ~en **a) die ~ eines Antrags/eines Falles** *usw.* dealing
with an application/handling a case
etc.; **b)** *(Adaption)* adaptation
beaufsichtigen *tr. V.* supervise;
look after ⟨*child*⟩
beauftragen *tr. V.* entrust
bebauen *tr. V.* build on; develop;
Bebauung die; ~, ~en **a)** development; **b)** *(Gebäude)* buildings *pl.*
beben *itr. V.* shake; **Beben** das; ~s,
~ *(Erd~)* earthquake
bebildern *tr. V.* illustrate
Becher der; ~s, ~ *(Glas~, Porzellan~)*
glass; tumbler; *(Plastik~)* beaker;
cup; *(Eis~)* *(aus Glas, Metall)* sundae
dish; *(aus Pappe)* tub; *(Joghurt~)* carton
Becken das; ~s, ~ **a)** *(Wasch~)* basin;
(Abwasch~) sink; *(Toiletten~)* pan; **b)**
(Anat.) pelvis; **c)** *Pl. (Musik)* cymbals
bedacht *Adj.* **auf etw.** *(Akk.)* **~ sein** be
intent on sth.; **bedächtig 1.** *Adj.* **a)**
deliberate; measured ⟨*steps, stride,
speech*⟩; **b)** *(besonnen)* thoughtful;
well-considered ⟨*words*⟩; **2.** *adv.* **a)**
deliberately; **b)** *(besonnen)* thoughtfully
bedanken *refl. V.* say thank you; **sich
bei jmdm. [für etw.] ~:** thank sb. [for
sth.]
Bedarf der; ~[e]s need (**an** + *Dat.* of);
requirement (**an** + *Dat.* for); *(Be-
darfsmenge)* needs *pl.;* requirements
pl.; **bei ~:** if required
bedauerlich *Adj.* regrettable; **be-
dauerlicher·weise** *Adv.* regrettably; **bedauern** *tr., itr. V.* **a)** feel
sorry for; **sie läßt sich gerne ~:** she
likes being pitied; **b)** *(schade finden)*
regret; **ich bedaure sehr, daß ...:** I am
very sorry that ...; **Bedauern** das; ~s
regret; **zu meinem ~:** to my regret;
bedauerns·wert *Adj. (geh.)* unfortunate ⟨*person*⟩
bedecken *tr. V.* cover; **bedeckt** *Adj.*
overcast ⟨*sky*⟩

bedenken *unr. tr. V.* **a)** consider; **b)**
(beachten) take into consideration;
Bedenken das; ~s, ~ reservation
(**gegen** about); **ohne ~:** without hesitation; **bedenken·los 1.** *Adj.* unhesit-
ating; *(skrupellos)* unscrupulous; **2.**
adv. without hesitation; *(skrupellos)*
unscrupulously; **bedenklich 1.** *Adj.*
a) dubious ⟨*methods, transactions,
etc.*⟩; **b)** *(bedrohlich)* alarming; **2.** *adv.*
alarmingly; **Bedenk·zeit** die; *o. Pl.*
time for reflection
bedeuten *tr. V.* **a)** mean; **was soll das
~?** what does that mean?; **b)** *(sein)*
represent; **das bedeutet ein Wagnis**
that is being really daring; **bedeutend 1.** *Adj.* **a)** important; **b)**
(groß) substantial; considerable ⟨*success*⟩; **2.** *adv.* considerably; **Bedeutung** die; ~, ~en **a)** meaning; **b)**
o. Pl. (Wichtigkeit) importance
bedeutungs-: **~los** *Adj.* insignificant; **~voll 1.** *Adj.* **a)** significant; **b)**
(vielsagend) meaningful; meaning
⟨*look*⟩; **2.** *adv.* meaningfully
bedienen 1. *tr. V.* **a)** serve; **werden Sie
schon bedient?** are you being served?;
b) *(handhaben)* operate ⟨*machine*⟩; **2.**
itr. V. serve; **3.** *refl. V.* help oneself;
sich selbst ~ *(im Geschäft, Restaurant
usw.)* serve oneself; **Bedienung** die;
~, ~en **a)** *o. Pl. (das Bedienen)* service;
~ inbegriffen service included; **b)** *o.
Pl. (das Handhaben)* operation; **c)**
(Servierer[in]) waiter/waitress; **Be-
dienungs·anleitung** die operating
instructions *pl.*
bedingen *tr. V.* cause; **Bedingung**
die; ~, ~en condition; **unter der ~,
daß ...:** on condition that ...; **bedin-
gungs·los** *Adj.* unconditional
bedrängen *tr. V.* **a)** besiege ⟨*town,
fortress, person*⟩; put ⟨*opposing player*⟩
under pressure; **b)** *(belästigen)* pester;
bedrohen *tr. V.* threaten; **bedrohlich 1.** *Adj. (unheilverkündend)* ominous; *(gefährlich)* dangerous; **2.** *adv.
(unheilverkündend)* ominously; *(gefährlich)* dangerously; **Bedrohung**
die threat (*Gen.* to)
bedrucken *tr. V.* print
bedrücken *tr. V.* depress
Beduine der; ~n, ~n Bed[o]uin
bedürfen *unr. itr. V.* **jmds./einer Sache ~** *(geh.)* require *or* need sb./sth.;
Bedürfnis das; ~ses, ~se need (**nach**
for); **das ~ haben, etw. zu tun** feel a
need to do sth.; **bedürftig** *Adj.*
needy

Beef·steak ['bi:f-] **das** [beef]steak; deutsches ~: ≈ beefburger

beehren *tr. V. (geh.)* honour

beeiden *tr. V.* ~, **daß** ...: swear [on oath] that ...; **eine Aussage** ~: swear to the truth of a statement

beeilen *refl. V.* hurry [up *(coll.)*]

beeindrucken *tr. V.* impress; **beeindruckend** *Adj.* impressive

beeinflussen *tr. V.* influence; **Beeinflussung die;** ~, ~en influencing

beeinträchtigen *tr. V.* restrict ⟨*sights, freedom*⟩; detract from ⟨*pleasure, enjoyment, value*⟩; spoil ⟨*appetite, good humour*⟩; impair ⟨*quality, reactions, efficiency, vision, hearing*⟩; damage, harm ⟨*sales, reputation*⟩

beenden *tr. V.* end; finish ⟨*piece of work etc.*⟩; complete ⟨*studies*⟩

beengen *tr. V.* restrict

beerben *tr. V.* **jmdn.** ~: inherit sb's estate

beerdigen *tr. V.* bury; **Beerdigung die;** ~, ~en burial; *(Trauerfeier)* funeral; **Beerdigungs·institut das** [firm *sing.* of] undertakers *pl.*

Beere die; ~, ~n berry

Beet das; ~[e]s, ~e *(Blumen~)* bed; *(Gemüse~)* plot

befahrbar *Adj.* passable; **befahren** *unr. tr. V.* **a)** drive on ⟨*road*⟩; drive across ⟨*bridge*⟩; use ⟨*railway line*⟩; **die Straße ist stark/wenig** ~: the road is heavily/little used; **eine stark** ~**e Straße** a busy road; **b)** sail ⟨*sea*⟩; navigate, sail up/down ⟨*river, canal*⟩

befallen *unr. tr. V.* **a)** overcome; ⟨*misfortune*⟩ befall; **von Panik/Angst** ~ **werden** be seized with panic/fear; **b)** ⟨*pests*⟩ attack

befangen 1. *Adj.* **a)** self-conscious ⟨*person*⟩; **b)** *(voreingenommen)* biased; **2.** *adv.* self-consciously; **Befangenheit die;** ~ **a)** self-consciousness; **b)** *(Voreingenommenheit)* bias

befassen *refl. V.* **sich mit etw.** ~: occupy oneself with sth.; ⟨*article, book*⟩ deal with sth.; *(etw. studieren)* study sth.

Befehl der; ~[e]s, ~e **a)** order; **b) den** ~ **über jmdn./etw. haben** be in command of sb./sth.; **befehlen 1.** *unr. tr., itr. V.* order; *(Milit.)* order; **man befahl ihm zu warten** he was told to wait; **2.** *unr. itr. V.* **über jmdn./etw.** ~: have command of *or* be in command of sb./sth.; **Befehls·haber der;** ~s, ~ *(Milit.)* commander

befestigen *tr. V.* **a)** fix; etw. **an der Wand** ~: fix sth. to the wall; **b)** *(haltbar machen)* stabilize ⟨*bank, embankment*⟩; make up ⟨*road, path, etc.*⟩; **c)** *(sichern)* fortify ⟨*town etc.*⟩; strengthen ⟨*border*⟩; **Befestigung die;** ~, ~en **a)** fixing; **b)** *(Milit.)* fortification

befeuchten *tr. V.* moisten; damp ⟨*hair, cloth*⟩

befiehlst, befiehlt *2., 3. Pers. Sg. Präsens v.* **befehlen**

befinden *unr. refl. V.* be; **Befinden das;** ~s health; *(eines Patienten)* condition

beflecken *tr. V.* stain

befohlen *2. Part. v.* **befehlen**

befolgen *tr. V.* follow, obey ⟨*instruction, grammatical rule*⟩; obey, comply with ⟨*law, regulation*⟩; follow ⟨*advice, suggestion*⟩

befördern *tr. V.* **a)** carry; transport; **b)** *(aufrücken lassen)* promote; **Beförderung die;** ~ **a)** *o. Pl.* carriage; transport; *(Personen~)* transport; **b)** *(das Aufrückenlassen)* promotion

befragen *tr. V.* **a)** question (über + *Akk.* about); **b)** *(konsultieren)* ask; **Befragung die;** ~, ~en **a)** questioning; **b)** *(Konsultation)* consultation; **c)** *(Umfrage)* opinion poll

befreien 1. *tr. V.* **a)** free; liberate ⟨*country, people*⟩ (von from); **b)** *(freistellen)* exempt (von from); **c)** **jmdn. von Schmerzen** ~: free sb. of pain; **2.** *refl. V.* free oneself (von from); **Befreier der** liberator; **Befreiung die;** ~ **a)** *s.* **befreien 1 a:** freeing; liberation; **b)** *(Freistellung)* exemption; **c) die** ~ **von Schmerzen** release from pain

befremden *tr. V.* **jmdn.** ~: put sb. off

befreunden *refl. V. s.* **anfreunden;** [gut *od.* eng] **befreundet sein** be [good *or* close] friends (mit with)

befriedigen *tr. V.* **a)** satisfy; gratify ⟨*lust*⟩; **b)** *(ausfüllen)* ⟨*job, occupation, etc.*⟩ fulfil; **c)** *(sexuell)* satisfy; **sich** [selbst] ~: masturbate; **befriedigend 1.** *Adj.* satisfactory; **2.** *adv.* satisfactorily; **Befriedigung die;** ~ **a)** *s.* **befriedigen a:** satisfaction; gratification; **b)** *(Genugtuung)* satisfaction

befristet *Adj.* temporary ⟨*visa*⟩; fixed-term ⟨*ban, contract*⟩

befruchten *tr. V.* fertilize ⟨*egg*⟩; pollinate ⟨*flower*⟩; impregnate ⟨*female*⟩; **Befruchtung die;** ~, ~en *s.* **befruchten:** fertilization; pollination; impregnation

Befugnis die; ~, ~se authority
befühlen tr. V. feel
Befund der (bes. Med.) result[s pl.]
befürchten tr. V. fear; **ich befürchte,
daß ...**: I am afraid that ...
befürworten tr. V. support
begabt Adj. talented; **Begabung**
die; ~, ~en talent
begann 1. u. 3. Pers. Sg. Prät. v. **beginnen**
begatten tr. V. mate with; ⟨man⟩ copulate with; **sich ~**: mate; ⟨persons⟩
copulate; **Begattung** die mating;
(bei Menschen) copulation
begeben unr. refl. V. (geh.) proceed;
make one's way; go; **sich zu Bett ~**:
retire to bed; **sich an die Arbeit ~**:
commence work
begegnen itr. V.; mit sein jmdm. ~:
meet sb.; **sich** (Dat.) ~: meet [each
other]; **Begegnung** die; ~, ~en a)
meeting; b) (Sport) match
begehen unr. tr. V. a) commit ⟨crime,
adultery, indiscretion, sin, suicide,
faux-pas, etc.⟩; make ⟨mistake⟩; **eine
[furchtbare] Dummheit ~**: do something [really] stupid; b) (geh.: feiern)
celebrate
begehren tr. V. desire; **begehrens·wert** Adj. desirable; **begehrlich** 1. Adj. greedy; 2. adv. greedily;
begehrt Adj. much sought-after
begeistern 1. tr. V. jmdn. [für etw.] ~:
fire sb. with enthusiasm [for sth.]; 2.
refl. V. get enthusiastic (für about);
begeistert 1. Adj. enthusiastic (von
about); 2. adv. enthusiastically; **Begeisterung** die; ~: enthusiasm
Begierde die; ~, ~n desire (nach for);
begierig 1. Adj. eager; 2. adv.
eagerly
begießen unr. tr. V. water ⟨plants⟩
Beginn der; ~[e]s beginning; [gleich]
zu ~: [right] at the beginning; **beginnen** 1. unr. itr. V. start; begin; **mit
dem Bau ~**: start or begin building;
dort beginnt der Wald the forest starts
there; 2. unr. tr. V. start; begin; start
⟨argument⟩; ~, **etw. zu tun** start to do
sth.
beglaubigen tr. V. certify; **Beglaubigung** die; ~, ~en certification
begleichen unr. tr. V. settle ⟨bill,
debt⟩; pay ⟨sum⟩
begleiten tr. V. accompany; **jmdn.
nach Hause ~**: see sb. home; **Begleiter** der; ~s, ~, **Begleiterin** die;
~, ~nen companion; (zum Schutz) escort; (Führer[in]) guide; **Begleitung**

die; ~, ~en a) o. Pl. er bot uns seine ~
an he offered to accompany us; **in ~
eines Erwachsenen** accompanied by an
adult; b) (Musik) accompaniment
beglückwünschen tr. V. congratulate (zu on)
begnadet Adj. (geh.) divinely gifted;
begnadigen tr. V. pardon; reprieve;
Begnadigung die; ~, ~en reprieving; (Straferlaß) pardon; reprieve
begnügen refl. V. content oneself
Begonie [be'go:niə] die; ~, ~n begonia
begonnen 2. Part. v. **beginnen**
begraben unr. tr. V. bury; **Begräbnis** das; ~ses, ~se burial; (~feier)
funeral
begreifen 1. unr. tr. V. understand; **er
konnte nicht ~, was geschehen war** he
could not grasp what had happened;
2. itr. V. understand; **schnell** od.
leicht/langsam od. **schwer ~**: be
quick/ slow on the uptake; **begreiflich** Adj. understandable
begrenzen tr. V. limit, restrict (auf +
Akk. to)
Begriff der a) concept; (Terminus)
term; b) (Auffassung) idea; **sich** (Dat.)
keinen ~ von etw. machen können not
be able to imagine sth.; **ein/kein ~
sein** be/not be well known; c) **im ~
sein** od. **stehen, etw. zu tun** be about to
do sth.; **begriffs·stutzig** Adj. (abwertend) obtuse
begründen tr. V. a) give reasons for;
b) (gründen) found; establish ⟨fame,
reputation⟩; **Begründer** der founder;
begründet Adj. well-founded; reasonable ⟨demand, objection, complaint⟩; **Begründung** die; ~, ~en
reason[s]; **mit der ~, daß ...**: on the
grounds that ...
begrüßen tr. V. a) greet; ⟨hostess,
host⟩ welcome; b) (fig.) welcome; **Begrüßung** die; ~, ~en greeting; (von
Gästen) welcoming; (Zeremonie) welcome (Gen. for)
begünstigen tr. V. favour
begutachten tr. V. a) examine and
report on; b) (ugs.) have a look at
begütert Adj. wealthy
begütigen tr. V. placate
behäbig 1. Adj. slow and ponderous;
2. adv. slowly and ponderously
behagen itr. V. etw. **behagt jmdm.** sb.
likes sth.; **Behagen** das; ~s pleasure; **behaglich** 1. Adj. comfortable;
2. adv. comfortably; **Behaglichkeit**
die; ~: comfortableness

behalten *unr. tr. V.* **a)** keep; etw. **für sich ~**: keep sth. to oneself; **b)** *(zurück~)* be left with ⟨*scar, defect, etc.*⟩; **c)** *(sich merken)* remember

Behälter der; ~s, ~ container; *(für Abfälle)* receptacle

behandeln *tr. V. (auch Med.)* treat; handle ⟨*matter, machine, device*⟩; deal with ⟨*subject, question etc.*⟩

Behandlung die; ~, ~en treatment

behängen *tr. V.* hang

beharren *itr. V.* **auf etw.** *(Dat.)* ~ *(etw. nicht aufgeben)* persist in sth.; *(auf etw. bestehen)* insist on sth.; **beharrlich 1.** *Adj.* dogged; **2.** *adv.* doggedly; **Beharrlichkeit** die; ~: doggedness

behauen *unr. tr. V.* hew

behaupten 1. *tr. V.* **a)** maintain; assert; ~, jmd. zu sein/etw. zu wissen claim to be sb./know sth.; **b)** *(verteidigen)* maintain ⟨*position*⟩; retain ⟨*record*⟩; **2.** *refl. V.* **a)** assert oneself; *(nicht untergehen)* hold one's ground; *(dableiben)* survive; **b)** *(Sport)* win through; **Behauptung** die; ~, ~en assertion

Behausung die; ~, ~en dwelling

beheben *unr. tr. V.* remove ⟨*danger, difficulty*⟩; repair ⟨*damage*⟩; remedy ⟨*abuse, defect*⟩; **Behebung** die; ~, ~en *s.* beheben: removal; repair; remedying

beheimatet *Adj.* **an einem Ort/in einem Land** *usw.* ~ **sein** be native to a place/to a country *etc.*

beheizen *tr. V.* heat

behelfen *unr. refl. V.* make do

behelfs·mäßig 1. *Adj.* makeshift; **2.** *adv.* in a makeshift way

behelligen *tr. V.* bother; *(zudringlich werden gegen)* pester

behend, behende 1. *Adj. (geschickt)* deft; *(flink)* nimble; **2.** *adv.; s. Adj.:* deftly; nimbly

beherbergen *tr. V.* accommodate

beherrschen 1. *tr. V.* **a)** control; rule ⟨*country, people*⟩; **b)** *(meistern)* control ⟨*vehicle, animal*⟩; be in control of ⟨*situation*⟩; **c)** *(bestimmen, dominieren)* dominate ⟨*townscape, landscape, discussions*⟩; **d)** *(zügeln)* control ⟨*feelings*⟩; control, curb ⟨*impatience*⟩; **e)** *(gut können)* have mastered ⟨*instrument, trade*⟩; have a good command of ⟨*language*⟩; **2.** *refl. V.* control oneself; **beherrscht 1.** *Adj.* self-controlled; **2.** with self-control; **Beherrschung** die; ~ **a)** control; *(eines Volks, Landes usw.)* rule; **b)** *(das Meistern)* control; **c)** *(Beherrschtheit)* self-control; **d)** *(das Können)* mastery

beherzigen *tr. V.* take ⟨*sth.*⟩ to heart

beherzt 1. *Adj.* spirited; **2.** *adv.* spiritedly

behilflich *Adj.* [jmdm.] ~ **sein** help [sb.] (bei with)

behindern *tr. V.* **a)** hinder; impede ⟨*movement*⟩; hold up ⟨*traffic*⟩; **b)** *(Sport, Verkehrsw.)* obstruct; **behindert** *Adj.* handicapped; **Behinderte** der/die; *adj. Dekl.* handicapped person; **die ~n** the handicapped; **WC für ~**: toilet for disabled persons; **Behinderung** die; ~, ~en **a)** hindrance; **b)** *(Sport, Verkehrsw.)* obstruction; **c)** *(Gebrechen)* handicap

Behörde die; ~, ~n authority; *(Amt, Abteilung)* department; **behördlich 1.** *Adj.* official; **2.** *adv.* officially

behüten *tr. V.* protect (**vor** + *Dat.* from); *(bewachen)* guard

behutsam 1. *Adj.* careful; **2.** *adv.* carefully

bei *Präp. mit Dat.* **a)** *(nahe)* near; *(dicht an, neben)* by; **wer steht da ~ ihm?** who is standing there with him?; **etw. ~ sich haben** have sth. with or on one; **sich ~ jmdm. entschuldigen** apologize to sb.; **b)** *(unter)* among; **war heute ein Brief für mich ~ der Post?** was there a letter for me in the post today?; **c)** *(an)* by; **jmdn. ~ der Hand nehmen** take sb. by the hand; **d)** *(im Wohn-/Lebens-/Arbeitsbereich von)*; **~ uns tut man das nicht** we don't do that; **~ mir [zu Hause]** at my house; **~ uns um die Ecke/gegenüber** round the corner from us/opposite us; **~ seinen Eltern leben** live with one's parents; **wir sind ~ ihr eingeladen** we have been invited to her house; **wir treffen uns ~ uns/Peter** we'll meet at our/Peter's place; **~ uns in der Firma** in our company; **~ Schmidt** *(auf Briefen)* c/o Schmidt; **~ einer Firma sein** be with a company; **~ jmdm./einem Verlag arbeiten** work for sb./a publishing house; **e)** *(im Bereich eines Vorgangs)* at; **~ einer Hochzeit/einem Empfang** *usw.* be at a wedding/reception *etc.*; **~ einem Unfall** in an accident; **f)** *(im Werk von)* **~ Goethe** in Goethe; **g)** *(im Falle von)* in the case of; **wie ~ den Römern** as with the Romans; **~ der Hauskatze** in the domestic cat; **h)** *(modal)* **~ Tag/Nacht** by day/night; **~ Tageslicht** by daylight; **~ Nebel in**

fog; i) *(im Falle des Auftretens von)* „~ Nässe **Schleudergefahr**" 'slippery when wet'; j) *(angesichts)* with; ~ dieser **Hitze** in this heat; ~ **deinen guten Augen/ihrem Talent** with your good eyesight/her talent; k) *(trotz)* ~ **all seinem Engagement/seinen Bemühungen** in spite of *or* despite *or* for all his commitment/efforts

bei‖**behalten** *unr. tr. V.* keep; retain; keep up ⟨*custom, habit*⟩; keep to ⟨*course, method*⟩; preserve, maintain ⟨*way of life; attitude*⟩

bei‖**bringen** *unr. tr. V.* a) jmdm. etw. ~: teach sb. sth.; b) *(ugs.: mitteilen)* jmdm. ~, daß ...: break it to sb. that ...; c) *(zufügen)* jmdm./sich etw. ~: inflict sth. on sb./oneself

Beichte die; ~, ~n confession *no def. art.;* **beichten** 1. *itr. V.* confess; 2. *tr. V. (auch fig.)* confess

Beicht-: ~**stuhl** der confessional; ~**vater** der father confessor

beid... *Indefinitpron. u. Zahlw.* 1. *Pl.* ~**e** both; *(der/die/das eine oder der/die/das andere)* either *sing.;* **die** ~**en** the two; **die/seine** ~**en Brüder** the/his two brothers; **die** ~**en ersten Strophen** the first two verses; **kennst du die** ~**en?** do you know those two?; **alle** ~**e** both of us/you/them; **ihr/euch** ~**e** you two; **ihr/euch** ~**e nicht** neither of you; **wir/uns** ~**e** the two of us/both of us; **er hat** ~**e Eltern verloren** he has lost both [his] parents; **mit** ~**en Händen** with both hands; **ich habe** ~**e gekannt** I knew both of them; **einer/eins von** ~**en** one of the two; **keiner/keins von** ~**en** neither [of them]; 2. *Neutr. Sg.;* ~**es** both *pl.; (das eine oder das andere)* either; ~**es ist möglich** either is possible; **ich glaube** ~**es/**~**es nicht** I believe both things/neither thing; **das ist** ~**es nicht richtig** neither of those is correct; **beiderlei** *Gattungsz., indekl.* ~ **Geschlechts** of both sexes; **beider · seits** 1. *Präp. mit Gen.* on both sides of; 2. *Adv.* on both sides **bei · einander** *Adv.* together; ~ **Trost suchen** seek comfort from each other **Bei · fahrer** der, **Bei · fahrerin** die a) passenger; b) *(berufsmäßig)* co-driver; *(im LKW)* driver's mate; **Beifahrer · sitz** der passenger seat; *(eines Motorrads)* pillion **Bei · fall** der; *o. Pl.* a) applause; b) *(Zustimmung)* approval; **bei · fällig** 1. *Adj.* approving; 2. *adv.* approvingly

beige [be:ʃ] *Adj.* beige; **Beige** das; ~, ~ *od. (ugs.)* ~s beige **Bei · geschmack** der: einen bitteren *usw.* ~ **haben** have a slightly bitter *etc.* taste [to it] **Bei · hilfe** die a) aid; *(Zuschuß)* allowance; b) *o. Pl. (Rechtsw.: Mithilfe)* aiding and abetting **Beil** das; ~[e]s, ~e axe; *(kleiner)* hatchet **Bei · lage** die a) *(Zeitungs~)* supplement; b) *(zu Speisen)* side-dish; *(Gemüse~)* vegetables *pl.* **bei · läufig** 1. *Adj.* casual; 2. *adv.* casually **bei‖legen** *tr. V.* a) enclose; b) *(schlichten)* settle ⟨*dispute etc.*⟩ **Bei · leid** das sympathy; |mein| herzliches *od.* aufrichtiges ~! please accept my sincere condolences **bei‖liegen** *unr. itr. V.* einem Brief ~: be enclosed with a letter; **bei · liegend** *Adj.* enclosed; ~ **senden wir ...:** please find enclosed ... **beim** *Präp. + Art.* a) = bei dem; b) ~ **Film sein** be in films; c) **er will** ~ **Arbeiten nicht gestört werden** he doesn't want to be disturbed when working; ~ **Duschen sein** be taking a shower **bei‖messen** *unr. tr. V.* attach **Bein** das; ~[e]s, ~e leg; **jmdm. ein** ~ **stellen** trip sb.; *(fig.)* put *or* throw a spanner *or (Amer.)* a monkey-wrench in sb.'s works; **wieder auf den** ~**en sein** be back on one's feet again **bei · nah[e]** *Adv.* almost **Bei · name** der epithet **Bein · bruch** der: das ist |doch| kein ~ *(ugs.)* it's not the end of the world **beinhalten** *tr. V. (Papierdt.)* involve -**beinig** *adj.* -legged **bei‖pflichten** *itr. V.* agree *(Dat.* with) **beirren** *tr. V.* sich durch nichts/von niemandem ~ **lassen** not be deterred by anything/anybody **beisammen** *Adv.* together; **beisammen‖haben** *unr. tr. V.* a) have got together; b) **er hat |sie| nicht alle beisammen** *(ugs.)* he's not all there *(coll.);* **Beisammen · sein** das get-together **Bei · schlaf** der sexual intercourse **Bei · sein** das: **in** jmds. ~: in the presence of sb. *or* in sb.'s presence **bei · seite** *Adv.* aside **Beis[e]l** das; ~s, ~ *od.* ~n *(österr.)* pub *(Brit. coll.);* bar *(Amer.)* **bei‖setzen** *tr. V.* lay to rest; inter ⟨*ashes*⟩; **Bei · setzung** die; ~, ~en funeral; burial

15*

Bei·spiel das example (für of); **zum ~:** for example; **mit gutem ~ vorangehen** set a good example; **beispielhaft** Adj. exemplary; **beispiel·los** Adj. unparalleled; **beispiels·weise** Adv. for example

beißen 1. unr. tr., itr. V. (auch fig.) bite; **2.** unr. refl. V. (ugs.) ⟨colours, clothes⟩ clash; **beißend** Adj. biting ⟨cold⟩; acrid ⟨smoke, fumes⟩; sharp ⟨frost⟩; **Beiß·zange** die s. Kneifzange

Bei·stand der o. Pl. (geh.: Hilfe) aid; **bei|stehen** unr. itr. V. jmdm. ~: aid sb.

bei|steuern tr. V. contribute

Beitrag der; ~[e]s, Beiträge contribution; (Versicherungs~) premium; (Mitglieds~) subscription; **bei|tragen** unr. tr., itr. V. contribute (zu to)

bei|treten unr. itr. V.; mit sein join ⟨union, club, etc.⟩; **einem Abkommen/ Pakt** accede to ⟨pact, agreement⟩; **Bei·tritt** der joining

Bei·wagen der side-car

Bei·werk das; o. Pl. accessories pl.

bei|wohnen itr. V. einer Sache (Dat.) ~ (geh.) be present at sth.

Beize die; ~, ~n (Holzbearb.) [wood]-stain

beizeiten Adv. in good time

beizen tr. V. (Holzbearb.) stain

bejahen [bəˈjaːən] tr. V. a) auch itr. answer ⟨sth.⟩ in the affirmative; b) (gutheißen) approve of; **das Leben ~:** have a positive or an affirmative attitude to life; **Bejahung** die; ~, ~en a) affirmative reply; b) (das Gutheißen) approval

bejammern tr. V. lament

bejubeln tr. V. cheer; acclaim

bekämpfen tr. V. a) fight against; b) combat ⟨disease, epidemic, pest, unemployment, crime, etc.⟩; **Bekämpfung** die; ~ a) fight (Gen. against); b) s. bekämpfen b: combating

bekannt Adj. well-known; b) **jmd./ etw. ist jmdm. ~:** sb. knows sb./sth.; **Darf ich ~ machen? Meine Eltern** may I introduce my parents?; **Bekannte** der/die; adj. Dekl. acquaintance

Bekannt·gabe die; ~: announcement; **bekannt|geben** unr. tr. V. announce

bekanntlich Adv. as is well known; **etw. ist ~ der Fall** sth. is known to be the case

bekannt|machen tr. V. announce; (der Öffentlichkeit) make public; **Be-**

kannt·machung die; ~, ~en announcement

Bekanntschaft die; ~, ~en acquaintance

bekannt|werden unr. itr. V.; mit sein (nur im Inf. und 2. Part. zusammengeschr.) become known

bekehren 1. tr. V. convert; **2.** refl. V. become converted; **Bekehrung** die; ~, ~en (auch fig.) conversion (zu to)

bekennen 1. unr. tr. V. a) confess; ~, **daß ...** admit that ...; b) (Rel.) profess; **2.** refl. V. **sich zum Islam ~:** profess Islam; **sich zu Buddha ~:** profess one's faith in Buddha; **sich zu seiner Schuld ~:** confess one's guilt; **sich schuldig/nicht schuldig ~:** confess/not confess one's guilt; (vor Gericht) plead guilty/not guilty; **Bekenntnis** das; ~ses, ~se a) confession; b) (Eintreten) **ein ~ zum Frieden** a declaration for peace; c) (Konfession) denomination

beklagen 1. tr. V. (geh.) a) (betrauern) mourn; b) (bedauern) lament; **2.** refl. V. complain

bekleckern tr. V. (ugs.) **etw./sich |mit Soße usw.| ~:** drop or spill sauce etc. down sth./oneself

bekleiden tr. V. a) clothe; **mit etw. bekleidet sein** be wearing sth.; b) (geh.: innehaben) occupy ⟨office, position⟩; **Bekleidung** die clothing; clothes pl.

beklemmend Adj. oppressive; **Beklemmung** die; ~, ~en oppressive feeling; **beklommen** Adj. uneasy; (stärker) apprehensive

bekloppt Adj. (salopp) barmy (Brit. sl.); loony (sl.)

beknien tr. V. (ugs.) beg

bekommen 1. unr. tr. V. a) get; get, receive ⟨money, letter, reply, news, orders⟩; (erreichen) catch ⟨train, bus, flight⟩; **was ~ Sie?** (im Geschäft) can I help you?; (im Lokal, Restaurant) what would you like?; **was ~ Sie |dafür|?** how much is that?; **Hunger/ Durst ~:** get hungry/thirsty; **Angst/ Mut ~:** become frightened/take heart; **er bekommt einen Bart** he's growing a beard; **sie bekommt eine Brust** her breasts are developing; **Zähne ~:** ⟨baby⟩ teethe; **sie bekommt ein Kind** she's expecting a baby; b) **etw. durch die Tür/ins Auto ~:** get sth. through the door/into the car; **2.** unr. V.; in der Funktion eines Hilfsverbs zur Umschreibung des Passivs get; **etw. geschenkt ~:** get [given] sth. or be given

sth. as a present; **3.** *unr. itr. V.; mit
sein* jmdm. gut ~: do sb. good; jmdm.
|gut| ~: ⟨*food, medicine*⟩ agree with
sb.; **wohl bekomm's!** your [very good]
health!
bekömmlich *Adj.* easily digestible
beköstigen *tr. V.* cater for
bekräftigen *tr. V.* reinforce ⟨*statement*⟩; reaffirm ⟨*promise*⟩
bekreuzigen *refl. V. (kath. Kirche)*
cross oneself
bekriegen *tr. V.* wage war on; *(fig.)*
fight; **sich** ~: be at war; *(fig.)* fight
bekümmern *tr. V.* jmdn. ~: cause sb.
worry; **bekümmert** *Adj.* worried;
(stärker) distressed
bekunden *tr. V.* express
belächeln *tr. V.* smile [pityingly/
tolerantly *etc.*] at
beladen *unr. tr. V.* load ⟨*ship*⟩; load
[up] ⟨*car, wagon*⟩; load up ⟨*horse, donkey*⟩
Belag der; ~|e|s, **Beläge a)** coating; **b)**
(Fußboden~) covering; *(Straßen~)*
surface; *(Brems~)* lining; **c)** *(von Kuchen, Scheibe Brot usw.)* topping; *(von
Sandwiches)* filling
belagern *tr. V. (auch fig.)* besiege;
Belagerung die; ~, ~en siege; *(fig.)*
besieging
Belang der; ~|e|s, ~e **a)** von/ohne ~
sein be of importance/of no importance; **b)** *Pl. (Interessen)* interests
belangen *tr. V. (Rechtsw.)* sue; *(strafrechtlich)* prosecute
belang·los *Adj. (trivial)* trivial; *(unerheblich)* of no importance (für for);
Belanglosigkeit die; ~, ~en unimportance; *(Trivialität)* triviality
belassen *unr. tr. V.* leave
belasten *tr. V.* **a)** etw. ~: put sth.
under strain; *(durch Gewicht)* put
weight on sth.; **b)** *(beeinträchtigen)*
pollute ⟨*atmosphere*⟩; put pressure on
⟨*environment*⟩; **c)** *(in Anspruch nehmen)* burden (mit with); **d)** jmdn. ~
⟨*responsibility, guilt*⟩ weigh upon sb.;
⟨*thought*⟩ weigh upon sb.'s mind; **e)**
(Rechtsw.) incriminate
belästigen *tr. V.* bother; *(sehr aufdringlich)* pester; *(sexuell)* molest
Belastung die; ~, ~en **a)** strain; *(das
Belasten)* straining; *(durch Gewicht)*
loading; *(Last)* load; **b)** die ~ der Atmosphäre/Umwelt durch Schadstoffe
the pollution of the atmosphere by
harmful substances/the pressure on
the environment caused by harmful
substances; **c)** *(Bürde, Sorge)* burden

belaufen *unr. refl. V.* sich auf ...*(Akk.)*
~: come to ...
belauschen *tr. V.* eavesdrop on
beleben 1. *tr. V.* enliven; stimulate
⟨*economy*⟩; **2.** *refl. V.* ⟨*market, economic activity*⟩ revive, pick up; **belebend 1.** *Adj.* invigorating; **2.** *adv.* ~
wirken have an invigorating effect;
belebt *Adj.* busy ⟨*street, crossing,
town, etc.*⟩
Beleg der; ~|e|s, ~e *(Beweisstück)*
piece of [supporting] documentary
evidence; *(Quittung)* receipt
belegen *tr. V.* **a)** *(Milit.: beschießen)*
bombard; *(mit Bomben)* attack; **b)**
(mit Belag versehen) cover ⟨*floor*⟩ (mit
with); fill ⟨*flan base, sandwich*⟩; top
⟨*open sandwich*⟩; **eine Scheibe Brot mit
Käse** ~: put some cheese on a slice of
bread; **c)** *(in Besitz nehmen)* occupy
⟨*seat, room, etc.*⟩; **d)** *(Hochschulw.)*
enrol for ⟨*seminar, lecture-course*⟩; **e)**
den ersten/letzten Platz ~ *(Sport)* take
first place/come last; **f)** *(nachweisen)*
prove; give a reference for ⟨*quotation*⟩
Belegschaft die; ~, ~en staff
belegt *Adj.* **a)** **ein** ~es **Brot** an open *or*
(Amer.) openface sandwich; *(zugeklappt)* a sandwich; **ein** ~es **Brötchen**
a roll with topping; an open-face roll
(Amer.); *(zugeklappt)* a filled roll; a
sandwich roll *(Amer.)*; **b)** *(mit Belag
bedeckt)* furred ⟨*tongue, tonsils*⟩; **c)**
(heiser) husky ⟨*voice*⟩; **d)** *(nicht mehr
frei)* ⟨*room, flat*⟩ occupied
belehren *tr. V.* teach; instruct; *(aufklären)* enlighten; *(informieren)* inform; **ich lasse micht gern** ~: I'm quite
willing to believe otherwise; **Belehrung die;** ~, ~en instruction; *(Zurechtweisung)* lecture
beleibt *Adj. (geh.)* portly
beleidigen *tr. V.* insult; **beleidigt**
Adj. insulted; *(gekränkt)* offended;
Beleidigung die; ~, ~en **a)** insult; **b)**
(Rechtsw.) (schriftlich) libel; *(mündlich)* slander
belesen *Adj.* well-read
beleuchten *tr. V.* light up; light
⟨*stairs, room, street, etc.*⟩; **Beleuchtung die;** ~, ~en **a)** lighting;
(Anstrahlung) illumination
beleumdet *Adj.* übel/gut ~ sein have
a bad/good reputation
Belgien ['bɛlgiən] *(das)*; ~s Belgium;
Belgier der; ~s, ~ Belgian; **belgisch** *Adj.* Belgian
belichten *tr. V. (Fot.)* expose; *itr.*
richtig/falsch/kurz ~: use the right/

wrong exposure/a short exposure time; **Belichtung die** *(Fot.)* exposure
Belieben das; ~s: **nach** ~: just as you/they *etc.* like
beliebig 1. *Adj.* any; **2.** *adv.* as you like/he likes *etc.;* ~ **lange/viele** as long/many as you like/he likes *etc.*
beliebt *Adj.* popular; favourite *attrib.;* **Beliebtheit die**; ~: popularity
beliefern *tr. V.* supply
bellen *itr. V.* bark
belohnen *tr. V.* reward ⟨*person, thing*⟩; **Belohnung die**; ~, ~en reward
belügen *unr. tr. V.* lie to
belustigen *tr. V.* amuse; **Belustigung die**; ~, ~en amusement
bemächtigen *refl. V.* **sich jmds./einer Sache** ~ *(geh.)* seize sb./sth.
bemalen *tr. V.* paint; *(verzieren)* decorate
bemängeln *tr. V.* find fault with
bemerkbar *Adj.* **sich** ~ **machen** attract attention [to oneself]; *(erkennbar werden)* become apparent; *(spürbar werden)* make itself felt; **bemerken** *tr. V.* **a)** *(wahrnehmen)* notice; **ich wurde nicht bemerkt** I was unobserved; **b)** *(äußern)* remark; **bemerkenswert 1.** *Adj.* remarkable; **2.** *adv.* remarkably; **Bemerkung die**; ~, ~en **a)** *(Äußerung)* remark; comment; **b)** *(Notiz)* note; *(Anmerkung)* comment
bemitleiden *tr. V.* pity; feel sorry for; **bemitleidens·wert** *Adj.* pitiable
bemogeln *tr. V. (ugs.)* cheat; diddle *(Brit. sl.)*
bemühen *refl. V.* make an effort; **sich** ~, **etw. zu tun** endeavour to do sth.; **sich um etw.** ~: try to obtain sth.; **sich um eine Stelle** ~: try to get a job; **sich um jmdn.** ~ *(kümmern)* seek to help sb.; **Bemühung die**; ~, ~en effort
benachbart *Adj.* neighbouring *attrib.*
benachrichtigen *tr. V.* notify ⟨von of⟩; **Benachrichtigung die**; ~, ~en notification
benachteiligen *tr. V.* put at a disadvantage; *(diskriminieren)* discriminate against
benehmen *unr. refl. V.* behave; **Benehmen das**; ~s behaviour; **kein** ~ **haben** have no manners *pl.*
beneiden *tr. V.* envy; **jmdn. um etw.** ~: envy sb. sth.; **beneidens·wert** *Adj.* enviable
Benelux·länder *Pl.* Benelux countries
benennen *unr. tr. V.* name

Bengel der; ~s, ~ *od. (nordd.)* ~s **a)** *(abwertend: junger Bursche)* young rascal; **b)** *(fam.: kleiner Junge)* little lad
benommen *Adj.* dazed; *(durch Fieber, Alkohol)* muzzy
benoten *tr. V.* mark *(Brit.)*; grade *(Amer.)*; **einen Test mit „gut"** ~: mark a test 'good' *(Brit.)*; assign a grade of 'good' to a test *(Amer.)*
benötigen *tr. V.* need; require
benutzen *tr. V.* use; **Benutzer der**; ~s, ~: user; **Benutzung die**; ~: use
Benzin das; ~s petrol *(Brit.)*; gasoline *(Amer.)*; gas *(Amer. coll.)*; *(Wasch~)* benzine
Benzol das; ~s, ~e *(Chemie)* benzene
beobachten *tr. V.* observe; watch; **Beobachter der**; ~s, ~: observer; **Beobachtung die**; ~, ~en observation
bepacken *tr. V.* load
bepflanzen *tr. V.* plant
bequem 1. *Adj.* **a)** comfortable; **b)** *(abwertend: träge)* idle; **2.** *adv.* **a)** comfortably; **b)** *(leicht)* easily; **bequemen** *refl. V.* **sich dazu** ~, **etw. zu tun** *(geh.)* condescend to do sth.; **Bequemlichkeit die**; ~ **a)** comfort; **b)** *(Trägheit)* idleness
berappen *tr., itr. V. (ugs.)* s. **blechen**
beraten 1. *unr. tr. V.* **a)** advise; **jmdn. gut/schlecht** ~: give sb. good/bad advice; **b)** *(besprechen)* discuss ⟨*plan, matter*⟩; **2.** *unr. itr. V.* **über etw.** *(Akk.)* ~: discuss sth. **3.** *unr. refl. V.* **sich mit jmdm.** ~, **ob** ...: discuss with sb. whether ...; **Berater der**; ~s, ~: adviser; **beratschlagen 1.** *tr. V.* discuss; **2.** *itr. V.* **über etw.** *(Akk.)* ~: discuss sth.; **Beratung die**; ~, ~en **a)** advice *no indef. art.; (durch Arzt, Rechtsanwalt)* consultation; **b)** *(Besprechung)* discussion
berauben *tr. V. (auch fig.)* rob ⟨Gen. of⟩
berauschen *(geh.)* **1.** *tr. V. (auch fig.)* intoxicate; **2.** *refl. V.* become intoxicated ⟨**an** + *Dat.* with⟩
berechnen *tr. V.* **a)** *(auch fig.)* calculate; predict ⟨*behaviour, consequences*⟩; **b)** *(anrechnen)* charge; **jmdm. 10 Mark für etw.** *od.* **jmdm. etw. mit 10 Mark** ~: charge sb. 10 marks for sth.; **jmdm. zuviel** ~: overcharge sb.; **Berechnung die a)** calculation; **b)** *o. Pl. (Eigennutz)* [calculating] self-interest
berechtigen *tr. V.* entitle; *itr. die*

Karte berechtigt zum Eintritt the ticket entitles the bearer to admission; **berechtigt** *Adj.* **a)** *(gerechtfertigt)* justified; **b)** *(befugt)* authorized; **Berechtigung die; ~, ~en a)** *(Befugnis)* entitlement; *(Recht)* right; **b)** *(Rechtmäßigkeit)* legitimacy

bereden *tr. V.* **a)** *(besprechen)* discuss; **b)** jmdn. **~, etw. zu tun** talk sb. into doing sth.

Bereich der; **~[e]s, ~e** area; **im privaten/staatlichen ~:** in the private/public sector

bereichern *refl. V.* get rich; **Bereicherung die; ~, ~en a)** money-making; **b)** *(Nutzen)* valuable acquisition

bereifen *tr. V.* put tyres on ⟨*car*⟩; put a tyre on ⟨*wheel*⟩; **Bereifung die; ~, ~en** [set *sing.* of] tyres *pl.*

bereinigen *tr. V.* clear up ⟨*misunderstanding*⟩; settle, resolve ⟨*dispute*⟩

bereit *Adj.* ready; **~ sein, etw. zu tun** be ready *or* willing to do sth.

bereiten *tr. V.* **a)** prepare; make ⟨*tea, coffee*⟩; **b)** *(verursachen)* cause ⟨*trouble, sorrow, difficulty, etc.*⟩

bereit-: ~|halten *unr. tr. V.* have ready; **~|legen** *tr. V.* lay out ready; **~|liegen** *unr. itr. V.* be ready

bereits *Adv.* already

Bereitschaft die; ~: readiness; willingness; **Bereitschafts·dienst** der: **~dienst haben** ⟨*doctor, nurse*⟩ be on call; ⟨*policeman, fireman*⟩ be on stand-by duty; ⟨*chemist's*⟩ be on rota duty *(for dispensing outside normal hours)*

bereit-: ~|stehen *unr. itr. V.* be ready; **~|stellen** *tr. V.* place ready; get ready ⟨*food, drinks*⟩; ready, make ⟨*money, funds*⟩ available; **~willig 1.** *Adj.* willing. **2.** *adv.* readily

bereuen 1. *tr. V.* regret; **2.** *itr. V.* be sorry; *(Rel.)* repent

Berg der; **~[e]s, ~e a)** hill; *(im Hochgebirge)* mountain; **b)** *(Haufen)* huge pile; *(von Akten, Abfall auch)* mountain

berg-, Berg-: ~ab [-'-] *Adv.* downhill; **~auf** [-'-] *Adv.* uphill; **~bahn die** mountain railway; *(Seilbahn)* mountain cableway; **~bau der;** *o. Pl.* mining

bergen *unr. tr. V.* **a)** rescue, save ⟨*person*⟩; salvage ⟨*ship, cargo, belongings*⟩; **b)** *(geh.: enthalten)* hold

Berg-: ~führer der mountain guide; **~hütte** die mountain hut

bergig *Adj.* hilly; *(mit hohen Bergen)* mountainous

Berg-: ~kristall der rock crystal; **~land** das hilly country *no indef. art; (mit hohen Bergen)* mountainous country *no indef. art.;* **~mann** der; *Pl.* **~leute** miner; **~station** die top station; **~steigen** das; **~s** mountaineering *no art.;* **~steiger** der mountaineer

Bergung die; **~, ~en a)** rescue; **b)** *(von Schiffen, Gut)* salvaging

Berg-: ~wacht die mountain rescue service; **~werk** das mine

Bericht der; **~[e]s, ~e** report; **berichten** *tr., itr. V.* report

Bericht-: ~erstatter der; **~s, ~:** reporter; **~erstattung** die reporting *no indef. art.*

berichtigen *tr. V.* correct; **Berichtigung** die; **~, ~en** correction

berieseln *tr. V.* **a)** *(bewässern)* irrigate; **b)** sich ständig mit Musik **~ lassen** *(ugs. abwertend)* constantly have music on in the background

Berlin (das); ~s Berlin; **Berliner 1.** *Adj.; nicht präd.* Berlin; **2. der; ~s, ~: a)** Berliner; **b)** *(~ Pfannkuchen)* [jam *(Brit.)* or *(Amer.)* jelly] doughnut; **berlinisch** *Adj.* Berlin *attrib.*

Bern (das); ~s Bern[e]

Bernhardiner der; **~s, ~:** St. Bernard [dog]

Bern·stein der; *o. Pl.* amber

bersten *unr. itr. V.; mit sein (geh.)* ⟨*ice*⟩ break up; ⟨*glass*⟩ shatter [into pieces]; ⟨*wall*⟩ crack up

berüchtigt *Adj.* notorious (**wegen** for); *(verrufen)* disreputable

berücksichtigen *tr. V.* take into account; consider ⟨*applicant, application, suggestion*⟩; **Berücksichtigung** die; **~: bei ~ aller Umstände** taking all the circumstances into account

Beruf der; **~[e]s, ~e** occupation; *(akademischer)* profession; *(handwerklicher)* trade; **was sind Sie von ~?** what do you do for a living?

¹berufen 1. *unr. tr. V.* **a)** *(einsetzen)* appoint; **b) berufe es nicht!** *(ugs.)* don't speak too soon!; **2.** *unr. refl. V.* **sich auf etw.** *(Akk.)* **~:** refer to sth.; **sich auf jmdn. ~:** quote *or* mention sb.'s name

²berufen *Adj.* **a)** competent; **aus ~em Munde** from somebody qualified to speak; **b) sich dazu ~ fühlen, etw. zu tun** feel called to do sth.

beruflich 1. *Adj.; nicht präd.* vocational ⟨*training etc.*⟩; *(bei akademischen Berufen)* professional ⟨*training etc.*⟩; **2.** *adv.* ~ **erfolgreich sein** be successful in one's career; **sich ~ weiterbilden** undertake further job training **berufs-, Berufs-:** ~**ausbildung** die vocational training; ~**beratung** die vocational guidance; ~**erfahrung** die; *o. Pl.* [professional] experience; ~**geheimnis** das professional secret; *(Schweigepflicht)* professional secrecy; ~**krankheit** die occupational disease; ~**leben** das working life; ~**schule** die vocational school; ~**soldat** der regular soldier; ~**sportler** der professional sportsman; ~**tätig** *Adj.* working *attrib.;* ~**tätige** der/die; *adj. Dekl.* working person; ~**tätige** *Pl.* working people; ~**verkehr** der rush-hour traffic

Berufung die; ~, ~en a) *(für ein Amt)* offer of an appointment (**auf, in, an** + *Akk.* to); **b)** *(innerer Auftrag)* vocation; **c)** *(das Sichberufen)* **unter** ~ *(Dat.)* **auf jmdn./etw.** referring *or* with reference to sb./sth.; **d)** *(Rechtsw.: Einspruch)* appeal; ~ **einlegen** lodge an appeal

beruhen *itr. V.* **auf etw.** *(Dat.)* ~: be based on sth.; **etw. auf sich ~ lassen** let sth. rest

beruhigen [bə'ruːɪgn] **1.** *tr. V.* calm [down]; pacify ⟨*child, baby*⟩; salve ⟨*conscience*⟩; (trösten) soothe; *(von einer Sorge befreien)* reassure; **2.** *refl. V.* ⟨*person*⟩ calm down; ⟨*sea*⟩ become calm; **Beruhigung** die; ~ *s.* **beruhigen 1:** calming [down]; pacifying; salving; soothing; reassurance; **Beruhigungs·mittel** das tranquillizer

berühmt *Adj.* famous; **berühmt-berüchtigt** *Adj.* notorious; **Berühmtheit** die; ~, ~en a) *o. Pl. (Ruhm)* fame; **b)** *(Mensch)* celebrity

berühren *tr. V.* a) touch; *(fig.)* touch on ⟨*topic, issue. etc.*⟩; **sich** ~ **:** touch; **b)** *(beeindrucken)* affect; **das berührt mich nicht** it's a matter of indifference to me; **Berührung** die; ~, ~en touch; **mit jmdm./etw. in** ~ *(Akk.)* **kommen** *(auch fig.)* come into contact with sb./sth.

besagen *tr. V.* say; *(bedeuten)* mean **besänftigen** *tr. V.* calm [down]; pacify; calm, soothe ⟨*temper*⟩

Besatz der *(Borte)* trimming *no indef. art.*

Besatzung die a) *(Mannschaft)* crew;

b) *(Milit.: Verteidigungstruppe)* garrison; **c)** *(Milit.: Okkupationstruppen)* occupying forces *pl.*

besaufen *unr. refl. V. (salopp)* get canned *(Brit. sl.)* or bombed *(Amer. sl.);* **Besäufnis** das; ~ses, ~se *(salopp)* booze-up *(Brit. sl.):* blast *(Amer. sl.)*

beschädigen *tr. V.* damage; **Beschädigung** die a) *o. Pl.* damaging; **b)** *(Schaden)* damage

¹**beschaffen** *tr. V.* obtain, get *(Dat. for)*

²**beschaffen** *Adj.* so ~ sein, daß ...: be such that ...; **Beschaffenheit** die; ~: properties *pl.*

Beschaffung die *s.* **beschaffen:** obtaining; getting

beschäftigen 1. *refl. V.* occupy oneself; **sich viel mit Musik/den Kindern** ~ : devote a great deal of one's time to music/the children; **sehr beschäftigt sein** be very busy; **2.** *tr. V.* a) *(geistig in Anspruch nehmen)* **jmdn.** ~ : preoccupy sb.; **b)** *(angestellt haben)* employ ⟨*workers, staff*⟩; **c)** *(zu tun geben)* occupy; **jmdn. mit etw.** ~ : give sb. sth. to occupy him/her; **Beschäftigte** der/die; *adj. Dekl.* employee; **Beschäftigung** die; ~, ~en a) *(Tätigkeit)* activity; **b)** *(Anstellung, Stelle)* job; **c)** *(mit einer Frage, einem Problem)* consideration (mit of); *(Studium)* study (mit of); **d)** *o. Pl. (von Arbeitskräften)* employment

beschämen *tr. V.* shame; **beschämend 1.** *Adj.* a) *(schändlich)* shameful; **b)** *(demütigend)* humiliating; **2.** *adv.* shamefully; **beschämt** *Adj.* ashamed; **Beschämung** die; ~: shame

beschatten *tr. V.* a) *(geh.)* shade; **b)** *(überwachen)* shadow

beschaulich 1. *Adj.* peaceful ⟨*life, manner, etc.*⟩; **2.** *adv.* peacefully

Bescheid der; ~[e]s, ~e a) *(Auskunft)* information; *(Antwort)* answer; reply; **jmdm.** ~ **geben** *od.* **sagen**[, **ob** ...] let sb. know or tell sb. [whether ...]; **sage bitte im Hotel** ~, **daß** ...: please let the hotel know that ...; [**über etw.** *(Akk.)*] ~ **wissen** know [about sth.]; **b)** *(Entscheidung)* decision

¹**bescheiden 1.** *unr. tr. V.* **jmdn./etw. abschlägig** ~ : turn sb./sth. down; **2.** *unr. refl. V. (geh.)* be content

²**bescheiden 1.** *Adj.* modest; **2.** *adv.* modestly; **Bescheidenheit** die; ~: modesty

bescheinigen *tr. V.* confirm ⟨*sth.*⟩ in
writing; **Bescheinigung** die; ~, ~en
written confirmation *no indef. art.;
(Schein, Attest)* certificate
beschenken *tr. V.* give ⟨*sb.*⟩ a pres-
ent/presents
bescheren *tr. V.* jmdn. |mit etw.| ~:
give sb. [sth. as] a Christmas present/
Christmas presents
Bescherung die; ~, ~en a) *(zu Weihnachten)* giving out of the Christmas
presents; b) **das ist ja eine schöne** ~
(ugs.) this is a pretty kettle of fish
beschießen *unr. tr. V.* fire at; *(mit Artillerie)* bombard
beschimpfen *tr. V.* abuse; swear at;
Beschimpfung die; ~, ~en insult;
~en abuse *sing.;* insults
Beschlag der a) fitting; b) **jmdn./etw.
mit** ~ **belegen** *od.* **in** ~ **nehmen** monopolize sb./sth.; ¹**beschlagen 1.** *unr.
tr. V.* shoe ⟨*horse*⟩; **2.** *unr. itr. V.; mit
sein* ⟨*window*⟩ mist up *(Brit.),* fog up
(Amer.); (durch Dampf) steam up
²**beschlagen** *Adj.* knowledgeable
Beschlag·nahme die; ~, ~n confiscation; **beschlag·nahmen** *tr. V.*
confiscate
beschleunigen 1. *tr. V.* accelerate;
speed up ⟨*work, delivery*⟩; quicken
⟨*pace, step[s], pulse*⟩; **2.** *refl. V.* ⟨*heart-
rate*⟩ increase; ⟨*pulse*⟩ quicken; **3.** *itr.
V.* ⟨*driver, car, etc.*⟩ accelerate; **Beschleunigung** die; ~, ~en *s.* beschleunigen **1**: acceleration; speeding
up; quickening
beschließen *unr. tr. V.* **a)** decide;
pass ⟨*law*⟩; ~, **etw. zu tun** decide *or* resolve to do sth.; **b)** *(beenden)* end
Beschluß der decision; *(gemeinsam
gefaßt)* resolution; **einen** ~ **fassen**
come to a decision/pass a resolution;
beschluß·fähig *Adj.* quorate; **Be-
schluß·fähigkeit** die; *o. Pl.*
presence of a quorum
beschmieren *tr. V.* etw./sich ~: get
sth./oneself in a mess
beschmutzen *tr. V.* make ⟨*sth.*⟩ dirty
beschneiden *unr. tr. V.* **a)** cut
⟨*hedge*⟩; prune ⟨*bush*⟩; cut back
⟨*tree*⟩; **einem Vogel die Flügel** ~: clip a
bird's wings; **b)** *(Med., Rel.)* circumcise; **Beschneidung** die; ~, ~en a)
s. beschneiden **a**: cutting; pruning;
cutting back; **b)** *(Med., Rel.)* circumcision
beschönigen *tr. V.* gloss over
beschränken 1. *tr. V.* restrict (**auf** +
Akk. to); **2.** *refl. V.* **sich auf etw.** *(Akk.)*

~: restrict oneself to sth.; **beschränkt 1.** *Adj.* **a)** *(dumm)* dullwitted; **b)** *(engstirnig)* narrowminded; **2.** *adv.* narrow-mindedly;
Beschränktheit die; ~: a) *(Dummheit)* lack of intelligence; b) *(Engstir-
nigkeit)* narrow-mindedness; **Beschränkung** die; ~, ~en restriction
beschreiben *unr. tr. V.* **a)** write on;
(vollschreiben) write ⟨*page, side, etc.*⟩;
b) *(darstellen)* describe; **Beschreibung** die; ~, ~en description
beschriften *tr. V.* label; inscribe
⟨*stone*⟩; letter ⟨*sign, label, etc.*⟩; *(mit
Adresse)* address
beschuldigen *tr. V.* accuse (*Gen.* of);
Beschuldigte der/die; *adj. Dekl.* accused; **Beschuldigung** die; ~, ~en
accusation
beschummeln *tr. V. (ugs.)* cheat;
diddle *(Brit. coll.)*
Beschuß der fire
beschützen *tr. V.* protect (**vor** + *Dat.*
from); **Beschützer** der; ~s, ~, **Be-
schützerin** die; ~, ~nen protector
Beschwerde die; ~, ~n a) complaint
(**gegen, über** + *Akk.* about); **b)** *Pl.
(Schmerz)* pain *sing.; (Leiden)* trouble
sing.
beschweren 1. *refl. V.* complain
(**über** + *Akk.,* **wegen** about); **2.** *tr. V.*
weight down; **beschwerlich** *Adj.*
arduous; *(ermüdend)* exhausting
beschwichtigen *tr. V.* pacify; mollify ⟨*anger etc.*⟩; **Beschwichtigung**
die; ~, ~en pacification; *(des Zorns
usw.)* mollification
beschwingt *Adj.* lively
beschwipst *Adj. (ugs.)* tipsy
beschwören *unr. tr. V.* **a)** swear to;
~, **daß ...**: swear that ...; **eine Aussage**
~: swear a statement on oath; **b)**
charm ⟨*snake*⟩; **c)** *(erscheinen lassen)*
invoke ⟨*spirit*⟩; **d)** *(bitten)* implore;
Beschwörung die; ~, ~en a) *(Zauberspruch)* spell; incantation; **b)** *s.* beschwören **c**: invoking; **c)** *(Bitte)* en-
treaty
beseitigen *tr. V.* remove; eliminate
⟨*error, difficulty*⟩; dispose of ⟨*rubbish*⟩; **Beseitigung** die; ~: *s.* beseitigen: removal; elimination; disposal
Besen der; ~s, ~ broom; **ich fress' einen** ~, **wenn das stimmt** *(salopp)* I'll eat
my hat if that's right *(coll.);* **neue** ~
kehren gut *(Spr.)* a new broom sweeps
clean *(prov.)*
besessen *Adj.* **a)** possessed; **b)** *(fig.)*
obsessive ⟨*gambler*⟩; **von einer Idee** ~

sein be obsessed with an idea; **Be-sessenheit** die; ~ a) possession; b) obsessiveness

besetzen tr. V. a) (mit Pelz, Spitzen) edge; trim; **mit Perlen besetzt** set with pearls; b) (belegen; auch Milit.: erobern) occupy; c) (vergeben) fill ⟨post, position, role, etc.⟩; **besetzt** Adj. occupied; ⟨table, seat⟩ taken pred.; (gefüllt) full; (Fernspr.) engaged; busy (Amer.); **Besetzung** die; ~, ~en a) (einer Stellung) filling; b) (Film, Theater usw.) cast; c) (Eroberung) occupation

besichtigen tr. V. see ⟨sights⟩; see the sights of ⟨town⟩; view ⟨house etc. for sale⟩; **Besichtigung** die; ~, ~en zur ~ der Stadt/des Schlosses/der Wohnung to see the sights of the town/to see the castle/to view the flat

besiedeln tr. V. settle
besiegen tr. V. defeat
besinnen unr. refl. V. a) think it over; b) sich [auf jmdn./etw.] ~: remember [sb./sth.]; **Besinnung** die; ~: consciousness; die ~ verlieren faint; [wieder] zur ~ kommen regain consciousness; **besinnungs·los** 1. Adj. unconscious; 2. adv. mindlessly

Besitz der a) property; b) (das Besitzen) possession; im ~ einer Sache (Gen.) sein be in possession of sth.; **besitzen** unr. tr. V. own; have ⟨quality, talent, etc.⟩; (nachdrücklicher) possess; **Besitzer** der; ~s, ~, **Besitzerin** die; ~, ~nen owner

besoffen Adj. (salopp) canned (Brit. sl.); bombed (Amer. sl.); **Besoffene** der/die; adj. Dekl. (salopp) drunk

besohlen tr. V. sole; neu ~: resole
besonder... Adj.; nicht präd. special; ein ~es Ereignis an unusual or a special event; keine ~e Leistung no great achievement; **Besonderheit** die; ~, ~en special feature; (Eigenart) peculiarity; **besonders** 1. Adv. particularly; 2. Adj.; nicht attr.; nur verneint (ugs.) nicht ~ sein be nothing special

besonnen 1. Adj. prudent; 2. adv. prudently; **Besonnenheit** die; ~: prudence

besorgen tr. V. a) get; (kaufen) buy; b) (erledigen) take care of; **Besorgnis** die; ~, ~se concern; **besorgt** 1. Adj. concerned (um about); 2. adv. with concern; **Besorgung** die; ~, ~en purchase

bespitzeln tr. V. spy on
besprechen unr. tr. V. discuss; (re-

zensieren) review; **Besprechung** die; ~, ~en discussion; (Konferenz) meeting; (Rezension) review

bespritzen tr. V. a) splash; (mit einem Wasserstrahl) spray; b) (beschmutzen) bespatter

besprühen tr. V. spray
besser 1. Adj. a) better; um so ~: so much the better; b) (sozial höher gestellt) superior; 2. adv. [immer] alles ~ wissen always know better; es ~ haben be better off; ~ gesagt to be [more] precise; 3. Adv. (lieber) das läßt du ~ sein od. (ugs.) bleiben you'd better not do that

besser|gehen unr. itr. V.; mit sein jmdm. geht es besser sb. feels better
bessern 1. refl. V. improve; ⟨person⟩ mend one's ways; 2. tr. V. improve; reform ⟨criminal⟩; **Besserung** die; ~: recovery; gute ~! get well soon

best... 1. Adj. a) best; bei ~er Gesundheit/Laune sein be in the best of health/spirits pl.; im ~en Falle at best; in den ~en Jahren, im ~en Alter in one's prime; ~e Grüße an ... (Akk.) best wishes to ...; mit den ~en Grüßen od. Wünschen with best wishes; (als Briefschluß) ≈ yours sincerely; b) es ist od. wäre das ~e, wenn ...: it would be best if ...; der/die/das nächste ~e ...: the first ... one comes across; einen Witz zum ~en geben entertain [those present] with a joke; das Beste vom Besten the very best; sein Bestes tun do one's best; zu deinem Besten for your benefit; 2. adv. am ~en best; 3. Adv. am ~en fährst du mit dem Zug it would be best for you to go by train

Bestand der a) o. Pl. existence, (Fort~) continued existence; b) (Vorrat) stock (an + Dat. of)

bestanden Adj. von od. mit etw. ~ sein have sth. growing on it; mit Tannen ~e Hügel fir-covered hills
beständig 1. Adj. a) nicht präd. constant; b) (gleichbleibend) constant; steadfast ⟨person⟩; settled ⟨weather⟩; c) (widerstandsfähig) resistant (gegen to); 2. adv. constantly; **Beständigkeit** die; ~ a) steadfastness; b) (Widerstandsfähigkeit) resistance (gegen to)

Bestand·teil der component
bestärken tr. V. confirm
bestätigen 1. tr. V. confirm; endorse ⟨document⟩; acknowledge ⟨receipt⟩; 2. refl. V. be confirmed; ⟨rumour⟩ prove to be true; **Bestätigung** die; ~, ~en

confirmation; *(des Empfangs)* acknowledgement; *(schriftlich)* letter of confirmation

bestatten *tr. V. (geh.)* inter *(formal);* bury; **Bestattung die;** ~, ~en *(geh.)* interment *(formal);* burial; *(Feierlichkeit)* funeral

bestäuben *tr. V.* a) dust; b) *(Biol.)* pollinate

bestaunen *tr. V.* marvel at

bestechen *unr. tr. V.* bribe; **bestechlich** *Adj.* corruptible; open to bribery *postpos.;* **Bestechung die;** ~, ~en bribery *no indef. art.;* **Bestechungs·geld das** bribe

Besteck das; ~|e|s, ~e cutlery setting; *(ugs.: Gesamtheit der Bestecke)* cutlery

bestehen 1. *unr. itr. V.* a) exist; **es besteht |die| Aussicht/Gefahr, daß ...:** there is a prospect/danger that ...; **noch besteht die Hoffnung, daß ...:** there is still hope that ...; b) *(fortdauern)* survive; last; c) **aus etw.** ~: consist of sth.; *(hergestellt sein)* be made of sth.; d) **auf etw.** *(Dat.)* ~: insist on sth.; **2.** *unr. tr. V.* pass *(test, examination);* **Bestehen das;** ~s existence; **die Firma feiert ihr 10jähriges** ~: the firm is celebrating its tenth anniversary

bestehen|bleiben *unr. itr. V.; mit sein* remain; *(regulation)* remain in force

bestehend *Adj.* existing; current *(conditions)*

bestehlen *unr. tr. V.* rob

besteigen *unr. tr. V.* a) climb; mount *(horse, bicycle);* ascend *(throne);* b) board *(ship, aircraft);* get on *(bus, train);* **Besteigung die** ascent

bestellen *tr. V.* a) *auch itr.* order (bei from); **würden Sie mir bitte ein Taxi** ~? would you order me a taxi?; b) *(reservieren lassen)* reserve *(tickets, table);* c) jmdn. |für 10 Uhr| **zu sich** ~: ask sb. to go/come to see one [at 10 o'clock]; d) *(ausrichten)* **jmdm. etw.** ~: tell sb. sth.; **bestell deinem Mann schöne Grüße von mir** give your husband my regards; **Bestellung die** a) order; b) *(Reservierung)* reservation

besten·falls *Adv.* at best; **bestens** *Adv.* extremely well

besteuern *tr. V.* tax

bestialisch 1. *Adj.* a) bestial; b) *nicht präd. (ugs.: schrecklich)* ghastly *(coll.);* **2.** *adv.* a) in a bestial manner; b) *(ugs.: schrecklich)* awfully *(coll.);* **Bestialität die;** ~: bestiality

besticken *tr. V.* embroider

Bestie ['bɛstiə] **die;** ~, ~n beast

bestimmen 1. *tr. V.* a) *(festsetzen)* decide on; fix *(price, time, etc.);* b) *(vorsehen)* intend; **das ist für dich bestimmt** that is meant for you; c) *(identifizieren)* identify; determine *(age, position);* define *(meaning);* d) *(prägen)* determine the character of; **2.** *itr. V.* a) make the decisions; b) **über jmdn.** ~: tell sb. what to do; |frei| **über etw.** *(Akk.)* ~: do as one wishes with sth.; **bestimmend 1.** *Adj.* decisive; **2.** *adv.* decisively; **bestimmt 1.** *Adj.* a) *(speziell)* particular; *(gewiß)* certain; *(genau)* definite; b) *(festgelegt)* fixed; given *(quantity);* c) *(Sprachw.)* definite *(article etc.);* d) *(entschieden)* firm; **2.** *adv.* a) *(deutlich)* clearly; *(genau)* precisely; b) *(entschieden)* firmly **3.** *Adv.* for certain; **du weißt es doch |ganz|** ~ **noch** I'm sure you must remember it; **ich habe das** ~ **liegengelassen** I must have left it behind; **Bestimmtheit die;** ~: firmness; *(im Auftreten)* decisiveness; **Bestimmung die** a) *o. Pl. (das Festsetzen)* fixing; b) *(Vorschrift)* regulation; c) *o. Pl. (Zweck)* purpose; d) *s.* **bestimmen 1 c:** identification; determination; definition; e) *(Sprachw.)* modifier; **adverbiale** ~: adverbial qualification

best·möglich *Adj.* best possible

bestrafen *tr. V.* punish (für, wegen for); **es wird mit Gefängnis bestraft** it is punishable by imprisonment; **Bestrafung die;** ~, ~en punishment

bestrahlen *tr. V.* a) illuminate; floodlight *(building);* b) *(Med.)* treat *(tumour, part of body)* using radiotherapy; **Bestrahlung die;** ~, ~en *(Med.)* radiation [treatment] *no indef. art.*

Bestreben das endeavour[s *pl.*]; **bestrebt** *Adj.:* ~ **sein, etw. zu tun** endeavour to do sth.; **Bestrebung die;** ~, ~en effort; *(Versuch)* attempt

bestreichen *unr. tr. V.* **A mit B** ~: spread B on A

bestreiten *unr. tr. V.* a) dispute; *(leugnen)* deny; b) *(finanzieren)* finance *(studies);* pay for *(studies, sb.'s keep);* meet *(costs, expenses);* c) *(gestalten)* carry *(programme, conversation, etc.)*

bestreuen *tr. V.* sprinkle

Bestseller der; ~s, ~: best seller

bestürzt 1. *Adj.* dismayed; **2.** *adv.* with dismay

Besuch der; ~[e]s, ~e **a)** visit (Gen.,
bei to); **ein ~ bei jmdm.** a visit to sb.;
(kurz) a call on sb.; **b)** *(Teilnahme)* attendance (Gen. at); **c)** *(Gast)* visitor;
(Gäste) visitors pl.; **~ haben** have vis-
itors/a visitor; **besuchen** tr. V. **a)**
visit; *(weniger formell)* go to see ⟨per-
son⟩; go to ⟨exhibition, theatre, museum, etc.⟩; *(zur Besichtigung)* go to
see ⟨church, exhibition, etc.⟩; **b) die
Schule/Universität ~:** go to school/
university; **Besucher** der; ~s, ~,
Besucherin die; ~, ~nen visitor;
besucht Adj. **gut/schlecht ~:** well/
poorly attended ⟨lecture, performance,
etc.⟩; much/little frequented ⟨restaur-
ant etc.⟩
betagt Adj. (geh.) elderly
betasten tr. V. feel [with one's fin-
gers]
betätigen 1. refl. V. occupy oneself;
sich politisch/körperlich ~: engage in
political/physical activity; **2.** tr. V.
operate ⟨lever, switch, flush, etc.⟩;
apply ⟨brake⟩; **Betätigung** die; ~,
~en: **a)** activity; **b)** o. Pl. s. betätigen
2: operation; application
betäuben tr. V. **a)** (Med.) anaesthet-
ize; deaden ⟨nerve⟩; **jmdn. örtlich ~:**
give sb. a local anaesthetic; **b)** *(unterdrücken)* deaden ⟨pain⟩; still ⟨unease,
fear⟩; **c)** *(benommen machen)* daze;
(mit einem Schlag) stun; **Betäubung**
die; ~, ~en: **a)** (Med.) anaesthetiza-
tion; *(Narkose)* anaesthesia; **b)** *(Benommenheit)* daze; **Betäubungsmittel das** narcotic; *(Med.)* anaesthetic
beteiligen 1. refl. V. take part (**an** +
Dat. in); **2.** tr. V. jmdn. |mit 10%| an
etw. (Dat.) ~: give sb. a [10%] share of
sth.; **beteiligt** Adj. **a)** involved (**an** +
Dat. in); **b)** *(finanziell)* **an einem Un-
ternehmen/am Gewinn ~ sein** have a
share in a business/in the profit; **Be-
teiligte der/die;** adj. Dekl. person involved; **Beteiligung** die; ~, ~en **a)**
participation (**an** + Dat. in); **b)** *(Anteil)* share (**an** + Dat. in)
beten 1. itr. V. pray (**für, um** for); **2.** tr.
V. say ⟨prayer⟩
beteuern tr. V. affirm; protest ⟨one's
innocence⟩; **Beteuerung** die; ~, ~en
s. beteuern: affirmation; protestation
Beton [be'tɔŋ, bes. österrr.: be'to:n]
der; ~s, ~s [-ɔŋs] od. (bes. österr.:) ~e
[-o:nə] concrete
betonen tr. V. **a)** stress ⟨word, syl-
lable⟩; **b)** *(hervorheben)* emphasize

betonieren tr. V. concrete; surface
⟨road etc.⟩ with concrete
betont 1. Adj. **a)** stressed; **b)** *(bewußt)*
studied; **2.** adv. studiedly; **Beto-
nung** die; ~, ~en **a)** stressing; **b)** *(Akzent)* stress; *(Intonation)* intonation;
c) *(Hervorhebung)* emphasis
betören tr. V. (geh.) captivate
betr. Abk. betreffs, betrifft re; **Betr.**
Abk. Betreff re
Betracht: jmdn./etw. in ~ ziehen consider sb./sth.; **jmdn./etw. außer ~ lassen** disregard sb./sth.; **betrachten**
tr. V. **a)** look at; **b) jmdn./etw. als etw.
~:** regard sb./sth. as sth.; **c)** *(beurteilen)* consider; **Betrachter** der; ~s,
~: observer
beträchtlich 1. Adj. considerable; **2.**
adv. considerably
Betrachtung die; ~, ~en **a)** contemplation; *(Untersuchung)* examination;
b) *(Überlegung)* reflection
Betrag der; ~[e]s, Beträge amount; „~
dankend erhalten" 'received with
thanks'; **betragen 1.** unr. itr. V. be;
(bei Geldsummen) come to; **2.** unr.
refl. V. behave; **Betragen das;** ~s behaviour
Betreff der; ~[e]s, ~e *(im Brief)* heading; **betreffen** unr. tr. V. concern;
⟨new rule, change, etc.⟩ affect; **betreffend** Adj. concerning; **der ~e
Sachbearbeiter** the person dealing
with this matter; **in dem ~en Fall** in
the case in question; **betreffs** Präp.
mit Gen. (Amtsspr., Kaufmannsspr.)
concerning
betreiben unr. tr. V. **a)** proceed with,
(energisch) press ahead with ⟨task,
case, etc.⟩; pursue ⟨policy, studies⟩;
carry on ⟨trade⟩; go in for ⟨sport⟩; **b)**
run ⟨business, shop⟩; **c)** *(in Betrieb halten)* operate
¹**betreten** unr. tr. V. *(hineintreten in)*
enter; *(treten auf)* step on to; *(begehen)* walk on ⟨carpet, grass, etc.⟩; „Betreten verboten" 'Keep off'; *(kein Eintritt)* 'Keep out'
²**betreten 1.** Adj. embarrassed; **2.**
adv. with embarrassment
betreuen tr. V. look after; care for
⟨invalid⟩; supervise ⟨youth group⟩; see
to the needs of ⟨tourists, sportsmen⟩;
Betreuung die; ~ care no indef. art.
Betrieb der; ~[e]s, ~e **a)** business;
(Firma) firm; **b)** o. Pl. *(das In-Funkti-
on-Sein)* operation; **außer ~ sein** not
operate; *(wegen Störung)* be out of
order; **in/außer ~ setzen** start up/stop

⟨*machine etc.*⟩; **c)** *o. Pl. (ugs.: Treiben)* bustle; *(Verkehr)* traffic; **es herrscht großer ~, es ist viel ~:** it's very busy; **betrieblich** *Adj.* firm's; company **Betriebs-: ~angehörige der/die** employee; **~anleitung die, ~anweisung die** operating instructions *pl.;* **~ausflug der** staff outing; **~ferien** *Pl.* firm's annual close-down *sing.;* **„Wegen ~ferien geschlossen"** 'closed for annual holidays'; **~klima das** working atmosphere; **~rat der a)** works committee; **b)** *(Person)* member of a/the works committee; **~wirt der** graduate in business management; **~wirtschaft die;** *o. Pl.* business management **betrinken** *unr. refl. V.* get drunk **betroffen 1.** *Adj.* upset; *(bestürzt)* dismayed; **2.** *adv.* in dismay; **Betroffenheit die;** *~:* dismay **betrüblich** *Adj.* gloomy; **betrübt 1.** *Adj.* sad; gloomy ⟨*face etc.*⟩; **2.** sadly; *(schwermütig)* gloomily **Betrug der; ~[e]s** deception; *(Delikt)* fraud; **betrügen 1.** *unr. tr. V.* deceive; be unfaithful to ⟨*husband, wife*⟩; *(Rechtsw.)* defraud; *(beim Spielen)* cheat; **jmdn. um 100 DM ~:** cheat *or (coll.)* do sb. out of 100 marks; *(arglistig)* swindle sb. out of 100 marks; **2.** *unr. itr. V.* cheat; *(bei Geschäften)* swindle people; **Betrüger der; ~s, ~:** swindler; *(Hochstapler)* con man *(coll.); (beim Spielen)* cheat; **Betrügerei die; ~, ~en** deception; *(beim Spielen usw.)* cheating; *(bei Geschäften)* swindling; **Betrügerin die; ~, ~nen** swindler; *(beim Spielen)* cheat **betrunken** *Adj.* drunken *attrib.;* drunk *pred.;* **Betrunkene der/die;** *adj. Dekl.* drunk **Bett das; ~[e]s, ~en a)** bed; **ins** *od.* **zu ~ gehen** go to bed; **die Kinder ins ~ bringen** put the children to bed; **b)** *(Feder~)* duvet **Bett-: ~bezug der** duvet cover; **~decke die** blanket; *(gesteppt)* quilt **Bettelei die; ~, ~en** begging *no art.;* **betteln** *itr. V.* beg (um for) **bett·lägerig** *Adj.* bedridden **Bett·laken das** sheet **Bettler der; ~s, ~, Bettlerin die; ~, ~nen** beggar **Bett-: ~ruhe die** bed rest; **~wäsche die** bed-linen; **~zeug das;** *o. Pl. (ugs.)* bedclothes *pl.* **betucht** *Adj. (ugs.)* well-heeled *(coll.);* well-off

betupfen *tr. V.* dab **Beuge die; ~, ~n** *(Turnen)* bend; **beugen 1.** *tr. V.* **a)** bend; bow ⟨*head*⟩; **b)** *(Sprachw.: flektieren)* inflect ⟨*word*⟩; **2.** *refl. V.* **a)** bend over; **sich nach vorn/hinten ~:** bend forwards/bend over backwards; **sich aus dem Fenster ~:** lean out of the window; **b)** *(sich fügen)* give way; **Beugung die; ~, ~en** *(Sprachw.)* inflexion **Beule die; ~, ~n** bump; *(Vertiefung)* dent; **beulen** *itr. V.* bulge **beunruhigen** *tr., refl. V.* worry **beurlauben** *tr. V.* **a)** **jmdn. [für zwei Tage] ~:** give sb. [two days'] leave of absence; **b)** *(suspendieren)* suspend **beurteilen** *tr. V.* judge; assess ⟨*situation etc.*⟩; **Beurteilung die; ~, ~en a)** judgement; *(einer Lage usw.)* assessment; **b)** *(Gutachten)* assessment **Beute die; ~, ~n** *(Gestohlenes)* haul; loot *no indef. art.;* **b)** *(von Raubtieren)* prey; *(eines Jägers)* bag **Beutel der; ~s, ~** bag; *(kleiner, für Tabak usw.)* pouch **bevölkern** *tr. V.* populate; **Bevölkerung die; ~, ~en** population; *(Volk)* people **bevollmächtigen** *tr. V.* authorize; **Bevollmächtigte der/die;** *adj. Dekl.* authorized representative **bevor** *Konj.* before; **~ du nicht unterschrieben hast** until you have signed; **bevor|stehen** *unr. itr. V.* be near; **unmittelbar ~:** be imminent; **jmdm. steht etw. bevor** sth. is in store for sb.; **bevorstehend** *Adj.* forthcoming; **unmittelbar ~:** imminent **bevorzugen** *tr. V.* **a)** *(vorziehen)* prefer (**vor** + *Dat.* to); **b)** *(begünstigen)* favour; give preference *or* preferential treatment to (**vor** + *Dat.* over); **bevorzugt 1.** *Adj.* favoured; *(privilegiert)* privileged; preferential ⟨*treatment*⟩; **2.** *adv.* **jmdn. ~ behandeln** give sb. preferential treatment; **Bevorzugung die; ~, ~en** *(Begünstigung)* preferential treatment **bewachen** *tr. V.* guard; **bewachter Parkplatz** car park with an attendant; **Bewacher der; ~s, ~:** guard; **Bewachung die; ~, ~en** guarding **bewaffnen: 1.** *tr. V.* arm; **2.** *refl. V. (auch fig.)* arm oneself (**mit** with); **Bewaffnung die; ~, ~en a)** arming; **b)** *(Waffen)* weapons *pl.* **bewahren** *tr. V.* **a)** protect (**vor** + *Dat.* from); **b)** *(erhalten)* **seine Fas-**

sung ~: retain one's composure; **Still-schweigen** ~: remain silent

bewähren *refl. V.* prove oneself/itself; **bewährt** *Adj.* proven *(method, design, etc.)*; well-tried *(recipe, cure)*; reliable *(worker)*; **Bewährung die;** ~, ~en *(Rechtsw.)* probation

bewaldet *Adj.* wooded

bewältigen *tr. V.* cope with; overcome *(difficulty, problem)*; cover *(distance)*; **Bewältigung die;** ~, ~en *s.* **bewältigen**: coping with; overcoming; covering

bewandert *Adj.* well-versed

Bewandtnis die; ~, ~se: **mit etw. hat es |s|eine eigene/besondere** ~: there's a [special] story behind sth.

bewässern *tr. V.* irrigate; **Bewässerung die;** ~, ~en irrigation

¹bewegen 1. *tr. V.* **a)** move; **b)** *(ergreifen)* move; **c)** *(innerlich beschäftigen)* preoccupy; 2. *refl. V.* move

²bewegen *unr. tr. V.* **jmdn. dazu ~, etw. zu tun** *(thing)* induce sb. to do sth.; *(person)* prevail upon sb. to do sth.; **Beweg·grund der** motive

beweglich *Adj.* **a)** movable; moving *(target)*; **b)** *(rege)* agile *(mind)*; **bewegt** *Adj.* eventful; *(unruhig)* turbulent; **Bewegung die;** ~, ~ **a)** movement; *(bes. Technik, Physik)* motion; **b)** *(körperliche* ~) exercise; **c)** *(Ergriffenheit)* emotion; **d)** *(Bestreben, Gruppe)* movement; **Bewegungs·freiheit die;** *o. Pl.* freedom of movement; **bewegungs·los** *Adj.* motionless

Beweis der; ~es, ~e proof *(Gen., für* of); **belastende** ~e incriminating evidence; **beweisbar** *Adj.* provable; **beweisen** *unr. tr. V.* prove; **Beweis·material das** evidence

bewenden *unr. V.* **es bei** *od.* **mit etw.** ~ **lassen** content oneself with sth.

bewerben *unr. refl. V.* apply **(bei** to, **um** for); **Bewerber der** applicant; **Bewerbung die** application

bewerfen *unr. tr. V.* **jmdn./etw. mit etw.** ~: throw sth. at sb./sth.

bewerten *tr. V.* assess; rate; *(dem Geldwert nach)* value **(mit** at); **Bewertung die** assessment; *(dem Geldwert nach)* valuation

bewilligen *tr. V.* grant; **Bewilligung die;** ~, ~en granting

bewirken *tr. V.* bring about; cause

bewirten *tr. V.* feed; **jmdn. mit etw.** ~: serve sb. sth.

bewirtschaften *tr. V.* **a)** manage

(estate, farm, restaurant, business, etc.); **b)** farm *(fields, land)*

Bewirtung die; ~, ~en provision of food and drink

bewog *1. u. 3. Pers. Sg. Prät. v.* **²bewegen**

bewohnbar *Adj.* habitable; **bewohnen** *tr. V.* inhabit, live in *(house, area)*; live in *(room, flat)*; **Bewohner der;** ~s, ~, **Bewohnerin die;** ~, ~nen *(eines Hauses, einer Wohnung)* occupant; *(einer Stadt, eines Gebietes)* inhabitant; **bewohnt** *Adj.* occupied *(house etc.)*; inhabited *(area)*

bewölken *refl. V.* cloud over; become overcast; **bewölkt** *Adj.* cloudy; overcast; **Bewölkung die;** ~, ~en cloud [cover]

Bewunderer der; ~s, ~, **Bewunderin die;** ~, ~nen admirer; **bewundern** *tr. V.* admire **(wegen, für** for); **bewunderns·wert** *Adj.* **a)** admirable; 2. *adv.* admirably; **Bewunderung die;** ~: admiration

bewußt 1. *Adj.* conscious *(reaction, behaviour, etc.)*; *(absichtlich)* deliberate *(lie, deception, attack, etc.)*; **etw. ist/wird jmdm.** ~: sb. is/becomes aware of sth.; **sb. realizes sth.; sich** *(Dat.)* **einer Sache** *(Gen.)* ~ **sein/werden** be/become aware of something; 2. *adv.* consciously; *(absichtlich)* deliberately; **bewußt·los** *Adj.* unconscious; **Bewußtlosigkeit die;** ~: unconsciousness; **Bewußt·sein das a)** consciousness; **das** ~ **verlieren/wiedererlangen** lose/regain consciousness; **bei vollem** ~ **sein** be fully conscious; **b)** *(deutliches Wissen)* awareness

bezahlbar *Adj.* affordable; **bezahlen** 1. *tr. V.* pay *(person, bill, taxes, rent, amount)*; pay for *(goods etc.)*; **das macht sich bezahlt** it pays off; 2. *itr. V.* pay; **Herr Ober, ich möchte** ~ *od.* **bitte** ~: waiter, the bill *or (Amer.)* check please; **Bezahlung die** payment; *(Lohn, Gehalt)* pay

bezaubernd 1. *Adj.* enchanting; 2. *adv.* enchantingly

bezeichnen *tr. V.* **a)** **jmdn./sich/etw. als etw.** ~: call sb./oneself/sth. sth.; **b)** *(Name, Wort sein für)* denote; **bezeichnend** *Adj.* characteristic *(für* of); **Bezeichnung die a)** marking; *(Angabe durch Zeichen)* indication; **b)** *(Name)* name

bezeugen *tr. V.* testify to

bezichtigen *tr. V.* accuse

beziehen 1. *unr. tr. V.* **a)** cover ⟨*seat, cushion, etc.*⟩; **die Betten frisch ~:** put clean sheets on the beds; **b)** *(einziehen in)* move into ⟨*house, office*⟩; **c)** *(Milit.)* take up ⟨*position, post*⟩; **d)** *(erhalten)* obtain ⟨*goods*⟩; take ⟨*newspaper*⟩; draw ⟨*pension, salary*⟩; **e)** *(in Beziehung setzen)* apply **(auf** + *Akk.* to); **2.** *unr. refl. V.* **a)** es/der Himmel bezieht sich it/the sky is clouding over *or* becoming overcast; **b) sich auf jmdn./ etw. ~** *(sich berufen auf)* ⟨*person, letter, etc.*⟩ refer to sb./sth.; *(betreffen)* ⟨*question, statement, etc.*⟩ relate to sb./sth.; **wir ~ uns auf Ihr Schreiben vom 28. 8.** with reference to your letter of 28 August; **Beziehung die a)** relation; *(Zusammenhang)* connection **(zu** with); **zwischen A und B besteht keine/eine ~:** there is no/a connection between A and B; **b)** *(Freundschaft, Liebes~)* relationship; **c)** *(Hinsicht)* respect; **in mancher ~:** in many respects; **beziehungs·weise** *Konj.* and ... respectively; *(oder)* or
Bezirk der; ~|e|s, ~e district
bezug: in ~ auf jmdn./etw. regarding sb./sth.
Bezug der a) *(für Kissen usw.)* cover; *(für Polstermöbel)* loose cover; slip-cover *(Amer.)*; *(für Betten)* duvet cover; *(für Kopfkissen)* pillowcase; **b)** *o. Pl. (Erwerb)* obtaining; *(Kauf)* purchase; **~ einer Zeitung** taking a newspaper; **c)** *Pl.* salary *sing.*; **d)** *(Papierdt.)* **mit** *od.* **unter ~ auf etw.** *(Akk.)* with reference to sth.; **~ nehmend auf unser Telex** with reference to our telex; **bezüglich** *Präp. mit Gen.* regarding
bezwecken *tr. V.* aim to achieve
bezweifeln *tr. V.* doubt
bezwingen *unr. tr. V.* conquer ⟨*enemy, mountain, pain, etc.*⟩; defeat ⟨*opponent*⟩; capture ⟨*fortress*⟩
BH [beː'haː] **der;** ~|s|, ~|s| *Abk.:* Büstenhalter bra
Bibel die; ~, ~n *(auch fig.)* Bible
Biber der; ~s, ~: beaver
Bibliothek die; ~, ~en library
biblisch *Adj.* biblical
Bidet [bi'deː] **das;** ~s, ~s bidet
bieder *Adj.* unsophisticated; *(langweilig)* stolid; *(treuherzig)* trusting
biegen 1. *unr. tr. V.* bend; **2.** *unr. refl. V.* bend; *(nachgeben)* give; **3.** *unr. itr. V.; mit sein* turn; **biegsam** *Adj.* flexible; pliable ⟨*material*⟩; **Biegung die;** ~, ~en bend

Biene die; ~, ~n bee
Bienen-: ~**honig der** bees' honey; ~**königin die** queen bee; ~**korb der** straw hive; ~**stock der** beehive
Bier das; ~|e|s, ~e beer
Bier-: ~**deckel der** beer-mat; ~**dose die** beer can; ~**faß das** beer-barrel; ~**flasche die** beer-bottle; ~**garten der** beer garden; ~**glas das** beer-glass; ~**kasten der** beer-crate; ~**zelt das** beer tent
Biest das; ~|e|s, ~er *(ugs. abwertend)* **a)** *(Tier, Gegenstand)* wretched thing; **b)** *(Mensch)* wretch
bieten 1. *unr. tr. V.* **a)** offer; put on ⟨*programme etc.*⟩; provide ⟨*shelter, guarantee, etc.*⟩; **b) ein schreckliches Bild ~:** present a terrible picture; **einen prächtigen Anblick ~:** be a splendid sight; **2.** *unr. refl. V.* **sich jmdm. ~:** present itself to sb.; **3.** *unr. itr. V.* bid
Bigamie die; ~: bigamy *no def. art.*
Bikini der; ~s, ~s bikini
Bilanz die; ~, ~en **a)** balance sheet; **b)** *(Ergebnis)* outcome; **~ ziehen** take stock
Bild das; ~|e|s, ~er **a)** picture; **b)** *(Anblick)* sight; **c)** *(Metapher)* image
bilden 1. *tr. V.* **a)** form **(aus** from); *(modellieren)* mould **(aus** from); **eine Gasse ~:** make a path; **sich** *(Dat.)* **ein Urteil ~:** form an opinion; **b)** *(ansammeln)* build up ⟨*fund, capital*⟩; **c)** *(darstellen)* be ⟨*exception etc.*⟩; **d)** *(erziehen)* educate; **2.** *refl. V.* **a)** form; **b)** *(lernen)* educate oneself
Bilder·buch das picture-book *(for children)*
Bild·hauer der sculptor
bild·hübsch *Adj.* really lovely; stunningly beautiful ⟨*girl*⟩
bildlich 1. *Adj.* pictorial; *(übertragen)* figurative; **2.** *adv.* pictorially; *(übertragen)* figuratively; **Bildnis** ['bɪltnɪs] **das;** ~ses, ~se portrait
Bild·schirm der *(Ferns., Informationst.)* screen; **Bildschirm·gerät das** VDU; visual display unit
bild·schön *Adj.* really lovely; stunningly beautiful ⟨*girl, woman*⟩
Bildung die; ~, ~en **a)** *(Erziehung)* education; *(Kultur)* culture; **b)** *(das Formen)* formation; **Bildungslücke die** gap in one's education
Billard ['bɪljart, *österr.:* bi'jaːɐ̯] **das;** ~s, ~e billiards
Billard-: ~**kugel die** billiard-ball; ~**stock der** billiard-cue; ~**tisch der** billiard-table

Billett [bɪl'jɛt] *das;* ~|e|s, ~e *od.* ~s *(schweiz., veralt.)* ticket

Billiarde *die;* ~, ~n thousand million million; quadrillion *(Amer.)*

billig 1. *Adj.* **a)** cheap; **b)** *(abwertend: primitiv)* cheap ⟨*trick*⟩; feeble ⟨*excuse*⟩; 2. *adv.* cheaply

billigen *tr. V.* approve; **Billigung** *die;* ~: approval

Billion *die;* ~, ~en million million; trillion *(Amer.)*

bimmeln *itr. V. (ugs.)* ring

bin *1. Pers. Sg. Präsens v.* ¹**sein**

Binde *die;* ~, ~n **a)** *(Verband)* bandage; *(Augen~)* blindfold; **b)** *(Arm~)* armband

Binde-: ~**gewebe** *das (Anat.)* connective tissue; ~**haut** *die (Anat.)* conjunctiva

binden 1. *unr. tr. V.* **a)** *(auch fig.)* tie; knot ⟨*tie*⟩; make up ⟨*wreath, bouquet*⟩; **jmdn. an sich** *(Akk.)* ~ *(fig.)* make sb. dependent on one; **b)** *(fesseln, festhalten, zusammenhalten, fig.: verpflichten, Buchw.)* bind; **c)** *(Kochk.: legieren)* thicken ⟨*sauce*⟩; 2. *unr. refl. V.* tie oneself down; **Binder** *der;* ~s, ~ tie; **Bindestrich** *der* hyphen; **Bind·faden** *der* string

Bindung *die;* ~, ~en **a)** *(Beziehung)* relationship (**an** + *Akk.* to); **b)** *(Verbundenheit)* attachment (**an** + *Akk.* to); **c)** *(Ski~)* binding

binnen *Präp. mit Dat. od. (geh.) Gen.* within

Binsen·weisheit *die* truism

bio-, Bio: ~**chemie** *die* biochemistry; ~**graph** *der;* ~en, ~en biographer; ~**graphie** *die;* ~, ~n biography; ~**graphisch** *Adj.* biographical; ~**loge** *der;* ~n, ~n biologist; ~**logie** *die;* ~: biology *no art.;* ~**logisch** *Adj.* **a)** biological; **b)** *(natürlich)* natural ⟨*medicine, cosmetic, etc.*⟩; ~**top** *der od. das;* ~s, ~e *(Biol.)* biotope

Birke *die;* ~, ~n birch[-tree]; *(Holz)* birch[wood]

Birma *(das);* ~s Burma

Birn·baum *der* pear-tree; **Birne** *die;* ~, ~n **a)** pear; **b)** *(Glüh~)* [light-]bulb; **c)** *(salopp: Kopf)* nut *(sl.)*

bis 1. *Präp. mit Akk.* **a)** *(zeitlich)* until; till; *(die ganze Zeit über und bis zu einem bestimmten Zeitpunkt)* up until; up till; *(nicht später als)* by; **b)** *(räumlich)* to; **dieser Zug fährt nur** ~ **Offenburg** this train only goes as far as Offenburg; ~ **5000 Mark** up to 5,000

marks; **c)** ~ **auf** *(einschließlich)* down to; *(mit Ausnahme von)* except for; 2. *Adv.* ~ **zu 6 Personen** up to six people. 3. *Konj.* **a)** *(nebenordnend)* to; **b)** *(unterordnend)* until; till; *(österr.: sobald)* when

Bisam·ratte *die* musk-rat

Bischof *der;* ~s, **Bischöfe** bishop; **bischöflich** *Adj.* episcopal

bis·her *Adv.* up to now; *(aber jetzt nicht mehr)* until now; till now; **bisherig** *Adj. (vorherig)* previous; *(momentan)* present

Biskaya [bɪs'ka:ja] *die;* ~: the Bay of Biscay

Biskuit [bɪs'kvi:t] *das od. der;* ~|e|s, ~s *od.* ~e **a)** sponge biscuit; **b)** *(~teig)* sponge

bis·lang *Adv.: s.* **bisher**

Bison *der;* ~s, ~s bison

Biß *der;* **Bisses, Bisse** bite

bißchen *indekl. Indefinitpron.* **a)** *adj.* **ein** ~ **Geld/Wasser** a bit of *or* a little money/a drop of *or* a little water; **ein/kein** ~ **Angst haben** be a bit/not a bit frightened; **b)** *adv.* **ein/kein** ~: a bit *or* a little/not a *or* one bit; **c)** *subst.* **ein** ~: a bit; a little; *(bei Flüssigkeiten)* a drop; a little; **das/kein** ~: the little [bit]/not a *or* one bit

Bissen *der;* ~s, ~: mouthful

bissig 1. *Adj.* **a)** ~ **sein** ⟨*dog*⟩ bite; **ein** ~**er Hund** a dog that bites; „**Vorsicht,** ~**er Hund**" 'beware of the dog'; **b)** *(fig.)* cutting ⟨*remark, tone, etc.*⟩; 2. *adv.* ⟨*say*⟩ cuttingly

Biß·wunde *die* bite

bist 2. *Pers. Sg. Präsens v.* ¹**sein**

Bistum ['bɪstuːm] *das;* ~s, **Bistümer** bishopric; diocese

bis·weilen *Adv. (geh.)* from time to time

bitte 1. *Adv.* please; 2. *Interj.* **a)** *(Bitte, Aufforderung)* please; **zwei Tassen Tee,** ~: two cups of tea, please; ~**|, nehmen Sie doch Platz|!** do take a seat; **Noch eine Tasse Tee?** – |**Ja|** ~! Another cup of tea? – Yes, please; **b)** *(Aufforderung, etw. entgegenzunehmen)* ~ |**schön** *od.* **sehr|!** there you are!; **c)** *(Ausdruck des Einverständnisses)* ~ |**gern|!** certainly; of course; **Entschuldigung!** – **Bitte!** [I'm] sorry! – That's all right!; **d)** ~ |**schön** *od.* **sehr|!** *(im Laden, Lokal)* yes, please?; **e)** |**wie|** ~? *(Nachfrage)* sorry; **f) Vielen Dank!** – **Bitte |schön** *od.* **sehr|!** Many thanks! – Not at all *or* you're welcome

Bjtte die; ~, ~n request; *(inständig)* plea; **bjtten** *unr. tr. V.* **a)** *auch itr.* ask **(um for)**; **darf ich Sie um Feuer/ein Glas Wasser ~?** could I ask you for a light/a glass of water, please?; **b)** *(einladen)* ask

bjtter 1. *Adj.* **a)** bitter; plain ⟨*chocolate*⟩; **b)** *(fig.)* *(verbittert)* bitter; **c)** *(schmerzlich)* bitter, painful, hard ⟨*loss*⟩; hard ⟨*time, fate, etc.*⟩; dire ⟨*need*⟩; desperate ⟨*poverty*⟩; grievous ⟨*injustice, harm*⟩; **2.** *adv. (sehr stark)* desperately; ⟨*regret*⟩ bitterly

bjtter-: ~böse 1. *Adj.* furious; **2.** *adv.* furiously; **~kalt** *Adj.; präd. getrennt geschr.* bitterly cold

bjtterlich 1. *Adj.* slightly bitter ⟨*taste*⟩. **2.** *adv. (heftig)* ⟨*cry, complain, etc.*⟩ bitterly; **bjtter·süß** *Adj. (auch fig.)* bitter-sweet

Bjtt·steller der; ~s, ~ petitioner

Bjwak das; ~s, ~s *(bes. Milit., Bergsteigen)* bivouac

bizarr 1. *Adj.* bizarre; **2.** *adv.* bizarrely

Bizeps der; ~|es|, ~e biceps

Blähung die; ~, ~en flatulence *no art., no pl.*

Blamage [bla'ma:ʒə] **die; ~, ~n** disgrace; **blamieren 1.** *tr. V.* disgrace; **2.** *refl. V.* disgrace oneself; *(sich lächerlich machen)* make a fool of oneself

blank *Adj.* shiny

Blanko-: ~scheck der *(auch fig.)* blank cheque; **~vollmacht die** *(auch fig.)* carte blanche

Bläschen ['blɛ:sçən] **das; ~s, ~ a)** [small] bubble; **b)** *(in der Haut)* [small] blister; **Blase die; ~, ~n a)** bubble; **b)** *(in der Haut)* blister; **c)** *(Harn~)* bladder; **Blase·balg der** bellows *pl.;* **blasen 1.** *unr. itr. V.* blow; **2.** *unr. tr. V.* **a)** blow; **b)** *(spielen)* play ⟨*musical instrument, tune, melody, etc.*⟩; **Bläser der; ~s, ~** *(Musik)* wind player

blasiert *(abwertend)* **1.** *Adj.* blasé; **2.** *adv.* in a blasé way

Blas-: ~instrument das wind instrument; **~kapelle die** brass band; **~musik die** brass-band music

Blasphemie [blasfe'mi:] **die; ~, ~n** blasphemy

Blas·rohr das blowpipe

blaß 1. *Adj.* pale; **2.** *adv.* palely; **Blässe die; ~:** paleness

Blatt das; ~|e|s, Blätter a) *(von Pflanzen)* leaf; **b)** *(Papier)* sheet; **c)** *(Buchseite usw.)* page; **etw. vom ~ spielen** sight-read sth.; **d)** *(Zeitung)* paper; **e)**

(Spielkarten) hand; **f)** *(am Werkzeug, Ruder)* blade; **Blättchen das; ~s, ~ a)** *(von Pflanzen)* [small] leaf; **b)** *(Papier)* [small] sheet; **blättern** *itr. V.* **in einem Buch ~:** leaf through a book; **Blätter·teig der** puff pastry

Blatt-: ~gold das; *o. Pl.* gold leaf; **~laus die** aphid

blau *Adj.* blue; **ein ~er Fleck** a bruise; **~ sein** *(fig. ugs.)* be tight *(coll.)*; **das Blaue vom Himmel herunterlügen** *(ugs.)* lie like anything; **Blau das; ~s, ~ od. (ugs.:) ~s** blue

blau-, Blau-: ~äugig *Adj.* **a)** blue-eyed; **b)** *(naiv)* naive; **~beere die** bilberry; **~grau** *Adj.* blue-grey; **~grün** *Adj.* blue-green

bläulich *Adj.* bluish

blau-, Blau-: ~licht das flashing blue light; **~|machen** *itr. V. (ugs.)* skip work; **~mann der;** *Pl.* **~männer** *(ugs.)* boiler suit; **~säure die;** *o. Pl. (Chemie)* prussic acid; **~stichig** *Adj. (Fot.)* with a blue cast *postpos., not pred.;* **~stichig sein** have a blue cast

Blazer ['ble:zɐ] **der; ~s, ~:** blazer

Blech das; ~|e|s, ~e a) sheet metal; *(Stück Blech)* metal sheet; **b)** *(Back~)* [baking] tray

Blech-: ~büchse die, ~dose die tin **blechen** *tr., itr. V. (ugs.)* cough up *(sl.)* **blechern** *Adj.* **1.** *(metallisch klingend)* tinny ⟨*sound, voice*⟩; **2.** *adv.* tinnily

Blech-: ~musik die *(abwertend)* brass-band music; **~napf der** metal bowl

Blechner der; ~s, ~ *(südd.) s.* **Klempner**

Blech-: ~schaden der *(Kfz-W.)* damage *no indef. art.* to the bodywork; **~trommel die** tin drum

blecken *tr. V.* **die Zähne ~:** bare one's/its teeth

Blei das; ~|e|s, ~e lead

Bleibe die; ~, ~n place to stay; **bleiben** *unr. itr. V.; mit sein* **a)** stay; remain; **~ Sie bitte am Apparat** hold the line please; **wo bleibt er so lange?** where has he got to?; **auf dem Weg ~:** keep to the path; **sitzen ~:** stay *or* remain sitting down *or* seated; **bei etw. ~:** *(fig.: an etw. festhalten)* keep to sth.; **b)** *(übrigbleiben)* be left; remain; **bleibend** *Adj.* lasting; permanent ⟨*damage*⟩; **bleiben|lassen** *unr. tr. V.* **etw. ~:** give sth. a miss

bleich *Adj.* pale; **¹bleichen** *tr. V.* bleach; **²bleichen** *regelm., veralt. auch unr. itr. V.* become bleached

blei-, Blei-: ~**frei** *Adj.* unleaded ⟨*fuel*⟩; ~**kristall das** lead crystal; ~**kugel** die lead ball; *(Geschoß)* lead bullet; ~**schwer** *Adj.* heavy as lead *postpos.;* ~**stift** der pencil; **mit** ~: in pencil; ~**stift·spitzer** der pencil-sharpener

Blende die; ~, ~**n a)** *(Lichtschutz)* shade; *(am Fenster)* blind; **b)** *(Optik, Film, Fot.)* diaphragm; *(Blendenzahl)* aperture setting; **blenden** 1. *tr. V.* **a)** *(auch fig.)* dazzle; **b)** *(blind machen)* blind; **2.** *itr. V.* ⟨*light*⟩ be dazzling; **blendend** 1. *Adj.* es geht mir ~: I feel wonderfully well; **2.** *adv.* wir haben uns ~ amüsiert we had a marvellous time

blich *1. u. 3. Pers. Sg. Prät. v.* ²**bleichen**
Blick der; ~|e|s, ~e **a)** look; *(flüchtig)* glance; **b)** *o. Pl. (Ausdruck)* look in one's eyes; **mit mißtrauischem** ~: with a suspicious look in one's eye; **c)** *(Aussicht)* view; **ein Zimmer mit** ~ **aufs Meer** a room with a sea view; **d)** *o. Pl. (Urteil|skraft|)* eye; **blicken** 1. *itr. V.* look; *(flüchtig)* glance; **2.** *tr. V.* **sich** ~ **lassen** put in an appearance
Blick-: ~**feld das** field of vision; ~**punkt** der view; ~**winkel** der **a)** angle of vision; **b)** *(fig.)* point of view; viewpoint
blieb *1. u. 3. Pers. Sg. Prät. v.* **bleiben**
blies *1. u. 3. Pers. Sg. Prät. v.* **blasen**
blind 1. *Adj.* **a)** *(auch fig.)* blind; ~ **werden** go blind; **b)** *(trübe)* clouded ⟨*glass*⟩; **c) ein** ~**er Passagier** a stowaway; **d)** ~**er Alarm** a false alarm; **2.** *adv.* **a)** *(ohne hinzusehen)* without looking; *(wahllos)* blindly; **b)** *(unkritisch)* ⟨*trust*⟩ implicitly; ⟨*obey*⟩ blindly; **Blind·darm** der **a)** caecum; **b)** *(volkst.: Wurmfortsatz)* appendix; **Blinde** der/die; *adj. Dekl.* blind person; blind man/woman; **die** ~**n** the blind; **Blinde·kuh** *o. Art.* blind man's buff
Blinden-: ~**hund** der guide-dog; ~**schrift** die Braille
Blindheit die; ~ *(auch fig.)* blindness; **blindlings** *Adv.* blindly; ⟨*trust*⟩ implicitly; **Blind·schleiche** die; ~, ~**n** slowworm; **blind·wütig** 1. *Adj.* raging ⟨*anger, hatred, fury, etc.*⟩; wild ⟨*rage*⟩; **2.** *adv.* in a blind rage
blinken 1. *itr. V.* **a)** ⟨*light, glass, crystal*⟩ flash; ⟨*star*⟩ twinkle; ⟨*metal, fish*⟩ gleam; **b)** *(Verkehrsw.)* indicate; **2.** *tr. V.* flash; **Blinker** der; ~**s,** ~ indicator [light]

Blink-: ~**licht das a)** flashing light; **b)** *s.* **Blinker;** ~**zeichen das** flashlight signal
blinzeln *itr. V.* blink; *(mit einem Auge, um ein Zeichen zu geben)* wink
Blitz der; ~**es,** ~**e a)** lightning *no indef. art.;* **ein** ~: a flash of lightning; **|schnell| wie der** ~: like lightning; **b)** *(~licht)* flash
blitz-, Blitz-: ~**ableiter** der lightning-conductor; ~**artig** 1. *Adj.* lightning; **2.** *adv.* like lightning; ⟨*disappear*⟩ in a flash; ~**blank** *Adj. (ugs.)* ~**blank |geputzt|** sparkling clean; brightly polished ⟨*shoes*⟩
blitzeblank *s.* **blitzblank; blitzen** *itr. V.* **a)** *unpers.* es blitzte *(einmal)* there was a flash of lightning; *(mehrmals)* there was lightning; **b)** *(glänzen)* ⟨*light, glass, crystal*⟩ flash; ⟨*metal*⟩ gleam
blitz-, Blitz-: ~**gerät das** flash [unit]; ~**licht das;** *Pl.* ~**lichter** flash[light]; ~**schnell** 1. *Adj.* lightning *attrib.;* ~**schnell sein** be like lightning; **2.** *adv.* like lightning; ⟨*disappear*⟩ in a flash; ~**start** der lightning start
Block der; ~|e|s, **Blöcke** *od.* ~**s a)** *Pl. nur* **Blöcke** *(Brocken)* block; **b)** *(Wohn~)* block; **c)** *Pl. nur* **Blöcke** *(Gruppierung von politischen Kräften, Staaten)* bloc; **d)** *(Schreib~)* pad
Blockade die; ~, ~**n** blockade
Block-: ~**flöte** die recorder; ~**haus das,** ~**hütte** die log cabin
blockieren *tr. V.* block; jam ⟨*telephone line*⟩; halt ⟨*traffic*⟩; lock ⟨*wheel, machine, etc.*⟩
Block·schrift die block capitals *pl.*
blöd[e] *(ugs.)* **1.** *Adj.* **a)** *(dumm)* stupid; idiotic *(coll.);* **b)** *(unangenehm)* stupid; **2.** *adv.* stupidly; idiotically *(coll.);* **Blödelei** die; ~, ~**en** silly joke; **blödeln** *itr. V.* make silly jokes; **Blödheit** die; ~, ~**en** stupidity
blöd-, Blöd-: ~**mann** der; *Pl.* ~**männer** *(salopp)* stupid idiot *(coll.);* ~**sinn** der; *o. Pl. (ugs.)* nonsense; **mach doch keinen** ~**sinn!** don't be stupid; ~**sinnig** *(ugs.)* 1. *Adj.* idiotic *(coll.);* 2. *adv.* idiotically *(coll.)*
blöken *itr. V.* ⟨*sheep*⟩ bleat; ⟨*cattle*⟩ low
blond *Adj.* fair-haired, blond ⟨*man, race*⟩; blonde ⟨*woman*⟩; blond/blonde, fair ⟨*hair*⟩; **Blondine** die; ~, ~**n** blonde
bloß 1. *Adj.* **a)** *(nackt)* naked; **b)** *(nichts als)* mere ⟨*words, promises, tri-*

*viality, suspicion, etc.⟩; der ~e Gedan-
ke daran the mere thought of it; 2.
Adv. (ugs.: nur) only; 3. Partikel was
hast du dir ~ dabei gedacht?* what on
earth were you thinking of?; **Blöße
die; ~: sich** *(Dat.)* **eine/keine ~ geben**
show a/not show any weakness;
bloß|stellen *tr. V.* show up; expose
⟨*swindler, criminal, etc.*⟩
Blouson [blu'zõ:] *das od.* **der; ~|s|, ~s**
blouson
blubbern *itr. V. (ugs.)* bubble
Bluejeans, Blue jeans ['blu:dʒi:ns]
Pl. od. **die; ~, ~:** [blue] jeans *pl.*
Blues [blu:s] **der; ~, ~:** blues *pl.*
Bluff der; ~s, ~s bluff; **bluffen** *tr., itr.
V.* bluff
blühen *itr. V.* **a)** ⟨*plant*⟩ flower, be in
flower *or* bloom; ⟨*flower*⟩ be in
bloom, be out; ⟨*tree*⟩ be in blossom;
~de Gärten gardens full of flowers; **b)**
(florieren) thrive; **c)** *(ugs.: bevorstehen)* **jmdm. ~:** be in store for sb.; **das
kann dir auch noch ~:** the same could
happen to you; **blühend** *Adj.* **a)**
(frisch, gesund) glowing ⟨*colour, complexion, etc.*⟩; radiant ⟨*health*⟩; **b)**
(übertrieben) vivid ⟨*imagination*⟩
Blümchen das; ~s, ~: [little] flower;
Blume die; ~, ~n a) flower; **b)** *(des
Weines)* bouquet; **c)** *(des Biers)* head
blumen-, Blumen-: **~beet das**
flower-bed; **~erde die** potting compost; **~geschäft das** florist's; **~ge-
schmückt** *Adj.* flower-bedecked;
adorned with flowers *postpos.;* **~ka-
sten der** flower-box; *(vor einem Fenster)* window box; **~kohl der** cauliflower; **~strauß der** bunch of
flowers; *(Bukett)* bouquet of flowers;
~topf der flowerpot; **~vase die**
[flower] vase; **~zwiebel die** bulb
Bluse die; ~, ~n blouse
Blut das; ~|e|s blood
blut-, Blut-: **~arm** *Adj. (Med.)* anaemic; **~armut die** *(Med.)* anaemia;
~bad das blood-bath; **~bahn die**
bloodstream; **~befleckt** *Adj.* blood-
stained; **~beschmiert** *Adj.* smeared
with blood *postpos.;* **~buche die** copper beech; **~druck der** blood pressure
Blüte die; ~, ~n a) flower; bloom; *(eines Baums)* blossom; **~n treiben**
flower; ⟨*tree*⟩ blossom; **b)** *(das Blühen)* flowering; *(Baum~)* blossoming
Blut·egel der leech; **bluten** *itr. V.*
bleed **(aus** from)
blüten-, Blüten-: **~blatt das** petal;

~honig der blossom honey; **~staub**
der pollen; **~weiß** *Adj.* sparkling
white
Bluter der; ~s, ~ *(Med.)* haemophiliac
Blut-: **~erguß der** haematoma; *(blauer Fleck)* bruise; **~fleck[en] der**
blood-stain; **~gefäß das** *(Anat.)*
blood-vessel; **~gerinnsel das** blood-
clot; **~gruppe die** blood group;
~hochdruck der high blood pressure; **~hund der** bloodhound
blutig a) bloody; **jmdn. ~ schlagen**
beat sb. to a pulp; **b)** *(fig. ugs.: völlig)*
complete ⟨*beginner, layman, etc.*⟩
blut-, Blut-: **~jung** *Adj.* very young;
~konserve die container of stored
blood; **~konserven** stored blood;
~körperchen das blood corpuscle;
rote/weiße ~körperchen red/white
corpuscles; **~krebs der** leukaemia;
~kreislauf der blood circulation;
~lache die pool of blood; **~leer** *Adj.*
bloodless; **~leere die** restricted
blood supply; **~orange die** blood
orange; **~probe die a)** *(~entnahme,
~untersuchung)* blood test; **b)** *(kleine
~menge)* blood sample; **~rache die**
blood revenge; **~rot** *Adj.* blood-red;
~rünstig 1. *Adj.* bloodthirsty; **2.
adv.** bloodthirstily; **~schande die**
incest; **~spende die** *(das Spenden)*
giving *no indef. art.* of blood; *(~men-
ge)* blood-donation; **~spender der**
blood-donor; **~spur die** trail of
blood; **~stillend** *Adj.* styptic
bluts-, Bluts-: **~tropfen der** drop of
blood; **~verwandt** *Adj.* related by
blood *postpos.;* **~verwandtschaft**
die blood relationship
Blut-: **~tat die** *(geh.)* bloody deed;
~transfusion die blood-transfusion
Blutung die; ~, ~en a) bleeding *no indef. art., no pl.;* **b)** *(Regel~)* period
blut-, Blut-: **~unterlaufen** *Adj.* suffused with blood *postpos.;* bloodshot
⟨*eyes*⟩; **~vergießen das; ~s** bloodshed; **~vergiftung die** bloodpoisoning *no indef. art., no pl.;*
~wurst die black pudding
Bö die; ~, ~en gust [of wind]
Bob der; ~, ~s bob[-sleigh]
Bob-: **~bahn die** bob[-sleigh] run;
~fahrer der bobber
¹Bock der; ~|e|s, Böcke a) *(Reh~, Ka-
ninchen~)* buck; *(Ziegen~)* billy-
goat; he-goat; *(Schafs~)* ram; **b)** *(Gestell)* trestle; **c)** *(Turngerät)* buck
²Bock das; ~s *(Bier)* bock [beer];
Bock·bier das bock [beer]

bocken *itr. V.* refuse to go on; *(vor einer Hürde)* refuse; *(sich aufbäumen)* buck; **bockig 1.** *Adj.* stubborn and awkward; *(coll.).* **2.** *adv.* stubbornly [and awkwardly]; **Bocks·horn das: sich ins ~horn jagen lassen** *(ugs.)* let oneself be browbeaten

Bock-: **~springen das** *(Turnen)* vaulting [over the buck]; **~wurst die** bockwurst

Boden der; **~s, Böden a)** *(Erd~)* ground; *(Fuß~)* floor; **am ~ zerstört** |sein| *(ugs.)* [be] shattered *(coll.);* **bleiben wir doch auf dem ~ der Tatsachen** *(fig.)* let's stick to the facts; **b)** *(unterste Fläche)* bottom; *(Torten~)* base; **c)** *(Dach~, Heu~)* loft

boden-, Boden-: **~belag** der floor-covering; **~frost** der ground frost; **~kammer** die attic; **~los** *Adj.* **a)** bottomless; **b)** *(ugs.: unerhört)* incredible *(foolishness, meanness, etc.);* **~nebel** der ground fog/mist; **~satz** der sediment; **~schätze** *Pl.* mineral resources

Boden·see der; *o. Pl.* Lake Constance

boden-, Boden-: **~ständig** *Adj.* indigenous *(culture, population, etc.);* **~turnen** das floor exercises *pl.;* **~welle** die bump

Bodybuilding [bɔdibɪldɪŋ] das; **~s** body-building *no art.*

Böe die; **~, ~n** *s.* Bö

bog *1. u. 3. Pers. Sg. Prät. v.* biegen

Bogen der; **~s, ~,** *(südd., österr.:)* Bögen **a)** curve; *(Math.)* arc; **b)** *(Archit.)* arch; **c)** *(Waffe, Musik: Geigen~ usw.)* bow; **d)** *(Papier~)* sheet

bogen-, Bogen-: **~fenster** das arched window; **~förmig** *Adj.* arched; **~schießen** das archery *no art.*

Boheme [bo'e:m] die; **~:** bohemian society; **Bohemien** [boe'mjɛ̃:] der; **~s, ~s** bohemian

Bohle die; **~, ~n** [thick] plank

Böhnchen das; **~s, ~:** [small] bean;

Bohne die; **~, ~n** bean; **nicht die ~** *(ugs.)* not one little bit

Bohnen-: **~eintopf** der bean stew; **~kaffee** der real coffee; **~kraut** das savory; **~stange** die *(auch ugs.: Mensch)* beanpole; **~stroh** das: **dumm wie ~stroh** *(ugs.)* as thick as two short planks *(coll.);* **~suppe** die bean soup

bohnern *tr., itr. V.* polish; **Bohner·wachs** das floor-polish

bohren 1. *tr. V.* **a)** bore; *(mit Bohrer, Bohrmaschine)* drill, bore ⟨hole⟩; sink ⟨well, shaft, pole, post etc.⟩ (in + Akk. into); **b)** *(bearbeiten)* drill ⟨wood, concrete, etc.⟩; **c)** *(drücken in)* poke (in + Akk. in[to]); **2.** *itr. V.* **a)** drill; **in der Nase ~:** pick one's nose; **nach Öl/Wasser** *usw.* **~:** drill for oil/water *etc.;* **b)** *(ugs.: drängen, fragen)* keep on; **3.** *refl. V.* bore its way; **bohrend** *Adj.* **a)** gnawing ⟨pain, hunger, remorse⟩; **b)** *(hartnäckig)* piercing ⟨look etc.⟩; probing ⟨question⟩; **Bohrer** der; **~s, ~** drill; **Bohr·turm** der derrick; **Bohrung die; ~, ~en** drill-hole

böig *Adj.* gusty

Boiler ['bɔylɐ] der; **~s, ~:** water-heater

Boje die; **~, ~n** buoy

Bolivien [bo'li:vjən] **(das); ~s** Bolivia

Böller·schuß der gun salute

Boll·werk das bulwark; *(fig.)* bulwark; bastion; stronghold

Bolschewik der; **~en, ~i,** *(abwertend:)* **~en** Bolshevik; **Bolschewismus** der; **~:** Bolshevism *no art.;* **Bolschewist** der; **~en, ~en** Bolshevist; **bolschewistisch** *Adj.* Bolshevik

bolzen *(ugs.)* itr. V. kick the ball about

Bolzen der; **~s, ~** bolt

bombardieren *tr. V.* **a)** bomb; **b)** *(fig. ugs.)* bombard; **Bombardierung** die; **~, ~en a)** *(Milit.)* bombing; **b)** *(fig. ugs.)* bombardment

bombastisch 1. *Adj.* bombastic; **2.** *adv.* bombastically

Bombe die; **~, ~n** bomb

Bomben-: **~angriff** der bomb attack; **~anschlag** der bomb attack; **~drohung** die bomb threat; **~erfolg** der *(ugs.)* smash hit *(sl.);* **~form** die *(ugs.)* top form

Bomber der; **~s, ~:** bomber

Bon [bɔŋ] der; **~s, ~s a)** voucher; coupon; **b)** *(Kassenzettel)* receipt

Bonbon [bɔŋ'bɔŋ] der *od. (österr. nur)* das; **~s, ~s** sweet *(Brit.);* candy *(Amer.);* *(fig.)* treat

bongen *tr. V. (ugs.)* ring up

Bongo das; **~|s|, ~s** *od.* die; **~, ~s** bongo [drum]

Bonmot [bõ'mo:] das; **~s, ~s** bon mot

Bonze der; **~n, ~n** bigwig *(coll.)*

Boom [bu:m] der; **~s, ~s** boom

Boot das; **~|e|s, ~e** boat

Boots-: **~fahrt** die boat trip; **~haus** das boathouse; **~steg** der landing-stage; **~verleih** der boat-hire

¹Bord das; **~|e|s, ~e** shelf

²Bord der; **~|e|s, ~e** *(eines Schiffes)*

side; **an** ~: on board; **über** ~: over-
board
Bordell das; ~s, ~e brothel
Bord·stein der kerb
Bordüre die; ~, ~n edging
borgen *tr. V.: s.* leihen
Borke die; ~, ~n bark
borniert 1. *Adj.* bigoted; 2. *adv.* in a
bigoted way
Börse die; ~, ~n stock market; *(Gebäude)* stock exchange
Börsen-: ~**krach der** stock-market
crash; ~**makler der** stockbroker
Borste die; ~, ~n bristle; **borstig**
Adj. bristly
Borte die; ~, ~n braiding *no indef.
art.*; edging *no indef. art.*
bös *s.* böse; **bös·artig** 1. *Adj.* **a)**
malicious *(person, remark, etc.)*; vicious ⟨*animal*⟩; **b)** *(Med.)* malignant;
2. *adv.* maliciously; **Bös·artigkeit
die a)** maliciousness; *(von Tieren)* vi-
ciousness; **b)** *(Med.)* malignancy
Böschung die; ~, ~en embankment
böse 1. *Adj.* **a)** wicked; evil; **b)** *(übel)*
bad ⟨*times, illness, dream, etc.*⟩; nasty
⟨*experience, affair, situation, trick, surprise, etc.*⟩; **c)** *(ugs.) (wütend)* mad
(coll.); (verärgert) cross *(coll.);* **d)**
(fam.: ungezogen) naughty; **f)** *(ugs.:
arg)* terrible *(coll.)* ⟨*pain, fall, shock,
disappointment, storm, etc.*⟩; 2. *adv.* **a)**
(übel)⟨*end*⟩ badly; **es war doch nicht ~
gemeint** I didn't mean it nastily; **b)**
(ugs.) (wütend) angrily; *(verärgert)*
crossly *(coll.);* **c)** *(ugs.: sehr)* terribly
(coll.); **boshaft** 1. *Adj.* malicious; 2.
adv. maliciously; **Boshaftigkeit
die**; ~, ~en **a)** *o. Pl.* maliciousness; **b)**
(Bemerkung) malicious remark; **Bosheit die**; ~, ~en **a)** *o. Pl.* malice; **b)**
(Bemerkung) malicious remark
Boß der; **Bosses, Bosse** *(ugs.)* boss
(coll.)
bös·willig 1. *Adj.* malicious; wilful
⟨*desertion*⟩; 2. *adv.* maliciously; wilfully ⟨*desert*⟩; **Bös·willigkeit die**;
~: malice; maliciousness
bot *1. u. 3. Pers. Sg. Prät. v.* bieten
Botanik die; ~ botany *no art.;* **botanisch** 1. *Adj.* botanical; 2. *adv.*
botanically
Bötchen das; ~s, ~ little boat
Bote der; ~n, ~n **a)** messenger; **b)**
(Laufbursche) errand-boy; **Botschaft die**; ~, ~en **a)** message; **b)**
(diplomatische Vertretung) embassy;
Botschafter der; ~s, ~: ambassador

Böttcher der; ~s, ~: cooper
Bottich der; ~s, ~e tub
Bouillon [bul'jɔŋ] **die**; ~, ~s bouillon
Boulevard [bulə'vaːɐ̯] **der**; ~s, ~s
boulevard
Bourgeoisie [bʊrʒoa'ziː] **die**; ~, ~n
bourgeoisie
Boutique [bu'tiːk] **die**; ~, ~s *od.* ~n
boutique
Bowle ['boːlə] **die**; ~, ~n punch *(made
of wine, champagne, sugar, and fruit or
spices)*
bowlen ['boːlən] *itr. V.* bowl; **Bowling** ['boːlɪŋ] **das**; ~s, ~s [ten-pin]
bowling; **Bowling·bahn die** bowl-
ing-alley
Box die; ~, ~en **a)** box; **b)** *(Lautsprecher)* speaker; **c)** *(Pferde-)* [loose] box;
d) *(Motorsport)* pit
boxen 1. *itr. V.* box; **gegen jmdn.** ~:
fight sb.; box [against] sb.; 2. *tr. V.*
punch; **Boxer der**; ~s, ~ *(Sportler,
Hund)* boxer
Box-: ~**handschuh der** boxing
glove; ~**kampf der** boxing match;
(im Streit) fist-fight; ~**ring der** boxing
ring; ~**sport der**; *o. Pl.* boxing *no art.*
Boy [bɔy] **der**; ~s, ~s servant; *(im Hotel)* page-boy
Boykott [bɔy'kɔt] **der**; ~[e]s, ~s boycott; **boykottieren** *tr. V.* boycott
¹**brach** *1. u. 3. Pers. Sg. Prät. v.* brechen
²**brach** *Adj.* fallow; *(auf Dauer)* uncul-
tivated
Brachial·gewalt die; *o. Pl.* brute
force
Brach·land das fallow [land]; *(auf
Dauer)* uncultivated land; **brach|lie-
gen** *unr. itr. V. (auch fig.)* lie fallow;
(auf Dauer) lie waste
brachte *1. u. 3. Pers. Sg. Prät. v.* bringen
Branche ['brãːʃə] **die**; ~, ~n [branch
of] industry
Brand der; ~[e]s, **Brände** fire; **beim ~
der Scheune** when the barn caught
fire; **etw. in ~ stecken** set fire to sth.
branden *itr. V. (geh.)* break
Branden·burg (das); ~s Brandenburg
brand-, Brand-: ~**marken** *tr. V.*
brand ⟨*person*⟩; denounce ⟨*thing*⟩;
~**neu** *Adj. (ugs.)* brand-new; ~**salbe
die** ointment for burns; ~**schaden
der** fire damage *no pl., no indef. art.;*
~**stelle die** burn; ~**stifter der** arsonist; ~**stiftung die** arson
Brandung die; ~, ~en surf

Brand·wunde die burn
brannte *1. u. 3. Pers. Sg. Prät. v.* **brennen**
Brannt·wein der spirits *pl.; (Sorte)*
spirit
Brasilianer der; ~s, ~, Brazilian;
brasilianisch *Adj.* Brazilian; **Brasilien** [bra'zi:liǝn] **(das)**; ~s Brazil
brät *3. Pers. Sg. Präsens v.* braten;
Brat·apfel der baked apple; **braten**
unr. tr., itr. V. fry; *(im Backofen)*
roast; **Braten** der; ~s, ~ **a)** joint; **b)** *o.
Pl.* roast [meat] *no indef. art.*
Braten-: ~**saft** der meat juice[s *pl.*];
~**soße** die gravy
Brat-: ~**fett** das [cooking] fat; ~**fisch**
der fried fish; ~**hähnchen** das,
(südd., österr.) ~**hendl** das roast
chicken; *(gegrillt)* broiled chicken;
~**hering** der fried herring; ~**kartoffeln** *Pl.* fried potatoes; home fries
(Amer.); ~**pfanne** die frying-pan;
~**spieß** der spit; ~**wurst** die [fried/
grilled] sausage
Brauch der; ~[e]s, **Bräuche** custom
brauchbar *Adj.* useful; *(benutzbar)*
usable; wearable 〈*clothes*〉;
brauchen 1. *tr. V.* **a)** *(benötigen)*
need; **b)** *(aufwenden müssen)* **mit dem
Auto braucht er zehn Minuten** it takes
him ten minutes by car; **wie lange
brauchst du dafür?** how long will it
take you?; *(im allgemeinen)* how long
does it take you?; **c)** *(benutzen, gebrauchen)* use; **ich könnte es gut** ~: I
could do with it; **2.** *mod. V.;* **2.** Part~:
need; **du brauchst nicht zu helfen** there
is no need [for you] to help; **du
brauchst doch nicht gleich zu weinen**
there's no need to start crying
Brauchtum ['brauxtu:m] **das**; ~s,
Brauchtümer custom
Braue die; ~, ~n [eye]brow
brauen *tr. V.* brew; **Brauerei** die; ~,
~en brewery
braun *Adj.* brown; ~ **werden** *(sonnen-
gebräunt)* get a tan; **Braun** das; ~s,
~, *(ugs.)* ~s brown; **Braun·bär** der
brown bear; **Bräune** die; ~: [sun]-
tan; **bräunen** *tr. V.* **a)** tan; **sich** ~: get
a tan; **b)** *(Kochk.)* brown; **braun·ge-
brannt** *Adj.* [sun-]tanned; **Braun-
kohle** die brown coal; lignite;
bräunlich *Adj.* brownish; **Bräu-
nung** die; ~, ~en browning
Braus *s.* **Saus**
Brause die; ~, ~n **a)** fizzy drink;
(~pulver) sherbet; **b)** *(veralt.: Dusche)*
shower; **brausen** 1. *itr. V.* **a)** 〈*wind,*

water, etc.〉 roar; **b)** *(sich schnell bewegen)* race; **c)** *auch refl.: s.* **duschen** 1; **2.**
tr. V. s. **duschen** 2
Brause-: ~**pulver** das sherbet; ~**tablette** die effervescent tablet
Braut die; ~, **Bräute** bride
Bräutigam der; ~s, ~e [bride]groom
Braut-: ~**jungfer** die bridesmaid;
~**kleid** das wedding dress; ~**paar**
das bride and groom
brav 1. *Adj.* **a)** *(artig)* good; **b)** *(redlich)*
honest; **2.** *adv.* **nun iß schön** ~ **deine
Suppe** be a good boy/girl and eat up
your soup
bravo ['bra:vo] *Interj.* bravo; **Bravo**
das; ~s, ~s cheer; **Bravo·ruf** der
cheer
BRD [be:|ɛr'de:] die; ~ *Abk.* **Bundesre-
publik Deutschland** FRG
Brech-: ~**bohne** die green bean;
~**eisen** das crowbar
brechen 1. *unr. tr. V.* **a)** break; **sich**
(Dat.) **den Arm/das Genick** ~: break
one's arm/neck; **b)** *(ablenken)* break
〈*waves*〉; refract 〈*light*〉; **c)** *(bezwingen)*
overcome 〈*resistance*〉; break 〈*will, silence, record, blockade, etc.*〉; **d)** *(nicht
einhalten)* break 〈*agreement, contract,
promise, the law, etc.*〉; **e)** *(ugs.: erbrechen)* bring up. **2.** *unr. itr. V.* **a)** *mit
sein* break; **brechend voll sein** be full
to bursting; **b)** *mit jmdm.* ~: break
with sb.; **c)** *mit sein durch etw.* ~:
break through sth.; **d)** *(ugs.: sich erbrechen)* throw up. **3.** *unr. refl. V.* 〈*waves
etc.*〉 break; 〈*rays etc.*〉 be refracted;
Brecher der; ~s, ~: breaker
Brech-: ~**mittel** das emetic; ~**reiz**
der nausea; ~**stange** die crowbar
Brei der; ~[e]s, ~e *(Hafer~)* porridge
(Brit.), oatmeal *(Amer.) no indef. art.;
(Reis~)* rice pudding; *(Grieß~)* semolina *no indef. art.;* **breiig** *Adj.*
mushy
breit 1. *Adj.* **a)** wide; broad, wide
〈*hips, face, shoulders, forehead, etc.*〉;
etw. ~ **machen** widen sth.; **die Beine**
~ **machen** open one's legs; **ein 5 cm**
~**er Saum** a hem 5 cm wide; **b)** *(groß)*
die ~**e Masse** the general public;
2. *adv.* ~ **gebaut** sturdily built;
breit·beinig 1. *Adj.* rolling 〈*gait*〉; **2.**
adv. with one's legs apart; **Breite**
die; ~, ~n **a)** *s.* **breit** 1 **a:** width;
breadth; **b)** *(Geogr.)* latitude;
breiten *(geh.) tr., refl. V.* spread
Breiten-: ~**grad** der degree of latitude; parallel *(~kreis);* ~**kreis** der
parallel

breit-, Breit-: ~|**machen** *refl. V. (ugs.)* **a)** take up room; **b)** *(sich ausbreiten)* be spreading; ~**schult[e]rig** *Adj.* broad-shouldered; ~**seite die** long side; *(eines Schiffes)* side; ~|**treten** *unr. tr. V. (ugs. abwertend)* go on about; ~**wand die** *(Kino)* big screen

Brems-: ~**backe die** brake-shoe; ~**belag der** brake lining

¹**Bremse die;** ~, ~n brake

²**Bremse die;** ~, ~n *(Insekt)* horse-fly

bremsen *tr. V.* **a)** *auch itr.* brake; **b)** *(fig.)* slow down ⟨*rate, development, production, etc.*⟩; restrict ⟨*imports etc.*⟩

Brems-: ~**klotz der** brake pad; ~**licht das;** *Pl.* ~**lichter** brake-light; ~**pedal das** brake-pedal; ~**spur die** skid-mark; ~**weg der** braking distance

brenn·bar *Adj.* combustible; **brennen** **1.** *unr. itr. V.* **a)** burn; ⟨*house etc.*⟩ be on fire; **schnell/leicht** ~: catch fire quickly/easily; **es brennt!** fire!; **b)** *(glühen)* be alight; **c)** *(leuchten)* be on; **das Licht** ~ **lassen** leave the light on; **d) die Sonne brannte** the sun was burning down; **e)** *(schmerzen)* ⟨*wound etc.*⟩ sting; ⟨*feet etc.*⟩ be sore; **f) darauf** ~, **etw. zu tun** be dying to do sth.; **2.** *unr. tr. V.* **a)** burn ⟨*hole, pattern, etc.*⟩; einem **Tier ein Zeichen ins Fell** ~: brand an animal; **b)** *(mit Hitze behandeln)* fire ⟨*porcelain etc.*⟩; distil ⟨*spirits*⟩; **c)** *(rösten)* roast ⟨*coffee-beans, almonds, etc.*⟩; **brennend** **1.** *Adj. (auch fig.)* burning; lighted ⟨*cigarette*⟩; urgent ⟨*topic*⟩; **2.** *adv.* **es interessiert mich** ~, **ob** ...: I'm dying to know whether ...; **Brennessel die;** ~, ~n stinging nettle

Brenn-: ~**glas das** burning-glass; ~**holz das;** *o. Pl.* firewood; ~**material das** fuel; ~**nessel die** *s.* **Brennessel;** ~**punkt der** focus; ~**spiritus der** methylated spirits; ~**stoff der** fuel

brenzlig *Adj.* **a)** ⟨*smell, taste, etc.*⟩ of burning *not pred.;* **b)** *(ugs.: gefährlich)* dicey *(sl.)*

Bresche die; ~, ~n gap; breach; |**für jmdn.|** **in die** ~ **springen** stand in [for sb.]

Brett das; ~|**e|s,** ~**er a)** board; *(lang und dick)* plank; *(Diele)* floorboard; **Schwarzes** ~: notice-board; **ein** ~ **vor dem Kopf haben** *(fig. ugs.)* be thick; **b)** *Pl. (Ski)* skis

Bretter-: ~**wand die** wooden partition; ~**zaun der** wooden fence

Brett·spiel das board game

Brezel die; ~, ~n pretzel

Bridge [brɪtʃ] **das;** ~: bridge

Brief der; ~|e|s, ~e letter

Brief-: ~**beschwerer der;** ~s, ~: paperweight; ~**block der;** *Pl.* ~**blocks** writing-pad; ~**bogen der** sheet of writing-paper; ~**freund der** pen-friend; pen-pal *(coll.);* ~**geheimnis das** privacy of the post; ~**karte die** correspondence card; ~**kasten der a)** post-box; **b)** *(privat)* letter-box; ~**kopf der a)** letter-heading; **b)** *(aufgedruckt)* letter-head; ~**kuvert das** *(veralt.) s.* ~**umschlag**

brieflich **1.** *Adj.* written; **2.** *adv.* by letter; **Brief·marke die** [postage] stamp

Briefmarken-: ~**album das** stamp-album; ~**sammler der** stamp-collector; ~**sammlung die** stamp-collection

Brief-: ~**öffner der** letter-opener; ~**papier das** writing-paper; ~**partner der,** ~**partnerin die** pen-friend; ~**schreiber der** [letter-]writer; ~**tasche die** wallet; ~**taube die** carrier pigeon; ~**träger der** postman; letter-carrier *(Amer.);* ~**trägerin die** postwoman; [female] letter-carrier *(Amer.);* ~**um·schlag der** envelope; ~**waage die** letter-scales *pl.;* ~**wahl die** postal vote; ~**wechsel der** correspondence

Bries das; ~es, ~e *(Kochk.)* sweetbreads *pl.*

briet *1. u. 3. Pers. Sg. Prät. v.* **braten**

Brigade die; ~, ~n *(Milit.)* brigade

Brikett das; ~s, ~s briquette

brillant [brɪ'jant] **1.** *Adj.* brilliant. **2.** *adv.* brilliantly; **Brillant der;** ~en, ~en brilliant

Brillant-: ~**ring der** *(brilliant-cut)* diamond ring; ~**schmuck der;** *o. Pl. (brilliant-cut)* diamond jewellery

Brillanz [brɪ'jants] **die;** ~ brilliance

Brille die; ~, ~n **a)** glasses *pl.;* spectacles *pl.;* **eine** ~: a pair of glasses *or* spectacles; **eine** ~ **tragen** wear glasses *or* spectacles; **b)** *(ugs.: Klosett~)* [lavatory] seat

Brillen-: ~**etui das,** ~**futteral das** glasses-case; spectacle-case; ~**glas das** [spectacle-]lens; ~**schlange die** spectacled cobra; ~**träger der** person who wears glasses; ~ **sein** wear glasses

Brimborium das; ~s *(ugs. abwertend)* hoo-ha *(coll.)*

bringen *unr. tr. V.* **a)** *(her~)* bring; *(hin~)* take; **jmdm. Glück/Unglück ~:** bring sb. [good] luck/bad luck; **jmdm. eine Nachricht ~:** bring sb. news; **b)** *(begleiten)* take; **jmdn. nach Hause/ zum Bahnhof ~:** take sb. home/to the station; **c) es zu etwas/nichts ~:** get somewhere/get nowhere; **d) jmdn. ins Gefängnis ~** ⟨*crime, misdeed*⟩ land sb. in gaol; **jmdn. wieder auf den rechten Weg ~** *(fig.)* get sb. back on the straight and narrow; **jmdn. zum La- chen/zur Verzweiflung ~:** make sb. laugh/drive sb. to despair; **jmdn. dazu ~, etw. zu tun** get sb. to do sth.; **etw. hinter sich ~** *(ugs.)* get sth. over and done with; **e) jmdn. um seinen Besitz ~:** do sb. out of his property; **f)** *(prä- sentieren)* present; *(veröffentlichen)* publish; *(senden)* broadcast; **g) ein Opfer ~:** make a sacrifice; **h) einen großen Gewinn/hohe Zinsen ~:** make a large profit/earn high interest; **i) das bringt es mit sich, daß ...:** that means that ...; **j)** *(verursachen)* cause
brisant *Adj.* explosive; **Brisanz die; ~:** explosiveness
Brise die; ~, ~n breeze
Britannien (das); ~s Britain; *(hist.)* Britannia; **Brite der; ~n, ~n** Briton; **die ~n** the British; **er ist [kein] ~:** he is [not] British; **Britin die; ~, ~nen** Briton; British girl/woman; **britisch** *Adj.* British; **die Britischen Inseln** the British Isles
bröckelig *Adj.* crumbly; **bröckeln** 1. *itr. V.* **a)** crumble; **b)** *mit sein von der Wand ~:* crumble away from the wall; 2. *tr. V.* crumble; **Brocken der; ~s, ~** *(von Brot)* hunk; *(von Fleisch)* chunk; *(von Lehm, Kohle, Erde)* lump; **ein paar ~ Englisch** *(fig.)* a smattering of English
brodeln *itr. V.* bubble
Broiler ['brɔylɐ] **der; ~s, ~** *(regional) s.* **Brathähnchen**
Brokat der; ~[e]s, ~e brocade
Brokkoli *Pl.* broccoli *sing.*
Brom·beere die blackberry
Bronchie ['brɔnçiə] **die; ~, ~n** bron- chial tube; **Bronchitis die; ~,** bron- chitis
Bronze ['brõːsə] **die; ~:** bronze; **Bronze·medaille die** bronze medal
Brosche die; ~, ~n brooch
Broschüre die; ~, ~n booklet
Brösel der; ~s, ~: breadcrumb; **brö- selig** *Adj.* crumbly; **bröseln** *itr. V.* crumble

Brot das; ~[e]s, ~e bread *no pl., no in- def. art.;* *(Laib ~)* loaf [of bread]; *(Scheibe ~)* slice [of bread]
Brot-: ~aufstrich der spread; **~be- lag der** topping; *(im zusammenge- klappten Brot)* filling
Brötchen das; ~s, ~: roll
Brot-: ~erwerb der way to earn a liv- ing; **~korb der** bread-basket; **~laib der** loaf [of bread]; **~messer das** bread-knife; **~rinde die** [bread] crust; **~zeit die** *(südd.)* **a)** *(Pause)* [tea-/ coffee-/lunch-]break; **b)** *o. Pl. (Vesper)* snack; *(Vesperbrot)* sandwiches *pl.*
Bruch der; ~[e]s, Brüche a) break; **in die Brüche gehen** *(zerbrechen)* get broken; *(fig.)* break up; **b)** *(Med.: Knochen~)* fracture; break; **c)** *(Med.: Eingeweide~)* hernia; **d)** *(fig.) (eines Versprechens)* breaking; *(eines Abkom- mens, Gesetzes)* violation; **e)** *(Math.)* fraction; **brüchig** *Adj.* **a)** brittle ⟨*rock, brickwork*⟩; **b)** *(fig.)* crumbling ⟨*relationship, marriage, etc.*⟩
Bruch-: ~landung die cräsh-landing; **~rechnen das** fractions *pl.;* **~strich der** fraction line; **~stück das** frag- ment; **~teil der** fraction; **im ~teil ei- ner Sekunde** in a split second
Brücke die; ~, ~n a) *(auch) (auch: Kommando~, Zahnmed., Bodenturnen, Rin- gen)* bridge; **b)** *(Landungs~)* gang- way; **c)** *(Teppich)* rug
Brücken-: ~bogen der arch [of a/the bridge]; **~geländer das** parapet
Bruder der; ~s, Brüder brother; **Brü- derchen das; ~s, ~:** little brother; **brüderlich** 1. *Adj.* brotherly; 2. *adv.* in a brotherly way; **Brüderlichkeit die; ~:** brotherliness; **Brüderschaft die; ~:** |mit jmdm.| **~ trinken** drink to close friendship [with sb.] *(agreeing to use the familiar 'du' form)*
Brühe die; ~, ~n a) stock; *(als Suppe)* clear soup; **b)** *(ugs. abwertend) (Ge- tränk)* muck; *(verschmutztes Wasser)* filthy water; **brühen** *tr. V.* **a)** blanch; **b)** *(auf~)* brew, make ⟨*tea*⟩; make ⟨*coffee*⟩
brüh-, Brüh-: ~warm *Adj.* **etw. ~warm weitererzählen** *(ugs.)* pass sth. on straight away; **~würfel der** stock cube
brüllen 1. *itr. V.* **a)** ⟨*bull, cow, etc.*⟩ bel- low; ⟨*lion, tiger, etc.*⟩ roar; **b)** *(ugs.) (schreien)* roar; *(weinen)* howl; 2. *tr. V.* yell
brummen *tr., itr. V.* **a)** ⟨*insect*⟩ buzz; ⟨*bear*⟩ growl; ⟨*engine etc.*⟩ drone; **b)**

(unmelodisch singen) drone; **c)** *(mürrisch sprechen)* mumble; **Brummer der; ~s, ~** *(ugs.)* **a)** *(Fliege)* bluebottle; **b)** *(Lkw)* heavy lorry *(Brit.) or* truck; **brummig** *Adj. (ugs.)* grumpy

Brumm-: ~**kreisel der** humming top; ~**schädel der** *(ugs.)* thick head

brünett *Adj.* dark-haired ⟨person⟩; dark ⟨hair⟩; **Brünette die; ~, ~n** brunette

Brunnen der; ~s, ~ a) well; **b)** *(Spring~)* fountain; **Brunnen·kresse die** watercress

Brunst die; ~, Brünste *(von männlichen Tieren)* rut; *(von weiblichen Tieren)* heat; **Brunst·zeit die** *(bei männlichen Tieren)* rutting season; *(bei weiblichen Tieren)* [season of] heat

brüsk 1. *Adj.* brusque; **2.** *adv.* brusquely; **brüskieren** *tr. V.* offend; *(stärker)* insult; *(schneiden)* snub

Brüssel (das); ~s Brussels

Brust die; ~, Brüste a) chest; **b)** *(der Frau)* breast; **c)** *(Hähnchen~)* breast; *(Rinder~)* brisket; **d)** *o. Pl. (~schwimmen)* breast-stroke

brüsten *refl. V.* sich mit etw. ~: boast about sth.

Brust-: ~**kasten** *(ugs.)* chest; ~**korb der** *(Anat.)* thorax *(Anat.)*; ~**krebs der** breast cancer; ~**schwimmen** *unr. itr. V.; nur im Inf.* do [the] breast-stroke; ~**schwimmen das** breast-stroke; ~**tasche die** breast pocket

Brüstung die; ~, ~en parapet; *(Balkon~)* balustrade

Brust·warze die nipple

Brut die; ~, ~en a) brooding; **b)** *(Jungtiere, auch fig. scherzh.: Kinder)* brood

brutal 1. *Adj.* brutal; violent ⟨attack, programme, etc.⟩; brute ⟨force, strength⟩; **2.** *adv.* brutally; **Brutalität die; ~, ~en a)** *o. Pl.* brutality; **b)** *(Handlung)* act of brutality

brüten *itr. V.* **a)** brood; **b)** *(grübeln)* ponder (über + *Dat.* over); **brütend·heiß** *Adj. (ugs.)* boiling hot; **Brüter der; ~s, ~** *(Kernphysik)* breeder

Brut-: ~**kasten der** incubator; ~**stätte die** *(auch fig.)* breeding-ground

brutto *Adv.* gross

Brutto-: ~**einkommen das** gross income; ~**gehalt das** gross salary; ~**sozialprodukt das** *(Wirtsch.)* gross national product

brutzeln 1. *itr. V.* sizzle. **2.** *tr. V. (ugs.)* fry [up]

Bub der; ~en, ~en *(südd., österr., schweiz.)* boy; lad; **Bube der; ~n, ~n** *(Kartenspiele)* jack; knave; **Bubi der; ~s, ~s a)** [little] boy *or* lad; **b)** *(salopp: Schnösel)* young lad

Buch das; ~[e]s, Bücher book; *(Dreh~)* script; über etw. *(Akk.)* ~ führen keep a record of sth.

Buch-: ~**binder der** bookbinder; ~**druck der;** *o. Pl.* letterpress printing

Buche die; ~, ~n a) beech[-tree]; **b)** *o. Pl. (Holz)* beech[wood]

Buch·ecker die beech-nut

buchen *tr. V.* **a)** enter; **b)** *(vorbestellen)* book

Bücher·brett das bookshelf

Bücherei die; ~, ~en library

Bücher-: ~**regal das** bookshelves *pl.*; ~**schrank der** bookcase; ~**wurm der** *(scherzh.)* bookworm

Buch-: ~**fink der** chaffinch; ~**führung die** bookkeeping; ~**halter der** bookkeeper; ~**haltung die a)** accountancy; **b)** *(Abteilung)* accounts department; ~**händler der** bookseller; ~**handlung die** bookshop; ~**klub der** book club; ~**laden der** bookshop; ~**messe die** book fair; ~**rücken der** spine

Buchs·baum ['bʊks-] **der** box[-tree]

Buchse ['bʊksə] **die; ~, ~n a)** *(Elektrot.)* socket; **b)** *(Technik)* bush

Büchse ['bʏksə] **die; ~, ~n a)** tin; **b)** *(ugs.: Sammel~)* [collecting-]box; **c)** *(Gewehr)* rifle; *(Schrot~)* shotgun; **Büchsen-** *s.* **Dosen-**

Buchstabe der; ~ns, ~n letter; *(Druckw.)* character; ein großer/kleiner ~: a capital [letter]/small letter; **buchstabieren** *tr. V.* spell; **buchstäblich** *Adv.* literally

Bucht die; ~, ~en bay

Buchung die; ~, ~en a) entry; **b)** *(Vorbestellung)* booking

Buckel der; ~s, ~ a) hump; einen ~ machen ⟨cat⟩ arch its back; ⟨person⟩ hunch one's shoulders; **b)** *(ugs.: Rücken)* back; rutsch mir den ~ runter! *(salopp)* get lost! *(sl.)*; **buckeln** *itr. V. (ugs.)* bow and scrape; vor jmdm. ~: kowtow to sb.

bücken *refl. V.* bend down

bucklig *Adj.* hunchbacked; **Bucklige der/die;** *adj. Dekl.* hunchback

¹Bückling der; ~s, ~e *(ugs. scherzh.: Verbeugung)* bow

²Bückling der; ~s, ~e *(Hering)* bloater

buddeln *itr., tr. V. (ugs.)* dig
Buddha ['bʊda] *der;* ~s, ~s Buddha;
Buddhismus *der;* ~: Buddhism *no art.;* **Buddhist** *der;* ~en, ~en Buddhist; **buddhistisch** *Adj.* Buddhist *attrib.*
Bude *die;* ~, ~n a) kiosk; *(Markt~)* stall; *(Jahrmarkts~)* booth; b) *(Bau~)* hut; c) *(ugs.) (Haus)* dump *(coll.); (Zimmer)* room; digs *pl. (Brit. coll.)*
Budget [by'dʒe:] *das;* ~s, ~s budget
Büfett *das;* ~[e]s, ~s *od.* ~e a) sideboard; b) *(Schanktisch)* bar; c) *(Verkaufstisch)* counter; d) **kaltes** ~: cold buffet
Büffel *der;* ~s, ~: buffalo
büffeln *(ugs.)* 1. *itr. V.* swot *(Brit. sl.);* cram; 2. *tr. V.* swot up *(Brit. sl.);* cram
Buffet [by'fe:] *das;* ~s, ~s *s.* Büfett
Bug *der;* ~[e]s, ~e *u.* Büge bow
Bügel *der;* ~s, ~ a) *(Kleider~)* hanger; b) *(Brillen~)* ear-piece; c) *(an einer Tasche, Geldbörse)* frame
bügel-, Bügel-: ~**brett** *das* ironing-board; ~**eisen** *das* iron; ~**falte** *die* [trouser] crease; ~**frei** *Adj.* non-iron
bügeln *tr., itr. V.* iron
bugsieren [bʊ'ksi:rən] *tr. V. (ugs.)* shift; manœuvre; steer *(person)*
buh *Interj.* boo; **Buh** *das;* ~s, ~s *(ugs.)* boo; **buhen** *itr. V. (ugs.)* boo
buhlen *itr. V. (geh. abwertend)* um jmds. Gunst ~: court sb.'s favour
Buh·mann *der; Pl.* Buhmänner *(ugs.)* whipping-boy
Bühne *die;* ~, ~n a) stage; b) *(Theater)* theatre
bühnen-, Bühnen-: ~**arbeiter** *der* stage-hand; ~**bildner** *der;* ~s, ~: stage designer; ~**reif** *Adj. ⟨play etc.⟩* ready for the stage; ⟨*imitation etc.*⟩ worthy of the stage; dramatic ⟨*entrance etc.*⟩
Buh·ruf *der* boo
buk *1. u. 3. Pers. Sg. Prät. v.* backen
Bukett *das;* ~s, ~s *od.* ~e *(geh.)* bouquet
Bulette *die;* ~, ~n *(bes. berl.)* rissole
Bulgare *der;* ~n, ~n Bulgarian; **Bulgarien** [bʊl'ga:riən] *(das);* ~s Bulgaria; **bulgarisch** *Adj.* Bulgarian
Bull-: ~**auge** *das* circular porthole; ~**dogge** *die* bulldog; ~**dozer** [-do:zɐ] *der;* ~s, ~: bulldozer
Bulle *der;* ~n, ~n a) bull; b) *(salopp: Polizist)* cop *(sl.);* **Bullen·hitze** *die (ugs.)* sweltering *or* boiling heat
Bulletin [byl'tɛ̃:] *das;* ~s, ~s bulletin
bullig 1. *Adj.* a) beefy ⟨*person, appear-*

ance, etc.⟩; chunky ⟨*car*⟩; b) *(drükkend)* sweltering ⟨*heat*⟩; 2. *adv.* ~ heiß boiling hot
Bull·terrier *der* bull-terrier
bum *Interj.* bang
Bumerang *der;* ~s, ~e *od.* ~s boomerang
Bummel *der;* ~s, ~ a) stroll (durch around); b) *(durch Lokale)* pub-crawl *(coll.);* **Bummelei** *die;* ~, ~en *(ugs.)* a) dawdling; b) *(Faulenzerei)* loafing about; **bummelig** *(ugs.)* 1. *Adj.* a) slow; b) *(nachlässig)* slipshod; 2. *adv.* a) slowly; b) *(nachlässig)* in a slipshod way; **bummeln** *itr. V.* a) *mit sein* stroll (durch around); durch die Kneipen ~: go on a pub-crawl *(Brit. coll.);* b) *(trödeln)* dawdle; c) *(faulenzen)* laze about
bums *Interj.* bang; **Bums** *der;* ~es, ~e *(ugs.)* bang; *(dumpfer)* thud; **bumsen** *itr. V. (ugs.)* a) bang; *(dumpfer)* thump; unpers. es bumste ganz furchtbar there was a terrible bang/thud; b) *mit sein (stoßen)* bang
¹**Bund** *der;* ~[e]s, Bünde a) *(Vereinigung)* association; *(Bündnis, Pakt)* alliance; b) *(föderativer Staat)* federation; c) *(an Röcken, Hosen)* waistband
²**Bund** *das;* ~[e]s, ~e bunch; **Bündchen** *das;* ~s, ~ band; **Bündel** *das;* ~s, ~ bundle; **bündeln** *tr. V.* bundle up ⟨*newspapers, old clothes, rags, etc.*⟩; tie ⟨*banknotes etc.*⟩ into bundles/a bundle; tie ⟨*flowers, radishes, carrots, etc.*⟩ into bunches/a bunch; sheave ⟨*straw, hay, etc.*⟩
Bundes- federal; *(in Namen, Titeln)* Federal
bundes-, Bundes-: ~**bürger** *der (veralt.)* West German citizen; ~**deutsch** *Adj. (veralt.)* West German; ~**land** *das* [federal] state; *(österr.)* province; ~**liga** *die* national division; ~**rat** *der* Bundesrat; ~**republik** *die* federal republic; die ~**republik Deutschland** The Federal Republic of Germany; ~**straße** *die* federal highway; ≈ A road *(Brit.);* ~**tag** *der* Bundestag
Bundestags-: ~**abgeordnete** *der/* die member of parliament; member of the Bundestag; ~**wahl** *die* parliamentary *or* general election
bundes-, Bundes-: ~**trainer** *der* national team manager; ~**wehr** *die* [Federal] Armed Forces *pl.;* ~**weit** *Adj., adv.* nation-wide

Bund-: ~**falten** *Pl.* pleats; ~**hose die** knee-breeches
bündig 1. *Adj.* **a)** succinct; **b)** *(schlüssig)* conclusive; **2.** *adv.* **a)** succinctly; **b)** *(schlüssig)* conclusively
Bündnis das; ~**ses,** ~**se** alliance
Bungalow ['bʊŋgalo] **der;** ~**s,** ~**s** bungalow
Bunker der; ~**s,** ~ **a)** bunker; **b)** *(Luftschutz~)* air-raid shelter
bunt 1. *Adj.* **a)** colourful; *(farbig)* coloured; ~**e Farben/Kleidung** bright colours/brightly coloured clothes; **b)** *(fig.)* varied *(programme etc.);* **2.** *adv.* **a)** colourfully; **b)** *(fig.)* **ein** ~ **gemischtes Programm** a varied programme
bunt-, Bunt-: ~**bemalt** *Adj.* brightly painted; ~**papier das** coloured paper; ~**specht der** spotted woodpecker; ~**stift der** coloured pencil/ crayon
Bürde die; ~, ~**n** *(geh.)* weight; load
Burg die; ~, ~**en a)** castle; **b)** *(Strand~)* wall of sand
Bürge der; ~**n,** ~**n** guarantor; **bürgen** *itr. V.* **a) für jmdn./etw.** ~: vouch for sb./sth.; **b)** *(fig.)* guarantee
Bürger der; ~**s,** ~, **Bürgerin die;** ~, ~**nen** citizen
Bürger-: ~**initiative die** citizens' action group; ~**krieg der** civil war
bürgerlich *Adj.* **a)** *nicht präd. (staats~)* civil *(rights, marriage, etc.);* civic *(duties);* **b)** *(dem Bürgertum zugehörig)* middle-class; **die** ~**e Küche** good plain cooking; **c)** *(Polit.)* non-socialist; *(nicht marxistisch)* non-Marxist
bürger-, Bürger-: ~**meister der** mayor; ~**nah** *Adj.* which/who reflects the general public's interests *postpos., not pred.;* ~**pflicht die** duty as a citizen; ~**steig der** pavement *(Brit.);* sidewalk *(Amer.)*
Bürgertum ['--tu:m] **das;** ~**s a)** middle class; **b)** *(Groß~)* bourgeoisie
Bürgin die; ~, ~**nen** *s.* **Bürge; Bürgschaft die;** ~, ~**en a)** guarantee; **b)** *(Betrag)* penalty
Büro das; ~**s,** ~**s** office
Büro-: ~**angestellte der/die** office-worker; ~**artikel der** item of office equipment; ~**haus das** office-block; ~**klammer die** paper-clip
Bürokrat der; ~**en,** ~**en** bureaucrat; **Bürokratie die;** ~, ~**n** bureaucracy; **bürokratisch** 1. *Adj.* bureaucratic; **2.** *adv.* bureaucratically
Bürschchen ['byrʃçən] **das;** ~, ~:

little fellow; **Bursche der;** ~**n,** ~**n a)** boy; lad; **b)** *(abwertend: Kerl)* guy *(sl.)*
burschikos 1. *Adj.* **a)** sporty ⟨*look, clothes*⟩; [tom]boyish ⟨*behaviour, girl, haircut*⟩; **b)** *(ungezwungen)* casual ⟨*comment, behaviour, etc.*⟩; **2.** *adv.* **a)** [tom]boyishly; **b)** *(ungezwungen)* in a colloquial way
Bürste die; ~, ~**n** brush; **bürsten** *tr. V.* brush
Bus der; ~**ses,** ~**se** bus; **Bus·bahnhof der** bus station
Busch der; ~**[e]s, Büsche** bush; **auf den** ~ **klopfen** *(fig. ugs.)* sound things out
Büschel das; ~**s,** ~: tuft; *(von Heu, Stroh)* handful
Busen der; ~**s,** ~ bust
Bus-: ~**fahrer der** bus-driver; ~**haltestelle die** bus-stop; ~**linie die** bus-route
Bussard der; ~**s,** ~**e** buzzard
Buße die; ~, ~**n** *(Rel.)* penance *no art.;* **büßen** 1. *tr. V.* **a)** atone for; **b)** *(fig.)* pay for; **2.** *itr. V.* **a) für etw.** ~: atone for sth.; **b)** *(fig.)* pay; **Buß·geld das** *(Rechtsw.)* fine
Büsten·halter der bra; brassière *(formal)*
Butan·gas das butane gas
Butt der; ~**[e]s,** ~**e** flounder; butt
Bütten·papier das handmade paper *(with deckle-edge)*
Butter die; ~: butter; **es ist alles in** ~ *(ugs.)* everything's fine
butter-, Butter-: ~**blume die** *(Sumpfdotterblume)* marsh marigold; *(Hahnenfuß)* buttercup; ~**brot das** slice of bread and butter; *(zugeklappt)* sandwich; ~**creme die** butter-cream; ~**milch die** buttermilk; ~**weich** *Adj.* beautifully soft
b.w. *Abk.* **bitte wenden** p.t.o.
bzw. *Abk.* **beziehungsweise**

C

c, C [tse:] **das;** ~, ~: **a)** *(Buchstabe)* c/C; **b)** *(Musik)* [key of] C
ca. *Abk.* **cirka** c.
Café das; ~**s,** ~**s** café

Cafeteria die; ~, ~s cafeteria
cal Abk. |Gramm|kalorie cal.
Callgirl ['kɔːlgəːl] das; ~s, ~s call-girl
Camp [kɛmp] das; ~s, ~s camp; campen itr. V. camp; Camping das; ~s camping
Camping-: ~bus der motor caravan; camper; ~platz der campsite; campground (Amer.)
Canasta das; ~s canasta
Caravan ['ka(:)ravan] der; ~s, ~s (Wohnwagen) caravan; trailer (Amer.)
Cayenne·pfeffer [ka'jɛn-] der cayenne [pepper]
CD [tseː'deː] die; ~, ~s CD
CDU [tseːdeː'|uː] die; ~ Abk. Christlich-Demokratische Union |Deutschlands| [German] Christian Democratic Party
C-Dur ['tseː-] das; ~: C major
Cello ['tʃɛlo] das; ~s, ~s od. Celli cello
Celsius o. Art. 20 Grad ~: 20 degrees Celsius or centigrade
Cembalo ['tʃɛmbalo] das; ~s, ~s od. Cembali harpsichord
Ceylon ['tsailɔn] (das); ~s (hist.) Ceylon (Hist.)
Champagner [ʃam'panjɐ] der; ~s, ~ champagne (from Champagne)
Champignon ['ʃampɪnjɔn] der; ~s, ~s mushroom
Chance ['ʃãːsə] die; ~, ~n a) chance; b) Pl. (Aussichten) prospects; |bei jmdm| ~n haben stand a chance [with sb.]
Chaos das; ~: chaos no art.
Charakter der; ~s, ~e [...'teːrə] character; charakterisieren tr. V. characterize; charakteristisch Adj. characteristic (für of); charakterlich 1. Adj. character attrib.; 2. adv. in [respect of] character; charakter·los Adj. unprincipled; (niederträchtig) despicable; (labil) spineless
charmant [ʃar'mant] 1. Adj. charming; 2. adv. charmingly; Charme [ʃarm] der; ~s charm
Charter- ['tʃartɐ-]: ~flug der charter flight; ~maschine die chartered aircraft
Chassis [ʃa'siː] das; ~ [ʃa'siː(s)], ~ [ʃa'siːs] chassis
Chauffeur [ʃo'føːɐ] der; ~s, ~e driver; (privat angestellt) chauffeur
Chef [ʃɛf] der; ~s, ~s, Chefin die; ~, ~nen (Leiter|in|) head; (der Polizei, des Generalstabs) chief; (einer Partei, Bande) leader; (Vorgesetzte[r]) superior; boss (coll.)

Chef-: ~koch der chef; head cook; ~sekretärin die director's secretary
Chemie die; ~ a) chemistry no art.; b) (ugs.: Chemikalien) chemicals pl.; Chemiker der; ~s, ~, Chemikerin die; ~, ~nen (graduate) chemist; chemisch 1. Adj. chemical; 2. adv. chemically
Chicorée ['ʃikore] der; ~s od. die; ~: chicory
Chiffon ['ʃifõ] der; ~s, ~s chiffon
Chiffre ['ʃifrə] die; ~, ~n a) (Zeichen) symbol; b) (Geheimzeichen) cipher; c) (in Annoncen) box number
Chile ['tʃiːle, 'çiːlə] (das); ~s Chile; Chilene [tʃi'leːnə, çi'leːnə] der; ~n, ~n, Chilenin die; ~, ~nen Chilean; chilenisch Adj. Chilean
Chili ['tʃiːli] der; ~s, ~es a) Pl. (Schoten) chillies; b) o. Pl. (Gewürz) chilli [powder]
China (das); ~s China; Chinese der; ~n, ~n, Chinesin die; ~, ~nen Chinese; chinesisch Adj. Chinese
Chip [tʃɪp] der; ~s, ~s a) (Spielmarke) chip; b) (Kartoffel~) [potato] crisp (Brit.) or (Amer.) chip; c) (Elektronik) [micro]chip
Chirurg der; ~en, ~en surgeon; Chirurgie die; ~, ~n a) o. Pl. surgery no art.; b) (Abteilung) surgical department; (Station) surgical ward; chirurgisch 1. Adj. surgical; 2. adv. surgically; by surgery
Chlor das; ~s chlorine; Chloroform das; ~s chloroform; Chlorophyll das; ~s chlorophyll
Cholera die; ~: cholera
cholerisch Adj. irascible; choleric ⟨temperament⟩
Cholesterin das; ~s cholesterol
Chor der; ~|e|s, Chöre ['køːrə] (auch Archit.) choir; (in Oper, Sinfonie, Theater; Komposition) chorus; im ~ rufen shout in chorus; Choral der; ~s, Choräle (Kirchenlied) chorale
Choreographie die; ~, ~n choreography
Chose ['ʃoːzə] die; ~, ~n (ugs.) stuff; die ganze ~: the whole lot (coll.) or (sl.) shoot
Chow-Chow [tʃau 'tʃau] der; ~s, ~s chow
Christ der; ~en, ~en Christian
Christ-: ~baum der (bes. südd.) Christmas tree; ~demokrat der (Politik) Christian Democrat
Christenheit die; ~ Christendom no art.; Christentum das; ~s Chris-

tianity *no art.; (Glaube)* Christian faith

Christin die; ~, ~**nen** Christian; **Christ·kind** das; *o. Pl.* Christ-child *(as bringer of Christmas gifts);* **christlich** 1. *Adj.* Christian. 2. *adv.* in a [truly] Christian spirit

Christ-: ~**messe** die *(kath. Rel.)* Christmas Mass; ~**mette** die *(kath. Rel.)* Christmas Mass; *(ev. Rel.)* midnight service [on Christmas Eve]; ~**rose** die Christmas rose; ~**stollen** der [German] Christmas loaf *(with candied fruit, almonds, etc.)*

Christus (der); ~ *od.* Christi Christ

Chrom das; ~s chromium

Chromosom das; ~s, ~en *(Biol.)* chromosome

Chronik die; ~, ~en chronicle; **chronisch** *Adj.* chronic

Chrysantheme die; ~, ~n chrysanthemum

City ['sɪti] die; ~, ~s city centre

clever ['klɛvɐ] 1. *Adj. (raffiniert)* shrewd; *(intelligent, geschickt)* clever; 2. *adv.: s. Adj.:* shrewdly; cleverly

Clique ['klɪkə] die; ~, ~n a) *(abwertend)* clique; b) *(Freundeskreis)* set; *(größere Gruppe)* crowd *(coll.)*

Clown [klaun] der; ~s, ~s clown

Club *s.* Klub

cm *Abk.:* Zentimeter cm.

Co. *Abk.:* Compagnie Co.

Cockpit das; ~s, ~s cockpit

Cocktail ['kɔkteɪl] der; ~s, ~s cocktail

Cognac Ⓦ der; ~s, ~s Cognac

Color- *(Fot.)* colour *(film, slide, etc.)*

Colt Ⓦ der; ~s, ~s Colt (P) [revolver]

Comic·heft *das* comic

Computer [kɔm'pju:tɐ] der; ~s, ~: computer

Container [kɔn'te:nɐ] der; ~s, ~: container; *(für Müll)* [refuse] skip

cool [ku:l] *(ugs.)* 1. *Adj.* cool; ~ bleiben keep one's cool *(sl.);* 2. *adv.* coolly *(coll.)*

Cord der; ~|e|s, ~e *od.* ~s cord; *(~samt)* corduroy

Corned beef ['kɔ:nd 'bi:f] das; ~ ~: corned beef

Couch [kautʃ] die, *(schweiz. auch:)* der; ~, ~es sofa

Coup [ku:] der; ~s, ~s coup

Coupon [ku'pō:] der; ~s, ~s coupon; voucher

Courage [ku'ra:ʒə] die; ~ *(ugs.)* courage

Cousin [ku'zɛ̃:] der; ~s, ~s, **Cousine** die; ~, ~n cousin

Cowboy ['kaubɔy] der; ~s, ~s cowboy

Credo *s.* Kredo

Creme [kre:m] die; ~, ~s, *(schweiz.:)* ~n cream

ČSFR [tʃe:|ɛs|ɛf'|ɛr] die; ~: die ~: Czechoslovakia

CSU [tse:|ɛs'|u:] die; ~ *Abk.:* Christlich-Soziale Union CSU

Curry ['kœri] das; ~s, ~s curry-powder

D

d, D [de:] das; ~, ~ a) *(Buchstabe)* d/D; b) *(Musik)* [key of] D

D *Abk.* Damen

da 1. *Adv.* a) *(dort)* there; da draußen/ drinnen/drüben/unten out/in/over/ down there; **da, wo** where; b) *(hier)* here; c) *(zeitlich)* then; *(in dem Augenblick)* at that moment; d) *(deshalb)* der Zug war schon weg, **da** habe ich den Bus genommen the train had already gone, so I took the bus; e) *(ugs.: in diesem Fall)* **da kann man nichts machen** there's nothing one can do about it; 2. *Konj. (weil)* as; since

da·bei *Adv.* a) with it/him/her/them; **nahe** ~: close by; b) *(währenddessen)* at the same time; *(bei diesem Anlaß)* then; on that occasion; **die ~ entstehenden Kosten** the expense involved; c) *(außerdem)* ~ **|auch|** what is more; d) *(hinsichtlich dessen)* about it/them; **was hast du dir denn ~ gedacht?** what 'were you thinking of?

dabei-: ~|**bleiben** *unr. itr. V.; mit sein* stay there; be there; ~|**haben** *unr. tr. V.* have with one; ~|**sein** *unr. itr. V.; mit sein (Zusschr. nur im Inf. u. 2. Part.)* a) *(anwesend sein)* be there; be present (**bei** at); *(teilnehmen)* take part (**bei** in); b) |**gerade**| ~**sein, etw. zu tun** be just doing sth.; ~|**stehen** *unr. itr. V.* stand there

da|bleiben *unr. itr. V.; mit sein* stay there; *(hier bleiben)* stay here

Dach das; ~|e|s, Dächer roof

Dach-: ~**decker** [~dɛkɐ] der; ~s, ~: roofer; ~**garten** der roof-garden; ~**kammer** die attic [room]; ~**luke**

die skylight; **~pappe** die roofing-
felt; **~rinne** die gutter

Dachs [daks] der; ~es, ~e badger

dachte *1. u. 3. Pers. Sg. Prät. v.* **denken**

Dach-: **~terrasse** die roof-terrace;
~ziegel der roof-tile

Dackel der; ~s, ~: dachshund

da·durch *Adv.* **a)** through it/them; **b)**
(durch diesen Umstand) as a result;
(durch dieses Mittel) by this [means]

da·für *Adv.* **a)** for it/them; ~, daß ...
(wenn man berücksichtigt, daß) con-
sidering that ...; *(damit)* so that ...; ~
sorgen [, daß ...] see to it [that ...]; **b)** ~
sein be in favour [of it]; **ein Beispiel ~
ist** ...: an example of this is ...; **c)** *(als
Gegenleistung)* in return [for it]; *(beim
Tausch)* in exchange; *(statt dessen)* instead

dafür|können *unr. tr. V.* **etwas/nichts
~:** be/not be responsible

dagegen *Adv.* **a)** against it/them; **etwas ~ haben** have sth. against it; **ich
habe nichts ~:** I've no objection; ~
sein be against it; **b)** *(im Vergleich dazu)* by *or* in comparison

da·heim *Adv. (bes. südd., österr.,
schweiz.)* **a)** *(zu Hause)* at home; *(nach
Präp.)* home; **b)** *(in der Heimat)* [back]
home

da·her *Adv.* **a)** from there; **b)** *(durch
diesen Umstand)* hence; **c)** *(deshalb)*
therefore; so

daher|kommen *unr. itr. V.* come
along

da·hin **a)** there; **b)** *(fig.)* ~ **mußte es
kommen** it had to come to that; **c) bis
~:** to there; *(zeitlich)* until then; **d)** ~
sein be *or* have gone; **e)** *(in diesem Sinne)* ~ [gehend], daß ...: to the effect
that ...

da·hinten *Adv.* over there

da·hinter *Adv.* behind it/them; *(folgend)* after it/them

Dahlie ['da:li̯ə] die; ~, ~n dahlia

da-: **~|lassen** *unr. tr. V. (ugs.)* leave
[there]; *(hier lassen)* leave here; **~|lie-
gen** *unr. itr. V.* lie there

dalli *Adv. (ugs.)* [~] ~! get a move on!

damalig *Adj.; nicht präd.* at that *or* the
time *postpos;* **damals** *Adv.* at that
time

Damast der; ~[e]s, ~e damask

Dame die; ~, ~n **a)** *(Frau)* lady; **b)**
(Schach, Kartenspiele) queen; **c)** *o. Pl.
(Spiel)* draughts *(Brit.)*; checkers
(Amer.)

Damen-: **~binde** die sanitary towel

(Brit.) or (Amer.) napkin; **~friseur**
der ladies' hairdresser; **~rad** das
lady's bicycle; **~toilette** die ladies'
toilet

da·mit **1.** *Adv.* **a)** with it/them; **b)**
(gleichzeitig) with that; **c)** *(daher)*
thus; **2.** *Konj.* so that

dämlich *(ugs. abwertend)* **1.** *Adj.*
stupid; **2.** *adv.* stupidly

Damm der; ~[e]s, **Dämme** embankment; levee *(Amer.); (Deich)* dike;
(Stau~) dam

dämmern *itr. V.* es dämmert *(morgens)* it is getting light; *(abends)* it is
getting dark; **Dämmerung** die; ~,
~en **a)** *(Abend~)* twilight; dusk; **b)**
(Morgen~) dawn

Dämon der; ~s, ~en [dε'mo:nən]
demon; **dämonisch** *Adj.* daemonic

Dampf der; ~[e]s, **Dämpfe** steam *no
pl., no indef. art ;* **dampfen** *itr. V.*
steam (vor + *Dat.* with)

dämpfen *tr. V.* **a)** *(garen)* steam ⟨fish,
vegetables, potatoes⟩; **b)** *(mildern)*
muffle ⟨sound⟩; cushion, absorb
⟨blow, impact, shock⟩

Dampfer der; ~s, ~: steamer

Dampf-: **~maschine** die steam engine; **~nudel** die *(südd., Kochk.)*
steamed yeast dumpling; **~walze die**
steamroller

da·nach *Adv.* **a)** *(zeitlich)* after it/that;
then; **b)** *(räumlich)* after it/them; **c)**
(entsprechend) in accordance with it/
them

Däne der; ~n, ~n Dane

da·neben *Adv.* **a)** beside him/her/it/
them *etc.;* **b)** *(im Vergleich dazu)* in
comparison

daneben-: **~|benehmen** *unr. refl. V.
(ugs.)* blot one's copybook (coll.);
~|gehen *unr. itr. V.; mit sein* miss
[the target]; **~|schießen** *unr. itr. V.*
miss [the target]

Dänemark (das); ~s Denmark; **Dänin** die; ~, ~nen Dane; Danish
woman/girl; **dänisch** *Adj.* Danish; *s.
auch* **deutsch, Deutsch**

dank *Präp. mit Dat. u. Gen.* thanks to;
Dank der; ~[e]s thanks *pl.; mit* [vielem
od. bestem] ~ **zurück** thanks for the
loan; *(bes. geschrieben)* returned with
thanks!; **vielen/besten/herzlichen ~!**
thank you very much; **dankbar** **1.**
Adj. grateful; *(anerkennend)* appreciative ⟨child, audience, etc.⟩; [jmdm.]
für etw. ~ sein be grateful [to sb.] for
sth.; **2.** *adv.* gratefully; **Dankbarkeit**
die; ~: gratitude; **danke** *Höflich-*

keitsformel thank you; *(ablehnend)* no, thank you; ~ **schön/sehr/vielmals** thank you very much; **danken 1.** *itr. V. (Dank aussprechen)* thank; **ich danke Ihnen vielmals** thank you very much; **na, ich danke!** *(ugs.)* no, 'thank you!; **2.** *tr. V.* [aber bitte,] nichts zu ~: don't mention it; **Danke·schön** das; ~s thank-you

dann *Adv.* **a)** then; **was ~?** what happens then?; **noch drei Tage, ~ ist Ostern** another three days and it will be Easter; **bis ~:** see you then; **~ und wann** now and then; **b)** *(in diesem Falle)* then; in that case; **~ will ich nicht weiter stören** in that case I won't disturb you any further; [na,] ~ **eben nicht!** in that case, forget it!; **nur ~, wenn ...:** only if ...

daran [da'ran] *Adv.* **a)** *(an dieser/diese Stelle, an diesem/diesen Gegenstand)* on it/them; **dicht ~:** close to it/them; **nahe ~ sein, etw. zu tun** be on the point of doing sth.; **b)** *(hinsichtlich dieser Sache)* about it/them; **~ ist nichts zu machen** there's nothing one can do about it; **kein Wort ~ ist wahr** not a word of it is true; **mir liegt viel ~:** it means a lot to me; **c)** **ich wäre beinahe ~ erstickt** I almost choked on it; **er ist ~ gestorben** he died of it

daran|setzen *tr. V.* devote *(energy etc.)* to it; summon up *(ambition)* for it; *(aufs Spiel setzen)* risk *(one's life, one's honour)* for it

darauf *Adv.* **a)** on it/them; *(oben ~)* on top of it/them; **b)** **er hat ~ geschossen** he shot at it/them; **c)** *(danach)* after that; **ein Jahr ~ / kurz ~ starb er** he died a year later/shortly afterwards

darauf-: ~**folgend** *Adj.* following; ~**hin** [--'-] *Adv.* **a)** thereupon; **b)** *(unter diesem Gesichtspunkt)* with a view to this/that

daraus *Adv.* **a)** from it/them; out of it/them; **b)** **mach dir nichts ~** don't worry about it; **was ist ~ geworden?** what has become of it?

darf *1. u. 3. Pers. Sg. Präsens v.* dürfen; **darfst** *2. Pers. Sg. Präsens v.* dürfen

darin *Adv.* **a)** in it/them; **b)** *(in dieser Hinsicht)* in that respect

dar|legen *tr. V.* explain; set forth *(reasons, facts)*

Darm der; ~[e]s, Därme intestines *pl.;* bowels *pl.*

dar|stellen *tr. V.* **a)** depict; portray; **etw. graphisch ~:** present sth. graphically; **b)** *(verkörpern)* play; act; **c)**

(schildern) describe *(person, incident, etc.)*; present *(matter, argument)*; **d)** *(sein, bedeuten)* represent

Darsteller der; ~s, ~ actor; **Darstellerin** die; ~, ~nen actress; **Darstellung** die **a)** representation; *(Schilderung)* portrayal ; *(Bild)* picture; graphische/schematische ~: diagram; *(Graph)* graph; **b)** *(Beschreibung, Bericht)* description; account

darüber *Adv.* **a)** over it/them; **b)** ~ **hinaus** in additon [to that]; *(noch obendrein)* what is more; **c)** *(über dieser/diese Angelegenheit)* about it/them; **d)** *(über diese Grenze, dieses Maß hinaus)* over [that]

darüber|stehen *unr. itr. V. (fig.)* be above such things

darum *Adv.* **a)** [a]round it/them; **b)** *(diesbezüglich)* **ich sorge mich ~:** I worry about it; **c)** ['--] *(deswegen)* for that reason

darunter *Adv.* **a)** *(unter dem Genannten/das Genannte)* under it/them; **b)** *(unter dieser Grenze, diesem Maß)* less; **Bewerber im Alter von 40 Jahren und ~:** applicants aged 40 and under

das 1. *best. Art. Nom. u. Akk.* the; **2.** *Demonstrativpron.* **a)** *attr.* **das Kind war es** it was 'that child; **b)** *alleinstehend* **das** [da] that one; **das** [hier] this one [here]; **3.** *Relativpron. (Mensch)* who; that; *(Sache, Tier)* which; that

da|sein *unr. itr. V.; mit sein; Zusschr. nur im Inf. u. Part.* **a)** be there; *(hier sein)* be here; **noch ~** *(übrig sein)* be left; **ist Herr X da?** is Mr X about *or* available?; **ich bin gleich wieder da** I'll be right back; **b)** *(fig.) (case)* occur; *(moment)* have arrived; *(situation)* have arisen

Da·sein das existence

da|sitzen *unr. itr. V.* sit there

dasjenige *s.* derjenige

daß *Konj.* **a)** that; **entschuldigen Sie bitte, ~ ich mich verspätet habe** please forgive me for being late; **ich verstehe nicht, ~ sie ihn geheiratet hat** I don't understand why she married him; **b)** *(nach Pronominaladverbien o. ä.)* [the fact] that; **das liegt daran, ~ du nicht aufgepaßt hast** that comes from your not paying attention; **c)** *(im Konsekutivsatz)* that; [so] ~: so that; **d)** *(im Finalsatz)* so that; **e)** *(im Ausruf)* ~ **mir das passieren mußte!** why did it have to [go and] happen to me!

dasselbe *s.* derselbe

da|stehen *unr. itr. V.* **a)** stand there;

b) *(fig.)* **gut ~:** be in a good position; |ganz| **allein ~:** be [all] alone in the world

Daten 1. *s.* **Datum; 2.** *Pl.* data

Daten-: ~schutz der data protection; **~verarbeitung die** data processing *no def. art.*

datieren *tr. V.* date

Dativ der; ~s, ~e *(Sprachw.)* dative [case]; **Dativ·objekt das** *(Sprachw.)* indirect object

Dattel die; ~, ~n date; **Dattel·palme die** date-palm

Datum das; ~s, Daten date

Dauer die; ~ a) length; **für die ~ eines Jahres** *od.* **von einem Jahr** for a period of one year; **b)** *(Fortbestehen)* **von ~ sein** last [long]; **auf die ~:** in the long run; **auf ~:** permanently

dauer-, Dauer-: ~auftrag der *(Bankw.)* standing order; **~haft 1.** *Adj.* **a)** [long-]lasting *(peace, friendship, etc.)*; **b)** *(haltbar)* durable; **2.** *adv.* lastingly; **~karte** die season ticket; **~lauf** der jogging *no art.;* **ein ~lauf** a jog

¹dauern *itr. V.* last; *(job etc.)* take; **einen Moment, es dauert nicht lange** just a minute, it won't take long

dauernd 1. *Adj.*constant *(noise, interruptions, etc.);* permanent *(institution);* **2.** *adv.* constantly; **er kommt ~ zu spät** he keeps on arriving late

Dauer-: ~stellung die permanent position; **~welle die** perm; **~wurst die** smoked sausage *(with good keeping properties, esp. salami)*

Daumen der; ~s, ~: thumb

Daune die; ~, ~n down [feather]; **~n** down *sing.*

davon *Adv.* **a)** *(von dieser Stelle entfernt, weg)* from it/them; *(von dort)* from there; *(mit Entfernungsangabe)* away [from it/them]; **b)** *(hinsichtlich dieser Sache)* about it/them; **c)** *(durch diese Angelegenheit verursacht)* by it/them; **das kommt ~!** *(ugs.)* [there you are,] that's what happens; **d) ich hätte gern ein halbes Pfund ~:** I would like half a pound of that/those; **e) ~ kann man nicht leben** you can't live on that

davon-: ~|fahren *unr. itr. V.; mit sein* leave; *(mit dem Auto)* drive off; *(mit dem Fahrrad, Motorrad)* ride off; **~|kommen** *unr. itr. V.; mit sein* get away; **~|laufen** *unr. itr. V.; mit sein* run away; **~|tragen** *unr. tr. V.* **a)** carry away; take away *(rubbish);* **b)** *(geh.: erringen)* gain *(a victory, fame);*

c) *(geh.: sich zuziehen)* receive *(injuries)*

da·vor *Adv.* **a)** in front of it/them; **b)** *(zeitlich)* before [it/them]

davor-: ~|liegen *unr. itr. V.* lie in front of it/them; **~|schieben 1.** *unr. tr. V.* push in front of it/them; **2.** *unr. refl. V.* move in front of it/them; **~|stehen** *unr. itr. V.* stand in front of it/them; **~|stellen 1.** *tr. V.* put in front of it/them; **2.** *refl. V.* plant oneself in front of it/them

da·zu *Adv.* **a)** *(zusätzlich zu dieser Sache)* with it/them; *(gleichzeitig)* at the same time; *(außerdem)* what is more; **b)** *(diesbezüglich)* about it/them; **c)** *(zu diesem Zweck)* for it; **d)** *(zu diesem Ergebnis)* to it; **~ reicht unser Geld nicht** we haven't enough money for that

dazu-: ~|geben *unr. tr. V.* add; **~|gehören** *tr. V.* belong to it/them; **~|kommen** *unr. itr. V.; mit sein* **a)** *(hinkommen)* arrive; **b)** *(hinzukommen)* **kommt noch etwas dazu?** is there anything else [you would like]?; **~ kommt daß...** *(fig.)* what's more,...; on top of that ...; **~|rechnen** *tr. V.* add on; **~|tun** *unr. tr. V.* *(ugs.)* add

da·zwischen *Adv.* in between; between them; *(darunter)* among them

dazwischen-: ~|kommen *unr. itr. V.; mit sein* **a)** **mit dem Finger ~kommen** get one's finger caught [in it]; **b)** *(es verhindern)* prevent it; **es ist mir etwas ~gekommen** I had problems; **~|reden** *itr. V.* interrupt

DDR [de:de:'|ɛr] **die; ~** *Abk.* *(1949–1990)* Deutsche Demokratische Republik GDR; East Germany *(in popular use)*

Debatte die; ~, ~n debate *(über + Akk.* on); **zur ~ stehen** be under discussion

Debüt [de'by:] **das; ~s, ~s** debut

Deck das; ~|e|s, ~s deck

Deck·bett das *s.* Oberbett; **Decke die; ~, ~n a)** *(Tisch~)* tablecloth; **b)** *(Woll~, Pferde~, fig.)* blanket; *(Reise~)* rug; **c)** *(Zimmer~)* ceiling

Deckel der; ~s, ~ a) lid; *(auf Flaschen, Gläsern usw.)* top; *(Schacht~, Uhr~, Buch~ usw.)* cover; **b)** *(Bier~)* beer-mat

decken 1. *tr. V.* **a)** **etw. über etw.** *(Akk.)* **~:** spread sth. over sth. **b)** roof *(house);* cover *(roof);* **c) den Tisch ~:** lay the table; **d)** *(schützen; Finanzw., Versicherungsw.)* cover; **e)** *(befriedigen)* meet *(need, demand);* **2.** *itr. V.*

(den Tisch ~) lay the table; **Deck-mantel** der; *o. Pl.* cover; **Deckung** die; ~, ~en a) *(Schutz; auch fig.)* cover *(esp. Mil.); (Boxen)* guard; *(bes. Fußball)* defence; **in ~ gehen** take cover; b) *(Befriedigung)* meeting; c) *(Finanzw., Versicherungsw.)* cover[ing]; **deckungs·gleich** *Adj. (Geom.)* congruent

defekt *Adj.* defective; faulty; **~ sein** have a defect; be faulty; *(nicht funktionieren)* not be working; **Defekt** der; **~[e]s, ~e** defect, fault (**an** + *Dat.* in)

defensiv 1. *Adj.* defensive; 2. *adv.* defensively; **Defensive die**; ~, ~n defensive; **in der ~:** on the defensive; **die ~** *(Sport)* defensive play

definieren *tr. V.* define; **Definition** die; ~, ~en definition

definitiv 1. *Adj.* definitive; 2. *adv.* finally

Defizit das; ~s, ~e a) deficit; b) *(Mangel)* deficiency

deformieren *tr. V.* a) *(verformen)* distort; b) *(entstellen)* deform *(also fig.)*

deftig *Adj. (ugs.)* a) [good] solid *attrib.* ⟨*meal etc.*⟩; [nice] big ⟨*sausage etc.*⟩; b) *(derb)* crude, coarse ⟨*joke, speech, etc.*⟩

Degen der; ~s, ~ a) *(Waffe)* [light] sword; b) *(Fechtsport)* épée

degradieren *tr. V.* demote

dehnbar *Adj.* a) *(elastisch)* ⟨*material etc.*⟩ that stretches *not pred.;* elastic ⟨*waistband etc.*⟩; **Dehnbarkeit die**; ~: elasticity; **dehnen** *tr., refl. V.* stretch

Deich der; **~[e]s, ~e** dike

Deichsel ['daɪksl] die; ~, ~n shaft; **deichseln** *tr. V. (ugs.)* fix

dein *Possessivpron.* your; **viele Grüße von Deinem Emil** with best wishes, yours Emil; **das Buch dort, ist das ~[e]s?** that book over there, is it yours?; **du und die Deinen** *(geh.)* you and yours; **deiner** *Gen. des Personalpronomens* **du** *(geh.)* of you; **deinerseits** *Adv. (von deiner Seite)* on your part; *(auf deiner Seite)* for your part; **deinet·wegen** *Adv.* because of you; *(für dich)* on your behalf; *(dir zuliebe)* for your sake

dekadent *Adj.* decadent; **Dekadenz** die; ~: decadence

deklamieren *tr., itr. V.* recite

Deklination die; ~, ~en *(Sprachw.)* declension; **deklinieren** *tr. V. (Sprachw.)* decline

Dekolleté [dekɔl'teː] das; ~s, ~s low[-cut] neckline; décolletage

Dekor das; ~s, ~s *od.* ~e decoration; *(Muster)* pattern; **Dekorateur** [dekora'tøːɐ̯] der; ~s, ~e, **Dekorateurin** die; ~, ~nen *(Schaufenster~)* window-dresser; *(von Innenräumen)* interior designer; **Dekoration** die; ~, ~en decorations *pl.; (Schaufenster~)* window display; **dekorativ** 1. *Adj.* decorative; 2. *adv.* decoratively; **dekorieren** *tr. V.* decorate ⟨*room etc.*⟩; dress ⟨*shop-window*⟩

Deko·stoff der furnishing fabric

Dekret das; **~[e]s, ~e** decree

Delegation die; ~, ~en delegation; **delegieren** *tr. V.* a) send as a delegate/as delegates; b) delegate ⟨*task etc.*⟩ (**an** + *Akk.* to); **Delegierte** der/die; *adj. Dekl.* delegate

delikat *Adj.* a) delicious; *(fein)* delicate ⟨*bouquet, aroma*⟩; b) *(heikel)* delicate; **Delikatesse** die; ~, ~n delicacy

Delikt das; **~[e]s, ~e** offence

Delinquent der; ~en, ~en offender

Delirium das; ~s, **Delirien** delirium

Delle die; ~, ~n *(ugs.)* dent

Delphin der; ~s, ~e dolphin

dem 1. *best. Art., Dat. Sg. v.* **¹der** 1 *u.* **das** 1 to the; *(nach Präp.)* the; 2. *Demonstrativpron., Dat. Sg. v.* **¹der** 2 *u.* **das** 2: a) *attr.* that; **gib es dem Mann** give it to 'that man; b) *alleinstehend* **gib es nicht dem, sondern dem da!** don't give it to him, give it to that man/child *etc.;* 3. *Relativpron., Dat. Sg. v.* **¹der** 3 *u.* **das** 3 *(Person)* that/whom; *(Sache)* that/which; **der Mann/das Kind, dem ich das Geld gab** the man/the child I gave the money to

Demagoge der; ~n, ~n demagogue

demagogisch *Adj.* demagogic

Dementi das; ~s, ~s denial; **dementieren** 1. *tr. V.* deny; 2. *itr. V.* deny it

dem-: **~entsprechend** 1. *Adj.* appropriate; 2. *adv.* accordingly; *(vor Adjektiven)* correspondingly; **~gemäß** *Adv.* a) *(infolgedessen)* consequently; b) *(entsprechend)* accordingly; **~jenigen** *s.* derjenige; **~nach** *Adv.* therefore; **~nächst** *Adv.* shortly

Demokrat der; ~en, ~en democrat; *(Parteimitglied)* Democrat; **Demokratie** die; ~, ~n democracy; **demokratisch** 1. *Adj.* democratic; 2. *adv.* democratically; **demokratisieren** *tr. V.* democratize

demolieren *tr. V.* wreck; smash up ⟨*furniture*⟩

Demonstrant der; ~en, ~en demonstrator; **Demonstrantin** die; ~, ~nen demonstrator; **Demonstration** die; ~, ~en demonstration (für in support of, gegen against); **demonstrativ** 1. *Adj.* a) pointed; b) *(Sprachw.)* demonstrative; 2. *adv.* pointedly; **Demonstrativ·pronomen** das *(Sprachw.)* demonstrative pronoun; **demonstrieren** 1. *itr. V.* demonstrate (für in support of, gegen against); 2. *tr. V.* demonstrate

dem·selben *s.* derselbe

Demut die; ~: humility; **demütig** 1. *Adj.* humble; 2. *adv.* humbly; **demütigen** 1. *tr. V.* humiliate; 2. *refl. V.* humble oneself; **Demütigung** die; ~, ~en humiliation

dem·zufolge *Adv.* consequently

¹den 1. *best. Art., Akk. Sg. v.* **¹der** 1: the; 2. *Demonstrativpron., Akk. Sg. v.* **¹der** 2: a) *attr.* that; **ich meine den Mann** I mean 'that man; b) *alleinstehend* **ich meine den [da]** I mean 'that one; 3. *Relativpron., Akk. Sg. v.* **¹der** 3 *(Person)* that/whom; *(Sache)* that/which; **der Mann, den ich gesehen habe** the man that I saw

²den 1. *best. Art., Dat. Pl. v.* **¹der** 1, **¹die** 1, **das** 1 the; 2. *Demonstrativpron. Dat. Pl. v.* **¹der** 2 a, **¹die** 2 a, **das** 2 a those.

denen 1. *Demonstrativpron., Dat. Pl. v.* **¹der** 2 b, **¹die** 2 b, **das** 2 b them; **gib es ~, nicht den anderen** give it to 'them, not to the others; 2. *Relativpron., Dat. Pl. v.* **¹der** 3, **¹die** 3, **das** 3 *(Personen)* that/whom; *(Sachen)* that/which; **die Menschen, ~ wir Geld gegeben haben** the people to whom we gave money; **die Tiere, ~ er geholfen hat** the animals that he helped

denjenigen *s.* derjenige

denkbar 1. *Adj.* conceivable; 2. *adv. (sehr, äußerst)* extremely; **denken** 1. *unr. itr. V.* think (an + *Akk.* of, über + *Akk.* about); **wie denkst du darüber?** what do you think about it?; what's your opinion of it?; **schlecht von jmdm. ~:** think badly of sb.; **denk daran, daß .../zu ...:** don't forget that .../to ...; **ich denke nicht daran!** no way!; not on your life!; **ich denke nicht daran, das zu tun** I've no intention of doing that; 2. *unr. tr. V.* think; **wer hätte das gedacht?** who would have thought it?; **eine gedachte Linie** an imaginary line; 3. *unr. refl. V.* a)

(sich vorstellen) imagine; b) **sich** *(Dat.)* **bei etw. etwas ~:** mean something by sth.; **ich habe mir nichts [Böses] dabei gedacht** I didn't mean any harm [by it]; **Denken** das; ~s thinking; *(Denkweise)* thought; **Denker** der; ~s, ~: thinker

denk-, Denk- ~faul *Adj.* mentally lazy; **~mal** das; **~mals, ~mäler** *od.* **~male** monument; **~vermögen** das ability to think [creatively]; **~würdig** *Adj.* memorable; **~zettel** der lesson

denn 1. *Konj. (kausal)* for; because; b) *(geh.: als)* than; 2. *Adv.* **es sei ~, ...:** unless ...; 3. *Partikel (in Fragesätzen)* **wie geht es dir ~?** tell me, how are you?; **wie heißt du ~?** tell me your name; **warum ~ nicht?** why ever not?

dennoch *Adv.* nevertheless

denselben *s.* derselbe

Denunziant der; ~en, ~en informer; grass *(sl.);* **denunzieren** *tr. V.* denounce; *(bei der Polizei)* inform against; grass on *(sl.)* (bei to)

Deo das; ~s, ~s, **Deodorant** das; ~s, ~s *(auch:)* ~e deodorant

Deponie die; ~, ~n tip. *(Brit.);* dump; **deponieren** *tr. V.* put; *(im Safe o. ä.)* deposit

Deportation die; ~, ~en transportation; *(ins Ausland)* deportation; **deportieren** *tr. V.* transport; *(ins Ausland)* deport; **Deportierte** der/die; *adj. Dekl.* transportee; *(ins Ausland)* deportee

Depot [de'po:] das; ~s, ~s a) depot; *(Lagerhaus)* warehouse; *(für Möbel usw.)* depository; *(im Freien, für Munition o. ä.)* dump; *(in einer Bank)* strong-room; safe deposit; b) *(hinterlegte Wertgegenstände)* deposits *pl.*

Depp der; ~en *(auch:)* ~s, ~en *(auch:)* ~e *(bes. südd., österr., schweiz. abwertend)* s. **Dummkopf**

Depression die; ~, ~en depression; **depressiv** 1. *Adj.* depressive; 2. *adv.* ~ **veranlagt sein** have a tendency towards depression; **deprimieren** *tr. V.* depress; **deprimierend** *Adj.* depressing; **deprimiert** 1. *Adj.* depressed; 2. *adv.* dejectedly

¹der 1. *best. Art. Nom.* the; **der Tod** death; **der „Faust"** 'Faust'; **der Bodensee/Mount Everest** Lake Constance/Mount Everest; **der Iran/Sudan** Iran/the Sudan; **der Mensch/Mann ist ...:** man is .../men are ...; 2. *Demonstrativpron.* a) *attr.* that; **der Mann war es** it was 'that man; b) *al-*

leinstehend he; **der war es** it was 'him;
der |da| *(Person)* that man/boy; *(Sa-
che)* that one; **der |hier|** *(Person)* this
man/boy; *(Sache)* this one; **3.** *Relativpron. (Person)* who/that; *(Sache)*
which/that; **der Mann, der da drüben
entlanggeht** the man walking along
over there; **4.** *Relativ- u. Demonstrativpron.* the one who
²**der 1.** *best. Art.* **a)** *Gen. Sg. v.* ¹**die 1:**
der Hut der Frau the woman's hat; **der
Henkel der Tasse** the handle of the
cup; **b)** *Dat. Sg. v.* ¹**die 1** to the; *(nach
Präp.)* the; **c)** *Gen. Pl. v.* ¹**der 1,** ¹**die 1,
das 1: das Haus der Freunde** our/their
etc. friends' house; **das Bellen der
Hunde** the barking of the dogs; **2.** *Demonstrativpron.* **a)** *Gen. Sg. v.* ¹**die 2:**
of the; of that; **b)** *Dat. Sg. v.* ¹**die 2**
attr. **der Frau |da/hier| gehört es** it be-
longs to that woman there/this
woman here; **c)** *Gen. Pl. v.* ¹**der 2 a,**
¹**die 2 a, das 2 a** of those; **3.** *Relativpron.; Dat. Sg. v.* ¹**die 3: die Frau, der
ich es gegeben habe** the woman I gave
it to; **die Katze, der er einen Tritt gab**
the cat [that] he kicked
der·art *Adv.* so; **es hat lange nicht
mehr ~ geregnet** it hasn't rained as
hard as that for a long time; **sie hat ~
geschrien, daß ...:** she screamed so
much that ...; **der·artig 1.** *Adj.* such;
2. *adv. s.* derart
derb 1. *Adj.* **a)** tough ⟨*material*⟩; stout,
⟨*shoes*⟩; **b)** *(kraftvoll, deftig)* earthy
⟨*scenes, humour*⟩; **2.** *adv.* **a)** strongly
⟨*made, woven, etc.*⟩; **b)** *(kraftvoll, deftig)* earthily
deren 1. *Relativpron.* **a)** *Gen. Sg. v.*
¹**die 3** *(Personen)* whose; *(Sachen)* of
which; **b)** *Gen. Pl. v.* ¹**der 3,** ¹**die 3, das
3** *(Personen)* whose; *(Sachen)* **Maßnahmen, ~ Folgen wir noch nicht ab-
sehen können** measures, the consequences of which we cannot yet
foresee; **2.** *Demonstrativpron.* **a)** *Gen.
Sg. v.* ¹**die 2: meine Tante, ihre Freundin und ~ Hund** my aunt, her friend
and 'her dog; **b)** *Gen. Pl. v.* ¹**der 2,** ¹**die
2, das 2: meine Verwandten und ~ Kin-
der** my relatives and their children
der·ent-: ~wegen *Adv.* **1.** *relativ (Personen)* because of whom; *(Sachen)*
because of which; **2.** *demonstrativ* because of them; **~willen** *Adv.* **um
~willen** *(Personen)* for whose sake;
(Sachen) for the sake of which
derer *Demonstrativpron.; Gen. Pl. v.*
¹**der 2,** ¹**die 2, das 2** of those

der·gleichen *indekl. Demonstrativpron.* **a)** *attr.* such; like that *postpos.,
not pred.;* **b)** *alleinstehend* that sort of
thing
**der·jenige, die·jenige, das·jeni-
ge** *Demonstrativpron.* **a)** *attr.* that; *Pl.*
those; **b)** *alleinstehend* that one; *Pl.*
those
derlei *indekl. Demonstrativpron.: s.*
dergleichen
der·maßen *Adv.* **~ schön** *usw.,*
daß ...: so beautiful *etc.* that ...
derselbe, dieselbe, dasselbe *Demonstrativpron.* **a)** *attr.* the same; **b)**
alleinstehend the same one; *Pl.* the
same people; **er sagt immer dasselbe**
he always says the same thing; **noch
einmal dasselbe, bitte** *(ugs.)* [the] same
again please
der·zeit *Adv.* at present; **der·zeitig**
Adj. present; current
des 1. *best. Art.; Gen. Sg. v.* ¹**der 1, das
1: die Mütze des Jungen** the boy's cap;
das Klingeln des Telefons the ringing
of the telephone; **2.** *Demonstrativpron.; Gen. Sg. v.* ¹**der 2, das 2: er ist
der Sohn des Mannes, der ...:** he's the
son of the man who ...
Deserteur [dezɛr'tøː̯ɐ̯] *der;* **~s, ~e**
deserter; **desertieren** *itr. V.; mit
sein* desert
des·gleichen *Adv.* likewise; **er ist
Arzt, ~ sein Sohn** he is a doctor, as is
his son
des·halb *Adv.* for that reason; **~ bin
ich zu dir gekommen** that is why I
came to you
Des·infektion die disinfection;
Desinfektions·mittel das disinfectant; **des·infizieren** *tr. V.* disin-
fect
Des·interesse das lack of interest
Despot [dɛs'poːt] *der;* **~en, ~en** despot; *(fig. abwertend)* tyrant; **despo-
tisch 1.** *Adj.* despotic; **2.** *adv.* des-
potically
des·selben *s.* derselbe
dessen 1. *Relativpron.; Gen. Sg. v.*
¹**der 3, das 3** *attr. (Person)* whose; *(Sache)* of which; **2.** *Demonstrativpron.;
Gen. Sg. v.* ¹**der 2, das 2: mein Onkel,
sein Sohn und ~ Hund** my uncle, his
son, and 'his dog
Dessert [dɛ'seːɐ̯] *das;* **~s, ~s** dessert
destillieren *tr. V. (Chemie)* distil
desto *Konj., vor Komp.* **je eher, ~ besser** the sooner the better
des·wegen *Adv. s.* deshalb
Detail [de'tai̯] *das;* **~s, ~s** detail; **de-**

tailliert 1. *Adj.* detailed; **2.** *adv.* in detail; **sehr ~:** in great detail

Detektiv der; ~s, ~e [private] detective

Detonation die; ~, ~en detonation; explosion

Deut *in* **keinen ~:** not one bit

deuten 1. *itr. V.* point; |mit dem Finger| auf jmdn./etw. ~: point [one's finger] at sb./sth.; **2.** *tr. V.* interpret

deutlich 1. *Adj.* clear; **2.** *adv.* clearly; **Deutlichkeit die; ~a)** clarity; **b)** *(Eindeutigkeit)* clearness

deutsch 1. *Adj.* German; **Deutsche Mark** Deutschmark; German mark; **auf** *od.* **in ~:** in German; **auf** |gut| **~** *(ugs.)* in plain English; **2.** *adv.* **~ sprechen/schreiben** speak/write German; **Deutsch das; ~|s|** German; **gutes/ fließend ~ sprechen** speak good/fluent German; **¹Deutsche der/die;** *adj. Dekl.* German; **~|r| sein** be German; **²Deutsche das;** *adj. Dekl.* **das ~:** German; **aus dem ~n/ins ~ übersetzen** translate from/into German; **Deutschland (das); ~s** Germany

deutsch-, Deutsch-: ~lehrer der German teacher; **~sprachig** *Adj.* **a)** German-speaking; **b)** German-language *attrib.;* **~unterricht der** German teaching; *(Unterrichtsstunde)* German lesson

Deutung die; ~, ~en interpretation

Devise die; ~, ~n motto; **Devisen** *Pl.* foreign currency *sing.*

Dezember der; ~s, ~: December

dezent 1. *Adj.* quiet *(colour, pattern, suit);* subdued *(lighting, music);* **2.** *adv.* discreetly; *(dress)* unostentatiously

dezimal *Adj.* decimal

Dezimal-: ~system das decimal system; **~zahl die** decimal [number]

dezimieren *tr. V.* decimate

dgl. *Abk.* dergleichen, desgleichen

d. h. *Abk.* das heißt i.e.

Di. *Abk.* Dienstag Tue[s].

Dia das; ~s, ~s slide

Diabetiker der; ~s, ~, Diabetikerin, die; ~, ~nen diabetic

Diagnose [dia'gno:zə] **die; ~, ~n** diagnosis

diagonal 1. *Adj.* diagonal; **2.** *adv.* diagonally; **Diagonale die; ~, ~n** diagonal

Dialekt der; ~|e|s, ~e dialect

Dialog der; ~|e|s, ~e dialogue

Diamant der; ~en, ~en diamond

diät *adv.* **~ kochen** cook according to a/one's diet; **~ essen** be on a diet; **Diät die; ~, ~en** diet; **eine ~ einhalten** keep to a diet; **Diäten** *Pl.* [parliamentary] allowance *sing.*

dich 1. *Akk. von* **du** you; **2.** *Akk. des Reflexivpron. der 2. Pers. Sg.* yourself

dicht 1. *Adj.* **a)** thick; dense *(forest, hedge, crowd);* heavy, dense *(traffic);* **b)** *(undurchlässig) (für Luft)* airtight; *(für Wasser)* watertight; **2.** *adv.* **a)** densely *(populated, wooded);* **b)** *(undurchlässig)* tightly; **c)** *mit Präp. (nahe)* **~ neben** right next to

dicht·besiedelt *Adj. (präd. getrennt geschrieben)* densely populated

Dichte die; ~ *(Physik, fig.)* density

dichten 1. *itr. V.* write poetry; **2.** *tr. V. (verfassen)* write; compose; **Dichter der; ~s, ~:** poet; *(Schriftsteller)* writer; author; **Dichterin die; ~, ~nen** poet[ess]; *(Schriftstellerin)* writer; author[ess]; **dichterisch** *Adj.* poetic; *(schriftstellerisch)* literary

dicht|machen *tr., itr. V. (ugs.)* shut; *(endgültig)* shut down

¹Dichtung die; ~, ~en seal; *(am Hahn usw.)* washer; *(am Vergaser, Zylinder usw.)* gasket

²Dichtung die; ~, ~en a) work of literature; *(in Versform)* poetic work; poem; **b)** *o. Pl. (Dichtkunst)* literature; *(in Versform)* poetry

dick 1. *Adj.* **a)** thick; stout *(tree);* fat *(person, legs, etc.);* swollen *(cheek, ankle, tonsils, etc.);* **~ werden** get fat; **5 cm ~ sein** be 5 cm thick; **b)** *(ugs.: groß)* big *(mistake);* hefty, *(coll.)* fat *(salary);* **2.** *adv.* thickly; **etw. ~ unterstreichen** underline sth. heavily; **sich ~ anziehen** wrap up warm[ly]; **etw. 5 cm ~ schneiden** cut sth. 5 cm. thick; **~ geschwollen** *(ugs.)* badly swollen; **¹Dicke die; ~:** thickness; *(von Menschen, Körperteilen)* fatness; **²Dicke der/die;** *adj. Dekl. (ugs.)* fatty *(coll.);* **dick·fellig** *(ugs.) Adj.* thick-skinned; **Dickicht** ['dıkıçt] **das; ~|e|s, ~e** thicket

dick-, Dick-: ~kopf der *(ugs.)* mule *(coll.);* **ein ~kopf sein** be stubborn as a mule; **einen ~kopf haben** be pig-headed; **~köpfig** *Adj. (ugs.)* pig-headed; **~milch die** sour milk

¹die 1. *best. Art. Nom.* the; **die Helga** *(ugs.)* Helga; **die Frau/Menschheit** women /Pl./mankind; **2.** *Demonstrativpron.* **a)** *attr.* **die Frau war es** it was 'that woman; **b)** *alleinstehend* she; **die war es** it was 'her; **die |da|** *(Person)* that woman/girl; *(Sache)* that one; **3.** *Relativpron. Nom. (Person)* who; that; *(Sache, Tier)* which; that; **4.** *Relativu. Demonstrativpron.* the one who **²die 1.** *best. Art.* **a)** *Akk. Sg. v.* **¹die** 1 the; **ich sah die Frau** I saw the women; **b)** *Nom. u. Akk. Pl. v.* **¹der** 1, **¹die** 1, **das** 1 the; **2.** *Demonstrativpron. Nom. u. Akk. Pl. v.* **¹der** 1, **¹die** 1, **das** 1: *attr.* **ich meine die Männer, die ...** I mean those men who ...; *alleinstehend* **ich meine die [da]** I mean 'them; **3.** *Relativpron.* **a)** *Akk. Sg. v.* **¹die** 3 *(Person)* who; *(Sache)* that; **b)** *Nom. u. Akk. Pl. v.* **¹der** 3, **¹die** 3, **das** 3 *(Personen)* whom; *(Sachen)* which; **die Männer, die ich gesehen habe** the men I saw

Dieb der; ~[e]s, ~e thief; **Diebin** die; ~, ~nen [woman] thief; **diebisch 1.** *Adj.* **a)** thieving; **b)** *(verstohlen)* mischievous; **2.** *adv.* mischievously; **Diebstahl** der; ~[e]s, Diebstähle theft

die·jenige *s.* derjenige

Diele die; ~, ~n hall[way]

dienen *itr. V.* serve; **womit kann ich ~?** what can I do for you?; **Diener** der; ~s, ~ servant; **einen ~ machen** *(ugs.)* bow; make a bow; **Dienerin** die; ~, ~nen maid; servant

dienlich *Adj.* helpful; **Dienst** der; ~[e]s, ~e **a)** *o. Pl. (Tätigkeit)* work; *(von Soldaten, Polizeibeamten, Krankenhauspersonal usw.)* duty; **seinen ~ antreten** start work/go on duty; **~ haben** be at work/on duty; ⟨doctor⟩ be on call; ⟨chemist⟩ be open; **b)** *(Arbeitsverhältnis)* post; **Major außer ~:** retired major; **c)** *o. Pl. (Tätigkeitsbereich)* service; *s. auch* **öffentlich; d)** *(Hilfe)* service

Diens·tag der Tuesday; **am ~:** on Tuesday; ~, **der 1. Juni** Tuesday, 1 June; **er kommt ~:** he is coming on Tuesday; **ab nächsten ~:** from next Tuesday [onwards]; **~ in einer Woche** a week on Tuesday; **~ vor einer Woche** a week last Tuesday; **diens·tags** *Adv.* on Tuesday[s]

dienst-, Dienst-: ~**bereit** *Adj.* ⟨chemist⟩ open *pred.;* ⟨doctor⟩ on call; ⟨dentist⟩ on duty; ~**bote** der servant; ~**eifrig** *Adj.* zealous; ~**frei** *Adj.* free ⟨time⟩; ~**geheimnis** das **a)** professional secret; *(im Staatsdienst)* official secret; **b)** *o. Pl.* professional secrecy; *(im Staatsdienst)* official secrecy; ~**grad** der *(Milit.)* rank; ~**leistung** die *(auch Wirtsch.)* service

dienstlich 1. *Adj.* business ⟨call⟩; *(im Staatsdienst)* official ⟨letter, call, etc.⟩; **2.** *adv.* on business; *(im Staatsdienst)* on official business

dienst-, Dienst-: ~**reise** die business trip; ~**stelle die** office; ~**wagen** der official car; *(Geschäftswagen)* company car; ~**weg** der official channels *pl.;* ~**zeit** die **a)** period of service; **b)** *(tägliche Arbeitszeit)* working hours *pl.*

dies *s.* dieser

dies·bezüglich *adv.* regarding this

diese *s.* dieser

Diesel der; ~[s], ~: diesel

die·selbe *s.* derselbe

Diesel·motor der diesel engine

dieser, diese, dieses, dies *Demonstrativpron.* **a)** *attr.* this; *Pl.* these; **b)** *alleinstehend* this one; *Pl.* these; **dies alles** all this; **dies und das,** *(geh.)* **dieses und jenes** this and that

diesig *Adj.* hazy

dies-: ~**mal** *Adv.* this time; ~**seits 1.** *Präp. mit Gen.* on this side of; **2.** *Adv.* ~**seits von** on this side of

Dietrich der; ~s, ~e picklock

diffamieren *tr. V.* defame; **Diffamierung** die; ~, ~en defamation

Differenz die; ~, ~en difference; *(Meinungsverschiedenheit)* difference [of opinion]; **differenziert** *Adj.* complex; subtly differentiated ⟨methods, colours⟩; sophisticated ⟨taste⟩

diffus *Adj. (Physik, Chemie)* diffuse; **b)** *(geh.)* vague; vague and confused ⟨idea, statement, etc.⟩; **2.** *adv.* in a vague and confused way

Digital- digital ⟨clock, display, etc.⟩

digitalisieren *tr. V. (DV)* digitalize

Diktat das; ~[e]s, ~e dictation

Diktator der; ~s, ~en dictator; **diktatorisch 1.** *Adj.* dictatorial; **2.** *adv.* dictatorially; **Diktatur** die; ~, ~en dictatorship

diktieren *tr. V.* dictate

Diktier·gerät das dictating machine

Dilemma das; ~s, ~s dilemma

Dilettant [dile'tant] der; ~en, ~en, **Dilettantin** die; ~, ~nen dilettante; **dilettantisch 1.** *Adj.* dilettante; amateurish; **2.** *adv.* amateurishly

Dill der; ~[e]s, ~e dill

Dimension die; ~, ~en *(Physik, fig.)* dimension

DIN [di:n] *Abk.* **Deutsche Industrie-Norm[en]** *German Industrial Standard[s];* DIN; **DIN-A4-Format** A4

¹**Ding** das; ~|e|s, ~e a) thing; b) *meist Pl.* **nach Lage der** ~e the way things are; **persönliche/private** ~e personal/private matters; **ein** ~ **der Unmöglichkeit sein** be quite impossible; **vor allen** ~en above all; c) **guter** ~e **sein** *(geh.)* be in good spirits; ²**Ding** das; ~|e|s, ~er *(ugs.)* thing; **das ist ja ein** ~! that's really something

Diözese die; ~, ~n diocese

Dipl.-Ing. *Abk.* **Diplomingenieur** *academically qualified engineer*

Diplom das; ~s, ~e ≈ [first] degree *(in a scientific or technical subject); (für einen Handwerksberuf)* diploma; **Diplom-:** qualified

Diplomat der; ~en, ~en, **Diplomatin die;** ~, ~nen diplomat; **diplomatisch** 1. *Adj.* diplomatic; 2. *adv.* diplomatically

dir 1. *Dat. von* **du** to you; *(nach Präp.)* you; **Freunde von** ~: friends of yours; 2. *Dat. des Reflexivpron. der 2. Pers. Sg.* yourself

direkt 1. *Adj.* direct; 2. *adv.* straight; directly; **etw.** ~ **übertragen** broadcast sth. live; **Direkt·flug der** direct flight

Direktion die; ~, ~en management; *(Büroräume)* managers' offices *pl.;* **Direktor** der; ~s, ~en, **Direktorin die;** ~, ~nen director; *(einer Schule)* headmaster/headmistress; *(einer Strafanstalt)* governor; *(einer Abteilung)* manager

Direkt·übertragung die live broadcast

Dirigent der; ~en, ~en conductor; **dirigieren** *tr. V.* a) *auch itr.* conduct; b) *(führen)* steer

Disco ['dɪsko:] **die;** ~, ~s disco

Diskette die; ~, ~n *(DV)* floppy disc

Diskont·satz der *(Finanzw.)* discount rate

Diskothek die; ~, ~en discothèque

Diskrepanz die; ~, ~en discrepancy

diskret 1. *Adj. (vertraulich)* confidential; *(taktvoll)* discreet; tactful; 2. *adv. (vertraulich)* confidentially; *(taktvoll)* discreetly; tactfully; **Diskretion die;** ~ a) *(Verschwiegenheit, Takt)* discretion; b) *(Unaufdringlichkeit)* discreetness

diskriminieren *tr. V.* discriminate against; **Diskriminierung die;** ~, ~en discrimination

Diskussion die; ~, ~en discussion; **zur** ~ **stehen** be under discussion

Diskussions-: ~**beitrag** der contribution to a/the discussion; ~**leiter** der chairman [of the discussion]

diskutieren 1. *itr. V.* **über etw.** *(Akk.)* ~: discuss sth.; 2. *tr. V.* discuss

disqualifizieren *tr. V.* disqualify

Distanz die; ~, ~en *(auch fig.)* distance; **distanzieren** *refl. V.* **sich von jmdm./etw.** ~ *(fig.)* dissociate oneself from sb./sth.; **distanziert** *Adj.* reserved

Distel die; ~, ~n thistle

Distel·fink der goldfinch

Disziplin die; ~, ~en discipline; *(Selbstbeherrschung)* [self-]discipline; **disziplinieren** 1. *tr. V.* discipline; 2. *refl. V.* discipline oneself; **diszipliniert** 1. *Adj.* well-disciplined; *(beherrscht)* disciplined; 2. *adv.* in a well-disciplined way; *(beherrscht)* in a disciplined way

divers... [di'vɛrs...] *Adj.; nicht präd.* various; *(mehrer...)* several

Dividende [divi'dɛndə] **die;** ~, ~n *(Wirtsch.)* dividend

dividieren *tr. V.* divide; **Division die;** ~, ~en *(auch Milit.)* division

DM *Abk.* **Deutsche Mark** DM

Do. *Abk.* **Donnerstag** Thur[s].

doch 1. *Konj.* but; 2. *Adv.* a) *(jedoch)* but; b) *(dennoch)* all the same; still; c) *(geh.: nämlich)* **wußte er** ~, **daß** ...: because he knew that ...; d) *(entgegen allen gegenteiligen Behauptungen, Annahmen)* **er war also** ~ **der Mörder!** so he 'was the murderer!; e) *(ohnehin)* in any case; 3. *Interj.* **Das stimmt nicht.** – **Doch!** That's not right. – [Oh] yes it is!; **Hast du keinen Hunger?** – **Doch!** Aren't you hungry? – Yes [I am]!; 4. *Partikel* a) *(Ungeduld ausdrückend)* **paß** ~ **auf!** [oh] do be careful!; **das ist** ~ **nicht zu glauben** that's just incredible; b) *(Zweifel ausdrückend)* **du hast** ~ **meinen Brief erhalten?** you did get my letter, didn't you?; c) *(Überraschung ausdrückend)* **das ist** ~ **Karl!** there's Karl! d) *(verstärkt Bejahung/Verneinung ausdrückend)* **gewiß/sicher** ~: [why] certainly; of course; **ja** ~: [yes,] all right; **nicht** ~! *(abwehrend)* [no,] don't!; e) *(Wunsch verstärkend)* **wäre es** ~ ...: if only it were ...

Docht der; ~|e|s, ~ wick

Dock das; ~s, ~s dock

Dogge die; ~, ~n: |deutsche| ~: Great Dane

Dogma das; ~s, **Dogmen** *(auch fig.)* dogma; **dogmatisch** *(Theol., auch fig.) Adj.* dogmatic

Dohle die; ~, ~n jackdaw

Doktor der; ~s, ~en *(auch ugs. Arzt)* doctor; *(Titel)* Doctor; **Doktor·arbeit** die doctoral thesis

Doktrin die; ~, ~en doctrine

Dokument das; ~|e|s, ~e document

Dokumentar·: ~**bericht** der documentary report; ~**film** der documentary [film]

Dokumentation die; ~, ~en *o. Pl.* documentation; b) *(Bericht)* documentary report

dokumentieren tr. V. a) document; *(fig.)* demonstrate; b) *(festhalten)* record

Dolch der; ~|e|s, ~e dagger

Dolde die; ~, ~n *(Bot.)* umbel

doll *(bes. nordd., salopp)* 1. *Adj.* a) *(ungewöhnlich)* incredible; b) *(großartig)* great *(coll.)*; 2. *adv.* a) *(großartig)* fantastically [well] *(coll.);* b) *(sehr)* ⟨hurt⟩ dreadfully *(coll.)*, like mad

Dollar der; ~|s|, ~s dollar; zwei ~: two dollars

dolmetschen *itr. V.* act as interpreter; **Dolmetscher** der; ~s, ~, **Dolmetscherin** die; ~, ~nen interpreter

Dom der; ~|e|s, ~e cathedral

dominieren *itr. V.* dominate

dominikanisch *Adj.* Dominican; die Dominikanische Republik the Dominican Republic

Domizil das; ~s, ~e *(geh.)* domicile; residence

Dom·pfaff der; ~en *od.* ~s, ~en *(Zool.)* bullfinch

Dompteur [dɔmp'tøːɐ] der; ~s, ~e, **Dompteuse** [dɔmp'tøːzə] die; ~, ~n tamer

Donau die; ~: Danube

Donner der; ~s, ~: thunder; **donnern** *itr. V.* a) *(unpers.)* thunder; b) *(fig.)* thunder; *(engine)* roar

Donners·tag der Thursday; *s. auch* Dienstag; **donnerstags** *Adv.* on Thursday[s]; *s. auch* dienstags

Donner·wetter das *(ugs.)* a) *(Krach)* row; b) ['--'--] zum ~ |noch einmal|! damn it!; ~! my word

doof *(ugs.)* 1. *Adj.* stupid; dumb *(coll.);* 2. *adv.* stupidly

Doppel das; ~s, ~ a) *(Kopie)* duplicate; copy; b) *(Sport)* doubles *sing. or pl.*

doppel-, Doppel-: ~**bett** das double bed; ~**bock** das extra-strong bock beer; ~**decker** der; ~s, ~: biplane; ~**deutig** [~dɔytɪç] 1. *Adj.* a) ambiguous; b) *(anzüglich)* suggestive; 2. *adv.* a) ambiguously; b) *(anzüglich)* suggestively; ~**fenster** das double-glazed window; ~**gänger** der; ~s, ~, ~**gängerin** die; ~, ~nen double; ~**kinn** das double chin; ~**punkt** der colon

doppelt 1. *Adj.* double; die ~e Menge twice the quantity; mit ~er Kraft arbeiten work with twice as much energy; 2. *adv.* ~ so groß/alt wie ...: twice as large/old as ...; sich ~ anstrengen try twice as hard; **Doppelte** das; *adj. Dekl.* das ~ bezahlen pay twice as much; pay double

Doppel-: ~**tür** die double door; ~**zentner** der 100 kilograms; ~**zimmer** das double room

Dorf das; ~|e|s, Dörfer village; auf dem ~: in the country; **Dorf·bewohner** der villager

Dorn der; ~|e|s, ~en thorn; jmdm. ein ~ im Auge sein annoy sb. intensely; **dornig** *Adj.* thorny; **Dorn·röschen** ⟨das⟩ the Sleeping Beauty

dörren *tr. V.* dry

Dörr-: ~**fleisch** das *(südd.)* lean bacon; ~**obst** das dried fruit

Dorsch der; ~|e|s, ~e cod

dort *Adv.* there; *s. auch* da 1 a

dort-: ~|**bleiben** *unr. itr. V.; mit sein* stay there; ~**her** *Adv.* |von| ~her from there; ~**hin** *Adv.* there

dortig *Adj.; nicht präd.* there

Dose die; ~, ~n a) *(Blech~)* tin; *(Pillen~)* box; *(Zucker~)* bowl; b) *(Konserven~)* can; tin *(Brit.);* *(Bier~)* can

dösen *itr. V. (ugs.)* doze

Dosen-: ~**bier** das canned beer; ~**milch** die canned *or (Brit.)* tinned milk; ~**öffner** der can opener; tin-opener *(Brit.)*

dosieren *tr. V.* etw. ~: measure out the required dose of sth.; **Dosis** die; ~, Dosen dose

Dotter der *od.* das; ~s, ~: yolk

Dotter·blume die marsh marigold

Dozent der; ~en, ~en, **Dozentin** die; ~, ~nen lecturer (für in)

Dr. *Abk.: Doktor* Dr

Drache der; ~n, ~n *(Myth.)* dragon; **Drachen** der; ~s, ~ a) kite; b) *(Fluggerät)* hang-glider

Dragée, Dragee [dra'ʒeː] das; ~s, ~s dragée

Draht der; ~|e|s, Drähte a) wire; b) *(Leitung)* wire; *(Telefonleitung)* line; wire; c) *(Telefonverbindung)* line

draht-, Draht-: ~**los** *(Nachrichtenw.)*

1. *Adj.* wireless; 2. *adv.* etw. ~los tele-
grafieren/übermitteln radio sth.;
~seil das [steel] cable; ~seil·bahn
die cable railway; ~zieher der *(fig.)*
wire puller

drall *Adj.* strapping ⟨girl⟩; full,
rounded ⟨cheeks, face, bottom⟩

Drama das; ~s, Dramen drama; *(fig.,
ugs.)* disaster; dramatisch 1. *Adj.*
dramatic. 2. *adv.* dramatically; dra-
matisieren *tr. V.* dramatize

dran *Adv. (ugs.)* a) häng das Schild ~!
put the sign up!; b) arm ~ sein be in a
bad way; gut/schlecht ~ sein be well
off/badly off; früh/spät ~ sein be
early/late; ich bin ~: it's my turn;
dran|bleiben *unr. itr. V.; mit sein
(ugs.) (am Telefon)* hang on *(coll.)*

drang *1. u. 3. Pers. Sg. Prät. v.* dringen

Drang der; ~[e]s, Dränge urge

dränge *1. u. 3. Pers. Sg. Konjunktiv II
v.* dringen

drängeln *(ugs.)* 1. *itr. V.* a) push [and
shove]; b) *(auf jmdn. einreden)* go on
(coll.); 2. *tr. V.* a) push; shove; b) *(einreden auf)* go on at *(coll.)*; 3. *refl. V.*
sich nach vorn ~: push one's way to
the front

drängen 1. *itr. V.* a) push; b) die Zeit
drängt time is pressing; 2. *tr. V.* a)
push; b) *(antreiben)* press; urge; 3.
refl. V. crowd

drangsalieren *tr. V. (quälen)* torment; *(plagen)* plague

dran-: ~|halten *unr. refl. V. (ugs.)* get
a move on *(coll.);* ~|kommen *unr. itr.
V.; mit sein (ugs.)* have one's turn;
~|nehmen *unr. tr. V. (ugs.) (beim Fri-
seur usw.)* see to; *(beim Arzt)* see

drastisch 1. *Adj.* drastic ⟨measure,
means⟩; 2. *adv.* drastically; ⟨punish⟩
severely

drauf *Adv. (ugs.)* on it

drauf-, Drauf-: ~gänger der daredevil; ~gängerisch *Adj.* daring;
~|gehen *unr. itr. V.; mit sein (ugs.)* a)
(umkommen) kick the bucket *(sl.);* b)
verbraucht werden) go *(für* on);
~|zahlen *(ugs.)* 1. *tr. V.* noch etwas/
1250 DM ~zahlen fork out *(sl.)* or pay
a bit more/an extra 1,250 marks; 2. *itr.
V. (Unkosten haben)* ich zahle dabei
noch ~: it's costing me money

draußen *Adv.* outside; hier/da ~: out
here/there; von/nach ~: from outside/
outside

Dreck der; ~[e]s a) *(ugs.)* dirt; *(sehr
viel)* filth; *(Schlamm)* mud; b) *(salopp
abwertend: Angelegenheit)* mach dei-

nen ~ allein do it yourself; das geht
dich einen [feuchten] ~ an *(salopp)*
none of your damned business *(sl.);* c)
(salopp abwertend: Zeug) junk *no indef. art.;* Dreck·arbeit die *(auch
fig.)* dirty work *no indef. art., no
pl./*dirty job; dreckig 1. *Adj.* a)
(ugs., auch fig.) dirty; *(sehr schmutzig)*
filthy; b) *(salopp: unverschämt)*
cheeky; 2. *adv.* a) es geht ihm ~ *(ugs.)*
he's in a bad way; b) *(salopp: unverschämt)* cheekily

Dreck-: ~sau die, ~schwein das
(derb) filthy swine

Dreh der; ~s, ~s *(ugs.)* a) den ~ her-
aushaben have [got] the knack; b) [so]
um den ~: about that

Dreh-: ~arbeiten *Pl. (Film)* shooting
sing. (zu of); ~bank die lathe;
~buch das screenplay; [film] script

drehen 1. *tr. V.* a) turn; b) *(formen)*
twist ⟨rope, thread⟩; roll ⟨cigarette⟩; c)
(Film) shoot ⟨scene⟩; film ⟨report⟩;
make; ⟨film⟩; 2. *itr. V.* a) ⟨car⟩ turn;
⟨wind⟩ change; b) an etw. *(Dat.)* ~:
turn sth.; c) *(Film)* film; 3. *refl. V.* a)
turn; b) *(ugs.: zum Gegenstand haben)*
sich um etw. ~: be about sth.

Dreh-: ~orgel die barrel-organ; ~re-
staurant das revolving restaurant;
~stuhl der swivel chair; ~tür die revolving door

Drehung die; ~, ~en turn; *(um einen
Mittelpunkt)* revolution

drei Kardinalz. three; Drei die; ~,
~en three; eine ~ schreiben *(Schulw.)*
get a C

drei-, Drei-: ~eck das; ~s, ~e
(Geom.) triangle; ~eckig *Adj.* triangular; ~ein·halb *Bruchz.* three and
a half

Dreier der; ~s, ~ *(ugs.)* three; dreier-
lei *Gattungsz.; indekl.* a) *attr.* three
kinds *or* sorts of; three different; b)
subst. three [different] things

drei-, Drei-: ~fach *Vervielfältigungsz.* triple; die ~fache Menge
three times the amount; ~fache das;
adj. Dekl. das ~fache kosten cost three
times as much; das ~fache von 3 ist 9
three times three is nine; ~hundert
Kardinalz. three hundred; ~jährig
Adj. (3 Jahre alt) three-year-old *attrib.; (3 Jahre dauernd)* three-year *attrib.;* ~kampf der *(Sport)* triathlon;
~klang der triad; ~köpfig *Adj.* ⟨fa-
mily, crew⟩ of three; ~mal *Adv.* three
times; ~malig *Adj.* eine ~malige
Wiederholung three repeats

drein *(ugs.) s.* darein
drein-: ~|blicken, ~|schauen *itr. V.* look
drei-, Drei-: ~rad das tricycle; ~satz der; rule of three; ~seitig *Adj.* three-sided ⟨*figure*⟩; three-page ⟨*letter, leaflet, etc.*⟩
dreißig *Kardinalz.* thirty; *s. auch* achtzig; **dreißigjährig** *Adj. (30 Jahre alt)* thirty-year-old *attrib.; (30 Jahre dauernd)* thirty-year *attrib.;* **dreißigst...** *Ordinalz.* thirtieth; **Dreißigstel** das; ~s, ~: thirtieth
dreist 1. *Adj.* brazen; barefaced ⟨*lie*⟩; 2. *adv.* brazenly
drei·stellig *Adj.* three-figure *attrib.*
Dreistigkeit die; ~, ~en a) *o. Pl.* brazenness; b) *(Handlung)* brazen act
drei-, Drei-: ~tausend *Kardinalz.* three thousand; ~teilig *Adj.* three-part *attrib.;* three-piece *attrib.* ⟨*suit*⟩; ~viertel *Bruchz.* three-quarters; ~viertel·stunde [---'--] die three-quarters of an hour; ~viertel·takt [-'---] der three-four time; ~zehn *Kardinalz.* thirteen; *s. auch* achtzehn
Dresche die; ~ *(salopp)* walloping *(sl.);* thrashing; **dreschen** 1. *unr. tr. V.* a) thresh; b) *(salopp: schlagen)* wallop *(sl.);* thrash; 2. *unr. itr. V.* thresh
dressieren *tr. V.* train ⟨*animal*⟩; **Dressur** die; ~, ~en training
Drill der; ~[e]s drilling; *(Milit.)* drill; **drillen** *tr. V. (auch Milit.)* drill
Drilling der; ~s, ~e triplet
drin *Adv. (ugs.)* a) in it; b) *s.* drinnen
dringen *unr. itr. V.* a) mit sein durch/ in etw. ~: penetrate sth.; b) *mit sein* in jmdn. ~ *(geh.)* press sb.; c) auf etw. *(Akk.)* ~: insist upon sth.; **dringend** 1. *Adj.* urgent; strong ⟨*suspicion, advice*⟩; 2. *adv.* urgently; ⟨*advise, suspect*⟩ strongly; ~ erforderlich essential; **dringlich** 1. *Adj.* urgent; 2. *adv.* urgently; **Dringlichkeit** die; ~: urgency
drinnen *Adv.* inside; *(im Haus)* indoors; inside
dritt *in* wir waren zu ~: there were three of us
dritt... *Ordinalz.* third; **Drittel** das, *(schweiz. meist* der); ~s, ~: third; **dritteln** *tr. V.* split *or* divide three ways; **drittens** *Adv.* thirdly
DRK [de:'ɛr'ka:] das; ~ *Abk.* Deutsches Rotes Kreuz German Red Cross
Dr. med. *Abk. doctor medicinae* MD
droben *Adv. (südd., österr., sonst geh.)* up there

Droge die; ~, ~n drug
drogen-: ~abhängig, ~süchtig *Adj.* addicted to drugs *postpos.*
Drogerie die; ~, ~n chemist's [shop] *(Brit.);* drugstore *(Amer.);* **Drogist** der; ~en, ~en, **Drogistin** die; ~, ~nen chemist *(Brit.);* druggist *(Amer.)*
drohen *itr., mod. V.* threaten; *(bevorstehen)* be threatening; jmdm. droht etw. sb. is threatened with sth.; **drohend** *Adj.* threatening; *(bevorstehend)* impending
Drohne die; ~, ~n drone
dröhnen *itr. V.* boom; ⟨*machine*⟩ roar
Drohung die; ~, ~en threat
drollig 1. *Adj.* funny; comical; *(niedlich)* sweet; cute *(Amer.);* 2. *adv.: s. Adj.:* comically; sweetly; cutely *(Amer.)*
Dromedar das; ~s, ~e dromedary
Drops der *od.* das; ~, ~: fruit *or (Brit.)* acid drop
drosch *1. u. 3. Pers. Sg. Prät. v.* dreschen
Drossel die; ~, ~n thrush
drosseln *tr. V.* a) turn down ⟨*heating, air-conditioning*⟩; throttle back ⟨*engine*⟩; b) *(herabsetzen)* reduce
Dr. phil. *Abk. doctor philosophiae* Dr
drüben *Adv.* dort *od.* da ~: over there; ~ auf der anderen Seite over on the other side
¹Druck der; ~[e]s, Drücke a) *(auch fig.)* pressure; b) *o. Pl.* ein ~ auf den Knopf a touch of the button; **²Druck** der; ~[e]s, ~e a) *o. Pl.* printing; in ~ gehen go to press; b) *(Produkt)* print; **Druck·buchstabe** der printed letter; **drucken** *tr., itr. V.* print
drücken 1. *tr. V.* a) press; press, push ⟨*button*⟩; squeeze ⟨*juice, pus*⟩ (aus out of); jmdm. die Hand ~: squeeze sb.'s hand; b) *(liebkosen)* jmdn. ~: hug [and squeeze] sb.; c) ⟨*shoe etc.*⟩ pinch; d) *(herabsetzen)* push down ⟨*price, rate*⟩; depress ⟨*sales*⟩; bring down ⟨*standard*⟩; 2. *itr. V.* a) press; auf den Knopf ~: press *or* push the button; ,,bitte ~": 'push'; b) *(Druck verursachen)* ⟨*shoe etc.*⟩ pinch; 3. *refl. V. (ugs.: sich entziehen)* shirk; sich vor etw. *(Dat.)* ~: get out of sth.; **drückend** *Adj.* heavy ⟨*debt, taxes*⟩; serious ⟨*worries*⟩; grinding ⟨*poverty*⟩; b) *(schwül)* oppressive
Drucker der; ~s, ~: printer; **Druckerei** die; ~, ~en printingworks; *(Firma)* printing-house; printer's

druck-, Druck-: ~fehler der misprint; printer's error; **~knopf** der press-stud *(Brit.);* snap-fastener; **~luft** die compressed air; **~mittel** das means of bringing pressure to bear (gegenüber on); **~reif 1.** *Adj.* ready for publication; *(~fertig)* ready for press; **2.** *adv.* ‹*speak*› in a polished manner; **~sache** die *(Postw.)* printed matter; **~schrift** die **a)** printed writing; **b)** *(Schriftart)* type[-face]; **c)** *(Schriftwerk)* pamphlet

drum *Adv. (ugs.)* **a)** *s.* **darum; b)** [a]round; **alles** *od.* **das** [ganze] **Drum und Dran** *(bei einer Mahlzeit)* all the trimmings; *(bei einer Feierlichkeit)* all the palaver that goes with it *(coll.);* **Drum·herum** das; **~s** everything that goes/went with it

drunter *Adv. (ugs.)* underneath; **es** *od.* **alles geht ~ und drüber** everything is topsy-turvy

Drüse die; **~, ~n** gland

Dschungel ['dʒʊŋl̩] der; **~s, ~** *(auch fig.)* jungle

dt. *Abk.* deutsch G.

Dtzd. *Abk.* Dutzend doz.

du *Personalpron.;* **2.** *Pers. Sg. Nom.* you; *(in Briefen)* **Du** you; **du zueinander sagen** use the familiar form in addressing one another; *s. auch (Gen.)* **deiner,** *(Dat.)* **dir,** *(Akk.)* **dich**

Dübel der; **~s, ~:** plug

ducken 1. *refl. V.* duck; **2.** *itr. V. (fig. abwertend)* humble oneself **(vor +** *Dat.* before)

Dudel·sack der bagpipes *pl.*

Duell das; **~s, ~e** duel; **duellieren** *refl. V.* fight a duel

Duett das; **~[e]s, ~e** *(Musik)* duet; **im ~ singen** sing a duet

Duft der; **~[e]s, Düfte** scent; *(von Parfüm, Blumen)* scent; fragrance; *(von Kaffee usw.)* aroma; **duften** *itr. V.* smell **(nach** of)

dulden *tr. V.* tolerate; put up with; **duldsam 1.** *Adj.* tolerant **(gegen** towards); **2.** *adv.* tolerantly

dumm, dümmer, dümmst... 1. *Adj.* **a)** stupid; **b)** *(unvernünftig)* foolish; **c)** *(ugs.: töricht, albern)* idiotic; silly; **d)** *(ugs.: unangenehm)* nasty *(feeling);* annoying ‹*habit*›; **das wird mir jetzt zu ~** *(ugs.)* I've had enough of it; **2.** *adv. (ugs.)* idiotically; **Dumme der/die;** *adj. Dekl.* fool; **der ~ sein** *(ugs.)* be the loser; **dummer·weise** *Adv.* **a)** unfortunately; *(ärgerlicherweise)* annoyingly; **b)** *(törichterweise)* foolishly;

Dummheit die; **~, ~en a)** *o. Pl.* stupidity; **b)** *(unkluge Handlung)* stupid thing; **Dumm·kopf** der *(ugs.)* nitwit *(coll.)*

dumpf 1. *Adj.* **a)** dull ‹*thud, rumble of thunder*›; muffled ‹*sound, thump*›; **b)** *(muffig)* musty; **c)** *(stumpfsinnig)* dull; **2.** *adv.* **a)** ‹*echo*› hollowly; **b)** *(stumpfsinnig)* apathetically

Düne die; **~, ~n** dune

düngen 1. *tr. V.* fertilize ‹*soil, lawn*›; spread fertilizer on ‹*field*›; scatter fertilizer around ‹*plants*›; **2.** *itr. V.* **gut ~** ‹*substance*› be a good fertilizer; **Dünger** der; **~s, ~:** fertilizer

dunkel 1. *Adj. (auch fig.)* dark; *(tief)* deep ‹*voice, note*›; *(undeutlich)* vague; **2.** *adv. (tief)* ‹*speak*› in a deep voice; **b)** *(undeutlich)* vaguely

Dünkel der; **~s** *(geh.)* arrogance; *(Einbildung)* conceit[edness]

dunkel-: ~blond *Adj.* light brown ‹*hair*›; ‹*person*› with light brown hair; **~häutig** *Adj.* dark-skinned

Dunkelheit die; **~:** darkness; **Dunkel·kammer** die dark-room; **dunkeln** *itr. V. (unpers.)* **es dunkelt** *(geh.)* it is growing dark; **Dunkel·ziffer** die number of unrecorded cases

dünn 1. *Adj.* thin; slim ‹*book*›; fine ‹*stocking*›; watery ‹*coffee, tea, beer*›; **2.** *adv.* thinly ‹*sliced, populated*›; lightly ‹*dressed*›

Dunst der; **~[e]s, Dünste a)** *o. Pl.* haze; *(Nebel)* mist; **b)** *(Geruch)* smell; **dünsten** *tr. V.* steam ‹*fish, vegetables*›; braise ‹*meat*›; stew ‹*fruit*›; **dunstig** *Adj.* hazy

Duo das; **~s, ~s** *(Musik)* duet; *(fig. scherzh.)* duo; pair

Duplikat das; **~[e]s, ~e** duplicate

Dur das; **~** *(Musik)* major [key]

durch 1. *Präp. mit Akk.* **a)** *(räumlich)* through; **b)** *(modal)* by; **~ Boten** by courier; **zehn** [geteilt] **~ zwei** ten divided by two; **2.** *Adv.* **a)** *(hin~)* **das ganze Jahr ~:** throughout the whole year; **b)** *(ugs.: vorbei)* **es war 3 Uhr ~:** it was gone 3 o'clock; **c) ~ und ~ naß/ überzeugt** wet through [and through]/completely totally convinced

durch|arbeiten 1. *tr. V.* work through; **2.** *itr. V.* work through; **die Nacht ~:** work through the night

durch·aus *Adv.* absolutely; perfectly; quite ‹*correct, possible, understandable*›; **das ist ~ richtig** that is entirely right; **~ nicht** by no means

durch|beißen *unr. tr. V.* bite through

durch|blättern *tr. V.* leaf through

Durch·blick der *(ugs.)* den |absoluten| ~ **haben** know [exactly] what's going on; **durch|blicken** *itr. V.* **a)** look through; **durch etw.** ~: look through sth.; **b)** ~ **lassen, daß .../wie ...**: hint that .../at how ...

Durch·blutung die; *o. Pl.* flow of blood (+ *Gen.* to); [blood-]circulation

¹**durch|bohren** *tr. V.* drill through ⟨*wall, plank*⟩; drill ⟨*hole*⟩; ²**durchbohren** *tr. V.* pierce

¹**durch|brechen** 1. *unr. tr. V.* etw. ~: break sth. in two; 2. *unr. itr. V.; mit sein* **a)** break in two; **b)** *(hervorkommen)* ⟨*sun*⟩ break through; **c)** *(einbrechen)* fall through ⟨*ice, floor, etc.*⟩; ²**durch·brechen** *unr. tr. V.* break through

durch|brennen *unr. itr. V.; mit sein* **a)** ⟨*heating coil, light bulb*⟩ burn out; ⟨*fuse*⟩ blow; **b)** *(ugs.: weglaufen) (von zu Hause)* run away; *(mit der Kasse, mit dem Geliebten/der Geliebten)* run off

durch|bringen *unr. tr. V.* get through; *(bei Wahlen)* **jmdn.** ~: get sb. elected; **seine Familie/sich** ~: support one's family/ oneself

Durch·bruch der *(fig.)* breakthrough

durch|drehen 1. *tr. V.* put ⟨*meat*⟩ through the mincer *or* ⟨*Amer.*⟩ grinder; 2. *itr. V.* auch *mit sein (ugs.)* crack up *(coll.)*

¹**durch|dringen** *unr. tr. V.; mit sein* ⟨*rain, sun*⟩ come through; ²**durchdringen** *unr. tr. V.* penetrate; **jmdn.** ~ ⟨*idea*⟩ take hold of sb. [completely]

durch·einander *Adv.* ~ **sein** ⟨*papers, desk, etc.*⟩ be in a muddle; *(verwirrt sein)* be confused; *(aufgeregt sein)* be flustered; **Durcheinander das;** ~s **a)** muddle; mess; **b)** *(Wirrwarr)* confusion

durcheinander|bringen *unr. tr. V.* **a)** get ⟨*room, flat*⟩ into a mess; get ⟨*papers, file*⟩ into a muddle; muddle up ⟨*papers, file*⟩; **b)** *(verwirren)* confuse; **c)** *(verwechseln)* confuse ⟨*names etc.*⟩; get ⟨*names etc.*⟩ mixed up

durch|fahren *unr. itr. V.; mit sein* **a)** |durch etw.| ~: drive through [sth.]; **b)** *(nicht anhalten)* go straight through; *(mit dem Auto)* drive straight through; **der Zug fährt |in H.| durch** the train doesn't stop [at H.]; **Durch·fahrt die a)** „~ **verboten"** 'no entry except for

access'; **auf der** ~ **sein** be passing through; **b)** *(Weg)* thoroughfare; „**bitte |die|** ~ **freihalten"** 'please do not obstruct'

Durch·fall der diarrhoea *no art.;* **durch|fallen** *unr. itr. V.; mit sein* **a)** fall through; **b)** *(ugs.: nicht bestehen)* fail

durch|finden *unr. refl. V.* find one's way through

durchführbar *Adj.* practicable; **durch|führen** 1. *tr. V.* carry out; put into effect ⟨*decision, programme*⟩; perform ⟨*operation*⟩; hold ⟨*meeting, election, examination*⟩; 2. *itr. V.* durch etw./unter etw. *(Dat.)* ~ ⟨*track, road*⟩ go through/under sth.; **Durch·führung** die carrying out; *(einer Operation)* performing; *(einer Versammlung, Wahl, Prüfung)* holding; *(eines Wettbewerbs)* staging

Durch·gang der **a)** passage[way]; „**kein** ~", „ ~ **verboten"** 'no thoroughfare'; **b)** *(Phase)* stage; *(einer Versuchsreihe)* run; *(Sport, Wahlen)* round

Durchgangs-: ~**straße die** through road; ~**verkehr der** through traffic

durch|geben *unr. tr. V.* announce ⟨*news*⟩; give ⟨*results, weather report*⟩; **eine Meldung im Radio/Fernsehen** ~: make an announcement on the radio/ on television

durch·gefroren *Adj.* frozen stiff; chilled to the bone

durch|gehen 1. *unr. itr. V.; mit sein* **a)** |durch etw.| ~: go *or* walk through [sth.]; **b)** *(hindurchdringen)* |durch etw.| ~: ⟨*rain, water*⟩ come through [sth.]; **c)** *(direkt zum Ziel führen)* ⟨*train etc.*⟩ go [right] through (bis to); ⟨*flight*⟩ go direct; **d)** *(andauern)* go on (bis zu until); **e)** *(hingenommen werden)* ⟨*discrepancy*⟩ be tolerated; ⟨*mistake, discourtesy*⟩ be allowed to pass; **jmdm. etw.** ~ **lassen** let sb. get away with sth. **f)** ⟨*horse*⟩ bolt; 2. *unr. tr. V.; mit sein* go through ⟨*newspaper, text*⟩

durch·gehend 1. *Adj.* **a)** continuous ⟨*line, pattern, etc.*⟩; constantly recurring ⟨*motif*⟩; **b)** *(direkt)* through ⟨*attrib.* ⟨*train, carriage*⟩; direct ⟨*flight, connection*⟩; 2. *adv.* ~ **geöffnet haben/bleiben** be/stay open all day

durch|greifen *unr. itr. V.* |hart| ~: take drastic measures *or* steps

durch|halten 1. *unr. itr. V.* hold out; *(bei einer schwierigen Aufgabe)* see it through; 2. *unr. tr. V.* stand

durch|hängen *unr. itr. V.* sag

durch|kämmen *tr. V.* **a)** comb ⟨*hair*⟩ through; **b)** *(durchsuchen)* comb ⟨*area etc.*⟩

durch|kommen *unr. itr. V.; mit sein* **a)** come through; *(mit Mühe)* get through; **b)** *(ugs.: beim Telefonieren)* get through; **c)** *(durchgehen, -fahren usw.)* **durch etw.** ~: come through sth.; **d)** *(ugs.: überleben)* pull through

¹durch|kreuzen *tr. V.* cross out; **²durch·kreuzen** *tr. V. (vereiteln)* frustrate

durch|lassen *unr. tr. V.* **a)** jmdn. |durch etw.| ~: let sb. through [sth.]; **b)** *(durchlässig sein)* let ⟨*light, water, etc.*⟩ through; **durchlässig** *Adj.* permeable; *(porös)* porous; *(undicht)* leaky; ⟨*raincoat, shoe*⟩ that lets in water

Durch·lauf der *(Sport, DV)* run; **¹durch|laufen** **1.** *unr. itr. V.; mit sein* **a)** |durch etw.| ~: run through [sth.]; *(durchrinnen)* trickle through [sth.]; **b)** *(passieren)* ⟨*runners*⟩ run *or* pass through; **c)** *(ohne Pause laufen)* run without stopping; **2.** *unr. tr. V.* go through ⟨*soles*⟩; **²durch·laufen** *unr. tr. V.* go through ⟨*phase, stage*⟩; **durchlaufend 1.** *Adj.* continuous; **2.** *adv.* ⟨*numbered, marked*⟩ in sequence

durch|lesen *unr. tr. V.* **etw.** |ganz| ~: read sth. [all the way] through

durch·leuchten *tr. V.* x-ray; *(fig.)* investigate ⟨*case, matter, problem, etc.*⟩ thoroughly

durch·löchern *tr. V.* make holes in

durch|machen *(ugs.)* **1.** *tr. V.* **a)** undergo ⟨*change*⟩; complete ⟨*training course*⟩; go through ⟨*stage, phase*⟩; serve ⟨*apprenticeship*⟩; **b)** *(erleiden)* go through; **c)** *(durcharbeiten)* work through ⟨*lunch-break etc.*⟩; **2.** *itr. V.* *(durcharbeiten)* work [right] through; *(durchfeiern)* celebrate all night/day *etc.*; keep going all night/day *etc.*

Durchmesser der; ~s, ~: diameter

durch|nehmen *unr. tr. V. (Schulw.: behandeln)* do

durch|probieren *tr. V.* taste ⟨*wines, cakes, etc.*⟩ one after another

durch·queren *tr. V.* cross; travel across ⟨*country*⟩; ⟨*train*⟩ go through ⟨*country*⟩

durch|rechnen *tr. V.* calculate ⟨*costs etc.*⟩ [down to the last penny]; check ⟨*bill*⟩ thoroughly

Durch·reise die journey through; **durch|reisen** *itr. V.; mit sein* travel

through; **Durchreise·visum** das transit visa

durch|reißen 1. *unr. tr. V.* **etw.** ~: tear sth. in two *or* in half; **2.** *unr. itr. V.; mit sein* ⟨*fabric, garment*⟩ rip, tear; ⟨*thread, rope*⟩ snap [in two]

durch|rosten *itr. V.; mit sein* rust through

durchs *Präp. + Art.* = **durch das**

Durch·sage die announcement; *(an eine bestimmte Person)* message

durchschaubar *Adj.* transparent; **leicht** ~ easy to see through; **durchschauen** *tr. V.* **a)** see through ⟨*person, plan, etc.*⟩; see ⟨*situation*⟩ clearly

durch|schlafen *unr. itr. V.* sleep [right] through

Durch·schlag der **a)** *(Kopie)* carbon [copy]; **b)** *(Küchengerät)* strainer; **durch|schlagen** *unr. tr. V.* **etw.** ~: chop sth. in two; **durchschlagend** *Adj.* resounding ⟨*success*⟩; decisive ⟨*effect, measures*⟩; conclusive ⟨*evidence*⟩

durch|schneiden *unr. tr. V.* cut through ⟨*thread, cable*⟩; cut ⟨*ribbon, sheet of paper*⟩ in two; cut ⟨*throat, umbilical cord*⟩; **etw. in der Mitte** ~: cut sth. in half; **Durch·schnitt** der average; **im** ~: on average; **über/unter dem** ~ **liegen** be above/below average; **durchschnittlich 1.** *Adj.* **a)** *nicht präd.* average ⟨*growth, performance, output*⟩; **b)** *(ugs.: nicht außergewöhnlich)* ordinary ⟨*life, person, etc.*⟩; **c)** *(mittelmäßig)* modest; ordinary ⟨*appearance*⟩; **2.** *adv.* ⟨*earn etc.*⟩ on [an] average; ~ **groß** of average height

Durchschnitts-: ~**alter** das average age; ~**geschwindigkeit** die average speed

Durch·schrift die carbon [copy]

durch|sehen 1. *unr. itr. V.* |durch etw.| ~: look through [sth.]; **2.** *unr. tr. V.* look through

durch|sein *unr. itr. V., mit sein; nur im Inf. u. Part. zusammengeschrieben* *(ugs.)* **a)** |durch etw.| ~: be through [sth.]; **b)** *(abgefahren sein)* ⟨*train, bus, etc.*⟩ have gone; **c)** *(fertig sein)* have finished; **durch etw.** ~: have got through sth.; **d)** ⟨*cheese*⟩ be ripe; ⟨*meat*⟩ be well done

durch|setzen 1. *tr. V.* carry through; achieve ⟨*objective*⟩; enforce ⟨*demand, claim*⟩; **2.** *refl. V.* assert oneself; ⟨*idea etc.*⟩ find *or* gain acceptance

Durch·sicht die: **nach** ~ **der Unterlagen** after looking *or* checking through the documents; **dụrchsichtig** *Adj.* *(auch fig.)* transparent

dụrch|sprechen *unr. tr. V.* talk ⟨*matter etc.*⟩ over; discuss ⟨*matter etc.*⟩ thoroughly

dụrch|stehen *unr. tr. V.* stand ⟨*pace, boring job*⟩; come through ⟨*difficult situation*⟩; get over ⟨*illness*⟩

dụrch|stellen *tr. V.* put ⟨*call*⟩ through (in + *Akk.*, **auf** + *Akk.* to)

dụrch|streichen *unr. tr. V.* cross out; *(in Formularen)* delete

durch·sụchen *tr. V.* search (**nach** for); search, scour ⟨*area*⟩ (**nach** for); **Durchsụchung** die; ~, ~en search

dụrch|treten *unr. tr. V.* press ⟨*clutch-, brake-pedal*⟩ right down

durchtrịeben *(abwertend)* 1. *Adj.* crafty; sly; 2. *adv.* craftily; slyly

durch·wạchsen *Adj.* ~er Speck streaky bacon

Dụrchwahl die; **a)** direct dialling; **mein Apparat hat keine ~:** I don't have an outside line; **b)** *s.* Durchwahlnummer; **dụrch|wählen** *itr. V.* **a)** dial direct; **b)** *(bei Nebenstellenanlagen)* dial straight through; **Dụrchwahl·nummer die** number of the/one's direct line

dụrch|zählen *tr. V.* count; count up

dụrch|ziehen 1. *unr. tr. V.* jmdn./etw. |durch etw.| ~: pull sb./sth. through [sth.]; **ein Gummiband |durch etw.| ~:** draw an elastic through [sth.]; 2. *unr. itr. V.; mit sein* pass through; ⟨*soldiers*⟩ march through

Dụrch·zug der o. Pl. draught

dụ̈rfen 1. *unr. Modalverb;* 2. *Part.* ~ **a)** etw. tun ~: be allowed to do sth.; **darf ich rauchen?** may I smoke?; **was darf es sein?** can I help you?; **b)** *Konjunktiv II + Inf.* **das dürfte der Grund sein** that is probably the reason; 2. *unr. tr., itr. V.* **er hat nicht gedurft** he was not allowed to; **dụrfte,** *1. u. 3. Pers. Sg. Prät. v.* dürfen; **dụ̈rfte** *1. u. 3. Pers. Sg. Konjunktiv II v.* dürfen

dụ̈rr *Adj.* **a)** withered; arid, barren ⟨*ground, earth*⟩; **b)** *(mager)* scrawny; **Dụ̈rre** die; ~, ~n drought

Dụrst der; ~|e|s thirst; ~ **haben** be thirsty; **ich habe ~ auf ein Bier** I could just drink a beer; **dụrstig** *Adj.* thirsty; **durst·stillend** *Adj.* thirst-quenching

Dụsche die; ~, ~n shower; **dụschen** *itr., refl. V.* have a shower

Dụ̈se die; ~, ~n *(Technik)* nozzle; *(eines Vergasers)* jet

Dụ̈sen-: ~**flugzeug das** jet aircraft; ~**motor der** jet engine

dụ̈ster 1. *Adj.* **a)** dark; gloomy; dim ⟨*light*⟩; **b)** *(fig.)* gloomy; sombre ⟨*colour, music*⟩; 2. *adv. (fig.)* gloomily

Dụtzend das; ~s, ~e dozen; **zwei ~:** two dozen; **dụtzend·weise** *Adv.* in [their] dozens *(coll.)*

dụzen *tr. V.* call ⟨*sb.*⟩ 'du' *(the familiar form of address)*

dynạmisch 1. *Adj.* **a)** *(auch fig.)* dynamic; 2. *adv.* dynamically

Dynamịt das; ~s dynamite

Dynạmo der; ~s, ~s dynamo

Dynastịe die; ~, ~n dynasty

D-Zug ['de:-] der express train

E

e, E [e:] das; ~, ~ **a)** *(Buchstabe)* e/E; **b)** *(Musik)* [key of] E

Ẹbbe die; ~, ~n ebb tide; *(Zustand)* low tide; **es ist ~:** the tide is out

eben 1. *Adj.* **a)** flat; **b)** *(glatt)* level; 2. *adv.* **a)** *(gerade jetzt)* just; **b)** *(kurz)* [for] a moment; **Ẹbene die,** ~, ~n **a)** plain; **in der ~:** on the plain; **b)** *(Geom., Physik)* plane; **c)** *(fig.)* level

ẹben·falls *Adv.* likewise; as well; **danke, ~:** thank you, [and] [the] same to you

Ẹben·holz das ebony

eben·so *Adv.* **a)** *mit Adjektiven* just as; **b)** *mit Verben* in exactly the same way

ebenso-: ~**gern** *Adv.* ~**gern mag ich Erdbeeren |wie ...|** I like strawberries just as much [as ...]; ~**gern würde ich an den Strand gehen** I would just as soon go to the beach; ~**gut** *Adv.* just as well; ~**sehr** *Adv.* **a)** *mit Adjektiven* just as; **b)** *mit Verben* just as much

Ẹber der; ~s, ~: boar

Ẹber·esche die rowan; mountain ash

ẹbnen *tr. V.* level ⟨*ground*⟩

Ẹcho das; ~s, ~s echo

ẹcht 1. *Adj.* **a)** genuine; real ⟨*love, friendship*⟩; **b)** *nicht präd. (typisch)* real, typical; 2. *adv.* **a)** *(ugs. verstärkend)* really; **b)** *(typisch)* typically

Eck-: ~**ball** der *(Sport)* corner[-kick/
-hit/-throw]; **einen** ~**ball treten** take a
corner; ~**bank** die corner seat
Ecke die; ~, ~**n** corner; **an der** ~: on
or at the corner; **um die** ~: round the
corner; **eckig** *Adj.* square; angular
Eck·zahn der canine tooth
edel *Adj.* **a)** *nicht präd.* thoroughbred
⟨*horse*⟩; species ⟨*rose*⟩; **b)** *(großmütig)*
noble[-minded], high-minded ⟨*per-
son*⟩; noble ⟨*thought, gesture, feelings,
deed*⟩; honourable ⟨*motive*⟩
Edel-: ~**metall** das precious metal;
~**stahl** der stainless steel; ~**stein** der
precious stone; gem[stone]
Edition die; ~, ~**en** edition
EDV *Abk.* **elektronische Datenverarbeitung** EDP
Efeu der; ~**s** ivy
Effekt der; ~[e]s, ~**e** effect; **effekt-
voll** *Adj.* effective; dramatic ⟨*pause,
gesture, entrance*⟩
EG ['e:'ge:] die; ~ *Abk.* **a) Europäische
Gemeinschaft** EC; **b) Erdgeschoß**
egal *Adj. nicht attr. (ugs.: einerlei)* es
ist jmdm. ~: it's all the same to sb.;
[ganz] ~, **wie/wer** *usw.* ...: no matter
how/who *etc.* ...
Egge die; ~, ~**n** harrow
ehe *Konj.* before
Ehe die; ~, ~**n** marriage
Ehe-: ~**bett** das marriage-bed; *(Doppelbett)* double bed; ~**frau** die wife;
(verheiratete Frau) married woman;
~**krach** der *(ugs.)* row; ~**leute** *Pl.*
married couple
ehelich *Adj.* marital; matrimonial;
conjugal ⟨*rights, duties*⟩; legitimate
⟨*child*⟩
ehemalig *Adj.* former
Ehe-: ~**mann** der; *Pl.* ~**männer** husband; *(verheirateter Mann)* married
man; ~**paar** das married couple
eher *Adv.* **a)** *(früher)* earlier; sooner;
b) *(lieber)* rather; sooner
Ehe-: ~**ring** der wedding-ring;
~**scheidung** die divorce
Ehre die; ~, ~**n** honour; jmdm. ~ an-
tun pay tribute to sb.; **ehren** *tr. V.* **a)**
honour; **Sehr geehrter Herr Mül-
ler!/Sehr geehrte Frau Müller!** Dear
Herr Müller/Dear Frau Müller; **b)**
(Ehre machen) deine Hilfsbereitschaft
ehrt dich your willingness to help does
you credit; **ehrenhaft** *Adj.* honourable
ehren-, **Ehren-:** ~**rührig** *Adj.*
defamatory ⟨*allegations*⟩; ~**sache**
die: das ist ~**sache** that is a point of

honour; ~**sache**! you can count on
me!; ~**voll** *Adj.* honourable; ~**wert**
Adj. (geh.) worthy; ~**wort** das; *pl.*
~**worte:** ~**wort** [!/?] word of honour
[!/?]
ehrerbietig *Adj. (geh.)* respectful
Ehr·furcht die reverence (**vor** + *Dat.*
for); **ehrfürchtig** *Adj.* reverent
ehr-, **Ehr-:** ~**gefühl** das; *o. Pl.* sense
of honour; ~**geiz** der ambition;
~**geizig** *Adj.* ambitious
ehrlich *Adj.* honest; genuine ⟨*concern,
desire, admiration*⟩; upright ⟨*character*⟩; **Ehrlichkeit** die; ~ *s.* ehrlich:
honesty; genuineness; uprightness
ehr·los *Adj.* dishonourable
Ehrung die; ~, ~**en:** die ~ der Preisträger the prize-giving *(Brit.) or
(Amer.)* awards ceremony; **bei der** ~
der Sieger when the winners were
awarded their medals/trophies
ehr·würdig *Adj.* venerable
Ei das; ~[e]s, ~**er** egg
Eiche die; ~, ~**n** oak[-tree]; *(Holz)*
oak[-wood]
Eichel die; ~, ~**n** acorn
eichen *tr. V.* calibrate ⟨*measuring instrument, thermometer*⟩; standardize
⟨*weights, measures, containers, products*⟩; adjust ⟨*weighing-scales*⟩
Eich·hörnchen das squirrel
Eid der; ~[e]s, ~**e** oath
Eidechse ['aidɛksə] die; ~, ~**n** lizard
eide·stattlich *Adj. (Rechtsw.)* eine
~**e Erklärung** a statutory declaration
Ei·dotter der *od.* das egg yolk
Eier-: ~**becher** der egg-cup; ~**kuchen** der pancake; *(Omelett)* omelette; ~**likör** der egg-liqueur;
~**stock** der *(Physiol., Zool.)* ovary;
~**uhr** die egg-timer
Eifer der; ~**s** eagerness
Eifer·sucht die jealousy (**auf** + *Akk.*
of); **eifer·süchtig** *Adj.* jealous (**auf**
+ *Akk.* of)
eifrig *Adj.* eager
Ei·gelb das; ~[e]s, ~**e** egg yolk
eigen *Adj.* own; *(selbständig)* separate
eigen-, **Eigen-:** ~**art** die *(Wesensart)*
particular nature; *(Zug)* peculiarity;
eine ~**art dieser Stadt** one of the characteristic features of this city; ~**artig**
Adj. peculiar; strange; odd; ~**hän-
dig 1.** *Adj.* personal ⟨*signature*⟩;
holographic ⟨*will, document*⟩; **2.** *adv.*
⟨*present, sign*⟩ personally; ~**heim** das
house of one's own
Eigenheit die; ~, ~**en** peculiarity
eigen-, **Eigen-:** ~**lob** das self-praise;

~**mächtig** *Adj.* unauthorized; ~**na-me** der proper name; ~**nützig** *Adj.* self-seeking; selfish ⟨*motive*⟩

eigens *Adv.* specially

Eigenschaft die; ~, ~en quality; characteristic; *(von Sachen, Stoffen)* property

Eigenschafts·wort das adjective

eigen-, Eigen-: ~**sinn** der; *o. Pl.* obstinacy; ~**sinnig** *Adj.* obstinate; ~**ständig** *Adj.* independent

eigentlich 1. *Adj. (wirklich)* actual; real; *(wahr)* true; *(ursprünglich)* original; 2. *Adv.* actually; 3. *Partikel* wie spät ist es ~? tell me, what time is it?; was willst du ~? what exactly do you want?

Eigen·tor das *(Ballspiele, fig.)* own goal

Eigentum das; ~s property; *(einschließlich Geld usw.)* assets *pl.*

Eigentümer der; ~s, ~: owner; *(Hotel~, Geschäfts~)* proprietor; **Eigentümerin** die; ~, ~nen owner; *(Hotel~, Geschäfts~)* proprietress; proprietor; **Eigentums·wohnung** die owner-occupied flat *(Brit.)*; condominium apartment *(Amer.)*

eigen·willig *Adj.* self-willed

eignen *refl. V.* be suitable; **Eignung** die; ~: suitability; seine ~ zum Fliegen his aptitude for flying

Eignungs-: ~**prüfung** die, ~**test** der aptitude test

Eil-: ~**bote** der special messenger; „durch *od.* per ~**boten"** *(veralt.)* 'express'; ~**brief** der express letter

Eile die; ~: hurry; in ~ sein be in a hurry; **eilen** *itr. V.* a) *mit sein* hurry; *(besonders schnell)* rush; b) *(dringend sein)* be urgent; „eilt!" 'urgent'; **eilig** 1. *Adj.* a) hurried; es ~ haben be in a hurry; b) *(dringend)* urgent; 2. *adv.* hurriedly; **Eil·zug** der semi-fast train

Eimer der; ~s, ~: bucket; *(Milch~)* pail; *(Abfall~)* bin; ein ~ [voll] Wasser a bucket of water; im ~ sein *(salopp)* be up the spout *(sl.)*

¹**ein** 1. *Kardinalz.* one; 2. *unbest. Art.* a/an; 3. *Indefinitpron; s.* irgendein a; *s. auch* einer

²**ein** *(elliptisch)* ~ – aus *(an Schaltern)* on – off

Einakter der; ~s, ~: one-act play

einander *reziprokes Pron.; Dat. u. Akk. (geh.)* each other; one another

ein|arbeiten *tr. V.* train *(employee)*

ein·armig *Adj.* one-armed

ein|äschern *tr. V.* cremate

ein|atmen *tr., itr. V.* breathe in

ein·äugig *Adj.* one-eyed

Ein·bahn·straße die one-way street

Ein·band der; *Pl.* -bände binding

Ein·bau der; ~s, ~ten fitting; *(eines Motors)* installation; **ein|bauen** *tr. V.* build in, fit; install ⟨*engine, motor*⟩; **Einbau·küche** die fitted kitchen

ein·beinig *Adj.* one-legged

ein|berufen *unr. tr. V.* summon; call; **Ein·berufung** die a) *(das Einberufen)* calling; b) *(zur Wehrpflicht)* call-up; conscription; draft *(Amer.)*

Einbett·zimmer das single room

ein|beziehen *unr. tr. V.* include

ein|biegen *unr. itr. V.; mit sein* turn

ein|bilden *refl. V.* a) sich *(Dat.)* etw. ~: imagine sth.; b) *(ugs.)* sich *(Dat.)* etwas ~: be conceited (**auf** + *Akk.* about); **Ein·bildung** die; ~, ~en a) imagination; b) *(falsche Vorstellung)* fantasy; c) *(Hochmut)* conceitedness

ein|binden *unr. tr. V.* bind ⟨*book*⟩; etw. neu ~: rebind sth.

ein|blenden *tr. V. (Rundf., Ferns., Film)* insert

Ein·blick der a) view; ~ in etw. *(Akk.)* haben be able to see into sth.; b) *(Durchsicht)* jmdm. ~ in etw. *(Akk.)* gewähren allow sb. to look at *or* examine sth.; c) *(Kenntnis)* insight

ein|brechen *unr. itr. V.* a) *mit haben od. sein* break in; in eine Bank ~: break into a bank; bei jmdm. ~: burgle sb.; b) *mit sein (einstürzen)* ⟨*roof, ceiling*⟩ cave in; c) *mit sein (durchbrechen)* fall through; **Einbrecher** der; ~s, ~: burglar

ein|bringen *unr. tr. V.* a) bring in ⟨*harvest*⟩; b) *(verschaffen)* Gewinn/Zinsen ~: yield a profit/bring in interest; jmdm. Ruhm ~: bring sb. fame; c) *(Parl.: vorlegen)* introduce ⟨*bill*⟩; d) invest ⟨*capital, money*⟩

Ein·bruch der a) burglary; ein ~ in eine Bank a break-in at a bank; b) *(das Einstürzen)* collapse

ein|bürgern 1. *tr. V.* naturalize; 2. *refl. V.* ⟨*custom, practice*⟩ become established; ⟨*person, plant, animal*⟩ become naturalized; **Einbürgerung** die; ~, ~en naturalization

Einbuße die loss; **ein|büßen** *tr. V.* lose; *(durch eigene Schuld)* forfeit

ein|checken *tr., itr. V. (Flugw.)* check in

ein|cremen *tr. V.* put cream on ⟨*hands etc.*⟩; sich ~: put cream on

ein|dämmen *tr. V. (fig.)* check; stem

ein|decken 1. *refl. V.* stock up; **2.** *tr.*
V. (ugs.: überhäufen) **jmdn. mit Arbeit
~:** swamp sb. with work

eindeutig *Adj.* clear; **Eindeutigkeit
die; ~, ~en** clarity

ein|dringen *unr. itr. V.; mit sein* in
etw. *(Akk.)* ~**:** penetrate into sth.; *(bullet)* pierce sth.; *(allmählich)* *(water,
sand, etc.)* seep into sth.; **ein · dringlich** *Adj.* urgent; impressive *(voice)*;
forceful, powerful *(words)*;
Eindringling der; ~s, ~e intruder

Ein · druck der; ~[e]s, Eindrücke im-
pression; **ein|drücken** *tr. V.* smash
in *(mudguard, bumper)*; stave in *(side
of ship)*; smash *(pier, column, support)*; break *(window)*; crush *(ribs)*;
flatten *(nose)*; **eindrucks · voll 1.**
Adj. impressive; **2.** *adv.* impressively

eine *s.* ¹**ein**

ein|ebnen *tr. V.* level

eineiig ['ain|aiiç] *Adj.* identical *(twins)*

ein · ein · halb *Bruchz.* one and a half;
~ Stunden an hour and a half

ein|engen *tr. V.* a) **jmdn. ~:** restrict
sb.'s movement[s]; b) *(fig.)* restrict

einer, eine, eines, eins Indefinitpron. *(man)* one; *(jemand)* someone;
somebody; *(fragend, verneint)*
anyone; anybody; **kaum einer** hardly
anybody; **ein[e]s ist sicher** one thing is
for sure

Einer der; ~s, ~ a) *(Math.)* unit; b)
(Sport) single sculler; **im ~:** in the
single sculls

einerlei *Adj.* **~, ob/wo/wer** *usw.* no
matter whether/where/who *etc.;* **es ist
~:** it makes no difference

Einerlei das; ~s monotony

einerseits *Adv.* on the one hand

ein · fach 1. *Adj.* a) simple; b) *(nicht
mehrfach)* single *(knot, ticket, journey)*; **2.** *Partikel* simply; just;
Einfachheit die; ~: simplicity

ein|fädeln 1. *tr. V.* thread **(in +** *Akk.*
into); **2.** *refl. V. (Verkehrsw.)* filter in

ein|fahren 1. *unr. itr. V.; mit sein*
come in *(train)* pull in; **in den Bahnhof ~:** pull into the station; **2.** *unr. tr.
V.* a) bring in *(harvest)*; b) *(beschädigen)* knock down *(wall)*; smash in
(mudguard); **Ein · fahrt die** a) *(das
Hineinfahren)* entry; **Vorsicht bei der
~ des Zuges!** stand clear [of the edge
of the platform], the train is ap-
proaching; b) *(Zufahrt)* entrance;
(Autobahn~) slip road; **„keine ~"** 'no
entry'

Ein · fall der a) *(Idee)* idea; b) *o. Pl.*

(Licht~) incidence *(Optics)*; **ein|fal-
len** *unr. itr. V.; mit sein* a) **jmdm. ~:**
occur to sb.; **was fällt dir denn ein!**
what do you think you're doing?; b)
(in Erinnerung kommen) **ihr Name
fällt mir nicht ein** I cannot think of her
name; **plötzlich fiel ihr ein, daß ...:**
suddenly she remembered that ...; c)
(von Licht) come in

einfalls-: ~los *Adj.* unimaginative;
lacking in ideas; **~reich** *Adj.* imaginative; full of ideas

Einfalt die; ~: simpleness; simple-
mindedness; **einfältig** *Adj.* simple;
naïve; naïve *(remarks)*

ein|fangen *unr. tr. V.* catch

ein|fassen *tr. V.* border; edge; frame
(picture); set *(gem)*; edge *(grave, lawn,
etc.)*; **Ein · fassung die** *s.* **einfassen:**
border; edging; frame; setting

ein|finden *unr. refl. V.* arrive; *(sich
treffen)* meet; *(crowd)* gather

ein|fliegen *unr. tr. V.* fly in

ein|flößen *tr. V.* a) **jmdm. Tee ~:** pour
tea into sb.'s mouth; b) *(fig.)* **jmdm.
Angst ~:** put fear into sb.

Ein · fluß der influence; **Einfluß · bereich der** sphere of influence;
einfluß · reich *Adj.* influential

ein · förmig *Adj.* monotonous

ein|frieren 1. *unr. itr. V.; mit sein*
freeze; *(pipes)* freeze up; **2.** *unr. tr. V.*
a) deep-freeze *(food)*; b) *(fig.)* freeze

ein|fügen *tr. V.* fit in; **etw. in etw.**
(Akk.) ~**:** fit sth. into sth.

ein|fühlen *refl. V.* **sich in jmdn. ~:** em-
pathize with sb.; **einfühlsam** *Adj.*
understanding; **Ein · fühlung die; ~:**
empathy **(in +** *Akk.* with)

Ein · fuhr die; ~, ~en *s.* Import;
ein|führen *tr. V.* a) *(als Neuerung)*
introduce *(fashion, method, technology)*; b) *(importieren)* import;
Ein · führung die introduction

Ein · gabe die petition; *(Beschwerde)*
complaint

Ein · gang der entrance; **„kein ~"** 'no
entry'; **ein · gängig** *Adj.* catchy;
eingangs *Adv.* at the beginning;
pedes

Eingangs-: ~halle die entrance hall;
(eines Hotels, Theaters) foyer; **~tür
die** *(von Kaufhaus, Hotel usw.)* [en-
trance] door; *(von Wohnung, Haus
usw.)* front door

ein · gebildet *Adj.* a) imaginary *(illness)*; b) *(arrogant)* conceited

Eingeborene der/die; *adj. Dekl. (veralt.)* native

ein|gehen 1. *unr. itr. V.; mit sein* a) arrive; b) *(fig.)* in die Geschichte ~: go down in history; c) *(schrumpfen)* shrink; d) auf eine Frage ~/nicht ~: go into *or* deal with/ignore a question; auf jmdn. ~: be responsive to sb.; auf jmdn. nicht ~: ignore sb.'s wishes; 2. *unr. tr. V.* enter into ⟨*contract, matrimony*⟩; take ⟨*risk*⟩; accept ⟨*obligation*⟩

eingehend *Adj.* detailed

Ein·gemachte das; ~n preserved fruit/vegetables

ein|gemeinden *tr. V.* incorporate ⟨*village*⟩ (in + *Akk.,* nach into)

ein·geschnappt *Adj. (ugs.)* huffy

Ein·geständnis das confession; admission; ein|gestehen *unr. tr. V.* admit

Eingeweide das; ~s, ~; *meist Pl.* entrails *pl.;* innards *pl.*

ein|gewöhnen *refl. V.* get used to one's new surroundings

ein|gießen *unr. tr., itr. V.* pour in

ein|gliedern *tr. V.* integrate (in + *Akk.* into); incorporate ⟨*village, company*⟩ (in + *Akk.* into); *(einordnen)* include (in + *Akk.* in)

ein|graben *unr. tr. V.* bury (in + *Akk.* in); sink ⟨*pile, pipe*⟩ (in + *Akk.* into)

ein|gravieren *tr. V.* engrave (in + *Akk.* on)

ein|greifen *unr. itr. V.* intervene (in + *Akk.* in); Ein·griff der a) intervention (in + *Akk.* in); b) *(Med.)* operation

ein|haken 1. *tr. V.* a) *(mit Haken befestigen)* fasten; b) sich ~: link arms; 2. *refl. V.* sich bei jmdm. ~: link arms with sb.

Ein·halt der: jmdm./einer Sache ~ gebieten *od.* tun *(geh.)* halt sb./sth.; ein|halten 1. *unr. tr. V.* keep ⟨*appointment*⟩; meet ⟨*deadline, commitments*⟩; keep to ⟨*diet, speed-limit, agreement*⟩; observe ⟨*regulation*⟩; 2. *unr. itr. V. (geh.)* stop

ein·heimisch *Adj.* native; home *attrib.* ⟨*team*⟩; Einheimische der/die; *adj. Dekl.* local

Einheit die; ~, ~en unity; einheitlich 1. *Adj.* unified; *(unterschiedslos)* uniform ⟨*dress*⟩; standard ⟨*procedure, practice*⟩; 2. *adv.* ~ gekleidet sein be dressed the same

einhellig 1. *Adj.* unanimous; 2. *adv.* unanimously

ein|holen 1. *tr. V.* a) catch up with ⟨*person, vehicle*⟩; b) make up ⟨*arrears, time*⟩; 2. *itr. V. (ugs.)* s. einkaufen 1

ein·hundert *Kardinalz. s.* hundert

einig *Adj.* sich *(Dat.)* ~ sein be agreed; sich *(Dat.)* ~ werden reach agreement

einig... *Indefinitpron. u. unbest. Zahlwort* some; ~e wenige a few; ~e hundert several hundred

einigen 1. *tr. V.* unite; 2. *refl. V.* reach an agreement

einigermaßen *Adv.* somewhat

Einigkeit die; ~ a) unity; b) *(Übereinstimmung)* agreement

ein·jährig *Adj.* one-year-old *attrib.;* one year old *pred.; (ein Jahr dauernd)* one-year *attrib.*

Ein·kauf der a) Einkäufe machen do some shopping; b) *(eingekaufte Ware)* purchase; c) *o. Pl. (Abteilung)* purchasing department; ein|kaufen 1. *itr. V.* shop; ~ gehen go shopping; 2. *tr. V.* buy; purchase; Ein·käufer der buyer; purchaser

Einkaufs-: ~bummel der [leisurely] shopping expedition; ~zentrum das shopping centre

ein|kehren *itr. V.; mit sein* stop; in einem Wirtshaus ~: stop at an inn

ein|klammern *tr. V.* etw. ~: put sth. in brackets; bracket sth.

Ein·klang der harmony; in *od.* im ~ stehen accord

ein|kleben *tr. V.* stick in

ein|kleiden *tr. V.* clothe

ein|klemmen *tr. V.* a) *(quetschen)* catch; b) *(fest einfügen)* clamp

ein|kochen *tr. V.* preserve ⟨*fruit etc.*⟩

Einkommen das; ~s, ~: income

ein|kreisen *tr. V.* a) etw. ~: put a circle round sth.; b) *(umzingeln)* surround

Einkünfte *Pl.* income *sing.;* feste ~: a regular income

¹ein|laden *unr. tr. V.* load ⟨*goods*⟩

²ein|laden *unr. tr. V.* invite ⟨*person*⟩ (zu for); einladend *Adj.* inviting; Ein·ladung die invitation

Ein·lage die a) *(in Brief)* enclosure; b) *(Kochk.)* vegetables, dumplings, etc. added to a clear soup; c) *(Schuh~)* arch-support; d) *(Programm~)* interlude

ein|lagern *tr. V.* store; lay in ⟨*stores*⟩

Einlaß der; Einlasses, Einlässe admission; ein|lassen *unr. tr. V.* a) *(hereinlassen)* admit; let in; b) *(einfüllen)* run ⟨*water*⟩

Ein·lauf der *(Med.)* enema; ein|laufen 1. *unr. itr. V.; mit sein* a) ⟨*ship*⟩ come in; b) *(kleiner werden)* shrink; 2. *unr. tr. V.* wear in ⟨*shoes*⟩

ein|leben *refl. V.* settle down

ein|legen *tr. V.* **a)** load ⟨*film*⟩; engage ⟨*gear*⟩; **b)** *(Kochk.)* pickle

ein|leiten *tr. V.* **a)** introduce; **b)** induce ⟨*birth*⟩; **c)** lead in; **etw. in etw.** *(Akk.)* ~: lead sth. into sth.; **Ein·leitung die a)** introduction; **b)** *(einer Geburt)* induction

ein|leuchten *itr. V.* jmdm. ~: be clear to sb.; **ein·leuchtend** *Adj.* plausible

ein|liefern *tr. V.* take ⟨*letter, person*⟩ (**bei, in** + **Abk. to**)

ein|lösen *tr. V.* cash ⟨*cheque*⟩

ein|machen *tr. V.* preserve ⟨*fruit etc.*⟩; *(in Gläser)* bottle

einmal **1.** *Adv.* **a)** once; **noch ~ so groß** |**wie**| twice as big [as]; **etw. noch ~ tun** do sth. again; **b)** ['-'-] *(später)* one day; *(früher)* once; **es war ~ ...**: once upon a time there was ...; **2.** *Partikel* **nicht ~**: not even; **wieder ~**: yet again; **Einmal·eins das**; ~: [multiplication] tables *pl.*; **einmalig 1.** *Adj.* **a)** unique; one-off ⟨*payment, purchase*⟩; **b)** *(ugs.)* fantastic *(coll.)*; **2.** *adv. (ugs.)* really fantastically *(coll.)*

Ein·marsch der a) entry; **b)** *(Besetzung)* invasion (**in** + **Akk.** of); **ein|marschieren** *itr. V.; mit sein* march in

ein|mischen *refl. V.* interfere (**in** + **Akk.** in)

einmütig 1. *Adj.* unanimous; **2.** *adv.* unanimously

ein|nähen *tr. V.* sew up

Einnahme die; ~, ~**en** **a)** income; *(Staats~)* revenue; *(Kassen~)* takings *pl.*; **b)** *(von Arzneimitteln)* taking; **c)** *(einer Stadt, Burg)* taking; **ein|nehmen** *unr. tr. V.* **a)** take; *(verdienen)* earn; **b)** *(ausfüllen)* take up ⟨*amount of room*⟩; **c)** *(beeinflussen)* jmdn. für sich ~: win sb. over

Ein·öde die barren waste

ein|ordnen 1. *tr. V.* arrange; put in order; **2.** *refl. V.* **a)** *(Verkehrsw.)* get into the correct lane; „**~**" 'get in lane'; **b)** *(sich einfügen)* fit in

ein|packen 1. *tr. V.* pack (**in** + **Akk.** in); *(einwickeln)* wrap [up]; **2.** *itr. V. (ugs.)* **er kann ~**: he's had it *(coll.)*

ein|parken *tr., itr. V.* park

ein|pflanzen *tr. V.* **a)** plant; **b)** *(Med., fig.)* implant

ein|prägen *tr. V.* **a)** stamp (**in** + **Akk.** into, on); **b)** *(fig.)* **sich** *(Dat.)* **etw. ~**: memorize sth.; **jmdm. etw. ~**: impress sth. on sb.; **einprägsam** *Adj.* easily remembered

ein|rahmen *tr. V.* frame

ein|räumen *tr. V.* **a)** put away; **b)** *(füllen)* **seinen Schrank ~**: put one's things away in one's cupboard; **ein Zimmer ~**: put the furniture into a room; **c)** *(zugestehen)* admit

ein|reden 1. *tr. V.* jmdm. etw. ~: talk sb. into believing sth.; **sich** *(Dat.)* ~, **daß ...**: persuade oneself that ...; **2.** *itr. V.* **auf jmdn. ~**: talk insistently to sb.

ein|regnen *refl. V.; unpers.* **es hat sich eingeregnet** it's begun to rain steadily.

ein|reiben *unr. tr. V.* rub ⟨*substance*⟩ in; **etw. mit Öl ~**: rub oil into sth.

ein|reichen *tr. V.* submit; lodge ⟨*complaint*⟩; tender ⟨*resignation*⟩

ein|reihen 1. *refl. V.* **sich in etw.** *(Akk.)* ~: join sth.; **2.** *tr. V.* jmdn. in eine Kategorie ~: place sb. in a category

Einreiher der; ~**s**, ~: single-breasted suit/jacket

Ein·reise die entry; **Einreise·erlaubnis die** entry permit; **ein|reisen** *itr. V.; mit sein* enter; **nach Schweden ~**: enter Sweden

ein|reißen 1. *unr. tr. V.* **a)** pull down ⟨*building*⟩; **b)** *(einen Riß machen in)* tear; rip; **2.** *unr. itr. V.; mit sein* tear; rip

ein|renken *tr. V.* **a)** *(Med.)* set; **b)** *(ugs.: bereinigen)* sort out

ein|richten 1. *refl. V.* **sich schön ~**: furnish one's home beautifully; **sich häuslich ~**: make oneself at home; **2.** *tr. V.* furnish ⟨*flat, house*⟩; fit out ⟨*shop*⟩; equip ⟨*laboratory*⟩; **Ein·richtung die a)** *o. Pl.* furnishing; **b)** *(Mobiliar)* furnishings *pl.*

ein|rollen 1. *tr. V.* roll up ⟨*carpet etc.*⟩; put ⟨*hair*⟩ in curlers; **2.** *itr. V.; mit sein* roll in

ein|rosten *itr. V.; mit sein* go rusty

ein|rücken 1. *itr. V.; mit sein (einmarschieren)* move in; **2.** *tr. V.* indent ⟨*line, heading, etc.*⟩

eins 1. *Kardinalz.* one; **es ist ~**: it is one o'clock; ~ **zu null** one-nil; ~ **zu ~**: one-all; „**~, zwei, drei!**" 'ready, steady, go'; **2.** *Adj.* **mir ist alles ~**: it's all the same to me; **3.** *Indefinitpron. s.* **irgendein a; Eins die**; ~, ~**en a)** one; **b)** *(Schulnote)* one; A

einsam *Adj.* **a)** lonely ⟨*person, decision*⟩; **b)** *(einzeln)* solitary ⟨*tree, wanderer*⟩; **c)** *(abgelegen)* isolated; **d)** *(menschenleer)* deserted; **Einsamkeit die**; ~ **a)** loneliness; **b)** *(Alleinsein)* solitude; **c)** *(Abgeschiedenheit)* isolation

ein|sammeln *tr. V.* **a)** *(auflesen)* pick up; gather up; **b)** *(sich aushändigen lassen)* collect in; collect ⟨tickets⟩

Ein·satz der a) *(aus Stoff)* inset; *(in Kochtopf, Nähkasten usw.)* compartment; **b)** *(Betrag)* stake; **c)** *(Gebrauch)* use; *(von Truppen)* deployment

Einsatz-: ~**befehl** der order to go into action; **den ~befehl haben** have operational command; ~**leiter der** head of operations; ~**wagen der** *(der Polizei)* police car; *(der Feuerwehr)* fire-engine; *(Notarztwagen)* ambulance

ein|saugen *unr. (auch regelm.) tr. V.* suck in; breathe [in] ⟨fresh air⟩

ein|schalten **1.** *tr. V.* **a)** switch on ⟨radio, TV, electricity, etc.⟩; **b)** *(fig.)* call in ⟨press, police, expert, etc.⟩; **2.** *refl. V.* **a)** switch [itself] on; **b)** *(eingreifen)* intervene **(in + Akk.** in)

ein|schärfen *tr. V.* **jmdm. etw.** ~: impress sth. [up]on sb.

ein|schätzen *tr. V.* judge ⟨person⟩; assess ⟨situation, income, damages⟩; *(schätzen)* estimate; **Ein·schätzung die** *s.* **einschätzen:** judging; assessment; estimation

ein|schenken *tr., itr. V.* **a)** *(eingießen)* pour [out]; **jmdm. etw.** ~: pour out sth. for sb.; **b)** *(füllen)* fill [up] ⟨glass, cup⟩

ein|scheren *itr. V.; mit sein* **auf eine Fahrspur** ~: get *or* move into a lane

ein|schicken *tr. V.* send in

ein|schieben *unr. tr. V.* **a)** push in; **b)** *(einfügen)* insert; put on ⟨trains, buses⟩

ein|schiffen *tr., refl. V.* embark

ein|schlafen *unr. itr. V.; mit sein* **a)** fall asleep; **b)** *(verhüll.: sterben)* pass away; **c)** *(gefühllos werden)* go to sleep; **ein|schläfern** *tr. V.* **a)** **jmdn.** ~: send sb. to sleep, *(betäuben)* put sb. to sleep; **b)** *(schmerzlos töten)* **ein Tier** ~: put an animal to sleep; **einschläfernd** **1.** *Adj.* soporific; **2.** *adv.* ~ **wirken** have a soporific effect

ein|schlagen **1.** *unr. tr. V.* **a)** knock in; **b)** *(zertrümmern)* smash [in]; **c)** *(einwickeln)* wrap up ⟨present⟩; cover ⟨book⟩; **2.** *unr. itr. V.* **a)** ⟨bomb⟩ land; ⟨lightning⟩ strike; **b)** **auf jmdn./etw.** ~: rain blows on sb./sth.

einschlägig **1.** *Adj.* specialist ⟨journal, shop⟩; relevant ⟨literature, passage⟩; **2.** *adv.* **er ist** ~ **vorbestraft** he has previous convictions for a similar offence/similar offences

ein|schleichen *unr. refl. V.* steal in

ein|schließen *unr. tr. V.* **a)** **etw. in etw.** *(Dat.)* ~: lock sth. up [in sth.]; **jmdn./sich** ~: lock sb./oneself in; **b)** *(umgeben)* surround; **einschließlich** **1.** *Präp. mit Gen.* including; ~ **der Unkosten** including expenses; **2.** *adv.* **bis ~ 30. Juni** up to and including 30 June

ein|schmeicheln *refl. V.* **sich bei jmdm.** ~: ingratiate oneself with sb.

ein|schmuggeln *tr. V.* smuggle in

ein|schneiden *unr. tr. V.* **a)** make a cut in; **b)** *(einritzen)* carve; **einschneidend** *Adj.* drastic

ein|schneien *itr. V.; mit sein* get snowed in

Ein·schnitt der cut

ein|schränken **1.** *tr. V.* **a)** reduce, curb ⟨expenditure, consumption⟩; **b)** *(einengen)* limit; restrict; **jmdn. in seinen Rechten** ~: limit *or* restrict sb.'s rights; **2.** *refl. V.* economize; **Einschränkung die** ~, ~**en a)** restriction; limitation; **b)** *(Vorbehalt)* reservation

ein|schreiben *unr. tr. V.* **a)** *(Postw.)* register ⟨letter⟩; **b)** *(eintragen)* **sich/ jmdn.** ~: enter one's/sb's name; **Ein·schreiben das** *(Postw.)* registered letter; **per** ~: by registered mail

ein|schreiten *unr. itr. V.* intervene

ein|schüchtern *tr. V.* intimidate

ein|schulen *tr. V.* **eingeschult werden** start school

ein|sehen *unr. tr. V.* **a)** *(überblicken)* see into; **b)** *(prüfend lesen)* look at; **c)** *(erkennen)* realize; **d)** *(begreifen)* see

ein|seifen *tr. V.* lather

ein·seitig **1.** *Adj.* **a)** on one side *postpos.*; **b)** *(tendenziös)* one-sided; **2.** *adv.* **a)** on one side; **b)** *(tendenziös)* one-sidedly

ein|senden *unr. (auch regelm.) tr. V.* send [in]

ein|setzen **1.** *tr. V.* **a)** *(hineinsetzen)* put in; **b)** put on ⟨special train etc.⟩; **c)** *(ernennen)* appoint; **d)** *(in Aktion treten lassen)* use; **e)** *(aufs Spiel setzen)* stake ⟨money⟩; **f)** *(riskieren)* risk; **2.** *itr. V.* begin; ⟨storm⟩ break. **3.** *refl. V.* *(sich engagieren)* **ich werde mich dafür** ~, **daß** ...: I shall do what I can to see that ...; **sich nicht genug** ~: ⟨pupil⟩ be lacking application; ⟨minister⟩ be lacking in commitment

Ein·sicht die a) view **(in + Akk.** into); **b)** *(Einblick)* ~ **in die Akten nehmen** take *or* have a look at the files; **c)** *(Erkenntnis)* insight; **einsichtig** *Adj.* **a)**

(verständnisvoll) understanding; **b)** *(verständlich)* comprehensible

Ein·siedler der hermit

ein·silbig *Adj.* **a)** monosyllabic ⟨*word*⟩; **b)** *(fig.)* taciturn ⟨*person*⟩

ein|sinken *unr. itr. V.* sink in

Einsitzer der; ~s, ~: single-seater; **einsitzig** *Adj.* single-seater *attrib.*

ein|spannen *tr. V.* harness ⟨*horse*⟩; put in ⟨*paper*⟩; fix ⟨*fabric*⟩; clamp ⟨*work*⟩

ein|sparen *tr. V.* save

ein|sperren *tr. V.* lock up

einsprachig *Adj.* monolingual

ein|springen *unr. itr. V.; mit sein* stand in; *(aushelfen)* step in and help out

ein|spritzen *tr. V.* inject; **jmdm. etw.** ~: inject sb. with sth.; **Einspritz·motor** der fuel-injection engine

Ein·spruch der objection (**gegen** to)

einspurig **1.** *Adj.* single-track ⟨*road*⟩; **2.** *adv.* die Autobahn ist nur ~ **befahrbar** only one lane of the motorway is open

einst *Adv. (geh.)* once

ein|stampfen *tr. V.* pulp ⟨*books*⟩

Ein·stand der: seinen ~ **geben** celebrate starting a new job

ein|stecken *tr. V.* **a)** put in; **b)** *(mitnehmen)* put ⟨*sth.*⟩ in one's pocket/bag *etc.*

ein|stehen *unr. itr. V.* **für jmdn.** ~: vouch for sb.; **für etw.** ~: take responsibility for sth.

ein|steigen *unr. itr. V.; mit sein* **a)** *(in ein Fahrzeug)* get in; **in ein Auto** ~: get into a car; **in den Bus** ~: get on the bus; **b)** *(eindringen)* climb in

einstellbar *Adj.* adjustable; **ein|stellen** **1.** *tr. V.* **a)** *(einordnen)* put away ⟨*books etc.*⟩; **b)** *(unterstellen)* put in ⟨*car, bicycle*⟩; **c)** *(beschäftigen)* take on ⟨*workers*⟩; **d)** *(regulieren)* adjust; **e)** *(beenden)* stop; call off ⟨*search, strike*⟩; **f)** *(Sport)* equal ⟨*record*⟩; **2.** *refl. V.* **a)** arrive; **b)** ⟨*pain, worry*⟩ begin; ⟨*success*⟩ come; ⟨*symptoms, consequences*⟩ appear; **c)** sich **auf etw.** *(Akk.)* ~: prepare oneself for sth.; **sich schnell auf neue Situationen** ~: adjust quickly to new situations

ein·stellig *Adj.* single-figure *attrib.*

Ein·stellung die **a)** *(von Arbeitskräften)* employment; **b)** *(Regulierung)* adjustment; **c)** *(Beendigung)* stopping; **d)** *(Sport)* die ~ **eines Rekordes** the equalling of a record; **e)** *(Ansicht)*

attitude; **ihre politische/religiöse** ~: her political/religious views *pl.*; **f)** *(Film)* take

Ein·stich der **a)** insertion; **b)** *(~stelle)* puncture; prick

Ein·stieg der; ~[e]s, ~e *(Eingang)* entrance; *(Tür)* door/doors

ein|stimmen **1.** *itr. V.* join in. **2.** *tr. V.* **jmdn. auf etw.** *(Akk.)* ~: get sb. in the [right] mood for sth.

einstimmig **1.** *Adj.* **a)** *(Musik)* for one voice; **b)** *(einmütig)* unanimous ⟨*decision, vote*⟩; **2.** *adv.* **a)** *(Musik)* in unison; **b)** *(einmütig)* unanimously

ein·stöckig *Adj.* single-storey *attrib.*

ein|studieren *tr. V.* rehearse

ein|stufen *tr. V.* classify; categorize

ein·stündig *Adj.* one-hour *attrib.*

ein|stürmen *itr. V.* **mit Fragen auf jmdn.** ~: besiege sb. with questions

Ein·sturz der collapse; **ein|stürzen** *itr. V.; mit sein* collapse

einst·weilen *Adv.* for the time being

eintägig *Adj.* one-day *attrib.*; **Eintags·fliege** die *(Zool.)* mayfly; *(fig. ugs.)* seven-day wonder

ein|tauchen **1.** *tr. V.* dip; *(untertauchen)* immerse; **2.** *itr. V.; mit sein* dive in; ⟨*submarine*⟩ dive

ein|tauschen *tr. V.* exchange (**gegen** for)

ein·tausend *Kardinalz.: s.* tausend

ein|teilen *tr. V.* **a)** divide up; classify ⟨*plants, species*⟩; **b)** *(disponieren, verplanen)* organize

einteilig *Adj.* one-piece

eintönig **1.** *Adj.* monotonous; **2.** *adv.* monotonously; **Eintönigkeit** die; ~: monotony

Ein·topf der stew

Ein·tracht die; *o. Pl.* harmony; **ein·trächtig** *Adj.* harmonious

Eintrag der; ~[e]s, **Einträge** entry; **ein|tragen** *unr. tr. V.* **a)** enter; **b)** *(Amtsspr.)* register

einträglich *Adj.* lucrative

ein|treffen *unr. itr. V.; mit sein* **a)** arrive; **b)** *(verwirklicht werden)* come true

ein|treiben *unr. tr. V.* collect ⟨*taxes, debts*⟩; *(durch Gerichtsverfahren)* recover ⟨*debts, money*⟩

ein|treten **1.** *unr. itr. V.; mit sein* **a)** enter; **bitte, treten Sie ein!** please come in; **b)** *(Mitglied werden)* **in einen Verein/einen Orden** ~: join a club/enter a religious order; **c)** *(Raumfahrt)* enter; **2.** *unr. tr. V.* kick in ⟨*door, window, etc.*⟩

ein|trichtern *tr. V. (salopp)* jmdm. etw. ~: drum sth. into sb.

Ein·tritt der a) entry; entrance; **vor dem ~ in die Verhandlungen** *(fig.)* before entering into negotiations; b) *(Beitritt)* der ~ in einen Verein/einen Orden joining a club/entering a religious order; c) *(von Raketen)* entry; d) *(Zugang, Eintrittsgeld)* admission; e) *(Beginn)* onset; ~ der Dunkelheit nightfall

Eintritts-: ~geld das admission fee; ~karte die admission ticket; ~preis der admission charge

ein|trocknen *itr. V.; mit sein* dry; ⟨water, toothpaste⟩ dry up; ⟨leather⟩ dry out; ⟨berry, fruit⟩ shrivel

ein|üben *tr. V.* practise

einverstanden *Adj.* ~ **sein** agree; **mit jmdm./etw.** ~ **sein** approve of sb./sth.

Ein·verständnis das consent

ein|wachsen *unr. itr. V.; mit sein* grow into the flesh; **eingewachsen** ingrown ⟨toe-nail⟩

Einwand der; ~[e]s, **Einwände** objection (gegen to)

Ein·wanderer der immigrant; **ein|wandern** *itr. V.; mit sein* immigrate (in + *Akk.* into); **Ein·wanderung** die immigration

einwand·frei 1. *Adj.* flawless; impeccable ⟨behaviour⟩; indisputable ⟨proof⟩; 2. *adv.* flawlessly; ⟨behave⟩ impeccably; ⟨prove⟩ beyond question

ein|wechseln *tr. V.* a) change ⟨money⟩; b) *(Sport)* substitute ⟨player⟩

ein|wecken *tr. V.* preserve; bottle

Ein·weg·flasche die non-returnable bottle

ein|weichen *tr. V.* soak

ein|weihen *tr. V.* open [officially] ⟨bridge, road⟩; dedicate ⟨monument⟩; **Einweihung** die; ~, ~en *s.* einweihen: [official] opening; dedication

ein|weisen *unr. tr. V.* a) *(in eine Tätigkeit)* introduce; b) *(in ein Amt)* install

ein|wenden *unr. tr. V. (auch regelm.) tr. V.* **dagegen läßt sich vieles** ~: there is a lot to be said against that

ein|werfen *unr. tr. V.* a) mail ⟨letter⟩; insert ⟨coin⟩; b) smash ⟨window⟩; c) throw in ⟨ball⟩; d) *(bemerken, sagen)* throw in ⟨remark⟩

ein|wickeln *tr. V.* wrap [up]

ein|willigen *itr. V.* agree (in + *Akk.* to); **Einwilligung** die; ~, ~en agreement

ein|winken *tr. V. (Verkehrsw.)* guide in ⟨aircraft, car⟩

ein|wirken a) *(beeinflussen)* **auf jmdn.** ~: influence sb.; b) *(eine Wirkung ausüben)* have an effect (**auf** + *Akk.* on); **Ein·wirkung** die *(Einfluß)* influence; *(Wirkung)* effect

Einwohner der; ~s, ~, **Einwohnerin** die; ~, ~nen inhabitant

Ein·wurf der a) insertion; *(von Briefen)* mailing; b) *(Ballspiele)* throw-in; c) *(Bemerkung)* interjection

Ein·zahl die; *o. Pl.* singular

ein|zahlen *tr. V.* pay in; **Ein·zahlung** die payment

ein|zäunen *tr. V.* fence in; enclose; **Einzäunung** die; ~, ~en fencing-in

ein|zeichnen *tr. V.* draw *or* mark in

einzeilig *Adj.* one-line *attrib.*

Einzel das; ~s, ~ *(Sport)* singles *pl.*

Einzel-: ~bett das single bed; ~fall der a) particular case; b) *(Ausnahme)* isolated case; ~gänger [-gɛŋɐ] der; ~s, ~: loner; ~haft die solitary confinement; ~handel der retail trade; ~händler der retailer

Einzelheit die; ~, ~en a) detail; b) *(einzelner Umstand)* particular

Einzel·kind das only child

einzeln *Adj.* a) *(für sich allein)* individual; b) *(alleinstehend)* solitary ⟨building, tree⟩; single ⟨lady, gentleman⟩; c) ~e *(wenige)* a few; *(einige)* some; d) *substantivisch* der/jeder ~e the/each individual; ~es some things *pl.*; **das Einzelne** the particular

Einzel-: ~teil das individual part; ~zelle die single cell; ~zimmer das single room

ein|ziehen 1. *unr. tr. V.* a) put in; thread in ⟨tape, elastic⟩; b) *(einholen)* haul in ⟨net⟩; c) *(einatmen)* breathe in ⟨scent, fresh air⟩; inhale ⟨smoke⟩; d) *(einberufen)* call up ⟨recruits⟩; e) *(beitreiben)* collect; 2. *unr. itr. V.; mit sein* a) ⟨liquid⟩ soak in; b) *(einkehren)* enter; c) *(in eine Wohnung)* move in

einzig 1. *Adj.* only; **kein** ~es **Wort** not a single word; 2. *adv.* a) *intensivierend bei Adj.* extraordinarily; b) *(ausschließlich)* only; **das** ~ **Wahre** the only thing; **einzig·artig** 1. *Adj.* unique; 2. *adv.* uniquely

Ein·zug der a) entry (**in** + *Akk.* into); b) *(in eine Wohnung)* move; **Einzugs·bereich** der catchment area

Eis das; ~es a) ice; b) *(Speise~)* icecream; **ein** ~ **am Stiel** an ice-lolly *(Brit.)* or *(Amer.)* ice pop

Eis-: ~bahn die ice-rink; ~bär der polar bear; ~becher der ice-cream sundae; ~**bein** das *(Kochk.)* knuckle of pork; ~**berg** der iceberg; ~**beutel** der ice-bag; ~**café** das ice-cream parlour

Ei·schnee der stiffly beaten egg-white

Eisen das; ~s, ~: iron

Eisen·bahn die **a)** railway; railroad *(Amer.)*; mit der ~ **fahren** go by train; **b)** *(Bahnstrecke)* railway line; railroad track *(Amer.)*; **Eisenbahner** der; ~s, ~: railwayman; railroader *(Amer.)*; **Eisenbahn·unglück** das train crash

Eisen-: ~**erz** das iron ore; ~**kette** die iron chain; ~**ring** der iron ring; ~**stange** die iron bar; ~**waren** *Pl.* ironmongery *sing.;* ~**zeit** die Iron Age

eisern 1. *Adj. (auch fig.)* iron; **2.** *adv.* resolutely; ⟨*save, train*⟩ with iron determination; ~ **durchgreifen** take drastic measures

eis-, Eis-: ~**fach** das freezing compartment; ~**frei** *Adj.* ice-free; ~**gekühlt** *Adj.* iced; ~**glatt** *Adj.* icy; ~**glätte** die black ice; ~**hockey** das ice hockey

eisig 1. *Adj.* **a)** icy ⟨*wind, cold*⟩; icy [cold] ⟨*water*⟩; **b)** *(fig.)* frosty; **2.** *adv.* **a)** ~ **kalt sein** be icy cold; **b)** *(fig.)* ⟨*smile*⟩ frostily; **eisig·kalt** *Adj. s.* eiskalt 1 a

eis-, Eis-: ~**kaffee** der iced coffee; ~**kalt 1.** *Adj.* **a)** ice-cold ⟨*drink*⟩; freezing cold ⟨*weather*⟩; **b)** *(gefühllos)* icy; ice-cold ⟨*look*⟩; **2.** *adv.* **es lief mir** ~**kalt über den Rücken** a cold shiver went down my spine; ~**kunstlauf** der figure skating; ~**kunst·läufer** der figure skater; ~**lauf** der ice-skating; ~|**laufen** *unr. itr. V.; mit sein* ice-skate; ~**laufen** das ice-skating; ~**läufer** der ice-skater; ~**schrank** der refrigerator; ~**sport** der ice sports *pl.;* ~**tanz** der *(Sport)* ice-dancing; ~**waffel** die [ice-cream] wafer; ~**wein** der *wine made from grapes frozen on the vine;* ~**würfel** der ice cube; ~**zapfen** der icicle; ~**zeit** die ice age

eitel *Adj.* vain; **Eitelkeit** die; ~, ~en vanity

Eiter der; ~s pus; **eitern** *itr. V.* suppurate; **eitrig** *Adj.* suppurating

Ei·weiß das **a)** egg-white; **b)** *(Protein)* protein

¹**Ekel** der; ~s revulsion; |**einen**| ~ **vor etw.** *(Dat.)* **haben** have a revulsion for

sth.; ²**Ekel** das; ~s, ~ *(ugs. abwertend)* horror; **er ist ein** |**altes**| ~: he is quite obnoxious; **ekelhaft** *Adj.* revolting ⟨*sight*⟩; horrible ⟨*weather, person*⟩ **ekeln 1.** *refl. V.* be disgusted; **sich vor etw.** *(Dat.)* ~: find sth. repulsive; **2.** *tr., itr. V. (unpers.)* **es ekelt mich** *od.* **mir ekelt davor** I find it revolting; **eklig** *Adj.* **a)** *s.* ekelhaft; **b)** *(ugs.: gemein)* nasty

Ekstase [ɛk'staːzə] die; ~, ~n ecstasy

Ekzem das; ~s, ~e *(Med.)* eczema

Elan der; ~s zest; vigour

elastisch *Adj.* elasticated ⟨*material*⟩; springy ⟨*surface*⟩; supple ⟨*person, body*⟩; **Elastizität** die; ~: elasticity; *(Federkraft)* springiness; *(Geschmeidigkeit)* suppleness

Elch der; ~|e|s, ~e elk; *(in Nordamerika)* moose

Elefant der; ~en, ~en elephant

elegant 1. *Adj.* elegant; **2.** *adv.* elegantly; **Eleganz** die; ~: elegance

elektrifizieren *tr. V.* electrify; **Elektrifizierung** die; ~, ~en electrification

Elektriker der; ~s, ~: electrician; **elektrisch 1.** *Adj.* electric; electrical ⟨*resistance, wiring, system*⟩; **2.** *adv.* ~ **kochen** cook with electricity; ~ **geladen sein** be electrically charged; **elektrisieren 1.** *tr. V. (Med.)* treat using electricity; **2.** *refl. V.* get an electric shock; **Elektrizität** die; ~ electricity

Elektrizitäts·werk das power station

Elektro-: ~**artikel** der electrical appliance; ~**auto** das electric car; ~**gerät** das electrical appliance; ~**geschäft** das electrical shop *or (Amer.)* store; ~**herd** der electric cooker; ~**mobil** das electric car; ~**motor** der electric motor

Elektron das; ~s, ~en [-'troːnən] electron

Elektronen-: ~[**ge**]**hirn** das *(ugs.)* electronic brain *(coll.);* ~**rechner** der electronic computer

Elektronik die; ~ **a)** electronics *sing., no art.;* **b)** *(Teile)* electronics *pl.;* **elektronisch 1.** *Adj.* electronic; **2.** *adv.* electronically

Elektro-: ~**rasierer** der electric shaver; ~**technik** die electrical engineering *no art.;* ~**techniker** der **a)** electronics engineer; **b)** *(Elektriker)* electrician

Element das; ~|e|s, ~e element; **ele-**

mentar *Adj.* **a)** *(grundlegend)* fundamental; **b)** *(einfach)* elementary ⟨*knowledge*⟩; **c)** *(naturhaft)* elemental ⟨*force*⟩; **Elementar·teilchen das** *(Physik)* elementary particle

elend *Adj.* wretched; miserable; **Elend das;** ~s misery

Elends-: ~**quartier das** slum [dwelling]; ~**viertel das** slum area

elf *Kardinalz.* eleven; **Elf die;** ~, ~**en a)** eleven; **b)** *(Sport)* team; side

Elfe die; ~, ~**n** fairy

Elfen·bein das ivory

Elfenbein-: ~**schnitzerei die** *o. Pl.* ivory-carving; ~**turm der** *(fig.)* ivory tower

Elf·meter der *(Fußball)* penalty; **einen** ~ **schießen** take a penalty; **Elfmeter·schießen das** *(Fußball)* durch ~**schießen** by *or* on penalties

eliminieren *tr. V.* eliminate

Elite die; ~, ~**n** élite

Ell·bogen der; ~s, ~: elbow

Elle die; ~, ~**n a)** *(Anat.)* ulna; **b)** *(frühere Längeneinheit)* cubit; **c)** *(veralt.: Maßstock)* ≈ yardstick; **Ellen·bogen** *s.* Ellbogen

Ellipse die; ~, ~**n** ellipse

Elsaß das; ~ *od.* **Elsasses** Alsace

Elster die; ~, ~**n** magpie

elterlich *Adj.* parental; **Eltern** *Pl.* parents *pl.*

eltern-, Eltern-: ~**abend der** *(Schulw.)* parents' evening; ~**haus das** home; ~**los** *Adj.* orphaned; ~**teil der** parent

Email [e'mai] **das;** ~s, ~s, **Emaille** [e'maljə] **das;** ~, ~**n** enamel

Emanzipation die; ~, ~**en** emancipation; **emanzipieren** *refl. V.* emancipate; **emanzipiert** *Adj.* emancipated

Embargo das; ~s, ~s embargo

Emblem das; ~s, ~e emblem

Embryo der; ~s, ~**nen** [-y'o:nən] *od.* ~s embryo

Emigrant der; ~**en**, ~**en** emigrant; *(Flüchtling)* emigré; **Emigration die;** ~, ~**en** *(das Emigrieren)* emigration; **emigrieren** *itr. V.; mit sein* emigrate

Emotion die; ~, ~**en** emotion; **emotional 1.** *Adj.* emotional; emotive ⟨*topic, question*⟩; **2.** *adv.* emotionally

Empfang der; ~[e]s, **Empfänge** reception; *(Entgegennahme)* receipt; **empfangen** *unr. tr. V.* receive; **Empfänger der;** ~s, ~ **a)** recipient; *(eines Briefs)* addressee; **b)** *(Empfangsgerät)* receiver

empfänglich *Adj.* **a)** receptive (für to); **b)** *(beeinflußbar)* susceptible; **Empfängnis die;** ~: conception; **Empfängnis·verhütung die** contraception

empfangs-, Empfangs-: ~**berechtigt** *Adj.* authorized to receive payment/goods *postpos.;* ~**chef der** head receptionist; ~**dame die** receptionist; ~**halle die** reception lobby

empfehlen 1. *unr. tr. V.* recommend; **2.** *unr. refl. V.* **a)** take one's leave; **b)** *unpers.* es empfiehlt sich, ... zu ...: it's advisable to ...; **empfehlens·wert** *Adj.* **a)** to be recommended *postpos.;* recommendable; **b)** *(ratsam)* advisable; **Empfehlung die;** ~, ~**en a)** recommendation; **b)** *(Empfehlungsschreiben)* letter of recommendation; **empfiehl** *Imperativ Sg. v.* empfehlen; **empfiehlst** *2. Pers. Sg. Präsens v.* empfehlen; **empfiehlt** *3. Pers. Sg. Präsens v.* empfehlen

empfinden *unr. tr. V.* **a)** *(wahrnehmen)* feel; **b)** *(auffassen)* etw. als Beleidigung ~: feel sth. to be an insult; **Empfinden das;** ~s feeling; für mein *od.* nach meinem ~: to my mind; **empfindlich 1.** *Adj.* **a)** sensitive; fast ⟨*film*⟩; **b)** *(leicht beleidigt)* sensitive; **c)** *(anfällig)* zart und ~: delicate; **d)** *(spürbar)* severe ⟨*punishment, shortage*⟩; **2.** *adv.* ~ auf etw. *(Akk.)* reagieren *(sensibel)* be susceptible to sth.; *(beleidigt)* react oversensitively to sth.; **Empfindlichkeit die;** ~, ~**en** *s.* empfindlich: sensitivity; severity; *(eines Films)* speed

empfindsam *Adj.* sensitive ⟨*nature*⟩; **Empfindung die;** ~, ~**en** *(Gefühl)* feeling

empfing *1. u. 3. Pers. Sg. Prät. v.* empfangen

empfohlen 1. *2. Part. v.* empfehlen; **2.** *Adj.* recommended

empirisch 1. *Adj.* empirical; **2.** *adv.* empirically

empor *Adv. (geh.)* upwards

Empore die; ~, ~**n** gallery

empören 1. *tr. V.* fill with indignation; outrage; **2.** *refl. V.* become indignant *or* outraged; **empörend** *Adj.* outrageous; **empört** *Adj.* outraged

emsig 1. *Adj.* industrious ⟨*person*⟩; bustling ⟨*activity*⟩; **2.** *adv.* industriously

Emu der; ~s, ~s *(Zool.)* emu

Ende das; ~s, ~**n** end; am ~ der Straße/Stadt at the end of the road/town; am/bis/gegen ~ des Monats at/by/towards the end of the month; ~ April at the end of April; zu ~ sein ⟨patience, war⟩ be at an end; ⟨school⟩ be over; ⟨film, game⟩ have finished; ~ gut, alles gut all's well that ends well (prov.); **enden** itr. V. **a)** end; ⟨programme⟩ finish; **b)** in der Gosse ~: end up in the gutter; (dort sterben) die in the gutter

end·gültig 1. Adj. final ⟨consent, decision⟩; conclusive ⟨evidence⟩; **2.** adv. das ist ~ vorbei that's all over and done with; sich ~ trennen separate for good

End-: ~kampf der (Sport) final; (Milit.) final battle; ~lauf der (Sport) final

endlich 1. Adv. **a)** (nach langer Zeit) at last; **b)** (schließlich) in the end; **2.** Adj. finite

end-, End-: ~los **1.** Adj. **a)** (ohne Ende) infinite; (ringförmig) continuous; **b)** (nicht enden wollend) endless; interminable ⟨speech⟩; **2.** adv. ~los lange dauern be interminably long; ~runde die (Sport) final; ~spiel das (Sport) final; ~spurt der (bes. Leichtathletik) final spurt; ~stadium das final stage; (Med.) terminal stage; ~station die terminus

Endung die; ~, ~en (Sprachw.) ending

Energie die; ~, ~n energy

Energie-: ~politik die energy policy; ~quelle die energy source; ~versorgung die energy supply

energisch 1. Adj. **a)** energetic ⟨person⟩; firm ⟨action⟩; **b)** forceful ⟨voice, words⟩; **2.** adv. **a)** energetically; ~ durchgreifen take drastic action; **b)** ⟨reject, say⟩ forcefully; ⟨stress⟩ emphatically; ⟨deny⟩ strenuously

eng [ɛŋ] **1.** Adj. **a)** (schmal) narrow **b)** (dicht) close ⟨writing⟩; **c)** (fest anliegend) close-fitting; **d)** (beschränkt) narrow; **e)** (nahe) close ⟨friend⟩; **2.** adv. **a)** (dicht) ~ [zusammen] sitzen/stehen sit/stand close together; **b)** (fest anliegend) ~ anliegen/sitzen fit closely; **c)** (beschränkt) etw. zu ~ auslegen interpret sth. too narrowly; **d)** (nahe) closely; **Enge** die; ~, ~n confinement

Engel der; ~s, ~: angel

eng·herzig Adj. petty

England (das); ~s England; **Engländer** der; ~s, ~: Englishman/English boy; er ist ~: he is English; die ~: the

English; **Engländerin** die; ~,·~nen Englishwoman/English girl; **englisch 1.** Adj. English; **die** ~e **Sprache/Literatur** the English language/English literature; **2.** adv. ~ sprechen speak English; **Englisch das;** ~[s] English

englisch-, Englisch-: ~lehrer der 'English teacher; ~sprachig Adj. **a)** English-language ⟨book, magazine⟩; **b)** (~ sprechend) English-speaking ⟨population, country⟩; ~unterricht der English teaching; (Unterrichtsstunde) English lesson

Eng·paß der **a)** defile; **b)** (fig.) bottleneck; **eng·stirnig** Adj. narrowminded

Enkel der; ~s, ~: grandson; **Enkelin** die; ~, ~nen granddaughter; **Enkel·kind** das grandchild

enorm 1. Adj. enormous ⟨sum, costs⟩; tremendous (coll.) ⟨effort⟩; immense ⟨strain⟩; **2.** adv. tremendously (coll.)

Ensemble [ã'sã:bļ] das ensemble; (Theater~) company

entarten itr. V.; mit sein degenerate **entbehren** tr. V. (verzichten auf) do without; **entbehrlich** Adj. dispensable; **Entbehrung** die; ~, ~en privation

entbinden 1. unr. tr. V. **a)** jmdn. von einem Versprechen ~: release sb. from a promise; seines Amtes od. von seinem Amt entbunden werden be relieved of [one's] office; **b)** jmdn. ~ (Med.) deliver sb.'s baby; **2.** unr. itr. V. give birth; **Entbindung** die (Med.) delivery

entblößen 1. refl. V. take one's clothes off; ⟨exhibitionist⟩ expose oneself; **2.** tr. V. uncover ⟨one's arm etc.⟩

entdecken tr. V. **a)** discover; **b)** (ausfindig machen) jmdn. ~: find sb.; etw. ~: find or discover sth.; **Entdecker** der; ~s, ~: discoverer; **Entdeckung** die; ~, ~en discovery

Ente die; ~, ~n duck

entehren tr. V. dishonour; ~d degrading

enteignen tr. V. expropriate; **Enteignung** die expropriation

enterben tr. V. disinherit

entern tr., itr. V. board ⟨ship⟩

entfachen tr. V. (geh.) **a)** kindle, light ⟨fire⟩; **b)** (fig.) provoke ⟨quarrel, argument⟩; arouse ⟨passion, enthusiasm⟩

entfallen unr. itr. V.; mit sein **a)** (aus dem Gedächtnis) es ist mir ~: it escapes me; **b)** *(zugeteilt werden)* **auf jmdn./etw. ~:** be allotted to sb./sth.; **c)** *(wegfallen)* lapse

entfalten 1. *tr. V.* **a)** open [up]; unfold ⟨*map etc.*⟩; **b)** *(fig.)* display ⟨*ability, talent*⟩; **2.** *refl. V.* **a)** open [up]; **b)** *(fig.)* ⟨*personality, talent, etc.*⟩ develop; **Entfaltung die; ~, ~en** *(fig.)* **a)** *(Entwicklung)* development; **b)** *s.* **entfalten 1 b:** display

entfernen 1. *tr. V.* remove; take out ⟨*tonsils etc.*⟩; **2.** *refl. V.* go away; **entfernt 1.** *Adj.* **a)** *(fern)* remote; **das ist od. liegt weit ~ von der Stadt** it is a long way from the town; **10 km/zwei Stunden ~:** 10 km/two hours away; **b)** slight ⟨*acquaintance*⟩; distant ⟨*relation*⟩; slight ⟨*resemblance*⟩; **2.** *adv.* **a)** *(fern)* remotely; **b)** slightly ⟨*acquainted*⟩; distantly ⟨*related*⟩; **Entfernung die; ~, ~en a)** *(Abstand)* distance; **b)** *(das Beseitigen)* removal

entfesseln *tr. V.* unleash

entflammen 1. *tr. V.* arouse ⟨*enthusiasm etc*⟩; **2.** *itr. V.; mit sein* flare up

entfliehen *unr. itr. V.; mit sein* escape; **jmdm. ~:** escape from sb.

entfremden 1. *tr. V.* **a) etw. seinem Zweck ~:** use sth. for a different purpose; **b)** *(Philos., Soziol.)* entfremdet alienated; **2.** *refl. V.* **sich jmdm./einer Sache ~:** become estranged from sb./unfamiliar with sth.; **Entfremdung die; ~, ~en** alienation; estrangement

entführen *tr. V.* kidnap ⟨*child etc.*⟩; hijack ⟨*plane, lorry, etc.*⟩; **Entführer der** *s.* **entführen:** kidnapper; hijacker; **Entführung die** *s.* **entführen:** kidnapping; hijacking

entgegen 1. *Adv.* towards; **2.** *Präp. mit Dat.* **~ meinem Wunsch** against my wishes; **~ dem Befehl** contrary to orders

entgegen-, Entgegen-: **~|bringen** *unr. tr. V.* *(fig.)* show ⟨*love, understanding*⟩; **~|fahren** *unr. itr. V.; mit sein* **jmdm. ~fahren** come/go to meet sb.; **~|gehen** *unr. itr. V.; mit sein* **a)** **jmdm. ~gehen** go to meet sb.; **b)** *(fig.)* be heading for ⟨*catastrophe, hard times*⟩; **~gesetzt 1.** *Adj.* **a)** *(umgekehrt)* opposite ⟨*end, direction*⟩; **b)** *(gegensätzlich)* opposing; **2.** *adv.* **genau ~gesetzt handeln/denken** do/think exactly the opposite; **~|kommen** *unr. itr. V.; mit sein* **jmdm. ~kommen** come to meet sb.; *(Zugeständnisse machen)* be accommodating towards sb.; **~kommen das** co-operation;

(Zugeständnis) concession; **~kommend** *Adj.* obliging; **~|nehmen** *unr. itr. V.* receive; **~|treten** *unr. itr. V.; mit sein* go/come up to; *(fig.)* stand up to ⟨*difficulties*⟩

entgegnen *tr. V.* retort; reply

entgehen *unr. itr. V.; mit sein* **a)** *(entkommen)* escape; **b) jmdm. entgeht etw. sb.** misses sth.

entgeistert *Adj.* dumbfounded

Entgelt das; ~|e|s, ~e payment; fee

entgiften *tr. V.* decontaminate ⟨*substance etc.*⟩; detoxicate ⟨*body etc.*⟩

entgleisen *itr. V.; mit sein* **a)** be derailed; **b)** *(fig.)* make a/some faux pas

entgräten *tr. V.* fillet

enthaaren *tr. V.* remove hair from; **Enthaarungs·mittel das** hair remover

¹enthalten 1. *unr. tr. V.* contain; **2.** *unr. refl. V.* **sich einer Sache** *(Gen.)* **~:** abstain from sth.; **sich der Stimme ~:** abstain; **²enthalten** *Adj.* **in etw.** *(Dat.)* **~ sein** be contained in sth.; **das ist im Preis ~:** that is included in the price; **enthaltsam 1.** *Adj.* abstemious; *(sexuell)* abstinent; **2.** *adv.* **~ leben** live in abstinence; **Enthaltsamkeit die; ~:** abstinence; **Enthaltung die** abstention

enthaupten *tr. V.* *(geh.)* behead

enthäuten *tr. V.* skin

entheben *unr. tr. V.* *(geh.)* relieve

enthemmt *Adj.* uninhibited

enthüllen *tr. V.* unveil ⟨*monument etc.*⟩; reveal ⟨*face, truth, secret*⟩; **Enthüllung die; ~, ~en** *s.* **enthüllen:** unveiling; revelation

Enthusiasmus [ɛntu'ziasmʊs] **der; ~:** enthusiasm; **enthusiastisch 1.** *Adj.* enthusiastic; **2.** *adv.* enthusiastically

entkalken *tr. V.* decalcify

entkleiden *tr. V.* *(geh.)* **a)** undress; **b)** *(berauben)* strip

entkommen *unr. itr. V.; mit sein* escape

entkorken *tr. V.* uncork ⟨*bottle*⟩

entkräften *tr. V.* **a)** weaken; **völlig ~:** exhaust; **b)** *(fig.)* refute ⟨*argument etc.*⟩; **Entkräftung die; ~, ~en** debility; **völlige ~:** exhaustion; **b)** *(fig.)* refutation

entladen 1. *unr. tr. V.* unload; **2.** *unr. refl. V.* **a)** ⟨*storm*⟩ break; **b)** *(fig.)* ⟨*anger etc.*⟩ erupt; ⟨*aggression etc.*⟩ be released

entlang 1. *Präp. mit Akk. u. Dat.* along; **2.** *Adv.* along; **hier/dort ~, bitte!** this/that way please!

entlang-: ~|**fahren** *unr. itr. V.; mit
sein* **a)** drive along; **b)** *(streichen)* go
along; ~|**gehen** *unr. itr. V.; mit sein
⟨person⟩* go *or* walk along; ~|**laufen**
unr. itr. V.; mit sein **a)** walk/run
along; **b)** *(verlaufen)* go *or* run along
entlarven *tr. V.* expose
entlassen *unr. tr. V.* **a)** *(aus dem Gefängnis)* release; *(aus dem Krankenhaus, der Armee)* discharge; **b)** *(aus einem Arbeitsverhältnis)* dismiss; *(wegen
Arbeitsmangels)* make redundant
(Brit.); lay off; **Entlassung** die; ~,
~en *s.* **entlassen:** release; discharge;
dismissal; redundancy *(Brit.);* laying
off
entlasten *tr. V.* **a)** relieve; **b)**
(Rechtsw.) exonerate ⟨*defendant*⟩;
Entlastung die; ~, ~en **a)** relief; **b)**
(Rechtsw.) exoneration; defence
entlaufen *unr. itr. V.; mit sein* run
away; **ein ~er Sträfling/Sklave** an es-
caped convict/a runaway slave
entlausen *tr. V.* delouse
entledigen *refl. V.* **sich jmds./einer
Sache** *(Gen.)* ~ *(geh.)* rid oneself of
sb./sth.
entleeren *tr. V.* empty; evacuate
⟨*bowels, bladder*⟩
entlegen *Adj.* remote
entleihen *unr. tr. V.* borrow
entlocken *tr. V. (geh.)* **jmdm. etw.** ~:
elicit sth. from sb.
entlohnen *tr.V.* pay; **Entlohnung**
die; ~, ~en payment; *(Lohn)* pay
entlüften *tr. V.* ventilate; **Entlüfter**
der; ~s, ~: ventilator
entmachten *tr. V.* deprive of power
entmilitarisieren *tr. V.* demilitarize
entmündigen *tr. V.* incapacitate;
Entmündigung die; ~, ~en incapa-
citation
entmutigen *tr. V.* discourage
Entnahme die; ~, ~n *(von Wasser)*
drawing; *(von Blut)* extraction
entnehmen *unr. tr. V.* **a)** etw. [einer
Sache *(Dat.)*] ~: take sth. [from sth.];
b) *(ersehen aus)* gather *(Dat.* from)
entnervend *Adj.* nerve-racking
entpuppen *refl. V.* **sich als etw./jmd.**
~: turn out to be sth./sb.
entrahmen *tr. V.* skim ⟨*milk*⟩
entreißen *unr. tr. V.* **jmdm. etw.** ~:
snatch sth. from sb.
entrichten *tr. V. (Amtsspr.)* pay ⟨*fee*⟩
entrümpeln *tr. V.* clear out; **Ent-
rümpelung** die; ~, ~en clear-out
entrüsten 1. *refl. V.* **sich [über etw.
(Akk.)]** ~: be indignant [at *or* about

sth.]; **2.** *tr. V. (empören)* **jmdn.** ~:
make sb. indignant; **Entrüstung** die
indignation *(über + Akk.* at, about)
Entsafter der; ~s, ~: juice-extractor
entsagen *itr. V.* **einer Sache** *(Dat.)* ~
(geh.) renounce sth.; **Entsagung**
die; ~, ~en *(geh.)* renunciation
entschädigen *tr. V.* compensate **(für**
for); **jmdn. für etw.** ~ *(fig.)* make up
for sth.; **Entschädigung** die compensation
entschärfen *tr. V.* defuse; tone down
⟨*discussion, criticism*⟩
entscheiden 1. *unr. refl. V.* **a)** decide;
b) *(unpers.)* **morgen entscheidet es sich,
ob ...:** I/we/you will know tomorrow
whether ...; **2.** *unr. itr. V.* **über etw.**
(Akk.) ~: settle sth; **3.** *unr. tr. V.* decide on ⟨*dispute*⟩; decide ⟨*outcome, result*⟩; **entscheidend 1.** *Adj.* crucial;
decisive ⟨*action*⟩; **2.** *adv.* **jmdn./etw.** ~
beeinflussen have a decisive influence
on sb./sth.; **Entscheidung** die decision
entschieden 1. *Adj.* **a)** *(entschlossen)*
determined; resolute; **b)** *(eindeutig)*
definite; **2.** *adv.* resolutely; **das geht** ~
zu weit that is going much too far
entschlafen *unr. itr. V.; mit sein* pass
away
entschließen *unr. refl. V.* decide;
Entschließung die resolution; **entschlossen** *Adj.* determined; **Entschlossenheit** die; ~: determination; **Entschluß** der decision
entschlüsseln *tr. V.* decipher
entschuldigen 1. *refl. V.* apologize;
2. *tr. V. (auch itr.)* V. excuse ⟨*person*⟩;
sich ~ **lassen** ask to be excused; ~ **Sie
[bitte]!** *(bei Fragen, Bitten)* excuse me;
(bedauernd) I'm sorry; **Entschuldigung** die; ~, ~en **a)** apology; **b)**
(Grund) excuse; **c)** *(Höflichkeitsfor-
mel)* ~! *(bei Fragen, Bitten)* excuse
me; *(bedauernd)* [I'm] sorry
entschwinden *unr. itr. V.; mit sein
(geh.)* disappear; vanish
entsetzen 1. *refl. V.* be horrified; **2.**
tr. V. horrify; **Entsetzen** das; ~s
horror; **entsetzlich 1.** *Adj.* **a)** horrible ⟨*accident, crime, etc.*⟩; **b)** *nicht
präd. (ugs.: stark)* terrible ⟨*thirst, hunger*⟩; **2.** *adv.* terribly *(coll.)*
entsinnen *unr. refl. V.* **sich jmds./ei-
ner Sache** ~: remember sb./sth.
entspannen 1. *tr. V.* relax; **2.** *refl. V.*
a) ⟨*person*⟩ relax; **b)** *(fig.) ⟨situation,
tension⟩* ease; **Entspannung** die; *o.
Pl.* **a)** relaxation; **b)** *(politisch)* easing

of tension; détente; **Entspªn-nungs·politik die** policy of détente
entsprechen *unr. itr. V.* **a)** *(überein-stimmen mit)* **einer Sache** *(Dat.)* ~: correspond to sth.; **b)** *(nachkommen)* **einem Wunsch** ~: comply with a request; **den Anforderungen** ~: meet the requirements; **entsprechend 1.** *Adj.* **a)** corresponding; *(angemessen)* appropriate; **b)** *nicht attr. (dem~)* in accordance *postpos.;* **2.** *adv.* **a)** *(ange-messen)* appropriately; **b)** *(dem~)* accordingly; **3.** *Präp. mit Dativ:* ~ **einer Sache** in accordance with sth.
entspringen *unr. itr. V.; mit sein* **a)** ⟨*river*⟩ rise; **b)** *(entstehen aus)* **einer Sache** *(Dat.)* ~: spring from sth.
entstehen *unr. itr. V.; mit sein* **a)** originate; ⟨*quarrel, friendship, etc.*⟩ arise; **b)** *(gebildet werden)* be formed (**aus** from, **durch** by); **c)** *(sich ergeben)* occur; *(als Folge)* result; **Entste-hung die;** ~: origin
entstehen *itr. V.* stone
entstellen *tr. V.* **a)** disfigure; **b)** *(ver-fälschen)* distort ⟨*text, facts*⟩; **Ent-stellung die a)** disfigurement; **b)** *(Verfälschung)* distortion
entstören *tr. V. (Elektrot.)* suppress ⟨*engine, electrical appliance*⟩
enttarnen *tr. V.* uncover
enttäuschen *tr. V.* disappoint; **ent-täuscht** *Adj.* disappointed; dashed ⟨*hopes*⟩; **Enttäuschung die** disappointment
entwachsen *unr. itr. V.; mit sein* **einer Sache** *(Dat.)* ~: grow out of sth.
entwaffnen *tr. V. (auch fig.)* disarm; **entwaffnend** *Adj.* disarming
entwarnen *itr. V.* sound the all-clear; **Entwarnung die** all-clear
entwässern *tr. V.* drain; **Entwäs-serung die;** ~, ~**en** drainage
entweder *Konj.:* ~ ... **oder** either ... or
entweichen *unr. itr. V.; mit sein* escape
entwenden *tr. V. (geh.)* purloin
entwerfen *unr. tr. V.* design ⟨*furni-ture, dress*⟩; draft ⟨*novel etc.*⟩; draw up ⟨*plans etc.*⟩
entwerten *tr. V.* **a)** cancel ⟨*ticket, postage stamp*⟩; **b)** devalue ⟨*currency*⟩
entwickeln 1. *refl. V.* develop; **2.** *tr. V.* produce ⟨*vapour, smell*⟩; display ⟨*ability, characteristic*⟩; develop ⟨*equipment, photograph, film*⟩; elaborate ⟨*theory, ideas*⟩; **Entwicklung die;** ~, ~**en a)** development; *(von Dämpfen usw.)* production; **in der** ~

sein ⟨*young person*⟩ be adolescent; **b)** *(Darlegung)* elaboration; **c)** *(Fot.)* developing
Entwicklungs-: ~**helfer der** development aid worker; ~**hilfe die** [development] aid; ~**land das;** *Pl.* ~**länder** developing country; ~**politik die** development aid policy
entwirren *tr. V.* disentangle
entwischen *itr. V.; mit sein (ugs.)* get away
entwöhnen *tr. V.* wean
entwürdigend *Adj.* degrading
Entwurf der a) design; **b)** *(Konzept)* draft
entwurzeln *tr. V.* uproot
entziehen 1. *unr. tr. V.* **a)** take away; **b)** *(nicht zugestehen)* withdraw; **2.** *unr. refl. V.* **sich seinen Pflichten** *(Dat.)* ~: evade one's duty; **das entzieht sich meiner Kontrolle** that is beyond my control; **Entziehung die a)** withdrawal; **b)** *(Entziehungskur)* withdrawal treatment *no indef. art.*
entziffern *tr. V.* decipher
entzückend *Adj.* delightful; **ent-zückt** *Adj.* delighted
Entzug der; ~[**e**]**s** withdrawal
entzündbar *Adj.* [in]flammable; **ent-zünden 1.** *tr. V.* light ⟨*fire*⟩; strike ⟨*match*⟩; **2.** *refl. V.* **a)** ignite; **b)** *(an-schwellen)* become inflamed; **ent-zündlich** *Adj.* **a)** [in]flammable ⟨*sub-stance*⟩; **b)** *(Med.)* inflammatory; **Entzündung die;** ~, ~**en** inflammation
entzwei *Adj. (geh.)* in pieces; **ent-zweien** *refl. V.* fall out; **ent-zwei**|**gehen** *unr. itr. V.; mit sein (geh.)* break
Enzian ['ɛntsia:n] **der;** ~**s,** ~**e** gentian
Enzyklika die; ~, **Enzykliken** encyclical
Enzyklopädie die; ~, ~**n** encyclopaedia; **enzyklopädisch** *Adj.* encyclopaedic
Epen *s.* **Epos**
Epidemie die; ~, ~**n** epidemic
Epilepsie die; ~, ~**n** *(Med.)* epilepsy *no art.;* **Epileptiker der;** ~**s,** ~: epileptic; **epileptisch** *Adj.* epileptic
episch *Adj.* epic
Episode die; ~, ~**n** episode
Epoche die; ~, ~**n** epoch
Epos ['e:pɔs] **das;** ~, **Epen** epic [poem]; epos
er *Personalpron. 3. Pers. Sg. Nom. Mask.* he; *(betont)* him; *(bei Dingen/ Tieren)* it; *s. auch* **ihm; ihn; seiner**

erạchten *tr. V. (geh.)* consider; etw. **als** *od.* **für seine Pflicht** ~: consider sth. [to be] one's duty

erạrbeiten *tr. V.* work for

Ẹrb·anlage die hereditary disposition

erbạrmen *refl. V. (geh.)* take pity *(Gen.* on); **Erbạrmen das;** ~s pity; **erbạrmlich 1.** *Adj.* **a)** *(elend)* wretched; **b)** *(unzulänglich)* pathetic; **c)** *(abwertend: gemein)* mean; wretched; **d)** *(sehr groß)* terrible ⟨*hunger, fear, etc.*⟩; **2.** *adv.* terribly

erbạuen 1. *tr. V.* **a)** build; **b)** *(geh.: erheben)* uplift; **2.** *refl. V.* **sich an etw.** *(Dat.)* ~: be uplifted by sth.; **Erbạuer der;** ~s, ~: architect

¹Ẹrbe das; ~s **a)** inheritance; **b)** *(Vermächtnis)* legacy; **²Ẹrbe der;** ~n ~n heir; **ẹrben** *tr. (auch itr.) V.* inherit

erbẹtteln *tr. V.* get by begging

erbẹuten *tr. V.* carry off, get away with ⟨*valuables, prey, etc.*⟩; capture ⟨*enemy plane, tank, etc.*⟩

Ẹrb-: ~**folge die** succession; ~**gut das** *(Biol.)* genetic make-up

Ẹrbin die; ~, ~**nen** heiress

erbịtten *unr. tr. V. (geh.)* request

erbịttern *tr. V.* enrage; **erbịttert 1.** *Adj.* bitter; **2.** *adv.* ~ **kämpfen** wage a bitter struggle

erblạssen *itr. V.; mit sein (geh.)* turn pale; blanch *(literary)*

erblẹichen *itr. V.; mit sein (geh.) s.* **erblassen**

ẹrblich *Adj.* hereditary ⟨*title, disease*⟩

erblịcken *tr. V. (geh.)* catch sight of; *(fig.)* see

erblịnden *itr. V.; mit sein* lose one's sight

erblühen *itr. V.; mit sein (geh.)* bloom; blossom

Ẹrb·masse die *(Biol.)* genetic make-up

erbọst *Adj.* furious

erbrẹchen 1. *unr. tr. V.* bring up ⟨*food*⟩; **2.** *unr. itr., refl. V.* vomit; **Erbrẹchen das;** ~s vomiting

erbrịngen *unr. tr. V.* produce

Ẹrbschaft die; ~, ~**en** inheritance; **Ẹrbschaft[s]·steuer die** estate *or* death duties *pl.*

Ẹrbse die; ~, ~**n** pea

Ẹrb-: ~**stück das** heirloom; ~**sünde die** original sin; ~**teil das** share of an/the inheritance

Ẹrd-: ~**achse die** earth's axis; ~**apfel der** *(bes. österr.) s.* **Kartoffel;** ~**beben das** earthquake; ~**beere die** strawberry; ~**boden der** ground; earth;

etw. **dem** ~**boden gleichmachen** raze sth. to the ground

Ẹrde die; ~, ~**n a)** *(Erdreich)* soil; earth; **b)** *o. Pl. (fester Boden)* ground; **c)** *o. Pl. (Welt)* earth; world; **d)** *o. Pl. (Planet)* Earth

erdẹnklich *Adj.* conceivable

Ẹrd-: ~**gas das** natural gas; ~**geschoß das** ground floor; first floor *(Amer.);* ~**kunde die** geography; ~**nuß die** peanut; ~**oberfläche die** earth's surface; ~**öl das** oil

erdöl-, Ẹrdöl-: ~**exportierend** *Adj.* oil-exporting ⟨*country*⟩; ~**gewinnung die** oil production; ~**leitung die** oil pipeline

erdrọsseln *tr. V.* strangle

erdrücken *tr. V.* **a)** crush; **b)** *(fig.: belasten)* overwhelm; **erdrückend** *Adj.* overwhelming; oppressive ⟨*heat, silence*⟩

Ẹrd-: ~**rutsch der** landslide; ~**teil der** continent

erdụlden *tr. V.* endure ⟨*sorrow, misfortune*⟩; tolerate ⟨*insults*⟩; *(über sich ergehen lassen)* undergo

ereifern *refl. V.* get excited

ereignen *refl. V.* happen; ⟨*accident, mishap*⟩ occur; **Ereignis das;** ~ses, ~**se** event; occurrence

Eremịt der; ~**en,** ~**en** hermit

erẹrbt *Adj.* inherited

¹erfạhren *unr. tr. V.* **a)** find out; learn; *(hören)* hear; **b)** *(geh.: erleben)* experience; *(erleiden)* suffer; **²erfạhren** *Adj.* experienced; **Erfạhrung die;** ~, ~**en** experience; ~**en sammeln** gain experience *sing.;* etw. **in** ~ **bringen** discover sth.; **erfạhrungs·gemäß** *Adv.* in our/my experience

erfạssen *tr. V.* **a)** *(mitreißen)* catch; **b)** *(begreifen)* grasp ⟨*situation, etc.*⟩; **c)** *(registrieren)* record; **Erfạssung die** registration

erfịnden *unr. tr. V.* invent; **das ist alles erfunden** it is pure fabrication; **Erfịnder der;** ~s, ~ **a)** inventor; **b)** *(Urheber)* creator; **erfịnderisch** *Adj.* inventive; *(schlau)* resourceful; **Erfịndung die;** ~, ~**en** invention

erflẹhen *tr. V. (geh.)* beg

Erfọlg der; ~**[e]s,** ~**e** success; **keinen** ~ **haben** be unsuccessful

erfọlgen *itr. V.; mit sein* take place; occur; **es erfolgte keine Reaktion** there was no reaction

erfọlg-: ~**los 1.** *Adj.* unsuccessful; **2.** *adv.* unsuccessfully; ~**reich 1.** *Adj.* successful; **2.** *adv.* successfully

Erfolgs·erlebnis das feeling of achievement

erfolg·versprechend *Adj.* promising

erforderlich *Adj.* required; necessary; **erfordern** *tr. V.* require; demand

erforschen *tr. V.* discover ⟨*facts, causes, etc.*⟩; explore ⟨*country*⟩; **Erforschung die** research (+ *Gen.* into); *(eines Landes usw.)* exploration

erfreuen 1. *tr. V.* please; **2.** *refl. V.* sich an etw. *(Dat.)* ~: take pleasure in sth.; **erfreulich** *Adj.* pleasant

erfrieren 1. *unr. itr. V.; mit sein* freeze to death; ⟨*plant, harvest, etc.*⟩ be damaged by frost; **2.** *unr. refl. V.* sich *(Dat.)* die Finger ~: get frostbite in one's fingers

erfrischen 1. *tr. (auch itr.) V.* refresh; **2.** *refl. V.* freshen oneself up; **erfrischend** *(auch fig.) Adj.* refreshing; **Erfrischung die**; ~, ~en *(auch fig.)* refreshment; **Erfrischungs·raum der** refreshment room

erfüllen 1. *tr. V.* grant ⟨*wish, request*⟩; fulfil ⟨*contract*⟩; carry out ⟨*duty*⟩; meet ⟨*condition*⟩; **2.** *refl. V.* ⟨*wish*⟩ come true; **Erfüllung die: in ~ gehen** come true

erfunden *Adj.* fictional ⟨*story*⟩

ergänzen *tr. V.* **a)** *(vervollständigen)* complete; *(erweitern)* add to; **b)** *(hinzufügen)* add ⟨*remark*⟩; **Ergänzung die**; ~, ~en **a)** *(Vervollständigung)* completion; *(Erweiterung)* enlargement; **b)** *(Zusatz)* addition; *(zu einem Gesetz)* amendment

ergattern *tr. V. (ugs.)* manage to grab

ergaunern *tr. V.* get by underhand means

¹ergeben 1. *unr. refl. V.* **a)** sich in etw. *(Akk.)* ~: submit to sth.; **b)** *(kapitulieren)* surrender *(Dat.* to); **c)** *(folgen, entstehen)* arise (aus from); **2.** *unr. tr. V.* result in; **²ergeben** *Adj.* **a)** *(zugeneigt)* devoted; **b)** *(resignierend)* mit ~er Miene with an expression of resignation; **Ergebnis das**; ~ses, ~se result; **ergebnis·los** *Adj.* fruitless

ergehen *unr. refl. V.* sich in etw. *(Dat.)* ~: indulge in sth.

ergiebig *Adj.* rich ⟨*deposits, resources*⟩; fertile ⟨*topic*⟩

ergötzen *(geh.)* **1.** *tr. V.* enthrall; **2.** *refl. V.* sich an etw. *(Dat.)* ~: be delighted by sth.

ergrauen *itr. V.; mit sein* go grey

ergreifen *unr. tr. V.* **a)** *(greifen)* grab;

b) *(festnehmen)* catch ⟨*thief etc.*⟩; **c)** *(fig.: erfassen)* seize; **d)** *(fig.: aufnehmen)* take up ⟨*career*⟩; take ⟨*initiative, opportunity*⟩; **e)** *(fig.: bewegen)* move; **ergreifend** *Adj.* moving; **ergriffen** *Adj.* moved

ergründen *tr. V.* ascertain; discover ⟨*cause*⟩

erhaben *Adj.* solemn ⟨*moment*⟩; awe-inspiring ⟨*sight*⟩; sublime ⟨*beauty*⟩; **über etw.** *(Akk.)* ~ **sein** be above sth.

Erhalt der; ~|e|s *(Amtsdt.)* receipt; **erhalten** *unr. tr. V.* **a)** receive ⟨*letter, news, gift*⟩; be given ⟨*order*⟩; get ⟨*good mark, impression*⟩; **b)** *(bewahren)* preserve ⟨*town, building*⟩; **erhältlich** *Adj.* obtainable; **Erhaltung die**; ~: preservation; *(des Friedens)* maintenance

erhängen *tr. V.* hang

erhärten *tr. V.* strengthen ⟨*suspicion, assumption*⟩; substantiate ⟨*claim*⟩

erheben 1. *unr. tr. V.* **a)** raise **b)** *(verlangen)* levy ⟨*tax*⟩; charge ⟨*fee*⟩; **2.** *unr. refl. V.* **a)** rise; **b)** *(rebellieren)* rise up (gegen against); **erhebend** *Adj.* uplifting; **erheblich 1.** *Adj.* considerable; **2.** *adv.* considerably

erheitern *tr. V.* jmdn. ~: cheer sb. up

erhellen *tr. V.* light up

erhitzen 1. *tr. V.* heat ⟨*liquid*⟩; jmdn. ~: make sb. hot; **2.** *refl. V.* heat up; ⟨*person*⟩ become hot

erhoffen *tr. V.* sich *(Dat.)* viel/wenig von etw. ~: expect a lot/little from sth.

erhöhen 1. *tr. V.* increase ⟨*prices, productivity, etc.*⟩; **2.** *refl. V.* ⟨*rent, prices*⟩ rise; **Erhöhung die**; ~, ~en increase *(Gen.* in)

erholen *refl. V. (auch fig.)* recover (von from); *(sich ausruhen)* have a rest; **erholsam** *Adj.* restful; **Erholung die**; ~: s. erholen: recovery; rest; ~ **brauchen** need a rest; **erholungs·bedürftig** *Adj.* in need of a rest *postpos.*

erhören *tr. V. (geh.)* hear

Erika die; ~, ~s *od.* **Eriken** *(Bot.)* erica

erinnern 1. *refl. V.* sich an jmdn./etw. ~: remember sb./sth.; **sich |daran|** ~, **daß ...**: remember *or* recall that ...; **2.** *tr. V.* jmdn. an etw./jmdn. ~: remind sb. of sth./sb.; **Erinnerung die**; ~, ~en memory (**an** + *Akk.* of); **etw. |noch gut| in** ~ **haben** [still] remember sth. [well]; **zur** ~ **an jmdn./etw.** in memory of sb./sth.

erjagen *tr. V.* **a)** catch; **b)** *(gewinnen)* win ⟨*fame*⟩; make ⟨*money, fortune*⟩

erkalten *tr. V.; mit sein* cool; **erkäl-**

ten *refl. V.* catch cold; **Erkältung die;** ~, ~en cold

erkämpfen *tr. V.* win; **den Sieg** ~: gain a victory

erkaufen *tr. V.* **a)** *(durch Opfer)* win; **b)** *(durch Geld)* buy

erkennbar *Adj.* recognizable; *(sichtbar)* visible; **erkennen** *unr. tr. V.* **a)** recognize; **b)** *(deutlich sehen)* make out; **erkenntlich** *Adj.* **a)** sich |für etw.| ~ zeigen show one's appreciation for sth.; **b)** *s.* erkennbar; **Erkenntnis die;** ~, ~se discovery; **zu der** ~ **kommen, daß** ...: come to the realization that ...

Erker *der;* ~s, ~: bay window; **Erker·fenster das** bay window

erklärbar *Adj.* explicable; **erklären** 1. *tr. V.* **a)** explain; **b)** *(mitteilen)* state; declare; **c) jmdn. für tot** ~: pronounce someone dead; **jmdn. zu etw.** ~: name sb. as sth; **2.** *refl. V.* **sich einverstanden/bereit** ~: declare oneself [to be] in agreement/willing; **erklärlich** *Adj.* understandable; **erklärt** *Adj.* declared; **Erklärung die;** ~, ~en **a)** *(Darlegung)* explanation; **b)** *(Mitteilung)* statement

erklimmen *unr. tr. V.* *(geh.)* climb

erklingen *unr. itr. V.; mit sein* ring out

erkranken *itr. V.; mit sein* become ill **(an** + *Dat.* with); **schwer erkrankt sein** be seriously ill; **Erkrankung die;** ~, ~en illness; *(eines Körperteils)* disease

erkunden *tr. V.* reconnoitre *(terrain)*; **erkundigen** *refl. V.* **sich nach jmdm./ etw.** ~: ask after sb./enquire about sth.; **Erkundigung die;** ~, ~en enquiry

erlahmen *itr. V.; mit sein* tire; *(strength)* flag

erlangen *tr. V.* gain; obtain *(credit, visa);* reach *(age)*

Erlaß *der; Erlasses, Erlasse* decree; **erlassen** *unr. tr. V.* **a)** enact *(law);* declare *(amnesty);* issue *(warrant);* **b)** *(verzichten auf)* remit *(sentence)*

erlauben 1. *tr. V.* **a)** allow; **b)** *(ermöglichen)* permit; **2.** *refl. V.* **sich** *(Dat.)* **etw.** ~: permit oneself sth.; **Erlaubnis die;** ~, ~se permission; *(Schriftstück)* permit

erläutern *tr. V.* explain; comment on *(picture etc.);* annotate *(text);* **Erläuterung die** explanation

Erle *die;* ~, ~n alder

erleben *tr. V.* experience; **etwas Schreckliches** ~: have a terrible experience; **er wird das nächste Jahr**

nicht mehr ~: he won't see next year; **du kannst was** ~! *(ugs.)* you won't know what's hit you!; **Erlebnis das;** ~ses, ~se experience

erledigen 1. *tr. V.* deal with *(task);* settle *(matter);* **ich muß noch einige Dinge erledigen** I must see to a few things; **sie hat alles pünktlich erledigt** she got everything done on time; **2.** *refl. V.(matter, problem)* resolve itself; **vieles erledigt sich von selbst** a lot of things sort them'selves out; **erledigt** *Adj.* closed *(case); (ugs.)* worn out *(person)*

erlegen *tr. V.* shoot *(animal)*

erleichtern *tr. V.* **a)** make easier; **b)** *(befreien)* relieve; **Erleichterung die;** ~, ~en **a)** zur ~ der Arbeit to make the work easier; **b)** *(Befreiung)* relief; **c)** *(Verbesserung, Milderung)* alleviation

erleiden *unr. tr. V.* suffer

erlernbar *Adj.* learnable; **erlernen** *tr. V.* learn

erlesen *Adj.* superior *(wine);* choice *(dish)*

erleuchten *tr. V.* **a)** light; **b)** *(geh.: mit Klarheit erfüllen)* inspire; **Erleuchtung die;** ~, ~en inspiration

erliegen *unr. itr. V.; mit sein* succumb *(Dat.* to); **einem Irrtum** ~: be misled; **einer Krankheit** *(Dat.)* ~: die from an illness

erlogen *Adj.* made up

Erlös *der;* ~es, ~e proceeds *pl.*

erlöschen *unr. itr. V.; mit sein (fire)* go out; **ein erloschener Vulkan** an extinct volcano

erlösen *tr. V.* save, rescue **(von** from); **Erlöser der;** ~s, ~ **a)** saviour; **b)** *(christl. Rel.)* redeemer; **Erlösung die** release **(von** from)

ermächtigen *tr. V.* authorize; **Ermächtigung die;** ~, ~en authorization

ermahnen *tr. V.* admonish; tell *(coll.); (warnen)* warn; **Ermahnung die** admonition; *(Warnung)* warning

Ermang[e]lung die; ~: **in** ~ (+ *Gen.*) *(geh.)* in the absence of

ermäßigen *tr. V.* reduce; **Ermäßigung die** reduction

ermatten *(geh.)* 1. *itr. V.; mit sein* become exhausted; **2.** *tr. V.* exhaust, tire

ermessen *unr. tr. V.* estimate, gauge; **Ermessen das;** ~s estimation

ermitteln 1. *tr. V.* ascertain *(facts);* discover *(culprit, address);* establish

⟨*identity, origin*⟩; decide ⟨*winner*⟩; calculate ⟨*quota, rates, data*⟩; **2.** *itr. V. (Rechtsw.)* investigate; **Ermittlung die; ~, ~en a)** *(das Ermitteln) s.* **ermitteln a:** ascertainment; discovery; establishment; **b)** *(Untersuchung)* investigation

ermöglichen *tr. V.* enable

ermorden *tr. V.* murder; **Ermordung die; ~, ~en** murder

ermüden 1. *itr. V.; mit sein* tire; **2.** *tr. V.* tire; make tired; **ermüdend** *Adj.* tiring; **Ermüdung die; ~, ~en** tiredness

ermuntern *tr. V.* encourage; **ermunternd** *Adj.* encouraging

ermutigen *tr. V.* encourage; **Ermutigung die; ~, ~en** encouragement

ernähren 1. *tr. V.* **a)** feed ⟨*young, child*⟩; **b)** *(unterhalten)* keep ⟨*family, wife*⟩; **2.** *refl. V.* feed oneself; **Ernährer der; ~s, ~, Ernährerin die; ~, ~nen** breadwinner; **Ernährung die; ~:** feeding; *(Nahrung)* diet

ernennen *unr. tr. V.* appoint; **Ernennung die** appointment **(zu as)**

erneuern *tr. V.* **a)** replace; **b)** *(wiederherstellen)* renovate ⟨*roof, building*⟩; *(fig.)* thoroughly reform ⟨*system*⟩; **Erneuerung die a)** replacement; **b)** *(Wiederherstellung)* renovation; **erneut 1.** *Adj.* renewed; **2.** *adv.* once again

erniedrigen *tr. V.* humiliate; **Erniedrigung die; ~, ~en** humiliation

ernst 1. *Adj.* **a)** serious; **b)** *(aufrichtig)* genuine ⟨*intention, offer*⟩; **c)** *(gefahrvoll)* serious ⟨*injury*⟩; grave ⟨*situation*⟩; **2.** *adv.* seriously

Ernst der; ~[e]s a) seriousness; **das ist mein |voller| ~:** I mean that [quite] seriously; **b)** *(Wirklichkeit)* **daraus wurde |blutiger/bitterer| ~:** it became [deadly] serious; **der ~ des Lebens** the serious side of life

ernst-, Ernst-: ~fall der: im ~: when the real thing happens; **~gemeint** *Adj. (präd. getrennt geschrieben)* serious; sincere ⟨*wish*⟩; **~haft 1.** *Adj.* serious; **2.** *adv.* seriously; **~haftigkeit die; ~:** seriousness

ernstlich 1. *Adj.* **a)** serious; **b)** *(aufrichtig)* genuine ⟨*wish*⟩; **2.** *adv.* **a)** seriously; **b)** *(aufrichtig)* genuinely ⟨*sorry, repentant*⟩

Ernte die; ~, ~n a) harvest; **b)** *(Ertrag)* crop; **die ~ einbringen** bring in the harvest; **Ernte·dank·fest das** harvest festival; **ernten** *tr. V.* harvest

ernüchtern *tr. V.* sober up; *(fig.)* bring down to earth; **~d** sobering; **Ernüchterung die; ~, ~en** *(fig.)* disillusionment

Eroberer der; ~s, ~, Eroberin die; ~, ~nen conqueror; **erobern** *tr. V.* **a)** conquer; take ⟨*town, fortress*⟩; seize ⟨*power*⟩; **Eroberung die; ~, ~en** conquest; *(einer Stadt, Festung)* taking

eröffnen *tr. V.* **a)** open; start ⟨*business, practice*⟩; **b)** *(mitteilen)* **jmdm. etw. ~:** reveal sth. to sb.; **c) ein Testament ~:** read a will; **Eröffnung die a)** opening; *(einer Sitzung)* start; **b)** *(Mitteilung)* revelation; **c)** *(Testaments~)* reading

erörtern *tr. V.* discuss; **Erörterung die; ~, ~en** discussion

Erotik die; ~: eroticism; **erotisch** *Adj.* erotic

Erpel der; ~s, ~: drake

erpicht *Adj. in* **auf etw.** *(Akk.)* **~ sein** be keen on sth.

erpressen *tr. V.* **a)** *(nötigen)* blackmail; **b)** *(erlangen)* extort ⟨*money etc.*⟩; **Erpresser der; ~s, ~:** blackmailer; **Erpressung die** blackmail *no indef. art.; (von Geld, Geständnis)* extortion

erproben *tr. V.* test ⟨*medicine*⟩ **(an +** *Akk.* **on)**

erraten *unr. tr. V.* guess

errechnen *tr. V.* calculate

erregen 1. *tr. V.* **a)** annoy; **b)** *(sexuell)* arouse; **c)** *(verursachen)* arouse; **2.** *refl. V.* get excited; **erregend** *Adj.* exciting; *(sexuell)* arousing; **Erreger der; ~s, ~** *(Med.)* pathogen; **erregt** *Adj.* excited; *(sexuell)* aroused; **Erregung die** excitement

erreichbar *Adj.* **a)** within reach *postpos.;* **b) der Ort ist mit dem Zug ~:** the place can be reached by train; **erreichen** *tr. V.* **a)** reach; **den Zug ~:** catch the train; **er ist telefonisch zu ~:** he can be contacted by telephone; **b)** *(durchsetzen)* achieve ⟨*goal, aim*⟩

errichten *tr. V.* **a)** build ⟨*house, bridge, etc.*⟩; **b)** *(aufstellen)* erect

erringen *unr. tr. V.* gain ⟨*victory*⟩; reach ⟨*first etc. place*⟩

erröten *itr. V.; mit sein* blush

Errungenschaft die; ~, ~en achievement

Ersatz der; ~es a) replacement; **b)** *(Entschädigung)* compensation

Ersatz-: ~kasse die private health insurance company; **~mann der;** *Pl.* **~männer, ~leute** replacement; *(Sport)*

substitute; ~**rad das** spare wheel; ~**reifen der** spare tyre; ~**teil das** *(bes. Technik)* spare part; spare *(Brit.)*
ersaufen *unr. itr. V.; mit sein (salopp)* drown; **ersäufen** *tr. V.* drown
erschaffen *unr. tr. V.* create; **Erschaffung die** creation
erscheinen *unr. itr. V.; mit sein* ⟨*book*⟩ be published; **Erscheinung die;** ~, ~**en a)** *(Vorgang)* phenomenon; **b)** *(äußere Gestalt)* appearance; **c)** *(Vision)* apparition; **eine** ~ **haben** see a vision
Erscheinungs-: ~**bild das** appearance; ~**form die** manifestation
erschießen *unr. tr. V.* shoot dead; **Erschießung die;** ~, ~**en** shooting
erschlaffen *itr. V.; mit sein* ⟨*muscle, limb*⟩ become limp; ⟨*skin*⟩ grow slack
¹**erschlagen** *unr. tr. V.* strike dead; kill; ²**erschlagen** *Adj. (ugs.)* **a)** *(erschöpft)* worn out; **b)** *(verblüfft)* **wie** ~ **sein** be flabbergasted *(coll.)* or thunderstruck
erschließen *unr. tr. V.* develop ⟨*area, building land*⟩; tap ⟨*resources*⟩
erschöpfen *tr. V.* exhaust; **erschöpfend** *Adj.* exhaustive; **erschöpft** *Adj.* exhausted; **Erschöpfung die** exhaustion
¹**erschrecken** *unr. itr. V.; mit sein* be startled; **vor etw.** *(Dat.)* od. **über etw.** *(Akk.)* ~: be startled by sth.; ²**erschrecken** *tr. V.* frighten; scare; ³**erschrecken** *unr. od. regelm. refl. V.* get a fright; **erschreckend** *Adj.* alarming; **erschrocken 1. 2. Part. v.** ¹**erschrecken; 2.** *Adj.* frightened
erschüttern *tr. V. (auch fig.)* shake; **erschütternd** *Adj.* deeply distressing; deeply shocking ⟨*conditions*⟩; **Erschütterung die;** ~, ~**en a)** vibration; *(der Erde)* tremor; **b)** *(Ergriffenheit)* shock; *(Trauer)* distress
erschweren *tr. V.* **etw.** ~: make sth. more difficult; **erschwerend 1.** *Adj.* complicating ⟨*factor*⟩; **2.** *adv.* **es kommt** ~ **hinzu, daß er ...:** to make matters worse he ...
erschwinglich *Adj.* reasonable
ersehen *unr. tr. V.* see; **aus etw. zu** ~ **sein** be evident from sth.
ersetzen *tr. V.* **a)** replace **(durch** by); **b)** *(erstatten)* reimburse ⟨*expenses*⟩; **jmdm. einen Schaden** ~: compensate sb. for damages
ersichtlich *Adj.* apparent
erspähen *tr. V. (geh.)* espy *(literary)*; catch sight of

ersparen *tr. V.* save; **Ersparnis die;** ~, ~**se** saving
ersprießlich *Adj. (geh.)* fruitful ⟨*contacts, collaboration*⟩
erst 1. *Adv.* **a)** *(zu~)* first; ~ **einmal** first [of all]; **b)** *(nicht eher als)* **eben** ~: only just; ~ **nächste Woche** not until next week; ~ **er war** ~ **zufrieden, als ...:** he was not satisfied until ...; **c)** *(nicht mehr als)* only; **2.** *Partikel* **so was lese ich gar nicht** ~: I dont even start reading that sort of stuff
erst... *Ordinalz.* **a)** first; **etw. das** ~**e Mal tun** do sth. for the first time; **am Ersten |des Monats|** on the first [of the month]; **als** ~**er/**~**e etw. tun** be the first to do sth.; **b)** *(best...)* **das** ~**e Hotel** the best hotel; **der/die Erste |der Klasse|** the top boy/girl [of the class]
erstarren *unr. V.; mit sein* ⟨*jelly, plaster*⟩ set; ⟨*limbs, fingers*⟩ grow stiff
erstatten *tr. V.* **a)** reimburse ⟨*expenses*⟩; **b) Anzeige gegen jmdn.** ~: report sb. [to the police]; **Erstattung die;** ~, ~**en** *(von Kosten)* reimbursement
Erst·aufführung die première
erstaunen *tr. V.* astonish; **Erstaunen das;** ~**s** astonishment; **erstaunlich 1.** *Adj.* astonishing; **2.** *adv.* astonishingly
Erst·ausgabe die first edition
erstechen *unr. tr. V.* stab [to death]
erstehen *(geh.)* **1.** *unr. tr. V. (kaufen)* purchase; **2.** *unr. itr. V.; mit sein* ⟨*difficulties, problems*⟩ arise
ersteigen *unr. tr. V.* climb
ersteigern *tr. V.* buy [at an auction]
erstellen *tr. V. (Papierdt.)* **a)** *(bauen)* build; **b)** *(anfertigen)* make ⟨*assessment*⟩; draw up ⟨*plan, report, list*⟩
erste·mal *Adv.* **das** ~: for the first time; **ersten·mal** *Adv.* **zum** ~: for the first time; **beim** ~: the first time
erstens *Adv.* firstly; in the first place;
erster... *Adj.* the former
erst·geboren *Adj.* first-born
ersticken 1. *itr. V.; mit sein* suffocate; *(sich verschlucken)* choke; **2.** *tr. V.* **a)** *(töten)* suffocate; **b)** smother ⟨*flames*⟩
erstklassig 1. *Adj.* first-class; **2.** *adv.* superbly; **erstmals** *Adv.* for the first time; **erstrangig** *Adj.* **a)** first-class; **b)** *(vordringlich)* of top priority *postpos.*
erstreben *tr. V.* strive for; **erstrebens·wert** *Adj.* ⟨*ideals etc.*⟩ worth striving for; desirable ⟨*situation*⟩
erstrecken *refl. V.* **a)** *(sich ausdeh-*

nen) stretch; **b)** *(dauern)* **sich über 10 Jahre** ~: carry on for 10 years

erstürmen *tr. V.* take by storm

ersuchen *tr. V. (geh.)* ask; **jmdn. ~, etw. zu tun** request sb. to do sth.

ertappen *tr. V.* catch ⟨*thief, burglar*⟩

erteilen *tr. V.* give ⟨*advice, information*⟩; give, grant ⟨*permission*⟩; **Erteilung die** giving; *(einer Genehmigung)* granting

ertönen *itr. V.; mit sein* sound

Ertrag der; ~**|e|s, Erträge a)** yield; **b)** *(Gewinn)* return

ertragen *unr. tr. V.* bear; **erträglich** *Adj.* tolerable; bearable ⟨*pain*⟩

ertrag·reich *Adj.* lucrative ⟨*business*⟩; productive ⟨*land, soil*⟩

ertränken *tr. V.* drown; **ertrinken** *unr. itr. V.; mit sein* be drowned; drown

erübrigen 1. *tr. V.* spare ⟨*money, time*⟩; **2.** *refl. V.* be unnecessary

erwachen *itr. V.; mit sein (geh.)* awake

Erwachen das; ~**s** *(auch fig.)* awakening

¹**erwachsen** *unr. itr. V.; mit sein* **a)** grow (**aus** out of); ⟨*rumour*⟩ spread; **b)** *(sich ergeben)* ⟨*difficulties, tasks*⟩ arise; ²**erwachsen** *Adj.* grown-up *attrib.*; ~ **sein** be grown up; **Erwachsene der/die;** *adj. Dekl.* adult; grown-up

erwägen *unr. tr. V.* consider; **Erwägung die;** ~, ~**en** consideration; **etw. in** ~ **ziehen** take sth. into consideration

erwählen *tr. V. (geh.)* choose

erwähnen *tr. V.* mention; **erwähnens·wert** *Adj.* worth mentioning *postpos.;* **Erwähnung die;** ~, ~**en** mention

erwärmen 1. *tr. V.* heat; **2.** *refl. V.* *(warm werden)* ⟨*air, water*⟩ warm up

erwarten *tr. V.* expect; **jmdn. am Bahnhof** ~: wait for sb. at the station; **Erwartung die;** ~, ~**en** expectation

erwartungs-: ~**gemäß** *Adv.* as expected; ~**voll** *Adj.* expectant

erwecken *tr. V.* **a)** *(auf~)* wake; **b)** *(erregen)* arouse ⟨*longing, pity*⟩

erweichen *tr. V.* soften

erweisen 1. *unr. tr. V.* **a)** prove; **b)** *(bezeigen)* **jmdm. Achtung** ~: show respect to sb.; **2.** *unr. refl. V.* **sich als etw.** ~: prove to be sth.

erweitern 1. *tr. V.* widen ⟨*river, road*⟩; expand ⟨*library, business*⟩; enlarge ⟨*collection*⟩; dilate ⟨*pupil, blood vessel*⟩; **2.** *refl. V.* ⟨*road, river*⟩ widen;

⟨*pupil, blood vessel*⟩ dilate; **Erweiterung die;** ~, ~**en** *s.* **erweitern:** widening; expansion; enlargement; dilation

Erwerb der; ~**|e|s a)** *(Aneignung)* acquisition; **b)** *(Kauf)* purchase; **erwerben** *unr. tr. V.* **a)** *(verdienen)* earn; **b)** *(sich aneignen)* gain; **c)** *(kaufen)* acquire

erwerbs-: ~**los** *Adj.: s.* **arbeitslos;** ~**tätig** *Adj.* gainfully employed; ~**unfähig** *Adj.* incapable of gainful employment *postpos.;* unable to work *postpos.*

Erwerbung die acquisition; *(Gekauftes)* purchase

erwidern *tr. V.* **a)** reply; **b)** *(reagieren auf)* return ⟨*greeting, visit*⟩; reciprocate ⟨*sb.'s feelings*⟩; **Erwiderung die;** ~, ~**en a)** reply (**auf** + *Akk.* to); **b)** *s.* **erwidern b:** return; reciprocation

erwiesen *Adj.* proved; proven ⟨*fact*⟩; **erwiesener·maßen** *Adv.* as has been proved

erwirken *tr. V.* obtain

erwirtschaften *tr. V.* **etw.** ~: obtain sth. by careful management

erwischen *tr. V. (ugs.)* **a)** catch ⟨*culprit, train, bus*⟩; **b)** *(greifen)* grab; **c)** *(bekommen)* manage to get; **d)** *(unpers.)* **es hat ihn erwischt** *(ugs.) (er ist tot)* he's bought it *(sl.); (er ist krank)* he's got it; *(er ist verletzt)* he's been hurt; *(scherzh.: er ist verliebt)* he's got it bad *(coll.)*

erwünscht *Adj.* wanted

erwürgen *tr. V.* strangle

Erz [ɛrts *od.* eːrts] **das;** ~**es,** ~**e** ore

erzählen *tr. V. (auch itr.)* tell ⟨*joke, story*⟩; **jmdm. etw.** ~: tell sb. sth.; **Erzähler der** story-teller; *(Autor)* writer [of stories]; narrative writer; **Erzählung die;** ~, ~**en** narration; *(Bericht)* account; *(Literaturw.)* story

Erz-: ~**bischof der** archbishop; ~**bistum das,** ~**diözese die** archbishopric; archdiocese; ~**engel der** archangel

erzeugen *tr. V.* produce; generate ⟨*electricity*⟩; **Erzeuger der;** ~**s,** ~ *(Vater)* father; **Erzeugnis das** product; **Erzeugung die** *(von Lebensmitteln usw.)* production; *(von Industriewaren)* manufacture; *(Strom~)* generation

Erz·feind der arch enemy

erziehen *unr. tr. V.* bring up; *(in der Schule)* educate; **ein Kind zu Sauberkeit und Ordnung** ~: bring a child up

to be clean and tidy; **Erzieher** der; ~s, ~, **Erzieherin** die; ~, ~nen educator; *(Pädagoge)* educationalist; *(Lehrer)* teacher; **Erziehung** die; o. *Pl.* upbringing; *(Schul~)* education; **Erziehungs·berechtigte** der/die; *adj. Dekl.* parent or [legal] guardian
erzielen *tr. V.* reach ⟨*agreement, compromise, speed*⟩; achieve ⟨*result, effect*⟩; make ⟨*profit*⟩; obtain ⟨*price*⟩
erzürnen *(geh.) tr. V.* anger; *(stärker)* incense
erzwingen *unr. tr. V.* force
es *Personalpron.; 3. Pers. Sg. Nom. u. Akk. Neutr.* **a)** *(s. auch Gen.* seiner; *Dat.* ihm) *(Sache)* it; *(weibliche Person)* she/her; *(männliche Person)* he/him; **b)** *ohne Bezug auf ein bestimmtes Subst., mit unpers. konstruierten Verben, als formales Satzglied* it; **ich bin es** it's me; **wir sind traurig, ihr seid es auch** we are sad, and so are you; **es sei denn, [daß]** ...: unless ...; **es ist genug!** that's enough; **es hat geklopft** there was a knock; **es klingelt** someone is ringing; **es wird schöner** the weather is improving; **es geht ihm gut/schlecht** he is well/unwell; **es wird gelacht** there is laughter; **es läßt sich aushalten** it is bearable; **er hat es gut** he has it good; **er meinte es gut** he meant well
Esche die; ~, ~n *(Bot.)* ash
Esel der; ~s, ~ **a)** donkey; ass; **b)** *(ugs.: Dummkopf)* ass *(coll.)*
Esels-: ~brücke die *(ugs.)* mnemonic; **~ohr** das *(ugs.: umgeknickte Stelle)* dog-ear
Eskalation die; ~, ~en escalation
Eskimo der; ~[s], ~[s] Eskimo
Eskorte die; ~, ~n escort; **eskortieren** *tr. V.* escort
Espe die; ~, ~n aspen
eßbar *Adj.* edible; **nicht ~:** inedible; **essen** *unr. tr., itr. V.* eat; **etw. gern ~:** like sth.; **sich satt ~:** eat one's fill; **gut ~:** have a good meal; *(immer)* eat well; **~ gehen** go out for a meal; **Essen** das; ~s, ~ *(Mahlzeit)* meal; *(Speise)* food; **[das] ~ machen/kochen** get/cook the meal
Essen[s]-: ~marke die meal-ticket; **~zeit** die mealtime
Essenz die; ~, ~en essence
Esser der; ~s, ~: **er ist ein schlechter ~:** he has a poor appetite
Essig der; ~s, ~e vinegar; **Essiggurke** die pickled gherkin
Eß-: ~kastanie die sweet chestnut; **~löffel** der *(Suppenlöffel)* soup-

spoon; *(für Nach-, Vorspeise)* dessertspoon; **~stäbchen** das chopstick; **~teller** der dinner plate; **~tisch** der dining-table; **~waren** *Pl.* food *sing.*; **~zimmer** das dining-room
Establishment [ɪs'tɛblɪʃmənt] das; ~s, ~s Establishment
Este der; ~n, ~n Estonian; **Est·land** (das); ~s Estonia
Estragon ['ɛstragɔn] der; ~s tarragon
Estrich ['ɛstrɪç] der; ~s, ~e composition floor
etablieren *tr. V.* establish; set up; **etabliert** *Adj.* established
Etage [e'taːʒə] die; ~, ~n floor; storey
Etappe die; ~, ~n stage
Etat [e'taː] der; ~s, ~s budget
etepetete [e:təpe'te:tə] *Adj. (ugs.)* fussy; finicky
Ethik die; ~, ~en **a)** ethics *sing.*; **b)** o. *Pl. (sittliche Normen)* ethics *pl.*; **ethisch** *Adj.* ethical
Etikett das; ~[e]s, ~en od. ~e od. ~s label; **Etikette** die; ~, ~n etiquette; **etikettieren** *tr. V.* label
etlich... *Indefinitpron. u. unbest. Zahlwort: Sg.* quite a lot of; *Pl.* quite a few
Etüde die; ~, ~n *(Musik)* étude
Etui [ɛt'viː] das; ~s, ~s case
etwa 1. *Adv.* **a)** *(ungefähr)* about; **~ so groß wie ...:** about as large as ...; **~ so** roughly like this; **b)** *(beispielsweise)* for example; 2. *Partikel* **störe ich ~?** am I disturbing you at all?; **etwaig...** ['ɛtva(ː)ɪg...] *Adj.* possible
etwas *Indefinitpron.* **a)** something; *(fragend, verneinend)* anything; **irgend ~:** something; **b)** *(Bedeutsames)* **aus ihm wird ~:** he'll make something of himself; **c)** *(ein Teil)* some; *(fragend, verneinend)* any; **~ von dem Geld** some of the money; **d)** *(ein wenig)* a little; **~ lauter/besser** a little louder/better
Etymologie die; ~, ~n etymology
euch 1. *Dat. u. Akk. Pl. des Personalpron.* **ihr** you; 2. *Dat. u. Akk. Pl. des Reflexivpron. der 2. Pers. Pl.* yourselves
¹euer *Possessivpron.* your; **Grüße von Eu[e]rer Helga/Eu[e]rem Hans** Best wishes, Yours, Helga/Hans; **²euer** *Gen. des Personalpron.* **ihr** *(geh.)* **wir werden ~ gedenken** we will remember you
Eule die; ~, ~n owl; **~n nach Athen tragen** carry coals to Newcastle
Eunuch der; ~en, ~en eunuch
Euphorie die; ~, ~n *(bes. Med., Psych.)* euphoria

eure *s.* ¹**euer**; **eurer·seits** *s.* deinerseits; **euret·wegen** *Adv. s.* deinetwegen

Eurocheque [ˈɔyroʃɛk] **der**; ~s, ~s
Eurocheque

Europa (das); ~s Europe

Europäer der; ~s, ~, **Europäerin**
die; ~, ~**nen** European; **europäisch**
Adj. European; **die Europäische Gemeinschaft** the European Community

Europa-: ~**meister der** *(Sport)* European champion; ~**meisterschaft**
die *(Sport)* **a)** *(Wettbewerb)* European
Championship; **b)** *(Sieg)* European
title; ~**parlament das**; *o. Pl.* European Parliament; ~**pokal der** *(Sport)*
European cup; ~**rat der**; *o. Pl.* Council of Europe; ~**straße die** European
long-distance road

Euro·scheck der *s.* Eurocheque

Euter das *od.* **der**; ~s, ~: udder

e.V., E.V. *Abk.* eingetragener Verein

ev. *Abk.* evangelisch ev.

evakuieren [evakuˈiːrən] *tr. V.* evacuate; **Evakuierung die**; ~, ~**en** evacuation

evangelisch [evaŋˈɡeːlɪʃ] *Adj.* Protestant; **Evangelium das**; ~s, Evan-
gelien **a)** *(auch fig.)* gospel; **b)** *(christl.
Rel.)* Gospel

eventuell [evɛnˈtuɛl] **1.** *Adj.* possible;
2. *adv.* possibly; perhaps

Evolution [evoluˈtsi̯oːn] **die**; ~, ~**en**
evolution

evtl. *Abk.* eventuell

EWG [eːveːˈɡeː] **die**; ~: EEC

ewig 1. *Adj.* eternal; *(abwertend)*
never-ending; **2.** *adv.* eternally; for
ever; **Ewigkeit die**; ~, ~**en a)** eternity; **b)** *(ugs.)* es dauert eine ~: it takes
ages *(coll.)*

ex *Adv.* *(ugs.)* etw. ex trinken drink sth.
down in one *(coll.)*; **Ex-** *(vor Personen-
bez.: vormalig)* ex-

exakt *Adj.* exact; precise

Examen das; ~s, ~ *od.* **Examina**
examination

Exekution die; ~, ~**en** execution;
Exekutive die; ~, ~**n** *(Rechtsw., Politik)* executive

Exempel das; ~s, ~: example; **Exemplar das**; ~s, ~**e** specimen; *(Buch,
Zeitung usw.)* copy

exerzieren *tr., itr. V.* drill

Exil das; ~s, ~**e** exile

Existenz die; ~, ~**en a)** existence; **b)**
(Lebensgrundlage) livelihood; **c)**
(Mensch) character

Existenz-: ~**grundlage die** basis of

one's livelihood; ~**minimum das**
subsistence level

existieren *itr. V.* exist

Exitus der; ~ *(Med.)* death

exkl. *Abk.* exklusiv[e] excl.

exklusiv 1. *Adj.* exclusive; **2.** *adv.* exclusively; **exklusive** *Präp.* + *Gen.*
exclusive of

Ex·kommunikation die excom-
munication

Exkursion die; ~, ~**en** study trip

exotisch 1. *Adj.* exotic; **2.** *adv.* ex-
otically

expandieren *tr., itr. V.* expand; **Expansion die**; ~, ~**en** expansion

Expedition die; ~, ~**en** expedition

Experiment das; ~[e]s, ~**e** experiment; **experimentell 1.** *Adj.* experimental; **2.** *adv.* experimentally;
experimentieren *itr. V.* experiment

Experte der; ~n, ~n, **Expertin die**;
~, ~**nen** expert (für in)

explodieren *itr. V.; mit sein (auch
fig.)* explode; *(costs)* rocket; **Explosion die**; ~, ~**en** explosion; **explosiv 1.** *Adj. (auch fig.)* explosive; **2.**
adv. explosively

Exponent der; ~**en**, ~**en** *(Math.)* exponent; **exponiert** *Adj.* exposed

Export der; ~[e]s, ~**e** export

Export-: ~**artikel der** export; ~**bier**
das export beer

Exporteur [ɛkspɔrˈtøːɐ̯] **der**; ~s, ~**e**
(Wirtsch.) exporter

Export-: ~**firma die** exporter; ~**handel der** export trade

exportieren *tr., itr. V.* export

Expreß·gut das express freight

Expressionismus der; ~: expres-
sionism *no art.;* **expressionistisch**
Adj. expressionist

extra *Adv.* **a)** *(gesondert)* ⟨pay⟩ separately; **b)** *(zusätzlich, besonders)* extra;
c) *(eigens)* especially; **Extra das**; ~s,
~s extra; **Extra·blatt das** special
edition

Extrakt der; ~[e]s, ~**e** extract

extravagant [-vaˈɡant] *Adj.* flamboyant; flamboyantly furnished ⟨flat⟩

extrem *Adj.* extreme; **Extrem das**;
~s, ~**e** extreme; **Extrem·fall der** extreme case; **Extremismus der**; ~:
extremism; **Extremist der**; ~**en**, ~**en**
extremist; **extremistisch** *Adj.* extremist

Exzellenz die; ~, ~**en** Excellency

exzentrisch 1. *Adj.* eccentric; **2.** *adv.*
eccentrically

Exzeß der; Exzesses, Exzesse excess

F

f, F [εf] das; ~, ~ a) *(Buchstabe)* f/F; b) *(Musik)* [key of] F
f. *Abk.* folgend f.
Fa. *Abk.* Firma
Fabel die; ~, ~n fable; *(Kern einer Handlung)* plot
fabelhaft 1. *Adj. (ugs.: großartig)* fantastic *(coll.);* **2.** *adv. (ugs.)* fantastically *(coll.)*
Fabrik die; ~, ~en factory
Fabrikant der; ~en, ~en manufacturer; **Fabrikat** das; ~|e|s, ~e product; *(Marke)* make; **Fabrikation** die; ~: production
Fabrik-: ~besitzer der factory-owner; ~direktor der works manager
fabrizieren *tr. V. (ugs. abwertend)* knock together *(coll.)*
Fach das; ~|e|s, Fächer a) compartment; *(für Post)* pigeon-hole; b) *(Studien~, Unterrichts~)* subject; *(Wissensgebiet)* field; *(Berufszweig)* trade; **ein Mann vom ~:** an expert
Fach-: ~arbeiter der skilled worker; ~arzt der specialist (für in); ~geschäft das specialist shop
fachlich *Adj.* specialist *(knowledge, work);* technical *(problem, explanation, experience)*
Fach-: ~mann der expert; ~werk das o. Pl. *(Bauweise)* half-timbered construction; ~werk·haus das half-timbered house
Fackel die; ~, ~n torch
fade *Adj.* insipid
Faden der; ~s, Fäden thread; **ein ~:** a piece of thread
faden·scheinig *Adj.* threadbare; flimsy *(excuse)*
Fagott das; ~|e|s, ~e bassoon
fähig *Adj.* a) *(begabt)* able; capable; b) zu etw. ~ sein be capable of sth.; **Fähigkeit** die; ~, ~en a) *meist Pl.* ability; capability; geistige ~en intellectual faculties; b) o. Pl. *(Imstandesein)* ability (zu to)

fahl *Adj.* pale; pallid; wan *(light)*
fahnden *itr. V.* search (nach for)
Fahne die; ~, ~n flag
Fahr·bahn die carriageway
Fähre die; ~, ~n ferry
fahren 1. *unr. itr. V.; mit sein* a) *(als Fahrzeuglenker)* drive; *(mit dem Fahrrad, Motorrad usw.)* ride; b) *(als Mitfahrer; mit öffentlichem Verkehrsmittel)* go (mit by); *(mit dem Aufzug/der Rolltreppe/der Seilbahn)* take the lift *(Brit.)* or *(Amer.)* elevator/escalator/cable-car; *(per Anhalter)* hitch-hike; c) *(reisen)* go; in Urlaub ~: go on holiday; d) *(los~)* go; leave; e) *(motor vehicle, train, lift, cable-car)* go; *(ship)* sail; mein Auto fährt nicht my car won't go; f) *(verkehren) (train etc.)* run; **2.** *unr. tr. V.* a) *(fortbewegen)* drive *(car, lorry, train, etc.);* ride *(bicycle, motor cycle);* b) 50/80 km/h ~: do 50/80 k.p.h.; hier muß man 50 km/h ~: you've got to keep to 50 k.p.h. here; sail *(boat);* Auto ~: drive [a car]; Kahn od. Boot/Kanu ~: go boating/canoeing; Ski ~: ski; U-Bahn ~: ride on the underground *(Brit.)* or *(Amer.)* subway; c) *(befördern)* take
Fahrenheit o. *Art.* 70 Grad ~: 70 degrees Fahrenheit
fahren|lassen *unr. tr. V.* let go; **Fahrer** der; ~s, ~: driver; **Fahrerflucht** die: ~ begehen fail to stop after [being involved in] an accident; **Fahrerin** die; ~, ~nen driver
Fahr-: ~gast der passenger; ~geld das fare
fahrig *Adj.* nervous
fahr-, Fahr-: ~karte die ticket; ~karten·automat der ticket machine; ~karten·schalter der ticket window; ~lässig **1.** *Adj.* negligent *(behaviour);* ~e Tötung/Körperverletzung *(Rechtsw.)* causing death/injury through [culpable] negligence; **2.** *adv.* negligently; ~lehrer der driving instructor
Fähr·mann der ferryman
Fahr-: ~plan der timetable; schedule *(Amer.);* ~preis der fare; ~prüfung die driving test; ~rad das bicycle; cycle; mit dem ~ fahren cycle; ride a bicycle; ~rad·ständer der bicycle rack; ~schein der ticket; ~schein·automat der ticket machine; ~schein·entwerter der ticket cancelling machine; ~schule die driving school; ~spur die traffic-lane
fährst 2. *Pers. Sg. Präsens v.* fahren

Fahr-: ~**stuhl der** lift *(Brit.);* elevator *(Amer.); (für Lasten)* hoist; ~**stunde die** driving lesson

Fahrt die; ~, ~**en a)** journey; **freie** ~ **haben** have a clear run; *(Schiffsreise)* voyage; *(kurze Reise, Ausflug)* trip; **b)** *o. Pl. (Geschwindigkeit)* **in voller** ~: at full speed; **fährt** *3. Pers. Sg. Präsens v.* **fahren**

Fährte die trail; jmds. ~ **verfolgen** track sb.

Fahrt·kosten *Pl. (für öffentliche Verkehrsmittel)* fare/fares; *(für Autoreisen)* travel costs; **Fahr·treppe die** escalator; **Fahrt·richtung die** direction; **in** ~ **parken** park in the direction of the traffic; **die** ~ **ändern** change direction; **fahr·tüchtig** *Adj.* ⟨*driver*⟩ fit to drive; ⟨*vehicle*⟩ roadworthy

Fahrt-: ~**wind der** airflow; ~**ziel das** destination

Fahr-: ~**werk das** *(Flugw.)* undercarriage; ~**zeit die** travelling time; ~**zeug das** vehicle; *(Luft~)* aircraft; *(Wasser~)* vessel

fair [fɛːɐ̯] **1.** *Adj.* fair **(gegen** to); **2.** *adv.* fairly

Fakten *s.* **Faktum; faktisch 1.** *Adj.* real; actual; **2.** *adv.* **das bedeutet** ~ ...: it means in effect ...

Faktor der; ~s, ~**en** *(auch Math.)* factor

Faktum das; ~s, **Fakten** fact

Fakultät die; ~, ~**en** *(Hochschulw.)* faculty

Falke der; ~**n,** ~**n** *(auch Politik fig.)* hawk

Fall der; ~|e|s, **Fälle a)** *(Sturz)* fall; **zu** ~ **kommen** have a fall; **jmdn. zu** ~ **bringen** *(fig.)* bring about sb.'s downfall; **b)** *(das Fallen)* descent; **der freie** ~: free fall; **c)** *(Ereignis; Rechtsw., Med., Grammatik)* case; *(zu erwartender Umstand)* eventuality; **es ist |nicht| der** ~: it is [not] the case; **gesetzt den** ~: assuming; **auf jeden** ~, **in jedem** ~, **auf alle Fälle** in any case; **auf keinen** ~: on no account; **Falle die;** ~, ~**n** *(auch fig.)* trap; **fallen** *unr. itr. V.; mit sein* **a)** fall; **etw.** ~ **lassen** drop sth.; **b)** *(hin~, stürzen)* fall [over]; **über einen Stein** ~: trip over a stone; **c)** ⟨*prices, light, glance, choise*⟩ fall; ⟨*temperature, water level*⟩ fall, drop; ⟨*fever*⟩ subside; ⟨*shot*⟩ be fired; **d)** *(im Kampf sterben)* die; fall *(literary);* **fällen** *tr. V.* **a)** fell ⟨*tree, timber*⟩; **b) ein Urteil** ~ ⟨*judge*⟩ pass sentence; ⟨*jury*⟩ return a verdict; **fällig** *Adj.* due; **falls** *(Konj.)*

a) *(wenn)* if; **b)** *(für den Fall, daß)* in case; **Fall·schirm der** parachute; **mit dem** ~ **abspringen** *(im Notfall)* parachute out; *(als Sport)* make a [parachute] jump

falsch 1. *Adj.* **a)** *(unecht, imitiert)* false ⟨*teeth, plait*⟩; imitation ⟨*jewellery*⟩; **b)** *(gefälscht)* forged; assumed ⟨*name*⟩; **c)** *(irrig, fehlerhaft)* wrong; **2.** *adv.* wrongly; **die Uhr geht** ~: the clock is wrong; **fälschen** *tr. V.* forge; **Fälscher der;** ~s, ~**forger; Falschgeld das** counterfeit money; **fälschlich 1.** *Adj.* false; **2.** *adv.* falsely; **Falsch·meldung die** false report; **Fälschung die;** ~, ~**en** fake

Falt·blatt das leaflet; *(in Zeitungen, Zeitschriften, Büchern)* insert; **Falte die;** ~, ~**n a)** crease; **b)** *(im Stoff)* fold; *(mit scharfer Kante)* pleat; **c)** *(Haut~)* wrinkle; **falten 1.** *tr. V.* fold; **die Hände** ~: fold one's hands; **2.** *refl. V. (auch Geol.)* fold; ⟨*skin*⟩ become wrinkled; **Falten·rock der** pleated skirt; **Falter der;** ~s, ~ *(Nacht~)* moth; *(Tag~)* butterfly; **faltig a)** *Adj.* ⟨*clothes*⟩ gathered [in folds]; wrinkled ⟨*skin, hands*⟩; **b)** *(zerknittert)* creased **-fältig** *Adj., adv.* -fold

familiär *Adj.* **a)** family ⟨*problems, worries*⟩; **b)** *(zwanglos)* familiar; informal; **Familie** [faˈmiːliə] **die;** ~, ~**n** family; ~ **Meyer** the Meyer family

Familien-: ~**angehörige der/die;** *adj. Dekl.* member of the family; ~**feier die** family party; ~**leben das;** *o. Pl.* family life; ~**name der** surname; ~**planung die;** *o. Pl.* family planning *no art.;* ~**stand der** marital status; ~**vater der:** ~**vater sein** be the father of a family; **ein guter** ~**vater** a good husband and father

Fan [fɛn] **der;** ~s, ~s fan

Fanatiker der; ~s, ~: fanatic; *(religiös)* fanatic; zealot; **fanatisch 1.** *Adj.* fanatical; **2.** *adv.* fanatically

fand *1. u. 3. Pers. Sg. Prät. v.* **finden**

Fanfare die; ~, ~**n** *(Signal)* fanfare

Fang der; ~|e|s, **Fänge a)** *(Tier~)* trapping; *(von Fischen)* catching; **b)** *(Beute)* bag; *(von Fischen)* catch; **fangen 1.** *unr. tr. V.* catch; capture ⟨*fugitive etc.*⟩; **2.** *unr. refl. V.* **a)** *(in eine Falle geraten)* be caught; **b)** *(wieder in die normale Lage kommen)* **sich |gerade| noch** ~: [just] manage to steady oneself; **Fang·frage die** catch question

Farb-: ~**bild das** *(Foto)* colour photo; ~**dia das** colour slide

Farbe die; ~, ~n a) colour; b) *(für Textilien)* dye; *(zum Malen, Anstreichen)* paint; ~n **mischen/auftragen** mix/apply paint; **farb·echt** *Adj.* colourfast; **färben 1.** *tr. V.* dye; **2.** *refl. V.* change colour; **sich schwarz/rot** *usw.* ~: turn black/red *etc;* **3.** *itr. V. (ugs.: ab~)* ⟨*material, blouse etc.*⟩ run; **-farben** *Adj.* coloured
farben-: ~**blind** *Adj.* colour-blind; ~**froh** *Adj.* colourful; ~**prächtig** *Adj.* vibrant with colour *postpos.*
Farb-: ~**fernsehen das** colour television; ~**fernseher der** *(ugs.)* colour telly *(coll.) or* television; ~**film der** colour film; ~**foto das** colour photo
farbig 1. *Adj.* a) coloured; b) *(bunt, auch fig.)* colourful; **2.** *adv.* colourfully; **-farbig** *Adj.* -coloured; **Farbige der/die;** *adj. Dekl.* coloured man/woman; *Pl.* coloured people
farblich 1. *Adj.* in colour *postpos.;* as regards colour *postpos;* **2.** *adv.* etw. ~ **abstimmen** match sth. in colour
farb-, Farb-: ~**los** *Adj. (auch fig.)* colourless; clear ⟨*varnish*⟩; neutral ⟨*shoe polish*⟩; ~**stift der** coloured pencil; ~**stoff der** a) *(Med., Biol.)* pigment; b) *(für Textilien)* dye; c) *(für Lebensmittel)* colouring; ~**ton der** shade
Färbung die; ~, ~en colouring
Farn der; ~[e]s, ~e, **Farn·kraut das** fern
Fasan der; ~[e]s, ~e[n] pheasant
Fasching der; ~s, ~e *od.* ~s [pre-Lent] carnival
Faschismus der; ~: fascism *no art.*
Faschist der; ~en, ~en fascist; **faschistisch** *Adj.* fascist
faseln *itr. V. (ugs. abwertend)* drivel
Faser die; ~, ~n fibre; **fasern** *itr. V.* fray
Faß das; Fasses, Fässer barrel; *(Öl~)* drum; *(kleines Bier~)* keg; *(kleines Sherry~ usw.)* cask; **Bier vom** ~: draught beer; **ein** ~ **ohne Boden** an endless drain on sb.'s resources
Fassade die; ~, ~n façade
faßbar *Adj.* a) tangible ⟨*results*⟩; b) *(verständlich)* comprehensible
Faß·bier das draught beer; beer on draught
fassen 1. *tr. V.* a) *(greifen)* grasp; take hold of; b) *(festnehmen)* catch ⟨*thief, culprit*⟩; c) *(aufnehmen können)* ⟨*hall, tank*⟩ hold; d) *(begreifen)* **ich kann es nicht** ~: I cannot take it in; e) **einen Entschluß** ~: make *or* take a decision; **2.** *itr. V.* a) *(greifen)* **nach etw.** ~: reach

for sth.; **in etw.** *(Akk.)* ~: put one's hand in sth.; **faßlich** *Adj.* comprehensible
Fasson [fa'sõ:] **die;** ~, ~s style; shape
Fassung die; ~, ~en a) *(Form)* version; b) *o. Pl. (Selbstbeherrschung)* composure; **die** ~ **bewahren** keep one's composure; **die** ~ **verlieren** lose one's self-control; **jmdn. aus der** ~ **bringen** upset sb.; c) *(für Glühlampen)* holder; **fassungs·los** *Adj.* stunned
fast *Adv.* almost; nearly; ~ **nie** hardly ever
fasten *itr. V.* fast; **Fast·nacht die** carnival
faszinieren *tr. V.* fascinate
fatal *Adj.* a) *(peinlich, mißlich)* awkward; b) *(verhängnisvoll)* fatal
fauchen *itr. V.* a) ⟨*cat*⟩ hiss; ⟨*tiger, person*⟩ snarl
faul *Adj.* a) *(verdorben)* rotten; bad ⟨*food, tooth*⟩; foul ⟨*water, air*⟩; b) *(träge)* lazy; **Fäule die;** ~: foulness; **faulen** *itr. V.; meist mit sein* rot; ⟨*water*⟩ go foul; ⟨*meat, fish*⟩ go off
faulenzen *itr. V.* laze about; loaf about *(derog.);* **Faulenzer der;** ~s, ~: idler; lazy-bones *sing. (coll.)*
Faulheit die; ~: laziness; **faulig** *Adj.* stagnating ⟨*water*⟩; ~ **schmecken/riechen** taste/smell off; **Fäulnis die;** ~: rottenness
Faul-: ~**pelz der** *(fam.)* lazy-bones *sing. (coll.);* ~**tier das** a) *(Zool.)* sloth; b) *(ugs.: Faulenzer) s.* ~**pelz**
Faust die; ~, **Fäuste** fist; **eine** ~ **machen** clench one's fist; **das paßt wie die** ~ **aufs Auge** *(ugs.) (paßt nicht)* that clashes horribly; *(paßt)* that matches perfectly; **auf eigene** ~: on one's own initiative; **Fäustchen das;** ~s, ~: **sich** *(Dat.)* **ins** ~ **lachen** laugh up one's sleeve; **faust·dick** *Adj.* as thick as a man's fist *postpos.;* *(fig.)* bare-faced ⟨*lie*⟩; **Fäustling der;** ~s, ~e mitten; **Faust·regel die** rule of thumb
Favorit [favo'ri:t] **der;** ~en, ~en favourite
Fax das; ~, ~[e]s fax; **faxen** *tr. V.* fax
Faxen *Pl. (ugs.)* fooling around
Fazit ['fa:tsɪt] **das;** ~s, ~s *od.* ~e result
Februar der; ~[s], ~e February
fechten *unr. itr., tr. V.* fence; **Fechter der;** ~s, ~: fencer
Feder die; ~, ~n a) *(Vogel~)* feather; b) *(zum Schreiben)* nib; c) *(Technik)* spring
feder-, Feder-: ~**ball der** a) *(Spiel)* badminton; b) *(Ball)* shuttlecock;

~**bett das** duvet *(Brit.)*; stuffed quilt *(Amer.)*; ~**führend** *Adj.* in charge *postpos.*; ~**halter der** fountain-pen; ~**leicht** *Adj.* ⟨*person*⟩ as light as a feather; featherweight ⟨*object*⟩; ~**lesen das: nicht viel** ~**lesen|s|** mit jmdm./etw. machen give sb./sth. short shrift

federn 1. *itr. V.* ⟨*springboard, floor, etc.*⟩ be springy; **2.** *tr. V.* *(mit einer Federung versehen)* spring; **das Bett ist gut gefedert** the bed is well-sprung; **Federung die;** ~, ~**en** *(Kfz-W.)* suspension

Fee die; ~, ~**n** fairy

Fege·feuer das purgatory; **fegen 1.** *tr. V.* a) *(bes. nordd.: säubern)* sweep; b) *(schnell entfernen)* brush; **2.** *itr. V.* sweep up

fehl *Adv.* ~ **am Platz|e| sein** be out of place; **Fehl·anzeige die:** ~! *(ugs.)* no chance! *(coll.)*; **fehlen** *itr. V.* a) *(nicht vorhanden sein)* **ihm fehlt das Geld** he has no money; b) *(ausbleiben)* be absent; c) *(verschwunden sein)* be missing; **in der Kasse fehlt Geld** money is missing from the till; d) *(vermißt werden)* **er/das wird mir** ~: I shall miss him/that; **ihm** ~ **noch zwei Punkte zum Sieg** he needs only two points to win; **es fehlte nicht viel, und ich wäre eingeschlafen** I all but fell asleep; **f)** unpers. *(mangeln)* **es fehlt an Lehrern** there is a lack of teachers; g) *(krank sein)* **was fehlt Ihnen?** what seems to be the matter?; **fehlt dir etwas?** is there something wrong?; **Fehler der;** ~**s,** ~ a) *(Irrtum)* mistake; error; *(Sport)* fault; b) *(schlechte Eigenschaft)* fault; **fehler·frei** *Adj.* faultless; **fehlerhaft** *Adj.* faulty; defective; imperfect ⟨*pronunciation*⟩; **Fehler·quelle die** source of error

fehl-, Fehl-: ~**geburt die** miscarriage; ~**schlag der** failure; ~|**schlagen** *unr. itr. V.; mit sein* fail; ~**start der** *(Leichtathletik)* false start; ~**tritt der** *(fig. geh.)* slip; ~**zündung die** *(Technik)* misfire

Feier die; ~, ~**n** a) *(Veranstaltung)* party; *(aus festlichem Anlaß)* celebration; b) *(Zeremonie)* ceremony; **Feier·abend der** *(Arbeitsschluß)* finishing time; **nach** ~: after work; ~ **machen** finish work; **feierlich 1.** *Adj.* ceremonial ⟨*act etc.*⟩; solemn ⟨*silence*⟩; **2.** *adv.* solemnly; ceremoniously; **Feierlichkeit die;** ~, ~**en** a) *o.*

Pl. solemnity; b) *meist Pl.* *(Veranstaltung)* celebration; **feiern 1.** *tr. V.* a) celebrate ⟨*birthday, wedding, etc.*⟩; b) acclaim ⟨*artist, sportsman, etc.*⟩; **2.** *itr. V.* celebrate

Feier·tag der holiday; **ein gesetzlicher/kirchlicher** ~ a public holiday/religious festival

feig[e] 1. *Adj.* cowardly; **2.** *adv.* in a cowardly way

Feige die; ~, ~**n** fig

Feigheit die; ~: cowardice; **Feigling der;** ~**s,** ~**e** coward

Feile die; ~, ~**n** file; **feilen** *tr., itr. V.* file

feilschen *itr. V.* haggle (**um** over)

fein 1. *Adj.* a) fine; finely-ground ⟨*flour*⟩; finely-granulated ⟨*sugar*⟩; b) *(hochwertig)* high-quality ⟨*fruit, soap, etc.*⟩; fine ⟨*silver, gold, etc.*⟩; fancy ⟨*cakes, pastries, etc.*⟩; c) *(ugs.: erfreulich)* great *(coll.)*; **2.** *adv.* ~ |**he**|**raussein** *(ugs.)* be sitting pretty *(coll.)*

Feind der; ~|**e**|**s,** ~**e** enemy; **feindlich 1.** *Adj.* a) hostile; b) *(Milit.)* enemy ⟨*attack, activity*⟩; **2.** *adv.* in a hostile manner; **Feindschaft die;** ~, ~**en** enmity; **feind·selig** *Adj.* hostile

Feinheit die; ~, ~**en** a) fineness; delicacy; b) *(Nuance)* subtlety

fein-, Fein-: ~**kost·geschäft das** delicatessen; ~|**machen** *refl. V.* *(ugs.)* dress up; ~**schmecker der;** ~**s,** ~ gourmet; ~**sinnig** *Adj.* sensitive and subtle; ~**waschmittel das** mild detergent

feist *Adj.* *(meist abwertend)* fat

Feld das; ~|**e**|**s,** ~**er** a) field; b) *(Sport: Spiel*~*)* pitch; field; c) *(auf Formularen)* box; space; *(auf Brettspielen)* space; *(auf dem Schachbrett)* square; d) *o. Pl.* *(Tätigkeitsbereich)* field; sphere

Feld-: ~**herr der** *(veralt.)* commander; ~**marschall der** Field Marshal; ~**salat der** corn salad; ~**stecher der** binoculars *pl.*; ~**webel der;** ~**s,** ~ *(Milit.)* sergeant; ~**weg der** path; track; ~**zug der** *(Milit., fig.)* campaign

Felge die; ~, ~**n** [wheel] rim

Fell das; ~|**e**|**s,** ~**e** a) *(Haarkleid)* fur; *(Pferde*~*, Hunde*~*, Katzen*~*)* coat; *(Schaf*~*)* fleece; b) *(Material)* fur; c) *(abgezogen)* hide; **ein dickes** ~ **haben** *(ugs.)* be thick-skinned

Fels der; ~**en,** ~**en** rock; **Felsen der;** ~**s,** ~: rock; *(an der Steilküste)* cliff; **felsen·fest** *Adj.* firm; unshakeable

⟨*opinion, belief*⟩; **felsig** *Adj.* rocky; **Fels·wand** die rock face

feminin *Adj.* feminine; **Feminismus** der; ~ feminism *no art.;* **Feministin** die; ~, ~nen feminist

Fenchel der; ~s fennel

Fenster das; ~s, ~: window

Fenster-: ~**bank** die window-sill; ~**laden** der [window] shutter; ~**leder** das wash-leather; ~**platz** der window-seat; ~**putzer** der window-cleaner; ~**rahmen** der window-frame; ~**scheibe** die window-pane

Ferien ['fe:riən] *Pl.* a) holiday[s *pl.*] *(Brit.);* vacation *(Amer.);* in die ~ fahren go on holiday/vacation; ~ **haben** have a *or* be on holiday/vacation; **Ferien·haus** das holiday/vacation house

Ferkel das; ~s, ~: piglet

fern 1. *Adj.* distant; **2.** *adv.* ~ von der Heimat far from home; **3.** *Präp. mit Dat. (geh.)* far [away] from; **fern|bleiben** *unr. itr. V.; mit sein (geh.)* stay away; **Ferne** die; ~, ~n distance; **ferner** *Adv.* furthermore

fern-, Fern-: ~**fahrer** der long-distance lorry-driver *(Brit.)* or *(Amer.)* trucker; ~**gespräch** das long-distance call; ~**glas** das binoculars *pl.;* ~|**halten** *unr. tr., refl. V.* keep away; ~**heizung** die district heating system; ~**licht** das *(Kfz-W.)* full beam; ~**melde·amt** das telephone exchange; ~**ost** *o. Art.* Far East; ~**rohr** das telescope; ~**ruf** der telephone number; ~**schreiben** das telex [message]; ~**schreiber** der telex [machine]

Fernseh-: ~**antenne** die television aerial *(Brit.)* or *(Amer.)* antenna; ~**apparat** der television [set]

fern|sehen *unr. itr. V.* watch television; **Fern·sehen** das; ~s television; im ~: on television; **Fern·seher** der; ~s, ~ *(ugs.)* telly *(Brit. coll.);* TV

Fernseh-: ~**gebühren** *Pl.* television licence fee; ~**gerät** das television [set]; ~**programm** das a) *(Sendungen)* television programmes *pl.;* b) *(Kanal)* television channel; c) *(Blatt, Programmheft)* television [programme] guide; ~**sendung** die television programme; ~**spiel** das television play; ~**zuschauer** der television viewer

Fern·sprecher der telephone

Fernsprech-: ~**gebühren** *Pl.* tele-

phone charges; ~**teilnehmer** der telephone subscriber; telephone customer *(Amer.)*

Fern-: ~**steuerung** die *(Technik)* remote control; ~**straße** die major road; ~**verkehr** der long-distance traffic; ~**zug** der long-distance train

Ferse die; ~, ~n heel

fertig *Adj.* a) finished ⟨*manuscript, picture, etc.*⟩; das Essen ist ~: lunch/dinner *etc.* is ready; |mit etw.| ~ sein/werden have finished/finish [sth.]; b) *(bereit, verfügbar)* ready (zu, für for); c) *(ugs.: erschöpft)* shattered *(coll.)*

fertig-, Fertig-: ~**bau** der; *Pl.* ~ten prefabricated building; ~**bauweise** die prefabricated construction; prefabrication ~|**bringen** *unr. tr. V.* manage

fertigen *tr. V.* make

Fertig-: ~**gericht** das ready-to-serve meal; ~**haus** das prefabricated house; prefab *(coll.)*

Fertigkeit die; ~, ~en skill

fertig-, Fertig-: ~|**machen** *tr. V. (ugs.)* finish ⟨*task, job, etc.*⟩; get ⟨*meals, beds*⟩ ready; jmdn. ~**machen** *(erschöpfen)* wear sb. out; *(durch Schikanen)* wear sb. down; *(deprimieren)* get sb. down; ~|**stellen** *tr. V.* complete; ~**stellung** die completion

Fessel die; ~, ~n fetter; shackle; *(Kette)* chain; **fesseln** *tr. V.* a) tie up; b) *(faszinieren)* ⟨*book*⟩ grip; ⟨*work, person*⟩ fascinate

fest 1. *Adj.* a) *(nicht flüssig od. gasförmig)* solid; b) firm ⟨*bandage*⟩; sound ⟨*sleep*⟩; sturdy ⟨*shoes*⟩; strong ⟨*fabric*⟩; solid ⟨*house, shell*⟩; steady ⟨*voice*⟩; der ~en Überzeugung sein, daß ...: be of the firm opinion that ...; c) *(dauernd)* permanent ⟨*address*⟩; fixed ⟨*income*⟩; **2.** *adv.* a) ⟨*tie, grip*⟩ tight[ly]; b) *(ugs. auch* ~e) ⟨*work*⟩ with a will; ⟨*eat*⟩ heartily; ⟨*sleep*⟩ soundly; c) ⟨*believe, be convinced*⟩ firmly; sich auf jmdn./etw. ~ verlassen rely one hundred per cent on sb./sth.; d) *(endgültig)* firmly; etw. ~ vereinbaren come to a firm arrangement about sth.; e) *(auf Dauer)* permanently; ~ befreundet sein be close friends; *(als Paar)* be going steady

Fest das; ~[e]s, ~e a) celebration; *(Party)* party; b) *(Feiertag)* festival; frohes ~! happy Christmas/Easter!

fest-: ~|**binden** *unr. tr. V.* tie [up]; ~|**bleiben** *unr. itr. V.; mit sein* stand firm; ~|**fahren** *unr. itr., refl. V. (itr. V.*

mit sein) get stuck; *(fig.)* get bogged down; ~|**halten 1.** *unr. tr. V.* **a)** *(halten, packen)* hold on to; **b)** *(nicht weiterleiten)* withhold ⟨*letter, parcel, etc.*⟩; **c)** *(verhaftet haben)* hold, detain ⟨*suspect*⟩; **2.** *unr. refl. V.* **sich an jmdm./ etw.** ~**halten** hold on to sb./sth.

festigen 1. *tr. V.* strengthen; consolidate ⟨*position*⟩; **2.** *refl. V.* ⟨*friendship, ties*⟩ become stronger

Festival ['fɛstivəl] *das;* ~s, ~s festival

fest-, Fest-: ~|**kleben** *tr., itr. V.; mit sein* stick **(an** + *Dat.* to); ~**land** *das; o. Pl. (Kontinent)* continent; *(im Gegensatz zu den Inseln)* mainland; ~|**legen** *tr. V.* **a)** fix ⟨*time, deadline, price*⟩; arrange ⟨*programme*⟩; **b)** *(verpflichten)* **sich [auf etw.** *(Akk.)]* ~**legen** |**lassen**| commit oneself [to sth.]; **jmdn. [auf etw.** *(Akk.)]* ~**legen** tie sb. down [to sth.]

festlich 1. *Adj.* festive ⟨*atmosphere*⟩; formal ⟨*dress*⟩; **2.** *adv.* festively; formally

fest-: ~|**machen** *tr. V.* **a)** *(befestigen)* fix; **b)** *(fest vereinbaren)* arrange ⟨*meeting etc.*⟩; ~|**nageln** *tr. V.* **a)** *(befestigen)* nail **(an** + *Dat.* to); **b)** *(ugs.: festlegen)* **jmdn. [auf etw.** *(Akk.)]* ~**nageln** tie sb. down [to sth.]; ~|**nehmen** *unr. tr. V.* arrest

Fest·rede *die* speech

fest-, Fest-: ~|**schnallen** *tr. V.* tie **(an** + *Dat.* to); ~|**sitzen** *unr. itr. V.* be stuck; ~|**stehen** *unr. itr. V.* ⟨*order, appointment, etc.*⟩ have been fixed; ⟨*decision*⟩ be definite; ⟨*fact*⟩ be certain; ~|**stellen** *tr. V.* **a)** establish ⟨*identity, age, facts*⟩; **b)** *(wahrnehmen)* detect; diagnose ⟨*illness*⟩; ~**stellung** *die* **a)** establishment; **b)** *(Wahrnehmung)* realization; **die** ~**stellung machen, daß ...:** realize that ...

Fest·tag *der* holiday; *(Ehrentag)* special day

Festung *die;* ~, ~en fortress

Fest·zelt *das* marquee

fest|ziehen *unr. tr. V.* pull tight

Fete *die;* ~, ~n *(ugs.)* party

fett 1. *Adj.* **a)** fatty ⟨*food*⟩; ~**er Speck** fat bacon; **b)** *(sehr dick)* fat; **2.** *adv.* ~ **essen** eat fatty foods; **Fett** *das;* ~|e|s, ~e fat; ~ **ansetzen** ⟨*animal*⟩ fatten up; ⟨*person*⟩ put on weight

fett-, Fett-: ~**arm** *Adj.* low-fat ⟨*food*⟩; low in fat *pred.;* ~**auge das** speck of fat; ~**fleck[en]** *der* grease mark; ~**gedruckt** *Adj. (präd. getrennt geschrieben)* bold

fettig *Adj.* greasy

fett-, Fett-: ~**leibig** *Adj.* obese; ~**leibigkeit die;** ~: obesity; ~**näpfchen das:** **ins** ~**näpfchen treten** *(scherzh.)* put one's foot in it; ~**reich** *Adj.* high-fat

Fetzen *der;* ~s, ~: scrap

feucht *Adj.* damp; humid ⟨*climate*⟩; **feucht·fröhlich** *Adj. (ugs. scherzh.)* merry ⟨*company*⟩; boozy *(coll.)* ⟨*evening*⟩; **Feuchtigkeit** *die* moisture

feucht-: ~**kalt** *Adj.* cold and damp; ~**warm** *Adj.* muggy

feudal *Adj.* **a)** feudal ⟨*system*⟩; **b)** aristocratic ⟨*regiment etc.*⟩; **c)** *(ugs.: vornehm)* plush ⟨*hotel etc.*⟩

Feuer *das;* ~s, ~ **a)** fire; **jmdm.** ~ **geben** give sb. a light; **b)** *(Brand)* fire; blaze; ~! fire!; **c)** *o. Pl. (Milit.)* **das** ~ **einstellen** cease fire

feuer-, Feuer-: ~**eifer** *der* enthusiasm; zest; ~**fest** *Adj.* heat-resistant ⟨*dish, plate*⟩; fire-proof ⟨*material*⟩; ~**gefährlich** *Adj.* [in]flammable; ~**holz** *das; o. Pl.* firewood; ~**leiter** *die (bei Häusern)* fire escape; *(beim* ~**wehrauto)** [fireman's] ladder; ~**löscher** *der;* ~s, ~: fire extinguisher; ~**melder** *der* fire alarm

feuern 1. *tr. V.* **a)** *(ugs.: entlassen)* fire *(coll.);* sack *(coll.);* **b)** *(ugs.: schleudern, werfen)* fling; **2.** *itr. V. (Milit.)* fire **(auf** + *Akk.* at)

feuer-, Feuer-: ~**rot** *Adj.* fiery red; ~**schlucker** *der* fire-eater; ~**sirene** *die* fire siren; ~**stein** *der* flint; ~**versicherung** *die* fire insurance; ~**waffe** *die* firearm; ~**wehr** *die;* ~, ~**en** fire service; ~**wehr·auto** *das* fire engine; ~**wehr·mann** *der; Pl.* ~**männer** *od.* ~**leute** fireman; ~**werk** *das* firework display; ~**werke** *pl.;* ~**werks·körper** *der* firework; ~**zeug** *das* lighter

Feuilleton [fœjə'tõ:] *das;* ~s, ~s arts section

feurig *Adj.* fiery

ff. *Abk.* **folgende [Seiten]** ff.

Ffm. *Abk.* **Frankfurt am Main**

Fiaker ['fi̯akɐ] *der;* ~s, ~ *(österr.)* cab

Fiasko *das;* ~s, ~s fiasco

Fibel *die;* ~, ~n reader; primer

ficht [fiçt] *Imperativ Sg. u. 3. Pers. Sg. Präsens v.* **fechten**

Fichte *die;* ~, ~n spruce

ficken *tr., itr. V. (vulg.)* fuck *(coarse)*

fidel *Adj. (ugs.)* jolly

Fieber *das;* ~s [high] temperature; *(über 38 °C)* fever; ~ **haben** have a

[high] temperature/a fever; **bei jmdm. ~ messen** take sb's temperature; **fieber·frei** *Adj.* ⟨*person*⟩ free from fever; **fieberhaft** *Adj.* feverish; **fieberig** *Adj.* feverish; **fiebern** *itr. V.* have a temperature; **Fieber·thermometer das** [clinical] thermometer; **fiebrig** *Adj.* feverish

Fiedel die; ~, ~n *(veralt., scherzh.)* fiddle

fiel *1. u. 3. Pers. Sg. Prät. v.* **fallen**

fiepen *itr. V.* ⟨*dog*⟩ whimper; ⟨*bird*⟩ cheep

fies 1. *Adj. (ugs.)* nasty ⟨*person, character*⟩; **2.** *adv.* in a nasty way

Figur die; ~, ~en a) *(einer Frau)* figure; *(eines Mannes)* physique; **b)** *(Bildwerk)* figure; **c)** *(geometrisches Gebilde)* shape

fiktiv *Adj.* fictitious

Filet [fi'le:] **das; ~s, ~s** fillet

Filiale die; ~, ~n branch

Filigran das; ~s, ~e filigree

Film der; ~[e]s, ~e a) *(Fot.)* film; **b)** *(Kino~)* film; movie *(Amer. coll.);* **filmen** *tr., itr. V.* film

Film-: ~kamera die film camera; *(Schmalfilmkamera)* cine-camera; **~produzent der** film producer; **~regisseur der** film director; **~schau·spieler der** film actor

Filter der, ~s, ~: filter; **filtern** *tr. V.* filter

Filter-: ~papier das filter paper; **~zigarette die** [filter-]tipped cigarette

Filz der; ~es, ~e felt

Fimmel der; ~s, ~: einen ~ für etw. haben *(ugs. abwertend)* have a thing about sth. *(coll.)*

Finale das; ~s, ~[s] a) *(Sport)* final; **b)** finale

Finanz die; ~: finance *no art.*

Finanz-: ~amt das a) *(Behörde)* ≈ Inland Revenue; **b)** *(Gebäude)* tax office; **~beamte der** tax officer

Finanzen *Pl.* finances; **finanziell** [finan'tsiɛl] *Adj.* financial; **finanzieren** *tr. V.* finance; **Finanzierung die; ~, ~en** financing

Finanz-: ~minister der minister of finance; **~politik die** *(des Staates, eines Unternehmens)* financial policy; *(allgemeine)* politics of finance

Findel·kind das foundling

finden *unr. tr. V.* find; **Freunde ~:** make friends; **Finder der; ~s, ~:** finder; *s. auch* **ehrlich 1 a; Finder·lohn der** reward [for finding sth.]; **findig** *Adj.* resourceful; **Findling der; ~s,**

~e a) *(Findelkind)* foundling; b) *(Geol.)* erratic block

fing *1. u. 3. Pers. Sg. Prät. v.* **fangen**

Finger der; ~s, ~: finger; **lange ~ machen** *(ugs.)* get itchy fingers

Finger-: ~abdruck der fingerprint; **~fertigkeit die;** *o. Pl.* dexterity; **~hut der** thimble

fingern *itr. V.* fiddle; **an etw.** *(Dat.)* **~:** fiddle with sth.; **nach etw. ~:** fumble [around] for sth.

Finger-: ~nagel der fingernail; **~spitze die** fingertip; **~spitzen·gefühl das;** *o. Pl.* feeling

fingieren *tr. V.* fake; **ein fingierter Name** a false name

Fink der; ~en, ~en finch

Finne der; ~n, ~n, Finnin die; ~, ~nen Finn; **finnisch** *Adj.* Finnish; **Finnland (das); ~s** Finland

finster 1. *Adj.* dark; dimly-lit ⟨*pub, district*⟩; **2.** *adv.* **jmdn. ~ ansehen** give sb. a black look; **Finsternis die; ~, ~se** darkness; *(auch bibl., fig.)* dark

Finte die; ~, ~n trick; **jmdn. durch eine ~ täuschen** deceive sb. by trickery

firm *Adj.* **in etw.** *(Dat.)* **~ sein** be well up in sth.

Firma die; ~, Firmen firm; company

Firmen-: ~inhaber der owner of the/a company; **~schild das** company's name plate; **~zeichen das** trademark

Firmung die; ~, ~en confirmation

First der; ~[e]s, ~e ridge

Fisch der; ~[e]s, ~e a) fish; **[fünf] ~e fangen** catch [five] fish; **kleine ~e** *(fig.)* small fry; **b)** *(Astrol.)* **die ~e** Pisces; **er ist [ein] ~:** he is a Piscean; **fischen 1.** *tr. V.* **a)** fish for; **b)** *(ugs.)* **etw. aus etw. ~:** fish sth. out of sth; **2.** *itr. V.* fish; **nach etw. ~:** fish for sth.; **Fischer der; ~s, ~** fisherman

Fischer·boot das fishing boat

Fischerei die; ~: fishing

Fisch-: ~fang der; *o. Pl.* **vom ~ leben** make a/one's living by fishing; **auf ~ gehen** go fishing; **~geschäft das** fishmonger's [shop] *(Brit.);* fish store *(Amer.);* **~grät[en]·muster das** *(Textilw.)* herringbone pattern; **~konserve die** canned fish; **~kutter der** fishing trawler; **~stäbchen das** *(Kochk.)* fish finger

Fiskus der; ~, Fisken *od.* **~se** Government *(as managing the State finances)*

Fittich der; ~[e]s, ~e *(dichter.)* wing

fix 1. *Adj. (ugs.)* quick; **ein ~er Bursche** a bright lad; **~ und fertig** quite finished; *(völlig erschöpft)* completely shattered *(coll.);* **2.** *adv. (ugs.)* quickly; **mach ~!** hurry up!

fixen *itr. V. (Drogenjargon)* fix *(sl.);* **Fixer der; ~s, ~** *(Drogenjargon)* fixer

fixieren *tr. V.* **a)** fix one's gaze on; **jmdn. scharf ~**: gaze sharply at sb.; **b)** *(geh.: schriftlich niederlegen)* take down

Fix·stern der *(Astron.)* fixed star

Fjord [fjɔrt] **der; ~|e|s, ~e** fiord

FKK [ɛf ka: 'ka:] *Abk.* Freikörperkultur nudism *no art.;* naturism *no art.;* **FKK-Strand der** nudist beach

flach *Adj.* **a)** flat; **b)** *(niedrig)* low; **c)** *(nicht tief)* shallow ⟨water, dish⟩; **Fläche die; ~, ~n a)** area; **b)** *(Ober~)* surface; **c)** *(Geom.)* area; *(einer dreidimensionalen Figur)* side

Flächen-: ~inhalt der area; **~maß das** unit of square measure

flach|fallen *itr. V.; mit sein (ugs.)* ⟨trip⟩ fall through; ⟨event⟩ be cancelled; **Flach·land das;** *o. Pl.* lowland

Flachs der; ~es flax

flachsen *itr. V. mit jmdm. ~ (ugs.)* joke with sb.

flackern *itr. V.* flicker

Fladen der; ~s, ~ *flat, round unleavened cake made with oat or barley flour*

Flagge die; ~, ~n flag; **flaggen** *itr. V.* put out the flags

flambieren *tr. V. (Kochk.)* flambé

Flamme die; ~, ~n a) flame; **b)** *(Brennstelle)* burner

Flanell der; ~s, ~e flannel

flanieren *itr. V.; mit Richtungsangabe mit sein* stroll

Flanke die; ~, ~n a) *(Weiche)* flank; **b)** *(Ballspiele: Vorlage)* centre; **c)** *(Teil des Spielfeldes)* wing

Flasche die; ~, ~n bottle; **eine ~ Wein** a bottle of wine; **dem Kind die ~ geben** feed the baby

Flaschen-: ~bier das bottled beer; **~öffner der** bottle-opener; **~zug der** block and tackle

flatterhaft *Adj.* fickle; **flattern** *itr. V. mit Richtungsangabe mit sein* flutter

flau *Adj.* **a)** slack ⟨breeze⟩; **b)** *(leicht übel)* queasy ⟨feeling⟩

Flaum der; ~|e|s fuzz

Flausch der; ~|e|s, ~e brushed wool; **flauschig** *Adj.* fluffy

Flause die; ~, ~n; *meist Pl. (ugs.)* **er hat nur ~n im Kopf** he can never think of anything sensible

Flaute die; ~, ~n a) *(Seemannsspr.)* calm; **b)** *(Kaufmannsspr.)* fall[-off] in trade

Flechte die; ~, ~n a) *(Bot.)* lichen; **b)** *(Med.)* eczema

flechten *unr. tr. V.* plait ⟨hair⟩; weave ⟨basket, mat⟩

Fleck der; ~|e|s, ~e a) stain; *(andersfarbige Stelle)* patch; **flecken** *itr. V.* stain; **flecken·los 1.** *Adj.* spotless; **2.** *adv.* spotlessly

Fleck·entferner der stain *or* spot remover

fleckig *Adj.* stained; blotchy ⟨face, skin⟩

Fleder·maus die bat

Flegel der; ~s, ~ *(abwertend)* lout; **flegelhaft** *Adj. (abwertend)* loutish

flehen ['fle:ən] *itr. V.* plead (um for)

Fleisch das; ~|e|s a) flesh; **b)** *(Nahrungsmittel)* meat; **Fleisch·brühe die** bouillon; consommé; **Fleischer der; ~s, ~**: butcher; **Fleischerei die; ~, ~en** butcher's shop

fleischig *Adj.* plump ⟨hands, face⟩; fleshy ⟨leaf, fruit⟩

Fleisch-: ~käse der meat loaf; **~klößchen das** small meat ball; **~pastete die** *(Kochk.)* pâté; **~salat der** *(Kochk.)* meat salad; **~vergiftung die** food poisoning [from meat]; **~waren** *Pl.* meat products; **~wolf der** mincer; **~wunde die** fleshwound; **~wurst die** pork sausage

Fleiß der; ~es hard work; *(Eigenschaft)* diligence; **fleißig 1.** *Adj.* hard-working; **2.** *adv.* hard; **~ lernen** learn as much as one can

flennen *itr. V. (ugs.)* blubber

fletschen *tr., itr. V.* **die Zähne** *od.* **mit den Zähnen ~**: bare one's teeth

Fleurop ⓦ ['flɔyrɔp] **die** Interflora **(P)**

flexibel 1. *Adj.* flexible; **2.** *adv.* flexibly

flicht *Imperativ Sg. u. 3. Pers. Sg. Präsens v.* flechten

flicken *tr. V.* mend; repair ⟨engine, cable⟩; **Flicken der; ~s, ~**: patch

Flick-: ~werk das; *o. Pl. (abwertend)* botched-up job; **~zeug das** repair kit

Flieder der; ~s, ~: lilac

Fliege die; ~, ~n a) fly; **b)** *(Schleife)* bow-tie; **fliegen 1.** *unr. itr. V.; mit sein* **a)** fly; **b)** *(ugs.: fallen)* **vom Pferd/ Fahrrad ~**: fall off a/the horse/bicycle; **c)** *(ugs.: entlassen werden)* get the sack *(coll.);* **von der Schule ~**: be chucked out [of the school] *(coll.);* **2.** *unr. tr. V.* fly

Fliegen-: ~**fenster das** wire-mesh window; ~**gewicht das** *(Schwerathletik)* flyweight; ~**pilz der** fly agaric; **Flieger der;** ~**s,** ~ pilot; **Fliegeralarm der** air-raid warning; **fliegerisch** *Adj.* aeronautical

fliehen ['fliːən] *unr. itr. V.; mit sein* flee (vor + *Dat.* from); *(aus dem Gefängnis usw.)* escape (**aus** from); **ins Ausland/über die Grenze** ~: flee the country/escape over the border

Flieh·kraft die *(Physik)* centrifugal force

Fliese die; ~, ~**n** tile

Fließ·band das conveyor belt; **am** ~**band arbeiten** *od. (ugs.)* **stehen** work on the assembly line

fließen *unr. itr. V.; mit sein* flow; ~**des Wasser** running water; **eine Sprache** ~**d sprechen** speak a language fluently

flimmern *itr. V.; mit Richtungsangabe mit sein* shimmer

flink 1. *Adj.* nimble *(fingers);* sharp *(eyes);* quick *(hands);* **2.** *adv.* quickly

Flinte die; ~, ~**n** shotgun; **die** ~ **ins Korn werfen** *(fig.)* throw in the towel

Flirt der; ~**s,** ~**s** flirtation; **flirten** *itr. V.* flirt

Flitter der; ~**s** frippery; trumpery

Flitter·wochen *Pl.* honeymoon *sing.*

flitzen *itr. V.; mit sein (ugs.)* shoot; dart; **Flitzer der;** ~**s,** ~ *(ugs.)* sporty job *(coll.)*

floaten ['floʊtn̩] *tr., itr. V. (Wirtsch.)* float

flocht *1. u. 3. Pers. Sg. Prät. v.* flechten

Flocke die; ~, ~**n a)** flake; **b)** *(Staub~)* piece of fluff; **flockig** *Adj.* fluffy

flog *1. u. 3. Pers. Sg. Prät. v.* fliegen

floh *1. u. 3. Pers. Sg. Prät. v.* fliehen

Floh der; ~**(e)s, Flöhe** flea

Floh-: ~**markt der** flea market; ~**zirkus der** flea-circus

Flora die; ~, **Floren** flora

Florett das; ~**(e)s,** ~**e** foil

florieren *itr. V.* flourish

Florist der; ~**en,** ~**en, Floristin die;** ~, ~**nen** [qualified] flower-arranger

Floskel die; ~, ~**n** cliché

floß *1. u. 3. Pers. Sg. Prät. v.* fließen

Floß das; ~**es, Flöße** raft

Flosse die; ~, ~**n a)** *(Zool., Flugw.)* fin; **b)** *(zum Tauchen)* flipper

flößen *tr., itr. V.* float

Flößer der; ~**s,** ~: raftsman

Flöte die; ~, ~**n** flute; *(Block~)* recorder; **flöten 1.** *itr. V.* *(bird)* flute; **2.** *tr. V.* whistle; **flöten|gehen** *unr. itr.*

V.; mit sein (ugs.) *(money)* go down the drain; *(time)* be wasted

flott 1. *Adj.* **a)** *(schwungvoll)* lively; **b)** *(schick)* smart; **2.** *adv.* *(work)* quickly; *(dance, write)* in a lively manner; *(be dressed)* smartly

Flotte die; ~, ~**n** fleet

flott|machen *tr. V.* refloat *(ship);* get *(car)* back on the road

Flöz das; ~**es,** ~**e** *(Bergbau)* seam

Fluch der; ~**(e)s, Flüche** curse; oath; **fluchen** *itr. V.* curse; swear

Flucht die; ~: flight; **flucht·artig 1.** *Adj.* hurried; hasty; **2.** *adv.* hurriedly; hastily; **flüchten 1.** *itr. V.; mit sein* **vor jmdm./etw.** ~: flee from sb./sth.; **vor der Polizei** ~: run away from the police; **2.** *refl. V.* take refuge; **flüchtig 1.** *Adj.* **a)** fugitive; **b)** cursory; superficial *(insight);* **2.** *adv.* **a)** *(oberflächlich)* cursorily; **b)** *(eilig)* hurriedly; **Flüchtigkeit die;** ~, ~**en** cursoriness;

Flüchtigkeits·fehler der slip; **Flüchtling der;** ~**s,** ~**e** refugee; **Flucht·weg der** escape route

Flug der; ~**(e)s, Flüge** flight

Flug-: ~**bahn die** trajectory; ~**blatt das** pamphlet; leaflet

Flügel der; ~**s,** ~ **a)** wing; **b)** *(Klavier)* grand piano

Flug·gast der [air] passenger

flügge *Adj.* fully-fledged

Flug-: ~**gesellschaft die** airline; ~**hafen der** airport; ~**linie die a)** *(Strecke)* air route; **b)** *(Gesellschaft)* airline; ~**lotse der** air traffic controller; ~**platz der** airfield; ~**schein der** air ticket; ~**verkehr der** air traffic

Flug·zeug das; ~**(e)s,** ~**e** aeroplane *(Brit.);* airplane *(Amer.);* aircraft

Flugzeug-: ~**absturz der** plane crash; ~**entführer der** [aircraft] hijacker; ~**entführung die** [aircraft] hijack[ing]; ~**träger der** aircraft carrier

Flunder die; ~, ~**n** flounder

flunkern *itr. V.* tell stories

Fluor das; ~**s** *(Chemie)* fluorine

¹**Flur der;** ~**(e)s,** ~**e** *(Korridor)* corridor; *(Diele)* [entrance] hall; **im/auf dem** ~: in the corridor/hall

²**Flur die;** ~, ~**en** farmland *no indef. art.*

Fluß der; Flusses, Flüsse river; *(fließende Bewegung)* flow

fluß-, Fluß-: ~**ab[wärts]** *Adv.* downstream; ~**auf[wärts]** *Adv.* upstream; ~**bett das** river bed

Flüßchen das; ~s, ~: small river
flüssig 1. *Adj.* a) liquid; b) *(fließend, geläufig)* fluent; 2. *adv.* ⟨*write, speak*⟩ fluently; **Flüssigkeit die; ~, ~en a)** liquid; *(auch Gas)* fluid; b) *(Geläufigkeit)* fluency; **flüssig|machen** *tr. V.* make available ⟨*money, funds*⟩
Fluß·pferd das hippopotamus
flüstern *itr., tr. V.* whisper
Flut die; ~, ~en a) *o. Pl.* tide; b) *meist Pl. (geh.: Wassermasse)* flood; **fluten** *itr. V.; mit sein (geh.)* flood; **Flut·licht** das; *o. Pl.* floodlight
focht *1. u. 3. Pers. Sg. Prät. v.* **fechten**
Föderalismus der; ~: federalism *no art.;* **föderalistisch** *Adj.* federalist
Fohlen das; ~s, ~: foal
Föhn der; ~[e]s, ~e föhn
Folge die; ~, ~n a) *(Auswirkung)* consequence; *(Ergebnis)* consequence; result; b) *(Aufeinander~)* succession; *(zusammengehörend)* sequence; c) *(Fortsetzung)(einer Sendung)* episode; *(eines Romans)* instalment; **Folgeerscheinung** die consequence; **folgen** *itr. V.; mit sein* follow; **jmdm. im Amt/in der Regierung ~:** succeed sb. in office/in government; **auf etw.** *(Akk.)* ~: follow sth.; **aus etw. ~:** follow from sth.; **folgend** *Adj.* der/die/das ~e the next in order; im ~en *od.* in ~em in [the course of] the following discussion/passage *etc.;* **folgendermaßen** *Adv.* as follows; *(so)* in the following way; **folge·richtig** 1. *Adj.* logical; consistent ⟨*behaviour, action*⟩; 2. *adv.* logically; ⟨*act, behave*⟩ consistently; **folgern** 1. *tr. V.* etw. aus etw. ~: infer sth. from sth.; 2. *itr. V.* richtig ~: draw a/the correct conclusion; **Folgerung die; ~, ~en** conclusion
folglich *Adv.* consequently; **folgsam** 1. *Adj.* obedient; 2. *adv.* obediently
Folie ['fo:liə] die; ~, ~n *(Metall~)* foil; *(Plastik~)* film
Folklore die; ~ a) folklore; b) *(Musik)* folk-music
Folter die; ~, ~n torture; **foltern** *tr. V.* torture; *(fig.)* torment; **Folterung** die; ~, ~en torture
Fön Ⓦ der; ~[e]s, ~e hair-drier
Fond [fõ:] der; ~s, ~s *(geh.)* back
Fonds [fõ:] der; ~ [fõ:(s)], ~ [fõ:s] fund
Fondue [fõ'dy:] die; ~, ~s *od.* das; ~s, ~s *(Kochk.)* fondue
fönen *tr. V.* blow-dry
Fontäne die; ~, ~n jet; *(Springbrunnen)* fountain

forcieren [fɔr'si:rən] *tr. V.* step up ⟨*production*⟩; intensify ⟨*efforts*⟩; push forward ⟨*developments*⟩
Förderer der; ~s, ~: patron
fordern *tr. V.* a) demand; b) *(in Anspruch nehmen)* make demands on
fördern *tr. V.* a) promote; patronize, support ⟨*artist, art*⟩; further ⟨*investigation*⟩; foster ⟨*talent, tendency*⟩; improve ⟨*appetite*⟩; aid ⟨*digestion, sleep*⟩; b) *(Bergbau, Technik)* mine ⟨*coal, ore*⟩; extract ⟨*oil*⟩
Forderung die; ~, ~en a) demand; b) *(Kaufmannsspr.)* claim **(an + Akk.** against)
Förderung die; ~, ~en a) *o. Pl. s.* **fördern a:** promotion; patronage; support; furthering; fostering; improvement; aiding; b) *(Bergbau, Technik)* output; *(das Fördern)* mining; *(von Erdöl)* extraction
Forelle die; ~, ~n trout
Form die; ~, ~en a) shape; **in ~ von Tabletten** in the form of tablets; b) *(bes. Sport: Verfassung)* form; **in ~ sein** be on form; c) *(vorgeformtes Modell)* mould; *(Back~)* baking tin; d) *(Darstellungs~, Umgangs~)* form
formal 1. *Adj.* formal; 2. *adv.* formally; **formalisieren** *tr. V.* formalize
Formalität die; ~, ~en formality
Format das; ~[e]s, ~e a) size; *(Buch~, Papier~, Bild~)* format; b) *o. Pl. (Persönlichkeit)* stature
formbar *Adj.* malleable
Formel die; ~, ~n formula
formell *Adj.* formal
formen *tr. V.* a) *(gestalten)* form; shape; b) *(bilden, prägen)* mould, form ⟨*character, personality*⟩; **Form·fehler** der irregularity
formieren *tr., refl. V.* form
förmlich 1. *Adj.* a) formal; b) *(regelrecht)* positive; 2. *adv.* a) formally; b) *(geradezu)* sich ~ fürchten be really afraid
form·los *Adj.* a) informal; b) *(gestaltlos)* shapeles
Form·sache die formality
Formular das; ~s, ~e form; **formulieren** *tr. V.* formulate; **Formulierung die; ~, ~en a)** *o. Pl. (das Formulieren)* formulation; *(eines Entwurfes, Gesetzes)* drafting; b) *(formulierter Text)* formulation
form·vollendet 1. *Adj.* perfectly executed ⟨*pirouette, bow, etc.*⟩; ⟨*poem*⟩ perfect in form; 2. *adv.* faultlessly
forsch *Adj.* forceful

forschen *itr. V.* **a) nach jmdm./etw. ~:**
search *or* look for sb./sth.; **b)** *(als Wissenschaftler)* research; **Forscher** der;
~s, **Forscherin** die; ~, ~nen researcher; **Forschung** die; ~, ~en research; **Forschungs·reisende** der/
die explorer

Forst der; ~|e|s, ~e|n| forest; **Förster**
der; ~s, ~: forest warden

Forst·wirtschaft die forestry

Forsythie [fɔr'zy:tsiə] die; ~, ~n for-
sythia

fort *Adv.* **a)** *s.* weg; **b)** *(weiter)* **und so
~:** and so on

fort-, Fort-: ~**an** [-'-] *Adv.* from now/
then on; ~**bestand** der; *o. Pl.* continuation; *(eines Staates)* continued
existence; ~|**bewegen** **1.** *tr. V.*
move; shift; **2.** *refl. V.* move [along];
~|**bleiben** *unr. itr. V.;* *mit sein* fail to
come; ~|**bringen** *unr. tr. V.: s.* weg-
bringen; ~|**dauern** *itr. V.* continue;
~|**fahren** **1.** *unr. itr. V.* **a)** *mit sein*
leave; **b)** *auch mit sein (weitermachen)*
continue; go on; **2.** *unr. tr. V.* drive
away; ~|**führen** *tr. V.* **a)** lead away;
b) *(fortsetzen)* continue; ~**gang** der;
o. Pl. **a)** departure (**aus** from); **b)** *(Wei-
terentwicklung)* progress; ~|**gehen**
unr. itr. V.; *mit sein* leave; geh ~! go
away!; ~**geschritten** *Adj.* advanced; ~**geschrittene** der/die;
adj. Dekl. advanced student/player;
~|**kommen** *unr. itr. V.;* *mit sein s.*
wegkommen a, b; ~|**laufen** *unr. itr.
V.;* *mit sein* **a)** *s.* weglaufen; **b)** *(sich
~setzen)* continue; ~**laufend 1.** *Adj.*
continuous; **2.** *adv.* continuously;
~|**pflanzen** *refl. V.* **a)** reproduce
[oneself/itself]; **b)** *(sich verbreiten)*
⟨idea, mood⟩ spread; ⟨sound, light⟩
travel; ~**pflanzung** die reproduc-
tion; ~|**schaffen** *tr. V.* take away;
~|**schreiten** *unr. itr. V.;* *mit sein* ⟨pro-
cess⟩ continue; ⟨time⟩ move on; ~
schritt der of progress; ~**schritte** progress *sing.;* **ein** ~**schritt** a step forward; ~**schrittlich 1.** *Adj.* progressive; **2.** *adv.* progressively;
~**schrittlichkeit** die; ~: progress-
iveness; ~|**setzen 1.** *tr. V.* continue;
2. *refl. V.* continue; ~**setzung** die; ~,
~en **a)** *(das ~setzen)* continuation; **b)**
(anschließender Teil) instalment;
~|**während 1.** *Adj.; nicht präd.*
continual; **2.** *adv.* continually;
~|**werfen** *unr. tr. V.: s.* wegwerfen

Foto das; ~s, ~s photo; ~s **machen**
take photos

Foto-: ~**album** das photo album;
~**apparat** der camera

fotogen *Adj.* photogenic **Foto·graf**
der; ~en, ~en photographer; **Foto-
grafie** die; ~, ~n **a)** *o. Pl.* photo-
graphy *no art.;* **b)** *(Lichtbild)* photograph; **fotografieren** *tr. V.* photograph; take a photograph/photo-
graphs of; **Fotografin** die; ~, ~nen
photographer

foto-, Foto-: ~**kopie** die photocopy;
~**kopieren** *tr., itr. V.* photocopy;
~**kopierer** der photocopier; ~**labor**
das photographic laboratory; ~**modell** das photographic model

Foul [faul] das; ~s, ~s *(Sport)* foul (**an**
+ *Dat.* on)

Foyer [fɔa'je:] das; ~s, ~s foyer

FPÖ *Abk.* Freiheitliche Partei Öster-
reichs

Fr. *Abk.* **a)** Franken SFr.; **b)** Frau; **c)**
Freitag Fri.

Fracht die; ~, ~en *(Schiffs~, Luft~)*
cargo; freight; *(Bahn~, LKW~)*
goods *pl.;* freight; **Frachter**
der; ~s, ~: freighter

Fracht-: ~**gut** das slow freight; slow
goods *pl.;* ~**schiff** das cargo ship

Frack der; ~|e|s, Fräcke tails *pl.;* even-
ing dress

Frage die; ~, ~n question; *(Angelegenheit)* issue; **in ~ kommen** be
possible; **das kommt nicht in ~** *(ugs.)*
that is out of the question; **Fragebogen** der questionnaire; *(Formular)*
form; **fragen 1.** *tr., itr. V.* **a)** ask; **b)**
(sich erkundigen) **nach etw. ~:** ask *or*
inquire about sth.; **c)** *(nachfragen)* ask
for; **2.** *refl. V.* **sich ~, ob ...:** wonder
whether ...; **Frage·zeichen** das
question mark; **fraglich** *Adj.* **a)**
doubtful; **b)** *nicht präd. (betreffend)* in
question *postpos.;* relevant

Fragment das; ~|e|s, ~e fragment

frag·würdig *Adj.* **a)** questionable; **b)**
(zwielichtig) dubious

Fraktion die; ~, ~en parliamentary
party; *(mit zwei Parteien)* parliamentary coalition

Fraktions- *(Parl.):* ~**führer** der
leader of the parliamentary party/
coalition; ~**zwang** der obligation to
vote in accordance with party policy

frank *Adv.* ~ **und frei** frankly and
openly; openly and honestly

Franken der; ~s ~: [Swiss] franc

Frankfurter die; ~, ~ *(Wurst)* frankfurter

frankieren *tr. V.* frank
Frank·reich (das); ~s France
Franse die; ~, ~n strand [of a/the fringe]
Franzose der; ~n, ~n Frenchman; **er ist ~:** he is French; **die ~n** the French; **Französin die; ~, ~nen** Frenchwoman; **französisch** *Adj.* French; **Französisch das; ~[s]** French
Fräse die; ~, ~n *(für Holz)* moulding machine; *(für Metall)* milling machine
fraß *1. u. 3. Pers. Sg. Prät. v.* fressen;
Fraß der; ~es *(derb)* muck
Fratze die; ~, ~n a) hideous face; **b)** *(ugs.: Grimasse)* grimace
Frau die; ~, ~en a) woman; **b)** *(Ehe~)* wife; **c)** *(Titel, Anrede)* ~ **Schulze** Mrs Schulze; *(in Briefen)* **Sehr geehrte ~ Schulze** Dear Madam; *(bei persönlicher Bekanntschaft)* Dear Mrs/Miss/ Ms Schulze
Frauen-: ~arzt der, ~ärztin die gynaecologist; **~bewegung die** *o. Pl.* women's movement; **~rechtlerin die; ~, ~nen** feminist; Women's Libber *(coll.)*
Fräulein das; ~s, ~ *(ugs. ~s)* **a)** *(junges ~)* young lady; *(ältliches ~)* spinster; **b)** *(Titel, Anrede)* ~ **Mayer/ Schulte** Miss Mayer/Schulte
fraulich **1.** *Adj.* feminine; **2.** *adv.* in a feminine way
frech **1.** *Adj.* **a)** impertinent; cheeky; bare-faced *(lie)*; **b)** *(keck, keß)* saucy; **2.** *adv.* impertinently; cheekily; **Frechheit die; ~, ~en a)** *o. Pl.* impertinence; cheek; **b)** *(Äußerung)* impertinent *or* cheeky remark
frei **1.** *Adj.* **a)** *(unabhängig)* free; **b)** *(nicht angestellt)* free-lance; **c)** *(ungezwungen)* free and easy; **d)** *(nicht mehr in Haft)* free; **e)** *(offen)* open; **f)** *(unbesetzt)* vacant; free; **g)** *(kostenlos)* free *(food, admission)*; **h)** *(verfügbar)* spare; free *(time)*; **2.** *adv.* freely
frei-, Frei-: ~bad das open-air swimming-pool; **~|bekommen** **1.** *unr. itr. V. (ugs.)* get time off; **2.** *unr. tr. V.* jmdn./etw. **~bekommen** get sb./ sth. released; **~beruflich** **1.** *Adj.* self-employed; free-lance; *(doctor, lawyer)* in private practice; **2.** *adv.* **~beruflich tätig sein/arbeiten** work free-lance/practise privately; **~betrag der** *(Steuerw.)* [tax] allowance
Freier der; ~s, ~ *(veralt.)* suitor
frei-, Frei-: ~exemplar das *(Buch)* free copy; *(Zeitung)* free issue; **~|geben** *unr. tr. V.* release; **~gebig** *Adj.*

generous; open-handed; **~gehege das** outdoor enclosure; **~gepäck das** baggage allowance; **~hafen der** free port; **~|halten** *unr. tr. V.* **a)** treat; **b)** *(offenhalten)* keep *(entrance, roadway)* clear; **Einfahrt ~halten!** no parking in front of entrance; **~handels·zone die** free-trade zone; **~händig** *adv.* *(cycle)* without holding on
Freiheit die; ~, ~en a) freedom; ~, **Gleichheit, Brüderlichkeit** Liberty, Equality, Fraternity; **b)** *(Vorrecht)* freedom; privilege; **freiheitlich** **1.** *Adj.* liberal *(philosophy, conscience)*; ~ **und demokratisch** free and democratic; **2.** *adv.* liberally
Freiheits-: ~beraubung die *(jur.)* wrongful detention; **~strafe die** term of imprisonment
frei-, Frei-: ~herr der baron; **~karte die** complimentary ticket; **~|kaufen** *tr. V.* ransom *(hostage)*; buy the freedom of *(slave)*; **~|kommen** *unr. itr. V.* **aus dem Gefängnis ~kommen** be released from prison; **~körper·kultur die;** *o. Pl.* nudism *no art.;* naturism *no art.;* **~|lassen** *unr. tr. V.* set free; release; **~|legen** *tr. V.* uncover
freilich *Adv.* of course
Frei·licht-: ~bühne die, ~theater das open-air theatre
frei-, Frei-: ~|machen **1.** *refl. V.* *(ugs.: frei nehmen)* take time off; **2.** *tr. V. (Postw.)* frank; **etw. mit 0,50 DM ~machen** put a 50-pfennig stamp on sth.; **~marke die** postage stamp; **~mütig** **1.** *Adj.* frank; **2.** *adv.* frankly; **~schaffend** *Adj.* free-lance; **~|schwimmen** *unr. refl. V.* **sich ~schwimmen** pass the 15-minute swimming test; **~|sprechen** *unr. tr. V.* **a)** *(Rechtsw.)* acquit; **b)** *(für unschuldig erklären)* exonerate (von from); **~spruch der** *(Rechtsw.)* acquittal; **~|stellen** *tr. V.* **a)** jmdm. etw. **~stellen** leave sth. up to sb.; **b)** *(befreien)* release *(person)*; jmdn. vom Wehrdienst **~stellen** exempt sb. from military service; **~stoß der** *(Fußball)* free kick
Frei·tag der Friday; *s. auch* **Dienstag, Dienstag-; freitags** *Adv.* on Friday[s]; *s. auch* **dienstags**
frei-, Frei-: ~tod der *(verhüll.)* suicide *no art.;* **~treppe die** [flight of] steps; **~übung die;** *meist Pl. (Sport)* keep-fit exercise; **~wild das** fair game; **~willig** **1.** *Adj.* voluntary

⟨*decision*⟩; optional ⟨*subject*⟩; **2.** *adv.*
voluntarily; **sich ~willig melden** volunteer; **~zeichen das** ringing tone;
~zeit die; *o. Pl.* spare time; **~zügig**
Adj. **a)** generous; **b)** *(gewagt, unmoralisch)* risqué ⟨*remark, film, dress*⟩;
~zügigkeit die generosity
fremd *Adj.* **a)** foreign; **b)** *(nicht eigen)*
other people's; of others *postpos.;* **c)**
(unbekannt) strange
fremd·artig *Adj.* strange
¹**Fremde der/die;** *adj. Dekl.* **a)**
stranger; **b)** *(Ausländer)* foreigner;
²**Fremde die;** ~ *(geh.)* die ~: foreign
parts *pl.*
Fremden-: **~führer der** tourist
guide; **~verkehr der** tourism *no art.;*
~zimmer das room
fremd-, Fremd-: **~|gehen** *unr. itr.*
V.; mit sein (ugs.) be unfaithful;
~herrschaft die foreign domination; **~ländisch** *Adj.* foreign; *(exotisch)* exotic
Fremdling der; ~s, ~e *(veralt.)*
stranger
fremd-, Fremd-: **~sprache die**
foreign language; **~sprachig** *Adj.*
bilingual/multilingual ⟨*staff, secretary*⟩; foreign ⟨*literature*⟩; foreign-language ⟨*edition, teaching*⟩; **~sprachlich** *Adj.* foreign-language ⟨*teaching*⟩; foreign ⟨*word*⟩; **~wort das;** *Pl.*
~wörter foreign word
frenetisch **1.** *Adj.* frenetic; **2.** *adv.*
frenetically
Frequenz die; ~, ~en *(Physik)* frequency; *(Med.: Puls~)* rate
Fresse die; ~, ~n *(derb)* **a)** *(Mund)*
gob *(sl.);* **b)** *(Gesicht)* mug *(sl.);* **fressen** **1.** *unr. tr. V.* **a)** ⟨*animal*⟩ eat; *(sich*
ernähren von) feed on; **b)** *(ugs.: verschlingen)* swallow up ⟨*money, time,*
distance⟩; drink ⟨*petrol*⟩; **c)** *(zerstören)*
eat away; **d)** *(derb: von Menschen)*
guzzle; **2.** *unr. itr. V. (von Tieren)* feed;
(derb: von Menschen) stuff one's face
(sl.); **Fressen das;** ~s **a)** *(für Hunde,*
Katzen usw.) food; *(für Vieh)* feed; **b)**
(derb: Essen) grub *(sl.);* **Fresserei**
die; ~, ~en *(derb)* guzzling
Freude die; ~, ~n joy; *(Vergnügen)*
pleasure; **~ an etw.** *(Dat.)* **haben** take
pleasure in sth.
Freuden-: **~haus das** house of pleasure; **~tag der** happy day; **freudestrahlend** *Adj.* beaming with joy;
freudig *Adj.* joyful; joyous ⟨*heart*⟩;
delightful ⟨*surprise*⟩; **freud·los** *Adj.*
joyless; **freuen** **1.** *refl. V.* be glad

(über + Akk. about); *(froh sein)* be
happy; **sich auf etw.** *(Akk.)* ~: look
forward to sth.; **2.** *tr. V.* please
Freund der; ~es, ~e **a)** friend; **b)** *(Verehrer, Geliebter)* boy-friend;
Freundin die; ~, ~nen **a)** friend; **b)**
(Geliebte) girl-friend; *(älter)* lady-friend; **freundlich** **1.** *Adj.* **a)** kind
⟨*face*⟩; friendly ⟨*reception*⟩; **b)** *(angenehm)* pleasant; **c)** *(freundschaftlich)*
friendly; **2.** *adv.* **jmdm. ~ danken**
thank sb. kindly; **Freundlichkeit**
die; ~: kindness; **Freundschaft die;**
~, ~en friendship; **mit jmdm. ~ schließen** make friends with sb.;
freundschaftlich **1.** *Adj.* friendly;
2. *adv.* in a friendly way
Frevel ['fre:fl] **der;** ~s, ~ *(geh., veralt.)*
crime; outrage
Friede der; ~ns, ~n *(älter, geh.)* s.
Frieden; Frieden der; ~s, ~: peace
Friedens-: **~forschung die** peace
studies *pl., no art.;* **~konferenz die**
peace conference; **~nobelpreis der**
Nobel Peace Prize; **~pfeife die** pipe
of peace; **~richter der** *lay magistrate*
dealing with minor offences; ≈ Justice
of the Peace; **~taube die** dove of
peace; **~verhandlungen** *Pl.* peace
negotiations; **~vertrag der** peace
treaty
fried·fertig *Adj.* peaceable ⟨*person,*
character⟩; **Fried·hof der** cemetery;
(Kirchhof) graveyard; **friedlich** **1.**
Adj. peaceful; **2.** *adv.* peacefully;
fried·liebend *Adj.* peace-loving
frieren *unr. itr. V.* **a)** be or feel cold; **b)**
mit sein (ge~) freeze
Frikadelle die; ~, ~n rissole
frisch **1.** *Adj.* fresh; new-laid ⟨*egg*⟩;
clean ⟨*linen, underwear*⟩; wet ⟨*paint*⟩;
2. *adv.* freshly; **Frische die;** ~ freshness; **geistige ~:** mental alertness;
körperliche ~: physical fitness;
Frisch·halte·beutel der airtight
bag
Friseur [fri'zø:ɐ̯] **der;** ~s, ~e, **Friseuse** [fri'zø:zə] **die;** ~, ~n hairdresser;
frisieren *tr. V.* **jmdn./sich ~:** do
sb.'s/one's hair; **sich ~ lassen** have
one's hair done
friß *Imperativ Sg. v.* fressen
frißt *2. u. 3. Pers. Sg. Präsens v.* fressen
Frist die; ~, ~en **a)** time; period; **die ~**
verlängern extend the deadline; **b)** *(begrenzter Aufschub)* extension
frist-: **~gemäß, ~gerecht** *Adj.,*
adv. within the specified time *postpos.; (bei Anmeldung usw.)* before the

closing date *postpos.; ~*los 1. *Adj.* instant; 2. *adv.* without notice
Frisur die; ~, ~en hairstyle
fritieren *tr. V.* deep-fry
frivol [fri'vo:l] *Adj.* **a)** *(schamlos)* suggestive *(remark, picture, etc.)*; risqué *(joke)*; earthy *(man)*; flighty *(woman)*; **b)** *(leichtfertig)* frivolous
froh *Adj.* **a)** happy; cheerful *(person, mood)*; good *(news)*; **b)** *(ugs.: erleichtert)* pleased, glad **(über** + *Akk.* about)
fröhlich *Adj.* cheerful; happy
Fröhlichkeit die; ~: cheerfulness; *(eines Festes, einer Feier)* gaiety
Froh·sinn der; *o. Pl.* cheerfulness; gaiety
fromm; ~er *od.* **frömmer,** ~st... *od.* **frömmst...** 1. *Adj.* pious, devout *(person)*; devout *(Christian)*; 2. *adv.* piously; **Frömmigkeit** die; ~: piety; devoutness
Fron·leichnam [fro:n-] *o. Art.* [the feast of] Corpus Christi
Front die; ~, ~en **a)** *(Gebäude~)* front; façade; **b)** *(Kampfgebiet)* front [line]; **frontal** 1. *Adj.* head-on *(collision)*; frontal *(attack)*; 2. *adv.* *(collide)* head-on; *(attack)* from the front; **Front·an·trieb** der *(Kfz-W.)* front-wheel drive
fror *1. u. 3. Pers. Sg. Prät. v.* frieren
Frosch der; ~[e]s, Frösche frog
Frosch-: ~**mann** der; *Pl.* ~**männer** frogman; ~**perspektive** die worm's-eye view; ~**schenkel** der frog's leg
Frost der; ~[e]s, Fröste frost; **Frostbeule** die chilblain; **frösteln** *itr. V.* feel chilly; **frostig** 1. *Adj. (auch fig.)* frosty; 2. *adv.* frostily; **Frost·schutz·mittel** das **a)** frost protection agent; **b)** *(Kfz-W.)* antifreeze
Frottee das u. der; ~s, ~s terry towelling; **Frottee·handtuch** das terry towel; **frottieren** *tr. V.* rub; towel
frotzeln 1. *tr. V.* tease; 2. *itr. V.* über jmdn./etw. ~: make fun of sb./sth.
Frucht die; ~, Früchte fruit; **fruchtbar** *Adj.* fertile; fruitful *(work, idea, etc.)*; **Fruchtbarkeit** die; ~: fertility; fruitfulness **Frucht·becher** der fruit sundae; **fruchten** *tr. V.* nichts ~: be no use; **fruchtig** *Adj.* fruity; **frucht·los** *Adj.* fruitless, vain *(efforts)*; **Frucht·saft** der fruit juice
früh 1. *Adj.* **a)** early; **b)** *(vorzeitig)* premature; 2. *adv.* early; **heute** ~: this

morning; **früh·auf: von** ~**auf** from early childhood on[wards]; **Frühaufsteher** der; ~s, ~: early riser; **Frühe** die; ~: **in aller** ~: at the crack of dawn; **früher** ['fry:ɐ] 1. *Adj., nicht präd.* **a)** *(vergangen)* earlier; former; **b)** *(ehemalig)* former *(owner, occupant, friend)*; 2. *adv.* formerly; ~ **war er ganz anders** he used to be quite different; **Früh·erkennung** die *(Med.)* early recognition
frühestens *Adv.* at the earliest; **Früh·geburt** die **a)** premature birth; **b)** *(Kind)* premature baby
Früh·jahr das spring; **Frühjahrs-müdigkeit** die springtime tiredness
Frühling der; ~s, ~e spring; **Frühlings·anfang** der first day of spring
früh-, Früh-: ~**reif** *Adj.* precocious *(child)*; ~**schoppen** der morning drink; *(um Mittag)* lunchtime drink; ~**sport** der early-morning exercise
Früh·stück das; ~s, ~e breakfast; **frühstücken** *itr. V.* have breakfast; **Frühstücks·pause** die morning break; coffee break
früh·zeitig 1. *Adj.* early; *(vorzeitig)* premature; 2. *adv.* early; *(vorzeitig)* prematurely
Frustration die; ~, ~en *(Psych.)* frustration; **frustrieren** *tr. V.* frustrate
Fuchs der; ~es, Füchse fox; **fuchsen** *tr. V.* annoy; vex; **fuchs·teufelswild** *Adj. (ugs.)* livid *(coll.)*
Fuchtel die; ~: **unter jmds.** ~ *(ugs.)* under sb.'s thumb; **fuchteln** *itr. V. (ugs.)* **mit etw.** ~: wave sth. about
Fuder das; ~s, ~: cart-load
¹Fuge die; ~, ~n joint; *(Zwischenraum)* gap; **²Fuge** die; ~, ~n *(Musik)* fugue
fügen 1. *tr. V.* place; set; **etw zu etw.** ~ *(fig.)* add sth. to sth.; 2. *refl. V.* **a)** *(sich ein~)* **sich in etw.** *(Akk.)* ~: fit into sth.; **b)** *(gehorchen)* **sich** ~: fall into line; **fügsam** *Adj.* obedient
fühlbar *Adj.* noticeable; **fühlen** 1. *tr., itr. V.* feel; 2. *refl. V.* **sich krank** ~: feel sick; **Fühler** der; ~s, ~: feeler; antenna; **Fühlungnahme** die; ~: initial contact
fuhr *1. u. 3. Pers. Sg. Prät. v.* fahren
Fuhre die; ~, ~n load
führen 1. *tr. V.* **a)** lead; **b)** *(verkaufen)* stock, sell *(goods)*; **c)** *(durch~)* Gespräche/Verhandlungen ~: hold conversations/negotiations; **eine glückliche Ehe** ~: be happily married; **d)** *(leiten)* manage, run *(company, business,*

pub, etc.>; lead *(party, country)*; command *(regiment)*; **e)** *(Amtsspr.)* drive *(train, motor, vehicle)*; **f)** *(als Kennzeichnung, Bezeichnung haben)* bear; **einen Titel/Künstlernamen ~:** have a title/use a stage name; **g)** *(angelegt haben)* keep *(diary, list, file)*; **h)** *(registrieren)* **jmdn. in einer Liste/Kartei ~:** have sb. on a list/on file; **i)** *(tragen)* **etw. bei** *od.* **mit sich ~:** have sth. on one; **eine Waffe/einen Ausweis bei sich ~:** carry a weapon/a pass; **2.** *itr. V.* **a)** lead; **b)** *(an der Spitze liegen)* lead; be ahead; **führend** *Adj.* leading; high-ranking *(official)*; prominent *(position)*

Führer der; ~s, ~ **a)** *(Leiter)* leader; **b)** *(Fremden~)* guide; **Führerin** die; ~, ~nen *s.* Führer; **führer·los** *1. Adj.* leaderless; *(ohne Lenker)* driverless *(car)*; **2.** *adv.: s.* 1; without a leader; without a driver; **Führer·schein** der driving licence *(Brit.);* driver's license *(Amer.);* **Führung** die; ~, ~en **a)** *o. Pl. s.* führen **1 d:** management; running; leadership; command; **b)** *(Fremden~)* guided tour; **c)** *o. Pl. (führende Position)* lead

Führungs-: ~**kraft** die manager; ~**spitze** die *(Politik)* top leadership; *(im Betrieb)* top management; ~**zeugnis** das *document issued by police certifying that holder has no criminal record*

Fuhr-: ~**unternehmer** der haulage contractor; ~**werk** das cart

Fülle die; ~ **a)** wealth; abundance; **b)** *(Körper~)* corpulence; **füllen** **1.** *tr. V.* fill; *(Kochk.)* stuff; **b)** *(fig.)* fill in *(gap, time)*; **2.** *refl. V. (voll werden)* fill [up]; **Füller** der; ~s, ~ *(ugs.)* [fountain-]pen; **Füll·federhalter** der fountain-pen; **füllig** *Adj.* corpulent, portly *(person)*; ample *(figure, bosom)*; **Füllung** die; ~, ~en stuffing; *(Kochk.; Zahnmed.)* filling; *(in Schokolade)* centre

fummeln *itr. V. (ugs.)* **a)** *(fingern)* fiddle; **b)** *(erotisch)* pet

Fund der; ~[e]s, ~e *(auch Archäol.)* find

Fundament das; ~[e]s, ~e **a)** *(Bauw.)* foundations *pl.;* **b)** *(Basis)* base; basis; **fundamental** *Adj.* fundamental

Fund-: ~**büro** das lost property office *(Brit.);* lost and found office *(Amer.);* ~**grube** die treasure-house; **fundieren** *tr. V.* underpin

fündig *Adj.* ~ **sein** yield something; ~ **werden** make a find; *(bei Bohrungen)* make a strike

Fund·ort der place *or* site where sth. is/was found

fünf *Kardinalz.* five; **Fünf** die; ~, ~en five; *(Schulnote)* E

fünf-, Fünf-: ~**eck** das; ~s, ~e pentagon; ~**fach** *Vervielfältigungsz.* fivefold; ~**fache** das; *adj. Dekl.* five times as much; ~**hundert** *Kardinalz.* five hundred; ~**kampf** der *(Sport)* pentathlon

Fünfling der; ~s, ~e quintuplet; quin *(coll.)*

fünf-: ~**mal** *Adv.* five times; ~**stellig** *Adj.* five-figure

fünft... *Ordinalz.* fifth; **Fünf·tagewoche** die five-day [working] week; **fünf·tausend** *Kardinalz.* five thousand

fünftel *Bruchz.* fifth; **Fünftel** das *(schweiz. meist* der); ~s, ~: fifth; **fünftens** *Adv.* fifthly; **fünf·zehn** *Kardinalz.* fifteen; **fünfzig** *Kardinalz.* fifty; **Fünfzig** die; ~: fifty; **fünfziger** *indekl. Adj.; nicht präd.* die ~ **Jahre** the fifties; **Fünfziger** der; ~s, ~ **a)** *(ugs.)* fifty-pfennig piece; **b)** *(50jähriger)* fifty-year-old; **fünfzigst...** *Ordinalz.* fiftieth

fungieren *itr. V.* **als etw. ~** *(person)* act as sth.; *(word etc.)* function as sth.

Funk der; ~s radio; **Funk·ausstellung** die radio and television exhibition

Funke der; ~ns, ~n *(auch fig.)* spark; **funkeln** *itr. V. (light, star)* twinkle; *(gold, diamonds)* glitter; *(eyes)* blaze

funken *tr. V.* radio; *(transmitter)* broadcast; **Funker** der; ~s, ~: radio operator

Funk-: ~**gerät** das radio set; *(tragbar)* walkie-talkie; ~**haus** das broadcasting centre; ~**kolleg** das radio-based [adult education] course; ~**sprech·gerät** das radiophone; *(tragbar)* walkie-talkie; ~**spruch** der radio signal; *(Nachricht)* radio message; ~**stille** die radio silence; ~**streife** die [police] radio patrol; ~**taxi** das radio taxi

Funktion die; ~, ~en function; **Funktionär** der; ~s, ~e official; functionary; **funktionieren** *itr. V.* work; function; **funktions·tüchtig** *Adj.* working; sound *(organ)*

Funk-: ~**turm** der radio tower; ~**verbindung** die radio contact

Funzel die; ~, ~n *(ugs.)* useless light
für 1. *Präp. mit Akk.* for; etw. ~ ungültig erklären declare sth. invalid *s. auch* was 1
Furche die; ~, ~n a) furrow; b) *(Wagenspur)* rut
Furcht die; ~: fear; ~ vor jmdm./etw. haben fear sb./sth.; **furchtbar** 1. *Adj.* a) dreadful; b) *(ugs.: unangenehm)* terrible *(coll.);* 2. *adv. (ugs.)* terribly *(coll.);* **fürchten** 1. *refl. V.* sich |vor jmdm./etw.| ~: be afraid *or* frightened [of sb./sth.]; 2. *tr. V.* be afraid of; ich fürchte, |daß| ...: I'm afraid [that] ...; **fürchterlich** *Adj. s.* furchtbar; **furcht·los** 1. *Adj.* fearless; 2. *adv.* fearlessly; **furchtsam** 1. *Adj.* timid; 2. *adv.* timidly
für·einander *Adv.* for one another; for each other
Furie ['fu:riə] die; ~, ~n Fury
Furnier das; ~s, ~e veneer
Für·sorge die; ~ a) care; b) *(veralt.: Sozialhilfe)* welfare; c) *(veralt.: Sozialamt)* social services *pl.;* **für·sorg·lich** 1. *Adj.* considerate; 2. *adv.* considerately
Für·sprache die support; **Für·sprecher** der advocate
Fürst der; ~en, ~en prince; **Fürstentum** das; ~s, Fürstentümer principality; **fürstlich** 1. *Adj.* a) royal; b) *(fig.: üppig)* lavish; 2. *adv.* lavishly
Furt die; ~, ~en ford
Furunkel der *od.* das; ~s, ~: boil; furuncle
Für·wort das; *Pl.* -wörter pronoun
Fusion die; ~, ~en amalgamation; *(von Konzernen)* merger; **fusionieren** *itr. V.* merge
Fuß der; ~es, Füße foot; *(einer Lampe, Säule)* base; *(von Möbeln)* leg; zu ~ gehen go on foot; walk; bei ~! heel!; *(fig.)* auf freiem ~ sein be at large; auf großem ~ leben live in great style
Fuß·ball der a) *o. Pl. (Ballspiel)* [Association] football; b) *(Ball)* football; **Fußballer** der; ~s, ~: footballer
Fußball-: ~platz der football ground; *(Spielfeld)* football pitch; ~spiel das a) football match; b) *o. Pl. (Sportart)* football *no art.;* ~spieler der football player
Fuß·boden der floor; **fußen** *itr. V.* auf etw. *(Dat.)* ~: be based on sth.; **Fuß·ende** das foot; **Fußgänger** der; ~s, ~, **Fußgängerin** die; ~, ~nen pedestrian

Fußgänger-: ~brücke die footbridge; ~übergang der, ~überweg der pedestrian crossing; ~unterführung die pedestrian subway; ~zone die pedestrian precinct
Fuß-: ~nagel der toe-nail; ~note die footnote; ~stapfen der; ~s, ~: footprint; ~tritt der kick; ~volk das a) *(hist.)* footmen *pl.;* b) *(abwertend: Untergeordnete)* lower ranks *pl.;* ~weg der footpath
futsch *Adj.(salopp)* ~ sein have gone for a burton *(Brit. sl.)*
¹**Futter** das; ~s *(Tiernahrung)* feed; *(für Pferde, Kühe)* fodder
²**Futter** das; ~s *(von Kleidungsstücken)* lining
Futteral das; ~s, ~e case
¹**füttern** *tr. V.* feed
²**füttern** *tr. V. (mit ²Futter ausstatten)* line
Fütterung die; ~, ~en feeding
Futur das; ~s, ~e *(Sprachw.)* future [tense]

G

g, G [ge:] das; ~, ~ a) *(Buchstabe)* g/G; b) *(Musik)* [key of] G
g *Abk.* a) **Gramm** g; b) **Groschen**
gab *1. u. 3. Pers. Sg. Prät. v.* geben
Gabe die; ~, ~n a) *(geh.: Geschenk, Talent)* gift; *(Almosen, Spende)* alms *pl.*
Gabel die; ~, ~n fork; *(Telefon~)* cradle; **gabeln** *refl. V.* fork; **Gabel·stapler** der; ~s, ~: fork-lift truck; **Gabelung** die; ~, ~en fork
Gaben·tisch der gift table
gackern *itr. V.* a) cluck; b) *(ugs.: lachen)* cackle
gaffen *itr. V. (abwertend)* gape; gawp *(coll.)*
Gag [gɛk] der; ~s, ~s a) *(Theater, Film)* gag; b) *(Besonderheit)* gimmick
Gage ['ga:ʒə] die; ~, ~n salary; *(für einzelnen Auftritt)* fee
gähnen *itr. V. (auch fig.)* yawn
Gala ['ga:la, *auch* 'gala] die; ~: formal dress

galant 1. *Adj.* gallant; *(amourös)* amorous; **2.** *adv.* gallantly

Gala·vorstellung die gala performance

Galeere die; ~, ~n galley

Galerie die; ~, ~n gallery

Galgen der gallows *sing.*

Galgen-: ~**frist** die reprieve; ~**humor** der gallows humour

Galle die; ~, ~n **a)** *(Gallenblase)* gall[-bladder]; **b)** *(Sekret) (bei Tieren)* gall; *(bei Menschen)* bile

Galopp der; ~s, ~s *od.* ~e gallop; **galoppieren** *itr. V.; meist mit sein* gallop

galt *1. u. 3. Pers. Sg. Prät. v.* **gelten**

galvanisch [gal'va:nɪʃ] *Adj.* galvanic

Gamasche die; ~, ~n gaiter; *(bis zum Knöchel reichend)* spat

Gambe die; ~, ~n *(Musik)* viola da gamba

Gamma·strahlen *Pl. (Physik, Med.)* gamma rays

gammelig *Adj. (ugs.)* **a)** bad; rotten; **b)** *(unordentlich)* scruffy; **gammeln** *itr. V.* **a)** *(ugs.)* go off; **b)** *(nichts tun)* loaf around; bum around *(Amer. coll.);* **Gammler** der; ~s, ~ *(ugs.)* drop-out *(coll.)*

gang: ~ und gäbe sein be quite usual

Gang der; ~[e]s, Gänge **a)** walk; gait; **b)** *(Besorgung)* errand; **c)** *o. Pl. (Verlauf)* course; **d)** *(Technik)* gear; **e)** *(Flur) (in Zügen, Gebäuden usw.)* corridor; *(Verbindungs~)* passage[-way]; *(im Theater, Kino, Flugzeug)* aisle; **f)** *(Kochk.)* course; **gangbar** *Adj.* passable; *(fig.)* practicable

Gängel·band das *in* jmdn. am ~ führen keep sb. in leading-reins; **gängeln** *tr. V. (ugs.)* jmdn. ~: boss sb. around

gängig *Adj.* **a)** *(üblich)* common; *(aktuell)* current; **b)** *(leicht verkäuflich)* popular

Gang·schaltung die *(Technik)* gear system; *(Art)* gear-change

Gangway ['gæŋweɪ] die; ~, ~s gangway

Ganove [ga'no:və] der; ~n, ~n *(ugs. abwertend)* crook *(coll.)*

Gans die; ~, Gänse goose

Gänse-: ~**blümchen** das daisy; ~**braten** der roast goose; ~**füßchen** das; *meist Pl. (ugs.) s.* **Anführungszeichen;** ~**haut** die *(fig.)* goose-flesh; goose pimples *pl.;* ~**marsch** *in* im ~marsch in single *or* Indian file

Gänserich der; ~s, ~e gander

ganz 1. *Adj.* **a)** *(gesamt)* whole; entire; den ~en Tag/das ~e Jahr all day/year; **b)** *(ugs.: alle)* die ~en Kinder/Leute/Gläser *usw.* all the children/people/glasses *etc.;* **c)** *(vollständig)* whole; **d)** *(ugs.: ziemlich [viel])* eine ~e Menge/ein ~er Haufen quite a lot/quite a pile; **e)** *(ugs.: unversehrt)* intact; etw. wieder ~ machen mend sth.; **2.** *adv.* quite; **Ganze** das; *adj. Dekl.* **a)** whole; **b)** *(alles)* das ~: the whole thing; **gänzlich** *Adv.* entirely

ganz-: ~**tägig** 1. *Adj.* all-day; eine ~tägige Arbeit a full-time job; **2.** *adv.* all day; ~**tags** *Adv.* ~ arbeiten work full-time

¹**gar** *Adj.* cooked; done *pred.*

²**gar** *Partikel* **a)** *(überhaupt)* ~ nicht [wahr] not [true] at all; ~ nichts nothing at all; ~ niemand *od.* keiner nobody at all; ~ keines not a single one; ~ kein Geld no money at all; **b)** *(südd., österr., schweiz.: verstärkend)* ~ zu only too; **c)** *(geh.: sogar)* even

Garage [ga'ra:ʒə] die; ~, ~n garage

Garant der; ~en, ~en guarantor; **Garantie** die; ~, ~n guarantee; **garantieren** 1. *tr. V.* guarantee; **2.** *itr. V.* für etw. ~: guarantee sth.; **garantiert** *Adv. (ugs.)* wir kommen ~ zu spät we're dead certain to arrive late *(coll.);* **Garantie·schein** der guarantee [certificate]

Garaus ['ga:ʀaus] jmdm. den ~ machen do sb. in *(coll.)*

Garbe die; ~, ~n **a)** sheaf; **b)** *(Geschoß~)* burst of fire

Garde die; ~, ~n guard

Garderobe die; ~, ~n **a)** *o. Pl.* wardrobe; clothes *pl.;* **b)** *(Flur~)* coatrack; **c)** *(im Theater o. ä.)* cloakroom; checkroom *(Amer.);* **Garderobenfrau** die cloakroom *or (Amer.)* checkroom attendant

Gardine die; ~, ~n **a)** net curtain; **b)** *(landsch., veralt.)* curtain

Gardinen-: ~**predigt** die *(ugs.)* telling-off *(coll.); (einer Ehefrau zu ihrem Mann)* curtain lecture; ~**stange** die curtain rail

garen *tr., itr. V.* cook

gären *regelm. (auch unr.) itr. V.* ferment; *(fig.)* seethe

Garn das; ~[e]s, ~e **a)** thread; *(Näh~)* cotton; **b)** *(Seew.)* yarn

Garnele die; ~, ~n shrimp

garnieren *tr. V.* **a)** decorate; **b)** *(Gastr.)* garnish

Garnison die; ~, ~en garrison

Garnitur die; ~, ~en **a)** set; *(Wäsche)* set of [matching] underwear; *(Möbel)* suite; **b)** *(ugs.)* **die erste/zweite ~:** the first/second-rate people *pl.*

garstig *Adj.* **a)** nasty; bad ‹*behaviour*›

Gärtchen das; ~s, ~: little garden;

Garten der; ~s, **Gärten** garden

Garten-: ~**arbeit** die gardening; ~**bau** der; *o. Pl.* horticulture; ~**fest** das garden party; ~**haus** das summer-house; ~**laube** die summer-house; garden house; ~**lokal** das beer garden; *(Restaurant)* open-air café; ~**schau** die horticultural show; ~**zwerg** der **a)** garden gnome; **b)** *(salopp abwertend)* little runt

Gärtner der; ~s, ~: gardener; **Gärtnerei** die; ~, ~en nursery; **Gärtnerin** die; ~, ~nen gardener

Gärung die; ~, ~en fermentation

Gas das; ~es, ~e **a)** gas; **b)** *(Treibstoff)* petrol *(Brit.)*; gasoline *(Amer.)*; gas *(Amer. coll.)*; ~ **wegnehmen** take one's foot off the accelerator; ~ **geben** accelerate; put one's foot down *(coll.)*

gas-, Gas-: ~**flasche** die gas-cylinder; *(für einen Herd, Ofen)* gas bottle; ~**förmig** *Adj.* gaseous; ~**hahn** der gas tap; ~**herd** der gas cooker; ~**leitung** die gas pipe; *(Hauptrohr)* gas main; ~**maske** die gas mask; ~**pedal** das accelerator [pedal]; gas pedal *(Amer.)*; ~**pistole** die pistol that fires gas cartridges

Gasse die; ~, ~n lane; *(österr.)* street; **Gassen·junge** der *(abwertend)* street urchin

Gast der; ~[e]s, **Gäste a)** guest; **b)** *(Besucher eines Lokals)* patron; **c)** *(Besucher)* visitor; **Gast·arbeiter** der immigrant *or* guest worker

Gäste-: ~**buch** das guest book; ~**zimmer** das *(privat)* guest room; spare room; *(im Hotel)* room

gast-, Gast-: ~**freundlich** *Adj.* hospitable; ~**freundschaft** die hospitality; ~**geber** der host; ~**geberin,** die hostess; ~**haus** das, ~**hof** der inn

gastieren *itr. V.* give a guest performance

gastlich *Adj.* hospitable; **Gastlichkeit** die; ~: hospitality

Gastronom der; ~en, ~en restaurateur; **Gastronomie** die; ~: catering *no art.*; *(Gaststättengewerbe)* restaurant trade

Gast-: ~**spiel** das guest performance; ~**stätte** die public house; *(Speiselokal)* restaurant; ~**wirt** der publican;

landlord; *(eines Restaurants)* [restaurant] proprietor; *(Pächter)* restaurant manager; ~**wirtschaft die** *s.* ~**stätte**

Gas-: ~**vergiftung** die gas-poisoning *no indef. art.*; ~**versorgung** die gas supply; ~**werk** das gasworks *sing.*; ~**zähler** der gas meter

Gatte der; ~n, ~n husband

Gatter das; ~s, ~ **a)** *(Zaun)* fence; *(Lattenzaun)* fence; paling; **b)** *(Tor)* gate;

Gattin die; ~, ~nen *(geh.)* wife

Gattung die; ~, ~en **a)** kind; sort; *(Kunst~)* genre; form; **b)** *(Biol.)* genus

Gaudi das; ~s *(bayr., österr.)* die; ~ *(ugs.)* bit of fun

Gaukler der; ~s, ~ **a)** *(veralt.: Taschenspieler)* itinerant entertainer; **b)** *(geh.: Betrüger)* charlatan

Gaul der; ~[e]s, **Gäule** nag *(derog.)*

Gaumen der; ~s, ~: palate

Gauner der; ~s, ~ *(abwertend)* crook *(coll.)*; rogue; **Gaunerei** die; ~, ~en swindle; **Gauner·sprache** die thieves' cant *or* Latin

Gaze ['ga:zə] die; ~, ~n gauze

geachtet *Adj.* respected

Geäst das; ~[e]s branches *pl.*

geb. *Abk.* **a)** geboren; **b)** geborene

Gebäck das; ~[e]s, ~e cakes and pastries *pl.*; *(Kekse)* biscuits *pl.*; *(Törtchen)* tarts *pl.*

gebacken 2. *Part. v.* **backen**

Gebälk das; ~[e]s, ~e beams *pl.*; *(Dach~)* rafters *pl.*

gebar 1. u. 3. *Pers. Sg. Prät. v.* **gebären**

Gebärde die; ~, ~n gesture; **gebärden** *refl. V.* behave

gebären *unr. tr. V.* bear; give birth to; *s. auch* geboren

Gebäude das; ~s, ~ **a)** building; **b)** *(Gefüge)* structure

gebaut *Adj.* **gut ~ sein** have a good figure

Gebein das; ~[e]s, ~e *Pl. (geh.)* bones *pl.*; *(sterbliche Reste)* [mortal] remains

Gebell das; ~[e]s barking; *(der Jagdhunde)* baying

geben 1. *unr. tr. V.* give; **jmdm. die Hand ~:** shake sb.'s hand; ~ **Sie mir bitte Herrn N.** please put me through to Mr N.; **Unterricht ~:** teach; **eins plus eins gibt zwei** one and one is *or* makes two; **etw. von sich ~:** utter sth.; **2.** *unr. tr. V. (unpers.)* **es gibt** there is/ are; *(coll.)*; **heute gibt's Fisch** we're having fish today; **morgen gibt es Schnee** it'll snow tomorrow; **3.** *unr. itr.*

V. **a)** *(Karten austeilen)* deal; **b)** *(Sport: aufschlagen)* serve; **4.** *unr. refl. V.* **a)** sich |natürlich/steif| ~: act *or* behave [naturally/stiffly]; **b)** das gibt sich noch it will get better
Gebet das; ~|e|s, ~e prayer
gebeten *2. Part. v.* **bitten**
Gebets-: ~mühle die prayer wheel; ~teppich der *(islam. Rel.)* prayer mat
gebiert *3. Pers. Sg. Präsens v.* gebären
Gebiet das; ~|e|s, ~e region; area; *(Staats~)* territory; *(Bereich, Fach)* field
gebieten *(geh.)* **a)** command; order; **b)** *(erfordern)* demand; **Gebieter** der; ~s, ~ *(veralt.)* master; **gebieterisch** *(geh.) Adj.* imperious; *(herrisch)* domineering; peremptory ⟨*tone*⟩
Gebilde das; ~s, ~: object; *(Bauwerk)* structure
gebildet *Adj.* educated
Gebirge das; ~s, ~: mountain range; im ~: in the mountains; **gebirgig** *Adj.* mountainous
Gebiß das; Gebisses, Gebisse **a)** set of teeth; teeth *pl.;* **b)** *(Zahnersatz)* denture; plate *(coll.); (für beide Kiefer)* dentures *pl.;* **gebissen** *2. Part. v.* beißen
geblasen *2. Part. v.* blasen
geblichen .*2. Part. v.* bleichen
geblümt *Adj.* flowered
Geblüt das; ~|e|s *(geh.)* blood
gebogen *2. Part. v.* biegen
geboren **1.** *2. Part. v.* gebären; **2.** *Adj.* blind/taub ~ sein be born blind/deaf; Frau Anna Schmitz ~e Meyer Mrs Anna Schmitz née Meyer
geborgen **1.** *2. Part. v.* bergen; **2.** *Adj.* safe; secure; **Geborgenheit** die; ~: security
geborsten *2. Part. v.* bersten
gebot *1. u. 3. Pers. Sg. Prät. v.* gebieten; **Gebot** das; ~|e|s, ~e **a)** *(Grundsatz)* precept; die Zehn ~e *(Rel.)* the Ten Commandments; **b)** *(Vorschrift)* regulation; **geboten** **1.** *2. Part. v.* bieten, gebieten; **2.** *Adj. (ratsam)* advisable; *(notwendig)* necessary
Gebr. *Abk.* Gebrüder Bros.
gebracht *2. Part. v.* bringen
gebrannt *2. Part. v.* brennen
gebraten *2. Part. v.* braten
Gebrauch der **a)** *o. Pl.* use; **b)** *meist Pl. (Brauch)* custom; **gebrauchen** *tr. V.* use; **gebräuchlich** *Adj.* **a)** normal; customary; **b)** *(häufig)* common
gebrauchs-, **Gebrauchs-:** ~an-

weisung die instructions *pl.* [for use]; ~fertig *Adj.* ready for use *pred.;* ~gegenstand der item of practical use
gebraucht *Adj.* second-hand; used ⟨*car*⟩ **Gebraucht·wagen** der used car
Gebrechen das; ~s, ~ *(geh.)* affliction; **gebrechlich** *Adj.* infirm; **Gebrechlichkeit** die; ~: infirmity
gebrochen **1.** *2. Part. v.* brechen; **2.** *Adj.* ~es Englisch/Deutsch broken English/German; **3.** *adv.* ~ Deutsch sprechen speak broken German
Gebrüder *Pl.:* die ~ Meyer Meyer Brothers
Gebrüll das; ~|e|s roaring
Gebrumm das; ~|e|s *(von Bären)* growling; *(von Flugzeugen, Bienen)* droning; *(von Insekten)* buzz[ing]
gebückt *Adj.* in ~er Haltung bending forward
Gebühr die; ~, ~en charge; *(Maut)* toll; *(Anwalts~)* fee
gebühren *(geh.) itr. V.* jmdm. gebührt Achtung *usw.* sb. deserves respect *etc.;* **gebührend** **1.** *Adj.* fitting; **2.** *adv.* fittingly
gebühren-, **Gebühren-:** ~ermäßigung die: reduction of charges/fees; ~frei **1.** *Adj.* free of charge *pred.;* **2.** *adv.* free of charge; ~pflichtig *Adj.* eine ~pflichtige Verwarnung a fine and a caution
gebunden **1.** *2. Part. v.* binden; **2.** *Adj. (verpflichtet)* bound
Geburt die; ~, ~en birth; **Geburten·kontrolle** die; *o. Pl.* birth control; **gebürtig** *Adj.* ein ~er Schwabe a Swabian by birth
Geburts-: ~anzeige die birth announcement; ~datum das date of birth; ~helfer der *(Arzt)* obstetrician; ~ort der place of birth; ~tag der birthday; jmdm. zum ~ gratulieren wish sb. many happy returns of the day; ~urkunde die birth certificate
Gebüsch das; ~|e|s, ~e bushes *pl.*
gedacht *2. Part. v.* denken, gedenken
Gedächtnis das; ~ses, ~se **a)** memory; **b)** *(Andenken)* memory
Gedächtnis-: ~lücke die gap in one's memory; ~schwund der loss of memory
gedämpft *Adj.* subdued ⟨*mood*⟩; subdued, soft ⟨*light*⟩; muffled ⟨*sound*⟩
Gedanke der; ~ns, ~n **a)** thought; der ~ an etw. *(Akk.)* the thought of sth.; **b)** *Pl. (Meinung)* ideas; **c)** *(Einfall)* idea

gedạnken-, Gedạnken-: ~**gang** der train of thought; ~**los 1.** *Adj.* unconsidered; *(zerstreut)* absentminded; **2.** *adv.* without thinking; *(zerstreut)* absent-mindedly; ~**losigkeit die** *(Zerstreutheit)* absentmindedness; *(Unüberlegtheit)* lack of thought; ~**strich der** dash; ~**verloren** *Adv.* lost in thought; ~**voll 1.** *Adj.* pensive; **2.** *adv.* pensively

gedạnklich 1. *Adj.* intellectual; **2.** *adv.* intellectually

Gedạrm das; ~|e|s, ~e intestines *pl.;* bowels *pl., (eines Tieres)* entrails *pl.*

Gedẹck das; ~|e|s, ~e a) place setting; cover; **b)** *(Menü)* set meal; **c)** *(Getränk)* drink [with a cover charge]

gedẹihen *unr. itr. V.; mit sein* **a)** thrive; **b)** *(fortschreiten)* progress

gedẹnken *unr. itr. V.* **a)** jmds./einer Sache ~ *(geh.)* remember sb./sth.; *(in einer Feier)* commemorate sb./sth.; **b)** etw. zu tun ~: intend to do *or* doing sth.

Gedẹnk·stätte die memorial

Gedịcht das; ~|e|s, ~e poem

gedịegen 1. *Adj.* solid *(furniture);* sound *(piece of work);* **2.** *adv.* ~ gebaut/verarbeitet solidly built/made

gedịeh *1. u. 3. Pers. Sg. Prät. v.* **gedeihen; gedịehen** *2. Part. v.* gedeihen

Gedrạ̈nge das; ~s pushing and shoving; *(Menge)* crush; crowd

gedrọschen *2. Part. v.* dreschen

gedrụngen 1. *2. Part. v.* dringen; **2.** *Adj.* stocky; thick-set

Gedụld die; ~: patience; **gedụlden** *refl. V.* be patient; **gedụldig 1.** *Adj.* patient; **2.** *adv.* patiently; **Gedụldsspiel das** puzzle

gedụrft *2. Part. v.* dürfen

geeịgnet *Adj.* suitable; *(richtig)* right

Gefạhr die; ~, ~en **a)** danger; *(Bedrohung)* danger; threat *(für* to); **bei** ~: in case of emergency; **b)** *(Risiko)* risk; **auf eigene** ~: at one's own risk; **gefạ̈hrden** *tr. V.* endanger; jeopardize *(enterprise, success, position, etc.)*

gefạhren *2. Part. v.* fahren

gefạ̈hrlich 1. *Adj.* dangerous; *(gewagt)* risky; **2.** *adv.* dangerously

gefạhr·los 1. *Adj.* safe; **2.** *adv.* safely

Gefạ̈hrt das; ~|e|s, ~e *(geh.)* vehicle

Gefạ̈hrte der; ~n, ~n, **Gefạ̈hrtin die;** ~, ~nen *(geh.)* companion; *(Ehemann/Ehefrau)* partner in life

Gefạ̈lle das; ~s, ~: slope; incline; *(einer Straße)* gradient

¹gefạllen *unr. itr. V.* **a)** das gefällt mir

|gut| I like it [a lot]; **b)** sich *(Dat.)* etw. ~ lassen put up with sth.

²gefạllen *2. Part. v.* fallen, gefallen

¹Gefạllen der; ~s, ~: favour

²Gefạllen das; ~s pleasure

Gefạllene der; *adj. Dekl.* soldier killed in action; **die** ~n the fallen

gefạ̈llig 1. *Adj.* **a)** obliging; helpful; **b)** *(anziehend)* pleasing; agreeable *(programme, behaviour);* **2.** *adv.* pleasingly; agreeably; **Gefạ̈lligkeit die;** ~, ~en favour; **gefạ̈lligst** *Adv.* *(ugs.)* kindly

gefạngen *2. Part. v.* fangen; **Gefạngene der/die;** *adj. Dekl.* prisoner

gefạngen-: ~|**halten** *unr. tr. V.* jmdn./ein Tier ~**halten** hold sb. prisoner/keep an animal in captivity; ~|**nehmen** *unr. tr. V.* jmdn. ~**nehmen** take sb. prisoner

Gefạngenschaft die; ~, ~en captivity

Gefạ̈ngnis das; ~ses, ~se **a)** prison; gaol; **b)** *(Strafe)* imprisonment

Gefạ̈ngnis-: ~**strafe die** prison sentence; ~**wärter der** [prison] warder

Gefạsel das; ~s *(ugs. abwertend)* twaddle *(coll.);* drivel *(derog.)*

Gefạ̈ß das; ~es, ~e **a)** vessel; container; **b)** *(Anat.)* vessel

gefạßt *Adj.* **a)** calm; composed; **b)** in auf etw. *(Akk.)* |nicht| ~ sein [not] be prepared for sth.

Gefẹcht das; ~|e|s, ~e battle

Gefịeder das; ~s, ~: plumage; feathers *pl.;* **gefịedert** *Adj.* feathered

geflịssentlich 1. *Adj.* deliberate; **2.** *adv.* deliberately

geflọchten *2. Part. v.* flechten

geflọgen *2. Part. v.* fliegen

geflọhen *2. Part. v.* fliehen

geflọssen *2. Part. v.* fließen

Geflụ̈gel das; ~s poultry

gefọchten *2. Part. v.* fechten

Gefọlge das; ~s, ~: entourage

gefrạgt *Adj.* in great demand *postpos.;* sought-after

gefrạ̈ßig *Adj.* *(abwertend)* greedy

Gefrẹite der; *adj. Dekl.* *(Milit.)* lance-corporal *(Brit.);* private first class *(Amer.);* *(Marine)* able seaman; *(Luftw.)* aircraftman first class *(Brit.);* airman third class *(Amer.)*

gefrẹssen *2. Part. v.* fressen

gefrịeren *unr. itr. V.; mit sein* freeze

gefrịer-, Gefrịer-: ~**fach das** freezing compartment; ~**punkt der** freezing-point; ~**schrank der** freezer;

~|trocknen *tr. V.; meist im Inf. u. 2.
Part.* freeze-dry
gefroren *2. Part. v.* frieren, gefrieren
Gefüge das; ~s, ~: structure; gefügig *Adj.* compliant; docile ⟨*animal*⟩
Gefühl das; ~s, ~e a) sensation; feeling; b) *(Gemütsverfassung)* feeling;
gefühl·los *Adj.* a) numb; b) *(herzlos,
kalt)* unfeeling
gefühls-, Gefühls-: ~betont *Adj.*
emotional; ~duselei die; ~ *(ugs. abwertend)* mawkishness; ~mäßig *Adj.*
emotional ⟨*reaction*⟩; ⟨*action*⟩ based
on emotion
gefühl·voll 1. *Adj.* sensitive; *(ausdrucksvoll)* expressive; 2. *adv.* sensitively; expressively
gefüllt *2. Part. v.* füllen
gefunden *2. Part. v.* finden; *s. auch*
Fressen b
gegangen *2. Part. v.* gehen
gegeben *2. Part. v.* geben
gegen *Präp. mit Akk.* a) against; ~
etw. stoßen knock into sth.; ein Mittel
~ Krebs a cure for cancer; ~ die Abmachung contrary to the agreement;
b) ~ Abend/Morgen towards evening/
dawn; ~ vier Uhr around 4 o'clock; c)
(im Vergleich zu) compared with; d)
(im Ausgleich für) for; ~ Quittung
against a receipt
Gegen-: ~angriff der counter-
attack; ~argument das counter-
argument; ~besuch der return visit
Gegend die; ~, ~en a) area; b) *(Kör-
perregion)* region
Gegen-: ~darstellung die: eine
~darstellung |der Sache| an account
[of the matter] from an opposing point
of view; ~druck der counter-
pressure
gegen·einander *Adv.* against each
other *or* one another
Gegen-: ~gewicht das counter-
weight; ein ~gewicht zu *od.* gegen etw.
bilden *(fig.)* counterbalance sth.;
~leistung die service in return;
~mittel das *(gegen Gift)* antidote;
(gegen Krankheit) remedy; ~probe
die cross-check; ~satz der a) *(Gegenteil)* opposite; b) *(Widerspruch)* conflict; ~sätzlich *Adj.* conflicting;
~seitig 1. *Adj. (wechselseitig)* mutual; 2. *adv.* sich ~seitig helfen/über-
bieten help/outdo each other *or* one
another; ~seitigkeit die reciprocity;
auf ~seitigkeit *(Dat.)* beruhen be mutual; ~spieler der opponent; *(Sport)*
opposite number

Gegen·stand der object; *(Thema)*
subject; topic; gegenständlich *Adj.
(Kunst)* representational; *(Philos.)* objective; gegenstands·los *Adj.* a)
(hinfällig) invalid; b) *(grundlos, unbegründet)* unfounded ⟨*accusation, complaint, jealousy*⟩; baseless ⟨*fear*⟩
gegen-, Gegen-: ~stimme die vote
against; ohne ~stimme unanimously;
~stück das companion piece; *(fig.)*
counterpart; ~teil das opposite; im
~teil on the contrary; ~teilig *Adj.*
opposite; contrary
gegen·über *Präp. mit Dat.* a) opposite; b) *(in bezug auf)* ~ jmdm. *od.*
jmdm. ~ freundlich sein be kind to sb.;
c) *(im Vergleich zu)* compared with
gegenüber-, Gegenüber-: ~|ste-
hen *unr. itr. V.* a) jmdm./einer Sache
~stehen stand facing sb./sth.; *(fig.)*
face sb./sth.; b) jmdm./einer Sache
feindlich/wohlwollend ~stehen be ill/
well disposed towards sb./sth.;
~|stellen *tr. V.* confront; ~stellung
die confrontation; b) *(Vergleich)* com-
parison; ~|treten *unr. itr. V.; mit sein*
jmdm./einer Sache treten *(auch fig.)*
face sb./sth.
Gegen·verkehr der oncoming traffic
Gegenwart die; ~ a) present; b) *(Anwesenheit)* presence; c) *(Grammatik)*
present [tense]; gegenwärtig 1. *Adj.*
present; 2. *adv.* at present; at the moment
Gegen-: ~wehr die; *o. Pl.* resistance;
~wind der head wind; ~zug der
(Brettspiele, fig.) countermove
gegessen *2. Part. v.* essen
geglichen *2. Part. v.* gleichen
geglitten *2. Part. v.* gleiten
Gegner der; ~s, ~ a) adversary; opponent; b) *(Sport)* opponent; gegne-
risch *Adj.* opposing; opponents'
⟨*goal*⟩
gegolten *2. Part. v.* gelten
gegoren *2. Part. v.* gären
gegossen *2. Part. v.* gießen
gegriffen *2. Part. v.* greifen
gehabt *2. Part. v.* haben
¹Gehalt der; ~|e|s, ~e a) meaning; b)
(Anteil) content
²Gehalt das, *österr. auch:* der; ~|e|s,
Gehälter salary
gehalten *2. Part. v.* halten
Gehalts-: ~empfänger der salary
earner; ~erhöhung die salary increase
gehalt·voll *Adj.* nutritious ⟨*food*⟩;
⟨*novel, speech*⟩ rich in substance

gehässig *Adj. (abwertend)* spiteful; **Gehässigkeit die; ~, ~en a)** *(Wesen)* spitefulness; **b)** *(Äußerung)* spiteful remark

gehauen 2. *Part. v.* **hauen**

gehäuft *Adj.* ein ~er Teelöffel/Eßlöffel a heaped teaspoon/tablespoon

Gehäuse das; ~s, ~ *(einer Maschine)* casing; housing; *(einer Kamera, Uhr)* case

geh·behindert *Adj.* able to walk only with difficulty *postpos.;* disabled

Gehege das; ~s, ~ a) *(Jägerspr.)* preserve; **b)** *(im Zoo)* enclosure

geheim 1. *Adj.* **a)** secret; **b)** *(mysteriös)* mysterious; 2. *adv.* ~ **abstimmen** vote by secret ballot

geheim-, Geheim-: ~**agent** der secret agent; ~**dienst** der secret service; ~|**halten** *unr. tr. V.* keep secret **Geheimnis das; ~ses, ~se** secret; **Geheimnis·tuerei die;** ~ *(ugs.)* secretiveness; **geheimnis·voll** *Adj.* mysterious

Geheiß das: auf jmds. ~ *(geh.)* at sb.'s behest

gehen *unr. itr. V.; mit sein* **a)** walk; go; **über die Straße** ~: cross the street; **b)** *(sich irgendwohin begeben)* go; **c)** *(regelmäßig besuchen)* attend; **d)** *(weg~)* go; leave; **e)** *(in Funktion sein)* work; **meine Uhr geht falsch** my watch is wrong; **f)** *(möglich sein)* **ja, das geht** yes, I/we can manage that; **das geht nicht** that can't be done; **g)** *(ugs.: gerade noch angehen)* **Hast du gut geschlafen? – Es geht** Did you sleep well? – Not too bad; **h)** *(sich entwickeln)* **der Laden/das Geschäft geht gut/gar nicht** the shop/business is doing well/not doing well at all; **i)** *(unpers.)* **wie geht es dir?** How are you?; **jmdm. geht es gut/schlecht** *(gesundheitlich)* sb. is well/not well; *(geschäftlich)* sb. is doing well/badly; **j)** *(unpers.) (sich um etw. handeln)* ; **worum geht es hier?** what is this all about?; 2. *unr. tr. V. (zurücklegen)* **10 km** ~: walk 10 km.

gehen|lassen *unr. refl. V. (sich nicht beherrschen)* lose control of oneself; *(sich vernachlässigen)* let oneself go

geheuer *Adj.* **a) in diesem Gebäude ist es nicht** ~: this building is eerie; **b) ihr war doch nicht |ganz|** ~: she felt [a little] uneasy; **c) die Sache ist |mir| nicht ganz** ~: [I feel] there's something odd about this business

Gehilfe der; ~**n,** ~**n** assistant

Gehirn das; ~|**e**|**s,** ~**e** brain

Gehirn-: ~**erschütterung die** concussion; ~**schlag der** stroke; ~**wäsche die** brainwashing *no indef. art.*

gehoben 1. 2. *Part. v.* **heben;** 2. *Adj.* **a)** higher; senior *⟨position⟩;* **b)** *(gewählt)* elevated, refined

geholfen 2. *Part. v.* **helfen**

Gehör das; ~|**e**|**s** [sense of] hearing

gehorchen *itr. V.* **jmdm.** ~: obey sb.

gehören 1. *itr. V.* **a) jmdm.** ~: belong to sb.; **b)** *(Teil eines Ganzen sein)* **zu jmds. Freunden/Aufgaben** ~: be one of sb.'s friends/part of sb.'s duties; **c)** *(passend sein)* **dein Roller gehört nicht in die Küche!** your scooter does not belong in the kitchen!; **d)** *(nötig sein)* **es hat viel Fleiß dazu gehört** it took a lot of hard work; **dazu gehört sehr viel** that takes a lot; 2. *refl. V. (sich schikken)* be fitting; **es gehört sich |nicht|, ... zu ...:** it is [not] good manners to ...;

gehörig 1. *Adj.* **a)** proper; **b)** *(ugs.: beträchtlich)* **ein** ~**er Schrecken/eine** ~**e Portion Mut** a good fright/a good deal of courage; 2. *adv. (ugs.: beträchtlich)* ~ **essen/trinken** eat/drink heartily

gehorsam *Adj.* obedient; **Gehorsam der;** ~**s** obedience

Geh·steig der pavement *(Brit.);* sidewalk *(Amer.)*

Geier der; ~**s,** ~: vulture

Geige die; ~, ~**n** violin

Geiger·zähler der *(Physik)* Geiger counter

geil *Adj. (oft abwertend: sexuell erregt)* randy; horny *(sl.);* *(lüstern)* lecherous

Geisel die; ~, ~**n** hostage

Geißel die; ~, ~**n** *(hist., auch fig.)* scourge

Geist der; ~|**e**|**s,** ~**er a)** *o. Pl. (Verstand)* mind; **b)** *o. Pl. (Scharfsinn)* wit; **c)** *o. Pl. (innere Einstellung)* spirit; **d)** *(denkender Mensch)* mind; intellect; **ein großer/kleiner** ~: a great mind/a person of limited intellect; **e)** *(überirdisches Wesen)* spirit; **der Heilige** ~ *(christl. Rel.)* the Holy Ghost *or* Spirit; **f)** *(Gespenst)* ghost; **Geisterfahrer der** *person driving on the wrong side of the road or the wrong carriageway;* **geisterhaft** *Adj.* ghostly; eerie *⟨atmosphere⟩*

geistes-, Geistes-: ~**abwesend** 1. *Adj.* absent-minded; 2. *adv.* absentmindedly; ~**blitz der** *(ugs.)* brainwave; ~**gegenwart die** presence of mind; ~**gegenwärtig** 1. *Adj.* quickwitted; 2. *adv.* with great presence of mind; ~**krank** *Adj.* mentally ill; ~**wissenschaften** *Pl.* arts; humanities; ~**zustand** der; *o. Pl.* mental state

geistig 1. *Adj.* a) intellectual; *(Psych.)* mental; b) alcoholic ⟨*drinks*⟩; 2. *adv.* intellectually; *(Psych.)* mentally; **geistlich** *Adj.* sacred ⟨*song, music*⟩; religious ⟨*order, book, writings*⟩; **Geistliche** der; *adj. Dekl.* clergyman

geist-: ~**los** *Adj.* dim-witted; *(trivial)* trivial; ~**reich** 1. *Adj.* witty; *(klug)* clever; 2. *adv.:* wittily; cleverly

Geiz der; ~**es** meanness; *(Knauserigkeit)* miserliness; **geizen** *itr. V.* be mean; **Geiz·hals** der *(abwertend)* skinflint; **geizig** *Adj.* mean; *(knauserig)* miserly

gekannt 2. *Part. v.* kennen
Gekicher das; ~s giggling
geklungen 2. *Part. v.* klingen
geknickt *Adj. (ugs.)* dejected
gekniffen 2. *Part. v.* kneifen
gekommen 2. *Part. v.* kommen
gekonnt 1. 2. *Part. v.* können; 2. *Adj.* accomplished; *(hervorragend ausgeführt)* masterly
gekrochen 2. *Part. v.* kriechen
gekünstelt 1. *Adj.* artificial; 2. *adv.* er lächelte ~: he gave a forced smile
Gelächter das; ~s, ~: laughter
geladen 2. *Part. v.* laden
Gelände das; ~s, ~ a) *(Landschaft)* ground; terrain; b) *(Grundstück)* site; *(von Schule, Krankenhaus usw.)* grounds *pl.*
Geländer das; ~s, ~: banisters *pl.;* handrail; *(am Balkon, an einer Brücke)* railing[s *pl.*]; *(aus Stein)* parapet
gelang 3. *Pers. Sg. Prät. v.* gelingen
gelangen *itr. V.; mit sein* **an etw.** *(Akk.)/***zu etw.** ~: reach sth.; *(fig.)* **zu Ansehen** ~: gain esteem
gelassen 1. 2. *Part. v.* lassen; 2. *Adj.* calm; *(gefaßt)* composed; **Gelassenheit** die; ~: calmness; *(Gefaßtheit)* composure
Gelatine [ʒela'ti:nə] die; ~: gelatine
gelaufen 2. *Part. v.* laufen
geläufig *Adj. (vertraut)* common ⟨*expression, concept*⟩
gelaunt **gut/schlecht** ~ **sein** be in a good/bad mood
gelb *Adj.* yellow; **Gelb** das; ~s, ~ *od. (ugs.)* ~s yellow; **gelblich** *Adj.* yellowish; yellowed ⟨*paper*⟩; sallow ⟨*skin*⟩; **Gelb·sucht** die; *o. Pl. (Med.)* jaundice

Geld das; ~es, ~er money; **großes** ~: large denominations *pl.;* **kleines/bares** ~: change/cash

geld-, Geld-: ~**automat** der cash dispenser ~**beutel** der *(bes. südd.)* purse; ~**börse** die purse; ~**gier** die avarice; ~**gierig** *Adj.* avaricious; ~**mittel** *Pl.* financial resources; ~**schein** der banknote; bill *(Amer.);* ~**schrank** der safe; ~**strafe** die fine; ~**stück** das coin; ~**wechsel** der exchanging of money; „~**wechsel**" 'bureau de change'

Gelee [ʒe'le:] der *od.* das; ~s, ~s jelly
gelegen 1. 2. *Part. v.* liegen; 2. *Adj.* a) *(passend)* convenient; **Gelegenheit** die; ~, ~**en** opportunity; *(Anlaß)* occasion

Gelegenheits-: ~**arbeit** die casual work; ~**kauf** der bargain
gelegentlich 1. *Adj.* occasional; 2. *adv.* occasionally
gelehrig *Adj.* ⟨*child*⟩ who is quick to learn; ⟨*animal*⟩ that is quick to learn; **gelehrt** *Adj.* learned; **Gelehrte** der/die; *adj. Dekl.* scholar
Geleit das; ~[e]s, ~e *(geh.)* **sie bot uns ihr** ~ **an** she offered to accompany us; **geleiten** *tr. V. (geh.)* escort; **Geleit·schutz** der *(Milit.)* escort
Gelenk das; ~[e]s, ~e joint; **gelenkig** 1. *Adj.* agile ⟨*person*⟩; supple ⟨*limb*⟩; 2. *adv.* agilely; **Gelenkigkeit** die; ~: agility; *(von Gliedmaßen)* suppleness
gelernt *Adj.* qualified
gelesen 2. *Part. v.* lesen
Geliebte der/die; *adj. Dekl.* lover/mistress
geliefert *Adj.:* ~ **sein** *(salopp)* have had it *(coll.)*
geliehen 2. *Part. v.* leihen
gelind[e] 1. *Adj.* mild; 2. *adv.* mildly; ~**e gesagt** to put it mildly
gelingen *unr. itr. V.; mit sein* succeed; **Gelingen** das; ~s success
gelitten 2. *Part. v.* leiden
gellen *itr. V.* a) *(hell schallen)* ring out; b) *(nachhallen)* ring
geloben *tr. V. (geh.)* vow; **das Gelobte Land** the Promised Land
gelogen 2. *Part. v.* lügen
gelöst *Adj.* relaxed
gelten 1. *unr. itr. V.* a) *(gültig sein)* valid; ⟨*banknote, coin*⟩ be legal tender; ⟨*law etc.*⟩ be in force; b) *(angesehen werden)* **als etw.** ~: be regarded as sth.; c) (+ *Dat.*) *(bestimmt sein für)* be directed at; 2. *unr. tr. V.* a) *(wert sein)* **sein Wort gilt viel/wenig** his word car-

ries a lot of/little weight; **b)** *unpers.* es
gilt, etw. zu tun it is essential to do
sth.; **geltend: etw.** ~ **machen** assert
sth.; **Geltung die;** ~ **a)** validity; **für
jmdn.** ~ **haben** apply to sb.; **b)** *(Wirkung)* recognition; **zur** ~ **kommen**
show to [its best] advantage; **Gel-
tungs·bedürfnis das** need for recognition
gelungen 1. *2. Part. v.* gelingen; **2.**
Adj. **a)** *(ugs.: spaßig)* priceless; **b)** *(ansprechend)* inspired
gemächlich [gəˈmɛ(ː)çlɪç] **1.** *Adj.* leisurely; **2.** *adv.* in a leisurely manner
gemacht *in* ein ~er **Mann sein** *(ugs.)*
be a made man
Gemahl der; ~s, ~e *(geh.)* consort;
husband; **Gemahlin die;** ~, ~nen
(geh.) consort; wife
Gemälde das; ~s, ~: painting
gemäß *Präp.* + *Dat.* in accordance
with
gemäßigt *Adj.* moderate; qualified
⟨optimism⟩; temperate ⟨climate⟩
gemein 1. *Adj.* **a)** vulgar ⟨joke, expres-
sion⟩; nasty ⟨person⟩; **b)** *(niederträchtig)* mean; dirty ⟨lie⟩; mean ⟨trick⟩; **2.**
adv. in a mean *or* nasty way
Gemeinde die; ~, ~n **a)** municipal-
ity; *(Bewohner)* community; **b)**
(Pfarr~) parish; **c)** *(versammelte Got-
tesdienstteilnahme)* congregation
Gemeinde-: ~**rat der a)** *(Gremium)*
local council; **b)** *(Mitglied)* local
councillor; ~**schwester die** district
nurse; ~**verwaltung die** local administration
gemein·gefährlich *Adj.* dangerous
to the public; **Gemein·gut das;** *o.
Pl. (geh.)* common property
Gemeinheit die; ~, ~en **a)** *o. Pl.*
meanness; **b)** *(Handlung)* mean trick
gemein·nützig *Adj.* serving the public good *postpos., not pred.; (wohltätig)*
charitable
gemeinsam 1. *Adj.* **a)** common ⟨inter-
ests, characteristics⟩; mutual ⟨ac-
quaintance, friend⟩; joint ⟨property,
account⟩; shared ⟨experience⟩; **b)** *(miteinander unternommen)* joint; **2.** *adv.*
together; **Gemeinsamkeit die;** ~,
~**en** common feature
Gemeinschaft die; ~, ~**en a)** community; **b)** *o. Pl. (Verbundenheit)*
coexistence; **gemeinschaftlich** *s.*
gemeinsam
gemein·verständlich *Adj.* generally comprehensible; **Gemein·wohl
das** public good

gemessen 1. *2. Part. v.* messen; **2.**
Adj. *(würdevoll)* measured ⟨steps,
tones, language⟩; deliberate ⟨words,
manner of speaking⟩
Gemetzel das; ~s, ~: massacre
gemieden *2. Part. v.* meiden
Gemisch das; ~|e|s, ~e mixture **(aus,
von** of)
gemocht *2. Part. v.* mögen
gemolken *2. Part. v.* melken
Gemse die; ~, ~n chamois
Gemurmel das; ~s murmuring
Gemüse das; ~s, ~: vegetables *pl.*
gemußt *2. Part. v.* müssen
Gemüt das; ~|e|s, ~er **a)** nature; **b)**
(Empfindungsvermögen) heart; **c)**
(Mensch) soul
gemütlich 1. *Adj.* snug; cosy; *(bequem)* comfortable; *(ungezwungen)*
informal; **2.** *adv.* cosily; *(bequem)*
comfortably; ~ **beisammensitzen** sit
pleasantly together; **Gemütlichkeit
die;** ~: snugness; *(Zwanglosigkeit)* in-
formality
gemüts·krank *Adj.* *(Med., Psych.)*
emotionally disturbed; **Ge-
müts·mensch der** *(ugs.)* even-tem-
pered person; **gemüt·voll** *Adj.*
warm-hearted; *(empfindsam)* sentimental
Gen das; ~s, ~e *(Biol.)* gene
genannt *2. Part. v.* nennen
genas *1. u. 3. Pers. Sg. Prät. v.* genesen
genau 1. *Adj.* **a)** *(exakt)* exact; precise; **b)** *(sorgfältig, gründlich)* meticulous, ⟨person⟩; careful ⟨study⟩; **2.** *adv.*
a) exactly; precisely; ~ **um 8⁰⁰** at 8
o'clock precisely; **b)** *(gerade, eben)*
just; **c)** *(als Verstärkung)* just; **d)** *(als
Zustimmung)* exactly; precisely; **e)**
(sorgfältig) ~ **arbeiten/etw.** ~ **durch-
denken** work/think sth. out meticulously
genau·genommen *Adv.* strictly
speaking
Genauigkeit die; ~ **a)** *(Exaktheit)*
exactness; precision; *(einer Waage)*
accuracy; **b)** *(Sorgfalt)* meticulousness; **genau·so** *Adv.* **a)** *mit Adjektiven* just as; **b)** *mit Verben* in exactly
the same way; *(in demselben Maße)*
just as much
genehm *Adj.* in jmdm. ~ **sein** *(geh.)*
(jmdm. passen) be convenient to sb.;
(jmdm. angenehm sein) be acceptable
to sb.
genehmigen *tr. V.* approve ⟨plan, al-
terations, application⟩; authorize
⟨stay⟩; grant ⟨request⟩; give per-

mission for ⟨*demonstration*⟩; **sich** *(Dat.)* etw. ~ *(ugs.)* treat oneself to sth.; **Genehmigung** die; ~, ~en **a)** *s.* **genehmigen**; approval; authorization; granting; permission (*Gen.* for); **b)** *(Schriftstück)* permit; *(Lizenz)* licence
geneigt *Adj.* in ~ sein, etw. **zu tun** be inclined to do sth.
General der; ~s, ~e *od.* **Generäle** general
General-: ~**direktor** der chairman; president *(Amer.)*; ~**probe** die *(auch fig.)* dress rehearsal; ~**streik** der general strike; ~**vertreter** der general representative
Generation die; ~, ~en generation; **Generations·konflikt** der generation gap
Generator der; ~s, ~en generator
generell 1. *Adj.* general; 2. *adv.* generally
genesen *unr. itr. V.; mit sein (geh.)* recover; **Genesung** die; ~, ~en *(geh.)* recovery
genetisch *(Biol.) Adj.* genetic
Genf (das); ~s Geneva; **Genfer** 1. der; ~s, ~: Genevese; 2. *Adj.* Genevese; der ~ See Lake Geneva
genial *Adj.* brillant; **Genialität** die; ~: genius
Genick das; ~[e]s, ~e back *or* nape of the neck
Genie [ʒe'ni:] das; ~s, ~s genius
genieren [ʒe'ni:rən] *refl. V.* be embarrassed
genießbar *Adj. (eßbar)* edible; *(trinkbar)* drinkable; **genießen** *unr. tr. V.* enjoy; **Genießer** der; ~s, ~: er ist ein richtiger ~: he is a regular 'bon viveur'
Genitale das; ~s, **Genitalien** [geni'ta:-liən], **Genital·organ** das genital organ
Genitiv der; ~s, ~e *(Sprachw.)* genitive [case]
genommen 2. *Part. v.* nehmen
genoß 1. u. 3. *Pers. Sg. Prät. v.* genießen
Genosse der; ~n, ~n comrade
genossen 2. *Part. v.* genießen
Genossenschaft die; ~, ~en cooperative; **Genossin** die; ~, ~nen comrade
genug *Adv.* enough
genügen *itr. V.* **a)** be enough; **b)** einer Sache *(Dat.)* ~: satisfy sth.; **genügend** 1. *Adj.* **a)** enough; **b)** *(befriedigend)* satisfactory; 2. *adv.* enough; **genügsam** *Adj.* modest

Genugtuung [-tu:ʊŋ] die; ~, ~en satisfaction
Genus das; ~, **Genera** *(Sprachw.)* gender
Genuß der; **Genusses, Genüsse a)** *o. Pl.* consumption; **b)** *(Wohlbehagen)* etw. mit ~ essen/lesen eat sth. with relish/enjoy reading sth.
genüßlich *Adv.* ⟨*eat, drink*⟩ with relish
Geograph der; ~en, ~en geographer; **Geographie** die; ~: geography *no art.;* **geographisch** *Adj.* geographic[al]
Geologe der; ~n, ~n geologist; **Geologie** die; ~: geology *no art.;* **geologisch** *Adj.* geological
Geometrie die; ~: geometry *no art.;* **geometrisch** *Adj.* geometric[al]
Gepäck das; ~[e]s luggage *(Brit.);* baggage *(Amer.); (am Flughafen)* baggage
Gepäck-: ~**annahme** die **a)** checking in the luggage/baggage; **b)** *(Schalter)* [in-counter of the] luggage office *(Brit.)* or baggage office *(Amer.); (zur Aufbewahrung)* [in-counter of the] left-luggage office *(Brit.)* or checkroom *(Amer.); (am Flughafen)* baggage check-in; ~**aufbewahrung** die left-luggage office *(Brit.);* checkroom *(Amer.); (Schließfächer)* luggage lockers *(Brit.);* baggage lockers *(Amer.);* ~**ausgabe** die [out-counter of the] luggage office *(Brit.)* or *(Amer.)* baggage office; *(zur Aufbewahrung)* [out-counter of the] left-luggage office *(Brit.)* or *(Amer.)* checkroom; *(am Flughafen)* baggage reclaim; ~**kontrolle** die baggage check; ~**netz** das luggage rack *(Brit.);* baggage rack *(Amer.);* ~**schalter** der *s.* ~**annahme b;** ~**schein** der luggage ticket *(Brit.);* baggage check *(Amer.);* ~**träger** der **a)** porter; **b)** *(am Fahrrad)* carrier; rack
gepfeffert *Adj. (ugs.)* steep *(coll.)* ⟨*price, rent, etc.*⟩
gepfiffen 2. *Part. v.* pfeifen
gepflegt *Adj.* **a)** well-groomed spruce ⟨*appearance*⟩; neat ⟨*clothing*⟩; **b)** *(hochwertig)* choice ⟨*food, drink*⟩
Gepflogenheit die; ~, ~en *(geh.)* custom; *(Gewohnheit)* habit
gepriesen 2. *Part. v.* preisen
gequält *Adj.* forced ⟨*smile, gaiety*⟩; pained ⟨*expression*⟩
gequollen 2. *Part. v.* quellen
gerade, *(ugs.)* **grade** 1. *Adj.* **a)**

straight; **b)** *(nicht schief)* upright; **c)** *(aufrichtig)* forthright; direct; **d)** *(Math.)* even ⟨*number*⟩; **2.** *Adv.* just; *(direkt)* right; **Gerade die;** ~n, ~n *(Geom.)* straight line

gerade-: ~**aus** *Adv.* straight ahead; ~|**biegen** *unr. tr. V.* **a)** bend straight; straighten [out]; **b)** *(ugs.: bereinigen)* straighten out; ~**heraus** [----'-] *(ugs.) Adv.* etw. ~**heraus sagen** say sth. straight out; ~**so** *Adv.* ~**so groß/lang wie ...:** just as big/long as ...; ~|**stehen** *unr. itr. V.* **a)** stand up straight; **b)** *(fig.: einstehen)* **für etw.** ~**stehen** accept responsibility for sth.; ~**zu** *Adv.* really; *(beinahe)* almost

Geranie [ge'ra:niə] **die;** ~, ~**n** geranium

gerann *3. Pers. Sg. Prät. v.* **gerinnen**

gerannt *2. Part. v.* **rennen**

gerät *3. Pers. Sg. Präsens v.* **geraten**

Gerät das; ~|e|s, ~e **a)** piece of equipment; *(Fernseher, Radio)* set; *(Garten~)* tool; **b)** *(Turnen)* piece of apparatus

¹**geraten** *unr. itr. V.; mit sein* **a)** *(gelangen)* get; **b)** *(werden)* turn out; *(gut ~)* turn out well

²**geraten 1.** *2. Part. v.* **raten,** ¹**geraten; 2.** *Adj.* advisable

Geratewohl: aufs ~ *(ugs.)* ⟨*select*⟩ at random; **wir fuhren aufs** ~ **los** *(ugs.)* we went for a drive just to see where we ended up

gerät *3. Pers. Sg. Präsens v.* ¹**geraten**

geraum *Adj. (geh.)* considerable

geräumig *Adj.* spacious ⟨*room*⟩; roomy ⟨*cupboard etc.*⟩

Geräusch das; ~|e|s, ~e sound; *(unerwünscht)* noise

geräusch-: ~**arm 1.** *Adj.* quiet; **2.** *adv.* quietly; ~**los 1.** *Adj.* silent; **2.** *adv.* **a)** silently; **b)** *(fig. ugs.)* without [any] fuss; ~**voll** *Adj.* noisy

gerben *tr. V.* tan ⟨*hides, skins*⟩

gerecht 1. *Adj.* just *(unparteiisch)* fair; **2.** *adv.* justly

gerechtfertigt *Adj.* justified

Gerechtigkeit die; ~: justice; **Gerechtigkeits·sinn der** sense of justice

Gerede das; ~s *(abwertend)* **a)** *(ugs.)* talk; **b)** *(Klatsch)* gossip

geregelt *Adj.* regular, steady ⟨*job*⟩

gereizt *Adj.* irritable

¹**Gericht das;** ~|e|s, ~e court; *(Richter)* bench; *(Gebäude)* court[-house]; **das Jüngste** ~ *(Rel.)* the Last Judgement

²**Gericht das;** ~|e|s, ~e dish

gerichtlich 1. *Adj.* judicial; legal ⟨*proceedings*⟩; **2.** *adv.* **jmdn.** ~ **verfolgen** take sb. to court

Gerichts-: ~**hof der** Court of Justice; ~**kosten** *Pl.* legal costs; ~**saal der** courtroom; ~**verfahren das** legal proceedings *pl.;* ~**vollzieher der;** ~s, ~: bailiff

gerieben *2. Part. v.* **reiben**

gering *Adj.* **a)** low; little ⟨*value*⟩; small ⟨*quantity, amount*⟩; short ⟨*distance, time*⟩; **b)** *(unbedeutend)* slight; minor ⟨*role*⟩

geringfügig 1. *Adj.* slight; minor ⟨*alteration, injury*⟩; trivial ⟨*amount, detail*⟩; **2.** *adv.* slightly; **Geringfügigkeit die;** ~, ~en triviality; **gering|schätzen** *tr. V.* think very little of ⟨*person, achievement*⟩; set little store by ⟨*success, riches*⟩; **geringschätzig** *Adj.* disdainful; disparaging ⟨*remark*⟩

gerinnen *unr. itr. V.; mit sein* ⟨*blood*⟩ clot; ⟨*milk*⟩ curdle

Gerippe das; ~s, ~: skeleton

gerippt *Adj.* ribbed; fluted ⟨*glass, column*⟩

gerissen 1. *2. Part. v.* **reißen; 2.** *Adj.* *(ugs.)* crafty

geritten *2. Part. v.* **reiten**

Germane der; ~n, ~n *(hist.)* ancient German; Teuton; **germanisch** *Adj.* *(auch fig.)* Germanic; Teutonic; **Germanistik die;** ~: German studies *pl.,* no art.

gern[e]; lieber, am liebsten *Adv.* **a)** **etw.** ~ **tun** like *or* enjoy doing sth.; **er spielt lieber Tennis als Golf** he prefers playing tennis to golf; **etw.** ~**/am liebsten essen** like sth./like sth. best; **ja,** ~**/aber** ~: yes, of course; certainly!; **b)** *(durchaus)* **das glaube ich** ~: I can well believe that

gerochen *2. Part. v.* **riechen**

Geröll das; ~s, ~e debris; *(größer)* boulders *pl.*

geronnen *2. Part. v.* **rinnen, gerinnen**

Gerste die; ~: barley; **Gerstenkorn das** *(Med.)* sty

Gerte die; ~, ~n switch

Geruch der; ~|e|s, Gerüche smell; *(von Blumen)* scent

Gerücht das; ~|e|s, ~e rumour

gerufen *2. Part. v.* **rufen**

geruhsam 1. *Adj.* peaceful; leisurely ⟨*stroll*⟩; **2.** *adv.* leisurely; quietly

Gerümpel das; ~s junk

gerungen *2. Part. v.* **ringen**

Gerüst das; ~|e|s, ~e scaffolding *no pl., no indef. art.*

gesamt *Adj*.whole; entire; **gesamt-deutsch** *Adj.* all-German; **Gesamt·eindruck der** general impression; **Gesamtheit die: die ~ der** Bevölkerung the entire population
Gesamt-: ~**schule die** comprehensive [school]; ~**werk das** œuvre; *(Bücher)* complete works *pl.*
gesandt *2. Part. v.* senden
Gesandte der/die; *adj. Dekl.* envoy; **Gesandtschaft die;** ~, ~**en** legation
Gesang der; ~|e|s, **Gesänge a)** singing; **b)** *(Lied)* song
Gesang-: ~**buch das** hymn-book; ~**verein der** choral society
Gesäß das; ~**es,** ~**e** backside; buttocks *pl.*
geschaffen *2. Part. v.* **schaffen 1**
Geschäft das; ~|e|s, ~**e a)** business; *(Transaktion)* [business] deal; **ein gutes ~ machen** make a good profit; **b)** *(Laden)* shop; store *(Amer.)*
Geschäfte·macher der *(abwertend)* profit-seeker
geschäftig *Adj.* bustling
geschäftlich 1. *Adj.* business *attrib.;* **2.** *adv.* on business
geschäfts-, Geschäfts-: ~**freund der** business associate; ~**führer der** manager; *(Vereinswesen)* secretary; ~**führung die;** *o. Pl.* management; ~**inhaber der** owner of the/a business; ~**jahr das** financial year; ~**kosten** *Pl.* **auf ~kosten** on expenses; ~**lage die** [business] position; ~**leitung die** *s.* ~**führung;** ~**leute** *s.* ~**mann;** ~**mann der;** *Pl.* ~**leute** businessman; ~**ordnung die** standing orders *pl.; (im Parlament)* [rules *pl.* of] procedure; ~**partner der** business partner; ~**reise die** business trip; ~**schluß der** closing-time; ~**stelle die** branch; *(einer Partei, eines Vereins)* office; ~**straße die** shopping-street; ~**tüchtig** *Adj.* able, ⟨*businessman, landlord, etc.*⟩; ~**viertel das** business quarter; *(Einkaufszentrum)* shopping district; ~**wagen der** company car; ~**zeit die** business hours *pl.; (im Büro)* office hours *pl.*
geschah *3. Pers. Sg. Prät. v.* **geschehen**
geschehen *unr. itr. V.; mit sein* happen; occur; *(ausgeführt werden)* be done; **jmdm. geschieht etw.** sth. happens to sb.
gescheit *Adj.* **a)** *(intelligent)* clever; **b)** *(ugs.: vernünftig)* sensible
Geschenk das; ~|e|s, ~**e** present; gift

Geschenk-: ~**artikel der** gift; ~**packung die** gift pack
Geschichte die; ~, ~**n a)** history; **b)** *(Erzählung)* story; **geschichtlich** *Adj.* **a)** historical; **b)** *(bedeutungsvoll)* historic
¹**Geschick das;** ~|e|s, ~**e** *(geh.)* fate
²**Geschick das;** ~|e|s skill; **Geschicklichkeit die;** ~: skilfulness; skill; **geschickt 1.** *Adj.* **a)** skilful; **b)** *(klug)* clever; adroit; **2.** *adv.* **a)** *(gewandt)* skilfully; **b)** *(klug)* cleverly; adroitly
geschieden *2. Part. v.* **scheiden**
geschienen *2. Part. v.* **scheinen**
Geschirr das; ~|e|s, ~**e a)** crockery; *(benutzt)* dishes *pl.;* **b)** *(für Zugtier)* harness
Geschirr-: ~**spül·maschine die** dishwasher; ~**tuch das;** *Pl.* -tücher tea-towel; dish towel *(Amer.)*
geschissen *2. Part. v.* **scheißen**
geschlafen *2. Part. v.* **schlafen**
geschlagen *2. Part. v.* **schlagen**
Geschlecht das; ~|e|s, ~**er a)** sex; **b)** *(Generation)* generation; **c)** *(Sippe)* family; **d)** *(Sprachw.)* gender; **geschlechtlich** *Adj.* sexual
geschlechts-, Geschlechts-: ~**krank** *Adj.* ⟨*person*⟩ suffering from VD; ~**krankheit die** venereal disease; ~**teil das** genitals *pl.;* ~**verkehr der** sexual intercourse; ~**wort das** *s.* **Artikel a**
geschlichen *2. Part. v.* **schleichen**
geschliffen 1. *2. Part. v.* **schleifen; 2.** *Adj.* polished
geschlossen 1. *2. Part. v.* **schließen; 2.** *Adj.* united ⟨*action, front*⟩; unified ⟨*procedure*⟩; **eine ~e Ortschaft** a built-up area
geschlungen *2. Part. v.* **schlingen**
Geschmack der; ~|e|s, **Geschmäcke** taste; **geschmacklos 1.** *Adj.* tasteless; **2.** *adv.* tastelessly; **Geschmacklosigkeit die;** ~, ~**en** lack of [good] taste; bad taste; *(Äußerung)* tasteless remark; **Geschmack[s]·sache die** *in* **das ist ~:** that is a question *or* matter of taste
geschmack·voll 1. *Adj.* tasteful. **2.** *adv.* tastefully
Geschmeide das; ~**s,** ~ *(geh.)* jewellery *no pl.*
geschmeidig 1. *Adj.* **a)** sleek ⟨*hair, fur*⟩; soft ⟨*leather, boots, skin*⟩; **b)** *(gelenkig)* supple ⟨*fingers*⟩; lithe ⟨*body, movement, person*⟩; **2.** *adv. (gelenkig)* agilely

geschmissen 2. *Part. v.* schmeißen
geschmolzen 2. *Part. v.* schmelzen
Geschnetzelte das; *adj. Dekl.: small, thin slices of meat [cooked in sauce]*
geschnitten 2. *Part. v.* schneiden
geschoben 2. *Part. v.* schieben
geschollen 2. *Part. v.* schallen
gescholten 2. *Part. v.* schelten
Geschöpf das; ~[e]s, ~e creature
geschoren 2. *Part. v.* scheren
¹**Geschoß das;** Geschosses, Geschosse projectile; *(Kugel)* bullet; *(Rakete)* missile
²**Geschoß das;** Geschosses, Geschosse floor; storey
geschossen 2. *Part. v.* schießen
geschraubt *Adj. (ugs.)* stilted
Geschrei das; ~s a) shouting; *(von Verletzten, Tieren)* screaming; screams *pl.; (ugs. fig)* fuss
geschrieben 2. *Part. v.* schreiben
geschrie[e]n 2. *Part. v.* schreien
geschritten 2. *Part. v.* schreiten
geschunden 2. *Part. v.* schinden
Geschütz das; ~es, ~e [big] gun; **Geschütz·feuer das** artillery-fire; shell-fire
geschützt *Adj.* sheltered
Geschwader das; ~s, ~ *(Marine)* squadron; *(Luftwaffe)* wing *(Brit.);* group *(Amer.)*
Geschwätz das; ~es *(ugs. abwertend)* prattling; *(Klatsch)* gossip; **geschwätzig** *Adj. (abwertend)* talkative
geschwiegen 2. *Part. v.* schweigen
geschwind *(bes. südd.)* 1. *Adj.* swift; quick; 2. *adv.* swiftly; quickly
Geschwindigkeit die; ~, ~en speed
Geschwindigkeits-: ~**begrenzung die,** ~**beschränkung die** speed limit
Geschwister *Pl.* brothers and sisters
geschwollen 1. 2. *Part. v.* schwellen; 2. *Adj.* a) swollen; b) *(fig. abwertend)* pompous; 3. *adv.* pompously
geschwommen 2. *Part. v.* schwimmen
geschworen 2. *Part. v.* schwören. **Geschworene der/die;** *adj. Dekl.* juror
Geschwulst die; ~, Geschwülste tumour
geschwunden 2. *Part. v.* schwinden
geschwungen 1. 2. *Part. v.* schwingen; 2. *Adj.* curved
Geschwür das; ~s, ~e ulcer; *(Furunkel)* boil
gesehen 2. *Part v.* sehen

Geselle der; ~n, ~n journeyman; *(Kerl)* fellow; **gesellen** *refl. V.* sich zu jmdm. ~: join sb.; **gesellig** *Adj.* sociable; ein ~er Abend/~es Beisammensein a convivial evening/a friendly get-together; **Geselligkeit die;** ~: die ~ lieben enjoy [good] company
Gesellschaft die; ~, ~en a) society; b) *(Veranstaltung)* party; c) *(Kreis von Menschen)* group of people; d) *(Wirtschaft)* company; **Gesellschafter der;** ~s, ~ a) ein guter ~ sein be good company; b) *(Wirtsch.)* partner; *(Teilhaber)* shareholder; **Gesellschafterin die;** ~, ~nen a) [lady] companion; b) *(Wirtsch.)* partner; *(Teilhaber)* shareholder; **gesellschaftlich** *Adj.* social
gesellschafts-, Gesellschafts-: ~**fähig** *Adj. (auch fig.)* socially acceptable; ~**ordnung die** social order; ~**reise die** group tour; ~**schicht die** stratum of society; ~**spiel das** party game
gesessen 2. *Part. v.* sitzen
Gesetz das; ~es, ~e a) law; *(geschrieben)* statute; b) *(Regel)* rule
Gesetz-: ~**buch das** statute-book; ~**geber der** legislator; *(Organ)* legislature; ~**gebung die;** ~: legislation
gesetzlich 1. *Adj.* legal; statutory ⟨holiday⟩; lawful ⟨heir, claim⟩; 2. *adv.* legally; **gesetz·mäßig 1.** *Adj.* a) law-governed; ~ sein be governed by or obey a [natural] law/[natural] laws; b) *(gesetzlich)* legal; *(rechtmäßig)* lawful; 2. *adv.* in accordance with a [natural] law/[natural] laws; **Gesetz·mäßigkeit die** a) conformity to a [natural] law/[natural] laws; b) *(Gesetzlichkeit)* legality; *(Rechtmäßigkeit)* lawfulness
gesetzt *Adj.* staid
gesetz·widrig *Adj.* illegal; unlawful
Gesicht das; ~[e]s, ~er face; *(fig.)* das ~ einer Stadt the appearance of a town
Gesichts-: ~**ausdruck der** expression; look; ~**creme die** face-cream; ~**punkt der** point of view; ~**wasser das** face-lotion; ~**züge** *Pl.* features
Gesindel das; ~s *(abwertend)* rabble
gesinnt *Adj.* christlich/sozial ~ [sein] [be] Christian-minded/public-spirited; jmdm. freundlich ~ sein be well-disposed towards sb.; **Gesinnung die;** ~, ~en [basic] convictions *pl.;* [fundamental] beliefs *pl.;* **gesin-**

nungs·los *(abwertend) Adj.* unprincipled; **Gesinnungs·wandel der** change of attitude
gesittet 1. *Adj.* well-behaved; well-mannered
gesogen *2. Part. v.* **saugen**
gesondert 1. *Adj.* separate; **2.** *adv.* separately
gesonnen *Adj.* ~ sein, etw. zu tun feel disposed to do sth.
gesotten *2. Part. v.* **sieden**
Gespann das; ~|e|s, ~e **a)** *(Zugtiere)* team; **b)** *(Wagen)* horse and carriage; **c)** *(Menschen)* couple; pair
gespannt *Adj.* **a)** eager; rapt ⟨*attention*⟩; ~ zuhören listen with rapt attention; **b)** tense ⟨*situation, atmosphere*⟩; strained ⟨*relationships*⟩
Gespenst das; ~|e|s, ~er **a)** ghost; **b)** *(geh.: Gefahr)* spectre
gespenstig, gespenstisch *Adj.* ghostly; eerie ⟨*building, atmosphere*⟩
gespie[e]n *2. Part. v.* **speien**
gesponnen *2. Part. v.* **spinnen**
Gespött das; ~|e|s mockery; ridicule
Gespräch das; ~|e|s, ~e conversation; *(Diskussion)* discussion; *(Telefon~)* call (mit to); **gesprächig** *Adj.* talkative
Gesprächs-: ~**partner der:** mein heutiger ~**partner wird X sein** today I shall be talking to X; ~**stoff der** topics *pl.* of conversation; ~**thema das** topic of conversation
gesprochen *2. Part. v.* **sprechen**
gesprossen *2. Part. v.* **sprießen**
gesprungen *2. Part. v.* **springen**
Gespür das; ~s feel
gest. *Abk.* gestorben d.
Gestalt die; ~, ~en **a)** build; **b)** *(Mensch, Persönlichkeit)* figure; **c)** *(in der Dichtung)* character; **d)** *(Form)* form; **gestalten** *tr. V.* fashion; lay out ⟨*public gardens*⟩; shape ⟨*character, personality*⟩; arrange ⟨*party, conference, etc.*⟩; **Gestaltung die;** ~, ~en *s.* gestalten: fashioning; laying out; arranging
gestand *1. u. 3. Pers. Sg. Prät. v.* **gestehen**
gestanden *2. Part. v.* **stehen, gestehen**
geständig *Adj.:* ~ sein have confessed; **Geständnis das;** ~ses, ~se confession
Gestank der; ~|e|s *(abwertend)* stench; stink
gestatten 1. *tr., itr. V.* permit; allow; ~ Sie, daß ich ...: may I ...?; **2.** *refl. V.* sich *(Dat.)* etw. ~: allow oneself sth.

Geste ['gɛstə, 'geːstə] **die;** ~, ~n *(auch fig.)* gesture
Gesteck das; ~|e|s, ~e flower arrangement
gestehen *tr., itr. V.* confess
Gestein das; ~|e|s, ~e rock
Gestell das; ~|e|s, ~e **a)** *(für Weinflaschen)* rack; *(zum Wäschetrocknen)* horse; **b)** *(Unterbau)* frame
gestern *Adv.* yesterday
gestiegen *2. Part. v.* **steigen**
gestikulieren *itr. V.* gesticulate
Gestirn das; ~|e|s, ~e star
gestochen 1. *2. Part. v.* **stechen; 2.** *Adj.* extremely neat ⟨*handwriting*⟩
gestohlen *2. Part. v.* **stehlen**
gestorben *2. Part. v.* **sterben**
gestoßen *2. Part. v.* **stoßen**
Gesträuch das; ~|e|s, ~e shrubbery; bushes *pl.*
gestreift *Adj.* striped
gestrichen 1. *2. Part. v.* **streichen; 2.** *Adj.* level ⟨*measure*⟩
gestrig *Adj.* yesterday's
gestritten *2. Part. v.* **streiten**
Gestrüpp das; ~|e|s, ~e undergrowth
gestunken *2. Part. v.* **stinken**
Gestüt das; ~|e|s, ~e stud[-farm]
Gesuch das; ~|e|s, ~e request (um for); *(Antrag)* application (um for); **gesucht** *Adj.* **a)** [much] sought-after; **b)** *(gekünstelt)* laboured
gesund; gesünder, *seltener:* ~er, **gesündest...,** *seltener:* ~est... *Adj.* healthy; wieder ~ werden get better; bleib ~! look after yourself!; **Gesundheit die;** ~: health; ~! *(ugs.)* bless you!; **gesundheitlich 1.** *Adj.; nicht präd.* ~e Betreuung health care; sein ~er Zustand [the state of] his health; **2.** *adv.* wie geht es Ihnen ~? how are you?
gesundheits-, Gesundheits-: ~**amt das** [local] public health department; ~**schädlich** *Adj.* detrimental to [one's] health *postpos.*; ~**zeugnis das** certificate of health; ~**zustand der** state of health
gesungen *2. Part. v.* **singen**
gesunken *2. Part. v.* **sinken**
getan *2. Part. v.* **tun**
Getier das; ~|e|s *(geh.)* animals *pl.*
Getöse das; ~s [thunderous] roar; *(von vielen Menschen)* din
getragen *2. Part. v.* **tragen**
Getränk das; ~|e|s, ~e drink; beverage *(formal)*
getrauen *refl. V.* dare
Getreide das; ~s grain

Getreide-: ~**anbau** der growing of cereals; ~**handel** der corn-trade

getrennt 1. *Adj.* separate; **2.** *adv.* ⟨*pay*⟩ separately; ⟨*sleep*⟩ in separate rooms

getreten 2. *Part. v.* treten

getreu 1. *Adj. (geh.)* exact; faithful ⟨*image*⟩; **2.** *adv. (geh.)* ⟨*report, describe*⟩ faithfully

Getriebe das; ~s, ~ gears *pl.; (in einer Maschine)* gear system; **getrieben 2.** *Part. v.* treiben

getroffen 2. *Part. v.* treffen, triefen

getrogen 2. *Part. v.* trügen

getrost 1. *Adj.* confident; **2.** *adv.* confidently; **du kannst es mir ~ glauben** you can take my word for it

getrunken 2. *Part. v.* trinken

Getto das; ~s, ~s ghetto

Getue das; ~s *(ugs. abwertend)* fuss (um about)

Getümmel das; ~s tumult

geübt *Adj.* accomplished; practised ⟨*eye, ear*⟩

Gewächs das; ~es, ~e plant; **gewachsen 1. 2.** *Part. v.* wachsen; **2. in jmdm./einer Sache ~ sein** be a match for sb./be equal to sth.

gewagt *Adj.* daring; *(gefährlich)* risky; *(fast anstößig)* risqué ⟨*joke etc.*⟩

gewählt *Adj.* refined; **2.** *adv.* in a refined manner

Gewähr die; ~: guarantee; **keine ~ übernehmen** be unable to guarantee sth.; **gewähren** *tr. V.* **a)** grant; give ⟨*pleasure, joy*⟩; **gewähr·leisten** *tr. V.* guarantee

Gewahrsam der; ~s **a)** *(Obhut)* safekeeping; **b)** *(Haft)* custody

Gewährs·mann der; *Pl.* ~**männer** *od.* ~**leute** informant; source

Gewalt die; ~, ~**en a)** power; **b)** *o. Pl. (Willkür)* force; **c)** *o. Pl. (körperliche Kraft)* force; violence; **Gewalt·anwendung** die use of force *or* violence; **Gewalten·teilung** die separation of powers; **gewaltig 1.** *Adj.* **a)** *(immens)* huge; **b)** *(imponierend)* mighty, huge, massive ⟨*building etc*⟩; monumental ⟨*literary work etc.*⟩; **2.** *adv. (ugs.)* very much; **gewalt·los 1.** *Adj.* non-violent; **2.** *adv.* without violence; **Gewalt·losigkeit** die; ~: non-violence; **gewaltsam 1.** *Adj.* forcible ⟨*expulsion*⟩; enforced ⟨*separation*⟩; violent ⟨*death*⟩; **2.** *adv.* forcibly; **gewalt·tätig** *Adj.* violent

Gewand das; ~|e|s, **Gewänder** *(geh.)* robe; gown

gewandt 1. 2. *Part. v.* wenden; **2.** *Adj.* skilful; *(körperlich)* agile; **3.** *adv.* skilfully; *(körperlich)* agilely; **Gewandtheit** die; ~: *s.* gewandt **2:** skill; skilfulness; agility

gewann *1. u. 3. Pers. Sg. Prät. v.* gewinnen

gewaschen 2. *Part. v.* waschen

Gewässer das; ~s, ~: stretch of water

Gewebe das; ~s, ~ **a)** *(Stoff)* fabric; **b)** *(Med., Biol.)* tissue

Gewehr das; ~|e|s, ~e rifle; *(Schrot~)* shotgun

Geweih das; ~|e|s, ~e antlers *pl.*

Gewerbe das; ~s, ~: business; *(Handel, Handwerk)* trade

Gewerbe-: ~**freiheit** die right to carry on a business *or* trade; ~**ordnung** die laws *pl.* governing trade and industry; ~**schein** der licence to carry on a business *or* trade; ~**treibende** der/die; \ *adj. Dekl.* tradesman/tradeswoman; ~**zweig** der branch of trade

gewerblich 1. *Adj.* commercial; business *attrib.; (industriell)* industrial; **2.** *adv.* ~ **sein** work; **gewerbs·mäßig** *Adj.* professional

Gewerkschaft die; ~, ~**en** trade union; **Gewerkschaft[l]er** der; ~s, ~: trade unionist; **gewerkschaftlich 1.** *Adj.* [trade] union *attrib.;* **2.** *adv.:* ~ **organisiert sein** belong to a [trade] union; **Gewerkschaftsfunktionär** der [trade] union official

gewesen 2. *Part. v.* ¹sein

gewichen 2. *Part. v.* weichen

Gewicht das; ~|e|s, ~e *(auch fig.)* weight; |nicht| ins ~ **fallen** be of [no] consequence; **Gewicht·heben** das; ~s weight-lifting; **gewichtig** *Adj.* weighty; **Gewichts·klasse** die *(Sport)* weight [division *or* class]

gewieft *Adj. (ugs.)* cunning

gewiesen 2. *Part. v.* weisen

gewillt *Adj. in* ~ |nicht| ~ **sein, etw. zu tun** be [un]willing to do sth.

Gewimmel das; ~s throng; *(von Insekten)* teeming mass

Gewinde das; ~s, ~ *(Technik)* thread

Gewinn der; ~|e|s, ~e **a)** profit; **b)** *(Preis einer Lotterie)* prize; *(beim Spiel)* winnings *pl.;* **c)** *(Sieg)* win; **Gewinn·beteiligung** die *(Wirtsch.)* profit-sharing; *(Betrag)* profit-sharing bonus; **gewinn·bringend** *Adj.* lucrative

gewinnen 1. *unr. tr. V.* win; gain

⟨*time, influence, validity, etc.*⟩; **2.** *unr.*
itr. V. win (**bei** at); **gewịnnend** *Adj.*
winning; **Gewịnner** der; ~s, ~: winner
Gewịnn-: **~spanne** die profit margin; **~sucht** die greed for profit;
~zahl die winning number
Gewịrr das; **~|e|s** a) tangle; b) *(Durcheinander)* ein ~ von Ästen a maze of branches
gewịß **1.** *Adj.* certain; **2.** *adv.* certainly
Gewịssen das; ~s, ~: conscience;
gewịssenhaft **1.** *Adj.* conscientious; **2.** *adv.* conscientiously; **gewịssen·los** *Adj.* unscrupulous; **Gewịssens·bisse** *Pl.* pangs of conscience
gewịssermạßen *Adv.* *(sozusagen)* as it were; *(in gewissem Sinne)* to a certain extent; **Gewịßheit** die; ~, ~en certainty
Gewịtter das; ~s, ~: thunderstorm; **Gewịtter·wolke** die thundercloud; **gewịttrig** *Adj.* thundery
gewịtzt *Adj.* shrewd
gewọben **2.** *Part. v.* weben
gewọgen **1.** **2.** *Part. v.* wiegen; **2.** *Adj.* *(geh.)* well disposed (+ *Dat.* towards)
gewöhnen **1.** *tr. V.* jmdn. an jmdn./ etw. ~: get sb. used to sb./sth.; accustom sb. to sb./sth.; **2.** *refl. V.* **sich an** jmdn./etw. ~: get used *or* get *or* become accustomed to sb./sth.; accustom oneself to sb./sth.; **Gewọhnheit** die; ~, ~en habit; **gewọhnheits·mäßig** **1.** *Adj.* habitual ⟨*drinker etc.*⟩; automatic ⟨*reaction etc.*⟩; **2.** *adv.* *(regelmäßig)* habitually; **gewöhnlich** **1.** *Adj.* a) normal; ordinary; b) *(gewohnt, üblich)* usual; c) *(abwertend: ordinär)* common; **2.** *adv.* a) |für| ~: usually; wie ~: as usual; b) *(abwertend: ordinär)* in a common way
gewọhnt *Adj.* a) usual; b) etw. *(Akk.)* ~ **sein** be used to sth.
Gewölbe das; ~s, ~: vault
gewọnnen **2.** *Part. v.* gewinnen
gewọrben **2.** *Part. v.* werben
gewọrfen **2.** *Part. v.* werfen
gewrụngen **2.** *Part. v.* wringen
Gewühl das; **~|e|s** milling crowd
gewụnden **2.** *Part. v.* winden
Gewürz das; **~es, ~e** spice; *(würzende Zutat)* seasoning
Gewürz-: **~gurke** die pickled gherkin; **~nelke** die clove
gewụßt **2.** *Part. v.* wissen

gez. *Abk.* gezeichnet sgd.
Gezeiten *Pl.* tides
gezielt **1.** *Adj.* specific ⟨*questions, measures, etc.*⟩; deliberate ⟨*insult, indiscretion*⟩; well-directed ⟨*advertising campaign*⟩; **2.** *adv.* ⟨*proceed, act*⟩ purposefully
geziemen *(geh. veralt.)* **1.** *itr. V.* jmdm. |nicht| ~: [ill] befit sb; **2.** *refl. V.* be proper; **sich für** jmdn. ~: befit sb.
geziert **1.** *Adj.* *(abwertend)* affected; **2.** *adv.* *(abwertend)* affectedly
gezogen **2.** *Part. v.* ziehen
Gezwitscher das; ~s twittering
gezwụngen **1.** **2.** *Part. v.* zwingen; **2.** *Adj.* forced; **gezwụngenermaßen** *Adv.* of necessity
gib *Imperativ Sg. Präsens v.* geben;
gibst **2.** *Pers. Sg. Präsens v.* geben;
gibt **3.** *Pers. Sg. Präsens v.* geben
Gicht die; ~: gout
Giebel der; ~s, ~: gable
Gier die; ~: greed (nach for); **gierig** **1.** *Adj.* greedy; **2.** *adv.* greedily
gießen **1.** *unr. tr. V.* a) pour (in + *Akk.* into, über + *Akk.* over); b) *(verschütten)* spill (über + *Akk.* over); c) *(begießen)* water; **2.** *(unpers., ugs.)* pour [with rain]
Gießer der; ~s, ~: caster; **Gießerei** die; ~, ~en foundry
Gift das; **~|e|s, ~e** a) poison; *(Schlangen~)* venom; **gift·grün** *Adj.* garish green; **giftig** *Adj.* poisonous; venomous ⟨*snake*⟩; toxic, poisonous ⟨*substance, gas, chemical*⟩; *(fig.)* venomous
Gift-: **~müll** der toxic waste; **~schlange** die venomous snake; **~zahn** der poison fang
Gigạnt der; ~en, ~en giant; **gigạntisch** *Adj.* gigantic
Gịlde die; ~, ~n *(hist.)* guild
gilt **3.** *Pers. Sg. Präsens v.* gelten
Gịmpel der; ~s, ~: bullfinch
Gin [dʒɪn] der; ~s gin
ging **1.** u. **3.** *Pers. Sg. Prät. v.* gehen
Gịnster der; ~s, ~: broom
Gịpfel der; ~s, ~: peak; *(höchster Punkt des Berges)* summit; *(fig.)* height; **Gịpfel·konferenz** die summit conference; **gịpfeln** *itr. V.* in etw. *(Dat.)* ~: culminate in sth.
Gips der; ~es, ~e plaster; gypsum *(Chem.)*; **Gips·abdruck** der plaster cast; **gịpsen** *tr. V.* plaster; put ⟨*leg, arm, etc.*⟩ in plaster; **Gips·verband** der plaster cast
Girạffe die; ~, ~n giraffe

Girlande die; ~, ~n festoon
Giro ['ʒi:ro] das; ~s, ~s, *österr. auch*
Giri *(Finanzw.)* giro; **Giro·konto**
das *(Finanzw.)* current account
gis, Gis das; ~, ~ *(Musik)* G sharp
Gischt der; ~|e|s, ~e *od.* die; ~, ~en
spray
Gitarre die; ~, ~n guitar
Gitter das; ~s, ~: bars *pl.; (vor Fen-
ster-, Türöffnungen)* grille; *(in der
Straßendecke, im Fußboden)* grating;
(Geländer) railing[s *pl.*]; **Gitter·fen-
ster** das barred window
Glacé·hand·schuh [gla'se:...] der
kid glove
Gladiole die; ~, ~n gladiolus
Glanz der; ~es **a)** *(von Licht, Sternen,
Augen)* brightness; *(von Haar, Metall,
Perlen, Leder usw.)* lustre; sheen; **b)**
(der Jugend, Schönheit) radiance; *(des
Adels usw.)* splendour; **glänzen** *itr.
V.* **a)** *(Glanz ausstrahlen)* shine; ⟨*hair,
metal, etc.*⟩ gleam; ⟨*elbows, trousers,
etc.*⟩ be shiny; **b)** *(Bewunderung erregen)* shine (**bei** at); **glänzend** *(ugs.)*
1. *Adj.* **a)** shining; gleaming ⟨*hair,
metal, etc.*⟩; shiny ⟨*elbows, trousers,
etc.*⟩; **b)** *(wundernswert)* brilliant;
splendid ⟨*references, marks, results,
etc.*⟩; **2.** *adv.* ~ **mit** jmdm. auskommen
get on very well with sb.; **es geht mir/
uns** ~: I am/we are very well
glanz-, Glanz-: ~leistung die *(auch
iron.)* brilliant performance; **~los**
Adj. dull; lacklustre; **~nummer** die
star turn; **~voll 1.** *Adj.* brilliant;
sparkling ⟨*variety number*⟩; **2.** *adv.*
brilliantly
Glas das; ~es, Gläser **a)** glass; **b)**
(Trinkgefäß) glass; **zwei** ~ *od.* Gläser
Wein two glasses of wine; **c)** *(Behälter)* jar; **Glas·bläser** der glass-
blower; **Gläschen** ['glɛːsçən] das;
~s, ~ **a)** [little] glass; **b)** *(kleines Gefäß)* [little] [glass] jar; **Glaser** der; ~s,
~: glazier; **gläsern** *Adj.* glass;
Glas·faser die; *meist Pl.* glass fibre;
glasieren *tr. V.* **a)** glaze; **b)** *(Kochk.)*
ice; glaze ⟨*meat*⟩; **glasig** *Adj.* **a)**
glassy; **b)** *(Kochk.)* transparent;
Glas·malerei die stained glass;
Glasur die; ~, ~en **a)** glaze; **b)**
(Kochk.) icing; *(auf Fleisch)* glaze
glatt 1. *Adj.* **a)** smooth; *(rutschig)* slippery; **b)** *(ugs.: offensichtlich)* downright ⟨*lie*⟩; outright ⟨*deception, fraud*⟩;
flat ⟨*refusal*⟩; **2.** *adv.* **a)** smoothly; **b)**
(ugs.: rückhaltlos) jmdm. etw. ~ ins
Gesicht sagen tell sb. sth. straight to

his/her face; ⟨*reject, deny*⟩ flatly;
Glätte die; ~: smoothness; *(Rut-
schigkeit)* slipperiness; **Glatt·eis** das
glaze; ice; *(auf der Straße)* black ice;
glätten *tr. V.* smooth out ⟨*piece of
paper, etc.*⟩; smooth [down] ⟨*feathers,
fur, etc.*⟩; plane ⟨*wood etc.*⟩
glatt-: ~|gehen *unr. itr. V.; mit sein
(ugs.)* go smoothly; **~weg** *Adv. (ugs.)*
etw. ~weg ablehnen/ignorieren turn
sth. down flat/simply ignore sth.; **das
ist ~weg erlogen/erfunden** that's a
downright lie/that's pure invention
Glatze die; ~, ~n bald head
Glaube der; ~ns faith (**an** + *Akk.* in);
(Überzeugung, Meinung) belief (**an** +
Akk. in); **glauben 1.** *tr. V. (meinen)*
think; **2.** *itr. V.* believe (**an** + *Akk.* in)
Glaubens-: ~bekenntnis das creed;
~freiheit die; *o. Pl.* religious freedom
glaubhaft 1. *Adj.* credible; **2.** *adv.*
convincingly; **gläubig 1.** *Adj.* devout; *(vertrauensvoll)* trusting; **2.** *adv.*
devoutly; *(vertrauensvoll)* trustingly;
Gläubige der/die; *adj. Dekl.* be-
liever; **Gläubiger** der; ~s, ~ creditor
glaub·würdig 1. *Adj.* credible; **2.**
adv. convincingly
gleich 1. *Adj.* **a)** *(identisch, von derselben Art)* same; *(~berechtigt, ~wertig,
Math.)* equal; **b)** *(ugs.: gleichgültig)* **es
ist mir völlig od. ganz** ~: I couldn't
care less *(coll.);* **ganz** ~, **wer anruft, ...:**
no matter who calls, ...; **2.** *adv.* **a)**
(übereinstimmend) ~ **groß/alt** *usw.*
sein be the same height/age *etc.;* ~
gut/schlecht *usw.* equally good/bad
etc.; **b)** *(in derselben Weise)* ~ **aufge-
baut/gekleidet** having the same struc-
ture/wearing identical clothes; **c)** *(sofort)* at once; straight away; *(bald)* in
a moment; **d)** *(räumlich)* right; just; ~
rechts/links immediately on the right/
left
gleich-, Gleich-: ~alt[e]rig
[~alt[ə]rɪç] *Adj.* of the same age (**mit**
as); **~artig 1.** *Adj.* of the same kind
postpos. (+ *Dat.* as); *(sehr ähnlich)*
very similar (+ *Dat.* to); **2.** *adv.* in the
same way; **~berechtigt** *Adj.* having
equal rights *postpos.;* **~berechtigte
Partner** equal partners; **~berechti-
gung** die equal rights *pl.;* **~|bleiben**
unr. itr. V.; mit sein remain the same;
⟨*speed, temperature, etc.*⟩ remain constant; **~bleibend** *Adj.* constant,
steady ⟨*temperature, speed, etc.*⟩;
gleichen *unr. itr. V.* jmdm./einer Sa-

che ~: be like *or* resemble sb./sth.; gleichermaßen *Adv.* equally
gleich-, Gleich-: ~falls *Adv. (auch)* also; *(ebenfalls)* likewise; danke ~falls! thank you, [and] the same to you; ~förmig 1. *Adj.* a) *(einheitlich)* uniform; b) *(monoton)* monotonous; 2. *adv.* a) *(einheitlich)* uniformly; b) *(monoton)* monotonously; ~geschlechtlich *Adj.* homosexual; ~gewicht das; *o. Pl.* balance; ~gewichts·störung die disturbance of one's sense of balance; ~gültig 1. *Adj.* indifferent (gegenüber towards); *(belanglos)* trivial; das ist mir |vollkommen| ~: it's a matter of [complete] indifference to me; 2. *adv.* indifferently; ~gültigkeit die indifference (gegenüber towards)
Gleichheit die; ~, ~en a) identity; *(Ähnlichkeit)* similarity; b) *o. Pl. (gleiche Rechte)* equality; Gleichheitszeichen das equals sign
gleich-, Gleich-: ~|kommen *unr. itr. V.; mit sein* a) *(entsprechen)* be tantamount to; b) *(die gleiche Leistung erreichen)* jmdm./einer Sache [an etw. *(Dat.)*] ~kommen equal sb./sth. [in sth.]; ~|machen *tr. V.* make equal; ~mäßig 1. *Adj.* regular *(interval, rhythm)*; uniform *(acceleration, distribution)*; even *(heat)*; 2. *adv. (breathe)* regularly; etw. ~mäßig verteilen/auftragen distribute sth. equally/apply sth. evenly; ~mut der equanimity
Gleichnis das; ~ses, ~se *(Allegorie)* allegory; *(Parabel)* parable; gleichsam *Adv. (geh.)* as it were
gleich-, Gleich-: ~|schalten *tr. V.* force into line; ~schenk[e]lig *Adj. (Math.)* isosceles; ~schritt der; *o. Pl.* marching in step; ~seitig *Adj. (Math.)* equilateral; ~|setzen *tr. V.* equate; ~|stellen *tr. V.* equate; ~strom der *(Elektrot.)* direct current
Gleichung die; ~, ~en equation
gleich-: ~wertig *Adj.* of the same value *postpos.;* ~wohl [-'- *od.* '--] *Adv.* nevertheless; ~zeitig 1. *Adj.* simultaneous; 2. *adv.* at the same time
Gleis das; ~es, ~e track; *(Bahnsteig)* platform; *(einzelne Schiene)* rail
gleiten *unr. itr. V.; mit sein* glide; *(hand)* slide; Gleit·flug der glide
Gletscher der; ~s, ~: glacier; Gletscher·spalte die crevasse
glich 1. u. 3. *Pers. Sg. Prät. v.* gleichen
Glied das; ~[e]s, ~er a) limb; *(Finger~, Zehen~)* joint; b) *(Ketten~, auch fig.)*

link; c) *(Teil eines Ganzen)* section; *(Mitglied)* member; gliedern 1. *tr. V.* structure; organize *(thoughts)*; 2. *refl. V.* sich in Gruppen/Abschnitte usw. ~: be divided into groups/sections *etc.;* Gliederung die; ~, ~en structure
Glied-: ~maße [-ma:sə] die; ~, ~n limb; ~satz der *(Sprachw.)* subordinate clause
glimmen *unr. od. regelm. itr. V.* glow; Glimm·stengel der *(ugs. scherzh.)* fag *(sl.);* ciggy *(coll.)*
glimpflich 1. *Adj.* a) der Unfall nahm ein ~es Ende the accident turned out not to be too serious; b) *(mild)* lenient *(sentence, punishment)*; 2. *adv.* a) *(ohne Schaden)* ~ davonkommen get off lightly; b) *(mild)* leniently
glitschig *Adj. (ugs.)* slippery
glitt 1. u. 3. *Pers. Sg. Prät. v.* gleiten
glitzern *itr. V. (star)* twinkle; *(diamond,· decorations)* sparkle; *(snow, eyes, tears)* glisten
global 1. *Adj.* a) global; world-wide; b) *(umfassend)* all-round *(education)*; overall *(control, planning, etc.)*; c) *(allgemein)* general; 2. *adv.* a) worldwide; b) *(umfassend)* in overall terms; c) *(allgemein)* in general terms; Globen s. Globus
Globetrotter der; ~s, ~: globetrotter
Globus der; ~ *od.* ~ses, Globen globe
Glöckchen das; ~s, ~: [little] bell; Glocke die; ~, ~n bell
Glocken-: ~blume die *(Bot.)* campanula; ~rock der widely flared skirt; ~spiel das a) carillon; *(mit einer Uhr gekoppelt auch)* chimes *pl.;* b) *(Instrument)* glockenspiel
glomm 1. u. 3. *Pers. Sg. Prät. v.* glimmen
Glorien·schein der glory; *(um den Kopf, fig.)* halo; glorifizieren *tr. V.* glorify; Glorifizierung die; ~, ~en glorification; glor·reich 1. *Adj.* glorious; 2. *adv.* gloriously
Glossar das; ~s, ~e glossary
Glosse die; ~, ~n commentary; *(spöttische Bemerkung)* sneering comment
glotzen *itr. V. (abwertend)* goggle; gawp *(coll.)*
Glück das; ~[e]s a) luck; |es ist| ein ~, daß...: it's lucky that...; |kein| ~ haben be [un]lucky; viel ~! [the] best of luck!; b) happiness
Glucke die; ~, ~n brood-hen
glücken *tr. V.; mit sein* succeed; etw. glückt jmdm. sb. is successful with sth.
gluckern *itr. V.* gurgle; glug

glücklich 1. *Adj.* **a)** happy (über + *Akk.* about); **b)** *(erfolgreich)* lucky ⟨*winner*⟩; successful ⟨*outcome*⟩; safe ⟨*journey*⟩; **c)** *(vorteilhaft)* fortunate; **2.** *adv.* **a)** *(erfolgreich)* successfully; **b)** *(vorteilhaft, zufrieden)* happily ⟨*chosen, married*⟩; **glücklicherweise** *Adv.* fortunately; luckily; **glück·selig 1.** *Adj.* blissfully happy; **2.** *adv.* blissfully; **Glück·seligkeit die**; ~: bliss
glucksen *itr. V.* **a)** *s.* gluckern; **b)** *(lachen)* chuckle
Glücks-: ~**klee** der four-leaf clover; ~**pfennig** der lucky penny; ~**pilz** der *(ugs.)* lucky devil *(coll.)*
Glück[s]·sache die: das ist ~: it's a matter of luck; **Glücks·spiel das** game of chance; **glück·strahlend** *Adj.* radiantly happy; **Glücks·zahl die** lucky number; **Glück·wunsch** der congratulations *pl.;* **herzlichen** ~ **zum Geburtstag!** happy birthday!
Glüh·birne die the light-bulb; **glühen** *itr. V.* glow; **glühend 1.** *Adj.* red-hot ⟨*metal etc.*⟩; blazing ⟨*heat*⟩; ardent ⟨*admirer etc.*⟩; passionate ⟨*words, letter, etc.*⟩; **2.** *adv.* **(love)** passionately; ⟨*admire*⟩ ardently; ~ **heiß** blazing hot; **Glüh·wein** der mulled wine
Glut die; ~, ~**en a)** embers *pl.;* **b)** *(geh.: Leidenschaft)* passion; **glut·rot** *Adj.* fiery red
Glyzerin das; ~s glycerine
GmbH *Abk.* **Gesellschaft mit beschränkter Haftung** ≈ p.l.c.
Gnade die; ~, ~**n** *(Gunst)* favour; *(Rel.)* grace; *(Milde)* mercy
gnaden-, Gnaden-: ~**brot das:** jmdm./einem Tier das ~**brot geben** keep sb./an animal in his/her/its old age; ~**frist die** reprieve; ~**gesuch das** plea for clemency; ~**los** *(auch fig.)* **1.** *Adj.* merciless; **2.** *adv.* mercilessly; ~**schuß** der coup de grâce *(by shooting)*
gnädig *Adj.* gracious; *(glimpflich)* lenient ⟨*sentence etc.*⟩
Gnom der; ~**en**, ~**en** gnome
Gockel der; ~s, ~ *(bes. südd., sonst ugs. scherzh.)* cock
Gold das; ~[e]s gold; **Gold·barren** der gold bar; **golden 1.** *Adj.* *(aus Gold)* gold; *(herrlich)* golden ⟨*days, memories, etc.*⟩; **2.** *adv.* like gold
Gold-: ~**grube die** *(auch fig.)* goldmine; ~**hamster** der golden hamster
goldig *Adj.* sweet
gold-, Gold-: ~**richtig** *(ugs.)* *Adj.*

absolutely right; ~**schmied** der goldsmith; ~**schnitt** der gilt; ~**währung, die** *(Wirtsch.)* currency tied to the gold standard
¹Golf der; ~[e]s, ~e gulf
²Golf das; ~s *(Sport)* golf
Golf-: ~**platz** der golf-course; ~**schläger** der golf club; ~**spieler** der, ~**spielerin** die golfer; ~**strom** der Gulf Stream
Gondel die; ~, ~**n** gondola; **gondeln** *itr. V.;* mit sein *(ugs.)* **a)** *(mit einem Boot)* cruise; **b)** *(reisen)* travel around; **c)** *(herumfahren)* cruise around
Gong der; ~s, ~s gong; **gongen** *itr. V.* es hat gegongt the gong has sounded
gönnen *tr. V.* jmdm. etw. ~: not begrudge sb. sth.; **sich/jmdm. etw. ~:** allow oneself/sb. sth.; **Gönner** der; ~s, ~: patron; **gönnerhaft** *(abwertend)* *Adj.* patronizing
gor *3. Pers. Sg. Prät. v.* gären
Göre die; ~, ~**n** *(nordd., oft abwertend)* kid *(coll.)*
Gorilla der; ~s, ~s gorilla
goß *1. u. 3. Pers. Sg. Prät. v.* gießen
Gosse die; ~, ~**n** gutter
Gotik die; ~ *(Stil)* Gothic [style]; *(Epoche)* Gothic period; **gotisch** *Adj.* Gothic
Gott der; ~es, Götter **a)** *o. Pl.; o. Art.* God; **grüß** [dich] ~! *(landsch.)* hello!; **um ~es Willen** *(bei Erschrecken)* for God's sake; *(bei einer Bitte)* for heaven's sake; **b)** *(übermenschliches Wesen)* god
Gottes-: ~**dienst** der service; ~**haus das** *(geh.)* house of God; ~**lästerung die** blasphemy
Gottheit die; ~, ~**en** deity; **Göttin die**; ~, ~**nen** goddess; **göttlich 1.** *Adj.* *(auch fig.)* divine; **2.** *adv.* divinely
gott-, Gott-: ~**lob** *adv.* thank goodness; ~**los 1.** *Adj.* **a)** ungodly ⟨*life etc.*⟩; impious ⟨*words, speech, etc.*⟩; **b)** *(Gott leugnend)* godless ⟨*theory etc.*⟩; **2.** *adv.* *(verwerflich)* irreverently; ~**vater** der God the Father; ~**vertrauen** das trust in God
Götze der; ~n, ~n *(auch fig.)* idol; **Götzen-:** ~**bild das** idol; ~**diener** der idolater
Gouverneur [guvɛr'nøːɐ̯] der; ~s, ~e governor
Grab das; ~[e]s, Gräber grave; **das Heilige** ~: the Holy Sepulchre; **das** ~

des Unbekannten Soldaten the tomb of the Unknown Warrior; **graben** *unr. tr., itr. V.* dig; **Graben** der; ~s, Gräben ditch; *(Schützen~)* trench; *(Festungs~)* moat

Grab-: ~**kammer** die burial chamber; ~**mal** das; *Pl.* ~mäler, *geh.* ~male monument; ~**stein** der gravestone

gräbst *2. Pers. Sg. Präsens v.* graben; **gräbt** *3. Pers. Sg. Präsens v.* graben

Gracht die; ~, ~en canal

Grad der; ~|e|s, ~e degree; *(Milit.)* rank; **Grad·messer** der gauge, yardstick (für of)

graduell 1. *Adj.* gradual; slight ⟨difference etc.⟩; 2. *adv.* gradually; ⟨different⟩ in degree; **graduiert** *Adj.* graduate; **ein** ~**er Ingenieur** an engineering graduate

Graf der; ~en, ~en count; *(britischer* ~*)* earl

Grafik *usw. s.* Graphik *usw.*

Gräfin die; ~, ~nen countess; **Grafschaft** die; ~, ~en a) count's land; *(in Großbritannien)* earldom; b) *(Verwaltungsbezirk)* county

Gram der; ~|e|s *(geh.)* grief; sorrow; **grämen** 1. *tr. V.* grieve; 2. *refl. V.* grieve (über + *Akk.*, um over)

Gramm das; ~s, ~e gram

Grammatik die; ~, ~en grammar; **grammatisch** 1. *Adj.* grammatical; 2. *adv.* grammatically

Grammophon Ⓦ das; ~s, ~e gramophone; phonograph *(Amer.)*

Granat der; ~|e|s, ~e *(Schmuckstein)* garnet; **Granat·apfel** der pomegranate

Granate die; ~, ~n shell; *(Hand~)* grenade

grandios 1. *Adj.* magnificent; 2. *adv.* magnificently

Granit der; ~s, ~e granite

grantig *(südd., österr. ugs.)* 1. *Adj.* bad-tempered; 2. *adv.* bad-temperedly

Graphik die; ~, ~en graphic art[s *pl.*]; *(Kunstwerk)* graphic; *(Druck)* print; **Graphiker** der; ~s, ~, **Graphikerin** die; ~, ~nen [graphic] designer; *(Künstler[in])* graphic artist; **graphisch** 1. *Adj.* graphic; 2. *adv.* graphically

Gras das; ~es, Gräser grass; **über etw.** *(Akk.)* ~ **wachsen lassen** *(ugs.)* let the dust settle on sth.; **grasen** *itr. V.* graze; **Gras·halm** der blade of grass

gräßlich 1. *Adj.* a) *(abscheulich)* horrible; terrible ⟨accident⟩; b) *(ugs.: un-*

angenehm) dreadful *(coll.);* c) *(ugs.: sehr stark)* terrible *(coll.);* 2. *adv.* a) *(abscheulich)* horribly; terribly; b) *(ugs.: unangenehm)* terribly *(coll.);* c) *(ugs.: sehr)* terribly *(coll.)*

Grat der; ~|e|s, ~e ridge

Gräte die; ~, ~n [fish-]bone

Gratifikation die; ~, ~en bonus

gratis *Adv.* free [of charge]; gratis

Grätsche die; ~, ~n *(Turnen)* straddle; *(Sprung)* straddle-vault

Gratulant der; ~en, ~en, **Gratulantin** die; ~, ~nen well-wisher; **Gratulation** die; ~, ~en congratulations *pl.;* **gratulieren** *itr. V.* jmdm. ~: congratulate sb.; **jmdm. zum Geburtstag** ~: wish sb. many happy returns [of the day]

grau *Adj.* grey; *(trostlos)* dreary; drab

[1]**grauen** *itr. V. (geh.)* **der Morgen/der Tag graut** morning/day is breaking

[2]**grauen** *itr. V. (unpers.)* **ihm graut |es| davor/vor ihr** he dreads [the thought of] it/he's terrified of her; **Grauen** das; ~s, ~: horror (vor + *Dat.* of); **grauen·haft** 1. *Adj.* horrifying; *(ugs.: sehr unangenehm)* terrible *(coll.);* 2. *adv.* horrifyingly; *(ugs.: sehr unangenehm)* terribly *(coll.)*

grau-: ~**haarig** *Adj.* grey-haired; ~**meliert** *Adj.* (präd. getrennt geschrieben) greying ⟨hair⟩

Graupe die; ~, ~n a) grain of pearl barley; b) *Pl. (Gericht)* pearl barley *sing.*

graupeln *itr. V. (unpers.)* **es graupelt** there's soft hail falling

grausam 1. *Adj.* a) cruel; b) *(furchtbar)* terrible; dreadful; 2. *adv.* a) cruelly; b) *(furchtbar)* terribly, dreadfully; **Grausamkeit** die; ~, ~en a) *o. Pl.* cruelty; b) *(Handlung)* act of cruelty

grausen 1. *tr., itr. V. (unpers.)* **es grauste ihm** od. **ihn davor/vor ihr** he dreaded it/he was terrified of her; 2. *refl. V.* **sich vor etw./jmdm.** ~: dread sth./be terrified of sb.; **Grausen** das; ~s horror; **grausig** *s.* grauenhaft

gravieren *tr. V.* engrave; **gravierend** *Adj.* serious, grave; **Gravierung** die; ~, ~en engraving

Gravitation die; ~ *(Physik, Astron.)* gravitation

Gravur [gra'vu:ɐ̯] die; ~, ~en engraving

Grazie ['gra:ʦiə] die; ~, ~n a) *o. Pl. (Anmut)* gracefulness; b) *Pl. (Myth.)* Graces

greifen 1. *unr. tr. V.* **a)** *(er~)* take hold of; grasp; *(rasch ~)* seize; **b)** *(fangen)* catch; 2. *unr. itr. V.* **a) in/unter/hinter etw./sich** *(Akk.)* ~: reach into/under/ behind sth./one; **nach etw.** ~: reach for sth.; *(hastig)* make a grab for sth.; **b)** *(Technik)* grip

Greis der; ~es, ~e old man; **Greisin** die; ~, ~nen old woman

grell 1. *Adj.* **a)** *(hell)* glaring, ⟨*light, sun, etc.*⟩; **b)** *(auffallend)* garish ⟨*colour etc.*⟩; loud ⟨*dress, pattern, etc.*⟩; **c)** *(schrill)* shrill, ⟨*cry, voice, etc.*⟩; 2. *adv.* **a)** *(hell)* with glaring brightness; **b)** *(auffallend)* **gegen** *od.* **von etw. ~ abstechen** contrast sharply with sth.; **c)** *(schrill)* shrilly

Gremium das; ~s, **Gremien** committee

Grenze die; ~, ~n **a)** boundary; *(Staats~)* border; *(gedachte Trennungslinie)* borderline; **b)** *(fig.)* limit; **grenzen** *itr. V.* **an etw.** *(Akk.)* ~: border [on] sth.; **grenzen·los** 1. *Adj.* boundless; *(fig.)* boundless, unbounded ⟨*joy, wonder, jealousy, grief, etc.*⟩; unlimited ⟨*wealth, power*⟩; limitless ⟨*patience, ambition*⟩; extreme ⟨*tiredness, anger, foolishness*⟩; 2. *adv.* endlessly; *(fig.)* beyond all measure; **Grenzen·losigkeit** die; ~: boundlessness

Grenz-: ~**übergang** der border crossing-point; ~**verkehr** der [cross-]border traffic

Greuel der; ~s, ~ **a)** etw./jmd. ist jmdm. ein ~: sb. loathes *or* detests sth./sb.; **b)** *meist Pl. (geh.) (~tat)* atrocity; **Greuel·tat** die atrocity; **greulich** 1. *Adj.* **a)** horrifying; **b)** *(unangenehm)* awful; 2. *adv.* **a)** horrifyingly; **b)** *(unangenehm)* terribly

Grieche der; ~n, ~n Greek; **Griechen·land** (das); ~s Greece; **griechisch** 1. *Adj.* Greek; 2. *adv.* ⟨*speak, write*⟩ in Greek; **Griechisch** das; ~|s| Greek *no art.*

griesgrämig 1. *Adj.* grumpy; 2. *adv.* in a grumpy manner

Grieß der; ~es, ~e semolina; **Grieß·brei** der semolina

griff *1. u. 3. Pers. Sg. Prät. v.* **greifen**; **Griff** der; ~|e|s, ~e **a)** grip; grasp; **b)** *(Knauf, Henkel)* handle; **griff·bereit** *Adj.* ready to hand *postpos.*

Griffel der; ~s, ~: slate-pencil

griffig *Adj.* **a)** *(handlich)* handy; **b)** *(gut greifend)* that grips well *postpos.*, not *pred.*; non-slip ⟨*surface, floor*⟩

Grill der; ~s, ~s grill; *(Rost)* barbecue

Grille die; ~, ~n **a)** cricket; **b)** *(sonderbarer Einfall)* whim

grillen 1. *tr. V.* grill; 2. *itr. V.* **im Garten** ~: have a barbecue in the garden

Grimasse die; ~, ~n grimace

grimmig 1. *Adj.* furious ⟨*person*⟩; grim ⟨*expression*⟩; 2. *adv.* grimly

grinsen *itr. V.* grin; *(höhnisch)* smirk

Grippe die; ~, ~n **a)** influenza; flu *(coll.)*; **b)** *(volkst.: Erkältung)* cold

Grips der; ~es brains *pl.*

grob 1. *Adj.* **a)** coarse; thick ⟨*wire*⟩; rough ⟨*work*⟩; **b)** *(ungefähr)* rough; **c)** *(schwerwiegend)* gross; flagrant ⟨*lie*⟩; **d)** *(barsch)* rude; 2. *adv.* **a)** coarsely; **b)** *(ungefähr)* roughly; **c)** *(schwerwiegend)* grossly; **d)** *(barsch)* rudely; **Grobheit** die; ~, ~en **a)** *o. Pl.* rudeness; **b)** *(Äußerung)* rude remark

Grobian der; ~|e|s, ~e lout

Grog der; ~s, ~s grog

grölen 1. *tr. V. (ugs. abwertend)* bawl [out]; roar, howl ⟨*approval*⟩; 2. *itr. V.* bawl

Groll der; ~|e|s *(geh.)* rancour; **grollen** *itr. V. (geh.)* **a)** |mit| jmdm. ~: bear a grudge against sb.; **b)** ⟨*thunder*⟩ rumble

Grönland (das); ~s Greenland

Gros [gro:] das; ~ [gro:s], ~ [gro:s] bulk

Groschen der; ~s, ~ **a)** *(österreichische Münze)* groschen; **b)** *(ugs.: Zehnpfennigstück)* ten-pfennig piece; *(fig.)* penny; cent *(Amer.)*

groß; größer, größt... 1. *Adj.* **a)** big, large; great ⟨*length, width, height*⟩; tall ⟨*person*⟩; wide ⟨*selection*⟩; 1 m² ~: 1 m² in area; **im ~en und ganzen** by and large; **b)** *(älter)* big ⟨*brother, sister*⟩; *(erwachsen)* grown-up; **c)** *(lange dauernd)* long, lengthy; **d)** intense ⟨*heat, cold*⟩; high ⟨*speed*⟩; great, major ⟨*event, artist, work*⟩; 2. *adv.* **ein Wort ~ schreiben** write a word with a capital; *(ugs.: besonders)* greatly; **groß·artig** 1. *Adj.* magnificent; 2. *adv.* magnificently

Großbritannien (das); ~s the United Kingdom; [Great] Britain

Groß·buchstabe der capital [letter]

Größe die; ~, ~n size; *(Höhe, Körper~)* height; *(fig.)* greatness; **die ~ der Katastrophe** the [full] extent of the catastrophe

Groß·eltern *Pl.* grandparents; **Größen·wahn** der delusions *pl.* of grandeur; **größer** *s.* **groß**

Groß-: ~**fahndung** die large-scale

search; ~**handel** der wholesale trade; ~**händler** der wholesaler; ~**industrielle** der/die; *adj. Dekl.* big industrialist

Grossist der; ~**en**, ~**en** *(Kaufmannsspr.)* wholesaler

groß-, Groß-: ~**macht** die great power; ~**maul** das *(ugs. abwertend)* big-mouth *(coll.);* ~**mut** die; ~: generosity; ~**mütig** *Adj.* generous; ~**mutter** die grandmother; ~**reinemachen** das *(ugs.)* thorough cleaning; ~|**schreiben** *unr. tr. V. (ugs.) in* ~**geschrieben werden** be stressed; *s. auch* **groß** 2; ~**spurig** *(abwertend)* 1. *Adj.* boastful; *(hochtrabend)* pretentious; 2. *adv.* boastfully; *(hochtrabend)* pretentiously; ~**stadt** die city; large town; ~**städter** der city-dweller

größt... *s.* **groß**; **Groß·teil** der **a)** *(Hauptteil)* major part; **b)** *(nicht unerheblicher Teil)* large part; **größtenteils** *Adv.* for the most part; **größt·möglich** *Adj.* greatest possible

groß-, Groß-: ~|**tun** *unr. itr. V.* boast; ~**vater** der grandfather; ~|**ziehen** *unr. tr. V.* bring up; raise; rear ⟨*animal*⟩; ~**zügig** 1. *Adj.* generous; grand and spacious ⟨*building, garden, etc.*⟩; 2. *adv.* **a)** generously; ~**zügigkeit** die generosity

grotesk 1. *Adj.* grotesque; 2. *adv.* grotesquely

Grotte die; ~, ~**n** grotto

grub *1. u. 3. Pers. Sg. Prät. v.* **graben; Grübchen** das; ~**s**, ~: dimple; **Grube** die; ~, ~**n** pit; *(Bergbau)* mine

grübeln *itr. V.* ponder (**über** + *Dat.* on, over)

Gruben·arbeiter der miner; mineworker

grüezi *Adv. (schweiz.)* hallo

Gruft die; ~, **Grüfte** vault; *(in einer Kirche)* crypt

grün *Adj.* green; **Grün** das; ~**s**, ~ *od.* *(ugs.)* ~**s** **a)** green; **b)** *o. Pl. (Pflanzen)* greenery; **Grün·anlage** die green space; *(Park)* park

Grund der; ~|**e**|**s**, **Gründe a)** ground; *(eines Gewässers)* bottom; **b)** *(Ursache, Veranlassung)* reason

Grund-: ~**besitz** der **a)** *(Eigentum an Land)* ownership of land; **b)** *(Land)* land; ~**buch** das land register

gründen 1. *tr. V.* **a)** found; set up, establish ⟨*business*⟩; start [up] ⟨*club*⟩; **b)** *(aufbauen)* base ⟨*plan, theory, etc.*⟩

(**auf** + *Akk.* on); 2. *itr. V.* **auf** *od.* **in etw.** *(Dat.)* ~: be based on sth. 3. *refl. V.* **sich auf etw.** *(Akk.)* ~: be based on sth.; **Gründer** der; ~**s**, ~, **Gründerin** die; ~, ~**nen:** founder

grundieren *tr. V.* prime

grund-, Grund-: ~**gesetz** das Basic Law; ~**kenntnis** die; *meist Pl.* basic knowledge *no pl.* (**in** + *Dat.* of); ~**lage** die basis; foundation; ~**legend** 1. *Adj.* fundamental, basic (**für** to); seminal ⟨*idea, work*⟩; 2. *adv.* fundamentally

gründlich 1. *Adj.* thorough; 2. *adv.* thoroughly; **Gründlichkeit** die; ~: thoroughness

grund·los 1. *Adj.* groundless; 2. *adv.* sich ~**los aufregen/ängstigen** be needlessly agitated/alarmed; **Grundnahrungs·mittel** das basic food[stuff]

Grün·donnerstag der Maundy Thursday

Grund-: ~**prinzip** das fundamental principle; ~**recht** das basic *or* constitutional right; ~**riß** der **a)** *(Bauw.)* [ground-] plan; **b)** *(Leitfaden)* outline; ~**satz** der principle

grund·sätzlich 1. *Adj.* **a)** fundamental ⟨*difference, question, etc.*⟩; **b)** *(aus Prinzip)* ⟨*opponent etc.*⟩ on principle; **c)** *(allgemein)* ⟨*agreement etc.*⟩ in principle; 2. *adv.* **a)** fundamentally; **b)** *(aus Prinzip)* on principle; **c)** *(allgemein)* in principle

Grund-: ~**schule** die primary school; ~**stein** der foundation-stone; ~**stück** das plot [of land]

Gründung die; ~, ~**en** *s.* **gründen** 1 a: foundation; setting up; establishing; starting [up]

Grund-: ~**wasser** das *(Geol.)* ground water; ~**zug** der essential feature

Grüne das; *adj. Dekl.* green; **im** ~**n/ins** ~: [out] in/into the country

Grün-: ~**fläche** die green space; *(im Park)* lawn; ~**span** der verdigris; ~**streifen** der central reservation *(grassed and often with trees and bushes)*

grunzen *tr., itr. V.* grunt

Gruppe die; ~, ~**n a)** group; **b)** *(Klassifizierung)* class; category

Gruppen-: ~**reise** die *(Touristik)* group travel *no pl., no art.;* ~**sieg** der *(Sport)* top place in the group

gruppieren 1. *tr. V.* arrange; 2. *refl. V.* form a group/groups; **Gruppierung** die; ~, ~**en** grouping

gruselig *Adj.* eerie; creepy; **gruseln**
1. *tr., itr. V. (unpers.)* es gruselt jmdn.
od. jmdm. sb.'s flesh creeps; 2. *refl. V.*
be frightened

Gruß der; ~es, Grüße a) greeting; *(Milit.)* salute; b) *(im Brief)* mit herzlichen
Grüßen [with] best wishes; **mit bestem
~/freundlichen Grüßen** yours sincerely; **grüßen** 1. *tr. V.* a) greet; *(Milit.)* salute; b) *(Grüße senden)* **grüße
deine Eltern** [ganz herzlich] von mir
please give your parents my [kindest]
regards; 2. *itr. V.* say hello; *(Milit.)* salute

Grütze die; ~, ~n groats *pl.; rote* ~:
red fruit pudding *(made with fruit
juice, fruit and cornflour, etc.)*

gucken *itr. V. (ugs.)* a) look; *(heimlich)* peep; b) *(hervorsehen)* stick out;
c) *(dreinschauen)* look; **Guck·loch
das** spy-hole

Guerilla [ge'rɪlja] die; ~, ~s guerrilla
war; *(Einheit)* guerrilla unit

Gulasch ['gʊlaʃ, 'gu:laʃ] das *od.* der;
~[e]s, ~e *od.* ~s goulash

Gulden der; ~s, ~: guilder

gültig *Adj.* valid; current ⟨note, coin⟩;
Gültigkeit die; ~: validity; ~ **haben/
erlangen** be/become valid

Gummi der *od.* das; ~s, ~[s] rubber

Gummi-: ~**band** das; *Pl.* ~bänder
rubber *or* elastic band; *(in Kleidung)*
elastic *no indef. art.;* ~**bärchen das**
jelly baby; ~**baum** der rubber plant

gummieren *tr. V.* gum

Gummi-: ~**handschuh** der rubber
glove; ~**knüppel** der [rubber]
truncheon; ~**sohle** die rubber sole;
~**stiefel** der rubber boot; *(für Regenwetter)* wellington [boot] *(Brit.)*

Gunst die; ~: favour; goodwill; **günstig** 1. *Adj.* favourable; propitious
⟨sign⟩; auspicious ⟨moment⟩; beneficial ⟨influence⟩; good; 2. *adv.* favourably; **etw. ~ beeinflussen** have *or* exert
a beneficial influence on sth.

Gurgel die; ~, ~n throat; **jmdm. die ~
zudrücken** throttle sb.; **gurgeln** *itr.
V.* gargle

Gurke die; ~, ~n cucumber; *(einge-
legt)* gherkin

gurren *itr. V. (auch fig.)* coo

Gurt der; ~[e]s, ~e strap; *(im Auto,
Flugzeug)* [seat-]belt; **Gürtel** der; ~s,
~: belt

Gürtel-: ~**linie** die waist[line]; ~**reifen** der radial[-ply] tyre

GUS [ge:|u:'|ɛs] *Abk.* **Gemeinschaft
Unabhängiger Staaten** CIS

Guß der; Gusses, Güsse a) *(das Gießen)* casting; b) *(ugs.: Regenschauer)*
downpour

Guß·eisen das cast iron; **guß·ei-
sern** *Adj.* cast-iron

gut; besser, best... 1. *Adj.* good; fine
⟨wine⟩; **ein ~es neues Jahr** a happy
new year; **mir ist nicht ~ :** I'm not feeling well; ~**en Appetit!** enjoy your
lunch/dinner *etc.!;* **eine ~e Stunde** [von
hier] a good hour [from here]; 2. *adv.*
a) well; b) *(mühelos)* easily; *s. auch*
besser, best...

Gut das; ~[e]s, **Güter a)** property; *(Be-
sitztum, auch fig.)* possession; b)
(landwirtschaftlicher Grundbesitz) estate; c) *(Fracht~, Ware)* item; **Güter**
goods; *(Fracht~)* freight *sing.;* goods
(Brit.);

gut-, Gut-: ~**achten das;** ~s, ~: [ex-
pert's] report; ~**artig** *Adj.* a) good-
natured; b) *(nicht gefährlich)* benign;
~**aussehend** *Adj.* good-looking;
~**bürgerlich** *Adj.* good middle-
class; ~**bürgerliche Küche** good plain
cooking; ~**dünken** das; ~s discretion

Güte die; ~: goodness; kindness;
(Qualität) quality

Güter-: ~**abfertigung** die a) *(Abfertigung von Waren)* dispatch of freight
or *(Brit.)* goods; b) *(Annahmestelle)*
freight or *(Brit.)* goods office;
~**bahnhof** der freight depot; goods
station *(Brit.);* ~**wagen** der goods
wagon *(Brit.);* freight car *(Amer.);*
~**zug** der goods train *(Brit.);* freight
train *(Amer.)*

gut-, Gut-: ~|**gehen** *unr. itr. V.; mit
sein* a) *(unpers.)* es geht jmdm. gut sb.
is well; b) *(~ ausgehen)* turn out well;
~**gelaunt** *Adj. (präd. getrennt geschrieben)* cheerful; ~**gemeint** *Adj.
(präd. getrennt geschrieben)* well-
meant; ~**gläubig** *Adj.* innocently
trusting; ~**haben das;** ~s, ~: credit
balance; ~|**heißen** *unr. tr. V.* ap-
prove of; ~**herzig** *Adj.* kind-hearted

gütig 1. *Adj.* kindly; 2. *adv.* ~ **lächeln**
give a kindly smile; **gütlich** *Adj.*
amicable

gut-, Gut-: ~|**machen** *tr. V.* make
good ⟨damage⟩; put right ⟨omission,
mistake, etc.⟩; ~**mütig** *Adj.* good-na-
tured; ~**mütigkeit die;** ~: good nature

Guts·besitzer der owner of a/the estate; landowner

gut-, Gut-: ~**schein** der voucher,

coupon (für, auf + *Akk.* for); ~|-
schreiben *unr. tr. V.* credit;
~**schrift** die credit
Guts·hof der estate; manor
gut-: ~|**tun** *unr. itr. V.* do good;
~**willig** 1. *Adj.* willing; *(entgegenkommend)* obliging; 2. *adv.* etw. ~**willig herausgeben/versprechen** hand sth.
over voluntarily/promise sth. willingly
Gymnasium das; ~s, **Gymnasien** ≈
grammar school
Gymnastik die; ~: physical exercises
pl.; (Turnen) gymnastics *sing.*
Gynäkologe der; ~n, ~n gynaecologist

H

h, H [ha:] das; ~, ~ a) *(Buchstabe)*
h/H; b) *(Musik)* [key of] B
h *Abk.* a) Uhr hrs; b) Stunde hr[s]
H *Abk.* a) Herren; b) Haltestelle
¹**ha** [ha(:)] *Interj.* a) *(Überraschung)* ah;
b) *(Triumph)* aha
²**ha** *Abk.* Hektar ha
Haar das; ~|e|s, ~e hair; **blonde** ~e *od.*
blondes ~ **haben** have fair hair; *(fig.)*
~**e auf den Zähnen haben** *(ugs.
scherzh.)* be a tough customer; **um ein**
~ *(ugs.)* very nearly
Haar-: ~**ausfall** der hair loss; ~**bürste** die hairbrush; ~**büschel** das tuft
of hair
haaren *itr. V.* moult; **Haares·breite**
die *in* um ~: by a hair's breadth;
Haar·festiger der setting lotion;
haar·genau *(ugs.)* 1. *Adj.* exact; 2.
adv. exactly; **haarig** *Adj.* hairy
haar-, Haar-: ~**klemme** die hair-
grip; ~**nadel** die hairpin; ~**na-
del·kurve** die hairpin bend;
~**schnitt** der haircut; *(modisch)* hairstyle; ~**spange** die hair-slide;
~**sträubend** *Adj.* a) *(grauenhaft)*
hair-raising; b) *(empörend)* outrageous; shocking; ~**teil** das hair-
piece; ~**wasch·mittel** das shampoo; ~**wasser** das; *Pl.* ~**wässer** hair
lotion

Habe die; ~ *(geh.)* possessions *pl.;*
haben 1. *unr. tr. V.* have; have got;
heute ~ **wir schönes Wetter** the
weather is fine today; **es gut/schlecht/
schwer** ~: have it good *(coll.)*/have a
bad time [of it]/have a difficult time;
du hast zu gehorchen you must obey;
das Jahr hat 12 Monate there are 12
months in a year; 2. *refl. V. (ugs.: sich
aufregen)* make a fuss; 3. *Hilfsverb*
have; **ich habe/hatte ihn eben gesehen**
I've/I'd just seen him; **er hat es gewußt**
he knew it; 4. *mod. V.* **du hast zu gehorchen** you must obey; **er hat sich
nicht einzumischen** he's not to interfere; **Haben** das; ~s, ~ *(Kaufmannsspr.)* credit; **Habe·nichts**
der; ~, ~e pauper; **Hab·gier** die *(abwertend)* greed; **hab·gierig** 1. *Adj.
(abwertend)* greedy; 2. *adv.* greedily
Habicht der; ~s, ~e hawk
Hab-: ~**seligkeiten** *Pl.* [meagre] belongings; ~**sucht** die; ~ *(abwertend)*
greed; avarice
Hachse die; ~, ~n *(südd.)* knuckle
Hack das; ~s *(ugs., bes. nordd.)*
mince; **Hack·braten** der meat loaf
¹**Hacke** die; ~, ~n hoe; *(Pickel)*
pick[axe]
²**Hacke** die; ~, ~n *(bes. nordd. u. md.)*
heel
hacken 1. *itr. V.* a) hoe; b) *(picken)*
peck; 2. *tr. V.* a) hoe ⟨garden, flower-
bed, etc.⟩; b) *(zerkleinern)* chop; chop
[up] ⟨meat, vegetables, etc.⟩
Hack·fleisch das minced meat;
mince
Häcksel der *od.* das; ~s *(Landw.)*
chaff
hadern *itr. V. (geh.)* mit etw. ~: be at
odds with sth.
Hafen der; ~s, **Häfen** harbour; port
Hafen-: ~**arbeiter** der dock-worker;
docker; ~**kneipe** die dockland pub
(Brit. coll.) or *(Amer.)* bar; ~**rundfahrt** die trip round the harbour;
~**stadt** die port; ~**viertel** das dock
area
Hafer der; ~s oats *pl.*
Hafer-: ~**brei** der porridge;
~**flocken** *Pl.* porridge oats
Haff das; ~|e|s, ~s *od.* ~e lagoon
Haft die; ~ a) *(Gewahrsam)* custody;
(aus politischen Gründen) detention;
b) *(Freiheitsstrafe)* imprisonment
-**haft** *Adj., adv.* -like
haftbar *Adj. (bes. Rechtsspr.)* für etw.
~ **sein** be liable for sth.; **Haft·befehl**
der *(Rechtsw.)* warrant [of arrest]

¹**haften** *itr. V.* stick; *(sich festsetzen)* ⟨*smell, dirt, etc.*⟩ cling (**an** + *Dat.* to)

²**haften** *itr. V.* für jmdn./etw. ~: be responsible for sb./liable for sth.; *(Rechtsw., Wirtsch.)* be liable

haften|bleiben *unr. itr. V.; mit sein* stick (**an/auf** + *Dat.* to); ⟨*smell, smoke*⟩ cling (**an/auf** + *Dat.* to); *(ugs.: im Gedächtnis bleiben)* stick

Häftling der; ~s, ~e prisoner

Haft·pflicht die liability (**für** for); **Haftpflicht·versicherung** die personal liability insurance; *(für Autofahrer)* third party insurance

Haft·schale die contact lens

Haftung die; ~, ~en liability; **Gesellschaft mit |un|beschränkter ~:** [un]limited [liability] company

Hagebutte die; ~, ~n **a)** *(Frucht)* rose-hip; **b)** *(ugs.: Heckenrose)* dog-rose

Hagel der; ~s, ~ *(auch fig.)* hail; **hageln** *itr. V., tr. V. (unpers.)* hail

hager *Adj.* gaunt

haha [ha'ha(:)] *Interj.* ha ha

Häher der; ~s, ~: jay

¹**Hahn** der; ~|e|s, **Hähne** cock; *(Wetter~)* weathercock

²**Hahn** der; ~|e|s, **Hähne**, *fachspr.:* ~en **a)** tap; faucet *(Amer.);* **b)** *(bei Waffen)* hammer

Hähnchen das; ~s, ~: chicken; **Hahnen·fuß** der buttercup

Hai der; ~s, ~e shark

Häkchen das; ~s, ~ **a)** [small] hook; **b)** *(Zeichen)* mark; *(beim Abhaken)* tick; **häkeln** *tr., itr. V.* crochet; **Häkel·nadel** die crochet-hook

haken **1.** *tr. V.* hook (**an** + *Akk.* on to); **2.** *itr. V. (klemmen)* be stuck; **Haken** der; ~s, ~ **a)** hook; **b)** *(Zeichen)* tick; **c)** *(ugs.: Schwierigkeit)* catch; **d)** *(Boxen)* hook; **Haken·kreuz das** swastika

halb **1.** *Adj. u. Bruchz.* half; **eine ~e Stunde/ein ~er Meter** half an hour/a metre; **zum ~en Preis** [at] half price; **~ Europa/die ~e Welt** half of Europe/half the world; **es ist ~ eins** it's half past twelve; **die ~e Wahrheit** half [of] the truth; **|noch| ein ~es Kind sein** be hardly more than a child; **2.** *adv.* ~ **voll/leer** half-full/-empty; **~ angezogen** half dressed; **Halb·dunkel das** semi-darkness; **Halbe** der *od.* die *od.* das; *adj. Dekl. (ugs.)* half litre *(of beer etc.);* **Halb·edelstein** der *(veralt.)* semi-precious stone

halber *Präp. mit Gen.; nachgestellt*

(wegen) on account of; *(um ... willen)* for the sake of

halb-, Halb-: ~**finale** das *(Sport)* semi-final; ~**gar** *Adj.* half-cooked; ~**gefror[e]ne das;** *adj. Dekl.* soft ice cream

halbieren *tr. V.* cut/tear ⟨*object*⟩ in half; halve ⟨*amount, number*⟩

halb-, Halb-: ~**insel** die peninsula; ~**jahr das** six months *pl.;* half year; ~**jährlich** **1.** *Adj.* six-monthly; **2.** *adv.* every six months; ~**kreis** der semicircle; ~**kugel** die hemisphere; ~**lang** *Adj.* mid-length ⟨*hair*⟩; mid-calf length ⟨*coat, dress, etc.*⟩; ~**links** ['-'-] *Adv.* *(Fußball)* ⟨*play*⟩ [at] inside left; ~**mast** *Adv.* at half-mast; ~**mond** der **a)** *(Mond)* half-moon; **b)** *(Figur)* crescent; ~**offen** *Adj. (präd. getrennt geschrieben)* half-open; ~**pension** die half-board; ~**rechts** ['-'-] *Adv.* *(Fußball)* ⟨*play*⟩ [at] inside right; ~**schuh** der shoe; ~**starke** der; *adj. Dekl. (ugs. abwertend)* [young] hooligan; ~**tags** *Adv.* ⟨*work*⟩ part-time; *(morgens/nachmittags)* ⟨*work*⟩ [in the] mornings/afternoons; ~**voll** *Adj. (präd. getrennt geschrieben)* half-full; ~**wegs** *Adv.* to some extent; ~**wüchsig** [~vy:ksɪç] *Adj.* adolescent; ~**wüchsige** der/die; *adj. Dekl.* adolescent; ~**zeit** die *(bes. Fußball)* **a)** half; **b)** *(Pause)* half-time

Halde die; ~, ~n *(Bergbau)* slag-heap

half *1. u. 3. Pers. Sg. Prät. v.* **helfen**

Hälfte die; ~, ~n **a)** half; **b)** *(ugs.: Teil)* part

¹**Halfter** der *od.* das; ~s, ~: halter

²**Halfter** die; ~, ~n; *auch das;* ~s, ~: holster

Hall der; ~|e|s, ~e **a)** *(geh.)* reverberation; **b)** *(Echo)* echo

Halle die; ~, ~n hall; *(Fabrik~)* shed; *(Hotel~, Theater~)* foyer

hallen *itr. V.* **a)** reverberate; ⟨*shot, bell, cry*⟩ ring out; **b)** *(widerhallen)* echo

Hallen- indoor ⟨*swimming-pool, handball*⟩

Hallig die; ~, ~en small low island *(particularly one of those off Schleswig-Holstein)*

hallo *Interj.* hello; **Hallo das;** ~s, ~s cheering

Halluzination die; ~, ~en hallucination

Halm der; ~|e|s, ~e stalk; stem

Hals der; ~es, **Hälse** *(Kehle)* throat; ~ **über Kopf** *(ugs.)* in a rush

Hals-: ~**ab·schneider** der *(ugs. ab-*

wertend) shark; ~**band** das; *Pl.*
~**bänder** *(für Tiere)* collar; ~**bruch**
der *s.* ~- **und Beinbruch**; ~**entzün-**
dung die inflammation of the throat;
~-**Nasen-Ohren-Arzt** der ear, nose,
and throat specialist; ~**schlagader**
die carotid [artery]; ~**schmerzen** *Pl.*
sore throat *sing.;* ~**starrig** [~ʃtarɪç]
Adj. (abwertend) stubborn; obstinate;
~**tuch** das cravat; ~- **und Bein-**
bruch *Interj. (scherzh.)* good luck;
~**weh** das *(ugs.) s.* ~**schmerzen**
halt *Interj.* stop; **Halt** der; ~|e|s, ~e
hold
haltbar *Adj.* **a)** ~ sein ⟨*food*⟩ keep
[well]; ~ **bis 5. 3.** use by 5 March; **b)**
(nicht verschleißend) hard-wearing
⟨*material, clothes*⟩; **c)** *(aufrechtzuer-*
halten) tenable ⟨*hypothesis etc.*⟩;
Haltbarkeit die; ~ *(Strapazierfähig-*
keit) durability
halten 1. *unr. tr. V.* **a)** *(auch Milit.)*
hold; **die Hand vor den Mund** ~: put
one's hand in front of one's mouth; **b)**
(Ballspiele) save ⟨*shot, penalty, etc.*⟩;
c) *(bewahren)* keep; *(beibehalten, auf-*
rechterhalten) keep up ⟨*speed etc.*⟩;
maintain ⟨*temperature, equilibrium*⟩;
d) *(erfüllen)* keep; **sein Wort/ein Ver-**
sprechen ~: keep one's word/a
promise; **e)** *(besitzen, beschäftigen, be-*
ziehen) keep ⟨*chickens etc.*⟩; take
⟨*newspaper, magazine, etc.*⟩; **f)** *(ein-*
schätzen) jmdn. **für reich/ehrlich** ~:
think sb. is rich/honest; **viel von**
jmdm.~: think a lot of sb.; **g)** *(ab~,*
veranstalten) give, ⟨*speech, lecture*⟩; **2.**
unr. itr. V. **a)** *(stehenbleiben)* stop; **b)**
(unverändert, an seinem Platz bleiben)
last; **c)** *(Sport)* save; **d)** *(beistehen)* **zu**
jmdm. ~: stand by sb.; **3.** *unr. refl. V.*
a) *(sich durchsetzen, behaupten)* **wir**
werden uns/die Stadt wird sich nicht
länger ~ **können** we/the town won't be
able to hold out much longer; **b)** *(sich*
bewähren) **sich gut** ~: do well; **c)** *(un-*
verändert bleiben) ⟨*weather, flowers,*
etc.⟩ last; ⟨*milk, meat, etc.*⟩ keep; **d)**
(Körperhaltung haben) **sich schlecht/**
gerade ~: hold oneself badly/straight;
e) *(bleiben)* **sich auf den Beinen/im**
Sattel ~: stay on one's feet/in the
saddle; **sich links/rechts** ~: keep [to
the] left/right; **sich an etw.** *(Akk.)* ~:
keep to sth.
Halter der; ~**s,** ~ **a)** *(Fahrzeug~)*
keeper; **b)** *(Tier~)* owner; **c)** *(Vorrich-*
tung) holder; **Halterung die;** ~, ~**en**
support

Halte-: ~**stelle** die stop; ~**verbot**
das **a)** „~**verbot**" 'no stopping'; **hier**
ist ~**verbot** this is a no-stopping zone;
b) *(Stelle)* no-stopping zone; ~**ver-**
bots·schild das no-stopping sign
-**haltig,** *(österr.)* -**hältig:** vit-
amin~/silber~ *usw.* containing vit-
amins/silver *etc. postpos., not pred.;*
vitamin~ sein contain vitamins
halt-: ~**los** *Adj.* **a)** *(labil)* ~**los sein** be
a weak character; **ein** ~**loser Mensch** a
weak character; **b)** *(unbegründet)* un-
founded; ~|**machen** *itr. V.* stop
Haltung die; ~, ~**en a)** *(Körper~)* posture; **b)** *(Pose)* manner; **c)** *(Einstel-*
lung) attitude; **d)** *(Fassung)* composure
Halunke der; ~**n,** ~**n** scoundrel; villain
Hamburger der; ~**s,** ~ *od.* ~**s** *(Frika-*
delle) hamburger
hämisch 1. *Adj.* malicious; **2.** *adv.*
maliciously
Hammel der; ~**s,** ~ **a)** wether; **b)**
(Fleisch) mutton; **Hammel·fleisch**
das mutton
Hammer der; ~**s,** **Hämmer a)** hammer; *(Holz~)* mallet; ~ **und Sichel**
hammer and sickle; **b)** *(Technik)* ram;
hämmern *itr., tr. V.* hammer
Hämorrhoiden [hɛmɔrɔˈiːdn̩] *Pl.*
(Med.) haemorrhoids; piles
Hampel·mann der; ~|**e|s,** **Hampel-**
männer a) jumping jack; **b)** *(ugs. ab-*
wertend) puppet
hampeln *itr. V. (ugs.)* jump about
Hamster der; ~**s,** ~: hamster
hamstern *tr., itr. V.* **a)** *(horten)* hoard;
b) *(Lebensmittel tauschen)* barter
goods for [food]
Hand die; ~, **Hände** hand; **jmdm. die** ~
geben shake sb.'s hand; ~ **und Fuß/**
weder ~ **noch Fuß haben** *(ugs.)* make
sense/no sense; **alle** *od.* **beide Hände**
damit voll haben, etw. **zu tun** *(ugs.)*
have one's hands full doing sth.; **die**
Hände in den Schoß legen sit back and
do nothing; **etw. aus der** ~ **geben** let
sth. out of one's hands; ~ **in** ~ **arbei-**
ten work hand in hand; **etw. zur** ~ **ha-**
ben have sth. handy; **zu Händen |von|**
Herrn Müller attention Herr Müller
Hand-: ~**arbeit die a)** handicraft;
etw. in ~**arbeit herstellen** make sth. by
hand; **b)** *(Gegenstand)* handmade article; **c)** *(Nadelarbeit)* [piece of] needlework; ~**ball** der handball; ~**besen**
der brush; ~**betrieb** der; *o. Pl.* manual operation; ~**bewegung** die **a)**

movement of the hand; **b)** *(Geste)* gesture; **~bremse die** handbrake; **~buch das** handbook; *(technisches ~buch)* manual

Händchen das; ~s, ~: [little] hand; **Hände** *s.* **Hand**

Hände-: **~druck der;** *Pl.* **~drücke** handshake; **~klatschen das;** ~s clapping

Handel der; ~s trade; **handeln 1.** *itr. V.* **a)** trade; deal; **b)** *(feilschen)* haggle; **c)** *(agieren)* act; **d)** *(sich verhalten)* behave; **e) von etw.** *od.* **über etw.** *(Akk.)* ~ ⟨*book, film, etc.*⟩ be about *or* deal with sth.; **2.** *refl. V. (unpers.)* **es handelt sich um ...:** it is a matter of ...; *(es dreht sich um)* it's about ...

handels-, Handels-: **~abkommen das** trade agreement; **~bank die** merchant bank; **~bilanz die a)** *(eines Betriebes)* balance-sheet; **b)** *(eines Staates)* balance of trade; **~einig, ~eins in mit jmdm. ~einig** *od.* **~eins werden/ sein** agree/have agreed terms with sb.; **~flotte die** merchant fleet; **~gesellschaft die** company; **~klasse die** grade; **~marine die** merchant navy; **~partner der** trading partner; **~register das** register of companies; **~schiff das** merchant ship; **~schule die** commercial college; **~straße die** *(hist.)* trade route; **~üblich** *Adj.* **~übliche Praktiken/Größen** standard business practices/standard [commercial] sizes; **~unternehmen das** trading concern; **~vertreter der** [sales] representative; travelling salesman/ saleswoman; **~vertretung die** trade mission; **~zentrum das** trading centre

hände·ringend *Adv. (ugs.: dringend)* ⟨*need*⟩ urgently; ⟨*search for sb./sth.*⟩ desperately

hand-, Hand-: **~feger der** brush; **~fest** *Adj.* robust; sturdy; substantial ⟨*meal etc.*⟩; **c)** solid ⟨*proof*⟩; concrete ⟨*suggestion*⟩; complete ⟨*lie*⟩; well-founded ⟨*argument*⟩; **~fläche die** palm [of one's/the hand]; flat of one's/the hand; **~gas das** *(Kfz-W.)* hand throttle; **~gearbeitet** *Adj.* hand-made; **~gelenk das** wrist; **~gemenge das** fight; **~gepäck das** hand-baggage; **~geschrieben** *Adj.* handwritten; **~granate die** handgrenade; **~greiflich** *Adj.* **a)** *(tätlich)* **~greiflich werden** start using one's fists; **b)** tangible ⟨*success, advantage, proof, etc.*⟩; palpable ⟨*contradiction,*

error⟩; obvious ⟨*fact*⟩; **~griff der a)** **mit einem ~griff/wenigen ~griffen** in one movement/without much trouble; *(schnell)* in no time at all/next to no time; **b)** *(am Koffer, an einem Werkzeug)* handle; **~habe die;** ~, **~n: eine [rechtliche] ~habe [gegen jmdn.]** a legal handle [against sb.]; **~haben** *tr. V.* **a)** handle; operate ⟨*device, machine*⟩; **b)** *(praktizieren)* implement ⟨*law etc.*⟩; **~habung die;** ~, **~en a)** handling; *(eines Gerätes, einer Maschine)* operation; **b)** *(Durchführung)* implementation

Handikap ['hɛndikɛp] **das;** ~s, ~s *(auch Sport)* handicap; **handikapen** ['hɛndikɛpn] *tr. V.* handicap

Hand-: **~käse der** *(landsch.)* small, hand-formed curd cheese; **~koffer der** [small] suitcase; **~kuß der** kiss on sb.'s hand; **~langer der;** ~s, ~ *(ungelernter·Arbeiter)* labourer; *(abwertend)* lackey; **~lauf der** handrail

Händler der; ~s, ~: trader

handlich *Adj.* handy; easily carried ⟨*parcel, suitcase*⟩; easily portable ⟨*television, camera*⟩

Handlung die; ~, **~en a)** *(Vorgehen)* action; *(Tat)* act; **b)** *(Fabel)* plot

handlungs-, Handlungs-: **~fähig** *Adj.* able to act *pred.;* working *attrib.* ⟨*majority*⟩; **~freiheit die;** *o. Pl.* freedom of action; **~reisende der/die** *s.* **Handelsvertreter;** **~weise die** conduct

hand-, Hand-: **puppe die** glove *or* hand puppet; **~schelle die** handcuff; **~schlag der** handshake; **~schrift die** handwriting; **~schriftlich 1.** *Adj.* hand-written; **2.** *adv.* by hand; **~schuh der** glove; **~schuhfach das** glove compartment; **~signiert** *Adj.* signed; **~spiegel der** hand-mirror; **~stand der** *(Turnen)* handstand; **~tasche die** handbag; **~tuch das;** *Pl.* -tücher towel; **~umdrehen: im ~umdrehen** in no time at all; **~voll die;** ~ *(auch fig.)* handful

Hand·werk das craft; *(als Beruf)* trade; **sein ~ kennen** *od.* **verstehen/beherrschen** know one's job; **Handwerker der;** ~s, ~: tradesman; **handwerklich** *Adj.* **ein ~er Beruf** a [skilled] trade; **Handwerks·zeug das** tools *pl.*

Hand·zeichen das sign [with one's hand]; *(eines Autofahrers)* hand signal; *(Abstimmung)* show of hands

Hanf der; ~[e]s hemp

Hang der; ~|e|s, **Hänge** slope; *(Neigung)* tendency
Hänge-: ~**brücke** die suspension bridge; ~**lampe** die pendant-light; ~**matte** die hammock
¹**hängen** *unr. itr. V.; südd., österr., schweiz. mit sein* hang (**an** + *Dat.* from); *(an einem Fahrzeug)* be hitched (**an** + *Dat.* to); ²**hängen 1.** *tr. V.* **a)** hang (**in/über** + *(Akk.)* in/over; **an/ auf** + *Akk.* on); *(befestigen)* hitch up (**an** + *Akk.* to); couple on ⟨*railway carriage, etc.*⟩ (**an** + *Akk.* to); **2.** *refl. V.* **a)** sich an etw. *(Akk.)* ~: hang on to sth.; **b)** *(sich festsetzen)* cling (**an** + *Akk.* to); **hängen|bleiben** *unr. itr. V.; mit sein (ugs.)* **a)** *(festgehalten werden)* [mit dem Ärmel *usw.*] **an/in** etw. *(Dat.)* ~: get one's sleeve *etc.* caught on/in sth.; **b)** *(verweilen)* get stuck *(coll.)*; **c)** *(haften)* **an/auf** etw. *(Dat.)* ~: stick to sth.; **hängend** *Adj.* hanging; **Hänge·schrank** der wall-cupboard
hänseln *tr. V.* tease
Hanse·stadt die Hanseatic city
Hantel die; ~, ~n *(Sport)(kurz)* dumbbell; *(lang)* barbell
hantieren *itr. V.* be busy
Häppchen das; ~s, ~ a) [small] morsel; **b)** *(Appetithappen)* canapé
Happen der; ~s, ~: morsel
happig *Adj. (ugs.)* ~e Preise fancy prices *(coll.)*
Happy-End ['hɛpi'|ɛnt] das; ~|s|, ~s happy ending
Harfe die; ~, ~n harp
Harke die; ~, ~n rake; **harken** *tr. V.* rake
harm·los 1. *Adj.* **a)** *(ungefährlich)* harmless; slight ⟨*injury, cold, etc.*⟩; mild ⟨*illness*⟩; safe ⟨*medicine, bend, road, etc.*⟩; **b)** *(arglos)* innocent; harmless ⟨*fun, pastime, etc.*⟩; **2.** *adv.* **a)** *(ungefährlich)* harmlessly; **b)** *(arglos)* innocently; **Harmlosigkeit** die; ~ **a)** *(Ungefährlichkeit)* harmlessness; *(einer Krankheit)* mildness; *(eines Medikamentes)* safety; **b)** *(Arglosigkeit, harmloses Verhalten)* innocence
Harmonie die; ~, ~n *(auch fig.)* harmony; **harmonieren** *itr. V.* **a)** harmonize; **b)** *(miteinander auskommen)* get on well
Harmonika die; ~, ~s *od.* **Harmoniken** harmonica
harmonisch 1. *Adj.* harmonious; *(Musik)* harmonic; **2.** *adv.* harmoniously; *(Musik)* harmonically

Harmonium das; ~s, **Harmonien** harmonium
Harn der; ~|e|s, ~e *(Med.)* urine; **Harn·blase** die bladder
Harnisch der; ~s, ~e armour
Harpune die; ~, ~n harpoon
harren *itr. V. (geh.)* jmds./einer Sache *od.* auf jmdn./etw. ~: await sb./sth.
harsch 1. *Adj.* **a)** *(vereist)* crusted; **b)** *(barsch)* harsh; **2.** *adv.* harshly; **Harsch** der; ~|e|s crusted snow
hart; härter, härtest... 1. *Adj.* **a)** hard; **b)** tough ⟨*situation, job*⟩; harsh ⟨*reality, truth*⟩; **c)** *(streng)* harsh ⟨*penalty, punishment, judgement*⟩; tough ⟨*measure, law, course*⟩; **d)** *(rauh)* rough ⟨*game, opponent*⟩; **2.** *adv.* hard chair; **a)** *(mühevoll)* ⟨*work*⟩ hard; **b)** *(streng)* harshly; **c)** *(nahe)* close (**an** + *Dat.* to); **Härte** die; ~, ~n **a)** *(auch Physik)* hardness; **b)** *(Widerstandsfähigkeit)* toughness; **c)** *(schwere Belastung)* hardship; **d)** *(Strenge)* harshness; **e)** *(Heftigkeit)* *(eines Aufpralls usw.)* force; *(eines Streits)* violence; **f)** *(Rauheit)* roughness; **Härte·fall** der **a)** case of hardship; **b)** *(ugs.: Person)* hardship case; **härten** *tr., itr. V.* harden; **härter** *s.* **hart; härtest...** *s.* **hart**
hart-, Hart-: ~**gekocht** *Adj.* hard-boiled ⟨*egg*⟩; ~**geld** das coins *pl.;* ~**herzig 1.** *Adj.* hard-hearted; **2.** *adv.* hard-heartedly; ~**herzigkeit** die; ~: hard-heartedness; ~**näckig 1.** *Adj.* **a)** *(eigensinnig)* obstinate; stubborn; **b)** *(ausdauernd)* dogged; **2.** *adv.* **a)** *(eigensinnig)* obstinately; stubbornly; **b)** *(ausdauernd)* doggedly; ~**näckigkeit** die; ~ **a)** *(Eigensinn)* obstinacy; stubbornness; **b)** *(Ausdauer)* doggedness; ~**wurst** die dry sausage
Harz das; ~es, ~e resin
Harzer Käse der; ~ ~s, ~ ~: Harz [Mountain] cheese
Haschee *(Kochk.)* das; ~s, ~s hash
¹**haschen** *tr. V. (veralt.)* catch
²**haschen** *itr. V. (ugs.)* smoke [hash] *(coll.)*
Häschen ['hɛːsçən] das; ~, ~: bunny
Haschisch das *od.* der; ~|s| hashish
Hase der; ~n, ~n **a)** hare; **b)** *(landsch.)* *s.* **Kaninchen**
Hasel·nuß die hazel-nut
Hasen-: ~**fuß** der *(spöttisch abwertend)* coward; chicken *(sl.);* ~**scharte** die *(Med.)* harelip
Haspel die; ~, ~n *(Technik) (für Garn)* reel; *(für ein Seil, Kabel)* drum

Haß der; **Hasses** hatred (**auf** + *Akk.*, gegen of, for); **hassen** *tr., itr. V.* hate; **haß·erfüllt** *Adj.* filled with hatred *postpos.*

häßlich 1. *Adj.* a) ugly; b) *(gemein)* nasty; c) *(unangenehm)* awful ⟨*weather, cold, situation, etc.*⟩; 2. *adv.* a) ⟨*dress*⟩ unattractively; b) *(gemein)* nastily; **Häßlichkeit die;** ~, ~**en** a) *o. Pl. (Aussehen)* ugliness; b) *o. Pl. (Gesinnung)* nastiness

hast 2. *Pers. Sg. Präsens v.* **haben**

Hast die; ~: haste; **hasten** *itr. V.; mit sein* hurry; **hastig** 1. *Adj.* hasty; hurried; 2. *adv.* hastily; hurriedly

hat 3. *Pers. Sg. Präsens v.* **haben**

hätscheln *tr. V.* caress

hatschi *Interj.* atishoo

hatte *1. u. 3. Pers. Sg. Prät. v.* **haben**; **hätte** *1. u. 3. Pers. Sg. Konjunktiv II v.* **haben**

Haube die; ~, ~**n** a) bonnet; *(einer Krankenschwester)* cap; b) *(Kfz-W.)* bonnet *(Brit.);* hood *(Amer.)*

Hauch der; ~|e|s, ~e *(geh.)* a) *(Atem, auch fig.)* breath; b) *(Luftzug)* breath of wind; c) *(leichter Duft)* delicate smell; d) *(dünne Schicht)* [gossamer-]thin layer; **hauch·dünn** *Adj.* gossamer-thin ⟨*material, dress*⟩; wafer-thin ⟨*layer, slice, majority*⟩; **hauchen** *itr. V.* breathe (**gegen, auf** + *Akk.* on)

Haue die; ~, ~**n** a) *(südd., österr.: Hacke)* hoe; b) *(ugs.: Prügel)* a hiding *(coll.);* **hauen** 1. *unr. tr. V.* a) *(ugs.: schlagen)* belt; clobber *(coll.);* b) *(ugs.: auf einen Körperteil)* belt *(coll.);* hit; c) *(herstellen)* carve ⟨*figure, statue, etc.*⟩ (**in** + *Akk.* in); 2. *unr. itr. V.* a) *(ugs.: prügeln)* **er haut immer gleich** he's quick to hit out; b) *(auf einen Körperteil)* belt *(coll.);* hit; c) *(ugs.: auf/gegen etw. schlagen)* thump; 3. *unr. refl. V. (ugs.: sich prügeln)* have a punch-up *(coll.)*

Haufen der; ~s, ~: heap; pile; *(Gruppe)* bunch *(coll.);* **häufen** 1. *tr. V.* heap, pile (**auf** + *Akk.* on to); *(aufheben)* hoard ⟨*money, supplies*⟩; 2. *refl. V. (sich mehren)* pile up

häufig 1. *Adj.* frequent; 2. *adv.* frequently; often; **Häufigkeit die;** ~, ~**en** frequency; **Häufung die;** ~, ~**en** increasing frequency

Haupt das; ~|e|s, **Häupter** *(geh., auch fig.)* head

haupt-, Haupt-: ~**bahnhof** der main station; ~**beruflich** 1. *Adj.* sei-

ne ~**berufliche Tätigkeit** his main occupation; 2. *adv.* **er ist** ~**beruflich als Elektriker tätig** his main occupation is that of electrician; ~**darsteller** der *(Theater, Film)* male lead; ~**darstellerin** die *(Theater, Film)* female lead; ~**eingang** der main entrance; ~**fach** das major; ~**figur** die main character; ~**film** der main feature; ~**gebäude** das main building; ~**gericht** das main course; ~**gewinn** der first prize

Häuptling der; ~s, ~e chief[tain]

haupt-, Haupt-: ~**mahlzeit** die main meal; ~**mann** der; *Pl.* ~**leute** *(Milit.)* captain; ~**person** die central figure; ~**postamt** das main post office; ~**quartier** das *(Milit., auch fig.)* headquarters *sing. or pl.;* ~**rolle** die main role; lead; ~**sache** die main thing; ~**sächlich** 1. *Adv.* mainly; principally; 2. *Adj.; nicht präd.* main; principal; ~**saison** die high season; ~**satz** der main clause; *(alleinstehend)* sentence; ~**schlagader** die aorta; ~**schul·abschluß** der ≈ secondary school leaving certificate; ~**schule** die ≈ secondary modern school; ~**stadt** die capital [city]; ~**städtisch** *Adj.* metropolitan; ~**straße** die main street; ~**verkehr** der the bulk of the traffic

Hauptverkehrs-: ~**straße** die main road; ~**zeit** die rush hour

Haupt-: ~**wache** die main police station; ~**wort** das *(Sprachw.)* noun

hau ruck *Interj.* heave[-ho]

Haus das; ~es, **Häuser** house; *(Amts-, Firmengebäude usw.)* building; *(Heim)* home; **nach** ~**e** home; **zu** ~**e** at home; **das erste** ~ **am Platze** the best hotel in the town

haus-, Haus-: ~**angestellte** der/die domestic servant; ~**apotheke** die medicine cabinet; ~**arbeit** die housework; *(Schulw.)* homework; ~**arrest** der house arrest; ~**arzt** der family doctor; ~**aufgabe** die homework; ~**backen** 1. *Adj.* plain; unadventurous ⟨*clothes*⟩; 2. *adv.* ⟨*dress*⟩ unadventurously; ~**besetzer** der squatter; ~**besitzer** der house-owner; *(Vermieter)* landlord; ~**besitzerin** die house-owner; *(Vermieterin)* landlady; ~**besuch** der house-call; ~**boot** das houseboat

Häuschen ['hɔysçən] das; ~s, ~: small house; **aus dem** ~ **sein** *(ugs.)* be over the moon *(coll.);* **hausen** *itr. V.*

(ugs. abwertend) live; b) *(Verwüstungen anrichten)* [furchtbar] ~: wreak havoc; **Häuser·block der** block [of houses]

haus-, Haus-: ~**flur der** hall[way]; *(im Obergeschoß)* landing; ~**frau die** housewife; **freund der a)** friend of the family; *(verhüll.: Liebhaber)* manfriend *(euphem.);* ~**friedensbruch der** *(Rechtsw.)* trespass; ~**gebrauch der** domestic use; **das reicht für den** ~**gebrauch** *(ugs.)* it's good enough to get by *(coll.);* ~**gehilfin die** [home] help; ~**gemacht** *Adj.* home-made

Haus·halt der a) household; b) *(Arbeit im* ~*)* housekeeping; **jmdm. den** ~ **führen** keep house for sb.; c) *(Politik)* budget; **haus|halten** *unr. itr. V.* be economical **(mit** with); **Haushälterin die;** ~, ~**nen** housekeeper

Haushalts-: ~**debatte, die** *(Politik)* budget debatte; ~**geld das;** *o. Pl.* housekeeping money; ~**jahr das** financial year; ~**kasse die** housekeeping money; ~**plan der** budget; ~**waren** *Pl.* household goods

Haus·herr der a) *(Familienoberhaupt)* head of the household; b) *(als Gastgeber)* host; c) *(Rechtsspr.)* *(Eigentümer)* owner; *(Mieter)* occupier; **haushoch 1.** *Adj.* as high as a house; *(fig.)* overwhelming; **2.** *adv. (fig.)* ~ **gewinnen** win hands down

hausieren *itr. V.* |mit etw.| ~: hawk [sth.]; peddle [sth.]; „Hausieren verboten" 'no hawkers'; **Hausierer der;** ~s, ~: pedlar; hawker

häuslich *Adj.* a) domestic; b) *(das Zuhause liebend)* home-loving

Hausmacher·art die: nach ~: home-made-style *attrib.*

Hausmanns·kost die plain cooking

Haus-: ~**marke die a)** house wine; b) *(ugs.: bevorzugtes Getränk)* favourite tipple *(coll.);* ~**meister der,** ~**meisterin die** caretaker; ~**mittel das** household remedy; ~**musik die** music at home; ~**nummer die** house number; ~**ordnung die** house rules *pl.;* ~**putz der** spring-clean; *(regelmäßig)* clean-out; ~**rat der** household goods *pl.;* ~**schlüssel der** front-door key; house-key; ~**schuh der** slipper **Haussuchung die;** ~, ~**en** house search; **Haussuchungs·befehl der** search warrant

Haus-: ~**tier das a)** pet; b) *(Nutztier)* domestic animal; ~**tür die** front door; ~**verbot das** ban on entering the

house/pub/restaurant *etc.;* ~**verwalter der** manager [of the block]; ~**wirt der** landlord; ~**wirtin die** landlady; ~**wirtschaft die;** *o. Pl.* domestic science and home economics

Haut die; ~, **Häute** skin; **aus der** ~ **fahren** *(ugs.)* go up the wall *(coll.);* **Haut·arzt der** skin specialist; **häuten 1.** *tr. V.* skin; flay; **2.** *refl. V.* shed its skin/their skins

haut-, Haut-: ~**eng** *Adj.* skin-tight; ~**farbe die** [skin] colour; ~**krankheit die** skin disease

Haxe die; ~, ~**n** *s.* Hachse

he *Interj. (ugs.)* hey

Heb·amme die midwife

Hebel der; ~s, ~: lever

heben *unr. tr. V.* **a)** lift; raise ⟨*baton, camera, glass*⟩; b) *(verbessern)* raise ⟨*standard, level*⟩; increase ⟨*turnover, self-confidence*⟩; improve ⟨*mood*⟩; enhance ⟨*standing*⟩; boost ⟨*morale*⟩

¹**hecheln** *itr. V. (ugs. abwertend)* gossip

²**hecheln** *itr. V.* pant [for breath]

Hecht der; ~|e|s, ~**e** pike; **Hecht·sprung der a)** *(Turnen)* Hecht vault; b) *(Schwimmen)* racing dive; *(vom Sprungturm)* pike-dive

Heck das; ~|e|s, ~**e** *od.* ~**s** stern; *(Flugzeug*~*)* tail; *(Auto*~*)* rear

Hecke die; ~, ~**n a)** hedge; b) *(wildwachsend)* thicket

Hecken-: ~**rose die** dogrose; ~**schütze der** sniper

Heck·scheibe die rear window

Heer das; ~|e|s, ~**e** armed forces *pl.;* *(für den Landkrieg, fig.)* army

Hefe die; ~, ~**n** yeast

¹**Heft das;** ~|e|s, ~**e** *(geh.)* haft; handle

²**Heft das;** ~|e|s, ~**e a)** *(bes. Schule)* exercise-book; b) *(Nummer einer Zeitschrift)* issue; **Heftchen das;** ~s, ~: book [of tickets/stamps *etc.*]; **heften 1.** *tr. V.* **a)** *(mit einer Nadel)* pin; *(mit einer Klammer)* clip; *(mit Klebstoff)* stick; b) *(Schneiderei)* tack; c) *(Buchbinderei)* stitch; *(mit Klammern)* staple; **2.** *refl. V.* **sich an jmds. Fersen** *(Akk.)* ~: stick hard on sb.'s heels

heftig 1. *Adj.* violent; heavy ⟨*rain, shower, blow*⟩; severe ⟨*pain*⟩; ⟨*person*⟩ with a violent temper; **2.** *adv.* ⟨*rain, snow, breathe*⟩ heavily; ⟨*hit*⟩ hard; ⟨*quarrel*⟩ violently

Heft-: ~**klammer die** staple; ~**pflaster das** sticking plaster; ~**zwecke die** *s.* Reißzwecke

hegen *tr. V.* **a)** *(bes. Forstw., Jagdw.)*

look after, tend; **b)** *(geh.: umsorgen)* look after; **c)** *(fig.)* feel ⟨contempt, hatred, mistrust⟩; cherish ⟨hope, wish, desire⟩; harbour ⟨grudge, suspicion⟩

Hehl der *od.* das: **kein|en| ~ aus etw. machen** make no secret of sth.; **Hehler** der; ~s, ~: receiver [of stolen goods]; **Hehlerei die;** ~, ~en *(Rechtsw.)* receiving [stolen goods] *no art.*

¹Heide der; ~n, ~n heathen

²Heide die; ~, ~n **a)** heath; *(~landschaft)* heathland; **Heide·kraut das;** *o. Pl.* heather

Heidel·beere die bilberry

heidnisch *Adj.* heathen

heikel *Adj.* **a)** *(schwierig)* delicate, ticklish ⟨matter, subject⟩; ticklish tricky ⟨problem, question, situation⟩; **b)** *(wählerisch)* fussy **(in bezug auf +** *Akk.* **about)**

heil *Adj. (nicht entzwei)* in one piece; **wieder ~ sein** ⟨injured part⟩ have healed [up]; **Heil das;** ~s a) *(Wohlergehen)* benefit; **b)** *(Rel.)* salvation; **Heiland der;** ~|e|s, ~e Saviour

Heil·anstalt die *(Anstalt für Kranke od. Süchtige)* sanatorium; *(psychiatrische Klinik)* mental hospital; **heilbar** *Adj.* curable

Heil·butt der halibut

heilen 1. *tr. V.* cure; heal ⟨wound⟩; **2.** *itr. V.; mit sein* ⟨wound⟩ heal [up]; ⟨fracture⟩ mend

heil·froh *Adj.* very glad

heilig *Adj.* **a)** holy; **die Heilige Schrift** the Holy Scriptures *pl.;* **der Heilige Abend** Christmas Eve **b)** *(geh.: unantastbar)* sacred ⟨right, tradition, cause, etc.⟩; **Heilig·abend der** Christmas Eve; **Heilige der/die;** *adj. Dekl.* saint; **heiligen** *tr. V.* keep ⟨tradition, Sabbath, etc.⟩; **der Zweck heiligt die Mittel** the end justifies the means; **Heiligen·schein der** gloriole; *(um den Kopf)* halo; **Heiligkeit die;** ~: holiness; **Heiligtum das;** ~s, Heiligtümer shrine

Heil-: ~**kraut das** medicinal herb; ~**mittel das** *(auch fig.)* remedy **(gegen** for); *(Medikament)* medicament; ~**praktiker der** non-medical practitioner

heilsam *Adj.* salutary; **Heils·armee die** Salvation Army; **Heilung die;** ~, ~en *(einer Wunde)* healing; *(von Krankheit, Kranken)* curing

Heim das; ~|e|s, ~e a) *(Zuhause)* home; **b)** *(Anstalt, Alters~)* home; *(für*

Obdachlose) hostel; **Heim·arbeit die** outwork

Heimat die; ~, ~en **a)** *(~ort)* home; home town/village; *(~land)* home; homeland; **b)** *(Ursprungsland)* natural habitat

Heimat-: ~**kunde die** local history, geography, and natural history; ~**land das** native land; *(fig.)* home

heimatlich *Adj.* native ⟨dialect⟩; nostalgic ⟨emotions⟩

heimat-, Heimat-: ~**los** *Adj.* homeless; ~**museum das** museum of local history; ~**ort der** home town/village; ~**vertriebene der/die;** *adj. Dekl.* expellee [from his/her homeland]

heim-, Heim-: ~|**bringen** *unr. tr. V.* **a)** jmdn. ~: take *or.* see sb. home; **b)** bring home; ~|**fahren 1.** *unr. itr. V.; mit sein* drive home; **2.** *unr. tr. V.* drive home; ~**fahrt die** journey home; *(mit dem Auto)* drive home; ~|**gehen** *unr. itr. V.; mit sein* go home

heimisch *Adj. (einheimisch)* indigenous, native ⟨plants, animals, etc.⟩ **(in** + *Dat.* to); domestic ⟨industry⟩; **sich ~ fühlen** feel at home; **~ werden [in (** + *Dat.)]* settle in[to]

heim-, Heim-: ~**kehr die;** ~: return home; homecoming; ~|**kehren** *itr. V.; mit sein* return home (**aus** from); ~|**kommen** *unr. itr. V.; mit sein* come home

heimlich 1. *Adj.* secret; **2.** *adv.* secretly; **Heimlichkeit die;** ~, ~en; *meist Pl.* secret

heim-, Heim-: ~**reise die** journey home; ~|**suchen** *tr. V.* ⟨storm, earthquake, epidemic⟩ strike; ⟨disease⟩ afflict; ⟨nightmares, doubts⟩ plague; ~**tückisch 1.** *Adj. (bösartig)* malicious; *(fig.)* insidious ⟨disease⟩; **2.** *adv.* maliciously; ~**wärts** *Adv. (nach Hause zu)* home; *(in Richtung Heimat)* homeward[s]; ~**weg der** way home-; ~**weh das** homesickness; ~**weh haben** be homesick (**nach** for); ~|**zahlen** *tr. V.* jmdm. etw. ~**zahlen** pay sb. back for sth.

Heinzel·männchen das brownie

Heirat die; ~, ~en marriage; **heiraten 1.** *itr. V.* get married; **2.** *tr. V.* marry

Heirats-: ~**antrag der:** jmdm. einen ~**antrag machen** propose to sb.; ~**anzeige die** announcement of a/the forthcoming marriage; ~**schwindler der** *person who makes a spurious offer of marriage for purposes of fraud*

heiser 1. *Adj.* hoarse; **2.** *adv.* in a hoarse voice; **Heiserkeit die;** ~ *s.* heiser: hoarseness
heiß 1. *Adj.* hot; **jmdm. ist** ~: sb. feels hot; **etw.** ~ **machen** heat sth. up; heated ⟨*debate, argument*⟩; fierce ⟨*fight, battle*⟩; ardent ⟨*wish, love*⟩; **ein** ~**es Thema** a controversial subject; **2.** *adv.* ⟨*fight*⟩ fiercely; ⟨*love*⟩ dearly; ⟨*long*⟩ fervently
heißen *unr. itr. V.* (*den Namen tragen*) be called; (*bedeuten*) mean; (*lauten*) ⟨*saying*⟩ go; (*unpers.*) **es heißt, daß ...:** they say that ...; **in dem Artikel heißt es ...:** in the article it says that ...
heiter *Adj.* cheerful; fine ⟨*weather, day*⟩; **Heiterkeit die;** ~ **a)** (*Frohsinn*) cheerfulness; **b)** (*Belustigung*) merriment
heizbar *Adj.* heated; **Heiz·decke die** electric blanket; **heizen 1.** *itr. V.* have the heating on; **2.** *tr. V.* heat ⟨*room etc.*⟩; **Heizer der;** ~**s,** ~ (*einer Lokomotive*) fireman; (*eines Schiffes*) stoker
Heiz-: ~**kissen das** heating pad; ~**körper der** radiator; ~**ofen der** stove; heater; ~**platte die** hotplate
Heizung die; ~, ~**en a)** [central] heating *no pl., no indef. art.;* **b)** (*ugs.: Heizkörper*) radiator
Hektar das *od.* **der;** ~**s,** ~**e** hectare
Hektik die; ~: hectic rush; (*des Lebens*) hectic pace; **hektisch** *Adj.* hectic
Held der; ~**en,** ~**en** hero; **heldenhaft 1.** *Adj.* heroic; **2.** *adv.* heroically; **Heldentum das;** ~**s** heroism; **Heldin die;** ~, ~**nen** heroine
helfen *unr. itr. V.* help; **jmdm. [bei etw.]** ~: help sb. [with sth.]; (*unpers.*) **es hilft nichts** it's no use *or* good; **Helfer der;** ~**s,** ~: helper; (*Mitarbeiter*) assistant; (*eines Verbrechens*) accomplice
Helikopter der; ~**s,** ~: helicopter
hell 1. *Adj.* **a)** (*von Licht erfüllt*) light; well-lit ⟨*stairs*⟩; **b)** (*klar*) bright ⟨*day, sky, etc.*⟩; **c)** (*viel Licht spendend*) bright ⟨*light, lamp, star, etc.*⟩; **d)** (*blaß*) light ⟨*colour*⟩; fair ⟨*skin, hair*⟩; light-coloured ⟨*clothes*⟩; **e)** (*akustisch*) high, clear ⟨*sound, voice*⟩; ringing ⟨*laugh*⟩; **f)** (*klug*) bright; **g)** (*ugs.: absolut*) sheer, utter ⟨*madness, foolishness, despair*⟩; **2.** *adv.* brightly
hell-: ~**blau** *Adj.* light blue; ~**blond** *Adj.* very fair; light blonde
Helle das; *adj. Dekl.* ≈ lager

Heller der; ~**s,** ~: heller; **bis auf den letzten** ~**/bis auf** ~ **und Pfennig** (*ugs.*) down to the last penny *or* (*Amer.*) cent
hell-: ~**grün** *Adj.* light green; ~**häutig** *Adj.* fair-skinned
Helligkeit die; ~, ~**en** (*auch Physik*) brightness
hell-, Hell-: ~**rot** *Adj.* light red; ~**sehen** *unr. itr. V.; nur im Inf.* ~**sehen können** have second sight; ~**seher der** clairvoyant; ~**wach** *Adj.* wide awake
Helm der; ~**[e]s,** ~**e** helmet
Hemd das; ~**[e]s,** ~**en** shirt; (*Unterhemd*) [under]vest; undershirt; **Hemds·ärmel der** shirt-sleeve
hemmen *tr. V.* **a)** (*verlangsamen*) slow [down]; **b)** (*aufhalten*) check; stem ⟨*flow*⟩; **c)** (*beeinträchtigen*) hinder; **Hemmung die;** ~, ~**en a)** (*Gehemmtheit*) inhibition; **b)** (*Bedenken*) scruple; **hemmungs·los 1.** *Adj.* unrestrained; **2.** *adv.* unrestrainedly
Hendl das; ~**s,** ~**[n]** (*bayr., österr.*) chicken; (*Brathähnchen*) [roast] chicken
Hengst der; ~**[e]s,** ~**e** (*Pferd*) stallion
Henkel der; ~**s,** ~: handle
Henker der; ~**s,** ~: hangman; (*Scharfrichter, auch fig.*) executioner
Henne die; ~, ~**n** hen
her [heːɐ̯] *Adv.* ~ **damit** give it to me; give it here (*coll.*); **vom Fenster** ~: from the window; **von ihrer Kindheit** ~: since childhood; **von der Konzeption** ~: as far as the basic design is concerned
herab *Adv.* down; **von oben** ~ (*fig.*) condescendingly
herab-: ~**|hängen** *unr. itr. V.* hang [down] (*von* from); ~**hängende Schultern** drooping shoulders; ~**|lassen 1.** *unr. tr. V.* let down; lower; **2.** *unr. refl. V.* (*iron.: bereit sein*) **sich** ~**lassen, etw. zu tun** condescend to do sth.; ~**|lassend 1.** *Adj.* condescending; patronizing (*zu* towards); **2.** *adv.* condescendingly; patronizingly; ~**|sehen** *unr. itr. V.* **auf jmdn.** ~**sehen** look down on sb.; ~**|setzen** *tr. V.* **a)** reduce; **b)** (*abwerten*) belittle
heran *Adv.* **an etw.** (*Akk.*) ~: right up to sth.
heran-, Heran-: ~**|bilden** *tr. V.* train [up]; (*auf der Schule, Universität*) educate; ~**|bringen** *unr. tr. V.* **a)** bring [up] (**an** + *Akk.,* **zu** to); **b)** (*vertraut machen*) **jmdn. an etw.** (*Akk.*) ~**bringen** introduce sb. to sth.; ~**|fahren**

unr. itr. V.; mit sein drive up (**an** + *Akk.* to); ~|**kommen** *unr. itr. V.; mit sein* **an etw.** *(Akk.)* ~**kommen** come near to sth.; *(erreichen)* reach sth.; *(erwerben)* obtain sth.; ~|**reifen** *itr. V.; mit sein* ⟨*fruit, crops*⟩ ripen; **zur Frau** ~**reifen** mature into a woman; ~|**treten** *unr. itr. V.; mit sein (sich wenden)* **an jmdn.** ~**treten** approach sb.; ~|**wachsen** *unr. itr. V.; mit sein* grow up; ~**wachsende der/die;** *adj. Dekl.* young person; ~|**ziehen** *unr. tr. V.* pull over; pull up ⟨*chair*⟩; **etw. zu sich** ~**ziehen** pull sth. towards one **herauf** *Adv.* up
herauf-: ~|**beschwören** *tr. V.* **a)** *(verursachen)* cause ⟨*disaster, war, crisis*⟩; **b)** *(erinnern)* evoke ⟨*memories etc.*⟩; ~|**kommen** *unr. itr. V.; mit sein (nach oben kommen)* come up; ~|**setzen** *tr. V.* increase, put up ⟨*prices, rents, interest rates, etc.*⟩
heraus *Adv.* ~ **aus den Federn!/dem Bett!** rise and shine!/out of bed!
heraus-: ~|**bekommen** *unr. tr. V.* **a)** *(entfernen)* get out (**aus** of); **b)** *(ugs.: lösen)* work out ⟨*problem, answer, etc.*⟩; solve ⟨*puzzle*⟩; **c)** *(ermitteln)* find out; **d)** *(als Wechselgeld bekommen)* **5 DM** ~**bekommen** get back 5 marks change; **ich bekomme noch 5 DM** ~: I still have 5 marks [change] to come; ~|**bringen** *unr. tr. V.* **a)** *(nach außen bringen)* bring out (**aus** of); **b)** *(nach draußen begleiten)* show out; **c)** *(veröffentlichen)* bring out; *(aufführen)* put on, stage ⟨*play*⟩; screen ⟨*film*⟩; **d)** *(auf den Markt bringen)* bring out; **e)** *(populär machen)* make widely known; ~|**fahren** **1.** *unr. itr. V.; mit sein* **a)** *(nach außen fahren)* **aus etw.** ~**fahren** drive/ride out of sth.; **b)** *(fahrend* ~*kommen)* come out; **2.** *unr. tr. V.* **den Wagen [aus dem Hof]** ~**fahren** drive the car out [of the yard]; **jmdn.** ~**fahren** drive sb. out (**zu** to); ~|**finden** **1.** *unr. tr. V.* find out; trace ⟨*fault*⟩; **2.** *unr. itr. V.* find one's way out (**aus** of); ~|**fordern** **1.** *tr. V.* **a)** *(auch Sport)* challenge; **b)** *(heraufbeschwören)* provoke ⟨*person, resistance, etc.*⟩; invite ⟨*criticism*⟩; court ⟨*danger*⟩; **2.** *itr. V.* **zu etw.** ~**fordern** provoke sth.; ~**forderung die** *(auch Sport)* challenge; *(Provokation)* provocation; ~|**geben** **1.** *unr. tr. V.* **a)** *(aushändigen)* hand over ⟨*property, person, hostage, etc.*⟩; *(zurückgeben)* give back; **b)** *(als Wechselgeld zurückgeben)* **5 DM/zuviel** ~**ge-**

ben give 5 marks/too much change; **c)** *(veröffentlichen)* publish; **d)** issue ⟨*stamp, coin, etc.*⟩; **2.** *itr. V.* give change; ~**geber der** publisher; *(Redakteur)* editor; ~|**gehen** *unr. itr. V.; mit sein* **a)** go out (**aus** of); **b)** *(sich entfernen lassen)* ⟨*stain etc.*⟩ come out; ~|**halten** *unr. refl. V.* keep out; ~|**hängen** *tr. V.* hang out (**aus** of); ~|**helfen** *unr. itr. V.* **jmdm.** ~**helfen** *(auch fig.)* help sb. out (**aus** of); ~|**holen** *tr. V.* **a)** *(nach außen holen)* bring out; **b)** *(ugs.: erwirken)* win ⟨*wage increase, advantage, etc.*⟩; ~|**kommen** *unr. itr. V.; mit sein* **a)** come out (**aus** of); **b)** *(erscheinen; ugs.: auf den Markt kommen, bekannt werden)* come out; ~|**nehmen** *unr. tr. V.* **a)** take out (**aus** of); **b)** *(ugs.: entfernen)* take out ⟨*appendix, tonsils, tooth, etc.*⟩; ~|**reden** *refl. V. (ugs.)* talk one's way out (**aus** of); ~|**reißen** *unr. tr. V.* **a)** tear out (**aus** of); pull up ⟨*plant*⟩; ~|**rutschen** *itr. V.; mit sein (ugs.)* ⟨*remark etc.*⟩ slip out; ~|**stellen** *refl. V.* **es stellte sich** ~, **daß** ...: it turned out that ...; ~|**suchen** *tr. V.* pick out; look out ⟨*file*⟩
herb *Adj.* [slightly] sharp ⟨*taste*⟩; dry ⟨*wine*⟩; [slightly] sharp ⟨*smell, perfume*⟩; bitter ⟨*disappointment*⟩; severe ⟨*face, features*⟩; austere ⟨*beauty*⟩; harsh ⟨*words, criticism*⟩
herbei-: ~|**eilen** *itr. V.; mit sein* hurry over; ~|**laufen** *unr. itr. V.; mit sein* come running up
Herberge die; ~, ~**n** *(veralt.: Gasthaus)* inn
her|bringen *unr. tr. V.* **etw.** ~: bring sth. [here]
Herbst der; ~[**e**]**s,** ~**e** autumn; fall *(Amer.);* s. auch **Frühling; Herbstanfang der** beginning of autumn; **herbstlich** *Adj.* autumn *attrib.;* autumnal
Herd der; ~[**e**]**s,** ~**e** cooker; *(fig.)* centre *(of disturbance/rebellion)*
Herde die; ~, ~**n** herd
herein-: ~|**bitten** *unr. tr. V.* **jmdn.** ~**bitten** ask *or* invite sb. in; ~|**brechen** *unr. itr. V.; mit sein (geh.)* ⟨*night, evening, dusk*⟩ fall; ⟨*winter*⟩ set in; ⟨*storm*⟩ strike, break; ~|**bringen** *unr. tr. V.* bring in; ~|**fallen** *unr. itr. V.; mit sein (ugs.)* be taken for a ride *(coll.);* be done *(coll.);* ~|**kommen** *unr. itr. V.; mit sein* come in; ~|**lassen** *unr. tr. V.* let in; ~|**legen** *tr. V. (ugs.)* **jmdn.** ~**legen** take sb. for a ride *(coll.)* (**mit, bei** with); ~|**platzen** *itr.*

V.; mit sein (ugs.) burst in; ~|**schnei-
en** *unr. itr. V.; mit sein (ugs.)* turn up
out of the blue *(coll.)*

her-, Her-: ~**fahrt** die journey here;
~|**fallen** *unr. itr. V.; mit sein* über
jmdn. ~**fallen** attack sb.; *(gierig zu essen beginnen)* über etw. *(Akk.)* ~**fallen**
fall upon sth.; ~**gang** der: der ~gang
der Ereignisse the sequence of events;
~|**geben** *unr. tr. V.* hand over; *(weg-
geben)* give away; ~|**gehen** *unr. itr.
V.; mit sein* neben/vor/hinter jmdm.
~**gehen** walk along beside/in front of/
behind sb.; ~|**haben** *unr. tr. V. (ugs.)*
wo hat er/sie das ~? where did he/she
get that from?; ~|**halten** *unr. itr. V.*
~**halten müssen** [für jmdn./etw.] be the
one to suffer [for sb./sth.]; ~|**hören**
itr. V. listen

Hering der; ~s, ~e a) herring; b) *(Zeltpflock)* peg

her-: ~|**kommen** *unr. itr. V.; mit sein*
come here; ~**kömmlich** *Adj.* conventional; traditional ⟨custom⟩

Herkunft die; ~, **Herkünfte** origin

her-: ~|**laufen** *unr. itr. V.; mit sein*
vor/hinter/neben jmdm. ~**laufen** run
[along] in front of/behind/alongside
sb.; *(nachlaufen)* hinter jmdm. ~**laufen**
run after sb.; *(fig.)* chase sb. up;
~|**leiten** *tr., refl. V.* derive (aus, von
from); ~|**machen** *(ugs.) refl. V.* sich
über etw. *(Akk.)* ~**machen** get stuck
into sth. *(coll.)*

Hermelin der; ~s, ~e *(Pelz)* ermine

hermetisch 1. *Adj.* hermetic; 2. *adv.*
hermetically

Heroin das; ~s heroin

Herr der; ~n, ~en a) *(Mann)* gentleman; b) *(Titel, Anrede)* ~ Schulze Mr
Schulze; Sehr geehrter ~ Schulze!
Dear Sir; *(bei persönlicher Bekanntschaft)* Dear Mr Schulze; meine ~en
gentlemen; c) *(Gebieter)* master

herren-, Herren-: ~**ausstatter** der
[gentle]men's outfitter; ~**los** *Adj.*
abandoned ⟨car, luggage⟩; stray ⟨dog,
cat⟩; ~**salon** der men's hairdressing
salon; ~**schuh** der man's shoe;
~**schuhe** men's shoes; ~**toilette** die
[gentle]men's toilet

Herr·gott der; ~s: der [liebe]/unser ~:
the Lord [God]; God; **Herrgottsfrühe** die *in* in aller ~: at the crack of
dawn

her|richten *tr. V. (bereitmachen)* get
⟨room, refreshments, etc.⟩ ready; arrange ⟨table⟩; *(in Ordnung bringen)*
renovate

Herrin die; ~, ~en mistress; **herrisch**
1. *Adj.* overbearing; imperious; 2.
adv. imperiously; **herrlich** 1. *Adj.*
marvellous; magnificent ⟨view,
clothes⟩; 2. *adv.* marvellously; **Herrlichkeit** die; ~, ~en a) *o. Pl. (Schönheit)* magnificence; splendour; b)
meist Pl. (herrliche Sache) marvellous
thing; **Herrschaft** die; ~, ~en a) *o.
Pl.* rule; *(Macht)* power; b) *Pl. (Damen u. Herren)* ladies and gentlemen;
herrschen *itr. V.* rule; ⟨monarch⟩
reign, rule; draußen ~ 30° Kälte it's
30° below outside; **Herrscher** der;
~s, ~: ruler; **herrsch·süchtig** *Adj.*
domineering

her-: ~|**rühren** *itr. V.* von jmdm./etw.
~**rühren** come from sb./stem from
sth.; ~|**sein** *unr. itr. V.; mit sein* einen
Monat/lange ~**sein** be a month/a long
time ago; es ist lange ~, daß wir ...: it
is a long time since we ...; von Köln
~**sein** be from Cologne; hinter jmdm.
(ugs.)/etw. ~**sein** be after sb./sth.;
~|**stellen** *tr. V.* produce

Her·steller der; ~s, ~: producer;
Her·stellung die production

herüber *Adv.* over

herum *Adv.* um ... ~ *(Richtung)*
round; *(Anordnung)* around; um
Weihnachten ~: around Christmas

herum-: ~|**ärgern** *refl. V. (ugs.)* sich
mit jmdm./etw. ~**ärgern** keep getting
annoyed with sb./sth.; ~|**drehen** 1.
tr. V. (ugs.) turn ⟨key⟩; turn over ⟨coin,
mattress, hand, etc.⟩; 2. *refl. V.* turn
[a]round; ~|**fahren** *(ugs.)* 1. *unr. itr.
V.; mit sein (sich plötzlich herumdre-
hen)* spin round; 2. *unr. tr. V.* jmdn. |in
der Stadt| ~**fahren** drive sb. around
the town; ~|**führen** 1. *tr. V.* jmdn. |in
der Stadt| ~**führen** show sb. around
the town; 2. *itr. V.* um etw. ~**führen**
⟨road etc.⟩ go round sth.; ~|**gehen**
unr. itr. V.; mit sein (vergehen) pass;
um etw. ~**gehen** go round sth.; etw.
~**gehen lassen** circulate sth.; pass;
~|**kommen** *unr. itr. V.; mit sein (ugs.)*
a) *(vermeiden können)* um etw. |nicht|
~**kommen** [not] be able to get out of
sth.; b) *(viel reisen)* get around *or*
about; in der Welt ~**kommen** see a lot
of the world; ~|**laufen** *unr. itr. V.; mit
sein* a) walk/*(schneller)* run around *or*
about; um etw. ~**laufen** go round sth.;
b) *(gekleidet sein)* wie ein Hippie ~**laufen** go about looking like a hippie;
~|**lungern** *itr. V. (salopp)* loaf
around; ~|**schlagen** *unr. refl. V.*

(ugs.) sich mit Problemen/Einwänden ~**schlagen** grapple with problems/ battle against objections; ~|**sein** *unr. itr. V.; mit sein; Zusammenschreibung nur im Inf. und Part. (ugs.) (vergangen sein)* have passed; ~|**sitzen** *unr. itr. V. (ugs.)* sit around *or* about; ~|**sprechen** *unr. refl. V.* get around *or* about; ~|**stöbern** *itr. V. (ugs.)* keep rummaging around *or* about (**in** + *Dat.* in); ~|**treiben** *unr. refl. V. (ugs. abwertend)* sich auf den Straßen/in Discos ~**treiben** hang around the streets/in discos; **sich in der Welt** ~**treiben** roam about the world

herunter *Adv.* **a)** *(nach unten)* down; **b)** *(fort)* off; ~ **vom Sofa!** [get] off the sofa!

herunter-: ~|**bringen** *unr. tr. V.* bring down; ~|**fallen** *unr. itr. V.; mit sein* fall down; **vom Tisch/Stuhl** ~**fallen** fall off the table/chair; ~|**gehen** *unr. itr. V.; mit sein* **a)** come down; **b)** *(niedriger werden)* ⟨*temperature*⟩ drop; ⟨*prices*⟩ come down, fall; ~**gekommen** 1. 2. *Part. v.* ~**kommen**; 2. *Adj.* poor ⟨*health*⟩; dilapidated ⟨*building*⟩; run-down ⟨*area*⟩; down and out ⟨*person*⟩; ~|**handeln** *tr. V. (ugs.)* **einen Preis** ~**handeln** beat down a price; ~|**hängen** *unr. itr. V.* hang down; ~|**hauen** *unr. tr. V. (ugs.)* **jmdm. eine** ~**hauen** give sb. a clout round the ear *(coll.)*; ~|**kommen** *unr. itr. V.; mit sein* **a)** come down; **b)** *(ugs.: verfallen)* go to the dogs *(coll.)*; ~|**lassen** *unr. tr. V.* lower; ~|**schlucken** *tr. V.* swallow; ~|**sein** *unr. itr. V.; mit sein; Zusammenschreibung nur im Inf. und Part. (ugs.)* be down; |**körperlich**| ~**sein** be in poor health; ~|**spielen** *tr. V. (ugs.)* play down *(coll.)*

hervor *Adv.* **aus ... ~**: out of

hervor-: ~|**heben** *unr. tr. V.* stress; ~**ragend** 1. *Adj.* outstanding[ly good]; 2. *adv.* ~**ragend geschult** outstandingly well trained; ~**ragend spielen/arbeiten** play/work outstandingly well; ~|**tun** *unr. refl. V.* distinguish oneself; *(wichtig tun)* show off

Herz das; ~ens, ~en **a)** heart; *(Kartenspiel)* hearts *pl.;* **von** ~en **kommen** come from the heart; **ein** ~ **für die Armen haben** feel for the poor; **ein** ~ **für Kinder haben** have a love of children; **schweren** ~ens with a heavy heart; **auf dem** ~en **haben** have sth. on one's mind; **es nicht übers** ~ **bringen, etw. zu tun** not have the heart to do sth.; **sich**

(Dat.) **etw. zu** ~en **nehmen** take sth. to heart; **Herz·anfall** der heart attack; **herzens·gut** ['--'-] *Adj.* kindhearted; **Herzens·lust** die: **nach** ~: to one's heart's content; **herzhaft** 1. *Adj.* hearty; *(nahrhaft)* hearty ⟨*meal*⟩; *(von kräftigem Geschmack)* tasty; 2. *adv.* heartily; *(nahrhaft)* **er ißt gern** ~: he likes to have a hearty meal

her|ziehen *unr. itr. V.; mit sein od. haben (ugs.)* **über jmdn./etw.** ~: run sb./ sth. down

herzig 1. *Adj.* sweet; delightful; 2. *adv.* sweetly; delightfully

herz-, Herz-: ~**infarkt** der heart attack; ~**klopfen** das; ~s: **jmd. hat** ~**klopfen** sb.'s heart is pounding; ~**krank** *Adj.* ⟨*person*⟩ with a heart condition

herzlich 1. *Adj.* warm ⟨*smile, reception*⟩; kind ⟨*words, regards*⟩; *(ehrlich gemeint)* sincere; ~**en Dank** many thanks; 2. *adv.* warmly; *(ehrlich gemeint)* sincerely; ⟨*congratulate*⟩ heartily; ~ **wenig** very *or (coll.)* precious little; **Herzlichkeit** die warmth; kindness; *(Aufrichtigkeit)* sincerity; **herz·los** 1. *Adj.* heartless; 2. *adv.* heartlessly

Herzog der; ~s, Herzöge duke; **Herzogin** die; ~, ~nen duchess

herz-, Herz-: ~**schlag** der heartbeat; *(Herzversagen)* heart failure; ~**schmerz** der; *meist Pl.* pain in the region of the heart; ~**transplantation** die *(Med.)* heart transplantation; ~**zerreißend** 1. *Adj.* heart-rending; 2. *adv.* heart-rendingly

Hessen (das); ~s Hesse

Hetze die; ~ **a)** [mad] rush; **b)** *o. Pl. (abwertend)* smear campaign; **hetzen** 1. *tr. V.* **a)** hunt; **b)** *(antreiben)* rush; 2. *itr. V.* **a)** *(in großer Eile sein)* rush; **b)** *mit sein (hasten)* rush; *(rennen)* dash; race; **Hetz·rede** die *(abwertend)* inflammatory speech

Heu das; ~[e]s hay

Heuchelei die; ~: hypocrisy; **heucheln** 1. *itr. V.* be a hypocrite; 2. *tr. V.* feign; **Heuchler** der; ~s, ~: hypocrite; **heuchlerisch** 1. *Adj.* hypocritical; 2. *adv.* hypocritically

heuer *Adv. (südd., österr., schweiz.)* this year

Heuer die; ~, ~n *(Seemannsspr.)* pay; wages *pl.*

Heu·ernte die **a)** hay harvest; **b)** *(Ertrag)* hay crop

heulen *itr. V.* **a)** howl; ⟨*siren etc.*⟩ wail; **b)** *(ugs.: weinen)* howl; bawl

Heurige der; *adj. Dekl. (bes. österr.)* **a)** *(Wein)* new wine; **b)** *(Weinlokal)* inn with new wine on tap

Heu-: ~**schnupfen** der hay fever; ~**schrecke** die grasshopper

heute *Adv.* today; ~ **früh** early this morning; ~ **morgen/abend** this morning/evening; ~ **mittag** [at] midday today; ~ **nacht** tonight; *(letzte Nacht)* last night; ~ **in einer Woche** a week [from] today; today week; ~ **vor einer Woche** a week ago today; **heutig** *Adj.* **a)** *(von diesem Tag)* today's; der ~**e Tag** today; **b)** *(gegenwärtig)* today's; of today *postpos.;* **in der** ~**en Zeit** nowadays; **heut·zu·tage** *Adv.* nowadays

Hexe die; ~, ~**n** witch; **hexen** *itr. V.* work magic

Hexen·schuß der; *o. Pl.* lumbago *no indef. art.;* **Hexerei** die; ~, ~**en** witchcraft; *(von Kunststücken usw.)* magic

hieb *1. u. 3. Pers. Sg. Prät. v.* **hauen;** **Hieb** der; ~**[e]s,** ~**e a)** *(Schlag)* blow; *(mit der Peitsche)* lash; **b)** *Pl. (ugs.: Prügel)* hiding *sing.;* **hieb·fest** *Adj.:* **hieb- und stichfest** watertight; cast-iron

hielt *1. u. 3. Pers. Sg. Prät. v.* **halten**

hier *Adv.* **a)** here; |**von**| ~ **oben/unten** [from] up/down here; **b)** *(jetzt)* now; **von** ~ **an** from now on

hieran *Adv.* here; **sich** ~ **festhalten** hold on to this; *(fig.)* **im Anschluß** ~: immediately after this

Hierarchie [hierar'çi:] die; ~, ~**n** hierarchy

hierauf *Adv.* **a)** on here; *(darauf)* on this; **wir werden** ~ **zurückkommen** we'll come back to this; **b)** *(danach)* after that; then; **c)** *(infolgedessen)* whereupon; **hieraus** *Adv.* out of here; *(aus dieser Tatsache, Quelle)* from this

hier-: ~|**behalten** *unr. tr. V.* jmdn./ etw. ~: keep sb./sth. here; ~**bei** *Adv.* **a)** *(bei dieser Gelegenheit)* **Diese Übung ist sehr schwierig. Man kann sich** ~ **leicht verletzen.** This exercise is very difficult. You can easily injure yourself doing it; **b)** *(bei der erwähnten Sache)* here; ~|**bleiben** *unr. itr. V.; mit sein* stay here; ~**durch** *Adv.* through here; *(auf Grund dieser Sache)* because of this; ~**für** *Adv.* for this

hier·her *Adv.* here; **ich gehe bis** ~ **und nicht weiter** I'm going this far and no further

hierher-: ~|**gehören** *itr. V.* belong here; *(hierfür wichtig sein)* be relevant [here]; ~|**kommen** *unr. itr. V.; mit sein* come here

hier·hin *Adv.* here; **bis** ~: up to here

hier-: ~**in** *Adv.* **a)** *(räumlich)* in here; **b)** in this; ~|**lassen** *unr. tr. V. etw.* ~: leave sth. here; ~**mit** *Adv.* with this/ these; ~**mit ist der Fall erledigt** that puts an end to the matter; ~**nach** *Adv. (anschließend)* after that

Hieroglyphe die; ~, ~**n** hieroglyph

hier-: ~**sein** *unr. itr. V.; mit sein; Zusammenschreibung nur im Inf. und Part.* be here; ~**über** *Adv.* **a)** *(über dem Erwähnten)* above here; *(über das Erwähnte)* over here; **b)** *(das Erwähnte betreffend)* about this/these; ~**von** *Adv.* of this/these; ~**zu** *Adv.* with this; *(hinsichtlich dieser Sache)* about this; ~**zu gehört/gehören ...:** this includes/these include; ~**zu reicht mein Geld nicht** I haven't got enough money for that; ~**zu·lande** *Adv.* [here] in this country

hiesig *Adj.; nicht präd.* local

hieß *1. u. 3. Pers. Sg. Prät. v.* **heißen**

Hi-Fi-Anlage ['haifi] die hi-fi system

Hilfe die; ~, ~**n a)** help; *(für Notleidende)* aid; relief; **zu** ~! help!; **b)** *(Hilfskraft)* help; *(im Geschäft)* assistant

Hilfe-: ~**leistung** die help; ~**ruf** der cry for help; ~**stellung** die *(Turnen)* jmdm. ~**stellung geben** act as spotter for sb.

hilflos **1.** *Adj.* helpless; **2.** *adv.* helplessly; **Hilflosigkeit** die; ~ helplessness

hilfs-, **Hilfs-:** ~**bedürftig** *Adj.* **a)** *(schwach)* in need of help *postpos.;* **b)** *(notleidend)* in need; needy; ~**bereit** *Adj.* helpful; ~**bereitschaft** die helpfulness; ~**kraft** die assistant; ~**mittel** das aid; ~**zeit·wort** das *(Sprachw.)* auxiliary [verb]

Himalaja der; ~[**s**]: der/im ~: the/in the Himalayas *pl.*

Him·beere die raspberry

Himmel der; ~**s,** ~**s;** sky; *(Rel.)* heaven; ~ **noch** [ein|**mal**! for Heaven's sake!

Himmel·bett das four-poster bed; **himmel·blau** *Adj.* sky-blue; clear blue ⟨*eyes*⟩

Himmels-: ~**richtung** die point of the compass; ~**schlüsselchen** das cowslip

himmel·weit *Adj.* enormous, vast ⟨*difference*⟩; **himmlisch** *Adj. (auch fig.)* heavenly

hin *Adv.* **a)** *(räumlich)* zur Straße ~ liegen face the road; **b)** *(zeitlich)* gegen Mittag ~: towards midday; **c)** *(in Verbindungen)* nach außen ~: outwardly; auf meinen Rat ~: on my advice; auf seine Bitte ~: at his request; **d)** *(in Wortpaaren)* ~ und zurück there and back; einmal Köln ~ und zurück a return [ticket] to Cologne; ~ und her to and fro; back and forth; ~ und wieder [every] now and then

hinab *Adv. s.* hinunter

hinab|- *s.* hinunter|-

hinauf *Adv.* up; bis ~ zu up to

hinauf-: ~|**fahren** *unr. itr. V.; mit sein* go up; *(im Auto)* drive up; *(mit einem Motorrad)* ride up; ~|**gehen** *unr. itr. V.; mit sein* **a)** *(nach oben gehen)* go up; **b)** *(nach oben führen)* lead up; **c)** *(ugs.: steigen)* ⟨*prices, taxes, etc.*⟩ go up; rise; ~|**klettern** *itr. V.; mit sein* climb up; ~|**steigen** *unr. itr. V.; mit sein* climb up; ~|**ziehen** 1. *unr. tr. V.* pull up; 2. *unr. itr. V.; mit sein* move up; 3. *unr. refl. V. (sich erstrecken)* stretch up

hinaus *Adv.* **a)** *(räumlich)* out; **b)** *(zeitlich)* auf Jahre ~: for years to come; **c)** *(etw. überschreitend)* über etw. *(Akk.)* ~: in addition to sth.

hinaus-: ~|**bringen** *unr. tr. V.* jmdn./ etw. ~bringen see sb. out/take sth. out (aus of); ~|**fahren** 1. *unr. itr. V.; mit sein* aus etw. ~fahren *(mit dem Auto)* drive out of sth.; *(mit dem Zweirad)* ride out of sth.; ⟨*car, bus*⟩ go out of sth.; ⟨*train*⟩ pull out of sth.; zum Flugplatz ~fahren drive out to the airport; 2. *unr. tr. V.* jmdn./etw. ~fahren drive sb./take sth. out; ~|**fallen** *unr. itr. V.; mit sein* fall out (aus of); ~|**finden** *unr. itr. V.* find one's way out (aus of); ~|**gehen** *unr. itr. V.; mit sein* **a)** go out (aus of); **b)** *(gerichtet sein)* das Zimmer geht nach Garten/nach Westen ~: the room looks out on to the garden/faces west; ~|**kommen** *unr. itr. V.; mit sein* come out (aus of); ~|**laufen** *unr. itr. V.; mit sein* **a)** run out (aus of); **b)** *(als Ergebnis haben)* auf etw. *(Akk.)* ~laufen lead to sth.; ~|**sehen** *unr. itr. V.* look out; zum Fenster ~sehen look out of the window; ~|**sein** *unr. itr. V.; mit sein* über etw. *(Akk.)* ~sein be past sth.; ~|**tragen** *unr. tr. V.* jmdn./etw. ~tragen carry

sb./sth. out; ~|**werfen** *unr. tr. V. (auch ugs. fig.)* throw out (aus of); ~|**ziehen** 1. *unr. tr. V.* **a)** *(nach draußen ziehen)* jmdn./etw. ~ziehen pull sb./sth. out (aus of); tow ⟨*ship*⟩ out; **b)** *(verzögern)* put off; delay; 2. *unr. refl. V.* be delayed; ~|**zögern** 1. *tr. V.* delay; 2. *refl. V.* be delayed

hin-, Hin-: ~|**blick** der *in* im *od.* in ~blick auf etw. *(Akk.) (wegen)* in view of; *(hinsichtlich)* with regard to; ~|**bringen** *unr. tr. V.* jmdn./etw. ~bringen take sb./sth. [there]; ~|**denken** *unr. itr. V.* wo denkst du hin? *(ugs.)* whatever are you thinking of?

hinderlich *Adj.* ~ sein get in the way; **hindern** *tr. V.* **a)** *(abhalten)* jmdn. ~: stop sb. (an + *Dat.* from); **b)** *(behindern)* hinder; **Hindernis** das; ~ses, ~se obstacle

hin|deuten *itr. V.* **a)** auf jmdn./etw. *od.* zu jmdn./etw. ~: point to sb./sth.; **b)** auf etw. *(Akk.)* ~ *(fig.)* point to sth.

hin·durch *Adv.* **a)** *(räumlich)* durch den Wald ~: through the wood; **b)** *(zeitlich)* das ganze Jahr ~: throughout the year

hinein *Adv.* **a)** *(räumlich)* in; in etw. *(Akk.)* ~: into sth.; **b)** *(zeitlich)* bis in den Morgen/tief in die Nacht ~: till morning/far into the night

hinein-: ~|**bringen** *unr. tr. V.* take in; ~|**fahren** *(mit dem Auto)* drive in; *(mit dem Zweirad)* ride in; in etw. *(Akk.)* ~fahren drive/ride into sth.; ~|**fallen** *unr. itr. V.; mit sein* fall in; in etw. *(Akk.)* ~fallen fall into sth.; ~|**gehen** *unr. itr. V.; mit sein* go in; in etw. *(Akk.)* ~gehen go into sth.; ~|**gucken** *itr. V. (ugs.)* look in; in etw. *(Akk.)* ~gucken look in[to] sth.; ~|**kommen** *unr. itr. V.; mit sein* **a)** come in; in etw. *(Akk.)* ~kommen come into sth.; **b)** *(gelangen, auch fig.)* get in; in etw. *(Akk.)* ~kommen get into sth.; ~|**reden** *itr. V.* jmdm. in seine Angelegenheiten/Entscheidungen usw. ~reden interfere in sb.'s affairs/ decisions *etc.*; ~|**sehen** *unr. itr. V.* look in; in etw. *(Akk.)* ~sehen look into sth.; ~|**versetzen** *refl. V.* sich in jmdn. *od.* jmds. Lage ~versetzen put oneself in sb.'s position

hin-, Hin-: ~|**fahren** 1. *unr. itr. V.; mit sein* go there; 2. *unr. tr. V.* jmdn. ~fahren drive sb. there; ~|**fahrt** die journey there; *(Seereise)* voyage out; ~|**fallen** *unr. itr. V.; mit sein* **a)** fall over; **b)** jmdm. fällt etw. ~: sb. drops

sth.; etw. ~fallen lassen drop sth.;
~fällig *Adj.* a) infirm; frail; b) *(un-
gültig)* invalid; ~|fliegen *unr. itr. V.;
mit sein* fly there; ~flug der outward
flight

hing *1. u. 3. Pers. Sg. Prät. v.* hängen
Hin·gabe die; ~: devotion; *(Eifer)*
dedication; Hingebung die; ~:
devotion; hingebungs·voll 1. *Adj.*
devoted; 2. *adv.* devotedly; with
devotion; *(listen)* with rapt attention;
(dance, play) with abandon
hin·gegen *Konj., Adv. (jedoch)* however; *(andererseits)* on the other hand
hin-: ~|gehen *unr. itr. V.; mit sein* a)
go [there]; zu jmdm./etw. ~gehen go to
sb./sth.; b) *(verstreichen)* *(time)* go by;
~|halten *unr. tr. V.* a) hold out; b)
(warten lassen) jmdn. ~halten keep sb.
waiting; ~|hören *itr. V.* listen
hinken ['hɪŋkn̩] *itr. V.* a) walk with a
limp; b) *mit sein (hinkend gehen)* limp
hin-: ~|kommen *unr. itr. V.; mit sein*
a) get there; b) *(an einen Ort gehören)*
go; belong; c) *(ugs.: stimmen)* be
right; ~länglich 1. *Adj.* sufficient;
(angemessen) adequate; 2. *adv.* sufficiently; *(angemessen)* adequately;
~|legen 1. *tr. V.* put; *(weglegen)* put
down; 2. *refl. V.* lie down; ~rei-
chend 1. *Adj.* sufficient; *(angemessen)* adequate; 2. *adv.* sufficiently;
(angemessen) adequately; ~reise die
journey there; *(mit dem Schiff)* voyage
out; ~reißend *Adj.* enchanting *(person, picture, view)*; captivating
(speaker, play); ~|richten *tr. V.* ex-
ecute; ~richtung die execution
Hinrichtungs·kommando das fir-
ing-squad
hin-, Hin-: ~|sehen *unr. itr. V.* look;
~|sein *unr. itr. V.; mit sein (nur im Inf.
u. Part. zusammengeschrieben) (ugs.)*
a) *(verloren sein)* be gone; b) *(nicht
mehr brauchbar sein)* have had it
(coll.); *(car)* be a write-off; c) *(salopp:
tot sein)* have snuffed it *(sl.)*; d) *(ugs.:
hingerissen sein)* von jmdm./etw. ganz
~sein be mad about sb./bowled over
by sth.; ~|setzen 1. *tr. V.* put; 2. *refl.
V.* sit down; ~sicht die; *o. Pl.* in gewisser ~sicht in a way/in some respect
or ways; in jeder ~sicht in every respect; in finanzieller ~sicht financially; ~sichtlich *Präp. mit Gen.
(Amtsspr.)* with regard to; *(in Anbe-
tracht)* in view of; ~|stellen 1. *tr. V.*
put; put up *(building)*; *(absetzen)* put
down; 2. *refl. V.* stand

hinten *Adv.* at the back; sich ~ anstellen join the back of the queue *(Brit.) or
(Amer.)* line; weiter ~: further back;
(in einem Buch) further on; die Adresse steht ~ auf dem Brief the address is
on the back of the envelope; nach ~
hinaus liegen/gehen be at the back; die
anderen sind ganz weit ~: the others
are a long way back

hinter 1. *Präp. mit Dat.* behind; *(nach)*
after; 3 km ~ der Grenze 3 km beyond
the frontier; eine Prüfung ~ sich haben
(fig.) have got an examination over
[and done] with; viele Enttäuschun-
gen/eine Krankheit ~ sich haben have
experienced many disappointments/
have got over an illness; 2. *Präp. mit
Akk.* behind

hinter... *Adj.; nicht präd.* back
hinter-, Hinter-: ~einander *Adv.* a)
(räumlich) one behind the other; b)
(zeitlich) one after another *or* the
other; ~gedanke der ulterior motive; ~gehen [--'--] *unr. tr. V.* deceive; ~grund der background;
~gründig 1. *Adj.* enigmatic; 2. *adv.*
enigmatically; ~halt der ambush;
~hältig 1. *Adj.* underhand; 2. *adv.* in
an underhand manner; ~her *Adv.*
(räumlich) behind; *(nachher)* afterwards; ~hof der courtyard; ~land
das hinterland; *(Milit.)* back area;
~lassen [--'--] *unr. tr. V.* leave; ~le-
gen [--'--] *tr. V.* deposit *(bei with)*;
~list die guile; deceit; ~listig *Adj.*
deceitful; ~mann der; *Pl.* ~männer
a) person behind; b) *(Gewährsmann)*
[secret] informant
Hintern der; ~s, ~ *(ugs.)* backside;
bottom
hinter-, Hinter-: ~rad das rear
wheel; ~teil das backside; behind;
~treffen das *(ugs.)* in ins ~treffen geraten *od.* kommen fall behind; ~trei-
ben [--'--] *unr. tr. V.* foil *(plan)*; prevent *(marriage, promotion)*; block
(law, investigation, reform); ~treppe
die back stairs *pl.*; ~tür die back
door; ~wäldler der; ~s, ~
(spött.) backwoodsman
hinüber *Adv.* over; across
Hin- und Rück·fahrt die journey
there and back; round trip *(Amer.)*
hinunter *Adv.* down
hinunter-: ~fahren 1. *unr. itr. V.;
mit sein* go down; *(mit dem Auto)*
drive down; *(mit dem Fahrrad)* ride
down; 2. *unr. tr. V.* jmdn./ein Auto/ei-
ne Ladung ~fahren drive sb. down/

drive a car down/take a load down;
~|**gehen** *unr. itr. V.; mit sein* go
down; ⟨*aircraft*⟩ descend; ~|**klettern**
itr. V.; mit sein climb down; ~|**rei-
chen 1.** *tr. V.* hand down; **2.** *itr. V.
(sich bis hinunter erstrecken)* reach
down (**bis auf** + *Akk.* to)
Hin·weg der way there
hin·węg *Adv.* **a)** *(geh.)* ~ **mit dir!**
away with you!; **b)** **über etw.** ~: over
sth.
hinwęg-: ~|**gehen** *unr. itr. V.; mit
sein* **über etw.** *(Akk.)* ~**gehen** pass over
sth.; ~|**kommen** *unr. itr. V.; mit sein*
über etw. *(Akk.)* ~**kommen** get over
sth.; ~|**setzen** *refl. V.* **sich über etw.**
(Akk.) ~**setzen** ignore sth.
Hinweis ['hɪnvaɪs] **der;** ~**es,** ~**e** hint;
unter ~ **auf** (+ *Akk.*) with reference
to
hin-: ~|**weisen 1.** *unr. itr. V.* **auf**
jmdn./etw. ~**weisen** point to sb./sth.;
2. *unr. tr. V.* **jmdn. auf etw.** *(Akk.)*
~**weisen** point sth. out to sb.; ~**wei-
send** *Adj. (Grammatik)* demonstrat-
ive; ~|**werfen** *unr. tr. V.* throw
down; ~|**ziehen 1.** *unr. tr. V.* pull,
draw (**zu** to, towards); **2.** *unr. itr. V.;
mit sein* **a)** *(umziehen)* move there; **wo
ist sie** ~**gezogen?** where did she move
to?; **3.** *unr. refl. V.* **a)** *(sich erstrecken)*
drag on (**über** + *Akk.* for); **b)** *(sich
verzögern)* be delayed
hinzu-: ~|**fügen** *tr. V.* add; ~|**kom-
men** *unr. itr. V.; mit sein* **a)** come
along; **b)** *(hinzugefügt werden)* **zu etw.**
~**kommen** be added to sth.; **es kommt
noch** ~, **daß** ... *(fig.)* there is also the
fact that...; ~|**tun** *unr. tr. V. (ugs.)* add
Hirn das; ~|e|**s,** ~**e a)** brain; **b)** *(Speise;
ugs.: Verstand)* brains *pl.*
Hirsch der; ~|e|**s,** ~**e** deer; *(Rothirsch)*
red deer; *(männlicher Rothirsch)* stag;
(Speise) venison
Hirse die; ~, ~**n** millet
Hirt der; ~**en,** ~**en, Hirte der;** ~**n,** ~**n**
herdsman; *(Schaf~)* shepherd
hissen *tr. V.* hoist
historisch *Adj.* **a)** historical; **b)** *(geschichtlich bedeutungsvoll)* historic
Hit der; ~|s|, ~**s** *(ugs.)* hit
Hitze die; ~: heat
hitze-, Hitze-: ~**beständig** *Adj.*
heat-resistant; ~**frei** *Adj.* ~**frei haben**
have the rest of the day off [school/
work] because of excessively hot
weather; ~**welle die** heat wave
hitzig *Adj.* **a)** hot-tempered; **b)** *(erregt)*
heated ⟨*discussion etc.*⟩

hitz-, Hitz-: ~**kopf der** hothead;
~**köpfig** *Adj.* hot-headed; ~**schlag
der** heat-stroke
hl *Abk.* Hektoliter hl
hob *1. u. 3. Pers. Sg. Prät. v.* **heben**
Hobby das; ~**s,** ~**s** hobby
Hobel der; ~**s,** ~ **a)** plane; **b)** *(Küchengerät)* [vegetable] slicer; **Ho-
bel·bank die** woodworker's bench;
hobeln *tr., itr. V.* **a)** plane; **b)** *(schneiden)* slice
hoch; höher, höchst... 1. *Adj.* high; tall
⟨*tree, mast*⟩; long ⟨*grass*⟩; deep ⟨*snow,
water*⟩; heavy ⟨*fine*⟩; large ⟨*sum,
amount*⟩; severe, extensive ⟨*damage*⟩;
senior ⟨*official, officer, post*⟩; high-
level ⟨*diplomacy, politics*⟩; **höchste Gefahr** extreme danger; **es ist höchste
Zeit, daß ...**: it is high time that...; **das
hohe C** top C; **vier** ~ **zwei** *(Math.)* four
to the power [of] two; four squared; **2.**
adv. (in großer Höhe) high; *(nach
oben)* up; *(zahlenmäßig viel, sehr)*
highly; ~ **verschuldet/versichert** heavily in debt/insured for a large sum [of
money]; **etw.** ~ **und heilig versprechen**
promise sth. faithfully; **Hoch das;**
~**s,** ~**s a)** *(Hochruf)* **ein |dreifaches|** ~
auf jmdn. ausbringen give three cheers
for sb.; **b)** *(Met.)* high
Hoch·achtung die great respect;
hochachtungs·voll *Adv. (Briefschluß)* yours faithfully
hoch-, Hoch-: ~**aktuell** *Adj.* highly
topical; ~**amt das** *(kath. Rel.)* high
mass; ~|**arbeiten** *refl. V.* work one's
way up; ~**begabt** *Adj. (präd. getrennt
geschrieben)* highly gifted; ~**betagt**
Adj. aged; ~**betrieb der;** *o. Pl. (ugs.)*
es herrschte ~ **betrieb im Geschäft** the
shop was at its busiest; ~**blüte die**
golden age; ~**burg die** stronghold;
~**deutsch** *Adj.* High German;
~**deutsch das,** ~**deutsche das**
High German; ~**druck der** *(Physik,
Met.)* high pressure; ~**empfindlich**
Adj. highly sensitive ⟨*instrument, device, material, etc.*⟩; fast ⟨*film*⟩; ex-
tremely delicate ⟨*fabric*⟩; ~|**fahren**
unr. itr. V.; mit sein **a)** *(ugs.)* go up;
(mit dem Auto) drive up; *(mit dem
Fahrrad, Motorrad)* ride up; **b)** *(auffahren)* start up; **aus dem Sessel** ~**fahren** start [up] from one's chair; **c)** *(aufbrausen)* flare up; ~**finanz die** high
finance; ~**fliegend** *Adj.* ambitious;
~**form die** top form; ~**gebirge das**
[high] mountains *pl.*; ~**gefühl das**
[feeling of] elation; ~|**gehen** *unr. itr.*

V.; mit sein (ugs.) go up; *(zornig werden)* blow one's top *(coll.);* explode; *(explodieren)* ⟨*bomb, mine*⟩ go off; **~genuß** der *in* ein ~genuß sein be a real delight; **~geschlossen** *Adj.* high-necked ⟨*dress*⟩; **~gestellt** *Adj.; nicht präd.* ⟨*person*⟩ in a high position; important ⟨*person*⟩; **~glanz** der: etw. auf ~glanz bringen give sth. a high polish; *(fig.)* make sth. spick and span; **~gradig** 1. *Adj.* extreme; 2. *adv.* extremely; ~|**halten** *unr. tr. V.* hold up; **~haus** das high-rise-building; ~|**heben** *unr. tr. V.* lift up; raise ⟨*arm, leg, hand*⟩; **~interessant** *Adj.* extremely interesting; **~kant** *Adv. (ugs.)* in jmdn. ~kant hinauswerfen chuck sb. out *(sl.);* throw sb. out on his/her ear *(coll.);* ~|**kommen** *unr. itr. V.; mit sein (ugs.)* come up; *(vorwärtskommen)* get on; ~|**krempeln** *tr. V.* roll up; ~|**leben** *itr. V. in* jmdn./ etw. ~leben lassen cheer sb./sth.; er lebe ~! three cheers for him; **~leistungs·sport** der top-level sport; **~modern** *Adj.* ultra-modern; **~mut** der arrogance; **~mütig** *Adj.* arrogant; **~näsig** *Adj. (abwertend)* stuckup; ~|**nehmen** *unr. tr. V. (ugs.: verspotten)* jmdn. ~nehmen pull sb.'s leg; **~ofen** der blast furnace; **~prozentig** *Adj.* high-proof ⟨*spirits*⟩; **~rechnung** die *(Statistik)* projection; **~ruf** der cheer; **~saison** die high season; ~|**schlagen** 1. *unr. tr. V.* turn up ⟨*collar, brim*⟩; 2. *unr. itr. V.; mit sein* ⟨*water, waves*⟩ surge up; ⟨*flames*⟩ leap up; **~schule** die college; *(Universität)* university

Hochsee·fischerei die deep-sea fishing *no art.*

hoch-, Hoch-: ~sitz der *(Jagdw.)* raised hide; **~sommer** der high summer; **~spannung** die *(Elektrot.)* high voltage; ~|**spielen** *tr. V.* blow up

höchst [høːçst] *Adv.* extremely; most; **höchst…** *s.* hoch

Hoch·stapler [~ˈʃtaːplɐ] der; ~s, ~ confidence trickster; con-man *(coll.); (Aufschneider)* fraud

höchstens *Adv.* at most; *(bestenfalls)* at best

Höchst-: ~fall der *in* im ~fall at [the] most; **~form** die *(bes. Sport)* peak form; **~geschwindigkeit** die top speed; *(Geschwindigkeitsbegrenzung)* speed limit

Hoch·stimmung die high spirits *pl.*

höchst-, Höchst-: ~leistung die

supreme performance; *(Ergebnis)* supreme achievement; **~maß** das: ein ~maß an etw. *(Dat.)* a very high degree of sth.; **~wahrscheinlich** *Adv.* very probably

hoch-, Hoch-: ~tour die: auf ~touren laufen run at full speed; *(intensiv betrieben werden)* be in full swing; **~trabend** *(abwertend)* 1. *Adj.* high-flown; 2. *adv.* in a high-flown manner; ~|**treiben** *unr. tr. V.* force up ⟨*prices etc.*⟩; **~verrat** der high treason; **~wasser** das *(Flut)* high tide; *(Überschwemmung)* flood; **~wertig** *Adj.* high-quality ⟨*goods*⟩; highly nutritious ⟨*food*⟩; **~würden** o. *Art.;* ~|**s|** *(veralt.)* Reverend Father

Hochzeit die; ~, ~en wedding

Hochzeits-: ~feier die wedding; **~nacht** die wedding night; **~reise** die honeymoon [trip]

Hocke die; ~, ~n a) *(Körperhaltung)* squat; crouch; b) *(Turnen)* squat vault; **hocken** 1. *itr. V.* a) mit haben *od. (südd.)* sein squat; crouch; b) mit haben *od. (südd.)* sein *(ugs.: sich aufhalten)* sit around; 2. *refl. V.* crouch down; **Hocker** der; ~s, ~: stool

Höcker der; ~s, ~: hump; *(auf der Nase)* bump; *(auf dem Schnabel)* knob

Hockey [ˈhɔki] das; ~s hockey

Hoden der; ~s, ~: testicle

Hof der; ~[e]s, Höfe a) courtyard; *(Schul~)* playground; *(Gefängnis~)* [prison] yard; b) *(Bauern~)* farm; c) *(Herrscher, Hofstaat)* court

Hof·dame die lady of the court; *(Begleiterin der Königin)* lady-in-waiting; **hof·fähig** *Adj.* presentable at court *pred.*

hoffen 1. *tr. V.* hope; 2. *itr. V.* hope; auf etw. *(Akk.)* ~: hope for sth.; *(Vertrauen setzen auf)* auf jmdn./etw. ~: put one's faith in sb./sth.; **hoffentlich** *Adv.* hopefully; ~! let's hope so; **Hoffnung** die; ~, ~en hope

hoffnungs-, Hoffnungs-: ~los 1. *Adj.* hopeless; despairing ⟨*person*⟩; 2. *adv.* hopelessly; **~losigkeit** die; ~: despair; *(der Lage)* hopelessness; **~voll** 1. *Adj.* a) hopeful; full of hope *pred.;* b) *(erfolgversprechend)* promising; 2. *adv.* a) full of hope; b) *(erfolgversprechend)* promisingly

höflich 1. *Adj.* polite; 2. *adv.* politely; **Höflichkeit** die; ~: politeness

hohe [ˈhoːə] *s.* hoch; **Höhe** [ˈhøːə] die; ~, ~n height; etw. in die ~ heben

lift sth. up; **das ist ja die ~**! *(fig. ugs.)* that's the limit
Hoheit die; **~**, **~en** sovereignty (über + *Akk.* over); **Seine/Ihre ~**: His/ Your Highness
Hoheits-: **~gebiet das** [sovereign] territory; **~gewässer das**; *meist Pl.* territorial waters
Höhen-: **~flug** der *(fig.)* flight; **~lage die** altitude; **~luft die**; *o. Pl.* mountain air; **~messer** der altimeter; **~sonne die** *(Med.)* sun lamp; **~unterschied der** difference in altitude
Höhepunkt der high point; *(einer Veranstaltung)* high spot; *(einer Laufbahn, des Ruhms)* pinnacle; *(Orgasmus)* climax
höher [ˈhøːɐ] *s.* **hoch**
hohl *Adj.* hollow; **Höhle die**; **~**, **~n a)** cave; *(größer)* cavern; **b)** *(Tierbau)* lair
Hohl-: **~maß das** measure of capacity; **~raum** der cavity; [hollow] space; **~spiegel der** concave mirror
Hohn der; **~|e|s** scorn; derision; **höhnen** *(geh.) itr. V.* jeer; **höhnisch 1.** *Adj.* scornful; **2.** *adv.* scornfully
Hokuspokus der; **~**: hocus-pocus; *(abwertend: Drum und Dran)* fuss
hold *Adj. (dichter. veralt.)* fair; lovely; lovely ⟨sight, smile⟩
holen 1. *tr. V.* **a)** fetch; get; **b)** *(ab~)* fetch; **c)** *(ugs.: erlangen)* get ⟨prize etc.⟩; carry off ⟨medal, trophy, etc.⟩; **2.** *refl. V. (ugs.: sich zuziehen)* catch; **sich** *(Dat.)* |beim Baden| **einen Schnupfen ~**: catch a cold [swimming]
Holland (das); **~s** Holland; **Holländer** der; **~s**, **~**: Dutchman; **holländisch** *Adj.* Dutch
Hölle die; **~**, **~n** hell *no art.*; **Höllenlärm** der *(ugs.)* diabolical noise or row *(coll.)*; **höllisch 1.** *Adj.* **a)** infernal; ⟨spirits, torments⟩ of hell; **b)** *(ugs.: sehr groß)* tremendous *(coll.)*; **2.** *adv. (ugs.: sehr)* hellishly *(coll.)*
Holm der; **~|e|s**, **~e a)** *(Turnen)* bar
holpern *itr. V. mit sein (fahren)* jolt; bump; **holprig** *Adj.* **a)** bumpy; rough; **b)** *(stockend)* halting ⟨speech⟩; clumsy ⟨verses, style, language, etc.⟩
Holunder der; **~s**, **~**: elder
Holz das; **~es**, **Hölzer** wood; *(Bau~, Tischler~)* timber; wood; **Holz·bein das** wooden leg; **hölzern** *Adj. (auch fig.)* wooden; **Holz·fäller** der woodcutter; lumberjack *(Amer.)*; **holzfrei** *Adj.* wood-free ⟨paper⟩; **holzig** *Adj.* woody

Holz-: **~klotz** der block of wood; *(als Spielzeug)* wooden block; **~kohle die** charcoal; **~kopf** der *(salopp abwertend)* blockhead; **~pantoffel** der clog; **~scheit das** piece of wood; *(Brenn~)* piece of firewood; **~schnitt** der **a)** *o. Pl.* woodcutting *no art.*; **b)** *(Blatt)* woodcut; **~schuh** der clog; **~stoß** der pile of wood; **~weg** der: **auf dem ~weg sein** be on the wrong track *(fig.)*; **~wolle die**; *o. Pl.* wood-wool; **~wurm** der woodworm
homogen *Adj.* homogeneous
homöopathisch *Adj.* homoeopathic
Homo·sexualität die; **~**: homosexuality; **homo·sexuell 1.** *Adj.* homosexual; **2.** *adv.* **~ veranlagt sein** have homosexual tendencies
Honig der; **~s**, **~e** honey; **Honig·kuchen** der honey cake; **Honig·wabe die** honeycomb
Honorar das; **~s**, **~e** fee; *(Autoren~)* royalty; **Honoratioren** [honoraˈtsioːrən] *Pl.* notabilities; **honorieren** *tr. V.* **a)** jmdn. **~**: pay sb. [a/his/her fee]; **b)** *(würdigen)* appreciate; *(belohnen)* reward
Hopfen der; **~s**, **~**: hop
hopp *Interj.* quick; look sharp; **hoppeln** *itr. V.; mit sein* hop; (über + *Akk.* across, over); **hoppla** *Interj.* oops; whoops; **hopsen** *itr. V.; mit sein (ugs.) (springen)* jump; *(hüpfen)* ⟨animal⟩ hop; ⟨child⟩ skip; ⟨ball⟩ bounce; **Hopser** der; **~s**, **~** *(ugs.)* [little] jump
Hör·apparat der hearing-aid; **hörbar 1.** *Adj.* audible; **2.** *adv.* audibly; *(geräuschvoll)* noisily; **horchen** *itr. V.* listen (auf + *Akk.* to); *(heimlich zuhören)* eavesdrop
Horde die; **~**, **~n** horde; *(von Halbstarken)* mob
hören 1. *tr. V.* hear; *(anhören)* listen to; **2.** *itr. V.* hear; *(zuhören)* listen; **auf jmdn./jmds. Rat ~**: listen to sb./sb.'s advice; **Hören·sagen das: vom ~**: from hearsay; **Hörer** der; **~s**, **~ a)** listener; **b)** *(Telefon~)* receiver
Hör-: **~fehler** der **a)** das war ein **~fehler** he/she *etc.* misheard; **b)** *(Schwerhörigkeit)* hearing defect; **~funk** der radio; **im ~funk** on the radio; **~gerät das** hearing-aid
hörig *Adj.*: jmdm. **~ sein** be submissively dependent on sb.; *(sexuell)* be sexually enslaved to sb.
Horizont der; **~|e|s**, **~e** *(auch Geol., fig.)* horizon; **horizontal 1.** *Adj.*

horizontal!; **2.** *adv.* horizontally; **Horizontale die;** ~, ~n a) *(Linie)* horizontal line; **b)** *o. Pl. (Lage)* **die** ~: the horizontal

Hormon das; ~s, ~e hormone

Horn das; ~|e|s, **Hörner** horn; **Hörnchen** das; ~s, ~ *(Gebäck)* croissant; **Horn·haut die a)** callus; hard skin *no indef. art.;* **b)** *(am Auge)* cornea

Hornisse die; ~, ~n hornet

Horoskop das; ~s, ~e horoscope

Hör·rohr das stethoscope

Horror der; ~s horror

Hör-: ~**saal** der lecture theatre *or* hall; ~**spiel** das radio play

Horst der; ~|e|s, ~e eyrie

Hort der; ~|e|s, ~e *s.* Kinderhort; **horten** *tr. V.* hoard; stockpile 〈*raw materials*〉

Hortensie die; ~, ~n hydrangea

Hör·weite die: in/außer ~weite in/ out of earshot

Höschen ['høːsçən] das; ~s, ~: trousers *pl.;* pair of trousers; *(kurzes* ~) shorts *pl.;* pair of shorts; **Hose die;** ~, ~n **a)** trousers *pl.;* pants *pl. (Amer.); (Unter~)* pants *pl.; (Freizeit~)* slacks *pl.; (Bund~)* breeches *pl.; (Reit~)* riding breeches *pl.;* **eine** ~: a pair of trousers/pants/slacks *etc.*

Hosen-: ~**an·zug** der trouser suit *(Brit.);* pant suit; ~**matz** der *(ugs. scherzh.)* toddler; ~**rock** der culottes *pl.;* ~**tasche** die trouser-pocket; pants pocket *(Amer.);* ~**träger** *Pl.* braces; suspenders *(Amer.);* pair of braces/suspenders

Hospital das; ~s, ~e *od.* **Hospitäler** hospital

Hostie ['hɔstiə] die; ~, ~n *(christl. Rel.)* host

Hotel das; ~s, ~s hotel; **Hotel·bar** die hotel bar; **Hotel garni** [~ gar'ni:] das; ~ ~, ~s ~s bed-and-breakfast hotel; **Hotelier** [hote'lie:] der; ~s, ~s hotelier

hüben *Adv.* over here

hübsch 1. *Adj.* pretty; nice 〈*area, flat, voice, tune, etc.*〉; nice-looking 〈*boy, person*〉; **ein** ~**es Sümmchen** *(ugs.)* a tidy sum *(coll.);* a nice little sum; **das ist eine** ~**e Geschichte** *(ugs. iron.)* this is a fine *or* pretty kettle of fish *(coll.);* **2.** *adv.* prettily; *(ugs.: sehr)* ~ **kalt** perishing cold

Hub·schrauber der; ~s, ~: helicopter

huckepack *Adv.* **jmdn.** ~ **tragen** *(ugs.)* give sb. a piggyback

hudeln *itr. V. (bes. südd., österr.)* be sloppy (bei in)

Huf der; ~|e|s, ~e hoof

Huf-: ~**eisen das** horseshoe; ~**schmied** der farrier

Hüfte die; ~, ~n hip

Hüft-: ~**gelenk** das *(Anat.)* hip-joint; ~**gürtel** der girdle

Hügel der; ~s, ~ hill; **hügelig** *Adj.* hilly

Huhn das; ~|e|s, **Hühner a)** chicken; *(Henne)* chicken; hen; **Hühnchen** das; ~s, ~: small chicken; **mit jmdm. |noch| ein** ~ **zu rupfen haben** *(ugs.)* [still] have a bone to pick with sb.

Hühner-: ~**auge** das *(am Fuß)* corn; ~**brühe** die chicken broth

hui [hui] *Interj.* whoosh

huldigen *itr. V.* **jmdm.** ~: pay tribute to sb.; **Huldigung** die; ~, ~en tribute

Hülle die; ~, ~n cover; **hüllen** *tr. V. (geh.)* wrap

Hülse die; ~, ~n **a)** case; **b)** *(Bot.)* pod

human *Adj.* humane; **Humanismus** der; ~: humanism; *(Epoche)* Humanism *no art.;* **humanitär** *Adj.* humanitarian

Humbug ['hʊmbʊk] der; ~s *(ugs.)* humbug

Hummel die; ~, ~n bumble-bee

Hummer der; ~s, ~: lobster

Humor der; ~s humour; *(Sinn für* ~) sense of humour; **den** ~ **nicht verlieren** remain good-humoured; **Humorist** der; ~en, ~en **a)** *(Autor)* humorist; **b)** *(Vortragskünstler)* comedian; **humoristisch** *Adj.* humorous

humor-: ~**los** *Adj.* humourless; ~**voll** *Adj.* humorous

humpeln *itr. V.* **a)** *auch mit sein* walk with a limp; **b)** *mit sein (sich* ~*d fortbewegen)* limp

Hund der; ~es, ~e **a)** dog; **auf den** ~ **kommen** *(ugs.)* go to the dogs *(coll.);* **vor die** ~**e gehen** *(ugs.)* go to the dogs *(coll.); (sterben)* kick the bucket *(sl.);* **b)** *(abwertend)* bastard *(coll.)*

hunde-, Hunde-: ~**elend** *Adj.; nicht attr. (ugs.)* [really] wretched *or* awful; ~**hütte** die [dog-]kennel; ~**kuchen** der dog-biscuit; ~**müde** *Adj.; nicht attr. (ugs.)* dog-tired; ~**rasse** die breed of dog

hundert *Kardinalz.* **a)** a *or* one hundred; **b)** *(ugs.: viele)* hundreds of; **¹Hundert** das; ~s, ~e hundred; **²Hundert** die; ~, ~en hundred; **Hunderter** der; ~s, ~ *(ugs.)* hundred-mark/-dollar *etc.* note; **hun-**

dert·mal *Adv.* a hundred times; **auch wenn du dich** ~ **beschwerst** *(ugs.)* however much you complain
Hundert-: ~**mark·schein** der hundred-mark note; ~**meter·lauf** der *(Leichtathletik)* hundred metres *sing.*
hundert·prozentig 1. *Adj.* a) *(von 100%)* [one-]hundred per cent *attrib.;* b) *(ugs.: völlig)* a hundred per cent; c) *(ugs.: ganz sicher)* absolutely reliable; 2. *adv. (ugs.)* **ich bin nicht** ~ **sicher** I'm not a hundred per cent sure; **hundertst...** ['hʊndɐtst...] *Ordinalz.* hundredth; **hundertstel** ['hʊndɐtstl] *Bruchz.* hundredth; **Hundertstel** das *(schweiz. meist* der); ~**s,** ~: hundredth; **hundert·tausend** *Kardinalz.* a *or* one hundred thousand
Hüne der; ~**n,** ~**n** giant; **Hünengrab** das megalithic tomb; *(Hügelgrab)* barrow
Hunger der; ~**s** a) ~ **bekommen/haben** get/be hungry; b) *(geh.: Verlangen)* hunger; *(nach Ruhm, Macht)* craving; **Hunger·kur** die starvation diet; **hungern** *itr. V.* go hungry; starve; **nach etw.** ~: *(fig.)* hunger for sth.; **Hungers·not** die famine; **Hunger·streik** der hunger-strike; **hungrig** *Adj. (auch geh. fig.)* hungry **(nach** for)
Hupe die; ~, ~**n** horn; **hupen** *itr. V.* sound one's horn; **dreimal** ~: hoot three times
hüpfen *itr. V.; mit sein* hop; ⟨ball⟩ bounce
Hürde die; ~, ~**n** hurdle; **Hürdenlauf** der *(Leichtathletik)* hurdling; *(Wettbewerb)* hurdles *pl.*
Hure die; ~, ~**n** *(abwertend)* whore; **huren** *itr. V. (abwertend)* whore
hurra *Interj.* hurray; hurrah; ~ **schreien** cheer; **Hurra** das; ~**s,** ~**s** cheer
hurtig 1. *Adj.* rapid; 2. *adv.* quickly
huschen *itr. V.; mit sein (lautlos u. leichtfüßig)* ⟨person⟩ steal; *(lautlos u. schnell)* dart; ⟨mouse, lizard, etc.⟩ dart; ⟨smile⟩ flit; ⟨light⟩ flash; ⟨shadow⟩ slide quickly
hüsteln *itr. V.* give a slight cough; **husten** 1. *itr. V.* cough; *(Husten haben)* have a cough; 2. *tr. V.* cough up ⟨blood, phlegm⟩; **Husten** der; ~**s,** ~: cough
Husten-: ~**bonbon** das cough-drop; ~**tropfen** *Pl.* cough-drops
¹**Hut** der; ~**es,** Hüte hat; *(fig.)* **da geht einem/mir der** ~ **hoch** *(ugs.)* it makes you/me mad *(coll.);* **das kann er sich** *(Dat.)* **an den** ~ **stecken** *(ugs. abwertend)* he can keep it *(coll.)*
²**Hut** die; ~ *(geh.)* keeping;. care; **auf der** ~ **sein** be on one's guard; **hüten** 1. *tr. V.* look after; tend ⟨sheep, cattle, etc.⟩; 2. *refl. V.* be on one's guard
Hut·schnur die *in* **das geht mir über die** ~ *(ugs.)* that's going too far
Hütte die; ~, ~**n** a) hut; *(ärmliches Haus)* shack; hut; b) *(Eisen~)* iron [and steel] works *sing. or pl.;* c) *(Jagd~)* [hunting-]lodge
Hütten-: ~**käse** der cottage cheese; ~**schuh** der slipper-sock
Hyäne die; ~, ~**n** hyena
Hyazinthe die; ~, ~**n** hyacinth
Hydrant der; ~**en,** ~**en** hydrant; **Hydraulik** die; ~ *(Technik)* a) *(Theorie)* hydraulics *sing., no art.;* b) *(Vorrichtungen)* hydraulics *pl.;* **hydraulisch** *(Technik)* 1. *Adj.* hydraulic; 2. *adv.* hydraulically; **Hydro·kultur** die; ~, ~**en** *(Gartenbau)* hydroponics *sing.*
Hygiene die; ~ a) *(Gesundheitspflege)* health care; b) *(Sauberkeit)* hygiene; **hygienisch** 1. *Adj.* hygienic; 2. *adv.* hygienically
Hymne ['hʏmnə] die; ~, ~**n** hymn; *(National~)* national anthem
Hypnose die; ~, ~**n** hypnosis; **hypnotisieren** *tr. V.* hypnotize
Hypochonder [hypo'xɔndɐ] der; ~**s,** ~: hypochondriac
Hypotenuse die; ~, ~**n** *(Math.)* hypotenuse
Hypothek die; ~, ~**en** *(Bankw.)* mortgage; *(fig.)* burden
Hypothese die; ~, ~**n** hypothesis; **hypothetisch** 1. *Adj.* hypothetical; 2. *adv.* hypothetically
Hysterie die; ~, ~**n** hysteria; **hysterisch** 1. *Adj.* hysterical; 2. *adv.* hysterically

I

i, I das; ~, ~: i/I; **das Tüpfelchen auf dem i** *(fig.)* the final touch
i *Interj.* ugh; **i bewahre, i wo** *(ugs.)* [good] heavens, no!

i. A. *Abk.* im Auftrag|e| p.p.
IC *Abk.* Intercity IC
ich *Personalpron.; 1. Pers. Sg. Nom.* I;
immer ~ *(ugs.)* [it's] always me; ~
nicht not me; **Menschen wie du und ~:**
people like you and me; *s. auch (Gen.)*
meiner, *(Dat.)* mir, *(Akk.)* mich
Ich das; ~|s|, ~|s| a) self; b) *(Psych.)*
ego
Ich-Form die; *o. Pl.* first person
ideal 1. *Adj.* ideal; 2. *adv.* ideally;
Ideal das; ~s, ~e ideal
Ideal-: ~**bild das** ideal; ~**fall der**
ideal case; ~**gewicht das** ideal
weight
idealisieren *tr. V.* idealize; **Idealis-**
mus der; ~ *(auch Philos.)* idealism;
Idealist der; ~en, ~en idealist;
idealistisch *(auch Philos.)* 1. *Adj.*
idealistic; 2. *adv.* idealistically; **Idee**
die; ~, ~n a) idea; b) *(ein bißchen)* ei-
ne ~: a shade; **eine ~ |Salz/Pfeffer|** a
touch [of salt/pepper]; **ideell** *Adj.*
non-material; *(geistig-seelisch)* spiritual; **ideen·los** *Adj.* [completely]
lacking in ideas *postpos.*
Identifikation [idɛntifikaˈtsi̯oːn] *die;*
~, ~en *(auch Psych.)* identification;
identifizieren 1. *tr. V.* identify; 2.
refl. V. (auch Psych.) sich mit jmdm./
etw. ~: identify with sb./sth.; **iden-**
tisch *Adj.* identical; **Identität die;**
~: identity
Ideologe der; ~n, ~n ideologue;
Ideologie die; ~, ~n [-iːɔn] ideology;
ideologisch 1. *Adj.* ideological; 2.
adv. ideologically
Idiot der; ~en, ~en *(auch ugs. abwer-*
tend) idiot; **Idioten·hügel der** *(ugs.*
scherzh.) nursery slope; **Idiotie die;**
~, ~n [-iːɔn] a) idiocy; b) *(ugs. abwer-*
tend: Dummheit) madness; **Idiotin**
die; ~, ~nen *(auch ugs. abwertend)*
idiotisch 1. *Adj.* a) *(Psych.)* severely
subnormal; b) *(ugs. abwertend)* idiotic; 2. *adv. (auch ugs. abwertend)*
idiotically
Idol das; ~s, ~e *(auch bild. Kunst)* idol
Idyll das; ~s, ~e idyll; **Idylle die;** ~,
~n idyll; **idyllisch** *Adj.* idyllic
Igel der; ~s, ~: hedgehog
Iglu der od. das; ~s, ~s igloo
Ignoranz [ignoˈrants] *die;* ~: ignorance; **ignorieren** *tr. V.* ignore
ihm *Dat. von* er, es: *(bei männlichen*
Personen) him; *(bei weiblichen Perso-*
nen) her; *(bei Dingen, Tieren)* it; **gib es**
~: give it to him; give him it; **Freunde**
von ~: friends of his

ihn *Akk. von* er *(bei männlichen Perso-*
nen) him; *(bei Dingen, Tieren)* it
ihnen *Dat. von* sie, *Pl.* them; **gib es ~:**
give it to them; give them it; **Freunde**
von ~: friends of theirs
Ihnen *Dat. von* Sie you; **ich habe es ~**
gegeben I gave it to you; **Freunde von**
~: friends of yours
¹**ihr** [iːɐ̯] *Dat. von* sie, *Sg. (bei Personen)*
her; *(bei Dingen, Tieren)* it
²**ihr,** *(in Briefen)* **Ihr** *Personalpron.; 2.*
Pers. Pl. Nom. you
³**ihr** *Possessivpron.* a) *Sg. (einer Person)*
her; *(eines Tieres, einer Sache)* its; b)
Pl. their
Ihr *Possessivpron. (Anrede)* your; ~
Hans Meier *(Briefschluß)* yours, Hans
Meier; **welcher Mantel ist ~er?** which
coat is yours?
ihrer a) *Gen. von* sie, *Sg. (geh.)* **wir ge-**
dachten ~: we remembered her; b)
Gen. von sie, *Pl. (geh.)* **wir werden ~**
gedenken we will remember them; **es**
waren ~ zwölf there were twelve of
them
Ihrer *Gen. von* Sie *(geh.)* **wir werden ~**
gedenken we will remember you
ihrerseits *Adv.* for her/their part;
(von ihr/ihnen) on her/their part
Ihrerseits *Adv. s.* deinerseits
ihres·gleichen *indekl. Pron.* people
pl. like her/them; *(abwertend)* the
likes of her/them
Ihresgleichen *indekl. Pron.* people
pl. like you; *(abwertend)* the likes of
you
ihret·wegen *Adv.: s.* meinetwegen:
because of her/them; for her/their
sake; about her/them; as far as she is/
they are concerned
Ihretwegen *Adv.: s.* deinetwegen
Ikone die; ~, ~n icon
illegal 1. *Adj.* illegal; 2. *adv.* illegally
Illegalität die; ~, ~en illegality; **ille-**
gitim [ˈɪlegitiːm] *Adj. (geh.)* illegitimate
illuminieren *tr. V.* illuminate
Illusion die; ~, ~en illusion; **illuso-**
risch *Adj.* illusory; *(zwecklos)* pointless
Illustration [ɪlʊstraˈtsi̯oːn] *die;* ~, ~en
illustration; **illustrieren** *tr. V.* illustrate; **Illustrierte die;** *adj. Dekl.* magazine
Iltis der; ~ses, ~se polecat; *(Pelz)* fitch
im *Präp. + Art.* a) = in dem; b) *(räum-*
lich) in the; **im Theater** at the theatre;
im Fernsehen on television; **im Bett** in
bed; c) *(zeitlich)* **im Mai** in May; **im**

letzten Jahr last year; **im Alter von ...** at the age of ...; **d)** *(Verlauf)* **etw. im Sitzen tun** do sth. [while] sitting down; **im Gehen sein** be going
Image ['ɪmɪtʃ] **das; ~[s], ~s** ['ɪmɪtʃs] image; **imaginär** *Adj. (geh., Math.)* imaginary
Imbiß der; Imbisses, Imbisse a) *(kleine Mahlzeit)* snack; **b)** *s.* **Imbißstube; Imbiß·stube** die café
Imitation die; ~, ~en imitation; **imitieren** *tr. V.* imitate
Imker der; ~s, ~: bee-keeper
Immatrikulation [ɪmatrikula'tsi̯o:n] **die; ~, ~en** *(Hochschulw.)* registration; **immatrikulieren** *tr., refl. V. (Hochschulw.)* register
immer *Adv.* **a)** always; **schon ~:** always; **~ wieder** time and time again; **~, wenn** every time that; **b) ~ +** *Komp.* **~ dunkler** darker and darker; **~ mehr** more and more; **c)** *(ugs.: jeweils)* **~ drei Stufen auf einmal** three steps at a time; **d)** *(auch)* **wo/wer/wann/wie [auch] ~:** wherever/whoever/whenever/however; **e)** *(verstärkend)* **~ noch, noch ~:** still; **f)** *(ugs.: bei Aufforderung)* **~ geradeaus!** keep [going] straight on
immer-, Immer-: ~fort *Adv.* all the time; **~grün** *Adj.* evergreen; **~grün das** periwinkle; **~hin** *Adv.* **a)** *(wenigstens)* at any rate; **b)** *(trotz allem)* all the same; **c)** *(schließlich)* after all; **~zu** *Adv. (ugs.)* the whole time
Immigrant der; ~en, ~en immigrant; **Immigration** [ɪmigra'tsi̯o:n] **die; ~, ~en** immigration; **immigrieren** *itr. V.; mit sein* immigrate
Immobilien *Pl.* property *sing.;* real estate *sing.*
immun a) *(Med., fig.)* immune **(gegen** to); **b)** *(Rechtsspr.)* **~ sein** have immunity; **Immunität die; ~, ~en a)** *(Med.)* immunity **(gegen** to); **b)** *(Rechtsspr.)* immunity **(gegen** from)
Imperativ der; ~s, ~e a) *(Sprachw.)* imperative; **b)** *(Philos.)* **[kategorischer] ~:** [categorical] imperative
Imperfekt das; ~s, ~e *(Sprachw.)* imperfect [tense]
Imperialismus der; ~: imperialism *no art.;* **imperialistisch** *Adj.* imperialistic
Imperium das; ~s, Imperien *(hist., fig.)* empire
impfen *tr. V.* vaccinate; inoculate
Impf-: ~paß der vaccination certificate; **~stoff der** vaccine

Impfung die; ~, ~en vaccination
implantieren *tr. V. (Med.)* implant
imponieren *itr. V.* impress; **imponierend 1.** *Adj.* impressive; **2.** *adv.* impressively
Import der; ~[e]s, ~e import; **Importeur** [ɪmpɔr'tøːɐ̯] **der; ~s, ~e** importer; **importieren** *tr., itr. V.* import
imposant 1. *Adj.* imposing; impressive ⟨*achievement*⟩; **2.** *adv.* imposingly
impotent *Adj.* impotent; **Impotenz die; ~:** impotence
imprägnieren *tr. V.* impregnate; *(wasserdicht machen)* waterproof
Improvisation die; ~, ~en improvisation; **improvisieren** *tr., itr. V.* improvise
Impuls der; ~es, ~e stimulus; *(innere Regung)* impulse; **impulsiv 1.** *Adj.* impulsive; **2.** *adv.* impulsively
imstande *Adv.* **~ sein, etw. zu tun** be able to do sth.
in 1. *Präp. mit Dat.* **a)** *(auf die Frage:* **wo?/wann?/wie?)** in; **er hat ~ Tübingen studiert** he studied at Tübingen; *s. auch* **im; 2.** *Präp. mit Akk. (auf die Frage: wohin?)* into; *s. auch* **ins**
In·anspruchnahme die; ~, ~n *(starke Belastung)* demands *pl.*
In·begriff der quintessence; **inbegriffen** *Adj.* included
In·betriebnahme die; ~, ~n, In·betriebsetzung die; ~, ~en *(Amtsspr.)* opening; *(von Maschinen)* bringing into service
In·brunst die; ~ *(geh.)* fervour; *(der Liebe)* ardour; **in·brünstig** *(geh.)* **1.** *Adj.* fervent; ardent ⟨*love*⟩; **2.** *adv.* fervently; ⟨*love*⟩ ardently
in·dem *Konj.* **a)** *(während)* while; *(gerade als)* as; **b)** *(dadurch, daß)* **~ man etw. tut** by doing sth.
Inder ['ɪndɐ] **der; ~s, ~:** Indian
in·dessen 1. *Konj. (geh.)* **a)** *(während)* while; **b)** *(wohingegen)* whereas; **2.** *Adv.* **a)** *(inzwischen)* meanwhile; in the mean time; **b)** *(jedoch)* however
Index der; ~ od. ~es, ~e od. Indizes a) *Pl.* **~e od. Indizes** *(Register)* index; **b)** *Pl.* **~e od.** *(kath. Kirche)* Index
Indianer der; ~s, ~: [American] Indian; **Indianer·häuptling der** Indian chief
Indien ['ɪndi̯ən] **(das)** India
in·different *Adj.* indifferent
Indikativ der; ~s, ~e [-i:və] *(Sprachw.)* indicative [mood]

in·direkt 1. *Adj.; nicht präd.* indirect;
2. *adv.* indirectly
indisch *Adj.* Indian
in·diskret *Adj.* indiscreet; In·dis-
kretion die; ~, ~en indiscretion
Individualist der; ~en, ~en *(geh.)* individualist; Individualität die; ~,
~en *(geh.)* a) *o. Pl.* individuality; b)
(Persönlichkeit) personality; individuell 1. *Adj.* individual; private *(property, vehicle, etc.)*; 2. *adv.* individu-
ally; Individuum das; ~s, Individuen
(auch Chemie, Biol.) individual
Indiz das; ~es, ~ien a) *(Rechtsw.)*
piece of circumstantial evidence;
~ien circumstantial evidence *sing.;* b)
(Anzeichen) sign (für of)
indoktrinieren *tr. V.* indoctrinate
Indonesien [ɪndoˈneːzi̯ən] (das) Indonesia; Indonesier der; ~s, ~ Indonesian; indonesisch *Adj.* Indonesian
industrialisieren *tr. V.* industrialize;
Industrialisierung die; ~: industri-
alization; Industrie die; ~, ~n industry
Industrie-: ~betrieb der industrial
firm; ~gebiet das industrial area;
~kaufmann der *person with three
years' business training employed on
the business side of an industrial company*
industriell 1. *Adj.* industrial; 2. *adv.*
industrially; Industrielle der/die;
adj. Dekl. industrialist
Industrie-: ~staat der industrial nation; ~stadt die industrial town;
~zweig der branch of industry
in·einander *Adv.* ~ verliebt sein be in
love with each other *or* one another;
~ verschlungene Ornamente inter-
twined decorations; ineinander|-
greifen *unr. itr. V.* mesh together
(lit. or fig.)
infam 1. *Adj.* disgraceful; 2. *adv.* disgracefully
Infanterie die; ~, ~n *(Milit.)* infantry
Infarkt der; ~[e]s, ~e *(Med.)* infarc-
tion
Infekt der; ~[e]s, ~e *(Med.)* infection
Infektion [ɪnfɛkˈtsi̯oːn] die; ~, ~en
(Med.) a) *(Ansteckung)* infection; b)
(ugs.: Entzündung) inflammation
Infektions-: ~gefahr die *(Med.)* risk
of infection; ~herd der *(Med.)* seat of
the/an infection; ~krankheit die
(Med.) infectious disease
Inferno das; ~s *(geh.)* inferno
Infinitiv der; ~s, ~e *(Sprachw.)* in-
finitive

infizieren 1. *tr. V.* infect; 2. *refl. V.*
become infected; sich bei jmdm. ~: be
infected by sb.
in flagranti *Adv. (geh.)* in flagrante
[delicto]
Inflation die; ~, ~en *(Wirtsch.)* inflation; *(Zeit der ~)* period of inflation
in·folge 1. *Präp.* + *Gen.* as a result
of; 2. *Adv.* ~ von etw. *(Dat.)* as a result
of sth.
infolge·dessen *Adv.* consequently
Informatik die; ~: computer science
no art.; Information die; ~, ~en a)
information *no pl., no indef. art.* (über
+ *Akk.* about, on); eine ~: [a piece of]
information; b) *(Büro)* information
bureau; *(Stand)* information desk
Informations-: ~material das in-
formational literature; ~quelle die
source of information
informativ *Adj.* informative; informieren 1. *tr. V.* inform (über + *Akk.*
about); 2. *refl. V.* inform oneself, find
out (über + *Akk.* about)
Infra·rot das; ~s *(Physik)* infra-red
radiation; Infra·struktur die infra-
structure
Infusion die; ~, ~en *(Med.)* infusion
Ing. *Abk.* Ingenieur; Ingenieur [ɪnʒe-
ˈni̯øːɐ̯] der; ~s, ~e [qualified] engineer
Ingwer der; ~s, ~ ginger
Inhaber der; ~s, ~ a) holder; b) *(Besitzer)* owner
inhaftieren *tr. V.* take into custody;
detain; Inhaftierung die; ~, ~en
detention
inhalieren *tr. V.* inhale
In·halt der; ~[e]s, ~e a) contents *pl.;*
b) *(einer Geschichte usw.)* content; c)
(bes. Math.) (Flächen~) area;
(Raum~) volume
Inhalts-: ~angabe die summary [of
contents]; synopsis; *(eines Films, Dra-
mas)* synopsis; ~verzeichnis das
table of contents; *(auf einem Paket)*
list of contents
in·human *Adj.* a) *(unmenschlich)* inhuman; b) *(rücksichtslos)* inhumane
Initiale die; ~, ~n initial [letter]
Initiative die; ~, ~n initiative; Initiator [iniˈtsi̯aːtor] der; ~s, ~en initiator;
(einer Organisation) founder
Injektion die; ~, ~en *(Med.)* injection; injizieren *tr. V. (Med.)* inject
inkl. *Abk.* inklusive incl.
inklusive [ɪnkluˈziːvə] 1. *Präp.* + *Gen.*
(bes. Kaufmannsspr.) including; 2.
Adv. inclusive
inkognito *Adv. (geh.)* incognito

in·kompetent *Adj.* incompetent; **In·kompetenz** die incompetence
in·konsequent 1. *Adj.* inconsistent; **2.** *adv.* inconsistently; **In·konsequenz** die inconsistency
in·korrekt 1. *Adj.* incorrect; **2.** *adv.* incorrectly
In·kraft·treten das; ~s: mit [dem] ~ des Gesetzes when the law comes/ came into force
In·land das; ~[e]s a) im ~: at home; b) *(Binnenland)* interior; inland; im/ins ~: inland; **inländisch** *Adj.* domestic; home-produced *(goods)*
Inlands-: ~markt der domestic market; ~porto das inland postage
in·mitten 1. *Präp.* + *Gen. (geh.)* in the midst of; **2.** *Adv.* ~ von in the midst of
inne|haben *unr. tr. V.* hold, occupy *(position)*; hold *(office)*
innen *Adv.* inside; *(auf/an der Innenseite)* on the inside
innen-, Innen-: ~architekt der interior designer; ~aufnahme die *(Fot.)* indoor photo[graph]; *(Film)* interior shot; ~einrichtung die furnishings *pl.*; ~hof der inner courtyard; ~leben das; *o. Pl.* a) [inner] thoughts and feelings *pl.*; b) *(oft scherzh.: Ausstattung)* inside; ~minister der Minister of the Interior; ≈ Home Secretary *(Brit.);* ≈ Secretary of the Interior *(Amer.);* ~politik die *(eines Staates)* home affairs *pl.; (einer Regierung)* domestic policy/policies *pl.;* ~politisch *s.* ~politik: **1.** *Adj.* ~politische Fragen matters of domestic policy; **2.** *adv.* as regards home affairs/domestic policy; ~stadt die town centre; downtown *(Amer.); (einer Großstadt)* city centre
inner... *Adj.* inner; *(inländisch; Med.)* internal; inside *(pocket, lane)*; **Innere** das; *adj. Dekl.; o. Pl.* inside; *(eines Gebäudes, Wagens, Schiffes)* interior; inside; *(eines Landes)* interior; **Innereien** *Pl.* entrails; *(Kochk.)* offal *sing.;* **inner·halb 1.** *Präp.* + *Gen.* a) within; ~ der Familie/Partei *(fig.)* within the family/party; b) *(binnen)* within; ~ einer Woche within a week; **2.** *Adv.* a) ~ von within; b) *(im Verlauf)* ~ von zwei Jahren within two years; **innerlich 1.** *Adj.* inner; **2.** *adv.* inwardly; **innerst...** *Adj.* innermost; **Innerste** das; *adj. Dekl.; o. Pl.* innermost being
inne|wohnen *itr. V. (geh.)* etw. wohnt

jmdm./einer Sache ~: sb./sth. possesses sth.
innig 1. *Adj.* deep *(affection, sympathy)*; fervent *(wish)*; intimate *(friendship); mein ~ster Dank* my sincerest thanks; **2.** *adv. (love)* with all one's heart; **Innigkeit** die; ~: depth; *(einer Beziehung)* intimacy
Innung ['ɪnʊŋ] die; ~, ~en [trade] guild
in·offiziell 1. *Adj.* unofficial; **2.** *adv.* unofficially
in puncto as regards
ins *Präp.* + *Art.* = in das
Insasse der; ~n, ~n a) *(Fahrgast)* passenger; b) *(Bewohner)* inmate
ins·besond[e]re *Adv.* particularly; in particular
In·schrift die inscription
Insekt [ɪn'zɛkt] das; ~s, ~en insect
Insel die; ~, ~n island
Inserat das; ~[e]s, ~e advertisement *(in a newspaper);* **Inserent** der; ~en, ~en advertiser; **inserieren** *itr.V.* advertise
ins·geheim *Adv.* secretly
ins·gesamt *Adv.* in all; altogether; *(alles in allem)* all in all
insofern 1. *Adv.* [ɪn'zo:fɐn] *(in dieser Hinsicht)* to this extent; **2.** *Konj.* [ɪnzo-'fɛrn] *(falls)* provided [that]
insoweit [ɪn'zo:vait/ɪnzo'vait] *Adv./ Konj. s.* **insofern**
in spe [ɪn 'spe:] future *attrib.; mein Schwiegersohn ~ ~:* my future son-in-law
Inspektion [ɪnspɛk'tsio:n] die; ~, ~en inspection; *(Kfz-W.)* service
Inspiration [ɪnspira'tsio:n] die; ~, ~en inspiration; **inspirieren** *tr. V.* inspire
inspizieren *tr. V.* inspect
Installateur [ɪnstala'tø:ɐ] der; ~s, ~e plumber; *(Gas~)* [gas-]fitter; *(Heizungs~)* heating engineer; *(Elektro~)* electrician; **Installation** [ɪnstala-'tsio:n] die; ~, ~en installation; *(Rohre)* plumbing *no pl.;* **installieren** *tr. V.* install
in·stand *Adv.* etw. ist gut/schlecht ~: sth. is in good/poor condition; etw. ~ halten keep sth. in good condition; etw. ~ setzen/bringen repair sth.; **In·stand·haltung** die maintenance
in·ständig 1. *Adj.* urgent; **2.** *adv.* urgently
Instanz [ɪn'stants] die; ~, ~en a) authority; b) *(Rechtsw.)* [die] erste/zweite/dritte ~: the court of original jurisdiction/the appeal court/the court of

final appeal; **durch alle ~en gehen** go through all the courts
Instinkt [ɪn'stɪŋkt] der; ~[e]s, ~e instinct; **instinktiv** 1. *Adj.* instinctive; 2. *adv.* instinctively
Institut das; ~[e]s, ~e a) institute; **Institution** [ɪnstitu'tsi̯oːn] die; ~, ~en *(auch fig.)* institution
Instruktion [ɪnstrʊk'tsi̯oːn] die; ~, ~en instruction
Instrument [ɪnstru'mɛnt] das; ~[e]s, ~e instrument; **instrumental** *(Musik)* 1. *Adj.* instrumental; 2. *adv.* instrumentally
Insulin das; ~s insulin
inszenieren *tr. V.* stage; put on; *(Regie führen bei)* direct; *(fig.) (einfädeln)* engineer; *(organisieren)* stage; **Inszenierung** die; ~, ~en staging; *(Regie)* direction; *(Aufführung)* production
intakt *Adj.* a) *(unbeschädigt)* intact; b) *(funktionsfähig)* in [proper] working order *postpos.;* healthy ‹*economy*›
integer *Adj.* **eine integre Persönlichkeit** a person of integrity; ~ **sein** be a person of integrity
Integral das; ~s, ~s *(Math.)* integral
integrieren *tr. V.* integrate
Intellekt der; ~[e]s intellect; **intellektuell** *Adj.* intellectual; **Intellektuelle** der/die; *adj. Dekl.* intellectual; **intelligent** 1. *Adj.* intelligent; 2. *adv.* intelligently; **Intelligenz** die; ~a) intelligence; b) *(Gesamtheit der Intellektuellen)* intelligentsia; **Intelligenz·quotient** der intelligence quotient
Intendant der; ~en, ~en *(Theater)* manager and artistic director; *(Fernseh~, Rundfunk~)* director-general
Intensität die; ~: intensity
intensiv 1. *Adj. (gründlich)* intensive *(kräftig)* intense; 2. *adv.* intensively; **intensivieren** *tr. V.* intensify; increase ‹*exports*›; strengthen ‹*connections*›; **Intensiv·station** die intensive-care unit
Intercity-Zug der inter-city train
interessant 1. *Adj.* interesting; 2. *adv.* ~ **schreiben** write in an interesting way; **interessanterweise** *Adv.* interestingly enough; **Interesse** das; ~s, ~ an interest; ~ **an jmdm./etw. haben** be interested in sb./sth.; **interesse·halber** *Adv.* out of interest; **Interessen·gebiet** das field of interest; **Interessent** der; ~en, ~en interested person; *(möglicher Käufer)* potential buyer; **Interessen·ver-**

band der [organized] interest group; **Interessen·vertretung die a)** representation; b) *(Vertreter von Interessen)* representative body; **interessieren** 1. *refl. V.* sich für jmdn./etw. ~: be interested in sb./sth. 2. *tr. V.* interest; **das interessiert mich nicht** I'm not interested [in it]; **interessiert** *Adj.* interested **(an** + *Dat.* in)
Interjektion [ɪntɛi̯ɛk'tsi̯oːn] die; ~, ~en *(Sprachw.)* interjection
Interkontinental·rakete die *(Milit.)* intercontinental ballistic missile
intern 1. *Adj.* internal; 2. *adv.* internally
Internat das; ~[e]s, ~e boarding-school
inter·national 1. *Adj.* international; 2. *adv.* internationally; **Inter·nationale** die; ~, ~n a) International; International; b) *(Lied)* Internationale
Internats-: ~**schüler** der, ~**schülerin** die boarding-school pupil; boarder
internieren *tr. V. (Milit.)* intern; **Internierung** die; ~, ~en internment
Internist der; ~en, ~en *(Med.)* internist
Interpol die; ~: Interpol *no art.*
Interpret der; ~en, ~en interpreter *(of music, text, events, etc.);* **Interpretation** [ɪntɛrpreta'tsi̯oːn] die; ~, ~en interpretation *(of music, text, events, etc.);* **interpretieren** *tr. V.* interpret ‹*music, texts, events, etc.*›; **Interpretin** die; ~, ~nen *s.* Interpret
Interpunktion [ɪntɛrpʊŋk'tsi̯oːn] die; ~ *(Sprachw.)* punctuation
Intervall [ɪntɛr'val] das; ~s, ~e *(Musik, Math.)* interval
intervenieren *itr. V. (geh., Politik)* intervene; **Intervention** [ɪntɛrvɛn'tsi̯oːn] die; ~, ~en *(geh., Politik)* intervention; *(Protest)* representations *pl.*
Interview [ɪntɐ'vi̯uː] das; ~s, ~s interview; **interviewen** [ɪntɐ'vi̯uːən] *tr. V.* interview
intim 1. *Adj.* intimate; 2. *adv.* ~ **befreundet sein** be intimate friends; **Intimität** [ɪntimi'tɛːt] die; ~, ~en intimacy; **Intim·sphäre** die private life
in·tolerant *Adj.* intolerant
intransitiv 1. *Adj. (Sprachw.)* intransitive; 2. *adv.* intransitively
Intrige [ɪn'triːgə] die; ~, ~n intrigue
Intuition [ɪntu̯i'tsi̯oːn] die; ~, ~en intuition; **intuitiv** 1. *Adj.* intuitive; 2. *adv.* intuitively

intus ['ɪntʊs] *in etw.* ~ **haben** *(ugs.) (begriffen haben)* have got sth. into one's head; *(gegessen od. getrunken haben)* have put sth. away *(coll.)*
Invalide der; *adj. Dekl.* invalid
Invasion die; ~, ~**en** invasion
Inventar das; ~**s**, ~**e** *(einer Firma)* fittings and equipment *pl.; (eines Hauses, Büros)* furnishings and fittings *pl.;* **Inventur** die; ~, ~**en** stocktaking
investieren *tr., itr. V. (auch fig.)* invest **(in** + *Akk.* in); **Investition** [ɪnvɛsti'tsi̯oːn] die; ~, ~**en** investment; **Investitions·güter** *Pl. (Wirtsch.)* capital goods; **Investor** [ɪn'vɛstɔr] der; ~**s**, ~**en** [-'toːrən] *(Wirtsch.)* investor
in·wie·fern *Adv.* in what way; *(bis zu welchem Grade)* to what extent; **in·wie·weit** *Adv.* to what extent
Inzest der; ~|**e|s**, ~**e** incest; **In·zucht** die; ~: inbreeding
in·zwischen *Adv.* **a)** *(seither)* in the meantime; since [then]; **b)** *(bis zu einem Zeitpunkt) (in der Gegenwart)* by now; *(in der Vergangenheit/Zukunft)* by then; **c)** *(währenddessen)* meanwhile
IOK [iːoːˈkaː] das; ~|s| Internationales Olympisches Komitee IOC
Ion das; ~**s**, ~**en** *(Physik, Chemie)* ion
Irak (das); ~**s** *od.* der; ~|s| Iraq; **Iraker** der; ~**s**, ~Iraqi; **irakisch** Iraqi
Iran (das); ~**s** *od.* der; ~|s| Iran; **Iraner** der; ~**s**, ~; **iranisch** *Adj.* Iranian
irden *Adj.* earthen[ware]; **irdisch** *Adj.* **a)** earthly; worldly ⟨*goods, pleasures, possessions*⟩; **b)** *(zur Erde gehörig)* terrestrial; **das** ~**e Leben** life on earth
Ire der; ~**n**, ~**n** Irishman
irgend *Adv.* **a)** ~ **jemand** someone; somebody; *(fragend, verneinend)* anyone; anybody; ~ **etwas** something; *(fragend, verneinend)* anything; ~ **so etwas** something like that; **b)** *(irgendwie)* **wenn** ~ **möglich** if at all possible
irgend-: ~**ein** *Indefinitpron.* **a)** *(attr.)* some; *(fragend, verneinend)* any; **b)** *(subst.)* ~**einer**/~**eine** someone; somebody; *(fragend, verneinend)* anyone; anybody; ~**eines** *od. (ugs.)* ~**eins** any one; ~**einmal** *Adv.* sometime; ~**wann** *Adv.* [at] some time [or other]; *(zu jeder beliebigen Zeit)* [at] any time; ~**was** *Indefinitpron. (ugs.)*

something [or other]; *(fragend, verneinend)* anything; ~**welch** *Indefinitpron.* some; *(fragend, verneinend)* any; ~**wer** *Indefinitpron. (ugs.)* somebody or other *(coll.); (fragend, verneinend)* anyone; anybody; ~**wie** *Adv.* somehow; ~**wo** *Adv.* somewhere; *(fragend, verneinend)* anywhere; ~**woher** *Adv.* from somewhere; *(fragend, verneinend)* from anywhere; ~**wohin** *Adv.* somewhere; *(fragend, verneinend)* anywhere
Irin die; ~, ~**nen** Irishwoman
Iris die; ~, ~ *(Bot., Anat.)* iris
irisch *Adj.* Irish; **Irland (das);** ~**s** Ireland
Ironie die; ~, ~**n** irony; **ironisch 1.** *Adj.* ironic; ironical; **2.** *adv.* ironically
irre 1. *Adj.* insane; **2.** *adv. (salopp)* terribly *(coll.);* **Irre** der/die; *adj. Dekl.* madman/madwoman; lunatic; *(fig.)* lunatic
irre|führen *tr. V.* mislead; *(täuschen)* deceive; **Irreführung die: eine bewußte** ~**führung** a deliberate attempt to mislead; ~**führung der Öffentlichkeit** misleading the public
irrelevant ['ɪrelevant] *Adj.* irrelevant *(für* to)
irre|machen *tr. V.* disconcert; put off; **irren 1.** *refl. V.* be mistaken; **Sie haben sich in der Nummer geirrt** you've got the wrong number; **2.** *itr. V.* **a) da** ~ **Sie** you are wrong there; **b)** *mit sein (ziellos umherstreifen)* wander
Irren-: ~**anstalt die** *(veralt. abwertend)* mental home; ~**haus das** *(abwertend)* [lunatic] asylum
Irr·fahrt die wandering; **irriger·weise** *Adv.* mistakenly
irritieren *tr., itr. V.* **a)** *(verwirren)* put off; **b)** *(stören)* disturb
irr-, Irr-: ~**licht das** will o' the wisp; ~**sinn** der; *o. Pl.* **a)** insanity; madness; **b)** *(ugs. abwertend)* lunacy; ~**sinnig 1.** *Adj.* **a)** *(geistig gestört)* insane; mad; *(absurd)* idiotic; **b)** *(ugs.: extrem)* terrible *(coll.);* terrific *(coll.)* ⟨*speed, heat, cold*⟩; **2.** *adv. (ugs.)* terribly *(coll.)*
Irrtum der; ~**s**, Irrtümer mistake; ~! wrong!; **im** ~ **sein** be wrong *or* mistaken; **irrtümlich 1.** *Adj.* incorrect; **2.** *adv.* by mistake
Ischias ['ɪʃi̯as] der *od.* das *od. Med.* die; ~: sciatica
Islam [ɪsˈlaːm *od.* ˈɪslam] der; ~|s|: der ~: Islam; **islamisch** *Adj.* Islamic

Island (das); ~s Iceland; **Isländer**
der; ~s, ~ Icelander; **isländisch**
Adj. Icelandic
Isolation die; ~, ~en *s.* Isolierung;
Isolator der; ~s, ~en insulator; **Iso-**
lier·band das; *Pl.* ~bänder insulating tape; **isolieren** *tr. V.* **a)** isolate;
b) *(Technik)* insulate ⟨*wiring, wall,*
etc.⟩; lag ⟨*boilers, pipes, etc.*⟩; **Iso-**
lier·station die *(Med.)* isolation
ward; **Isolierung die**; ~, ~en **a)**
isolation; **b)** *(Technik) s.* isolieren **b:**
insulation; lagging
Isotop das; ~s, ~e isotope
Israel ['ɪsraeːl] **(das)**; ~s Israel; **Israe-**
li der; ~|s|, ~|s|/**die**; ~, ~|s| Israeli; **is-**
raelisch *Adj.* Israeli; **Israelit der**;
~en, ~en Israelite; **israelitisch** *Adj.*
Israelite
iß *Imperativ Sg. v.* essen
ißt *2. u. 3. Pers. Sg. Präsens v.* essen
ist *3. Pers. Sg. Präsens v.* sein
Italien [i'taːliən] **(das)**; ~s Italy; **Ita-**
liener [ita'liːenɐ] der; ~s, ~: Italian;
italienisch *Adj.* Italian
I-Tüpfel[chen] das; ~s, ~: final
touch; **bis aufs |letzte|** ~: down to the
last detail
i. V. [iː'faʊ] *Abk.* in Vertretung

J

j, J [jɔt, *österr.*: jeː] **das**; ~, ~: j/J
ja *1. Interj.* yes; *(nachgestellt: nicht*
wahr?) won't you/doesn't it *etc.*?; **2.**
Partikel **Sie wissen ja, daß ...:** you
know, of course, that ...; **da seid ihr ja!**
there you are!; **Ja das**; ~|s|, ~|s| yes;
mit ~ **stimmen** vote yes
Jacht die; ~, ~en yacht
Jacke die; ~, ~n jacket; *(gestrickt)*
cardigan; **Jacken·kleid das** dress
and jacket combination; **Jacket-**
krone ['dʒɛkɪt-] **die** *(Zahnmed.)*
jacket crown; **Jackett** [ʒa'kɛt] **das**;
~s, ~s jacket
Jade die; ~: jade
Jagd die; ~, ~en **a)** *o. Pl.* die ~: shooting; hunting; **auf die** ~ **gehen** go hunt-
ing/shooting; **b)** *(Veranstaltung)*

shoot; *(Hetzjagd)* hunt; **c)** *(Verfol-*
gung) hunt; *(Verfolgungsjagd)* chase;
auf jmdn./etw. ~ **machen** hunt for sb./
sth.
Jagd-: ~**beute die** bag; kill; ~**bom-**
ber der *(Luftwaffe)* fighter-bomber;
~**flieger der** *(Luftwaffe)* fighter pilot;
~**flugzeug das** *(Luftwaffe)* fighter
aircraft; ~**gewehr das** sporting gun;
~**horn das** hunting-horn; ~**hund der**
gun-dog; ~**hütte die** shooting box;
~**revier das** preserve; shoot;
~**schein der** game licence; ~**wurst**
die chasseur sausage; ~**zeit die** open
season
jagen 1. *tr. V.* **a)** hunt ⟨*game, fugitive,*
criminal, etc.⟩; shoot ⟨*game, game*
birds⟩; *(hetzen)* chase ⟨*fugitive, crim-*
inal, etc.⟩; **b)** *(treiben)* drive; **jmdn. aus**
dem Haus ~: throw sb. out of the
house; **2.** *itr. V. (die Jagd ausüben)* go
shooting *or* hunting; **Jäger der**; ~s,
~: **a)** hunter; **b)** *(Milit.)* rifleman; **c)**
(Soldatenspr.: Jagdflugzeug) fighter;
Jäger·hut der huntsman's hat
Jäger-: ~**latein das** *(scherzh.)*
[hunter's] tall story/stories; **das ist das**
reinste ~**latein** that's all wild exaggeration; ~**rock der** hunting jacket;
~**schnitzel das** *(Kochk.)* escalope
chasseur
Jaguar der; ~s, ~e jaguar
jäh [jɛː] **1.** *Adj. (geh.)* **a)** sudden; abrupt
⟨*change, movement, stop*⟩; sudden,
sharp ⟨*pain*⟩; **b)** *(steil)* steep; precipitous; **2.** *adv.* **a)** ⟨*change*⟩ abruptly; **b)**
(steil) ⟨*fall, drop*⟩ steeply; **jählings**
Adv. (geh.) **a)** *(plötzlich)* ⟨*change, end,*
stop⟩ suddenly, abruptly; ⟨*die*⟩ suddenly; **b)** *(steil)* steeply
Jahr das; ~|e|s, ~e year; **ein halbes** ~:
six months; **im** ~|e| **1908** in [the year]
1908; **er ist zwanzig** ~e **|alt|** he is
twenty years old; **Kinder bis zu zwölf**
~**en** children up to the age of twelve;
zwischen den ~**en** between Christmas
and the New Year; **jahr·aus** *Adv.* ~,
jahrein year in, year out; **jahre·lang**
1. *Adj.; nicht präd.* [many] years of;
long-standing ⟨*feud, friendship*⟩; **2.**
adv. for [many] years
jähren *refl. V.* **heute jährt sich zum**
zehntenmal, daß ...: it is ten years ago
today that ...
Jahres-: ~**bilanz die** *(Wirtsch., Kauf-*
mannsspr.) annual balance [of ac-
counts]; *(Dokument)* annual balance
sheet; ~**einkommen das** annual income; ~**ende das** end of the year;

~frist; *o. Art.; o. Pl.* in *od.* **innerhalb**
od. **binnen** ~**frist** within [a period of] a
or one year; ~**hälfte die: die erste/**
zweite ~**hälfte** the first/secound half
or six months of the year; ~**karte die**
yearly season ticket; ~**tag der** anniversary; ~**urlaub der** annual holiday *or (formal)* leave *or (Amer.)* vacation; ~**wechsel der** turn of the year;
zum ~**wechsel die besten Wünsche** best
wishes for the New Year; ~**zahl die**
date; ~**zeit die** season
Jahr·gang der a) *(Altersklasse)* year;
der ~ **1900** those born in 1900; b) *(ei-*
nes Weines) vintage; c) *(einer Zeit-*
schrift) set [of issues] for a/the year;
Jahr·hundert das century; **Jahr-**
hundert·wende die turn of the century; -**jährig** a) *(... Jahre alt)* ein elf-
jähriges **Kind** an eleven-year-old
child; b) *(... Jahre dauernd)*
... year's/years'; **nach vierjähriger Vor-**
bereitung after four years' preparation; **mit dreijähriger Verspätung**
three years late; **jährlich 1.** *Adj.;*
nicht präd. annual; yearly; **2.** *adv.* annually; yearly; **zweimal** ~: twice a
year
Jahr-: ~**markt der** fair; fun-fair;
~**tausend das** thousand years; mil-
lennium; ~**zehnt das** decade
jahrzehnte·lang 1. *Adj.; nicht präd.*
decades of ⟨*practice, experience, etc.*⟩;
2. *adv.* for decades
Jäh·zorn der violent anger; **jäh·zor-**
nig 1. *Adj.* violent-tempered; **2.** *adv.*
in a blind rage
ja·ja *Part. (ugs.)* a) *(seufzend)* ~[, so ist
das Leben] o well[, that's life]; b) *(un-*
geduldig) ~[, ich komme schon]! all
right, all right[, I'm coming]!
Jalousie [ʒalu'ziː] **die;** ~, ~**n** Venetian
blind
Jamaika (das); -**s** Jamaica; **Jamai-**
kaner der; ~**s,** ~Jamaican
Jammer der; ~**s** [mournful] wailing;
(Elend) misery; **jämmerlich 1.** *Adj.*
pitiful; b) wretched ⟨*appearance, ex-*
istence, etc.⟩; paltry, meagre ⟨*quant-*
ity⟩; **2.** *adv.* pitifully; **jammern** *itr.*
V. wail; *(sich beklagen)* moan; **jam-**
mer·schade *Adj.; nicht attr. (ugs.)*
es ist ~**schade, daß ...:** it's a crying
shame that ...; **es ist** ~**schade um ihn**
it's a great pity about him
Janker der; ~**s,** ~ *(südd., österr.)* Alpine jacket
Januar der; ~[**s**], ~**e** January
Japan (das); ~**s** Japan; **Japaner der;**

~**s,** ~Japanese; **japanisch** *Adj.* Jap-
anese
japsen *itr. V. (ugs.)* pant
Jargon [jar'gõ:] **der;** ~**s,** ~**s** jargon
Jasmin der; ~**s,** ~**e** jasmine
Ja·stimme die yes-vote
jäten *tr., itr. V.* weed; **Unkraut** ~:
weed
Jauche die; ~, ~**n** liquid manure;
Jauche·grube die liquid-manure
reservoir
jauchzen *itr. V.* cheer; **vor Freude** ~:
shout for joy; **Jauchzer der;** ~**s,** ~:
cry of delight
jaulen *itr. V.* howl
Jause die; ~, ~**n** *(österr.)* a) snack; eine ~ **machen** have a snack; b) *(Nach-*
mittagskaffee) [afternoon] tea
ja·wohl *Part.* certainly; **Ja·wort das**
consent; **jmdm. das** ~ **geben** consent
to marry sb.
Jazz [dʒæz *od.* dʒɛs *od.* jats] **der;** ~:
jazz; **Jazz·keller der** jazz cellar
¹je 1. *Adv.* a) *(jemals)* ever; **mehr/bes-**
ser denn je more/better than ever; b)
(jeweils) **je zehn Personen** ten people
at a time; **sie kosten je 30 DM** they
cost 30 DM each; c) *(entsprechend)* **je**
nach Gewicht according to weight; **2.**
Präp. mit Akk. per; for each; **3.** *Konj.*
je länger, je lieber the longer the better; **je nachdem** it all depends
²je *Interj.* **ach je, wie schade!** oh dear,
what a shame!
Jeans [dʒiːnz] *Pl. od.* **die;** ~, ~: jeans
pl.; denims *pl.*
jede *s.* jeder; **jeden·falls** *Adv.* a) in
any case; b) *(zumindest)* at any rate;
jeder, jede, jedes *Indefinitpron. u.*
unbest. Zahlwort **1.** *attr.* a) *(alle)*
every; b) *(alle einzeln)* each; c) *(jegli-*
cher) all; **2.** *alleinstehend* a) *(alle)*
everyone; everybody; b) *(alle einzeln)*
jedes der Kinder each of the children
jeder-: ~**mann** *Indefinitpron. u. un-*
best. Zahlwort; nur alleinstehend
everyone; everybody; ~**zeit** *Adv.* [at]
any time
jedes *s.* jeder; **jedes·mal** *Adv.* every
time
je·doch *Konj., Adv.* however
je·her [od. '-'-] *Adv.* **seit** *od.* **von** ~: always; since time immemorial
jemals *Adv.* ever
jemand *Indefinitpron.* someone;
somebody; *(fragend, verneinend)*
anyone; anybody
Jemen (das); ~**s** *od.* **der;** ~[**s**] Yemen
jener, jene, jenes *Demonstrativpron.*

(geh.) **1.** *attr.* that; *(im Pl.)* those; **2.** *alleinstehend* that one; *(im Pl.)* those **jenseits 1.** *Präp. mit Gen.* on the other side of; *(in größerer Entfernung)* beyond; **2.** *Adv.* on the other side; ~ **vom Rhein** on the other side of the Rhine; **Jenseits das;** ~: hereafter; beyond
¹**Jersey** ['dʒøːɐ̯zi] **der;** ~|s|, ~s *(Textilind.)* jersey
²**Jersey das;** ~s, ~s *(Sport: Trikot)* jersey
Jesus (der); Jesu Jesus
Jet [dʒɛt] **der;** ~|s|, ~s jet; **mit einem ~ fliegen/reisen** fly/travel by jet
jetzig *Adj.; nicht präd.* current
jetzt *Adv.* **a)** just now; **bis** ~: up to now; **bis ~ noch nicht** not yet; **von ~ an** *od.* **ab** from now on[wards]; **erst ~** *od.* ~ **erst** only just; **schon** ~: already; **b)** *(heutzutage)* now; nowadays
jeweilig *Adj.; nicht präd.* **a)** *(in einem bestimmten Fall)* particular; **b)** *(zu einer bestimmten Zeit)* current; of the time *postpos., not pred.;* **c)** *(zugehörig, zugewiesen)* respective; **jeweils** *Adv.* **a)** *(jedesmal)* ~ **am ersten/letzten Mittwoch des Monats** on the first/last Wednesday of each month; **b)** *(zur Zeit)* at the time
Jg. *Abk.* **Jahrgang**
Jh. *Abk.* **Jahrhundert** c.
jiddisch ['jɪdɪʃ] *Adj.* Yiddish
Job [dʒɔp] **der;** ~s, ~s *(ugs.; auch DV)* job; **jobben** [dʒɔbn̩] *itr. V. (ugs.)* do a job/jobs
Joch das; ~|e|s, ~e yoke
Jockei, Jockey ['dʒɔke *od.* 'dʒɔki] **der;** ~s, ~s jockey
Jod [joːt] **das;** ~|e|s iodine
jodeln *itr., tr. V.* yodel
jod·haltig *Adj.* iodiferous
Joga der *od.* **das;** ~|s| yoga
joggen ['dʒɔgn̩] *itr. V.; mit Richtungsangabe mit sein* jog
Joghurt ['joːgʊrt] **der** *od.* **das;** ~|s|, ~|s| yoghurt; **Joghurt·becher der** yoghurt pot *(Brit.)* or *(Amer.)* container
Johannis·beere die currant; **rote/ weiße/schwarze** ~n redcurrants/white currants/blackcurrants
johlen *itr. V.* yell; *(vor Wut)* howl
Joint [dʒɔɪnt] **der;** ~s, ~s *(ugs.)* joint *(sl.)*
Jolle die; ~, ~n keel-centre-board yawl
Jongleur [ʒɔŋˈløːɐ̯] **der;** ~s, ~e juggler; **jonglieren** *tr., itr. V.* juggle
Joppe die; ~, ~n heavy jacket
Jordanien (das); ~s Jordan; **Jorda-**

nier der; ~s, ~: Jordanian; **jordanisch** *Adj.* Jordanian
Jot das; ~, ~: j, J
Journalismus der; ~: journalism *no art.;* **Journalist der;** ~en, ~en journalist; **journalistisch 1.** *Adj.; nicht präd.* journalistic; **eine ~e Ausbildung** a training in journalism; **2.** *adv.* journalistically; ~ **tätig sein** be a journalist
jr. *Abk.* **junior** Jr.
Jubel der; ~s rejoicing; jubilation; *(laut)* cheering; **jubeln** *itr. V.* cheer; **über etw.** *(Akk.)* ~: rejoice over sth.; **Jubilar der;** ~s, ~e man celebrating his anniversary/birthday; **Jubiläum das;** ~s, **Jubiläen** anniversary; *(eines Monarchen)* jubilee; **jubilieren** *itr. V. (geh.)* jubilate *(literary);* rejoice
juchzen ['jʊxtsn̩] *itr. V. (ugs.)* shout with glee
jucken 1. *tr., itr. V.* **a) mir juckt die Haut** I itch; **es juckt mich hier** I've got an itch here; **b)** *(Juckreiz verursachen)* irritate; **2.** *tr. V. (reizen, verlocken)* **es juckt mich, das zu tun** I am itching to do it; **3.** *refl. V. (ugs.: sich kratzen)* scratch; **Juck·reiz der** itch
Jude der; ~n, ~n Jew; **Juden·stern der** *(ns.)* Star of David; **Judentum das;** ~s **a)** *(Volk)* Jewry; Jews *pl.;* **b)** *(Kultur u. Religion)* Judaism; **Jüdin die;** ~, ~nen Jewess; **jüdisch** *Adj.* Jewish
Judo ['juːdo] **das;** ~|s| judo *no art.*
Jugend die; ~ **a)** youth; **b)** *(Jugendliche)* young people
jugend-, Jugend-: ~**amt das** youth office *(agency responsible for education and welfare of young people);* ~**arrest der** detention in a community home; ~**bewegung die** *(hist.)* [German] youth Movement; ~**buch das** book for young people; ~**frei** *Adj.* ⟨film, book, etc.⟩ suitable for persons under 18; **nicht** ~**frei** ⟨film⟩ not U-certificate *pred.;* ~**gefährdend** *Adj.* liable to have an undesirable influence on the moral development of young people *postpos.;* ~**heim das** youth centre; ~**herberge die** youth hostel; ~**kriminalität die** juvenile delinquency
jugendlich 1. *Adj.* **a)** *nicht präd.* young ⟨offender, customer, etc.⟩; **b)** *(für Jugendliche charakteristisch)* youthful; **Jugendliche der/die;** *adj. Dekl.* young person; **die** ~**n** the young people

Jugend-: ~**liebe** die sweetheart of one's youth; ~**schutz** der protection of young people; ~**schutz·gesetz** das laws *pl.* protecting young people; ~**sprache** die young people's language *no art.*; ~**stil** der art nouveau; *(in Deutschland)* Jugendstil; ~**strafe** die youth custody sentence; ~**sünde** die youthful folly; ~**zeit** die youth; ~**zentrum** das youth centre
Jugo·slawe der Yugoslav; **Jugoslawien (das)**; ~s Yugoslavia; **jugo·slawisch** *Adj.* Yugoslav[ian]
Julei der; ~|s|, ~s *s.* Juli
Juli der; ~|s|, ~s July; *s. auch* April
jung *Adj.*; jünger, jüngst... **a)** young; new ⟨*project, undertaking, sport, marriage, etc.*⟩; **b)** *(letzt...)* recent; **in jüngster Zeit** recently
¹Junge der; ~n, ~n *od. (ugs.)* Jung|en|s boy; **²Junge** das; *adj. Dekl.* **ein** ~**s** one of the young; ~ **kriegen** give birth to young; **jungen** *itr. V.* give birth; ⟨*cat*⟩ have kittens; ⟨*dog*⟩ have pups; **jungenhaft** *Adj.* boyish; **jünger** *Adj.* youngish; **sie ist noch** ~: she is still quite young; *s. auch* **jung; Jünger** der; ~s, ~: follower; **Jungfer** die; ~, ~n *(abwertend: ältere ledige Frau)* spinster; **Jungfern·fahrt** die maiden voyage; **Jungfern·häutchen** das hymen; **Jung·frau** die **a)** virgin; **b)** *(Astrol.)* Virgo; **jung·fräulich** *Adj. (geh., auch fig.)* virgin; **Jung·geselle** der bachelor; **Jung·gesellin** die; ~, ~**nen** bachelor girl
Jüngling der; ~s, ~e *(geh., spött.)* youth; boy; **jüngst** *Adv. (geh.)* recently; **jüngst...** *s.* jung; **Jüngste** der/die; *adj. Dekl.* youngest [one]
Jung-: ~**verheiratete** der/die; *adj. Dekl.*, young married man/woman; **die** ~**verheirateten** the newly-weds; ~**wähler** der first-time voter
Juni der; ~|s|, ~s June; *s. auch* April
junior *indekl. Adj.; nach Personennamen* junior; **Junior** der; ~s, ~en **a)** *(oft scherzh.)* junior *(joc.)*; **b)** *(Kaufmannsspr.)* junior partner; **Junior·chef** der owner's *or (coll.)* boss's son
Juno der; ~|s|, ~s *s.* Juni
Junta ['xʊnta] die; ~, **Junten** junta
Jura *o. Art., o. Pl.* law; ~ **studieren** read Law; **Jurist** der; ~en, ~en, **Juristin** die; ~, ~**nen** lawyer; jurist; **juristisch** *Adj.* legal
Jury [ʒy'ri:] die; ~, ~s **a)** *(Preisrichter)* panel [of judges]; jury; **b)** *(Sachverständige)* panel [of experts]

Justiz die; ~: justice; *(Behörden)* judiciary
Justiz-: ~**irrtum** der miscarriage of justice; ~**minister** der Minister of Justice; ~**vollzugs·anstalt** die *(Amtsspr.)* penal institution *(formal);* prison
Jute ['ju:tə] die; ~: jute
Juwel das *od.* der; ~s, ~en piece of jewellery; *(Edelstein)* jewel; **Juwelier** [juvə'li:ɐ̯] der; ~s jeweller; **Juwelier·geschäft** das jeweller's shop
Jux der; ~es, ~e *(ugs.)* joke

K

k, K [ka:] das; ~, ~: k/K
Kabarett das; ~s, ~s *od.* ~e **a)** satirical revue; **b)** *(Ensemble)* cabaret act; **Kabarettist** der; ~en, ~en revue performer
kabbeln *refl. V. (ugs.)* bicker (mit with)
Kabel das; ~s, ~: cable; *(für kleineres Gerät)* flex
Kabeljau der; ~s, ~e *od.* ~s cod
kabeln *tr., itr. V. (veralt.)* cable
Kabine die; ~, ~n **a)** cabin; **b)** *(Umkleideraum, abgeteilter Raum)* cubicle; **c)** *(einer Seilbahn)* [cable-]car; *(einer Seilbahn)* ~e Cabinet
Kabinett das; ~s, ~s car; **d)** *(Astron.)* Virgo; **jung·fräulich** *Kabinett* das; ~s, ~s car
Kabrio das; ~s, ~s, **Kabriolett** das; ~s, ~s convertible
Kachel die; ~, ~n [glazed] tile; **kacheln** *tr. V.* tile
Kadaver der; ~s, ~: carcass
Kader der *od. (schweiz.)* das; ~s, ~ cadre; **b)** *(Sport)* squad
Käfer der; ~s, ~: beetle
Kaff das; ~s, ~s *od.* **Käffer** *(ugs. abwertend)* dump *(coll.)*
Kaffee ['kafe *od. (österr.)* ka'fe:] der; ~s, ~s **a)** coffee; **b)** *(Nachmittags~)* afternoon coffee; ~ **trinken** have afternoon coffee
Kaffee-: ~**kanne** die coffee-pot; ~**kränzchen** das *(veralt.)* **a)** *(Zusammentreffen)* coffee afternoon; **b)** *(Gruppe)* coffee circle; ~**maschine**

die coffee-maker; ~**mühle die** coffee-grinder; ~**satz der** coffee-grounds *pl.;* ~**tante die** *(ugs. scherzh.)* coffee addict

Käfig der; ~s, ~e cage

kahl *Adj.* a) *(ohne Haare)* bald; b) *(ohne Grün, schmucklos)* bare

kahl-, Kahl-: ~|**fressen** *unr. tr. V.* etw. ~fressen strip sth. bare; ~**köpfig** *Adj.* bald[-headed]; ~|**scheren** *unr. tr. V.* jmdn. ~scheren shave sb.'s head; ~**schlag der** a) clear-felling *no indef. art.;* b) *(Waldfläche)* clear-felled area

Kahn der; ~|e|s, **Kähne** a) *(Ruder~)* rowing-boat; *(Stech~)* punt; b) *(Lastschiff)* barge

Kai der; ~s, ~s quay

Kaiser der; ~s, ~: emperor; **Kaiserin die;** ~, ~**nen** empress

Kaiser-: ~**krone die** imperial crown; ~**reich das** empire; ~**schnitt der** Caesarean section

Kajüte die; ~, ~n *(Seemannsspr.)* cabin

Kakao [ka'kau] **der;** ~s, ~s cocoa

Kakerlak der; ~s *od.* ~en, ~en cockroach

Kaktus der; ~, **Kakteen** cactus

Kalauer der; ~s, ~: corny joke *(coll.); (Wortspiel)* atrocious *or (coll.)* corny pun

Kalb das; ~|e|s, **Kälber** a) calf; b) *(ugs.: ~fleisch)* veal; **kalben** *itr. V.* calve; **Kalb·fleisch das** veal

Kalbs-: ~**braten der** *(Kochk.)* roast veal *no indef. art.; (Gericht)* roast of veal; ~**leder das** calfskin; ~**schnitzel das** veal cutlet

Kalender der; ~s, ~: calendar; *(Taschen~)* diary; **Kalender·jahr das** calendar year

Kalesche die; ~, ~n *(hist.)* barouche

Kali das; ~s, ~s potash

Kaliber das; ~s, ~: a) *(Technik, Waffenkunde)* calibre; b) *(ugs., oft abwertend)* sort; kind

Kalifornien [kali'fɔrniən] **(das)** ~s California

Kalium *(Chemie)* **das;** ~s potassium

Kalk der; ~|e|s, ~e calcium carbonate; *(Baustoff)* lime; quicklime; **kalken** *tr. V.* whitewash

Kalk-: ~**mangel der;** *o. Pl.* calcium deficiency; ~**stein der** limestone

Kalkül das *od.* **der;** ~s, ~e *(geh.)* calculation; **Kalkulation die;** ~, ~en *(auch Wirtsch.)* calculation; **kalkulieren** *tr. V.* calculate ⟨cost, price⟩; cost ⟨product, article⟩

Kalorie die; ~, ~n calorie; **kalorien·arm 1.** *Adj.* low-calorie *attrib.;* ~arm sein be low in calories; **2.** *adv.* ~arm kochen cook low-calorie meals

kalt; kälter, kältest... **1.** *Adj.* cold; frosty ⟨atmosphere, smile⟩; **2.** *adv.* a) ~ **duschen** have a cold shower **Getränke/Sekt** ~ **stellen** cool drinks/chill champagne; b) *(nüchtern)* coldly; c) *(abweisend, unfreundlich)* frostily

kalt-, Kalt-: ~|**bleiben** *unr. itr. V.;* mit sein remain unmoved; ~**blütig 1.** *Adj.* a) cool-headed; b) *(abwertend: skrupellos)* cold-blooded; **2.** *adv.* a) coolly; b) *(abwertend: skrupellos)* cold-bloodedly; ~**blütigkeit die;** ~: *s.* ~blütig **a, b:** cool-headedness; cold-bloodedness

Kälte die; ~ cold; *(fig.)* coldness

Kälte-: ~**einbruch der** *(Met.)* sudden onset of cold weather; ~**grad der** degree of frost

kälter *s.* **kalt; kältest...** *s.* **kalt; Kälte·welle die** cold spell

kalt-, Kalt-: ~**herzig** *Adj.* cold-hearted; ~**lächelnd** *Adv. (ugs. abwertend)* etw. ~lächelnd tun take callous pleasure in doing sth.; ~|**lassen** *unr. tr. V. (ugs.)* jmdn. ~lassen leave sb. unmoved; *(nicht interessieren)* leave sb. cold *(coll.);* ~|**machen** *tr. V. (salopp)* jmdn. ~machen do sb. in *(sl.);* ~**miete die** rent exclusive of heating; ~**schale die** *cold sweet soup made with fruit, beer, wine, or milk;* ~**schnäuzig** [~ʃnɔytsɪç] *(ugs.)* **1.** *Adj.* cold and insensitive; *(frech)* insolent; **2.** *adv.* coldly and insensitively; *(frech)* insolently; ~|**stellen** *tr. V. (ugs.)* jmdn. ~stellen put sb. out of the way *(coll. joc.)*

kam *1. u. 3. Pers. Prät. v.* **kommen**

Kambodscha [kam'bɔdʒa] **(das);** ~s Cambodia

käme *1. u. 3. Pers. Konjunktiv II v.* **kommen**

Kamel das; ~s, ~e camel

Kamera die; ~, ~s camera

Kamerad der; ~en, ~en companion; *(Freund)* friend; *(Mitschüler)* mate; *(Soldat)* comrade; *(Sport)* team-mate; **Kameradschaft die;** ~: comradeship; **kameradschaftlich 1.** *Adj.* comradely; **2.** *adv.* in a comradely way

Kamera·mann der *Pl.* ~**männer** *od.* ~**leute** cameraman

Kamerun ['kaməruːn] **(das);** ~s Cameroon; the Cameroons *pl.*

Kamille die; ~, ~n camomile
Kamin der, *schweiz.:* das; ~s, ~e fireplace; **Kamin·feger** der *(bes. südd.)* s. Schornsteinfeger
Kamm der; ~[e]s, **Kämme** a) comb; b) *(bei Hühnern usw.)* comb; c) *(Gebirgs~)* ridge; **kämmen** *tr. V.* comb
Kammer die; ~, ~n a) store-room; b) *(Biol., Med., Technik, Waffenkunde)* chamber; c) *(Parl.)* chamber
Kammer-: ~**diener** der *(veralt.)* valet; ~**jäger** der pest controller; ~**musik** die; *o. Pl.* chamber music; ~**sänger** der *title awarded to singer of outstanding merit;* ~**zofe** die *(veralt.)* lady's maid
Kamm·garn das worsted
Kampagne [kam'panjə] die; ~, ~n campaign
Kampf der; ~[e]s, **Kämpfe** a) *(militärisch)* battle (um for); b) *(zwischen persönlichen Gegnern)* fight; *(fig.)* struggle; c) *(Wett~)* contest; *(Boxen)* contest; bout; d) *(Einsatz aller Mittel)* fight (um, für for; gegen against); **kampf·bereit** *Adj.* ready to fight *postpos.;* ⟨army, troops⟩ ready for battle; **kämpfen** *itr. V.* a) fight; b) *(Sport: sich messen)* ⟨team⟩ play; ⟨wrestler, boxer⟩ fight
Kampfer der; ~s camphor
Kämpfer der; ~s, ~, **Kämpferin** die; ~, ~nen fighter
kampf-, Kampf-: ~**fähig** *Adj.* ⟨troops⟩ fit for action; ⟨boxer etc.⟩ fit to fight; ~**handlungen** *Pl.* fighting *sing.;* ~**richter** der *(Sport)* judge; ~**unfähig** *Adj.* ⟨troops⟩ unfit for action; ⟨boxer etc.⟩ unfit to fight
kampieren *itr. V.* camp
Kanada (das); ~s Canada; **Kanadier** [ka'na:diɐ] der; ~s, ~ Canadian; **kanadisch** *Adj.* Canadian
Kanal der; ~s, **Kanäle** a) canal; b) *(Geogr.)* der ~: the [English] Channel; c) *(für Abwässer)* sewer; d) *(zur Entwässerung, Bewässerung)* channel; *(Graben)* ditch; e) *(Rundf., Ferns., Weg der Information)* channel; **Kanalisation** die; ~, ~en sewerage system; sewers *pl.;* **kanalisieren** *tr. V.* a) *(lenken)* channel ⟨energies, goods, etc.⟩; b) *(schiffbar machen)* canalize
Kanaren *Pl.* Canaries; **Kanarien·vogel** [ka'na:riən-] der canary; **Kanarische Inseln** *Pl.* Canary Islands
Kandare die; ~, ~n curb bit; **jmdn. an die** ~ **nehmen** *(fig.)* take sb. in hand

Kandidat der; ~en, ~en a) candidate; b) *(beim Quiz usw.)* contestant; **Kandidatur** die; ~, ~en candidature (auf + *Akk.* for); **kandidieren** *itr. V.* stand [as a candidate] (für for)
kandieren *tr. V.* candy; **kandiert** crystallized ⟨orange, petal⟩; glacé ⟨cherry, pear⟩; candied ⟨peel⟩; **Kandis** der; ~, **Kandis·zucker** der rock candy
Känguruh ['kɛŋguru] das; ~s, ~s kangaroo
Kaninchen das; ~s, ~: rabbit
Kanister der; ~s, ~: can; [metal/plastic] container
kann *1. u. 3. Pers. Sg. Präsens v.* **können**
Kännchen das; ~s, ~: [small] pot; *(für Milch)* [small] jug; **Kanne** die; ~, ~n a) pot; *(für Milch, Wein, Wasser)* jug; b) *(Henkel~)* can; *(für Milch)* pail; *(beim Melken)* churn
kannst *2. Pers. Sg. Präsens v.* **können**
kannte *1. u. 3. Pers. Sg. Prät. v.* **kennen**
Kanon der; ~s, ~s canon
Kanone die; ~, ~n cannon; *(fig. ugs.: Könner)* ace
Kantate die; ~, ~n *(Musik)* cantata
Kante die; ~, ~n edge; **kantig** *Adj.* square-cut ⟨timber, stone⟩; rough-edged ⟨rock⟩; angular ⟨face⟩; square ⟨chin⟩
Kantine die; ~, ~n canteen
Kanton der; ~s, ~e canton
Kantor der; ~s, ~en choirmaster and organist
Kanu das; ~s, ~s canoe
Kanüle die; ~, ~n *(Med.)* cannula
Kanzel die; ~, ~n a) pulpit; b) *(Flugw.)* cockpit
Kanzlei die; ~, ~en a) *(veralt.: Büro)* office; b) *(Anwalts~)* chambers *pl. (of barrister);* office *(of lawyer)*
Kanzler der; ~s, ~ chancellor
Kap das; ~s, ~s cape
Kapazität die; ~, ~en a) capacity; b) *(Experte)* expert
Kapelle die; ~, ~n a) *(Archit.)* chapel; b) *(Musik~)* band; [light] orchestra
Kapell·meister der bandmaster; *(im Orchester)* conductor; *(im Theater usw.)* musical director
Kaper die; ~, ~n caper *usu. in pl.*
kapern *tr. V.* a) *(hist.)* capture; b) *(ugs.)* jmdn. |für etw.| ~ : rope sb. in[to sth.]
kapieren *(ugs.)* 1. *tr. V. (ugs.)* get *(coll.);* 2. *itr. V.* **kapiert?** got it? *(coll.)*

Kapital das; ~s, ~e *od.* ~ien a) capital; b) *(fig.)* asset; **Kapitalismus** der; ~: capitalism *no art.;* **Kapitalist** der; ~en, ~en capitalist; **kapitalistisch** *Adj.* capitalistic

Kapital·verbrechen das serious offence; *(mit Todesstrafe bedroht)* capital offence

Kapitän der; ~s, ~e *(Seew.)* captain

Kapitel das; ~s, ~: chapter

Kapitulation die; ~, ~en surrender; capitulation; **seine ~ erklären** admit defeat; **kapitulieren** *itr. V.* a) surrender; capitulate; b) *(fig.: aufgeben)* give up; **vor etw.** *(Dat.)* ~: give up in the face of sth.

Kaplan der; ~s, **Kapläne** *(kath. Kirche)* chaplain; *(Hilfsgeistlicher)* curate

Kappe die; ~, ~n cap

kappen *tr. V.* a) *(Seemannsspr.)* cut; b) *(beschneiden)* cut back ⟨hedge etc.⟩; *(abschneiden)* cut off ⟨branches etc.⟩

Käppi das; ~s, ~s garrison cap

Kapsel die; ~, ~n capsule

Kapstadt (das) Cape Town

kaputt *Adj.* a) broken; **das Telefon ist ~:** the phone is not working; b) *(ugs.: erschöpft)* shattered *(coll.)*

kaputt-: ~|**gehen** *unr. itr. V.; mit sein (ugs.) (entzweigehen)* break; ⟨machine⟩ break down, *(sl.)* pack up; ⟨light-bulb⟩ go; *(zerbrechen)* be smashed; ~|**lachen** *refl. V. (ugs.)* kill oneself [laughing] *(coll.);* ~|**machen** (ugs.) 1. *tr. V.* break; spoil ⟨sth. made with effort⟩; ruin ⟨clothes, furniture, etc.⟩; finish ⟨person⟩ off; 2. *refl. V.* wear oneself out

Kapuze die; ~, ~n hood; *(bei Mönchen)* cowl; hood; **Kapuziner** der; ~s, ~: Capuchin [friar]

Karabiner der; ~s, ~: carbine

Karaffe die; ~, ~n carafe; *(mit Glasstöpsel)* decanter

Karambolage [karambo'la:ʒə] die; ~, ~n *(ugs.)* crash; collision

Karamel der *(schweiz.: das)*; ~s caramel; **Karamel·bonbon** der *od.* das caramel [toffee]

Karat das; ~|e|s, ~e carat

Karate das; ~|s| karate

Karawane die; ~, ~n caravan

Kardinal der; ~s, **Kardinäle** *(kath. Kirche)* cardinal

Kardinal-: ~**tugend** die; *meist Pl.* cardinal virtue; ~**zahl** die cardinal [number]

Karenz die; ~, ~en, **Karenz·zeit** die waiting period

Kar·freitag der Good Friday

karg 1. *Adj.* meagre ⟨wages etc.⟩; frugal ⟨meal etc.⟩; poor ⟨light, accommodation⟩; *(wenig fruchtbar)* barren; 2. *adv.* ~ **bemessen sein** ⟨helping⟩ be mingy *(Brit. coll.);* ⟨supply⟩ be scanty; ~ **leben** live frugally; **kärglich** 1. *Adj.* meagre, poor ⟨wages etc.⟩; poor ⟨light⟩; frugal ⟨meal⟩; scanty ⟨supply⟩; 2. *adv.* poorly ⟨lit, paid, rewarded⟩

karibisch *Adj.* Caribbean

kariert *Adj.* check, checked ⟨material, pattern⟩; check ⟨jacket etc.⟩; squared ⟨paper⟩

Karies ['ka:riɛs] die; ~: caries

Karikatur die; ~, ~en cartoon; *(Porträt)* caricature; **Karikaturist** der; ~en, ~en cartoonist; *(Porträtist)* caricaturist; **karikieren** *tr. V.* caricature

karitativ *Adj.* charitable

Karl [karl] (der) Charles; ~ **der Große** Charlemagne

Karneval ['karnəval] der; ~s, ~e *od.* ~s carnival; ~ **feiern** join in the carnival festivities

Karnickel das; ~s, ~ *(landsch.)* rabbit

Kärnten (das); ~s Carinthia

Karo das; ~s, ~s a) square; *(auf der Spitze stehend)* diamond; b) *o. Pl.* ⟨~muster⟩ check; c) *o. Art.; o. Pl.* *(Kartenspiel: Farbe)* diamonds *pl.;* d) *(Kartenspiel: Karte)* diamond; **Karo·as** das ace of diamonds

Karosse die; ~, ~n [state-]coach; **Karosserie** die; ~, ~n bodywork

Karotte die; ~, ~n small carrot

Karpaten *Pl.* Carpathians; Carpathian Mountains

Karpfen der; ~s, ~: carp

Karre die; ~, ~n *(bes. nordd.)* a) *s.* **Karren**; b) *(abwertend: Fahrzeug)* [old] heap *(coll.)*

Karree das; ~s, ~s: **ums ~ gehen/fahren** walk/drive round the block

karren *tr. V.* a) cart; b) *(salopp: mit einem Auto)* run *(coll.);* **Karren** der; ~s, ~ *(bes. südd., österr.)* cart; *(zweirädrig)* barrow

Karriere [ka'riɛ:rə] die; ~, ~n career; ~ **machen** make a [successful] career for oneself

Kar·samstag der Easter Saturday

Karte die; ~, ~n card; *(Speise~)* menu; *(Fahr~, Flug~, Eintritts~)* ticket; *(Land~)* map; **alles auf eine ~ setzen** stake everything on one chance; **Kartei** die; ~, ~en card file

Kartei-: ~**karte** die file card; ~**kasten** der file-card box

Kartell das; ~s, ~e *(Wirtsch., Politik)* cartel

Kartell-: ~**amt** das *government body concerned with the control and supervision of cartels;* ≈ Monopolies and Mergers Commission *(Brit.);* ~**gesetz** das *law relating to cartels;* ≈ monopolies law *(Brit.)*

Karten-: ~**haus** das house of cards; ~**spiel** das **a)** *(Spiel mit Karten)* cardgame; **b)** *(Satz Spielkarten)* pack *or (Amer.)* deck [of cards]; ~**vor·verkauf** der; *o. Pl.* advance booking

Kartoffel die; ~, ~n potato

Kartoffel-: ~**brei** der mashed potatoes *pl.; mash (coll.);* ~**chips** Pl. [potato] crisps *(Brit.) or (Amer.)* chips; ~**käfer** der Colorado beetle; ~**kloß** der potato dumpling; ~**puffer** der potato pancake *(made from grated raw potatoes);* ~**püree** das; *s.* ~**brei**

Karton [kar'tɔŋ] der; ~s, ~s **a)** *(Pappe)* card[board]; **b)** *(Schachtel)* cardboard box

Karussell das; ~s, ~s *od.* ~e merrygo-round; carousel *(Amer.); (kleineres)* roundabout

Kar·woche die Holy Week

Karzinom das; ~s, ~e *(Med.)* carcinoma

kaschieren *tr. V.* conceal; hide; disguise *⟨fault⟩*

¹**Kaschmir** (das); ~s Kashmir; ²**Kaschmir** der; ~s, ~e *(Textilw.)* cashmere

Käse der; ~s, ~: cheese; *(ugs. abwertend: Unsinn)* rubbish

Käse-: ~**blatt** das *(salopp abwertend)* rag; ~**glocke** die cheese dome

Kaserne die; ~, ~n barracks *sing. or pl.*

käse·weiß *Adj. (ugs.)* [as] white as a sheet; **käsig** *Adj. (ugs.)* pasty; pale

Kasino das; ~s, ~s **a)** *(Spiel~)* casino; **b)** *(Offiziers~)* [officers'] mess; **c)** *(Speiseraum)* canteen

Kasko·versicherung die *(Voll~)* comprehensive insurance; *(Teil~)* insurance against theft, fire, or act of God

Kasper der; ~s, ~: ≈ Punch; *(fig. ugs.)* clown; **Kasperl** das; ~s, ~[n] *(österr.),* **Kasperle** das *od.* der; ~s, ~: *s.* Kasper

Kasper-: ~**puppe** die ≈ Punch and Judy puppet; ~**theater** das ≈ Punch and Judy show; *(Puppenbühne)* ≈ Punch and Judy theatre

Kasse die; ~, ~n a) cash-box; *(Regi-*

strier~) till; **b)** *(Ort zum Bezahlen)* cash desk; *(im Supermarkt)* checkout; *(in einer Bank)* counter; **c)** *(Kassenraum)* cashier's office; **d)** *(Theater~, Kino~)* box-office

Kasseler das; ~s smoked loin of pork

Kassen-: ~**arzt** der *doctor who treats members of health insurance schemes;* ~**bon** der sales slip; receipt; ~**patient** der *patient who is a member of a health insurance scheme;* ~**zettel** der *s.* ~**bon**

Kassette die; ~, ~n a) box; case; b) *(mit Büchern, Schallplatten)* boxed set; *(Tonband~, Film~)* cassette; **Kassetten·recorder** der cassette recorder

kassieren 1. *tr. V.* **a)** collect; **b)** *(ugs.: wegnehmen)* confiscate; take away *⟨driving licence⟩;* 2. *itr. V.* **a) bei jmdm.** ~: give sb. his/her bill *or (Amer.)* check; *(ohne Rechnung)* settle up with sb.; **darf ich bei Ihnen ~?** would you like your bill?/can I settle up with you?; **Kassierer** der; ~s, ~, **Kassiererin** die; ~, ~nen cashier; *(bei einem Verein)* treasurer

Kastanie [kas'ta:niə] die; ~, ~n chestnut; **kastanien·braun** *Adj.* chestnut

Kästchen das; ~s, ~ **a)** small box; **b)** *(vorgedrucktes Quadrat)* square; *(auf Fragebögen)* box

Kaste die; ~, ~n caste

kasteien *refl. V.* **a)** *(als Bußübung)* chastise oneself; **b)** *(sich Entbehrungen auferlegen)* deny oneself; **Kasteiung** die; ~, ~en **a)** *(als Bußübung)* self-chastisement; **b)** *(Auferlegung von Entbehrungen)* self-denial

Kastell das; ~s, ~e **a)** *(hist.: röm. Lager)* fort; **b)** *(Burg)* castle

Kasten der; ~s, Kästen **a)** box; *(für Flaschen)* crate; **b)** *(ugs.: Briefkasten)* post-box; **c)** *(ugs. abwertend) (Gebäude)* barracks *sing. or pl.; (Auto)* heap *(coll.); (fig. ugs.)* etw. **auf dem ~ haben** have got it up top *(coll.);* **Kastenbrot** das tin[-loaf]

Kastration [kastra'tsjo:n] die; ~, ~en castration; **kastrieren** *tr. V.* castrate

Katalog der; ~[e]s, ~e *(auch fig.)* catalogue; **katalogisieren** *tr. V.* catalogue

Katalysator der; ~s, ~en [-za'to:rən] *(Chemie, fig.)* catalyst; *(Kfz-W.)* catalytic converter

katapultieren *tr. V. (auch fig.)* catapult; eject *⟨pilot⟩*

Katarrh [ka'tar] der; ~s, ~e *(Med.)* catarrh

katastrophal [katastro'fa:l] 1. *Adj.* disastrous; *(stärker)* catastrophic; 2. *adv.* disastrously; *(stärker)* catastrophically; **Katastrophe** [katas-'tro:fǝ] die; ~, ~n *(Unglück)* disaster; *(stärker, auch Literaturw.)* catastrophe

Katastrophen-: ~alarm der disaster alert; ~gebiet das disaster area; ~schutz der *(Organisation)* emergency services *pl.; (Maßnahmen)* disaster procedures *pl.*

Kategorie die; ~, ~n category; **kategorisch** 1. *Adj.* categorical; 2. *adv.* categorically

Kater der; ~s, ~ a) tom-cat; b) *(ugs.)* hangover

Kathedrale die; ~, ~n cathedral

Katholik der; ~en, ~en, **Katholikin** die; ~, ~nen [Roman] Catholic; **katholisch** *Adj.* [Roman] Catholic; **Katholizismus** der; ~: [Roman] Catholicism *no art.*

Kätzchen das; ~s, ~ a) little cat; pussy; *(junge Katze)* kitten; b) *meist Pl.* catkin; **Katze** die; ~, ~n cat

katzen-, Katzen-: ~auge das reflector; Cat's-eye (P); ~jammer der a) *(Kater)* hangover; b) *(fig.)* mood of depression; ~musik die *(ugs. abwertend)* terrible row *(coll.);* ~sprung der stone's throw; ~wäsche die *(ugs.)* ~wäsche machen have a lick and a promise *(coll.)*

Kauderwelsch das; ~[s] gibberish *no indef. art.*

kauen *tr., itr. V.* chew; [die] Nägel ~: bite one's nails

kauern 1. *itr., refl. V.* crouch [down]; *(ängstlich)* cower

Kauf der; ~[e]s, Käufe a) *(das Kaufen)* buying; purchasing *(formal);* b) *(das Gekaufte)* purchase; **kaufen** 1. *tr. V.* buy; purchase; 2. *itr. V. (einkaufen)* shop; **Käufer** der; ~s, ~: buyer; purchaser *(formal)*

Kauf-: ~haus das department store; ~kraft die *(Wirtsch.)* a) *(Wert des Geldes)* purchasing power; b) *(Zahlungsfähigkeit)* spending power

käuflich 1. *Adj.* a) for sale *postpos.;* b) *(bestechlich)* venal; ~ sein be easily bought; 2. *adv.* etw. ~ erwerben/erstehen purchase sth.; **Kauf·mann** der; *Pl.* **Kaufleute** a) *(Geschäftsmann)* businessman; *(Händler)* trader; b) *(Besitzer)* shopkeeper; *(eines Lebens-*

mittelladens) grocer; **kaufmännisch** *Adj.* commercial; business *attrib.;* **Kauf·preis** der purchase price

Kau·gummi der *od.* das; ~s, ~s chewing gum

Kaukasus der; ~: the Caucasus

Kaulquappe die; ~, ~n tadpole

kaum *Adv.* hardly; scarcely; ~ hatte er Platz genommen, als ...: no sooner had he sat down than ...

kausal *Adj. (geh., Sprachw.)* causal

Kau·tabak der chewing tobacco

Kaution [kau'tsio:n] die; ~, ~en a) *(bei Freilassung eines Gefangenen)* bail; b) *(beim Mieten einer Wohnung)* deposit

Kautschuk der; ~s, ~e rubber

Kauz der; ~es, Käuze a) *(Wald~)* tawny owl; *(Stein~)* little owl; b) *(Sonderling)* strange fellow; oddball *(coll.)*

Kavalier [kava'li:ɐ] der; ~s, ~e gentleman; **Kavaliers·delikt** das trifling offence

Kavallerie die; ~, ~n *(Milit. hist.)* cavalry; **Kavallerist** der; ~en, ~en cavalryman

Kaviar ['ka:viar] der; ~s, ~e caviare

kcal *Abk.* **Kilo|gramm|kalorie** kcal

keck 1. *Adj.* a) cheeky; saucy *(Brit.);* b) *(veralt.: verwegen)* bold; c) *(flott)* jaunty, pert ⟨hat etc.⟩; 2. *adv.* a) cheekily; saucily *(Brit.);* b) *(veralt.: verwegen)* boldly; c) *(flott)* jauntily; **Keckheit** die; ~, ~en a) cheek; sauce *(Brit.);* b) *(veralt.: Kühnheit)* boldness

Kegel der; ~s, ~ a) cone; b) *(Spielfigur)* skittle; *(beim Bowling)* pin; **Kegel·bahn** die skittle alley; **kegelförmig** *Adj.* conical; **kegeln** 1. *itr. V.* play skittles *or* ninepins; 2. *tr. V.* eine Partie ~: play a game of skittles *or* ninepins; eine Neun ~: score a nine

Kehle die; ~, ~n throat; **Kehl·kopf** der *(Anat.)* larynx

Kehre die; ~, ~n sharp bend; **[1]kehren** 1. *tr. V.* turn; 2. *refl. V.* turn

[2]kehren 1. *itr. V. (bes. südd.)* sweep; do the sweeping; 2. *tr. V.* sweep; *(mit einem Handfeger)* brush; **Kehricht** der *od.* das; ~s *(schweiz.: Müll)* refuse; garbage *(Amer.)*

Kehr·seite die a) back; *(einer Münze, Medaille)* reverse; *(scherzh.) (Gesäß)* backside; b) *(nachteiliger Aspekt)* drawback; disadvantage; **kehrt|machen** *itr. V. (ugs.)* turn [round and go] back

keifen *itr. V. (abwertend)* nag

Keil der; ~|e|s, ~e a) *(zum Spalten)* wedge; b) *(zum Festklemmen)* chock; *(unter einer Tür)* wedge; **keilen** *refl. V. (ugs.: sich prügeln)* fight; scrap; **Keiler** der; ~s, ~ *(Jägerspr.)* wild boar; **Keilerei** die; ~, ~en *(ugs.)* punch-up *(coll.);* fight

Keil-: ~**riemen** der *(Technik)* V-belt; ~**schrift** die cuneiform script

Keim der; ~|e|s, ~e *(Bot.)* shoot; *(Biol.)* embryo; **keimen** *itr. V.* germinate; *(fig.) ⟨hope⟩* stir; **keim·frei** *Adj.* germ-free; sterile; **Keim·zelle** die nucleus

kein *Indefinitpron.* a) no; b) *(ugs.: nicht ganz, nicht einmal)* less than; **kein...** *Indefinitpron.* ~**er/**~**e** nobody; no one; ~**s** von beiden neither [of them]; **keinerlei** *indekl. unbest. Gattungsz.* no ... what[so]ever

keines-: ~**falls** *Adv.* on no account; ~**wegs** *Adv.* by no means

kein·mal *Adv.* not [even] once

Keks der; ~ *od.* ~es, ~ *od.* ~e biscuit *(Brit.);* cookie *(Amer.)*

Kelch der; ~|e|s, ~e goblet; *(Rel.)* chalice

Kelle die; ~, ~n a) ladle; b) *(Signalstab)* signalling disc; c) *(Maurer~)* trowel

Keller der; ~s, ~: cellar; *(~geschoß)* basement; **Keller·assel** die woodlouse; **Kellerei** die; ~, ~en winery; *(Kellerräume)* [wine] cellars *pl.;* **Keller·geschoß** das basement

Kellner der; ~s, ~: waiter; **kellnern** *itr. V. (ugs.)* work as a waiter/waitress

Kelte der; ~n, ~n Celt

Kelter die; ~, ~n winepress; **keltern** *tr. V.* press *⟨grapes etc.⟩*

keltisch *Adj.* Celtic

Kenia (das) ~s Kenya; **Kenianer** der; ~s, ~: Kenyan

kennen *unr. tr. V.* a) know; b) *(bekannt sein mit)* know; **kennen|lernen** *tr. V.* get to know; *(erstmals begegnen)* meet; *(in Berührung gebracht werden mit)* come to know; **Kenner** der; ~s, ~: expert (+ *Gen.* on); *(von Wein, Speisen)* connoisseur; **Kennerblick** der expert eye; **mit** ~: with an expert eye; **Kenn·marke** die [police] identification badge; ≈ [police] warrant card *or (Amer.)* ID card; **kenntlich** *Adj.:* ~ sein be recognizable (an by); **etw./jmdn.** ~ **machen** mark sth./make sb. [easily] identifiable; **Kenntnis** die; ~, ~se knowledge

kenn-, Kenn-: ~**wort** das; *Pl.* ~wörter code-word; *(Parole)* password; code-word; ~**zahl** die index; ~**zeichen** das a) sign; b) *(Erkennungszeichen)* badge; *(auf einem Behälter, einer Ware usw.)* label; *(am Fahrzeug)* registration number; ~**zeichnen** *tr. V.* a) mark; label; mark *⟨way⟩;* b) *(charakterisieren)* characterize; ~**zeichnend** *Adj.* typical, characteristic (für of)

kentern *itr. V. mit sein* capsize

Keramik die; ~, ~en *o. Pl.* ceramics *pl.;* pottery; *(~gegenstand)* piece of pottery

Kerbe die; ~, ~n notch

Kerbel der; ~s chervil

Kerb·holz das: etwas auf dem ~holz haben *(ugs.)* have done a job *(sl.)*

Kerker der; ~s, ~ *(hist.)* dungeons *pl.; (einzelne Zelle)* dungeon

Kerl der; ~s, ~e *(nordd., md. auch:* ~s) *(ugs.)* fellow *(coll.);* bloke *(Brit. sl.)*

Kern der; ~|e|s, ~e pip; *(von Steinobst)* stone; *(von Nüssen usw.)* kernel; *(Atom~)* nucleus; *(fig.)* der ~ einer **Sache** the heart of a matter; **der harte** ~: the hard core

kern-, Kern-: ~**energie** die nuclear energy *no art.;* ~**gehäuse** das core; ~**gesund** *Adj.* fit as a fiddle *pred.*

kernig *Adj.* earthy *⟨language⟩;* forceful *⟨speech⟩;* pithy *⟨saying⟩*

kern-, Kern-: ~**kraft** die nuclear power; ~**kraftwerk** das nuclear power station *or* plant; ~**los** *Adj.* seedless; ~**obst** das pomaceous fruit; ~**physik** die nuclear physics *sing., no art.;* ~**reaktor** der nuclear reactor; ~**seife** die washing soap; ~**spaltung** die *(Physik)* nuclear fission *no art.;* ~**waffe** die; *meist Pl.* nuclear weapon

Kerze die; ~, ~n candle

kerzen-, Kerzen-: ~**gerade,** *(ugs.)* ~**grade** 1. *Adj.* dead straight; 2. *adv.* bolt upright; ~**halter** der candleholder; ~**leuchter** der candlestick

keß 1. *Adj.* a) pert; jaunty *⟨hat, dress, etc.⟩;* b) *(frech)* cheeky; 2. *adv.* a) *(flott)* jauntily; b) *(frech)* cheekily

Kessel der; ~s, ~ a) kettle; *(zum Kochen)* pot; *(Wasch~)* copper; b) *(Berg~)* basin-shaped valley; c) *(Milit.)* encircled area

Kessel-: ~**stein** der; *o. Pl.* scale; ~**treiben** das *(Hetzkampagne)* witchhunt

Kette die; ~, ~n chain; *(Hals~)* neck-

lace; *(von Ereignissen)* string; **ketten**
tr. V. chain (**an** + *Akk.* to)
Ketten-: ~**hund** der guard-dog *(kept
on a chain);* ~**raucher** der chain-
smoker
Ketzer der; ~s, ~ *(auch fig.)* heretic;
Ketzerei die; ~, ~en *(auch fig.)* heresy
keuchen *itr. V.* gasp for breath;
Keuch·husten der whooping cough
no art.
Keule die; ~, ~n a) club; b) *(Kochk.)*
leg
keusch 1. *Adj.* chaste; 2. *adv.* ~ leben
lead a chaste life; **Keuschheit** die; ~
chastity
Kfz [kaːɛfˈtsɛt] *Abk.* **Kraftfahrzeug**
kg *Abk.* **Kilogramm** kg
KG *Abk.* **Kommanditgesellschaft**
kichern *itr. V.* giggle
kicken *(ugs.)* 1. *itr. V.* play football; 2.
tr. V. kick
kidnappen [ˈkɪtnɛpn̩] *tr. V.* kidnap;
Kidnapper der; ~s, ~: kidnapper
Kiebitz der; ~es, ~e lapwing; peewit
¹**Kiefer** der; ~s, ~: jaw; *(~knochen)*
jaw-bone
²**Kiefer** die; ~, ~n pine[tree]
Kiefer·höhle die *(Anat.)* maxillary
sinus
Kiefern·holz das pine[-wood]
Kiel der; ~[e]s, ~e keel; **kiel·holen** *tr.
V. (Seemannsspr.)* keel-haul *(person);*
Kiel·wasser das wake
Kieme die; ~, ~n; *meist Pl.* gill
Kien der; ~[e]s resinous wood
Kies der; ~es, ~e gravel; *(auf dem
Strand)* shingle; **Kiesel** der; ~s, ~:
pebble; **Kiesel·stein** der pebble
Kies-: ~**grube** die gravel pit; ~**weg**
der gravel path
kiffen *itr. V. (ugs.)* smoke pot *(sl.)* or
grass *(sl.);* **Kiffer** der; ~s, ~ *(ugs.)*
pot-head *(sl.)*
kikeriki [kikəriˈkiː] *Interj. (Kinderspr.)*
cock-a-doodle-doo
Killer der; ~s, ~ *(salopp)* killer; *(gegen
Bezahlung)* hit man *(sl.)*
Kilo das; ~s, ~[s] kilo; **Kilo·gramm**
das kilogram; **Kilometer** der; ~s, ~:
kilometre; **kilometer·lang** 1. *Adj.*
miles long *pred.;* 2. *adv.* for miles [and
miles]; **Kilometer·stand** der mileage reading
Kimme die; ~, ~n sighting notch
Kimono der; ~s, ~s kimono
Kind das; ~[e]s, ~er a) child; **ein** ~ **er-
warten** be expecting; |~**er,|** ~**er!** my
goodness!

Kinder-: ~**arzt** der paediatrician;
~**bett** das cot; *(für größeres Kind)*
child's bed; ~**dorf** das children's village
Kinderei die; ~, ~en childishness *no
indef. art., no pl.*
kinder-, Kinder-: ~**feindlich** *Adj.*
hostile to children *pred.;* ~**freundlich** *Adj.* fond of children *pred.;*
(town, resort) which caters for children; *(planning, policy)* which caters
for the needs of children; ~**garten**
der nursery school; ~**gärtnerin** die
nusery-school teacher; ~**heilkunde**
die paediatrics *sing., no art.;* ~**hort**
der day-home for schoolchildren;
~**lähmung** die poliomyelitis;
~**leicht** *(ugs.) Adj.* childishly simple;
dead easy; **das ist** ~**leicht** it's kid's
stuff *(coll.);* it's child's play; ~**lieb**
Adj. fond of children *pred.;* ~**los** *Adj.*
childless; ~**reich** *Adj.* with many
children *postpos., not pred.;* ~**sterb-
lichkeit** die child mortality; ~**stube**
die; *o. Pl.* eine gute/schlechte ~**stube**
gehabt haben have been well/badly
brought up; ~**teller** der *(auf der Spei-
sekarte)* children's menu; ~**wagen**
der pram *(Brit.);* baby carriage
(Amer.); (Sportwagen) push-chair
(Brit.); stroller *(Amer.)*
Kindes-: ~**alter** das; *o. Pl.* childhood; ~**mißhandlung** die
(Rechtsw.) child abuse
Kindheit die; ~: childhood; **kindisch** 1. *Adj.* childish, infantile;
naïve *(ideas);* 2. *adv.* childishly;
kindlich 1. *Adj.* childlike; 2. *adv. (behave)* in a childlike way
Kinkerlitzchen *Pl. (ugs.)* trifles
Kinn das; ~[e]s, ~e chin
Kinn-: ~**haken** der hook to the chin;
~**lade** die jaw
Kino das; ~s, ~s cinema *(Brit.);* movie
theater *(Amer.);* **Kino·karte** die
cinema ticket *(Brit.);* movie ticket
(Amer.)
Kiosk der; ~[e]s, ~e kiosk
¹**Kippe** die; ~, ~n *(ugs.)* cigarette end;
dog-end *(sl.)*
²**Kippe** die; ~, ~n a) *(Bergmannsspr.)*
slag-heap; **etw. steht auf der** ~ *(fig.)*
it's touch and go with sth.; *(etw. ist
noch nicht entschieden)* sth. hangs in
the balance; **kippen** 1. *tr. V.* a) tip
[up]; b) *(ausschütten)* tip [out]; 2. *itr.
V.; mit sein* tip over; *(top-heavy object)*
topple over; *(person)* topple; *(boat)*
overturn; *(car)* roll over

Kipp-: ~**fenster das** horizontally pivoted window; ~**schalter der** tumbler switch

Kirche die; ~, ~n church; **in die ~ gehen** go to church

Kirchen-: ~**fest das** church festival; ~**lied das** hymn; ~**musik die** church music; ~**steuer die** church tax

Kirch·hof der *(veralt.)* churchyard; **kirchlich** 1. *Adj.* ecclesiastical; church *attrib.* ⟨*wedding, funeral*⟩; 2. *adv.* ~ **getraut/begraben werden** have a church wedding/funeral

Kirch-: ~**turm der** [church] steeple; *(ohne Turmspitze)* church tower; ~**weih die;** ~, ~**en** fair *(held on the anniversary of the consecration of a church)*

Kirmes die; ~, **Kirmessen** *(bes. md., niederd.) s.* **Kirchweih**

Kirsch·baum der cherry[-tree]; **Kirsche die;** ~, ~n cherry

Kirsch-: ~**torte die** cherry gateau; *(mit Tortenboden)* cherry flan; ~**wasser das** kirsch

Kissen das; ~s, ~: cushion; *(Kopf~)* pillow

Kiste die; ~, ~n box; *(Truhe)* chest; *(Latten~)* crate

Kitsch der; ~[e]s kitsch; **kitschig** *Adj.* kitschy

Kitt der; ~[e]s, ~e putty; *(für Porzellan, Kacheln usw.)* cement

Kittchen das; ~s, ~ *(ugs.)* clink *(sl.)*

Kittel der; ~s, ~ **a)** overall; *(eines Arztes usw.)* white coat; **b)** *(hemdartige Bluse)* smock

kitten *tr. V.* cement [together]

Kitz das; ~es, ~e *(Reh~)* fawn; *(Ziegen~, Gemsen~)* kid

kitzeln *tr., itr. V.* tickle; **kitzlig** *Adj. (auch fig.)* ticklish

KKW [ka:ka:'|ve:] *Abk.* **Kernkraftwerk**

Klacks der; ~es, ~e *(ugs.)* dollop *(coll.); (~ Senf)* dab

Kladde die; ~, ~n rough book

Kladderadatsch der; ~[e]s, ~e *(ugs.)* unholy mess *(coll.)*

klaffen *itr. V.* yawn; ⟨*hole, wound*⟩ gape; **kläffen** *itr. V. (abwertend)* yap

Klafter ['klaftɐ] **der** *od.* **das;** ~s, ~ *(Raummaß für Holz)* cord

Klage die; ~, ~n **a)** *(Äußerung der Trauer)* lament; **b)** *(Beschwerde)* complaint; **c)** *(Rechtsw.)* action; *(im Strafrecht)* charge; **klagen** 1. *itr. V.* **a)** *(geh.: jammern)* wail; *(stöhnend)* moan; **b)** *(sich beschweren)* complain (**über** + *Akk.* about); **c)** *(bei Gericht)*

take legal action; 2. *tr. V.* **jmdm. sein Leid/seine Not ~:** pour out one's sorrows *pl.*/troubles *pl.;* **Kläger der;** ~s, ~, **Klägerin die;** ~, ~nen *(im Zivilrecht)* plaintiff; *(im Strafrecht)* prosecuting party; *(bei einer Scheidung)* petitioner; **kläglich** *Adj.* **a)** *(mitleiderregend)* pitiful; **b)** *(minderwertig)* pathetic; **c)** *(erbärmlich)* despicable ⟨*behaviour, role, compromise*⟩; pathetic ⟨*result, defeat*⟩

Klamauk der; ~s *(ugs. abwertend)* fuss; *(Lärm, Krach)* row *(coll.)*

klamm *Adj.* **a)** *(feucht)* cold and damp; **b)** *(steif)* numb; **Klammer die;** ~, ~n *(Wäsche~)* peg; *(Haar~)* [hair-]grip; *(Zahn~)* brace; *(Büro~)* paper-clip; *(Heft~)* staple; *(Schriftzeichen)* bracket; **klammern** 1. *refl. V.* **sich an jmdn./etw.** ~ *(auch fig.)* cling to sb./sth.; 2. *tr. V.* **a) eine Wunde ~:** close a wound with a clip/clips; **b)** *(mit einer Büroklammer)* clip; *(mit einer Heftmaschine)* staple; *(mit Wäscheklammern)* peg

Klamotten *Pl. (salopp) (Kleidung)* gear *sing. (sl.); (Kram)* stuff *sing.*

Klampfe die; ~, ~n *(volkst.: Gitarre)* guitar

klang *1. u. 3. Pers. Sg. Prät. v.* **klingen**

Klang der; ~[e]s, **Klänge a)** *(Ton)* sound; **b)** *(~farbe)* tone

Klapp·bett das folding bed; **Klappe die;** ~, ~n **a)** [hinged] lid; *(am LKW)* tail-gate; *(seitlich)* side-gate; *(am Kombiwagen)* back; *(am Ofen)* [drop-] door; **b)** *(an Musikinstrumenten)* key; *(an einer Trompete)* valve; **c)** *(Filmjargon)* clapper-board; **d)** *(salopp: Mund)* trap *(sl.);* **klappen** 1. *tr. V.* **nach oben/unten ~:** turn up/down ⟨*collar, hat-brim*⟩; lift up/put down ⟨*lid*⟩; **nach vorne/hinten ~:** tilt forward/back ⟨*seat*⟩; 2. *itr. V.* **a)** ⟨*door, shutter*⟩ bang; **b)** *(stoßen)* bang; **c)** *(ugs.: gelingen)* work out all right; **klapperig** *Adj.* rickety; **klappern** *itr. V.* **a)** rattle; **b)** *(ein Klappern erzeugen)* make a clatter; **Klapperschlange die** rattlesnake; **klapprig** *Adj.* rickety

Klapp-: ~**sitz der** tip-up seat; ~**stuhl der** folding chair

Klaps der; ~es, ~e *(ugs.)* smack; slap; **Klaps·mühle die** *(salopp)* loony-bin *(sl.)*

klar 1. *Adj.* **a)** clear; straight ⟨*question, answer*⟩; **sich** *(Dat.)* **über etw.** *(Akk.)* **im ~en sein** realize sth.; **b)** *nicht attr.*

(fertig) ready; **2.** *adv.* clearly; **Klär-anlage die** sewage treatment plant; **Klare der;** ~n, ~n schnapps; **klären 1.** *tr. V.* **a)** settle ⟨*question, issue, matter*⟩; clarify ⟨*situation*⟩; clear up ⟨*case, affair, misunderstanding*⟩; **b)** *(reinigen)* purify; treat ⟨*effluent, sewage*⟩; **2.** *refl. V.* **a)** ⟨*situation*⟩ become clear; ⟨*question, issue, matter*⟩ be settled; **b)** *(rein werden)* ⟨*liquid, sky*⟩ clear; ⟨*weather*⟩ clear [up]; **klar|gehen** *unr. itr. V.; mit sein (ugs.)* go OK *(coll.);* **Klarheit die;** ~: clarity; **sich** *(Dat.)* **über etw.** *(Akk.)* ~ **verschaffen** clarify sth.

Klarinette die; ~, ~n clarinet

klar-: ~**|machen** *tr. V.* **a)** *(ugs.)* make clear; **b)** *(Seemannsspr.)* get ready; ~**|sehen** *unr. itr. V.* understand the matter

Klarsicht·folie die transparent film; **klar|stellen** *tr. V.* clear up; clarify; **Klar·text der** *(auch DV)* clear text; **im** ~**text** *(fig.)* in plain language; **Klärung die;** ~, ~**en a)** clarification; **b)** *(Reinigung)* purification; *(von Abwässern)* treatment; **klar|werden** *unr. V.; mit sein; nur im Inf. und Part. zusammengeschrieben* **1.** *refl. V.* **sich** *(Dat.)* **über etw.** *(Akk.)* ~: realize sth.; **2.** *itr. V.* **jmdm. wird etw. klar** sth. becomes clear to sb.

klasse *(ugs.)* **1.** *indekl. Adj.* great *(coll.);* **2.** *adv.* marvellously; **Klasse die;** ~, ~**n a)** *(Schul~)* class; *(Raum)* class-room; *(Stufe)* year; grade *(Amer.);* **b)** *(Sport)* league; *(Boxen)* division; **c)** *(Fahrzeug~, Boots~, Qualitätsstufe)* class

klassen-, Klassen-: ~**arbeit die** *(Schulw.)* [written] class test; ~**gesellschaft die** *(Soziol.)* class society; ~**kampf der** *(marx.)* class struggle; ~**lehrer der,** ~**lehrerin die** *(Schulw.)* class teacher; ~**los** *Adj. (Soziol.)* classless; ~**sprecher der,** ~**sprecherin die** *(Schulw.)* class spokesman; ~**treffen das** *(Schulw.)* class reunion; ~**ziel das** *(Schulw.)* required standard *(for pupils in a particular class);* ~**zimmer das** *(Schulw.)* class-room

klassifizieren *tr. V.* classify **(als** as); **Klassifizierung die;** ~, ~**en** classification; **Klassik die;** ~ **a)** *(Antike)* classical antiquity *no art.;* **b)** *(Zeit kultureller Höchstleistung)* classical period

Klassiker der; ~**s,** ~: classical writer/composer; **klassisch** *Adj.* classical; *(vollendet, zeitlos; auch iron.)* classic; **Klassizismus der;** ~: classicism

Klatsch der; ~**[e]s,** ~**e a)** *o. Pl. (ugs. abwertend)* gossip; **b)** *(Geräusch)* smack; **Klatsch·base die** *(ugs. abwertend)* gossip; **klatschen** *itr. V.* **a)** *auch mit sein* ⟨*waves, wet sails*⟩ slap; **b)** *(mit den Händen; applaudieren)* clap; **c)** *(schlagen)* slap; **d)** *(ugs. abwertend: reden)* gossip **(über** + *Akk.* about); **klatschhaft** *Adj.* gossipy; fond of gossip *pred.;* **Klatsch·mohn der** corn-poppy; **klatsch·naß** *Adj. (ugs.)* sopping wet; dripping wet ⟨*hair*⟩

Klaue die; ~, ~**n a)** claw; *(von Raubvögeln)* talon; *(salopp: Hand)* mitt *(sl.);* **b)** *o. Pl. (salopp abwertend: Schrift)* scrawl; **klauen** *(ugs.)* **1.** *tr. V.* pinch *(sl.);* **jmdm. etw.** ~: pinch sth. from sb.; **2.** *itr. V.* pinch *(sl.)* things

Klause die; ~, ~**n** hermitage; *(Klosterzelle)* cell; **Klausel die;** ~, ~**n** clause; *(Bedingung)* condition; *(Vorbehalt)* proviso

Klavier [kla'viːɐ] **das;** ~**s,** ~**e** piano

Klebe·folie die adhesive film; **kleben 1.** *itr. V.* **a)** stick **(an** + *Dat.* to); **b)** *(ugs.: klebrig sein)* be sticky **(von, vor** + *Dat.* with); **2.** *tr. V.* **a)** *(befestigen)* stick; *(mit Klebstoff)* glue; **jmdm. eine** ~ *(salopp)* belt sb. one *(coll.);* **b)** *(reparieren)* stick *or* glue ⟨*vase etc.*⟩ back together; **Kleber der;** ~**s,** ~: adhesive; glue; **klebrig** *Adj.* sticky

Kleb-: ~**stoff der** adhesive; glue; ~**streifen der** adhesive *or* sticky tape

kleckern *itr. V.* make a mess; **Klecks der;** ~**es,** ~**e a)** stain; *(nicht aufgesogen)* blob; *(Tintenfleck)* [ink-] blot; **b)** *(ugs.: kleine Menge)* spot; *(von Senf, Mayonnaise)* dab; **klecksen** *itr. V.* **a)** make a stain/stains; *(mit Tinte)* make a blot/blots; ⟨*pen*⟩ blot; **b)** *(ugs. abwertend: schlecht malen)* daub

Klee der; ~**s** clover; **Klee·blatt das** clover-leaf

Kleid das; ~**es,** ~**er a)** dress; **b)** *Pl. (Kleidung)* clothes; **kleiden 1.** *refl. V.* dress; **2.** *tr. V.* **a)** dress; **b)** *(jmdm. stehen)* suit

Kleider-: ~**bügel der** clothes-hanger; coat-hanger; ~**bürste die** clothes-brush; ~**haken der** coat-hook; ~**schrank der** wardrobe; ~**ständer der** coat-stand

kleidsam *Adj.* becoming; **Kleidung die;** ~: clothes *pl.*

Kleidungs·stück das garment
klein 1. *Adj.* **a)** little; small; **er ist ~er
als ich** he is shorter than me; **b)** *(jung)*
little; **von ~ auf** from an early age; **c)**
(von kurzer Dauer) little, short ⟨*while*⟩;
short ⟨*walk, break, holiday*⟩; brief
⟨*moment*⟩; **d)** *(von geringer Menge)*
small; low ⟨*price*⟩; **~es Geld haben**
have some [small] change; **e)** *(von geringem Ausmaß)* small ⟨*party, gift*⟩;
scant ⟨*attention*⟩; slight ⟨*cold, indisposition, mistake, irregularity*⟩; minor
⟨*event, error*⟩; **f)** *(unbedeutend)* lowly
⟨*employee*⟩; minor ⟨*official*⟩; **~ anfangen** *(ugs.)* start off in a small way; **2.**
adv. **die Heizung ~/~er einstellen** turn
the heating down low/lower; **ein Wort
~ schreiben** write a word with a small
initial letter
klein-, Klein-: ~anzeige die *(Zeitungsw.)* small *or* classified advertisement; **~asien (das)** Asia Minor;
~bürgerlich *Adj.* **a)** *(das Kleinbür-
gertum betreffend)* lower middle-
class; **b)** *(abwertend: spießbürgerlich)*
petit bourgeois
¹Kleine der; *adj. Dekl.* **a)** *(kleiner Junge)* little boy; **b)** *(ugs. Anrede)* little
man; **²Kleine** die; *adj. Dekl.* **a)** *(kleines Mädchen)* little girl; **b)** *(ugs. Anrede)* love; *(abwertend)* little madam
klein-, Klein-: ~familie die *(Soziol.)*
nuclear family; **~geld das;** *o. Pl.*
[small] change; **~gläubig** sceptical
Kleinigkeit die; ~, ~en small thing;
(Einzelheit) [small] detail; **ich habe
noch eine ~ zu erledigen** I still have a
small matter to attend to; **eine ~ essen**
have a [small] bite to eat; **eine ~ für
jmdn. sein** be no trouble for sb.
klein-, Klein-: ~kind das small
child; **~kram** der *(ugs.)* odds and
ends *pl.; (unbedeutende Dinge)* trivial
matters *pl.;* **~|kriegen** *tr. V. (ugs.)* **a)**
(zerkleinern) crush [to pieces]; **b)** *(zerstören)* smash; break; **c)** *(aufbrau-
chen)* get through; **d) jmdn. ~kriegen**
get sb. down *(coll.); (durch Drohun-
gen)* intimidate sb.; *(gefügig machen)*
bring sb. into line; **~laut** 1. *Adj.* subdued; *(verlegen)* sheepish; **2.** *adv.* in a
subdued fashion; *(verlegen)* sheep-
ishly
kleinlich *(abwertend)* 1. *Adj.* pernick-
ety; *(ohne Großzügigkeit)* mean; *(engstirnig)* small-minded; petty; **2.** *adv.*
meticulously
Kleinod das; **~[e]s, ~e** od. **~ien** *(geh.)*
a) *(Schmuckstück)* piece of jewellery;

(Edelstein) jewel; **b)** *(Kostbarkeit)*
gem
klein-, Klein-: ~|schneiden *unr. tr.
V.* cut into small pieces; chop up ⟨*onion*⟩ [small]; **~stadt die** small town;
~städter der small-town dweller
Kleinste der/die/das; *adj. Dekl.*
youngest boy/girl/child
klein|stellen *tr. V.* turn down [low]
Kleister der; **~s, ~:** paste
Klementine die; ~, ~n clementine
Klemme die; ~, ~n clip; **in der ~ sein**
od. **sitzen** *(ugs.)* be in a fix *(coll.);*
klemmen 1. *tr. V.* **a)** *(befestigen)*
tuck; stick *(coll.);* **b)** *(quetschen)* **sich**
(Dat.) **den Fuß/die Hand ~:** get one's
foot/hand caught *or* trapped; **2.** *refl.
V.* **sich hinter etw.** *(Akk.)* **~** *(fig. ugs.)*
put some hard work into sth.; **3.** *itr. V.*
⟨*door, drawer, etc.*⟩ stick
Klempner der; **~s, ~:** tinsmith; *(~
und Installateur)* plumber
Kleptomanie die; ~ *(Psych.)* kleptomania *no art.*
klerikal *Adj. (auch abwertend)* clerical; church ⟨*property*⟩; **Klerus der;**
~: clergy
Klette die; ~, ~n bur; *(Pflanze)* bur-
dock
klettern *itr. V.; mit sein (auch fig.)*
climb; **auf einen Baum ~:** climb a
tree; **Kletter·pflanze die** creeper;
(Bot.) climbing plant; climber
klicken *itr. V.* click
Klient der; **~en, ~en, Klientin die; ~,
~nen** client
Klima das; ~s, ~s *od.* **Klimate** climate; **Klima·an·lage die** air-conditioning *no indef. art.;* **klimatisch**
Adj. climatic; **klimatisieren** *tr. V.*
air-condition; **Klima·wechsel der**
change of climate
Klimm·zug der *(Turnen)* pull-up
klimpern 1. *itr. V.* jingle; **2.** *tr. V. (ugs.
abwertend)* plunk out ⟨*tune etc.*⟩
Klinge die; ~, ~n blade
Klingel die; ~, ~n bell
Klingel-: ~beutel der offertory-bag;
collection-bag; **~knopf der** bell-push
klingeln *itr. V.* ring; ⟨*alarm clock*⟩ go
off; **es klingelt** *(an der Tür)* there is a
ring at the door; *(Telefon)* the telephone is ringing
klingen *unr. itr. V.* sound; **die Glok-
ken klangen** the bells were ringing
Klinik die; ~, ~en hospital; *(speziali-
siert)* clinic
Klinke die; ~, ~n door-handle
Klinker der; **~s, ~:** [Dutch] clinker

klipp *Adv.:* ~ **und klar** *(ugs.)* quite plainly

Klippe die; ~, ~n rock

klirren *itr. V.* clink; ⟨*weapons in fight*⟩ clash; ⟨*window-pane*⟩ rattle; ⟨*chains, spurs*⟩ rattle; ⟨*harness*⟩ jingle

Klischee das; ~s, ~s cliché

klitsch·naß *Adj. (ugs.)* sopping wet; *(tropfnaß)* dripping wet

klitze·klein *Adj. (ugs.)* teeny[-weeny] *(coll.)*

Klo das; ~s, ~s *(ugs.)* loo *(Brit. coll.)*; john *(Amer. coll.)*

Kloake die; ~, ~n cesspit; *(Kanal)* sewer

klobig *Adj.* heavy and clumsy [-looking] ⟨*shoes, furniture*⟩; bulky ⟨*figure*⟩; *(plump)* clumsy

Klo·papier das *(ugs.)* loo-paper *(Brit. coll.)*; toilet-paper

klopfen 1. *itr. V.* a) *(schlagen)* knock; b) *(pulsieren)* ⟨*heart*⟩ beat; ⟨*pulse*⟩ throb; 2. *tr. V.* beat ⟨*carpet*⟩

Klöppel der; ~s, ~ *(Glocken~)* clapper; **klöppeln** *tr., itr. V.* [etw.] ~: make [sth. in] pillow-lace

Klops der; ~es, ~e *(nordostd.)* meat ball

Klosett das; ~s, ~s *od.* ~e lavatory

Kloß der; ~es, **Klöße** dumpling; *(Fleisch~)* meat ball

Kloster das; ~s, **Klöster** *(Mönchs~)* monastery; *(Nonnen~)* convent

Klotz der; ~es, **Klötze** block [of wood]; *(Stück eines Baumstamms)* log

Klub der; ~s, ~s club; **Klub·sessel** der club chair

¹**Kluft** die; ~, ~en *(ugs.)* gear *(coll.)*; *(Uniform)* garb

²**Kluft** die; ~, **Klüfte** *(veralt.)* *(Spalte)* cleft; *(im Gletscher)* crevasse; *(Abgrund)* chasm; *(fig.)* gulf

klug; **klüger**, **klügst...** *Adj.* clever; bright ⟨*child, pupil*⟩; intelligent ⟨*eyes*⟩; *(vernünftig)* wise; sound ⟨*advice*⟩; *(geschickt)* shrewd ⟨*politician, negotiator, question*⟩; astute ⟨*businessman*⟩; **klüger** *s.* klug; **Klugheit** die; ~ *s.* klug: cleverness; brightness; intelligence; wisdom; soundness; shrewdness; astuteness; **klügst...** *s.* klug

klumpen *itr. V.* go lumpy; **Klumpen** der; ~s, ~: lump; **ein** ~ **Gold** a gold nugget

km *Abk.* Kilometer km.

knabbern 1. *tr. V.* nibble; 2. *itr. V.* **an** etw. *(Dat.)* ~: nibble [at] sth.

Knabe der; ~n, ~n *(geh. veralt./ südd., österr., schweiz.)* boy; *(ugs.: Bursche)* chap *(coll.)*; **knabenhaft** 1. *Adj.* boyish; 2. *adv.* boyishly

Knäcke·brot das crispbread; *(Scheibe)* slice of crispbread; **knacken** 1. *itr. V.* a) ⟨*bed, floor, etc.*⟩ creak; b) *mit sein (ugs.: zerbrechen)* snap; ⟨*window*⟩ crack; 2. *tr. V.* a) crack ⟨*nut, shell*⟩; *(salopp: aufbrechen)* crack ⟨*safe*⟩ [open]; break into ⟨*car, bank, etc.*⟩; **knackig** *Adj.* a) crisp; b) *(ugs.: attraktiv)* delectable; **Knacks** der; ~es, ~e *(ugs.)* crack; *(fig.: Defekt)* **einen** ~ **bekommen** ⟨*person*⟩ have a breakdown; ⟨*health*⟩ suffer

Knall der; ~[e]s, ~e bang; **knallen** 1. *itr. V.* a) ⟨*shot*⟩ ring out; ⟨*firework*⟩ go bang; ⟨*cork*⟩ pop; ⟨*door*⟩ slam; ⟨*whip, rifle*⟩ crack; **mit der Tür** ~: slam the door; b) *(ugs.: schießen)* shoot, fire *(auf + Akk.* at); c) *(Ballspiele ugs.)* **aufs Tor** ~: belt the ball/puck at the goal *(coll.)*; 2. *tr. V.* a) *(ugs.)* slam down; *(werfen)* sling *(coll.)*; b) *(ugs.: schlagen)* jmdm. **eine** ~ *(salopp)* belt sb. one *(coll.)*

knall-: ~**hart** *(ugs.)* 1. *Adj.* very tough ⟨*demands, measures, etc.*⟩; ⟨*person*⟩ as hard as nails; 2. *adv.* brutally; **gegen etw. ~hart vorgehen** take very tough action against sth.; ~**rot** *Adj.* bright *or* vivid red; **sie wurde ~rot** she turned as red as a beetroot

knapp 1. *Adj.* a) meagre; narrow ⟨*victory, lead*⟩; narrow, bare ⟨*majority*⟩; **die Vorräte wurden** ~: supplies ran short; **vor einer ~en Stunde** just under an hour ago; b) *(eng)* tight-fitting ⟨*garment*⟩; *(zu eng)* tight ⟨*garment*⟩; c) *(kurz)* terse ⟨*reply, greeting*⟩; succinct ⟨*description, account, report*⟩; 2. *adv.* a) ~ **bemessen sein** be meagre, ⟨*time*⟩ be limited; ~ **gewinnen/verlieren** win/ lose narrowly; **er ist ~ fünfzig** he is just this side of fifty; b) *(eng)* ~ **sitzen** fit tightly; *(zu eng)* be a tight fit; c) *(kurz)* ⟨*reply*⟩ tersely; ⟨*describe, summarize*⟩ succinctly; **Knappheit** die; ~ a) *(Mangel)* shortage *(an + Dat.* of); b) *(Kürze)* *(einer Antwort, eines Grußes)* terseness; *(einer Beschreibung, eines Berichts)* succinctness

knarren *itr. V.* creak

Knast der; ~[e]s, **Knäste** *od.* ~e *(ugs.)* a) *o. Pl. (Strafe)* bird *(sl.)*; time; b) *(Gefängnis)* clink *(sl.)*; prison

knattern *itr. V.* clatter; ⟨*sail*⟩ flap; ⟨*radio*⟩ crackle

Knäuel der *od.* das; ~s, ~ ball; *(wirres ~)* tangle

Knauf der; ~[e]s, **Knäufe** knob; *(eines Schwertes, Dolches)* pommel

knauserig *Adj. (ugs. abwertend)* stingy; tight-fisted; **knausern** *itr. V. (ugs. abwertend)* be stingy; skimp

knautschen *(ugs.)* 1. *tr. V.* crumple; crease ⟨*dress*⟩; 2. *itr. V.* ⟨*dress, material*⟩ crease

Knebel der; ~s, ~ a) gag; b) *(Griff)* toggle; **knebeln** *tr. V.* gag

Knecht der; ~[e]s, ~e farm-labourer; **knechten** *tr. V. (geh.)* reduce to slavery; enslave; *(unterdrücken)* oppress; **Knechtschaft** die; ~, ~en *(geh.)* bondage; slavery

kneifen 1. *unr. tr., itr. V.* pinch; 2. *unr. itr. V.* a) ⟨*clothes*⟩ be too tight; b) *(ugs.: sich drücken)* chicken *(sl.)* out (vor + *Dat.* of); **Kneif·zange** die pincers *pl.*

Kneipe die; ~, ~n *(ugs.)* pub *(Brit. coll.)*; bar *(Amer.)*

kneippen *itr. V. (ugs.)* take a Kneipp cure; **Kneipp·kur** die Kneipp cure

kneten *tr. V.* a) *(bearbeiten)* knead ⟨*dough, muscles*⟩; work ⟨*clay*⟩; b) *(formen)* model ⟨*figure*⟩; **Knet·masse** die Plasticine (P)

Knick der; ~[e]s, ~e sharp bend; *(Falz)* crease; **knicken** 1. *tr. V.* a) *(brechen)* snap; b) *(falten)* crease ⟨*page, paper, etc.*⟩; 2. *itr. V.; mit sein* snap

Knicks der; ~es, ~e curtsy; **knicksen** *itr. V.* curtsy (vor + *Dat.* to)

Knie das; ~s, ~ ['kni:(ə)] a) knee; b) *(Biegung)* sharp bend

knie-, Knie-: ~beuge die kneebend; ~fall der: einen ~fall tun *od.* machen *(auch fig.)* go down on one's knees (vor + *Dat.* before); ~kehle die hollow of the knee

knien ['kni:(ə)n] 1. *itr. V.* kneel; 2. *refl. V.* kneel [down]

Knie-: ~scheibe die kneecap; ~strumpf der knee-length sock

Kniff der; ~[e]s, ~e a) pinch; b) *(Falte)* crease; c) *(Kunstgriff)* trick

knipsen *tr. V.* a) *(entwerten)* clip; punch; b) *(fotografieren)* take a snap[shot] of

Knirps der; ~es, ~e a) (Ⓦ Taschenschirm) telescopic umbrella; b) *(ugs.: Junge)* nipper *(coll.)*

knirschen *itr. V.* crunch; **mit den Zähnen** ~ grind one's teeth

knistern *itr. V.* rustle; ⟨*wood, fire*⟩ crackle

knittern *tr., itr. V.* crease; crumple

knobeln *itr. V. (mit Würfeln)* play dice

Knob·lauch der garlic; **Knob·lauch·zehe** die clove of garlic

Knöchel der; ~s, ~: ankle; *(am Finger)* knuckle; **Knochen** der; ~s, ~: bone

knochen-, Knochen-: ~bau der; *o. Pl.* bone structure; ~bruch der fracture; ~hart *Adj. (ugs.)* rock-hard; ~mark das bone marrow

knochig *Adj.* bony

Knödel der; ~s, ~ *(bes. südd., österr.)* dumpling

Knolle die; ~, ~n tuber

Knopf der; ~[e]s, **Knöpfe** button; *(Knauf)* knob; **knöpfen** *tr. V.* button [up]; **Knopf·loch** das buttonhole

Knorpel der; ~s, ~ *(Anat.)* cartilage; *(im Steak o. ä.)* gristle

knorrig *Adj.* gnarled

Knospe die; ~, ~n bud; **knospen** *itr. V.* bud

knoten *tr. V.* knot; **Knoten** der; ~s, ~: knot; *(Haartracht)* bun; knot; *(Med.)* lump; **Knoten·punkt** der junction; intersection

knuffen *tr. V.* poke

Knüller der; ~s, ~ *(ugs.)* sensation; *(Angebot, Verkaufsartikel)* sensational offer

knüpfen *tr. V.* a) tie (an + *Akk.* to); Bedingungen an etw. *(Akk.)* ~ attach conditions to sth.; b) *(durch Knoten herstellen)* knot; make ⟨*net*⟩;

Knüppel der; ~s, ~ cudgel; *(Polizei~)* truncheon; **knüppel·dick** *Adv. (ugs.)* **es kam** ~**dick** it was one disaster after the other; **Knüppel·schaltung** die *(Kfz-W.)* floor[-type] gearchange

knurren 1. *itr. V.* a) ⟨*animal*⟩ growl; *(wütend)* snarl; *(fig.)* ⟨*stomach*⟩ rumble; b) *(murren)* grumble (**über** + *Akk.* about)

knusprig *Adj.* crisp; crusty ⟨*bread, roll*⟩

knutschen *(ugs.)* 1. *tr. V.* smooch with *(coll.); (sexuell berühren)* pet; **sich** ~: smooch *(coll.)*/pet; 2. *itr. V.* smooch *(coll.); (sich sexuell berühren)* pet

k. o. [ka:'|o:] *Adj.; nicht attr.* a) *(Boxen)* jmdn. k. o. schlagen knock sb. out; b) *(ugs.: übermüdet)* all in *(coll.)*

koalieren *itr. V. (Politik)* form a coalition (**mit** with); **Koalition** die; ~, ~en coalition

Kobalt das; ~s *(Chemie)* cobalt

Kobold der; ~[e]s, ~e goblin

Kobra die; ~, ~s cobra

Koch der; ~[e]s, **Köche** cook; *(Küchenchef)* chef; **Koch·buch** das cookery book *(Brit.);* cookbook *(Amer.);* **kochen** 1. *tr. V.* **a)** boil; *(zubereiten)* cook ⟨*meal*⟩*;* make ⟨*purée, jam*⟩*;* Tee ~: make some tea; **b)** *(waschen)* boil; 2. *itr. V.* **a)** *(Speisen zubereiten)* cook; **b)** *(sieden)* ⟨*water, milk, etc.*⟩ boil; **Kocher** der; ~s, ~ [small] stove; *(Kochplatte)* hotplate

Köcher der; ~s, ~ *(für Pfeile)* quiver

Köchin die; ~, ~nen cook

Koch-: ~**löffel** der wooden spoon; ~**nische** die kitchenette; ~**topf** der [cooking] pot

Köder der; ~s, ~: bait; **ködern** *tr. V.* lure

Koffein das; ~s caffeine; **koffeinfrei** *Adj.* decaffeinated

Koffer der; ~s, ~: [suit]case

Koffer-: ~**kuli** der luggage trolley; ~**radio** das portable radio; ~**raum** der boot *(Brit.);* trunk *(Amer.)*

Kognak ['kɔnjak] der; ~s, ~s brandy; *s. auch* **Cognac**

Kohl der; ~[e]s **a)** cabbage; **b)** *(ugs. abwertend: Unsinn)* rubbish; rot *(sl.);* **Kohl·dampf** der; *o. Pl. (salopp)* [einen] ~ haben be ravenously hungry

Kohle die; ~, ~n coal; [1]**kohlen** *itr. V.* smoulder; ⟨*wick*⟩ smoke

[2]**kohlen** *itr. V. (fam.) (lügen)* tell fibs; *(übertreiben)* exaggerate

Kohlen-: ~**grube** die coal-mine; ~**händler** der coal merchant ~**monoxyd** [--'---] das *(Chemie)* carbon monoxide; ~**säure** die carbonic acid; ~**stoff** der; *o. Pl.* carbon

Kohle·papier das carbon paper

Köhler der; ~s, ~: charcoal burner

Kohl-: ~**kopf** der [head of] cabbage; ~**rübe** die swede

Koitus der; ~, **Koitus** *(geh.)* sexual intercourse; coitus *(formal)*

Koje die; ~, ~n **a)** *(Seemannsspr.)* bunk; berth; **b)** *(Ausstellungsstand)* stand

Kokain das; ~s cocaine

kokett 1. *Adj.* coquettish; 2. *adv.* coquettishly

Kokos·nuß die coconut

Koks der; ~es coke

Kolben der; ~s, ~ **a)** *(Technik)* piston; **b)** *(Chemie: Glas~)* flask; **c)** *(Teil des Gewehrs)* butt

Kolchose [kɔl'ço:zə] die; ~, ~n kolkhoz; Soviet collective farm

Kolibri der; ~s, ~s humming-bird

Kolik die; ~, ~en colic

Kollaborateur [kɔlabora'tø:ɐ̯] der; ~s, ~e collaborator

Kollaps der; ~es, ~e collapse

Kolleg das; ~s, ~s lecture

Kollege der; ~n, ~n colleague; **kollegial** 1. *Adj.* helpful and considerate; 2. *adv.* ⟨*act etc.*⟩ like a good colleague/good colleagues; **Kollegium** das; ~s, **Kollegien a)** *(Gruppe)* group; *(unmittelbar zusammenarbeitend)* team; **b)** *(Lehrkörper)* [teaching] staff

Kollekte die; ~, ~n collection; **Kollektion** [kɔlɛk'tsio:n] die; ~, ~en collection; *(Sortiment)* range; **kollektiv** 1. *Adj.* collective; 2. *adv.* collectively

kollidieren *itr. V.* **a)** *mit sein* collide; **b)** *(fig.)* conflict

Kollier [kɔ'lie:] das; ~s, ~s necklace

Kollision die; ~, ~en collision

Köln (das); ~s Cologne; **Kölner** 1. *indekl. Adj.* Cologne *attrib.; (in Köln)* in Cologne *postpos., not pred;* ⟨*suburb, archbishop, mayor, speciality*⟩ of Cologne; 2. der; ~s, ~: inhabitant of Cologne; *(von Geburt)* native of Cologne; **Kölnerin** die; ~, ~nen *s.* **Kölner** 2

Kolonialismus der; ~: colonialism *no art.;* **Kolonie** die; ~, ~n colony; **kolonisieren** *tr. V.* colonize

Kolonne die; ~, ~n column

Koloß der; **Kolosses, Kolosse** *(auch fig. ugs.)* giant; **kolossal** 1. *Adj.* **a)** colossal; gigantic; **b)** *(ugs.: sehr groß)* tremendous *(coll.);* incredible *(coll.)* ⟨*rubbish, nonsense*⟩; 2. *adv. (ugs.)* tremendously *(coll.)*

Kolumbianer der; ~s, ~: Colombian; **Kolumbien** [ko'lʊmbjən] **(das);** ~s Colombia

Kombination die; ~, ~en **a)** combination; **b)** *(gedankliche Verknüpfung)* deduction; piece of reasoning; **c)** *(Kleidungsstücke)* ensemble; suit; *(Herren~)* suit; **kombinieren** 1. *tr. V.* combine; 2. *itr. V.* deduce; reason

Kombi-: ~**wagen** der estate [car]; station wagon *(Amer.);* ~**zange** die combination pliers *pl.*

Komet der; ~en, ~en comet

Komfort der; ~s comfort; **komfortabel** 1. *Adj.* comfortable; 2. *adv.* comfortably

Komik die; ~: comic effect; *(komisches Element)* comic element; **Komiker** der; ~s, ~ **a)** *(Vortragskünstler)* comedian; **b)** *(Darsteller)* comic actor; **komisch** *Adj.* **a)** comical; funny; **b)** *(seltsam)* funny

Komitee das; ~s, ~s committee
Komma das; ~s, ~s *od.* ~ta comma;
(Math.) decimal point; **zwei** ~ **acht**
two point eight
Kommandant der; ~en, ~en *(Milit.)*
commanding officer; **Kommandeur**
[kɔman'døːɐ̯] der; ~s, ~e *(Milit.) s.*
Kommandant; kommandieren 1. *tr.*
V. **a)** command; be in command of;
order ‹*retreat, advance*›; **b)** *(ugs.)*
jmdn. ~: boss sb. about *(coll.)*; **2.** *itr.*
V. (ugs.) boss people about *(coll.)*
Kommandit · gesellschaft die
(Wirtsch.) limited partnership
Kommando das; ~s, ~·s command
kommen *unr. itr. V.; mit sein* **a)** come;
angelaufen ~: come running along;
(auf jmdn. zu) come running up; **b)**
(gelangen, geraten) get; **unter ein Auto**
~: be knocked down by a car; **wie**
kommst du darauf? what gives you
that idea?; **c)** ~ **lassen** *(bestellen)*
order ‹*taxi*›; **den Arzt/die Polizei** ~
lassen send for a doctor/the police; **d)**
(aufgenommen werden) **zur Schule/**
aufs Gymnasium ~: start school/
grammar school; **e)** *(auftauchen)*
‹*seeds, plants*› come up; ‹*buds,*
flowers› come out; ‹*teeth*› come
through; **f)** *(seinen festen Platz haben)*
go; belong; **in die Schublade**~: go *or*
belong in the drawer; *(seinen Platz er-*
halten) **in die Mannschaft** ~: get into
the team; **auf den ersten Platz** ~: go
into first place; **g)** *(Gelegenheit haben)*
dazu ~, **etw. zu tun** get round to doing
sth.; **h)** *(sich ereignen)* come about;
wie kommt es, daß ...: how is it that ...;
how come that ... *(coll.)*; **i)** *(etw. erlan-*
gen) **zu Geld** ~: become wealthy; **zu**
Erfolg/Ruhm *usw.* ~: gain success/
fame *etc.*
kommend *Adj.* **a)** *(folgend)* next; **b)**
(mit großer Zukunft) der ~e **Mann/**
Meister the coming man/future champion
Kommentar der; ~s, ~e commentary; *(Stellungnahme)* comment; **kein**
~! no comment!; **Kommentator**
der; ~s, ~en commentator; **kom-**
mentieren *tr. V.* **a)** *(erläutern)* furnish with a commentary ‹*text, work*›;
b) *(Stellung nehmen zu)* comment on
kommerziell 1. *Adj.* commercial; **2.**
adv. commercially
Kommiß der; Kommisses *(Solda-*
tenspr.) army; **Kommissar** der; ~s,
~e **a)** *(Beamter der Polizei)* detective
superintendent; **b)** *(staatlicher Beauf-*

tragter) commissioner; **Kommissi-**
on die; ~, ~en **a)** *(Gremium)* committee; *(Prüfungs~)* commission; **b)** etw.
in ~ **nehmen/haben/geben** *(Wirtsch.)*
take/have sth. on commission/give
sth. to a dealer for sale on commission
Kommode die; ~, ~n chest of drawers
kommunal *Adj.* local; *(bei einer städ-*
tischen Gemeinde) municipal; local;
Kommunal · wahl die local [govern-
ment] elections *pl.*; **Kommunikati-**
on ['kɔmunika'tsɨoːn] die; ~, ~en
(Sprachw., Soziol.) communication;
Kommunion die; ~, ~en *(kath. Kir-*
che) [Holy] Communion; **Kommuni-**
qué [kɔmyni'keː] das; ~s, ~s communiqué; **Kommunismus** der; ~:
communism; **Kommunist** der; ~en,
~en communist; **kommunistisch 1.**
Adj. communist; **2.** *adv.* Communist-
‹*influenced, led, ruled, etc.*›; **kommu-**
nizieren *itr. V.* **a)** *(geh.)* communicate; **b)** *(kath. Kirche)* receive [Holy]
Communion
Komödiant der; ~en, ~en *(veralt.)*
actor; player; *(abwertend: Heuchler)*
play-actor; **Komödie** [ko'møːdɨə]
die; ~, ~n comedy; *(Theater)* comedy
theatre
Kompagnon [kɔmpan'jõː] der; ~s, ~s
(Wirtsch.) partner; associate
kompakt *Adj.* solid
Kompanie die; ~, ~n company
Komparativ der; ~s, ~e *(Sprachw.)*
comparative
Kompaß der; Kompasses, Kompasse
compass
kompensieren *tr. V.* etw. mit etw. *od.*
durch etw. ~: compensate for sth. by
sth.
kompetent *Adj.* competent; **Kom-**
petenz die; ~, ~en competence; *(bes.*
Rechtsw.) authority
komplett 1. *Adj.* complete; **2.** *adv.*
fully ‹*furnished, equipped*›; *(ugs.: ganz*
und gar) completely
Komplex der; ~es, ~e *(auch Psych.)*
complex
Komplikation [kɔmplika'tsɨoːn] die;
~, ~en *(auch Med.)* complication
Kompliment das; ~[e]s, ~e compliment
Komplize der; ~n, ~n *(abwertend)* accomplice
komplizieren *tr. V.* complicate;
kompliziert 1. *Adj.* complicated; **2.**
adv. ~ **aufgebaut sein** have a complicated *or* complex structure

Komplott das; ~|e|s, ~e plot; conspiracy
komponieren tr., itr. V. compose; **Komponist** der; ~en, ~en composer; **Komposition** [kɔmpozi'tsi̯oːn] die; ~, ~en composition; **Kompost** der; ~|e|s, ~e compost; **Kompott** das; ~|e|s, ~e stewed fruit; compote
Kompresse die; ~, ~n *(Med.)* **a)** *(Umschlag)* [wet] compress; **b)** *(Mull)* [gauze] pad; **Kompressor** der; ~s, ~en *(Technik)* compressor
Kompromiß der; **Kompromisses, Kompromisse** compromise
kompromiß-, Kompromiß-: ~**bereit** *Adj.* willing to compromise *pred.; ~***los** 1. *Adj.* uncompromising; 2. *adv.* uncompromisingly; ~**vorschlag** der compromise proposal
kompromittieren tr. V. compromise
Kondensation [kɔndɛnza'tsi̯oːn] die; ~, ~en *(Physik, Chemie)* condensation; **Kondensator** der; ~s, ~en *(Elektrot.)* capacitor; **kondensieren** tr., itr. V. *(itr. auch mit sein) (Physik, Chemie)* condense
Kondens-: ~**milch** die condensed milk; ~**streifen** der condensation trail; ~**wasser** das condensation
Kondition [kɔndi'tsi̯oːn] die; ~, ~en condition; **Konditional·satz** der *(Sprachw.)* conditional clause; **Konditions·training** das fitness training
Konditor der; ~s, ~en pastry-cook; **Konditorei** die; ~, ~en cake-shop; *(Lokal)* café
kondolieren itr. V. offer one's condolences; jmdm. |zu jmds. Tod| ~: offer one's condolences to sb. [on sb.'s death]
Kondom das *od.* der; ~s, ~e condom
Konfekt das; ~|e|s **a)** confectionery; sweets *pl. (Brit.);* candies *pl. (Amer.);* **b)** *(bes. südd., österr., schweiz.: Teegebäck)* [small] fancy biscuits *pl. (Brit.)* or *(Amer.)* cookies *pl.*
Konfektion die; ~, ~en ready-made garments *pl.*
Konferenz die; ~, ~en conference; *(Besprechung)* meeting; **konferieren** 1. itr. V. confer **(über** + *Akk.* on, about)
Konfession die; ~, ~en denomination; **konfessionell** 1. *Adj.; nicht präd.* denominational; 2. *adv.* as regards denomination; ~ |un|gebunden sein have [no] denominational ties
Konfetti das; ~|s| confetti

Konfirmand der; ~en, ~en *(ev. Rel.)* confirmand; **Konfirmation** [kɔnfırma'tsi̯oːn] die; ~, ~en *(ev. Rel.)* confirmation; **konfirmieren** tr. V. *(ev. Rel.)* confirm
konfiszieren tr. V. *(bes. Rechtsw.)* confiscate
Konfitüre die; ~, ~n jam
Konflikt der; ~|e|s, ~e conflict
Konföderation die; ~, ~en confederation
konform *Adj.* concurring *attrib.; ~* gehen be in agreement; **Konformist** der; ~en, ~en conformist
Konfrontation die; ~, ~en confrontation; **konfrontieren** tr. V. confront
konfus 1. *Adj.* confused; 2. *adv.* in a confused fashion
¹Kongo der; ~|s| *(Fluß)* Congo; **²Kongo** (das); ~s *od.* der; ~|s| *(Staat)* the Congo
Kongreß der; **Kongresses, Kongresse** congress; conference; der ~ *(USA):* Congress; **Kongreß·halle** die conference hall
König der; ~s, ~e king; **Königin** die; ~, ~nen queen; **königlich** 1. *Adj.* **a)** royal; **b)** *(vornehm)* regal; **c)** *(reichlich)* princely ⟨gift, salary, wage⟩; 2. *adv.* ⟨pay⟩ handsomely; *(ugs.: außerordentlich)* ⟨enjoy oneself⟩ immensely *(coll.);* **König·reich** das kingdom; **Königs·haus** das royal house; **Königtum** das; ~s, Königtümer **a)** o. *Pl. (Monarchie)* monarchy; **b)** *(veralt.: Reich)* kingdom
Konjugation [kɔnjuga'tsi̯oːn] die; ~, ~en *(Sprachw.)* conjugation; **konjugieren** tr. V. *(Sprachw.)* conjugate; **Konjunktion** [kɔnjʊŋk'tsi̯oːn] die; ~, ~en *(Sprachw.)* conjunction; **Konjunktiv** der; ~s, ~e *(Sprachw.)* subjunctive; **Konjunktur** die; ~, ~en *(Wirtsch.)* **a)** *(wirtschaftliche Lage)* [level of] economic activity; economy; *(Tendenz)* economic trend; **b)** *(Hoch~)* boom; *(Aufschwung)* upturn [in the economy]; **konjunkturell** *Adj.* economic; **Konjunktur·politik** die *(Wirtsch.)* measures *pl.* aimed at avoiding violent fluctuations in the economy
konkav *(Optik)* 1. *Adj.* concave; 2. *adv.* concavely
konkret 1. *Adj.* concrete; 2. *adv.* in concrete terms
Konkurrent der; ~en, ~en, **Konkurrentin** die; ~, ~nen *(Sport, Wirtsch.)*

competitor; **Konkurrenz die; ~, ~en** *(Sport, Wirtsch.)* competition; **konkurrenz·fähig** *Adj.* competitive; **Konkurrenz·kampf der** competition; *(zwischen zwei Menschen)* rivalry; **konkurrieren** *itr. V.* compete; **Konkurs der; ~es, ~e a)** *(Bankrott)* bankruptcy; **b)** *(gerichtliches Verfahren)* bankruptcy proceedings *pl.* **können 1.** *unr. Modalverb; 2. Part.* ~ **a)** be able to; **er kann gut reden/tanzen** he is a good talker/dancer; **ich kann nicht schlafen** I cannot *or (coll.)* can't sleep; **kann das explodieren?** could it explode?; **man kann nie wissen** you never know; **es kann sein, daß ...:** it could be that ...; **kann ich Ihnen helfen?** can I help you?; **b)** *(Grund haben)* **du kannst ganz ruhig sein** you don't have to worry; **das kann man wohl sagen!** you could well say that; **c)** *(dürfen)* **kann ich gehen?** can I go?; ~ **wir mit|kommen|?** can we come too?; **2.** *unr. tr. V. (beherrschen)* know ⟨language⟩; be able to play ⟨game⟩; **sie kann das |gut|** she can do that [well]; **etw./nichts für etw.~:** be/not be responsible for sth.; **3.** *unr. itr. V.* **a)** *(fähig sein)* **er kann nicht anders** there's nothing else he can do; *(es ist seine Art)* he can't help it *(coll.)*; **b)** *(Zeit haben)* **ich kann heute nicht** I can't today *(coll.)*; **c)** *(ugs.: Kraft haben)* **kannst du noch |weiter|?** can you go on?; **d)** *(ugs.: umgehen ~)* **|gut| mit jmdm.** ~: get on [well] with sb.; **Können das; ~s** ability; **Könner der; ~s, ~:** expert; **konnte** *1. u. 3. Pers. Sg. Prät. v.* **können; könnte** *1. u. 3. Pers. Sg. Konjunktiv II v.* **können**

konsequent 1. *Adj.* consistent; *(folgerichtig)* logical; **2.** *adv.* consistently; *(folgerichtig)* logically; **Konsequenz die; ~, ~en a)** *(Folge)* consequence; **b)** *o. Pl. (Unbeirrbarkeit)* determination **konservativ 1.** *Adj.* conservative; **2.** *adv.* conservatively; **Konservative der/die;** *adj. Dekl.* conservative; **Konservatorium das; ~s, Konservatorien** conservatoire; conservatory *(Amer.);* **Konserve die; ~, ~n a)** *(Büchse)* can; tin *(Brit.);* **b)** *(konservierte Lebensmittel)* preserved food; *(in Dosen)* canned *or (Brit.)* tinned food **Konserven-: ~büchse die, ~dose die** can; tin *(Brit.)* **konservieren** *tr. V.* preserve; conserve ⟨work of art⟩; **Konservierung**

die; ~, ~en preservation; **Konservierungs·mittel das** preservative **konsolidieren** *tr. V.* consolidate **Konsonant der; ~en, ~en** consonant **Konsortium** [kɔn'zɔrtsiʊm] **das; ~s, Konsortien** *(Wirtsch.)* consortium **konspirativ** [kɔnspira'ti:f] *Adj.* conspiratorial **konstant** [kɔn'stant] **1.** *Adj.* **a)** constant; **b)** *(beharrlich)* persistent; **2.** *adv.* **a)** constantly; **b)** *(beharrlich)* persistently **Konstellation** [kɔnstɛla'tsio:n] **die; ~, ~en a)** *(von Parteien usw.)* grouping; *(von Umständen)* combination; **b)** *(Astron., Astrol.)* constellation **konstituieren** [kɔnstitu'i:rən] **1.** *tr. V. (gründen)* constitute; set up; **2.** *refl. V.* be constituted; **Konstitution** [kɔnstitu'tsio:n] **die; ~, ~en** constitution **konstruieren** [kɔnstru'i:rən] *tr. V.* **a)** *(entwerfen)* design; **b)** *(aufbauen, Geom., Sprachw.)* construct; **c)** *(abwertend)* fabricate; **Konstrukteur** [kɔnstrʊk'tø:ɐ̯] **der; ~s, ~e** designer; design engineer; **Konstruktion** [kɔnstrʊk'tsio:n] **die; ~, ~en a)** *(Aufbau, Geom., Sprachw.)* construction; *(das Entwerfen)* designing; **b)** *(Entwurf)* design; *(Bau)* construction; **konstruktiv 1.** *Adj.* constructive; **2.** *adv.* constructively **Konsul der; ~s, ~n** *(Dipl., hist.)* consul; **Konsulat das; ~|e|s, ~e** *(Dipl., hist.)* consulate; **konsultieren** *tr. V. (auch fig.)* consult **Konsum der; ~s** consumption; **Konsument der; ~en, ~en** consumer; **Konsum·gesellschaft die** consumer society; **konsumieren** *tr. V.* consume **Kontakt der; ~|e|s, ~e** contact; **mit od. zu jmdm.** ~ **haben/halten** be/remain in contact with sb. **Kontakt-: ~linse die** contact lens; **~mann der;** *Pl.:* **~männer od. ~leute** *(Agent)* contact **Konten** *s.* **Konto kontern** *tr., itr. V. (Boxen, auch fig.)* counter; *(Ballspiele)* counter-attack; **Konter·revolution die** counterrevolution **Kontinent der; ~|e|s, ~e** continent; **kontinental** *Adj.* continental **Kontingent das; ~|e|s, ~e** quota **kontinuierlich 1.** *Adj.* steady; **2.** *adv.* steadily; **Kontinuität die;** ~: continuity **Konto das; ~s, Konten od. Konti** account; **ein laufendes** ~: a current account

Konto-: ~**aus·zug der** *(Bankw.)* [bank] statement; ~**nummer die** account number

Kontor das; ~**s,** ~**e** branch; *(einer Reederei)* office

Konto·stand der *(Bankw.)* balance; state of an/one's account

kontra 1. *Präp. mit Akk. (Rechtsspr., auch fig.)* versus; **2.** *Adv.* against

Kontra das; ~**s,** ~**s** *(Kartenspiele)* double; **jmdm.** ~ **geben** *(fig. ugs.)* flatly contradict sb.

Kontrahent der; ~**en,** ~**en** adversary; opponent

konträr *Adj.* contrary; opposite; **Kontrast der;** ~**[e]s,** ~**e** contrast

Kontroll·abschnitt der stub; **Kontrolle die;** ~, ~**n a)** *(Überwachung)* surveillance; **b)** *(Überprüfung)* check; *(bei Waren, bei Lebensmitteln)* inspection; **c)** *(Herrschaft)* control; **die** ~ **über etw.** *(Akk.)* **verlieren** lose control of sth.; **Kontrolleur** [kɔntrɔ'løːɐ̯] **der;** ~**s,** ~**e** inspector; **Kontroll-gang der** tour of inspection; *(eines Nachtwächters)* round; *(eines Polizisten)* patrol; **kontrollieren** *tr. V.* **a)** *(überwachen)* check; monitor; **b)** *(überprüfen)* check; inspect ⟨*goods, food*⟩; **c)** *(beherrschen)* control; **Kontrollturm der** control tower

Kontroverse [kɔntro'vɛr] **die;** ~, ~**n** controversy **(um, über** + *Akk.* about)

Kontur die; ~, ~**en;** *meist Pl.* contour; outline

Konvention [kɔnvɛn'tsi̯oːn] **die;** ~, ~**en** convention; **konventionell 1.** *Adj.* **a)** conventional; **b)** *(förmlich)* formal; **2.** *adv.* **a)** conventionally; **b)** *(förmlich)* formally

Konversation [kɔnvɛrza'tsi̯oːn] **die;** ~, ~**en** conversation; **Konversations·lexikon das** encyclopaedia

konvertieren [kɔnvɛr'tiːrən] *itr. V.; auch mit sein (Rel.)* be converted

konvex [kɔn'vɛks] *(Optik)* **1.** *Adj.* convex; **2.** *adv.* convexly

Konvoi [kɔn'vɔy] **der;** ~**s,** ~**s** *(bes. Milit.)* convoy

Konzentration [kɔntsɛntra'tsi̯oːn] **die;** ~, ~**en** concentration

Konzentrations-: ~**fähigkeit die;** *o. Pl.* ability to concentrate; ~**lager das** *(bes. ns.)* concentration camp

konzentrieren 1. *refl., tr. V.* concentrate; **sich auf etw.** *(Akk.)* ~: concentrate on sth.; **konzentriert 1.** *Adj.*

concentrated; **2.** *adv.* with concentration

Konzept das; ~**[e]s,** ~**e a)** [rough] draft; **b)** *(Programm)* programme; *(Plan)* plan

Konzern der; ~**[e]s,** ~**e** *(Wirtsch.)* group [of companies]

Konzert das; ~**[e]s,** ~**e a)** *(Komposition)* concerto; **b)** *(Veranstaltung)* concert; **Konzert·saal der** concert-hall

Konzession die; ~, ~**en a)** *(Amtsspr.)* licence; **b)** *(Zugeständnis)* concession

Konzil das; ~**s,** ~**e** *od.* ~**ien** *(kath. Kirche)* council

konzipieren *tr. V.* draft; design ⟨*device, car, etc.*⟩

kooperativ 1. *Adj.* co-operative; **2.** *adv.* co-operatively; **kooperieren** *tr. V.* co-operate

Koordinate die; ~, ~**n** coordinate; **Koordinaten·system das** *(Math.)* system of coordinates; **koordinieren** *tr. V.* coordinate

Kopenhagen (das); ~**s** Copenhagen

Kopf der; ~**[e]s,** **Köpfe a)** head; **ein** ~ **Salat** a lettuce; ~ **an** ~: shoulder to shoulder; *(im Wettlauf)* neck and neck; *(fig.)* **nicht wissen, wo einem der** ~ **steht** not know whether one is coming or going; ~ **hoch!** chin up!; **den** ~ **hängen lassen** become disheartened; **b)** *(Person)* person; **ein kluger/fähiger** ~ **sein** be a clever/able man/woman; **pro** ~: per head; **die führenden Köpfe der Wirtschaft** the leading minds in the field of economics; **c)** *(Wille)* **seinen** ~ **durchsetzen** make sb. do what one wants; **d)** *(Verstand)* mind; head; **sich** *(Dat.)* **den** ~ **zerbrechen** *(ugs.)* rack one's brains **(über** + *Akk.* over)

Kopf-: ~**bahn·hof der** terminal station; ~**bedeckung die** headgear; **ohne** ~**bedeckung** without anything on one's head

Köpfchen das; ~**s,** ~: brains *pl.;* ~ **muß man haben** you've got to have it up here *(coll.);* **köpfen** *tr. V.* **a)** decapitate; *(hinrichten)* behead; **b)** *(Fußball)* head

Kopf-: ~**ende das** head end; ~**haut die** [skin of the] scalp; ~**hörer der** headphones *pl.;* ~**kissen das** pillow; ~**lastig** *Adj.* down by the head *pred.;* ~**los 1.** *Adj.* rash; *(in Panik)* panic-stricken; **2.** *adv.* rashly; ~**los davon-rennen** flee in panic; ~**rechnen** *itr. V.; nur im Inf. gebr.* do mental arithmetic; ~**rechnen das** mental arithmetic; ~**salat der** head lettuce;

~**schmerz** der; *meist Pl.* headache; ~**schmerzen haben** have a headache *sing.;* ~**sprung** der header; ~**stand** der headstand; ~|**stehen** *unr. itr. V. (ugs.: überrascht sein)* be bowled over; ~**stein·pflaster** das cobblestones *pl.;* ~**tuch** das headscarf; ~**weh** das; *o. Pl. (ugs.)* headache; ~**weh haben** have a headache; ~**zerbrechen** das; ~s: etw. bereitet *od.* macht jmdm. ~**zerbrechen** sb. has to rack his/her brains about sth.; *(etw. macht jmdm. Sorgen)* sth. is a worry to sb.

Kopie die; ~, ~n copy; *(Durchschrift)* carbon copy; *(Fotokopie)* photocopy; *(Fot., Film)* print; **kopieren** *tr. V.* copy; *(fotokopieren)* photocopy; *(Fot., Film)* print; **Kopier·gerät** das photocopier

¹**Koppel** das; ~s, ~, *österr.:* die; ~, ~n *(Gürtel)* [leather] belt *(as part of a uniform);* ²**Koppel** die; ~, ~n paddock

koppeln *tr. V.* couple (**an** + *Akk.* to); dock ⟨*spacecraft*⟩

Koppelung *s.* **Kopplung; Kopplung** die; ~, ~en coupling; *(Raumf.)* docking

kopulieren *itr. V.* copulate

Koralle die; ~, ~n coral

Koran der; ~s, ~e Koran

Korb der; ~es, Körbe a) basket; b) jmdm. einen ~ geben turn sb. down; **Korb·ball** der; *o. Pl.* netball

Kord der; ~|e|s a) corduroy; cord; b) *s.* Kordsamt

Kordel die; ~, ~n cord

Kord·samt der cord velvet

Korea (das); ~s Korea; **Koreaner** der; ~s, ~: Korean; **koreanisch** *Adj.* Korean

Korinthe die; ~, ~n currant

Kork der; ~s, ~e cork; **Korken** der; ~s, ~: cork; **Korken·zieher** der corkscrew

¹**Korn** das; ~|e|s, Körner a) *(Frucht)* grain; *(Getreide~)* grain [of corn]; *(Pfeffer~)* corn; b) *o. Pl. (Getreide)* corn; grain; c) *(Salz~, Sand~)* grain; *(Hagel~)* stone; ²**Korn** der; ~|e|s, ~ *(ugs.)* corn schnapps; corn liquor *(Amer.);* **Korn·blume** die cornflower; **Körnchen** das; ~s, ~: tiny grain; *(von Sand usw.)* [tiny] grain; granule; **Körner** *s.* Korn; **Korn·feld** das cornfield; **körnig** *Adj.* granular

Korona die; ~, Koronen crowd *(coll.)*

Körper der; ~s, ~: body

körper-, Körper-: ~**bau** der; *o. Pl.* physique; ~**behindert** *Adj.* physic-

ally handicapped; ~**behinderte** der/die physically handicapped person; ~**behinderte** *Pl.* physically handicapped people; ~**geruch** der body odour; BO *(coll.);* ~**größe** die height körperlich 1. *Adj.* physical; 2. *adv.* physically

Körper-: ~**pflege** die body care *no art.;* ~**spray** der *od.* das deodorant spray; ~**teil** der part of the/one's body; ~**verletzung** die *(Rechtsw.)* bodily harm *no indef. art.*

Korps [koːɐ̯] das; ~ [koːɐ̯(s)], ~ [koːɐ̯s] a) *(Milit.)* corps; b) *(Studentenverbindung)* student duelling society

korpulent *Adj.* corpulent

korrekt 1. *Adj.* correct; 2. *adv.* correctly; **korrekter·weise** *Adv.* to be [strictly] correct; **Korrektheit** die; ~: correctness; **Korrektor** der; ~s, ~en [-'toːrən] proof-reader; **Korrektur** die; ~, ~en correction

Korrespondent der; ~en, ~en correspondent; **Korrespondenz** die; ~, ~en correspondence; **korrespondieren** *itr. V.* correspond (**mit** with)

Korridor der; ~s, ~e corridor

korrigieren *tr. V.* correct; revise ⟨*opinion, view*⟩

korrupt *Adj.* corrupt; **Korruption** [kɔrʊpˈtsi̯oːn] die; ~, ~en corruption

Korsett das; ~s, ~s *od.* ~e corset

Korsika (das); ~s Corsica

koscher *Adj.* kosher

Kose-: ~**form** die familiar form; ~**name** der pet name

Kosinus der; ~, ~ *od.* ~se *(Math.)* cosine

Kosmetik die; ~ a) beauty culture *no art.;* b) *(fig.)* cosmetic procedures *pl.;* **Kosmetikerin** die; ~, ~nen cosmetician; beautician; **kosmetisch** 1. *Adj. (auch fig.)* cosmetic; 2. *adv.* jmdn. ~ beraten give sb. advice on beauty care; **sich** ~ **behandeln lassen** have beauty treatment

kosmisch *Adj.* cosmic ⟨*ray, dust, etc.*⟩; space ⟨*age, station, research, etc.*⟩; meteoric ⟨*iron*⟩; **Kosmos** der; ~: cosmos

Kost die; ~: food; ~ **und Logis** board and lodging

kostbar 1. *Adj.* valuable; precious ⟨*time*⟩; 2. *adv.* expensively ⟨*dressed*⟩; luxuriously ⟨*decorated*⟩; **Kostbarkeit** die; ~, ~en a) *(Sache)* treasure; b) *o. Pl. (Eigenschaft)* value

¹**kosten** 1. *tr. V.* a) taste; try; 2. *itr. V. (probieren)* have a taste

²kosten *tr. V.* **a)** cost; **b)** *(erfordern)* take; cost ⟨*lives*⟩; **Kosten** *Pl.* cost *sing.;* costs; *(Auslagen)* expenses; *(Rechtsw.)* costs

kosten-, Kosten-: ~**deckend** *Adj.* that covers/cover [one's] costs *postpos., not pred.;* ~**erstattung** die reimbursement of costs; ~**los** 1. *Adj.* free; 2. *adv.* free of charge; ~**pflichtig** *(Rechtsw.)* 1. *Adj.* eine ~pflichtige Verwarnung a fine and a caution; 2. *adv.* eine Klage ~pflichtig abweisen dismiss a case with costs; ein Auto ~pflichtig abschleppen tow a car away at the owner's expense; ~**voran·schlag** der estimate

Kost·geld das payment for [one's] board

köstlich 1. *Adj.* delicious; *(unterhaltsam)* delightful; 2. *adv.* ⟨*taste*⟩ delicious; **sich ~ amüsieren/unterhalten** enjoy oneself enormously *(coll.);* **Köstlichkeit** die; ~, ~en *(Sache)* delicacy

Kost·probe die; ~, ~n taste

kost·spielig *Adj.* costly

Kostüm das; ~s, ~e **a)** suit; **b)** *(Theater~, Verkleidung)* costume; **kostümieren** *tr. V.* dress up

Kot der; ~[e]s, ~e excrement

Kotangens der; ~, ~ *(Math.)* cotangent

Kotelett [kɔt'lɛt] **das;** ~s, ~s chop; *(vom Nacken)* cutlet; **Koteletten** *Pl.* side-whiskers

Köter der; ~s, ~ *(abwertend)* cur

Kot·flügel der *(Kfz-W.)* wing

kotzen *itr. V. (derb)* puke *(coarse)*

KP [ka:'pe:] *Abk.* **Kommunistische Partei** CP

Krabbe die; ~, ~n **a)** *(Zool.)* crab; **b)** *(ugs.: Garnele)* shrimp; *(größer)* prawn; **krabbeln** 1. *itr. V.; mit sein* crawl; 2. *tr. V. (ugs.: kraulen)* tickle

Krach der; ~[e]s, Kräche **a)** *o. Pl. (Lärm)* noise; row; **b)** *(lautes Geräusch)* crash; **c)** *(ugs.: Streit)* row; **krachen** 1. *itr. V.* **a)** *(Krach auslösen)* ⟨*thunder*⟩ crash; ⟨*shot*⟩ ring out; **b)** *mit sein (ugs.: bersten)* ⟨*ice*⟩ crack; ⟨*bed*⟩ collapse; **c)** *mit sein (ugs.: mit Krach auftreffen)* crash; 2. *refl. V. (ugs.)* row *(coll.);* **krächzen** *itr. V.* ⟨*raven, crow*⟩ caw; ⟨*parrot*⟩ squawk; ⟨*person*⟩ croak

kraft *Präp. + Gen. (Amtsspr.)* ~ |meines| Amtes by virtue of my office; ~ Gesetzes by law; **Kraft die;** ~, Kräfte strength; *(Wirksamkeit)* power; *(Physik)* force; *(Arbeits~)* employee; **mit**

letzter ~: with one's last ounce of strength; **aus eigener ~:** by one's own efforts; **mit vereinten Kräften werden wir ...:** if we join forces *or* combine our efforts we will ...; **außer ~ setzen** repeal ⟨*law*⟩; countermand ⟨*order*⟩; **außer ~ sein/treten** no longer be/cease to be in force; **in ~ treten/sein/bleiben** come into/be in/remain in force

Kraft-: ~**aufwand** der effort; ~**brühe** die strong meat broth; ~**fahrer** der driver; motorist; ~**fahrzeug das** motor vehicle

Kraftfahrzeug-: ~**brief** der vehicle registration document; log-book *(Brit.);* ~**schein** der vehicle registration document; ~**steuer** die vehicle tax

kräftig 1. *Adj.* strong; vigorous ⟨*plant, shoot*⟩; powerful, hefty ⟨*blow, kick, etc.*⟩; nourishing ⟨*soup, bread, meal, etc.*⟩; 2. *adv.* powerfully ⟨*built*⟩; ⟨*rain, snow*⟩ heavily; ⟨*eat*⟩ heartily; **kräftigen** *tr. V.* ⟨*holiday, air, etc.*⟩ invigorate; ⟨*food etc.*⟩ fortify

kraft-, Kraft-: ~**meier** der; ~s, ~ *(ugs.: abwertend)* muscleman; ~**probe** die trial of strength; ~**rad das** *(Amtsspr.)* motorcycle; ~**stoff** der *(Kfz-W.)* fuel; ~**stoff·verbrauch** der fuel consumption; ~**voll** 1. *Adj.* powerful; 2. *adv.* powerfully; ~**wagen** der motor vehicle; ~**werk das** power station

Kragen der; ~s, ~, *südd., österr. u. schweiz. auch:* Krägen collar; **Kragen·weite** die collar size

Krähe ['krɛːə] die; ~, ~n crow; **krähen** *itr. V. (auch fig.)* crow; **Krähen·füße** *Pl. (ugs.)* crow's feet

krakeelen *itr. V. (ugs.)* kick up a row *(coll.)*

krakeln *tr., itr. V. (ugs.)* scrawl; **krakelig** *Adj. (ugs. abwertend)* scrawly

Kralle die; ~, ~n claw; **krallen** 1. *refl. V.* **sich an etw. (Akk.)** ~ ⟨*cat*⟩ dig its claws into sth.; ⟨*person*⟩ clutch sth. [tightly]; 2. *tr. V. (fest greifen)* **die Finger in/um etw. (Akk.)** ~: dig one's fingers into sth./clutch sth. [tightly] with one's fingers

Kram der; ~[e]s *(ugs.)* **a)** stuff; *(Gerümpel)* junk; **b)** *(Angelegenheit)* affair; **kramen** 1. *itr. V.* **in etw. (Dat.)** ~: rummage about in sth.; 2. *tr. V. (ugs.)* **etw. aus etw.** ~: fish *(coll.)* sth. out of sth.; **Krämer der;** ~s, ~: grocer; **Kram·laden der** *(ugs. abwertend)* junk shop

Krampf der; ~|e|s, **Krämpfe a)** cramp; *(Zuckung)* spasm; **b)** *o. Pl.* painful strain; *(sinnloses Tun)* senseless waste of effort; **Krampf·ader die** varicose vein; **krampfhaft 1.** *Adj.* convulsive; *(verbissen)* desperate; **2.** *adv.* convulsively; *(verbissen)* desperately
Kran der; ~|e|s, **Kräne a)** crane; **b)** *(südwestd.: Wasserhahn)* tap; faucet *(Amer.)*
Kranich der; ~s, ~e crane
krank; kränker, kränkst... *Adj.* ill *usu. pred.;* sick; bad ⟨*leg, tooth*⟩; diseased ⟨*plant, organ*⟩; *(fig.)* ailing ⟨*economy, business*⟩; ~ **werden** be taken ill; jmdn. ~ **schreiben** give sb. a medical certificate; **Kranke der/die;** *adj. Dekl.* sick man/woman; *(Patient)* patient; **kränkeln** *itr. V.* be in poor health; **kränken** *tr. V.* jmdn. ~: hurt sb. *or* sb.'s feelings
Kranken-: ~**geld** das sickness benefit; ~**haus das** hospital; ~**kasse die** health insurance scheme; *(Körperschaft)* health insurance institution; *(privat)* health insurance company; ~**pfleger** der male nurse; ~**schein** der health insurance certificate; ~**schwester** die nurse; ~**versicherung die a)** *(Versicherung)* health insurance; **b)** *(Unternehmen)* health insurance company; ~**wagen** der ambulance
krank|feiern *itr. V. (ugs.)* skive off work *(sl.)* [pretending to be ill]; **kränker** *s.* krank; **krankhaft 1.** *Adj.* pathological; morbid ⟨*growth, state, swelling, etc.*⟩; **2.** *adv.* pathologically; morbidly ⟨*swollen, sensitive*⟩; **Krankheit die;** ~, ~**en a)** illness; *(bestimmte Art, von Pflanzen, Organen)* disease; **b)** *o. Pl. (Zeit des Krankseins)* illness; **Krankheits·erreger** der pathogen; **kränklich** *Adj.* ailing; **kränkst...** *s.* krank; **Kränkung die;** ~, ~**en:** eine ~: an injury to one's/sb.'s feelings
Kranz der; ~es, **Kränze** wreath; garland; *(auf einem Grab usw.)* wreath; **Kränzchen das;** ~s, ~: coffee circle; coffee klatch *(Amer.)*
Krapfen der; ~s, ~: doughnut
kraß 1. *Adj.* blatant ⟨*case*⟩; flagrant ⟨*injustice*⟩; stark ⟨*contrast*⟩; complete ⟨*contradiction*⟩; sharp ⟨*difference*⟩; out-and-out ⟨*egoist*⟩; **2.** *adv.* sich ~ **ausdrücken** put sth. bluntly; sich von etw. ~ **unterscheiden** be in stark contrast to sth.
Krater der; ~s, ~: crater

Kratz·bürste die *(ugs. scherzh.)* prickly so-and-so; **kratzen 1.** *tr. V.* scratch; *(entfernen)* scrape; **2.** *itr. V.* **a)** scratch; **b)** *(jucken)* itch; **Kratzer** der; ~s, ~ *(ugs.)* scratch; **kratzig** *Adj.* itchy ⟨*material*⟩
Kraul das; ~s *(Sport)* crawl; ¹**kraulen 1.** *itr. V.* do the crawl; **2.** *tr. V.; auch mit sein* eine Strecke ~: cover a distance using the crawl
²**kraulen** *tr. V.* jmdm. das Kinn ~: tickle sb. under the chin; jmdn. in den Haaren ~: run one's fingers through sb.'s hair
kraus *Adj.* creased ⟨*skirt etc.*⟩; frizzy ⟨*hair*⟩; **Krause die;** ~, ~**n** *(Kragen)* ruff; *(am Ärmel)* ruffle
kräuseln 1. *tr. V.* ruffle ⟨*water, surface*⟩; gather ⟨*material etc.*⟩; frizz ⟨*hair*⟩; **2.** *refl. V.* ⟨*hair*⟩ go frizzy; ⟨*water*⟩ ripple; ⟨*smoke*⟩ curl up
Kraut das; ~|e|s, **Kräuter a)** herb; **b)** *o. Pl. (bes. südd., österr.: Kohl)* cabbage
Krawall der; ~s, ~e **a)** riot; **b)** *o. Pl. (ugs.: Lärm)* row *(coll.)*
Krawatte die; ~, ~**n** tie
kreativ 1. *Adj.* creative; **2.** *adv.* ~ **veranlagt sein** have a creative bent
Kreatur die; ~, ~**en** creature
Krebs der; ~es, ~e **a)** crustacean; *(Fluß~)* crayfish; *(Krabbe)* crab; **b)** *(Krankheit)* cancer
krebs-, Krebs-: ~**erregend,** ~**erzeugend** *Adj.* carcinogenic; ~**krank** *Adj.* ~krank sein have cancer; ~**rot** *Adj.* as red as a lobster *postpos.*
Kredit der; ~|e|s, ~e credit; *(Darlehen)* loan; **Kredit·karte die** credit card; mit ~**karte bezahlen** pay by credit card; **kredit·würdig** *Adj. (Finanzw.)* credit-worthy
Kreide die; ~, ~**n** chalk; **kreide-bleich** *Adj.* as white as a sheet *postpos.;* **Kreide·felsen** der chalk cliff
kreieren [kre'i:rən] *tr. V.* create
Kreis der; ~es, ~e circle; *(Verwaltungsbezirk)* district; *(Wahl~)* ward; **Kreis·bahn die** orbit
kreischen *itr. V.* screech; ⟨*door*⟩ creak
Kreisel der; ~s, ~ *(Kinderspielzeug)* top; *(ugs.: Kreisverkehr)* roundabout; **kreisen** *itr. V.; auch mit sein* ⟨*planet*⟩ revolve (um around); ⟨*satellite etc.*⟩ orbit; ⟨*aircraft, bird*⟩ circle
kreis-, Kreis-: ~**förmig** *Adj.* circular; ~**lauf** der *(Physiol.)* circulation; *(der Natur, des Lebens usw.)* cycle;

~lauf·störungen *Pl. (Med.)* circulatory trouble *sing.;* ~rund *Adj.* [perfectly] round; ~säge die circular saw **Kreiß·saal** der *(Med.)* delivery room **Kreis-:** ~stadt die chief town of a/the district; ~verkehr der roundabout **Krem** die; ~, ~s *s.* Creme **Krematorium** das; ~s, **Krematorien** crematorium **kremig** *s.* cremig **Krempe** die; ~, ~n brim **Krempel** der; ~s *(ugs. abwertend)* stuff; *(Gerümpel)* junk **krepieren** *itr. V.; mit sein (salopp)* ⟨*person*⟩ snuff it *(sl.)* **Krepp** der; ~s, ~s *od.* ~e crêpe **Kresse** die; ~, ~n *(Bot.)* cress **Kreta (das)** ~s Crete **Kreuz** das; ~es, ~e a) cross; *(Kreuzzeichen)* sign of the cross; b) *(Teil des Rückens)* small of the back; **jmdn. aufs ~ legen** *(salopp)* take sb. for a ride *(sl.);* c) *o. Art., o. Pl. (Kartenspiel) (Farbe)* clubs *pl.; (Karte)* club; d) *(Autobahn)* interchange; e) *(Musik)* sharp; **kreuzen** 1. *tr. V. (auch Biol.)* cross; 2. *refl. V.* a) *(überschneiden)* cross; b) *(zuwiderlaufen)* clash (**mit** with); 3. *itr. V.; mit haben od. sein (fahren)* cruise **Kreuz-:** ~fahrer der *(hist.)* crusader; ~fahrt die cruise; ~feuer das *(Milit., auch fig.)* cross-fire; ~gang der cloister **kreuzigen** *tr. V.* crucify; **Kreuzigung die;** ~, ~en crucifixion **Kreuz-:** ~otter die adder; [common] viper; ~ritter der *(hist.)* crusader; ~schmerzen *Pl.* pain *sing.* in the small of the back **Kreuzung die;** ~, ~en a) crossroads *sing.;* b) *(Biol.)* crossing; cross-breeding; *(Ergebnis)* cross **kreuz-, Kreuz-:** ~verhör das cross-examination; ~weise crosswise; ~wort·rätsel das crossword [puzzle]; ~zug der *(hist., fig.)* crusade **kribbelig** *Adj. (ugs.) (vor Ungeduld)* fidgety; *(nervös)* edgy; **kribbeln** *itr. V. (jucken)* tickle; *(prickeln)* tingle **kriechen** *unr. itr. V.* a) *mit sein* ⟨*insect, baby*⟩ crawl; ⟨*plant*⟩ creep; ⟨*person, animal*⟩ creep, crawl; b) *auch mit sein (fig. abwertend)* crawl (**vor** + *Dat.* to); **Kriecher** der; ~s, ~ *(abwertend)* crawler; **Kriech·spur** die *(Verkehrsw.)* crawler lane **Krieg** der; ~[e]s, ~e war **kriegen** *tr. V. (ugs.)* get; *(erreichen)* catch ⟨*train, bus, etc.*⟩

Krieger der; ~s, ~: warrior; **kriegerisch** *Adj.* a) *(kampflustig)* warlike; b) *(militärisch)* military; **eine ~e Auseinandersetzung** an armed conflict **kriegs-, Kriegs-:** ~beil das tomahawk; **das ~beil begraben** *(scherzh.)* bury the hatchet; ~bemalung die *(Völkerk.)* war-paint; ~beschädigt *Adj.* war-disabled; ~beschädigte der/die war invalid; ~dienst der a) *(im Krieg)* active service; b) *(Wehrdienst)* military service; **den ~dienst verweigern** be a conscientious objector; ~dienst·verweigerer der conscientious objector; ~erklärung die declaration of war; ~gefangene der prisoner of war; POW; ~gefangenschaft die captivity; ~schiff das warship; ~verbrechen das *(Rechtsw.)* war crime **Krimi** der; ~[s], ~[s] *(ugs.)* crime thriller; **Kriminal·beamte** der [plain-clothes] detective; **Kriminalität die;** ~: crime *no art.* **Kriminal-:** ~polizei die criminal investigation department; ~roman der crime novel; *(mit Detektiv als Held)* detective novel **kriminell** 1. *Adj.* criminal; 2. *adv.* ~ **veranlagt sein** have criminal tendencies; ~ **handeln** act illegally; **Kriminelle der/die;** *adj. Dekl.* criminal **Krimskrams** der; ~[es] *(ugs.)* stuff **Kringel** der; ~s, ~ *(Kreis)* [small] ring; *(Kritzelei)* round squiggle; *(Gebäck)* [ring-shaped] biscuit; **kringeln** *refl. V.* curl [up]; ⟨*hair*⟩ go curly; **sich ~ [vor Lachen]** *(ugs.)* kill oneself [laughing] *(coll.)* **Kripo** die; ~ *(ugs.)* **die ~:** ≈ the CID **Krippe** die; ~, ~n a) *(Futtertrog)* manger; crib; b) *(Weihnachts~)* model of a nativity scene; c) *(Kinder~)* crèche **Krise** die; ~, ~n *(auch Med.)* crisis; **kriseln** *itr. V. (unpers.)* **es kriselt in ihrer Ehe/in der Partei** their marriage is in trouble/the party is in a state of crisis; **Krisen·herd** der trouble spot ¹**Kristall** der; ~s, ~e crystal; ²**Kristall** das; ~s crystal *no indef. art.* **Kriterium** das; ~s, **Kriterien** criterion **Kritik** die; ~, ~en a) criticism *no indef. art.* (**an** + *Dat.* of); **an jmdm./etw. ~ üben** criticize sb./sth.; b) *(Besprechung)* review; **Kritiker** der; ~s, ~: critic; **kritik·los** 1. *Adj.* uncritical; 2. *adv.* uncritically; **kritisch** 1. *Adj.* critical; 2. *adv.* critically; **kritisieren**

tr. V. criticize; review ⟨*book, play, etc.*⟩

kritzeln 1. *itr. V. (schreiben)* scribble; *(zeichnen)* doodle; **2.** *tr. V.* scribble

Kroatien [kro'a:tsjən] **(das); ~s** Croatia; **kroatisch** *Adj.* Croatian

kroch *1. u. 3. Pers. Sg. Prät. v.* **kriechen**

Krokant der; ~s praline

Krokette die; ~, ~n *(Kochk.)* croquette

Krokodil das; ~s, ~e crocodile; **Krokodils·tränen** *Pl. (ugs.)* crocodile tears

Krokus der; ~, ~ *od.* **~se** crocus

Krone die; ~, ~n crown; (eines Baumes) top; crown; *(einer Welle)* crest; **die ~ der Schöpfung** the pride of creation; **krönen** *tr. V. (auch fig.)* crown; **Kronen·korken der** crown cork

Kron-: ~juwel das *od.* **der;** *meist Pl.* **die ~juwelen** the crown jewels; **~leuchter der** chandelier; **~prinz der** crown prince

Krönung die; ~, ~en coronation; *(fig.)* culmination; **Kron·zeuge der** *(Rechtsw.)* person who turns Queen's/King's evidence; **als ~ auftreten** turn Queen's/King's evidence

Kropf der; ~[e]s, Kröpfe *(Med.)* goitre

Kröte die; ~, ~n a) toad; **b)** *Pl. (salopp: Geld)* **ein paar/eine ganze Menge ~n verdienen** earn a few bob *(Brit. sl.)*/a fair old whack *(sl.)*

Krücke die; ~, ~n crutch; **Krückstock der** walking-stick

Krug der; ~[e]s, Krüge jug; *(größer)* pitcher; *(Bier~)* mug

Krume die; ~, ~n crumb; **Krümel der; ~s, ~:** crumb; **krümeln** *itr. V.* **a)** crumble; **b)** *(Krümel machen)* make crumbs

krumm 1. *Adj.* **a)** bent ⟨*nail, back*⟩; crooked ⟨*stick, branch, etc.*⟩; bandy ⟨*legs*⟩; **b)** *nicht präd. (ugs.: unrechtmäßig)* crooked; **2.** *adv.* crookedly; **krümmen 1.** *tr. V.* bend; **2.** *refl. V.* **a)** *(sich winden)* writhe; **b)** *(krumm verlaufen)* ⟨*road, path, river*⟩ bend

krumm-: ~|lachen *refl. V. (ugs.)* **sich über etw.** *(Akk.)* **~lachen** fall about laughing over sth.; **~|nehmen** *unr. tr. V. (ugs.)* **etw. ~nehmen** take sth. the wrong way

Krümmung die; ~, ~en bend

Krüppel der; ~s, ~: cripple

Kruste die; ~, ~n crust; *(vom Braten)* crisp

Kruzifix das; ~es, ~e crucifix

Krypta die; ~, Krypten *(Archit.)* crypt

Kuba (das); ~s Cuba; **Kubaner der; ~s, ~:** Cuban

Kübel der; ~s, ~: pail

Kubik- cubic ⟨*metre, foot, etc.*⟩

Küche die; ~, ~n kitchen; *(Einrichtung)* kitchen furniture *no indef. art.; (Kochk.)* cooking; cuisine; **kalte/warme ~:** cold/hot food

Kuchen der; ~s, ~: cake; *(Obst~)* flan; *(Torte)* gateau

Kuchen-: ~form die cake-tin; **~gabel die** pastry-fork

Küchen·gerät das kitchen utensil; *(als Kollektivum)* kitchen utensils *pl.*

Kuckuck der; ~s, ~e a) cuckoo; **zum ~ [noch mal]!** *(salopp)* for crying out loud! *(coll.)*; **b)** *(scherzh.: Pfandsiegel)* bailiff's seal *(placed on distrained goods)*; **Kuckucks·uhr die** cuckoo clock .

Kufe die; ~, ~n runner; *(von Flugzeugen, Hubschraubern)* skid

Kugel die; ~, ~n a) ball; *(Geom.)* sphere; *(Kegeln)* bowl; *(beim Kugelstoßen)* shot; **b)** *(ugs.: Geschoß)* bullet; **Kugel·lager das** *(Technik)* ball-bearing; **kugeln** *tr. V.* roll; **2.** *refl. V.* **sich [vor Lachen] ~** *(ugs.)* double *or* roll up [laughing]

kugel-, Kugel-: ~rund [--'-] *Adj.* round as a ball *postpos.; (scherzh.: dick)* rotund; tubby; **~schreiber der** ball-pen; Biro **(P); ~sicher** *Adj.* bullet-proof; **~stoßen das; ~s** shot[-put]; *(Disziplin)* putting the shot *no art.*

Kuh die; ~, Kühe cow

Kuh-: ~fladen der cow-pat; **~haut die: das geht auf keine ~haut** *(fig. salopp)* it's absolutely staggering

kühl 1. *Adj.* cool; **etw. ~ lagern** keep sth. in a cool place; **2.** *adv.* coolly

Kuhle die; ~, ~n *(ugs.)* hollow

Kühle die; ~: coolness

kühlen *tr. V.* cool; chill ⟨*wine*⟩; refrigerate ⟨*food*⟩; **2.** *itr. V.* ⟨*cold compress, ointment, breeze, etc.*⟩ have a cooling effect; **Kühler der; ~s, ~ a)** *(am Auto)* radiator; *(~haube)* bonnet *(Brit.)*; hood *(Amer.)*; **b)** *(Sekt~)* ice-bucket; **Kühler·haube die** bonnet *(Brit.)*; hood *(Amer.)*

Kühl-: ~schrank der refrigerator; fridge *(Brit. coll.)*; icebox *(Amer.)*; **~truhe die** [chest] freezer; *(im Lebensmittelgeschäft)* freezer [cabinet]

Kühlung die; ~, ~en cooling; *(Vor-*

richtung) cooling system; *(für Lebensmittel)* refrigeration system; **Kühl·wasser das** cooling water **kühn 1.** *Adj.* bold; *(dreist)* audacious; **2.** *adv.* boldly; *(gewagt)* daringly; *(dreist)* audaciously; **Kühnheit die;** ~: boldness; *(Gewagtheit)* daringness; *(Dreistigkeit)* audacity **Kuh·stall der** cowshed **Küken das;** ~s, ~: chick **kulant** *Adj.* obliging; fair ⟨terms⟩; **Kulanz die;** ~: willingness to oblige **Kuli der;** ~s, ~s **a)** coolie; **b)** *(ugs.)* ball-point; Biro (P) **kulinarisch** *Adj.* culinary **Kulisse die;** ~, ~n piece of scenery; flat; *(Hintergrund)* backdrop; **die ~n** the scenery *sing.* **kullern** *(ugs.)* *itr. V. mit sein* roll **Kult der;** ~|e|s, ~e *(auch fig.)* cult; **kultivieren** *tr. V. (auch fig.)* cultivate; **kultiviert 1.** *Adj.* cultured; *(vornehm)* refined; **2.** *adv.* in a cultured manner; *(vornehm)* in a refined manner; **Kultur die;** ~, ~en **a)** *o. Pl.* culture; *(kultivierte Lebensart)* refinement; **ein Mensch von ~:** a cultured person; **b)** *(Zivilisation, Lebensform)* civilization **Kultur-:** ~**abkommen das** cultural agreement; ~**austausch der** cultural exchange; ~**beutel der** sponge-bag *(Brit.);* toilet-bag **kulturell 1.** *Adj.* cultural; **2.** *adv.* culturally **Kultur-:** ~**film der** documentary film; ~**geschichte die a)** *o. Pl.* history of civilization; *(einer bestimmten Kultur)* cultural history; ~**politik die** cultural and educational policy **Kultus·minister der** minister for education and cultural affairs **Kümmel der;** ~s, ~: caraway [seed]; *(Branntwein)* kümmel **Kummer der;** ~s sorrow; grief; *(Ärger, Sorgen)* trouble; ~ **um** *od.* **über jmdn.** grief for sb.; **jmdm. ~ machen** give sb. trouble; **kümmerlich** *Adj.* **a)** *(schwächlich)* puny; stunted ⟨vegetation, plants⟩; **b)** *(ärmlich)* wretched; miserable; **c)** *(abwertend: gering)* miserable; meagre ⟨knowledge, left-overs⟩; **kümmern 1.** *refl. V.* **a) sich um jmdn./etw.** ~: take care of sb./sth.; **b)** *(sich befassen mit)* **sich nicht um Politik** ~: not be interested in politics; **2.** *tr. V.* concern **Kumpan der;** ~s, ~e *(ugs.)* **a)** pal *(coll.);* buddy *(coll.);* **b)** *(abwertend:*

Mittäter) accomplice; **Kumpel der;** ~s, ~ **a)** *(Bergmannsspr.)* miner; **b)** *(salopp: Kamerad)* pal *(coll.);* buddy *(coll.)* **kündbar** *Adj.* terminable ⟨contract⟩; redeemable ⟨loan, mortgage⟩; **¹Kunde der;** ~n, ~n customer; *(eines Architekten-, Anwaltbüros, einer Versicherung usw.)* client **²Kunde die;** ~ *(geh.)* tidings *pl. (literary);* **Kunden·dienst der** *o. Pl.* service to customers; *(Wartung)* after-sales service; **Kundgebung die;** ~, ~en rally; **kundig** *Adj. (kenntnisreich)* knowledgeable; *(sachverständig)* expert; **kündigen 1.** *tr. V.* cancel ⟨subscription, membership⟩; terminate ⟨contract, agreement⟩; **seine Stellung ~:** hand in one's notice (**bei** to); **2.** *unr. itr. V.* **a)** *(ein Mietverhältnis beenden)* ⟨tenant⟩ give notice; **jmdm. ~** ⟨landlord⟩ give sb. notice to quit; **zum 1. Juli ~:** give notice for 1 July; **b)** *(ein Arbeitsverhältnis beenden)* ⟨employee⟩ hand in one's notice (**bei** to); **jmdm. ~** ⟨employer⟩ give sb. his/her notice; **Kündigung die;** ~, ~en **a)** *(der Mitgliedschaft, eines Abonnements)* cancellation; *(eines Vertrags)* termination; **b)** *(eines Arbeitsverhältnisses)* **jmdm. die ~ aussprechen** give sb. his/her notice; **Kundin die;** ~, ~nen customer/client; **Kundschaft die;** ~, ~en *o. Pl.; s.* **¹Kunde a:** customers *pl.;* clientele; **Kundschafter der;** ~s, ~: scout; **kund|tun** *(geh.)* *unr. tr. V.* announce **künftig 1.** *Adj.* future; **2.** *adv.* in future **Kunst die;** ~, **Künste a)** art; **b)** *(das Können)* skill; **die ärztliche ~:** medical skill; **das ist keine ~!** *(ugs.)* there's nothing 'to it **kunst-, Kunst-:** ~**aus·stellung die** art exhibition; ~**buch das** art book; ~**erzieher der,** ~**erzieherin die** art teacher; ~**faser die** synthetic fibre; ~**führer der** guide to cultural and artistic monuments [of an/the area]; ~**genuß der** enjoyment of art; *(Ereignis)* artistic treat; ~**gerecht 1.** *Adj.* expert; **2.** *adv.* expertly; ~**geschichte die** *o. Pl.* art history; ~**geschichtlich 1.** *Adj.* art historical ⟨studies, evidence, expertise⟩; ⟨work⟩ on art history; **2.** *adv.* ~**geschichtlich interessiert/versiert** interested/well versed in art history; ~**gewerbe das** arts and crafts *pl.;* ~**griff der** trick; dodge;

~**halle** die art gallery; ~**händler** der [fine-]art dealer; ~**handwerk** das craftwork; ~**kritiker** der art critic; ~**leder** imitation leather

Künstler der; ~s, ~, **Künstlerin** die; ~, ~**nen** a) artist; *(Zirkus~, Varieté~)* artiste; b) *(Könner)* genius (in + *Dat.* at); **künstlerisch** 1. *Adj.* artistic; 2. *adv.* artistically; **Künstler·name** der stage-name; **künstlich** 1. *Adj.* a) artificial; b) *(gezwungen)* forced ⟨*laugh, cheerfulness, etc.*⟩; 2. *adv.* artificially

kunst-, Kunst-: ~**los** *Adj.* plain; ~**post·karte** die art postcard; ~**sammler** der art collector; ~**sammlung** die art collection; ~**stoff** der synthetic material; plastic; ~**stück** das trick; **das ist kein** ~**stück** *(ugs.)* it's no great feat; ~**turnen** das gymnastics *sing.;* ~**voll** 1. *Adj.* ornate and artistic; *(kompliziert)* elaborate; 2. *adv.* a) ornately *or* elaborately and artistically; b) *(geschickt)* skilfully; ~**werk** das work of art

kunter·bunt 1. *Adj.* multi-coloured; *(abwechslungsreich)* varied; *(ungeordnet)* jumbled ⟨*confusion, muddle, etc.*⟩; 2. *adv.* ⟨*painted, printed*⟩ in many colours; ~ **durcheinander sein** be higgledy-piggledy

Kupfer das; ~s a) copper; b) *(~geschirr)* copperware; *(~geld)* coppers *pl.*

Kupfer-: ~**geld** das coppers *pl.;* ~**stich** der a) *o. Pl.* copperplate engraving *no art.;* b) *(Blatt)* copperplate print *or* engraving

Kuppe die; ~, ~**n** a) [rounded] hilltop; b) *(Finger~)* tip; end

Kuppel die; ~, ~**n** dome; *(kleiner)* cupola

Kuppelei die; ~: procuring; **kuppeln** *itr. V.* operate the clutch; **Kuppelung** *s.* **Kupplung; Kuppler** der; ~s, ~: procurer; **Kupplerin** die; ~, ~**nen** procuress; **Kupplung** die; ~, ~**en** a) *(Kfz-W.)* clutch; b) *(Technik: Vorrichtung zum Verbinden)* coupling

Kur die; ~, ~**en** [health] cure; *(ohne Aufenthalt im Badeort)* course of treatment

Kür die; ~, ~**en** *(Eiskunstlauf)* free programme; *(Turnen)* optional exercises *pl.*

Kurbel die; ~, ~**n** crank [handle]; *(an Spieldosen, Grammophonen)* winder; *(an einem Brunnen)* [winding-]handle; **kurbeln** *tr. V.* etw. nach oben/unten

~: wind sth. up/down; **Kurbel·welle** die *(Technik)* crankshaft

Kürbis der; ~ses, ~se pumpkin

Kurde der; ~n, ~n Kurd

Kur-: ~**fürst** der *(hist.)* Elector; ~**gast** der visitor to a/the spa; *(Patient)* patient at a/the spa

Kurier der; ~s, ~e courier

kurieren *tr. V. (auch fig.)* cure (**von** of)

kurios 1. *Adj.* curious; 2. *adv.* curiously; strangely; oddly; **Kuriosität** die; ~, ~**en** a) *o. Pl.* strangeness; b) *(Gegenstand)* curiosity; curio

Kur-: ~**konzert** das concert [at a spa]; ~**ort** der spa; ~**pfuscher** der *(ugs. abwertend)* quack

Kurs der; ~es, ~e a) *(Richtung)* course; **ein harter/weicher** ~ *(fig.)* a hard/soft line; b) *(von Wertpapieren)* price; *(von Devisen)* exchange rate; **der** ~ **des Dollars** the dollar rate; c) *(Lehrgang)* course; *(Teilnehmer)* class

Kürschner der; ~s, ~: furrier

kursieren *itr. V.; auch mit sein* circulate; **Kurs·teilnehmer** der course participant; **Kursus** der; ~, Kurse *s.* Kurs; **Kurs·wagen** der *(Eisenb.)* through carriage

Kur·taxe die visitors' tax *(at a spa)*

Kurve die; ~, ~**n** a) *(einer Straße)* bend; b) *(Geom.)* curve; c) *(in der Statistik, Temperatur~ usw.)* graph; **kurven** *itr. V.; mit sein* a) ⟨*aircraft*⟩ circle; ⟨*tanks etc.*⟩ circle [round]; b) *(ugs.: fahren)* drive around; **kurven·reich** *Adj.* winding; twisting

kurz; kürzer, kürzest... 1. *Adj.* short; *(zeitlich; knapp)* short, brief; quick ⟨*look*⟩; 2. *adv.* a) *(zeitlich)* briefly; *(knapp)* ~ **gesagt** in a word; b) *(wenig)* just; ~ **vor/hinter der Kreuzung** just before/past the crossroads; ~ **vor/nach Pfingsten** just before/after Whitsun; **Kurz·arbeit** die short-time working; **kurz·ärm[e]lig** *Adj.* short-sleeved; **Kürze** die; ~ a) shortness; b) *(geringe Dauer)* shortness; brevity; **in** ~: shortly; c) *(Knappheit)* brevity; **Kürzel** das; ~s, ~: shorthand symbol; **kürzen** *tr. V.* shorten; abridge ⟨*article, book*⟩; cut ⟨*pension, budget*⟩; **kürzer** *s.* kurz; **kurzer·hand** *Adv.* without more ado; **kürzest...** *s.* kurz

kurz-, Kurz-: ~**fristig** 1. *Adj.* a) ⟨*refusal, resignation, etc.*⟩ at short notice; b) *(für kurze Zeit)* short-term; 2. *adv.* a) at short notice; b) *(für kurze Zeit)* for a short time; *(auf kurze Sicht)* in

the short term; *(in kurzer Zeit)* without delay; **~geschichte die** short story; **~lebig** *Adj. (auch fig.)* short-lived
kürzlich *Adv.* recently; not long ago
kurz-, Kurz-: ~**parker der** short-stay *(Brit.) or* short-term parker; ~**schluß der** *(Elektrot.)* short-circuit; ~**sichtig** *(auch fig.)* **1.** *Adj.* short-sighted; **2.** *adv.* short-sightedly
Kürzung die; ~, ~**en** cut
kurz-, Kurz-: ~**waren** *Pl.* haberdashery *sing. (Brit.);* notions *(Amer.);* ~**welle die** *(Physik, Rundf.)* short wave; ~**zeitig 1.** *Adj.* brief; **2.** *adv.* briefly
kuscheln *refl. V.* **sich an jmdn.** ~: snuggle up to sb.
kuschen *itr. V.* knuckle under (**vor** + *Dat.* to)
Kusine die; ~, ~**n** *s.* Cousine
Kuß der; Kusses, Küsse kiss; **kußecht** *Adj.* kissproof; **küssen** *tr., itr. V.* kiss; **Kuß · hand die:** jmdm. **eine** ~ **zuwerfen** blow sb. a kiss; **mit** ~ *(ugs.)* gladly
Küste die; ~, ~**n** coast; **Küsten · wache die** coastguard [service]
Küster der; ~**s,** ~: sexton
Kutsche die; ~, ~**n** coach; **Kutscher der;** ~**s,** ~: coach-driver; **kutschieren** *itr. V.; mit sein* drive, ride [in a coach]; **2.** *tr. V.* **jmdn.** ~: drive sb. [in a coach]
Kutte die; ~, ~**n** [monk's/nun's] habit
Kutter der; ~**s,** ~: cutter
Kuvert [ku've:ɐ̯] **das;** ~**s,** ~**s** envelope; *(geh.: Gedeck)* cover
Kuwait [ku'vait] **(das);** ~**s** Kuwait
Kybernetik die; ~: cybernetics *sing.*

L

l, L [ɛl] **das;** ~, ~: l/L
l *Abk.* Liter l.
laben *(geh.)* **1.** *tr. V.* **jmdn.** ~: give sb. refreshment; **2.** *refl. V.* refresh oneself (**an** + *Dat.,* **mit** with)
labil *Adj.* **a)** *(Med.)* delicate ‹constitution, health›; poor ‹circulation›; **b)**

(auch Psych.) unstable ‹person, character, situation, etc.›
Labor das; ~**s,** ~**s,** *auch:* ~**e** laboratory; **Laboratorium das;** ~**s, Laboratorien** laboratory
Labyrinth das; ~**[e]s,** ~**e** maze; labyrinth
¹Lache die; ~, ~**n** *(ugs.)* laugh
²Lache ['la(:)xə] **die;** ~, ~**n** puddle; *(von Blut, Öl)* pool
lächeln *itr. V.* smile (**über** + *Akk.* at); **Lächeln das;** ~**s** smile; **lachen 1.** *itr. V.* laugh (**über** + *Akk.* at); **2.** *tr. V.* **was gibt es denn zu** ~? what's so funny?; **Lachen das;** ~**s** laughter; **ein lautes** ~: a loud laugh; **lächerlich 1.** *Adj.* ridiculous; ludicrous ‹argument, statement›; **2.** *adv.* ridiculously; **Lächerlichkeit die;** ~: ridiculousness; *(von Argumenten, Behauptungen usw.)* ludicrousness; **lachhaft** *Adj.* ridiculous
Lachs der; ~**es,** ~**e** salmon
Lack der; ~**[e]s,** ~**e a)** varnish; *(für Metall, Lackarbeiten)* lacquer; **lackieren** *tr. V.* varnish; spray ‹car›; **Lack · leder das** patent leather
Lade die; ~, ~**n** *(landsch.)* drawer; **Lade · hemmung die** jam; **¹laden 1.** *unr. tr. V.* load; *(Physik)* charge; **2.** *unr. itr. V.* load [up]
²laden *unr. tr. V.* **a)** *(Rechtsspr.)* summon; **b)** *(geh.: ein~)* invite
Laden der; ~**s, Läden a)** shop; store *(Amer.);* **der** ~ **läuft** *(ugs.)* business is good; **b)** *(Fenster~)* shutter
Laden-: ~**diebstahl der** shop-lifting; ~**schluß der** shop *or (Amer.)* store closing-time; ~**tisch der** [shop-] counter
Lade-: ~**rampe die** loading ramp; ~**raum der** *(beim Auto)* luggage-space; *(beim Flugzeug, Schiff)* hold; *(bei LKWs)* payload space
lädieren *tr. V.* damage
lädst 2. *Pers. Sg. Präsens v.* **laden;** **lädt 3.** *Pers. Sg. Präsens v.* **laden**
Ladung die; ~, ~**en a)** *(Schiffs~, Flugzeug~)* cargo; *(LKW~)* load; **b)** *(beim Sprengen, Schießen; Physik)* charge; **c)** *(Rechtsspr.: Vor~)* summons *sing.*
lag 1. u. 3. *Pers. Sg. Prät. v.* **liegen; Lage die;** ~, ~**n a)** situation; **eine gute** ~ **haben** be well situated; **b)** *(Art des Liegens)* position; **c)** *(Situation)* situation; **Lage · plan der** map of the area; **Lager das;** ~**s,** ~ **a)** camp; **b)** store-room; *(in Geschäften, Betrieben)* stock-room; **c)** *(Warenbestand)* stock

Lager-: ~**feuer das** camp-fire; ~**halle die** warehouse
lagern 1. *tr. V.* **a)** store; **b)** *(hinlegen)* lay down; **2.** *itr. V.* **a)** camp; **b)** *(liegen)* lie; ⟨*foodstuffs, medicines, etc.*⟩ be kept
Lager-: ~**platz der** campsite; ~**raum** store-room; *(im Geschäft, Betrieb)* stock-room
Lagerung die; ~, ~**en** storage
Lagune die; ~, ~**n** lagoon
lahm *Adj.* **a)** *(gelähmt)* lame; *(ugs.: unbeweglich)* stiff; **b)** *(ugs.: unzureichend)* lame ⟨*excuse, explanation, etc.*⟩; **c)** *(ugs. abwertend: matt)* dreary; **lahmen** *itr. V.* be lame; **lähmen** *tr. V.* paralyse; *(fig.)* paralyse ⟨*economy, industry*⟩; bring ⟨*traffic*⟩ to a standstill; **Lähmung die;** ~, ~**en** paralysis; *(fig.) (der Wirtschaft, Industrie)* paralysis; **zu einer** ~ **des Verkehrs führen** bring traffic to a standstill
Laib der; ~**|e|s,** ~**e** loaf; **ein |halber|** ~ **Brot** [half] a loaf of bread
Laich der; ~**|e|s,** ~**e** spawn; **laichen** *itr. V.* spawn
Laie der; ~**n,** ~**n** *(Mann)* layman; *(Frau)* laywoman
Lakai der; ~**en,** ~**en** lackey; liveried footman
Lake die; ~, ~**n** brine
Laken das; ~**s,** ~ *(bes. nordd.)* sheet
Lakritze die; ~, ~**n** liquorice
lallen *tr., itr. V.* ⟨*baby*⟩ babble; ⟨*drunk/ drowsy person*⟩ mumble
Lamelle die; ~, ~**n** *(einer Jalousie)* slat; *(eines Heizkörpers)* rib
lamentieren *itr. V. (ugs.)* moan (über + *Akk.* about)
Lametta das; ~**s** lametta
Lamm das; ~**|e|s, Lämmer** lamb
lamm-, Lamm-: ~**fell das** lambskin; ~**fleisch das** lamb; ~**fromm 1.** *Adj.* ⟨*person*⟩ as meek as a [little] lamb; **2.** *adv.* ⟨*answer*⟩ like a lamb
Lampe die; ~, ~**n** light; *(Tisch*~, *Öl*~, *Signal*~*)* lamp
Lampen-: ~**fieber das** stage fright; ~**schirm der** [lamp]shade
Lampion [lamˈpiɔŋ] **der;** ~**s,** ~**s** Chinese lantern
Land das; ~**es, Länder** *od. (veralt.)* ~**e a)** *o. Pl.* land *no indef. art.; (dörfliche Gegend)* country *no indef. art.;* **an** ~: ashore; **auf dem** ~ **wohnen** live in the country; **b)** *(Staat)* country; **c)** *(Bundesland)* Land; state; *(österr.)* province; **Land·bevölkerung die** rural population

Lande-: ~**an·flug der** *(Flugw.)* [landing] approach; ~**bahn die** *(Flugw.)* [landing] runway
landen 1. *itr. V.; mit sein* **a)** land; *(ankommen)* arrive; **b)** *(ugs.: gelangen)* land up; **2.** *tr. V.* **a)** land ⟨*aircraft, troops, passengers, fish, etc.*⟩; **b)** *(ugs.: zustande bringen)* pull off ⟨*victory, coup*⟩; have ⟨*smash hit*⟩
Ländereien *Pl.* estates
Länder-: ~**kampf der** *(Sport)* international match; ~**spiel das** *(Sport)* international [match]
Landes-: ~**innere das** interior [of the country]; ~**kunde die;** *o. Pl.* regional studies *pl., no art.;* ~**regierung die** government of a/the Land/province; ~**sprache die** language of the country; ~**tracht die** national costume *or* dress; ~**verrat der** *(Rechtsw.)* treason; ~**währung die** currency of a/the country
land-, Land-: ~**flucht die** migration from the countryside [to the towns]; ~**gewinnung die** reclamation of land; ~**haus das** country house; ~**karte die** map; ~**kreis der** district; ~**läufig** *Adj.* widely accepted
ländlich *Adj.* rural; country *attrib.* ⟨*life*⟩
Land-: ~**plage die** *(fig.)* pest; nuisance; ~**ratte die** *(ugs.)* landlubber
Landschaft die; ~, ~**en** landscape; *(ländliche Gegend)* countryside; **landschaftlich 1.** *Adj.* regional; **2.** *adv.* ~ **herrlich gelegen sein** be in a glorious natural setting
Lands·mann der; *Pl.* ~**leute** fellow-countryman; compatriot
Land-: ~**straße die** country road; *(im Gegensatz zur Autobahn)* ordinary road; ~**streicher der** tramp; ~**strich der** area; ~**tag der** Landtag; state parliament; *(österr.)* provincial parliament; **Landung die;** ~, ~**en** landing; **Landungs·brücke die** [floating] landing-stage
land-, Land-: ~**weg der** overland route; **auf dem** ~**weg** overland; ~**wirt der** farmer; ~**wirtschaft die** *o. Pl.* agriculture *no art.;* farming *no art.;* ~**wirtschaftlich 1.** *Adj.* agricultural; **2.** *adv.* ~ **genutzt werden** be used for agricultural purposes; ~**zunge die** *(Geogr.)* tongue of land
lang; länger, längst... 1. *Adj.* long; *(ugs.: groß)* tall; **2.** *adv.* [for] a long time; **eine Sekunde/mehrere Stunden** ~: for a second/several hours

lang-: **~ärm[e]lig** *Adj.* long-sleeved; **~atmig** 1. *Adj.* long-winded; 2. *adv.* long-windedly; ⟨*relate*⟩ at great length **lange; länger, am längsten** *Adv.* **a)** a long time; **bist du schon ~ hier?** have you been here long?; **b)** *(bei weitem)* **ich bin noch ~ nicht fertig** I'm nowhere near finished; **hier is es ~ nicht so schön** it isn't nearly as nice here; **Länge die; ~, ~n** length; *(Geogr.)* longitude

langen *(ugs.)* 1. *itr. V.* **a)** be enough; **b)** *(greifen)* reach **(in** + *Akk.* into; **auf** + *Akk.* on to; **nach** for); 2. *tr. V.* **jmdm. eine ~** *(ugs.)* give sb. a clout [around the ear] *(coll.)*

Längen·grad der *(Geogr.)* degree of longitude

länger 1. *s.* **lang, lange;** 2. *Adj.* **seit ~er Zeit** for quite some time

Lange·weile die; ~ *od.* **Langenweile** boredom; **~ haben** be bored

lang-, Lang-: **~fristig** 1. *Adj.* longterm; long-dated ⟨*loan*⟩; 2. *adv.* on a long-term basis; **~jährig** *Adj.* ⟨*customer, friend*⟩ of many years' standing; long-standing ⟨*friendship*⟩; **~jährige Erfahrung** many years of experience; **~lauf** der *(Skisport)* crosscountry

länglich *Adj.* oblong; **längs** 1. *Präp.* + *Gen. od. (selten) Dat.* along; 2. *Adv.* lengthways; **Längs·achse die** longitudinal axis

langsam 1. *Adj.* slow; 2. *adv.* **a)** slowly; **~, aber sicher** *(ugs.)* slowly but surely; **b)** *(allmählich)* gradually

Lang-: **~schläfer der** late riser; **~spiel·platte die** long-playing record; LP

Längs·schnitt der longitudinal section

längst *Adv.* **a)** *(schon lange)* a long time ago; **b)** *(bei weitem)* **hier ist es ~ nicht so schön** it isn't nearly as nice here; **längst... s. lang; längstens** *Adv. (ugs.) (höchstens)* at [the] most; *(spätestens)* at the latest

Languste die; ~, ~n spiny lobster

lang-, Lang-: **~weilen** 1. *tr. V.* bore; 2. *refl. V.* be bored; **~weilig** 1. *Adj.* boring; dull ⟨*place*⟩; 2. *adv.* boringly; **~welle die** *(Physik, Rundf.)* long wave; **~wierig** *Adj.* lengthy; prolonged ⟨*search*⟩

Lanze die; ~, ~n lance; *(zum Werfen)* spear

Laos ['la:ɔs] **(das); Laos'** Laos; **Laote** [la'o:tə] der; **~n, ~n** Laotian

lapidar 1. *Adj. (kurz, aber wirkungsvoll)* succinct; *(knapp)* terse; 2. *adv.* succinctly/tersely

Lappalie die; ~, ~n trifle

Lappe der; ~n, ~n Lapp

Lappen der; ~s, ~: cloth; *(Fetzen)* rag; *(Wasch~)* flannel

läppisch *Adj.* silly

Lapp·land (das) Lapland

Lärche die; ~, ~n larch

Lärm der; ~[e]s noise; *(Krach)* din; row *(coll.)*; **Lärm·belästigung die** disturbance caused by noise; **lärmen** *itr. V.* make a noise *or (coll.)* row

Larve die; ~, ~n grub; larva

las *1. u. 3. Pers. Sg. Prät. v.* lesen

lasch 1. *Adj.* limp ⟨*handshake*⟩; feeble ⟨*action, measure*⟩; lax ⟨*upbringing*⟩; 2. *adv. s. Adj.:* limply; feebly; laxly

Lasche die; ~, ~n *(Gürtel~)* loop; *(eines Briefumschlags)* flap; *(Schuh~)* tongue

Laser ['leɪzə] der; **~s, ~** *(Physik)* laser

laß *Imperativ Sg. v.* lassen; **lassen** 1. *unr. tr. V.* **a)** mit *Inf.* + *Akk. (2. Part. ~) (veranlassen)* **etw. tun/machen/bauen/waschen ~:** have *or* get sth. done/made/built/washed; **jmdn. warten ~:** keep sb. waiting; **jmdn. grüßen ~:** send one's regards to sb.; **jmdn. kommen/rufen ~:** send for sb.; **b)** mit *Inf.* + *Akk. (2. Part. ~) (erlauben)* **jmdn. etw. tun ~:** let sb. do sth.; allow sb. to do sth.; **c)** *(belassen)* **jmdn. in Frieden ~:** leave sb. in peace; **d)** *(hinein~/heraus~)* let *or* allow **(in** + *Akk.* into, **aus** out of); **e)** *(unterlassen)* stop; **f)** *(zurück~; bleiben ~)* leave; **g)** *(überlassen)* **jmdm. etw. ~:** let sb. have sth.; **h)** *(als Aufforderung)* **laß/laßt uns gehen/fahren!** let's go!; **i)** *(verlieren)* lose; *(ausgeben)* spend; 2. *unr. refl. V.* **die Tür läßt sich leicht öffnen** the door opens easily; **das läßt sich nicht beweisen** it can't be proved; 3. *unr. itr. V.* **a)** *(ugs.)* **Laß mal. Ich mache das schon** Leave it. I'll do it; **b)** *(veranlassen)* **ich lasse bitten** would you ask him/her/them to come in

lässig 1. *Adj.* casual; 2. *adv.* casually

läßt *3. Pers. Sg. Präsens v.* lassen

Last die; ~, ~en load; *(Gewicht)* weight; *(Bürde)* burden; **lasten** *itr. V.* be a burden; **auf jmdm./etw. ~:** weigh heavily [up]on sb./sth.; **¹Laster** der; **~s, ~** *(ugs.: Lkw)* truck; lorry *(Brit.)*

²Laster das; ~s, ~: vice; **lasterhaft** *Adj. (abwertend)* depraved; **lästern**

1. *itr. V. (abwertend)* über jmdn./etw.
~: make malicious remarks about sb./
sth.; **2.** *tr. V. (veralt.)* blaspheme
against
lästig *Adj.* tiresome; troublesome ⟨*illness, cough, etc.*⟩
Last-: ~**schrift die** debit; ~**wagen**
der truck; lorry *(Brit.)*
Lasur die; ~, ~**en** varnish; *(farbig)*
glaze
Latein das; ~s Latin; **Latein·ameri-
ka (das)** Latin America; **lateinisch**
Adj. Latin
latent *Adj.* latent
Laterne die; ~, ~**n a)** *(Leuchte)* lamp;
lantern *(Naut.);* **b)** *(Straßen~)* street
light; **Laternen·pfahl der** lamppost
Latrine die; ~, ~**n** latrine
latschen *itr. V.; mit sein (salopp)*
trudge; *(schlurfend)* slouch; **Latschen der;** ~**s,** ~ *(ugs.)* old worn-out
shoe/slipper
Latte die; ~, ~**n a)** lath; *(Zaun~)*
pale; **b)** *(Sport: Quer~ des Tores)*
[cross]bar; **c)** *(Leichtathletik)* bar;
Latten·zaun der paling fence
Latz der; ~**es,** Lätze bib; **Lätzchen
das;** ~**s,** ~: bib
lau *Adj.* tepid, lukewarm ⟨*water etc.*⟩;
mild ⟨*wind, air, evening, etc.*⟩
Laub das; ~[e]s leaves *pl.;* dichtes ~:
thick foliage; **Laub·baum der**
broad-leaved tree
Laube die; ~, ~**n** summer-house;
(überdeckter Sitzplatz) bower; arbour
Laub-: ~**frosch der** tree frog; ~**säge
die** fretsaw; ~**wald der** deciduous
wood/forest
Lauch der; ~[e]s *(Porree)* leek
Lauer die; ~: auf der ~ liegen *od.* sein
(ugs.) jmdm. auflauern) lie in wait;
lauern *itr. V. (auch fig.)* lurk
Lauf der; ~[e]s, Läufe **a)** *o. Pl.* running; **b)** *(Sport: Wettrennen)* heat; **c)** *o.
Pl. (Ver~)* course; **im** ~[e] der Zeit in
the course of time; **im** ~[e] der Jahre/
des Tages over the years/during the
day; **d)** *(von Schußwaffen)* barrel;
Lauf·bahn die a) *(Werdegang)*
career; **b)** *(Leichtathletik)* running-
track; **laufen 1.** *unr. itr. V.; mit sein*
a) run; *(beim Eislauf)* skate; *(beim
Ski~)* ski; *(gehen)* go; *(zu Fuß gehen)*
walk; **in** *(Akk.)*/**gegen etw.** ~: walk
into sth.; **dauernd zum Arzt** ~ *(ugs.)*
keep running to the doctor; **b)** *(im
Gang sein)* ⟨*machine*⟩ be running; ⟨*radio, television, etc.*⟩ be on; *(funktionie-*

ren) ⟨*machine*⟩ run; ⟨*radio, television,
etc.*⟩ work; **c)** *(gelten)* ⟨*contract, agreement, engagement, etc.*⟩ run; **d)** *(gespielt werden)* ⟨*programme, play, etc.*⟩
be on; **2.** *unr. tr. u. itr. V.* **a)** *mit sein
(zurücklegen) (zu Fuß)* walk; *(rennen)*
run; **b)** *mit sein (erzielen)* einen Rekord
~: set up a record; **c)** *mit haben od.
sein* Ski/Schlittschuh/Rollschuh ~:
ski/skate/roller-skate; **laufend 1.**
Adj. **a)** *(ständig)* regular ⟨*interest, income*⟩; recurring ⟨*costs*⟩; **b)** *(gegenwärtig)* current ⟨*issue, year, month,
etc.*⟩; **2.** *adv.* constantly; ⟨*increase*⟩
steadily; **Läufer der;** ~**s,** ~ **a)** *(Sport)*
runner; *(Handball; Fußball veralt.)*
half-back; **b)** *(Teppich) (long narrow)*
carpet; **Lauf·feuer das** brush fire;
wie ein ~: like wildfire
Lauf-: ~**masche die** ladder; ~**paß
der:** er hat seiner Freundin den ~**paß**
gegeben *(ugs.)* he finished with his
girl-friend *(coll.);* ~**schritt der: im**
~**schritt, marsch, marsch!** at the
double, quick march!
läufst *2. Pers. Sg. Präsens v.* laufen;
Lauf·stall der playpen; **läuft** *3.
Pers. Sg. Präsens v.* laufen
Lauge die; ~, ~**n a)** soapy water; **b)**
(Chemie) alkaline solution; **Lau-
gen·brezel die** *(südd.)* pretzel
Laune die; ~, ~**n** mood; **launenhaft**
Adj. temperamental; *(unberechenbar)*
capricious; **launig** witty; **launisch**
Adj.: s. launenhaft
Laus die; ~, Läuse louse
Laus·bub der little rascal
lauschen *itr. V.* **a)** *(horchen)* listen;
b) *(zuhören)* listen [attentively];
Lauscher der; ~**s,** ~: eavesdropper;
lauschig *Adj.* cosy, snug ⟨*corner*⟩
lausig 1. *Adj. (ugs.)* **a)** *(abwertend: unangenehm, schäbig)* lousy *(sl.);* rotten
(coll.); **b)** *(sehr groß)* perishing *(Brit.
sl.),* freezing ⟨*cold*⟩; terrible *(coll.)*
⟨*heat*⟩; **2.** *adv.* terribly *(coll.)*
¹**laut 1.** *Adj.* loud; *(geräuschvoll)*
noisy; **2.** *adv.* loudly; *(geräuschvoll)*
noisily
²**laut** *Präp. + Gen. od. Dat. (Amtsspr.)*
according to
Laut der; ~[e]s, ~**e** sound
Laute die; ~, ~**n** lute
lauten *itr. V.* ⟨*answer, instruction, slogan*⟩ be, run; ⟨*letter, passage, etc.*⟩
read, go; ⟨*law*⟩ state; **läuten 1.** *tr., itr.
V.* ring; ⟨*alarm clock*⟩ go off; **2.** *itr. V.
(bes. südd.: klingeln)* ring; **es läutete**
the bell rang *or* went **(zu for)**

¹**lauter** *Adj. (geh.)* honourable ⟨*person, intentions, etc.*⟩; honest ⟨*truth*⟩
²**lauter** *indekl. Adj.* nothing but; sheer ⟨*nonsense, joy, etc.*⟩
läutern *tr. V. (geh.)* reform ⟨*character*⟩; purify ⟨*soul*⟩; **Läuterung** die; ~, ~en *(geh.)* reformation; *(der Seele)* purification
laut·hals *Adv.* at the top of one's voice; ~ **lachen** roar with laughter
lautlich 1. *Adj.* phonetic; 2. *adv.* phonetically
laut-, Laut-: ~**los** 1. *Adj.* silent; soundless; *(wortlos)* silent; 2. *adv.* silently; soundlessly; ~**schrift** die *(Phon.)* phonetic alphabet; *(Umschrift)* phonetic transcription; ~**sprecher** der loudspeaker; *(einer Stereoanlage usw.)* speaker; ~**stark** 1. *Adj.* loud; vociferous, loud ⟨*protest*⟩; 2. *adv.* loudly; ⟨*protest*⟩ vociferously; ~**stärke** die volume
lau·warm *Adj.* lukewarm
Lava die; ~, **Laven** *(Geol.)* lava
Lavendel der; ~s, ~: lavender
Lawine die; ~, ~n *(auch fig.)* avalanche; **eine** ~ **von Protesten** *(fig.)* a storm of protest; **Lawinen·gefahr** die danger of avalanches
lax 1. *Adj.* lax; 2. *adv.* laxly
Lazarett das; ~[e]s, ~e military hospital
leben *itr. V.* live; *(lebendig sein)* be alive; **leb[e] wohl!** farewell!; **von seiner Rente/seinem Gehalt** ~: live on one's pension/salary; **Leben** das; ~s, ~ **a)** life; **das** ~: life; **sich** *(Dat.)* **das** ~ **nehmen** take one's [own] life; **am** ~ **sein/bleiben** be/stay alive; **ums** ~ **kommen** lose one's life; **b)** *(Betriebsamkeit)* **auf dem Markt herrschte ein reges** ~: the market was bustling with activity; **das** ~ **auf der Straße** the comings and goings in the street; **lebend** *Adj.* living; live ⟨*animal*⟩; **lebendig** 1. *Adj.* living; *(lebhaft)* lively; 2. *adv. (lebhaft)* in a lively way
lebens-, Lebens-: ~**abend** der *(geh.)* evening of one's life *(literary)*; ~**art** die **a)** way of life; **b)** *o. Pl. (Umgangsformen)* manners *pl.*; ~**aufgabe** die life's work; ~**bejahend** *Adj.* ⟨*person*⟩ with a positive attitude to life; ~**bereich** der area of life; ~**dauer** die life-span; ~**ende** das end [of one's life]; ~**erinnerungen** *Pl.* memories of one's life; *(aufgezeichnet)* memoirs; ~**erwartung** die life expectancy; ~**fähig** *Adj. (auch fig.)*

viable; ~**freude** die; *o. Pl.* zest for life; ~**froh** *Adj.* full of zest for life *postpos.*; ~**gefahr** die mortal danger; „**Achtung,** ~**gefahr!**" 'danger'; ~**gefährlich** 1. *Adj.* highly dangerous; critical ⟨*injury*⟩; 2. *adv.* critically ⟨*injured, ill*⟩; ~**geister** *Pl.* **jmds.** ~**geister [wieder] wecken** put new life into sb.; ~**groß** *Adj.* life-size; ~**größe** die: **eine Statue in** ~**größe** a life-size statue
Lebenshaltungs·kosten *Pl.* cost of living *sing.*
lebens-, Lebens-: ~**jahr** das year of [one's] life; ~**kraft** die vitality; ~**künstler** der: **ein [echter/wahrer]** ~**künstler** a person who always knows how to make the best of things; ~**lage** die situation [in life]; ~**länglich** 1. *Adj.* ~**länglicher Freiheitsentzug** life imprisonment; 2. *adv.* **jmdn.** ~**länglich gefangenhalten** keep sb. imprisoned for life; ~**lauf** der curriculum vitae; c.v.; ~**lustig** *Adj.* ⟨*person*⟩ full the joys of life
Lebens·mittel das; *meist Pl.* food[stuff]; ~ *Pl.* food *sing.*; **Lebensmittel·geschäft** das food shop
lebens-: ~**müde** *Adj.* weary of life *pred.*; ~**notwendig** *Adj.* essential; ~**raum** der **a)** *(Umkreis)* lebensraum; **b)** *(Biol.)* s. **Biotop**; ~**retter** der rescuer; ~**standard** der standard of living; ~**unterhalt** der: **seinen** ~**unterhalt verdienen/bestreiten** earn one's living/support oneself; ~**versicherung** die life insurance; ~**wandel** der way of life; ~**weg** der [journey through] life; ~**weise** die way of life; ~**zeichen** das sign of life; ~**zeit** die life[-span]; **auf** ~**zeit** for life
Leber die; ~, ~n liver
Leber-: ~**fleck** der liver spot; ~**käse** der; *o. Pl.* meat loaf made with mincemeat, [minced liver,] eggs, and spices; ~**tran** der fish-liver oil; *(des Kabeljaus)* cod-liver oil; ~**wurst** die liver sausage
Lebe-: ~**wesen** das living being; ~**wohl** [--'-] das; ~[e]s, ~ *od.* ~e *(geh.)* farewell
lebhaft 1. *Adj.* **a)** lively; busy ⟨*traffic*⟩; brisk ⟨*business*⟩; **b)** *(deutlich)* vivid ⟨*idea, picture, etc.*⟩; **c)** *(kräftig)* bright ⟨*colour*⟩; vigorous ⟨*applause, opposition*⟩. 2. *adv.* **a)** in a lively way; **b)** *(deutlich)* vividly; **c)** *(kräftig)* brightly ⟨*coloured*⟩

leb-, Leb-: ~**kuchen** der ≈ gingerbread; ~**los** *Adj.* lifeless; ~**zeiten**
Pl. **bei** *od.* **zu** jmds. ~**zeiten** during
sb.'s lifetime
lechzen *itr. V. (geh.)* **nach einem**
Trunk ~: long for a drink; **nach Rache**
usw. ~: thirst for revenge *etc.*
leck *Adj.* leaky; ~ **sein** leak; **Leck**
das; ~|e|s, ~s leak
¹**lecken 1.** *tr. V.* lick; **2.** *itr. V.* **an etw.**
(Dat.) ~: lick sth.
²**lecken** *itr. V. (leck sein)* leak
lecker *Adj.* tasty ⟨*meal*⟩; delicious
⟨*cake etc.*⟩; good ⟨*smell, taste*⟩; **Lek-**
ker·bissen der delicacy; **Leckerei**
die; ~, ~**en** *(ugs.)* dainty; *(Süßigkeit)*
sweet [meat]
led. *Abk.* ledig
Leder das; ~**s,** ~: leather; **Leder-**
waren *Pl.* leather goods
ledig *Adj.* single; **eine** ~**e Mutter** an
unmarried mother; **Ledige** der/die;
adj. Dekl. single person; **lediglich**
Adj. merely
leer *Adj.* empty; clean ⟨*sheet of paper*⟩;
Leere die; ~ *(auch fig.)* emptiness;
leeren *tr., refl. V.* empty
leer-, Leer-: ~**gefegt** *Adj.* deserted
⟨*street, town*⟩; **wie** ~**gefegt** deserted;
~**lauf** der; *o. Pl.* **im** ~**lauf den Berg**
hinunterfahren ⟨*driver*⟩ coast down the
hill in neutral; ⟨*cyclist*⟩ freewheel
down the hill; ~**stehend** *Adj.* empty,
unoccupied; ~**taste** die space-bar
Leerung die; ~, ~**en** emptying; *(von*
Briefkästen) collection
Lefze die; ~, ~**n** lip
legal 1. *Adj.* legal; **2.** *adv.* legally; **le-**
galisieren *tr. V.* legalize; **Legalität**
die; ~: legality
legen 1. *tr. V.* **a)** lay [down]; **b)** *(verle-*
gen) lay ⟨*pipe, cable, carpet, tiles,*
etc.⟩; **2.** *tr., itr. V.* ⟨*hen*⟩ lay; **3.** *refl. V.*
a) lie down; **b)** *(nachlassen)* die down;
abate; ⟨*enthusiasm*⟩ wear off, subside
legendär *Adj.* legendary
Legende die; ~, ~**n** legend
leger [le'ʒeːɐ̯] **1.** *Adj.* casual; **2.** *adv.*
casually
legieren *tr. V.* alloy; **Legierung** die;
~, ~**en** alloy
Legislative die; ~, ~**n** *(Politik)* legislature; **Legislatur·periode** die
legislative period; **legitim** *Adj.* legitimate; **Legitimation** [legitima-
'tsioːn] die; ~, ~**en a)** legitimation; **b)**
(Ausweis) proof of identity; **legiti-**
mieren 1. *tr. V.* **a)** *(rechtfertigen)* justify; **b)** *(bevollmächtigen)* authorize; **c)**

(für legitim erklären) legitimize ⟨*child,*
relationship⟩; **2.** *refl. V.* show proof of
one's identity
Lehm der; ~**s** loam; *(Ton)* clay
Lehne die; ~, ~**n** *(Rücken~)* back;
(Arm~) arm; **lehnen 1.** *tr., refl. V.*
lean ⟨**an** + *Akk.,* **gegen** against⟩; **2.** *itr.*
V. be leaning ⟨**an** + *Dat.* against⟩;
Lehn·stuhl der armchair
Lehr·buch das textbook
Lehre die; ~, ~**n a)** apprenticeship; **b)**
(Weltanschauung) doctrine; **c)** *(Theo-*
rie, Wissenschaft) theory; **d)** *(Erfah-*
rung) lesson; **lehren** *tr., itr. V.* teach;
Lehrer der; ~**s,** ~ *(auch fig.)* teacher;
(Ausbilder) instructor; **Lehrerin** die;
~, ~**nen** teacher
Lehr-: ~**gang** der course (**für, in** +
Dat. in); ~**jahr** das year as an apprentice; ~**körper** der *(Amtsspr.)*
teaching staff; faculty *(Amer.)*
Lehrling der; ~**s,** ~**e** apprentice; *(in*
kaufmännischen Berufen) trainee
lehr-, Lehr-: ~**reich** *Adj.* informative; ~**stelle** die apprenticeship; *(in*
kaufmännischen Berufen) trainee
post; ~**stoff** der *(Schulw.)* syllabus
Leib der; ~|e|s, ~**er** *(geh.)* body;
Leib·gericht das favourite dish;
leibhaftig *Adj.* in person *postpos.;*
(echt) real; **leiblich** *Adj.* physical
⟨*well-being*⟩; *(blutsverwandt)* real
Leib-: ~**schmerzen** *Pl.* abdominal
pain *sing.;* ~**wächter** der bodyguard
Leiche die; ~, ~**n** [dead] body;
corpse; **leichen·blaß** *Adj.* deathly
pale; **Leichnam** der; ~**s,** ~**e** *(geh.)*
body
leicht 1. *Adj.* light; lightweight ⟨*suit,*
material⟩; easy ⟨*task, question, job,*
etc.⟩; slight ⟨*accent, illness, wound,*
doubt, etc.⟩; mild ⟨*cigar, cigarette*⟩; **2.**
adv. lightly ⟨*built*⟩; *(einfach, schnell,*
spielend) easily; *(geringfügig)* slightly
leicht-, Leicht-: ~**athletik** die
[track and field] athletics *sing.;* ~**fal-**
len *unr. itr. V.;* *mit sein* be easy; **das**
fällt mir ~: its easy for me; ~**fertig 1.**
Adj. careless ⟨*behaviour, person*⟩; rash
⟨*promise*⟩; ill-considered, slapdash
⟨*plan*⟩; **2.** *adv.* carelessly; ~**gläubig**
Adj. gullible
Leichtigkeit die; ~ *(geringes Ge-*
wicht) lightness; *(Mühelosigkeit)* ease
leicht-, Leicht-: ~|**machen** *tr. V.*
jmdm./sich etw. ~**machen** make sth.
easy for sb./oneself; ~|**nehmen** *unr.*
tr. V. etw. ~**nehmen** make light of sth.;
~**sinn** der; *o. Pl.* carelessness *no in-*

def. art.; (mit Gefahr verbunden) recklessness *no indef. art.;* **~sinnig 1.** *Adj.* careless; *(sich, andere gefährdend)* reckless; *(fahrlässig)* negligent; **2.** *adv.* carelessly; *(gefährlich)* recklessly; *(promise)* rashly; **~verletzt** *Adj.; präd. getrennt geschrieben* slightly injured

leid *Adj.; nicht attr.* **a)** es tut mir ~ [, daß ...] I'm sorry [that ...]; er tut mir ~: I feel sorry for him; **b)** *(überdrüssig)* etw./jmdn. ~ sein/werden *(ugs.)* be/get fed up with sth./sb. *(coll.);* **Leid** das; **~[e]s a)** *(Schmerz)* suffering; *(Kummer)* grief; sorrow; **b)** *(Unrecht)* wrong; *(Böses)* harm; **leiden 1.** *unr. itr. V.* suffer **(an, unter** + *Dat.* from); **2.** *unr. tr. V.* **a)** jmdn. [gut] ~ können *od.* mögen like sb.; **b)** *(geh.: ertragen müssen)* suffer *(hunger, thirst, etc.);* **Leiden** das; **~s, ~ a)** *(Krankheit)* illness; *(Gebrechen)* complaint; **b)** *(Qual)* suffering; **leidend** *Adj.* **a)** *(krank)* ailing; **b)** *(schmerzvoll)* strained *(voice);* martyred *(expression)*

Leidenschaft die; ~, ~en passion **(zu, für** for); **leidenschaftlich 1.** *Adj.* passionate; vehement *(protest);* **2.** *adv.* passionately; *(eifrig)* dedicatedly; etw. ~ gern tun adore doing sth.

leider *Adv.* unfortunately; **leidig** *Adj.* tiresome; **leidlich** *Adj.* reasonable

Leier die; ~, ~n lyre

leihen *unr. tr. V.* **a)** jmdm. etw. ~: lend sb. sth.; **b)** *(entleihen)* borrow

Leih-: ~gebühr die hire *or (Amer.)* rental charge; *(bei Büchern)* borrowing fee; **~haus** das pawnbroker's; pawnshop; **~mutter** die surrogate mother; **~wagen** der hire *or (Amer.)* rental car

Leim der; ~[e]s glue; **leimen** *tr. V.* glue **(an** + *Akk.* to)

Leine die; ~, ~n rope; *(Wäsche~, Angel~)* line; *(Hunde~)* lead *(esp. Brit.);* leash; **Leinen** das; **~s a)** *(Gewebe)* linen; **b)** *(Buchw.)* cloth; **Lein·wand** die **a)** *o. Pl.* linen; *(grob)* canvas; **b)** *(des Malers)* canvas; **c)** *(für Filme und Dias)* screen

leise 1. *Adj.* **a)** quiet; soft *(steps, music, etc.);* **b)** *(leicht)* faint; slight; slight, gentle *(touch);* **2.** *adv.* **a)** quietly; **b)** *(leicht; kaum merklich)* slightly; *(touch, rain)* gently

Leiste die; ~, ~n strip; *(Holz~)* batten; *(profiliert)* moulding

leisten 1. *tr. V.* do *(work); (schaffen)* achieve *(a lot, nothing);* jmdm. Hilfe ~: help sb.; **2.** *refl. V. (ugs.)* sich *(Dat.)* etw. ~: treat oneself to sth.; sich *(Dat.)* etw. [nicht] ~ können [not] be able to afford sth.; **Leistung** die; ~, ~en **a)** *o. Pl. (Qualität bzw. Quantität der Arbeit)* performance; **b)** *(Errungenschaft)* achievement; *(im Sport)* performance; **c)** *o. Pl. (Leistungsvermögen, Physik: Arbeits~)* power; **d)** *(Zahlung, Zuwendung)* payment; *(Versicherungsw.)* benefit; **e)** *(Dienst~)* service

leistungs-, Leistungs-: ~fähig *Adj.* capable *(person); (körperlich)* able-bodied; **~gesellschaft** die competitive society; **~prinzip** das; *o. Pl.* competitive principle; **~sport** der competitive sport *no art.*

Leit·artikel der *(Zeitungsw.)* leading article; **leiten** *tr. V.* **a)** *(anführen)* lead; head; be head of *(school); (verantwortlich sein für)* be in charge of *(project, expedition, etc.);* manage *(factory, enterprise); (den Vorsitz führen bei)* chair; conduct *(orchestra, choir);* **~der Angestellter** manager; **b)** *(begleiten, führen)* lead; **c)** *(lenken)* direct; route *(traffic); (um~)* divert; **¹Leiter** der; ~s, ~: leader; *(einer Abteilung)* head; *(eines Instituts)* director; *(einer Schule)* head teacher; headmaster *(Brit.);* principal *(esp. Amer.); (Vorsitzender)* chair[man]

²Leiter die; ~, ~n ladder

Leiterin die; ~, ~nen *s.* **¹Leiter;** *(einer Schule)* head teacher; headmistress *(Brit.);* principal *(esp. Amer.)*

Leit·planke die crash barrier; guardrail *(Amer.)*

Leitung die; ~, ~en **a)** *o. Pl. s.* leiten a: leading; heading; being in charge of; management; chairing; **b)** *o. Pl. (einer Expedition usw.)* leadership; *(Verantwortung)* responsibility (*Gen.* for); *(eines Betriebes, Unternehmens)* management; *(einer Sitzung, Diskussion)* chairmanship; **c)** *(leitende Personen)* management; *(einer Schule)* head and senior staff; **d)** *(Rohr~)* pipe; *(Haupt~)* main; **e)** *(Draht, Kabel)* cable; *(für ein Gerät)* lead; **f)** *(Telefon~)* line

Leitungs·wasser das tap-water

Lektion [lɛk'tsi̯o:n] die; ~, ~en lesson; **Lektüre** die; ~, **~n a)** *o. Pl.* reading; **b)** *(Lesestoff)* reading [matter]

Lende die; ~, ~n loin

lenken tr. V. a) auch itr. steer; be at the controls of ⟨aircraft⟩; guide ⟨missile⟩; (fahren) drive ⟨car etc.⟩; b) direct ⟨thoughts etc.⟩ (auf + Akk. to); turn ⟨attention⟩ (auf + Akk. to); c) (kontrollieren) control ⟨person, press, economy⟩; govern ⟨state⟩; **Lenker** der; ~s, ~ a) handlebars pl.; b) (Fahrer) driver
Lenk-: ~rad das steering-wheel; ~stange die handlebars pl.
Lenz der; ~es, ~e (dichter. veralt.) spring
Leopard der; ~en, ~en leopard
Lepra die; ~: leprosy no art.
Lerche die; ~, ~n lark
lernen 1. itr. V. study; (als Lehrling) train; 2. tr. V. learn (aus from)
lesbar Adj. legible; (klar) lucid ⟨style⟩; (verständlich) comprehensible
Lesbe die; ~, ~n (ugs.) Lesbian; **Lesbierin** ['lɛsbiərɪn] die; ~, ~nen Lesbian; **lesbisch** Adj. Lesbian
Lese·buch das reader; ¹**lesen** unr. tr., itr. V. read; ²**lesen** unr. tr. V. a) pick ⟨grapes, berries, fruit⟩; gather ⟨firewood⟩; Ähren ~: glean [ears of corn]; b) (aussondern) pick over; **Leser** der; ~s, ~, **Leserin** die; ~, ~nen reader; **leserlich** 1. Adj. legible; 2. adv. legibly; **Lese·zeichen** das bookmark; **Lesung** die; ~, ~en reading
Lette der; ~n, ~n, **Lettin** die; ~, ~nen Latvian; **lettisch** Adj. Latvian; Lettish ⟨language⟩; **Lett·land** (das); ~s Latvia
Letzt: zu guter ~: in the end; **letzt...** Adj. last; ~en Endes in the end; (äußerst...) ultimate; (neuest...) latest ⟨news⟩; **letzte·mal:** das ~: [the] last time; **letzen·mal:** beim ~: last time; zum ~: for the last time; **letzter...** Adj. latter; **letztlich** Adv. ultimately; in the end
Leuchte die; ~, ~n light; **leuchten** itr. V. a) ⟨moon, sun, star, etc.⟩ be shining; ⟨fire, face⟩ glow; b) shine a/the light; jmdm. ~: light the way for sb.; **leuchtend** Adj. a) shining ⟨eyes⟩; brilliant ⟨colours⟩; bright ⟨blue, red, etc.⟩; b) (großartig) shining ⟨example⟩; **Leuchter** der; ~s, ~: candelabrum; (für eine Kerze) candlestick
Leucht-: ~reklame die neon sign; ~turm der lighthouse; ~ziffer-blatt das luminous dial
leugnen 1. tr. V. deny; 2. itr. V. deny it

Leukämie die; ~, ~n (Med.) leuk-aemia
Leumund der; ~[e]s (geh.) reputation
Leute Pl. people; die reichen/alten ~: the rich/the old
Leutnant der; ~s, ~s second lieutenant (Milit.)
leut·selig 1. Adj. affable; 2. adv. affably
Lexikon das; ~s, Lexika od. Lexiken encyclopaedia (Gen., für of)
Libanese der; ~n, ~n, **Libanesin** die; ~, ~nen Lebanese; **Libanon** (das) od. der; ~s Lebanon
Libelle die; ~, ~n dragon-fly
liberal 1. Adj. liberal; 2. adv. liberally; **Liberale** der/die; adj. Dekl. liberal; **liberalisieren** tr. V. liberalize; relax ⟨import controls⟩
Libero der; ~s, ~s (Fußball) sweeper
Libyen (das); ~s Libya; **libysch** Adj. Libyan
licht Adj. a) light; b) (dünn bewachsen) sparse; thin; **Licht** das; ~[e]s, ~er a) o. Pl. light; b) (elektrisches ~) light; c) Pl. auch ~e (Kerze) candle; **Licht-bild** das [small] photograph (for passport etc.); **licht·empfindlich** Adj. sensitive to light; ¹**lichten** 1. tr. V. thin out ⟨trees etc.⟩; 2. refl. V. ⟨trees⟩ thin out; ⟨hair⟩ grow thin; ⟨fog, mist⟩ lift
²**lichten** tr. V. (Seemannsspr.) den/die Anker ~: weigh anchor
lichterloh 1. Adj. blazing ⟨fire⟩; leaping ⟨flames⟩; 2. adv. ~ brennen be blazing fiercely
Licht-: ~hupe die headlight flasher; ~reklame die neon sign; ~schalter der light-switch
Lichtung die; ~, ~en clearing
Lid das; ~[e]s, ~er eyelid
lieb 1. Adj. a) (liebevoll) kind ⟨words, gesture⟩; b) (liebenswert) likeable; nice; (stärker) lovable ⟨child, girl, pet⟩; ~ aussehen look sweet or (Amer.) cute; c) (artig) good ⟨child, dog⟩; d) (geschätzt) dear; sein liebstes Spielzeug his favourite toy; ~er Hans/~e Else! (am Briefanfang) dear Hans/Else; e) (angenehm) welcome; es wäre mir ~/~er, wenn ...: I should be glad/should prefer it if ...; 2. adv. a) (liebenswert) kindly; b) (artig) nicely; **Liebe** die; ~, ~n a) o. Pl. love; ~ zu jmdm./zu etw. love for sb./of sth.; aus ~ [zu jmdm.] for love [of sb.]; tu mir die ~ und ...: do me a favour and ...; mit ~: lovingly; with loving care; b) (ugs.:

geliebter Mensch) love; **Liebelei** die; ~, ~en flirtation; **lieben 1.** *tr. V.* **a)** jmdn. ~: love sb.; *(sexuell)* make love to sb.; **sich** ~: be in love; *(sexuell)* make love; **b)** etw. ~: be fond of sth.; *(stärker)* love sth.; **2.** *itr. V.* be in love; **liebend** *Adv.* etw. ~ **gern tun** [simply] love doing sth.; **liebenswürdig** *Adj.* kind; charming *(smile)*; **lieber** *Adv.* **a)** *s.* **gern; b)** better; **laß das** ~: better not do that **Liebes**~: ~**brief** der love-letter; ~**paar das** courting couple; ~**roman** der romantic novel **liebe·voll 1.** *Adj.* loving *attrib.* *(care)*; affectionate *(embrace, gesture, person)*; **2.** *adv.* lovingly; affectionately; *(mit Sorgfalt)* lovingly; **lieb|haben** *unr. tr. V.* love; *(gern haben)* be fond of; **Liebhaber** der; ~s, ~ **a)** lover; **b)** *(Interessierter, Anhänger)* enthusiast *(Gen.* for); *(Sammler)* collector; **lieblich 1.** *Adj.* **a)** charming; *(angenehm)* sweet *(scent, sound)*; **2.** *adv.* sweetly; *(angenehm)* pleasingly; **Liebling** der; ~s, ~e *(bes. als Anrede)* darling; *(bevorzugte Person)* favourite; **Lieblings-** favourite; **lieb·los 1.** *Adj.* loveless. **2.** *adv.* **a)** without affection; **b)** *(ohne Sorgfalt)* without proper care; **liebsten: am** ~: *s.* **gern Liechtenstein (das);** ~s Liechtenstein **Lied** das; ~[e]s, ~er song **liederlich** *Adj.* slovenly; messy *(hairstyle, person)* **Lieder-:** ~**macher** der; ~s, ~, ~**macherin** die; ~, ~**nen** singer-songwriter **lief** *1. u. 3. Pers. Sg. Prät. v.* **laufen Lieferant** der; ~en, ~en supplier; **lieferbar** *Adj.* available; *(vorrätig)* in stock; **liefern** *tr. V.* **a)** *(bringen)* deliver **(an** + *Akk.* to); *(zur Verfügung stellen)* supply. **b)** *(hervorbringen)* produce; provide *(eggs, honey, examples, raw material, etc.)* **Liefer-:** ~**schein** der delivery note; ~**termin** der delivery date **Lieferung** die; ~, ~en delivery **Liefer-:** ~**wagen** der [delivery] van; ~**zeit** die delivery time **Liege** die; ~, ~n day-bed; *(zum Ausklappen)* bed-settee; *(als Gartenmöbel)* sun-lounger; **liegen** *unr. itr. V.* lie; *(person)* be lying down; *(sich befinden)* be; *(object)* be [lying]; *(town, house, etc.)* be [situated]; **im Bett** ~:

lie in bed; **das liegt an ihm** *od.* **bei ihm** it is up to him; *(ist seine Schuld)* it is his fault; **es liegt mir nicht** it doesn't suit me; *(es spricht mich nicht an)* it doesn't appeal to me; *(ich mag es nicht)* I don't like it; **daran liegt ihm viel/wenig/nichts** he sets great/little/no store by that **liegen-:** ~|**bleiben** *unr. itr. V.; mit sein* **a)** stay [lying]; **[im Bett]** ~: stay in bed; **b)** *(things)* stay, be left; *(vergessen werden)* be left behind; *(nicht erledigt werden)* be left undone; ~|**lassen** *unr. tr. V.* **a)** leave; *(vergessen)* leave [behind]; **b)** *(unerledigt lassen)* leave *(work)* undone; leave *(letters)* unposted/unopened **Liege-:** ~**stuhl** der deck-chair; ~**wagen** der couchette car **lieh** *1. u. 3. Pers. Sg. Prät. v.* **leihen lies** *Imperativ Sg. v.* **lesen ließ** *1. u. 3. Pers. Sg. Prät. v.* **lassen liest** *3. Pers. Sg. Präsens v.* **lesen Lift** der; ~[e]s, ~e *od.* ~s **a)** lift *(Brit.);* elevator *(Amer.);* **b)** *Pl.:* ~e *(Ski~, Sessel~)* lift **Liga** die; ~, **Ligen** league; *(Sport)* division **Likör** der; ~s, ~e liqueur **lila** *indekl. Adj.* mauve; *(dunkel~)* purple; **Lila** das; ~s *od. (ugs.)* ~s mauve; *(Dunkel~)* purple **Lilie** ['li:liə] die; ~, ~n lily **Liliputaner** der; ~s, ~: dwarf **Limit** das; ~s, ~s limit **Limo** die, *auch:* das; ~, ~[s] *(ugs.)* fizzy drink; **Limonade** die; ~, ~n fizzy drink; *(Zitronen~)* lemonade **Linde** die; ~, ~n lime[-tree] **lindern** *tr. V.* relieve *(suffering, pain);* slake *(thirst)* **Lineal** das; ~s, ~e ruler **Linie** ['li:niə] die; ~, ~n line; *(Verkehrsstrecke)* route; **die** ~ **12** *(Verkehrsw.)* the number 12; **auf die [schlanke]** ~ **achten** *(ugs. scherzh.)* watch one's figure; **auf der ganzen** ~ *(fig.)* all along the line **linien-, Linien-:** ~**bus** der regular bus; ~**flug** der scheduled flight; ~**richter** der *(Fußball usw.)* linesman; *(Tennis)* line judge; *(Rugby)* touch judge; ~**treu 1.** *Adj.* loyal to the party line *postpos.;* **2.** *adv.* *(act)* in accordance with the party line **linieren, liniieren** *tr. V.* rule **link...** *Adj.* **a)** left; **b)** *(innen, nicht sichtbar)* wrong, reverse *(side);* **c)** *(in der Politik)* left-wing; **linkisch 1.**

Adj. awkward; **2.** *adv.* awkwardly; **links** *Adv.* on the left; *(Politik)* on the left wing

links-, Links-: **~abbieger** der *(Verkehrsw.)* motorist/cyclist/car *etc.* turning left; **~außen der;** ~, ~ *(Ballspiele)* left wing; outside left; **~händer der;** ~s, ~: left-hander; **~kurve die** left-hand bend; **~verkehr der** driving *no art.* on the left

Linoleum das; ~s linoleum; lino

Linse die; ~, ~n a) *(Bot., Kochk.)* lentil; b) *(Med., Optik)* lens

Lippe die; ~, ~n lip; **Lippen·stift der** lipstick

liquid *Adj. (Wirtsch.)* liquid ⟨*funds, resources*⟩; solvent ⟨*business*⟩; **liquidieren** *(verhüll.: töten; Wirtsch.)* liquidate

lispeln *itr. V.* lisp

Lissabon (das); ~s Lisbon

List die; ~, ~en a) [cunning] trick; b) *(listige Art) o. Pl.* cunning

Liste die; ~, ~n list; **schwarze ~:** blacklist

listig 1. *Adj.* cunning; crafty; **2.** *adv.* cunningly; craftily

Litauen (das); ~s Lithuania; **Litauer der;** ~s, ~: Lithuanian; **litauisch** *Adj.* Lithuanian

Liter der, *auch:* **das;** ~s, ~: litre

literarisch *Adj.* literary; **Literatur die;** ~, ~en literature

Litfaß·säule die advertising column

Lithographie die; ~, ~n *(Druck)* lithograph

litt *1. u. 3. Pers. Sg. Prät. v.* leiden

Litze die; ~, ~n braid

Lizenz die; ~, ~en licence

Lkw, LKW [ɛlka:'ve:] **der;** ~[s], ~[s] *Abk.* Lastkraftwagen truck; lorry *(Brit.)*

Lob das; ~[e]s, ~e praise *no indef. art.*

Lobby ['lɔbi] **die;** ~, ~s *od.* **Lobbies** lobby

loben *tr.V.* praise; **löblich** *Adj.* commendable; **Lob·lied das** song of praise

Loch das; ~[e]s, **Löcher** hole; **lochen** *tr. V.* punch holes/a hole in; punch ⟨*ticket*⟩; **Locher der;** ~s, ~: punch; **löcherig** *Adj.* full of holes *pred.*

Locke die; ~, ~n curl

locken *tr. V.* a) lure; b) *(reizen)* tempt

Locken·wickler der [hair] curler

locker 1. *Adj.* loose; *(entspannt)* relaxed ⟨*position, muscles*⟩; slack ⟨*rope, rein*⟩; **2.** *adv.* ~ sitzen ⟨*tooth, screw, nail*⟩ be loose; *(entspannt, ungezwun-*

gen) loosely; **locker|lassen** *unr. itr. V.* *(ugs.)* **nicht ~:** not give up; **lockern 1.** *tr. V.* loosen; slacken [off] ⟨*rope etc.*⟩; relax ⟨*muscles, limbs*⟩; **2.** *refl. V.* ⟨*brick, tooth, etc.*⟩ work itself loose; ⟨*person*⟩ loosen up

lockig *Adj.* curly

Lock·vogel der decoy

Loden·mantel der loden coat

Löffel der; ~s, ~: spoon; *(als Maßangabe)* spoonful; *(Jägerspr.)* ear; **löffeln** *tr. V.* spoon [up]

log *1. u. 3. Pers. Sg. Prät. v.* lügen

Logarithmus der; ~, **Logarithmen** *(Math.)* logarithm; log

Loge ['lo:ʒə] **die;** ~, ~n box; **logieren** *itr. V. (veralt.)* stay

Logik die; ~: logic; **logisch 1.** *Adj.* logical; **2.** *adv.* logically

Lohn der; ~[e]s, **Löhne** a) wage[s *pl.*]; pay *no indef. art., no pl.;* b) *o. Pl. (Belohnung)* reward; **Lohn·büro das** payroll office

lohnen 1. *refl., itr. V.* be worth it; **2.** *tr. V.* be worth; **lohnend** *Adj.* rewarding

Lohn·steuer die income tax; **Lohnsteuer·karte die** income-tax card; **Lohn·tüte die** pay-packet *(Brit.);* wage packet

Lokal das; ~s, ~e pub *(Brit. coll.);* bar *(Amer.);* *(Speise~)* restaurant; **Lokalität die;** ~, ~en locality

Lokal-: **~blatt das** local paper; **~termin der** *(Rechtsspr.)* visit to the scene [of the crime]

Lokomotive [lokomo'ti:və] **die;** ~, ~n locomotive; **Lokomotiv·führer der** engine-driver *(Brit.);* engineer *(Amer.)*

Lokus der; ~ *od.* ~ses, ~ *od.* ~se *(salopp)* loo *(Brit. coll.);* john *(Amer. coll.)*

London (das); ~s London; **Londoner 1.** *indekl. Adj.* London; **2. der;** ~s, ~: Londoner

Lorbeer der; ~s, ~en a) laurel; b) *(Gewürz)* bay-leaf

Lore die; ~, ~n car; *(kleiner)* tub

los 1. *Adj.* a) *(gelöst, ab)* off; b) **es ist etwas ~:** there is something going on; c) jmdn./etw. ~ **sein** be rid of sb./sth.; **2.** *Adv. (als Aufforderung)* come on!

Los das; ~es, ~e a) lot; b) *(Lotterie~)* ticket

Lösch·blatt das piece of blotting-paper; **löschen** *tr. V.* a) put out; extinguish; **seinen Durst ~** *(fig.)* quench one's thirst; b) *(tilgen)* delete ⟨*entry*⟩; erase ⟨*recording, memory, etc.*⟩; **Lösch·papier das** blotting paper

lose 1. *Adj.* loose; **2.** *adv.* loosely
Löse·geld das ransom
losen *itr. V.* draw lots (**um** for)
lösen 1. *tr. V.* **a)** remove ‹*stamp, wallpaper*›; *etw.* **von** *etw.* ~: remove sth. from sth.; **b)** *(lockern)* undo ‹*screw, belt, tie*›; **c)** *(klären)* solve; resolve ‹*contradiction, conflict*›; **d)** *(annullieren)* break off ‹*engagement*›; cancel ‹*contract*›; sever ‹*relationship*›; **e)** *(kaufen)* buy, obtain ‹*ticket*›; **2.** *refl. V.* **a)** *(lose werden)* come off; *(sich lockern)* ‹*wallpaper, plaster*› come off; ‹*packing, screw*› come loose; **b)** *(sich klären)* ‹*puzzle, problem*› be solved; **c)** *(sich auflösen)* dissolve
los-: ~|**fahren** *unr. itr. V.; mit sein* set off; *(wegfahren)* move off; ~|**gehen** *unr. itr. V.; mit sein* **a)** *(aufbrechen)* set off; **b)** *(ugs.: beginnen)* start; **c)** *(ugs.: abgehen)* ‹*button, handle, etc.*› come off; ~|**kommen** *unr. itr. V.; mit sein (ugs.)* **a)** get away; **b)** *(freikommen)* get free; ~|**lassen** *unr. tr. V.* **a)** *(nicht festhalten)* let go of; **b)** *(freilassen)* let ‹*person, animal*› go; ~|**legen** *itr. V. (ugs.)* get going
löslich *Adj.* soluble
los-: ~|**machen 1.** *tr. V. (ugs.)* let ‹*animal*› loose; untie ‹*string, line, rope*›; unhitch ‹*trailer*›; ~|**reißen** *unr. refl. V.* break free *or* loose; ~|**sagen** *refl. V.* sich von jmdm./etw. ~sagen break with sb./sth.; ~|**schlagen** *unr. itr. V. (bes. Milit.)* attack; launch one's attack
Losung die; ~, ~en slogan; *(Milit.: Kennwort)* password
Lösung die; ~, ~en **a)** solution (*Gen.*, für to); **b)** *s.* lösen 1 d: breaking off; cancellation; severing
los|werden *unr. tr. V.; mit sein* get rid of
Lot das; ~|e|s, ~e plumb[-bob]; |nicht| im ~ sein be [out of] plumb
löten *tr. V.* solder
Lotion [lo'tsi̯oːn] die; ~, ~en lotion
Lotse der; ~n, ~n *(Seew.)* pilot; **lotsen** *tr. V.* guide
Lotterie die; ~, ~n lottery; **Lotto** das; ~s, ~s national lottery
Lotto-: ~**schein** der national-lottery coupon; ~**zahlen** *Pl.* winning national-lottery numbers
Löwe der; ~n, ~n a) lion; b) *(Astrol.)* Leo; the Lion
Löwen-: ~**anteil** der lion's share, ~**mäulchen** das snapdragon; ~**zahn** der dandelion

Löwin die; ~, ~nen lioness
loyal [lo̯a'jaːl] **1.** *Adj.* loyal; **2.** *adv.* loyally; **Loyalität** die; ~: loyalty
LP [ɛl'peː] die; ~, ~|s| *Abk.* **Langspielplatte** LP
Luchs der; ~es, ~e lynx
Lücke die; ~, ~n gap; **Lücken·büßer** der; ~s, ~ *(ugs.)* stopgap; **lückenhaft** *Adj.* sketchy; **lückenlos** *Adj.* complete
lud *1. u. 3. Pers. Sg. Prät. v.* laden
Luft die; ~, Lüfte air; **an die frische ~ gehen** get out in[to] the fresh air; **die ~ anhalten** hold one's breath; **tief ~ holen** take a deep breath; **in die ~ gehen** *(fig. ugs.)* blow one's top *(coll.)*
luft-, Luft-: ~**ballon** der balloon; ~**brücke** die airlift; ~**dicht** *Adj.* airtight; ~**druck** der a) *(Physik)* air pressure; b) *(Druckwelle)* blast
lüften 1. *tr. V.* **a)** air ‹*room, clothes, etc.*›; **b)** raise ‹*hat*›; **c)** disclose ‹*secret*›; **2.** *itr. V.* air the room/house *etc.*
luft-, Luft-: ~**fahrt** die; *o. Pl.* aviation *no art.*; ~**feuchtigkeit** die [atmospheric] humidity; ~**gekühlt** *Adj.* air-cooled; ~**gewehr** das air rifle; airgun
luftig *Adj.* airy ‹*room, building, etc.*›; light ‹*clothes*›
Luftkissen·boot das hovercraft
luft-, Luft-: ~**leer** *Adj.* ein ~leerer Raum a vacuum; ~**linie** die *o. Pl.* 1 000 km ~linie 1,000 km. as the crow flies; ~**loch** das air-hole; ~**matratze** die air-bed; air mattress; Lilo (P); ~**pirat** der [aircraft] hijacker; ~**post** die airmail; **etw. per** *od.* **mit** ~**post schicken** send sth. [by] airmail; ~**pumpe** die air pump; *(für Fahrrad)* [bicycle-]pump; ~**röhre** die *(Anat.)* windpipe; ~**schiff** das airship; ~**schloß** das castle in the air; ~**schutz** der air-raid protection *no art.*; ~**schutz·keller** der air-raid shelter; ~**verschmutzung** die air pollution; ~**waffe** die air force
Lüge die; ~, ~n lie; **lügen 1.** *itr., tr. V.* lie; **das ist gelogen!** that's a lie!; **Lügner** der; ~s, ~: liar
Luke die; ~, ~n *(Dach~)* skylight; *(bei Schiffen)* hatch; *(Keller~)* trap-door
lukrativ 1. *Adj.* lucrative; **2.** *adv.* lucratively
Lümmel der; ~s, ~: lout; *(ugs., fam.: Bengel)* rascal
Lump der; ~en, ~en scoundrel; **lumpen** *(ugs.)* tr. V. **sich nicht ~ lassen** splash out *(coll.)*; **Lumpen** der; ~s,

~: rag; **Lumpen·sammler der** rag-and-bone man
Lunge die; ~, ~n lungs *pl.*
Lungen-: ~**entzündung die** pneumonia *no indef. art.;* ~**krebs der** lung cancer; ~**zug der** inhalation
Lunte die; ~, ~n fuse; match
Lupe die; ~, ~n magnifying glass
Lurch der; ~|e|s, ~e amphibian
Lust die; ~ a) ~ **haben,** etw. zu tun feel like doing sth.; b) *(Vergnügen)* pleasure; joy; **lustig 1.** *Adj.* a) merry; jolly; enjoyable ⟨*time*⟩; b) *(komisch)* funny; **2.** *adv.* a) merrily; b) *(komisch)* funnily
lust-, Lust-: ~**los 1.** *Adj.* listless; **2.** *adv.* listlessly; ~**spiel das** comedy
lutherisch *Adj.* Lutheran
lutschen 1. *tr. V.* suck; **2.** *itr. V.* suck; **an** etw. *(Dat.)* ~: suck sth.
Luxemburg (das); ~s Luxembourg
luxuriös 1. *Adj.* luxurious; **2.** *adv.* luxuriously; **Luxus der;** ~: luxury
Lymph·knoten der lymph node
lynchen *tr. V.* lynch
Lyrik die; ~: lyric poetry; **lyrisch** *Adj.* lyrical; lyric ⟨*poetry*⟩
Lyzeum das; ~s, Lyzeen girls' high school

M

m, M [ɛm] **das; ~, ~:** m/M
m *Abk.* Meter m
machen 1. *tr. V.* a) make; **aus Plastik/ Holz** *usw.* **gemacht** made of plastic/ wood *etc.;* **sich** *(Dat.)* etw. ~ **lassen** have sth. made; **etw. aus** jmdm. ~: make sb. into sth.; **jmdn. zum Präsidenten** *usw.* ~: make sb. president *etc.;* **jmdn./sich |einen| Kaffee** ~: make [some] coffee for sb./oneself; b) *(verursachen)* **jmdm. Arbeit** ~: make [extra] work for sb.; **das macht das Wetter** that's [because of] the weather; c) *(ausführen)* do ⟨*job, repair, etc.*⟩; **einen Spaziergang** ~: go for a walk; **eine Reise** ~: go on a journey; **einen Besuch |bei jmdm.|** ~: pay [sb.] a visit; d) *(tun)* do; **was machst du da?**

what are you doing?; **so etwas macht man nicht** that [just] isn't done; e) **was macht ...?** *(wie ist es um ... bestellt?)* how is ...?; **was macht die Gesundheit/ Arbeit?** how are you keeping/ how ist the job [getting on]?; f) *(ergeben) (beim Rechnen)* be; *(bei Geldbeträgen)* come to; **zwei mal zwei macht vier** two times two is four; **das macht 12 DM** that is 12 marks; *(Endsumme)* that comes to 12 marks; g) *(schaden)* **was macht das schon?** what does it matter?; **macht nichts!** *(ugs.)* it doesn't matter; h) *(teilnehmen an)* **einen Kursus** *od.* **Lehrgang** ~: take a course; i) **mach's gut!** *(ugs.)* look after yourself!; *(auf Wiedersehen)* so long!; **2.** *refl. V.* a) **sich an etw.** *(Akk.)* ~: get down to sth.; b) *(ugs.: sich entwickeln)* do well; c) **mach dir nichts daraus!** *(ugs.)* don't let it bother you; **3.** *itr. V.* a) **mach schon!** *(ugs.)* get a move on! *(coll.);* b) **das macht hungrig/durstig** it makes you hungry/thirsty; **das macht dick** it's fattening; **Machenschaften** *Pl.* *(abwertend)* wheeling and dealing *sing.*
Macht die; ~, Mächte power; **an die ~ kommen** come to power; **Macht·haber der;** ~s, ~: ruler; **mächtig 1.** *Adj.* a) powerful; b) *(beeindruckend groß)* mighty; **2.** *adv.* *(ugs.)* terribly *(coll.)*
macht-, Macht-: ~**kampf der** power struggle; ~**los** *Adj.* powerless; **gegen** etw. ~**los sein** be powerless in the face of sth.; ~**probe die** trial of strength
Mädchen das; ~s, ~ a) girl; b) *(Haus~)* maid; **mädchenhaft** *Adj.* girlish; **Mädchen·name der** a) girl's name; b) *(Name vor der Ehe)* maiden name
Made die; ~, ~n maggot; **madig** *Adj.* maggoty; **jmdn./etw.** ~ **machen** *(ugs.)* run sb./sth. down
Madonna die; ~, Madonnen madonna
mag *1. u. 3. Pers. Sg. Präsens v.* **mögen**
Magazin das; ~s, ~e a) *(Lager)* store; *(für Waren)* stock-room; b) *(für Patronen, Dias, Film* usw.; *Zeitschrift)* magazine
Magen der; ~s, Mägen *od.* ~: stomach
magen-, Magen-: ~**bitter der;** ~s, ~: bitters *pl.;* ~**schmerzen** *Pl.* stomach-ache *sing.*
mager *Adj.* a) thin; b) *(fettarm)* low-fat; low in fat *pred.;* lean ⟨*meat*⟩; c)

(fig.) poor ⟨*soil, harvest*⟩; meagre ⟨*profit, increase, success, report, etc.*⟩; thin ⟨*programme*⟩

Mager-: ~**milch** die skim[med] milk; ~**quark** der low-fat curd cheese

Magie die; ~: magic; **Magier** ['ma:gi̯ɐ] der; ~s, ~ *(auch fig.)* magician; **magisch** *Adj.* magic ⟨*powers*⟩; *(geheimnisvoll)* magical

Magistrat der; ~|e|s, ~e City Council

Magnet der; ~en *od.* ~|e|s, ~e magnet; **magnetisch** 1. *Adj.* magnetic; 2. *adv.* magnetically; **Magnetismus** der; ~: magnetism; **Magnet·nadel** die [compass] needle

Mahagoni das; ~s mahogany

Mäh·drescher der combine harvester; **mähen** 1. *tr. V.* mow; cut ⟨*corn*⟩; 2. *itr. V.* mow; *(Getreide* ~*)* reap

Mahl das; ~|e|s, **Mähler** *(geh.)* meal; repast *(formal)*

mahlen *unr. tr., itr. V.* grind

Mahl·zeit meal

Mähne die; ~, ~n mane

mahnen *tr. V.* urge; remind ⟨*debtor*⟩

Mahn-: ~**mal** das memorial *(erected as a warning to future generations);* ~**schreiben** das reminder

Mahnung die; ~, ~en a) exhortation; *(Warnung)* admonition; b) *s.* **Mahnschreiben**

Mai der; ~|e|s *od.* ~: May

Mai~: ~**baum** der maypole; ~**glöckchen** das lily of the valley; ~**käfer** der May-bug

Mais der; ~es maize; corn *(esp. Amer.); (als Gericht)* sweet corn; **Mais·kolben** der corn-cob; *(als Gericht)* corn on the cob

Majestät die; ~, ~en a) *(Titel)* Majesty; **Eure** ~: Your Majesty; b) *o. Pl. (geh.)* majesty; **majestätisch** 1. *Adj.* majestic; 2. *adv.* majestically

Major der; ~s, ~e *(Milit.)* major

Majoran der; ~s, ~e marjoram

makaber *Adj.* macabre

Makedonien [make'do:ni̯ən] **(das);** ~s Macedonia

Makel der; ~s, ~ *(geh.)* a) *(Schmach)* stigma; b) *(Fehler)* blemish; **makel·los** 1. *Adj.* flawless; spotless ⟨*white, cleanness*⟩; 2. *adv.* immaculately; spotlessly ⟨*clean*⟩

Make-up [me:k'|ap] das; ~s, ~s make-up

Makkaroni *Pl.* macaroni *sing.*

Makler der; ~s, ~: estate agent *(Brit.);* realtor *(Amer.)*

Makrele die; ~, ~n mackerel

Makrone die; ~, ~n macaroon

mal 1. *Adv.* times; *(bei Flächen)* by; 2. *Partikel* **komm** ~ **her!** come here!; ¹**Mal** das; ~|e|s, ~e time; **mit einem** ~|e| all at once; ²**Mal** das; ~|e|s, ~e *od.* **Mäler** mark; *(Muttermal)* birthmark; *(braun)* mole

Malaie der; ~n, ~n Malay; **Malaysia (das);** ~s Malaysia

Mal·buch das colouring-book; **malen** *tr., itr. V.* paint; decorate ⟨*flat, room, walls*⟩; **Maler** der; ~s, ~: painter; **Malerei** die; ~, ~en painting; **malerisch** 1. *Adj.* picturesque; 2. *adv.* picturesquely

mal|nehmen *unr. tr., itr. V.* multiply *(mit by)*

Malz·bier das malt beer

Mama die; ~, ~s *(fam.)* mamma; **Mami** die; ~, ~s *(fam.)* mummy *(Brit. coll.);* mommy *(Amer. coll.)*

Mammut das; ~s, ~e *od.* ~s mammoth

man *Indefinitpron. im Nom.* one; you *2nd person; (irgend jemand)* somebody; *(die Behörden; die Leute dort)* they *pl.; (die Menschen im allgemeinen)* people *pl;* ~ **hat mir gesagt ...:** I was told ...

Management ['mænɪdʒmənt] das; ~s, ~s management; **managen** ['mɛnɪdʒn̩] *tr. V.* a) *(ugs.)* fix; organize; b) *(betreuen)* manage ⟨*singer, artist, player*⟩; **Manager** ['mɛnɪdʒɐ] der; ~s, ~: manager; *(eines Fußballvereins)* club secretary

manch *Indefinitpron.* a) *attr.* many a; **in** |so| ~**er** Beziehung in many respects; b) *alleinstehend* ~**er** many a person/man; ~**e** *Pl.* some; *(viele)* many; |so| ~**es** a number of things; *(allerhand Verschiedenes)* all kinds of things; **mancherlei** *unbest. Gattungsz.* a) *attr.* various; a number of; b) *alleinstehend* various things; **manch·mal** *Adv.* sometimes

Mandant der; ~en, ~en client

Mandarine die; ~, ~n mandarin [orange]

Mandel die; ~, ~n a) almond; b) *(Anat.)* tonsil; **Mandel·entzündung** die tonsillitis *no indef. art.*

Manege [ma'ne:ʒə] die; ~, ~n *(im Zirkus)* ring; *(in der Reitschule)* arena

¹**Mangel** der; ~s, **Mängel** a) *o. Pl. (Fehlen)* lack **(an** + *Dat.* of); *(Knappheit)* shortage, lack **(an** + *Dat.* of); b) *(Fehler)* defect

²**Mangel** die; ~, ~n [large] mangle

mangelhaft 1. *Adj.* faulty ⟨*goods, German, English, etc.*⟩*; (unzulänglich)* inadequate ⟨*knowledge, lighting*⟩*; (Schulw.)* **die** Note „~" the mark 'unsatisfactory'; *(bei Prüfungen)* the fail mark; **2.** *adv.* faultily; *(unzulänglich)* inadequately; **¹mangeln** *itr. V.; unpers.* **es mangelt an etw.** *(Dat.) (etw. fehlt)* there is a lack of sth.; *(etw. ist unzureichend vorhanden)* there is a shortage of sth.; **jmdm./einer Sache mangelt es an etw.** *(Dat.)* sb./sth. lacks sth.

²mangeln *tr. V.* mangle

mangels *Präp. mit Gen.* in the absence of

Manie die; ~, ~n mania

Manier die; ~, ~en **a)** manner; **b)** *Pl. (Umgangsformen)* manners; **manierlich 1.** *Adj.* **a)** *(fam.)* well-mannered; well-behaved ⟨*child*⟩*; **b)** *(ugs.: einigermaßen gut)* decent; **2.** *adv.* **a)** *(fam.)* nicely; **b)** *(ugs.: einigermaßen gut)* **ganz/recht** ~: quite/really nicely

Manifest das; ~|e|s, ~e manifesto

Maniküre die; ~: manicure; **maniküren** *tr. V.* manicure

manipulieren *tr. V.* manipulate; rig ⟨*election result etc.*⟩

Manko das; ~s, ~s shortcoming; deficiency

Mann der; ~|e|s, **Männer a)** man; **b)** *(Ehemann)* husband; **Männchen das;** ~s, ~ **a)** little man; **b)** *(Tier~)* male; ~ **machen** ⟨*animal*⟩ sit up and beg

Mannequin ['manəkɛ̃] **das;** ~s, ~s mannequin; [fashion] model

mannig·fach *Adj.* multifarious

männlich 1. *Adj.* **a)** male; **b)** *s.* **maskulin 1; 2.** *adv.* in a masculine way; **Mannschaft die;** ~, ~en *(Sport, auch fig.)* team; *(Schiffs-, Flugzeugbesatzung)* crew; *(Milit.)* unit

Manöver das; ~s, ~ **a)** *(Milit.)* exercise; ~ *Pl.* manœuvres; **b)** *(Bewegung; fig. abwertend: Trick)* manœuvre; **manövrieren** *itr., tr. V.* manœuvre

Mansarde die; ~, ~n attic; *(Zimmer)* attic room

Manschette die; ~, ~n cuff; **Manschetten·knopf der** cuff-link

Mantel der; ~s, **Mäntel** coat

Manuskript das; ~|e|s, ~e **a)** manuscript; *(Typoskript)* typescript; **b)** *(Notizen)* notes *pl.*

Mappe die; ~, ~n **a)** folder; **b)** *(Aktentasche)* briefcase; *(Schul~)* schoolbag

Marathon·lauf [...tɔn...] **der** marathon

Märchen das; ~s, ~: fairy story; fairy-tale; *(ugs.: Lüge)* [tall] story *(coll.);* **Märchen·buch das** book of fairy stories; **märchenhaft 1.** *Adj.* magical; **2.** *adv.* magically; *(ugs.)* fantastically *(coll.)*

Margarine die; ~: margarine

Margerite die; ~, ~n ox-eye daisy

Maria (die); ~s *od. (Rel.)* **Mariä** Mary; **Marien·käfer der** ladybird

Marihuana das; ~s marijuana

Marinade die; ~, ~n *(Kochk.)* marinade; *(Salatsauce)* [marinade] dressing

Marine die; ~, ~n fleet; *(Kriegs~)* navy

Marionette die; ~, ~n puppet; marionette; **Marionetten·theater das** puppet theatre

¹Mark die; ~, ~: mark; **Deutsche** ~: Deutschmark

²Mark das; ~|e|s **a)** *(Knochen~)* marrow; **b)** *(Frucht~)* pulp

markant *Adj.* striking; prominent ⟨*figure, nose, chin*⟩*; clear-cut ⟨*features, profile*⟩

Marke die; ~, ~n **a)** *(Waren~)* brand; *(Fabrikat)* make; **b)** *(Brief~, Rabatt~, Beitrags~)* stamp; **c)** *(Essen~)* meal-ticket; **d)** *(Erkennungs~)* [identification] disc; *(Dienst~)* [police] identification badge; ≈ warrant card *(Brit.)* or *(Amer.)* ID card

Marken-: ~**artikel der** proprietary or *(Brit.)* branded article; ~**zeichen das** trade mark

markieren *tr. V.* **a)** mark; **b)** *(ugs.: vortäuschen)* sham ⟨*illness, breakdown, etc.*⟩*; **2.** *itr. V. (ugs.: simulieren)* put it on *(coll.);* **Markierung die;** ~, ~en marking

Markt der; ~|e|s, **Märkte** market; *(~platz)* market-place or -square; **freitags ist** ~: Friday is market-day

Markt-: ~**forschung die** market research *no def. art.;* ~**frau die** marketwoman; ~**halle die** covered market; ~**lücke die** gap in the market; ~**platz der** market-place; ~**stand der** market stall; ~**wirtschaft die** market economy

Marmelade die; ~, ~n jam; *(Orangen~)* marmalade

Marmor der; ~s marble

Marokkaner der; ~s, ~: Moroccan; **marokkanisch** *Adj.* Moroccan; **Marokko (das);** ~s Morocco

Maro̱ne die; ~, ~n [sweet] chestnut

Ma̱rs der; ~: Mars *no def. art.*

Ma̱rsch der; ~[e]s, Märsche march; *(Wanderung)* [long] walk; **marschie̱ren** *itr. V.; mit sein* march; *(wandern)* walk

Ma̱rs·mensch der Martian

Ma̱rter die; ~, ~n *(geh.)* torture; *(seelisch)* torment; **ma̱rtern** *tr. V. (geh.)* torture

Mä̱rtyrer der; ~s, ~: martyr; **Marty̱rium** das; ~s, Marty̱rien martyrdom

Marxi̱smus der; ~: Marxism *no art.;* **Marxi̱st** der; ~en, ~en Marxist; **marxi̱stisch** *Adj.* Marxist

Mä̱rz der; ~[es] March

Marzipan das; ~s marzipan

Ma̱sche die; ~, ~n stitch; *(Lauf~)* run; ladder *(Brit.); (beim Netz)* mesh; **Ma̱schen·draht** der wire netting

Maschi̱ne die; ~, ~n a) *(auch ugs.: Motorrad)* machine; b) *(ugs.: Automotor)* engine; c) *(Flugzeug)* [aero]plane; d) *(Schreib~)* typewriter; **maschi̱ne·geschrieben** *Adj.* typewritten; **maschine̱ll** 1. *Adj.* machine *attrib.;* by machine *postpos.;* 2. *adv.* by machine; ~ **hergestellt** machine-made

Maschi̱nen-: ~**gewehr** das machine-gun; ~**pistole** die sub-machine-gun

maschi̱ne|schreiben *unr. itr. V.; nur im Inf. u. Part.* type

Ma̱sern *Pl.* measles *sing. or pl.*

Ma̱serung die; ~, ~en [wavy] grain

Ma̱ske die; ~, ~n mask; **Ma̱sken·ball** der masked ball; **Maske̱rade** die; ~, ~n *(fancy-dress)* costume; **maskie̱ren** 1. *tr. V.* mask; 2. *refl. V.* put on a mask/masks

Masko̱ttchen das; ~s, ~: [lucky] mascot

maskuli̱n [*auch* '---] 1. *Adj. (auch Sprachw.)* masculine; 2. *adv.* in a masculine way

maß *1. u. 3. Pers. Sg. Prät. v.* me̱ssen; **¹Maß** das; ~es, ~e a) measure (für of); *(fig.)* das ~ ist voll enough is enough; b) *(Größe)* measurement; c) *(Grad)* degree (an + *Dat.* of); in großem/gewissem ~e to a great/certain extent; **²Maß** die; ~, ~[e] *(bayr., österr.)* litre [of beer]

Massage [ma'sa:ʒə] die; ~, ~n massage

Massaker das; ~s, ~: massacre

Maß-: ~**anzug** der made-to-measure suit; ~**arbeit** die a) custom-made item; *(Kleidungsstück)* made-to-

measure item; b) *(genaue Arbeit)* neat work

Ma̱sse die; ~, ~n a) mass; b) *(Gemisch)* mixture

Maß·einheit die unit of measurement

Ma̱ssen·grab das mass grave; **ma̱ssenhaft** 1. *Adj.; nicht präd.* in huge numbers *postpos.;* 2. *adv.* on a huge scale

ma̱ssen-, Ma̱ssen-: ~**karambolage** die multiple crash; ~**medium** das mass medium; ~**mörder** der mass murderer; ~**produktion** die mass production; ~**weise** *Adv.* in huge numbers

Masseur [ma'søː̰] der; ~s, ~e masseur; **Masse̱urin** die; ~, ~nen, **Masse̱use** [ma'søːzə] die; ~, ~n masseuse

maß·gebend, maß·geblich 1. *Adj.* authoritative ⟨book, expert, opinion⟩; definitive ⟨text⟩; influential ⟨person, circles, etc.⟩; decisive ⟨factor, influence, etc.⟩; 2. *adv.* ⟨influence⟩ to a considerable extent; *(entscheidend)* decisively; **maß|halten** *unr. itr. V.* exercise moderation

massie̱ren *tr. V.* massage

mä̱ßig 1. *Adj.* moderate; *(mittel~)* mediocre; 2. *adv.* in moderation; moderately ⟨gifted, talented⟩; *(mittel~)* indifferently; **mä̱ßigen** *refl. V. (geh.)* a) practise or exercise moderation; b) *(sich beherrschen)* control or restrain oneself; **Mä̱ßigkeit** die; ~: moderation; **Mä̱ßigung** die; ~: moderation

massi̱v 1. *Adj.* a) solid; b) *(heftig)* massive ⟨demand⟩; crude ⟨accusation, threat⟩; strong ⟨attack, criticism, pressure⟩; 2. *adv.* ⟨attack⟩ strongly; ⟨accuse, threaten⟩ crudely

maß-, Maß-; ~**krug** der *(südd., österr.)* litre beer-mug; *(aus Steingut)* stein; ~**los** 1. *Adj.* extreme; gross ⟨exaggeration, insult⟩; excessive ⟨demand, claim⟩; boundless ⟨ambition, greed, sorrow, joy⟩; 2. *adv.* extremely; ⟨exaggerate⟩ grossly; ~**nahme** die; ~, ~n measure; ~**regel** die regulation; *(Maßnahme)* measure; ~**regeln** *tr. V. (zurechtweisen)* reprimand; *(bestrafen)* discipline; ~**stab** der a) standard; b) *(einer Karte, eines Modells usw.)* scale; ~**voll** 1. *Adj.* moderate; 2. *adv.* in moderation

Ma̱st der; ~[e]s, ~en, *auch:* ~e *(Schiffs~, Antennen~)* mast; *(Stange,*

Fahnen~) pole; *(Hochspannungs~)* pylon

mästen *tr. V.* fatten

masturbieren *itr., tr. V.* masturbate

Match [mɛtʃ] das *od.* der; ~|e|s, ~s *od.* ~e match

Material das; ~s, ~ien material; *(Bau~; Hilfsmittel)* materials *pl.;* **Materialismus** der; ~: materialism; **Materialist** der; ~en, ~en materialist; **materialistisch** 1. *Adj.* materialistic; 2. *adv.* materialistically; **Materie** die; ~, ~n a) matter; b) *(geh.: Thema, Gegenstand)* subject-matter; **materiell** 1. *Adj. (finanziell)* financial; 2. *adv.* materially; *(finanziell)* financially

Mathematik die; ~: mathematics *sing., no art.;* **mathematisch** 1. *Adj.* mathematical; 2. *adv.* mathematically

Matjes der; ~, ~: matie [herring]

Matratze die; ~, ~n mattress

Matrose der; ~n, ~n sailor; seaman

Matsch der; ~|e|s *(ugs.)* mud; *(breiiger Schmutz)* sludge; *(Schnee~)* slush; **matschig** *Adj. (ugs.)* a) muddy; slushy ⟨snow⟩; b) *(weich)* mushy; squashy ⟨fruit⟩

matt 1. *Adj.* a) weak; feeble ⟨applause, reaction⟩; b) *(glanzlos)* matt; dull ⟨metal, mirror, etc.⟩; c) *(undurchsichtig)* frosted ⟨glass⟩; pearl ⟨light-bulb⟩; d) subdued; *(Schach)* checkmated; ~! checkmate!; 2. *adv.* a) *(kraftlos)* weakly; b) *(mäßig)* ⟨protest, contradict⟩ feebly

Matte die; ~, ~n mat

Matt·scheibe die *(ugs.)* telly *(Brit. coll.);* box *(coll.)*

Mätzchen das; ~s, ~: ~ **machen** *(ugs.)* fod about *or* around

Mauer die; ~, ~n wall; **mauern** 1. *tr. V.* build; 2. *itr. V.* lay bricks; **Mauer·werk** das a) masonry; *(aus Ziegeln)* brickwork; b) *(Mauern)* walls *pl.*

Maul das; ~|e|s, Mäuler *(von Tieren)* mouth; *(derb: Mund)* gob *(sl.)*

Maul-: ~**esel** der the mule; ~**korb** der *(auch fig.)* muzzle; ~**tier** das mule; ~**wurf** der mole

Maurer der; ~s, ~: bricklayer

Maus die; ~, Mäuse mouse

Mauschelei die; ~, ~en *(ugs. abwertend)* shady wheeling and dealing *no indef. art.;* **mauscheln** *itr. V. (ugs. abwertend)* engage in shady wheeling and dealing

Mäuschen das; ~s, ~: little mouse;

mäuschen·still *Adj.* ~ **sein** be as quiet as a mouse; **Mause·falle** die mousetrap

Maut die; ~, ~en toll

maximal 1. *Adj.* maximum; 2. *adv.* ~ zulässige Geschwindigkeit maximum permitted speed; **Maxime** die; ~, ~n maxim; **Maximum** das; ~s, Maxima maximum (**an** + *Dat.* of)

Mayonnaise [majoˈnɛːzə] die; ~, ~n mayonnaise

Mäzen der; ~s, ~e *(geh.)* patron

MdB, M.d.B. *Abk.* Mitglied des Bundestages Member of the Bundestag

m.E. *Abk.* meines Erachtens in my opinion *or* view

Mechanik die; ~: mechanics *sing., no art.;* **Mechaniker** der; ~s, ~: mechanic; **mechanisch** 1. *Adj.* mechanical; power *attrib.* ⟨loom, press⟩; 2. *adv.* mechanically; **Mechanismus** der; ~, Mechanismen mechanism

meckern *itr. V.* a) *(auch fig.)* bleat; b) *(ugs.: nörgeln)* grumble; moan

Mecklenburg-Vorpommern (das); ~s Mecklenburg-Western Pomerania

Medaille [meˈdaljə] die; ~, ~n medal; **Medaillon** [medaljˈjõː] das; ~s, ~s a) locket; b) *(Kochk., bild. Kunst)* medallion

Medikament das; ~|e|s, ~e medicine; *(Droge)* drug

meditieren *itr. V.* meditate (**über** + *Akk.* [up]on)

Medium das; ~s, Medien medium

Medizin die; ~, ~en medicine; **Mediziner** der; ~s, ~: doctor; *(Student)* medical student; **medizinisch** 1. *Adj.* medical; medicinal ⟨bath etc.⟩; medicated ⟨toothpaste, soap, etc.⟩; 2. *adv.* medically

Meer das; ~|e|s, ~e *(auch fig.)* sea; **am** ~: by the sea; **Meer·enge** die straits *pl.;* strait

Meeres-: ~**bucht** die bay; ~**früchte** *Pl. (Kochk.)* seafood *sing.;* ~**spiegel** der sea-level

Meer-: ~**jungfrau** die mermaid; ~**rettich** der horse-radish; ~**schweinchen** das guinea-pig

Megaphon das; ~s, ~e megaphone; loud hailer

Mehl das; ~|e|s flour; **mehlig** *Adj.* a) floury; b) mealy ⟨potato, apple, etc.⟩

mehr 1. *Indefinitpron.* more; 2. *Adv.* a) more; b) **nicht** ~: not ... any more; no longer; **es war niemand** ~ **da** there was no one left; **das wird nie** ~ **vorkommen** it will never happen again; **da ist**

nichts ~ zu machen there is nothing
more to be done
mehr-: ~bändig *Adj.* in several vol-
umes *postpos.;* ~deutig 1. *Adj.* ambiguous; 2. *adv.* ambiguously
mehren *(geh.) refl. V.* increase; mehrer... *Indefinitpron. u. unbest. Zahlwort* a) *attr.* several; b) *alleinstehend*
~e several people; ~es several things
pl.; mehr·fach 1. *Adj.* multiple;
(wiederholt) repeated; 2. *adv.* several
times; *(wiederholt)* repeatedly;
Mehrheit die; ~, ~en majority
mehr-, Mehr-: ~jährig *Adj.* lasting
several years *postpos.;* ~malig *Adj.;
nicht präd.* repeated; ~mals *Adv.*
several times; *(wiederholt)* repeatedly;
~sprachig *Adj.* multilingual;
~stimmig *(Musik)* 1. *Adj.* for several
voices *postpos.;* ein ~stimmiges Lied a
part-song; 2. *adv.* ~stimmig singen
sing in harmony; ~teilig *Adj.* in several parts *postpos.;* ~wert der
(Wirtsch.) surplus value; ~wert-
steuer die *(Wirtsch.)* value added tax
(Brit.); VAT *(Brit.);* sales tax *(Amer.);*
~zahl die; *o. Pl.* a) *(Sprachw.)* plural;
b) *(Mehrheit)* majority
meiden *unr. tr. V. (geh.)* avoid
Meile die; ~, ~n mile
mein *Possessivpron.* my; ~e Damen
und Herren ladies and gentlemen; das
Buch dort, ist das ~[e]s? that book over
there, is it mine?
Mein·eid der perjury *no indef. art.;*
einen ~ schwören commit perjury
meinen 1. *itr. V.* think; 2. *tr. V.* a)
think; b) *(sagen wollen, im Sinn haben)* mean; c) *(beabsichtigen)* mean;
intend; es gut mit jmdm. ~: mean well
by sb.; d) *(sagen)* say
meiner *Gen. von* ich *(geh.)* gedenkt ~:
remember me; erbarme dich ~: have
mercy upon me; meinerseits *Adv.*
for my part; ganz ~: the pleasure is
[all] mine; meinetwegen *Adv.* a)
because of me; *(mir zuliebe)* for my
sake; *(um mich)* about me; b) *[auch
--'--] (von mir aus)* as far as I'm concerned; ~! if you like
Meinung die; ~, ~en opinion (zu on,
über + *Akk.* about); meiner ~ nach in
my opinion; ganz meine ~: I agree entirely; einer ~ sein be of the same
opinion
Meinungs-: ~forschung die opinion research; ~freiheit die freedom
to form and express one's own opin-
ions; *(Redefreiheit)* freedom of

speech; ~umfrage die [public] opinion poll; ~verschiedenheit die difference of opinion
Meise die; ~, ~n tit[mouse]
Meißel der; ~s, ~: chisel; meißeln
tr. V. chisel; carve ⟨*statue, sculpture*⟩
with a chisel
meist *Adv.* mostly; meist... *Indefinitpron. u. unbest. Zahlw.* most; die
~en Leute ...: most people ...; am ~en
most; meistens *Adv. s.* meist
Meister der; ~s, ~ a) master; b)
(Werk~, Polier) foreman; c) *(Sport)*
champion; meisterhaft 1. *Adj.*
masterly; 2. *adv.* in a masterly manner; meistern *tr. V.* master;
Meisterschaft die; ~, ~en a) *o. Pl.*
mastery; b) *(Sport)* championship
Meister-: ~stück das masterpiece
(an + *Dat.* of); ~titel der *(Sport)*
championship [title]; ~werk das
masterpiece (an + *Dat.* of)
Melancholie [melaŋko:'li:] die; ~ *(Ge-
mütszustand)* melancholy; *(Psych.)*
melancholia; melancholisch 1.
Adj. melancholy; melancholy, melancholic ⟨*person, temperament*⟩; 2. *adv.*
melancholically
melden 1. *tr. V.* report; *(registrieren
lassen)* register ⟨*birth, death, etc.*⟩
(*Dat.* with); 2. *refl. V.* a) report; b)
(am Telefon) answer; c) *(ums Wort bitten)* put one's hand up; d) *(von sich
hören lassen)* get in touch (bei with);
Meldung die; ~, ~en a) report;
(Nachricht) piece of news; b) *(Wort~)*
request to speak
meliert *Adj.* mottled; [grau] ~es Haar
hair streaked with grey
melken *regelm. (auch unr.) tr. V.* milk
Melodie die; ~, ~n melody; *(Weise)*
tune; melodisch 1. *Adj.* melodic; 2.
adv. melodically
Melone die; ~, ~n a) melon; b) *(ugs.:
Hut)* bowler [hat]
Membran die; ~, ~en a) *(Technik)*
diaphragm; b) *(Biol., Chemie)* membrane
Memoiren [me'mŏa:rən] *Pl.* memoirs
Menge die; ~, ~n a) quantity;
amount; b) *(große ~)* lot *(coll.);* eine ~
(ugs.) lots [of it/them] *(coll.);* c) *(Men-
schen~)* crowd; d) *(Math.)* set
Mengen-: ~lehre die; *o. Pl.* set theory *no art.;* ~rabatt der bulk discount
Mensa die; ~, ~s *od.* Mensen refectory *(of university, college)*
Mensch der; ~en, ~en a) *(Gattung)*

der ~: man; die ~en man *sing.;*
human beings; mankind *sing.;* b)
(Person) person; man/woman; ~en
people
menschen-, Menschen-: ~**affe**
der anthropoid [ape]; ~**auflauf** der
crowd [of people]; ~**feind** der misan-
thropist; ~**fresser** der *(ugs.)* cannibal; ~**freund** der philanthropist;
~**handel** der trade *or* traffic in
human beings; ~**kenner** der judge of
human nature; ~**kenntnis die;** *o. Pl.*
ability to judge human nature; ~**leben** das life; ~**leer** *Adj.* deserted;
~**menge** die crowd [of people];
~**recht** das human right; ~**schlag**
der breed [of people]; ~**seele die:**
keine ~seele not a [living] soul
Menschens·kind: ~! *(salopp) (erstaunt)* good heavens; good grief;
(vorwurfsvoll) for heaven's sake
menschen·unwürdig 1. *Adj.* ⟨ac-
commodation⟩ unfit for human habitation; ⟨conditions⟩ unfit for human
beings; ⟨behaviour⟩ unworthy of a
human being; 2. *adv.* ⟨treat⟩ in a degrading and inhumane way; ⟨live, be
housed⟩ in conditions unfit for human
beings; **Menschen·verstand** der
human intellect; **Menschheit die;**
~: mankind *no art.;* humanity *no art.;*
human race; **menschlich** 1. *Adj.* a)
human; b) *(annehmbar)* civilized; c)
(human) humane ⟨person, treatment,
etc.⟩; 2. *adv.* a) er ist mir ~ sympathisch I like him as a person; b)
(human) humanely; **Menschlich-
keit** die humanity *no art.*
Mensen *s.* Mensa
Mentalität die; ~, ~en mentality
Menü das; ~s, ~s *(auch DV)* menu
merkbar 1. *Adj.* noticeable; 2. *adv.*
noticeably; **Merk·blatt** leaflet;
merken 1. *tr. V.* notice; 2. *refl. V.*
sich *(Dat.)* etw. ~: remember sth.;
merklich *s.* merkbar; **Merkmal**
das; ~s, ~e feature
Merkur der; ~s Mercury
merkwürdig 1. *Adj.* strange; odd; 2.
adv. strangely; oddly
meßbar *Adj.* measurable
¹**Messe die;** ~, ~n *(Gottesdienst, Musik)* mass
²**Messe die;** ~, ~n *(Ausstellung)*
[trade] fair
messen 1. *unr. tr. V.* a) *auch itr.*
measure; b) *(beurteilen)* judge **(nach
by)**; 2. *unr. refl. V. (geh.)* compete (mit
with)

Messer das; ~s, ~: knife
messer-, Messer-: ~**scharf** 1. *Adj.*
razor-sharp; *(fig.)* incisive ⟨logic⟩;
razor-sharp ⟨wit, intellect⟩; 2. *adv. (fig.
ugs.)* ⟨argue⟩ incisively; ~**stich** der
knife-thrust; *(Wunde)* knife-wound
Messias der; ~, ~se Messiah
Messing das; ~s brass
Messung die; ~, ~en measurement
Metall das; ~s, ~e metal; **Metall·in-
dustrie die** metal-processing and
metal-working industries *pl.;* **metallisch** *Adj.* metallic; metal *attrib.,* metallic ⟨conductor⟩
Metapher die; ~, ~n metaphor
Meta·physik die; ~: metaphysics
sing., no art.
Meteor der; ~s, ~e meteor; **Meteo-
rit** der; ~en *od.* ~s, ~e[n] meteorite
Meteorologe der; ~n, ~n meteorologist; **Meteorologie die;** ~: meteorology *no art.*
Meter der *od.* das; ~s, ~: metre
meter-, Meter-: ~**dick** *Adj. (sehr
dick)* metres thick *postpos.;* ~**hoch**
Adj. metres high *postpos.;* ⟨snow⟩
metres deep; ~**maß** das tape-
measure; *(Stab)* [metre] rule
Methode die; ~, ~n method; **methodisch** 1. *Adj.* methodological;
(nach einer Methode vorgehend) methodical; 2. *adv.* methodologically;
(nach einer Methode) methodically
Metier [me'tie:] **das;** ~s, ~s profession
Metrik die; ~, ~en metrics
Metropole die; ~, ~n metropolis
Mett·wurst die soft smoked sausage
made of minced pork and beef
Metzger der; ~s, ~ *(bes. westmd.,
südd., schweiz.)* butcher; **Metzgerei
die;** ~, ~en *(bes. westmd., südd.,
schweiz.)* butcher's [shop]
Meute die; ~, ~n a) *(Jägerspr.)* pack;
b) *(ugs. abwertend)* mob; **Meuterei
die;** ~, ~en mutiny; **meutern** *itr. V.*
a) mutiny; ⟨prisoners⟩ riot; b) *(ugs.:
Unwillen äußern)* moan
Mexikaner der; ~s, ~: Mexican;
mexikanisch *Adj.* Mexican; **Mexiko (das);** ~s Mexico
MEZ *Abk.* mitteleuropäische Zeit CET
mg *Abk.* Milligramm mg
MG [ɛm'ge:] **das;** ~s, ~s *Abk.* Maschinengewehr
Mi. *Abk.* Mittwoch Wed.
miau *Interj.* miaow; **miauen** *itr. V.*
miaow
mich 1. *Akk. von* ich me; 2. *Akk. des
Reflexivpron. der 1.Pers. Sg.* myself

mick[e]rig *Adj. (ugs.)* miserable; measly *(sl.);* puny ⟨*person*⟩
mied *l. u. 3. Pers. Sg. Prät. v.* meiden
Mieder·waren *Pl.* corsetry *sing.*
Miene die; ~, ~n expression
mies *(ugs.)* **1.** *Adj.* lousy *(sl.);* **2.** *adv.* lousily *(sl.)*
Mies·muschel die [common] mussel
Miete die; ~, ~n rent; *(für ein Auto, Boot)* hire charge; **zur ~ wohnen** live in rented accommodation; **mieten** *tr. V.* rent; *(für kürzere Zeit)* hire; **Mieter der; ~s, ~:** tenant; **Miets·haus das** block of rented flats *(Brit.)* or *(Amer.)* apartments
Miet-: **~vertrag der** tenancy agreement; **~wagen der** hire-car
Migräne die; ~, ~n migraine
mikro-, Mikro- micro-
Mikrobe die; ~, ~n microbe
mikro-, Mikro-: **~film der** microfilm; **~phon** [--'-] **das; ~s, ~e** microphone; **~skop** [--'-] **das; ~s, ~e** microscope; **~skopisch** --'--] **1.** *Adj.* microscopic; **2.** *adv.* microscopically
Milbe die; ~, ~n mite
Milch die; ~: milk; **Milch·flasche die** milk-bottle; **milchig 1.** *Adj.* milky; **2.** *adv.* **~ weiß** milky-white
Milch-: **~kaffee der** coffee with plenty of milk; **~kännchen das** milk-jug; **~reis der** rice pudding; **~straße die** Milky Way; Galaxy
mild, milde 1. *Adj.* mild; lenient ⟨*judge, judgement*⟩; soft ⟨*light*⟩; smooth ⟨*brandy*⟩; **2.** *adv. (gütig)* leniently; *(gelinde)* mildly; **Milde die; ~:** mildness; *(Güte)* leniency; **mildern** *tr. V.* moderate; mitigate ⟨*punishment*⟩; **Milderung die; ~:** *s.* **mildern:** moderation; mitigation
Milieu [mi'ljø:] **das; ~s, ~s** environment
militant *Adj.* militant; **¹Militär das; ~s** armed forces *pl.;* military; *(Soldaten)* soldiers *pl.;* **²Militär der; ~s, ~s** [high-ranking military] officer
Militär-: **~dienst der** military service; **~diktatur die** military dictatorship
militärisch *Adj.* military; **militarisieren** *tr. V.* militarize; **Military** ['mɪlɪtərɪ] **die; ~, ~s** *(Reiten)* three-day event; **Miliz die; ~, ~en** militia; *(Polizei)* police
Mill. *Abk.* Million m.
milli- Milli-
Milliarde die; ~, ~n billion
Milli-: **~gramm das** milligram;

~meter der *od.* **das** millimetre; **~meter·papier das** [graph] paper ruled in millimetre squares
Million die; ~, ~en million; **Millionär der; ~s, ~e** millionaire
Millionen-: **~schaden der** damage *no pl., no indef. art.* running into millions; **~stadt die** town with over a million inhabitants
millionst... *Ordinalz.* millionth
Milz die; ~: spleen
Mimik die; ~: gestures and facial expressions *pl.*
Mimose die; ~, ~n a) mimosa; **b)** *(fig.)* over-sensitive person
minder *Adv. (geh.)* less; **minder...** *Adj.* inferior ⟨*goods, brand*⟩; **minder·bemittelt** *Adj.* without much money *postpos., not pred.;* **~bemittelt** sein not have much money; geistig **~bemittelt** *(fig. salopp abwertend)* not all that bright *(coll.);* **Minderheit die; ~, ~en** minority
minder·jährig *Adj.* ⟨*child etc.*⟩ who is/was a minor; **Minder·jährige der/die;** *adj. Dekl.* minor; **mindern** *tr. V. (geh.)* reduce; **Minderung die; ~, ~en** reduction *(Gen.* in); **minderwertig** *Adj.* inferior; **mindest...** *Adj.* least; *(geringst...)* slightest; **das ist das ~e, was du tun kannst** it is the least you can do; **mindestens** *Adv.* at least
Mine die; ~, ~n a) *(Bergwerk, Sprengkörper)* mine; **b)** *(Bleistift~)* lead; *(Kugelschreiber~, Filzschreiber~)* refill
Mineral das; ~s, ~e *od.* **Mineralien** mineral; **Mineralogie die; ~:** mineralogy *no art.*
Mineral-: **~öl das** mineral oil; **~wasser das** mineral water
Mini das; ~s, ~s *(Mode)* mini *(coll.);* **Mini-** mini-; **Miniatur die; ~, ~en** miniature
minimal 1. *Adj.* minimal; marginal ⟨*advantage, lead*⟩; very slight ⟨*benefit, profit*⟩; **2.** *adv.* minimally; **Minimum das; ~s, Minima** minimum (**an +** *Dat.* of)
Minister der; ~s, ~: minister (**für** for); *(eines britischen Hauptministeriums)* Secretary of State (**für** for); *(eines amerikanischen Hauptministeriums)* Secretary (**für** of); **Ministerium das; ~s, Ministerien** Ministry; Department *(Amer.);* **Minister·präsident der a)** *(eines deutschen Bundeslandes)* minister-president; **b)** *(Pre-*

mierminister) Prime Minister; **Ministrant** der; ~en, ~en *(kath. Kirche)* server

Minorität die; ~, ~en *s.* Minderheit

minus *Konj., Adv. (bes. Math.)* minus; **Minus** das; ~: deficit; **Minuszeichen** das minus sign

Minute die; ~, ~n minute; **minuten·lang** 1. *Adj.* lasting [for] several minutes *postpos.;* 2. *adv.* for several minutes; **Minuten·zeiger** der minute-hand

Mio. *Abk.* Million[en] m.

mir 1. *Dat. von* ich to me; *(nach Präpositionen)* me; **Freunde von ~:** friends of mine; **gehen wir zu ~:** let's got to my place; **von ~ aus** as far as I'm concerned; 2. *Dat. des Reflexivpron. der 1. Pers. Sg.* myself

Mirabelle die; ~, ~n mirabelle

Misch-: ~**brot** das bread made from wheat and rye flour; ~**ehe** die mixed marriage

mischen 1. *tr. V.* mix; 2. *refl. V.* **a)** *(sich ver~)* mix (**mit** with); ⟨*smell, scent*⟩ blend (**mit** with); **b)** *(sich ein~)* **sich in etw.** *(Akk.)* ~: interfere in sth.; **Misch·farbe** die non-primary colour; **Mischling** der; ~s, ~e halfcaste; **Mischmasch** der; ~[e]s, ~e *(ugs., meist abwertend)* hotchpotch; mishmash; **Mischung** die; ~, ~en mixture; *(Tee~, Kaffee~, Tabak~)* blend; *(Pralinen~)* assortment; **Misch·wald** der mixed [deciduous and coniferous] forest

miserabel *(ugs.)* 1. *Adj.* dreadful *(coll.);* 2. *adv.* dreadfully *(coll.);* **ihm geht es gesundheitlich ~:** he's in a bad way; **Misere** die; ~, ~n *(geh.)* wretched *or* dreadful state; *(Elend)* misery; *(Not)* distress

miß *Imperativ Sg. v.* messen

miß·achten *tr. V.* **a)** *(ignorieren)* disregard; ignore; **b)** *(geringschätzen)* be contemptuous of

miß·billigen *tr. V.* disapprove of; **Miß·billigung** die disapproval

Miß·brauch der *s.* mißbrauchen: abuse; misuse; **miß·brauchen** *tr. V.* abuse; misuse; abuse ⟨*trust*⟩

missen *tr. V. (geh.)* jmdn./etw. nicht ~ mögen not want to be without sb./sth.

Miß·erfolg der failure

Misse·tat die *(geh. veralt.)* misdeed

miß·fallen *unr. itr. V.* etw. mißfällt jmdm. sb. dislikes sth.; **Mißfallen** das; ~s displeasure; *(Mißbilligung)* disapproval

Miß·geschick das mishap

miß·glücken *itr. V.; mit sein* fail

miß·gönnen *tr. V.* jmdm. etw. ~: begrudge sb. sth.

Miß·griff der error of judgement

miß·handeln *tr. V.* maltreat; **Mißhandlung** die maltreatment

Mission die; ~, ~en mission; **Missionar** der; ~s, ~e, missionary

Miß·kredit der in jmdn./etw. in ~ bringen bring sb./sth. into discredit

mißlang *1. u. 3. Pers. Sg. Prät. v.* mißlingen

mißliebig *Adj.* unpopular

mißlingen *unr. itr. V.; mit sein* fail; **Mißlingen** das; ~s failure; **mißlungen** 2. *Part. v.* mißlingen

Miß·mut der ill humour *no indef. art.;* **miß·mutig** 1. *Adj.* badtempered; sullen ⟨*face*⟩; 2. *adv.* badtemperedly

Miß·stand der deplorable state of affairs *no pl.*

mißt 2. *u. 3. Pers. Sg. Präsens v.* messen

miß·trauen *itr. V.* jmdm./einer Sache ~: mistrust *or* distrust sb./sth.; **Mißtrauen** das; ~s mistrust, distrust (gegen of); **mißtrauisch** 1. *Adj.* mistrustful; distrustful; 2. *adv.* mistrustfully; distrustfully

miß·verständlich 1. *Adj.* unclear; ⟨*formulation, concept, etc.*⟩ that could be misunderstood; 2. *adv.* ⟨*express oneself, describe*⟩ in a way that could be misunderstood; **Miß·verständnis** das misunderstanding; **miß·verstehen**[1] *unr. tr. V.* misunderstand

Mist der; ~[e]s **a)** dung; *(Dünger)* manure; *(mit Stroh usw. gemischt)* muck; **b)** *(~haufen)* dung/manure/ muck heap; **c)** *(ugs. abwertend) (Unsinn)* rubbish *no indef. art.; (Minderwertiges)* junk *no indef. art.*

Mistel die; ~, ~n mistletoe

Mist·haufen der dung/manure/ muck heap

mit 1. *Präp. mit Dat.* with; **ein Zimmer ~ Frühstück** a room with breakfast included; **~ 50 [km/h] fahren** drive at 50 [k.p.h]; **~ der Bahn/dem Auto fahren** go by train/car; **~ 20 [Jahren]** at [the age of] twenty; 2. *Adv.* **a)** too; as well; **b) seine Arbeit war ~ am besten** *(ugs.)* his work was among the best

Mit·arbeit die; *o. Pl.* collaboration

---

[1] *ich mißverstehe, mißverstanden, mißzuverstehen*

(bei/an + Dat. on); *(Mithilfe)* assistance (bei, in + *Dat.* in); *(Beteiligung)* participation (in + *Dat.* in); **mịt|arbeiten** *itr. V.* collaborate (bei/an + *Dat.* on) *(sich beteiligen)* participate (in + *Dat.* in); **Mịt·arbeiter der a)** collaborator; **freier ~:** free-lance worker; **b)** *(Angestellter)* employee

mịt|bekommen *unr. tr. V.* **a)** etw. ~: be given sth. to take with one; **b)** *(wahrnehmen)* be aware of; *(durch Hören, Sehen)* hear/see

mịt|bestimmen 1. *itr. V.* have a say; **2.** *tr. V.* have an influence on; **Mịtbestimmung die;** *o. Pl.* participation (bei in); *(der Arbeitnehmer)* codetermination

mịt|bringen *unr. tr. V.* **a)** etw. ~: bring sth. with one; jmdm./sich etw. ~: bring sth. with one for sb./bring sth. back for oneself; **b)** *(haben)* have *⟨ability, gift, etc.⟩;* **Mịtbringsel das; ~s, ~:** [small] present; *(Andenken)* [small] souvenir

mit·einạnder *Adv.* **a)** with each other *or* one another; ~ sprechen talk to each other *or* one another; **b)** *(gemeinsam)* together

mịt|erleben *tr. V.* **a)** witness *⟨events etc.⟩;* **b)** *(mitmachen)* be alive during

mịt|fahren *unr. itr. V.; mit sein* bei jmdm. |im Auto| ~: go/travel with sb. [in his/her car]; *(mitgenommen werden)* get a lift with sb. [in his/her car]

mịt·fühlend 1. *Adj.* sympathetic; **2.** *adv.* sympathetically

mịt|führen *tr. V.* **a)** *(Amtsspr.: bei sich tragen)* etw. ~: carry sth. [with one]; **b)** *(transportieren)* *⟨river, stream⟩* carry along

mịt|geben *unr. tr. V.* jmdm. etw. ~: give sb. sth. to take with him/her; *(fig.)* provide sb. with sth.

Mịt·gefühl das; *o. Pl.* sympathy

mịt|gehen *unr. itr. V.; mit sein* **a)** go too; mit jmdm. ~: go with sb.; **b)** *(sich mitreißen lassen)* begeistert ~: respond enthusiastically

Mịt·gift die; ~, ~en *(veralt.)* dowry

Mịt·glied das member *(Gen.,* in + *Dat.* of)

mịt|halten *unr. itr. V.* keep up (bei in, mit with)

Mịt·hilfe die; *o. Pl.* help; assistance

mịt|hören 1. *tr. V.* listen to; *(zufällig)* overhear *⟨conversation, argument, etc.⟩; (abhören)* listen in on; **2.** *itr. V.* listen; *(zufällig)* overhear

mịt|kommen *unr. itr. V.; mit sein* **a)**

come too; **kommst du mit?** are you coming [with me/us]?; **b)** *(Schritt halten)* keep up

Mịt·läufer der *(abwertend)* [mere] supporter

Mịt·laut der consonant

Mịt·leid das pity, compassion (mit for); *(Mitgefühl)* sympathy (mit for); **Mịt·leidenschaft die:** jmdn./etw. in ~ ziehen affect sb./sth.; **mịt·leidig 1.** *Adj.* compassionate; *(mitfühlend)* sympathetic; **2.** *adv.* compassionately; *(mitfühlend)* sympathetically

mịt|machen 1. *tr. V.* **a)** *(teilnehmen an)* go on *⟨trip⟩;* join in *⟨joke⟩;* follow *⟨fashion⟩;* fight in *⟨war⟩;* do *⟨course, seminar⟩;* das mache ich nicht mit *(ugs.)* I can't go along with it; **b)** *(ugs.: erleiden)* zwei Weltkriege/viele Bombenangriffe mitgemacht haben have been through two world wars/many bomb attacks; **2.** *itr. V.* **a)** *(sich beteiligen)* join in; **b)** *(ugs.: funktionieren)* mein Herz/Kreislauf macht nicht mit my heart/circulation can't take it

Mịt·mensch der fellow human being

mịt|nehmen *unr. tr. V.* **a)** jmdn. ~: take sb. with one; etw. ~: take sth. with one; *(verhüll.: stehlen)* walk off with sth. *(coll.); (kaufen)* take sth.; **Essen/Getränke zum Mitnehmen** food/drinks to take away *or (Amer.)* to go; **b)** *(in Mitleidenschaft ziehen)* jmdn. ~: take it out of sb.

mịt|reden *itr. V.* **a)** join in the conversation; **b)** *(mitbestimmen)* have a say

Mịt·reisende der/die fellow passenger

mịt|reißen *unr. tr. V.* die Begeisterung/seine Rede hat alle Zuhörer mitgerissen the audience was carried away with enthusiasm/by his speech

mit·sạmt *Präp. mit Dat.* together with

Mịt·schuld die share of the blame *or* responsibility (an + *Dat.* for)

Mịt·schüler der, Mịt·schülerin die schoolfellow

mịt|spielen *itr. V.* **a)** join in the game; **b)** in einem Film ~: be in a film; in einem Orchester/in *od.* bei einem Fußballverein ~: play in an orchestra/for a football club; **Mịt·spieler der, Mịt·spielerin die** player; *(in derselben Mannschaft)* team-mate

mịttag *Adv.* heute/Montag ~: at midday today/on Monday; **Mịttag der; ~s, ~e a)** midday *no art.;* gegen ~: around midday; zu ~ essen have

lunch; **b)** *o. Pl. (ugs.: Mittagspause)*
lunch-hour; **Mittag·essen das**
lunch; **mittags** *Adv.* at midday; **12
Uhr ~:** 12 noon
Mittags-: **~pause** die lunch-hour;
~ruhe die period of quiet after lunch;
~zeit die a) *o. Pl. (Zeit gegen 12 Uhr)*
lunch-time *no art.;* **b)** *(~pause)* lunch-
hour
Mitte die; **~, ~n** middle; *(eines Krei-
ses, einer Kugel, Stadt)* centre; **~ des
Monats/Jahres** in the middle of the
month/year
mit|teilen *tr. V.* jmdm. etw. **~:** tell sb.
sth.; *(informieren)* inform sb. of sth.;
mitteilsam *Adj.* communicative;
(gesprächig) talkative; **Mit·teilung
die** communication; *(Bekanntgabe)*
announcement
Mittel das; ~s, ~ a) means; *(Methode)*
way; method; *(Werbe~, Propagan-
da~ usw.)* device *(Gen.* for); **mit allen
~n versuchen, etw. zu tun** try by every
means to do sth.; **b)** *(Arznei)* **ein ~ gegen Husten** *usw.* a cure for coughs
etc.; **c)** *Pl. (Geld~)* funds; *(Privat~)*
means
Mittel·alter das; *o. Pl.* Middle Ages
pl.; **mittel·alterlich** *Adj.* medieval
mittelbar 1. *Adj.* indirect; **2.** *adv.* indirectly
mittel-, Mittel-: **~ding das;** *o. Pl.*
ein ~ding sein be something in between; **~europa (das)** Central
Europe; **~finger der** middle finger;
~gebirge das low mountains *pl.;*
~linie die centre line; *(Fußball)* half-
way line; **~los** *Adj.* without means
postpos.; **~mäßig** *Adj.* mediocre;
~meer das Mediterranean [Sea];
~punkt der a) *(Geom.)* centre; *(einer
Strecke)* midpoint; **b)** *(Mensch/Sache
im Zentrum)* centre of attention;
~scheitel der centre parting;
~schule die *s.* Realschule; **~stand
der;** *o. Pl.* middle class; **~weg der**
middle course; **~welle die** *(Physik,
Rundf.)* medium wave
mitten *Adv.* **~ an/auf etw.** *(Akk./Dat.)*
in the middle of sth.; **~ durch die
Stadt** right through the town
mitten-: **~drin** *Adv.* [right] in the
middle; **~durch** *Adv.* [right] through
the middle
Mitter·nacht die; *o. Pl.* midnight *no
art.;* **Mitternachts·sonne die** midnight sun
mittler... *Adj.* middle; moderate
⟨*speed*⟩; medium-sized ⟨*company,*

town⟩; medium ⟨*quality, size*⟩; *(durchschnittlich)* average
mittler·weile *Adv.* since then; *(bis
jetzt)* by now; *(unterdessen)* in the
meantime
Mittwoch der; ~[e]s, ~e Wednesday;
mittwochs *Adv.* on Wednesday[s]
mit·unter *Adv.* from time to time
mit·wirken *itr. V.* **an etw.** *(Dat.)*/**bei
etw. ~:** collaborate on/be involved in
sth.; **in einem Orchester/Theaterstück
~:** play in an orchestra/act *or* appear
in a play; **Mitwirkende der/die** *adj.
Dekl. (an einer Sendung)* participant;
(in einer Show) performer; *(in einem
Theaterstück)* actor
Mit·wisser der; ~s ~: ~ einer Sache
(Gen.) **sein** be an accessory to sth.
mixen *tr. V.* mix; **sich** *(Dat.)* **einen
Drink ~:** fix oneself a drink; **Mixer
der; ~s, ~ a)** *(Bar~)* barman; bar-
tender·*(Amer.);* **b)** *(Gerät)* blender *or*
liquidizer
mm *Abk.* Millimeter mm.
Mo. *Abk.* Montag Mon.
Mob der; ~s *(abwertend)* mob
Möbel das; ~s, ~ a) *Pl.* furniture
sing., no indef. art.; **b)** piece of furniture; **Möbel·wagen der** furniture
van; removal van; **mobil** *Adj.* **a)**
mobile; **~ machen** mobilize; **b)** *(ugs.)
(lebendig)* lively; **Mobiliar das; ~s**
furnishings *pl.;* **mobilisieren** *tr. V.*
a) *(Milit., fig.)* mobilize; **b)** *(aktivieren)* activate; **Mobilmachung die;
~, ~en** mobilization; **Mobil·telefon
das** cellular phone; **möblieren** *tr. V.*
furnish
mochte *1. u. 3. Pers. Sg. Prät. v.* **mögen; möchte** *1. u. 3. Pers. Sg. Konjunktiv II v.* mögen
Mode die; ~, ~n fashion; **Mode·far-
be die** fashionable colour
Modell das; ~s, ~e *(auch fig.)* model;
jmdm. **~ sitzen** *od.* stehen sit for sb.;
modellieren *tr. V.* model, mould
⟨*figures, objects*⟩; mould ⟨*clay, wax*⟩;
Modell·kleid das model dress
Moden·schau die fashion show
Moder der; ~s mould; *(~geruch)* mus-
tiness
Moderation die; ~, ~en *(Rundf.,
Ferns.)* presentation; **Moderator
der; ~s, ~en, Moderatorin die; ~,
~nen** *(Rundf., Ferns.)* presenter; **moderieren** *tr. V. (Rundf., Ferns.)* present ⟨*programme*⟩
¹modern *itr. V.; auch mit sein* go
mouldy

²mod**e**rn 1. *Adj.* modern; *(modisch)* fashionable; 2. *adv.* in a modern manner; *(modisch)* fashionably; **modernisieren** *tr. V.* modernize

Mode-: ~**schöpfer** der couturier; ~**schöpferin** die couturière; ~**wort** das; *Pl.* ~**wörter** vogue-word; ~**zeitschrift** die fashion magazine

modifizieren *tr. V. (geh.)* modify

m**o**disch 1. *Adj.* fashionable; 2. *adv.* fashionably

Mofa das; ~s, ~s [low-powered] moped

Mogelei die; ~, ~en *(ugs.)* cheating *no pl.;* **mogeln** *itr. V.* cheat

mögen 1. *unr. Modalverb; 2. Part.* ~: a) *(wollen)* want to; **das hätte ich sehen** ~: I would have liked to see that; b) *(geh.:* sollen) **das mag genügen** that should be enough; c) *(Vermutung, Möglichkeit)* **sie mag/mochte vierzig sein** she must be/must have been [about] forty; **|das| mag sein** maybe; d) *Konjunktiv II (den Wunsch haben)* **ich/ sie möchte gern wissen ...**: I would/she would like to know ...; 2. *unr. tr. V.* like; **sie mag keine Rosen** she does not like roses; **sie ~ sich** they're fond of one another; **möchten Sie ein Glas Wein?** would you like a glass of wine?; **ich möchte lieber Tee** I would prefer tea; 3. *unr. itr. V.* a) *(es wollen)* like to; b) **ich möchte nach Hause** I want to go home; **er möchte zu Herrn A** he would like to see Mr A

möglich *Adj.* possible; **es war ihm nicht ~ |zu kommen|** he was unable [to come]; **alles ~e** *(ugs.)* all sorts of things; **|das ist doch| nicht ~!** impossible!; **sein ~stes tun** do one's utmost; **möglicherweise** *Adv.* possibly; **Möglichkeit** die; ~, ~en a) possibility; *(Methode)* way; **es besteht die ~, daß ...**: there is a possibility that ...; b) *(Gelegenheit)* opportunity; chance; **möglichst** *Adv.* a) if [at all] possible; b) **~ schnell** as fast as possible

Moha**mmed (der)** Muhammad; **Mohammedaner** der; ~s, ~: Muslim; Muhammadan; **mohammedanisch** *Adj.* Muslim; Muhammadan

Mohn der; ~s poppy; *(Samen)* poppy seed; *(auf Brot, Kuchen)* poppy seeds *pl.*

Mohn-: ~**blume** die poppy; ~**brötchen** das poppy-seed roll; ~**kuchen** der poppy-seed cake

Möhre die; ~, ~n carrot

Mohren·kopf der chocolate marshmallow

Mohr·rübe die carrot

mokieren *refl. V. (geh.)* **sich über etw.** *(Akk.)* ~: scoff at sth.; **sich über jmdn.** ~: mock sb.

Mokka der; ~s strong black coffee

Molch der; ~|e|s, ~e newt

Mole die; ~, ~n [harbour] mole

Molekül das; ~s, ~e molecule

molk *1. u. 3. Pers. Sg. Prät. v.* **melken**;

Molkerei die; ~, ~en dairy

Moll das; ~ *(Musik)* minor [key]

mollig 1. *Adj.* a) *(rundlich)* plump; b) *(warm)* snug; 2. *adv.* snugly; **~ warm** warm and snug

¹**Moment** der; ~|e|s, ~e moment; **jeden ~** *(ugs.)* [at] any moment; **im ~:** at the moment; ²**Moment** das; ~|e|s, ~e factor, element (für in); **momentan** 1. *Adj.* a) present; b) *(vorübergehend)* temporary; *(flüchtig)* momentary; 2. *adv.* a) at present; b) *(vorübergehend)* temporarily

Monaco (das); ~s Monaco

Monarch der; ~en, ~en monarch;

Monarchie die; ~, ~n monarchy;

Monarchin die; ~, ~nen monarch

Monat der; ~s, ~e month; **im ~ April** in the month of April; **monatelang** 1. *Adj.* lasting for months *postpos., not pred.;* 2. *adv.* for months [on end]; **monatlich** 1. *Adj.* monthly; 2. *adv.* every month; *(pro Monat)* per month

Monats-: ~**erste** der first [day] of the month; ~**hälfte** die half of the month; ~**karte** die monthly season-ticket; ~**letzte** der last day of the month

Mönch der; ~|e|s, ~e monk

Mond der; ~|e|s, ~e moon; **auf** *od.* **hinter dem ~ leben** *(fig. ugs.)* be a bit behind the times *(coll.);* **nach dem ~ gehen** *(ugs.)* ⟨clock, watch⟩ be hopelessly wrong

Mond-: ~**finsternis** die eclipse of the moon; ~**landung** die moon landing

Mongole der; ~n, ~n a) Mongol; b) *(Bewohner der Mongolei)* Mongolian; **Mongolei** die; ~: Mongolia

Monitor der; ~s, ~en monitor

Mono·gramm das; ~s, ~e monogram; **Monographie** die; ~, ~n monograph

Monolog der; ~s, ~e monologue

Monopol das; ~s, ~e monopoly (**auf** + *Akk.,* für in, of)

monoton 1. *Adj.* monotonous; 2. *adv.*

monotonously; **Monotonie die; ~,**
~n monotony
Monster das; ~s, ~: monster; *(häß-*
lich) [hideous] brute; **Monstren** *s.*
Monstrum; monströs *Adj.* monstrous; **Monstrum das; ~s, Mon-**
stren a) monster; **b)** *(Sache)* hulking
great thing *(coll.)*
Mon·tag der Monday
Montage [mɔn'ta:ʒə] **die; ~, ~n a)**
(Zusammenbau) assembly; *(Einbau)*
installation; *(Aufstellen)* erection;
(Anbringen) fitting **(an** + *Akk. od.*
Dat. to); mounting **(auf** + *Akk. od.*
Dat. on); **b)** *(Film, bild. Kunst, Litera-*
turw.) montage
montags *Adv.* on Monday[s]
montieren *tr. V.* **a)** *(zusammenbauen)*
assemble **(aus** from); erect ⟨building⟩;
b) *(anbringen)* fit **(an** + *Akk. od. Dat.*
to; **auf** + *Akk. od. Dat.* on); *(einbau-*
en) install **(in** + *Akk.* in); *(befestigen)*
fix **(an** + *Akk. od. Dat.* to)
Monument das; ~|e|s, ~e monument;
monumental *Adj.* monumental
Moor das; ~|e|s, ~e bog; *(Bruch)*
marsh
Moos das; ~es, ~e moss
Moped ['mo:pɛt] **das; ~s, ~s** moped
Mops der; ~es, Möpse pug [dog]; *(sa-*
lopp: dicke Person) podge *(coll.)*
Moral die; ~ a) *(Norm)* morality; **b)**
(Sittlichkeit) morals *pl.;* **c)** *(Selbstver-*
trauen) morale; **d)** *(Lehre)* moral;
moralisch 1. *Adj.* **a)** moral; **b)** *(tu-*
gendhaft) virtuous; **2.** *adv.* **a)** morally;
b) *(tugendhaft)* virtuously; **morali-**
sieren *itr. V. (geh.)* moralize; **Mora-**
list der; ~en, ~en moralist
Morast der; ~|e|s, ~e od. Moräste a)
bog; swamp; **b)** *o. Pl. (Schlamm)* mud
Mord der; ~|e|s, ~e murder **(an** +
Dat. of); *(durch ein Attentat)* assassination; **einen ~ begehen** commit murder; **morden** *tr., itr. V.* murder;
Mörder der; ~s, ~: murderer *(esp.*
Law); killer; *(politischer ~)* assassin;
Mörderin die; ~, ~nen murderer;
murderess; *(politische ~)* assassin;
mörderisch 1. *Adj.* **a)** murderous; **2.**
adv. (ugs.) dreadfully *(coll.);* **Mord-**
fall der murder case; **mords-,**
Mords- *(ugs.)* terrific *(coll.)*
Mord-: ~verdacht der suspicion of
murder; **~versuch der** attempted
murder; *(Attentat)* assassination attempt; **~waffe die** murder weapon
morgen *Adv.* **a)** tomorrow; **~ in einer**
Woche tomorrow week; a week to-

morrow; **~ um diese Zeit** this time tomorrow; **bis ~!** until tomorrow!; see
you tomorrow!; **b)** *(am Morgen)* **heute**
~: this morning; |am| **Sonntag ~**: on
Sunday morning; **Morgen der; ~s,**
~: morning; **am ~**: in the morning;
am folgenden *od.* **nächsten ~**: next
morning; **früh am ~, am frühen ~**:
early in the morning; **morgendlich**
Adj. morning
Morgen-: ~grauen das daybreak;
~mantel der dressing-gown; **~rot**
das *(geh.)* rosy dawn
morgens *Adv.* in the morning; *(jeden*
Morgen) every morning; **Dienstag** *od.*
dienstags ~: on Tuesday morning[s];
von ~ bis abends from morning to
evening; **morgig** *Adj.* tomorrow's
Morphium das; ~s morphine; **mor-**
phium·süchtig *Adj.* addicted to
morphine *pred.*
morsch *Adj. (auch fig.)* rotten
Mörser der; ~s, ~ *(Gefäß, Geschütz)*
mortar
Mörtel der; ~s mortar
Mosaik das; ~s, ~en *od.* **~e** mosaic
Mosambik (das); ~s Mozambique
Moschee die; ~, ~n mosque
Moschus der; ~: musk
Mosel die; ~: Moselle; **Mosel·wein**
der Moselle [wine]
Moskau (das); ~s Moscow; **Mos-**
kauer 1. *indekl. Adj.* Moscow *attrib.;*
2. der; ~s, ~: Muscovite
Moskito der; ~s, ~s mosquito
Moslem der; ~s, ~s Muslim; **mosle-**
misch *Adj.* Muslim
Most der; ~|e|s, ~e a) [cloudy fer-
mented] fruit-juice; **b)** *(landsch.: neuer*
Wein) new wine; **Mostrich der; ~s**
(nordostd.) mustard
Motel das; ~s, ~s motel
Motiv das; ~s, ~e a) motive; **b)**
(fachspr.: Thema) motif; theme; *(bild.*
Kunst) subject
Motor der; ~s, ~en engine; *(Elek-*
tro~) motor; **Motor·haube die**
(Kfz-W.) bonnet *(Brit.);* hood *(Amer.);*
motorisieren *tr. V.* motorize; **Mo-**
tor·rad das motor cycle; **Motor-**
rad·fahrer der motor-cyclist
Motor-: ~roller der motor scooter;
~schaden der engine trouble *no in-*
def. art.
Motte die; ~, ~n moth; **Motten·ku-**
gel die moth-ball
Motto das; ~s, ~s motto; *(Schlag-*
wort) slogan
Möwe die; ~, ~n gull

Mrd. *Abk.* **Milliarde** bn.

Mücke die; ~, ~n midge; *(größer)* mosquito; **Mücken·stich** der midge/mosquito bite

Mucks der; ~es, ~e *(ugs.)* murmur [of protest]; keinen ~ sagen not utter a [single] word

müde 1. *Adj.* tired; *(ermattet)* weary; *(schläfrig)* sleepy; jmdn./etw. od. jmds./einer Sache ~ sein *(geh.)* be tired of sb./sth.; 2. *adv.* wearily; *(schläfrig)* sleepily; **Müdigkeit** die; ~: tiredness

muffelig *(ugs.)* 1. *Adj.* grumpy; 2. *adv.* grumpily

muffig *Adj.* musty

Mühe die; ~, ~n trouble; sich *(Dat.)* mit jmdm./etw. ~ geben take [great] pains over sb./sth.; mit Müh und Not with great difficulty; **mühelos** 1. *Adj.* effortless; 2. *adv.* effortlessly; **mühe·voll** *Adj.* laborious; painstaking ⟨work⟩

Mühle die; ~, ~n a) mill; *(Kaffee~)* [coffee-] grinder; b) *(Spiel)* o. Art., o. *Pl.* nine men's morris

Mühsal die; ~, ~e *(geh.)* tribulation; *(Strapaze)* hardship; **mühsam** 1. *Adj.* laborious; 2. *adv.* laboriously; **müh·selig** *(geh.)* 1. *Adj.* laborious; arduous ⟨journey, life⟩; 2. *adv.* with [great] difficulty

Mulde die; ~, ~n hollow

Mull der; ~[e]s *(Stoff)* mull; *(Verband~)* gauze

Müll der; ~s refuse; rubbish; garbage *(Amer.)*; trash *(Amer.)*; *(Industrie~)* [industrial] waste

Mull·binde die gauze bandage

Müller der; ~s, ~: miller

Müll-: ~halde die refuse dump; ~mann der; *Pl.* ~männer *(ugs.)* dustman *(Brit.)*; garbage man *(Amer.)*; ~sack der refuse bag; ~schlucker der rubbish or *(Amer.)* garbage chute; ~tonne die dustbin *(Brit.)*; garbage or trash can *(Amer.)*; ~wagen der dust-cart *(Brit.)*; garbage truck *(Amer.)*

mulmig *Adj. (ugs.)* uneasy

Multiplikation die; ~, ~en *(Math.)* multiplication; **multiplizieren** *tr. V.* multiply (mit by)

Mumie ['mu:mi̯ə] die; ~, ~n mummy

Mumm der; ~s *(ugs.) (Mut)* guts *pl.* *(coll.)*; *(Tatkraft)* drive; zap *(sl.)*; *(Kraft)* muscle-power

Mumps der od. die; ~: mumps *sing.*

München (das); ~s Munich;

Münch[e]ner 1. *indekl. Adj.* Munich *attrib.;* 2. der; ~s, ~: inhabitant/native of Munich

Mund der; ~[e]s, **Münder** mouth; er küßte sie auf den ~: he kissed her on the lips; mit vollem ~ sprechen speak with one's mouth full; den ~ nicht aufmachen *(fig. ugs.)* not say anything; den od. seinen ~ halten *(ugs.) (zu sprechen aufhören)* shut up *(coll.);* *(nichts sagen)* not say anything; *(nichts verraten)* keep quiet (über + Akk. about); sie ist nicht auf den ~ gefallen *(fig. ugs.)* she's never at a loss for words; **Mund·art** die dialect

münden *itr. V.; mit sein* in etw. Akk. ~: ⟨river⟩ flow into sth.; ⟨corridor, street⟩ lead into sth.

mund-, Mund-: ~faul *Adj. (ugs.)* uncommunicative; ~gerecht *Adj.* bite-sized; ~geruch der bad breath *no indef. art.;* ~harmonika die mouth-organ

mündig *Adj.* of age *pred.;* ~ werden come of age

mündlich 1. *Adj.* oral; 2. *adv.* orally; **Mund·stück** das mouthpiece; *(bei Zigaretten)* tip; **mund·tot** *Adj.* jmdn. ~ machen silence sb.; **Mündung** die; ~, ~en a) mouth; *(größere Trichter~)* estuary; b) *(bei Feuerwaffen)* muzzle

Mund-zu-Mund-Beatmung die mouth-to-mouth resuscitation

Munition die; ~: ammunition

munkeln *tr., itr. V. (ugs.)* man munkelt, daß ...: there is a rumour that ...

Münster das; ~s, ~: minster; *(Dom)* cathedral

munter 1. *Adj.* a) cheerful; *(lebhaft)* lively ⟨eyes, game⟩; b) *(wach)* awake; 2. *adv.* cheerfully; **Munterkeit** die; ~: cheerfulness

Münz·automat der slot-machine; **Münze** die; ~, ~n coin

Münz-: ~fernsprecher der payphone; pay station *(Amer.);* ~tankstelle die coin-in-the-slot petrol *(Brit.)* or *(Amer.)* gas station; ~wechsler der change machine

mürbe *Adj.* crumbly ⟨biscuit, cake, etc.⟩; tender ⟨meat⟩; soft ⟨fruit⟩; jmdn. ~ machen *(fig.)* wear sb. down

Murmel die; ~, ~n marble

murmeln *tr., itr. V.* mumble; mutter; *(sehr leise)* murmur

Murmel·tier das marmot

murren *itr. V.* grumble; **mürrisch** 1. *Adj.* grumpy; 2. *adv.* grumpily

Mus das od. der; ~es, ~e purée
Muschel die; ~, ~n a) mussel; *(Schale)* [mussel-]shell; b) *(am Telefon)* *(Hör~)* ear-piece; *(Sprech~)* mouthpiece
Muse die; ~, ~n muse
Museum das; ~s, Museen museum
Musik die; ~, ~en music; **musikalisch** 1. *Adj.* musical; 2. *adv.* musically; **Musikant** der; ~en, ~en musician; **Musik·box** die juke-box; **Musiker** der; ~s, ~, **Musikerin** die; ~, ~nen musician
Musik-: ~**hochschule** die college of music; ~**instrument** das musical instrument; ~**stunde** die music-lesson
musisch 1. *Adj.* artistic; *(education)* in the arts; 2. *adv.* artistically; **musizieren** *itr. V.* play music; *(bes. unter Laien)* make music
Muskat der; ~[e]s, ~e nutmeg; **Muskat·nuß** die nutmeg
Muskel der; ~s, ~n muscle
Muskel-: ~**kater** der stiff muscles *pl.; ~***protz** der *(ugs.)* muscleman
Muskulatur die; ~, ~en musculature; muscular system; **muskulös** *Adj.* muscular
Müsli das; ~s, ~s muesli
muß *1. u. 3. Pers. Sg. Präsens v.* müssen; **Muß** das; ~: necessity; must *(coll.)*
Muße die; ~: leisure
müssen 1. *unr. Modalverb;* 2. *Part.* ~ a) have to; **er muß es tun** he must do it; he has to or *(coll.)* has got to do it; **das muß 1968 gewesen sein** it must have been in 1968; **er muß gleich hier sein** he will be here at any moment; b) *Konjunktiv II* **es müßte doch möglich sein** it ought to be possible; **reich müßte man sein!** how nice it would be to be rich!; 2. *unr. itr. V.* **ich muß nach Hause** I have to or must go home; **ich muß mal** *(fam.)* I need to spend a penny *(Brit. coll.)* or *(Amer. coll.)* go to the john
müßig 1. *Adj.* idle *(person); (hours, weeks, life)* of leisure; 2. *adv.* idly; **Müßig·gang** der *o. Pl.* leisure; *(Untätigkeit)* idleness
müßte *1. u. 3. Pers. Sg. Prät. v.* müssen
Muster das; ~s, ~ a) *(Vorlage)* pattern; b) *(Vorbild)* model **(an** + *Dat.* of); c) *(Verzierung)* pattern; d) *(Warenprobe)* sample; **muster·gültig** 1. *Adj.* exemplary; impeccable *(order);* 2. *adv.* in an exemplary fashion
mustern *tr. V.* a) eye; b) *(Milit.: ärzt-*

lich untersuchen) jmdn. ~: give sb. his medical; **Musterung** die; ~, ~en a) scrutiny; b) *(Milit.: von Wehrpflichtigen)* medical examination; medical
Mut der; ~[e]s courage; **mutig** 1. *Adj.* brave; 2. *adv.* bravely; **mut·los** *Adj.* dejected; *(entmutigt)* disheartened; **Mut·losigkeit** die; ~: dejection
mutmaßlich *Adj.* supposed; suspected *(murderer etc.)*
Mut·probe die test of courage
[1]**Mutter** die; ~, Mütter mother; [2]**Mutter** die; ~, ~n nut; **mütterlich** 1. *Adj.* a) maternal *(line, love, instincts, etc.);* b) *(fürsorglich)* motherly *(woman, care);* 2. *adv.* in a motherly way; **mütterlicher·seits** *Adv.* on the/his/her *etc.* mother's side
Mutter-: ~**liebe** die motherly love *no art.; ~***mal** das; *Pl.* ~**male** birthmark
Mutterschaft die; ~: motherhood
mutter-, Mutter-: ~**seelen·allein** *Adj.* all alone; ~**söhnchen** das mummy's or *(Amer.)* mama's boy; ~**sprache** die mother tongue; ~**tag** der; *o. Pl.* Mother's Day *no def. art.*
Mutti die; ~, ~s mummy *(Brit. coll.);* mum *(Brit. coll.);* mommy *(Amer. coll.);* mom *(Amer. coll.)*
mut·willig 1. *Adj.* wilful; wanton *(destruction);* 2. *adv.* wilfully
Mütze die; ~, ~n cap
MW *Abk. (Rundf.)* Mittelwelle MW
Mw.-St., MwSt. *Abk.* Mehrwertsteuer VAT
mysteriös 1. *Adj.* mysterious; 2. *adv.* mysteriously; **Mystik** die; ~: mysticism
Mythologie die; ~, ~n mythology; **Mythos** der; ~, Mythen myth

N

n, N [ɛn] das; ~, ~: n/N
N *Abk.* Nord[en] N
na *Interj. (ugs.)* well; **na so [et]was!** well I never!; **na und?** *(wennschon)* so what?; *(beschwichtigend)* **na, na, na!** now, now, come along; *(triumphierend)* **na also!** there you are!; *(unsi-*

cher) **na, ich weiß nicht** hmm, I'm not sure; *(ärgerlich)* **na, was soll das denn?** now what's all this about?; *(drohend)* **na warte!** just [you] wait!

Nabel der; ~s, ~: navel; **Nabelschnur** die umbilical cord

nach 1. *Präp. mit Dat.* **a)** *(räumlich)* to; **der Zug ~ München** the train for Munich *or* the Munich train; **~ Hause gehen** go home; **~ Osten |zu|** eastwards; [towards the] east; **b)** *(zeitlich)* after; **zehn |Minuten| ~ zwei** ten [minutes] past two; **c)** *(mit bestimmten Verben, bezeichnet das Ziel der Handlung)* for; **d)** *(bezeichnet [räumliche und zeitliche] Reihenfolge)* after; **~ Ihnen/dir!** after you; **e)** *(gemäß)* according to; **~ meiner Ansicht** *od.* **Meinung, meiner Ansicht** *od.* **Meinung ~:** in my view *or* opinion;**~ der neusten Mode gekleidet** dressed in [accordance with] the latest fashion; **dem Gesetz ~:** in accordance with the law; by law; **~ etw. schmecken/riechen** taste/smell of sth.; **2.** *Adv.* **a)** *(räumlich)* **|alle| mir ~!** [everybody] follow me!; **b)** *(zeitlich)* **~ und ~:** little by little; gradually; **~ wie vor** still

nach|ahmen *tr. V.* imitate; **Nachahmung** die; ~, ~en imitation

Nachbar der; ~n , ~n neighbour; **Nachbar·haus** das house next door; **Nachbarin** die; ~, ~nen neighbour; **Nachbarschaft** die; ~ **a)** the whole neighbourhood; **b)** *(Beziehungen)* **gute ~:** good neighbourliness; **c)** *(Gegend)* neighbourhood; *(Nähe)* vicinity

nach|bestellen *tr. V.* |noch| etw. ~: order more of sth.; *(shop)* reorder sth.

Nach·bildung die **a)** *o. Pl.* copying; **b)** *(Gegenstand)* copy

nach|blicken *tr. V. (geh.)* jmdm./einer Sache ~: gaze after sb./sth.

nach|datieren *tr. V.* backdate

nach·dem *Konj.* **a)** after; **b)** *s.* ¹je 3 b

nach|denken *unr. itr. V.* think; **denk mal |gut od. scharf| nach** have a [good] think; **Nach·denken** das thought; **nachdenklich** 1. *Adj.* thoughtful; 2. *adv.* thoughtfully

Nach·druck der; *Pl.* ~e **a)** *o. Pl.* **mit ~:** emphatically; **b)** *(Druckw.)* reprint; **nachdrücklich** 1. *Adj.* emphatic; 2. *adv.* emphatically

nach|eifern *itr. V.* jmdm. ~: emulate sb.

nach·einander *Adv.* one after the other

nach|empfinden *unr. tr. V.* empathize with *(feeling)*; share *(delight, sorrow)*

Nach·erzählung die retelling [of a story]; *(Schulw.)* reproduction

Nachfahr der; ~en , ~en *(geh.)* descendant

Nach·folge die succession; **Nachfolger** der; ~s, ~, **Nachfolgerin** die; ~, ~nen successor

Nach·forschung die investigation

Nach·frage die demand (nach for)

nach|fühlen *tr. V.* empathize with

nach|füllen *tr. V.* top up; **Salz/Wein ~:** put [some] more salt/wine in

nach|geben *unr. itr. V.* give way

Nach·gebühr die excess postage

nach|gehen *unr. itr. V.; mit sein* **a)** jmdm./einer Sache ~: follow sb./sth.; einer Sache ~ *(fig.)* look into a matter; einem Beruf ~: practise a profession; **b)** *(nicht aus dem Kopf gehen)* jmdm. ~: remain on sb.'s mind; **c)** *(clock, watch)* be slow; |um| **eine Stunde ~:** be an hour slow

Nach·geschmack der after-taste

nach·giebig *Adj.* indulgent; **Nachgiebigkeit** die; ~: indulgence

nach·haltig 1. *Adj.* lasting; 2. *adv.* *(auf längere Zeit)* for a long time

Nach·hause·weg der way home

nach|helfen *unr. itr. V.* help

nach·her *[auch: '--]* *Adv.* afterwards; *(später)* later [on]; **bis ~!** see you later!

Nachhilfe·unterricht der coaching

nach|holen *tr. V. (nachträglich erledigen)* catch up on *(work, sleep)*; make up for *(working hours missed)*

Nachkomme der; ~n, ~n descendant; **nach|kommen** *unr. itr. V.; mit sein* follow [later]; come [on] later; **Nachkommenschaft** die; ~: descendants *pl.*; **Nachkömmling** der; ~s, ~e much younger child *(than the rest)*

Nach·kriegs- post-war *(generation, period, etc.)*

Nach·laß der; Nachlasses, Nachlasse *od.* Nachlässe **a)** estate; **b)** *(Kaufmannsspr.: Rabatt)* discount; **nach| lassen** 1. *unr. itr. V.* let up; *(pain, stress, pressure)* ease; *(effect)* wear off; *(interest, enthusiasm, strength, courage)* wane; *(health, hearing, memory)* deteriorate; *(business)* drop off; 2. *unr. tr. V. (Kaufmannsspr.)* give a discount of; **nach·lässig** 1. *Adj.* careless; 2. *adv.* carelessly; **Nachlässigkeit** die; ~, ~en carelessness

nach|laufen *unr. itr. V.; mit sein*
jmdm./einer Sache ~: run after sb./
sth.
nach|lesen *unr. tr. V.* look up
nach|lösen 1. *tr. V.* **eine Fahrkarte** ~:
buy a ticket [on the train, bus, etc.]; 2.
itr. V. pay the excess [fare]
nach|machen *tr. V. (auch tun)* copy;
(imitieren) imitate; *(genauso herstellen)* reproduce ⟨*period furniture etc.*⟩;
forge ⟨*signature*⟩
nach·mittag *Adv.* **heute** ~: this afternoon; |**am**| **Sonntag** ~: on Sunday
afternoon; **Nach·mittag** der afternoon; **am** ~: in the afternoon; **am späten** ~: late in the afternoon; **nachmittags** *Adv.* in the afternoon; **dienstags** *od.* **Dienstag** ~: on Tuesday
afternoons; **um vier Uhr** ~: at four in
the afternoon; at 4 p.m.
Nachnahme die; ~, ~n: **per** ~: cash
on delivery; COD
Nach·name der surname
nachprüfbar *Adj.* verifiable; **nach|-
prüfen** *tr., itr. V.* check
nach|rechnen *tr. V.* check ⟨*figures*⟩
Nach·rede die: **üble** ~: malicious
gossip; *(Rechtsw.)* defamation [of
character]
Nachricht die; ~, ~en a) news *no pl.;*
eine ~ **hinterlassen** leave a message; b)
Pl. (Ferns., Rundf.) news *sing.;* ~en
hören listen to the news
Nachrichten-: ~**sprecher** der,
~**sprecherin** die news-reader
nach|rücken *itr. V.; mit sein* move up
Nach·ruf der; ~|e|s, ~e obituary (**auf**
+ *Akk.* of); **nach|rufen** *unr. tr., itr.*
V. **jmdm.** |**etw.**| ~: call [sth.] after sb.
nach|sagen *tr. V.* a) *(wiederholen)* repeat; b) **man sagt ihm nach, er sei ...:**
he is said to be ...; **jmdm. Schlechtes** ~:
speak ill of sb.
Nach·saison die late season
nach|schicken *tr. V.* a) *(durch die
Post o. ä.)* forward; b) **jmdm. jmdn.** ~:
send sb. after sb.
nach|schlagen 1. *unr. tr. V.* look up;
2. *unr. itr. V.* **im Lexikon/Wörterbuch**
~: consult the encyclopaedia/dictionary; **Nachschlage·werk** das work
of reference
Nach·schlüssel der duplicate key
Nach·schub der *(Milit.)* a) supply (**an**
+ *Dat.* of); b) *(~material)* supplies
pl. (**an** + *Dat.* of)
nach|sehen 1. *unr. itr. V.* a) **jmdm./einer Sache** ~: gaze after sb./sth.; b)
(kontrollieren) check; c) *(nachschla-*

gen) have a look; 2. *unr. tr. V.* **a)**
(nachlesen) look up; b) *(überprüfen)*
check [over]
nach|senden *unr. od. regelm. tr. V.*
forward
Nach·sicht die leniency; **nachsichtig** 1. *Adj.* lenient (**gegen, mit** towards); 2. *adv.* leniently
nach|sitzen *unr. itr. V.* be in detention; |**eine Stunde**| ~ **müssen** have [an
hour's] detention
Nach·speise die dessert; sweet
Nach·spiel das: **die Sache wird noch
ein** ~ **haben** this affair will have repercussions; **ein gerichtliches** ~ **haben**
result in court proceedings
nach|sprechen *unr. tr. V.* |**jmdm.**|
etw. ~: repeat sth. [after sb.]
nächst... 1. *Sup. zu* **nahe;** 2. *Adj.*
next; *(kürzest)* shortest ⟨*way*⟩; **am** ~**en
Tag** the next day; **beim** ~**en Mal, das**
~**e Mal** the next time; **der** ~**e bitte!**
next [one], please; **wer kommt als** ~**er
dran?** whose turn is it next?; **Nächste** der; ~**n,** ~**n** *(geh.)* neighbour;
Nächsten·liebe die charity [to
one's neighbour]; **nächstens** *Adv.* **a)**
shortly; b) *(ugs.: wenn es so weitergeht)* if it goes on like this
nächst-: ~**liegend** *Adj.; nicht präd.*
first, immediate ⟨*problem*⟩; [most] obvious ⟨*explanation etc.*⟩; ~**möglich**
Adj. earliest possible
nach|suchen *itr. V. (geh.)* **um etw.** ~:
request sth.; *(bes. schriftlich)* apply for
sth.
nacht *Adv.* **gestern/morgen/Dienstag**
~: last night/tomorrow night/on
Tuesday night; **heute** ~: tonight;
Nacht die; ~, **Nächte** night; **bei** ~, **in
der** ~: at night[-time]; **über** ~ **bleiben**
stay overnight
Nacht-: ~**arbeit** die; *o. Pl.* night
work *no art.;* ~**dienst** der night duty;
~**dienst haben** be on night duty;
⟨*chemist's shop*⟩ be open late
Nach·teil der disadvantage; **nachteilig** 1. *Adj.* detrimental; harmful; 2.
adv. detrimentally; harmfully
Nacht-: ~**essen** das *(bes. südd.,
schweiz.)* s. **Abendessen;** ~**hemd** das
night-shirt
Nachtigall die; ~, ~en nightingale
Nach·tisch der; *o. Pl.* dessert; sweet
nächtlich *Adj.* nocturnal; night ⟨*sky*⟩;
⟨*darkness, stillness*⟩ of the night;
Nacht·lokal das night-spot (coll.)
nach|tragen *unr. tr. V. (schriftlich ergänzen)* insert; add; **nach·tragend**

Adj. unforgiving; *(rachsüchtig)* vindictive; **nachträglich 1.** *Adj.* later; subsequent ⟨*apology*⟩; *(verspätet)* belated ⟨*greetings, apology*⟩; **2.** *adv.* afterwards; subsequently; *(verspätet)* belatedly

nach|trauern *itr. V.* jmdm./einer Sache ~: bemoan the passing of sb./sth. **Nacht·ruhe die** night's sleep; **nachts** *Adv.* at night; **Montag** *od.* montags ~: on Monday nights; **um 3 Uhr** ~: at 3 o'clock in the morning **Nacht-:** ~**schicht die** night-shift; ~**schwester die** night nurse; ~**tisch der** bedside table; ~**tischlampe die** bedside light; ~**topf der** chamber-pot; ~**wächter der** night-watchman

Nach·untersuchung die follow-up examination; check-up

nach|vollziehen *unr. tr. V.* reconstruct; *(begreifen)* comprehend

nach|wachsen *unr. itr. V.; mit sein* |wieder| ~: grow again

Nach·wehen *Pl. (Med.)* afterpains; *(fig. geh.)* unpleasant after-effects

Nachweis der; ~es, ~e proof *no indef. art.* (*Gen.,* über + *Akk.* of); *(Zeugnis)* certificate (über + *Akk.* of); **nachweisbar 1.** *Adj.* demonstrable ⟨*fact, truth, error, defect, guilt*⟩; detectable ⟨*substance, chemical*⟩; **2.** *adv.* demonstrably; **nach|weisen** *unr. tr. V.* prove; **nachweislich** *Adv.* as can be proved

nach|winken *itr. V.* jmdm./einer Sache ~: wave after sb./sth.

Nach·wirkung die after-effect

Nach·wort das; *Pl.* ~worte afterword

Nach·wuchs der; *o. Pl* **a)** *(fam.: Kind[er])* offspring; **b)** *(junge Kräfte)* new blood; *(für eine Branche usw.)* new recruits *pl.; (in der Ausbildung)* trainees *pl.*

nach|zahlen *tr., itr. V.* **a)** pay later; **b)** *(zusätzlich zahlen)* **25 DM** ~: pay another 25 marks

nach|zählen *tr., itr. V.* [re]count

Nach·zahlung die additional payment

Nachzügler der straggler; *(spät Ankommender)* latecomer

Nackedei der; ~s, ~s *(fam. scherzh.)* |kleiner| ~: naked little thing

Nacken der; ~s, ~: back *or* nape of the neck; *(Hals)* neck

nackt *Adj.* naked; bare ⟨*feet, legs, arms, skin, fists*⟩; *(fig.)* plain ⟨*truth, fact*⟩; bare ⟨*existence*⟩; **Nackt·ba-**

de·strand der nudist beach; **Nackte der/die;** *adj. Dekl.* naked man/woman; **Nackt·foto das** nude photo

Nadel die; ~, ~n needle; *(Steck~, Hut~, Haar~)* pin

Nadel-: ~**baum der** conifer; coniferous tree; ~**wald der** coniferous forest

Nagel der; ~s, Nägel nail; **den** ~ **auf den Kopf treffen** *(fig. ugs.)* hit the nail on the head *(coll.)*

Nagel-: ~**bürste die** nailbrush; ~**feile die** nail-file; ~**lack der** nail varnish *(Brit.);* nail polish

nageln *tr. V.* nail (**an** + *Akk.* to, **auf** + *Akk.* on); *(Med.)* pin; **nagel·neu** *Adj. (ugs.)* brand-new; **Nagel·schere die** nail-scissors *pl.*

nagen 1. *itr. V.* gnaw; **an etw.** *(Dat.)* ~: gnaw [at] sth.; **2.** *tr. V.* gnaw off; **ein Loch ins Holz** ~: gnaw a hole in the wood

nah *s.* **nahe**

Nah·aufnahme die *(Fot.)* close-up [photograph]

nahe ['na:ə]; **näher** ['nɛ:ɐ], **nächst...** **1.** *Adj.* **a)** *(räumlich)* near *pred.;* close *pred.;* nearby *attrib.;* **b)** *(zeitlich)* imminent; near *pred.;* **c)** *(eng)* close ⟨*relationship etc.*⟩; **2.** *adv.* **a)** *(räumlich)* ~ **an** (+ *Dat./Akk.*), ~ **bei** close to; ~ **gelegen** nearby; **von** ~**m** from close up; **b)** *(zeitlich)* ~ **an die achtzig** *(ugs.)* pushing eighty *(coll.);* **c)** *(eng)* closely; **3.** *Präp. mit Dat. (geh.)* near; close to; **Nähe die;** ~: closeness

nahe-: ~**bei** *Adv.* nearby; close by; ~**|gehen** *unr. itr. V.; mit sein* jmdm. ~gehen affect sb. deeply; ~**|kommen** *unr. itr. V.; mit sein* einer Sache *(Dat.)* ~kommen come close to sth.; ⟨*amount*⟩ approximate to sth.; jmdm./sich [menschlich] ~kommen get to know sb./one another well; ~**|legen** *tr. V.* suggest; give rise to ⟨*suspicion, supposition, thought*⟩; ~**|liegen** *unr. itr. V.* ⟨*thought*⟩ suggest itself; ⟨*suspicion, question*⟩ arise; ~**liegend** *Adj.* obvious ⟨*reason, solution*⟩

nähen 1. *itr. V.* sew; *(Kleider machen)* make clothes; **2.** *tr. V.* **a)** sew ⟨*seam, hem*⟩; make ⟨*dress etc.*⟩; **b)** *(Med.)* stitch

näher 1. *Komp. zu* **nahe; 2.** *Adj.* **a)** *(kürzer)* shorter ⟨*way, road*⟩; **b)** *(genauer)* more precise ⟨*information*⟩; closer ⟨*investigation, inspection*⟩; **3.** *adv.* **a) bitte treten Sie** ~! please come in/nearer/this way; **b)** *(genauer)* more closely; *(im einzelnen)* in [more] detail

näher|kommen *unr. itr. V.; mit sein* jmdm. |menschlich| ~kommen get on closer terms with sb.; **nähern** *refl. V.* approach; sich jmdm./einer Sache ~: approach sb./sth.

nahe-: ~|stehen *unr. itr. V.* jmdm. ~stehen be on intimate terms with sb.; ~zu *Adv.* almost; nearly; *(mit Zahlenangabe)* close on

Näh-: ~garn das [sewing] cotton; ~kasten der sewing-box

nahm *1. u. 3. Pers. Sg. Prät. v.* nehmen

Näh-: ~maschine die sewing-machine; ~nadel die sewing-needle

nähren *1. tr. V.* feed (mit on); *2. refl. V. (geh.)* sich von etw. ~: live on sth.; ⟨animal⟩ feed on sth.; **nahrhaft** *Adj.* nourishing; **Nahrung die;** ~: food; **Nahrungs·mittel das** food [item]; ~mittel *Pl.* foodstuffs; **Nähr·wert der** nutritional value

Näh·seide die sewing silk

Naht die; ~, Nähte seam

Nah-: ~verkehr der local traffic; ~verkehrs·zug der local train

Näh·zeug das sewing things *pl.*

naiv *1. Adj.* naïve; *2. adv.* naïvely; **Naivität die;** ~: naïvety

Name der; ~ns, ~n name; **namens** *Adv.* by the name of

Namens-: ~schild das a) *(an Türen usw.)* name-plate; b) *(zum Anstecken)* name-badge; ~tag der name-day

namentlich *1. Adj.* by name *postpos.; 2. adv.* by name; *3. Adv. (besonders)* particularly; **namhaft** *Adj.* a) *(berühmt)* noted; b) *(ansehnlich)* noteworthy ⟨sum, difference⟩; notable ⟨contribution, opportunity⟩; **nämlich** *Adv.* a) er kann nicht kommen, er ist ~ krank he cannot come, as he is ill; b) *(und zwar)* namely

nannte *1. u. 3. Pers. Sg. Prät. v.* nennen

nanu *Interj.* ~, was machst du denn hier? hello, what are you doing here?; ~, Sie gehen schon? what, you're going already?

Napf der; ~|e|s, Näpfe bowl *(esp. for animal's food)*

Narbe die; ~, ~n scar; **narbig** *Adj.* scarred

Narkose die; ~, ~n *(Med.)* narcosis

Narr der; ~en, ~en fool; **Narrenfreiheit die** freedom to do as one pleases; **Närrin die;** ~, ~nen fool; **närrisch** *1. Adj.* crazy; carnival-crazy ⟨season⟩; *2. adv.* crazily

Narzisse die; ~, ~n narcissus

naschen *1. itr. V. (Süßes essen)* eat sweet things; *(heimlich essen)* have a nibble; *2. tr. V.* eat ⟨sweets, chocolate, etc.⟩; er hat Milch genascht he has been at the milk; **naschhaft** *Adj.* sweet-toothed; ~ sein have a sweet tooth

Nase die; ~, ~n nose; die ~ voll haben *(ugs.)* have had enough

Nasen-: ~bluten das; ~s bleeding from the nose; ~loch das nostril; ~tropfen *Pl.* nose-drops

nase·weis *1. Adj.* precocious; pert ⟨remark, reply⟩; *2. adv.* precociously; **Nas·horn das** rhinoceros

naß; nasser *od.* nässer, nassest... *od.* nässest...: *Adj.* wet; sich/das Bett ~ machen wet oneself/one's bed; **Nässe die;** ~: wetness; **naß·kalt** *Adj.* cold and wet; **Naß·rasur die** wet shaving *no art.*

Nation die; ~, ~en nation; **national** *1. Adj.* a) national; *2. adv.* nationally

National-: ~elf die *(Fußball)* national side; ~hymne die national anthem

Nationalismus der; ~: nationalism *usu. no art.;* **nationalistisch** *1. Adj.* nationalist; nationalistic; *2. adv.* nationalistically; **Nationalität die;** ~, ~en nationality

national-, National-: ~mannschaft die national team; ~sozialismus der National Socialism; ~sozialist der National Socialist; ~sozialistisch *Adj.* National Socialist

NATO, Nato die; ~: NATO, Nato *no art.*

Natron das; ~s |doppeltkohlensaures| ~: sodium bicarbonate; |kohlensaures| ~: sodium carbonate

Natter die; ~, ~n colubrid

Natur die; ~, ~en nature; die freie ~: [the] open countryside; **Naturalien** [natu'ra:liən] *Pl.* natural produce *sing. (used as payment);* in ~ *(Dat.)* bezahlen pay in kind; **Naturalismus der;** ~: naturalism; **naturalistisch** *1. Adj.* naturalistic; *2. adv.* naturalistically; **Naturell das;** ~s, ~e temperament

natur-, Natur-: ~erscheinung die natural phenomenon; ~farben *Adj.* natural-coloured; ~freund der nature-lover; ~gemäß *Adv.* naturally; ~geschichte die; *o. Pl.* natural history; ~gesetz das law of nature; ~getreu *1. Adj.* lifelike ⟨portrait, imitation⟩; faithful ⟨reproduction⟩; *2. adv.* ⟨draw⟩ true to life; ⟨reproduce⟩

faithfully; ~**heilkunde** die naturo-
pathy *no art.;* ~**katastrophe** die
natural disaster

natürlich 1. *Adj.* natural; 2. *adv.*
⟨*laugh, behave*⟩ naturally; 3. *Adv.* a)
(selbstverständlich, wie erwartet)
naturally; of course; b) *(zwar)* of
course; **Natürlichkeit** die; ~: naturalness

Natur-: ~**park** der ≈ national park;
~**produkt** das natural product;
~**schutz** der [nature] conservation;
~**schutz·gebiet** das nature reserve;
~**verbunden** *Adj.* ⟨*person*⟩ in tune
with nature; ~**volk** das primitive
people; ~**wissenschaft** die natural
science *no art.;* ~**wissenschaftler**
der [natural] scientist; ~**wissenschaftlich** 1. *Adj.* scientific; 2. *adv.*
scientifically; ~**wunder** das miracle
or wonder of nature

Navigation die; ~: navigation *no art.*

n. Chr. *Abk.* nach Christus AD

Neandertaler der; ~s, ~: Neander-
thal man

Nebel der; ~s, ~: fog; *(weniger dicht)*
mist; **nebelig** *s.* neblig

Nebel-: ~**scheinwerfer** der fog-
lamp; ~**wand** die wall of fog

neben 1. *Präp. mit Dat.* a) *(Lage)* next
to; beside; b) *(außer)* apart from;
aside from *(Amer.);* c) *(verglichen mit)*
beside; 2. *Präp. mit Akk. (Richtung)*
next to; beside; **neben·an** *Adv.* next
door; **neben·bei** *Adv.* a) ⟨*work*⟩ on
the side; *(zusätzlich)* as well; b) *(beiläufig)* ⟨*remark, ask*⟩ by the way;
⟨*mention*⟩ in passing

neben-, **Neben**-: ~**beruf** der second
job; sideline; ~**beruflich** 1. *Adj.* eine
~**berufliche Tätigkeit** a second job; 2.
adv. on the side; **er arbeitet** ~**beruflich als Übersetzer** he translates as a
sideline; ~**beschäftigung** die second job; sideline; ~**buhler** der,
~**buhlerin** die rival

neben·einander *Adv.* a) next to each
other; *(fig.: zusammen)* ⟨*live, exist*⟩
side by side; ~ **wohnen** live next door
to each other; b) *(gleichzeitig)*
together

nebeneinander-: ~|**legen** *tr. V.* lay
or place ⟨*objects*⟩ side by side; ~|**set-
zen** *tr. V.* put *or* place ⟨*persons, ob-
jects*⟩ next to each other; ~|**sitzen**
unr. itr. V. sit next to each other;
~|**stellen** *tr. V.* put *or* place ⟨*tables,
chairs, etc.*⟩ next to each other

Neben-: ~**erwerb** der secondary oc-

cupation; ~**fach** das subsidiary subject; minor *(Amer.);* ~**fluß** der tributary; ~**gebäude** das a) annexe; out-
building; b) *(Nachbargebäude)* neighbouring building; ~**geräusch** das
background noise; ~**haus** das house
next door

neben·her *Adv. s.* nebenbei

nebenher-: ~|**fahren** *unr. itr. V.; mit
sein* drive/ride alongside; ~|**gehen**
unr. itr. V.; mit sein walk alongside

neben-, **Neben**-: ~**kosten** *Pl.* a) additional costs; b) *(bei Mieten)* heating,
lighting, and services; ~**produkt** das
by-product; ~**rolle** die supporting
role; ~**sache** die minor matter; ~**sachen** inessentials; ~**sächlich** *Adj.* of
minor importance *postpos.;* unimportant; minor ⟨*detail*⟩; ~**satz** der
(Sprachw.) subordinate clause;
~**straße** die side street; ~**tätigkeit**
die second job; sideline; ~**tisch** der
next table; ~**verdienst** der additional income; ~**wirkung** die side-
effect; ~**zimmer** das next room

neblig *Adj.* foggy; *(weniger dicht)*
misty

Necessaire [nesɛ'sɛːɐ̯] das; ~s, ~s
sponge-bag *(Brit.);* toilet bag *(Amer.)*

necken *tr. V.* tease; **Neckerei** die;
~: teasing

nee *(ugs.)* no; nope *(Amer. coll.)*

Neffe der; ~n, ~n nephew

negativ 1. *Adj.* negative; 2. *adv.* ⟨*answer*⟩ in the negative; **Negativ** das;
~s, ~e *(Fot.)* negative

Neger der; ~s, ~: Negro; **Negerin**
die; ~, ~nen Negress

nehmen *unr. tr. V.* take; **sich** *(Dat.)*
etw. ~: take sth.; *(sich bedienen)* help
oneself to sth.; **auf sich** *(Akk.)* ~: take
on ⟨*responsibility, burden*⟩; **jmdm./ei-
ner Sache etw.** ~: deprive sb./sth. of
sth.; **was nehmen Sie dafür?** how much
do you charge for it?

Neid der; ~[e]s envy; jealousy;
neiden *tr. V. (geh.)* **jmdm. etw.** ~:
envy sb. [for] sth.; **neidisch** 1. *Adj.*
envious; 2. *adv.* enviously

neigen 1. *tr. V.* tip; tilt; incline ⟨*head,
upper part of body*⟩; 2. *refl. V.:* ⟨*person*⟩ lean; ⟨*ship*⟩ heel over, list;
⟨*scales*⟩ tip; 3. *itr. V.* a) **zu Erkältun-
gen/Krankheiten** ~: be prone to
colds/illnesses; b) *(tendieren)* tend;
Neigung die; ~, ~en a) *(Vorliebe)* inclination; b) *o. Pl. (Tendenz)* tendency

nein *Interj.* no; **Nein** das; ~[s], ~[s]
no; **Nein·stimme** die no-vote

Nektar der; ~s, ~e *(Bot.)* nectar; **Nektarine** die; ~, ~n nectarine

Nelke die; ~, ~n a) pink; *(Dianthus caryophyllus)* carnation; b) *(Gewürz)* clove

nennen 1. *unr. tr. V.* a) call; b) *(angeben)* give ⟨name, date of birth, address, reason, price, etc.⟩; c) *(anführen)* give ⟨example⟩; *(erwähnen)* mention ⟨person, name⟩; 2. *unr. refl. V.* ⟨person, thing⟩ be called

neo-, Neo-: neo-

Neon das; ~s neon

Neon-: ~licht das neon light; ~röhre die neon tube

Nepal (das); ~s Nepal

Nepp der; ~s *(ugs. abwertend)* daylight robbery *no art.*; rip-off *(sl.)*; **Nepplokal** das *(ugs. abwertend)* clip-joint *(sl.)*

Nerv der; ~s, ~en nerve; die ~en verlieren lose control [of oneself]; jmdm. auf die ~en gehen *od.* fallen get on sb.'s nerves

nerven-, Nerven-: ~aufreibend *Adj.* nerve-racking; ~bündel das *(ugs.)* bundle of nerves *(coll.)*; ~gift das neurotoxin; ~heilanstalt die *(veralt.)* psychiatric hospital; ~krank *Adj.* ⟨person⟩ suffering from a nervous disease; ~probe die mental trial; ~säge die *(salopp)* pain in the neck *(coll.)*; ~zusammenbruch der nervous breakdown

nervlich *Adj.* nervous ⟨strain⟩; **nervös** 1. *Adj. (auch Med.)* nervous; jittery ⟨person⟩; 2. *adv.* nervously; **Nervosität** die; ~ nervousness; **nervtötend** *Adj.* nerve-racking ⟨wait⟩; soul-destroying ⟨activity, work⟩

Nerz der; ~es, ~e mink; **Nerzmantel** der mink coat

Nessel die; ~, ~n nettle

Nest das; ~[e]s, ~er a) nest; b) *(fam.: Bett)* bed; c) *(ugs. abwertend: kleiner Ort)* little place

nett 1. *Adj.* nice; *(freundlich)* kind; 2. *adv.* nicely; *(freundlich)* nicely; kindly; **netterweise** *Adv.* kindly

netto *Adv.* ⟨weigh, earn, etc.⟩ net

Netto-: ~einkommen das net income; ~gehalt das net salary

Netz das; ~es, ~e a) net; *(Einkaufs~)* string bag; *(Gepäck~)* [luggage-]rack; b) *(Spinnen~)* web; c) *(Verteiler~, Verkehrs~ usw.)* network; *(für Strom, Wasser, Gas)* mains *pl.*; **Netzhaut** die *(Anat.)* retina

neu 1. *Adj.* new; die ~este Mode the latest fashion; das ist mir ~: that is news to me; der/die Neue the new man/woman/boy/girl; 2. *adv.* a) ~ tapeziert/gestrichen repapered/repainted; sich ~ einrichten refurnish one's home; b) *(gerade erst)* diese Ware ist ~ eingetroffen this item has just come in; **neuartig** *Adj.* new; **Neubau** der; *Pl.* Neubauten new house/building; **Neubauwohnung** die flat *(Brit.)* or *(Amer.)* apartment in a new block/house

neuerdings *Adv.* er trägt ~ eine Brille he has recently started wearing glasses; **neueröffnet** *Adj.* a) newly-opened; b) *(wiedereröffnet)* reopened; **Neueröffnung** die a) opening; b) *(Wiedereröffnung)* reopening; **Neuerung** die; ~, ~en innovation; **neugeboren** *Adj.* newborn; **Neugier, Neugierde** die; ~: curiosity; *(Wißbegierde)* inquisitiveness; **neugierig** 1. *Adj.* curious; inquisitive; inquisitive ⟨person⟩; ich bin ~, was er dazu sagt I'm curious to know what he'll say about it; 2. *adv.* ⟨ask⟩ inquisitively; ⟨peer⟩ nosily *(coll. derog.)*; **Neuheit** die; ~, ~en a) *o. Pl.* novelty; b) *(Neues)* new product/gadget/article *etc.*; **Neuigkeit** die; ~, ~en piece of news; ~en news *sing.*; **Neujahr** das New Year's Day; **Neuland** das *(fig.)* new ground; **neulich** *Adv.* recently; ~ morgens the other morning; **Neuling** der; ~s, ~e newcomer; *(auf einem Gebiet)* novice; **Neumond** der new moon

neun *Kardinalz.* nine; **Neun** die; ~, ~en nine

neun-: ~hundert *Kardinalz.* nine hundred; ~jährig *Adj. (9 Jahre alt)* nine-year-old *attrib.*; *(9 Jahre dauernd)* nine-year *attrib.*; ~mal *Adv.* nine times

neunt... *Ordinalz.* ninth

neuntausend *Kardinalz.* nine thousand; **Neuntel** das *(schweiz. meist* der*)*; ~s, ~: ninth; **neuntens** *Adv.* ninthly; **neunzehn** *Kardinalz.* nineteen; **neunzig** *Kardinalz.* ninety; **neunziger** *indekl. Adj.; nicht präd.* die ~ Jahre the nineties; **neunzigst...** *Ordinalz.* ninetieth

neureich *Adj.* nouveau riche

Neurose die; ~, ~n neurosis; **neurotisch** *Adj.* neurotic

Neuseeland (das); ~s New Zealand; **Neuseeländer** der; ~s, ~: New Zealander

neutral 1. *Adj.* neutral; 2. *adv.* sich ~ verhalten remain neutral; **Neutralität die**; ~, ~en neutrality; **Neutron das**; ~s, ~en neutron; **Neutrum das**; ~s, **Neutra** *(österr. nur so) od.* **Neutren** *(Sprachw.)* neuter

neu-, Neu-: ~**wert** der value when new; ~**wertig** *Adj.* as new; ~**zeit die**; o, *Pl.* modern age; ~**zeitlich** *Adj.* modern

nicht *Adv.* **a)** not; ~! [no,] don't!; ~|wahr|? isn't it/he/she *etc.*; don't you/we/they *etc.*; **du magst das,** ~ |wahr|? you like that, don't you?; **was du** ~ **sagst!** you don't say!

nicht-, Nicht-: non-
Nicht·angriffs·pakt der non-aggression pact

Nichte die; ~, ~n niece

nichtig *Adj.* **a)** *(geh.)* vain 〈*things, pleasures, etc.*〉; trivial 〈*reason*〉; **b)** *(Rechtsspr.)* void; **Nicht·raucher** der non-smoker; „~raucher" 'no smoking'; **nicht·rostend** *Adj.* non-rusting 〈*blade*〉; stainless 〈*steel*〉; **nichts** *Indefinitpron.* nothing; **ich möchte** ~: I don't want anything

nichts-, Nichts-: ~**nutz** der; ~es, ~e *(veralt.)* good-for-nothing; ~**nutzig** *Adj. (veralt.)* good-for-nothing *attrib.*; worthless 〈*existence*〉; ~**sagend** 1. *Adj.* empty; *(fig.: ausdruckslos)* expressionless 〈*face*〉; 2. *adv.* meaninglessly 〈*formulated*〉; ~**tun das** idleness *no art.*

Nickel das; ~s nickel
nicken *itr. V.* nod
nie *Adv.* never

nieder 1. *Adj.; nicht präd.* lower 〈*class, intelligence*〉; minor 〈*official*〉; lowly 〈*family, origins, birth*〉; menial 〈*task*〉; 2. *Adv.* down

nieder-, Nieder-: ~**gang** der fall; decline; ~|**gehen** *unr. itr. V.; mit sein* 〈*plane etc., rain, avalanche*〉 come down; ~**geschlagen** *Adj.* dejected; ~**geschlagenheit die**; ~: dejection; ~**lage die** defeat

Nieder·lande *Pl.:* **die** ~: the Netherlands; **Niederländer der**; ~s, ~: Dutchman; **Niederländerin die**; ~, ~nen Dutchwoman; **niederländisch** *Adj.* Dutch; Netherlands *attrib.* 〈*government, embassy, etc.*〉

nieder-, Nieder-: ~|**lassen** *unr. refl. V.* **a)** set up in business; 〈*doctor, lawyer*〉 set up in practice; **b)** *(seinen Wohnsitz nehmen)* settle; ~**lassung die**; ~, ~en *(Wirtsch.)* branch; ~|**le-**

gen *tr. V.* **a)** *(geh.: hinlegen)* lay *or* put down; lay 〈*wreath*〉; **b)** *(fig.)* resign [from] 〈*office*〉; relinquish 〈*command*〉

Nieder·sachsen (das) Lower Saxony

nieder-, Nieder-: ~**schlag** der precipitation; ~|**schlagen** *unr. tr. V.* **a)** jmdn. ~schlagen knock sb. down; **b)** *(beenden)* suppress, put down 〈*revolt, uprising, etc.*〉; **c)** *(senken)* lower 〈*eyes, eyelids*〉; ~**trächtig** 1. *Adj.* malicious 〈*person, slander, lie, etc.*〉; *(verachtenswert)* despicable 〈*person*〉; base 〈*misrepresentation, slander, lie*〉; 2. *adv.* 〈*betray, lie, treat*〉 in a despicable way; ~**trächtigkeit die**; ~, ~en **a)** o. *Pl. s.* ~trächtig 1: maliciousness; despicableness; baseness; **b)** *(gemeine Handlung)* despicable act

Niederung die; ~, ~en low-lying area; *(an Flußläufen, Küsten)* flats *pl.; (Tal)* valley

niedlich 1. *Adj.* sweet; cute *(Amer. coll.)*; 2. *adv.* sweetly

niedrig 1. *Adj.* low; lowly 〈*origins, birth*〉; base 〈*instinct, desire, emotion*〉; vile 〈*motive*〉; 2. *adv.* 〈*hang, fly*〉 low

niemals *Adv.* never; **niemand** *Indefinitpron.* nobody; no one

Niere die; ~, ~n kidney
Nieren-: ~**entzündung** die nephritis; ~**stein** der kidney stone

Niesel·regen der drizzle
niesen *itr. V.* sneeze

¹**Niete die**; ~, ~n **a)** *(Los)* blank; **b)** *(ugs.: Mensch)* dead loss *(coll.)* (in + *Dat.* at)

²**Niete die**; ~, ~n rivet; **nieten** *tr. V.* rivet

Nikolaus·tag der St Nicholas' Day
Nikotin das; ~s nicotine; **nikotin·arm** *Adj.* low-nicotine *attrib.;* low in nicotine *pred.*

Nil der; ~|s| Nile; **Nil·pferd das** hippopotamus

nimm *Imperativ Sg. v.* nehmen
nippen *itr. V.* sip

nirgends, nirgend·wo *Adv.* nowhere

Nische die; ~, ~n niche; *(Erweiterung eines Raumes)* recess

nisten *itr. V.* nest
Nitrat das; ~|e|s, ~e nitrate
Niveau [ni'vo:] **das**; ~s, ~s level; *(Qualitäts~)* standard

Nixe die; ~, ~n nixie; *(mit Fischschwanz)* mermaid

nobel *Adj.* **a)** *(geh.)* noble;

noble[-minded] ⟨*person*⟩; b) *(oft spött.: luxuriös)* elegant; posh *(coll.)*

Nobel·preis der Nobel prize

noch 1. *Adv.* a) *[(wie) bisher)* still; ~ nicht not yet; sie sind immer ~ nicht da they're still not here; **ich habe Großvater** ~ **gekannt** I'm old enough to have known grandfather; **er hat** ~ **Glück gehabt** he was lucky; **das geht** ~: that's [still] all right; b) *(als Rest einer Menge)* **ich habe |nur|** ~ **zehn Mark** I've [only] ten marks left; **es sind** ~ **10 km bis zur Grenze** it's another 10 km. to the border; c) *(bevor etw. anderes geschieht)* just; **ich will** ~ **|schnell| duschen** I just want to have a [quick] shower; d) *(irgendwann einmal)* some time; one day; **er wird** ~ **anrufen/kommen** he will still call/come; e) *(womöglich)* if you're/he's *etc.* not careful; **du kommst** ~ **zu spät!** you'll be late if you're not careful; f) *(drückt eine geringe zeitliche Distanz aus)* only; **gestern habe ich ihn** ~ **gesehen** I saw him only yesterday; g) *(nicht später als)* ~ **am selben Abend** the [very] same evening; h) *(außerdem, zusätzlich)* **wer war** ~ **da?** who else was there?; ~ **etwas Kaffee?** [would you like] some more coffee?; **Geld/Kleider** *usw.* ~ **und** ~ heaps and heaps of money/clothes *etc. (coll.)*; i) **er ist** ~ **größer |als Karl|** he is even taller [than Karl]; **er will** ~ **mehr haben** he wants even more; **jeder** ~ **so dumme Mensch versteht das** anyone, however stupid, can understand that; j) **wie heißt s¹e |doch|** ~**?** [now] what's her name again?; 2. *Partikel* **das ist** ~ **Qualität!** that's what I call quality; **der wird sich** ~ **wundern** *(ugs.)* he's in for a surprise; **er kann** ~ **nicht einmal lesen** he can't even read; 3. *Konj. (und auch nicht)* nor; **weder ...** ~ **noch** neither ... nor; **noch·mals** *Adv.* again

Nominativ der; ~s, ~e *(Sprachw.)* nominative [case]

Nonne die; ~, ~n nun

Nord *o. Art.; o. Pl. (bes. Seemannsspr., Met.)* s. Norden

nord-, Nord-: ~**afrika** (das) North Africa; ~**amerika** (das) North America; ~**deutsch** *Adj.* North German

Norden der; ~s north; **der** ~: the North; **nach** ~: northwards; **Nordirland** (das) Northern Ireland; **nordisch** *Adj.* Nordic; **Nord·kap** das North Cape; **nördlich** 1. *Adj.* a) *(im* Norden gelegen)* northern; b) *(nach, aus dem Norden)* northerly; c) *(aus dem Norden kommend, für den Norden typisch)* Northern; 2. *adv.* northwards; ~ **von ...**: [to the] north of ...; 3. *Präp. mit Gen.* [to the] north of; **Nord·pol** ['--] der North Pole; **Nord·rhein-Westfalen** (das); ~s North Rhine-Westphalia; **Nord·see** die; *o. Pl.* North Sea; **nord·wärts** *Adv.* northwards; **Nord·wind** der northerly wind

Nörgelei die; ~ *(abwertend) o. Pl.* grumbling; **nörgeln** *itr. V. (abwertend)* moan, grumble **(an** + *Dat.* about)

Norm die; ~, ~en a) norm; b) *(geforderte Arbeitsleistung)* quota; c) *(Sport)* qualifying standard; d) *(technische, industrielle* ~) standard; **normal** 1. *Adj.* normal; 2. *adv.* normally; **Normal·benzin** das ≈ two-star petrol *(Brit.)*; regular *(Amer.)*; **normalerweise** *Adv.* normally; **normalisieren** 1. *tr. V.* normalize; 2. *refl. V.* return to normal

Normandie die; ~: Normandy

normen *tr. V.,* **normieren** *tr. V.* standardize

Norwegen (das); ~s Norway; **Norweger** der; ~s, ~, **Norwegerin** die; ~, ~nen Norwegian; **norwegisch** *Adj.* Norwegian

Nostalgie die; ~: nostalgia

Not die; ~, Nöte a) *(Gefahr)* **in** ~ **sein** be in desperate straits; b) *o. Pl. (Mangel, Armut)* need; poverty [and hardship]; ~ **leiden** suffer poverty [and hardship]; **in** ~ **geraten/sein** encounter hard times/be suffering want [and deprivation]; c) *o. Pl. (Verzweiflung)* distress; d) *(Sorge, Mühe)* trouble; **mit knapper** ~: by the skin of one's teeth; f) *o. Pl. (veralt.: Notwendigkeit)* necessity; **zur** ~: if need be

Notar der; ~s, ~e notary; **Notariat** das; ~|e|s, ~e a) *(Amt)* notaryship; b) *(Kanzlei)* notary's office

not-, Not-: ~**arzt** der doctor on [emergency] call; ~**ausgang** der emergency exit; ~**bremse** die emergency brake; ~**dienst** der s. Bereitschaftsdienst; ~**dürftig** 1. *Adj.* makeshift ⟨*shelter, repair*⟩; scanty ⟨*cover, clothing*⟩; 2. *adv.* scantily ⟨*clothed*⟩

Note die; ~, ~n a) *(Zeichen)* note; b) *Pl. (Text)* music *sing.*; c) *(Schul*~) mark; d) *(Eislauf, Turnen)* score

not-, Not-: ~**fall** der a) emergency; b)

im ~**fall** *(nötigenfalls)* if need be; ~**falls** *Adv.* if need be; ~**gedrungen** *Adv.* of necessity

notieren 1. *tr. V.* [sich *(Dat.)*] etw. ~: make a note of sth.; 2. *itr. V. (Börsenw., Wirtsch.)* be quoted (mit at)

nötig 1. *Adj.* necessary; etw./jmdn. ~ **haben** need sth./sb.; 2. *adv.* er braucht ~ Hilfe he is in urgent need of help; **nötigen** *tr. V.* compel; force; *(Rechtsspr.)* coerce

Notiz die; ~, ~en note; *(Zeitungs~)* brief report; von jmdm./etw. [keine] ~ **nehmen** take [no] notice of sb./sth.

Notiz-: ~block der; *Pl.* ~blocks, *schweiz.:* ~blöcke notepad; ~**buch** das notebook

not-, Not-: ~lage die serious difficulties *pl.;* ~**landen**[1] *itr. V.; mit sein* do an emergency landing; ~**landung** die emergency landing; ~**leidend** *Adj.* needy; ~**lösung** die stopgap; ~**lüge** die evasive lie; *(aus Rücksichtnahme)* white lie

notorisch 1. *Adj.* notorious; 2. *adv.* notoriously

Not-: ~ruf der a) *(Hilferuf)* emergency call; *(eines Schiffes)* Mayday call; b) *(Nummer)* emergency number; ~**ruf·nummer** die emergency number; ~**ruf·säule** die emergency telephone *(mounted in a pillar);* ~**stand** der crisis; *(Staatsrecht)* state of emergency; ~**unterkunft** die emergency accommodation *no pl., no indef. art.;* ~**wehr** die self-defence

not·wendig *Adj.* necessary; **Notwendigkeit** die; ~, ~en necessity

Nougat ['nu:gat] der; *auch* das; ~s nougat

Novelle die; ~, ~n *(Literaturw.)* novella

November der; ~[s], ~: November

Nr. *Abk.* Nummer No

Nu der: im Nu in no time

Nuance ['nゔã:sə] die; ~, ~n nuance; *(Grad)* shade

nüchtern 1. *Adj. (nicht betrunken; realistisch)* sober; *(ungeschminkt)* bare, plain *(fact);* der Patient muß ~ sein the patient's stomach must be empty; 2. *adv.* soberly

nuckeln *(ugs.) itr. V.* suck (an + *Dat.* at)

Nudel die; ~, ~n piece of spaghetti/vermicelli/tortellini *etc.; (als Suppen-*

einlage) noodle; ~n *(Teigwaren)* pasta *sing.; (als Suppeneinlage)* noodles

nuklear 1. *Adj.* nuclear; 2. *adv.* ~ **angetrieben** nuclear-powered

null *Kardinalz.* nought; ~ **Komma sechs** [nought] point six; **gegen** ~ **Uhr** around twelve midnight; **Null** die; ~, ~en a) nought; zero; in ~ **Komma nichts** *(ugs.)* in less than no time; **gleich** ~ **sein** *(fig.)* be practically zero; **auf** ~ **stehen** *(indicator, needle, etc.)* be at zero; b) *(ugs.: Versager)* failure; dead loss *(coll.);* **Null·punkt** der zero

numerieren *tr. V.* number; **Numerierung** die; ~, ~en numbering; **Nummer** die; ~, ~n a) number; ein **Wagen mit** [einer] **Münchner** ~: a car with a Munich registration; **ich bin unter der** ~ 24 26 79 **zu erreichen** I can be reached on 24 26 79; b) *(Ausgabe)* issue; c) *(Größe)* size; **Nummern·schild** das number-plate; license plate *(Amer.)*

nun 1. *Adv.* now; 2. *Partikel* now; **das hast du** ~ **davon!** it serves you right!; **kommst du** ~ **mit oder nicht?** now are you coming or not?; ~ **gut** [well,] all right; ~, ~! now, come on; ~ **ja** ...: well, yes ...

nur 1. *Adv.* a) *(nicht mehr als)* only; just; b) *(ausschließlich)* only; **nicht** ~ ..., **sondern auch** ...: not only ..., but also ...; ~ **zu seinem Spaß** just for fun; 2. *Konj.* but; **ich kann dir das Buch leihen,** ~ **nicht heute** I can lend you the book, only not today; 3. *Partikel* wenn er ~ **hier wäre** if only he were here; ~ **zu!** go ahead; **laß dich** ~ **nicht erwischen** just don't let me/them *etc.* catch you; **was sollen wir** ~ **tun?** what on earth are we going to do?; **so schnell er** ~ **konnte** just as fast as he could

Nürnberg (das); ~s Nuremberg

Nuß die; ~, Nüsse a) nut; **Nuß·baum** der walnut-tree; **Nuß·knacker** der nutcrackers *pl.*

Nutte die; ~, ~n *(derb)* tart *(sl.);* hooker *(Amer. sl.)*

nutz-: ~bar *Adj.* usable; exploitable, utilizable ⟨*mineral resources, invention*⟩; cultivatable ⟨*land, soil*⟩; ~**bringend** 1. *Adj.* useful; *(gewinnbringend)* profitable; 2. *adv.* profitably

nutzen 1. *tr. V.* a) use; exploit, utilize ⟨*natural resources*⟩; cultivate ⟨*land, soil*⟩; harness ⟨*energy source*⟩; exploit ⟨*advantage*⟩; b) *(be~, aus~)* use; make use of; 2. *itr. V. s.* **nützen** 1;

---

[1] *ich notlande, notgelandet, notzulanden*

Nutzen der; ~s a) benefit; [jmdm.] von ~ sein be of use [to sb.]; b) *(Profit)* profit; **nützen** 1. *itr. V.* be of use *(Dat.* to); **nichts ~:** be no use; 2. *tr. V. s.* nutzen 1; **nützlich** *Adj.* useful; **nutzlos** 1. *Adj.* useless; *(vergeblich)* vain *attrib.;* in vain *pred.;* 2. *adv.* uselessly; *(vergeblich)* in vain; **Nutz·losigkeit die;** ~: uselessness; *(Vergeblichkeit)* futility; **Nutznießer der;** ~s, ~, **Nutznießerin die;** ~, ~nen beneficiary; **Nutzung die;** ~, ~en use; *(des Landes, des Bodens)* cultivation; *(von Bodenschätzen)* exploitation; *(einer Energiequelle)* harnessing

Nylon ⓦ ['nailɔn] **das;** ~s nylon

Nymphe die; ~, ~n *(Myth., Zool.)* nymph

Nymphomanin die; ~, ~nen *(Psych.)* nymphomaniac

O

o, O das; ~, ~: o/O

O *Abk.* Ost[en] E

ö, Ö das; ~, ~: o/O umlaut

o. ä. *Abk.* oder ähnlich[es] or similar

Oase die; ~, ~n *(auch fig.)* oasis

ob *Konj.* a) whether; b) **und ob!** of course!

OB *Abk.* Oberbürgermeister

Obacht die; ~ *(bes. südd.)* caution; ~ **auf jmdn./etw. geben** take care of sb./ sth.; *(aufmerksam sein)* pay attention to sb./sth.

Obdach das; ~[e]s *(geh.)* shelter; **obdach·los** *Adj.* homeless; **Obdachlose der/die;** *adj. Dekl.* homeless person/man/woman; **die** ~**n** the homeless

Obduktion die; ~, ~en *(Med., Rechtsw.)* post-mortem [examination]; autopsy

O-Beine *Pl.* bandy legs; bow-legs

oben *Adv.* a) hier/dort ~: up here/ there; **weiter** ~: further up; **nach** ~: upwards; **von** ~: from above; **von** ~ **herab** *(fig.)* condescendingly; b) *(im Gebäude)* upstairs; **nach** ~: upstairs;

c) *(am oberen Ende, zum oberen Ende hin)* at the top; **nach** ~ [hin] towards the top; **von** ~: from the top; c) *(an der Oberseite)* on top; d) *(in einer Hierarchie, Rangfolge)* at the top; e) *([weiter] vorn im Text)* above; **oben·genannt** *Adj.* above-mentioned

ober... *Adj.* upper *attrib.;* top *attrib.*

Ober der; ~s, ~: waiter; **Herr** ~! waiter!

Ober-: ~**arm der** upper arm; ~**bekleidung die** outer clothing; ~**bürgermeister der** mayor

Ober·fläche die surface; *(Flächeninhalt)* surface area; **oberflächlich** 1. *Adj.* superficial; 2. *adv.* superficially

ober·halb 1. *Adv.* above; ~ **von** above; 2. *Präp. mit Gen.* above

Ober-: ~**haupt das** head; *(einer Verschwörung)* leader; ~**hemd das** shirt; ~**kiefer der** upper jaw; ~**körper der** upper part of the body; ~**schenkel der** thigh; ~**schicht die** *(Soziol.)* upper class; ~**schule die** secondary school; ~**seite die** top

oberst... *s.* ober...

Ober·teil das *od.* **der** top [part]; *(eines Bikinis, Anzugs, Kleids usw.)* top [half]

ob·gleich *Konj. s.* obwohl

obig *Adj.* above

Objekt das; ~s, ~e object; *(Kaufmannsspr.: Immobilie)* property; **objektiv** 1. *Adj.* objective; 2. *adv.* objectively; **Objektiv das;** ~s, ~e lens; **Objektivität die;** ~: objectivity

Obrigkeit die; ~, ~en authorities *pl.*

ob·schon *Konj. (geh.)* although

Obst das, ~[e]s fruit

Obst-: ~**baum der** fruit-tree; ~**garten der** orchard; ~**kuchen der** fruit flan; ~**saft der** fruit juice

obszön 1. *Adj.* obscene; 2. *adv.* obscenely; **Obszönität die;** ~, ~en obscenity

ob·wohl *Konj.* although; though

Ochse ['ɔksə] **der;** ~n, ~n a) ox; bullock; b) *(salopp)* numskull *(coll.);* **Ochsen·schwanz·suppe die** oxtail soup

od. *Abk.* oder

öde *Adj.* a) deserted; desolate ⟨area, landscape⟩; b) *(unfruchtbar)* barren; c) *(langweilig)* tedious; dreary ⟨life, time, existence⟩; **Öde die;** ~: *s.* öde a–c: desertedness; desolateness; barrenness; tediousness; dreariness

oder *Konj.* or; *(in Fragen)* **er ist doch hier,** ~**?** he is here, isn't he? *(zweifelnd)* he is here – or isn't he?

OEZ *Abk.* osteuropäische Zeit EET
Ofen der; ~s, **Öfen** heater; *(Kohle~)*
stove; *(Back~)* oven; *(Brenn~, Trok-
ken~)* kiln; **Ofen·rohr** das [stove]
flue
offen 1. *Adj.* **a)** open; **ein ~es Hemd** a
shirt with the collar unfastened; ~ **haben** *od.* **sein** be open; ~**es Licht** a
naked light; **b)** *(frei)* vacant ⟨*job,
post*⟩; **c)** *(ungewiß, ungeklärt)* open
⟨*question*⟩; uncertain ⟨*result*⟩; **d)** *(noch
nicht bezahlt)* outstanding ⟨*bill*⟩; **e)**
(freimütig, aufrichtig) frank [and
open] ⟨*person*⟩; frank, candid ⟨*look,
opinion, reply*⟩; 2. *adv.* openly; ~ **gesagt** frankly; to be frank; **offen·bar**
1. *Adj.* obvious; 2. *adv.* obviously;
Offenbarung die; ~, ~**en** revela-
tion; **offen|bleiben** *unr. itr. V.; mit
sein* **a)** stay open; **b)** *(ungeklärt bleiben)* remain open; ⟨*decision*⟩ be left
open; **Offen·heit** die; ~: *s.* offen e:
frankness [and openness]; candour
offen-: ~**kundig** 1. *Adj.* obvious; 2.
adv. obviously; ~**lassen** *unr. tr. V.*
etw. ~**lassen** leave sth. open; ~**sichtlich** 1. *Adj.* obvious; 2. *adv.* obviously
offensiv 1. *Adj.* **a)** offensive; **b)**
(Sport) attacking; 2. *adv.* **a)** offens-
ively; **b)** *(Sport)* ~ **spielen** play an attacking game; **Offensive** die; ~, ~**n**
(auch Sport) offensive
offen|stehen *unr. itr. V.* be open
öffentlich 1. *Adj.* public; state *attrib.,*
[state-] maintained ⟨*school*⟩; **der** ~**e**
Dienst the civil service; 2. *adv.* publicly; ⟨*perform, appear*⟩ in public; **Öffentlichkeit** die; ~: public
offiziell 1. *Adj.* official; 2. *adv.* officially
Offizier der; ~s, ~**e** officer
öffnen 1. *tr. V.* open; turn on ⟨*tap*⟩;
undo ⟨*coat, blouse, button, zip*⟩; 2. *itr.
V.* **a)** [jmdm.] ~: open the door [to sb.];
b) *(geöffnet werden)* ⟨*shop, bank, etc.*⟩
open; 3. *refl. V.* open; **Öffner** der;
~s, ~: opener; **Öffnung** die; ~, ~**en**
opening; **Öffnungs·zeiten** *Pl.*
opening times
oft *Adv.* öfter, **am öftesten** often; **wie
oft soll ich dir noch sagen, daß ...?** how
many [more] times do I have to tell
you that ...?; **öfter** *Adv.* now and
then; **oftmals** *Adv.* often; frequently
OG *Abk.* Obergeschoß
ohne 1. *Präp. mit Akk.* without; ~
mich! [you can] count me out!; ~ **weiteres** *(leicht, einfach)* easily; *(ohne Ein-*

wand) readily; 2. *Konj.* ~ **zu zögern**
without hesitation; **ohne·hin** *Adv.*
anyway
Ohnmacht die; ~, ~**en a)** faint; **in** ~
fallen faint; **b)** *(Machtlosigkeit)*
powerlessness; impotence; **ohnmächtig** 1. *Adj.* **a)** unconscious; ~
werden faint; ~ **sein** have fainted; **b)**
(machtlos) powerless; impotent; 2.
adv. impotently; ~ **zusehen** watch
helplessly
Ohr das; ~|e|s, ~**en** ear; **gute/schlechte**
~**en haben** have good/poor hearing
sing.; **jmdn. übers** ~ **hauen** *(fig. ugs.)*
put one over on sb. *(coll.);* **Öhr** das,
~|e|s, ~**e** eye; **Ohren·schmerz** der
earache; ~**schmerzen haben** have [an]
earache *sing.*
ohr-, Ohr-: ~**feige** die box on the
ears; ~**feigen** *tr. V.* jmdn. ~**feigen**
box sb.'s ears; **ich könnte mich ~fei-
gen!** *(ugs.)* I could kick myself!;
~**läppchen** das ear-lobe; ~**ring** der
ear-ring
okay [o'ke] *(ugs.) Interj., Adj., adv.* OK
(coll.); okay *(coll.)*
öko-, Öko-: eco-
Ökologie die; ~: ecology; **ökologisch** 1. *Adj.* ecological; 2. *adv.* ecologically
ökonomisch 1. *Adj.* **a)** economic; **b)**
(sparsam) economical; 2. *adv.* economically
Oktober der; ~|s|, ~: October
Öl das; ~|e|s, ~**e** oil; **in Öl malen** paint
in oils; **ölen** *tr. V.* oil; **Öl·farbe** die
a) oil-based paint; **b)** *(zum Malen)* oil-
paint; **ölig** *Adj.* oily
Olive die; ~, ~**n** olive
Öl-: ~**ofen** der oil heater; ~**sardine**
die sardine in oil; **eine Dose** ~**n** a tin of
sardines; ~**wechsel** der *(bes. Kfz-
W.)* oil-change
Olympiade die; ~, ~**n** Olympic
Games *pl.;* Olympics *pl.;* **Olympia-
stadion** das Olympic stadium;
olympisch *Adj.* Olympic; **die Olym-
pischen Spiele** the Olympic Games;
the Olympics
Oma die; ~, ~**s** *(fam.)* granny *(coll./
child lang.)*
Omelett [ɔm[ə]'lɛt] das; ~|e|s, ~**e** *od.*
~**s** omelette
Omnibus der; ~**ses**, ~**se** omnibus
(formal); *(Privat- und Reisebus auch)*
coach
Onkel der; ~s, ~ *od. (ugs.)* ~**s** uncle
OP [o:'pe:] der; ~|s|, ~|s| *Abk.* Operati-
onssaal

Opa der; ~s, ~s *(fam.)* grandad *(coll./ child lang.)*

Opal der; ~s, ~e opal

OPEC ['o:pɛk] die; ~ *Abk.* OPEC

Oper die; ~, ~n opera; *(Opernhaus)* Opera; opera-house

Operation die; ~, ~en operation; **Operations·saal** der operating-theatre *(Brit.) or* -room

Operette die; ~, ~n operetta

operieren 1. *tr. V.* operate on ⟨*patient*⟩; 2. *itr. V.* operate

Opern·glas das opera-glass[es *pl.*]

Opfer das; ~s, ~: a) sacrifice; b) *(Geschädigter)* victim; **opfern** *tr. V. (auch fig.)* sacrifice; offer up ⟨*fruit, produce, etc.*⟩

Opium das; ~s opium

opponieren *itr. V.* **gegen** jmdn./etw. ~: oppose sb./sth.; **Opposition** die; ~, ~en opposition; **oppositionell** *Adj.* opposition *attrib.* ⟨*group, movement, etc.*⟩; ⟨*newspaper, writer, artist, etc.*⟩ opposed to the government

Optik die; ~: optics *sing., no art.;* **Optiker** der; ~s, ~: optician

optimal 1. *Adj.* optimal; optimum *attrib;* 2. *adv.* jmdn. ~ **beraten** give sb. the best possible advice; **Optimismus** der; ~: optimism; **Optimist** der; ~en, ~en, **Optimistin** die; ~, ~nen optimist; **optimistisch** 1. *Adj.* optimistic; 2. *adv.* optimistically

optisch 1. *Adj.* optical; visual ⟨*impression*⟩; eine ~e Täuschung an optical illusion; 2. *adv.* optically; visually ⟨*impressive, effective*⟩

orange [o'rã:ʒ(ə)] *indekl. Adj.* orange; **Orange** die; ~, ~n orange

Orangen-: ~**marmelade** die orange marmalade; ~**saft** der orange-juice

Orchester [ɔr'kɛstɐ] das; ~s, ~: orchestra

Orden der; ~s, ~ a) order; b) *(Ehrenzeichen)* decoration

ordentlich 1. *Adj.* a) [neat and] tidy; neat ⟨*handwriting, clothes*⟩; b) *(anständig)* respectable; proper ⟨*manners*⟩; c) *(planmäßig)* ordinary ⟨*meeting*⟩; ~es Mitglied full member; d) *(ugs.: richtig)* proper; real; ein ~es Stück Kuchen a nice big piece of cake; e) *(ugs.: recht gut)* decent ⟨*wine, flat, marks, etc.*⟩; ganz ~: pretty good; 2. *adv.* a) tidily; neatly; ⟨*write*⟩ neatly; b) *(anständig)* properly; c) *(ugs.: gehörig)* ~ feiern have a real good celebration *(coll.);* d) *(ugs.: recht gut)* ⟨*ski, speak, etc.*⟩ really well

Ordinal·zahl die ordinal [number]; **ordinär** 1. *Adj.* vulgar; 2. *adv.* vulgarly; **Ordinate** die; ~, ~n *(Math.)* ordinate

ordnen *tr. V.* arrange; **sein Leben/seine Finanzen** ~: straighten out one's life/put one's finances in order; **Ordner** der; ~s, ~: file; **Ordnung** die; ~, ~en order; *(geregelter Ablauf)* routine; ~ **halten** keep things tidy; **in** ~ **sein** *(ugs.)* be OK *(coll.) or* all right; **hier ist etw. nicht in** ~: there's something wrong here; **sie ist in** ~ *(ugs.)* she's OK *(coll.);* **in** ~! *(ugs.)* OK! *(coll.);* all right!

ordnungs-, Ordnungs-: ~**gemäß** 1. *Adj.* ⟨*conduct etc.*⟩ in accordance with the regulations; 2. *adv.* in accordance with the regulations; ~**halber** *Adv.* as a matter of form; ~**widrig** *(Rechtsw.)* 1. *Adj.* ⟨*actions, behaviour, etc.*⟩ contravening the regulations; illegal ⟨*parking*⟩; 2. *adv.* ~**widrig parken** park illegally; ~**zahl** die ordinal [number]

Organ das; ~s, ~e organ; *(ugs.: Stimme)* voice; **Organisation** die; ~, ~en organization; **Organisator** der; ~s, ~en organizer; **organisatorisch** *Adj.* organizational; **organisch** 1. *Adj.* organic; 2. *adv.* organically; **organisieren** 1. *tr. V.* organize; 2. *itr. V.* gut ~ **können** be a good organizer; 3. *refl. V.* organize; **Organismus** der; **Organismen** organism

Organist der; ~en, ~en, **Organistin** die; ~, ~nen organist

Orgasmus der; ~, **Orgasmen** orgasm

Orgel die; ~, ~n organ

Orgie ['ɔrgiə] die; ~, ~n *(auch fig.)* orgy

Orient ['o:riɛnt] der; ~s Middle East and south-western Asia *(including Afghanistan and Nepal);* der **Vordere** ~: the Middle East; **orientalisch** *Adj.* oriental; **orientieren** 1. *refl. V.* a) get one's bearings; b) sich über etw. *(Akk.)* ~ *(fig.)* inform oneself about sth.; c) sich an etw. *(Dat.)* ~ *(fig.)* be oriented towards sth.; ⟨*policy, advertising*⟩ be geared towards sth; 2. *tr. V. (unterrichten)* inform ⟨über + *Akk.* about⟩; **Orientierung** die; ~ a) die ~ verlieren lose one's bearings; b) *(Unterrichtung)* zu Ihrer ~: for your information; **Orientierungs·sinn** der sense of direction

original 1. *Adj.* original; 2. *adv.* ~ **italienischer Espresso** genuine Italian espresso coffee; **etw.** ~ **übertragen** broadcast sth. live; **Original das**; ~s, ~e original; **Original·fassung die** original version; **Originalität die**; ~: originality; **originell 1.** *Adj.* original; **2.** *adv.* with originality

Orkan der; ~|e|s, ~e hurricane

Ornament das; ~|e|s, ~e ornament

¹**Ort der**; ~|e|s, ~e place; (Dorf) village; (Stadt) town; **an** ~ **und Stelle** there and then; ²**Ort: vor** ~ *(fig.)* on the spot

Orthographie die; ~; ~n orthography; **orthographisch 1.** *Adj.* orthographic; ~e **Fehler** spelling mistakes; **2.** *adv.* orthographically; **Orthopäde der**; ~n, ~n orthopaedic specialist; **orthopädisch 1.** *Adj.* orthopaedic; **2.** *adv.* orthopaedically

örtlich 1. *Adj.* (auch Med.) local; **2.** *adv.* (auch Med.) locally; ~ **betäubt werden** be given a local anaesthetic; **Ortschaft die**; ~, ~en (Dorf) village; (Stadt) town

Orts-: ~**gespräch das** (Fernspr.) local call; ~**name der** place-name; ~**netz·kennzahl die** (Fernspr.) dialling code; area code (Amer.)

Öse die; ~, ~n eye

Ossi der; ~s, ~s (salopp) East German

Ost o. Art.; o. Pl. (bes. Seemannsspr., Met.) s. **Osten**

ost-, Ost-: ~**block der**; o. Pl. Eastern bloc; ~**deutsch** *Adj.* Eastern German; (hist.: auf die DDR bezogen) East German; ~**deutschland (das)** Eastern Germany; (hist.: DDR) East Germany

Osten der; ~s east; **der** ~: the East; **der Ferne** ~: the Far East; **der Nahe** ~: the Middle East

Oster-: ~**ei das** Easter egg; ~**glocke die** daffodil; ~**hase der** Easter hare (said to bring children their Easter Eggs)

Ostern das; ~, ~: Easter; **Frohe** od. **Fröhliche** ~: Happy Easter!; **zu** ~: at Easter

Österreich (das); ~s Austria; **Österreicher der**; ~s, Österreicherin **die** ~, ~nen Austrian; **österreichisch** *Adj.* Austrian

Ost·europa (das) Eastern Europe; **östlich 1.** *Adj.* **a)** (im Osten gelegen) eastern; **b)** (nach, aus dem Osten) easterly; **c)** (aus dem Osten kommend, für den Osten typisch; Politik) Eastern; ⟨influence, policies⟩ of the East; **2.** *adv.* eastwards; ~ **von** ...: [to the] east of ...;

3. *Präp. mit Gen.* [to the] east of; **Ost·see die**; o. Pl. Baltic [Sea]; **ost·wärts** *Adv.* eastwards; **Ost·wind der** easterly wind

¹**Otter der**; ~s, ~ (Fisch~) otter

²**Otter die**; ~, ~n (Viper) adder; viper

Otto·motor der Otto engine

Ouvertüre [uvɛrˈtyːrə] **die**; ~, ~n (auch fig.) overture (Gen. to)

oval *Adj.* oval

Ozean der; ~s, ~e ocean; **Ozean·dampfer der** ocean liner

Ozon der od. **das**; ~s ozone

P

p, P [pe] **das**; ~, ~: p/P

paar *indekl. Indefinitpron.* **ein** ~ ...: a few ...; (zwei od. drei) a couple of ...; **Paar das**; ~|e|s, ~e pair; (Mann und Frau) couple; **ein** ~ **Würstchen** two sausages; **paaren** refl. V. ⟨animals⟩ mate; ⟨people⟩ copulate; **Paar·lauf der** pairs pl.; **paar·mal** Adv. **ein** ~**mal** a few times; (zwei- oder dreimal) a couple of times; **paar·weise** Adv. in pairs

Pacht die; ~, ~en **a)** lease; **etw. in** ~ **nehmen** lease sth.; **etw. in** ~ **haben** have sth. on lease; **etw. in** ~ **geben** lease sth.; **pachten** tr. V. lease; **Pächter der**; ~s, ~, **Pächterin die** ~, ~nen leaseholder; (eines Hofes) tenant

¹**Pack der**; ~|e|s, ~e od. **Päcke a)** pack; **b)** s. **Packen**; ²**Pack das**; ~|e|s (ugs. abwertend) rabble; **Päckchen das**; ~s, ~ **a)** package; (auch Postw.) small parcel; (Bündel) packet; **b)** s. **Packung a; packen 1.** tr. V. **a)** pack; **b)** (fassen) grab [hold of]; (fig.) **Furcht packte ihn/er wurde von Furcht gepackt** he was seized with fear; **2.** itr. V. (Koffer usw. ~) pack; **Packen der**; ~s, ~: pile; (zusammengeschnürt) bundle; (von Geldscheinen) wad; **Pack·papier das** [stout] wrapping-paper; **Packung die**; ~, ~en **a)** packet; pack (esp. Amer.); **b)** (Med., Kosmetik) pack

Pädagoge der; ~n, ~n *(Erzieher, Lehrer)* teacher; *(Wissenschaftler)* educationalist; **pädagogisch** 1. *Adj.* educational; **seine ~en Fähigkeiten** his teaching ability *sing.;* 2. *adv.* educationally ⟨*sound, wrong*⟩

Paddel das; ~s, ~: paddle; **Paddel·boot** das canoe; **paddeln** *itr. V.; mit sein* paddle; *(als Sport)* canoe

paffen 1. *tr. V.* puff at ⟨*pipe etc.*⟩; 2. *itr. V.* puff away

Page ['pa:ʒə] der; ~n, ~n bellboy

Paket das; ~[e]s, ~e pile; *(zusammengeschnürt)* bundle; *(Eingepacktes, Post~)* parcel; *(Packung)* packet; pack *(esp. Amer.)*

Paket-: ~**karte** die parcel dispatch form; ~**schalter** der parcels counter

Pakistan (das); ~s Pakistan; **Pakistaner** der; ~s, ~, **Pakistani** der; ~[s], ~[s] Pakistani; **pakistanisch** *Adj.* Pakistani

Pakt der; ~[e]s, ~e pact; **paktieren** *itr. V.* make *or* do a deal/deals

Palast der; ~[e]s, **Paläste** palace

Palästina (das); ~s Palestine; **Palästinenser** der; ~s, ~: Palestinian; **palästinensisch** *Adj.* Palestinian

Palette die; ~, ~n palette

Palme die; ~, ~n palm[-tree]

Pampelmuse die; ~, ~n grapefruit

Panama (das); ~s Panama; **Panama·kanal** der; *o. Pl.* Panama Canal

panieren *tr. V.* bread; coat ⟨*sth.*⟩ with breadcrumbs; **Panier·mehl** das breadcrumbs *pl.*

Panik die; ~, ~en panic; **panisch** *Adj.* panic *attrib.* ⟨*fear, terror*⟩; panic-stricken ⟨*flight*⟩;

Panne die; ~, ~n a) breakdown; *(Reifen~)* puncture; flat [tyre]; b) *(Mißgeschick)* mishap; **Pannen·dienst** der breakdown service

Panorama das; ~s, **Panoramen** panorama

Panther der; ~s, ~: panther

Pantoffel der; ~s, ~n backless slipper

Pantomime die; ~, ~n mime

Panzer der; ~s, ~ a) *(Milit.)* tank; b) *(Zool.)* armour *no indef. art.; (von Schildkröten, Krebsen)* shell

Panzer-: ~**glas** das bullet-proof glass; ~**schrank** der safe

Papa der; ~s, ~s *(ugs.)* daddy *(coll.)*

Papagei der; ~en *od.* ~s, ~[e]n parrot

Papi der; ~s, ~s *(ugs.)* daddy *(coll.)*

Papier das; ~s, ~e a) paper; b) *Pl. (Ausweis[e])* [identity] papers; c) *(Finanzw.: Wert~)* security

Papier-: ~**geld** das paper money; ~**korb** der waste-paper basket

Pappe die; ~, ~n cardboard

Pappel die; ~, ~n poplar

päppeln *tr. V.* feed up

Papp·karton der cardboard box

Paprika der; ~s, ~[s] a) pepper; b) *o. Pl. (Gewürz)* paprika

Papst der; ~[e]s, **Päpste** pope; **päpstlich** *Adj.* papal

Parabel die; ~, ~n a) *(bes. Literaturw.)* parable; b) *(Math.)* parabola

Parade die; ~, ~n parade

Paradies das; ~es, ~e paradise; **paradiesisch** *Adj.* paradisical; *(herrlich)* heavenly

paradox *Adj.* paradoxical

Paragraph der; ~en, ~en section; *(in Vertrag)* clause

parallel 1. *Adj.* parallel; 2. *adv.* ~ **verlaufen** run parallel (mit, zu to); **Parallele** die; ~, ~n parallel; **Parallelogramm** das; ~s, ~e parallelogram; **Parallel·straße** die street running parallel *(Gen.* to)

Para·nuß die Brazil-nut

Parasit der; ~en, ~en *(auch fig.)* parasite

parat *Adj.* ready

Parfum [par'fœ:], **Parfüm** das; ~s, ~s perfume; **Parfümerie** die; ~, ~en perfumery; **parfümieren** *tr. V.* perfume

Pariser 1. *indekl. Adj.* Parisian; Paris *attrib.;* 2. der; ~s, ~ Parisian; **Pariserin** die; ~, ~nen Parisian

Parität die; ~, ~en parity

Park der; ~s, ~s park; *(Schloß~ usw.)* grounds *pl.*

Parka der; ~s, ~s parka

parken *tr., itr. V.* park; „**Parken verboten!**" 'No Parking'

Parkett das; ~[e]s, ~e a) parquet floor; b) *(Theater)* [front] stalls *pl.;* parquet *(Amer.)*

Park-: ~**gebühr** die parking-fee; ~**haus** das multi-storey car-park; ~**lücke** die parking-space; ~**platz** der car-park; parking lot *(Amer.); (für ein einzelnes Fahrzeug)* parking-space; ~**scheibe** die parking-disc; ~**schein** der car-park ticket; ~**uhr** die parking-meter; ~**verbot** das ban on parking; **im ~verbot stehen** be parked illegally; ~**verbots·schild** das no-parking sign

Parlament das; ~[e]s, ~e parliament; **Parlamentarier** der; ~s, ~, **Parlamentarierin** die; ~, ~nen member of

parliament; **parlamentarisch** *Adj.*
parliamentary
Parodie die; ~, ~n parody (**auf** +
Akk. of)
Parole die; ~, ~n a) *(Wahlspruch)*
motto; *(Schlagwort)* slogan; b) *(bes.
Milit.: Kennwort)* password
Partei die; ~, ~en a) *(Politik,
Rechtsw.)* party; b) *(Gruppe, Mann-
schaft)* side; **für jmdn.** ~ **ergreifen** *od.*
nehmen side with sb.; **parteiisch 1.**
Adj. biased; **2.** *adv.* in a biased man-
ner; **partei·los** *Adj. (Politik)* inde-
pendent ⟨*MP*⟩; **Partei·tag** der party
conference *or (Amer.)* convention
Parterre das; ~s, ~s ground floor;
first floor *(Amer.)*
Partie die; ~, ~n a) part; b) *(Spiel,
Sport: Runde)* game; *(Golf)* round; c)
eine gute ~ |**für jmdn.**| **sein** be a good
match [for sb.]
Partisan der; ~s *od.* ~en, ~en, **Parti-
sanin** die, ~, ~nen guerrilla; *(gegen
Besatzungstruppen im Krieg)* partisan
Partitur die; ~, ~en *(Musik)* score
Partizip das; ~s, ~ien [-'tsi:piən]
(Sprachw.) participle
Partner der; ~s, ~, **Partnerin** die; ~,
~nen partner; **Partnerschaft** die; ~,
~en partnership; **partnerschaft-
lich 1.** *Adj.* ⟨*co-operation etc.*⟩ on a
partnership basis; **2.** *adv.* in a spirit of
partnership; **Partner·stadt** die twin
town *(Brit.);* sister city *or* town
(Amer.)
Party ['pa:ɐti] die; ~, ~s *od.* **Parties**
party
Parzelle die; ~, ~n [small] plot [of
land]
Paß der; **Passes**, **Pässe** a) *(Reise~)*
passport; b) *(Gebirgs~; Ballspiele)*
pass
passabel 1. *Adj.* reasonable; presentable ⟨*appearance*⟩; **2.** *adv.* reasonably
well
Passage [pa'sa:ʒə] die; ~, ~n a) [shop-
ping] arcade; b) *(Abschnitt)* passage;
Passagier [pasa'ʒi:ɐ] der; ~s, ~e
passenger; **blinder** ~: stowaway
Passagier-: ~**dampfer** der passenger steamer; ~**flugzeug** das passenger aircraft; ~**liste** die passenger
list
Paß·amt das passport office
Passant der; ~en, ~en, **Passantin**
die; ~, ~nen passer-by
Paß·bild das passport photograph
Pässe *s.* **Paß**
passen *itr. V.* a) *(die richtige Größe/*

Form haben) fit; b) *(geeignet sein)* be
suitable (**auf** + *Akk.*, **zu** for); *(harmonieren)* ⟨*colour etc.*⟩ match; **zu etw./
jmdm.** ~: go well with sth./be well
suited to sb.; **zueinander** ~ ⟨*things*⟩ go
well together; ⟨*two people*⟩ be suited to
each other; c) *(genehm sein)* **jmdm.** ~
⟨*time*⟩ suit sb.; d) *(Kartenspiel)* pass;
passend *Adj.* a) *(geeignet)* suitable
⟨*dress, present, etc.*⟩; right ⟨*words, expression, moment*⟩; b) *(harmonierend)*
matching ⟨*shoes etc.*⟩
Paß·foto das *s.* **Paßbild**
passierbar *Adj.* passable ⟨*road*⟩; nav-
igable ⟨*river*⟩; negotiable ⟨*path*⟩; **passieren 1.** *tr. V.* pass; **die Grenze** ~:
cross the border; **2.** *itr. V.; mit sein*
happen
Passion die; ~, ~en a) passion; b)
(christl. Rel.) Passion
passioniert *Adj.* passionate ⟨*collector, card-player, huntsman*⟩
passiv 1. *Adj.* passive; **2.** *adv.* pass-
ively; **Passiv** das; ~s, ~e *(Sprachw.)*
passive; **Passivität** die; ~: passivity
Paß-: ~**kontrolle** die passport
check; ~**zwang** der obligation to
carry a passport
Paste die; ~, ~n paste
Pastell das; ~|e|s, ~e a) *(Farbton)* pas-
tel shade; b) *o. Pl. (Maltechnik)* pastel
no art.
Pastell-: ~**farbe** die pastel colour;
~**ton** der pastel shade
Pastete die; ~, ~n a) *(gefüllte* ~*)* vol-
au-vent; b) *(in einer Schüssel o. ä. ge-
gart)* pâté; *(in einer Hülle aus Teig gebacken)* pie
pasteurisieren [pastøri'zi:rən] *tr. V.*
pasteurize
Pastille die; ~, ~n pastille
Pastor der; ~s, ~en, **Pastorin** die; ~,
~nen pastor
Pate der; ~n, ~n godfather; *(männlich
od. weiblich)* godparent
Paten-: ~**kind** das godchild; ~**onkel**
der godfather; ~**stadt** die *s.* **Partnerstadt**
patent *(ugs.)* **1.** *Adj.* a) *(tüchtig)* capable; b) *(zweckmäßig)* ingenious; **2.**
adv. ingeniously; neatly ⟨*solved*⟩; **Pa-
tent** das; ~|e|s, ~e a) *(Schutz)* patent;
etw. zum *od.* **als** ~ **anmelden** apply for
a patent for sth.; b) *(Erfindung)* [pa-
tented] invention
Paten·tante die godmother
patentieren *tr. V.* patent; **Patent-
lösung** die patent remedy (**für, zu**
for)

Pater der; ~s, ~ od. **Patres** *(kath. Kirche)* Father; **Paternoster** der; ~s, ~ *(Aufzug)* paternoster [lift]

pathetisch 1. *Adj.* emotional *(speech, manner)*; melodramatic *(gesture)*; pompous *(voice)*; **2.** *adv.* emotionally; *(dramatisch)* [melo]dramatically; **Pathos das**; ~: emotionalism

Patient [pa'tsi̯ɛnt] der; ~en, ~en, **Patientin** die; ~, ~nen patient

Patin die; ~, ~nen godmother

Patres *s.* **Pater**

Patriot der; ~en, ~en, **Patriotin** die; ~, ~nen patriot; **patriotisch 1.** *Adj.* patriotic; **2.** *adv.* patriotically; **Patriotismus der**; ~: patriotism

Patrone die; ~, ~n cartridge

Patrouille [pa'trʊljə] die; ~, ~n patrol; **patrouillieren** [patrʊl'jiːrən] *itr. V.; auch mit sein* be on patrol

Patsche die; ~, ~n *(ugs.) s.* **Klemme**; **patschen** *itr. V., mit sein (ugs.)* splash; **patsch·naß** *Adj. (ugs.)* sopping wet

patzig *(ugs.)* **1.** *Adj.* snotty *(coll.)*; *(frech)* cheeky; **2.** *adv.* snottily *(coll.)*; *(frech)* cheekily

Pauke die; ~, ~n kettledrum; **auf die ~ hauen** *(ugs.) (feiern)* paint the town red *(sl.)*; *(sich lautstark äußern)* come right out with it

pausbäckig *Adj.* chubby-faced; chubby *(face)*

pauschal 1. *Adj.* **a)** all-inclusive *(price, settlement)*; **b)** *(verallgemeinernd)* sweeping *(judgement, criticism, statement)*; indiscriminate *(prejudice)*; wholesale *(discrimination)*; **2.** *adv.* **a)** *(cost)* all in all; *(pay)* in a lump sum; **b)** *(ohne zu differenzieren)* wholesale

Pauschale die; ~, ~n flat-rate payment

Pauschal-: ~**preis** der flat rate; *(Inklusivpreis)* all-in price; ~**reise** die package holiday; *(mit mehreren Reisezielen)* package tour

Pause die; ~, ~n break; *(Ruhe~)* rest; *(Theater)* interval *(Brit.)*; intermission *(Amer.)*

pausen *tr. V.* trace; *(eine Lichtpause machen)* Photostat *(Brit. P)*

pausen·los 1. *Adj.;* incessant *(noise, moaning, questioning)*; continous *(work, operation)*; **2.** *adv.* incessantly; *(work)* non-stop

Pavian ['paːvi̯aːn] der; ~s, ~e baboon

Pavillon ['pavɪljɔn] der; ~s, ~s pavilion

Pazifik der; ~s Pacific; **pazifisch** *Adj.* Pacific *(area)*; **der Pazifische Ozean** the Pacific Ocean

Pech das; ~[e]s, ~e **a)** pitch; **b)** *o. Pl. (Mißgeschick)* bad luck; **pech·schwarz** *Adj. (ugs.)* jet-black

Pedal das; ~s, ~e pedal

Pediküre die; ~, ~n pedicure; **pediküren** *tr. V.* pedicure

Pegel der; ~s, ~ **a)** water-level indicator; *(Tide~)* tide-gauge; **b)** *(Wasserstand)* water-level

peilen *tr. V.* take a bearing on *(transmitter, fixed point)*

Pein die; ~ *(geh.)* torment; **peinigen** *tr. V. (geh.)* torment; *(foltern)* torture; **peinlich 1.** *Adj.* **a)** embarrassing; awkward *(question, position, pause)*; **es ist mir sehr ~:** I feel very bad *(coll.)* or embarrassed about it; **b)** *(äußerst genau)* meticulous; **2.** *adv.* **a)** unpleasantly *(surprised)*; **b)** *(überaus [genau])* meticulously; **Peinlichkeit** die; ~, ~en **a)** *o. Pl.* embarrassment; **die ~ der Situation** the awkwardness of the situation; **b)** *o. Pl. (Genauigkeit)* meticulousness; **c)** *(peinliche Situation)* embarrassing situation

Peitsche die; ~, ~n whip; **peitschen** *tr. V.* whip; *(fig.) (storm, waves, rain)* lash

Pelikan der; ~s, ~e pelican

Pelle die; ~, ~n *(bes. nordd.)* skin; *(abgeschält)* peel; **pellen** *(bes. nordd.)* *tr., refl. V.* peel; **Pell·kartoffel** die potato boiled in its skin

Pelz der; ~es, ~e **a)** fur; coat; *(des toten Tieres)* skin; pelt; **b)** *o. Pl. (Material)* fur; *(~mantel)* fur coat; **Pelz·mantel** der fur coat

Pendel das; ~s, ~: pendulum

pendeln *itr. V.* **a)** swing [to and fro]; *(mit weniger Bewegung)* dangle; **b)** *mit sein (bus, ferry, etc.)* operate a shuttle service; *(person)* commute

penetrant 1. *Adj.* **a)** penetrating *(smell, taste)*; overpowering *(stink, perfume)*; **b)** *(aufdringlich)* pushing, *(coll.)* pushy *(person)*; overbearing *(tone, manner)*; aggressive *(question)*; **2.** *adv.* **a)** overpoweringly; **b)** *(aufdringlich)* overbearingly

penibel 1. *Adj.* over-meticulous *(person)*; *(pedantisch)* pedantic; **2.** *adv.* painstakingly; over-meticulously *(dressed)*

Penis der; ~, ~se penis

Penner der; ~s, ~ *(salopp)* tramp *(Brit.)*; hobo *(Amer.)*

Pęnsen s. Pensum
Pension [pã'zịo:n] die; ~, ~en a) o. Pl.
(Ruhestand) in ~ gehen retire; in ~
sein be retired; b) (Ruhegehalt) [retire-
ment] pension; c) (Haus für
[Ferien]gäste) guest-house; d) o. Pl.
(Unterkunft u. Verpflegung) board;
Pensionär [pãzịo'nɛ:ɐ̯] der; ~s, ~e,
Pensionärin die; ~, ~nen retired
civil servant; **pensionieren** tr. V.
pension off; retire; sich |vorzeitig] ~
lassen take [early] retirement; **Pen-
sionierung** die; ~, ~en retirement
Pęnsum das; ~s, Pęnsen work quota
per Präp. mit Akk. a) (mittels) by; ~
Adresse X care of X; c/o X; b) (Kaufmannsspr.: [bis] zum) by; (am) on; c)
(Kaufmannsspr.: pro) per
perfękt 1. Adj. a) perfect ⟨crime,
host⟩; faultless ⟨English, French, etc.⟩;
b) ~ sein (ugs.: abgeschlossen, fertig
sein) be finalized; **2.** adv. perfectly;
Pęrfekt das; ~s (Sprachw.) perfect
Pergamęnt·papier das grease-proof
paper
Periǫde die; ~, ~n period
Pęrle die; ~, ~n a) (auch fig.) pearl; b)
(aus Holz, Glas o. ä.) bead; **Pęrlmutt**
das; ~s mother-of-pearl
Perlon Ⓦ das; ~s ≈ nylon
Pęrser der; ~s, ~ a) Persian; b) s. Per-
serteppich; **Pęrserin** die; ~, ~nen
Persian; **Pęrser·teppich** der Persian carpet; **Persiǎner** der; ~s, ~
(~mantel) Persian lamb coat; **Pęr-
sien (das)**; ~s Persia; **pęrsisch** Adj.
Persian
Persǫn die; ~, ~en person; (in der
Dichtung, im Film) character; **Perso-
nạl** das; ~s (in einem Betrieb o. ä.)
staff; (im Haushalt) domestic staff pl.;
Personạl·ausweis der identity
card; **Personạlien** Pl. personal par-
ticulars; **Personạl·pronomen** das
(Sprachw.) personal pronoun
Persǫnen-: ~kraftwagen der (bes.
Amtsspr.) private car or (Amer.) automobile; ~name der personal name;
~wagen der (Auto) [private] car;
automobile (Amer.); (im Unterschied
zum Lastwagen) passenger car or
(Amer.) automobile; ~zug der stopping train
persönlich 1. Adj. personal; ~ werden get personal; **2.** adv. personally;
(auf Briefen) 'private [and confiden-
tial]'; **Persönlichkeit** die; ~, ~en a)
personality; b) (Mensch) person of
character; eine ~ sein have a strong

personality; ~en des öffentlichen Le-
bens public figures
Perspektịve die; ~, ~n perspective;
(Blickwinkel) angle; (Zukunftsaus-
sicht) prospect
Peru (das); ~s Peru; **Peruạner** der;
~s, ~: Peruvian; **peruạnisch** Adj.
Peruvian
Perücke die; ~, ~n wig
pervęrs Adj. perverted
Pessimịsmus der; ~: pessimism;
Pessimịst der; ~en, ~en, **Pessimị-
stin** die; ~, ~nen pessimist; **pessi-
mịstisch 1.** Adj. pessimistic; **2.** adv.
pessimistically
Pęst die; ~: plague
Petersilie [petɐ'zi:lịǝ] die; ~: parsley
Petroleum [pe'tro:leʊm] das; ~s par-
affin (Brit.); kerosene (Amer.)
Pętrus (der); **Pętri** (christl. Rel.: Apo-
stel) St Peter
Pf Abk. Pfennig
Pfad der; ~|e|s, ~e path
Pfad-: ~finder der Scout; ~finderin
die; ~, ~nen Guide (Brit.); girl scout
(Amer.)
Pfaffe der; ~n, ~n (abwertend) cleric;
Holy Joe (derog.)
Pfahl der; ~|e|s, Pfähle post; stake
Pfand das; ~|e|s, Pfänder a) security;
pledge (esp. fig.); b) (für Flaschen
usw.) deposit (auf + Dat. on); **pfän-
den** tr. V. seize [under distress] (Law)
⟨goods, chattels⟩; attach ⟨wages etc.⟩
(Law); **Pfänder** s. Pfand; **Pfän-
dung** die; ~, ~en seizure; distraint
(Law); (von Geldsummen, Vermögens-
rechten) attachment (Law)
Pfanne die; ~, ~n [frying-]pan;
Pfann·kuchen der a) pancake; b)
(Berliner ~) doughnut
Pfarrei die; ~, ~en a) (Bezirk) parish;
b) (Dienststelle) parish office; c) s.
Pfarrhaus; **Pfarrer** der; ~s, ~ pastor;
(anglikanisch) vicar; (von Freikirchen)
minister; **Pfarrerin** die; ~, ~nen
[woman] pastor; (in Freikirchen)
[woman] minister; **Pfarr·haus** das
vicarage; (katholisch) presbytery; (in
Schottland) manse
Pfau der; ~|e|s, ~en peacock;
Pfauen·auge das peacock butterfly
Pfd. Abk. Pfund lb.
Pfęffer der; ~s, ~: pepper; **Pfęffer·-
kuchen** der ≈ gingerbread; **Pfęf-
ferminz** o. Art., indekl. peppermint;
Pfęffer·minze die peppermint
[plant]; **Pfęfferminz·tee** der peppermint tea

pfeffern *tr. V.* season with pepper
Pfeife die; ~, ~n pipe; *(Triller~)*
whistle; **pfeifen 1.** *unr. itr. V.*
whistle; ⟨*bird*⟩ sing; *(auf einer Triller-*
pfeife o.ä.) ⟨*policeman, referee, etc.*⟩
blow one's whistle; **auf jmdn./etw.** ~
(ugs.) not give a damn about sb./sth.;
2. *unr. tr. V.* whistle ⟨*tune etc.*⟩; ⟨*bird*⟩
sing ⟨*song*⟩; *(auf einer Pfeife)* pipe,
play ⟨*tune etc.*⟩
Pfeil der; ~|e|s, ~e arrow
Pfeiler der; ~s, ~: pillar; *(Brücken~)*
pier
Pfennig der; ~s, ~e pfennig; **es kostet**
20 ~: it costs 20 pfennig[s]
pferchen *tr. V.* cram; pack
Pferd das; ~|e|s, ~e horse; *(Schachfi-*
gur) knight; **mit ihr kann man ~e steh-**
len *(ugs.)* she's game for anything
Pferde-: ~**rennen das** horse-race;
(Sportart) horse-racing; ~**schwanz**
der *(Frisur)* pony-tail; ~**stall** der
stable
pfiff *1. u. 3. Pers. Sg. Prät. v.* pfeifen
Pfiff der; ~|e|s, ~e **a)** whistle; **b)**
(ugs.: besonderer Reiz) style
Pfifferling der; ~s, ~e chanterelle;
keinen *od.* **nicht einen** ~ **wert sein**
(ugs.) be not worth a bean *(sl.)*
pfiffig 1. *Adj.* smart; bright ⟨*idea*⟩;
artful ⟨*smile, expression*⟩; **2.** *adv.* art-
fully
Pfingsten das; ~, ~: Whitsun
Pfingst-: ~**montag** der Whit Monday *no def. art.;* ~**sonntag** der Whit
Sunday *no def. art.*
Pfirsich der; ~s, ~e peach
Pflanze die; ~, ~n plant; **pflanzen**
tr. V. plant; **Pflanzen·öl** das vegetable oil; **pflanzlich** *Adj.* plant *attrib.*
⟨*life, motif*⟩; vegetable ⟨*dye, fat*⟩
Pflaster das; ~s, ~ **a)** *(Straßen~)*
road surface; *(auf dem Gehsteig)*
pavement; **ein teures/gefährliches** ~
(ugs.) an expensive/dangerous place
or spot to be; **b)** *(Wund~)* sticking-
plaster; **pflastern** *tr. (auch itr.) V.*
surface; *(mit Kopfsteinpflaster, Stein-*
platten) pave; **Pflaster·stein** der
paving-stone; *(Kopfstein)* cobble-
stone
Pflaume die; ~, ~n plum; **getrocknete**
~**n** [dried] prunes
Pflege die; ~: care; *(Maschinen~,*
Fahrzeug~) maintenance; *(fig.: von*
Beziehungen, Kunst, Sprache) cultivation; **jmdn./etw. in** ~ *(Akk.)* **nehmen**
look after sb./sth.
pflege-, Pflege-: ~**eltern** *Pl.* foster-

parents; ~**fall** der: **ein** ~ **sein** be in
[permanent] need of nursing; ~**kind**
das foster-child; ~**leicht** *Adj.* easy-
care *attrib.* ⟨*textiles, flooring*⟩
pflegen 1. *tr. V.* look after; care for;
take care of ⟨*skin, teeth, floor*⟩; look
after ⟨*bicycle, car, machine*⟩; look
after, tend ⟨*garden, plants*⟩; cultivate
⟨*relations, arts, interests*⟩; foster ⟨*con-*
tacts, co-operation⟩; pursue ⟨*hobby*⟩;
2. *mod. V.* etw. zu tun ~: usually do
sth.; **Pfleger** der; ~s, ~ **a)** *(Kran-*
ken~) [male] nurse; **b)** *(Tier~)*
keeper; **Pflegerin** die; ~, ~nen **a)**
(Kranken~) nurse; **b)** *(Tier~)* keeper
Pflicht die; ~, ~en duty
pflicht-, Pflicht-: ~**bewußt 1.** *Adj.*
conscientious; **2.** *adv.* with a sense of
duty; ~**bewußtsein das,** ~**gefühl**
das; *o. Pl.* sense of duty; ~**übung** die
(fig.) ritual exercise
Pflock der; ~|e|s, Pflöcke peg
pflücken *tr. V.* pick
Pflug der; ~|e|s, Pflüge plough; **pflü-**
gen *tr., itr. V.* plough
Pforte die; ~, ~n *(Tor)* gate; *(Tür)*
door; *(Eingang)* entrance; **Pförtner**
der; ~s, ~ porter; *(eines Wohnblocks,*
Büros) door-keeper; *(am Tor)* gate-
keeper
Pfosten der; ~s, ~ post
Pfote die; ~, ~n paw
Pfropf der; ~|e|s, ~e blockage;
pfropfen *tr. V. (ugs.)* cram; stuff; **ge-**
pfropft voll crammed [full]; packed;
Pfropfen der stopper; *(Korken)*
cork; *(für Fässer)* bung
pfui *Interj.* ugh; ~ **rufen** boo
Pfund das; ~|e|s, ~e pound
Pfütze die; ~, ~n puddle
Phänomen das; ~s, ~e phenomenon
Phantasie die; ~, ~n **a)** *o. Pl.* imagination; **b)** *meist Pl. (Produkt der* ~*)*
fantasy; **phantasie·los 1.** *Adj.* unimaginative; **2.** *adv.* unimaginatively;
phantasie·voll 1. *Adj.* imaginative;
2. *adv.* imaginatively; **phantastisch**
1. *Adj.* **a)** fantastic; ⟨*idea*⟩ divorced
from reality; **b)** *(ugs.: großartig)* fantastic *(coll.);* **2.** *adv. (ugs.)* fantastically
(coll.)
Phase die; ~, ~n phase
Philosoph der; ~en, ~en philosopher; **Philosophie** die; ~, ~n
philosophy; **philosophieren** *itr.*
(auch tr.) V. philosophize; **philoso-**
phisch 1. *Adj.* philosophical; ⟨*dic-*
tionary, principles⟩ of philosophy; **2.**
adv. philosophically

Photo 652

Photo das; ~s, ~s s. Foto
Phrase die; ~, ~n *(abwertend)* [empty] phrase; cliché
Physik die; ~: physics *sing., no art.;* **physikalisch** *Adj.* physics *attrib.* ⟨*experiment, formula, research, institute*⟩; physical ⟨*map, process*⟩; **Physiker** der; ~s, ~ physicist; **physisch** 1. *Adj.* physical; 2. *adv.* physically
Pianist der; ~en, ~en, **Pianistin** die; ~, ~nen pianist
Pickel der; ~s, ~: pimple
picken 1. *itr. V.* peck (**nach** at; **an** + *Akk.,* **gegen** on, against); 2. *tr. V.* ⟨*bird*⟩ peck; *(ugs.)* ⟨*person*⟩ pick
Picknick das; ~s, ~e *od.* ~s picnic
piep[s]en *itr. V. (ugs.)* squeak; ⟨*small bird*⟩ cheep
Pietät [pie'tɛːt] die; ~: respect; *(Ehrfurcht)* reverence
Pik das; ~|s|, ~|s| *(Kartenspiel)* **a)** *(Farbe)* spades *pl.*; **b)** *(Karte)* spade
pikant 1. *Adj.* **a)** piquant; **b)** *(fig.: witzig)* ironical; **c)** *(verhüll.: schlüpfrig)* racy ⟨*joke, story*⟩; 2. *adv.* piquantly ⟨*seasoned*⟩
pikiert 1. *Adj.* piqued; 2. *adv.* ⟨*reply, say*⟩ in an aggrieved tone
Pilger der; ~s, ~: pilgrim; **pilgern** *itr. V.* go on a pilgrimage
Pille die; ~, ~n pill
Pilot der; ~en, ~en pilot
Pils das; ~, ~: Pils
Pilz der; ~es, ~e fungus; *(Speise~, auch fig.)* mushroom
Pinguin der; ~s, ~e penguin
Pinie ['piːni̯ə] die; ~, ~n [stone- *or* umbrella] pine
pinkeln *itr. V. (salopp)* pee *(coll.)*
Pinsel der; ~s, ~: brush; *(Mal~)* paintbrush
Pinzette die; ~, ~n tweezers *pl.*
Pionier der; ~s, ~e *(Milit.)* sapper; *(fig.: Wegbereiter)* pioneer
Pirat der; ~en, ~en pirate
pissen *itr. V. (derb)* piss *(coarse)*
Pistazie [pɪs'taːtsi̯ə] die; ~, ~n pistachio
Piste die; ~, ~n *(Ski~)* piste; *(Renn~)* course; *(Flugw.)* runway
Pistole die; ~, ~n pistol
Pizza die; ~, ~s *od.* **Pizzen** pizza
Pkw, PKW ['peːkaːveː] der; ~|s|, ~|s| [private] car; automobile *(Amer.)*
plädieren *itr. V. (Rechtsw.)* plead (**auf** + *Akk.* for); *(fig.)* argue; **Plädoyer** [plɛdo̯a'jeː] das; ~s, ~s *(Rechtsw.)* summing up *(for the defence/prosecution); (fig.)* plea

Plage die; ~, ~n **a)** nuisance; **b)** *(ugs.: Mühe)* bother; trouble; **plagen** 1. *tr. V.* **a)** torment; **b)** *(ugs.: bedrängen)* harass; *(mit Bitten, Fragen)* pester; 2. *refl. V.* **a)** *(sich abmühen)* slave away; **b)** *(leiden)* **sich mit etw.** ~: be bothered by sth.
Plakat das; ~|e|s, ~e poster; **Plakette** die; ~, ~n badge
Plan der; ~|e|s, **Pläne a)** plan; **b)** *(Karte)* map; plan
Plane die; ~, ~n tarpaulin
planen *tr., itr. V.* plan
Planet der; ~en, ~en planet
planieren *tr. V.* level; grade; **Planier·raupe** die bulldozer
Planke die; ~, ~n plank
plan-: ~los 1. *Adj.* aimless; *(ohne System)* unsystematic; 2. *adv. s.* 1: aimlessly; unsystematically; **~mäßig** 1. *Adj.* **a)** scheduled ⟨*service, steamer*⟩; **~mäßige Ankunft/Abfahrt** scheduled time of arrival/departure; **b)** *(systematisch)* systematic; 2. *adv.* **a)** *(wie geplant)* according to plan; *(pünktlich)* on schedule; **b)** *(systematisch)* systematically
Plansch·becken das paddling-pool; **planschen** *itr. V.* splash [about]
Plantage [plan'taːʒə] die; ~, ~n plantation
Planung die; ~, ~en planning; **Plan·wirtschaft** die planned economy
¹**Plastik** die; ~, ~en sculpture; ²**Plastik** das; ~s *(ugs.)* plastic
Plastik-: ~beutel der, **~tüte** die plastic bag
Platane die; ~, ~n plane-tree
Platin das; ~s platinum
plätschern *itr. V.* **a)** splash; **b)** *mit sein* (~*d auftreffen)* splash (**an** + *Akk.,* **gegen** against); **plätschern** *itr. V.* **a)** splash; ⟨*rain*⟩ patter; ⟨*stream*⟩ burble; **b)** *mit sein* ⟨*stream*⟩ burble along
platt *Adj.* flat; **ein Platter** *(ugs.)* a flat *(coll.)*
platt·deutsch *Adj.* Low German
Platte die; ~, ~n **a)** *(Stein~)* slab; *(Metall~)* plate; sheet; *(Span~, Hartfaser~ usw.)* board; *(Tisch~)* [table-]top; *(Grab~)* [memorial] slab; **b)** *(Koch~)* hotplate; **c)** *(Schall~)* [gramophone] record; **d)** *(Teller)* plate; *(zum Servieren, aus Metall)* dish; **kalte ~:** selection of cold meats [and cheese]; **Platten·spieler** der record-player; **Platt·fuß** der **a)** flat foot; **b)** *(ugs.: Reifenpanne)* flat *(coll.)*

Platz der; ~es, **Plätze a)** square; **b)** *(Sport~)* ground; *(Spielfeld)* field; *(Tennis~, Volleyball~ usw.)* court; *(Golf~)* course; **c)** *(Stelle, wo jmd., etw. hingehört)* place; **nicht** *od.* **fehl am ~|e| sein** *(fig.)* be out of place; **d)** *(Sitz~)* seat; *(am Tisch, Steh~ usw.)* place; **~ nehmen** sit down; **e)** *(bes. Sport: Plazierung)* place; **f)** *(Ort)* place; **am ~ :** in the town/village; **g)** *o. Pl. (Raum)* space; room; **~ machen** make room *(Dat.* for); **Plätzchen** das; ~s, **~ a)** little place; **b)** *(Keks)* biscuit *(Brit.);* cookie *(Amer.)*

platzen *itr. V.;* **mit sein a)** burst; *(explodieren)* explode; **b)** *(ugs.: scheitern)* fall through; **der Wechsel/das Treffen ist geplatzt** the bill has bounced *(sl.)*/the meeting is off; **c) in eine Versammlung ~** *(ugs.)* burst into a meeting

Platz-: **~karte die** reserved-seat ticket; **~konzert das** open-air concert *(by a military or brass band);* **~mangel der** lack of space; **~regen** der cloudburst; **~wunde die** lacerated wound

plaudern *itr. V.* chat

plausibel *Adj.* plausible

pleite *(ugs.)* **~ sein** ⟨person⟩ be broke *(coll.);* ⟨company⟩ have gone bust *(coll.);* **~ gehen** go bust *(coll.);* **Pleite** die; ~, **~n** *(ugs.)* **a)** *(Bankrott)* bankruptcy *no def. art.;* **~ machen** go bust *(coll.);* **b)** *(Mißerfolg)* wash-out *(sl.)*

Plissee das; ~s, **~s** accordion pleats *pl.*

Plombe die; ~, **~n a)** *(Siegel)* [lead] seal; **b)** *(veralt.: Zahnfüllung)* filling; **plombieren** *tr. V.* **a)** *(versiegeln)* seal; **b)** *(veralt.)* fill ⟨tooth⟩

plötzlich 1. *Adj.* sudden; **2.** *adv.* suddenly

plump 1. *Adj.* **a)** *(dick)* plump; *(unförmig)* ungainly ⟨shape⟩; *(rundlich)* bulbous; **b)** *(schwerfällig)* clumsy ⟨movements, style⟩; **c)** *(fig.)* *(dreist)* crude ⟨lie, deception, trick⟩; *(leicht durchschaubar)* blatantly obvious; *(unbeholfen)* clumsy ⟨excuse, advances⟩; crude ⟨joke, forgery⟩; **2.** *adv.* **a)** *(schwerfällig)* clumsily; **b)** *(fig.)* in a blatantly obvious manner

plündern *itr., tr. V.* **a)** loot; plunder ⟨town⟩; **b)** *(scherzh.)* raid ⟨larder, fridge, account⟩

Plural der; ~s, **~e** plural

plus *Konj., Adv.* plus; **Plus** das; ~ **:** surplus; *(Vorteil)* advantage

Plüsch der; ~|e|s, **~e** plush

Plusquam·perfekt das pluperfect [tense]

PLZ *Abk.* Postleitzahl

Po der; ~s, **~s** *(ugs.)* bottom

Pöbel der; ~s rabble

pochen *itr. V. (klopfen)* knock **(gegen/an** + *Akk.* at, on); *(geh.: pulsieren)* ⟨heart⟩ pound

Pocken *Pl.* smallpox *sing.*

Podest das *od.* der; ~|e|s, **~e** rostrum; **Podium** das; ~s, **Podien** *(Plattform)* platform; *(Bühne)* stage; *(trittartige Erhöhung)* rostrum

Poesie die; ~ **:** poetry; **Poet** der; ~en, **~en** *(veralt.)* poet; bard *(literary);* **poetisch 1.** *Adj.* poetic[al]; **2.** *adv.* poetically

Pointe ['poɛ̃ːtə] die; ~, **~n** *(eines Witzes)* punch line; *(einer Geschichte)* point; *(eines Sketches)* curtain line

Pokal der; ~s, **~e a)** *(Trinkgefäß)* goblet; **b)** *(Siegestrophäe, ~wettbewerb)* cup

Pökel·fleisch das salt meat; **pökeln** *tr. V.* salt

Poker das *od.* der; ~s poker; **pokern** *itr. V.* play poker

Pol der; ~s, **~e** pole

Pole der; ~n, **~n** Pole

polemisch 1. *Adj.* polemic[al]; **2.** *adv.* polemically

Polen das; ~s Poland

Police [po'liːsə] die; ~, **~n** *(Versicherungsw.)* policy

polieren *tr. V.* polish

Poli·klinik die out-patients' clinic

Polin die; ~n, **~nen** Pole

Politik die; ~, **~en a)** *o. Pl.* politics *sing., no art.;* **b)** *(eine spezielle ~)* policy; **Politiker** der; ~s, ~, **Politikerin** die; ~, **~nen** politician; **politisch 1.** *Adj.* political; **2.** *adv.* politically; **politisieren 1.** *itr. V.* talk politics; **2.** *tr. V.* make politically active

Politur die; ~, **~en** polish

Polizei die; ~, **~en** police *pl.*

Polizei-: **~auto das** police car; **~beamte der** police officer; **~kontrolle die** police check

polizeilich 1. *Adj.* police; **~e Meldepflicht** obligation to register with the police; **2.** *adv.* by the police

Polizei-: **~präsidium das** police headquarters *sing. or pl.;* **~revier das** police station; **~streife die** police patrol; **~stunde die** closing time; **~wache die** police station

Polizist der; ~en, **~en** policeman

polnisch *Adj.* Polish

Polster das; ~s, ~: upholstery *no pl.,
no indef. art.;* **Polster·möbel** *Pl.*
upholstered furniture *sing.;* **polstern** *tr. V.* upholster *(furniture)*

poltern *itr. V.* **a)** crash about; **b)** *mit
sein* der Karren polterte über das Pflaster the cart clattered over the cobble-
stones

Polyp der; ~en, ~en *(Zool., Med.)*
polyp

Pommern (das); ~s Pomerania

Pommes frites [pom'frit] *Pl.* chips
(Brit.); French fries *(Amer.)*

pompös 1. *Adj.* grandiose; 2. *adv.*
grandiosely

¹Pony ['poni] das; ~s, ~s pony; **²Pony**
der; ~s, ~s *(Frisur)* fringe

Popeline·mantel der poplin coat

populär 1. *Adj.* popular (bei with); 2.
adv. popularly; **Popularität** die; ~:
popularity

Pore die; ~, ~n pore

Pornographie die; ~: pornography

Porree der; ~s leek

Portal das; ~s, ~e portal

Portemonnaie [portmɔ'ne:] das; ~s,
~s purse

Porti *Pl. s.* Porto

Portier [por'tie:] der; ~s, ~s, *österr.:*
[por'ti:ɐ] der; ~s, ~e porter

Portion [por'tsio:n] die; ~, ~en **a)**
(beim Essen) portion; helping; **b)**
(ugs.: Anteil) amount

Porto das; ~s, ~s *od.* **Porti** postage
(für on, for)

Portugal (das); ~s Portugal; **Portugiese** der; ~n, ~n Portuguese; **portugiesisch** *Adj.* Portuguese

Portwein der port

Porzellan das; ~s porcelain; china

Posaune die; ~, ~n trombone

Position [pozi'tsio:n] die; ~, ~en position; **positiv** 1. *Adj.* positive; 2. *adv.*
positively; **Positiv** das; ~s, ~e *(Fot.)*
positive

Possessiv·pronomen das
(Sprachw.) possessive pronoun

Post die; ~, ~en **a)** post *(Brit.);* mail;
etw. mit der *od.* per ~ schicken send
sth. by post *or* mail; **b)** *(~amt)* post
office

Post-: ~amt das post office; ~an-
weisung die postal remittance form;
~auto das mail van; ~bote der
(ugs.) postman *(Brit.);* mailman
(Amer.)

Posten der; ~s, ~ **a)** post; **b)** *(bes. Milit.: Wachmann)* sentry

post-, Post-: ~fach das post-office
or PO box; *(im Büro, Hotel o. ä.)* pigeon-hole; ~karte die postcard;
~lagernd *Adj., adv.* poste restante;
general delivery *(Amer.);* ~leitzahl
die postcode; Zip code *(Amer.);*
~stempel der *(Abdruck)* postmark;
~wendend *Adv.* by return [of post]

potent *Adj.* potent; **Potenz** die; ~,
~en **a)** *o. Pl.* potency; **b)** *(Math.)*
power; **potenzieren** *tr. V. (Math.)*
mit 5 ~: raise to the power [of] 5

Pracht die; ~: splendour; **prächtig,
pracht·voll** 1. *Adj.* splendid; 2. *adv.*
splendidly

prädestiniert *Adj.* predestined

Prädikat das; ~[e]s, ~e **a)** *(Auszeichnung)* rating; **b)** *(Sprachw.)* predicate

Prag (das); ~s Prague

prägen *tr. V.* **a)** emboss; **b)** mint
(coin); **c)** *(fig.: beeinflussen)* shape

prägnant 1. *Adj.* concise; succinct; 2.
adv. concisely; succinctly

Prägung die; ~, ~en embossing; *(von
Münzen)* minting

prahlen *itr. V.* boast, brag (mit about)

Praktik die; ~, ~en practice; **Praktika** *s.* Praktikum; **Praktikant** der;
~en, ~en, **Praktikantin** die; ~, ~nen
a) *(in einem Betrieb)* student trainee;
b) *(an der Hochschule)* physics/chem-
istry student *(doing a period of practical training);* **Praktikum** das; ~s,
Praktika period of practical training;
praktisch 1. *Adj.* practical; ~er Arzt
general practitioner; 2. *adv.* practically; *(auf die Praxis bezogen; wirklich)*
in practice; **praktizieren** *tr. V.* practise

Praline die; ~, ~n [filled] chocolate

prall *Adj.* **a)** hard *(ball);* bulging *(sack,
wallet, bag);* big strong *attrib. (thighs,
muscles, calves);* well-rounded
(breasts); **b)** *(intensiv)* blazing *(sun);*
prallen *itr. V.; mit sein* crash (gegen/
auf/an + Akk. into); collide (gegen/
auf/an + Akk. with)

Prämie ['prɛ:mi̯ə] die; ~, ~n **a)** *(Lei-
stungs~; Wirtschaft)* bonus; *(Belohnung)* reward; *(Spar~, Versiche-
rungs~)* premium; **b)** *(einer Lotterie)*
[extra] prize; **prämieren** *tr. V.* award
a prize to *(person, film);* give an award
for *(best essay etc.)*

Pranger der; ~s, ~ *(hist.)* pillory

Pranke die; ~, ~n paw

Präparat das; ~[e]s, ~e preparation

Präposition die; ~, ~en *(Sprachw.)*
preposition

Prärie die; ~, ~n prairie

Präsens ['prɛːzɛns] das; ~ *(Sprachw.)* present [tense]; **präsentieren** *tr. V.* present

Präservativ das; ~s, ~e condom

Präsident der; ~en, ~en; **Präsidentin** die; ~, ~nen president; **Präsidium** das; ~s, Präsidien a) committee; b) *(Vorsitz)* chairmanship; c) *(Polizei~)* police headquarters *sing. or pl.*

prasseln *itr. V.* pelt down; ⟨shots⟩ clatter; ⟨fire⟩ crackle

prassen *itr. V.* live extravagantly; *(schlemmen)* feast

Präteritum das; ~s *(Sprachw.)* preterite [tense]

Praxis die; ~, Praxen a) *o. Pl. (im Unterschied zur Theorie)* practice *no art.; (Erfahrung)* [practical] experience; b) *(eines Arztes, Anwalts usw.)* practice; *(~räume) (eines Arztes)* surgery *(Brit.);* office *(Amer.); (eines Anwalts usw.)* office

präzise 1. *Adj.* precise; 2. *adv.* precisely; **Präzision** die; ~: precision

predigen 1. *itr. V.* deliver a/the sermon; 2. *tr. V.* preach; **Prediger** der; ~s, ~: preacher; **Predigt** die; ~, ~en sermon

Preis der; ~es, ~e a) *(Kauf~)* price (für of); b) *(Belohnung)* prize; **Preis·aus·schreiben** das [prize] competition

Preisel·beere die cowberry; cranberry *(Gastr.)*

preisen *unr. tr. V. (geh.)* praise

preis-, Preis-: ~**günstig** 1. *Adj.* ⟨goods⟩ available at unusually low prices; **das ist [sehr]** ~**günstig** that is [very] good value; 2. *adv.* at a low price; ~**nachlaß** der price reduction; ~**schild** das price-tag; ~**steigerung** die increase in prices; ~**träger der** prizewinner; ~**verleihung** die presentation [of prizes/awards]; ~**wert** 1. *Adj.* good value *pred.;* 2. *adv.* ⟨eat⟩ at a reasonable price; **dort kann man** ~**wert einkaufen** you get good value for money there

Prellung die; ~, ~en bruise

Premiere [prəˈmi̯eːrə] die; ~, ~n opening night

Presse die; ~, ~n a) press; *(Zitronen~)* squeezer; b) *o. Pl. (Zeitungen)* press

Presse-: ~**freiheit** die freedom of the press; ~**meldung** die press report

pressen *tr. V.* press

Preß·luft-: ~**bohrer** der pneumatic

drill; ~**hammer** der pneumatic hammer

Prestige [prɛsˈtiːʒə] das; ~s prestige

prickeln *itr. V.* tingle

pries *1. u. 3. Pers. Sg. Prät. v.* preisen

Priester der; ~s, ~: priest; **Priesterin** die; ~, ~nen priestess

prima *(ugs.)* 1. *indekl. Adj.* great *(coll.);* 2. *adv.* ⟨taste⟩ great *(coll.);* ⟨sleep⟩ fantastically well *(coll.)*

primär 1. *Adj.* primary; 2. *adv.* primarily

Primel die; ~, ~n primula; *(Schlüsselblume)* cowslip

primitiv 1. *Adj.* primitive; *(einfach, schlicht)* simple; 2. *adv.* primitively; *(einfach, schlicht)* in a simple manner

Prinz der; ~en, ~en prince; **Prinzessin** die; ~, ~nen princess

Prinzip das; ~s, ~ien [-ˈt̯siːpi̯ən] principle; **aus** ~: on principle; **prinzipiell** 1. *Adj.* in principle *postpos., not pred.;* ⟨rejection⟩ on principle; 2. *adv. (im Prinzip)* in principle; *(aus Prinzip)* ɔn principle

Prise die; ~, ~n pinch

privat 1. *Adj.* private; *(persönlich)* personal; 2. *adv.* privately

Privat-: ~**adresse** die private *or* home address; ~**angelegenheit** die private matter; ~**besitz** der private property; ~**eigentum** das private property; ~**leben** das; *o. Pl.* private life; ~**lehrer** der private tutor; ~**patient** der private patient; ~**unterricht** der private tuition

pro *Präp. mit Akk.* per; ~ **Stück** each; a piece

pro-: pro-; ~**westlich/~kommunistisch** pro-western/pro-communist

Probe die; ~, ~n a) test; b) *(Muster, Teststück)* sample; c) *(Theater~, Orchester~)* rehearsal

Probe-: ~**fahrt** die trial run; *(vor dem Kauf, nach einer Reparatur)* test drive; ~**jahr** das probationary year

proben *tr., itr. V.* rehearse; **probeweise** *Adv.* ⟨employ⟩ on a trial basis; **Probe·zeit** die probationary period; **probieren** 1. *tr. V.* a) try; have a go at; b) *(kosten)* taste; try; c) *(aus~)* try out; *(an~)* try on ⟨clothes, shoes⟩; 2. *itr. V.* a) *(versuchen)* try; b) *(kosten)* have a taste

Problem das; ~s, ~e problem; **problematisch** *Adj.* problematic[al]; **problem·los** 1. *Adj.* problem-free; 2. *adv.* without any problems

Produkt das; ~[e]s, ~e *(auch Math.,*

fig.) product; **Produktion** die; ~, ~en production; **produktiv** 1. productive; prolific ⟨*writer, artist, etc.*⟩; 2. *adv.* ⟨*work, co-operate*⟩ productively; **Produktivität** die; ~: productivity; **Produzent** der; ~en, ~en producer; **produzieren** *tr. V.* produce
Prof. *Abk.* Professor Prof.; **professionell** 1. *Adj.* professional; 2. *adv.* professionally; **Professor** der; ~s, ~en; **Professorin** die; ~, ~nen professor; **Profi** der; ~s, ~s *(ugs.)* pro *(coll.)*
Profil das; ~s, ~e a) *(Seitenansicht)* profile; **im** ~: in profile; b) *(von Reifen, Schuhsohlen)* tread
Profit der; ~[e]s, ~e profit; **profitieren** *itr. V.* profit **(von, bei** by)
Prognose die; ~, ~n prognosis; *(Wetter~, Wirtschafts~)* forecast
Programm das; ~s, ~e a) programme; program *(Amer., Computing); (Ferns.: Sender)* channel
Programm-: ~**heft** das programme; ~**hinweis** der programme announcement
programmieren *tr. V.* a) *(DV)* program; b) *(auf etw. festlegen)* programme
Programm-: ~**vorschau** die *(im Fernsehen)* preview [of the week's/evening's *etc.* viewing]; *(im Kino)* trailers *pl.;* ~**zeitschrift** die radio and television magazine
progressiv 1. *Adj.* progressive; 2. *adv.* progressively
Projekt das; ~[e]s, ~e project; **Projektor** der; ~s, ~en projector; **projizieren** *tr. V. (Optik)* project
proklamieren *tr. V.* proclaim
Prolet der; ~en, ~en *(abwertend)* peasant; **Proletariat** das; ~[e]s proletariat; **Proletarier** [proleˈtaːri̯ɐ] der; ~s, ~: proletarian; **proletarisch** *Adj.* proletarian
Promenade die; ~, ~n promenade
Promille das; ~s, ~: [part] per thousand; **er fährt nur ohne** ~ *(ugs.)* he never drinks and drives; **er hatte 1,8** ~: he had a blood alcohol level of 1.8 per thousand; **Promille·grenze** die *(ugs.)* legal [alcohol] limit
prominent *Adj.* prominent; **Prominenz** die; ~: prominent figures *pl.*
prompt 1. *Adj.* prompt; 2. *adv.* a) promptly; b) *(ugs., meist iron.: wie erwartet)* [and] sure enough
Pronomen das; ~s, ~ *od.* **Pronomina** *(Sprachw.)* pronoun

Propaganda die; ~: propaganda; **propagieren** *tr. V.* propagate
Propan·gas das; *o. Pl.* propane
Propeller der; ~s, ~ propeller
Prophet der; ~en, ~en prophet; **prophezeien** *tr. V.* prophesy *(Dat.* for); predict ⟨*result, weather*⟩
Proportion die; ~, ~en proportion
Prosa die; ~: prose
prosit *Interj.* your [very good] health; ~ **Neujahr!** happy New Year!
Prospekt der *od. (bes. österr.)* das ~[e]s, ~e *(Werbeschrift)* brochure; *(Werbezettel)* leaflet
prost *Interj. (ugs.)* cheers *(Brit. coll.)*
Prostituierte die/der; *adj. Dekl.* prostitute; **Prostitution** die; ~: prostitution *no art.*
Protest der; ~[e]s, ~e protest; **Protestant** der; ~en, ~en, **Protestantin** die; ~, ~nen Protestant; **protestantisch** *Adj.* Protestant; **protestieren** *itr. V.* protest, make a protest **(gegen** against, about); **Protest·kundgebung** die protest rally
Prothese die; ~, ~n artificial limb; prosthesis *(Med.); (Zahn~)* set of dentures; dentures *pl.*
Protokoll das; ~s, ~e a) *(wörtlich mitgeschrieben)* transcript; *(Ergebnis~)* minutes *pl.; (bei Gericht)* record; **etw. zu** ~ **geben** make a statement about sth.; b) *(diplomatisches Zeremoniell)* protocol; **protokollieren** 1. *tr. V.* take down; take the minutes of ⟨*meeting*⟩; minute ⟨*remark*⟩; 2. *itr. V.* take the minutes; *(bei Gericht)* keep the record
Proviant der; ~s, ~e provisions *pl.*
Provinz die; ~, ~en province; **provinziell** 1. *Adj.* provincial; 2. *adv.* provincially
Provision die; ~, ~en *(Kaufmannsspr.)* commission; **provisorisch** 1. *Adj.* provisional; temporary; 2. *adv.* temporarily
Provokation die; ~, ~en provocation; **provozieren** *tr. V.* provoke
Prozedur die; ~, ~en procedure
Prozent das; ~[e]s, ~e a) *nach Zahlenangaben Pl. ungebeugt* per cent *sing.;* **fünf** ~: five per cent; b) *Pl. (ugs.: Gewinnanteil)* share *sing.* of the profits; *(Rabatt)* discount *sing.;* **auf etw.** *(Akk.)* ~**e bekommen** get a discount on sth.; **-prozentig** *adj.* -per-cent
Prozent-: ~**rechnung** die percentage calculation; ~**satz** der percentage

prozentual 1. *Adj.* percentage; 2. *adv.* ~ **am Gewinn beteiligt sein** have a percentage share in the profits
Prozeß der; Prozesses, Prozesse **a)** trial; *(Fall)* [court] case; **einen ~ gewinnen/verlieren** win/lose a case; **b)** *(Vorgang)* process; **prozessieren** *itr. V.* go to court; **gegen jmdn.** ~: bring an action against sb.; **Prozeß·kosten** *Pl.* legal costs
prüde *(abwertend)* 1. *Adj.* prudish; 2. prudishly
prüfen *tr. V.* **a)** *auch itr.* examine *⟨pupil, student, etc.⟩*; **mündlich/schriftlich geprüft werden** have an oral/a written examination; **b)** *(untersuchen)* examine **(auf** + *Akk.* for); check *⟨device, machine, calculation⟩* **(auf** + *Akk.* for); investigate *⟨complaint⟩; (testen)* test **(auf** + *Akk.* for); **c)** *(kontrollieren)* check *⟨accounts, books⟩;* **d)** *(vor einer Entscheidung)* check *⟨price⟩;* examine *⟨offer⟩;* consider *⟨application⟩;* **Prüfer** der; ~s, ~, **Prüferin** die; ~, ~nen **a)** inspector; *(Buch~)* **b)** *(im Examen)* examiner; **Prüfung die;** ~, ~en **a)** examination; exam *(coll.);* **eine ~ machen** *od.* **ablegen** take an examination; **b)** *s.* **prüfen b–d**: examination; check; investigation; test; consideration
Prügel *Pl. (Schläge)* beating *sing.; (als Strafe für Kinder)* hiding *(coll.);* **prügeln** 1. *tr. (auch itr.)* V. beat; 2. *refl. V.* **sich ~**: fight; **sich mit jmdm. [um etw.]** ~: fight sb. [over *or* for sth.]
Prunk der; ~|e|s splendour; magnificence
PS [peːˈʔɛs] das; ~, ~: *Abk.* **Pferdestärke** h.p.
Psalm der; ~s, ~en psalm
Psychiater der; ~s, ~: psychiatrist; **Psychiatrie** die; ~ psychiatry *no art.;* **psychisch** 1. *Adj.* psychological; mental *⟨process, illness⟩;* 2. *adv.* psychologically; ~ **gesund/krank sein** be mentally fit/ill
psycho-, Psycho- [psyːço-]: ~**loge** der; ~n, ~n psychologist; ~**logie die;** ~: psychology; ~**login die** psychologist; ~**logisch** 1. *Adj.* psychological; 2. *adv.* psychologically
Pubertät die; ~: puberty
Publikum das; ~s **a)** *(Zuschauer, Zuhörer)* audience; *(bei Sportveranstaltungen)* crowd; **b)** *(Kreis von Interessierten)* public; *(eines Schriftstellers)* readership; **c)** *(Besucher)* clientele; **publizieren** *tr. (auch itr.) V.* publish

Pudding der; ~s, ~e *od.* ~s thick, usually flavoured, milk-based dessert; ≈ blancmange
Pudel der; ~s, ~ poodle
Puder der; ~s, ~: powder; **Puderdose die** powder compact; **pudern** *tr. V.* powder; **Puder·zucker der** icing sugar *(Brit.);* confectioners' sugar *(Amer.)*
¹Puff der; ~|e|s, Püffe *(ugs.)* **a)** *(Stoß)* thump; *(leichter/kräftiger Stoß mit dem Ellenbogen)* nudge/dig; **b)** *(Knall)* bang; **²Puff** der *od.* das; ~s, ~s *(salopp: Bordell)* knocking-shop *(Brit. sl.);* brothel; **puffen** *(ugs.) tr. V.: s.* **¹Puff a**: thump; nudge; dig
Pulli der; ~s, ~s *(ugs.),* **Pullover der;** ~s, ~: pullover; sweater; **Pullunder der;** ~s, ~: slipover
Puls der; ~es, ~e pulse; **Puls·ader die** artery
Pult das; ~|e|s, ~e desk; *(Lese~)* lectern
Pulver das; ~s, ~ powder
pumm[e]lig *Adj. (ugs.)* chubby
Pumpe die; ~, ~n pump; **pumpen** *tr., itr. V.* **a)** *(auch fig.)* pump; **b)** *(salopp) s.* **leihen a, b**
Punkt der; ~|e|s, ~e **a)** *(Tupfen)* dot; *(größer)* spot; **b)** *(Satzzeichen)* full stop; **c)** *(I-Punkt)* dot; **d)** *(Stelle)* point; **ein schwacher/wunder ~** *(fig.)* a weak/sore point; **e)** *(Gegenstand, Thema, Abschnitt)* point; *(einer Tagesordnung)* item; **f)** *(Bewertungs~)* point; *(bei einer Prüfung)* mark
pünktlich 1. *Adj.* punctual; 2. *adv.* punctually; on time; **Pünktlichkeit die;** ~: punctuality
Punsch der; ~|e|s, ~e *od.* Pünsche punch
Pupille die; ~, ~n pupil
Puppe die; ~, ~n **a)** doll[y]; **b)** *(Marionette)* puppet; marionette
Puppen-: ~**stube die** doll's house; dollhouse *(Amer.);* ~**wagen der** doll's pram
pur *Adj.* **a)** *(rein)* pure; **b)** *(unvermischt)* neat *⟨whisky etc.⟩;* straight
Püree das; ~s, ~s **a)** purée; **b)** *s.* **Kartoffelbrei**
Purpur der; ~s crimson
Puste die; ~ *(salopp)* puff; breath
Pustel die; ~, ~n pimple; pustule *(Med.)*
pusten *(ugs.) tr., itr. V.* blow
Pute die; ~, ~n turkey hen; *(als Braten)* turkey; **Puter der;** ~s, ~: turkeycock; *(als Braten)* turkey

Putsch der; ~[e]s, ~e putsch; coup [d'état]; **putschen** itr. V. organize a putsch or coup

Putz der; ~es plaster; *(für Außenmauern)* rendering; **putzen** tr. V. **a)** *(blank reiben)* polish; **b)** *(säubern)* clean; groom ⟨horse⟩; [sich *(Dat.)*] die Zähne/die Nase ~: clean or brush one's teeth/blow one's nose; **c)** *auch itr. (saubermachen)* clean ⟨room, shop, etc.⟩; ~ **gehen** work as a cleaner; **d)** *(vorbereiten)* wash and prepare ⟨vegetables⟩; **Putz·frau** die cleaner

Puzzle ['pazl] das; ~s, ~s, **Puzzlespiel** das jigsaw [puzzle]

Pyjama [py'dʒaːma] der *(österr., schweiz. auch:* das); ~s, ~s pyjamas *pl.*

Pyramide die; ~, ~n pyramid

Q

q, Q [kuː] das; ~, ~: q, Q

Quadrat das; ~[e]s, ~e square; **quadratisch** Adj. square; **Quadratmeter** der od. das square metre

quaken itr. V. ⟨duck⟩ quack; ⟨frog⟩ croak

Qual die; ~, ~en **a)** o. Pl. torment; **b)** meist Pl. *(Schmerzen)* agony; ~en pain sing.; agony sing.; *(seelisch)* torment sing.; **quälen** tr. V. **a)** torment ⟨person, animal⟩; be cruel to ⟨animal⟩; *(foltern)* torture; **b)** *(plagen)* ⟨cough etc.⟩ plague; *(belästigen)* pester; **Quälerei** die; ~, ~en **a)** torment; *(Folter)* torture; *(Grausamkeit)* cruelty; **b)** *(das Belästigen)* pestering

Qualifikation die; ~, ~en **a)** *(Ausbildung)* qualifikations pl.; **b)** *(Sport)* qualification; **qualifizieren** refl. V. **a)** gain qualifications; **b)** *(Sport)* qualify

Qualität die; ~, ~en quality; **qualitativ** **1.** Adj. qualitative; ⟨difference, change⟩ in quality; **2.** adv. with regard to quality; **Qualitäts·erzeugnis** das quality product

Qualle die; ~, ~n jellyfish

Qualm der; ~[e]s [thick] smoke; **qualmen** itr. V. **a)** give off clouds of [thick] smoke; **b)** *(ugs.: rauchen)* puff away

qual·voll 1. Adj. agonizing; **2.** adv. agonizingly

Quantität die; ~, ~en quantity; **Quantum** das; ~s, **Quanten** quota **(an** + Dat. of); *(Dosis)* dose

Quarantäne [karan'tɛːnə] die; ~, ~n quarantine

Quark der; ~s quark

Quartal das; ~s, ~e quarter [of the year]

Quartett das; ~[e]s, ~e **a)** quartet; **b)** *(Spiel)* ≈ Happy Families; *(Satz von vier Karten)* set [of four]

Quartier das; ~s, ~e accommodation no indef. art.; accommodations pl. *(Amer.);* place to stay; *(Mil.)* quarters pl.

Quarz der; ~es, ~e quartz

quasi Adv. [so] ~: more or less; *(so gut wie)* as good as

Quaste die; ~, ~n tassel

Quatsch der; ~[e]s *(ugs.)* **a)** *(Äußerung)* rubbish; **b)** *(Handlung)* nonsense; *(Unfug)* messing about; **laß den** ~: stop that nonsense

Queck·silber das mercury

Quelle die; ~, ~n spring; *(eines Flusses; fig.)* source; **quellen** unr. itr. V.; mit sein **a)** ⟨liquid⟩ gush, stream; *(aus der Erde)* well up; ⟨smoke⟩ billow; **b)** *(sich ausdehnen)* swell [up]

quer Adv. sideways; *(schräg)* diagonally; *(rechtwinklig)* at right angles; ~ **durch/über** (+ Akk.) straight through/across

quer-, Quer-: ~**achse** die transverse axis; ~**schnitt** der *(auch fig.)* cross-section; ~**schnitt[s]·gelähmt** Adj. *(Med.)* paraplegic; ~**straße** die intersecting road

quetschen tr. V. crush; **sich** *(Dat.)* die Hand ~: get one's hand caught

quietschen itr. V. squeak; ⟨brakes, tyres⟩ squeal, screech; *(ugs.)* ⟨person⟩ squeal, shriek

Quirl der; ~[e]s, ~e long-handled blender with a star-shaped head

quitt Adj. *(ugs.)* quits

Quitte die; ~, ~n quince

quittieren tr. V. **a)** *auch itr.* acknowledge, confirm ⟨receipt, condition⟩; give a receipt for ⟨sum, invoice⟩; **b)** etw. mit etw. ~: react or respond to sth. with sth.; **Quittung** die; ~, ~en **a)** receipt; **b)** *(fig.)* come-uppance *(coll.)*

Quiz [kvɪs] **das**; ~, ~: quiz
quoll *1. u. 3. Pers. Sg. Prät. v.* quellen
Quote die; ~, ~n proportion; **Quoten·regelung die** *requirement that women should be adequately represented*

R

r, R [ɛr] **das**; ~, ~: r, R
Rabatt der; ~|e|s, ~e discount
Rabatte die; ~, ~n border
Rabe der; ~n, ~n raven
rabiat 1. *Adj.* violent; brutal; ruthless ⟨*methods*⟩; **2.** *adv. (gewalttätig)* violently; brutally
Rache die; ~: revenge; |an jmdm.| ~ **nehmen** take revenge [on sb.]
Rachen der; ~s, ~ **a)** *(Schlund)* pharynx *(Anat.);* **b)** *(Maul)* mouth; maw *(literary); (fig.)* jaws *pl.*
rächen 1. *tr. V.* avenge ⟨*person, crime*⟩; take revenge for ⟨*insult, crime*⟩; **2.** *refl. V.* **a)** take one's revenge; **b)** ⟨*mistake etc.*⟩ take its/their toll
Rachitis die; ~ *(Med.)* rickets *sing.*
Rach·sucht die; *o. Pl. (geh.)* lust for revenge; **rach·süchtig** *(geh.)* **1.** *Adj.* vengeful; **2.** *adv.* vengefully
Rad das; ~es, Räder ['rɛːdɐ] **a)** wheel; **das fünfte ~ am Wagen sein** *(fig. ugs.)* be superfluous; **b)** *(Fahr~)* bicycle; bike *(coll.)*
Radar der *od.* **das**; ~s radar
Radar: ~**falle die** *(ugs.)* [radar] speed trap; ~**kontrolle die** [radar] speed check
rad-, Rad-: **dampfer der** paddle-steamer; ~|**fahren** *unr. itr. V.*; *mit sein* cycle; ride a bicycle *or (coll.)* bike; ~**fahrer der** cyclist
Radien *s.* Radius
radieren *tr. (auch itr.) V.* erase; **Radier·gummi der** rubber [eraser]
Radieschen das; ~s, ~: radish
radikal 1. *Adj.* radical; drastic ⟨*measure, method, cure*⟩; **2.** *adv.* radically; *(vollständig)* totally; **Radikalismus der**; ~: radicalism

Radio das *(südd., schweiz. auch:* der); ~s, ~s radio; ~ **hören** listen to the radio; **Radio·wecker der** radio alarm clock
Radius der; ~, Radien radius
Rad·kappe die hub-cap
Radler der; ~s, ~: cyclist
Rad-: ~**rennbahn die** cycle-racing track; ~**rennen das** cycle race; *(Sport)* cycle-racing; ~**sport der** cycling *no def. art.;* ~**tour die** cycling tour; ~**weg der** cycle-path *or* -track
raffen *tr. V.* **a)** snatch; rake in *(coll.)* ⟨*money*⟩; **etw. |an sich| ~:** seize sth.; *(eilig)* snatch sth.; **b)** gather ⟨*material, curtain*⟩
Raffinerie die; ~, ~n refinery; **Raffinesse die**; ~, ~n **a)** *o. Pl. (Schlauheit)* guile; ingenuity; **b)** *meist Pl. (Finesse)* refinement; **raffiniert** 1. *Adj.* **a)** ingenious ⟨*plan, design*⟩; *(verfeinert)* refined, subtle ⟨*colour, scheme, effect*⟩; sophisticated ⟨*dish, cut (of clothes)*⟩; **b)** *(gerissen)* cunning ⟨*person, trick*⟩; **2.** *adv.* **a)** ingeniously; *(verfeinert)* with great refinement/sophistication; **b)** *(gerissen)* cunningly
Rage ['raːʒə] **die**; ~ *(ugs.)* fury
ragen *itr. V.* **a)** *(vertikal)* rise [up]; ⟨*mountains*⟩ tower up; **b)** *(horizontal)* project, stick out (**in** + *Akk.* into; **über** + *Akk.* over)
Ragout [ra'guː] **das**; ~s, ~s ragout
Rahm der; ~|e|s cream
rahmen *tr. V.* frame; **Rahmen der**; ~s, ~ **a)** frame; *(Fahrgestell)* chassis; **b)** *(fig.)* framework
Rakete die; ~, ~n rocket; *(Lenkflugkörper)* missile
rammen *tr. V.* ram
Rampe die; ~, ~n **a)** *(Lade-)* [loading] platform; **b)** *(schiefe Fläche)* ramp; **Rampen·licht das: im ~ |der Öffentlichkeit| stehen** be in the limelight
Ramsch der; ~|e|s, ~e *(ugs.)* **a)** *(Ware)* trashy goods *pl.;* **b)** *(Kram)* junk
ran *Adv. (ugs.)* **a)** *s.* heran; **b)** *(fang|t| an)* off you go; *(fangen wir an)* let's go; **c)** *(greif|t| an)* go at him/them!
Rand der; ~|e|s, Ränder **a)** edge; *(Einfassung)* border; *(Hut~)* brim; *(Brillen~, Gefäß~, Krater~)* rim; *(eines Abgrunds)* brink; *(auf einem Schriftstück)* margin; *(Weg~)* verge; *(Stadt~)* outskirts *pl.;* **b)** *(Schmutz~)* mark; *(rund)* ring
randalieren *itr. V.* riot

Rạnd·bemerkung die marginal note *or* comment

rạng *1. u. 3. Pers. Sg. Prät. v.* **ringen**

Rạng der; ~[e]s, **Ränge a)** rank; *(in der Gesellschaft)* status; **b)** *(im Theater)* circle; **erster** ~: dress circle; **zweiter** ~: upper circle; **dritter** ~: gallery

rangieren [raŋ'ʒiːrən] *tr. V.* shunt *⟨trucks etc.⟩;* switch *⟨cars⟩ (Amer.)*

Rạng·ordnung die order of precedence; *(Verhaltensf.)* pecking order

Rạnke die; ~, ~n *(Bot.)* tendril; **rạnken** *refl. V.* climb, grow **(an** + *Dat.* up, **über** + *Akk.* over)

rạnn *1. u. 3. Pers. Sg. Prät. v.* **rinnen**

rạnnte *1. u. 3. Pers. Sg. Prät. v.* **rennen**

Rạnzen der; ~s, ~: satchel

rạnzig *Adj.* rancid

Rạppe der; ~n, ~n black horse

Rạppen der; ~s, ~: [Swiss] centime

Rạps der; ~es *(Bot.)* rape

rạr *Adj.* scarce; *(selten)* rare; **Rarität** die; ~, ~en rarity

rasạnt *(ugs.)* **1.** *Adj.* tremendously fast *(coll.) ⟨car, horse, etc.⟩;* **2.** *adv.* at terrific speed *(coll.)*

rạsch **1.** *Adj.* quick; speedy, swift *⟨end, action, decision, progress⟩;* **2.** *adv.* quickly; *⟨decide, end, proceed⟩* swiftly, rapidly

rạscheln *itr. V.* rustle; *⟨mouse etc.⟩* make a rustling noise

rạsen *itr. V.* **a)** *mit sein (ugs.: eilen)* dash *or* rush [along]; *(fahren)* tear *or* race along; *(fig.) ⟨pulse⟩* race; **b)** *(toben) ⟨person⟩* rage

Rạsen der; ~s, ~: grass *no indef. art.; (gepflegte ~fläche)* lawn

rạsend 1. *Adj.* **a)** *(sehr schnell)* breakneck *attrib. ⟨speed⟩;* **b)** *(tobend)* raging; **c)** *(heftig)* violent; **2.** *adv. (ugs.)* incredibly *(coll.)*

Rạsen·mäher der; ~s, ~: lawnmower

Raserẹi die; ~, ~en *(ugs.)* tearing along *no art.*

Rasier·apparat der [safety] razor; *(elektrisch)* electric shaver; **rasieren** *tr. V.* shave; **sich** ~: shave; **sich naß/ trocken/elektrisch** ~: have a wet shave/ have a dry shave/use an electric shaver

Rasier-: ~**klinge** die razor-blade; ~**wasser** das aftershave; *(vor der Rasur)* pre-shave lotion

Rạsse die; ~, ~n **a)** breed; **b)** *(Menschen~)* race

Rạssel die; ~, ~n rattle; **rạsseln** *itr. V.* rattle

Rạssen-: ~**haß** der racial hatred *no art.;* ~**trennung** die; *o. Pl.* racial segregation *no art.*

Rassịsmus der; ~: racism; racialism; **Rassịst** der; ~en, ~en racist; racialist

Rạst die; ~, ~en rest; ~ **machen** stop for a break; **rạsten** *itr. V.* rest; take a rest *or* break

Rạst-: ~**haus** das roadside café; *(an der Autobahn)* motorway restaurant; ~**platz der a)** place to rest; **b)** *(an Autobahnen)* parking place *(with benches and WCs);* picnic area; ~**stätte** die service area

Rasụr die; ~, ~en shave

Rat der; ~[e]s, **Räte a)** *o. Pl.* advice; **ein** ~: a word of advice; **b)** *(Gremium)* council

rät *3. Pers. Sg. Präsens v.* **raten**

Rạte die; ~, ~n **a)** *(Teilbetrag)* instalment; **etw. auf** ~n **kaufen** buy sth. by instalments *or (Brit.)* on hire purchase *or (Amer.)* on the installment plan; **b)** *(Statistik)* rate

raten **1.** *unr. itr. V.* **a)** jmdm. ~: advise sb.; **b)** *(schätzen)* guess; **2.** *tr. V.* **a)** jmdm. ~, etw. zu tun advise sb. to do sth.; **b)** *(er~)* guess

Raten·zahlung die payment by instalments

Rat·haus das town hall!

Ration die; ~, ~en ration; **rational** *Adj.* rational; **rationalisieren** *tr., itr. V.* rationalize

rationẹll 1. *Adj.* efficient; *(wirtschaftlich)* economic; **2.** *adv.* efficiently; *(wirtschaftlich)* economically; **rationieren** *tr. V.* ration

rat·los 1. *Adj.* baffled; helpless *⟨look⟩;* **2.** *adv.* helplessly; **Rat·losigkeit** die; ~: helplessness; **ratsam** *Adj.; nicht attr.* advisable; **Rat·schlag** der [piece of] advice

Rätsel das; ~s, ~ **a)** riddle; *(Bilder~, Kreuzwort~ usw.)* puzzle; **b)** *(Geheimnis)* mystery; **rätselhaft 1.** *Adj.* mysterious; *(unergründlich)* enigmatic; **2.** *adv.* mysteriously; *(unergründlich)* enigmatically

Rạtte die; ~, ~n *(auch fig.)* rat

Raub der; ~[e]s **a)** robbery; **b)** *(Beute)* stolen goods *pl.;* **rauben** *tr. V.* steal; kidnap *⟨person⟩;* jmdm. etw. ~: rob sb. of sth.; *(geh.: wegnehmen)* deprive sb. of sth.; **Räuber** der; ~s, ~: robber

Raub-: ~**fisch** der predatory fish; ~**mord** der *(Rechtsw.)* murder **(an** + *Dat.* of) in the course of a robbery *or* with robbery as motive; ~**tier** das

predator; ~**überfall** der robbery (**auf**
+ *Akk.* of); ~**vogel** der bird of prey
Rauch der; ~|e|s smoke; **rauchen** 1.
itr. V. smoke; 2. *tr. (auch itr.) V.*
smoke ⟨*cigarette, pipe, etc.*⟩; „**Rauchen
verboten**" 'No smoking'; **Raucher**
der; ~s, ~: smoker; **Raucher·abteil**
das smoking-compartment; smoker;
Raucherin die; ~, ~nen smoker;
räuchern *tr. V.* smoke ⟨*meat, fish*⟩;
rauchig *Adj.* smoky; husky ⟨*voice*⟩;
Rauch·verbot das ban on smoking
räudig *Adj.* mangy
rauf *Adv. (ugs.)* up; ~ **mit euch!** up you
go!; *s. auch* **herauf; hinauf**
raufen 1. *itr., refl. V.* fight; 2. *tr. V.*
sich *(Dat.)* **die Haare/den Bart** ~: tear
one's hair/at one's beard
rauh 1. *Adj.* **a)** *(nicht glatt)* rough; **b)**
(nicht mild) harsh ⟨*climate, winter*⟩;
raw ⟨*wind*⟩; **c)** *(kratzig)* husky, hoarse
⟨*voice*⟩; **d)** *(entzündet)* sore ⟨*throat*⟩; **e)**
(grob, nicht feinfühlig) rough; harsh
⟨*words, tone*⟩; 2. *adv.* **a)** *(kratzig)*
⟨*speak etc.*⟩ huskily, hoarsely; **b)**
(grob, nicht feinfühlig) roughly
Rauh-: ~**faser·tapete** die woodchip
wallpaper; ~**reif** der hoar-frost
Raum der; ~|e|s, **Räume a)** *(Wohn~,
Nutz~)* room; **b)** *(Gebiet)* area; region; **c)** *o. Pl. (Platz)* room; space;
räumen *tr. V.* **a)** clear [away]; clear
⟨*snow*⟩; **b)** *(an einen Ort)* clear; move;
c) *(frei machen)* clear ⟨*street, building,
warehouse, stocks, etc.*⟩; **d)** *(verlassen)*
vacate; **Raum·fahrt** die; ~: space
travel; **räumlich** 1. *Adj.* **a)** spatial;
aus ~**en Gründen** for reasons of space;
b) *(dreidimensional)* three-dimen-
sional; stereoscopic ⟨*vision*⟩; 2. *adv.*
a) spatially; **b)** *(dreidimensional)*
three-dimensionally; **Raum·schiff**
das spaceship; **Räumung** die; ~, ~en
a) clearing; **b)** *(das Verlassen)* vacation; vacating; **c)** *(wegen Gefahr)*
evacuation; **d)** *(eines Lagers)* clearance
raunen *tr., itr. V. (geh.)* whisper
Raupe die; ~, ~n caterpillar
raus *Adv. (ugs.)* out; ~ **mit euch!** out
you go!; *s. auch* **heraus; hinaus**
Rausch der; ~|e|s, **Räusche a)** state of
drunkenness; **b)** *(starkes Gefühl)*
transport; **der** ~ **der Geschwindigkeit**
the exhilaration *or* thrill of speed;
rauschen *itr. V.* ⟨*water, wind, torrent*⟩ rush; ⟨*trees, leaves*⟩ rustle; ⟨*skirt,
curtains, silk*⟩ swish; ⟨*waterfall, strong
wind*⟩ roar; ⟨*rain*⟩ pour down;

Rausch·gift das drug; narcotic; ~
nehmen take drugs; be on drugs
räuspern *refl. V.* clear one's throat
raus|schmeißen *unr. tr. V. (ugs.)*
chuck *(coll.)* ⟨*objects*⟩ out *or* away;
give ⟨*employee*⟩ the push *(coll.) or* sack
(coll.); chuck *(coll.) or* throw ⟨*customer, drunk, tenant*⟩ out (**aus** of)
Raute die; ~, ~n *(Geom.)* rhombus
Razzia die; ~, **Razzien** raid
reagieren *itr. V.* react (**auf** + *Akk.*
to); **Reaktion** die; ~, ~en reaction
(**auf** + *Akk.* to); **reaktionär** *Adj.* reactionary; **Reaktionär** der; ~s, ~e
reactionary; **Reaktor** der; ~s, ~en
[-'toːrən] reactor
real 1. *Adj.* real; 2. *adv.* actually; **rea-
lisieren** *tr. V. (geh.)* realize; **Realismus** der; ~: realism; **Realist** der;
~en, ~en realist; **realistisch** 1. *Adj.*
realistic; 2. *adv.* realistically; **Realität** die; ~, ~en reality
Rebe die; ~, ~n **a)** vine shoot; **b)**
(Weinstock) [grape] vine
Rebell der; ~en, ~en rebel; **rebellieren** *itr. V.* rebel (**gegen** against);
Rebellion die; ~, ~en rebellion; **rebellisch** *Adj.* rebellious
Reb-: ~**huhn** das partridge; ~**stock**
der vine
rechen *tr. V. (bes. südd.)* rake; **Rechen** der; ~s, ~ *(bes. südd.)* rake
Rechen-: ~**fehler** der arithmetical
error; ~**maschine** die calculator
Rechenschaft die; ~: account;
jmdn. für etw. zur ~ **ziehen** call *or*
bring sb. to account for sth.
rechnen 1. *tr. V.* **a)** eine Aufgabe ~:
work out a problem; **b)** *(veranschlagen)* reckon; estimate; **gut/rund gerechnet** at a generous/rough estimate;
c) *(berücksichtigen)* take into account;
d) *(einbeziehen)* count; 2. *itr. V.* **a)** do
or make a calculation/calculations;
gut/schlecht ~ **können** be good/bad at
figures; **b)** *(zählen)* reckon; **c)** *(ugs.:
berechnen)* calculate; estimate; **d)**
(wirtschaften) budget carefully; **e)** **auf**
jmdn./etw. *od.* mit jmdm./etw. ~:
count on sb./sth.; **f)** mit etw. ~ *(etw.
einkalkulieren)* reckon with sth.; *(etw.
erwarten)* expect sth.; **Rechnen das;**
~s arithmetic; **Rechner** der; ~s, ~:
calculator; *(Computer)* computer;
rechnerisch *Adj.* arithmetical;
Rechnung die; ~, ~en **a)** calculation; **b)** *(schriftliche Kosten~)* bill; in-
voice *(Commerc.);* |jmdm.| etw. in ~
stellen charge [sb.] for sth.

recht 1. *Adj.* **a)** *(geeignet, richtig)* right; **b)** *(gesetzmäßig, anständig)* right; proper; ~ **und billig** right and proper; **c)** *(wunschgemäß)* **jmdm.** ~ **sein** be all right with sb.; **d)** *(wirklich, echt)* real; 2. *adv.* **a)** *(geeignet)* **du kommst gerade** ~: you are just in time; **b)** *(richtig)* correctly; **c)** *(gesetzmäßig, anständig)* properly; **d)** *(wunschgemäß)* **es jmdm.** ~ **machen** please sb.; **e)** *(wirklich, echt)* really; **f)** *(ziemlich)* quite; rather; *s. auch* **Recht d**; **recht...** *Adj.* **a)** right; right[-hand] ⟨*edge*⟩; **b)** *(außen, sichtbar)* right ⟨*side*⟩; **c)** *(in der Politik)* right-wing; **Recht** das; ~|e|s, ~e **a)** *(Rechtsordnung)* law; **b)** *(Rechtsanspruch)* right; **sein** ~ **fordern** *od.* **verlangen** demand one's rights; **c)** *o. Pl. (Berechtigung)* right **(auf** + *Akk.* to); **gleiches** ~ **für alle!** equal rights for all!; **im** ~ **sein** be in the right; **zu** ~: rightly; **d) recht haben** be right; **jmdm. recht geben** admit that sb. is right

recht·fertigen *tr. V.* justify **(vor +** *Dat.* to); **Recht·fertigung** die justification

rechtlich 1. *Adj.* legal; 2. *adv.* legally; **recht·los** *Adj.* without rights *postpos.;* **rechtmäßig** 1. *Adj.* lawful; rightful; legitimate ⟨*claim*⟩; 2. *adv.* lawfully; rightfully; **Rechtmäßigkeit** die; ~: legality; *(eines Anspruchs)* legitimacy

rechts *Adv.* **a)** on the right; **von** ~: from the right; **b)** *(Politik)* on the right wing

Rechts-: ~**abbieger** der *(Verkehrsw.)* motorist/cyclist/car *etc.* turning right; ~**anwalt** der, ~**anwältin** die lawyer; solicitor *(Brit.);* attorney *(Amer.); (vor Gericht)* barrister *(Brit.);* attorney[-at-law] *(Amer.);* advocate *(Scot.);* ~**außen** [-'--] der; ~, ~ *(Ballspiele)* right wing; outside right

recht-, Recht-: ~**schaffen** 1. *Adj.* honest; 2. *adv.* honestly; ~**schreibfehler** der spelling mistake; ~**schreibung** die orthography

rechts-, Rechts-: ~**händer** der; ~s, ~: right-hander; ~**kräftig** *(Rechtsw.)* 1. *Adj.* final [and absolute] ⟨*decision, verdict, etc.*⟩; 2. *adv.* **jmdn.** ~**kräftig verurteilen** pass a final sentence on sb.; ~**kurve** die right-hand bend

Recht·sprechung die; ~, ~en administration of justice; *(eines Gerichts)* jurisdiction

rechts-, Rechts-: ~**staat** der [constitutional] state founded on the rule of law; ~**staatlich** *Adj.* founded on the rule of law *postpos.;* ~**verkehr** der driving *no art.* on the right; ~**widrig** 1. *Adj.* unlawful; 2. *adv.* unlawfully

recht-: ~**wink[e]lig** *Adj.* right-angled; ~**zeitig** 1. *Adj.* timely; *(pünktlich)* punctual; 2. *adv.* in time; *(pünktlich)* on time

Reck das; ~|e|s, ~e *od.* ~s horizontal bar

recken 1. *tr. V.* stretch; 2. *refl. V.* stretch oneself

Redakteur [redak'tøːɐ̯] der; ~s, ~e, **Redakteurin** die; ~, ~nen editor; **Redaktion** die; ~, ~en **a)** *(Redakteure)* editorial staff; **b)** *(Büro)* editorial department *or* office/offices *pl.*

Rede die; ~, ~n **a)** *(Ansprache)* address; speech; **eine** ~ **halten** give *or* make a speech; **b)** *o. Pl. (Vortrag)* rhetoric; **c)** *(Äußerung, Ansicht)* **nicht der** ~ **wert sein** be not worth mentioning; **jmdn. zur** ~ **stellen** make someone explain himself/herself; **reden** 1. *tr. V.* talk; **Unsinn** ~: talk nonsense; **kein Wort** ~: not say *or* speak a word; 2. *itr. V.* **a)** *(sprechen)* talk; speak; **viel/wenig** ~: talk a lot *(coll.)*/not talk much; **b)** *(sich äußern, eine Rede halten)* speak; **gut** ~ **können** be a good speaker; **c)** *(sich unterhalten)* talk; **mit jmdm./über jmdn.** ~: talk to/about sb.; **Redens·art** die **a)** expression; *(Sprichwort)* saying; **b)** *Pl. (Phrase)* empty *or* meaningless words

Rede·wendung die *(Sprachw.)* idiom

redlich 1. *Adj.* honest; 2. *adv.* honestly; **Redlichkeit** die; ~: honesty

Redner der; ~s, ~, **Rednerin** die; ~, ~nen **a)** speaker; **b)** *(Rhetoriker)* orator; **red·selig** *Adj.* talkative

reduzieren 1. *tr. V.* reduce **(auf +** *Akk.* to); 2. *refl. V.* decrease; diminish

Reeder der; ~s, ~: shipowner; **Reederei** die; ~, ~en shipping firm

reell 1. *Adj.* honest, straight ⟨*person, deal, etc.*⟩; sound, solid ⟨*business, firm, etc.*⟩; straight ⟨*offer*⟩; 2. *adv.* honestly

Reet das; ~s *(nordd.)* reeds *pl.*

Referat das; ~|e|s, ~e **a)** paper; **b)** *(kurzer schriftlicher Bericht)* report; **referieren** *itr. V.* **über etw.** *(Akk.)* ~: present a paper on sth.; *(zusammenfassend)* give a report on sth.

reflektieren *tr. V.* reflect
Reflex der; ~es, ~e reflex; **Reflexiv·pronomen** das *(Sprachw.)* reflexive pronoun
Reform die; ~, ~en reform; **Reform·haus** das health-food shop; **reformieren** *tr. V.* reform
Refrain [rə'frɛ̃:] der; ~s, ~s chorus
Regal das; ~s, ~e [set *sing.* of] shelves *pl.*
rege 1. *Adj.* a) *(betriebsam)* busy ⟨*traffic*⟩; brisk ⟨*demand, trade, business, etc.*⟩; b) *(lebhaft)* lively; keen ⟨*interest*⟩; 2. *adv.* a) *(betriebsam)* actively; b) *(lebhaft)* actively
Regel die; ~, ~n a) rule; **nach allen ~n der Kunst** *(fig.)* well and truly; b) rule; custom; **die ~ sein** be the rule; **in der** *od.* **aller ~**: as a rule; c) *(Menstruation)* period; **regel·mäßig** 1. *Adj.* regular; 2. *adv.* regularly; **Regel·mäßigkeit** die regularity; **regeln** 1. *tr. V.* a) settle ⟨*matter, question, etc.*⟩; put ⟨*finances, affairs, etc.*⟩ in order; b) *(einstellen, regulieren)* regulate; *(steuern)* control; 2. *refl. V.* take care of itself; **Regelung** die; ~, ~en a) *o. Pl. s.* regeln 1a, b: settlement; putting in order; regulation; control; b) *(Vorschrift)* regulation
regen 1. *tr. V. (geh.)* move; 2. *refl. V.* a) *(sich bewegen)* move; b) *(geh.)* ⟨*hope, doubt, desire, conscience*⟩ stir
Regen der; ~s, ~ a) rain; **vom** *od.* **aus dem ~ in die Traufe kommen** *(fig.)* jump out of the frying-pan into the fire; b) *(fig.)* shower
Regen-: ~**bogen** der rainbow; ~**mantel** der raincoat; mackintosh; ~**schirm** der umbrella; ~**tag** der rainy day; ~**wetter** das; *o. Pl.* wet weather; ~**wolke** die rain cloud; ~**wurm** der earthworm
Regie [re'ʒi:] die; ~ a) *(Theater, Film, Ferns., Rundf.)* direction; b) *(Leitung, Verwaltung)* management
regieren 1. *itr. V.* rule *(über + Akk.* over)*; ⟨*party, administration*⟩ govern; 2. *tr. V.* rule; govern; ⟨*monarch*⟩ reign over; **Regierung** die; ~, ~en a) *o. Pl.* *(Herrschaft)* rule; *(eines Monarchen)* reign; b) *(Kabinett)* government; **Regierungs·sitz** der seat of government
Regiment das; ~[e]s, ~e *od.* ~er a) *Pl.* ~e *(Herrschaft)* rule; b) *Pl.* ~er *(Milit.)* regiment
Region die; ~, ~en region; **regional** 1. *Adj.* regional; 2. *adv.* regionally

Regisseur [reʒɪ'sø:ɐ̯] der; ~s, ~e, **Regisseurin** die; ~, ~nen director
Register das; ~s, ~ a) index; b) *(amtliche Liste)* register; c) *(Musik) (bei Instrumenten)* register; *(Orgel~)* stop; **registrieren** *tr. V.* a) register; b) *(bewußt wahrnehmen)* note; register
Regler der; ~s, ~ *(Technik)* regulator; *(Kybernetik)* control
reg·los *Adj.* motionless
regnen 1. *itr., tr. V. (unpers.)* rain; **es regnet** it is raining; 2. *itr. V.; mit sein (fig.)* rain down; **regnerisch** *Adj.* rainy
regulär *Adj.* a) proper; normal ⟨*working hours*⟩; b) *(normal, üblich)* normal; **regulieren** *tr. V.* regulate; **Regulierung** die; ~, ~en regulation
Regung die; ~, ~en *(geh.: Gefühl)* stirring; **regungs·los** *Adj.* motionless
Reh das; ~[e]s, ~e roe-deer
Reh-: ~**bock** der roebuck; ~**kitz** das fawn [of a/the roe-deer]
Reibe die; ~, ~n, **Reib·eisen** das grater; **reiben** 1. *unr. tr. V.* a) rub; b) *(zerkleinern)* grate; 2. *unr. itr. V.* rub *(an + Dat.* on)*; **Reibung** die; ~, ~en *(Physik, fig.)* friction; **reibungs·los** 1. *Adj.* smooth; 2. *adv.* smoothly
reich 1. *Adj.* a) *(vermögend)* rich; b) *(prächtig)* costly ⟨*goods, gifts*⟩; rich ⟨*décor, finery*⟩; c) *(üppig)* rich; abundant ⟨*harvest*⟩; abundant ⟨*mineral resources*⟩; ~ **an etw.** *(Dat.)* be rich in sth.; d) *(vielfältig)* rich ⟨*collection, possibilities*⟩; wide, large ⟨*selection, choice*⟩; wide ⟨*knowledge, experience*⟩; 2. *adv.* richly
Reich das; ~[e]s, ~e a) empire; *(König~)* kingdom; realm; **das |Deutsche| ~** *(hist.)* the German Reich *or* Empire; **das Dritte ~** *(hist.)* the Third Reich; b) *(fig.)* realm
reichen 1. *itr. V.* a) *(aus~)* be enough; **das Geld reicht nicht** I/we *etc.* haven't got enough money; **jetzt reicht's mir aber!** now I've had enough!; **danke, es reicht** that's enough, thank you; b) *(sich erstrecken)* reach; ⟨*forest, fields, etc.*⟩ extend; 2. *tr. V.* a) pass; hand; **jmdm. die Hand ~**: hold out one's hand to sb.; **sich** *(Dat.)* **die Hand ~**: shake hands; b) *(servieren)* serve ⟨*food, drink*⟩
reich·haltig *Adj.* extensive; varied ⟨*programme*⟩; substantial ⟨*meal*⟩; **reichlich** 1. *Adj.* large; ample ⟨*space, time*⟩; good ⟨*hour, year*⟩; 2. *adv.* a) amply; b) *(mehr als)* over; more than;

c) *(ugs.: ziemlich, sehr)* a bit too ⟨*cheeky, dear, late*⟩; **Reichtum** der; ~s, **Reichtümer a)** *o. Pl.* wealth (**an** + *Dat.* of); **b)** *Pl. (Vermögenswerte)* riches

Reich·weite die reach; *(eines Geschützes, Senders, Flugzeugs)* range

reif *Adj.* **a)** ripe ⟨*fruit, grain, cheese*⟩; mature ⟨*brandy, cheese*⟩; ~ **für etw. sein** *(ugs.)* be ready for sth.; **b)** *(erwachsen, ausgewogen)* mature

¹Reif der; ~[e]s hoar-frost

²Reif der; ~[e]s, ~e *(geh.)* ring; *(Arm~)* bracelet; *(Diadem)* circlet

Reife die; ~ **a)** ripeness; *(von Menschen, Gedanken, Produkten)* maturity; **b)** *(Reifung)* ripening; **reifen** **1.** *itr. V.; mit sein* **a)** ⟨*fruit, cereal, cheese*⟩ ripen; **b)** *(geh.: älter, reifer werden)* mature (**zu** into); **c)** ⟨*idea, plan, decision*⟩ mature; **2.** *tr. V.* ripen ⟨*fruit, cereal*⟩;

Reifen der; ~s, ~ **a)** hoop; **b)** *(Gummi~)* tyre; **c)** *s.* **²Reif**

Reifen-: ~**panne** die puncture; ~**wechsel** der tyre change

reiflich **1.** *Adj.* [very] careful; **2.** *adv.* [very] carefully

Reigen der; ~s, ~ **a)** round dance; **b)** *(fig.)* **den ~ eröffnen** start off

Reihe die; ~, ~n **a)** row; **in Reih und Glied** *(Milit.)* in rank and file; **aus der ~ tanzen** *(fig. ugs.)* be different; **b)** *o. Pl. (Reihenfolge)* series; **er/sie usw. ist an der ~:** it's his/her *etc.* turn; **der ~ nach, nach der ~:** in turn; **c)** *(größere Anzahl)* number; **reihen** *(geh.) tr. V.* string; thread

Reihen-: ~**folge** die order; ~**haus** das terraced house

Reiher der; ~s, ~: heron

Reim der; ~[e]s, ~e rhyme; **reimen** **1.** *itr. V.* make up rhymes; **2.** *tr., refl. V.* rhyme (**auf** + *Akk.* with)

¹rein *Adv. (ugs.)* ~ **mit dir!** in you go/come!

²rein **1.** *Adj.* **a)** *(unvermischt)* pure; **b)** *(nichts anderes als)* pure; sheer; plain, unvarnished ⟨*truth*⟩; **c)** *(frisch, sauber)* clean; fresh ⟨*clothes, sheet of paper, etc.*⟩; pure, clean ⟨*water, air*⟩; clear ⟨*complexion*⟩; **etw. ins ~e schreiben** make a fair copy of sth.; **etw. ins ~e bringen** clear sth. up; **2.** *Adv.* purely; ~ **gar nichts** *(ugs.)* absolutely nothing

Rein·fall der *(ugs.)* let-down

Rein·gewinn der net profit

Reinheit die; ~ **a)** purity; **b)** *(Sauberkeit)* cleanness; *(des Wassers, der*

Luft) purity; *(der Haut)* clearness;

reinigen *tr. V.* clean; purify ⟨*effluents, air, water, etc.*⟩; **Kleider** [**chemisch**] ~ **lassen** have clothes [dry-] cleaned; **Reinigung** die; ~, ~**en a)** *s.* reinigen: cleaning; purification; drycleaning; **b)** *(Betrieb)* [dry-]cleaner's;

reinlich *Adj.* cleanly; **Reinlichkeit** die; ~: cleanliness

rein·rassig *Adj.* thoroughbred ⟨*animal*⟩; **Rein·schrift** die fair copy

Reis der; ~es rice

Reise die; ~, ~n journey; *(kürzere Fahrt, Geschäfts~)* trip; *(Ausflug)* outing; trip; *(Schiffs~)* voyage; **eine ~ machen** go on a trip/an outing; **auf ~n sein** travel; *(nicht zu Hause sein)* be away; **glückliche** *od.* **gute ~!** have a good journey

Reise-: ~**an·denken** das souvenir; ~**büro** das travel agent's; travel agency; ~**bus** der coach; ~**führer** der **a)** *(~leiter)* courier; **b)** *(Buch)* guidebook; ~**führerin** die courier; ~**gepäck** das luggage *(Brit.)*; baggage *(Amer.)*; *(am Flughafen)* baggage; ~**gesellschaft** die **a)** *(~gruppe)* party of tourists; **b)** *(ugs.: ~veranstalter)* tour operator; ~**kosten** *Pl.* travel expenses; ~**leiter** der, ~**leiterin** die courier

reisen *itr. V.; mit sein* **a)** travel; **b)** *(ab~)* leave; set off; **Reisende** der/die; *adj. Dekl.* traveller; *(Fahrgast)* passenger

Reise-: ~**paß** der passport; ~**scheck** der traveller's cheque; ~**tasche** die hold-all; ~**verkehr** der holiday traffic; ~**ziel** das destination

Reisig das; ~s brushwood

Reiß·brett das drawing-board

reißen 1. *unr. tr. V.* **a)** tear; *(in Stücke)* tear up; **b)** *(ziehen an)* pull; *(heftig)* yank *(coll.)*; **c)** *(werfen, ziehen)* jmdn. **zu Boden/in die Tiefe ~:** knock sb. to the ground/drag sb. down into the depths; **d)** *(töten)* ⟨*wolf, lion, etc.*⟩ kill ⟨*prey*⟩; **e)** **etw. an sich ~** *(fig.)* seize sth.; **2.** *unr. itr. V.* **a)** *mit sein* ⟨*paper, fabric*⟩ tear, rip; ⟨*rope, thread*⟩ break, snap; ⟨*film*⟩ break; ⟨*muscle*⟩ tear; **b)** *(ziehen)* **an etw.** *(Dat.)* ~: pull at sth.; **3.** *unr. refl. V. (ugs.: sich bemühen um)* **sie ~ sich um die Eintrittskarten** they are fighting each other to get tickets; **reißend** *Adj.* rapacious ⟨*animal*⟩; raging ⟨*torrent*⟩; ~**en Absatz finden** sell like hot cakes

Reiß-: ~**leine** die *(Flugw.)* rip-cord;

~nagel der s.; **~zwecke**; **~verschluß** der zip [fastener]; **~zwecke** die drawing-pin *(Brit.)*; thumbtack *(Amer.)*

reiten 1. *unr. itr. V.; meist mit sein* ride; **2.** *unr. tr. V.; auch mit sein* ride; **Schritt/Trab/Galopp** ~: ride at a walk/trot/gallop; **Reiten** das; ~s riding *no art.;* **Reiter** der; ~s, ~, **Reiterin** die; ~, ~nen rider

Reit-: **~hose** die riding breeches *pl.;* **~pferd** das saddle-horse; **~stiefel** der riding boot

Reiz der; ~es, ~e **a)** *(Physiol.)* stimulus; **b)** *(Anziehungskraft)* attraction; appeal *no pl.; (des Verbotenen, der Ferne usw.)* lure; **c)** *(Zauber)* charm; **reizbar** *Adj.* irritable; **Reizbarkeit** die; ~: irritability; **reizen 1.** *tr. V.* **a)** annoy; tease ⟨*animal*⟩*; (herausfordern, provozieren)* provoke; s. *auch* **gereizt; b)** *(Physiol.)* irritate; **c)** *(Interesse erregen bei)* jmdn. ~: attract sb.; appeal to sb.; **d)** *(Kartenspiele)* bid; **2.** *itr. V. (Kartenspiele)* bid; **reizend 1.** *Adj.* charming; delightful, lovely ⟨*child*⟩*; * **2.** *adv.* charmingly; **reizlos** *Adj.* unattractive; ⟨landscape, scenery⟩ lacking in charm; **reizvoll** *Adj.* **a)** *(hübsch)* charming; **b)** *(interessant)* attractive

rekeln *refl. V. (ugs.)* stretch

Reklamation [reklama'tsi̯o:n] die; ~, ~en complaint *(wegen* about); **Reklame** die; ~, ~n **a)** *o. Pl.* advertising *no indef. art.;* ~ für jmdn./etw. machen promote sb./advertise *or* promote sth.; **b)** *(ugs.: Werbemittel)* advert *(Brit. coll.);* ad *(coll.); (im Fernsehen, Radio auch)* commercial; **reklamieren 1.** *itr. V.* complain; **2.** *tr. V.* **a)** complain about **(bei** to, **wegen** on account of); **b)** *(beanspruchen)* claim

rekonstruieren *tr. V.* reconstruct

Rekord der; ~[e]s, ~e record

Rekrut der; ~en, ~en *(Milit.)* recruit

Rektor der; ~s, ~en **a)** *(einer Schule)* head[master]; **b)** *(Universitäts~)* Rector; ≈ Vice-Chancellor *(Brit.); (einer Fachhochschule)* principal; **Rektorin** die; ~, ~nen **a)** *(einer Schule)* head[mistress]; **b)** s. **Rektor b**

Relation die; ~, ~en relation; **relativ 1.** *Adj.* relative; **2.** *adv.* relatively

Relativ-: **~pronomen** das *(Sprachw.)* relative pronoun; **~satz** der *(Sprachw.)* relative clause

Relief das; ~s, ~s *od.* ~e relief

Religion die; ~, ~en religion; **religi-**

ös 1. *Adj.* religious; **2.** *adv.* in a religious manner

Relikt das; ~[e], ~e relic

Reling die; ~, ~s *od.* ~e [deck-]rail

Reliquie die; ~, ~n relic

Remis das; ~ [rə'mi:(s)], ~ [rə'mi:s] *(bes. Schach)* draw

Ren das; ~s, ~s *od.* ~e reindeer

Rendezvous [rãde'vu:] das; ~ [...'vu:(s)], ~ ['rãde'vu:s] rendezvous

Renn·bahn die *(Sport)* race-track; *(für Pferde)* racecourse; **rennen** *unr. itr. V.; mit sein* run; **an/gegen jmdn./ etw.** ~: run *or* bang into sb./sth.; **Rennen** das; ~s, ~: running; *(Pferde~, Auto~)* racing; *(Wettbewerb)* race

Renn-: **~fahrer** der racing driver; **~pferd** das racehorse; **~rad** das racing cycle; **~wagen** der racing car

renommiert *Adj.* renowned

renovieren *tr. V.* renovate; redecorate ⟨*room, flat*⟩*;* **Renovierung** die; ~, ~en renovation; *(eines Zimmers, einer Wohnung)* redecoration

rentabel 1. *Adj.* profitable; **2.** *adv.* profitably

Rente die; ~, ~n **a)** pension; **b)** *(Kapitalertrag)* annuity

Ren·tier das reindeer

rentieren *refl. V.* be profitable; ⟨*equipment, machinery*⟩ pay its way

Rentner der; ~s, ~, **Rentnerin** die; ~, ~nen pensioner

Reparatur die; ~, ~en repair **(an** + *Dat.* to)

Reparatur·werkstatt die repair [work]shop; *(für Autos)* garage

reparieren *tr. V.* repair; mend

Repertoire [repɛ'to̯a:ɐ̯] das; ~s, ~s repertoire

Report der; ~[e]s, ~e, **Reportage** [repɔr'ta:ʒə] die; ~, ~n report; **Reporter** der; ~s, ~, **Reporterin** die; ~, ~nen reporter

Repräsentant der; ~en, ~en, **Repräsentantin** die; ~, ~nen representative; **repräsentativ** *Adj.* representative; **repräsentieren** *tr. V.* represent

Repressalie die; ~, ~n repressive measure

Reproduktion die reproduction; **reproduzieren** *tr. V.* reproduce

Reptil das; ~s, ~ien reptile

Republik die; ~, ~en republic; **republikanisch** *Adj.* republican

Reservat das; ~[e]s, ~e **a)** reservation; **b)** *(Naturschutzgebiet)* reserve; **Reserve** die; ~, ~n reserve

Reserve-: ~**rad das** spare wheel; ~**reifen der** spare tyre

reservieren tr. V. reserve; **Reservoir** [rezɛr'vọa:ɐ̯] **das;** ~s, ~e (auch fig.) reservoir (**an** + Dat. of)

Residẹnz die; ~, ~**en a)** residence; **b)** (Hauptstadt) [royal] capital

Resignatiọn die; ~, ~**en** resignation; **resignieren** itr. V. give up

resolụt 1. Adj. resolute; **2.** adv. resolutely; **Resolutiọn die;** ~, ~**en** resolution

Resonạnz die; ~, ~**en** resonance

Respẹkt der; ~|e|s **a)** (Achtung) respect (**vor** + Dat. for); **b)** (Furcht) jmdm. ~ **einflößen** intimidate sb.; **respektieren** tr. V. respect; **respẹkt·los 1.** Adj. disrespectful; **2.** adv. disrespectfully; **Respẹktlosigkeit die;** ~: disrespectfulness; **respẹkt·voll 1.** Adj. respectful; **2.** adv. respectfully

Ressort [rɛ'soːɐ̯] **das;** ~s, ~s area of responsibility; (Abteilung) department

Rẹst der; ~|e|s, ~e **a)** rest; **ein** ~ **von a** little bit of; **b)** (Endstück) remnant; **c)** (Math.) remainder

Restaurant [rɛsto'rãː] **das;** ~s, ~s restaurant; **restaurieren** tr. V. restore

rẹstlich Adj. remaining; **rẹst·los 1.** Adj. complete; **2.** adv. completely

Resultạt das; ~|e|s, ~e result

Retọrte die; ~, ~**n** retort

rẹtten 1. tr. V. save; (vor Gefahr) save; rescue; (befreien) rescue; **jmdm. das Leben** ~ : save sb.'s life; **2.** refl. V. (fliehen) escape (**aus** from); **Rẹtter der;** ~s, ~, **Rẹtterin die;** ~, ~**nen** rescuer

Rẹttich der; ~s, ~e radish

Rẹttung die rescue; (vor Zerstörung) saving

rẹttungs-, Rẹttungs-: ~**boot das** lifeboat; ~**hubschrauber der** rescue helicopter; ~**los 1.** Adj. hopeless; inevitable ⟨disaster⟩; **2.** adv. hopelessly; ~**ring der** lifebelt

Reue die; ~ : remorse (**über** + Akk. for); (Rel.) repentance; **reuen** tr. V. etw. reut jmdn. sb. regrets sth.; **reu·mütig** Adj. remorseful; repentant ⟨sinner⟩

Reuse die; ~, ~**n** fish-trap

Revạnche [re'vãː ʃ(ə)] **die;** ~, ~**n** revenge; (Sport) return match/fight/ game; **revanchieren** refl. V. **a)** get one's revenge, (coll.) get one's own back (**bei** on); **b) sich bei jmdm. für eine Einladung** ~ (ugs.) return sb.'s invitation

Revers [rə'veːɐ̯] **das** od. (österr.) **der;** ~ [rə'veːɐ̯(s)], ~ [rə'veːɐ̯s] lapel

Revier das; ~s, ~e **a)** (Aufgabenbereich) province; **b)** (Zool.) territory; **c)** (Polizei~) (Dienststelle) [police] station; (Bereich) district; (des einzelnen Polizisten) beat

Revisiọn die; ~, ~**en a)** revision; (Änderung) amendment; **b)** (Rechtsw.) appeal [on a point/points of law]; ~ **einlegen, in die** ~ **gehen** lodge an appeal [on a point/points of law]

Revọlte die; ~, ~**n** revolt; **Revolutiọn die;** ~, ~**en** (auch fig.) revolution; **revolutionär 1.** Adj. revolutionary; **2.** adv. in a revolutionary way; **Revolutionär der;** ~s, ~e, **Revolutionärin die;** ~, ~**nen** revolutionary

Revọlver der; ~s, ~ : revolver

Rezẹpt das; ~|e|s, ~e **a)** (Med.) prescription; **b)** (Anleitung) recipe; **Rezeptiọn die;** ~, ~**en** reception no art.; **rezẹpt·pflichtig** Adj. ⟨drug etc.⟩ obtainable only on prescription

R-Gespräch ['ɛr-] **das** reverse-charge call (Brit.); collect call (Amer.)

Rhabạrber der; ~s rhubarb

Rhein der; ~|e|s Rhine; **rheinisch** Adj. Rhenish; ⟨speciality etc.⟩ of the Rhine region; **Rhein·land das;** ~|e|s Rhineland; **Rheinland-Pfạlz (die)**; ~': the Rhineland-Palatinate

Rhetọrik die; ~, ~**en** rhetoric

Rheuma das; ~s (ugs.) rheumatism; **rheumạtisch** (Med.) **1.** Adj. rheumatic; **2.** adv. rheumatically; **Rheumatịsmus der;** ~, **Rheumatịsmen** (Med.) rheumatism

Rhinọzeros das; ~|ses|, ~se rhinoceros; rhino (coll.)

Rhododendron der od. **das;** ~s, **Rhododendren** rhododendron

rhythmisch 1. Adj. rhythmical; rhythmic; **2.** adv. rhythmically; **Rhythmus der;** ~, **Rhythmen** (auch fig.) rhythm

richten 1. tr. V. **a)** direct ⟨gaze⟩ (**auf** + Akk. at, towards); turn ⟨eyes, gaze⟩ (**auf** + Akk. towards); point ⟨torch, telescope, gun⟩ (**auf** + Akk. at); aim ⟨gun, missile, telescope, searchlight⟩ (**auf** + Akk. on); (fig.) direct ⟨activity, attention⟩ (**auf** + Akk. towards); address ⟨letter, remarks, words⟩ (**an** + Akk. to); level ⟨criticism⟩ (**an** + Akk. at); **b)** (gerade~) straighten; **c)** (aburteilen) judge; (verurteilen) condemn; s. auch **zugrunde a; 2.** refl. V. **a)** (sich hinwenden) **sich auf jmdn./etw.** ~

(auch fig.) be directed towards sb./ sth.; **b)** *sich an jmdn./etw.* ~ ⟨*person*⟩ turn on sb./sth.; ⟨*appeal, explanation*⟩ be directed at sb./sth.; **sich gegen jmdn./etw.** ~ ⟨*person*⟩ criticize sb./ sth.; ⟨*criticism, accusations, etc.*⟩ be aimed *or* levelled at sb./sth.; **c)** *(sich orientieren)* **sich nach jmdm./jmds. Wünschen** ~: fit in with sb./sb.'s wishes; **d)** *(abhängen)* **sich nach jmdm./etw.** ~: depend on sb./sth.; **3.** *itr. V. (urteilen)* judge; **Richter** der; ~s, ~, **Richterin** die; ~, ~nen judge **Richt·geschwindigkeit** die recommended maximum speed
richtig 1. *Adj.* **a)** right; *(zutreffend)* right; correct; accurate ⟨*prophecy, premonition*⟩; **b)** *(ordentlich)* proper; **c)** *(wirklich, echt)* real; **2.** *adv.* **a)** right; correctly; **b)** *(ordentlich)* properly; **c)** *(richtiggehend)* really
richtig|stellen *tr. V.* correct
Richt-: ~**linie** die guideline; ~**schnur** die; *Pl.* ~**schnuren** *(fig.)* guiding principle
Richtung die; ~, ~en **a)** direction; **b)** *(fig.: Tendenz)* movement; trend
rieb *1. u. 3. Pers. Sg. Prät. v.* **reiben**
riechen 1. *unr. tr. V.* **a)** smell; **b)** *(wittern)* ⟨*dog etc.*⟩ pick up the scent of; **2.** *unr. itr. V.* **a)** smell; **an jmdm./etw.** ~: smell sb./sth.; **b)** *(einen Geruch haben)* smell (**nach** of)
rief *1. u. 3. Pers. Sg. Prät. v.* **rufen**
Riegel der; ~s, ~ **a)** bolt; **b) ein** ~ **Schokolade** a bar of chocolate
Riemen der; ~s, ~ **a)** strap; *(Treib~, Gürtel)* belt; **sich am** ~ **reißen** *(ugs.)* pull oneself together; get a grip on oneself; **b)** *(Ruder)* [long] oar
Riese der; ~n, ~n giant
rieseln *itr. V.; mit Richtungsangabe mit sein* trickle [down]; ⟨*snow*⟩ fall gently
Riesen- giant; enormous ⟨*selection, profit, portion*⟩; tremendous *(coll.)* ⟨*effort, rejoicing, success*⟩; terrific *(coll.)*, terrible *(coll.)* ⟨*stupidity, scandal, fuss*⟩
riesen·groß *Adj.* enormous; huge; terrific *(coll.)* ⟨*surprise*⟩; **Riesen-schritt** der giant stride; **riesig 1.** *Adj.* enormous; huge; vast ⟨*country*⟩; tremendous ⟨*effort, progress*⟩; **2.** *adv.* *(ugs.)* tremendously *(coll.)*; terribly *(coll.)*
Riesling der; ~s, ~e Riesling
riet *1. u. 3. Pers. Sg. Prät. v.* **raten**
Riff das; ~[e]s, ~e reef
Rille die; ~, ~n groove

Rind das; ~[e]s, ~er **a)** cow; *(Stier)* bull; ~er cattle *pl.*; **b)** *(~fleisch)* beef
Rinde die; ~, ~n **a)** *(Baum~)* bark; **b)** *(Brot~)* crust; *(Käse~)* rind
Rinder·braten der roast beef *no indef. art.; (roh)* roasting beef *no indef. art.*
Rind-: ~**fleisch** das beef; ~**vieh** das cattle *pl.*
Ring der; ~[e]s, ~e ring; **Ringel·natter** die ring-snake
ringen 1. *unr. tr. V. (Sport, fig.)* wrestle; *(fig.: kämpfen)* struggle, fight (**um** for; **gegen, mit** with); **nach Luft** ~: struggle for breath; **2.** *unr. itr. V.* **die Hände** ~: wring one's hands; **Ringen** das; ~s *(Sport)* wrestling *no art.*
Ring-: ~**finger** der ring-finger; ~**kampf** der **a)** [stand-up] fight; **b)** *(Sport)* wrestling bout
rings *Adv.* all around; **rings·herum** *Adv.* all around [it/them *etc.*]
Ring·straße die ring road
rings-: ~**um**, ~**umher** *Adv.* all around
Rinne die; ~, ~n channel; *(Dach~, Rinnstein)* gutter; *(Abfluß)* drainpipe; **rinnen** *unr. itr. V.; mit sein* run; **Rinn·stein** der gutter
Rippchen das; ~s, ~ *(Kochk. südd.)* rib [of pork]; **Rippe** die; ~, ~n rib
Risiko das; ~s, Risiken risk; **riskant 1.** *Adj.* risky; **2.** *adv.* riskily; **riskieren** *tr. V.* risk
riß *1. u. 3. Pers. Sg. Prät. v.* **reißen**
Riß der; **Risses**, **Risse** tear; *(Spalt, Sprung)* crack; **rissig** *Adj.* cracked; chapped ⟨*lips*⟩
ritt *1. u. 3. Pers. Sg. Prät. v.* **reiten**
Ritt der; ~[e]s, ~e ride; **Ritter** der; ~s, ~: knight; **Ritter·sporn** der delphinium; **rittlings** *Adv.* astride
Ritze die; ~, ~n crack; [narrow] gap; **ritzen** *tr. V.* scratch
Rivale der; ~n, ~n, **Rivalin** die; ~, ~nen rival; **Rivalität** die; ~, ~en rivalry *no indef. art.*
Robbe die; ~, ~n seal
Robe die; ~, ~n robe; *(schwarz)* gown
Roboter der; ~s, ~: robot
robust *Adj.* robust
roch *1. u. 3. Pers. Sg. Prät. v.* **riechen**
Rochade die; ~, ~n *(Schach)* castling
röcheln *itr. V.* ⟨*dying person*⟩ give the death-rattle
Rock der; ~[e]s, Röcke skirt
Rodel·bahn die toboggan-run; *(Sport)* luge-run; **rodeln** *itr. V.; mit sein* sledge; toboggan

roden *tr. V.* clear ⟨*wood, land*⟩; *(aus-graben)* grub up ⟨*tree*⟩
Rogen der; ~s, ~: roe
Roggen der; ~s rye
Roggen-: ~**brot das** rye bread; **ein** ~**brot** a loaf of rye bread; ~**brötchen das** rye-bread roll
roh 1. *Adj.* **a)** raw ⟨*food*⟩; unboiled ⟨*milk*⟩; unfinished ⟨*wood*⟩; **b)** *(ungenau)* rough; **c)** *(brutal)* brutish; brute *attrib.* ⟨*force*⟩; **2.** *adv.* **a)** *(ungenau)* roughly; **b)** *(brutal)* brutishly; *(grausam)* callously; *(grob)* coarsely
Roh-: ~**bau** der shell [of a/the building]; ~**kost** die raw fruit and vegetables *pl.;* ~**material das** raw material; ~**öl das** crude oil
Rohr das; ~|e|s, ~e **a)** *(Leitungs~)* pipe; *(als Bauteil)* tube; **b)** *o. Pl. (Röhricht)* reeds *pl.;* **c)** *o. Pl. (Werkstoff)* reed; **Röhre die;** ~, ~n tube; *(Elektronen~)* valve *(Brit.);* tube *(Amer.)*
Roh·stoff der raw material
Rokoko das; ~|s| rococo
Rolladen der; ~s, **Rolläden** [roller] shutter; **Roll·bahn die** *(Flugw.)* taxiway; **Rolle die;** ~, ~n **a)** *(Spule)* reel; **b)** *(zylindrischer [Hohl]körper; Zusammengerolltes)* roll; **c)** *(Walze)* roller; **d)** *(Rad)* [small] wheel; *(an Möbeln usw.)* castor; *(für Gardine, Schiebetür usw.)* runner; **e)** *(Turnen, Kunstflug)* roll; **f)** *(Theater, Film usw., fig.)* role; part; *(Soziol.)* role; **es spielt keine** ~: it is of no importance; *(es macht nichts aus)* it doesn't matter; **rollen 1.** *tr. V.* roll; **2.** *itr. V.* **a)** *mit sein* ⟨*ball, wheel, etc.*⟩ roll; ⟨*vehicle*⟩ move; ⟨*aircraft*⟩ taxi; **Roller** der; ~s, ~: scooter
Roll-: ~**feld das** runway[s] and taxiway[s]; ~**kragen** der polo-neck; ~**laden** der s. **Rolladen;** ~**mops** der rollmops; ~**schuh** der roller-skate; ~**schuh laufen** roller-skate; ~**splitt** der loose chippings *pl.;* ~**stuhl** der wheelchair; ~**treppe** die escalator
Rom *(das);* ~s Rome
Roman der; ~s, ~e novel
Romantik die; ~: romanticism; **die** ~: Romanticism; **romantisch 1.** *Adj.* romantic; **2.** *adv.* romantically
Romanze die; ~, ~n romance
Römer der; ~s, ~: Roman
römisch-katholisch *Adj.* Roman Catholic
röntgen *tr. V.* X-ray
Röntgen-: ~**aufnahme die,** ~**bild das** X-ray [image/photograph *or* picture]; ~**strahlen** *Pl.* X-rays

rosa 1. *indekl. Adj.* pink; **2.** *adv.* pink; **Rosa das;** ~s, ~ *od.* ~s pink; **Rose die;** ~, ~n rose
rosé 1. *indekl. Adj.* pale pink; **Rosé** der; ~s, ~s rosé [wine]
Rosen-: ~**kohl** der; *o. Pl.* [Brussels] sprouts *pl.;* ~**kranz** der *(kath. Kirche)* rosary; **einen** ~**kranz beten** say a rosary; ~**montag der** the day before Shrove Tuesday
rosig *Adj.* **a)** rosy; pink ⟨*piglet etc.*⟩; **b)** *(fig.)* rosy; optimistic ⟨*mood*⟩
Rosine die; ~, ~n raisin
Rosmarin der; ~s rosemary
Roß das; Rosses, Rosse *od.* **Rösser** horse; steed *(poet./joc.);* **hoch zu** ~: on horseback; **auf dem** *od.* **seinem hohen** ~ **sitzen** *(fig.)* be on one's high horse
¹Rost der; ~|e|s, ~e **a)** *(Gitter)* grating; *(eines Ofens, einer Feuerstelle)* grate; *(Brat~)* grill; **b)** *(Bett~)* base
²Rost der; -|e|s rust
Rost-: ~**braten der** grilled steak; ~**bratwurst die** grilled sausage
rosten *itr. V.; auch mit sein* rust
rösten ['rœstn̩, 'ro:stn̩] *tr. V.* roast; toast ⟨*bread*⟩
rost·frei *Adj.* stainless ⟨*steel*⟩
Rösti die; ~ *(schweiz. Kochk.)* thinly sliced fried potatoes *pl.*
rostig *Adj.* rusty
rot 1. *Adj.* red; ~ **werden** turn red; ⟨*person*⟩ blush; ⟨*traffic-light*⟩ change to red; **2.** *adv.* red; **Rot das;** ~s, ~ *od.* ~s red; **Rot·barsch** der rose-fish; **Röte die;** ~: red[ness]; **röten 1.** *tr. V.* redden; **2.** *refl. V.* go *or* turn red; **rot·haarig** *Adj.* red-haired; **Rothirsch** der red deer
rotieren *itr. V.* **a)** rotate; **b)** *(ugs.: hektisch sein)* get into a flap *(coll.)*
Rot-: ~**käppchen (das)** Little Red Riding Hood; ~**kehlchen das;** ~s, ~: robin [redbreast]; ~**kohl** der, *(bes. südd., österr.)* ~**kraut das** red cabbage
rötlich *Adj.* reddish; **Rot·stift der** red pencil; **Rötung die;** ~, ~en reddening; **Rot·wein** der red wine
Rotz der; ~es *(salopp)* snot *(sl.)*
Rouge [ru:ʒ] **das;** ~s, ~s rouge
Roulade [ru:la:də] **die;** ~, ~n *(Kochk.)* [beef/veal/pork] olive
Route ['ru:tə] **die;** ~, ~n route; **Routine** [ru'ti:nə] **die;** ~ **a)** *(Erfahrung)* experience; *(Übung)* practice; **b)** *(Gewohnheit)* routine *no def. art.*
Rübe die; ~, ~n turnip; **rote** ~: beetroot; **gelbe** ~ *(südd.)* carrot

rüber *Adv. (ugs.)* over
Rubin der; ~s, ~e ruby
Rubrik die; ~, ~en column; *(fig.: Kategorie)* category
Ruck der; ~[e]s, ~e jerk
Rück·blick der look back (**auf** + *Akk.* at); retrospective view (**auf** + *Akk.* of)
rücken *itr., tr. V.* move
Rücken der; ~s, ~: back; *(Buch~)* spine
Rücken-: ~**deckung** die **a)** *(bes. Milit.)* rear cover; **b)** *(fig.)* backing; ~**lehne** die [chair/seat] back; ~**mark** das *(Anat.)* spinal cord; ~**schmerzen** *Pl.* backache *sing.;* ~**schwimmen** das backstroke; ~**wind** der tail wind
rück-, Rück-: ~|**erstatten** *tr. V.; nur im Inf. u. 2. Part.* repay; ~**erstattung** die repayment; ~**fahrkarte** die, ~**fahrschein** der return [ticket]; ~**fahrt** die return journey; ~**fall** der *(Med., auch fig.)* relapse; ~**fällig** *Adj. (Med., auch fig.)* relapsed *(patient, alcoholic, etc.);* ~**fällig werden** have a relapse; *(alcoholic etc.)* go back to one's old ways; *(criminal)* commit a second offence; ~**flug** der return flight; ~**frage** die query; ~**gabe** die return; ~**gang** der drop, fall *(Gen.* in); ~**gängig** *Adj.* ~**gängig machen** cancel *(agreement, decision, etc.);* ~**grat** das spine; *(bes. fig.)* backbone; ~**halt** der support; backing; ~**halt·los 1.** *Adj.* unreserved, unqualified *(support);* **2.** *adv.* unreservedly; ~**kehr** die ~: return; ~**lage** die savings *pl.;* ~**läufig** *Adj.* decreasing *(number);* declining *(economic growth etc.);* falling *(rate, production, etc.);* ~**licht** das rear- or taillight
rücklings *Adv.* on one's back
Rück-: ~**nahme** die taking back; ~**reise** die return journey; ~**ruf** der *(Fernspr.)* return call
Ruck·sack der rucksack; *(Touren~)* back-pack
rück-, Rück-: ~**schlag** der set-back; ~**schritt** der retrograde step; ~**seite** die back; *(einer Münze usw.)* reverse; far side; ~**sicht** die consideration; ~**sicht auf jmdn. nehmen** show consideration for *or* towards sb.; ~**sicht·nahme** die; ~: consideration; ~**sichts·los 1.** *Adj.* inconsiderate; thoughtless; *(verantwortungslos)* reckless *(driver); (schonungslos)* ruthless; **2.** *adv. s. Adj:* inconsiderately;

recklessly; ruthlessly; ~**sichts·losigkeit** die; ~, ~en *s.* rücksichtslos : lack of consideration; recklessness; ruthlessness; ~**sichts·voll 1.** *Adj.* considerate; **2.** *adv.* considerately; ~**sitz** der back seat; ~**spiegel** der rear-view mirror; ~**sprache** die consultation; ~**stand** der **a)** *(Rest)* residue; **b)** *(ausstehende Zahlung)* arrears *pl.;* **c)** *(Zurückbleiben hinter dem gesetzten Ziel)* backlog; *(bes. Sport: hinter dem Gegner)* deficit; |mit etw.| im ~**stand sein/in** ~**stand** *(Akk.)* geraten be/get behind [with sth.]; ~**ständig** *Adj.* **a)** backward; *(schon länger fällig)* outstanding *(payment, amount); (wages)* still owing; ~**strahler** der reflector; ~**tritt** der resignation (**von** from); *(von einer Kandidatur, einem Vertrag usw.)* withdrawal (**von** from)
rückwärts *Adv.* backwards; **Rückwärts·gang** der *(Kfz-W.)* reverse [gear]
rück-, Rück-: ~**weg** der return journey; ~**wirkend 1.** *Adj.* retrospective; backdated *(pay increase);* **2.** retrospectively; ~**zahlung** die repayment; ~**zug** der retreat
Rüde der; ~n, ~n [male] dog
Rudel das; ~s, ~: herd; *(von Wölfen, Hunden)* pack
Ruder das; ~s, ~ **a)** *(Riemen)* oar; **b)** *(Steuer~)* rudder; **Ruder·boot** das row-boat; rowing-boat *(Brit.);* **rudern 1.** *itr. V.; mit sein* row; **2.** *tr. V.* row
Ruf der; ~[e]s, ~e **a)** call; *(Schrei)* shout; cry; *(Tierlaut)* call; **b)** *o. Pl. (fig.: Forderung)* call (**nach** for); **c)** *o. Pl. (Telefonnummer)* telephone [number]; **d)** *(Leumund)* reputation; **rufen 1.** *unr. itr. V.* call (**nach** for); *(schreien)* shout (**nach** for); *(animal)* call; **2.** *unr. tr. V.* **a)** *(aus~)* call; *(schreien)* shout; **b)** *(herbei~, an~)* **jmdn.** ~: call sb.; **jmdn. zu Hilfe** ~: call to sb. to help
Ruf-: ~**name** der first name *(by which one is generally known);* ~**nummer** die telephone number
Rüge die; ~, ~n reprimand; **rügen** *tr. V.* reprimand *(person)* (**wegen** for); censure *(carelessness etc.)*
Ruhe die; ~ **a)** *(Stille)* silence; ~ [bitte]! quiet *or* silence [please]!; **b)** *(Ungestörtheit)* peace; **jmdn. mit etw. in** ~ **lassen** stop bothering sb. with sth.; **c)** *(Unbewegtheit)* rest; **d)** *(Erholung)* rest *no def. art.;* **e)** *(Gelassenheit)*

calm[ness]; composure; [die] ~ **bewah-ren/die** ~ **verlieren** keep calm/lose one's composure; **in [aller]** ~: [really] calmly; **ruhe·los 1.** *Adj.* restless; **2.** *adv.* restlessly; **ruhen** *itr. V.* **a)** *(aus~)* rest; **b)** *(geh.: schlafen)* sleep; **c)** *(stillstehen)* ⟨*work, business*⟩ have stopped; ⟨*production, firm*⟩ be at a standstill

Ruhe-: ~**pause** die break; ~**stand** der; *o. Pl.* retirement; ~**störung** die disturbance; *(Rechtsw.)* disturbance of the peace; ~**tag** der closing day; „Dienstag ~**tag**" 'closed on Tuesdays'

ruhig 1. *Adj.* **a)** *(still, leise)* quiet; **b)** *(friedlich, ungestört)* peaceful ⟨*times, life, valley, etc.*⟩; quiet ⟨*talk, reflection, life*⟩; **c)** *(unbewegt)* calm ⟨*sea, weather*⟩; still ⟨*air*⟩; *(fig.)* peaceful ⟨*melody*⟩; *(gleichmäßig)* steady ⟨*breathing, hand, steps*⟩; smooth ⟨*flight, crossing*⟩; **d)** *(gelassen)* calm ⟨*voice etc.*⟩; quiet, calm ⟨*person*⟩; **2.** *adv.* **a)** *(still, leise)* quietly; **sich ~ verhalten** keep quiet; **b)** *(friedlich, ohne Störungen)* peacefully; *(ohne Zwischenfälle)* uneventfully; ⟨*work, think*⟩ in peace; **c)** *(unbewegt)* ⟨*sit, lie, stand*⟩ still; *(gleichmäßig)* ⟨*burn, breathe*⟩ steadily; ⟨*run, fly*⟩ smoothly; **d)** *(gelassen)* ⟨*speak, watch, sit*⟩ calmly; **3.** *Adv.* by all means

Ruhm der; ~[e]s fame; **rühmen 1.** *tr. V.* praise; **2.** *refl. V.* boast (+ *Gen.* about; **ruhm·reich** *Adj.* glorious ⟨*victory, history*⟩; celebrated ⟨*general, army, victory*⟩

Ruhr die; ~, ~**en** dysentery *no art.*

Rühr·ei das scrambled egg[s *pl.*]; **rühren 1.** *tr. V.* **a)** *(um~)* stir; (ein~) stir ⟨*egg, powder, etc.*⟩ ⟨**an, in** + *Akk.* into⟩; **b)** *(bewegen)* move ⟨*limb, fingers, etc.*⟩; **c)** *(fig.)* move; touch; **2.** *itr. V.* **a)** *(um~)* stir; **b)** *(geh.: her~)* das rührt daher, daß ...: that stems from the fact that ...; **3.** *refl. V.* **a)** *(sich bewegen)* move; **b)** *(Milit.)* **rührt euch!** at ease!; **rührend 1.** *Adj.* touching; **2.** *adv.* touchingly; **rühr·selig 1.** *Adj.* **a)** emotional ⟨*person*⟩; **b)** *(allzu gefühlvoll)* over-sentimental; **2.** *adv.* in an over-sentimental manner; **Rührung** die; ~: emotion

Ruine die; ~, ~**n** ruin; **ruinieren** *tr. V.* ruin

rülpsen *itr. V. (ugs.)* burp

rum *Adv. (ugs.) s.* **herum**

Rum der; ~s, ~s rum

Rumäne der; ~**n**, ~**n** Romanian; **Ru-**

mänien (das); ~s Romania; **rumänisch** *Adj.* Romanian

Rummel der; ~s *(ugs.)* **a)** commotion; *(Aufhebens)* fuss (**um** about); **b)** *(Jahrmarkt)* fair

Rumpf der; ~[e]s, **Rümpfe a)** trunk [of the body]; **b)** *(beim Schiff)* hull; **c)** *(beim Flugzeug)* fuselage

rümpfen *tr. V.* die Nase [bei etw.] ~: wrinkle one's nose [at sth.]; über jmdn./etw. die Nase rümpfen *(fig.)* look down one's nose at sb./turn up one's nose at sth.

rund 1. *Adj.* **a)** round; **b)** *(dicklich)* plump ⟨*arms etc.*⟩; chubby ⟨*cheeks*⟩; fat ⟨*stomach*⟩; **c)** *(ugs.: ganz)* round ⟨*dozen, number, etc.*⟩; **2.** *Adv.* **a)** *(ugs.: etwa)* about; **b)** ~ **um** jmdn./etw. [all] around sb./sth.; **Rund·blick** der panorama; view in all directions; **Runde** die; ~, ~**n a)** *(Sport: Strecke)* lap; **b)** *(Sport: Durchgang usw.)* round; **über die** ~**n kommen** *(fig. ugs.)* get by; manage; **c)** *(Personenkreis)* circle; *(Gesellschaft)* company; **d)** *(Rundgang)* round; **e)** *(Lage)* round

rund-, Rund-: ~**erneuern** *tr. V. (Kfz-W.)* remould; ~**fahrt** die tour (**durch** of); ~**funk** der **a)** radio; **b)** *(Einrichtung, Gebäude)* radio station

Rundfunk-: ~**anstalt** die broadcasting corporation; ~**gerät** das radio set; ~**sendung** die radio programme; ~**sprecher** der radio announcer

rund-, Rund-: ~**gang** der round (**durch** of); ~**herum** *Adv.* **a)** *(ringsum)* all around; **b)** *(völlig)* completely

rundlich *Adj.* **a)** roundish; **b)** *(mollig)* plump

Rund-: ~**reise** die [circular] tour (**durch** of); ~**weg** der circular path *or* walk

runter *Adv. (ugs.)* ~ [da]! get off [there]; *s. auch* **herunter; hinunter**

Runzel die; ~, ~**n** wrinkle; **runz[e]lig** *Adj.* wrinkled; **runzeln** *tr. V.* die Stirn/die Brauen ~: wrinkle one's brow/knit one's brows; *(ärgerlich)* frown

rupfen *tr. V.* **a)** pluck ⟨*goose, hen, etc.*⟩; **b)** *(abreißen)* pull up ⟨*weeds, grass*⟩; pull off ⟨*leaves etc.*⟩

Rüsche die; ~, ~**n** ruche; frill

Ruß der; ~**es** soot

Russe der; ~**n**, ~**n** Russian

Rüssel der; ~**s**, ~ *(des Elefanten)* trunk; *(des Schweins)* snout; *(bei Insekten u. ä.)* proboscis

rußen *itr. V.* give off sooty smoke
Russin die; ~, ~**nen** Russian; **russisch** 1. *Adj.* Russian; 2. *adv. (auf~)* in Russian; **Russisch das;** ~[s] Russian; **Ruß·land (das);** ~s Russia
rüsten *itr. V.* arm
rüstig 1. *Adj.* sprightly; active
rustikal 1. *Adj.* country-style *(food, inn, clothes, etc.);* rustic *(furniture);* 2. *adv.* in [a] country style
Rüstung die; ~, ~**en a)** armament *no art.; (Waffen)* arms *pl.;* weapons *pl.;* **b)** *(hist.)* suit of armour
Rüstungs-: ~**industrie** die armaments *or* arms industry; ~**kontrolle** die arms control; ~**stopp** der arms freeze
Rute die; ~, ~**n** switch; *(Birken~, Angel~, Wünschel~)* rod
Rutsch·bahn die slide; **rutschen** *itr. V.; mit sein* slide; *(clutch, carpet)* slip; **rutschig** *Adj.* slippery
rütteln *tr., itr. V.* shake

S

s, S [ɛs] das; ~, ~: s, S
s *Abk.* Sekunde sec.; s.
S *Abk.* **a)** Süden S.; **b)** *(österr.)* Schilling Sch.
s. *Abk.* siehe
S. *Abk.* Seite p.
Sa. *Abk.* Samstag Sat.
Saal der; ~[e]s, **Säle a)** hall; *(Ball~)* ballroom; **b)** *(Publikum)* audience
Saar·land das; ~[e]s Saarland; Saar *(esp. Hist.)*
Saat die; ~, ~**en a)** *(das Gesäte)* [young] crops *pl.;* **b)** *o. Pl. (das Säen)* sowing; **c)** *(Samenkörner)* seed[s *pl.*]
Säbel der; ~s, ~: sabre
Sabotage [zabo'taːʒə] die; ~, ~**n** sabotage *no art.;* **sabotieren** *tr. V.* sabotage
sach·dienlich *Adj.* useful; **Sache** die; ~, ~**n a)** *Pl.* things; **b)** *(Angelegenheit)* matter; business *(esp. derog.);* **zur** ~ **kommen** come to the point; **c)** *(Rechts~)* case; **d)** *o. Pl. (Anliegen)* cause

sach-, Sach-: ~**gemäß,** ~**gerecht** 1. *Adj.* proper; correct; 2. *adv.* properly; correctly; ~**kenntnis** die expertise; ~**kundig** 1. *Adj.* with a knowledge of the subject *postpos., not pred.;* 2. *adv.* expertly
sachlich 1. *Adj.* **a)** *(objektiv)* objective; *(nüchtern)* functional *(building style, etc.);* matter-of-fact *(letter etc.);* **b)** *nicht präd. (sachbezogen)* factual *(error);* 2. *adv. (objektiv)* objectively; *(state)* as a matter of fact; *(nüchtern)* *(furnished)* in a functional style; *(written)* in a matter-of-fact way; **b)** *(sachbezogen)* factually *(wrong);* **sächlich** *Adj. (Sprachw.)* neuter; **Sach·schaden** der damage [to property] *no indef. art.*
Sachse der; ~**n,** ~**n** Saxon; **Sachsen-Anhalt (das);** ~s Saxony-Anhalt
sacht, sachte 1. *Adj.* **a)** *(behutsam)* gentle; **b)** *(leise)* quiet; 2. *adv.* **a)** gently; **b)** *(leise)* quietly
Sach-: ~**verhalt** der; ~[e]s, ~**e** facts *pl.* [of the matter]; ~**verstand** der expertise; grasp of the subject
Sack der; ~[e]s, **Säcke** sack; *(aus Papier, Kunststoff)* bag
Sack-: ~**gasse** die cul-de-sac; ~**hüpfen das;** ~s sack race
Sadismus der; ~: sadism *no art.;* **Sadist** der; ~**en,** ~**en, Sadistin** die; ~, ~**nen** sadist; **sadistisch** 1. *Adj.* sadistic; 2. *adv.* sadistically
säen *tr. (auch itr.) V.* sow
Saft der; ~[e]s, **Säfte a)** juice; **b)** *(in Pflanzen)* sap; **saftig** *Adj.* **a)** juicy; sappy *(stem);* lush *(meadow, green);* **b)** *(ugs.)* hefty *(slap, blow);* steep *(coll.) (prices, bill);* crude *(joke, song, etc.);* strongly-worded *(letter etc.)*
Sage die; ~, ~**n** legend; *(bes. nordische)* saga
Säge die; ~, ~**n** saw
sagen 1. *tr. V.* **a)** say; **was ich noch** ~ **wollte** [oh] by the way; **unter uns gesagt** between you and me; **b)** *(mitteilen)* jmdm. etw. ~: say sth. to sb.; *(zur Information)* tell sb. sth.; **c)** *(nennen)* **zu jmdm./etw. X** ~: call sb./sth. X; **d)** *(anordnen, befehlen)* tell; 2. *refl. V.* **sich** *(Dat.)* **etw.** ~: say sth. to oneself
sägen *tr., itr. V.* saw
sah *1. u. 3. Pers. Sg. Prät. v.* sehen
Sahne die; ~: cream
Saison [zɛˈzõː] die; ~, ~s season
Saite die; ~, ~**n** string; **Saiten·instrument das** stringed instrument

Sakko der od. das; ~s, ~s jacket
Sakrament das; ~|e|s, ~e sacrament;
  Sakristei die; ~, ~en sacristy
Salami die; ~, ~|s| salami
Salat der; ~|e|s, ~e a) salad; b) o. Pl.
  |grüner| ~: lettuce; ein Kopf ~: a [head
  of] lettuce
Salat-: ~besteck das salad-servers
  pl.; ~soße die salad-dressing
Salbe die; ~, ~n ointment
Salbei der od. die; ~: sage
Saldo der; ~s, ~s od. **Saldi** (Buchf., Fi-
  nanzw.) balance
Säle s. Saal
Salmiak der od. das; ~: sal ammoniac
Salon [za'lõ:] der; ~s, ~s a) (Raum)
  drawing-room; b) (Geschäft) [hair-
  etc.] salon
salopp 1. Adj. casual (clothes); informal (behaviour); 2. adv. (dress)
  casually
Salto der; ~s, ~s od. **Salti** somersault;
  (beim Turnen auch) salto
salutieren itr. V. (bes. Milit.) salute
Salve die; ~, ~n (Milit.) salvo; (aus
  Gewehren) volley
Salz das; ~es, ~e salt; **salzen** tr. V.
  salt; **salzig** Adj. salty
Salz-: ~kartoffel die; meist Pl.
  boiled potato; ~säure die; o. Pl.
  (Chemie) hydrochloric acid; ~stan-
  ge die salt stick; ~streuer der; ~s,
  ~: salt-sprinkler; salt-shaker (Amer.);
  ~wasser das; Pl. ~wässer a) o. Pl.
  (zum Kochen) salted water; b) (Meerwasser) salt water
Sambia (das); ~s Zambia
Samen der; ~s, ~ a) (~korn) seed; b)
  o. Pl. (~körner) seed[s pl.]; c) o. Pl.
  (Sperma) sperm; semen
sammeln 1. tr. (auch itr.) V. a) collect;
  gather (honey, firewood, fig.: experi-
  ences, impressions, etc.); gather, pick
  (berries etc.); b) (zusammenkommen
  lassen) gather (people) [together]; assemble (people); cause (light rays) to
  converge; 2. refl. V. gather [together];
  Sammler der; ~s, ~: collector;
  Sammlung die; ~, ~en collection;
  b) |innere| ~: composure
Samstag der; ~|e|s, ~e Saturday; s.
  auch Dienstag; Dienstag-; **sams-
  tags** Adv. on Saturdays
samt 1. Präp. mit Dat. together with;
  2. Adv. ~ und sonders one and all
Samt der; ~|e|s, ~e velvet
sämtlich Indefinitpron. u. unbest.
  Zahlwort all the
Sand der; ~|e|s sand

Sandale die; ~, ~n sandal
sandig Adj. sandy
Sand-: ~kasten der [child's] sand-
  pit; sand-box (Amer.); ~kuchen der
  Madeira cake; ~mann der, ~männ-
  chen der; o. Pl. sandman; ~stein
  der sandstone; ~strand der sandy
  beach
sandte 1. u. 3. Pers. Sg. Prät. v. senden
sanft 1. Adj. gentle; (leise) soft; (friedlich) peaceful; 2. adv. gently; (leise)
  softly; (friedlich) peacefully
sang 1. u. 3. Pers. Sg. Prät. v. singen;
  Sänger der; ~s, ~, **Sängerin** die; ~,
  ~nen singer
sanieren 1. tr. V. a) redevelop (area);
  rehabilitate (building); (renovieren)
  renovate [and improve] (flat etc.); b)
  (Wirtsch.) restore (firm) to profitability; 2. refl. V. (company etc.) restore itself to profitability; (person) get oneself out of the red; **Sanierung** die;
  ~, ~en a) s. sanieren a: redevelop-
  ment; rehabilitation; renovation; b)
  restoration to profitability; **sanitär**
  Adj. sanitary; **Sanitäter** der; ~s, ~:
  first-aid man; (im Krankenwagen)
  ambulance man
sank 1. u. 3. Pers. Sg. Prät. v. sinken
sann 1. u. 3. Pers. Sg. Prät. v. sinnen
Saphir der; ~s, ~e sapphire
Sardelle die; ~, ~n anchovy
Sardine die; ~, ~n sardine
Sarg der; ~|e|s, Särge coffin
saß 1. u. 3. Pers. Sg. Prät. v. sitzen
Satan der (bibl.) Satan no def. art.
Satellit der; ~en, ~en satellite
Satire die; ~, ~n satire
satt Adj. a) full [up] pred.; well-fed;
  sich ~ essen/trinken eat/drink· as
  much as one wants; eat/drink one's
  fill; b) jmdn./etw. ~ haben (ugs.) be
  fed up with sb./sth. (coll.)
Sattel der; ~s, Sättel a) saddle; **satteln** 1. tr. V. saddle; 2. itr. V. saddle
  the/one's horse
sättigen itr. V. be filling
Sattler der; ~s, ~: saddler; (allgemein) leather-worker
Satz der; ~es, Sätze a) (sprachliche
  Einheit) sentence; b) (Musik) movement; c) (Tennis, Volleyball) set;
  (Tischtennis, Badminton) game; d)
  (Sprung) leap; jump; e) (Amtsspr.: Tarif) rate; f) (Set) set; g) (Boden~) sediment; (von Kaffee) grounds pl.
Satzung die; ~, ~en articles of association pl.; statutes pl.
Satz·zeichen das punctuation mark

Sau die; ~, **Säue a)** *(weibliches Schwein)* sow; **b)** *(bes. südd.: Schwein)* pig

sauber 1. *Adj.* **a)** clean; **b)** *(sorgfältig)* neat; **2.** *adv.* **a)** *(sorgfältig)* neatly; **b)** *(fehlerlos)* |sehr| ~: |quite| perfectly; **Sauberkeit** die; ~: cleanness; **sauber|machen 1.** *tr. V.* clean; **2.** *itr. V.* clean; do the cleaning; **säubern** *tr. V.* clean; **Säuberung** die; ~, ~en cleaning

Sauce *s.* Soße

Saudi [zaudi] der; ~s, ~s Saudi; **Saudi-Arabien (das)** Saudi Arabia

sauer 1. *Adj.* **a)** sour; pickled ⟨*herring, gherkin, etc.*⟩; acid[ic] ⟨*wine, vinegar*⟩; **saurer Regen** acid rain; **b)** *(ugs.: verärgert)* cross, annoyed **(auf + Akk.** with); **2.** *adv.* in vinegar; **Sauer·braten** der braised beef marinated in vinegar and herbs; sauerbraten *(Amer.)*

Sauerei die; ~, ~en *(salopp abwertend)* **a)** *(Unflätigkeit)* obscenity **b)** *(Gemeinheit)* bloody scandal *(sl.)*

Sauer-: ~**kirsche** die sour cherry; ~**kraut** das *o. Pl.* sauerkraut

säuerlich *Adj.* |leicht| ~: slightly sour; slightly sharp ⟨*sauce*⟩

Sauer-: ~**stoff** der; *o. Pl.* oxygen; ~**stoffgerät** das oxygen apparatus; ~**stoffmangel** der; *o. Pl.* lack of oxygen; ~**teig** der leaven

saufen 1. *unr. itr. V. (salopp: trinken)* drink; swig *(coll.)*; *(Alkohol trinken)* drink; booze *(coll.)*; **2.** *unr. tr. V. (salopp: trinken)* drink; **Säufer** der; ~s, ~ *(salopp)* boozer *(coll.)*; **säuft 3. Pers. Sg. Präsens v.** saufen

saugen 1. *tr. V.* **a)** *auch unr.* suck; **b)** *auch itr. (staub~)* vacuum; hoover *(coll.)*; **2.** *regelm. (auch unr.) itr. V.* **an etw.** *(Dat.)* ~: suck [at] sth.; **3.** *unr. (auch regelm.) refl. V.* **sich voll etw.** ~: become soaked with sth.; **säugen** *tr. V.* suckle; **Säuge·tier** das *(Zool.)* mammal; **Säugling** der; ~s, ~e baby; **Säuglings·pflege** die baby care

Säule die; ~, ~n column; *(nur als Stütze, auch fig.)* pillar

Saum der; ~|e|s, **Säume** hem; **säumen** *tr. V.* hem; *(fig. geh.)* line

säumig *(geh.) Adj.* tardy

Sauna die; ~, ~s *od.* **Saunen** sauna

Säure die; ~, ~n **a)** *o. Pl. (von Früchten)* sourness; *(von Wein, Essig)* acidity; *(von Soßen)* sharpness; **b)** *(Chemie)* acid; **Saure·gurken·zeit** die *(ugs.)* silly season *(Brit.)*

Saus: **in** ~ **und Braus leben** live the high life

säuseln 1. *itr. V.* ⟨*leaves, branches, etc.*⟩ rustle; ⟨*wind*⟩ murmur; **2.** *tr. V. (iron.: sagen)* whisper; **sausen** *itr. V.* **a)** ⟨*wind*⟩ whistle; ⟨*storm*⟩ roar; ⟨*head, ears*⟩ buzz; **b)** *mit sein* ⟨*person*⟩ rush; ⟨*vehicle*⟩ roar; **c)** *mit sein* ⟨*whip, bullet, etc.*⟩ whistle

Savanne [za'vanə] die; ~, ~n savannah

Saxophon das; ~s, ~e saxophone

S-Bahn ['εs-] die city and suburban railway

SB- [εs'be:-] self-service *(attrib.)*

Schabe die; ~, ~n cockroach

schaben *tr., itr. V.* scrape; **Schaber** der; ~s, ~: scraper

schäbig 1. *Adj.* **a)** *(abgenutzt)* shabby; **b)** *(jämmerlich, gering)* pathetic; **c)** *(gemein)* shabby; **2.** *adv.* **a)** *(abgenutzt)* shabbily; **b)** *(jämmerlich)* miserably; **c)** *(gemein)* meanly

Schach das; ~s, ~s **a)** *o. Pl. (Spiel)* chess; **b)** *(Stellung)* check; **jmdn./etw. in** ~ **halten** *(ugs. fig.)* keep sb./sth. in check

Schach-: ~**brett** das chessboard; ~**figur** die chess piece; ~**spiel** das **a)** *o. Pl. (Spiel)* chess; *(das Spielen)* chess-playing; **b)** *(Brett und Figuren)* chess set

Schacht der; ~|e|s, **Schächte** shaft

Schachtel die; ~, ~n **a)** box; **eine** ~ **Zigaretten** a packet *or (Amer.)* pack of cigarettes; **b)** **alte** ~ *(salopp abwertend)* old bag *(sl.)*

schade *Adj.* |ach, wie| ~! |what a| pity *or* shame; |es ist| ~ **um jmdn./etw.** it's a pity *or* shame about sb./sth.; **für jmdn./für** *od.* **zu etw. zu** ~ **sein** be too good for sb./sth.

Schädel der; ~s, ~: skull; *(Kopf)* head; **Schädel·bruch** der *(Med.)* skull fracture

schaden *itr. V.* **jmdm./einer Sache** ~: damage *or* harm sb./sth.; **Schaden** der; ~s, **Schäden a)** damage *no pl., no indef. art.;* **ein kleiner/großer** ~: little/ major damage; **b)** *(Nachteil)* disadvantage

schaden-, Schaden-: ~**ersatz** der *(Rechtsw.)* damages *pl.;* ~**freude** die *o. Pl.* malicious pleasure; ~**froh 1.** *Adj.* gloating; ~**froh sein** gloat; **2.** *adv.* with malicious pleasure

schadhaft *Adj.* defective; **schädigen** *tr. V.* damage ⟨*health, reputation, interests*⟩; harm, hurt ⟨*person*⟩; cause

losses to ⟨*firm, industry, etc.*⟩; **Schä-
digung die;** ~, ~en damage *no pl., no
indef. art.* (*Gen.* to); **schädlich** *Adj.*
harmful; **Schädling der;** ~s, ~e pest
Schaf das; ~|e|s, ~e a) sheep; b) (*ugs.:
Dummkopf*) twit (*Brit. sl.*);
Schaf·bock der ram; **Schäfchen
das;** ~s, ~: [little] sheep; (*Lamm*)
lamb; **Schäfer der;** ~s, ~: shepherd;
Schäfer·hund der sheep-dog; |deut-
scher| ~: Alsatian; **Schaf·fell das**
sheepskin
schaffen 1. *unr. tr. V.* a) create; b)
auch regelm. (*herstellen*) create ⟨*conditions, jobs, situation, etc.*⟩; make
⟨*room, space, fortune*⟩; 2. *tr. V.* a) (*bewältigen*) manage; **es** ~, **etw. zu tun**
manage to do sth.; b) (*ugs.: erschöpfen*) wear out; c) **etw. aus etw./in etw.**
(*Akk.*) ~: get sth. out of/into sth.; 3.
itr. V. a) (*südd.: arbeiten*) work; b) **sich**
(*Dat.*) **zu** ~ **machen** busy oneself;
jmdm. zu ~ **machen** cause sb. trouble
Schaffner der; ~s ~ (*im Bus*)
conductor; (*im Zug*) guard (*Brit.*);
conductor (*Amer.*); **Schaffnerin die;**
~, ~nen (*im Bus*) conductress (*Brit.*);
(*im Zug*) guard (*Brit.*); conductress
(*Amer.*)
Schaffung die; ~: creation
Schafott das; ~|e|s, ~e scaffold
Schafs·käse der sheep's milk
cheese; **Schaf·wolle die** sheep's
wool
Schakal der; ~s, ~e jackal
schal *Adj.* stale ⟨*drink, taste, smell,
joke*⟩; empty ⟨*words, feeling*⟩
Schal der; ~s, ~s *od.* ~e scarf
Schale die; ~, ~n a) (*Obst~*) skin;
(*abgeschälte* ~) peel *no pl.*; b) (*Nuß~,
Eier~*) shell; c) (*Schüssel*) bowl; (*flacher*) dish; d) **sich in** ~ **werfen** *od.*
schmeißen (*ugs.*) get dressed [up] to
the nines; **schälen** 1. *tr. V.* peel
⟨*fruit, vegetable*⟩; shell ⟨*egg, nut, pea*⟩;
2. *refl. V.* peel
Schall der; ~|e|s, ~e *od.* Schälle
sound; **Schall·dämpfer der** a)
silencer; b) (*Musik*) mute; **schalldicht** *Adj.* sound-proof; **schallen**
regelm. (*auch unr.*) *itr. V.* ring out;
~**des Gelächter** ringing laughter
Schall-: ~**geschwindigkeit die**
speed *or* velocity of sound; ~**platte
die** record
Schalotte die; ~, ~n shallot
schalt *1. u. 3. Pers. Sg. Prät. v.* schelten
schalten 1. *tr. V.* switch; 2. *itr. V.* a)

(*Schalter betätigen*) switch, turn (**auf**
+ *Akk.* to); b) ⟨*machine*⟩ switch (**auf**
+ *Akk.* to); c) (*im Auto*) change
[gear]; d) ~ **und walten** manage one's
affairs; e) (*ugs.: begreifen*) twig (*coll.*);
catch on (*coll.*); **Schalter der;** ~s, ~
a) switch; b) (*Post~, Bank~ usw.*)
counter
Schalter-: ~**beamte der** counter
clerk; (*im Bahnhof*) ticket clerk;
~**halle die** hall; (*im Bahnhof*) book-
ing-hall (*Brit.*); ticket office
Schaltjahr das leap year; **Schaltung die;** ~, ~en (*Elektrot.*) circuit;
wiring system
Scham die; ~: shame; **schämen** *refl.
V.* be ashamed (*Gen.,* **für, wegen** of);
Scham·gefühl das; *o. Pl.* sense of
shame; **schamhaft** 1. *Adj.* bashful;
2. *adv.* bashfully; **scham·los** 1. *Adj.*
a) (*skrupellos, dreist*) shameless; b)
(*unanständig*) indecent; shameless
⟨*person*⟩; 2. *adv.* a) (*skrupellos, dreist*)
shamelessly; b) (*unanständig*) indecently
Schande die; ~: disgrace; **schändlich** 1. *Adj.* disgraceful; 2. *adv.* disgracefully
Schar die; ~, ~en crowd; horde;
scharen·weise *Adv.* in swarms *or*
hordes
scharf; schärfer, schärfst... 1.
Adj. a) sharp; b) (*stark gewürzt, brennend, stechend*) hot; strong ⟨*drink, vinegar, etc.*⟩; caustic ⟨*chemical*⟩; pungent ⟨*smell*⟩; c) (*durchdringend*) shrill;
(*hell*) harsh; (*kalt*) biting ⟨*cold, wind,
etc.*⟩; sharp ⟨*frost*⟩; d) (*deutlich wahrnehmend*) keen; e) (*schnell*) fast; hard
⟨*ride, gallop, etc.*⟩; f) (*explosiv*) live;
(*Ballspiele*) powerful ⟨*shot*⟩; g) **das** ~**e**
S (*bes. österr.*) the German letter 'ß';
h) ~ **auf jmdn./etw. sein** (*ugs.*) really
fancy sb. (*coll.*)/be really keen on sth;
2. *adv.* a) ~ **würzen/abschmecken** sea-
son/flavour highly; ~ **riechen** smell
pungent; b) (*durchdringend*) shrilly;
(*hell*) harshly; (*kalt*) bitingly; c) (*deutlich wahrnehmend*) ⟨*listen, watch, etc.*⟩
closely, intently; ⟨*think, consider, etc.*⟩
hard; d) (*deutlich hervortretend*)
sharply; e) (*schonungslos*) ⟨*attack, criticize, etc.*⟩ sharply, strongly; ⟨*watch,
observe, etc.*⟩ closely; f) (*schnell*) fast;
~ **bremsen** brake hard *or* sharply;
Schärfe die; ~ a) sharpness; b) (*von
Geschmack*) hotness; (*von Chemikalien*) causticity; (*von Geruch*) pungency; c) (*Intensität*) shrillness; (*des

Frostes) sharpness; **schärfen 1.** *tr. V.* *(auch fig.)* sharpen; **2.** *refl. V.* become sharper *or* keener

scharf-: ~kantig *Adj.* sharp-edged; **~sichtig** *Adj.* sharp-sighted; perspicacious; **~sinnig 1.** *Adj.* astute; **2.** *adv.* astutely

Scharlach der; ~s *(Med.)* scarlet fever

Scharnier das; ~s, ~e hinge

scharren *itr. V.* **a)** scrape; **b)** *(wühlen)* scratch; **2.** *tr. V.* scrape, scratch out *(hole, hollow, etc.)*

Schaschlik der *od.* **das; ~s, ~s** *(Kochk.)* shashlik

Schatten der; ~s, ~ a) shadow; **b)** *o. Pl. (schattige Stelle)* shade; **schattig** *Adj.* shady

Schatz der; ~es, Schätze treasure *no indef. art.;* **schätzen 1.** *tr. V.* **a)** estimate; **sich glücklich ~:** deem oneself lucky; **b)** *(ugs.: annehmen)* reckon; **c)** *(würdigen, hochachten)* **jmdn. ~:** hold sb. in high esteem; **2.** *itr. V.* guess; **Schätzung die; ~, ~en** estimate

Schau die; ~, ~en a) *(Ausstellung)* exhibition; **b)** *(Vorführung)* show; **c) zur ~ stellen** *(ausstellen)* exhibit; display; *(offen zeigen)* display

Schauder der; ~s, ~: shiver; **schauderhaft 1.** *Adj.* terrible; **2.** *adv.* terribly; **schaudern** *itr. V.* **a)** *(vor Kälte)* shiver; **b)** *(vor Angst)* shudder

schauen *(bes. südd., österr., schweiz.)* **1.** *itr. V.* **a)** look; **b)** *(sich kümmern um)* **nach jmdm./etw. ~:** take *or* have a look at sb./sth.; **c)** *(achten)* **auf etw.** *(Akk.)* ~: set store by sth.; **d)** *(ugs.: sich bemühen)* **schau, daß du ...:** see *or* mind that you ...; **e)** *(nachsehen)* have a look; **2.** *tr. V.* **Fernsehen ~:** watch television

Schauer der; ~s, ~: shower

Schauer·geschichte die horror story; **schauerlich 1.** *Adj.* **a)** horrifying; **b)** *(ugs.: fürchterlich)* terrible *(coll.);* **2.** *(ugs.: fürchterlich)* terribly *(coll.)*

Schaufel die; ~, ~n shovel; *(Kehr~)* dustpan; **schaufeln** *tr. V.* shovel; *(graben)* dig

Schau·fenster das shop-window; **Schaufenster·bummel der: einen ~ machen** go window-shopping

Schaukel die; ~, ~n a) swing; **b)** *(Wippe)* see-saw; **schaukeln 1.** *itr. V.* **a)** swing; *(im Schaukelstuhl)* rock; **b)**

(sich hin und her bewegen) sway [to and fro]; *(sich auf und ab bewegen)* ⟨*ship, boat*⟩ pitch and toss; ⟨*vehicle*⟩ bump [up and down]; **2.** *tr. V.* rock

Schaukel-: ~pferd das rocking-horse; **~stuhl der** rocking-chair

Schau·lustige der/die; *adj. Dekl.* curious onlooker

Schaum der; ~s, Schäume a) foam; *(von Seife usw.)* lather; *(von Getränken, Suppen usw.)* froth; **b)** *(Geifer)* foam; froth; **schäumen** *itr. V.* foam; froth; ⟨*soap etc.*⟩ lather; ⟨*beer, fizzy drink, etc.*⟩ froth [up]

Schaum-: ~gummi der foam rubber; **~wein der** sparkling wine

Schau-: ~spiel das a) *o. Pl. (Drama)* drama *no art.;* **b)** *(ernstes Stück)* play; **c)** *(geh.: Anblick)* spectacle; **~spieler der** actor; **~spielerin die** actress; **~steller der; ~s, ~:** showman

Scheck der; ~s, ~s cheque; **Scheckheft das** cheque-book; **Scheck·karte die** cheque card

scheel *(ugs.)* **1.** *Adj.* disapproving; *(neidisch)* envious; jealous; **2.** *adv.* disapprovingly; *(neidisch)* enviously; jealously

Scheibe die; ~, ~n a) disc; **b)** *(abgeschnittene ~)* slice; **c)** *(Glas~)* pane [of glass]; *(Fenster~)* [window-]pane; **Scheiben·wischer der** windscreen-wiper

Scheide die; ~, ~n a) sheath; **b)** *(Anat.)* vagina

scheiden *unr. tr. V.* dissolve ⟨*marriage*⟩; divorce ⟨*married couple*⟩; **sich ~ lassen** get divorced *or* get a divorce; **Scheidung die; ~, ~en** divorce

Schein der; ~|e|s, ~e a) *o. Pl. (Licht~)* light; **b)** *o. Pl. (An~)* appearances *pl., no art.;* *(Täuschung)* pretence; **etw. nur zum ~ tun** [only] pretend to do sth.; make a show of doing sth.; **c)** *(Geld~)* note; **scheinbar 1.** *Adj.* apparent; seeming; **2.** *adv.* seemingly; **scheinen** *unr. itr. V.* **a)** shine; **b)** *(den Eindruck erwecken)* seem; appear; **mir scheint, |daß| ...:** it seems *or* appears to me that ...

schein-, Schein-: ~heilig 1. *Adj.* hypocritical; **2.** *adv.* hypocritically; **~werfer der** floodlight; *(am Auto)* headlight

Scheiße die; ~ *(derb)* shit *(coarse);* crap *(coarse);* **scheißen** *unr. itr. V.* *(derb)* [have *or* *(Amer.)* take a] shit *(coarse);* crap *(coarse);* have a crap *(coarse)*

Scheitel der; ~s, ~: parting;
scheiteln tr. V. part ⟨hair⟩
scheitern itr. V.; mit sein fail; ⟨talks,
marriage⟩ break down; ⟨plan, project⟩
fail, fall through
Schelle die; ~, ~n bell; **schellen** itr.
V. (westd.) s. **klingeln**
Schell·fisch der haddock
Schelm der; ~|e|s, ~e rascal; rogue;
schelmisch 1. Adj. roguish; 2. adv.
roguishly
Schelte die; ~, ~n (geh.) scolding;
schelten (südd., geh.) 1. unr. itr. V.
auf od. über jmdn./etw. ~: moan
about sb./sth.; 2. unr. tr. V. scold
Schema das; ~s, ~s od. ~ta od.
Schemen pattern; **schematisch** 1.
Adj. a) diagrammatic; b) (mechanisch)
mechanical; 2. adv. a) in diagram
form; b) (mechanisch) mechanically
Schemel der; ~s, ~ a) stool; b)
(südd.: Fußbank) footstool
Schenkel der; ~s, ~: thigh
schenken tr. V. a) give; jmdm. etw.
|zum Geburtstag| ~: give sb. sth. or
sth. to sb. [as a birthday present or for
his/her birthday]; b) (ugs.: erlassen)
jmdm./sich etw. ~: spare sb./oneself
sth.
Scherbe die; ~, ~n fragment
Schere die; ~, ~n a) scissors pl.; eine
~: a pair of scissors; b) (Zool.) claw;
¹**scheren** unr. tr. V. crop; (von Haar
befreien) shear, clip ⟨sheep⟩
²**scheren** tr., refl. V. sich um jmdn./
etw. nicht ~: not care about sb./sth.;
Scherereien Pl. (ugs.) trouble no pl.
Scherz der; ~es, ~e joke; **scherzen**
itr. V. joke; **scherzhaft** 1. Adj. jocular; 2. adv. jocularly
scheu 1. Adj. shy; timid ⟨animal⟩;
(ehrfürchtig) awed; 2. adv. a) shyly; b)
(von Tieren) timidly; **Scheu** die; ~ a)
shyness; (Ehrfurcht) awe; b) (von Tieren) timidity
scheuchen tr. V. shoo; drive
scheuen 1. tr. V. shrink from; shun
⟨people, light, company, etc.⟩; 2. refl.
V. sich vor etw. (Dat.) ~: be afraid of
or shrink from sth. 3. itr. V. ⟨horse⟩
shy (vor + Dat. at)
scheuern 1. tr., itr. V. a) (reinigen)
scour; scrub; b) (reiben) rub; chafe; 2.
tr. V. (reiben an) rub
Scheuer-: ~pulver das scouring
powder; ~tuch das; Pl. ~tücher
scouring cloth
Scheune die; ~, ~n barn
Scheusal das; ~s, ~e monster;

scheußlich 1. Adj. a) dreadful; b)
(ugs.: äußerst unangenehm) dreadful
(coll.); ghastly (coll.) ⟨weather, taste,
smell⟩; 2. adv. a) dreadfully; b) (ugs.:
sehr) dreadfully (coll.)
Schi usw.: s. **Ski** usw.
Schicht die; ~, ~en a) (Lage) layer;
(Geol.) stratum; (von Farbe) coat;
(sehr dünn) film; b) (Gesellschafts~)
stratum; c) (Arbeits~) shift; ~ arbeiten work shifts; be on shift work;
schichten tr. V. stack
schick 1. Adj. a) stylish; chic ⟨clothes,
fashions⟩; smart ⟨woman, girl, man⟩;
b) (ugs.: großartig, toll) great (coll.);
fantastic (coll.); 2. adv. a) stylishly;
smartly ⟨furnished, decorated⟩
schicken 1. tr. V. send; jmdm. etw. ~,
etw. an jmdn. ~: send sth. to sb.; send
sb. sth.; 2. itr. V. nach jmdm. ~: send
for sb; 3. refl. V. (veralt.: sich ziemen)
be proper or fitting
Schicksal das; ~s, ~e: |das| ~: fate;
destiny; (schweres Los) fate; **Schick-
sals·schlag** der stroke of fate
Schiebe·dach das sunroof;
schieben 1. unr. tr. V. a) push; b)
(stecken) put; c) etw. auf jmdn./etw. ~:
blame sb./sth. for sth.; 2. unr. refl. V.
sich durch die Menge ~: push one's
way through the crowd; 3. unr. itr. V.
push; (heftig) shove; **Schiebe·tür**
die sliding door; **Schiebung** die; ~,
~en (ugs.) a) shady deal; b) (o. Pl.: Begünstigung) pulling strings
schied 1. u. 3. Pers. Sg. Prät. v. **scheiden**
Schieds·richter der referee; (Tennis,
Hockey, Kricket) umpire
schief 1. Adj. a) (schräg) leaning ⟨wall,
fence, post⟩; (nicht parallel) crooked;
sloping ⟨surface⟩; worn[-down]
⟨heels⟩; b) (fig.: verzerrt) distorted
⟨picture, presentation, view, impres-
sion⟩; false ⟨comparison⟩; 2. adv. a)
(schräg) das Bild hängt/der Teppich
liegt ~: the picture/carpet is crooked;
der Tisch steht ~: the table isn't level;
b) (fig.: verzerrt) etw. ~ darstellen give
a distorted account of sth.
Schiefer der; ~s (Gestein) slate
schief-: ~|gehen, ~|laufen unr. itr.
V.; mit sein (ugs.) go wrong
schielen itr. V. a) squint; auf dem
rechten Auge ~: have a squint in one's
right eye; b) (ugs.: blicken) look out of
the corner of one's eye
schien 1. u. 3. Pers. Sg. Prät. v. **scheinen**

Schien·bein das shinbone; **Schiene** die; ~, ~n a) rail; b) *(Gleit~)* runner; c) *(Med.: Stütze)* splint; **schienen** tr. V. jmds. Arm/ Bein ~: put sb.'s arm/leg in a splint/ splints

schießen 1. *unr. itr. V.* a) shoot; auf jmdn./etw. ~: shoot/fire at sb./sth.; b) *mit sein (fließen, heraus~)* gush; *(spritzen)* spurt; c) *mit sein (schnell wachsen)* shoot up; 2. *unr. tr. V.* a) shoot; fire *(bullet, missile, rocket)*; b) *(Fußball)* score *(goal)*; c) *(ugs.: fotografieren)* einige Aufnahmen ~: take a few snaps; **Schießerei** die; ~, ~en a) shooting *no indef. art., no pl.*; b) *(Schußwechsel)* gun-battle

Schiff das; ~|e|s, ~e a) ship; mit dem ~: by ship *or* sea; b) *(Archit.: Kirchen~) (Mittel~)* nave; *(Quer~)* transept; *(Seiten~)* aisle; **Schiffahrt** die; *o. Pl.* shipping *no indef. art.; (Schiffahrtskunde)* navigation

Schiff-: ~**bruch** der *(veralt.)* shipwreck; ~**brüchige** der/die; *adj. Dekl.* shipwrecked man/woman

Schiffer der; ~s, ~: boatman; *(eines Lastkahns)* bargee; *(Kapitän)* skipper

Schiffs-: ~**arzt** der ship's doctor; ~**brücke** die pontoon bridge; ~**junge** der ship's boy; ~**reise** die voyage; *(Vergnügungsreise)* cruise; ~**verkehr** der shipping traffic

Schikane die; ~, ~n a) harassment *no indef. art.;* b) mit allen ~n *(ugs.) (kitchen, house)* with all mod cons *(Brit. coll.); (car, bicycle, stereo)* with all the extras; **schikanieren** tr. V. jmdn. ~: harass sb.

¹**Schild** der; ~|e|s, ~e shield; ²**Schild** das; ~|e|s, ~er sign; *(Nummern~)* number-plate; *(Namens~)* nameplate; *(auf Denkmälern, Gebäuden usw.)* plaque; *(Etikett)* label; **schildern** tr. V. describe; **Schild·kröte** die tortoise; *(Seeschildkröte)* turtle

Schilf das; ~|e|s a) reed; b) *o. Pl. (Röhricht)* reeds *pl.*

schillern *itr. V.* shimmer

Schilling der; ~s, ~e schilling

schilt *3. Pers. Sg. Präsens v.* schelten

Schimmel der; ~s, ~ a) *o. Pl.* mould; *(auf Leder, Papier)* mildew; b) *(Pferd)* white horse; **schimmelig** *Adj.* mouldy; mildewy *(paper, leather)*; **schimmeln** *itr. V.; auch mit sein* go mouldy; *(leather, paper)* get covered with mildew

Schimmer der; ~s *(Schein)* gleam; *(von Seide)* shimmer; sheen; keinen ~ |von etw.| haben *(ugs.)* not have the faintest idea [about sth.] *(coll.);* **schimmern** *itr. V.* gleam; *(water, sea)* glisten, shimmer; *(metal)* glint, gleam; *(silk etc.)* shimmer

schimmlig *s.* schimmelig

Schimpanse der; ~n, ~n chimpanzee

schimpfen 1. *itr. V.* a) carry on *(coll.)* (auf, über + Akk. about); *(meckern)* grumble, moan (auf, über + Akk. at); b) mit jmdm. ~: tell sb. off; scold sb.; 2. *tr. V.* jmdn. ~: tell sb. off; **Schimpf·wort** das *(Beleidigung)* insult; *(derbes Wort)* swear-word

schinden *unr. tr. V.* maltreat; illtreat; Zeit ~ *(ugs.)* play for time

Schinken der; ~s, ~ ham; **Schinken·speck** der bacon

Schippe die; ~, ~n *(Schaufel)* shovel

Schirm der; ~|e|s, ~e umbrella; brolly *(Brit. coll.); (Sonnen~)* sunshade

Schirm-: ~**herr** der patron; ~**herrin** die patroness; ~**herrschaft** die patronage; ~**ständer** der umbrella stand

schiß *1. u. 3. Pers. Sg. Prät. v.* scheißen

Schlacht die; ~, ~en battle; **schlachten** tr. V. *(auch itr.)* V. slaughter; kill *(rabbit, chicken, etc.);* **Schlachter** der; ~s, ~ *(nordd.)* butcher; **Schlachterei** die; ~, ~en *(nordd.)* butcher's [shop]

Schlacht-: ~**hof** der abattoir; ~**vieh** das animals *pl.* kept for meat; *(kurz vor der Schlachtung)* animals *pl.* for slaughter

Schlacke die; ~, ~n cinders *pl.; (Hochofen~)* slag

Schlaf der; ~|e|s sleep; einen leichten/ festen/gesunden ~ haben be a light/ heavy/good sleeper; **Schlaf·an·zug** der pyjamas *pl.;* **Schläfchen** das; ~s, ~: nap; snooze *(coll.)*

Schläfe die; ~, ~n temple

schlafen *unr. itr. V.* a) *(auch fig.)* sleep; tief *od.* fest ~: be sound asleep; lange ~: sleep for a long time; *(am Morgen)* sleep in; ~ gehen go to bed; b) *(ugs.: nicht aufpassen)* be asleep; **Schläfer** der; ~s, ~: sleeper

schlaff 1. *Adj.* a) slack; flabby *(stomach, muscles);* b) *(schlapp, matt)* limp *(body, hand, handshake);* shaky *(knees);* 2. *adv.* a) slackly; b) *(schlapp, matt)* limply

Schlaf-: ~**gelegenheit** die place to sleep; ~**mittel** das sleep-inducing drug

schläfrig 1. *Adj.* sleepy; 2. *adv.* sleep-ily
Schlaf-: ~**saal** der dormitory; ~**sack** sleeping-bag
schläft 3. *Pers. Sg. Präsens v.* schlafen
Schlaf-: ~**tablette** die sleeping-pill; ~**wagen** der sleeping-car; sleeper; ~**zimmer** das bedroom
Schlag der; ~|e|s, Schläge a) blow; *(Faust~)* punch; *(Klaps)* slap; *(Tennis~, Golf~)* stroke; shot; ~ **auf** ~ *(fig.)* in quick succession; b) *(Auf~, Aufprall)* bang; *(dumpf)* thud; *(Klopfen)* knock; c) *o. Pl. (des Herzens, Pulses)* beating; *(eines Pendels)* swinging; d) *(einzelne rhythmische Bewegung) (Herz~, Puls~, Takt~)* beat; *(eines Pendels)* swing; e) *o. Pl. (Töne) (einer Uhr)* striking; *(einer Glocke)* ringing; f) *(einzelner Ton) (Stunden~)* stroke; *(Glocken~)* ring; ~ **acht Uhr** on the stroke of eight
schlag-, Schlag-: ~**ader** die artery; ~**anfall** der stroke; ~**artig** 1. *Adj.* very sudden; 2. *adv.* quite suddenly; ~**baum** der barrier
schlagen 1. *unr. tr. V.* a) hit; beat; strike; *(mit der Faust)* punch; hit; *(mit der flachen Hand)* slap; b) *(mit Richtungsangabe)* hit *(ball)*; **einen Nagel in etw.** *(Akk.)* ~: knock a nail into sth.; c) *(rühren)* beat *(mixture)*; whip *(cream)*; *(mit einem Schneebesen)* whisk; d) *(läuten)* *(clock)* strike; *(bell)* ring; e) *(legen)* throw; f) *(einwickeln)* wrap **(in** + *Akk.* in); g) *(besiegen, übertreffen)* beat; 2. *unr. itr. V.* a) er schlug mit der Faust auf den Tisch he beat the table with his fist; b) **mit den Flügeln ~** *(bird)* beat or flap its wings; c) *mit sein (prallen)* bang; **mit dem Kopf auf etw.** *(Akk.)/gegen etw.* ~: bang one's head on/against sth.; d) *mit sein* jmdm. **auf den Magen ~**: affect sb.'s stomach; e) *(pulsieren)* *(heart, pulse)* beat; *(heftig)* *(heart)* pound; *(pulse)* throb; f) *(läuten)* *(clock)* strike; *(bell)* ring; 3. *unr. refl. V.* fight; **sich mit jmdm.** ~: fight with sb.; **Schlager** der; ~s, ~ a) pop song; b) *(Erfolg) (Buch)* best seller; *(Ware)* best-selling line; *(Film, Stück, Lied)* hit
Schläger der; ~s, ~ a) *(Raufbold)* tough; thug; b) *(Tennis~, Federball~, Squash~)* racket; *(Tischtennis~, Kriket~)* bat; *([Eis]hockey~, Polo~)* stick; *(Golf~)* club; **Schlägerei** die; ~, ~en brawl; fight
Schlager·sänger der pop singer

schlag-, Schlag-: ~**fertig** *Adj.* quick-witted *(reply)*; *(person)* who is quick at repartee; ~**fertigkeit** die; *o. Pl.* quickness at repartee; ~**loch** das pothole; ~**obers** das; ~ *(österr.)*, ~**rahm** der *(bes. südd., österr., schweiz.)*, ~**sahne** die whipping cream; *(geschlagen)* whipped cream; ~**zeile** die headline; ~**zeug** das drums *pl.*
schlaksig *(ugs.) Adj.* gangling; lanky
Schlamassel der *od.* das; ~s *(ugs.)* mess
Schlamm der; ~|e|s, ~e *od.* Schlämme a) mud; b) *(Schlick)* sludge; **schlammig** *Adj.* a) muddy; b) *(schlickig)* sludgy; muddy
Schlamperei die; ~, ~en *(ugs. abwertend)* sloppiness; **schlampig** *(ugs. abwertend)* 1. *Adj.* a) *(liederlich)* slovenly; b) *(nachlässig)* sloppy; slipshod *(work)*; 2. *adv.* a) *(liederlich)* in a slovenly way; b) *(nachlässig)* sloppily
schlang 1. *u.* 3. *Pers. Sg. Prät. v.* schlingen; **Schlange** die; ~, ~n a) snake; b) *(Menschen~)* queue; line *(Amer.)*; ~ **stehen** queue; stand in line *(Amer.)*; c) *(Auto~)* tailback *(Brit.)*; backup *(Amer.)*; **schlängeln** refl. V. *(snake)* wind [its way]; *(road)* wind, snake [its way]; **Schlangen·linie** die wavy line
schlank *Adj.* slim *(person)*; slim, slender *(build, figure)*; **Schlankheitskur** die slimming diet
schlapp *Adj.* a) worn out; tired out; *(wegen Schwüle)* listless; *(wegen Krankheit)* run-down; b) *(ugs.: ohne Schwung)* wet *(sl.)*; feeble; c) slack *(rope, cable)*; loose *(skin)*; flabby *(stomach, muscles)*; **Schlappe** die; ~, ~n setback; **schlapp|machen** itr. V. *(ugs.)* flag; *(zusammenbrechen)* flake out *(coll.)*; *(aufgeben)* give up
schlau 1. *Adj.* a) shrewd; astute; *(gerissen)* wily; crafty; cunning; b) *(ugs.. gescheit)* clever; bright; smart; **aus jmdm. nicht ~ werden** *(ugs.)* not be able to make sb. out; 2. *adv.* shrewdly; astutely; *(gerissen)* craftily; cunningly
Schlauch der; ~|e|s, Schläuche a) hose; b) *(Fahrrad~, Auto~)* tube; **Schlauch·boot** das rubber dinghy; inflatable [dinghy]; **schlauchen** *(ugs.) tr., auch itr. V.* jmdn. ~: take it out of sb.; **schlauch·los** *Adj.* tubeless *(tyre)*
Schläue die; ~: shrewdness; astute-

ness; *(Gerissenheit)* wiliness; craftiness; cunning

Schlaufe die; ~, ~n loop

schlecht 1. *Adj.* **a)** bad; poor, bad *(food, quality, style, harvest, health, circulation)*; poor *(salary, eater, appetite)*; poor-quality *(goods)*; bad, weak *(eyes)*; **um jmdn./mit etw. steht es ~:** sb./sth. is in a bad way; **b)** *(böse)* bad; wicked; **c)** *nicht attr. (ungenießbar)* off; **das Fleisch ist ~ geworden** meat has gone off; **2.** *adv.* **a)** badly; **er sieht/hört ~:** his sight is poor/he has poor hearing; **über jmdn.** *od.* **von jmdm. ~ sprechen** speak ill of sb.; **b)** *(schwer)* **heute geht es ~:** today is difficult; **c) ~ und recht, mehr ~ als recht** after a fashion

schlecht-: ~**bezahlt** *Adj. (präd. getrennt geschrieben)* badly *or* poorly paid; ~**|gehen** *unr. itr. V.; unpers.; mit sein* **es geht ihr/mir ~:** she is/I am doing badly; *(gesundheitlich)* she is/I am ill *or* unwell *or* poorly; ~**gelaunt** *Adj. (präd. getrennt geschrieben)* bad-tempered; ~**|machen** *tr. V.* **jmdn.** ~**machen** run sb. down; disparage sb.

schlecken *(bes. südd., österr.) tr. V.* lap up

schleichen 1. *unr. itr. V.; mit sein* creep; *(heimlich)* creep; sneak; *(cat)* slink, creep; *(langsam fahren)* crawl along; **2.** *unr. refl. V.* creep; sneak; *(cat)* slink, creep; **schleichend** *Adj.* insidious *(disease)*; slow[-acting] *(poison)*; creeping *(inflation)*; gradual *(crisis)*

Schleier der; ~s, ~: veil; **schleierhaft** *Adj.* **jmdm.** ~**haft sein/bleiben** be/remain a mystery to sb.

Schleife die; ~, ~n **a)** bow; *(Fliege)* bow-tie; **b)** *(starke Biegung)* loop

¹**schleifen** *unr. tr. V.* grind; cut *(diamond, glass)*; *(mit Schleifpapier usw.)* sand; *(schärfen)* sharpen

²**schleifen** 1. *tr. V.* **a)** *(auch fig.)* drag; **b)** *(niederreißen)* raze *(sth.)* [to the ground]; **2.** *itr. V.; auch mit sein* drag; **die Kupplung ~ lassen** *(Kfz-W.)* slip the clutch

Schleim der; ~[e]s, ~e mucus; *(im Hals)* phlegm; *(von Schnecken)* slime; **schleimig** *Adj. (auch fig.)* slimy; *(Physiol., Zool.)* mucous

schlemmen *itr. V.* have a feast; **Schlemmer** der; ~s, ~: gourmet

schlendern *itr. V.; mit sein* stroll

Schlenker der; ~s, ~ *(ugs.)* swerve; **einen ~ machen** swerve

schlenkern *tr., itr. V.* swing; **mit den Armen ~:** swing one's arms

Schleppe die; ~, ~n train; **schleppen** 1. *tr. V.* **a)** *(ziehen)* tow *(vehicle, ship)*; **b)** *(tragen)* carry; lug; **c)** *(ugs.: mitnehmen)* drag; **2.** *refl. V.* drag *or* haul oneself; **Schlepper** der; ~s, ~ **a)** *(Schiff)* tug; **b)** *(Traktor)* tractor

Schlepp-: ~**lift** der T-bar [lift]; ~**tau** das tow-line

Schleuder die; ~, ~n sling; *(mit Gummiband)* catapult *(Brit.)*; slingshot *(Amer.)*; **schleudern** 1. *tr. V.* hurl; **2.** *itr. V.; mit sein* *(vehicle)* skid

schleunigst *Adv.* **a)** *(auf der Stelle)* at once; immediately; straight away; **b)** *(eilends)* hastily; with all haste

Schleuse die; ~, ~n **a)** sluice[-gate]; **b)** *(Schiffs~)* lock

schlich *1. u. 3. Pers. Sg. Prät. v.* **schleichen**

schlicht 1. *Adj.* **a)** simple; plain *(pattern, furniture)*; **b)** *(unkompliziert)* simple, unsophisticated *(person, view, etc.)*; **2.** *adv.* simply; simply, plainly *(dressed, furnished)*

schlichten 1. *tr. V.* settle *(argument etc.)*; settle *(industrial dispute etc.)* by mediation; **2.** *itr. V.* mediate

Schlick der; ~[e]s, ~e silt

schlief *1. u. 3. Pers. Sg. Prät. v.* **schlafen**

Schließe die; ~, ~n clasp; *(Schnalle)* buckle; **schließen** 1. *unr. tr. V.* **a)** close; shut; turn off *(tap)*; fasten *(belt, bracelet)*; do up *(button, zip)*; close *(street, route, border, electrical circuit)*; fill, close *(gap)*; **b)** *(außer Betrieb setzen)* close [down] *(shop, school)*; **c)** *(ein~)* **etw./jmdn./sich in etw. (Akk.) ~:** lock sth./sb./oneself in sth.; **d)** *(beenden)* close *(meeting, proceedings, debate)*; end, conclude *(letter, speech, lecture)*; **e)** *(eingehen, vereinbaren)* conclude *(treaty, pact, cease-fire, agreement)*; reach *(settlement, compromise)*; enter into *(contract)*; **f)** *(folgern)* infer **(aus** from); **2.** *unr. itr. V.* **a)** close, shut; **b)** *(enden)* end; conclude; **c)** *(aus etw.)* **auf etw. (Akk.) ~:** infer sth. [from sth.]; **3.** *unr. refl. V.* *(door, window)* close, shut; *(wound, circle)* close; **Schließ · fach** das locker; *(bei der Post)* PO box; *(bei der Bank)* safe-deposit box; **schließlich** *Adv.* **a)** finally; in the end; **b)** *(immerhin, doch)* after all

schliff *1. u. 3. Pers. Sg. Prät. v.* **schleifen**

Schliff der; ~|e|s, ~e a) *o. Pl.* cutting; *(von Messern, Sensen usw.)* sharpening; b) *(Art, wie etw. geschliffen wird)* cut; *(von Messern, Scheren usw.)* edge; c) *o. Pl.* **einem Brief/Text** *usw.* **den letzten ~ geben** put the finishing touches *pl.* to a letter/text *etc.*

schlimm 1. *Adj.* a) grave, serious ⟨*error, mistake, accusation, offence*⟩; bad, serious ⟨*error, mistake*⟩; b) *(übel)* bad; nasty, bad ⟨*experience*⟩; |**das ist alles| halb so ~:** it's not as bad as all that; **ist nicht ~!** [it] doesn't matter; **2.** *adv.* **~ d|a|ran sein** be in a bad way; *(in einer ~en Situation)* be in dire straits; **schlimmsten·falls** *Adv.* if the worst comes to the worst

Schlinge die; ~, ~n a) loop; *(für den Arm)* sling; *(zum Aufhängen)* noose; b) *(Fanggerät)* snare

schlingen 1. *unr. tr. V.* **etw. um etw. ~:** loop sth. round sth.; **2.** *unr. refl. V.* **sich um etw. ~:** wind itself round sth; **3.** *unr. itr. V.* bolt one's food

schlingern *itr. V.; mit sein* ⟨*ship, boat*⟩ roll; ⟨*train, vehicle*⟩ lurch from side to side

Schlips der; ~es, ~e tie

Schlitten der; ~s, ~: sledge; sled; *(Pferde~)* sleigh; *(Rodel~)* toboggan; **~ fahren** go tobogganing

schlittern *itr. V.* slide

Schlitt-: **~schuh** der [ice-]skate; **~schuh laufen** *od.* **fahren** [ice-]skate; **~schuh·laufen das** [ice-]skating *no art.;* **~schuh·läufer** der [ice-]skater

Schlitz der; ·es, ~e a) slit; *(Briefkasten~, Automaten~)* slot; b) *(Hosen~)* flies *pl.;* fly

schloß *1. u. 3. Pers. Sg. Prät. v.* **schließen**

Schloß das; Schlosses, Schlösser a) lock; *(Vorhänge~)* padlock; **hinter ~ und Riegel** *(ugs.)* behind bars; b) *(Verschluß)* clasp; c) *(Wohngebäude)* castle; *(Palast)* palace; *(Herrschaftshaus)* mansion

Schlosser der; ~s, ~: metalworker; *(Maschinen~)* fitter; *(für Schlösser)* locksmith; *(Auto~)* mechanic

Schlot der; ~|e|s, ~e *od.* Schlöte chimney[-stack]; *(eines Schiffes)* funnel

schlottern *itr. V.* a) shake; b) ⟨*clothes*⟩ hang loose

Schlucht die; ~, ~en ravine

schluchzen *itr. V.* sob

Schluck der; ~|e|s, ~e *od.* Schlücke swallow; mouthful; *(großer ~)* gulp; *(kleiner ~)* sip; **Schluck·auf** der; ~s

hiccups *pl.;* **Schlückchen** das; ~s, ~: sip; **schlucken 1.** *tr. V.* swallow; **etw. hastig ~:** gulp sth. down; **2.** *itr. V.* swallow; **Schlucker** der; ~s, ~: **armer ~** *(ugs.)* poor devil *or (Brit. coll.)* blighter

schluderig *s.* **schludrig; schludern** *itr. V.* *(ugs.)* work sloppily; **schludrig** *(ugs.)* **1.** *Adj.* a) slipshod ⟨*work, examination*⟩; botched ⟨*job*⟩; slapdash ⟨*person, work*⟩; b) *(schlampig [aussehend])* scruffy; **2.** *adv.* a) in a slipshod *or* slapdash way; b) *(schlampig)* scruffily

schlug *1. u. 3. Pers. Sg. Prät. v.* **schlagen**

Schlummer der; ~s *(geh.)* slumber *(poet./rhet.);* **schlummern** *itr. V.* *(geh.)* slumber *(poet./rhet.)*

Schlund der; ~|e|s, Schlünde [back of the] throat; pharynx *(Anat.)*

schlüpfen *itr. V.; mit sein* slip; **|aus dem Ei| ~:** ⟨*chick*⟩ hatch out

Schlüpfer der; ~s, ~ *(für Damen)* knickers *pl. (Brit.);* panties *pl.; (für Herren)* [under]pants *pl. or* trunks *pl.*

schlüpfrig *Adj.* a) slippery; b) *(anstößig)* lewd

schlurfen *itr. V.; mit sein* shuffle

schlürfen 1. *tr. V.* slurp [up] *(coll.);* **2.** *itr. V.* slurp *(coll.)*

Schluß der; Schlusses, Schlüsse a) end; *(eines Vortrags o. ä.)* conclusion; *(eines Buchs, Schauspiels usw.)* ending; **am** *od.* **zum ~:** at the end; *(schließlich)* in the end; b) *(Folgerung)* conclusion

Schlüssel der; ~s, ~: key

Schlüssel-: **~bein** das collar-bone; clavicle *(Anat.);* **~blume** die cowslip; *(Primel)* primula; **~bund** der *od.* das bunch of keys; **~loch** das keyhole

schlüssig 1. *Adj.* a) conclusive ⟨*proof, evidence*⟩; convincing, logical ⟨*argument, conclusion*⟩; b) **sich** *(Dat.)* **~ werden** make up one's mind; **2.** *adv.* conclusively

Schluß-: **~licht** das; *Pl.* ~lichter tail-or rear-light; **~strich** der [bottom] line; **~verkauf** der [end-of-season] sale[s *pl.*]

schmächtig *Adj.* slight

schmackhaft *Adj.* tasty

schmal; **~er** *od.* schmäler, **~st...** *od.* schmälst... *Adj.* narrow; slim, slender ⟨*hips, hands, figure, etc.*⟩; thin ⟨*lips, face, nose, etc.*⟩; **schmälern** *tr. V.* diminish; restrict ⟨*rights*⟩

¹**Schmalz** das; ~es dripping; *(Schwei-*

ne~) lard; **²Schmalz der;** ~es *(abwertend)* schmaltz *(coll.);* **Schmalz·brot das** slice of bread and dripping; **schmalzig** *(abwertend)* 1. *Adj.* schmaltzy *(coll.);* 2. *adv.* with slushy sentimentality

schmarotzen *itr. V. (fig.)* sponge; free-load *(sl.)*

Schmarren der; ~s, ~ *(österr., auch südd.)* pancake broken up with a fork after frying

schmatzen *itr. V.* smack one's lips; *(geräuschvoll essen)* eat noisily

Schmaus der; ~es, Schmäuse *(veralt., scherzh.)* [good] spread *(coll.)*

schmecken 1. *itr. V.* taste **(nach** of); |gut| ~: taste good; **schmeckt es |dir|?** are you enjoying it *or* your meal?; 2. *tr. V.* taste; *(kosten)* sample

schmeicheln *itr. V.* jmdm. ~: flatter sb.; **Schmeichler der;** ~s, ~: flatterer

schmeißen *(ugs.)* 1. *unr. tr. V.* chuck *(coll.);* sling *(coll.); (schleudern)* fling; hurl; 2. *unr. refl. V.* throw oneself; *(mit Wucht)* hurl oneself; 3. *unr. itr. V.* **mit etw. |nach jmdm.|** ~: chuck sth. [at sb.] *(coll.)*

Schmeiß·fliege die blowfly; *(blaue* ~*)* bluebottle

schmelzen 1. *unr. itr. V.; mit sein* melt; *(fig.)* ⟨*doubts, apprehension, etc.*⟩ dissolve, fade away; 2. *unr. tr. V.* melt; smelt ⟨*ore*⟩*; render ⟨fat⟩;* **Schmelz·käse der** processed cheese

Schmerz der; ~es, ~en a) *(physisch)* pain; *(dumpf u. anhaltend)* ache; **wo haben Sie** ~**en?** where does it hurt?; ~**en haben** be in pain; b) *(psychisch)* pain; *(Kummer)* grief; **schmerz-empfindlich** *Adj.* sensitive to pain *pred.;* **schmerzen** 1. *tr. V.* jmdn. ~: hurt sb.; *(jmdm. Kummer bereiten)* grieve sb.; cause sb. sorrow; 2. *itr. V.* hurt; **schmerzhaft** *Adj.* painful; **schmerzlich** 1. *Adj.* painful; distressing; 2. *adv.* painfully; **schmerz-, Schmerz-:** ~**los** 1. *Adj.* painless; 2. *adv.* painlessly; ~**stillend** *Adj.* pain-killing; ~**tablette die** pain-killing tablet

Schmetterling der; ~s, ~e butterfly

schmettern 1. *tr. V.* a) hurl **(an** + *Akk.* at, **gegen** against); b) *(laut spielen, singen usw.)* blare out ⟨*march, music*⟩; ⟨*person*⟩ sing lustily ⟨*song*⟩; c) *(Tennis usw.)* smash ⟨*ball*⟩; 2. *itr. V.* ⟨*trumpet, music, etc.*⟩ blare out

Schmied der; ~|e|s, ~e blacksmith; **Schmiede die;** ~, ~en smithy; forge; **schmieden** *tr. V. (auch fig.)* forge

schmiegen 1. *refl. V.* snuggle, nestle **(in** + *Akk.* in); **sich an jmdn.** ~: snuggle [close] up to sb.; 2. *tr. V.* press **(an** + *Akk.* against)

schmieren 1. *tr. V.* a) lubricate; b) *(streichen)* spread ⟨*butter, jam, etc.*⟩ **(auf** + *Akk.* on); **Brote** ~: spread slices of bread; 2. *itr. V.* a) ⟨*oil, grease*⟩ lubricate; b) *(ugs: unsauber schreiben)* ⟨*person*⟩ scrawl, scribble; ⟨*pen, ink*⟩ smudge, make smudges; **schmierig** *Adj.* greasy; **Schmier-seife die** soft soap

schmilzt *2. u. 3. Pers. Sg. Präsens v.* **schmelzen**

Schminke die; ~, ~n make-up; **schminken** 1. *tr. V.* make up ⟨*face, eyes*⟩; 2. *refl. V.* make oneself up

Schmirgel·papier das emery-paper; *(Sandpapier)* sandpaper

schmiß *1. u. 3. Pers. Sg. Prät. v.* **schmeißen**

Schmöker der; ~s, ~ *(ugs.)* lightweight adventure story/romance; **schmökern** *(ugs.)* 1. *itr. V.* bury oneself in a book; 2. *tr. V.* bury oneself in ⟨*book*⟩

schmollen *itr. V.* sulk; **Schmoll-mund der** pouting mouth

schmolz *1. u. 3. Pers. Sg. Prät. v.* **schmelzen**

Schmor·braten der braised beef; **schmoren** 1. *tr. V.* braise; 2. *itr. V.* a) braise; b) *(ugs.: schwitzen)* swelter

schmuck *Adj.* attractive

Schmuck der; ~|e|s a) *(~stücke)* jewelry; jewellery *(esp. Brit.);* b) *s.* ~**stück;** c) *(Zierde)* decoration

schmücken *tr. V.* decorate; embellish ⟨*writings, speech*⟩

schmuck-, Schmuck-: ~**kästchen das,** ~**kasten der** jewelry *or (esp. Brit.)* jewellery box; ~**los** *Adj.* plain; bare ⟨*room*⟩; ~**stück das** piece of jewelry *or (esp. Brit.)* jewellery

schmuddelig *Adj. (ugs.)* grubby; mucky *(coll.); (schmutzig u. unordentlich)* messy; grotty *(Brit. sl.)*

Schmuggel der; ~s smuggling *no art.;* **schmuggeln** *tr., itr. V.* smuggle **(in** + *Akk.* into; **aus** out of); **Schmuggler der;** ~s, ~: smuggler

schmunzeln *itr. V.* smile to oneself

schmusen *itr. V. (ugs.)* cuddle; ⟨*couple*⟩ kiss and cuddle

Schmutz der; ~es dirt; *(Schlamm)* mud; **schmutzen** *itr. V.* get dirty; **schmutzig** *Adj.* dirty

Schnabel der; ~s, Schnäbel a) beak; b) *(ugs.: Mund)* gob *(sl.)*

Schnake die; ~, ~n a) daddy-long-legs; b) *(bes. südd.: Stechmücke)* mosquito

Schnalle die; ~, ~n *(Gürtel~)* buckle; **schnallen** *tr. V.* a) *(mit einer Schnalle festziehen)* buckle ⟨shoe, belt⟩; fasten ⟨strap⟩; b) *(mit Riemen/Gurten befestigen)* strap (auf + Akk. on to)

schnalzen *itr. V.* |mit der Zunge/den Fingern| ~: click one's tongue/snap one's fingers

schnappen 1. *itr. V.* nach jmdm./etw. ~ ⟨animal⟩ snap at sb./sth.; nach Luft ~: gasp for breath; 2. *tr. V.*⟨dog, bird, etc.⟩ snatch; [sich *(Dat.)*] jmdn./etw. ~ *(ugs.)* ⟨person⟩ grab sb./sth.; *(mit raschem Zugriff)* snatch sb./sth.; **Schnapp·schuß** der snapshot

Schnaps der; ~es, Schnäpse a) spirit; *(Klarer)* schnapps; b) *o. Pl. (Spirituosen)* spirits *pl.*

schnarchen *itr. V.* snore

schnattern *itr. V.* a) ⟨goose etc.⟩ cackle, gaggle; b) *(ugs.: eifrig schwatzen)* jabber [away]; chatter

schnauben *itr. V.* snort (vor with)

schnaufen *itr. V.* puff (vor with)

Schnauze die; ~, ~n a) *(von Tieren)* muzzle; *(der Maus usw.)* snout; *(Maul)* mouth; b) *(derb: Mund)* gob *(sl.);* |halt die| ~! shut your trap! *(sl.);* **schnauzen** *tr., itr. V. (ugs.)* bark; *(ärgerlich)* snap; snarl

Schnecke die snail; *(Nackt~)* slug; **Schnecken·haus das** snail-shell

Schnee der; ~s snow

Schnee-: ~ball der snowball; ~besen der whisk; ~flocke die snowflake; ~gestöber das snow flurry; ~glöckchen das snowdrop; ~kette die snow-chain; ~matsch der slush; ~pflug der snow-plough; ~sturm der snowstorm

Schneewittchen (das) Snow White

Schneide die; ~, ~n [cutting] edge; **schneiden** 1. *unr. itr. V.* cut (in + Akk. into); 2. *unr. tr. V.* a) cut; (in Scheiben) slice ⟨bread, sausage, etc.⟩; *(klein ~)* cut up, chop ⟨wood, vegetables⟩; *(stutzen)* prune ⟨tree, bush⟩; trim ⟨beard⟩; cut, mow ⟨grass⟩; sich *(Dat.)* die Haare ~ lassen have one's hair cut; b) eine Kurve ~: cut a corner **Schneider** der; ~s, ~: tailor; *(Da-*

men~) dressmaker; **Schneiderei** die; ~, ~en tailor's shop; *(Damen~)* dressmaker's shop; **Schneiderin** die; ~, ~nen *s.* Schneider; **schneidern** *tr. V.* make; make, tailor ⟨suit⟩

Schneide·zahn der incisor

schneien 1. *itr., tr. V. (unpers.)* snow; es schneit it is snowing; 2. *itr. V.; mit sein (fig.)* rain down; fall like snow

Schneise die; ~, ~n *(Wald~)* aisle; *(als Feuerschutz)* firebreak

schnell 1. *Adj.* quick ⟨journey, decision, service, etc.⟩; fast ⟨car, skis, road, track, etc.⟩; quick, swift ⟨progress, movement, blow, action⟩; 2. *adv.* quickly; ⟨drive, move, etc.⟩ fast, quickly; ⟨spread⟩ quickly, rapidly; *(bald)* soon ⟨sold, past, etc.⟩; mach ~! *(ugs.)* move it! *(coll.);* **schnellen** *itr. V.; mit sein* shoot ⟨aus + Dat. out of; in + Akk. into⟩; **Schnelligkeit** die; ~, ~en speed; **Schnell·imbiß** der snack-bar; **schnellstens** *Adv.* as quickly as possible

Schnell-: ~straße die expressway; ~zug der express [train]

Schnepfe die; ~, ~n snipe

schneuzen 1. *tr. V.* sich *(Dat.)*/einem Kind die Nase ~: blow one's/a child's nose; 2. *refl. V.* blow one's nose

schnippeln *(ugs.)* 1. *itr. V.* snip [away] (an + Dat. at); 2. *tr. V.* shred ⟨vegetables⟩; chop ⟨beans etc.⟩ [finely]

schnippen 1. *itr. V.* snap one's fingers (nach at); 2. *tr. V.* flick (von off, from)

schnippisch 1. *Adj.* pert ⟨reply, tone, etc.⟩; 2. *adv.* pertly

Schnipsel der *od.* das; ~s, ~: scrap; *(Papier~, Stoff~)* snippet; shred

schnipseln *s.* schnippeln

schnitt *1. u. 3. Pers. Sg. Prät. v.* schneiden

Schnitt der; ~[e]s, ~e a) cut; b) *(das Mähen) (von Gras)* mowing; *(von Getreide)* harvest

Schnitt-: ~blume die cut flower; ~bohne die French bean

Schnitte die; ~, ~n slice; eine ~ [Brot] a slice of bread; **schnittig** 1. *Adj.* stylish, smart ⟨suit, appearance, etc.⟩; *(sportlich)* racy ⟨car, yacht, etc.⟩; 2. *adv.* stylishly; *(sportlich)* racily

Schnitt-: ~lauch der chives *pl.;* ~wunde die cut; *(lang u. tief)* gash

Schnitzel das; ~s, ~ a) *(Fleisch)* [veal/pork] escalope; b) *(von Papier)* scrap; *(von Holz)* shaving; **schnitzeln** *tr. V.*

chop up ⟨*vegetables*⟩ [into small pieces]; shred ⟨*cabbage*⟩; **schnitzen** *tr., itr. V.* carve

schnodderig *(ugs.)* 1. *Adj.* brash; 2. *adv.* brashly

schnöde *(geh.)* 1. *Adj.* a) *(verachtenswert)* contemptible; b) *(gemein)* contemptuous, scornful ⟨*glance, reply, etc.*⟩. 2. *adv. (gemein)* contemptuously; ⟨*exploit, misuse*⟩ flagrantly

Schnörkel der; ~s, ~: scroll; *(der Handschrift, in der Rede)* flourish

schnorren *tr., itr. V. (ugs.)* scrounge *(coll.)* (bei, von + *Dat.* off); **Schnorrer der;** ~s, ~ *(ugs.)* scrounger *(coll.)*

schnüffeln *itr. V.* a) sniff; b) *(ugs.: spionieren)* snoop [about] *(coll.);* **Schnüffler der;** ~s, ~ *(ugs.)* Nosey Parker; *(Spion)* snooper *(coll.)*

schnupfen 1. *tr. V.* sniff; **Tabak** ~: take snuff; 2. *itr. V.* take snuff; **Schnupfen der;** ~s, ~: [head] cold; **Schnupf·tabak der** snuff

schnuppe: das/er ist mir ~/**mir völlig** ~ *(ugs.)* I don't care/I couldn't care less about it/him *(coll.)*

schnuppern *itr. V.* sniff; **an etw.** *(Dat.)* ~: sniff sth.

Schnur die; ~, **Schnüre** a) *(Bindfaden)* piece of string; *(Kordel)* piece of cord; b) *(ugs.: Kabel)* flex *(Brit.);* lead; cord *(Amer.);* **schnüren** *tr. V.* tie ⟨*bundle, string, etc.*⟩; tie, lace up ⟨*shoe, corset, etc.*⟩

Schnurr·bart der moustache; **schnurren** *itr. V.* ⟨*cat*⟩ purr; ⟨*machine*⟩ hum

Schnür-: ~**schuh der** lace-up shoe; ~**senkel der;** ~s, ~ *(bes. nordd.)* [shoe-]lace; *(für Stiefel)* bootlace

schob *1. u. 3. Pers. Prät. v.* schieben

Schock der; ~[e]s, ~s shock; **schockieren** *tr. V.* shock; **über etw.** *(Akk.)* schockiert sein be shocked at sth.

Schöffe der; ~n, ~n lay judge *(acting together with another lay judge and a professional judge);* **Schöffen·gericht das** *court presided over by a professional judge and two lay judges*

Schokolade die; ~, ~n a) chocolate; b) *(Getränk)* [drinking] chocolate

Schokolade[n]-: ~**eis das** chocolate ice-cream; ~**guß der** chocolate icing; ~**pudding der** chocolate blancmange; ~**torte die** chocolate cake *or* gateau

scholl *1. u. 3. Pers. Sg. Prät. v.* schallen

Scholle die; ~, ~n a) *(Erd~)* clod [of

earth]; b) *(Eis~)* [ice-]floe; c) *(Fisch)* plaice

schon 1. *Adv.* a) *(bereits) (oft nicht übersetzt)* already; *(in Fragen)* yet; **wie lange bist du** ~ **hier?** how long have you been here?; b) *(fast gleichzeitig)* there and then; c) *(jetzt)* ~ |mal| now; *(inzwischen)* meanwhile; d) *(selbst, sogar)* even; *(nur)* only; e) *(ohne Ergänzung, ohne weiteren Zusatz)* on its own; |allein| ~ **der Gedanke daran** the mere thought of it; ~ **deshalb** for this reason alone; f) *(wohl)* really; **Lust hätte ich** ~, **aber** ...: I'd certainly like to, but ...; 2. *Partikel* a) *(ugs. ungeduldig: endlich)* **nun komm** ~! come on!; hurry up!; b) *(beruhigend: bestimmt)* all right; c) *(durchaus)* **das ist** ~ **möglich** that is quite possible

schön 1. *Adj.* a) beautiful; handsome ⟨*youth, man*⟩; b) *(angenehm)* pleasant, nice ⟨*day, holiday, dream, relaxation, etc.*⟩; fine ⟨*weather*⟩; *(nett)* nice; **das war eine** ~**e Zeit** those were wonderful days; c) *(gut)* good; d) *(in Höflichkeitsformeln)* ~**e Grüße** best wishes; **recht** ~**en Dank für** ...: thank you very much for ...; e) ~! *(ugs.: einverstanden)* OK *(coll.);* all right; f) *(iron.: leer)* ~**e Worte** fine[-sounding] words; *(schmeichlerisch)* honeyed words; g) *(ugs.: beträchtlich)* handsome, *(coll.)* tidy ⟨*sum, fortune, profit*⟩; considerable ⟨*quantity, distance*⟩; pretty good ⟨*pension*⟩; h) *(iron.: unerfreulich)* nice *(coll. iron.);* **das sind ja** ~**e Aussichten!** this is a fine look-out *sing. (iron.);* 2. *adv.* a) beautifully; b) *(angenehm, erfreulich)* nicely; ~ **warm/weich/langsam** nice and warm/soft/slow; c) *(gut)* well; d) *(in Höflichkeitsformeln)* **bitte** ~, **können Sie mir sagen,** ...: excuse me, could you tell me ...; e) *(iron.)* **wie es so** ~ **heißt, wie man so** ~ **sagt** as they say; f) *(ugs.: beträchtlich)* really; *(vor einem Adjektiv)* pretty; **ganz** ~ **arbeiten müssen** have to work jolly hard *(Brit. coll.);* 3. *Partikel (ugs.)* **bleib** ~ **liegen!** lie there and be good

schonen 1. *tr. V.* treat ⟨*clothes, books, furniture, etc.*⟩ with care; *(schützen)* protect ⟨*hands, furniture*⟩; *(nicht strapazieren)* spare ⟨*voice, eyes, etc.*⟩; conserve ⟨*strength*⟩; 2. *refl. V.* take things easy

Schönheit die; ~, ~en beauty

Schönheits-: ~**chirurgie die** cosmetic surgery *no art.;* ~**pflege die** beauty care *no art.*

Schon·kost die light food
schön|machen *(ugs.)* **1.** *tr. V.*
smarten ⟨*person, thing*⟩ up; make ⟨*person, thing*⟩ look nice; **2.** *refl. V.*
smarten oneself up
schonungs|los 1. *Adj.* unsparing,
ruthless ⟨*criticism etc.*⟩; blunt ⟨*frankness*⟩; **2.** *adv.* unsparingly; ⟨*say*⟩ without mincing one's words
Schopf der; ~[e]s, **Schöpfe** shock of
hair
schöpfen *tr. V.* **a)** scoop [up] ⟨*water,
liquid*⟩; *(mit einer Kelle)* ladle ⟨*soup*⟩;
b) *(geh.: einatmen)* draw, take ⟨*breath*⟩
Schöpfer der; ~s, ~: creator; *(Gott)*
Creator; **schöpferisch 1.** *Adj.* creative; **2.** *adv.* creatively
Schöpf-: ~**kelle** die, ~**löffel** der
ladle
Schöpfung die; ~, ~en *(geh.)* creation; **die** ~ *(die Welt)* Creation
Schoppen der; ~s, ~: [quarter-litre/
half-litre] glass of wine/beer
schor *1. u. 3. Pers. Sg. Prät. v.* scheren
Schorf der; ~[e]s, ~e scab
Schorn·stein der chimney; *(Lokomotiv~, Schiffs~)* funnel; **Schornstein·feger** der; ~s, ~: chimney-sweep
schoß *1. u. 3. Pers. Sg. Prät. v.* schießen
Schoß der; ~es, **Schöße** lap
Schote die; ~, ~n pod
Schotte der; ~n, ~n Scot; Scotsman;
die ~n the Scots; the Scottish;
Schotten·rock der tartan skirt;
(Kilt) kilt; **Schottin** die; ~, ~nen
Scot; Scotswoman; **schottisch** *Adj.*
Scottish; ~**er Whisky** Scotch whisky;
Schottland (das); ~s Scotland
schräg 1. *Adj.* diagonal ⟨*line, beam,
cut, etc.*⟩; sloping ⟨*surface, roof, wall,
side, etc.*⟩; slanting, slanted ⟨*writing,
eyes, etc.*⟩; tilted ⟨*position of the head
etc., axis*⟩; **2.** *adv.* at an angle; *(diagonal)* diagonally; **Schräge** die; ~,
~n **a)** *(schräge Fläche)* sloping surface; **b)** *(Neigung)* slope
schrak *1. u. 3. Pers. Sg. Prät. v.*
schrecken
Schramme die; ~, ~n scratch;
schrammen *tr. V.* scratch
Schrank der; ~[e]s, **Schränke** cupboard; closet *(Amer.)*; *(Glas~; kleiner
Wand~)* cabinet; *(Kleider~)* wardrobe; *(Bücher~)* bookcase;
Schränkchen das; ~s, ~: cabinet
Schranke die; ~, ~n **a)** *(auch fig.)*
barrier; **b)** *(fig.: Grenze)* limit

Schraube die; ~, ~n bolt; *(Holz~,
Blech~)* screw; **schrauben** *tr. V.* **a)**
s. **Schraube:** bolt/screw **(an, auf +
Akk.** on to); **b)** *(drehen)* screw ⟨*nut,
hook, light-bulb, etc.*⟩ **(auf + Akk.** on
to; **in + Akk.** into)
Schrauben-: ~**schlüssel** der spanner; ~**zieher** der; ~s, ~: screwdriver
Schraub·verschluß der screw-top
Schreber·garten der ≈ allotment
(cultivated primarily as a garden)
Schreck der; ~[e]s, ~e fright; scare;
(Schock) shock; **jmdm. einen** ~ **einjagen** give sb. a fright; **schrecken** *regelm. (auch unr.)* *itr. V.* start [up]; **aus
dem Schlaf** ~: awake with a start;
start from one's sleep; **Schrecken**
der; ~s, ~: fright; scare; *(Entsetzen)*
horror; *(große Angst)* terror; **jmdm. einen** ~ **einjagen** give sb. a fright;
schreckhaft *Adj.* easily scared; ~:
schrecklich 1. *Adj.* terrible; **2.** *adv.*
terribly
Schrei der; ~[e]s, ~e cry; *(lauter Ruf)*
shout; *(durchdringend)* yell; *(gellend)*
scream; *(kreischend)* shriek
Schreib·block der; *Pl.* ~**blocks** *od.*
~**blöcke** writing-pad
schreiben 1. *unr. itr. V.* write; *(mit der
Schreibmaschine)* type; **an einem Roman usw.** ~: be writing a novel *etc.*;
jmdm. od. an jmdn. ~: write to sb.; **2.**
unr. tr. V. **a)** write; *(mit der Schreibmaschine)* type; **wie schreibt man dieses Wort?** how is this word spelt?; **3.**
unr. refl. V. be spelt; **Schreiben** das;
~s, ~ **a)** *o. Pl.* writing *no def. art.;* **b)**
(Brief) letter; **Schreiber** der; ~s, ~:
writer; *(Verfasser)* author; **Schreiberin** die; ~, ~en writer; *(Verfasserin)*
authoress
Schreib-: ~**maschine** die typewriter; ~**maschinen·papier** das
typing paper; ~**papier** das writing-paper; ~**tisch** der desk
Schreibung die; ~, ~en spelling
Schreib-: ~**waren** *Pl.* stationery
sing.; ~**waren·geschäft** das stationer's
schreien *unr. itr. V.* ⟨*person*⟩ cry [out];
(laut rufen/sprechen) shout; *(durchdringend)* yell; *(gellend)* scream;
⟨*baby*⟩ yell, bawl; **zum Schreien sein**
(ugs.) be a scream *(sl.)*
Schreiner der; ~s, ~ *(bes. südd.) s.*
Tischler
schreiten *unr. itr. V.; mit sein (geh.)*
walk; *(mit großen Schritten)* stride
schrickst *2. Pers. Sg. Präsens v.*

schrecken; **schrickt** *3. Pers. Sg. Präsens v.* schrecken
schrie *1. u. 3. Pers. Sg. Prät. v.* schreien
schrieb *1. u. 3. Pers. Sg. Prät. v.* schreiben; **Schrieb** der; ~[e]s, ~e *(ugs.)* missive *(coll.)*
Schrift die; ~, ~en a) *(System)* script; *(Alphabet)* alphabet; b) *(Hand~)* [hand]writing; c) *(Werk)* work; **schriftlich** 1. *Adj.* written; 2. *adv.* in writing
Schrift-: ~**steller** der; ~s, ~: writer; ~**stück** das [official] document; ~**wechsel** der correspondence
schrill 1. *Adj.* shrill; 2. *adv.* shrilly; **schrillen** *itr. V.* shrill; sound shrilly
schritt *1. u. 3. Pers. Sg. Prät. v.* schreiten; **Schritt** der; ~[e]s, ~e a) step; einen ~ machen *od.* tun take a step; b) *Pl. (Geräusch)* footsteps; c) *(Entfernung)* pace; d) *(Gleich~)* aus dem ~ kommen get out of step; e) *o. Pl. (Gangart)* walk; seinen ~ verlangsamen/beschleunigen slow/quicken one's pace; [mit jmdm./etw.] ~ halten *(auch fig.)* keep up *or* keep pace [with sb./sth.]; f) *(~geschwindigkeit)* walking pace; „~ fahren" 'dead slow'; g) *(fig.: Maßnahme)* step; measure; **Schritt·geschwindigkeit** die walking pace
schroff 1. *Adj.* a) precipitous *(rock etc.)*; b) *(plötzlich)* sudden *(transition, change)*; *(kraß)* stark *(contrast)*; c) *(barsch)* curt *(refusal, manner)*; brusque *(manner, behaviour, tone)*; 2. *adv.* a) *(rise, drop)* sheer; *(fall away)* precipitously; b) *(plötzlich, unvermittelt)* suddenly; c) *(barsch)* curtly; *(interrupt)* abruptly; *(treat)* brusquely
schröpfen *tr. V. (ugs.)* fleece
Schrot der *od.* das; ~[e]s, ~e a) coarse meal; *(aus Getreide)* whole meal *(Brit.)*; whole grain; b) *(Munition)* shot; **schroten** *tr. V.* grind *(grain etc.)* [coarsely]; crush *(malt)* [coarsely]
Schrot-: ~**flinte** die shotgun; ~**kugel** die pellet
Schrott der; ~[e]s, ~e a) scrap [-metal]; ein Auto zu ~ fahren *(ugs.)* write a car off; b) *o. Pl. (salopp fig.)* rubbish; **schrott·reif** *Adj.* ready for the scrap-heap *postpos.*
schrubben *tr. (auch itr.) V.* scrub; **Schrubber** der; ~s, ~: [long-handled] scrubbing-brush
Schrulle die; ~, ~n cranky idea; *(Marotte)* quirk

schrumpelig *Adj. (ugs.)* wrinkly; **schrumpeln** *itr. V.; mit sein (ugs.)* *(skin)* go wrinkled; *(apple etc.)* shrivel
schrumpfen *itr. V.; mit sein* shrink; *(metal, rock)* contract; *(apple etc.)* shrivel; *(skin)* go wrinkled; *(abnehmen)* decrease; *(supplies, capital, hopes)* dwindle
Schub der; ~[e]s, Schübe a) *(Physik: ~kraft)* thrust; b) *(Med.: Phase)* phase; stage; c) *(Gruppe, Anzahl)* batch
Schuber der; ~s, ~: slip-case
Schub-: ~**karre** die, ~**karren** der wheelbarrow; ~**lade** die drawer
Schubs der; ~es, ~e *(ugs.)* shove; **schubsen** *tr. (auch itr.) V. (ugs.)* push; shove
schüchtern 1. *Adj.* a) shy *(person, smile, etc.)*; shy, timid *(voice, knock, etc.)*; b) *(fig.: zaghaft)* tentative, cautious *(attempt, beginnings, etc.)*; 2. *adv.* shyly; *(knock, ask, etc.)* timidly; **Schüchternheit** die; ~: shyness
Schuft der; ~[e]s, ~e scoundrel
schuften *(ugs.) itr. V.* slave away
Schuh der; ~[e]s, ~e shoe; *(hoher ~, Stiefel)* boot; jmdm. etw. in die ~e schieben *(fig. ugs.)* pin the blame for sth. on sb.
Schuh-: ~**creme** die shoe-polish; ~**größe** die shoe size; welche ~**größe** hast du? what size shoe[s] do you take?; ~**macher** der; ~s, ~: shoemaker; ~**sohle** die sole [of a/one's shoe]
Schul-: ~**abschluß** der school-leaving qualification; ~**buch** das school-book; ~**bus** der school bus
schuld *s.* Schuld b; **Schuld** die; ~, ~en a) *o. Pl.* guilt; er ist sich *(Dat.)* keiner ~ bewußt he is not conscious of having done any wrong; b) *o. Pl. (Verantwortlichkeit)* blame; es ist [nicht] seine ~: it is [not] his fault; [an etw. *(Dat.)*] schuld haben *od.* sein be to blame [for sth.]; c) *(Verpflichtung zur Rückzahlung)* debt; 5000 Mark ~en haben have debts of 5,000 marks, owe 5,000 marks; **schuld·bewußt** 1. *Adj.* guilty *(look, face, etc.)*; 2. *adv.* guiltily; **schulden** *tr. V.* owe; was schulde ich Ihnen? how much do I owe you?; **Schuld·gefühl** das feeling of guilt; **schuldig** *Adj.* a) guilty; der [an dem Unfall] ~e Autofahrer the driver to blame [for the accident]; b) jmdm. etw. ~ sein/bleiben owe sb. sth.; c) *(gebührend)* due; proper; **Schuldige**

der/die; *adj. Dekl.* guilty person; *(im Strafprozeß)* guilty party; **schuld·los** *Adj.* innocent (**an** + *Dat.* of); **Schuld·spruch** der verdict of guilty

Schule die; ~, ~n **a)** school; **zur** *od.* **in die ~ gehen, die ~ besuchen** go to school; **auf** *od.* **in der ~:** at school; **schulen** *tr. V.* train; **Schüler** der; ~s, ~: pupil; *(Schuljunge)* schoolboy; **Schülerin** die; ~, ~nen pupil; *(Schulmädchen)* schoolgirl

schul-, Schul-: ~**ferien** *Pl.* school holidays *or (Amer.)* vacation *sing.;* ~**frei** *Adj.* *(day)* off school; ~**hof** der school yard; ~**jahr** das **a)** school year; **b)** *(Klasse)* year; ~**junge** der schoolboy; ~**kind** das schoolchild; ~**klasse** die [school] class; ~**mädchen** das schoolgirl; ~**ranzen** der [school] satchel; ~**tag** der school day; ~**tasche** die school-bag; *(Ranzen)* [school] satchel

Schulter die; ~, ~n shoulder; **jmdm. auf die ~ klopfen** pat sb. on the shoulder *or (fig.)* back; **Schulterblatt** das *(Anat.)* shoulder-blade; **schultern** *tr. V.* shoulder; **das Gewehr ~:** shoulder arms

Schul-: ~**weg** der way to school; ~**zeit** die school-days *pl.*

schummerig *Adj.* dim ⟨light etc.⟩; dimly lit ⟨room etc.⟩

Schund der; ~[e]s trash

Schuppe die; ~, ~n **a)** scale; **b)** *Pl.* *(auf dem Kopf)* dandruff *sing.; (auf der Haut)* flaking skin *sing.;* **schuppen** 1. *tr. V.* scale ⟨fish⟩; 2. *refl. V.* ⟨skin⟩ flake; ⟨person⟩ have flaking skin

Schuppen der; ~s, ~ **a)** shed; **b)** *(ugs.: Lokal)* joint *(sl.)*

schüren *tr. V.* **a)** poke ⟨fire⟩; **b)** *(fig.)* stir up ⟨hatred, envy, etc.⟩

schürfen 1. *itr. V.* scrape; 2. *tr. V.* **a)** **sich** *(Dat.)* **das Knie** *usw.* **~:** graze one's knee *etc.;* **b)** *(Bergbau)* mine ⟨ore etc.⟩ open-cast *or (Amer.)* opencut; **Schürf·wunde** die graze; abrasion

Schurke der; ~n, ~n rogue

Schur·wolle die new wool

Schürze die; ~, ~n apron; *(Frauen~, Latz~)* pinafore

Schuß der; **Schusses, Schüsse a)** shot (**auf** + *Akk.* at); **weit** *od.* **weitab vom ~** *(fig. ugs.)* well away from the action; **b)** *(Menge Munition/Schießpulver)* round; **drei ~ Munition** three rounds of ammunition; **c)** *(~wunde)* gunshot

wound; **d)** *(kleine Menge)* dash; **e)** *(Drogenjargon)* shot; fix *(sl.);* **f)** *(Skisport)* schuss; ~ **fahren** schuss; **g)** *(ugs.)* etw. **in ~ bringen/halten** get sth. into/keep sth. in [good] shape

Schüssel die; ~, ~n bowl; *(flacher)* dish

schusselig *(ugs.)* 1. *Adj.* scatterbrained; 2. *adv.* in a scatter-brained way

Schuß-: ~**linie** die line of fire; **in die/jmds. ~linie geraten** *od.* **kommen** *(auch fig.)* come under fire/come under fire from sb.; ~**verletzung** die gunshot wound; ~**waffe** die weapon *(firing a projectile); (Gewehr usw.)* firearm

Schuster der; ~s, ~ *(ugs.)* shoemaker; *(Flick~)* shoe-repairer

Schutt der; ~[e]s rubble; „~ abladen verboten" 'no tipping'; 'no dumping'

Schüttel·frost der [violent] shivering fit

schütteln 1. *tr. V.* **a)** shake; **den Kopf** [**über etw.** *(Akk.)*] ~: shake one's head [over sth.]; **jmdm. die Hand** ~: shake sb.'s hand; shake sb. by the hand; **b)** *(unpers.)* **es schüttelte ihn** [**vor Kälte**] he was shaking [with *or* from cold]; 2. *refl. V.* shake oneself/itself; 3. *itr. V.* **mit dem Kopf** ~: shake one's head

schütten 1. *tr. V.* pour ⟨liquid, flour, etc.⟩; *(unabsichtlich)* spill ⟨liquid, flour, etc.⟩; tip ⟨rubbish, coal, etc.⟩; 2. *itr. V.* *(unpers.)* *(ugs.: regnen)* pour [down]

schütter *Adj.* sparse; thin

Schutz der; ~es protection (**vor** + *Dat.*, **gegen** against); *(Zuflucht)* refuge

schutz-, Schutz-: ~**bedürftig** *Adj.* in need of protection *postpos.;* ~**blech** das mudguard; ~**brief** der *(Kfz-W.)* travel insurance; *(Dokument)* travel insurance certificate

Schütze der; ~n, ~n **a)** marksman; **b)** *(Fußball usw.: Tor~)* scorer; **c)** *(Milit.: einfacher Soldat)* private; **d)** *(Astrol.)* Sagittarius

schützen 1. *tr. V.* protect (**vor** + *Dat.* from, **gegen** against); safeguard ⟨interest, property, etc.⟩ (**vor** + *Dat.* from); gesetzlich registered [as a trade-mark]; 2. *itr. V.* provide *or* give protection (**vor** + *Dat.* from, **gegen** against); *(vor Wind, Regen)* give shelter (**vor** + *Dat.* from)

Schützen·fest das *shooting competition with fair*

Schutz·engel der guardian angel

Schützen-: ~graben der trench; ~panzer der armoured personnel carrier; ~verein der rifle club
Schutz-: ~helm der helmet; *(bei Motorradfahrern usw.)* crash-helmet; *(bei Bauarbeitern usw.)* safety helmet; ~hütte die a) *(Unterstand)* shelter; b) *(Berghütte)* mountain hut; ~impfung die vaccination
Schützling der; ~s, ~e protégé; *(Anvertrauter)* charge
schutz-, Schutz-: ~los *Adj.* defenceless; ~mann der; *Pl.* ~männer *od.* ~leute *(ugs. veralt.)* [police] constable; copper *(Brit. coll.)*; ~patron der patron saint; ~suchend *Adj.* seeking protection *postpos.*; ~umschlag der dust-jacket
schwabbelig *Adj.* flabby 〈*stomach, person, etc.*〉; wobbly 〈*jelly etc.*〉; schwabbeln *itr. V. (ugs.)* wobble
Schwabe der; ~n, ~n Swabian; Schwaben (das); ~s Swabia; Schwäbin die; ~, ~nen Swabian; schwäbisch *Adj.* Swabian
schwach; schwächer, schwächst... 1. *Adj.* a) weak; weak, delicate 〈*child, woman*〉; frail 〈*invalid, old person*〉; low-powered 〈*engine, bulb, amplifier, etc.*〉; weak, poor 〈*eyesight, memory, etc.*〉; poor 〈*hearing*〉; delicate 〈*health, constitution*〉; ~ werden grow weak; *(fig.: schwanken)* weaken; *(fig.: nachgeben)* give in; b) *(nicht gut)* poor 〈*pupil, player, performance, result, etc.*〉; weak 〈*argument, opponent, play, film, etc.*〉; c) *(gering, niedrig)* poor, low 〈*attendance etc.*〉; slight 〈*effect, resistance, gradient, etc.*〉; light 〈*wind, rain, current*〉; faint 〈*voice, pressure, hope, smile, smell*〉; weak, faint 〈*pulse*〉; faint, dim 〈*light*〉; pale 〈*colour*〉; d) *(wenig konzentriert)* weak 〈*solution, coffee, poison, etc.*〉; e) *(Sprachw.)* weak; 2. *adv.* a) weakly; b) *(nicht gut)* poorly; c) *(in geringem Maße)* poorly 〈*attended, developed*〉; slightly 〈*poisonous, sweetened, inclined*〉; 〈*rain*〉 slightly; 〈*remember, glow, smile*〉 faintly; d) *(Sprachw.)* ~ gebeugt weak; Schwäche die; ~, ~n weakness; eine ~ für jmdn./etw. haben have a soft spot for sb./a weakness for sth.; Schwäche·anfall der sudden feeling of faintness; schwächen *tr. V.* weaken; schwächlich *Adj.* weakly 〈*person*〉; frail 〈*old person, constitution*〉; Schwächling der; ~s, ~e weakling

schwach-, Schwach-: ~sinn der; *o. Pl.* a) *(Med.)* mental deficiency; b) *(ugs.)* [idiotic *(coll.)*] rubbish; ~sinnig 1. *Adj.* a) *(Med.)* mentally deficient; b) *(ugs.)* idiotic *(coll.)*, nonsensical 〈*measure, policy, etc.*〉; rubbishy 〈*film etc.*〉; 2. *adv. (ugs.)* idiotically *(coll.)*; stupidly
schwafeln *(ugs.)* 1. *itr. V.* rabbit on *(Brit. sl.)*, waffle (von about); 2. *tr. V.* blether 〈*nonsense*〉
Schwager der; ~s, Schwäger brother-in-law; Schwägerin die; ~, ~nen sister-in-law
Schwalbe die; ~, ~n swallow
Schwall der; ~[e]s, ~e torrent
schwamm 1. u. 3. Pers. Sg. Prät. v. schwimmen
Schwamm der; ~[e]s, Schwämme a) sponge; ~ drüber! *(ugs.)* [let's] forget it; b) *(südd., österr.: Pilz)* mushroom; Schwammerl das; ~s, ~[n] *(bayr., österr.)* mushroom; schwammig 1. *Adj.* a) spongy; b) *(aufgedunsen)* flabby, bloated 〈*face, body, etc.*〉; 2. *adv. (unpräzise)* vaguely
Schwan der; ~[e]s, Schwäne swan
schwand 1. u. 3. Pers. Sg. Prät. v. schwinden
schwang 1. u. 3. Pers. Sg. Prät. v. schwingen
schwanger *Adj.* pregnant (von by); Schwangere die; *adj. Dekl.* expectant mother; pregnant woman; schwängern *tr. V.* make 〈*woman*〉 pregnant; Schwangerschaft die; ~, ~en pregnancy
Schwank der; ~[e]s, Schwänke comic tale; *(auf der Bühne)* farce
schwanken *itr. V.; mit Richtungsangabe mit sein* a) sway; 〈*boat*〉 rock; *(heftiger)* roll; 〈*ground, floor*〉 shake; b) *(fig.: unbeständig sein)* 〈*prices, temperature, etc.*〉 fluctuate; 〈*number, usage, etc.*〉 vary; c) *(fig.: unentschieden sein)* waver; *(zögern)* hesitate
Schwanz der; ~es, Schwänze a) tail; b) *(salopp: Penis)* prick *(coarse)*; cock *(coarse)*
schwänzeln *itr. V.* wag its tail/their tails
schwänzen *tr. V., itr. V. (ugs.)* skip, cut 〈*lesson etc.*〉; [die Schule] ~: play truant *or (Amer.)* hookey
schwappen *itr. V.* slosh
Schwarm der; ~[e]s, Schwärme a) swarm; b) *(fam.: Angebetete[r])* idol; heart-throb; schwärmen *itr. V.* a) *mit Richtungsangabe mit sein* swarm;

b) *(begeistert sein)* für jmdn./etw. ~:
be mad about *or* really keen on sb./
sth.; **von etw.** ~: go into raptures
about sth.; **schwärmerisch 1.** *Adj.*
rapturous; **2.** *adv.* rapturously

Schwarte die; ~, ~n a) rind; b) *(ugs.:
dickes Buch)* tome

schwarz; schwärzer, schwärzest... 1.
Adj. **a)** black; Black ⟨*person*⟩;
filthy[-black] ⟨*hands, finger-nails,
etc.*⟩; **mir wurde ~ vor den Augen**
everything went black; **der ~e Erdteil**
od. **Kontinent** the Dark Continent;
das Schwarze Meer the Black Sea; **ins
Schwarze treffen** *(fig.)* hit the nail on
the head; *(illegal)* illicit ⟨*deal, exchange, etc.*⟩; **der ~e Markt** the black
market; **2.** *adv. (illegal)* illegally;
Schwarz das; ~[e]s, ~: black

Schwarz·brot das black bread

Schwarze der/die; *adj. Dekl.* Black;
schwärzen *tr. V.* blacken

schwarz-, Schwarz-: ~|**fahren**
unr. itr. V.; mit sein dodge paying the
fare; ~**fahrer** der fare-dodger;
~**haarig** *Adj.* black-haired; ~**handel** der black market (mit in); *(Tätigkeit)* black marketeering (mit in);
~**markt** der black market; ~|**sehen**
unr. itr. V. **a)** *(pessimistisch sein)* look
on the black side; be pessimistic (**für**
about; **b)** *(schwarz fernsehen)* watch
television without a licence; ~**seher**
der **a)** *(ugs.)* pessimist; **b)** *(jmd, der
schwarz fernsieht)* [television] licence
dodger; ~**wald** der; ~|e|s Black
Forest; **schwarz·weiß** *Adj.* black
and white; **Schwarzweiß·foto** das
black and white photo; **Schwarz-
wurzel** die black salsify

schwatzen, *(bes. südd.)* **schwätzen**
1. *itr. V.* chat; *(über belanglose Dinge)*
chatter; natter *(coll.)*; **2.** *tr. V.* say; talk
⟨*nonsense, rubbish*⟩; **Schwätzer** der;
~s, ~: chatterbox; *(klatschhafter
Mensch)* gossip; **schwatzhaft** *Adj.*
talkative; *(klatschhaft)* gossipy

Schwebe die: **in der ~ sein/bleiben**
(fig.) be/remain in the balance

Schwebe-: ~**bahn** die cableway;
~**balken** der *(Turnen)* [balance] beam

schweben *itr. V.* **a)** ⟨*bird, balloon,
etc.*⟩ hover; ⟨*cloud, balloon, mist*⟩
hang; **in Gefahr ~** *(fig.)* be in danger;
b) *mit sein (durch die Luft)* float

Schwede der; ~n, ~n Swede;
Schweden (das); ~s Sweden;
Schwedin die; ~, ~nen Swede;
schwedisch *Adj.* Swedish

Schwefel der; ~s sulphur

Schweif der; ~|e|s, ~e tail;
schweifen *itr. V.; mit sein (geh.;
auch fig.)* wander

Schweige·geld das hush money

schweigen *unr. itr. V.* remain *or* stay
silent; say nothing; **ganz zu ~ von ...:**
not to mention ...; **Schweigen** das;
~s silence; **schweigsam** *Adj.* silent;
quiet

Schwein das; ~|e|s, ~e a) pig; b) *o. Pl.
(Fleisch)* pork; **c)** *(salopp: gemeiner
Mensch)* swine; *(Schmutzfink)* mucky
devil *(coll.)*; mucky pig *(coll.)*; **d)** *(salopp: Mensch)* **ein armes ~:** a poor
devil; **kein ~ war da** there wasn't a
bloody *(Brit. sl.) or (coll.)* damn soul
there; **e)** *(ugs.: Glück)* |großes| ~ **haben**
have a [big] stroke of luck; *(davonkommen)* get away with it *(coll.)*

Schweine-: ~**braten** der roast pork
no indef. art.; ~**fleisch** das pork;
~**kotelett** das *(Kochk.)* pork chop

Schweinerei die; ~, ~en *(ugs.)* **a)**
(Schmutz) mess; **b)** *(Gemeinheit)*
mean *or* dirty trick

Schweine-: ~**schnitzel** das escalope of pork; ~**stall** der *(auch fig.)*
pigsty; pigpen *(Amer.)*

schweinisch *(ugs.) Adj.* **a)** *(schmutzig)* filthy; **b)** *(unanständig)* dirty;
smutty

Schweins·leder das pigskin

Schweiß der; ~es sweat; **mir brach
der ~ aus** I broke out in a sweat

Schweiß·brenner der welding
torch; **schweißen** *tr., itr. V.* weld;
Schweißer der; ~s, ~: welder

Schweiß-: ~**fuß** sweaty foot; ~**perle** die bead of sweat

Schweiz die; ~: Switzerland *no art.*;
Schweizer der; ~s, ~: Swiss;
schweizer·deutsch *Adj.* Swiss
German; **Schweizerin** die; ~, ~nen
Swiss; **schweizerisch** *Adj.* Swiss

schwelen *(auch fig.)* smoulder

schwelgen *itr. V.* feast

Schwelle die; ~, ~n a) threshold; b)
(Eisenbahn~) sleeper *(Brit.)*; [cross-]
tie *(Amer.)*

schwellen *unr. itr. V.; mit sein* swell;
⟨*limb, face, cheek, etc.*⟩ swell [up];
Schwellung die; ~, ~en swelling

Schwemme die; ~, ~n glut (**an** +
Dat. of)

Schwengel der; ~s, ~ a) *(Glocken~)*
clapper; b) *(Pumpen~)* handle

schwenken 1. *tr. V.* **a)** swing; wave
⟨*flag, handkerchief*⟩; b) *(spülen)* rinse;

2. *itr. V.; mit sein ⟨marching column⟩* swing, wheel; ⟨camera⟩ pan; ⟨path, road, car⟩ swing

schwer 1. *Adj.* **a)** heavy; **2 Kilo ~ sein** weigh two kilos; **b)** *(mühevoll)* heavy ⟨work⟩; hard, tough ⟨job⟩; hard ⟨day⟩; difficult ⟨birth⟩; **es ~/nicht ~ haben** have it hard/easy; **c)** *(schlimm)* severe ⟨shock, disappointment, strain, storm⟩; serious, grave ⟨wrong, injustice, error, illness, blow, reservation⟩; serious ⟨accident, injury⟩; heavy ⟨punishment, strain, loss, blow⟩; **2.** *adv.* **a)** heavily ⟨built, laden, armed⟩; **~ tragen** be carrying sth. heavy [with difficulty]; **b)** ⟨work⟩ hard; ⟨breathe⟩ heavily; **~ hören** be hard of hearing; **c)** *(schwierig)* with difficulty; **d)** *(sehr)* seriously ⟨injured⟩; greatly, deeply ⟨disappointed⟩; ⟨punish⟩ severely, heavily; **~ verunglücken** have a serious accident

Schwer-: **~arbeiter** der worker engaged in heavy physical work; **~behinderte** der/die severely handicapped person; *(körperlich auch)* severely disabled person; **die ~behinderten** the severely handicapped/disabled; **~beschädigte** der/die; *adj. Dekl.* severely disabled person

Schwere die; **~ a)** weight; **b)** *(Schwerkraft)* gravity; **c)** *s.* **schwer 1 c:** severity; seriousness; gravity; heaviness; **schwere·los** *Adj.* weightless; **Schwerelosigkeit** die; **~:** weightlessness

schwer-, Schwer-: **~|fallen** *unr. itr. V.; mit sein* **jmdm. fällt etw. ~:** sb. finds sth. difficult; **~fällig 1.** *Adj. (auch fig.)* ponderous; cumbersome ⟨bureaucracy, procedure⟩; **2.** *adv.* ponderously; **~gewicht** das **a)** *(Sport)* heavyweight; **b)** *o. Pl. (Schwerpunkt)* main focus; **~hörig** *Adj.* hard of hearing *pred.;* **~industrie** die heavy industry; **~kraft** die; *o. Pl.* gravity; **~krank** *Adj.; präd. getrennt geschrieben* seriously ill

schwerlich *Adv.* hardly

schwer-, Schwer-: **~|machen** *tr. V.* **jmdm./sich etw. ~machen** make sth. difficult for sb./oneself; **~metall** das heavy metal; **~mütig 1.** *Adj.* melancholic; **2.** *adv.* melancholically; **~|nehmen** *unr. tr. V.* take ⟨sth.⟩ seriously; **~punkt** der centre of gravity; *(fig.)* main focus; *(Hauptgewicht)* main stress

Schwert das; **~[e]s,** **~er** sword; **Schwert·lilie** die iris

schwer-, Schwer-: **~|tun** *unr. refl. V. (ugs.)* **sich mit** *od.* **bei etw. ~tun** *(ugs.)* have trouble with sth.; **~verbrecher** der serious offender; **~verdaulich** *Adj.; präd. getrennt geschrieben (auch fig.)* hard to digest *pred.;* **~verletzt** *Adj.; präd. getrennt geschrieben* seriously injured; **~wiegend** *Adj.* serious; momentous ⟨decision⟩

Schwester die; **~, ~n a)** sister; **b)** *(Kranken~)* nurse; **schwesterlich 1.** *Adj.* sisterly; **2.** *adv.* **~ handeln** act in a sisterly way

schwieg *1. u. 3. Pers. Prät. v.* **schweigen**

Schwieger-: **~eltern** *Pl.* parents-in-law; **~mutter** die mother-in-law; **~sohn** der son-in-law; **~tochter** die daughter-in-law; **~vater** der father-in-law

Schwiele die; **~, ~n** callus; **~n an den Händen** horny hands

schwierig *Adj.* difficult; **Schwierigkeit** die; **~, ~en** difficulty

Schwimm-: **~bad** das swimming-baths *pl. (Brit.);* swimming-pool; **~becken** das swimming-pool

schwimmen 1. *unr. itr. V.* **a)** *meist mit sein* swim; **b)** *meist mit sein (treiben, nicht untergehen)* float; **c)** *(ugs.: unsicher sein)* be all at sea; **ins Schwimmen geraten** start to flounder; **2.** *unr. tr. V.; auch mit sein* swim; **Schwimmen** das; **~:** swimming *no art.;* **Schwimmer** der; **~s, ~ a)** swimmer; **b)** *(Technik)* float

Schwimm-: **~flosse** die flipper; **~lehrer** der swimming instructor; **~weste** die life-jacket

Schwindel der; **~s a)** dizziness; giddiness; **b)** *(Betrug)* swindle; *(Lüge)* lie; **schwindel·frei** *Adj.* **~ sein** have a head for heights; **schwindelig** *s.* **schwindlig; schwindeln** *itr. V.* **a)** *(unpers.)* **mich** *od.* **mir schwindelt** I feel dizzy *or* giddy; **b)** *(lügen)* tell fibs

schwinden *unr. itr. V.; mit sein* fade; ⟨supplies, money⟩ run out; ⟨effect⟩ wear off; ⟨fear, mistrust⟩ lessen; ⟨powers, influence⟩ wane

Schwindler der; **~s, ~** *(Lügner)* liar; *(Betrüger)* swindler; *(Hochstapler)* con man *(coll.)*

schwindlig *Adj.* dizzy; giddy; **jmdm. wird es ~:** sb. gets dizzy *or* giddy

schwingen 1. *unr. itr. V.* **a)** *mit sein* swing; **b)** *(vibrieren)* vibrate; **2.** *unr. tr. V.* swing; wave ⟨flag, wand⟩; brandish ⟨*sword, axe, etc.*⟩; **3.** *unr. refl. V.* **sich aufs Pferd/Fahrrad** ~: leap on to one's horse/bicycle; **Schwingung die;** ~, ~**en a)** swinging; *(Vibration)* vibration; **b)** *(Physik)* oscillation

Schwips der; ~**es,** ~**e** *(ugs.)* **einen** ~ **haben** be tipsy

schwirren *itr. V. mit sein* ⟨*arrow, bullet, etc.*⟩ whiz; ⟨*bird*⟩ whirr; ⟨*insect*⟩ buzz

schwitzen *itr. V. (auch fig.)* sweat

schwor *1. u. 3. Pers. Sg. Prät. v.* **schwören; schwören 1.** *unr. tr., itr. V.* swear ⟨*fidelity, friendship*⟩; swear, take ⟨*oath*⟩; **2.** *unr. itr. V.* swear an/the oath

schwul *Adj. (ugs.)* gay *(coll.)*

schwül *Adj.* sultry; close

Schwule der; *adj. Dekl. (ugs.)* gay *(coll.); (abwertend)* queer *(sl.)*

Schwüle die; ~: sultriness

schwülstig 1. *Adj.* bombastic; pompous; over-ornate ⟨*art, architecture*⟩; **2.** *adv.* bombastically; pompously

Schwund der; ~|e|s decrease, drop *(Gen.* in); *(an Interesse)* waning; falling off

Schwung der; ~|e|s, **Schwünge a)** *(Bewegung)* swing; **b)** *(Linie)* sweep; **c)** *o. Pl. (Geschwindigkeit)* momentum; ~ **holen** build *or* get up momentum; **d)** *o. Pl. (Antrieb)* drive; energy; **e)** *o. Pl. (mitreißende Wirkung)* sparkle; **schwung·haft** *Adj.* thriving; brisk, flourishing ⟨*trade, business*⟩; **schwung·voll a)** lively; **b)** *(kraftvoll)* vigorous; sweeping ⟨*movement, gesture*⟩; bold ⟨*handwriting, line, stroke*⟩; **2.** *adv.* spiritedly; *(kraftvoll)* with great vigour

Schwur der; ~|e|s, **Schwüre a)** *(Gelöbnis)* vow; **b)** *(Eid)* oath; **Schwur·gericht das** *court with a jury*

sechs *Kardinalz.* six; **Sechs die;** ~, ~**en** six

sechs-, Sechs-: ~**eck das** hexagon; ~**eckig** *Adj.* hexagonal; ~**fach** *Vervielfältigungsz.* sixfold; ~**hundert** *Kardinalz.* six hundred; ~**mal** *Adv.* six times

sechst... *Ordinalz.* sixth

sechs·tausend *Kardinalz.* six thousand

sechstel *Bruchz.* sixth; **Sechstel das,** *schweiz. meist* **der;** ~**s,** ~: sixth; **sechstens** *Adv.* sixthly; **sechzehn** *Kardinalz.* sixteen; **sechzig** *Kardinalz.* sixty; **sechzigst...** *Ordinalz.* sixtieth

SED [ɛse:'de:] **die;** ~: *Abk. (ehem. DDR)* **Sozialistische Einheitspartei Deutschlands** Socialist Unity Party of Germany

¹See der; ~**s,** ~**n** lake; **²See die;** ~: **die** ~: the sea; **an die** ~ **fahren** go to the seaside; **auf hoher** ~: on the high seas

See-: ~**bad das** seaside health resort; ~**fahrt die** *o. Pl.* seafaring *no art.;* sea travel *no art.;* ~**gang der;** *o. Pl.* leichter/starker *od.* hoher *od.* schwerer ~**gang** light/heavy *or* rough sea; ~**hund der** [common] seal; *(Pelz)* seal[skin]; ~**igel der** sea-urchin; ~**krank** *Adj.* seasick; ~**krankheit die;** *o. Pl.* seasickness; ~**lachs der** pollack

Seele die; ~, ~**n** soul; *(Psyche)* mind; **seelen·ruhig 1.** *Adj.* calm; **2.** *adv.* calmly; **seelisch 1.** *Adj.* psychological ⟨*cause, damage, tension*⟩; mental ⟨*equilibrium, breakdown, illness, health*⟩; **2.** *adv.* ~ **bedingt sein** have psychological causes; ~ **krank** mentally ill; **Seel·sorge die;** *o. Pl.* pastoral care; **Seelsorger der;** ~**s,** ~: pastoral worker; *(Geistlicher)* pastor

See-: ~**macht die** sea power; ~**mann der;** *Pl.* ~**leute** seaman; sailor; ~**meile die** nautical mile; ~**not die;** *o. Pl.* distress [at sea]; **in** ~ **geraten** get into difficulties *pl.;* ~**pferd[chen] das** sea-horse; ~**räuber der** pirate; ~**reise die** voyage; *(Kreuzfahrt)* cruise; ~**rose die** waterlily; ~**stern der** starfish; ~**tüchtig** *Adj.* seaworthy; ~**zunge die** sole

Segel das; ~**s,** ~: sail

Segel-: ~**boot das** sailing-boat; ~**flieger der** glider pilot; ~**flugzeug das** glider

segeln *itr. V.; mit sein* sail

Segel-: ~**schiff das** sailing ship; ~**tuch das** sailcloth

Segen der; ~**s,** ~: blessing; *(Gebet in der Messe)* benediction

Segler der; ~**s,** ~: yachtsman

segnen *tr. V.* bless

sehen 1. *unr. itr. V.* **a)** see; **schlecht/ gut** ~: have bad/good eyesight; **mal** ~, **wir wollen** *od.* **werden** ~ *(ugs.)* we'll see; **siehste!** *(ugs.)* there, you see!; **b)** *(hin~)* look **(auf** + *Akk.* at); **sieh mal** *od.* **doch!** look!; **siehe da!** lo and behold!; **2.** *unr. tr. V.* **a)** *(auch fig.)* see; **jmdn./etw. |nicht| zu** ~ **bekommen** [not] get to see sb./sth.; **ich habe ihn kommen |ge|**~: I saw him coming; **b)** *(an~)* watch ⟨*television programme*⟩;

sehens·wert *Adj.* worth seeing *postpos.*; **Sehens·würdigkeit** die; ~, ~en sight; **Seher** der; ~s, ~: seer; prophet; **Seh·fehler** der sight defect

Sehne die; ~, ~n a) tendon; b) *(Bogen~)* string

sehnen *refl. V.* sich nach jmdm./etw. ~: long *or* yearn for sb./sth.

sehnig *Adj.* a) stringy ⟨*meat*⟩; b) *(kräftig)* sinewy ⟨*figure, legs, etc.*⟩

sehnlichst 1. *Adj.* das ist mein ~es Verlangen/mein ~er Wunsch that's what I long for most/that's my dearest wish; **2.** *adv.* etw. ~ herbeiwünschen look forward longingly to sth.; **Sehn·sucht** die longing; ~ nach jmdm. haben long to see sb.; **sehn·süchtig** *Adj.* longing *attrib.*, yearning *attrib.* ⟨*desire, look, gaze, etc.*⟩

sehr *Adv.* a) mit *Adj. u. Adv.* very; ~ viel a great deal; jmdn. ~ gern haben like sb. a lot *(coll.)* or a great deal; b) *mit Verben* very much; greatly; **danke** ~! thank you *or* thanks [very much]; **bitte** ~, Ihr Steak! here's your steak, sir/madam

Seh·test der eye test

sei *1. u. 3. Pers. Sg. Präsens Konjunktiv u. Imperativ Sg. v.* sein

seicht 1. *Adj. (auch fig.)* shallow; **2.** *adv. (fig.)* shallowly

seid *2. Pers. Pl. Präsens u. Imperativ Pl. v.* sein

Seide die; ~, ~n silk

Seidel das; ~s, ~: beer-mug

seiden *Adj.; nicht präd.* silk; **Seiden·papier** das tissue paper; **seidig 1.** *Adj.* silky; **2.** *adv.* silkily

Seife die; ~, ~n soap

Seifen-: ~blase die soap bubble; ~schale die soap-dish; ~schaum der; *o. Pl.* lather

Seil das; ~s, ~e rope; *(Draht~)* cable

Seil-: ~bahn die cableway; ~tänzer der tightrope-walker; ~winde die cable winch

¹sein 1. *unr. itr. V.* be; *(existieren)* be; exist; *(sich ereignen)* be; happen; **wie dem auch sei** be that as it may; **er ist Schwede/Lehrer** he is Swedish *or* a Swede/a teacher; **bist du es?** is that you?; **mir ist kalt/besser** I am *or* feel cold/better; **mir ist schlecht** I feel sick; **drei und vier ist** *od. (ugs.)* **sind sieben** three and four is *or* makes seven; **es ist drei Uhr/Mai/Winter** it is three o'clock/May/winter; **er ist aus Berlin** he is *or* comes from Berlin; **was**

darf es ~? *(im Geschäft)* what can I get you?; **es war einmal ein Prinz** once upon a time there was a prince; **2.** *mod. V. (in der Funktion von* können/ müssen + *Passiv)* **es ist niemand zu sehen** there's no one to be seen; **das war zu erwarten** that was to be expected; **die Schmerzen sind kaum zu ertragen** the pain is hardly bearable; **die Richtlinien sind strengstens zu beachten** the guidelines are to be strictly followed; **3.** *Hilfsverb* a) *(zur Bildung des Perfekts usw. im Aktiv)* have; **er ist gestorben** he has died; b) *(zur Bildung des Perfekts usw. im Passiv und des Zustandspassivs)* be; **wir sind gerettet worden/wir waren gerettet** we were saved

²sein *Possessivpron. (einer männlichen Person)* his; *(einer weiblichen Person)* her; *(einer Sache, eines Tiers)* its; *(nach man)* one's; his *(Amer.)*

seiner *(geh.) Gen. von* er: **sich ~ erbarmen** have pity on him; **~ gedenken** remember him

seiner-: ~seits *Adv.* for his part; *(von ihm)* on his part; ~zeit *Adv.* at that time

seines·gleichen *indekl. Pron.* his own kind

seinet·wegen *Adv. s.* meinetwegen: because of him; for his sake; about him; as far as he is concerned

Seismo·graph der; ~en, ~en seismograph

seit 1. *Präp. mit Dat. (Zeitpunkt)* since; *(Zeitspanne)* for; **ich bin ~ zwei Wochen hier** I've been here [for] two weeks; **2.** *Konj.* since; ~ **du hier wohnst** since you have been living here; **seit·dem 1.** *Adv.* since then; **2.** *Konj. s.* seit 2

Seite die; ~, ~n a) side; zur *od.* auf die ~ gehen move aside *or* to one side; ~ an ~: side by side; jmdm. zur ~ stehen stand by sb.; von allen ~n *(auch fig.)* from all sides; nach allen ~n in all directions; *(fig.)* on all sides; b) *(Buch~, Zeitungs~)* page

Seiten-: ~ansicht die side view; ~hieb der *(fig.)* side-swipe *(auf* + *Akk.* at); ~ruder das *(Flugw.)* rudder **seitens** *Präp. mit Gen. (Papierdt.)* on the part of

Seiten-: ~sprung der infidelity; ~straße die side-street; ~wind der; *o. Pl.* side wind; cross-wind; ~zahl die a) page number; b) *(Anzahl der Seiten)* number of pages

seit·her *Adv.* since then
seitlich 1. *Adj.* at the side *(postpos.);*
2. *adv. (an der Seite)* at the side; *(von
der Seite)* from the side; *(nach der Seite)* to the side; **seit·wärts** *Adv.* sideways
Sekretär der; ~s, ~e a) secretary; b)
(Schreibschrank) bureau *(Brit.);* **Se-
kretariat** das; ~[e]s, ~e [secret-
ary's/secretaries'] office; **Sekretärin**
die; ~, ~nen secretary
Sekt der; ~[e]s, ~e high-quality sparkling wine; ≈ champagne
Sekte die; ~, ~n sect
sekundär 1. *Adj.* secondary; 2. *adv.*
secondarily; **Sekunde** die; ~, ~n a)
(auch Math., Musik) second; b) *(ugs.:
Augenblick)* second; moment; **Se-
kunden·zeiger** der second hand
selb... *Demonstrativpron.* same; **sel-
ber** *indekl. Demonstrativpron. s.*
selbst 1; **selbst 1.** *indekl. Demonstrativpron.* myself / yourself / himself /
herself / itself / ourselves / yourselves
/ themselves; **von** ~: automatically; 2.
Adv. even
Selbst·achtung die self-respect
selb·ständig 1. *Adj.* independent;
self-employed *⟨business man, tradesman, etc.⟩;* **sich ~ machen** set up on
one's own; 2. *adv.* independently; ~
denken think for oneself; **Selbstän-
digkeit** die; ~: independence
selbst-, Selbst-: ~**auslöser** der
(Fot.) delayed-action shutter release;
~**bedienung** die self-service *no art.;*
~**befriedigung** die masturbation *no
art.;* ~**beherrschung** die self-control *no art.;* ~**bewußt 1.** *Adj.* self-
confident; 2. *adv.* self-confidently;
~**bewußtsein** das self-confidence
no art.; ~**erkenntnis** die; *o. Pl.* self-
knowledge *no art.;* ~**gefällig 1.** *Adj.*
self-satisfied; smug; 2. *adv.* smugly;
~**gefälligkeit** die; *o. Pl.* self-satis-
faction; smugness; ~**gemacht** *Adj.*
home-made; ~**gespräch** das conversation with oneself; ~**los 1.** *Adj.* self-
less; 2. *adv.* selflessly; unselfishly;
~**mord** der suicide *no art.;* ~**mörder**
der suicide; ~**sicher 1.** *Adj.* self-confident; 2. *adv.* in a self-confident
manner; ~**süchtig 1.** *Adj.* selfish; 2.
adv. selfishly; ~**tätig 1.** *Adj.* automatic; 2. *adv.* automatically; ~**verständlich 1.** *Adj.* natural; **etw. für
~verständlich halten** regard sth. as a
matter of course; *(für gegeben hinneh-
men)* take sth. for granted; 2. *adv.*

naturally; of course; ~**vertrauen** das
self-confidence; ~**verwaltung** die
self-government *no art.;* ~**zweck**
der; *o. Pl.* end in itself
selig 1. *Adj.* **a)** *(Rel.)* blessed; b) *(tot)*
late [lamented]; **c)** *(glücklich)* blissful
⟨idleness, slumber, etc.⟩; blissfully
happy *⟨person⟩;* 2. *adv.* blissfully;
Seligkeit die; ~, ~en bliss *no pl.;*
[blissful] happiness *no pl.*
Sellerie der; ~s, ~[s] *od.* die; ~, ~:
celeriac; *(Stangen~)* celery
selten 1. *Adj.* rare; infrequent *⟨visit,
visitor⟩;* 2. *adv.* **a)** rarely; b) *(sehr)* exceptionally; uncommonly; **Selten-
heit** die; ~, ~en rarity; **Selten-
heits·wert** der; ~[es] rarity value
Selters·wasser das seltzer [water]
seltsam 1. *Adj.* strange; odd; 2. *adv.*
strangely
Semester das; ~s, ~: semester
Semikolon das; ~s, ~s semicolon
Seminar das; ~s, ~e **a)** seminar (über
+ *Akk.* on); b) *(Institut)* department
Semmel die; ~, ~n *(bes. österr., bayr.,
ostmd.)* [bread] roll; **Semmel·knö-
del** der *(bayr., österr.)* bread dumpling
Senat der; ~[e]s, ~e senate; **Senator**
der; ~s, ~en
¹**senden** *unr. (auch regelm.) tr. V.
(geh.)* send
²**senden** *regelm. (schweiz. unr.) tr., itr.
V.* broadcast *⟨programme, play, etc.⟩;*
transmit *⟨signals, Morse, etc.⟩;* **Sender** der; ~s, ~: [broadcasting] station; *(Anlage)* transmitter
Sende-: ~**reihe** die series [of pro-
grammes]; ~**schluß** der close-down
Sendung die; ~, ~en **a)** consignment;
b) *(Rundf., Ferns.)* programme
Senf der; ~[e]s, ~e mustard
senior *indekl. Adj.; nach Personennamen* senior; **Senior** der; ~s, ~en **a)**
(Kaufmannsspr.) senior partner; b)
(Sport) senior [player]; **c)** *(Rentner)*
senior citizen; **Senioren·heim** das
home for the elderly
Senke die; ~, ~n hollow; **senken 1.**
tr. V. lower; 2. *refl. V. ⟨curtain, barrier,
etc.⟩* fall, come down; *⟨ground, building, road⟩* subside, sink; *⟨water-level⟩*
fall, sink
senk-, Senk-: ~**fuß** der flat foot;
~**recht 1.** *Adj.* vertical; **~ zu etw.** perpendicular to sth.; 2. *adv.* vertically;
~**rechte** die vertical; *(Geom.: Gerade)* perpendicular
Sensation die; ~, ~en sensation;

sensationell 1. *Adj.* sensational; 2. *adv.* sensationally

Sense die; ~, ~n scythe

sensibel 1. *Adj.* sensitive; 2. *adv.* sensitively; **Sensibilität** die; ~: sensitivity

sentimental 1. *Adj.* sentimental; 2. *adv.* sentimentally; **Sentimentalität** die; ~, ~en sentimentality

separat 1. *Adj.* separate; self-contained ⟨*flat etc.*⟩; 2. *adv.* separately

September der; ~|s|, ~: September

Serbe der; ~n, ~n Serb; Serbian; **Serbien** (das); ~s Serbia; **serbisch** *Adj.* Serbian

Serenade die; ~, ~n serenade

Serie die; ~, ~n series; **serien·mäßig** 1. *Adj.* standard ⟨*product, model, etc.*⟩; 2. *adv.* **a**) ~ gefertigt *od.* gebaut produced in series; **b**) *(nicht als Sonderausstattung)* ⟨*fitted, supplied, etc.*⟩ as standard

seriös *Adj.* respectable ⟨*person, hotel, etc.*⟩; trustworthy ⟨*firm, partner, etc.*⟩; serious ⟨*offer, applicant, artist, etc.*⟩

Serpentine die; ~, ~n hairpin bend

Serum das; ~s, Seren serum

¹**Service** [zɛr'viːs] das; ~, ~: [dinner *etc.*] service; ²**Service** ['zøːɐvɪs] der; ~, ~s ['zøːɐvɪsɪs] *(Bedienung, Kundendienst)* service; **servieren** *tr. V.* serve; **Serviererin** die; ~, ~nen waitress; **Serviette** [zɛr'vi̯ɛtə] die; ~, ~n napkin; serviette *(Brit.)*

Servo·lenkung die power [-assisted] steering *no indef. art.*

Sesam der; ~s sesame seeds *pl.*

Sessel der; ~s, ~ **a**) armchair; **b**) *(österr.: Stuhl)* chair; **Sessel·lift** der chair-lift

seßhaft *Adj.* settled; ~ werden settle down

Set das *od.* der; ~|s|, ~s **a**) set, combination **(aus** of); **b**) *(Deckchen)* table- *or* place-mat

setzen 1. *refl. V.* **a**) sit [down]; sich Sie sich sit down; take a seat; sich aufs Sofa *usw.* ~: sit on the sofa *etc.*; **b**) ⟨*coffee, froth, etc.*⟩ settle; ⟨*sediment*⟩ sink to the bottom; 2. *tr. V.* **a**) put; **b**) *(einpflanzen)* plant ⟨*tomatoes, potatoes, etc.*⟩; **c**) *(aufziehen)* hoist ⟨*flag etc.*⟩; set ⟨*sails, navigation lights*⟩; **d**) *(Druckw.)* set ⟨*manuscript etc.*⟩; 3. *itr. V.* **a**) *meist mit sein (springen)* leap, jump; **b**) *über einen Fluß* ~ *(mit einer Fähre o. ä.)* cross a river; **c**) *(beim Wetten)* bet; *auf ein Pferd/auf Rot* ~: back a horse/put one's money on red; **Setzer** der; ~s, ~, **Setzerin** die; ~, ~nen *(Druckw.)* [type]setter; **Setzling** der; ~s, ~e seedling

Seuche die; ~, ~n epidemic

seufzen *itr., tr. V.* sigh; **Seufzer** der; ~s, ~: sigh

Sex der; ~|es| sex *no art.*; **Sexualität** die; ~: sexuality *no art.*; **sexuell** 1. *Adj.* sexual; 2. *adv.* sexually

sezieren *tr. V.* dissect ⟨*corpse*⟩

sfr., *(schweiz. nur:)* **sFr.** *Abk.* Schweizer Franken

Shampoo [ʃam'puː], **Shampoon** [ʃam'poːn] das; ~s, ~s shampoo

Sherry ['ʃɛrɪ] der; ~s, ~s sherry

Show [ʃoʊ] die; ~, ~s show

siamesisch *Adj.* Siamese; **Siam·katze** die Siamese cat

Sibirien (das); ~s Siberia

sich *Reflexivpron. der 3. Pers. Sg. und Pl. Akk. und Dat.* **a**) himself/herself/itself/themselves; *(auf man bezogen)* oneself; *(auf das Anredepronomen* Sie *bezogen)* yourself/yourselves; ~ **freuen/wundern/schämen/täuschen** be pleased/surprised/ashamed/mistaken; ~ **sorgen** worry; **b**) *(reziprok)* one another, each other

Sichel die; ~, ~n sickle

sicher 1. *Adj.* **a**) safe ⟨*road, procedure, etc.*⟩; secure ⟨*job, investment, etc.*⟩; **b**) reliable ⟨*evidence, source*⟩; certain ⟨*proof*⟩; reliable, sure ⟨*judgment, taste, etc.*⟩; **c**) *(selbstbewußt)* [self-]assured ⟨*person, manner*⟩; **d**) *(gewiß)* certain; sure; 2. *adv.* **a**) safely; **b**) *(zuverlässig)* reliably; ~ **|Auto| fahren** be a safe driver; **c**) *(selbstbewußt)* [self-]confidently; 3. *Adv.* certainly; **sicher|gehen** *unr. itr. V.; mit sein* play safe; **Sicherheit** die; ~, ~en **a**) *o. Pl.* safety; *(der Öffentlichkeit)* security; **jmdn./etw. in** ~ [**vor etw.** *(Dat.)*] **bringen** save *or* rescue sb./sth. [from sth.]; **b**) *o. Pl. (Gewißheit)* certainty; **c**) *(Wirtsch.: Bürgschaft)* security

sicherheits-, Sicherheits-: ~**abstand** der *(Verkehrsw.)* safe distance between vehicles; ~**gurt** der seatbelt; ~**halber** *Adv.* to be on the safe side; ~**nadel** die safety-pin; ~**schloß** das safety lock

sicherlich *Adv.* certainly; **sichern** *tr. V.* make ⟨*door etc.*⟩ secure; *(garantieren)* safeguard ⟨*rights, peace*⟩; *(schützen)* protect ⟨*rights etc.*⟩; **sich** *(Dat.)* **etw.** ~: secure sth.; **sicher|stellen** *tr. V.* **a**) impound ⟨*goods, vehicle*⟩; **b**) guarantee ⟨*supply, freedom, etc.*⟩; **Si-cherung die**; ~, ~**en a)** *o. Pl.* safeguarding; *(das Schützen)* protection; **b)** *(Elektrot.)* fuse; **c)** *(techn. Vorrichtung)* safety-catch

Sicht die; ~: view **(auf + *Akk.*, in +** *Akk.* of); **gute** *od.* **klare/schlechte** ~: good/poor visibility; **sichtbar 1.** *Adj.* visible; *(fig.)* apparent ⟨*reason*⟩; **2.** *adv.* visibly; **sichten** *tr. V.* sight; **sichtlich 1.** *Adj.* obvious; evident; **2.** *adv.* obviously; evidently; visibly ⟨*impressed*⟩

Sicht-: ~**verhältnisse** *Pl.* visibility *sing.*; ~**vermerk der** visa; ~**weite die** visibility *no art.*; **außer/in** ~**weite sein** be out of/in sight

sickern *itr. V.; mit sein* seep; *(spärlich fließen)* trickle

sie 1. *Personalpron.; 3. Pers. Sg. Nom. Fem.* she; *(betont)* her; *(bei Dingen, Tieren)* it; s. auch ¹**ihr; ihrer a.; 2.** *Personalpron.; 3. Pers. Pl. Nom.* they; *(betont)* them; *s. auch* **ihnen; ihrer b; 3.** *Akk. von* **sie 1** her; *(bei Dingen, Tieren)* it; **4.** *Akk. von* **sie 2 a** them

Sie *Personalpron.; 3. Pers. Pl. Nom. u. Akk; Anrede an eine od. mehrere Personen* you; *s. auch* **Ihnen; Ihrer**

Sieb das; ~⟨e⟩s, ~e sieve; *(für Tee)* strainer; ¹**sieben** *tr. V.* **a)** sieve ⟨*flour etc.*⟩; riddle ⟨*sand, gravel, etc.*⟩; **b)** *(auswählen)* screen ⟨*candidates*⟩

²**sieben** *Kardinalz.* seven; **Sieben die;** ~, ~**en** seven

sieben-, Sieben-: ~**fach** *Vervielfältigungsz.* sevenfold; ~**mal** *Adj.* seven times; ~**sachen** *Pl. (ugs.)* **meine/deine** *usw.* ~**sachen** my/your *etc.* belongings *or (coll.)* bits and pieces

siebt... *Ordinalz.* seventh; **siebtel** *Bruchz.* seventh; **Siebtel das,** *schweiz. meist der;* ~s, ~: seventh; **siebtens** *Adv.* seventhly; **siebzehn** *Kardinalz.* seventeen; **siebzig** *Kardinalz.* seventy; **siebzigst...** *Ordinalz.* seventieth

siedeln *itr. V.* settle

sieden *unr. od. regelm. itr. V.* boil; **Siede·punkt der** *(auch fig.)* boiling-point

Siedler der; ~s, ~: settler; **Siedlung die;** ~, ~**en a)** *(Wohngebiet)* [housing] estate; **b)** *(Niederlassung)* settlement

Sieg der; ~⟨e⟩s, ~e victory, *(bes. Sport)* win (**über +** *Akk.* over)

Siegel das; ~s, ~: seal; *(von Behörden)* stamp

siegen *itr. V.* win; **über jmdn.** ~: gain

or win a victory over sb.; *(bes. Sport)* win against sb.; beat sb.; **Sieger der;** ~s, ~: winner; *(Mannschaft)* winners *pl.*; *(einer Schlacht)* victor; **Sieger-ehrung die** presentation ceremony; awards ceremony; **sieges·sicher 1.** *Adj.* confident of victory *pred.*; **2.** *adv.* confident of victory; **siegreich** *Adj.* victorious; winning ⟨*team*⟩; successful ⟨*campaign*⟩

sieh, siehe *Imperativ Sg. v.* sehen; **siehst** *2. Pers. Sg. Präsens v.* sehen; **sieht** *3. Pers. Sg. Präsens v.* sehen

Signal das; ~s, ~e signal; **signalisieren** *tr. V.* indicate ⟨*danger, change, etc.*⟩

Signatur die; ~, ~**en a)** initials *pl.*; *(Kürzel)* abbreviated signature; *(des Künstlers)* autograph; **b)** *(Unterschrift)* signature; **c)** *(in einer Bibliothek)* shelf-mark; **signieren** *tr. V.* sign; autograph ⟨*one's own work*⟩

Silbe die; ~, ~**n** syllable

Silber das; ~s **a)** silver; **b)** *(silbernes Gerät)* silver[ware]; **Silber·medaille die** silver medal; **silbern 1.** *Adj.* silver; silvery ⟨*moonlight, shade, gleam, etc.*⟩; **2.** *adv.* ⟨*shine, shimmer, etc.*⟩ with a silvery lustre; **Silber·papier das** silver paper

Silhouette [zi'lu̯ɛtə] **die;** ~, ~**n** silhouette

Silo der *od.* **das;** ~s, ~s silo

Silvester der *od.* **das;** ~s, ~: New Year's Eve

Simbabwe (das); ~s Zimbabwe

simpel 1. *Adj.* **a)** simple ⟨*question, task*⟩; **b)** *(beschränkt)* simple-minded ⟨*person*⟩; simple ⟨*mind*⟩; **2.** *adv.* **a)** simply; **b)** *(beschränkt)* in a simple-minded manner; **Simpel der;** ~s, ~ *(bes. südd. ugs.)* simpleton; fool

Sims der *od.* **das;** ~es, ~e ledge; sill; *(Kamin*~*)* mantelpiece

Simulant der; ~en, ~en malingerer; **simulieren 1.** *tr. V.* feign, sham ⟨*illness, emotion, etc.*⟩; simulate ⟨*situation, condition, etc.*⟩; **2.** *itr. V.* feign illness

simultan 1. *Adj.* simultaneous; **2.** *adv.* simultaneously

sind *1. u. 3. Pers. Pl. Präsens v.* ¹**sein**

Sinfonie die; ~, ~**n** symphony; **Sinfonie·orchester das** symphony orchestra

singen *unr. tr., itr. V.* sing

Singular der; ~s singular

Sing·vogel der songbird

sinken *unr. itr. V.; mit sein* **a)** ⟨*ship,*

sun⟩ sink, go down; ⟨*plane, balloon*⟩ descend, go down; **b)** *(nieder~)* fall; **c)** *(niedriger werden)* ⟨*temperature, level*⟩ fall, drop; **d)** *(an Wert verlieren; nachlassen; abnehmen)* fall, go down **Sinn** der; ~|e|s, ~e **a)** sense; **b)** *Pl. (geh.: Bewußtsein)* senses; mind *sing.;* **nicht bei** ~**en sein** be out of one's senses *or* mind; **c)** *o. Pl. (Gefühl, Verständnis)* feeling; **d)** *o. Pl. (~gehalt, Bedeutung)* meaning; **e)** *(Ziel u. Zweck)* point; **Sinn·bild** das symbol **Sinnes-:** ~**organ** das sense-organ; sensory organ; ~**täuschung** die trick of the senses

sinn·gemäß 1. *Adj.* **eine** ~**e** Übersetzung a translation which conveys the general sense; **2.** *adv.* etw. ~ übersetzen/wiedergeben translate the general sense of sth./give the gist of sth.; **sinnlich** *Adj.* sensory ⟨*impression, perception, stimulus*⟩; sensual ⟨*love, mouth*⟩; sensuous ⟨*pleasure, passion*⟩; **Sinnlichkeit** die; ~: sensuality; **sinn·los 1.** *Adj.* **a)** senseless; **b)** *(zwecklos)* pointless; **2.** *adv.* **a)** senselessly; **b)** *(zwecklos)* pointlessly; **Sinnlosigkeit** die; ~ **a)** senselessness; **b)** *(Zwecklosigkeit)* pointlessness; **sinn·voll 1.** *Adj.* **a)** *(vernünftig)* sensible; **b)** *(einen Sinn ergebend)* meaningful; **2.** *adv.* **a)** *(vernünftig)* sensibly; **b)** *(einen Sinn ergebend)* meaningfully

Sint·flut die Flood; Deluge; **sint-flut·artig 1.** *Adj.* torrential; **2.** *adv.* in torrents

Sippe die; ~, ~n **a)** *(Völkerk.)* sib; **b)** *(ugs.: Verwandtschaft)* clan; **Sipp-schaft** die; ~, ~en *(ugs.)* s. Sippe b

Sirene die; ~, ~n siren

Sirup der; ~s, ~e syrup

Sitte die; ~, ~n **a)** *(Brauch)* custom; tradition; **b)** *(moralische Norm)* common decency; **c)** *Pl. (Benehmen)* manners; **sittlich 1.** *Adj.* moral; **2.** *adv.* morally; **Sittlichkeit** die; *o. Pl.* morality

Sittlichkeits-: ~**verbrechen** das sexual crime; ~**verbrecher** der sex offender

Situation die; ~, ~en situation

Sitz der; ~es, ~e **a)** seat; **b)** *(Verwaltungs~)* headquarters *sing. or pl.;* **c)** *(von Kleidungsstücken)* fit

sitzen *unr. itr. V.; südd., österr., schweiz. mit sein* **a)** sit; **b)** *(sein)* be; **c)** *([gut] passen)* fit

sitzen-: ~|**bleiben** *unr. itr. V. (ugs.)*

a) *(nicht versetzt werden)* stay down [a year]; **b)** *(unverheiratet bleiben)* be left on the shelf; **c)** **auf etw.** *(Dat.)* ~**blei-ben** *(für etw. keinen Käufer finden)* be left *or (coll.)* stuck with sth.; ~|**lassen** *unr. tr. V. (ugs.)* **a)** *(nicht heiraten)* jilt; **b)** *(im Stich lassen)* leave in the lurch; **c)** etw. **nicht auf sich** *(Dat.)* ~**lassen** not take sth.

Sitzplatz der seat; **Sitzung** die; ~, ~**en** meeting; *(Parlaments~)* sitting; session; **Sitzungs·saal** der conference hall

Skala die; ~, **Skalen** scale

Skalp der; ~s, ~e scalp

Skalpell das; ~s, ~e scalpel

skalpieren *tr. V.* scalp

Skandal der; ~s, ~e scandal; **skan-dalös** *Adj.* scandalous

Skandinavien (das); ~s Scandinavia; **Skandinavier** der; ~s, ~: Scandinavian; **skandinavisch** *Adj.* Scandinavian

Skat der; ~|e|s, ~e *od.* ~s skat

Skelett das; ~|e|s, ~e skeleton

Skepsis die; ~: scepticism; **skep-tisch 1.** *Adj.* sceptical; **2.** *adv.* sceptically

Ski [ʃiː] der; ~s, ~**er** *od.* ~: ski; ~ **lau-fen** *od.* **fahren** ski

Ski-: ~**läufer** der skier; ~**lehrer** der ski-instructor; ~**lift** der ski-lift; ~**springen** das; ~s ski-jumping *no art.*

Skizze die; ~, ~n sketch; **Skiz-zen·block** der sketch-pad; **skiz-zieren** *tr. V.* sketch

Sklave der; ~n, ~n slave; **Skla-ven·händler** der slave-trader; **Sklaverei** die; ~: slavery *no art.;* **Sklavin** die; ~, ~**nen** slave; **skla-visch 1.** *Adj.* slavish; **2.** *adv.* slavishly

Skonto der *od.* das; ~s, ~s *(Kauf-mannsspr.)* [cash] discount

Skorbut der; ~|e|s scurvy *no art.*

Skorpion der; ~s, ~e scorpion

Skrupel der; ~s, ~: scruple; **skru-pel·los 1.** *Adj.* unscrupulous; **2.** *adv.* unscrupulously; **Skrupellosigkeit** die; ~: unscrupulousness

Skulptur die; ~, ~**en** sculpture

Slalom der; ~s, ~s slalom

Slawe der; ~n, ~n Slav; **slawisch** *Adj.* Slav[ic]; Slavonic

Slip der; ~s, ~s briefs *pl.*

Slowake der; ~n, ~n Slovak; **Slo-wakei** die; ~: Slovakia *no art.*

Smaragd der; ~|e|s, ~e emerald

Smoking der; ~s, ~s dinner-jacket or (Amer.) tuxedo and dark trousers

so 1. Adv. **a)** (auf diese Weise; in, von dieser Art) like this/that; this/that way; **weiter so!** carry on in the same way!; **b)** (dermaßen, überaus) so; **c)** (genauso) as; **so gut ich konnte** as best I could; **d)** (ugs.: solch) such; **so ein Idiot!** what an idiot!; **so einer/eine/eins** one like that; **e)** betont (eine Zäsur ausdrückend) right; OK (coll.); **g)** (ugs.: schätzungsweise) about; 2. Konj. **so daß** ... (damit) so that ...; (und deshalb) and so ...; 3. Partikel **a)** just; **ach, das hab' ich nur so gesagt** oh, I didn't mean anything by that; **b)** (in Aufforderungssätzen verstärkend) **komm doch** come on now

So. Abk. Sonntag Sun.

s. o. Abk. siehe oben

sobald Konj. as soon as

Socke die; ~, ~n sock

Sockel der; ~s, ~ **a)** (einer Säule, Statue) plinth; **b)** (unterer Teil eines Hauses, Schrankes) base

Soda·wasser das; Pl. **Sodawässer** soda; soda-water

Sod·brennen das; ~s heartburn

so·eben Adv. just

Sofa das; ~s, ~s sofa; settee

so·fern Konj. provided [that]

soff 1. u. 3. Pers. Sg. Prät. v. saufen

so·fort Adv. immediately; at once; **sofortig** Adj. (unmittelbar) immediate

sog 1. u. 3. Pers. Sg. Prät. v. saugen;

Sog der; ~[e]s, ~e suction; (bei Schiffen) wake; (bei Fahr-, Flugzeugen) slip-stream; (von Wasser, auch fig.) current

so·gar Adv. even

so·genannt Adj. so-called

so·gleich Adv. immediately; at once

Sohle die; ~, ~n **a)** (Schuh~) sole; (Einlege~) insole; **b)** (Fuß~) sole [of the foot]

Sohn der; ~es, **Söhne** son

Soja·: ~bohne die soy[a] bean; **~soße** die soy[a] sauce

so·lang[e] Konj. so or as long as

Solarium das; ~s, **Solarien** solarium

solch Demonstrativpron. **a)** attr. such; **das macht ~en Spaß!** it's so much fun!; **b)** alleinstehend **~e wie die** people like that

Sold der; ~[e]s, ~e [military] pay

Soldat der; ~en, ~en soldier; **Soldaten·friedhof** der military or war cemetery; **Soldatin** die; ~, ~nen [fe-

male or woman] soldier; **soldatisch** 1. Adj. military (discipline, expression, etc.); soldierly (figure, virtue); 2. adv. in a military manner

Söldner der; ~s, ~: mercenary

solidarisch 1. Adj. **~es Verhalten zeigen** show one's solidarity; 2. adv. **~ handeln/sich ~ verhalten** act in/show solidarity; **solidarisieren** refl. V. show [one's] solidarity; **Solidarität** die; ~: solidarity

solide 1. Adj. **a)** solid; sturdy (shoes, material); [good-]quality (goods); **b)** (gut fundiert) sound (work, education, knowledge); solid (firm); **c)** (anständig) respectable (person, life, profession); 2. adv. **a)** solidly (built); sturdily (made); **b)** (gut fundiert) soundly (educated, constructed); **c)** (anständig) (live) respectably, steadily

Solist der; ~en, ~en soloist

Soll das; ~[s], ~[s] **a)** (Bankw.) debit; **b)** (Arbeits~) quota; **sein ~ erfüllen** od. **erreichen** achieve one's target

sollen 1. unr. Modalverb; 2. Part. ~ **a)** (bei Aufforderung, Anweisung, Auftrag) **was soll ich als nächstes tun?** what should I do next?; [sagen Sie ihm,] er soll hereinkommen tell him to come in; **b)** (bei Wunsch, Absicht, Vorhaben) **das sollte ein Witz sein** that was meant to be a joke; **was soll denn das heißen?** what is that supposed to mean?; **c)** (bei Ratlosigkeit) **was soll ich nur machen?** what am I to do?; **d)** (Notwendigkeit ausdrückend) **man soll so etwas nicht unterschätzen** it shouldn't be taken so lightly; **e)** häufig im Konjunktiv II (Erwartung, Wünschenswertes ausdrückend) **du solltest dich schämen** you ought to be ashamed of yourself; **das hättest du besser nicht tun ~:** it would have been better if you hadn't done that; **f)** (jmdm. beschieden sein) **er sollte seine Heimat nicht wiedersehen** he was never to see his homeland again; **g)** im Konjunktiv II (eine Möglichkeit ausdrückend) **wenn du ihn sehen solltest, sage ihm bitte ...:** if you should see him, please tell him ...; **h)** im Präsens (sich für die Wahrheit nicht verbürgend) **das Restaurant soll sehr teuer sein** the restaurant is supposed or said to be very expensive; **i)** im Konjunktiv II (Zweifel ausdrückend) **sollte das sein Ernst sein?** is he really being serious?; **j)** (können) **mir soll es gleich sein** it's all the same to me; 2. tr., itr.

V. **was soll das?** what's the idea?; **was soll ich dort?** what would I do there? **Solo das;** ~s, ~s *od.* **Soli** solo
so·mit [auch: '--] *Adv.* consequently; therefore
Sommer der; ~s, ~: summer
Sommer·ferien *Pl.* summer holidays; **sommerlich** 1. *Adj.* summer; summery (*warmth, weather*); summer's *attrib.* (*day, evening*); 2. *adv.* **es war ~ warm** it was as warm as summer
sommer-, Sommer-: ~**reifen** der standard tyre; ~**schluß·verkauf** der summer sale/sales; ~**sprosse** die freckle; ~**sprossig** *Adj.* freckled; ~**zeit** die (*Uhrzeit*) summer time
Sonate die; ~, ~n (*Musik*) sonata
Sonde die; ~, ~n probe; (*zur Ernährung*) tube
Sonder·angebot das special offer; **sonderbar** 1. *Adj.* strange; odd; 2. *adv.* strangely; oddly; **Sonder·fall** der special case
sonder·gleichen *Adv., nachgestellt* **eine Frechheit/Unverschämtheit ~:** the height of cheek/impudence
sonderlich *Adv.* particularly; **Sonderling** der; ~s, ~e strange *or* odd person; **Sonder·müll** der hazardous waste
¹**sondern** *tr. V.* (*geh.*) separate (**von** from)
²**sondern** *Konj.* but; **nicht nur ...,** ~ [**auch**] **...:** not only ... but also ...
Sonder-: ~**schule** die special school; ~**zug** der special train
sondieren *tr. V.* sound out
Sonett das; ~[e]s, ~e sonnet
Sonn·abend der (*bes. nordd.*) Saturday; **sonn·abends** *Adv.* on Saturday[s]
Sonne die; ~, ~n sun; (*Licht der ~*) sun[light]; **sonnen** *refl. V.* sun oneself
sonnen-, Sonnen-: ~**aufgang** der sunrise; ~**baden** *itr. V.* sunbathe; ~**blume** die sunflower; ~**brand** der sunburn *no indef. art.;* ~**brille** die sun-glasses *pl.;* ~**energie** die solar energy; ~**finsternis** die solar eclipse; ~**hut** der sun-hat; ~**licht** das sunlight; ~**öl** das sun-oil; ~**schein** der *o. Pl.* sunshine; ~**schirm** der sunshade; ~**stich** der sunstroke *no indef. art.;* ~**strahl** der ray of sun[shine]; ~**uhr** die sundial; ~**untergang** der sunset
sonnig *Adj.* sunny
Sonn·tag der Sunday; **sonn·täg-**

lich 1. *Adj.* Sunday *attrib.;* 2. *adv.* ~ **gekleidet** dressed in one's Sunday best; **sonntags** *Adv.* on Sunday[s]
sonst *Adv.* **a)** der ~ so freundliche **Mann ...:** the man, who is/was usually so friendly, ...; **alles war wie ~:** everything was [the same] as usual; ~ **noch was?** (*ugs., auch iron.*) anything else?; **wer/was/wie/wo |denn|** ~**?** who/what/how/where else?; **b)** (*andernfalls*) otherwise; or; **sonstig...** *Adj.; nicht präd.* other; further
sonst-: ~**was** *Indefinitpron.* (*ugs.*) anything else; ~**wer** *Indefinitpron.* (*ugs.*) somebody else; (*fragend, verneinend*) anybody else; ~**wo** *Adv.* (*ugs.*) somewhere else; (*fragend, verneinend*) anywhere else
so·oft *Konj.* whenever
Sopran der; ~s, ~e (*Musik*) soprano (*im Chor*) sopranos *pl.;* **Sopranistin** die; ~, ~nen soprano
Sorge die; ~, ~n worry; **keine ~!** don't [you] worry!; **sorgen** 1. *refl. V.* worry (**um** about); 2. *itr. V.* **für jmdn./etw. ~:** take care of sb./sth.
sorgen-, Sorgen-: ~**frei** 1. *Adj.* carefree; 2. *adv.* ~**frei leben** live in a carefree manner; ~**kind** das (*auch fig.*) problem child; ~**voll** 1. *Adj.* worried; 2. *adv.* worriedly
Sorg·falt die; ~: care; **sorg·fältig** 1. *Adj.* careful; 2. *adv.* carefully
sorg·los 1. *Adj.* **a)** (*ohne Sorgfalt*) careless; **b)** (*unbekümmert*) carefree; 2. *adv.* ~ **mit etw. umgehen** treat sth. carelessly; **Sorglosigkeit** die; ~ **a)** (*Mangel an Sorgfalt*) carelessness; **b)** (*Unbekümmertheit*) carefreeness; **sorgsam** 1. *Adj.* careful; 2. *adv.* carefully
Sorte die; ~, ~n **a)** sort; type; kind; **b)** *Pl.* (*Devisen*) foreign currency *sing.*
sortieren *tr. V.* sort [out] (*pictures, letters, washing, etc.*); grade (*goods etc.*)
Sortiment das; ~[e]s, ~e range (**an** + *Dat.* of)
so·sehr *Konj.* however much
Soße die; ~, ~n sauce; (*Braten~*) gravy; sauce; (*Salat~*) dressing
sott *1. u. 3. Pers. Sg. Prät. v.* **sieden**
Souffleur [zu'flø:ɐ̯] der; ~s, ~e, **Souffleuse** [zu'flø:zə] die; ~, ~n prompter; **soufflieren** [zu'fli:rən] *tr. V.* prompt
Souvenir [suvə'ni:ɐ̯] das; ~s, ~s souvenir
souverän [zuvə'rɛ:n] *Adj.* sovereign; **Souveränität** die; ~: sovereignty

so·viel 1. *Konj.* as *or* so far as; 2. *Indefinitpron.* ~ **wie** *od.* **als** as much as; **halb/doppelt** ~: half/twice as much
so·weit 1. *Konj.* **a)** as *or* so far as; **b)** *(in dem Maße, wie)* [in] so far as; 2. *Adv.* by and large; *(bis jetzt)* up to now; ~ **sein** *(ugs.)* be ready
so·wenig *Indefinitpron.* ~ **wie** *od.* **als** möglich as little as possible
so·wie *Konj.* **a)** *(und)* as well as; **b)** *(sobald)* as soon as
so·wie·so *Adv.* anyway
sowjetisch *Adj.* Soviet
Sowjet·union die *(1922–1991)* Soviet Union
so·wohl *Konj.* ~ ... **als** *od.* **wie** |auch|...: both ... and ...; ... as well as ...
sozial 1. *Adj.* social; 2. *adv.* socially
sozial-, Sozial-: ~**abgaben** *Pl.* social welfare contributions; ~**arbeiter der** social worker; ~**demokrat der** Social Democrat; ~**demokratisch** *Adj.* social democratic; ~**hilfe die** social welfare
Sozialismus der; ~: socialism *no art.;* **Sozialist der;** ~**en,** ~**en, Sozialistin die;** ~, ~**nen** socialist; **sozialistisch** 1. *Adj.* socialist; 2. ~ **regierte Länder** countries with socialist governments
Sozial-: ~**politik die** social policy; ~**produkt das** *(Wirtsch.)* national product; ~**staat der** welfare state
Soziologe der; ~**n,** ~**n** sociologist; **Soziologie die;** ~: sociology; **soziologisch** 1. *Adj.* sociological; 2. *adv.* sociologically
Sozius der; ~, ~**se a)** *Pl. auch:* **Sozii** *(Wirtsch.: Teilhaber)* partner; **b)** *(beim Motorrad)* pillion
so·zu·sagen *Adv.* as it were
Spachtel der; ~**s,** ~ *od.* **die;** ~, ~**n** putty-knife; *(zum Malen)* palette-knife; **spachteln** *tr. V.* **a)** stop, fill ⟨*hole, crack, etc.*⟩; smooth over ⟨*wall, panel, surface, etc.*⟩; **b)** *(ugs.: essen)* put away *(coll.)* ⟨*food, meal*⟩
Spagat der *od.* **das;** ~|**e|s,** ~**e** splits *pl.*
Spaghetti *Pl.* spaghetti *sing.*
spähen *itr. V.* peer; *(durch ein Loch, eine Ritze usw.)* peep; **Späher der;** ~**s,** ~ *(Milit.)* scout; *(Posten)* lookout; *(Spitzel)* informer
Spalier das; ~**s,** ~**e a)** trellis; **b)** *(Ehren~)* guard of honour; ~ **stehen** line the route; ⟨*soldiers*⟩ form a guard of honour
Spalt der; ~|**e|s,** ~**e** opening; *(im Fels)* fissure; crevice; *(zwischen Vorhängen)*

chink; gap; *(langer Riß)* crack; **Spalte die;** ~, ~**n a)** crack; *(Fels~)* crevice **b)** *(Druckw.)* column; **spalten** *unr.* *(auch regelm.) tr., refl. V.* split
Span der; ~|**e|s, Späne** *(Hobel~)* shaving
Span·ferkel das sucking pig
Spange die; ~, ~**n** clasp; *(Haar~)* hair-slide *(Brit.);* barrette *(Amer.);* *(Arm~)* bracelet; bangle
Spaniel ['ʃpa:niəl] **der;** ~**s,** ~**s** spaniel
Spanien ['ʃpa:niən] **(das);** ~**s** Spain; **Spanier der;** ~**s,** ~: Spaniard; **spanisch** *Adj.* Spanish
Span·korb der chip basket; chip
spann *1. u. 3. P. Sing. Prät. v.* **spinnen**
spannen 1. *tr. V.* **a)** tighten ⟨*violin string, violin bow, etc.*⟩; draw ⟨*bow*⟩; tension ⟨*spring, tennis net, drumhead, saw-blade*⟩; stretch ⟨*fabric, shoe, etc.*⟩; draw *or* pull ⟨*line*⟩ tight *or* taut; flex ⟨*muscle*⟩; cock ⟨*gun, camera shutter*⟩; **b)** *(befestigen)* put up ⟨*washing-line*⟩; stretch ⟨*net, wire, tarpaulin, etc.*⟩ (über + *Akk.* over); **c)** *(schirren)* harness (vor, an + *Akk.* to); 2. *refl. V.* **a)** become *or* go taut; ⟨*muscles*⟩ tense; **b)** *(geh.: sich wölben)* **sich über etw.** *(Akk.)* ~: span sth.; 3. *itr. V.* ⟨*clothing*⟩ be [too] tight; ⟨*skin*⟩ be taut; **spannend** 1. *Adj.* exciting; *(stärker)* thrilling; 2. *adv.* excitingly; *(stärker)* thrillingly; **Spannung die;** ~, ~**en a)** *o. Pl.* excitement; *(Neugier)* suspense; **b)** *o. Pl. (eines Romans, Films usw.)* suspense; **c)** *(Zwistigkeit, Nervosität)* tension; **d)** *(Elektrot.)* voltage;
Spann·weite die [wing-]span
Spar·buch das savings book
sparen 1. *tr. V.* save; 2. *itr. V.* **a)** save; **für** *od.* **auf etw.** *(Akk.)* ~: save up for sth.; **b)** *(sparsam wirtschaften)* economize (**mit** on); **an etw.** *(Dat.)* ~: be sparing with sth.; *(beim Einkauf)* economize on sth.; **Sparer der;** ~**s,** ~: saver
Spargel der; ~**s,** ~, *schweiz. auch* **die;** ~, ~**n** asparagus *no pl., no indef. art.*
Spar-: ~**groschen der** *(ugs.)* nest-egg; savings *pl.;* ~**kasse die** savings bank; ~**konto das** savings *or* deposit account
spärlich 1. *Adj.* sparse ⟨*vegetation, beard, growth*⟩; thin ⟨*hair, applause*⟩; scanty ⟨*left-overs, knowledge, news, evidence, clothing*⟩; poor ⟨*lighting*⟩; 2. *adv.* sparsely, thinly ⟨*populated, covered*⟩; poorly ⟨*lit, attended*⟩; scantily ⟨*dressed*⟩

sparsam 1. *Adj.* thrifty ⟨*person*⟩; *(wirtschaftlich)* economical; **mit etw. ~ sein** be economical with sth.; **2.** *adv.* **~ mit der Butter/dem Papier umgehen** use butter/paper sparingly; economize on butter/paper; **Sparsamkeit die; ~:** thrift[iness]; *(Wirtschaftlichkeit)* economicalness

Sparte die; ~, ~n a) *(Teilbereich)* area; *(eines Geschäfts)* line [of business]; **b)** *(Rubrik)* section

Spaß der; ~es, Späße a) *o. Pl. (Vergnügen)* fun; **~ an etw.** *(Dat.)* **haben** enjoy sth.; [jmdm.] **~ machen** be fun [for sb.]; **viel ~!** have a good time!; **b)** *(Scherz)* joke; *(Streich)* prank; **er macht nur ~:** he's only joking; **~ beiseite!** joking aside; **~ muß sein!** there's no harm in a joke; **~ verstehen** be able to take a joke; **im** *od.* **zum** *od.* **aus ~:** as a joke; for fun; **spaßen** *itr. V.* **a)** *(Spaß machen)* joke; **b) er läßt nicht mit sich ~:** he won't stand for any nonsense; **mit ihm/damit ist nicht zu ~:** he/it is not to be trifled with; **spaßes·halber** *Adv.* for the fun of it; for fun; **spaßig** *Adj.* funny; comical; amusing

spät 1. *Adj.* late; **wie ~ ist es?** what time is it?; **2.** *adv.* late; **~ am Abend** late in the evening

Spaten der; ~s, ~: spade

später 1. *Adj.* **a)** later ⟨*years, generations, etc.*⟩; **b)** *(zukünftig)* future ⟨*owner, wife, etc.*⟩; **2.** *Adv.* later; **spätestens** *Adv.* at the latest

Spatz der; ~en, ~en a) sparrow; **b)** *(fam.: Liebling)* pet

Spätzle *Pl.* spaetzle; kind of noodles

spazieren *itr. V.; mit sein* stroll

spazieren-: ~|fahren 1. *unr. itr. V.; mit sein* go for a ride; **2.** *tr. V.* **ein Kind** |im Kinderwagen| **~fahren** take a baby for a walk [in a pram]; **~|gehen** *unr. itr. V.; mit sein* go for a walk

Spazier-: ~gang der walk; **~gänger der; ~s, ~:** person out for a walk

SPD [εspe:'de:] *der;* **~** *Abk.* **Sozialdemokratische Partei Deutschlands** SPD

Specht der; ~|e|s, ~e woodpecker

Speck der; ~|e|s, ~e a) bacon fat; *(Schinken~)* bacon; **b)** *(ugs. scherzh.: Fettpolster)* fat; flab *(sl.)*; **speckig** *Adj.* greasy

Spediteur [ʃpedi'tø:ɐ̯] *der;* **~s, ~e** carrier; haulage contractor; *(Möbel~)* furniture-remover

Speer der; ~|e|s, ~e a) spear; **b)** *(Sportgerät)* javelin

Speichel der; ~s saliva

Speicher der; ~s, ~ a) storehouse; *(Lagerhaus)* warehouse; **b)** *(südd.: Dachboden)* loft; **c)** *(Elektronik)* memory; **speichern** *tr. V.* store

speien *(geh.) unr. tr., itr. V.* spit

Speise die; ~, ~n a) *(Gericht)* dish; **b)** *o. Pl. (geh.: Nahrung)* food

Speise-: ~gaststätte die restaurant; **~kammer die** larder; **~karte die** menu; **~lokal das** restaurant

speisen *(geh.)* **1.** *itr. V.* eat; *(dinieren)* dine; **2.** *tr. V.* eat; *(dinieren)* dine on

Speise-: ~saal der dining-hall; *(im Hotel, in einer Villa usw.)* dining-room; **~wagen der** restaurant car *(Brit.);* **~zettel der** menu

Spektakel der; ~s, ~ *(ugs.) (Lärm)* row *(coll.);* rumpus *(coll.);* **spektakulär 1.** *Adj.* spectacular; **2.** *adv.* spectacularly

Spekulation die; ~, ~en speculation; **spekulieren** *itr. V.* **a)** *(ugs.)* **darauf ~, etw. tun zu können** count on being able to do sth.; **b)** *(Wirtsch.)* speculate **(mit in)**

Spelunke die; ~, ~n *(ugs. abwertend)* dive *(coll.)*

Spelze die; ~, ~n *(des Getreidekorns)* husk

Spende die; ~, ~n donation; contribution; **spenden** *tr., itr. V.* **a)** donate; give; **b)** *(fig. geh.)* give ⟨*light*⟩; afford, give ⟨*shade*⟩; give off ⟨*heat*⟩; **Spender der; ~s, ~, Spenderin die; ~, ~nen** donor; donator; **spendieren** *tr. V.* *(ugs.)* get, buy ⟨*drink, meal, etc.*⟩; stand ⟨*round*⟩

Spengler der; ~s, ~ *(südd., österr., schweiz.) s.* Klempner

Sperling der; ~s, ~e sparrow

Sperma das; ~s, Spermen sperm; semen

sperr·angel·weit *Adv. (ugs.)* **~ offen** *od.* **geöffnet** wide open

Sperre die; ~, ~n a) barrier; *(Straßen~)* road-block; *(Milit.)* obstacle; **b)** *(fig.)* ban; *(Handels~)* embargo; *(Import~, Export~)* blockade; *(Nachrichten~)* [news] black-out; **sperren 1.** *tr. V.* **a)** close; close off ⟨*area*⟩; block ⟨*entrance, access, etc.*⟩; lock ⟨*mechanism etc.*⟩; **b)** cut off ⟨*water, gas, electricity, etc.*⟩; **c)** *(Bankw.)* stop ⟨*cheque, overdraft facility*⟩; freeze ⟨*bank account*⟩; **d)** *(ein~)* **ein Tier/ jmdn. in etw.** *(Akk.)* **~** shut an animal/sb. in sth.; **e)** *(Sport: von der Teilnahme ausschließen)* ban; **f)** *(Druckw.: spationieren)* print ⟨*word,*

text) with the letters spaced; **2**. *refl. V.*
sich [**gegen etw.**] ~: balk [at sth.];
Sperr·holz das plywood; **sperrig**
Adj. unwieldy

Sperr-: ~**müll der** bulky refuse *(for
which there is a separate collection service)*; ~**sitz der** *(im Kino)* seat in the
back stalls; *(im Zirkus)* front seat; *(im
Theater)* seat in the front stalls;
~**stunde die** closing time

Spesen *Pl.* expenses; **auf ~**: on expenses

Spezi der; ~**s**, ~**[s]** *(südd., österr.,
schweiz. ugs.)* [bosom] pal *(coll.)*;
chum *(coll.)*

spezialisieren *refl. V.* specialize (**auf**
+ *Akk.* in); **Spezialist der**; ~**en**, ~**en**
specialist; **Spezialität die**; ~, ~**en**
speciality; **speziell 1**. *Adj.* special;
specific *(question, problem, etc.)*; **2**.
Adv. especially; *(eigens)* specially;
spezifisch 1. *Adj.* specific; characteristic *(smell, style)*; **2**. *adv.* specifically

spicken *tr. V.* lard

spie *1. u. 3. Pers. Sg. Prät. v.* speien

Spiegel der; ~**s**, ~ **a)** mirror; **b)** *(Was-
ser-, fig.: Konzentration)* level

spiegel-, Spiegel-: ~**bild das** reflection; ~**blank** *Adj.* shining; ~**ei das**
fried egg; ~**glatt** *Adj.* like glass *postpos.*; as smooth as glass *postpos.*

spiegeln 1. *itr. V.* **a)** *(glänzen)* shine;
gleam; **b)** *(als Spiegel wirken)* reflect
the light; **2**. *tr. V.* reflect; mirror; **3**.
refl. V. be mirrored *or* reflected

Spiegel·reflex·kamera die reflex
camera

Spiel das; ~**[e]s**, ~**e a)** play; **b)**
(Glücks-; Gesellschafts-) game;
(Wett-) game; match; **auf dem ~ stehen** be at stake; **etw. aufs ~ setzen** put
sth. at stake; risk sth.; **Spiel·bank
die**; *Pl.* ...**banken** casino; **spielen 1**.
itr. V. **a)** play; **auf der Gitarre ~**: play
the guitar; **um Geld ~**: play for
money; **b)** *(als Schauspieler)* act; perform; **c) der Roman/Film spielt im 17.
Jahrhundert/in Berlin** the novel/film
is set in the 17th century/in Berlin; **d)**
(fig.) **das Blau spielt ins Violette** the
blue is tinged with purple; **2**. *tr. V.* **a)**
play; **Cowboy ~**: play at being a cowboy; **Geige** *usw.* **~**: play the violin
etc.; **b)** *(aufführen, vorführen)* put on
(play); show *(film)*; perform *(piece of
music)*; play *(record)*; **den Beleidig-
ten/Unschuldigen ~** *(fig.)* act of-
fended/play the innocent; **spielend**

Adv. easily; **Spieler der**; ~**s**, ~:
player; *(Glücks-)* gambler; **Spiele-
rei die**; ~, ~**en a)** *o. Pl.* playing *no
art.*; *(im Glücksspiel)* gambling *no art.*;
b) eine ~ mit Worten/Zahlen playing
[around] with words/numbers;
Spielerin die; ~, ~**nen** *s.* Spieler

Spiel-: ~**feld das** field; pitch *(Brit.)*;
(Tennis, Squash, Volleyball usw.)
court; ~**film der** feature film; ~**kamerad der** playmate; ~**karte die**
playing-card; ~**plan der** programme;
~**platz der** playground; ~**raum der**
room to move *(fig.)*; scope; latitude;
~**sachen** *Pl.* toys; ~**verderber der**;
~**s**, ~: spoil-sport; ~**waren** *Pl.*
~**zeug das a)** toy; *(fig.)* toy; play-
thing; **b)** *o. Pl.* *(~sachen, ~waren)* toys
pl.

Spieß der; ~**es**, ~**e a)** *(Waffe)* spear;
den ~ umdrehen *od.* **umkehren** *(ugs.)*
turn the tables; **b)** *(Brat-)* spit; **c)**
(Fleisch-) kebab; **d)** *(Soldatenspr.)*
[company] sergeant-major

Spießer der; ~**s**, ~ *(abwertend)* [petit]
bourgeois; **spießig** *(abwertend)* **1**.
Adj. [petit] bourgeois; **2**. *adv.* *(think,
behave, etc.)* in a [petit] bourgeois way

Spinat der; ~**[e]s**, ~**e** spinach

Spind der *od.* **das**; ~**[e]s**, ~**e** locker

Spindel die; ~, ~**n** spindle

Spinne die; ~, ~**n** spider; **spinnen 1**.
unr. tr. V. **a)** spin *(fig.)*; plot *(intrigue)*; think up *(idea)*; hatch *(plot)*; **2**.
unr. itr. V. **a)** spin; **b)** *(ugs.: verrückt
sein)* be crazy *or* *(sl.)* nuts; **Spin-
nen·netz das** spider's web; **Spin-
ner der**; ~**s**, ~ **a)** *(Beruf)* spinner; **b)**
(ugs. abwertend) nut-case *(sl.)*; idiot;
Spinnerei die; ~, ~**en** spinning mill;
Spinnerin die; ~, ~**nen** *s.* Spinner
Spinn-: ~**rad das** spinning-wheel;
~**webe die**; ~, ~**n** cobweb

Spion der; ~**s**, ~**e a)** spy; **b)** *(Guckloch)* spyhole; **Spionage** [ʃpio'na:ʒə]
die; ~: spying; espionage; **spionieren** *itr. V.* spy; **Spionin die**; ~,
~**nen** spy

Spirale die; ~, ~**n** spiral

Spiral·feder die coil spring

Spirituose die; ~, ~**n** spirit *usu. in pl.*

Spiritus der; ~, ~**se** spirit; ethyl alcohol

Spiritus·kocher der spirit stove

Spital das; ~**s**, **Spitäler** *(bes. österr.,
schweiz.)* hospital

spitz 1. *Adj.* **a)** pointed; sharp *(pencil,
needle, stone, etc.)*; fine *(pen nib)*; *(Geom.)* acute *(angle)*; **b)** *(schrill)* shrill

⟨cry etc.⟩; c) *(boshaft)* cutting ⟨remark etc.⟩; **2.** adv. **a)** ~ **zulaufen** taper to a point; ~ **zulaufend** pointed; **b)** *(boshaft)* cuttingly
Spitz der; ~es, ~e spitz
spitz-, Spitz-: ~**bart** der goatee; ~**bube** der *(scherzh.: Schlingel)* rascal; ~**bübisch 1.** Adj. mischievous; **2.** adv. mischievously
spitze indekl. Adj. *(ugs.)* s. **klasse;**
Spitze die; ~, ~n **a)** point; *(Pfeil~, Horn~ usw.)* tip; **b)** *(Turm~, Baum~, Mast~ usw.)* top; *(eines Berges)* summit; **c)** *(Zigarren~, Haar~, Zweig~)* end; *(Schuh~)* toe; *(Finger~, Nasen~)* tip; **d)** *(vorderes Ende)* front; **an der ~ liegen** *(Sport)* be in the lead or in front; **e)** *(führende Position)* top; **f)** *(einer Firma, Organisation usw.)* head; *(einer Hierarchie)* top; *(leitende Gruppe)* management; **g)** *(Höchstwert)* maximum; peak; **h)** **[absolute/einsame]** ~ **sein** *(ugs.)* be [absolutely] great *(coll.)*; **i)** *(fig.: Angriff)* dig **(gegen** at); **j)** *(Textilwesen)* lace
Spitzel der; ~s, ~: informer
spitzen tr. V. sharpen ⟨pencil⟩; purse ⟨lips, mouth⟩; prick up ⟨ears⟩
Spitzen-: ~**erzeugnis das** top-quality product; ~**klasse die** top class; ~**qualität die** top quality; ~**sportler** top sportsman
spitz-, Spitz-: ~**findig** Adj. hairsplitting; ~**hacke** die pick; ~**|kriegen** tr. V. *(ugs.)* tumble to *(coll.)*; ~**name** der nickname
Spleen [ʃpliːn] der; ~s, ~e od. ~s strange habit; eccentricity
Splitt der; ~|e|s, ~e [stone] chippings pl.; *(zum Streuen)* grit
Splitter der; ~s, ~: splinter; *(Granat~, Bomben~)* splinter; **splittern** itr. V. **a)** *(Splitter bilden)* splinter; **b)** *mit sein (in Splitter zerbrechen)* ⟨glass, windscreen, etc.⟩ shatter; **splitternackt** Adj. *(ugs.)* stark naked; starkers pred. *(Brit. sl.)*; **Splitter·partei** die splinter party
sponsern tr. V. sponsor; **Sponsor** der; ~s, ~en sponsor
spontan 1. Adj. spontaneous; **2.** adv. spontaneously
sporadisch 1. Adj. sporadic; **2.** adv. sporadically
Spore die; ~, ~n spore
Sporn der; ~|e|s, Sporen *(des Reiters)* spur; **einem Pferd die Sporen geben** spur a horse
Sport der; ~|e|s **a)** sport; *(als Unter-*

richtsfach) sport; PE; ~ **treiben** do sport; **b)** *(Hobby, Zeitvertreib)* hobby; pastime
Sport-: ~**fest** das sports festival; *(einer Schule)* sports day; ~**flugzeug das** sports plane; ~**geist** der; o. Pl. sportsmanship; ~**journalist** der sports journalist; ~**kleidung** die sportswear
Sportler der; ~s, ~: sportsman; **Sportlerin** die; ~, ~nen sportswoman; **sportlich 1.** Adj. **a)** sporting attrib.; **b)** *(fair)* sportsmanlike; sporting; **c)** *(fig.: flott, rasant)* sporty ⟨car, driving, etc.⟩; **d)** *(zu sportlicher Leistung fähig)* sporty, athletic ⟨person⟩; **e)** *(jugendlich wirkend)* sporty, smart but casual ⟨clothes⟩; smart but practical ⟨hair-style⟩; **2.** adv. **a)** as far as sport is concerned; **b)** *(fair)* sportingly; **c)** *(fig.: flott, rasant)* in a sporty manner
Sport-: ~**platz** der sports field; *(einer Schule)* playing field/fields pl.; ~**schuh** der sports shoe; ~**stadion das** [sports] stadium; ~**verein** der sports club; ~**wagen** der **a)** *(Auto)* sports car; **b)** *(Kinderwagen)* pushchair *(Brit.)*; stroller *(Amer.)*
Spott der; ~|e|s mockery; *(höhnischer)* ridicule; derision; **spott·billig** Adj., adv. *(ugs.)* dirt cheap; **spötteln** itr. V. mock [gently]; poke or make [gentle] fun; **spotten** itr. V. **a)** mock; poke or make fun; *(höhnischer)* ridicule; be derisive; **b)** **einer Sache** *(Gen.)* ~: be contemptuous of or scorn sth.; **Spötter** der; ~s, ~: mocker; **spöttisch 1.** Adj. mocking; *(höhnischer)* derisive; **2.** adv. mockingly; **Spott·preis** der *(ugs.)* ridiculously low price
sprach *1. u. 3. Pers. Sg. Prät. v.* **sprechen; Sprache** die; ~, ~n **a)** language; **in englischer ~:** in English; **b)** *(Sprechweise)* way of speaking; speech; *(Stil)* style; **c)** etw. **zur ~ bringen** bring sth. up; raise sth.; **heraus mit der ~!** come on, out with it!; **Sprachen·schule** die language school
Sprach-: ~**fehler** der speech impediment or defect; ~**führer** der phrasebook; ~**kenntnisse** Pl. knowledge sing. of a language/languages; ~**kurs** der language course
sprachlich 1. Adj. linguistic; **2.** adv. linguistically
sprach-, Sprach-: ~**los** Adj. *(über-*

rascht) speechless; ~**rohr** das *(Repräsentant)* spokesman; *(Propagandist)* mouthpiece; ~**unterricht** der language teaching
sprang *1. u. 3. Pers. Sg. Prät. v.* **springen**
Spray [ʃpreː] das *od.* der; ~s, ~s spray; **Spray·dose** die aerosol [can]; **sprayen** *tr., itr. V.* spray
Sprech-: ~**anlage** die intercom *(coll.);* ~**chor** der chorus
sprechen *1. unr. itr. V.* speak (über + *Akk.* about; von about, of); *(sich unterhalten, sich besprechen auch)* talk (über + *Akk.,* von about); *⟨parrot etc.⟩* talk; **deutsch/flüsternd** ~: speak German/in a whisper; **für/gegen etw.** ~: speak in favour of/against sth.; **mit jmdm.** ~: speak *or* talk with *or* to sb.; **mit wem spreche ich?** who is speaking please?; *2. unr. tr. V.* **a)** speak *⟨language, dialect⟩;* say *⟨word, sentence⟩;* „**Hier spricht man Deutsch**" 'German spoken'; **b)** *(rezitieren)* say, recite *⟨poem, text⟩;* say *⟨prayer⟩;* **c)** **jmdn.** ~: speak to sb.; **d)** *(aus~)* pronounce *⟨name, word, etc.⟩;* **Sprecher** der; ~s, ~ **a)** spokesman; **b)** *(Ansager)* announcer; *(Nachrichten~)* newscaster; news-reader; **c)** *(Kommentator, Erzähler)* narrator
sprech-, Sprech-: ~**funk·gerät** das radio-telephone; *(Walkie-talkie)* walkie-talkie; ~**stunde** die consultation hours *pl.; (eines Arztes)* surgery; ~**stunden·hilfe** die *(eines Arztes)* receptionist; *(eines Zahnarztes)* assistant; ~**zimmer** das consulting-room
spreizen *tr. V.* spread *⟨fingers, toes, etc.⟩;* **die Beine** ~: spread one's legs apart; open one's legs
Spreiz·fuß der *(Med.)* spread foot
sprengen *tr. V.* **a)** blow up; blast *⟨rock⟩;* **etw. in die Luft** ~: blow sth. up; **b)** *(gewaltsam öffnen, aufbrechen)* force [open] *⟨door⟩;* force *⟨lock⟩;* burst, break *⟨bonds, chains⟩; (fig.)* break up *⟨meeting, demonstration⟩;* **c)** *(be~)* water *⟨flower-bed, lawn⟩;* sprinkle *⟨street, washing⟩* with water; *(verspritzen)* sprinkle; *(mit dem Schlauch)* spray
Sprenkel der; ~s, ~: spot; dot; speckle; **sprenkeln** *tr. V.* sprinkle spots of *⟨colour⟩;* sprinkle *⟨water⟩*
Spreu die; ~: chaff
sprich *Imperativ Sg. v.* **sprechen;** **sprichst** *2. Pers. Sg. Präsens v.* **sprechen; spricht** *3. Pers. Sg. Präsens v.*

sprechen; Sprich·wort das; *Pl.* Sprichwörter proverb
sprießen *unr. itr. V.; mit sein ⟨leaf, bud⟩* shoot, sprout; *⟨seedlings⟩* come *or* spring up; *⟨beard⟩* sprout
Spring·brunnen der fountain; **springen** *1. unr. itr. V.* **a)** *mit sein (auch Sport)* jump; *(mit Schwung)* leap; spring; jump; *⟨frog, flea⟩* hop, jump; *(sich in Sprüngen fortbewegen)* bound; **b)** *mit sein (fig.) ⟨pointer, milometer, etc.⟩* jump **(auf** + *Akk.* to); *⟨traffic-lights⟩* change **(auf** + *Akk.* to); *⟨spark⟩* leap; *⟨ball⟩* bounce; **c)** *mit sein ⟨string, glass, porcelain, etc.⟩* break; *(Risse, Sprünge bekommen)* crack; *2. unr. tr. V.; auch mit sein (Sport)* perform *⟨somersault, twist dive, etc.⟩*
Springer der; ~s, ~ **a)** *(Sport)* jumper; **b)** *(Schachfigur)* knight
spring·lebendig *Adj.* extremely lively; full of beans *pred. (coll.)*
Spring·reiten das show-jumping no art.
sprinten *itr. (auch tr.) V.; mit sein* sprint; **Sprinter** der; ~s, ~, **Sprinterin** die; ~, ~**nen** *(Sport)* sprinter
Sprit der; ~[e]s, ~**e a)** *(ugs.: Treibstoff)* gas *(Amer. coll.);* juice *(sl.);* petrol *(Brit.);* **b)** *(ugs.: Schnaps)* shorts *pl.*
Spritze die; ~, ~**n a)** syringe; **b)** *(Injektion)* injection; **c)** *(Feuer~)* hose; *(Löschfahrzeug)* fire engine
spritzen *1. tr. V.* **a)** *(versprühen)* spray; *(ver~)* splash; *(in Form eines Strahls)* spray, squirt *⟨water, foam, etc.⟩;* pipe *⟨cream etc.⟩;* **b)** *(be~, besprühen)* water *⟨lawn, tennis-court⟩;* water, spray *⟨street, yard⟩;* spray *⟨plants, crops, etc.⟩; (mit Lack)* spray *⟨car etc.⟩;* **jmdn. naß** ~: splash sb.; *(mit Wasserpistole, Schlauch)* spray sb.; **c)** *(injizieren)* inject *⟨drug etc.⟩; (ugs.: einer Injektion unterziehen)* **jmdn./sich** ~: give sb. an injection/inject oneself; *2. itr. V.; mit Richtungsangabe mit sein ⟨hot fat⟩* spit; *⟨mud etc.⟩* spatter; *⟨blood, water⟩* spurt; **Spritzer** der; ~s, ~ *(kleiner Tropfen)* splash; *(von Farbe)* splash; spot; **spritzig** *1. Adj.* **a)** sparkling *⟨wine⟩;* tangy *⟨fragrance, perfume⟩;* **b)** lively *⟨show, music, article⟩;* sparkling *⟨performance⟩;* racy *⟨style⟩;* nippy *(coll.);* zippy *⟨car, engine⟩;* agile *⟨person⟩;* *2. adv.* sparklingly *⟨produced, performed, etc.⟩;* racily *⟨written⟩;* **Spritz·tour** die *(ugs.)* spin

spröd, spröde *Adj.* **a)** brittle ⟨*glass, plastic, etc.*⟩; dry ⟨*hair, lips, etc.*⟩; *(rissig)* chapped ⟨*lips, skin*⟩; *(rauh)* rough ⟨*skin*⟩; **b)** *(fig.: abweisend)* aloof ⟨*person, manner, nature*⟩

sproß *1. u. 3. Pers. Sg. Prät. v.* **sprießen; Sproß** der; **Sprosses, Sprosse** *(Bot.)* shoot

Sprosse die; ~, ~n **a)** *(auch fig.)* rung; **b)** *(eines Fensters)* glazing bar

Sprößling der; ~s, ~e *(ugs. scherzh.)* offspring; **seine** ~e his offspring *pl.*

Sprotte die; ~, ~n sprat

Spruch der; ~[e]s, **Sprüche** *(Wahl~)* motto; *(Sinn~)* maxim; *(Aus~)* saying; aphorism; *(Zitat)* quotation; **spruch·reif** *Adj.* **das ist noch nicht** ~: that's not definite, so people mustn't start talking about it yet

Sprudel der; ~s, ~ **a)** sparkling mineral water; **b)** *(österr.)* fizzy drink; **sprudeln** *itr. V.; mit sein* bubble; ⟨*lemonade, champagne, etc.*⟩ fizz, effervesce; **Sprudel·wasser das;** *Pl.* **-wässer** sparkling mineral water

Sprüh·dose die aerosol [can]; **sprühen 1.** *tr. V.* spray; **2.** *itr. V.; mit Richtungsangabe mit sein* ⟨*sparks, spray*⟩ fly; *(fig.)* ⟨*eyes*⟩ sparkle (**vor** + *Dat.* with); ⟨*intellect, wit*⟩ sparkle

Sprüh·regen der drizzle; fine rain

Sprung der; ~[e]s, **Sprünge a)** *(auch Sport)* jump; *(schwungvoll)* leap; *(Satz)* bound; *(fig.)* leap; **keine großen Sprünge machen können** *(fig. ugs.)* not be able to afford many luxuries; **auf dem** ~[e] **sein** *(fig. ugs.)* be in a rush; **b)** *(ugs.: kurze Entfernung)* stone's throw; **c)** *(Riß)* crack

Sprung·brett das *(auch fig.)* springboard; **sprunghaft 1.** *Adj.* **a)** erratic ⟨*person, character, manner*⟩; disjointed ⟨*conversation, thoughts*⟩; **b)** *(unvermittelt)* sudden; **c)** *(ruckartig)* rapid ⟨*change*⟩; sharp ⟨*increase*⟩; **2.** *adv.; s.* 1 b–c: disjointedly; suddenly; rapidly; sharply

Spucke die; ~: spit; **spucken 1.** *itr. V.* spit; **in die Hände** ~ *(fig.: an die Arbeit gehen)* go to work with a will; **2.** *tr. V.* spit; cough up ⟨*blood, phlegm*⟩

Spuk der; ~[e]s, ~e [ghostly *or* supernatural] manifestation; **spuken** *itr. V.; unpers.* **hier/in dem Haus spukt es** this place/the house is haunted

Spule die; ~, ~n spool; *(für Tonband, Film)* spool; reel

Spüle die; ~, ~n sink unit; *(Becken)* sink

spulen *tr., itr. V.* spool; *(am Tonbandgerät)* wind

spülen 1. *tr. V.* **a)** rinse; bathe ⟨*wound*⟩; **b)** *(landsch.: abwaschen)* wash up ⟨*dishes, glasses, etc.*⟩; **Geschirr** ~: wash up; **2.** *itr. V.* **a)** *(beim WC)* flush [the toilet]; **b)** *(den Mund ausspülen)* rinse out [one's mouth]; **c)** *(landsch.) s.* **abwaschen 2**

Spül-: ~**maschine** die dishwasher; ~**mittel das** washing-up liquid

Spur die; ~, ~**en a)** *(Abdruck im Boden)* track; *(Folge von Abdrücken)* tracks *pl.*; **eine heiße** ~ *(fig.)* a hot trail; **jmdm./einer Sache auf der** ~ **sein** be on to the track *or* trail of sb./sth.; **b)** *(Anzeichen)* trace; *(eines Verbrechens)* clue *(Gen.* to); **c)** *(sehr kleine Menge; auch fig.)* trace; **d)** *(Verkehrsw.: Fahr~)* lane; **die** ~ **wechseln** change lanes

spürbar 1. *Adj.* noticeable; distinct, perceptible ⟨*improvement*⟩; evident ⟨*relief, embarrassment*⟩; **2.** *adv.* noticeably; perceptibly; *(sichtlich)* clearly ⟨*relieved, on edge*⟩; **spüren** *tr. V.* feel; *(instinktiv)* sense

spur·los 1. *Adj.* total, complete ⟨*disappearance*⟩; **2.** *adv.* ⟨*disappear*⟩ completely *or* without trace

Spür·sinn der; *o. Pl. (feiner Instinkt)* intuition

Spurt der; ~[e]s, ~s *od.* ~e spurt; **spurten** *itr. V.* **a)** *mit Richtungsangabe mit sein* spurt; **b)** *mit sein (ugs.: schnell laufen)* sprint

sputen *refl. V. (veralt.)* make haste

St. *Abk.* **a) Sankt** St.; **b) Stück**

Staat der; ~[e]s, ~en state; **staatlich 1.** *Adj.* state *attrib.;* ⟨*power, unity, etc.*⟩ of the state; state-owned ⟨*factory etc.*⟩; **2.** *adv.* by the state; ~ **anerkannt/geprüft** state-approved/-certified

staats-, Staats-: ~**angehörige** der/die national; ~**angehörigkeit** die nationality; ~**anwalt** der public prosecutor; ~**bürger** der citizen; **er ist deutscher** ~**bürger** he is a German citizen *or* national; ~**bürgerlich** *Adj.* civil ⟨*rights*⟩; civic ⟨*duties, loyalty*⟩; ⟨*education, attitude*⟩ as a citizen; ~**bürgerschaft die** *s.* ~**angehörigkeit;** ~**grenze** die state frontier *or* border; ~**mann** der; *Pl.* -**män-ner** statesman; ~**oberhaupt das** head of state; ~**präsident** der [state] president

Stab der; ~[e]s, **Stäbe a)** rod; *(länger)*

pole; *(eines Käfigs, Gitters, Geländers)* bar; **b)** *(Milit.)* staff; **c)** *(Team)* team
stabil 1. *Adj.* sturdy ‹*chair, cupboard*›; robust, sound ‹*health*›; stable ‹*prices, government, economy, etc.*›; **2.** *adv.* ~ gebaut solidly built; **stabilisieren 1.** *tr. V.* stabilize; **2.** *refl. V.* **a)** stabilize; **b)** ‹*health, circulation, etc.*› become stronger

Stab·lampe die torch *(Brit.);* flashlight *(Amer.)*

Stabs·arzt der *(Milit.)* medical officer, MO *(with the rank of captain)*

stach *1. u. 3. Pers. Sg. Prät. v.* **stechen**

Stachel der; ~s, ~n **a)** spine; *(Dorn)* thorn; **b)** *(Gift~)* sting; **c)** *(spitzes Metallstück)* spike; *(an ~draht)* barb

Stachel-: ~**beere** die gooseberry; ~**draht** der barbed wire

stachelig *Adj.* prickly

Stadion das; ~s, **Stadien** stadium

Stadium das; ~s, **Stadien** stage

Stadt die; ~, **Städte a)** town; *(Groß~)* city; **die** ~ **Basel** the city of Basel; **in die** ~ **gehen** go into town; go downtown *(Amer.);* **b)** *(Verwaltung)* town council; *(in der Großstadt)* city council; city hall *no art. (Amer.)*

Stadt-: ~**bahn** die urban railway; ~**bummel** der *(ugs.)* **einen** ~**bummel machen** take a stroll through the town/city centre

Städter der; ~s, ~, **Städterin** die; ~, ~**nen a)** town-dweller; *(Großstädter, -städterin)* city-dweller; **b)** *(Stadtmensch)* townie *(coll.)*

Stadt-: ~**führer** der town/city guidebook; ~**gespräch** das: ~**gespräch sein** be the talk of the town

städtisch 1. *Adj.* **a)** *(kommunal)* municipal; **b)** *(urban)* urban ‹*life, way of life, etc.*›; **2.** *adv. (kommunal)* municipally

Stadt-: ~**mauer** die town/city wall; ~**mitte** die town centre; *(einer Großstadt)* city centre; downtown area *(Amer.);* ~**park** der municipal park; ~**plan** der [town/city] street plan *or* map; ~**rand** der outskirts *pl.* of the town/city; **am** ~: on the outskirts of the town/city; ~**rundfahrt** die sightseeing tour round a/the town/city; ~**teil** der district; part [of a/the town]; ~**tor** das town/city gate; ~**viertel** das district

Staffel die; ~, ~**n a)** *(Sport: Mannschaft)* relay team; **b)** *(Sport: ~lauf)* relay race; **c)** *(Luftwaffe: Einheit)* flight; **d)** *(Eskorte)* escort formation

Staffelei die; ~, ~**en** easel

stahl *1. u. 3. Pers. Sg. Prät. v.* **stehlen**

Stahl der; ~[e]s, **Stähle** *od.* ~**e** steel

Stahl-: ~**beton** der reinforced concrete; ~**blech** das sheet steel

stählern *Adj.; nicht präd.* steel

stak *1. u. 3. Pers. Sg. Prät. v.* **stecken**

Stall der; ~[e]s, **Ställe** *(Pferde~, Renn~)* stable; *(Kuh~)* cowshed; *(Hühner~)* [chicken-]coop; *(Schweine~)* [pig]sty; *(für Kaninchen, Kleintiere)* hutch; *(für Schafe)* pen; **Stallung** die; ~, ~**en** *(Pferdestall)* stable; *(Kuhstall)* cow-shed; *(Schweinestall)* [pig]sty

Stamm der; ~[e]s, **Stämme a)** *(Baum~)* trunk; **b)** *(Volks~)* tribe; **Stamm·baum** der family tree; *(eines Tieres)* pedigree

stammeln *tr., itr. V.* stammer

stammen *itr. V.* come **(aus, von** from); *(datieren)* date **(aus, von** from)

Stamm-: ~**gast** der *(im Lokal/Hotel)* regular customer/visitor; regular *(coll.);* ~**tisch** der **a)** *(Tisch)* regulars' table *(coll.);* **b)** *(~tischrunde)* group of regulars *(coll.);* **c)** *(Treffen)* gettogether with the regulars *(coll.)*

stampfen 1. *itr. V.* **a)** *(laut auftreten)* stamp; **b)** *mit sein (sich fortbewegen)* tramp; *(mit schweren Schritten)* trudge; **2.** *tr. V.* **a)** mit den Füßen den Rhythmus ~: tap the rhythm with one's feet; **b)** *(fest~)* compress; **c)** *(zerkleinern)* mash ‹*potatoes*›

stand *1. u. 3. Pers. Sg. Prät. v.* **stehen**

Stand der; ~[e]s, **Stände a)** *o. Pl. (das Stehen)* standing position; |bei jmdm. *od.* gegen jmdm.| einen schweren ~ haben *(fig.)* have a tough time [of it] [with sb.]; **b)** *(~ort)* position; **c)** *(Verkaufs~; Box für ein Pferd)* stall; *(Messe~, Informations~)* stand; *(Zeitungs~)* [newspaper] kiosk; **d)** *o. Pl. (erreichte Stufe; Zustand)* state; **etw. auf den neu[e]sten** ~ **bringen** bring sth. up to date; **e)** *(des Wassers, Flusses)* level; *(des Thermometers, Zählers, Barometers)* reading; *(der Kasse, Finanzen)* state; *(eines Himmelskörpers)* position; **f)** *o. Pl. (Familien~)* status; **g)** *(Gesellschaftsschicht)* class; *(Berufs~)* trade; *(Ärzte, Rechtsanwälte)* [professional] state

Standard der; ~s, ~s standard

Ständchen das; ~s, ~: serenade; **jmdm. ein** ~ **bringen** serenade sb.

Ständer der; ~s, ~: stand; *(Kleider~)* coat-stand; *(Wäsche~)* clothes-horse

standes-, Standes-: ~amt das registry office; ~amtlich 1. *Adj.; nicht präd.* registry office ⟨*wedding, document*⟩; 2. *adv.* ~amtlich heiraten get married in a registry office; ~beamte der registrar
stand-, Stand-: ~fest *Adj.* steady; stable; strong ⟨*stalk, stem*⟩; ~haft 1. *Adj.* steadfast; 2. *adv.* steadfastly; ~haftigkeit die; ~: steadfastness; ~|halten *unr. itr. V.* stand firm; einer Sache *(Dat.)* ~halten withstand sth.
ständig 1. *Adj.* constant ⟨*noise, worry, pressure, etc.*⟩; permanent ⟨*residence, correspondent, staff, member, etc.*⟩; standing ⟨*committee*⟩; regular ⟨*income*⟩; 2. *adv.* constantly
Stand-: ~licht das *(Kfz-W.)* sidelights *pl.;* ~ort der; *Pl.* ~orte a) position; *(eines Betriebes o.ä.)* location; site; b) *(Milit.: Garnison)* garrison; base; ~punkt der *(fig.)* point of view; viewpoint; auf dem ~punkt stehen, daß ...: take the view that ...; ~spur die *(Verkehrsw.)* hard shoulder; ~uhr die grandfather clock
Stange die; ~, ~n pole; *(aus Metall)* bar; *(dünner)* rod; *(Kleider~)* rail; *(Vogel~)* perch; ein Anzug von der ~ *(ugs.)* an off-the-peg-suit
Stangen-: ~brot das French bread; ~spargel der asparagus spears *pl.*
stank *1. u. 3. Pers. Sg. Prät. v.* stinken
Stapel der; ~s, ~: pile; ein ~ Holz a pile or stack of wood; **stapeln** 1. *tr. V.* pile up; stack; 2. *refl. V.* pile up
stapfen *itr. V.; mit sein* tramp
¹Star der; ~|e|s, ~e *od. (schweiz.)* ~en *(Vogel)* starling
²Star der; ~s, ~s *(berühmte Persönlichkeit)* star
³Star der; ~|e|s *(Med.)* grauer ~: cataract; grüner ~: glaucoma
starb *1. u. 3. Pers. Sg. Prät. v.* sterben
stark stärker, stärkst... 1. *Adj.* a) strong; potent ⟨*drink, medicine, etc.*⟩; powerful ⟨*engine, lens, voice, etc.*⟩; *(ausgezeichnet)* excellent; s. *auch* Stück c; b) *(dick)* thick; stout ⟨*rope, string*⟩; *(verhüll.: korpulent)* well-built *(euphem.);* c) *(zahlenmäßig groß, umfangreich)* sizeable, large; big ⟨*demand*⟩; eine 100 Mann ~e Truppe a 100-strong unit; d) *(heftig, intensiv)* heavy; severe ⟨*frost, pain*⟩; strong ⟨*impression, current, resistance, dislike*⟩; grave ⟨*doubt, reservations*⟩; great ⟨*exaggeration, interest*⟩; loud ⟨*applause*⟩; e) *(Jugendspr.: großartig)* great *(coll.);*

fantastic *(coll.);* 2. *adv.* a) *(sehr, überaus, intensiv)* *(mit Adj.)* very; heavily ⟨*indebted, stressed*⟩; greatly ⟨*increased, reduced, enlarged*⟩; strongly ⟨*emphasized, characterized*⟩; badly ⟨*damaged, worn, affected*⟩; *(mit Verb)*; heavily; *(exaggerate, impress)* greatly; ⟨*enlarge, reduce, increase*⟩ considerably; ⟨*support, oppose, suspect*⟩ strongly; ⟨*remind*⟩ very much; ~ erkältet sein have a heavy or bad cold; b) *(Jugendspr.: großartig)* fantastically *(coll.);* **Stark·bier** das strong beer; **Stärke** die; ~, ~n a) *o. Pl.* strength; *(eines Motors)* power; *(einer Glühbirne)* wattage; b) *(Dicke)* thickness; *(Technik)* gauge; c) *o. Pl. (zahlenmäßige Größe)* strength; d) *(besondere Fähigkeit, Vorteil)* strength; jmds. ~/nicht jmds. ~ sein be sb.'s forte/not be sb.'s strong point; e) *(Intensität)* strength; *(von Sturm, Schmerzen, Abneigung)* intensity; *(von Frost)* severity; *(von Lärm, Verkehr)* volume; f) *(organischer Stoff)* starch; **stärken** 1. *tr. V.* a) strengthen; boost ⟨*power, prestige*⟩; ⟨*drink, food, etc.*⟩ fortify ⟨*person*⟩; b) *(steif machen)* starch ⟨*washing etc.*⟩; 2. *refl. V.* refresh oneself; **Stärkung** die; ~, ~en a) *o. Pl.* strengthening; b) *(Erfrischung)* refreshment
starr 1. *Adj.* a) rigid; *(steif)* stiff (vor + *Dat.* with); fixed ⟨*expression, smile, stare*⟩; b) *(nicht abwandelbar)* inflexible, rigid ⟨*law, rule, principle*⟩; c) *(unnachgiebig)* inflexible ⟨*person, attitude, etc.*⟩; 2. *adv.* rigidly; *(steif)* stiffly
starren *itr. V.* a) stare (in + *Akk.* into, auf, an, gegen + *Akk.* at); jmdm. ins Gesicht ~: stare sb. in the face; b) vor/von Schmutz ~: be filthy
Starr·sinn der; *o. Pl.* pig-headedness
starr·sinnig *Adj.* pig-headed
Start der; ~|e|s, ~s start; *(eines Flugzeugs)* take-off; *(einer Rakete)* launch; **Start·bahn** die [take-off] runway; **start·bereit** *Adj.* ready to start *postpos.;* ⟨*aircraft*⟩ ready for take-off; **starten** 1. *itr. V.; mit sein* a) start; ⟨*aircraft*⟩ take off; ⟨*rocket*⟩ blast off, be launched; b) *(den Motor anlassen)* start the engine; 2. *tr. V.* start; launch ⟨*rocket, satellite, attack*⟩; start [up] ⟨*engine, machine, car*⟩
Station die; ~, ~en a) station; b) *(Haltestelle)* stop; c) *(Zwischen~, Aufenthalt)* stopover; ~ machen stop over or

off; **d)** *(Kranken~)* ward; **stationär**
1. *Adj. (Med.)* ⟨*treatment*⟩ in hospital,
as an in-patient; **2.** *adv. (Med.)* in hospital; jmdn. ~ **behandeln** treat sb. as
an in-patient; **stationieren** *tr. V.*
station ⟨*troops*⟩; deploy ⟨*weapons,*
bombers, etc.⟩
Stations-: ~**arzt** der ward doctor;
~**schwester** die ward sister; ~**taste**
die *(Rundf.)* preset [tuning] button;
preset
Statistik die; ~: statistics *sing., no*
art.
statt 1. *Präp. mit Gen.* instead of; ~
dessen instead [of this]; **2.** *Konj.: s.* **an-**
statt
statt-: ~|**finden** *unr. itr. V.* take
place; ⟨*process, development*⟩ occur;
~**haft** *Adj.* permissible
stattlich 1. a) well-built; imposing
⟨*figure, stature, building, etc.*⟩; fine
⟨*farm, estate*⟩; impressive ⟨*trousseau,*
collection⟩; **b)** *(beträchtlich)* considerable; **2.** *adv.* impressively
Statue die; ~, ~n statue
Statur die; ~, ~en build
Status der; ~, ~ ['ʃtaːtuːs] status
Statut das; ~|e|s, ~en statute
Stau der; ~|e|s, ~s *od.* ~e **a)** build-up;
b) *(von Fahrzeugen)* tailback *(Brit.)*;
backup *(Amer.)*
Staub der; ~|e|s dust; ~ **wischen** dust;
~ **saugen** vacuum *or (Brit. coll.)*
hoover; **sich aus dem** ~|e| **machen** *(fig.*
ugs.) make oneself scarce *(coll.)*;
stauben *itr. V.* cause dust; **staubig**
Adj. dusty
staub-, Staub-: ~**saugen** *itr., tr. V.*
vacuum, *(Brit. coll.)* hoover; ~**sau-**
ger der vacuum cleaner; Hoover
(Brit. P); ~**tuch** das; *Pl.* ~**tücher**
duster
Staude die; ~, ~n *(Bot.)* herbaceous
perennial
stauen 1. *tr. V.* dam [up] ⟨*stream,*
river⟩; staunch ⟨*blood*⟩; **2.** *refl. V.* ⟨*wa-*
ter, blood, etc.⟩ accumulate, build up;
⟨*people*⟩ form a crowd; ⟨*traffic*⟩ form a
tailback/tailbacks *(Brit.)* or *(Amer.)*
backup/backups
staunen *itr. V.* be amazed *or* as-
tonished (**über** + *Akk.* at); *(beein-*
druckt sein) marvel (**über** + *Akk.* at);
~**d** with *or* in amazement; **Staunen**
das; ~s amazement (**über** + *Akk.* at);
(Bewunderung) wonderment
Stauung die; ~, ~en **a)** *(eines Bachs,*
Flusses) damming; *(des Blutes, Was-*
sers) stemming the flow; *(das Sich-*

stauen) build-up; **b)** *(Verkehrsstau)*
tailback *(Brit.)*; backup *(Amer.)*; jam
Std. *Abk.* **Stunde** hr.
stechen 1. *unr. itr. V.* **a)** prick; ⟨*wasp,*
bee⟩ sting; ⟨*mosquito*⟩ bite; **b)** *(hin-*
ein~) **mit etw. in etw.** *(Akk.)* ~: stick
or jab sth. into sth.; **2.** *unr. tr. V. (mit*
dem Messer, Schwert) stab; *(mit der*
Nadel, mit einem Dorn usw.) prick;
⟨*bee, wasp*⟩ sting; ⟨*mosquito*⟩ bite; **sich**
in den Finger ~: prick one's finger
Stech-: ~**mücke** die mosquito; gnat;
~**uhr** die time clock
Steck-: ~**brief** der description [of
a/the wanted person]; *(Plakat)*
'wanted' poster; ~**dose** die socket;
power point
stecken 1. *tr. V.* **a)** put; **b)** *(mit Na-*
deln) pin ⟨*hem, lining, etc.*⟩; pin [on]
⟨*badge*⟩; pin up ⟨*hair*⟩; **2.** *itr. V.* be; **wo**
steckt meine Brille? *(ugs.)* where have
my glasses got to *or* gone?; **hinter etw.**
(Dat.) ~ *(fig. ugs.)* be behind sth.
stecken-, Stecken-: ~|**bleiben**
unr. itr. V.; mit sein get stuck; ~|**las-**
sen *unr. tr. V.* leave; ~**pferd das a)**
(Spielzeug) hobby-horse; **b)** *(Liebha-*
berei) hobby
Stecker der; ~s, ~: plug; **Steck·na-**
del die pin
Steg der; ~|e|s, ~e *(Brücke)* [narrow]
bridge; *(Laufbrett)* gangplank;
(Boots~) landing-stage
Steg·reif der: aus dem ~: impromptu
stehen *unr. itr. V.; südd., österr.,*
schweiz. mit sein **a)** stand; **b)** *(sich be-*
finden) be; ⟨*upright object, building*⟩
stand; **c)** *(einen bestimmten Stand ha-*
ben) **auf etw.** ~ ⟨*needle, hand*⟩
point to sth.; **das Barometer steht tief/**
auf Regen the barometer is reading
low/indicating rain; **das Spiel/es steht**
1:1 *(Sport)* the score is one all; **die Sa-**
che steht gut/schlecht things are going
well/badly; **d)** *(einen bestimmten*
Kurs, Wert haben) ⟨*currency*⟩ stand
(bei at); **wie steht das Pfund?** what is
the rate for the pound?; **e)** *(nicht in*
Bewegung sein) be stationary; ⟨*machi-*
ne etc.⟩ be at a standstill; **meine Uhr**
steht my watch has stopped; **f)** *(ge-*
schrieben, gedruckt sein) be; **in der**
Zeitung steht, daß ...: it says in the
paper that ...; **g)** *(Sprachw.: gebraucht*
werden) ⟨*subjunctive etc.*⟩ occur; be
found; **h)** jmdm. |**gut**| ~ ⟨*dress etc.*⟩ suit
sb. [well]
stehen: ~|**bleiben** *unr. itr. V.; mit*
sein **a)** stop; ⟨*traffic*⟩ come to a stand-

still; **b)** *(stehengelassen werden)* stay; be left; *(zurückgelassen werden)* be left behind; *(der Zerstörung entgehen)* ⟨*building*⟩ be left standing; ~**|lassen** *unr. tr. V.* **a)** leave; **b)** *(vergessen)* leave [behind]

Steh·lampe die standard lamp *(Brit.);* floor lamp *(Amer.)*

stehlen *unr. tr., itr. V.* steal; *s. auch* **gestohlen 2**

Steh·platz der *(im Theater usw.)* standing place; *(im Bus)* space to stand

Steiermark die; ~: Styria *no art.*

steif 1. *Adj.* stiff; *(förmlich)* stiff; formal; **2.** *adv.* stiffly

steigen 1. *unr. itr. V.; mit sein* **a)** climb; ⟨*mist, smoke, sun*⟩ rise; ⟨*balloon*⟩ climb, rise; **auf die Leiter** ~: get on to the ladder; **in den/aus dem Bus/ Zug** ~: board *or* get on/get off *or* out of the bus/train; **b)** *(ansteigen, zunehmen)* rise; ⟨*price, cost, salary, output*⟩ increase, rise; ⟨*debts, tension*⟩ increase, mount; ⟨*chances*⟩ improve; **2.** *unr. tr. V.; mit sein* climb ⟨*stairs, steps*⟩; **Steiger der;** ~s, ~ *(Bergbau)* overman

steigern 1. *tr. V.* **a)** increase ⟨*speed, value, sales, consumption, etc.*⟩ **(auf +** *Akk.* to); step up ⟨*demands, production, etc.*⟩; raise ⟨*standards, requirements*⟩; *(verstärken)* intensify ⟨*fear, tension*⟩; heighten ⟨*effect*⟩; **b)** *(Sprachw.)* compare ⟨*adjective*⟩; **2.** *refl. V.* ⟨*confusion, speed, profit, etc.*⟩ increase; ⟨*pain, excitement, tension, etc.*⟩ become more intense; ⟨*costs*⟩ escalate; ⟨*effect*⟩ be heightened; **Steigerung die;** ~, ~**en a)** increase *(Gen.* in); *(Verstärkung)* intensification; *(einer Wirkung)* heightening; *(Verbesserung)* improvement *(Gen.* in); *(bes. Sport: Leistungs~)* improvement [in performance]; **b)** *(Sprachw.)* comparison

Steigung die; ~, ~**en** gradient

steil 1. *Adj.* steep; meteoric ⟨*career*⟩; rapid ⟨*rise*⟩; **2.** *adv.* steeply; **Steil·hang der** steep escarpment

Stein der; ~**[e]s,** ~**e** stone; *(Fels)* rock; *(Bau~)* [stone]block; **mir fällt ein** ~ **vom Herzen** that's a weight off my mind; **Stein·bock der a)** ibex; **b)** *(Astrol.)* Capricorn; the Goat; **steinern** *Adj.* stone; **Stein·gut das** earthenware; **stein·hart** *Adj.* rockhard; **steinig** *Adj.* stony

Stein-: ~**kohle die** [hard] coal;

~**metz der;** ~**en,** ~**en** stonemason; ~**obst das** stone-fruit; ~**pilz der** cep; ~**schlag der** rock fall; „**Achtung ~schlag**" 'beware falling rocks'; ~**zeit die** Stone Age; *(fig.)* stone age

Steiß·bein das *(Anat.)* coccyx

Stelle die; ~, ~**n a)** place; **an jmds.** ~ **treten** take sb.'s place; **ich an deiner** ~ **...:** ... if I were you; **an achter** ~ **liegen** be in eighth place; **die erste** ~ **hinter** *od.* **nach dem Komma** *(Math.)* the first decimal place; **an** ~ **(+** *Gen.*) instead of; **auf der** ~: immediately; **b)** *(begrenzter Bereich)* patch; *(am Körper)* spot; **c)** *(Passage)* passage; *(Punkt im Ablauf einer Rede usw.)* point; **d)** *(Arbeits~)* job; post; **eine freie** ~: a vacancy; **e)** *(Dienst~)* office; *(Behörde)* authority; **stellen 1.** *tr. V.* **a)** put; *(mit Sorgfalt)* place; *(aufrecht hin~)* stand; **b)** *(ein~)* set ⟨*points, clock, scales*⟩; **den Wecker auf 6 Uhr** ~: set the alarm for 6 o'clock; **die Heizung höher/niedriger** ~: turn the heating up/down; **c)** *(bereit~)* provide; **d) jmdn. besser** ~: ⟨*firm*⟩ improve sb.'s pay; **gut/schlecht/besser gestellt** comfortably/badly/better off; **e)** *verblaßt* put ⟨*question*⟩; set ⟨*task, topic, condition*⟩; make ⟨*application, demand, request*⟩; **jmdm. eine Frage** ~: ask sb. a question; **2.** *refl. V.* **a)** place oneself; **sich auf die Zehenspitzen** ~: stand on tiptoe; **b) sich schlafend/taub/tot** *usw.* ~: feign sleep/ deafness/death *etc.;* pretend to be asleep/deaf/dead *etc.*

stellen-, Stellen-: ~**angebot das** offer of a job; *(Inserat)* job advertisement; „**~angebote**" 'situations vacant'; ~**gesuch das** 'situation wanted' advertisement; ~**weise** *Adv.* in places

Stellung die; ~, ~**en** position; **zu etw.** ~ **nehmen** express one's opinion on sth.; **Stellungnahme die;** ~, ~**n** opinion; *(kurze Äußerung)* statement; **Stell·vertreter der** deputy

Stelze die; ~, ~**n** stilt; **stelzen** *itr. V.; mit sein* strut; stalk

stemmen 1. *tr. V.* **a)** *(hoch~)* lift [above one's head]; **b)** *(drücken)* brace ⟨*feet, knees*⟩ **(gegen** against); **2.** *refl. V.* **sich gegen etw.** ~: brace oneself against sth.

Stempel der; ~**s,** ~: stamp; *(Post~)* postmark; **stempeln** *tr. V.* stamp ⟨*passport, form*⟩; postmark ⟨*letter*⟩; cancel ⟨*postage stamp*⟩

Stengel der; ~s, ~: stem; stalk
steno-, Steno-: ~gramm das shorthand text; ~graph der; ~en, ~en
stenographer; ~graphie die; ~, ~n
stenography *no art.*; shorthand *no
art.*; ~graphieren *itr. V.* do shorthand; ~typistin die shorthand typist
Stepp·decke die quilt
Steppe die; ~, ~n steppe
steppen *tr. (auch itr.) V.* backstitch
sterben *unr. itr. V.; mit sein* die; **im
Sterben liegen** lie dying; **ster-
bens·krank** *Adj.* mortally ill;
sterblich *Adj.* mortal
stereo *Adv.* in stereo; **Stereo** das; ~s
stereo; **Stereo·anlage** die stereo
[system]
steril *Adj.* sterile
Sterling ['stɛːlɪŋ]: **Pfund** ~: pound/
pounds sterling
Stern der; ~[e]s, ~e star; **Sternchen**
das; ~s, ~ *(Druckw.)* asterisk;
Stern·schnuppe die; ~, ~n shooting star
Stethoskop [ʃteto'skoːp] das; ~s, ~e
(Med.) stethoscope
¹**Steuer** das; ~s, ~: [steering-]wheel;
(von Schiffen) helm; ²**Steuer** die; ~,
~n tax
steuer-, Steuer-: ~berater der tax
consultant *or* adviser; ~bord das *od.
österr.* der; *o. Pl. (Seew., Flugw.)* starboard; ~erklärung die tax return;
~frei *Adj.* tax-free; ~mann der; *Pl.*
~leute *od.* ~männer *(Rudersport)* cox
steuern 1. *tr. V. (fahren)* steer; *(fliegen)* pilot, fly *(aircraft)*; fly *(course)*;
2. *itr. V.* **a)** be at the wheel; *(auf dem
Schiff)* be at the helm; **b)** *mit sein
(Kurs nehmen, ugs.: sich hinbewegen,
auch fig.)* head; **Steuerung** die; ~,
~en **a)** *(System)* controls *pl.*; **b)** *o. Pl.
s.* steuern 1: steering; piloting; flying
Steward ['stju:ɐt] der; ~s, ~s steward;
Stewardeß ['stju:ɐdɛs] die; ~, Ste-
wardessen stewardess
stich *Imper. Sg. v.* stechen
Stich der; ~[e]s, ~e **a)** *(mit einer Waffe)*
stab; **b)** *(Dornen~, Nadel~)* prick;
(von Wespe, Biene usw.) sting; *(Mük-
ken~ usw.)* bite; **c)** *(~wunde)* stab
wound; **d)** *(beim Nähen)* stitch; **e)**
(Schmerz) stabbing *or* shooting pain;
f) *(Kartenspiel)* trick; **g)** jmdn./etw. im
~ lassen leave sb. in the lurch/aban-
don sth.; **sticheln** *itr. V.* make snide
remarks *(coll.)* **(gegen** about)
stich-, Stich-: ~flamme die tongue
of flame; ~haltig *Adj.* sound *(argu-*

ment, reason); valid *(assertion, reply)*;
conclusive *(evidence)*; ~probe die
[random] sample; *(bei Kontrollen)*
spot check
stichst 2. *Pers. Sg. Präsens v.* stechen;
sticht 3. *Pers. Sg. Präsens v.* stechen
Stich-: ~tag der set date; deadline;
~wunde die stab wound
sticken 1. *itr. V.* do embroidery; 2. *tr.
V.* embroider; **Stickerei** die; ~, ~en
embroidery *no pl.; (gestickte Arbeit)*
piece of embroidery; **Stick·garn**
das embroidery thread
stickig *Adj.* stuffy; stale *(air)*;
Stick·stoff der nitrogen
Stief- step *(brother, child, mother, etc.)*
Stiefel der; ~s, ~ boot
Stief·mütterchen das *(Bot.)* pansy;
stief·mütterlich 1. *Adj.* poor,
shabby *(treatment)*; 2. *adv.* ~ behandeln treat *(person)* poorly *or* shabbily;
neglect *(pet, flowers, doll, problem)*
stieg 1. *u.* 3. *Pers. Sg. Prät. v.* steigen
Stieglitz der; ~es, ~e goldfinch
stiehl *Imp. Sg. v.* stehlen; **stiehlst**
2. *Pers. Sg. Präsens v.* stehlen; **stiehlt**
3. *Pers. Sg. Präsens v.* stehlen
Stiel der; ~[e]s, ~e *(Griff)* handle; *(Be-
sen~)* [broom-]stick; *(für Süßigkeiten)*
stick; *(bei Gläsern)* stem; *(bei Blumen)*
stem; *(an Obst usw.)* stalk
Stier der; ~[e]s, ~e bull
stieren *itr. V.* stare [vacantly] **(auf +
Akk.** at)
Stier·kampf der bullfight
stieß 1. *u.* 3. *Pers. Sg. Prät. v.* stoßen
Stift der; ~[e]s, ~e **a)** *(aus Metall)* pin;
(aus Holz) peg; **b)** *(Blei~)* pencil;
(Mal~) crayon; *(Schreib~)* pen
stiften *tr. V.* **a)** found, establish
(monastery, hospital, etc.); endow
(prize, scholarship); *(als Spende)* donate, give **(für** to); **b)** *(herbeiführen)*
cause, create *(unrest, confusion, strife,
etc.)*; bring about *(peace, order, etc.)*;
arrange *(marriage)*; **Stifter** der; ~s,
~: founder; *(Spender)* donor
Stift·zahn der *(Zahnmed.)* post
crown
Stil der; ~[e]s, ~e style; **stilistisch**
1. *Adj.* stylistic; 2. *adv.* stylistically
still 1. *Adj.* quiet; *(ohne Geräusche)* silent; still; *(reglos)* still; *(wortlos)* silent; *(heimlich)* secret; **der Stille Ozean** the Pacific [Ocean]; 2. *adv.* quietly;
(geräuschlos) silently; *(wortlos)* in
silence; **Stille** die; ~: quiet; *(Ge-
räuschlosigkeit)* silence; stillness;
stillegen *tr. V.* close *or* shut down;

close ⟨*railway line*⟩; **stillen 1.** *tr. V.* **a)**
ein Kind ~ : breast-feed a baby; **b)** *(be-*
friedigen) satisfy; quench ⟨*thirst*⟩; **c)**
(eindämmen) stop ⟨*bleeding, tears,*
pain⟩; **2.** *itr. V.* breast-feed
still-, Still-: ~|**halten** *unr. itr. V.*
keep *or* stay still; ~|**legen** *s.* **stille-**
gen; ~**schweigen das** silence;
~**schweigen bewahren** maintain
silence; keep silent; ~**schweigend**
1. *Adj.* silent; *(ohne Abmachung)* tacit
⟨*assumption, agreement*⟩; **2.** *adv.* in
silence; *(ohne Abmachung)* tacitly;
~|**sitzen** *unr. itr. V.* sit still; ~**stand**
der; *o. Pl.* standstill; ~|**stehen** *unr.*
itr. V. **a)** *(factory, machine)* stand idle;
⟨*traffic*⟩ be at a standstill; ⟨*heart etc.*⟩
stop; **b)** *(Milit.)* stand to attention
Stimm·bruch der: er ist im ~ : his
voice is breaking; **Stimme die;** ~, ~**n**
a) voice; **b)** *(bei Wahlen)* vote
stimmen 1. *itr. V.* **a)** be right *or* correct; **stimmt es, daß ...?** is it true
that ...?; **b)** *(seine Stimme geben)* vote;
mit Ja ~ : vote yes *or* in favour; **2.** *tr.*
V. **a)** *(in eine Stimmung versetzen)*
make; **b)** *(Musik)* tune ⟨*instrument*⟩
Stimm-: ~**enthaltung die** abstention; ~**recht das** right to vote
Stimmung die; ~, ~**en a)** mood; **b)**
(Atmosphäre) atmosphere
Stink·bombe die stink-bomb; **stin-**
ken *unr. itr. V.* stink (**nach** of); **stin-**
kig *Adj.* *(salopp abwertend)* stinking;
smelly
stirb *Imp. Sg. v.* **sterben; stirbst**
2. *Pers. Sg. Präsens v.* **sterben; stirbt**
3. *Pers. Sg. Präsens v.* **sterben**
Stirn die; ~, ~**en** forehead; brow
stöbern *itr. V.* *(ugs.)* rummage
stochern *itr. V.* poke
¹**Stock der;** ~|**e|s, Stöcke a)** stick; *(Zei-*
ge~*)* pointer; stick; *(Takt*~*)* baton;
(Ski~*)* pole; stick; **b)** *(Pflanze) (Ro-*
sen~*)* [rose-]bush; *(Reb*~*)* vine;
²**Stock der;** ~|**e|s,** ~ *(Etage)* floor;
storey; **in welchem** ~**?** on which
floor?; **stock·dunkel** *Adj.* *(ugs.)*
pitch-dark; **stocken** *itr. V.* **a)** ⟨*traf-*
fic⟩ be held up; ⟨*conversation, produc-*
tion⟩ stop; ⟨*business*⟩ slacken; ⟨*jour-*
ney⟩ be interrupted; **b)** *(innehalten)*
falter; **stock·finster** *Adj.* *(ugs.)*
pitch-dark
-**stöckig** -storey *attr.;* -storeyed
Stockung die; ~, ~**en** hold-up *(Gen.*
in); **Stockwerk das** floor; storey
Stoff der; ~|**e|s,** ~**e a)** material; fabric;
b) *(Materie)* substance; **c)** *o. Pl. (Phi-*

los.) matter; **d)** *(Thema)* subject[-mat-
ter]; *(Gesprächsthema)* topic; **Stoff-**
wechsel der; *o. Pl.* metabolism
stöhnen *itr. V.* moan; *(vor Schmerz)*
groan
Stola die; ~, **Stolen** shawl; *(Pelz*~*)*
stole
Stollen der; ~**s,** ~ **a)** *(Kuchen)* Stollen; **b)** *(Bergbau)* gallery; **c)** *(bei Sport-*
schuhen) stud
stolpern *itr. V.; mit sein* stumble; trip
stolz 1. *Adj.* proud (**auf** + *Akk.* of);
eine ~**e Summe** *(ugs.)* a tidy sum; **2.**
adv. proudly; **Stolz der;** ~**es** pride
(**auf** + *Akk.* in); **stolzieren** *itr. V.;*
mit sein strut
stop *Interj.* stop; *(Verkehrsw.)* halt
stopfen *tr. V.* **a)** darn; **b)** *(hineintun)*
stuff; **c)** *(füllen)* stuff ⟨*cushion, quilt,*
etc.⟩; fill ⟨*pipe*⟩; plug, stop [up] ⟨*hole,*
leak⟩
Stopf-: ~**garn das** darning-cotton;
~**nadel die** darning-needle
Stopp der; ~**s,** ~**s** stop; *(Einstellung)*
freeze *(Gen.* on)
Stoppel die; ~, ~**n** stubble *no pl.;*
stoppelig *Adj.* stubbly
stoppen *tr., itr. V.* stop
Stopp-: ~**licht das;** *Pl.* ~**er** stop-
light; ~**schild das** stop sign; ~**uhr**
die stop-watch
Stöpsel der; ~**s,** ~ plug
Stör der; ~**s,** ~**e** sturgeon
Storch der; ~|**e|s, Störche** stork
stören 1. *tr. V.* **a)** disturb; disrupt
⟨*court proceedings, lecture, church ser-*
vice, etc.⟩; interfere with ⟨*transmitter,*
reception⟩; **b)** *(mißfallen)* bother; **2.**
itr. V. **a)** disturb; **b)** *(Unruhe stiften)*
make *or* cause trouble; **3.** *refl. V.* **sich**
an jmdm./etw. ~ : take exception to
sb./sth.; **Störenfried der;** ~|**e|s,** ~**e**
trouble-maker
störrisch 1. *Adj.* stubborn; **2.** *adv.*
stubbornly
Störung die; ~, ~**en a)** disturbance;
(einer Gerichtsverhandlung, Vorlesung,
eines Gottesdienstes usw.) disruption;
bitte entschuldigen Sie die ~, **aber ...:**
I'm sorry to bother you, but ...; **b) eine**
technische ~ : a technical fault
Stoß der; ~**es, Stöße a)** *(mit der Faust)*
punch; *(mit dem Fuß)* kick; *(mit dem*
Kopf, den Hörnern) butt; *(mit dem Ell-*
bogen) dig; **b)** *(mit einer Waffe) (Stich)*
thrust; *(Schlag)* blow; **c)** *(beim*
Schwimmen, Rudern) stroke; **d)** *(Sta-*
pel) pile; stack; **stoßen 1.** *unr. tr. V.*
a) *auch itr. (mit der Faust)* punch; *(mit*

dem Fuß) kick; *(mit dem Kopf, den Hörnern)* butt; *(mit dem Ellbogen)* dig; b) *(hineintreiben)* plunge, thrust ⟨*dagger, knife*⟩; push ⟨*stick, pole*⟩; c) *(schleudern)* push; **die Kugel ~:** put the shot; **2.** *unr. itr. V.* **a)** *mit sein (auftreffen)* bump *(gegen* into); **mit dem Kopf gegen etw. ~:** bump one's head on sth.; b) *mit sein (fig.)* **auf etw.** *(Akk.) ~ (etw. entdecken)* come upon sth.; **auf Ablehnung ~** *(abgelehnt werden)* meet with disapproval; **c)** *(grenzen)* **an etw.** *(Akk.) ~* ⟨*room, property, etc.*⟩ be [right] next to sth.; **3.** *unr. refl. V.* bump *or* knock oneself; **sich an etw.** *(Dat.) ~ (fig.)* object to sth.

Stoß-: **~seufzer** der heartfelt groan; **~stange** die bumper

stößt *3. Pers. Sg. Präsens v.* stoßen; **stoß·weise** *Adv.* **a)** spasmodically; b) *(in Stapeln)* by the pile; in piles

Stotterer der; **~s, ~:** stutterer; **stottern 1.** *itr. V.* stutter; **2.** *tr. V.* stutter [out]

Str. *Abk.* Straße St./Rd.

stracks *Adv.* **a)** *(direkt)* straight; **b)** *(sofort)* straight away

straf·bar *Adj.* punishable; **Strafe die; ~, ~n** punishment; *(Rechtsspr.)* penalty; *(Freiheits~)* sentence; *(Geld~)* fine; **strafen** *tr. V.* punish

straff 1. *Adj.* **a)** tight, taut ⟨*rope, lines, etc.*⟩; firm ⟨*breasts, skin*⟩; **b)** *(energisch)* strict ⟨*organization, planning, etc.*⟩; strict ⟨*discipline, leadership, etc.*⟩; **2.** *adv.* **a)** |zu| ~ sitzen ⟨*clothes*⟩ be [too] tight; b) *(energisch)* tightly, strictly

straf·fällig *Adj.* ~ werden commit a criminal offence

straffen *tr. V.* **a)** tighten; firm ⟨*skin*⟩; **b)** *(fig.)* tighten up ⟨*text, procedure, organization, etc.*⟩

straf-, Straf-: **~frei** *Adj.* **~frei ausgehen** go unpunished; **~gefangene** der/die prisoner; **~gesetz·buch** das penal code

sträflich 1. *Adj.* criminal; **2.** *adv.* criminally; **Sträfling** der; **~s, ~e** prisoner

straf-, Straf-: **~los** *Adj.* unpunished; **~tat** die criminal offence; **~täter** der offender; **~zettel** der *(ugs.)* [parking-, speeding-, *etc.*] ticket

Strahl der; **~|e|s, ~en** *(auch Phys., Math., fig.)* ray; *(von Scheinwerfern, Taschenlampen)* beam; *(von Flüssigkeit)* jet; **strahlen** *itr. V.* **a)** shine; **bei ~dem Wetter/Sonnenschein** in glori-

ous sunny weather/in glorious sunshine; **~d weiß** sparkling white; **b)** *(glänzen)* sparkle; **c)** *(lächeln)* beam *(vor + Dat.* with); **Strahler der; ~s, ~ a)** radiator; **b)** *(Heiz~)* radiant heater; **Strahlung die; ~, ~en** radiation

Strähne die; **~, ~n** strand; **eine graue ~:** a grey streak; **strähnig 1.** *Adj.* straggly ⟨*hair*⟩; **2.** *adv.* in strands

stramm 1. *Adj.* **a)** *(straff)* tight, taut ⟨*rope, line, etc.*⟩; tight ⟨*clothes*⟩; **b)** *(kräftig)* strapping ⟨*girl, boy*⟩; sturdy ⟨*legs, body*⟩; **c)** *(gerade)* upright, erect ⟨*posture, etc.*⟩; **2.** *adv.* **a)** *(straff)* tightly; **b)** *(kräftig)* sturdily ⟨*built*⟩

strampeln *itr. V.* ⟨*baby*⟩ kick [his/her feet]

Strand der; **~|e|s, Strände** beach; **am ~:** on the beach; **Strand·bad** das bathing beach *(on river, lake)*; **stranden** *itr. V.; mit sein* ⟨*ship*⟩ run aground; **Strand·korb** der basket chair

Strang der; **~|e|s, Stränge** rope

Strapaze die; **~, ~n** strain *no pl.*; **strapazieren** *tr. V.* be a strain on ⟨*person, nerves*⟩; **strapazier·fähig** *Adj.* hard-wearing ⟨*clothes, shoes*⟩; durable ⟨*material*⟩

Straße die; **~, ~n** *(in Ortschaften)* street; road; *(außerhalb)* road

Straßen-: **~bahn** die tram *(Brit.)*; streetcar *(Amer.)*; **~ecke** die street corner; **~feger** der *(bes. nordd.)* road-sweeper; **~graben** der ditch [at the side of the road]; **~karte** die road-map; **~sperre** die road-block

sträuben 1. *tr. V.* ruffle [up] ⟨*feathers*⟩; bristle ⟨*fur, hair*⟩; **2.** *refl. V.* ⟨*hair, fur*⟩ bristle, stand on end; ⟨*feathers*⟩ become ruffled; **b)** *(sich widersetzen)* resist

Strauch der; **~|e|s, Sträucher** shrub; **straucheln** *itr. V.; mit sein (geh.)* stumble

¹Strauß der; **~es, Sträuße** bunch of flowers; bouquet [of flowers]

²Strauß der; **~es, ~e** *(Vogel)* ostrich; **Sträußchen** das; **~s, ~:** posy

streben *itr. V.* **a)** *mit sein* make one's way briskly; **b)** *(trachten)* strive *(nach* for); **Streber** der; **~s; ~** *(abwertend)* pushy person *(coll.)*; *(in der Schule)* swot *(Brit. sl.)*; grind *(Amer. sl.)*; **strebsam** *Adj.* ambitious and industrious

Strecke die; **~, ~n** distance; *(Abschnitt, Route)* route; *(Eisenbahn~)*

line; **strecken** 1. *tr. V. (gerade machen)* stretch ⟨*arms, legs*⟩; *(dehnen)* stretch [out] ⟨*arms, legs, etc.*⟩; **den Kopf aus dem Fenster** ~: stick one's head out of the window *(coll.);* **2.** *refl. V.* stretch out; **strecken·weise** *Adv.* in places; *(fig.: zeitweise)* at times

Streich der; ~|e|s, ~e trick; prank; jmdm. einen ~ spielen play a trick on sb.; **streicheln** *tr. V.* stroke; **streichen** 1. *unr. tr. V.* **a)** stroke; b) *(an~)* paint; „frisch gestrichen" 'wet paint'; c) *(auftragen)* spread ⟨*butter, jam, ointment, etc.*⟩; *(be~)* ein Brötchen mit Butter/mit Honig ~: butter a roll/spread honey on a roll; d) *(aus~, tilgen)* delete; cancel ⟨*train, flight*⟩; **2.** *unr. itr. V.* **a)** stroke; jmdm. über den Kopf ~: stroke sb.'s head; b) *(an~)* paint

Streich-: ~holz das match; ~**instrument** das string[ed] instrument; ~**käse** der cheese spread; ~**wurst** die [soft] sausage for spreading; ≈ meat spread

Streife die; ~, ~n **a)** *(Personen)* patrol; **b)** *(Streifengang)* patrol; **streifen** 1. *tr. V.* **a)** *(leicht berühren)* touch; ⟨*shot*⟩ graze; **b)** *(kurz behandeln)* touch [up]on ⟨*problem, subject, etc.*⟩; c) den Ring vom Finger ~: slip the ring off one's finger; die Ärmel nach oben ~: pull/push up one's sleeves; **2.** *itr. V. mit sein* roam; **Streifen** der; ~s, ~ **a)** stripe; **b)** *(Stück, Abschnitt)* strip; **Streifen·wagen** der patrol car; **streifig** *Adj.* streaky

Streik der; ~|e|s, ~s strike; **Streik·brecher** der strike-breaker; blackleg *(derog.);* **streiken** *itr. V.* **a)** strike; be on strike; *(in den Streik treten)* come out *or* go on strike; strike; **b)** *(ugs.: nicht mitmachen)* go on strike; **c)** *(ugs.: nicht funktionieren)* pack up *(coll.);* **Streikende** der/die; *adj. Dekl.* striker; **Streik·posten** der picket

Streit der; ~|e|s, ~e *(Zank)* quarrel; *(Auseinandersetzung)* dispute; argument; **streiten** *unr. itr., refl. V.* quarrel; argue; *(sich zanken)* quarrel; **Streiterei** die; ~, ~en arguing *no pl., no indef. art.; (Gezänk)* quarrelling *no pl.;* **Streitigkeit** die; ~, ~en *meist Pl.* **a)** quarrel; argument; **b)** *(Streitfall)* dispute

streng 1. *Adj.* **a)** strict; severe ⟨*punish-*

ment⟩; stringent, strict ⟨*rule, regulation, etc.*⟩; stringent ⟨*measure*⟩; rigorous ⟨*examination, check, test, etc.*⟩; stern ⟨*reprimand, look*⟩; absolute ⟨*discretion*⟩; complete ⟨*rest*⟩; **b)** *(schmucklos, herb)* austere, severe ⟨*cut, collar, style, etc.*⟩; severe ⟨*face, features, hairstyle, etc.*⟩; **c)** *(durchdringend)* pungent, sharp ⟨*taste, smell*⟩; **d)** *(rauh)* severe ⟨*winter*⟩; sharp, severe ⟨*frost*⟩; **2.** *adv.* ⟨*mark, judge, etc.*⟩ strictly, severely; ⟨*punish*⟩ severely; ⟨*look, reprimand*⟩ sternly; ⟨*smell*⟩ strongly; **Strenge** die; ~ **a)** *s.* streng a: strictness; severity; stringency; rigour; sternness; **b)** *(von [Gesichts]zügen)* severity; **c)** *(von Geruch, Geschmack)* pungency; sharpness; **d)** *s.* streng d: severity; sharpness; **strengstens** *Adv.* [most] strictly

Streß der; Stresses stress

Streu die; ~, ~en straw; **streuen** *tr. V.* **a)** spread ⟨*manure, sand, grit*⟩; sprinkle ⟨*salt, herbs, etc.*⟩; strew, scatter ⟨*flowers*⟩; **b)** *auch itr.* die Straßen |mit Sand/Salz| ~: grit/salt the roads

streunen *itr. V.; meist mit sein* wander *or* roam about *or* around; ~de Katzen/Hunde stray cats/dogs

Streusel·kuchen der streusel cake

strich 1. u. 3. Pers. Sg. Prät. v. streichen

Strich der; ~|e|s, ~e *(Linie)* line; *(Gedanken~)* dash; *(Schräg~)* diagonal; *(Binde~, Trennungs~)* hyphen; auf den ~ gehen *(salopp)* walk the streets; **stricheln** *tr. V.* **a)** sketch in [with short lines]; **b)** *(schraffieren)* hatch

Strich-: ~**junge** der *(salopp)* [young] male prostitute; ~**mädchen** das *(salopp)* street-walker; hooker *(Amer. sl.)*; ~**punkt** der semicolon

Strick der; ~|e|s, ~e cord; *(Seil)* rope; **stricken** *tr., itr. V.* knit

Strick-: ~**jacke** die cardigan; ~**nadel** die knitting-needle; ~**zeug** das knitting

striegeln *tr. V.* groom ⟨*horse*⟩

strikt 1. *Adj.* strict; **2.** *adv.* strictly

Strippe die; ~, ~n *(ugs.)* string; an der ~ hängen *(fig.)* be on the phone *(coll.);* *(dauernd)* hog the phone *(coll.)*

Stripperin die; ~, ~nen *(ugs.)* stripper

stritt 1. u. 3. Pers. Sg. Prät. v. streiten; **strittig** *Adj.* contentious ⟨*point, problem*⟩; disputed ⟨*territory*⟩; ⟨*question*⟩ in dispute, at issue

Stroh das; ~|e|s straw

Stroh-: ~**blume** die a) *(Immortelle)* immortelle; b) *(Korbblütler)* strawflower; ~**halm** der straw; ~**witwe** die *(ugs. scherzh.)* grass widow; ~**witwer** der *(ugs. scherzh.)* grass widower

Strolch der; ~|e|s, ~e *(fam. scherzh.: Junge)* rascal

Strom der; ~|e|s, Ströme river; *(fig.)* stream; *(Strömung; Elektrizität)* current; *(~versorgung)* electricity; **unter** ~ **stehen** be live

strom-: ~**abwärts** *Adv.* downstream; ~**auf[wärts]** *Adv.* upstream

strömen *itr. V.; mit sein* stream; **Strömung** die; ~, ~en current; *(Met.)* airstream; *(fig.)* trend

Strophe die; ~, ~n verse; *(einer Ode)* strophe

strotzen *itr. V.* von *od.* vor etw. *(Dat.)* ~: be full of sth.; **von** *od.* **vor Gesundheit** ~: be bursting with health

strubbelig *Adj.* tousled

Strudel der; ~s, ~ a) whirlpool; b) *(bes. südd., österr.: Gebäck)* strudel

Strumpf der; ~|e|s, Strümpfe stocking; *(Socke, Knie~)* sock

Strumpf-: ~**band das** garter; *(Straps)* suspender *(Brit.);* garter *(Amer.);* ~**hose die** tights *pl. (Brit.);* pantyhose *(esp. Amer.)*

Strunk der; ~|e|s, Strünke stem; stalk; *(Baum~)* stump

struppig *Adj.* shaggy; tangled, tousled *(hair)*

Stube die; ~, ~n a) *(veralt.: Wohnraum)* [living-]room; parlour *(dated);* b) *Milit.)* [barrack-]room; **Stubenfliege** die [common] house-fly

Stück das; ~|e|s, ~e a) piece; *(kleines)* bit; *(Teil, Abschnitt)* part; **ein** ~ **Kuchen** a piece *or* slice of cake; **ein** ~ **Zucker/Seife** a lump of sugar/ a piece *or* bar of soap; **im** *od.* **am** ~: unsliced *(sausage, cheese, etc.);* b) *(Einzel~)* item; *(Exemplar)* specimen; **ich nehme 5** ~: I'll take five [of them]; **30 Pfennig das** ~: thirty pfennigs each; ~ **für** ~: piece by piece; *(eins nach dem andern)* one by one; **das ist [ja] ein starkes** ~ *(ugs.)* that's a bit much; **ein faules/freches** ~ *(salopp)* a lazy/cheeky thing *or* devil; c) *(Bühnen~)* play; *(Musik~)* piece; **Stückchen das;** ~s, ~: [little] piece; bit; **stückeln** *tr. V.* put together *(sleeve, curtain)* with patches **Student** der; ~en, ~en, **Studentin** die; ~, ~nen a) student; b) *(österr.: Schüler)* [secondary-school] pupil; **Studie** ['ʃtuːdiə] **die;** ~, ~n study

Studien-: ~**aufenthalt** der study visit (**in** + *Dat.* to); ~**freund** der university/college friend; ~**reise die** study trip

studieren *tr., itr. V.* study; **Studierende** der/die; adj. Dekl. student; **Studio das;** ~s, ~s studio; **Studium das;** ~s, **Studien** study; *(Studiengang)* course of study

Stufe die; ~, ~n a) step; *(einer Treppe)* stair; „**Vorsicht,** ~!" 'mind the step'; b) *(Raketen~, Geol., fig.: Stadium)* stage; *(Niveau)* level; *(Steigerungs~, Grad)* degree; *(Rang)* grade

Stuhl der; ~|e|s, Stühle chair

Stuhl-: ~**gang** der; *o. Pl.* bowel movement[s]; *(Kot)* stool; ~**lehne die** *(Rückenlehne)* chair-back; *(Armlehne)* chair-arm

stülpen *tr. V.* etw. auf *od.* über etw. *(Akk.)* ~: pull/put sth. on to *or* over sth.

stumm *Adj.* dumb *(person); (schweigsam)* silent; *(wortlos)* wordless; mute *(glance, gesture);* **Stumme der/die;** *adj. Dekl.* mute; **die** ~**n** the dumb

Stummel der; ~s, ~: stump; *(Bleistift~)* stub; *(Zigaretten-/Zigarren~)* [cigarette-/cigar-]butt

Stümper der; ~s, ~: botcher; bungler; **stümperhaft 1.** *Adj.* incompetent; botched *(job); (laienhaft)* amateurish *(attempt, drawing);* **2.** *adv.* incompetently; *(laienhaft)* amateurishly; **stümpern** *itr. V.* work incompetently; *(pfuschen)* bungle

stumpf *Adj.* a) blunt *(pin, needle, knife, etc.);* b) *(glanzlos, matt)* dull *(paint, hair, metal, colour, etc.);* **Stumpf der;** ~|e|s, Stümpfe stump

Stumpf-sinn der; *o. Pl.* a) apathy; b) *(Monotonie)* monotony; tedium; **stumpf-sinnig 1.** *Adj.* a) apathetic; vacant *(look);* b) *(monoton)* tedious; souldestroying *(job, work);* **2.** *adv.* a) apathetically; *(stare)* vacantly; b) *(monoton)* tediously

Stunde die; ~, ~n hour; *(Unterrichts~)* lesson; **eine** ~ **Aufenthalt/ Pause** an hour's stop/break; a stop/ break of an hour

stünde *1. u. 3. Pers. Sg. Konjunktiv II v. stehen*

stunden *tr. V.* jmdm. einen Betrag usw. ~: allow sb. to defer payment of a sum *etc.*

stunden-, Stunden-: ~**kilometer** der kilometre per hour; k.p.h.; ~**lang 1.** *Adj.* lasting hours *postpos.;* **2.** *adv.*

for hours; ~**lohn der** hourly wage; ~**plan der** timetable; ~**zeiger der** hour-hand

-**stündig** *adj.* -hour; -**stündlich** *adj.* -hourly; **zwei~/halb~**: two-hourly/ half-hourly; *adv.* every two hours/ half an hour; **stündlich** *Adj., adv.* hourly

Stups der; ~**es,** ~**e** *(ugs.)* push; shove; *(leicht)* nudge; **stupsen** *tr. V. (ugs.)* push; shove; *(leicht)* nudge; **Stups·nase die** snub nose

stur *(ugs.)* **1.** *Adj.* **a)** obstinate; dogged ⟨*insistence*⟩; *(phlegmatisch)* dour; **b)** *(unbeirrbar)* dogged; persistent; **c)** *(stumpfsinnig)* tedious; **2.** *adv.* **a)** obstinately; **b)** *(unbeirrbar)* doggedly; **c)** *(stumpfsinnig)* tediously; ⟨*learn, copy*⟩ mechanically

stürbe *1. u. 3. Pers. Sg. Konjunktiv II v.* sterben

Sturheit die; ~ *(ugs.)* **a)** obstinacy; *(phlegmatisches Wesen)* dourness; **b)** *(Stumpfsinnigkeit)* deadly monotony

Sturm der; ~**[e]s, Stürme a)** storm; *(heftiger Wind)* gale; **b)** *(Milit.)* assault **(auf** + *Akk.* on); ~ **klingeln** ring the [door]bell like mad; **stürmen 1.** *itr. V.* **a)** *unpers.* **es stürmt [heftig]** it's blowing a gale; **b)** *mit sein (rennen)* rush; *(verärgert)* storm; **2.** *tr. V. (Milit.)* storm ⟨*town, position, etc.*⟩; *(fig.)* besiege ⟨*booking-office, shop, etc.*⟩; **Stürmer der:** ~**s,** ~ *(Sport)* striker; forward; **stürmisch 1.** *Adj.* **a)** stormy; *(fig.)* tempestuous, turbulent; **b)** *(ungestüm)* tumultuous ⟨*applause, welcome, reception*⟩; wild ⟨*enthusiasm*⟩; passionate ⟨*lover, embrace, temperament*⟩; vehement ⟨*protest*⟩; **2.** *adv.* ⟨*protest*⟩ vehemently; ⟨*embrace*⟩ impetuously, passionately; ⟨*demand*⟩ clamorously; ⟨*applaud*⟩ wildly

Sturz der; -es, Stürze a) fall; *(Unfall)* accident; **b)** *(fig.: von Preis, Temperatur usw.)* [sharp] fall, drop *(Gen.* in); **c)** *(Verlust des Amtes, der Macht)* fall; *(Absetzung)* overthrow; *(Amtsenthebung)* removal from office; **stürzen 1.** *itr. V.; mit sein* **a)** fall; *(fig.)* ⟨*temperature, exchange rate, etc.*⟩ drop [sharply]; ⟨*prices*⟩ tumble; ⟨*government*⟩ fall, collapse; **b)** *(laufen)* rush; dash; **c)** *(fließen)* stream; pour; **2.** *refl. V.* **sich auf jmdn./etw.** ~ *(auch fig.)* pounce on sb./sth.; **sich in etw.** *(Akk.)* ~: throw oneself into sth.; **3.** *tr. V.* **a)** throw; *(mit Wucht)* hurl; **b)** *(umdrehen)* upturn ⟨*mould*⟩; turn out ⟨*pud-*

ding, cake, etc.⟩; **c)** *(des Amtes entheben)* oust ⟨*person*⟩ [from office]; *(gewaltsam)* overthrow ⟨*leader, government*⟩; **Sturz·helm der** crash-helmet

Stute die; ~, ~**n** mare

Stütze die; ~, ~**n** *(auch fig.)* support

¹**stutzen** *itr. V.* stop short

²**stutzen** *tr. V.* trim; dock ⟨*tail*⟩; clip ⟨*ear, hedge, wing*⟩; prune ⟨*tree, bush*⟩

stützen 1. *tr. V.* support; *(mit Pfosten o. ä.)* prop up; *(aufstützen)* rest ⟨*head, hands, arms, etc.*⟩; **2.** *refl. V.* **sich auf jmdn./etw.** ~: lean *or* support oneself on sb./sth.

stutzig *Adj.* ~ **werden** begin to wonder; **jmdn.** ~ **machen** make sb. wonder

s.u. *Abk.* **siehe unten** see below

Subjekt das; ~**[e]s,** ~**e a)** subject; **b)** *(abwertend: Mensch)* creature; **subjektiv 1.** *Adj.* subjective; **2.** *adv.* subjectively; **Subjektivität die;** ~: subjectivity

Substantiv das; ~**s,** ~**e** *(Sprachw.)* noun; **Substanz die;** ~, ~**en a)** *(auch fig.)* substance; **b)** *(Grundbestand)* **die** ~: the reserves *pl.*

sub·tropisch *Adj.* subtropical

Suche die; ~, ~**n** search **(nach** for); **auf der** ~ **[nach jmdm./etw.]** sein be looking/*(intensiver)* searching [for sb./ sth.]; **suchen 1.** *tr. V.* **a)** look for; *(intensiver)* search for; **,,Leerzimmer gesucht"** 'unfurnished room wanted'; **b)** *(bedacht sein auf, sich wünschen)* seek ⟨*protection, advice, company, warmth, etc.*⟩; look for ⟨*adventure*⟩; **2.** *itr. V.* search; **nach jmdm./etw.** ~: look/ search for sb./sth.

Sucht die; ~, **Süchte** *od.* ~**en a)** addiction **(nach** to); **[bei jmdm.] zur** ~ **werden** *(auch fig.)* become addictive [in sb.'s case]; **b)** *Pl.* **Süchte** *(übermäßiges Verlangen)* craving **(nach** for); **süchtig** *Adj.* **a)** addicted; **b)** *(fig.)* **nach etw.** ~ **sein** be obsessed with sth.

Süd *o. Art.; o. Pl. (bes. Seemannsspr., Met.) s.* **Süden**

Süd-: ~**afrika (das)** South Africa; ~**amerika (das)** South America

Sudan (das); ~**s** *od.* **der;** ~**s** Sudan

Süden der; ~**s** south; **der** ~: the South; **Süd·frucht die** tropical [or sub-tropical] fruit; **Südländer der;** ~**s,** ~: Southern European; **südländisch** *Adj.* Southern [European]; Latin ⟨*temperament*⟩; ~ **aussehen** have Latin looks; **südlich 1.** *Adj.* **a)** southern; **b)** *(nach, von Süden)* southerly; **c)** *(aus dem Süden)* Southern; **2.** *adv.*

southwards; **3.** *Präp. mit Gen.* [to the] south of

süd-, Süd-: ~**pol** der South Pole; ~**see** die; ~: die ~: the South Seas *pl.;* ~**see·insel** die South Sea island; ~**tirol (das)** South Tirol ~**wärts** *Adv.* southwards; ~**wind** der south *or* southerly wind

Sues·kanal ['zuːɛs-] der; ~s Suez Canal

Sühne die; ~, ~**n** *(geh.)* atonement; expiation; **sühnen** *tr., itr. V.* [für] etw. ~: atone for *or* pay the penalty for sth.

Sultanine die; ~, ~**n** sultana

Sülze die; ~, ~**n a)** diced meat/fish in aspic; *(vom Schweinskopf)* brawn; **b)** *(Aspik)* aspic

Summe die; ~, ~**n** sum

summen 1. *itr. V.* hum; *(lauter, heller)* buzz; **2.** *tr. V.* hum ⟨tune, song, etc.⟩

summieren *refl. V.* add up **(auf +** *Akk.* to)

Sumpf der; ~[e]s, **Sümpfe** marsh; *(bes. in den Tropen)* swamp; **sumpfig** *Adj.* marshy

Sund der; ~[e]s, ~**e** *(Geogr.)* sound

Sünde die; ~, ~**n** sin; *(fig.)* misdeed; transgression; **Sünden·bock** der *(ugs.)* scapegoat; **Sünder** der; ~s, ~, **Sünderin** die; ~, ~**nen** sinner; **sün·digen** *itr. V.* sin

Super das; ~s, ~: four star *(Brit.);* premium *(Amer.);* **super-** ultra-⟨long, high, fast, modern, masculine, etc.⟩; **Super-** super-⟨hero, figure, car, group, etc.⟩; terrific *(coll.),* tremendous *(coll.)* ⟨success, offer, chance, idea, etc.⟩; **Superlativ** ['zuːpɐlatiːf] der; ~s, ~**e** *(Sprachw.)* superlative; **Super·markt** der supermarket

Suppe die; ~; ~**n** soup; **Suppen·löffel** der soup-spoon

Surf·brett ['səːf-] **das** surf-board; **surfen** ['səːfn̩] *itr. V.* surf; **Surfer** ['səːfɐ] der; ~s, ~: surfer

surren *itr. V.* **a)** *(summen)* hum; ⟨camera, fan⟩ whirr; **b)** *mit sein (schwirren)* whirr

suspekt 1. *Adj.* suspicious; jmdm. ~ sein arouse sb.'s suspicions; **2.** *adv.* suspiciously

süß 1. *Adj.* sweet; **2.** *adv.* sweetly; **sü·ßen** *tr. V.* sweeten; **Süßigkeit** die; ~, ~**en** sweet *(Brit.);* candy *(Amer.);* ~**en** sweets *(Brit.);* candy *sing. (Amer.);* *(als Ware)* confectionery *sing.;* **süßlich 1.** *Adj.* **a)** [slightly] sweet; on the sweet side *pred.;* **b)** *(sen-*

timental) sickly mawkish; **2.** *adv.* ⟨write, paint⟩ mawkishly

süß-, Süß-: ~**most** der unfermented fruit juice; ~**sauer 1.** *Adj.* sweet-and-sour; *(fig.)* wry ⟨smile, face⟩; **2.** *adv.* **a)** etw. ~**sauer zubereiten** give sth. a sweet-and-sour flavour; **b)** *(fig.)* ⟨smile⟩ wryly; ~**speise** die sweet; dessert; ~**stoff** der sweetener; ~**wasser das;** *Pl.* ~**wasser** fresh water

svw. *Abk.* soviel wie

Symbol das; ~s, ~**e** symbol; **symbo·lisch 1.** *Adj.* symbolic; **2.** *adv.* symbolically

Sympathie [zʏmpaˈtiː] die; ~, ~**n** sympathy (für with); **sympathisch 1.** *Adj.* congenial, likeable ⟨person, manner⟩; appealing ⟨voice, appearance, material⟩; **2.** *adv.* in an appealing way; *(angenehm)* agreeably

Symphonie *usw. s.* Sinfonie *usw.*

Synagoge die; ~, ~**n** synagogue

Syrer der; ~s, ~, **Syrerin** die; ~, ~**nen** Syrian; **Syrien** ['zyːriən] **(das)**; ~s Syria; **syrisch** *Adj.* Syrian

System das; ~, ~**e** system; **syste·matisch 1.** *Adj.* systematic; **2.** *adv.* systematically

Szene ['stseːnə] die; ~, ~**n** *(auch fig.)* scene

T

t, T [teː] das; ~, ~: t, T

t *Abk.* Tonne t

Tab. *Abk.* Tabelle

Tabak ['ta(ː)bak] der; ~s, ~e tobacco; **Tabaks·pfeife** die [tobacco-]pipe

Tabelle die; ~, ~**n** table

Tabernakel das *od.* der; ~s, ~: tabernacle

Tablett das; ~[e]s, ~s *od.* ~e tray; **Ta·blette** die; ~, ~**n** tablet

tabu *Adj.* taboo; **Tabu** das; ~s, ~s taboo

Tacho der; ~s, ~s *(ugs.)* speedo *(coll.);* **Tacho·meter** der *od.* das speedometer

Tadel der; ~s, ~ **a)** censure; **b)** *(im*

Klassenbuch) black mark; **tadel·los 1.** *Adj.* impeccable; immaculate ⟨*hair, clothing, suit, etc.*⟩; perfect ⟨*condition, teeth, pronunciation, German, etc.*⟩; **2.** *adv.* ⟨*dress*⟩ impeccably; ⟨*fit, speak, etc.*⟩ perfectly; ⟨*live, behave, etc.*⟩ irreproachably; **tadeln** *tr. V.* jmdn. |für *od.* wegen etw.| ~: rebuke sb. [for sth.]

Tafel die; ~, ~n a) *(Schiefer~)* slate; *(Wand~)* blackboard; **b)** *(plattenförmiges Stück)* slab; **eine ~ Schokolade** a bar of chocolate; **c)** *(Gedenk~)* plaque; **d)** *(geh.: festlicher Tisch)* table; **Täfelchen das;** ~s, ~: *s.* Tafel b: [small] slab; [small] bar; **tafeln** *itr. V. (geh.)* feast; **täfeln** *tr. V.* panel

Tafel-: ~**spitz** der *(österr.)* boiled fillet of beef; ~**wasser** das; *Pl.* ~wässer [bottled] mineral water; ~**wein** der table wine

Taft der; ~|e|s, ~e taffeta

Tag der; ~|e|s, ~e day; **am** ~|e| during the day[time]; **guten** ~! hello; *(bei Vorstellung)* how do you do?; **an diesem** ~: on this day; **dreimal am** ~: three times a day; **am folgenden** ~: the next day; **eines** ~es one day; some day; **tag·aus** *Adv.* ~, **tagein** day in, day out; day after day; **Tage·buch das** diary; **tag·ein** *Adv. s.* tagaus; **tage·lang 1.** *Adj.* lasting for days *postpos.;* **nach** ~em Regen after days of rain; **2.** *adv.* for days [on end]; **tagen** *itr. V.* meet; **das Gericht/Parlament tagt** the court/parliament is in session

Tages-: ~**karte** die a) *(Gastron.)* menu of the day; **b)** *(Fahr-, Eintrittskarte)* day ticket; ~**kasse** die a) boxoffice *(open during the day);* **b)** *(~einnahme)* day's takings *pl.;* ~**licht** das; *o. Pl.* daylight; ~**zeit** die time of day; ~**zeitung die** daily newspaper

-**tägig a)** *(... Tage alt)* **ein sechstägiges Küken** a six-day-old chick; **b)** *(... Tage dauernd)* **nach dreitägiger Vorbereitung** after three days' preparation; **täglich 1.** *Adj.* daily; **2.** *adv.* every day; **zweimal** ~: twice a day; ~ **drei Tabletten einnehmen** take three tablets daily; **tags** *Adv.* **a)** by day; in the daytime; **b)** ~ **zuvor/davor** the day before; ~ **darauf** the next *or* following day; the day after; **tags·über** *Adv.* during the day; **tag·täglich 1.** *Adj.* day-to-day; daily; **2.** *adv.* every single day; **Tagung** die; ~, ~en conference

Taifun der; ~s, ~e typhoon

Taille ['taljə] die; ~, ~n waist

Taiwan (das); ~s Taiwan

Takt der; ~|e|s, ~e a) *(Musik)* time; *(Einheit)* bar; measure *(Amer.);* **aus dem** ~ **kommen** lose the beat; **b)** *o. Pl. (rhythmischer Bewegungsablauf)* rhythm; **c)** *o. Pl. (Feingefühl)* tact

Taktik die; ~, ~en: |eine| ~: tactics *pl.;* **taktisch 1.** *Adj.* tactical; **2.** *adv.* tactically

takt-: ~**los 1.** *Adj.* tactless; **2.** *adv.* tactlessly; ~**voll 1.** *Adj.* tactful; **2.** *adv.* tactfully

Tal das; ~|e|s, **Täler** valley

Talent das; ~|e|s, ~e talent (**zu, für** for); *(Mensch)* talented person

Talg der; ~|e|s, ~e suet; *(zur Herstellung von Seife, Kerzen usw.)* tallow

Talisman der; ~s, ~e talisman

Tampon der; ~s, ~s tampon

Tamtam das; ~s *(ugs. abwertend)* |großes| ~: [a big] fuss

Tang der; ~|e|s, ~e seaweed

Tangente die; ~, ~n *(Math.)* tangent

Tank der; ~s, ~s tank; **tanken** *tr., itr. V.* fill up; **Öl** ~: fill up with oil

Tank-: ~**säule** die petrol-pump *(Brit.);* gasoline pump *(Amer.);* ~**stelle** die petrol station *(Brit.);* gas station *(Amer.);* ~**wart** der; ~s, ~e petrol-pump attendant *(Brit.)*

Tanne die; ~, ~n fir[-tree]

Tannen-: ~**baum** der *(ugs.)* fir-tree; *(Weihnachtsbaum)* Christmas tree; ~**grün** das; *o. Pl.* fir sprigs *pl.;* ~**zweig** der fir branch

Tansania [tan'zaːnia] **(das);** ~s Tanzania

Tante die; ~, ~n a) aunt; **b)** *(Kinderspr.: Frau)* lady; **c)** *(ugs.: Frau)* woman

Tanz der; ~es, **Tänze** dance

Tanz-: ~**abend** der evening dance; ~**bar** die night-spot *(coll.)* with dancing; ~**café** das coffee-house with dancing

tanzen *itr., tr. V.* dance; **Tänzer** der; ~s, ~, **Tänzerin** die; ~, ~nen dancer; *(Ballett~)* ballet-dancer

Tanz-: ~**fläche** die dance-floor; ~**lokal** das café/restaurant with dancing; ~**orchester** das dance band; ~**stunde** die a) *(~kurs)* dancing-class; **b)** *(einzelne Stunde)* dancing lesson

Tapete die; ~, ~n wallpaper; **tapezieren** *tr. V.* [wall]paper

tapfer 1. *Adj.* brave; **2.** *adv.* bravely; **Tapferkeit** die; ~: courage; bravery

tappen *itr. V.* **a)** *mit sein)* patter; **b)** *(tastend greifen)* grope (**nach** for); **Taps**

der; ~es, ~e *(ugs. abwertend)* clumsy oaf

Tarif der; ~s, ~e charge; *(Post~, Wasser~)* rate; *(Verkehrs~)* fares *pl.; (Zoll~)* tariff; *(Lohn~)* [wage] rate; *(Gehalts~)* [salary] scale

tarnen 1. *tr., itr. V.* camouflage; 2. *refl. V.* camouflage oneself

Tasche die; ~, ~n bag; *(in Kleidung, Rucksack usw.)* pocket; **jmdm. auf der ~ liegen** *(fig. ugs.)* live off sb.

Taschen-: ~**buch** das paperback; ~**lampe** die [pocket] torch *(Brit.) or (Amer.)* flashlight; ~**messer** das penknife; ~**rechner** der pocket calculator; ~**tuch** das; *Pl.* ~**tücher** handkerchief; ~**uhr** die pocket-watch

Tasse die; ~, ~n cup

Taste die; ~, ~n a) *(eines Musikinstruments, einer Schreibmaschine)* key; b) *(Fuß~)* pedal [key]; c) *(am Telefon, Radio, Fernsehgerät, Taschenrechner usw.)* button; **tasten** 1. *itr. V. (fühlend suchen)* grope, feel **(nach** for); 2. *refl. V. (sich tastend bewegen)* grope or feel one's way; **Tasten·telefon** das push-button telephone

tat *1. u. 3. Pers. Sg. Prät. v.* **tun; Tat** die; ~, ~en act; *(das Tun)* action; **eine gute ~:** a good deed; **in der ~** *(verstärkend)* actually; *(zustimmend)* indeed

Tatar das; ~[s] steak tartare

Täter der; ~s, ~, **Täterin** die; ~, ~nen culprit; **tätig** *Adj.* a) ~ **sein** work; b) *(rührig, aktiv)* active; **tätigen** *tr. V. (Kaufmannsspr., Papierdt.)* transact ⟨business, deal, etc.⟩; **Tätigkeit** die; ~, ~en activity; *(Arbeit)* job; **Tatkraft** die energy; drive; **tat·kräftig** 1. *Adj.* energetic ⟨person⟩; 2. *adv.* energetically

tätowieren *tr. V.* tattoo; **Tätowierung** die; ~, ~en tattoo

Tat·sache die fact; **tatsächlich** 1. *Adj.* actual; real; 2. *adv.* actually; really

tätscheln *tr. V.* pat

Tatze die; ~, ~n paw

¹**Tau** der; ~[e]s dew

²**Tau** das; ~[e]s, ~e *(Seil)* rope

taub *Adj.* a) deaf; b) *(wie abgestorben)* numb; c) *(leer, unbefruchtet usw.)* empty ⟨nut⟩; dead ⟨rock⟩

¹**Taube** die; ~, ~n pigeon; *(Turtel~; auch Politik fig.)* dove

²**Taube** der/die; *adj. Dekl.* deaf person; deaf man/woman; **die** ~**n** the deaf; **Taubheit** die; ~: deafness; **taub·stumm** *Adj.* deaf and dumb;

Taub·stumme der/die; *adj. Dekl.* deaf mute

tauchen 1. *itr. V.* a) *auch mit sein* dive **(nach** for); b) *mit sein (ein~)* dive; *(auf~)* rise; emerge; 2. *tr. V.* a) *(ein~)* dip; b) *(unter~)* duck; **Taucher** der; ~s, ~, **Taucherin** die; ~, ~nen diver; *(mit Flossen und Atemgerät)* skindiver; **Tauch·sieder** der; ~s, ~: portable immersion heater

tauen 1. *itr. V.* a) *unpers.* **es taut** it's thawing; b) *mit sein (schmelzen)* melt; 2. *tr. V.* melt; thaw

Taufe die; ~, ~n *(christl. Rel.)* a) *o. Pl. (Sakrament)* baptism; b) *(Zeremonie)* christening; baptism; **taufen** *tr. V.* a) baptize; b) *(einen Namen geben)* christen

taugen *itr. V.* **nichts/nicht viel/etwas ~:** be no/not much/some good *or* use; **tauglich** *Adj.* |**nicht**| ~: [un]suitable; *(für Militärdienst)* fit [for service]

Taumel der; ~s a) [feeling of] dizziness; b) *(Rausch)* frenzy; fever; **taumelig** *Adj.* dizzy; giddy; **taumeln** *itr. V.* a) *auch mit sein (wanken)* reel, sway **(vor** + *Dat.* with); b) *mit sein (sich ~d bewegen)* stagger

Tausch der; ~|e|s, ~e exchange; **ein guter/schlechter ~:** a good/bad deal; **tauschen** 1. *tr. V.* exchange **(gegen** for); **sie tauschten die Plätze** they changed places; 2. *itr. V.* **mit jmdm. ~** *(fig.)* change places with sb.

täuschen 1. *tr. V.* deceive; **wenn mich nicht alles täuscht** unless I'm completely mistaken; 2. *itr. V.* be deceptive; 3. *refl. V.* be wrong *or* mistaken **(in** + *Dat.* about); **täuschend** 1. *Adj.* remarkable, striking ⟨similarity, imitation⟩; 2. *adv.* remarkably; **Täuschung** die; ~, ~en deception; *(Selbst~)* delusion

tausend *Kardinalz.* a) *a or* one thousand; b) *(ugs.: sehr viele)* thousands of; ~ **Dank/Küsse** a thousand thanks/kisses; **Tausend** das; ~s, ~e *od.* ~ a) *nicht in Verbindung mit Kardinalzahlen; Pl.:* ~ thousand; b) *Pl. (eine unbestimmte große Zahl)* thousands; **tausend·ein[s]** *Kardinalz.* a *or* one thousand and one; **Tausender** der; ~s, ~ *(ugs.) (Tausendmarkschein usw.)* thousand-mark/-dollar *etc.* note; *(Betrag)* thousand marks/dollars *etc.;* **tausenderlei** *Gattungsz.; indekl. (ugs.)* a thousand and one different ⟨answers, kinds, etc.⟩; **tausend·mal** *Adv.* a thousand times; **Tausend-**

mark·schein der thousand-mark note; **tausendst...** *Ordinalz.* thousandth; *s. auch* **acht...; tausendstel** *Bruchz.* thousandth; **Tausendstel** das *(schweiz. meist* der); ~s, ~: thousandth

Tau·wetter das thaw

Taxi das; ~s, ~s taxi; **Taxi·fahrer** der taxi-driver

Tb, Tbc [te:'be:, te:be:'tse:] die; ~ *Abk.* Tuberkulose TB

Technik die; ~, ~en **a)** *o. Pl.* technology; *(Studienfach)* engineering *no art.;* **b)** *o. Pl. (technische Ausrüstung)* equipment; **c)** *(Arbeitsweise, Verfahren)* technique; **Techniker** der; ~s, ~, **Technikerin** die; ~, ~nen technical expert; **technisch** ['tɛçnɪʃ] **1.** *Adj.* technical; technological ⟨*progress, age*⟩; **2.** *adv.* technically; technologically ⟨*advanced*⟩; **Technologie** die; ~, ~n technology

TEE [te:|e:'|e:] der; ~|s|, ~|s| *Abk.* Trans-Europ-Express TEE

Tee der; ~s, ~s tea

Tee-: ~**beutel** der tea-bag; ~**kanne** die teapot; ~**löffel** der teaspoon; ~**sieb** das tea-strainer; ~**tasse** die teacup

Teich der; ~|e|s, ~e pond

Teig der; ~|e|s, ~e dough; *(Kuchen~, Biskuit~)* pastry; *(Pfannkuchen~, Waffel~)* batter; **Teig·waren** *Pl.* pasta *sing.*

Teil a) der; ~|e|s, ~e part; **fünfter ~:** fifth; **b)** der *od.* das; ~|e|s, ~e *(Anteil; Beitrag)* share; **c)** der; ~|e|s, ~e *(beteiligte Person[en]; Rechtssw.: Partei)* party; **d)** das; ~|e|s, ~e *(Einzel~)* part; **teil·bar** *Adj.* divisible **(durch** by); **Teilchen** das; ~s, ~ **a)** *(kleines Stück)* [small] part; **b)** *(Partikel)* particle; **teilen 1.** *tr. V.* **a)** divide **(durch** by); **b)** *(auf~; teilhaben [lassen] an)* share **(unter** + *Dat.* among); **2.** *refl. V.* sich *(Dat.)* etw. |mit jmdm.| ~ : share sth. [with sb.]; **teil|haben** *unr. itr. V.* share **(an** + *Dat.* in); **Teil·kaskoversicherung** die insurance giving limited cover

Teilnahme die; ~, ~n **a)** participation **(an** + *Dat.* in); ~ **an einem Kurs** attendance at a course; **b)** *(Interesse)* interest **(an** + *Dat.* in); **c)** *(geh.: Mitgefühl)* sympathy; **teilnahms·los** *Adj.* indifferent; **Teilnahmslosigkeit** die indifference; **teilnahms·voll 1.** *Adj.* compassionate; **2.** *adv.* compassionately; **teil|nehmen** *unr. itr. V.*

[an etw. *(Dat.)*] ~ : take part [in sth.]; |an einem **Lehrgang**| ~ : attend [a course]; **Teilnehmer** der; ~s, ~ **a)** participant *(Gen.,* **an** + *Dat.* in); *(bei Wettbewerb auch)* competitor, contestant **(an** + *Dat.* in); **b)** *(Fernspr.)* subscriber

teils *Adv.* partly; **Teilung** die; ~, ~en division; **teil·weise 1.** *Adv.* partly; **2.** *adj.* partial; **Teilzeit·arbeit** die part-time work *no indef. art.*

Teint [tɛ̃:] der; ~s, ~s complexion

Telefon ['te:lefo:n, *auch* tele'fo:n] das; ~s, ~e telephone; phone *(coll.);* **ans** ~ **gehen** answer the [tele]phone

Telefon-: ~**anruf** der [tele]phone call; ~**anschluß** der telephone; line; ~**apparat** der telephone

Telefonat das; ~|e|s, ~e telephone call

Telefon-: ~**buch** das [tele]phone book *or* directory; ~**gespräch** das telephone conversation

telefonieren *itr. V.* make a [tele]phone call; **mit jmdm.** ~ : talk to sb. [on the telephone]; **telefonisch 1.** *Adj.* telephone; **2.** *adv.* by telephone; **Telefonist** der; ~en, ~en, **Telefonistin** die; ~, ~nen telephonist; *(in einer Firma)* switchboard operator

Telefon-: ~**nummer** die [tele]phone number; ~**verzeichnis** das telephone list; ~**zelle** die [tele]phonebooth *or* (Brit.) -box; call-box (Brit.)

Telegraf der; ~en, ~en telegraph; **Telegrafie** die; ~ : telegraphy *no art.;* **telegrafieren** *itr., tr. V.* telegraph; **telegrafisch 1.** *Adj.* telegraphic; **2.** *adv.* by telegraph *or* telegram

Telegramm das telegram

Tele·objektiv das *(Fot.)* telephoto lens

Teller der; ~s, ~ : plate

Temperament das; ~|e|s, ~e **a)** *(Wesensart)* temperament; **b)** *o. Pl. (Schwung)* **eine Frau mit** ~ : a woman with spirit; **das** ~ **geht oft mit mir durch** I often lose my temper; **temperament·voll** *Adj.* spirited ⟨*person, speech, dance, etc.*⟩

Temperatur die; ~, ~en temperature

Temperatur-: ~**anstieg** der rise in temperature; ~**rückgang** der drop *or* fall in temperature

Tempo das; ~s, ~s *od.* Tempi **a)** *Pl.* ~s speed; **b)** *(Musik)* tempo; time

Tempus das; ~, Tempora *(Sprachw.)* tense

Tendenz die; ~, ~en trend; **tendieren** itr. V. tend (**zu** towards)
Teneriffa (das); ~s Tenerife
Tennis das; ~: tennis no art.
Tennis-: ~**ball** der tennis-ball;
~**platz** der tennis-court; ~**schläger**
der tennis-racket; ~**spieler** der tennis-player
Tenor der; ~s, Tenöre, (österr. auch:)
~**e** (Musik) tenor; (im Chor) tenors
pl.; tenor voices pl.
Teppich der; ~s, ~e carpet; (kleiner)
rug; **Teppich·boden** der fitted carpet
Termin der; ~s, ~e date; (Anmeldung)
appointment; (Verabredung) engagement; (Rechtsw.) hearing; **Terminal**
['tø:ɐminəl] das; ~s, ~s terminal; **Ter-
min·kalender** der appointments
book
Terpentin das, (österr. meist:) der; ~s
a) (Harz) turpentine; **b)** (ugs.: Terpen-
tinöl) turps sing. (coll.); **Terpentin-
öl** das oil of turpentine
Terrain [tɛ'rɛ:] das; ~s, ~s terrain
Terrasse die; ~, ~n terrace
Terrier ['tɛriɐ] der; ~s, ~: terrier
Terrine die; ~, ~n tureen
Territorium das; ~s, Territorien territory
Terror der; ~s terrorism no art.; **terrorisieren** tr. V. **a)** terrorize; **b)** (ugs.:
belästigen) pester; **Terrorist** der;
~en, ~en terrorist
Terz die; ~, ~en (Musik) third
Test der; ~[e]s, ~s od. ~e test
Testament das; ~[e]s, ~e **a)** will; **b)**
(christl. Rel.) Testament
testen tr. V. test (**auf** + Akk. for)
teuer 1. Adj. expensive; dear usu.
pred.; **wie ~ war das?** how much did
that cost?; **2.** adv. expensively;
dearly; **etw. ~ kaufen/verkaufen** pay a
great deal for sth./sell sth. at a high
price; **Teuerung** die; ~, ~en rise in
prices
Teufel der; ~s, ~: devil; **teuflisch** 1.
Adj. **a)** devilish, fiendish ⟨plan, trick,
etc.⟩; diabolical ⟨laughter, pleasure,
etc.⟩; **b)** (ugs.: groß, intensiv) terrible
(coll.); dreadful (coll.); **2.** adv. **a)** dia-
bolically; **b)** (ugs.) terribly (coll.)
Text der; ~[e]s, ~e text; (Wortlaut)
wording; (eines Theaterstücks) script;
(einer Oper) libretto; (eines Liedes,
Chansons usw.) words pl.; (eines
Schlagers) words pl.; lyrics pl.; (zu einer Abbildung) caption; **texten** tr. V.
write ⟨song, advertisement, etc.⟩

Textilien Pl. **a)** textiles; **b)** (Fertigwa-
ren) textile goods
Thailand (das); ~s Thailand
Theater das; ~s, ~ **a)** theatre; **ins ~
gehen** go to the theatre; **im ~:** at the
theatre; ~ **spielen** act; (fig.) play-act;
pretend; **b)** o. Pl. (fig. ugs.) fuss
Theater-: ~**abonnement** das
theatre subscription [ticket]; ~**stück**
das [stage] play
Theke die; ~, ~n **a)** (Schanktisch) bar;
b) (Ladentisch) counter
Thema das; ~s, Themen subject;
topic; (einer Abhandlung) subject;
theme; (Leitgedanke) theme
Themse die; ~: Thames
Theologe der; ~n, ~n theologian;
Theologie die; ~, ~n theology no
art.; **theologisch** 1. Adj. theological; **2.** adv. theologically
Theorie die; ~, ~n theory
Therapeut der; ~en, ~en, **Thera-
peutin** die; ~, ~nen therapist; thera-
peutist; **therapeutisch** 1. Adj.
therapeutic; **2.** adv. therapeutically
Therapie die; ~, ~n therapy (**gegen**
for)
Thermo·meter das (österr. u.
schweiz. der od. das) thermometer;
Thermos·flasche ⓦ die Thermos
flask (P); vacuum flask; **Thermostat** der; ~[e]s od. ~en, ~e od. ~en
thermostat
Thron der; ~[e]s, ~e throne
Thun·fisch der tuna
Thüringen (das); ~s Thuringia; **Thü-
ringer Wald** der Thuringian Forest
Thymian der; ~s, ~e thyme
ticken itr. V. tick
tief 1. Adj. (auch fig.) deep; (niedrig)
low; low ⟨neckline, bow⟩; deep; intense ⟨pain, suffering⟩; **2.** adv. deep;
(niedrig) low; (intensiv) deeply;
⟨stoop, bow⟩ low; ⟨breathe, inhale⟩
deeply; **Tief** das; ~s, ~s (Met.) low
tief-, Tief-: ~**bewegt** Adj. (präd. getrennt geschrieben) deeply moved;
~**blau** Adj. deep blue; ~**druck** der;
o. Pl. (Met.) low pressure
Tiefe die; ~, ~n depth; **in die ~ stürzen**
plunge into the depths
tief-, Tief-: ~**garage** die underground car park; ~**greifend; tiefer
greifend, am tiefsten greifend** od.
tiefstgreifend 1. Adj. profound; profound, deep ⟨crisis⟩; far-reaching ⟨im-
provement⟩; **2.** adv. profoundly;
~**gründig** Adj. profound; ~**kühlen**
tr. V. [deep-]freeze

Tief·kühl-: ~**fach** das freezer [compartment]; ~**kost** die frozen food
tief-, Tief-: ~**punkt** der low [point]; ~**see** die *(Geogr.)* deep sea; ~**sinnig** 1. *Adj.* profound; 2. *adv.* profoundly
Tiegel der; ~**s,** ~ *(zum Kochen)* pan; *(Schmelz~)* crucible; *(Behälter)* pot
Tier das; ~|e|s, ~e animal
Tier-: ~**arzt** der veterinary surgeon; vet; ~**garten** der zoo; zoological garden; ~**heim** das animal home
tierisch 1. *Adj.* a) animal *attrib.*; savage ⟨*cruelty, crime*⟩; b) *(ugs.: unerträglich groß)* terrible *(coll.);* ~**er** Ernst deadly seriousness; 2. *adv.* a) ⟨*roar*⟩ like an animal; savagely ⟨*cruel*⟩; b) *(ugs.: unerträglich)* terribly *(coll.)*
tier-, Tier-: ~**kreis** der; *o. Pl. (Astron., Astrol.)* zodiac; ~**kreis·zeichen** das *(Astron., Astrol.)* sign of the zodiac; ~**lieb** *Adj.* animal-loving *attrib.;* fond of animals *postpos.;* ~**park** der zoo; ~**pfleger** der animal-keeper; ~**quälerei** [---'-] die cruelty to animals; ~**reich** das; *o. Pl.* animal kingdom
Tiger der; ~**s,** ~: tiger
tilgen *tr. V.* a) *(geh.)* delete ⟨*word, letter, error*⟩; erase ⟨*record, endorsement*⟩; *(fig.)* wipe out ⟨*shame, guilt, traces*⟩; b) *(Wirtsch., Bankw.)* repay; pay off
Tilsiter der; ~**s,** ~: Tilsit [cheese]
Tinte die; ~, ~**n** ink; **in der** ~ **sitzen** *(ugs.)* be in the soup *(coll.);* **Tinten·fisch** der cuttlefish; *(Krake)* octopus
Tip der; ~**s,** ~**s** a) *(ugs.)* tip; b) *(bei Toto, Lotto usw.)* tip; **tip·pen** 1. *itr. V.* a) **an/gegen etw.** *(Akk.)* ~: tap sth.; b) *(ugs.: maschineschreiben)* type; c) *(wetten)* do the pools/lottery *etc.;* **im Lotto** ~: do the lottery; 2. *tr. V.* a) tap; b) *(ugs.: mit der Maschine schreiben)* type; c) *(setzen auf)* choose; **sechs Richtige** ~: make six correct selections
tipp·topp *(ugs.)* 1. *Adj. (tadellos)* immaculate; *(erstklassig)* tip-top; 2. *adv.* immaculately
Tirol (das); ~**s** [the] Tyrol; **Tiroler** der; ~**s,** ~, **Tirolerin** die; ~, ~**nen** Tyrolese; Tyrolean
Tisch der; ~|e|s, ~e table; **reinen** ~ **machen** *(ugs.)* sort things out
Tisch-: ~**dame** die dinner partner; ~**decke** die table-cloth; ~**gebet** das grace; ~**herr** der dinner partner; ~**lampe** die table-lamp

Tischler der; ~**s,** ~: joiner; *(bes. Kunst~)* cabinet-maker; **Tischlerei** die; ~, ~**en** a) *(Werkstatt)* joiner's/cabinet-maker's [workshop]; b) *o. Pl. (Handwerk)* joinery/cabinet-making
Tisch-: ~**nachbar** der person next to one [at table]; ~**platte** die table-top; ~**tennis** das table tennis; ~**tuch** das; *Pl.* ~**tücher** table-cloth; ~**wäsche** die table-linen; ~**wein** der table wine; ~**zeit** die lunch-time
Titel der; ~**s,** ~ a) title; b) *(ugs.: Musikstück, Song usw.)* number
Titel-: ~**bild** das cover picture; ~**blatt** das title-page; ~**rolle** die title-role; ~**seite** die a) *(einer Zeitung, Zeitschrift)* [front] cover; b) *(eines Buchs)* title-page
titulieren *tr. V.* call
tja [tja(:)] *Interj.* [yes] well; *(Resignation ausdrückend)* oh, well
Toast [to:st] der; ~|e|s, ~e *od.* ~s toast; **Toast·brot** das; *o. Pl.* [sliced white] bread for toasting; **toasten** *tr. V.* toast; **Toaster** der; ~**s,** ~: toaster
toben *itr. V.* a) go wild **(vor +** *Dat.* with); *(fig.)* ⟨*storm, sea, battle*⟩ rage; b) *(tollen)* romp *or* charge about; c) **mit sein** *(laufen)* charge
Tochter die; ~, **Töchter** daughter
Tod der; ~|e|s, ~e death; **eines natürlichen/gewaltsamen** ~**es sterben** die a natural/violent death; **jmdn. zum** ~**e verurteilen** sentence sb. to death; **tod·ernst** 1. *Adj.* deadly serious; 2. *adv.* deadly seriously
Todes-: ~**anzeige** die a) *(in einer Zeitung)* death notice; b) *(Karte)* card announcing a person's death; ~**fall** der death; *(in der Familie)* bereavement; ~**nachricht** die news of his/her/their *etc.* death; ~**opfer** das death; fatality; ~**strafe** die death penalty; ~**ursache** die cause of death; ~**urteil** das death sentence
Tod·feind der deadly enemy; **tod·krank** *Adj.* critically ill; **tödlich** 1. *Adj.* a) fatal ⟨*accident, illness, outcome, etc.*⟩; lethal, deadly ⟨*poison, bite, shot, trap, etc.*⟩; lethal ⟨*dose*⟩; b) *(sehr groß, ausgeprägt)* deadly ⟨*hatred, seriousness, certainty, boredom*⟩; 2. *adv.* a) fatally; b) *(sehr)* terribly *(coll.)*
tod-, Tod-: ~**müde** *Adj.* dead tired; ~**sicher** *(ugs.)* 1. *Adj.* sure-fire *(coll.);* 2. *adv.* for certain *or* sure; ~**sünde** die *(auch fig.)* deadly *or* mortal sin; ~**unglücklich** *Adj. (ugs.)* extremely *or* desperately unhappy

Toilette [tŏa'lɛtə] **die;** ~, ~n toilet
Toiletten·papier das toilet paper
toi, toi, toi ['tɔy 'tɔy 'tɔy] *Interj.* good
luck!; *(unberufen!)* touch wood!
Tokio (das); ~s Tokyo
tolerant 1. *Adj.* tolerant **(gegen** of); 2.
adv. tolerantly; **Toleranz die;** ~:
tolerance; **tolerieren** *tr. V.* tolerate
toll 1. *Adj.* **a)** *(ugs.) (großartig)* great
(coll.); fantastic *(coll.);* *(erstaunlich)*
amazing; *(heftig, groß)* enormous ⟨*respect*⟩; terrific *(coll.)* ⟨*noise, storm*⟩; **b)**
(wild) wild; 2. *adv.* **a)** *(ugs.: großartig)*
terrifically well *(coll.);* **b)** *(ugs.: heftig)*
⟨*rain, snow*⟩ like billy-o *(coll.);* **c)**
(wild) **bei dem Fest ging es** ~ **zu** it was a
wild party; **tollen** *itr. V.* **a)** romp
about; **b)** *mit sein* romp
toll-, Toll-: ~**kühn** 1. *Adj.* daredevil
attrib.; daring; 2. *adv.* daringly;
~**wut die** rabies *sing.;* ~**wütig** *Adj.*
rabid
Tolpatsch der; ~|e|s, ~e *(ugs.)* clumsy
or awkward creature; **tolpatschig**
(ugs.) 1. *Adj.* clumsy; awkward; 2.
adv. clumsily; awkwardly
Tölpel der; ~s, ~: fool; **tölpelhaft** 1.
Adj. foolish; 2. *adv.* foolishly
Tomate die; ~, ~n tomato; **Toma-
ten·mark das** tomato purée
Tombola die; ~, ~s raffle
¹Ton der; ~|e|s, ~e clay
²Ton der; ~|e|s, **Töne a)** *(auch Physik,
Musik; beim Telefon)* tone; *(Klang)*
note; **b)** *(Film, Ferns. usw., ~ wiedergabe)* sound; **c)** *(ugs.: Äußerung)* word;
d) *(Farb~)* shade; **e)** *(Akzent)* stress
ton-, Ton-: ~**angebend** *Adj.* predominant; ~**art die a)** *(Musik)* key; **b)**
(fig.) tone; ~**band das;** *Pl.* ~**bänder**
tape
Ton·band·gerät das tape recorder
tönen 1. *itr. V. (geh.)* sound; ⟨*bell*⟩
sound, ring; *(schallen, widerhallen)* resound; 2. *tr. V. (färben)* tint
Ton·fall der tone; *(Intonation)* intonation
Tonne die; ~, ~n **a)** *(Behälter)* drum;
(Müll~) bin; *(Regen~)* water-butt; **b)**
(Gewicht) tonne; **tonnen·weise**
Adv., adj. by the ton
Tönung die; ~, ~en tint; shade
Topf der; ~es, **Töpfe a)** pot; *(Braten~,
Schmor~)* casserole; *(Stielkasserolle)*
saucepan; **b)** *(zur Aufbewahrung)* pot;
c) *(Krug)* jug; **d)** *(Nacht~)* chamber
pot; *(für Kinder)* potty *(Brit. coll.);* **e)**
(Blumen~) [flower]pot; **Topf·blume
die** [flowering] pot plant

Töpfchen das; ~s, ~: potty *(Brit.
coll.);* **Töpfer der;** ~s, ~: potter;
Töpferei die; ~, ~en **a)** *o. Pl. (Handwerk)* pottery *no art.;* **b)** *(Werkstatt)*
pottery; potter's workshop; **c)** *(Erzeugnis)* piece of pottery; ~**en** pottery
sing.
Topf-: ~**lappen der** oven cloth;
~**pflanze die** pot plant
Tor das; ~|e|s, ~e **a)** gate; *(einer Gara-
ge, Scheune)* door; *(fig.)* gateway; **b)**
(Ballspiele) goal; **c)** *(Ski)* gate
Torf der; ~|e|s, ~e peat
Torheit die; ~, ~en *(geh.)* **a)** *o. Pl.*
foolishness; **b)** *(Handlung)* foolish act
Tor·hüter der *(Ballspiele)* goalkeeper
töricht *(geh.)* 1. *Adj.* foolish; 2. *adv.*
foolishly
torkeln *itr. V.; mit sein* stagger
Tor·mann der; *Pl.* ~**männer** *od.* ~**leute** *(Ballspiele)* goalkeeper
Tornister [tɔr'nɪstɐ] **der;** ~s, ~: knapsack; *(Schulranzen)* satchel
torpedieren *tr. V. (Milit., fig.)* torpedo; **Torpedo das;** ~s, ~s torpedo
Törtchen das; ~s, ~: tartlet; **Torte
die;** ~, ~n *(Creme~, Sahne~)* gateau;
(Obst~) [fruit] flan
Torten-: ~**boden der** flan case; *(ohne
Rand)* flan base; ~**guß der** glaze;
~**heber der** cake-slice
Tortur die; ~, ~en **a)** ordeal; **b)** *(veralt.: Folter)* torture
Tor-: ~**wart der;** ~|e|s, ~e *(Ballspiele)*
goalkeeper; ~**weg der** gateway
tosen *itr. V.* roar; ⟨*storm*⟩ rage
tot *Adj.* dead; ~ **umfallen** drop dead
total 1. *Adj.* total; 2. *adv.* totally; **totalitär** *(Politik)* 1. *Adj.* totalitarian; 2.
adv. in a totalitarian way; ⟨*organized,
run*⟩ along totalitarian lines; **To-
tal·schaden der** *(Versicherungsw.)*
an beiden Fahrzeugen entstand ~: both
vehicles were a write-off
tot|ärgern *refl. V. (ugs.)* get livid
(coll.); **Tote der/die;** *adj. Dekl.* dead
person; **die** ~**n** the dead; **töten** *tr., itr.
V.* kill; deaden ⟨*nerve etc.*⟩
toten-, Toten-: ~**blaß,** ~**bleich**
Adj. deathly pale; ~**gräber der**
grave-digger; ~**kopf der a)** skull; **b)**
(als Symbol) death's head; *(mit gekreuzten Knochen)* skull and cross-
bones; ~**schädel der** skull; ~**still**
Adj. deathly quiet; ~**stille die**
deathly silence; ~**wache die** vigil by
the body
tot-, Tot-: ~|**fahren** *unr. tr. V.* [run
over and] kill; ~**geboren** *Adj. (präd.*

getrennt geschrieben) stillborn; ~**ge-burt** die still birth; ~|**lachen** *refl. V. (ugs.)* kill oneself laughing; **zum Tot-lachen sein** be killing *(coll.)*
Toto das *od.* der; ~s, ~s a) *(Pferde~)* tote *(sl.)*; **im ~**: on the tote; b) *(Fuß-ball~)* [football] pools *pl.*; |**im**| ~ **spie-len** do the pools; **Toto·schein der** pools coupon/*(sl.)* tote ticket
tot-, Tot-: ~|**schießen** *unr. tr. V. (ugs.)* jmdn. ~**schießen** shoot sb. dead; ~**schlag der** *(Rechtsw.)* man-slaughter *no indef. art.;* ~|**schlagen** *unr. tr. V.* beat to death; ~|**stellen** *refl. V.* pretend to be dead; play dead; ~|**treten** *unr. tr. V.* trample *(person)* to death; step on and kill *(insect)*
Tötung die; ~, ~en killing; **fahrlässige** ~ *(Rechtsspr.)* manslaughter by culp-able negligence
Toupet [tu'pe:] das; ~s, ~s toupee; **toupieren** [tu'pi:rən] *tr. V.* back-comb
Tour [tu:ɐ̯] die; ~, ~en tour **(durch** of); *(kürzere Fahrt, Ausflug)* trip; *(mit dem Auto)* drive; *(mit dem Fahrrad)* ride; *(feste Strecke)* route; **in einer ~** *(ugs.)* the whole time; **Tourismus** [tu'rıs-mʊs] der; ~: tourism *no art.;* **Tourist** der; ~en, ~en tourist; **Touristen-klasse** die tourist class; **Touristin** die; ~, ~nen tourist
Tournee [tʊr'ne:] die; ~, ~s *od.* ~n [tʊr'ne:ən] tour; **auf ~ sein/gehen** be/go on tour
Trab der; ~[e]s trot; **im ~**: at a trot; **im ~ reiten** trot; **traben** *itr. V.; mit sein (auch ugs.: laufen)* trot
Tracht die; ~, ~en a) *(Volks~)* na-tional costume; *(Berufs~)* uniform; b) **eine ~ Prügel** a thrashing; *(als Strafe)* a hiding
trachten *itr. V. (geh.)* strive **(nach** for, after)
Tradition die; ~, ~en tradition; **tra-ditionell** 1. *Adj.* traditional; 2. *adv.* traditionally
traf *1. u. 3. Pers. Sg. Prät. v.* treffen; **träfe** *1. u. 3. Pers. Sg. Konjunktiv II v.* treffen
Trafik die; ~, ~en *(österr.)* tobaccon-ist's [shop]
Trag·bahre die stretcher; **tragbar** *Adj.* a) portable; b) wearable *(clothes)*; c) *(finanziell)* supportable *(cost, debt, etc.)*; d) *(erträglich)* bear-able; tolerable
träge 1. *Adj.* a) sluggish; 2. *adv.* sluggishly

tragen 1. *unr. tr. V.* a) carry; b) *(brin-gen)* take; c) *(ertragen)* bear *(fate, des-tiny)*; bear, endure *(suffering)*; d) *(hal-ten)* hold; **einen/den linken Arm in der Schlinge ~**: have one's arm/one's left arm in a sling; e) *(von unten stützen)* support; f) *(belastbar sein durch)* be able to carry *or* take *(weight)*; g) *(übernehmen, aufkommen für)* bear, carry *(costs etc.)*; take *(blame, respons-ibility, consequences)*; h) *(am Körper)* wear *(clothes, wig, glasses, jewellery, etc.)*; have *(false teeth, beard, etc.)*; j) *(hervorbringen)* *(tree)* bear *(fruit)*; *(field)* produce *(crops)*; 2. *unr. itr. V.* a) carry; b) *(am Körper)* **man trägt** |**wieder**| **kurz/lang** short/long skirts are in fashion [again]; c) **der Baum trägt gut** the tree produces a good crop; **tragend** *Adj. (Stabilität gebend)* load-bearing; supporting *(wall, col-umn, function, etc.)*
Träger der; ~s, ~ a) porter; b) *(Zei-tungs~)* paper boy/girl; delivery boy/girl; c) *(Bauw.)* girder; [supporting] beam; d) *(an Kleidung)* strap; *(Ho-sen~)* braces *pl.*; e) *(Inhaber) (eines Amts)* holder; *(eines Namens, Titels)* bearer; *(eines Preises)* winner; **Trä-gerin** die; ~, ~nen *s.* Träger a, b, e
Trage·tasche die carrier-bag
Trag-: ~**fähigkeit** die load-bearing capacity; ~**fläche** die wing; ~**flü-gel·boot das** hydrofoil
Trägheit die; ~, ~en sluggishness
Tragik die; ~: tragedy; **tragi·ko-misch** 1. *Adj.* tragicomic; 2. *adv.* tragicomically; **tragisch** 1. *Adj.* tragic; **das ist nicht** |**so**| ~ *(ugs.)* it's not the end of the world *(coll.);* 2. *adv.* tragically; **Tragödie** die; ~, ~n tra-gedy
Trag·weite die; *o. Pl.* consequences *pl.*
Trainer ['trɛ:nɐ] der; ~s, ~: coach; trainer; *(einer Fußballmannschaft)* manager; **trainieren** 1. *tr. V.* a) train; coach *(swimmer, tennis-player)*; manage *(football team)*; exercise *(muscles etc.)*; b) *(üben, einüben)* prac-tise *(exercise, jump, etc.)*; **Fußball ~**: do football training; 2. *itr. V.* train; **Training** ['trɛ:nıŋ] das; ~s, ~s train-ing *no indef. art.*
Trainings-: ~**anzug** der track suit; ~**hose** die track-suit bottoms *pl.*
Trakt der; ~[e]s, ~e section; *(Flügel)* wing; **Traktor** der; ~s, ~en tractor

trällern *itr., tr. V.* warble

trampeln 1. *itr. V.* **a)** |mit den Füßen| ~: stamp one's feet; **b)** *mit sein (treten)* trample (**auf** + *Akk.* on); **2.** *tr. V.* trample; **Trampel·pfad der** [beaten] path

trampen ['trɛmpn̩] *itr. V. mit sein* hitch-hike

Tramway ['tramve] **die**; ~, ~s *(österr.)* tram *(Brit.);* streetcar *(Amer.)*

Tran der; ~|e|s train-oil

tranchieren [trãˈʃiːrən] *tr. V.* carve

Träne die; ~, ~n tear; ~n lachen laugh till one cries; **tränen** *itr. V.* ⟨eyes⟩ water

tranig *Adj. (ugs. abwertend: langsam)* sluggish; slow

trank *1. u. 3. Pers. Sg. Prät. v.* trinken; **Tränke die**; ~, ~n watering-place; **tränken** *tr. V.* **a)** water; **b)** *(sich vollsaugen lassen)* soak

Transfer der; ~s, ~s *(bes. Wirtsch., Sport)* transfer

Trans·formator der; ~s, ~en transformer

Transistor der; ~s, ~en transistor

Transit [tranˈziːt, *auch:* 'tranzɪt] **das**; ~s, ~s transit visa; **transitiv** *(Sprachw.)* **1.** *Adj.* transitive; **2.** *adv.* transitively; **Transit·verkehr der** transit traffic

transparent *Adj.* transparent; *(Licht durchlassend)* translucent; **Transparent das**; ~|e|s, ~e *(Spruchband)* banner; *(Bild)* transparency; **Transparenz die**; ~ transparency

Transport der; ~|e|s, ~e **a)** transportation; **b)** *(beförderte Lebewesen od. Sachen) (mit dem Zug)* train-load; *(mit mehreren Fahrzeugen)* convoy; *(Fracht)* consignment; **transportabel** *Adj.* transportable; *(tragbar)* portable; **Transporteur** [...'tøːɐ̯] **der**; ~s, ~e carrier; **transport·fähig** *Adj.* moveable; **transportieren** *tr. V.* transport ⟨goods, people⟩; move ⟨patient⟩; **Transport·kosten** *Pl.* carriage *sing.;* transport costs

Transvestit der; ~en, ~en transvestite

Trapez das; ~es, ~e **a)** *(Geom.)* trapezium *(Brit.);* trapezoid *(Amer.);* **b)** *(im Zirkus o. ä.)* trapeze

trappeln *itr. V.; mit sein* patter [along]; ⟨feet⟩ patter; ⟨hoofs⟩ go clip-clop

Trara das; ~s *(ugs.)* razzmatazz *(coll.)*

trat *1. u. 3. Pers. Sg. Prät. v.* treten

Tratsch der; ~|e|s *(ugs.)* gossip; tittle-tattle; **tratschen** *itr. V. (ugs.)* gossip; *(schwatzen)* chatter

Traube die; ~, ~n **a)** *(Beeren)* bunch; *(von Johannisbeeren o. ä.)* cluster; **b)** *(Wein~)* grape; **c)** *(Menschenmenge)* bunch; cluster

trauen 1. *itr. V.* jmdm./einer Sache ~: trust sb./sth.; **2.** *refl. V.* dare; **3.** *tr. V. (verheiraten)* ⟨vicar, registrar, *etc.*⟩ marry

Trauer die; ~ **a)** grief (**über** + *Akk.* over); *(um einen Toten)* mourning (**um** + *Akk.* for); **b)** *(~zeit)* [period of] mourning; **c)** ~ **tragen** be in mourning

Trauer-: ~**fall der** bereavement; ~**feier die** memorial ceremony; *(beim Begräbnis)* funeral ceremony; ~**karte die** [pre-printed] card of condolence; ~**kleidung die** mourning clothes *pl.*

trauern *itr. V.* mourn; **um jmdn.** ~: mourn for sb.

Trauer-: ~**spiel das** tragedy; *(fig. ugs.)* deplorable business; ~**weide die** weeping willow

träufeln *tr. V.* [let] trickle (**in** + *Akk.* into); drip ⟨ear-drops *etc.*⟩

Traum der; ~|e|s, Träume ['trɔymə] dream; **träumen 1.** *itr. V.* dream (**von** of, about); *(unaufmerksam sein)* [day-] dream; **2.** *tr. V.* dream; **Träumer der**; ~s, ~, **Träumerin die**; ~, ~nen dreamer; **träumerisch 1.** *Adj.* dreamy; **2.** *adv.* dreamily; **traumhaft** *(ugs.)* **1.** *Adj.* marvellous; fabulous *(coll.);* **2.** *adv.* fabulously *(coll.)*

traurig 1. *Adj.* **a)** sad; unhappy ⟨childhood, youth⟩; painful ⟨duty⟩; **b)** *(kümmerlich)* sorry ⟨state *etc.*⟩; miserable ⟨result⟩; **2.** *adv.* sadly; **Traurigkeit die**; ~: sadness; sorrow

Trau-: ~**ring der** wedding-ring; ~**schein der** marriage certificate; **Trauung die**; ~, ~en wedding [ceremony]; **Trau·zeuge der** witness *(at wedding ceremony)*

Trecker der; ~s, ~: tractor

Treff der; ~s, ~s *(ugs.)* rendezvous; *(Ort)* meeting-place; **treffen 1.** *unr. tr. V.* **a)** hit; ⟨punch, blow, object⟩ strike; **ihn trifft keine Schuld** he is in no way to blame; **b)** *(erschüttern)* affect [deeply]; *(verletzen)* hurt; **c)** *(begegnen)* meet; **d)** *(vorfinden)* come upon, find ⟨anomalies *etc.*⟩; **es gut/schlecht** ~: be *or* strike lucky/be unlucky; **e)** *(als Funktionsverb)* make ⟨arrangements, choice, preparations, de-*

cision, etc.); **2.** *unr. itr. V.* **a)** ⟨*person, shot, etc.*⟩ hit the target; **nicht ~**: miss [the target]; **b)** *mit sein auf etw. (Akk.)* **~**: come upon sth.; **auf Widerstand/ Ablehnung/Schwierigkeiten ~**: meet with ·resistance/rejection/difficulties; **3.** *unr. refl. V.* **a) sich mit jmdm. ~**: meet sb.; **b)** *unpers.* **es trifft sich gut/ schlecht** it is convenient/inconvenient; **Treffen das; ~s, ~**: meeting; **treffend 1.** *Adj.* apt; **2.** *adv.* aptly; **Treffer der; ~s, ~ a)** *(Milit., Boxen, Fechten usw.)* hit; *(Schlag)* blow; *(Ballspiele)* goal; **b)** *(Gewinn)* win; *(Los)* winner; **trefflich** *(geh.)* **1.** *Adj.* excellent; splendid ⟨*person*⟩; **2.** *adv.* excellently; splendidly
treff-, Treff-: **~punkt der** meeting-place; **~sicher 1.** *Adj.* accurate ⟨*language, mode of expression*⟩; unerring ⟨*judgement*⟩; **2.** *adv.* accurately; **~sicherheit die;** *o. Pl.* accuracy
Treib·eis das drift-ice
treiben 1. *unr. tr. V.* **a)** drive; **b)** *(sich beschäftigen mit)* do in for ⟨*farming, cattle-breeding, etc.*⟩; study ⟨*French etc.*⟩; carry on, pursue ⟨*studies, trade, craft*⟩; **viel Sport ~**: do a lot of sport; **es wüst/übel/toll ~** *(ugs.)* lead a dissolute/bad life/live it up; **2.** *unr. itr. V. meist, mit Richtungsangabe nur, mit sein* drift; **Treiben das; ~s a)** *(Durcheinander)* bustle; **b)** *(Tun)* activities *pl.;* doings *pl.*
Treib-: **~haus das** hothouse; **~haus- effekt der** greenhouse effect; **~stoff der** fuel
Trenchcoat ['trɛntʃkoʊt] **der; ~[s], ~s** trench coat
Trend der; ~s, ~s trend **(zu +** *Dat.* towards); *(Mode)* vogue
trennen 1. *tr. V.* **a)** separate **(von** from); sever ⟨*head, arm*⟩; **b)** *(auf~)* unpick ⟨*dress, seam*⟩; **c)** *(teilen)* divide ⟨*word, parts of a room etc., fig.: people*⟩; **2.** *refl. V.* **a)** *(voneinander weggehen)* part [company]; **b)** *(eine Partnerschaft auflösen)* ⟨*couple, partners*⟩ split up; **c) sich von etw. ~**: part with sth.; **Trennung die; ~, ~en** *(von Menschen)* separation **(von** from); *(von Gegenständen)* parting; *(von Wörtern)* division
trepp- ~ab *Adv.* down the stairs; **~auf** *Adv.* up the stairs
Treppe die; ~, ~n staircase; [flight *sing.* of] stairs *pl.; (im Freien, auf der Bühne)* [flight *sing.* of] steps *pl.*
Treppen-: **~absatz der** half-landing;

~geländer das banisters *pl.;* **~haus das** stair-well; **~stufe die** stair; *(im Freien)* step
Tresen der; ~s, ~ *(bes. nordd.)* bar; *(Ladentisch)* counter
Tresor der; ~s, ~e safe
Tret·boot das pedalo; **treten 1.** *unr. itr. V.* **a)** *mit sein* step **(in +** *Akk.* into, **auf +** *Akk.* on to); **b)** *(seinen Fuß setzen)* **auf etw.** *(Akk.)* **~** tread on sth.; **c)** *(ausschlagen)* kick; **2.** *unr. tr. V.* **a)** *(Tritt versetzen)* kick ⟨*person, ball, etc.*⟩; **b)** *(trampeln)* trample ⟨*path*⟩; **c)** *(mit dem Fuß niederdrücken)* step on ⟨*brake, pedal*⟩; operate ⟨*bellows, clutch*⟩
treu 1. *Adj.* faithful; loyal; faithful ⟨*husband, wife*⟩; loyal ⟨*ally, subject*⟩; **jmdm. ~ sein** be true to sb.; **sich selbst** *(Dat.)***/seinem Glauben ~ bleiben** be true to oneself/one's faith; **2.** *adv.* faithfully; loyally; **Treue die; ~ a)** loyalty; *(von [Ehe]partnern)* fidelity; **b)** *(Genauigkeit)* accuracy
treu-, Treu-: **~hand[anstalt] die** *o. Pl. (Wirtschaft)* German privatization agency; **~herzig 1.** *Adj.* ingenuous; *(naiv)* naïve; *(unschuldig)* innocent; **2.** *adv.* ingenuously; *(naiv)* naïvely; *(unschuldig)* innocently; **~los 1.** *Adj.* disloyal, faithless ⟨*friend, person*⟩; unfaithful ⟨*husband, wife, lover*⟩; **2.** *adv.* faithlessly
Tribunal das; ~s, ~e tribunal; **Tribüne die; ~, ~n** [grand]stand
Trichter der; ~s, ~ funnel
Trick der; ~s, ~s trick; *(fig.: List)* ploy
trieb *1. u. 3. Pers. Sg. Prät. v.* treiben; **Trieb der; ~[e]s, ~e a)** *(innerer Antrieb)* impulse; *(Drang)* urge; *(Verlangen)* [compulsive] desire; **b)** *(Sproß)* shoot
trieb-, Trieb-: **~feder die** mainspring; *(fig.)* driving *or* motivating force; **~haft 1.** *Adj.* compulsive; carnal ⟨*sensuality*⟩; **2.** *adv.* compulsively; **~wagen der** *(Eisenb.)* railcar
triefen *unr. od. regelm. itr. V.* **a)** *mit sein (fließen) (in Tropfen)* drip; *(in kleinen Rinnsalen)* trickle; **b)** *(naß sein)* be dripping wet; ⟨*nose*⟩ run
triff *Imperativ Sg. v.* treffen; **trifft** *3. Pers. Sg. Präsens v.* treffen
triftig *Adj.* good ⟨*reason, excuse*⟩; valid, convincing ⟨*motive, argument*⟩
¹Trikot [tri'ko] **der** *od.* **das; ~s, ~s** *(Stoff)* cotton jersey; **²Trikot das; ~s, ~** *(ärmellos)* singlet; *(eines Tänzers)* leotard; *(eines Fußballspielers)* shirt

Triller der; ~s, ~: trill; **trillern** 1. *itr. V.* trill; 2. *tr. V.* warble ⟨*song*⟩; **Triller·pfeife** die police/referee's whistle

Trimm-dich-Pfad der keep-fit trail; **trimmen** *tr. V. (durch Sport)* get ⟨*person*⟩ into shape

trinken 1. *unr. itr. V.* drink; **auf jmdn./ etw.** ~: drink to sb./sth.; 2. *unr. tr. V.* drink; **einen Kaffee/ein Bier** ~: have a coffee/beer; **Trinker** der; ~s, ~: alcoholic; **Trinkerei** die; ~, ~en drinking *no art.*

Trink-: ~**geld** das tip; ~**wasser** das; *Pl.* ~**wässer** drinking-water; „**kein** ~**wasser**" 'not for drinking'

Trio das; ~s, ~s *(Musik, fig.)* trio

trippeln *itr. V.; mit sein* trip; ⟨*child*⟩ patter

trist *Adj.* dreary; dismal

tritt *Imperativ Sg. u. 3. Pers. Sg. Präsens v.* **treten**; **Tritt** der; ~|e|s, ~e *(Schritt; Trittbrett)* step; *(Fuß~)* kick; **Tritt·brett** das step

Triumph der; ~|e|s, ~e triumph; **triumphieren** *itr. V.* a) exult; b) *(siegen)* be triumphant; triumph *(lit. or fig.)* (**über** + *Akk.* over)

trivial 1. *Adj.* a) *(platt)* banal; trite; *(unbedeutend)* trivial; b) *(alltäglich)* humdrum ⟨*life, career*⟩; 2. *adv. (platt)* banally; ⟨*say etc.*⟩ tritely

trocken 1. *Adj. (auch fig.)* dry; 2. *adv.* drily; **Trocken·haube** die [hood-type] hair-drier; **Trockenheit** die; ~, ~en a) *o. Pl.* dryness; b) *(Dürreperiode)* drought

trocken-, Trocken-: ~|**legen** *tr. V.* a) ein Baby ~legen change a baby's nappies *(Brit.)* or *(Amer.)* diapers; b) *(entwässern)* drain ⟨*marsh, pond, etc.*⟩; ~**milch** die dried milk; ~|**reiben** *unr. tr. V.* rub ⟨*hair, child, etc.*⟩ dry; wipe ⟨*crockery, window, etc.*⟩ dry

trocknen 1. *itr. V.; meist mit sein* dry; 2. *tr. V.* dry

Tröddel die; ~, ~n tassel

Trödel der; ~s *(ugs.)* junk; *(für den Flohmarkt)* jumble; **trödeln** *itr. V.* a) *(ugs.)* dawdle (**mit** over); b) *mit sein (ugs.: schlendern)* saunter; **Trödler** der; ~s, ~ *(ugs.)* junk-dealer

troff *1. u. 3. Pers. Sg. Prät. v.* **triefen**

trog *1. u. 3. Pers. Sg. Prät. v.* **trügen**

Trog der; ~|e|s, Tröge trough

trollen *(ugs.) refl. V.* push off *(coll.)*

Trommel die; ~, ~n drum; **trommeln** 1. *itr. V.* a) beat the drum; *(als Beruf, Hobby usw.)* play the drums; b)

([auf etw.] schlagen, auftreffen) drum (**auf** + *Akk.* on, **an** + *Akk.* against); **Trommel·wirbel** der drum-roll; **Trommler** der; ~s, ~drummer

Trompete die; ~, ~n trumpet; **trompeten** 1. *itr. V.* play the trumpet; *(fig.)* ⟨*elephant*⟩ trumpet; 2. *tr. V.* play ⟨*piece*⟩ on the trumpet; **Trompeter** der; ~s, ~trumpeter

Tropen *Pl.* tropics; **Tropen-** tropical; **Tropen·helm** der sun-helmet

Tropf der; ~|e|s, ~e *(Med.)* drip; **Tröpfchen** das; ~s, ~: droplet; *(kleine Menge)* drop; **tröpfeln** 1. *itr. V.* **a)** *mit sein* drip (**auf** + *Akk.* on to, **aus,** von from); b) *unpers. (ugs.: leicht regnen)* es tröpfelt it's spitting [with rain]; 2. *tr. V.* let ⟨*sth.*⟩ drip (**in** + *Akk.* into, **auf** + *Akk.* on to); **tropfen** 1. *itr. V.; mit Richtungsangabe mit sein* drip; ⟨*tears*⟩ fall; *unpers.* es tropft [**vom Dach** *usw.*] water is dripping from the roof *etc.*; 2. *tr. V.* let ⟨*sth.*⟩ drip (**in** + *Akk.* into, **auf** + *Akk.* on to); **Tropfen** der; ~s, ~ drop; **ein guter/edler** ~: a good/fine vintage; **Tropfstein·höhle** die limestone cave with stalactites and/or stalagmites

Trophäe die; ~, ~n *(hist., Jagd, Sport)* trophy

tropisch *Adj.* tropical

Troß der; Trosses, Trosse a) *(Milit.)* baggage train; b) *(Gefolge)* retinue; *(fig.: Zug)* procession [of hangers-on]

Trost der; ~|e|s consolation; *(bes. geistlich)* comfort; **nicht |ganz od. recht| bei** ~ **sein** *(ugs.)* be out of one's mind; **trösten** 1. *tr. V.* comfort, console (**mit** with); 2. *refl. V.* console oneself; **tröstlich** *Adj.* comforting; **trost·los** *Adj.* **a)** hopeless; *(verzweifelt)* in despair *postpos.*; b) *(deprimierend, öde)* miserable; dreary; hopeless ⟨*situation*⟩; **Trost·preis** der consolation prize

Trott der; ~|e|s, ~e trot; *(fig.)* routine

Trottel der; ~s, ~ *(ugs.)* fool; **trottelig** *(ugs.)* 1. *Adj.* doddery; 2. *adv.* in a feeble-minded way

trotten *itr. V.; mit sein* trot [along]

trotz *Präp. mit Gen., seltener mit Dat.* in spite of; despite; **Trotz** der; ~es defiance; **trotz·dem** [*auch:* '-'-] *Adv.* nevertheless; **trotzen** *itr. V.* a) *(geh.: widerstehen)* jmdm./einer Sache ~ *(auch fig.)* defy sb./sth.; b) *(trotzig sein)* be contrary; **trotzig** 1. *Adj.* defiant; *(widerspenstig)* contrary; difficult ⟨*child*⟩; 2. *adv.* defiantly

trüb[e] 1. *Adj.* **a)** *(nicht klar)* murky ‹*stream, water*›; cloudy ‹*liquid, wine, juice*›; *(schlammig)* muddy ‹*puddle*›; *(schmutzig)* dirty ‹*glass, window-pane*›; dull ‹*eyes*›; **b)** *(nicht hell)* dim ‹*light*›; dull, dismal ‹*day, weather*›; grey, overcast ‹*sky*›; 2. *adv.* ‹*shine, light*› dimly

Trubel der; ~s [hustle and] bustle

trüben 1. *tr. V.* **a)** make ‹*liquid*› cloudy; cloud ‹*liquid*›; **b)** *(beeinträchtigen)* dampen ‹*mood*›; mar ‹*relationship*›; cloud ‹*judgement*›; 2. *refl. V.* ‹*liquid*› become cloudy; ‹*eyes*› become dull; ‹*sky*› darken; **Trübsal** die; ~, ~e *(geh.)* **a)** *(Leiden)* affliction; **b)** *o. Pl. (Kummer)* grief; ~ **blasen** *(ugs.)* mope (**wegen** over, about)

trüb-, Trüb-: ~**selig** 1. *Adj.* **a)** *(öde)* dreary, depressing ‹*place, area, colour*›; **b)** *(traurig)* gloomy; 2. *adv. (traurig)* gloomily; ~**sinn** der; *o. Pl.* melancholy; ~**sinnig** 1. *Adj.* melancholy; 2. *adv.* gloomily

Trübung die; ~, ~**en a)** clouding; *(des Auges)* dimming; **b)** *(Beeinträchtigung)* deterioration; *(der Stimmung)* dampening

trudeln *itr. V.* mit sein roll

Trüffel die; ~, ~n truffle

trug *1. u. 3. Pers. Prät. v.* **tragen**; **trüge** *1. u. 3. Pers. Sg. Konjunktiv II v.* **tragen**

trügen 1. *unr. tr. V.* deceive; 2. *unr. itr. V.* be deceptive; ‹*feeling, deception*› be a delusion; **trügerisch** 1. *Adj.* deceptive; false ‹*hope, sign, etc.*›; treacherous ‹*ice*›; 2. *adv.* deceptively

Truhe die; ~, ~n chest

Trümmer *Pl. (eines Gebäudes)* rubble *sing.; (Ruinen)* ruins; *(eines Flugzeugs usw.)* wreckage *sing.; (kleinere Teile)* debris *sing.;* **Trümmer·haufen** der pile *or* heap of rubble

Trumpf der; ~[e]s, Trümpfe *(auch fig.)* trump [card]; *(Farbe)* trumps *pl.;* ~ **sein** *(fig.: Mode sein)* be the in thing; **trumpfen** *itr. V.* play a trump

Trunk der; ~[e]s, Trünke *(geh.) (Getränk)* drink; beverage *(formal);* **Trunkenheit** die; ~: drunkenness; ~ **am Steuer** drunken driving; **Trunk·sucht** die; *o. Pl.* alcoholism *no art.*

Trupp der; ~s, ~s troop; *(von Arbeitern, Gefangenen)* gang; *(von Soldaten, Polizisten)* squad; **Truppe** die; ~, ~n **a)** *(Einheit der Streitkräfte)* unit; **b)** *Pl. (Soldaten)* troops; **c)** *o. Pl. (Streit-*

kräfte) [armed] forces *pl.; (Heer)* army; **d)** *(Gruppe von Schauspielern, Artisten)* troupe; *(von Sportlern)* squad

Trut·hahn der turkey [cock]

tschau *Interj. (ugs.)* ciao *(coll.)*

Tscheche der; ~n, ~n Czech; **tschechisch** *Adj.* Czech; **Tschechoslowakei** die; ~: Czechoslovakia *no art.;* **tschechoslowakisch** *Adj.* Czechoslovak[iaɲ]

tschüs *Interj. (ugs.)* bye *(coll.)*

Tsd. *Abk.* Tausend

T-Shirt ['tiːʃəːt] das; ~s, ~s T-shirt

Tube die; ~, ~n tube

Tuberkulose die; ~, ~n *(Med.)* tuberculosis *no art.*

Tuch das; ~[e]s, Tücher *od.* ~e **a)** *Pl.* Tücher cloth; *(Kopf~, Hals~)* scarf; **b)** *Pl.* ~e *(Gewebe)* cloth

tüchtig 1. *Adj.* **a)** efficient; *(fähig)* capable, competent (**in** + *Dat.* at); **b)** *(ugs.: beträchtlich)* sizeable ‹*piece, portion*›; big ‹*gulp*›; hearty ‹*eater, appetite*›; 2. *adv.* **a)** efficiently; *(fähig)* competently; **b)** *(ugs.: sehr)* really ‹*cold, warm*›; ‹*snow, rain*› good and proper *(coll.);* ‹*eat*› heartily; **Tüchtigkeit** die; ~: efficiency; *(Fähigkeit)* ability; competence; *(Fleiß)* industry

Tücke die; ~, ~n **a)** *o. Pl. (Hinterhältigkeit)* deceit[fulness]; *(List)* guile; **b)** *meist Pl. ([verborgene] Gefahr/Schwierigkeit)* [hidden] danger/difficulty

tuckern *itr. V.; mit Richtungsangabe mit sein* chug

tückisch 1. *Adj.* **a)** *(hinterhältig)* wily; *(betrügerisch)* deceitful; **b)** *(gefährlich)* treacherous ‹*bend, slope, spot, etc.*›; 2. *adv.* craftily

tüfteln *itr. V. (ugs.)* fiddle (**an** + *Dat.* with); do finicky work (**an** + *Dat.* on); *(geistig)* rack one's brains (**an** + *Dat.* over)

Tugend die; ~, ~en virtue; **tugendhaft** 1. *Adj.* virtuous; 2. *adv.* virtuously

Tüll der; ~s, ~e tulle

Tülle die; ~, ~n *(bes. nordd.)* spout

Tulpe die; ~, ~n tulip

tummeln *refl. V.* romp [about]; **Tummel·platz** der *(auch fig.)* playground

Tumor der; ~s, ~en *(Med.)* tumour

Tümpel der; ~s, ~: pond

Tumult der; ~[e]s, ~e tumult; commotion; *(Protest)* uproar

tun 1. *unr. tr. V.* **a)** *(so etwas tut man nicht* that is just not done; [etwas] mit etw./jmdm. zu ~ haben be concerned

with sth./have dealings with sb.; **b)** *als
Funktionsverb* make ⟨*remark, catch,
etc.*⟩; take ⟨*step, jump*⟩; do ⟨*deed*⟩; **c)**
(bewirken) work, perform ⟨*miracle*⟩;
d) *(an~)* jmdm. etw. ~: do sth. to sb.;
e) es ~ *(ugs.: genügen)* be good
enough; **f)** *(ugs.: irgendwohin bringen)*
put; **2.** *unr. itr. V.* **a)** *(ugs.: funktionieren)* work; **b) freundlich/geheimnisvoll**
~: pretend to be *or (coll.)* act friendly/
act mysteriously; **3.** *unr. refl. V.; unpers.* es hat sich einiges getan quite a
bit has happened

Tünche die; ~, ~n distemper; wash;
|weiße| ~: whitewash; **tünchen** *tr.
(auch itr.) V.* distemper; weiß ~:
whitewash

Tunell das; ~s, ~s *(südd., österr.,
schweiz.) s.* **Tunnel**

Tunesien [tu'ne:ziən] (das); ~s Tunisia; **tunesisch** *Adj.* Tunisian

Tunke die; ~, ~n *(bes. ostmd.)* sauce;
(Bratensoße) gravy; **tunken** *tr. V.
(bes. ostmd.)* dip

Tunnel der; ~s, ~ *od.* ~s tunnel

tupfen *tr. V.* **a)** dab; **b)** *(mit Tupfen
versehen)* dot; **Tupfen** der; ~s, ~:
dot; *(größer)* spot; **Tupfer** der; ~s, ~
(Med.) swab

Tür die; ~, ~en door; *(Garten~)* gate;
an die ~ gehen *(öffnen)* [go and]
answer the door; **vor die ~ gehen** go
outside

Turban der; ~s, ~e turban

Turbine die; ~, ~n turbine

turbulent 1. *Adj. (auch fachspr.)* turbulent; **2.** *adv. (auch fachspr.)* turbu-
lently

Tür·griff der door-handle

Türke der; ~n, ~n Turk; **Türkei** die;
~: Turkey *no art.*

türkis *indekl. Adj.* turquoise; **Türkis**
der; ~es, ~e turquoise

türkisch *Adj.* Turkish

Tür·klinke die door-handle

Turm der; ~|e|s, **Türme a)** tower; *(spit-
zer Kirch~)* spire; steeple; **b)** *(Schach)*
rook; **c)** *(Sprung~)* diving-platform;
Türmchen das; ~s, ~: turret; **¹tür-
men 1.** *tr. V. (stapeln)* stack up; *(häufen)* pile up; **2.** *refl. V.* be piled up;
⟨*clouds*⟩ gather

²türmen *itr. V.; mit sein (salopp)* scar-
per *(Brit. sl.)*

Turm·falke der kestrel

turnen 1. *itr. V.* do gymnastics;
(Schulw.) do gym; **2.** *tr. V.* do, perform ⟨*exercise, routine*⟩; **Turnen** das;
~s gymnastics *sing., no art.; (Schulw.)*

gym *no art.;* PE *no art.;* **Turner** der;
~s, ~, **Turnerin** die; ~, ~nen gymnast

Turn-: ~**halle** die gymnasium;
~**hemd** das [gym] singlet; ~**hose** die
gym shorts *pl.*

Turnier das; ~s, ~e *(auch hist.)* tournament; *(Reit~)* show; *(Tanz~)* competition

Turn·schuh der gym shoe

Turnus der; ~, ~se regular cycle

Turn·verein der gymnastics club

Tusch der; ~|e|s, ~e fanfare

Tusche die; ~, ~n Indian *(Brit.) or
(Amer.)* India ink

tuscheln *itr., tr. V.* whisper

Tüte die; ~, ~n bag

tuten *itr. V.* hoot; ⟨*siren, [fog-]horn*⟩
sound

Typ der; ~s, ~en **a)** type; **b)** *Gen. auch*
~en *(ugs.: Mann)* bloke *(Brit. sl.);* **Type** die; ~, ~n *(Druck~, Schreibma-
schinen~)* type

Typhus der; ~ typhoid [fever]

typisch 1. *Adj.* typical (für of); **2.** *adv.*
typically

Tyrann der; ~en, ~en *(auch fig.)* tyrant; **Tyrannei** die; ~, ~en *(auch fig.)*
tyranny; **tyrannisch 1.** *Adj.* tyrannical; **2.** *adv.* tyrannically; **tyranni-
sieren** *tr. V.* tyrannize

U

u, U [u:] das; ~, ~: u, U

ü, Ü [y:] das; ~, ~: u umlaut

u. *Abk.* und

u. a. *Abk.* **unter anderem**

U-Bahn die underground *(Brit.);* subway *(Amer.); (bes. in London)* tube;
U-Bahn-Station die underground
station *(Brit.);* subway station
(Amer.); (bes. in London) tube station

übel *Adj.* **a)** foul, nasty ⟨*smell,
weather*⟩; bad, nasty ⟨*headache, cold,
taste*⟩; nasty ⟨*consequences, situation*⟩; sorry ⟨*state, affair*⟩; foul,
(coll.) filthy ⟨*mood*⟩; **nicht** ~ *(ugs.)* not
bad at all; **b)** *(unwohl)* jmdm. ist/wird
~: sb. feels sick; **c)** *(verwerflich)* bad;

wicked; nasty, dirty ⟨*trick*⟩. **Übel** das; **~s, ~** evil; **Übelkeit** die; **~, ~en** nausea

übel|nehmen *unr. tr. V.* jmdm. etw. **~:** hold sth. against sb.; etw. **~:** take offence at sth.; **Übel·täter** der wrongdoer

üben *tr. V.* **a)** *(auch itr.)* practise; rehearse ⟨*scene, play*⟩; practise on ⟨*musical instrument*⟩; **b)** *(trainieren, schulen)* exercise ⟨*fingers*⟩; train ⟨*memory*⟩

über 1. *Präp. mit Dat.* **a)** *(Lage, Standort)* over; above; *(in einer Rangfolge)* above; **~** jmdm. wohnen live above sb.; **zehn Grad ~ Null** ten degrees above zero; **sie trug eine Jacke ~ dem Kleid** she wore a jacket over her dress; **b)** *(während)* during; **~ dem Lesen/der Arbeit einschlafen** fall asleep over one's book/magazine *etc./*over one's work; **2.** *Präp. mit Akk.* **a)** *(Richtung)* over; *(quer hinüber)* across; **~ Ulm nach Stuttgart** via Ulm to Stuttgart; **b)** *(während)* over; *(für die Dauer von)* for; **c)** *(betreffend)* about; **~ etw. reden/schreiben** talk/write about sth.; **ein Scheck/eine Rechnung ~ 1 000 Mark** a cheque/bill for 1,000 marks; **d) Kinder ~ 10 Jahre** children over ten [years of age]; **2.** *Adv.* **a)** *(mehr als)* over; **b) ~ und ~:** all over

über·all [*od.* --'-] *Adv.* **a)** everywhere; **b)** *(bei jeder Gelegenheit)* always

über·anstrengen *tr. V.* overtax ⟨*person, energy*⟩; strain ⟨*eyes, nerves, heart*⟩; **sich ~:** over-exert oneself

über·arbeiten 1. *tr. V.* rework; revise ⟨*text, edition*⟩; **2.** *refl. V.* overwork

über·aus *Adv. (geh.)* extremely

über·backen *unr. tr. V.* etw. mit Käse usw. **~:** top sth. with cheese *etc.* and brown it lightly [under the grill/in a hot oven]

überbelichten[1] *tr. V. (Fot.)* overexpose

über·bieten *unr. tr. V.* **a)** outbid (um by); **b)** *(übertreffen)* surpass; outdo ⟨*rival*⟩; break ⟨*record*⟩ (um by); exceed ⟨*target*⟩ (um by)

Über·blick der **a)** view; einen guten **~ über etw.** *(Akk.)* haben have a good view over sth.; **b)** *(Abriß)* survey; **c)** *o. Pl. (Einblick)* overall view; **über·blicken** *tr. V. s.* übersehen a, b

über·bringen *unr. tr. V.* deliver; convey ⟨*greetings, congratulations*⟩

über·brücken *tr. V.* bridge ⟨*gap, gulf*⟩; reconcile ⟨*difference*⟩; **Überbrückung** die; **~, ~en** *(fig.)* bridging; *(von Gegensätzen)* reconciliation

überdacht *Adj.* covered ⟨*terrace, station platform, etc.*⟩

über·dauern *tr. V.* survive ⟨*war, separation, hardship*⟩.

über·dies *Adv.* moreover

Über·druck der; *Pl.* **~drücke** excess pressure

Überdruß der; **Überdrusses** surfeit (an + *Dat.* of); **überdrüssig** *Adj.* jmds./einer Sache **~** sein/werden be/grow tired of sb./sth.

über·eilen *tr. V.* rush; **übereilt** overhasty

über·einander *Adv.* **a)** one on top of the other; **b)** ⟨*talk etc.*⟩ about each other

übereinander-: ~|legen *tr. V.* Holzscheite usw. **~legen** lay pieces of wood *etc.* one on top of the other; **~|schlagen** *unr. tr. V.* die Arme/Beine **~schlagen** fold one's arms/cross one's legs

überein|kommen *unr. itr. V.; mit sein* agree; come to an agreement; **Übereinkommen** das; **~, ~, Übereinkunft** die; **~, Übereinkünfte** agreement

überein|stimmen *itr. V.* **a)** *(einer Meinung sein)* agree (in + *Dat.* on); **b)** *(sich gleichen)* ⟨*colours, styles*⟩ match; ⟨*figures, statements, reports, results*⟩ tally, agree; ⟨*views, opinions*⟩ coincide; **Überein·stimmung** die **a)** agreement (in + *Dat.* on; *Gen.* between)

über·empfindlich 1. *Adj.* oversensitive (gegen to); *(Med.)* hypersensitive (gegen to). **2.** *adv.* oversensitively; *(Med.)* hypersensitively

[1]über|fahren 1. *unr. tr. V.* jmdn. **~:** ferry *or* take sb. over; **2.** *unr. itr. V.; mit sein* cross over; **[2]über·fahren** *unr. tr. V.* **a)** run over; **b)** *(hinwegfahren über)* cross; go over ⟨*crossroads*⟩; **Über·fahrt** die crossing (über + *Akk.* of)

Über·fall der attack (auf + *Akk.* on); *(aus dem Hinterhalt)* ambush (auf + *Akk.* on); *(mit vorgehaltener Waffe)* hold-up; *(auf eine Bank o.ä.)* raid (auf + *Akk.* on); **über·fallen** *unr. tr. V.* **a)** attack; raid ⟨*bank, enemy position, village, etc.*⟩; *(hinterrücks)* ambush; *(mit vorgehaltener Waffe)* hold

---

[1] *ich überbelichte, überbelichtet, überzubelichten*

up; b) *(überkommen)* ⟨*tiredness, home-
sickness, fear*⟩ come over; **über·fäl-
lig** *Adj.* overdue
über·fliegen *unr. tr. V.* **a)** fly over;
overfly *(formal);* **b)** *(flüchtig lesen)*
skim [through]
über·flügeln *tr. V.* outshine; outstrip
Über·fluß der; *o. Pl.* abundance **(an**
+ *Dat.* of); *(Wohlstand)* affluence;
über·flüssig *Adj.* superfluous; unnecessary ⟨*purchase, words, work*⟩
über·fluten *tr. V. (auch fig.)* flood
über·fordern *tr. V.* jmdn. |mit etw.| ~:
overtax sb. [with sth.]; ask *or* demand
too much of sb. [with sth.]
¹über|führen *tr. V.* transfer; **²über-
führen** *tr. V.* **a)** *s.* **¹überführen**; **b)**
jmdn. |eines Verbrechens| ~: find sb.
guilty [of a crime]; convict sb. [of a
crime]; **Über·führung** die **a)** transfer; **b)** *(eines Verdächtigen)* conviction; **c)** *(Brücke)* bridge; *(Hochstraße)*
overpass; *(Fußgänger~)* [foot-]bridge
über·füllt *Adj.* crammed full **(von**
with); *(mit Menschen)* overcrowded
(von with); over-subscribed ⟨*course*⟩
Über·gabe die **a)** handing over **(an** +
Akk. to); *(von Macht)* handing over;
b) *(Auslieferung an den Gegner)* surrender **(an** + *Akk.* to)
Über·gang der **a)** crossing; **b)** *(Stelle
zum Überqueren)* crossing; *(Bahn~)*
level crossing *(Brit.);* grade crossing
(Amer.); *(Grenz~)* crossing-point; **c)**
(Wechsel, Überleitung) transition **(zu,
auf** + *Akk.* to)
über·geben 1. *unr. tr. V.* **a)** hand
over; pass ⟨*baton*⟩; **b)** *(übereignen)*
transfer, make over *(Dat.* to); **c)** *(ausliefern)* surrender *(Dat.*, **an** + *Akk.*
to); **d) eine Straße dem Verkehr** ~:
open a road to traffic; **2.** *unr. refl. V.*
(sich erbrechen) vomit
¹über|gehen *unr. itr. V.; mit sein* **a)**
pass; **b) zu etw.** ~: go over to sth.; **c) in
etw.** *(Akk.)* ~ *(zu etw. werden)* turn
into sth.
²über·gehen *unr. tr. V.* **a)** *(nicht beachten)* ignore; **b)** *(auslassen, überspringen)* skip [over]; **c)** *(nicht berücksichtigen)* pass over
über·geordnet *Adj.* higher ⟨*court,
authority, position*⟩; greater ⟨*significance*⟩; superordinate ⟨*concept*⟩
Über·gewicht das **a)** excess weight;
(von Person) overweight; **b)** *(fig.)*
predominance
über·glücklich *Adj.* blissfully
happy; *(hoch erfreut)* overjoyed

über|greifen *unr. itr. V.* **auf etw.**
(Akk.) ~: spread to sth.
Über·griff der *(unrechtmäßiger Eingriff)* encroachment (**auf** + *Akk.* on);
infringement (**auf** + *Akk.* of); *(Angriff)* attack (**auf** + *Akk.* on)
Über·größe die outsize
überhand|nehmen *unr. itr. V.* get
out of hand; ⟨*attacks, muggings, etc.*⟩
increase alarmingly; ⟨*weeds*⟩ run riot
über|hängen *tr. V.* sich *(Dat.)* eine
Jacke ~: put a jacket round one's
shoulders; sich *(Dat.)* das Gewehr/die
Tasche ~: hang the rifle/bag over
one's shoulder
über·häufen *tr. V.* jmdn. mit etw. ~:
heap *or* shower sth. on sb.
überhaupt *Adv.* **a)** in general; **b)** ~
nicht not at all; ~ keine Zeit haben
have no time at all; ~ nichts nothing
at all
überheblich 1. *Adj.* arrogant; supercilious ⟨*grin*⟩; **2.** *adv.* arrogantly;
⟨*grin*⟩ superciliously
Überheblichkeit die; ~: arrogance
über·holen 1. *tr. V.* **a)** overtake *(esp.
Brit.);* pass *(esp. Amer.);* **b)** *(übertreffen)* outstrip; **c)** *(wieder instand setzen)* overhaul; **2.** *itr. V.* overtake *(esp.
Brit.);* pass *(esp. Amer.);* **Überholspur** die overtaking lane *(esp. Brit.);*
pass lane *(esp. Amer.);* **überholt** *Adj.*
(veraltet) outdated; **Überholung**
die; ~, ~en overhaul
Überhol·verbot das prohibition of
overtaking
über·hören *tr. V.* not hear
über·irdisch 1. *Adj.* celestial;
heavenly; *(übernatürlich)* supernatural; **2.** *adv.* celestially; *(übernatürlich)* supernaturally
über|kochen *itr. V.; mit sein (auch fig.
ugs.)* boil over
über·kommen *unr. tr. V.* Mitleid/
Ekel/Furcht überkam mich I was overcome by pity/revulsion/fear
über·laden *unr. tr. V. (auch fig.)* overload
über·lassen *unr. tr. V.* **a)** jmdm. etw.
~: let sb. have sth.; **b)** sich *(Dat.)*
selbst ~ sein be left to one's own de-
vices; **c)** etw. jmdm. ~ *(etw. jmdn. ent-
scheiden/tun lassen)* leave sth. to sb.
über·lasten *tr. V.* overload; overtax
⟨*person*⟩; *(mit Arbeit)* overwork ⟨*person*⟩
Über·lauf der overflow; **¹über|lau-
fen** *unr. itr. V.; mit sein* **a)** overflow;
b) *(auf die gegnerische Seite überwech-*

seln) defect; ⟨*partisan*⟩ go over to the other side; ²**über·laufen** *unr. tr. V.* seize; **ein Frösteln/Schauer überlief mich, es überlief mich ǀeisǀkalt** a cold shiver ran down my spine; ³**über-laufen** *Adj.* overcrowded; **Über-läufer der** *(auch fig.)* defector
über·leben *tr. V.* survive; **Über·le-bende der/die;** *adj. Dekl.* survivor
¹**überǀlegen** *tr. V.* jmdm. etw. ~: put sth. over sb.; ²**über·legen 1.** *tr. V.* consider; think about; **es sich anders ~:** change one's mind; **2.** *itr. V.* think; ³**überlegen 1.** *Adj.* **a)** superior; clear, convincing ⟨*win, victory*⟩; **jmdm. ~ sein** be superior to sb. (**an** + *Dat.* in); **b)** *(herablassend)* supercilious; **2.** *adv.* **a)** in a superior manner; ⟨*play*⟩ much the better: ⟨*win, argue*⟩ convincingly; **b)** *(herablassend)* superciliously; **Überlegenheit die;** ~ superiority; **überlegt 1.** *Adj.* carefully considered; **2.** *adv.* in a carefully considered way; **Überlegung die;** ~, ~**en a)** *o. Pl.* thought; **b)** *(Gedanke)* idea; ~**en** *(Gedankengang)* thoughts
über·liefern *tr. V.* hand down; **Über·lieferung die** tradition
überlisten *tr. V.* outwit
überm *Präp.* + *Art.* = **über dem**
Über·macht die; *o. Pl.* superior strength; *(zahlenmäßig)* superior numbers *pl.*
über·mannen *tr. V.* overcome
Über·maß das; *o. Pl.* excessive amount, excess (**an** + *Dat.* of); **über·mäßig 1.** *Adj.* excessive; **2.** *adv.* excessively
über·menschlich *Adj.* superhuman
über·mitteln *tr. V.* send; *(als Mittler weitergeben)* pass on, convey ⟨*greetings, regards, etc.*⟩
über·morgen *Adv.* the day after tomorrow
Übermüdung die; ~: overtiredness
Über·mut der high spirits *pl.;* **über-mütig 1.** *Adj.* high-spirited; **2.** *adv.* high-spiritedly
über·nächst... *Adj.* im ~**en Jahr,** ~**es Jahr** the year after next; **am** ~**en Tag** two days later
über·nachten *itr. V.* stay overnight; **übernächtigt** *Adj.* ⟨*person*⟩ tired or worn out [through lack of sleep]; tired ⟨*face, look, etc.*⟩; **Übernachtung die;** ~, ~**en** overnight stay; ~ **und Frühstück** bed and breakfast
Übernahme die; ~ *(von Waren, einer Sendung)* taking delivery *no art.; (ei-*

ner Idee usw.) adoption, taking over *no indef. art.; (der Macht, einer Praxis usw.)* take over
über·natürlich *Adj.* supernatural
über·nehmen 1. *unr. tr. V.* take delivery of ⟨*goods, consignment*⟩; take over ⟨*power, practice, business, etc.*⟩; take on ⟨*job, position, etc.*⟩; undertake to pay ⟨*costs*⟩; **b)** *(sich zu eigen machen)* adopt ⟨*ideas, methods, subject, etc.*⟩ (**von** from); borrow ⟨*word, phrase*⟩ (**von** from); **2.** *unr. refl. V.* overdo things *or* it; **sich mit etw. ~:** take on too much with sth.
über·prüfen *tr. V.* check (**auf** + *Akk.* for); review ⟨*issue, situation, results*⟩; **Über·prüfung die a)** *o. Pl.* checking *no indef. art.* (**auf** + *Akk.* for); **b)** *(Kontrolle)* check; *(einer Lage, Frage usw.)* review
über·queren *tr. V.* cross
über·ragen *tr. V.* **a)** jmdn./etw. ~: tower above sb./sth.; **b)** *(übertreffen)* **jmdn. an etw.** *(Dat.)* ~: be head and shoulders above sb. in sth.; **überra-gend 1.** *Adj.* outstanding; **2.** *adv.* outstandingly
überraschen *tr. V.* surprise; **Über-raschung die;** ~, ~**en** surprise
über·reden *tr. V.* persuade
über·reichen *tr. V.* ǀjmdm.ǀ etw. ~: present sth. [to sb.]
über·rumpeln *tr. V.* jmdn. ~: take sb. by surprise
über·runden *tr. V.* **a)** *(Sport)* lap; **b)** *(übertreffen)* outstrip
übers *Präp.* + *Art.* = **über das**
Überschall-: ~**flugzeug das** supersonic aircraft; ~**geschwindigkeit die** supersonic speed
über·schätzen *tr. V.* overestimate; overrate ⟨*artist, talent, etc.*⟩
überschaubar *Adj.* **eine** ~**e Menge/ Zahl** a manageable quantity/number
Über·schlag der a) rough calculation *or* estimate; **b)** *(Turnen)* handspring; **c)** *s.* **Looping;** ¹**überǀschlagen 1.** *unr. tr. V.* **die Beine** ~: cross one's legs; **2.** *unr. itr. V.; mit sein* ⟨*wave*⟩ break; ²**über·schlagen 1.** *unr. tr. V.* **a)** skip ⟨*chapter, page, etc.*⟩; **b)** *(ungefähr berechnen)* calculate *or* estimate roughly; **2.** *unr. refl. V.* go head over heels; ⟨*car*⟩ turn over
überǀschnappen *itr. V.; mit sein (ugs.)* go crazy
über·schneiden *unr. refl. V.* cross, intersect; *(fig.)* overlap
über·schreiben *unr. tr. V.* **a)** entitle;

head ⟨*chapter, section*⟩; **b)** etw. jmdm. od. auf jmdm. ~: transfer sth. to sb.
über·schreiten *unr. itr. V.* cross; *(fig.)* exceed
Über·schrift die heading; *(in einer Zeitung)* headline; *(Titel)* title
Über·schuß der surplus (an + *Dat.* of); **überschüssig** *Adj.* surplus
über·schütten *tr. V.* cover
Überschwang der; ~[e]s exuberance
über·schwemmen *tr. V. (auch fig.)* flood; **Überschwemmung** die; ~, ~en flood; *(das Überschwemmen)* flooding *no pl.*
über·schwenglich 1. *Adj.* effusive ⟨*words etc.*⟩; wild ⟨*joy, enthusiasm*⟩; **2.** *adv.* effusively
Über·see o. *Art.* aus od. von ~: from overseas; **in/nach** ~: overseas
über·sehen *unr. tr. V.* **a)** look out over; **b)** *(abschätzen)* assess ⟨*damage, situation, consequences, etc.*⟩; **c)** *(nicht sehen)* overlook; miss; miss ⟨*turning, signpost*⟩; **d)** *(ignorieren)* ignore
über·senden *unr. (auch regelm.) tr. V.* send
¹**über|setzen 1.** *tr. V.* ferry over; **2.** *itr. V.; auch mit sein* cross [over]; ²**übersetzen** *tr., itr. V. (auch fig.)* translate; **Über·setzer** der, **Übersetzerin** die; ~, ~nen translator; **Übersetzung** die; ~, ~en translation
Über·sicht die **a)** o. *Pl.* overall view, overview (über + *Akk.* of); **b)** *(Darstellung)* survey; *(Tabelle)* summary; **über·sichtlich 1.** *Adj.* clear; ⟨*crossroads*⟩ which allows a clear view; **2.** *adv.* clearly
¹**über|siedeln**, ²**über·siedeln** *itr. V.; mit sein* move (**nach** to)
über·spielen *tr. V.* **a)** *(hinweggehen über)* cover up; smooth over ⟨*difficult situation*⟩; **b)** *(aufnehmen)* [auf ein Tonband] ~: transfer ⟨*record*⟩ to tape; put ⟨*record*⟩ on tape
über·spitzen *tr. V.* etw. ~: push *or* carry sth. too far
über·springen *unr. tr. V.* **a)** jump ⟨*obstacle*⟩; **b)** *(auslassen)* miss out
¹**über|stehen** *unr. itr. V.; südd., österr., schweiz. mit sein* jut out
²**über·stehen** *unr. tr. V.* come through ⟨*danger, war, operation*⟩; get over ⟨*illness*⟩
über·steigen *unr. tr. V.* **a)** climb over; **b)** *(fig.)* exceed
über·stimmen *tr. V.* outvote
Über·stunde die: ~n machen do overtime

über·stürzen 1. *tr. V.* rush; **2.** *refl. V.* rush; *(rasch aufeinanderfolgen)* ⟨*events, news, etc.*⟩ come thick and fast; **überstürzt 1.** *Adj.* hurried ⟨*escape, departure*⟩; over-hasty ⟨*decision*⟩; **2.** *adv.* ⟨*decide, act*⟩ over-hastily; ⟨*depart*⟩ hurriedly
übertölpeln *tr. V.* dupe; con *(coll.)*
über·tönen *tr. V.* drown out
Übertrag der; ~[e]s, **Überträge** *(bes. Buchf.)* carry-over; **über·tragbar** *Adj.* transferable (**auf** + *Akk.* to); *(auf etw. anderes anwendbar)* applicable (**auf** + *Akk.* to); *(übersetzbar)* translatable; *(ansteckend)* infectious ⟨*disease*⟩; **über·tragen** *unr. tr. V.* **a)** transfer (**auf** + *Akk.* to); transmit ⟨*power, torque, etc.*⟩ (**auf** + *Akk.* to); communicate ⟨*disease, illness*⟩ (**auf** + *Akk.* to); carry over ⟨*subtotal*⟩; *(auf etw. anderes anwenden)* apply (**auf** + *Akk.* to); *(übersetzen)* translate; **b)** *(senden)* broadcast ⟨*concert, event, match, etc.*⟩; *(im Fernsehen)* televise; **c)** *(geben)* jmdm. Aufgaben/Pflichten *usw.* ~: hand over tasks/duties *etc.* to sb.; *(anvertrauen)* entrust sb. with tasks/duties *etc.;* **Übertragung** die; ~, ~en **a)** *s.* übertragen **a:** transference; transmission; communication; carrying over; application; translation; **b)** *(das Senden)* broadcasting; *(Sendung)* broadcast; *(im Fernsehen)* televising/television broadcast
über·treffen *unr. tr. V.* **a)** surpass, outdo (**an** + *Dat.* in); break ⟨*record*⟩; **b)** *(übersteigen)* exceed
über·treiben *unr. tr. V.* **a)** *auch itr.* exaggerate; **b)** *(zu weit treiben)* overdo; **Übertreibung** die; ~, ~en exaggeration
¹**über|treten** *unr. itr. V.; mit sein* change sides; **zum Katholizismus/Islam** ~: convert to Catholicism/Islam; ²**über·treten** *unr. tr. V.* contravene ⟨*law*⟩; violate ⟨*regulation, prohibition*⟩; **Übertretung** die; ~, ~en **a)** *s.* ²übertreten: contravention; violation; **b)** *(Vergehen)* misdemeanour
übertrieben *Adj.* **1.** exaggerated; *(übermäßig)* excessive ⟨*care, thrift, etc.*⟩; **2.** *adv.* excessively
Über·tritt der change of allegiance; switch (**zu** to); *(Rel.)* conversion (**zu** to)
über·trumpfen *tr. V.* outdo
über·vor·teilen *tr. V.* cheat
über·wachen *tr. V.* keep under sur-

veillance ⟨*suspect, agent, area, etc.*⟩; supervise ⟨*factory, workers, process*⟩; control ⟨*traffic*⟩; monitor ⟨*progress, production process, experiment, patient*⟩; **Überwachung** die; ~, ~en *s.* **überwachen:** surveillance; supervision; controlling; monitoring

überwältigen *tr. V.* **a)** overpower; **b)** *(fig.)* ⟨*sleep, emotion, fear, etc.*⟩ overcome; ⟨*sight, impressions, beauty, etc.*⟩ overwhelm; **überwältigend 1.** *Adj.* overwhelming ⟨*sight, impression, victory, majority, etc.*⟩; overpowering ⟨*smell*⟩; stunning ⟨*beauty*⟩; **2.** *adv.* stunningly ⟨*beautiful*⟩

über·weisen *unr. tr. V.* **a)** transfer ⟨*money*⟩ (**an, auf** + *Akk.* to); **b)** refer ⟨*patient*⟩ (**an** + *Akk.* to); **Überweisung** die **a)** *o. Pl.* transfer (**an, auf** + *Akk.* to); **b)** *(Summe)* remittance; **c)** *(eines Patienten)* referral (**an** + *Akk.* to)

überwiegend 1. [*auch* --'--] *Adj.* overwhelming; **2.** *adv.* mainly

über·winden 1. *unr. tr. V.* overcome; get past ⟨*stage*⟩; **2.** *unr. refl. V.* overcome one's reluctance; **sich** |dazu| ~, **etw. zu tun** bring oneself to do sth.; **Über·windung** die **a)** *s.* überwinden **1:** overcoming; getting past; **b)** *(das Sichüberwinden)* **es war eine große ~ für ihn** it cost him a great effort

Über·zahl die; *o. Pl.* majority; **überzählig** *Adj.* surplus

überzeugen 1. *tr. V.* convince; **2.** *itr. V.* be convincing; **überzeugend 1.** *Adj.* convincing; **2.** *adv.* convincingly; **überzeugt** *Adj.* convinced; **Über·zeugung** die *(feste Meinung)* conviction

¹**über|ziehen** *unr. tr. V.* pull on; ²**über·ziehen** *unr. tr. V.* **a)** etw. mit etw. ~: cover sth. with sth.; **b)** overdraw ⟨*account*⟩ (um by); **Überzug** der **a)** *(Beschichtung)* coating; **b)** *(Bezug)* cover

üblich *Adj.* usual; *(normal)* normal; *(gebräuchlich)* customary

U-Boot das submarine; sub *(coll.)*

übrig *Adj.* remaining *attrib.; (ander...)* other; **alle ~en Gäste ...:** all the other guests ...; **im ~en** besides; **es ist etwas ~:** there is some left; **übrig|bleiben** *unr. itr. V.; mit sein* be left; ⟨*food, drink*⟩ be left over; **übrigens** *Adv.* by the way; **übrig|lassen** *unr. tr. V.* leave; leave ⟨*food, drink*⟩ over

Übung die; ~, ~en **a)** exercise; **b)** *o. Pl.* *(das Üben, Geübtsein)* practice

UdSSR [u:de:|ɛs|ɛs|'ɛr] *Abk.* **die;** ~ *(1922–1991)* **Union der Sozialistischen Sowjetrepubliken** USSR

Ufer das; ~s, ~: bank; *(des Meers)* shore

UG *Abk.* Untergeschoß

Uganda (das); ~s Uganda

Uhr die; ~, ~en **a)** clock; *(Armband~, Taschen~)* watch; *(Wasser~, Gas~)* meter; *(an Meßinstrumenten)* dial; gauge; **auf die** *od.* **nach der ~** look at the time; **rund um die ~** *(ugs.)* round the clock; **b)** *o. Pl.* **acht ~:** eight o'clock; **wieviel ~ ist es?** what's the time?; what time is it?

Uhr-: ~**armband** das watch-strap; ~**kette** die watch-chain; ~**macher** der watchmaker/clockmaker; ~**werk** das clock/watch mechanism; ~**zeiger** der clock-/watch-hand; ~**zeiger·sinn** der: **im/entgegen dem ~zeigersinn** clockwise/anticlockwise; ~**zeit** die time; **jmdn. nach der ~zeit fragen** ask sb. the time

Uhu der; ~s, ~s eagle owl

Ukraine die; ~: Ukraine; **Ukrainer** der; ~s, ~, **Ukrainerin** die; ~, ~nen Ukrainian

UKW [u:ka:'ve:] *o. Art.; Abk.* Ultrakurzwelle VHF; **UKW-Sender** der VHF station; ≈ FM station

Ulk der; ~s, ~e lark *(coll.); (Streich)* trick; [practical] joke; **ulkig** *(ugs.)* **1.** *Adj.* funny; **2.** *adv.* in a funny way

Ulme die; ~, ~n elm

Ultimatum das; ~s, **Ultimaten** ultimatum

Ultra·kurz·welle die ultra-short wave; *(Rundf.: Wellenbereich)* very high frequency; VHF

Ultra·schall der *(Physik, Med.)* ultrasound; **ultra·violett** *Adj.* ultraviolet

um 1. *Präp. mit Akk.* **a)** *(räumlich)* [a]round; **um die Ecke** round the corner; **b)** *(zeitlich) (genau)* at; *(etwa)* around [about]; **c) Tag um Tag/Stunde um Stunde** day after day/hour after hour; **d)** *(bei Maß- u. Mengenangaben)* by; **2.** *Adv.* around; about; **um |die| 10 Mark/50 Personen |herum|** around *or* about ten marks/50 people; **3.** *Konj.* **a)** *(final)* **um ... zu** [in order] to; **b)** *(konsekutiv)* **er ist groß genug/ist noch zu klein, um ... zu ...:** he is big enough/is still too young to ...; **c) je ... um so** the ..., the; **um so besser/schlimmer!** all the better/worse!

um|ändern *tr. V.* change; revise ⟨*text, novel*⟩; alter ⟨*garment*⟩

umạrmen tr. V. embrace; *(an sich drücken)* hug; **Umạrmung die; ~, ~en** embrace; hug

Ụm·bau der; ~[e]s, ~ten s. **umbauen:** rebuilding; alteration; conversion; *(fig.)* reorganization; **ụm|bauen** tr., auch itr. V. rebuild; *(leicht ändern)* alter; *(zu etw. anderem)* convert (**zu** into); *(fig.)* reorganize ⟨*system, administration, etc.*⟩

ụm|benennen unr. tr. V. change the name of; rename

ụm|biegen 1. unr. tr. V. bend; **2.** unr. itr. V.; *mit sein* turn

ụm|binden unr. tr. V. put on

ụm|blättern 1. tr. V. turn [over]; **2.** itr. V. turn the page/pages

ụm|blicken refl. V. **a)** look around; **b)** *(zurückblicken)* [turn to] look back (**nach** at)

ụm|bringen unr. tr. V. kill

Ụm·bruch der a) radical change; *(Umwälzung)* upheaval; **b)** o. Pl. *(Druckw.)* make-up; *(Ergebnis)* page proofs pl.

ụm|buchen 1. tr. V. change (**auf** + Akk. to); **2.** itr. V. change one's booking (**auf** + Akk. to)

ụm|drehen 1. tr. V. turn round; turn over ⟨*coin, hand, etc.*⟩; turn ⟨*key*⟩; **2.** refl. V. turn round; *(den Kopf wenden)* turn one's head; **3.** itr. V.; *auch mit sein (ugs.: umkehren)* turn back; *(ugs.: wenden)* turn round; **Ụm·drehung die** turn; *(eines Motors usw.)* revolution; rev *(coll.)*

um·einạnder Adv. sich ~ kümmern/ sorgen take care of/worry about each other *or* one another

¹ụm|fahren unr. tr. V. knock down; **²um·fạhren** unr. tr. V. go round; make a detour round ⟨*obstruction etc.*⟩; *(im Auto)* drive round; *(im Schiff)* sail round; *(auf einer Umgehungsstraße)* bypass ⟨*town, village, etc.*⟩

ụm|fallen unr. itr. V.; *mit sein* **a)** fall over; **b)** *(zusammenbrechen)* collapse; **tot ~:** fall down dead

Ụm·fang der a) circumference; *(eines Quadrats usw.)* perimeter; *(eines Baums, Menschen usw.)* girth; **b)** *(Größe)* size; **c)** *(Ausmaß)* extent; **ụm·fang·reich** Adj. extensive; substantial ⟨*book*⟩

um·fạssen tr. V. **a)** grasp; *(umarmen)* embrace; **b)** *(enthalten)* contain; *(einschließen)* include; span, cover ⟨*period*⟩; **umfạssend 1.** Adj. full ⟨*re-*

ply, information, survey, confession⟩; extensive, wide ⟨*knowledge, powers*⟩; **2.** adv. ⟨*inform*⟩ fully

ụm|formen tr. V. reshape; revise ⟨*poem, novel*⟩; transform ⟨*person*⟩

Ụm·frage die survey; *(Politik)* opinion poll

ụm|füllen tr. V. etw. in etw. *(Akk.)* ~: transfer sth. into sth.

Ụm·gang der; o. Pl. **a)** *(gesellschaftlicher Verkehr)* contact; **b)** *(das Umgehen)* **den ~ mit Pferden lernen** learn how to handle horses; **ụmgänglich** Adj. affable; *(gesellig)* sociable

Ụmgangs-: ~**form die** gute/schlechte/keine ~**formen haben** have good/bad/no manners; ~**sprache die** colloquial language

um·geben unr. tr. V. **a)** surround; ⟨*hedge, fence, wall, etc.*⟩ enclose; **b)** **etw. mit etw.** ~: surround sth. with sth.; *(einfrieden)* enclose sth. with sth.; **Umgebung die; ~, ~en** surroundings pl.; *(Nachbarschaft)* neighbourhood; *(eines Ortes)* surrounding area

¹ụm|gehen unr. itr. V.; *mit sein* **a)** *(im Umlauf sein)* ⟨*list, rumour, etc.*⟩ go round, circulate; ⟨*illness, infection*⟩ go round; **b)** *(spuken)* **hier geht ein Gespenst um** this place is haunted; **c)** *(behandeln)* **mit jmdm. freundlich/liebevoll usw. ~:** treat sb. kindly/lovingly etc.; **er kann mit Geld nicht ~:** he can't handle money

²um·gehen unr. tr. V. **a)** go round; make a detour round; *(auf einer Umgehungsstraße)* bypass ⟨*town etc.*⟩; **b)** *(vermeiden)* avoid; evade ⟨*question, issue*⟩; **c)** *(nicht befolgen)* circumvent ⟨*law, restriction, etc.*⟩; evade ⟨*obligation, duty*⟩; **ụmgehend 1.** Adj. immediate; **2.** adv. immediately; **Umgehung die; ~, ~en a)** durch ~ der Innenstadt by bypassing *or* avoiding the town centre; **b)** s. **²umgehen c:** circumvention; evasion; **Umgehungs·straße die** bypass

umgekehrt 1. Adj. inverse ⟨*ratio, proportion*⟩; reverse ⟨*order*⟩; opposite ⟨*sign*⟩; **2.** adv. inversely ⟨*proportional*⟩

ụm|graben unr. tr. V. dig over

Ụm·hang der cape; **ụm|hängen** tr. V. **a)** etw. ~: hang sth. somewhere else; **b)** jmdm./sich einen Mantel/eine Decke ~: drape a coat/blanket round sb.'s/one's shoulders

ụm|hauen unr. tr. V. fell; *(fig.)* knock down

um·her *Adv.* around
umher-: *s.* **herum-**
um|hören *refl. V.* keep one's ears
open; *(direkt fragen)* ask around
um·jubeln *tr. V.* cheer
um|kehren 1. *itr. V.; mit sein* turn
back; 2. *tr. V.* turn upside down; turn
over ⟨*sheet of paper*⟩; *(nach links drehen)* turn ⟨*garment etc.*⟩ inside out;
(nach rechts drehen) turn ⟨*garment
etc.*⟩ right side out
um|kippen 1. *itr. V.; mit sein* a) fall
over; ⟨*boat*⟩ capsize, turn over;
⟨*vehicle*⟩ overturn; b) *(ugs.: ohnmächtig werden)* keel over; 2. *tr. V.* tip
over; knock over ⟨*lamp, vase, glass,
cup*⟩; capsize ⟨*boat*⟩; turn ⟨*boat*⟩ over;
overturn ⟨*vehicle*⟩
um|klappen *tr. V.* fold down
Umkleide·kabine die changing-
cubicle
um|knicken *itr. V.; mit sein* a) |mit
dem Fuß| ~: go over on one's ankle; b)
bend; ⟨*branch*⟩ bend and snap
um|kommen *unr. itr. V.; mit sein* die;
(bei einem Unglück, durch Gewalt) get
killed; die; ⟨*food*⟩ go off
Um·kreis der *o. Pl.* surrounding area;
im ~ von 5 km within a radius of 5
km.; **um·kreisen** *tr. V.* circle;
⟨*spacecraft, satellite*⟩ orbit; ⟨*planet*⟩ revolve [a]round
Um·lauf der a) *(von Planeten)* revolution; b) *o. Pl. (Zirkulation)* circulation; in *od.* im ~ sein be circulating;
⟨*coin, banknote*⟩ be in circulation; in ~
bringen circulate; bring ⟨*coin, banknote*⟩ into circulation; **Umlauf-
bahn** die *(Astron., Raumf.)* orbit
Um·laut der *(Sprachw.)* umlaut
um|legen *tr. V.* a) *(um einen Körper-
teil)* put on; b) *(verlegen)* transfer ⟨*patient, telephone call*⟩; c) *(salopp: ermorden)* jmdn. ~: bump sb. off *(sl.)*
um|leiten divert; **Um·leitung** die
diversion
umliegend *Adj.* surrounding ⟨*area*⟩;
(nahe) nearby ⟨*building*⟩
um|räumen 1. *tr. V.* rearrange; 2. *itr.
V.* rearrange things
um|rechnen *tr. V.* convert (in + Akk.
into)
¹um|reißen *unr. tr. V.* pull ⟨*mast, tree*⟩
down; knock ⟨*person*⟩ down; ⟨*wind*⟩
tear ⟨*tent etc.*⟩ down
²um·reißen *unr. tr. V.* outline; summarize ⟨*subject, problem, situation*⟩
um|rennen *unr. tr. V.* [run into and]
knock down

um·ringen *tr. V.* surround
Um·riß der *(auch fig.)* outline
um|rühren *tr. (auch itr.) V.* stir
um|rüsten *tr. V. (Technik)* convert
(auf + Akk. to, zu into)
ums [ʊms] *Präp. + Art.* a) = um das;
b) ~ Leben kommen lose one's life
um|satteln *itr. V. (ugs.)* change jobs;
⟨*student*⟩ change courses
Um·satz der turnover; *(Verkauf)* sales
pl. (an + *Dat.* of); ~ machen *(ugs.)*
make money
um|säumen *tr. V.* hem
um|schalten 1. *tr. V. (auch. fig.)*
switch [over] (auf + Akk. to); move
⟨*lever*⟩; 2. *itr. V.* switch *or* change over
(auf + Akk. to)
Um·schlag der a) cover; b) *(Brief~)*
envelope; c) *(Schutz~)* jacket; *(einer
Broschüre, eines Heftes)* cover; d)
(Med.: Wickel) compress; *(warm)*
poultice; **um|schlagen** 1. *unr. tr. V.*
a) turn up ⟨*sleeve, collar, trousers*⟩;
turn over ⟨*page*⟩; b) *(umladen, verladen)* turn round, trans-ship ⟨*goods*⟩;
2. *unr. itr. V.; mit sein* change (in +
Akk. into); ⟨*wind*⟩ veer [round]
¹um|schreiben *unr. tr. V.* rewrite;
²um·schreiben *unr. tr. V.* a) *(in
Worte fassen)* describe; *(definieren)*
define ⟨*meaning, sb.'s task, etc.*⟩; *(pa-
raphrasieren)* paraphrase ⟨*word, expression*⟩; b) *(Sprachw.)* construct (mit
with); **Um·schreibung** die description; *(Definition)* definition; *(Verhül-
lung)* circumlocution (Gen. for);
Um·schrift die *(Sprachw.)* transcription
um|schulen 1. *tr. V. (beruflich)* re-
train; 2. *itr. V.* retrain (auf + Akk. as)
um|schütten *tr. V.* a) pour [into an-
other container]; decant ⟨*liquid*⟩; b)
(verschütten) spill
Um·schwung der complete change;
(in der Politik usw.) U-turn
um|sehen *unr. refl. V.* a) look; sich im
Zimmer ~: look [a]round the room; b)
(zurücksehen) look round *or* back
umseitig *Adj., adv.* overleaf
um|setzen *tr. V.* a) move; *(auf ande-
ren Posten usw.)* move, transfer (in +
Akk. to); *(umpflanzen)* transplant; *(in
anderen Topf)* repot; b) *(verwirklichen)*
implement ⟨*plan*⟩; translate ⟨*plan, intention, etc.*⟩ into action *or* reality;
realize ⟨*ideas*⟩; c) *(Wirtsch.)* turn over,
have a turnover of ⟨*x marks etc.*⟩; sell
⟨*shares, goods*⟩
Um·sicht die; *o. Pl.* circumspection;

ụm·sichtig 1. *Adj.* circumspect; 2. *adv.* circumspectly

ụm|siedeln 1. *tr. V.* resettle; 2. *itr. V.; mit sein* move (in + *Akk.*, nach to)

um·sọnst *Adv.* a) *(unentgeltlich)* free; for nothing; b) *(vergebens)* in vain

Ụm·stand der a) *(Gegebenheit)* circumstance; *(Tatsache)* fact; unter Umständen possibly; b) *(Aufwand)* business; macht keine |großen| Umstände please don't go to any bother

ụmständlich 1. *Adj.* involved, elaborate ⟨procedure, method, description, explanation, etc.⟩; elaborate, laborious ⟨preparation, check, etc.⟩; awkward, difficult ⟨journey, job⟩; *(weitschweifig)* long-winded; *(Umstände machend)* awkward ⟨person⟩; 2. *adv.* in an involved or roundabout way; *(weitschweifig)* at great length

Ụmstands·kleid das maternity dress

ụmstehend *Adj.* standing round *postpos.*

ụm|steigen *unr. itr. V.* change (in + *Akk.* [on] to)

¹ụm|stellen 1. *tr. V.* a) rearrange, change round ⟨furniture, books, etc.⟩; reorder ⟨words etc.⟩; transpose ⟨two words⟩; b) *(anders einstellen)* reset ⟨lever, switch, points, clock⟩; c) *(ändern)* change or switch over (auf + *Akk.* to); 2. *refl. V.* adjust (auf + *Akk.* to);

²um·stellen *tr. V.* surround

ụm|stimmen *tr. V.* win ⟨person⟩ round

ụm|stoßen *unr. tr. V.* a) knock over; b) *(rückgängig machen)* change ⟨plan, decision⟩; *(zunichte machen)* upset, wreck ⟨plan, theory⟩

umstrịtten *Adj.* disputed; controversial ⟨book, author, policy, etc.⟩

Ụm·sturz der coup; ụm|stürzen 1. *tr. V.* overturn; *(fig.)* topple, overthrow ⟨political system, government⟩; 2. *itr. V.* overturn; ⟨wall, building, chimney⟩ fall down; ụmstürzlerisch *Adj.* subversive

Ụm·tausch der exchange; ụm|tauschen *tr. V.* exchange ⟨goods, article⟩ (gegen for); change ⟨dollars, pounds, etc.⟩ (in + *Akk.* into)

Ụm·trunk der communal drink

ụm|tun *unr. refl. V. (ugs.)* look [a]round; sich nach etw. ~: be on the look-out for sth.

ụm|wandeln *tr. V.* convert ⟨substance, building, etc.⟩ (in + *Akk.* into); *(ändern)* change; alter

Ụm·weg der detour

Ụm·welt die a) environment; b) *(Menschen)* people *pl.* around sb.

umwelt-, Ụmwelt-: ~bedingt *Adj.* caused by the or one's environment *postpos.;* ~freundlich 1. *Adj.* environment-friendly; 2. *adv.* in an ecologically desirable way; ~schutz der environmental protection *no art.;* ~schützer der environmentalist; conservationist; ~verschmutzung die pollution [of the environment]

ụm|wenden *regelm. (auch unr.) tr. V.* a) turn over ⟨page, joint, etc.⟩; b) turn round ⟨vehicle, horse⟩

ụm|werfen *unr. tr. V.* a) knock over; knock ⟨person⟩ down or over; *(fig. ugs.: aus der Fassung bringen)* bowl ⟨person⟩ over; stun ⟨person⟩; b) *(fig. ugs.: umstoßen)* knock ⟨plan⟩ on the head *(coll.);* ụmwerfend *(ugs.)* 1. *Adj.* fantastic *(coll.);* stunning *(coll.);* 2. *adv.* fantastically [well] *(coll.);* brilliantly

um·wịckeln *tr. V.* wrap; bind; *(mit einem Verband)* bandage

Umzäunung die ~, ~en fence, fencing (*Gen.* round)

ụm|ziehen 1. *unr. itr. V.; mit sein* move (an + *Akk.*, in + *Akk.*, nach to); 2. *unr. tr. V.* jmdn. ~: change sb. or get sb. changed; sich ~: change or get changed

um·zịngeln *tr. V.* surround; encircle

Ụm·zug der a) move; *(von Möbeln)* removal; b) *(Festzug)* procession

UN [u:'ɛn] *Pl.* UN *sing.*

unabänderlich 1. *Adj.* unalterable; irrevocable ⟨decision⟩; 2. *adv.* irrevocably

ụnabhängig 1. *Adj.* independent (von of); *(unbeeinflußt)* unaffected (von by); 2. *adv.* independently (von of); ~ davon, ob .../was .../wo ... *usw.* irrespective or regardless of whether .../ what .../where ... *etc.;* Ụnabhängigkeit die independence

unabkömmlich *Adj.* indispensable; sie ist im Moment ~: she is otherwise engaged

ụnablässig 1. *Adj.* incessant; 2. *adv.* incessantly

ụnabsichtlich 1. *Adj.* unintentional; 2. *adv.* unintentionally

unabwẹndbar *Adj.* inevitable

ụnachtsam 1. *Adj.* a) inattentive; b) *(nicht sorgfältig)* careless; 2. *adv. (ohne Sorgfalt)* carelessly; Ụnachtsamkeit die; ~ a) inattentiveness; b) *(mangelnde Sorgfalt)* carelessness

unangebracht *Adj.* inappropriate

unangefochten *Adj.* unchallenged; *(Rechtsw.)* uncontested ‹*verdict, will, etc.*›

unangenehm 1. *Adj.* unpleasant (*Dat.* for); *(peinlich)* embarrassing ‹*question, situation*›; **2.** *adv.* unpleasantly

unannehmbar *Adj.* unacceptable; **Unannehmlichkeit die** trouble

unansehnlich *Adj.* unprepossessing; plain ‹*girl*›

unanständig 1. *Adj.* improper; *(anstößig)* indecent; dirty ‹*joke*›; rude ‹*word, song*›; **2.** *adv.* improperly; **Unanständigkeit die** impropriety; indecency; *(Obszönität)* obscenity

unappetitlich 1. *Adj.* unappetizing; *(fig.)* unsavoury ‹*joke*›; disgusting ‹*wash-basin, nails, etc.*›; **2.** *adv.* unappetizingly

Unart die bad habit; **unartig** *Adj.* naughty

unästhetisch *Adj.* unpleasant ‹*sight etc.*›; ugly ‹*building etc.*›

unauffällig 1. *Adj.* inconspicuous; unobtrusive ‹*scar, defect, skill, behaviour, surveillance, etc.*›; discreet ‹*signal, elegance*›; **2.** *adv.* inconspicuously; unobtrusively

unaufgefordert *Adv.* without being asked

unaufhaltsam 1. *Adj.* inexorable; **2.** *adv.* inexorably

unaufmerksam *Adj.* inattentive (**gegenüber** to); careless ‹*driver*›

unaufrichtig *Adj.* insincere; **Unaufrichtigkeit die** insincerity

unausbleiblich *Adj.* inevitable

unbändig 1. *Adj.* **a)** boisterous; **b)** *(überaus groß/stark)* unbridled; **2.** *adv.* **a)** wildly; **b)** *(sehr, äußerst)* unrestrainedly; tremendously *(coll.)*

unbarmherzig *Adj.* merciless

unbeabsichtigt 1. *Adj.* unintentional; **2.** *adv.* unintentionally

unbeachtet *Adj.* unnoticed

unbedenklich *adv.* without second thoughts

unbedeutend 1. *Adj.* insignificant; minor ‹*artist, poet*›; slight, minor ‹*improvement, change, error*›; **2.** *adv.* slightly

unbedingt 1. *Adj.* absolute; **2.** *adv.* absolutely; **3.** *Adv.* *(auf jeden Fall)* whatever happens

unbefangen *Adj.* **a)** *(ungehemmt)* uninhibited; **b)** *(unvoreingenommen)* impartial

unbefristet 1. *Adj.* for an indefinite period *postpos.;* indefinite ‹*strike*›; unlimited ‹*visa*›; **2.** *adv.* for an indefinite period

unbefugt 1. *Adj.* unauthorized; **2.** *adv.* without authorization

unbegreiflich *Adj.* incomprehensible (*Dat.*, **für** to); incredible ‹*love, goodness, stupidity, carelessness, etc.*›

unbegrenzt 1. *Adj.* unlimited; **2.** *adv.* ‹*stay, keep, etc.*› indefinitely

Unbehagen das uneasiness, disquiet; *(Sorge)* concern (**an** + *Dat.* about); **unbehaglich 1.** *Adj.* uneasy ‹*feeling, atmosphere*›; uncomfortable ‹*thought, room*›; **2.** *adv.* uneasily

unbeholfen 1. *Adj.* clumsy; **2.** *adv.* clumsily

unbekannt *Adj.* **a)** unknown; *(nicht vertraut)* unfamiliar; unidentified ‹*caller, donor*›; „**Empfänger ~**" 'not known at this address'; **b)** *(nicht vielen bekannt)* little known; obscure ‹*poet, painter, etc.*›; ¹**Unbekannte der/die;** *adj. Dekl.* unknown *or* unidentified man/woman; *(Fremde[r])* stranger; ²**Unbekannte die;** *adj. Dekl. (Math.; auch fig.)* unknown

unbekleidet *Adj.* without any clothes on *postpos.;* bare ‹*torso etc.*›; naked ‹*corpse*›

unbekümmert 1. *Adj.* carefree; *(ohne Bedenken, lässig)* casual; **2.** *adv.* **a)** in a carefree way; **b)** *(ohne Bedenken)* without caring *or* worrying

unbeleuchtet *Adj.* unlit ‹*street, corridor, etc.*›; ‹*vehicle*› without [any] lights

unbeliebt *Adj.* unpopular (**bei** with)

unbemannt *Adj.* unmanned

unbemerkt *Adj., adv.* unnoticed

unbenutzt *Adj.* unused

unbequem 1. *Adj.* **a)** uncomfortable; **b)** *(lästig)* awkward, embarrassing ‹*question, opinion*›; troublesome ‹*politician etc.*›; unpleasant ‹*criticism, truth, etc.*›; **2.** *adv.* uncomfortably

unberechenbar 1. *Adj.* unpredictable; **2.** *adv.* unpredictably

unberechtigt *Adj.* **a)** *(ungerechtfertigt)* unjustified; **b)** *(unbefugt)* unauthorized

unberührt *Adj.* untouched; **sie ist noch ~:** she is still a virgin

unbeschrankt *Adj.* ‹*crossing*› without gates, with no gates

unbeschreiblich 1. *Adj.* indescribable; unimaginable ‹*fear, beauty*›; ‹*fear, beauty*› beyond description; **2.**

adv. indescribably ⟨*beautiful*⟩; unbelievably ⟨*busy*⟩

unbesorgt *Adj.* unconcerned; **seien Sie ~**: don't [you] worry

unbeständig *Adj.* changeable ⟨*weather*⟩; fickle ⟨*lover etc.*⟩

unbestimmt 1. *Adj.* **a)** indefinite; indeterminate ⟨*age, number*⟩; *(ungewiß)* uncertain; **b)** *(ungenau)* vague; **c)** *(Sprachw.)* indefinite ⟨*article, pronoun*⟩; 2. *adv. (ungenau)* vaguely

unbewacht *Adj.* unsupervised; unattended ⟨*car-park*⟩

unbewaffnet *Adj.* unarmed

unbeweglich *Adj.* motionless; still ⟨*air, water*⟩; fixed ⟨*gaze, expression*⟩

unbewußt *Adj.* unconscious

unbrauchbar *Adj.* unusable; *(untauglich)* useless ⟨*method, person*⟩

und *Konj.* and; *(folglich)* [and] so; **ich ~ tanzen?** what, me dance?; **sei so gut ~ mach das Fenster zu** be so good as to shut the window

Undank der ingratitude; **undankbar** *Adj.* ungrateful ⟨*person, behaviour*⟩

undeutlich 1. *Adj.* unclear; indistinct; *(ungenau)* vague ⟨*idea, memory, etc.*⟩; 2. *adv.* indistinctly; *(ungenau)* vaguely

undicht *Adj.* leaky; leaking; **~e** Fenster windows which do not fit tightly

undurchführbar *Adj.* impracticable

undurchlässig *Adj.* impermeable; *(wasserdicht)* watertight; waterproof; *(luftdicht)* airtight

unehelich *Adj.* illegitimate ⟨*child*⟩; unmarried ⟨*mother*⟩

unehrlich 1. *Adj.* dishonest; 2. *adv.* dishonestly; by dishonest means

uneigennützig *Adj.* unselfish

uneinig *Adj.* ⟨*party*⟩ divided by disagreement; **[sich** *(Dat.)]* **~ sein** disagree; **Uneinigkeit die** disagreement (**in** + *Dat.* on); **uneins** *Adj.; nicht attr.* **~ sein** be divided (**in** + *Dat.* on); ⟨*persons*⟩ be at variance *or* at cross purposes (**in** + *Dat.* over)

unempfindlich *Adj.* **a)** insensitive (**gegen** to); **b)** *(immun)* immune (**gegen** to, against); **c)** *(strapazierfähig)* hard-wearing

unendlich 1. *Adj.* infinite; boundless; *(zeitlich)* endless; *(Math.)* infinite; 2. *adv.* infinitely ⟨*lovable, sad*⟩; immeasurably ⟨*happy*⟩; ⟨*happy*⟩ beyond measure

unentbehrlich *Adj.* indispensable (*Dat.*, **für** to)

unentgeltlich [*od.* '----] 1. *Adj.* free;

2. *adv.* free of charge; ⟨*work*⟩ for nothing, without pay

unentschieden 1. *Adj.* unsettled; undecided ⟨*question*⟩; *(Sport, Schach)* drawn; 2. *adv.* **~ spielen** draw

unentwegt [*od.* --'-] 1. *Adj.* **a)** *(beharrlich)* persistent ⟨*fighter, champion, efforts*⟩; **b)** *(unaufhörlich)* constant; incessant; 2. *adv.* **a)** *(beharrlich)* persistently; **b)** *(unaufhörlich)* constantly; incessantly

unerbittlich 1. *Adj. (auch fig.)* inexorable; unsparing ⟨*critic*⟩; relentless ⟨*battle, struggle*⟩; implacable ⟨*hate, enemy*⟩; 2. *adv. (auch fig.)* inexorably

unerfahren *Adj.* inexperienced

unerfreulich 1. *Adj.* unpleasant; bad ⟨*news*⟩; 2. *adv.* unpleasantly

unerheblich *Adj.* insignificant

unerhört 1. *Adj. (empörend)* outrageous; 2. *adv.* outrageously

unerlaubt 1. *Adj.* unauthorized; 2. *adv.* without authorization

unermüdlich 1. *Adj.* tireless, untiring (**bei, in** + *Dat.* in); 2. *adv.* tirelessly

unerreichbar *Adj.* inaccessible; *(fig.)* unattainable; **unerreicht** *Adj.* unequalled

unerschöpflich *Adj.* inexhaustible

unersetzlich *Adj.* irreplaceable

unerträglich [*od.* '----] *Adj.* unbearable; intolerable ⟨*situation, conditions, etc.*⟩

unerwartet 1. *Adj.* unexpected; **es kam für alle ~**: it came as a surprise to everybody; 2. *adv.* unexpectedly

unerwünscht *Adj.* unwanted; unwelcome ⟨*interruption, visit, visitor*⟩; undesirable ⟨*side-effects*⟩

unfähig *Adj.* **a)** **~ sein, etw. zu tun** *(ständig)* be incapable of doing sth.; *(momentan)* be unable to do sth.; **b)** *(inkompetent)* incompetent

unfair 1. *Adj.* unfair (**gegen** to); 2. *adv.* unfairly

Un·fall der accident

Unfall-: **~arzt** der casualty doctor; **~stelle** die scene of an/the accident; **~versicherung** die accident insurance

unförmig *Adj.* shapeless; huge ⟨*legs, hands, body*⟩; bulky, ungainly ⟨*shape, shoes, etc.*⟩

unfrei *Adj.* not free *pred.*; subject, dependent ⟨*people*⟩; ⟨*life*⟩ of bondage; **unfreiwillig** 1. *Adj.* involuntary; *(erzwungen)* enforced ⟨*stay*⟩; *(nicht beabsichtigt)* unintended ⟨*publicity, joke, humour*⟩; 2. *adv.* involuntarily; without wanting to; *(unbeabsichtigt)* unintentionally

unfreundlich 1. *Adj.* unfriendly (**zu, gegen** to); unkind ⟨*words, remark*⟩; **2.** *adv.* in an unfriendly way

unfrisiert *Adj.* ungroomed ⟨*hair*⟩

unfruchtbar *Adj.* infertile; *(fig.)* unproductive; **Unfruchtbarkeit die** infertility; *(fig.)* unproductiveness

Unfug der; ~**[e]s a)** [piece of] mischief; **grober** ~: public nuisance; **b)** *(Unsinn)* nonsense

Ungar der; ~**n,** ~**n** Hungarian; **ungarisch** *Adj.* Hungarian; **Ungarn (das);** ~**s** Hungary

ungeachtet *Präp. mit Gen. (geh.)* notwithstanding; despite

ungebildet *Adj.* uneducated

ungebräuchlich *Adj.* uncommon; rare; rarely used ⟨*method, process*⟩

ungedeckt *Adj.* uncovered ⟨*cheque*⟩

Ungeduld die impatience; **ungeduldig 1.** *Adj.* impatient; **2.** *adv.* impatiently

ungeeignet *Adj.* unsuitable; *(für eine Aufgabe)* unsuited (**für, zu** to, for)

ungefähr 1. *Adj.* approximate; rough ⟨*idea, outline*⟩; **2.** *adv.* approximately; roughly

ungefährlich *Adj.* safe; harmless ⟨*animal, person, illness, etc.*⟩

ungeheizt *Adj.* unheated

ungeheuer 1. *Adj.* enormous; tremendous ⟨*strength, energy, effort, enthusiasm, fear, success, pressure, etc.*⟩; vast, immense ⟨*fortune, knowledge*⟩; *(schrecklich)* terrible *(coll.)*, terrific *(coll.)* ⟨*pain, rage*⟩; **2.** *adv.* tremendously; terribly *(coll.)* ⟨*difficult, clever*⟩; **Ungeheuer das;** ~**s,** ~ *(auch fig.)* monster

ungehindert *Adj.* unimpeded

ungehörig 1. *Adj.* improper; *(frech)* impertinent; **2.** *adv.* improperly; *(frech)* impertinently

ungehorsam *Adj.* disobedient (**gegenüber** to); **Ungehorsam der** disobedience (**gegenüber** to)

ungekürzt *Adj.* unabridged ⟨*edition, book*⟩; uncut ⟨*film, speech*⟩

ungelegen 1. *Adj.* **das kommt mir sehr** ~/**nicht** ~: that is very inconvenient *or* awkward/quite convenient for me; **2.** *adv.* inconveniently

ungelernt *Adj.* unskilled

ungemütlich 1. *Adj.* uninviting, cheerless ⟨*room, flat*⟩; uncomfortable, unfriendly ⟨*atmosphere*⟩; **2.** *adv.* uncomfortably ⟨*furnished*⟩

ungenau 1. *Adj.* inaccurate; imprecise, inexact ⟨*definition, formulation, etc.*⟩; *(undeutlich)* vague ⟨*memory, idea, impression*⟩; **2.** *adv.* inaccurately; ⟨*define*⟩ imprecisely, inexactly; ⟨*remember*⟩ vaguely

ungeniert ['ʊnʒeniːɐ̯t] **1.** *Adj.* free and easy; uninhibited; **2.** *adv.* openly; ⟨*yawn*⟩ unconcernedly; ⟨*undress etc.*⟩ without any embarrassment

ungenießbar *Adj. (nicht eßbar)* inedible; *(nicht trinkbar)* undrinkable; *(fig. ugs.)* unbearable

ungenügend 1. *Adj.* inadequate; **die Note** „~"/**ein Ungenügend** *(Schulw.)* the/an 'unsatisfactory' [mark]; **2.** *adv.* inadequately

ungepflegt *Adj.* neglected ⟨*garden, park, car, etc.*⟩; unkempt ⟨*person, appearance, hair*⟩; uncared-for ⟨*hands*⟩

ungerade *Adj.* odd ⟨*number*⟩

ungerecht 1. *Adj.* unjust, unfair (**gegen, zu, gegenüber** to); **2.** *adv.* unjustly; unfairly; **Ungerechtigkeit die;** ~, ~**en** injustice

ungern *Adv.* reluctantly; **etw.** ~ **tun** not like *or* dislike doing sth.

ungeschält *Adj.* unpeeled ⟨*fruit*⟩

ungeschickt 1. *Adj.* clumsy; awkward; **2.** *adv.* clumsily; awkwardly

ungesetzlich 1. *Adj.* unlawful; illegal; **2.** *adv.* unlawfully; illegally

ungestempelt *Adj.* uncancelled ⟨*stamp*⟩

ungestört *Adj.* undisturbed; uninterrupted ⟨*development*⟩

ungesund *Adj. (auch fig.)* unhealthy

Ungetüm das; ~**s,** ~**e** monster

ungewiß *Adj.* uncertain; **über etw.** *(Akk.)* **im ungewissen sein** be uncertain *or* unsure about sth.; **Ungewißheit die** uncertainty

ungewöhnlich 1. *Adj.* **a)** unusual; **b)** *(sehr groß)* exceptional ⟨*strength, beauty, ability, etc.*⟩; outstanding ⟨*achievement, success*⟩; **2.** *adv.* **a)** ⟨*behave*⟩ abnormally, strangely; **b)** *(enorm)* exceptionally

ungewohnt 1. *Adj.* unaccustomed; *(nicht vertraut)* unfamiliar ⟨*method, work, surroundings, etc.*⟩; **2.** *adv.* unusually

Ungeziefer das; ~**s** vermin *pl.*

ungezogen 1. *Adj.* naughty; badly behaved; bad ⟨*behaviour*⟩; *(frech)* cheeky; **2.** *adv.* naughtily; ⟨*behave*⟩ badly

ungläubig 1. *Adj.* **a)** disbelieving; **b)** *(Rel.)* unbelieving; **2.** *adv.* in disbelief; **unglaublich 1.** *Adj.* incredible; **2.** *adv.* *(ugs.: äußerst)* incredibly *(coll.);* **unglaubwürdig** *Adj.* implausible; untrustworthy, unreliable ⟨*witness etc.*⟩

ungleich 1. *Adj.* unequal; odd, unmatching ⟨*socks, gloves, etc.*⟩; *(unähnlich)* dissimilar; **2.** *adv.* **a)** unequally; **b)** *(ungleichmäßig)* unevenly

Unglück das; ~[e]s, ~e **a)** *(Unfall)* accident; *(Flugzeug*~, *Zug*~*)* crash; accident; **b)** *o. Pl. (Not)* misfortune; *(Leid)* suffering; **c)** *(Pech)* bad luck; ~ **haben** be unlucky; **das bringt** ~: that's unlucky; **d)** *(Schicksalsschlag)* misfortune; **unglücklich 1.** *Adj.* **a)** unhappy; **b)** *(nicht vom Glück begünstigt)* unfortunate ⟨*person*⟩; *(bedauernswert, arm)* hapless ⟨*person, animal*⟩; **c)** *(ungünstig, ungeschickt)* unfortunate ⟨*moment, combination, meeting, etc.*⟩; unhappy ⟨*end, choice, solution*⟩; **2.** *adv.* **a)** unhappily; **b)** *(ungünstig)* unfortunately; *(ungeschickt)* unhappily, clumsily ⟨*translated, expressed*⟩; **unglücklicherweise** *Adv.* unfortunately; **Unglücks·fall der** accident

ungültig *Adj.* invalid; void *(esp. Law)*; spoilt ⟨*vote, ballot-paper*⟩; disallowed ⟨*goal*⟩

ungünstig 1. *Adj.* **a)** unfavourable; unfortunate, bad ⟨*shape, layout*⟩; **b)** *(unpassend)* inconvenient ⟨*time*⟩; *(ungeeignet)* inappropriate, inconvenient ⟨*time, place*⟩; **2.** *adv.* **a)** unfavourably; badly ⟨*designed, laid out*⟩; **b)** *(unpassend)* inconveniently

Unheil das disaster; **unheilbar 1.** *Adj.* incurable; **2.** *adv.* incurably; **unheil·voll** *Adj.* disastrous; *(verhängnisvoll)* fateful

unheimlich 1. *Adj.* **a)** eerie; **b)** *(ugs.) (schrecklich)* terrible *(coll.)* ⟨*hunger, headache, etc.*⟩ terrific *(coll.)* ⟨*fun etc.*⟩; **2.** *adv.* **a)** eerily; **b)** *(ugs.: äußerst)* terribly *(coll.);* incredibly *(coll.)* ⟨*quick, long*⟩

unhöflich 1. *Adj.* impolite; **2.** *adv.* impolitely; **Unhöflichkeit die** impoliteness

unhygienisch 1. *Adj.* unhygienic; **2.** *adv.* unhygienically

Uniform die; ~, ~en uniform

uninteressant *Adj.* uninteresting; *(nicht von Belang)* of no interest *postpos.;* unimportant

Union [u'nio:n] **die;** ~, ~en union

Universität die; ~, ~en university

Universum das; ~s universe

Unkenntnis die; *o. Pl.* ignorance

unklar *Adj.* unclear; **sich** *(Dat.)* **über etw.** *(Akk.)* **im** ~**en sein** be unclear *or* unsure about sth.

Unkosten *Pl.* **a)** [extra] expense *sing.;* expenses; **b)** *(ugs.: Ausgaben)* costs; expenditure *sing.*

Unkraut das weeds *pl.*

unleserlich 1. *Adj.* illegible; **2.** *adv.* illegibly

unmäßig 1. *Adj.* immoderate; excessive; **2.** *adv.* excessively; ⟨*eat, drink*⟩ to excess

Unmensch der brute; **unmenschlich 1.** *Adj.* **a)** inhuman; brutal; appalling ⟨*conditions*⟩; **b)** *(entsetzlich)* appalling; **2.** *adv.* **a)** in an inhuman way; **b)** *(entsetzlich)* appallingly *(coll.)*

unmißverständlich 1. *Adj.* **a)** *(eindeutig)* unambiguous; **b)** *(offen, direkt)* blunt ⟨*answer, refusal*⟩; unequivocal ⟨*language*⟩; **2.** *adv.* **a)** *(eindeutig)* unambiguously; **b)** *(offen, direkt)* bluntly; unequivocally

unmittelbar 1. *Adj.* immediate; direct ⟨*contact, connection, influence, etc.*⟩; **2.** *adv.* immediately; directly

unmöbliert *Adj.* unfurnished

unmodern 1. *Adj.* old-fashioned; *(nicht modisch)* unfashionable; **2.** *adv.* in an old-fashioned way; *(nicht modisch)* unfashionably

unmöglich 1. *Adj.* impossible; *(ugs.: seltsam)* incredible; **2.** *adv. (ugs.) (behave)* impossibly; ⟨*dress*⟩ ridiculously; **3.** *Adv. (ugs.)* **ich/es usw. kann** ~ ...: I/it *etc.* can't possibly ...

unmoralisch 1. *Adj.* immoral; **2.** *adv.* immorally

unmündig *Adj.* under-age

unnatürlich 1. *Adj.* unnatural; forced ⟨*laugh*⟩; **2.** *adv.* unnaturally; ⟨*laugh*⟩ in a forced way; ⟨*speak*⟩ affectedly

unnötig 1. *Adj.* unnecessary; **2.** *adv.* unnecessarily

UNO ['u:no] **die;** ~: UN

unordentlich 1. *Adj.* **a)** untidy; **b)** *(ungeregelt)* disorderly ⟨*life*⟩; **2.** *adv.* untidily; ⟨*tie, treat, etc.*⟩ carelessly; **Unordnung die** disorder; mess

unparteiisch 1. *Adj.* impartial; **2.** *adv.* impartially

unpassend 1. *Adj.* inappropriate; unsuitable ⟨*dress etc.*⟩; **2.** *adv.* inappropriately; unsuitably ⟨*dressed etc.*⟩

unpersönlich 1. *Adj.* impersonal; distant, aloof ⟨*person*⟩; **2.** *adv.* impersonally; ⟨*answer, write*⟩ in impersonal terms

unpraktisch 1. *Adj.* unpractical; **2.** *adv.* in an unpractical way

unpünktlich 1. *Adj.* unpunctual ⟨*person*⟩; late, unpunctual ⟨*payment*⟩; **2.** *adv.* late

Unrecht das; *o. Pl.* wrong; **zu ~:** wrongly; **unrecht haben** be wrong; **jmdm. unrecht tun** do sb. an injustice; **unrechtmäßig 1.** *Adj.* unlawful; **2.** *adv.* unlawfully

unregelmäßig 1. *Adj.* irregular; **2.** *adv.* irregularly

unreif *Adj.* **a)** unripe; **b)** *(nicht erwachsen)* immature

Unruhe die *(auch fig.)* unrest; *(Lärm)* noise; *(Unrast)* restlessness; *(Besorgnis)* anxiety; **unruhig 1.** *Adj.* **a)** restless; *(besorgt)* anxious; unsettled, troubled ⟨*time*⟩; **b)** *(laut)* noisy; **c)** *(ungleichmäßig)* uneven ⟨*breathing, pulse, etc.*⟩; fitful ⟨*sleep*⟩; disturbed ⟨*night*⟩; **2.** *adv.* **a)** restlessly; *(besorgt)* anxiously; **b)** *(ungleichmäßig)* unevenly; ⟨*sleep*⟩ fitfully

uns 1. a) *Akk. von* **wir** us; **b)** *Dat. von* **wir; gib es ~:** give it to us; **bei ~:** at our home *or (coll.)* place; **2.** *Reflexivpron. der 1. Pers. Pl.* **a)** *refl.* ourselves; **b)** *reziprok* one another

unsachlich 1. *Adj.* unobjective; **2.** *adv.* without objectivity

unsauber 1. *Adj.* **a)** dirty; **b)** *(nachlässig)* untidy; sloppy; **2.** *adv. (nachlässig)* untidily

unschädlich *Adj.* harmless

unscharf *Adj.* blurred ⟨*photo, picture*⟩

unscheinbar *Adj.* inconspicuous

Unschuld die; *o. Pl.* innocence; **unschuldig 1.** *Adj.* innocent; **2.** *adv.* innocently

unselbständig *Adj.* dependent [on other people]

[1]unser *Possessivpron. der 1. Pers. Pl.* our; **das ist ~s** that is ours; **[2]unser** *Gen. von* **wir** *(geh.)* of us; **in ~ aller/ beider Interesse** in the interest of all/ both of us; **unser·einer, unser· eins** *Indefinitpron. (ugs.)* the likes of us *pl.;* our sort *(coll.);* **unserer·seits** *Adv.* for our part; *(von uns)* on our part; **unser[e]s·gleichen** *indekl. Indefinitpron.* people *pl.* like us; **unsert·wegen** *Adv., s.* meinetwegen: because of us; for our sake; about us; as far as we are concerned

unsicher 1. *Adj.* uncertain; *(nicht selbstsicher)* insecure; **2.** *adv.* ⟨*walk, stand, etc.*⟩ unsteadily; *(nicht selbstsicher)* ⟨*smile, look*⟩ diffidently

unsichtbar *Adj.* invisible (**für** to)

Unsinn der nonsense; **~ machen** mess *or* fool about; **unsinnig** *Adj.* nonsensical ⟨*statement, talk, etc.*⟩; absurd, ridiculous ⟨*demand etc.*⟩

Unsitte die bad habit; **unsittlich 1.** *Adj.* indecent; **2.** *adv.* indecently

unsr... *s.* **[1]unser**

unsterblich *Adj.* immortal

unsympathisch *Adj.* uncongenial, disagreeable ⟨*person*⟩; unpleasant ⟨*characteristic, nature, voice*⟩

Untat die misdeed; evil deed

untauglich *Adj.* unsuitable; *(für Militärdienst)* unfit [for service] *postpos.*

unten *Adv.* **a)** down; **hier/da ~:** down here/there; **von ~:** from below; **b)** *(in Gebäuden)* downstairs; **nach ~:** downstairs; **c)** *(am unteren Ende, zum unteren Ende hin)* at the bottom; **~ [links] auf der Seite/im Schrank** at the bottom [left] of the page/cupboard; **d)** *(an der Unterseite)* underneath; **e)** *(im Text)* below; **unten·genannt** *Adj.* undermentioned *(Brit.);* mentioned below *postpos.*

unter 1. *Präp. mit Dat. (Lage, Standort)* under; *(zwischen)* among[st]; **Mengen ~ 100 Stück** quantities of less than 100; **~ Angst/Tränen** in *or* out of fear/in tears; **2.** *Präp. mit Akk.* under; *(zwischen)* among[st]; **~ Null sinken** drop below zero; **3.** *Adv.* less than; **~ 30 [Jahre alt] sein** be under 30 [years of age]

unter... *Adj.* lower; bottom; *(ganz unten)* bottom; *(in der Rangfolge o. ä.)* lower

Unter·arm der forearm; **unterbe· lichten[1]** *tr. V. (Fot.)* underexpose

unter·bleiben *unr. itr. V.; mit sein* etw. unterbleibt sth. does not occur *or* happen; **unter·brechen** *unr. tr. V.* interrupt; break ⟨*journey, silence*⟩; **Unter·brechung die** *s.* unterbrecher: interruption; break *(Gen.* in)

unter|bringen *unr. tr. V.* **a)** put up; **b)** *(beherbergen)* put up; **Unterbringung die** **~, ~en** accommodation *no indef. art.*

unter·der·hand *Adv.* on the quiet **unter·dessen** *s.* inzwischen; **unterdrücken** *tr. V.* suppress; hold back ⟨*comment, question, answer, criticism, etc.*⟩; oppress ⟨*minority etc.*⟩; **Unterdrückung die** **~, ~en a)** *(das Unter-*

----

[1] *ich unterbelichte, unterbelichtet, unterzubelichten*

drücken) suppression; **b)** *(das Unter-drücktwerden, -sein)* oppression

unter·einander *Adv.* **a)** *(räumlich)* one below the other; **b)** *(miteinander)* among[st] ourselves/themselves *etc.*

unter·ernährt *Adj.* undernourished;

Unter·ernährung die malnutrition

Unter·führung die underpass; *(für Fußgänger)* subway *(Brit.);* [pedestrian] underpass *(Amer.)*

unter-, Unter-: ~**gang der a)** *(Sonnen~, Mond~ usw.)* setting; **b)** *(von Schiffen)* sinking; **c)** *(das Zugrundegehen)* decline; ~|**gehen** *unr. itr. V.; mit sein* **a)** ⟨*sun, star, etc.*⟩ set; ⟨*ship*⟩ sink, go down; ⟨*person*⟩ drown, go under; **b)** *(zugrunde gehen)* come to an end; ~**geordnet** *Adj.* secondary ⟨*role, importance, etc.*⟩; subordinate ⟨*position, post, etc.*⟩; ~**gewicht das;** *o. Pl.* underweight; ~**grund der** *o. Pl. (bes. Politik)* underground

Untergrund·bahn die underground [railway] *(Brit.);* subway *(Amer.)*

unter-, Unter-: ~|**haken** *tr. V. (ugs.)* jmdn. ~haken take sb.'s arm; ~**halb** **1.** *Adv.* below; ~**halb von** below; **2.** *Präp. mit Gen.* below; ~**halt der;** *o. Pl.* **a)** living; **b)** *(~haltszahlung)* maintenance; **c)** *(Instandhaltung[skosten])* upkeep; ~**halten** **1.** *unr. tr. V.* **a)** support; **b)** *(instand halten)* maintain ⟨*building*⟩; **c)** *(betreiben)* run, keep ⟨*car, hotel*⟩; **d)** *(pflegen)* maintain, keep up ⟨*contact, correspondence*⟩; **e)** entertain ⟨*guest, audience*⟩; **2.** *unr. refl. V.* **a)** talk; converse; **b)** *(sich vergnügen)* enjoy oneself; ~**haltsam** *Adj.* entertaining; ~**haltung die a)** *o. Pl. (Versorgung)* support; **b)** *o. Pl. (Instandhaltung)* maintenance; **c)** *(Gespräch)* conversation; **e)** *(Zeitvertreib)* entertainment; ~**händler der** *(bes. Politik)* negotiator; ~**hemd das** vest *(Brit.);* undershirt *(Amer.);* ~**hose die** *(Herren~)* briefs *pl.;* [under]pants *pl.;* *(Damen~)* panties; knickers *(Brit.);* ~**irdisch 1.** *Adj.* underground; **2.** *adv.* underground; ~**kiefer der** lower jaw; ~|**kommen** *unr. itr. V.; mit sein* find accommodation

unter·kühlt *Adj.* ~ **sein** be suffering from hypothermia *or* exposure

Unter-: ~**kunft die;** ~, ~**künfte** accommodation *no indef. art.;* lodging *no indef. art.;* ~**kunft und Frühstück** bed and breakfast; ~**kunft und Verpflegung** board and lodging; ~**lage die a)** *(Schreib~)* pad; *(für eine*

Schreibmaschine usw.) mat; **b)** *Pl.* documents; papers

unter-: ~**lassen** *unr. tr. V.* refrain from [doing]; ~**laufen** *unr. itr. V.; mit sein* occur; **jmdm. ist ein Fehler/Irrtum** ~: sb. made a mistake; ~**legen** *Adj.* inferior; **jmdm.** ~ **sein** be inferior to sb. **(an** + *Dat.* in)

Unter·leib der lower abdomen

unter·liegen *unr. itr. V.* **a)** *mit sein (besiegt werden)* lose; be beaten *or* defeated; **b)** *(unterworfen sein)* be subject to

unterm *Präp.* + *Art.* = **unter dem**

unter·mauern *tr. V. (mit Argumenten, Fakten absichern)* back up

Unter-: ~**miete die** subtenancy; sublease; ~**mieter der** subtenant; lodger

untern *(ugs.) Präp.* + *Art.* = **unter den**

unter-, Unter-: ~**nehmen** *unr. tr. V.* **a)** *(durchführen)* undertake; make; take ⟨*steps*⟩; **b)** etwas ~**nehmen** do something; ~**nehmen das;** ~**nehmens, ~nehmen a)** *(Vorhaben)* enterprise; **b)** *(Firma)* concern; ~**nehmer der;** ~**nehmers, ~nehmer** employer; ~**nehmungs·lustig** *Adj.* active; **sie ist sehr ~nehmungslustig** she is always out doing things

Unter·offizier der a) non-commissioned officer; **b)** *(Dienstgrad)* corporal

unter·ordnen 1. *tr. V.* subordinate; **2.** *refl. V.* accept a subordinate role

Unterredung die; ~, ~**en** discussion

Unterricht der; ~[e]s, ~e instruction; *(Schul~)* teaching; *(Schulstunden)* classes *pl.;* **unterrichten 1.** *tr. V.* **a)** teach; **b)** *(informieren)* inform **(über** + *Akk.* of, about); **2.** *itr. V. (Unterricht geben)* teach; **3.** *refl. V. (sich informieren)* inform oneself **(über** + *Akk.* about); **Unterrichts·stunde die** lesson; period

Unter·rock der [half] slip

unter|rühren *tr. V.* stir in

unters *Präp.* + *Art.* = **unter das**

unter·sagen *tr. V.* forbid; prohibit

Unter·satz der *s.* Untersetzer

unter-, Unter-: ~**schätzen** *tr. V.* underestimate ⟨*amount, effect, etc.*⟩; underrate ⟨*talent, ability, etc.*⟩; ~**scheiden 1.** *unr. tr. V.* distinguish; **2.** *unr. refl. V.* differ **(durch** in, **von** from); ~**scheidung die** *(Vorgang)* differentiation; *(Resultat)* distinction

Unter-: ~**schenkel der** shank; lower leg; ~**schicht die** *(Soziol.)* lower class

Ụnter·schied der; ~|e|s, ~e difference; **unterschiedlich 1.** *Adj.* different; *(uneinheitlich)* variable; varying; **2.** *adv.* |sehr/ganz| ~: in [very/quite] different ways; **unterschieds·los 1.** *Adj.* uniform; equal ⟨*treatment*⟩; **2.** *adv.* ⟨*treat*⟩ equally; *(ohne Benachteiligung)* without discrimination

unter·schlagen *unr. tr. V.* embezzle ⟨*money, funds, etc.*⟩; *(unterdrücken)* intercept ⟨*letter*⟩; withhold ⟨*fact, news, information, etc.*⟩

Ụnter·schlupf der; ~|e|s, ~e shelter; *(Versteck)* hiding-place; hide-out; **unter|schlüpfen** *itr. V.; mit sein (ugs.)* hide out

unter·schreiben *unr. itr., tr. V.* sign; **Ụnter·schrift** die signature; *(Bild~)* caption

Unter-: ~**see·boot** das submarine; ~**setzer** der mat; *(für Gläser)* coaster **untersẹtzt** *Adj.* stocky

Ụnter·stand der *(Schutzbunker)* dugout; *(Unterschlupf)* shelter

unter|stehen 1. *unr. itr. V.* jmdm. ~: be subordinate *or* answerable to sb.; **2.** *unr. refl. V.* dare

¹**unter|stellen 1.** *tr. V. (zur Aufbewahrung)* keep; store ⟨*furniture*⟩; **2.** *refl. V.* take shelter

²**unter·stellen** *tr. V.* **a)** jmdm. eine Abteilung ~: put sb. in charge of a department; **die Behörde ist dem Ministerium unterstellt** the office is under the ministry; **b)** *(unterschieben)* **jmdm. böse Absichten** *usw.* ~: insinuate that sb.'s intentions *etc.* are bad; **Unterstẹllung die** *(falsche Behauptung)* insinuation

unter·streichen *unr. tr. V.* **a)** underline; **b)** *(hervorheben)* emphasize

unter·stützen *tr. V.* support; **Unter·stützung die a)** support; **b)** *(finanzielle Hilfe)* allowance; *(für Arbeitslose)* [unemployment] benefit *no art.*

unter·suchen *tr. V.* examine; *(überprüfen)* test **(auf** + *Akk.* for); *(aufzuklären suchen)* investigate; *(durchsuchen)* search **(auf** + *Akk.,* **nach** for); **Untersuchung die;** ~, ~ **en a)** *s.* **untersuchen:** examination; test; investigation; search; **b)** *(wissenschaftliche Arbeit)* study; **Untersuchungs·haft die** imprisonment *or* detention while awaiting trial

Ụnter·tasse die saucer

unter|tauchen 1. *itr. V.; mit sein* **a)** *(im Wasser)* dive [under]; **b)** *(verschwinden)* disappear; **2.** *tr. V.* duck

Ụnter·teil das *od.* der bottom part; **unter·teilen** *tr. V.* divide; *(gliedern)* subdivide

unter·treiben *unr. itr. V.* play things down

Ụnter·wäsche die underwear

unterwẹgs *Adv.* on the way; *(nicht zu Hause)* out [and about]

unter·weisen *unr. tr. V. (geh.)* instruct

Ụnter·welt die; ~: underworld

unter·werfen 1. *unr. tr. V.* **a)** subjugate ⟨*people, country*⟩; **b)** *(unterziehen)* subject *(Dat.* to); **2.** *unr. refl. V.* sich |jmdm./einer Sache| ~: submit [to sb./sth.]; **unterwürfig 1.** *Adj.* obsequious; **2.** *adv.* obsequiously

unter·zeichnen *tr. V.* sign

unter·ziehen 1. *unr. tr. V.* **etw. einer Untersuchung/Überprüfung** *(Dat.)* ~: examine/check sth.; **2.** *unr. refl. V.* **sich einer Operation** *(Dat.)* ~: undergo *or* have an operation

untrạgbar *Adj.* unbearable

ụntreu *Adj.* disloyal; *(in der Ehe, Liebe)* unfaithful; **Ụntreue die** disloyalty; *(in der Ehe, Liebe)* unfaithfulness

untröstlich *Adj.* inconsolable

Ụntugend die bad habit

ụnüberlegt 1. *Adj.* rash; **2.** *adv.* rashly

unübersẹhbar 1. *Adj.* **a)** *(offenkundig)* conspicuous; **b)** *(sehr groß)* enormous; **2.** *adv. (sehr)* extremely

ụnübersichtlich 1. *Adj.* unclear; confusing ⟨*arrangement*⟩; blind ⟨*bend*⟩; broken ⟨*country etc.*⟩; **2.** *adv.* unclearly; confusingly ⟨*arranged*⟩

unübertrẹfflich 1. *Adj.* superb; **2.** *adv.* superbly; **unübertrọffen** *Adj.* unsurpassed

unumgänglich *Adj.* [absolutely] necessary

unumwụnden 1. *Adj.* frank; **2.** *adv.* frankly; openly

ụnunterbrochen 1. *Adj.* incessant; **2.** *adv.* incessantly

unveränderlich *Adj.* unchangeable

unverạntwortlich 1. *Adj.* irresponsible; **2.** *adv.* irresponsibly

unverbẹsserlich *Adj.* incorrigible

ụnverbindlich 1. *Adj.* **a)** not binding *pred.;* without obligation *postpos;* **b)** *(reserviert)* non-committal ⟨*answer, words*⟩; impersonal ⟨*attitude, person*⟩; **2.** *adv.* ⟨*send, reserve*⟩ without obligation

unverblümt 1. *Adj.* blunt; **2.** *adv.* bluntly

unverbraucht *Adj.* untouched; unspent ⟨*energy*⟩; fresh ⟨*air*⟩

unverdaut *Adj.* undigested

unverdorben *Adj.* unspoilt

unverfroren *Adj.* insolent; impudent

unvergänglich *Adj.* immortal ⟨*fame*⟩; unchanging ⟨*beauty*⟩; abiding ⟨*recollection*⟩

unvergeßlich *Adj.* unforgettable

unvergleichlich 1. *Adj.* incomparable; **2.** *adv.* incomparably

unverheiratet *Adj.* unmarried

unverhofft 1. *Adj.* unexpected; **2.** *adv.* unexpectedly

unverkäuflich *Adj.* **diese Vase ist** ~ : this vase is not for sale; *(nicht absetzbar)* unsaleable

unvermeidlich *Adj.* unavoidable; *(sich als Folge ergebend)* inevitable

Unvermögen das lack of ability

unvermutet 1. *Adj.* unexpected; **2.** *adv.* unexpectedly

unvernünftig *Adj.* stupid; foolish

unverrichtet *Adj.* ~**er Dinge** without having achieved anything

unverschämt 1. *Adj.* **a)** impertinent ⟨*person, manner, words, etc.*⟩; barefaced ⟨*lie*⟩; **b)** *(ugs.: sehr groß)* outrageous ⟨*price, luck, etc.*⟩; **2.** *adv.* impertinently; ⟨*lie*⟩ barefacedly; blatantly; **Unverschämtheit die;** ~**, ~en** impertinence

unversehens *Adv.* suddenly

unversehrt *Adj.* unscathed; *(unbeschädigt)* undamaged

unverständlich *Adj.* incomprehensible; **Unverständnis das** lack of understanding

unverträglich *Adj.* **a)** quarrelsome; **b)** incompatible ⟨*blood groups, medicines, transplant tissue*⟩

unverwechselbar *Adj.* unmistakable; distinctive

unverwüstlich *Adj.* indestructible

unverzeihlich *Adj.* unforgivable

unverzüglich 1. *Adj.* prompt; **2.** *adv.* promptly

unvollkommen 1. *Adj.* **a)** imperfect; **b)** *(unvollständig)* incomplete; **2.** *adv.* **a)** imperfectly; **b)** *(unvollständig)* incompletely; **Unvollkommenheit die a)** imperfectness; **b)** *(Unvollständigkeit)* incompleteness

unvollständig *Adj.* incomplete; **Unvollständigkeit die** incompleteness

unvorhergesehen *Adj.* unforeseen; unexpected ⟨*visit*⟩

unvorsichtig 1. *Adj.* careless; *(unüberlegt)* rash; **2.** *adv.* carelessly; *(unüberlegt)* rashly

unvorstellbar 1. *Adj.* inconceivable; **2.** *adv.* unimaginably

unvorteilhaft *Adj.* **a)** unattractive ⟨*figure, appearance*⟩; **b)** *(ohne Vorteil)* unfavourable, poor ⟨*purchase, exchange*⟩; unprofitable ⟨*business*⟩

Unwahrheit die a) *o. Pl.* untruthfulness; **b)** *(Äußerung)* untruth; **unwahrscheinlich 1.** *Adj.* **a)** improbable; unlikely; **b)** *(ugs.: sehr viel)* incredible *(coll.)*; **2.** *adv. (ugs.: sehr)* incredibly *(coll.)*

unweiblich *Adj.* unfeminine

unweigerlich 1. *Adj.* inevitable; **2.** *adv.* inevitably

Unwetter das [thunder]storm

unwichtig *Adj.* unimportant

unwiderruflich 1. *Adj.* irrevocable; **2.** *adv.* irrevocably

unwiderstehlich *Adj.* irresistible

Unwille[n] der; *o. Pl.* displeasure

unwillig 1. *Adj.* indignant; *(widerwillig)* unwilling; **2.** *adv.* indignantly; *(widerwillig)* unwillingly

unwillkürlich 1. *Adj.* **a)** spontaneous ⟨*cry, sigh*⟩; instinctive ⟨*reaction, movement, etc.*⟩; **b)** *(Physiol.)* involuntary ⟨*movement etc.*⟩; **2.** *adv.* **a)** ⟨*shout etc.*⟩ spontaneously; ⟨*react, move, etc.*⟩ instinctively; **b)** *(Physiol.)* ⟨*move etc.*⟩ involuntarily

unwirklich *(geh.) Adj.* unreal

unwirsch 1. *Adj.* surly; ill-natured; **2.** *adv.* ill-naturedly

unwirtschaftlich 1. *Adj.* uneconomic ⟨*procedure etc.*⟩; *(nicht sparsam)* uneconomical ⟨*driving etc.*⟩; **2.** *adv.* ⟨*work, drive, etc.*⟩ uneconomically

Unwissenheit die; ~ : ignorance; **unwissentlich 1.** *Adj.* unconscious; **2.** *adv.* unknowingly; unwittingly

unwohl *Adv.* unwell; **mir ist** ~ : I don't feel well; **Unwohlsein das;** ~**s** indisposition

unwürdig *Adj.* **a)** undignified ⟨*person, behaviour*⟩; degrading ⟨*treatment*⟩; **b)** *(unangemessen)* unworthy

unzählig *Adj.* innumerable; countless

Unze die; ~**, ~n** ounce

unzeitgemäß *Adj.* anachronistic

unzerbrechlich *Adj.* unbreakable

unzertrennlich *Adj.* inseparable

Unzucht die: ~ **treiben** fornicate; **gewerbsmäßige** ~ : prostitution; **unzüchtig 1.** *Adj.* obscene ⟨*letter, ges-*

ture⟩; **2.** *adv.* ⟨*touch, approach, etc.*⟩ indecently; ⟨*speak*⟩ obscenely

ụnzufrieden *Adj.* dissatisfied; *(stärker)* unhappy; **Ụnzufriedenheit die** dissatisfaction; *(stärker)* unhappiness

ụnzugänglich *Adj.* inaccessible ⟨*area, building, etc.*⟩; unapproachable ⟨*character, person, etc.*⟩

ụnzulänglich *(geh.)* **1.** *Adj.* insufficient; **2.** *adv.* insufficiently

ụnzumutbar *Adj.* unreasonable

ụnzurechnungsfähig *Adj.* not responsible for one's actions *pred.; (geistesgestört)* of unsound mind *postpos.*

ụnzustellbar *Adj. (Postw.)* „~": 'not known [at this address]'

ụnzutreffend *Adj.* inappropriate; *(falsch)* incorrect

ụnzuverlässig *Adj.* unreliable; **Ụnzuverlässigkeit die** unreliability

ụnzweckmäßig 1. *Adj.* unsuitable; *(unpraktisch)* impractical; **2.** *adv.* unsuitably; *(unpraktisch)* impractically

ụ̈ppig 1. *Adj.* lush ⟨*vegetation*⟩; thick ⟨*hair, beard*⟩; full ⟨*bosom, lips*⟩; voluptuous ⟨*figure, woman*⟩; *(fig.)* sumptuous, opulent ⟨*meal*⟩; **2.** *adv.* luxuriantly; *(fig.)* sumptuously

Ur·abstimmung die [*esp.* strike] ballot

Urạl der; ~[s] Urals *pl.;* Ural Mountains *pl.*

ur·alt *Adj.* very old; ancient

Urạn das; ~s uranium

urbar *Adj.* ein Stück Land ~ **machen** cultivate a piece of land

Ụr·einwohner der native inhabitant; **Ụr·enkel der** great-grandson; **Ụr·groß·eltern** *Pl.* great-grandparents

Ụr·heber der; ~s, ~ originator; initiator; *(bes. Rechtsspr.: Verfasser, Autor)* author

urig *Adj.* natural ⟨*person*⟩; real ⟨*beer*⟩; cosy ⟨*pub*⟩

Urịn der; ~s, ~e *(Med.)* urine; **urinieren** *itr. V.* urinate

Ụr·kunde die; ~, ~n document; *(Bescheinigung, Sieger~, Diplom~ usw.)* certificate

Ụrlaub der; ~[e]s, ~e holiday[s] *(Brit.)*; vacation; *(bes. Milit.)* leave

Ụrlaubs-: ~**reise die** holiday [trip]; ~**zeit die** holiday period *or* season

Ụrne die; ~, ~n urn; *(Wahl~)* [ballot-]box

Ụr·sache die cause

Ụr·sprung der origin; **ụr·sprünglich 1.** *Adj.* **a)** original ⟨*plan, price, form, material, etc.*⟩; **b)** *(natürlich)*

natural; **2.** *adv.* **a)** originally; **b)** *(natürlich)* naturally

Ụrteil das; ~s, ~e judgement; *(Strafe)* sentence; *(Gerichts~)* verdict; **urteilen** *itr. V.* form an opinion; judge; über etw./jmdn. ~: judge sth./sb.; **Ụrteils·vermögen das;** *o. Pl.* competence to judge

Ụr·wald der primeval forest; *(tropisch)* jungle

USA [u:|ɛs'|a:] *Pl.* USA

usw. *Abk.* und so weiter etc.

Utensịl das; ~s, ~ien [... jən] piece of equipment; ~**ien** equipment *sing.*

Utopie̱ die; ~, ~n utopian dream; **utọpisch** *Adj.* utopian

UV *Abk.* Ultraviolett UV

V

v, V [vau̯] **das;** ~, ~: v, V

v. *Abk.* von

vage̱ 1. *Adj.* vague; **2.** *adv.* vaguely

vakuum·verpackt *Adj.* vacuum-packed

Vanịlle [va'nɪljə] **die;** ~: vanilla; **Vanịlle·zucker der** vanilla sugar

variạbel 1. *Adj.* variable; **2.** *adv.* variably

variie̱ren *tr., itr. V.* vary

Vase̱ ['va:zə] **die;** ~, ~n vase

Vater der; ~s, Väter father; **Gott** ~: God the Father; **Vater·land das;** *Pl.* ~länder fatherland; **väterlich 1.** *Adj.* **a)** paternal ⟨*line, love, instincts, etc.*⟩; **b)** *(fürsorglich)* fatherly; **2.** *adv.* in a fatherly way; **väterlicherseits** *Adv.* on the/his/her *etc.* father's side; **Vaterschaft die;** ~, ~en fatherhood; **Vaterunser das;** ~s, ~: Lord's Prayer; **Vati der;** ~s, ~s *(fam.)* dad[dy] *(coll.)*

Vatikạn [vati'ka:n] **der;** ~s Vatican

v. Chr. *Abk.* vor Christus BC

Vegetarier [vege'ta:riɐ] **der;** ~s, ~: vegetarian; **vegetạrisch 1.** *Adj.* vegetarian; **2.** *adv.* er ißt *od.* lebt ~: he is a vegetarian; **Vegetatio̱n die;** ~, ~en vegetation *no indef. art.;* **vegetie̱ren** *itr. V.* vegetate

Veilchen das; ~s, ~: violet
Vene ['ve:nə] die; ~, ~n vein
Venedig [ve'ne:dɪç] (das); ~s Venice
Venezolaner [venetso'la:nɐ] der; ~s, ~: Venezuelan; **venezolanisch** Adj. Venezuelan; **Venezuela** (das); ~s Venezuela
Ventil [vɛn'ti:l] das; ~s, ~e valve; **Ventilator** [vɛnti'la:tɔr] der; ~s, ~en ventilator
Venus ['ve:nʊs] die; ~: Venus no def. art.
verabreden 1. tr. V. arrange; 2. refl. V. sich im Park/zum Tennis/für den folgenden Abend ~: arrange to meet in the park/for tennis/next evening; **Verabredung** die; ~, ~en a) arrangement; b) (verabredete Zusammenkunft) appointment; eine ~ absagen call off a meeting
verabscheuen tr. V. detest; loathe
verabschieden 1. tr. V. a) say goodbye to; b) (aus dem Dienst) retire ⟨general, civil servant, etc.⟩; 2. refl. V. sich [von jmdm.] ~: say goodbye [to sb.]; **Verabschiedung** die; ~, ~en a) leave-taking; b) (aus dem Dienst) retirement
verachten tr. V. despise; **verächtlich** 1. Adj. a) contemptuous; b) (verachtenswürdig) contemptible; 2. adv. contemptuously; **Verachtung** die; ~: contempt
verallgemeinern tr., itr. V. generalize; **Verallgemeinerung** die; ~, ~en generalization
veralten itr. V.; mit sein become obsolete
Veranda [ve'randa] die; ~, Veranden veranda; porch
veränderlich Adj. changeable; **verändern** tr., refl. V. change; **Veränderung** die change ⟨Gen. in⟩
verängstigen tr. V. frighten; scare
verankern tr. V. fix ⟨tent, mast, pole, etc.⟩; (mit einem Anker) anchor
veranlagen tr.V. (Steuerw.) assess ⟨mit at⟩; **veranlagt** Adj. künstlerisch/praktisch ~ sein have an artistic bent/be practically minded; **Veranlagung** die; ~, ~en [pre]disposition
veranlassen tr. V. cause; induce; ~, daß ... see to it that ... **Veranlassung** die; ~, ~en reason
veranschaulichen tr. V. illustrate
veranschlagen tr. V. estimate ⟨mit at⟩
veranstalten tr. V. organize; hold,

give ⟨party⟩; hold ⟨auction⟩; do ⟨survey⟩; **Veranstalter** der; ~s, ~ organizer; **Veranstaltung** die; ~, ~en a) (das Veranstalten) organizing; organization; b) (etw., was veranstaltet wird) event
verantworten 1. tr. V. etw. ~: take responsibility for sth.; 2. refl. V. sich für etw. ~: answer for sth.; sich vor jmdm. ~: answer to sb.; **verantwortlich** Adj. responsible; **Verantwortung** die; ~, ~en responsibility ⟨für for⟩
verantwortungs-: ~bewußt Adj. responsible; ~los Adj. irresponsible; ~voll Adj. responsible
verarbeiten tr. V. use; etw. zu etw. ~: make sth. into sth.; (geistig bewältigen) assimilate ⟨film, experience, impressions⟩
verärgern tr. V. annoy
verarzten tr. V. (ugs.) patch up (coll.) ⟨person⟩; fix (coll.) ⟨wound etc.⟩
veräußern tr. V. dispose of ⟨property⟩
Verb [vɛrp] das; ~s, ~en verb
Verband der a) (Binde) bandage; dressing; b) (von Vereinen, Clubs o. ä.) association
Verband[s]-: ~kasten der first-aid-box; ~material das dressing materials pl.
Verband·zeug das first-aid things pl.
Verbannung die; ~, ~en banishment
verbergen unr. tr. V. hide; conceal
verbessern 1. tr. V. a) improve; reform ⟨schooling, world⟩; b) (korrigieren) correct; 2. refl. V. a) improve; b) [beruflich] aufsteigen) better oneself; **Verbesserung** die a) improvement; b) (Korrektur) correction
verbeugen refl. V. bow ⟨vor + Dat. to⟩; **Verbeugung** die; ~, ~en bow
verbieten unr. tr. V. a) forbid; jmdm. etw.~: forbid sb. sth.; „Betreten des Rasens/Rauchen verboten" 'keep off the grass'/'no smoking'; b) (für unzulässig erklären) ban
verbinden 1. unr. tr. V. a) (bandagieren) bandage; dress; b) (zubinden) bind; jmdm. die Augen ~: blindfold sb.; c) (zusammenfügen) join; d) (in Beziehung bringen) connect ⟨durch by⟩; link ⟨towns, lakes, etc.⟩ ⟨durch by⟩; e) (verknüpfen) combine ⟨abilities, qualities, etc.⟩; f) auch itr. (telefonisch) jmdn. [mit jmdm.] ~: put sb. through [to sb.]; 2. unr. refl. V. a) (auch Chemie) combine ⟨mit with⟩; b) (sich zusammentun) join [together]; join

forces; **verbindlich 1.** *Adj.* **a)** friendly; **b)** *(bindend)* obligatory; compulsory; binding ⟨*agreement, decision, etc.*⟩; **2.** *adv.* **a)** *(freundlich)* in a friendly manner; **b)** ~ **zusagen** definitely agree; **jmdm. etw.** ~ **zusagen** make sb. a firm offer of sth.; **Verbindung die a)** *(das Verknüpfen)* linking; **b)** *(Zusammenhalt)* join; connection; **c)** *(verknüpfende Strecke)* link; **d)** *(durch Telefon, Funk, Verkehrs~)* connection (**nach** to); **e)** *(Kombination)* combination; **in** ~ **mit etw.** in conjunction with sth.; **f)** *(Kontakt)* contact; **sich mit jmdm. in** ~ **setzen** get in touch *or* contact with sb.; **g)** *(Zusammenhang)* connection
verbissen 1. *Adj.* dogged; doggedly determined; **2.** *adv.* doggedly
verbitten *unr. refl. V.* **sich** *(Dat.)* **etw.** ~: refuse to tolerate sth.
verbittern *tr. V.* embitter
verblassen *itr. V.; mit sein (auch fig. geh.)* fade
Verbleib der; ~|e|s *(geh.)* whereabouts *pl.;* **verbleiben** *unr. itr. V.; mit sein* remain; **wie seid ihr verblieben?** what did you arrange?
Verblendung die; ~, ~en blindness
verblüffen *tr. (auch itr.) V.* amaze; **verblüffend 1.** *Adj.* amazing; **2.** *adv.* amazingly
verblühen *itr. V.; mit sein (auch fig.)* fade
verbluten *itr. (auch refl.) V.; mit sein* bleed to death
verbohrt *Adj.* pigheaded
verborgen *Adj. (abgelegen)* secluded; *(nicht sichtbar)* hidden
Verbot das; ~|e|s, ~e ban (*Gen.,* **von** on); **Verbots·schild das;** *Pl.* ~**schilder** sign *(prohibiting sth.); (Verkehrsw.)* prohibitive sign
Verbrauch der; ~|e|s consumption; (**von, an** + *Dat.* of); **verbrauchen** *tr. V.* use; consume ⟨*food, drink*⟩; use up ⟨*provisions*⟩; spend ⟨*money*⟩; consume, use ⟨*fuel*⟩; *(fig.)* use up ⟨*strength, energy*⟩; **Verbraucher der;** ~s, ~: consumer
Verbrechen das; ~s, ~: crime (**an** + *Dat.,* **gegen** against); **Verbrecher der;** ~s, ~: criminal; **verbrecherisch** *Adj.* criminal
verbreiten 1. *tr. V.* spread; radiate ⟨*optimism, calm, etc.*⟩; **2.** *refl. V.* spread; **Verbreitung die;** ~, ~en **a)** *s.* verbreiten 1: spreading; radiation; **b)** *(Ausbreitung)* spread

verbrennen 1. *unr. itr. V.; mit sein* burn; **2.** *tr. V.* burn; cremate ⟨*dead person*⟩; **sich** *(Dat.)* **den Mund** ~ *(fig.)* say too much; **Verbrennung die;** ~, ~en **a)** *s.* verbrennen 2: burning; cremation; **b)** *(Wunde)* burn
verbringen *unr. tr. V.* spend
verbummeln *tr. V. (ugs.)* **a)** waste ⟨*time*⟩; **b)** *(vergessen)* forget [all] about; clean forget; *(verlieren)* lose
verbünden *refl. V.* form an alliance; **Verbündete der/die;** *adj. Dekl.* ally
verbüßen *tr. V.* serve ⟨*sentence*⟩
Verdacht der; ~|e|s, ~e *od.* Verdächte suspicion; **verdächtig 1.** *Adj.* suspicious; **2.** *adv.* suspiciously; **Verdächtige der/die;** *adj. Dekl.* suspect;
verdächtigen *tr. V.* suspect
verdammen *tr. V.* condemn; *(Rel.)* damn ⟨*sinner*⟩
verdampfen 1. *itr. V.; mit sein* evaporate; **2.** *tr. V.* evaporate
verdanken *tr. V.* **jmdm./einer Sache etw.** ~: owe sth. to sb./sth.
verdarb *1. u. 3. Pers. Sg. Prät. v.* **verderben**
verdattert *(ugs.) Adj.* flabbergasted; *(verwirrt)* dazed; stunned
verdauen 1. *tr. V. (auch fig.)* digest; **2.** *itr. V.* digest [one's food]; **verdaulich** *Adj.* digestible; **Verdauung die;** ~: digestion
Verdeck das; ~|e|s, ~e top; hood *(Brit.); (bei Kinderwagen)* hood; **verdecken** *tr. V.* hide; cover
verderben 1. *unr. itr. V.; mit sein* go bad *or* off, spoil; **2.** *unr. tr. V.* spoil; *(stärker)* ruin; spoil ⟨*appetite, enjoyment, fun, etc.*⟩; **3.** *unr. refl. V.* **sich** *(Dat.)* **den Magen/die Augen** ~: give oneself an upset stomach/ruin one's eyesight; **Verderben das;** ~s ruin; **verderblich** *Adj.* perishable ⟨*food*⟩; pernicious ⟨*influence, effect, etc.*⟩
verdeutlichen *tr. V.* **etw.** ~: make sth. clear; *(erklären)* explain sth.
verdichten *refl. V.* ⟨*fog, smoke*⟩ thicken, become thicker; *(fig.)* ⟨*suspicion, rumour*⟩ grow; *(feeling)* intensify
verdienen 1. *tr. V.* **a)** earn; **b)** *(wert sein)* deserve; **2.** *itr. V.* **beide Eheleute** ~: husband and wife are both earning; **Verdiener der;** ~s, ~: wage-earner; **¹Verdienst der** income; earnings *pl.;* **²Verdienst das;** ~|e|s, ~e merit
verdienst·voll 1. *Adj.* commendable; ⟨*person*⟩ of outstanding merit; **2.** *adv.* commendably; **verdient** *Adj.*

⟨person⟩ of outstanding merit; **sich um etw. ~ machen** render outstanding services to sth.
verdoppeln 1. *tr. V.* double; *(fig.)* double, redouble ⟨*efforts etc.*⟩; **2.** *refl. V.* double
verdorben *2. Part. v.* verderben
verdorren *itr. V.; mit sein* wither [and die]; ⟨*meadow*⟩ scorch
verdrängen *tr. V.* **a)** drive out ⟨*inhabitants*⟩; *(fig.: ersetzen)* displace; **b)** *(Psych.)* repress; *(bewußt)* suppress
verdrehen *tr. V.* **a)** twist ⟨*joint*⟩; roll ⟨*eyes*⟩; **b)** *(ugs. abwertend: entstellen)* twist ⟨*words, facts, etc.*⟩
verdrießen *unr. tr. V. (geh.)* irritate; annoy; **verdrießlich 1.** *Adj.* morose; **2.** *adv.* morosely; **verdroß** *1. u. 3. Pers. Sg. Prät. v.* verdrießen; **verdrossen 1.** *Adj. (mißmutig)* morose; *(mißmutig und lustlos)* sullen; **2.** *adv. (mißmutig)* morosely; *(mißmutig und lustlos)* sullenly; **Verdruß der;** Ver**drusses,** Verdrusse annoyance
verdunkeln *tr. V.* darken; *(vollständig)* black out ⟨*room, house, etc.*⟩
Verdunk[e]lung die; ~, ~en darkening; *(vollständig)* black-out
verdünnen *tr. V.* dilute
verdunsten *itr. V.; mit sein* evaporate; **Verdunstung die; ~:** evaporation
verdursten *itr. V.; mit sein* die of thirst
verdutzt *Adj.* taken aback *pred.;* nonplussed; *(verwirrt)* baffled
verehren *tr. V.* **a)** venerate; **b)** *(geh.: bewundern)* admire; *(ehrerbietig lieben)* worship; **Verehrer der; ~s, ~,** **Verehrerin die; ~, ~en** admirer; **Verehrung die; o. Pl.** **a)** veneration; **b)** *(Bewunderung)* admiration
vereidigen *tr. V.* swear in; **Vereidigung die; ~, ~en** swearing in
Verein der; ~s, ~e organization; *(der Kunstfreunde usw.)* association; society; *(Sport~)* club; **vereinbar** *Adj.; nicht attr.* compatible; **vereinbaren** *tr. V.* agree; arrange ⟨*meeting etc.*⟩; **Vereinbarung die; ~, ~en** **a)** agreeing; *(eines Termins usw.)* arranging; **b)** *(Abmachung)* agreement
vereinfachen *tr. V.* simplify
vereinheitlichen *tr. V.* standardize
vereinigen *tr., refl. V.* unite; *(in der Wirtschaft)* merge; **vereinigt** *Adj.* united; **Vereinigung die** **a)** organization; **b)** *(das Vereinigen)* uniting; *(von Unternehmen)* merging

vereinzelt 1. *Adj.; nicht präd.* occasional; **2.** *adv. (zeitlich)* occasionally; *(örtlich)* here and there
vereisen *itr. V.; mit sein* freeze *or* ice over; ⟨*wing*⟩ ice up; ⟨*lock*⟩ freeze up
vereiteln *tr. V.* thwart
vereitern *itr. V.; mit sein* go septic
verenden *itr. V.; mit sein* perish; die
verengen *refl. V.* narrow; ⟨*pupils*⟩ contract
vererben *tr. V.* leave, bequeath ⟨*property*⟩ (*Dat.,* **an** + *Akk.* to)
Vererbung die; ~, ~en heredity *no art.*
verfahren 1. *unr. refl. V.* lose one's way; **2.** *unr. itr. V.; mit sein* proceed; **Verfahren das; ~s, ~** **a)** procedure; *(Technik)* process; *(Methode)* method; **b)** *(Rechtsw.)* proceedings *pl.*
Verfall der; o. Pl. **a)** decay; *(fig.: der Preise, einer Währung)* collapse; **b)** *(Auflösung)* decline; **verfallen** *unr. itr. V.; mit sein* **a)** *(baufällig werden)* fall into disrepair; **b)** *(körperlich)* ⟨*strength*⟩ decline; **c)** *(untergehen)* ⟨*empire*⟩ decline; ⟨*morals, morale*⟩ deteriorate; **d)** *(ungültig werden)* expire
verfassen *tr. V.* write; draw up ⟨*resolution*⟩; **Verfasser der; ~s, ~,** **Verfasserin die; ~, ~nen** writer; *(eines Buchs, Artikels usw.)* author; writer; **Verfassung die a)** *(Politik)* constitution; **b)** *o. Pl. (Zustand)* state [of health/mind]; **in guter/schlechter ~ sein** be in good/poor shape
verfaulen *itr. V.; mit sein* rot
verfehlen *tr. V.* miss; **Verfehlung die; ~, ~en** misdemeanour; *(Rel.: Sünde)* transgression
verfeinden *refl. V.* **sich ~ mit** make an enemy of
verfeinern *tr. V.* improve; refine ⟨*method, procedure*⟩
verfertigen *tr. V.* produce
verfilmen *tr. V.* film; make a film of; **Verfilmung die; ~, ~en a)** *(das Verfilmen)* filming; **b)** *(Film)* film [version]
verflixt *(ugs.)* **1.** *Adj.* **a)** *(ärgerlich)* awkward, unpleasant ⟨*situation, business, etc.*⟩; **b)** *(verdammt)* blasted *(Brit.)*; blessed; confounded; **~ [noch mal]!** [damn and] blast! *(Brit. coll.);* **c)** *nicht präd. (sehr groß)* **er hat ~es Glück gehabt** he was damned lucky *(coll.);* **2.** *adv. (sehr)* damned *(coll.)*
verflossen *Adj. (ugs.)* former
verfluchen *tr. V.* curse; **verflucht 1.**

Adj. (salopp) damned *(coll.);* bloody *(Brit. sl.);* ~ |**noch mal**|! damn [it]! *(coll.);* **2.** *adv. (sehr)* damned *(coll.)* **verfolgen** *tr. V.* pursue; hunt, track ‹*animal*›; etw. |strafrechtlich| ~: prosecute sth.; **Verfolgung die;** ~, ~en pursuit; *(eines Ziels, Plans usw.)* pursuance

verfressen *Adj. (salopp)* greedy **verfügen 1.** *tr. V. (anordnen)* order; *(dekretieren)* decree; **2.** *itr. V.* über etw. *(Akk.)* |frei| ~ können be free to decide what to do with sth.; über etw. *(Akk.)* ~ *(etw. haben)* have sth. at one's disposal; **Verfügung die;** ~, ~en **a)** *(Anordnung)* order; *(Dekret)* decree; **b)** *o. Pl. (Disposition)* **etw. zur** ~ **haben** have sth. at one's disposal; **jmdm. etw. zur** ~ **stellen** put sth. at sb.'s disposal

verführen *tr. V.* **a)** *(verleiten)* tempt; **b)** *(sexuell)* seduce; **Verführer der** seducer; **verführerisch 1.** *Adj.* **a)** *(verlockend)* tempting; **b)** *(aufreizend)* seductive; **2.** *adv.* **a)** *(verlockend)* temptingly; **b)** *(aufreizend)* seductively; **Verführung die a)** temptation; **b)** *(sexuell)* seduction

vergangen 1. *Adj.* **a)** *(vorüber, vorbei)* bygone, former ‹*times, years, etc.*›; **b)** *(letzt...)* last ‹*year, week, etc.*›; **Vergangenheit die;** ~ **a)** past; **b)** *(Grammatik: Präteritum)* past tense; **vergänglich** *Adj.* transient; transitory; ephemeral; **Vergänglichkeit die;** ~: transience

Vergaser der; ~s, ~: carburettor **vergaß** *1. u. 3. Pers. Sg. Prät. v.* vergessen

vergeben *unr. tr. V.* **a)** *auch itr. (geh.: verzeihen)* forgive; **jmdm. etw.** ~: forgive sb. [for] sth.; **b)** throw away ‹*chance, goal, etc.*›; **c)** *(geben)* place ‹*order*› (an + Akk. with); award ‹*grant, prize*› (an + Akk. to); **vergebens 1.** *Adv.* in vain; vainly; **2.** *adj.* **es war** ~: it was of *or* to no avail; **vergeblich 1.** *Adj.* futile; vain, futile ‹*attempt, efforts*›; **2.** *adv.* in vain; **Vergebung die;** ~, ~en *(geh.)* forgiveness

vergehen *unr. itr. V.; mit sein* ‹*time*› pass [by], go by; ‹*pain*› wear off, pass; ‹*pleasure*› fade; **Vergehen das;** ~s, ~: crime; *(Rechtsspr.)* offence **vergelten** *unr. tr. V.* repay **vergessen 1.** *unr. tr. (auch itr.) V.* forget; **Vergessenheit die;** ~: oblivion; **vergeßlich** *Adj.* forgetful

vergeuden *tr. V.* waste; **Vergeudung die;** ~, ~en waste **vergewaltigen** *tr. V.* rape; **Vergewaltigung die;** ~, ~en rape **vergewissern** *refl. V.* make sure *(Gen.* of*)* **vergießen** *unr. tr. V.* spill; **Tränen** ~: shed tears **vergiften** *tr. V. (auch fig.)* poison; **Vergiftung die;** ~, ~en poisoning **vergiß** *Imper. Sg. v.* vergessen; **Vergiß·mein·nicht das;** ~|e|s, ~|e| forget-me-not; **vergißt** *2. u. 3. Pers. Sg. Präs. v.* vergessen

Vergleich der; ~|e|s, ~e **a)** comparison; **b)** *(Rechtsw.)* settlement; **vergleichbar** *Adj.* comparable; **vergleichen** *tr. V.* compare; **Vergleichs·form die** *(Sprachw.)* comparative/superlative form

vergnügen *refl. V.* enjoy oneself; have a good time; **Vergnügen das;** ~s, ~: pleasure; *(Spaß)* fun; **viel** ~! *(auch iron.)* have fun!; **vergnügt 1.** *Adj.* cheerful; **2.** *adv.* cheerfully; **Vergnügungs·viertel das** pleasure district

vergolden *tr. V.* gold-plate ‹*jewellery etc.*›; *(mit Blattgold)* gild **vergraben** *unr. tr. V.* bury **vergrämt** *Adj.* care-worn **vergreifen** *unr. refl. V.* **sich an jmdm.** ~: assault sb.; **vergriffen** *Adj.* out of print *pred.*

vergrößern 1. *tr. V.* **a)** *(erweitern)* extend ‹*room, area, building, etc.*›; **b)** *(vermehren)* increase; **c)** *(größer reproduzieren)* enlarge ‹*photograph etc.*›; **2.** *refl. V.* **a)** *(größer werden)* ‹*firm, business, etc.*› expand; **b)** *(zunehmen)* increase; **3.** *itr. V.* ‹*lens etc.*› magnify; **Vergrößerung die;** ~, ~en **a)** *s.* vergrößern **1, 2**: extension; increase; enlargement; expansion; **b)** *(Foto)* enlargement; **Vergrößerungs·glas das** magnifying glass

Vergünstigung die; ~, ~en privilege **vergüten** *tr. V.* **a)** *(erstatten)* **jmdm. etw.** ~: reimburse sb. for sth.; **b)** *(bes. Papierdt.: bezahlen)* remunerate, pay for ‹*work, services*›; **Vergütung die;** ~, ~en **a)** *(Rückerstattung)* reimbursement; **b)** *(Geldsumme)* remuneration **verhaften** *tr. V.* arrest; **Sie sind verhaftet** you are under arrest; **Verhaftung die;** ~, ~en arrest **verhalten** *unr. refl. V.* **a)** behave; *(reagieren)* react; **b)** *(beschaffen sein)* be; **Verhalten das;** ~s behaviour

Verhaltens·weise die behaviour;
Verhältnis das; ~ses, ~se a) ein ~
von drei zu eins a ratio of three to one;
b) *(persönliche Beziehung)* relationship (zu with); mit jmdm. ein ~ haben
(ugs.) have an affair with sb.; c) *Pl.*
(Umstände) conditions; **verhält-
nis·mäßig** *Adv.* relatively; com-
paratively; **Verhältnis·wort** das;
Pl. ~wörter *(Sprachw.)* preposition
verhandeln 1. *itr. V.* a) negotiate
(über + *Akk.* about); b) *(strafrechtlich)* try a case; *(zivilrechtlich)* hear a
case; 2. *tr. V.* a) etw. ~: negotiate over
sth.; b) *(strafrechtlich)* try ⟨case⟩; *(zivilrechtlich)* hear ⟨case⟩; **Verhandlung**
die a) ~en negotiations; b) *(strafrechtlich)* trial; *(zivilrechtlich)* hearing; die
~ gegen X the trial of X
verhängen *tr. V.* impose ⟨fine, punish-
ment⟩ (über + *Akk.* on); declare
⟨state of emergency, state of siege⟩;
(Sport) award, give ⟨penalty etc.⟩;
Verhängnis das; ~ses, ~se undoing;
verhängnis·voll *Adj.* disastrous
verharmlosen *tr. V.* play down
verharren *itr. V. (geh.)* remain
verhärten 1. *tr. V.* harden; make ⟨per-
son⟩ hard; 2. *refl. V.* ⟨tissue⟩ become
hardened
verhaßt *Adj.* hated; detested
verhätscheln *tr. V. (ugs.)* pamper
verhauen *(ugs.) unr. tr. V.* beat up;
(als Strafe) beat
verheben *unr. refl. V.* do oneself an
injury [while lifting sth.]
verheeren *tr. V.* devastate; lay waste
[to]; **verheerend** *Adj.* a) devastating; b) *(ugs.: scheußlich)* ghastly *(coll.)*
verhehlen *tr. V. (geh.)* conceal (*Dat.*
from)
verheilen *itr. V.; mit sein* ⟨wound⟩
heal [up]
verheimlichen *tr. V.* [jmdm.] etw. ~:
keep sth. secret [from sb.]
verheiraten *refl. V.* get married; sich
mit jmdm. ~: marry sb.; get married to
sb.; **Verheiratete** der/die; *adj. Dekl.*
married person; married man/
woman; **Verheiratung** die; ~, ~en
marriage
verhelfen *unr. itr. V.* jmdm./einer Sache zu etw. ~: help sb./sth. to get/
achieve sth.
verherrlichen *tr. V.* glorify
verheult *Adj. (ugs.)* ⟨eyes⟩ red from
crying; ⟨face⟩ puffy *or* swollen from
crying
verhexen *tr. V. (auch fig.)* bewitch

verhindern *tr. V.* prevent; **Verhinderung** die; ~, ~en prevention
verhöhnen *tr. V.* mock
Verhör das; ~[e]s, ~e interrogation;
questioning; *(bei Gericht)* examination; **verhören** 1. *tr. V.* interrogate;
question; *(bei Gericht)* examine; 2.
refl. V. mishear
verhüllen *tr. V.* cover; *(fig.)* disguise
verhungern *itr. V.; mit sein* die of
starvation; starve [to death]
verhüten *tr. V.* prevent; **Verhütung**
die; ~, ~en prevention; *(Empfäng-
nis~)* contraception; **Verhütungsmittel** das contraceptive
verirren *refl. V.* a) get lost; lose one's
way; ⟨animal⟩ stray; b) *(irgendwohin
gelangen)* stray (in, an + *Akk.* into)
verjagen *tr. V.* chase away
verkalken *refl. V.; mit sein* a) ⟨tissue⟩
calcify; ⟨arteries⟩ become hardened;
b) *(ugs.: senil werden)* become senile
Verkauf der sale; **verkaufen** *tr. V.*
(auch fig.) sell *(Dat.,* an + *Akk.* to);
„zu ~" 'for sale'; **Verkäufer** der,
Verkäuferin die a) seller; vendor
(formal); b) *(Berufsbez.)* sales *or* shop
assistant; *(im Außendienst)* salesman/
saleswoman; **verkäuflich** *Adj. (zum
Verkauf geeignet)* saleable; *(zum Verkauf bestimmt)* for sale *postpos.;* **ver-
kaufs·offen** *Adj.* der ~e Samstag
Saturday on which the shops are open
all day; **Verkaufs·preis** der retail
price
Verkehr der; ~s a) traffic; b) *(Kontakt)* contact; communication; c) *(Ge-
schlechts~)* intercourse; **verkehren**
itr. V. a) auch mit sein *(fahren)* run;
⟨aircraft⟩ fly; b) *(in Kontakt stehen)*
mit jmdm. ~: associate with sb.; c) *(zu
Gast sein)* bei jmdm. ~: visit sb. regularly
Verkehrs-: ~**ampel** die traffic lights
pl.; ~**aufkommen** das volume of
traffic; ~**hindernis** das obstruction
to traffic; ~**knotenpunkt** der [traf-
fic] junction; ~**kontrolle** die traffic
check; ~**meldung** die traffic announcement; ~**mittel** das means of
transport; die öffentlichen ~**mittel**
public transport *sing.;* ~**schild** das;
Pl. ~**schilder** traffic sign; road sign;
~**teilnehmer** der road-user; ~**unfall** der road accident; ~**zeichen** das
traffic sign; road sign
verkehrt 1. *Adj.* wrong; 2. *adv.*
wrongly; **alles** ~ **machen** do everything wrong

verkennen *unr. tr. V.* fail to recognize; misjudge ⟨*situation*⟩

verklagen *tr. V.* sue; take to court; **eine Firma auf Schadenersatz ~:** sue a company for damages

verkleben 1. *itr. V.; mit sein* stick together; **2.** *tr. V. (zukleben)* seal up ⟨*hole*⟩; *(festkleben)* stick [down] ⟨*floorcovering etc.*⟩

verkleiden *tr. V.* disguise; *(kostümieren)* dress up; **sich ~:** disguise oneself/dress [oneself] up; **Verkleidung die a)** *o. Pl.* disguising; *(das Kostümieren)* dressing up; **b)** *(Kleidung)* disguise; *(bei einer Party)* fancy dress

verkleinern 1. *tr. V.* **a)** make smaller; **b)** *(verringern)* reduce ⟨*size, number, etc.*⟩; **c)** *(kleiner reproduzieren)* reduce ⟨*photograph etc.*⟩; **2.** *refl. V.* become smaller; ⟨*number*⟩ decrease; **Verkleinerungs·form die** *(Sprachw.)* diminutive form

verknoten *tr. V.* tie; knot

verknüpfen *tr. V.* **a)** *(knoten)* tie; knot; **b)** *(in Beziehung setzen)* link

verkochen *itr. V.; mit sein* boil away

verkohlen *itr. V.* char

¹verkommen *unr. itr. V.; mit sein* go to the dogs; *(moralisch, sittlich)* go to the bad; **²verkommen** *Adj.* depraved

verköstigen *tr. V.* feed; provide with meals

verkraften *tr. V.* cope with

verkrampfen *refl. V.* ⟨*muscle*⟩ become cramped; ⟨*person*⟩ tense up; **Verkrampfung die;** ~, ~en tenseness; tension

verkriechen *unr. refl. V.* ⟨*animal*⟩ creep [away]; ⟨*person*⟩ hide [oneself away]

verkrümmt *Adj.* bent ⟨*person*⟩; crooked ⟨*finger*⟩; curved ⟨*spine*⟩; **Verkrümmung die** crookedness

verkrüppeln *tr. V.* cripple

verkümmern *itr. V.; mit sein* ⟨*person, animal*⟩ go into a decline; ⟨*plant etc.*⟩ become stunted; ⟨*talent, emotional life, etc.*⟩ wither away

verkünden *tr. V.* announce; pronounce ⟨*judgement*⟩; promulgate ⟨*law, decree*⟩; **verkündigen** *tr. V. (geh.)* announce; proclaim; **Verkündigung die** announcement; proclamation

verkürzen *tr. V.* **a)** *(verringern)* reduce; *(abkürzen)* shorten; **b)** *(abbrechen)* cut short ⟨*stay, life*⟩; put an end to, end ⟨*suffering*⟩

verladen *unr. tr. V.* load

Verlag der; ~[e]s, ~e publishing house *or* firm; publisher's

verlagern *tr. V.* shift; *(an einen anderen Ort)* move; *(fig.)* transfer; shift ⟨*emphasis*⟩

verlangen *tr. V.* demand; *(nötig haben)* ⟨*task etc.*⟩ require, call for ⟨*patience, knowledge, experience, skill, etc.*⟩; *(berechnen)* charge; *(sehen/sprechen wollen)* ask for; **du wirst am Telefon verlangt** you're wanted on the phone *(coll.)*; **Verlangen das;** ~s, ~ **a)** desire (**nach** for); **b) auf ~:** on request

verlängern *tr. V.* extend; lengthen; make longer ⟨*skirt, sleeve, etc.*⟩; renew ⟨*passport, driving-licence, etc.*⟩

Verlängerung die; ~, ~en *s.* verlängern: extension; lengthening; renewal

verlangsamen *tr. V.* **das Tempo/seine Schritte ~:** reduce speed/slacken one's pace; slow down

¹verlassen 1. *unr. refl. V.* rely, depend (**auf** + *Akk.* on); **2.** *unr. tr. V.* leave; **²verlassen** *Adj.* deserted ⟨*street etc.*⟩; empty ⟨*house*⟩; *(öd)* desolate ⟨*region etc.*⟩

verläßlich 1. *Adj.* reliable; **2.** *adv.* reliably

Verlauf der; ~[e]s, Verläufe course; **verlaufen 1.** *unr. itr. V.; mit sein* **a)** *(sich erstrecken)* run; **b)** *(ablaufen)* ⟨*test, rehearsal, etc.*⟩ go; ⟨*party etc.*⟩ go off; **2.** *unr. refl. V.* get lost; lose one's way; **Verlaufs·form die** *(Sprachw.)* progressive *or* continuous form

verlautbaren *tr. V.* announce [officially]; **verlauten** *itr. V.; mit sein* be reported; **wie verlautet** according to reports

verleben *tr. V.* spend; **verlebt** *Adj.* dissipated

¹verlegen *tr. V.* **a)** mislay; **b)** *(verschieben)* postpone (**auf** + *Akk.* until); *(vor~)* bring forward (**auf** + *Akk.* to); **einen Termin ~:** alter an appointment; **c)** *(verlagern)* move; transfer ⟨*patient*⟩; **d)** *(legen)* lay ⟨*cable, pipe, carpet, etc.*⟩; **²verlegen 1.** *Adj.* embarrassed; **2.** *adv.* in embarrassment; **Verlegenheit die;** ~, ~en **a)** *o. Pl. (Befangenheit)* embarrassment; **jmdn. in ~ bringen** embarrass sb.; **b)** *(Unannehmlichkeit)* embarrassing situation

Verleger der; ~s, ~, **Verlegerin die;** ~, ~nen publisher

Verleih der; ~[e]s, ~e **a)** *o. Pl.* hiring out; *(von Autos)* renting *or* hiring out;

b) *(Unternehmen)* hire firm; *(Film~)* distribution company; *(Video~)* video library; *(Auto~)* rental *or* hire firm; **verleihen** *unr. tr. V.* **a)** hire out; rent *or* hire out ⟨*car*⟩; *(umsonst)* lend [out]; **b)** *(überreichen)* award; confer ⟨*award, honour*⟩
Verleihung die; ~, ~en **a)** *s.* verleihen **a:** hiring out; renting out; lending [out]; **b)** *s.* verleihen **b:** awarding; conferring; *(Zeremonie)* award; conferment
verleiten *tr. V.* jmdn. dazu ~, etw. zu tun lead *or* induce sb. to do sth.
verlernen *tr. V.* forget
verlesen 1. *unr. tr. V.* read out; **2.** *unr. refl. V. (falsch lesen)* make a mistake/ mistakes in reading
verletzen *tr. V.* **a)** injure; *(durch Schuß, Stich)* wound; **b)** *(kränken)* hurt ⟨*person, feelings*⟩; **c)** *(verstoßen gegen)* violate; infringe ⟨*regulation*⟩; break ⟨*agreement, law*⟩; **verletzlich** *Adj.* vulnerable; **Verletzte** der/die; *adj. Dekl.* casualty; *(durch Schuß, Stich)* wounded person; **Verletzung** die; ~, ~en **a)** *(Wunde)* injury; **b)** *(Kränkung)* hurting; **c)** *s.* verletzen **c:** violation; infringement; breaking
verleugnen *tr. V.* deny; disown ⟨*friend, relation*⟩
verleumden *tr. V.* slander; *(schriftlich)* libel; **Verleumdung** die; ~, ~en slander; *(in Schriftform)* libel
verlieben *refl. V.* fall in love (**in** + *Akk.* with); **Verliebte** der/die; *adj. Dekl.* lover
verlieren *unr. tr., itr. V.* lose; **Verlierer** der; ~s, ~: loser
verloben *refl. V.* get engaged; **verlobt sein** be engaged; **Verlobte** der/die; *adj. Dekl.* fiancé/fiancée
verlockend *Adj.* tempting; **Verlockung** die temptation
verlogen *Adj.* lying, mendacious ⟨*person*⟩; false ⟨*morality etc.*⟩
verlor *1. u. 3. Pers. Sg. Prät. v.* verlieren; **verloren** *2. Part. v.* verlieren; **verloren|gehen** *unr. itr. V.; mit sein* get lost
verlosen *tr. V.* raffle; **Verlosung** die; ~, ~en raffle; draw
verlottern *itr. V.; mit sein* ⟨*person*⟩ go to seed
Verlust der; ~|e|s, ~e loss (**an** + *Dat.* of)
vermachen *tr. V.* jmdm. etw. ~: leave *or* bequeath sth. to sb.; *(fig.: schenken, überlassen)* give sth. to sb.

vermählen *refl. V. (geh.)* sich |jmdm. *od.* mit jmdm.| ~: marry *or* wed [sb.]; **Vermählung** die; ~, ~en *(geh.)* **a)** marriage; **b)** *(Fest)* wedding ceremony
vermehren 1. *tr. V.* increase (**um** by); **2.** *refl. V.* **a)** increase; **b)** *(sich fortpflanzen)* reproduce; **Vermehrung** die; ~, ~en **a)** increase (*Gen.* in); **b)** *(Fortpflanzung)* reproduction
vermeiden *unr. tr. V.* avoid
vermeintlich *Adj.* supposed
vermengen *tr. V.* mix (**miteinander** together)
Vermerk der; ~|e|s, ~e note; *(amtlich)* remark; **vermerken** *tr. V.* make a note of; note [down]; *(in Akten, Wachbuch usw.)* record
¹vermessen *unr. tr. V.* measure; survey ⟨*land, site*⟩; **²vermessen** *Adj. (geh.)* presumptuous
vermieten *tr. V. (auch itr.) V.* rent [out], let [out] (**an** + *Akk.* to); hire [out] ⟨*boat, car, etc.*⟩; „Zimmer zu ~“ 'room to let'; **Vermieter** der landlord; **Vermieterin** die landlady
vermindern 1. *tr. V.* reduce; decrease; reduce, lessen ⟨*danger, stress*⟩; lower ⟨*resistance*⟩; reduce ⟨*debt*⟩; **2.** *refl. V.* decrease; ⟨*resistance*⟩ diminish
vermischen 1. *tr. V.* mix (**miteinander** together); blend ⟨*teas, tobaccos, etc.*⟩; **2.** *refl. V.* mix; *(fig.)* mingle; ⟨*races, animals*⟩ interbreed; **Vermischung** die *s.* vermischen: mixing; blending; *(fig.)* mingling
vermissen *tr. V.* **a)** miss; **b)** *(nicht haben)* ich vermisse meinen Ausweis my identity card is missing; **Vermißte** der/die; *adj. Dekl.* missing person
vermitteln 1. *itr. V.* mediate, act as [a] mediator (**in** + *Dat.* in); **2.** *tr. V.* **a)** *(herbeiführen)* arrange; negotiate ⟨*transaction, cease-fire, compromise*⟩; **b)** *(besorgen)* jmdm. eine Stelle ~: find sb. a job; **c)** *(weitergeben)* impart ⟨*knowledge, insight, values, etc.*⟩; communicate, ⟨*message, information, etc.*⟩; convey ⟨*feeling*⟩; pass on ⟨*experience*⟩; **Vermittler** der; ~s, ~ **a)** *(Mittler)* mediator; **b)** *s.* vermitteln **2 c:** imparter; communicator; conveyer; **c)** *(von Berufs wegen)* agent; **Vermittlung** die; ~, ~en **a)** *(Schlichtung)* mediation; **b)** *s.* vermitteln **2 a:** arrangement; negotiation; **c)** *s.* vermitteln **2 c:** imparting; communicating; conveying; **d)** *(Telefonzentrale)* exchange; *(in einer Firma)* switchboard

vermögen *(geh.) unr. tr. V.* **etw. zu tun**
~: be able to do sth.; be capable of
doing sth.; **Vermögen das;** ~s, ~ a)
o. Pl. (geh.: Fähigkeit) ability; b) *(Besitz)* fortune; **er hat** ~: he has money;
vermögend *Adj.* wealthy; well-off;
Vermögen[s]·steuer die wealth
tax
vermummen *tr. V.* wrap up
[warmly]; *(verbergen)* disguise
vermuten *tr. V.* suspect; **das ist zu** ~:
that is what one would suppose *or* expect; we may assume that; **vermutlich 1.** *Adj.* probable; **2.** *Adv.* presumably; *(wahrscheinlich)* probably;
Vermutung die; ~, ~en supposition
vernachlässigen *tr. V.* neglect; *(unberücksichtigt lassen)* ignore; disregard; **Vernachlässigung die;** ~, ~en
neglect
vernarben *itr. V.; mit sein* [form a]
scar; heal *(lit. or fig.)*
vernehmbar *Adj. (geh.)* audible;
vernehmen *unr. tr. V.* a) *(geh.: hören, erfahren)* hear; b) *(verhören)*
question; **vernehmlich 1.** *Adj.*
[clearly] audible; **2.** *adv.* audibly;
Vernehmung die; ~, ~en questioning
verneigen *refl. V. (geh.)* bow (**vor** +
Dat. to, *(literary)* before)
verneinen *tr. (auch itr.) V.* a) say 'no'
to *(question)*; answer *(question)* in the
negative; b) *(Sprachw.)* negate; **Verneinung die;** ~, ~en *(Sprachw.)*
negation
vernichten *tr. V.* destroy; exterminate *(pests, vermin)*; **Vernichtung
die;** ~, ~en destruction; *(von Schädlingen)* extermination
Vernunft die; ~: reason; **vernünftig
1.** *Adj.* a) sensible; b) *(ugs.: ordentlich, richtig)* decent; **2.** *adv.* a) sensibly; b)
(ugs.: ordentlich, richtig) (talk, eat)
properly; *(dress)* sensibly
veröffentlichen *tr. V.* publish; **Veröffentlichung die;** ~, ~en publication
verordnen *tr. V.* [jmdm. etw.] ~: prescribe [sth. for sb.]; **Verordnung die**
prescribing
verpachten *tr. V.* lease
verpacken *tr. V.* pack; wrap up
(present, parcel); **Verpackung die a)**
o.Pl. packing; b) *(Umhüllung)* packaging *no pl.;* wrapping
verpassen *tr. V.* miss
verpflanzen *tr. V. (auch Med.)* transplant; graft *(skin)*

verpflegen *tr. V.* cater for; feed;
Verpflegung die; ~, ~en a) *o.Pl.*
catering *no indef. art. (Gen.* for); b)
(Nahrung) food; **Unterkunft und** ~:
board and lodging
verpflichten 1. *tr. V.* a) oblige; commit; *(festlegen, binden)* bind; b) *(einstellen, engagieren)* engage *(manager,
actor, etc.)*; **2.** *refl. V.* undertake;
promise; **sich vertraglich** ~: sign a
contract; **Verpflichtung die;** ~, ~en
a) obligation; commitment; b) *(Engagement)* engaging; engagement
verprügeln *tr. V.* beat up; *(zur Strafe)*
thrash
Verputz der plaster; *(auf Außenwänden)* rendering; **verputzen** *tr. V.*
plaster; render *(outside wall)*
verquollen *Adj.* swollen
Verrat der; ~[e]s betrayal (**an** + *Dat.*
of); **verraten** *unr. tr. V.* a) betray (**an**
+ *Akk.* to); b) *(ugs.: mitteilen)* jmdm.
den Grund *usw.* ~: tell sb. the reason
etc.; c) *(erkennen lassen)* show, betray
(feelings, surprise, fear, etc.); show *(influence, talent)*; **Verräter der;** ~s, ~:
traitor; **Verräterin die;** ~, ~en traitress; **verräterisch** *Adj.* treacherous
(plan, purpose, act, etc.)
verrechnen 1. *tr. V.* include *(amount
etc.)*; *(gutschreiben)* credit *(cheque
etc.)* to another account; **2.** *refl. V.*
miscalculate; **Verrechnungsscheck der** crossed cheque
verregnen *itr. V.; mit sein* be spoilt *or*
ruined by rain
verreiben *unr. tr. V.* rub in
verreisen *itr. V.; mit sein* go away
verrenken *tr. V.* dislocate; **Verrenkung die;** ~, ~en dislocation
verrichten *tr. V.* perform
verriegeln *tr. V.* bolt
verringern 1. *tr. V.* reduce; **2.** *refl. V.*
decrease; **Verringerung die;** ~: reduction; decrease *(Gen., von in)*
verrosten *itr. V.; mit sein* rust; **verrostet** rusty
verrückt *(ugs.)* **1.** *Adj.* a) mad; ~ **werden** go mad *or* insane; b) *(überspannt,
ausgefallen)* crazy *(idea, fashion,
prank, day, etc.)*; **2.** *adv.* crazily; *(behave)* crazily *or* like a madman; *(dress
etc.)* in a mad *or* crazy way; **Verrückte der/die;** *adj. Dekl. (ugs.)*
madman/madwoman; lunatic
verrühren *tr. V.* stir together; mix
verrutschen *itr. V.* slip
Vers der; ~es, ~e verse
versagen *itr. V.* fail; *(machine, en-*

gine⟩ stop [working]; **menschliches Versagen** human error; **Versager der; ~s, ~**: failure

versalzen *unr. tr. V.* put too much salt in/on; *(fig. ugs.)* spoil

versammeln *tr., refl. V.* assemble; **Versammlung die a)** meeting; **b)** *(Gremium)* assembly

versäumen *tr. V.* **a)** *(verpassen)* miss; lose ⟨*time, sleep*⟩; **b)** *(vernachlässigen, unterlassen)* neglect ⟨*duty, task*⟩

verschaffen *tr. V.* **jmdm. etw. ~**: provide sb. with sth.; get sb. sth.; **sich** *(Dat.)* **etw. ~**: get hold of sth.; obtain sth.

verschämt [fɛɐ̯ʃɛːmt] **1.** *Adj.* bashful; **2.** *adv.* bashfully

verschenken *tr. V.* give away

verscheuchen *tr. V.* chase away

verschieben 1. *unr. tr. V.* **a)** shift; move; **b)** *(aufschieben)* put off, postpone (**auf** + *Akk.* till); **2.** *unr. refl. V.* be postponed (**um** for); ⟨*start*⟩ be put back *or* delayed (**um** by); **Verschiebung die** postponement

verschieden 1. *Adj.* **a)** different (**von** from); **b)** *(vielfältig)* various; **die ~sten** ...: all sorts of ...; **die ~en** ...: the various ...; **c)** **~es** various things *pl.*; **2.** *adv.* differently; **verschieden·artig 1.** *Adj.* different in kind *pred.*; *(mehr als zwei)* diverse; **2.** *adv.* diversely; **Verschiedenheit die; ~, ~en** difference; *(unter mehreren)* diversity; **verschiedentlich** *Adv.* on various occasions

verschimmeln *itr. V.; mit sein* go mouldy; **verschimmelt** mouldy

¹verschlafen 1. *unr. itr. (auch refl.)V.* oversleep; **2.** *unr. tr. V.* **a)** *(schlafend verbringen)* sleep through ⟨*morning, journey, etc.*⟩; **b)** *(versäumen)* not wake up in time for ⟨*appointment*⟩; not wake up in time to catch ⟨*train, bus*⟩; **c)** *(ugs.: vergessen)* forget about ⟨*appointment etc.*⟩; **²verschlafen** *Adj.* half-asleep; *(fig.)* sleepy ⟨*town*⟩

Verschlag der shed

¹verschlagen *unr. tr. V.* **die Seite ~**: lose one's place *or* page; **jmdm. die Sprache ~**: leave sb. speechless; **²verschlagen 1.** *Adj.* sly; shifty; **2.** *adv.* slyly; shiftily

verschlechtern 1. *tr. V.* make worse; **2.** *refl. V.* get worse; deteriorate; **Verschlechterung die; ~, ~en** worsening, deterioration (*Gen.* in)

Verschleiß der; ~es, ~e a) wear *no*

indef. art.; **b)** *(Verbrauch)* consumption (**an** + *Dat.* of); **verschleißen 1.** *unr. itr. V.; mit sein* wear out; **2.** *unr. tr. V.* wear out; *(fig.)* run dowr., ruin ⟨*one's nerves, one's health*⟩; use up ⟨*energy, ability, etc.*⟩

verschleppen *tr. V.* **a)** carry off; take away ⟨*person*⟩; **b)** *(weiterverbreiten)* carry, spread ⟨*disease, bacteria, mud, etc.*⟩; **c)** *(verzögern)* delay; *(in die Länge ziehen)* draw out; let ⟨*illness*⟩ drag on [and get worse]

verschleudern *tr. V.* **a)** sell dirt cheap; *(mit Verlust)* sell at a loss; **b)** *(verschwenden)* squander

verschließbar *Adj.* closable; lockable ⟨*suitcase, drawer, etc.*⟩; |luftdicht| **~**: sealable ⟨*container etc.*⟩; **verschließen** *unr. tr. V.* **a)** close; stop, *(mit einem Korken)* cork ⟨*bottle*⟩; **b)** *(abschließen)* lock; lock up ⟨*house etc.*⟩; **c)** *(wegschließen)* lock away (**in** + *Dat. od. Akk.* in)

verschlimmern 1. *tr. V.* make worse; **2.** *refl. V.* get worse; ⟨*position, conditions*⟩ deteriorate, worsen

verschlingen *unr. tr. V.* **a)** [inter]twine ⟨*threads etc.*⟩ (**zu** into); **b)** *(essen, fressen)* devour ⟨*food*⟩; *(fig.)* devour ⟨*novel, money, etc.*⟩

verschlissen 2. Part. v. verschleißen 2

verschlossen *Adj. (wortkarg)* taciturn; *(zurückhaltend)* reserved

verschlucken 1. *tr. V.* swallow; **2.** *refl. V.* choke

Verschluß der *(am BH, an Schmuck usw.)* fastener; fastening; *(an Taschen, Schmuck)* clasp; *(an Schuhen, Gürteln)* buckle; *(am Schrank, Fenster, Koffer usw.)* catch; *(an Flaschen)* top; *(Stöpsel)* stopper

verschmähen *tr. V. (geh.)* spurn

verschmerzen *tr. V.* get over

verschmieren *tr. V.* smear ⟨*window etc.*⟩; *(beim Schreiben)* mess up ⟨*paper*⟩; scrawl all over ⟨*page*⟩; smudge ⟨*ink*⟩

verschmitzt 1. *Adj.* mischievous; **2.** *adv.* mischievously

verschmutzen 1. *itr. V.; mit sein* get dirty; ⟨*river etc.*⟩ become polluted; **2.** *tr. V.* dirty; soil; pollute ⟨*air, water, etc.*⟩; **Verschmutzung die; ~, ~en** *(der Umwelt)* pollution; *(von Stoffen, Teppichen usw.)* soiling

verschnaufen *itr. (auch refl.) V.* have *or* take a breather

verschneit *Adj.* snow-covered *attrib.;* covered with snow *postpos.*

verschnörkelt *Adj.* ornate
verschnüren *tr. V.* tie up
verschollen *Adj.* missing
verschonen *tr. V.* spare; **jmdn. mit
etw. ~:** spare sb. sth.
verschränken *tr. V.* fold ⟨*arms*⟩;
cross ⟨*legs*⟩; clasp ⟨*hands*⟩
verschreiben 1. *unr. tr. V. (Med.: verordnen)* prescribe; 2. *unr. refl. V.* **a)**
make a slip of the pen; **b) sich einer
Sache** *(Dat.)* **~:** devote oneself to sth.;
verschreibungs·pflichtig *Adj.*
available only on prescription *postpos.*
verschrie[e]n *Adj.* notorious **(wegen**
for)
verschulden 1. *tr. V.* be to blame for
⟨*accident, death, etc.*⟩; 2. *refl. V.* get
into debt; **Verschulden das;** **~s**
guilt; **durch eigenes ~:** through one's
own fault; **verschuldet** *Adj.* in debt
postpos. **(bei** to); **hoch ~:** deeply in
debt
verschütten *tr. V.* **a)** spill; **b)** *(begraben)* bury ⟨*person*⟩ [alive]
verschwägert *Adj.* related by marriage *postpos.*
verschweigen *unr. tr. V.* conceal
(*Dat.* from)
verschwenden *tr. V.* waste **(an** +
Akk. on); **Verschwender der; ~s, ~**
(von Geld) spendthrift; *(von Dingen)*
wasteful person; **verschwende-
risch** 1. *Adj.* wasteful ⟨*person*⟩; ⟨*life*⟩
of extravagance; 2. *adv.* wastefully;
Verschwendung die; ~, ~en waste-
fulness; extravagance
verschwiegen *Adj.* discreet; *(still,
einsam)* secluded; **Verschwiegenheit die; ~:** secrecy; *(Diskretion)* discretion
verschwimmen *unr. itr. V.; mit sein*
blur
verschwinden *unr. itr. V.; mit sein*
disappear; vanish; **verschwinde [hier]!**
off with you!; go away!; hop it! *(sl.);*
ich muß mal ~ *(ugs. verhüll.)* I have to
pay a visit *(coll.) or (Brit. coll.)* spend a
penny
verschwommen 1. *Adj.* blurred
⟨*photograph, vision*⟩; blurred, hazy
⟨*outline*⟩; vague, woolly ⟨*idea, concept, formulation, etc.*⟩; 2. *adv.*
vaguely; ⟨*remember*⟩ hazily
versehen 1. *unr. tr. V.* **a)** *(ausstatten)*
provide; equip ⟨*car, factory, machine,
etc.*⟩; **b)** *(ausüben, besorgen)* perform
⟨*duty etc.*⟩; 2. *unr. refl. V.* make a slip;
slip up; **Versehen das; ~s, ~:** over-

sight; slip; **aus ~:** by mistake; inadvertently; **versehentlich** 1. *Adv.* by
mistake; inadvertently; 2. *adj.; nicht
präd.* inadvertent
Versehrte der/die; *adj. Dekl.* disabled person; **die ~n** the disabled
versenden *unr. tr. V. (auch regelm.) tr. V.*
send ⟨*letter, parcel*⟩; send out ⟨*invita-
tions*⟩; dispatch ⟨*goods*⟩
versetzen 1. *tr. V.* **a)** move; transfer,
move ⟨*employee*⟩; *(in die nächsthöhere
Klasse)* move ⟨*pupil*⟩ up, *(Amer.)* promote ⟨*pupil*⟩ **(in** + *Akk.* to); *(umpflanzen)* transplant, move ⟨*plant*⟩; *(fig.)*
transport **(in** + *Akk.* to); **b)** *(nicht ge-
radlinig anordnen)* stagger; **c)** *(verpfänden)* pawn; **d)** *(verkaufen)* sell; **e)**
(ugs.: vergeblich warten lassen) stand
⟨*person*⟩ up *(coll.);* **f)** *(vermischen)*
mix; **g)** *(erwidern)* retort; **h) etw. in Be-
wegung/Tätigkeit ~:** set sth. in mo-
tion/operation; **jmdn. in die Lage ~,
etw. zu tun** put sb. in a position to do
sth.; **jmdm. einen Stoß/Fußtritt/
Schlag** *usw.* **~:** give sb. a push/kick/
deal sb. a blow *etc.*; 2. *refl. V.* **sich in
jmds. Lage** *(Akk.)* **~:** put oneself in
sb.'s position *or* place; **Versetzung
die; ~, ~en** *(eines Schülers)* moving
up, *(Amer.)* promotion **(in** + *Akk.* to);
(eines Angestellten) transfer
verseuchen *tr. V. (auch fig.)* contaminate; **radioaktiv ~:** contaminate with
radioactivity
versichern *tr. V.* **a)** assert ⟨*sth.*⟩; **b)**
(vertraglich schützen) insure **(bei**
with); **Versicherte der/die;** *adj.
Dekl.* insured [person]; **Versicherung die a)** *(Beteuerung)* assurance;
b) *(Schutz durch Vertrag)* insurance;
(Vertrag) insurance [policy] **(über** +
Akk. for); *(Gesellschaft)* insurance
[company]
Versicherungs-: ~beitrag der insurance premium; **~gesellschaft
die** insurance company; **~police die**
insurance policy
versickern *itr. V.; mit sein* ⟨*river etc.*⟩
drain *or* seep away
versiegeln *tr. V.* seal
versiegen *itr. V.; mit sein (geh.)* dry
up; run dry
versinken *unr. itr. V.; mit sein* sink;
im Schlamm ~: sink into the mud
versöhnen 1. *refl. V.* **sich [miteinan-
der] ~:** become reconciled; **sich mit
jmdm. ~:** make it up with sb.; 2. *tr. V.*
reconcile; **Versöhnung die; ~, ~en**
reconciliation

versonnen 1. *Adj.* dreamy; **2.** *adv.* dreamily

versọrgen *tr. V.* **a)** supply; **b)** *(unterhalten, ernähren)* provide for ⟨children, family⟩; **c)** *(sorgen für)* look after; jmdn. ärztlich ~: give sb. medical care; *(kurzzeitig)* give sb. medical attention; **Versọrger der;** ~s, ~, **Versọrgerin die;** ~, ~nen breadwinner; **Versọrgung die;** ~, ~en a) o. *Pl.* supply[ing]; **b)** *(Unterhaltung, Ernährung)* support[ing]; **c)** *(Bedienung, Pflege)* care; ärztliche ~: medical care *or* treatment; *(kurzzeitig)* medical attention

Verspạnnung die *(Med.: der Muskulatur)* tension

verspäten *refl. V.* be late; **verspätet** *Adj.* late ⟨arrival etc.⟩; belated ⟨greetings, thanks⟩; ~ eintreffen arrive late; **Verspätung die;** ~, ~en lateness; *(verspätetes Eintreffen)* late arrival; |fünf Minuten| ~ haben be [five minutes] late

versperren *tr. V.* block; obstruct ⟨view⟩

verspielen *tr. V.* gamble away; *(fig.)* squander, throw away ⟨opportunity, chance⟩; forfeit ⟨right, credibility, etc⟩; **verspielt 1.** *Adj.* *(auch fig.)* playful; fanciful, fantastic ⟨form, design, etc.⟩; **2.** *adv.* playfully *(lit. or fig.)*; ⟨dress, designed⟩ fancifully, fantastically

verspọtten *tr. V.* mock; ridicule

versprechen 1. *unr. tr. V.* promise; sich *(Dat.)* etw. von etw./jmdm. ~: hope for sth. *or* to get sth. from sth./sb.; **2.** *unr. refl. V.* make a slip/slips of the tongue; **Versprechen das;** ~s, ~, **Versprechung die;** ~, ~en promise

versprühen *tr. V.* spray

verspüren *tr. V.* feel

Verstạnd der; ~|e|s *(Fähigkeit zu denken)* reason *no art.*; *(Fähigkeit, Begriffe zu bilden)* mind; *(Vernunft)* [common] sense *no art.*; hast du denn den ~ verloren? *(ugs.)* have you taken leave of your senses?; **verständig 1.** *Adj.* sensible; **2.** *adv.* sensibly

verständigen 1. *tr. V.* notify, inform (von, über + *Akk.* of); **2.** *refl. V.* **a)** make oneself understood; sich mit jmdm. ~: communicate with sb.; **b)** *(sich einigen)* sich |mit jmdm.| über/auf etw. *(Akk.)* ~: come to an understanding [with sb.] about *or.* on sth.; **Verständigkeit die;** ~: understanding; intelligence; **Verständigung die;** ~,

~en **a)** notification; **b)** *(das Sichverständlichmachen)* communication *no art.*; **c)** *(Einigung)* understanding; **Verständigungs·schwierigkeit die** difficulty of communication; **verständlich 1.** *Adj.* **a)** comprehensible; *(deutlich)* clear ⟨pronunciation, presentation, etc.⟩; sich ~ machen make oneself understood; jmdm. etw. ~ machen make sth. clear to sb.; **b)** *(begreiflich, verzeihlich)* understandable; **2.** *adv.* comprehensibly; *(deutlich)* ⟨speak, express oneself, present⟩ clearly; **verständlicher·weise** *Adv.* understandably; **Verständlichkeit die;** ~: comprehensibility; clarity; **Verständnis das;** ~ses, ~se understanding; ich habe volles ~ dafür, daß ...: I fully understand that ...; für die Unannehmlichkeiten bitten wir um |Ihr| ~: we apologize for the inconvenience caused

verständnis-: ~los **1.** *Adj.* uncomprehending; **2.** *adv.* uncomprehendingly; ~voll **1.** *Adj.* understanding; **2.** *adv.* understandingly

verstärken 1. *tr. V.* **a)** strengthen; **b)** *(zahlenmäßig)* reinforce ⟨troops etc.⟩ (um by); enlarge ⟨orchestra, choir⟩ (um by); **c)** *(intensiver machen)* intensify, increase ⟨effort, contrast⟩; strengthen, increase ⟨impression, suspicion⟩; *(größer machen)* increase ⟨pressure, voltage, effect, etc.⟩; *(lauter machen)* amplify ⟨signal, sound, guitar, etc.⟩; **2.** *refl. V.* increase; **Verstärker der;** ~s, ~: amplifier; **Verstärkung die;** ~, ~en **a)** strengthening; **b)** *(zahlenmäßig)* reinforcement *(esp. Mil.)*; **c)** *(Zunahme)* increase ⟨Gen. in⟩; *(der Lautstärke)* amplification; **d)** *(zusätzliche Person[en])* reinforcements *pl.*

verstauben *itr. V.; mit sein* get dusty; gather dust *(lit. or fig.)*

verstauchen *tr. V.* sprain; sich *(Dat.)* den Fuß/die Hand ~: sprain one's ankle/wrist; **Verstauchung die;** ~, ~en sprain

verstauen *tr. V.* pack (in + *Dat. od.* Akk. in[to]); *(bes. im Boot/Auto)* stow (in + *Dat. od. Akk.* in)

Verstẹck das; ~|e|s, ~e hiding-place: ~ spielen play hide-and-seek; **verstẹcken 1.** *tr. V.* hide (vor + *Dat.* from); **2.** *refl. V.* sich |vor jmdm./etw.| ~: hide [from sb./sth.]; **verstẹckt** *Adj.* hidden; *(heimlich)* secret ⟨malice, activity, etc.⟩; disguised ⟨foul⟩

verstehen 1. *unr. tr. V.* understand;

wie soll ich das ~? how am I to interpret that?; **jmdn./etw. falsch ~:** misunderstand sb./sth.; **2.** *unr. refl. V.* **sich mit jmdm. ~:** get on with sb.; **das versteht sich |von selbst|** that goes without saying
versteigern *tr. V.* auction; **etw. ~ lassen** put sth. up for auction; **Versteigerung die** auction
verstellbar *Adj.* adjustable; **verstellen 1.** *tr. V.* **a)** *(falsch plazieren)* misplace; **b)** *(anders einstellen)* adjust ⟨*seat etc.*⟩; alter [the adjustment of] ⟨*mirror etc.*⟩; reset ⟨*alarm clock, points, etc.*⟩; **c)** *(versperren)* block, obstruct; **d)** *(zur Täuschung verändern)* disguise ⟨*voice, handwriting*⟩; **2.** *refl. V.* pretend; **Verstellung die** pretence; *(der Stimme, Schrift)* disguising
verstimmen *tr. V.* put ⟨*person*⟩ in a bad mood; *(verärgern)* annoy; **verstimmt** *Adj.* **a)** *(Musik)* out of tune *pred.;* **b)** *(verärgert)* put out, peeved, disgruntled (**über** + *Akk.* by, about); **ein ~er Magen** an upset stomach; **Verstimmung die** bad mood
verstohlen 1. *Adj.* furtive; **2.** *adv.* furtively
verstopfen 1. *tr. V.* block; **verstopft sein** ⟨*pipe, drain, jet, nose, etc.*⟩ be blocked (**durch,** von with); **2.** *itr. V.; mit sein* become blocked; **Verstopfung die;** ~, ~en *(Med.)* constipation
verstorben *Adj.* late; **Verstorbene der/die;** *adj. Dekl. (geh.)* deceased
verstören *tr. V.* distress; **verstört** *Adj.* distraught
Verstoß der violation (**gegen** of); **verstoßen 1.** *unr. tr. V.* disown; **2.** *unr. itr. V.* **gegen etw. ~:** infringe sth.
verstreichen 1. *unr. tr. V.* apply, put on ⟨*paint*⟩; spread ⟨*butter etc.*⟩; **2.** *unr. itr. V.; mit sein (geh.)* ⟨*time*⟩ pass [by]
verstreuen *tr. V.* scatter; put down ⟨*bird food, salt*⟩; *(versehentlich)* spill
verstricken 1. *tr. V.* **jmdn. in etw.** *(Akk.)* ~: involve sb. in sth.; draw sb. into sth.; **2.** *refl. V.* **sich in etw.** *(Akk.)* ~: become entangled *or* caught up in sth.
verstümmeln *tr. V.* mutilate; *(fig.)* garble ⟨*report*⟩; chop, mutilate ⟨*text*⟩
verstummen *itr. V.; mit sein (geh.)* fall silent; ⟨*music, noise, conversation*⟩ cease
Versuch der; ~|e|s, ~e attempt; *(Experiment)* experiment (**an** + *Dat.* on); *(Probe)* test; **versuchen** *tr. V.* **a)** try; attempt; **b)** *(probieren)* try ⟨*cake etc.*⟩

versündigen *refl. V.* **sich an jmdm./etw. ~:** sin against sb./sth.
versüßen *tr. V.* **jmdm./sich etw. ~** *(fig.)* make sth. more pleasant for sb./oneself
vertauschen *tr. V.* exchange; switch; reverse ⟨*roles, poles*⟩; **etw. mit** *od.* **gegen etw. ~:** exchange sth. for sth.
verteidigen *tr. V.* defend; **Verteidiger der;** ~s, ~, **Verteidigerin, die;** ~, ~nen *(auch Sport)* defender; *(Rechtsw.)* defence counsel; **Verteidigung die,** ~, ~en defence; **Verteidigungs·minister der** minister of defence
verteilen *tr. V.* distribute, hand out ⟨*leaflets, prizes, etc.*⟩ (**an** + *Akk.* to, **unter** + *Akk.* among); share [out], distribute ⟨*money, food*⟩ (**an** + *Akk.* to, **unter** + *Akk.* among); allocate ⟨*work*⟩; distribute ⟨*weight etc.*⟩ (**auf** + *Akk.* over); spread ⟨*cost*⟩ (**auf** + *Akk.* among); distribute, spread ⟨*butter, seed, dirt, etc.*⟩; **Verteilung die** distribution; *(der Rollen, der Arbeit)* allocation
verteuern 1. *tr. V.* make ⟨*goods*⟩ more expensive; **2.** *refl. V.* become more expensive
verteufeln *tr. V.* condemn; denigrate
vertiefen 1. *tr. V.* *(auch fig.)* deepen (**um** by); **2.** *refl. V.* **sich ~ in** (+ *Akk.*) bury oneself in ⟨*book, work, etc.*⟩; **in etw.** *(Akk.)* **vertieft sein** be engrossed in sth.; **Vertiefung die;** ~, ~en *(Muldě)* depression; hollow
vertikal 1. *Adj.* vertical; **2.** *adv.* vertically; **Vertikale die;** ~; ~n *s.* **Senkrechte**
vertilgen *tr. V.* **a)** *(vernichten)* exterminate ⟨*vermin*⟩; kill off ⟨*weeds*⟩; **b)** *(ugs.: verzehren)* devour, *(joc.)* demolish ⟨*food*⟩
vertonen *tr. V.* set ⟨*text, poem*⟩ to music; **Vertonung die;** ~, ~en setting
Vertrag der; ~|e|s, **Verträge** contract; *(zwischen Staaten)* treaty; **vertragen 1.** *unr. tr. V.* endure; tolerate *(esp. Med.);* *(aushalten, leiden können)* stand; bear; **ich vertrage keinen Kaffee** coffee disagrees with me; **2.** *unr. refl. V.* **sich mit jmdm. ~:** get on *or* along with sb.; *(passen)* **sich mit etw. ~:** go with sth.; **verträglich 1.** *Adj.* contractual; **2.** *adv.* contractually; by contract; **verträglich** *Adj.* **a)** digestible ⟨*food*⟩; **b)** *(umgänglich)* good-natured; easy to get on with *pred.*

vertrauen itr. V. jmdm./einer Sache ~: trust sb./sth.; **auf etw.** (Akk.) ~: [put one's] trust in sth.; **Vertrauen das;** ~s trust; confidence; **jmdn. ins ~ ziehen** take sb. into one's confidence; **vertrauen·erweckend** Adj. inspiring

vertrauens-, Vertrauens-: ~**bruch der** breach of trust; ~**person die** person in a position of trust; ~**sache die** matter or question of trust; ~**selig** Adj. all too trusting; ~**voll 1.** Adj. trusting ⟨relationship⟩; ⟨collaboration, co-operation⟩ based on trust; (zuversichtlich) confident; **2.** adv. trustingly; (zuversichtlich) confidently; ~**würdig** Adj. trustworthy

vertraulich 1. Adj. **a)** confidential; **b)** (freundschaftlich, intim) familiar ⟨manner, tone, etc.⟩; intimate ⟨conversation⟩; **2.** adv. **a)** confidentially; **b)** (freundschaftlich, intim) in a familiar way; **Vertraulichkeit die;** ~, ~**en a)** o. Pl. confidentiality; **b)** (vertrauliche Information) confidence; **c)** o. Pl. (distanzloses Verhalten) familiarity; (Intimität) intimacy; **vertraut** Adj. **a)** close ⟨friend etc.⟩; intimate ⟨circle, conversation, etc.⟩; **b)** (bekannt) familiar; **jmdn./sich mit etw. ~ machen** familiarize sb./oneself with sth.; **Vertraute der/die;** adj. Dekl. close friend

vertreiben unr. tr. V. **a)** drive out (aus of); drive away ⟨animal, smoke, clouds⟩ (aus from); fight off ⟨tiredness, troubles⟩; **b)** (verkaufen) sell

vertreten 1. unr. tr. V. **a)** stand in or deputize for ⟨colleague etc.⟩; ⟨teacher⟩ cover for ⟨colleague⟩; **b)** (eintreten für, repräsentieren) represent ⟨person, firm, interests, constituency, country, etc.⟩; (Rechtsw.) act for ⟨person, prosecution, etc.⟩; ~ **sein** be represented; **c)** (einstehen für, verfechten) support ⟨point of view, principle⟩; hold ⟨opinion⟩; advocate ⟨thesis etc.⟩; **2.** unr. refl. V. **sich** (Dat.) **die Füße** od. **Beine ~** (ugs.) stretch one's legs; **Vertreter der;** ~s, ~ **a)** (Stell~) deputy; standin; **b)** (Interessen~, Repräsentant) representative; (Handels~) sales representative; commercial traveller; **c)** (Verfechter, Anhänger) supporter; advocate; **Vertretung die;** ~, ~**en** deputy; (Delegierte[r]) representative; (Delegation) delegation (Handels~) [sales] agency; **eine diplomatische ~:** a diplomatic mission

Vertriebene der/die; adj. Dekl. expellee [from his/her homeland]

vertrocknen itr. V.; mit sein dry up

vertrödeln tr. V. (ugs. abwertend) dawdle away, waste ⟨time⟩

vertrösten tr. V. put ⟨person⟩ off (**auf** + Akk. until)

vertun 1. unr. tr. V. waste; **2.** unr. refl. V. (ugs.) make a slip

vertuschen tr. V. hush up ⟨scandal etc.⟩; keep ⟨truth etc.⟩ secret

verübeln tr. V. **jmdm. eine Äußerung** usw. ~: take sb.'s remark etc. amiss

verüben tr. V. commit ⟨crime etc.⟩

verunglücken itr. V.; mit sein have an accident; ⟨car etc.⟩ be involved in an accident; **mit dem Auto/Flugzeug ~:** be in a car/an air accident or crash; **Verunglückte der/die;** adj. Dekl. accident victim; casualty

verunreinigen tr. V. pollute; contaminate ⟨water, milk, flour, oil⟩

verunsichern tr. V. **jmdn.** ~: make sb. feel unsure or uncertain

verunstalten tr. V. disfigure

verursachen tr. V. cause

verurteilen tr. V. pass sentence on; sentence; (fig.) condemn ⟨behaviour, action⟩; **jmdn. zum Tode ~:** sentence or condemn sb. to death; **Verurteilte der/die;** adj. Dekl. convicted man/woman; **Verurteilung die;** ~, ~**en** sentencing; (fig.) condemnation

vervollkommnen tr. V. perfect

vervollständigen tr. V. complete

verwachsen Adj. deformed

verwählen refl. V. misdial

verwahren 1. tr. V. keep [safe]; **2.** refl. V. protest; **verwahrlosen** itr. V.; mit sein get in a bad state; ⟨house, building⟩ fall into disrepair; ⟨garden, hedge⟩ become overgrown; ⟨person⟩ let oneself go; **verwahrlost** neglected; overgrown ⟨hedge, garden⟩; dilapidated ⟨house, building⟩; unkempt ⟨person, appearance, etc.⟩; (in der Kleidung) ragged ⟨person⟩; **Verwahrlosung die;** ~: (eines Gebäudes) dilapidation; (einer Person) advancing decrepitude

verwaisen itr. V. be orphaned

verwalten tr. V. **a)** administer ⟨estate, property⟩; run ⟨house⟩; hold ⟨money⟩ in trust; **b)** (leiten) run, manage ⟨hostel, kindergarten, etc.⟩; (regieren) administer ⟨area, colony, etc.⟩; govern ⟨country⟩; **Verwalter der;** ~s, ~, **Verwalterin die;** ~, ~**nen** administrator; (eines Amts usw.) manager; (ei-

nes Nachlasses) trustee; **Verwaltung die;** ~, ~**en a)** administration; *(eines Landes)* government; *(eines Amtes)* tenure; *(einer Aufgabe)* performance; **b)** *(Organ)* administration

verwandeln 1. *tr. V.* convert (**in +** *Akk.*, **zu** into); *(völlig verändern)* transform (**in +** *Akk.*, **zu** into); **2.** *refl. V.* **sich in etw.** *(Akk.) od.* **zu etw.** ~: turn *or* change into sth.; *(bei chemischen Vorgängen usw.)* be converted into sth.; **Verwandlung die;** ~, ~**en** conversion (**in +** *Akk.*, **zu** into); *(völlige Veränderung, das Sichverwandeln)* transformation (**in +** *Akk.*, **zu** into)

¹**verwandt 2.** *Part. v.* **verwenden**

²**verwandt** *Adj.* related (**mit** to); *(fig.)* similar ⟨*views, ideas, forms*⟩; **Verwandte der/die;** *adj. Dekl.* relative; relation; **Verwandtschaft die;** ~, ~**en a)** relationship (**mit** to); *(fig.)* affinity; **b)** *o. Pl. (Verwandte)* relatives *pl.*; relations *pl.*; **die ganze** ~: all one's relatives; **verwandtschaftlich** *Adj.* family ⟨*ties, relationships, etc.*⟩

verwarnen *tr. V.* warn, caution (**wegen** for); **Verwarnung die;** ~, ~**en** warning; caution

verwechseln *tr. V.* **a)** |miteinander| ~: confuse ⟨*two things/people*⟩; **etw. mit etw./jmdn. mit jmdm.** ~: mistake sth. for sth./sb. for sb.; confuse sth. with sth./sb. with sb.; **b)** *(vertauschen)* mix up; **Verwechslung die;** ~, ~**en a)** [case of] confusion; **b)** *(Vertauschung)* mixing up; **eine** ~: a mix-up

verwegen 1. *Adj.* daring; *(auch fig.)* audacious; **2.** *adv. (auch fig.)* audaciously; **Verwegenheit die;** ~: daring; *(auch fig.)* audacity

verwehren *tr. V.* **jmdm. etw.** ~: refuse *or* deny sb. sth.

Verwehung die; ~, ~**en** [snow]drift

verweigern *tr. V.* refuse; **Verweigerung die;** ~, ~**en** refusal

Verweis der; ~**es**, ~**e a)** reference (**auf +** *Akk.* to); *(Quer~)* cross-reference; **b)** *(Tadel)* reprimand; **verweisen** *unr. tr. V.* **a) jmdn./einen Fall** *usw.* **an jmdn./etw.** ~ *(auch Rechtsspr.)* refer sb./a case *etc.* to sb./sth.; **b)** *(wegschikken)* **jmdn. von der Schule/aus dem Saal** ~: expel sb. from the school/ send sb. out of the room; **einen Spieler vom Platz** ~: send a player off [the field]; **c)** *auch itr. (hinweisen)* |**jmdn.**| **auf etw.** *(Akk.)* ~: refer [sb.] to sth.

verwelken *itr. V.; mit sein* wilt

verwendbar *Adj.* usable; **Verwend-**

barkeit die; ~: usability; **verwenden** *unr. od. regelm. tr. V.* **a)** use (**zu**, **für** for); **b)** *(aufwenden)* spend ⟨*time*⟩ (**auf +** *Akk.* on); **Verwendung die;** ~, ~**en** use

verwerfen *unr. tr. V.* reject; dismiss ⟨*thought*⟩; **verwerflich** *(geh.)* **1.** *Adj.* reprehensible; **2.** *adv.* reprehensibly

verwertbar *Adj.* utilizable; usable; **verwerten** *tr. V.* utilize, use (**zu** for); make use of ⟨*suggestion, experience, knowledge, etc.*⟩

verwesen *itr. V.; mit sein* decompose; **Verwesung die;** ~: decomposition

verwickeln 1. *refl. V.* get tangled up *or* entangled; **sich in etw.** *(Akk. od. Dat.)* ~: get caught [up] in sth.; **2.** *tr. V.* involve; **Verwicklung die;** ~, ~**en** complication

verwildern *itr. V.* ⟨*garden*⟩ become overgrown; ⟨*domestic animal*⟩ return to the wild

verwirklichen 1. *tr. V.* realize ⟨*dream*⟩; realize, put into practice ⟨*plan, proposal, idea, etc.*⟩; carry out ⟨*project, intention*⟩; **2.** *refl. V.* ⟨*hope, dream*⟩ be realized; **Verwirklichung die;** ~, ~**en** realization; *(eines Wunsches, einer Hoffnung)* fulfilment

verwirren *tr. (auch itr.) V.* confuse; **verwirrt** confused; ~**d** bewildering; **Verwirrung die;** ~, ~**en** confusion

verwischen *tr. V.* smudge ⟨*signature, writing, etc.*⟩; smear ⟨*paint*⟩; *(fig.)* cover up ⟨*tracks*⟩

verwitwet *Adj.* widowed

verwöhnen *tr. V.* spoil; **verwöhnt** *Adj.* spoilt; *(anspruchsvoll)* discriminating; ⟨*taste, palate*⟩ of a gourmet

verworren *Adj.* confused, muddled ⟨*ideas, situation, etc.*⟩

verwunden *tr. V.* wound; injure; **Verwundete der/die;** *adj. Dekl.* casualty; **die** ~**n** the wounded; **Verwundung die;** ~, ~**en** wound

verwünschen *tr. V.* curse

verwüsten *tr. V.* devastate; **Verwüstung die;** ~, ~**en** devastation

verzählen *refl. V.* miscount

verzaubern *tr. V.* cast a spell on; bewitch; *(fig.)* enchant; **jmdn. in etw.** *(Akk.)* ~: transform sb. into sth.

Verzehr der; ~**[e]s** consumption; **verzehren** *tr. V.* consume

Verzeichnis das; ~**ses**, ~**se** list; *(Register)* index

verzeihen *unr. tr., itr. V.* forgive; *(entschuldigen)* excuse ⟨*behaviour, re-*

mark, etc.⟩; ~ **Sie** [bitte], **können Sie mir sagen ...?** excuse me, could you tell me ...?; **Verzeihung die;** ~: forgiveness; ~! sorry!; **jmdn. um ~ bitten** apologize to sb.

verzerren 1. *tr. V.* **a)** contort ⟨*face etc.*⟩ (zu into); **b)** *(akustisch, optisch)* distort ⟨*sound, image*⟩; **etw. verzerrt darstellen** *(fig.)* present a distorted account *or* picture of sth.

Verzicht der; ~[e]s, ~e **a)** renunciation **(auf** + *Akk.* of); **b)** *(auf Reichtum, ein Amt usw.)* relinquishment **(auf** + *Akk.* of); **verzichten** *itr. V.* do without; ~ **auf** (+ *Akk.*) do without; *(sich enthalten)* refrain from; *(aufgeben)* give up ⟨*share, smoking, job, etc.*⟩; renounce ⟨*inheritance*⟩; relinquish ⟨*right, privilege*⟩; *(opfern)* sacrifice ⟨*holiday, salary*⟩

¹**verziehen 2.** *Part. v.* **verzeihen**
²**verziehen 1.** *unr. tr. V.* **a)** screw up ⟨*face, mouth, etc.*⟩; **b)** *(schlecht erziehen)* spoil; **2.** *unr. refl. V.* **a)** *(aus der Form geraten)* go out of shape; ⟨*wood*⟩ warp; **b)** *(wegziehen)* ⟨*clouds, storm*⟩ move away, pass over; ⟨*fog, mist*⟩ disperse; **c)** *(ugs.: weggehen)* take oneself off; **3.** *unr. itr. V.; mit sein* move [away]; **"Empfänger** [unbekannt] **verzogen"** 'no longer at this address'

verzieren *tr. V.* decorate; **Verzierung die;** ~, ~en decoration

verzögern 1. *tr. V.* **a)** delay (um by); **b)** *(verlangsamen)* slow down; **2.** *refl. V.* be delayed (um by); **Verzögerung die;** ~, ~en delay *(Gen.* in); *(Verlangsamung)* slowing down

Verzug der; ~[e]s delay; **im ~ sein/in ~ kommen** be/fall behind

verzweifeln *itr. V.; mit sein* despair; **über etw./jmdn.** ~: despair at sth./of sb.; **verzweifelt 1.** *Adj.* despairing ⟨*person*⟩; desperate ⟨*situation, attempt, effort, struggle, etc*⟩; ~ **sein** be in despair; **2.** *adv.* desperately; **Verzweiflung die;** ~ despair

verzweigen *refl. V.* branch [out]

Veteran [vete'ra:n] **der;** ~en, ~en *(auch fig.)* veteran

Vetter der; ~s, ~n cousin

vgl. *Abk.* vergleiche cf.

v. H. *Abk.* vom **Hundert** per cent

via ['vi:a] *Präp.* via

Viadukt [via'dʊkt] **das** *od.* **der;** ~[e]s, ~e viaduct

vibrieren [vi'bri:rən] *itr. V.* vibrate

video-, Video- ['vi:deo-]: video; **Video das;** ~s, ~s *(ugs.)* video

Vieh das; ~[e]s **a)** *(Nutztiere)* livestock *sing. or pl.;* **b)** *(Rind~)* cattle *pl.;* **Vieh·zucht die;** *o. Pl.* [live]stock/cattle breeding *no art.*

viel 1. *Indefinitpron. u. unbest. Zahlw.* **a)** *Sg.* a great deal of; a lot of *(coll.);* **wie/nicht/zu** ~: how/not/too much; ~[es] *(vielerlei)* much; **der** ~**e Regen** all the rain; **um** ~**es jünger** a great deal younger; **b)** *Pl.* many; **gleich** ~[e] the same number of; **die** ~**en Menschen** all the people; **2.** *Adv.* **a)** *(oft, lange)* a great deal; a lot *(coll.);* **b)** *(wesentlich)* much; a great deal; a lot *(coll.);* ~ **zu klein** much too small; **vielerlei** *indekl. unbest. Gattungsz.* **a)** *attr.* many different; all kinds *or* sorts of; **b)** *subst.* all kinds of things

viel-, Viel-: ~**fach 1.** *Adj.* **a)** multiple; **die** ~**fache Menge** many times the amount; **b)** *(vielfältig)* many kinds of; **2.** *adv.* many times; ~**falt die;** ~: diversity; ~**fältig 1.** *Adj.* many and diverse; **2.** *adv.* in many different ways

vielleicht *Adv.* perhaps; maybe

viel-: ~**mals** *Adv.* **ich bitte** ~**mals um Entschuldigung** I'm very sorry; **danke** ~**mals** thank you very much; ~**mehr** [*od.* -'-] *Konj. u. Adv.* rather; ~**sagend 1.** *Adj.* meaningful; **2.** *adv.* meaningfully; ~**seitig** *Adj.* versatile ⟨*person*⟩; ~**versprechend 1.** *Adj.* [very] promising; **2.** *adv.* [very] promisingly

vier *Kardinalz.* four; **Vier die;** ~, ~en four; **eine** ~ **schreiben/bekommen** *(Schulw.)* get a D

vier-, Vier-: *(s. auch* **acht-, Acht-**): ~**beiner der;** ~s, ~ *(ugs.)* four-legged friend; ~**beinig** *Adj.* four-legged; ~**eck das** quadrilateral; *(Rechteck)* rectangle; *(Quadrat)* square; ~**eckig** *Adj.* quadrilateral; *(rechteckig)* rectangular; ~**fach** *Vervielfältigungsz.* fourfold; quadruple; ~**fache das;** *adj. Dekl.* **um das** ~**fache:** fourfold; by four times the amount; ~**hundert** *Kardinalz.* four hundred

Vierling der; ~s, ~e quadruplet

vier-, Vier-: ~**mal** *Adv.* four times; ~**spurig** *Adj.* four-lane ⟨*road, motorway*⟩; ~**spurig sein** have four lanes; ~**stellig** *Adj.* four-figure *attrib.;* ~**sterne·hotel** [-'----] **das** four-star hotel

viert... *Ordinalz.* fourth; **viertausend** *Kardinalz.* four thousand; **viertel** ['fɪrtl̩] *Bruchz.* quarter; **ein** ~

Pfund a quarter of a pound; **Viertel** ['firtl] **das** *(schweiz. meist* der); ~s, ~ **a)** quarter; ~ **vor/nach eins** [a] quarter to/ past one; **drei** ~: three-quarters; **b)** *(Stadtteil)* quarter; district

viertel-, Viertel-: ~**finale das** *(Sport)* quarter-final; ~**jahr das** three months *pl.;* ~**jährlich 1.** *Adj.* quarterly; **2.** *adv.* quarterly; ~**liter der** quarter of a litre; ~**note die** *(Musik)* crotchet *(Brit.);* quarter note *(Amer.);* ~**pfund das** quarter [of a] pound; ~**stunde die** quarter of an hour; ~**stündig** *Adj.* quarter-of-an-hour; ~**stündlich 1.** *Adj.* every quarter of an hour *postpos.;* **2.** *adv.* every quarter of an hour

viertens *Adv.* fourthly; **viertürig** *Adj.* four-door *attrib.;* ~ **sein** have four doors

Vierwaldstätter See, *(schweiz.:)* **Vierwaldstättersee** der Lake Lucerne

vier- ['fir-]: ~**zehn** *Kardinalz.* fourteen; ~**zehn·tägig** *Adj.* two-week; ~**zehn·täglich 1.** *Adj.* fortnightly; **2.** *adv.* fortnightly

vierzig ['firtsiç] *Kardinalz.* forty; *s. auch* **achtzig; vierzigst ...** *Ordinalz.* fortieth; *s. auch* **acht ...**

Vikar der; ~s, ~e **a)** *(kath. Kirche)* locum tenens; **b)** *(ev. Kirche)* ≈ [trainee] curate

Villa ['vila] **die;** ~, **Villen** villa; **Villen·viertel das** exclusive residential district

violett [vio'lɛt] purple; violet; **Violett das;** ~s, ~e *od. ugs.* ~s purple; violet; *(im Spektrum)* violet

Violine [vio'li:nə] **die;** ~, ~**n** *(Musik)* violin

Viper ['vi:pɐ] **die;** ~, ~**n** viper; adder

Viren *s.* **Virus**

Virtuose [vɪr'tuo:zə] der; ~n, ~n virtuoso; **Virtuosität die;** ~: virtuosity

Virus ['vi:rʊs] **das;** ~, **Viren** virus

Visa *s.* **Visum; Visen** *s.* **Visum**

Visier [vi'zi:ɐ] **das;** ~s, ~e *(am Helm)* visor; *(an der Waffe)* backsight

Vision [vi'zio:n] **die;** ~, ~**en** vision

Visite [vi'zi:tə] **die;** ~, ~**n** round; ~ **machen** do one's round; **Visiten·karte die** visiting-card

Visum ['vi:zʊm] **das;** ~s, **Visa** *od.* **Visen** visa

Vitamin [vita'mi:n] **das;** ~s, ~e vitamin

vitamin-, Vitamin-: ~**arm** *Adj.* low in vitamins *postpos.;* ~**mangel** der;

o. Pl. vitamin deficiency; ~**reich** *Adj.* rich in vitamins *postpos.*

Vitrine [vi'tri:nə] **die;** ~, ~**n** display case; *(Möbel)* display cabinet

Vize- vice-

Vogel der; ~s, **Vögel** bird; **einen ~ haben** *(salopp)* be off one's rocker *(sl.)*

Vogel-: ~**käfig** der birdcage; ~**nest das** bird's nest; ~**perspektive die** bird's eye view; ~**scheuche die;** ~, ~**n** scarecrow

Vokabel [vo'ka:bl] **die;** ~, ~**n** word; ~**n** vocabulary *sing.*

Vokal [vo'ka:l] der; ~s, ~e *(Sprachw.)* vowel

Volk das; ~[e]s, **Völker** people

volks-, Volks-: ~**abstimmung die** plebiscite; ~**eigen** *Adj. (ehem. DDR)* publicly *or* nationally owned; ~**entscheid** der *(Politik)* referendum; ~**fest das** public festival; *(Jahrmarkt)* fair; ~**hochschule die** adult education centre; ~**kunde die** folklore; ~**lied das** folk-song; ~**musik die** folk-music; ~**polizei die;** *o. Pl. (ehem. DDR)* People's Police; ~**republik die** People's Republic; ~**stamm** der tribe; ~**tanz** der folk-dance; ~**tracht die** traditional costume; *(eines Landes)* national costume

volkstümlich 1. *Adj.* popular; **2.** *adv.* ~ **schreiben** write in terms readily comprehensible to the layman; **Volks·wirtschaft die** national economy; *(Fach)* economics *sing., no art.;* **volks·wirtschaftlich 1.** *Adj.* economic; **2.** *adv.* economically

voll 1. *Adj.* full; ample ⟨bosom⟩; *(salopp: betrunken)* plastered *(sl.);* ~ **von** *od.* **mit etw. sein** be full of sth.; **jmdn. nicht für ~ nehmen** not take sb. seriously; **2.** *adv.* fully; ~ **und ganz** completely; **voll·auf** [*od.* '--] *Adv.* completely; **vollaufen** *unr. itr. V., trennbar* fill up; **etw. ~ lassen** fill sth. [up]

voll-, Voll-: ~**automatisch 1.** *Adj.* fully automatic; **2.** *adv.* fully automatically; ~**bad das** bath; ~**bart der** full beard; ~**bringen** [-'--] *unr. tr. V. (geh.)* accomplish; achieve

voll·enden *tr. V.* complete; **voll·endet 1.** *Adj.* accomplished ⟨performance⟩; perfect ⟨gentleman, host, manners, reproduction⟩; **2.** *adv.* ⟨play⟩ in an accomplished manner; **vollends** *Adv.* completely; **Voll·endung die** completion; **voller** *indekl. Adj.* full of; ~ **Flecken** covered with stains

Volley·ball ['vɔlibal] der volleyball

voll-, Voll-: ~**führen** [-'--] tr. V. perform; ~|**füllen** tr. V. fill up; ~**gas** das; o. Pl. ~**gas geben** put one's foot down; **mit** ~**gas** at full throttle; ~|**gießen** unr. tr. V. fill [up]

völlig 1. Adj. complete; total; 2. adv. completely; totally; **du hast** ~ **recht** you are absolutely right

voll-, Voll-: ~**jährig** Adj. of age pred.; ~**jährig werden** come of age; ~**jährigkeit die**; ~: majority no art.; ~**kasko·versicherung die** fully comprehensive insurance

voll·kommen 1. Adj. **a)** [-'-- od. '---] (vollendet) perfect; **b)** ['---] (vollständig) complete; total; 2. ['---] adv. completely; totally

voll-, Voll-: ~**korn·brot** das wholemeal (Brit.) or (Amer.) wholewheat bread; ~|**laufen** s. vollaufen; ~|**machen** tr. V. fill up; [**sich** ⟨Dat.⟩] **die Hosen/Windeln** ~**machen** (ugs.) mess one's pants/nappy; ~**macht die**; ~, ~**en a)** authority; **b)** (Urkunde) power of attorney; ~**milch die** full-cream milk; ~**milch·schokolade die** full-cream milk chocolate; ~**mond der**; o. Pl. full moon; ~**pension die**; meist o. Art.; o. Pl. full board no art.; ~**ständig** 1. Adj. complete; full ⟨text, address, etc.⟩; 2. adv. completely; ⟨list⟩ in full; ~**ständigkeit die**; ~: completeness; ~**strecken** [-'--] tr. V. enforce ⟨penalty, fine, law⟩; carry out ⟨sentence⟩ (**an** + Dat. on); ~|**tanken** tr. (auch itr.) V. fill up; **bitte** ~**tanken** fill it up, please; ~**treffer der** direct hit; **ein** ~**treffer sein** (fig.) hit the bull's eye; ~**zählig** Adj. complete

voll·ziehen unr. tr. V. carry out (**an** + Dat. on); execute, carry out ⟨order⟩; perform ⟨sacrifice, ceremony, sexual intercourse⟩; **Voll·zug der** s. vollziehen: carrying out; execution; performance

Volt [vɔlt] das; ~ od. ~|e|s, ~: (Physik, Elektrot.) volt

Volumen [vo'luːmən] das; ~s, ~: volume

vom Präp. + Art. **a)** = von dem; **b)** (räumlich) from the; **links/rechts** ~ **Eingang** to the left/right of the entrance; ~ **Stuhl aufspringen** jump up out of one's chair; **c)** (zeitlich) ~ **Morgen bis zum Abend** from morning till night; ~ **ersten Januar an** [as] from the first of January; **d)** (zur Angabe der Ursache) **das kommt** ~ **Rauchen/Alko-**

hol that comes from smoking/drinking alcohol; **jmdn.** ~ **Sehen kennen** know sb. by sight; **von** Präp. mit Dat. **a)** (räumlich) from; **nördlich/südlich** ~ **Mannheim** to the north/south of Mannheim; **rechts/links** ~ **mir** on my right/left; ~ **hier an** od. (ugs.) **ab** from here on[ward]; ~ **Mannheim aus** from Mannheim; **b)** (zeitlich) from; ~**jetzt an** od. (ugs.) **ab** from now on; ~ **heute/ morgen an** [as] from today/tomorrow; starting today/tomorrow; **in der Nacht** ~ **Freitag auf** od. **zu Samstag** during Friday night; **das Brot ist** ~ **gestern** it's yesterday's bread; **c)** (anstelle eines Genitivs) of; **acht** ~ **hundert/zehn** eight out of a hundred/ten; **d)** (zur Angabe des Urhebers, der Ursache, beim Passiv) by; **der Roman ist** ~ **Fontane** the novel is by Fontane; **müde** ~ **der Arbeit sein** be tired from work[ing]; **sie hat ein Kind** ~ **ihm** she has a child by him; **e)** (zur Angabe von Eigenschaften) of; **eine Fahrt** ~ **drei Stunden** a three-hour drive; **von·einander** Adv. from each other or one another; **vonstatten** Adv. ~ **gehen** proceed

vor 1. Präp. mit Dat. **a)** (räumlich) in front of; (weiter vorn) ahead of; in front of; (nicht ganz so weit wie) before; (außerhalb) outside; **kurz** ~ **der Abzweigung** just before the turn-off; ~ **der Stadt** outside the town; **etw.** ~ **sich haben** (fig.) have sth. before one; **das liegt noch** ~ **mir** (fig.) I still have that to come or have that ahead of me; **b)** (zeitlich) before; **es ist fünf [Minuten]** ~ **sieben** it is five [minutes] to seven; **c)** (bei Reihenfolge, Rangordnung) before; **knapp** ~ **jmdm. siegen** win just ahead or in front of sb.; **d)** (auf Grund von) with; ~ **Freude strahlen** beam with joy; ~ **Hunger/Durst umkommen** (ugs.) die of hunger/thirst; **e)** ~ **fünf Minuten/10 Jahren/Wochen** usw. five minutes/ten years/weeks ago; **heute** ~ **einer Woche** a week ago today; 2. Präp. mit Akk. in front of; ~ **sich hin** to oneself

Vor·abend der evening before; (fig.) eve

vor·an Adv. forward[s] ahead; first

voran-: ~|**gehen** unr. itr. V.; mit sein **a)** go first; **b)** (Fortschritte machen) make progress; ~|**kommen** unr. itr. V.; mit sein **a)** make headway; **b)** (Fortschritte machen) make progress

Vor·arbeiter der foreman

vor·aus 1. [-'-] Präp. mit Dat., nachge-

stellt in front; **jmdm./seiner Zeit ~ sein** *(fig.)* be ahead of sb./one's time; **2.** *Adv.* **im ~** ['--] in advance

voraus-, Voraus-: **~|gehen** *unr. itr. V.; mit sein* **a)** go [on] ahead; **b)** *(zeitlich)* **einem Ereignis ~gehen** precede an event; **~sage** *tr. V.* **Vorhersage**; **~|sagen** *tr. V.* predict; **~|sehen** *unr. tr. V.* foresee; **~|setzen** *tr. V.* **a)** *(als gegeben ansehen)* assume; **~gesetzt, |daß|** ...: provided [that] ...; **b)** *(erfordern)* require ⟨*skill, experience, etc.*⟩; presuppose ⟨*good organization, planning, etc.*⟩; **~setzung die;** **~, ~en a)** *(Annahme)* assumption; *(Prämisse)* premiss; **b)** *(Vorbedingung)* prerequisite; **unter der ~setzung, daß ...:** on condition *or* on the pre-condition that ...; **~sichtlich 1.** *Adj.* anticipated; **2.** *adv.* probably

Vor·bau der; *Pl.* **~ten** porch

Vorbehalt der; ~|e|s, ~e reservation; **unter dem ~, daß ...:** with the reservation that ...; **vor|behalten** *unr. tr. V.* **sich** *(Dat.)* **etw. ~:** reserve oneself sth.; „Änderungen **~**" 'subject to alterations'

vor·bei *Adv.* **a)** *(räumlich)* past; by; **an etw.** *(Dat.)* **~:** past sth.; **b)** *(zeitlich)* past; over; *(beendet)* finished; over; **es ist acht Uhr ~** *(ugs.)* it is past *or* gone eight o'clock

vorbei-: **~|fahren 1.** *unr. itr. V.; mit sein* **a)** drive/ride past; pass; **an jmdm. ~fahren** drive/ride past *or* pass sb.; **b)** *(ugs.: einen kurzen Besuch machen)* **|bei jmdm./der Post| ~fahren** drop in *(coll.)* [at sb.'s/at the post office]; **~|gehen** *unr. itr. V.; mit sein* **a)** pass; go past; **an jmdm./etw. ~gehen** pass *or* go past sb./sth.; **der Schuß ist ~gegangen** the shot missed; **b)** *(ugs.: einen kurzen Besuch machen)* **|bei jmdm./der Post| ~gehen** drop in *(coll.)* [at sb.'s/at the post office]; **c)** *(vergehen)* pass; **~|kommen** *unr. itr. V.; mit sein* pass; **an etw.** *(Dat.)* **~kommen** pass sth.; **~|reden** *itr. V.* **an etw.** *(Dat.)* **~reden** talk round sth. without getting to the point; **aneinander ~reden** talk at cross purposes; **~|schießen** *unr. itr. V.* miss

vor|bereiten *tr. V.* prepare; **jmdn./ sich auf** *od.* **für etw. ~:** prepare sb./ oneself for sth.; **Vor·bereitung die; ~, ~en** preparation; **~en |für etw.| treffen** make preparations for sth.

vor|bestellen *tr. V.* order in advance; **Vor·bestellung die** advance order

vor·bestraft *Adj.* with a previous conviction/previous convictions *postpos., not pred.*

vor|beugen 1. *tr. V.* bend ⟨*head, upper body*⟩ forward; **sich ~:** lean forward; **2.** *itr. V.* **einer Sache** *(Dat.)* *od.* **gegen etw. ~:** prevent sth.; **Vor·beugung die** prevention **(gegen of)**; **zur ~:** as a preventive

Vor·bild das model; **jmdm. ein gutes ~ sein** be a good example to sb.; **vor·bildlich 1.** *Adj.* exemplary; **2.** *adv.* in an exemplary way

vor|bringen *unr. tr. V.* say; **eine Forderung/ein Anliegen ~:** make a demand/express a desire; **Argumente ~:** present arguments

vor·christlich *Adj.* pre-Christian

vor|datieren *tr. V.* postdate

vorder... *Adj.* front; **der Vordere Orient** the Middle East

Vorder-: **~grund der** foreground; **im ~grund stehen** *(fig.)* be prominent *or* to the fore; **~mann der;** *Pl.* **~männer** person in front; **jmdn. auf ~mann bringen** *(ugs.)* lick sb. into shape

vor|drängen *refl. V.* push [one's way] forward *or* to the front; *(fig.)* push oneself forward

vor|dringen *unr. itr. V.; mit sein* push forward; advance

vor·dringlich 1. *Adj.* **a)** priority *attrib.* ⟨*treatment*⟩; **b)** *(dringlich)* urgent; **2.** *adv.* **a)** as a matter of priority; **b)** *(dringlich)* as a matter of urgency

Vor·druck der; *Pl.* **Vordrucke** form

vor·eilig 1. *Adj.* rash; **2.** *adv.* rashly

vor·einander *Adv.* **a)** one in front of the other; **b)** *(einer dem anderen gegenüber)* opposite each other; face to face; **c) Angst ~ haben** be afraid of each other

vor·eingenommen *Adj.* prejudiced; biased; **für/gegen jmdn. ~ sein** be prejudiced in sb.'s favour/against sb.

vorenthalten[1] *unr. tr. V.* **jmdm. etw. ~:** withhold sth. from sb.

vor·erst [*od.* '-'-] *Adv.* for the present

Vorfahr der; ~en, ~en forefather; **vor|fahren** *unr. itr. V.; mit sein* **a)** *(ankommen)* drive/ride up; **b)** *(weiter nach vorn fahren)* ⟨*person*⟩ drive *or* move forward; ⟨*car*⟩ move forward; **c)** *(vorausfahren)* drive *or* go on ahead; **Vor·fahrt die;** *o. Pl.* right of way; „~ beachten/gewähren" 'give way'

---

[1] *ich enthalte vor (od. seltener: vorenthalte), vorenthalten, vorzuenthalten*

Vorfahrt[s]-: ~**schild** das right-of-way sign; ~**straße** die main road

Vor·fall der incident; occurrence; **vor|fallen** unr. itr. V.; mit sein a) (sich ereignen) happen; occur; b) (nach vorn fallen) fall forward

vor|finden unr. tr. V. find

Vor·freude die anticipation

vor|führen tr. V. show ⟨film, slides, etc.⟩; present ⟨circus act, programme⟩; perform ⟨play, trick, routine⟩; (demonstrieren) demonstrate; jmdn. dem Richter ~: bring sb. before the judge; **Vor·führung** die show; (eines Theaterstücks) performance

Vor·gang der occurrence; (Amtsspr.) file; **Vorgänger** der; ~s, ~, **Vorgängerin** die; ~, ~nen predecessor

Vor·garten der front garden

vor|geben unr. tr. V. pretend

Vor·gebirge das promontory

vor·gefaßt Adj. preconceived

vor|gehen unr. itr. V.; mit sein a) (ugs.: nach vorn gehen) go forward; b) (vorausgehen) go on ahead; jmdn. ~ lassen let sb. go first; c) ⟨clock⟩ be fast; d) (einschreiten) gegen jmdn./etw. ~: take action against sb./sth.; e) (verfahren) proceed; f) (sich abspielen) happen; go on; g) (Vorrang haben) have priority; come first

Vor·geschmack der; o. Pl. foretaste

Vor·gesetzte der/die; adj. Dekl. superior

vor·gestern Adv. the day before yesterday

vor|greifen unr. itr. V. jmdm. ~: anticipate sb. or jump in ahead of sb.

vor|haben unr. tr. V. intend; (geplant haben) plan; **Vor·haben** das; ~s, ~: plan; (Projekt) project

Vor·halle die entrance hall; (eines Theaters, Hotels) foyer

vor|halten unr. tr. V. a) hold up; mit vorgehaltener Schußwaffe at gunpoint; b) (zum Vorwurf machen) jmdm. etw. ~: reproach sb. for sth.; **Vorhaltungen** Pl. jmdm. [wegen etw.] ~ machen reproach sb. [for sth.]

vorhanden Adj. existing; (verfügbar) available; ~ sein exist or be in existence/be available

Vor·hang der (auch Theater) curtain; **Vorhänge·schloß** das padlock

Vor·haut die foreskin

vor·her [od. -'-] beforehand; (davor) before; **vorher|gehen** unr. itr. V.; mit sein in den ~den Wochen in the preceding weeks

Vor·herrschaft die supremacy; **vorherrschen** itr. V. predominate

vorher-, Vorher-: ~**sage** die prediction; (des Wetters) forecast; ~|**sagen** tr. V. predict; forecast ⟨weather⟩; ~|**sehen** unr. tr. V. s. voraussehen

vor·hin [od. -'-] Adv. a short time or while ago

vorig... Adj. last

Vor·jahr das previous year; **vor·jährig** Adj. of the previous year

Vor·kämpfer der pioneer

Vorkehrungen Pl. precautions

Vor·kenntnis die background knowledge

vor|kommen unr. itr. V.; mit sein a) (sich ereignen) happen; b) (vorhanden sein) occur; c) (erscheinen) seem; das Lied kommt mir bekannt vor I seem to know the song; **Vorkommnis** das; ~ses, ~se incident; occurrence

vor|laden unr. tr. V. summon; **Vorladung** die summons

Vor·lage die a) o. Pl.; s. vorlegen: presentation; showing; production; submission; tabling; b) (Entwurf) draft; c) (Muster) pattern; (Modell) model

Vor·läufer der precursor; forerunner; **vor·läufig** 1. Adj. temporary; provisional; interim ⟨order, agreement⟩; 2. adv. for the time being

vor·laut 1. Adj. forward; 2. adv. forwardly

vor|legen tr. V. present; show, produce ⟨certificate, identity card, etc.⟩; show ⟨sample⟩; submit ⟨evidence⟩; table ⟨parliamentary bill⟩

vor|lesen unr. tr., itr. V. read aloud or out; read ⟨story, poem, etc.⟩ aloud; jmdn. [etw.] ~: read [sth.] to sb.; **Vor·lesung** die lecture; (~sreihe) series or course of lectures

vor·letzt... Adj. last but one; penultimate ⟨page, episode, etc.⟩

Vor·liebe die preference; **vor·lieb|nehmen** unr. itr. V. mit jmdm./etw. ~: put up with sb./sth.; (sich begnügen) make do with sb./sth.

vor|liegen unr. itr. V. jmdm. ~: be with sb.; die Ergebnisse liegen uns noch nicht vor we do not have the results yet; im ~den Fall in the present case

vorm Präp. + Art. a) = vor dem; b) (räumlich) in front of the; c) (zeitlich bei Reihenfolge) before the

vor|machen tr. V. (ugs.) jmdm. etw. ~: show sb. sth.; (vortäuschen) ki⟨(coll.) or fool sb.

vormalig *Adj.* former; **vormals** *Adv.* formerly

Vor·marsch der *(auch fig.)* advance

vor|merken *tr. V.* make a note of; **ich habe Sie für den Kurs vorgemerkt** I've put you down for the course

vor·mittag *Adv.* **heute/morgen/Freitag ~:** this/tomorrow/Friday morning; **Vor·mittag** der morning; **vormittags** *Adv.* in the morning

Vor·mund der; *Pl.* **Vormunde** *od.* **Vormünder** guardian

vorn[e] *Adv.* at the front; **nach ~:** to the front; **von ~:** from the front; **noch einmal von ~ anfangen** start afresh; **von ~ bis hinten** *(ugs.)* from beginning to end

vornehm 1. *Adj. (nobel; adelig)* noble; *(kultiviert)* distinguished; *(elegant)* exclusive *⟨district, hotel, restaurant, resort⟩;* elegant *⟨villa, clothes⟩;* 2. *adv.* nobly; *(elegant)* elegantly

vor|nehmen *unr. refl. V.* **sich** *(Dat.)* **etw. ~:** plan sth.; **sich** *(Dat.)* **~, mit dem Rauchen aufzuhören** resolve to give up smoking

vorn-: **~herein** *in* **von ~herein** from the outset; **~über** *Adv.* forwards

Vor·ort der suburb

Vor·rang der; *o. Pl.* **a)** priority (vor + *Dat.* over); **b)** *(bes. österr.: Vorfahrt)* right of way

Vor·rat der supply, stock (**an** + *Dat.* of); **vorrätig** *Adj.* in stock *postpos.*

Vor·recht das privilege

Vor·richtung die device

vor|rücken 1. *tr. V.* move forward; advance *⟨chess piece⟩;* 2. *itr. V.; mit sein* move forward; **auf den 5. Platz ~:** move up to fifth place

Vor·ruhestand der early retirement

vors *Präp. + Art.* = vor das

vor|sagen *tr. V.* **a)** *auch itr.* **jmdm.|die Antwort| ~:** tell sb. the answer; *(flüsternd)* whisper the answer to sb.; **b)** *(aufsagen)* recite

Vor·saison die start of the season; early [part of the] season

Vor·satz der intention; **vorsätzlich** 1. *Adj.* intentional; wilful *⟨murder, arson, etc.⟩;* 2. *adv.* intentionally

Vor·schau die preview

Vor·schein der: **zum ~ kommen** appear; *(entdeckt werden)* come to light

vor|schieben *unr. tr. V.* **a)** push *⟨bolt⟩* across; **b)** *(nach vorn schieben)* push forward

vor|schießen *unr. tr. V.* **jmdm. Geld ~:** advance sb. money

Vor·schlag der suggestion; proposal; **vor|schlagen** *unr. tr. V.* **|jmdm.| etw. ~:** suggest *or* propose sth. [to sb.]

vor·schreiben *unr. tr. V.* stipulate, set *⟨conditions⟩;* lay down *⟨rules⟩;* prescribe *⟨dose⟩;* **Vor·schrift** die instruction; order; *(gesetzliche od. amtliche Bestimmung)* regulation; **vorschrifts·mäßig** 1. *Adj.* correct; proper; 2. *adv.* correctly; properly

Vor·schuß der advance

vor|sehen 1. *unr. tr. V.* **a)** plan; **etw. für/als etw. ~:** intend sth. for/as sth.; **b)** *⟨law, plan, contract, etc.⟩* provide for; 2. *unr. refl. V.* **sich |vor jmdm./etw.| ~:** be careful [of sb./sth.]

vor|setzen *tr. V.* **jmdm. etw. ~:** serve sb. sth.; *(fig.)* serve *or* dish sb. up sth.

Vor·sicht die; *o. Pl.* care; *(bei Risiko, Gefahr)* caution; **zur ~:** as a precaution; **~!** be careful!; „**~, Stufe!**" 'mind the step!'; **vorsichtig** 1. *Adj.* careful; *(bei Risiko, Gefahr)* cautious; **sei ~!** be careful!; take care!; 2. *adv.* carefully; with care; **vorsichts·halber** *Adv.* as a precaution; to be on the safe side; **Vorsichts·maßnahme** die precautionary measure; precaution

Vor·silbe die [monosyllabic] prefix

vor|singen *unr. tr. V.* **|jmdm.| etw. ~:** sing sth. [to sb.]

Vor·sitz der chairmanship; **Vorsitzende** der/die; *adj. Dekl.* chair[person]; *(bes. Mann)* chairman; *(Frau auch)* chairwoman

Vor·sorge die; *o. Pl.* precautions *pl.;* *(für den Todesfall, Krankheit, Alter)* provisions *pl.;* **vor|sorgen** *itr. V.* **für etw. ~:** make provisions for sth.; provide for sth.; **Vorsorge·untersuchung** die *(Med.)* medical check-up; **vorsorglich** *adv.* as a precaution

Vor·spann der *(Film, Ferns.)* opening credits *pl.*

Vor·speise die starter; hors d'œuvre

Vor·spiel das *(Theater)* prologue; *(Musik)* prelude; **vor|spielen** *tr. V.* **a)** play *⟨piece of music⟩* (*Dat.* to, for); act out, perform *⟨scene⟩* (*Dat.* for, in front of) **b)** *(vorspiegeln)* **jmdm. etw. ~:** feign sth. to sb.

vor|sprechen 1. *unr. tr. V.* **a)** *(zum Nachsprechen)* **jmdm. etw. ~:** pronounce *or* say sth. first for sb.; **b)** *(zur Prüfung)* recite; 2. *unr. itr. V.* audition

Vor·sprung der lead (vor + *Dat.* over)

Vor·stadt die suburb

Vor·stand der *(einer Firma)* board [of directors]; *(eines·Vereins, einer Gesellschaft)* executive committee; *(einer Partei)* executive

vor|stehen *unr. itr. V.* **a)** project, jut out; ⟨*teeth, chin*⟩ stick out; ~de Zähne buck-teeth; projecting teeth; **b)** *(geh.: leiten)* **einer Institution** ~: be the head of an institution

vor|stellen **1.** *tr. V.* jmdn./sich jmdm. ~: introduce sb./oneself to sb.; *(bei Bewerbung)* sich ~: come/go for [an] interview; **die Uhr |um eine Stunde|** ~: put the clock forward [one hour]; **2.** *refl. V.* sich *(Dat.)* etw. ~: imagine sth.; **Vor·stellung die a)** *(Begriff)* idea; **b)** *o. Pl. (Phantasie)* imagination; **c)** *(Aufführung)* performance; *(im Kino)* showing

Vor·stoß der advance; **vor|stoßen** *unr. itr. V.; mit sein* advance; push forward

Vor·strafe die previous conviction

vor|strecken *tr. V.* stretch ⟨*arm, hand*⟩ out; advance ⟨*money, sum*⟩

Vor·tag der day before

vor|täuschen *tr. V.* feign; simulate ⟨*reality etc.*⟩; fake ⟨*crime*⟩

Vor·teil [*od.* 'fɔrtaɪl] der advantage; **vorteilhaft 1.** *Adj.* advantageous; **2.** *adv.* advantageously

Vortrag der; ~|e|s, **Vorträge** talk; *(wissenschaftlich)* lecture; **einen** ~ **halten** give a talk/lecture; **vor|tragen** *unr. tr. V.* **a)** sing ⟨*song*⟩; perform, play ⟨*piece of music*⟩; recite ⟨*poem*⟩; **b)** *(darlegen)* present ⟨*case, matter, request, demands*⟩; lodge, make ⟨*complaint*⟩; express ⟨*wish, desire*⟩

vor·trefflich 1. *Adj.* excellent; **2.** *adv.* excellently

vorüber *Adv.* over; *(räumlich)* past; **vorüber|gehen** *unr. itr. V.; mit sein* **a)** go *or* walk past; pass by; **an jmdm./ etw.** ~: go past sb./sth.; pass sb./sth.; *(achtlos)* pass sb./sth. by; **b)** *(vergehen)* pass; ⟨*pain*⟩ go; **vorübergehend 1.** *Adj.* temporary; passing ⟨*interest, infatuation*⟩; brief ⟨*illness, stay*⟩; **2.** *adv.* temporarily; *(für kurze Zeit)* for a short time; briefly

Vor·urteil das bias; *(voreilige Schlußfolgerung)* prejudice

Vor·vergangenheit die *(Sprachw.)* pluperfect

Vor·verkauf der advance sale of tickets

vor|verlegen *tr. V. (zeitlich)* bring forward (**auf** + *Akk.* to; **um** by)

Vorwahl die, **Vorwähl·nummer** die *(Fernspr.)* dialling code

Vorwand der; ~|e|s, **Vorwände** pretext; *(Ausrede)* excuse

vor·wärts *Adv.* forwards; *(weiter)* onwards; **vorwärts|kommen** *unr. itr. V.; mit sein* make progress; *(im Beruf, Leben)* get on; get ahead

vor·weg *Adv.* beforehand; **vorweg|nehmen** *unr. tr. V.* anticipate

vor|weisen *unr. tr. V.* produce

vor|werfen *unr. tr. V.* jmdm. etw. ~: reproach sb. with sth.; *(beschuldigen)* accuse sb. of sth.

vor·wiegend *Adv.* mainly

vor·witzig *Adj.* bumptious; pert ⟨*child*⟩

Vor·wort das; *Pl.* ~e foreword

Vor·wurf der reproach; *(Beschuldigung)* accusation; **vorwurfs·voll 1.** *Adj.* reproachful; **2.** *adv.* reproachfully

Vor·zeichen das **a)** *(Omen)* omen; **b)** *(Math.)* [algebraic] sign

vor|zeigen *tr. V.* produce; show

Vor·zeit die prehistory; **vorzeitig 1.** *Adj.* premature; early ⟨*retirement*⟩; **2.** *adv.* prematurely

vor|ziehen *unr. tr. V.* prefer

Vor·zimmer das outer office

Vor·zug der **a)** *o. Pl.* preference (gegenüber over); **b)** *(gute Eigenschaft)* good quality; merit; **vorzüglich 1.** *Adj.* excellent; first-rate; **2.** *adv.* excellently

vulgär 1. *Adj.* vulgar; **2.** *adv.* in a vulgar way

Vulkan [vʊl'kaːn] der; ~s, ~e volcano; **vulkanisch** *Adj.* volcanic; **vulkanisieren** *tr. V.* vulcanize

v.u.Z. *Abk.* vor unserer Zeit|rechnung| BC

w, W [veː] das; ~s, ~: w, W

W *Abk.* **a)** West, Westen W.; **b)** Watt W.

Waage die; ~, ~n [pair *sing.* of] scales *pl.;* **waage·recht 1.** *Adj.* horizontal;

2. *adv.* horizontally; **Waage·rechte die** horizontal; **Waag·schale die** scale pan

Wabe die; ~, ~n honeycomb

wach 1. *Adj.* awake; **2.** *adv.* alertly; attentively; **Wache die;** ~, ~n **a)** *(Milit.)* guard *or* sentry duty; *(Seew.)* watch [duty]; **b)** *(Wächter, Milit.)* guard; *(Seew.)* watch; **c)** *(Polizei~)* police station; **wachen** *itr. V. (geh.)* be awake; **bei jmdm.** ~: stay up at sb.'s bedside; sit up with sb.; **Wachhund** der guard-dog

Wacholder der; ~s, ~: juniper

Wach·posten der *(Milit.)* guard

Wachs das; ~es, ~e wax

wachsam *Adj.* watchful; vigilant

¹wachsen *unr. itr. V.; mit sein* grow

²wachsen *tr. V.* wax

Wachs-: ~**figur die** waxwork; ~**figuren·kabinett das** waxworks *sing. or pl.;* waxworks museum

wächst 2. u. 3. Pers. Sg. Präsens v. wachsen; **Wachstum das;** ~s growth

Wachtel die; ~, ~n quail

Wächter der; ~s, ~: guard; *(Nacht~, Turm~)* watchman; *(Park~)* [park-] keeper; **Wach[t]·turm der** watchtower

wackelig *Adj.* **a)** wobbly ‹chair, table, etc.›; loose ‹tooth›; **b)** *(ugs.: kraftlos, schwach)* frail; **Wackel·kontakt der** *(Elektrot.)* loose connection; **wackeln** *itr. V.* wobble; ‹tooth etc.› be loose; ‹house, window, etc.› shake; **mit dem Kopf/den Ohren** ~: waggle one's head/ears

wacker *(veralt.)* **1.** *Adj.* upright; **2.** *adv.* valiantly; **sich** ~ **halten** put up a good show

Wade die; ~, ~n *(Anat.)* calf; **Waden·krampf der** cramp in one's calf

Waffe die; ~, ~n weapon

Waffel die; ~, ~n waffle; *(dünne ~, Eis~)* wafer; *(Eistüte)* cone

Waffen-: ~**gewalt die;** *o. Pl.* mit ~**gewalt** by force of arms; ~**handel der** arms trade; ~**händler der** arms dealer; ~**schein der** firearms licence; ~**stillstand der** armistice

Wage·mut der daring; **wage·mutig** *Adj.* daring; **wagen 1.** *tr. V.* risk; |es| ~, etw. zu tun dare to do sth.; **2.** *refl. V.* sich irgendwohin/nicht irgendwohin ~: venture somewhere/not dare to go somewhere

Wagen der; ~s, ~: *(PKW)* car; *(Pferde~)* cart; *(Eisenbahn~) (Personen~)* coach; *(Güter~)* truck; *(Straßen-*

bahn~) car; *(Kinder~, Puppen~)* pram *(Brit.);* baby carriage *(Amer.); (Sport~)* push-chair *(Brit.);* stroller *(Amer.);* **Wagen·heber der** jack; **Waggon** [va'gɔŋ, *südd., österr.:* va'goːn] **der;** ~s, ~s, *südd., österr.:* ~s, ~e wagon; truck *(Brit.);* car *(Amer.)*

waghalsig 1. *Adj.* daring; *(leichtsinnig)* reckless; **2.** *adv.* daringly; ‹speculate› riskily; *(leichtsinnig)* recklessly; **Wagnis das;** ~ses, ~se daring exploit *or* feat; *(Risiko)* risk

Wahl die; ~, ~en **a)** *o. Pl.* choice; **eine/ seine** ~ **treffen** make a/one's choice; **b)** *(in ein Gremium, Amt usw.)* election; **geheime** ~: secret ballot; **wahl·berechtigt** *Adj.* eligible *or* entitled to vote *postpos.;* **Wahl·beteiligung die** turn-out; **wählen 1.** *tr. V.* **a)** choose; *(aus~)* select; **b)** *(Fernspr.)* dial ‹number›; **c)** *(durch Stimmabgabe)* elect; **d)** *(stimmen für)* vote for *‹party, candidate›;* **2.** *itr. V.* **a)** choose; **b)** *(Fernspr.)* dial; **c)** *(stimmen)* vote; **Wähler der;** ~s, ~: voter; **Wahl·ergebnis das** election result; **Wählerin die;** ~, ~nen voter; **wählerisch** *Adj.* choosy; particular (**in** + *Dat.* about)

wahl-, Wahl-: ~**gang der** ballot; ~**geheimnis das** secrecy of the ballot; ~**kabine die** polling-booth; ~**kampf der** election campaign; ~**kreis der** constituency; ~**lokal das** polling-station; ~**los 1.** *Adj.* indiscriminate; **2.** *adv.* indiscriminately; ~**recht das** *o. Pl.* right to vote

Wähl·scheibe die *(Fernspr.)* dial

Wahl-: ~**sieg der** election victory; ~**spruch der** motto; ~**urne die** ballot-box

Wahn der; ~|e|s mania delusion; **Wahn·sinn der;** *o. Pl.* **a)** insanity; madness; **b)** *(ugs.: Unvernunft)* madness; lunacy; **wahnsinnig 1.** *Adj.* **a)** *(geistesgestört)* insane; mad; **b)** *(ugs.: ganz unvernünftig)* mad; crazy; **c)** *(ugs.: groß, heftig, intensiv)* terrific *(coll.)* ‹effort, speed, etc.›; terrible *(coll.)* ‹fright, job, pain›; **2.** *adv. (ugs.)* incredibly *(coll.);* terribly *(coll.)*

wahr *Adj.* **a)** true; **nicht** ~? *translation depends on preceding verb-form;* **du hast Hunger, nicht** ~? you're hungry, aren't you?; **nicht** ~, **er weiß es doch?** he does know, doesn't he?; **b)** *(wirklich)* real ‹reason, motive, feelings, joy, etc.›; actual ‹culprit›; *(echt)* true, real ‹friend, friendship, love, art›

wahren *tr. V. (geh.)* preserve ⟨*balance, equality, neutrality, etc.*⟩; maintain ⟨*authority, right*⟩; *(verteidigen)* defend

währen *itr. V. (geh.)* last; **während** **1.** *Konj.* **a)** *(zeitlich)* while; **b)** *(adversativ)* whereas; **2.** *Präp. mit Gen.* during; *(über einen Zeitraum von)* for

wahr|haben *unr. tr. V. in etw.* **nicht ~ wollen** not want to admit sth.; **wahrhaft** *(geh.)* **1.** *Adj.* true; **2.** *adv.* truly; **wahrhaftig** **1.** *Adj. (geh.)* truthful ⟨*person*⟩; **2.** *adv.* really; genuinely; **Wahrheit die;** ~, ~en truth; **wahrheits·getreu 1.** *Adj.* truthful; faithful ⟨*account*⟩; **2.** *adv.* truthfully; ⟨*portray*⟩ faithfully

wahr|nehmen *unr. tr. V.* **a)** *(mit den Sinnen erfassen)* perceive; *(spüren)* feel; detect ⟨*sound, smell*⟩; *(bemerken)* notice; *(erkennen, ausmachen)* make out; **b)** *(nutzen)* take advantage of ⟨*opportunity*⟩; exploit ⟨*advantage*⟩; exercise ⟨*right*⟩; **c)** *(vertreten)* look after ⟨*sb.'s interests, affairs*⟩; **d)** *(erfüllen, ausführen)* carry out, perform ⟨*function, task, duty*⟩; fulfil ⟨*responsibility*⟩; **Wahrnehmung die;** ~, ~en **a)** perception; *(eines Sachverhalts)* awareness; *(eines Geruchs, eines Tons)* detection; **b)** *(Nutzung) (eines Rechts)* exercise; *(einer Gelegenheit, eines Vorteils)* exploitation; **c)** *(Vertretung)* representation; **d)** *(einer Funktion, Aufgabe, Pflicht)* performance; execution; *(einer Verantwortung)* fulfilment

wahr·sagen 1. *itr. V.* tell fortunes; **2.** *tr. V.* predict, foretell ⟨*future*⟩; **Wahrsager der;** ~s, ~, **Wahrsagerin die;** ~, ~nen fortune-teller

wahrscheinlich 1. *Adj.* probable; likely; **2.** *adv.* probably; **Wahrscheinlichkeit die;** ~, ~en probability; likelihood

Währung die; ~, ~en currency; **Währungs·reform die** currency reform

Wahr·zeichen das symbol; *(einer Stadt, einer Landschaft)* [most famous] landmark

Waise die; ~, ~n orphan; **Waisen·haus das** orphanage

Wal der; ~[e]s, ~e whale

Wald der; ~[e]s, **Wälder** wood; *(größer)* forest; **Wald·brand der** forest fire; **Wäldchen das** copse; **Wald-meister der;** *o. pl. (Bot.)* woodruff

Waliser der; ~s, ~: Welshman; **Wa-liserin die;** ~, ~nen Welshwoman; **walisisch** *Adj.* Welsh

Wall der; ~[e]s, **Wälle** earthwork; embankment; rampart *(esp. Mil.)*

Wall-: ~fahrer der pilgrim; ~fahrt die pilgrimage

Wal·nuß die walnut

Wal·roß das; *Pl.* -rosse walrus

walten *itr. V. (geh.)* ⟨*good sense, good spirit*⟩ prevail; ⟨*peace, silence, harmony, etc.*⟩ reign

Walze die; ~, ~n roller; *(Straßen~)* [road-]roller; *(Schreib~)* platen; **walzen** *tr. V.* roll ⟨*field, road, steel, etc.*⟩; **wälzen 1.** *tr. V.* roll; heave ⟨*heavy object*⟩; *(fig.)* shove ⟨*blame, responsibility*⟩ **(auf** + *Akk.* on); **etw. in Mehl** *usw.* ~ *(Kochk.)* toss sth. in flour *etc.*; **Probleme** ~ *(fig. ugs.)* mull over problems; **2.** *refl. V.* roll; *(auf der Stelle)* roll about *or* around; *(im Krampf, vor Schmerzen)* writhe around; **Walzer der;** ~s, ~: waltz

wand *1. u. 3. Pers. Sg. Prät. v.* winden

Wand die; ~, **Wände** wall; *(Trenn~)* partition; *(bewegliche Trenn~)* screen; *(eines Behälters, Schiffs)* side

Wandel der; ~s change; **wandeln** *refl., tr. V.* change **(in** + *Akk.* into)

Wanderer der; ~s, ~: rambler; hiker; **Wander·karte die** rambler's [path] map; **wandern** *itr. V.; mit sein* **a)** hike; ramble; **b)** *(ugs.: gehen; fig.)* wander *(lit. or fig.)*; **c)** *(ziehen, reisen)* travel; *(ziellos)* roam; ⟨*exhibition, circus, theatre*⟩ tour, travel; ⟨*animal, people, tribe*⟩ migrate

Wanderung die; ~, ~en **a)** hike; walking tour; **eine ~ machen** go on a hike/tour/trek; **b)** *(Zool., Soziol.)* migration

Wander·weg der footpath *(constructed for ramblers)*

Wandlung die; ~, ~en change; *(grundlegend)* transformation

Wand-: ~malerei die *(Bild)* mural; ~schrank der wall cupboard *or (Amer.)* closet

wandte *1. u. 3. Pers. Prät. v.* wenden

Wange die; ~, ~n *(geh.)* cheek

wankelmütig *Adj. (geh.)* vacillating; **wanken** *itr. V.* **a)** sway; ⟨*person*⟩ totter; *(unter einer Last)* stagger; **b)** *mit sein (unsicher gehen)* stagger; totter

wann *Adv.* when; **seit ~ wohnst du dort?** how long have you been living there?

Wanne die; ~, ~n bath[tub]

Wanze die; ~, ~n bug *(coll.)*

Wappen das; ~s, ~: coat of arms

war *1. u. 3. Pers. Sg. Prät. v.* sein

warb *1. u. 3. Pers. Sg. Prät. v.* **werben**
ward *(geh.) 1. u. 3. Pers. Sg. Prät. v.*
werden
Ware die; ~, ~n a) ~[n] goods *pl.;* b)
(einzelne ~) article; commodity
(Econ., fig.); (Erzeugnis) product
Waren-: ~**haus** das department
store; ~**lager** das *(einer Fabrik o.ä.)*
stores *pl.; (eines Geschäftes)* stock-
room; *(größer)* warehouse; ~**muster**
das, ~**probe** die sample; ~**zeichen**
das trade mark
warf *1. u. 3. Pers. Sg. Prät. v.* **werfen**
warm; **wärmer, wärmst** ... 1. *Adj. (auch
fig.)* warm; hot ⟨*meal, food, bath,
spring*⟩; das Essen ~ **machen** heat up
the food; „~" *(auf Wasserhahn)* 'hot';
keen, lively ⟨*interest*⟩; 2. *adv.* warmly;
~ **essen/duschen** have a hot meal/
shower; **Wärme** die; ~: warmth;
(Hitze; auch Physik) heat; **wärmen** 1.
tr. V. warm; *(aufwärmen)* warm up
⟨*food, drink*⟩; 2. *itr. V.* be warm;
(warm halten) keep one warm;
Wärm·flasche die hot-water bottle
Warm·wasser-: ~**bereiter** der; ~s,
~: water-heater; ~**heizung** die hot-
water heating
Warn-: ~**blinkanlage** die *(Kfz-W.)*
hazard warning lights *pl.;* ~**dreieck**
das *(Kfz-W.)* hazard warning triangle
warnen *tr. (auch itr.) V.* warn (vor +
Dat. of, about); jmdn. [davor] ~, etw.
zu tun warn sb. against doing sth.
Warn-: ~**schild** das warning sign;
~**schuß** der warning shot; ~**signal**
das warning signal; ~**streik** der
token strike
Warnung die; ~, ~en warning (vor +
Dat. of, about)
Warschau (das); ~s Warsaw
Warte-: ~**halle** die waiting room;
(Flugw.) departure lounge; ~**liste** die
waiting list
warten 1. *itr. V.* wait (auf + *Akk.*
for); 2. *tr. V.* service ⟨*car etc.*⟩
Wärter der; ~s, ~: attendant; *(Tier~,
Zoo~, Leuchtturm~)* keeper; *(Kran-
ken~)* orderly; *(Gefängnis~)* warder
Warte-: ~**saal** der waiting-room;
~**zimmer** das waiting-room
Wartung die; ~, ~en service; *(das
Warten)* servicing; *(Instandhaltung)*
maintenance
warum *Adv.* why
Warze die; ~, ~n wart; *(Brust~)*
nipple
was 1. *Interrogativpron. Nom. u. Akk.
u. (nach Präp.) Dat. Neutr.;* ~ kostet

das? what *or* how much does that
cost?; **ach** ~! *(ugs.)* oh, come on!; ~
für ein .../~ **für** ...: what sort *or* kind
of ...; 2. *Relativpron. Nom. u. Akk. u.
(nach Präp.) Dat. Neutr.;* |das,| ~:
what; **alles,** ~ ...: everything *or* all
that ...; **vieles/nichts/etwas,** ~ ...:
much/nothing/something that ...; ~
mich betrifft, |so| ...: as far as I'm con-
cerned, ...; 3. *Indefinitpron. Nom. u.
Akk. u. (nach Präp.) Dat. Neutr. (ugs.)*
s. **etwas**; 4. *Adv. (ugs.) (warum, wozu)*
why; what ... for
Wasch-: ~**anlage** die car-wash;
~**automat** der washing-machine;
~**becken** das wash-basin
Wäsche die; ~, ~n a) *o. Pl. (zu wa-
schende Textilien)* washing; *(für die
Wäscherei)* laundry; b) *o. Pl. (Unter~)*
underwear; c) *(das Waschen)* washing
no pl.; (einmalig) wash; **in der** ~ **sein**
be in the wash; **wasch·echt** *Adj.* a)
colour-fast ⟨*textile, clothes*⟩; fast ⟨*colour*⟩; b) *(fig.)* genuine
Wäsche-: ~**klammer** die clothes-
peg *(Brit.);* clothes-pin *(Amer.);*
~**korb** der laundry-basket; ~**leine**
die clothes-line
waschen 1. *unr. tr.V.* wash; sich ~:
wash [oneself]; have a wash; **Wäsche**
~: do the/some washing; 2. *unr. itr.
V.* do the washing; **Wäscherei** die;
~, ~en laundry
Wäsche-: ~**schleuder** die spin-
drier; ~**trockner** der a) *(Maschine)*
tumble-drier; b) *(Gestell)* clothes-airer
Wasch-: ~**gelegenheit** die washing
facilities *pl.;* ~**küche** die laundry-
room; ~**lappen** der [face] flannel;
washcloth *(Amer.);* ~**maschine** die
washing-machine; ~**mittel** das detergent; ~**pulver** das washing-powder;
~**straße** die [automatic] car-wash
wäscht *3. Pers. Sg. Präsens v.* **waschen**
Wasser das; ~s, ~/**Wässer** a) *o. Pl.*
water; b) *(Mineral~, Tafel~)* mineral
water; *(Heil~)* water; c) *o. Pl. (Gewässer)* **ein fließendes/stehendes** ~: a
moving/stagnant stretch of water; d)
o. Pl. (Urin) water; urine; ~ **lassen**
pass water
wasser-, **Wasser**-: ~**ball** der a)
beach-ball; b) *o. Pl. (Spiel)* water
polo; ~**dicht** *Adj.* waterproof ⟨*clothing, watch, etc.*⟩; watertight ⟨*container, seal, etc.*⟩; ~**fall** der waterfall;
~**farbe** die water-colour; ~**hahn** der
water-tap; faucet *(Amer.)*
wässerig *s.* **wäßrig**

Wạsser-: ~**kessel** der kettle; ~**leitung** die water-pipe; *(Hauptleitung)*
water-main

wạssern *itr. V.; mit sein* land [on the
water]; **wạssern** *tr. V.* soak; *(Phot.)*
wash ⟨*negative, print*⟩

wạsser-, Wạsser-: ~**pflanze** die
aquatic plant; ~**rohr** das water-pipe;
~**schlauch** der [water-]hose;
~**schutz·polizei** die river/lake
police; [1]~**ski** der water-ski; ~ **fahren**
water-ski; [2]~**ski** das; ~**s** water-skiing
no art.; ~**spiegel** der **a)** *(Oberfläche)*
surface [of the water]; **b)** *(Niveau)*
water-level; ~**sport** der water-sport
no art.; ~**spülung** die flush

Wạsser·stoff der; *o. Pl.* hydrogen;
Wạsser·stoff·bombe die hydrogen bomb

Wạsser-: ~**strahl** der jet of water;
~**straße** die waterway; ~**temperatur** die water-temperature; ~**tiefe** die
depth of the water; ~**tropfen** der
drop of water; ~**turm** der water-
tower; ~**werfer** der water-cannon;
~**werk** das waterworks *sing.;* ~**zeichen** das watermark

wäßrig *Adj.* watery

waten *itr. V.; mit sein* wade

wạtscheln *itr. V.; mit sein* waddle

[1]**Wạtt** das; ~|e|s, ~en mud-flats *pl.*

[2]**Wạtt** das; ~s, ~ *(Technik, Physik)*
watt

Wạtte die; ~, ~n cotton wool; **Wạt-
te·bausch** der wad of cotton wool

Wạtten·meer das tidal shallows *pl.*

wattiert *Adj.* quilted; padded ⟨*shoulder etc., envelope*⟩

WC [ve:'tse:] das; ~|s|, ~|s| toilet; WC

weben *tr., itr. V.* weave; **Weber** der;
~s, ~: weaver; **Web·stuhl** der loom

Wechsel der; ~s, ~ **a)** *(das Auswechseln)* change; *(Geld~)* exchange; **b)**
(Aufeinanderfolge) alternation; **im** ~:
alternately; *(bei mehr als zwei)* in rotation; **c)** *(das Überwechseln)* move;
(Sport) transfer; **d)** *(Bankw.)* bill of
exchange (**über** + *Akk.* for)

wechsel-, Wechsel-: ~**geld** das; *o.
Pl.* change; ~**haft** *Adj.* changeable;
~**jahre** *Pl.* change of life *sing.;*
menopause *sing.;* ~**kurs** der exchange rate

wechseln **1.** *tr. V.* **a)** change; **das
Hemd** ~: change one's shirt; **die Wohnung** ~: move home; **b)** *([aus]tau-
schen)* exchange ⟨*letters, glances,
etc.*⟩; **c)** *(um~)* change ⟨*money, note,
etc.*⟩ (**in** + *Akk.* into); **2.** *itr. V.* change

wechsel-, Wechsel-: ~**seitig** **1.**
Adj. mutual; **2.** *adv.* mutually;
~**strom** der *(Elektrot.)* alternating
current; ~**stube** die bureau de
change; ~**wirkung** die interaction

wecken *tr. V.* jmdn. |aus dem Schlaf|
~: wake sb. [up]; *(fig.: hervorrufen)*
arouse ⟨*interest, curiosity, anger*⟩;
Wecker der; ~s, ~ alarm clock

wedeln *itr. V.* ⟨*tail*⟩ wag; |mit dem
Schwanz| ~ ⟨*dog*⟩ wag its tail

weder *Konj.* ~ **A noch B** neither A nor
B

weg *Adv.* away; *(verschwunden, ~ge-
gangen)* gone; **er ist schon seit einer
Stunde** ~: he left an hour ago; **weit** ~:
far away; a long way away

Weg der; ~|e|s,~e **a)** *(Fuß~)* path;
(Feld~) track; **b)** *(Zugang)* way; *(Passage, Durchgang)* passage; **sich** *(Dat.)*
einen ~ **durch etw. bahnen** clear a path
or way through sth.; **c)** *(Route, Verbindung)* way; route; **d)** *(Strecke, Entfernung)* distance; *(Gang)* walk; *(Reise)*
journey; **auf dem kürzesten** ~: by the
shortest route; **auf halbem** ~|e| *(auch
fig.)* half-way; **sich auf den** ~ **machen**
set off; **etw. in die** ~**e leiten** get sth.
under way; **e)** *(ugs.: Besorgung)* errand; **f)** *(Methode)* way; *(Mittel)*
means

weg-: ~|**bleiben** *unr. itr. V.; mit sein*
(nicht kommen) stay away; *(nicht nach
Hause kommen)* stay out; ~|**bringen**
unr. tr. V. take away; *(zur Reparatur,
Wartung usw.)* take in

wegen *Präp. mit Gen.* **a)** because of;
~ **Umbau|s| geschlossen** closed for al-
terations; **b)** *(um... willen)* for the sake
of; ~ **der Kinder/** *(ugs.)* **dir** for the children's/your sake; **c)** *(bezüglich)*
about; regarding

weg-: ~|**fahren** **1.** *unr. itr. V.; mit sein*
a) leave; *(im Auto)* drive off; *(losfahren)* set off; **b)** *(irgendwohin fahren)* go
away; **2.** *unr. tr. V.* drive away; *(mit
dem Handwagen usw.)* take away;
~|**fallen** *unr. itr. V.; mit sein* be dis-
continued; *(nicht mehr zutreffen)* no
longer apply; ~|**fliegen** *unr. itr. V.;
mit sein* fly away; *(~geblasen werden)*
fly off; ~|**gehen** *unr. itr. V.* **a)** leave;
(ugs.: ausgehen) go out; *(ugs.:* ~**ziehen)* move away; **b)** *(verschwinden)*
⟨*spot, fog, etc.*⟩ go away; **c)** *(sich entfer-
nen lassen)* ⟨*stain*⟩ come out; ~|**jagen**
tr. V. chase away; ~|**kommen** *unr.
itr. V.; mit sein* **a)** get away; **b)** *(abhanden kommen)* go missing; **c)** **gut/**

schlecht *usw.* [bei etw.] ~**kommen**
(ugs.) come off well/badly *etc.* [in
sth.]; ~|**kriegen** *tr. V.* get rid of ⟨cold,
pain, *etc.*⟩; get out, get rid of ⟨stain⟩;
~|**lassen** *unr. tr. V.* **a)** jmdn. ~**lassen**
let sb. go; *(ausgehen lassen)* let sb. go
out; **b)** *(auslassen)* leave out; omit;
~|**laufen** *unr. itr. V.*; *mit sein* run
away **(von,** *vor* + *Dat.* from); ~|**le-
gen** *tr. V.* put aside; *(an seinen Platz
legen)* put away; ~|**nehmen** *unr. tr.
V.* **a)** take away; move ⟨head, arm⟩; **b)**
jmdm. etw. ~**nehmen** take sth. away
from sb.; ~|**schicken** *tr. V.* **a)** send
off ⟨letter, parcel⟩; **b)** send ⟨person⟩
away; ~|**schmeißen** *unr. tr. V. (ugs.)*
chuck away *(coll.)*; ~|**schütten** *tr. V.*
pour away; ~|**sehen** *unr. itr. V.* look
away; ~|**stellen** *tr. V.* put away; *(bei-
seite stellen)* put aside; ~|**stoßen** *unr.
tr. V.* push *or* shove away; ~|**tragen**
unr. tr. V. carry away
Wegweiser *der;* ~s, ~ signpost
weg-: ~|**werfen** *unr. tr. V. (auch fig.)*
throw away; ~**werfend** *Adj.* dis-
missive ⟨gesture, remark⟩; ~|**wi-
schen** *tr. V.* wipe away; ~|**ziehen** 1.
unr. tr. V. pull away; draw back ⟨cur-
tain⟩; pull off ⟨blanket⟩; 2. *unr. itr. V.;
mit sein* **a)** *(umziehen)* move away; **b)**
(wandern) ⟨animals, nomads, *etc.*⟩
leave [on their migration]
weh *(ugs.)* 1. *Adj.* sore; 2. *adv.* ~ **tun**
hurt; **mir tut der Magen/Kopf** ~**:** my
stomach/head is aching *or* hurts;
jmdm./sich ~ **tun** hurt sb./oneself;
Wehe *die;* ~, ~**n:** ~**n haben** have
contractions; **in den** ~**n liegen** be in labour
wehen *itr. V.* **a)** *(blasen)* blow; **b)** *(flattern)* flutter
weh-, Weh-: ~**leidig** *(abwertend)* 1.
Adj. (überempfindlich) soft; *(weinerlich)* whining *attrib.;* 2. *adv.* self-
pityingly; *(weinerlich)* whiningly;
~**mut die;** ~ *(geh.)* wistful nostalgia;
~**mütig** *Adj.* wistfully nostalgic
¹**Wehr die;** ~, ~**en sich** [gegen jmdn./
etw.] **zur** ~ **setzen** make a stand
[against sb./sth.]; resist [sb./sth.];
²**Wehr das;** ~|e|s, ~e weir
Wehr·dienst *der; o. Pl.* military service *no art.;* **seinen** ~ **ableisten** do
one's military service
Wehr·dienst-: ~**verweigerer** *der;*
~s, ~: conscientious objector; ~**verweigerung die** conscientious objection
wehren *refl. V.* defend oneself

wehr-, Wehr-: ~**los** *Adj.* defenceless; ~**pflicht die;** *o. Pl.* military service; **die allgemeine** ~**pflicht** compulsory military service; ~**pflichtig**
Adj. liable for military service *postpos.*
Weib das; ~|e|s, ~er **a)** *(veralt., ugs.)*
woman; female *(derog.);* **Weibchen
das;** ~s, ~ female; **weiblich** 1. *Adj.*
a) female; **b)** *(für die Frau typisch;
Sprachw.)* feminine; 2. *adv.* femin-
inely
weich 1. *Adj. (auch fig.)* soft; **ein** ~**es
Ei** a soft-boiled egg; 2. *adv.* softly
¹**Weiche die;** ~, ~**n** *(Flanke)* flank
²**Weiche die;** ~, ~**n** points *pl. (Brit.);*
switch *(Amer.)*
weichen *unr. itr. V.; mit sein* move;
vor jmdm./einer Sache ~**:** give way to
sb./sth.
weich·gekocht *Adj. (präd. getrennt
geschrieben)* soft-boiled ⟨egg⟩;
weichlich 1. *Adj.* soft; *(ohne innere
Festigkeit)* weak; 2. *adv.* softly
¹**Weide die;** ~, ~**n** willow
²**Weide die;** ~, ~**n** pasture; **weiden**
itr., tr. V. graze
Weiden·kätzchen das willow catkin
weigern *refl. V.* refuse; **Weigerung
die;** ~, ~**en** refusal
Weih·bischof *der (kath. Kirche)* suf-
fragan bishop; **Weihe die;** ~, ~**n**
(Rel.) consecration; *(kath. Kirche:
Priester~, Bischofs~)* ordination;
weihen *tr. V.* **a)** *(Rel.)* consecrate;
(zueignen) dedicate (*Dat.* to); **b)** *(kath.
Kirche: ordinieren)* ordain
Weiher *der;* ~s, ~: [small] pond
Weihnachten das; ~, ~**:** Christmas;
frohe *od.* **fröhliche** *od.* **gesegnete** ~**!**
Merry *or* Happy Christmas!;
weihnachtlich *Adj.* Christmassy
Weihnachts-: ~**baum** *der* Christmas tree; ~**feiertag** *der:* **der erste/
zweite** ~**feiertag** Christmas Day/Box-
ing Day; ~**fest das** Christmas; ~**geschenk das** Christmas present *or*
gift; ~**lied das** Christmas carol;
~**mann** *der; Pl.* ~**männer** Father
Christmas; Santa Claus; ~**markt der**
Christmas fair; ~**zeit die** Christmas
time
Weih-: ~**rauch** *der* incense; ~**wasser das** *(kath. Kirche)* holy water
weil *Konj.* because
Weile die; ~**:** while; **weilen** *itr. V.
(geh.) (ver~)* stay; *(sein)* be
Wein der; ~|e|s, ~e wine
Wein-: ~**berg** *der* vineyard; ~**brand**
der brandy

weinen *itr. V.* cry (**über** + *Akk.* over, about); *(aus Trauer, Kummer)* cry, weep (**um** for); **weinerlich 1.** *Adj.* tearful; weepy; **2.** *adv.* tearfully

wein-, Wein-: ~**essig** der wine vinegar; ~**flasche** winebottle; ~**glas** das wineglass; ~**handlung** die winemerchant's; ~**karte** die wine-list; ~**lokal** das wine bar; ~**probe** die wine-tasting [session]; ~**rot** *Adj.* wine-red; ~**stube** die wine bar; ~**traube** die grape

weise 1. *Adj.* wise; **2.** *adv.* wisely

Weise die; ~, ~**n a)** *(Art, Verfahren)* way; **b)** *(Melodie)* tune; melody

weisen 1. *unr. tr. V. (geh.: zeigen)* show; **jmdn. aus dem Zimmer** ~: send sb. out of the room; **2.** *unr. itr. V. (irgendwohin zeigen)* point

Weisheit die; ~, ~**en a)** *o. Pl.* wisdom; **b)** *(Erkenntnis)* wise insight; *(Spruch)* wise saying; **Weisheits·zahn** der wisdom tooth; **weis|machen** *tr. V. (ugs.)* **das kannst du mir nicht** ~! you can't expect me to swallow that!

¹**weiß** *1. u. 3. Pers. Sg. Präsens v.* **wissen**

²**weiß** *Adj.* white; **Weiß** das; ~|e|s, ~: white

weis·sagen *tr. V.* prophesy; **Weissagung** die; ~, ~**en** prophecy

Weiß-: ~**bier** das weiss beer; ~**brot** das white bread; ~**dorn** der hawthorn

Weiße der/die; *adj. Dekl.* white; white man/woman; **weißen** *tr. V.* paint white; *(tünchen)* whitewash

weiß-, Weiß-: ~**gold** das white gold; ~**herbst** der ≈ rosé wine; ~**kohl** der, *(bes. südd., österr.)* ~**kraut** das white cabbage

weißlich *Adj.* whitish

weißt *2. Pers. Sg. Präsens v.* **wissen**

Weiß-: ~**wein** der white wine; ~**wurst** die veal sausage

Weisung die; ~, ~**en** *(geh., sonst Amtsspr.)* instruction; *(Direktive)* directive

weit 1. *Adj.* wide; long *(way)*; **jmdm. zu** ~ **sein** *(clothes)* be too loose on sb.; **2.** *adv.* **a)** *(räumlich ausgedehnt)* ~ **geöffnet** wide open; ~ **und breit war niemand zu sehen** there was no one to be seen anywhere; **b)** *(lang)* far; ~**er** further; farther; **am** ~**esten** [the] furthest or farthest; ~ **|entfernt** *od.* **weg| wohnen** live a long way away *or* off; live far away; **von** ~**em** from a distance; **das geht zu** ~ *(fig.)* that is going too

far; **c)** *(zeitlich entfernt)* ~ **nach Mitternacht** well past midnight; **d)** *(in der Entwicklung)* far; **Weit·blick** der; *o. Pl.* far-sightedness; **Weite** die; ~, ~**n a)** *(räumliche Ausdehnung)* expanse; **b)** *(bes. Sport: Entfernung)* distance; **c)** *(eines Kleidungsstückes)* width; **weiten 1.** *tr. V.* widen; **2.** *refl. V.* widen; *(pupil)* dilate; **weiter** *Adv.* **a)** *s.* **weit** 2; **b)** **und so** ~: and so on; **c)** *(~hin, anschließend)* then; **d)** *(außerdem, sonst)* ~ **nichts** nothing more *or* else; **weiter...** *Adj.* further; **bis auf** ~**es** for the time being; *s. auch* **ohne**

weiter-, Weiter-: ~|**bringen** *unr. tr. V.* **die Diskussion brachte uns nicht** ~: the discussion did not get us any further [forward]; ~|**erzählen** *tr. V.* **a)** continue telling; *itr.* **erzähl weiter!** do carry *or* go on; **b)** *(~sagen)* pass on; ~|**fahren** *unr. itr. V.; mit sein* continue [on one's way]; *(~ reisen)* travel on; ~|**führen** *tr., itr. V.* continue; ~|**geben** *unr. tr. V.* pass on; ~|**gehen** *unr. itr. V.; mit sein* go on; **bitte** ~**gehen!** please move along *or* keep moving!; ~**hin** *Adv.* **a)** *(immer noch)* still; **b)** *(künftig)* in future; **c)** *(außerdem)* in addition; ~|**kommen** *unr. itr. V.; mit sein* **a)** get further; **b)** *(Fortschritte machen)* make progress; **im Beruf** ~**kommen** get on in one's career; ~|**machen** *(ugs.) itr. V.* carry on; go on; ~|**reichen** *tr. V.* pass on; ~|**sagen** *tr. V.* pass on; ~|**sehen** *unr. itr. V.* see; ~|**verarbeiten** *tr. V.* process; ~**verarbeitende** processing

weit-, Weit-: ~**gehend 1.** *Adj.* extensive, wide, sweeping *(powers)*; far-reaching *(support, concessions, etc.)*; wide *(support, agreement, etc.)*; general *(renunciation)*; **2.** *adv.* to a large *or* great extent; ~**gereist** *Adj.* widely travelled; ~**hin** *Adv.* for miles around; ~**läufig 1.** *Adj.* **a)** *(ausgedehnt)* extensive; *(geräumig)* spacious; **b)** *(entfernt)* distant; **2.** *adv.* **a)** *(ausgedehnt)* spaciously; **b)** *(entfernt)* distantly; ~**räumig 1.** *Adj.* spacious *(room, area, etc.)*; wide *(gap, space)*; **2.** *adv.* spaciously; ~**reichend 1.** *Adj. (fig.)* far-reaching *(importance, consequences)*; sweeping *(changes, powers)*; extensive *(relations, influence)*; **2.** *adv.* extensively; ~**sichtig** *Adj.* long-sighted; ~**sichtigkeit** die; ~ long-sightedness; ~**sprung** der *(Sport)* long jump *(Brit.)*; broad jump *(Amer.)*; ~**verbreitet** *Adj.* widespread; common; common ⟨*plant, animal*⟩; **~winkel·objektiv das** wide-angle lens

Weizen der; ~s wheat

welch 1. *Interrogativpron. (bei Wahl aus einer unbegrenzten Menge)* what; *(bei Wahl aus einer begrenzten Menge) (adj.)* which; *(subst.)* which one; **2.** *Relativpron. (bei Menschen)* who; *(bei Sachen)* which; **3.** *Indefinitpron.* some; *(in Fragen)* any

welk *Adj.* withered ⟨*skin, hands, etc.*⟩; wilted ⟨*leaves, flower*⟩; limp ⟨*lettuce*⟩; **welken** *itr. V.; mit sein* ⟨*plant, flower*⟩ wilt

Well·blech das corrugated iron; **Welle die; ~, ~n a)** *(auch fig.)* wave; *(Rundf.: ~nlänge)* wavelength; **b)** *(Technik)* shaft

wellen-, Wellen-: ~bad das artificial wave pool; **~brecher der** breakwater; **~gang der;** *o. Pl.* swell; **bei starkem ~gang** in heavy seas; **~länge die** wavelength; **~sittich der** budgerigar

Well·fleisch das boiled belly pork; **wellig** *Adj.* wavy ⟨*hair*⟩; undulating ⟨*scenery, hills, etc.*⟩; uneven ⟨*surface, track, etc.*⟩; **Well·pappe die** corrugated cardboard

Welt die; ~, ~en a) *o. Pl.* world; **auf der ~:** in the world; **die Alte/Neue ~:** the Old/New World; **die dritte/vierte ~** the Third/Fourth World; **auf die** *od.* **zur ~ kommen** be born; **alle ~** *(fig. ugs.)* the whole world; everybody; **b)** *(~all)* universe

welt-, Welt-: ~all das universe; **~anschauung die** world-view; **~ausstellung die** world fair; **~berühmt** *Adj.* world-famous

Welten·bummler der; ~s, ~ globetrotter

welt-, Welt-: ~fremd 1. *Adj.* unworldly; **2.** *adv.* unrealistically; **~frieden der** world peace; **~karte die** map of the world; **~krieg der** world war; **der erste/zweite ~krieg** the First/Second World War

weltlich *Adj.* **a)** worldly; **b)** *(nicht geistlich)* secular

welt-, Welt-: ~literatur die world literature *no art.;* **~macht die** world power; **~markt der** *(Wirtsch.)* world market; **~meister der** world champion; **~meisterschaft die** world championship; **~raum der** space *no art.;* **~reise die** world tour; **~rekord der** world record; **~stadt die** cosmo-

politan city; **~weit 1.** *Adj.* worldwide; **2.** *adv.* throughout the world; **~wirtschaft die** world economy

wem *Dat. von* **wer 1.** *Interrogativpron.* to whom; who ... to; **mit/von/zu ~:** with/from/to whom; who ... with/ from/to; **2.** *Relativpron.* the person to whom ...; the person who ... to; **3.** *Indefinitpron. (ugs.: jemandem)* to somebody *or* someone; *(fragend od. verneint)* to anybody *or* anyone

wen *Akk. von* **wer 1.** *Interrogativpron.* whom; who *(coll.);* **an/für ~:** to/for whom ...; who ... to/for; **2.** *Relativpron.* the person whom; **3.** *Indefinitpron. (ugs.: jemanden)* somebody; someone; *(fragend od. verneint)* anybody; anyone

Wende die; ~, ~n change **(zu** for); **Wende·kreis der a)** *(Geogr.)* tropic; **b)** *(Kfz-W.)* turning circle; **Wendel·treppe die** spiral staircase; **¹wenden 1.** *tr., auch itr. V. (auf die andere Seite)* turn [over]; *(in die entgegengesetzte Richtung)* turn [round]; **bitte ~!** please turn over; **2.** *itr. V.* turn [round]; **3.** *refl. V.* **sich zum Besseren/ Schlechteren ~:** take a turn for the better/worse; **²wenden 1.** *unr. (auch regelm.) tr. V.* turn; **2.** *unr. (auch regelm.) refl. V.* **a)** ⟨*person*⟩ turn; **b)** *(sich richten)* **sich an jmdn. [um Rat]** turn to sb. [for advice]; **wendig 1.** *Adj.* **a)** agile; manœuvrable ⟨*vehicle, boat, etc.*⟩; **b)** *(gewandt)* astute; **2.** *adv.* **a)** *(beweglich)* agilely; **b)** *(gewandt)* astutely; **Wendung die; ~, ~en a)** *(Änderung der Richtung)* turn; **b)** *(Veränderung)* change

wenig 1. *Indefinitpron. u. unbest. Zahlw.* **a)** *Sing.* little; **das ist ~:** that isn't much; **zu ~ Zeit/Geld haben** not have enough time/money; **ein Exemplar/50 Mark zu ~:** one copy too few/ 50 marks too little; **b)** *Pl.* a few; **mit ~en Worten** in a few words; **2.** *Adv.* little; **~ mehr** not much more; **weniger 1.** *Komp. von* **wenig;** *Indefinitpron. u. unbest. Zahlw.* (+ *Sg.*) less; (+ *Pl.*) fewer; **immer ~:** less and less; **2.** *Komp. von* **wenig;** *Adv.* less; **das ist ~ angenehm/erfreulich/schön** that is not very pleasant/pleasing/nice; *s. auch* **mehr 1; 3.** *Konj.* less; **fünf ~ drei** five, take away three; **wenigst... 1.** *Sup. von* **wenig;** *Indefinitpron. u. unbest. Zahlw.* least; **am ~en** least; **2.** *Sup. von* **wenig; am ~en** the least; **wenigstens** *Adv.* at least

wenn *Konj.* **a)** *(konditional)* if; **außer ~:** unless; **~ es nicht anders geht** if there's no other way; **b)** *(temporal)* when; **jedesmal, od. immer, ~:** whenever; **c)** *(konzessiv)* **wenn ... auch** even though; **d)** *(in Wunschsätzen)* if only

wer *Nom. Mask. u. Fem.; s. auch (Gen.)* **wessen;** *(Dat.)* **wem;** *(Akk.)* **wen** **1.** *Interrogativpron.* who; **~ von ...:** which of; **2.** *Relativpron.* the person who; *(jeder, der)* anyone *or* anybody who; **3.** *Indefinitpron. (ugs.: jemand)* someone; *(in Fragen, Konditionalsätzen)* anyone; anybody

Werbe-: **~agentur die** advertising agency; **~fernsehen das** television commercials *pl.;* **~funk der** radio commercials *pl.*

werben **1.** *unr. itr. V.* advertise; **für etw. ~:** advertise sth.; **2.** *unr. tr. V.* attract ⟨*readers, customers, etc.*⟩; recruit ⟨*soldiers, members, etc.*⟩; **Werbung die;** **~:** advertising; **für etw. ~ machen** advertise sth.

Werde·gang der career; **werden 1.** *unr. itr. V.; mit sein* become; get; **älter ~:** get *or* grow old[er]; **wahnsinnig od. verrückt ~:** go mad; **das muß anders ~:** things have to change; **wach ~:** wake up; **rot ~:** go *or* turn red; **Arzt/Professor ~:** become a doctor/professor; **zu etw. ~:** become sth.; **es wird [höchste] Zeit** it is [high] time; **es wird 10 Uhr** it is nearly 10 o'clock; **es wird Herbst** autumn is coming; **sind die Fotos [etwas] geworden?** *(ugs.)* have the photos turned out [well]?; **2.** *Hilfsverb;* **2.** *Part.* **worden a)** *(zur Bildung des Futurs)* **wir ~ uns um ihn kümmern** we will take care of him; **es wird gleich regnen** it is going to rain any minute; **es wird um die 80 Mark kosten** *(ich vermute, es kostet um die 80 Mark)* it will cost around 80 marks; **b)** *(zur Bildung des Passivs)* **du wirst gerufen** you are being called; **er wurde gebeten** he was asked

werfen **1.** *unr. tr. V.* throw; drop ⟨*bombs*⟩; **2.** *unr. itr. V.* **a)** throw; **mit etw. ~:** throw sth.; **b)** *(Junge kriegen)* give birth; ⟨*dog, cat*⟩ litter; **3.** *unr. refl. V.* throw oneself; **sich vor einen Zug ~:** throw oneself under a train

Werft die; **~, ~en** shipyard

Werk das; **~[e]s, ~e** **a)** work; **b)** *(Betrieb, Fabrik)* factory; works *sing. or pl.;* **ab ~:** ex works

Werk·bank die; *Pl.* **~bänke** workbench

Werk[s]-: **~angehörige der/die** factory *or* works employee; **~arzt der** factory *or* works doctor

werk-, Werk-: **~statt die;** **~statt, ~stätten** workshop; *(Kfz-W.)* garage; **~stoff der** material; **~tag der** working day; workday; **~tags** *Adv.* on weekdays; **~tätig** *Adj.* working; **~tätige der/die;** *adj. Dekl.* worker; **~zeug das;** *Pl.* **~zeuge** *(auch fig.)* tool

Werkzeug·kasten der tool-box

Wermut der; **~[e]s, ~s a)** *(Pflanze)* wormwood; **b)** *(Wein)* vermouth

wert *Adj. (geh.)* esteemed; *(als Anrede)* my dear ...; **etw./nichts ~ sein** be worth sth./be worthless; **Wert der;** **~[e]s, ~e** value; **im ~[e] von ...:** worth ...; **~ auf etw.** *(Akk.)* **legen** set great store by *or* on sth.; **wert·beständig** *Adj.* of lasting value *postpos.;* **werten** *tr., itr. V.* judge; assess

wert-, Wert-: **~gegenstand der** valuable object; **~gegenstände** valuables; **~los** *Adj.* worthless; valueless; **~papier das** *(Wirtsch.)* security; **~sache die** valuable item; **~sachen** valuables; **~sendung die** *(Postw.)* registered item

Wertung die; **~, ~en** judgement; **wert·voll** *Adj.* valuable; *(moralisch)* estimable

Wesen das; **~s** nature; **wesentlich 1.** *Adj.* fundamental (für to); **im ~en** essentially; **2.** *adv. (erheblich)* considerably; much

wes·halb *Adv. s.* **warum**

Wespe die; **~, ~n** wasp

wessen *Interrogativpron.* **a)** *Gen. von* **wer** whose; **b)** *Gen. von* **was: ~ wird er beschuldigt?** what is he accused of?

Wessi der; **~s, ~s** *(salopp)* West German

West *o. Art.; o. Pl. (bes. Seemannsspr., Met.) s.* **Westen; west·deutsch** *Adj.* Western German; *(hist.: auf die alte BRD bezogen)* West German; **West·deutschland (das)** Western Germany; *(hist.: alte BRD)* West Germany

Weste die; **~, ~n** waistcoat *(Brit.);* vest *(Amer.)*

Westen der; **~s** west; **der ~:** the West; **Western der;** **~[s], ~:** western; **West·europa (das)** Western Europe; **Westfalen (das); ~s** Westphalia; **westfälisch** *Adj.* Westphalian; **West·indien (das)** the West Indies *pl.;* **westlich 1.** *Adj.* **a)** western; **b)** *(nach Westen)* westerly; **c)** *(aus*

dem Westen) Western; **2.** *adv.* westwards; **3.** *Präp. mit Gen.* [to the] west of; **wẹst·wärts** *Adv.* [to the] west; **Wẹst·wind** der west[erly] wind
wes·wẹgen *Adv. s.* **warum**
Wẹtt·bewerb der; ~|e|s, ~e a) competition; b) *o. Pl. (Wirtsch.)* competition *no indef. art.;* **Wẹtte** die; ~, ~n bet; **eine** ~ |mit jmdm.| abschließen make a bet [with sb.]; **mit jmdm. um die** ~ laufen race sb.; **wẹtt·eifern** *itr. V.* mit jmdm. |um etw.| ~: compete with sb. [for sth.]; **wẹtten** *itr. V.* bet; **mit jmdm.** ~: have a bet with sb.; mit jmdm. um etw. ~: bet sb. sth.
Wẹtter das; ~s weather
Wẹtter-: ~**aussichten** *Pl.* weather outlook *sing.;* ~**bericht** der weather report; *(Vorhersage)* weather forecast; ~**karte** die weather-chart; weathermap; ~**lage** die weather situation; ~**vorhersage** die weather forecast; ~**warte** die weather station
wẹtt-, Wẹtt-: ~**kampf** der competition; ~**lauf** der race; ~|**machen** *tr. V.* make up for (**durch** with); ~**rennen** das race; ~**rüsten** das; ~s arms race; ~**streit** der contest
wẹtzen *tr. V.* sharpen; whet
WEZ *Abk.* **Westeuropäische Zeit** GMT
Whiskey ['vɪski] der; ~s ~s whiskey; **Whisky** ['vɪski] der; ~s, ~s whisky
wịch *1. u. 3. Pers. Sg. Prät. v.* **weichen**
wịchtig *Adj.* important; **Wịchtigkeit** die; ~ importance
Wịcke die; ~, ~n vetch; *(im Garten)* sweet pea
Wịckel der; ~s, ~: compress; **wịckeln** *tr. V.* wind; *(ein~)* wrap (**in** + *Akk.* in); *(aus~)* unwrap (**aus** + *Dat.* from); *(ab~)* unwind (**von** from); **ein Kind** ~: change a baby's nappy
Wịdder der; ~s, ~: a) ram; b) *(Astrol.)* Aries
wider *Präp. mit Akk. (geh.)* against
wider-: ~**fahren** *unr. itr. V.; mit sein (geh.)* etw. ~**fährt** jmdm. sth. happens to sb.; ~**legen** *tr. V.* etw. ~**legen** refute sth.; jmdn. ~**legen** prove sb. wrong
wịderlich 1. *Adj.* revolting; repulsive *(person, behaviour, etc.);* awful *(headache etc.);* **2.** *adv.* revoltingly; *(behave)* in a repugnant *or* repulsive manner; awfully *(cold, sweet, etc.)*
wider-, Wider-: ~**rede** die: keine ~**rede!** don't argue!; ~**ruf** der retraction; |**bis**| **auf** ~**ruf** until revoked; ~**rufen** [--'--] *unr. tr., auch itr. V.* re-

tract *(statement, claim, confession, etc.);* ~**setzen** [--'--] *refl. V.* sich jmdm./einer Sache ~**setzen** oppose sb./sth.; ~**spenstig 1.** *Adj.* unruly; stubborn *(horse, mule, etc.);* **2.** *adv.* wilfully; ~|**spiegeln**, ~**spiegeln** [--'--] **1.** *tr. V.* mirror; *(fig.)* reflect; **2.** *refl. V.* be mirrored; *(fig.)* be reflected; ~**sprechen** [--'--] *unr. itr. V.* contradict; ~**spruch der** a) *o. Pl. (Widerrede, Protest)* opposition; protest; b) *(etw. Unvereinbares)* contradiction; ~**sprüchlich** *Adj.* contradictory *(news, statements, etc.);* inconsistent *(behaviour, attitude, etc.)*
Wider·stand der a) resistance (**gegen** to); b) *(Hindernis)* opposition
widerstands: ~**fähig** *Adj.* robust; resistant *(material etc.);* hardy *(animal, plant);* ~**los** *Adj., adv.* without resistance *postpos.*
wider-: ~**stehen** [--'--] *unr. itr. V.* a) *(nicht nachgeben)* |jmdm./einer Sache| ~**stehen** resist [sb./sth.]; b) *(standhalten)* jmdm./einer Sache ~**stehen** withstand sb./sth.; ~**streben** [--'--] *itr. V.* etw. ~**strebt** jmdm. sb. dislikes *or* detests sth.; ~**wärtig 1.** *Adj.* revolting, repugnant *(smell, taste, etc.);* offensive *(person, behaviour, etc.);* **2.** *adv.* *(behave etc.)* in an offensive manner; ~**wille** der aversion (**gegen** to); ~**willig** *adv.* reluctantly; unwillingly
wịdmen 1. *tr. V.* a) dedicate; b) *(verwenden für/auf)* devote; **2.** *refl. V.* sich jmdm./einer Sache ~: attend to sb./sth.; *(ausschließlich)* devote oneself to sb./sth.; **Wịdmung** die; ~, ~en dedication (**an** + *Akk.* to)
widrig *Adj.* unfavourable; adverse
wie 1. *Interrogativadv.* how; ~ |**bitte**|? [I beg your] pardon?; ~ **spät ist es?** what time is it?; **2.** *Relativadv.* ~ **er es tut** the way *or* manner in which he does it; **3.** *Konj.* a) *Vergleichspartikel* as; |**so**| ... ~ ...: as ... as ...; **ich fühlte mich** ~ ...: I felt as if I were ...; „N" ~ „**Nordpol**" N for November; b) *(zum Beispiel)* like; such as; c) *(und, sowie)* as well as; both
wieder *Adv.* again; **alles ist** ~ **beim alten** everything is back as it was before; **ich bin gleich** ~ **da** I'll be right back *(coll.)*
wieder-, Wieder-: ~|**bekommen** *unr. tr. V.* get back; ~|**beleben** *tr. V.* revive, resuscitate *(person);* ~**belebungs·versuch** der attempt at resuscitation; ~|**erkennen** *unr. tr. V.*

recognize; ~|**finden** *unr. tr. V.* find
again; ~**gabe die** *(Bericht)* report;
(Übersetzung) rendering; *(Reproduktion)* reproduction; ~|**geben** *unr. tr. V.*
a) *(zurückgeben)* give back; **b)** *(berichten)* report; *(wiederholen)* repeat
wieder·gut|machen *tr. V.* make
good; put right; **den Schaden** ~ *(bezahlen)* pay for the damage
wieder|haben *untr. tr. V. (auch fig.)*
have back
wieder-: ~**her|stellen** *tr. V.* **a)** re-
establish ⟨*contact, peace*⟩; **b)** *(reparieren)* restore ⟨*building*⟩; ~**holen 1.** *tr.
V.* repeat; *(repetieren)* revise ⟨*lesson,
vocabulary, etc.*⟩; **2.** *refl. V.* **a)** *(wieder
dasselbe sagen)* repeat oneself; **b)** *(erneut geschehen)* happen again; **c)** *(wiederkehren)* be repeated; recur
wieder|holen *tr. V.* fetch *or* get back
wiederholt 1. *Adj.* repeated; **2.** *adv.*
repeatedly; **Wiederholung die;** ~,
~**en** repetition; *(eines Fußballspiels
usw.)* replay; *(einer Sendung)* repeat;
(einer Aufführung) repeat performance; *(von Lernstoff)* revision
Wieder·hören das:|auf| ~! goodbye!
(at end of telephone call)
wieder-, Wieder-: ~**kehr die;** ~
(geh.) return; ~|**kehren** *itr. V.; mit
sein (geh.)* return; ~|**kommen** *unr.
itr. V.; mit sein* **a)** *(zurückkommen)* return; come back; **b)** *(noch einmal kommen)* come back *or* again; **c)** *(sich
noch einmal ereignen)* ⟨*opportunity,
past*⟩ come again; ~|**kriegen** *tr. V.
(ugs.)* get back; ~**schauen das:|auf|**
~**schauen!** *(südd., österr.)* goodbye!;
~|**sehen** *unr. tr. V.* see again; ~**se-
hen das;** ~**s,** ~: reunion; **|auf|** ~**se-
hen!** goodbye!; ~**um** *Adv.* **a)** *(erneut)*
again; **b)** *(andererseits)* on the other
hand; ~**wahl die** re-election;
~|**wählen** *tr. V.* re-elect
Wiege die; ~, ~**n** *(auch fig.)* cradle
¹**wiegen** *unr. itr., tr. V.* ⟨*weigh*⟩
²**wiegen** *tr. V.* rock; shake ⟨*head*⟩
Wiegen·lied das lullaby; cradle-song
wiehern *itr. V.* whinny; *(lauter)* neigh
Wien (das); ~**s** Vienna; ¹**Wiener der;**
~**s,** ~: Viennese; ²**Wiener** *Adj.* Viennese; *s. auch* Würstchen; **Wienerin
die;** ~, ~**nen** Viennese; **wienerisch**
Adj. Viennese
wies *1. u. 3. Pers. Sg. Prät. v.* weisen
Wiese die; ~, ~**n** meadow; *(Rasen)*
lawn
wie·so *Interrogativadv.* why
wie·viel [*od.* '--] *Interrogativpron.*

(+ *Sg.*) how much; (+ *Pl.*) how
many; ~ **Uhr ist es?** what time is it?
wie·viel·mal [*od.* -'--] *Interrogativadv.* how many times
wievielt... [*od.* '--] *Interrogativadj.*
der ~e Band? which number volume?;
der Wievielte ist heute? what is the
date today?
wie·weit *Interrogativadv.* to what extent; how far
wild 1. *Adj. (auch fig.)* wild; *(wütend)*
furious ⟨*cursing, shouting, etc.*⟩; ~**es
Parken** illegal parking; ~**er Streik**
wildcat strike; ~ **auf etw./jmdn.** sein
(ugs.) be mad *or* crazy about sth./sb.
(coll.); ~ **werden** get furious; **jmdn.**
machen infuriate sb.; **2.** *adv.* **a)**
wildly; **wie** ~ *(ugs.)* like mad *(coll.);* **b)**
(ordnungswidrig) illegally; **Wild das;**
~**|e|s a)** *(Tiere, Fleisch)* game; **b)** *(ein-
zelnes Tier)* [wild] animal; **Wild·bret**
[~brɛt] **das;**~**s** *(geh.)* game; **Wilde
der/die;** *adj. Dekl.* savage; **Wilderer
der;** ~**s,** ~: poacher; **wild·fremd**
Adj. completely strange; ~**e Leute**
complete strangers; **Wildheit die;** ~:
wildness; **Wild·leder das** suede;
Wildnis die; ~, ~**se** wilderness
Wild-: ~**schwein das** wild boar;
~**wechsel der** *o. Pl.* game crossing;
~**west·film der** western
will [vɪl] *1. u. 3. Pers. Sg. Präsens v.*
wollen
Wille der; ~**ns** will; *(Wunsch)* wish
willen *Präp. mit Gen.* **um jmds./einer
Sache** ~: for sb.'s/sth.'s sake; **Willen
der;** ~**s** *s.* Wille; **willen·los 1.** *Adj.*
will-less; **2.** *adv.* will-lessly; **willens**
Adj. ~ **sein, etw. zu tun** *(geh.)* be willing to do sth.; **willens·stark** *Adj.*
strong-willed; **willentlich 1.** *Adj.*
deliberate; **2.** *adv.* deliberately; on
purpose; **willig 1.** *Adj.* willing; **2.**
adv. willingly
will·kommen *Adj.* welcome; **jmdn.**
~ **heißen** welcome sb.
Will·kür die; ~: arbitrary use of
power; *(Handlung o. ä.)* arbitrariness;
willkürlich 1. *Adj.* arbitrary; *(vom
Willen gesteuert)* voluntary ⟨*muscle,
movement, etc.*⟩; **2.** *adv.* arbitrarily;
(vom Willen gesteuert) voluntarily
wimmeln *itr. V.* **von Fehlern** ~: be
teeming with mistakes
wimmern *itr. V.* whimper
Wimpel der; ~**s,** ~: pennant
Wimper die; ~, ~**n** [eye]lash
Wind der; ~**|e|s,** ~**e** wind; **Wind-
beutel der** cream puff

Winde die; ~, ~n winch
Windel die; ~, ~n nappy *(Brit.);* diaper *(Amer.);* **Windel·höschen** das nappy pants *pl.*
winden 1. *unr. tr. V. (geh.)* make ‹*wreath, garland*›; etw. um etw. ~: wind sth. around sth.; 2. *unr. refl. V.* ‹*plant, tendrils*› wind (**um** around); ‹*snake*› coil [itself], wind itself (**um** around); **sich vor Schmerzen~**: writhe in pain
Windes·eile die: **in ~**: in next to no time; **Wind·hund** der greyhound; **windig** *Adj.* windy
Wind-: **~mühle** die windmill; **~pocken** *Pl.* chicken-pox *sing.;* **~schutz·scheibe** die windscreen *(Brit.);* windshield *(Amer.);* **~stärke** die: ~stärke 7/9 *usw.* wind force 7/9 *etc.;* **~still** *Adj.* windless; still; **~stoß** der gust of wind; **~surfing** das windsurfing *no art.*
Windung die; ~, ~en a) bend; b) *(spiralförmiger Verlauf)* spiral; *(einer Spule o. ä.)* winding
Wink der; ~[e]s, ~e sign; *(Hinweis)* hint; *(Ratschlag)* tip; hint
Winkel der; ~s, ~ a) *(Math.)* angle; **toter ~**: blind spot; b) *(Ecke; auch fig.)* corner; **winkelig** *Adj.* twisty ‹*streets*›
winken 1. *itr. V.* a) wave; **mit etw. ~**: wave sth.; b) *(auffordern heranzukommen)* jmdm. ~: beckon sb. over; **einem Taxi ~**: hail a taxi; 2. *tr. V.* beckon; **jmdn. zu sich ~**: beckon sb. over [to one]
winklig *Adj. s.* winkelig
winseln *itr. V.* ‹*dog*› whimper
Winter der; ~s, ~: winter; **Winteranfang** der beginning of winter; **winterlich** 1. *Adj.* wintry; winter *attrib.* ‹*clothing, break*›; 2. *adv.* ~ **kalt** cold and wintry
Winter-: **~reifen** der winter tyre; **~schlußverkauf** der winter sale[s *pl.*]; **~sport** der winter sports *pl.;* **~zeit** die; *o. Pl.* winter-time
Winzer der; ~s, ~winegrower
winzig 1. *Adj.* tiny; 2. *adv.* ~ **klein** tiny; minute
Wipfel der; ~s, ~: tree-top
Wippe die; ~, ~n see-saw; **wippen** *itr. V.* bob up and down; *(hin und her)* bob about; *(auf einer Wippe)* see-saw
wir Personalpron.; 1. Pers. Pl. Nom. we; *s. auch (Gen.)* unser; *(Dat.)* uns; *(Akk.)* uns
wirb *Imperativ Sg. v.* werben

Wirbel der; ~s, ~ a) *(kreisende Bewegung) (im Wasser)* whirlpool; *(in der Luft)* whirlwind; *(kleiner)* eddy; *(von Rauch, beim Tanz)* whirl; b) *(Trubel)* hurly-burly; c) *(Aufsehen)* fuss; d) *(Anat.)* vertebra; **wirbeln** 1. *itr. V.* **mit sein** whirl; ‹*water, snowflakes*› swirl; 2. *tr. V.* swirl ‹*leaves, dust*›; whirl ‹*dancer*›
Wirbel-: **~säule** die spinal column; **~sturm** der cyclone
wirbt 3. *Pers. Sg. Präsens v.* werben
wird 3. *Pers. Sg. Präsens v.* werden
wirf *Imperativ Sg. v.* werfen; **wirft** 3. *Pers. Sg. Präsens v.* werfen
wirken *itr. V.* a) *(eine Wirkung haben)* have an effect; **gegen etw. ~**: be effective against sth.; b) *(erscheinen)* seem; appear
wirklich 1. *Adj.* real; 2. *Adv.* really; **Wirklichkeit** die; ~, ~en reality
wirksam 1. *Adj.* effective; 2. *adv.* effectively; **Wirksamkeit** die; ~: effectiveness; **Wirk·stoff** der active agent; **Wirkung** die; ~, ~en effect (**auf** + *Akk.* on); **mit ~ vom 1. Juli** *(Amtsspr.)* with effect from 1 July
wirkungs-: **~los** 1. *Adj.* ineffective; 2. *adv.* ineffectively; **~voll** 1. *Adj.* effective; 2. *adv.* effectively
wirr *Adj. (unordentlich)* tousled ‹*hair, beard*›; tangled ‹*ropes, roots*›; *(unklar, verwirrt)* confused; **Wirren** *Pl.* turmoil *sing.;* **Wirrwarr** der; ~s chaos; *(von Stimmen)* clamour
Wirsing der; ~s, **Wirsingkohl** der savoy [cabbage]
Wirt der; ~[e]s, ~e landlord; **Wirtin** die; ~, ~nen landlady
Wirtschaft die; ~, ~en a) economy; *(Geschäftsleben)* commerce and industry; b) *(Gast~)* public house; pub *(Brit. coll.);* bar *(Amer.);* c) *(Haushalt)* household; d) *o. Pl. (ugs. abwertend: Unordnung)* mess; shambles *sing.;* **wirtschaften** *itr. V.* **mit dem Geld gut ~**: manage one's money well; **mit Verlust/Gewinn ~**: run at a loss/profit; **wirtschaftlich** 1. *Adj.* a) economic; b) *(finanziell)* financial; c) *(sparsam, rentabel)* economical; 2. *adv.; s. Adj.:* economically; financially; **Wirtschaftlichkeit** die; ~: economic viability
Wirtschafts-: **~hilfe** die economic aid *no indef. art.;* **~krise** die economic crisis; **~minister** der minister for economic affairs; **~politik** die economic policy

Wirts: ~**haus das** pub *(Brit. coll.);*
~**leute** *Pl.* landlord and landlady
Wisch der; ~|e|s, ~e *(salopp)* piece *or*
bit of paper; **wischen** *itr., tr. V.*
wipe; **Staub** ~: do the dusting; dust
wispern *itr., tr. V.* whisper
wiß-, Wiß-: ~**begier,** ~**begierde
die;** *o. Pl.* thirst for knowledge; ~**begierig** *Adj.* eager for knowledge;
⟨*child*⟩ eager to learn
wissen 1. *unr. tr. V.* know; **von jmdm./
etw. nichts |mehr|** ~ **wollen** want to
have nothing [more] to do with sb./
sth.; **2.** *unr. itr. V.* **von etw./um etw.** ~:
know about sth.; **Wissen das;** ~s
knowledge; **meines/unseres** ~**s** to my/
our knowledge; **Wissenschaft die;**
~, ~**en** science; **Wissenschaftler
der;** ~s ~, **Wissenschaftlerin die;**
~, ~**nen** academic; *(Natur~)* scientist; **wissenschaftlich 1.** *Adj.* scholarly; *(natur~)* scientific; **2.** *adv.* in a
scholarly manner; *(natur~)* scientifically; **wissens·wert** *Adj.* ~ **sein** be
worth knowing; **wissentlich 1.** *Adj.*
deliberate; **2.** *adv.* knowingly; deliberately
wittern 1. *itr. V.* sniff the air; **2.** *tr. V.*
get wind of; *(fig.: ahnen)* sense; **Wit-
terung die;** ~, ~**en a)** *(Wetter)*
weather *no indef. art;* **b)** *(Jägerspr.)
(Geruchssinn)* sense of smell; *(Geruch)*
scent
Witwe die; ~, ~**n** widow; ~ **werden** be
widowed; **Witwer der;** ~s, ~: widower
Witz der; ~**es,** ~**e** joke
Witz-: ~**blatt das** humorous magazine; ~**bold der;** ~**es,** ~**e** joker
witzig 1. *Adj.* funny; **2.** *adv.* amus-
ingly; **witz·los** *Adj.* **a)** dull; **b)** *(ugs.:
sinnlos)* pointless
wo 1. *Adv.* where; **2.** *Konj.* **a)** *(da, weil)*
seeing that; **b)** *(obwohl)* although;
when; **wo·anders** *Adv.* somewhere
else; **wo·bei** *Adv.* **a)** *(interrogativ)* ~
hast du sie ertappt? what did you
catch her doing?; **b)** *(relativisch)* **er
gab sechs Schüsse ab,** ~ **einer der Täter
getötet wurde** he fired six shots - one
of the criminals was killed
Woche die; ~, ~**n** week; **in dieser/der
nächsten/der letzten** ~: this/next/last
week; **heute in/vor einer** ~: a week
today/a week ago today
wochen-, Wochen-: ~**bett das; im**
~**bett liegen** be lying in; ~**ende das**
weekend; ~**lang 1.** *Adj.* lasting weeks
postpos; **2.** *adv.* for weeks [on end];

~**tag der** weekday *(including Saturday);* ~**tags** *Adv.* on weekdays [and
Saturdays]
wöchentlich *Adj., adv.* weekly; **Wo-
chen·zeitung die** weekly newspaper; -**wöchig a)** *(... Wochen alt)*
... -week-old; **b)** *(... Wochen dauernd)*
... week's/weeks'; ...-week; **Wöchne-
rin die;** ~, ~**nen** woman who has just
given birth
Wodka der; ~s, ~s vodka
wo·durch *Adv.* **a)** *(interrogativ)* how;
b) *(relativisch)* as a result of which;
wo·für *Adv.* **a)** *(interrogativ)* for
what; **b)** *(relativisch)* for which
wog *1. u. 3. Pers. Sg. Prät. v.* **wiegen**
Woge die; ~, ~**n** wave
wo·gegen 1. *Adv.* **a)** *(interrogativ)*
against what; what ... against; **b)** *(relativisch)* against which; which ...
against; **2.** *Konj.* whereas
wogen *itr. V. (geh.)* ⟨*sea*⟩ surge; *(fig.)*
⟨*corn*⟩ wave
wo·her *Adv.* **a)** *(interrogativ)* where ...
from; ~ **weißt du das?** how do you
know that?; **b)** *(relativisch)* where ...
from; **wo·hin** *Adv.* **a)** *(interrogativ)*
where [... to]; **b)** *(relativisch)* where;
wo·hingegen *Konj.* whereas
wohl 1. *Adv.* **a)** well; **jmdm. ist nicht** ~,
jmd. fühlt sich nicht ~: sb. does not
feel well; **b)** *(behaglich)* at ease;
happy; **leb** ~!/**leben Sie** ~! farewell!;
c) *(durchaus)* well; **d)** *(ungefähr)*
about; **2.** *Partikel* probably; ~ **kaum**
hardly; **Wohl das;** ~|e|s welfare; **auf
jmds.** ~ **trinken** drink sb.'s health; **zum**
~! cheers!
wohl-, Wohl-: ~**auf** [-'-] *Adj.(geh.)*
~**auf sein** be well; ~**befinden das**
well-being; ~**behagen das** sense of
well-being; ~**behalten** *Adj.* safe and
well ⟨*person*⟩; undamaged ⟨*thing*⟩;
~**fahrts·staat der** welfare state;
~**gefallen das** pleasure; ~**gemerkt**
Adv. please note; ~**habend** *Adj.*
prosperous
wohlig 1. *Adj.*pleasant; agreeable; **2.**
adv. ⟨*sigh, purr, etc.*⟩ with pleasure
wohl, Wohl-: ~**klang der** *(geh.)* melodious sound; ~**schmeckend** *Adj.*
(geh.) delicious; ~**stand der;** *o. Pl.*
prosperity; ~**stands·gesellschaft
die** *o. Pl.* affluent society; ~**tat die a)**
(gute Tat) good deed; *(Gefallen)* favour; **b)** *o. Pl. (Genuß)* blissful relief;
~**tätig** *Adj.* charitable; ~**tuend** *Adj.*
agreeable; ~|**tun** *unr. itr. V.* **etw. tut
jmdm.** ~: sth. does sb. good; ~**ver-**

dient *Adj.* well-earned; **~weislich** *Adv.* deliberately; **~wollen das; ~s** goodwill; **~wollend 1.** *Adj.* benevolent; favourable ⟨*judgement, opinion*⟩; **2.** *adv.* benevolently; ⟨*judge, consider*⟩ favourably

Wohn·anhänger der caravan; trailer *(Amer.);* **wohnen** *itr. V.* live; *(kurzfristig)* stay

wohn-, Wohn-: **~gemeinschaft die** group sharing a flat *(Brit.) or (Amer.)* apartment/house; **~haft** *Adj.* resident **(in + *Dat.* in);** **~heim** das *(für Alte, Behinderte)* home; *(für Obdachlose, Lehrlinge)* hostel; *(für Studenten)* hall of residence

wohnlich *Adj.* homely

Wohn-: **~mobil das; ~s, ~e** motor home; **~ort der;** *Pl.* **~e** place of residence; **~sitz der** place of residence; **ohne festen ~sitz** of no fixed abode

Wohnung die; ~, ~en a) flat *(Brit.);* apartment *(Amer.);* **b)** *o. Pl. (Unterkunft)* lodging

Wohn-: **~verhältnisse** *Pl.* living conditions; **~wagen der** caravan; trailer *(Amer.);* **~zimmer das** living-room

wölben 1. *tr. V.* curve; vault, arch ⟨*roof, ceiling*⟩; **2.** *refl. V.* curve; ⟨*bridge, ceiling*⟩ arch; **Wölbung die; ~, ~en** curve; *(einer Decke)* arch; vault

Wolf der; ~[e]s, Wölfe wolf

Wolke die; ~, ~n cloud

wolken-, Wolken-: ~bruch der; *Pl.* **~brüche** cloudburst; **~bruch·artig** *Adj.* torrential; **~kratzer der** skyscraper; **~los** *Adj.* cloudless

wolkig *Adj.* cloudy

Wolle die; ~, ~n wool; **¹wollen** *Adj.* woollen

²wollen 1. *unr. Modalverb;* **2.** *Part.* **~ etw. tun ~** *(den Wunsch haben, etw. zu tun)* want to do sth.; *(die Absicht haben, etw. zu tun)* be going to do sth.; **die Wunde will nicht heilen** the wound [just] won't heal; **2.** *unr. itr. V.* **du mußt nur ~, dann ...** you only have to want to enough, then ... **ganz wie du willst** just as you like; *(ugs.)* **ich will nach Hause** I want to go home; **zu wem ~ Sie?** whom do you want to see?; **3.** *unr. tr. V.* want; **das habe ich nicht gewollt** I never meant that to happen

wo·mit *Adv.* **a)** *(interrogativ)* **~ schreibst du?** what do you write with?; **b)** *(relativisch)* **~ du schreibst**

which *or* that you write with; *(more formal)* with which you write; **womöglich** *Adv.* possibly; **wo·nach** *Adv.* **a)** *(interrogativ)* after what; **what ... after; ~ suchst du?** what are you looking for?; **b)** *(relativisch)* after which; which ... after

Wonne die; ~, ~n *(geh.)* bliss *no pl.;* ecstasy; *(etw., was Freude macht)* joy; **wonnig** *Adj.* sweet

woran *Adv.* **a)** *(interrogativ)* **~ denkst du?** what are you thinking of?; **b)** *(relativisch)* **nichts, ~ man sich anlehnen könnte** nothing one could lean against; **worauf a)** *(interrogativ)* **~ wartest du?** what are you waiting for?; **b)** *(relativisch)* **etwas, ~ man sich verlassen kann** something one can rely on; **c)** *(relativisch: woraufhin)* whereupon

woraus *Adv.* **a)** *(interrogativ)* **~ schließt du das?** what do you infer that from?; **b)** *(relativisch)* **es gab nichts, ~ wir den Wein hätten trinken können** there was nothing for us to drink the wine out of

worden *2. Part. v.* werden 2

worin *Adv.* **a)** *(interrogativ)* in what; what ... in; **b)** *(relativisch)* in which; which ... in

Wort das; ~[e]s, Wörter/~e a) *Pl.* **Wörter,** *(auch:)* **~e** word; **~ für ~:** word for word; **DM 1000 (in ~en: tausend)** DM 1,000 (in words: one thousand); **b)** *Pl.* **~e** *(Äußerung)* word; **mir fehlen die ~e** I'm lost for words; **Dr. Meyer hat das ~:** it's Dr Meyer's turn to speak; **c)** *Pl.* **~e** *(Spruch)* saying; *(Zitat)* quotation; **d)** *Pl.* **~e** *(geh.: Text)* words *pl.;* **in ~ und Bild** in words and pictures; **e)** *Pl.* **~e** *(Versprechen)* word; **[sein] ~ halten** keep one's word; **wort·brüchig** *Adj.* **~ werden** break one's word; **Wörter·buch das** dictionary

wort-, Wort-: ~getreu *Adj.* word-for-word; **~karg 1.** *Adj.* taciturn ⟨*person*⟩; **2.** *adv.* taciturnly; **~laut der** wording; **im [vollen] ~laut** verbatim

wörtlich 1. *Adj.* **a)** word-for-word; **b)** *(der eigentlichen Bedeutung entsprechend)* literal; **2.** *adv.: s. Adj.:* word for word; literally

wort-, Wort-: ~los 1. *Adj.* silent; wordless; **2.** *adv.* without saying a word; **~spiel das** play on words; pun; **~wechsel der** exchange of words; **~wörtlich** *Adj.* word-for-word

worüber *Adv.* **a)** *(interrogativ)* over what ...; what ... over; **b)** *(relativisch)* over which; which ... over; **worum** *Adv.* **a)** *(interrogativ)* around what; what ... around; **b)** *(relativisch)* around which; which ... around; **worunter** *Adv.* **a)** *(interrogativ)* under what; what ... under; **b)** *(relativisch)* under which; which ... under; **wo·von** *Adv.* **a)** *(interrogativ)* from where; where ... from; **b)** *(relativisch)* from which; which ... from; **wo·vor** *Adv.* **a)** *(interrogativ)* in front of what; what ... in front of; **b)** *(relativisch)* in front of which; which ... in front of; **wo·zu** *Adv.* **a)** *(interrogativ)* to what; what ... to; *(wofür)* what ... for; **b)** *(relativisch)* ~ **du dich auch entschließt** whatever you decide on

Wrack das; ~|e|s, ~s *od.* ~e wreck
wrang *1. und 3. Pers. Sg. Prät. v.* **wringen; wringen** *unr. tr. V. (bes. nordd.)* wring
Wucher der; ~s profiteering; *(beim Verleihen von Geld)* usury; **wuchern** *itr. V.* **a)** *auch mit sein* ⟨*plants, weeds, etc.*⟩ proliferate, run wild; **b)** *(Wucher treiben)* |mit etw.| ~: profiteer [on sth.]; *(beim Verleihen von Geld)* lend [sth.] at extortionate interest rates; **Wucherung** die; ~, ~en growth
wuchs *1. und 3. Pers. Sg. Prät. v.* **wachsen; Wuchs** der; ~es *(Gestalt)* stature
Wucht die; ~ force; *(von Schlägen)* power; weight; **wuchtig 1.** *Adj.* **a)** *(voller Wucht)* powerful; mighty; **b)** *(schwer, massig)* massive; **2.** *adv.* powerfully
wühlen 1. *itr. V.* **a)** dig; *(mit der Schnauze, dem Schnabel)* root (**nach** for); ⟨*mole*⟩ tunnel, burrow; **b)** *(ugs.: suchen)* rummage [around] (**nach** for); **2.** *tr. V.* burrow; tunnel out ⟨*burrow*⟩
wulstig *Adj.* bulging
wund *Adj.* sore; **Wunde** die; ~, ~n wound
wunder *Adv. (ugs.)* **er denkt, er sei ~ wer** he thinks he's really something; **Wunder** das; ~s, ~ **a)** miracle; ~ **wirken** *(fig. ugs.)* work wonders; **ein/kein** ~ **sein** *(ugs.)* be a/no wonder; **b)** *(etw. Erstaunliches)* wonder; **wunderbar 1.** *Adj.* **a)** miraculous; **b)** *(sehr schön, herrlich)* wonderful; marvellous; **2.** *adv.* *(sehr schön, herrlich)* wonderfully; marvellously; **b)** *(ugs.: sehr)* wonderfully
Wunder-: ~**kerze** die sparkler; ~**kind** das child prodigy

wunderlich 1. *Adj.* strange; odd; **2.** *adv.* strangely; oddly; **wundern 1.** *tr. V.* surprise; **mich wundert** *od.* **es wundert mich, daß** ...: I'm surprised that ...; **2.** *refl. V.* **sich über jmdn./etw.** ~: be surprised at sb./sth.
wunder-: ~**schön 1.** *Adj.* simply beautiful; *(herrlich)* simply wonderful; **2.** *adv.* quite beautifully; ~**voll 1.** *Adj.* wonderful; **2.** *adv.* wonderfully
wund|liegen *unr. refl. V.* get bedsores (**an** + *Dat.* on); **Wund·starrkrampf** der *(Med.)* tetanus
Wunsch der; ~|e|s, Wünsche wish (**nach** to have); *(Sehnen)* desire (**nach** for); **haben Sie** |sonst| **noch einen** ~? will there be anything else?; **auf jmds.** ~: at sb.'s wish; **mit den besten/herzlichsten Wünschen** with best/warmest wishes; **wünschen** *tr. V.* **a)** **sich** *(Dat.)* **etw.** ~: want sth.; *(im stillen)* wish for sth.; **b)** *(in formelhaften Wünschen)* wish; **jmdm. alles Gute/frohe Ostern** ~: wish sb. all the best/a happy Easter; **c)** *auch itr. V. (begehren)* want; **was** ~ **Sie?, Sie** ~? *(im Lokal)* what would you like?; *(in einem Geschäft)* can I help you?
Wunsch-: ~**kind** das wanted child; ~**konzert** das request concert; *(im Rundfunk)* request programme; ~**zettel** der *(zum Geburtstag o. ä.)* list of presents one would like
wurde *1. u. 3. Pers. Sg. Prät. v.* **werden; würde** *1. u. 3. Pers. Sg. Konjunktiv II v.* **werden**
Würde die; ~ dignity; **würde·los 1.** *Adj.* undignified; *(schimpflich)* disgraceful; **2.** *adv.* in an undignified way; *(schimpflich)* disgracefully; **Würdenträger** der dignitary; **würde·voll 1.** *Adj.* dignified; **2.** *adv.* with dignity; **würdig 1.** *Adj.* **a)** dignified; **b)** *(wert)* worthy; **2.** *adv.* **a)** with dignity; **b)** *(angemessen)* worthily; **würdigen** *tr. V.* **a)** *(anerkennen, beachten)* recognize; *(schätzen)* appreciate; *(lobend hervorheben)* acknowledge; **b)** *(für wert halten)* **jmdn. keines Blickes/keiner Antwort** ~: not deign to look at/answer sb.
Wurf der; ~|e|s, Würfe **a)** throw; *(beim Kegeln)* bowl; **b)** *o. Pl. (das Werfen)* throwing/pitching/bowling; **c)** *(Zool.)* litter
Würfel der; ~s, ~ cube; *(Spiel~)* dice; die *(formal)*; **Würfel·becher** der dice-cup; **würfeln 1.** *itr. V.* throw the dice; **um etw.** ~: play dice for sth.; **2.**

tr. V. **a)** throw; **b)** *(in Würfel schnei-*
den) dice
Würfel-: ~**spiel** das dice; *(Brettspiel)*
dice game; ~**zucker** der; *o. Pl.* cube
sugar
würgen 1. *tr. V.* strangle; throttle; **2.**
itr. V. (Brechreiz haben) retch
Wurm der; ~|e|s, **Würmer** worm; *(Ma-*
de) maggot; **wurmig** *Adj.,* **wurm-**
stichig *Adj.* worm-eaten; *(madig)*
maggoty
Wurst die; ~, **Würste** sausage; **es geht**
um die ~ *(fig. ugs.)* the crunch has
come; **jmdm. ist jmd./etw. ~** *(ugs.)* sb.
doesn't care about sb./sth.; **Würst-**
chen das; ~**s,** ~ **a)** [small] sausage;
Frankfurter/Wiener ~: frankfurter/
wienerwurst; **b)** *(fig. ugs.)* nobody;
(hilfloser Mensch) poor soul; **Würst-**
chen·bude die sausage-stand
Würze die; ~, ~**n** spice; seasoning
Wurzel die; ~, ~**n** *(auch fig.)* root;
wurzeln *itr. V.* take root
würzen *tr. V.* season; **würzig** *Adj.*
tasty; full-flavoured ⟨*beer, wine*⟩; aromatic ⟨*fragrance*⟩; tangy ⟨*air*⟩
wusch *1. u. 3. Pers. Sg. Prät. v.* **wa-**
schen
wußte *1. und 3. Pers. Sg. Prät. v.* **wis-**
sen; wüßte *1. und 3. Pers. Sg. Kon-*
junktiv II v. **wissen**
wüst 1. *Adj.* **a)** *(öde)* desolate; **b)** *(un-*
ordentlich) chaotic; **c)** *(ungezügelt)*
wild; *(unanständig)* rude; **2.** *adv.* **a)**
(unordentlich) chaotically; **b)** *(ungezü-*
gelt) wildly
Wüste die; ~, ~**n** desert
Wut die; ~: rage; fury; **wüten** *itr. V.*
(auch fig.) rage; *(zerstören)* wreak
havoc; **wütend 1.** *Adj.* furious;
angry ⟨*voice, mob*⟩; **2.** *adv.* furiously;
in a fury

X

¹**x, X** [ıks] das; ~, ~: x, X
²**x** *unbest. Zahlwort (ugs.)* umpteen
(coll.)
x-Achse die *(Math.)* x-axis
X-Beine *Pl.* knock-knees

x-beliebig *Adj. (ugs.)* **irgendein** ~**er/**
irgendeine ~**e/irgendein** ~**es** any old
(coll. attrib.); **jeder** ~**e Ort** any old
place *(coll.)*
x-fach 1. *Vervielfältigungsz.* **die** ~**e**
Menge *(Math.)* x times the amount;
(ugs.) umpteen times the amount
(coll.); **2.** *adv. (ugs.)* ~ **erprobt sein**
⟨*tested etc.*⟩ umpteen times *(coll.);*
x-mal *Adv. (ugs.)* umpteen times
(coll.)
x-t... *Ordinalz. (ugs.)* umpteenth *(coll.)*

Y

y, Y [ˈʏpsilɔn] das; ~, ~: y, Y
y-Achse die *(Math.)* y-axis
Yacht *s.* **Jacht**
Yoga *s.* **Joga**
Ypsilon das; ~|s|, ~s y, Y; *(im griechi-*
schen Alphabet) upsilon

Z

z, Z [tsɛt] das; ~, ~: z, Z
Zacke die; ~, ~**n** point; peak; *(einer*
Säge, eines Kamms) tooth; *(einer Ga-*
bel, Harke) prong; **Zacken** der; ~**s,**
~ *s.* **Zacke**
zaghaft 1. *Adj.* timid; *(zögernd)*
hesitant; **2.** *adv.* timidly; *(zögernd)*
hesitantly; **Zaghaftigkeit die;** ~:
timidity; *(Zögern)* hesitancy
zäh 1. *Adj.* **a)** tough; heavy ⟨*dough,*
soil⟩; *(dickflüssig)* glutinous; viscous
⟨*oil*⟩; **b)** *(widerstandsfähig)* tough ⟨*per-*
son⟩; **c)** *(beharrlich)* tenacious; tough
⟨*negotiations*⟩; dogged ⟨*resistance*⟩; **2.**
adv. (beharrlich) tenaciously; ⟨*resist*⟩
doggedly; **Zähigkeit die;** ~ **a)** *(Wi-*
derstandsfähigkeit) toughness; **b)** *(Be-*

harrlichkeit) tenacity; **mit** ~: ten-aciously

Zahl die; ~, ~en number; *(Ziffer)* numeral; *(Zahlenangabe, Geldmenge)* figure; **in den roten/schwarzen** ~en in the red/black; **zahlbar** *Adj. (Kaufmannsspr.)* payable; **zahlen** 1. *tr. V.* pay (**an** + *Akk.* to); 2. *itr. V.* pay; ~ **bitte!** *(im Lokal)* [can I/we have] the bill, please!; **zählen** 1. *itr. V.* **a)** count; **zu einer Gruppe** *usw.* ~ : be one of *or* belong to a group *etc.;* **b) auf jmdn./etw.** ~ : count on sb./sth.; 2. *tr. V.* count; **jmdn. zu seinen Freunden** ~: count sb. among one's friends

zahl-, Zahl-: ~**karte** die *(Postw.)* paying-in slip; ~**los** *Adj.* countless; ~**reich** *Adj.* numerous

Zahlung die; ~, ~en payment; **Zählung** die; ~, ~en counting; **eine** ~: a count; **Zahlungs·mittel** das means of payment; **Zahl·wort** das; *Pl.* ~**wörter** *(Sprachw.)* numeral

zahm 1. *Adj.* tame; 2. *adv.* tamely; **zähmen** *tr. V. (auch fig.)* tame

Zahn der; ~[e]s, **Zähne** tooth; *(Raubtier~)* fang; *(an einer Briefmarke usw.)* serration

Zahn-: ~**arzt** der dentist; *(mit chirurgischer Ausbildung)* dental surgeon; ~**bürste** die toothbrush

zahnen *itr. V.* 〈*baby*〉 be teething

zahn-, Zahn-: ~**fleisch** das gum; *(als Ganzes)* gums *pl.;* ~**los** *Adj.* toothless; ~**lücke** die gap in one's teeth; ~**pasta** die; ~, ~**pasten** toothpaste; ~**prothese** die dentures *pl.;* [set *sing.* of] false teeth *pl.;* ~**schmerzen** *Pl.* toothache *sing.;* ~**stocher** der; ~s, ~: toothpick; ~**weh** das; *o. Pl. (ugs.)* toothache

Zange die; ~, ~n **a)** *(Werkzeug)* pliers *pl.; (Eiswürfel~, Zucker~)* tongs *pl.; (Geburts~)* forceps *pl.; (Kneif~)* pincers *pl.;* **eine** ~: a pair of pliers/tongs/forceps/pincers; **b)** *(bei Tieren)* pincer

Zank der; ~[e]s squabble; row; **zanken** *refl. (auch itr.) V.* squabble, bicker (**um** *od.* **über** + *Akk.* over); **zänkisch** *Adj.* quarrelsome

Zäpfchen das; ~s, ~ suppository; **zapfen** *tr. V.* tap, draw 〈*beer, wine*〉; **Zapfen** der; ~s, ~ **a)** *(Bot.)* cone; **b)** *(Stöpsel)* bung; **Zapf·säule** die petrol-pump *(Brit.);* gasoline pump *(Amer.)*

zappeln *itr. V.* wriggle; 〈*child*〉 fidget

Zar der; ~en, ~en *(hist.)* Tsar; **Zarin** die; ~, ~nen *(hist.)* Tsarina

zart 1. *Adj. (auch fig.)* delicate; soft 〈*skin*〉; tender 〈*bud, shoot; meat, vegetables*〉; fine 〈*biscuits*〉; gentle 〈*kiss, touch*〉; soft 〈*pastel colours*〉; 2. *adv. (empfindlich)* delicately; 〈*kiss, touch*〉 gently; **zärtlich** 1. *Adj.* tender; 2. *adv.* tenderly; **Zärtlichkeit** die; ~, ~en **a)** *o. Pl. (Zuneigung)* tenderness; affection; **b)** *meist Pl. (Liebkosung)* caress

Zauber der; ~s, ~ **a)** *(auch fig.)* magic; *(Bann)* [magic] spell; **b)** *o. Pl. (ugs. abwertend: Aufheben)* fuss; **Zauberei** die; ~, ~en **a)** *o. Pl. (das Zaubern)* magic; **b)** *(Zaubertrick)* magic trick; **Zauberer** der; ~s, ~: magician; **zauber·haft** 1. *Adj.* enchanting; 2. *adv.* enchantingly; **Zauberin** die; ~, ~nen **a)** sorceress; **b)** *(Zauberkünstlerin)* conjurer; **Zauber·künstler** der conjurer; magician; **zaubern** 1. *itr. V.* **a)** do magic; **b)** *(Zaubertricks ausführen)* do conjuring tricks; 2. *tr. V. (auch fig.)* conjure

zaudern *itr. V. (geh.)* delay

Zaum der; ~[e]s, **Zäume** bridle; **zäumen** *tr. V.* bridle; **Zaum·zeug** das bridle

Zaun der; ~[e]s, **Zäune** fence; **Zaun·könig** der wren

z. B. *Abk.* zum Beispiel e.g.

ZDF [tsɛtdeːˈʔɛf] das; ~ *Abk.* Zweites Deutsches Fernsehen Second German Television Channel

Zebra das; ~s, ~s zebra; **Zebra·streifen** der zebra crossing *(Brit.);* pedestrian crossing

Zeche die; ~, ~n **a)** *(Rechnung)* bill *(Brit.);* check *(Amer.);* **b)** *(Bergwerk)* pit; mine; **zechen** *itr. V. (veralt., scherzh.)* tipple

Zeh der; ~s, ~en, **Zehe** die; ~, ~n **a)** toe; **b)** *(Knoblauch~)* clove; **Zehen·spitze** die: **auf** ~n on tiptoe

zehn *Kardinalz.* ten; **Zehn** die; ~, ~en ten; **Zehner** der; ~s, ~ **a)** *(ugs.: Geldschein, Münze)* ten; **b)** *(ugs.: Autobus)* number ten; **c)** *(Math.)* ten; **zehn·fach** *Vervielfältigungsz.* tenfold; **Zehnfache** das; *adj. Dekl.* das ~: ten times as much

zehn-, Zehn-: ~**kampf** der *(Sport)* decathlon; ~**mal** *Adv.* ten times; ~**mark·schein** der ten-mark note; ~**pfennig·**[**brief**]**marke** die ten-pfennig stamp; ~**pfennig·stück** das ten-pfennig piece

zehnt... *Ordinalz.* tenth; **zehn·tausend** *Kardinalz.* ten thousand;

zehntel *Bruchz.* tenth; **Zehntel das** (*schweiz. meist* der); ~s, ~: tenth; **zehntens** *Adv.* tenthly

zehren *itr. V. von etw.* ~: live on *or* off sth.

Zeichen das; ~s, ~ sign; (*Markierung*) mark; (*Chemie, Math., auf Landkarten usw.*) symbol; jmdm. ein ~ geben signal to sb.

Zeichen-: ~**setzung** die punctuation; ~**sprache** die sign language

zeichnen 1. *tr. V.* draw; (*fig.*) portray (*character*); 2. *itr. V.* draw; **Zeichner** der; ~s, ~, **Zeichnerin** die; ~, ~**nen** graphic artist; (*Technik*) draughtsman/-woman; **Zeichnung** die; ~, ~**en** drawing

Zeige·finger der index finger; forefinger; **zeigen** 1. *itr. V.* point; 2. *tr. V.* show; 3. *refl. V.* a) (*sich sehen lassen*) appear; b) (*sich erweisen*) prove to be; es wird sich ~, ...: time will tell ...; **Zeiger** der; ~s, ~: pointer; (*Uhr*~) hand

Zeile die; ~, ~n line; (*Reihe*) row

zeit *Präp. mit Gen.* ~ meines *usw.*/unseres *usw.* Lebens all my *etc.* life/our *etc.* lives; **Zeit** die; ~, ~en a) *o. Pl.* time *no art.*; mit der ~: with *or* in time; (*allmählich*) gradually; b) (~*punkt*) time; zur ~: at the moment; c) (~*abschnitt, Lebensabschnitt*) time; period; (*Geschichtsabschnitt*) age; period; d) (*Sprachw.*) tense

zeit-, Zeit-: ~**alter** das age; era; ~**gemäß** *Adj.* (*modern*) up-to-date; (*aktuell*) topical (*theme*); contemporary (*views*); ; ~**genosse** der, ~**genossin** die contemporary; ~**genössisch** *Adj.* contemporary; ~**geschehen das**: das [aktuelle] ~geschehen current events *pl.*

zeitig *Adj., adv.* early

Zeit·lang die: eine ~: for a while; **zeit·lebens** *Adv.* all one's life; **zeitlich** 1. *Adj.* (*length, interval*) in time; chronological (*order, sequence*); 2. *adv.* with regard to time

zeit-, Zeit-: ~**los** 1. *Adj.* timeless; classic (*fashion, shape*); 2. *adv.* timelessly; ~**lupe** die; *o. Pl.* slow motion; ~**punkt** der moment; ~**raubend** *Adj.* time-consuming; ~**raum** der period; ~**schrift** die magazine; (*bes. wissenschaftlich*) journal; periodical; ~**spanne** die period

Zeitung die; ~, ~**en** [news]paper; **Zeitungs·notiz** die newspaper item

zeit-, ~Zeit-: ~**verschwendung**

die waste of time; ~**vertreib** der; ~[e]s, ~e pastime; **zum** ~**vertreib** to pass the time; ~**weilig** 1. *Adj.* temporary; 2. *adv.* temporarily; ~**weise** *Adv.* (*gelegentlich*) occasionally; (*von Zeit zu Zeit*) from time to time; ~**wort das**; *Pl.* ~**wörter** (*Sprachw.*) verb

Zelle die; ~, ~n cell

Zelluloid [tsɛlu'lɔyt] **das**; ~[e]s celluloid

Zelt das; ~[e]s, ~e tent; (*Fest*~) marquee; (*Zirkus*~) big top; **zelten** *itr. V.* camp

Zelt-: ~**lager** das camp; ~**plane** die tarpaulin

Zement der; ~[e]s, ~e cement

Zensur die; ~, ~**en** mark; grade (*Amer.*)

Zenti- [tsɛnti-]: ~**meter** der, *auch:* das centimetre; ~**meter·maß** das [centimetre] measuring-tape

Zentner der; ~s, ~ a) metric hundredweight; b) (*österr., schweiz.*) *s.* **Doppelzentner**

zentral 1. *Adj.* central; 2. *adv.* centrally; **Zentrale** die; ~, ~n a) (*zentrale Stelle*) head *or* central office; (*der Polizei, einer Partei*) headquarters *sing.* or *pl.*; (*Funk*~) control centre; b) (*Telefon*~) [telephone] exchange; (*eines Hotels, einer Firma o. ä.*) switchboard; **Zentral·heizung** die central heating

Zentren *s.* **Zentrum**

Zentrifugal·kraft die (*Physik*) centrifugal force; **Zentrifuge** die; ~, ~n centrifuge

Zentrum das; ~s, **Zentren** centre; im ~: at the centre; (*im Stadt*~) in the town/city centre

Zeppelin der; ~s, ~e Zeppelin

Zepter das, *auch:* der; ~s, ~: sceptre

zerbeißen *unr. tr. V.* bite in two

zerbersten *unr. itr. V.; mit sein* burst apart

zerbrechen 1. *unr. itr. V.; mit sein* break [into pieces]; smash [to pieces]; (*glass*) shatter; (*fig.*) (*marriage, relationship*) break up; 2. *unr. tr. V.* break; smash, shatter (*dishes, glass*); **zerbrechlich** *Adj.* fragile; (*fig.*) frail

zerbröckeln 1. *itr. V.; mit sein* crumble away; 2. *tr. V.* break into small pieces

zerdrücken *tr. V.* mash

Zeremonie die; ~, ~n ceremony; (*fig.*) ritual; **Zeremoniell das**; ~s, ~e ceremonial

zerfallen *unr. itr. V.; mit sein* a) (*auch*

fig.) disintegrate (**in** + *Akk.,* **zu** into); ⟨*building*⟩ fall into ruin, decay; ⟨*corpse*⟩ decompose, decay

zerfetzen *tr. V.* rip *or* tear to pieces; *(fig.)* tear apart ⟨*body, limb*⟩

zerfleischen *tr. V.* tear ⟨*person, animal*⟩ limb from limb

zerfressen *unr. tr. V.* **a)** eat away; ⟨*moth etc.*⟩ eat holes in; **b)** *(zersetzen)* corrode ⟨*metal*⟩; eat away ⟨*bone*⟩

zergehen *unr. itr. V.; mit sein* melt; *(in Wasser, im Mund)* ⟨*tablet etc.*⟩ dissolve

zerhacken *tr. V.* chop up (**zu** into)

zerhauen *unr. tr. V.* chop up

zerkleinern *tr. V.* chop up *(zermahlen)* crush ⟨*rock etc.*⟩

zerknautschen *tr. V. (ugs.)* crumple

zerknirscht 1. *Adj.* remorseful; **2.** *adv.* remorsefully

zerknittern *tr. V.* crease; crumple

zerknüllen *tr. V.* crumple up [into a ball]

zerkratzen *tr. V.* scratch

zerkrümeln *tr. V.* crumble up

zerlegen *tr. V.* **a)** dismantle; take to pieces; **b)** *(zerschneiden)* cut up ⟨*animal, meat*⟩; carve ⟨*joint*⟩

zerplatzen *itr. V.; mit sein* burst

Zerr·bild das distorted image

zerreiben *unr. tr. V.* crush

zerreißen 1. *unr. tr. V.* **a)** tear up; *(in kleine Stücke)* tear to pieces; break ⟨*thread*⟩; **b)** *(beschädigen)* tear ⟨*stocking, trousers, etc.*⟩ (**an** + *Dat.* on); **2.** *unr. itr. V.; mit sein* ⟨*thread, string, rope*⟩ break; ⟨*paper, cloth, etc.*⟩ tear

zerren 1. *tr. V.* **a)** drag; **b)** sich *(Dat.)* einen Muskel/eine Sehne ~: pull a muscle/tendon; **2.** *itr. V.* **an etw.** *(Dat.)* ~: tug *or* pull at sth.; **Zerrung** die; ~, ~en pulled muscle/tendon

zerrütten *tr. V.* ruin; shatter ⟨*nerves*⟩

zerschellen *itr. V.; mit sein* be dashed *or* smashed to pieces

zerschlagen 1. *unr. tr. V.* smash ⟨*plate, windscreen, etc.*⟩; smash up ⟨*furniture*⟩; *(fig.)* smash ⟨*spy ring etc.*⟩; **2.** *unr. refl. V.* ⟨*plan, deal*⟩ fall through

zerschmettern *tr. V.* smash; shatter ⟨*glass, leg, bone*⟩

zerschneiden *unr. tr. V.* cut; *(in Stücke)* cut up; *(in zwei Teile)* cut in two

zersetzen *tr. V.* corrode ⟨*metal*⟩; decompose ⟨*organism*⟩

zersplittern *itr. V.; mit sein* ⟨*wood, bone*⟩ splinter; ⟨*glass*⟩ shatter

zerspringen *unr. itr. V.; mit sein* shatter; *(Sprünge bekommen)* crack

zerstäuben *tr. V.* spray

zerstören *tr. V.* destroy; ⟨*hooligan*⟩ smash up, vandalize; *(fig.)* ruin ⟨*health, life*⟩; **Zerstörung** die *s.* zerstören: destruction; smashing up; vandalization; *(fig.)* ruin[ation]

zerstreuen 1. *tr. V.* scatter; disperse ⟨*crowd*⟩; jmdn./sich ~ *(ablenken)* take sb.'s/one's mind off things; **2.** *refl. V.* disperse; *(schneller)* scatter; **zerstreut 1.** *Adj.* distracted; *(vergeßlich)* absent-minded; **2.** *adv.* absentmindedly; **Zerstreuung** die; ~, ~en *(Ablenkung)* diversion

zerstückeln *tr. V.* break ⟨*sth.*⟩ up into small pieces; *(zerschneiden)* cut *or* chop ⟨*sth.*⟩ up into small pieces; dismember ⟨*corpse*⟩

zerteilen *tr. V.* divide into pieces; *(zerschneiden)* cut into pieces; cut up

Zertifikat das; ~[e]s, ~e certificate

zertrampeln *tr. V.* trample all over ⟨*flower-bed etc.*⟩; trample ⟨*child etc.*⟩ underfoot

zertreten *unr. tr. V.* stamp on; stamp out ⟨*cigarette, match*⟩

zertrümmern *tr. V.* smash; smash, shatter ⟨*glass*⟩; smash up ⟨*furniture*⟩; wreck ⟨*car, boat*⟩; reduce ⟨*building*⟩ to ruins

Zerwürfnis das; ~ses, ~se *(geh.)* quarrel; dispute; *(Bruch)* rift

zerzausen *tr. V.* ruffle; **zerzaust aussehen** look dishevelled

zetern *itr. V.* scold [shrilly]; *(sich beklagen)* moan (**über** + *Akk.* about)

Zettel der; ~s, ~: slip *or* piece of paper; *(mit einigen Zeilen)* note; *(Bekanntmachung)* notice; *(Formular)* form; *(Kassen~)* receipt; *(Hand~)* leaflet

Zeug das; ~[e]s, ~e **a)** *o. Pl. (ugs.)* stuff; **dummes** ~: nonsense; rubbish; **b)** *(Kleidung)* things *pl.*; **Zeuge** der; ~n, ~n witness

zeugen *tr. V.* procreate; ⟨*man*⟩ father ⟨*child*⟩

Zeugen·aussage die testimony; **Zeugin** die; ~, ~nen witness; **Zeugnis** das; ~ses, ~se **a)** *(Schulw.)* report; **b)** *(Arbeits~)* reference; testimonial; **c)** *(Gutachten)* certificate

Zeugung die; ~, ~en procreation; *(eines Kindes)* fathering; **zeugungsfähig** *Adj.* fertile

z. Hd. *Abk.* zu Händen attn.

Zickzack der; ~[e]s, ~e zigzag

Ziege die; ~, ~n goat; *(Schimpfwort: Frau)* cow *(sl. derog.)*

Ziegel der; ~s, ~ brick; *(Dach~)* tile;
Ziegel·stein der brick
Ziegen-: ~bock der he- *or* billy-goat;
~käse der goat's cheese
ziehen 1. *unr. tr. V.* **a)** pull; *(sanfter)*
draw; *(zerren)* tug; *(schleppen)* drag;
etw. nach sich ~ *(fig.)* result in sth.; entail sth.; **b)** *(heraus~)* extract *(tooth)*;
take out, remove *(stitches)*; draw
(cord, sword, pistol); **den Hut** ~: raise
one's hat; **die |Quadrat|wurzel** ~
(Math.) extract the square root; **c)**
(dehnen) stretch *(elastic etc.)*; stretch
out *(sheets etc.)*; **d)** *(Gesichtspartien
bewegen)* make *(face, grimace)*; **e)** *(bei
Brettspielen)* move *(chess-man etc.)*; **f)**
(zeichnen) draw *(line etc.)*; **g)** *(anlegen)* dig *(trench)*; build *(wall)*; erect
(fence); put up *(washing-line)*; run,
lay *(cable, wires)*; draw *(frontier)*; **h)**
(auf~) grow *(plants, flowers)*; breed
(animals); 2. *unr. itr. V.* **a)** *(reißen)*
pull; **an etw.** *(Dat.)* ~: pull on sth.; **b)**
(funktionieren) *(stove, pipe, chimney)*
draw; **c)** *mit sein (um~)* move **(nach,
in + Akk.** to); **d)** *mit sein (gehen)* go;
(marschieren) march; *(umherstreifen)*
roam; *(weggehen)* go away; leave;
(fog, clouds) drift; **e)** *(saugen)* draw;
an einer Zigarette/Pfeife ~: draw on a
cigarette/pipe; **f)** *(tea, coffee)* draw; **g)**
(Kochk.) simmer; **h)** *unpers.* **es zieht**
there's a draught; 3. *unr. refl. V.*
(road) run, stretch; *(frontier)* run;
Zieh·harmonika die piano accordion; **Ziehung** die; ~, ~en draw
Ziel das; ~|e|s, ~e **a)** destination; **b)**
(Sport) finish; *(~linie)* finishing-line;
(Pferderennen) finishing-post; **c)**
(~scheibe; auch Milit.) target; **d)**
(Zweck) aim; goal; **sein** ~ **erreichen**
achieve one's objective *or* aim;
ziel·bewußt 1. *Adj.* determined; 2.
adv. determinedly; **zielen** *itr. V.* aim
(auf + Akk., at); *(fig.)* **auf jmdn./etw.**
~ *(reproach, efforts, etc.)* be aimed at
sb./sth.
ziel-, Ziel-: ~los 1. *Adj.* aimless; 2.
adv. aimlessly; ~scheibe die *(auch
fig.)* target *(Gen.* for); ~strebig 1.
Adj. **a)** purposeful; **b)** *(energisch)*
single-minded *(person)*; 2. *adv.* **a)**
purposefully; **b)** *(energisch)* single-
mindedly
ziemlich 1. *Adj. (ugs.)* fair, sizeable
(quantity, number); 2. *adv.* **a)** quite;
fairly; **b)** *(ugs.: fast)* pretty well
Zierde die; ~, ~n *(auch fig.)* ornament; **zieren** *refl. V.* be coy; **zierlich**

1. *Adj.* dainty; petite, dainty *(woman,
figure)*; 2. *adv.* daintily
Ziffer die; ~, ~n numeral; *(in einer
mehrstelligen Zahl)* digit; figure; **Zif-
fer·blatt** das dial; face
-zig, zig *unbest. Zahlwort (ugs.)* umpteen *(coll.)*
Zigarette die; ~, ~n cigarette; **Ziga-
rillo** der *od.* das; ~, ~s cigarillo;
small cigar; **Zigarre** die; ~, ~n cigar
Zigeuner der; ~s, ~, **Zigeunerin**
die; ~, ~nen gypsy
zig·mal *Adv. (ugs.)* umpteen times
(coll.); **zig·tausend** *unbest. Zahlwort (ugs.)* umpteen thousand *(coll.)*
Zimmer das; ~s, ~: room; **Zimmer-
mädchen** das chambermaid
zimmern *tr. V.* make *(shelves etc.)*;
Zimmer·suche die room-hunt
zimperlich 1. *Adj.* timid; *(leicht angeekelt)* squeamish; *(prüde)* prissy; 2.
adv.: s. Adj.: timidly; squeamishly;
prissily
Zimt der; ~|e|s, ~e cinnamon
Zink das; ~|e|s zinc
Zinke die; ~, ~n prong; *(eines Kam-
mes)* tooth
Zinn das; ~|e|s tin; *(Gegenstände)*
pewter[ware]
Zins der; ~es, ~en interest; **Zin-
ses·zins** der compound interest
zins·los 1. *Adj.* interest-free; 2. *adv.*
free of interest; **Zins·satz** der interest rate
Zipfel der; ~s, ~ *(einer Decke, eines
Tisch-, Handtuchs usw.)* corner;
(Wurst~, eines Halstuchs) [tail-]end;
Zipfel·mütze die [long-]pointed cap
zirka *Adv.* about; approximately
Zirkulation die, ~, ~en circulation;
zirkulieren *itr. V.; auch mit sein* circulate
Zirkus der; ~, ~se **a)** circus; **b)** *(ugs.)*
o. Pl. (Trubel) hustle and bustle;
(Krach) to-do
zirpen *itr. V.* chirp
zischeln *tr. V.* whisper angrily
zischen *itr. V.* **a)** hiss; *(hot fat)* sizzle;
b) *mit sein* hiss
Zitat das; ~|e|s, ~e quotation **(aus**
from)
zitieren *tr., itr. V.* **a)** quote;
(Rechtsspr.) cite; **b)** *(rufen)* summon
Zitronat das; ~|e|s candied lemon-
peel; **Zitrone** die; ~, ~n lemon
Zitronen-: ~limonade die lemonade; ~presse die lemon-squeezer;
~saft der lemon-juice
Zitrus·frucht die citrus fruit

zittern *itr. V.* tremble **(vor** + *Dat.*
with); *(vor Kälte)* shiver; *(beben)*
⟨*walls, windows*⟩ shake; **vor jmdm./**
etw. ~: be terrified of sb./sth.; **zittrig**
Adj. shaky; doddery ⟨*old man*⟩
Zitze die; ~, ~n teat
zivil 1. *Adj.* **a)** civilian; non-military
⟨*purposes*⟩; civil ⟨*aviation, marriage,
law, defence*⟩; **b)** *(annehmbar)* decent;
2. *adv.* *(annehmbar)* decently; **Zivil**
das; ~s civilian clothes *pl.*; **Zivil·be-**
völkerung die civilian population;
Zivilisation [tsiviliza'tsjo:n] die; ~,
~en civilization; **zivilisieren** *tr. V.*
civilize; **zivilisiert** 1. *Adj.* civilized;
2. *adv.* in a civilized way; **Zivilist**
der; ~en, ~en civilian; **Zivil·klei-**
dung die civilian clothes *pl.*
Zofe die; ~, ~n *(hist.)* lady's maid
zog *1. u. 3. Pers. Sg. Prät. v.* ziehen
zögern *itr. V.* hesitate; **ohne zu ~:**
without hesitation
Zoll der; ~|e|s, Zölle **a)** [customs] duty;
b) *o. Pl. (Behörde)* customs *pl.*
zoll-, Zoll-: ~**amt das** customs house
or office; ~**beamte der** customs officer; ~**frei** 1. *Adj.* duty-free; free of
duty *pred.*; 2. *adv.* free of duty;
~**kontrolle die** customs examination
or check; ~**stock der** folding rule
Zone die; ~, ~n zone
Zoo der; ~s, ~s zoo; **Zoologe** der;
~n, ~n zoologist; **Zoologie** die; ~:
zoology *no art.*; **zoologisch** *Adj.*
zoological; ~**er Garten** zoological
gardens *pl.*
Zoom das; ~s, ~s *(Film, Fot.: Objektiv)* zoom; **Zoom·objektiv das**
(Film, Fot.) zoom lens
Zopf der; ~|e|s, Zöpfe plait; *(am Hin-
terkopf)* pigtail
Zorn der; ~|e|s anger; *(stärker)* wrath;
fury; **zornig** 1. *Adj.* furious; 2. *adv.*
furiously
Zote die; ~, ~n dirty joke; **zotig** 1.
Adj. smutty; dirty ⟨*joke*⟩; 2. *adv.*
smuttily
zottig *Adj.* shaggy
zu 1. *Präp. mit Dat.* **a)** *(Richtung)* to;
zu ... hin towards ...; **b)** *(zusammen
mit)* with; **zu dem Käse gab es Wein**
there was wine with the cheese; **c)**
(Lage) at; **zu beiden Seiten** on both
sides; **d)** *(zeitlich)* at; **zu Weihnachten**
at Christmas; **e)** *(Art u. Weise)* **zu meiner Zufriedenheit/Überraschung** to
my satisfaction/surprise; *(bei Men-
genangaben o. ä)* **zu Dutzenden/zweien**
by the dozen/in twos; **f)** *(ein Zahlen-*

verhältnis ausdrückend) **ein Verhältnis
von 3 zu 1** a ratio of 3 to 1; **g)** *(einen
Preis zuordnend)* at; for; **h)** *(Zweck)*
for; **i)** *(Ziel, Ergebnis)* into; **zu etw.
werden** turn into sth.; **j)** *(über)* about;
on; **sich zu etw. äußern** comment on
sth.; **k)** *(gegenüber)* **freundlich/häßlich
zu jmdm. sein** be friendly/nasty to sb.;
s. auch **zum; zur;** 2. *Adv.* **a)** *(allzu)*
too; **zu sehr** too much; **b)** *nachgestellt
(Richtung)* towards; 3. *Konj.* **a)** *(mit
Infinitiv)* to; **was gibt's da zu lachen?**
what is there to laugh about?; **b)** *(mit
1. Part.)* **die zu erledigende Post** the
letters *pl.* to be dealt with
Zubehör das; ~|e|s, ~e *od.* schweiz.
~den accessories *pl.*; *(eines Staubsau-
gers, Mixers o. ä.)* attachments *pl.*;
(Ausstattung) equipment
zu|bereiten *tr. V.* prepare ⟨*meal etc.*⟩;
make up ⟨*medicine, ointment*⟩; *(kochen)* cook ⟨*fish, meat, etc.*⟩
zu|billigen *tr. V.* **jmdm. etw. ~:** grant
or allow sb. sth.
zu|binden *unr. tr. V.* tie [up]
zu|blinzeln *itr. V.* **jmdm. ~:** wink at
sb.
zu|bringen *unr. tr. V.* spend; **Zu-
bringer der;** ~s, ~ **a)** *(Straße)* access
road; **b)** *(Verkehrsmittel)* shuttle
Zucht die; ~, ~en **a)** breeding; *(von
Pflanzen)* cultivation; **ein Pferd aus
deutscher ~:** a German-bred horse; **b)**
o. Pl. (geh.: Disziplin) discipline;
züchten *tr. V. (auch fig.)* breed; cultivate ⟨*plants*⟩; culture ⟨*bacteria,
pearls*⟩; **Züchter der;** ~s, ~, **Züch-
terin die;** ~, ~nen breeder; *(von
Pflanzen)* grower [of new varieties];
Züchtung die; ~, ~en **a)** breeding;
(von Pflanzen) cultivation; **b)** *(Zucht-
ergebnis)* strain
zucken *itr. V.;* mit Richtungsangabe
mit sein twitch; ⟨*body, arm, leg, etc.*⟩
jerk; *(vor Schreck)* start; ⟨*flames*⟩
flicker; **mit den Achseln/Schultern ~:**
shrug one's shoulders; **zücken** *tr. V.*
draw ⟨*sword, dagger, knife*⟩
Zucker der; ~s, ~ **a)** sugar; **b)** *o. Pl.
(ugs.: ~krankheit)* diabetes; **~ haben**
be a diabetic
zucker-, Zucker-: ~**dose die** sugar
bowl; ~**hut der** sugar loaf; ~**krank**
Adj. diabetic
zuckern *tr. V.* sugar
Zuckung die; ~, ~en twitch
zu|decken *tr. V.* cover up; cover
[over] ⟨*well, ditch*⟩; **jmdn./sich ~:** tuck
sb./oneself up

zu|drehen *tr. V.* **a)** *(abdrehen)* turn off; **b)** *(zuwenden)* jmdm. den Rücken ~: turn one's back on sb.

zu·dringlich 1. *Adj.* pushy *(coll.)*, pushing 〈*person, manner*〉; *(sexuell)* importunate 〈*person, manner*〉; prying 〈*glance*〉; **2.** *adv.* importunately; **Zudringlichkeit** die; ~, ~en **a)** *o. Pl.* pushiness *(coll.)*; *(in sexueller Hinsicht)* importunate manner; **b)** *(Handlung)* ~en insistent advances *or* attentions

zu|drücken *tr. V.* press shut; push 〈*door*〉 shut; jmdm. die Kehle ~: choke *or* throttle sb.

zu·einander *Adv.* to one another

zu·erst *Adv.* **a)** first; **b)** *(anfangs)* at first; to start with; **c)** *(erstmals)* first

Zu·fahrt die **a)** *o. Pl.* access [for vehicles]; **b)** *(Straße, Weg)* access road; *(zum Haus)* driveway; **Zufahrts·straße** die access road

Zu·fall der chance; *(zufälliges Zusammentreffen von Ereignissen)* coincidence; durch ~: by chance; **zu|fallen** *unr. itr. V.; mit sein* **a)** 〈*door etc.*〉 slam shut; 〈*eyes*〉 close; **b)** *(zukommen)* jmdm. ~ 〈*task*〉 fall to sb.; 〈*prize, inheritance*〉 go to sb.; **zu·fällig 1.** *Adj.* accidental; chance *attrib.* 〈*meeting, acquaintance*〉; random 〈*selection*〉; **2.** *adv.* by chance; wissen Sie ~, wie spät es ist? *(ugs.)* do you by any chance know the time?; **Zufallstreffer** der fluke

zu|fassen *itr. V.* make a snatch *or* grab

zu|fliegen *unr. itr. V.; mit sein (ugs.)* 〈*door, window, etc.*〉 slam shut

Zu·flucht die refuge (vor + *Dat.* from); *(vor Unwetter o. ä.)* shelter (vor + *Dat.* from); **Zufluchts·ort** der place of refuge; sanctuary

Zu·fluß der **a)** *o. Pl. (das Zufließen)* inflow; supply; *(fig.)* influx; **b)** *(Gewässer)* feeder stream/river

zu|flüstern *tr. V.* jmdm. etw. ~: whisper sth. to sb.

zu·folge *Präp. mit Dat.; nachgestellt* according to

zu·frieden 1. *Adj.* contented; *(befriedigt)* satisfied; mit etw. ~ sein be satisfied with sth.; **2.** *adv.* contentedly; **zufrieden|geben** *unr. refl. V.* be satisfied; **Zufriedenheit** die; ~: contentment; *(Befriedigung)* satisfaction; **zufrieden|stellen** *tr. V.* satisfy; **zufriedenstellend 1.** *Adj.* satisfactory; **2.** *adv.* satisfactorily

zu|frieren *unr. itr. V.; mit sein* freeze over

zu|fügen *tr. V.* jmdm. etw. ~: inflict sth. on sb.; jmdm. Schaden/[ein] Unrecht ~: do sb. harm/an injustice

Zufuhr die; ~: supply; *(Material)* supplies *pl.*; **zu|führen 1.** *itr. V.* auf etw. *(Akk.)* ~: lead towards sth.; **2.** *tr. V.* **a)** *(zuleiten)* einer Sache *(Dat.)* etw. ~: supply sth. to sth.; **b)** *(bringen)* einer Partei Mitglieder ~: bring new members to a party

Zug der; ~[e]s, Züge **a)** *(Bahn)* train; **b)** *(Kolonne)* column; *(Umzug)* procession; *(Demonstrations~)* march; **c)** *(das Ziehen)* pull; traction *(Phys.)*; **d)** *(Vorrichtung)* pull; **e)** *(Wanderung)* migration; **f)** *(beim Brettspiel)* move; **g)** *(Schluck)* swig *(coll.)*; mouthful; *(großer Schluck)* gulp; das Glas auf einen *od.* in einem ~ leeren empty the glass at one go; **h)** *(beim Rauchen)* pull; drag *(coll.)*; **i)** *(Atem~)* breath; **j)** *o. Pl. (Zugluft; beim Ofen)* draught; **k)** *(Gesichts~)* feature; *(Wesens~)* characteristic; trait

Zu·gabe die **a)** *(Geschenk)* [free] gift; **b)** *(im Konzert, Theater)* encore

Zu·gang der **a)** *(Weg, auch fig.)* access; *(Eingang)* entrance; **b)** *o. Pl. (das Hinzukommen) (von Personen)* intake; *(von Patienten)* admission; *(Zuwachs)* increase (von in); zu·gange: ~ sein *(ugs.)* be busy *or* occupied; **zugänglich** *Adj.* **a)** accessible; *(geöffnet)* open; **b)** *(zur Verfügung stehend)* available *(Dat.,* für to); *(verständlich)* accessible *(Dat.,* für to); **c)** *(aufgeschlossen)* approachable 〈*person*〉

zu·geben *unr. tr. V.* admit; admit to 〈*deed, crime*〉

zu·gegen *Adj.* ~ sein be present

zu|gehen *unr. itr. V.; mit sein* **a)** auf jmdn./etw. ~: approach sb./sth.; **b)** jmdm. ~ *(zugeschickt werden)* be sent to sb.; ~ *(ugs.: sich schließen)* close; shut; die Tür geht nicht zu the door will not shut

Zügel der; ~s, ~: rein; **zügel·los** *(fig.)* **1.** *Adj.* unrestrained; unbridled 〈*rage, passion*〉; **2.** *adv.* without restraint; **zügeln** *tr. V.* rein [in] 〈*horse*〉; *(fig.)* curb, restrain 〈*desire etc.*〉

zu|gesellen *refl. V.* sich jmdm./einer Sache ~: join sb./sth.

Zu·geständnis das concession; **zu·gestehen** *unr. tr. V.* admit; concede

zu·getan *Adj.* jmdm. [herzlich] ~ sein *(geh.)* be [very] attached to sb.

zugig *Adj.* draughty, *(im Freien)* windy ⟨*corner etc.*⟩

zügig 1. *Adj.* speedy; rapid; 2. *adv.* speedily; rapidly

zu·gleich *Adv.* at the same time

Zug·luft die; *o. Pl.* draught

zu|greifen *unr. itr. V.* **a)** take hold; **b)** *(sich bedienen)* help oneself; **c)** *(fleißig arbeiten)* [hart *od.* kräftig] ~: [really] knuckle down to it; **Zu·griff** der *(Zugang)* access (**auf** + *Akk.* to)

zu·grunde *Adv.* **a)** ~ gehen *(sterben)* die (**an** + *Dat.* of); *(zerstört werden)* be destroyed (**an** + *Dat.* by); ~ richten destroy; *(finanziell)* ruin ⟨*company, person*⟩; **b)** etw. einer Sache *(Dat.)* ~ legen base sth. on sth.; etw. liegt einer Sache ~: sth. is based on sth.

zu|gucken *itr. V.* *(ugs.)* s. zusehen

zu·gunsten 1. *Präp. mit Gen.* in favour of; 2. *Adv.* ~ von in favour of

zu·gute *Adv.* jmdm. seine Unerfahrenheit *usw.* ~ halten *(geh.)* make allowances for sb.'s inexperience *etc.;* sich *(Dat.)* etwas/viel auf etw. *(Akk.)* ~ tun *od.* halten *(geh.)* be proud/very proud of sth.; jmdm./einer Sache ~ kommen stand sb./sth. in good stead

zu|haben *unr. itr. V.* *(ugs.)* ⟨*shop, office*⟩ be shut *or* closed

zu|halten *unr. tr. V.* hold closed; *(nicht öffnen)* keep closed

zu|hängen *tr. V.* cover ⟨*window, cage*⟩

zu|hauen *(ugs.)* 1. *unr. itr. V.* bang *or* slam ⟨*door, window*⟩ shut; 2. *unr. itr. V.* hit *or* strike out

Zu·hause das; ~s home

zu|hören *itr. V.* jmdm./einer Sache ~: listen to sb./sth.; **Zu·hörer** der, **Zu·hörerin** die listener

zu|kleben *tr. V.* seal ⟨*letter, envelope*⟩

zu|knallen *(ugs.)* 1. *tr. V.* slam; 2. *itr. V.; mit sein* slam

zu|knöpfen *tr. V.* button up

zu|kommen *itr. V.; mit sein* auf jmdn. ~: approach sb.

Zukunft die; ~: future

Zulage die extra pay *no indef. art.;* additional allowance *no indef. art.*

zu|lassen *unr. tr. V.* **a)** allow; permit; **b)** *(teilnehmen lassen)* admit; **c)** *(mit einer Lizenz usw. versehen)* jmdn. als Arzt ~: register sb. as a doctor; **d)** *(Kfz-W.)* register ⟨*vehicle*⟩; **e)** *(geschlossen lassen)* leave closed *or* shut ⟨*door, window, etc.*⟩; **zu·lässig** *Adj.* permissible; admissible ⟨*appeal*⟩; **Zulassung** die; ~, ~en registration

Zu·lauf der *o. Pl.* ~ haben ⟨*shop, restaurant, etc.*⟩ enjoy a large clientele; ⟨*doctor, lawyer*⟩ have a large practice; **zu|laufen** *unr. itr. V.; mit sein* **a)** auf jmdn./etw. ~ *(auch fig.)* run towards sb./sth.; **b)** jmdm. ~ ⟨*cat, dog, etc.*⟩ adopt sb. as a new owner

zu|legen *refl. V.* sich *(Dat.)* etw. ~: get oneself sth.

zu·letzt *Adv.* **a)** last [of all]; **b)** *(als letzter/letzte/letztes)* last; **c)** *(fig.: am wenigsten)* least of all; **d)** *(schließlich, am Ende)* in the end; **bis** ~: [right up] to *or* until the end

zum *Präp.* + *Art.* **a)** = zu dem; **b)** *(räumlich: Richtung)* to the; **c)** *(räumlich: Lage)* etw. ~ Fenster hinauswerfen throw sth. out of the window; **d)** *(Hinzufügung)* Milch ~ Tee nehmen take milk with [one's] tea **e)** *(zeitlich)* at the; spätestens ~ 15. April by 15 April at the latest; **f)** *(Zweck)* ~ Spaß/Vergnügen for fun/pleasure; **g)** *(Folge)* ~ Ärger seines Vaters to the annoyance of his father

zu|machen *tr. V.* close; fasten, do up ⟨*dress*⟩; seal ⟨*envelope, letter*⟩; turn off ⟨*tap*⟩; put the top on ⟨*bottle*⟩; *(stillegen)* close *or* shut down ⟨*factory, mine, etc.*⟩

zu·mal 1. *Adv.* especially; particularly; 2. *Konj.* especially *or* particularly since

zumindest *Adv.* at least

zu·mute *Adj.* jmdm. ist unbehaglich *usw.* ~: sb. feels uncomfortable *etc.;* mir war nicht danach ~: I didn't feel like it *or* in the mood

zu|muten *tr. V.* jmdm. etw. ~ *(abverlangen)* expect *or* ask sth. of sb.; *(antun)* expect sb. to put up with sth.; **Zumutung** die; ~, ~en unreasonable demand; eine ~ sein be unreasonable

zu·nächst *Adv.* **a)** *(als erstes)* first; *(anfangs)* at first; **b)** *(im Moment, vorläufig)* for the moment

Zunahme die; ~, ~n increase *(Gen., sn + Dat. in)*

Zu·name der surname; last name

zünden 1. *tr. V.* ignite ⟨*gas, fuel, etc.*⟩; detonate ⟨*bomb, explosive device, etc.*⟩; let off ⟨*fireworks*⟩; fire ⟨*rocket*⟩; 2. *itr. V.* ⟨*rocket, engine*⟩ fire; ⟨*lighter, match*⟩ light; ⟨*gas, fuel, explosive*⟩ ignite

Zünd-: ~holz das *(bes. südd., österr.)* match; ~schlüssel der *(Kfz-W.)* ignition key

Zündung die; ~, ~en **a)** s. zünden 1:

ignition; detonation; letting off; firing; b) *(Kfz-W.: Anlage)* ignition
zu|nehmen *unr. itr. V.* **a)** increase **(an + *Dat.* in)**; ⟨*moon*⟩ wax; **b)** *(schwerer werden)* put on *or* gain weight
Zu·neigung die; ~, **-en** affection
Zunge die; ~, **-n** tongue; [jmdm.] die ~ **herausstrecken** put one's tongue out [at sb.]
zu·nichte *Adj.* etw. ~ **machen** ruin sth.
zu·oberst *Adv.* [right] on [the] top
zupfen 1. *itr. V.* **an etw.** *(Dat.)* ~: pluck *or* pull at sth.; **2.** *tr. V.* **a)** etw. **aus/von** *usw.* etw. ~: pull sth. out of/ from *etc.* sth.; **b)** *(auszupfen)* pull out; pluck ⟨*eyebrows*⟩; **c)** pluck ⟨*string, guitar, tune*⟩; **d)** **jmdn. am Ärmel** ~: pull *or* tug [at] sb.'s sleeve
zur *Präp. + Art.* **a)** = **zu der; b)** *(räumlich, fig.: Richtung)* to the; ~ **Schule/ Arbeit gehen** go to school/work; **c)** *(räumlich: Lage)* ~ **Tür hereinkommen** come [in] through the door; **d)** *(Zusammengehörigkeit, Hinzufügung)* with; **e)** *(zeitlich)* at the; ~ **Zeit** at the moment; at present; **f)** *(Zweck)* ~ **Entschuldigung** by way of [an] excuse; **g)** *(Folge)* ~ **vollen Zufriedenheit** to the complete satisfaction
zurechnungs·fähig *Adj.* sound of mind *pred.*
zurecht-: ~|**finden** *unr. refl. V.* find one's way [around]; ~|**kommen** *unr. itr. V.; mit sein* get on (mit with); ~|**legen** *tr. V.* lay out [ready]; **jmdm. etw.** ~**legen** lay sth. out ready for sb.; ~|**machen** *tr. V. (ugs.)* **a)** *(vorbereiten)* get ready; **b)** *(herrichten)* do up; **c)** **jmdn./sich** ~: get sb. ready/get [oneself] ready; *(schminken)* make sb. up/put on one's make-up; ~|**weisen** *unr. tr. V.* rebuke; reprimand ⟨*pupil, subordinate, etc.*⟩
zu|reden *itr. V.* **jmdm.** ~: persuade sb.; *(ermutigen)* encourage sb.
Zürich (das); ~s Zurich
zu·rück *Adv.* back; *(weiter hinten)* behind; **einen Schritt** ~: a step backwards; ~! get *or* go back!
zurück-, Zurück-: ~|**behalten** *unr. tr. V.* **a)** keep [back]; retain; **b)** be left with ⟨*scar, heart defect, etc.*⟩; ~|**bekommen** *unr. itr. V.* get back; **Sie bekommen 10 Mark** ~: you get 10 marks change; ~|**bleiben** *unr. itr. V.; mit sein* **a)** remain; **b)** *(nicht mithalten)* lag behind; *(fig.)* fall behind; **c)** *(bleiben)* remain; ~|**erstatten** *tr. V.* refund;

jmdm. etw. ~**erstatten** refund sth. to sb.; ~|**fahren** *unr. itr. V.; mit sein* **a)** go back; return; **b)** *(nach hinten fahren)* go back[wards]; ~|**fallen** *unr. itr. V.; mit sein* **a)** *(in Rückstand geraten)* fall behind; **b)** *(auf einen niedrigeren Rang)* drop **(auf + *Akk.* to)**; **c)** **an jmdn.** ~**fallen** ⟨*property*⟩ revert to sb.; **d)** **auf jmdn.** ~**fallen** ⟨*actions, behaviour*⟩ reflect [up]on sb.; ~|**fliegen** *unr. itr. V.; mit sein* fly back; ~|**führen** *tr. V.* etw. **auf etw.** *(Akk.)* ~**führen** attribute sth. to sth.; ~|**geben** *unr. tr. V.* give back; return; take back ⟨*defective goods*⟩; ~|**gehen** *unr. itr. V.; mit sein* **a)** go back; return; **b)** *(nach hinten)* go back; **c)** *(verschwinden)* disappear; ⟨*swelling, inflammation*⟩ go down; ⟨*pain*⟩ subside; **d)** *(sich verringern)* decrease; ⟨*fever*⟩ abate; ⟨*flood*⟩ subside; ⟨*business*⟩ fall off; **e)** *(zurückgeschickt werden)* be returned *or* sent back; ~|**greifen** *unr. itr. V.* **auf jmdn./etw.** ~**greifen** fall back on sb./sth.; ~|**halten 1.** *unr. tr. V.* **a)** **jmdn.** ~**halten** hold sb. back; *(von etw. abhalten)* stop sb.; **b)** *(am Vordringen hindern)* keep back ⟨*crowd, mob, etc.*⟩; **c)** *(behalten)* withhold ⟨*news, letter, etc.*⟩; **d)** *(nicht austreten lassen)* hold back ⟨*tears etc.*⟩; **2.** *unr. refl. V.* restrain *or* control oneself; **sich in einer Diskussion** ~**halten** keep in the background in a discussion; ~**haltend 1.** *Adj.* **a)** reserved; **b)** *(kühl, reserviert)* cool, restrained ⟨*reception, response*⟩; **c)** *(Wirtsch.: schwach)* slack ⟨*demand*⟩; **2.** *adv.* ⟨*behave*⟩ with reserve *or* restraint; *(kühl, reserviert)* coolly; ~**haltung die;** *o. Pl.* reserve; *(Kühle, Reserviertheit)* coolness; *(Wirtsch.)* caution; ~|**kehren** *itr. V.; mit sein* return; come back; ~|**kommen** *unr. itr. V.; mit sein* come back; return; *(zurückgelangen)* get back; ~**kommen auf** **(+ *Akk.*)** come back to ⟨*subject, question, point, etc.*⟩; ~|**kriegen** *tr. V. s.* ~**bekommen;** ~|**lassen** *unr. tr. V.* leave; ~|**legen** *tr. V.* **a)** put back; **b)** *(reservieren)* put aside, keep ⟨*Dat., für* for⟩; **c)** *(sparen)* put away; **d)** *(hinter sich bringen)* cover ⟨*distance*⟩; ~|**lehnen** *refl. V.* lean back; ~|**nehmen** *unr. tr. V. (auch fig. widerrufen)* take back; ~|**rufen** *unr. tr. V.* **a)** call back; recall ⟨*ambassador*⟩; **b)** *auch itr. (telefonisch)* call *or (Brit.)* ring back; ~|**schicken** *tr. V.* send back ~|**schrecken** *regelm., veralt. unr. itr.*

V.; mit sein vor etw. (Dat.) ~**schrecken** *(fig.)* shrink from sth.; **er schreckt vor nichts** ~: he will stop at nothing; ~|**senden** *unr. od. regelm. tr. V. (geh.)* s. ~**schicken;** ~|**treten** *unr. itr. V.; mit sein* step back; *(von einem Amt)* resign; step down; *(government)* resign; *(von einem Vertrag usw.)* withdraw (**von** from); back out (**von** of); *(fig.: in den Hintergrund treten)* become less important; ~|**weisen** *unr. tr. V.* reject *(proposal, question, demand, application, etc.)*; turn down, refuse *(offer, request, help, etc.)*; turn away *(petitioner, unwelcome guest)*; repudiate *(accusation, claim, etc.)*; ~|**werfen** *unr. tr. V.* throw back; reflect *(light, sound)*; repulse *(enemy)*; *(fig.: in einer Entwicklung)* set back; ~|**zahlen** *tr. V.* pay back; ~|**ziehen** 1. *unr. tr. V.* **a)** pull back; draw back *(bolt, curtains, one's hand, etc.)*; **b)** *(abziehen, zurückbeordern)* withdraw *(troops)*; recall *(ambassador)*; **c)** *(rückgängig machen)* withdraw; cancel *(order, instruction)*; 2. *unr. refl. V.* withdraw

Zu·ruf *der* shout; **zu|rufen** *unr. tr. V.* **jmdm. etw.** ~: shout sth. to sb.

Zu·sage *die* **a)** *(auf eine Einladung hin)* acceptance; *(auf eine Stellenbewerbung hin)* offer; **b)** *(Versprechen)* promise; undertaking; **zu|sagen** 1. *itr. V.* **a)** accept; **b) jmdm.** ~ *(gefallen)* appeal to sb.; 2. *tr. V.* promise

zusammen *Adv.* together

zusammen-, Zusammen-: ~|**arbeiten** *itr. V.* co-operate; ~|**binden** *unr. tr. V.* tie together; ~|**brechen** *unr. itr. V.; mit sein* collapse; *(fig.)(order, communications, system, telephone network)* break down; *(traffic)* come to a standstill; ~**bruch** *der* collapse; *(fig., auch psychisch, nervlich)* breakdown; ~|**drücken** *tr. V.* press together; ~|**fahren** *unr. itr. V.; mit sein (~zucken)* start; jump; ~|**fallen** *unr. itr. V.; mit sein* **a)** collapse; **b)** *(zeitlich)* ~**fallen** coincide; ~|**fassen** *tr. V.* summarize; ~**fassung** *die* summary; ~|**fegen** *tr. V. (bes. nordd.)* sweep together; ~|**fließen** *unr. itr. V.; mit sein (rivers, streams)* flow into each other; ~**fluß** *der* confluence; ~|**fügen** *tr. V.* fit together; ~|**führen** *tr. V.* bring together; ~|**gehören** *itr. V.* belong together; ~**gehörig** *Adj.* [closely] related *or* connected *(subjects, problems, etc.)*; matching *attrib.*

(pieces of tea service, cutlery, etc.) ~**gehörigkeit** *die*; ~: **ein starkes Ge** **fühl der** ~**gehörigkeit** a strong sense of belonging together; ~**hang** *der* con nection; *(einer Geschichte, Rede)* co herence; *(Kontext)* context; ~|**hän gen** *unr. itr. V.* **a)** be joined [together]; **b) mit etw.** ~**hängen** *(fig.* be related to sth.; *(durch etw. [mit] ver ursacht sein)* be the result of sth. ~|**kehren** *tr. V. (bes. südd.) s.* ~**fegen** ~**klappbar** *Adj.* folding; ~|**klapper** *tr. V.* fold up; ~|**kommen** *unr. itr. V. mit sein* **a)** meet; **mit jmdm.** ~**komme** meet sb.; **b)** *(zueinanderkommen; auc fig.)* get together; *(gleichzeitig auftre ten)* occur *or* happen together ~**kunft** *die;* ~, ~**künfte** meeting ~|**laufen** *unr. itr. V.; mit sein* **a** *(people, crowd)* gather, congregate; **b** *(rivers, streams)* flow into each other join up; ~|**leben** *itr. V.* live together ~|**leben** *das; o. Pl.* living together *n art.;* ~|**legen** 1. *tr. V.* **a)** put *or* gathe together; **b)** *(zusammenfalten)* fold [up]; **c)** *(miteinander verbinden)* amal gamate, merge *(classes, departments etc.)*; combine *(events)*; **d)** put *(pa tients, guests, etc.)* together [in th same room]; 2. *itr. V.* club together ~|**nehmen** 1. *unr. tr. V.* **a)** summor up *(courage, strength, understanding)* 2. *unr. refl. V.* get *or* take a grip or oneself; **nimm dich** ~! pull yoursel together!; ~|**passen** *itr. V.* g together; *(persons)* be suited to eacl other; ~**prall** *der;* ~|**e|s,** ~e collision ~|**prallen** *itr. V.; mit sein* collide (**mi** with); ~|**sein** *unr. itr. V.; mit sein* Zusschr. nur im Inf. u. Part. **a)** b together; **b)** *(zusammenleben)* be or live together; ~|**setzen** 1. *tr. V.* pu together; 2. *refl. V.* **a) sich aus etw.** ~**setzen** be made up *or* composed of sth.; **b)** *(sich zueinander setzen)* sit together; *(zu einem Gespräch)* ge together; ~|**stehen** *unr. itr. V.* stand together; ~|**stellen** *tr. V.* pu together; draw up *(list)*; ~**stoß** *der* collision; *(fig.)* clash (**mit** with); ~|**stoßen** *unr. itr. V.; mit sein* collide (**mit** with); ~|**treffen** *unr. itr. V.; mi* *sein* meet; **mit jmdm.** ~**treffen** mee sb.; *(zeitlich)* coincide; ~|**zählen** *tr V.* add up; ~|**zucken** *itr. V.; mit sein* start; jump

Zu·satz *der* addition; *(Zugesetztes, Additiv)* additive; **zusätzlich** 1. *Adj.* additional; 2. *adv.* in addition

zu|schauen *itr. V. (südd., österr., schweiz.) s.* zusehen; **Zu·schauer der, Zu·schauerin die;** ~, ~nen spectator; *(im Theater, Kino)* member of the audience; *(an einer Unfallstelle)* onlooker; *(Fernseh~)* viewer; **die** ~: *(im Theater, Kino)* the audience *sing.*

zu|schicken *tr. V.* send

zu|schieben *unr. tr. V.* **a)** push ⟨*drawer, door*⟩ shut; **b)** *(fig.)* **jmdm. die Schuld** ~: lay the blame on sb.

Zu·schlag der a) additional *or* extra charge; *(für Nacht-; Feiertagsarbeit usw.)* additional *or* extra payment; **b)** *(Eisenb.)* supplement ticket; **zu|-schlagen 1.** *unr. tr. V.* bang *or* slam ⟨*door, window, etc.*⟩ shut; close ⟨*book*⟩; *(heftig)* slam ⟨*book*⟩ shut; **2.** *unr. itr. V.* **a)** *mit sein* ⟨*door, trap*⟩ slam *or* bang shut; **b)** *(einen Schlag führen)* throw a blow/blows; *(losschlagen)* hit *or* strike out; *(fig.)* ⟨*army, police, murderer*⟩ strike

zu|schließen **1.** *unr. tr. V.* lock; **2.** *unr. itr. V.* lock up

zu|schnüren *tr. V.* tie up

zu|schrauben *tr. V.* screw the lid *or* top on ⟨*jar, flask*⟩; screw ⟨*lid, top*⟩ on

Zu·schrift die letter; *(auf eine Anzeige)* reply

Zu·schuß der contribution (**zu** towards)

zu|sehen *unr. itr. V.* **a)** watch; **jmdm. [beim Arbeiten** *usw.*] ~: watch sb. [working *etc.*]; **b)** *(dafür sorgen)* make sure; see to it

zu|senden *unr. od. regelm. tr. V.: s.* zuschicken; **Zu·sendung die** sending

zu|spitzen *refl. V.* become aggravated

zu|sprechen **1.** *unr. tr. V.* **a)** **er sprach ihr Trost/Mut zu** his words gave her comfort/courage; **b)** **jmdm. ein Erbe** *usw.* ~: award sb. an inheritance *etc.*; **2.** *unr. itr. V.* **jmdm. ermutigend/tröstend** *usw.* ~: speak encouragingly/comfortingly to sb.

Zu·stand der a) condition; *(bes. abwertend)* state; **b)** *(Stand der Dinge)* state of affairs; **zu·stande** *Adv.* **etw. ~ bringen** [manage to] bring about sth.; **~ kommen** come into being; *(geschehen)* take place; **zu·ständig** *Adj.* appropriate relevant ⟨*authority, office, etc.*⟩; **[für etw.]** ~ **sein** *(verantwortlich)* be responsible [for sth.]

zu|stehen *unr. itr. V.* **etw. steht jmdm. zu** sb. is entitled to sth.

zu|steigen *unr. itr. V.; mit sein* get on;

ist noch jemand zugestiegen? *(im Bus)* ≈ any more fares, please?; *(im Zug)* ≈ tickets, please!

zu|stellen *tr. V.* deliver ⟨*letter, parcel, etc.*⟩

zu|stimmen *itr. V.* agree; **jmdm. [in einem Punkt]** ~: agree with sb. [on a point]; **einer Sache** *(Dat.)* ~: agree to sth.; **Zu·stimmung die** *(Billigung)* approval (**zu** of); *(Einverständnis)* agreement (**zu** to, with)

zu|stoßen *unr. itr. V.; mit sein* **jmdm.** ~: happen to sb.

Zu·tat die ingredient

zu·teil *Adv.* **jmdm./einer Sache ~ werden** *(geh.)* be granted to sb./sth.; **zu|teilen** *tr. V.* **jmdm. jmdn./etw.** ~: allot *or* assign sb./sth. to sb.; **jmdm. seine Portion** ~: mete out his/her share to sb.

zu|tragen *unr. refl. V. (geh.)* occur; **zuträglich** *Adj.* healthy ⟨*climate*⟩; **jmdm./einer Sache ~ sein** be good for sb./sth.; be beneficial to sb./sth.

zu|trauen *tr. V.* **jmdm. etw.** ~: believe sb. [is] capable of [doing] sth.; **sich** *(Dat.)* **etw.** ~: think one can do *or* is capable of doing sth.; **Zutrauen das;** ~s confidence, trust (**zu** in); **zutraulich 1.** *Adj.* trusting; **2.** *adv.* trustingly; **Zutraulichkeit die;** ~: trust[fulness]

zu|treffen *unr. itr. V.* **a)** be correct; **b)** **auf** *od.* **für jmdn./etw.** ~: apply to sb./ sth.; **zutreffend 1.** *Adj.* **a)** correct; **b)** *(geltend)* applicable; relevant; **2.** *adv.* correctly

zu|trinken *unr. itr. V.* **jmdm.** ~: raise one's glass and drink to sb.

Zu·tritt der entry; admittance; **,,kein ~", ,,~ verboten"** 'no entry'; 'no admittance'; **~ [zu etw.] haben** have access [to sth.]

zu·unterst *Adv.* right at the bottom

zuverlässig 1. *Adj.* reliable; *(verläßlich)* dependable ⟨*person*⟩; **2.** *adv.* reliably; **Zuverlässigkeit die;** ~: reliability; *(Verläßlichkeit)* dependability

zuversichtlich 1. *Adj.* confident; **2.** *adv.* confidently

zuviel 1. *indekl. Indefinitpron.* too much; *(ugs.: zu viele)* too many; **2.** *adv.* too much

zu·vor *Adv.* before

zuvor|kommen *unr. itr. V.; mit sein* **a)** **jmdm.** ~: beat sb. to it; **b)** **einer Sache** *(Dat.)* ~: anticipate sth.; **zuvorkommend 1.** *Adj.* obliging; *(höflich)* courteous; **2.** *adv.* obligingly; *(höf-lich)* courteously

zu·weilen *Adv. (geh.)* now and again

zu|weisen *unr. tr. V.* jmdm. etw. ~ : allocate *or* allot sb. sth.

zu|wenden *unr. od. regelm. refl. V.* sich jmdm./einer Sache ~ *(auch fig.)* turn to sb./sth.

zu·wenig **1.** *indekl. Indefinitpron.* too little; *(ugs.: zu wenige)* too few; **2.** *adv.* too little

zuwider *Adj.* jmdm. ~ sein be repugnant to sb.

zu|winken *itr. V.* jmdm./einander ~ : wave to sb./one another

zu|zahlen *tr. V.* pay ⟨five marks etc.⟩ extra

zu|ziehen **1.** *unr. tr. V.* pull ⟨door⟩ shut; draw ⟨curtain⟩; do up ⟨zip⟩; **2.** *unr. refl. V.* sich *(Dat.)* eine Krankheit ~ : catch an illness; **3.** *unr. itr. V.; mit sein* move into the area

zuzüglich *Präp. mit Gen.* plus

zwang *1. u. 3. Pers. Sg. Prät. v.* zwingen; **Zwang** *der;* ~|e|s, Zwänge **a)** compulsion; **b)** *(unwiderstehlicher Drang)* irresistible urge; **zwängen** **1.** *tr. V.* squeeze; **2.** *refl. V.* squeeze [oneself]; **zwanglos** **1.** *Adj.* **a)** informal; casual ⟨behaviour⟩; **b)** *(unregelmäßig)* haphazard ⟨arrangement⟩; **2.** *adv.* **a)** informally; **b)** *(unregelmäßig)* haphazardly ⟨arranged⟩; **Zwangs·lage** **die** predicament; **zwangs·läufig** **1.** *Adj.* inevitable; **2.** *adv.* inevitably

zwanzig *Kardinalz.* twenty; *s. auch* achtzig; **zwanziger** *indekl. Adj.; nicht präd.* **die** ~ Jahre the twenties; **Zwanzig·mark·schein** **der** twenty-mark note; **zwanzigst ...** *Ordinalz.* twentieth

zwar *Adv.* **a)** admittedly; **b)** und ~ : to be precise

Zweck *der;* ~|e|s, ~e purpose; *(Sinn)* point; es hat keinen ~ : it's pointless; es hat keinen ~, das zu tun there is no point in doing that

zweck-, Zweck-: ~los *Adj.* pointless; ~mäßig **1.** *Adj.* appropriate; expedient ⟨behaviour, action⟩; functional ⟨building, fittings, furniture⟩; **2.** *adv.* appropriately ⟨arranged, clothed⟩; ⟨act⟩ expediently; ⟨equip, furnish⟩ functionally; ~mäßigkeit **die** appropriateness; *(einer Handlung)* expediency; *(eines Gebäudes)* functionalism

zwecks *Präp. mit Gen. (Papierdt.)* for the purpose of

zwei *Kardinalz.* two; *s. auch* ¹acht; **Zwei** **die;** ~, ~en **a)** *(Zahl)* two; **b)** *(Schulnote)* B

zwei-, Zwei-: ~bettzimmer **das** twin-bedded room; ~deutig **1.** *Adj.* ambiguous; *(fig.: schlüpfrig)* suggestive ⟨remark, joke⟩; **2.** *adv.* ambiguously; *(fig.)* suggestively; ~deutigkeit **die;** ~, ~en ambiguity; *(fig.)* suggestiveness; ~dimensional **1.** *Adj.* two-dimensional; **2.** *adv.* two-dimensionally; ~ein·halb *Bruchz.* two and a half

zweierlei *Gattungsz.; indekl.* **a)** *attr.* two sorts *or* kinds of; two different ⟨sizes, kinds, etc.⟩; odd ⟨socks, gloves⟩; **b)** *(alleinstehend)* two [different] things; **zwei·fach** *Vervielfältigungsz.* double; *(~mal)* twice; **Zwei·fache** **das;** *adj. Dekl.* das ~ : twice as much

Zweifel *der;* ~s, ~ : doubt (an + *Dat.* about); etw. in ~ ziehen question sth.; **zweifelhaft** *Adj.* **a)** doubtful; **b)** *(fragwürdig)* dubious; *(suspekt)* suspicious; **zweifel·los** *Adv.* undoubtedly; **zweifeln** *itr. V.* doubt; an jmdm./etw. ~ : doubt sb./sth.; have doubts about sb./sth.

Zweig *der;* ~|e|s, ~e [small] branch; *(meist ohne Blätter)* twig

zwei-, Zwei-: ~hundert *Kardinalz.* two hundred; ~mal *Adv.* twice; ~mark·stück **das** two-mark piece; ~pfennig·stück **das** two-pfennig piece; ~reiher **der** double-breasted suit/coat/jacket; ~schneidig *Adj.* double-edged; ~sprachig **1.** *Adj.* bilingual; ⟨sign⟩ in two languages; **2.** *adv.* bilingually; ⟨written⟩ in two languages; ⟨published⟩ in a bilingual edition; ~spurig *Adj.* **a)** two-lane ⟨road⟩; **b)** two-track ⟨vehicle⟩; **c)** two- *or* twin-track ⟨recording⟩; ~stellig *Adj.* two-figure *attrib.* ⟨number, sum⟩; ~stöckig *Adj.* two-storey *attrib.;* ~stöckig sein have two storeys

zweit ... *Ordinalz.* second; jeder ~e every other one; *s. auch* erst...

zwei·tägig *Adj. (2 Tage alt)* two-day-old *attrib.; (2 Tage dauernd)* two-day *attrib.;* **zweit·ältest ...** *Adj.* second oldest; **zwei·tausend** *Kardinalz.* two thousand; **zweit·best...** *Adj.* second best

zweite·mal *Adv.* das ~ : for the second time; **zweiten·mal** *Adv.* zum ~ : for the second time; beim ~ : the second time [round]; **zweitens** *Adv* secondly; in the second place; **Zwei-te[r]-Klasse-Abteil das** second-class compartment; **zweit·rangig** *Adj.* of secondary importance *postpos.; (~klassig)* second-rate; **zweitürig** *Adj.* two-door ⟨*car*⟩

Zweit-: ~**wagen der** second car; ~**wohnung die** second home

Zwei·zimmerwohnung die two-room flat *(Brit.) or (Amer.)* apartment

Zwerg der; ~|e|s, ~e dwarf; *(Garten~)* gnome

Zwetsche die; ~, ~n damson plum

Zwieback der; ~|e|s, ~e *od.* Zwiebäcke rusk; *(unzählbar)* rusks *pl.*

Zwiebel die; ~, ~n onion; *(Blumen~)* bulb

zwie-, Zwie-: ~**gespräch das** *(geh.)* dialogue; ~**spalt der;** ~|e|s, ~e *od.* ~spälte [inner] conflict; ~**spältig** *Adj.* conflicting ⟨*mood, feelings*⟩; discordant ⟨*impression*⟩; *(widersprüchlich)* contradictory ⟨*nature, attitude, person, etc.*⟩

Zwilling der; ~s, ~e twin

Zwillings-: ~**bruder der** twin brother; ~**paar das** pair of twins; ~**schwester die** twin sister

zwingen 1. *unr. tr. V.* force; jmdn. zu etw. ~, jmdn. |dazu| ~, etw. zu tun force *or* compel sb. to do sth.; **zwingend** *Adj.* compelling ⟨*reason, logic*⟩; conclusive ⟨*proof, argument*⟩; imperative ⟨*necessity*⟩

zwinkern *itr. V.* |mit den Augen| ~: blink; *(als Zeichen)* wink

Zwirn der; ~|e|s, ~e [strong] thread *or* yarn

zwischen *Präp. mit Dat./Akk.* between; *(mitten unter)* among[st]

zwischen-, Zwischen-: ~**durch** [-'-] *Adv.* **a)** *(zeitlich)* between times; *(zwischen zwei Zeitpunkten)* in between; *(von Zeit zu Zeit)* from time to time; ~**fall der** incident; ~|**landen** *itr. V.; mit sein* in X ~landen land in X on the way; ~**mahlzeit die** snack [between meals]; ~**menschlich 1.** *Adj.* interpersonal ⟨*relations*⟩; ⟨*contacts*⟩ between people; **2.** *adv.* on a personal level; ~**raum der** space; gap; *(Lücke)* gap; ~**zeit die** interim

Zwist der; ~|e|s, ~e *(geh.)* strife *no indef. art.; (Fehde)* feud; dispute; **Zwistigkeit die;** ~, ~en *(geh.)* dispute

zwitschern *itr. (auch tr.) V.* chirp

Zwitter der; ~s, ~ *(Biol.)* hermaphrodite

zwo *Kardinalz. (ugs.; bes. zur Verdeutlichung)* two

zwölf *Kardinalz.* twelve; ~ Uhr mittags/nachts [twelve o'clock] midday/midnight; *s. auch* ¹**acht; zwölft...** *Ordinalz.* twelfth; *s. auch* **acht...; zwölftel** *Bruchz.* twelfth; *s. auch* **achtel; Zwölftel das** *(schweiz. meist* der) ~s, ~: twelfth

zwot... *Ordinalz. (ugs.; bes. bei Datumsangaben)* second; **zwotens** *Adv. (ugs.)* secondly

Zylinder [ts̱i'lɪndɐ] **der;** ~s, ~ **a)** cylinder; **b)** *(Hut)* top hat; **zylindrisch 1.** *Adj.* cylindrical; **2.** *adv.* cylindrically

zynisch 1. *Adj.* cynical; **2.** *adv.* cynically

Zynismus der; ~: cynicism

Zypern (das); ~s Cyprus; **Zyprer der;** ~s, ~, **Zyprerin die;** ~, ~nen Cypriot

Zypresse die; ~, ~n cypress

Zypriot der; ~en, ~en, **Zypriotin die;** ~, ~nen Cypriot; **zypriotisch, zyprisch** *Adj.* Cypriot

Zyste die; ~, ~n *(Med.)* cyst

Englische unregelmäßige Verben

Ein Sternchen (*) weist darauf hin, daß die korrekte Form von der jeweiligen Bedeutung abhängt.

Infinitive	Past Tense	Past Participle	Infinitive	Past Tense	Past Participle
Infinitiv	*Präteritum*	*2. Partizip*	*Infinitiv*	*Präteritum*	*2. Partizip*
arise	arose	arisen	flee	fled	fled
awake	awoke	awoken	fling	flung	flung
be	was *sing.*, were *pl.*	been	floodlight	floodlit	floodlit
			fly	flew	flown
bear	bore	borne	forbid	forbade, forbad	forbidden
beat	beat	beaten			
become	became	become	forecast	forecast, forecasted	forecast, forecasted
begin	began	begun			
bend	bent	bent	foretell	foretold	foretold
bet	bet, betted	bet, betted	forget	forgot	forgotten
bid	*bade, bid	*bidden, bid	forgive	forgave	forgiven
bind	bound	bound	forsake	forsook	forsaken
bite	bit	bitten	freeze	froze	frozen
bleed	bled	bled	get	got	got, *(Amer.)* gotten
blow	blew	blown			
break	broke	broken	give	gave	given
breed	bred	bred	go	went	gone
bring	brought	brought	grind	ground	ground
broadcast	broadcast	broadcast	grow	grew	grown
build	built	built	hang	*hung, hanged	*hung, hanged
burn	burnt, burned	burnt, burned			
burst	burst	burst	have	had	had
bust	bust, busted	bust, busted	hear	heard	heard
buy	bought	bought	hew	hewed	hewn, hewed
cast	cast	cast	hide	hid	hidden
catch	caught	caught	hit	hit	hit
choose	chose	chosen	hold	held	held
cling	clung	clung	hurt	hurt	hurt
come	came	come	keep	kept	kept
cost	*cost, costed	*cost, costed	kneel	knelt, *(esp. Amer.)* kneeled	knelt, *(esp. Amer.)* kneeled
creep	crept	crept			
cut	cut	cut			
deal	dealt	dealt	know	knew	known
dig	dug	dug	lay	laid	laid
dive	dived, *(Amer.)* dove	dived	lead	led	led
			lean	leaned, *(Brit.)* leant	leaned, *(Brit.)* leant
do	did	done			
draw	drew	drawn	leap	leapt, leaped	leapt, leaped
dream	dreamt, dreamed	dreamt, dreamed	learn	learnt, learned	learnt, learned
drink	drank	drunk	leave	left	left
drive	drove	driven	lend	lent	lent
dwell	dwelt	dwelt	let	let	let
eat	ate	eaten	²lie	lay	lain
fall	fell	fallen	light	lit, lighted	lit, lighted
feed	fed	fed	lose	lost	lost
feel	felt	felt	make	made	made
fight	fought	fought	mean	meant	meant
find	found	found	meet	met	met

Infinitive	Past Tense	Past Participle	Infinitive	Past Tense	Past Participle
Infinitiv	*Präteritum*	*2. Partizip*	*Infinitiv*	*Präteritum*	*2. Partizip*
mow	mowed	mown, mowed	spend	spent	spent
			spill	spilt, spilled	spilt, spilled
overhang	overhung	overhung	spin	spun	spun
pay	paid	paid	spit	spat, spit	spat, spit
prove	proved	proved, proven	split	split	split
			spoil	spoilt, spoiled	spoilt, spoiled
put	put	put			
quit	quitted, *(Amer.)* quit	quitted, *(Amer.)* quit	spread	spread	spread
			spring	sprang, *(Amer.)* sprung	sprung
read [ri:d]	read [red]	read [red]			
rid	rid	rid			
ride	rode	ridden	stand	stood	stood
²ring	rang	rung	steal	stole	stolen
rise	rose	risen	stick	stuck	stuck
run	ran	run	sting	stung	stung
saw	sawed	sawn, sawed	stink	stank, stunk	stunk
say	said	said	strew	strewed	strewed, strewn
see	saw	seen			
seek	sought	sought	stride	strode	stridden
sell	sold	sold	strike	struck	struck
send	sent	sent	string	strung	strung
set	set	set	strive	strove	striven
sew	sewed	sewn, sewed	sublet	sublet	sublet
shake	shook	shaken	swear	swore	sworn
shear	sheared	shorn, sheared	sweep	swept	swept
			swell	swelled	swollen, swelled
shed	shed	shed			
shine	shone	shone	swim	swam	swum
shit	shitted, shit	shitted, shit	swing	swung	swung
shoe	shod	shod	take	took	taken
shoot	shot	shot	teach	taught	taught
show	showed	shown	tear	tore	torn
shrink	shrank	shrunk	tell	told	told
shut	shut	shut	think	thought	thought
sing	sang	sung	thrive	thrived, throve	thrived, thriven
sink	sank, sunk	sunk			
sit	sat	sat	throw	threw	thrown
slay	slew	slain	thrust	thrust	thrust
sleep	slept	slept	tread	trod	trodden, trod
slide	slid	slid	understand	understood	understood
sling	slung	slung	undo	undid	undone
slink	slunk	slunk	wake	woke	woken
slit	slit	slit	wear	wore	worn
smell	smelt, smelled	smelt, smelled	¹weave	wove	woven
			weep	wept	wept
sow	sowed	sown, sowed	wet	wet, wetted	wet, wetted
speak	spoke	spoken	win	won	won
speed	*sped, speeded	*sped, speeded	²wind [waɪnd]	wound [waʊnd]	wound [waʊnd]
			wring	wrung	wrung
spell	spelled, *(Brit.)* spelt	spelled, *(Brit.)* spelt	write	wrote	written

German irregular verbs

Irregular and partly irregular verbs are listed alphabetically by infinitive. 1st, 2nd, and 3rd person present and imperative forms are given after the infinitive, and preterite subjunctive forms after the preterite indicative, where they take an umlaut, change *e* to *i*, etc.

Verbs with a raised number in the German-English section of the Dictionary have the same number in this list.

Compound verbs (including verbs with prefixes) are only given if a) they do not take the same forms as the corresponding simple verb, e.g. *befehlen*, or b) there is no corresponding simple verb, e.g. *bewegen*.

An asterisk (*) indicates a verb which is also conjugated regularly.

Infinitive *Infinitiv*	Preterite *Präteritum*	Past Participle *2. Partizip*
abwägen	wog (wöge) ab	abgewogen
backen (du bäckst, er bäckt; *auch:* du backst, er backt)	backte, *älter:* buk (büke)	gebacken
befehlen (du befiehlst, er befiehlt; befiehl!)	befahl (beföhle, befähle)	befohlen
beginnen	begann (begänne, *seltener:* begönne)	begonnen
beißen	biß	gebissen
bergen (du birgst, er birgt; birg!)	barg (bärge)	geborgen
bersten (du birst, er birst; birst!)	barst (bärste)	geborsten
besinnen	besann (besänne)	besonnen
²bewegen	bewog (bewöge)	bewogen
biegen	bog (böge)	gebogen
bieten	bot (böte)	geboten
binden	band (bände)	gebunden
bitten	bat (bäte)	gebeten
blasen (du bläst, er bläst)	blies	geblasen
bleiben	blieb	geblieben
bleichen*	blich	geblichen
braten (du brätst, er brät)	briet	gebraten
brechen (du brichst, er bricht; brich!)	brach (bräche)	gebrochen
brennen	brannte (brennte)	gebrannt
bringen	brachte (brächte)	gebracht
denken	dachte (dächte)	gedacht
dreschen (du drischst, er drischt; drisch!)	drosch (drösche)	gedroschen
dringen	drang (dränge)	gedrungen
dürfen (ich darf, du darfst, er darf)	durfte (dürfte)	gedurft
empfehlen (du empfiehlst, er empfiehlt; empfiehl!)	empfahl (empföhle, *seltener:* empfähle)	empfohlen
erklimmen	erklomm (erklömme)	erklommen
erlöschen (du erlischst, er erlischt; erlisch!)	erlosch (erlösche)	erloschen
erschallen*	erscholl (erschölle)	erschollen
·³erschrecken (du erschrickst, er erschrickt; erschrick!)	erschrak (erschräke)	erschrocken
erwägen	erwog (erwöge)	erwogen

Infinitive *Infinitiv*	Preterite *Präteritum*	Past Participle *2. Partizip*
essen (du ißt, er ißt; iß!)	aß (äße)	gegessen
fahren (du fährst, er fährt)	fuhr (führe)	gefahren
fallen (du fällst, er fällt)	fiel	gefallen
fangen (du fängst, er fängt)	fing	gefangen
fechten (du fichtst, er ficht; ficht!)	focht (föchte)	gefochten
finden	fand (fände)	gefunden
flechten (du flichtst, er flicht; flicht!)	flocht (flöchte)	geflochten
fliegen	flog (flöge)	geflogen
fliehen	floh (flöhe)	geflohen
fließen	floß (flösse)	geflossen
fressen (du frißt, er frißt; friß!)	fraß (fräße)	gefressen
frieren	fror (fröre)	gefroren
gären*	gor (göre)	gegoren
gebären (*geh.:* du gebierst, sie gebiert; gebier!)	gebar (gebäre)	geboren
geben (du gibst, er gibt; gib!)	gab (gäbe)	gegeben
gedeihen	gedieh	gediehen
gehen	ging	gegangen
gelingen	gelang (gelänge)	gelungen
gelten (du giltst, er gilt; gilt!)	galt (gölte, gälte)	gegolten
genesen	genas (genäse)	genesen
genießen	genoß (genösse)	genossen
geschehen (es geschieht)	geschah (geschähe)	geschehen
gewínnen	gewann (gewönne, gewänne)	gewonnen
gießen	goß (gösse)	gegossen
gleichen	glich	geglichen
gleiten	glitt	geglitten
glimmen	glomm (glömme)	geglommen
graben (du gräbst, er gräbt)	grub (grübe)	gegraben
greifen	griff	gegriffen
haben (du hast, er hat)	hatte (hätte)	gehabt
halten (du hältst, er hält)	hielt	gehalten
[1]hängen	hing	gehangen
hauen	haute, *geh.:* hieb	gehauen
heben	hob (höbe)	gehoben
heißen	hieß	geheißen
helfen (du hilfst, er hilft; hilf!)	half (hülfe, *selten:* hälfe)	geholfen
kennen	kannte (kennte)	gekannt
klingen	klang (klänge)	geklungen
kneifen	kniff	gekniffen
kommen	kam (käme)	gekommen
können (ich kann, du kannst, er kann)	konnte (könnte)	gekonnt
kriechen	kroch (kröche)	gekrochen
[1,2]laden (du lädst, er lädt)	lud (lüde)	geladen
lassen (du läßt, er läßt)	ließ	gelassen
laufen (du läufst, er läuft)	lief	gelaufen
leiden	litt	gelitten
leihen	lieh	geliehen
[1,2]lesen (du liest, er liest; lies!)	las (läse)	gelesen
liegen	lag (läge)	gelegen
lügen	log (löge)	gelogen
mahlen	mahlte	gemahlen
meiden	mied	gemieden

Infinitive *Infinitiv*	Preterite *Präteritum*	Past Participle *2. Partizip*
melken* (du milkst, er milkt; milk!; du melkst, er melkt; melke!)	molk (mölke)	gemolken
messen (du mißt, er mißt; miß!)	maß (mäße)	gemessen
mißlingen	mißlang (mißlänge)	mißlungen
mögen (ich mag, du magst, er mag)	mochte (möchte)	gemocht
müssen (ich muß, du mußt, er muß)	mußte (müßte)	gemußt
nehmen (du nimmst, er nimmt; nimm!)	nahm (nähme)	genommen
nennen	nannte (nennte)	genannt
pfeifen	pfiff	gepfiffen
preisen	pries	gepriesen
quellen (du quillst, er quillt; quill!)	quoll (quölle)	gequollen
raten (du rätst, er rät)	riet	geraten
reiben	rieb	gerieben
reißen	riß	gerissen
reiten	ritt	geritten
rennen	rannte (rennte)	gerannt
riechen	roch (röche)	gerochen
ringen	rang (ränge)	gerungen
rinnen	rann (ränne, *seltener:* rönne)	geronnen
rufen	rief	gerufen
salzen*	salzte	gesalzen
saufen (du säufst, er säuft)	soff (söffe)	gesoffen
saugen*	sog (söge)	gesogen
schaffen*	schuf (schüfe)	geschaffen
schallen*	scholl (schölle)	geschallt
scheiden	schied	geschieden
scheinen	schien	geschienen
scheißen	schiß	geschissen
schelten (du schiltst, er schilt; schilt!)	schalt (schölte)	gescholten
¹scheren	schor (schöre)	geschoren
schieben	schob (schöbe)	geschoben
schießen	schoß (schösse)	geschossen
schinden	schindete	geschunden
schlafen (du schläfst, er schläft)	schlief	geschlafen
schlagen (du schlägst, er schlägt)	schlug (schlüge)	geschlagen
schleichen	schlich	geschlichen
¹schleifen	schliff	geschliffen
schließen	schloß (schlösse)	geschlossen
schlingen	schlang (schlänge)	geschlungen
schmeißen	schmiß	geschmissen
schmelzen (du schmilzt, er schmilzt; schmilz!)	schmolz	geschmolzen
schneiden	schnitt	geschnitten
schrecken* (du schrickst, er schrickt; schrick!)	schrak (schräke)	geschreckt
schreiben	schrieb	geschrieben
schreien	schrie	geschrie[e]n
schreiten	schritt	geschritten
schweigen	schwieg	geschwiegen
schwellen (du schwillst, er schwillt; schwill!)	schwoll (schwölle)	geschwollen
schwimmen	schwamm (schwömme, *seltener:* schwämme)	geschwommen

| Infinitive | Preterite | Past Participle |
Infinitiv	*Präteritum*	*2. Partizip*
schwinden	schwand (schwände)	geschwunden
schwingen	schwang (schwänge)	geschwungen
schwören	schwor (schwüre)	geschworen
sehen (du siehst, er sieht; sieh[e]!)	sah (sähe)	gesehen
sein (ich bin, du bist, er ist, wir sind, ihr seid, sie sind; sei!)	war (wäre)	gewesen
senden*	sandte (sendete)	gesandt
sieden*	sott (sötte)	gesotten
singen	sang (sänge)	gesungen
sinken	sank (sänke)	gesunken
sitzen	saß (säße)	gesessen
sollen (ich soll, du sollst, er soll)	sollte	gesollt
spalten*	spaltete	gespalten
speien	spie	gespie[e]n
spinnen	spann (spönne, spänne)	gesponnen
sprechen (du sprichst, er spricht; sprich!)	sprach (spräche)	gesprochen
sprießen	sproß (sprösse)	gesprossen
springen	sprang	gesprungen
stechen (du stichst, er sticht; stich!)	stach (stäche)	gestochen
stehen	stand (stünde, *auch:* stände)	gestanden
stehlen (du stiehlst, er stiehlt; stiehl!)	stahl (stähle, *seltener:* stöhle)	gestohlen
steigen	stieg	gestiegen
sterben (du stirbst, er stirbt; stirb!)	starb (stürbe)	gestorben
stinken	stank (stänke)	gestunken
stoßen (du stößt, er stößt)	stieß	gestoßen
streichen	strich	gestrichen
streiten	stritt	gestritten
tragen (du trägst, er trägt)	trug (trüge)	getragen
treffen (du triffst; er trifft; triff!)	traf (träfe)	getroffen
treiben	trieb	getrieben
treten (du trittst, er tritt; tritt!)	trat (träte)	getreten
triefen*	troff (tröffe)	getroffen
trinken	trank (tränke)	getrunken
trügen	trog (tröge)	getrogen
tun	tat (täte)	getan
verderben (du verdirbst, er verdirbt; verdirb!)	verdarb (verdürbe)	verdorben
verdrießen	verdroß (verdrösse)	verdrossen
vergessen (du vergißt, er vergißt, vergiß!)	vergaß (vergäße)	vergessen
verlieren	verlor (verlöre)	verloren
verschleißen*	verschliß	verschlissen
verzeihen	verzieh	verziehen
¹wachsen (du wächst, er wächst)	wuchs (wüchse)	gewachsen
waschen (du wäschst, er wäscht)	wusch (wüsche)	gewaschen
weichen	wich	gewichen
weisen	wies	gewiesen
²wenden*	wandte (wendete)	gewandt
werben (du wirbst, er wirbt; wirb!)	warb (würbe)	geworben
werden (du wirst, er wird; werde!)	wurde, *dichter.:* ward (würde)	geworden; *als Hilfsv.:* worden
werfen (du wirfst, er wirft; wirf!)	warf (würfe)	geworfen
¹wiegen	wog (wöge)	gewogen

Infinitive *Infinitiv*	Preterite *Präteritum*	Past Participle *2. Partizip*
winden	wand (wände)	gewunden
wissen (ich weiß, du weißt, er weiß)	wußte (wüßte)	gewußt
wollen (ich will, du willst, er will)	wollte	gewollt
wringen	wrang (wränge)	gewrungen
ziehen	zog (zöge)	gezogen
zwingen	zwang (zwänge)	gezwungen

Weights and Measures / Maße und Gewichte

Weight / Gewichte

1,000 milligrams (mg) *1 000 Milligramm (mg)*	= 1 gram (g) *= 1 Gramm (g)*	= 15.43 grains
1,000 grams *1 000 Gramm*	= 1 kilogram (kg) *= 1 Kilogramm (kg)*	= 2.205 pounds
1,000 kilograms *1 000 Kilogramm*	= 1 tonne (t) *= 1 Tonne (t)*	= 19.684 hundredweight
	1 grain (gr.)	= 0.065 g
437½ grains	= 1 ounce (oz.)	= 28.35 g
16 ounces	= 1 pound (lb.)	= 0.454 kg
14 pounds	= 1 stone (st.)	= 6.35 kg
112 pounds	= 1 hundredweight	= 50.8 kg
20 hundredweight	= 1 ton (t.)	= 1,016.05 kg

Length / Längenmaße

10 millimetres (mm) *10 Millimeter (mm)*	= 1 centimetre (cm) *= 1 Zentimeter (cm)*	= 0.394 inch
100 centimetres *100 Zentimeter*	= 1 metre (m) *= 1 Meter (m)*	= 39.4 inches / 1.094 yards
1,000 metres *1 000 Meter*	= 1 kilometre (km) *= 1 Kilometer (km)*	= 0.6214 mile ≈ ⅝ mile
	1 inch (in.)	= 25.4 mm
12 inches	= 1 foot (ft.)	= 30.48 cm
3 feet	= 1 yard (yd.)	= 0.914 m
220 yards	= 1 furlong	= 201.17 m
8 furlongs	= 1 mile (m.)	= 1.609 km
,760 yards	= 1 mile	= 1.609 km

Square measure / Flächenmaße

100 square metres (sq. m)	= 1 are	= 0.025 acre
100 Quadratmeter (m²)	= *1 Ar (a)*	
100 ares	= 1 hectare (ha)	= 2.471 acres
100 Ar	= *1 Hektar (ha)*	
100 hectares	= 1 square kilometre (sq. km)	= 0.386 square miles
100 Hektar	= *1 Quadratkilometer (km²)*	

	1 square inch	=	6.452 cm²
144 square inches	= 1 square foot	=	929.03 cm²
9 square feet	= 1 square yard	=	0.836 m²
4,840 square yards	= 1 acre	=	0.405 ha
640 acres	= 1 square mile	=	2.59 k²/ 259 ha

Cubic measure / Raummaße

1 cubic centimetre (cc)		= 0.06 cubic inches
1 Kubikzentimeter (cm³)		
1,000,000 cubic centimetres	= 1 cubic metre (cu. m)	= 35.714 cubic feet /
1 000 000 Kubikzentimeter	= *1 Kubikmeter (m³)*	1.307 cubic yards

	1 cubic inch	=	16.4 cm³
1,728 cubic inches	= 1 cubic foot	=	0.028 m³
27 cubic feet	= 1 cubic yard	=	0.764 m³

Capacity / Hohlmaße

10 millilitres (ml)	= 1 centilitre (cl)	
10 Milliliter (ml)	= *1 Zentiliter (cl)*	
100 centilitres	= 1 litre (l)	= 1.76 pints (2.1 US pints)/ 0.22 gallons (0.264 US gallons)
100 Zentiliter	= *1 Liter (l)*	

4 gills	= 1 pint (pt.) (1.201 US pints)	= 0.568 l
2 pints	= 1 quart (qt.) (1.201 US quarts)	= 1.136 l
4 quarts	= 1 gallon (gal.) (1.201 US gallons)	= 4.546 l

Revisions to German spelling / die neue Regelung der Rechtschreibung

In July 1996, after much debate, wide-ranging changes to the spelling of German were agreed and ratified by the governments of Germany, Austria, and Switzerland. The following list, whilst not all-encompassing, details those changes which may be of interest to the user of this dictionary. It is worth noting that although these reforms are valid immediately, they will not be expected to be reflected in all written texts until 2005. Until that date, both old and new spellings will be acceptable.

The following list contains words which are not included in the A–Z text of this dictionary. Nonetheless, it is the editors' view that the learner of German will gain a better overview of the systematic changes involved by studying a more comprehensive list of words affected by the reforms.

alt	neu
A	
[gestern, heute, morgen] abend	[gestern, heute, morgen] Abend
aberhundert	*auch:* Aberhundert
Aberhunderte	*auch:* aberhunderte
abertausend	*auch:* Abertausend
Abertausende	*auch:* abertausende
Abfluß	Abfluss
abgeblaßt	abgeblasst
Abguß	Abguss
Ablaß	Ablass
Abriß	Abriss
Abschluß	Abschluss
Abschuß	Abschuss
absein	ab sein
Abszeß	Abszess
abwärtsgehen	abwärts gehen
in acht nehmen	in Acht nehmen
außer acht lassen	außer Acht lassen
8achser	8-Achser
der/die achte, den/die ich sehe	der/die Achte, den/die ich sehe

alt	neu
jeder/jede achte kommt mit	jeder/jede Achte kommt mit
achtgeben	Acht geben
achthaben	Acht haben
8jährig	8-jährig
der/die 8jährige	der/die 8-Jährige
8mal	8-mal
achtmillionenmal	acht Millionen Mal
8tonner	8-Tonner
achtunggebietend	Achtung gebietend
über Achtzig	über achtzig
Mitte [der] Achtzig	Mitte [der] achtzig
in die Achtzig kommen	in die achtzig kommen
die achtziger Jahre	*auch:* die Achtzigerjahre*
die Achtzigerjahre	*auch:* die achtziger Jahre
ackerbautreibende Völker	Ackerbau treibende Völker
Action-painting	Actionpainting
	auch: Action-Painting
ade sagen	*auch:* Ade sagen*
Aderlaß	Aderlass
Adhäsionsverschluß	Adhäsionsverschluss
Adreßbuch	Adressbuch
afro-amerikanisch	afroamerikanisch
afro-asiatisch	afroasiatisch
Afro-Look	Afrolook
After-shave	Aftershave
ich habe ähnliches erlebt	ich habe Ähnliches erlebt
und/oder ähnliches (u. ä./o. ä.)	und/oder Ähnliches (u. Ä./o. Ä.)
Alkoholmißbrauch	Alkoholmissbrauch
alleinerziehend	allein erziehend
alleinseligmachend	allein selig machend
alleinstehend	allein stehend
es ist das allerbeste, daß ...	es ist das Allerbeste, dass ...
im allgemeinen	im Allgemeinen
allgemeingültig	allgemein gültig
allgemeinverständlich	allgemein verständlich
allzubald	allzu bald

alt	neu
allzufrüh	allzu früh
allzugern	allzu gern
allzulange	allzu lange
allzuoft	allzu oft
allzusehr	allzu sehr
allzuviel	allzu viel
allzuweit	allzu weit
Alma mater	Alma Mater
Alpdruck	*auch:* Albdruck
Alptraum	*auch:* Albtraum
als daß	als dass
aus alt mach neu	aus Alt mach Neu
für alt und jung	für Alt und Jung
er ist immer der alte geblieben	er ist immer der Alte geblieben
alles beim alten lassen	alles beim Alten lassen
Alter ego	Alter Ego
altwienerisch	alt-wienerisch
Amboß	Amboss
Anbiß	Anbiss
andersdenkend	anders denkend
andersgeartet	anders geartet
anderslautend	anders lautend
aneinanderfügen	aneinander fügen
aneinandergeraten	aneinander geraten
aneinandergrenzen	aneinander grenzen
aneinanderlegen	aneinander legen
aneinanderreihen	aneinander reihen
angepaßt	angepasst
Angepaßtheit	Angepasstheit
Anglo-Amerikaner	Angloamerikaner
jmdm. angst machen	jmdm. Angst machen
anheimfallen	anheim fallen
anheimstellen	anheim stellen
Anlaß	Anlass
anläßlich	anlässlich
Anriß	Anriss

alt	neu
Anschiß	Anschiss
Anschluß	Anschluss
ansein	an sein
der Archimedische Punkt	der archimedische Punkt
im argen liegen	im Argen liegen
bei arm und reich	bei Arm und Reich
Armee-Einheit	*auch:* Armeeeinheit
Aschantinuß	Aschantinuss
As	Ass
aufeinanderbeißen	aufeinander beißen
aufeinanderfolgen	aufeinander folgen
aufeinandertreffen	aufeinander treffen
aufgepaßt!	aufgepasst!
aufgerauht	aufgeraut
Aufguß	Aufguss
Auflösungsprozeß	Auflösungsprozess
aufrauhen	aufrauen
Aufriß	Aufriss
Aufschluß	Aufschluss
aufschlußreich	aufschlussreich
ein aufsehenerregendes Ereignis	ein Aufsehen erregendes Ereignis
aufsein	auf sein
auf seiten	aufseiten
	auch: auf Seiten
der aufsichtführende Lehrer	der Aufsicht führende Lehrer
aufwärtsgehen	aufwärts gehen
aufwendig	*auch:* aufwändig
auseinanderbiegen	auseinander biegen
auseinanderfallen	auseinander fallen
auseinandergehen	auseinander gehen
auseinanderhalten	auseinander halten
auseinanderleben	auseinander leben
auseinanderreißen	auseinander reißen
auseinandersetzen	auseinander setzen
Ausfluß	Ausfluss
Ausguß	Ausguss

alt	neu
Ausschluß	Ausschluss
Ausschuß	Ausschuss
aussein	aus sein
aufs äußerste gespannt	*auch:* aufs Äußerste gespannt
außerstande	*auch:* außer Stande

B

alt	neu
Bajonettverschluß	Bajonettverschluss
Ballettänzerin	Balletttänzerin
	auch: Ballett-Tänzerin
Ballokal	Balllokal
	auch: Ball-Lokal
Bänderriß	Bänderriss
jmdm. [angst und] bange machen	jmdm. [Angst und] Bange machen
bankrott gehen	Bankrott gehen
Baroneß	Baroness
baselstädtisch	basel-städtisch
baß erstaunt	bass erstaunt
Baß	Bass
Baßgeige	Bassgeige
Baßsänger	Basssänger
	auch: Bass-Sänger
Baukostenzuschuß	Baukostenzuschuss
beeinflußbar	beeinflussbar
Beeinflußbarkeit	Beeinflussbarkeit
beeinflußt	beeinflusst
befaßt	befasst
Begrüßungskuß	Begrüßungskuss
behende	behände
Behendigkeit	Behändigkeit
beieinanderhaben	beieinander haben
beieinandersein	beieinander sein
beieinandersitzen	beieinander sitzen
beieinanderstehen	beieinander stehen
beifallheischend	Beifall heischend
beisammensein	beisammen sein

alt	neu
Beischluß	Beischluss
belemmert	belämmert
jeder beliebige	jeder Beliebige
Beschiß	Beschiss
Beschluß	Beschluss
beschlußfähig	beschlussfähig
Beschlußfassung	Beschlussfassung
Beschuß	Beschuss
ich will im besonderen erwähnen ...	ich will im Besonderen erwähnen ...
bessergehen	besser gehen
es ist das beste, wenn ...	es ist das Beste, wenn ...
aufs beste geregelt sein	*auch:* aufs Beste geregelt sein
zum besten geben	zum Besten geben
zum besten haben/halten	zum Besten haben/halten
das erste beste	das erste Beste
bestehenbleiben	bestehen bleiben
Bestelliste	Bestellliste
	auch: Bestell-Liste
bestgehaßt	bestgehasst
bestußt	bestusst
Betelnuß	Betelnuss
um ein beträchtliches höher	um ein Beträchtliches höher
in betreff	in Betreff
betreßt	betresst
Bettuch *[zu: Bett]*	Betttuch
	auch: Bett-Tuch
bevorschußt	bevorschusst
bewußt	bewusst
bewußtlos	bewusstlos
Bewußtlosigkeit	Bewusstlosigkeit
Bewußtsein	Bewusstsein
in bezug auf	in Bezug auf
bezuschußt	bezuschusst
Bibliographie	*auch:* Bibliografie
Bierfaß	Bierfass

alt	neu
die Bismarckschen Sozialgesetze	die bismarckschen Sozialgesetze
	auch: die Bismarck'schen
	Sozialgesetze
Biß	Biss
bißchen	bisschen
du sollst bitte sagen	*auch:* du sollst Bitte sagen*
es ist bitter kalt	es ist bitterkalt
Bittag	Bitttag
	auch: Bitt-Tag
Blackout	*auch:* Black-out*
blankpoliert	blank poliert
blaß	blass
Bläßhuhn/Bleßhuhn	Blässhuhn/Blesshuhn
bläßlich	blässlich
blaßrosa	blassrosa
Blattschuß	Blattschuss
der blaue Planet *[die Erde]*	der Blaue Planet
blaugestreift	blau gestreift
bläulichgrün	bläulich grün
bleibenlassen	bleiben lassen
blendendweiß	blendend weiß
blondgefärbt	blond gefärbt
Bluterguß	Bluterguss
Bonbonniere	*auch:* Bonboniere
Börsentip	Börsentipp
im bösen wie im guten	im Bösen wie im Guten
Boß	Boss
Bouclé	*auch:* Buklee
braungebrannt	braun gebrannt
bräunlichgelb	bräunlich gelb
des langen und breiten	des Langen und Breiten
breitgefächert	breit gefächert
Brennessel	Brennnessel
	auch: Brenn-Nessel
Bruderkuß	Bruderkuss
Brummbaß	Brummbass

807

alt	neu
brütendheiß	brütend heiß
buntgefiedert	bunt gefiedert
buntschillernd	bunt schillernd
Büroschluß	Büroschluss
Butterfaß	Butterfass

C

Cashewnuß	Cashewnuss
Centre Court	Centrecourt
	auch: Centre-Court
Chansonnier	*auch:* Chansonier
Choreographie	*auch:* Choreografie
Cleverneß	Cleverness
Comeback	*auch:* Come-back*
Common sense	Commonsense
	auch: Common Sense
Corned beef	Cornedbeef
	auch: Corned Beef
Corpus delicti	Corpus Delicti
Countdown	*auch:* Count-down*

D

dabeisein	dabei sein
Dachgeschoß	Dachgeschoss *[in Österreich weiterhin mit ß]*
dahinterklemmen	dahinter klemmen
dahinterkommen	dahinter kommen
Dampfschiffahrt	Dampfschifffahrt
Danaidenfaß	Danaidenfass
darauffolgend	darauf folgend
Darmverschluß	Darmverschluss
darüberstehen	darüber stehen
dasein	da sein
daß	dass
daß-Satz	dass-Satz
	auch: Dasssatz

alt	neu
datenverarbeitend	Daten verarbeitend
Dein *[in Briefen]*	dein
mein und dein verwechseln	Mein und Dein verwechseln
die Deinen	*auch:* die deinen
die Deinigen	*auch:* die deinigen
Dekolleté	*auch:* Dekolletee
Delikateßgurke	Delikatessgurke
Delikateßsenf	Delikatesssenf
	auch: Delikatess-Senf
Delphin	*auch:* Delfin
Denkprozeß	Denkprozess
wir haben derartiges nicht bemerkt	wir haben Derartiges nicht bemerkt
dessenungeachtet	dessen ungeachtet
des weiteren	des Weiteren
auf deutsch	auf Deutsch
deutschsprechend	Deutsch sprechend
das d'Hondtsche System	das d'hondtsche System
	auch: das d'Hondt'sche System
diät leben	Diät leben
Dich *[in Briefen]*	dich
dichtbehaart	dicht behaart
dichtgedrängt	dicht gedrängt
Differential	*auch:* Differenzial*
Diktaphon	*auch:* Diktafon
Dir *[in Briefen]*	dir
Doppelpaß	Doppelpass
dortbleiben	dort bleiben
dortzulande	*auch:* dort zu Lande
draufsein	drauf sein
Dreß	Dress
etwas aufs dringendste fordern	*auch:* etwas aufs Dringendste fordern
drinsein	drin sein
jeder dritte, der mitwollte	jeder Dritte, der mitwollte
zum dritten	zum Dritten

alt	neu
die dritte Welt	die Dritte Welt
drückendheiß	drückend heiß
Du *[in Briefen]*	du
auf du und du stehen	auf Du und Du stehen
im dunkeln tappen	im Dunkeln tappen
im dunkeln bleiben	im Dunkeln bleiben
dünnbesiedelt	dünn besiedelt
Dünnschiß	Dünnschiss
durcheinanderbringen	durcheinander bringen
durcheinandergeraten	durcheinander geraten
durcheinanderlaufen	durcheinander laufen
Durchfluß	Durchfluss
Durchlaß	Durchlass
durchnumerieren	durchnummerieren
Durchschuß	Durchschuss
durchsein	durch sein
dußlig	dusslig
Dußligkeit	Dussligkeit
Dutzende Reklamationen	*auch:* dutzende Reklamationen
Dutzende von Reklamationen	*auch:* dutzende von Reklamationen

E

alt	neu
ebensogut	ebenso gut
ebensosehr	ebenso sehr
ebensoviel	ebenso viel
ebensowenig	ebenso wenig
an Eides Statt	an Eides statt
sein eigen nennen	sein Eigen nennen
sich zu eigen machen	sich zu Eigen machen
einbleuen	einbläuen
aufs eindringlichste warnen	*auch:* aufs Eindringlichste warnen
das einfachste ist, wenn ...	das Einfachste ist, wenn ...
Einfluß	Einfluss
einflußreich	einflussreich

alt	neu
aufs eingehendste untersuchen	*auch:* aufs Eingehendste untersuchen
einiggehen	einig gehen
Einlaß	Einlass
einläßlich	einlässlich
Einriß	Einriss
Einschluß	Einschluss
Einschuß	Einschuss
Einschußstelle	Einschussstelle
	auch: Einschuss-Stelle
Einsendeschluß	Einsendeschluss
einwärtsgebogen	einwärts gebogen
der/die/das einzelne kann ...	der/die/das Einzelne kann ...
jeder einzelne von uns	jeder Einzelne von uns
bis ins einzelne geregelt	bis ins Einzelne geregelt
ins einzelne gehend	ins Einzelne gehend
einzelnstehend	einzeln stehend
der/die/das einzige wäre ...	der/die/das Einzige wäre ...
kein einziger war gekommen	kein Einziger war gekommen
er als einziger/sie als einzige hatte ...	er als Einziger/sie als Einzige hatte ...
das einzigartige ist, daß ...	das Einzigartige ist, dass ...
Eisenguß	Eisenguss
die eisenverarbeitende Industrie	die Eisen verarbeitende Industrie
eisigkalt	eisig kalt
eislaufen	Eis laufen
Eisschnellauf	Eisschnelllauf
Eisschnelläufer	Eisschnellläufer
energiebewußt	energiebewusst
aufs engste verflochten	*auch:* aufs Engste verflochten
engbefreundet	eng befreundet
engbedruckt	eng bedruckt
Engpaß	Engpass
nicht im entferntesten beabsichtigen	*auch:* nicht im Entferntesten beabsichtigen

alt	neu
auf das entschiedenste zurückweisen	*auch:* auf das Entschiedenste zurückweisen
Entschluß	Entschluss
ein Entweder-Oder gibt es hier nicht	ein Entweder-oder gibt es hier nicht
Entwicklungsprozeß	Entwicklungsprozess
erblaßt	erblasst
Erdgeschoß	Erdgeschoss *[in Österreich weiterhin mit ß]*
Erdnuß	Erdnuss
die erdölexportierenden Länder	die Erdöl exportierenden Länder
erfaßbar	erfassbar
erfaßt	erfasst
Erguß	Erguss
erholungsuchende Großstädter	Erholung suchende Großstädter
Erlaß	Erlass
ermeßbar	ermessbar
ernstgemeint	ernst gemeint
ernstzunehmend	ernst zu nehmend
erpreßbar	erpressbar
nicht den erstbesten nehmen	nicht den Erstbesten nehmen
der erste, der gekommen ist	der Erste, der gekommen ist
das reicht fürs erste	das reicht fürs Erste
zum ersten, zum zweiten, zum dritten	zum Ersten, zum Zweiten, zum Dritten
die Erste Hilfe	die erste Hilfe
das erstemal	das erste Mal
zum erstenmal	zum ersten Mal
Erstkläßler	Erstklässler
die Erstplazierten	die Erstplatzierten
eßbar	essbar
Eßbesteck	Essbesteck
Eßecke	Essecke
essentiell	*auch:* essenziell*
Eßlöffel	Esslöffel
eßlöffelweise	esslöffelweise

alt	neu
Eßtisch	Esstisch
etlichemal	etliche Mal
Euch *[in Briefen]*	euch
Euer *[in Briefen]*	euer
die Euren	*auch:* die euren
die Eurigen	*auch:* die eurigen
Existentialismus	*auch:* Existenzialismus*
existentialistisch	*auch:* existenzialistisch*
existentiell	*auch:* existenziell*
Exportüberschuß	Exportüberschuss
Exposé	*auch:* Exposee
expreß	express
Expreßreinigung	Expressreinigung
Expreßzug	Expresszug
Exzeß	Exzess
F	
Fabrikationsprozeß	Fabrikationsprozess
fahrenlassen	fahren lassen
Fairneß	Fairness
Fair play	Fairplay
	auch: Fair Play
fallenlassen	fallen lassen
Fallinie	Falllinie
	auch: Fall-Linie
Fallout	*auch:* Fall-out*
Familienanschluß	Familienanschluss
Fangschuß	Fangschuss
Faß	Fass
faßbar	fassbar
Faßbier	Fassbier
Fäßchen	Fässchen
faßlich	fasslich
du faßt	du fasst
Fast food	Fastfood
	auch: Fast Food

alt	neu
Faxanschluß	Faxanschluss
Feedback	*auch:* Feed-back*
Fehlpaß	Fehlpass
Fehlschuß	Fehlschuss
jmdm. feind sein	jmdm. Feind sein
feingemahlen	fein gemahlen
fernliegen	fern liegen
fertigbringen	fertig bringen
fertigstellen	fertig stellen
Fertigungsprozeß	Fertigungsprozess
festangestellt	fest angestellt
festumrissen	fest umrissen
festverwurzelt	fest verwurzelt
fettgedruckt	fett gedruckt
feuerspeiende Drachen	Feuer speiende Drachen
die fischverarbeitende Industrie	die Fisch verarbeitende Industrie
Fitneß	Fitness
Flachschuß	Flachschuss
fleischfressende Pflanzen	Fleisch fressende Pflanzen
Flohbiß	Flohbiss
das Bier floß in Strömen	das Bier floss in Strömen
flötengehen	flöten gehen
Fluß	Fluss
flußabwärts	flussabwärts
flußaufwärts	flussaufwärts
Flußbett	Flussbett
Flüßchen	Flüsschen
Flußdiagramm	Flussdiagramm
flüssigmachen	flüssig machen
Flußsand	Flusssand
	auch: Fluss-Sand
Flußschiffahrt	Flussschifffahrt
	auch: Fluss-Schifffahrt
Flußspat	Flussspat
	auch: Fluss-Spat
die Haare fönen	die Haare föhnen

folgendes ist zu beachten	Folgendes ist zu beachten
wie im folgenden erläutert	wie im Folgenden erläutert
Fraktionsausschuß	Fraktionsausschuss
Fraktionsbeschluß	Fraktionsbeschluss
Free climbing .	Freeclimbing
	auch: Free Climbing
Free Jazz	*auch:* Freejazz
Freßgier	Fressgier
Freßpaket	Fresspaket
Freßsack	Fresssack
	auch: Fress-Sack
Friedensschluß	Friedensschluss
frischgebacken	frisch gebacken
fritieren	frittieren
frohgelaunt	froh gelaunt
frühverstorben	früh verstorben
Full-time-Job	Fulltimejob
	auch: Full-Time-Job
Fünfpaß	Fünfpass
funkensprühend	Funken sprühend
Funkmeßtechnik	Funkmesstechnik
fürbaß	fürbass
fürliebnehmen	fürlieb nehmen
Fußballänderspiel	Fußballländerspiel
	auch: Fußball-Länderspiel

G

Gangsterboß	Gangsterboss
im ganzen gesehen	im Ganzen gesehen
im großen und ganzen	im Großen und Ganzen
Gärungsprozeß	Gärungsprozess
Gäßchen	Gässchen
gefangenhalten	gefangen halten
gefangennehmen	gefangen nehmen
gefaßt	gefasst
gefirnißt	gefirnisst

alt	neu
es ist das gegebene, schnell zu handeln	es ist das Gegebene, schnell zu handeln
gegeneinanderprallen	gegeneinander prallen
gegeneinanderstoßen	gegeneinander stoßen
von allen gehaßt	von allen gehasst
geheimhalten	geheim halten
gehenlassen	gehen lassen
Gelaß	Gelass
gutgelaunt	gut gelaunt
gelblichgrün	gelblich grün
Gemse	Gämse
wir haben gemußt	wir haben gemusst
die Wunde hat genäßt	die Wunde hat genässt
aufs genaueste festgelegt	*auch:* aufs Genaueste festgelegt
genaugenommen	genau genommen
genausogut	genauso gut
genausowenig	genauso wenig
Generalbaß	Generalbass
sie genoß den Sonnenschein	sie genoss den Sonnenschein
Genuß	Genuss
genüßlich	genüsslich
Genußmittel	Genussmittel
genußsüchtig	genusssüchtig
Geographie	*auch:* Geografie
es hat gut gepaßt	es hat gut gepasst
wir haben gepraßt	wir haben geprasst
frisch gepreßter Saft	frisch gepresster Saft
geradehalten	gerade halten
geradesitzen	gerade sitzen
geradestellen	gerade stellen
Gerichtsbeschluß	Gerichtsbeschluss
um ein geringes weniger	um ein Geringes weniger
es geht ihn nicht das geringste an	es geht ihn nicht das Geringste an
nicht im geringsten stören	nicht im Geringsten stören
geringachten	gering achten
geringschätzen	gering schätzen

alt	neu
Geruchsverschluß	Geruchsverschluss
Geschäftsschluß	Geschäftsschluss
er wurde geschaßt	er wurde geschasst
Geschichtsbewußtsein	Geschichtsbewusstsein
Geschirreiniger	Geschirreiniger
	auch: Geschirr-Reiniger
Geschoß	Geschoss *[in Österreich*
	weiterhin mit ß]
gestern abend/morgen/nacht	gestern Abend/Morgen/Nacht
alle waren gestreßt	alle waren gestresst
getrenntlebend	getrennt lebend
Gewinnummer	Gewinnnummer
	auch: Gewinn-Nummer
gewiß	gewiss
Gewissensbiß	Gewissensbiss
Gewißheit	Gewissheit
gewißlich	gewisslich
ich habe es gewußt	ich habe es gewusst
Ginkgo	*auch:* Ginko
Glacéhandschuh	*auch:* Glaceehandschuh
glänzendschwarz	glänzend schwarz
glattgehen	glatt gehen
glatthobeln	glatt hobeln
glattschleifen	glatt schleifen
glattstreichen	glatt streichen
das gleiche tun	das Gleiche tun
aufs gleiche hinauskommen	aufs Gleiche hinauskommen
gleich und gleich gesellt sich gern	Geich und Gleich gesellt sich gern
gleichlautend	gleich lautend
Gleisanschluß	Gleisanschluss
Glimmstengel	Glimmstängel
glühendheiß	glühend heiß
Gnadenerlaß	Gnadenerlass
die Goetheschen Dramen	die goetheschen Dramen
	auch: die Goethe'schen Dramen
Graphit	*auch:* Grafit

817

alt	neu
Graphologie	*auch:* Grafologie
gräßlich	grässlich
graugestreift	grau gestreift
grellbeleuchtet	grell beleuchtet
Grenzfluß	Grenzfluss
Greuel	Gräuel
greulich	gräulich
griffest	grifffest
jmdn. aufs gröbste beleidigen	*auch:* jmdn. aufs Gröbste beleidigen
grobgemahlen	grob gemahlen
ein Programm für groß und klein	ein Programm für Groß und Klein
im großen und ganzen	im Großen und Ganzen
das größte wäre, wenn ...	das Größte wäre, wenn ...
Großschiffahrtsweg	Großschifffahrtsweg
groß schreiben *[mit großem Anfangsbuchstaben]*	großschreiben
grünlichgelb	grünlich gelb
Guß	Guss
Gußeisen	Gusseisen
gußeisern	gusseisern
guten Tag sagen	*auch:* Guten Tag sagen*
es im guten versuchen	es im Guten versuchen
gutaussehend	gut aussehend
gutbezahlt	gut bezahlt
gutgehen	gut gehen
gutgehend	gut gehend
gutgelaunt	gut gelaunt
gutgemeint	gut gemeint
guttun	gut tun
gutunterrichtet	gut unterrichtet

H

alt	neu
haftenbleiben	haften bleiben
haltmachen	Halt machen
Hämorrhoide	*auch:* Hämorride

alt	neu
händchenhaltend	Händchen haltend
handeltreibend	Handel treibend
Handkuß	Handkuss
Handout	*auch:* Hand-out*
hängenbleiben	hängen bleiben
hängenlassen	hängen lassen
Happy-End	Happyend
	auch: Happy End
Haraß	Harass
Hard cover	Hardcover
	auch: Hard Cover
Hard-cover-Einband	Hardcovereinband
	auch: Hard-Cover-Einband
hartgekocht	hart gekocht
Haselnuß	Haselnuss
Haselnußstrauch	Haselnussstrauch
	auch: Haselnuss-Strauch
Haß	Hass
haßerfüllt	hasserfüllt
häßlich	hässlich
Häßlichkeit	Hässlichkeit
Haßliebe	Hassliebe
du haßt	du hasst
Hauptschulabschluß	Hauptschulabschluss
nach Hause	*in Österreich und der Schweiz*
	auch: nachhause
zu Hause	*in Österreich und der Schweiz*
	auch: zuhause
haushalten	*auch:* Haus halten
Haushaltsausschuß	Haushaltsausschuss
Hawaii-Insel	*auch:* Hawaiiinsel
heiligsprechen	heilig sprechen
Heilungsprozeß	Heilungsprozess
heimlichtun	heimlich tun
heißbegehrt	heiß begehrt
heißgeliebt	heiß geliebt

alt	neu
heißumkämpft	heiß umkämpft
helleuchtend	hell leuchtend
hellicht	helllicht
hellila	helllila
hellodernd	hell lodernd
heransein	heran sein
heraussein	heraus sein
herbstlichgelb	herbstlich gelb
Heringsfaß	Heringsfass
hersein	her sein
herumsein	herum sein
heruntersein	herunter sein
Herzas	Herzass
jmdn. auf das herzlichste begrüßen	*auch:* jmdn. auf das Herzlichste begrüßen
heute abend/mittag/nacht	heute Abend/Mittag/Nacht
Hexenschuß	Hexenschuss
hierbleiben	hier bleiben
hierlassen	hier lassen
hiersein	hier sein
hierzulande	*auch:* hier zu Lande
High-Fidelity	Highfidelity
	auch: High Fidelity
High-Society	Highsociety
	auch: High Society
hilfesuchend	Hilfe suchend
hinaussein	hinaus sein
es wurde etwas hineingeheimnißt	es wurde etwas hineingeheimnisst
hinsein	hin sein
hintereinanderfahren	hintereinander fahren
hintereinandergehen	hintereinander gehen
hintereinanderschalten	hintereinander schalten
hinterhersein	hinterher sein
hinübersein	hinüber sein
er hißt die Flagge	er hisst die Flagge

alt	neu
Hochgenuß	Hochgenuss
Hochschulabschluß	Hochschulabschluss
aufs höchste erfreut sein	*auch:* aufs Höchste erfreut sein
hofhalten	Hof halten
die Hohe Schule	die hohe Schule
hohnlachen	*auch:* Hohn lachen
das holzverarbeitende Gewerbe	das Holz verarbeitende Gewerbe
Hosteß	Hostess
Hot dog	Hotdog
	auch: Hot Dog
ein paar hundert	*auch:* ein paar Hundert
viele Hunderte	*auch:* viele hunderte
Hunderte von Zuschauern	*auch:* hunderte von Zuschauern
Hungers sterben	hungers sterben
hurra schreien	*auch:* Hurra schreien*

I

auch Ihr seid herzlich eingeladen *[in Briefen]*	auch ihr seid herzlich eingeladen
im allgemeinen	im Allgemeinen
im besonderen	im Besonderen
Imbiß	Imbiss
Imbißstand	Imbissstand
	auch: Imbiss-Stand
im einzelnen	im Einzelnen
im nachhinein	im Nachhinein
Impfpaß	Impfpass
imstande	*auch:* im Stande
im übrigen	im Übrigen
im voraus	im Voraus
im vorhinein	im Vorhinein
in betreff	in Betreff
in bezug auf	in Bezug auf
Indizes	*auch:* Indices
Indizienprozeß	Indizienprozess

821

alt	neu
ineinanderfließen	ineinander fließen
ineinandergreifen	ineinander greifen
inessentiell	*auch:* inessenziell*
Informationsfluß	Informationsfluss
in Frage stellen	*auch:* infrage stellen
in Frage kommen	*auch:* infrage kommen
innesein	inne sein
insektenfressende Pflanzen	Insekten fressende Pflanzen
instand halten	*auch:* in Stand halten
instand setzen	*auch:* in Stand setzen
I-Punkt	i-Punkt
irgend etwas	irgendetwas
irgend jemand	irgendjemand
I-Tüpfelchen	i-Tüpfelchen

J

alt	neu
ja sagen	*auch:* Ja sagen*
Jagdschloß	Jagdschloss
Jäheit	Jähheit
Jahresabschluß	Jahresabschluss
2jährig, 3jährig, 4jährig ...	2-jährig, 3-jährig, 4-jährig ...
ein 2jähriger, 3jähriger, 4jähriger kann das noch nicht verstehen	ein 2-Jähriger, 3-Jähriger, 4-Jähriger kann das noch nicht verstehen
Jaß	Jass
du jaßt	du jasst
Jauchefaß	Jauchefass
jedesmal	jedes Mal
Job-sharing	Jobsharing
Joghurt	*auch:* Jogurt
Joint-venture	Jointventure
	auch: Joint Venture
Judaskuß	Judaskuss
Julierpaß	Julierpass
Jumbo-Jet	Jumbojet
für jung und alt	für Jung und Alt

K

alt	neu
Kabelanschluß	Kabelanschluss
Kabinettsbeschluß	Kabinettsbeschluss
Kaffee-Ernte	*auch:* Kaffeeernte
Kaffee-Ersatz	*auch:* Kaffeeersatz
Kalligraphie	*auch:* Kalligrafie
kalorienbewußt	kalorienbewusst
kaltlächelnd	kalt lächelnd
Kameraverschluß	Kameraverschluss
Kammacher	Kammmacher
	auch: Kamm-Macher
Kämmaschine	Kämmmaschine
	auch: Kämm-Maschine
Kammuschel	Kammmuschel
	auch: Kamm-Muschel
Känguruh	Känguru
Kanonenschuß	Kanonenschuss
Kapselriß	Kapselriss
Karamel	Karamell
karamelisieren	karamellisieren
2karäter, 3karäter, 4karäter ...	2-Karäter, 3-Karäter, 4-Karäter ...
2karätig, 3karätig, 4karätig ...	2-karätig, 3-karätig, 4-karätig ...
Karoas	Karoass
Kartographie	*auch:* Kartografie
Kaßler	Kassler
Katarrh	*auch:* Katarr
kegelschieben	Kegel schieben
Kellergeschoß	Kellergeschoss *[in Österreich weiterhin mit ß]*
kennenlernen	kennen lernen
Kennummer	Kennnummer
	auch: Kenn-Nummer
die Keplerschen Gesetze	die keplerschen Gesetze
	auch: die Kepler'schen Gesetze
keß	kess
Keßheit	Kessheit

alt	neu
Ketchup	*auch:* Ketschup*
Kickdown	*auch:* Kick-down*
Kick-off	*auch:* Kickoff*
an Kindes Statt	an Kindes statt
Kindesmißhandlung	Kindesmisshandlung
Kißchen	Kisschen
sich über etwas im klaren sein	sich über etwas im Klaren sein
klardenkend	klar denkend
klarsehen	klar sehen
klarwerden	klar werden
Klassenbewußtsein	Klassenbewusstsein
Klassenhaß	Klassenhass
klatschnaß	klatschnass
Klausenpaß	Klausenpass
klebenbleiben	kleben bleiben
Klee-Einsaat	*auch:* Kleeeinsaat
Klee-Ernte	*auch:* Kleeernte
bis ins kleinste geregelt	bis ins Kleinste geregelt
ein Staat im kleinen	ein Staat im Kleinen
ein Programm für groß und klein	ein Programm für Groß und Klein
kleingedruckt	klein gedruckt
kleinschneiden	klein schneiden
klein schreiben *[mit kleinem Anfangsbuchstaben]*	kleinschreiben
Klemmappe	Klemmmappe *auch:* Klemm-Mappe
Klettverschluß	Klettverschluss
klitschnaß	klitschnass
es wäre das klügste, wenn ...	es wäre das Klügste, wenn ...
knapphalten	knapp halten
Knockout	*auch:* Knock-out*
kochendheiß	kochend heiß
kohleführende Flöze	Kohle führende Flöze
Kolanuß	Kolanuss
Kollektivbewußtsein	Kollektivbewusstsein
Kolophonium	*auch:* Kolofonium

Koloß	Koloss
Kombinationsschloß	Kombinationsschloss
Kommiß	Kommiss
Kommißbrot	Kommissbrot
Kommißstiefel	Kommissstiefel
	auch: Kommiss-Stiefel
Kommuniqué	*auch:* Kommunikee
Kompaß	Kompass
kompreß	kompress
Kompromiß	Kompromiss
kompromißbereit	kompromissbereit
kompromißlos	kompromisslos
Kompromißlösung	Kompromisslösung
Komteß	Komtess
Konferenzbeschluß	Konferenzbeschluss
Kongreß	Kongress
Kongreßhalle	Kongresshalle
Kongreßsaal	Kongresssaal
	auch: Kongress-Saal
Kongreßstadt	Kongressstadt
	auch: Kongress-Stadt
Königsschloß	Königsschloss
Kontrabaß	Kontrabass
Kontrollampe	Kontrolllampe
	auch: Kontroll-Lampe
Kontrolliste	Kontrollliste
	auch: Kontroll-Liste
Kopfnuß	Kopfnuss
Kopfschuß	Kopfschuss
kopfstehen	Kopf stehen
Koppelschloß	Koppelschloss
krank schreiben	krankschreiben
kraß	krass
Kraßheit	Krassheit
krebserregende Substanzen	Krebs erregende Substanzen
Kreiselkompaß	Kreiselkompass

alt	neu
Kreppapier	Krepppapier
	auch: Krepp-Papier
Kreuzas	Kreuzass
die kriegführenden Parteien	die Krieg führenden Parteien
Kriminalprozeß	Kriminalprozess
Kristallüster	Kristalllüster
	auch: Kristall-Lüster
kroß	kross
krummnehmen	krumm nehmen
KSZE-Schlußakte	KSZE-Schlussakte
Kunststoffolie	Kunststofffolie
	auch: Kunststoff-Folie
Küraß	Kürass
den kürzeren ziehen	den Kürzeren ziehen
kürzertreten	kürzer treten
kurzgebraten	kurz gebraten
kurzhalten	kurz halten
Kurzpaß	Kurzpass
Kurzschluß	Kurzschluss
kurztreten	kurz treten
Kuß	Kuss
Küßchen	Küsschen
kußecht	kussecht
Kußhand	Kusshand
du/er/sie küßt	du/er/sie küsst
Küstenschiffahrt	Küstenschifffahrt
Kwaß	Kwass
L	
Ladenschluß	Ladenschluss
die La-Fontaineschen Fabeln	die la-fontaineschen Fabeln
	auch: die la-Fontaine'schen Fabeln
Lamé	*auch:* Lamee
Lamellenverschluß	Lamellenverschluss

826

alt	neu
etwas des langen und breiten erklären	etwas des Langen und Breiten erklären
langgestreckt	lang gestreckt
länglichrund	länglich rund
langstengelig	langstängelig
langziehen	lang ziehen
Lapsus linguae	Lapsus Linguae
läßlich	lässlich
du läßt	du lässt
zu Lasten	*auch:* zulasten
Lattenschuß	Lattenschuss
laubtragende Bäume	Laub tragende Bäume
auf dem laufenden sein	auf dem Laufenden sein
laufenlassen	laufen lassen
Laufpaß	Laufpass
Layout	*auch:* Lay-out*
Lebensgenuß	Lebensgenuss
Leberabszeß	Leberabszess
die lederverarbeitende Industrie	die Leder verarbeitende Industrie
leerstehend	leer stehend
leichenblaß	leichenblass
es ist mir ein leichtes, das zu tun	es ist mir ein Leichtes, das zu tun
leichtentzündlich	leicht entzündlich
leichtfallen	leicht fallen
leichtmachen	leicht machen
leichtnehmen	leicht nehmen
leichtverderblich	leicht verderblich
leichtverständlich	leicht verständlich
jmdm. leid tun	jmdm. Leid tun
Lenkradschloß	Lenkradschloss
Lernprozeß	Lernprozess
der letzte, der gekommen ist	der Letzte, der gekommen ist
als letzter fertig sein	als Letzter fertig sein
das letzte, was sie tun würde	das Letzte, was sie tun würde
bis ins letzte geklärt	bis ins Letzte geklärt
letzteres trifft zu	Letzteres trifft zu

alt	neu
zum letztenmal	zum letzten Mal
leuchtendblau	leuchtend blau
Lichtmeß	Lichtmess
es wäre uns das liebste, wenn ...	es wäre uns das Liebste, wenn ...
liebenlernen	lieben lernen
liebgewinnen	lieb gewinnen
liebhaben	lieb haben
liegenbleiben	liegen bleiben
liegenlassen	liegen lassen
Live-Mitschnitt	*auch:* Livemitschnitt
Lizentiat	*auch:* Lizenziat*
Lorbaß	Lorbass
Löß	*auch:* Löss *[bei Aussprache mit kurzem ö]*
Lößboden	*auch:* Lössboden *[bei Aussprache mit kurzem ö]*
Lößschicht	*auch:* Lössschicht oder Löss-Schicht *[bei Aussprache mit kurzem ö]*
Lötschenpaß	Lötschenpass
Love-Story	*auch:* Lovestory
Luftschiffahrt	Luftschifffahrt
Luftschloß	Luftschloss

M

alt	neu
Magistratsbeschluß	Magistratsbeschluss
2mal, 3mal, 4mal ...	2-mal, 3-mal, 4-mal ...
Malaise	*auch:* Maläse
Marschkompaß	Marschkompass
maschineschreiben	Maschine schreiben
maßhalten	Maß halten
Matrizes	*auch:* Matrices
Maulkorberlaß	Maulkorberlass
Megaphon	*auch:* Megafon
Mehrheitsbeschluß	Mehrheitsbeschluss
Meldeschluß	Meldeschluss

alt	neu
Meniskusriß	Meniskusriss
wir haben das menschenmögliche getan	wir haben das Menschenmögliche getan
Mesner	*auch:* Messner
Meßband	Messband
meßbar	messbar
Meßbecher	Messbecher
Meßbuch	Messbuch
Meßdaten	Messdaten
Meßdiener	Messdiener
Meßfühler	Messfühler
Meßgewand	Messgewand
Meßinstrument	Messinstrument
Meßopfer	Messopfer
Meßstab	Messstab
	auch: Mess-Stab
Meßtischblatt	Messtischblatt
Metallguß	Metallguss
Metallegierung	Metalllegierung
	auch: Metall-Legierung
die metallverarbeitende Industrie	die Metall verarbeitende Industrie
Midlife-crisis	Midlifecrisis
	auch: Midlife-Crisis
Milchgebiß	Milchgebiss
millionenmal	Millionen Mal
Milzriß	Milzriss
nicht im mindesten	nicht im Mindesten
mißachten	missachten
Mißbildung	Missbildung
mißbilligen	missbilligen
Mißbrauch	Missbrauch
Mißerfolg	Misserfolg
Mißernte	Missernte
mißfallen	missfallen
Mißfallenskundgebung	Missfallenskundgebung
Mißgeburt	Missgeburt

alt	neu
Mißgeschick	Missgeschick
mißglücken	missglücken
Mißgunst	Missgunst
mißgünstig	missgünstig
Mißklang	Missklang
Mißkredit	Misskredit
mißlich	misslich
mißlingen	misslingen
mißmutig	missmutig
mißraten	missraten
Mißstand	Missstand
Mißtrauen	Misstrauen
mißtrauisch	misstrauisch
Mißverständnis	Missverständnis
Mißwirtschaft	Misswirtschaft
mit Hilfe	*auch:* mithilfe
[gestern, heute, morgen] mittag	[gestern, heute, morgen] Mittag
Mixed Pickles	*auch:* Mixedpickles*
modebewußt	modebewusst
wir sprachen über alles mögliche	wir sprachen über alles Mögliche
sein möglichstes tun	sein Möglichstes tun
3monatig, 4monatig, 5monatig ...	3-monatig, 4-monatig, 5-monatig ...
3monatlich, 4monatlich, 5monatlich ...	3-monatlich, 4-monatlich, 5-monatlich ...
Monographie	*auch:* Monografie
Mop	Mopp
Mordprozeß	Mordprozess
morgen abend, mittag, nacht	morgen Abend, Mittag, Nacht
[gestern, heute] morgen	[gestern, heute] Morgen
Moto-Cross	*auch:* Motocross
Mückenschiß	Mückenschiss
Mulläppchen	Mullläppchen
	auch: Mull-Läppchen
Multiple-choice-Verfahren	Multiplechoiceverfahren
	auch: Multiple-Choice-Verfahren

alt	neu
Muskatnuß	Muskatnuss
Muskelriß	Muskelriss
ich muß	ich muss
du mußt	du musst
ich müßte	ich müsste
du müßtest	du müsstest
Mußheirat	Mussheirat
müßiggehen	müßig gehen
Musterprozeß	Musterprozess
Myrrhe	*auch:* Myrre

N

alt	neu
nachfolgendes gilt auch ...	Nachfolgendes gilt auch ...
nach Hause	*in Österreich und der*
	Schweiz auch: nachhause
im nachhinein	im Nachhinein
Nachlaß	Nachlass
Nachlaßverwalter	Nachlassverwalter
[gestern, heute, morgen]	[gestern, heute, morgen]
nachmittag	Nachmittag
Nachschuß	Nachschuss
der nächste, bitte!	der Nächste, bitte!
als nächstes wollen wir ...	als Nächstes wollen wir ...
im nachstehenden heißt es ...	im Nachstehenden heißt es ...
[gestern, heute, morgen] nacht	[gestern, heute, morgen] Nacht
nahebringen	nahe bringen
nahelegen	nahe legen
naheliegen	nahe liegen
naheliegend	nahe liegend
etwas des näheren erläutern	etwas des Näheren erläutern
näherliegen	näher liegen
nahestehen	nahe stehen
nahestehend	nahe stehend
Narziß	Narziss
Narzißmus	Narzissmus
narzißtisch	narzisstisch

alt	neu
naß	nass
naßforsch	nassforsch
naßgeschwitzt	nass geschwitzt
naßkalt	nasskalt
Naßrasur	Nassrasur
Naßschnee	Nassschnee
	auch: Nass-Schnee
nationalbewußt	nationalbewusst
Nationaldreß	Nationaldress
Nebelschlußleuchte	Nebelschlussleuchte
Nebenanschluß	Nebenanschluss
nebeneinandersitzen	nebeneinander sitzen
nebeneinanderstehen	nebeneinander stehen
nebeneinanderstellen	nebeneinander stellen
Nebenfluß	Nebenfluss
im nebenstehenden wird gezeigt ...	im Nebenstehenden wird gezeigt ...
Necessaire	*auch:* Nessessär
Negligé	*auch:* Negligee
nein sagen	*auch:* Nein sagen*
Netzanschluß	Netzanschluss
es aufs neue versuchen	es aufs Neue versuchen
auf ein neues!	auf ein Neues!
neueröffnet	neu eröffnet
New Yorker	*auch:* New-Yorker
nichtrostend	*auch:* nicht rostend
Nichtseßhafte	Nichtsesshafte
nichtssagend	nichts sagend
No-future-Generation	No-Future-Generation
die notleidende Bevölkerung	die Not leidende Bevölkerung
in Null Komma nichts	in null Komma nichts
das Thermometer steht auf Null	das Thermometer steht auf null
Nullage	Nulllage
	auch: Null-Lage
Nulleiter	Nullleiter
	auch: Null-Leiter

alt	neu
Nullösung	Nulllösung
	auch: Null-Lösung
numerieren	nummerieren
Numerierung	Nummerierung
Nuß	Nuss
Nüßchen	Nüsschen
Nußknacker	Nussknacker
Nußschale	Nussschale
	auch: Nuss-Schale
Nußschinken	Nussschinken
	auch: Nuss-Schinken
Nußschokolade	Nussschokolade
	auch: Nuss-Schokolade
Nußstrudel	Nussstrudel
	auch: Nuss-Strudel
Nußtorte	Nusstorte

O

O-beinig	*auch:* o-beinig
obenerwähnt	oben erwähnt
obenstehend	oben stehend
Obergeschoß	Obergeschoss *[in Österreich weiterhin mit ß]*
offenbleiben	offen bleiben
offenlassen	offen lassen
offenstehen	offen stehen
O-förmig	*auch:* o-förmig
des öfteren	des Öfteren
Ölmeßstab	Ölmessstab
Ordonnanz	*auch:* Ordonanz
Orthographie	*auch:* Orthografie

P

Panther	*auch:* Panter
die papierverarbeitende Industrie	die Papier verarbeitende Industrie
Pappmaché	*auch:* Pappmaschee

alt	neu
parallellaufend	parallel laufend
parallelschalten	parallel schalten
Paranuß	Paranuss
Parlamentsbeschluß	Parlamentsbeschluss
Parnaß	Parnass
Parteikongreß	Parteikongress
Parteitagsbeschluß	Parteitagsbeschluss
Paß	Pass
Paßbild	Passbild
passé	*auch:* passee
Paßform	Passform
Paßgang	Passgang
paßgerecht	passgerecht
Paßkontrolle	Passkontrolle
Paßstelle	Passstelle
	auch: Pass-Stelle
Paßstraße	Passstraße
	auch: Pass-Straße
Paßwort	Passwort
Patentverschluß	Patentverschluss
patschnaß	patschnass
Perkussionsschloß	Perkussionsschloss
Personenschiffahrt	Personenschifffahrt
Petitionsausschuß	Petitionsausschuss
Pfeffernuß	Pfeffernuss
Pferdegebiß	Pferdegebiss
pflichtbewußt	pflichtbewusst
Pflichtbewußtsein	Pflichtbewusstsein
Pfostenschuß	Pfostenschuss
Pikas	Pikass
Pimpernuß	Pimpernuss
er pißt	er pisst
Pistolenschuß	Pistolenschuss
pitschnaß	pitschnass
Platitüde	Plattitüde
	auch: Platitude

alt	neu
Playback	*auch:* Play-back*
plazieren	platzieren
pleite gehen	Pleite gehen
polyphon	*auch:* polyfon
Pornographie	*auch:* Pornografie
Portemonnaie	*auch:* Portmonee
Potemkinsche Dörfer	potemkinsche Dörfer
	auch: Potemkin'sche Dörfer
potentiell	*auch:* potenziell*
potthäßlich	potthässlich
Poussierstengel	Poussierstängel
präferentiell	*auch:* präferenziell*
er praßt	er prasst
preisbewußt	preisbewusst
Preisnachlaß	Preisnachlass
Preßform	Pressform
Preßluftbohrer	Pressluftbohrer
Preßsack	Presssack
	auch: Press-Sack
Preßschlag	Pressschlag
	auch: Press-Schlag
Preßspan	Pressspan
	auch: Press-Span
du preßt	du presst
Preßwehe	Presswehe
Prinzeßbohne	Prinzessbohne
privatversichert	privat versichert
probefahren	Probe fahren
Problembewußtsein	Problembewusstsein
Produktionsprozeß	Produktionsprozess
Profeß	Profess
Programmusik	Programmmusik
	auch: Programm-Musik
Progreß	Progress
Prozeß	Prozess
Prozeßkosten	Prozesskosten

alt	neu
Prozeßbevollmächtigte	Prozessbevollmächtigte
prozeßführend	prozessführend
Prozeßkosten	Prozesskosten
Prozeßrechner	Prozessrechner
pudelnaß	pudelnass
Pulverfaß	Pulverfass
pußlig	pusslig

Q

alt	neu
Quadrophonie	*auch:* Quadrofonie
qualitätsbewußt	qualitätsbewusst
Quartalsabschluß	Quartalsabschluss
Quellfluß	Quellfluss
Quentchen	Quäntchen
Querpaß	Querpass
Quickstep	Quickstepp

R

alt	neu
radfahren	Rad fahren
Radikalenerlaß	Radikalenerlass
radschlagen	Rad schlagen
Rammaschine	Rammmaschine
	auch: Ramm-Maschine
zu Rande kommen	*auch:* zurande kommen
Rassenhaß	Rassenhass
ich raßle mit den Ketten	ich rassle mit den Ketten
zu Rate ziehen	*auch:* zurate ziehen
Räterußland	Räterussland
Ratsbeschluß	Ratsbeschluss
Ratschluß	Ratschluss
Rauchfaß	Rauchfass
rauh	rau
rauhbeinig	raubeinig
Rauhfasertapete	Raufasertapete
Rauhfrost	Raufrost
Rauhhaardackel	Rauhaardackel

alt	neu
Rauhnächte	Raunächte
Rauhputz	Rauputz
Rauhreif	Raureif
Rausschmiß	Rausschmiss
recht haben	Recht haben
recht behalten	Recht behalten
recht bekommen	Recht bekommen
jmdm. recht geben	jmdm. Recht geben
Rechtens sein	rechtens sein
Rechtsbewußtsein	Rechtsbewusstsein
Redaktionsschluß	Redaktionsschluss
Regenguß	Regenguss
regennaß	regennass
Regreß	Regress
Regreßanspruch	Regressanspruch
Regreßpflicht	Regresspflicht
regreßpflichtig	regresspflichtig
reichgeschmückt	reich geschmückt
reichverziert	reich verziert
Reifungsprozeß	Reifungsprozess
Reisepaß	Reisepass
Reißverschluß	Reißverschluss
Reißverschlußsystem	Reißverschlusssystem
	auch: Reißverschluss-System
Reschenpaß	Reschenpass
Rettungsschuß	Rettungsschuss
Rezeß	Rezess
Rhein-Main-Donau-Großschiffahrtsweg	Rhein-Main-Donau-Großschifffahrtsweg
das ist genau das richtige für mich	das ist genau das Richtige für mich
mit etwas richtigliegen	mit etwas richtig liegen
richtigstellen	richtig stellen
Riß	Riss
rißfest	rissfest
Roheit	Rohheit

alt	neu
Rolladen	Rollladen
	auch: Roll-Laden
Rommé	*auch:* Rommee
rosigweiß	rosig weiß
Roß	Ross
Roßbreiten	Rossbreiten
Roßhaarmatratze	Rosshaarmatratze
Roßkastanie	Rosskastanie
Roßkur	Rosskur
Rößl	Rössl
Roßtäuscherei	Rosstäuscherei
der rote Planet *[Mars]*	der Rote Planet
rotgestreift	rot gestreift
rotglühend	rot glühend
rötlichbraun	rötlich braun
die Rubensschen Gemälde	die rubensschen Gemälde
	auch: die Rubens'schen
	Gemälde
Rückfluß	Rückfluss
Rückpaß	Rückpass
Rückschluß	Rückschluss
rückwärtsgewandt	rückwärts gewandt
Ruhegenuß	Ruhegenuss
ruhenlassen	ruhen lassen
ruhigstellen	ruhig stellen
Runderlaß	Runderlass
Rußland	Russland

S

alt	neu
Säbelraßler	Säbelrassler
Saisonnier	*auch:* Saisonier
Saisonschluß	Saisonschluss
Salutschuß	Salutschuss
Salzfaß	Salzfass
Samenerguß	Samenerguss
Sammelanschluß	Sammelanschluss

alt	neu
Sankt Gallener	*auch:* Sankt-Gallener
sanktgallisch	sankt-gallisch
Sanmarinese	San-Marinese
sanmarinesisch	san-marinesisch
sauberhalten	sauber halten
saubermachen	sauber machen
sausenlassen	sausen lassen
Saxophon	*auch:* Saxofon
sein Schäfchen ins trockene bringen	sein Schäfchen ins Trockene bringen
Schalenguß	Schalenguss
Schallehre	Schalllehre *auch:* Schall-Lehre
Schalloch	Schallloch *auch:* Schall-Loch
Schalterschluß	Schalterschluss
etwas auf das schärfste verurteilen	*auch:* etwas auf das Schärfste verurteilen
er schaßte ihn	er schasste ihn
ein schattenspendender Baum	ein Schatten spendender Baum
schätzenlernen	schätzen lernen
Schauprozeß	Schauprozess
Scheidungsprozeß	Scheidungsprozess
schießenlassen	schießen lassen
Schiffahrt	Schifffahrt *auch:* Schiff-Fahrt
Schippenas	Schippenass
Schiß	Schiss
Schlachtroß	Schlachtross
Schlagfluß	Schlagfluss
Schlammasse	Schlammmasse *auch:* Schlamm-Masse
schlechtgehen	schlecht gehen
schlechtgelaunt	schlecht gelaunt
das schlimmste ist, daß ...	das Schlimmste ist, dass ...

alt	neu
sie haben ihn auf das schlimmste getäuscht	*auch:* sie haben ihn auf das Schlimmste getäuscht
er schliß Federn	er schliss Federn
Schlitzverschluß	Schlitzverschluss
Schloß	Schloss
Schlößchen	Schlösschen
Schloßherr	Schlossherr
Schloßpark	Schlosspark
Schluß	Schluss
Schlußbemerkung	Schlussbemerkung
schlußendlich	schlussendlich
schlußfolgern	schlussfolgern
Schlußfolgerung	Schlussfolgerung
Schlußlicht	Schlusslicht
Schlußpfiff	Schlusspfiff
Schlußpunkt	Schlusspunkt
Schlußsatz	Schlusssatz *auch:* Schluss-Satz
Schlußspurt	Schlussspurt *auch:* Schluss-Spurt
Schlußstrich	Schlussstrich *auch:* Schluss-Strich
Schlußverkauf	Schlussverkauf
Schlußwort	Schlusswort
Schmerfluß	Schmerfluss
sie schmiß mit Steinen	sie schmiss mit Steinen
Schmiß	Schmiss
Schmuckblattelegramm	Schmuckblatttelegramm *auch:* Schmuckblatt-Telegramm
schmutziggrau	schmutzig grau
Schnappschloß	Schnappschloss
Schnappschuß	Schnappschuss
Schnee-Eifel	*auch:* Schneeeifel
Schnee-Eule	*auch:* Schneeeule
Schneewächte	Schneewechte
Schnellimbiß	Schnellimbiss

alt	neu
Schnelläufer	Schnellläufer
	auch: Schnell-Läufer
schnellebig	schnelllebig
Schnellebigkeit	Schnelllebigkeit
Schnellschuß	Schnellschuss
Schnepper	*auch:* Schnäpper
schneppern	*auch:* schnäppern
schneuzen	schnäuzen
Schokoladenguß	Schokoladenguss
aufs schönste übereinstimmen	*auch:* aufs Schönste übereinstimmen
er schoß	er schoss
Schoß *[einer Pflanze]*	Schoss
schräglaufend	schräg laufend
Schraubverschluß	Schraubverschluss
schreckensblaß	schreckensblass
Schreckschußpistole	Schreckschusspistole
Schrittempo	Schritttempo
	auch: Schritt-Tempo
Schrotschuß	Schrotschuss
Schulabschluß	Schulabschluss
an etwas schuld haben	an etwas Schuld haben
sich etwas zuschulden kommen lassen	*auch:* sich etwas zu Schulden kommen lassen
schuldbewußt	schuldbewusst
Schuldenerlaß	Schuldenerlass
Schulschluß	Schulschluss
Schulstreß	Schulstress
Schulterschluß	Schulterschluss
Schuß	Schuss
schußbereit	schussbereit
schußfest	schussfest
schußlig	schusslig
Schußlinie	Schusslinie
Schußschwäche	Schussschwäche
	auch: Schuss-Schwäche

alt	neu
Schußwaffe	Schusswaffe
Schußwechsel	Schusswechsel
schwachbetont	schwach betont
schwachbevölkert	schwach bevölkert
aus schwarz weiß machen	aus Schwarz Weiß machen
Schwarze Magie	schwarze Magie
schwarzgefärbt	schwarz gefärbt
schwarzrotgolden	*auch:* schwarz-rot-golden
schwerfallen	schwer fallen
schwernehmen	schwer nehmen
schwertun	schwer tun
schwerverständlich	schwer verständlich
Schwimmeister	Schwimmmeister
	auch: Schwimm-Meister
Science-fiction	Sciencefiction
	auch: Science-Fiction
Sechspaß	Sechspass
See-Elefant	*auch:* Seeelefant
jedem das Seine	*auch:* jedem das seine
das Seine beitragen	*auch:* das seine beitragen
die Seinen	*auch:* die seinen
die Seinigen	*auch:* die seinigen
seinlassen	sein lassen
Seismograph	*auch:* Seismograf
auf seiten	aufseiten
	auch: auf Seiten
von seiten	vonseiten
	auch: von Seiten
selbständig	*auch:* selbstständig
Selbständigkeit	*auch:* Selbstständigkeit
selbstbewußt	selbstbewusst
Selbstbewußtsein	Selbstbewusstsein
selbsternannt	selbst ernannt
selbstgebacken	selbst gebacken
selbstgemacht	selbst gemacht
selbstgestrickt	selbst gestrickt

Selbstschuß	Selbstschuss
selbstverdient	selbst verdient
seligpreisen	selig preisen
seligsprechen	selig sprechen
Senatsbeschluß	Senatsbeschluss
Sendeschluß	Sendeschluss
Sendungsbewußtsein	Sendungsbewusstsein
Sensationsprozeß	Sensationsprozess
Séparée	*auch:* Separee
sequentiell	*auch:* sequenziell*
seßhaft	sesshaft
Seßhaftigkeit	Sesshaftigkeit
S-förmig	*auch:* s-förmig
die Shakespeareschen Sonette	die shakespeareschen Sonette
	auch: die Shakespeare'schen Sonette
Short story	Shortstory
	auch: Short Story
Showbusineß	Showbusiness
Showdown	*auch:* Show-down*
Shrimp	*auch:* Schrimp
auf Nummer Sicher gehen	*auch:* auf Nummer sicher gehen
das sicherste ist, wenn ...	das Sicherste ist, wenn ...
Sicherheitsschloß	Sicherheitsschloss
Sicherheitsverschluß	Sicherheitsverschluss
siedendheiß	siedend heiß
siegesbewußt	siegesbewusst
siegesgewiß	siegesgewiss
Simplonpaß	Simplonpass
die Singende Säge	die singende Säge
Siphonverschluß	Siphonverschluss
sitzenbleiben	sitzen bleiben
sitzenlassen	sitzen lassen
Skipaß	Skipass
Small talk	Smalltalk
	auch: Small Talk

843

alt	neu
so daß	sodass
	auch: so dass
Sommerschlußverkauf	Sommerschlussverkauf
alles sonstige besprechen wir morgen	alles Sonstige besprechen wir morgen
Soufflé	*auch:* Soufflee
soviel du willst	so viel du willst
soviel wie	so viel wie
noch einmal soviel	noch einmal so viel
es ist soweit	es ist so weit
soweit wie möglich	so weit wie möglich
ich kann das sowenig wie du	ich kann das so wenig wie du
Sowjetrußland	Sowjetrussland
hier gilt kein Sowohl-Als-auch	hier gilt kein Sowohl-als-auch
Spaghetti	*auch:* Spagetti
Spantenriß	Spantenriss
spazierenfahren	spazieren fahren
spazierengehen	spazieren gehen
Speichelfluß	Speichelfluss
Sperrad	Sperrrad
	auch: Sperr-Rad
Sperriegel	Sperrriegel
	auch: Sperr-Riegel
Spliß	Spliss
du splißt	du splisst
eine sporenbildende Pflanze	eine Sporen bildende Pflanze
Sportdreß	Sportdress
Sprenggeschoß	Sprenggeschoss *[in Österreich weiterhin mit ß]*
Spritzguß	Spritzguss
es sproß neues Grün	es spross neues Grün
Sproß	Spross
Sproßachse	Sprossachse
SpRößchen	Sprösschen
Sprößling	Sprössling
staatenbildende Insekten	Staaten bildende Insekten

alt	neu
Stahlroß	Stahlross
Stallaterne	Stalllaterne
	auch: Stall-Laterne
Stammutter	Stammmutter
	auch: Stamm-Mutter
standesbewußt	standesbewusst
Standesbewußtsein	Standesbewusstsein
Startschuß	Startschuss
steckenbleiben	stecken bleiben
steckenlassen	stecken lassen
Steckschloß	Steckschloss
Steckschuß	Steckschuss
stehenbleiben	stehen bleiben
stehenlassen	stehen lassen
Stehimbiß	Stehimbiss
Steilpaß	Steilpass
Stemmeißel	Stemmmeißel
	auch: Stemm-Meißel
Stendelwurz	Ständelwurz
Stengel	Stängel
Step	Stepp
Steptanz	Stepptanz
Stereophonie	*auch:* Stereofonie
Steuererlaß	Steuererlass
Steuermeßbetrag	Steuermessbetrag
Stewardeß	Stewardess
stiftengehen	stiften gehen
etwas im stillen vorbereiten	etwas im Stillen vorbereiten
Stilleben	Stillleben
	auch: Still-Leben
stillegen	stilllegen
Stillegung	Stilllegung
Stoffarbe	Stofffarbe
	auch: Stoff-Farbe
Stoffetzen	Stofffetzen
	auch: Stoff-Fetzen

alt	neu
Stoffülle	Stofffülle
	auch: Stoff-Fülle
Stop	Stopp
Straferlaß	Straferlass
Strafprozeß	Strafprozess
Strafprozeßordnung	Strafprozessordnung
Straß	Strass
Streifschuß	Streifschuss
Streitroß	Streitross
strenggenommen	streng genommen
strengnehmen	streng nehmen
aufs strengste unterschieden	*auch:* aufs Strengste unterschieden
Streß	Stress
der Lärm streßt	der Lärm stresst
Streßsituation	Stresssituation
	auch: Stress-Situation
2stündig, 3stündig, 4stündig ...	2-stündig, 3-stündig, 4-stündig ...
2stündlich, 3stündlich, 4stündlich ...	2-stündlich, 3-stündlich, 4-stündlich ...
Stuß	Stuss
substantiell	*auch:* substanziell*
Sustenpaß	Sustenpass
T	
Tablettenmißbrauch	Tablettenmissbrauch
tabula rasa machen	Tabula rasa machen
zutage treten	*auch:* zu Tage treten
2tägig, 3tägig, 4tägig ...	2-tägig, 3-tägig, 4-tägig ...
Tankschloß	Tankschloss
Tarifabschluß	Tarifabschluss
Täßchen	Tässchen
ein paar tausend	*auch:* ein paar Tausend
Tausende von Zuschauern	*auch:* tausende von Zuschauern
T-bone-Steak	T-Bone-Steak
Tee-Ei	*auch:* Teeei

alt	neu
Tee-Ernte	*auch:* Teeernte
Teerfaß	Teerfass
Telephon	Telefon
Telephonanschluß	Telefonanschluss
Thunfisch	*auch:* Tunfisch
Tie-Break	*auch:* Tiebreak
aufs tiefste gekränkt	*auch:* aufs Tiefste gekränkt
tiefbewegt	tief bewegt
tiefempfunden	tief empfunden
tiefverschneit	tief verschneit
Tintenfaß	Tintenfass
Tip	Tipp
todblaß	todblass
Todesschuß	Todesschuss
Tolpatsch	Tollpatsch
tolpatschig	tollpatschig
Tomatenketchup	*auch:* Tomatenketschup
Topographie	*auch:* Topografie
Torschlußpanik	Torschlusspanik
Torschuß	Torschuss
totenblaß	totenblass
totgeboren	tot geboren
traditionsbewußt	traditionsbewusst
Tränenfluß	Tränenfluss
tränennaß	tränennass
Traß	Trass
Trekking	*auch:* Trecking
treuergeben	treu ergeben
triefnaß	triefnass
auf dem trockenen sitzen	auf dem Trockenen sitzen
sein Schäfchen ins trockene bringen	sein Schäfchen ins Trockene bringen
tropfnaß	tropfnass
Troß	Tross
im trüben fischen	im Trüben fischen
Truchseß	Truchsess

alt	neu
Trugschluß	Trugschluss
Trumpfas	Trumpfass
Tuffelsen	Tufffelsen
	auch: Tuff-Felsen
Türschloß	Türschloss

U

alt	neu
übelgelaunt	übel gelaunt
übelnehmen	übel nehmen
übelriechend	übel riechend
Überbiß	Überbiss
Überdruß	Überdruss
übereinanderlegen	übereinander legen
übereinanderliegen	übereinander liegen
übereinanderwerfen	übereinander werfen
Überfluß	Überfluss
Überflußgesellschaft	Überflussgesellschaft
Überguß	Überguss
überhandnehmen	überhand nehmen
übermorgen abend, nachmittag	übermorgen Abend, Nachmittag
Überschuß	Überschuss
überschwenglich	überschwänglich
überwächtet	überwechtet
ein übriges tun	ein Übriges tun
im übrigen wissen wir doch alle ...	im Übrigen wissen wir doch alle ...
alles übrige später	alles Übrige später
die übrigen kommen nach	die Übrigen kommen nach
übrigbehalten	übrig behalten
übrigbleiben	übrig bleiben
übriglassen	übrig lassen
U-förmig	*auch:* u-förmig
Ultima ratio	Ultima Ratio
Umdenkprozeß	Umdenkprozess
die Liste umfaßt alles Wichtige	die Liste umfasst alles Wichtige
Umriß	Umriss
Umrißzeichnung	Umrisszeichnung

alt	neu
Umschichtungsprozeß	Umschichtungsprozess
Umschluß	Umschluss
umsein	um sein
um so [mehr, größer, weniger ...]	umso [mehr, größer, weniger ...]
Umstellungsprozeß	Umstellungsprozess
Umwandlungsprozeß	Umwandlungsprozess
Umwelteinfluß	Umwelteinfluss
sich ins unabsehbare ausweiten	sich ins Unabsehbare ausweiten
unangepaßt	unangepasst
Unangepaßtheit	Unangepasstheit
unbeeinflußbar	unbeeinflussbar
unbeeinflußt	unbeeinflusst
Anzeige gegen Unbekannt	Anzeige gegen unbekannt
unbewußt	unbewusst
und ähnliches (u. ä.)	und Ähnliches (u. Ä.)
unendlichemal	unendliche Mal
unerläßlich	unerlässlich
unermeßlich	unermesslich
Unfairneß	Unfairness
unfaßbar	unfassbar
unfaßlich	unfasslich
ungewiß	ungewiss
Ungewißheit	Ungewissheit
unigefärbt	uni gefärbt
im unklaren bleiben	im Unklaren bleiben
im unklaren lassen	im Unklaren lassen
unmißverständlich	unmissverständlich
unpäßlich	unpässlich
Unpäßlichkeit	Unpässlichkeit
unplaziert	unplatziert
unrecht haben	Unrecht haben
unrecht behalten	Unrecht behalten
unrecht bekommen	Unrecht bekommen
Unrechtsbewußtsein	Unrechtsbewusstsein
unselbständig	*auch:* unselbstständig
Unselbständigkeit	*auch:* Unselbstständigkeit

alt	neu
die Unseren	*auch:* die unseren
die Unsrigen	*auch:* die unsrigen
untenerwähnt	unten erwähnt
untenstehend	unten stehend
unterbewußt	unterbewusst
Unterbewußtsein	Unterbewusstsein
unterderhand	unter der Hand
untereinanderstehen	untereinander stehen
Untergeschoß	Untergeschoss *[in Österreich weiterhin mit ß]*
ohne Unterlaß	ohne Unterlass
Untersuchungsausschuß	Untersuchungsausschuss
unvergeßlich	unvergesslich
unerläßlich	unerlässlich
unzähligemal	unzählige Mal

V

alt	neu
va banque spielen	*auch:* Vabanque spielen
Varieté	*auch:* Varietee
veranlaßt	veranlasst
verantwortungsbewußt	verantwortungsbewusst
Verantwortungsbewußtsein	Verantwortungsbewusstsein
Verbiß	Verbiss
verblaßt	verblasst
verbleuen	verbläuen
im verborgenen blühen	im Verborgenen blühen
das verdroß uns	das verdross uns
Verdruß	Verdruss
du verfaßt	du verfasst
vergeßlich	vergesslich
Vergeßlichkeit	Vergesslichkeit
Vergißmeinnicht	Vergissmeinnicht
du vergißt	du vergisst
verhaßt	verhasst
auf jmdn. ist Verlaß	auf jmdn. ist Verlass
verläßlich	verlässlich

alt	neu
Verläßlichkeit	Verlässlichkeit
verlorengehen	verloren gehen
vermißt	vermisst
Vermißtenanzeige	Vermisstenanzeige
er hat den Zug verpaßt	er hat den Zug verpasst
das Geld wurde verpraßt	das Geld wurde verprasst
Verriß	Verriss
verschiedenes war noch unklar	Verschiedenes war noch unklar
verschiedenemal	verschiedene Mal
Verschiß	Verschiss
Verschluß	Verschluss
Verschlußkappe	Verschlusskappe
Verschlußsache	Verschlusssache
	auch: Verschluss-Sache
verselbständigen	*auch:* verselbstständigen
Versorgungsengpaß	Versorgungsengpass
Vertragsabschluß	Vertragsabschluss
Vertragsschluß	Vertragsschluss
V-förmig	*auch:* v-förmig
Vibraphon	*auch:* Vibrafon
viel zuviel	viel zu viel
viel zuwenig	viel zu wenig
vielbefahren	viel befahren
vielgelesen	viel gelesen
Vierpaß	Vierpass
aus dem vollen schöpfen	aus dem Vollen schöpfen
voneinandergehen	voneinander gehen
von seiten	vonseiten
	auch: von Seiten
vorangehendes gilt auch ...	Vorangehendes gilt auch ...
im vorangehenden heißt es ...	im Vorangehenden heißt es ...
im voraus	im Voraus
vorgefaßt	vorgefasst
vorgestern abend, mittag, morgen	vorgestern Abend, Mittag, Morgen
Vorhängeschloß	Vorhängeschloss

alt	neu
vorhergehendes gilt auch ...	Vorhergehendes gilt auch ...
im vorhergehenden heißt es ...	im Vorhergehenden heißt es ...
im vorhinein	im Vorhinein
das vorige gilt auch ...	das Vorige gilt auch ...
im vorigen heißt es ...	im Vorigen heißt es ...
Vorlegeschloß	Vorlegeschloss
vorliebnehmen	vorlieb nehmen
[gestern, heute, morgen]	[gestern, heute, morgen]
vormittag	Vormittag
Vorschlußrunde	Vorschlussrunde
Vorschuß	Vorschuss
Vorschußlorbeeren	Vorschusslorbeeren
vorstehendes gilt auch ...	Vorstehendes gilt auch ...
im vorstehenden heißt es ...	im Vorstehenden heißt es ...
vorwärtsgehen	vorwärts gehen
vorwärtskommen	vorwärts kommen

W

alt	neu
ein wachestehender Soldat	ein Wache stehender Soldat
Wachsabguß	Wachsabguss
Wächte	Wechte
Waggon	*auch:* Wagon
Wahlausschuß	Wahlausschuss
Walkie-talkie	Walkie-Talkie
Walnuß	Walnuss
Walroß	Walross
Wandlungsprozeß	Wandlungsprozess
Warnschuß	Warnschuss
Wasserschloß	Wasserschloss
wäßrig	wässrig
Wehrpaß	Wehrpass
weichgekocht	weich gekocht
Weinfaß	Weinfass
aus schwarz weiß machen	aus Schwarz Weiß machen
weißgekleidet	weiß gekleidet
Weißrußland	Weißrussland

alt	neu
des weiteren wurde gesagt ...	des Weiteren wurde gesagt ...
weitgereist	weit gereist
weitreichend	weit reichend
weitverbreitet	weit verbreitet
Werkstattage	Werkstatttage
	auch: Werkstatt-Tage
Werkstofforschung	Werkstoffforschung
	auch: Werkstoff-Forschung
es besteht im wesentlichen aus ...	es besteht im Wesentlichen aus ...
Wetteufel	Wettteufel
	auch: Wett-Teufel
Wetturnen	Wettturnen
	auch: Wett-Turnen
widereinanderstoßen	widereinander stoßen
wieviel	wie viel
Winterschlußverkauf	Winterschlussverkauf
Wißbegierde	Wissbegierde
wißbegierig	wissbegierig
ihr wißt	ihr wisst
du wußtest	du wusstest
wir wüßten gern ...	wir wüssten gern ...
Witterungseinfluß	Witterungseinfluss
Wollappen	Wolllappen
	auch: Woll-Lappen
Wollaus	Wolllaus
	auch: Woll-Laus
als ob er wunder was getan hätte	als ob er Wunder was getan hätte
sich wundliegen	sich wund liegen
Wurfgeschoß	Wurfgeschoss *[in Österreich weiterhin mit ß]*

X, Y

alt	neu
X-beinig	*auch:* x-beinig
X-förmig	*auch:* x-förmig
zum x-tenmal	zum x-ten Mal

alt	neu
Z	
Zäheit	Zähheit
Zahlenschloß	Zahlenschloss
Zäpfchen-R	*auch:* Zäpfchen-r
Zaubernuß	Zaubernuss
Zechenstillegung	Zechenstilllegung
Zeilengußmaschine	Zeilengussmaschine
2zeilig, 3zeilig, 4zeilig ...	2-zeilig, 3-zeilig, 4-zeilig ...
eine Zeitlang	eine Zeit lang
zur Zeit *[derzeit]*	zurzeit
Zellehre	Zelllehre
	auch: Zell-Lehre
Zellstoffabrik	Zellstofffabrik
	auch: Zellstoff-Fabrik
Zersetzungsprozeß	Zersetzungsprozess
zielbewußt	zielbewusst
Zierat	Zierrat
zigtausend	*auch:* Zigtausend
Zigtausende	*auch:* zigtausende
Zippverschluß	Zippverschluss
Zirkelschluß	Zirkelschluss
Zivilprozeß	Zivilprozess
Zivilprozeßordnung	Zivilprozessordnung
Zoo-Orchester	*auch:* Zooorchester
sich zu eigen machen	sich zu Eigen machen
zueinanderfinden	zueinander finden
Zufluß	Zufluss
sich zufriedengeben	sich zufrieden geben
zufriedenlassen	zufrieden lassen
zufriedenstellen	zufrieden stellen
zugrunde gehen	*auch:* zu Grunde gehen
zugrunde legen	*auch:* zu Grunde legen
zugrunde liegen	*auch:* zu Grunde liegen
zugrundeliegend	zugrunde liegend
	auch: zu Grunde liegend
zugrunde richten	*auch:* zu Grunde richten

alt	neu
zugunsten	*auch:* zu Gunsten
zu Hause	*in Österreich und der Schweiz*
	auch: zuhause
bei uns zulande	bei uns zu Lande
zulasten	*auch:* zu Lasten
jmdm. etwas zuleide tun	*auch:* jmdm. etwas zu Leide tun
zumute sein	*auch:* zu Mute sein
Zündschloß	Zündschloss
Zungenkuß	Zungenkuss
Zungen-R	*auch:* Zungen-r
sich etwas zunutze machen	*auch:* sich etwas zu Nutze machen
jmdm. zupaß kommen	jmdm. zupass kommen
zugepreßt	zugepresst
zu Rande kommen	*auch:* zurande kommen
jmdn. zu Rate ziehen	*auch:* jmdn. zurate ziehen
sie hat zurückgemußt	sie hat zurückgemusst
zur Zeit *[derzeit]*	zurzeit
Zusammenfluß	Zusammenfluss
zusammengefaßt	zusammengefasst
zusammengepaßt	zusammengepasst
zusammengepreßt	zusammengepresst
Zusammenschluß	Zusammenschluss
zusammensein	zusammen sein
zuschanden werden	*auch:* zu Schanden werden
sich etwas zuschulden kommen	*auch:* sich etwas zu Schulden
lassen	kommen lassen
Zuschuß	Zuschuss
Zuschußbetrieb	Zuschussbetrieb
zusein	zu sein
zustande bringen	*auch:* zu Stande bringen
zustande kommen	*auch:* zu Stande kommen
zutage fördern	*auch:* zu Tage fördern
zutage treten	*auch:* zu Tage treten
zuungunsten	*auch:* zu Ungunsten
zuviel	zu viel
zuwege bringen	*auch:* zu Wege bringen

alt	neu
zuwenig	zu wenig
die zwanziger Jahre	*auch:* die Zwanzigerjahre*
die Zwanzigerjahre	*auch:* die zwanziger Jahre
das Zweite Gesicht	das zweite Gesicht
er hat wie kein zweiter gearbeitet	er hat wie kein Zweiter gearbeitet
jeder zweite war krank	jeder Zweite war krank
Zweitkläßler	Zweitklässler
Zwischengeschoß	Zwischengeschoss *[in Österreich weiterhin mit ß]*